KV-026-894

THE
ALL ENGLAND
LAW REPORTS

Incorporating the

**LAW TIMES
REPORTS**

**LAW JOURNAL
REPORTS**

1967
VOLUME 1

Consulting Editor for Taxation Cases
CYRIL KING, Q.C.
Bencher of the Middle Temple

Editor
J. T. EDGERLEY
of the Inner Temple and Lincoln's Inn, Barrister-at-Law

**LONDON
BUTTERWORTHS**

ENGLAND:	BUTTERWORTH & CO. (PUBLISHERS) LTD.
	LONDON: 88 Kingsway, W.C.2
AUSTRALIA:	BUTTERWORTH & CO. (AUSTRALIA) LTD.
	SYDNEY: 20 Loftus Street
	MELBOURNE: 473 Bourke Street
	BRISBANE: 240 Queen Street
CANADA:	BUTTERWORTH & CO. (CANADA) LTD.
	TORONTO: 1367 Danforth Avenue, 6
NEW ZEALAND:	BUTTERWORTH & CO. (NEW ZEALAND) LTD.
	WELLINGTON: 49/51 Ballance Street
	AUCKLAND: 35 High Street
SOUTH AFRICA:	BUTTERWORTH & CO. (SOUTH AFRICA) LTD.
	DURBAN: 33/35 Beach Grove

©

Butterworth & Co. (Publishers) Ltd.

1967

Printed in Great Britain by R. J. Acford, Ltd., Industrial Estate, Chichester, Sussex.

HOUSE OF LORDS

THE LORD HIGH CHANCELLOR OF GREAT BRITAIN: THE RT. HON. LORD GARDINER

LORDS OF APPEAL IN ORDINARY

THE RT. HON. LORD REID	THE RT. HON. LORD PEARCE
THE RT. HON. LORD MORRIS OF	THE RT. HON. LORD UPJOHN
BORTH-Y-GEST	THE RT. HON. LORD DONOVAN
THE RT. HON. LORD HODSON	THE RT. HON. LORD WILBERFORCE
THE RT. HON. LORD GUEST	THE RT. HON. LORD PEARSON

COURT OF APPEAL

THE LORD HIGH CHANCELLOR OF GREAT BRITAIN

LORD CHIEF JUSTICE OF ENGLAND: THE RT. HON. LORD PARKER

MASTER OF THE ROLLS: THE RT. HON. LORD DENNING

PRESIDENT OF THE PROBATE, DIVORCE AND ADMIRALTY DIVISION:
THE RT. HON. SIR JOCELYN SIMON

THE RT. HON. LORD JUSTICE SELLERS	THE RT. HON. LORD JUSTICE RUSSELL
THE RT. HON. LORD JUSTICE WILLMER	THE RT. HON. LORD JUSTICE SALMON
THE RT. HON. LORD JUSTICE HARMAN	THE RT. HON. LORD JUSTICE WINN
THE RT. HON. LORD JUSTICE DANCKWERTS	
THE RT. HON. LORD JUSTICE DAVIES	THE RT. HON. LORD JUSTICE SACHS
THE RT. HON. LORD JUSTICE DIPLOCK	THE RT. HON. LORD JUSTICE EDMUND DAVIES

CHANCERY DIVISION

THE LORD HIGH CHANCELLOR OF GREAT BRITAIN

THE HON. MR. JUSTICE LLOYD-JACOB	THE HON. MR. JUSTICE PLOWMAN
THE HON. MR. JUSTICE CROSS	THE HON. MR. JUSTICE UNGOED-THOMAS
THE HON. MR. JUSTICE BUCKLEY	THE HON. MR. JUSTICE STAMP
THE HON. MR. JUSTICE PENNYCUICK	THE HON. MR. JUSTICE GOFF

QUEEN'S BENCH DIVISION

LORD CHIEF JUSTICE OF ENGLAND: THE RT. HON. LORD PARKER

THE HON. MR. JUSTICE STABLE	THE HON. MR. JUSTICE ROSKILL
THE HON. MR. JUSTICE HAVERS	THE HON. MR. JUSTICE LYELL
THE HON. MR. JUSTICE GLYN-JONES	THE HON. MR. JUSTICE JOHN STEPHENSON
THE HON. MR. JUSTICE ASHWORTH	THE HON. MR. JUSTICE MILMO
THE HON. MR. JUSTICE HINCHCLIFFE	THE HON. MR. JUSTICE CANTLEY
THE HON. MR. JUSTICE PAULL	THE HON. MR. JUSTICE BROWNE
THE HON. MR. JUSTICE MELFORD STEVENSON	THE HON. MR. JUSTICE WALLER
THE HON. MR. JUSTICE THESIGER	THE HON. MR. JUSTICE LAWRENCE
THE HON. MR. JUSTICE PHILLIMORE	(died February 3, 1967)
THE HON. MR. JUSTICE FENTON ATKINSON	THE HON. MR. JUSTICE JAMES
THE HON. MR. JUSTICE NIELD	THE HON. MR. JUSTICE BLAIN
THE HON. MR. JUSTICE HOWARD	THE HON. MR. JUSTICE CUSACK
THE HON. MR. JUSTICE VEALE	THE HON. MR. JUSTICE CHAPMAN
THE HON. MR. JUSTICE MEGAW	THE HON. MR. JUSTICE WILLIS
THE HON. MR. JUSTICE LAWTON	THE HON. MR. JUSTICE SWANWICK
THE HON. MR. JUSTICE WIDGERY	THE HON. MR. JUSTICE DONALDSON
THE HON. MR. JUSTICE MACKENNA	THE HON. MR. JUSTICE GEOFFREY LANE
THE HON. MR. JUSTICE MOCATTA	THE HON. MR. JUSTICE O'CONNOR
THE HON. MR. JUSTICE THOMPSON	THE HON. MR. JUSTICE CRICHTON
THE HON. MR. JUSTICE BRABIN	(appointed April 3, 1967)

PROBATE, DIVORCE AND ADMIRALTY DIVISION

PRESIDENT: THE RT. HON. SIR JOCELYN SIMON

THE HON. MR. JUSTICE KARMINSKI	THE HON. MR. JUSTICE FAULKS
THE HON. MR. JUSTICE WRANGHAM	THE HON. MR. JUSTICE STIRLING
THE HON. MR. JUSTICE LLOYD-JONES	THE HON. MR. JUSTICE CUMMING-BRUCE
THE HON. MR. JUSTICE CAIRNS	THE HON. MR. JUSTICE LATEY
THE HON. MR. JUSTICE BAKER	THE HON. MR. JUSTICE PARK
THE HON. MR. JUSTICE ORMROD	THE HON. MRS. JUSTICE LANE
THE HON. MR. JUSTICE REES	THE HON. MR. JUSTICE ORR
THE HON. MR. JUSTICE PAYNE	THE HON. MR. JUSTICE BRANDON

REPORTERS

HOUSE OF LORDS	KATHLEEN O'BRIEN	Barrister-at-Law
PRIVY COUNCIL	KATHLEEN O'BRIEN	Barrister-at-Law
COURT OF APPEAL [CIVIL DIVISION]	F. GUTTMAN, ESQ. F. A. AMIES, ESQ. HENRY SUMMERFIELD, ESQ.	Barristers-at-Law
COURT OF APPEAL [CRIMINAL DIVISION]	N. P. METCALFE, ESQ.	Barrister-at-Law
COURTS-MARTIAL APPEALS	N. P. METCALFE, ESQ.	Barrister-at-Law
CHANCERY DIVISION	JENIFER SANDELL JACQUELINE METCALFE	Barristers-at-Law
QUEEN'S BENCH DIVISION and COURTS OF ASSIZE	M. DENISE CHORLTON J. M. COLLINS, ESQ. MARY COLTON K. B. EDWARDS, ESQ. T. M. EVANS, ESQ. S. A. HATTEEA, ESQ. D. M. HUGHES, ESQ. LAURENCE H. KINGSLEY, ESQ. GWYNEDD LEWIS DEIRDRE McKINNEY K. DIANA PHILLIPS KAUSHALYA PURIE	Barristers-at-Law
RATING CASES	F. A. AMIES, ESQ.	Barrister-at-Law
REVENUE CASES	F. A. AMIES, ESQ.	Barrister-at-Law
PROBATE AND DIVORCE	ALICE BLOOMFIELD	Barrister-at-Law
ADMIRALTY	N. P. METCALFE, ESQ.	Barrister-at-Law
RESTRICTIVE PRACTICES COURT	MARY COLTON	Barrister-at-Law

CITATION

These reports are cited thus:

[1967] 1 All E.R.

REFERENCES

These reports contain references, which follow after the headnotes, to the following major works of legal reference described in the manner indicated below—

HALSBURY'S LAWS OF ENGLAND, SIMONDS EDITION

The reference 2 HALSBURY'S LAWS (3rd Edn.) 20, para. 48, refers to paragraph 48 on page 20 of Volume 2 of the third edition of Halsbury's Laws of England, of which Viscount Simonds is Editor-in-Chief.

HALSBURY'S STATUTES OF ENGLAND, SECOND EDITION

The reference 26 HALSBURY'S STATUTES (2nd Edn.) 138, refers to page 138 of Volume 26 of the second edition of Halsbury's Statutes.

ENGLISH AND EMPIRE DIGEST

The reference 41 DIGEST 290, *1492*, refers to case No. 1492 on page 290 of Volume 41 of the Digest.

There are three cumulative supplements to the Digest, described as Digest Supp., 2nd Digest Supp. and 3rd Digest Supp.; of these the first two include cases up to December 31, 1939, and December 31, 1951, respectively.

The reference 31 DIGEST (Repl.) 244, *3794*, refers to case No. 3794 on page 244 of Digest Replacement Volume 31.

The reference DIGEST (Cont. Vol. A) 287, *2666a*, refers to case No. 2666a on page 287 of Digest Continuation Volume A.

HALSBURY'S STATUTORY INSTRUMENTS

The reference 12 HALSBURY'S STATUTORY INSTRUMENTS 124, refers to page 124 of Volume 12 of Halsbury's Statutory Instruments, first edition.

A reference to a volume as " 1st Re-issue " refers to the first re-issue of the appropriate volume of Halsbury's Statutory Instruments.

ENCYCLOPAEDIA OF FORMS AND PRECEDENTS

The reference 15 ENCY. FORMS & PRECEDENTS (3rd Edn.) 938, Form 231, refers to Form 231 on page 938 of Volume 15 of the third edition, and the reference 7 ENCY. FORMS & PRECEDENTS (4th Edn.) 247, Form 12, refers to Form 12 on page 247 of Volume 7 of the fourth edition, of the Encyclopaedia of Forms and Precedents.

CASES REPORTED

IN VOLUME 1

INDEX

CASES NOTED

STATUTES, ETC., NOTED

WORDS AND PHRASES

CORRIGENDA

[1966] 3 All E.R.

p. 865. JEFFS v. NEW ZEALAND DAIRY PRODUCTION AND MARKETING BOARD AND OTHERS. Counsel for the appellants: read " *P. B. Temm* " instead of " *P. B. Tenn* ".

p. 944. GREEN v. MINISTER OF HOUSING AND LOCAL GOVERNMENT. Line G.5: for " notes " read " report ".

[1967] 1 All E.R.

p. 37. DU SAUTOY v. SYMES. Line C.2: for " relevant entry did come to light " read " relevant entry did not come to light ".

p. 42. HOUSE v. HAUGHTON BROTHERS (WORCESTER), LTD. Agents for *Duggan, Elton & James*: for " *Kingsley Wood & Co.* " read " *Barlow, Lyde & Gilbert* ".

p. 190. BAILEY v. PURSER. Counsel for the respondent: read " *Ronald Bernstein* " instead of " *S. N. Bernstein* ".

p. 259. JOLLIFFE v. EXETER CORPORATION. Counsel for the plaintiff: read " *D. P. Kerrigan, Q.C.,* and *A. B. Dawson* for the plaintiff " instead of as printed.

p. 561. R. v. KENT JUSTICES. Counsel: read " *Sir Peter Rawlinson, Q.C.,* and *J. P. Harris* for the applicants. *J. H. R. Newey* and *A. O. R. Vick* for the respondents " instead of as printed.

p. 743. PARKASHO v. SINGH. Lines C.1, H.5, I.2: for " counsel for the wife " read " counsel for the husband ".

p. 750. DIN v. NATIONAL ASSISTANCE BOARD. Lines I.2 and 3: for the words from " repealed, however " to " and Sch. 8 ", substitute " repealed (see 1965 (c. 55), s. 1 and Schedule) and replaced by National Insurance Act 1965, s. 113 (1), National Insurance (Industrial Injuries) Act 1965, s. 86 (5) and Family Allowances Act 1965, s. 17 (9) ".

p. 836. ALFRED F. BECKETT, LTD. v. LYONS. Line E.5: for " therefore " read " theretofore "; p. 837, line B.1: for " trespassers " read " trespasses "; p. 837, line I.7: for " right claimed by the defendants " read " plaintiffs' action "; p. 838, line H.3: for " descriptive " read " prescriptive ".

p. 945. RADZIEJ v. RADZIEJ. Counsel for the wife: read " *J. M. Collins (C. R. Sinclair-Morris with him*) " instead of " *S. Morris* ".

p. 1021. ANGEL v. BUSHELL. Counsel for the defendants: read " *David Hirst, Q.C.,* and *Richard Hartley* " instead of as printed.

THE
ALL ENGLAND
LAW REPORTS

INCORPORATING THE

LAW TIMES REPORTS

AND THE

LAW JOURNAL REPORTS

Dicta of LORD UPJOHN at 9, 10, 11
explained in Re VANDERVELL'S
TRUSTS [1974] 1 All ER 47

VANDERVELL v. INLAND REVENUE COMMISSIONERS.

[HOUSE OF LORDS (Lord Reid, Lord Pearce, Lord Upjohn, Lord Donovan and Lord Wilberforce), June 15, 16, 20, November 24, 1966.]

Surtax—Settlement—Income of property of which settlor claims to have " divested himself absolutely "—Property or income becoming payable to him or applicable for his benefit—Gift of shares to college, they granting a purchase option to trustee company—Dividends to provide funds for chair in pharmacology— Intent—Beneficial trusts of option not defined—Whether resulting trust inferred from primary facts or established in law on the evidence—Income Tax Act, 1952 (15 & 16 Geo. 6 & 1 Eliz. 2 c. 10), s. 415 (1) (d), (2).

Equity—Equitable interest—Transfer—Writing—Transfer of legal interest of bare trustee of shares in a company, beneficial owner intending gift of them— Whether any need for separate written transfer of equitable interest—Law of Property Act, 1925 (15 & 16 Geo. 5 c. 20), s. 53 (1) (c).

In 1958 the taxpayer, who controlled a very successful private company, decided to give £150,000 to the Royal College of Surgeons to found a chair of pharmacology. The company's issued ordinary share capital was (i) five hundred thousand ordinary shares, substantially all of which were held by the taxpayer; (ii) one hundred thousand " A " ordinary shares held by a bank as nominee for the taxpayer and (iii) 2,600,000 " B " ordinary shares, of which the taxpayer held 546,692 and the remaining 2,053,308 were held by V.T., Ltd. as trustees of a family settlement. Only the first class of shares carried voting rights. In order to achieve his purpose the taxpayer, through R. his financial adviser, suggested giving to the college the one hundred thousand " A " ordinary shares, intending to pass to the college both the legal and beneficial interest in them. Subsequently, on the advice of R. and by way of second thoughts in order to avoid any future difficulties if the company were to be converted into a public company, the taxpayer acceded to R.'s suggestion that the college should give an option to V.T., Ltd. to purchase the shares for £5,000 within five years. In November, 1958, R. delivered to the college the transfer by the bank of the " A " ordinary shares and an option deed. The college sealed these deeds and were registered as owners of the shares. Dividends on the " A " shares, amounting to £145,000 less tax at the standard rate, were paid to the college. On Oct. 11, 1961, V.T., Ltd. exercised the option. The £5,000 was paid to the college. The taxpayer was assessed to surtax on the basis that the dividends in the years 1958-59 and 1959-60 which, with the £5,000 on the exercise of the option, made up the gift to the college, were his income or were required to be treated as his income under s. 415 of the Income Tax Act, 1952. It was not disputed that there was a settlement within the meaning of s. 411 (2) of that Act. The taxpayer contended that he had by the settlement within s. 411 (2)

B

divested himself absolutely of the property and thus came within the   A
exception provided by s. 415 (1) (d) and (2)*.

Held: (i) (LORD REID and LORD DONOVAN dissenting) the option to
purchase the " A " shares was vested in the trustee company in 1958, either
(per LORD UPJOHN and LORD PEARCE) as a matter of inference from the
primary facts on such trusts as might be declared subsequently, or (per
LORD WILBERFORCE) as a matter of interpretation of the evidence on trusts   B
which were undefined, and on either basis the consequence in law was that
the option was held on a resulting trust for the taxpayer; accordingly the
taxpayer had failed to divest himself absolutely of the property which was the
source of the dividends paid to the college, and had not brought himself
within the exempting provisions of s. 415 (1) (d), (2) of the Income Tax Act,
1952, with the consequence that the assessments should stand (see p. 11,   C
letters A and C, p. 6, letter E, p. 17, letter I, and p. 18, letter C, post).

(ii) since a transfer of the " A " shares had been executed by the bank,
which was nominee for the taxpayer, and had been delivered on the taxpayer's behalf to the college, which became registered as owners of the shares,
there had been no need for a separate transfer of the taxpayer's equitable
interest in the " A " shares and s. 53 (1) (c) of the Law of Property Act, 1925,   D
had no application (see p. 7, letters G and I, p. 6, letter E, p. 4, letter I,
p. 11, letters D and E, and p. 18, letter H, post).

Per LORD UPJOHN: I do not agree that prima facie a transfer of the legal
estate carries with it the absolute beneficial interest in the property transferred; this plainly is not so, e.g., the transfer may be on a change of trustee;
it is a matter of intention in each case. If the intention of the beneficial   E
owner in directing the trustee to transfer the legal estate to " X " is that
" X " should be beneficial owner, I can see no reason for any further document, or further words in the document assigning the legal estate, also
expressly transferring the beneficial interest (see p. 7, letter F, post).

Decision of the COURT OF APPEAL ([1965] 2 All E.R. 37) affirmed, but on
rather different reasoning.   F

[Editorial Note. The House of Lords did not decide that the doctrine of
resulting trust applies to an option to purchase shares in a company (see p. 9,
letter I, post).

As to a settlor's liability for surtax on income of settlement property, see 20
HALSBURY'S LAWS (3rd Edn.) 587, 588, paras. 1151-1153.   G

As to the incidents of a beneficial interest in property, see 14 HALSBURY'S
LAWS (3rd Edn.) 554, 555, paras. 1035, 1036.

As to resulting trusts on voluntary conveyances, see 38 HALSBURY'S LAWS
(2nd Edn.) 867, 868, para. 1461; and for cases on the subject, see 47 DIGEST
(Repl.) 122-127, *876-927*.

For the Law of Property Act, 1925, s. 53 (1) (c), see 20 HALSBURY'S STATUTES   H
(2nd Edn.) 551.

For the Income Tax Act, 1952, s. 415 (1), (2), see 31 HALSBURY'S STATUTES
(2nd Edn.) 395.]

---

* Section 415 provides, so far as is material: " (1) Where, during the life of the settlor,
income arising under a settlement . . . is . . . payable to or applicable for the benefit of   I
any person other than the settlor, then, unless . . . the income . . . —(d) is income from
property of which the settlor has divested himself absolutely by the settlement . . . the
income shall be treated for the purposes of surtax as the income of the settlor . . .
" (2) The settlor shall not be deemed for the purposes of this section to have divested
himself absolutely of any property if that property or any income therefrom or any
property directly or indirectly representing proceeds of, or of income from, that property
or any income therefrom is, or will or may become, payable to or applicable for his
benefit in any circumstances whatsoever. " Subsection (2) was amended by the Finance Act 1965, s. 12 (2) and (4), in relation to settlements made after Apr. 7, 1965; but
the alteration appears to be immaterial as respects the ratio decidendi of this case.

A Cases referred to:

    Curteis' Trusts, Re, (1872), L.R. 14 Eq. 217; 41 L.J.Ch. 631; 26 L.J. 863;
        47 Digest (Repl.) 107, *773*.

    Fowkes v. *Pascoe*, [1874-80] All E.R. Rep. 521; (1875), 10 Ch. App. 343;
        44 L.J.Ch. 367; 32 L.T. 545; 20 Digest (Repl.) 486, *1953*.

    Grey v. *Inland Revenue Comrs.*, [1959] 3 All E.R. 603; [1960] A.C. 1; [1959]
B   3 W.L.R. 759; 47 Digest (Repl.) 17, *49*.

    Oughtred v. *Inland Revenue Comrs.*, [1958] 1 All E.R. 252; [1958] Ch. 383;
        [1958] 2 W.L.R. 174; *revsd.* C.A., [1958] 2 All E.R. 443; [1958] Ch. 678;
        [1958] 3 W.L.R. 64; *affd.* H.L., [1959] 3 All E.R. 623; [1960] A.C. 206;
        [1959] 3 W.L.R. 898; 47 Digest (Repl.) 17, *47*.

    Rose, Re, Midland Bank Executor & Trustee Co., Ltd. v. *Rose*, [1948] 2 All E.R.
C   971; [1949] Ch. 78; [1949] L.J.R. 208; 23 Digest (Repl.) 392, *4625*.

    Standing v. *Bowring*, [1881-85] All E.R. Rep. 702; (1885), 31 Ch.D. 282; 55
        L.J.Ch. 218; 54 L.T. 191; 47 Digest (Repl.) 123, *894*.

Appeal.

    This was an appeal by the taxpayer, Guy Anthony Vandervell, from an order
of the Court of Appeal (WILLMER, HARMAN and DIPLOCK, L.JJ.), dated Feb. 26,
D 1965, and reported [1965] 2 All E.R. 37, dismissing an appeal by the taxpayer
from an order of the Chancery Division (PLOWMAN, J.), dated Mar. 16, 1964,
whereby an appeal by the taxpayer on a Case Stated by the Special Commissioners
of Income Tax was dismissed and the determination of the commissioners dated
Dec. 7, 1962, was upheld but for different reasons. The taxpayer had appealed to
the Special Commissioners against additional assessments to surtax made upon
E him for 1958-59 and 1959-60 in the amounts of £162,500 and £87,500 respectively.
The assessments were made on the footing that certain dividends paid to the
Royal College of Surgeons on one hundred thousand " A " ordinary shares in
Vandervell Products, Ltd. (a private company of which the taxpayer was chair-
man, managing director and principal shareholder), were the income of the
taxpayer or fell to be treated as his income by virtue of s. 404 or s. 415 of the
F Income Tax Act, 1952. The facts found by the Special Commissioners are set out
in the opinion of LORD DONOVAN at p. 12, letters B to E, post.

    Sir Lionel Heald, Q.C., Viscount Bledisloe, Q.C., and *W. T. Elverston* for the
taxpayer.

    E. I. Goulding, Q.C., J. R. Philips and *J. P. Warner* for the Crown.

G   Their lordships took time for consideration.

    November 24. The following opinions were delivered.

    LORD REID: My lords, this case provides yet another illustration of the
folly of entering into an important transaction of an unusual character without
first obtaining expert advice regarding tax liabilities which it may create. In
H 1958 the taxpayer decided to give £150,000 to the Royal College of Surgeons to
found a chair of pharmacology. By reason of the method by which this gift was
made, however, additional assessments to surtax amounting to £250,000 have
been made on the taxpayer for the years 1958-59 and 1959-60, and, if this appeal
fails, there is a possibility of further additional assessments.

    The taxpayer is chairman, managing director and principal shareholder of a
I very successful engineering company. The capital structure of the company is
unusual. Besides certain preference shares there were three classes of ordinary
shares: first there were five hundred thousand ordinary shares substantially all of
which were owned by the taxpayer; secondly there were one hundred thousand
" A " ordinary shares held by a bank as trustee for the taxpayer when this gift
was made; and thirdly there were 2,600,000 " B " ordinary shares o¹which over
two million were held by Vandervell Trustees, Ltd., as trustees of a family
settlement. Only the first of these three classes of shares carried any voting
rights but the articles permitted the company (which was controlled by the

taxpayer) to resolve that the whole of the profit to be distributed in any year   A
might be paid as dividends on any one of these three classes of shares to the
exclusion of the other two.

The taxpayer decided to make this gift to the Royal College of Surgeons by
causing the bank to transfer to them the one hundred thousand " A " ordinary
shares and then causing the company to declare dividends on these shares amounting to £150,000. It then occurred to his financial adviser, Mr. Robins, however,   B
that if the taxpayer's company were to be floated as a public company there might
be difficulties if these shares remained registered in the name of the college, so he
advised that there should be an option to acquire these shares from the college
after they had received the £150,000 in dividends. The taxpayer agreed to this and
gave Mr. Robins carte blanche to make whatever arrangements he thought fit.
The taxpayer did not want to have these " A " ordinary shares because of possible   C
estate duty questions on his death, and he wished to make the gift by causing the
company to pay it in dividends because of the possibility of surtax directions if
the company did not distribute enough of its profits. It is clear that both he and
Mr. Robins intended that he should have no further rights to or in respect of
the shares or the dividends.

Many of the arrangements were made orally. The only relevant documents are   D
(i) a letter of Nov. 14, 1958, from the taxpayer to Mr. Robins in which he said:
" I have decided to give to the college the one hundred thousand ' A ' shares in
Vandervell Products, Ltd."; (ii) a letter of Nov. 19 from Mr. Robins' firm to the
college in these terms:

> " We have pleasure in advising you that our client Mr. G. A. Vandervell
> has, in response to your appeal, decided to make available to you the sum   E
> of £150,000 (one hundred and fifty thousand pounds) to establish and
> maintain a chair in pharmacology.
> " You will receive between now and Mar. 31, 1959, dividends totalling
> £145,000 gross on shares in Vandervell Products, Ltd. which our client
> now owns and will transfer to you. The balance of £5,000 will be paid to you
> when the option to purchase the shares is exercised."   F

(iii) a transfer of the shares by the bank to the college dated Nov. 26; (iv) an
option deed of Dec. 1 granted by the college giving to Vandervell Trustees, Ltd.
an option to purchase the shares for £5,000 and (v) a letter of Oct. 11, 1961, from
their agent to the college exercising the option and enclosing £5,000.

The assessment was made under s. 415 of the Income Tax Act, 1952. That   G
section provides that where income arising under a settlement is payable to a
person other than the settlor, then, unless it is income from property of which the
settlor has divested himself absolutely by the settlement, the income shall be
treated for the purposes of surtax as the income of the settlor. Section 411 (2)
provides that " settlement " includes any agreement or arrangement. It is not
disputed that there was a settlement within the meaning of this section. It is   H
found in the Case Stated that it consisted of the transfer of the shares, the granting
of the option and the declaration of the dividends received by the college. The
question at issue is whether the taxpayer by the settlement divested himself
absolutely of the shares which were transferred to the college. The Crown maintain that he did not for two reasons. In the first place they found on s. 53 of the
Law of Property Act, 1925. Secondly they maintain that when Vandervell   I
Trustees, Ltd. received the option from the college, they held it on a resulting
trust for the taxpayer. The Court of Appeal (1) rejected the first of these grounds,
but held that there was a resulting trust and therefore the assessment was
validly made under s. 415.

I agree that the Crown's first argument is unsound; but their second argument
raises questions of difficulty. It is clear that the taxpayer did not wish to retain
any right of any kind with regard to these shares, but he gave full authority to

---

(1) [1965] 2 All E.R. 37; [1966] Ch. 261.

A Mr. Robins to make the necessary arrangements. It is, I think, equally clear that Mr. Robins, in making the arrangements, did not intend that any right in respect of the shares should be reserved to the taxpayer. The argument is that, whatever he intended, the result of what he did in law caused Vandervell Trustees, Ltd. to hold the option given to them on a resulting trust for the taxpayer. So it is necessary to determine precisely what was the nature of this company's right

B to the option.

The law with regard to resulting trusts is not in doubt. It is stated conveniently in UNDERHILL ON TRUSTS (11th Edn.) at p. 172 and in LEWIN ON TRUSTS (16th Edn.) at p. 115. UNDERHILL says:

" When it appears to have been the intention of the donor that the donee should not take beneficially there will be a resulting trust in favour of the

C donor."

LEWIN says that the general rule is that whenever " it appears to have been the intention of the donor that the grantee, devisee or legatee was not to take beneficially " there will be a resulting trust. The basis of the rule is, I think, that the beneficial interest must belong to or be held for somebody: so, if it was not

D to belong to the donee or be held by him in trust for somebody, it must remain with the donor.

The only difficulty is with regard to the word " beneficially ". The argument for the Crown is that there was no intention that the trust company or any of its three directors and shareholders should gain financially from the option and therefore the company was not intended to take beneficially. It is, I think,

E however, quite common for a testator to give to a legatee an absolute and unfettered right to property, although his hope and belief is that the legatee will not retain it for his own benefit but will use it in a manner which he thinks is in accordance with the wishes of the testator. In such a case the legatee takes the property beneficially. There is no resulting trust. If the legatee chooses to disregard any moral obligation there may be and put the property in his own pocket,

F he is free to do so, and the testator's representatives have no legal remedy. In a popular sense the testator may be said to trust the legatee, but there is no trust in law. The same can apply to a donation inter vivos, and I think that that is what happened in this case.

It is true that the taxpayer's case has hitherto been based on other, and to my mind unsound, arguments; but I do not see anything to prevent this point from

G being taken now, and it would be rather surprising if the Inland Revenue sought to take a technical objection to its being considered.

On the face of the documents the trustee company took an absolute and unfettered right to the option and therefore the existence of a resulting trust must depend on inference from the facts. As the option was part of the settlement or arrangement, I shall assume that it was provided by the taxpayer. Then the

H question is—can it be inferred that he, or Mr. Robins as his agent, did not intend that the trustee company should take it " beneficially " in the sense which I have explained: or is the correct inference that he, or Mr. Robins, intended that the trustee company, or its three directors, should have the right to decide how to use it and what to do with the shares if the option was exercised?

I find no difficulty in holding that the latter is the correct inference from the

I facts set out in the Case Stated. The Crown found on para. 9 (2) of the Case:

" The directors and shareholders of the trustee company never considered that the option . . . could be turned to account in such a way as to benefit them personally."

They emphasise the word " could " in this finding as meaning that the directors and shareholders recognised that they had no legal right to do this. If the word had been " would " there would be no difficulty, and the next sub-paragraph shows that the directors thought that they and not the taxpayer had the right to

decide on what trusts they should hold the shares if the option was exercised. **A**
The directors were not lawyers and clearly knew nothing about the legal position;
but in any event it is the intention of the donor and not the belief of the donee
that matters.

There is nothing in the facts found to suggest that Mr. Robins intended that the
taxpayer should have any legal control over the option or the way in which it was
exercised. Moreover, I see nothing surprising in Mr. Robins being content to rely **B**
on his belief that the directors of the trust company would act in the best interests
of the taxpayer and his company. As trustees of the family settlement they
already held over two million shares in the taxpayer's company over which he
had no control; but clearly it was in the interests of the beneficiaries of this
settlement that the trustees should co-operate in everything which would be
beneficial to the taxpayer's company. So it was reasonable to expect that the **C**
trust company would co-operate as regards these shares and, that being so, it was
equally reasonable to expect that that company would co-operate in regard to the
shares to be acquired by the exercise of the option. There would have been no
point in the taxpayer's retaining legal control of these one hundred thousand
shares when he had no control over the other two million, and I can find no ground
for holding that there was any intention to limit the legal right of the trust com- **D**
pany to deal with the option or the shares acquired by its exercise in whatever
way they might think fit. If that is right, then there can be no resulting trust.

I would allow this appeal.

LORD PEARCE: My Lords, I agree with the opinion of my noble and
learned friend, LORD UPJOHN, and would dismiss the appeal.
E

LORD UPJOHN: My Lords, the facts are fully set out in the Case Stated
and in the judgments in the courts below (2) and I shall be brief in my reference
to them. The claim by the Crown against the taxpayer is founded on the
provisions of s. 404 and s. 415 of the Income Tax Act, 1952, but in argument has
turned on s. 415 (1). If and so far as the commissioners determined the matter
under s. 415 (2) by giving an impossibly wide construction to the concluding **F**
words thereof—" payable to him or applicable for his benefit in any circumstances
whatever "—the Crown do not seek to support it. The whole question, as counsel
for the taxpayer submitted, depends on the application of principles of equity to
the facts and inferences from the primary facts which should properly be drawn
in this case.

There are two points to be considered, completely different, each in a watertight **G**
compartment. On the first point it is not necessary to do more than state that at
the beginning of the relevant history the taxpayer was beneficially entitled to
one hundred thousand " A " ordinary shares in Vandervell Products, Ltd. (a
company owned and controlled by him through a holding of other ordinary shares)
which stood in the name of the National Provincial Bank, Ltd. as bare trustee for
him. In September, 1958, the taxpayer directed the bank to transfer those shares **H**
to the Royal College of Surgeons with the intention of passing to the college not
only the legal but beneficial interest in them. I can ignore for the moment the
fact that contemporaneously the college gave an option to a third party to acquire
these shares for £5,000. In the court of first instance it was contended that such
direction was given in writing by the taxpayer, but this has now rightly been
abandoned. The transfer to the college was effected by the bank on a common **I**
form transfer (pursuant to art. 91 of the company's articles of association) in
consideration of 10s. and the college were duly registered as holders in the books
of the company.

The question is whether, notwithstanding the plainly expressed intention of
the taxpayer by himself or his agents, the absence of writing prevented any
equitable or beneficial interest in the shares passing to the college so that contrary

---

(2) [1965] 2 All E.R. 37; [1966] Ch. 261, 273.

A to his wishes and understanding they remained bare trustees for him. This depends entirely on the true construction of s. 53 (1) (c) of the Law of Property Act, 1925, which the Crown maintain makes writing necessary to pass the beneficial interest. This section was generally thought to re-enact s. 9 of the Statute of Frauds, and that section had never been applied to a trust of an equitable interest of pure personalty. Before the cases of *Grey* v. *Inland Revenue*

B *Comrs.* (3) and *Oughtred* v. *Inland Revenue Comrs.* (4), both in your lordships' House, this argument would have been quite untenable.

It was shown in those cases that the Law of Property Act, 1925, was not re-enacting s. 9 but that it had been amended by the Law of Property Act, 1924. The relevant words of s. 53 are:

C "... a disposition of an equitable interest or trust subsisting at the time of the disposition must be in writing signed by the person disposing of the same ..."

Those words were applied in *Grey* v. *Inland Revenue Comrs.* (3) and *Oughtred* v. *Inland Revenue Comrs.* (4) to cases where the legal estate remained outstanding in a trustee and the beneficial owner was dealing and dealing only with the equitable estate. That is understandable; the object of the section, as was the object of the

D old Statute of Frauds, is to prevent hidden oral transactions in equitable interests in fraud of those truly entitled, and making it difficult, if not impossible, for the trustees to ascertain who are in truth his beneficiaries. When the beneficial owner, however, owns the whole beneficial estate and is in a position to give directions to his bare trustee with regard to the legal as well as the equitable estate there can be no possible ground for invoking the section where the beneficial

E owner wants to deal with the legal estate as well as the equitable estate.

I cannot agree with DIPLOCK, L.J., (5) that prima facie a transfer of the legal estate carries with it the absolute beneficial interest in the property transferred; this plainly is not so, e.g., the transfer may be on a change of trustee; it is a matter of intention in each case. If, however, the intention of the beneficial owner in directing the trustee to transfer the legal estate to X is that X should

F be the beneficial owner, I can see no reason for any further document or further words in the document assigning the legal estate also expressly transferring the beneficial interest; the greater includes the less. X may be wise to secure some evidence that the beneficial owner intended him to take the beneficial interest in case his beneficial title is challenged at a later date but it certainly cannot, in my opinion, be a statutory requirement that to effect its passing there must be

G some writing under s. 53 (1) (c).

Counsel for the Crown admitted that where the legal and beneficial estate was vested in the legal owner and he desired to transfer the whole legal and beneficial estate to another he did not have to do more than transfer the legal estate and he did not have to comply with s. 53 (1) (c); and I can see no difference between that case and this.

H As I have said, that section is, in my opinion, directed to cases where dealings with the equitable estate are divorced from the legal estate and I do not think any of their lordships in *Grey* v. *Inland Revenue Comrs.* (3) and *Oughtred* v. *Inland Revenue Comrs.* (4) had in mind the case before your lordships. To hold the contrary would make assignments unnecessarily complicated; if there had to be assignments in express terms of both legal and equitable interests that would

I make the section more productive of injustice than the supposed evils it was intended to prevent.

I think that the Court of Appeal (6) reached a correct conclusion on this point, which was not raised before PLOWMAN, J.

I turn, then, to the second point.

(3) [1959] 3 All E.R. 603; [1960] A.C. 1.
(4) [1959] 3 All E.R. 623; [1960] A.C. 206.
(5) [1965] 2 All E.R. at p. 44, letter B; [1966] Ch. at p. 287.
(6) [1965] 2 All E.R. 37; [1966] Ch. 261.

My lords, we have had much argument on the law of resulting trusts. I do not A
think that any question of the principles of law to be applied gives rise to any
difficulty or is in doubt (except possibly as to their application to an option to
purchase). I believe that all your lordships and the judges in the court below are
at one on the general principles. The difficulty, and it is very great, lies in the
application of those well-settled principles to the facts of the case.

So I will be as brief as I can on the principles. Where A transfers, or directs a B
trustee for him to transfer, the legal estate in property to B otherwise than for
valuable consideration it is a question of the intention of A in making the transfer
whether B is to take beneficially or on trust and, if the latter, on what trusts.
If, as a matter of construction of the document transferring the legal estate, it is
possible to discern A's intentions, that is an end of the matter, and no extraneous
evidence is admissible to correct and qualify his intentions so ascertained. If, C
however, as in this case (a common form share transfer), the document is silent,
then there is said to arise a resulting trust in favour of A; but this is only a
presumption and is easily rebutted. All the relevant facts and circumstances can
be considered in order to ascertain A's intentions with a view to rebutting this
presumption. As LINDLEY, L.J., said in *Standing* v. *Bowring* (7):

> " Trusts are neither created nor implied by law to defeat the intentions of D
> donors or settlors; they are created or implied, or are held to result in
> favour of donors or settlors, in order to carry out and give effect to their
> true intentions, expressed or implied."

The law was well stated by MELLISH, L.J., in *Fowkes* v. *Pascoe* (8):

> " Now, SIR GEORGE JESSEL, M.R., appears to have thought that because E
> the presumption that it was a trust and not a gift must prevail if there were
> no evidence to rebut the presumption, therefore when there was evidence to
> rebut the presumption he ought not to consider the probability or improbabil-
> ity of the circumstances of the case, and whether the presumption was really
> true or not, but ought to decide the case on the ground that the evidence of
> Pascoe and his wife taken alone was not satisfactory. But, in my opinion, F
> when there is once evidence to rebut the presumption, the court is put in the
> same position as a jury would be, and then we cannot give such influence to
> the presumption in point of law as to disregard the circumstances of the
> investment, and to say that neither the circumstances nor the evidence are
> sufficient to rebut the presumption."

JAMES, L.J., in the same case (9) also pointed out in effect that it was really a G
jury matter, on the basis, I may add, of weighing the evidence on the balance of
probabilities. A very good example of this is to be found in the case of *Re Curteis'
Trusts* (10) where SIR JAMES BACON, V.-C., (11) without any direct evidence as
to the intention of the settlor, drew a commonsense deduction as to what he must
have intended. In reality the so-called presumption of a resulting trust is no
more than a long stop to provide the answer when the relevant facts and H
circumstances fail to yield a solution.

The doctrine of resulting trust, however, plays another very important part in
our law and, in my opinion, is decisive of this case.

If " A " intends to give away all his beneficial interest in a piece of property
and thinks that he has done so, but, by some mistake or accident or failure to
comply with the requirements of the law, he has failed to do so, either wholly or I
partially, there will, by operation of law, be a resulting trust for him of the
beneficial interest which he has failed effectually to dispose of. If the beneficial
interest was in " A " and he fails to give it away effectively to another or others
or on charitable trusts, it must remain in him. Early references to equity, like

---

(7) [1881-85] All E.R. Rep. 702 at p. 706; (1885), 31 Ch.D. 282 at p. 289.
(8) (1875), 10 Ch. App. 343 at p. 352; [1874-80] All E.R. Rep. 521 at p. 527.
(9) [1874-80] All E.R. Rep. at p. 524; (1875), 10 Ch. App. at p. 349.
(10) (1872), L.R. 14 Eq. 217.   (11) (1872), L.R. 14 Eq. at p. 221.

A nature, abhorring a vacuum, are delightful but unnecessary. Let me give an example close to this case.

" A ", the beneficial owner, informs his trustees that he wants forthwith to get rid of his interest in the property and instructs him to hold the property forthwith on such trusts as he will hereafter direct; that beneficial interest, notwithstanding the expressed intention and belief of " A " that he has thereby parted with his

B whole beneficial interest in the property, will inevitably remain in him for he has not given the property away effectively to or for the benefit of others. As Plowman, J., said:

" As I see it a man does not cease to own property simply by saying ' I don't want it '. If he tries to give it away the question must always be has he succeeded in doing so or not."

C I must now apply these really elementary principles to the facts of this case.

The college were in terms the grantors of the option dated Dec. 1, 1958, to Vandervell Trustees, Ltd. (the " trustee company ") enabling them to exercise an option within five years to acquire these one hundred thousand " A " shares in Vandervell Products, Ltd. for £5,000 but I, for my part, cannot doubt that the real grantor was the taxpayer. True he himself wanted to give the whole

D beneficial interest in the shares to the college and, indeed, thought that he had done so. It was Mr. Robins who for the reasons set out in para. 9 (1) of the Case Stated introduced the idea of an option. So, on Nov. 5, 1958, Mr. Robins asked the secretary of the college whether the college would be prepared to give this option to the trustee company. This question was, however, a matter of courtesy; at this time the college had no legal or beneficial interest in the shares and they

E could only comply with it. They did so in due course, and in fact they were not in the least degree interested in the ultimate fate of the shares after they had received the promised dividends. In law I cannot doubt, however, that it was the taxpayer acting by his agent, Mr. Robins, who procured the college to grant the option to the trustee company.

In the courts below (12) it seems to have been assumed that in these circum-

F stances the trustee company, unless they took beneficially, held the option to acquire the shares on a resulting trust for the taxpayer. We are, of course, only concerned with the option and not with its ultimate exercise. My lords, I am by no means convinced that any such presumption arises in the case of an option to purchase. I asked in vain for any authority on the point.

The grant of an option to purchase is very different from a grant of a legal

G estate in some real or personal property without consideration to a person nominated by the beneficial owner. The grantee of an option has not, in reality, an estate in the property. Of course, he has an interest in it which can be measured by saying that he can obtain an injunction preventing the grantor from parting with the property except subject to the option, and in this case, having regard to the express terms of cl. 2, from parting with the property at all; and that he can

H enforce the option against all subsequent owners except purchasers for value without notice. Essentially, however, an option confers no more than a con-tractual right to acquire property on payment of a consideration, and that seems to me a very different thing from the ordinary case where the doctrine of a resulting trust has been applied. However, it is a question of intention whether the taxpayer and the trustee company intended that the option should be held

I by the trustee company beneficially or as a trustee and, if the latter, on what trusts. As the option deed is itself quite silent on this point all the relevant facts and circumstances must be looked at to solve this question. As I think the facts and circumstances are sufficient for this purpose without resort to this long stop presumption, it is unnecessary finally to decide whether the doctrine of resulting trust does apply to an option.

On this vital question whether the trustee company held the option beneficially

(12) [1965] 2 All E.R. 37; [1966] Ch. 261, 273.

or as trustee and, if the latter, on what trusts, my mind has fluctuated; it is a very A
difficult matter to decide what is the proper inference to draw from the known
facts.

There are, as I see it, three possibilities. 1. That the trustee company was
intended to take as trustee for the children's settlement of Dec. 30, 1949. 2.
That the trustee company should take beneficially, the taxpayer relying on his
three friends and advisers, Messrs. Robins, Green and Jobson, the directors and B
holders of all the shares in the trustee company, to carry out his wishes which
from time to time should be intimated to them in the way of a gentleman's
agreement, but having no power at law to enforce them. 3. That the trustee
company should hold as trustee on such trusts as he or the trustee company
should from time to time declare.

With regard to the first possibility it was but faintly argued that there was a C
trust for the children's settlement but, like all your lordships, I can see no ground
for it; cl. 11 of the settlement was relied on, but it does not seem to me to have
anything to do with it, so I dismiss this possibility. It is the choice between
possibilities 2 and 3 that has caused me so much difficulty. Part of the difficulty
has been caused by the fact that Mr. Jobson, the solicitor, does not seem to have
been brought into the picture at any relevant date, and the other advisers of the D
taxpayer do not seem to have appreciated the vital distinction in the legal
result between possibilities 2 and 3. Indeed, the matter does not seem to have
been canvassed to any great extent before the Special Commissioners; certainly
no direct finding was made on these points, and no contention to the effect that
the trustee company took beneficially appears in the taxpayer's contentions set
out in para. 13 of the Case Stated. Neither party asked this House to remit this E
matter to the commissioners to make a finding on the vital facts, and so your
lordships have to draw your own conclusions as to the proper inference to be
drawn from the primary facts.

On the one hand, there are some findings of the commissioners which might
lead to the inference that the transfer to the trustee company was beneficial—
see, for example, para. 14 (5), but then the concluding words of para. 14 (9) were F
to the contrary and so, on the whole, was para. 14 (6). What has influenced me
in the end is that throughout the correspondence in 1961 the taxpayer's advisers
were contending that the trustee company took the shares as trustees and that
before PLOWMAN, J., this was conceded. He said " No one suggests that the
trustee company took it otherwise than on trust ".

While the Court of Appeal (13) assumed that there was a resulting trust of the G
option for the taxpayer—they did not decide it on that ground alone. DIPLOCK,
L.J., said (14): " It is next contended that the trustee company took the option
beneficially. This also seems to me to fly in the face of the evidence "—which he
then examined in some detail. WILLMER, L.J., in the next judgment said (15):

> " Later—prompted, I suspect, by certain observations made by members
> of this court—the argument was developed that the trustee company should H
> be regarded as taking the option beneficially."

He also examined the evidence and came to the conclusion that there was no
intention to give any beneficial interest to the trustee company. HARMAN, L.J.,
came to the same conclusion (16).

My lords, this question is really one of inference from primary facts, but having I
regard to the way in which the matter has developed I should be reluctant to
differ from the courts below, and I do not think that the question whether the
doctrine of resulting trust applies to options, on the facts of this case in the least
degree invalidates the reasoning of the Court of Appeal (13) or its' conclusions on
this point.

---

(13) [1965] 2 All E.R. 37; [1966] Ch. 261.
(14) [1965] 2 All E.R. at p. 45, letter I; [1966] Ch. at p. 290.
(15) [1965] 2 All E.R. at p. 47, letter D; [1966] Ch. at pp. 292, 293.
(16) [1965] 2 All E.R. at p. 49, letter D; [1966] Ch. at p. 296.

A　　I agree with the conclusions of the Court of Appeal (17) and PLOWMAN, J.,
that the intention was that the trustee company should hold on such trusts as
might thereafter be declared.

That is sufficient to dispose of the appeal, but one question was debated in the
Court of Appeal (17), though not before your lordships, and that is whether the
option was held by the trustee company on such trusts as the trustee company

B　in its discretion should declare or as the taxpayer should declare. Once it is
established that the trustee company held solely as trustee that, as the Court
of Appeal (17) held, matters not. The taxpayer could at any time revoke that
discretion, if he had vested it in the trustee company.

Then, for the reasons I have given earlier, it follows that until these trusts
should be declared there was a resulting trust for the taxpayer. This is fatal to

C　his case, and I would dismiss the appeal.

LORD DONOVAN: My Lords, s. 53 (1) (c) of the Law of Property Act,
1925, enacts that the disposition of an equitable interest must be in writing signed
by the person disposing of it, or by his agent thereunto lawfully authorised in
writing or by will. This clearly refers to the disposition of an equitable interest as
such. If, owning the entire estate, legal and beneficial, in a piece of property, and

D　desiring to transfer that entire estate to another, I do so by means of a disposition
which ex facie deals only with the legal estate, it would be ridiculous to argue that
s. 53 (1) (c) has not been complied with, and that therefore the legal estate alone
has passed. The present case, it is true, is different in its facts in that the legal
and equitable estates in the shares were in separate ownership: but when the
taxpayer, being competent to do so, instructed the bank to transfer the shares to

E　the college, and made it abundantly clear that he wanted to pass, by means of that
transfer, his own beneficial, or equitable, interest, plus the bank's legal interest,
he achieved the same result as if there had been no separation of the interests.
The transfer thus made pursuant to his intentions and instructions was a disposition not of the equitable interest alone, but of the entire estate in the shares.
In such a case I see no room for the operation of s. 53 (1) (c).

F　　The Special Commissioners decided the case against the taxpayer on a construction of s. 415 (2) of the Income Tax Act, 1952, which the Crown did not seek to
support. The commissioners construed the words " in any circumstances whatsoever " appearing in that subsection to mean " in any circumstances whatsoever
that are practicable and possible ". This qualification hardly restricts the relevant
words at all, and would, indeed, embrace acts which were unlawful—a construc-

G　tion which must be rejected. But proceeding on it the Special Commissioners
found that the taxpayer could have set up further trusts with the trustee company
as trustee, for any objects he might wish, including himself. Accordingly, he had
not divested himself absolutely of the shares within the meaning of s. 415.

The Crown, before your lordships, agreed that the words in s. 415 (2) " in
any circumstances whatsoever " must receive some limitation of meaning: and

H　submitted that they connoted only such circumstances as, on a reasonable
construction of the settlement or arrangements, were within its contemplated
scope. With this, I would agree. But applying that test the result is, I think,
adverse to the Crown. I do not think that any such benefit as the commissioners
specify was within the contemplated scope of the arrangement.

That leaves the question of a resulting trust in the option, and this, indeed, is

I　not easy. The courts below (17) have held that such a trust existed—(a) because
the taxpayer caused the option right to be transferred to the trust company
without consideration and without declaring express trusts in respect of it; (b)
because he has not rebutted the presumption of a resulting trust to himself
which thus arises.

Both these propositions need to be carefully considered not only because of
the heavy fiscal consequences to the taxpayer himself, but also because the result

(17) [1965] 2 All E.R. 37; [1966] Ch. 261.

follows, if the propositions are sound, that there was a complete breach of trust   A
when the shares were ultimately acquired for £5,000 taken out of the children's
settlement, and settled on the terms of that disposition. Whatever the taxpayer
may have done since, there is no evidence that he consented at the time.

First, then, who provided the option? If one looks at the option deed itself,
it was the college and nobody else; but it is said that the taxpayer through his
agent stipulated for the option as a condition of the gift, and so must be regarded   B
as the grantor vis-à-vis the trust company. The Special Commissioners (before
whom this contention of a resulting trust was not advanced by the Crown) found
the following facts: (i) On Sept. 29, 1958, through his adviser Mr. Robins, the
taxpayer suggested a gift to the college of one hundred thousand " A " shares,
the dividend on which would provide the intended sum of £150,000. (ii) A few
days later, Mr. Robins suggested to the taxpayer that the college should give   C
an option on the shares to the trustee company, and the taxpayer agreed. (iii)
On Nov. 6, 1958, the college was asked by Mr. Robins whether the college would
agree to give the option to the trustee company. (iv) On Nov. 14, 1958, the
taxpayer wrote to Mr. Robins saying ". . . I have decided to give to the college
the one hundred thousand ' A ' shares . . ." (v) On Nov. 18, 1958, the college
informed Mr. Robins that it was prepared to grant the option. (vi) On Nov. 19,   D
1958, Mr. Robins handed to the college an executed transfer of the shares and the
option deed for sealing by the college. (vii) The college returned the transfer duly
sealed by itself to Mr. Robins on Nov. 25, 1958, for registration, and also the
option deed likewise sealed by the college. (viii) The whole purpose of the option
was to avoid the difficulty which might otherwise arise on a public flotation if
the college remained the registered holder of shares in the company. The taxpayer   E
having decided that the shares should not in that event remain in the hands of
the college did not interest himself further in the option.

The Special Commissioners, no doubt because the question of a resulting trust
was not raised before them, make no express finding on whether the taxpayer
provided the option. Both the courts below (18), however, state it as a fact. I
agree that it is an easy conclusion to draw. My doubt is whether it is not too   F
easy. If the taxpayer had said or represented to the college by himself or through
his agent that, if there were no option granted, then there would be no gift, the
conclusion would be clearly right. Supposing, however, the college were left free
to decide, and that the taxpayer's attitude was " I have already decided to give
you the shares and that will still be done; but without making it a condition of
the gift, I would like you to give the option. Will you do so? " Who, in that   G
case, would be the donor of the option to the trustee company, the college having
decided of its own free will to give it? Clearly, I should have thought, the
college.

As between these two alternatives, how does the evidence stand? There is
nothing, I venture to think, to enable anyone to come down firmly on one side
or the other; yet the Crown must show that the taxpayer was the donor of the   H
option, if they are to succeed in the contention of a resulting trust to him. The
facts which occasion my doubt are that originally the taxpayer had no thought
of an option: that when the idea was put into his mind he did not ask for the
option to be granted to himself: that after the college was first asked for the
option, but before it had decided to grant it, the taxpayer wrote to Mr. Robins
saying that he had decided to give the shares to the college and making no mention   I
of any condition: and that from start to finish there is no hint in the evidence of
" No option—no gift ". This has been simply inferred, and the inference is, in
my opinion, to say the least, doubtful. Unless, however, the taxpayer is shown,
despite the language of the option deed, to be the donor of it, the contention of a
resulting trust to him fails in limine. Indeed, if the college were the donor of the
option, there would be no resulting trust to anybody, for the transaction would

---

(18) [1965] 2 All E.R. 37; [1966] Ch. 261.

A not make sense except on the view that the trust company was to be the absolute owner.

I proceed to consider that question, however, on the footing that I am mistaken in my doubts whether the taxpayer granted the option, and that in fact he did so.

It was argued on his behalf that the onus is on the Crown to establish a resulting trust in the taxpayer's favour. It is the Crown who are asserting it, in the face

B of a deed which uses the language of an absolute grant. In this particular case where pure personality was transferred under seal to a stranger alone, and there is no hint on the face of the deed of any trust, I think that the proposition is correct; but I doubt in the end whether here it makes any difference to the ultimate result. Evidence bearing on the matter is in the Case Stated and its accompanying documents, and the problem now is to say whether that evidence,

C fairly considered, establishes a resulting trust with that reasonable certainty which is required if fiscal burdens are to follow.

The purpose of the option was to enable the one hundred thousand shares given to the college to be recovered so as to facilitate a possible future flotation of the shares in Vandervell Products, Ltd. This purpose would be achieved whether the taxpayer himself was entitled to the option, or whether it were in the hands of

D some other person whose co-operation, in the event of such a flotation, could be relied on. This would certainly be true of the trust company. Leaving aside the fact that its directors were friends and advisers of the taxpayer, it itself held over two million ordinary shares in Vandervell Products, Ltd. on the trusts of the children's settlement; and a smooth public flotation would, therefore, be of advantage to it, as well as to the taxpayer. (It is perhaps as well to recall that

E the one hundred thousand shares, the subject-matter of the option, had no voting rights, and no dividend rights save such as the taxpayer, in his capacity as controlling shareholder, chose to accord.)

At the outset, therefore, it is difficult to discern any compelling reason why the taxpayer should *not* let the trust company own the option absolutely. On the contrary, there are some compelling reasons why he should not own the option

F himself whether pursuant to a resulting trust or otherwise. It is obvious that the college was to get its £150,000 not by a straightforward cash payment of that sum by the taxpayer, but by substantial contributions from the public purse. (I say this, not in criticism, but because it is relevant to the case.) Thus the dividends which were to amount to £145,000 were to be gross dividends from which tax would be deducted at source. The tax would be recovered from the

G Revenue by the college as a charity. Then the declaration of such dividends was to be a protection for the taxpayer against a heavy liability for surtax which might otherwise fall on him under the provisions of ss. 245 et seq. of the Income Tax Act, 1952. These advantages would never accrue if the taxpayer retained the right to recover the shares back for himself by means of the option right. The college would not be entitled to repayment of tax, and the dividends

H of £145,000 gross would be liable to surtax as the taxpayer's own income. The persons acting for the taxpayer were not children in these matters: and while accountants are not lawyers (and should not try to be) there is one thing that is part of the general knowledge of every experienced accountant today; namely, that if you give property away, expecting to save tax thereby, you must reserve no right to get it back. When this consideration is added to the fact that it would

I seem to suit the taxpayer's purpose to give the option to the trust company outright, it is clear that one must walk a little warily on the path leading to a resulting trust.

It is, however, said by the Crown (in effect) that the accountant advising the taxpayer, while no doubt astute enough to avoid a direct grant of the option to his client, nevertheless, through an imperfect knowledge of the law of trusts, unwittingly saddled him with the beneficial ownership. This, of course, is the issue. The Crown relies on these circumstances. (i) Before the Special Commissioners there was no contention that there had been an outright gift of the

option to the trust company. (ii) It is found in the Case Stated that the directors A
and shareholders in the trust company never considered that the option could be
turned to account so as to benefit them personally. (iii) It had not been agreed
between the taxpayer's accountant and his solicitor (both directors of the trust
company) for what purpose the trustee company held the option. The accountant
considered that if, when the option was exercised, the trust company were
trustee of more than one settlement, the directors would consider the interests B
of the beneficiaries thereunder before deciding for what purpose to exercise the
option. In the meantime it was assumed that the trustees held the option for the
purposes of the 1949 children's settlement.

The point that the taxpayer never contended for an outright gift of the option
to the trust company, when the case was before the Special Commissioners, is a
legitimate one to make, and has to be borne in mind. It is certainly not con- C
clusive, however, any more than is the circumstance that before the Special
Commissioners the Crown never contended for a resulting trust. The circumstance
that the directors and shareholders of the trust company never considered that
the option right could be turned to account for their benefit is also a factor to be
taken into account.

If the true situation were that the option was granted to the company as a D
trustee on trusts to be decided hereafter that would be an end of the matter; but
why no mention of this in any document connected with the transaction, or in
any of the domestic records of the company? The company would have to agree
to such an arrangement, and there is no evidence, so far as I can see, that it ever
did. Moreover, there was no real reason why it should. From a practical point
of view, absolute ownership of the option by the trustee company would be no E
obstacle in the event of a public flotation of the Vandervell shares.

On the question of the purpose for which the trustee company held the option,
the accountant seems to have laboured for some time under a basic misconception.
Writing to the Revenue in 1961 his firm said that the trustee company could only
hold shares which came to them on trust: and, when the Revenue corrected this
view by referring to the company's memorandum of association, the accountant F
lamely replied: "Your view is probably correct." The misconception may,
however, have coloured other observations by the accountant which induced the
view that the option itself was held on trust.

In all the circumstances I should not feel safe in relying on the accountant's
various statements, whether favourable or unfavourable to the taxpayer.
Looking at the situation objectively I find an outright grant of the option to the G
trust company. For the purpose which the parties had in mind this was, in
the circumstances, both rational and acceptable. There was no reason why the
option should be held in trust for the taxpayer either expressly or by implication.
On the contrary, there were weighty reasons why it should not. The taxpayer
himself clearly considered that he had parted with the shares for good, and had H
no residual hold on them. On these facts, wherever the onus of proof may lie, I
should feel no confidence in drawing the conclusion of a resulting trust. I incline,
indeed, more to the view that the trust company owned the option absolutely.

During the course of the argument I suggested that the option might be caught
by cl. 1 of the children's settlement so as to be held on the trusts thereof. As a
result of the examination of this possibility which followed, I am, like your I
lordships, satisfied that it is not so.

The assessments on the taxpayer were made under the provisions of s. 404 (2)
of the Income Tax Act, 1952, as well as under s. 415, though the argument has
proceeded throughout mainly on the latter section. This is understandable. I
see no ground on which the assessments could be confirmed under s. 404 (2) if
they had to be discharged under s. 415.

I would allow the appeal.

A	　**LORD WILBERFORCE:** My Lords, this appeal, apart from the point which arises under s. 53 (1) (c) of the Law of Property Act, 1925, involves, in my opinion, no question of principle or of law. It depends on the interpretation one places on the facts as found. The Special Commissioners, PLOWMAN, J., and the Court of Appeal (19) have all taken a view of those facts adverse to the taxpayer, which though they may somewhat differ in expression coincide in

B	substance. This is that he failed to divest himself of all interest in the option, which in turn controlled the shares in Vandervell Products, Ltd., the subject of the gift. If it were not that there is a division of opinion in this House, I should think it sufficient to state my concurrence with the judgments of the Court of Appeal (19), since I can find no basis on which to arrive at a different factual conclusion which is that, while the taxpayer desired to make a certain amount of

C	income available to the Royal College of Surgeons through a gift of shares, he has failed to bring about that total divestiture of the source of that income which is required if he is to escape taxation on it. The strict requirements of s. 415 of the Income Tax Act, 1952, have thus not been satisfied. I must now endeavour to indicate my reasons for this opinion.

　　The taxpayer's plans first began to take shape in the summer of 1958. Having

D	formed the wish to give £150,000 to found a chair at the Royal College of Surgeons and having consulted his experts, he had decided by September to make over to the college the one hundred thousand " A " shares in his manufacturing company, Vandervell Products, Ltd. The advantage of so doing were threefold: first, the taxpayer, as the controlling shareholder in the company, could vote the necessary £150,000, or whatever sum he ultimately decided to give by way of dividend on

E	the " A " shares, as and when he pleased; secondly, the distribution of these dividends might help him to avoid a surtax assessment in respect of non-distributed profits of the company; thirdly, there might be a saving of estate duty.

　　The idea of the option came to Mr. Robins, the taxpayer's personal friend and financial adviser, as second thoughts. He was concerned about a possible public

F	flotation of the manufacturing company, and so as to avoid possible difficulties he thought " that it would not be desirable to give the shares outright to the college "—one may note at once some inherent hazards in the idea, or at least in the words in which he expressed it. So in November, 1958, he put to the college (and they accepted) the proposal that the college should grant an option to resell the shares to a company called Vandervell Trustee, Ltd., for £5,000. It was

G	explained in a letter of Nov. 19, 1958, that the taxpayer had decided to make £150,000 available to the college and that £145,000 (gross) would be paid by way of dividend on the shares in Vandervell Products, Ltd., the balance of £5,000 to be paid when the option should be exercised. The transaction was completed by transfer of the shares and the grant of the option on or about Nov. 25, 1958.

　　The critical question is whether the grant of the option prevented the taxpayer

H	from having divested himself absolutely of the shares. Obviously this depends on ascertaining to whom the option beneficially belonged and this was the issue which was enquired into by the Special Commissioners, to which evidence was directed, and on which findings were made. The effect of this evidence and the Special Commissioners' conclusions on it appear in the Case Stated and may be summarised as follows: The option was to be granted (and was granted) to

I	Vandervell Trustees, Ltd. "the only large shareholder apart from [the taxpayer] ". This company is a private company, with a capital of £100 held by Mr. Robins, Mr. Jobson (the taxpayer's solicitor) and Mr. Green (Mr. Robins' partner), which three gentlemen were also the directors of the company having taken office at the taxpayer's request. The trustee company has power by its memorandum to carry on a wide range of business activity but its principal object is to act as trustee. At all material times it had only three activities: (i) as trustee of a settlement of Dec. 30, 1949, of which the taxpayer's children were the

---

(19) [1965] 2 All E.R. 37; [1966] Ch. 261.

main beneficiaries, in which capacity it held 2,053,308 " B " shares in the A
manufacturing company; (ii) as trustee of a savings fund set up by
the manufacturing company; (iii) as grantee of the option.

The deed by which the option was granted merely states that it was granted
by the college to the trustee company. In what capacity did the trustee company
receive it? It has never been suggested that it received the option as trustee of
the savings fund, because no part of that fund could, under the rules, be invested B
in shares of the manufacturing company. So there are left three alternatives:
(i) that the option was held on the trusts of the 1949 settlement; (ii) that the
option was held on trusts not at the time determined, but to be decided on at a
later date; (iii) that the option was held by the trustee company free from any
trust and (at most) subject to an understanding that it or the shares when it was
exercised would be disposed of in a suitable manner.   C

The Special Commissioners held an oral hearing in order to decide on this
question. Before they did so, there was some correspondence which was of some
significance, because it gave shape to the issues as the commissioners had to
decide them. On Dec. 29, 1960, the inspector of taxes asked on what trusts
Vandervell Trustees, Ltd. intended to hold the shares on exercise of the option
(it was not exercised till 1961). The reply, from the taxpayer's accountants, was D
" it will be for Vandervell Trustees, Ltd. to elect *on what trusts* they shall hold
the shares if the option be exercised ". On Apr. 6, 1961, the inspector asked why
Vandervell Trustees, Ltd. would in the event of the option being exercised have
to hold the shares on trust. The answer to this was:

" Vandervell Trustees, Ltd. are a trustee company with no business of their
own. Therefore, any shares coming to them could only be held *on trust*. If E
this option is exercised it is probable that they would be held on the trusts
of [the children's settlement of 1949]."

So the expressed contention at this stage was that the option was held on trust:
indeed no alternative was in contemplation and the issue was whether the trust
was such that Mr. Vandervell benefited or could benefit under it.

With this preliminary statement of position, the hearing before the commis- F
sioners took place. Both the taxpayer and Mr. Robins gave evidence, and it
seems clear that in their evidence they adhered to what they had maintained in
the letters. The commissioners, in their statement of facts, fully reviewed the
history of the matter; they brought out the following salient points: (i) The
whole purpose of the option was to avoid difficulties in the event of a public
flotation which might arise if the college was the holder of shares in the company. G
The trustee company was considered the suitable person to hold the shares. The
taxpayer considered that he had parted with the shares and gave Mr. Robins carte
blanche to make what arrangements he thought fit. (ii) The directors and shareholders of the trustee company never considered that the option or their shares
in the trustee company could be turned to account in such a way as to benefit
them personally. (iii) It was not formally agreed between Mr. Jobson (the solicitor) H
and Mr. Robins for what purpose the trustee company held the option; each of
them assumed that it was held for the purposes of the 1949 settlement. Both of
them, however, had in mind that it might be exercised for the purpose of a
proposed new trust for employees. Then—I quote—

" the evidence of Mr. Robins on this point (which we accepted) was that I
if, when the time came to exercise the option, the trustee company should
have been trustee of other settlements besides the 1949 children's settlement,
the directors of the trustee company would have considered the rights and
interests of the beneficiaries before deciding for what purpose to exercise
the option."

The commissioners then stated (as is usual) the contentions of the parties. The
only positive contention formulated by the taxpayer as to the ownership of the
option was that the trustee company took the option as trustee of the 1949

A settlement. The findings of the commissioners were: (a) that the trustee company was not free to deal with the option, or the shares, in any way it wished, but held the option and would hold the shares as a trustee; (b) that when the trustee company acquired the option it was not finally settled for what objects it would hold the shares if the option should be exercised. There was a strong possibility that they would be held on the trusts of the 1949 settlement but this was not

B bound to happen: other trusts might be set up, under which the taxpayer might be a beneficiary, and there was nothing to prevent the trustee company from applying the shares for the purposes of those trusts.

On these findings it was, in my opinion, at once clear that the taxpayer's contention that the option became subject to the trusts of the children's settlement of 1949 must fail, for the reason that it was not the intention of the settlor,

C or of his plenipotentiary, Mr. Robins, at the time the option was exercised that this should be so. I need not elaborate this point since I understand that there is no disagreement about it. This was the taxpayer's main (if not the sole) contention before the commissioners and PLOWMAN, J., and it remained his first contention on this appeal. The alternative which I have numbered (iii) (see p. 16, letter C, ante) and which is expressed in the printed case as being that the option was

D held by the trustee company in equity as well as in law as the absolute owner thereof for the purposes of its business, is, of course, one which the taxpayer is entitled to put forward, as a contention of law, at any stage, provided that it is consistent with the facts as found by the commissioners. It is on that contention that the taxpayer ultimately fell back. For my part, I cannot find that it is so consistent.

E I would be disposed to agree that it might be wrong to put too much weight on the commissioners' finding which I have quoted under (b) (see letter A, supra) or at least on its literal wording—and possibly the Court of Appeal (20) did so; but it still cannot be disregarded altogether. I might accept that the taxpayer should not be bound by the opinions held by Mr. Robins and Mr. Jobson—they may have misapprehended the legal situation; but it still remains the case that there

F was evidence, from Mr. Robins himself, of his contemporary intentions. Moreover making all allowances, the evidence fairly read to my mind admits fairly of one interpretation only, put on it by all who have so far considered it, that the option was vested in the trustee company as a trustee, and that this was the intention of Mr. Robins at the time when it was granted.

Correspondingly, the evidence points clearly away from any conclusion that

G the trustee company held beneficially, or for the purpose of its business. It had no business, no function, except as a trustee; no assets, except as a trustee. The £5,000 to be paid if the option was to be exercised was, as a term of the arrangement between the taxpayer and the college, part of the £150,000 benefaction; how could that come from the company's own resources? To extract from the findings a conclusion that the trustee company was to hold free from any trust

H but possibly subject to some understanding or gentleman's agreement seems to me, rather than even a benevolent interpretation of the evidence, a reconstruction of it. I may add that had this contention been put forward at the hearing before the Special Commissioners the Revenue might well have been tempted to explore, by cross-examination, the real control of the trustee company and to argue that the case came within s. 415 (2) of the Income Tax Act, 1952.

I If, then, as I think, both the first two alternatives fail, there remains only the third, which, to my mind, corresponds exactly with Mr. Robins' intentions, namely, that the option was held by the trustee company on trusts which were undefined, or in the air.

As to the consequences, there has been some difference and possibly lack of clarity below. The commissioners held that the initially undefined trusts could be defined later in a way which might benefit the taxpayer, and they found the benefit to the taxpayer in this circumstance. The Court of Appeal (20), starting

---

(20) [1965] 2 All E.R. 37; [1966] Ch. 261.

from the fact that the trustee company took the option as a volunteer, thought A
that this was a case where the presumption of a resulting trust arose and was not
displaced. For my part, I prefer a slightly different and simpler approach. The
transaction has been investigated on the evidence of the settlor and his agent and
the facts have been found. There is no need, nor room, as I see it, to invoke a
presumption. The conclusion, on the facts found, is simply that the option was
vested in the trustee company as a trustee on trusts, not defined at the time, B
possibly to be defined later. The equitable, or beneficial interest, however, cannot
remain in the air: the consequence in law must be that it remains in the settlor.
There is no need to consider some of the more refined intellectualities of the
doctrine of resulting trust, nor to speculate whether, in possible circumstances,
the shares might be applicable for the taxpayer's benefit: he had, as the direct
result of the option and of the failure to place the beneficial interest in it securely C
away from him, not divested himself absolutely of the shares which it controlled.

There remains the alternative point taken by the Crown that in any event, by
virtue of s. 53 (1) (c) of the Law of Property Act, 1925, the taxpayer never
effectively disposed of the beneficial interest in the shares to the Royal College of
Surgeons. This argument I cannot accept. Section 53 (1) (c), a successor to the
dormant s. 9 of the Statute of Frauds, has recently received a new lease of life as an D
instrument in the hands of the revenue. The subsection, which has twice recently
brought litigants to this House (*Grey* v. *Inland Revenue Comrs.* (21), *Oughtred* v.
Inland Revenue Comrs. (22)), is certainly not easy to apply to the varied transactions in equitable interests which now occur. However, in this case no problem
arises. The shares in question, the one hundred thousand " A " shares in Vandervell Products, Ltd., were, prior to Nov. 14, 1958, registered in the name of the E
National Provincial Bank, Ltd., on trust for the taxpayer absolutely. On Nov. 14,
1958, the taxpayer's solicitor received from the bank a blank transfer of the
shares, executed by the bank, and the share certificate. So at this stage the
taxpayer was the absolute master of the shares and only needed to insert his
name as transferee in the transfer and to register it to become the full legal owner.
He was also the owner in equity. On Nov. 19, 1958, the solicitor (or Mr. Robins— F
the Case is ambiguous) on behalf of the taxpayer, who intended to make a gift,
handed the transfer to the college which, in due course, sealed it and obtained
registration of the shares in the college's name. The case should then be regarded
as one in which the taxpayer himself has, with the intention to make a gift, put
the college in a position to become the legal owner of the shares, which the college
in fact became. If the taxpayer had died before the college had obtained registra- G
tion, it is clear on the principle of *Re Rose, Midland Bank Executor & Trustee Co.,
Ltd.* v. *Rose* (23) that the gift would have been complete, on the basis that he had
done everything in his power to transfer the legal interest, with an intention to
give, to the college. No separate transfer, therefore, of the equitable interest ever
came to or needed to be made and there is no room for the operation of the subsection. What the position would have been had there simply been an oral H
direction to the legal owner (viz., the bank) to transfer the shares to the college,
followed by such a transfer, but without any document in writing signed by the
taxpayer as equitable owner, is not a matter which calls for consideration here.
The Crown's argument on this point fails but, for the reasons earlier given, I
would dismiss the appeal.

Appeal dismissed. I

Solicitors: *Culross & Co.* (for the taxpayer); *Solicitor of Inland Revenue.*

[*Reported by* KATHLEEN J. H. O'BRIEN, *Barrister-at-Law.*]

---

(21) [1959] 3 All E.R. 603; [1960] A.C. 1.
(22) [1959] 3 All E.R. 623; [1960] A.C. 206.
(23) [1948] 2 All E.R. 971; [1949] Ch. 78.

A

TROW v. IND COOPE, LTD. AND ANOTHER.
TROW v. IND COOPE (WEST MIDLANDS), LTD.
AND ANOTHER.

[QUEEN'S BENCH DIVISION (Blain, J.), October 31, 1966.]

B *Time—Computation—Duration of specified period—Period " beginning with
the date of . . ."—Writ of summons issued on Sept. 10, 1965, and served on
Sept. 10, 1966—Validity of writ for the purpose of service for twelve months
beginning with the date of its issue—Whether service out of time—R.S.C.,
Ord. 6, r. 8 (1).*

In computing the period for which a writ remains valid, by virtue of R.S.C.,
C   Ord. 6, r. 8 (1), for the purpose of service, the period of " twelve months
beginning with the date of its issue " is a period that includes the day on
which the writ is issued; and accordingly in the present case the service on
Sept. 10, 1966, of writs issued on Sept. 10, 1965, was invalid (see p. 24, letter
B, post).

Hare v. *Gocher* ([1962] 2 All E.R. 763) applied.
D   *Goldsmiths' Co.* v. *West Metropolitan Ry. Co.* ([1900-03] All E.R. Rep. 667)
distinguished.

[As to the inclusion or exclusion of first and last days in the computation of
prescribed periods of time, see 37 HALSBURY'S LAWS (3rd Edn.) 92-99, paras.
161-173; and for cases on the subject, see 45 DIGEST (Repl.) 252-257, *195-250*.
As to the service and renewal of writs within the proper time, see 24 HALS-
E   BURY'S LAWS (3rd Edn.) 199, 200, para. 357, and 30 ibid., p. 303, para. 558; and
for cases on the subject, see 32 DIGEST (Repl.) 623, 624, *2001-2013*, DIGEST
(Practice) 311, 312, *358-368*, and 3rd DIGEST SUPP.]

Cases referred to:

Baker v. *Bowketts Cakes, Ltd.*, [1966] 2 All E.R. 290; [1966] 1 W.L.R. 861.
F   *Goldsmiths' Co.* v. *West Metropolitan Ry. Co.*, [1900-03] All E.R. Rep. 667;
[1904] 1 K.B. 1; 72 L.J.K.B. 931; 89 L.T. 428; 68 J.P. 41; 45 Digest
(Repl.) 257, *247*.
Hare v. *Gocher*, [1962] 2 All E.R. 763; [1962] 2 Q.B. 641; [1962] 3 W.L.R. 339;
126 J.P. 395; 45 Digest (Repl.) 257, *250*.
North, Re, Ex p. Hasluck, [1895] 2 Q.B. 264; 64 L.J.Q.B. 694; 59 J.P. 724;
G   sub nom. *Re North, Ex p. Parkinson*, 72 L.T. 854; 45 Digest (Repl.)
252, *197*.
Rodriguez v. *Parker*, [1966] 2 All E.R. 349; [1966] 3 W.L.R. 546.

Interlocutory Appeals.

These were two appeals by defendants to the judge in chambers from decisions
of the district registrar of Hanley, Stoke-on-Trent, that writs in two actions for
H   personal injuries which were issued on Sept. 10, 1965, by the plaintiff, Christina
Trow (married woman), against Ind Coope, Ltd., and John Murphy in the first
action, and against Ind Coope (West Midlands), Ltd., and the said John Murphy
in the second action, were not served out of time under R.S.C., Ord. 6, r. 8 (1)
when served on the defendant Murphy in the first action and on both defendants
in the second action on Sept. 10, 1966.   The appeals were heard in chambers
I   and the judgment, which (at the invitation of counsel) dealt with both appeals
together was delivered in open court.   The facts are set out in the judgment.

S. Tumim for the defendants.
W. G. Wingate, Q.C., and *G. Slynn* for the plaintiff.

Cur. adv. vult.

Oct. 31.   **BLAIN, J.:** In the first action, that is to say 1965 T. No. 521,
where the defendants are named as Ind Coope, Ltd. and John Murphy, Ind
Coope, Ltd. and John Murphy are sued for damages in respect of personal injuries

Affirmed. C.A. [1967] 2 All E.R. 900.

alleged to have been sustained by the plaintiff through their negligence or breaches A
of statutory duty on Sept. 11, 1962.   The second action is by the same plaintiff
against Ind Coope (West Midlands), Ltd. and the same John Murphy; the
plaintiff sues those two defendants, the different defendant company though the
same individual defendant, for what appears to be precisely the same thing,
namely damages sustained through negligence or breach of statutory duty on the
same date and, I suppose, in respect of the same accident.   Why there should B
be two separate actions, and particularly how there could be two such separate
actions against the defendant Murphy I do not know, but in these interlocutory
appeals it is not pertinent to enquire.

The cause of action is alleged to have arisen on Sept. 11, 1962, although writs
were issued on Sept. 10, 1965, the last day before expiry of the period limited
by the Statute of Limitations.   In the first action the writ was served on the C
defendant Murphy on Sept. 10, 1966; the date of service, if any, on the defendant
company is not material to these appeals.   In the second action the writ was
served on both the defendant company and the defendant Murphy also on Sept.
10, 1966.   I was informed that in each case service was at an earlier time of day
on Sept. 10, 1966, than the time of day on which the writs had been issued on
Sept. 10, 1965.   In the first action the defendant Murphy, and in the second D
action both defendants, applied by summons to the district registrar of Hanley,
Stoke-on-Trent, for an order that the service of the writ and all subsequent
proceedings be set aside on the grounds that the writ was not served during the
period of twelve months beginning with the date of its issue.   In passing, the
form of summons originally sought an order that the writ of summons itself be
set aside, but I have agreed to treat this as an application to set aside service, E
and I propose to deal with it as an application accordingly.

The district registrar dismissed both applications and these are appeals by the
defendant Murphy in the first action and by both defendants in the second action
against those decisions.   I will deal with the two appeals as one, as I was invited
to do.   R.S.C., Ord. 6, r. 8 (1) provides as follows:

" For the purpose of service, a writ . . . is valid in the first instance for F
twelve months beginning with the date of its issue . . ."

I do not think that I need read any more of that rule.   The full question in issue
is the interpretation of the words " twelve months beginning with the date of
its issue ", and the key words are first of all the word " beginning " and secondly,
the word " date ".   It is, I think, conceded on the one hand that if the word G
" time " were substituted for the word " date " then the writs were still valid
when served, whereas if the word " day " were substituted for the word " date ",
then the writs were no longer valid when served.   I say that I think that is
conceded, because nothing else was argued.   I do not wish to embarrass either
party if they feel that they have not made a binding concession, and I certainly
do not approach it as that. H

On behalf of the plaintiff reference was made to a sentence in the judgment of
LORD DENNING, M.R., in the case of *Baker* v. *Bowketts Cakes, Ltd.* (1), where
LORD DENNING, M.R., said:

" Now a writ is only valid in the first instance for twelve months.   So this
writ was only valid from May 28, 1964, until May 28, 1965."

That statement seems to accord with the view, if it were being so decided, that I
the word " date " in the writ is the equivalent to the word " time ".   In the same
case, however, HARMAN, L.J., said (2):

" Now it is true that you may wait until the 364th day of the third year
before issuing your writ and until the 364th day of one year more before
serving it and you will still be in time."

(1) [1966] 2 All E.R. 290 at p. 291.
(2) [1966] 2 All E.R. at p. 293.

A HARMAN, L.J.'s statement would seem to accord with the view that the word
" date " in the writ is equivalent to the word " day " and not the word " time ".
Both of those statements were obiter and I do not imagine that any argument had
been addressed to the Court of Appeal on the point which is in question today.
Reference was also made by counsel for the plaintiff to the case of *Rodriguez* v.
Parker (3), where one can find, on successive pages, two single lined statements
B by NIELD, J., the first being a statement of fact, where he said (4): " The writ
in the action was issued on June 11, 1964 ", and the second statement where he
said (5): " There was no reply to that letter, and on June 11, 1965, the period
of one year from the date of the issue of the writ expired." Putting those two
sentences together, they would appear to accord with the view that the word
" time " should be substituted for the word " date ". That, too, was obiter, there
C having been, so far as I can ascertain, no discussion about it or reason to define
the precise date of expiry of the period in question on that occasion. I do not need
to emphasise that no disrespect is intended to my lords who were dealing with
those cases when I say that the contexts of these dicta are such that I do not regard
them as decisive of the point now in issue.

Counsel for the plaintiff also referred me to the provisions of R.S.C., Ord. 3,
D r. 2, which reads in part as follows:

" (1) Any period of time fixed by these rules or by any judgment, order
or direction for doing any act shall be reckoned in accordance with the
following provisions of this rule. (2) Where the act is required to be done
within a specified period after or from a specified date, the period begins
immediately after that date. (3) Where the act is required to be done within
E or not less than a specified period before a specified date, the period ends
immediately before that date. (4) Where the act is required to be done a
specified number of clear days before or after a specified date, at least that
number of days must intervene between the day on which the act is done
and that date."

F Those rules, he says, are of general application and show the basis for calculation
of any period fixed by the rules. I make two comments about R.S.C., Ord. 3,
r. 2; first, that paras. (2), (3) and (4) are all dealing with acts " required
to be done "; they deal with mandatory compliance with orders, not with
circumstances where nothing is required to be done, and there is no mandate.
For example, if the court orders somebody to leave premises or to abate a nuisance
G by a certain date, that is mandatory, and very serious consequences may follow
if the order is disobeyed. In the cases with which I am dealing, there is no obligation, indeed there is no obligation in any case to issue a writ and no obligation
to serve a writ that has been issued. That is the first comment which I make.
The second is perhaps of more importance, namely, that whilst these rules under
R.S.C., Ord. 3, r. 2, are of general application they do not purport to apply to a
H case where there is some statutory or equivalent timetable elsewhere laid down
for the circumstances of the particular case. The paragraph in the 1966 edition
of the ANNUAL PRACTICE (6), where the cases on that Order and rule are to be
found, which paragraph is headed " Exceptions " is, in my view, correct, I
quote:

" Nevertheless in construing any statute or instrument, ' the rational mode
I of computation is to have regard in each case to the purpose for which the
computation is to be made '."

That is a quotation from LORD ESHER, M.R., in his judgment in the case of
Re North, Ex p. Hasluck (7). The note goes on to say: " In a contract for a year's

---

(3) [1966] 2 All E.R. 349.   (4) [1966] 2 All E.R. at p. 351, letter G.
(5) [1966] 2 All E.R. at p. 352, letter D.
(6) See at p. 22 of the ANNUAL PRACTICE, 1966, and p. 11 of Vol. 1, The SUPREME
COURT PRACTICE, 1967, notes to R.S.C., Ord. 3, r. 2.
(7) [1895] 2 Q.B. 264 at p. 269.

service commencing on a certain day, the servant is considered to serve the whole   A
of that day ", that is to say the first day. It then goes on: " In a sentence of
imprisonment, the whole of the day on which the imprisonment first takes place
is part of the sentence ", and then comes the most relevant passage (8):

" If an Act, which receives the Royal Assent on July 28 (sic), is to come
into force ' at the expiration of one month beginning with the date on
which it is passed ', that date is included in the computation of the period,   B
and the Act comes into force immediately after midnight August 28/29;
and similarly if it provides that ' no offence shall be committed at any time
within the period of two months beginning with the commencement of
this Act ', that period ends at midnight October 28."

The case of *Hare* v. *Gocher* (9) there referred to is a case where a phrase comparable   C
with the one which I have to construe in the Order occurs in an Act of Parliament, the Caravan Sites and Control of Development Act, 1960. It is perhaps
convenient first to read s. 14 of the Act. Section 14, so far as material, provides:

" No offence shall be committed under s. 1 of this Act in respect of an
existing site at any time within the period of two months beginning with the   D
commencement of this Act, and if within that period the occupier of an
existing site duly makes an application under this Part of this Act for a site
licence, no offence shall be committed under s. 1 of this Act in respect of the
existing site at any time after the expiration of the said period, and before a
site licence is first issued in respect of that existing site."

Then s. 50 (4) reads: E

" This Act shall come into force at the expiration of a period of one month
beginning with the date on which it is passed."

The phrase " beginning with the date " is the important phrase for today's
purposes (10). In *Hare* v. *Gocher* (11) the headnote, which appears to be accurate,
said that at noon on Oct. 29, 1960, the defendant, the occupier of land on which   F
there was an existing caravan site, delivered an application for a site licence to
the licensing authority, under s. 14 of the Caravan Sites and Control of Development Act, 1960. On Sept. 21, 1961, an information was preferred against the
defendant alleging that he had permitted part of his land to be used as a caravan
site without a site licence, contrary to s. 1 of the Act of 1960. At the hearing, the
issue before the justices was whether the defendant had made his application   G
within the two months' period " beginning with the commencement of this Act ".
By s. 50 (4) the Act of 1960 was to come into force " at the expiration . . . of one
month beginning with the date on which it is passed ". The Act of 1960 received
the Royal Assent on July 29, 1960. The justices held that the two months' period
elapsed at midnight on Oct. 28, 1960, and convicted the defendant. The defendant
appealed and it was held that the wording of s. 14 and s. 50 (4) of the Caravan   H
Sites and Control of Development Act, 1960, had been adopted by the legislature
to prevent the construction that the period of time should exclude the date
from which time commenced to run; accordingly, the date on which the Act of
1960 received the Royal Assent was to be included in the computation and therefore the Act of 1960 commenced immediately after midnight of August 28/29,

I

(8) The date July 28 is stated in error in the note quoted: the Caravan Sites and
Control of Development Act, 1960, received the Royal Assent on July 29, 1960. This
date is correctly given in *Hare* v. *Gocher* ([1962] 2 All E.R. 763 at p. 765, letters F, G;
[1962] 2 Q.B. 641 at p. 646).
(9) [1962] 2 All E.R. 763; [1962] 2 Q.B. 641.
(10) The Caravan Sites and Control of Development Act, 1960, s. 1, s. 14 and s. 50,
are set out in 40 HALSBURY's STATUTES (2nd Edn.) 1068, 1077, 1102.
(11) [1962] 2 All E.R. 763; [1962] 2 Q.B. 641.

A 1960, and the period of two months in which the defendant had to apply for a site licence ended at midnight on Oct. 28, 1960. The defendant was therefore twelve hours late in delivering his application and was rightly convicted. WINN, J., delivered the only judgment of any length, and he said (12):

B " This is an appeal by Case Stated by justices for the borough of King's Lynn in respect of their adjudication as a magistrates' court . . . by which they convicted the appellant of an offence under s. 1 (1) of the Caravan Sites and Control of Development Act, 1960 . . . [His LORDSHIP then read s. 1 (1), stated the facts and continued:] Section 14 provides: ' No offence shall be committed under s. 1 of this Act in respect of an existing site at any time within the period of two months beginning with the commencement of this Act, and if within that period the occupier of an existing site duly makes an applica-

C tion under this Part of this Act for a site licence, no offence shall be committed under s. 1 of this Act in respect of the existing site at any time after the expiration of the said period, and before a site licence is first issued in respect of that existing site.'

" The contest between the parties was whether or not the application made by the appellant was made in time, that is to say, made ' within the period

D of two months beginning with the commencement of this Act '. ' The commencement of this Act ' is defined by s. 50 (4) in these words: ' This Act shall come into force at the expiration of a period of one month beginning with the date on which it is passed.' That phrase, and the phrase ' within the period of two months beginning with the commencement of this Act ', fall to be considered on this appeal.

E " In my judgment, it is not necessary, for the purposes of this case, to consider in any detail earlier decisions of the Court of Appeal, the Divisional Court and other courts which have construed the meaning of similar but by no means identical words. I refer to Goldsmiths' Co. v. West Metropolitan Ry. Co. (13), to emphasise that the words that there fell to be considered

F were these: ' The powers of the company for the compulsory purchase of lands for the purposes of this Act (14) shall cease after the expiration of three years from the passing of this Act.' The judgments of SIR RICHARD HENN COLLINS, M.R., and MATHEW, L.J., make it clear that, in their judgment, the general rule, if any, to be applied, as from the date of that decision for the construction of such words, subject to controlling terms which would

G indicate a contrary intention, is that the first day of the period referred to should be excluded in the computation. There are later decisions, which I think that it is unnecessary to consider for the purposes of this judgment, so I pass at once to emphasise that, in this case, one had the words ' beginning with the commencement of this Act '. It is submitted by counsel for the respondent, as I think correctly, that these words are to be taken to have been

H adopted in order to avoid equivocation, and to exclude the application for the purposes of this statute of the rule which, in Goldsmiths' Co. v. West Metropolitan Ry. Co. (13), was said to be the general rule insofar as any general rule could be accepted as existing."

The appeal was dismissed and the justices' decision upheld.

I The distinction is quite clear, namely, that in the Act (14) which fell for consideration in the Goldsmiths' case (13) the words were " three years from the passing of this Act "; whereas in the Caravan Sites and Control of Development Act, 1960, with which the court was dealing in Hare v. Gocher (15), the words

---

(12) [1962] 2 All E.R. at pp. 764, 765; [1962] 2 Q.B. at pp. 644-646.
(13) [1900-03] All E.R. Rep. 667; [1904] 1 K.B. 1.
(14) Section 29 of the West Metropolitan Railway Act, 1899 (repealed).
(15) [1962] 2 All E.R. 763; [1962] 2 Q.B. 641.

were " beginning with the date ", and it so happens that these words " beginning **A** with the date ", of the significance of which I must assume that the makers of the Rules of the Supreme Court were fully conscious, form the phrase that we find in R.S.C., Ord. 6, r. 8 (1), which says: ". . . a writ . . . is valid in the first instance for twelve months beginning with the date of its issue." The difference seems to be that where a statute reads " from the passing of this Act ", the day on which the Act is passed is excluded in computing the period, whereas where **B** the words are " beginning with the date of the passing of this Act ", the day on which the Royal Assent is given is included in computing the period.

I can find no distinction between the words in s. 50 (4) of the Caravan Sites and Control of Development Act, 1960, and the phrase in R.S.C., Ord. 6, r. 8 (1), and accordingly I allow these appeals and order that service be set aside. The service was out of time; it will be set aside, the plaintiff paying the costs of these **C** proceedings before me and before the district registrar.

I have already indicated, before adjourning into open court for this judgment, that I would give leave to appeal, and there is one matter which I think particularly is of some importance and which I consider should be amended if my decision is correct. The note on the prescribed form of writ in general use is wrong (16), and unless what I have decided is reversed, no doubt consideration will be **D** given to the question whether it should be altered in some way in future. That is because of the effect it could have, particularly on laymen who get writs served on them and who do not have the benefit of legal advice, in whose case it could be a very important matter. It is primarily for that reason that I felt it right to adjourn into open court for the purposes of giving judgment.

E
Appeals allowed.

Solicitors: *Preston, Lane-Claypon & O'Kelly*, agents for *Hollinshead & Moody*, Stoke-on-Trent (for the defendants); *Waterhouse & Co.*, agents for *Nelson & Steele*, Kidsgrove, Staffs. (for the plaintiff).

[*Reported by* K. DIANA PHILLIPS, *Barrister-at-Law.*] **F**

G

H

I

_____

(16) The note reads: " This writ may not be served more than twelve calendar months after the above date unless renewed by order of the Court." The " above date " is the date of issue of the writ. The note is in the prescribed form, No. 1 of App. A to the R.S.C., incorporated by reference in form No. 2 (THE SUPREME COURT PRACTICE 1967, Vol. 2, pp. 1, 3).

A   DU SAUTOY v. SYMES AND OTHERS.

[CHANCERY DIVISION (Cross, J.), October 13, 14, 17, 1966.]

Option—Purchase—Freehold—Duration—Clause conferring option and also right of pre-emption—Whether option continued after failure to exercise right of pre-emption.

B *Option—Purchase—Freehold—Land charge—Registration as estate contract—Official certificate of search obtained by subsequent purchaser of land showing no entry in respect of option—Application for search containing insufficiently clear description of land—Whether certificate conclusive in favour of purchaser—Whether option-holder entitled to specific performance against purchaser—Land Charges Act, 1925 (15 & 16 Geo. 5 c. 22), s. 17 (3).*

C *Specific Performance—Delay—Action not brought to trial quickly—Right of pre-emption offered but not exercised—Twenty-one year option exercised subsequently—Whether specific performance would be granted or plaintiff left to remedy in damages.*

On the sale of the agricultural land of Reddings Farm (which comprised some 226 acres) in the parish of Tillingham, Essex, to the second to fifth
D defendants the vendor reserved an option, contained in cl. 14 of the conditions of sale, as follows—" The vendor shall have the right at any time within twenty-one years from the date hereof upon giving to the purchasers one month's notice in writing to repurchase from the purchasers or their successors in title the easternmost portion of enclosure No. 174 having an area of twenty acres for the sum of £1,000 and if the purchasers shall within
E the period aforesaid desire to sell the same they shall first offer it to the vendor who shall notify the purchasers within one month if he desires to purchase ". In September, 1958, registration under the Land Charges Act, 1925, was effected in respect of cl. 14 on the vendor's behalf against the names of the second to fifth defendants. The entries on the register gave, under the heading " Parish or Place ", the word " Tillingham ", and under
F the heading " Short Description of land (if practicable) " the description " Ordnance Survey 174 ". This was a correct description. The conveyance to the second to fifth defendants on Oct. 16, 1958, did not refer to cl. 14. In June, 1959, the vendor conveyed the farmhouse of Reddings Farm, which had not been included in the sale of the agricultural land, to the plaintiff; and by a separate deed the vendor assigned to the plaintiff
G the benefit of cl. 14. Notice of this assignment was given by the plaintiff to the second to fifth defendants. On Aug. 29, 1962, the second to fifth defendants informed the plaintiff that they were proposing to sell Reddings farm land, and enquired whether the plaintiff desired to exercise his right to re-purchase the twenty acres under cl. 14. The plaintiff did not notify the second to fifth defendants within one month of his desire to re-purchase.
H On Sept. 25, 1962, the solicitors for the prospective purchaser (the first defendant*), who was contemplating buying, in addition to Reddings Farm, fields Nos. 87 and 118 in the adjoining parish of Asheldham, applied for an official search in the land charges register for entries under the names of the second to fifth defendants. The application made for search, so far as material to the description of the land, was " for any subsisting entries . . .
I affecting land in the county of *Essex* parish of *Tillingham and Asheldham*†, place or district of *Tillingham and Asheldham* known as *O.S. Field Nos. 87 and 118 Asheldham and Reddings Farm, Tillingham* ". The official certificate of search, dated Sept. 26, 1962, read " no subsisting entries ". On Oct. 5, 1962, the plaintiff notified the solicitors for the second to fifth defendants

---

* The first defendant and his father were in partnership; the land was conveyed to the first defendant, the purchase price being paid out of partnership money; see p. 29, letter D, post.
† The italic type shows the words inserted in the printed form of application.

that he wished to purchase the twenty acres. On Oct. 15, the farm land   A
(including enclosure No. 174) was conveyed by the second to fifth defendants
to the first defendant.   On Jan. 15, 1963, the plaintiff, purporting to act
under the first part of cl. 14, gave the defendants by letters one month's
notice to re-purchase the field.   On Jan. 25, 1963, the plaintiff issued a
writ against the defendants claiming (as against the first defendant) specific
performance of a contract for re-purchase or pre-emption by virtue of cl. 14   B
and (as against the second to fifth defendants) damages for breach of contract.   Pleadings were closed on Apr. 25, 1963, but the action was not set
down until application to strike out was made by the first defendant, and in
February, 1966, an order was made for trial on or before Mar. 4, 1966.

   Held: (i) on the true construction of cl. 14, (a) cl. 14 conferred two rights,
viz., an option to re-purchase and a right of pre-emption, and the first right   C
continued to subsist notwithstanding that the second had lapsed (see p. 33,
letter H, post);   and (b) the personal liability of the second to fifth defendants
to the plaintiff under cl. 14 did not come to an end when, having offered
the plaintiff pre-emption, they sold the land including the twenty acres
(see p. 34, letters D and G, post).

   Wright v. *Dean* ([1948] 2 All E.R. 415) distinguished.   D

   (ii) although, as a matter of construction of the Land Charges Act, 1925,
a certificate of search duly obtained in respect of particular land and showing
no subsisting entry was conclusive by virtue of s. 17 (3)* of the absence of
registration at its date against the names mentioned, yet a purchaser was
not protected by s. 17 (3) unless the application for search gave no reasonable scope for misunderstanding as to, e.g., the land in question; in the   E
present case the description of the land in the application for search was
such that it might well have been read as relating only to fields Nos. 87
and 118, and not as relating first to those fields and secondly to Reddings
Farm, with the consequence that the plaintiff was not debarred from, but
was entitled to, relief against the first defendant (see p. 35, letter H, p. 36,
letters B and D, and p. 37, letters A and C, post).   F

   Stock v. *Wanstead & Woodford Borough Council* ([1961] 2 All E.R. 433)
applied.

   (iii) the case was not one in which the plaintiff should be refused specific,
performance and left to his remedy in damages, notwithstanding the delay
in bringing the action to trial; the plaintiff was entitled to choose and to be
granted the remedy of specific performance against the first defendant,   G
and accordingly was not also entitled to damages against the second to
fifth defendants (see p. 37, letter D, p. 38, letter A, post).

   The incidence of costs in such circumstances, as between the first defendant
on the one hand and the second to fifth defendants on the other hand,
considered (see p. 38, letter G, post).

   [As to the effect of registration under the Land Charges Act, 1925, see 23   H
HALSBURY'S LAWS (3rd Edn.) 60, 61, para. 113; as to the conclusiveness of an
official certificate of search, see ibid., p. 98, para. 205; and for a case on that
subject, see 35 DIGEST (Repl.) 312, *285.*

   For the Land Charges Act, 1925, s. 10 (1), s. 13 (2), s. 16, s. 17 (3), see 20
HALSBURY'S STATUTES (2nd Edn.) 1076, 1087, 1093, 1094.

   For the Law of Property Act, 1925, s. 198, see 20 HALSBURY'S STATUTES   I
(2nd Edn.) 821.

   For the Law of Property (Amendment) Act, 1926, s. 4 (2), see 20 HALSBURY'S
STATUTES (2nd Edn.) 901.]

Cases referred to:

   Hertford (*Marquis*) v. *Boore, Aston* v. *Boore*, (1801), 5 Ves. 719;   31 E.R.
      823; 44 Digest (Repl.) 111, *915.*

---

* Section 17 (3) is set out at p. 35, letter E, post.

A　　*Stock* v. *Wanstead and Woodford Borough Council,* [1961] 2 All E.R. 433;
　　　[1962] 2 Q.B. 479; [1961] 2 W.L.R. 868; 35 Digest (Repl.) 312, *285.*
　　Wright v. *Dean,* [1948] 2 All E.R. 415; [1948] Ch. 686; [1948] L.J.R. 1571;
　　　30 Digest (Repl.) 501, *1430.*

Action.

B　　This was an action brought by writ issued on Jan. 25, 1963, by the plaintiff,
Edward Masfen Collingwood Du Sautoy, against the defendants, Lionel Holbrook
Symes, Bertram George Robinson, Joseph Edward Robinson, Ernest Henry
Robinson and George Robinson. By an agreement in writing dated Sept. 5,
1958, the second to fifth defendants agreed to purchase from Charles Wilfred
Douglas-Brown certain land in Tillingham, Essex for £11,000. The provisions
C　of cl. 14 (which is set out at p. 28, letter F, post) of the special conditions applic-
able to the agreement were registered as a land charge class C (iv) under the
Land Charges Act, 1925, against the second defendant on Sept. 15, 1958, and
against the third to fifth defendants on Sept. 12, 1958. In his statement of claim
delivered on Feb. 18, 1963, the plaintiff claimed against the first defendant (1)
specific performance of the contract constituted by the option or alternatively
D　the right of first refusal contained in the agreement in writing dated Sept. 5,
1958, together with a letter dated Aug. 29, 1962 (whereby the second to fifth
defendants gave notice to the plaintiff that they were proposing to sell the land
the subject matter of the option and right of first refusal to one B. R. Symes
and enquired whether the plaintiff desired to re-purchase the same), and an oral
communication of about Sept. 3, 1962, whereby, the plaintiff purported to
E　exercise the said option or right of first refusal by verbal notice to the second
to fifth defendants; alternatively, (2) specific performance of the contract
constituted by the said option and by a letter dated Jan. 15, 1963, from his
solicitors to the first defendants' solicitors, whereby the plaintiff purported to
exercise the option vested in him to purchase the land therein comprised for
£1,000; (3) all necessary accounts, directions and enquiries; (4) damages in
F　addition to or in lieu of specific performance. The plaintiff claimed against the
second to fifth defendants damages for breach of contract.

　　The first defendant by his defence, delivered on Apr. 2, 1963, pleaded that
if, which was denied, the plaintiff became legally entitled to exercise the said
rights or either of them against the remaining defendants, then the said rights
had ceased to be exercisable, against him on, among others, the grounds specified
G　in para. 7 of his defence. By para. 6 of his defence the first defendant pleaded
that there was no such option as alleged by the plaintiff which then affected
the relevant land and was binding on him and stated that in this connexion
he would rely on (i) an application by his solicitors for an official search in the
alphabetical index to the registers kept under the Land Charges Act, 1925, and
the Law of Property (Amendment) Act, 1926, for any subsisting entries made
H　under a series of names, addresses and descriptions including those of the second
to fifth defendants affecting land therein specified and described, including land
the subject of the proceedings; and (ii) on the official certificate dated Sept. 26,
1962, revealing no subsisting entries. He pleaded that by statute that certificate
was conclusive in his favour and that the option and right of pre-emption were
void against him. In the alternative, he contended that the option became
I　spent and ceased to have effect on the expiry of one month from the date of
the dispatch or receipt of the letter dated Aug. 29, 1962, and that the purported
exercise of such option by the letter dated Jan. 15, 1963, was a nullity.

　　The second, third, fourth and fifth defendants by their joint defence delivered
on Mar. 28, 1963, pleaded that the plaintiff had not validly or effectually
exercised his rights in the manner alleged in the statement of claim or at all,
and that they were entitled to sell the land the subject-matter of cl. 14 because
the plaintiff had not prior to the delivery of the conveyance validly or effectually
exercised the option or right of first refusal.

At the hearing, the plaintiff abandoned the contention that he had exercised A
any right given to him by cl. 14 within the period of one month. The facts and
relevant statutory provisions are set out in the judgment.

The authority, statutory provisions, rules and cases noted below* were cited
during the argument in addition to those referred to in the judgment.

Raymond Walton, Q.C., and *M. W. Jacomb* for the plaintiff.
Charles Sparrow, Q.C., and *B. T. Buckle* for the first defendant.   B
J. L. Knox for the second, third, fourth and fifth defendants.

CROSS, J.: On Sept. 5, 1958, a Mr. Douglas-Brown, who owned a house
and a farm called Reddings in the parish of Tillingham in Essex, consisting of
some 226 acres, contracted to sell the agricultural land to the second, third,
fourth and fifth defendants in this action, Bertram George Robinson, Joseph C
Edward Robinson, Earnest Henry Robinson and George Robinson, who were
farmers in the neighbourhood, retaining the house and garden in his own ownership. Mr. Douglas-Brown had originally intended to sell both the house and
the agricultural land together by auction, and the contract for the sale of the
farmland to the Robinsons was in fact contained in a copy of the auction
particulars and conditions of sale which were amended and extended to deal D
with the changed position; that is to say, the exclusion of the house. One of
the alterations was the insertion of a clause which is cl. 14 in the conditions
of sale, which gave Mr. Douglas-Brown an option to repurchase part of a field,
No. 174 on the ordnance plan, on which the plan on the contract was based,
which lay immediately to the north of the house and garden. The clause ran
as follows: E

"The vendor [that is, Mr. Douglas-Brown] shall have the right at any
time within twenty-one years from the date hereof upon giving to the
purchasers one month's notice in writing to repurchase from the purchasers
or their successors in title the easternmost portion of enclosure No. 174
having an area of twenty acres for the sum of £1,000 and if the purchasers
shall within the period aforesaid desire to sell the same they shall first F
offer it to the vendor who shall notify the purchasers within one month
if he desires to purchase."

Mr. Douglas-Brown registered cl. 14 in the land charges register as an estate
contract against the third, fourth and fifth defendants on Sept. 12 and against
the second defendant on Sept. 15. In each case the entry on the register gave G
under the heading " County ", Essex, under the heading " Parish or Place ",
Tillingham, and under the heading " Short Description of Land (If practicable) ",
" Ordnance Survey 174 ". The contract of sale was completed by a conveyance
on Oct. 16, 1958, which conveyed the agricultural lands under the description
of " Reddings Farm ", including the part of Ordnance Survey No. 174 which was
the subject of cl. 14; but the conveyance did not contain any reference to the H
option.

On June 6, 1959, Mr. Douglas-Brown conveyed Reddings—that is to say, the
house and grounds—to the plaintiff, Edward Du Sautoy; and on the same day,
by a separate deed, he assigned to him the benefit of cl. 14, and on June 11,
1959, the plaintiff gave notice of the assignment to the second to fifth defendants.
In the pleadings the point was taken that cl. 14 was personal to Mr. Douglas- I
Brown, but that point was, in my judgment quite rightly, abandoned at the
hearing, and it is conceded that the plaintiff acquired the benefit of it.

---

* 1957 Conveyancer and Property Lawyer, New Series, vol. 21, p. 89; Administration
of Estates Act, 1925, s. 36 (6), (7); Settled Land Act, 1925, ss. 35 (3), 110 (1)-(5); Land
Charges Rules, 1925, rr. 1, 6, 9; and Forms L.C. 4, 11; Land Charges Rules (No. 2),
1940; *Bath* v. *Bowles*, (1905), 93 L.T. 801; *Goffin* v. *Houlder*, (1920), 90 L.J.Ch. 488;
Re Duce and Boots Cash Chemists (Southern), Ltd.'s Contract, [1937] 3 All E.R. 788;
[1937] Ch. 642; *Stromdale & Ball, Ltd.* v. *Burden*, [1952] 1 All E.R. 59; [1952] Ch. 223;
Re Button's Lease, [1963] 3 All E.R. 708; [1964] Ch. 263.

A   On Aug. 29, 1962, Messrs. Crick & Freeman, the solicitors acting for the second to fifth defendants, wrote to Messrs. Webber & Williams, the solicitors acting for the plaintiff, a letter in the following terms:

" *Re : Reddings Farm, Tillingham.*

B
" We act for Messrs. Robinson Bros., the owners of the above farm, and we write to you on behalf of your client, Mr. E. M. C. Du Sautoy, of Reddings, Tillingham aforesaid. We refer to your notice, dated June 11, 1959, when you informed us that your client had taken an assignment of the benefit of an agreement dated Sept. 5, 1958, and made between Wilfred Douglas-Brown of the one part and our clients of the other part, whereby your client had the right to repurchase twenty acres of land, part of enclosure No. 174, for the parish of Tillingham, at any time within twenty-one years from the original agreement, and providing that we should give you notice on any sale. We inform you our clients are proposing to sell this farm to Mr. B. R. Symes and we shall be glad to know whether your client wishes to exercise the right to repurchase this twenty-acre field."

C

Mr. B. R. Symes is the father of the first defendant, Lionel Holbrook Symes.
On Oct. 15, the second to fifth defendant's conveyed Reddings Farm to the first defendant. He and his father were partners, and the purchase price was paid out of the partnership money.

D

Messrs. Webber & Williams did not answer the letter of Aug. 29 until Oct. 5, which was more than a month after its receipt. They then wrote to Messrs. Crick & Freeman in the following terms:

E   " Referring to your letter of Aug. 29, for which we thank you, we confirm that [the plaintiff] wishes to purchase the twenty acres in question, and we shall be glad if you will please let us have the abstract of title."

It is alleged in the statement of claim that the plaintiff exercised his option or right of pre-emption under cl. 14 verbally on or about Sept. 2 or 3, 1962. In their defence the second to fifth defendants deny that he exercised it in that way or, in fact, that he could exercise it in that way. At the hearing, however, the plaintiff abandoned the contention that he had exercised any right given to him by cl. 14 within the period of one month from the letter of Aug. 29. So there is no question of his having any rights under the second part of cl. 14.

F

During the period between Aug. 29 and Oct. 5 certain correspondence took place between Messrs. Crick & Freeman, the solicitors acting for the second to fifth defendants, and Messrs. F. H. Bright & Sons, the solicitors acting for the Symes, and I must refer to some parts of that correspondence. On Aug. 30, Messrs. Crick & Freeman wrote as follows:

G

" We enclose herewith a plan of the land proposed to be sold to your client, but we are unable to let you have a contract at this stage as there is a right for the present owner of Reddings Farm [the plaintiff], to re-purchase part of Ordnance Survey field No. 174, amounting to twenty acres, shown on the plan, and we have written to his solicitors to know whether he wishes to repurchase this field. As soon as we have information as to this we will let you have a draft contract for approval."

H

Then, after some letters to which I need not refer, Messrs. Crick & Freeman wrote on Sept. 19 a letter of which I will read the following part:

I

" We have asked our clients to let us know next Tuesday if it will be in order for your client [that is, the Symes] to have possession of this farm, excluding the twenty-acre field, part of Ordnance Survey field No. 174, pending hearing from [the plaintiff], on the balance of the purchase money being deposited [the deposit, of course, had already been paid] it being understood that if [the plaintiff] proceeds then the purchase money will have to be reduced rateably. [The plaintiff] must give us a reply by the 30th instant, as the month's notice expires then. The right of [the plaintiff] is

to purchase this field at any time within twenty-one years from Sept. 5,   A
1958, at the price of £1,000."

On Sept. 20 Messrs. Bright & Sons answered:

" As you know we ourselves would prefer to complete the matter before
the end of this month. ... On the assumption that we will be receiving
from you an abstract of title within the next day or so we see no reason   B
why the sale of the whole of the farm other than field No. 174 could not be
completed and this field left until the notice served on [the plaintiff] has
expired."

Then on Sept. 21, Messrs. Crick & Freeman wrote a letter to Messrs. F. H. Bright
& Sons, the material parts of which are as follows:

" We have heard nothing further from [the plaintiff's] solicitors and now   C
enclose herewith abstract of title in two parts with ten electricity wayleave
consents."

On Sept. 25, Messrs. Bright & Sons applied for an official search, which I must set
out in some detail, distinguishing between what is printed on the official form
and what was inserted by the solicitors. As the number of names against which   D
they wished to search was too great to be inserted on one form, they used two
forms, but apart from the names each form was filled up in exactly the same
way. The first form, document " H ", runs as follows:

" *Application for official search.*
"We hereby apply for an official search to be made in the alphabetical
index to the registers kept under the above Acts [that is, the Land Charges   E
Act, 1925 and the Law of Property (Amendment) Act, 1926] for any subsisting entries therein under the undermentioned names, addresses and descriptions affecting land in the County of [then the solicitors have inserted
' Essex '] parish of [then they have inserted ' Tillingham and Asheldham ']
under place or district of [then they have put ' Tillingham and Asheldham ']
known as [then they have put ' O.S. Field Nos. 87 and 118 Asheldham and   F
Reddings Farm, Tillingham] '."

I should have said that there was a proposal on foot at this time that the Symes
should buy from the Robinsons, as well as Reddings Farm, two fields in the
adjoining parish of Asheldham, Nos. 87 and 118. Then there come the names:
" Surname, Christian names, All addresses ", and on the first form, after a
number of other names who were people on the earlier title, one finds " Bertram   G
George Robinson " and " Joseph Edward Robinson ". Bertram George's
address is " Asheldham, The Old School House, Dengie " and Joseph Edward's
" 30, South Street, Tillingham; Rushes Farm, Asheldham; 6 Council Houses,
Tillingham." Then on the next form the particulars inserted in the opening
part are exactly the same, and the names include the names of the remaining
Robinsons, Ernest Henry and George. As I have said, the only reason for using   H
the two forms was that there were too many names to put on the one form.

On the top of the first form the Land Registry affixed a stamp to the following
effect:

" No subsisting entries. H.M. Land Registry, London, Sept. 26, 1962
[that is the day after it was sent and the day it was received]. Protection
ends Oct. 16, 1962."   I

On the back of the second form they stamped this:

" No subsisting entries clearly affecting but the following entries which
may or may not relate thereto appear. [and] H.M. Land Registry, London,
Sept. 26, 1962. Protection ends Oct. 16, 1962."

The entries set out on the second form relate to a number of Robinsons who
are not the Robinsons in question in this case and to a number of matters which
have nothing whatever to do with this contract.

A　　On Sept. 27, Messrs. Bright & Sons wrote to Messrs. Crick & Freeman as follows:

> "We write to inform you that we have written to our client asking him
> to let us have a remittance for £14,400 which we propose to put on deposit
> in our joint names. This figure is made up of the balance purchase
> money on Reddings, less a further £1,800 in respect of the twenty acres

B

> connected with the option at £90 per acre, being in round figures the purchase
> price. We enclose the replies to the official search which we have received
> which reveals certain entries which we assume are not applicable. [They
> were, of course, the entries on the second form.] However, we would be
> grateful if you would endorse the search accordingly."

C　On Oct. 1, Messrs. Crick & Freeman replied:

> "We thank you for your letter of the 27th ultimo with enclosures as
> stated. We have heard nothing from [the plaintiff] or his solicitors and,
> therefore, the month has elapsed and our clients are in a position to sell to
> your clients the remainder of field No. 174. In the circumstances we shall
> be glad if you will arrange to have a further £1,800 placed on deposit, bring-

D

> ing the total on deposit in respect of this purchase up to £16,200. We
> return herewith your search duly certified as requested, and we are assuming
> that you are not taking possession of O.S. Field No. 118 for the parish of
> Asheldham."

—that was one of the fields which, as I said, it was contemplated might be sold
at the same time as Reddings. On Oct. 2, Messrs. Bright & Sons answer, stating

E

that they have put the purchase money on deposit. Then they wrote this:

> "There is only one point upon which we are not clear and this is in
> connexion with the option in favour of [the plaintiff]. We understand that
> the notice which you gave to his solicitors has now expired, and we assume
> that he declined to exercise his rights. From our land charges search it

F

> appears that this option is not registered, and it, therefore, seems to us that
> it will not be enforceable in future against our client. However, we would
> be grateful of your comment."

On Oct. 3, Messrs. Crick & Freeman answered that in a long letter in which
they set out the facts, cl. 14 of the original contract, the notice which they had
received from the plaintiffs of the assignment that gave him the benefit of

G

the option, but did not commit themselves positively one way or the other as
to what rights, if any, the plaintiff might have. Then on Oct. 5 there comes the
letter to which I have already referred, a letter out of time, from the plaintiff's
solicitors purporting to exercise the right of pre-emption after the expiry of one
month. That letter was acknowledged by Messrs. Crick & Freeman by a letter
to which I need not refer.

H　　On Oct. 15, as I have already said, the sale by the Robinsons to Mr. Symes
was completed. The conveyance was, in fact, dated Sept. 29, which was wrong,
but I need not enter into the reasons or possible reasons for that wrong date
because it has no bearing on this case. On Oct. 16, Messrs. Crick & Freeman
answered Messrs. Webber & Williams' letter of Oct. 5 in these terms:

I

> "With reference to your letter of the 5th instant as the acknowledgment
> of our notice, incorporated in our letter of Aug. 29 last, was not received
> within the month, in accordance with the agreement of Sept. 5, 1958, our
> clients proceeded to sell this property to [the first defendant], and you
> should now communicate with his solicitors, Messrs. F. H. Bright & Sons,
> at West Square, Maldon."

On Oct. 17, in answer to a telephone call from Mr. Williams, Messrs. Bright
& Sons sent him copies of the official search certificates to show the plaintiff
that they had in fact searched and found nothing.

On Nov. 7, Messrs. Webber & Williams wrote a letter to Messrs. Bright &   A
Sons, a copy of which was sent to Messrs. Crick & Freeman, in the following
terms:

"*Re Enclosure No. 174 on Ordnance Survey Map, Tillingham, Essex.*

"We understand from Messrs. Crick & Freeman that their clients Messrs.
Robinson have recently conveyed the above mentioned field to your client
[the first defendant]. The easternmost portion of this field has at all times   B
since Sept. 5, 1958, been subject to an option, the benefit of which has since
June 6, 1959, been vested in our client [the plaintiff] . . . [they set out the
terms of the option] . . . This option was duly registered as a land charge,
class C (iv) against the above mentioned enclosure of land. We understand
from you that prior to acquiring this land you made an official search upon   C
behalf of your client which revealed no subsisting entries, but if this is so
we do not think that the search can have been made against the right
parcel of land, because we ourselves have recently searched to confirm the
entries against the above parcel of land, and obtained a correct affirmative
answer. Pursuant to the second branch of the said option, the Messrs.
Robinson duly gave notice to our client through ourselves on Aug. 29, 1962,   D
that they were proposing to sell the land to you, and required to know
whether our client wished to exercise his right to purchase the above
mentioned field. Our client verbally intimated to one Mr. J. E. Robinson on
behalf of the Messrs. Robinson, on or about Sept. 3, 1962 (i.e. within the one
month limited by the option) that he did desire to purchase. As there is no
specific method of notification laid down in the option, such verbal notification was in our view quite sufficient. Our client's exercise of the option was   E
confirmed by our letter of Oct. 5, 1962, which was of course outside the
month [that point about the verbal exercise is not now relied on]. Our client
could, of course, simply rely upon the contract constituted by the notification under the offer and his acceptance thereof. Purely, however, as a
matter of precaution, and without prejudice to our client's contentions
as set out in the preceding paragraph, we have advised him that in order   F
to put the matter beyond doubt he should now exercise the option under
the first part thereof. Will you therefore please on behalf of your client
[the first defendant] accept this letter as being the one month's notice in
writing to repurchase the easternmost portion of field No. 174 on the
Ordnance Survey map, Tillingham, Essex, from your client as being the
successor in title of the original purchasers therein named."   G

The defendants refused to accept the contention advanced in this letter. As
there was some doubt whether Messrs. Bright & Sons had on Nov. 7, authority
to accept notice on behalf of the first defendant, Messrs. Webber & Williams,
on behalf of the plaintiff, exercised, or purported to exercise, the option conferred
by cl. 14, again on Jan. 15 by letter sent both to Messrs. Bright & Sons, acting   H
for the first defendant, and to Messrs. Crick & Freeman, acting for the second to
fifth defendants. I do not think that I need refer in detail to those letters.
There is no doubt that if the option under cl. 14 was exercisable those letters
effectively exercised it.

Then the writ was issued in the action by the plaintiff against Mr. Symes as
the first defendant and the Robinsons as the second to the fifth defendants on   I
Jan. 25, 1963. The pleadings were closed as long ago as April, 1963.

In view of the concessions made by both sides at the hearing there are now
only three points to be decided. The first point is: does cl. 14 confer one right
or two rights; that is to say, having, as is now conceded, failed to exercise such
right as he had within the month from the letter announcing the intended sale,
did the plaintiff continue to have an option which he could continue to exercise
after the sale? That is a matter of construction of the clause. The second
question, which raises matters of general law, is this: if the plaintiff had any

A such right, is he precluded from getting specific performance against the first
defendant, by reason of the negative certificate of official search issued from
the Land Registry under the Land Charges Act, 1925, in answer to the search
asked for by the first defendant's solicitors? The third point, which again is a
question of construction of the agreement, is: if the plaintiff had the option
under cl. 14, but cannot get specific performance against the first defendant
B because of the effect of the search, can he get damages against the second to
fifth defendants because he is not getting the field? It is agreed that if he can
the measure would be the value of the land in question at the date of the
exercise of the option less £1,000.

There is one more document to which I should perhaps refer. On June 23,
1965—that is, pending the proceedings—the London agents of the plaintiff's
C solicitors applied for an official search against the names of the second to fifth
defendants for entries affecting land described as " In the County of Essex,
Parish of Tillingham, known as Reddings Farm ", and in answer to that request,
on June 24, they received an official certificate disclosing a number of entries,
including the four entries registered by Mr. Douglas-Brown in September, 1958,
in respect of the option under cl. 14.

D   I now come to the question of construction. In support of the view that cl.
14 confers only a single right it is said that if there are two rights it is difficult,
if not impossible, to see what was the point of conferring the right of pre-emption
contained in the latter part of the clause. The option, it is said, is the larger
right of the two, and it cannot have been meant to continue notwithstanding
a sale. Surely, it is said, what was intended was that, though the option was to
E continue for twenty-one years if the second to fifth defendants or their successors
in their farming business remained in possession, if they sold to a stranger the
option-holder would have to make up his mind there and then whether or not
he wanted the land. Of course that construction involves reading the second
half of the clause, which in fact is introduced by the word " and ", which prima
facie adds something, as a proviso drastically limiting the right given by the
F first part. Moreover, it involves reading the words " successors in title ", which
prima facie would include successors by purchase in a somewhat unnatural and
limited sense. Further, to my mind, it is not so absurd as the defendants say
that it is for Mr. Douglas-Brown to have wanted the right of pre-emption as well
as the option. After all, he appears to have known the second to fifth defendants,
who were local farmers, and he may well have thought that he would never
G require to exercise the option under cl. 14 as long as they were carrying on their
farming business at Reddings Farm. On the other hand, he might well wish to
exercise it because the land was near his house if they proposed to sell it to a
stranger, unless he was satisfied as to the character and intentions of the purchaser. He might, therefore, well like to be told of any contemplated sale so that
he could have a chance to exercise the option before the sale went through rather
H than have to exercise it after the sale against the purchaser if he proved unsatisfactory. Be that as it may, those considerations lead me to decide the first
question against the defendants; that is to say, I hold that there were here
two rights given, and that, though the second right has undoubtedly gone
because it was not exercised within the month, the first one subsisted.

Although it is taking the matter out of the logical order, it is convenient to
I deal with the third point, which is also a question of construction, now, before
I deal with the second point which raises different matters. On the footing that
cl. 14 confers two rights, as I have held that it does, then it is said on behalf
of the second to fifth defendants that their personal liability to the plaintiff
must come to an end when they sell the land, having previously offered it to the
option-holder as required by the second part of cl. 14. They say that they have
done everything that they are required to do, and it is simply a matter between
the plaintiff and the first defendant. They agree that if they sold the land without first offering it to the option-holder, and he for some reason could not

exercise the option against the purchaser—because, for example, it had not been A
registered—they would then be liable in damages for the breach of the second
part of cl. 14; but they say that, if they have offered the land to him before
the sale, they have done everything which can be reasonably required of them
and they must be relieved of any further liability. In considering that argument,
one must bear in mind the nature of the right conferred by the first part of
cl. 14. It was, as I see it, an irrevocable offer by the second to fifth defendants B
to Mr. Douglas-Brown and his assigns which could be accepted at any time
within twenty-one years, and which, when it was accepted, would result in a
contract between the second to fifth defendants and the person who accepted the
offer. It also created by the grant of the option what may be described as a contingent burden on the land which would become an actual burden when the offer
was accepted, if the land was then in the hands of the second to fifth defendants or C
a purchaser from them with notice; but, though if the second to fifth defendants
had parted with the land and the purchaser had notice the contract could be
specifically enforced in equity against the land in the hands of the purchaser, the
contract which came into existence on the exercise of the option would, as I see it,
still be a contract between the acceptor and the second to fifth defendants. Therefore, prima facie, if for any reason specific performance could not be obtained D
against the purchaser—because, for instance, the option under cl. 14 had not been
registered—the second to fifth defendants would be liable in damages. No doubt
that liability might be excluded by appropriate words in the contract, and, from
the point of view of the second to fifth defendants, at all events, it might not be
unreasonable to exclude it; but, to my mind, the mere fact that cl. 14 as well
as granting the option also contains this rather curious right of pre-emption is E
not sufficient to amount to such an exclusion. On this part of the case the plaintiff relies, naturally, on the decision of WYNN-PARRY, J., in the case of *Wright*
v. *Dean* (1). It is fair to say that that case is distinguishable, because there
the document granting the option did not make any express reference to the
possibility of the sale of the land by the grantor as cl. 14 does; but although
it certainly is possible that if the minds of the parties had been directed to the F
point the clause would have expressly relieved the second to fifth defendants of
any personal liability after they had sold the land, it does not seem to me that
the clause does so. I think that it would be wrong to read the grant of the right
of pre-emption as achieving that result.

I now come to the second question, which involves a consideration of some
parts of the property legislation of 1925. Section 10 (1) of the Land Charges G
Act, 1925, provides that the rights granted by cl. 14 could be registered as land
charges under class C (iv), which I need not read in detail, and they were so
registered. Section 198 (1) of the Law of Property Act, 1925, which was passed
at the same time as the Land Charges Act, 1925, provides:

    " The registration of any instrument or matter under the provisions of
    the Land Charges Act, 1925, or any enactment which it replaces, in any H
    register kept at the land registry or elsewhere, shall be deemed to constitute
    actual notice of such instrument or matter, and of the fact of such registr-
    ation, to all persons and for all purposes connected with the land affected,
    as from the date of registration or other prescribed date and so long as the
    registration continues in force."

 I
If the rights had not been registered before the completion of the purchase
they would have been void against the first defendant even though he had in
fact actual notice of them. That appears from s. 13 (2) of the Land Charges Act,
1925 (which again I do not think that I need read) and from s. 199 (1) of the Law
of Property Act, 1925. Those sections have no application here, however, because
the option was registered. So at this point one has this: that the registration
constituted actual notice to the first defendant of the option under cl. 14.

(1) [1948] 2 All E.R. 415; [1948] Ch. 686.

A   Now I must turn to the provisions as to searches in the register. Section 4 (2) of the Law of Property (Amendment) Act, 1926, which was passed a year later, provides as follows:

" Where a purchaser has obtained an official certificate of the result of search, any entry which is made in the register after the date of the certificate and before the completion of the purchase, and is not made
B   pursuant to a priority notice entered on the register before the certificate is issued, shall not, if the purchase is completed before the expiration of the second day after the date of the certificate, affect the purchaser."

The period of two days has now been extended by the rules (2) made under sub-s. (4) to fourteen days. Those provisions do not have any direct bearing
C   on this case, because there is no question here of a priority notice, but they do afford an example of a case in which the general effect of s. 198 (1)—that is to say, that registration amounts to actual notice—is qualified by other statutory provisions.

Finally I must come to Part 7 of the Land Charges Act, 1925, which is headed: " Searches and Official Searches ", and I must read s. 16 and part of s. 17.

D   " 16. Any person may search in any register or index kept in pursuance of this Act on paying the prescribed fee.

" 17. (1) Where any person requires search to be made at the registry for entries of any matters or documents, whereof entries are required or allowed to be made in the registry by this Act, he may on payment of the pre-scribed fee lodge at the registry a requisition in that behalf. (2) The registrar
E   shall thereupon make the search required, and shall issue a certificate setting forth the result thereof. (3) In favour of a purchaser or an intending purchaser, as against persons interested under or in respect of matters or documents whereof entries are required or allowed as aforesaid, the certificate, according to the tenor thereof, shall be conclusive, affirmatively or negatively, as the case may be. (4) Every requisition under this section
F   shall be in writing, signed by the person making the same, specifying the name against which he desires search to be made, or in relation to which he requires a certificate of result of search, and other sufficient particulars."

Subsection (5) deals with misconduct by the officials in the registry, to which I need not refer; and I do not think that I need refer to sub-s. (6). Subsections (7), (8) and (9) provide:
G
" (7) Where a solicitor obtains a certificate of result of search under this section, he shall not be answerable in respect of any loss that may arise from error in the certificate. (8) Where the solicitor is acting for trustees, executors, agents, or other persons in a fiduciary position, those persons also shall not be so answerable. (9) Where such persons obtain such a certificate without a solicitor, they shall also be protected in like manner."
H
The first defendant, of course, relies on s. 17 (3). He says that, in view of it, the plaintiff cannot allege against him that the option was registered, though in fact it was. If mistakes are made by those who conduct official searches, either the person entitled to the registered charge or the purchaser must suffer, and in view of the affection for purchasers shown in the property legislation,
I   it does not surprise me to find that the loss is made to fall on the chargee and not the purchaser. It is said, however, that one would have expected s. 198 (1) of the Law of Property Act, 1925, to contain some warning that actual registra-tion will not prevail against a negative certificate. Of course, the qualification is introduced in the Act of 1926 a year later and could not have been foreseen in 1925; but the Law of Property Act and the Land Charges Act were passed in 1925, and one would have expected to find some warning in s. 198 (1) that

(2) I.e., the Land Charges Rules, 1940 (S.R. & O. 1940 No. 1998); 18 HALSBURY'S STATUTORY INSTRUMENTS (First Re-Issue) 280.

there might be circumstances in which actual registration would not avail the A
person who registered.

Again, it is said that if sub-s. (3) of s. 17 means what it appears to mean,
it is hard to see the point of sub-s. (7) and sub-s. (8). If the certificate is to
prevail over the facts, why should any loss arise from errors in it? Counsel
for the plaintiff, who made the point about s. 198 and about sub-s. (7) and
sub-s. (8), was unable, however, to suggest any meaning to sub-s. (3) other B
than the meaning contended for by the first defendant; and even apart from
authority, I would have come to the conclusion that on this aspect of the case
the first defendant was right. In point of fact, however, a decision to that
effect was given by MELFORD STEVENSON, J., in the Queen's Bench Division
in the case of *Stock* v. *Wanstead and Woodford Borough Council* (3), which I
should have followed even had I entertained any doubts on the matter, which C
I do not.

It does not, however, follow from this that the second question must be decided
in favour of the first defendant. One must ask oneself: of what is the certificate
conclusive between the purchaser and the owner of the charge? As I see it, it
is conclusive that on that date there was no entry on the register against the
names mentioned in the application which affected the lands mentioned in the D
application other than those entries set out on the second form, which admittedly
do not include this option at all. But the certificate cannot protect the first
defendant if he applied for a search against the wrong names or in respect of
the wrong lands. That seems to me to be plain. No question arises here about
the names. The application set out the names of the second to fifth defendants
quite correctly; but the matter is not so clear when one comes to the description E
of the lands affected. It is apparent from the application that the solicitors
acting for the first defendant combined in a single form applications for searches
against the same names in respect of lands in two different parishes; that is to say,
against fields Nos. 87 and 118 in the parish of Asheldham and against Reddings
Farm in the parish of Tillingham. So far as I know, they were perfectly at
liberty to do that if they chose; but to do that increased the risk of some mistake F
being made, especially if the application does not confine itself, as it is entitled to
do, to referring to the county and parish, but goes on to give a description of the
lands which does not distinguish between the lands in each parish. It was submitted by counsel for the first defendant that the words " known as O.S. field
Nos. 87 and 118 Asheldham and Reddings Farm, Tillingham " need not have
been put in—which is quite true—and that, therefore, I can ignore them; but I G
do not think that I can do that. The first defendant must be judged, as I see it,
on the application which he made. Even if his solicitors had left out those words,
it might have been said that the application was misleading to the extent that it
referred simply to the parish of Tillingham and Asheldham instead of the parishes
of Tillingham and Asheldham. That would have been a small point, however,
and I do not suppose for one moment that in that case the certificate would H
have failed to disclose the option registered in respect of lands in the parish of
Tillingham, which was the description in the registration of the option. What
probably caused the mistake was the single description of both sets of lands
starting with the words: " O.S. field Nos. 87 and 118 ". It is easy for us who
know the facts to see that the application was referring to two separate matters,
first, to O.S. fields Nos. 87 and 118 in the parish of Asheldham and secondly, I
to Reddings Farm in the parish of Tillingham, and if the gentleman who conducted the search had read it in that way he would have got on to the registered
option, as he did at once in answer to the application made by the plaintiff in
1965 which referred to lands in the County of Essex, parish of Tillingham, known
as Reddings Farm. It was, however, easy for the searcher to think that the
lands affected by the application put in by the first defendant's solicitors were

(3) [1961] 2 All E.R. 433; [1962] 2 Q.B. 479.

A simply ordnance survey fields Nos. 87 and 118, which were part of a farm with
the rather curious name of Asheldham and Reddings Farm in the parish of
Tillingham. If he read it in that way, he would not disclose the option, because
the option under cl. 14, although registered as affecting land in the County of
Essex in the parish of Tillingham, described the land specifically and accurately as
ordnance survey No. 174.   That, of course, is only conjecture on my part and it
B may be that the mistake arose in some other way for which the first defendant's
solicitors were not in any way responsible.   But it is enough to say that it
may have arisen in the way that I suggest.   It is a strong thing to take away the
vested right which the owner of a charge acquires by registering it, and, in my
judgment, a purchaser can only rely on s. 17 (3), which I have construed in the
way suggested by the first defendant, if the form of his application gave no
C reasonable scope for misunderstanding and the blame for the fact that the
relevant entry did come to light rests fairly and squarely on the officials in the
registry.   There was scope for misunderstanding here and, therefore, I hold that
the plaintiff is prima facie entitled as against the first defendant to an order for
specific performance of the option conferred by cl. 14.

As the plaintiff is entitled to specific performance against the first defendant,
D obviously he cannot be entitled to damages against the second to fifth defendants.
[His Lordship heard argument whether he should grant only damages.]

Charles Sparrow, Q.C.: A note to the report of *Marquis of Hertford* v. *Boore* (4)
reads:

". . . The parties differed as to the construction of the agreement; and
E the bill was delayed for seven years.   Lord Alvanley, M.R., observed
that Lord Kenyon was the first, who set himself against the idea, that had
prevailed, that, when an agreement was entered into, either party might
come at any time: but that it is now perfectly known that a party cannot
call upon a Court of Equity for a specific performance, unless he has shown
himself ready, desirous, prompt and eager."

F I take my stand on that last phrase—the plaintiff must have shown himself
ready, desirous, prompt and eager.   My submission is that the plaintiff failed to
take up his right to the land at the time of the sale to the first defendant, when
it would have caused no trouble to give effect to it.   He chose not to do so.
Subsequently he started proceedings in January, 1963.   Pleadings closed in April,
1963.   The summons for directions was first heard in July, 1963.   Nothing further
G happened on that summons until Feb. 4, 1966, when an order was made for
trial on or before Mar. 4.   It was only under threat to strike out the action that
the defendants were able to get the matter heard.

Raymond Walton, Q.C.: The plaintiff started his action for specific performance
promptly.   If the first defendant found that the action was not going fast enough,
he had a remedy under the rules.   That cannot effect the plaintiff's substantive
H right at the hearing, at any rate when there is nothing amounting to
abandonment of his right.   The first defendant has not been prejudiced.

Charles Sparrow, Q.C.: The true test is that the plaintiff must be shown to have
been ready, desirous, prompt and eager.   He is asking for the purely equitable
relief of specific performance.   The question is not whether he abandoned his
I right.

CROSS, J.: In this case the writ was issued promptly, and I do not think
that the fact that the plaintiff was making alternative claims under both branches
of cl. 14, one of which he has subsequently abandoned, can affect the right
to specific performance, though it may have some bearing on the question of
costs.   It is said, however, that there was great delay in bringing the action to trial.
I have not been taken through the correspondence in detail, but what I gather

(4) (1800), 5 Ves. 719 at p. 720.

is alleged by the first defendant is that, though there was some negotiation in A
the early stages, from about October, 1964, the delay in bringing the action
to trial was the fault of the plaintiff. Assuming that to be so, however, I do
not think that it is sufficient to justify me in refusing to grant him specific performance and instead to grant damages under Lord Cairns' Act (5).   I can
conceive of a case where, though an action is started promptly, nevertheless,
by his conduct the plaintiff has lulled the defendant into a belief that he is B
going to ask for damages only and not specific performance; but it would need
a clear case to make that out, and no such case has been made out here.   Therefore, I make the order for specific performance.

[Argument followed on costs.]

Raymond Walton, Q.C.: The plaintiff is entitled to costs against both the first C
defendant and the second to fifth defendants. I do not dispute that if there has
been any increase in costs due to the joinder of the abandoned claim, the costs
awarded to the plaintiff should be mitigated in respect of that.

Charles Sparrow, Q.C.: I submit that the first defendant ought not to pay the
costs of the second to fifth defendants. In the ANNUAL PRACTICE, 1966, p. 1999/
230, it is stated that a " Bullock order " will not be made where the plaintiff's D
doubt is as to the law not the facts; and here the question has been one of law.
The plaintiff has established two remedies and has elected for one, viz., specific
performance against the first defendant.

J. L. Knox: The joinder of the abandoned claim is of capital importance in
regard to the position of the second to fifth defendants as to costs. That issue has E
been principally responsible for them being represented.   It is not disputed
that the plaintiff is entitled to damages against the second to fifth defendants,
but he is only so entitled if he does not get specific performance against the first
defendant, and he has elected for and obtained that remedy.   The origin of
the whole of this matter is the answer that was received from the original search.
That was an incorrect search put in on behalf of the first defendant.   F

CROSS, J.: On the whole I think that the plaintiff is entitled to costs
against both the first defendant and the second to fifth defendants separately,
mitigated in each case, by the making of an allowance for the costs of the issue
which the plaintiff raised and which he abandoned.   There should be a set-
off against the plaintiff in regard to the costs of that issue.   The proportion in
which the first defendant on the one hand and the second to fifth defendants G
on the other hand should bear the costs should reflect the fact that to some
extent the chief cause of the trouble was the form of the application for search.
Accordingly two-thirds of the plaintiff's costs should be borne by the first
defendant and one-third by the second to fifth defendants.

Order for specific performance and costs accordingly. H

Solicitors: *Gilmore, Tylee & Co.*, agents for *Webber & Williams*, Ampthill,
Beds. (for the plaintiff); *Beaumont, Son & Rigden*, agents for *F. H. Bright &
Sons*, Maldon, Essex (for the first defendant); *Gard, Lyell, Bridgman & Co.*,
agents for *Crick & Freeman*, Maldon, Essex (for the second to fifth defendants).

[*Reported by* JACQUELINE METCALFE, *Barrister-at-Law.*] I

---

(5) I.e., the Chancery Amendment Act, 1858.

A

HOUSE *v.* HAUGHTON BROTHERS (WORCESTER), LTD.

[COURT OF APPEAL, CIVIL DIVISION (Danckwerts and Winn, L.JJ.), November 18, 1966.]

B
Court of Appeal—Evidence—Further evidence—Matters known to witness but not known to those who called him as a witness—No examination at trial on such matters—Whether evidence regarded as available at trial—Matter important to the issue that was to be decided—New trial granted.

The plaintiff while employed by the defendants suffered injury by falling through the floor of a building. He alleged against the defendants that they were in breach of reg. 7 (2) of the Construction (General Provisions) Regula-
C
tions, 1961, by not having provided sufficient means of support, it being agreed that three scaffold boards would have satisfied the regulations. The plaintiff gave evidence that the defendants provided no board but that he himself fetched one from their yard. Other witnesses were called for the plaintiff, and a director of the defendants gave evidence for them. It was not suggested in examination or cross-examination of witnesses that in the
D
interval of twenty-four hours between the accident and the arrival of the factory inspector additional boards had been delivered. When the factory inspector arrived he found boards either on the premises or in the yard. Judgment having been given for the defendants, four witnesses on behalf of the plaintiff who were present or available at the trial made statements that boards were brought on the scene after the accident and before the factory
E
inspector arrived. On appeal by the plaintiff and application by him that this fresh evidence should be admitted.

Held: in so far as evidence which a witness could have given was not known at the trial to those who caused him to be called as witness, then, assuming that the solicitors who interviewed him to see what evidence he could give did so carefully, that evidence, and in respect of it the witness,
F
were to be regarded as not having been available at the trial; accordingly in the present case evidence concerning the bringing of additional boards after the accident would be treated as not having been available at the trial, and, as that matter was of essential importance, a new trial would be ordered (see p. 41, letter F, and p. 42, letter B, post).

Ladd v. *Marshall* ([1954] 3 All E.R. 745) applied.
G
Appeal allowed.

[As to the power of the Court of Appeal to receive further evidence, see 30 HALSBURY'S LAWS (3rd Edn.) 408, 409, para. 884: as to the grounds of new trial, see ibid., pp. 475, 476, para. 891; and for cases on fresh evidence on appeal, see DIGEST (Practice) 775-778, *3396-3420.*

For the Construction (General Provisions) Regulations, 1961, reg. 7 (2), see
H
8 HALSBURY'S STATUTORY INSTRUMENTS (First Re-Issue) 265.]

Case referred to:
Ladd v. *Marshall,*]1954] 3 All E.R. 745; [1954] 1 W.L.R. 1489; 3rd Digest Supp.

Appeal.
I
This was an appeal by the plaintiff by notice dated Jan. 21, 1966, from a judgment of Mr. Commissioner NORMAN RICHARDS, Q.C., on Dec. 13, 1965, dismissing his action for damages for personal injuries and assessing the damages that he would have awarded at £1,135 4s. 4d.; the plaintiff sought an order that the judgment should be set aside and that judgment should be entered for him. By notice of motion dated Jan. 27, 1966, the plaintiff applied for liberty to adduce further evidence for witnesses and to read such evidence on the appeal.

The plaintiff appeared in person.

E. B. Gibbens, Q.C., and *O. B. Popplewell* for the defendants.

WINN, L.J., delivered the first judgment at the invitation of DANCKWERTS, A
L.J.: The plaintiff suffered injuries by falling through the floor of a building. He
was engaged at the time in the employment of the defendant company in
removing, inter alia, at the exact time when his accident happened, rotten floorboards in order that he might lay a fresh floor. The boards gave way, or one
board gave way, or he suffered a slip as the result of the one scaffold board on
which he was then resting his weight across the joists of the floor tipping and B
letting him down through the floor. He was not using more than one board. The
issue, so far as any live issue survived at the trial among those which, having
been raised on the pleadings, clearly could not stand up on the evidence, was
whether or not the defendants had, in accordance with their duty under reg. 7 (2)
of the Construction (General Provisions), Regulations, 1961 (1), which were in
force at the relevant time, provided him with means of support, other than a C
ladder, suitable and sufficient for the purpose when he could not safely work
from the ground or from any permanent structure. The defendants agreed that
three boards would be the proper requirement for providing a working platform
in these conditions. The court thinks that that is clearly right.

The issue, therefore, was: had the defendants provided three scaffold boards
or had they failed to do so? The plaintiff said that they had not provided any D
but that he himself went and fetched one and did not feel disposed, for good or
poor reasons, to fetch more than one himself from the firm's yard. Witnesses
were called by the plaintiff, including a man called Webster and a man called
Nicholls, and we are told, and of course accept it, that a man called Morgan, who
was the cathedral gardener, was also available as a witness in court. Those
witnesses said nothing about any provision of scaffold boards having been made E
in the interval of time between the occurrence of the plaintiff's accident, which
was roundabout noon on one day, and caused him to be taken to and detained in
hospital, and the arrival of the factory inspector, which was some twenty-four
hours later. They were not asked any questions to lead their evidence to any such
matter. They gave their evidence on other questions, and it is right to take note
of the correct submission of counsel for the third defendants that one of them, F
Mr. Webster, was clearly not believed or his evidence was not accepted by the
judge on an issue of fact. Not only was there no attempt made to lead the evidence
of the witnesses who were called to the matter which I have mentioned, but no
cross-examination of Mr. Allen, the employer, was directed to the question
whether or not he had delivered additional scaffold boards after the accident and
before the factory inspector arrived.   G

Very quickly indeed after judgment had been pronounced by the commissioner
against the plaintiff, Mr. Webster and Mr. Nicholls, and in due course Mr. Morgan
and one Bozward, tendered statements on the matter explaining that they had
come forward to give such information because they had been shocked and
surprised to find that the plaintiff had lost his action, they having thought, until
judgment was given against him, that he could " easily collect some damages H
from the insurance company ", as they put it themselves. The effect of their
evidence, as shown in the statements which they have signed (and I deliberately
do not go into any detail at all) is an allegation that Mr. Allen delivered additional
scaffold boards in the interval of time which I have already indicated: it is said
that as a result the commissioner was misled into believing the statement that
the number of scaffold boards provided handy for use in this building, whether I
they were at any material time across the joists or across the beams in the roof,
was the same number as those which the factory inspector found somewhere on
the premises or in the yard when he arrived. It seems to this court that that
matter is of the most essential importance in this case. If it were to be established
that Mr. Allen did make this further delivery in the period of time which I have
indicated, then there might be much greater strength than the commissioner,

(1) S.I. 1961 No. 1580.

A naturally enough, attributed to the plaintiff's case on the issue of whether or not adequate scaffolding boards were timeously provided.

The court has, of course, been referred once again to the case of *Ladd* v. *Marshall* (2), a decision of this court where, laying down the relevant principles so far only as was requisite for the purposes of that case, DENNING, L.J., said (3):

B   " It is very rare that application is made to this court for a new trial on the ground that a witness has told a lie."

This case is not precisely the same as that. This is a case of suppressio veri which may or may not in the circumstances have amounted to a suggestio falsi, but it is not shown that a lie was told by either of the witnesses at the trial; for the sake of their employment they were discreet. DENNING, L.J., continued (3):

C   " The principles to be applied are the same as those always applied when fresh evidence is sought to be introduced. In order to justify the reception of fresh evidence or a new trial, three conditions must be fulfilled: first, it must be shown that the evidence could not have been obtained with reasonable diligence for use at the trial . . ."

D That is very often in my own experience paraphrased by saying it must be shown that the witness was not available at the trial. I venture to think that had the mind of DENNING, L.J., been then specifically directed to the point, he might well have added by way of amplification what I myself deliberately now add: that the evidence or witness may not have been available or the evidence " could not have been obtained with reasonable diligence for use at the trial " where,

E although the witness is called at the trial, is physically present in the witness box and gives evidence about some matters relevant in that trial, he has not told the party who caused him to be called as a witness or that party's solicitors, what he, the witness, is able to say about some issue in the trial. In that situation his evidence on that issue " cannot have been obtained with reasonable diligence ", if it can be assumed that the solicitors are not shown to have been careless or

F neglectful or dilatory in the manner in which they interviewed the witness to see what evidence could be given by him at the trial. Equally in this case, on the question whether he or his evidence was available, for myself I say that in so far as the evidence which he could have given was not known to those who caused him to be called as a witness, then quoad such evidence, neither he nor that evidence was available.

G Then DENNING, L.J., went on to state two other criteria (4):

     ". . . second, the evidence must be such that, if given, it would probably have an important influence on the result of the case, although it need not be decisive . . ."

I have already expressed my view that that condition is satisfied in the instant case.

H   ". . . third, the evidence must be such as is presumably to be believed, or in other words, it must be apparently credible, although it need not be incontrovertible."

I have expressed the view that while the evidence of these witnesses, if given on a retrial, may be open to quite a lot of criticism and it may well be proper to

I probe closely their reasons for not having given such evidence at the first trial, I do not myself see that their evidence is necessarily not credible. DENNING, L.J., went on to say (5):

     ". . . some good reason must be shown why a lie was told in the first instance, and good ground given for thinking the witness will tell the truth on the second occasion."

---

(2) [1954] 3 All E.R. 745.   (3) [1954] 3 All E.R. at p. 748, letter A.
(4) [1954] 3 All E.R. at p. 748, letter B.   (5) [1954] 3 All E.R. at p. 748, letter C.

I think those criteria do not bar the allowance of a new trial in the circumstances   A
which are before the court.

For the reasons which I have endeavoured shortly to indicate, I am of opinion
that a new trial should be ordered.

DANCKWERTS, L.J.: I am of the same opinion. For the reasons which
have been stated by WINN, L.J., I think that there should be a new trial in this   B
case.

Appeal allowed; New trial ordered. Leave to appeal to the House of Lords refused.

Solicitors: *Kingsley Wood & Co.*, agents for *Duggan, Elton & James*,
Birmingham (for the defendants).

[*Reported by* F. GUTTMAN, ESQ., *Barrister-at-Law.*]   C

SHOP AND STORE DEVELOPMENTS, LTD.
v. INLAND REVENUE COMMISSIONERS.

D

[HOUSE OF LORDS (Lord Reid, Lord Morris of Borth-y-Gest, Lord Hodson, Lord
Guest and Lord Wilberforce), October 27, 31, December 8, 1966.]

*Stamp Duty—Transfer of property from one associated company to another—
Consideration for the transfer—Transfer to associated company in return*   E
*for allotment of shares—Sale of shares by associated company to issuing
house, which was not an associated company—Payment for allotment made
out of proceeds of public issue—Whether the phrase " consideration for the
transfer " extended to include cash obtained for shares sold to issuing house—
Finance Act, 1930 (20 & 21 Geo. 5 c. 28), s. 42 (1)—Finance Act, 1938*
(1 & 2 Geo. 6 c. 46), s. 50 (1) (a).   F

*Stamp Duty—Repayment—Interest on overpaid duty—Amount of duty refunded
to Revenue pending appeal to House of Lords—Appeal allowed—Interest
five per cent.—No retroactive operation of enactment—Finance Act 1965
(c. 25), s. 91.*

A " property company " and a " clothing company " were associated
companies. In pursuance of or in connexion with what was admittedly   G
an " arrangement " within s. 50* of the Finance Act, 1938, certain property
of the clothing company was transferred to the property company, the
consideration expressed in the transfer being the issuing to the clothing
company of a renounceable letter of allotment for 2,920,000 5s. shares in the
property company. This transfer was only one step in an elaborate scheme,
the purpose of which was, by means of a public issue of shares of the property   H
company, to enable a family to realise a substantial sum of money for shares
that they held. The clothing company sold 1,200,000 of the 2,920,000 shares
to an issuing house (which was not an associated company) for £385,000
with a view to the 1,200,000 shares being issued to the public, which in due

---

* Section 50, so far as relevant, is printed at p. 44, letter H, post.   Section 42 of   I
the Finance Act, 1930, so far as material, provides: " (1) Stamp duty under the
heading ' Conveyance of Transfer on Sale ' in Sch. 1 to the Stamp Act, 1891, shall not
be chargeable on an instrument to which this section applies: . . . (2) This section
applies to any instrument as respects which it is shown to the satisfaction of the Commissioners of Inland Revenue—(a) that the effect thereof is to convey or transfer a beneficial
interest in property from one company with limited liability to another such company;
and (b) that either—(i) one of the companies is beneficial owner of not less than ninety
per cent. of the issued share capital of the other company, or (ii) not less than ninety
per cent. of the issued share capital of each of the companies is in the beneficial
ownership of a third company with limited liability."

A   course was successfully done.   No stamp duty was payable on the renuncia-
tion of the allotment of the 1,200,000 shares.   The ultimate result was that
the clothing company had got 1,720,000 shares of the property company and
£385,000 in return for what it had transferred.

On adjudication, ad valorem stamp duty was assessed on the transfer
at £19,693.   This sum was paid by the property company on Feb. 7, 1962.
B   On Apr. 13, 1965, the company's appeal from the adjudication was allowed.
On July 23, 1965, the Commissioners of Inland Revenue repaid the £19,693.
On Nov. 2, 1965, an appeal to the Court of Appeal was allowed, and on
Jan. 24, 1966, the duty was paid back to the commissioners.

On appeal from the Court of Appeal's decision that the £385,000 was part
of the consideration received by the clothing company for the property
C   transferred by it, with the consequence, as that sum was not received from an
associated company, that the transfer was excepted by s. 50 (1) (*a*) of the
Finance Act, 1938, from the exemption from ad valorem stamp duty that
it otherwise would have had under s. 42 of the Finance Act, 1930,

Held: (i) (LORD REID and LORD GUEST dissenting) the words " consideration for the transfer " in s. 50 (1) (*a*) of the Finance Act, 1938, referred
D   to that which was taken by the transferor under the transfer alone, and
not to the quid pro quo which ultimately was the transferor's as a result of
the whole " arrangement " in pursuance of or in connexion with which the
transfer was executed; in the present case the " consideration for the transfer "
was, therefore, the 2,920,000 shares in the property company, and as
all of these were provided by that company, which was a company associated
E   with the clothing company, s. 50 (1) (*a*) of the Act of 1938 did not exclude
the transfer from exemption under s. 42 of the Act of 1930, and the ad
valorem stamp duty must be refunded to the property company (see p. 48,
letter I, p. 49, letter B, p. 50, letter G, p. 53, letters E and F, and p. 55,
letter D, post).

(ii) (LORD GUEST expressing no opinion on this point) the ad valorem
F   stamp duty to be repaid under (i) should be repaid with interest at five per
cent. from Jan. 24, 1966, but no interest could be awarded under s. 91* of
the Finance Act 1965 in respect of the period between the initial payment of
the duty and its repayment to the property company on July 23, 1965, since
to award interest for that period would be to give retroactive operation to
s. 91 (see p. 45, letter H, p. 49, letter D, p. 51, letter B, and p. 55,
G   letter F, post).

Decision of the COURT OF APPEAL ([1965] 3 All E.R. 893) reversed.

[As to relief from stamp duty on conveyances or transfers on sale between
associated companies, see 33 HALSBURY'S LAWS (3rd Edn.) 318, 319, para. 556;
and for a case on the subject, see 39 DIGEST (Repl.) 321, *653*.

For the Finance Act, 1927, s. 55, see 21 HALSBURY'S STATUTES (2nd Edn.) 935.
H   For the Finance Act, 1930, s. 42 (1), and the Finance Act, 1938, s. 50 (1), see
21 HALSBURY'S STATUTES (2nd Edn.) 959, *1196*.

For the Finance Act 1965, s. 91, see 45 HALSBURY'S STATUTES (2nd Edn.) 1398.]

Case referred to:

Holmleigh (Holdings), Ltd. v. *Inland Revenue Comrs.*, (1958), 37 A.T.C. 406.

Appeal.

I   This was an appeal by Shop and Store Developments, Ltd. (" the property
company ") from an order of the Court of Appeal (LORD DENNING, M.R.,
DANCKWERTS and WINN, L.JJ.) dated Nov. 2, 1965 and reported [1965] 3 All E.R.
893, allowing an appeal by the Crown from an order of the Chancery Division
(PENNYCUICK, J.) dated Apr. 13, 1965 and reported [1965] 2 All E.R. 684, in favour
of the appellant property company on a Case Stated by the Commissioners

*
* Section 91 is printed at p. 55, letter E, post.   It came into operation on Aug. 5,
1965.

of Inland Revenue, under s. 13 of the Stamp Act, 1891, for the opinion of the A
court as to the stamp duty chargeable on five instruments presented to them
by the property company for adjudication under s. 12 of the Act of 1891. The
commissioners found that the instruments were chargeable to stamp duty ad
valorem, as conveyances on sale, in an aggregate sum of £19,693. The five instruments comprised: (a) three transfers of registered land made by Greenwood
(Hosiers & Outfitters), Ltd., a clothing company (hereinafter referred to as " the B
clothing company "), to the property company; (b) an assignment by the clothing
company to the property company of a leasehold interest in property; and (c) a
conveyance by the clothing company to the property company of further
properties.

The facts are fully stated in the report [1965] 3 All E.R. 893, and are set out in
the opinion of LORD MORRIS OF BORTH-Y-GEST at pp. 45 and 46, letters I to C, C
et seq., post.

R. P. S. Instone for the property company.
Peter Foster, Q.C., and *J. P. Warner* for the Crown.

Their lordships took time for consideration.

December 8. The following opinions were delivered. D

LORD REID: My Lords, a family who owned the shares of two companies,
referred to as the clothing company and the property company, wished to turn
the property company (who are the appellants) into a public company, to issue
a number of its shares for sale to the public, to obtain a stock exchange quotation
and to get out of the proceeds a sum of over £250,000. An elaborate scheme was E
put into operation to achieve this. The only parts of it which I need consider
were first a sale of certain property by the clothing company (the transferor)
to the property company (the transferee) for which the transferee gave to the
transferor allotment letters for 2,920,000 new shares of the transferee and
secondly a sale by the transferor of allotment letters for 1,200,000 of these shares to
underwriters, Investment Registry, Ltd., for £385,000. So as a result of carrying F
out the arrangement the transferor company had parted with the property and
had acquired 1,720,000 shares and £385,000.

The question in this case is whether the instrument conveying the property
from the transferor company to the transferee, the appellant, is exempt from
stamp duty. It would have been exempt under s. 42 of the Finance Act, 1930,
because these two companies were associated in such a way as to comply with
that section. The scope of that section was restricted, however, by s. 50 of the G
Finance Act, 1938, the relevant part of which is in these terms:

" 50.—(1) Section 42 of the Finance Act, 1930 (which relieves from stamp
duty any instrument the effect whereof is to convey or transfer a beneficial
interest in property from one associated company to another, in this section
respectively referred to as the ' transferor ' and ' transferee ') shall not apply H
to any such instrument, unless it is shown to the satisfaction of the Commissioners of Inland Revenue that the instrument was not executed in pursuance
of or in connexion with an arrangement whereunder—(a) the consideration
for the transfer or conveyance was to to be provided directly or indirectly by
a person other than a company which at the time of the execution of the
instrument was associated with either the transferor or the transferee; ..." I

Admittedly this instrument was executed in pursuance of the arrangement to
which I have referred. So we must determine what was the consideration
under the arrangement for the transfer. The property company says that it
was the allotment letters for 2,920,000 shares. The Crown says that it was that
which under the arrangement the transferor received and kept as a result of the
transfer of its property. The case for the property company is that we must
isolate that part or stage of the arrangement which consisted of the sale of the
property and see what the transferor got at that stage. The case for the Crown

A is that we must take the arrangement as a whole and see what the transferor got as a result of the transfer, when the arrangement was completed. If the property company is right on this short point, this appeal succeeds, because the consideration would then be the 2,920,000 shares all of which were provided by the associated company, the transferee. If the Crown is right the appeal fails because the consideration would then be the 1,720,000 shares which the transferor retained

B plus the £385,000 which was paid to them by the underwriters for the other 1,200,000 shares, and the underwriters were not an associated company.

I think that the Crown is right. Admittedly " consideration " in this context does not have its technical meaning in the law of contract. Under this section consideration is to include anything provided directly by persons other than the transferee. Nevertheless something directly provided by a person other

C than the transferee is something which does not move from the transferee, and which would therefore not be consideration in the technical sense. The meaning of the word " consideration " in this context must therefore be determined from the context, and the general scheme of the section.

As I understand it the reason for this exemption is that, when the whole transaction is between closely associated companies, what is in effect an exchange

D between them of property for shares or money is more a matter of internal administration than a sale in the ordinary sense. If outside money is brought in as part of the arrangement, however, then the arrangement ceases to be confined to internal administration and there is no longer any adequate reason for the exemption from stamp duty. If that were right and the section were well drafted, then one would not expect the exemption to apply to the present

E case. An essential feature of this arrangement was that a large sum was to come to the companies and the family who owned them from outside sources: in the first instance from the underwriters, and ultimately from the public who purchased these 1,200,000 shares. The issuing of the allotment letters by the transferee to the transferor company was only part of the machinery which made this possible.

F Turning to the words of the section and bearing in mind that consideration has no technical meaning here but merely means what the transferor got, the question is—what under the arrangement did the transferor get for the transfer? I do not think that it involves any stretching of the language to hold that the transferor got shares and money. On the other hand it would, I think, be an unreasonable result if we had to hold that all depended on the stage of the

G arrangement at which the outside money came to the transferor. If it came at the stage of the transfer of the property, then it would admittedly destroy the exemption but if it came at the next stage it would not. I would only accept that if the words were not reasonably capable of any other meaning. I do not think that the words " for the transfer " are so rigid and compelling as to require that result. In my view it is a natural use of ordinary language to say that

H under this arrangement the transferor company got the shares and the money " for " the transfer of its property.

I would therefore dismiss this appeal; but if the appeal is allowed I agree with your lordships' views as to the amount of interest to be awarded.

LORD MORRIS OF BORTH-Y-GEST: My Lords, this appeal raises

I questions concerning the effect of s. 50 of the Finance Act, 1938, in its application to the facts set out in the Case Stated. I need not re-state those facts, but for purposes of referring to them it will be convenient to describe the appellant company as " the property company " and to describe Greenwoods (Hosiers and Outfitters), Ltd. as " the clothing company ". After the sale on Nov. 2, 1959, by members of the Greenwood family to the clothing company of 1,078,800 shares of 5s. each in the property company for the sum of £269,700 the clothing company then became the beneficial owner of not less than ninety per cent. of the issued share capital of the property company. At that time the issued share capital of the

property company consisted of 1,080,000 ordinary shares of 5s. each. There- A
after, though also on Nov. 2, 1959, an agreement was signed between the clothing
company and the property company whereby the clothing company agreed to
sell a number of freehold and leasehold properties to the property company.
The transfer was to be completed on the same day. The price was £984,571.
That sum was to be satisfied by the issue to the clothing company (or its nominees)
of renounceable letters of allotment in respect of a further 2,920,000 ordinary B
shares of 5s. each in the capital of the property company. There were five
instruments (all dated Nov. 2, 1959), in respect of the properties (three being
transfers of registered land, one an assignment of leasehold interests set out in a
schedule thereto, and one a conveyance of properties set out in a schedule
thereto). These were the adjudicated instruments. If they fell to be assessed
to conveyance or transfer on sale duty then the instruments were chargeable C
with sums of duty which in total amount to £19,693.

Had there been no qualification of s. 42 of the Finance Act, 1930, it would
seem clear that the instruments would not be chargeable. By that section there
is relief from transfer stamp duty on instruments as respects which it is shown
to the satisfaction of the commissioners that the effect thereof is to convey or
transfer a beneficial interest in property from one company with limited liability D
to another such company and if (inter alia) one of the companies is beneficial
owner of not less than ninety per cent. of the issued share capital of the other
company. It is the measure of the restriction on that relief that now calls for
consideration. The restriction was imposed by s. 50 of the Finance Act, 1938.
As a result of the restriction s. 42 of the Finance Act, 1930, is made not to apply
to the instruments now in question unless it is shown to the satisfaction of the E
commissioners that the instruments were not

> " executed in pursuance of or in connexion with an arrangement where-
> under—(a) the consideration for the transfer or conveyance was to be
> provided directly or indirectly by a person other than a company which at
> the time of the execution of the instrument was associated with either "

F

the clothing company or the property company. For another company to be
" associated " either with the clothing company or the property company there
would have to be satisfaction of the requirements of s. 50 (2). It is sufficient for
present purposes to remember that Investment Registry, Ltd. was not an
associated company.

That company (Investment Registry, Ltd.) was an issuing house. I will G
refer to it as "I.R.". The clothing company by an agreement also made on Nov. 2,
agreed to sell 1,200,000 of the ordinary shares in the property company (being
part of the 2,920,000 shares) to I.R. The sale was at a price of 6s. 5d. per share.
The price was to be paid within ten days after obtaining permission to deal in
and a quotation for the whole of the issued share capital of the property company.
The purchase by I.R. of the shares was made conditional on the granting by the H
Council of The Stock Exchange, London, of permission to deal in and quotation
for the whole of the issued share capital of the property company. An application for such permission had been made on behalf of the property company on
Oct. 27. As the purchase price of the properties sold by the clothing company
was £984,571 and as the clothing company agreed with the property company
that the sum was to be satisfied by the issue of 2,920,000 shares it follows that I
the price put on the shares by the clothing company and the property company
was a price of 6s. 9d. per share.

The next stage to be carried out, in what was by common consent a carefully
planned series of transactions which must be regarded as an " arrangement ",
was that I.R. prepared for an offer of sale of the 1,200,000 shares to the public.
The property company had in fact issued to the clothing company a single
renounceable letter of allotment in respect of the 2,920,000 shares in the property
company. So that the sale by the clothing company to I.R. of the 1,200,000

A   shares might be completed the letter of allotment in respect of the 2,920,000 shares was split into two letters, one for 1,720,000 in favour of the clothing company and one for 1,200,000 which was delivered to I.R.   On Nov. 6, the permission of the Council of the Stock Exchange, London, was given to deal in the shares. On Nov. 9, I.R. offered the shares to the public at the price of 6s. 9d. per share. The offer was successful.   I.R. paid £385,000 (being the price of the 1,200,000

B   shares) to the clothing company.   Thereafter (on Nov. 17) the clothing company paid to the members of the Greenwood family the sum of £269,700 which had remained owing in respect of the 1,078,800 shares which (at a price representing 5s. per share) the clothing company had bought.

If the series of transactions or the " arrangement " is surveyed it will be seen that the members of the Greenwood family finished up with a considerable

C   sum of money: the property company finished up owning properties which they had bought for £984,571 (and which properties they in fact leased back to the clothing company): the clothing company finished up holding 1,078,800 shares in the property company (which it had bought at 5s. per share), 1,720,000 shares in the property company (taken at a price of 6s. 9d. per share), and a considerable sum in money: members of the public finished up holding 1,200,000 shares in the

D   property company which had been issued at a price of 6s. 9d. per share.

The adjudicated instruments having been assessed to duty in sums amounting in the aggregate to £19,693 the property company paid that amount on Feb. 7, 1962, and required the commissioners to state and sign a Case pursuant to s. 13 of the Stamp Act, 1891.   The Case was stated and signed on Sept. 22, 1964.   The main question for the opinion of the court was framed as being whether the adjudi-

E   cated instruments were chargeable with the ad valorem duty assessed by the commissioners.   The matter came up for argument before PENNYCUICK, J. (1), on Mar. 17, 1965.   In a reserved judgment delivered on Apr. 13, 1965, the learned judge allowed the appeal.   It was declared that the adjudicated instruments were not chargeable with stamp duty and re-payment of the duty was ordered.   Re-payment was made on July 23, 1965.   The commissioners appealed

F   to the Court of Appeal (2) (LORD DENNING, M.R., DANCKWERTS and WINN, L.JJ.) who heard argument on Nov. 1 and 2, 1965, and by their judgments given on the latter date allowed the appeal and ordered that the sum of £19,693 stamp duty should be repaid to the commissioners.   That was done on Jan. 24, 1966.

My lords, the decision in this case calls for a full and fair application of particular statutory language to particular facts as found.   The desirability or the unde-

G   sirability of one conclusion as compared with another cannot furnish a guide in reaching a decision.   The result reached must be that which is directed by that which is enacted.

It is first necessary to consider whether the instruments now being considered were " executed in pursuance of or in connexion with an arrangement ".   I think that they clearly were.   It is manifest, and, as the Case Stated records,

H   it was common ground, that the various transactions which took place on Nov. 2, 1959, were all planned in advance.   It was at an early staged envisaged that there would be a public flotation of shares, which would be effected by an offer to the public of the renounced letters of allotment purchased by I.R. from the clothing company.   Discussions had taken place with I.R., although it is clear that I.R. were not contractually obliged to do anything prior to the time when,

I   on Nov. 2, 1959, they agreed to buy the 1,200,000 shares from the clothing company.   The money realised by I.R. after offering the 1,200,000 shares to the public at a price of 6s. 9d. enabled I.R. to pay the clothing company the sum of £385,000 (the price of the 1,200,000 shares at 6s. 5d.).   The receipt by the clothing company from I.R. of that sum of £385,000 enabled the clothing company to pay the sum of £269,700 (as it did on Nov. 17) to the members of the Greenwood family for the 1,078,800 shares in the property company which the clothing

(1) [1965] 2 All E.R. 684; [1966] Ch. 108.
(2) [1965] 3 All E.R. 893; [1966] Ch. at p. 123.

company bought on Nov. 2, 1959. So there was before Nov. 2, 1959, a pre-   A
existing "arrangement". The adjudicated instruments were executed in
pursuance of or in connexion with the arrangement. It is not necessary to
consider whether the parties concerned were, before Nov. 2, 1959, in any way
contractually obliged to proceed to carry out what had been discussed or arranged.

Accepting, therefore, that the adjudicated instruments were executed in
pursuance of or in connexion with an arrangement, it next becomes necessary   B
to decide whether under that arrangement the consideration for the transfers
and conveyance of the property was to be provided either directly or indirectly
by a person or company other than the property company. The clothing company sold its properties to the property company. If it is asked what did the
clothing company get in return the answer and, as it seems to me, the complete
answer, must be that it got 2,920,000 shares in the property company. The   C
fact that the issue of the consideration shares was to take place by means of a
renounceable allotment letter or letters makes no difference. The property
company was an "associated" company in the sense prescribed by statute.
If the question is posed—were the consideration shares provided by I.R. or
provided by the public?—it is manifest that the answer must be "No". The
words "directly or indirectly" must be given full effect. It seems clear that   D
just as the shares were not provided directly save by the property company so,
equally, they were not provided indirectly by anyone else. If, therefore, the
shares were the consideration for the transfer I would think that the commissioners ought to have been satisfied that the property company was not
deprived of the relief given to it by s. 42 of the Finance Act, 1930. The enquiry
is then raised whether there was some other consideration than the shares and   E
as to the meaning in the context of the word "consideration".

It is necessary to bear fully in mind what were the results of the transactions
comprising the arrangement. I have referred to them above and I have set
out how the various parties would stand when the arrangement was carried out.
As a result of selling its properties the clothing company would have obtained
shares, some of which it would sell so that the shares could get a stock exchange   F
quotation and so that it could receive money. In anticipation of the receipt
of that money it had incurred a debt on a prior purchase of shares. The final
result which all concerned planned and projected was designed to be satisfactory
for the property company, for the Greenwood family, for the clothing company
and for some members of the public. When all this is recognised, however, and
stated the question still has to be asked and answered: what was the consideration   G
for the transfer or conveyance of the properties which the clothing company
transferred or conveyed? This is not the same as the question: how would it
stand when the whole arrangement was completed? At that time in respect of
or consequential on the transfer of its properties and as a result of the arrangement the clothing company would have a number of shares in the property
company and a sum of money. The money would have come to it from I.R.,   H
who were not an "associated" company. I cannot think, however, that such
money can be regarded as being part of the consideration for the transfer or
conveyance by the clothing company.

The duty that was assessed on the adjudicated instruments was assessed
pursuant to s. 55 of the Stamp Act, 1891. Section 55 (1) of that Act provides
that where the consideration or any part of the consideration for a conveyance on   I
sale consists of any stock or marketable security the conveyance is to be charged
with ad valorem duty in respect of the value of the stock or security. It seems
to me that both in that section and in s. 50 of the Finance Act, 1938, the word
"consideration" denotes that which is received. What the clothing company
received or what it got when it transferred or conveyed its properties to the
property company was shares in the property company. The shares had a
value of 6s. 9d. per share. Those facts are not changed by the circumstance
that in a different and separate transaction it sold some of the shares to someone

A else at a price of 6s. 5d. per share. There is all the difference between what the clothing company got and what it did with what it got. The question who provided the consideration on the different and separate sale does not arise. The money which the clothing company received came as a result of the realisation by it of a part of what it received for its properties but, in my view, no part of what it received for the transfer or conveyance was provided either directly

B or indirectly by any person or company other than the property company. In agreement with PENNYCUICK, J. (3) I recognise that the words " directly or indirectly " cast a wide net, but I also agree with him that if company A sells property to company B in consideration of full-paid shares in company B and if company A, even pursuant to a pre-arranged plan, then sells some of the shares to C, it cannot be said that C has provided directly or indirectly the con-

C sideration for the sale of the property by company A to company B. For these reasons I feel impelled to the conclusion that the answer to the question raised in the Case Stated should be that the adjudicated instruments are not chargeable with the ad valorem duty assessed. I consider, therefore, that the duty paid should again be repaid, and in exercise of the power given by s. 91 of the Finance Act, 1965, I consider that it should be repaid with interest at five per cent. as

D from Jan. 24, 1966.

I would allow the appeal.

LORD HODSON: My Lords, the question is, what was the consideration for the transfer of certain property by the clothing company (the transferor) and the property company (the transferee) under the arrangement for that

E transfer?

The transferee gave to the transferor in exchange for the property renounceable allotment letters for 2,920,000 new shares of the transferee. Did the transferor company give anything else? In my opinion, it did not do so. True, it was part of the arrangement that the transferor should sell 1,200,000 of these shares to Investment Registry, who acted as underwriters, at the price of £385,000.

F The shares were afterwards passed on to the public. However extended the meaning which one gives to the word " consideration ", I cannot see that it was other than the allotment letters which were provided by and could only be granted by the property company. This consideration was provided directly and was not provided indirectly by anyone else. There is no deeming provision to draw into the net the arrangement by which money was to be raised by dis-

G posing of the shares. There was no restriction on the transferor's right to dispose of the shares.

This is said to be too technical a view, but the words used in the Acts should not be stretched against the taxpayer. Parliament could, for example, have provided against the sale of the shares until a time limit had expired. This was done in s. 55 (6) of the Finance Act, 1927, where an exemption was deemed not

H to have been allowed when a company within a period of two years ceased in certain circumstances to be the beneficial owner of shares.

Reliance was placed on some obiter dicta by HARMAN, J., in favour of the Commissioners of Inland Revenue in *Holmleigh (Holdings), Ltd.* v. *Inland Revenue Comrs.* (4) where a parallel situation arose. He said:

I " The appellants' argument here was that the only consideration for the transfer to Hale was the issue of the Hale shares and that therefore no consideration was provided by an outsider. I cannot accept this too technical view. In fact this transaction should, as I have said, be regarded as one step in the performance of the whole agreement. The share consideration provided by Hale was not intended to rest where it was : this indeed is shown by the fact that it was never vested in Flatau, but by that company's direction was issued direct to the vendor shareholders. The only

---

(3) [1965] 2 All E.R. at p. 690, letters F, G ; [1966] Ch. at p. 120.
(4) (1958), 37 A.T.C. 406 at p. 410.

explanation of this—and a sufficient one—is that the vendor shareholders $\qquad$ A
were already bound by the sale agreement to buy the shares from Flatau.
They therefore, or at one remove G.U.S., provided the consideration."

That the sale agreement was an " arrangement " within the section was not
denied.   These dicta were accepted by the Court of Appeal (5) in this case but,
with all respect to HARMAN, J., I cannot agree that what happened to the shares
after the transfer renders the proceeds of sale part of the consideration at one $\qquad$ B
remove or at all.   There is admittedly no distinction to be drawn between this
case and the *Holmleigh* case (6) by reason of the existence of a binding agreement
in the latter case, whereas there was no binding agreement with Investment
Registry, Ltd., in this case.   If the consideration for the transfer was provided
under a relevant arrangement it matters not that there was no consideration for
the arrangement.   No doubt it was an essential element in the arrangement $\qquad$ C
that cash should be raised by the sale of allotment letters, but it does not follow
that the consideration for the transfer was other than what it was stated to be.
See the agreement for sale dated Nov. 2, 1959.   Paragraph 2 reads, so far as
material:

> " The purchase price for the said properties shall be the sum of £984,571 $\qquad$ D
> which shall be satisfied by the issue to the vendor or its nominees of renounce-
> able letters of allotment for 2,920,000 ordinary shares of 5s. each in the
> capital of the purchaser . . ."

This was what happened and it matters not that in the hands of the recipient
the consideration stated in the agreement ultimately took a different form.
They sold the shares which they had received but, in the ordinary use of language, $\qquad$ E
it cannot be said that the consideration was provided directly or indirectly
either by Investment Registry, Ltd. or the members of the public who ultimately
subscribed for the shares.   Cash was ultimately provided by the sale of the
shares but not as consideration for the sale of the properties.

This interpretation is consistent with the apparent object of s. 50 of the Finance
Act, 1938, which is to restrict the exemption given by s. 42 of the Finance Act, $\qquad$ F
1930, to those cases where the consideration which would otherwise attract
stamp duty originates within the relevant group of companies.

Whatever extended meaning is given to " consideration " it must represent
a quid pro quo for that which passed by the transfer or conveyance.   I agree
with the conclusion at which PENNYCUICK, J., arrived.   He said (7):

> " The words ' directly ' or ' indirectly ' cast a wide net, but in the case $\qquad$ G
> where, under an arrangement, company A sells property to company B in
> consideration of fully-paid shares in company B, and then sells those shares
> to C, I do not myself see how, on any ordinary use of language, C can be said
> to have provided directly or indirectly the consideration for the sale of the
> property by company A to company B."

I would allow the appeal. $\qquad$ H

The appellants claim interest on the duty which will be repayable to them
(£19,693).   They paid the duty to the commissioners on Feb. 7, 1962.   PENNY-
CUICK, J. (8) gave judgment in favour of the appellants on Apr. 13, 1965, and
the commissioners repaid the duty on July 23, 1965.   By s. 91 of the Finance
Act 1965, it is provided:

> " Where under s. 13 (4) of the Stamp Act, 1891 (appeals against assess- $\qquad$ I
> ment of stamp duty) a court orders any sum to be repaid by the Commis-
> sioners of Inland Revenue the court may order it to be repaid with such
> interest as the court may determine."

---

(5) [1965] 3 All E.R. 893; [1966] Ch. at p. 123.
(6) (1958), 37 A.T.C. 406.
(7) [1965] 2 All E.R. at p. 690, letter F; [1966] Ch. at p. 120, letter F.
(8) [1965] 2 All E.R. at p. 687; [1966] Ch. at p. 119.

A   This Act of 1965 came into force on Aug. 5, 1965. On Jan. 24, 1966, the appellants, following the judgment of the Court of Appeal (9), repaid the duty to the commissioners. The property company should receive interest at the appropriate rate (five per cent. per annum) from Jan. 24, 1966, to the date of repayment but, in my opinion, interest cannot be awarded in respect of the earlier period before the Finance Act 1965, was passed. This would be to give retro-

B   spective effect to the legislation in a matter of substance not merely of procedure and is not to be done unless the statute itself so directs.

LORD GUEST: My lords, where the consideration for a conveyance on sale consists of any stock, ad valorem stamp duty is chargeable under s. 55 of the Stamp Act, 1891, on the conveyance. By s. 42 of the Finance Act, 1930, no stamp duty is chargeable on any instrument the effect of which is to transfer

C   a beneficial interest from one company to another where one of such companies is the beneficial owner of not less than ninety per cent. of the issued share capital of the other.   This exemption from stamp duty is taken away in certain circumstances which are detailed in s. 50 of the Finance Act, 1938, which, so far as material, is in the following terms:

D   " (1) Section 42 of the Finance Act, 1930 . . . shall not apply to any such instrument, unless it is shown to the satisfaction of the Commissioners of Inland Revenue that the instrument was not executed in pursuance of or in connexion with an arrangement whereunder—(a) the consideration for the transfer or conveyance was to be provided directly or indirectly by a person other than a company which at the time of the execution of the instrument

E   was associated with either the transferor or the transferee; . . ."

The adjudicated instruments were five conveyances of property from Greenwoods (Hosiers & Outfitters), Ltd. (known as the " clothing company ") to the property company executed on Nov. 2, 1959. The Commissioners of Inland Revenue assessed the adjudicated instruments to duty in the aggregate sum of £19,693, based on the total values of the properties. On a Case Stated PENNYCUICK, J.,

F   (10) found in favour of the property company, but his decision was reversed on appeal by the Court of Appeal (9).   If the property company is not entitled to the relief claimed, there is no dispute as to the amount of duty payable. The effect of the arrangement pursuant to which the adjudicated instruments were executed was one for providing cash for the shareholders of the property company (who with their relatives owned all the issued shares of the clothing company)

G   by means of an offer of shares for sale to the public. The arrangement was carried into effect by the following stages:

" (a) The property company allotted to its members 1,048,000 ordinary shares of 5s. each credited as fully paid up by the capitalisation of reserves; these shares together with all but 1,200 of its previously-issued shares were sold by the allottees to the clothing company for the aggregate sum of

H   £269,700 payable in cash; and the clothing company was registered as the holder of all the shares so sold.

" It is accepted by the commissioners that at the conclusion of this stage the two companies were related in manner prescribed by s. 42 of the Finance Act, 1930.

" (b) Thereupon the clothing company agreed to sell to the property

I   company certain freehold and leasehold properties which it owned for the sum of £984,571 (being the sum at which such properties had recently been professionally valued) to be satisfied by the issue of renounceable allotment letters for 2,920,000 ordinary shares of 5s. each in the capital of the property company credited as fully paid up.

" Such shares were thereby accorded a value (to the nearest farthing) of 6s. 9d. each.

(9) [1965] 3 All E.R. 893; [1966] Ch. at p. 123.
(10) [1965] 2 All E.R. 684; [1966] Ch. 108.

" (c) The clothing company sold to an issuing house 1,200,000 of the last-   **A**
mentioned shares at the price of 6s. 5d. per share; such shares were offered
for sale to the public by the issuing house (which bore certain of the expenses
in connexion therewith) at 6s. 9d. per share; the offer was over-subscribed
and out of the proceeds the issuing house paid the clothing company for the
shares so sold to it; and the clothing company in turn out of the same money
paid the sum of £269,700 payable by it for the shares of the property company   **B**
purchased at stage (a)."

All these stages took place on one day, Nov. 2, 1959.

The question is whether the property company has shown that the adjudicated
instruments were not executed in pursuance of or in connexion with an arrangement whereunder the consideration for the transfer or conveyance was to be   **C**
provided directly or indirectly by a person other than an associated company
within the meaning of s. 50 of the Finance Act, 1938. At the first stage in the
arrangement above referred to it was agreed that the two companies were related
in the manner prescribed by s. 42 of the Finance Act, 1930, and that the property
company were entitled to the exemption therein provided unless excluded by
s. 50 of the Act of 1938. The contention for the property company was that in   **D**
deciding whether consideration for the transfer or conveyance had been provided
by a person other than the associated company attention must solely be directed
to the conveyance itself. This was provided by an associated company, and s. 50
of the Act of 1938 did not accordingly deprive the property company of the
relief afforded by s. 42 of the Finance Act, 1930. What required to be examined
was what was the consideration for the transfer, not what was the consideration   **E**
receivable under the arrangement. This construction, in my opinion, ignores
these words in the section—

" the instrument was not executed in pursuance of or in connexion with
an arrangement whereunder—(a) the consideration for the transfer or
conveyance was to be provided . . ."

The onus is on the property company to show that the circumstances provided   **F**
in s. 50 do not apply. Section 50 must be looked at as a whole, and the whole
arrangement must be examined to see who provided the consideration for the
transfer under the arrangement. The " consideration " is not confined to its
strict legal meaning in the law of contract. It means the quid pro quo received by
the transferor under the arrangement; not the consideration moving from the
transferee, but the consideration moving to the transferor. In these circum-   **G**
stances what must be looked at is what was the consideration under the
arrangement as a whole at the end of the day. So viewed I have no hesitation in
holding that the consideration for the transfer or conveyance under the arrangement was not limited to the shares in the property company. Under the arrangement a substantial benefit was to be provided not by the property company but   **H**
by the issuing house. As DANCKWERTS, L.J., (11) put it: " indirectly, if not
directly, the issuing house were providing an essential part of the consideration
for the transfer of " properties of the property company.

It was said that to give effect to the Crown's contention would mean that
" consideration " would have different meanings in s. 50 of the Finance Act,
1938, and in s. 55 of the Stamp Act, 1891. I see no reason why this should not be   **I**
so. The " consideration " in s. 55 is the yardstick for assessing the stamp duty
on the relevant conveyance: the " consideration " under s. 50 is one item in the
determination of the question whether the exemption allowed in s. 42 of the
Finance Act, 1930, is to apply to the transaction. The one section is a taxing
section: the other section is an exempting section.

Finally, I am impressed by the argument that if the property company's

---

(11) [1965] 3 All E.R. at p. 899, letter G; [1966] Ch. at p. 132, letter D.

A   contention were to be upheld it might lead to the wholesale evasion of the provisions of the Stamp Act, 1891, referred to by LORD DENNING, M.R. (12). If I were forced to the conclusion on a proper consideration of s. 50 that the appellants had preserved their exemption under s. 42 of the Finance Act, 1930, then I would agree that it was a matter for the legislature to step in to prevent the abuse. I am not, however, so constrained and on a proper construction of

B   s. 50 I would hold that the property company was not entitled to the relief claimed.

    I would dismiss the appeal.

    LORD WILBERFORCE: My Lords, I do not believe that it is necessary to state more than the following outline facts. The appellant ("the property

C   company") on Nov. 2, 1959, agreed to acquire from an associated company certain freehold and leasehold properties for £984,571 to be satisfied by the allotment to the associated company of 2,920,000 ordinary shares of the property company credited as fully paid up: arithmetically this conferred on the allotted shares a value of 6s. 9d. each. Allotment letters in renounceable form were duly issued. Shortly afterwards the associated company sold 1,200,000 of these shares

D   to an issuing house at a price, paid in cash, of £385,000 representing 6s. 5d. per share, and the issuing house made an issue to the public. It is admitted that these transactions were part of a single arrangement. The question for decision is this: whether the instruments of transfer of the freehold and leasehold properties were executed in pursuance of or in connexion with an arrangement whereunder the consideration for the transfer was to be provided directly or indirectly by the

E   issuing house or (though this raises the same point) the public.

    There are two contending views as to the meaning of the relevant part of s. 50 of the Finance Act, 1938, which is incorporated in the statement that I have made of the question. The first is that one should read "consideration for the transfer" as referring to that consideration which was taken by the transferor company under the transfer alone—which in this case would be the

F   2,920,000 fully paid shares in the associated transferee company. The second would be to read the words as referring to the ultimate consideration or quid pro quo which found its way to the transferor under, i.e., as a result of, the arrangement as a whole.

    The first interpretation, which involves the success of the property company's claim to exemption from stamp duty in respect of the transfer(s), was accepted

G   by PENNYCUICK, J., (13): the second, which involves the contrary result, was accepted by the Court of Appeal (14).

    The reasons which induce me to prefer the former of these two interpretations are the following. In the first place, the phrase " consideration for the transfer or conveyance " seems to me to refer clearly and naturally to that which passed to the transferor company " for " the transferred properties. The earlier portion

H   of s. 50 itself, in its reference to s. 42 of the Finance Act, 1930, speaks of an instrument " the effect whereof is to convey or transfer a beneficial interest in property from one associated company to another ", and the words in para. (*a*) are an evident reference back to these words.

    So, just as it is clear that the initial part is directing attention to the instrument of transfer as between the two associated companies, so one would naturally

I   expect to find the same thought expressed in para. (*a*).

    The Crown's case against this depends on the words " an arrangement whereunder ": the Crown says that para. (*a*) is not concerned merely with the consideration for the transfer but with the consideration for the transfer under the arrangement. This is quite right, but I do not see that it assists the Crown's

---

(12) [1965] 3 All E.R. at pp. 897, 898; [1966] Ch. at pp. 129, 130.
(13) [1965] 2 All E.R. 684; [1966] Ch. 108.
(14) [1965] 3 All E.R. 893; [1966] Ch. at p. 123.

argument. The addition of the reference to the arrangement does nothing to alter   A
the basic requirement that the consideration must be for the transfer. It does not
achieve what, if the Crown is to succeed it must achieve, namely, to substitute
for the consideration for the transfer the consideration receivable under the
arrangement as a whole.

The relevance of the arrangement in the argument is established, in my opinion,
by the words " provided directly or indirectly by a person other than " an   B
associated company; but these do nothing to assist the Crown. It is said that
they show at least that " consideration " must be given a wider meaning than
that which it bears in the ordinary law of contract and that, therefore, one may
look outside the contractual document. Perhaps this is true in a sense, but only
in the sense that the ultimate source of the consideration may be sought in what
has been arranged. The meaning of " consideration " remains the same. Con-   C
sideration payable by, or moving from, one party to a contract to another, may
quite well be provided by an outside party and still be, as between the contracting
parties, the consideration for the contract. The outside party may give or lend
money to the contracting party, so as to enable him to pay for what he has
bought, and effect can be given to the words " directly " or " indirectly " by
supposing that the provider is, in the one case, not an associated company or,   D
in the other case, an associated company which in turn gets the money from an
outsider. Secondly, the argument for reading " consideration for the transfer "
in a normal contractual sense becomes all the stronger when it is recalled that it
is the consideration for the transfer which (under this very terminology) forms
the basis for the stamp duty charge (see Stamp Act, 1891, s. 1, s. 55; Schedule,
sub tit., " Conveyance or transfer on sale "). Apart from the terminological   E
argument for reading the two expressions in the same way, not conclusive but
surely strong, it seems strange to rest the test for exemption from stamp duty on
consideration in one sense and the charge on consideration in another sense—to
say in fact that the consideration for the purpose of s. 50 (1) (a) was 1,720,000
shares (valued at 6s. 9d. each) plus cash equal to 6s. 5d. for 1,200,000 shares,
whereas, for the purposes of stamping, the consideration is 2,920,000 shares   F
at 6s. 9d.

Thirdly, if one asks: " for what were 1,200,000 shares plus £385,000 (the quid
pro quo under the arrangement, according to the Crown) the consideration ", the
answer, to my mind, is not " the transfer ", which must mean the transfer of
the properties, but is " the transfer of the properties followed by a sale of 1,200,000
shares "—a point made by PENNYCUICK, J., (15) and, in my opinion, unanswered   G
by the Crown.

Finally, a general consideration of the scheme of the sections and the implications of the rival arguments, decidedly, to my mind, supports the property
company. The property company's construction, on the one hand, gives quite
an intelligible scope to s. 50. Section 42 of the Finance Act, 1930, having conferred
stamp duty exemption on transfers of property within a group (an expression I   H
use to refer to companies associated as the statute prescribes), s. 50 would remove
this exemption in cases where either the property transferred (sub-s. (1) (b)) or
the consideration for it (sub-s. (1) (a)) comes from a source outside the group.

The Crown's construction, on the other hand, would impose a tax liability in
cases where a purely intra-group transaction is followed (as part of an arrangement) by a disposition of the, or part of the, property or consideration transferred.   I
One may ask two questions as to this: first, if it was intended to restrict the
exemption to cases where the transferred property or the consideration rests with
the original holder, why should not this be so stated, as it has been when such an
objective is desired—see, for example, Finance Act, 1927, s. 55 (6) (b). Secondly,
what is the policy to which, or (to use the prejudicial word) the mischief against
which, such legislation could be directed? If the consideration in this case had

---

(15) [1965] 2 All E.R. at p. 690, letter E; [1966] Ch. at p. 120.

A been either real property, or (more strikingly) registered shares, why should exemption be denied to the intra-group transfer merely because the consideration is sold on? The second transfer would itself attract full ad valorem duty, so no duty would be lost. One can imagine many cases of intra-group transfers carried out with the object of subsequent charges, purchases, or sales, and in all such cases, if the Crown is right, not only would duty be payable on those

B transactions, but, given an arrangement, on the intra-group transfer as well.

In this particular case, admittedly, tax will be lost if the property company succeeds, but it is worth considering just why it is lost. The reason is that instead of issuing registered shares as consideration, renounceable allotment letters were used which, subject to certain conditions, can be transferred free of stamp duty. In other words, the loss of duty does not arise from the sub-transfer of the

C consideration under the arrangement, but from the special character of the consideration. Apart from that, transactions such as the present would involve no loss of duty, which once more confirms that they are not the target at which the section aims.

I agree with the judgment of PENNYCUICK, J., (16) and would restore it by allowing the appeal and directing that the duty be repaid.

D There remains one further question. The Finance Act 1965, s. 91, which came into effect on Aug. 5, 1965, has, since the decision of PENNYCUICK, J., (16) altered the law by providing that interest may be awarded on duty repaid: its terms are:

" 91. Where under s. 13 (4) of the Stamp Act, 1891 (appeals against assessment of stamp duty) a court orders any sum to be repaid by the
E Commissioners of Inland Revenue, the court may order it to be repaid with such interest as the court may determine."

When the Court of Appeal (17) allowed the appeal from the decision of PENNY-CUICK, J., (16) the property company, on Jan. 24, 1966, repaid the duty claimed (£19,693) to the commissioners. It would clearly be right, under the section, that

F the duty should now be repaid with interest from that date to the date of repayment, and it is not disputed that the appropriate rate would be five per cent. per annum. In my opinion, however, interest cannot be awarded in respect of the period between the original payment of the duty and its repayment to the property company on July 23, 1965, following the decision of PENNYCUICK, J., (16) in its favour. To make such an order would amount to giving retrospective effect to legislation of a substantive character which, unless the statute itself so

G directs, cannot be done.

Appeal allowed.

Solicitors: *Ward, Bowie & Co.*, agents for *Lee & Priestley*, Bradford (for the property company, the appellant); *Solicitor of Inland Revenue.*

[*Reported by* KATHLEEN J. O'BRIEN, *Barrister-at-Law.*]

H

I

---

(16) [1965] 2 All E.R. 684; [1966] Ch. 108.
(17) [1965] 3 All E.R. 893; [1966] Ch. at p. 123.

A

Re RAMPGILL MILL, LTD.

[CHANCERY DIVISION (Plowman, J.), November 10, 11, 22, 1966.]

Company—Winding-up—Wages—Preferential creditor—Advances for payment of wages—No wages account—Arrangement by lending bank with another bank for company to cash cheques (principally wages cheques) locally—Money withdrawn for wages debited to general account of company with lending bank—Whether lending bank entitled to priority for money advanced by bank and applied in paying wages—Companies Act, 1948 (11 & 12 Geo. 6 c. 38), s. 319 (4).

B

On transfer of a company's account to L. Bank, Ltd., the bank agreed to give overdraft facilities and arranged for " cheques to be drawn in respect of wages " at another bank at Alston, as L. Bank, Ltd. had no branch there. No account was opened by the company with the other bank at Alston, but the cheques were debited to the company's general account with L. Bank, Ltd. at Newcastle. It was common ground that, within the agreed financial limit, cheques could be cashed at Alston for any purpose, but that the arrangement for cashing cheques there was made with wages in mind. About fourteen months later the company went into a creditor's voluntary liquidation. Of the moneys owing to L. Bank, Ltd. by the company on overdraft, £2,161 11s. 6d. had been used by the company for paying wages. The liquidator did not accept that L. Bank, Ltd. was entitled to priority for this sum under s. 319 (4)* of the Companies Act, 1948, his view being based on the ground that the money was not advanced " for that purpose " within sub-s. (4), viz., for the purpose of paying wages.

C

D

E

Held: the company's overdraft was provided by L. Bank, Ltd. for the purpose of enabling the company to meet its commitments, and, so far as money provided under the Alston arrangement was concerned, the reason for the arrangement existing was to provide money for wages, which, therefore, was the commitment for which that money was provided; accordingly the £2,161 11s. 6d. was advanced for the purpose of paying wages within s. 319 (4) of the Companies Act, 1948, and L. Bank, Ltd. was entitled to priority in respect of that sum (see p. 60, letter I, to p. 61, letter A, post).

F

Re Primrose (Builders) Ltd. ([1950] 2 All E.R. 334) applied.

[As to preference in winding-up for money advanced for wages or salary of a clerk or servant, see 6 HALSBURY'S LAWS (3rd Edn.) 666, 667, para. 1316; and for cases on the subject, see 10 DIGEST (Repl.) 994-996, *6836-6851*.

G

For the Companies Act, 1948, s. 319, see 3 HALSBURY'S STATUTES (2nd Edn.) 698.]

Case referred to:

Primrose (Builders), Ltd., Re, [1950] 2 All E.R. 334; [1950] Ch. 561; 10 Digest (Repl.) 996, *6851*.

H

Adjourned Summons.

This was an application by originating summons dated Dec. 20, 1965 by Lloyds Bank, Ltd., claiming to be a preferential creditor of Rampgill Mill, Ltd. (" the company "), a company in a creditors' voluntary liquidation, asking that the decision of Anthony Morgan Boyd, the liquidator of the company in rejecting the proof of the applicant for £7,000 0s. 11d. as being preferential to the extent of £2,228 0s. 6d. be varied and that the liquidator be ordered to admit such proof as preferential to the extent of £2,161 11s. 6d. as having been advanced by the bank for the purpose of paying wages within s. 319 of the Companies Act, 1948. The facts and relevant statutory provisions are set out in the judgment.

I

---

* Section 319 (4), so far as material, is set out at p. 57, letter E, post.

A   The cases noted below* were cited in argument in addition to the case referred to in the judgment.

R. A. K. *Wright* for the bank, the applicant.
C. H. L. *Bathurst* for the liquidator.

Cur. adv. vult.

B   Nov. 22. **PLOWMAN, J.**, read the following judgment: This is an application by Lloyds Bank, Ltd. (which I shall call " the bank ") against the rejection by the liquidator of Rampgill Mill, Ltd. (which I shall call " the company ") of the bank's claim to priority in the liquidation of the company for moneys advanced by the bank to the company which were used by it to pay wages. The company went into liquidation on Dec. 18, 1964, and the winding up is a
C   creditors' voluntary winding-up.

The bank's claim to be a preferential creditor is based on s. 319 of the Companies Act, 1948, which, so far as material, provides as follows. First of all, sub-s. (1) (*b*) of the section says:

D   " (1) In a winding up there shall be paid in priority to all other debts . . . (*b*) all wages or salary (whether or not earned wholly or in part by way of commission) of any clerk or servant in respect of services rendered to the company during four months next before the relevant date and all wages (whether payable for time or for piece work) of any workman or labourer in respect of services so rendered . . ."

Then, sub-s. (4) of the section provides as follows:

E   " (4) Where any payment has been made—(*a*) to any clerk, servant, workman or labourer in the employment of a company, on account of wages or salary; . . . out of money advanced by some person for that purpose, the person by whom the money was advanced shall in a winding-up have a right of priority in respect of the money so advanced and paid up to the amount by which the sum in respect of which the clerk, servant, workman
F   or labourer, or other person in his right, would have been entitled to priority in the winding-up has been diminished by reason of the payment having been made."

The sum for which the bank claims priority is £2,161 11s. 6d. It is common ground that, out of the moneys advanced by the bank to the company on overdraft and not repaid, the company did use that sum in the payment of wages
G   during the relevant period. The dispute, however, is whether the sum in question was advanced by the bank " for that purpose " within the meaning of s. 319, sub-s. (4).

The relevant facts are as follows. In October, 1963, the company, which carried on its business at Alston, in Cumberland, and banked at the Hexham Branch of Martins Bank, Ltd., decided to transfer its account to the Newcastle-
H   upon-Tyne Branch of Lloyds Bank, Ltd. On Oct. 11, 1963, a discussion took place at the company's mill between Mr. Tingle, the assistant manager of that branch, and Mr. Deas, the managing director of the company, as a result of which, on Oct. 14, Mr. Tingle wrote to Mr. Deas a letter, which included the following sentence:

I   " As promised when I saw you on Friday, I am writing to confirm our conversation when I agreed that the bank would allow overdraft facilities up to a maximum of £5,000 on the account of Rampgill Mill, Ltd. for the next twelve months subject to the usual banking conditions."

On Oct. 16, Mr. Deas wrote to the bank accepting the proposed overdraft arrangements and referred to a matter which had clearly come up for discussion

---

* *Cumming* v. *Shand*, (1860), 5 H. & N. 95; *Fleming* v. *Bank of New Zealand,* [1900] A.C. 577; *Re E. J. Morel (1934), Ltd.,* [1961] 1 All E.R. 796; [1962] Ch. 21; *Re James R. Rutherford & Sons, Ltd.,* [1964] 3 All E.R. 137.

on Oct. 11—namely, the question of wages cheques.   In his letter, Mr. Deas   A
said this:

" Dear Mr. Tingle, Thank you for your letter of Oct. 14 with regard to
overdraft arrangements, which we are pleased to accept.   The question of
Settlingstones guaranteeing any borrowings in excess of £5,000 will be
dealt with at their next board meeting on Nov. 11, and thereafter I shall
write you further.   In the meantime, I enclose: (1) Formal application   B
from this company to open an account with your bank . . . (2) Specimen
signatures of the directors and secretary.   It is our intention to utilise the
account as from Monday next, Oct. 20.   At the outset, of course, the account
will be on overdraft, but as we have already told you we shall be closing
our account with Martins Bank, Ltd., Hexham, on Oct. 31, and the balance
outstanding at that date will be transferred to your branch.   The first wages   C
drawing against the account will be next week and as you have no branch
in Alston we would ask you to make the necessary arrangements for cheques
to be honoured at the Midland Bank instead."

On the same day, Mr. Tingle replied to Mr. Deas saying:

" I write to thank you for your letter of Oct. 16 enclosing our authority 7   D
in connection with the above new account, together with the necessary
specimen signatures.   I note that it is your intention to utilise this account
from Monday next, Oct. 20, and I will arrange for you to be supplied with a
crossed cheque book suitably printed, and I will also make arrangements
for cheques to be drawn in respect of wages at the Midland Bank, Alston,
up to a maximum of £500 in any one week.   Please let me know if this   E
figure is not sufficient for your requirements.   Incidentally, I hope I am
right in assuming that the wages will be withdrawn at the Midland Bank,
Alston, by either Mr. Banks or Mr. Swales and it is not your intention
that both should attend to collect the cash."

The bank accordingly arranged for the company to be able to draw up to £500   F
per week at the Alston Branch of the Midland Bank by cheque drawn on their
account with the bank at Newcastle.   No account was opened by the company
with the Midland Bank.   The cheques so drawn were debited to the company's
general account at the bank in exactly the same way as any other cheques
drawn on it.   It is common ground that within the limit of £500 per week there
was no restriction on the purpose for which cheques could be cashed at Alston,   G
but it is also common ground that the arrangement was made with wages in
mind.

In fact, in the period from Oct. 17, 1963, when the company's account with
the bank was opened, to Dec. 21, 1964, when it was closed following on the
liquidation, the company drew a total of £51,414 1s. 8d. from the bank, of which
about thirty per cent.—namely, £15,669 15s. 6d.—was in respect of cheques   H
cashed at the Alston Branch of the Midland Bank.   The money drawn at Alston
included not only wages but also a small element (about ten per cent.) for
national insurance stamps and, on at least one occasion, a small sum of petty
cash.   It is however conceded on behalf of the liquidator that this does not affect
the question which I have to decide, and the sum of £2,161 11s. 6d. is agreed
to be the sum used for wages for which the bank is entitled to priority if it is   I
entitled to any priority at all.

The liquidator denies that it is, and his argument, in a nutshell, is set out
in his solicitors' letter dated May 7, 1965.   In that letter, after referring to
s. 319 (4), they say:

" It is, therefore, essential to the bank's right of priority that the money
was advanced *for the purpose* of being paid to a servant on account of wages.
There is no doubt that the company drew money for this purpose, but the
test is whether the bank had this purpose in making the advance.   The bank

A have so far produced no evidence to the liquidator that the sum in respect
of which they claim priority was advanced to the company *for the purpose*
of being paid to a servant on account of wages."

The question, therefore, which I have to decide is whether the sum of £2,161
11s. 6d. was advanced by the bank for the purpose of paying wages.

B In the majority of cases in which a bank claims the benefit of s. 319 (4), there
is no dispute because the bank will have insisted on a wages account being
opened and operated in such a way as to leave the bank with an unquestionable
claim to the maximum priority afforded by the section; but there was no wages
account in this case, and the money used for wages was drawn within the general
overall limit of the overdraft which the bank had agreed to permit.

C Only one comparable case appears to have come before the court—namely, the
case of *Re Primrose (Builders), Ltd.* (1). Two points arose in that case, with only
one of which I am concerned here, but, so far as relevant to the present case,
the facts in *Re Primrose (Builders), Ltd.* (1) were these. Primrose (Builders),
Ltd. opened a current account with National Provincial Bank, Ltd., and were
permitted to overdraw up to a stated limit. In July, 1948, National Provincial
Bank, Ltd., told the company that, in the absence of further credits, drawing
D must be restricted to payments for wages. Between January and May, 1949,
when the winding-up order was made, the company presented nine cheques,
made out in the first two cases to " cash " and in the remainder to " wages ".
The details of the manner in which payment was required were written on the
backs of the cheques, and on every occasion the bank manager or his assistant
declined to honour the cheque until he was satisfied that a payment or payments
E substantially equal to or exceeding the amount for which the cheque was drawn
would shortly be paid in. National Provincial Bank, Ltd., lodged a proof in the
winding-up for the money said to have been advanced to the company for the
purpose of paying wages, that proof was rejected by the liquidator and National
Provincial Bank, Ltd. appealed. It is, I think, instructive to see what the
arguments of counsel were in that case. Counsel for the National Provincial
F Bank, Ltd. argued as follows (2):

" In order to qualify as a preferential creditor under s. 319 (4), it is not
necessary to show that payments made for wages were paid in pursuance
of an agreement to that end, or that they were made with a view to becoming
a preferential creditor. It is only necessary to show that the advances were
in fact made for the purposes specified in the subsection. Whether the
G cheques were made out to ' cash ' or to ' wages ', they were intended for the
purpose of paying wages and the bank in fact advanced the money for that
purpose. If an account with a bank is in debit and the bank honour a cheque
made payable to wages or made payable to cash in such circumstances that it
is evident that the bank knew that it was to be used for paying wages,
then, unless there is evidence to the contrary, it must be assumed that
H the cheque is in fact used for the purpose of paying wages. In this case the
evidence supports that assumption. The account was carried on as an
ordinary current account as between banker and customer; pass sheets
were issued regularly to the company; and no objection was ever taken
to the form of the account."

I Counsel for the liquidator argued as follows (3):

" In order to qualify under s. 319, (4), the advance must be made
with a purpose directly related to the object or purpose of the person
seeking to draw the money. That is the meaning of ' purpose ' in that
subsection. [He referred to the definition of ' purpose ' in the OXFORD
ENGLISH DICTIONARY and STROUD'S JUDICIAL DICTIONARY (2nd edn.).]
The bank had a purely commercial basis in making these advances: they

(1) [1950] 2 All E.R. 334; [1950] Ch. 561.
(2) [1950] Ch. at p. 563.   (3) [1950] Ch. at p. 564.

were not made for the ' purpose ' of paying wages. The bank may have
expected that, in the ordinary course of business, some of the money which
they advanced would be spent on wages; but they had no real ' purpose ',
in making the advance, that it should be so spent."

WYNN-PARRY, J.'s judgment, so far as it deals with the point with which I
am concerned, is as follows. He said (4):

" It is to be observed, in regard to [sub-s. (4)], that there is no obligation on
the person seeking to rank as a preferential creditor to show that the money
advanced for the purposes specified in paras. (*a*) and (*b*) of that subsection
was so advanced pursuant to any agreement or arrangement, nor, in my view,
is it incumbent on such person to assert and prove that his aim in so advancing such money was with a view to becoming a preferential creditor. If he
satisfies the conditions in the subsection, . . . he achieves the priority given by
the section."

Then, at the end of his judgment, WYNN-PARRY, J., said (5):

" In those circumstances . . . the conditions of the Companies Act, 1948,
s. 319 (4), are fulfilled by the bank, because it is agreed to the extent of the
figure which I have mentioned, viz. £2,524 9s. 11d., that the moneys advanced
by the bank, in the circumstances to which I have referred, were applied
in the payment of wages, and I find as a fact that those moneys were advanced
by the bank for that purpose."

Counsel for the liquidator seeks to distinguish that case in a way that I shall
mention in a moment, and submits that the bank can only say that it made a
particular advance for a particular purpose if it (i) had a discretion whether or
not to make that particular advance, (ii) exercised that discretion in relation to
the advance and (iii) decided to make the advance because, so far as it knew, the
money was to be used for that purpose. He submits that where, as here, the bank
has agreed to allow a general borrowing up to a certain limit and a cheque is
cashed within that limit and without further managerial thought, there is no
exercise of a discretion, and that therefore the bank can have no purpose in view.
He proposes the " discretion " test as a halfway house between, on the one hand,
an agreement or arrangement (which *Re Primrose (Builders), Ltd.* (6) decided was
unnecessary) and, on the other, the view that the bank makes an advance for a
purpose whenever it knows the customer's purpose in drawing the money in
question. He submits that the existence of the arrangement for drawing money
at Alston is wholly irrelevant to the problem in issue, and that the problem would
have been exactly the same if the money had been drawn at Newcastle. He
distinguishes *Re Primrose (Builders), Ltd.* (6) on the ground that there unlike
the present case, the facts satisfied the "discretion" test since, as I have already
indicated, on every occasion on which a cheque for wages was drawn the bank
made it a condition that it should be satisfied that an equivalent sum of money
would shortly be paid in.

In my judgment, counsel for the liquidator seeks to apply too rigid a test.
The object of s. 319 (4), as I see it, was to establish a principle of subrogation in
favour of banks (although its operation is not, of course, confined to banks),
and the subsection should, therefore, in my judgment, be given a benevolent
construction rather than one which narrows the limits of its operation. WYNN-
PARRY, J., in the *Primrose* case (6), appears to have taken a similar view, and to
have accepted counsel for the bank's argument and tacitly rejected that of counsel
for the liquidator. He treated the question as being ultimately one of fact.

In the present case, the bank clearly had a purpose in advancing money to
the company—namely, the purpose of enabling it to meet its commitments. I
then ask myself, " what commitments? ", and my answer, so far as the money

(4) [1950] 2 All E.R. at p. 335; [1950] Ch. at p. 565.
(5) [1950] 2 All E.R. at p. 337; [1950] Ch. at p. 567.
(6) [1950] 2 All E.R. 334; [1950] Ch. 561.

A provided under the Alston arrangement is concerned, is wages, which were the whole raison d'être of that arrangement. I therefore find as a fact that the sum in question, £2,161 11s. 6d., was advanced for the purpose of paying wages, and accordingly I propose to make an order as asked by para. (1) of the summons.

Order accordingly. Leave to appeal.

B   Solicitors: *Cameron, Kemm, Nordon & Co.* (for the bank, the applicant); *Dickinson, Miller & Turnbull* (for the liquidator).

[*Reported by* JACQUELINE METCALFE, *Barrister-at-Law.*]

C   GOULSTON DISCOUNT CO., LTD. *v.* CLARK.

[COURT OF APPEAL, CIVIL DIVISION (Lord Denning, M.R., Danckwerts and Diplock, L.JJ.), October 25, 1966.]

Hire-Purchase—Indemnity—Recourse agreement—Construction of "Specific Indemnity and Repurchase Undertaking" by motor dealer—Construed as
D   *indemnity—Finance company terminated hiring for hirer's failure to pay instalments on hire-purchase of car—Car re-sold—Finance company entitled to recover whole loss from dealer.*

By an agreement headed "Specific Indemnity and Repurchase Undertaking" a motor car dealer agreed with a finance company that, in consideration of the finance company's entering into a hire-purchase agreement with one W. in respect of a car, the dealers would "indemnify [the finance
E   company] against any loss that you may suffer by reason of the fact that the hirer under the [hire-purchase contract] for any cause whatsoever does not pay the amounts which he would if he completed his agreement by exercising the option to purchase". The hirer defaulted. The finance company terminated the hiring, re-took the car and sold it. They were unable to
F   recover £157* (part of the hire-purchase price of £458) from W. They brought an action against the dealer for indemnity against the loss that they suffered owing to the hirer's default. On appeal from judgment for £74 16s. 10d., given on the basis that the agreement should be construed as a guarantee and that the dealer's liability was accordingly limited to the hirer's liability and thus to the instalments in arrear when the hiring was terminated,
G   **Held:** the recourse agreement was one of indemnity and not a guarantee; the finance company were, therefore, entitled to indemnity against their loss and the dealer was liable for the £157 (see p. 63, letter I, and p. 64, letters B, D and G, post).

Unity Finance, Ltd. v. *Woodcock* ([1963] 2 All E.R. 270) distinguished.
H   Appeal allowed.

[As to recourse agreements, see 19 HALSBURY'S LAWS (3rd Edn.) 529, para. 850, and as to a finance company's right to damages on termination of the hire-purchase contract, see 19 HALSBURY'S LAWS (3rd Edn.) 550, para. 891; and for cases on these subjects, see, respectively, 26 DIGEST (Repl.) 664, *29*, 668, *42*, and DIGEST (Cont. Vol. A) 650-652, *77a-81b*.]

I Cases referred to:

Financings, Ltd. v. *Baldock*, [1963] 1 All E.R. 443; [1963] 2 Q.B. 104; [1963] 2 W.L.R. 359; Digest (Cont. Vol. A) 650, *77d*.

Unity Finance, Ltd. v. *Woodcock*, [1963] 2 All E.R. 270; [1963] 1 W.L.R. 455; Digest (Cont. Vol. A) 628, *18a*.

---

* The calculation by which the £157 was reached made allowance for accelerated payment of instalments after the date of termination. The finance company could not recover by action against the hirer more than the arrears of instalments prior to the date of termination of the hire-purchase contract, see p. 63, letter B, post.

Appeal.   A

This was an appeal by the plaintiff finance company, Goulston Discount Co., Ltd., from a decision of His Honour JUDGE HILLARD, given on June 15, 1966, at Trowbridge county court, awarding the plaintiffs £74 16s. 10d. under a recourse agreement. The following statement of facts is taken substantially from the judgment of the county court judge.

The plaintiffs entered into a hire-purchase agreement, dated Nov. 3, 1964, with   B
one Webb, under which Webb agreed to hire a Jaguar motor car. The hire-purchase price was £458. The agreement provided for an initial deposit of £100; for twenty-four monthly instalments of £14 17s. 6d. commencing on Dec. 3, 1964, and for an option to purchase at £1. Mr. Webb paid the deposit and the first instalment of £14 17s. 6d., but failed to pay the instalments due in January and February. On Feb. 17, 1965, the plaintiff served on Mr. Webb a notice of   C
default. No further payment was made, and on May 28 the plaintiffs terminated the hiring and took possession of the car. This they did under cl. 10 of the agreement which provided that—

" If the hirer shall fail to pay any sum due hereunder . . . the [finance company] may thereupon and without notice terminate the hiring and/or this agreement, and may, subject only to the restriction of the [finance   D
company's] rights to recover contained in the statutory notice hereto [where applicable] retake possession of the goods . . .''

At the hearing before the county court judge it was conceded on behalf of the plaintiffs that as against Mr. Webb the plaintiffs' claim fell to be decided in the light of the decision in *Financings, Ltd.* v. *Baldock**, with the result that the   E
plaintiffs were entitled as against him only to the unpaid instalments prior to the date of termination, amounting to £74 7s. 6d. and interest thereon in accordance with cl. 2 calculated up to May 3, 1965, amounting to 9s. 4d. The plaintiffs re-sold the car for £155, which the county court judge found to have been the best price obtainable. The plaintiffs then brought the county court action claiming £156 5s., calculated by deducting from the hire-purchase price the   F
amount of the deposit and the first instalment paid by Mr. Webb, the amount realised on the sale of the vehicle, and by making an allowance of £31 17s. 6d. for accelerated payment. The defendant filed a defence in person alleging only that the trade price at the time of sale was £225, but he did not appear at the hearing. After considering authorities, the county court judge found that the agreement must be construed as a contract of guarantee. Accordingly he   G
held that the defendant was liable under the recourse agreement for the amount of the five unpaid instalments prior to the date of termination of the hiring together with the interest of 9s. 4d.

The authority and the case noted below† were cited during the argument in addition to the cases referred to in the judgments.

Greville Janner for the plaintiffs, the finance company.   H
The respondent dealer did not appear and was not represented.

LORD DENNING, M.R.: In this case in November, 1964, a customer called Webb went to a dealer, the defendant, Mr. Clark, at Southwick in Wiltshire. He wanted to get a Jaguar car. The cash price was £400. He had not the money to pay, but he had an old car worth £100. So he got the Jaguar on hire-purchase terms in the usual way. He handed the old car to the defendant   I
in part exchange. That represented £100. Then the defendant sold the Jaguar to the plaintiff finance company, Goulston Discount Co., Ltd., for £400, giving credit for £100. Then the plaintiffs paid £300 in cash to the defendant, and thus became owners of the Jaguar car. The plaintiffs then let out the Jaguar car on

---

* [1963] 1 All E.R. 443; [1963] 2 Q.B. 104.
   † GUEST ON HIRE PURCHASE, paras. 392, 393, 441, 442; *Western Credit, Ltd.* v. *Alberry*, [1964] 2 All E.R. 938.

A hire-purchase terms to the customer on instalments payable over two years. These instalments were calculated so as to cover the £300 and there was to be added, of course, the finance charge of £57. There was the usual option to purchase of £1. So the total hire-purchase price was £458 and the customer had the car. The customer paid the first instalment, and then he defaulted. The car was re-taken and eventually sold by the plaintiffs for £155.

B Owing to the decision of this court in *Financings, Ltd.* v. *Baldock* (1) the plaintiffs could only sue the hirer for the arrears of the instalments. They could not get anything more from him. So they came down on the defendant. He had signed a specific recourse agreement, i.e., a recourse agreement in respect of this very car. The question in the case is whether that is an agreement of guarantee or of indemnity. If it is a guarantee, the defendant is under no more liability than the hirer, i.e., to pay the arrears; but if it is an indemnity, he will

C be liable to pay the whole of the hire-purchase price. This is what the agreement says:

> " In consideration of your entering into a hire-purchase agreement with Raymond Harry Webb . . . I agree to indemnify you against any loss you
D may suffer by reason of the fact that the hirer under the said agreement for any cause whatsoever does not pay the amounts which he would if he completed his agreement by exercising the option to purchase. The date of loss shall be any date you notify me after termination of any of the said agreement or the hiring thereunder. Loss shall mean the difference between the total amount the hirer would have had to pay to acquire title to the goods under the hire-purchase agreement, plus your expenses, less payments
E received by you. If an indemnity is also given to you by any other person my indemnity shall not be a joint indemnity but an indemnity against default of that indemnifier. On payment by me to you of the loss I shall be entitled to your rights in respect of the hirer, the goods and any other indemnifier or guarantor. No time or indulgence shown by you to the
F hirer or any indemnifier or guarantor shall in any way affect this indemnity."

That was signed on Nov. 4, 1964. On the face of it, the defendant, who has had £400 for the car, is saying to the plaintiffs: " If you let the hirer have this car, I will make sure that it is purchased at the hire-purchase price. If he defaults, I will indemnify you against any deficiency on that price on the understanding, of course, that I shall in return get the car and all your rights." That seems to
G me a very reasonable and sensible agreement. I have no doubt that it is an indemnity and not a guarantee.

The only difficulty is the decision of this court in *Unity Finance, Ltd.* v. *Woodcock* (2). The judge felt that on that case he was bound to hold that this agreement here was a guarantee. I can well understand the judge taking that view, seeing what was said in that case; but on reading the case again, I think that
H the decision should be based on illegality. The finance company there had acted quite illegally. They had repossessed the car in breach of the statute when more than one-third had been paid. On so doing the hire-purchase agreement came to an end altogether. There was no hire-purchase price and no sums payable under the agreement. Yet by the action they were seeking to be paid the full amount which by the statute they had forfeited. They were seeking
I indemnity from the consequences of their own illegal act. That they could not be allowed to do. That is the ground on which the decision should rest. The case should not be taken as establishing that all these recourse agreements are contracts of guarantee and not indemnity. Quite the contrary. A simple specific recourse agreement, such as that before us here, is clearly a contract of indemnity and not a guarantee.

---

(1) [1963] 1 All E.R. 443; [1963] 2 Q.B. 104.
(2) [1963] 2 All E.R. 270.

The defendant wanted to sell this Jaguar car. He sold it to the plaintiffs for A £400, and was paid for it. The evidence shows that the plaintiffs would not have bought the car from him unless he had agreed that, in case the hirer defaulted, he would indemnify them. That was a very sensible agreement. The defendant ought to honour it. When the hirer defaulted, the defendant could have had the car if he had wanted it; but he did not take it over and it was resold for a reasonable sum. The defendant must indemnify the plaintiffs against B their loss. I would allow the appeal accordingly.

DANCKWERTS, L.J.: I agree. It seems to me a particularly plain case. The document which is relevant in the present case is described as a " specific indemnity and repurchase undertaking ". By the operative words the defendant agrees to indemnify the plaintiffs, the finance company, against loss. " Loss " C is defined, and the only references to a guarantor are in two places where it is referring to some document which may be entered into by some other party. In its terms the document is quite plainly an indemnity and not a guarantee.

We have been referred to a number of cases in regard to the matter, but they all seem to me to differ in their circumstances or in the wording of the documents and really do not assist one way or the other in the present case. The learned D county court judge, as LORD DENNING, M.R., has said, misled himself by reference to the case of *Unity Finance, Ltd.* v. *Woodcock* (3). In my view that case is not really material to the present because the circumstances were different and this case stands on its own wording. In my opinion it is not a guarantee but an indemnity. Accordingly I also would allow the appeal.

DIPLOCK, L.J.: I agree that this document is clearly an indemnity and E not a guarantee. I did at one time feel some difficulty whether I was entitled to say that, in view of the decision in *Unity Finance, Ltd.* v. *Woodcock* (3). It does appear, however, that in the argument in that case, so far as one can discover from the report, the question was not closely canvassed whether the document in that case, which was a recourse agreement in somewhat different terms from this, was an indemnity or a guarantee. Examining closely, as we have done F now, the rationes decidendi of the judgments, I have come to the conclusion that the only common ratio decidendi in that case was that the hire-purchase agreement had been terminated by force (4) of s. 11 of the Hire Purchase Act, 1938, and a statutory release of all liability of the hirer under the agreement had been effected by that section. I do not think, therefore, that *Unity Finance, Ltd.* v. *Woodcock* (3) binds me to hold that this agreement, which is clearly an indemnity G and not a guarantee, is in law a guarantee; and I am fortified in the feeling that I am not so bound by the judgments which have been delivered by my lords, who were also parties to the decision in *Unity Finance, Ltd.* v. *Woodcock* (3).

Appeal allowed.

Solicitors: *Sidney Davidson & Co.* (for the plaintiffs, the finance company). H

[*Reported by* F. GUTTMAN, ESQ., *Barrister-at-Law.*]

I

---

(3) [1963] 2 All E.R. 270.
(4) Section 11 of the Act of 1938 has been repealed; see now s. 34 of the Hire-Purchase Act 1965; 45 HALSBURY'S STATUTES (2nd Edn.) 1444.

A   ASKINEX, LTD. *v.* GREEN AND OTHERS.

[COURT OF APPEAL, CIVIL DIVISION (Lord Denning, M.R., Diplock and Russell, L.JJ.), July 18, 19, 20, 21, November 14, 1966.]

Moneylender—Memorandum—Interest—Rate of interest—Alternative statutory
  requirements—Actual or notional rate—Total interest, as defined in statute,
B *spread over period of repayment of loan in order to compute actual rate stated*
  —Whether compliance with the alternative statutory requirement for statement
  of an actual rate—Moneylenders Act, 1927 (17 & 18 Geo. 5 c. 21), s. 6 (2),
  s. 15 (1), Sch. 1.

  A memorandum of agreement with the plaintiffs, who were moneylenders, was signed by G. agreeing to repay a loan of £25,000 over a period of ten
C years by 120 monthly instalments of £208 6s. 8d. The rate of interest was stated to be 26.776860 per cent. per annum, and it was provided that the interest should be paid by 120 monthly instalments of £281 5s. less income tax. The memorandum did not state that the rate of interest was calculated in accordance with Sch. 1 to the Moneylenders Act, 1927. The defendant, R., was liable to the moneylenders by way of indemnity for the performance
D of the borrower's obligations. It was admitted that the interest was not excessive and that the transaction was not harsh or unconscionable. "Interest" by definition (s. 15 (1)* of the Act of 1927) included any amount in excess of the principal, payable to a moneylender in respect of a loan. In the present case the principal was £25,000 and the statutory "interest" (which was not the payment of £281 5s. monthly) worked out at a total
E amount of £33,750. This sum spread over ten years at simple interest represented a rate of 26.776860 per cent. per annum. Section 6 (2)† of the Act of 1927 required that the memorandum should state either (a) the actual rate of interest, viz., " the interest charged on the loan expressed in terms of a rate per cent. per annum " or (b) a notional rate, viz., " the rate per cent. per annum represented by the interest charged as calculated in
F accordance with the provisions of Sch. 1 to this Act ". If alternative (b), the notional rate, were chosen the memorandum was required (by s. 6 (2)) to state that the rate was calculated in accordance with the provisions of Sch. 1.

  Held (DIPLOCK, L.J., dissenting): the interest charged on the loan in the present case was capable of being stated as an actual rate in accordance with
G alternative (a) and was correctly so stated, with the consequence that the memorandum was sufficient and repayment of the loan was enforceable (see p. 70, letter E, and p. 79, letter G, post).

  Parkfield Trust, Ltd. v. *Curtis* ([1934] All E.R. Rep. 43) and *Mason & Wood, Ltd.* v. *Greene* ([1936] 2 All E.R. 509) distinguished.

H *Moneylender—Memorandum—Collateral transactions not stated—Whether memo-*
  randum sufficient—Moneylenders Act, 1927 (17 & 18 Geo. 5 c. 21), s. 6 (2).

  R. applied to moneylenders to procure a loan (£25,000) for G., in respect of which loan R. became liable to indemnify the moneylenders. The moneylenders required that R. should obtain for them the financing of another transaction (£12,000) and should agree to indemnify them against
I any losses in respect of a separate transaction with K. In a subsequent action by the moneylenders in respect of repayment of the loan to G., R. contended that the memorandum of agreement in respect of G.'s loan should have contained the terms in respect of the £12,000 transaction and the transaction with K.

  Held: G. not being a party to either the £12,000 transaction or the transaction with K., the sums payable in respect of these transactions were

---

 * Section 15 (1), so far as material, is set out at p. 68, letter H, post.
 † Section 6 (2), so far as material, is set out at p. 68, letter G, post.

not " interest " (within s. 15 (1) of the Moneylenders Act, 1927) charged on   A
the loan to G., nor were they payable by G.; accordingly they did not have
to be mentioned in the statutory memorandum in respect of the loan to G.
(see p. 70, letter I, p. 72, letter I, and p. 79, letter H, post).

    Appeal allowed.

[As to the form of memorandum of a moneylenders' contract, see 27 HALS-
BURY'S LAWS (3rd Edn.) 32, para. 50; as to the calculation of the rate of interest, B
see ibid., p. 37, para. 65; and for cases on the subjects, see 35 DIGEST (Repl.)
241-243, *401-426.*

    For the Moneylenders' Act, 1927, s. 6 (2), s. 15 (2), Sch. 1, see 16 HALSBURY'S
STATUTES (2nd Edn.) 386, 397, 401.]

Cases referred to:

    Mason & Wood, Ltd. v. *Greene,* [1936] 2 All E.R. 509; [1936] 2 K.B. 370; C
        105 L.J.K.B. 774; 155 L.T. 11; 35 Digest (Repl.) 244, *432.*

    Mutual Loan Fund Association, Ltd. v. *Sanderson,* [1937] 1 All E.R. 380;
        35 Digest (Repl.) 243, *426.*

    Parkfield Trust, Ltd. v. *Curtis,* [1934] All E.R. Rep. 43; [1934] 1 K.B. 685;
        103 L.J.K.B. 609; 150 L.T. 436; 35 Digest (Repl.) 244, *430.*

Appeal.
                                                                                                      D

This was an appeal by the plaintiffs, Askinex, Ltd., from a decision of His
Honour JUDGE BLOCK given at the Mayor's and City of London Court on Apr. 5,
1966, that judgment should be entered for the defendants, that the bills of
exchange, the legal charges and mortgages described in the counterclaim of the
defendants were unenforceable and be delivered up by the plaintiffs to the defen- E
dants, and that the plaintiffs be restrained from seeking to enforce any of the said
securities. The plaintiffs, who were licensed moneylenders, had claimed by
their particulars of claim £380 12s. due under two bills of exchange for £208 6s. 8d.
and £172 5s. 4d., representing an instalment of capital and an instalment of
interest respectively, which became due on Oct. 6, 1965, in respect of a loan of
£25,000 granted by the plaintiffs to the first defendant. To secure repayment of F
the principal of, and interest on, the loan, the first defendant, Frank Green,
gave to the plaintiffs 120 bills of exchange, each for £208 6s. 8d. in respect of
principal, and 120 bills of exchange each for £172 5s. 4d. in respect of interest
payments after allowing for deduction of income tax thereon at 7s. 9d. in the
pound. These bills of exchange were drawn by his wife, the second defendant,
Joan Beryl Green, were accepted by the first defendant and were endorsed by G
the second, third and fourth defendants, viz., Mrs. Green, Verland Investments,
Ltd. and John Augustus Rudland. The two bills of exchange for £208 6s. 8d.
and £172 5s. 4d. were not met on presentment and had not been paid. The
amount that had been repaid of the loan, excluding interest, as pleaded in the
particulars of claim dated Nov. 29, 1965, was £2,063 6s. 8d. and, if interest were
included, was £3,783 14s. 2d. The defendants pleaded that the memorandum H
of loan did not comply with s. 6 (2) of the Moneylenders Act, 1927, in that (a)
the rate of interest was calculated in accordance with the provisions of Sch. 1 to
the Act of 1927, but that fact was not stated in the memorandum and (b) the
memorandum did not state all the terms of the contract for the loan. The
defendants counterclaimed for declarations that the bills of exchange, legal
charge and mortgage, concerned, were unenforceable and for delivery up to them,
and for an injunction to restrain the plaintiffs from seeking to enforce any of I
these securities.

    Desmond Ackner, Q.C., Mark Littman, Q.C., and *R. L. Johnson* for the plaintiffs,
the moneylenders.

    S. N. McKinnon for the first and second defendants.

    Leonard Caplan, Q.C., and *G. V. Owen* for the third and fourth defendants.

                                                           Cur. adv. vult.

Nov. 14. The following judgments were read.

A   **LORD DENNING, M.R.:** Mr. Frank Green has been to sea as a purser. In 1964 he was minded to get a hotel. He saw an advertisement saying that the George Hotel at Crewkerne in Somerset was for sale. He had not got the money to buy it. So he got in touch with a Mr. Rudland, who describes himself as a business transfer specialist. Mr. Rudland has several companies which he controls. Mr. Rudland, through one of his companies, Verland Investments,

B   Ltd., agreed to buy the freehold of the hotel, together with the goodwill, fixtures and fittings for £32,000. Then Verland Investments, Ltd. let the hotel on lease to Mr. Green for forty years at a rent of £2,000 a year, but Mr. Green had to pay a premium of £22,500 for this lease. Verland Investments, Ltd. also agreed to sell the goodwill, fixtures and fittings to Mr. Green for £11,500.

In order to raise the cash, Mr. Rudland went to registered moneylenders

C   called Askinex, Ltd., with whom he had done a good deal of business already. He arranged for the moneylenders to lend £25,000 to Mr. Green; but the moneylenders had other matters outstanding with Mr. Rudland. One of these was the King transaction. Mr. Rudland had introduced to the moneylenders a Mrs. King to whom they had lent £3,000 or £4,000 and she had fallen behind in her payments. The moneylenders told Mr. Rudland that they would not go ahead

D   with the George Hotel transaction unless he agreed to indemnify them against loss on their loan to Mrs. King. So Mr. Rudland signed a deed of indemnity. He was afterwards called on to pay three instalments under this indemnity. Another matter was the £12,000 transaction. The moneylenders discovered that Mr. Rudland had arranged to borrow £12,000 from other moneylenders called Reputable Finance, Ltd., and charge the freehold of the George Hotel to

E   those other moneylenders. When they learned of this, the moneylenders told Mr. Rudland that he was to cancel those arrangements with the other moneylenders and borrow £12,000 from them, and charge the freehold to them. Unless he did so, the loan to Mr. Green would not be forthcoming. Mr. Rudland felt obliged to do this. He cancelled the arrangements with the other moneylenders (and paid them £149 13s. for their abortive work), and the moneylenders

F   lent £12,000 to him or his company at a substantial rate of interest. The judge found that the moneylenders by pressure forced Mr. Rudland to enter into those two transactions, the King indemnity and the £12,000 loan.

Once Mr. Rudland had satisfied the moneylenders on those two matters, they lent Mr. Green the £25,000. He signed a memorandum of agreement dated Nov. 6, 1964, by which he agreed to repay the £25,000 by monthly instal-

G   ments of £208 6s. 8d. over a period of ten years, and also interest by monthly instalments of £281 5s. less tax over ten years. He signed 120 bills of exchange for the instalments and they were endorsed by his wife, Mrs. Green, and Mr. Rudland and Mr. Rudland's company, Verland Investments, Ltd. The memorandum of agreement was in these terms:

H   " 1. The amount to be advanced shall be £25,000.

" 2. The said sum shall be advanced on Nov. 6, 1964.

" 3. The rate of interest payable (as well after as before any judgment) shall be 26.776860 per centum per annum.

" 4. The said principal sum shall be repaid by 120 equal monthly instalments of £208 6s. 8d. commencing on Dec. 6, 1964, and thereafter on the same date of each successive month until the whole amount shall have been

I   repaid.

" 5. The said interest shall be paid by 120 equal monthly instalments of £281 5s. less income tax at the standard rate at the date hereof commencing on the said Dec. 6, 1964 and thereafter on the same date of each successive month until the whole amount shall have been paid."

When Mr. Green received the £25,000 he used it to acquire the lease of the George Hotel from Mr. Rudland's company and he charged the lease to the moneylenders to secure the loan.

Mr. Green went into occupation of the hotel, but unfortunately it was not a **A** success. He got into difficulties and on July 26, 1965, he assigned the lease, goodwill and the other things to Mr. Rudland. In return Mr. Rudland agreed to indemnify Mr. Green against his liability to the moneylenders. So the George Hotel and its business became the property of Mr. Rudland. Mr. Rudland is also liable (as between him and Mr. Green) to pay off the moneylenders. Mr. Rudland has not paid them. The moneylenders now sue for one of the instalments. **B** The judge has held that they have not complied with the Moneylenders Acts, 1900 and 1927, and can recover nothing. The moneylenders appeal to this court.

1. *Does the memorandum show the rate of interest?*

The Acts require the moneylenders to show the rate of interest charged on the loans. The reasons are twofold: first, so that the borrower can know what he **C** is being charged; secondly, because if the rate be more than forty-eight per cent. per annum, it is presumed to be excessive and that the transaction is harsh and unconscionable; see s. 10 (1) of the Moneylenders Act, 1927.

This memorandum does purport to show the rate of interest. It states it to be 26.776860. Such a figure, given to the sixth decimal place, is obviously the result of a mathematical calculation. The borrower says that that rate was **D** calculated in accordance with the provisions of Sch. 1 to the Act of 1927: and that fact should have been stated. The figure of 26.776860 ought, he says, to have been followed by the significant words " as calculated in accordance with the provisions of Sch. 1 to the Act of 1927 " and that the omission of those words is fatal to the memorandum. He relies on the cases in this court of *Parkfield Trust, Ltd.* v. *Curtis* (1) and *Mason & Wood, Ltd.* v. *Greene* (2). This is a highly **E** technical defence. The borrower admits that the interest was not excessive and the transaction was not harsh or unconscionable. Yet he says that he can escape payment owing to the omission of those words. If the defence is good, the real beneficiary is Mr. Rudland, who will get the George Hotel at Crewkerne without having to pay the price. The judge has held that the defence is good. The moneylenders appeal to this court. **F**

The case depends on the true application to this case of s. 6 (2) of the Act of 1927. That is the section which compels the moneylenders to show the rate of interest. It provides that the note or memorandum shall show

">. . . either the interest charged on the loan expressed in terms of a rate per cent. per annum, or the rate per cent. per annum represented by the **G** interest charged as calculated in accordance with the provisions of Sch. 1 to this Act."

In applying this section it is important to remember the definition of " interest " and " principal ". Section 15 (1) provides that:

" ' Interest ' . . . includes any amount, by whatsoever name called, in excess of the principal, paid or payable to a moneylender in consideration **H** of or otherwise in respect of a loan; ' principal ' means in relation to a loan the amount actually lent to the borrower."

In this case the " principal " was £25,000. The " interest " was the excess over £25,000 payable by the borrower. It comes to £33,750. This must be steadily borne in mind. The " interest charged on the loan " was not the payment of £281 5s. a month. It was the *total sum* of £33,750. It must also be borne in **I** mind that we are only concerned with simple interest. The Act of 1927 prohibits compound interest; see s. 7.

With this introduction, I turn now to s. 6 (2). It gives the moneylender a choice between two alternatives, which I will call alternatives (A) and (B). The choice is between stating an *actual* rate and a *deemed* rate. The first alternative

(1) [1934] All E.R. Rep. 43; [1934] 1 K.B. 685.
(2) [1936] 2 All E.R. 509; [1936] 2 K.B. 370.

A   (A) applies when the interest charged on the loan (i.e., the *total* amount payable in money over the full period) is *capable* of being expressed in terms of a *simple actual* rate per cent. per annum over that period. In such a case the moneylender satisfies the statute by stating that rate in the memorandum. The second alternative (B) applies when the *total* sum of interest is *not* capable of being expressed in terms of a single actual rate per cent. per annum, with the result

B   that resort must be had to a *deemed* rate. In this second alternative the moneylender has to ascertain the *deemed* rate by making the calculation prescribed in Sch. 1 and he must state in the memorandum that it is " calculated in accordance with the provisions in Sch. 1 " to the Act of 1927.

These two alternatives can best be explained by taking an illustration of each. To illustrate the first alternative (A), I would take the case where a moneylender

C   makes a loan of £24,000 repayable over ten years at £200 a month, and meanwhile interest to be payable at the rate of twenty-five per cent. per annum on the balance outstanding from time to time. Under such a contract, the principal is reduced by £200 a month. So the interest gets less each month. The interest payable for the first month is £500 (twenty-five per cent. per annum on £24,000 for one month). The interest payable for the second month is £495 16s. 8d.

D   (twenty-five per cent. per annum on £23,800 for one month); and so on. The interest is reduced by £4 3s. 4d. each month. The interest payable for the last month is £4 3s. 4d. (twenty-five per cent. per annum on £200 for one month). The *total* sum payable for interest over the ten years comes to £30,250. That is the " interest charged on the loan "; but it is capable of being expressed in terms of an actual rate per cent. per annum, namely, twenty-five per cent. per

E   annum. The moneylender satisfies the statute by expressing the interest as twenty-five per cent. per annum. To illustrate the second alternative (B), I would take the case where a moneylender makes a loan of £24,000 repayable with interest over ten years at £450 a month. Each instalment is payable in a lump sum to include both principal and interest without splitting them up (similar to hire-purchase transactions where the monthly instalments are not

F   split up). Under such a contract it is impossible to calculate an *actual* rate of interest: for the simple reason that you do not know how much is paid off the principal each month and how much off the interest. Suppose that during the first five years each instalment of £450 was split up into £350 off the principal and £100 off the interest; and that during the second five years it was £50 off the principal and £400 off the interest. You cannot express that transaction in

G   terms of a single rate per cent. per annum over the whole ten years. Faced with this difficulty, Sch. 1 tells the moneylender how to calculate the *deemed* rate. On making that calculation, the result is a *deemed* rate of 24.13 per cent. He puts that figure in the memorandum and adds the words " as calculated in accordance with the provisions of Sch. 1 ". If he chooses this alternative, he must insert those words, or words to the like effect.

H   In the present case the moneylenders assert that they have chosen the first alternative (A). They say that the *total* interest of £33,750 is capable of being expressed in terms of an *actual* rate per cent. per annum, namely, 26.776860 per cent. per annum. Although the figure of 26.776860 is the result of calculation, I think that this contention is right. It is precisely the same as the illustration which I took in (A) above. The transaction can be expressed in these simple

I   terms: it is a loan of £25,000 repayable over ten years at £208 6s. 8d. a month, and meanwhile interest to be paid at the rate of 26.776860 per cent. per annum on the amount outstanding from time to time. It can be verified by simple arithmetic. The interest payable for the first month is £557 17s. (26.776860 per cent. per annum on £25,000 for one month). The interest payable for the second month is £553 4s. (26.776860 per cent. per annum on £24,791 13s. 4d. for one month). As the principal is reduced by £208 6s. 8d. each month, so the interest is less by £4 13s. each month. The interest payable for the last month is £4 13s. The *total* sum payable for interest over the ten years comes to £33,750.

That is the " interest charged on the loan ".   It can be expressed in terms of a
rate per cent. per annum, namely 26.776860 per cent. per annum.

The borrower and guarantors in this case admit in the pleadings that " the
rate per centum per annum of interest charged on the said loan was 26.776860 ":
and their counsel expressly admitted it at the Bar.   But they sought to say,
nevertheless, that the moneylenders did not choose the first alternative (A).
The borrowers said that the moneylenders chose the second alternative (B).
The rate of 26.776860 per cent. per annum was calculated, they say, in accordance
with the provisions of Sch. 1 because the formula used by the moneylenders is,
to all intents and purposes, the same as the formula contained in Sch. 1.   Hence
the borrowers say that the memorandum ought to have contained the words
" as calculated in accordance with the provisions of Sch. 1 "; and as it did
not contain those words, it is bad.

I think that there is a fallacy in this argument.   I agree that the formula
used by the moneylenders gives in this case the same result as the formula in
Sch. 1.   I set out in an appendix the two formulae; but the calculation in this
case gives the *actual* rate of interest, and not the *deemed* rate.   Inasmuch as
it gives the *actual* rate, it is sufficient for the moneylender to show that *actual*
rate without adding the magic words " as calculated in accordance with the
provisions of Sch. 1 ".

In my judgment, therefore, the interest charged on the loan, namely, £33,750
over the ten years, was capable of being expressed in terms of a rate per centum
per annum, namely, 26.776860: and the moneylenders satisfied the first alternative (A) in s. 6 (2) by saying in the memorandum that " the rate of interest
payable . . . shall be 26.776860 per centum per annum ".

2.   *Did the memorandum contain all the terms of the contract?*

By the statute, the memorandum must contain all the terms of the contract,
i.e., of the " contract for the repayment " by the borrower of the money and
interest; see s. 6 (1) and (2) of the Act of 1927.

The borrower contended in the court below that the memorandum should have
contained the terms relating to the King transaction and the £12,000 transaction.
The judge has so held.   He said that it was a term of the contract that " the
borrower would procure " that the guarantor (Mr. Rudland or his company)
would borrow the £12,000 from the moneylenders and that he would further
indemnify the moneylenders against any losses in the King transaction.   The
defendants in this court did not seek to support the judge's reasoning.   It was,
I fear, mistaken.   There was no agreement whatever by Mr. Green to *procure*
the guarantor to do anything in regard to the King transaction or the £12,000
transaction.   Those were transactions between the moneylenders and Mr.
Rudland to which Mr. Green was not a party.   They were collateral to the
contract of loan and formed no part of it.

The defendants did, however, seek to pray in aid these transactions by a
different line of argument.   They said that these transactions gave the moneylenders, by an indirect means, an increase in the " interest " charged on the
loan: and should, therefore, have been included in the calculation of interest,
which they were not.   The defendants say that the sums payable to the moneylenders on the King indemnity, and the interest payable on the £12,000 loan,
were amounts " by whatsoever name called, in excess of the principal, paid or
payable to a moneylender in consideration of *or otherwise* in respect of a loan ",
see s. 15.

I cannot accept this contention.   These amounts were not paid " in respect of
the loan " to Mr. Green.   They were paid in respect of the King transaction and
the £12,000 transaction.   Moreover, s. 6 is concerned with interest paid " by
him ", i.e., by the borrower; see s. 6 (1): and not payments by other persons.
These amounts cannot be regarded as part of the interest paid or payable by
Mr. Green.   They do not need, therefore, to be included in the calculation of
interest.   The moneylenders have not broken the statute.

3. *Conclusion*

The real defendant here is Mr. Rudland.   He is obviously a business man of great experience in financial matters.   He has negotiated numerous loans with moneylenders and must know the ropes.   He got money from these money-lenders with which to buy the George Hotel at Crewkerne: and now he seeks to get out of paying them.   He takes two technical points on the Moneylenders Acts.   Neither of them is good.   I would allow this appeal and give judgment for the moneylenders.

I have set out the mathematics in an appendix.   It is not fit to read aloud or at all.

APPENDIX

1. *The Moneylenders' Figure*

The moneylenders made their calculations in this way.   They took the loan of £25,000.   It was repayable over ten years.   They decided to charge interest at a " flat rate " of $13\frac{1}{2}$ per cent. per annum.   That meant that they charged $13\frac{1}{2}$ per cent. per annum on the full sum of £25,000 as if it were outstanding for the whole of the ten years.   That comes to £3,375 a year for ten years, thus making £33,750 altogether over the ten years by way of interest.

The moneylenders decided, however, that both principal and interest should be paid by equal monthly instalments over the ten years, that is, over 120 months. In order to arrive at the instalments, they divided the £25,000 principal by 120. That made £208 6s. 8d. a month payable off the principal.   Then they divided the £33,750 interest by 120.   That made £281 5s. a month payable off the interest.   From which tax would have to be deducted by the payer.

The moneylenders had then to express the interest of £33,750 in terms of a rate per cent. per annum.   To do this, they applied an algebraic formula: $F \times \dfrac{2n}{n+1}$ where F denotes the flat rate; and n denotes the number of months during which the loan was to be outstanding.   On the figures in this case the calculation was $13\frac{1}{2} \times \dfrac{2 \times 120}{120 + 1}$.   That comes to 26.776860.   That gives the required rate per cent. per annum.

2. *Schedule 1 Formula*

Let P = The principal, i.e. the amount actually lent to the borrower.

I = The interest, i.e. the total amount, in excess of the principal, payable to the moneylender over the whole period.

n = The number of months over which the principal and interest are repayable by equal monthly instalments.

At the end of each month, therefore, the instalment payable is:

$$\frac{P}{n} \text{ off the principal; and } \frac{I}{n} \text{ off the interest.}$$

Under Sch. 1, the first step is to make the s. 15 (2) apportionment.   To do this you take each monthly instalment and appropriate it to principal and interest in the proportion of P to I.   Now the first monthly instalment is: $\left(\dfrac{P}{n} + \dfrac{I}{n}\right)$.   When you appropriate that to principal and interest, it is $\dfrac{P}{n}$ for principal and $\dfrac{I}{n}$ for interest.

The next step is to apply para. 1 of Sch. 1 so as to ascertain the amount of principal taken to be outstanding at the time.   During the first month it is P. During the second month it is $P - \dfrac{P}{n}$.   During the third month $P - \dfrac{2P}{n}$; and so forth.

The next step is to apply para. 2 of Sch. 1.   You multiply each of those amounts of principal by the number of calendar months during which they have been outstanding. Each has been outstanding for only one month.   So you multiply each by one. So you get P for the first month: $P - \dfrac{P}{n}$ for the second month; and so on. Then you add all those together. That is:

$$P + \left(P - \frac{P}{n}\right) + \left(P - \frac{2P}{n}\right) + \ldots\ldots \left(P - \frac{(n-1)P}{n}\right)$$

That comes to: $nP - \dfrac{P}{n}(1 + 2 + 3 \ldots\ldots (n-1)$

That comes to: $nP - \dfrac{P}{n} \times \dfrac{n(n-1)}{2}$

That comes to: $\dfrac{P(n+1)}{2}$

The third step is to apply para. 3 of Sch. 1. You take the total amount of interest (I) and divide it by 1/12th of $\dfrac{P(n+1)}{2}$ and multiply the quotient by 100.

That is:

$$\frac{I \times 100}{\dfrac{1}{12} \times \dfrac{P(n+1)}{2}}$$

That comes to: $\dfrac{2400\,I}{P(n+1)}$

So the rate per cent. per annum is: $\dfrac{2400\,I}{P(n+1)}$

3. The Moneylender's Formula

The moneylender gets his rate per cent. per annum by taking the flat rate of interest (which I will call F) and multiplying it by $\dfrac{2n}{n+1}$.

Now F (the flat rate) is the rate of interest which would be paid if the whole principal (P) remained outstanding during the whole of the n months. The moneylender desires to get that amount of interest. For each month the interest payments payable would be: $\dfrac{F}{12 \times 100} \times P$

At the end of n months the total interest payable would be: $\dfrac{nF}{1200} \times P$

The moneylender wants that amount of interest to be paid to him. So $\dfrac{nFP}{1200} = I$.

With the result that: $F = \dfrac{1200\,I}{nP}$

To get the rate per cent. per annum the moneylender takes F, which equals $\dfrac{1200\,I}{nP}$ and multiplies it by $\dfrac{2n}{n+1}$. This gives the result of: $\dfrac{2400\,I}{P(n+1)}$.

4. Result of Formulae

It is plain, therefore, that the Sch. 1 formula gives the same result as the moneylender's formula, namely: $\dfrac{2400\,I}{P(n+1)}$ which is: $\dfrac{2400 \times 33750}{25000 \times 121}$. That comes to 26.776860.

DIPLOCK, L.J.: On the issue whether the memorandum contained all the terms of the contract, I agree with what LORD DENNING, M.R., has said in the latter part of his judgment and have nothing to add. On the main question of law about the way in which the rate of interest is stated in the memorandum, however, I am afraid that I differ from everyone else concerned in this appeal except the judge of the Mayor's and City of London Court, whose judgment on this point

I myself would uphold. Fortunately I can do so with a clear conscience for my dissent will not result in what, if either of my brethren agreed with me, would be a wholly unmeritorious victory for the defendants.

Two earlier decisions of this court in *Parkfield Trust, Ltd.* v. *Curtis* (3) and *Mason & Wood, Ltd.* v. *Greene* (4) have laid it down that where the rate per cent. per annum of the interest charged shown in the memorandum is that " represented by the interest charged as calculated in accordance with Sch. 1 " to the Moneylenders Act, 1927 and is not " the interest charged on the loan expressed in terms of a rate per cent. per annum ", s. 6 of the Act of 1927 makes the contract unenforceable unless the memorandum also states that the rate per cent. per annum so shown is calculated in accordance with the provisions of the Act. These decisions are binding on us and, even if they were not, I should, for reasons which will appear, find them persuasive and follow them.

What is said by the moneylenders in this case is that as the contract expressly appropriates each of the monthly repayments to principal and interest in the same proportions as are specified in s. 15 (2) of the Act of 1927, the calculation in Sch. 1 does itself give " the interest charged on the loan expressed in terms of a rate per cent. per annum ". Therefore, the two permissible methods of showing the rate per cent. per annum of interest coincide and it is unnecessary to state in the memorandum that the rate per cent. per annum of the interest charged was calculated in accordance with the provisions of Sch. 1. If I could agree with LORD DENNING, M.R., in accepting the premise, I should accept the conclusion too and allow the appeal. The accuracy of the premise depends on combined questions of law and mathematics and it is with equal diffidence that I differ from LORD DENNING, M.R., in both those branches of learning. But differ I must.

The question of law is the true construction of the phrase " the interest charged on the loan expressed in terms of a rate per cent. per annum " in s. 6 (2) of the Moneylenders Act, 1927, which requires that the note or memorandum of the contract shall show inter alia:

". . . the amount of the principal of the loan, and, *either* the interest charged on the loan expressed in terms of a rate per cent. per annum, *or* the rate per cent. per annum represented by the interest charged as calculated in accordance with the provisions of Sch. 1 to this Act."

It is to be observed that what has to be shown as a rate per cent. per annum is under the first option " the interest charged on the loan ", but under the second option " the interest charged " simpliciter: and a similar dichotomy between " the interest charged on the loan " and " the interest charged " is to be found in s. 15 (2) which reads as follows:

" Where by a contract for the loan of money by a moneylender the interest charged on the loan is not expressed in terms of a rate, any amount paid or payable to the moneylender under the contract (other than simple interest charged in accordance with the proviso to s. 7 of this Act) shall be appropriated to principal and interest in the proportion that the principal bears to the total amount of the interest, and the rate per cent. per annum represented by the interest charged as calculated in accordance with the provisions of Sch. 1 to this Act shall be deemed to be the rate of interest charged on the loan."

This subsection also makes it clear that the options are mutually exclusive and both subsections suggest that the draftsman at any rate thought that as a matter of mathematics, the alternative permitted methods of calculating the rate per cent. per annum to be shown in the note or memorandum of the contract led to different results.

The expressions " interest " and " principal " are defined in s. 15 (1) as follows:

---

(3) [1934] All E.R. Rep. 43; [1934] 1 K.B. 685.
(4) [1936] 2 All E.R. 509; [1936] 2 K.B. 370.

" ' Interest ' does not include any sum lawfully charged in accordance
with the provisions of this Act by a moneylender for or on account of costs,
charges, or expenses, but save as aforesaid, includes any amount, by whatsoever name called, in excess of the principal, paid or payable to a moneylender in consideration of or otherwise in respect of a loan. ' Principal '
means in relation to a loan the amount actually lent to the borrower."

The effect of this definition of " interest " is that the expression " the interest
charged ", which appears in each of the options in s. 6 (2), means a lump sum of
money representing (where, as in the present case, nothing is charged on account
of costs, charges or expenses) the difference between the total amount payable
under the contract to the moneylender and the amount actually lent by the
moneylender to the borrower.   It is a figure arrived at by a simple subtraction
sum.   It is independent of the duration of the contract, of the amount of any
individual instalments by which the loan is repayable and the intervals between
them and of any description, whether as " interest " or " principal ", which the
contract applies to any instalment or part of an instalment.   It is this lump
sum which, under the first option, must be expressed as the rate per cent. per
annum at which interest is charged " on the loan "; or, under the second option,
at the figure resulting from the calculation made in accordance with Sch. 1 to the
Act of 1927 irrespective of what that figure represents in terms of mathematical
concepts.

If the first option is exercised, however, the only guide how the calculation is
to be made is contained in the words in which the required result of the calculation
is described, and these words do involve mathematical concepts.   " Interest "
is " money paid for the use of money lent " (SHORTER OXFORD DICTIONARY),
and if " interest charged on the loan " is to be expressed in terms of a rate in
relation to time (viz., per annum), the interest must be treated as accruing from
day to day and if it is to be expressed as a single rate, it must be treated as accruing
at a uniform rate throughout the contract.   It follows that where the contract
provides for payment by the borrower of the total amount of principal and
interest by periodic instalments, the " interest charged on the loan ", if it is to
be capable of being expressed in terms of a single rate, must be treated as accruing
at a uniform rate during the periods between successive instalments.   This is
possible mathematically only if the sum paid in each instalment is treated as
consisting as to part of interest at the expressed rate per cent. per annum for the
period since the date on which the previous instalment was paid on the amount
of principal outstanding since that date, and as to the remainder of repayment
of principal; from which it follows that the actual sum, payable as interest on
the principal outstanding in respect of each period, diminishes progressively
in each successive instalment as more and more of the principal is repaid.   Consequently if the periodic instalments by which the loan is repayable are of equal
amounts payable at equal intervals, the proportion of each instalment to be
treated as repayment of principal increases, and the proportion to be treated
as payment of interest correspondingly decreases in each successive instalment.
If the amount of each instalment, the length of the intervals between instalments
and the amount actually lent are known, it is possible, although laborious, to
calculate the rate per cent. per annum at which interest is charged on the loan.
This method of appropriating the total amount of each instalment between
interest and principal is the only one which enables one to express in terms of a
single rate per cent. per annum the actual yield which the moneylender obtains on
his investment.   The rate per cent. per annum so calculated is that which is
referred to in such cases as *Parkfield Trust, Ltd.* v. *Curtis* (5), *Mason & Wood, Ltd.*
v. *Greene* (6) and *Mutual Loan Fund Association, Ltd.* v. *Sanderson* (7), as the
" true interest " or " actual interest ".   It is in my view what is meant by the

---

(5) [1934] All E.R. Rep. 43; [1934] 1 K.B. 685.
(6) [1936] 2 All E.R. 509; [1936] 2 K.B. 370.   (7) [1937] 1 All E.R. 380.

expression in s. 6 (2) of the Act of 1927, " the interest charged *on the loan* expressed in terms of a rate per cent. per annum ".

The calculation which is to be made if the second option is exercised does entail a different method of appropriating the total amount of each instalment between interest and principal. The same proportion of each instalment is appropriated to interest instead of a series of different proportions diminishing with each successive instalment. If the periods between successive instalments are equal, the interest charged during the periods between successive instalments is at an increasing rate per cent. per annum on the principal outstanding during each successive period. It cannot be expressed as a single rate. The calculation in Sch. 1, as a matter of mathematics, gives the weighted average of the various rates at which interest is charged on the various amounts of principal outstanding during each successive interval. Where the instalments are of equal amounts, payable at equal intervals, the calculation of such weighted average can be shortened by making use of the elementary mathematical proposition that the sum of an arithmetical progression of successive prime numbers from 1 to n. is $n \times (n + 1) \div 2$, and can be expressed algebraically in a number of alternative formulae, all of which are mathematically equivalent to one another. In his appendix LORD DENNING, M.R., has demonstrated the mathematical equivalence of two such formulae. Two more are to be found in documents in evidence in this case. I should add that where a loan is payable in more than one instalment and the intervals between instalments are equal, it is mathematically impossible that the result of this calculation provided for in the second option should be the same as the result of the calculation which I have already indicated is in my judgment called for in the first option.

What the moneylenders have done in the present case is to appropriate expressly by the terms of the contract the total amount of each instalment to principal and interest in the same proportions as the statutory appropriation used for the purpose of the calculation provided for in the second option. That they have chosen to call particular instalments or parts thereof by the name of " interest " cannot, in view of the statutory definition of " interest " which I have already cited, affect their rights under the Act of 1927. Their proposition thus involves the contention that in any case in which the total amount of each instalment is appropriated to principal and interest in the proportions set out in s. 15 (2) of the Act of 1927, whether the appropriation is by the operation of that subsection itself or by the express terms of the contract, the calculation provided for in Sch. 1 does give the " interest charged on the loan expressed in terms of a rate per cent. per annum ".

The first answer to this proposition is in my view to be found in the terms of s. 15 (2) of the Act of 1927 itself. The appropriation and calculation there provided for is only to be made where by the contract " the interest charged on the loan " is not expressed in terms of a rate. If that appropriation and calculation, however, does itself actually express in terms of a rate per cent. per annum " the interest charged on the loan " instead of merely being deemed to do so, as the subsection itself says, the circumstances contemplated by the subsection in which alone the calculation provided for in Sch. 1 falls to be made (viz., where by the contract the interest charged on the loan is *not* expressed as a rate) can never occur in respect of an enforceable contract, for by s. 6 (2) the terms of the contract must include an undertaking by the borrower to pay interest at a rate per cent. per annum calculated in one or other of the ways there specified, by both of which, according to this proposition, " the interest charged on the loan " *is* expressed in terms of a rate.

The moneylenders seek, however, to justify the proposition by reference to the provisions of s. 7 of the Act of 1927 which make a moneylending contract illegal " in so far as it provides directly or indirectly for the payment of compound interest ". Although interest at a rate per cent. per annum on the loan (i.e., the amount of principal from time to time outstanding) accrues from day to day, there

is nothing in the Act of 1927, so they suggest, to prevent the parties from agreeing
that the due date of payment of the whole or any part of the interest which has
accrued shall be referred to some later date and if this is done, the Act itself
provides that no interest can be charged on the accrued interest for the period of
deferment. Thus, it is contended, where the parties expressly agree on the
rate of interest to be charged on the loan, and also provide expressly by their
contract for the appropriation of specified proportions of each instalment to
principal and interest respectively, it is not necessary that the sum comprised
in each successive instalment which is expressed to be paid by way of interest
should be the same as the interest calculated at the agreed rate per cent. per
annum for the period since the last instalment on the principal outstanding
during that period. It is sufficient if the interest which has so accrued is paid
either as part of the instalment payable at the end of the period in respect of
which it has accrued or as part of any subsequent instalment. Accordingly
when the parties do agree on a rate of interest to be charged on the loan and on
the appropriation to interest of a proportion of the total amount of any instalment which is less in the case of the earlier instalments and greater in the case
of the later instalments than interest calculated at the agreed rate per cent. per
annum on the amount of principal outstanding since the payment of the last
preceding instalment, they are (since payment of interest on interest is illegal) to
be assumed to have agreed that any such deficit represents accrued interest,
the payment of which is agreed to be deferred and any such excess represents
a deferred payment of interest which has earlier accrued. If this assumption
can properly be made, it is true, as a matter of mathematics, that where the
total amount of each successive instalment is apportioned to principal and
interest in the proportions specified in s. 15 (2), which in the present case was done
under the express terms of the contract, the agreed rate per cent. per annum
charged on the loan can be arrived at by the calculation provided for in Sch. 1
or any other formula which is the mathematical equivalent of that calculation.
It is mathematically the same as the weighted average of the rates at which
interest accrues due between successive instalments.

This ingenious proposition is merely a more elaborate way of saying that
contrary to what the draftsman of the Act of 1927 obviously thought, the calculation of a rate of interest in accordance with the provisions of Sch. 1 *always*
gives the interest charged on the loan expressed in terms of a rate per cent. per
annum. The basic fallacy in it is that it ignores the true nature of interest
expressed as a rate.

Interest is by definition money paid for the use of money lent. Where it is
charged on a loan at a rate per cent. per annum, it must be treated as accruing
from day to day to the principal on which it is charged throughout the period
during which the borrower has the use of the principal and as payable together
with the principal to which it has accrued and not otherwise. Unless it is so
treated, the money paid for use of the principal can be expressed at a variety of
rates per cent. per annum by attaching different labels to the repayments made by
the borrower to the lender. To take a simple example, a loan of £100 repayable by
two annual instalments of £100 each. The true rate of interest is approximately
sixty-two per cent. Yet if the moneylenders proposition is correct, this could
be expressed as a rate per cent. per annum of one hundred per cent. by calling
the whole of the first instalment " principal " and the whole of the second
instalment " interest ", or of 66⅔ per cent. by calling £50 of each instalment
" principal " and £50 " interest ". Or assume that the £100 loan is repayable by
a first instalment of £100 at the end of one year and a second instalment at the
end of the third year instead of the second year. Obviously the borrower is
paying less for the use of the £100 lent to him than in the first example. The
true rate of interest is in fact fifty per cent. Yet if the defendants' proposition
is correct, the rate of interest could be expressed as a rate per cent. per annum
of one hundred per cent., as in the first example, simply by describing the whole

A of the first instalment as " principal " and the whole of the second instalment as " interest ".   Incidentally, this is one of the rare cases where the calculation in accordance with Sch. 1 would give the true rate of interest.   It cannot have been the intention of the Act of 1927 that the rate per cent. per annum to be shown in the note or memorandum of the contract should depend on the name by which the moneylender has chosen to call the whole or part of particular instal-

B ments payable by the borrower. The definition of " interest " in s. 15 (1) expressly so provides.

The object of the requirement in s. 6 (2), that the rate of interest shall be shown in the note or memorandum, is, at least in part, to enable the borrower and the court to see whether the " interest charged " exceeds the rate of forty-eight per cent. per annum and so gives rise to the prima facie presumption that

C the transaction is harsh and unconscionable.   This provision would be irrational unless the Act of 1927 also requires the rate of interest shown in the note or memorandum of every moneylender's contract to be calculated on a comparable and known basis.   The Act of 1927 in fact provides for two and only two alternative bases on which the rate of interest may be calculated.   Only in very rare cases do the alternative calculations give the same result.   A fair

D comparison can, therefore, only be made if the note or memorandum also shows by which of the two alternative methods the rate per cent. per annum shown was calculated.   This, as I read their judgments, is why the Court of Appeal in *Parkfield Trust, Ltd.* v. *Curtis* (8) and *Mason & Wood, Ltd.* v. *Greene* (9) construed s. 6 (2) as requiring the note or memorandum to show on which of the two the rate per cent. per annum of interest was calculated; and, with respect, I think

E that they were right.

The contract in the present case, which was itself the memorandum under s. 6 (2) of the Act of 1927, provided for repayment of the principal and interest by 120 equal monthly instalments and by its terms expressly allocated the total amount of each instalment as between interest and principal in the same proportions as the statutory allocation laid down in s. 15 (2) of the Act of 1927.   The

F interest charged on the amount of principal outstanding during each period was, therefore, charged at a different rate per cent. per annum in respect of each of the 120 monthly periods and was incapable of being expressed in terms of a single uniform rate per cent. per annum.   The memorandum stated: " The rate of interest payable . . . shall be 26.776860 per cent. per annum ".   The evidence showed that this was in fact the weighted average of the various different rates

G of interest charged in each of the 120 months.   It was calculated in accordance with the provisions of Sch. 1 to the Act of 1927 by one or other of several equivalent formulae in which that method can be expressed algebraically when payment is by equal instalments at equal intervals; but the memorandum did not show that this was the method used.   The true rate of " interest charged on the loan " was not 26.776860 per cent. per annum but was 22.404963 per cent.

H per annum.   The contract must accordingly be held to be unenforceable in accordance with those authorities unless the defendants have deprived themselves of the right to rely on this defence by the admission in the pleadings and at the hearing to which I referred at the outset.

It was stated in the particulars of claim, inter alia—" The rate per centum per annum of interest charged on the said loan was 26.776860 "—and this was

I admitted in the defence.   Had the admission stood alone, it could, I think, have been treated as an admission of fact without any obligation lying on the court to enquire whether it was based on the true construction of the Act of 1927 or not.   The admission is followed, however, by a positive averment that

" The rate of interest charged by the plaintiffs was calculated in accordance with the provisions of Sch. 1 to the Act of 1927 but the said interest was not so stated."

(8) [1934] All E.R. Rep. 43; [1934] 1 K.B. 685.
(9) [1936] 2 All E.R. 509; [1936] 2 K.B. 370.

This averment is inconsistent with the admission, for, as I have pointed out, **A** it is mathematically certain that where, as in this case, a loan is repayable by periodic instalments of equal amounts at equal intervals the rate per cent. per annum of interest charged calculated in accordance with the provisions of Sch. 1 to the Act of 1927 cannot be the same as " interest charged on the loan " expressed in terms of a rate per cent. per annum on the true construction of that phrase in the Act of 1927.   Although I am far from saying that this court is bound to **B** take judicial notice of all mathematical propositions, however complicated, the inaccuracy of the admission in the present case can be so easily and plainly demonstrated by applying the rate of 26.776860 per cent. per annum to the total amount of principal, viz. £25,000 outstanding during the first month.   This is about £560 which is greater than the total amount of the instalment then payable, viz. £491 11s. 8d., so that at this rate of interest the principal would never be **C** repaid.   I do not think that we can shut our eyes to this.

It has been pleaded and proved in evidence that the rate of interest shown in the memorandum was calculated in accordance with the provisions of Sch. 1 to the Act of 1927, and we must, I think, treat the admissions as being based on an erroneous construction of the Act of 1927—as was, indeed, apparent in the explanation of it which was ultimately given by counsel for the defendants **D** at the hearing before us while expressing his adherence to it.

Despite the admission, I should, therefore, feel bound to dismiss this appeal, though I would do so with great reluctance, for the result would be that the defendants would escape their just indebtedness on a technical point wholly devoid of merit on which they and their advisers seem to have stumbled by accident.   The interest charged on the loan expressed in terms of a rate per **E** cent. per annum, if they had not apportioned the instalments as between principal and interest, would have been less than that stated.   Alternatively, the plaintiffs could have added the words " calculated in accordance with the provisions of Sch. 1 to the Moneylenders Act, 1927 ".

I am glad that this is a dissenting judgment, and so cannot affect the result of this appeal.   **F**

RUSSELL, L.J.: The Moneylenders Act, 1927, has a number of phrases referring to interest on a loan.   Section 5 (4) deals with a document emanating from a moneylender purporting to indicate the terms of interest on which he is willing to make a particular loan: such document is required either to

> ". . . express the interest proposed to be charged in the terms of a rate **G** per cent. per annum or show the rate per cent. per annum represented by the interest proposed to be charged as calculated in accordance with the provisions of Sch. 1."

Failure is an offence.   Suppose that a moneylender says to a proposed borrower: " I will lend you £2,000 for two years.   I will charge you interest on the loan **H** at the rate of thirty per cent. per annum—a total of £1,200.   I realise that your financial prospects will make it difficult for you to pay the interest as well as the principal by the end of two years.   Therefore, I will postpone your obligation to pay the interest until the end of three years."   I do not think that such a document would be an offence under s. 5.

Is there any difference between the phrase " the interest . . . to be charged ", **I** and " the interest to be charged on the loan", or " the interest charged on the loan "?   I should not have thought so.

The proviso to s. 7 refers to " the interest charged *in respect of* the loan ". Section 8 (1) (*a*) in requiring information to be given on request to the borrower, says that must include " the rate per cent. per annum of interest *charged* ". Section 9 (2) (*b*) uses the phrase " where *the interest* is not expressed by the contract for the loan in terms of a rate ".   Section 10 (1) refers to occasions when " the interest *charged* exceeds the rate of forty-eight per cent. per annum ".

A Section 13 (1) uses the phrase " money lent . . . or of any interest *in respect* thereof ". By s. 14 (1) (*a*) a pawnbroker has an obligation, without alternative, to state " the interest charged on the loan expressed in terms of a rate per cent. per annum ". These considerations make it difficult for me to attach any special significance to the phrase " the interest charged on the loan expressed in terms of a rate per cent. per annum ".

B   Let me suppose a contract for the loan of £12,000 repayable by twelve equal monthly instalments of £1,000 starting one month after the date of the loan. Suppose that the contract further provides that the interest charged on the loan shall be at the rate of thirty per cent. per annum to accrue due and be payable on the same twelve monthly dates. I apprehend that this could be correctly stated in the contract as involving twelve payments of interest of the following

C amounts: (i) £300, (ii) £275, (iii) £250, (iv) £225, (v) £200, (vi) £175, (vii) £150, (viii) £125, (ix) £100, (x) £75, (xi) £50, (xii) £25: a total of £1,950. It seems to me that such a contract would show, and correctly, the interest charged on the loan expressed in terms of a rate per cent. per annum.

     Suppose, however, that the same contract merely said that the interest should *accrue due* on the same twelve dates, and set out the figures above stated, and

D went on to provide " notwithstanding that the interest charged on the loan should *accrue due* on the date and in the amounts stated, the obligation to *pay* the first seven of such amounts shall be postponed to such an extent (both in time and amount) as will only oblige the borrower to pay on each of the said twelve dates the sum of £162 10s. (1/12th of £1,950) ". I do not myself see why such a provision should falsify the statement that the interest charged on the

E loan is at the rate of thirty per cent. per annum.

     Now let the same contract be expressed in shorter terms: simply saying that the interest charged on the loan shall be at the rate of thirty per cent. per annum, but that the interest shall be *paid* in twelve equal instalments (on the said monthly dates) of £162 10s. I cannot see that this shorter version is relevantly different from the longer version. Nor do I see how it is relevantly different

F from the contract of loan with which we are concerned.

     I can see no mischief resulting from this approach. Both the court and the borrower are told the rate per cent. per annum of interest. To *postpone* the obligation to pay part of some of the instalments of interest does not seem to be a matter of grievance for the borrower, or to be calculated to confuse him or the court as to the rate of interest that has to be paid.

G   Accordingly I agree with LORD DENNING, M.R., that this is not a case in which it was necessary that the contract should refer to Sch. 1. I have an uneasy feeling that on this point my judgment is to that of DIPLOCK, L.J., as Watson was to Holmes, and that it may merit the sub-title " Rattle of a Simple Man "; but there it is.

     On the other aspect of the case I agree with both my brethren that the contract

H included all the terms of the loan.

     Accordingly, I agree with LORD DENNING, M.R., that the appeal should be allowed.

Appeal allowed. Leave to appeal to the House of Lords refused.

     Solicitors: *Alfred Neale & Co.*, Croydon (for the plaintiffs, the moneylenders);
I *Radcliffes & Co.* (for the first and second defendants); *Philip Taylor & Co.* (for the third and fourth defendants).

[*Reported by* F. GUTTMAN, ESQ., *Barrister-at-Law.*]

MAWAZ KHAN AND ANOTHER v. REGINAM.   A

[PRIVY COUNCIL (Lord Hodson, Lord Pearce and Lord Pearson), October 4, 5, November, 7, 1966.]

Privy Council—Hong Kong—Criminal law—Evidence—Admissibility—Hearsay
—Statements of two accused setting up same alibi—Each statement made to
police by one accused in the absence of the other—Evidence of statements   B
admitted to show that accused were acting in concert in concocting alibi.

The appellants were charged with the murder of A. on Feb. 10, 1965.
The Crown relied on circumstantial evidence connecting both appellants
with the crime and in addition on statements made at the police station
by each of the appellants in the absence of the other, in which they both
set up an alibi that they were elsewhere, viz., at the Ocean Club, on the   C
night in question and in which they explained their injuries as having been
sustained in a fight between them.   Evidence of these statements was
admitted as relevant to show that the appellants fabricated a joint story
and that they had co-operated in this after the alleged crime.   Neither
appellant gave evidence at his trial.   On appeal against conviction the
main ground of appeal was that the statement of one accused made in the   D
absence of the other had been wrongly admitted against the other.

Held: the statement of each appellant had not been admitted for the
purpose of proving the truth of the facts stated, but in order to show, by
reason of the fact that the statement was made, that the appellants were
acting in concert and that such action indicated a common guilt; for this
purpose the statements had been admissible without breach of the hearsay   E
rule, and the appeal would be dismissed (see p. 82, letter H, and p. 83,
letters B and F, post).

Subramaniam v. *Public Prosecutor* ([1956] 1 W.L.R. 965) applied.
Appeal dismissed.

[As to the rule against hearsay, see 15 HALSBURY'S LAWS (3rd Edn.) 294,
para. 533; and for cases on the subject, see 14 DIGEST (Repl.) 507, 508, *4909-4924*;   F
and for cases on statements made in the absence of the accused, see 14 DIGEST
(Repl.) 445, 446, *4326-4329.*

As to admissibility of relevant facts to show guilty knowledge, see 10
HALSBURY'S LAWS (3rd Edn.) 440, para. 815; and for cases on the subject see
14 DIGEST (Repl.) *426, 4129-4134.*]

Cases referred to: G

R. v. *Rudd*, (1948), 32 Cr. App. Rep. 138; 14 Digest (Repl.) 531, *5152.*
R. v. *Wattam*, (1952), 36 Cr. App. Rep. 72; 14 Digest (Repl.) 515, *4986.*
Subramaniam v. *Public Prosecutor*, [1956] 1 W.L.R. 965; Digest (Cont. Vol. A)
    522, *495a.*

Appeal.   H
This was an appeal in forma pauperis, by special leave, from a judgment of
the Supreme Court of Hong Kong in its appellate jurisdiction (HOGAN, C.J.
and RIGBY, A.J., BRIGGS, A.J. dissenting), dated Aug. 23, 1965, dismissing
the appeals of both appellants, Mawaz Khan (alias Fazal Karim) and Amanat
Khan, against their conviction by the Supreme Court in its original criminal
jurisdiction (HUGGINS, J. and a jury) on May 5, 1965, for the offence of murder,   I
in respect of which they were each sentenced to death.

E. F. Gratiaen, Q.C., and *E. Cotran* for the appellants.
J. G. Le Quesne, Q.C., and *N. R. Macdougal* (of the Hong Kong bar) for the
Crown.

LORD HODSON: This is an appeal from a judgment of the Supreme
Court of Hong Kong (HOGAN, C.J., RIGBY, A.J., and BRIGGS, A.J.), dated
Aug. 23, 1965, dismissing the appeals of both appellants against their conviction

A for murder, by the Supreme Court sitting in its criminal jurisdiction with a jury on May 5, 1965. Both were sentenced to death; each made statements, but neither gave evidence in the witness-box.

The main ground of appeal is that the trial judge erred in ruling that a statement made by one accused person in the absence of another could be used for any purpose or in any way against the other. To admit such a statement would,
B it is said, violate the " hearsay " rule.

Before considering the facts of this case it is convenient to state what is meant by the "hearsay" rule, for contravention of the rule makes evidence inadmissible. The accepted text books on the law of evidence are at one in saying that such statements are inadmissible to prove truth of the matters stated. WIGMORE ON EVIDENCE (3rd Edn.) vol. 6, p. 178 puts the matter clearly
C in this way:

" The prohibition of the hearsay rule, then, does not apply to all words or utterances merely as such. If this fundamental principle is clearly realised, its application is a comparatively simple matter. The hearsay rule excludes extrajudicial utterances only when offered for a special purpose, namely, as assertions to evidence the truth of the matter asserted."

D
The rule has been stated to the same effect by their lordships in the case of *Subramaniam* v. *Public Prosecutor* (1):

" Evidence of a statement made to a witness by a person who is not himself called as a witness may or may not be hearsay. It is hearsay and inadmissible when the object of the evidence is to establish the truth of
E what is contained in the statement. It is not hearsay and is admissible when it is proposed to establish by the evidence, not the truth of the statement, but the fact that it was made."

The appellants were charged with the murder of one Said Afzal on Feb. 10, 1965. He was a Pakistani watchman and his body was found on the following morning with no less than forty-nine wounds in it, pointing to the fact that
F he had been savagely stabbed and hacked to death.

The case for the prosecution rested on circumstantial evidence which may be summarized as follows:—(a) One Farid Khan testified that in 1958 in his village of Haider in West Pakistan he had seen the deceased stab and kill one Wassal Khan, at a time when the appellants were living in the same village. The deceased had served a term of imprisonment before coming to Hong Kong and
G among the possessions of the second appellant was found a photograph of a girl on the back of which was written the name " Wassal Khan " and the words " West Pakistan ". A possible motive for the killing of the deceased was revenge for his having killed Wassal Khan. (b) Some evidence of bloodstains on the clothing and shoes of the second appellant: this was of group B and group O; the blood group of the deceased was group B, that of the first appellant group
H O. These stains could not be accounted for by the statements of the two appellants that they sustained injuries in a fight with one another which would account for the blood. (c) A small ring was found at the scene of the crime; a photograph of the second appellant taken about a month before the incident shows him wearing a small ring on his signet finger, although he was not wearing that ring when interviewed by the police after the incident. (d) At the scene of the crime
I the police found a number of shoe impressions, three of which were clear enough to be photographed. One impression corresponded with the rubber heel of the shoes the deceased was wearing. Among the belongings of the second appellant was found a pair of rubber-heeled shoes. A comparison of a heel impression found at the scene of the crime showed six similar points of comparison with one of this pair of shoes. The heels of these shoes were identical with one another. In the same way five points of similarity were to be seen

---

(1) [1956] 1 W.L.R. 965 at p. 970.

by comparing a third heel impression found at the scene of the crime with the **A** right heel impression of shoes taken from the first appellant. Of particular significance was an impression on the floor corresponding with a nail hammered into the right heel of the pair of shoes belonging to the first appellant. In that the shoes of two persons were involved there was thus a double coincidence.

This circumstantial evidence connected both appellants with the scene of the crime, but the Crown relied strongly on the fact that each of the appellants **B** had in their respective statements sought to set up a joint alibi which was demonstrated to be false. Each of the appellants separately told the police that they were at a place called the Ocean Club on the night in question, and endeavoured to explain their injuries as having been sustained in a fight between them and as having no connexion with the killing of the deceased. Many of the details of their statements were contradicted by the evidence of witnesses. The **C** statement of each appellant was used against him, the judge directing the jury:

"A statement which is made by an accused person in the absence of the other is not evidence against the other. It is evidence against the maker of the statement but against him only."

No complaint was made of this direction, but the judge went on to say: **D**

"The Crown's case here is not that these statements are true and that what one says ought to be considered as evidence of what actually happened. What the Crown say is that these statements have been shown to be a tissue of lies and that they disclose an attempt to fabricate a joint story. Now, members of the jury, if you come to that conclusion, then the fabrication of a joint story would be evidence against both. It would be **E** evidence that they had co-operated after the alleged crime."

It was submitted that the direction of the judge that a statement made by one accused person in the absence of the other is not evidence against that other was nullified by the further direction that the jury were entitled to compare the statements, and, if they came to the conclusion that they were false, that would be evidence that they had co-operated after the alleged crime and jointly **F** concocted the story out of a sense of guilt.

Their lordships are of opinion that this submission, which appealed to one member of the Court of Appeal and no doubt impressed HOGAN, C.J. and RIGBY, A.J., when they made reference to the importance of the question involved, ought not to be sustained. Their lordships agree with HOGAN, C.J., and RIGBY, A.J., in accepting the generality of the proposition maintained by the text writers **G** (2) and to be found in *Subramaniam's* case (3) that a statement is not hearsay and is admissible when it is proposed to establish by the evidence not the truth of the statement but the fact that it was made. Not only therefore can the statements of each appellant be used against each appellant individually, as the learned judge directed, but they can, without any breach of the hearsay rule, be used, not for the purpose of establishing the truth of the assertions contained therein but **H** for the purpose of asking the jury to hold the assertions false and to draw inferences from their falsity. The statements were relevant as tending to show that the makers were acting in concert and that such action indicated a common guilt. This is a factor to be taken into account in conjunction with the circumstantial evidence to which reference has been made in determining the guilt or innocence of the accused persons. Telling lies to the police when **I** enquiries are being made about a crime is of great significance, but as OLIVER, J. pointed out in *R.* v. *Wattam* (4):

"There must be something more than the telling of lies to the police before a man is convicted of any crime, let alone murder."

---

(2) See, e.g., 15 HALSBURY'S LAWS (3rd Edn.) 294, para. 533, published in 1956, and, subsequently, *R.* v. *Willis* ([1960] 1 All E.R. 331).
(3) [1965] 1 W.L.R. 965.   (4) (1952), 36 Cr. App. Rep. 72 at p. 76.

A It was contended before your lordships that, even if the statements were admissible to show the concoction of a false story by the appellants, there was insufficient weight in the circumstantial evidence to call for an answer, hence the telling of lies carried no weight. Their lordships do not accept this contention. There was weight in the circumstantial evidence which called for an explanation. The concerted attempt to give a false explanation by way of
B alibi was evidence of guilt to be taken into consideration with the other evidence given in the case. It is an additional factor to be taken into consideration with all other relevant evidence. It is in their lordships' opinion immaterial that the appellants were not charged with conspiracy. No such charge would be likely to be added to the charge of murder. What is found against the appellants is that the statements were concocted for the purpose of escaping from the con-
C sequences of their crime and, if false, are admissible to show guilt. As has been said: " The recourse to falsehood leads fairly to an inference of guilt." The misapprehension which arose in the case and caused BRIGGS, A.J., to take the view that the statement could not be put to the use which the Crown proposed was based on the judgment of HUMPHREYS, J. in R. v. Rudd (5), when he said:

D   " Ever since this court was established it has been the invariable rule to state the law in the same way—that, while a statement made in the absence of the accused person by one of his co-defendants cannot be evidence against him, if a co-defendant goes into the witness-box and gives evidence in the course of a joint trial, then what he says becomes evidence for all the purposes of the case including the purpose of being evidence against his co-defendant."

E
The question there was whether the evidence given by an accused person in the witness-box was admissible against his co-accused. The answer was in the affirmative, and the statement made by the judge about statements outside the trial was made only to show the distinction between this and sworn evidence. The sweeping statement about statements made outside the trial is of course
F generally true but there are exceptions to it as, for example, if the statements are part of the res gestae or made by a combination in furtherance of a common design. The conclusion in the case however lends no support to the contention put forward by the appellants.

Their lordships are of opinion that there was no misdirection of the jury, and will accordingly humbly advise Her Majesty that the appeal be dismissed.

G   *Appeal dismissed.*

Solicitors: *T. L. Wilson & Co.* (for the appellants); *Charles Russell & Co.* (for the Crown).

[*Reported by* KATHLEEN J. H. O'BRIEN, *Barrister-at-Law.*]

H

I

---

(5) (1948), 32 Cr. App. Rep. 138 at p. 140.

BATES v. INLAND REVENUE COMMISSIONERS.

[House of Lords (Lord Reid, Lord Morris of Borth-y-Gest, Lord Guest, Lord Upjohn and Lord Wilberforce), October 11, 12, 13, 17, December 8, 1966.]

Income Tax—Settlement—Sums paid to settlor otherwise than as income—
Body corporate connected with a settlement—Loans to settlor by body corporate
—Amount of a loan paid direct to settlor deemed to be income paid to him
by trustees of settlement—Available income—Deduction of past capital pay-
ments—Method of computation—Income Tax Act, 1952 (15 & 16 Geo. 6 & 1
Eliz. 2 c. 10), s. 408 (1), (2), (7), s. 411 (4).

In 1948 the taxpayer made an irrevocable settlement of shares in a
company of which he was a director on trust for accumulation of the dividends for the benefit of children of his.   The company was one to which
s. 245 of the Income Tax Act, 1952, applied, but no direction deeming income
to be income of members of the company had been made at any material
time.   The company's financial year began at the beginning of April.
It was the taxpayer's practice to have a current account with the company,
the debit balance on which he paid up at the end of each financial year.
On Apr. 5, 1954, the company debited £9,100 to this account.   This sum was
a loan to the taxpayer.   It was paid by cheque drawn in his favour*, which
he paid into his bank account. He was assessed to surtax on the basis that this
loan of £9,100 was to be treated as his income by virtue of s. 408 (1)†, with
the consequence that he would be liable to be taxed on the appropriate
" amount of income available ", on the ground that the company was a body
corporate connected with the settlement within the terms of the definition of
that phrase in s. 411 (4)‡.

Under s. 408 (2) (*a*) the amount of income available up to the end of a
year of assessment was to be the aggregate amount of income arising under
the settlement less the amount of any other capital sums paid to the settlor
in a relevant year before the year in which the sum in question was paid.
In the year 1951-52 the sum of £8,586 was lent by the company to the
taxpayer.   It was not disputed§ that in that year the company was not a
body corporate connected with the settlement within the definition of
s. 411 (4).

Held: (i) in regard to the year of assesment 1953-54 the company was a
body corporate connected with the settlement (as defined in s. 411 (4) of the
Income Tax Act, 1952), because s. 411 (4) (*b*) required it to be assumed that
the company had not distributed its income for the year of assessment 1953-
54 and, on that assumption, the income of the company could have been
apportioned to members (viz., to the trustees) with the consequence that
the definition in s. 411 (4) was satisfied (see p. 90, letter A, p. 92, letters E
and F, p. 94, letter B, p. 96, letter B, and p. 99, letter B, post).

(ii) the payment of the £9,100 was a payment of a capital sum within
s. 408 (7) and, accordingly, was to be treated by virtue of s. 408 (1) as having
been paid by the trustees of the settlement, not by the company, and as
being the income of the taxpayer to the extent to which that sum fell within
the amount of income available up to the end of the year of assessment
1953-54 (see p. 90, letters D and H, p. 92, letter H, p. 94, letter G, and p.
99, letter C, post).

---

* In other years of additional assessment (with one exception, not relevant to
this appeal) the cheque was drawn in favour of the bank.   Before Plowman, J., and
before the Court of Appeal it became common ground that the outcome of the case, in its
particular circumstances, would be financially the same whether there was or was not
legal distinction where the cheque was drawn in favour of the bank, which was creditor
on the taxpayer's overdraft at the relevant time (compare per Lord Denning, M.R.,
[1965] 3 All E.R. at p. 70, letter D, and per Lord Reid at p. 91, letter H, post).
† Section 408 (1), (2) is set out at p. 87, letters E to I, post.
‡ Section 411 (4) is set out at p. 88, letter E, post.
§ See p. 96, letter E, and p. 99, letter G, post; cf. p. 93, letter C, post.

A   (iii) as it was not shown that the sum of £8,586 was paid by a body corporate connected with the settlement within the definition in s. 411 (4) (*b*) in the year of assessment 1951-52, that sum could not be treated as having been paid by the trustees and, therefore, it was not deductible in computing the amount of income available under s. 408 (2) (*a*), that is to say, it was not deductible in assessing the taxpayer in regard to the £9,100 (see p. 91,

B   letter D, p. 93, letter E, p. 94, letter H, p. 96, letter E, and p. 99, letter H, post).

Decision of the COURT OF APPEAL (sub nom. *Inland Revenue Comrs.* v. *Bates* [1965] 3 All E.R. 64) affirmed on holdings (i) and (iii) of that report.

[Editorial Note. Only surtax was assessed, although on the strict wording of
C   s. 408 (1) the amount available of the £9,100 was to be regarded as income for the purposes of income tax and would thus be liable also to income tax at the standard rate; the purpose of limiting the assessment to surtax was to mitigate the injustice of the enactment by administrative practice, but in law, it seems, income tax at the standard rate would have been exigible (see p. 90, letter C, post). A further inequity inherent in the statutory mode of computation was not
D   sought to be enforced (cf., p. 90, letter E, post), and so the mode of computing assessment for the year 1953-54 and subsequent years of assessment was a method that is not legally binding, but rests on administrative discretion (cf., p. 96, letter H, post). In three financial years payments were made to the appellant's bank, not direct to him, and it is stated by LORD REID that these payments would not fall within s. 408 (1), (7) (see p. 91, letter G, post); this view is not that taken
E   by the majority in the Court of Appeal (see [1965] 3 All E.R. at p. 65, holding (ii)), and the point was apparently not in issue on the appeal.

The Income Tax Act, 1925, s. 411 has been amended by the Finance Act 1965, s. 79, Sch. 18, Pt. 2, para. 15 (1); 45 HALSBURY'S STATUTES (2nd Edn.) 623, 738.

As to capital sums paid to a settlor treated as his income, see 20 HALSBURY'S LAWS (3rd Edn.) 586, 587, paras. 1147-1150; and for a case on the subject, see
F   28 DIGEST (Repl.) 287, *1268.*

For the Income Tax Act, 1952, s. 408 (1), (2), (3) and (7) and s. 411 (4), see 31 HALSBURY'S STATUTES (2nd Edn.) 385, 386, 389.]

Cases referred to:
Fattorini, Ltd. v. *Inland Revenue Comrs.*, [1942] 1 All E.R. 619; [1942] A.C. 643; 111 L.J.K.B. 546; 167 L.T. 45; 24 Tax Cas. 328; 28 Digest
G   (Repl.) 366, *1607.*
Potts' Executors v. *Inland Revenue Comrs.*, [1951] 1 All E.R. 76; [1951] A.C. 443; 28 Digest (Repl.) 287, *1268.*

Appeal.
This was an appeal by the taxpayer, Geoffrey Booth Bates, from an order of
H   the Court of Appeal (LORD DENNING, M.R., DAVIES and RUSSELL, L.JJ.) dated June 2, 1965 and reported [1965] 3 All E.R. 64, allowing an appeal by the Crown from an order of the Chancery Division (PLOWMAN, J.) dated May 15, 1964, whereby an appeal by the Crown by way of Case Stated from a determination of the Special Commissioners of Income Tax dated Apr. 30, 1962, was dismissed. The additional assessments to surtax in question were made under
I   Part 18 of the Income Tax Act, 1952 and in particular under s. 408 on the taxpayer for the years 1953-54, 1954-55 and 1955-56, in the sums £3,607, £3,165 and £2,709 respectively.

The following is a summary of the facts found by the Special Commissioners as set out in the Case Stated. The taxpayer was at all material times a director of Thomas Ambler & Sons, Ltd., a company which was incorporated on Apr. 2, 1948. On Aug. 7, 1948, the taxpayer made an irrevocable settlement in favour of his infant daughters and caused sixty thousand ordinary shares of the company to be allotted to and registered in the names of the trustees of the settlement credited as fully paid, such shares being subscribed for in cash by the taxpayer. The settle- **A** ment provided for the division of the trust fund into three equal parts and that one-third of the income should be accumulated for each daughter until she attained the age of twenty-six, when her share of the capital and accumulation should be paid to her. By further deeds made on Oct. 4, 1948 and Nov. 10, 1950 the shareholding of the trustees was increased to eighty-six thousand ordinary shares. The company, which was a trading company to which the provisions of **B** s. 245 of the Income Tax Act, 1952 applied, paid no ordinary (as distinct from preference) dividends from the date of its incorporation to Mar. 31, 1952. Its financial year ended on Mar. 31. For the years ending Mar. 31, 1953, 1954, 1955 and 1956 ordinary dividends were paid at the rate of ten per cent., ten per cent., fourteen per cent., and fourteen per cent. respectively. In respect of the years ending Mar. 31, 1953 and 1954, additional dividends of 6.6 per cent. and four per **C** cent. respectively were paid pursuant to an agreement with the Special Commissioners. No direction was made by the Special Commissioners under the provisions of s. 245 in respect of any of the years material to this appeal. Income received by the trustees of the settlement from the settled shares amounted to £3,610, £3,158 and £3,201 in respect of the years 1953-54, 1954-55 and 1955-56. The dividends from the shares of the company were the only settlement income. **D**

The taxpayer had had a current account with the company since its incorporation and that account was overdrawn for most of the years until about June, 1954. The taxpayer however was a person of substance and could at any time have paid off his indebtedness to the company without embarrassment. The state of his account was principally due to large items debited at the commencement of each accounting period of the company to his current account in respect of cheques **E** paid to the taxpayer or to the bank by the company for the credit of the taxpayer's current account with the bank, which was overdrawn on each such occasion. The debit balances of the taxpayer's current account at his bank were: Apr. 6, 1950, £8,289; Apr. 27, 1951, £11,406; Apr. 4, 1952, £10,315; Apr. 8, 1953, £9,957; Apr. 5, 1954, £9,032. The cheques so drawn by the company were Apr. 6, 1950 (part cheque), £8,286; Apr. 28, 1951 (part cheque), **F** £8,000; Apr. 4, 1952, £10,158; Apr. 8, 1953, £10,100; Apr. 5, 1954, £9,100. During each accounting period the taxpayer's current account with the company was credited, inter alia, with his salary and dividends received and at the end of each accounting period of the company with a substantial cheque drawn by the taxpayer on the bank, the effect of which was to place the taxpayer's current account with the company in credit on the date to which the accounts of the **G** company were made up each year, i.e., Mar. 31. The taxpayer was assessed to surtax in the additional assessments on the basis that the capital sums loaned by the company to him constituted income of the taxpayer as settlor of the settlement to the extent of the income available under the settlement for the year in question under s. 408 (1), (2) of the Act of 1952.

Heyworth Talbot, Q.C., H. Major Allen, Q.C., and *B. Pinson* for the taxpayer. **H**
Viscount Bledisloe, Q.C., J. R. Philips and *J. P. Warner* for the Crown.

Their lordships took time for consideration.

December 8. The following opinions were delivered.

LORD REID: My Lords, this is an appeal against additional assessments **I** to surtax in the years 1953-54, 1954-55 and 1955-56 laid under Part 8 of the Income Tax Act, 1952 and in particular under s. 408 thereof. The taxpayer was a director and shareholder of a company Thomas Ambler & Sons, Ltd. to which the provisions of Chapter III of Part 9 applied. In 1948 he made an irrevocable settlement in favour of his children in which accumulation of the trust income was directed, and he conveyed to the trustees of the settlement some of his shares in that company. It was his practice to have a current account with that company. From time to time sums accruing to him were paid in and sums

A owing by him were paid by the company and debited to this account. There was generally a considerable balance owing by him, but at the end of each financial year of the company he paid to them enough to meet this balance, thereby creating a large overdraft from his bank, and at the beginning of the next year the company paid out enough to cover that overdraft from his bank. In April of 1950, 1951 and 1953 this was done by the company paying a sum direct to

B the bank but in 1952 and 1954 it was done by the company drawing cheques in favour of the taxpayer, which he paid into his account with the bank. We are particularly concerned with a payment of £9,100 made by the company to the taxpayer on Apr. 5, 1954. I have no doubt that this was a sum paid by way of loan within the meaning of s. 408 (7).

The case against the taxpayer is that s. 408 requires that the sum of £9,100

C shall be treated as the income of the taxpayer to the extent therein provided. The section requires that any loan to the settlor by " any body corporate connected with the settlement " shall be treated as having been paid by the trustees of the settlement, and the definition in s. 411 (4) of " body corporate connected with the settlement " is so wide that in my opinion it must be held to include this company, although there was in fact no connexion whatever between the

D company and the settlement beyond the fact that the settlement trustees held some shares of the company, and the taxpayer had no intention of gaining any tax advantage, and in fact gained none, by taking this loan from the company.

This startling proposition makes it necessary to examine these statutory provisions with some care. They are as follows:

E   " 408. (1) Any capital sum paid directly or indirectly in any relevant year of assessment by the trustees of a settlement to which this section applies to the settlor shall—

   " (*a*) to the extent to which the amount of that sum falls within the amount of income available up to the end of that year, be treated for all the purposes of this Act as the income of the settlor for that year; (*b*) to

F   the extent to which the amount of that sum exceeds the amount of income available up to the end of that year but falls within the amount of the income available up to the end of the next following year, be treated for the purposes aforesaid as the income of the settlor for the next following year,

and so on.

G   " (2) For the purposes of sub-s. (1) of this section, the amount of income available up to the end of any year shall, in relation to any capital sum paid as aforesaid, be taken to be the aggregate amount of income arising under the settlement in that year and any previous relevant year which has not been distributed, less—(*a*) the amount of any other capital sums paid to the settlor in any relevant year before that sum was paid; and (*b*) so much of

H   any income arising under the settlement in that year and any previous relevant year which has not been distributed as is shown to consist of income which has been treated as income of the settlor by virtue of s. 404 of this Act; and (*c*) any income arising under the settlement in that year and any previous relevant year which has been treated as the income of the settlor by virtue of s. 405 of this Act; and (*d*) any sums paid by virtue or in conse-

I   quence of the settlement, to the extent that they are not allowable, by virtue of the last preceding section, as deductions in computing the settlor's income for that year or any previous relevant year; and (*e*) an amount equal to tax at the standard rate on—(i) the aggregate amount of income arising under the settlement in that year and any previous relevant year which has not been distributed, less (ii) the aggregate amount of the income and sums referred to in paras. (*b*), (*c*) and (*d*) of this subsection.

   " (3) For the purpose of this section, any capital sum paid to the settlor in

any year of assessment by any body corporate connected with the settle-   A
ment in that year shall be treated as having been paid by the trustees of the
settlement in that year.

"(4) Where the whole or any part of any sum is treated by virtue of this
section as income of the settlor for any year, it shall be treated as income
of such an amount as, after deduction of tax at the standard rate for that
year, would be equal to that sum or that part thereof.   B

"(5) Tax chargeable at the standard rate by virtue of this section shall
be charged under Case VI of Sch. D.

"(6) In computing the liability to income tax of a settlor chargeable by
virtue of this section, the same deductions and reliefs shall be allowed as
would have been allowed if the amount treated as his income by virtue of
this section had been received by him as income.   C

"(7) This section applies to any settlement wherever made, and whether
made before or after the passing of this Act, and in this section—'capital
sum' means—

    (i) any sum paid by way of loan or repayment of a loan; and

    (ii) any other sum paid otherwise than as income, being a sum which is
    not paid for full consideration in money or money's worth,   D

but does not include any sum which could not have become payable to the
settlor except in one of the events specified in the proviso to sub-s. (2) of
s. 405 of this Act; and 'relevant year' means any year of assessment after
the year 1937-38; and references to sums paid to the settlor include references to sums paid to the wife or husband of the settlor.   E

"411 (4) For the purposes of this Chapter, a body corporate shall be deemed
to be connected with a settlement in any year of assessment if any of the
income thereof for any year or period ending in that year of assessment—
(a) has been apportioned to the trustees of or a beneficiary under the settlement under Chapter III of Part 9 of this Act, or could have been so apportioned if the body corporate had been incorporated in the United Kingdom;
or (b) could have been so apportioned if the income of the body corporate   F
for that year or period had not been distributed to the members thereof and,
in the case of a body corporate incorporated outside the United Kingdom,
if the body corporate had been incorporated in the United Kingdom."

These provisions were first enacted in 1938. The mischief against which they
were directed appears to have been that some taxpayers, intending to avoid   G
paying surtax, transferred to trustees of settlements shares in companies controlled by them: then they borrowed money from the trustees, who used the
dividends on these shares to make the loans. In that way the settlors got
possession of the income from the shares which they had settled in the form
of capital payments which did not attract surtax; and if the trustees were
complacent the settlors might never repay these "loans".   H

The reason why some companies were brought in appears to have been that
some settlors had devised rather more elaborate schemes. A settlor might form
a company, controlled by him, to which he transferred assets yielding income.
He would then put the whole, or the greater part, of the shares of that company
in the settlement, and then he would cause that company to lend to him the
whole or a part of its income thereby diminishing the dividends which would   I
otherwise have gone to the settlement trustees. He would not repay these
loans during his lifetime and in that way he would receive and enjoy the income
of the assets which he had transferred to the company without being liable to
pay surtax in respect of it.

Of course it was necessary to stop that kind of tax evasion and of course it
was necessary to try to anticipate and forestall more complicated variations of
this plan. This was an early example, however, of legislation directed against
tax evasion and experience has shown that in at least one respect it is too narrow

A —see *Potts' Executors* v. *Inland Revenue Comrs.* (1) to which I shall return—and in other respects it is too wide. Its provisions suffer from two glaring defects. In the first place they impose heavy liabilities in respect of many kinds of ordinary and innocent transactions, which no laymen and indeed few lawyers not familiar with this section would ever imagine could be caught in this way—in short they are a trap. Secondly they are framed in such a way that their
B plain meaning in many cases leads to a result which RUSSELL, L.J. (2), has rightly called monstrous.

Normally when we construe a statute we are attempting to discover the intention of Parliament from the words used in the Act; but here it is obvious, and indeed admitted, that Parliament could never have intended some of the results which are inescapable if certain of the provisions of the section are not to
C be disregarded. We cannot apply a statutory provision, however, in one way in cases where it creates injustice and in a different way in cases where it serves to defeat attempts to evade tax.

The first and main question in this case involves the construction of s. 411 (4). I have tried to explain why it was necessary to bring in companies controlled by settlors and used in aiding schemes for tax evasion, and this subsection is
D intended to do that. The fact that it is so widely drawn as to be a trap for the innocent does not in my judgment entitle a court to attribute to any of its provisions a strained or unnatural meaning so as to make it impotent in those cases where tax evasion is attempted. It applies to companies subject to surtax directions which would be followed by apportionment of the whole income for the year where that is directed. There is no difficulty about para. (*a*). If in
E any year there has been apportionment of any part of the company's income to the settlement trustees (or a beneficiary), the subsection applies. The difficulty is in para. (*b*). This requires that there could have been such an apportionment " if the income " of the company " had not been distributed to the members ". There can be apportionment if, and only if, the Special Commissioners are of opinion that a reasonable part of the company's income has not been distributed.
F So it appears to me that the natural meaning of the words which I have quoted is—if a reasonable part of the income had not been distributed. We are to look at the year retrospectively: if there was no apportionment we are to enquire whether there could have been apportionment, and there could have been apportionment in that case but in no other. If that is right it is not disputed that if a reasonable part of the company's income had not been distributed in the year
G when the loan of £9,100 was made there could have been apportionment. In fact a reasonable part must have been held to have been distributed and no apportionment was made of that year's income, but that is immaterial.

The argument for the taxpayer was that " the income " must mean the whole income, and that to hold that it means a reasonable part of the income or that part which in fact was distributed involves writing in words which are not there;
H but in my view " the income " must take its meaning from the context. The expression is capable of meaning " the whole income ", or " income " without the article " the ", or " part of the income ", or such part of the income as the context indicates to be relevant; and to give the words the meaning " the whole income " would make nonsense of the paragraph. It would only apply if the whole of the company's actual income from all sources had in fact been
I distributed, but not if only ninety per cent. had been distributed. The taxpayer admits that that would be so unreasonable that no one could possibly have intended that to be the test. It may not be easy to see why para. (*b*) is there at all, but we are not entitled either to disregard it or to attribute an absurd meaning to it if it is susceptible of a reasonable meaning, as I think that it is. I should add that I get no assistance either way from the references in para. (*a*) and para. (*b*) to bodies corporate not incorporated in the United Kingdom. So I

---

(1) [1951] 1 All E.R. 76; [1951] A.C. 443.
(2) [1965] 3 All E.R. 64 at p. 75, letter I.

hold that for the relevant year the company must by reason of s. 411 (4) be   A
deemed to be connected with the settlement made by the taxpayer.

I now turn to s. 408 under which the assessments have been made.   By sub-s.
(3) a loan to the settlor by a company connected with the settlement in the
year in which it was made must be treated as having been made by the trustees
of the settlement in that year.   So the £9,100 must be treated as having been
paid by the trustees to the taxpayer on the last day of the year 1953-54, although   B
in fact they did not have such a sum available.   Then sub-s. (1) provides that
such a payment—to an extent which I shall deal with later—shall be treated
for all purposes of the Income Tax Act, 1952, as the income of the settlor for
that year.   That clearly means that he must pay both income tax and surtax
on it; but this is only an assessment to surtax.   Counsel for the Crown admitted
that it had been their practice not to demand income tax in these cases because   C
that would be wholly unjust and involve double taxation: but they were unable
to suggest any construction of the words of the section which could justify this.

The next point is the extent to which the loan is to be regarded as the settlor's
income in any year.   Subsection (1) (*a*) deals with the first year, 1953-54.   For
that year the assessment is £3,607: that can be reconciled with the words of the
Act of 1952.   For the next year, however, the assessment of £3,165 has been   D
arrived at by a method which bears no relation to the method prescribed by the
Act of 1952.   That is admitted and again the reason is given that to follow the
prescribed method would lead to injustice and double taxation.   The draftsman
has chosen such a complicated method that he has obviously failed to realise
the absurd results to which it leads in all but the simplest cases and I think in
almost every case where the trust income has to be accumulated; so the Crown   E
have taken it on themselves to disregard the statute and substitute a method
which they think fair and, if I understood counsel rightly, in accord with the
spirit of the Act of 1952.   I can, I hope, explain the difference in this way.
Suppose loans of £20,000 are made by the connected company in year 1 which is
the first in which the trustees receive income.   That, after making the calculations in sub-s. (2) (*b*) and (*e*) is £3,000.   That £3,000 is added to the settlor's   F
income for year 1.   It is the calculation directed for year 2 which gives rise to
the absurdity.   Suppose the trust income in year 2 to be £2,000, then the " income available " up to the end of year 2 is the sum of the incomes of years 1 and 2,
i.e., £5,000, because there was a direction to accumulate.   And if in year 3 there
is a trust income of £3,000 the " income available " at the end of that year is
the sum of the incomes for years 1, 2 and 3, i.e., £8,000.   In year 2 £5,000 will be   G
treated as the income of the settlor and in year 3 £8,000 will be treated as his
income, so although the trust income for the three years was only £8,000 in all,
the settlor's income for these years will be regarded as increased by £3,000 plus
£5,000 plus £8,000, i.e., £16,000, or double the whole trust income.   It is not
surprising that RUSSELL, L.J. (3) called this " monstrous " and that the Crown
refuse to apply sub-s. (2) as it stands and have devised a scheme which appears to   H
avoid this particular injustice.   Nevertheless the fact that the Crown have chosen
to assess for a smaller sum than the terms of the section would appear to justify
does not entitle us to hold that the assessment is bad.

Then the taxpayer argued that he is entitled to a statutory deduction which
has not been taken into account.   Section 408 (2) (*a*) requires that before ascertaining the " income available " for treatment as the income of the settlor in   I
any year there must be deducted the amount of any other capital sum, i.e., loan,
paid to the settlor in any " relevant year " before the year in which this loan of
£9,100 was paid to him.   By definition in s. 408 (7) " relevant year " simply
means any financial year after 1937-38; and a loan of £8,586 was paid by the
company to the taxpayer in an earlier year, 1951-52.   The answer of the Crown
is twofold.   First it is said that in 1951-52 this company was not a company

(3) [1965] 3 All E.R. at p. 75, letter I.

A connected with the settlement. I do not think that the facts found in the Stated Case enable us to determine that matter, and, although this was raised in argument, neither party asked for a remit to enable further facts to be stated. So I pass to the Crown's second answer. It is said that if this sum had to be brought in under s. 408 (2) (*a*) it would also have to be brought in under s. 408 (1) so that the taxpayer in the end would be no better off. This the taxpayer denies.

B It is pointed out that whereas s. 408 (2) (*a*) refers to a sum paid " in any relevant year ", s. 408 (1) refers to a sum paid " in any relevant year of assessment ". It was argued that although 1951-52 was a " relevant year " it was not " a relevant year of assessment ", because on the facts there could have been no assessment under this section in that year. It is of course an elementary principle of drafting that different expressions should not be used in different places in

C the same section to express the same meaning. So there is a presumption that these two expressions do not mean the same thing; but that is only a presumption, and if it is applied in this case it leads to an absurd result. So I am forced to the conclusion that this difference of phraseology is only another example of the thoroughly bad draftsmanship of this section. I must therefore decide this point against the taxpayer.

D Before I conclude I must again draw attention to the very unsatisfactory state in which the law has been allowed to remain since the decision by this House in 1950 of *Potts'* case (4). In that case the question was whether sums paid by a company connected with the settlement to creditors of the settlor to discharge his debts fell within the scope of this section. It was argued (5) by the Crown that a decision against them " would make it so easy to circumvent

E the Act as to render it useless for its object ". LORD NORMAND said (6):

" Courts of law are not concerned with extrinsic circumstances, such as that the provisions of s. 40 [of the Finance Act, 1938; now s. 408 of the Act of 1952] as I have construed them are of little value because they may easily be evaded by those who have the will to evade them, or that persons who contract genuine loans or receive repayment of genuine loans without

F any purpose of evasion and without in fact evading any liability to tax are as likely to be taxed under s. 40 as persons who contrive elaborate schemes of pretended loans for the purpose of evasion."

When the case was decided against the Crown, however, nothing was done to amend the section. In the present case it appears that in five different years

G payments were made by the company for the purpose of discharging the taxpayer's debt to his bank. In three cases these payments were made direct to the bank, and *Potts'* case (4) shows that they were not caught by s. 408; but it so happened that in the other two years the payments were made by cheques drawn in favour of the taxpayer and not in favour of the bank. It is this fortuitous circumstance alone that has brought the taxpayer within the scope of

H s. 408 and imposed on him tax liability for several thousands of pounds. This case may well afford ammunition to that body of opinion which holds that redrafting of the Income Tax Act, 1952, ought to be taken out of the hands of those at present responsible.

With regret I must move that this appeal be dismissed.

I **LORD MORRIS OF BORTH-Y-GEST:** My Lords, during the fiscal year 1953-54 a cheque for £9,100 payable to the taxpayer was drawn by Thomas Ambler & Sons, Ltd. It was recorded in a ledger account kept by that company. That ledger account contained entries of sums paid either to or on the instructions of the taxpayer and also contained entries of sums received or held by the company for the credit of the taxpayer. When the cheque for £9,100 was received by the taxpayer, the account showed that no money was owed to him

---

(4) [1951] 1 All E.R. 76; [1951] A.C. 443.   (5) [1951] A.C. at p. 450.
 (6) [1951] 1 All E.R. at p. 83, letter E; [1951] A.C. at p. 459.

or was held for him by the company.   There was a balance owing to the company.   **A**
I think that it must follow that the sum of £9,100 was a loan by the company
to the taxpayer.   It was none the less a loan because of the existence of a number
of transactions as shown in the account.   The substance of the matter was that
during a year the company paid some sums for the taxpayer or paid sums to
him and that at the close of a year the taxpayer who was a man of substance,
paid to the company the balance of what was owing to them.   The payment of   **B**
£9,100 was nothing less than a loan.   It was a " capital sum " within the meaning
of s. 408 of the Income Tax Act, 1952.   It was paid directly to the taxpayer.
He was the settlor of certain settlements in favour of his children.   They were
settlements to which s. 408 applied (see s. 408 (7)).   The capital sum was paid
in a " relevant year of assessment " (see s. 408 (1)) for I read that phrase to refer
to any year of assessment after the year 1937-38.   If the capital sum was paid   **C**
to the taxpayer in 1953-54 by any body corporate connected with the settlement
in the year 1953-54 then it must be treated as having been paid by the trustees
of the settlement in 1953-54 (see s. 408 (3).)   The sum of £9,100 was paid by
Thomas Ambler & Sons, Ltd.   If that company was in 1953-54 a body corporate
connected with the settlement then the £9,100 must be treated as having been
paid by the trustees of the settlement in 1953-54.   If so treated then to the extent   **D**
to which the £9,100 falls " within the amount of income available " up to the
end of 1953-54 it must be treated (for all the purposes of the Income Tax Act,
1952) as the income of the taxpayer for 1953-54.

Before considering the " amount of income available " up to the end of 1953-54
it is necessary to decide whether Thomas Ambler & Sons, Ltd. was in 1953-54 a
body corporate connected with the settlements.   It must be deemed to be such   **E**
if (see s. 411 (4) (*b*)) the income of the company could have been apportioned to
the trustees of the settlement (or to a beneficiary under the settlement) under
Chapter III of Part 9 of the Income Tax Act, 1952, if the income of the company
for 1953-54 had not been distributed to the members of the company.   This,
I think, requires that it should first be assumed that in the year 1953-54 the
company had not distributed its income, and that the question should then be   **F**
asked whether in that eventuality there could have been a direction which
would have had the result that an apportionment of the actual income from all
sources of the company would have been made by the Special Commissioners in
accordance with the respective interests of the members.   In the Case Stated
it is recorded that for the year to Mar. 31, 1954, the company paid a dividend of
ten per cent. and that in respect of that year a further additional dividend of   **G**
four per cent. was paid with the agreement of the Special Commissioners.   Those
dividends were paid to the trustees of the settlements in respect of the shares
which they held.   From the facts as found I think that it follows that the
income of the company for the year 1953-54 could have been apportioned if the
income for that year had not been distributed to members .   The result is that
the company was deemed to be connected with the settlement in the year of   **H**
assessment 1953-54.   The capital sum of £9,100 paid to the taxpayer in that
year must be treated as having been paid by the trustees of the settlement.   It
must, therefore (see s. 408 (1) (*a*)) be treated as the income of the settlor for the
year 1953-54 to the extent to which it was within the amount of income available
up to the end of that year.

The amount of such income available is to be calculated in accordance with   **I**
s. 408 (2).   First, a figure must be ascertained of the aggregate amount of income
arising under the settlement in the particular year and any previous year of
assessment after 1937-38 which had not been distributed.   Certain deductions
are to be made, and thereafter there is to be a grossing up.

In the years with which we are concerned the income arising under the settlement remained undistributed.   From the aggregate of the amount of such
income one of the deductions that falls to be made is of the amount of any " other
capital sums " paid to the settlor in any relevant year before the capital sum

A   which is being treated as the income of the settlor was paid. On Apr. 4, 1952, the taxpayer received a loan from the company of £8,586. Should that sum be deducted in making the calculation under s. 408 (2)? If it should, the result would be that the " income available " would be nil. The loan would only be a capital sum within the calculation if it was paid by a body corporate connected with the settlement in the year in which the sum was paid by way of loan. The

B   inquiry becomes, therefore, whether in the year of assessment 1951-52 the income of the company could have been apportioned under Chapter III of Part 9 of the Act of 1952 if the income of the company for that year had not been distributed to the members. In the year 1951-52 some preference dividends were paid, but the company paid no ordinary dividends. If the question is posed whether (on the assumption that in 1951-52 the company had not dis-

C   tributed its income) the income for that year could have been apportioned under Chapter III of Part 9 of the Act of 1952, there are indications that the answer would be in the negative, though it may be that the available information does not suffice to give a positive answer without a remission. If the Crown's contention is correct, that the test posed by sub-s. (4) (*b*) is factual and that the relevant question is whether the distributions that were in fact made by the body

D   corporate for the relevant period were such as to prevent the making of a direction and apportionment for that period, then it is agreed that in that event, having regard to the figures disclosed by the accounts, the company cannot be regarded as a body corporate connected with the settlement for the year of assessment 1951-52. I would prefer the Crown's contention to that of the taxpayer's and in all the circumstances I do not consider that a remission is necessary. I do

E   not think that it is shown that the sum of £8,586 was paid by a body corporate connected with the settlement in the year in which it was paid.

We are not concerned with precise figures but, on the views which I have expressed, I see no escape from the conclusion that in the year 1953-54 the taxpayer was assessable in the manner contended for by the Crown. By an application of s. 408 (1) (*b*) and on the facts and figures as found, I think it follows that

F   the taxpayer was also assessable for the two later years.

I would add my concurrence with the view that it is a matter of regret that the statutory provisions now under consideration have been allowed to remain in an unsatisfactory state.

I would dismiss the appeal.

G   **LORD GUEST:** My Lords, the controversy between the taxpayer and the Crown centred on s. 408 and s. 411 of the Income Tax Act, 1952. The first question is whether the company which made the loans to the taxpayer is a " body corporate connected with the settlement " within the meaning of s. 411 (4) of the Act. This subsection reads:

H   " (4) For the purposes of this Chapter, a body corporate shall be deemed to be connected with a settlement in any year of assessment if any of the income thereof for any year or period ending in that year of assessment—

" (*a*) has been apportioned to the trustees of or a beneficiary under the settlement under Chapter III of Part 9 of this Act, or could have been so apportioned if the body corporate had been incorporated in the United Kingdom; or

I   " (*b*) could have been so apportioned if the income of the body corporate for that year or period had not been distributed to the members thereof and, in the case of a body corporate incorporated outside the United Kingdom, if the body corporate had been incorporated in the United Kingdom."

The meaning of this subsection is obscure, but after mature consideration I have come to the view that the construction contended for by the Crown is correct. The taxpayer's construction involved reading before the word " income " where it appears in para. (*b*) " the whole of the ". This would mean that the

first limb of the paragraph would only operate if the whole of the income had   A
not been distributed to the members; but not so if a portion, however small,
had been distributed.   This would lead to such a nonsensical result that I decline
to accept it.   The Crown's contention is that the test posed by the section is
factual and that the relevant question is whether the distributions which in fact
were made were such as to prevent an apportionment under the relevant section
of the Income Tax Act, 1952.   If this is the proper test the company is a body   B
corporate connected with the settlement for the years 1953-54, 1954-55, 1955-56.
The rationale of this construction appears to be that sub-s. (4) (a) deals with the
company where an actual apportionment has been made and the income has
thereby become the income of the members.   Subsection (4) (b) provides for
the case where, but for the distribution, there would have been an apportionment;
in other words, where the distribution which in fact been made has prevented   C
an apportionment and the income has also gone to the members.

This construction of the subsection has an important bearing on the question
of the amount of the income available under s. 408 (2), but I will pass for the
moment to the question whether the loans in question were capital sums within
the meaning of s. 408 (7) which is in the following terms:

   " ' capital sum ' means—
      " (i) any sum paid by way of loan or repayment of a loan; and
      " (ii) any other sum paid otherwise than as income, being a sum which
   is not paid for full consideration in money or money's worth,"

D

It was argued for the taxpayer that the expression " being a sum which is not
paid for full consideration in money or money's worth " qualified not only the   E
opening words of para. (ii) but also the whole of para. (i) so that the subsection
would read " any sum paid by way of loan or repayment of a loan being a sum
which is not paid for full consideration in money or money's worth ".   In my view,
this is not a tenable construction and involves a contradiction in terms.   A loan is
made in respect of an obligation to repay and could not by its very sense be " for
full consideration in money or money's worth ".   An obligation to repay is   F
not " money or money's worth ".   Next it was suggested that these sums were
not loans, but were payments passing in the course of a running account between
the company and the taxpayer.   Even if they were, the sums were, in my opinion,
none the less loans.   I pose the rhetorical question—" If those sums were not loans,
what were they? "   I accordingly reach the conclusion that the payments made
by the company to the taxpayer were capital sums within the meaning of s. 408 (7)   G
and, therefore, caught by s. 408 (1).

The last point concerns the contention for the taxpayer that in calculating
the income available in s. 408 (2) a deduction fell to be made under sub-s. (2) (a)
of £8,586 being the net sum paid to the taxpayer by the company in 1951-52.
The parties are agreed that, assuming the Crown's construction of s. 411 (4) is
sound, which I think that it is, the company was not during that period " a body   H
corporate connected with the settlement " within the meaning of s. 411 (4).   The
deduction is accordingly not admissible.

I would dismiss the appeal.

   LORD UPJOHN: My Lords, the taxpayer was a substantial holder of
shares in a private company called Thomas Ambler and Sons, Ltd., of which at   I
all material times he was a director.   It was a trading company to which Chapter
III of Part 9 of the Income Tax Act, 1952, is applicable, that is to say, it was what
is commonly called a " surtax " company.   The most important section of that
chapter is s. 245.   In 1948 the taxpayer made a settlement of sixty thousand
of his shares in the company on trusts under which for the relevant years of
assessment the trustees were bound to accumulate the income.   The company's
financial year began on Apr. 1, and on Apr. 5, 1954, it made a substantial payment of £9,100 to the taxpayer.   The Crown seeks to tax this sum as income of

A the taxpayer for surtax purposes spread over a number of years, the relevant
years of assessment being 1953-54, 1954-55 and 1955-56. The Crown does so
in reliance on certain legislative provisions originally enacted in 1938 and now to
be found in s. 408 to s. 411 of the Income Tax Act, 1952.

Section 408 provided that in certain circumstances (satisfied here) any capital
sum paid by trustees of a settlement to the settlor should be treated as income
B of the settlor to the extent (putting it very briefly) of the available income of the
settlement. Realising, however, that the ingenious might devise schemes
whereby payments might be made to them by a company rather than by trustees,
s. 408 (3) provided that

C
".. . any capital sum paid to the settlor in any year of assessment by any
body corporate connected with the settlement in that year shall be treated
as having been paid by the trustees of the settlement in that year."

The first and most important question, therefore, is whether the company,
having made this payment, is a body corporate connected with the settlement.
That depends on s. 411 (4) of the Act of 1952 which defines a body corporate
connected with a settlement. The draftsman of the Act of 1952 realised that
D the companies aimed at would in all probability be surtax companies so he
expressly defined a connected company by reference to Chapter III of Part 9
of the Act of 1952. Now, s. 245 empowered the Special Commissioners to apportion the income of a surtax company among its members where it appeared to
them that the company had not distributed to its members a reasonable part
of its income for its financial year and s. 411 (4) must be read in the light of that
E provision. Paragraph (*a*) is clear enough; a company is a connected company
if any of its income has been apportioned to the trustees of the settlement under
s. 245 in that year. Paragraph (*b*) provided that a company is a connected
company if any of its income " could have been so apportioned if the income of
the body corporate for that year or period had not been distributed to the
members thereof ". The whole difficulty of construction of this paragraph, to my
F mind, is caused by the use of the words " the income ". If the phraseology
employed had been " could have been so apportioned, if a reasonable part of the
income of the body corporate had not been distributed to the members thereof " I
would think there could be no possible doubt about the construction of the section.
It would be reflecting s. 245, and dealing with the purely factual case where there
could have been an apportionment but for the fact that the body corporate
G had distributed sufficient of its income to prevent an apportionment. I cannot
myself think that the draftsman of this section was dealing in any way with a
hypothetical case, but was dealing with a purely factual case.

The taxpayer, however, seizing on the phrase " the income " has argued that
the natural meaning of " the income " is the whole income, and therefore if the
company distributes not the one hundred per cent. of its income but only ninety-
nine per cent. it escapes from the consequences of para. (*b*). All of your lordships
H and the Court of Appeal (7) reached the conclusion that such a construction must
lead to such a ludicrous result that Parliament cannot have intended it. I
entirely agree. For my part, I am not satisfied that the natural meaning of the
words " the income " is necessarily the whole income. It must entirely depend
on the context in which that phrase is found. Again, for my part, I have no
I difficulty, as para. (*b*) is obviously echoing s. 245, in thinking that the section
should be read so as to make a company a connected company if it has prevented
an apportionment which could otherwise have been directed by a reasonable
body of Special Commissioners by reason of the fact that it has distributed
a reasonable part of its actual income to its members. Apparently the draftsman of the subsection deliberately excluded from the definition of a connected
company those companies who made no or only a very small distribution to
their members but justified this on the grounds of commercial prudence, so as

(7) [1965] 3 All E.R. 64.

to prevent the Special Commissioners from saying that a reasonable part of its A
income has not been distributed and those fortunate companies whose accounts
had escaped the vigilance of the Special Commissioners who failed to make an
apportionment. The law was altered to include all surtax companies in 1965, (8).

Accordingly, as it is admitted that the company in the relevant year did distribute a reasonable part of its income in order to prevent an apportionment
(by a perfectly proper arrangement with the commissioners), it follows that for B
that year the company was deemed to be connected with the settlement. Accordingly if proved to be payment of a capital sum, the payment of £9,100 paid by
the company to the taxpayer must be treated as having been paid by the trustees
of the settlement in that year.

The definition of a " capital sum " includes (by s. 408 (7) (i)) " any sum paid
by way of loan or repayment of a loan ". It is perfectly clear that this sum was C
so paid as a loan: that was the practice of the taxpayer and his brother. Shortly
after the commencement of each financial year of the company they caused to
be paid to themselves substantial sums which they repaid just before the end of
that financial year. The particular cheque of £9,100 was dated Apr. 5, 1954,
and was made payable to the taxpayer. It was plainly a payment to him for
he could dispose of the cheque and its proceeds in any way he pleased; the case D
of *Potts' Executors* v. *Inland Revenue Comrs.* (9), where payments were made not
directly to the settlor, but to his creditors, is plainly distinguishable.

The final question that arises is whether a sum of £8,586 paid by the company
to the taxpayer in the year 1951-52 is a proper deduction for the purposes of
s. 408 (2) (*a*). The taxpayer would have been on strong grounds, in my view,
in saying that that sum could be so deducted, apart from the fact that it seems E
to be common ground that in 1951-52 the company was not a connected company
because neither sub-s. (4) (*a*) nor sub-s. (4) (*b*) of s. 411 applied to it. Accordingly
a payment made by the company to the taxpayer in that year cannot be treated
as having been paid by the trustees of the settlement in that earlier year; it
follows that sub-s. (2) (*a*) has no application and, accordingly, the sum is not
deductible.   F

My lords, I only desire to refer briefly to a more general aspect of this matter.
First, the monstrous result of this series of sections, which has been so clearly
set out by LORD REID (10) in his speech; putting it very shortly, if a large capital
sum was paid and that had to be spread over income of the settlement for, say,
five years, it would follow that the income available in the settlement in the first
year would be taken into account five times and would be taxed five times over; G
income available in the second year taxed four times over and so on. Such a
result cannot of course have been intended: but that seems to be the perfectly
plain result of the provisions of s. 408 (2). It is regrettable, especially having
regard to the decision in *Potts' Executors* v. *Inland Revenue Comrs.* (9), now
sixteen years ago, that it has not been thought fit to amend this section. Instead,
the Commissioners of Inland Revenue, realising the monstrous result of giving H
effect to the true construction of the section, have in fact worked out what they
consider to be an equitable way of operating it which seems to them to result in
a fair system of taxation. I am quite unable to understand on what principle
they can properly do so and, like LORD REID, I hope this matter may receive
some consideration in the proper place.

For these reasons I would dismiss the appeal.   I

LORD WILBERFORCE: My Lords, the taxpayer has been additionally
assessed to surtax in respect of three sums of £3,610, £3,158 and £3,201 for the
years 1953-54, 1954-55 and 1955-56. These assessments were made under
s. 408 of the Income Tax Act, 1952, on the basis that the taxpayer received capital

(8) See the Finance Act 1965, s. 79, Sch. 18, Pt. 2, para. 15 (1);   45 HALSBURY'S
STATUTES (2nd Edn.) 623, 738.
(9) [1951] 1 All E.R. 76; [1951] A.C. 443.   (10) See p. 90, letters D to H, ante.

A sums from a body corporate connected with an accumulation settlement made for the benefit of his children on Aug. 7, 1948. He appeals against the assessment on three grounds: (1) that the company from which he received payments was not a body corporate connected with the settlement in the relevant years; (2) that such payments as were made to him by the company were not capital sums within the meaning of s. 408 (7); (3) that in any event on a correct

B computation of the figures his liability under the section is nil.

1. *The body corporate.* The company in question was a trading company named Thomas Ambler & Sons, Ltd. incorporated on Apr. 2, 1948. It had a preference and ordinary share capital of equal nominal amounts. The trustees of the settlement held ordinary shares in it and the taxpayer was a director. It paid no ordinary dividends from its incorporation down to Mar. 31, 1952,

C but for the accounting years ending on Mar. 31, 1953, 1954, 1955 and 1956 ordinary dividends were paid of amounts accepted by the Special Commissioners as sufficient to avoid a surtax direction under s. 245 of the Income Tax Act, 1952.

In relation to these facts it is necessary to consider the definition of a body corporate connected with a settlement provided in s. 411 (4) of the Act. It is as follows:

D   " (4) For the purposes of this Chapter a body corporate shall be deemed to be connected with a settlement in any year of assessment if any of the income thereof for any year or period ending in that year of assessment—

  " (*a*) has been apportioned to the trustees of or a beneficiary under the settlement under Chapter III of Part 9 of this Act, or could have been so apportioned if the body corporate had been incorporated in the

E   United Kingdom; or

  " (*b*) could have been so apportioned if the income of the body corporate for that year or period had not been distributed to the members thereof and, in the case of a body corporate incorporated outside the United Kingdom, if the body corporate had been incorporated in the United Kingdom."

F Since no apportionment was made in any of the three years para. (*a*) does not apply; if at all the case comes under para. (*b*).

In order to see what the subsection may mean, it is necessary to have in mind the main provisions of s. 245 of the Act of 1952, found in Chapter III of Part 9. These must be considered as they stood at the time of the Finance Act, 1938, from which s. 408 and s. 411 were derived, and therefore without certain special

G provisions later added with regard to investment companies (see the Finance Act, 1939, s. 14, and the Income Tax Act, 1952, s. 262). They provided that if it appeared to the Special Commissioners that a company had not distributed to its members in such a way as to make the amount distributed liable to be returned for surtax, a reasonable part of its actual income for the year, they might direct that " the said income of the company " should be deemed to be the income of the

H members and the amount thereof should be apportioned among the members. There were a number of elaborate provisions of a consequential character but I need not refer to them here.

The significant points to notice about this legislation are (i) that it is for the Special Commissioners to determine, in the light of all that they know about the company's business and its requirements, whether in any year a reasonable part

I of its income has been distributed, (ii) that if they so decide that a direction is appropriate, the direction must extend to the whole income of the company. But the section does not say or suggest that, in order to avoid a direction, *the whole* of the company's income must be *distributed,* but only what the commissioners decide to be, in the circumstances, a reasonable part. There may be circumstances in which it is reasonable to make no distribution at all (see *Fattorini, Ltd.* v. *Inland Revenue Comrs.* (11).)

---

(11) [1942] 1 All E.R. 619; [1942] A.C. 643.

Returning to s. 411 (4), the taxpayer's main contention was that the words **A**
" if the income of the body corporate for that year or period had not been distributed " mean " if *the whole* income " etc.   If this were right, the subsection
would not apply to the company here because, in each relevant year, an apportionment was avoided by a distribution of less than the whole of the income. Though
there is much that is doubtful about the subsection I am clear that it cannot
mean that.   In the first place, a test dependent on a total distribution is incon- **B**
sistent with the statutory scheme, which (as it stood in 1938) depended on a
reasonable distribution: it could only fit the case—exceptional if existent at all—
where a reasonable distribution was a total distribution.   Secondly, as was well
pointed out in the Court of Appeal (12), this interpretation would introduce a
distinction between cases of one hundred per cent. distribution, which would be
within the section, and those of (say) ninety per cent. which would not.   There **C**
would be no reasonable logic either in the inclusion of one case or the exclusion of
the other. Like the Court of Appeal (12), therefore, I would not accept this
meaning if there is any reasonable alternative.

In the search for another interpretation the first clue is, I think, provided by
the references, equally in the body of s. 411 (4), in para. (*a*) and in para. (*b*), to
the actual year of assessment. These suggest that the test to be applied is to some **D**
extent a factual test, related to the position in the year in question, not one
wholly hypothetical, related to the nature or structure of the company irrespective
of what it does. But one is not entitled to look solely at the actual facts, because
some hypothesis is certainly introduced by the words " if the income " etc.:
the difficulty is to see what this hypothesis is. That which was put forward by the
Crown can be reflected in the following paraphrase: " The income could have **E**
been so apportioned but for the fact that the income of the body corporate, which
was actually distributed, was distributed." This presupposes that a distribution
was made in the relevant year and that it is possible to say that it was this
distribution that prevented an apportionment being made.

This interpretation has the attraction of a clear and direct application to the
facts of this case, for in the relevant years it was shown that discussion took place **F**
with the Special Commissioners as to the amount of the distribution with the
result that no apportionment was made. It was no doubt mainly this that made
it acceptable to the Court of Appeal (12).

For myself, while I find this meaning clearly preferable to that suggested by the
taxpayer, I am not wholly satisfied with it. I am unable to discern, and counsel
for the Crown was unable to suggest, any convincing reason of taxation policy **G**
why the test of connectedness for this purpose should be based on the making of
such a distribution as in fact has prevented an apportionment being made. One
could think, on the contrary, that the policy of the section would require that a
taxpayer who obtains loans or other capital payments from a company which
makes an insufficient distribution should be liable to a surtax assessment, and this **H**
whether or not an apportionment of income has actually been made. The
interpretation which I would prefer is not, perhaps, very different, but it would
take a different hypothesis as the starting point. It would take as the test of
connectedness that the income could have been so apportioned on the assumption
that the income of the body corporate which was in fact distributed was not distributed. In other words, I would read the subsection as directing one to disregard **I**
any distribution made, to assume that it was not made, and then to ask whether,
by commissioners acting reasonably in the light of all the relevant facts about the
company, an apportionment could have been made. This seems to produce an
intelligible fiscal scheme. Taken together with para. (*a*) it brings within the subsection all (qualified) companies, whether in the relevant year they have abstained

---

(12) [1965] 3 All E.R. 65.

A from distribution, or made any distribution, with the sole exception of a company as to which no body of commissioners could (which I take to mean " could reasonably ") have directed an apportionment in the absence of any distribution at all. Such cases are not uncommon and are typified by the company whose affairs were considered in the case of *Fattorini* (13), and very probably by the company in this case in some years prior to 1953.

B   Not to tax a settlor in respect of loans made by such a company seems reasonable enough because no surtax has been escaped: to tax all other cases seems, if not fair, at least logical. There is no doubt that if this is the test, it was satisfied by the company in each of the three years 1953-54 to 1955-56, so that the Crown's argument succeeds on this point.

C   2. *The capital sums.* The facts as to these are set out in para. 6 of the Case Stated. There can be no dispute, in my opinion, that in 1953-54 the taxpayer received a loan or loans from the company amounting to £9,100 which rank as " capital sums " within the meaning of s. 408 (7). It may well be in fact that he received other sums of a similar character, but this one sum is enough to justify the assessments and it is unnecessary to reach any conclusion as to any additional amounts.

D   3. *The computation.* The taxpayer's contention is that, even assuming points (2) and (3) against him, the assessments made are not justified on the figures. His argument can be simply identified (though fully to explain it would require some detailed arithmetic) by saying that he claims that, against the figures of assessment in 1953-54, he is entitled to subtract a sum of £8,586 which represents a net capital sum (viz. a loan) paid to him in the previous year 1951-52. That

E such a payment was made is proved.

    The provision under which this deduction is claimed is s. 408 (2) (*a*) which refers to " any other capital sums paid to the settlor in any relevant year before that sum was paid ". To qualify as a deduction the capital sum in question must be paid to him either by the trustees of the settlement or (and this is the claim

F here) by a body corporate connected with the settlement.

    The Crown's first answer to this is that in 1951-52 the company which made the payment (Thomas Ambler & Sons, Ltd.) was not such a body corporate, or at least that the taxpayer has not shown that it was. The facts, so far as proved, are that although profits were made in that year, the only distribution made was of a dividend on the company's preference share capital, and it may safely be

G inferred that the Special Commissioners, who considered the company's affairs in the next following year, thought that this was a reasonable distribution to have made. On the Crown's interpretation of s. 411 (4) (*b*), it is agreed by both sides that the company was not a connected body corporate in that year and, although no finding has been made which would cover the alternative interpretation which

H I would prefer, it seems unlikely that any different result would follow, and no remission for such a finding to be made was requested on the taxpayer's behalf.

    The conclusion must, therefore, be that the taxpayer does not succeed in the initial step of showing that the sum for which deduction is claimed was paid by a body corporate connected with the settlement. Consequently this third contention fails in limine and it is unnecessary to deal with some difficult points as to the

I meaning of " any relevant year of assessment " in s. 408 (1) and " any relevant year " in s. 408 (2), or with certain computation anomalies which would arise in recalculating the assessments. I must, however, state my opinion that it seems clear that there are in several respects grave defects in s. 408 (2), particularly with regard to the aggregation of income, which are over-ripe for correction. The Crown has very fairly not taken advantage of these deficiencies which might,

---

(13) [1942] 1 All E.R. 619; [1942] A.C. 643.

indeed, lead to exorbitant surtax claims but, in matters of taxation, administrative moderation, though not to be discouraged, is, except in the short term, no real substitute for legislative clarity and precision.

I would dismiss the appeal.

Appeal dismissed.

Solicitors: *Blundell, Baker & Co.*, agents for *Wade & Cox*, Bradford (for the taxpayer); *Solicitor of Inland Revenue.*

[*Reported by* KATHLEEN J. H. O'BRIEN, *Barrister-at-Law.*]

Dictum of LORD PARKER CJ at 102
applied in JEMMISON v PRIDDLE
[1972] 1 All ER 539

Distinguished in BAYLE v ROSIER
[1977] 2 All ER 160

WARE *v.* FOX.
FOX *v.* DINGLEY AND ANOTHER.

[QUEEN'S BENCH DIVISION (Lord Parker, C.J., Salmon, L.J., and Widgery, J.), November 17, 1966.]

WARE *v.* FOX

Drugs—Dangerous drugs—Cannabis—Information charging managing premises for purpose of smoking cannabis or for purpose of dealing in cannabis— Whether bad for duplicity—Dangerous Drugs Act 1965 (c. 15), s. 5 (a), (b).

The appellant was convicted on an information charging him with being concerned in the management of certain premises which were used for the purpose of smoking cannabis or cannabis resin *or* for the purpose of dealing in cannabis or cannabis resin, contrary to s. 5* of the Dangerous Drugs Act 1965. On appeal on the ground that the information was bad for duplicity,

Held: being concerned in the management of premises used for the purpose of smoking cannabis or cannabis resin, and being concerned in the management of premises used for the purpose of dealing in cannabis or cannabis resin, were offences relating to two different activities and thus were separate offences; accordingly the information had been bad for duplicity and the conviction would be quashed (see p. 102, letter I, and p. 103, letters B and F, post), and similarly para. (a) of s. 5 created two separate offences.

Dictum of LORD PARKER, C.J., in *Mallon* v. *Allon* ([1963] 2 All E.R. at p. 846) applied.

Appeal allowed.

FOX *v.* DINGLEY AND ANOTHER

Drugs—Dangerous drugs—Cannabis—Information charging managing premises for purpose of smoking and dealing in cannabis—Whether bad for duplicity —Dangerous Drugs Act 1965 (c. 15), s. 5 (b).

An information against the respondents charging that they were concerned in the management of certain premises which were used for the purpose of smoking *and* dealing in cannabis and cannabis resin, contrary to s. 5 (b)* of the Dangerous Drugs Act 1965, was dismissed on a submission that the information was bad for duplicity. On appeal by the prosecutor,

Held: for the reason stated at letter F above, para. (b) of s. 5 of the Act of 1965 created two separate offences and the information was bad for duplicity, the only difference from the case of *Ware* v. *Fox*, supra, being that the two activities were charged in the conjunctive, not disjunctive, form (see p. 104, letters D and G, post).

Dictum of LORD PARKER, C.J., in *Mallon* v. *Allon* ([1963] 2 All E.R. at p. 846) applied.

Appeal dismissed.

---

* Section 5 is set out at p. 102, letter G, post.

A   [As to offences under the Dangerous Drugs Acts, see 26 HALSBURY'S LAWS (3rd Edn.) 215, para. 4817.

For the Dangerous Drugs Act 1965, s. 5, see 45 HALSBURY'S STATUTES (2nd Edn.) 895.]

Cases referred to:

B   *Mallon* v. *Allon*, [1963] 3 All E.R. 843; [1964] 1 Q.B. 385; [1963] 3 W.L.R. 1053; 128 J.P. 81; Digest (Cont. Vol. A) 624, *482Ad.*

Thomson v. *Knights*, [1947] 1 All E.R. 112; [1947] K.B. 336; [1947] L.J.R. 445; 176 L.T. 367; 111 J.P. 43; 45 Digest (Repl.) 95, *327.*

R. v. *Clow*, [1963] 2 All E.R. 216; [1965] 1 Q.B. 598; [1963] 3 W.L.R. 84; 127 J.P. 371; 47 Cr. App. Rep. 136; Digest (Cont. Vol. A) 351, *2165a.*

C   WARE *v.* FOX

Case Stated.

This was a Case Stated by justices for the city of Cambridge in respect of their adjudication as a magistrates' court, sitting at Cambridge on Feb. 22, 1966. On Nov. 11, 1965, an information was preferred by the respondent, Harry Frederick Fox, an inspector of police of the city of Cambridge, against the
D   appellant, David Thomas Sidney Ware, charging that on either Aug. 6 or 7, 1965, at and in the city, he was concerned in the management of certain premises situate at 26/27, Clarendon Street, which were used for the purpose of smoking cannabis or cannabis resin or for the purpose of dealing in cannabis or cannabis resin, contrary to s. 5 of the Dangerous Drugs Act 1965. The appellant did not give evidence before the justices and no evidence was called on his behalf.
E   The following facts were found. The premises at 26/27, Clarendon Street were at all material times in the occupation of a number of persons who were tenants of separate flats or rooms thereat. The appellant had a financial interest in the premises under an arrangement started in December, 1964, and continued until Aug. 7, 1965. He at all material times looked after them in that he collected the rents from the tenants on his own behalf paying a head rent of £22 per week
F   to the owner; he re-let rooms which became vacant; and he attended at the premises virtually daily and attempted to maintain proper order thereat in that he visited the premises frequently, often late at night in order to try to maintain order and that this was done as a result of persistent complaints from neighbours, and that he arranged for a colleague from the Bell School of Languages to become a lodger there to assist in the maintenance of order. The appellant did not himself
G   live at the premises. On Aug. 7, 1965, at 2.45 a.m., one Richard Wilson was stopped by a police officer in Clarendon Street. He had come from the premises and he was in possession of a matchbox containing cannabis resin but could not remember where it came from. On Aug. 7, 1965, at 7.15 a.m., police officers entered the premises and executed a search warrant issued under the Dangerous Drugs Act 1965. The appellant was not on the premises when the search warrant
H   was executed, and there was no evidence that he had been on the premises on either Aug. 6 or 7, 1965. On Aug. 7, 1965, when the search warrant was executed there was found on the premises: (i) a quantity of flowering tops of cannabis sativa from which the resin had not been extracted found in the trousers pocket of one Lindo in the room occupied by him; (ii) a quantity of cigarette ash found in the room of Lindo; (iii) a quantity of crude cannabis resin found in a dressing
I   gown pocket in the basement flat occupied by one Dowle; (iv) a pipe which had been used for smoking cannabis found in Dowle's flat; (v) some cigarette ends containing cannabis found in the room of one Clark; (vi) some dust in a drawer in a room occupied by one Whittaker which contained a small fragment of cannabis plant; (vii) a tin containing a small quantity of tobacco with a microscopic piece of cannabis with it found in the room of one Youngblutt; (viii) three pipes which had been used for the purpose of smoking cannbis found in the room of one Powell. Lindo, Dowle, Clark, Whittaker, Youngblutt and Powell were all tenants of rooms in the premises.

At the conclusion of the evidence called by the respondent before the justices A
it was contended on behalf of the appellant that there was no evidence before
the court to justify conviction on the information, and in particular that there
was no evidence of cannabis or cannabis resin having been smoked or dealt in
on the premises either on Aug. 6 or 7, 1965.   The justices were of the opinion
that it was proper to infer from the primary facts as found by them that cannabis
or cannabis resin had been smoked or dealt in on the premises either on Aug. B
6 or 7, 1965, and they so found.   The following matters arose: (i) whether
premises were used for the purpose of smoking or dealing in cannabis or cannabis
resin within the meaning of s. 5 of the Dangerous Drugs Act 1965, by reason only
of the fact that cannabis or cannabis resin had been smoked or dealt in thereon;
(ii) whether a person was concerned in the management of premises within the
meaning of s. 5 if his concern in the management was only such as on the C
justices' findings of fact the appellant had;   (iii) whether s. 5 created an absolute
offence without proof of mens rea or knowledge on the part of the person concerned in the management.   The justices were of the opinion that, as a matter
of law, all those questions should be answered in the affirmative.   They, therefore,
convicted the appellant and imposed a fine of £50, and the appellant now appealed.
On the appeal the question arose whether the information was bad for duplicity, D
in that it charged separate offences not consisting of one single act and whether the
conviction was also bad.   No submission that the information was defective was
made to the justices.

J. C. G. Burge, Q.C., and *A. L. Figgis* for the appellant.
J. C. C. Blofeld for the respondent.
E

LORD PARKER, C.J.: This is an appeal by way of Case Stated from a
decision of justices for the city of Cambridge, who convicted the appellant on
an information which alleged as follows: that the appellant on a day in August,
1965, at and in the city was concerned in the management of certain premises
situate at 26/27, Clarendon Street, which were used for the purpose of smoking
cannabis or cannabis resin or for the purpose of dealing in cannabis or cannabis F
resin, contrary to s. 5 of the Dangerous Drugs Act 1965.   The justices heard the
evidence and in the end convicted the appellant.   Before this court the point
is taken, and, as I understand it, is taken for the first time, that this information
was bad for duplicity.   The fact that it has not been taken before is clearly not
conclusive, because this is a matter which goes to jurisdiction.   Section 5 of the
Act of 1965 provides as follows, and it is important to consider its exact wording: G

" If a person—(a) being the occupier of any premises, permits those
premises to be used for the purpose of smoking cannabis or cannabis resin
or of dealing in cannabis or cannabis resin (whether by sale or otherwise);
or (b) is concerned in the management of any premises used for any such
purpose as aforesaid; he shall be guilty of an offence against this Act."
H

It is, in my judgment, clear that at any rate there are two offences here,
those described in para. (a) in relation to the occupier and those in para. (b) in
respect of the manager.   It is submitted, however, that the matter goes further,
and that in each of those paras. (a) and (b) there are two separate offences.
I find it easiest to approach the matter by considering what would have been the
position if this information had been laid under para. (a).   If laid under para. (a), I
it would, as it seems to me, allege a user for two completely different activities,
one for the purpose of smoking and the other for the purpose of dealing.   Prima
facie, therefore, it is alleging two separate offences.   It is quite different from the
sort of case which alleges one activity achieved in one of two different respects.
A number of cases have been referred to in this connexion, each one depending
on the exact wording of the statute.   There are cases relating to " drink or
drugs ", to " wilfully or negligently " and the many cases under the Road
Traffic Acts dealing with dangerous driving.   Here I am quite satisfied in my

A own mind that both para. (*a*) and para. (*b*) each contain two offences relating to two different activities. Moreover, this is dealing with quite a different case from that in which there is a single incident, a piece of dangerous driving. This is dealing with an activity over a period, a user of premises for certain purposes. Finally, as it seems to me, it is relevant to consider the question of penalty. Read as two separate offences, if both were proved, there could be a penalty

B on each, but more important, if only one were proved, it might result in quite a different penalty from the other. No doubt if two men who were perhaps West Indians were found smoking cannabis it might call for an apparently small sentence, but on the other hand if those two men in the presence of the manager were actively engaged in peddling and dealing, it might call for a completely different penalty.

C I find it unnecessary to refer to the many cases on this matter. It is, perhaps, just worth referring to a passage in *Mallon* v. *Allon* (1), dealing with a very different matter, namely, a breach of rules made under the Gaming and Betting Act, 1960. It was alleged that the appellants in that case unlawfully admitted and allowed a person to remain on the betting office premises, which was contrary to a rule which said that no person apparently under the age of eighteen years

D should be admitted to or allowed to remain on those premises. In giving judgment and after referring to *Thomson* v. *Knights* (2), dealing with drink or drugs, and another case (3), I said this (4):

" In both those cases, however, it is quite clear that what was being considered was a single act, in the one case driving, in the other case failing to comply with conditions. The expressions ' wilfully or negligently ' and

E ' drink or drugs ' were merely descriptive of the particular act complained of. This is a case, as it seems to this court, which is quite different. There are two separate acts, first of all admitting a person, and, secondly, allowing him to remain after he has got on to the premises, and in those circumstances it seems perfectly clear that these are two separate offences."

F It seems to me that what I said in that case applies equally in the present case. In my judgment, this point, to which the justices were not referred, is fatal in this case, and, accordingly, the appeal must be allowed and the conviction quashed.

SALMON, L.J.: I agree.

WIDGERY, J.: I agree.

G *Appeal allowed. Conviction quashed.*

FOX *v.* DINGLEY AND ANOTHER

Case Stated.

This was a Case Stated by the justices for the city of Cambridge in respect of their adjudication as a magistrates' court sitting at Cambridge on Mar. 25,

H 1966. On Mar. 17, 1966, an information was preferred by the appellant, Harry Frederick Fox, then an inspector of police of the Mid-Anglia Constabulary, charging that on Feb. 27, 1966, in the city of Cambridge, the respondents, Stuart Dingley and Pamela Greta Ann Dingley, were concerned in the management of certain premises, namely, the Alley Club, Falcon Yard, which were used for the purpose of smoking and dealing in cannabis and cannabis resin, contrary to

I s. 5 (*b*) of the Dangerous Drugs Act 1965.

At the conclusion of the case a submission was made on behalf of the respondents that the information was bad for duplicity in that it charged the respondents with separate offences in the same information. The justices were of

(1) [1963] 3 All E.R. 843; [1964] 1 Q.B. 385.
(2) [1947] 1 All E.R. 112; [1947] K.B. 336.
(3) *G. Newton, Ltd.* v. *Smith, W. C. Standerwick, Ltd.* v. *Smith*, [1962] 2 All E.R. 19; [1962] 2 Q.B. 278.
(4) [1963] 3 All E.R. at p. 846; [1964] 1 Q.B. at p. 392.

the opinion that, as a matter of law, the information was bad for duplicity. **A**
They, therefore, upheld the submission and dismissed the information. They
did not, therefore, adjudicate on the respondents' solicitors' submission on the
facts nor on the further submission at law which were made on behalf of the
respondents. The appellant now appealed.

J. C. C. Blofeld for the appellant.
M. Dyer for the respondents.   **B**

   LORD PARKER, C.J.: This is another appeal by way of Case Stated
from a decision of justices at Cambridge who on this occasion dismissed an
information preferred by the appellant, an inspector of police, against the
respondents which alleged that they were concerned in the management of
certain premises which were used for the purpose of smoking and dealing in **C**
cannabis and cannabis resin, contrary to s. 5 (*b*) of the Dangerous Drugs Act 1965.
In this case a submission was made that the information was bad for duplicity
and that was upheld by the justices. As this court has already decided in the
previous case, also an appeal from a decision of justices for the city of Cambridge,
the provisions in both para. (*a*) and para. (*b*) of s. 5 of the Dangerous Drugs
Act 1965, comprise two separate offences of using premises for the purposes of **D**
smoking and using premises for the purposes of dealing. The only difference
between this case and the last is that those two activities are put in the conjunctive form and not disjunctive. In my judgment, these magistrates were
right.

   This case is governed really by *Mallon* v. *Allon* (5), where I said in giving
judgment that   **E**

   " It is then contended, in the alternative, that granted that that is so,
   the informations here took the form not of disjunctive but of conjunctive
   expressions. The informations read, ' unlawfully admit and allow ', and
   in that connexion reference is made to the case of *R.* v. *Clow* (6), where it
   was held that an indictment charging the driving of a motor vehicle on a **F**
   road ' at a speed and in a manner which was dangerous ' was not bad for
   duplicity. That, however, again was a case in which the charge related to
   a single incident, a single piece of driving. Here, as I have said, there are
   two incidents involved, one the admission of the person and the other the
   allowing to remain."

In my judgment, the justices here came to a correct decision and I would dismiss **G**
this appeal.

   SALMON, L.J.: I agree.

   WIDGERY, J.: I agree.

                                                         Appeal dismissed.
                                                                            H
   Solicitors: *Francis & Co.*, Cambridge (for the appellant Ware); *Waterhouse &
Co.*, agents for *Few & Kester*, Cambridge (for Fox); *Crossman & Co.*, Cambridge
(for the respondents Stuart Dingley and Pamela Greta Anne Dingley).

                  [*Reported by* N. P. METCALFE, ESQ., *Barrister-at-Law.*]

                                                                            I

---

(5) [1963] 3 All E.R. at p. 846; [1964] 1 Q.B. at p. 392.
(6) [1963] 2 All E.R. 216; [1965] 1 Q.B. 598.

A

Re BELLING (*deceased*).

LONDON BOROUGH OF ENFIELD *v.* PUBLIC TRUSTEE AND OTHERS.

Applied in HAXWELL
UDC [1973] 2 AII ER 1022   v   BARTON

B

[CHANCERY DIVISION (Pennycuick, J.), November 4, 10, 1966.]

Charity—Uncertainty—Intention to create charitable trust—Document not clearly showing dispositive intention—Testator signed document expressing desire to build on his land, and provide funds for, a technical college to be built in conjunction with borough council—Executors entered into contract for sale of land—Action brought by council for declaration of charitable trust and

C

injunction—Whether council had locus standi to sue to establish charitable trust.

A testator, who had made a will, executed a document in testamentary form on Jan. 15, 1965, in which he stated that he wished to bring his life's work to a suitable and lasting conclusion by building a technical college for the electrical industry and accommodation for teachers on his property known as Owls Hall Farm at Enfield. The document stated that the

D

college would be built in conjunction with the Enfield council's planning department, their existing technical college and any other departments which would give practical help; and that the number of houses built (as teachers' accommodation) could be shared with the Enfield council. The document stated that £1,000,000 would be available for the purpose in July. The

E

testator died on Feb. 8, 1965. The document was admitted to probate as a third codicil to his will. Considering that this third codicil was merely a statement of intention, the Treasury Solicitor, after consulting counsel for the Attorney-General, wrote to the executors' solicitors that the Attorney-General did not claim that it constituted a charitable gift. On the other hand the plaintiff, the London Borough of Enfield (" the council ") was

F

advised that the testator had prima facie established a valid charitable trust. The executors having accepted an offer by a purchaser to buy Owls Hall Farm, the council issued a writ claiming a declaration that on the true construction of the third codicil Owls Hall Farm and £1,000,000 were held on valid charitable trusts, an injunction and other relief. The council had been refused authority under s. 28 (2)* of the Charities Act, 1960, to take

G

proceedings. On motion by the council for an injunction.

Held: the motion would be dismissed for the following reasons—

(i) having regard to the fact that under the Education Act, 1944, responsibility for independent educational charities was not among the duties imposed on local education authorities, that the general duty of protecting property given for charitable purposes was the Sovereign's as parens patriae, the Attorney-General being the proper party to sue, and that the former

H

powers of the Charity Commissioners in regard to educational charities were vested in the Secretary of State†, the council had not, in principle, locus standi to initiate the present proceedings (see p. 110, letter G, post).

Dictum of PEARSON, J., in *Strickland* v. *Weldon* ((1885), 28 Ch.D. at p. 430) applied.

I

Dictum of PICKFORD, L.J., in *Guaranty Trust Co. of New York* v. *Hannay & Co.* ([1914-15] All E.R. Rep. at p. 35) distinguished.

(ii) as the definition of " charity proceedings " in s. 28 (8) of the Charities Act, 1960, did not cover proceedings by way of construction of a testamentary document to determine whether a provision was effective to create a

---

* Section 28 (2) is set out at p. 111, letter E, post.

† The functions of the Minister of Education under the Charities Act, 1960, were transferred to the Secretary of State for Education and Science by the Secretary of State for Education and Science Order 1964, S.I. 1964 No. 490.

charitable trust, the council could not be authorised by the court under   A
s. 28 (5) to bring such proceedings (see p. 111, letter H, and p. 112, letter A,
post).

Rendall v. *Blair* ((1890), 45 Ch.D. 139) applied.

[As to the Attorney-General's being the appropriate party to sue to protect
property given to charity, see 4 HALSBURY'S LAWS (3rd Edn.) 446, para. 926;
and for cases on the subject, see 8 DIGEST (Repl.) 517-520, *2472-2516.*   B

As to the need for a clear charitable intention to create a charitable trust,
see 4 HALSBURY'S LAWS (3rd Edn.) 267-269, para. 562; and for cases on the
subject, see 8 DIGEST (Repl.) 387-393, *804-861.*

For the Education Act, 1944, s. 7, see 8 HALSBURY'S STATUTES (2nd Edn.) 152.

For the Charities Act, 1960, s. 28, see 40 HALSBURY'S STATUTES (3rd Edn.)
159.]   C

Cases referred to:

Guaranty Trust Co. of New York v. *Hannay & Co.,* [1914-15] All E.R. Rep. 24;
     [1915] 2 K.B. 536; 84 L.J.K.B. 1465; 113 L.T. 98; 30 Digest (Repl.)
     174, *239.*

London Association of Shipowners and Brokers, Ltd. v. *London and India Docks*   D
     Joint Committee, [1891-94] All E.R. Rep. 462; [1892] 3 Ch. 242; 62
     L.J.Ch. 294; 67 L.T. 238; 30 Digest (Repl.) 172, *229.*

Rendall v. *Blair,* (1890), 45 Ch.D. 139; 59 L.J.Ch. 641; 63 L.T. 265; 8 Digest
     (Repl.) 514, *2417.*

Roberts (Charles) & Co., Ltd. v. *British Railways Board,* [1964] 3 All E.R.
     651; [1965] 1 W.L.R. 396; 3rd Digest Supp.   E

Shum's Trusts, Re, Prichard v. *Richardson,* (1904), 91 L.T. 192; 8 Digest
     (Repl.) 575, *2440.*

Strickland v. *Weldon,* (1885), 28 Ch.D. 426; 54 L.J.Ch. 452; 52 L.T. 247;
     8 Digest (Repl.) 518, *2483.*

Motion.

The plaintiff corporation, the London Borough of Enfield (" the council ")   F
issued a writ on Oct. 21, 1966, claiming (i) a declaration that on the true construction of the third codicil dated Jan. 15, 1966, to the will of Charles Reginald Belling,
deceased, the freehold land and premises, Owls Hall Farm at Enfield in Greater
London and the sum of £1,000,000 were held on valid charitable trusts, namely
trusts for the foundation and endowment of a scientific technological college at
Enfield for the electrical industry; (ii) administration of the trusts; (iii) if   G
necessary a scheme for the administration of the charity, and (iv) an injunction
to restrain the first four defendants or any of them as personal representatives
of the deceased from conveying or otherwise disposing of or from taking any
steps to convey or otherwise dispose of the land and premises or any part thereof
otherwise than in due execution of the trusts and for the purposes of the charity.
On the same date a notice of motion was given for an interlocutory injunction in   H
substantially the same terms as para. (iv) of the writ. The defendants were the
Public Trustee, Harold Percy Aston, Richard Eric Belling, John William Mayo
who were the personal representatives of the deceased, and Her Majesty's
Attorney-General. The facts are set out in the judgment.

The cases noted below* were cited during the argument in addition to those
referred to in the judgment.   I

Charles Sparrow, Q.C., and *P. J. Millett* for the plaintiff council.

J. A. Brightman, Q.C., and *J. W. Brunyate* for the defendant executors.

Cur. adv. vult.

Nov. 10. **PENNYCUICK, J.:** By this motion the plaintiff corporation, the
Mayor, Aldermen and Burgesses of the London Borough of Enfield, to whom I

* *Dance* v. *Goldingham,* (1873), 8 Ch. App. 902; *Re Barrance, Barrance* v. *Ellis,*
1910] 2 Ch. 419.

A will refer as " the council ", seeks an injunction restraining the first four defendants, as the personal representatives of one Charles Reginald Belling, from
disposing of certain land known as Owls Hall Farm in the borough of Enfield.

The testator made a will, with which I am not now concerned. On Jan. 15,
1965, he executed a document in testamentary form on which the present question
turns. It is a very odd document and I must, I think, read it in full. It says:

B
" Written on Friday, Jan. 15. Being on a cruise towards the Caribbean
Islands, and having time available I have decided to write another codicil to
my will in connexion with a matter I have given a lot of thought to and in
fact discussed with several of Belling & Co.'s directors on several occasions.
The subject matter is the building of a scientific technological college for the

C electrical industry at Enfield and the people I have already had discussions
with about it are my wife, Mr. Robert Belling, Mr. Runton, Mr. Aston, Mr.
Hawkins, Mr. Coldwell, Mr. Dean, who are already directors of Belling & Co.
and know my wishes fairly well. The broad idea is to bring my life's work to a
suitable and lasting conclusion and one which will be useful to the industry
I have worked in and made what money I have got in.

D " As we are continually reading about the advantage of technical staff
in this country to carry out such fundamental work as is necessary in
converting the original ideas which we in this country seemed to be blessed
with into practical working appliances, it would seem that any additional
help which we can obtain from technical training colleges and the like would
obviously be one of the best possible steps to take and so prevent as far as

E possible other countries from exploiting our brains (which we seem to have
for new and novel ideas) to our disadvantage, especially as competition is
getting very keen.

" To get down to tin tacks. The best idea which has arisen so far is that I
should use a part of my farm known as O.H.F. [that is Owls Hall Farm]
for the purpose, and where the present farmhouse is situated, build the

F technical school in its place and as I have some sixty acres freehold on this side
of the main road, i.e., the road from Chase Side Enfield to Cuffley and Northaw,
to also build perhaps some forty smallish houses so that the teachers and the
necessary staff can be found and accommodated (otherwise we should never
get the teaching staff).

" We should be quite happy to share the number of houses which might
G eventually be built with the Enfield U.D.C. so that any ill feeling in the
district can be avoided. Our own particular people the B.E.A.M.A. and the
engineering union will probably want some say in the disposal of perhaps one
or two houses.

" As a first start our own dwg. office will be preparing a prospective view
of the general position as it might appear from the ridge along the top of our
H field near Fountains Farm. The college itself we should of course build in
conjunction with the Enfield council's planning department; their existing
technical college and any other departments who would give real practical
and useful help. The money which will be made over for this idea to be
carried out will be £1,000,000 sterling in cash which will be available in early
July, operations would be started immediately then."

I The testator died on Feb. 8, 1965. The document which I have read was admitted
to probate as a third codicil with the will on Mar. 22, 1965. The testator left an
estate of approximately £2,700,000 gross less duty of approximately £1,000,000.

Correspondence took place between the solicitors acting for the executors and
the Treasury Solicitor. On May 28, 1965, the solicitors acting for the executors
wrote to the Treasury Solicitor enclosing a copy of the document of Jan. 15, 1965,
and expressing their own view that it had no dispositive effect. On June 9, the
Treasury Solicitor replied:

A

" I have now consulted counsel for H.M. Attorney-General who considers that the testamentary document of Jan. 15 was merely a statement of intention by the testator. In these circumstances the Attorney-General does not propose to claim that this document constituted a charitable gift."

There later ensued a more lengthy correspondence between the town clerk for the council and his solicitors on the one side and the solicitors for the executors on the other side. I will not read most of that correspondence and it will be sufficient to say that on Feb. 22, 1966, the solicitors for the council wrote:

" With further reference to this matter our client's counsel . . . [and he names him], now advises that (i) In his opinion the testator had, prima facie established a valid charitable trust for the establishment of a technical college. (ii) The council should communicate at once with the Treasury Solicitor (as agent for the Attorney-General) with a view to early proceedings to determine the validity of the gift. We shall be glad therefore to know that you agree to submit this matter to the court."

In reply the solicitors for the executors informed the solicitors for the council that they had already consulted the Treasury Solicitor and referred to the correspondence which I have read. The letter concluded:

" Having regard to the views of counsel for H.M. Attorney-General, the executors can see no reason to take the matter any further."

To that letter the solicitors for the council replied, acknowledging the letter and stating, " upon which we are communicating with our professional client, and on hearing from him we will again contact you." Nothing further was done by the council until Oct. 13 as I will mention.

The executors proceeded to advertise the Owls Hall Farm property for sale by auction on Oct. 27. Advertisements were inserted in the local and national newspapers. From Aug. 18 onwards there were in all twelve advertisements in the local newspapers and eleven advertisements in national newspapers. The auction was fixed for Oct. 27. The executors considered a number of offers to purchase by private treaty including one by Mr. Bartlett who offered to purchase for £35,560. On Oct. 13, Messrs. Knight, Frank & Rutley, the agents representing the executors in this matter, wrote advising acceptance of Mr. Bartlett's offer. On the same day, by coincidence, that is to say, Oct. 13, 1966, the solicitors for the council wrote to the solicitors for the executors in these terms:

" With further reference to this matter our clients, the London Borough of Enfield, were concerned to learn that your clients were offering Owls Hall Farm for sale by public auction having regard to the pending claim in regard to the validity of the codicil."

As I have said, that was the first communication from the solicitors to the council since their letter of Mar. 1. The very next day, Oct. 14, the executors signed a contract with Mr. Bartlett for the purchase of Owls Hall Farm at the price of £35,560, the date for completion being Nov. 28, 1966.

The council issued the writ in the present action on Oct. 21, 1966. The relief sought by the writ is as follows:

" (i) A declaration that upon the true construction of the third codicil dated Jan. 15, 1966, to the will of the above-named deceased the freehold land and premises Owls Hall Farm at Enfield in Greater London and the sum of £1,000,000 are held upon valid charitable trusts, namely trusts for the foundation and endowment of a scientific technological college at Enfield for the electrical industry. (ii) Administration of the said trusts. (iii) If necessary a scheme for the administration of the said charity. (iv) An injunction to restrain the first four defendants or any of them as personal representatives of the said deceased from conveying or otherwise disposing of or from taking any steps to convey or otherwise dispose of the land and premises aforesaid

A   or of any part thereof otherwise than in due execution of the said trusts and for the purposes of the said charity."

On the same date notice of the present motion was given, the relief sought being an injunction in substantially the same terms as that sought by para. (iv) in the writ. On the motion an affidavit was sworn by Mr. Platten, the town clerk of the council, which contains the following paragraph:

B

" The Enfield Borough Council is the local education authority for Enfield, and as such it is vitally interested in the charity constituted by the testator's third codicil. Moreover, it is the body designated by the testator both as a potential recipient of his bounty and as a participant in his scheme (for his reference to the Enfield U.D.C.—which does not exist—is plainly a mistake).

C   The council is anxious, therefore, that the testator's scheme should be implemented, and his testamentary wishes, as expressed in his last codicil, duly carried into effect."

An affidavit in answer was sworn by Mr. Aston, the second named executor, in which he set out in detail the history of the matter, the reasons for approving of the sale to Mr. Bartlett and certain matters relating to the testator's estate. There

D   is no suggestion that the proceeds of Owls Hall Farm are needed for the purpose of administration.

The document signed by the testator on Jan. 15, 1965, is in very unusual language if intended to create a binding trust, and it may well be that the executors and their counsel are right in the view that it has no dispositive effect. The fact remains that the testator executed the document in testamentary form, and I

E   am not prepared to hold that it is so manifestly ineffective to create a charitable trust that the executors could properly deal with the Owls Hall property without regard to the document, if a request to seek a decision of the court on it were made by someone having a locus standi in the matter. Indeed, counsel for the executors accepts that they would have been bound to comply with such a request if made by the Attorney-General.

F   The real question on the present motion is, it seems to me, whether the council has such a locus standi. When a testator creates, or purports to create, a new charitable trust, in contradistinction to making a gift to an existing charity, he does not seek to confer a beneficial interest on any person. He seeks to dedicate part of his estate to a purpose and, in legal theory, the Sovereign, as parens patriae, has the right to compel the testator's personal representatives to set

G   aside the assets directed or required to meet that purpose. In this connexion the Attorney-General acts on behalf of the Sovereign and in the ordinary course the Attorney-General takes whatever steps may be necessary, including the institution or defence of proceedings by originating summons, for the construction of a will alleged to create a charitable trust. On this point I refer to *Strickland* v. *Weldon* (1), where PEARSON, J., said:

H   " The Attorney-General is the only person who can really represent a charity and sue on its behalf . . ."

For a concise statement of principle I refer to 4 HALSBURY'S LAWS OF ENGLAND (3rd Edn.) 446, para. 926, where it says:

" As a rule the Attorney-General is a necessary party to all actions

I   relating to charities. It is the duty of the Queen, as parens patriae, to protect property devoted to charitable uses, and that duty is executed by the Attorney-General as the officer who represents the Crown for all forensic purposes. He represents the beneficial interest, in other words the objects, of the charity."

No case has been cited to me in which anyone, other than the Attorney-General, has been admitted to institute proceedings of this type and it is difficult to see

_____

(1) (1885), 28 Ch.D. 426 at p. 430.

how, apart from some statutory provision, anyone other than the Attorney- A
General could so assume the mantle of the Sovereign. The position is, of course,
different where a party claims some beneficial interest for himself, for example,
an annuity out of property otherwise devoted to charity.

Counsel for the plaintiff council contended that the council had the necessary
locus standi to institute these proceedings on two grounds, namely, first, that the
council is named in and interested under the codicil, and, second, that it B
is the local authority responsible for education in its area. As regards the first
ground, the testator, in the document of Jan. 15, merely indicates a desire, in two
passages, that the building of certain houses, and the building of the college itself,
should be carried out in conjunction with the council, and that the council should
give help in the matter. I do not think that this desire, even if it represented a
direction binding on the executors, could be treated as conferring on the council C
any interest in the testator's estate such as would give it the necessary locus standi
to institute proceedings. The council is concerned in the matter merely in an
advisory or co-operative capacity if called in by the trustees.

The second ground raises a question of some general importance which might
merit further consideration than it could receive on an interlocutory motion. I
was not taken through the provisions of the Education Act, 1944, and will refer D
only briefly to them. Section 7 of the Education Act, 1944, is in these terms:

" The statutory system of public education shall be organised in three
progressive stages to be known as primary education, secondary education,
and further education; and it shall be the duty of the local education
authority for every area, so far as their powers extend, to contribute towards
the spiritual, moral, mental and physical development of the community by E
securing that efficient education throughout those stages shall be available
to meet the needs of the population of their area."

That section is very wide, but the whole of the second sentence is qualified by
the words " so far as their powers extend ". Under the succeeding sections of the
Act of 1944 it is the duty of the local education authority to secure that there F
shall be available for their area sufficient schools for providing primary and
secondary education and also to secure the provision for their area of adequate
facilities for further education. A great number of further powers and duties is
conferred on local education authorities; but there appears to be no provision
in the Act of 1944—and certainly I have not been referred to any—whereby a
local education authority has responsibility for independent educational charities G
in its area. It will be remembered that the powers formerly vested in the charity
commissioners with regard to educational charities are now vested in the Secretary of State for Education. I do not see how in the circumstances a local authority
can be said as such to have any interest in the establishment of an educational
charity so as to support legal proceedings by way of the construction of a will.

I conclude then in principle that the council has no locus standi to institute H
these proceedings. No case has been cited in which a local authority has in fact
been admitted to institute comparable proceedings.

Counsel for the plaintiff council placed great reliance on *Guaranty Trust Co.
of New York* v. *Hannay & Co.* (2) in the Court of Appeal, and the earlier case of
London Association of Shipowners and Brokers, Ltd. v. *London and India Docks
Joint Committee* (3). I do not think, however, that those cases help him. The I
principle underlying the majority judgment in the *Guaranty Trust* case (2) is
concisely stated by PICKFORD, L.J., in the following terms (4):

" I think, therefore, that the effect of the rule is to give a general power
to make a declaration whether there be a cause of action or not; and at the

---

(2) [1914-15] All E.R. Rep. 24; [1915] 2 K.B. 536.
(3) [1891-94] All E.R. Rep. 462; [1892] 3 Ch. 242.
(4) [1914-15] All E.R. Rep. at p. 35; [1915] 2 K.B. at p. 562.

A   instance of any party who is interested in the subject-matter of the declaration. It does not extend to enable any stranger to the transaction to go and ask the court to express its opinion in order to help him in other transactions. Whether it extends to a declaration that the plaintiff is not liable in an action intended, or proceeding is a matter I shall discuss in dealing with this particular case."

B   In both the cases which were cited the plaintiff was clearly interested in the subject-matter of the transaction, in the one case as a person affected by the regulations sought to be impugned and in the other case as a party to the contract sought to be construed. Here the whole question is whether the council has a necessary interest in the subject-matter of the declaration sought; and for the reasons which I have given I do not think that it has that interest.

C   Counsel for the plaintiff council also referred to *Charles Roberts & Co., Ltd.* v. *British Railways Board* (5), but that was a case of ultra vires and does not seem to me to have any significant bearing on the present point.

Counsel for the plaintiff council advanced an alternative contention based on s. 28 of the Charities Act, 1960. So far as is material that section is in the following terms:

D   " (1) Charity proceedings may be taken with reference to a charity either by the charity, or by any of the charity trustees, or by any person interested in the charity, or by any two or more inhabitants of the area of the charity, if it is a local charity, but not by any other person.

" (2) Subject to the following provision of this section, no charity proceedings relating to a charity (other than an exempt charity) shall be entertained
E   or proceeded with in any court unless the taking of the proceedings is authorised by order of the commissioners . . .

" (5) Where the foregoing provisions of this section require the taking of charity proceedings to be authorised by an order of the commissioners, the proceedings may nevertheless be entertained or proceeded with if after the order had been applied for and refused leave to take the proceedings was
F   obtained from one of the judges of the High Court attached to the Chancery Division.

" (8) In this section 'charity proceedings' means proceedings in any court in England or Wales brought under the court's jurisdiction with respect to charities, or brought under the court's jurisdiction with respect to trusts in relation to the administration of a trust for charitable purposes."

G   I am told that the council has in fact applied to the Secretary of State under sub-s. (2) for authority to bring these proceedings and that that application was refused. The council now invites me to treat as before me an application for leave under sub-s. (5). It seems to me that the definition in sub-s. (8) does not cover proceedings by way of the construction of a will in order to determine whether a provision in the will is effective to create a charitable trust. Such
H   proceedings are brought neither under the court's jurisdiction as to charities nor under the court's jurisdiction with respect to trusts in relation to the administration of a trust for charitable purposes. This view derives support from a number of decisions under s. 17 of the Charitable Trusts Act, 1853, which was the statutory predecessor, albeit in entirely different terms, of s. 28 of the Act of 1960. It
I   was well established under s. 17 of the Act of 1853 that the section related exclusively to administration (see *Rendall* v. *Blair* (6), per BOWEN, L.J., and per FRY, L.J. (7)). The last line of the latter judgment is: " In my opinion the section relates exclusively to administration." See also *Re Shum's Trusts, Prichard* v. *Richardson* (8), where it was held that no consent under the Act of 1853 was required where a trustee applied by summons to determine whether or not the trust was charitable. Here, it seems to me, if the council had any locus

---

(5) [1964] 3 All E.R. 651.   (6) (1890), 45 Ch.D. 139 at p. 154.
(7) (1890), 45 Ch.D. at p. 160.   (8) (1904), 91 L.T. 192.

standi it could have brought these proceedings without any leave under s. 28; **A**
conversely, if it has not a locus standi the requisite authority cannot be conferred
under s. 28.

The question arose whether Mr. Bartlett, the purchaser from the executors,
was a necessary party to this action. I think it unnecessary in the circumstances
to pursue that question.

There was considerable argument whether, having regard to the point of time **B**
at which this motion was brought, an injunction ought in any event to be granted
at the instance of the council. I think it right to say that I should not have been
disposed to refuse an injunction on this ground, but I need not express a concluded decision on this point.

I propose to dismiss the motion on the grounds that I have stated.

Motion dismissed. **C**

Solicitors: *T. D. Jones & Co.* (for the plaintiff council); *Linklaters & Paines*
(for the defendant executors).

[*Reported by* JENIFER SANDELL, *Barrister-at-Law.*]

Overruled in IMPERIAL TOBACCO v   ————   **D**
A-G [1979] 2 All ER 592 [1980] 1 All E.R. 866

DIRECTOR OF PUBLIC PROSECUTIONS *v.* BRADFUTE
AND ASSOCIATES, LTD.

[QUEEN'S BENCH DIVISION (Lord Parker, C.J., Glyn-Jones and Widgery, JJ.), **E**
November 10, 1966.]

*Gaming—Lottery—Advertisement—Distribution of advertisement of lottery—Bingo
prize competition—Label attached to tin of proprietary cat food—Label containing bingo card of sixteen digits with prize values which might be won
if line completed from adjoining rectangle containing eighteen digits—No
skill required to complete line—Matter of luck in obtaining a winning label—* **F**
*Easy puzzle then to be solved before competitor could claim prize—Element
of skill in solving this—Whether scheme one entire scheme severable into two
stages—Whether scheme involved a lottery—Betting, Gaming and Lotteries
Act* 1963 (*c.* 2), *s.* 42 (1) (*c*) (i).

The respondents printed and distributed an advertisement in the form of a
label attached to tins of a proprietary cat food. On the outside of the label **G**
were the words " Play World's Biggest £30,000 Bingo. Your card is inside
the label ". On the other side of the label was a provision for the so-called
playing of Bingo—" the world's biggest Bingo—£30,000 in big cash prizes ".
There was then set out a square comprising a Bingo card of sixteen digits,
and opposite each line horizontally and vertically were the prize values
which might be won if the line were completed—they went from £1 up to **H**
£1,000. There was another rectangle containing eighteen digits, and the so-
called play consisted of going through the numbers in the rectangle and striking off any similar numbers that appeared in the square with the sixteen
digits. If by this means a line were completed, the holder of the label or the
card was entitled to claim the prize set out at the end of that line. Before
the prize was paid the customer had to solve a puzzle, which consisted of a **I**
geometrical diagram; the person applying for the prize had to state the number of triangles that appeared in that geometrical figure. On appeal by the
prosecution against the dismissal of an information against the respondents
of causing to be printed for the purpose of publication or distribution an
advertisement of a lottery, contrary to s. 42 (1) (*c*) (i)* of the Betting, Gaming
and Lotteries Act 1963,

---

* Section 42 (1) is set out at p. 114, letter G, post.

A   **Held:** the scheme in the present case was severable into two stages, the first, the obtaining of a label which would enable the Bingo card to be completed in one line, was one purely of luck and the second, the puzzle, involved a little skill; since no skill was required for the first stage and the right obtained thereby was something of value and thus constituted in itself a prize, the scheme involved in its first stage a lottery, viz., a distribution of

B   prizes, the winning labels, by chance; accordingly the case would be remitted with a direction to convict (see p. 115, letter H, and p. 116, letters D and G, post).

   Kerslake v. *Knight* ([1925] All E.R. Rep. 679) applied.

   Appeal allowed.

   [As to what is a lottery, see 18 HALSBURY'S LAWS (3rd Edn.) 238, 239, para.

C   460; and for cases on the subject, see 25 DIGEST (Repl.) 493-495, *511-527,*
   511-513, *614-622.*

   As to offences in connexion with unlawful lotteries, see 18 HALSBURY'S LAWS (3rd Edn.) 241, 242, para. 464; and for cases on the subject, see 25 DIGEST (Repl.) 498, *545-553.*

   For the Betting, Gaming and Lotteries Act 1963, s. 42, see 43 HALSBURY'S

D   STATUTES (2nd Edn.) 352.]

   Cases referred to:

   Kerslake v. *Knight,* [1925] All E.R. Rep. 679; 94 L.J.K.B. 919; 133 L.T. 606;
       89 J.P. 142; 41 T.L.R. 555; 25 Digest (Repl.) 495, *527.*

   Scott v. *Director of Public Prosecutions,* [1914-15] All E.R. Rep. 825; [1914]
       2 K.B. 868; 83 L.J.K.B. 1025; 111 L.T. 59; 78 J.P. 267; 25 Digest

E   (Repl.) 513, *621.*

   Case Stated.

   This was a Case Stated by JOHN AUBREY-FLETCHER, ESQ., one of the stipendiary magistrates of the metropolis in respect of his adjudication as a magistrates' court sitting at Great Marlborough Street on Mar. 4, 1966. On Jan. 26, 1966, an information was preferred by George Bentley, a police officer on behalf of

F   the Director of Public Prosecutions, against the respondents, Bradfute & Associates, Ltd., charging that, on or before Nov. 27, 1965, in the Inner London Area, they caused to be printed for the purpose of publication or distribution an advertisement of a lottery contrary to s. 42 (1) (c) (i) of the Betting, Gaming and Lotteries Act 1963. The following facts were found. At all material times the respondents were a limited liability company. On Nov. 27, 1965, a product

G   called Kit-E-Kat was on sale to the public packed in tins to which labels were specially attached. On Nov. 27, 1965, George Bentley purchased in a shop a tin of Kit-E-Kat to which was attached such a label. On the outside of the label appeared the words " Play World's Biggest £30,000 Bingo. Your card is inside the label ". On the inside of the label appeared (i) a rectangle containing eighteen differently numbered boxes; (ii) a square containing sixteen differently numbered

H   boxes and (iii) a puzzle. If by deleting on the square any numbers that appeared in the rectangle, an horizontal or vertical line on the square was thereby completely deleted, and if the puzzle was then correctly solved, the competitor was entitled to a prize of the value indicated at the beginning of the deleted line. The deleting of the numbers on the square that appeared in the rectangle did not require the exercise of skill. The solving of the puzzle required the exercise of some skill.

I   The respondents caused the label to be printed and distributed. The label was an advertisement.

   It was contended on behalf of the appellant before the metropolitan magistrate that (a) (i) a label with a " winning " line was itself a saleable commodity and, therefore, itself a prize, because it gave the holder the opportunity to get a sum of money, subject to solving the puzzle, and (ii) the distribution of labels with a " winning line " was purely by chance and was, therefore, a lottery; (b) the puzzle was merely a test and was in no sense competitive; (c) in any event, skill in solving the puzzle in no way influenced the amount of the prizes won, which ranged from £1 to £1,000; (d) the reality of the scheme was that whether the **A** buyer of a tin got a prize at all, and the value of the prize, depended on pure chance, subject only to passing a test before claiming the prize. It was contended on behalf of the respondents before the metropolitan magistrate that (a) the " prize ", in the ordinary acceptance of that word, was the monetary sum capable of being gained by a successful entrant and the appellant's dichotomy was artificial; (b) the scheme was, and was to be considered as, a whole so that **B** success required the double qualification of the exercise of the requisite degree of skill and the possession of the requisite luck; and not as two competitions with separate prizes, one capable of being won only with luck and the other with skill; (c) there was an ingredient of skill and an ingredient of luck needed to obtain a prize, and as skill thus played some part in determining the distribution there had been no offence; (d) it was for the appellant to establish clearly and **C** beyond doubt that the scheme was a lottery, and this he had not done.

The magistrate was of the opinion that the contention of the respondents was correct and dismissed the information and the appellant now appealed.

The cases noted below* were cited during the argument in addition to those referred to in the judgment of LORD PARKER, C.J.

J. H. Buzzard, J. C. Mathew and *T. F. L. Cassel* for the appellant.   **D**
Leonard Caplan, Q.C., and *Norman C. Tapp* for the respondents.

LORD PARKER, C.J.: This is an appeal by way of Case Stated from a decision of one of the stipendiary magistrates of the metropolis sitting at Great Marlborough Street, who dismissed an information preferred by the appellant, the Director of Public Prosecutions, against the respondents, a company called **E** Bradfute & Associates, Ltd., alleging that the respondents caused to be printed for the purpose of publication or distribution an advertisement of a lottery, contrary to s. 42 (1) (c) (i) of the Betting, Gaming and Lotteries Act 1963. It is convenient to refer to the only statutory provisions which are relevant here, namely, s. 41 and s. 42 of the Act of 1963. Section 41 provides that: " Subject to the provisions of this Act, all lotteries are unlawful ". By s. 42 (1), it is pro- vided, so far as it is material here, that: **F**

" Subject to the provisions of this section, every person who in connexion with any lottery promoted or proposed to be promoted either in Great Britain or elsewhere . . . (c) prints, publishes or distributes, or has in his possession for the purpose of publication or distribution—(i) any advertise- ment of the lottery . . ."   **G**

[HIS LORDSHIP stated the facts, and continued:] The sole question here is whether the advertisement, because undoubtedly it was an advertisement, was the advertisement of a lottery. " Lottery ", as is well known, is not defined any- where, but can be taken to bear its dictionary meaning as adopted by the courts, that is, a distribution of prizes by lot or chance. Any skill other than a mere colourable skill which is involved will prevent the scheme from being a lottery. **H** As ATKIN, J., said in *Scott* v. *Director of Public Prosecutions* (1):

" Any kind of skill or dexterity, whether bodily or mental, in which persons can compete would prevent a scheme from being a lottery if the result depended partly upon such skill or dexterity."

The argument for the respondents, which was accepted by the magistrate in dismissing the information, was really this, that the scheme here is a scheme **I** to be considered as a whole and as an entire scheme, and that success in the scheme involved two things, a requisite degree of luck in getting a label which will enable the Bingo card to be completed in one line, and also the requisite degree of skill to solve the puzzle, and that, in those circumstances, it cannot be said to

---

* *Taylor* v. *Smetton*, (1883), 11 Q.B.D. 207; *Barratt* v. *Burden*, (1893), 63 L.J.M.C. 33; *Hall* v. *Cox*, [1899] 1 Q.B. 198; *Moore* v. *Elphick*, [1945] 2 All E.R. 155; *R.* v. *Young*, (1957), 24 W.W.R. 83.
(1) [1914-15] All E.R. Rep. 825 at p. 834; [1914] 2 K.B. 868 at p. 880.

A be a lottery. That was the contention which the learned magistrate accepted, and which has given rise to this appeal. Before this court, counsel for the appellant has taken a number of points, only one of which I think it is necessary for me to deal with, and that is this, that the only proper reading of the scheme here is that it involves two stages, one of pure luck and one of some skill, and that, if one looks at the first stage, the stage of pure luck, one finds something which can

B properly be described as a prize, and, accordingly, before one ever gets to the second stage there is a lottery. In my judgment, it is quite clear that a prize need not be a sum of money; it can of course be an article, a commodity, and, in my judgment, can be anything which can be sold, or indeed anything which can be said to be of value. Counsel for the appellant says that, if one were the lucky holder of such a card and had completed a line opposite which was printed £1,000, then one

C clearly had something of some considerable value, and indeed the easier the puzzle the greater the value of what he would describe as the prize. There is little authority on this matter, and for my part I am not going to be tempted to go into a number of other possible situations in order to decide whether they amount to lotteries or not. It seems to me that the only thing here is to look at the facts of the individual case under consideration.

D That a right to obtain a sum of money subject to a test, or subject to undertaking some service, is a prize seems to me quite clear as a matter of principle, and, indeed, was so treated in *Kerslake* v. *Knight* (2). There the manager of a newspaper furnished a supply of numbered tickets to certain tradesmen who happened to advertise in his newspaper, and every purchaser at the tradesmen's shops received a ticket. Once a week the counterfoils of the distributed tickets

E were taken by the manager's servants to the newspaper office, and seventeen numbers were drawn; the holder of one of those tickets then became entitled to a prize on giving an undertaking to exhibit a card bearing the name of the newspaper in their windows for a certain period. Undoubtedly the real decision of the court was that the service to be rendered, which it is said prevented this from being a lottery, was merely colourable. As LORD HEWART, C.J., said (3):

F   " It was said that the ticket was not a ticket in a lottery because of the service. In this case the service was a colourable part of the scheme, and could be rendered nugatory."

Then he goes on, obiter, it is true (3):

      " But even if it had been substantial, it was clear that the chance of rendering that service for money was as much a prize as if a book or any other article had been offered."

G

Accordingly, as it seems to me, the sole question is whether counsel for the appellant is right in saying that, if one looks at the facts of this case, one should not treat it as one entire scheme but as severable in the way which I have indicated. For my part I feel on the facts of this case that it is quite impossible to contend

H that this is one entire scheme. It seems to me that the right obtained by getting the winning label constituted a prize in itself, and that that really is the end of this case. I confess that I am influenced in coming to that conclusion by two considerations. One is that such skill as there is in solving the puzzle has nothing whatever to do with the value of the prize: it is, as it were, a mere condition which has to be fulfilled before the prize is paid; and secondly, because in this case

I in solving the puzzle the holder of the card is not competing with anybody. If he does not solve the puzzle, nobody else is going to get the prize; he is not competing with anybody else. Whether those two matters can be said of themselves to prevent this being a lottery, I need not consider, but they certainly influence me considerably in the approach to this scheme. In my judgment, the only possible conclusion here on the primary facts is that this scheme constituted a lottery, and, accordingly, I would send the case back to the magistrate with a direction to convict.

GLYN-JONES, J.: I agree. The puzzle which the fortunate purchaser of A a tin of Kit-E-Kat containing a label on which he can fill up one of the lines in what is called the Bingo card is a regular pentagon within which three lines are drawn, and it is possible to count eleven triangles made by those lines in the boundaries of the pentagon. By pure luck and nothing else the purchaser may find himself in possession of a label where the numbers are such that he can scratch out four numbers in a line under the figure " £1,000 ". If he does not know what a B triangle is, of course, he will have some difficulty in solving the puzzle, but I should have thought that any man of the intelligence of a fourth form schoolboy who was prepared to take a certain amount of trouble and care would know that he could count the number of triangles quite easily, and all he had to do to win £1,000 would be to count the number of triangles. It seems to me that a sensible man would pay many hundreds of pounds for such an opportunity, and to say in those cir- C cumstances that the label is not a prize seems to me to be nonsense; if it is not a prize, I do not know what is.

This court has had occasion from time to time in the past to pronounce on the question whether a given scheme is a lottery or not. All these schemes have differed, and all of them have differed as far as I can see from this one. Save to the extent that we are bound to apply, as we do, any principles which emerged D from the variety of decisions in the past, decisions on other schemes are of no assistance to us. I must say that I entirely agree with what has fallen from LORD PARKER, C.J., and I think that this appeal should be allowed.

WIDGERY, J.: I agree with both judgments. I am impressed by counsel for the respondents' argument that one should not be too astute to separate E what is in truth a compound scheme in order to isolate some part which depends on chance only with a view to saying that the whole scheme is a lottery. There are some schemes, however, and I am of the view that this is one, which, although they appear at first sight to be a single and united scheme, are in fact readily separable, and, when separated, show that a lottery exists. For the reasons given by my brothers, I am quite satisfied that, when the lucky recipient F of a card which had the appropriate numbers to draw a prize of £1,000 opened her label and observed that fact, she would be prepared at once to go round and tell her neighbours to rejoice, because she had won a prize, and she would do that because she would know perfectly well that, although the solution of the puzzle is not by any means a trivial matter, and not one which all of us would guarantee to get right immediately, it is a puzzle which quite obviously she could get solved, and the possibility of her not getting a prize did not exist at all. G

For the reasons already given in the other judgments, and for that reason, I am quite satisfied myself that, in this case, the ticket was a prize, the prizes were distributed entirely by lot, the scheme was a lottery, the decision below was wrong, and that the Case should be sent back, as LORD PARKER, C.J., has said.

Appeal allowed.   Case remitted.   Leave to appeal to the House of Lords refused. H

Solicitors: *Director of Public Prosecutions* (for the appellant); *Durrant, Cooper & Hambling* (for the respondents).

[*Reported by* N. P. METCALFE, ESQ., *Barrister-at-Law.*]

Applied in BELVOIR FINANCE STAPLETON [1970] 3 All ER 664 v

WICKHAM HOLDINGS, LTD. v. BROOKE HOUSE MOTORS, LTD.

[COURT OF APPEAL, CIVIL DIVISION (Lord Denning, M.R., Danckwerts and Winn, L.JJ.), November 8, 1966.]

Hire-purchase—Damages—Sale of goods by hirer—Measure of damages in conversion or detinue—Two-thirds of hire-purchase price already paid—Whether full value of goods recoverable by finance company.

By a hire-purchase agreement dated Oct. 28, 1964, a finance company let a Rover motor car to P. The total hire-purchase price was £889. P. paid in all £615 10s. In June, 1965, he went to motor dealers to trade in the Rover for another car. The dealers on June 11, 1965, enquired of the finance company the " settlement figure " for the Rover. They were told that it was £274 10s., but that the finance company would accept £270, if the sum were paid within seven days. This was confirmed in writing by the finance company. The dealers accepted the Rover from P., making him an allowance in part payment of another car; by an oversight, however, the dealers failed to pay the £270 to the finance company. The finance company, when it learnt of the sale of the Rover, notified P. that they terminated the hire-purchase agreement for his breach of the agreement by selling the car, demanded the return of the car and sued the dealers for its return or its value and for damages for its detention. On appeal by the dealers against an award to the finance company for £440, being the trade value of the car (£365) and £75 damages for detention,

Held: the finance company was entitled to recover as damages in conversion only what it had lost by reason of the wrongful act in selling the car; the amount of this loss was £274 10s., and that was the amount recoverable as damages, less any subsequent payment of instalments (see p. 120, letter I, p. 121, letters A and I, and p. 122, letter H, post).

Belsize Motor Supply Co. v. *Cox* ([1911-13] All E.R. Rep. 1084) applied.

United Dominions Trust (Commercial), Ltd. v. *Parkway Motors, Ltd.* ([1955] 2 All E.R. 557) disapproved.

Appeal allowed.

[As to the parties' rights on repudiation by a hirer of a hire-purchase agreement, see 19 HALSBURY'S LAWS (3rd Edn.) 550, 551, para. 891; and for cases on the subject and as to damages, see 26 DIGEST (Repl.) 669-671, *50-61.*

As to the measure of damages in actions of trover and detinue, see 38 HALSBURY'S LAWS (3rd Edn.) 791-793, paras. 1317, 1318; as to the measure of damages where the plaintiff has a limited interest, see ibid., 796, para. 1324; and for cases on the subject, see 46 DIGEST (Repl.) 512-515, *583-605.*]

Cases referred to:

Belsize Motor Supply Co. v. *Cox,* [1911-13] All E.R. Rep. 1084; [1914] 1 K.B. 244; 83 L.J.K.B. 261; 110 L.T. 151; 26 Digest (Repl.) 660, *16.*

Edmondson v. *Nuttall,* (1864), 17 C.B.N.S. 280; 34 L.J.C.P. 102; 114 E.R. 113; 46 Digest (Repl.) 514, *596.*

United Dominions Trust (Commercial), Ltd. v. *Parkway Motors, Ltd.,* [1955] 2 All E.R. 557; [1955] 1 W.L.R. 719; 26 Digest (Repl.) 669, *53.*

Appeal.

This was an appeal in an action brought by Wickham Holdings, Ltd. against Brooke House Motors Ltd., who were proprietors of Starnes Motors, by writ issued on Sept. 16, 1965. The plaintiff, which was a finance company, by its statement of claim endorsed on the writ alleged that it was the owner of a Rover motor car, index number 9789 PU, which it hired to Derek Edward Pattinson, subject to the terms of a hire-purchase agreement dated Oct. 28, 1964. The finance company alleged that Mr. Pattinson wrongly and without its consent parted with the possession of the motor car to the defendants. The finance

Distinguished in CHUBB CASH LTD v J CRILLEY & SON [1983] 2 All ER 294

company alleged that the defendants were detaining the motor car notwith- A
standing a specific request in writing dated Sept. 6, 1965, to deliver it up.   The
finance company claimed the return of the motor car or its value, and damages
for its detention.   By their defence delivered on Oct. 15, 1965, the defendants
denied that the finance company was the owner of the motor car and after pleading various matters, briefly referred to in the judgment at p. 119, letters G to I, post;
the defendants denied that the finance company was entitled to the motor car   B
or to damages for its illegal detention, and averred that the finance company
was entitled only to such moneys as were payable under the hire-purchase
agreement, which sums they had at all times been ready and willing to pay.
At the trial of the action on June 17, 1966, FENTON ATKINSON, J., awarded the
finance company £440 damages.   By notice of appeal served on July 27, 1966,
the defendants sought an order that this judgment should be set aside and that   C
judgment should be entered for the defendants on the grounds, among others,
that the judge had erred in law in holding that the defendants illegally detained
the motor car and in holding that the finance company was entitled to the motor
car or its value, and in holding that the defendants were liable to the finance
company in the sum of £440 based on the trade value of the motor car at the
time of the judgment together with a sum in respect of general damages for   D
illegal detention.

Douglas Draycott, Q.C., and *John A. Baker* for the defendants, the dealers.
P. Sheridan for the plaintiffs, the finance company.

LORD DENNING, M.R.: In October, 1964, Mr. Pattinson got a Rover
three litre on hire-purchase from a finance company called Wickham Holdings,
Ltd. The cash price of it was £834. The finance charges were £54. The option   E
fee was £1. So the total hire-purchase price was £889. He paid £234 cash
down. He had to pay the balance over the next twelve months at £54 10s. a
month, the first instalment being on Nov. 28, 1964. The hire-purchase agreement had all the usual clauses on the back. Mr. Pattinson paid the first seven
months instalments quite regularly up to May 28, 1965, amounting to £381 10s.
So altogether he had paid £234 cash down and £381 10s. instalments, making   F
£615 10s. on this Rover car out of a total hire-purchase price of £889.   So he had
paid three-quarters of the price: and was well up to date.

Early in June, 1965, Mr. Pattinson thought he would trade the Rover in for
another car. He went to a firm of dealers called Starnes Motors, who were owned
by Brooke House Motors, Ltd. On July 11, 1965, these dealers telephoned to the
finance company and asked the company what was the " settlement figure " for   G
the Rover. The finance company said that the amount required to complete
was £274 10s., but it would accept £270 for settlement within seven days. The
finance company confirmed this in writing to the dealers saying:

" Re:—D. E. Pattinson, Rover—9789 PU. We confirm our telephone
coversation that the amount required to complete the above account is £270,   H
providing this sum is received within the next seven days."

On receipt of this information, the dealers entered into a transaction with Mr.
Pattinson. They let him have another car and accepted this Rover car in part
exchange, making him an allowance for it. They did some repairs to the Rover
costing £50, and later sold it. But meanwhile the dealers had made an unfortunate mistake.   They had intended to send the £270 to the finance company   I
within the seven days; but they overlooked it. They mislaid the letter from
the finance company and never sent the £270. It appears that the director was
on holiday. They were very rushed and forgot all about it.

The finance company soon found out what had happened, and determined to
take advantage of it. The finance company claimed that Mr. Pattinson, by
selling the Rover to the dealers, had broken the hire-purchase agreement, and
that the finance company was entitled to take the car. On July 23, 1965, the
finance company wrote to Mr. Pattinson saying:

" From information received it would appear that you have disposed of our vehicle and as this is a serious breach of our agreement we hereby give you formal notice terminating the hiring."

On Sept. 2, 1965, they sent along some " car snatchers " to the dealers to try and get the car; but of course it had gone.   The dealers had resold it.   Then for the first time the dealers realised their mistake.   They telephoned the finance company and offered £270, and sent a cheque for that sum.   The finance company refused it.   The dealers asked: " What do you want? "   The finance company replied: " The car or its trade value."   A few days later the dealers offered not only the £270 but £15 or £20 more, but the finance company refused to accept it.   On Sept. 16, 1965, the finance company issued a writ against the dealers claiming the return of the Rover car, or its value, and damages for its detention.   The dealers offered £274 10s. and paid it into court.   The judge held that the car belonged to the finance company, and that the finance company was entitled to its trade value as at the date of judgment;   £415 less the £50 which the dealers had expended for repairs, making £365.   Then he added £75 damages for detention.   Together the total sum he awarded was £440.   The dealers appeal to this court and say that the finance company should only recover the £274 10s.

The case raises the important question: what is the proper measure of damages when the hirer resells the car?   The finance company relies on cl. 12 in the hire-purchase agreement:

" That neither the option of purchase, nor any other rights or interests under this agreement, nor the vehicle or any interest therein, shall be disposed of or be assignable on the part of the hirer or by anyone claiming under him, and any assignment or disposition or attempted assignment or disposition of the same shall be void, and shall render nugatory and absolutely determine the hirer's rights under this agreement."

The finance company says that, when Mr. Pattinson traded in the Rover car to the dealers (without the £270 having been paid in settlement), his rights in the agreement and in the car automatically determined: that thenceforward the car belonged absolutely to the finance company without any rights in Mr. Pattinson or anyone else; and that accordingly the finance company can recover the car or its full value.   It does not matter that the finance company has already received £615 10s. (three-quarters of its value).   The finance company can, it says, recover the full value of the car as damages in detinue or in conversion, without giving any credit for what the finance company has already received.

The dealers say, first, that the finance company waived the clause forbidding assignment.   They rely on the practice in the trade which they state in the pleadings:

" Further that notwithstanding any alleged terms purporting to restrict the rights of the said Derek Edward Pattinson to part with possession of the car, that it is, and has been for as long as the devices of hire-purchase agreements have been in operation, a recognised mercantile practice for persons in positions similar to the said Pattinson to sell their cars subject to the payments by the purchasers of outstanding charges.   Further it is a recognised mercantile practice for purchasers to telephone finance houses and acquaint them with the fact of a sale and obtain by telephone what is called ' a settlement figure ' which is the amount due to such finance houses, less a rebate by reason of speedier payment than is in the agreement provided."

That practice was admitted by the finance company in its reply.   The dealers say that on the faith of this practice and their telephone conversation of June 11, 1965, and the letter, they bought the car from Mr. Pattinson, and that this amounted to a binding waiver or estoppel.   I have some doubt about this.   If there was any waiver, it was conditional on the money being paid, namely, £270 within seven days, or £274 10s. within a reasonable time.   No such sum was paid or tendered within due time.

Even so, there remains the important question: what is the proper measure of damage? It is a familiar situation. The hirer of a motor car, who has got it on hire-purchase wrongfully sells it to someone else. The hiring is thereupon automatically determined. The finance company claims the return of the car and damages for detention or, alternatively, damages for conversion. In such a case the finance company in my opinion is not entitled to the full value of the car. The finance company is only entitled to what it has lost by the wrongful act of the defendant. I am well aware, of course, that prima facie in conversion the measure of damages is the value of the goods at the date of the conversion. That does not apply, however, where the plaintiff, immediately prior to the conversion, has only a limited interest in the goods: see *Edmondson* v. *Nuttall* (1), per WILLES, J. Take this case. The hirer had a most valuable interest in the car. He had paid already £615 10s. towards the purchase price and had the right to buy it outright on paying another £274 10s. The interest of the finance company was limited correspondingly. Its interest was limited to securing the payment of the outstanding £274 10s. It is entitled to be compensated for the loss of that interest, and no more. This was so held by CHANNELL, J., in the well known case of *Belsize Motor Supply Co.* v. *Cox* (2). As WINN, L.J., pointed out in the course of the argument, immediately prior to the wrongful sale, the high probability was that the finance company would only get out of this transaction another £274 10s.; either because Mr. Pattinson would complete the purchase, or because a purchaser would pay the " settlement figure ". That is all that the finance company has lost and all that it should recover. It would be most unjust that the finance company should recover twice as much as it has lost.

As against this view, we were referred to *United Dominions Trust (Commercial), Ltd.* v. *Parkway Motors, Ltd.* (3). In that case the hire-purchase price of a van was £626 3s. The hirer paid £529 19s. and resold it when the outstanding balance was only £96 4s. The finance company refused to accept this £96 and claimed the full value of the van, £350. McNAIR, J., awarded them the £350. That was four times as much as the finance company had lost. He was referred to the *Belsize* case (2), but distinguished it on this ground. In the *Belsize* case (2) the hire-purchase agreement contained a simple prohibition that " the hirer shall not re-let sell or part with the possession " of the goods. In the *United Dominions Trust* case (3), it contained a prohibition that the hirer " shall not sell, offer for sale, assign or charge the goods or the benefit of the agreement ". The only distinction is that in the *United Dominions Trust* case (3) the printed form contained the extra words " or the benefit of the agreement ". This distinction, said McNAIR, J., made all the difference: and entitled him to award the finance company the full value of the van. I must confess that this distinction drawn by McNAIR, J., is too fine for me. I cannot subscribe to it. And I am glad to see that in the latest edition of MAYNE AND McGREGOR ON DAMAGES (12th Edn.), p. 611, note 46, it is said that the distinction " seems inconsistent with the principles of the earlier cases ". The same was said in SALMOND ON TORTS (13th Edn.), p. 284, note 76. I think that the *United Dominions Trust* case (3) was wrongly decided.

I base my decision on this. In a hire-purchase transaction there are two proprietary interests, the finance company's interest and the hirer's interest. If the hirer wrongfully sells the goods or the benefit of the agreement, in breach of the agreement, then the finance company are entitled to recover what they have lost by reason of his wrongful act. That is normally the balance outstanding on the hire-purchase price; but they are not entitled to more than they have lost.

I would, therefore, allow the appeal. The judgment below should be varied

---

(1) (1864), 17 C.B.N.S. 280 at p. 294.
(2) [1911-13] All E.R. Rep. 1084; [1914] 1 K.B. 244.
(3) [1955] 2 All E.R. 557.

by substituting for the figure of £440, the sum of £274 10s.   We were told, however, that the finance company has claimed another instalment of £54 10s. from
Mr. Pattinson, and has received it.   So this must come off too.

DANCKWERTS, L.J.: I agree.   It is clear, of course, that at the time of
the incident which has given rise to the present controversy, the hirer of the car
had paid something like £615 10s. against the hire-purchase price of £889.   He
apparently was doing a deal of some sort with the defendants, Brooke House
Motors, Ltd.   What happened, as found by the judge, was that, when an enquiry
was made of the finance company, a Mr. Dulson checked up from a file and said
that the amount required to complete was £274 10s., but that he would accept
£270 for settlement within seven days.   He was asked to confirm the figure and
Mr. Dulson indicated that he would confirm it in writing.   He then wrote the
letter of June 11, 1965, which is in these terms:

" We confirm our telephone conversation that the amount required to
complete the above account is £270, providing this sum is received within
the next seven days."

As I construe that letter, it is not simply confirmation of the figure of £270 but
is confirmation of the conversation which took place on that day, as indeed the
letter says.   Therefore, it also includes the agreement or suggestion, whichever
one likes to call it, that £274 10s. would be accepted in completion of the hire-
purchase agreement.   Unfortunately, a mistake was made.   It is quite clear that
the dealers intended to take up the transaction and they acted on that by acquiring
the car from the hirer.

Now it seems to me that in those circumstances there was a representation on
behalf of the finance company which was acted on by the dealers, and the
finance company is not in a position, therefore, to go back on the terms which
they quoted.   Whether it is put on the ground of estoppel or on the ground of
waiver, it does not matter very much: it comes to very much the same thing.
The result was to waive the provisions of cl. 12 and cl. 15 of the hire-purchase
agreement.   The dealers quite clearly were ready and willing to pay the sum
which was required to be paid, and although no doubt the matter depended on
due payment, the dealers were ready to perform that condition; and even if the
statement was conditional on payment, they were ready and willing to carry out
the matter by proper payment.   So it seems to me that the finance company
was not entitled to refuse the sum tendered on behalf of the dealers.   When the
dealers' manager came, he was prepared to pay more than £270 if necessary,
but that was refused by the finance company.

Then the finance company attempted to terminate the hire-purchase agreement by a notice on July 23.   In view of having waived the terms of the hire-
purchase agreement, the finance company had in my view no right to do that.
It is quite clear that at all times the finance company knew that it was dealing
with dealers and that the dealers were preparing to purchase the car.   It would
be monstrous if the finance company could go back on that interview and sue
now on the terms that the hire-purchase agreement was at an end.

I also agree that it would be quite wrong that the finance company should be
entitled to recover more than the amount of its loss by non-payment of the sum
required to complete the payment on the hire-purchase agreement.   The loss in
case of non-performance could only be the amount which had not been paid and
the finance company should not be entitled to recover £440, or in other words
about twice the amount of its real loss.

As regards the decision of McNair, J., in United Dominions Trust (Commercial),
Ltd. v. Parkway Motors, Ltd. (4), I agree with Lord Denning, M.R., that the
distinction which the judge drew in that case was not well founded, and I think,
therefore, that it was wrongly decided.   I would also allow the appeal.

(4) [1955] 2 All E.R. 557.

WINN, L.J.: I agree that this appeal should be allowed. I must confess
that I entertain more doubt than my lords about the suggested invalidity of the
decision of McNair, J., in *United Dominions Trust (Commercial), Ltd.* v. *Parkway
Motors, Ltd.* (5). I prefer not to express any opinion myself about the correctness
of that decision, but I do not think that it matters in the present case.

Very briefly, since I do not intend to go into this matter at any length, I
express the opinion, for myself, that it is right for the court, as indeed counsel on
both sides have invited the court, to pay attention to the business reality of this
transaction and to have regard to what the men concerned in the telephone
conversation and the writer of the letter of June 11, which partially but only
partially confirmed that conversation, were thinking about and minded to state.
It is quite clear, I think, that one of the reasons why dealers, or individuals, to
whom a car is offered for sale and who are told or discover that it is or has been
the subject of a hire-purchase agreement, get in touch at once with the finance
company which is party to the agreement, is to find out whether or not the
agreement is still in force and valid or whether the finance company is minded
to terminate it and to treat the hirer's original rights under it as no longer
subsisting.

It follows then that the substance of the conversation which took place and
led to the letter was really this: " Is there an account in Mr. Pattinson's name
relating to Rover No. so and so which can be cleared by a payment? If so,
what is the amount required to settle the account? ": to which the answer, as the
judge has found, was: " £274 10s. but we are quite ready to take £270 providing
we get it within seven days. " The dealers were rather pleased no doubt to get that
reduction, though it was a small reduction. The person speaking for the dealers
said: " Will you confirm that figure of £270 to me? ". That is all that the letter
purports to do: it confirms that £270 will be accepted providing it is received
within seven days. It does not refer to £274 10s., but the effect of the intimation,
taken as a whole, received by the dealers is: " Yes, it is all in order: there is an
account which can be cleared for £274 10s.: you can treat this car, therefore,
as one which, subject to the clearance of the account by payment of that amount
within a reasonable time, or, if you prefer it, £270 within seven days, you can
safely deal with and get a good title and pass a good title in respect of the car ".
I do not find in the judge's findings of fact about the telephone conversation or
in this letter any stipulation either of a condition precedent that payment should
be made, that payment should be received, or that any cheque sent should be
cleared and the proceeds collected before any dealing took place with regard to
the car by the dealers with Mr. Pattinson: nor any condition subsequent to the
effect that, if no payment of £274 10s. was received within a reasonable time, any
intervening dealings would be tortious vis-à-vis the finance company in its
proprietary interest in respect of this car.

I agree entirely with what has been said by my lords about the measure of
damages and think that the right approach is for the court to ask itself: what
would have been the value of this car to this finance company on a balance of
probabilities in all the prevailing circumstances had not this mistake so unfortunately been made by someone in the dealers' office? It would have been,
I think, £274 10s.

Accordingly, I am in favour of allowing this appeal.

Appeal allowed. Leave to appeal to House of Lords refused.

Solicitors: *Beach & Beach* (for the defendants, the dealers); *Montague and
Cox & Cardale* (for the plaintiffs, the finance company).

[*Reported by* F. GUTTMAN, ESQ., *Barrister-at-Law.*]

---

(5) [1955] 2 All E.R. 557.

DAVIS *v.* DAVIS.

[COURT OF APPEAL, CIVIL DIVISION (Willmer, Harman and Salmon, L.JJ.),
October 21, 24, 1966.]

*Divorce—Maintenance of wife—Lump sum payment—Alternative or additional
to annual sum—Factors to be regarded—Wife's fortune, husband's ability
to pay, parties' conduct—Wealthy husband—Wife had no assets nor income—
Judge's discretion—Principle on which Court of Appeal may interfere with
exercise of discretion—Matrimonial Causes Act* 1965 (c. 72), s. 16 (1).

The husband was divorced by the wife on the ground of cruelty. He
was the chairman of the Rank Organisation and director of several other
companies. His net capital assets were worth not less than £400,000 and
his income was between £27,000 and £40,000 a year. The wife had married
the husband in 1954, giving up her career as an actress (she was at the
peak of that career, being then in her middle thirties), but she had no savings
and no income. Each party had two children by a previous marriage, all
four having been accepted as children of the family but being substantially
grown up at the time of the divorce. The allegations of cruelty in the wife's
divorce petition, which was undefended, showed the husband in a very
bad light; but the wife had had an adulterous association with one man,
which had occurred, according to her discretion statement, only after she
had been reduced to a state of considerable depression by her husband's
conduct. The wife was awarded maintenance at the rate of £8,500 a year
less tax, of which £4,500 was to be secured, and also a lump sum payment
of £10,000, increased on appeal to £15,000, under s. 16 (1)* of the Matrimonial
Causes Act 1965. On a further appeal in respect of the lump sum payment,

Held: (i) the same matters were to be taken into consideration in determining what was a reasonable lump sum payment to be ordered under
para. (*c*) of s. 16 (1) of the Matrimonial Causes Act 1965 as were to be
taken into consideration for the purposes of determining a sum to be secured
under para. (*a*) of that subsection (see p. 125, letter C, p. 127, letter I, and
p. 128, letter C, post).

(ii) although it would not be right for the Court of Appeal to interfere
unless it were satisfied that the judge had arrived at a wholly erroneous
estimate (see p. 126, letter E, post), yet, applying the considerations mentioned in para. (*a*) of s. 16 (1) to the circumstances of the present case, and
having regard to the wife's accustomed standard of living during marriage
and the prospective cost of establishing a new home, the amount awarded
by the judge had been so much too little that the Court of Appeal would
interfere and a lump sum payment of £25,000 would be ordered (see p. 127,
letters A, H and I, and p. 128, letter C, post).

Appeal allowed.

[As to the amount of maintenance in divorce see 12 HALSBURY'S LAWS
(3rd Edn.) 436-438, para. 982; and for cases on the subject see 27 DIGEST (Repl.)
616-620, *5765-5791.*

For the Matrimonial Causes Act 1965, s. 16 (1), see 45 HALSBURY'S STATUTES
(2nd Edn.) 468.]

Cases referred to:
> *N. v. N.*, [1928] All E.R. Rep. 462; 138 L.T. 693; 27 Digest (Repl.) 618,
> *5772.*
> *Schlesinger* v. *Schlesinger*, [1960] 1 All E.R. 721; [1960] P. 191: [1960] 3
> W.L.R. 83; Digest (Cont. Vol. A) 786, *5660a.*

Interlocutory Appeal.

This was an appeal by the wife against an order of ORR, J., made on July 29,
1966, varying an order of Mr. Registrar TOWNLEY-MILLERS made on June 27,

---

* Section 16 (1) is set out at p. 124, letter I, to p. 125, letter A, post.

Principle stated by WILLMER, L.J.,
at p. 126, *applied in* HAKLUYTT *v.*
HAKLUYTT. [1968] 2 All E.R. 863.

Dictum of WILLMER LJ at 126 applied
in MILLWARD v MILLWARD [1971]
3 All ER 526

1966. By the registrar's order the husband was ordered to pay or cause to be
paid to the wife maintenance for herself in the lump sum of £10,000 and also
as from Oct. 14, 1965, further maintenance for herself during their joint lives
until further order at the rate of £8,500 per annum less tax payable monthly,
of which sum £4,500 per annum was to be secured to the wife for her life until
further order on security to be agreed or referred to a registrar in default of
agreement. The order was varied by the judge who substituted the sum of £15,000
for the lump sum of £10,000. The grounds of appeal were that the lump sum
as so varied was insufficient because the judge did not take properly into account
the amount of the husband's assets, the lack of the wife's assets, the financial
sacrifice made by the wife in giving up her career, the amount needed by the
wife in order to re-establish herself on an appropriate scale bearing in mind the
scale at which the parties lived during the marriage, the amount with which the
husband would be left after making the payment of the lump sum to the wife,
and the general circumstances of the case; and further that the judge did not
look at the matter from an equitable point of view, as he ought to have done.

G. H. Crispin, Q.C., and Joseph Jackson for the wife.
Sir Peter Rawlinson, Q.C., and F. M. Drake for the husband.

WILLMER, L.J.: This is an appeal by leave of this court from an interlocutory order made in chambers by ORR, J., on appeal from an order of Mr.
Registrar TOWNLEY-MILLERS, relating to the maintenance of a wife by her
divorced husband. The question at issue relates to the award of a lump sum
to the wife in addition to maintenance and secured provision. The wife's application was made in pursuance of s. 16 (1) of the Matrimonial Causes Act 1965.

The husband is an extremely wealthy man, being chairman of the Rank
Organisation and a director of a number of other companies. He enjoys a very
substantial income and is also possessed of very large capital assets. The wife
was therefore clearly entitled to expect an order for maintenance on a very
liberal scale. In fact the registrar ordered maintenance at the rate of £8,500
a year less tax, of which he directed that £4,500 a year should be secured. In
addition he made an order for a lump sum payment of £10,000. The wife was
satisfied with the order for maintenance and secured provision, but appealed
to the judge against the lump sum award of £10,000. It was her case that in
all the circumstances she was entitled to such a capital sum as would enable
her to set herself up by buying and furnishing a house, and providing herself
with a car. For this purpose it was submitted that £10,000 was much too low,
having regard to the standard of living to which she was accustomed. The
judge said that he differed with reluctance from the registrar, but nevertheless
increased the lump sum award to £15,000. It appears from the note of his reasons,
which has been placed before us, that he was acceding to the contention that
the wife should be able to buy a house, but was not prepared to take into account
the cost of acquiring a car. The wife now appeals to this court, contending that
the figure of £15,000 is still much too low to enable her to set herself up in
accordance with a reasonable standard of living.

Until recently the court had no power to make an award of a capital sum
for maintenance. The power was first conferred by s. 5 (1) of the Matrimonial
Causes Act 1963, and is now contained in s. 16 (1) of the consolidating Act of
1965, which provides:

"(1) On granting a decree of divorce or at any time thereafter (whether
before or after the decree is made absolute), the court may, if it thinks fit
and subject to sub-s. (3) of this section, make one or more of the following
orders—(a) an order requiring the husband to secure to the wife, to the
satisfaction of the court, such lump or annual sum for any term not exceeding
her life as the court thinks reasonable having regard to her fortune (if any),
his ability and the conduct of the parties; (b) an order requiring the husband

A   to pay to the wife during their joint lives such monthly or weekly sum for
her maintenance as the court thinks reasonable; (*c*) an order requiring the
husband to pay to the wife such lump sum as the court thinks reasonable."

We have been informed that this is the first case in which the question of a
lump sum payment has arisen for determination, at any rate in this court. It
therefore falls to us to determine for the first time what are the considerations
B   by which the court should be guided.

    It is to be observed that in para. (*a*) of the subsection the word " reasonable "
is qualified by the words " having regard to her fortune (if any), his ability
and the conduct of the parties "; but no such qualification appears in para. (*b*)
and para. (*c*). Nevertheless, I am of opinion that as a matter of construction
the same matters must be taken into consideration under para. (*b*) and para. (*c*)
C   as have to be considered under para. (*a*) in determining what is reasonable.
Subject to that, Parliament has given us no guidance as to the circumstances
in which a lump sum should be awarded, or as to the matters to be taken into
account in assessing the amount. In those circumstances I will deal first with
the three matters to which I have already referred, viz., the fortune of the wife,
the husband's ability to pay and the conduct of the parties.

D   For this purpose it is necessary to refer briefly to the history of the marriage.
This took place on Mar. 3, 1954. At that time the wife was a woman in her
middle thirties and the husband was a man about fourteen years older. At
the time of the marriage the wife was at the peak of her career as an actress,
and this career she gave up in order to marry the husband. She had been married
before and had two children, then aged eight and six years old respectively.
E   In the case of the husband this was his fifth marriage. He also had two children
from a previous marriage, their ages at the time of this marriage being five
and four years respectively. All four of these children were accepted by both
parents as " children of the family ". They are all now substantially grown up,
and since the separation the wife's own two children have stayed with her,
and the husband's own children have stayed with him. As to the wife's children,
F   the elder, who is a boy, is now training for a career as a chartered accountant;
the younger, a girl, is training as a model.

    The wife, although she had enjoyed a successful career as an actress, and no
doubt had been earning a substantial income, does not appear to have saved
anything. At the time of the marriage she did not have, and she still does
not have, any capital assets of her own, apart from her jewellery and furs.
G   The husband, as I have said, was and is an extremely wealthy man. There
was no agreement as to the exact details of his resources, nor do I think that
the precise figures matter; it is sufficient to say that he enjoys an income
variously stated as ranging between £27,000 and £40,000 a year, which is derived
partly from what he earns and partly from investments. It is admitted that
his net capital assets are worth not less than £400,000. His assets include a
H   substantial estate in Kent, where the matrimonial home was established, and
for the rest consist in shares, largely in companies of which he is a director.
He has also no doubt enjoyed a number of the " fringe benefits " often enjoyed
by people in his position, such as the use of cars belonging to one or other of
his companies. He also had the use of a flat in London belonging to the Rank
Organisation, for which he pays what appears to me to be the very moderate
I   rent of £450 a year. It is in this flat that the wife is now residing, but it is clear
that she has no security of tenure. So much for the fortune of the wife and the
husband's ability to pay.

    As to the conduct of the parties, the wife's petition was on the ground of
cruelty. The petition is a lengthy document setting out a number of grave
allegations, some of them of an extremely unpleasant nature. I do not think
that it is necessary in this judgment to refer to them in detail. The husband
filed no answer, but allowed the case to go undefended; a decree nisi was pronounced on July 13, 1965, and that has since been made absolute. The husband

must therefore be taken to admit the substantial truth of the wife's allegations; and if they be only approximately true they do undoubtedly show up the husband in a very bad light.

The wife herself, however, was not without fault, as she had to ask for the discretion of the court to be exercised in her favour. She filed the usual discretion statement, and that described an adulterous association which she had had with one man, beginning about the end of 1962 and continuing for a year or so. That was at a time when she was still living with the husband; but, as she said in her discretion statement, it was only after she had been reduced to a state of considerable depression in consequence of the husband's conduct. The registrar, we are told, was disposed to take a lenient view of the wife's behaviour when compared with the conduct of which she accused the husband. On this appeal it has not been suggested that we should do otherwise than take a reasonably lenient view of the wife's adultery, having regard to all the circumstances; but it is clearly a factor which has to be taken into consideration in relation to her claim for maintenance.

Bearing those considerations in mind, I come to the question: did the judge award a proper sum by way of lump sum payment? The only guidance to be obtained from the words of the statute is that the sum must be such " as the court thinks reasonable having regard to " the matters to which I have already referred. It seems to me that in those circumstances the question is one very much for the discretion of the judge who has to deal with it. I do not think that it would be right for this court to interfere unless satisfied that the judge below arrived at a wholly erroneous figure. In my judgment an appeal against the quantum of a lump sum award should be approached in very much the same way as an appeal against an award of damages.

It is to be observed from the terms of the section (1) that a lump sum payment may be ordered either in lieu of or in addition to maintenance. As a practical matter, it is clear that an order for a lump sum payment can only properly be made against a husband possessed of sufficient capital assets to justify it. It is not to be expected, therefore, that the question is likely to arise except in relatively rare cases. In the present case there can be no doubt that the husband is in a position to make a substantial capital payment; but, in assessing his capacity to do so, regard must be had to the fact that quite a substantial part of his capital assets must be tied up in order to serve as security for the secured provision of £4,500 a year.

The real difficulty which I have felt is to ascertain what the legislature had in mind in making this provision for a lump sum payment, either alternative to or coupled with an order for maintenance. I apprehend that one type of case in which a lump sum payment might be appropriate would be one where there was a wealthy husband whose wife desired to set herself up in business. In such a case, assuming that the wife was a woman who had experience in business, it could well be reasonable and appropriate that a lump sum payment should be made; but that is not this case. What is suggested here is that the wife, who while living with her husband has been accustomed to a high standard of living, playing the part of wife to the chairman of a large commercial organisation, should be entitled to such a lump sum payment as will enable her to set herself up in a home commensurate with that to which she has been accustomed.

There is no doubt that, in assessing an ordinary claim for maintenance, it is proper to have regard to the standard of living to which the wife was accustomed during the marriage; that appears from the dictum of LORD MERRIVALE, P., in N. v. N. (2), which was cited and followed by SACHS, J., in *Schlesinger* v. *Schlesinger* (3), I see no reason why the same should not apply to a claim made

(1) The words " in lieu of, or in addition to " an order for maintenance in s. 5 (1) of the Matrimonial Causes Act 1963, 43 HALSBURY'S STATUTES (2nd Edn.) 439, are not reproduced in s. 16 (1) of the Act of 1965.
(2) [1928] All E.R. Rep. 462 at p. 466.
(3) [1960] 1 All E.R. 721 at p. 725; [1960] P. 191 at p. 197.

A under the Act of 1965 for a lump sum payment. If the wife has been accustomed during the marriage to live in a luxuriously appointed house, I think that she is entitled to ask for a lump sum payment of such an amount as will provide her with a standard of living commensurate with that to which she has been accustomed. I use the word " commensurate ", for it must be obvious that she can hardly expect exactly equivalent accommodation; it would be not

B " reasonable " to award enough for that.

It has been argued on the other side that it would not be " reasonable " to award any larger amount than that already ordered by way of a lump sum in addition to the very large award of maintenance. It has been suggested that Parliament really intended that the two forms of relief should be alternative, leaving the wife to opt for that which better suits her case. Here it is said that

C the wife in effect opted for a very large annual sum by way of maintenance, and consequently should not expect to receive any larger amount by way of lump sum payment. I do not think that this argument has much force in view of the words of the section, which specifically empowers the court to award *both* maintenance *and* a lump sum. Moreover, while the rate of maintenance looks on the face of it very large, this is to some extent illusory having regard to the

D incidence of taxation. We were indeed informed that after deduction of income tax and surtax, the sum awarded for maintenance would leave little more than £3,000 a year in the hands of the wife. Clearly she could not be in a position to make any substantial contribution out of her maintenance to the cost of setting up a new home.

Is the sum awarded by the judge then " reasonable " having regard to what

E the wife is entitled to expect? Such evidence as is before the court confirms, what I think must be common knowledge, that £15,000 does not go very far towards purchasing house property in the sort of neighbourhood where a woman with this background can reasonably expect to live. Moreover, the expenses of setting up a home do not stop at the purchase of a property, for when it is purchased it will probably require decoration, and will certainly require furnishing. It is

F true that in other proceedings the wife is claiming as her own some of the furniture from the matrimonial home. We have been told that negotiations are in progress which may lead to some agreement with regard to this. Even assuming, however, that the wife does get a substantial quantity of furniture from this source, it would, I think, be closing one's eyes to reality not to recognise that setting up a new home is bound to be an expensive adventure. Moreover,

G I think there is force in the contention that the lump sum to be awarded should, if possible, be sufficient to leave something over, after establishing a new home, by way of liquid capital which can be used, for instance, for buying a car or for dealing with any emergency that may arise, or even to put by for use on a rainy day. If that is what is " reasonable " in circumstances such as those in the present case, I think it must be obvious that £15,000 is too little, and so much

H too little that this court is bound to interfere. In my judgment the award of £15,000 should be increased to one of £25,000.

I should have been disposed to award rather more had it not been for the fact of the wife's own misconduct. Since, however, as I have pointed out, the relevant section of the Act of 1965 is in my judgment to be read as requiring the court to take into consideration the conduct of the parties, the award must, I think,

I be somewhat lower than it otherwise might have been. In those circumstances I would allow the appeal and substitute an order for a lump sum payment of £25,000.

HARMAN, L.J.: I agree. The only importance of this matter, except to the parties, is the attention to be paid to s. 16 of the Matrimonial Causes Act 1965, which we are told has not come before the court (in public, at any rate) hitherto. Section 16 (1), in mentioning " one or more of the following orders ", rules out the possibility that paras. (*a*), (*b*) and (*c*) which follow are alternative.

They may be aggregate. That is clear enough. Nevertheless, it seems to me A right to say that the amount any one of them, or the burden that any one of them casts on the husband must have its effect on the amount of any other of them. Thirdly, I agree with WILLMER, L.J., in thinking that the words " reasonable having regard to her fortune (if any), his ability and the conduct of the parties " must be read into para. (b) and para. (c), though for some reason not apparent to me the draftsman has omitted them. Here there can be no B doubt that the wife has no fortune, and that the husband has ample ability; and therefore one is left with " the conduct of the parties ", as to which I say no more than that I agree with my lord. As to the rest, WILLMER, L.J., has so fully covered the grounds that it would be otiose for me to repeat them in such terms as I could command. I would allow the appeal.

C

　　SALMON, L.J.: I agree.

Appeal allowed. Order below varied by substituting the sum of £25,000 for £15,000.

Solicitors: *M. A. Jacobs & Sons* (for the wife); *Summer & Co.* (for the husband).

[*Reported by* F. A. AMIES, ESQ., *Barrister-at-Law*.]

D

E

PRACTICE DIRECTION.

House of Lords—Appeal—Law reports—List of authorities.

　　Counsel and agents engaged in House of Lords appeals are informed that the House of Lords library has five sets of the following:—Law Reports from F 1866, the English Reports, All England Reports, Criminal Appeal Reports, Reports of Patent Cases, Session Cases, Tax Cases, Weekly Law Reports, Statutes.

　　Where it is desired to refer to reports shown on the above list, it will suffice to submit lists of authorities as has been done in the past.

　　In cases where it is desired to refer to reports not shown on the above list, counsel and agents should set out these Reports separately on their lists of G authorities, *indicating clearly the particular passage to which reference is to be made.* Arrangements will then be made for photostat copies of these passages to be made, which will be available to their Lordships at the hearing of the appeal. In appeals in which it is proposed to cite a large number of passages which require to be photostatically copied, every effort should be made to lodge the list of authorities in the Judicial Office not less than seven days before the H hearing of the appeal.

　　Direction 30 amended accordingly.

DAVID STEPHENS,
Nov. 8, 1966.　　　　　　　　　　　　　　　　　　　Clerk of the Parliaments.

A   DUKE OF BUCCLEUCH AND ANOTHER
     v. INLAND REVENUE COMMISSIONERS.

[HOUSE OF LORDS (Lord Reid, Lord Morris of Borth-y-Gest, Lord Hodson,
   Lord Guest and Lord Wilberforce), October 24, 25 and 26, December 20,
   1966.]

B *Estate Duty—Valuation—Landed estate—Price that the property would fetch
     if sold in the open market at the deceased's death—Division of large estate
     into units and notional sale of each unit separately—Such division not an
     artificial division, but a proper one having regard to reality—Value of estate
     on the basis of realisation in many separate units substantially higher than
     its value if sold as a whole—Principal value of estate for estate duty purposes*
C *properly estimated on the basis of realisation in many separate units—
     Finance Act, 1894 (57 & 58 Vict. c. 30), s. 7 (5)—Finance (1909-10) Act,
     1910 (10 Edw. 7 c. 8), s. 60 (2).*

       Settled property became subject to estate duty on the death of the
   deceased. The property was shares in a company which were to be valued
   by reference to the company's assets. The assets included ten landed estates,
D comprising in all 119,000 acres of land. One of these estates was taken as a
   test; it comprised some 20,000 acres and was valued by the Inland Revenue
   Commissioners on a basis of being sold in 486* separate units. If it were
   sold as one whole, or if the compact main area of land were sold as an entity
   and only outlying areas of land were split off from it, the value would be
   about twenty per cent. less, since only a land developer or speculator
E would be likely to buy such a quantity of land. The appeal was determined
   on the basis that the division of the estate into 486 units was a natural and
   proper division, not an artificial division, having regard to the state of
   affairs actually existing on the estate. There was expert evidence that an
   actual realisation of the estate so divided would not be possible, owing to the
   number of units to be sold, within a reasonable time† (of the order of
F twelve months) after the death. The settlement trustees accordingly contended that the estate sold should be valued under s. 7 (5)‡ of the Finance
   Act, 1894, on the basis that it was realised substantially as one whole, viz.,
   as fetching only the lower price which a land developer might be expected to
   pay. By s. 60 (2) of the Finance (1909-10) Act, 1910, the estimate of value
   at the death was not to be reduced on account of all properties being assumed
G to be placed on the market at one time§.

       Held: the contention that it would be impossible actually to realise
   the estate, if sold in many separate lots, within a reasonable time after
   the death and that therefore the estate should be valued as substantially
   one whole, was in conflict with the scheme of the Finance Act, 1894, which
   required a hypothetical market to be assumed and which did not provide for
H any reduction in the value of a unit or the total of their values on account
   of the multiplicity of similar units to be realised or of the expenses of sales
   of the units; accordingly, as the appeal must be decided on the basis that
   at the date of the death the estate might properly be regarded as composed
   of 486 units of valuation, the principal value of the estate for the purposes
   of estate duty should be computed at the aggregate of the prices that these
I units would fetch if sold separately at the date of the death (see p. 135,
   letters D and F, p. 138, letter G, p. 139, letter E, p. 141, letter D, p. 143,
   letter H, p. 145, letter D, p. 147, letter C, and p. 148, letter H, post).

   * The figure of 486 represents the number of units into which so much of the estate
as was a compact estate in England was divided for the purpose of valuation; the total
number of units, 532, includes forty-six units which could be " hived off " as outlying
units.
      † The suggested period for such a realisation was seven years.
      ‡ The relevant terms of s. 7 (5) are printed at p. 131, letter E, post.
      § See, e.g., p. 139, letter I, post.

Earl of Ellesmere v. *Inland Revenue Comrs.* ([1918] 2 K.B. 735) considered and explained and dictum of SANKEY, J., as reported in 119 L.T. at p. 573, questioned.

Per LORD WILBERFORCE: the wording of the Finance Act, 1894, s. 7 (5) requires the gross open market price, i.e., what the purchaser pays, and not what the vendor ultimately receives, to be taken as the valuation figure; moreover, in making the valuation it is not legitimate to arrive at a higher price by supposing that expenditure, by way, e.g., of repair or improvement on the property has been made: but I do not think that this section neces- sarily prevents account being taken of the cost of lotting an estate, by which I mean preparing adequate separate particulars of existing units, or, in relation to moveables, cataloguing a collection (see p. 148, letters C and D, post; cf. p. 139, letter E, and p. 140, letter I, post).

Decision of the COURT OF APPEAL ([1965] 3 All E.R. 458) affirmed.

[**Editorial Note.** Elaborate sub-division of an estate into separate artificial units, if that course would increase the gross value, is not permissible (see, e.g., p. 134, letter B, p. 143, letter B, and p. 145, letter C, post).

As to the principal value of property for estate duty purposes, see 15 HALS- BURY'S LAWS (3rd Edn.) 71, 72, paras. 143-146; and for cases on the subject, see 21 DIGEST (Repl.) 55-58, *214-227*.

For the Finance Act, 1894, s. 7 (5), see 9 HALSBURY'S STATUTES (2nd Edn.) 362; and for the Finance (1909-10) Act, 1910, s. 60, see ibid., p. 404.]

Cases referred to:

Ellesmere (Earl) v. *Inland Revenue Comrs.*, [1918] 2 K.B. 735; 88 L.J.K.B. 337; 119 L.T. 568; 21 Digest (Repl.) 56, *211*.

Inland Revenue Comrs. v. *Crossman, Inland Revenue Comrs.* v. *Mann*, [1936] 1 All E.R. 762; [1937] A.C. 26; sub nom. *Re Crossman, Re Paulin*, 105 L.J.K.B. 450; 154 L.T. 570; 21 Digest (Repl.) 56, *219*.

Inland Revenue Comrs. v. *Marr's Trustees*, (1906), 44 Sc.L.R. 647.

Appeal.

This was an appeal by the appellants, Walter John Montague Douglas, Duke of Buccleuch, and Mary Alice Gascoyne, Dowager Duchess of Devonshire, trustees of the Chatsworth Settlement, from an order of the Court of Appeal (LORD DENNING, M.R., DANCKWERTS and WINN, L.JJ.), dated July 23, 1965, dismissing an appeal by the appellants from a decision of the Lands Tribunal (Erskine Simes, Esq., Q.C., H. P. Hobbs, Esq., and R. C. G. Fennell, Esq.), given on Jan. 15, 1965, determining the total value for estate duty purposes of ten estates in England owned by Chatsworth Estates Co., Ltd., at £3,176,646. Estate duty became chargeable on the estates in consequence of the death of the tenth Duke of Devonshire on Nov. 26, 1950. In an interim decision on May 4, 1964, the Lands Tribunal determined the value of one of the estates, the Hardwick Estate. The tribunal held that the value of the estate should be estimated on the basis that it was sold in 532 separate units, on which basis the respondent Inland Revenue Commissioners had valued it at £868,129. The tribunal found alternatively, however, that if forty-six units were sold as separate units, these comprising outlying portions of land, and if the remaining 486 units, which formed together a compact area, were sold as a single entity, they would realise £537,966 (twenty per cent. less than if the 486 separate units were sold separately at an aggregate of £672,458) making the total value only £733,637. On this alternative basis of sale substantially as one whole, for which the trustees contended, the value of the ten estates at the date of the death would have been £2,743,760.

Sir Andrew Clark, Q.C., R. E. Megarry, Q.C., and *W. J. Glover* for the trustees.
Sir Milner Holland, Q.C., W. L. Roots, Q.C., J. R. Phillips and *J. P. Warner* for the commissioners.

A   Their lordships took time for consideration.

December 20.   The following opinions were delivered.

LORD REID: My Lords, the appellants are trustees of a settlement made
by the tenth Duke of Devonshire in 1946.   The duke died on Nov. 26, 1950,
within five years of making the settlement and estate duty is admittedly payable
B   on the whole of the settled property.   This case is concerned with shares of the
Chatsworth Estates Co., Ltd., and admittedly they must be valued with reference
to the company's assets.   These included 119,000 acres of land in England.   In
1961 the respondents, the Commissioners of Inland Revenue, determined the
value of this land to be £3,176, 646.   The trustees appealed to the Lands Tribunal
maintaining that the valuation ought to be £2,743,760.   The tribunal upheld
C   the determination of the Commissioners and stated a Case for the decision of the
Court of Appeal (1), the question of law being: "Whether upon the findings of
fact we came to a correct decision in law."   On July 23, 1965, the Court of
Appeal (1) by a majority dismissed the appeal.

It is not very easy to determine what were the findings of fact of the tribunal
or to state precisely the question of law which must now be decided.   I think it
D   best first to state the relevant law, as I understand it, and then to attempt to
discover whether and if so where the tribunal misdirected themselves.   Section 7
of the Finance Act, 1894, provides that in determining the value of " an estate "
certain deductions are to be made.   Estate there means the whole estate.   Then
s. 7 (5) provides:

" The principal value of any property shall be estimated to be the price
E   which, in the opinion of the commissioners, such property would fetch if
sold in the open market at the time of the death of the deceased;"

In my view " any property " does not refer to the whole estate of the deceased.
His estate generally consists of a wide variety of different kinds of property—
land, chattels, and incorporeal rights—and it would clearly be impossible to
value it as a whole.   The context shows that " any property " must mean any
F   part of the estate which it is proper to treat as a unit for valuation purposes.
This case turns on the determination of what are the correct principles to apply
in subdividing an estate into units for valuation purposes, and it shows how
greatly the total value of the estate may differ according to how it has been
subdivided.   The statute is silent as to the proper methods of division.

Subsection (5) only applies after the division has been made, but I think that
G   it throws some light on this matter.   It requires an estimate of the price which a
particular unit would fetch if sold in a certain way, so one must envisage a hypothetical sale of the actual unit; and that sale must be supposed to have taken
place " in the open market " and " at the time of the death ".   The subsection
must mean the price which the property *would have fetched* if sold at the time
of the death.   I agree with the argument of the commissioners that " at the
H   time of the death " points to a definite time—the day on which the death occurred:
it does not mean within a reasonable time after the death.   No doubt the words
" at the time of " are capable of such a meaning, but I see nothing to recommend
this meaning in this context.   The value of some kinds of property fluctuates
from day to day and there at least a particular day must be taken.

There was some argument about the meaning of " in the open market ".
I   Originally no doubt when one wanted to sell a particular item of property one
took it to a market where buyers of that kind of property congregated.   Then
the owner received offers and accepted what he thought was the best offer that
he was likely to get; and for some kinds of property that is still done.   But
this phrase must also be applied to other kinds of property where that is
impossible.   In my view the phrase requires that the seller must take—or here
be supposed to have taken—such steps as are reasonable to attract as much

(1) [1965] 3 All E.R. 458;   [1966] 1 Q.B. 851.

competition as possible for the particular piece of property which is to be sold. **A** Sometimes this will be by sale by auction, sometimes otherwise. I suppose that the biggest open market is the stock exchange, where there is no auction. And there may be two kinds of market commonly used by owners wishing to sell a particular kind of property. For example it is common knowledge that many owners of houses first publish the fact that they wish to sell and then await offers: they only put the property up for auction as a last resort. I see **B** no reason for holding that in proper cases the former method could not be regarded as sale in the open market. Here, however, what must be envisaged is sale in the open market on a particular day. So there is no room for supposing that the owner would do as many prudent owners do—withdraw the property if he does not get a sufficient offer and wait until a time when he can get a better offer. The commissioners must estimate what the property would probably **C** have fetched on that particular day if it had then been exposed for sale, no doubt after such advance publicity as would have been reasonable.

I am confirmed in my opinion by the fact that the Act of 1894 permits no deduction from the price fetched of the expenses involved in the sale (except in the case of property abroad under s. 7 (3)). It is notorious that the rough and ready provisions of many sections of this Act can lead to great injustice **D** with estate duty at its present level; but one must construe the Act keeping in mind that the maximum rate of duty which it provided was eight per cent. Parliament—or the liberal government of the time—seems to have thought that it was best to keep the scheme simple and to omit things which justice would seem to require, if the practical difference with a low rate of duty would in most cases be negligible or would at worst be small. I find it impossible to suppose **E** that they can have contemplated that the kinds of hypothetical sale which they envisaged would involve heavy expenses. In applying the provisions of any Act one must always try to find a construction which is not unreasonable.

With these matters in view I turn to consider the main question of law in this case—how the whole estate of the deceased should be divided into units for separate valuation. Generally the estate will consist of what one may call **F** natural units—units or parcels of property which can be easily identified without there being any substantial difficulty or expense in carving them out of the whole estate. In my opinion it is implicit in the scheme of the Finance Act, 1894, that s. 7 (5) should be applied to each of such units, and there is no justification for requiring elaborate subdivision of natural units on the ground that if that had been done before the hypothetical sale the total price for the natural unit **G** would have been increased. We must take the estate as it was when the deceased died; often the price which a piece of property would fetch would be considerably enhanced by small expense in minor repair or cleaning, which would make the property more attractive to the eye of the buyer. Admittedly that cannot be supposed to have been done; and I can see no more justification for requiring the supposition that natural units have been subdivided. This subsection applies **H** to all kinds of property. A library was instanced by WINN, L.J. (2). Generally there would be little difficulty, delay or expense in getting someone knowledgeable to pick out valuable books for separate valuation, and I would therefore regard such books as natural units. Suppose, however, that the deceased had bought a miscellaneous and mixed lot of surplus stores intending to sort out and arrange them in saleable lots. That might involve a great deal of work, **I** time and expense, and I see no justification for requiring the supposition that that had been done and then valuing the saleable lots that would have emerged.

It is sometimes said that the estate must be supposed to have been realised in such a way that the best possible prices were obtained for its parts. But that cannot be a universal rule. Suppose that the owner of a wholesale business dies possessed of a large quantity of hardware or clothing or whatever he deals

---

(2) See [1965] 3 All E.R. at p. 464, letters B, C; [1966] 1 Q.B. at p. 876.

A   in. It would have been possible by extensive advertising to obtain offers for small lots at something near retail prices. So it would have been possible to realise the stock at much more than wholesale prices. It would not have been reasonable and it would not have been economic, but it would have been possible. Counsel for the commissioners did not contend that that would be a proper method of valuation; but that necessarily amounts to an admission that there

B   is no universal rule that the best possible prices at the date of death must be taken.

    I have said that this Act applies rough and ready methods. It is vain to apply theoretical logic. The question of what units to value is a practical question to be solved by commonsense. So if the commissioners apply the right criteria there is no appeal; but in this case it is difficult to discover whether the

C   commissioners or the tribunal have applied the right criteria.

    The matter has been made more difficult by misconceptions about what seems to be the only authority, the case of the *Earl of Ellesmere* v. *Inland Revenue Comrs.* (3). We were invited to consider the report in the Law Times series; but I find that there is a notable discrepancy between the two reports, which I feel sure that counsel would have drawn to our attention had they been aware

D   of it. I find that in the Court of Appeal (4) LORD DENNING, M.R., adopted and gave great weight to a passage from the judgment of SANKEY, J., as reported in the Law Times, which is absent from the report in the Law Reports. I do not know what the practice was in 1918, but I suspect that the judgment in the Law Reports may have been revised by the learned judge and that the judgment in the Law Times was not. The report in the Law Reports appears over the initials

E   of the senior King's Bench reporter named in the title page of the volume, and I cannot believe that an experienced reporter would have cut out this passage without the authority of the judge himself. I think that it goes too far and on second thoughts SANKEY, J., may well have thought the same.

    The facts were that on the death of the late Earl his successor was advised by an eminent firm to sell as one lot an estate of 2,200 acres which comprised

F   a variety of agricultural holdings, business premises and woodlands. In 1915 it fetched £68,000. The purchaser resold in lots. By 1917 he had realised £65,000 and he still had unsold parts worth £16,000. The referee held the value at the date of death to be £75,618. Before SANKEY, J., the commissioners contended that, having regard to the varied character of the property and the fact that it did not all lie together, the price realised by a sale in one lot could not represent

G   the true value. SANKEY, J., said that there might be many cases where a sale to a single purchaser could not realise the price which the property would fetch in the open market. He instanced an owner selling as one lot a colliery and a draper's shop, and gave instances where the owner sold in one lot because he wanted money quickly. Then he said (5):

H   " But it does not at all follow that the price which he obtains under such circumstances is ' the price which it would fetch if sold in the open market '. What is meant by those words is the best possible price that is obtainable and what that is is largely, if not entirely, a question of fact. I can readily conceive cases in which a sale of the whole property in one lot would realise the true market price, but I can equally imagine cases in which it would not. Here the referee held that because the property was of a mis-

I   cellaneous character and not lying in a ring fence the price paid by the single purchaser was not the true value. I think he was entitled so to hold, and that the contention as to misdirection fails."

    I see nothing wrong with the decision, and, subject to what I have said about the best possible price, I would quarrel with nothing in the passage which I have quoted from the Law Reports. But in the Law Times there is interpolated

(3) [1918] 2 K.B. 735; 119 L.T. 568.
(4) See [1965] 3 All E.R. at p. 461; [1966] 1 Q.B. at p. 871.
(5) [1918] 2 K.B. at p. 740.

in that passage the passage, quoted by LORD DENNING, M.R., that the property **A**
must be sold "in such a manner and subject to such conditions as might reasonably be calculated to obtain for the vendor the best price for the property",
and this has been taken to justify elaborate and expensive subdivision of
natural units if that course would increase the gross price. If SANKEY, J.,
did delete this passage when he revised his judgment, I think that he was wise;
but it was strongly founded on by the commissioners in argument and it may **B**
well have misled the tribunal. They quote it in full in their interim decision.

The property assessed includes ten estates in England, and the commissioners
did not determine their valuation until eleven years after the duke's death.
They proceeded on the basis that these ten estates had to be notionally divided
into some 3,500 units and that each of these units had to be valued separately.
All that we learn from the tribunal about the way in which the estates were so **C**
divided is contained in a sentence in a letter from the commissioners and in a
short paragraph in the interim decision (6). The letter states that the valuation
had been made on the basis of such lotting of the whole property as was calculated
to produce the best price. Before the tribunal the Hardwick Estate (some
20,000 acres) alone was investigated, it being taken as typical. With regard
to it the tribunal say: **D**

> "For the purposes of arriving at the valuation, the estate had been
> divided into some 532 separate units, each unit representing a lot which,
> in the [commissioners'] view, would have commanded the best market
> price if sold on the date of the duke's death."

If the dubious passage in the judgment of SANKEY, J., were right if given the
meaning for which the commissioners contend, there would be no need to say **E**
more; and it must be said in fairness to the tribunal that the argument as
then presented for the trustees did not raise the method of lotting. So we do
not know whether or not substantially all the units which were valued separately
were what I have called natural units, nor do we know how much time, work
or expense was involved in the lotting or would have been involved if the owner
of these estates had decided to sell them in these units. What we do know **F**
is that the tribunal quote and apparently accept evidence of one of the trustees'
witnesses " that it would have been impossible to sell all the individual units
within a reasonable time of the date of death, and [he] took the view it would
take at least seven years". The commissioners' witness said that it would be
impossible to sell all the units within a year, but he did not say how long he
thought that it would take. The argument for the trustees before the tribunal **G**
and their first argument before your lordships was that this by itself was enough
to show that the commissioners' method must be wrong. For reasons which I
shall state in a moment I cannot accept that argument. Before I could reach
any decision in favour of the trustees I should at least have to know how far
this delay of seven years would have been caused by initial difficulties of lotting
and drawing up conditions of sale for these numerous lots, how far it would **H**
have been caused by the lack of sufficient professional men with the necessary
skill, and how far it would have been caused by a desire not to flood the market.

The ten estates to be valued were each managed as a separate unit at the
time of the Duke's death, and the trustees maintain that each should now be
valued as a single unit, subject to the excision and separate valuation of a
number of outlying parts, which were easily severable. The tribunal have **I**
found that, if that is the proper method of dividing the property for valuation,
the total value of these estates would be some £433,000 lower than the commission's valuation based on separate valuation of smaller units. The reason
for this large difference is that only speculators or property developers or
investors would be interested in buying entire estates. A buyer who intended to
resell the estate in small lots would have to incur the trouble and expense involved

(6) The interim decision was a decision given on May 4, 1964, relating to the Hardwick
Estate and assessing its value on the basis of its being sold in 532 separate units.

A   in dividing up the estate, he would have to lie out of his money for a long time, and he would expect to make a reasonable profit. He might therefore pay for the estate only some eighty per cent. of the total amount which he would expect to realise from re-selling it in small lots.

    The trustees say that the true value of these estates at the date of death must be the amount which would be realised within a reasonable time. If the commis-

B   sioners' values could only be realised over a period of seven years and after incurring much expense which is not a permissible deduction, then the basis of their valuation must be wrong. We cannot approach the problem in that general way, however just and attractive it may seem; and if we could look at the problem broadly, there is another side to it. If the deceased owned only two or three farms, then it could not be disputed that the proper method of valuation

C   would be to suppose each farm to have been sold as a separate unit; so what justification can there be for valuing a particular farm in one way if the deceased had owned few others but in another way if he had owned a great many. I do not think that we can decide the question on general arguments of this kind. We must go back to s. 7 (5) of the Finance Act, 1894.

    If I am right in thinking that s. 7 (5) is dealing one by one with the units into

D   which the estate has already been divided, then the hypothetical sale which it envisages must be a supposed sale of one unit in the conditions which in fact existed at the date of the death. To add one unit to those which in fact were then for sale would not have disturbed the market. If, however, we had to suppose that a large number of the units owned by the deceased had been put on the market simultaneously, the conditions which in fact existed would have

E   been materially altered and prices would have dropped. This is expressly dealt with by s. 60 (2) of the Finance (1909-10) Act, 1910, but I doubt whether this subsection did more than express what was already implicit in the Act of 1894.

    It must follow that the fact that it would have taken a long time to sell separately the units of a large estate is irrelevant insofar as that delay would have been caused by the need to avoid flooding the market. And insofar as delay

F   would have been caused by there not being enough qualified professional men to make the necessary preparations for a very large number of separate sales within a short period, that factor must, I think, be equally irrelevant. So in my view we come back to the question with which I have already dealt—whether the estates were so easily separable into large numbers of units that these units can be regarded as what I have called natural units.

G   This matter was never separately investigated by the tribunal, because the trustees did not raise it as a separate point. I think that the problem could be approached in this way. Suppose that each of these 532 units had been separately owned. Then, if the owner of one of them had died, it would have cost his executor an appreciable percentage of its value to sell it, say on the average X per cent.; but that would not have been a permissible deduction. So if the owner of 532

H   units dies his executors cannot object insofar as the cost of realisation amounts to X per cent. of the total value of the units; but insofar as it exceeds that amount they have a legitimate grievance. As the Act of 1894 deals with such problems in a rough and ready way, they would have to tolerate a moderate excess. If, however, there were a great excess caused by initial difficulty and cost in dividing the estate into lots, that would be evidence—it might be strong evidence—that these units were not truly natural units.

I   In a case such as the present I should not regard it as fatal to the trustees' case that this point was not taken before the tribunal. I should be prepared to consider whether justice required a remit for further findings; but in this case it seems to me obvious, from the facts already in the Case, that the factor which I have tried to describe could not have accounted for the greater part of the difference between the valuations of the trustees and the commissioners. So I do not think that this is a case in which the exceptional course of making such a remit would be justified. I must therefore move that the appeal be dismissed.

LORD MORRIS OF BORTH-Y-GEST: My Lords, after the death of **A** the tenth Duke of Devonshire, who died on Nov. 26, 1950, it became necessary for estate duty purposes to value as at that date the shares in the Chatsworth Estates Co., Ltd.   By virtue of s. 55 of the Finance Act, 1940, (7) the principal value of the shares fell to be estimated by reference to the net value of the assets of the company.   Amongst the many and various assets were real and leasehold properties.   The principal value of the assets had to be estimated in accordance **B** with the provisions of s. 7 (5) of the Finance Act, 1894.   By that subsection:

"The principal value of any property shall be estimated to be the value which, in the opinion of the commissioners, such property would fetch if sold in the open market at the time of the death of the deceased."

By letter dated Nov. 3, 1961, the Commissioners of Inland Revenue informed **C** the trustees of the Chatsworth settlement of the values as determined by the commissioners.   Included in the figures which in the aggregate gave the principal value of the shares there was a figure of £3,450,874 which was the principal value of the real and leasehold property.   The real and leasehold properties were (save as to property in Scotland valued at £274,228) in various part of England. The value of the properties in England was, therefore, determined to be £3,176,646. **D**

Pursuant to s. 1 (3) of the Lands Tribunal Act, 1949, the trustees (the appellants) exercised their right to appeal to the Lands Tribunal against the commissioners' determination.   The appeal appears to have been limited to a consideration of the values of those assets which consisted of real and leasehold properties. In England those properties amounted to some 119,000 acres or 186 square miles.   In a schedule sent by the commissioners with their letter of Nov. 3, 1961, **E** the properties were divided into ten estates.   The values had been arrived at by adding together the separate valuations of the various units comprising the various estates.   In all there were in England some 3,521 units into which the commissioners had divided the estate.   One of the ten estates was called the Hardwick Estate.   Its total acreage was 20,635.   Its valuation was fixed at £868,129.   That sum represented the total of the separate valuations of 532 separate units.   For **F** the purposes of argument before the tribunal the parties agreed to consider that estate in particular in the hope that, if an interim decision were given in relation to that estate, it might be possible to agree values in respect of the other estates in dispute.   After a hearing on five days in February, 1964, the tribunal gave an interim decision on May 4, 1964.   In the course of it they recorded the points raised and their findings.   On the basis of that decision and in the light of it the parties agreed the values of the other English properties.   That enabled the **G** tribunal to give their decision.   The decision was dated Jan. 15, 1965.   By that decision they fixed the value of the English real and leasehold properties under the statutory provisions as being £3,176,646—which was the figure as determined by the commissioners.   They held, however, that if on appeal the basis should be accepted alternative to that which they upheld, then the total valuation should be £2,743,760 rather than £3,176,646.   Those figures exclude the property **H** in Scotland.   By s. 3 (4) of the Lands Tribunal Act, 1949, a decision of the tribunal is final, but a person aggrieved by the decision as being erroneous in point of law may require a Case to be stated.   The tribunal were asked to state a Case. They did so on Apr. 12, 1965.   It is important to endeavour to ascertain what is the point of law which is raised.   In the Case Stated the tribunal record and set out the grounds of appeal which the trustees had raised against the deter- **I** mination by the commissioners of £3,450,874 and they referred to their interim award (dated May 4, 1964) as containing the facts proved or admitted and the contentions advanced.   The point of law was stated as being whether on their findings of fact they came to the correct decision in law.

It becomes necessary, therefore, to study the interim decision of May 4, 1964, in order to see what were the findings of fact and to see what were the contentions

(7) 9 HALSBURY'S STATUTES (2nd Edn.) 483.

A advanced which raised any question of law and to see from their interim and
final decisions what their findings were. The facts as found, beyond those to
which I have already referred, appear to be as follows:

(a) The Hardwick Estate comprised principally farms with farm buildings
but there were also small holdings, allotments, gardens, agricultural land, woodlands, residential property, sporting rights, ground rents, licensed houses, leases
B of quarries and collieries and the land upon which the Staveley Ironworks stand.

(b) The area of the Hardwick Estate was 20,635 acres:

> " For the purposes of arriving at the valuation, the estate had been
> divided into some 532 separate units, each unit representing a lot which,
> in the [commissioners'] view, would have commanded the best market price
> if sold on the date of the duke's death " (8).

C
Detailed tables showing the particulars in respect of each unit were produced
in evidence before the tribunal. I can find nothing in the decision of the tribunal
which suggests that the units were artificial or unnatural or irrational or which
suggests that it was contended that the actual division into units which
was adopted was objectionable or was objected to. In the case of properties
having a total area of 20,635 acres which were being managed and looked after
D as one estate it would be reasonable to assume that any division into separate
units or lots would be made so as to accord with the realities affecting the features
of and the locations of the properties. If it had been desired to suggest that
the method of division into separate units had been arbitrary or unreasonable,
a finding to that effect would have been sought from the tribunal. The decisions
of the tribunal contained no such suggestion.
E
(c) The valuations of the units as asessed by the commissioners were sound
and were correct provided always that the units were to be separately valued.
The valuation on the commissioners' basis was made on the assumption that each
of the units had been sold in the open market at the time of death at a price
which might reasonably have been expected to be paid for that lot at that time.
Such prices were based on prices obtained on the sale of comparable properties
F and the general level of prices for lots of the particular kind as at the date of
the death.

The contentions raised by the trustees would appear to have been as follows:

(i) The basis of valuation was wrong in that the sum of £3,450,874 represented
the aggregate of the individual values of each separate unit on the basis that
there would have been a purchaser prepared at the time of death to give the full
G open market value for each such unit.

(ii) The £3,450,874 should be reduced so as to take account of the impossibility
of offering for sale at the time of death all the real and leasehold property except
as a whole or as individual estates. The only purchaser on a sale in the open
market at the time of death would have been an investor or a speculator: any
such person would only have paid a reduced price because he would have to
H safeguard himself against the risks and delays and uncertainties affecting re-sale
or re-sales, would also have to provide for the costs of re-sale or re-sales and
would have to provide for his profit on re-sale or re-sales.

(iii) The sum of £3,450,874 could only have been realised by an orderly disposal
of the units over a considerable period of time and, to arrive at a price which
the property would be expected to fetch at the time of death, deductions would
I have to be made to cover deferment to probable dates of sales and to cover
uncertainties as to conditions at the dates of such sales and to cover the costs
of preparing for such sales.

(iv) " The time of death " should be construed as meaning within a reasonable
period after the date of death. In fact and in practice the sale of an estate such,
for example, as the Hardwick Estate could only have been realised within a

---

(8) The quotation is from the Lands Tribunal's interim decision of May 4, 1964.

reasonable period (which it was said would be one year), if the bulk of the estate **A**
were sold in one block.

The findings of the tribunal would appear to have been as follows:

1. The price which would have been obtained for the Hardwick Estate
would have been higher if it were sold in separate lots than if sold as a
whole to an investor or speculator.

2. The price to be ascertained is that which the property would fetch **B**
at the time at which the death occurred and not that which would have
resulted from a sale consequent on death.

3. The valuations as at the time of death of the various separate items
were correct.

Accordingly, the tribunal decided that the value of the Hardwick Estate arrived **C**
at under the statutory provisions was £868,129. On that basis the value of the
real and leasehold property in England was £3,176,646. In the event of their
being wrong in law the tribunal proceeded to fix the value of the Hardwick
Estate on an alternative basis. On the alternative basis the value of the Hardwick
Estate was £733,637: on that basis the value of the real and leasehold property
in England was £2,743,760. **D**

The point of law which emerges, therefore, is whether the basis taken was
correct or whether the alternative basis was correct. To appreciate precisely
the point of law raised it is important to quote what the tribunal state was the
alternative basis which was put forward. They say:

" If we are wrong in law and what ought to be assumed are the circumstances of an actual sale taking place within a reasonably short time from **E**
the time of the death, and, that preparations for this sale would be commenced at the time of the death, then we agree that in order to secure the
best open market price within such a time the properties would have to be
sold in the manner put forward by the [trustees], that is to say, each estate
would have to be sold as a whole, and the only properties extracted would
be those which could, thereby, individually produce a higher price and yet **F**
at the same time leave the large unit no less attractive for sale."

My Lords, I think that the tribunal were right in not accepting such a basis.
In a number of respects it disobeys the directions given by s. 7 (5) of the Finance
Act, 1894. The value of any property must be estimated to be the price which,
in the opinion of the commissioners, the property would fetch if sold in the open **G**
market at the time of the death of the deceased. " At the time of the death "
must not be paraphrased or altered so as to read " within a reasonably short
time of the death ". It follows from this that the section is envisaging a hypothetical sale at the time of the death. This is quite inconsistent with a notion that the
value of a piece of property is to be estimated by postulating that preparations
for an actual sale would be commenced at, but after, the time of death, and **H**
that a sale would later follow after such preparations. This is not what the
section, which is in effect a valuation section, envisages. The section prescribes
the criterion for valuation.

The Case Stated contains a summary of some of the evidence given before the
tribunal. There was evidence to the effect that with an estate of the size of the
Hardwick Estate, containing, as it did, some 20,000 acres, it would in practice **I**
take several years to effect the sale of it by selling 532 separate units. There was
evidence that if it were desired to sell the whole estate within a period of about
a year the only way in which in practice this could be achieved would be (after
separating a few easily disposable units) to sell the main part of the property
as a whole with the result that the only purchaser would be one out of a limited
class of investors or speculators. Such a person would only pay a sum which
would be some twenty per cent. less than the aggregate amount which he would
consider that he would be able to secure at later dates after arranging for the

division of the property into units and after allowing for all the expenses to which he would be put and after allowing for his profit.

In my view, the considerations to which this evidence pointed were quite irrelevant. It stands to reason that it would have been impossible in fact to sell the Hardwick Estate after the death of the duke but on the day of his death, i.e., Nov. 26, 1950. It would have been impossible there and then to sell it either as a whole or in separate units: equally, it would have been impossible there and then to sell some forty-six separate units and to sell the remainder as one entity. Furthermore, it would have been quite impossible there and then to sell, either as an entity or as a series of entities, all the various estates in England. Their total area was just under 119,000 acres or 186 square miles. All this merely serves to emphasise that s. 7 (5) is a valuable subsection in that it points to a time by reference to which, and a basis on which, values are to be estimated. When the section speaks of the value of " any property " or of " the property " an indication is, perhaps, given that each item of property in an estate must be valued. The principles on which value is estimated do not vary according as an estate consists or one item of property or of several items of property or of tens of thousands of items of property.

The basis propounded by the trustees before the Lands Tribunal was, I think, rightly rejected for a further reason. The value of a property is to be estimated to be the price which it would " fetch " if sold in the open market at the time of the death of the deceased. This points to the price which a purchaser would pay. The net amount that a vendor would receive would be less. There would be costs of and incidental to a sale. It would seem to be harsh or even unjust that allowances cannot be made in respect of them; but the words of the statute must be followed. A valuation would be on an entirely different basis if related to such figure as would be likely to be realised in fact and in practice if there was a sale at as early a date after the death as was practicable, and if the units of property comprising what had been administered as a large estate could only at such time be sold to an investor or speculator.

It was submitted that the valuation ought to have been made on the basis of taking the property as it was at the time of death and not on some altered basis. For management purposes the properties now being considered were doubtless referred to as an estate. When all in one ownership they could conveniently, and no doubt desirably, all be looked after as one estate. But by being divided into separate viable units the properties were not physically altered. The fact that in the section there is a reference to " the property " cannot mean that, if many properties are in one ownership, then they must only be conceived of as one property. It must be beyond question that it would take a very considerable time with an " estate " of twenty thousand acres to arrange for sales in the open market of the units or items or lots comprising it and to arrange for their separate descriptions. Unless, however, the units as arranged for valuation purposes can be characterised as unreal or spurious or artificial their classification becomes a reasonable and necessary and essential part of the process of valuing. That in reality and in practice sales of nearly 120,000 acres could not suddenly have been arranged to take place on Nov. 26, 1950, is irrelevant. Equally is it irrelevant that fair prices could not be obtained if the property market were suddenly deluged. Section 60 (2) of the Finance (1909-10) Act, 1910, postulates that an estimate of value " according to the market price at the time of the death " is not to be reduced on account of the estimate being made on the assumption that the whole property (which I think must mean all the properties) is to be placed on the market at one and the same time. The stipulation that an estimate must be made of the value which a property would fetch if sold in the open market does not, in my view, require an assumption that the highest possible price will be realised. It involves that an estimate should be made of the price which would be realised under the reasonable, competitive conditions of an open market on a particular date. I see no fault in what the tribunal found had been

the assumption of the commissioners in making their valuations, i.e., that each
of the units had been sold in the open market at the time of death at a price
which might reasonably have been expected to be paid for that lot at that time,
such expectation being based on prices obtained on the sale of comparable
properties and the general level of prices for lots of the particular kind at the date
of death.

On the point of law raised I consider that the Lands Tribunal were right in
rejecting the alternative basis that they set out, and I consider that on their
findings of fact they came to a correct decision in law.

I would dismiss the appeal.

LORD HODSON: My Lords, the question at issue between the parties
relates to the valuation of the Hardwick Estate, part of the real and leasehold
property owned by the Chatsworth Estate Co., Ltd., for the purpose of ascertaining
the estate duty payable in consequence of the death of the tenth Duke of Devonshire who died on Nov. 26, 1950. The appellants, who are the trustees of the
Chatsworth settlement, maintain that the Lands Tribunal were wrong in law
in taking as a basis for the valuation of the estate a division into some 532
separate units (less forty-six " hived off " in one piece), each unit representing a
lot which, in the view of the Commissioners of Inland Revenue, would have
commanded the best market price if sold at the date of the duke's death. The
trustees agreed the value to be attributed to the individual units if valued on the
basis adopted by the commissioners but contended that the commissioners' basis
was wrong, in that it was not legitimate to divide the estate into separate lots.
Their contention was that the Hardwick Estate and the other nine English
estates subject to the settlement must be regarded as being offered for sale
without lotting in the condition in which they were at the time of death. On this
assumption the only purchasers would be investors or speculators and the price
which such persons would be willing to pay would be much lower. The separation
into lots had never been made or contemplated and, although the lots could
properly be valued individually, to do so, including making ready for sale, etc.,
would take several years and involve considerable expense. Accordingly, the
assumption should be one of a sale in one unit, as the Hardwick Estate physically
was, so that a price would be obtainable of some twenty per cent. less than the
price obtainable by the valuation of the commissioners.

The question depends on the construction of s. 7 (5) of the Finance Act, 1894,
which reads:

" (5) The principal value of any property shall be estimated to be the
price which, in the opinion of the commissioners, such property would fetch
if sold in the open market at the time of the death of the deceased;"

It is to be observed that the section does not contemplate an actual sale or even
the possibility of sale. Notional sale only is envisaged, as was made plain by the
decision of your lordships in the case of *Inland Revenue Comrs.* v. *Crossman* (9).

It is further to be observed from the terms of the section itself that no deduction
is permissible to cover the expenses of sale or of making ready for sale. If there
were doubt about this it is set at rest by the language of s. 7 (3) of the Act of
1894, which permits an allowance to be made where additional expense in realising
property has been incurred because of the property being situate out of the United
Kingdom. This, in my opinion, makes inadmissible the argument of the trustees
that the method of valuation adopted by the commissioners should not be
accepted because of the expense involved in making ready for sale and in selling
in lots. Further, no deduction can be made in respect of the length of time
which an actual orderly disposal of the various units might take. This, in my
opinion, follows from the language of s. 7 (5) which speaks of " the time of the

---

(9) [1936] 1 All E.R. 762; [1937] A.C. 26.

death of the deceased " as the moment of the hypothetical sale. I cannot, there-fore, accept the argument for the trustees that these reductions should be made so as to reflect the price which could be obtained within a reasonable time of death. This involves an extended construction of the words " the time of the death ", which I do not think is admissible in the context in which they appear.

In my opinion, the tribunal were entitled to find as a fact, as they did, that the permissible units of valuation were those which, in the case of the Hardwick Estate, were 532 in all. If they were entitled to sub-divide and were not compelled to treat the English estates as indivisible, there is no objection taken to the figures reached, for the trustees agree the values attributed to the individual units, if valued on the basis adopted by the commissioners.

The case for the trustees has never been that the sub-division into units was artificial. On the contrary, they have argued that the valuation was objectionable owing to the impossibility of realisation within a reasonable time. I agree with my noble and learned friend, LORD WILBERFORCE, that the fact that one estate may be capable of division into one hundred units and another not is not to be taken into account simply because of the practical difficulty of organising sales. This would be to treat an owner of a large estate more favourably than the owner of a small one. Accepting as I do the commissioners' contention that no deduction in respect of the expenses of sale or making ready for sale is permissible, I do not see any room for further enquiry as to the way in which the value of each individual unit was reached. The Revenue rely on the case of the *Earl of Ellesmere* v. *Inland Revenue Comrs.* (10), but I do not think that it should be taken as laying down any principle according to which a particular estate ought to be regarded as one whole for valuation or regarded as divisible into portions. My noble and learned friend, LORD REID, has drawn attention (11) to the variation in the report of the case in the Law Reports as compared with that in the Law Times, but on either version I remain of the same opinion.

I would dismiss the appeal.

LORD GUEST: My Lords, the tenth Duke of Devonshire died on Nov. 26, 1950. The duke had some four years and eight months previously transferred to the appellant trustees nearly all his shares in Chatsworth Estates Co., Ltd., which owned a considerable amount of real and leasehold property in England. By virtue of s. 55 of the Finance Act, 1940, the value of the shares in the company falls to be estimated by reference to the net value of the assets of the company. The estates are, therefore, to be treated as if they had passed on the death of the duke in terms of s. 1 of the Finance Act, 1894.

At the date of the duke's death the company owned some 186 square miles or 119,000 acres of real and leasehold property divided into ten estates. The Commissioners of Inland Revenue determined the value of the real and leasehold property at £3,176,646, the value attributable to the Hardwick Estate, consisting of 20,635 acres, being £868,129. The values were arrived at by the addition of separate valuations for each of 3,787 units, the division of the Hardwick Estate being into 532 units. The appeal of the trustees against the determination of the commissioners was dismissed by the Lands Tribunal, but the tribunal stated that if the tribunal were wrong in law the alternative value would be £2,743,760. The tribunal stated a question of law for the Court of Appeal who sustained the determination of the tribunal (12). Before the tribunal the Hardwick Estate was taken by the parties as a typical example on the facts of which the correct principle could be decided and then applied to the other estates. The figure contended for by the trustees for the valuation of the Hardwick Estate was £732,637 whereas the figure in the commissioners' determination was £868,129. Owing to the agreement of the parties to take the Hardwick Estate as typical

---

(10) [1918] 2 K.B. 735; 119 L.T. 568.   (11) See p. 133, letter I, to p. 134, letter A, ante.
(12) [1965] 3 All E.R. 458; [1965] 1 Q.B. 851.

the difference between the commissioners and the trustees as to the value of all
the estates belonging to the company amounts to £432,886.

The statutory provisions governing the principal value for estate duty purposes
are contained in s. 7 (5) of the Finance Act, 1894:

"The principal value of any property shall be estimated to be the price
which, in the opinion of the commissioners, such property would fetch if
sold in the open market at the time of the death of the deceased;"

Before discussing the construction of the subsection it is necessary to appreciate
the way in which the case was conducted before the tribunal. The estate was of a
miscellaneous and varied character consisting principally of farms with farm
buildings, but there were also smallholdings, allotments, gardens, agricultural
land, woodlands, residential property, sporting rights, ground rents, licensed
houses, leases of quarries and colliery lands and the land on which the Staveley
Ironworks stand. Out of the 532 units on which the commissioners' determination
had been based the trustees agreed that forty-six were separate and could easily
and expeditiously be disposed of separately. As regards the remaining 486 units
the commissioners contended that the total value of these units should be the
aggregate of the valuations of each of these units. The trustees while conceding
that the forty-six separate units could properly be valued separately by themselves, contended that the division and making ready for sale of the remaining
block would take several years and involve considerable expense, and that
accordingly for the purpose of estimating the principal value the whole of this
block should be assumed to be sold as one unit. Sold in this way the price obtainable, it was argued, would be some twenty per cent. less than the price obtainable
by the method of sale contended for by the commissioners.

The terms of s. 7 (5) of the Finance Act, 1894, have already been quoted. The
value of property under this subsection is to be taken to be at its market value at
the date of the death of the deceased. Some things, I think, are reasonably clear.
The words " price . . . such property would fetch " in s. 7 (5) mean that it is not
the price which the vendor would have received but is what the purchaser would
have paid to be put into the shoes of the deceased. This means that the costs of
realisation do not form a legitimate deduction in arriving at the valuation. Such
a result must follow from the provisions of s. 7 (3) which allows a deduction of five
per cent. in arriving at the value of foreign properties. The doctrine expressio
unius exclusio alterius applies and indicates that costs of realisation are not
permissible deductions in arriving at the valuation of properties within the
United Kingdom. " At the time of the death " means at the moment of death,
not within a reasonable time after the death. Further, the subsection does not
require the envisagement of an actual sale. In fact it is irrelevant in arriving at the
valuation to consider what would have been the circumstances attending an
actual sale. So far the construction of s. 7 (5) is, I think, reasonably clear.

But the contest between the trustees and the commissioners before the tribunal
was whether the full value of the aggregate of the values of each unit should be
taken or whether the aggregate should be reduced by some percentage deduction.
This was the only issue before the tribunal, as is shown by the table of figures
produced. Section 7 (5) of the Act of 1894 prescribes a method of valuation in
order to ascertain the " principal value " of the estate in s. 1. I do not find any
assistance from s. 1 in deciding into what units an estate is to be divided for
purposes of valuation. This is a question of circumstances. Different properties
will require different methods of valuation under the section. Different properties
may require to be split into different units. A man owns a manor house, agricultural land, leases of farms, pictures, a library, a factory and some villages. To
decide the market value of such an estate the property may have to be split up
into several separate units of valuation. There may have to be sub-units; for
instance, the library may require to be examined in order to see whether the whole
should be valued together or whether some individual books possess a value
which necessitates their separate valuation. Similarly, a village might require

A the separate valuation of each house, each licensed house, each hall, as these
would normally be sold separately. These are entirely questions of fact to be
decided by the tribunal. The question of law is, what is the proper method of
valuation of each of these units of valuation? It was argued before this House
that the tribunal had in the present case artificially divided the Hardwick Estate
into 532 mythical lots and then had valued each lot, the addition of the individual
B values making up the aggregate valuation. If I had thought that such method
had been adopted, I should have come to the conclusion that the tribunal had
erred in law in their valuation and that this method of valuation was not in
accordance with s. 7 (5) of the Act of 1894; but I am not so satisfied.

The commissioners having issued their determination of value, it was for the
trustees to displace this valuation before the tribunal. I can detect no evidence
C in the interim decision of the tribunal that the commissioners had divided the
estate into artificial lots or that the tribunal had done so in arriving at their valuation; there was no evidence that the units into which the estate had been divided
were other than proper units of valuation. The commissioners' basis of valuation
was made " on the assumption that each of the units had been sold in the open
market at the time of death at a price which might reasonably have been expected
D to be paid for that lot at that time. Such prices being based on prices obtained
on the sale of comparable properties and the general level of prices for lots of that
kind at that time ". There was in fact no dispute between the parties as to what
units were to be taken as, nor as to the valuation of, the individual units of valuation. The trustees' basis of valuation is not very easy to understand. Mr. Strathon,
a valuer called for the trustees, expressed the view that it would be impossible
E within a year after death to sell all the individual units separately and that the
only way to sell such an estate within a reasonable period would be to " hive off "
certain individual units which could be sold readily as separate units and to offer
the remainder of the estate as one unit which would attract an investor. He had
deducted twenty per cent. from " the sum of the prices agreed on the revenue
basis for the units comprised in the larger unit ". His calculation of the figure
F of twenty per cent. is not clear. Mr. Strutt, another valuer for the trustees,
said that it would have been impossible to sell all the individual units within a
period of seven years of the date of death. His valuation was based on the view
that a " speculator " would be the most likely buyer, and the result of his calculations approximated very closely to Mr. Strathon's. Neither of these witnesses
indicated that the division into units which they accepted for their valuation
G was unnatural or artificial. In fact it was the basis of their valuation in arriving
at the aggregate figure which they then reduced to provide for the " investor " or
" speculative element ".

The only question for this House appears to be whether the tribunal erred in
law in not accepting the trustees' method of valuation and in preferring the
commissioners' method. The trustees' method of valuation was, in my opinion,
H not in accordance with the terms of s. 7 (5). It is not necessary to assume an actual
sale: a hypothetical market must be assumed for all the items of property at the
date of death. The impossibility of putting the property on the market at the
time of death or of actually realising the open market price is irrelevant. In
other words, one does not have to assume that the property had actually to be
sold; the assumption is that it is sold at the moment of death.

I   The authorities relied on by the commissioners included *Inland Revenue Comrs.*
v. *Crossman* (13). This case is important because it shows that items of property
must be valued even though there is no open market for them. The existence of
an open market is not a condition of liability: s. 7 (5) merely prescribes the open
market as the measure of value (see per VISCOUNT HAILSHAM, L.C. (14). The case
of *Earl of Ellesmere* v. *Inland Revenue Comrs.* (15) was strongly relied on by the

(13) [1936] 1 All E.R. 762; [1937] A.C. 26.
(14) [1936] 1 All E.R. at p. 770; [1937] A.C. at pp. 41, 42.
(15) [1918] 2 K.B. 735; 119 L.T. 568.

commissioners and also finds a place in the interim decision of the tribunal and A in the judgment of LORD DENNING, M.R. (16). This was the case of the valuation of a miscellaneous property of some two thousand acres where the successor to the third Earl of Ellesmere, contrary to advice received by him from surveyors, sold his estate to a speculator in one lot for £68,000. The surveyors had advised him that he would obtain less for the estates if he sold in one lot than if he sold it in individual lots. The speculator re-sold a portion of the property for £65,000 and B the remainder was worth about £16,000. The commissioners valued the property at £77,000 on the principle that the market price was the price which the property would have realised if it had been divided up and sold in lots. The referee upheld the commissioners' contention with a slight reduction on the valuation. An appeal to SANKEY, J., failed. It will be seen that on its facts this case closely resembles the present. A property of a varied and miscellaneous character actually C sold as one lot, but the price obtained was not taken as the value but the value was the aggregate of the values of the separate lots. The decision of SANKEY, J., was that the referee had acted on the correct principle in arriving at his decision and that there was evidence on which he could properly find the principal value of the property at the sum which he had fixed. SANKEY, J., said (17):

" Now the Act of 1894 says that the value of the property shall be estim- D ated to be the price which it would fetch if sold in the open market. That, in my opinion, does not necessarily mean the price which it would fetch if sold to a single purchaser. There may be many cases where a sale to a single purchaser cannot realise ' the price which it would fetch if sold in the open market '. Take the case of an owner having property including a colliery and a draper's shop. It is conceivable that if the colliery and the draper's shop E were sold separately the best possible price might be obtained for each. On the other hand a purchaser who was anxious to buy the draper's shop might not wish to be encumbered with a colliery, and vice versa, and con- sequently if the owner insisted upon selling the whole property to one purchaser he would not obtain the market price which the Act contemplates. So, too, with regard to property of the same character situate in different F areas. It may well be that if in such case the vendor insists upon the different parts being all sold to the same person he will not get as good a price as if he allowed different persons to buy the portions situate in the different districts. No doubt a sale in one lot of a varied property such as that in the present case may be highly convenient to the vendor. He may want to get the money quickly; he may not care to risk an auction. He may be going abroad, or G may be called up to serve in the Army, and it may be of great importance to him to sell at once. But it does not at all follow that the price which he obtains under such circumstances is ' the price which it would fetch if sold in the open market '. What is meant by those words is the best possible price that is obtainable, and what that is is largely, if not entirely, a question of fact. I can readily conceive cases in which a sale of the whole property in H one lot would realise the true market price, but I can equally imagine cases in which it would not. Here the referee held that because the property was of a miscellaneous character and not lying in a ring fence the price paid by the single purchaser was not the true value. I think he was entitled so to hold, and that the contention as to misdirection fails."

With respect to the learned judge I entirely agree. The market value of property I is the best price that can be obtained for the property in the open market.

My noble and learned friend, LORD REID, has discovered that the passage in the judgment of SANKEY, J., which occurs in the Law Times report (18) to this effect:

" I am of opinion that according to the true construction of s. 7 (5) of the

(16) [1965] 3 All E.R. at p. 461; [1966] 1 Q.B. at p. 871.
(17) [1918] 2 K.B. at pp. 739, 740. (18) (1918), 119 L.T. at p. 573.

Finance Act, 1894, and s. 60 (2) of the Finance (1909-10) Act, 1910, the principal value means the price which the property would have fetched on the death of the deceased in the open market if it had been then sold in such a manner and subject to such conditions as might reasonably be calculated to obtain for the vendor the best price for the property; but I am satisfied that this is largely, if not entirely, a question of fact for the referee."

does not appear in the official report (19). In fact the entire judgment appears to have been substantially re-written. It is true that the passage excised from the Law Times is referred to by the tribunal, and by the Court of Appeal (20) and is founded on by the commissioners in support of their contention that the property must be divided into saleable lots to arrive at its value. As I have said there is, in my opinion, no justification for an artificial division of the property into separate lots in order to arrive at a higher value and the passage quoted from Sankey, J., in the Law Times would not afford justification for such a method of valuation. I do not, however, think that the *Ellesmere* case (21) was a case of artificial division and I can find no suggestion in the present case that any such artificial division of the Hardwick Estate was made.

I would dismiss the appeal.

LORD WILBERFORCE: My Lords, the Finance Act, 1894, requires that for the assessment of estate duty a valuation must be made of all the property passing or deemed to pass on the death. The Act lays down the principles of valuation: when the valuations have been completed and all the necessary adjustments have been made, the duty is levied at the appropriate rate. Although the basis for valuation is the market price at the time of death, the Act does not require that any property forming part of the estate should actually be sold: in fact, some sales will be necessary, but this is no concern of the Commissioners of Inland Revenue. The Act of 1894 does not require the valuers to step as it were into the shoes of the deceased or of his executors, or take account of the practical difficulties or delays inherent in any realisation except to the extent that these may help to fix the market price at the time of death.

When, as is usually the case, the estate consists of an aggregate of items of property, each item must be separately valued, and it is not difficult to see that problems may arise as to the manner in which the separate units of valuation are to be ascertained or in which individual items are to be grouped into units of valuation. These problems must necessarily be resolved, as they are in practice, in a commonsense way. The estate is to be taken as it is found: it is not to be supposed, in order to obtain higher figures of valuation, that any substantial expense is to be incurred or work done in organising the estate into units: on the other hand, some practical grouping or classification, such as can reasonably be carried out without undue expenditure of time or effort, by a prudent man concerned to obtain the most favourable price, may be supposed.

Questions of subdivision or grouping must commonly occur in relation to the larger landed estates, which may consist of farms, houses, allotments, woodlands, accommodation lands and incorporeal rights. The case of the *Earl of Ellesmere v. Inland Revenue Comrs.* (21) was concerned with such an estate, and it appears that the method there approved by the court has been adopted and followed generally as a working rule. The decision can be accepted as a sound and useful decision in the kind of situation to which it relates, but the limits of its application must be understood. The estate there was an aggregate of separate units, the division of which was apparent and which had been accepted immediately after the owner's death by his successors: the question for decision was whether the commissioners were bound to accept for valuation purposes the figure obtained through the actual sale of the estate as a whole or whether it was permissible to

(19) [1918] 2 K.B. at p. 738.   (20) [1965] 3 All E.R. 458; [1966] 1 Q.B. 851.
(21) [1918] 2 K.B. 735; 119 L.T. 568.

value the units. It did not involve and does not assist on any question whether a particular " estate " ought to be regarded as one whole, or whether, for valuation, it may be regarded as divisible into portions and, if the latter, how many portions, or how they may be grouped. The judgment of SANKEY, J., with or without the passage quoted by LORD DENNING, M.R., and, as my noble and learned friend, LORD REID, points out, omitted from the Law Reports, must be read in this light.

Another illustration of the working of this principle but of a kind converse to the *Ellesmere* case (22) is the Scottish decision of *Inland Revenue Comrs.* v. *Marr's Trustees* (23). This related to a herd of cattle. A valuation had been made of the herd as a whole and it was objected that a separate value should have been taken for each head. The Lord Ordinary rejected the objection on the basis that a choice between herd valuation and head valuation was a pure finding of fact.

The Act of 1894 entrusts the task of valuation to the Commissioners of Inland Revenue, from whom an appeal lies, in matters affecting land, to the Lands Tribunal. It is for these bodies to fix the units of valuation according to the principles which I have endeavoured to indicate, and then to value each unit. Their decisions, being findings of fact, can only be reviewed for misdirection or other error in law. I now proceed to examine the findings in this case.

This appeal relates to the Hardwick Estate, selected as a case typical of the other estates belonging to the Chatsworth Estates Co., Ltd. But the term " Hardwick Estate " is merely a term of convenience used to describe a considerable aggregate of separate and disparate properties. In their interim decision the tribunal describe it in these terms:

" The estate comprises principally farms with farm buildings, but there are also small holdings, allotments, gardens, agricultural land, woodlands, residential property, sporting rights, ground rents, licensed houses, leases of quarries and colliery lands and the land upon which the Staveley Ironworks stand."

They continue with the following passage:

" For the purposes of arriving at the valuation, the estate had been divided into some 532 separate units, each unit representing a lot which, in the [commissioners'] view, would have commanded the best market price if sold on the date of the duke's death.

" Detailed tables showing the particulars in respect of each unit were produced in evidence and summarized tables were also produced at the hearing.

"The [trustees] agree the values attributed to the individual units if valued upon the basis adopted by the [commissioners], a basis which they do not accept as that which should be applied.

" The dispute between the parties is as to the basis of valuation to be adopted in the light of the statutory provisions which are applicable."

Together with a subsequent reference to unity of management, which I do not find of assistance, this is all the finding the decision contains. There is a reference in a letter written by the Solicitor of Inland Revenue on Feb. 14, 1952, to " such lotting of the whole property as was calculated to produce the best price ". This is scanty material indeed, and I have anxiously considered whether the whole case ought not to be remitted for further findings—a depressing result fifteen years after the relevant date. In the end, however, I have come to the conclusion that this course should not be taken. The finding states the divisibility, in the opinion of the tribunal, of the " estate " into 532 units; a figure arrived at, it is seen, after inspection of maps and other data as well as of the locality. It was open to the trustees to contest the appropriateness of this division and to submit either that the " estate " should be regarded as one whole or that any division of it should be into fewer or different units; for example, that it should be regarded as consisting of outlying portions—of which there were forty-six

(22) [1918] 2 K.B. 735; 119 L.T. 568.   (23) (1906), 44 Sc. L.R. 647.

identifiable parcels—plus a central indivisible nucleus. As the interim decision shows, they did not do this. Their case was quite a different one. It was that it was impossible to realise the estate, as so divided, within a " reasonable time ": that, if one is to suppose disposition within a " reasonable time " (of the order of twelve months from the death) the only disposition which could be made was of the outlying portions in lots, and of the remainder as a whole. The alternative basis of valuation suggested by them is on this hypothesis, treating the remainder as suitable for sale only to a speculator or investor. The evidence given by their two experts, as recorded in the interim decision, was to this effect: it was directed to the impossibility of realisation of the individual units within a year or a reasonable time. Neither is recorded as saying that the suggested division into 532 units was artificial, or that it did not correspond with reality or with the state of affairs actually existing at the date of death. So, unsatisfied though I must remain as to the completeness of the factual findings presented to us, I think that we are obliged to deal with this case on the footing that the Hardwick Estate as existing at the date of death may properly and reasonably be regarded as composed of 532 units of valuation.

The next stage is to enquire what figure or figures result from this. The commissioners' valuation is stated to be " on the assumption that each of the units had been sold in the open market at the time of death at a price which might reasonably have been expected to be paid for that lot at that time. Such prices being based on prices obtained on the sale of comparable properties and the general level of prices for lots of that kind at that time." After so arriving at the values of individual units, the commissioners simply aggregate them to form a total figure for the " estate ". The trustees' objection is that the aggregation takes no account of the impossibility of offering all the " estate " at the time of death except as a whole, or as a whole after " hiving off " outlying portions. The commissioners' figure, they contend, could only have been achieved " by an orderly disposal of the various units which would have taken a very considerable time ", and so deductions should be allowed to cover " deferment to probable dates of sales, uncertainties as to conditions at the dates of such sales and costs of preparing for such sales ". The evidence of their experts, as recorded in the interim decision, was directed to showing the impossibility of disposal by lots in " a reasonable time " and the commissioners' expert agreed with this. Both the trustees' experts said that the only sale possible in a reasonable time was by " hiving off " outlying portions and selling the core as one unit to an investor or speculator. The evidence did not establish positively what a " reasonable time " would be, nor did the tribunal make any finding as to this matter.

My lords, it must be clear that, if the principles of statutory valuation are as I have stated earlier in this opinion, the trustees' argument cannot succeed, based as it is on suppositions relevant to some actual sale which may have to be made. This is in conflict with the scheme of the Finance Act, 1894. Once a figure has been arrived at for the value of a unit, that is the relevant " principal " value: the Act of 1894 does not provide for any reduction in the value either of any one unit or of the total of their values on account of the multiplicity of similar units: indeed, s. 60 (2) of the Finance (1909-10) Act, 1910, contains an explicit prohibition of any reduction to take account of any lower price which might result from placing them all on the market at one and the same time. The nature of the " impossibility " of disposing of the units of this estate in a reasonable time is not explained in the evidence, but whatever it is I am of opinion that no allowance for it is warranted by the legislation. If it is a matter of mere numbers and the practical or administrative difficulty in organising sales, to allow a deduction would mean treating differently the owner of one hundred units (say separate farms) from the owner of one, and that cannot be right. If it is a matter of flooding the market, that is something which under positive enactment cannot be taken account of (Finance (1909-10) Act, 1910, s. 60 (2)). If it is a matter of finding a purchaser for any individual property, which may take time, that is something which ought to be reflected in the individual valuations of that property. We were not informed about this one way or the other, and I am left with some uneasiness whether due allowance has been made for this factor. Again the issue was not joined on this point, but on the admissibility or otherwise of a deduction on account of the time which, it was claimed, would be involved in disposing of so many units of property. This, in my view, is inadmissible.

There remains one other matter as to which I feel much difficulty. The trustees claim, in general terms, that, even if the commissioners' basis of valuation is correct, a deduction should be allowed for the extra expense of realisation in individual lots. The commissioners dispute this, contending that expenses of sale are in law not deductible. The wording of the Finance Act, 1894, s. 7 (5), adequate perhaps when it was passed, but with the great increase of rates of duty now severe and even unjust, requires the gross open market price, i.e., what the purchaser pays, and not what the vendor ultimately receives, to be taken as the valuation figure. Moreover, as I have already stated, in making the valuation it is not legitimate to arrive at a higher price by supposing that expenditure, by way, for example, of repair or improvement on the property, has been made. But I do not think that this is the end of the matter, or that the section necessarily prevents account being taken of the cost of lotting an estate, by which I mean preparing adequate separate particulars of existing units, or, in relation to movables, cataloguing a collection. These are matters which may very well enter directly into the value of the property: an uncatalogued collection may be worth less than a catalogued collection; an estate as to which no particulars exist as to the individual units may be worth less than one fully equipped with maps, valuations and records. The injustice of making no allowance for the difference can be seen if one supposes that the deceased had himself caused the catalogue or particulars to be made before his death: in such a case the expense of so doing, which may be quite considerable, would have been withdrawn from his estate. So I would see no reason why, in a suitable case, the commissioners might not treat that aggregate as worth somewhat less than the total of the individual values on account of the absence of a catalogue or of necessary particulars. In referring to a suitable case, I have in mind an estate which, taking it as it is found at the date of death, can fairly be said to be made up of an aggregate of units or items, suitable for separate disposal: if, in order for this to be possible, expenditure on the estate itself is required, then it would not be right to treat the estate as anything but an indivisible whole.

We do not know in the present case whether there was or was not such an absence of detailed description of the individual units as would fairly be reflected in a diminution of value of the aggregate: the trustees, whose interest it would have been so to contend, do not seem to have called any specific evidence to the point. But in general terms they made the claim and I would have thought it appropriate to remit the matter to the tribunal for a finding of fact on this limited point. Apart from it—and I understand that this step does not commend itself to your lordships—I have come to the conclusion that the appeal must be dismissed.

Appeal dismissed.

Solicitors: *Currey & Co.* (for the trustees); *Solicitor of Inland Revenue.*

[*Reported by* KATHLEEN J. H. O'BRIEN, *Barrister-at-Law.*]

A   VENN *v.* NATIONAL COAL BOARD.

[SHEFFIELD ASSIZES (Veale, J.), June 9, 10, 13, 14, 15, 1966.]

Coal Mining—Statutory duty—Breach—Security of working place—Support of every place where any mineral is worked—" Working place "—Market man in drawing-off shift removing prop from support bar—Whether a working
B *place ceases, by reason of danger and intention that falls should occur, to be a working place—Long wall face—" Proper" control of movement of strata in mine—Mines and Quarries Act, 1954 (2 & 3 Eliz. 2 c. 70), s. 48 (1), s. 49 (1), (5), s. 53.*

The word " proper " in s. 49 (5)* of the Mines and Quarries Act, 1954, (which describes the system of support that is to be provided and maintained,
C as being a system " consistent with the proper control of movement of the strata in the mine ") means " such control as will result in security ". Security, in that connexion, means " a physical condition of stability which will ordinarily result in safety " (dictum of LORD RADCLIFFE in *Brown* v. *National Coal Board* ([1962] 1 All E.R. at p. 85) applied); the support rules† must, therefore, be consistent with such control of movement of strata in
D the mine as will ordinarily result in safety (see p. 154, letter G, post).

The plaintiff was employed by the defendants at their colliery as a market man, i.e., he was an experienced underground worker who had been trained in different types of underground working, and was available to do such work as he was detailed on any particular occasion to do. The plaintiff was sent with G. on the night drawing-off shift to a coal face to which
E neither of them had been before, to fill coal which had not been filled off and after that to help with the drawing-off. Support at the face was by means of bars, props, sylvester props, chocks and lids. At the beginning of a filling shift, over the conveyor belt at the face, there was a row of bars four feet apart, the bars being at right angles to the face and each bar being supported on two props, the face prop (nearer to the face) and the gob prop
F (nearer to the waste). Instead of the normal sylvester props or lining props, forming a row in line with the gob props at the waste edge (the object of which was to form a breaking off line) chocks were to be used instead of every alternate sylvester or lining prop. By the time when the drawing-off shift began, a new line of bars, each being supported by two props, had been set against the face and over the conveyor belt. During the drawing-off
G shift the bars and props set on the previous filling shift had to be withdrawn working in the direction of the mother gate, and the chocks and sylvester props had to be advanced. Having filled the coal, they proceeded with the drawing-off. The plaintiff would advance either the sylvester prop or the chock between the bars and then draw the gob side prop of the bar with his sylvester. Having done that, he would draw the remaining prop under that
H bar. The plaintiff advanced a chock (No. 1) before dealing with the bars on either side of it and then came to another chock (No. 3) between two further bars (A and B). Because of the way that supports had been set, after removing chock No. 3 he had no alternative but to leave it unadvanced. Leaving the pieces of chock No. 3 ready to replace when they had withdrawn the bar, the plaintiff and G. advanced chock No. 2. Having drawn the gob
I prop under bar B the sylvester chain slipped off and the gob prop became loose and was lying in a diagonal position under bar B. To his left was a remaining prop under bar B and the bar itself on top of it, to his right was bar A, standing on two props and untouched, and quite close to him there was the gob prop of the face line of bars. The plaintiff reached forward to

---

* Section 49, so far as material, is set out at p. 154, letters E and F, post.
† Viz., rules made under or by virtue of provisions of the Mines and Quarries Act, 1954, relating to support, which precede s. 54 (see ibid., s. 54 (1)). They are rules made by the manager of the mine.

Followed in HAMMOND v NATIONAL COAL BOARD [1984] 3 All ER 321

Distinguished in ROBSON *v.* NAT. COAL BD. [1968] 3 All E.R. 159.

pull the loose prop out by hooking the hook of the chain on to the flange of   **A**
the prop, when a stone over six feet long fell from the roof, reeled out the
remaining prop of bar B and the gob prop of bar A, bent bar A and fell
across his back.   In an action against the defendants for damages for
personal injuries the plaintiff alleged, inter alia, breaches of statutory
duty under s. 48 (1)* (duty to secure safety of working places), s. 49 (1)†
and s. 53‡ of the Mines and Quarries Act, 1954. The court found that there   **B**
were substantial breaches of s. 49 (1) and s. 53 (see p. 155, letter C, post),
which, however, would not entitle the plaintiff to succeed unless the statutory
duty applied to the place where the plaintiff was injured and unless the
breaches caused the accident.

Held: (i) the words " every place where any mineral is worked " in
para. (*a*) of sub-s. (1) of s. 49 did not include a place that was not a " working   **C**
place " (see p. 155, letter E, post);   and a working place was a place where
a man not only was working but also had been set to work or in which he
might be expected to be, and did not ipso facto cease to be a working place
merely because an element of danger arose there (see p. 156, letters A and E,
post).

Dicta of LORD THANKERTON in *Lochgelly Iron & Coal Co., Ltd.* v. *McMullan*   **D**
([1934] A.C. at p. 16) and LORD DENNING in *Gough* v. *National Coal Board*
([1959] 2 All E.R. at p. 174) applied.

(ii) although in the present case an area from which props and bars were
wholly withdrawn would cease to be part of the working place, for it was
the intention that falls should occur there, yet at the time of the accident
the area between bar A and bar B was still part of the plaintiff's working   **E**
place, for only the gob prop of bar B had been removed and no fall was yet
intended to occur, nor should a fall have occurred if the system had been
so carried out as to enable the plaintiff to advance and erect the chock;   the
remaining prop and the bar had still to be withdrawn, and the area remained
the working place of the plaintiff either for that reason or because the
defendants should have contemplated that the plaintiff might well do what he   **F**
did (see p. 157, letters B and F, and p. 158, letter E, post); accordingly the
defendants were liable to the plaintiff for breach of statutory duty under
s. 48 (1) and s. 49 (1) (see p. 160, letter B, post).

(iii) the defendants were also in breach of statutory duty under s. 53 of the
Act of 1954, since the fact that the plaintiff could not advance chock
No. 3 was a direct result of breaches of the support rules and those breaches   **G**
were a cause of the accident (see p. 160, letters B and D, post).

Per CURIAM: I take it to be clear that a manager is not automatically
guilty of a contravention if a fall occurs. Nevertheless, the fact of a fall is
some evidence of a breach of s. 48 (1). Should there be, in any case, no other
evidence at all, I have no doubt but that the plaintiff would be held to have
established his case (see p. 154, letter C, post).   **H**

[As to security of roads and working places in a mine, see 26 HALSBURY'S
LAWS (3rd Edn.) 658, 659, para. 1271; and for cases on the subject, see 33 DIGEST
(Repl.) 899-902, *1322-1334.*

As to mine deputies' duties as to support, see 26 HALSBURY'S LAWS (3rd Edn.)
661, para. 1275.   **I**

---

* Section 48 (1), so far as material, is set out at p. 153, letter E, post.
† Section 49, so far as material, is set out at p. 154, letters E and F, post.
‡ Section 53, so far as material, provides: " It shall be the duty of every person
employed at a mine who is appointed for the purpose of fulfilling any requirements
imposed with respect to the mine by virtue of para. (*a*) of sub-s. (1) of s. 12 of the Act,
to ensure to the best of his ability . . . that there are duly set any supports which appear
to him to be necessary in addition to those set in pursuance of the requirements imposed
by or by virtue of the said provisions."

A   For the Mines and Quarries Act, 1954, s. 48, s. 49, s. 52, s. 53 and s. 157, see 34 HALSBURY'S STATUTES (2nd Edn.) 555, 556, 558, 627.

For the Coal and Other Mines (Support) Regulations, 1956, see 14 HALSBURY'S STATUTORY INSTRUMENTS (First Re-Issue) 57.]

Cases referred to:

B   *Beiscak* v. *National Coal Board*, [1965] 1 All E.R. 895; [1965] 1 W.L.R. 518; 3rd Digest Supp.

Brown v. *National Coal Board*, [1962] 1 All E.R. 81; [1962] A.C. 574; [1962] 2 W.L.R. 269; 33 Digest (Repl.) 895, *1302.*

Gough v. *National Coal Board*, [1958] 1 All E.R. 754; [1959] 1 Q.B. 189; [1958] 2 W.L.R. 735; *revsd.* H.L., [1959] 2 All E.R. 164; [1959] A.C. 698; [1959] 2 W.L.R. 658; 33 Digest (Repl.) 901, *1333.*

C   *Lochgelly Iron & Coal Co., Ltd.* v. *McMullan*, [1934] A.C. 1; 102 L.J.P.C. 123; 149 L.T. 526; 33 Digest (Repl.) 899, *1323.*

Soar v. *National Coal Board*, [1965] 2 All E.R. 318; [1965] 1 W.L.R. 886; 3rd Digest Supp.

Stein (John G.) & Co., Ltd. v. *O'Hanlon*, [1965] 1 All E.R. 547; [1965] A.C. 890; [1965] 2 W.L.R. 496; 3rd Digest Supp.

D
Action.

This was an action by the plaintiff, Leonard Raymond Venn, for damages for personal injuries suffered while in the defendants' employment at 4's North District of the Silkstone Seam of Manvers Main Colliery on June 15, 1962. The plaintiff was employed by the defendants as a market man, i.e., he E   was an experienced underground worker who had been trained in different types of underground working, and was available to do such work as he was detailed on any particular occasion to do. 4's North District was a double unit, long wall face. The right hand face, with which the action was concerned, was some 130 yards in length. On this face support was by means of bars, props, sylvester (or lining) props, chocks and lids. The bars were six feet six F   inches long, four inches wide and $1\frac{1}{2}$ inches high; face props were two feet nine inches long and $3\frac{1}{2}$ inches square; gob props two feet two inches long and $3\frac{1}{4}$ inches square; sylvester props two feet three inches long and four inches square; and lids five inches square and two inches thick. Chocks were two feet square and with their wider area gave more support than props. The method of utilising these supports was laid down in the manager's support rules, supplied G   to employees in accordance with s. 54 (6) of the Mines and Quarries Act, 1954.

At the beginning of a filling shift, over the conveyor belt at the face, there was a row of bars four feet apart, the bars being at right angles to the face and each bar being supported on two props, namely, the face prop nearer the face and the gob prop nearer the waste (or gob or goaf). The support rules required that between each bar and in line with the gob props at the waste edge there should be H   set sylvester props as lining props, forming a row, the object of which was to form a breaking off line so that the roof might have some sort of fulcrum as it subsided in the waste; but with respect to the face in question there was an instruction to the deputies that chocks must be used instead of every alternate lining or sylvester prop.

The face and belt would have advanced during the filling shift and by the time I   of the drawing-off shift a new line of bars each supported by its two props would have been set against the face and over the conveyor belt. There remained in the positions in which they were originally set the bars and props set on the previous filling shift and these had in each cycle to be withdrawn during the drawing-off shift. The drawers-off would work from right to left in the direction of the mother gate and remove these bars and props and also advance the chocks and sylvester props or lining props until at the end of the drawing-off shift the position would be as previously described for the filling shift. In addition to the use of top lids on the props, the practice was to set

the face props on one foot lid and the gob props on two foot lids. The roof in **A**
4's North District was one where considerable convergence occurred. By the
time when the next filling shift came round the total height at the face props had
sunk by some four inches, though the precise amount varied. The convergence
was taken up by the lids crushing and the foot lids sinking into the floor. Alongside the face props at the end of the next filling shift would be set the gob props
of a new set of bars. Because of the convergence, the shorter gob props plus **B**
two foot lids were of adequate height. If the convergence was not as much as
four inches, only two foot lids under the new gob props would make these props
too short and the only way suggested by the evidence of gaining the required
height would be by utilising a third foot lid; and if a prop were to be set on three
lids it was recognised as undoubtedly bad practice and made for unstable support.
The floor was a fireclay or spavin floor which did to some extent get soft if there **C**
were water about. Water was used on the cutting shift. At the place where
the plaintiff's accident occurred there was a swilly, or saucer-like depression, some
four or five yards long, where water would tend to accumulate.

On the drawing-off shift of the night of June 14, 1962, the plaintiff and another
market man named Grindle, neither of whom had been on that face before, were sent
with other men to fill coal which had not been filled off (which they did), and after **D**
that to help with the drawing-off. The plaintiff and Grindle as they worked
towards the mother gate had to work through the swilly. The props had in
each case a lid between the top of the prop and the bar that it supported, but they
had on occasions been made up to the required height with foot lids, not only
two, but on occasions three or even four. There were sylvester props and also
some chocks instead of sylvester props, but the chocks were not set at regular **E**
intervals, and occasionally there was a space between bars where, instead of a
sylvester prop or chock, there was nothing at all. The tools supplied to the
plaintiff consisted of a sylvester and chain and a seven pound hammer with two
feet three inches shaft. Drawing-off proceeded. Between bars the plaintiff
advanced either the sylvester prop, if a sylvester prop was there, or a chock if a
chock was there. Having advanced the prop or chock, he then drew the gob **F**
side prop of the bar with his sylvester. Having done that, he would then draw
the remaining prop under that bar. Drawing a prop when weight had come on it
required considerable exertion, but when the plaintiff and Grindle got to the area
near the swilly the props came out, as he put it, " easy, without any undue
effort ". Near the place where the accident happened the plaintiff advanced a
chock (described on the plans as chock No. 1) before dealing with the bars on **G**
either side of it. He then came to a place where there was a chock referred to
as No. 3 which was between two bars called A and B. Normally it would have
been his duty to advance that chock as he had advanced chock No. 1, but,
because of the way that supports had been set, after removing it he had no
alternative but to leave that chock unadvanced. Leaving the pieces of chock
No. 3 ready to replace when they had withdrawn the bar, the plaintiff and Grindle **H**
went to chock No. 2 a little further along the face and advanced that chock.
The time then came when the sylvester chain, having been attached to the gob
prop under bar B, was drawn by the plaintiff and that gob prop came out without
much effort. All the way along the face as the plaintiff had worked from bar
to bar, when a gob prop had been removed the remaining bar and the prop
itself had stood; and when the gob prop under bar B was removed bar B and the **I**
the remaining prop stood. However, the sylvester chain slipped off and the
gob prop became loose and was lying in a diagonal position under bar B. The
plaintiff had no five foot hammer with which to fish it out. He went to a position
between bar B and bar A (which was the next undrawn bar in the direction of
the mother gate) and reached forward to pull the prop out by hooking the hook
of the chain on to the flange of the prop. He was convinced that the roof where
he was was well supported. To his right was bar A, standing on two props and
untouched; to his left was a remaining prop under bar B, and the bar itself on

A top of it, and quite close to him was the gob prop of the face line of bars.   As he was reaching forward, a stone over six feet long fell from the roof and, as it fell, it reeled out the remaining prop of bar B, reeled out the gob prop of bar A, bent bar A and fell across his back.

The plaintiff alleged that his injuries were caused by the negligence and/or breach of statutory duty of the defendants, their servants or agents of s. 48 (1),

B s. 49 (1), s. 51 (3) and s. 53 of the Mines and Quarries Act, 1954, reg. 2 of the Coal and Other Mines (Managers and Officials) Regulations, 1956, and reg. 2 (1) of the Coal and Other Mines (Support) Regulations, 1956*. The defendants denied that they were negligent or in breach of statutory duty, and alleged that the accident was caused wholly or partly by the fault of the plaintiff in various respects, which included the following as para. (a)—"He went under a part of the roof, outside

C his proper working place, which as he well knew was not properly supported ".

D. J. Clarkson and *S. P. Grenfell* for the plaintiff.
D. S. Forrester-Paton, Q.C., and *S. W. Williamson* for the defendants.

VEALE, J., stated the facts, referred to the correspondence and, having stated that he accepted the plaintiff's evidence, continued: These being the facts,

D what is the law applicable?   The plaintiff alleges in particular breaches of s. 48 and of s. 49 of the Mines and Quarries Act, 1954.   The well-known words of s. 48 (1) are as follows:

" It shall be the duty of the manager of every mine to take, with respect to every road and working place in the mine, such steps by way of controlling movement of the strata in the mine and supporting the roof and sides of the

E road or working place as may be necessary for keeping the road or working place secure . . ."

The duty under s. 48 of the Mines and Quarries Act, 1954, is not so stringent as the former duty under s. 49 of the Coal Mines Act, 1911. The present duty under the Act of 1954 is imposed on the manager personally, but, as was said by LORD

F DENNING in *Brown* v. *National Coal Board* (1):

" No doubt he [that is the manager] cannot see to it all himself.   He has to do it by overmen and by deputies.   But he is responsible for them and, if they fail to take the necessary steps, he himself is guilty of a contravention of the Act."

The extent of the duty imposed on the manager by s. 48 (1) has been put in

G various ways.   Since the decision of the House of Lords in *Brown's* case (2), a manager is not

"automatically guilty of having failed to take the necessary steps by the bare circumstances of insecurity coming about or a fall taking place "

(per LORD RADCLIFFE (3)).   LORD REID'S words were (4):

H ". . . a duty to exercise care and skill—the highest degree of care and skill that a competent manager could exercise."

Section 48 (1) imports foreseeability; as LORD DENNING said (5):

" ' Keeping ' the road secure does not mean that the manager must ensure that there shall never be a fall, however unforeseeable.   He can only

I ' take steps ' against foreseeable danger . . . The manager must take steps

---

* See the Coal and Other Mines (Managers and Officials) Order, 1956 (S.I. 1956 No. 1758) and the Coal and Other Mines (Support) Order, 1956 (S.I. 1956 No. 1763). The respective Regulations are contained in Sch. 1 to the apposite Order; 14 HALSBURY'S STATUTORY INSTRUMENTS (First Re-Issue) 21, 57.
(1) [1962] 1 All E.R. 81 at p. 90; [1962] A.C. 574 at p. 597.
(2) [1962] 1 All E.R. 81; [1962] A.C. 574.
(3) [1962] 1 All E.R. at p. 86; [1962] A.C. at p. 591.
(4) [1962] 1 All E.R. at p. 83; [1962] A.C. at p. 587.
(5) [1962] 1 All E.R. at p. 91; [1962] A.C. at p. 598.

to guard the workmen against those foreseeable dangers which are a   A
possible cause of injury in circumstances which may reasonably be expected
to occur."

These last words of LORD DENNING were emphasised when, as Master of the
Rolls, he gave judgment in *Soar* v. *National Coal Board* (6), a case in which the
defendants succeeded because the fall in that case was not a

B

" danger such as to be a possible cause of injury in circumstances which
might reasonably be expected to occur."

On the other hand, if it is known, or appreciated, or should be known or appreciated, that insecurity may arise, the manager's duty to control the strata or
to support is absolute, and in such circumstances the manager, and through
him the defendants, will be liable if a fall occurs, as is shown by the speeches of C
their lordships in *John G. Stein & Co., Ltd.* v. *O'Hanlon* (7).   I take it to be clear
that a manager is not automatically guilty of a contravention if a fall occurs.
Nevertheless, the fact of a fall is *some* evidence of a breach of s. 48 (1).   Should
there be, in any case, no other evidence at all, I have no doubt but that the
plaintiff would be held to have established his case.   For my part, I do not think
that in most cases it makes any real difference whether one approaches this kind D
of problem by saying that a fall of roof raises a prima facie case of a breach of
s. 48 (1) on the part of the manager, or whether one says that the onus is on the
manager in the first place, as was held by KARMINSKI, J., in *Beiscak* v. *National
Coal Board* (8).   That, then, is the general law, if I may call it such, relating to
s. 48.

By s. 49 (1):   E

" Subject to the provisions of this section, in every mine . . . there shall
be provided and maintained systematic support for the roof and sides of—
(*a*) every place where any mineral is worked; . . ."

Paragraph (*b*), para. (*c*) and para. (*d*) refer to other places in the mine.   By
sub-s. (5) of that section:
                                                                        F
" For the purposes of this section references to provision and maintenance
of systematic support shall, as respects any mine, be construed as references
to provision and maintenance of support in accordance with a system
specified in rules to be made by the manager of the mine, being a system
consistent with the proper control of movement of the strata in the mine."

I take the word " proper " in s. 49 (5) to mean " such control as will result in G
security ".   Security, in this connexion, means " a physical condition of stability
which will ordinarily result in safety ".   This definition of secure, originally
given by MCNAIR, J., in the Court of Appeal in *Gough* v. *National Coal Board* (9),
was expressly adopted by LORD RADCLIFFE, in *Brown's* case (10).   The support
rules must, therefore, be consistent with such control of movement of strata in
the mine as will ordinarily result in safety.   H

What was the position at this face?   I think that I may claim to have had as
judge, and perhaps more particularly as counsel, appearing for both injured
workmen and for the National Coal Board, substantial experience of coal mining
accidents.   I am deeply conscious that a little learning is a dangerous thing,
and I must not try this case on the experience which I have had of other cases;
but I have certainly never yet heard a deputy describe the support on his face I
as deplorable, the safety officer describe it as deplorable, or an under-manager
describe it as disgraceful, and the expert witness agreeing with both those
adjectives, as has been done in this case.   The supports were not regular, they
were not in pairs, the bars were not parallel, no steps whatever were taken to

(6) [1965] 2 All E.R. 318 at p. 321.   (7) [1965] 1 All E.R. 547; [1965] A.C. 890.
(8) [1965] 1 All E.R. 895.
(9) [1958] 1 All E.R. 754 at p. 762, letter A;   [1959] 1 Q.B. 189 at p. 200.
(10) [1962] 1 All E.R. at p. 85, letter H;   [1962] A.C. at p. 590.

A see that market men, quite new to the face, had the necessary chains or long hammer. In addition, despite an express instruction to the deputies that alternate lining props were to be replaced by chocks, which give a greater support, the deputy Hirst himself told me that they were in fact placed either alternately or two lining props per chock.   More than that, I accept the plaintiff's evidence that there were on occasions gaps when there was neither chock nor lining prop

B (which, indeed, is borne out by the defendants' own plan).   The support position was such that the drawers-off could not advance a chock as they ought to have been able to do.   In the circumstances, perhaps, " deplorable " and " disgraceful " are under-statements.   There were very substantial breaches of s. 49 (1) and of s. 53 by the deputies; but this does not avail the plaintiff if those breaches did not cause this accident, nor if the statutory duties did not apply to

C the place where he was injured.   This is the real point of this case.

    The defendants contend that they were at the relevant place under no duty to support at all, either by statute or at common law.   Under s. 48 (1) the manager's duty is to take " with respect to every road and working place ", such steps as may be necessary for keeping the road or working place secure. " Secure " means, as I have already said, physical conditions of stability, which

D ordinarily result in safety.   In *Gough* v. *National Coal Board* (11), LORD REID used the words: " in such a state that there will be no danger from accidental falls."   The important words relied on by the defendants are " working place ". Under s. 49 (1), the defendants' duty is to maintain a systematic support for the roof and sides of, inter alia, " every place where any mineral is worked ".   The defendants say that " every place where any mineral is worked " cannot include

E a place which is not a working place.   In this I think that they are right.   What, then, is a working place?   The expression " working place " was not defined in the Coal Mines Act, 1911, nor is it defined in the Act of 1954.   In *Lochgelly Iron & Coal Co., Ltd.* v. *McMullan* (12), LORD THANKERTON said:

> ". . . in the absence of any definition of the term in the statute, I see no reason against giving it the ordinary sense of a place where a miner is set

F   to work by his employers . . . ."

    LORD MACMILLAN (13) used the words " any place where a miner is set to work ". In *Gough* v. *National Coal Board* (14), LORD DENNING said, " Working place means, I think, every place at which men are working or may be expected to work ".   In my judgment, the phrase " working place " has the same meaning under the Act of 1954, as it had under the Act of 1911.   It will usually be the

G place where a man is in fact working, but this will not necessarily always be the case.   The area of a working place will vary very much with the work.   Fillers have their stint or stall, packers have their pack hole, but cutter men or belt men could have the whole length of a long wall face as a working place.   Further, I think that a working place may unexpectedly extend beyond the usual ambit. One would not, for example, expect a cutter man normally to be on the goaf

H side of the belt, but, if he should see a gobside prop in an unstable position, his working place would include the area required to make it stable; and the employers could not say that it was unexpected that such a man would be in such a position, and that he was, therefore, out of a working place.   He would have a duty to reset the prop.

    Neither in the *Lochgelly* case (15) nor in the *Gough* case (16) was it necessary

I to consider the full implications of the phrase " working place ", as it is necessary for me to do in this case.   LORD THANKERTON and LORD MACMILLAN used (17) the words " set to work by his employers ".   LORD DENNING in *Gough's* case (14) used the word, " at which men are working or may be expected to work ".

---

(11) [1959] 2 All E.R. 164 at p. 170; [1959] A.C. 698 at p. 711.
(12) [1934] A.C. 1 at p. 16.   (13) [1934] A.C. at p. 19.
(14) [1959] 2 All E.R. at p. 174; [1959] A.C. at p. 716.
(15) [1934] A.C. 1.   (16) [1959] 2 All E.R. 164; [1959] A.C. 698.
                (17) [1934] A.C. at pp. 16, 19.

It is not the place where the man is actually working which is the acid test; **A**
it is the place where he is actually working which is also the place where he has
been " set to work ", or " in which he may be expected to be ". It includes all
places where the man is properly working, all places where, in the particular
circumstances of the particular colliery, the employers would or should contemplate that the man might well be working. It is not a question of deciding the
scope of the employment; the decision of the problem which sometimes arises **B**
in a different kind of case—namely, was the workman improperly doing something which he was employed to do, or was he doing something which he was not
employed to do at all?—does not help. Circumstances vary enormously, and
it is a question of fact in each case. Could, for instance, the defendants argue
that a filler who left his stall, his working place, in order to pass the time of day
with another filler in another working place, had no remedy under s. 48 (1) if **C**
the roof fell? Of course not, for it would still be *a* working place, though not
the working place of the injured man. At the other extreme, the workman
who kept tools in the goaf unknown to his employers could not possibly argue
that the goaf was part of his working place because he kept his tools there. On
the other hand, if the employers—if one can imagine such a thing—permitted
the practice of keeping tools in the goaf, they would be setting the workman to **D**
work in the goaf, in that he would properly go to and from it in the course of his
work. Even the goaf, in such extreme circumstances, would be part of the
working place. I appreciate that this kind of example may have little basis in
reality, but I do not think that part of a working place ipso facto ceases to be
part of a working place if an element of danger arises therein. It depends on all
the circumstances, including, of course, the degree of danger. The sudden **E**
discovery of instability of a roof in a working place, for instance, by means of
jowling, might involve great danger, but the working place would not at once
cease to be a working place. On the other hand, if a discovered danger were
fenced off and workmen withdrawn, it would no longer be in the working place.

There was certainly no express prohibition in the support rules at Manvers
Main Colliery against entry by drawers-off into what I may call the disputed **F**
area—that is, the area between bars A and B. General instruction No. 2 in
those support rules, reproducing in substance s. 52 (1) of the Act of 1954,
refers to withdrawal " from a position of safety "—and the plaintiff thought that
he was in a position of safety. Mr. Gregson (18) says that he was, or should have
been. Mr. Marshall (19) says that he was not. I have to consider the meaning
of working place as applied to drawers-off. At the beginning of a drawing-off **G**
shift, the whole length of props and bars between the belt in its new position and
the goaf, is the working place of the drawers-off. The object of drawing-off,
or removing entirely that line of props and bars, is part of the technique of
mining at a long wall face. It is part of the process of control of strata. Seams
vary, roofs and strata vary, different roofs behave in different ways. Sometimes
strip packs are built between the roadside packs at intervals along the face. **H**
These are permanent and the roof comes down eventually in between them.
The system at Manvers Main Colliery in 4's North District in the Silkstone seam
was " total caving ". There were no strip packs. Instead there was a system
of lining props and alternate chocks, set between each bar at the goaf end, which
formed a strong line of support as a breaking-off line. Hence the support rules
specifically provide for the drawers-off to advance the sylvester lining props—or **I**
chocks used in substitution, although chocks are not mentioned in the rules—
before withdrawing any supports. A new breaking-off line was thereby formed
and, as props and bars were drawn, the area which they had protected would
become part of the waste until, on completion, the whole area was goaf. It
follows that the working place of the drawers-off as they carried out this system

---

(18) A mining consultant called by the plaintiff.
(19) Under-manager at the colliery at the time of the accident.

from right to left towards the mother gate, got steadily smaller. The problem, the vital problem, which lies at the heart of this case, the problem which is, I think, of considerable general importance, is where exactly and when exactly does the admitted working place cease to be a working place?

Everybody who knows anything at all about coal mining knows that the first thing every underground worker is taught is that one must never go under unsupported roof. This was, of course, well known to the plaintiff, who was an experienced market man. The area from which props and bars was wholly withdrawn clearly ceased to be part of the working place. The intention was that falls should occur there; indeed, that the whole roof should come down. The area under props and bars still standing clearly remained part of the working place, and certainly no falls were intended there while the supports stood. The disputed area is the area between two bars at a point of time in the operation, when the goaf prop only of the next bar in turn has been drawn. The distance between each row of props should be four feet six inches. The distance between adjoining props in the same row should be four feet. I am concerned, therefore, with an area four feet six inches by four feet, and only three feet two inches high. When does this area cease to be part of the working place? I am quite clear that, on withdrawal of the goaf prop, no fall was intended in this area; but the defendants say that this area was destined to be complete waste in a very short time, that it is notorious that any disturbance of support is liable to cause falls of roof, that the whole four feet six inches area therefore became a danger area, and so obvious a danger area that it at once ceased to be part of the working place. They say that the object of the drawing-off was to bring down the roof at the breaking-off line. They point to a second chain for the sylvester being compulsory as emphasising the danger.

The plaintiff points to the support in fact still existing. Assuming, says counsel for the plaintiff, that the supports had been properly set in the first place, the area was bounded by a bar properly set on two props and a bar standing firm on one prop. In addition, the waste end prop of the next bar was close at hand. This was still, he says, perfectly good support, or should have been. It was not intended that any of this roof should fall at this moment; nor should it, nor would it, says counsel for the plaintiff, have fallen, if the supports had been properly set, and certainly not if the system had been carried out in such a way as to permit the plaintiff to erect the chock which he was unable to advance. A prop or chock, according to Mr. Gregson, gives support for an area of some two feet radius round it, and Mr. Palframan (20) agreed; and the plaintiff would have been substantially touching a prop on either side of him, but rather behind him. The danger on removing one leg of a bar, so the argument goes, is that the weight may come on that end of the bar and thereby cause the other prop to reel, but it is said that no real danger is to be anticipated to a man in the position of the plaintiff if weight comes on in the area of the standing prop, for the bar is then but an extended lid.

Counsel for the defendants puts his case in this way. He says: either when an area is made insecure it ceases to be part of the working place altogether, or s. 52 (1) (which is in substance reproduced in the support rules) involves (21) an implied exception to the manager's obligation under s. 48 (1).

I think that " working place " must be construed in a broad, commonsense way, and although in very many cases it may very well be that the circumstances of a particular seam in a particular mine may render a particular fall impossible to prevent on withdrawal of a gob prop, that does not alter the words " working place ". If the circumstances are such that it is impossible to prevent a fall, the defendants have their escape under s. 157. I ask myself: what was the work that the plaintiff was doing? What had still to be done in that area of

---

(20) Under-manager of the seam at the time of the accident.
(21) Section 52 is set out at p. 159, letter D, post.

four feet six inches by four feet ?   Only the gob leg of the bar was down. Assuming the chain had not slipped, what else had to be done?   The bar still stood; it had to be removed.   The chain must be put round the remaining prop, and that prop and the bar must be removed from what would thereafter certainly be a danger area.   Was the bar not in the working place?   Was the prop not in the working place?   And how put the chain round the prop without going, technically at all events, outside the working place, if the defendants are right? The remaining prop under bar B had still to be withdrawn, and of course it was not as reliable as it was before the gob leg was drawn; but even Mr. Marshall does not include this prop in the " waste ".   And if the danger was all that great, why is there not a requirement in the support rules that a spare chain be attached to that prop?   If this remaining prop had not become part of the waste, why had it ceased to be part of the working place?   And if this prop was still part of the working place, why should not the plaintiff, who was close to one of the two props, properly supporting a bar, not be still in the working place?   Further, if potential danger is the definitive factor, how does one define its area?   The evidence is that, on withdrawal of the gob leg, a whole series of bars might reel out.   Are they all outside the working place, or are only so many outside it, and if so, how many?   The degree and extent of this danger is unforeseeable, although it is foreseeable that potential danger may exist in any roof of any seam at any time.   The technique of mining lies partly in controlling the dangerous potential.

I hold that the disputed area between the bars was still part of the plaintiff's working place.   I should have made this finding if every support had been regularly and properly set, including the advancing of the chock. It was none the less a working place because the supports were irregularly set and the chock could not be advanced.   Further, if I am wrong on general principles, I hold that, in the particular circumstances of this seam in this pit, it was a working place, because the defendants should have contemplated that the plaintiff might well do just what he did do.   Support discipline on this face was shockingly slack, and, in particular, the attention paid to drawing-off was such that the defendants took no steps to insist on two chains when two chains were compulsory by the rules, nor had they provided a long hammer.   Of course the removal of the goaf end prop increased the danger of a fall. Of course it is wise not to go under a bar from which a prop has been removed.   Of course some falls might not be preventable.   Any disturbance of support increases the risk; but the real risk, the serious risk, is, I think, the risk which I have already mentioned—weight coming on at the unsupported end of the bar, or flushing in the waste.   Of course one uses a sylvester from the safest place one can find, i.e., up against the face; but none of these considerations make me believe that what I have called the disputed area is no longer part of the working place.   Because any disturbance of support creates some risk, and because safety precautions will take into account this risk (for instance by the provision of two sylvester chains), it does not, in my judgment, therefore follow that an unintended fall inside a working place becomes an intended fall outside a working place.   One possible course open to the plaintiff was to set a catch prop, or another prop under the bar.   In my view, it is idle to contend that, in those circumstances, it would not have been a working place.   If the plaintiff was going outside his working place in doing what he did, I do not follow why the safety committee should be so concerned—as they obviously were from the minutes of their meeting—with what should have been the proper support of the area of fall.

I should mention a further point. Counsel for the defendants relies on the Coal and Other Mines (Support) Regulations, 1956 (22), and in particular on the definition of " face working " in reg. 17 (1).   That definition reads as follows:

" ' Face working ' in relation to a working face at which supports are

(22) See the Coal and Other Mines (Support) Order, 1956, S.I. 1956 No. 1763. The regulations are in Sch. 1 to the Order.

systematically withdrawn means all that part of the mine between the face
and the front line of the packs, if any, or the last row of supports for the
time being maintained, whichever is farther from the face . . ."

I need not read the rest of the definition. It is said that the words " the last
row of supports for the time being maintained " would exclude the whole of
bar B in this case, for it was no longer being maintained after the goaf prop
was drawn, and it was not, therefore, part of the face working for the purposes
of these regulations. The expression " face working " is used in reg. 3 (1)
(setting props), reg. 8 (1) (permitted intervals between supports) and reg. 11 (3)
(postponing bar setting because of the cutter path), and " face working " has
its prescribed meaning in reg. 17 (1) for these purposes. I am not concerned,
however, with any of these purposes; I am concerned with the words " working
place " in relation to a drawer-off, and I do not think that this definition is of
great assistance. Indeed, I am not sure that it does not equally assist the plaintiff, as the front prop with the bar over it was being maintained.

I am not impressed by counsel for the defendants' alternative argument.
Section 52 reads as follows:

" (1) No person shall withdraw support from the roof or sides of any
place in a mine otherwise than by a method or device by which he does so
from a position of safety.

" (2) Where it is part of the system of work at a place in a mine to withdraw
from the waste or from under the roof adjoining the waste support provided
in compliance with a requirement to provide it imposed by or by virtue of
s. 49 or 50 of this Act, no person shall, at that place, otherwise than in
accordance with a system specified in rules to be made by the manager of
the mine, withdraw as aforesaid support so provided."

This, as I understand it, is primarily directed to the normal method of withdrawal
of support, for instance by a sylvester, and a sylvester must be anchored in a
position of safety. The object is to protect a man withdrawing from what may
fall during the act of withdrawal. What does " position of safety " mean in
this connexion? I think that it means a position where one is reasonably entitled
to regard support as secure. Again quoting McNair, J. (23)—" a physical condition of stability which will ordinarily result in safety ". If there were to be a
slipe or slickenside against the face, the drawer-off beneath would not be in a
position of safety in fact, though I think that, if the support was such as would
ordinarily result in safety, the place would be " secure " in law, and the man
consequently (in law) in a position of safety. One therefore has to take into
account the extent of foreseeability of the risk; but none of these considerations
lead me to read into s. 48 a limitation of the express obligation in that section
relating to roads and working places. I repeat: if the circumstances are such
that it is impossible to prevent a fall, the defendants have their escape under
s. 157.

Counsel for the defendants further submitted that, even assuming the disputed
area to be a working place, and assuming a duty to take necessary steps, the
plaintiff had still not proved causation in that, by going into the disputed area,
the plaintiff had made it impossible for the manager to take steps, and his duty
then had, as it were, a new incidence. It may be—I do not decide it—that, in
some circumstances in relation to some falls there may be something in this argument, though, again, s. 157 would be a shield. I do not think that it can be
validly advanced in this case, where a stone over six feet long reeled out a bar
on two props, as well as a bar on one prop. This is not putting an impossibly
harsh obligation on the defendants. I have no doubt that in many if not the
majority of cases the defendants would have a complete and easy defence under
s. 157, in that in those cases it would be impracticable to avoid or to prevent the

(23) [1958] 1 All E.R. at p. 762; [1959] 1 Q.B. at p. 200.

contravention, and the man who goes out into the proximity of the drawn prop **A**
would have only himself to blame. But it is, perhaps, not without significance
in this case that s. 157 has not been pleaded by the defendants. If it had, I should
have had no hesitation at all on the facts in holding that the defendants had not,
in the circumstances, discharged the onus of bringing themselves within its
provisions.

I hold the defendants liable under both s. 48 (1) and s. 49 (1). There were **B**
breaches of both sections which caused this accident. I also hold that there was
a breach of s. 53. I find as a fact, as the safety committee in effect found as a
fact, that the fall would probably not have occurred if the plaintiff had been able
to advance the chock. Mr. Marshall was a formidable witness, but he gave evidence as to theory, and as to what this face ought to have been. He had no
first-hand knowledge of it, and I am dealing with this face as it in fact was. The **C**
safety committee comprised the manager and the safety officer, and their view
was that the fall would probably not have occurred, if the plaintiff had been able
to advance the chock. I am certainly not convinced of the contrary. That the
plaintiff could not advance the chock was a direct result of breaches of the support
rules, and I hold that those breaches were a cause of this accident. I think that
the probabilities are, though perhaps in the circumstances it is not necessary **D**
to make any express finding on it, that the gob prop of bar A was insecure on
three lids, and that the face prop of bar B was not as firm as it should be. I accept
that three foot lids were on occasion used. I find that this was not a fall which
could be described as being an everyday occurrence in drawing-off; it was a fall
which *should* not have occurred, and which *would* not have occurred if the supports
had been as stable as they should have been, quite apart from the absence of the **E**
chock which the plaintiff could not advance. As I have said, Mr. Marshall's
evidence was very helpful, and he gave it admirably, but he had no first-hand
knowledge of this face, and he was talking of it as it ought to have been and not
as I find that it was in fact.

That is not an end of the case. The defendants allege contributory negligence
against the plaintiff. I will not further lengthen this judgment by reading the **F**
allegations of contributory negligence set out in the defence. Suffice it to say that
I regard some of them, which have very properly been abandoned, as quite
astonishing. The allegation of substance made against the plaintiff is in para.
(a), (24). The plaintiff did not go outside his working place, though he knew that
risk in part of it was incurred. He agreed in cross-examination that withdrawing
a gob prop to a certain extent reduces support. He agreed that, when a support is **G**
withdrawn, an area of roof is liable to break. He agreed that, when gob props
were withdrawn, the roof sometimes broke immediately. He knew the reason for
two chains, he knew that the rules required two chains, and he knew that he was
just beyond the breaking-off line. Nevertheless, it was his duty to recover timber
if he could properly do so. I am not surprised, in all the circumstances of this
case, that he did what he did do, despite his frank admissions in cross-examination. **H**
Mr. Gregson saw nothing improper in what he did. The burden of proving
contributory negligence is on the defendants, and, on the whole, I am not satisfied
that they have done so in the circumstances of this case. In many cases a man
would have only himself to blame if he was hit by, for instance, a small fall.
The plaintiff knew he was taking *a* risk, but not that he was taking *this* risk.
My findings in this case do not mean that drawers-off are to be encouraged to go **I**
near withdrawn supports—quite the reverse; but I accept that the plaintiff
was very close to the remaining supports. In any event, if I were to be wrong and
some blame should be imputed to the plaintiff, I would hold that it was only
relatively a small percentage. As I have said more than once, support discipline
on this face was quite deplorable.

In my judgment, therefore, the plaintiff is entitled to succeed in this action.
I have had the advantage of reading the medical reports which have been set

(24) See p. 153, letter C, ante.

A before me. The special damages are agreed at £962 18s. 6d., and, I hope taking into account all the things that I should take into account, I think that the proper figure to award as general damages is the sum of £1,500. There will, therefore, be judgment for the plaintiff for £2,462 18s. 6d.

Judgment for the plaintiff.

B Solicitors: *Raley & Pratt,* Barnsley (for the plaintiff); *C. M. H. Glover,* Doncaster (for the defendants).

[*Reported by* G. M. SMAILES, ESQ., *Barrister-at-Law.*]

C

Re N. (infants).

[CHANCERY DIVISION (Stamp, J.), November 17, 18, 21, 22, 1966.]

Injunction—Sunday—Dies non juridicus—Interim injunction granted as emergency measure on a Sunday to prevent father abducting children on terms
D *that summons to make them wards of court be issued on the next day—Whether granting of injunction was excepted from judicial acts not to be done on a Sunday—Title of order for injunction—R.S.C., Ord. 29, r. 1.*
Practice—Title of proceedings—Injunction before issue of originating process.
Ward of Court—Jurisdiction—Injunction—Interim injunction—Originating process not yet issued—Whether inherent jurisdiction to grant injunction
E *before issue of originating process restricted by Law Reform (Miscellaneous Provisions) Act, 1949 (12, 13 & 14 Geo. 6 c. 100), s. 9.*

On Sunday, Oct. 16, 1966, the mother of two infant children who, by agreement between the parents, had been sent to a school in Switzerland, applied to a High Court judge, assigned to the Queen's Bench Division, at his private residence for an order to prevent the father of the infants removing
F them from Switzerland and taking them to Australia, where he was resident. The judge granted the injunction on the terms that an originating summons should be issued on the following day. On the following day the mother issued an originating summons, to which the father was defendant, and by which she asked that the infants should become wards of court. Questions having arisen whether the order for the injunction, made on a Sunday,
G could be entered, application was made to the court for directions.

Held: the order for the injunction was validly made and should be drawn up in the Chancery Division, entitled in the matter of an intended action to make infants wards of court (see p. 169, letter G, post), for the following reasons—

(i) in a case of emergency, as the present case was, an interlocutory
H injunction being an act in exercise of the equitable jurisdiction originally of the Lord Chancellor, could be granted validly on a Sunday, although that day was a dies non juridicus, as the granting of an injunction was within the class of judicial acts which were excepted from the general rule of the common law that a judicial act could not be done on Sunday (see p. 164, letter G, and p. 166, letters C and F, post).
I Judgment of LORD MANSFIELD in *Swann v. Broome* ((1764), 3 Burr. 1595) considered.

Dictum of LORD ELDON, L.C., in *Crowley's Case* ((1818), 2 Swan. at p. 48) applied.

(ii) under R.S.C., Ord. 29, r. 1*, a judge of the High Court could grant an injunction in an urgent case before the writ or originating summons was issued on terms providing for its issue (see p. 167, letter E, post).

---

* R.S.C., Ord. 29, r. 1, is printed at p. 167, letters C and D, post.

(iii) although after s. 9* of the Law Reform (Miscellaneous Provisions) **A**
Act, 1949, came into force an infant did not become a ward of court until
an application to the court was made for the purpose, and although the
summons to make the infants wards of court had not been issued when
the injunction was granted, yet the court's inherent jurisdiction to make
an order for the protection of an infant before wardship proceedings had
been begun was not thereby destroyed (see p. 168, letters B to D, and p.   **B**
169, letter D, post).

Dicta of KAY, J., in *Brown* v. *Collins* ((1883), 25 Ch.D. at p. 60) applied.

Re E. (*an infant*) ([1955] 3 All E.R. 174) criticised.

[As to Sunday being a dies non juridicus, see 37 HALSBURY'S LAWS (3rd Edn.)
88, para. 155, text and note (*p*); and for cases on the subject, see 45 DIGEST
(Repl.) 247, *138-150*, 249, *172-183*.   **C**

As to granting an injunction before the issue of a writ, see 21 HALSBURY'S
LAWS (3rd Edn.) 412, para. 863; and for cases on the subject, see 28 DIGEST
(Repl.) 880, 881, *1061-1063*.

For the Law Reform (Miscellaneous Provisions) Act, 1949, s. 9, see 28
HALSBURY'S STATUTES (2nd Edn.) 777.]

Cases referred to: **D**

Barnardo v. *McHugh*, [1891-94] All E.R. Rep. 825; [1891] A.C. 388; 61
    L.J.Q.B. 721; 65 L.T. 423; 55 J.P. 628; 16 Digest (Repl.) 307, *837*.

Broome v. *Swan*, (1766), 6 Bro. Parl. Cas. 333; 2 E.R. 1115; *affg.* sub nom.
    Swann v. *Broome*, (1764), 3 Burr. 1595; 45 Digest (Repl.) 247, *149*.

Brown v. *Collins*, (1883), 25 Ch.D. 56; 49 L.T. 329; 16 Digest (Repl.) 209, *986*.

Chanoch v. *Hertz*, (1888), 4 T.L.R. 331; 28 Digest (Repl.) 883, *1094*.   **E**

Crowley's Case, (1818), 2 Swan. 1; Buck, 264; 36 E.R. 514; 16 Digest (Repl.)
    298, *706*.

E. (*an infant*), *Re*, [1955] 3 All E.R. 174; [1956] Ch. 23; [1955] 3 W.L.R. 493;
    28 Digest (Repl.) 607, *1171*.

Fynn, *Re*, (1848), 2 De G. & Sm. 457; 12 L.T.O.S. 143; 64 E.R. 205; 28 Digest
    (Repl.) 618, *1221*.   **F**

Harrison v. *Smith*, (1829), 9 B. & C. 243; 7 L.J.O.S.K.B. 171; 109 E.R. 91;
    45 Digest (Repl.) 247, *150*.

Mackalley's Case, (1611), 9 Co. Rep. 65b; Cro. Jac. 279; 77 E.R. 828; 45 Digest
    (Repl.) 247, *138*.

McGrath (*Infants*), *Re*, [1892] 2 Ch. 496; 61 L.J.Ch. 549; 66 L.T. 850; *affd.*
    C.A., [1893] 1 Ch. 143; 62 L.J.Ch. 208; 67 L.T. 636; 28 Digest (Repl.) **G**
    644, *1373*.

Spence, *Re*, (1847), 2 Ph. 247; 16 L.J.Ch. 309; 9 L.T.O.S. 241; 41 E.R. 937;
    28 Digest (Repl.) 630, *1314*.

Thorneloe v. *Skoines*, (1873), L.R. 16 Eq. 126; 42 L.J.Ch. 788; 28 Digest
    (Repl.) 882, *1091*.

Young v. *Brassey*, (1875), 1 Ch.D. 277; 45 L.J.Ch. 142; 28 Digest (Repl.) **H**
    880, *1063*.

Adjourned Summons.

The mother, Mrs. N., and the father, Mr. N., were married in 1950. There
were two children of the marriage. The mother resided in London and the
father resided in Australia. By agreement between the parties the children
were placed in a school in Switzerland. On Oct. 15, 1966, the father, without **I**
prior notification to the mother removed the children from the school. On
Sunday, Oct. 16, CHAPMAN, J., on the application of the mother made an order
that the father should return the children to their school, if the children were
still in Switzerland, or if the children were not in Switzerland that he should
bring them into and should not remove them from the jurisdiction of the English
court. On Oct. 17, 1966, the mother applied by originating summons seeking
an order that the infants be made wards of court and be returned to her care and

---

* Section 9, so far as material, is printed at p. 168, letter A, post.

A control.   On Oct. 18, 1966, wardship proceedings were begun in Australia
and of these the mother was notified and arrangements were made for service
on her.

The authorities and the cases noted below* were cited during the argument in
addition to those referred to in the judgment.

   G. M. Godfrey for the mother.
B   *J. E. Vinelott* appeared as amicus curiae.

   STAMP, J., read the following judgment: On Sunday, Oct. 16, 1966, application was made by the mother of two infants, who had been sent to school in
Switzerland, to a High Court judge at his private residence, for an order designed
to prevent the father of the infants removing them from Switzerland and taking
C them to Australia.   If ever an urgent action was required to prevent children
being snatched and taken to the other side of the world it was on that day,
—though, in the event, the stable-door was not closed until after the horses had
been stolen—and naturally the judge granted an injunction against the father
designed to prevent the threatened acts.   He did so on the terms that an originating summons should be issued on the following day.   In fact, as might be
D expected, an originating summons was issued on the following day by the mother,
being plaintiff, and making the father defendant, asking that the infants should
become wards of court, and other relief.

   Thereafter, the mother's legal advisers sought to have the order of CHAPMAN,
J., made on the Sunday, passed and entered.   The officers of this court responsible
for these matters felt difficulty in acting on such an order and application was
E made to me on behalf of the mother for an appropriate direction.   The matter
was mentioned to me by counsel then acting on behalf of the mother on, I think,
two occasions and on it appearing, as counsel pointed out to me, that there were
questions arising which were not without difficulty, it was arranged that the
court should have the assistance of the Official Solicitor as amicus curiae.   This
court has had that assistance in full measure and is most indebted to counsel on
F both sides now appearing before me.

   The first point taken by counsel appearing as amicus curiae, is that Sunday is
a dies non juridicus on which no judicial act can lawfully be done, that the order
is a nullity and cannot be properly passed and entered.   The authorities show,
beyond doubt, that at common law, Sunday, like other holy days, was a dies
non juridicus.   See *Mackalley's Case* (1), a case decided in 1611, which was
G considered to be of so much importance that all the judges in England were
called together to consider whether a man could lawfully be arrested on Sunday
and where, according to the report, it was held that (2)

   " . . . no judicial act ought to be done on that day, but ministerial acts may
   be lawfully executed on a Sunday;   for otherwise peradventure they can
   never be executed."

H See also *Swann* v. *Broome* (3), where LORD MANSFIELD held that by law a valid
judgment could not possibly be given on a Sunday and, therefore, a judgment
could not be supposed to have been given; and see per LORD COKE in his Second
Institute, p. 264, where he said:

   " In the common law, there be dies jurdici and dies non jurdici.   Dies
I non juridici sunt dies Dominici, the Lord's days, throughout the whole
   year."

---

* 7 COMYNS' DIGEST 405; 2 DANIELL'S CHANCERY PRACTICE (8th Edn.) 1406; 1
SETON'S JUDGMENTS AND ORDERS (7th Edn.) 515; *Carr* v. *Morice*, (1873), L.R. 16 Eq.
125; *Campara* v. *Webb*, (1874), 22 W.R. 622; *Ex p. McPhail*, (1879), 12 Ch.D. 632;
Re A.B. (*an infant*), (1885), 1 T.L.R. 657; *Quinn* v. *Leathem*, [1900-03] All E.R. Rep. 1;
[1901] A.C. 495; *A.-G. of Canada* v. *Hirsch*, (1960), 24 D.L.R. 94; *Official Solicitor* v. *K.*,
[1963] 3 All E.R. 191; [1965] A.C. 201; *Re W.* (*an infant*), [1963] 3 All E.R. 459; [1964]
Ch. 202.   (1) (1611), 9 Co. Rep. 65b.
   (2) (1611), 9 Co. Rep. at 66b.   (3) (1764), 3 Burr. 1595.

Again, in BLACKSTONE'S COMMENTARIES (21st Edn.) it is said at p. 277:   **A**

">. . . no proceedings can be held, or judgment can be given, or supposed
to be given, on the Sunday,"

and see also *Harrison* v. *Smith* (4), where it was held that a judgment for want
of a plea could not be signed on a dies non juridicus at common law.   It is clear
that at common law Sunday was not to be profaned by the tumult of forensic   **B**
litigations.

I accept the submission that acts which, in the language of common lawyers,
were described as judicial acts could not, and, subject to statute providing to the
contrary, cannot now, be lawfully done on Sunday.   I also accept the further
submission of counsel appearing as amicus curiae that the making of an order
restraining the doing of an act by way of interlocutory injunction is, in the   **C**
language of lawyers of today, properly described as a judicial act; and although
the contrary argument might, perhaps, succeed if it was material, I will assume
in favour of counsel appearing as amicus curiae, without so deciding, that an
injunction for the protection of an infant, made by a judge in the exercise of
what is called the paternal jurisdiction over infants, delegated to him from the
Crown through the Lord Chancellor, is in no different case: that is to say, it is,   **D**
in the language of today, a judicial act.

It does not, however, in my judgment, follow that because today a particular
act is, in the language of lawyers, properly described as a judicial act it was such
an act as was, or is, covered by the ancient rule.   Although today the granting
of an interlocutory injunction is, no doubt, a judicial and not an administrative
act, an injunction is a creature of equity: a creature of the jurisdiction exercised   **E**
by the Lord Chancellor to give a remedy which the common lawyers in the
common law courts could not give.   The courts of common law might give a
remedy when the wrong had been done, but until the Common Law Procedure
Act, 1852, they could not interfere to prevent it.   Such interference was, however,
an early subject of the Lord Chancellor's jurisdiction (see HOLDSWORTH'S "A
HISTORY OF ENGLISH LAW " (5th Edn.), Vol. 1, at p. 458) and, in my judgment,   **F**
what I have to consider is whether the granting of an injunction ex parte by
way of interlocutory relief to prevent a party acting in such and such a way until
such and such a time, is to be regarded as a judicial act within the meaning of
and for the purposes of the common law rule that no judicial act may lawfully
be done on a dies non juridicus, or whether the granting of an interlocutory
injunction is a judicial act which is excepted from that rule.   **G**

It is at this point that the judgment of LORD MANSFIELD in *Swann* v. *Broome* (5)
assumes a vital importance, for the decision in that case, that no judicial act
could be done on Sunday, was founded, to some extent, on the posthumous works
of SIR HENRY SPELMAN, 1564-1641, published, I think, in 1693, under a heading
entitled " THE ORIGINAL OF THE TERMS "; and in view of what was said in
Swann v. *Broome* (5) I must, I think, treat that work as authoritative on the   **H**
question which I have to decide.

SIR HENRY SPELMAN, in his work (6), specifies classes of acts which could be
done on a dies non juridicus, and if the granting of an interlocutory injunction by a
judge as a matter of urgency to preserve the status quo pending the ascertainment of the rights of the parties is an act falling within that classification, then,
in my judgment, it matters not whether the act is to be regarded as an administra-   **I**
tive, as distinct from a judicial, act—a distinction which was regarded in
Mackalley's Case (7) as a vital decision—or as a judicial act falling within
the exception to the general rule; for the line dividing the judicial act from the
administrative act, at the beginning of the seventeenth century, was, I think, so

(4) (1829), 9 B. & C. 243.   (5) (1764), 3 Burr. 1595.
(6) See under the heading " The Original of the Terms " at p. 94.
(7) (1611), 9 Co. Rep. 65b.

A far as the Chancery was concerned, drawn at a very different point from that at which it would be drawn today.

The chapter of SIR HENRY SPELMAN's work in which the list of exceptions occurs is chapter 3, which is headed " Why some law business may be done on days exempted ". It reads:

B " In the mean time let us see, why some law business may be done on days exempted, and sometimes on Sunday it self, notwithstanding any thing before mentioned. For as in term-time some days are exempted from term business, and some portion of the day from sitting in courts; so in the vacation-time and days exempted, some law business may be performed by express permission of the Canon Law ..."

C It then recites an extract from " the Georgics ". It goes on:

" The Synod of Medard admitteth matters de pace et concordia, to be dispatched both on holy-days and on Sunday it self: the laws of Hen. I. matters of concord and doing fealty to the Lord: the decree of Gregory IX. cases of necessity and doing piety, according to that of Prosper ..."

D He then recites a passage from the works of Prosper, and goes on:

" The rule is verified by our Saviour's healing on the sabbath. Out of these and such other autorities of the laws ecclesiastical and civil, cited in the glosses, the canonists have collected these cases, wherein judges may proceed legally upon the days prohibited, or do the things herein following."

E Then there follows a list of matters on which judges may proceed legally on the days prohibited. I do not refer to them all, but among these cases, according to SIR HENRY SPELMAN, were:

" For matters of peace and concord, by reason whereof our judges take the acknowledgment of fines, statutes, recognizances, &c. upon any day, even the sabbath-day (tho' it were better then forborn, if necessity require it not). For suppressing of traitors, thieves, and notorious offenders, which **F** may otherwise trouble the peace of the common-wealth, and endanger the kingdom ... For saving that which otherwise would perish: a work of necessity. For doing that, which time overslip, cannot be done: As for making appeals within the time limited, &c. For taking the benefit of a witness that otherwise would be lost, as by death or departure. For making the son sui juris: as if, amongst us, the Lord should discharge his ward of **G** wardship. [He goes on, after some further remarks, to say this:] Upon these reasons the Admiral-Court is always open; for that strangers and merchants and sea-faring-men, must take the opportunity of tides and of winds, and other necessities; and cannot without ruine or great prejudice attend the solemnity of courts and dilatory pleadings. The marshal's court also for military matters ... [He deals with that and then goes on:] So **H** likewise the Chancery, being a court of piety, is said to be always open: but I take this to be understood as it is officina brevium and consistorium aequi et boni; not where it is praetorium, juris communis, and proceedeth in course of the common law. As for the Star-chamber, it is in lieu of that which was in ancient time the counsel-chamber, and specula Regni, the watch-tower of the kingdom: where the barons and other of the king's **I** counsel us'd to meet ad prospiciendam fovendamque remp. to discover, prevent, and suppress all dangers and enormities occurrent, and to provide for the safety and good of the kingdom. It was necessary therefore that this session should not only be daily open, but (as is said of the house of fame) Nocte dieque patens; for an evil may happen in the night, that would be too late to prevent in the morning."

There has been some debate before me as to the meaning of consistorium aequi et boni and praetorium juris communis, it being common ground that officina brevium is the writ office of Chancery, which was, we know, always open. It is to be observed that by SPELMAN's time there were, in the Chancery, two courts:

" '. . . one ordinary, wherein the Lord Chancellor . . . proceeds according to the right line of the laws and statutes of the realm . . . another extra-ordinary, according to the rule of equity.' "

(See HOLDSWORTH's " A HISTORY OF ENGLISH LAW " (5th Edn.), Vol. 1, at p. 451, quoting COKE's FOURTH INSTITUTE). I have been given no reason to doubt that the consistorium aequi et boni to which SPELMAN refers was the court extra-ordinary wherein the Lord Chancellor proceeded according to the rule of equity and that the praetorium juris communis was the court ordinary wherein the Lord Chancellor proceeded according to the right line of the laws and statutes of the realm. It follows, I think, that in SIR HENRY SPELMAN's opinion the Lord Chancellor, in exercising the equitable jurisdiction, could act on a dies non juridicus, and since an interlocutory injunction is an act which derived from the equitable jurisdiction of the Chancellor it was, and is, in my judgment, an act which could and can be done by a judge on a Sunday. I am assisted in that conclusion by passages from LORD ELDON, L.C.'s judgment in *Crowley's Case* (8), and, in particular, a passage, where he said (9):

" ' The like writ ' (of habeas corpus) ' is to be granted out of the Court of Chancery, either in the time of the term (as in the King's Bench), or in the vacation, for the court of Chancery is officina justiciae, and is ever open, and never adjourned, so as the subject, being wrongfully imprisoned, may have justice for the liberty of his person, as well in the vacation time, as in the term.' "

The equitable jurisdiction, of course, can now be exercised by all the judges of the High Court and where the rules of equity and rules of common law in any way differ the rules of equity are to be followed and prevail. In my judgment, therefore, an interlocutory injunction, granted as an emergency measure before the party against whom it is granted is before the court, is within the acts which may be done on ". . . even the sabbath-day (tho' it were better then forborn, if necessity require it not) ".

The second point taken against the validity of the order is that no injunction can be granted nor other order made except in proceedings which have been commenced by writ or originating summons: and, of course, the originating summons had not been issued when the order in question in this case was made. Attention is called to the moment of time when, under the Rules of the Supreme Court, a writ or originating summons is issued. The position in that respect is now, and has been since 1963, that the issue of a writ or originating summons takes place on its being sealed by an officer of the office out of which it was issued. Prior to that the position had, for many years, been governed by a rule which provided that every writ should be sealed by the proper officer and should thereupon be deemed to be issued. It does not seem to me that the position was altered by this slight change of wording and, in my judgment, proceedings by writ or originating summons were not commenced until the writ or originating summons had been sealed by the proper officer. Nevertheless, the judges, relying on *Chanoch* v. *Hertz* (10), granted any injunctions in urgent cases where, on account of the office being closed, the writ was not issued, the writ being retained by the judge or registrar, if he was available, and passed to the central office at the earliest opportunity with instructions to treat it as issued at the time it passed into official custody.

On occasions, the judges, in such circumstances, no doubt relying on *Thorneloe* v. *Skoines* (11), have adopted the somewhat different practice, which was relied

---

(8) (1818), 2 Swan. 1.
(9) (1818), 2 Swan. at p. 48. LORD ELDON is quoting from LORD COKE's writing in SECOND INSTITUTES 53, on Magna Charta.
(10) (1888), 4 T.L.R. 331.   (11) (1873), L.R. 16 Eq. 126.

A on in this case, of requiring an undertaking to issue the writ (or originating summons) immediately it is possible to do so without the writ coming into the custody of the judge or registrar and, in those cases, the practice has been, so I am told, at any rate in the Queen's Bench Division, to date the writ with the date on which it is actually issued and to add a note that it is to be treated as issued as at the date of the undertaking.

B In my judgment, I am, by the effect of the new R.S.C., Ord. 29, r. 1 (3), which, I think, gives effect to both practices, relieved from the task of considering whether as a matter of logic either of the practices to which I have referred can be reconciled with the rule, if such a rule there ever was, that no injunction can be granted except in proceedings which have been commenced by the issue of a writ or originating summons. R.S.C., Ord. 29, r. 1, provides as follows

C   " (1) An application for the grant of an injunction may be made by any party to a cause or matter before or after the trial of the cause or matter, whether or not a claim for the injunction was included in that party's writ, originating summons, counterclaim or third party notice, as the case may be.

       " (2) Where the applicant is the plaintiff and the case is one of urgency such application may be made ex parte on affidavit, but, except as aforesaid, D such application must be made by motion or summons.

       " (3) The plaintiff may not make such an application before the issue of the writ or originating summons by which the cause or matter is to be begun except where the case is one of urgency, and in that case the injunction applied for may be granted on terms providing for the issue of the writ or summons and such other terms, if any, as the court thinks fit."

E In my judgment, a judge can now, pursuant to that rule, clearly grant an injunction, where the case is one of urgency, before the writ or originating summons is issued, on terms providing for its issue, which was precisely what was done in this case. It is, no doubt, desirable that the writ or originating summons should be left with the judge or in the custody of the court so that there can be as little doubt as possible that it will be issued. It is also, in my view, most desirable F that where this cannot be done the terms imposed should be such as to require that the writ or summons be so drawn that if it had been issued the injunction could have been granted. So far as regards the title to the order, I am told by the registrar that in a case where the proceedings had not been issued and a judge, on a Saturday, granted an injunction he directed that the order should be headed " In the matter of an intended action between A and B ..." etc., and that G there is no difficulty in passing and entering an order in that form (compare *Young* v. *Brassey* (12)).

    Finally, it was submitted that the inherent jurisdiction of this court over infants has been restricted by the Law Reform (Miscellaneous Provisions) Act, 1949, to infants who have become wards of court, whereas the children in this case had not become wards of court at the date of the order in question. *Re E.* H *(an infant)* (13) is relied on for this purpose and it is also urged that the undertaking given to the judge who made the order in this case was not an undertaking to issue a summons to make the children wards of court but merely an undertaking to issue a summons. I will deal with the second part of the contention first by calling attention to the fact that the originating summons, when issued on the following day, did ask that the children should be made wards of court, and I I shall presume, until the contrary is shown to be the case, which it is not, that what ought to have been done was, in fact, done and that the undertaking given was an undertaking to that effect.

    The substantial point taken by counsel appearing as amicus curiae on this part of the case rests, however, on s. 9 of the Law Reform (Miscellaneous Provisions) Act, 1949. That section provides:

(12) (1875), 1 Ch.D. 277.
(13) [1955] 3 All E.R. 174; [1956] Ch. 23.

" (1) Subject to the provisions of this section, no infant shall be made a ward of court except by virtue of an order to that effect made by the court. (2) Where application is made for such an order in respect of an infant, the infant shall become a ward of court on the making of the application, but shall cease to be a ward of court at the expiration of such period as may be prescribed by rules of court unless within that period an order has been made in accordance with the application."

As the infant does not, since the passing of that section, become a ward of court until an application is made for that purpose and since the application is not made until the summons is issued, it follows, so the argument runs, that no order for the protection of an infant can be made until after the summons is issued. In *Re E. (an infant)* (14), ROXBURGH, J., certainly used language which can and, I think, should be construed as indicating that the jurisdiction of this court in respect of an infant could in no case be invoked until after he had become a ward of court, and if it was the law that before 1949 this court could only intervene to protect an infant after something had been done to make him a ward of court then, subject to the effect of the new R.S.C., Ord. 29, the conclusion for which counsel appearing as amicus curiae contends would be, so it seems to me, almost irresistible. In my judgment, however, this was never the law before 1949. Awkward questions sometimes arose whether a child was or was not a ward. He might have become so almost by accident, as when proceedings were taken for the administration of property in which he was interested, such proceedings not being designed in the least to make the infant a ward of court. This was very awkward, because the effect of the infant becoming a ward of court was that he or she could not be taken out of the jurisdiction without the leave of the court and could not marry without the leave of the court; and I have no doubt whatsoever that many infants were married and taken out of the jurisdiction of the court without their parents being aware that a contempt of court was being committed. One of the purposes of s. 9 may well have been to avoid these inconvenient results, and I cannot accept the conclusion that s. 9 had the far-reaching consequences suggested by ROXBURGH, J. The term " ward of court " meant, strictly, or properly, " a person under the care of a guardian appointed by the court " (see SIMPSON ON " THE LAW OF INFANTS " (4th Edn.) at p. 165). The editor of that work adds:

". . . but the term has been extended to infants who are brought under the authority of the court by an application to it on their behalf, though no guardian is appointed by the court."

That it was never the case that this court could not interfere to protect an infant except after the infant had become a ward of court is, in my judgment, indicated by such cases as *Re Spence* (15) and in *Re McGrath (infants)* (16), and it is, perhaps, convenient that I should call attention to a passage in the judgment of NORTH, J., in the latter case, where he said (17):

" ' This court interferes for the protection of infants, quâ infants, by virtue of the prerogative which belongs to the Crown as parens patriae, and the exercise of which is delegated to the Great Seal.' "

That passage was quoted with approval by LORD HALSBURY, L.C., in *Barnardo* v. *McHugh* (18). Again, in *Brown* v. *Collins*, KAY, J., said (19):

" Undoubtedly, we use the words ' ward of court ' in such a case in rather a special sense. In one sense all British subjects who are infants are wards of court, because they are subject to that sort of parental jurisdiction which

---

(14) [1955] 3 All E.R. 174; [1956] Ch. 23.   (15) (1847), 2 Ph. 247.
(16) [1892] 2 Ch. 496.   (17) [1892] 2 Ch. at p. 511.
(18) [1891-94] All E.R. Rep. 825 at p. 827; [1891] A.C. 388 at p. 395.
(19) (1883), 25 Ch.D. 56 at p. 60.

A is intrusted to the court in this country, and which has been administered continually by the courts of the Chancery Division. It may be exercised as it has been in many cases, such as *Re Fynn* (20) and *Re Spence* (21) whether they have property or not, although, of course, where the infant has no property it makes it extremely difficult to exercise the jurisdiction at all . . ."

B Then KAY, J., added (22):

" The jurisdiction exists from the fact that the infant is a British subject, and the Chancery Division has always exercised that parental jurisdiction over British subjects who are infants."

In my judgment, this court, before 1949, had jurisdiction to make an order **C** for the protection of an infant before any other wardship proceedings had been commenced. No doubt the effect of such an order usually, if not always, would have been to make the child a ward of court and, no doubt, by the effect of the Act of 1949 this will no longer be the result. Wardship was the result of, and not the ground for, the exercise of the jurisdiction and I am bound to say that in view of the cases to which I have referred (which do not appear to have been **D** cited to ROXBURGH, J. (23)), I find considerable difficulty in accepting the view of ROXBURGH, J., that the effect of the Act of 1949 is to destroy the inherent jurisdiction of this court over infants in this country.

I do not, however, feel it necessary to disregard the decision of ROXBURGH, J. however much I may feel a difficulty in following it, because I hold that the necessary authority to make an order such as was made in this case is to be found **E** in the terms of R.S.C., Ord. 29, r. 1, itself, which, in my judgment, applies, for there is nothing to exclude it, alike to an injunction to protect the person of an infant before the summons is issued, as it applies to other cases. It would be a remarkable defect in our law and procedure if an injunction could be granted to protect the property of an infant, in anticipation of a writ to be issued by the infant, acting by his next friend, asking for administration of his property, but **F** no injunction could be granted to protect the infant's person. In my judgment there is no such anomaly in our law.

Subject to what the Official Solicitor suggests, the order will be drawn up in the following form, and in the Chancery Division. It will be drawn up— " In the matter of . . ." the infants, naming them, and " In the matter of an intended action between . . ." the mother and the father, ". . . to make the said **G** infants wards of court ". The order will be dated on the day on which the judge made it. I am told that that will create no difficulties.

Order accordingly.

Solicitors: *Kingsley, Napley & Co.* (for the mother); *Official Solicitor.*

[*Reported by* JENIFER SANDELL, *Barrister-at-Law.*]

H

I

---

(20) (1848), 2 De G. & Sm. 457.   (21) (1847), 2 Ph. 247.
(22) (1883), 25 Ch.D. at p. 61.
(23) I.e., in *Re E.* (*an infant*), [1955] 3 All E.R. 174; [1956] Ch. 23.

NOTE.

R. *v.* ANDREWS.

[COURT OF APPEAL, CRIMINAL DIVISION (Lord Parker, C.J., Salmon, L.J., and Blain, J.), December 8, 1966.]

Criminal Law—Indictment—Joinder of counts—Driving while disqualified for holding licence—Joinder with a different offence relating to a motor vehicle, or to driving it, permissible — If prejudicial, counsel to apply before arraignment for separate trials.

Criminal Law—Verdict—Inconsistent verdicts—No absolute rule that first verdict of guilty will be set aside.

[**Editorial Note.** As to having two indictments where separate trials of two charges would be ordered, see *Connelly* v. *Director of Public Prosecutions*, [1964] 2 All E.R. 401, per LORD DEVLIN at p. 446, letters C and D, and per LORD PEARCE at p. 451, letters B, C and G.

As to joinder of several offences and separate trials, see 10 HALSBURY'S LAWS (3rd Edn.) 391, 392, paras. 708, 709; and for cases on the subject, see 14 DIGEST (Repl.) 256-258, *2228-2249.*]

Case referred to:

R. v. *Pomeroy*, (1935), 25 Cr. App. Rep. 147.

Appeal.

This was an appeal by Joseph Andrews against his conviction at Inner London Sessions on July 28, 1966, of receiving a stolen motor car. The facts were that a Morris Mini Traveller car was stolen from outside its owner's house on Feb. 27 or Feb. 28, 1966. On Mar. 18 three police officers saw the car pass them and turn into a street where it stopped. Three men got out, two from the passengers' door and one from the driver's door, and the police evidence was that the man who got out of the driver's door was the appellant. He was only about twenty-five feet away. He was a local man who lived near the police station and had been known for years to the police. After walking away the men were brought back and all denied having anything to do with the car; the appellant said— " I haven't seen it before. We've got nothing to do with it." The prosecution was conducted on the basis that, before the jury found that the appellant had possession and control of the car, they must be satisfied that he had been the driver when it had recently been in motion. Joint control of the car by all three men was not left to the jury. The appellant gave evidence and called witnesses to show that he was in the neighbourhood but had left a Mr. Bellding's house only a minute or two before and could not have been the driver of the car. The jury, after an absence of one hour and twenty-five minutes, convicted the appellant of receiving.

On Aug. 2, 1966, the appellant was tried at Inner London Sessions for driving a car while disqualified. The same evidence in substance as before was given on behalf of the prosecution, and again the issue rested on the accuracy of police observation that it was the appellant who got out of the driver's side of the car. On this occasion the appellant was found not guilty.

T. G. Ashmore for the appellant.

D. B. Watling for the Crown.

LORD PARKER, C.J., after stating the facts, continued: This court does not wish it to be thought that whenever there are two verdicts, one following the other, which appear to be inconsistent, it will inevitably follow that the verdict of guilty will be set aside. Clearly it is necessary to look at the facts of each case. In the present case, however, it seems, from the fact that the jury were absent for one hour and twenty-five minutes, that they may have been puzzled on the question of receiving and may have been satisfied that all three men were in control of the stolen car, and that, therefore, it was unnecessary that they (the jury) should be satisfied that the appellant was the driver. The matter, however, was not really put to the jury in that way, and, that being so, the verdict of guilty in the first trial ought not to be allowed to stand and should be quashed.

Before leaving this case, the court would like to comment on what we are told is the practice at Inner London Sessions, when a charge of driving whilst disqualified is made together with another charge, whether it be a motoring offence such as dangerous driving or taking and driving away, or, indeed, as in this case, receiving. It has become the inevitable practice, so we are told, to have two indictments and two trials. It may be that that practice has evolved as a result of the decision of the Court of Criminal Appeal in *R. v. Pomeroy* (1). In that case there were two charges in one indictment, one of dangerous driving and the other of driving when disqualified, and they were tried together. GODDARD, J., in giving the judgment of the court, said (2):

" While it was possible in law to adopt that course, it is, in the opinion of the court, undesirable that that course should be adopted in a case such as the present, because, although no details were given with regard to the reason why the appellant was disqualified for holding a licence, the mere mention of the fact that he was disqualified might, and probably would, indicate to the jury that he had been convicted of some motoring offence of a more or less serious character ... In the present case, however, there has been no miscarriage of justice, because the appellant's defence was not that he was not driving dangerously, but that he was not the driver of the car in question."

Finally GODDARD, J., said (2):

" Further, though the appellant was defended by counsel of experience, no application was made to the court that the two counts should be tried separately, and it is too late to take such a point on appeal."

This court is quite satisfied that when the defence is that the accused was, as in that case, not the driver or, as in this case, was not there at all, the joinder of the other count of driving whilst disqualified cannot prejudice the accused in any way. Moreover, it is difficult to think that there could be any prejudice where the other offence is not a driving offence at all but, as in this case, a receiving case. The court is of the opinion that it would be proper in every case to draft the indictment containing the two counts, one of which being driving whilst disqualified. It is then perfectly open for counsel for the accused before arraignment to take the point, if it be a good point, that his client may on the particular facts of that case be prejudiced by the joinder and ask for separate trials. It seems to the court that in that way no injustice whatever could be done to an accused and at the same time what happened in the present case could not possibly arise.

Appeal allowed; conviction quashed.

Solicitors: *Registrar of Criminal Appeals* (for the appellant); *Solicitor for the Metropolitan Police* (for the Crown).

[*Reported by* N. P. METCALFE, ESQ., *Barrister-at-Law.*]

---

(1) (1935), 25 Cr. App. Rep. 147.   (2) (1935), 25 Cr. App. Rep. at p. 149.

PEAK TRAILER & CHASSIS, LTD. v. JACKSON.

[QUEEN'S BENCH DIVISION (Lord Parker, C.J., Glyn-Jones and Widgery, JJ.),
November 8, 1966.]

*Road Traffic—Articulated vehicle—Overall length—Length exceeding thirteen
metres—Whether normally used for conveying indivisible loads of exceptional
length—Meaning of " normally used "—Forty-six out of 177 loads carried
in a period of twelve months not indivisible loads of exceptional length—Motor
Vehicles (Construction and Use) Regulations 1963 (S.I. 1963 No. 1646),
reg. 7 (1) as amended by the Motor Vehicles (Construction and Use) (Amendment) (No. 2) Regulations 1964 (S.I. 1964 No. 1169), reg. 4.*

An articulated lorry belonging to the appellants had an overall length
exceeding thirteen metres. Regulation 7 (1)* of the Motor Vehicles (Construction and Use) Regulations 1963 enacted that the overall length should
not exceed thirteen metres, but, by proviso (b), that prohibition did not
apply in the case of an articulated vehicle constructed and normally used
for the conveyance of indivisible loads of exceptional length. Out of 177
journeys over a period of twelve months forty-six were journeys carrying a
load of a length that could be accommodated in a vehicle thirteen metres long
without any rearward projection beyond the tailboard. On appeal against
conviction of contravening reg. 7 (1),

Held: the use of the lorry for loads of which forty-six out of 177 were loads
which were not indivisible loads of exceptional length showed that journeys
with short loads were not abnormal; accordingly the lorry was not normally
used, within proviso (b) of reg. 7 (1), for conveying indivisible loads of
exceptional length, with the consequence that the conviction should stand
(see p. 176, letters F and H, post).

Appeal dismissed.

[As to the maximum length of articulated vehicles, see 33 HALSBURY'S LAWS
(3rd Edn.) 422, para. 694, notes (m) and (o); and for a case on the subject, see
45 DIGEST (Repl.) 76, *233*.]

Case Stated.

This was a Case Stated by justices for the petty sessional division of Howden-
shire in the East Riding of Yorkshire, in respect of their adjudication as a magistrates' court sitting at Howden on Dec. 23, 1965, whereby they convicted the
appellants, Peak Trailer & Chassis, Ltd., for an offence under reg. 7 (1) of the
Motor Vehicles (Construction & Use) Regulations 1963, as amended. On
Aug. 1, 1965, an information was preferred by the respondent, Gordon Jackson,
against the appellants that on Mar. 11, 1965, they used on a road called Boothferry Road at Howden an articulated lorry which exceeded thirteen metres in
length contrary to reg. 7.

The following facts were found. On Mar. 11, 1965, at a Ministry of Transport
check at Boothferry Bridge at Howden an articulated motor lorry No. AMB 684 B
belonging to the appellants was stopped by a police officer. The overall length of
the lorry was fifty feet nine inches, which comprised the standard motor unit
of ten feet nine inches (usable with any trailer) and the trailer of forty feet.
The lorry at the time was carrying fifteen caravan chassis arranged in three stacks
each containing five chassis, which constituted obviously a divisible load. The

---

* Regulation 7 (1) as amended by the Motor Vehicles (Construction and Use) (Amendment) (No. 2) Regulations 1964, provides, so far as material: " The overall length of
an articulated vehicle shall not exceed thirteen metres: Provided that . . . (b) This
paragraph shall not apply in the case of an articulated vehicle constructed and normally
used for the conveyance of indivisible loads of exceptional length—(i) if each wheel of
the vehicle is fitted with a pneumatic tyre, or (ii) if each wheel of the vehicle is not so
fitted but the vehicle is not driven at a speed exceeding twelve miles an hour." The
explanatory note to the amending regulations interprets thirteen metres as
approximately forty-two feet seven inches.

Dictum of WIDGERY J at 176 applied
in R v EASTLEIGH BC [1983]
2 All ER 481

A   police officer saw the same vehicle on Apr. 13, 1965, on the A.63 at Stockbridge roundabout at Elloughton when it was carrying a similar load of small chassis. He saw this vehicle on other occasions on all of which it was carrying similar loads which were divisible.   The permitted overhang from all vehicles was three feet six inches.   The officer did not recall ever seeing the lorry with an overhanging load.   According to reg. 7 (1), the maximum permitted length of an articulated

B   vehicle was forty-two feet seven inches.   Deducting the motor unit of ten feet nine inches the maximum length of the trailer was thirty-one feet ten inches. The maximum length of the load was therefore thirty-one feet ten inches plus three feet six inches overhang if necessary making a total possible length of load of thirty-five feet four inches (reg. 106 (6) (*b*)*.)

The appellants manufactured chassis frames and sold them to builders of cara-

C   vans including seven customers in Hull. About thirty per cent. were sold for the export trade.   The appellants' chassis varied from seven feet to forty-eight feet three inches in length plus in each case a tow bar of three feet, making total lengths varying from ten feet to fifty-one feet three inches. At least fifty per cent. of the chassis manufactured would be over thirty feet.   To deliver these, the appellants owned sixteen or eighteen vehicles including the specially long vehicle No. AMB

D   684B and two others similar.   They had no vehicle of exactly thirteen metres. The vehicle in question had been specially made for the purpose of carrying long chassis.   On the statement made by the appellants' general manager in his evidence-in-chief, the appellants could not store many chassis at their factory and must deliver as quickly as possible whether the appropriate wagon for delivery was available or not.

E   By agreement between the parties, the present respondent put in as evidence a document headed " Peak Trailer & Chassis, Ltd. List of consignments despatched by trailer No. AMB 684B from Oct. 1, 1964, to date ". The date of the last entry on this list was Oct. 7, 1965. This list was from the log sheets of vehicles and a book in their office from which invoices are made out. It was only about ninety-five per cent. complete. The journey of Apr. 13, 1965, mentioned by the Police

F   Officer was not included in the list.

It was contended before the justices on behalf of the appellants that they were not guilty of the offence because of the wording of proviso (*b*) of reg. 7 (1), which in effect said that an articulated vehicle might exceed thirteen metres or forty-two feet seven inches if it were " constructed and normally used for the conveyance of indivisible loads of exceptional length " subject to certain conditions as to wheels and speed, which conditions were satisfied. The list of journeys made by

G   the vehicle in question (though admitted to be not hundred per cent. complete) showed 177 journeys between Oct. 1, 1964 and Oct. 7, 1965. On seventy-seven of these journeys the vehicle was carrying several chassis each over thirty-five feet four inches in length. These chassis could not be carried on a vehicle of ordinary maximum length without excessive overhang requiring special markings. On a

H   further fifty-four of the journeys the vehicle was carrying chassis of a length which if carried on a vehicle of normal permitted length would have had to overhang varying distances up to the three feet six inches permitted. The appellants considered it undesirable that their chassis should overhang the carrying vehicle at all and therefore used the motor unit AMB 684B with the extra long trailer, the subject of the charge. The appellants argued that because these 131 journeys, i.e.,

I   _____

* Regulation 106 (6) (*b*) provides, so far as material: " Subject to the following provisions of this regulation, no load shall be carried on a vehicle— . . . (*b*) where the load has a rearward projection exceeding three feet six inches in length but not exceeding ten feet in length, unless the condition specified in para. 4 Sch. 6 [to these regulations] has been complied with."

Schedule 6, para. 4 reads: " The condition referred to . . . is that steps shall have been taken to render the relevant projection clearly visible to other persons using the road within a reasonable distance, in the case of a forward projection, from the front thereof or, in the case of a rearward projection, from the rear thereof and, in either case, from either side thereof."

seventy-seven plus fifty-four, formed a majority of the total 177 journeys in the **A**
year, the vehicle was being " normally " used for the conveyance of the indivisible
loads. A load overhanging a vehicle of maximum length was of exceptional
length. The description of a vehicle as being " normally used " for carrying
loads of exceptional length was not rendered incorrect because the journey it
made for other purposes were not confined to return journeys when empty or
with other loads. " Normal " meant " usually ". It was contended on behalf **B**
of the respondent that the seventy-seven journeys made when the vehicles was
carrying chassis each over thirty-five feet four inches in length were all properly
made, but the remaining hundred journeys were made with loads which did not
need a vehicle of exceptional length as permitted under reg. 7.

The respondent argued that the " normal " use of the vehicle was when it was
used for the seventy-seven journeys only. Forty-six journeys could have been **C**
made on vehicles of normal length without taking advantage of the three feet
six inches overhang provision while fifty-four journeys could have been similarly
made though there might have been overhang as permitted.

The justices were of the opinion: (a) That the load carried by the vehicle on
Mar. 11, 1965, was obviously divisible and could have been divided without undue
expense or risk of damage and carried on vehicles of normal length. (b) That the **D**
proviso (b) in reg. 7 (1) was intended to allow on the roads certain vehicles which
were specially constructed to carry outsize indivisible loads which could not
otherwise be carried because of their length. (c) That the word " normally " in
the said proviso (b) must be read with " constructed " and " used ". Such vehicles
would at times have to be "used " without a load at all, as when returning empty
from delivering an outsize indivisible load. The word " normally " was intended **E**
to give permission for a vehicle so to return empty—or perhaps with some small
load on such return journey—without infringing the regulation. (d) That if the
appellants' argument as to " normal use " were correct, reg. 7, which was intended
to restrict on the road the number of vehicles beyond a certain size, would be
pointless, for by following a certain course of operation with their vehicles, the
appellants could virtually make their own law and any " outsize " vehicle could **F**
be used with impunity to carry any divisible or composite load which could
otherwise be carried on a vehicle of normal size.

Consequently the justices rejected the " List of Consignments " as irrelevant
to the issue, found the appellants guilty and fined them £5 with £2 witnesses'
costs.

The question for the opinion of the High Court was whether they were correct in **G**
rejecting the appellants' contention based on the evidence of the " List of
Consignments " and in their interpretation of the said reg. 7 (1) (b).

R. *Wood* for the appellants.
B. H. *Anns* for the respondent.

WIDGERY, J., delivered the first judgment at the invitation of LORD **H**
PARKER, C.J., in which, after stating the nature of the appeal, briefly summarising
the facts and referring to the evidence, he continued: The only issue in this matter
before the magistrates was whether the proviso to reg. 7 (1) of the Motor Vehicles
(Construction and Use) Regulations 1963 applied so as to exclude this vehicle
of the appellants from the regulation, because quite clearly the vehicle was an
articulated vehicle noticeably in excess of thirteen metres in length. The evidence **I**
put before the magistrates to deal with the application of the proviso was perhaps
not wholly satisfactory in character, but it was put forward with the consent of
both parties and I approach it on the basis that it is entirely reliable and true.

The evidence consisted of a schedule of journeys undertaken by this lorry over
a period of approximately twelve months from October, 1964 to October, 1965.
It was not said to be a complete list but it was thought to be about ninety-five
per cent. complete. From this list certain calculations have been made and the
result can be expressed in this way, that of the 177 journeys shown in the list or

A schedule, seventy-seven were journeys when the vehicle was carrying an indivisible load which was too long to be accommodated on what one might call a standard length articulated lorry of not more than thirteen metres in length, even
if allowances were made for the three feet six inches rearward projection which
is allowed (1) as a matter of course and without permission in regard to the load of
all vehicles of this kind. Thus in seventy-seven of the 177 journeys, there was an
B indivisible load so long that it could not be carried on a vehicle of standard
length, even if allowance were made for the three feet six inches backward projection of the load, which is, as I see it, a normal feature. Fifty-four of the journeys
included in the total of 177 were journeys where the vehicle was carrying an
indivisible load in the form of a caravan chassis of such length that it could be
carried on a standard length vehicle of thirteen metres, provided that advantage
C was taken of the facility for three feet six inches rearward projection of the load.
In other words in these fifty-four cases, the indivisible load would not fit entirely
within a standard length vehicle but could be so accommodated if advantage
were taken of the three feet six inches rearward projection permitted. Finally,
of the remaining journeys, some forty-six in total, the load carried by this vehicle
was one which could be carried on a vehicle of standard length without any
D rearward projection of the load beyond the tailboard at all. That material was
put before the justices in order that they could answer the question which is
inherent in the proviso as to what was the normal use of this vehicle.

It is to be observed that, in order to come within the proviso, the vehicle must be
one constructed and normally used for the conveyance of indivisible loads of
exceptional length. The draftsman of the regulations, no doubt advisedly, has
E not attempted to define "exceptional length" in relation to loads and there
has been some argument on that matter in this court. All that I feel convinced
about as a result of that argument is that a load which will fit entirely within the
confines of an articulated lorry of standard length, namely thirteen metres,
is not a load of exceptional length. Whether one can regard as a load of exceptional
length, a load which cannot be entirely confined in a standard vehicle but must
F protrude to the rear by an amount up to three feet six inches is, I find, more
difficult. I am inclined to think that, if the case really turned on it, I should
be minded to say such loads were not of exceptional length because, as I see it,
the permitted projection of three feet six inches is an entirely normal, un-
exceptional thing, but I find it unnecessary to decide that point and the only
matter on which I rest my opinion with conviction is that if the load will accommo-
G date itself entirely within a standard length lorry, it is not a load of exceptional
length. Accordingly, on any view, forty-six of the loads carried out of the total of
177, to which I have referred, were not loads of exceptional length.

Then one moves to the second feature of the proviso, namely the phrase
"normal use". The magistrates, with the advantage of the information to which
I have referred, were required to decide whether this vehicle was normally used
H for the carriage of indivisible loads of exceptional length, and what they said about
it was this:

"that the word 'normally' in the said proviso (*b*) must be read with
'constructed' and 'used'. Such vehicles will at times have to be 'used'
without a load at all as when returning empty from delivering an outsize
indivisible load. The word 'normally' is intended to give permission for a
I vehicle to so return empty—or perhaps with some small load on such return
journey—without infringing the regulation."

They went on to say that in consequence of taking that view they rejected the
schedule of journeys to which I have referred as being irrelevant to the issue and
the question which is posed for the opinion of this court is whether they were right
in rejecting the appellants' contention based on this schedule.

---

(1) See the Motor Vehicles (Construction and Use) Regulations, 1963, reg. 106 (6) (*b*),
printed in footnote *, p. 173, ante.

The appellants' argument below, and in substance their argument today, is **A** that when one looks at the figures to which I have referred, they show a situation on which at least it was open to the justices to say that this vehicle was normally used for the conveyance of loads of exceptional length. It is recognised by counsel for the appellants that on any view, if he is to succeed, the matter must go back so that the justices can consider whether that argument is sound or not, but in my judgment it is not necessary to send the case back for reasons which I will **B** now endeavour to explain.

The justices maybe have applied a somewhat too narrow test. They are saying in effect that a vehicle cannot be normally used for the carriage of indivisible loads of exceptional length unless it is always used, either on its outward or homeward journey, for such a load. They imply that normality in this sense means that on every return journey, one leg of the journey, as it were, should be involved **C** with a load of exceptional length, and they consider that other loads can be carried only when the vehicle would otherwise be coming home light. If that is what they say, for my part I think that it may be unduly strict, but I do not propose to offer any further opinion in regard to it except that I would not recommend it for use hereafter when similar problems arise. It seems to me what one really has to ask oneself here is whether the figures do disclose clearly, one way or the other, **D** the answer to the question: was this vehicle normally used for loads of exceptional length?

In my view the word " normally " has a perfectly ordinary meaning which would be given to it by ordinary people in everyday use as a man might say " I normally get to the office every morning at 9.30 but this morning I was delayed by fog and only arrived at 10 o'clock ". In using the word " normally ", one is **E** referring to something which is in contradistinction to abnormal or exceptional. One cannot speak of the use of this lorry as being normal for loads of exceptional length, unless the carriage of other loads is an abnormal and exceptional feature of its life and use. It seems to me on the figures with which we have been supplied in this case, and taking the view most favourable to the appellants that only forty-six out of the 177 journeys were journeys in which exceptionally long loads **F** were not involved, that it is unarguable that journeys with short loads are abnormal or exceptional. In order to show that the use of the lorry is normally for long loads, it is not enough to say it is so used more often than not. It is necessary to go much further than that and it would be right in any given case for the tribunal to consider whether the use for other than long loads was so exceptional and abnormal as to justify the conclusion that use for long loads was the normal **G** use.

I, for my part, find it unnecessary to send this case back to the magistrates because I am satisfied that any magistrate, properly instructed, would be bound to hold if the vehicle was used for short loads on forty-six out of 177 journeys that its normal use is not for exceptionally long loads. Accordingly, my view is that the magistrates were right, although I base my conclusion on somewhat **H** different reasons, and the appeal should be dismissed.

    GLYN-JONES, J.: I entirely agree; so entirely that I do not think it necessary to add anything further.

    LORD PARKER, C.J.: I also agree.

                                                    Appeal dismissed. **I**

    Solicitors: *Robbins, Olivey & Lake*, for the appellants; *Jaques & Co.*, agents for *Bailey & Haigh*, Selby, for the respondents.

                                  [*Reported by* S. A. HATTEEA, ESQ., *Barrister-at-Law.*]

A   COMMISSIONERS OF CUSTOMS AND EXCISE
v. HARZ AND ANOTHER.

[HOUSE OF LORDS (Lord Reid, Lord Morris of Borth-y-Gest, Lord Hodson, Lord Pearce and Lord Wilberforce), November 7, 8, 9, 10, 14, 15, 16, 17, 21, 22 and December 20, 1966.]

B   *Criminal Law—Evidence—Admissibility—Confession—Inducement—Evidence of statements made to investigating officers tendered at a trial on charges of conspiracy to defraud customs—Statements induced by threat of prosecution for not answering questions put by investigating officers—Threat thus of prosecution for a different offence than that in issue at trial—Finance Act, 1946 (9 & 10 Geo. 6 c. 64), s. 20 (4)—Purchase Tax Act 1963 (c. 9), s. 33 (5).*

C   *Criminal Law—Evidence—Admissibility—Admission—Whether any difference in principle in admissibility of full confession or admission falling short of a full confession.*

Criminal Law—No miscarriage of justice—Power to dismiss appeal—Re-trial following trial at which jury disagreed—Appellate court not precluded from applying proviso—Test to be applied—Criminal Appeal Act, 1907
D   *(7 Edw. 7 c. 23), s. 4 (1) proviso.*

The principle that a confession or statement by an accused is not admissible in evidence at his trial if it was induced by a threat or promise, applies equally where the inducement does not relate to the charge or contemplated charge as where the inducement does so relate (see p. 182, letter I, p. 185, letters B and D, and p. 187, letter G, post).

E   Test stated by LORD SUMNER in *Ibrahim* v. *Regem* ([1914-15] All E.R. Rep. at p. 877) applied.

R. v. *Joyce* ([1957] 3 All E.R. 623) not applied.

In the course of investigating suspected fraudulent failure by a company to pay purchase tax customs officers, who had lawfully inspected books of the company and had found them meagre and defective, subjected the
F   appellant H. to interrogation lasting more than three hours, during which he made incriminating admissions. The power to interrogate was said to be derived from s. 20 (3)* of the Finance Act, 1946 (or, after Apr. 1, 1963†, under s. 24 (6) of the Purchase Tax Act 1963). H., whose solicitor was present, believed that there was power (by virtue of s. 33 (5) of the Act of 1963) to prosecute H. if he did not answer, and, but for this, H. would not
G   have answered. At the subsequent trial of H. and others on charges of conspiracy to cheat and defraud the customs of purchase tax evidence of the oral admissions was received. There were two trials, the first was a trial lasting forty days at which the jury disagreed, and the second was a re-trial lasting fifty-four days. H. was convicted on five counts of an indictment containing seven counts. At the re-trial H.'s admissions were an essential
H   part of the prosecution case, and were introduced at the outset of the re-trial, being preceded by argument on their admissibility, which took place in the absence of the jury and lasted four days. On appeal against conviction, on the ground that the admissions ought not to have been received in evidence,

Held: (i) the admissions were inadmissible in evidence because—

(a) the relevant enactment did not confer power to subject a trader to
I   prolonged interrogation in the nature of cross-examination, and accordingly H.'s admissions made in the course of the interrogation were not rendered admissible by the statute (see p. 181, letter I, p. 185, letter D, and p. 187 letter G, post).

(b) the admissions would not have been made if H. had not been told that he must answer the customs officers' questions forthwith and that if he refused to answer them he would be prosecuted, and thus they were made

---

* For the terms of the enactment, see p. 181, letters A and B, post.
† Interviews with customs officers took place between Feb. 27 and Nov. 26, 1963. A principal interview was on Aug. 22, 1963.

Considered in DEOKINANAN *v.* R. [1968] 2 All E.R. 346.

Applied in EMI RECORDS LTD *v* SPILLANE [1986] 2 All ER 1016

Applied in BANK OF ENGLAND *v* RILEY [1992] 1 All ER 769

Applied in RE JEFFREY S LEVITT LTD [1992] 2 All ER 509

under threat; accordingly, being admissions, not real evidence, and not A being voluntarily made, they were not admissible at common law (see p. 180, letter I, p. 182, letter C, p. 185, letter D, p. 187, letter G, post).

(c) there was no difference, for the purposes of the rule that a confession was not admissible unless it was voluntarily made, between a full confession and an admission falling short of a full confession (see p. 182, letters D and F, p. 185, letter D, and p. 187, letter G, post).   B

(ii) the circumstance that there had been a first trial at which the jury disagreed did not automatically preclude an appellate court from applying the proviso to s. 4 (1) of the Criminal Appeal Act, 1907; in the present case, however, the proviso should not be applied because the inadmissible evidence had been depended on by the prosecution and was a feature of their case, and it could not be said with confidence that a reasonable jury, properly C directed, would have convicted without having heard the inadmissible evidence (see p. 186, letter B, p. 185, letter C, and p. 187, letters E to G, post).

Stirland v. *Director of Public Prosecutions* ([1944] 2 All E.R. 13) applied.

Dictum of ASHWORTH, J., in *R.* v. *Johnson* ([1961] 3 All E.R. at p. 971) not applied.

PER CURIAM: where, in a statute which confers power to require informa- D tion from a person, there is no express provision that incriminating answers may be used against him, the question whether they are admissible in evidence subsequently depends on the proper construction of the statute; incriminating answers to proper demands under the enactment relevant to the present case (s. 24 (6) of the Purchase Tax Act 1963) would, it seems, be admissible in evidence (see p. 181, letter F, p. 185, letter D, and p. 187, E letter G, post).

Decision of the COURT OF CRIMINAL APPEAL (sub nom. *R.* v. *Harz, R.* v. *Power*, [1966] 3 All E.R. 433) affirmed.

[As to admissions or confessions by a defendant before trial, see 10 HALSBURY'S LAWS (3rd Edn.) 469, 470, paras. 860-862; 473-475, paras. 866, 867; and for cases on the subject, see 14 DIGEST (Repl.) 468, 469, *4508-4527*, 480-486, *4578-* F *4649*.

As to the admissibility of evidence wrongfully obtained, see 15 HALSBURY'S LAWS (3rd Edn.) 266, 267, para. 487.

For the Finance Act, 1946, s. 20, see 21 HALSBURY'S STATUTES (2nd Edn.) 1321.

For the Purchase Tax Act 1963, s. 24, see 43 HALSBURY'S STATUTES (2nd Edn.) 1038, 1047.   G

For the Criminal Appeal Act, 1907, s. 4 (1), see 5 HALSBURY'S STATUTES (2nd Edn.) 929; the amending provisions of s. 4 of the Criminal Appeal Act 1966 (see HALSBURY'S STATUTES INTERIM SERVICE) came into operation on Oct. 1, 1966, by virtue of the Criminal Appeal Act 1966 (Commencement No. 1) Order 1966, S.I. 1966 No. 1018.]   H

Cases referred to:

Ibrahim v. *Regem*, [1914-15] All E.R. Rep. 874; [1914] A.C. 599; 83 L.J.P.C. 185; 111 L.T. 20; 14 Digest (Repl.) 468, *4513*.

R. v. *Gilham*, (1828), 1 Mood. C.C. 186; 14 Digest (Repl.) 484, *4623*.

R. v. *Green*, (1834), 6 C. & P. 655; 14 Digest (Repl.) 485, *4639*.

R. v. *Johnson*, [1961] 3 All E.R. 969; [1961] 1 W.L.R. 1478; 126 J.P. 40; I 46 Cr. App. Rep. 55; Digest (Cont. Vol. A) 373, *4777c*.

R. v. *Joyce*, [1957] 3 All E.R. 623; [1958] 1 W.L.R. 140; 122 J.P. 53; 42 Cr. App. Rep. 19; Digest (Cont. Vol. A) 372, *4638a*.

R. v. *Lloyd*, (1834), 6 C. & P. 393; 14 Digest (Repl.) 485, *4640*.

R. v. *Manning*, [1961] Crim. L.R. 561.

R. v. *Shuter* (Nov. 26, 1965), unreported.

R. v. *Smith*, [1959] 2 All E.R. 193; [1959] 2 Q.B. 35; [1959] 2 W.L.R. 623; 123 J.P. 295; 43 Cr. App. Rep. 121; Digest (Cont. Vol. A) 369, *4517a*.

A   *R.* v. *Thornton*, (1824), 1 Mood. C.C. 27; 14 Digest (Repl.) 485, *4628.*
   Stirland v. *Director of Public Prosecutions*, [1944] 2 All E.R. 13; [1944] A.C. 315;
      113 L.J.K.B. 394; 171 L.T. 78; 109 J.P. 1; sub nom. *R.* v. *Stirland*,
      30 Cr. App. Rep. 40; 14 Digest (Repl.) 511, *4949.*

   Appeal.
   This was an appeal by the Commissioners of Customs and Excise pursuant to
B the certificate and leave of the Court of Criminal Appeal given under s. 1 (2) of
   the Administration of Justice Act, 1960, to appeal from two orders of that
   court, both dated July 8, 1966, made on the appeals of the present respondents
   and reported [1966] 3 All E.R. 433, against convictions of conspiracy to cheat
   and defraud the commissioners of purchase tax. The respondent Harz and
   the respondent Power had appealed to the Court of Criminal Appeal against their
C convictions at the Central Criminal Court before JUDGE KILNER BROWN, Q.C.,
   Harz having been convicted on five counts and Power having been convicted
   on three counts. They were indicted with seven other individuals and seven
   companies. There was a trial followed by a re-trial. The trial lasted forty
   days and at the end of it the jury disagreed; the re-trial lasted fifty-four days
   and ended on Dec. 17, 1965. The sentences were passed on Dec. 20, 1965, Harz
D being sentenced to five years' imprisonment in all and Power being sentenced
   to eighteen months' imprisonment in all. On allowing the appeals against
   conviction the Court of Criminal Appeal certified that a point of law of general
   public importance was involved in the decision to allow the appeals, viz., whether
   in a trial for conspiracy to evade payment of purchase tax oral admissions made
   by an accused person to customs officials in consequence of a threat to prosecute
E for a statutory offence under the Finance Act, 1946, or the Purchase Tax Act
   1963, should be received in evidence. The commissioners appealed accordingly.

   *The Solicitor-General (Sir Dingle Foot, Q.C.), Sebag Shaw, Q.C., R. D. L. Du
   Cann* and *D. W. T. Price* for the commissioners.
   M. Waters and *P. N. Brandt* for the respondent Harz.
F *R. J. C. V. Prendergast* for the respondent Power.

   Their Lordships took time for consideration.

   Dec. 20.   The following opinions were read.

   LORD REID: My Lords, the respondents Harz and Power were convicted
   at the Central Criminal Court on Dec. 17, 1965, and Harz was sentenced to five
G years and Powers to eighteen months' imprisonment. They were alleged to
   have cheated and defrauded the appellants, the Commissioners of Customs and
   Excise, of some £119,000 of purchase tax. The respondents had been indicted
   together with seven other individuals and seven companies and there were seven
   counts of conspiracy in the indictment. The trial lasted fifty-four days. The main
   question raised in their appeal to the Court of Criminal Appeal (1) was whether
H answers given by them in the course of interrogations by customs officers were
   admissible in evidence. At the trial this question had been argued for four days
   before the trial judge before the case was opened to the jury and he had held
   the evidence to be admissible. The Court of Criminal Appeal by a majority
   (CANTLEY and BLAIN, JJ.; THESIGER, J., dissenting) held the evidence to be
   inadmissible and they quashed the convictions (1).
I   The main facts can be stated briefly. Harz owned most of the shares of a
   company, Harry Lee & Co., Ltd., and it is not disputed that he was aware of
   and responsible for all its activities. Power was associated with him, and it is
   not argued that the case against him can be differentiated from the case against
   Harz, so I shall not deal separately with it. This company dealt largely in
   toilet goods and toys, many of these commodities being chargeable with purchase
   tax under the Finance Act, 1940, now replaced by the Purchase Tax Act 1963.

   (1) [1966] 3 All E.R. 433.

The general scheme of the Act is that purchase tax is not payable until a registered A
dealer—generally a wholesaler—sells chargeable goods to someone who is not a
registered dealer—generally, but not necessarily, a retailer.   On such a sale the
registered dealer must account for the purchase tax to the commissioners.
Harry Lee & Co., Ltd. was a registered dealer.   It is not disputed that during the
period covered by these charges this company bought at least £750,000 of chargeable goods on which purchase tax had not been paid, that at the end of the B
period the amount still in its possession was negligible, and that it only paid
purchase tax in respect of some £250,000 of these goods.   The allegation is that
purchase tax ought to have been paid on substantially the whole of the £750,000
worth of goods and that the accused have fraudulently failed to account for
purchase tax on the balance of about £500,000 worth of goods.

When customs officers made demands to inspect the books of the company, C
they found them to be meagre and defective and in all the counts it is alleged
that the fraud was committed " by means of the falsification, concealment and
destruction of invoices, records, books of account, purchase tax returns and
other documents ".   Broadly speaking the method alleged was this.   Harz was
not himself a registered dealer, and he controlled or had interests in various
companies in various parts of England which were not registered dealers.   So D
when the company sold chargeable goods to any of them the company ought to
have accounted for purchase tax on these goods.   But it is said that on these
occasions the company only included in the invoices a comparatively small part
of the goods actually sold and delivered.   The rest was simply paid for in cash
and all documents relating to it were destroyed as soon as possible.   For these
concealed sales the company would obtain prices appropriate for goods in respect E
of which they had paid purchase tax, and in this way the company would receive
and keep as profits the money which it ought to have accounted for as tax; and
I should add that it is alleged that some other customers of the company lent
itself to this fraudulent scheme by accepting invoices which only included a
part of the goods which they had bought.

The fact that so many documents had disappeared made it difficult to prove F
that more goods had been sold to non-registered dealers than appeared from
the invoices.   When, however, raids were made on premises of the purchasers,
some papers were found which indicated that for some recent transactions the
invoice did not disclose all that had been purchased.   Without his own admissions there was nothing to connect Harz with these papers, and for that reason
these admissions were essential for the proof of at least some of the counts.   G

On Feb. 27, 1963, customs officers took possession of a number of Lee's books
and began to question Harz and others.   Harz said " We are not talking " but
the officers told him that he would be prosecuted if he did not answer. He gave
certain answers on that occasion.   On subsequent occasions, the last being in
August, he and his solicitor who was present continued to believe that there
was power to prosecute if he did not answer and in the course of long interroga- H
tions one of which lasted more than three hours he made certain incriminating
admissions.   I am of opinion that it must be held that this threat of prosecution
was intended by the customs officers to apply and was thought by Harz to apply
on all these occasions, and that this is a typical case of a suspected person being
induced by a threat to make incriminating admissions.   I think that it is clear
that Harz would not have made these admissions if he had not been told that I
he must answer the officers' questions there and then and that if he refused he
would be prosecuted.

In my opinion the officers had no right to require Harz to submit to this prolonged interrogation, and he could not have been prosecuted if he had refused
to answer.   The officers' power to interrogate was said to be derived from the
Finance Act, 1946, s. 20 (3) (now replaced by s. 24 (6) of the Purchase Tax Act
1963) which provides as follows:

" Every person concerned with the purchase or importation of goods or with the application of goods to any process of manufacture or with dealings with imported goods should furnish to the commissioners within such time and in such form as they may require information relating to the goods or to the purchase or importation thereof or to the application of any process of manufacture thereto or to dealings therewith as they may specify, and shall, upon demand made by any officer or other persons authorised in that behalf by the commissioners, produce any books or accounts or other documents of whatever nature relating thereto for inspection by that officer or person at such time and place as that officer or person may require."

There is here a clear distinction between the right of an officer to demand production of documents and the right of the commissioners to require information to be furnished at such time and in such manner as they may require. The right of the officer is to require immediate production of documents, and, if the trader fails to produce documents in his possession of the kind demanded, he can be prosecuted. No doubt the officer can ask questions relating to documents of the kinds which he has demanded, and the trader's answer or refusal to answer may be admissible in evidence; but the prosecution will not be for refusal to answer questions, it will be for refusal to produce documents, and I can see nothing to require the trader to give answers which may incriminate him.

The right of the commissioners to require information is quite different. If a demand for information is made in the proper manner the trader is bound to answer the demand within the time and in the form required whether or not the answer may tend to incriminate him, and if he fails to comply with the demand he can be prosecuted. If he answers falsely he can be prosecuted for that, and, if he answers in such a manner as to incriminate himself, I can see no reason why his answer should not be used against him. Some statutes expressly provide that incriminating answers may be used against the person who gives them and some statutes expressly provide that they may not. Where, as here, there is no such express provision the question whether such answers are admissible evidence must depend on the proper construction of the particular statute. Although I need not decide the point, it seems to me to be reasonably clear that incriminating answers to a proper demand under this section must be admissible if the statutory provision is to achieve its obvious purpose.

If the admissions with which the appeal is concerned had been obtained by a proper exercise of this power of the commissioners, they might well have been admissible in evidence in this prosecution. It was argued in the first place that the officers who conducted the interrogation had not been properly authorised by the commissioners to exercise their powers. Probably they had not, but I need not pursue that because I think that the respondents succeed in their second argument. The trader is only bound to furnish information within such time and in such form as the commissioners require. The information will often be complicated, and the commissioners can be relied on to fix a reasonable time. If the information required is simple and easily provided, the time required may be short. I do not think, however, that this entitles the commissioners to send a representative to confront the trader, put questions to him orally and demand oral answers on the spot; and I am certainly of opinion that it does not entitle them to send their representative to subject the trader to a prolonged interrogation in the nature of a cross-examination. This provision is in sharp contrast with provisions which expressly entitle officers to question persons with regard to particular matters, e.g., to question passengers entering the country with regard to their luggage. When it is intended that officers shall obtain information by asking oral questions that is made plain in the statute. The Solicitor-General was asked whether he was aware of any other case in which a government department claimed the right to send a representative to interrogate a person for hours on end under the sanction that he would be prosecuted, if he failed to answer

any question, and that any incriminating answer which he might give under
threat of prosecution for failing to answer could be used in evidence against him.
He was unable to cite any parallel case. I am not to be taken as saying that
every inquisitorial procedure is inherently objectionable: this case may indicate
the contrary. If, however, any such procedure were introduced, it would certainly contain safeguards which are absent from the procedure which the
commissioners support in this case.

As there is no statutory provision making these statements admissible in
evidence against the accused, I must now consider whether they were admissible
at common law. The commissioners' first argument was that relevant evidence is
always admissible, even where the prosecution obtained it by illegal means.
There is authority to that effect where the evidence is real evidence—some
object like a blood stained knife, which was only discovered because the accused
was compelled by illegal means to say where it was hidden; but that has no
application to confessions which for some three centuries have been held to be
inadmissible unless they are free and voluntary.

Then it was argued that there is a difference between confessions and admissions
which fall short of a full confession. A difference of that kind appears to be
recognised in some other countries. In India and Ceylon legislative enactments
severely limit the admissibility of confessions, and the courts have construed these
enactments as not preventing the admission in evidence of other incriminating
statements obtained by fair means, though not in the manner required for
confessions; and for some reason not made clear in argument some such distinction appears to be recognised at least in some States in the United States. But
there appears to be no English case for more than a century in which an admission
induced by a threat or promise has been admitted in evidence where a full
confession would have been excluded. If such a case had occurred since appeal to
the Court of Criminal Appeal became possible, I find it very difficult to believe
that there would not have been an appeal. I can see no justification in principle
for the distinction. In similar circumstances one man induced by a threat makes
a full confession and another induced by the same threat makes one or more
incriminating admissions. Unless the law is to be reduced to a mere collection
of unrelated rules, I see no distinction between these cases; and it is noteworthy
that the new Judges' Rules published in 1964 (2) make no such distinction.
They are clear and emphatic:

" (e) That it is a fundamental condition of the admissibility in evidence
against any person, equally of any oral answer given by that person to a
question put by a police officer and of *any statement* made by that person,
that it shall have been voluntary in the sense that it has not been obtained
from him by fear of prejudice or hope of advantage, exercised or held out
by a person in authority, or by oppression. The principle set out in para. (e)
above is overriding and applicable in all cases."

The italics are mine.

I must now deal a little more fully with the next argument, because it was
accepted by THESIGER, J., and forms the basis of his dissent. It is said that if
the threat or promise which induced the statement related to the charge or
contemplated charge against the accused, the statement is not admissible; but
that if it related to something else, the statement is admissible. This distinction
does appear in some, but by no means all, modern text books and it has a very
curious history. There is no mention of it in the earlier works of authority—
HALE'S PLEAS OF THE CROWN, chapter 38; HAWKINS' PLEAS OF THE CROWN,
chapter 46; EAST'S PLEAS OF THE CROWN, chapter 16. Apparently it first appears
in the 1840's. JOY states (CONFESSIONS, p. 12):

---

(2) See [1964] 1 All E.R. 237. The matter quoted at (e) above is taken from the note
in the introduction in App. A before the rules are set out; see [1964] 1 All E.R. 237,
footnote.

" But the threat or inducement held out must have reference to the prisoner's escape from the charge and be such as would lead him to suppose it will be better for him to admit himself to be guilty of an offence which he never committed."

And TAYLOR ON EVIDENCE (1848 Edn.) p. 592, says:

" We come now to the nature of the inducement: and here it may be laid down as a general rule that in order to exclude a confession, the inducement whether it be in the shape of a promise, a threat, or mere advice must have reference to the prisoner's escape from the criminal charge against him."

This is merely an inference which those learned writers draw from a few cases, none of which appears to me to warrant it. The most striking is *R.* v. *Lloyd* (3). There the inducement was that the gaoler would let the prisoner see his wife, and PATTERSON, J., without giving any reason held that that did not make the confession inadmissible. The report is short and we do not know all the circumstances. He may well have thought the inducement too small to matter. Suppose, however, that the wife had been at death's door: I can imagine no inducement more likely to lead to a false confession, and I cannot believe that in such a case PATTERSON, J., would have held it to be admissible. Yet the rule invented by these learned authors would mean that the confession would have been admissible. Then there are cases cited where no inducement was held out at all, e.g., in *R.* v. *Green* (4) the man offered to confess if his handcuffs were removed. There is also *R.* v. *Gilham* (5), where after much argument it was held that a confession following on spiritual exhortation was admissible, but all the argument was quite unnecessary if there had been any rule of the kind suggested. Then there is cited *R.* v. *Thornton* (6), a decision which would certainly not be followed today, where a constable in a manner " calculated to intimidate " obtained a confession from a boy.

This " rule " was not adopted by ARCHBOLD (7) or STARKIE (8) but it has been adopted by some later writers. ROSCOE'S CRIMINAL EVIDENCE (1862 Edn.) p. 41 rightly says " Upon this point there are but few authorities ", and the author does not seem enthusiastic for the rule. SIR J. STEPHEN in his DIGEST OF THE LAW OF EVIDENCE (9) simply says that the inducement must have reference to the charge against the accused person. PHIPSON writing in 1892 (10) simply cites TAYLOR (11), STEPHEN (12) and RUSSELL (13) as his authorities. I get little from RUSSELL. Later authors do no more than copy those who preceded them.

There appears to have been no judicial consideration of this " rule " for more than a century after it was first formulated; but in *R.* v. *Joyce* (14) SLADE, J., based his judgment on the rule as stated in KENNY (15). I doubt whether he need have done. The constable had only said " I need to take a statement from you ". Unless he misled the man into thinking that he was bound to make a statement and would suffer in some way if he refused, I would not regard that as involving any threat or inducement at all. The only case in the Court of Criminal Appeal brought to our notice was *R.* v. *Shuter* (16). There FENTON ATKINSON, J., said:

(3) (1834), 6 C. & P. 393.   (4) (1834), 6 C. & P. 655.
(5) (1828), 1 Mood. C.C. 186.   (6) (1832), 1 Mood. C.C. 27.
(7) See ARCHBOLD'S PLEADING AND EVIDENCE IN CRIMINAL CASES (18th Edn., 1875) 239.
(8) A Practical Treatise on the LAW OF EVIDENCE by THOMAS STARKIE (1824), Vol. 2, pp. 48, 49.
(9) (1876), art. 22 (Vol. 1, p. 32).
(10) See PHIPSON THE LAW OF EVIDENCE (4th Edn., 1907) 244.
(11) See TAYLOR ON THE LAW OF EVIDENCE (9th Edn., 1895), pp. 567, 568, ss. 879-881.
(12) A DIGEST OF THE LAW OF EVIDENCE by JAMES FITZJAMES STEPHEN, Q.C. (1876), Vol. 1, p. 32.
(13) The reference seems to be to *R.* v. *Warner*, cited in 3 RUSSELL ON CRIME (6th Edn.) 489n.   (14) [1957] 3 All E.R. 623; 42 Cr. App. Rep. 19.
(15) KENNY'S OUTLINES OF CRIMINAL LAW.   (16) (Nov. 26, 1965), unreported.

" In our view inducement will not vitiate a confession when the proferred
benefit has no bearing on the course of the prosecution and on this point
the text book writers speak with one voice."

Research in preparing the present case shows that there are notable exceptions.
Then he quoted KENNY and other text books, *R.* v. *Lloyd* (17) and *R.* v. *Joyce* (18)
being the only decided cases which he cited; and then he said " That principle
must have been acted upon times without number for very many years past ".
I would venture to doubt that. Appeal has been easy for nearly sixty years, and,
unless counsel have been very much less astute than I would suppose, I can
scarcely think that many opportunities to appeal on this matter can have been
missed.

One suggested justification of this rule appears to be that the tendency to
exclude confessions which followed on some vague threat or inducement had been
carried much too far, and that the formula set out in many text books affords a
useful and time-honoured way of limiting this tendency.   The common law,
however, should proceed by the rational development of principles and not by
the elaboration of rules or formulae. I do not think that it is possible to reconcile
all the very numerous judicial statements on rejection of confessions, but two
lines of thought appear to underlie them: first, that a statement made in response
to a threat or promise may be untrue or at least untrustworthy; and secondly,
that nemo tenetur seipsum prodere. It is true that many of the so-called inducements have been so vague that no reasonable man would have been influenced by
them, but one must remember that not all accused are reasonable men or women:
they may be very ignorant and terrified by the predicament in which they find
themselves. So it may have been right to err on the safe side.   If, however, the
tendency to reject confessions is thought to have been carried too far, it cannot
be proper to try to redress the balance by engrafting on the general principle an
illogical exception which at best can only operate sporadically leaving the mischief
untouched in the great majority of cases.

That the alleged rule or formula is illogical and unreasonable I have no doubt.
Suppose that a daughter is accused of shop lifting and later her mother is detected
in a similar offence, perhaps at a different branch, where the mother is brought
before the manager of the shop. He might induce her to confess by telling her
that she must tell him the truth and it will be worse for her if she does not: or
the inducement might be that, if she will tell the truth, he will drop proceedings
against the daughter. Obviously the latter would in most cases be far the more
powerful inducement and far the more likely to lead to an untrue confession; but
if this rule were right the former inducement would make the confession
inadmissible, and the latter would not.   The law of England cannot be so
ridiculous as that.

In *R.* v. *Smith* (19) a soldier was accused of murder during a barrack room fight.
Soon after the fight the sergeant major put his company on parade and said
that they would be kept there until he learned who was responsible. After a time
Smith confessed. The inducement clearly was that, if the culprit confessed, his
comrades would be released. It had nothing to do with any impending charge;
but it was held sufficient to make the confession inadmissible. LORD PARKER, C.J.,
said (20):

" It has always been a fundamental principle of the courts and something
quite apart from the Judges' Rules that a prisoner's confession outside the
court is only admissible if it is voluntary. In deciding whether an admission
is voluntary the court has been at pains to hold that even the most gentle, if
I may put it that way, threat or slight inducement will taint a confession."

This case must have been wrongly decided if the alleged rule exists.

(17) (1834), 6 C. & P. 393.   (18) [1957] 3 All E.R. 623;   42 Cr. App. Rep. 19.
(19) [1959] 2 All E.R. 193; [1959] 2 Q.B. 35.
(20) [1959] 2 All E.R. at p. 195; [1959] 2 Q.B. at p. 39.

In the well known statement of the general principle by LORD SUMNER in *Ibrahim* v. *Regem* (21) this rule is omitted; and, perhaps more important, it is omitted from the passage from the Judges' Rules which I have already quoted (22). I do not think that these omissions are likely to have been due to mere oversight. So I come without hesitation to the conclusion that this alleged rule should not be adopted, indeed that it never has been part of the law of England.

These convictions must therefore be quashed unless it is proper to apply the proviso to s. 4 of the Criminal Appeal Act, 1907, as amended by s. 4 of the Criminal Appeal Act 1966. I agree with my noble and learned friend LORD MORRIS OF BORTH-Y-GEST that the fact that the jury disagreed at the first trial would not prevent the application of the proviso; and with some regret I feel compelled to agree with his reasons why the proviso should not be applied in the circumstances of this case. I would therefore dismiss this appeal.

LORD MORRIS OF BORTH-Y-GEST: My Lords, I have had the advantage of reading the speech of my noble and learned friend, LORD REID, and I am in agreement with it. I will add only a few words in regard to the question whether the proviso to s. 4 (1) of the Criminal Appeal Act, 1907, should be applied. That proviso in its present form is as follows:

" Provided that the court may, notwithstanding that they [i.e., the Court of Appeal, Criminal Division] are of opinion that the point raised in the appeal might be decided in favour of the appellant, dismiss the appeal if they consider that no miscarriage of justice has actually occurred."

It was submitted by the Solicitor-General that apart from the impugned statements there was ample evidence to support the convictions, and that in the Court of Criminal Appeal (23) the proviso should have been applied and should if necessary be applied in this House. In the Court of Criminal Appeal (23) the learned judges expressed themselves only briefly in regard to it. Though in the view formed by THESIGER, J., the application of the proviso was not required he said that he appreciated (24) " that in the light of previous decisions its application would be difficult in this case, although the words of the proviso taken by themselves seem wide enough to cover the situation that has arisen ". CANTLEY, J., said (24) that the case was not one " where the court would be entitled to apply the proviso ". BLAIN, J., recorded (25) that the court had " felt itself unable to apply the proviso ". It would appear that the " previous decisions " which influenced the court were two decisions in the Court of Criminal Appeal in 1961. The first was *R.* v. *Manning* (26) in which the Court of Criminal Appeal said:

". . . the court has come to the conclusion that it would be unsafe in this case to allow the conviction to stand. There can, as it seems to this court, be no question of applying the proviso to s. 4 (1) of the Criminal Appeal Act, 1907, because this was the second trial. At the first trial, when given proper directions and with no interjections of this sort, the jury disagreed."

The second decision was *R.* v. *Johnson* (27). In that case the passage just set out was cited, and in quashing a conviction and refusing to apply the proviso the court said:

" This court has no reason in the world to suppose that the first trial was not properly conducted or that the summing-up was not free from criticism and yet the jury disagreed. It would be quite wrong to apply the proviso in this case and, accordingly, the court has no other course open to it than to quash the conviction and thereby allow the appeal."

It would seem to be clear that the reason why in the present case the Court of Criminal Appeal did not in their judgments proceed to express any view whether

(21) [1914-15] All E.R. Rep. 874 at p. 877; [1914] A.C. 599 at p. 609.
(22) See p. 182, letter G, ante.   (23) [1966] 3 All E.R. 433.
(24) [1966] 3 All E.R. at p. 454.   (25) [1966] 3 All E.R. at p. 458.
(26) [1961] Crim. L.R. 561.   (27) [1961] 3 All E.R. 969; 46 Cr. App. Rep. 55.

on a consideration of the facts the proviso should be applied was because they felt
bound by the reasoning in the two cited judgments. They considered that the
reasoning applied in the present case because there had been an earlier trial in
which the jury had disagreed.

My lords, I cannot think that the mere circumstance that there has been a
first trial in which the jury disagreed should automatically preclude the application of the proviso, if there is an appeal following on conviction in a second trial.
The reasons why a jury fail to agree either to convict or to acquit are in normal
circumstances not known. No firm conclusion can ordinarily be drawn merely
from the fact of a disagreement. There could be cases where nearly everyone on
a jury considered that guilt was proved, and where the contrary view was held
irrationally or perversely or possibly for discreditable reasons. Why, it may be
asked, should an application of the proviso be ruled out automatically or almost
automatically in such a case. Evidence not presented with clarity, but in confused
manner, in a first trial might be presented with greater clarity and with abundant
candour in a second trial. Though the circumstance that on a first trial a jury
has disagreed will be noted by the Court of Criminal Appeal if considering the
proviso after a conviction in a second trial there should, in my view, be no
replacement or abandonment of the principle of the approach indicated in
Stirland v. *Director of Public Prosecutions* (28). In his speech in that case VISCOUNT
SIMON, L.C., in referring to the proviso, said (29) that it assumed a situation
where " a reasonable jury, after being properly directed, would, on the evidence
properly admissible, without doubt convict ".

It is to be observed that the test to be followed is not that of seeking to assess
what the particular jury that heard the case would or must have done if it had
only heard a revised version of the evidence. For the purpose of the test the
appellate court must assume a reasonable jury, and must then ask whether such
a reasonable jury, hearing only the admissible evidence, could if properly directed
have failed to convict.

If in the present case the impugned evidence is to be excluded, the process in
invoking the proviso becomes that of considering whether a reasonable jury who
had heard only the admissible evidence would, after a proper direction in a
summing-up, without doubt have convicted. When it is remembered that in the
present case there were originally seven counts and that the jury were occupied
for approximately fifty-four days, it seems manifest that the task of re-creating
the structure of the prosecution case as it would have been without the evidence
now being eliminated may be beset with particular difficulty. In this connexion
it cannot be forgotten that the prosecution at the outset of the second trial made
the submission that, for the presentment of the case in a form of opening that
they would consider desirable, they needed to introduce the statements whose
admissibility was in question. As a consequence there was a sort of trial before
the trial in the absence of the jury. That lasted, we are told, four days. The issue
of admissibility was debated. The prosecution then opened the case and introduced the statements. They introduced them as an essential part of their case.
Thereafter they were woven into the fabric of the prosecution case. It is, of
course, possible for the prosecution to suggest—as indeed they do—that they
would or should have achieved the same result (i.e., of securing convictions) even
if the trial had proceeded on the different basis that would have resulted if the
statements had never been before a jury. There is, however, all the difference
between envisaging what the picture before a jury would have been if there had
merely been some measure of elimination, and envisaging what the picture would
have been if it had had to be quite differently painted.

There were originally seven counts in the indictment and Harz was concerned
in all of them. Count 3 was not proceeded with and courts 4 to 7 were described

A in the summing-up as counts 3 to 6 respectively. Between all six counts there was some inter-relation. It is accepted by the prosecution that they depended, so far as count 4 was concerned, on the evidence of the August interview and that without that evidence the application of the proviso could not be invoked. That was the count that introduced Green and Russell, Ltd. In regard to count 6 (which introduced Ross) it would not be safe for present purposes to place too

B much dependence on the ability of the witness Tansley to observe sufficiently and the evidence linking Harz with the discrepancies is somewhat slender. In regard to counts 2 and 3 (which introduced the associated companies) the case against Harz rested considerably on the basis that he was implicated because he exercised certain general supervisory functions, though he said that he did not have control over the companies.

C   The case in regard to count 1 was that there were very large purchases of chargeable goods and that by a disposal of quantities of them through unregistered sources there were extensive evasions of payment of purchase tax. That there was a wide gap seems clear. The Crown's case was that there was ample proof, implicating Harz, that chargeable goods professedly sold to registered traders had in fact been disposed of through unregistered sources. They contended that

D the jury must have rejected the evidence which suggested that large quantities of goods had been sold to a man named Reynolds. Manifestly, the case was one of very grave suspicion, but the question now arising is whether on a survey of the admissible evidence, but eliminating from it all the impugned evidence, it can be said that a reasonable jury properly directed would without doubt have convicted. The case was one of much complexity. The hearing was lengthy. There

E was a mass of detail. The inadmissible evidence was depended on by the prosecution. It was a part and feature of their case. Its impact recurred at many points. It does not seem to me that it can be said with confidence that, had there been a hearing without it, a reasonable jury properly directed would without doubt have convicted.

F   **LORD HODSON:** My Lords, I have had the benefit of reading the opinions of my noble and learned friends LORD REID and LORD MORRIS OF BORTH-Y-GEST, with which I agree.

       LORD PEARCE: My Lords, I have had the benefit of reading the opinions of my noble and learned friends LORD REID and LORD MORRIS OF BORTH-Y-GEST, with which I agree.

G   **LORD WILBERFORCE:** My Lords, having had the benefit of reading the opinions prepared by my noble and learned friends, LORD REID and LORD MORRIS OF BORTH-Y-GEST, I find myself entirely in agreement with each of them and for the reasons there stated would dismiss the appeal.

Appeal dismissed.

H   Solicitors: *Solicitor, Customs & Excise* (for the commissioners); *Tarlo, Lyons & Aukin* (for the respondent Harz); *Barnett & Barnett* (for the respondent Power).

[*Reported by* KATHLEEN J. H. O'BRIEN, *Barrister-at-Law.*]

BAILEY v. PURSER.

[QUEEN'S BENCH DIVISION (Lord Parker, C.J., Widgery and O'Connor, JJ.),
November 24, 1966.]

*Agriculture—Notice to quit—Consent of tribunal—Greater hardship—Financial
considerations relevant to deceased landlord's estate and his widow's position
—Whether " hardship " was confined to hardship referable to possession and
use of agricultural holding—Agricultural Holdings Act, 1948 (11 & 12
Geo. 6 c. 63), s. 25 (1), as substituted by Agriculture Act, 1958 (6 & 7 Eliz. 2
c. 71), s. 3 (2).*

" Hardship " in s. 25 (1) (d)* of the Agricultural Holdings Act, 1948 (as
substituted by the Agriculture Act, 1958, s. 3 (2)) is not confined to hardship
referable to possession or use of the agricultural holding nor is the meaning
of the word limited in any way; accordingly the Agricultural Land Tribunal
can give consent under s. 25 (1) (d) to a notice to quit where the greater
hardship that would be caused to the landlord by withholding consent is
attributable to the financial situation of the landlord and, on his death, of his
widow and his estate (see p. 190, letter F, p. 191, letter I, and p. 192, letter
A, post).

[As to consent to a notice to quit an agricultural holding, see 1 HALSBURY'S
LAWS (3rd Edn.) 284, 285, para. 601; and for cases on the subject, see 2 DIGEST
(Repl.) 14-16, *61-68.*

For the Agricultural Holdings Act, 1948, s. 25 (as originally enacted), s. 30,
see 28 HALSBURY'S STATUTES (2nd Edn.) 48, 55.

For the Agricultural Holdings Act, 1948, s. 25 (1), as substituted by the
Agricultural Act, 1958, s. 3 (2), see 38 HALSBURY'S STATUTES (2nd Edn.) 70,
and SUPPLEMENT (amended texts).]

Case Stated.

This is a special Case Stated for the opinion of the High Court pursuant to s. 6
of the Agricultural (Miscellaneous Provisions) Act, 1954†, as amended by the
Agricultural Land Tribunal, Eastern Area, with regard to their decision made on
Mar. 7, 1966, and issued on Apr. 2, 1966, consenting to the operation of a notice to
quit dated Feb. 3, 1965, on the ground that greater hardship would be caused by
withholding consent than by giving it. The following facts were found. In 1955
the appellant, George H. Purser, became tenant of the deceased, William Henry
Bailey, of Slate Hall Farm, Therfield, Hertfordshire (hereinafter called " the
holding ") and of an adjoining farm known as Five House Farm. The appellant
purchased the freehold of Five House Farm in 1959 and he had at all times since
1955 farmed both farms as one unit. In 1963 a notice to quit the holding was
served on the appellant. The validity of such notice to quit was one of the issues
in an action pending in the Queen's Bench Division of the High Court of Justice
the short title and reference to the record whereof was *Bailey* v. *Purser*, 1964 B.
No. 4113. By a notice dated Feb. 3, 1965, the deceased gave the appellant
notice to quit the holding on Feb. 4, 1966, or at the end of the year of the tenancy
which would expire next after the end of twelve months from the date of the
serving of the notice. A counter-notice by the appellant was served on Mar. 1,
1965. The validity of this notice to quit was not challenged by the appellant.
On July 6, 1965, the deceased applied to the Agricultural Land Tribunal, Eastern
Area, under s. 24 of the Agricultural Holdings Act, 1948 (as amended by the
Agriculture Act, 1958) for the consent of the tribunal to the operation of the
notice to quit. On Sept. 14, 1965, the chairman of the tribunal under r. 33 of
the Schedule to the Agricultural Land Tribunals and Notices to Quit Order, 1959‡,
accepted the said application for consideration by the tribunal notwithstanding
that the same was made out of time. The deceased died on Nov. 17, 1965.

* Section 25 (1) (d), as substituted, is set out at p. 190, letter B, post.
† 34 HALSBURY'S STATUTES (2nd Edn.) 8.
‡ S.I. 1959 No. 81, as amended. For rr. 33, see 1 HALSBURY'S STATUTORY INSTRU-
MENTS (Second Re-Issue) 111.

Affirmed. C.A. [1967] 2 All E.R. 189.

A   On Jan. 27, 1966, letters of administration to the estate of the deceased limited to the application pending before the tribunal were granted out of the principal probate registry to the respondent, Ernest J. Bailey. The application was partly heard on Jan. 31, 1966, when it was adjourned to, and the hearing was concluded on, Mar. 7, 1966. Neither at the date of the first nor of the adjourned hearing had probate of the will of the deceased or any letters of administration

B   other than letters of administration limited to the application pending before the tribunal been granted to the respondent or to any other person. The effect of the dispositions of the deceased's will were summarised as follows:—(i) legacies were given of £1,000 to the widow and of £500 to each of two daughters of the deceased, (ii) the widow was given an annuity of £750 per annum, and (iii) the residue of the estate was given to the respondent. The liabilities of the deceased's

C   estate were substantial and interest at the rate of about £1,340 per annum was accruing on secured debts. If the assets set out in the estate duty affidavit were realised, there was a prospect of a surplus of about £1,500 which would enable at least some of the bequests in the will to be fulfilled.

     The tribunal took into account in reaching its decision all the circumstances of the case on which its discretion could be exercised, including the following

D   matters. (i) That, as counsel for the appellant conceded, hardship could be said to be inflicted on the estate of the deceased and on those entitled under it if the holding continued to be occupied by a tenant when interest on the secured liabilities of the deceased's estate at about £1,340 per annum would greatly exceed the amount of the rent which, currently, was £341 16s. per annum. The secured liabilities of the deceased's estate were charged on the holding, which was

E   the only asset of the estate on which any money could be secured or borrowed. The financial position of the estate was such that no further borrowing was possible. (ii) That, as counsel for the appellant conceded, the situation of the deceased's very elderly widow could amount to hardship in that, unless the farm was sold, it would be impossible for the deceased's estate to be administered, and for the widow, now living on national assistance, to receive the benefit to which

F   she was entitled from the estate. (iii) That, as counsel for the appellant conceded, the stigma of the deceased dying insolvent could constitute hardship to the estate of the deceased and, in a different way, to the members of the family. (iv) That hardship could be said to be inflicted on the respondent, who was an undischarged bankrupt, if he bore the burden, in his bankruptcy, of the debts of his father, the deceased, as contingent liabilities when such liabilities might in

G   whole or in part be liquidated if the farm were sold. (v) That in accordance with the decision in *Hart* v. *Frampton** referred to by counsel for the appellant, the degrees of hardship must be carefully considered in relation to those by whom they were or might be borne. (vi) That, as counsel for the appellant submitted, only in exceptional cases should the tribunal consent to the operation of a notice to quit, the effect of which consent would probably be to enable the landlord to

H   sell the holding.

     The questions of law which the tribunal referred to the High Court were the following: (a) whether on the true construction of s. 25 of the Agricultural Holdings Act, 1948, as amended by the Agriculture Act, 1958, the circumstances referred to by the tribunal were capable of being taken into consideration with all the other factors in the case in arriving at a decision whether there was " hard-

I   ship " within the meaning or for the purposes of para. (*d*) of s. 25 (1) of the Agricultural Holdings Act, 1948, amended as aforesaid; and (b) whether under and on the true construction of the Agricultural Holdings Act, 1948, as amended, and in particular s. 25 and s. 30 thereof, it was within the jurisdiction or competence of the tribunal to consent to the operation of a notice to quit when the probable result would be that, although there was no existing contract for the sale of the holding, the landlord would sell the holding in due course.

---

* [1947] 2 All E.R. 604.

J. W. Mills, Q.C., and *J. A. R. Finlay* for the appellant.   A
L. A. Blundell, Q.C., and *S. N. Bernstein* for the respondent.

LORD PARKER, C.J.: This is an appeal by way of Case Stated from a
decision of the Agricultural Land Tribunal, Eastern Area, by which they consented to a notice to quit served on one George H. Purser, the appellant before
this court. The ground on which the tribunal consented to the notice was the
ground which is to be found in s. 25 (1) (*d*) of the Agricultural Holdings Act, 1948,   B
as substituted by s. 3 (2) of the Agriculture Act, 1958, namely

" that greater hardship would be caused by withholding than by giving
consent to the operation of the notice."

The facts can be very shortly stated here because the point that emerges is really
a pure point of law, namely the construction of those words to which I have just   C
referred—s. 25 (1) (*d*) as amended.

It appears that the holding in question was Slate Hall Farm, a farm of eighty-
two acres of which up to Nov. 17, 1965, one William Henry Bailey was the
landlord, and of which the appellant was and is the tenant. On Feb. 3, 1965 Mr.
William Henry Bailey gave the tenant a notice to quit to expire on Feb. 4, 1966.
He further set in motion the procedure for the obtaining of consent to that notice   D
to quit which was required under the Act of 1948, but before the matter was
dealt with he died on Nov. 17, 1965.

His son, Ernest J. Bailey, the respondent, obtained limited administration of
the estate for the sole purpose of these proceedings, and the reason put forward
for there being a greater hardship in refusing consent than by granting it, was
the state of that estate. The estate was insolvent, or nearly insolvent. Unless   E
this property was sold with vacant possession there was nothing whatever for
the beneficiaries under the will, and particularly nothing for Mrs. Bailey, the
widow, who was forced to live on national assistance. In addition the respondent,
who was himself bankrupt, had guaranteed his father's debts. The question that
then arises in this case is whether hardship in the statute is confined, as is urged
before this court, to hardship referable to possession of the holding or use of the   F
holding or whether it is hardship at large, which will enable the financial consideration of the landlord or those representing the landlord to be taken into
consideration. Counsel for the appellant has put forward another point, which,
I think, he concedes is really involved in that first point, which he puts in this
way: that consent cannot be given under the statute to enable a landlord to sell
with vacant possession purely for financial considerations.   G

In putting this matter before the court, counsel for the appellant summarises
his contentions under six heads. He says in the first instance, what is undoubtedly
true, that what falls to be considered is a number of provisions in the Agricultural
Holdings Act, 1948, dealing with agricultural matters in which, in the first
instance under the earlier legislation the consent of the Minister of Agriculture
and Fisheries had to be obtained, and as amended, the consent of the Agricultural   H
Land Tribunal. He says that both the Minister of Agriculture, Fisheries and
Food, and the tribunal are fully competent and fit to decide matters of hardship
dealing with what one may call general agricultural matters, possession and use
of the holding, but are not the sort of tribunal which one would expect to decide
matters of hardship at large. He refers secondly to the exact wording of the
provision that greater hardship would be caused by withholding than by giving   I
consent to the operation of the notice, by which he contends that Parliament
meant " caused by in the one instant being kept out of possession and deprived
of the use of his own land, and on the other side, the tenant's side, being deprived
of his possession and use of the holding which he then had ". Thirdly, he points
out that this provision in para. (*d*) not only comes in a subsection dealing with
grounds, all of which are directed to the purpose for which the land is intended to
be used, agricultural purposes quite generally, but it comes as the fourth of five,
sandwiched in between those that deal purely with agricultural matters. I find

A   it unnecessary to read those provisions in detail, but that generally can be said
to be the fact.

Fourthly counsel for the appellant says that as a matter of history his contention is borne out. If one looks at the amended section in the Agriculture Act,
1958, s. 3 (2), it is found that broadly speaking the provisions originally set out in
s. 25 (1) of the Agriculture Holdings Act, 1948, are continued with a slight re-
B   arrangement in form, but with para. (c) and para. (d) of s. 25 (1) in its original form
merged, as he would put it, into the provision that appears in para. (d) now, and he
says that if one goes back to the original s. 25 and para. (c) and para. (d) thereof, it
is patent that para. (c) and para. (d) are themselves dealing with what I may call
agricultural purposes. For my part I find very great difficulty in obtaining any
help from the history of this matter. Paragraph (c) and para. (d) have been
C   wholly replaced; the Act of 1958 was an amending Act, and it is to be observed
that the original para. (c) has gone in its entirety and the original para. (d) has
been enlarged in its scope by the deletion of the restrictions or conditions there
set out which operated to limit its scope. Whether the hardship in the original
para. (c) and para. (d) were confined in the way suggested by counsel for the
appellant I am by no means clear; certainly as it seems to me that the words
D   " greater hardship " in the original para. (d) were not limited in any way save
by the conditions precedent to the operation of the paragraph. In any event,
however, as I have already said, one of those paragraphs has completely gone,
one has been widened in scope, and bearing in mind that the Act of 1958 is an
amending Act, I can derive no help from the history.

Fifthly, counsel for the appellant refers to s. 25 (5) of the Act of 1948, which is
E   still in force as amended (1), and which provides that:

> " Where the Agricultural Land Tribunal consent under the last fore-
> going section to the operation of a notice to quit, the tribunal may impose
> such conditions as appear to the tribunal requisite for securing that the
> land to which the notice relates will be used for the purpose for which the
> landlord proposes to terminate the tenancy."

F

Again I myself can get no help from a provision empowering conditions to be
imposed when the ground for the obtaining of the consent is the purpose for
which the landlord intends to use it. That does not mean that there cannot be
other grounds that do not involve a purpose.

Finally, counsel for the appellant refers to s. 30 of the Act of 1948, which deals
G   with the position when a contract to sell the land is entered into during the
currency of a notice to quit. That section provides that, in default of agreement
or the machinery there laid down, the notice to quit shall be of no effect. I can
get no help from that because in the first instance I find it very difficult to understand, and I gather I am not alone in thinking that. In Jackson's Agricultural
Holdings (11th Edn.) p. 70 the author says:

H   " Its purpose has been thought to be to prevent an owner from giving
> notice to quit in order to sell with vacant possession, but judges have
> professed themselves unable to discover its true object, or the mischief which
> it was intended to remedy."

In the second place it seems to me that it is dealing with an entirely different
I   situation, and really casts little, if any, light on the question here which has to be
determined.

In the end, therefore, I am left just looking at the words in para. (d), words
which are wholly unrestricted as a matter of language, and I can find no possible
ground for limiting the word " hardship " in any way. For those reasons which
I have stated shortly, I think the tribunal came to a right decision in law, and I
would dismiss this appeal.

---

(1) By the Agriculture Act, 1958, s. 8 (1), Sch. 1, Pt. 1, para. 6 (b).

WIDGERY, J.: I entirely agree, and there is nothing which I can usefully   A
add.

O'CONNOR, J.: I agree.

Appeal dismissed. Leave to appeal to the Court of Appeal granted.

Solicitors: *Pollard, Thomas & George Martin* (for the appellant); *I. A. Landy, Laufer & Co.* (for the respondent).

                                                                            B

[*Reported by* S. A. HATTEEA, ESQ., *Barrister-at-Law.*]

Re GRIERSON, OLDHAM & ADAMS, LTD.   C

[CHANCERY DIVISION (Plowman, J.), November 2, 3, 1966.]

Company—Scheme of arrangement—Transfer of shares to transferee company —Acquisition of shares of dissentients—Unfairness—Burden of proof— Factors—Fairness to body of shareholders as a whole—More generous to preference than to ordinary shareholders—Offer price exceeding market price   D *—Acceptance by holders of ninety-nine per cent. of shares—Take-over bid— Companies Act, 1948 (11 & 12 Geo. 6 c. 38), s. 209 (1).*

G., Ltd. had an issued share capital of 3,785,292 ordinary shares of 2s. each, fifty thousand five per cent. first cum. preference shares of £1 each and 50,500 7½ per cent. second cum. preference shares of £1 each. H., Ltd. made an offer for G., Ltd.'s shares. This was announced in the press in   E mid-September, 1965. The price offered for the first cum. preference was 17s. per share, for the second cum. preference was 23s. per share, and for each ordinary share was 6s. The middle market price of the ordinary shares in mid-September, 1965, was 5s. 9d. per share. The offer for the preference shares was about 3s. in excess of the market value of each such share. Shareholders holding some seventy-five per cent. of the ordinary   F shares had signified their intentions to accept the offer at the date when it was circularised, and acceptances bringing the total above ninety-nine per cent. of the ordinary shares were received. The applicants, each of whom held two thousand ordinary shares, declined the offer, and, having received notice of intention to acquire their shares pursuant to s. 209* of the Companies Act, 1948, applied to the court for a declaration that H., Ltd. was not   G entitled to acquire their shares, alleging that the offer was unfair. There had been a substantial rise in the profits of G., Ltd. in the period ending Mar. 31, 1965. The ordinary share dividend had remained constant for the years 1962-65, and the prices of the ordinary shares had been as high in 1960 as 7s. 6d., in 1961 as 9s. 9d., in 1962 as 8s. 3d., in 1963 as 7s. 7d., in 1964 as 7s. 6d., and in 1965 as 7s. 3d.; in each of these years also the lowest price   H had been below 6s. Goodwill was valued in G., Ltd.'s balance sheet at £1 and the company's freehold and leasehold properties were entered at 1959 values or at cost, part one way and part another.

Held: (i) the test of fairness was whether the offer was fair to the offerees, the body of shareholders, as a whole, not to the applicants individually; the onus (which was a heavy one as the acquisition was of shares and the   I price offered was above market price) was on the applicants to prove that the offer was obviously and convincingly unfair, and it was not enough to show only that the scheme was open to criticism or capable of improvement (see p. 197, letters G and H, p. 198, letter D, and p. 200, letter A, post).

Re Sussex Brick Co., Ltd. ([1960] 1 All E.R. 772) explained and applied. *Re Hoare & Co., Ltd.* ([1933] All E.R. Rep. 105) applied.

---

* Section 209 (1), so far as material, is set out at p. 194, letters B to D, post.

(ii) the applicants failed to discharge the onus of proof that was on them, having regard particularly to the facts that holders of over ninety-nine per cent. of the ordinary shares had accepted the offer and that the price offered exceeded the market price (see p. 201, letters F and G, post); moreover (a) the fact that the preference shareholders were treated more generously did not render the offer to the ordinary shareholders unfair, and (b) the element of acquisition of control of G., Ltd. was one which should not be taken into account by way of addition in computing the value of the ordinary shares (see p. 201, letter C, and p. 200, letter G, post).

Short v. *Treasury Comrs.* ([1947] 2 All E.R. 298) considered.

[As to the powers to acquire shares of dissenting shareholders, see 6 HALS-BURY'S LAWS (3rd Edn.) 774, 775, para. 1561; and for cases on the subject, see 10 DIGEST (Repl.) 1093-1096, *7559-7574.*

For the Companies Act, 1948, s. 209, see 3 HALSBURY'S STATUTES (2nd Edn.) 628.]

Cases referred to:

Bugle Press, Ltd., Re, Re Houses and Estates, Ltd., [1960] 1 All E.R. 768; [1961] Ch. 270; [1960] 2 W.L.R. 658; *affd.* C.A., [1960] 3 All E.R. 791; [1961] Ch. at p. 270; [1960] 3 W.L.R. 956; Digest (Cont. Vol. A) 198, *7574c.*

Hoare & Co., Ltd., Re, [1933] All E.R. Rep. 105; 150 L.T. 374; 10 Digest (Repl.) 1095, *7572.*

Press Caps, Ltd., Re, [1949] 1 All E.R. 1013; [1949] Ch. 434; [1949] L.J.R. 1460; 10 Digest (Repl.) 1095, *7574.*

Short v. *Treasury Comrs.,* [1947] 2 All E.R. 298; [1948] 1 K.B. 116; *affd.* H.L., [1948] 2 All E.R. 509; [1948] A.C. 534; [1949] L.J.R. 143; 17 Digest (Repl.) 481, *280.*

Sussex Brick Co., Ltd., Re, [1960] 1 All E.R. 772, n.; [1961] Ch. 289, n.; [1960] 2 W.L.R. 665, n.; Digest (Cont. Vol. A) 198, *7574b.*

Adjourned Summons.

This was an application by originating summons dated Feb. 28, 1966, by John Selwyn Cecil Gurney-Champion and Philip Gilbert Lightfoot (" the applicants ") members of Grierson Oldham & Adams, Ltd. (" the company ") for an order under s. 209 of the Companies Act, 1948, declaring that the respondents, John Holt & Co. (Liverpool), Ltd. was neither entitled nor bound to acquire the shares of the applicants in the company or any of them on the terms of the scheme or contract dated Sept. 27, 1965, notwithstanding that it had been approved by holders of nine-tenths in value of the ordinary shares of the company. The facts are set out in the judgment.

The cases noted below* were cited during the argument in addition to those referred to in the judgment.

The applicants appeared in person.

R. B. S. Instone for the respondents.

PLOWMAN, J.: This is a summons asking for an order under s. 209 of the Companies Act, 1948, declaring that the respondents, John Holt & Co. (Liverpool), Ltd., are neither entitled to nor bound to acquire the shares of the applicants in Grierson, Oldham & Adams, Ltd., or any of them on the terms of the scheme or contract dated Sept. 27, 1965, notwithstanding that it had been approved by holders of nine-tenths in value of the shares of Grierson, Oldham & Adams, Ltd.

The two applicants in this case are Mr. Gurney-Champion, a solicitor, and Mr. Lightfoot. They have appeared in person on this application. Mr. Gurney-Champion has conducted his case, if I may say so, with great propriety and

---

* *Re Castner-Kellner Alkali Co., Ltd.,* [1930] 2 Ch. 349; *Re Evertite Locknuts (1938), Ltd.,* [1945] 1 All E.R. 401; [1945] Ch. 220; *Dean* v. *Prince,* [1954] 1 All E.R. 749; [1954] Ch. 409; *Re Fras. Hinde & Sons, Ltd.,* (1966), The Times, Apr. 23.

ability, and Mr. Lightfoot has been happy to stand or fall with Mr. Gurney-Champion and has not argued the matter before me separately.

Section 209 (1), under which this application is made, provides as far as material as follows:

" Where a scheme or contract involving the transfer of shares or any class of shares in a company (in this section referred to as ' the transferor company ') to another company, whether a company within the meaning of this Act or not (in this section referred to as ' the transferee company '), has, within four months after the making of the offer in that behalf by the transferee company been approved by the holders of not less than nine-tenths in value of the shares whose transfer is involved (other than shares already held at the date of the offer by, or by a nominee for, the transferee company or its subsidiary), the transferee company may, at any time within two months after the expiration of the said four months, give notice in the prescribed manner to any dissenting shareholder that it desires to acquire his shares, and when such a notice is given the transferee company shall, unless on an application made by the dissenting shareholder within one month from the date on which the notice was given the court thinks fit to order otherwise, be entitled and bound to acquire those shares on the terms on which, under the scheme or contract, the shares of the approving shareholders are to be transferred to the transferee company . . ."

Grierson, Oldham & Adams, Ltd. (which I will call " the company ") was incorporated in the year 1894, and its business is that of shippers of wines and spirits. At all material times its issued share capital had consisted of 3,785,292 ordinary shares of 2s. each and 100,500 preference shares of £1 each; and the preference shares were divided into two classes—fifty thousand five per cent. first cumulative preference and 50,500 7½ per cent. second cumulative preference.

Mr. Gurney-Champion holds two thousand ordinary shares in the company. He bought those shares at various times during the first half of 1963, and in order to avoid a loss on his investment he needs to sell the shares for not less than 6s. 7½d. each. Mr. Lightfoot also holds two thousand ordinary shares in the company which he bought in 1959 at the price of 6s. 9d., disregarding expenses. Those two holdings aggregate four thousand ordinary shares, representing, in fact, something less than · 1 per cent. of the ordinary shareholding of the company.

The respondents to the summons, John Holt & Co. (Liverpool), Ltd. (which I will call " Holts ") are also in the wine and spirit business, although they have other businesses as well, including that of shipping.

In the autumn of 1965, Holts made an offer through Lazards for the whole of the issued share capital of the company; and that offer was announced to the press on Sept. 15, 1965, and on Sept. 27, a circular was sent out in the usual way to all the company's shareholders, and a copy of that circular was in evidence. I propose to read one or two extracts from that circular. Paragraph 1 is headed " The Offer ", and states as follows:

" On behalf of Holts we offer to acquire the whole of the issued share capital of Griersons, consisting of fifty thousand five per cent. first cumulative preference shares of £1 each, 50,500 7½ per cent. second cumulative preference shares of £1 each and 3,785,292 ordinary shares of 2s. each, upon the following terms and conditions:

" A. For each of the five per cent. first cumulative
preference shares of £1, holders are offered   ..   17s. in cash,
free of all expenses

" For each of the 7½ per cent. second cumulative
preference shares of £1, holders are offered   ..   23s. in cash
free of all expenses

" For each of the ordinary shares of 2s., holders
are offered   ..   .. 6s. in cash
free of all
expenses."

The same paragraph goes on to state, among other things, that the offer is

" conditional upon irrevocable acceptances being received in accordance
with the instructions set out below not later than 3 p.m. on Oct. 18, 1965
(or such later date, not being later than Nov. 18, 1965, as Holts may decide),
in respect of not less than ninety per cent. (or such lesser percentage as
Holts may decide) of the total nominal amount of the issued share capital
of Griersons."

And then Lazards set out a letter which they received from the company's
chairman which includes the following passage:

" The directors of Griersons and their advisers, S. G. Warburg & Co., Ltd.,
consider the offer to be fair and reasonable. The directors of Griersons
therefore unanimously recommend acceptance of the offer which they
intend to accept in respect of the shares which they own or control. These
shares together with those of certain other shareholders who have also
signified their intention of accepting the offer, amount in the aggregate to
2,871,798 ordinary shares, which is approximately 75·8 per cent. of the
ordinary share capital."

In the next paragraph there is reference to Stock Exchange prices. The
paragraph states:

" The middle market quotations of the five per cent. first cumulative
preference shares, the $7\frac{1}{2}$ per cent. second cumulative preference shares
and the ordinary shares of Griersons, as shown in the daily official list of
the Stock Exchange, London, on Sept. 14, 1965 (the last dealing day before
the announcement of this offer), on Sept. 23, 1965 (the latest practicable date
before the printing of this letter), and on the last dealing day of each of the
last six months, are shown below, together with, in the case of the ordinary
shares, the highest and lowest prices at which dealings were marked in the
daily official list during each of the last six months."

All I propose to refer to in the table which follows is the fact that the middle
market quotation for the ordinary shares on Sept. 14 was 5s. 9d. and on Sept. 23
it was also 5s. 9d. In para. 5 it is stated that

" The directors of Griersons and their families are beneficially interested
in an aggregate of 1,764,580 ordinary shares of Griersons."

In para. 6 it is said that

" The following information is given in the appendices overleaf:—I. A
summary of the audited consolidated balance sheet of Griersons as at
Mar. 31, 1965. II. A statement of the profits of Griersons for each of the
last five years.
" The annual report and accounts of Griersons for the year ended Mar. 31,
1965, have been posted to you today."

So that the accounts for the previous financial year and the circular went out
on the same day.

Turning to the appendices, I would draw attention to the fact that the second
appendix shows that the profits of the company had been going up since the
fifteen months ending Mar. 31, 1961, and they had had a substantial rise in the
period ending Mar. 31, 1965; the ordinary share dividend remained constant
for 1962, 1963, 1964 and 1965 at fifteen per cent. So that from that circular it
appears that ordinary shareholders were being offered 6s. a share as against a
middle market price of 5s. 9d., that is to say, they were being offered 3d. a share
above the relevant Stock Exchange price.

Holts' offer was accepted by holders of more than ninety-nine per cent. of the shares in the company, but it was not accepted by the applicants. Accordingly on Jan. 28, 1966, Holts served a notice on each of the applicants pursuant to s. 209 to the effect that it desired to acquire their shares and that unless they applied to the court on or before Feb. 28, 1966, and the court otherwise ordered, Holts would be entitled and bound to acquire their shares on the terms of the offer; and the summons which is before me now was in fact issued on the last day, namely, Feb. 28, 1966.

Now, the contentions which are put forward by the applicants in this case fall under two main heads. In the first place it is said that the price of 6s. a share is unfair, taking into account the assets and future prospects of the company and the advantages which will accrue to Holts by the take-over; and secondly, it is said that it is unfair to the applicants that they should be compelled to sell their shares at a loss. Before considering those contentions in more detail, there are two or three general observations which I should make and which I think are justified by the authorities on this section to which I have been referred.

The first general observation is that the onus of proof here is fairly and squarely on the applicants, and, indeed, they accept that that is so. The onus of proof is on them to establish, if they can, that the offer was unfair. In *Re Hoare & Co. Ltd.* (1), MAUGHAM, J., had this to say (2):

" I have some hesitation in expressing my view as to when the court should think fit to order otherwise. I think, however, the view of the legislature is that where not less than nine-tenths of the shareholders in the transferor company approve the scheme or accept the offer, prima facie, at any rate, the offer must be taken to be a proper one, and in default of an application by the dissenting shareholders, which include those who do not assent, the shares of the dissentients may be acquired on the original terms by the transferee company. Accordingly, I think it is manifest that the reasons for inducing the court to ' order otherwise ' are reasons which must be supplied by the dissentients who take the step of making an application to the court, and that the onus is on them of giving a reason why their shares should not be acquired by the transferee company.

" One conclusion which I draw from that fact is that the mere circumstance that the sale or exchange is compulsory is one which ought not to influence the court. It has been called an expropriation, but I do not regard that phrase as being very apt in the circumstances of the case. The other conclusion I draw is this, that again prima facie the court ought to regard the scheme as a fair one inasmuch as it seems to me impossible to suppose that the court, in the absence of very strong grounds, is to be entitled to set up its own view of the fairness of the scheme in opposition to so very large a majority of the shareholders who are concerned. Accordingly, without expressing a final opinion on the matter, because there may be special circumstances in special cases, I am unable to see that I have any right to order otherwise in such a case as I have before me, unless it is affirmatively established that, notwithstanding the views of a very large majority of shareholders, the scheme is unfair. There may be other grounds, but I see no other grounds available in the present case for the interference of the court."

These remarks with regard to the onus of proof have been applied in later cases. I notice, for example, that at first instance in *Re Bugle Press, Ltd., Re Houses and Estates, Ltd.* (3), to which I have been referred, BUCKLEY, J.. whose decision was upheld by the Court of Appeal (4), said this (5):

---

(1) [1933] All E.R. Rep. 105.   (2) [1933] All E.R. Rep. at p. 107.
(3) [1960] 1 All E.R. 768; [1961] Ch.. 270.
(4) [1960] 3 All E.R. 791; [1961] Ch. at p. 270.
(5) [1960] 1 All E.R. at p. 771; [1961] Ch. at p. 276.

A " In the ordinary case of an offer under s. 209, where the ninety per cent. majority who accept the offer are unconnected with the persons who are concerned with making the offer, the court pays the greatest attention to the views of that majority. In all commercial matters, where commercial people are much better able to judge of their own affairs than the court is able to do, the court is accustomed to pay the greatest attention to what

B commercial people who are concerned with the transaction in fact decide. It has been recognised in a number of authorities to which I have been referred—Re Hoare & Co., Ltd. (6), a decision of MAUGHAM, J.; Re Press Caps, Ltd. (7); and a decision of VAISEY, J., in Re Sussex Brick Co., Ltd. (8)— that where there is a large majority of shareholders who are only concerned to see that they get what they consider to be a fair price for their shares,

C and who are in favour of accepting the offer, the burden is a heavy one on the dissentient shareholder to show that the offer is not one which he ought reasonably to accept."

The second general observation which seems to me to be relevant is this: that, since this is not a case of a purchase of assets, but is a case of a purchase of shares, the market price on the Stock Exchange of those shares is cogent

D evidence of their true value; not conclusive evidence, of course, but cogent evidence. In another of the cases which was mentioned, Re Press Caps, Ltd. (9), WYNN-PARRY, J., who was sitting on this occasion as a member of the Court of Appeal, had this to say on that topic (10):

" A valuation is only an expression of opinion. It may be made on one

E of a number of bases, but the final test of what is the value of a thing is what it will fetch if sold. In some cases a sale has to take place, as one knows who exercises the administrative jurisdiction of the Chancery Division, but if there exists a market, as, for instance, the Stock Exchange in the case of shares in respect of which there is a quotation or in respect of which there is permission to deal, there may be no need to sell, and prima facie the

F stock exchange markings can be taken as a satisfactory indication of the value of the shares in question. For that reason alone it appears to me, with respect, that the view of MAUGHAM, J. (11), as to where the onus lies under the section is justified. It therefore follows that to succeed the applicants must go behind the Stock Exchange prices, and that undoubtedly, is a heavy task."

G In this case the applicants have set out to discharge a formidable onus, bearing in mind not only that the offer price was above the Stock Exchange price, but also that holders of over ninety-nine per cent. of the ordinary shares accepted it.

The third general observation which arises out of the arguments that have been put forward here concerns the question whether the test of the fairness of the offer

H is whether it is fair to the individual shareholder or whether it is fair to the body of shareholders as a whole In my judgment, the test of fairness is whether the offer is fair to the offerees as a body and not whether it is fair to a particular shareholder in the peculiar circumstances of his own case. Mr. Gurney-Champion, I think, suggested that the contrary was the true view, and he referred in support of that submission to certain remarks made by VAISEY, J.,

I in Re Sussex Brick Co., Ltd. (8). VAISEY, J., said this (12):

---

(6) [1933] All E.R. Rep. 105.   (7) [1949] 1 All E.R. 1013; [1949] Ch. 434.
(8) [1960] 1 All E.R. 772, n.; [1961] Ch. 289, n.
(9) [1949] 1 All E.R. 1013; [1949] Ch. 434.
(10) [1949] 1 All E.R. at p. 1018; [1949] Ch. at p. 447.
(11) In Re Hoare & Co., Ltd., [1933] All E.R. Rep. at p. 107; see p. 196, letters E to I, ante.
(12) [1960] 1 All E.R. at p. 773, n.; [1961] Ch. at p. 290, n.

"The matter has been considered in more than one case, and the considerations which govern it are well stated by MAUGHAM, J., in *Re Hoare & Co., Ltd.* (13). Summarising the judgment it really comes to this: that the applicant, taking advantage of s. 209 has, in effect, to show that the scheme is unfair to him, and that is the yardstick which is accepted and adopted as the criterion whether a shareholder may get out of the provisions of the section for the acquisition of his shares. It is admitted that unless the scheme is unfair to the applicant, he is not entitled under the section to obtain a declaration that he is not bound to transfer his shares."

Mr. Gurney-Champion naturally seized on that passage in support of the contention that he was putting forward. When VAISEY, J.'s judgment is read as a whole, however, and when MAUGHAM, J.'s judgment is also read, (because in the passage to which I have been referred VAISEY, J., was only purporting to summarise what MAUGHAM, J., said) I do not think that VAISEY, J., was intending to suggest that the test of fairness was an individual test to be applied to each dissenting shareholder separately. It would quite obviously be impossible, at any rate, in most cases, for the offeror to know the circumstances of every individual shareholder; and, therefore, to frame an offer which would necessarily be fair to every individual shareholder in the peculiar circumstances of his case.

The other general observation is one which arises from *Re Sussex Brick Co., Ltd.* (14). It is this, that the fact that the applicants may be able to demonstrate that the scheme is open to criticism or is capable of improvement is not enough to discharge the onus of proof which lies on them. VAISEY, J., had this to say (15):

"The applicant set out certain criticisms in his affidavit which undoubtedly show that a good case could be made out for the formulation of a better scheme, a fairer scheme, of a scheme which would have been more attractive to the shareholders, if they could have understood the implications of the criticisms. I have no doubt at all that a better scheme might have been evolved; but is that enough? Is it necessary to establish the validity of such an offer as put forward in the present case? A better and fairer offer might have been made, but the fact that the offer that was made is not one hundred per cent. fair or right is not the kind of unfairness with which MAUGHAM, J., was dealing in *Re Hoare & Co., Ltd.* (13). I think that the scheme must be obviously unfair, patently unfair, unfair to the meanest intelligence. I do not think that merely finding items in the scheme or details of the scheme which are open to valid criticism is enough. A scheme can be effective to bind a dissenting shareholder without complying to the extent of one hundred per cent. with the highest possible standards of fairness, equity and reason."

Towards the end of his judgment, VAISEY, J., said (16):

"It must be affirmatively established that, notwithstanding the view of the majority, the scheme is unfair, and that is a different thing from saying that it must be established that the scheme is not a very fair or not a fair one: a scheme has to be shown affirmatively, patently, obviously and convincingly to be unfair."

Now, after stating these general observations, let me refer in a little more detail to some of the points which have been put forward on the part of the applicants. They have complained that the market price was substantially higher than 6s. a share for a number of years; and the evidence is that in 1959 the shares went as high as 7s. 3d.; in 1960, 7s. 6d.; 1961, 9s. 9d.; 1962, 8s. 3d.; 1963, 7s. 7d.; 1964, 7s. 6d.; 1965, 7s. 3d: equally, as Mr. Gurney-Champion said, in each of those years the lowest price for the shares was under 6s. However that

(13) [1933] All E.R. Rep. 105.   (14) [1960] 1 All E.R. 772, n.; [1961] Ch. 289, n.
(15) [1960] 1 All E.R. at p. 774, n.; [1961] Ch. at pp. 291, n., 292, n.
(16) [1961] Ch. at p. 293, n.; [1960] 1 All E.R. at p. 774, n.

A may be, it seems to me that the real point is this—was 6s. a fair price at the time
when the offer was made, namely, in September, 1965?

Mr. Gurney-Champion then says that September, 1965, when the offer was
made was a time when the shares were temporarily depressed; that the future
prospects were good, and that the market price is not really a reliable guide
in this case, particularly having regard to the fact that the accounts for the year

B ending Mar. 31, 1965, which showed a substantial increase in profits were published simultaneously with the offer so that the market had no opportunity to
adjust itself to the latest results.   In answer to that, it has to be remembered
that shareholders had three weeks in which to make up their minds whether
to accept the offer or not; and it cannot be said that during that three weeks there
was no time for the market to react, in which ever way it was likely to react in

C the particular circumstances of this case; nor can it be said that three weeks
did not give the shareholders ample time in which to form their own view of
the question whether 6s. was a fair offer in the light of the accounts with which
they were furnished at the same time.   It is perfectly true that holders of 75·8 per
cent. of the ordinary shares had already accepted the offer, but, of course,
holders of another 14·2 per cent. of the ordinary shares would have to accept

D before Holts could get the ninety per cent. acceptances which would enable
them to operate the provisions of s. 209.

It is said that in the company's balance sheet the goodwill of the parent
company is shown at a figure of £1 and that the freehold and leasehold properties
have been valued either at 1959 values or at cost, part one way and part another;
and it is said that those figures do not indicate the true value of either the good-

E will or fixed assets.   There seems to me to be a number of answers to that contention.   First of all, as I have indicated earlier on, this is not a question of a
purchase of assets, but a question of the purchase of shares.   Secondly, the
balance sheet does not purport to offer a current valuation of either the goodwill
or of the fixed assets.   It makes it perfectly plain what the basis is on which the
properties are put in at those figures.   Anybody looking at the balance sheet

F with ordinary intelligence would know that £1 is not being put forward as
representing the value of the goodwill and that the figures in the balance sheet
are not being put forward as the current value of the assets in question.   There
is also another point in relation to the matter that I am considering which counsel
for the respondents pointed out, namely, that the balance sheet showed that the
company had reserves totalling almost exactly the same amount as the amount

G of the issued ordinary share capital which would give each ordinary share a net
book value of twice its value, that is to say, each 2s. ordinary share would have
a net book value of 4s., and counsel points out that the offer is fifty per cent. in
excess of that value of 4s. and 2s. a share represents something like an additional
£380,000 which Holts are paying for the ordinary shares.   It seems to me that
that is a matter which has to be balanced against any question of undervaluation.

H   Then, it is said that the price of 6s. a share does not reflect the advantages
accruing to Holts by their obtaining complete control of the company.   Now,
I agree with counsel that that might possibly be used as an argument to justify
paying a shareholder with a controlling interest a larger price for the shares than
the price paid to minority holders.   In my judgment, however, it is not unfair
to offer a minority shareholder the value of what he possesses, i.e., a minority

I shareholding.   The same argument was put to the Court of Appeal in *Re Press
Caps, Ltd.* (17) to which I have been referred, and although the Court of Appeal
did not find it necessary to pronounce conclusively on that argument, it is quite
clear that it did not find any favour in the Court of Appeal.   In this connexion,
counsel referred me to the case of *Short* v. *Treasury Comrs.* (18).   That was a
case where the Minister of Aircraft Production made an order under the defence
regulations, transferring all the shares in Short Brothers (Rochester and Bedford),

(17) [1949] 1 All E.R. 1013; [1949] Ch. 434.
(18) [1947] 2 All E.R. 298; [1948] 1 K.B. 116.

Ltd. to nominees, and the question was how much the Treasury had to pay,   **A**
and that depended on a provision in the appropriate regulations, which were
the Defence (General) Regulations, 1939, (19) reg. 78 (5), which said:

" The price to be paid by a competent authority in respect of any shares
transferred by virtue of such an order as aforesaid shall be such price as may
be specified in an order made by the Treasury, being a price which, in the
opinion of the Treasury, is not less than the value of those shares as between   **B**
a willing buyer and a willing seller on the date of the order made by that
authority . . ."

The decision in that case is set out in the headnote (20) which I will read:

" Inasmuch as the expression ' as between a willing buyer and a willing
seller ' in reg. 78 (5) of the Defence (General) Regulations, 1939, imports,   **C**
when construed according to its ordinary and natural meaning, the conception of a separate bargain of sale by an individual seller to an individual
buyer, a shareholder of an undertaking taken over under reg. 55 of the
Regulations of 1939 is prima facie entitled, under reg. 78, to be paid for his
shareholding only on the basis of the value of a single share, and no account
is to be taken, in assessing the compensation payable to him, of the fact that   **D**
the competent authority in acquiring all the shares is acquiring, in addition,
the exclusive control of the undertaking; for to add to each parcel of shares,
as sold separately, a rateable proportion of the added or ' control ' value of
the totality of the shares would be to add to each holding an item of value
which the shareholder, as an individual, did not, in fact, possess. Moreover,
as shareholders are not, in the eye of the law, part-owners of the undertaking,   **E**
they are also not entitled to have their shares valued by the method of
apportioning among all the shares in the undertaking the value of the undertaking as a whole."

Mr. Gurney-Champion very fairly pointed out, however, that that case really
turned on the construction of the provision in the defence regulations as to the
meaning of " as between a willing buyer and a willing seller ", and I agree that   **F**
it is not of very much assistance in the present case in determining a different
question, namely, whether the offer of 6s. was fair or not.   On general principle,
however, and quite irrespective of *Short* v. *Treasury Comrs.* (21), in my judgment,
the element of control is not one which ought to have been taken into account
as an additional item of value in the offer of these shares.

Then Mr. Gurney-Champion submitted that it was unfair that he should   **G**
be compelled to sell these shares at a loss, particularly having regard to the fact
that the loss would be one which was not available for capital gains tax purposes,
for the reason that he had bought the shares before Apr. 6, 1965, and on that
day the price of the shares was less than the purchase price.   Now, if I am right
in thinking that the question of unfairness has to be judged without reference
to the particular circumstances of the applicant, then, it seems to me that this   **H**
argument is irrelevant, and I am bound to reject it.   What the court is concerned
with is the fairness of the offer as a whole.

I should add a word or two about the affidavit of Mrs. Letts which has been
made in this matter.   She has some expert knowledge of share valuations.   I
have already covered a good many of the points which she makes in that affidavit
in dealing with the points put forward by Mr. Gurney-Champion.   There are,   **I**
perhaps, two points to which I should specifically refer.   In para. 6 (c) she states:

" The price offered for the ordinary shares would appear to be inadequate
in relation to the price offered for the preference shares.   If the prospects
for the preference shares warranted a price of approximately 3s. in excess
of the middle market price at the time that the offer was made, then it seems

(19) S.R. & O. 1939 No. 927, as amended.   (20) [1948] I K.B. 116.
          (21) [1947] 2 All E.R. 298; [1948] 1 K.B. 116.

A reasonable to assume that the ordinary shares warranted a price in excess
of 3d. over the middle market price, particularly bearing in mind the good
results for the year to Mar. 31, 1965, which it is reasonable to assume would
have had a much greater effect on the price of the ordinary shares than
they would have had on the preference shares if the market had had an
opportunity of reflecting these results before the bid was announced."

B In reply to that, counsel for the respondents says: " Fair enough; that is fair
comment. On the figures the preference shareholders were dealt with propor-
tionately better than the ordinary shareholders." Counsel says, however, and
this is really the answer to the point, that the question is not whether the preference shareholders were dealt with generously, but whether the ordinary shareholders were dealt with fairly; and whether the preference shareholders were

C dealt with over generously I do not know. I do not know what considerations
led to the offer being made to them at the figure at which it was made; but the
mere fact that they were dealt with generously, and that the ordinary shareholders were dealt with less generously or not generously at all, does not mean
that the ordinary shareholders were not dealt with fairly.

The other point on Mrs. Letts' affidavit is in para. 6 (e) where, after referring

D to a number of matters, she states:

" Taking all these factors into account I am of the opinion that the offer
price is inadequate and that an adequate price would be not less than 7s. an
ordinary share, a price which the shares have exceeded in the market during
each one of the last five years."

E Let us assume that by " adequate price " she really means the same thing as a
fair price. I have no doubt that that is her honest opinion, but the question of
value is obviously one about which opinions may differ. Against her opinion
I have to set off what seems to me to be the two overwhelming factors in this
case, namely, that ninety-nine plus per cent. of the ordinary shareholders regarded
this offer as a fair offer which they were prepared to accept and did accept.

F The other matter is that in point of fact the offer to the ordinary shareholders
was one which did exceed the Stock Exchange price. It is possible to criticise,
in cases like this, figures, offers and balance sheets and argue about matters
of fairness and unfairness; but that is what makes the task of dissentients
who come to the court under this section a very difficult task, one which, so
far as reported cases go, they have never succeeded in discharging. They have

G not succeeded, except in *Re Bugle Press, Ltd.* (22), which is a different case that
really lies outside the scheme of s. 209; and, although I have sympathy for the
applicants, who naturally did not want to face a loss on their investments, I
have no doubt in the end that they have failed, like others before them, to
discharge this heavy onus of proof, and, that being so, I am bound to dismiss
this application.

H There are one or two points to add. First of all, the respondents, Holts,
concede that the applicants are entitled to interest on the purchase money for
their shares as from the expiration of the notice which Holts gave under
s. 209 (1); that is to say, as from Mar. 1, 1966, the notice expiring on Feb. 28.
I think the appropriate rate of interest in the circumstances would be five per
cent.; and, therefore, the order should provide for that matter. The other

I point is the question of costs. The respondents do not ask for costs, and I think
the proper thing to do in the circumstances is to make no order as to costs.

Summons dismissed.

Solicitors: *Gurney-Champion & Co.*, Portsmouth (for the applicants); *Linklaters & Paines* (for the respondents).

[*Reported by* JACQUELINE METCALFE, *Barrister-at-Law.*]

(22) [1960] 3 All E.R. 791; [1961] Ch. at p. 270.

A

Re S. (infants).

[CHANCERY DIVISION (Cross, J.), November 7, 8, 9, 10, 16, 1966.]

*Ward of Court—Evidence—Expert evidence of psychiatrist or educational psycho-
logist—Education of ward, a boy aged thirteen and a half, at English school
—Broken marriage—Mother re-married to an American and living in
California—Mother wishing boy to continue education in America and live
with her—Official Solicitor's report—Ordinary case of broken home—Ward
wishing to continue at school in England—Whether necessary that there should
be expert examination of ward by educational psychologist or psychiatrist—
Court's consent to such examination required.*

In the wardship proceedings the ward's mother, who had divorced the
father and had re-married and was living in California, applied for an order
that the ward (their son, then aged thirteen and a half), who was at a school
chosen by her in England, should go to California, should live with her
and should continue his education there.   The ward did not wish to go to
be educated in California.   The father wanted him to continue his education
in England.   In the wardship proceedings custody had been given to the
father (who was over sixty, retired, and who had a flat in London and
another in the south of France) and care and control had been given to the
mother.   The Official Solicitor, who was joined in the proceedings by the
Master's direction to represent the ward, interviewed the ward and his form
mistress at the school.   He filed statements and submissions.   These
included his views that the ward was a quiet, phlegmatic type of boy, was
well settled into his school life and that the ward's relations with both his
parents were good; and included his conclusion that it would not be in the
ward's best interests to interrupt the continuity of his education for some
completely new foreign system to which he would doubtless take some time
to adjust.   Finally, the Official Solicitor stated that in his view it was
totally unnecessary, as the ward seemed a very normal boy, that he should
be subjected, as the mother had suggested, either to a psychiatric report or
to a test by an industrial psychological institute.   In the Official Solicitor's
view any introduction of psychiatric processes would tend to make the
ward a psychiatric case.   Evidence was filed, on the mother's behalf,
by a consultant physician who specialised in child guidance.   There was
cross-examination, and the judge saw the ward in his private room.   The
consultant's evidence included a statement that there was a comparatively
large number of backward children at the ward's school, that there was
doubt whether the ward was made to work as hard as he should, that the
ward's objection to going to an American school with its intensely competitive atmosphere needed looking into and, by way of reply to the Official
Solicitor's view that the ward was a quiet, phlegmatic type of boy, that it
was far more important to know what might be the hidden effects of the
break-up of family life in the ward's case.   The consultant expressed the
view that the question of the extent to which the ward's apparent phlegm
concealed anxiety which could be harmful was a very important medical
problem, which he was surprised had not been the subject of proper investigation.   The school, where the ward was, was a school that specialised in the
education of backward children, and of which the consultant approved.

Held: this was an ordinary case of a broken marriage and home, and,
although such cases were tragic for the children involved, there was no reason
to dissent from the view of the Official Solicitor that expert examination of
the child by a psychiatrist or educational psychologist was not necessary in
this case; in all the circumstances of the present case the existing arrangements
for the ward's education would not be changed (see p. 207, letter A, p. 209,
letter C, and p. 210, letter C, post).

Per CUR: Psychiatric examination of a child with a view to the report

B

C

D

E

F

G

H

I

Dictum of CROSS J at 209 applied in
RE J (MINOR: ABDUCTION: WARD OF COURT)
[1989] 3 All ER 590

Dictum of CROSS, J., *at p.* 209,
applied in Re L. [1967] 2 All E.R.
1110.

Dictum of CROSS, J., *at p.* 209,
applied in BEEDLES *v.* BEEDLES.
[1968] 3 All E.R. 170.

A being put in evidence was an important step which, in relation to a ward of court, should not be taken without the court's consent, and, if the parents disagreed on whether such examination was necessary and on the psychiatrist, the Official Solicitor should be appointed guardian ad litem and should decide, subject to the court's view, whether such examination was needed, and, if it was, should instruct the psychiatrist (see p. 209, letters

B C to E, and G, post).

[As to the court's control over the residence and education of wards of court, see 21 HALSBURY'S LAWS (3rd Edn.) 218, 219, paras. 481, 482; and for cases on the subject, see 28 DIGEST (Repl.) 709-711, *2175-2199* (residence) and 712, *2208-2220* (education).]

. **Adjourned Summons.**

C This was an application by summons issued on Apr. 19, 1966, by the mother of an infant ward (a son, Howard, born in 1953 and about thirteen and a half years old at the hearing) asking (i) that Howard might be sent out to her in California and live with her and be educated there, and (ii) that his wardship in this country might be brought to an end. At the hearing the mother did not propose that the wardship should be brought to an end; instead she suggested

D that Howard should continue to be a ward in this country, but should go to day school in California and come back to this country for part of his holidays to see his father. The following statement of fact is summarised from the judgment.

Howard's father and mother were married in 1945; there were two children, a son Tony, who was born in 1949, and the ward, Howard. In the summer of 1964 the mother met K., an American. In May, 1965, she left the father, taking

E Howard with her. The father started the present proceedings under which Howard became a ward of court. The mother petitioned for divorce on the ground of alleged cruelty; the divorce suit was not contested. She obtained a decree nisi on July 20, 1965, which was made absolute on Oct. 20. On Oct. 21 she married K. Neither the father nor the mother alleged that the other's behaviour, bad though it might have been, had been such as to render him or

F her unfit to look after Howard. His Lordship (CROSS, J.) said that he was not called on to express any opinion whether the father or the mother was telling the truth with regard to the events that led to the breakdown of the marriage. After the breakdown of the marriage the father, who was over sixty and a man of means who had retired, sold the matrimonial home. He had a flat in London, and another flat in the south of France. In the

G autumn of 1965 the mother went to live in California. The eldest son, Tony, having taken his " O " level examinations, went with his father's consent to California to attend a course of training. Some friction developed between Tony and his step-father; and the father set him up with a flat of his own in California. The mother said that since then relations had improved and that Tony had meals with her and K. almost every day. Howard went to California

H in the summer of 1965 for his holidays. On his return to England he went to a co-educational school chosen by the mother. On Oct. 17, 1965, an order was made by consent in the wardship proceedings giving custody to the father and care and control to the mother and it was directed that until further order Howard should stay at this school, the father paying the fees and a weekly sum for maintenance. It was thought that Howard would spend his holidays, or most

I of them, with his mother. He went out to California in the Christmas holidays and it was arranged that he should go there for the Easter holidays. At that time, in the belief that there would be no opposition from the father, the mother's solicitors obtained an appointment for Apr. 18, 1966, to obtain an order discharging the wardship. However, Howard got measles and did not go to California. He also made it clear to his father that he wanted to go on being educated in England and did not want to go to live in California. In view of this the father retracted any such provisional consent as it could be said that he might have given to the mother's proposal that Howard should continue his education

in California.   On Apr. 19, 1966, the mother issued the present summons asking A
for the relief mentioned at p. 203, letter C, ante.

Charles Sparrow, Q.C., and *Betty Knightly* for the mother.
J. Monckton for the father.
John K. Wood for the Official Solicitor.

Cur. adv. vult.   B

Nov. 16.   **CROSS, J.,** read the following judgment in which he stated
the nature of the application and the facts, which have previously been summarised and continued: After the mother had filed evidence in support of her
summons and the father had filed evidence in answer, the master on June 7
directed that the Official Solicitor should be joined to represent the ward, Howard.
The Official Solicitor interviewed the father, Howard and his form mistress at C
school, and filed a statement of fact and submissions on July 21 part of which
I must read.   He says:

"The urgent question for consideration is whether Howard should go
to [a certain school in California which he specifies] and live with the mother
(who has re-married and is permanently in residence in Santa Barbara) as
proposed by her, or whether he should remain at his present school as D
proposed by the father."

Howard, who is just thirteen, struck the Official Solicitor as a quiet, phlegmatic
type of boy who does not seem to be overtly affected by the break-up of his
parents' marriage.   According to the boy's form mistress he is academically
about average or slightly below.   The report continues:
E
"He is well settled and integrated into boarding school life at his present
school, he seems happy and is popular at school, he has plenty of friends
and enters readily into any fun that is going on.   His relations with both
his parents seems reasonably good.   The father visits him at school and
maintains regular contact with him by telephone.   There is every chance of
Howard achieving adequate 'O' levels in due course, though it is doubtful F
at present if he is 'A' level material.   Howard himself is quite emphatic
that he does not wish to leave his present school and complete his education
in the United States of America.   He is happy to spend his summer holidays
in California with the mother and step-father and this has been arranged.
Short Christmas and Easter holidays he is to spend with his father, who has
a flat at Dulwich and another in the South of France.   Howard is an English G
boy and his education so far has been at English schools.   He has been at
his present school, which was selected for him by the mother, for a year."

Then he gives the name of the school and some details about it which I need not
read, and continues:

"In the Official Solicitor's view it would not be in Howard's best interests H
to interrupt the continuity of his education for some completely new foreign
system to which he would doubtless take some time to adjust.   Obviously
the question of Howard's care and control is very much wrapped up with
that of his education.   The mother has asserted in her evidence that the
father is not a fit and proper person to have care and control of a boy of
thirteen owing to the fact that the marriage was dissolved on the grounds I
of the father's cruelty [that was not persisted in here].   The Official Solicitor
is unable to comment on this as he has not been supplied with a copy of the
divorce petition particularising the cruelty [that is before me].   However,
the fact that the parents' marriage lasted for a period of twenty years would
not seem to indicate that the father's conduct was such as to disqualify him
from looking after his son adequately in the short holidays, particularly as
the boy's relationship with him appears to be a good one.   The mother's
other reason for prosposing a change of schools to the United States of

America is the desirability of reuniting Howard with his elder brother Anthony. Anthony is now seventeen and the Official Solicitor has been given to understand that he has, in fact, left the mother and step-father's household and is now living in a flat of his own near the college at which he is studying photography."

After saying that he would not support the proposed change of school against Howard's own express wishes, the Official Solicitor says:

" There is one final point with which the Official Solicitor feels he should deal and that is the mother's suggestion that Howard should be subjected either to a psychiatric report or to a test by an industrial psychological institute. In the Official Solicitor's view the first is totally unnecessary as Howard seemed a very normal boy and any introduction to psychiatric processes would tend to have the reverse effect and make him a psychiatric case. The second is quite inappropriate for a boy of Howard's age."

Howard spent the summer holidays or the greater part of them in California this year with the mother and he returned to school in this country at the end of September. On Nov. 3 the mother filed an affidavit in reply to the father's evidence and the Official Solicitor's statement and supported her evidence by an affidavit by Dr. S., a consultant physician at a London hospital, who specialises in child guidance. The mother, Dr. S. and the father were cross-examined on their affidavits and I saw the boy myself in my private room.

The mother's wish that Howard should make his home with her is readily understandable. While she is in California and Howard is at boarding school in this country she is cut off from him. She does not believe that the father is either willing or able to keep in touch with him sufficiently during the school term. She worries that he may not be properly clothed, fed or looked after. If she lived in England she could keep an eye on him, ringing him up at school, taking him out at week-ends and so on, but this is impossible from California. I have no doubt that she genuinely believes that it is in Howard's best interests that he should live with her and be educated in California.

The father thinks that the mother tends to over-mother the boy and is unnecessarily fussy over his clothes and food and so on. He considers that he will be able to keep an eye on the boy when he is at school. He rings him up from time to time and sometimes has him out for the week-end, although he thinks that the mother would like the child taken out for many more week-ends than is really good for him and than the school approves of. He wants the boy to take his " O " levels over here, if possible, rather than start schooling in America at this stage, although he is ready enough to consider sending him to college in America later on if he wants to go. The fact that there was friction between Tony and his step-father makes the father doubt the wisdom of sending Howard to the same household. Undoubtedly the father's chief objection is that Howard himself does not wish to go. The reason the ward himself gave me for wishing to stay at school here and visit his mother for part of the holidays, rather than go to live with her in California, is, firstly, that he has settled down in an English school where he is very happy and has made friends. He does not want the upheaval of change. Secondly, he does not get on particularly well with the youngest K. child, a boy called Peter, who is the same age as he is, but more advanced. He was quite emphatic that he did not want to go to the same school as Peter and he was by no means enthusiastic about the idea of living in the same home as Peter, but going to some other school. He says that he and Peter were always arguing and the impression I got was that he saw quite enough of Peter in the summer holidays without having him round his neck the whole time.

I turn now to consider the evidence of Dr. S. who did not have an opportunity of seeing the ward. His evidence is primarily in a letter written by him to the mother's solicitors after considering the documentary evidence in the case, but he amplified his views in examination-in-chief and cross-examination.   I do not propose to read the whole letter, but I will give what I hope is a fair summary of his views, although not in the same order as he presents them.   In para. (C) of his letter he expresses the view that, although children of broken homes are often sent to boarding schools because that is a solution which is acceptable to both parents, it is often an unsound solution and it would appear on the face of it to be an especially unsound solution in this case.   The mother lives abroad and Howard, if he is at boarding school here, has no real home and is in fact a mere visitor during the holidays wherever he goes, whether to his father or mother.

In para. (B) of his letter Dr. S. comments on the school at which Howard is at present, of which he has some professional knowledge. He says that, given that Howard has to go to a boarding school in this country, he has as good, if not a better, chance of being reasonably happy at that school as anywhere else, but he says that there are a comparatively large number of pupils at the school who are backward and present educational problems and he expresses some doubt whether Howard is being made to work as hard as he should.   In this connexion he makes the following comment on Howard's unwillingness to leave the school:

"I think that Howard's reported opposition to going to the American school needs looking into.   It should be remembered that Howard has been to America and has no doubt talked with his step-brother Peter who attends the school.   Those who are familiar with the American educational system, especially the private school side of it, are generally impressed by the earnestness and the competitiveness of the atmosphere in these schools. After the family break up Howard has made himself a reasonably comfortable adjustment in his pleasant English school with its tolerant atmosphere, its easy educational demands and its strong sense of community.   It does not surprise me that he cannot face yet another total change of educational environment and go as an outsider to the most intensely competitive school atmosphere that exists anywhere.   Whether it is in the ultimate interest of his educational and moral development to let him have his own way in this matter is a different matter, which, I would submit, needs to be judged against the background of the total life offered to the boy by the respective proposals for his future."

Then finally I come to para. (A), which is perhaps the most important part of the letter.   Dr. S. puts the question: "Has Howard suffered harm from the experiences of the last six years? "   The answer is:

"The only available independent view, that of the Official Solicitor, July, 1966, is that Howard is ' a quiet, phlegmatic type of boy who does not seem to be overtly affected by the break-up of his parents' marriage '. With respect, it must be said that it is far more important to know what may be the hidden effects of the break-up of family life in Howard's case.   To what extent does Howard's apparent phlegm conceal anxiety which could be harmful?   This is a very important medical problem and I am frankly surprised that it has not been the subject of a proper investigation.   For Howard's sake one must be concerned not only with the anxiety that he shows, but with the total person."

Then Dr. S. ends his report as follows:

"To recapitulate, there are a number of unresolved questions which, in my opinion, require proper attention: (i) it is not known to what degree Howard has or has not been adversely affected by the family break-up and by his subsequent experiences; and no attempt has been made to make a professional assessment of these matters. (ii) It is not known whether Howard is backward at school or not; nor what is his potential level of capacity; nor whether the school curriculum he is following is in the least relevant to his needs. (iii) It is not known from where, if anywhere, Howard is gaining experience of how to live as a member of a family, how to develop intimate and durable human relationships. Does he derive this experience from the artificial social group of the boarding school, from his fifty-nine year old father during parts of the school holidays, or from his temporary visits to the other family in a foreign culture during other holiday times? These are all matters deserving thorough study by someone experienced in and duly qualified to make such studies. I do not understand why the Official Solicitor opposed the obtaining of a psychiatric report. Surely the authorities concerned cannot be unaware of public medical and educational policy and practice in regard to the assessment of childern's problems of living in the event of family breakdown and what is usually done to judge their performance at school or elsewhere under these and other disadvantageous circumstances? Is it not realised that every education authority in the country employs the services of child psychiatrists and educational psychologists, to a very considerable extent, in the elucidation of problems similar to those presented by Howard; that the Education Act, 1944, has established the duty of educational authorities to provide for the right of every parent and child to receive these services at public expense if they desire; and that under the National Health Service Acts nation-wide facilities for such consultations are provided? I, myself, for the past eighteen years have been in charge of a department of a well-known London teaching hospital which is mainly devoted to problems of this order. In this context of public action the Official Solicitor's view that a psychiatric report is ' totally unnecessary as Howard seemed a very normal boy and an introduction to psychiatric processes would tend to have the reverse effect and make him a psychiatric case ' is nothing short of astonishing. The serious issue here is that this boy is being denied a service which is available for all children as a normal part of medical provisions for the community, and designed to prevent the very problems that the Official Solicitor fears it may create."

What Dr. S. is saying there is in effect this: Not having had an opportunity to see the boy, I cannot express a concluded opinion, but, on the face of it, the advantages of his living with the mother and Mr. K. and their family in California are very great and I do not think that the court ought to rely on the boy's unwillingness to go as any reason for not sending him without having a report on him by some qualified expert.

It is only recently that it has become common for the evidence of a psychiatrist or educational psychologist to be tendered in wardship cases, and I think that the time has now come when the question in what circumstances such evidence ought to be admitted and how, if it is admitted, such evidence should be given should be thoroughly explored in the light of experience gained in the last few years. It would plainly be wrong for a single judge of first instance to purport to lay down any rules on the subject. On the other hand, in view of Dr. S.'s criticism of the Official Solicitor's decision, I am bound to say something on the matter in the context of the facts of this particular case.

The first point which I would make is that this is a perfectly ordinary case of a broken home. Almost all such cases are tragic; for the children of a broken home will generally have lived for some time in a household in which father and mother are at loggerheads and they will often have been present at—or even participated in—quarrels between their parents. One can very well understand that such children will be, as Dr. S. put it, " vulnerable ". In this case, however, even if one accepts the mother's evidence in toto, there were no unusual features which would lead anyone to think that this ward has been subjected to any exceptional strain which would differentiate his case from the case of most other children of broken homes.

The second point that I would make is that although the marriage broke up and the child was made a ward as long ago as May, 1965, it was not until a year afterwards, that is the summer of 1966, that it occurred to anyone that Howard ought to be examined by a psychiatrist. When his parents agreed to the order of Oct. 17, 1965, neither of them suggested to the court that its ward needed the attention of a psychiatrist. The school to which Howard was sent is one of which Dr. S. approves and which specialises in the education of backward and difficult children. One would suppose that the masters and mistresses at such an establishment would be more alive than those at more old fashioned institutions to the desirability of having the children examined by psychiatrists if there seemed to be the least need to do so, yet no such suggestion was made by them with regard to Howard. The first time it was suggested was when the mother found her wish to have Howard to live with her in California thwarted by his wish to stay here.

Next I must say something about the Official Solicitor. He and the members of his staff who assist in these cases are laymen and consequently, if it is right to say that no layman, however experienced, is capable of judging whether or not a child of a broken home is or is not in need of examination by a psychiatrist or an educational psychologist, then the Official Solicitor must be unfit to take such a decision. But if one does not take this rather extreme view, there can be few laymen in this country better qualified to answer such a question than the Official Solicitor. Each year he interviews the children and parents involved in very many cases of broken homes, and he is well aware of the benefits which can be derived in some cases from an examination by a psychiatrist. He frequently arranges for such examinations, and I can myself recall several cases in which I have been greatly assisted by a psychiatrist's report on the ward. There is an old fashioned flavour about the words " Chancery " and " Official Solicitor " and, as the evidence in wardship cases is, very rightly, given in private, it is perhaps inevitable that people should think that we live in the past and have no time for psychiatrists and such new-fangled nonsense. But that is simply not true, and it is in order to show, if I can, that it is not true that I am giving my judgment in this case in open court.

When I first read Dr. S.'s report, I thought that he was saying that, as children of broken homes might be suffering from latent disturbances not observable by unqualified persons, all such children ought to be professionally examined. Such a view, whether or not one agrees with it, is perfectly intelligible. Its realisation would of course entail great expense. The parties in this case are wealthy people, but in many wardship cases they are legally aided. Nevertheless, if it be the fact that the welfare of children of broken homes requires that they all be examined by experts, it may be said that the welfare state should foot the bill in so far as the parents are unable to do so. Dr. S. however, when examined on his letter, did not maintain that view. He agreed that a sufficiently experienced layman might be able to judge rightly whether or not a child of a broken home needed to be professionally examined. But he said that there were danger signals which ought to warn the layman in question that an examination by a professional was called for. When asked what were the danger signals in this case to which the Official Solicitor seemed not to have paid sufficient attention, he instanced first that Howard was said to be lazy, and, secondly, that his father in giving reasons for his opposition to his going to live with the K.'s in California had said:

" Howard is a boy whom it is difficult to draw out, he has friends in his school and where he used to live, especially Mrs. R. and her family, but I think it might be difficult for him to acquire new friends in an alien environment."

To my mind this is giving with one hand and taking away with the other. If such very common characteristics as laziness and a measure of shyness or reserve

A are to count as danger signals, then it would seem to me that only in the very rarest cases could a layman be justified in taking on himself to say that a child of a broken home did not need to be examined by a psychiatrist. One can, perhaps, imagine some brisk young extrovert whose whole demeanour testified beyond peradventure that the family dissensions had not taken a feather off him; but he would be a rare bird.

B I think therefore that Dr. S. would have been logically on stronger ground if he had adhered to the view, which I believe he holds in his heart of hearts, that all children of broken homes ought to be professionally examined. It may be that that will be the law one day, but as things are the Official Solicitor and the court have a discretion in the matter and, bearing in mind the various considerations which I have mentioned, I see no reason whatever for dissenting from the

C view of the Official Solicitor that no such examination was needed in this case.

Though they are not strictly necessary for my decision in this case I venture to add a few further observations on this topic. When a child is made a ward no important step in the child's life can be taken without the court's consent. To my mind the examination of the ward by a psychiatrist with a view to the report being put in evidence in the case is such a step. If both sides agree that an

D examination is necessary and agree on the person or persons to conduct it then normally no doubt there would be no reason for the court to refuse to follow their wishes. If they disagree, however, then it would seem right that the official solicitor should be appointed guardian ad litem of the ward—as was done in this case—and that he should decide, subject to the views of the judge, whether or not an examination is needed. Further if he decides that it is needed

E then, as it seems to me, he should instruct the psychiatrist or psychiatrists in question so as to ensure that he or they have all the relevant material and can see both parents. I have no doubt that the psychiatrists who give evidence in wardship cases are persons of the highest integrity, but if they are instructed on behalf of one party their views are bound to be coloured to some extent by that party's views. Further if they are ordinary human beings, as I hope and

F believe that they are, they can hardly help having some faint desire that their side should win just because it is their side. I am not, of course, suggesting that there should be anything in the nature of a panel of court experts whose views would be in any sense sacrosanct. Any psychiatrist instructed by the Official Solicitor can be cross-examined. Further the Official Solicitor himself is in no way committed to accepting the views which he expressed or precluded from

G obtaining a second and possibly contrary opinion. My suggestion is simply directed to ensuring that psychiatrists who give evidence in wardship cases should receive unbiased instructions, and I repeat that the views which I am expressing are merely tentative. I fully realise that others as qualified, or better qualified, to judge may dissent from them.

Finally I come back to the present case. Prima facie, and apart from the

H wishes of the ward, there is obviously something to be said for the view that the parents being situated as they are it would be better for the ward to live with his mother in California and to go to school there. The educational arguments in favour of his staying in England though appreciable, are not overwhelming. Howard is of very average intelligence, his intelligence quotient is about 115 and he is not a good worker. I have no reason for thinking that

I he would be better taught here than he would be in California, although one may doubt whether Dr. S. is right in thinking that the highly competitive spirit which he says exists in American private schools, and of which he appears to approve, would suit Howard. In favour of his education here it may be said that if he is going to make a living in England he ought to get " O " levels here. It is by no means clear, however, that he will get as many, if any, " O " levels here and, when the time comes, he may want to earn his living out of England. So, if he wanted to go to live with the mother, I should be inclined to think that it would be right to take the educational risks involved. But although Howard

I

is fond of the mother and willing to spend holidays with her in California, he definitely wishes to continue his education here. There are occasions when the wishes expressed by a boy of thirteen and a half may count for very little. In many cases it is unfortunately plain that they are reflections of the wishes of one of the parents which have been assiduously instilled into the ward and are not anything which could be called an independent exercise of his own will. Sometimes again the ward's wishes, although genuinely his own, are so plainly contrary to his long term interest that the court may feel justified in disregarding them. Neither of these things can be said here. Nobody suggests that the ward's wish to stay at school here owes anything to any pressure of the father. It is his own considered opinion formed with knowledge of the K. household in California. His reasons are perfectly sensible reasons, which I can well appreciate. In the result I can see no reason to change the existing arrangements and therefore I dismiss the mother's summons.

Summons dismissed.

Solicitors: *T. L. Wilson & Co.* (for the mother); *Groos, Guest, Lowden & Hazell* (for the father); *Official Solicitor.*

[*Reported by* JACQUELINE METCALFE, *Barrister-at-Law.*]

MINISTER OF SOCIAL SECURITY *v.* AMALGAMATED ENGINEERING UNION.

[HOUSE OF LORDS (Lord Reid, Lord Morris of Borth-y-Gest, Lord Hodson, Lord Guest and Lord Wilberforce), November 1, 2, 3, December 20, 1966.]

Industrial Injury—Medical appeal tribunal—Jurisdiction—Scope of jurisdiction —Finding by statutory authority (deputy commissioner) on claim for injury benefit that injured workman suffered personal injury caused by accident— Subsequent application by workman for disablement benefit—Whether medical appeal tribunal bound to accept finding of statutory authority that injury was caused by accident—Whether tribunal's jurisdiction confined to question of loss of faculty as result of injury—National Insurance (Industrial Injuries) Act, 1946 (9 & 10 Geo. 6 c. 62), s. 7 (1), s. 36 (as amended), s. 49 (4).

On Aug. 3, 1961, a workman, who was insured under the National Insurance Acts, lifted and moved a very heavy flagstone in the course of his employment. While so doing, he felt pain in his chest, which became very acute. In due course it was found that he had a small hiatus hernia. He claimed industrial injury benefit, payable under s. 7 (1) (*a*) of the National Insurance (Industrial Injuries) Act, 1946, to an insured person who is incapable of work as a result of " personal injury caused . . . by accident arising out of and in the course of his [insurable] employment ". The insurance officer refused the workman's claim. On Mar. 4, 1963, on appeal by the workman, a deputy industrial injuries commissioner decided, pursuant to s. 36 (2)* of the Act of 1946, that, on Aug. 3, 1961, the workman had suffered injury by accident arising out of and in the course of his insurable employment, thus entitling him to injury benefit. Subsequently, the workman claimed disablement benefit in respect of the period after that for which he was held entitled to injury benefit, disablement benefit being a benefit payable under s. 7 (1) (*b*)† of the Act of 1946 to an insured person who suffered from loss of physical or mental faculty " as the result of the injury ". On Aug. 6, 1963, a medical appeal tribunal, concerned pursuant to s. 36 (1) (*c*) (i)‡ of the

---

* Section 36 (2), (3), is set out at p. 213, letter B, post.
† Section 7 (1) (*b*) is set out at p. 218, letter C, post.
‡ Section 36 (1) (*c*) is set out at p. 218, letter H, post.

Distinguished in R. *v.* NAT. INSUR- ANCE COMR. [1969] 2 All E.R. 631

Distinguished in R. *v.* NAT. INSUR- ANCE COMR. [1970] 1 All E.R. 109.

Followed in JONES *v.* SEC OF STATE FOR SOCIAL SERVICES [1972] 1 All E.R. 145

A   Act of 1946 with the question whether the relevant accident had resulted in a loss of faculty, decided that it " was not satisfied that the hiatus hernia was either caused or aggravated by the relevant accident ". The subsequent decision of a deputy industrial injuries commissioner upholding the medical appeal tribunal was quashed by the Court of Appeal. On appeal,

    Held (LORD WILBERFORCE dissenting): the determination of the deputy

B   industrial injuries commissioner on the claim for injury benefit that the claimant had suffered personal injury caused by accident arising out of his employment was final and conclusive (by virtue of s. 36 (3) and s. 49 (4)* of the National Insurance (Industrial Injuries) Act, 1946) not only for the purpose of the claim to injury benefit but also for the purpose of the subsequent claim to disablement benefit; thus the medical appeal tribunal in

C   deciding (in effect) that the claimant had not suffered personal injury caused by accident arising out of his employment had disregarded the determination of the commissioner and had thereby exceeded its jurisdiction for his determination was binding on the medical appeal tribunal, and accordingly the second commissioner's decision upholding the tribunal had been rightly quashed (see p. 216, letter C, p. 217, letters A and H, p. 219, letters F to H,

D   p. 221, letter D, and p. 212, letter B, post).

    Decision of the COURT OF APPEAL (sub nom. *R.* v. *Deputy Industrial Injuries Comr., Ex parte Amalgamated Engineering Union; Re Dowling* [1966] 1 All E.R. 705) affirmed.

    [**Editorial Note.** In the present case the circumstances were such that a decision what caused the claimant's injury also resolved the question whether

E   there was an industrial accident at all, which latter question was one within the purview of an insurance officer under s. 36 (2) of the Act of 1946; the circumstances were thus exceptional in that the accident and causation by accident of the injury were not separable questions (cf. p. 215, letter H, and p. 219, letter E, post).

    The National Insurance (Industrial Injuries) Act, 1946, s. 7, s. 36 and s. 49,

F   have been repealed by the Statute Law Revision (Consequential Repeals) Act 1965, and replaced by the National Insurance (Industrial Injuries) Act 1965 (see particularly s. 5, ss. 35-37 and s. 48).

    As to the finality of an insurance commissioner's decision, see 27 HALSBURY'S LAWS (3rd Edn.) 682, para. 1233, and as to the determination of Industrial Injuries claims and questions, see ibid., pp. 853-866, paras. 1495-1513.

G   For the National Insurance (Industrial Injuries) Act, 1946, s. 7, s. 36 and s. 49, see 16 HALSBURY'S STATUTES (2nd Edn.) 814, 844, 855.

    For the National Insurance (Industrial Injuries) Act 1965, see 45 HALSBURY'S STATUTES (2nd Edn.) 1094.]

Case referred to:

H   *Fenton* v. *Thorley (J.) & Co., Ltd.,* [1903] A.C. 443; 72 L.J.K.B. 787; 89 L.T. 314; 34 Digest (Repl.) 359, *2727.*

    Appeal.

    This was an appeal by the Minister of Social Security from an order of the Court of Appeal (LORD DENNING, M.R., DAVIES and SALMON, L.JJ.), dated Dec. 15, 1965, and reported [1966] 1 All E.R. 705, allowing an appeal by the

I   respondents, the Amalgamated Engineering Union, from an order of the Queen's Bench Divisional Court (LORD PARKER, C.J., SACHS and BROWNE, JJ.), dated May 20, 1965, dismissing a motion for certiorari by the respondent union to bring up and quash a decision of Mr. D. NELIGAN, Deputy Industrial Injuries Commissioner, dated Oct. 16, 1964, dismissing the respondent union's appeal from a decision of the medical appeal tribunal, dated Aug. 6, 1963, that they were not satisfied that a hernia suffered by a member of the respondent union, Mr. Ellis Dowling, was caused or aggravated by an industrial accident which he had

—————————————————————————————
   * Section 36 (3) and s. 49 (4) are set out at p. 219, letter G, and p. 221, letter A, post.

suffered on Aug. 3, 1961, as had been found by Mr. H. I. NELSON, Q.C., Deputy   A
Industrial Injuries Commissioner, on Mar. 4, 1963. The facts are set out in the
opinion of LORD MORRIS OF BORTH-Y-GEST.

H. A. P. *Fisher*, Q.C., and *Nigel Bridge* for the appellant.
P. R. *Pain*, Q.C., and S. J. *Waldman* for the respondents.

Their Lordships took time for consideration.

B

Dec. 20. The following opinions were delivered.

LORD REID: My Lords, I have read the speech of my noble and learned
friend, LORD HODSON.   I agree with it and have nothing to add.   I would,
therefore, dismiss this appeal.

LORD MORRIS OF BORTH-Y-GEST: My Lords, the important issues   C
which are raised in these proceedings relate to a claim to disablement benefit
made by Mr. Ellis Dowling, the claimant, who was an insured person.   On
Aug. 3, 1961, he was working as a labourer at a holiday camp.   In the course of
his work he was required to lift a granite flagstone (measuring three feet by two
feet and of a thickness of two to two-and-a-half inches) and to place it over a
manhole.   While so doing, he felt pain in his chest which became very acute.   D
He felt " a terrible pressure " in his chest of a nature which he had never previously
experienced.   He went to the works surgery and thence to his own doctor who
ordered him to bed.   In due course it was found that he had a small hiatus hernia.
He claimed injury benefit pursuant to the National Insurance (Industrial Injuries)
Act, 1946, as then, with certain amendments, in force.   He had to bring his claim
within s. 7 (1).   That section provides that, subject to the provisions of the Act,   E
where an insured person suffers personal injury caused by accident arising out of
and in the course of his employment, being insurable employment, then (*a*) injury
benefit is payable to him if during a certain period he is, as a result of the injury,
incapable of work, (*b*) disablement benefit is payable to him if after that period
he suffers, as a result of the injury, from loss of physical or mental faculty to an
extent defined and assessed in accordance with provisions of the Act, (*c*) if death   F
results from the injury a death benefit is payable to certain persons as provided
by the Act.   There was no doubt that Mr. Dowling was an insured person and that
he was in insurable employment.   On his claim for injury benefit a question
arose whether he had suffered personal injury caused by accident arising out of
and in the course of his employment.   That question had to be determined.   The
Act contains elaborate provisions relating to the determination of questions and   G
claims.

By s. 36 (1) (*a*) (as amended (1)), certain questions are to be determined by the
Minister; by s. 36 (1) (*b*) (as amended (1)), certain questions are to be determined
in the way that questions would be determined in respect of an allowance under
the Family Allowances Act, 1945; by s. 36 (1) (*c*) (as amended (1)), certain questions are to be determined by a medical board or a medical appeal tribunal.   The   H
questions to be determined under s. 36 (1) (*c*) are as follows—(i) whether the relevant accident has resulted in a loss of faculty: a relevant accident in relation
to any benefit means the accident in respect of which the benefit is claimed
or payable (see s. 88 (1)); (ii) at what degree the extent of disablement resulting
from a loss of faculty is to be assessed and what period is to be taken into account
by the assessment.   Those questions are " disablement questions " (see s. 36 (5)).   I
Questions under s. 36 (1) are " special questions " (see s. 36 (5)).   On the claim
of Mr. Dowling for injury benefit no " special question " arose.   The question or

(1) Section 36 (1) was amended by the National Insurance (Industrial Injuries) Act,
1953, s. 8, Sch. 2, paras. 1 (1), 2 (5); 33 HALSBURY'S STATUTES (2nd Edn.) 446, 448;
and the Family Allowances and National Insurance Act, 1956, s. 2 (1), Schedule, para. 12;
36 ibid., 640, 652. See now, as regards paras. (*a*), (*b*) and (*c*) referred to in the text,
s. 35 (1), s. 36 and s. 37, respectively, of the National Insurance (Industrial Injuries)
Act 1965; 45 ibid., 1125, 1127.

questions that did arise fell to be determined in the first place by the insurance officer. From him there was an appeal. It is provided by s. 36 (2) as follows:

" Subject to the foregoing provisions of this section, any claim for benefit and any question arising in connexion with a claim for or award of benefit shall be determined by an insurance officer, a local appeal tribunal or the commissioner appointed or constituted in accordance with the following provisions of this Act."

This is followed by sub-s. (3), which provides (2):

" Except as provided by this Part of this Act any decision of a claim or question as provided by the foregoing provisions of this section shall be final."

Mr. Dowling's claim for injury benefit had, therefore, to be determined by the insurance officer. His functions within the scheme of the machinery prescribed by the Act are manifestly of great importance. The insurance officer decided that Mr. Dowling did not succeed in his claim. An appeal to the local appeal tribunal (who were assisted by a medical assessor) failed. There was then an appeal to the commissioner. The appeal was heard on Feb. 12, 1963, by the Deputy Industrial Injuries Commissioner, Mr. H. I. NELSON, Q.C. There was an oral hearing before him. Mr. Dowling was represented by counsel, while on the other hand submissions were made by a representative of the insurance officer. In his decision the commissioner pointed out that the problem to be solved was whether the hernia which Mr. Dowling developed was related to the work which he did on Aug. 3, 1961. The commissioner pointed out that that was a matter of medical evidence. He heard the oral evidence of Dr. Capper. Dr. Capper, a consultant chest physician, had examined Mr. Dowling on May 29, and July 3, 1962. He had presented a report dated July 3, 1962, in which he had expressed the opinion that the hiatus hernia was probably traumatic in origin and that the trauma had occurred while doing the work on Aug. 3, 1961, which I have described. After Dr. Capper had presented his written report of July 3, 1962, that report had been submitted by a senior medical officer of the Ministry of Pensions and National Insurance to a consultant surgeon, Mr. d'Abreu. Mr. d'Abreu sent a written report dated Nov. 5, 1962, in which he expressed the view that Mr. Dowling's hernia was due to natural causes, and was neither caused nor materially aggravated by the heavy work which Mr. Dowling had been doing on Aug. 3, 1961. Mr. d'Abreu's report was before the commissioner, but Mr. d'Abreu was not a witness. Dr. Capper in his oral evidence explained in detail why he disagreed with Mr. d'Abreu's report. The representative of the insurance officer said that he did not propose to call a senior medical officer of the Ministry who was present, but would leave the matter for decision whether there had been a physiological change. The commissioner gave his decision in writing on Mar. 4, 1963. His decision was that, on Aug. 3, 1961, Mr. Dowling had suffered injury by accident arising out of and in the course of his insurable employment. In a careful review of the case he recorded his reasons for accepting the view of Dr. Capper.

Mr. Dowling was, therefore, entitled to injury benefit. His claim succeeded. As a result of the provision in s. 36 (3), the decision of the commissioner as to his claim was final. That involved that Mr. Dowling had established that he had suffered personal injury caused by accident arising out of and in the course of his employment. As to most of the facts there had been little dispute. There was no doubt that Mr. Dowling had a hernia. The question that arose was whether it was due to natural causes, in which case it was not caused by accident arising out of and in the course of his employment, or whether it was caused by, or materially aggravated by, lifting a heavy flagstone, in which case it was caused

---

(2) Section 36 (3) was amended by the Family Allowances and National Insurance Act, 1959, s. 1 (5), Schedule, Part 1; 39 HALSBURY'S STATUTES (2nd Edn.) 905, 909. See now the National Insurance (Industrial Injuries) Act 1965, s. 50 (1); 45 ibid., 1136.

by accident arising out of and in the course of his employment. The commissioner had to decide. After weighing the evidence he came to a conclusion which involved that the hernia was caused by accident arising out of and in the course of his employment.

Mr. Dowling claimed disablement benefit in respect of the period after that, for which he was held entitled to injury benefit. Reverting to s. 7 (1) of the Act, it is seen that (subject to the provisions of the Act) where an insured person suffers personal injury caused by accident arising out of and in the course of his employment (being insurable employment) then disablement benefit is payable to him if (after the injury benefit period) he suffers, as the result of the injury, from loss of physical or mental faculty. It would seem natural to suppose that, having obtained a decision that he had suffered personal injury caused by accident arising out of and in the course of his employment, the only further matters that would arise in relation to a claim for disablement benefit would be whether the accident had resulted in a loss of faculty and as to the degree of disablement and for what period should it be assessed. These were " disablement questions " (see s. 36 (5)). They were to be determined by a medical board or medical appeal tribunal (see s. 36 (1) (c)). Accordingly, Mr. Dowling's claim for disablement benefit was considered by a medical board. They presented a report which was dated Apr. 29, 1963, in which they decided that the accident had not resulted in a loss of physical or mental faculty. Their reasons for that finding were expressed under the heading " Remarks " as follows:

" The commissioner's decision is noted. The board have studied the reports from Mr. d'Abreu and Dr. Capper. They find Dr. Capper's report and reasoning unconvincing and accept that from Mr. d'Abreu which they consider is more in keeping with informed surgical opinion at the present time."

That meant that they refused to accept the commissioner's decision. It meant that they were saying that Mr. Dowling had not suffered personal injury by accident, although the commissioner had decided that Mr. Dowling had suffered personal injury by accident. It involved that Mr. Dowling ought not to have had any injury benefit. It means that, being asked to say whether the accident had resulted in a loss of faculty, they decided, in complete reversal of the commissioner's decision, that there never had been an accident. They decided, contrary to what the commissioner had found, that the hernia (as to the existence of which no question arises) was due to natural causes. There was an appeal to the medical appeal tribunal on Aug. 6, 1963. This tribunal confirmed the decision of the medical board. They accepted (i) that the symptoms of which Mr. Dowling complained were due to hiatus hernia and (ii) that the condition was a disabling one; but, after considering (a) the history of the onset of the symptoms, (b) the opinion of Dr. Capper and (c) the opinion of Mr. d'Abreu, they said that, on the balance of probabilities, they were " not satisfied that the hiatus hernia was either caused or aggravated by the relevant accident ". That question, again, was the very question which it had been the duty of Mr. NELSON to consider and decide. He had decided that Mr. Dowling had suffered personal injury by accident. The medical board and the medical appeal tribunal purported to overrule his decision. Being invited to determine whether the accident in respect of which disablement benefit was claimed had resulted in a loss of faculty, they decided that there never had been an accident. This must be the result of their decision. If Mr. Dowling's hernia was not the result of lifting the flagstone, then it followed that there was no injury by accident; in other words, that there was nothing which within the scheme of the Act could be regarded as an accident.

Mr. Dowling is a member of the Amalgamated Engineering Union, the respondents. They applied, pursuant to reg. 13C (4) of the National Insurance (Industrial

Injuries) (Determination of Claims and Questions) Regulations, 1948 (as added) (3), for leave to appeal against the decision of the medical appeal tribunal (who had refused to give leave) to the commissioner.   The application came before the deputy commissioner, Mr. NELIGAN, who gave leave and then heard the question of law arising on the appeal as provided (3) by reg. 13G (2) (see s. 2 (1) of the Family Allowances and National Insurance Act, 1959, (4)).   After hearing arguments and considering the various statutory provisions, Mr. NELIGAN in a careful decision recorded his reasons for coming to the conclusion that the medical appeal tribunal's decision was not erroneous in point of law.   He dismissed the appeal. The respondents applied by motion to the Divisional Court of the Queen's Bench Division for an order of certiorari to remove Mr. NELIGAN's decision and to quash it. Substantially the motion was based on the ground that it should have been held that the medical appeal tribunal had erred in law and had exceeded its jurisdiction. The Divisional Court dismissed the motion.   The respondents appealed to the Court of Appeal (5) who, on Dec. 15, 1965, by a majority (LORD DENNING, M.R., and SALMON, L.J., DAVIES, L.J., dissenting) allowed the appeal.   Appeal is now brought to this House.

My lords, the difficult questions which call for decision in this case may, perhaps, owe their origin to the rather special circumstances.   In an ordinary case it may be easy to isolate some event or occurrence or incident which can properly be described as an accident.   It will then be necessary to decide whether the accident arose out of and in the course of an insured person's employment and to decide whether personal injury has been caused by such an accident.   If, on a claim for injury benefit, an issue is raised as to these matters, it will have to be decided by the insurance officer or on appeal from him by a local appeal tribunal or on appeal by the commissioner.   Any decision of the commissioner (if the matter reaches him) in regard to a claim for injury benefit will be final (s. 36 (3) of the Act of 1946).   Any decision of the commissioner whether there ever was an accident will, in my view, be final.   So also, in my view, any decision of his whether personal injury was caused by any such accident.   When, however, a disablement question arises, such a question must be determined by a medical board or a medical appeal tribunal.   There may be a question whether a relevant accident (i.e., the accident in respect of which disablement benefit is claimed) has resulted in a loss of faculty.   Such a question will call for the use of medical expertise.   The medical board starts, however, with a determination that there has been an accident.   This seems to be implicit in the wording of s. 36 (1) (c). The fact that there was an accident will have been determined, and determined finally, before the medical board ever embarks on a determination.   The questions for the medical board will be (i) has the accident (which, as has been finally held, did in fact happen) resulted in a loss of faculty?   (ii) at what degree is the extent of disablement resulting from a loss of faculty to be assessed and what period is to be taken into account by the assessment?   These questions the medical board are free to decide; but they cannot go back behind their own starting point and say that there never was an accident at all and say that it was quite wrong for injury benefit ever to have been paid.   The present case is exceptional because a decision as to what caused the injury complained of also resolved the question whether there was an accident at all.   If Mr. Dowling was caused to suffer a hernia as a result of lifting the heavy flagstone, then he suffered personal injury by accident.   If his lifting of the heavy flagstone was nothing at all to do with his hernia, then he never suffered personal injury by accident all.   On the claim for disablement benefit, the disablement questions only came before a

---

(3) S.I. 1948 No. 1299 as amended.   Regulation 13C and reg. 13G were added by S.I. 1959 No. 1596.

(4) 39 HALSBURY'S STATUTES (2nd Edn.) 905.   Section 2 (1) was repealed by the Statute Law Revision (Consequential Repeals) Act 1965, and replaced by s. 42 of the National Insurance (Industrial Injuries) Act 1965;   45 ibid., 1131.

(5) [1966] 1 All E.R. 705.

medical board after a finding that there had been a " relevant accident ".   If
there had never been a claim for injury benefit but only a claim for disablement
benefit, the question whether there had been a relevant accident would have to
be decided by an insurance officer, a local appeal tribunal or the commissioner.
A medical board would not be called on until after there was a determination that
there had been an accident. A medical board could not reverse a determination
which was a prerequisite to their being convened. The view of Mr. NELIGAN
was that the decision of Mr. NELSON provided Mr. Dowling with, so to speak,
a " ticket of admission " to the medical board. With respect, I should think that
Mr. NELSON's decision fixed for the medical board a datum line or starting point
which it was not for them to question. Being invited on the basis that there was
an accident, it was not open to them to say that there never had been one at all.
I consider, therefore, that they and the medical appeal tribunal exceeded their
jurisdiction.

Though the present case could, in my view, be decided in favour of the respondents for the reason which I have stated, the further question is raised whether a
medical board, though accepting that there had been an accident, could decide
that no personal injury was thereby caused. It is said that both the language
of s. 12 (1), as substituted (6), i.e.

" an insured person shall be entitled to disablement benefit if he suffers
as the result of the relevant accident from loss of physical or mental
faculty . . ."

and the language of s. 36 (1) (c), i.e., " any question—(i) whether the relevant
accident has resulted in a loss of faculty ", point to the conclusion that, though a
medical board must accept that there has been an accident, it is quite free to
decide whether any personal injury was caused and, accordingly, may decide
that an accident has not resulted in a loss of faculty for the reason that it has
not resulted in any injury at all. So, in the present case, it is said that the medical
board's decision could be supported by saying that Mr. Dowling had an accident
in that he over-exerted himself and that it was open to the medical board to hold
that he had not suffered any personal injury and, accordingly, to hold that the
relevant accident had not resulted in a loss of faculty. My Lords, I am unable to
accept this view. The general scheme of the Act is outlined in s. 7. That section
shows that benefit may be of three descriptions. There may be injury benefit;
there may be disablement benefit; there may be death benefit. To qualify for
any one or more of these the opening words of the section must be satisfied, i.e.,

" Subject to the provisions of this Act, where an insured person suffers
personal injury caused on or after the appointed day by accident arising out
of and in the course of his employment, being insurable employment, then
. . ."

The word " then " tends to show that injury benefit, disablement benefit and
death benefit can only become payable where the conditions denoted by the
quoted words are satisfied.   Any questions whether a person was an insured
person and whether he suffered personal injury caused by accident and whether
that arose out of and in the course of his employment and whether his employment was insurable employment are for determination otherwise than by a medical
board or a medical appeal tribunal; but if once injury by accident is established
(and once the other factors are established), then there may be injury benefit.
That will only be if, during a certain period, he is " as the result of the injury "
incapable of work (see s. 7 (1) (a)). Again, once injury by accident is established
(and the other factors), then there may be disablement benefit. That will only
be if at a time not within an injury benefit period he suffers " as the result of
the injury " from loss of physical or mental faculty (see s. 7 (1) (b)). Whether he

(6) By the National Insurance (Industrial Injuries) Act, 1953, s. 3 (1); 33 HALSBURY'S
STATUTES (2nd Edn.) 441. See now, as regards the words cited, the National Insurance
(Industrial Injuries) Act 1965 s. 12 (1); 45 ibid., 1104.

does so suffer a loss of faculty " as the result of the injury " will be a question for determination by a medical board; but, in my view, the statutory language shows that they are only concerned with questions whether loss of faculty is the result of injury. They start with the premise that there has been injury caused by accident. They cannot say that there has been no injury. That will have been determined before they are invited to act.

This conclusion is, in my view, in no way invalidated by a consideration of the language of either s. 36 (1) (*c*) or of s. 12 (1). The medical board is concerned with the relevant accident, i.e., the accident in respect of which any variety of benefit is claimed, but it has no jurisdiction to decide that there was no personal injury caused by accident. The medical board will have to decide whether a loss of faculty has resulted and the degree of the extent of the disablement which results and the period to be taken into account. Reverting to s. 7, it is also to be observed that a death benefit will be payable only after injury by accident is established (and the other factors), and if the death of the insured person " results from the injury ".

The conclusions that I have expressed are, in my view, supported by a consideration of the provisions of s. 49, (7). Section 49 (1) provides that where, in connexion with any claim for benefit, it is determined that the relevant accident was or was not an industrial accident (see s. 49 (5)), an express declaration of that fact is to be recorded. It is provided by sub-s. (5) that, for the purposes of the section,

> " an accident whereby a person suffers personal injury shall be deemed, in relation to him, to be an industrial accident if—(*a*) it arises out of and in the course of his employment; (*b*) that employment is insurable employment; and (*c*) payment of benefit is not, under the provisions of Part 2 of this Act, precluded because the accident happened while he was outside Great Britain . . ."

In my view, Mr. NELSON's decision was a determination (within sub-s. (1)) that the relevant accident (Mr. Dowling's accident) was an industrial accident. Mr. NELSON in his decision declared as follows:

> " My decision is that on Aug. 3, 1961, the claimant suffered personal injury by accident arising out of and in the course of his insurable employment."

Section 49 (4) provides that, subject to provisions as to appeal and review,

> " any declaration under this section that an accident was or was not an industrial accident shall be conclusive for the purposes of any claim for benefit in respect of that accident . . ."

The result, in my view, was that Mr. NELSON's determination that Mr. Dowling suffered personal injury by accident arising out of and in the course of his insurable employment was conclusive for the purposes of " any claim for benefit in respect of that accident ". The claim for disablement benefit was a claim for benefit in respect of the accident to Mr. Dowling in respect of which Mr. NELSON made his determination. Accordingly, I consider that the medical board and the medical appeal tribunal exceeded their jurisdiction.

I would dismiss the appeal.

LORD HODSON: My Lords, this appeal by the Minister of Social Security raises a difficult question under the National Insurance (Industrial Injuries) Act, 1946, to which I shall refer as " the Act ". The Act was passed in substitution for the Workmen's Compensation Acts, 1925-1945, to provide a system of insurance against personal injury caused by accident arising out of and in the course of a person's employment and for purposes connected therewith.

There have been a series of appeals arising out of a single occurrence in which a Mr. Dowling, the claimant (now represented by the respondents, the Amalgamated Engineering Union), who is a workman insured under the National Insurance

---

(7) See now the National Insurance (Industrial Injuries) Act 1965, s. 48; 45 HALSBURY'S STATUTES (2nd Edn.) 1135.

Acts, lifted a heavy flagstone in the course of his employment. While so doing he felt a pain in his chest, because of which he was sent home from work. He returned to light work on Sept. 2, 1961, but thereafter suffered pain in his chest after exertion and so remained off work from October, 1961, onwards. Subsequently he remained disabled for heavy work. He was found to be suffering from hiatus hernia and claimed industrial benefit payable under s. 7 (1) of the Act which reads as follows:

" Subject to the provisions of this Act, where an insured person suffers personal injury caused on or after the appointed day by accident arising out of and in the course of his employment, being insurable employment, then—(a) industrial injury benefit (in this Act referred to as ' injury benefit ') shall be payable to the insured person if during such period as is hereinafter provided he is, as the result of the injury, incapable of work; (b) industrial disablement benefit (in this Act referred to as ' disablement benefit ') shall be payable to the insured person if at a time not falling within the said period he suffers, as the result of the injury, from such loss of physical or mental faculty as is hereinafter provided . . ."

Mr. Dowling first claimed industrial injury benefit under s. 7 (1) (a) on the ground that he was incapable of work as a result of personal injury caused by accident arising out of and in the course of his employment. The insurance officer refused the claim, finding that the hernia was due to natural causes and not caused or aggravated by moving the flagstone. The claim came up for the determination of the Deputy Industrial Injuries Commissioner, Mr. H. I. NELSON, Q.C., who gave his decision on Mar. 4, 1963, pursuant to s. 36 (2) of the Act. This section provides:

" Subject to the foregoing provisions of this section, any claim for benefit and any question arising in connexion with a claim for or award of benefit shall be determined by an insurance officer, a local appeal tribunal or the commissioner . . ."

The commissioner decided that the claimant suffered personal injury by accident arising out of and in the course of his employment, thus entitling him to injury benefit for the statutory period of six months. There was a direct conflict of medical evidence. On the one hand, a surgeon, Mr. d'Abreu, gave as his opinion, in a written report, that the hiatus hernia was due to natural causes and was neither caused nor materially aggravated by the accident described. On the other hand, a physician, Dr. Capper, gave oral evidence which convinced the commissioner. Dr. Capper held the opposite opinion to that held by Mr. D'Abreu, saying that, in his view, the hernia was traumatic in origin.

Mr. Dowling subsequently claimed disablement benefit under s. 7 (1) (b) of the Act for a period beginning after the expiration of the six months for which the injury benefit was awarded. This claim was resisted by the insurance officer on the same ground, and the matter came for determination by the medical appeal tribunal, pursuant to s. 36 (1) (c) of the Act (as amended (8)), which provides:

" any question—(i) whether the relevant accident has resulted in a loss of faculty; . . . (iii) at what degree the extent of disablement resulting from a loss of faculty is to be assessed, and what period is to be taken into account by the assessment; shall be determined by a medical board or medical appeal tribunal . . ."

This tribunal had exactly the same material before it as had the deputy commissioner, but came to an opposite conclusion, regarding, as they said, the opinion of Mr. d'Abreu as more in keeping with informed surgical opinion at the present time. The decision of the medical appeal tribunal was upheld by Mr. D. NELIGAN, another deputy industrial injuries commissioner, on Oct. 16, 1964. He took the view that, although the decision of Mr. NELSON was final for the purposes of the

(8) See note (1), p. 212, ante.

injury benefit, it did no more so far as the claim for disablement benefit went than to give the claimant, so to speak, " a ticket of admission " to the medical board who had to decide for themselves the question committed to them by the statute. This decision was upheld by the Divisional Court on an application for an order of certiorari, but was reversed by the Court of Appeal (9) which, by a majority consisting of LORD DENNING, M.R., and SALMON, L.J. (DAVIES, L.J., dissenting), held that the medical tribunal was wrong in law in disregarding the finding of Mr. NELSON which was final and conclusive and binding on the tribunal. The decision of Mr. NELIGAN was, accordingly, quashed.

It is a condition of every claim to benefit, whether injury, disablement or death benefit, that the insured person should have suffered personal injury by accident arising out of and in the course of his or her employment (see s. 7 (1) of the Act). Under s. 36 of the Act, there is a division of labour for the determination of questions arising under the Act. Some questions are determined by the Minister (see s. 36 (1) (*a*) and (*b*) (as amended (10)), but any claim for benefit or any question arising in connexion with a claim must be determined by an insurance officer, with a right of appeal to a local appeal tribunal and ultimately to a commissioner (s. 36 (2)). Some questions the insurance officer is bound to refer to the medical board. These include questions whether the accident has resulted in a loss of faculty and the extent of disablement resulting from a loss of faculty (see s. 36 (1) (*c*)). There may be overlapping, but in the ordinary case no difficulty will arise. The Act speaks of personal injury caused by accident, treating injury and accident as different things. By s. 88 (1), " relevant accident " and " relevant injury " means respectively, in relation to any benefit, the accident and injury in respect of which the benefit is claimed or payable; and " relevant loss of faculty " means the loss of faculty resulting from the relevant injury. In the ordinary case where accident and injury are separate, there is no difficulty, but here the accident and the injury are the same. There would be no accident but for the injury. The problem in this case is to determine whether the decision of Mr. Commissioner NELSON stands, or whether it is cancelled by the subsequent decision of the medical tribunal. In my judgment, the " question " which the commissioner had to decide was one arising in connexion with a claim for benefit within the language of s. 36 (2) of the Act. In order to ascertain whether there was an accident, he had to resolve the conflict of medical testimony and, in doing so, he was acting within his jurisdiction. His decision is, accordingly, final according to the terms of s. 36 (3) of the Act (as amended (11)), which provides:

" Except as provided by this Part of this Act any decision of a claim or question as provided by the foregoing provisions of this section shall be final."

There is no reason to limit the meaning of the word " final ", as the Minister seeks to do, to the particular claim which is being dealt with. The claims for injury and disablement benefit are linked together and in the normal case they follow one another.

It is contended that the policy which the Act reveals is one of segregation of medical questions so that they may be decided by skilled persons and not by a lay tribunal. It has been pointed out, however, that there are many places in the Act where medical questions fall to be determined by the statutory authority, for s. 36 (3) comes into play only when the extent of the disablement has to be settled. Whether there is incapacity to work as a result of a relevant injury may be a medical question. Under s. 7 (1) (*c*) of the Act, entitlement to death benefit may depend on medical evidence. Section 13 of the Act deals with increase of disablement pension on account of unemployability and may require medical evidence. The like applies to s. 14 of the Act dealing with cases of special hardship. Section 15 of the Act, providing for increases of disablement pension

---

(9) [1966] 1 All E.R. 705.   (10) See note (1), p. 212, ante.
                    (11) See note (2), p. 213, ante.

where constant attendance is required, is a matter for the Minister under s. 36 (1) (a) (v) of the Act, and may give rise to the need for medical evidence. Further, it may be said that an experienced legal commissioner is well qualified to determine questions of fact and weigh the evidence of medical or other expert witnesses, and that it is desirable that there should be finality even if there may occasionally be cases where it may be thought that a wrong answer to a question was given in the first place. This is a commonplace in all litigation.

The use of the words accident and injury in the Act presents difficulties. Clearly they are intended to be kept separate in contrast to their use in the old Workmen's Compensation Acts, but it must be remembered that, for the purposes of the Act, accidents are not relevant unless they are followed by injury caused thereby, and I cannot gain any assistance from the omission of the word " injury " or the substitution of the word " accident " for the word " injury " in s. 12 (1) of the Act (as amended (12) by the National Insurance (Industrial Injuries) Act, 1953), which deals with disablement benefit. An insured person is entitled to this benefit if he suffers as a result of the relevant accident from loss of faculty, but this means that the accident must have caused an injury. The cases where the accident and the injury are in fact the same do not fit readily into the language of the Act, which is more apt to provide for those cases, and only those cases, where the injury is severable from the accident.

It is objected that the medical authorities are left with no function in such a case as this if the injury and accident are treated as a compound expression, for the finding that the hernia was traumatic takes away their function. Reliance is placed on s. 12 (2) (b) (i) of the Act, which says that disability shall be treated as having been incurred as a result of the relevant loss of faculty except in so far as the claimant

" would in any case have been subject thereto as the result of a congenital defect or of an injury or disease received or contracted before the relevant accident."

This, as LORD DENNING, M.R., pointed out (13), cannot be raised here if the commissioner's decision is final, but it does no more than provide an illustration of that which I mentioned earlier, namely, that the correct result may not be achieved in all cases. The medical authorities would, of course, always be concerned with the case of the man whose disability had lessened or increased or whose disability had disappeared altogether. They could be concerned also with other injuries than that first considered by the insurance officer. I do not find that s. 12 (2) (b) (i) provides an obstacle in the way of Mr. Dowling's claim for disablement benefit.

Much discussion has ranged round the language of s. 49 of the Act. This section is concerned with declarations that an accident is an industrial accident. The section and, indeed, the Act itself, always deals with real accidents and not with hypothetical accidents, and I cannot accept the contention of the Minister that this declaration, to which the claimant is entitled, is only a declaration that, if there were an accident, it would be an industrial one. Such a declaration would be of scant value to a claimant who, while having had his declaration recorded, would be put in the position at a much later date, when his evidence might no longer be available and records destroyed, of trying to establish the necessary facts to support his claim. I accept the submission of the respondents that, in this Act, accident and injury are considered together, and what is being considered is personal injury by accident. Section 49 (2) refers to " any person suffering personal injury by accident " as being entitled to a declaration, and it seems that the industrial accident in the section connotes the injury suffered thereby. Section 49 (4) provides:

" Subject to the provisions of this Part of this Act as to appeal and

(12) See s. 3 of the Act of 1953; 33 HALSBURY'S STATUTES (2nd Edn.) 441.
(13) [1966] 1 All E.R. at p. 710.

A review, any declaration under this section that an accident was or was not an industrial accident shall be conclusive for the purposes of any claim for benefit in respect of that accident, whether or not the claimant is the person at whose instance the declaration was made."

B The last words are important, for if the claimant were the widow seeking a death benefit under the Act the declaration to the limited effect contended for by the Minister might well be valueless. LORD PARKER, C.J., thought that the accident itself must be found in the declaration, but the injury caused thereby can be left outside the scope of the declaration as being an injury alleged and not established. With all respect to him, I cannot agree that what is being covered by the declaration is hypothetical whether as to accidents or injuries. The practical question under the Act always is " did the claimant suffer an accident causing personal

C injury? ". Sometimes in the Act the eye of the draftsman may be on accident rather than on an injury, but it is always accident involving an individual person and one causing him personal injury which falls to be considered in dealing with claims for benefit. True that the language of s. 49 (4) is different from that in s. 36 (3), but " conclusive " for the purposes of any claim for benefit is no less strong language than the phrase " any decision of a claim or question . . . shall

D be final " in the last mentioned subsection.

I would dismiss the appeal.

LORD GUEST: My Lords, I have had the advantage of reading the opinion of my noble and learned friend, LORD HODSON, and I am in agreement with it.

E **LORD WILBERFORCE:** My Lords, the question raised in this appeal is as to the respective responsibilities, under the National Insurance (Industrial Injuries) Act, 1946, of medical boards and medical appeal tribunals, on the one hand, and insurance officers, local appeal tribunals and the industrial injuries commissioner, on the other hand. The learned judges in the courts below have reached different conclusions, the Divisional Court of the Queen's Bench Division

F and DAVIES, L.J., taking one view, the majority of the Court of Appeal (14) another. Your lordships, as I understand, support the conclusion of the majority of the Court of Appeal (14), but for somewhat different reasons from those there expressed. Regretting as I do to find myself in disagreement, since the matter is of general importance, I must explain why I think that the appeal should be allowed.

G The purpose of the Act is to provide benefit in cases where insured persons suffer personal injury by accident arising out of and in the course of their employment. This basic and general objective is stated (as such) in s. 7 (1) of the Act. The types of benefit with which we are here concerned are injury benefit and disablement benefit. Injury benefit is payable during a limited period in respect of incapacity for work. The claim is determined by an insurance officer, who is entitled, but not

H bound, to obtain a medical report. The precise question which he has to decide is whether, and in respect of how many days during the specified period, the claimant, as a result of the relevant *injury*, is incapable of work (s. 11). An appeal lies from his decision to a local appeal tribunal (which may have a medical assessor without power of decision), and ultimately to the commissioner. These bodies, generally, I refer to as " statutory authorities ". Disablement benefit is

I payable in respect of loss of physical or mental faculty and is not available until after the period of incapacity for work; it may be payable for an indefinite period. The question whether the relevant *accident* has resulted in a loss of faculty and as to the degree of disablement, obviously a question calling for expert diagnosis, has to be determined by a medical board consisting of two or more medical practitioners. This board may (as it did in this case) have before it any medical report obtained by the insurance officer, and may (as it did in this case) examine

(14) [1966] 1 All E.R. 705.

the claimant for itself. The Act (15) provides that the disability is to be treated as   A
having been incurred as a result of the relevant loss of faculty unless the claimant
would in any case have been subject thereto as a result of a congenital defect or
of an injury or disease contracted before or after (but not directly attributable to)
the accident.   There is an appeal from a medical board to a medical appeal
tribunal, which consists of a chairman and two medical practitioners.   These
bodies, generally, I refer to as " medical authorities ".   B

I need not restate the course of the proceedings in the present case.   The
effect of them is that, on an essentially medical question, namely, whether his
hernia was traumatic or congenital, the claimant obtained a decision in his
favour, on appeal, from a statutory authority, namely, Mr. H. I. NELSON, Q.C.,
deciding judicially between conflicting medical evidence, but an adverse decision
from two concurrent medical authorities.   Whether he was fortunate in the   C
first case or unfortunate in the second is not a matter which can be decided here—
the multiplicity of instances certainly seems to justify some complaint; but the
question for us is a general question of law, whether the medical authorities
exceeded their powers in deciding as they did.   The consequence of the decision
of the Court of Appeal (16) is that a medical board, on whom the duty is expressly
cast of deciding whether the relevant accident has resulted in a loss of faculty   D
(s. 36 (1) (c) (i)), is prevented from applying its expert knowledge to the case by
virtue of a decision reached by an insurance officer or other statutory authority
for the limited purpose of granting injury benefit.   Since there may be many
cases in which an insurance officer may (for the purpose of dealing with an
injury benefit claim) consider the medical aspect of a claim, it is obvious that
this conclusion severely reduces the sphere of responsibility of the medical   E
boards; indeed, as I understand the view of the matter which is to gain acceptance,
the medical boards are in all cases bound to accept an insurance officer's finding,
whether reached with or without a medical report, that, for the purpose of injury
benefit, the claimant has sustained personal injury arising from accident.   A
medical board, in such cases, will find their powers limited to an assessment of
the degree and period of disability which, as medical men, they may consider,   F
or know, not to arise from accident at all.   It does not require emphasis to
show that this places the medical men who serve on these boards in a most
unsatisfactory position.   It is equally not clear that such a result is in the
interest of claimants, who may, if the powers of medical authorities are to be
reduced in this way, find the right to have their cases reviewed diminished.

The issue as to the respective spheres of competence of the two sets of authori-   G
ties is of a broad character related to the whole structure of the Act. I propose
to examine it in this way.   In my opinion, the examination does not support the
conclusion that the medical authorities are so circumscribed as the claimant
suggests.   (i) There is in the Act one section which explicitly defines the respective responsibilities and competences of the various authorities—namely, s. 36.
It assigns separate tasks (in this order) to the Minister (sub-ss. 1 (a) and (b) (as   H
amended (17))), to medical authorities (sub-s. (1) (c) (as amended (17))) and to
statutory authorities (sub-s. (2)). Subsection (1) (c) entrusts to medical authorities
decisions on the question whether the relevant accident has resulted in a loss of
faculty, which is called a " disablement question ", a species of the genus " special
question ".   Section 36 (2) entrusts decisions on claims for benefit and questions
arising in connexion therewith to statutory authorities, but is expressly made   I
subject to the preceding subsection. I cannot, therefore, follow the argument
that the statutory authorities have, in respect of disablement questions, any
priority over medical authorities, or their decisions on such questions any effect
binding on the medical authorities, or that they have some kind of overriding

---

(15) See s. 12 (2) (b); 16 HALSBURY'S STATUTES (2nd Edn.) 820. That enactment has
been repealed and is replaced by the National Insurance (Industrial Injuries) Act 1965,
Sch. 4, para. 1 (b); 45 ibid., 1179.

(16) [1966] 1 All E.R. 705.   (17) See note (1), p. 212, ante.

A   jurisdiction, the medical authorities being cast in a subordinate role. The section, on the contrary, shows that the medical authorities have a prior and unqualified competence in their field. (ii) The procedure by which claims are dealt with is that all claims for benefit must be submitted to an insurance officer (s. 45). If no " special question " arises, he may deal with the claim or may refer it to a local appeal tribunal (s. 45 (3)). If he is of opinion that a " special

B   question " arises, he must refer it for decision by the appropriate authority. Machinery exists for enabling other questions to be postponed until a " special question " has been decided (s. 48). Again, this shows that the authorities who are competent as to " special questions " (which include medical authorities) are fully responsible in their own sphere. (iii) Section 12 (1) (as substituted (18)) lays down the principles on which disablement benefit may be granted, excluding

C   (inter alia) cases of congenital defect. I do not see how this directive can be carried out if the medical board is prevented from giving effect to its view that the case is one of congenital defect by the fact that the insurance officer has reached a different conclusion.

    I find nothing in other provisions of the Act which prevents the medical authorities from exercising the jurisdiction—or rather, discharging the duty—

D   cast on them. (a) Section 36 (3) (as amended),

    " Except as provided by this Part of this Act any decision of a claim or question as provided by the foregoing provisions of this section shall be final,"

    I do not read as applying here. Insofar as the commissioner's decision was on

E   a claim, the claim was for injury benefit—it is not final on any other claim; insofar as it was a decision on a " question ", by sub-s. (2), it is made " subject to the foregoing provisions of the section ", i.e., to sub-s. (1) (c) which confers jurisdiction as to disablement questions on medical authorities. In either case, that the word " final " refers merely to the claim under consideration is surely shown by the contrasting words in s. 49 (4) " conclusive for the purposes of any

F   claim for benefit "; s. 36 (3), in other words, is merely saying that a decision as to a matter within the jurisdiction of a particular authority is final; it throws no light on the division of jurisdiction between competing authorities. (b) Section 7 has been invoked to support an argument that a decision of the statutory authorities involves ipso facto a finding that the claimant has suffered personal injury by accident and that this becomes, as it were, an unassailable substratum

G   at all later stages. I do not so read the section. It does no more than state the general objective of the Act and the general conditions for benefit. The Act is not, at this stage, concerned with jurisdiction or competence at all; it has merely laid down the ground plan; its subdivision comes later. There are other arguments of lesser weight based on linguistic considerations and on s. 49 of the Act which I shall take up later. So far, I have examined the division of

H   jurisdiction between the medical and the statutory authorities on the structure of the Act. It is next necessary to see how the suggested division works in practical application.

    It is natural to take first the straightforward case of injury occurring to an insured person through some identifiable external event, such as where a man is struck by a piece of machinery, or by a moving stone—a case which I may describe

I   (with reservation of later analysis) as accident plus injury. Here the " accident ", constituted by an unforeseen happening in nature or at least the physical world, can, perhaps, be segregated as a cause from the physiological injury to the man arising as an effect. There is no difficulty in seeing how the Act deals with such cases. The happening of the accident is a matter for investigation by the statutory authorities, who also decide whether it was an industrial accident. Thereafter the medical authorities decide whether an accident (the happening

---

    (18) By the National Insurance (Industrial Injuries) Act, 1953, s. 3 (1); 33 HALSBURY'S STATUTES (2nd Edn.) 441.

of which they must accept as a datum) has resulted in a loss of faculty; this is   A just what s. 12 says, and the same is stated in terms in s. 36 (1) (c) (" whether the relevant accident has resulted in a loss of faculty "). The same sequence of decision is provided for in s. 49, which, as was possible under the Workmen's Compensation Acts, enables a declaration of the fact that an accident was an industrial accident to be made. The section is clear and definite; the declaration relates to the accident—the nature of the accident—and nothing else (see sub-s. (2)   B in particular).

How, then, can it be said that the medical authorities have not the full responsibility for determining the question of loss of faculty? The argument is that they have not, because the statutory authorities have to identify the nature of the injury—their finding on this matter being conclusive. I am quite unable to accept this. All the three relevant sections refer—as the datum from which the medical   C authorities are to start—to the relevant *accident* (s. 12 (1) (as substituted), s. 36 (1) (c) and s. 49); to give effect to the argument, these would have to be rewritten so as to refer to " relevant *injury* ". But this contention, in itself sufficiently implausible, becomes even more difficult to agree to when it is seen that the expression " relevant injury " originally appearing in s. 12 (1) was amended (19) to " relevant accident " by the amending Act of 1953. The Court of Appeal (20)   D appreciated this difficulty, and took the bold course of holding that injury and accident were convertible terms in the Act. I do not understand that your lordships are able to accept this—nor am I; the distinction between them is too deliberately clear. But if the distinction is accepted, then, any basis for holding the medical authorities bound by the statutory authorities' finding on injury, at least in a normal case, can only rest on s. 36 (3), a foundation equally   E unsound. I reach, therefore, this point, I must say, without difficulty—that, in the case of accident plus injury, the medical authorities are fully responsible for dealing with questions of disablement unfettered by any finding as to injury which the statutory authorities may have made. So it would follow that the present appeal must succeed unless some special argument can be found related to the particularity of the present case. I turn now to this point.   F

In fact, it is said that there was no separate, external, physical mishap or accident causing, as an effect, a physical injury, and it is this suggestion which has given rise to some perplexity. It has enabled it to be said that here the " accident " *is* " the injury ", or " the injury " *is* " the accident ", so that a finding that there has been " an accident " or " accident " carries with it a finding that there has been " the injury ". The medical board, it is said, nor-   G mally starts from the datum of " the accident " but in this case the datum is " the injury "; they cannot negative the injury without destroying the very basis of their own jurisdiction. The first reflection which this line of thought suggests is that it would be strange if the Act had not this kind of situation in mind. Not only is this kind of compound accident-injury common enough in industrial work, but its existence was recognised and its character analysed by   H this House under the Workmen's Compensation Act in 1903 (*Fenton* v. *J. Thorley & Co., Ltd.* (21)). How, then, should one suppose that the legislature intended to deal with it? There seems to be two alternatives; either to suppose that the Act intended to apply the same jurisdictional scheme as to cases of accident plus injury, or to suppose that in this type of case a different principle applies involving a telescoping of the jurisdictions so that a finding of " accident " is also   I a finding of " injury ". Acceptance of this would enable the respondents to succeed in this appeal, but on narrower grounds than those which your lordships suggest.

My lords, I venture to suggest that the inclination should be towards the former alternative—if workable. Not only would it fit best with what appears to be the scheme of the Act in the generality of cases, but it would appear to

---

(19) See note (18), p. 223, ante.   (20) [1966] 1 All E.R. 705.

(21) [1903] A.C. 443.

give in practice a more satisfactory solution. For it is surely this type of case, where the chain of events is physiological in origin and ultimate result, that calls for the application of medical expertise; correspondingly, it is the least suitable for a binding decision to be made by a non-medical authority on, at best, a medical report. Is there, then, any insuperable difficulty in so resolving the complex, accident-injury, as to make it possible to assign the appropriate juris-dictional competence to separate elements of it? Is there, indeed, any greater difficulty here than exists in which I have called the normal case of accident plus injury? I would suggest, on the contrary, that in principle the two categories are only superficially different and that, for the operational purposes of the Act, the same kind of analysis is both possible and required. In all cases what the Act has to deal with is a complex event, or of events, compounded of the impact of something in the external world on physical organs or vice versa. Where a body (say a stone) swings and crushes a man, it is not the swinging stone that is the accident, but its impact in an unexpected and (generally) damaging manner on a body—the compound happening.   Is there any the less an accident because a workman tries to stop its movement and strains himself in so doing? Is there any the less an accident because a workman struggles with the stone's inertia instead of with its momentum?   Would it become more of an accident if the stone had been fortuitously immobilised by frost?   These kinds of situations shade into one another, and the principle of analysis must be the same. Linguistic-ally one may find difficulty in some accident-injury cases in saying that one thing is the accident and another the injury, but even here, if one changes the linguistic form, and says, as one may, that the workman was " accidentally injured " or (to take the expression of Lord Macnaghten in *Fenton's* case (22)) that the man had " met with an accident ", one can perceive the two elements, the physiological change and the unforeseen impact of the physical world. Just as with the perplexing nexus " cause " and " effect ", one is faced here with merging concepts which, for an immediate practical purpose, the law requires to be segregated, the question in law being whether this is what the Act, for its own purposes, requires and whether, in the working of the Act, some intelligible division can be made.   We find in fact (i) that the Act has (relevantly) two dis-tinct objectives: to ascertain (a) " what happened " and the connexion of that with the workman's employment, and (b) what effect was produced on the workman's physical or mental faculties, and (ii) that it has set up separate mechanisms to determine these facts.   The respondents' arguments would have us allow what are in the end logical perplexities to obscure both the Act's scheme and its working.

I shall not prolong this argument by carrying it through the various provisions of the Act; in my opinion, there is no difficulty in working out the scheme of s. 49.   The analysis which has already been made of the various provisions of the Act is enough to show, without re-statement, that there is no difficulty in assigning to the statutory authorities responsibility for determining the accidental character of the mishap, and its connexion with the employment, while leaving it fully open to the medical authorities to decide on loss of faculty.   I conclude in the opinion that nothing in the general scheme of the Act or in the particular circumstances of this case should prevent the medical authorities from performing their statutory task and that the Divisional Court was right in refusing to quash their decision.   I would allow the appeal.

Appeal dismissed.

Solicitors: *Solicitor, Ministry of Social Security* (for the appellant); *W. M. Thompson* (for the respondents).

[*Reported by* Kathleen O'Brien, *Barrister-at-Law.*]

---

(22) [1903] A.C. at p. 446.

Re K. (H.) (an infant).

[QUEEN'S BENCH DIVISION (Lord Parker, C.J., Salmon, L.J., and Blain, J.),
December 2, 7, 1966.]

*Commonwealth Immigrant—Admission—Discretion of immigration officer—Duty
to act fairly—Child under sixteen of Commonwealth citizen—Dispute over
age of immigrant—Examination by immigration officers and medical officer
who formed view immigrant was over sixteen years old—Refusal of admission
—Whether rules of natural justice apply—Mandamus, not certiorari nor
habeas corpus, appropriate remedy if further investigation to be ordered—
Commonwealth Immigrants Act, 1962 (10 & 11 Eliz. 2 c. 21), s. 2 (2) (b),
s. 3 (1), Sch. 1, paras. 1 (1), 2 (1), (3).*

A.R., a native of Pakistan and a Commonwealth citizen to whom s. 1 of
the Commonwealth Immigrants Act, 1962, applied, had settled in England
in 1961, leaving his wife and family in West Pakistan. Intending to visit them
and return with his eldest son, H.K., he forwarded to the Pakistan High
Commission in England a sworn declaration dated June 8, 1966, stating that
H.K. was 15½ years old and that it was his intention to be responsible for
and maintain H.K. in England. On Oct. 18, 1966, a passport was issued in
Pakistan to H.K., his date of birth being given as Feb. 29, 1951 (a non-
existent date). On Nov. 21, 1966, A.R., having been to Pakistan, arrived at
London Airport with H.K., where they were interviewed by the immigration
authorities. The immigration officer who first saw them formed the view H.K.
was sixteen years old or more. He therefore sent H.K. to the medical officer
whose opinion was that H.K. was seventeen plus. Both A.R. and H.K. were
then interviewed separately through interpreters and, finally, by the chief
immigration officer, who, exercising his powers under s. 3 (1)* of, and Sch. 1,
paras. 1 and 2† to, the Commonwealth Immigrants Act, 1962, caused a
formal notice in writing dated Nov. 21, 1966, to be served on H.K. pursuant
to s. 2‡ of, and Sch. 1, para. 2 (1) to, the Act of 1962, refusing him admission.
On the next day it appeared that H.K. had in his possession a school leaving
certificate in arabic script and modern English figures which, by translation,
seemed to show that H.K. was born on Feb. 29, 1951. There was evidence
before the court that there was no compulsory registration of births in
Pakistan. On motion for habeas corpus to secure H.K.'s release from the
custody of the chief immigration officer and for an order of certiorari to
quash that officer's decision refusing H.K. admission to the United Kingdom,

Held: (i) an immigration officer in exercising his discretion to refuse
admission to the United Kingdom under s. 2 (1) of the Commonwealth
Immigrants Act, 1962, was bound to act impartially and fairly, and to that
extent was bound to act in accordance with the rules of natural justice,
but he was not bound to hold any full scale inquiry or to adopt judicial
procedure (see p. 231, letter D, p. 230, letter I, p. 232, letter I, to p. 233,
letter A, p. 233, letter D, and p. 235, letter A, post).

Shareef v. *Comr. for Registration of Indian and Pakistani Residents* ([1966]
A.C. 47) and dictum of LORD RADCLIFFE in *Nakkuda Ali* v. *M. F. de S.
Jayaratne* ([1951] A.C. at p. 81) considered and distinguished.

(ii) the burden was on the applicant for entry to the United Kingdom
to satisfy the immigration authorities of the matters mentioned in s. 2 (2)
of the Act of 1962, and both A.R. and H.K. had been given ample opportunity so to do; accordingly no case justifying the issue of habeas corpus
or certiorari had been made out (see p. 232, letters C and H, and p. 234,
letters C, F and G, post).

---

* Section 3 (1), so far as material, is set out at p. 228, letter E, post.

† Schedule 1, paras. 1 and 2, so far as material, are set out at p. 228, letters F to I,
post.

‡ Section 2, so far as material, is set out at p. 227, letter I, and p. 228, letter B, post.

Considered in Re A. (AN INFANT),
[1968] 2 All E.R. 145.

Followed and dictum of LORD PARKER,
C.J., at p. 231, distinguished in
SCHMIDT v. HOME OFFICE. [1968] 3
All E.R. 795.

Dictum of LORD PARKER CJ at 231
applied in R v GAMING BOARD [1970]
2 All ER 528

Dictum of LORD PARKER CJ at 231
applied in R v BIRMINGHAM CITY
JUSTICE [1970] 3 All ER 945

Dictum of LORD PARKER CJ at
231 applied in R v SEC OF STATE,
EX PARTE PERESTRELLO [1980] 3 All
ER 28

Per CURIAM: even if further opportunity to satisfy the immigration authorities ought to have been given to A.R. or H.K., the appropriate prerogative order would have been mandamus not certiorari (see p. 232, letter E, p. 234, letter B, and p. 235, letter B, post).

[As to the control of immigration of Commonwealth citizens and examination of immigrants, see SUPPLEMENT to 5 HALSBURY'S LAWS (3rd Edn.) title COMMON-WEALTH AND DEPENDENCIES, paras. 1513, 1514.

As to powers of immigration officers, see 1 HALSBURY'S LAWS (3rd Edn.) 513, 514, para. 992.

For the Commonwealth Immigrants Act, 1962, s. 2, s. 3, Sch. 1, see 42 HALSBURY'S STATUTES (2nd Edn.) 5, 7, 21.]

Cases referred to:

> *Liversidge* v. *Anderson*, [1941] 3 All E.R. 338; [1942] A.C. 206; 110 L.J.K.B. 724; 116 L.T. 1; 17 Digest (Repl.) 422, *27*.
>
> *Nakkuda Ali* v. *M. F. de S. Jayaratne*, [1951] A.C. 66; 8 Digest (Repl.) 802, *562*.
>
> *Shareef* v. *Comr. for Registration of Indian and Pakistani Residents*, [1966] A.C. 47; [1965] 3 W.L.R. 704; 3rd Digest Supp.

Motion for habeas corpus and certiorari.

This was a motion by Abdul Rehman for a writ of habeas corpus to secure the release of one H.K., an infant, detained by the chief immigration officer at London Airport with a view to H.K. being returned to Pakistan; and, further, for an order of certiorari to quash the decision of the chief immigration officer dated Nov. 21, 1966, and made on behalf of the Home Secretary, whereby it was decided that H.K. should be refused admission to the United Kingdom. The facts are set out in the judgments of LORD PARKER, C.J.

E. F. N. Gratiaen, Q.C., and *L. J. Blom-Cooper* for the applicant.
Nigel Bridge for the respondent, the chief immigration officer.

LORD PARKER, C.J.: The applicant, Abdul Rehman, a native of Pakistan, came to this country in 1961 and settled and engaged in work at Bradford. He left behind, so he says, in West Pakistan his family, said to consist of his wife and five children, one of whom, the eldest, is the infant H.K. said to have been born in February, 1951. Earlier this year the applicant was minded to visit his family in Pakistan and to bring back to this country H.K. With this in view, he forwarded to the office of the High Commission for Pakistan a sworn declaration dated June 8, 1966, in which he gave particulars of H.K. as being his son and as being $15\frac{1}{2}$ years of age, and he undertook to be responsible for the son's maintenance and expenses in coming to and in this country. That declaration was in due course sent to the passport authorities in Rawalpindi, recommending them to issue a passport to H.K., subject to verification of his age and of his relationship with the applicant. In due course, on Oct. 18, a passport was issued in Rawalpindi to H.K., his date of birth being given as Feb. 29, 1951. In passing, it is to be observed that this was an impossible date as 1951 was not a leap year. The applicant in fact had gone to Pakistan as he intended and on Nov. 21 he and H.K. arrived by air at London Airport and were interviewed by the immigration authorities.

Before describing what then happened, it is convenient to look at the relevant legislation. By s. 2 (1) of the Commonwealth Immigrants Act, 1962, it is provided as follows:

" Subject to the following provisions of this section, an immigration officer may, on the examination under this Part of this Act of any Commonwealth citizen to whom s. 1 of this Act applies who enters or seeks to enter the United Kingdom—(*a*) refuse him admission into the United Kingdom; or (*b*) admit him into the United Kingdom subject to a condition restricting the period for which he may remain there, with or without conditions for restricting his employment or occupation there."

Pausing there, both the applicant and H.K. are undoubtedly Commonwealth citizens to whom the Act of 1962 applies and that subsection on its face gives the immigration authorities complete unfettered discretion whether to admit them or not, and whether, if admission is granted, it should be on conditions. Section 2 (2) provides as follows:

" The power to refuse admission or admit subject to conditions under this section shall not be exercised . . . in the case of any person who satisfies an immigration officer that he . . . (a) is ordinarily resident in the United Kingdom or was so resident at any time within the past two years; or (b) is the . . . child under sixteen years of age, of a Commonwealth citizen who is resident in the United Kingdom . . ."

I have read only the relevant words, but it becomes perfectly clear from what I have read that the applicant could not possibly be refused entry or made the subject of conditions because he was ordinarily resident in the United Kingdom or at any rate was so resident within the past two years. Equally, there was no power to refuse to admit H.K. or to impose any conditions on his entry, if he satisfied an immigration officer that he was the child of a Commonwealth citizen and was under sixteen years of age. In other words, sub-s. (2) is fettering the absolute discretion which there would otherwise be under sub-s. (1). Section 3 (1) provides that:

" The provisions of Part 1 of Sch. 1 to this Act shall have effect with respect to . . . (b) the exercise by immigration officers of their powers of refusal of admission or admission subject to conditions under s. 2 of this Act, and the cancellation, variation and duration of such refusals and conditions."

Turning then to Sch. 1 to the Act of 1962, para. 1 provides that:

" (1) Subject to the provisions of this paragraph, an immigration officer may examine any person who lands or seeks to land in the United Kingdom for the purpose of ascertaining whether that person is or is not a Commonwealth citizen subject to control under Part 1 of this Act, and if so for the purpose of determining what action, if any, should be taken in his case under the said Part 1; and it shall be the duty of every such person to furnish to an immigration officer such information in his possession as that officer may reasonably require for the purpose of his functions under this paragraph.

" (2) A person shall not be required to submit to examination under this paragraph after the expiration of the period of twenty-four hours from the time when he lands in the United Kingdom unless, upon being examined within that period, he is required in writing by an immigration officer to submit to further examination."

Paragraph 2 is dealing with the general provisions as to refusal of admission and provides:

" (1) The power of an immigration officer under s. 2 of this Act to refuse admission into the United Kingdom or to admit into the United Kingdom subject to conditions shall be exercised by notice in writing; and subject to sub-para. (2) of this paragraph, any such notice shall be given by being delivered by the immigration officer to the person to whom it relates.

" (3) Subject to the following provisions of this Schedule, a notice under this paragraph shall not be given to any person unless he has been examined in pursuance of para. 1 of this Schedule, and shall not be given to any person later than twelve hours after the conclusion of his examination (including any further examination) in pursuance of that paragraph."

Accordingly, it is clear that the period that can elapse before a notice is given will, subject to any question of further examination, be no more than thirty-six hours from the time of landing. By para. 2 (4) it is provided:

A   " A notice refusing a person admission into the United Kingdom may at
    any time be cancelled by a subsequent notice in writing given to him by an
    immigration officer . . ."

That indeed is a provision that one would expect because quite clearly the
immigration officer must have authority, must have jurisdiction, to reconsider
his decision at any time before the immigrant is actually admitted to the United

B   Kingdom or physically removed from it.

To return to the events at London Airport, the applicant and H.K. were met
by Mr. Mottram, an immigration officer employed by the Home Office at London
Airport. Turning to his affidavit, one finds in para. 2 the inception of what
happened. He says:

C   " On Nov. 21, 1966, I was on duty at the immigration control, No. 3
    building, when two persons approached my position at the control. They
    each presented a passport. The elder person had a passport in the name of
    [the applicant], and the younger in the name of [H.K.]. The older person
    appeared to have been ordinarily resident in the United Kingdom within
    the past two years. I saw from the passport of the younger person that he
D   was stated to be the son of [the applicant], that the photograph matched the
    appearance of the bearer, but the date of birth was expressed to be
    ' 29.2.1951 '. [Mr. Mottram adds:] I did not at the time notice that this was
    a non-existent date but my suspicions were aroused because the bearer
    appeared to be well over the age of fifteen years,"

E   that is to say, sixteen years or more. Having formed that impression, he sent
    H.K. along to the port medical officer with a form requiring the officer to
    estimate the age. According to Mr. Mottram, some half an hour later H.K.
    returned with this form on which the medical officer had endorsed " seventeen
    years +. The two third molars of lower jaw are well erupted." Following that,
    Mr. Mottram caused both of them, both the applicant and H.K., to be inter-
    viewed, and interviewed separately, and for that purpose had an interpreter,
F   in the first instance a Mr. Ross and later a Mr. Irons. It is quite clear that what
    happened as a result of these interviews increased Mr. Mottram's suspicions.
    It is unnecessary to go into the details, but at one time he understood that the
    applicant was saying that the present age of his wife was twenty years.
    Finally, he referred the matter to the chief immigration officer, Mr. Collison.

G   Mr. Collison apparently then took over the conduct of the interviews, and he
    sets out in his affidavit and there is set out in the affidavit of the interpreter,
    Mr. Irons, the answers which they obtained. It is enough to say that again
    those answers apparently increased Mr. Collison's suspicions. He was surprised
    at the absence of relatives, bearing in mind that this was a Pakistani family,
    both saying apparently that there were no uncles, aunts or cousins at all and
H   matters of that sort. In the end, it is quite clear that Mr. Collison made up his
    mind that he was not satisfied by H.K. or the applicant that H.K. was under
    sixteen years of age, and accordingly he caused that information to be conveyed
    to H.K. and a formal notice in writing to be served refusing admission. Accord-
    ingly, it was on the afternoon or evening of Nov. 21 that a decision refusing
    admission was made. It is pointed out to me that the notice also stated that
    he would be removed from the United Kingdom at noon on the following day,
I   Nov. 22.

Now on Nov. 22 in the morning, according to Mr. Collison, he read in the paper
something to the effect that H.K. had in his possession a school leaving certificate.
There is some doubt—one cannot put it higher than that—whether the presence
of a school leaving certificate could have come to the notice of Mr. Collison
through a newspaper, but, at any rate he was minded to inquire whether there
was a school leaving certificate on that morning, and it is not suggested that he
had any knowledge of such a certificate when he arrived at his decision on the

evening of Nov. 21.   According to Mr. Collison what happened was this.   He A
says:

> "I, therefore, accompanied by Mr. Irons [the interpreter] interviewed
> H.K., and asked him if he had such a certificate.   H.K. produced from his
> outside breast pocket a folded piece of paper, which he opened and showed to
> me, and which appeared to contain arabic script and modern English figures.
> I asked H.K. to read out the headings on the said paper, as Mr. Irons was B
> unable to read the script.   H.K. said that one such heading showed that he
> had left school on Mar. 31, 1965, but he was unable to make sense of the
> other headings.   H.K. then replaced the said piece of paper in his pocket,
> and at no time has it been in my possession."

Further questions followed as a result of which Mr. Collison, so far from cancel- C
ling the notice, was confirmed in his opinion and further had doubts whether
H.K. was the son of the applicant.   Pausing there, this court has seen a translation of that school leaving certificate and it appears to say that the date of birth
of H.K. was the date stated in the passport, Feb. 29, 1951, and it may well be that
the date on the passport was taken from this school leaving certificate.   Meanwhile, about noon on Nov. 22, proceedings were taken by way of an application D
to the judge in chambers for a writ of habeas corpus, and meanwhile also
Mr. Collison had undertaken that H.K. would not be removed pending that
application until Nov. 23.

Those are the facts up to the time of the application, and counsel for the applicant submits that in deciding whether or not he is satisfied as to the matter set
out in the subsection—in this case whether he is satisfied that the boy is under E
sixteen—an immigration officer is acting in a judicial or quasi-judicial capacity
and must conform to the rules of natural justice.   Subject to there being due
compliance with those rules, counsel admits that the decision of the immigration
officer cannot be challenged and that this court should not interfere.   He does,
however, maintain that the rules of natural justice require that before reaching
his decision the immigration officer must give the immigrant an opportunity F
to satisfy him and if, as in this case, he has formed an impression that the immigrant is sixteen or more, he must give the immigrant an opportunity to remove
that impression.   He claims that if that opportunity had been given evidence
would have been provided such as has been produced before us in these proceedings, which evidence he claims would have satisfied the officer.   Having regard
to the course which these proceedings have taken, it is unnecessary and I think G
indeed inadvisable to comment on that further evidence.   It is enough to say
that there has been produced to us medical evidence, evidence from medical
experts, to the effect that the conclusion reached by the port medical officer may
not be right or at any rate the grounds on which that report was made are incon-
clusive.   There is also evidence now that there being no births registration in
Pakistan the date of birth on the school leaving certificate is generally regarded as H
some evidence at any rate, if not strong evidence, of the date of birth, and finally
there is the evidence of the applicant himself and of friends of his and of the
surrounding circumstances which counsel for the applicant would say show that
H.K. is the applicant's son.   All this, it is said, if proper inquiries had been
made by the immigration officer, would have come to light and would have
resulted in the immigration officer being satisfied of the matters in the section. I
On one thing I myself am quite clear, and that is that even if an immigration
officer is required to act judicially or quasi-judicially, he is not under any duty
to hold a full-scale inquiry or to adopt judicial process and procedure.   The
burden here under the Act of 1962 is on the immigrant to satisfy the immigration
officer and the provisions of the schedule to which I have referred quite clearly
show that it is impossible and therefore not contemplated that an immigration
officer should hold any inquiry of that sort.

A   The court was referred by counsel for the applicant to *Shareef* v. *Comr. for Registration of Indian and Pakistani Residents* (1), a decision of the Judicial Committee. It is unnecessary to consider that in any detail, but that was a case where the commissioner of registration of Indian and Pakistani residents was specifically required by the statute to hold an inquiry and specific provision was made for the serving of notices and for hearings. That is a clear case where

B   not only was the commissioner acting judicially or quasi-judicially but also he was required to adopt the judicial processes envisaged by the statute. This, as it seems to me, is a very different case, and I doubt whether it can be said that the immigration authorities are acting in a judicial or quasi-judicial capacity as those terms are generally understood. At the same time, however, I myself think that even if an immigration officer is not acting in a judicial or quasi-judicial capacity,

C   he must at any rate give the immigrant an opportunity of satisfying him of the matters in the subsection, and for that purpose let the immigrant know what his immediate impression is so that the immigrant can disabuse him. That is not, as I see it, a question of acting or being required to act judicially, but of being required to act fairly. Good administration and an honest or bona fide decision must, as it seems to me, require not merely impartiality, nor merely bringing

D   one's mind to bear on the problem, but of acting fairly, and to the limited extent that the circumstances of any particular case allow, and within the legislative framework under which the administrator is working, only to that limited extent do the so-called rules of natural justice apply, which in a case such as this is merely a duty to act fairly. I appreciate that in saying that it may be said that one is going further than is permitted on the decided cases because heretofore

E   at any rate the decisions of the courts do seem to have drawn a strict line in these matters according to whether there is or is not a duty to act judicially or quasi-judicially. It has sometimes been said that if there is no duty to act judicially or quasi-judicially there is no power in the court whatever to interfere. I observe that in the well-known case of *Nakkuda Ali* v. *M. F. de S. Jayaratne* (2), again a decision of the Privy Council, the court were considering this sort of case. There

F   the controller of textiles in Ceylon was empowered to revoke licences where the controller had reasonable grounds to believe that any dealer was unfit to be allowed to continue as a dealer. Those were the words to be considered in that case which are of course different from those in the present case. LORD RADCLIFFE when giving the advice of the Judicial Committee, however, began by distinguishing that case from *Liversidge* v. *Anderson* (3) and went on to consider the position

G   of the controller in law. He said (4):

> " In truth, when he cancels a licence he is not determining a question: he is taking executive action to withdraw a privilege because he believes, and has reasonable grounds to believe, that the holder is unfit to retain it . . . the power conferred on the controller . . . stands by itself on the bare words of the regulation and, if the mere requirement that the controller

H   > must have reasonable grounds of belief is insufficient to oblige him to act judicially, there is nothing else in the context or conditions of his jurisdiction that suggests that he must regulate his action by analogy to judicial rules."

Having come to that decision, LORD RADCLIFFE then went on in effect to deal with the position if that was wrong, and if the controller was acting in a judicial

I   capacity. Later he said (5):

> " It is impossible to see in this any departure from natural justice. The respondent had before him ample material that would warrant a belief that the appellant had been instrumental in getting the interpolations made and securing for himself a larger credit at the bank than he was entitled to. Nor did the procedure adopted fail to give the appellant the essentials that

(1) [1966] A.C. 47.   (2) [1951] A.C. 66.
(3) [1941] 3 All E.R. 338; [1942] A.C. 206.   (4) [1951] A.C. at pp. 78, 79.
                        (5) [1952] A.C. at pp. 81, 82.

justice would require, assuming the respondent to have been under a duty to   **A**
act judicially.''

That might be understood as saying that if there was no duty to act judicially
then it would be impossible to interfere, even if the applicant had not been given
the essentials that justice requires. I very much doubt however whether it
was intended to say any more than that there is no duty to invoke judicial
process unless there is a duty to act judicially. I do not understand him to be   **B**
saying that if there is no duty to act judicially then there is no duty even to be
fair. When however that has been said, it seems to me impossible in the present
case to say that the decision made on the evening of Nov. 21 was not arrived at,
as I put it, fairly. It is impossible to believe other than that both the applicant
and H.K. knew full well of what they had to satisfy the authorities. They were,
as it seems to me, given ample opportunity to do so, and the fact that the officer   **C**
was not satisfied is not, as is admitted, a matter for this court.

Counsel for the applicant, however, goes on to contend that if after a decision
has been made information reaches the authorities that might on investigation
cause them to cancel the decision they are under a duty to let the immigrant
know what it is and enable him to deal with it and thus persuade the authorities
to cancel the notice. Having listened with care to what counsel for the applicant   **D**
has said and the way in which he puts it, it seems to me that even if that submission is correct, this would not be a matter for habeas corpus or certiorari at
all. The decision under which H.K. is held is the decision arrived at on Nov. 21.
Even if it can be said that the presence of this school certificate ought to have
been inquired into more closely by the immigration officer, and that further
opportunity ought to have been given to the applicant to satisfy the immigration   **E**
officer that the notice should be cancelled, it seems to me to be entirely a matter
for mandamus, and could not be a matter for certiorari.

It was as a result of arriving at that, at any rate provisional, conclusion that
this court last week decided to adjourn this application. Counsel for the applicant
had frankly said that all he could ask for was for the immigration authorities to
reconsider the matter with a view to cancellation in the light of all the evidence   **F**
now produced before this court, and the immigration authorities, through their
counsel, frankly said that that was what they were going to do. That being so,
the court thought it was proper to adjourn the case until today and retain, as it
were, seizin of it. Today the court has been told that no decision has yet been
come to. It appears that further information even beyond what has been submitted to this court is now available and not only that but the matter is having   **G**
the personal attention of the Home Secretary. Accordingly, it seems to me that
counsel for the applicant has had even more than he hoped for, and that there
is no reason why this court should retain any further control over it. In those
circumstances, it seemed right this morning that we should dispose of this case
by giving judgment.

Accordingly for the reasons that I have endeavoured to state, I would dismiss   **H**
both the application for habeas corpus and the application for certiorari.

    SALMON, L.J.: I agree. The power conferred on the immigration officer
by s. 2 (1) of the Commonwealth Immigrants Act, 1962, to refuse admission into
the United Kingdom to a Commonwealth citizen is not unfettered. It is fettered
by sub-s. (2) which enacts in effect that the immigration officer shall not refuse   **I**
admission in the case of any person who satisfies him—and I am merely referring
to the words which are relevant to this case—that he is a child under sixteen
years of age of a Commonwealth citizen who is resident in the United Kingdom
with whom he enters or seeks to enter the United Kingdom. I have no doubt
at all that in exercising his powers under that section, the immigration officer is
obliged to act in accordance with the principles of natural justice. That does not
of course mean that he has to adopt judicial procedures or hold a formal inquiry,
still less that he has to hold anything in the nature of a trial, but he must act, **as**

A LORD PARKER, C.J., has said, fairly in accordance with the ordinary principles
of natural justice. If for example, and this I am sure would never arise, it could
be shown that when he made an order refusing admission he was biased or had
acted capriciously or dishonestly, this court would have power to intervene by the
prerogative writ. There are, as LORD PARKER, C.J., has said, a good many cases
in which the view has been expressed that unless a person exercising a power is
B acting in a judicial or quasi-judicial capacity the courts cannot intervene. An
immigration officer is acting in an administrative rather than in a judicial capacity.
What however is a quasi-judicial capacity has, so far as I know, never been
exhaustively defined. It seems to me to cover at any rate a case where the
circumstances in which a person who is called on to exercise a statutory power
and make a decision affecting basic rights of others are such that the law
C impliedly imposes on him a duty to act fairly. When Parliament passed the
Commonwealth Immigrants Act, 1962, it deprived Commonwealth citizens of
their right of unrestricted entry into the United Kingdom. It laid down conditions under which they might enter, and left it to the immigration officers to
decide whether such conditions existed. Their decisions are of vital importance
to the immigrants since their whole future may be affected. In my judgment
D it is implicit in the statute that the authorities in exercising these powers and
making decisions must act fairly in accordance with the principles of natural
justice.

Counsel for the applicant has not suggested, nor would it be possible to suggest
on the evidence before this court, that when on Nov. 21, 1966, the immigration
officer refused permission to H.K. to enter the United Kingdom, he acted other-
E wise than in accordance with the rules of natural justice. It is quite plain that
no one could say that, on the material then before him, as a fair man he must
have been satisfied that H.K. was under sixteen years of age. The material
before him did not satisfy him, and I for one am not at all surprised. Therefore,
the refusal made and the notice served on Nov. 21 are unimpeachable. It follows
that H.K.'s detention pending his removal abroad was lawful.
F Schedule 1, para. 2 (4) to the Act of 1962 provides that:

" A notice refusing a person admission into the United Kingdom may at
any time be cancelled by a subsequent notice in writing given to him by an
immigration officer; and where a notice under this subparagraph cancelling
such a notice is given to any person at any time, the immigration officer may,
notwithstanding anything in sub-para. (3) of this paragraph, at the same
G time give to that person a notice admitting him into the United Kingdom
subject to conditions under s. 2 of this Act."

The Act of 1962 clearly contemplates that the immigration officer who has
exercised his power under s. 2 may change his mind as, for example, when he
has decided to refuse entry on somewhat tenuous material put before him and then
H finds that there is other material which leads to the conclusion that he should
allow entry.

On Nov. 22 it came to the notice of the chief immigration officer, Mr. Collison,
that H.K. was said to have with him a school leaving certificate, which was of
importance in that it might provide strong evidence as to the boy's age. The
school leaving certificate in Pakistan does show or purports to show H.K.'s age,
I and it is a particularly important document since, as I understand it, there are
no birth certificates in Pakistan. So very fairly and properly he went to see H.K.
and asked for his school leaving certificate, but due I think to the fact that the
interpreter whom he had with him was not as adept as he might have been in
deciphering Urdu and H.K. was unable to explain what was on the certificate,
Mr. Collison was quite unable to derive any assistance from it. The complaint
made by counsel for the applicant is that he ought not to have left it at that; he
ought to have taken steps to have had the certificate properly translated and
then applied his mind to it and considered whether or not this provided sufficient

evidence to justify him in changing his original decision. Counsel complains A
that in point of fact he took no further steps in relation to that certificate.
Whether that argument is sound or not, it cannot avail counsel for the applicant
in these proceedings. The refusal of Nov. 21 is admitted to have been properly
made and the detention of the boy after that order was lawful. It was still
lawful on Nov. 22. Now if Mr. Collison had done everything that counsel says
that he ought to have done, he would still have kept H.K. lawfully in detention B
whilst these further investigations were being pursued. So it is quite plain that
the most that this applicant could have hoped for in respect of the occurrence
of Nov. 22—and I express no view whether he would have obtained it—would
have been an order for mandamus. On no possible view could habeas corpus
have gone in respect of what happened on Nov. 21 or Nov. 22, nor could certiorari
have gone in respect of the decision of Nov. 21 because when it was made it was C
unimpeachable.

Accordingly, the application in this case is quite hopeless. Although it fails,
counsel for the applicant can perhaps properly regard it as a triumph from a
practical point of view. It has had the effect of this matter being considered at a
very high level indeed. As soon as the matter was drawn to the attention of the
authorities they expressed their willingness to consider any fresh material which D
might be put before them. They have now fully considered an accurate translation of the school leaving certificate. Indeed they have re-investigated the matter
most thoroughly. They came to the conclusion after that further investigation
that nothing more could be done and that the original decision should stand.
At the last moment, however, a cable has arrived from Pakistan suggesting that
there is a medical certificate from the district medical officer of the district E
in which this boy was born testifying that he is under sixteen years of age, and
very fairly and properly, as of course one would expect, the authorities have said
that until that further evidence arrives in this country, providing it arrives in a
reasonable time, no further steps will be taken to remove the boy. So either in
the end as a result of this application he will be admitted or if he is removed
he will at any rate have the satisfaction of knowing that every possible step has F
been taken and every relevant matter investigated in order to arrive at a just
conclusion. I agree that the applications for habeas corpus and certiorari should
be refused.

BLAIN, J.: I agree. It is not suggested now at any rate that the decision
to refuse admission come to on Nov. 21, 1966, was a decision which can be G
attacked in the light of the information then available to the immigration officer,
and in the light of the consideration which he then gave to that information.
That of itself is sufficient to mean that the application for leave to issue a writ of
habeas corpus and the application for leave to issue an order of certiorari must
fail. The case has however thrown up important considerations of what may
happen after that first decision has been taken, a decision which the statute H
really contemplates would have to be taken within a very short time. Section
3 (1) of the Commonwealth Immigrants Act, 1962, provides thus:

"The provisions of Part 1 of Sch. 1 to this Act shall have effect with
respect to . . . (b) the exercise by immigration officers of their powers of
refusal of admission or admission subject to conditions under s. 2 of this
Act, and the cancellation, variation and duration of such refusals and I
conditions."

It is the question of cancellation which has given rise to further discussion in this
court, and the relevant sub-paragraph of Sch. 1—para. 2 (4)—reads, in so far as
it needs to be read:

"A notice refusing a person admission into the United Kingdom may at
any time be cancelled by a subsequent notice in writing given to him by an
immigration officer . . .",

A and then there follow further administrative provisions for carrying that out. I would only say that an immigration officer having assumed the jurisdiction granted by those provisions is in a position where it is his duty to exercise that assumed jurisdiction, whether it be administrative, executive or quasi-judicial, fairly, by which I mean applying his mind dispassionately to a fair analysis of the particular problem and the information available to him in analysing it. If in

B any hypothetical case, and in any real case, this court was satisfied that an immigration officer was not so doing, then in my view mandamus would lie. That is not the position in this case nor indeed is the court in this case moved for leave to issue an order of mandamus. I need say no more than that I agree with what has fallen from my lords.

Motion dismissed.

C   Solicitors: *Lawford & Co.* (for the applicant); *Treasury Solicitor.*

[*Reported by* N. P. METCALFE, ESQ., *Barrister-at-Law.*]

D   DEVON COUNTY COUNCIL *v.* HAWKINS.

[QUEEN'S BENCH DIVISION (Lord Parker, C.J., Glyn-Jones and Widgery, JJ.), November 9, 1966.]

Road Traffic—Driving licence—Refusal by licensing authority to grant, being satisfied on inquiry that applicant suffering from prescribed disease—Appli-
E   *cant suffering from epilepsy which did not show itself while controlled by drugs—Whether applicant suffering from prescribed disease—Road Traffic Act, 1960 (8 & 9 Eliz. 2 c. 16), s. 100 (2).*

The respondent had suffered periodic epileptic fits in the past amounting to about ten or eleven since 1958, the last being in December, 1963. At the time of the last attack he had ceased on his own initiative to take the drugs
F   prescribed for him by his doctors which were designed to prevent recurrence of the attacks. Since the last attack he had continued to take the prescribed drugs, of which he was able to obtain further supplies as necessary by seeing his doctor about every two or three months. So long as he regularly continued to take the drugs, the chance of another attack of epilepsy was practically eliminated. The licensing authority refused the respondent a
G   driving licence on the ground that he was suffering from epilepsy and s. 100 (2)* of the Road Traffic Act, 1960, required them to refuse it. On appeal from a decision of the justices ordering a driving licence to be issued,

Held: so long as drugs were necessary to prevent the manifestation of a disease, the disease remained; accordingly the respondent was suffering from epilepsy within the meaning of s. 100 (2) of the Road Traffic Act, 1960, and
H   must be refused a driving licence (see p. 237, letters G and H, post).

Appeal allowed.

[As to physical fitness of applicants for driving licences, see 33 HALSBURY'S LAWS (3rd Edn.) 454, 455, para. 774; and for cases on the subject, see 45 DIGEST (Repl.) 79, 80, *255, 256.*

For the Road Traffic Act, 1960, s. 100, see 40 HALSBURY'S STATUTES (2nd
I Edn.) 804.]

Case Stated.

This was a Case Stated by justices for the County of Devon in respect of their adjudication as a magistrates' court sitting at Moretonhampstead on Feb. 21, 1966.

On Feb. 21, 1966, an appeal was lodged by the respondent, George Roy Hawkins, being a person aggrieved, against the decision of the appellants,

---

* Section 100 (2) is set out at p. 236, letter H, post.

Devon County Council, as the licensing authority, not to grant the respondent A a driving licence in the exercise of their powers under s. 100 (2) of the Road Traffic Act, 1960. The following facts were found to be proved: On his application in the prescribed form for the issue to him of a driving licence, the respondent in answer to question five thereof: " Have you ever been refused a licence by a council or had one revoked? If not write No but otherwise name the council and give the date and the reason " wrote: " Yes, Devon County Council, January, B 1964, suffered from blackout." Further, in answer to question six: " Do you suffer from either of the following diseases or disabilities which are specified below for the purposes of s. 100 of the Road Traffic Act, 1960? (i) Epilepsy . . .? " the respondent wrote " No ". The respondent had suffered periodic epileptic fits in the past amounting to about ten or eleven since 1958, the last being in December, 1963, and at the time of this last attack he had ceased on his own C initiative for about two months to take the drugs prescribed for him by his doctors which were designed to prevent recurrence of the attacks. Since the last attack the respondent had continued to take the prescribed drugs of which he was able to obtain further supplies as necessary by seeing his doctor about every two or three months. So long as he regularly continued to take the drugs, the chance of another attack of epilepsy was practically eliminated. D

It was contended by the appellants that, so long as it was necessary for a person to be under treatment for a disease or disability, whether the treatment was curative or preventative, then that person must be held to be suffering from that disease or disability. It was contended by the respondent that he was not suffering from any disease or disability specified in the application form.

The justices accepted the contention of the respondent that he was not suffering E from any specified disease or disability on the facts as found by them, allowed his appeal and ordered that a licence should be issued to him; and the appellants appealed.

The cases noted below* were cited during the argument.

T. G. Field-Fisher for the appellants.
Quentin Edwards for the respondent.   F

LORD PARKER, C.J., having stated the nature of the appeal, continued: It is convenient to look first at s. 100 of the Road Traffic Act, 1960. Subsection (1) provides that:

> " On an application for the grant of a licence the applicant shall make a G declaration in the prescribed form as to whether or not he is suffering from any such disease or physical disability as may be specified in the form . . ."

The form is no doubt well known to most people. A number of questions are asked in regard to diseases and disabilities. One of them is—" Do you suffer from epilepsy or from sudden attacks of disabling giddiness or fainting ?"; to that the respondent answered " No ". Section 100 (2) goes on to provide that: H

> " If from the declaration it appears that the applicant is suffering from any such disease or disability as aforesaid, or if on inquiry into other information the licensing authority are satisfied that the applicant is suffering from any such disease or disability, then subject to the following provisions of this section the licensing authority shall refuse to grant the licence."   I

In the present case, albeit the answer to the question put to the respondent was " No ", the licensing authority, the present appellants, on inquiries thereafter made, were satisfied that he suffered from epilepsy, and accordingly it became their duty to refuse, and they did refuse, the grant of a licence. Section 103 gives a right of appeal to a person aggrieved by the refusal. It provides that:

---

* *R. v. Cumberland Justices, Ex p. Hepworth*, [1931] All E.R. Rep. 717; *R. v. City of Cardiff Justices, Ex p. Cardiff City Council*, [1962] 1 All E.R. 751; [1962] 2 Q.B. 436.

" A person who is aggrieved by the refusal under s. 100 of this Act of a licensing authority to grant a licence or by the revocation thereunder of a licence, or by the refusal under the last foregoing section of a licensing authority to grant a licence, may, after giving the licensing authority notice of his intention so to do, appeal—(*a*) if he resides in England or Wales, to a magistrates' court acting for the petty sessions area in which he resides, (*b*) if he resides in Scotland, to the sheriff within whose jurisdiction he resides, and on any such appeal the court or sheriff may make such order as it or he thinks fit and an order so made shall be binding on the licensing authority."

On appeal to the magistrates, evidence was given from which the justices found as follows:

" The respondent had suffered periodic epileptic fits in the past amounting to about ten or eleven since 1958, the last being in December, 1963, and at the time of this last attack he had ceased on his own initiative for about two months to take the drugs prescribed for him by his doctors which are designed to prevent recurrence of the attacks. Since the last attack the respondent had continued to take the prescribed drugs, of which he was able to obtain further supplies as necessary by seeing his doctor about every two or three months. So long as he regularly continued to take the said drugs, the chance of another attack of epilepsy was practically eliminated."

Those were the facts found by the justices, what one might call the primary facts, and on that they reached this conclusion:

" We accepted the contention of the respondent that he was not suffering from any specified disease or disability on the facts as found by us, allowed his appeal and ordered that a licence should be issued to him."

The contention put forward by the appellants to this appeal is that the magistrates, properly directing themselves as to the law, could not on these facts find that the respondent was not suffering from epilepsy. It is said, and said with much force, that so long as it is necessary for a person to be under treatment for a disease or disability, then that person must be held to be suffering from that disease or disability. In my judgment, that is right. The respondent, as it seems to me, was suffering from a condition which no doubt is properly termed a disease, a condition of epilepsy, whereby he was subject to attacks, and, as the facts show, these drugs prevent those attacks, in other words prevent the disease from manifesting itself, and, so long as drugs are necessary to prevent the manifestation of disease, the disease in my judgment remains. Of course, a time may come when drugs are really unnecessary, when it can be said that the respondent is cured, but here on the evidence it appears that as recently as 1963 manifestations occurred when he had ceased on his own initiative to take the drugs.

In my judgment, the justices here came to a conclusion which they were not entitled to reach on the evidence, and I would allow this appeal and send the Case back to the justices with a direction that they should disallow the appeal to them.

GLYN-JONES, J.: I agree.

WIDGERY, J.: I also agree.

Appeal allowed.   Case remitted.

Solicitors: *Sharpe, Pritchard & Co.*, agents for *H. G. Godsall*, Exeter (for the appellants); *Robbins, Olivey & Lake* (for the respondent).

[*Reported by* S. A. Hatteea, Esq., *Barrister-at-Law.*]

NOTE.

Re HENRY WOOD NATIONAL MEMORIAL TRUSTS.
ARMSTRONG AND OTHERS *v.* MOISEIWITSCH AND OTHERS.

[CHANCERY DIVISION (Stamp, J.), April 27, 1966.]

Charity—Cy-près doctrine—Property given for a specific charitable purpose
which failed—Resulting trust for donors—" Reasonable " advertisements
and inquiries for donors, leading to application cy-près under Charities
Act, 1960 (8 & 9 Eliz. 2 c. 58), s. 14 (1) (a).

[As to the failure of a charitable purpose, see 4 HALSBURY'S LAWS (3rd Edn.)
319-322, paras. 658-660; and for cases on the subject, see 8 DIGEST (Repl.)
421, *1112-1117.*

For the Charities Act, 1960, s. 14, see 40 HALSBURY'S STATUTES (2nd Edn.)
139.]

Adjourned Summons.

In May, 1941, Queen's Hall, where the Henry Wood promenade concerts
were performed, was destroyed by enemy action.   In October, 1943, an announcement was made in the press that a national appeal was to be made, that a number
of concerts were to be organised, that the proceeds would go into a general fund
and that it would be left to Sir Henry Wood to decide the appropriate musical
cause to which the fund should be devoted.   Not only Sir Henry Wood's seventy-
fifth birthday but also the fiftieth season of the promenade concerts was to fall
in March, 1944.   The appeal was launched on Feb. 25, 1944, and its object was
then stated to be the provision of a concert hall to be named after Sir Henry
Wood.   A fund was established from contributions and the proceeds of cash
collections, concerts, rentals, sales of diaries and photographs and kindred
activities.   By a trust deed dated May 6, 1946, the trustees in whom the fund
was vested declared that they held it in trust ". . . for improving and extending
the knowledge and appreciation of good music amongst the general public . . ."
and, in particular, by establishing and maintaining a concert hall.   By 1952
it had become fairly clear that the fund would be inadequate to build a concert
hall without outside assistance.   The Government put forward proposals at
the end of 1948 which had to be abandoned in 1955, and other projects later
investigated by the trustees for a redevelopment of the Queen's Hall site proved
to be ineffective.

The trustees took out a summons on May 1, 1964, for the determination of the
destination of the assets in the fund and they asked, amongst other things,
whether the assets (a) were held on the trusts of the deed dated May 6, 1946, or
(b) fell to be dealt with as having been given only for a specific charitable purpose
which had failed; or (c) were held in trust to provide a music centre (alternatively
a music centre chosen by Sir Henry Wood) ; or (d) were held in trust for charitable
purposes generally or on some other and, if so, what trusts.

The summons was heard by STAMP, J., on Oct. 7 and 8, 1965, and he gave
judgment on Oct. 28, making a declaration in the terms of (b) on the summons
but, in considering a submission by counsel for the trustees on question (a) that
they had power to declare the trusts to which the contributions should be subject,
based on the rule stated by SIR HERBERT COZENS-HARDY, M.R., in *A.-G.* v.
Mathieson*, STAMP, J., said that it would be undesirable in the context of the
case before him to attempt to formulate or define the limits of that power but
that, if the money given in response to the appeal of Feb. 25, 1944, was, prior to
the declaration of trust on May 6, 1946, held for a specific charitable object, the
declaration of trust did not, in his judgment, affect the consequential rights of
the contributors.   He held that the particular charitable purpose for which the

* [1907] 2 Ch. 383 at p. 394.

fund was intended failed ab initio, and that subject to s. 14* of the Charities Act, 1960, the fund, so far as arising from identifiable sources, was held on resulting trusts for the donors. He declared the resulting trust accordingly, but the declaration did not extend to moneys received before Feb. 25, 1944, from donors who had no knowledge of the terms of the appeal made on that day, and the declaration did not extend to moneys received after May 6, 1946, from persons who were aware of the terms of the trust deed of that date or were aware that the objects of the trusts declared by that deed were not confined to providing a new concert hall. He declared returnable the assets representing contributions of those other donors whose gifts did not come within s. 14 (2) of the Act of 1960 and exceeded two guineas or, if anonymous, ten guineas, unless they executed written disclaimers of their right to have these assets returned to them, or unless, after such advertisements and inquiries as were reasonable, these donors could not be identified or could not be found.

On Apr. 27, 1966, the summons came on for hearing on a further question, viz., for directions as to what advertisements and further inquiries would be reasonable under s. 14 (1) (a) of the Charities Act, 1960.

P. W. E. Taylor for the trustees.

P. R. Oliver, Q.C., for the personal representatives of two contributors.

B. J. H. Clauson for the Attorney-General.

STAMP, J.: The following notices, together with inquiries already made, would constitute reasonable advertisements and inquiries for identifying and finding donors who have not disclaimed, viz.—notices inviting a donor who does not wish to give such a written disclaimer to notify his name and address in writing to the designated agents of the trustees, so as to be received by them before a specified date not less than two months after publication or posting of the notice, such a notice to be inserted in two issues of each of the following newspapers, namely, *The Times, The Daily Telegraph* and *The Scotsman,* and to be sent by ordinary post to the address, as recorded in the books and papers of the trustees, of every donor who made any such gift and has such a recorded address (not being an address of a formation or unit of Her Majesty's Forces) but who has not already given such a written disclaimer.

There will be an order that other inquiries, so far as may be necessary, should be made as to what gifts made after May 6, 1946 (the date of the trust deed), were made for the purposes of that deed.

Order accordingly.

Solicitors: *Rubinstein, Nash & Co.* (for the trustees); *Stanley Attenborough & Co.* (for the personal representatives of two contributors); *Treasury Solicitor.*

[*Reported by* Jenifer Sandell, *Barrister-at-Law.*]

---

* Section 14, so far as material, provides: "(1) Property given for specific charitable purposes which fail shall be applicable cy-près as if given for charitable purposes generally, where it belongs—(a) to a donor who, after such advertisements and inquiries as are reasonable, cannot be identified or cannot be found; or (b) to a donor who has executed a written disclaimer of his right to have the property returned. (2) For the purpose of this section property shall be conclusively presumed (without any advertisement or inquiry) to belong to donors who cannot be identified, in so far as it consists—(a) of the proceeds of cash collections made by means of collecting boxes or by other means not adapted for distinguishing one gift from another; or (b) of the proceeds of any lottery, competition, entertainment, sale or similar money-raising activity, after allowing for property given to provide prizes or articles for sale or otherwise to enable the activity to be undertaken. (3) The court may by order direct that property not falling within sub-s. (2) above shall for the purposes of this section be treated (without any advertisement or inquiry) as belonging to donors who cannot be identified, where it appears to the court either—(a) that it would be unreasonable, having regard to the amounts likely to be returned to the donors, to incur expense with a view to returning the property; or (b) that it would be unreasonable, having regard to the nature, circumstances and amount of the gifts, and to the lapse of time since the gifts were made, for the donors to expect the property to be returned."

Cancelled by PRACTICE DIRECTION
[1972] 3 All ER 704

PRACTICE DIRECTION.

PROBATE, DIVORCE AND ADMIRALTY DIVISION (DIVORCE).

Divorce—Practice—Agreement or arrangement between parties—Lodgment of copy of terms—Order approving terms—When terms may be incorporated in decree—Practice if terms, not previously approved, are produced at trial— Matrimonial Causes Act 1965 (c. 72), s. 5 (2).

In cases where an agreement has been come to in pursuance of s. 5 (2) of the Matrimonial Causes Act 1965 (1) and the terms of the agreement have been approved by the judge on an application to him by summons, it has been observed that the practice is growing of asking the trial judge to embody these terms in the decree nisi in the form of an order.

The inclusion of terms in a decree will usually be justified only where they are such as to be liable to subsequent variation or enforcement. Thus, where it is intended:

(a) that a party should submit to an order which it is within the statutory power of the court to make, or

(b) that a party should submit to an undertaking to the court which, in the event of non-compliance, is to be enforceable by attachment,

the order or undertaking must be fully set out in the decree. With this type of undertaking, care should be taken to see that it is in sufficiently precise terms to be enforceable.

Other terms, including undertakings too general to be enforceable by attachment, will be sufficiently dealt with if there is an order approving them (which will desirably, although not necessarily, have been obtained before the hearing of the suit (2)) a copy of the terms being lodged and placed on the court file.

The President has directed that in London cases where it is proposed to ask the judge to incorporate in a decree an order embodying the terms of an agreement or any part of them, the terms should, at least one week before the hearing of the summons for approval, be submitted to the court registrar so that he can consider the appropriate form of order.

Where terms of agreement which have not been previously approved are produced at the hearing of the suit, then if they meet with the approval of the judge, he should be asked to leave open the manner of their incorporation in the decree, so that the court registrar has an opportunity of considering them.

Dec. 22, 1966.

COMPTON MILLER
Senior Registrar.

---

(1) 45 HALSBURY'S STATUTES (2nd Edn.) 452.
(2) See *Allford* v. *Allford*, [1964] 3 All E.R. 220; [1965] P. 117.

A

DUNGATE *v.* LEE.

[CHANCERY DIVISION (Buckley, J.), November 7, 8, 9, 10, 29, 1966.]

Betting—Licensed betting office—Partnership—Defendant partner alone held betting office licence—Plaintiff partner had no bookmaker's permit—Plaintiff partner did not take bets over counter of office—Legality of partnership—

B

Dissolution of partnership—Betting and Gaming Act, 1960 (8 & 9 *Eliz.* 2 *c.* 60), *s.* 2, *s.* 3 (1)—*Betting, Gaming and Lotteries Act* 1963 (*c.* 60), *s.* 2, *s.* 3 (1).*

The plaintiff and the defendant agreed to set up a bookmaking business together in Newhaven. They both agreed to contribute £500 to it. It was agreed initially (so the court found) that the defendant should give up his employment to devote all his time to it, that the plaintiff would continue

C

his own business, which was in London, and should give part time assistance at the betting office, that the defendant should draw £10 a week from the betting office but that the plaintiff should draw nothing, that the profits remaining after the defendant's £10 weekly should be retained in the business and that the plaintiff and defendant should ultimately share equally

D

in the retained profits. The lease and other contracts were to be in the defendant's sole name, and only one betting office licence was to be obtained which was to be in the defendant's name. It was also agreed initially, as the court found, that the defendant should, and the plaintiff should not, deal with clients over the counter, the intention being that the business should be conducted without conflict with s. 3 (1)* of the Betting and Gaming

E

Act, 1960. The plaintiff did not obtain a bookmaker's permit. There was no agreement, before business commenced, between the plaintiff and defendant precisely what each should do. The business opened on Nov. 6, 1961. During the next eighteen weeks the plaintiff attended at the office on fifty-five out of eighty-one racing days. The defendant attended on all eighty-one days. The plaintiff never dealt with clients over the counter, though he did to some extent handle credit betting by telephone, which

F

may have amounted to acting as a bookmaker in that respect. He recorded bets on field sheets, made out winnings' slips, and wrote up the accounts. There was friction between the parties and on Mar. 12, 1962, a new agreement was reached to the effect that the plaintiff would attend on every racing day and draw £3 a day and the defendant should draw £23 a week. On July 23, 1962, the plaintiff gave the defendant notice that he terminated the associa-

G

tion.   On July 8, 1963, the plaintiff issued a writ claiming a declaration that a partnership between him and the defendant had been dissolved as from July 23, 1962, and to have the affairs of the partnership wound up.   In his defence the defendant pleaded that any partnership would have been contrary to the provisions of Part 1 of the Act of 1960 and void for illegality.

H

Held: although the Betting and Gaming Act, 1960, required that every partner who acted as a bookmaker should have a bookmaker's permit, it did not require that every partner in a bookmaker's business should have a bookmakers' permit; in the present case the plaintiff and defendant had not decided before the business was started, what their respective functions should be otherwise than that the defendant should, and the plaintiff should

I

not, deal with clients over the counter of the betting office, and accordingly any partnership between the plaintiff would not be illegal by reason of the Act of 1960, with the consequence that, as the relationship between the plaintiff and the defendant had all the characteristics of a partnership, the plaintiff was entitled to the relief that he sought (see p. 250, letters B, C and D, and p. 248, letter F, post).

[**Editorial Note.** The relevant provisions of the Betting and Gaming Act, 1960, were repealed by the Betting, Gaming and Lotteries Act 1963, which

* Section 3 (1) is printed at p. 249, letters F and G, post.

came into force on Mar. 28, 1963. Section 2 and s. 3 (1) of the Act of 1963 repro- ⌐
duce, so far as relevant, s. 2 and s. 3 (1) of the Act of 1960.

As to a bookmaker's permit, see SUPPLEMENT to 18 HALSBURY'S LAWS (3rd
Edn.), title GAMING AND WAGERING, para. 384 B.

For s. 2, s. 3, and s. 28 of and para. 17 of Sch. 1 to, the Betting and Gaming
Act, 1960, see 40 HALSBURY'S STATUTES (2nd Edn.) 335, 359, 368; and for
s. 2 and s. 3 of the Betting, Gaming and Lotteries Act 1963, see 43 HALSBURY'S ⌐
STATUTES (2nd Edn.) 314, 315.]

Action.

This was an action by the plaintiff, Arthur Cyril Dungate, begun by writ
dated July 8, 1963, claiming a declaration that the partnership between him and
the defendant, Alan Albert Lee, constituted by an oral agreement made on or
about July, 1961, as varied by a further agreement made on or about Mar. 12, C
1962, had been dissolved as from July 23, 1962, and that the affairs of partnership
might be wound up.   The facts are set out in the judgment.

The authority and cases noted below* were cited during the argument.

M. D. Sherrard for the plaintiff.
G. T. Hesketh for the defendant.

Cur. adv. vult.   D

Nov. 29.   **BUCKLEY, J.,** read the following judgment: This is a sad
story of two close and affectionate friends whose friendship has foundered as a
result of their embarking together on a business venture with insufficient capital
and without appreciating the strain which carrying on the business would
impose on them.   E

Before the second world war the defendant was, for a time, a bookmaker by
profession.   Subsequently, for a number of years, he was employed in the
railway police and was so employed when he met the plaintiff.   The plaintiff
is an insurance broker carrying on business single-handed, or virtually so, through
a private limited company in which he holds ninety-nine per cent. of the shares.
His office is, and was at the relevant times, in the Haymarket in London.   The   F
plaintiff and the defendant first met in 1954 and soon became intimate friends.
At the time with which I am concerned the plaintiff lived at Saltdean, which is
not far from Newhaven, and the defendant lived at Newhaven.

The defendant had it in mind that he would go back into the bookmaking
business if the law was altered in such a way as to make betting offices legal.
The Betting and Gaming Act, 1960, received the Royal Assent on July 29, 1960.   G
The relevant provisions of the Act of 1960, that is, those which legalised licensed
betting offices and required bookmakers to hold bookmaker's permits, came into
operation on May 1, 1961.   Early in 1961 the defendant suggested to the plaintiff
that the plaintiff should join him in a bookmaking business.   This idea pleased
the plaintiff and from that time onwards it was frequently discussed between
them.   H

The defendant had no capital, but on retirement from the railway police
would become entitled to a superannuation payment of about £450.   This would
have been insufficient to enable him to start a betting office on his own.   The
plaintiff and the defendant agreed that they would each put £500 into such a
business.   The plaintiff was unwilling to give up his insurance broking business
and, indeed, the parties were agreed that to start with they could not both make   I
a living out of the betting office business.   The idea was that a betting office
should be opened in Newhaven and the defendant was of the opinion that a
betting office in Newhaven would never be likely to produce enough profit to

---

* 28 HALSBURY'S LAWS (3rd Edn.) 494, 495, para. 949;   *Thwaites* v. *Coulthwaite*,
[1896] 1 Ch. 496;   *Saffery* v. *Mayer*, [1901] 1 K.B. 11;   *Keen* v. *Price*, [1914] 2 Ch. 98;
Jeffrey v. *Bamford*, [1921] 2 K.B. 351;   *Miles* v. *Clarke*, [1953] 1 All E.R. 779;   *St. John
Shipping Corpn.* v. *Joseph Rank, Ltd.*, [1956] 3 All E.R. 683;   [1957] 1 Q.B. 267;   *Re
Trepca Mines, Ltd.*, [1962] 3 All E.R. 351;   [1963] Ch. 199.

support two families. The plaintiff accepted this view and accordingly the discussions proceeded on the footing that for a time, at any rate, the plaintiff would continue his existing business in London and should attend only part-time at the betting office. The defendant had his eye on premises at 4A, High Street, Newhaven, as suitable for use as a betting office. On July 21, 1961, an estate agent, of whom the defendant had earlier made enquiries about these premises, wrote to the defendant saying that someone else was interested in acquiring them. This spurred the plaintiff and the defendant into making an offer for the premises which was successful. It was at or about this time that the parties finally agreed that they would embark together on the betting office venture, although, as the discussions had been of a friendly and informal nature, it is now hard to say just when a concluded agreement was reached.

It was agreed between them that each of them would contribute £500 to the venture; that the defendant should give up his employment as a policeman and devote himself whole time to the betting office business; that the plaintiff should for the time being continue his London business and should only give part time assistance at the betting office; that the defendant should draw £10 a week only from the betting office business and the plaintiff should draw nothing, and that the profits of the betting office business, beyond the defendant's drawings, should be retained in the business. It was further agreed that the lease and such contracts as that with the Exchange Telegraph Co. and with the G.P.O. for a telephone, should be in the defendant's sole name; that the betting office licence should be obtained in his name only, and that one bookmaker's permit only should be obtained, namely, by the defendant. It was no part of this agreement, as alleged in the defence, that the business would or might be transferred to a limited company. Such a possibility was discussed at a later stage, but not initially.

The principal issue in this action is whether the parties thereby became partners or not. The defendant's contention is that the agreement was that he should be sole owner of the business until the plaintiff should give up his London business and devote himself whole time to the betting office business, whereupon they would become partners in equal shares. The plaintiff, on the other hand, says that there was no such term of the agreement and that they were both equal partners in the betting office business from the start. The defendant says that he had understood from a Home Office circular that it would be illegal for two persons to be partners in a betting office business without their both holding bookmakers permits and that he was therefore concerned to see that he and the plaintiff did not enter into partnership while he, the defendant, alone held a bookmaker's permit. No such circular was produced in evidence. If there was such a circular —and I have no reason to suppose that there was not—it cannot, I think, if it was accurate, have stated the position in nearly such wide terms as the defendant says that he understood. I shall have to deal with this point later.

I am satisfied that the defendant did, as a result of something he had seen in some circular or other document, believe that so long as he alone held a bookmaker's permit it was desirable that the business should be conducted by him and in his sole name, and undesirable that the plaintiff's connexion with or interest in the business as a principal should be apparent. I am also satisfied that there was no agreement between the parties, express or implied, negativing the possibility of a partnership existing between them from the start. In particular, I do not accept the defendant's evidence to the effect that he and the plaintiff agreed that they should not become partners unless and until the plaintiff gave up his London business and came into the betting office business full time. The defendant may well have thought that, matters being arranged as they were, he and the plaintiff were not technically partners. It is my task, however, to decide whether the arrangement was in fact such as to constitute them partners. Before considering this I will complete the history. The parties together visited the estate agent and went to look at the premises at 4A, High Street, Newhaven,

which in due course became the betting office. Together they prepared the
draft of a new rule book containing the rules which were to regulate the business
with clients of the betting office. During the defendant's absence on holiday
the plaintiff affixed to the premises the necessary notice of the application (1) for a
betting office licence. When the day came for the hearing of that application,
and of the application for a bookmaker's permit in the defendant's name, the
plaintiff and the defendant each provided £50, being one half of the cost of the
permit. I am not clear how the cost of the licence was provided, but this
amounted only to £1. The plaintiff's wife provided some curtains for the office,
and she and the defendant's wife together chose the wallpaper to be used for
redecorating it.

The business opened on Nov. 6, 1961, and during the next eighteen weeks the
plaintiff attended at the office on fifty-five out of eighty-one racing days. The
defendant attended on all eighty-one days. On the days when the plaintiff
attended at the betting office he would leave home in time to catch a train at
Brighton at 6.30 in the morning, travel to London and give some attention to his
business in the Haymarket, catch an 11 a.m. train back to Brighton and reach the
betting office before the time of the first race. He would then remain at the
betting office until it closed. When the plaintiff attended at the betting office,
the defendant used to deal with clients over the counter; the plaintiff did not
do so. The plaintiff's jobs were to record the bets placed on what are known as
field sheets, which show the state of the book on each race, to deal with any
credit betting placed by telephone, to fill out slips showing what each winning
client was entitled to receive and to write up the books of account of the business.
Although the functions of the plaintiff and the defendant were in practice divided
in this way, there was not any antecedent agreement between them as to precisely
what either of them should do.

A profit and loss account of the business for the period Nov. 6, 1961, to Feb. 10,
1962, and a balance sheet as at the latter date, were prepared by a Mr. Mossman,
a professional accountant employed for the purpose. In the profit and loss
account the £10 per week drawn by the defendant, as well as £30 which the plaintiff
had drawn with the defendant's consent to meet Christmas expenses, and a
further 10s. which the plaintiff had drawn on one occasion at the defendant's
insistence, were all described as " partners' salaries ". The account showed a
net profit for the period of £392 13s. 9d. which after deduction of the so-called
" partners' salaries " left a residual profit of £222 3s. 9d., half of which was
credited in the balance sheet to the capital account of each of the plaintiff and
the defendant. The defendant raised objections as to the description " partners'
salaries ", but none to the division of the residual profit. The reason why he
raised what objections he did raise was that he feared that some competitor
might see these accounts and make trouble with the authorities about the business
being carried on by partners with only one bookmaker's permit. The division
of the residual profit did not worry the defendant, because, as he told me, it
had been agreed that all the profits should be retained in the business and would
eventually be shared between the plaintiff and himself.

It is evident that when he prepared these accounts, Mr. Mossman believed that
there was a partnership in existence. At a later stage Mr. Mossman prepared
another set of accounts of the business for the period Nov. 6, 1961, to May 5, 1962.
These were prepared on the footing that the defendant was sole proprietor of
the business. The plaintiff is shown as a creditor on the loan account in a
sum of £500, his contribution to the business, and the whole net profit for the
period, amounting to £1,188 5s. 9d., is credited to the defendant's capital account.
That these accounts were framed in this way was, I have no doubt, due either to
instructions given to Mr. Mossman by the defendant or to the objections which

(1) See the Betting and Gaming Act, 1960, Sch. 1, para. 60; 40 HALSBURY'S STATUTES
(2nd Edn.) 364; now replaced by the Betting, Gaming and Lotteries Act 1963, Sch. 1,
para. 6; 43 ibid., 373.

the defendant had raised to the form of the earlier accounts. The plaintiff saw these later accounts, but raised no objection to them.

A bank account for the business was opened in the defendant's sole name. Into this account the plaintiff paid £450, the balance of his £500 contribution. It seems that the defendant never contributed the whole of his £500, his contribution having in fact been £451. A contract was entered into with the Exchange Telegraph Co. and also with the G.P.O. for a telephone for the office. These contracts were in the defendant's sole name. I think that the contracts for other public facilities, such as electricity, were also in the defendant's name. The opening of the bank account and the making of these contracts in the defendant's name alone were effected with the plaintiff's knowledge and approval. The plaintiff arranged the insurances in respect of the office premises.

Daily summary sheets of each day's business were prepared and the defendant was supplied with copies of all these. On Saturdays the defendant's wife used to help in the betting office without payment and the plaintiff's wife, who having young children to care for could not attend at the office, used to prepare an evening meal for all four of them. The two ladies used to buy the food for this meal in alternate weeks. Originally on days when the plaintiff did not attend the office the defendant carried on the business alone, although the plaintiff was available for discussion on the telephone if necessary. Later a girl was employed to help in the office. I have no doubt that both parties were working very hard. The plaintiff particularly was subject to a régime which exposed him to very great physical strain and which was certainly not advantageous to his London business.

There was some friction between the plaintiff and the defendant about the policy to be adopted as to hedging bets, the plaintiff favouring a more cautious line and the defendant a more adventurous one. In the course of time these strains and stresses rendered the relations between the parties less harmonious. The defendant was frequently pressing the plaintiff to give up his London business and devote himself whole time to the betting office. This the plaintiff was, for economic reasons, unable to do unless he could obtain a living from the betting office. The plaintiff, however, was willing to devote more time to the betting office and less to his London business, so as to give the defendant more assistance and support provided he could draw something from the betting office business.

On Mar. 12, 1962, he and the defendant reached a new agreement to the effect that the plaintiff would attend at the office on every day when there was racing, reaching the office before racing started; that he should be entitled to draw £3 for each day on which he so attended; that the defendant should thenceforth draw £23 per week, that is, £5 more than the plaintiff would draw in a six day week, and that if on any racing day the plaintiff was unable to attend he should draw nothing for that day, but the defendant should be entitled to draw an extra £3. The plaintiff would continue to attend to his London business so far as this arrangement would permit.

Thereafter the business was carried on as before, but subject to the variation agreed on Mar. 12. Unfortunately, this did not put an end to the differences between the parties. The plaintiff was working under even greater strain than before. The differences about hedging continued and later in March the defendant agreed that all matters relating to hedging should be under the exclusive control of the plaintiff. This was a consequence of a threat by the plaintiff to put an end to the association between the defendant and himself. It is, I think, a cogent indication that the plaintiff was already at that time someone with a share in the business and not merely a man with a prospect of becoming a partner.

Naturally, the new régime which required the plaintiff to give more time to the betting office business did not favour his insurance agency business. By April he was in difficulties with the mortgage payments on his house. In May, 1962, after discussion with the defendant and with the defendant's acquiescence,

the plaintiff drew £120 from the betting office business bank account to help him
meet these liabilities.

Unfortunately, friction continued and on July 23, 1962, the plaintiff informed
the defendant orally of his intention to sever relations with the defendant in
the betting office business. On the same day the plaintiff's solicitors wrote the
defendant a letter which was perhaps couched in rather carefully chosen terms:

" Dear Sir, We have been consulted by our client [the plaintiff] of 20,
Linchmere Avenue, Saltdean, Sussex, regarding his business arrangements
and investments with your firm. Our client has requested us to notify you
that owing to your attitude regarding his London commitments, full details
of which you are already aware, he is compelled to terminate his association
with you as from Saturday, July 21, 1962.

" Our client is, of course, entitled to his share of the goodwill and profits
of the business as well as return of his investments. We are at the moment
looking into this matter and as soon as we have ascertained the amount
due to our client we will write you further."

The defendant on that date paid £350 to the plaintiff out of the business bank
account, making, with the sums of £30 and £120 already drawn by the plaintiff,
the total of his £500 contribution. At the insistence of the defendant the plaintiff
agreed to help him in the office during July 23, in consideration of a payment of
£5, a sum which the plaintiff says he stipulated for to distinguish this payment
from the £3 a day which he had been drawing under the agreement of Mar. 12, 1962.
Thereafter the plaintiff took no part in the business of the betting office.

On Aug. 1, 1962, accountants acting for the plaintiff put forward a claim to the
defendant on the basis that the plaintiff was entitled to a half share of the profits.
On Aug. 8, 1962, solicitors for the defendant replied saying that they could see
no justification for any further claim against the defendant but without preferring
any reasons for this view, or any more specific reply to the letter of Aug. 1. The
correspondence then hung fire for some weeks and it was not until Oct. 19, 1962,
that the accountants acting for the defendant wrote a letter in substance denying
the existence of a partnership. This letter contained a number of inaccuracies.
Amongst other things, it was alleged in para. 2 (a) of the letter that it had been
agreed that the defendant would carry on the business for the time being and that
the plaintiff would take steps to dispose of his London business and make himself
available to take a full time part in the running of the betting office business
as soon as possible and at any rate to be fully available as soon as the flat racing
season started in March, 1962, when it was expected that the business would
expand considerably. I find nothing in the evidence to justify that suggestion
that there was any agreement that the plaintiff should dispose of his London
business by March, 1962. In para. 2 (b) of the letter it alleges:

" It was further agreed that providing the business prospered, a company
would be formed to take over the business and that [the plaintiff] should
have an interest in the company on terms to be agreed."

The evidence indicates that that was not the subject-matter of the initial agreement between the parties at all, although there was some discussion of the possibility of the formation of a company in April, 1962. In para. 2 (c) of the letter
it alleges:

" In the meantime [the plaintiff] should assist when possible and make
himself available not later than March, 1962, to assist full time in the
development of the business."

Again that was no part of the original agreement between the parties. The letter
goes on to say in para. 4:

" [The plaintiff], however, failed to carry out his part of his verbal agreement in that (a) he did not dispose of his London business as he had originally
agreed to do. (b) He was consequently not available to devote his full

time and efforts to the running and building up of the betting office business.
(c) He attended at the office at weekends only during the winter period and
for half days only for a period from mid-March to mid-July, eighteen weeks
in all during which time he was paid at the rate of £18 per week or £3 per
half day's attendance."

It is now clear, from what has been said by the defendant in the witness box, that
the plaintiff fully honoured his obligations with regard to attending at the betting
office in accordance with what had been agreed between himself and the defendant
throughout the period of the association of the parties.   The letter goes on:

" (d) He eventually, after some pressure from [the defendant], admitted
that he was insolvent and therefore was unable to become a director of the
proposed company.   [There is no foundation whatever for that allegation
apparent from the evidence.]   This position must have existed to a very
great extent at the time the betting office business was first discussed,
although at that time he made no mention of this to [the defendant]."

That also seems to be an unjustifiable comment.   At the end of the letter the
accountants say:

" With regard to the question as to whether [the plaintiff] is entitled
to a share of the profits of the business for the period Nov. 6, 1961, to July 23,
1962, here again, in view of [the plaintiff's] complete failure to devote the
whole of his time to the running of the business from March onwards, the
claim that he has a right to one half share of the profits for the period is
unrealistic and unacceptable.   There is no legal liability on [the defendant]
to pay to [the plaintiff] any share of the profits."

The writ was issued on July 8, 1963.   The plaintiff claims a declaration that a
partnership between the plaintiff and the defendant constituted by the initial
agreement between them and the subsequent agreement of Mar. 12, 1962, has
been dissolved as from July 23, 1962, and to have the affairs of such partnership
wound up.

The defendant by his defence alleged in para. 2 that it was part of the agreement
between himself and the plaintiff that,

" If the plaintiff within a reasonable time gave up his said business in
London and agreed to work full time in the said business, the defendant
would take the plaintiff into the said business as an equal partner or the
business would be transferred to and carried on by a limited company
in which the plaintiff and the defendant would be equal shareholders.
. . .   In pursuance of the agreement set out in para. 2 hereof the defendant
duly obtained premises at 4A, High Street, Newhaven, for the purposes of the
said business and duly applied to the Lewes magistrates' court and was
granted a permit for the said business."

In para. 4 of the defence it is alleged:

" Shortly after the defendant started the said business the plaintiff
ceased to attend at the business premises except on Saturday."

This allegation, which is clearly quite unjustified, has been abandoned at the trial
and the defendant has very fairly conceded that both before and after the agreement on Mar. 12, 1962, the plaintiff fully honoured his obligations as to attending
at the betting office.   Paragraph 6 of the defence is in these terms:

" On or about Mar. 24, 1962, shortly before the start of the flat racing
season the defendant pressed the plaintiff to give up his business in London
and to work whole time in the defendant's said business.   On or about Mar.
26, 1962, the plaintiff informed the defendant that he had made up his
mind to take no further part in the defendant's said business and to devote
his whole time and attention to his London business.   The plaintiff took no
part in the defendant's said business after July 21, 1962."

The reference there to Mar. 26, 1962, is a reference to the occasion when it was agreed the plaintiff should have sole control of all matters relating to hedging. The defendant in para. 8 disputes the existence of any partnership.

The substance of the defendant's case is that any agreement for a partnership was conditional on the plaintiff within a reasonable time giving up his London business and working full time at the betting office. With this condition the defendant says that the plaintiff never complied, so that there was never a partnership. Alternatively, the defendant alleges in para. 10 of the defence that at all material times the defendant held a bookmaker's permit and the plaintiff never held such a permit, which is quite accurate.

> " The defendant will contend that any partnership between the plaintiff
> and the defendant in a bookmaking business as alleged in the statement of
> claim or at all would have been contrary to the provisions of Part 1 of the
> Betting and Gaming Act, 1960, and void for illegality."

As I have already said, I do not accept the defendant's evidence as to the conditional nature of any agreement for a partnership. The conduct of the parties in the early stages of the venture is really only consistent with the view that this was from the beginning a joint venture to which both the plaintiff and the defendant were contributing both capital and effort. There is no question but that it was embarked on with a view to profit. I am satisfied, and I find as a fact, that by their initial agreement the parties agreed that they would share equally the profits of the business remaining after the defendant had drawn his £10 per week, although all such profits would for the time being be retained in the business to build up a working capital. In March, 1962, the arrangement as to the drawings which each party was to be permitted to make before the equally divisible profits were ascertained was varied, but otherwise the relationship between them remained substantially the same. I may add that throughout the period of their association the plaintiff and the defendant were accustomed to address one another in conversation and letters—no doubt somewhat facetiously —as " partner ", " pard " and " mate ".

The relationship between the plaintiff and the defendant had, in my judgment, all the characteristics of a partnership and, unless such partnership was illegal, the plaintiff is, in my judgment, entitled to the relief which he seeks.

A contract of partnership is illegal if the purpose for which the partnership is intended to be formed is illegal or if, although that purpose is one which could be attained by legal means, it is the intention of the parties that it shall be attained in an illegal way. There is, of course, nothing illegal about the carrying on of a betting office business with due regard to the Betting and Gaming Act, 1960, nor anything illegal about forming a partnership to carry on such a business with due regard to the requirements of the Act of 1960. I have no doubt that a great number of such partnerships exists. The question is whether a partnership formed to carry on a betting office business with the intention that only one partner shall obtain a bookmaker's permit offends against the Act of 1960, or whether, if this is not universally true, the circumstances of the present case were such that the partners intended to achieve the object for which the partnership was formed in a manner which offends against the Act of 1960. Section 2 of the Act of 1960 provides :

> " (1) No person shall act as a bookmaker on his own account unless he
> is the holder of a permit authorising him so to act (in this Act referred to as a
> ' bookmaker's permit ') which is for the time being in force; and if any
> person acts as a bookmaker in contravention of this subsection he shall be
> guilty of an offence."

Then there is an exception with regard to pool bets with which I am not concerned. Section 28 is the interpretation section and in sub-s. (1) there is a definition of " the board " meaning the Racecourse Betting Control Board and " bookmaker " as meaning

" any person other than the board who, whether on his own account or as servant or agent to any other person, carries on, whether occasionally or regularly, the business of receiving or negotiating bets or conducting pool betting operations, or who by way of business in any manner holds himself out, or permits himself to be held out, as a person who receives or negotiates bets or conducts such operations, so, however, that a person shall not be deemed to be a bookmaker by reason only of the fact—(a) that he carries on, or is employed in, sponsored pool betting business; or (b) that he operates, or is employed in operating, a totalisator; and the expression ' bookmaking ' shall be construed accordingly."

Section 2 further provides that

" (2) Schedule 1 to the Act shall have effect for the purposes of book-maker's permits."

When one turns to Sch. 1 one finds that it contains a group of paragraphs headed " Grounds for refusal to grant or renew bookmaker's or betting agency permit ". Paragraph 17 reads:

" In the case of an application for the grant or renewal of a bookmaker's permit, and subject to para. 19 of this Schedule, the appropriate authority may refuse the application if— ... (b) the authority are satisfied that, if the permit were to be granted or renewed, the business to which it relates would be managed by, or carried on for the benefit of, a person other than the applicant, being a person who would himself be refused the grant or renewal of such a permit either under para. 16 of this Schedule or under sub-para. (a) of this paragraph."

It is apparent from this that the fact that a permit applied for would, if granted, relate to a business carried on for the benefit of some person other than the applicant would not be a ground for refusing the application unless that other person was someone who would himself be refused the grant of a permit either under para. 16 or para. 17 (a) of Sch. 1. Section 3 (1) of the Act of 1960 provides:

" No person shall by way of business receive or negotiate bets as servant or agent to another bookmaker or to the board unless—(a) he has attained the age of twenty-one years; and (b) he is authorised in that behalf in writing in the prescribed form by that other bookmaker or, as the case may be, by the board; and (c) in the case of a person acting as servant or agent to another bookmaker, that other bookmaker is the holder of a bookmaker's permit or betting agency permit: Provided that this subsection shall not apply to any person who is the holder of such a permit as aforesaid, or who receives or negotiates bets as aforesaid on premises occupied by the holder of such a permit or by the board."

Anyone who, in the way of business and whether on his own account or as servant or agent of another, receives or negotiates bets or conducts pool betting operations, or holds himself out or permits himself to be held out as doing so, acts as a book-maker. This he may not do on his own account without a permit, but he will not require a permit if he does this as servant or agent of another bookmaker who holds a permit if he, the servant or agent, has attained the age of twenty-one and is only authorised in accordance with s. 3 (1) (b) or, if he receives or negotiates the bets as servant or agent of another bookmaker who holds a permit and on premises occupied by that other bookmaker. It would seem that the proviso to s. 3 (1) may be capable of having a wider effect than I have attributed to it, but I do not think that I am concerned with that.

Counsel for the defendant has submitted that in the present case the agreement was that the plaintiff and the defendant should both work in the business. This is correct. Counsel for the defendant goes on to say that in taking bets in the course of working in the business the plaintiff was not acting as servant or as agent for the defendant, but was acting on his own account and on account of the defendant, and that so far as he was doing so on his own account he was not acting as a servant or agent at all.

Counsel for the plaintiff, on the other hand, has submitted that the evidence establishes that the business was carried on under the managerial control of the defendant and the plaintiff was merely giving assistance. He says, further, that if the plaintiff had in fact carried on business as a bookmaker on his own account this has been purely incidental and not in pursuance of any term of the partnership agreement.

In my judgment, the Act of 1960 does not require that every partner in a bookmaker's business must obtain a permit, although it appears to me that it does require that every partner in a bookmaker's business who acts as a book-maker in the course of that business must have a permit. There would, I think, be nothing wrong in A holding a bookmaker's permit and B holding no such permit carrying on a bookmaking business in partnership, A alone being actively engaged in the conduct of the business and B contributing the capital but taking no active part in the business. Nor do I think that there would be anything wrong if B, instead of taking no active part in the conduct of the business, con-fined his activities in the business to activities other than receiving or negotiating bets or conducting pool betting operations; in other words, so long as B did not act as a bookmaker. He might, for instance, confine his participation in the business to keeping accounts and records.

If I am right in this view, the further question arises whether in this particular case the partnership agreement was one which required the plaintiff to act as a bookmaker in the conduct of the business or was entered into with a common intention on the part of the plaintiff and the defendant that the plaintiff would act as a bookmaker in the conduct of the business without a permit.

I have already found as a fact that there was no agreement between the parties antecedent to the opening of the business as to precisely what either of them should do, and accordingly the partnership agreement was not one which specific-ally required the plaintiff to act as a bookmaker in the conduct of the business. The greater part of the plaintiff's activities in the business did not constitute acting as a bookmaker within the meaning of the Act of 1960. In so far as the plaintiff handled credit betting placed by telephone it appears to me that he may have acted as a bookmaker and may have been in breach of the Act of 1960 in so doing without a bookmaker's permit; but the evidence does not establish that the partnership agreement was entered into on the basis—that is, with a common intention—that the plaintiff should perform this particular function. As I have indicated, the defendant was anxious that the arrangement between the plaintiff and himself should be such that, having regard to their intention that initially only the defendant should hold a permit, the business should be so conducted as to avoid conflict with the provisions of the Act of 1960. Had either of the parties appreciated that by handling the credit betting without a permit the plaintiff was or might be committing an offence under the Act of 1960, I have no doubt whatever that they would have rearranged their method of conducting their business so as to avoid this result.

I have formed the view on the evidence, and I find, that the parties had not before the business was started decided what their respective functions should be otherwise than that the defendant should and the plaintiff should not deal with clients over the counter of the betting office. It follows that in my judgment the partnership agreement was not in conflict with the provisions of the Act of 1960. Any infringement of the Act of 1960 that may have occurred in the conduct of the business after the establishment of partnership cannot in these circumstances have any bearing on the validity of the partnership agreement.

Accordingly, the defence based on illegality, in my judgment, fails.

Declaration that a partnership existed between plaintiff and defendant as alleged in statement of claim and that such partnership was dissolved as from July 23, 1962. Order for usual accounts and inquiries.

Solicitors: *Philip Ross, Elliston & Co.* (for the plaintiff); *Edwin Coe & Calder Woods* (for the defendant).

[Reported by JENIFER SANDELL, Barrister-at-Law.]

STAMP *v.* UNITED DOMINIONS TRUST (COMMERCIAL), LTD.

[QUEEN'S BENCH DIVISION (Lord Parker, C.J., Salmon, L.J., and Widgery, J.), November 17, 18, 1966.]

Criminal Law—Restitution order—Discretion—Circumstances in which discretionary power might or should not be exercised by a criminal court—Competing claim by third party—Magistrates' Courts Act, 1952 (15 & 16 Geo. 6 & 1 Eliz. 2 c. 55), s. 33 (1)—Larceny Act, 1916 (6 & 7 Geo. 5 c. 50), s. 45 (1).

Criminal Law—Restitution order—Jurisdiction—Order not made on day of conviction—Possession of property by third party no bar—Magistrates' Courts Act, 1952 (15 & 16 Geo. 6 & 1 Eliz. 2 c. 55), s. 33—Larceny Act, 1916 (6 & 7 Geo. 5 c. 50), s. 45 (1).

Hire-Purchase—Larceny of goods—Restitution order in favour of finance company —Sale of motor vehicle to trade purchaser when hire-purchase agreement still subsisting—Purchaser not buying in good faith—Hire-Purchase Act 1964 (c. 53), s. 27 (2), s. 29 (2).

M. had possession of a motor car as hirer under a hire-purchase agreement made in March, 1965. In about June, 1965, when hire-purchase instalments were still running, he sold it to the appellant. On Oct. 21, 1965, M. was convicted in summary proceedings before justices of larceny as bailee of the car; application was then made by the respondent finance company for a restitution order in respect of the car, but the court adjourned the matter for notice to be given to the appellant. On Jan. 5, 1966, the respondents applied by complaint for the restitution order by virtue of s. 33* of the Magistrates' Courts Act, 1952, and s. 45† of the Larceny Act, 1916; and on Feb. 10 the justices made the order. At that time the amount owing to the respondents in respect of the car was £1,693 6s. 8d. At the time of the appellant's purchase of the car he was carrying on a business of purchasing motor vehicles and offering them for sale and was a trade purchaser within s. 29 (2) of the Hire-Purchase Act 1964, and, so the justices found, was not a private purchaser nor a purchaser in good faith within s. 27 (2)‡. On appeal,

Held: (i) the justices had jurisdiction under s. 33 of the Magistrates' Courts Act, 1952, to make the restitution order notwithstanding (a) that the car was in the possession of a third person, the appellant, and (b) that the order was made on a day subsequent to the date of conviction, having regard to the fact that an application was made on the date of conviction (see p. 254, letters F and G, p. 256, letter E, and p. 257, letter G, post).

R. v. *Macklin* ((1850), 5 Cox, C.C. 216) and *Vilmont* v. *Bentley* ((1886), 18 Q.B.D. 322) applied.

(ii) the justices had a discretion whether to make the restitution order and in the present case their order should stand, particularly as their finding that the appellant was not a purchaser in good faith precluded him from maintaining a claim under s. 27 (2) of the Hire-Purchase Act 1964; but criminal courts (whether courts of assize, quarter sessions or courts of

---

* Section 33 (1) is set out at p. 254, letter A, post.
† Section 45, so far as material, is set out at p. 254, letter B, post.
‡ Section 27 (2), so far as material, is set out at p. 256, letter B, post.

summary jurisdiction) should not normally exercise their discretionary power to make orders for the restitution of property where there were serious competing claims involving third parties (see p. 255, letter G, p. 256, letters D and H, and p. 257, letters F and H, post).

Appeal dismissed.

[**Editorial Note.** There was no material in the Case Stated on which argument could be based that the prosecution had been a police prosecution and that therefore the case should be regarded as being outside s. 45 (1) of the Larceny Act, 1916, on the ground that the offender would not have been prosecuted to conviction by or on behalf of the owner of the property (see p. 255, letter I, post).

As to restitution of stolen property, see 10 HALSBURY's LAWS (3rd Edn.) 816-819, paras. 1579-1581; and for cases on the subject, see 14 DIGEST (Repl.) 594-597, *5914-5945.*

As to offences by hirers of goods under hire-purchase agreements, see 19 HALSBURY's LAWS, 556, 557, paras. 901, 903 and SUPPLEMENT, para. 877A; and for cases on the subject, see 26 DIGEST (Repl.) 670, *56, 57.*

For the Larceny Act, 1916, s. 45, see 5 HALSBURY's STATUTES (2nd Edn.) 1040.

For the Magistrates' Courts Act, 1952, s. 33, see 32 HALSBURY's STATUTES (2nd Edn.) 451.

For the Hire-Purchase Act 1964, s. 27, s. 29 (2), see 44 HALSBURY's STATUTES (2nd Edn.) 1082, 1085.]

Cases referred to:

Leicester & Co. v. *Cherryman,* [1904-07] All E.R. Rep. 794; [1907] 2 K.B. 101; 76 L.J.K.B. 678; 96 L.T. 784; 71 J.P. 301; 14 Digest (Repl.) 598, *5964.*

R. v. *Macklin,* (1850), 5 Cox, C.C. 216; 15 J.P. 518; 14 Digest (Repl.) 594, *5916.*

Vilmont v. *Bentley,* (1886), 18 Q.B.D. 322; 56 L.J.Q.B. 128; 56 L.T. 318; 51 J.P. 436; *affd.* H.L., sub nom. *Bentley* v. *Vilmont,* (1887), 12 App. Cas. 471; 14 Digest (Repl.) 597, *5945.*

Case Stated.

This was a Case Stated by justices for the borough of Lowestoft in respect of their adjudication as a magistrates' court at Lowestoft on Feb. 10, 1966. On Jan. 5, 1966, a complaint was made by the respondent finance company, United Dominions Trust (Commercial), Ltd., against the appellant Ronald Stamp that the appellant was in possession of an E type Jaguar motor car bearing reg. no. CEX 300C, having acquired it from Brian Nicholas Mingay in June, 1965, of which car the respondents were the lawful owners. Mingay was convicted of larceny of the car on Oct. 21, 1965, at the Lowestoft magistrates' court but the appellant had retained possession of the car. The respondents applied, by virtue of s. 45 of the Larceny Act, 1916, for an order that the said motor car be returned to them, under s. 33 of the Magistrates' Courts Act, 1952.

The following facts were found: Brian Nicholas Mingay entered into a hire-purchase agreement with the respondents on Mar. 23, 1965, in respect of the Jaguar motor car. The cash price was £2,022 17s. 11d. The car was obtained from Mann Egerton & Co., Ltd., Lowestoft. The hire-purchase agreement was never terminated, and the amount owing to the respondents was £1,693 6s. 8d. The car was severely damaged in June, 1965, on a race track at Snetterton, Norfolk. Subsequently the appellant purchased the car from Mingay and paid him £750. Mingay appeared before the Lowestoft borough justices on Oct. 21, 1965, and, having consented to summary trial, was convicted of larceny of the car. At the time of the said disposition of the car to him the appellant was carrying on a business which consisted wholly or partly of purchasing motor vehicles for the purpose of offering them or exposing them for sale, and was accordingly a trade purchaser within the meaning of s. 29 (2) of the Hire-Purchase Act 1964. It was contended on behalf of the appellant before the justices that

A they had no jurisdiction to hear the application, as it was not made at the time
of the conviction of Mingay; that it was wrong for the court to hear an application of such a nature, which involved complex matters of fact and law, and that
the remedy under s. 45 of the Larceny Act, 1916 was discretionary and should
be refused in difficult cases. If the appellant was wrong in his contention, then
the effect of the Hire-Purchase Act 1964, as applied to the transaction between
B Mingay and the appellant, was that the limit of £2,000 referred to in s. 21 of the
Act of 1964 did not restrict the operation of s. 27 of the Act of 1964, so that if
there was evidence of essential elements under s. 27 to pass a good title in the said
car to the appellant, the appellant acquired a good title as against the respondents
and the court had no power to order restitution under the Larceny Act, 1916. If
the court decided that at the time of the disposition of the car to him the appellant
C was a person carrying on a business which consisted wholly or partly of purchasing
motor vehicles for the purpose of offering them or exposing them for sale he should
still be treated as a private purchaser for the purpose of s. 27 of the Hire-Purchase
Act 1964, if he acquired the car for his own use and not for sale. It was contended
on behalf of the respondents before the justices that the court had power to hear
the application notwithstanding that such hearing took place on a date subsequent
D to the conviction of Mingay, because the respondents had made an application to
the justices at the time of the said conviction and the court deferred dealing
with the matter so that notice of the application should be given to the appellant.
It was also contended that s. 45 of the Larceny Act, 1916 was not affected by
s. 27 of the Hire-Purchase Act 1964 and that a distinction must be drawn between
the larceny of a motor vehicle and the sale of a motor vehicle.

E The justices were of the opinion that they had jurisdiction to hear the application, as oral application was made to the court at the time of the conviction of
Mingay which the court directed should be made on notice to the appellant.
Whether they should entertain the application or leave the respondents to their
civil remedies was within their discretion, which they exercised by dealing with
the application. The court found there was no dispute that up to March, 1965, the
F appellant was a person carrying on a business which consisted wholly or partly
of purchasing motor vehicles for the purpose of offering or exposing them for
sale and there was a strong probability that at the time of the disposition of the
said motor car to him the appellant had not ceased to carry on such a business.
They further found that he was not a purchaser in good faith as he had on his
own admission noticed that Mingay owed money on the vehicle and he had shut
G his eyes to the possibility that there was a hire-purchase agreement. They found
that he was a trade purchaser within the meaning of s. 29 (2) of the Hire-Purchase
Act 1964, and held that he could not at the same time be both a trade purchaser
and a private purchaser. The justices were of the opinion that they had the power
to make the order for restitution of the motor car to the respondents, and made
the order.

H
M. *Dyer* for the appellant.

J. M. *Rankin* for the respondents.

WIDGERY, J., delivered the first judgment at the invitation of LORD
PARKER, C.J., in which, after having stated the nature of the proceedings and
I reviewed the facts, he said: The submissions which are made today by counsel
for the appellant fall into two main groups. In the first instance he contends that
the justices had no jurisdiction to make this restitution order, either because there
were third parties involved, or because, if they had jurisdiction to make a
restitution order at all, they should have made it on the occasion when Mr.
Mingay was convicted, namely in October, 1965, and not on Feb. 10, 1966, some
six months later.

The jurisdiction of magistrates to make a restitution order comes in the first
instance from the Magistrates' Courts Act, 1952, s. 33 (1), which provides:

" Where any person has been summarily convicted under this Act of an offence that is not a summary offence, the court may make the like order for the restitution of property as might have been made by the court before which the offender would have been tried had he been tried on indictment."

One goes from there to the powers which exist after trial on indictment, and these are found in s. 45 of the Larceny Act, 1916:

" (1) If any person guilty of any such felony or misdemeanour as is mentioned in this Act . . . is prosecuted to conviction by or on behalf of the owner of such property, the property shall be restored to the owner or his representative. (2) In every case in this section referred to the court before whom such offender is convicted shall have power to award from time to time writs of restitution for the said property or to order the restitution thereof in a summary manner."

Then certain provisos are added to which I need not refer. Subsection (3) throws some light on the matters before this court, where it provides that:

" On the restitution of any stolen property if it appears to the court by the evidence that the offender has sold the stolen property to any person, and that such person has had no knowledge that the same was stolen, and that any moneys have been taken from the offender on his apprehension, the court may, on the application of such purchaser, order that out of such moneys a sum not exceeding the amount of the proceeds of such sale be delivered to the said purchaser."

It is unnecessary in my judgment to do more than point out that within the section itself one finds, in sub-s. (3), that it is clearly contemplated that a restitution order may be made although the goods have left the possession of the principal offender and have gone into the hands of a third party. Not only is there a positive internal indication that the section applies in that way, but there is certainly nothing to the contrary in any of the three subsections to which I have referred, and in my judgment there is no substance whatever in the submission of counsel for the appellant that the justices lacked jurisdiction to make an order of this kind merely because the goods in question had ceased to be in the possession of the offender whose conviction made the making of the order possible.

Equally, as it seems to me, there is no substance in the other submission of counsel for the appellant that the jurisdiction of the magistrates was dependent on their making their order on the day when the conviction was entered, and as part, as it were, of those proceedings. It is true that s. 45 contemplates that restitution orders shall sometimes be made in a summary form, and no doubt frequently will be made at the close of the prosecution itself. Here, however, the matter having been raised at that time, the justices took the step of adjourning in order to give the third party an opportunity of being heard, and I can see nothing at all in the section to indicate that that is wrong.

There is some support in authority for the view which I have expressed. First of all in *R.* v. *Macklin* (1) there was an arraignment of a prisoner on several indictments to which he pleaded guilty, and then an application was made by counsel for the prosecution to the court for an order on several pawnbrokers into whose hands the stolen goods had come. Counsel appeared for the pawnbrokers, and claimed to be heard on behalf of the pawnbrokers. ALDERSON, B., said (2):

" I do not think I ought to object to hear what the pawnbrokers have to say against this application, and if I ought to hear them, I do not see why I should not hear their counsel."

Indeed, the matter was argued out between the three parties and that forms an admirable precedent for the kind of proceeding which took place in the present case.

---

(1) (1850), 5 Cox, C.C. 216.   (2) (1850), 5 Cox, C.C. at p. 216.

A There is some further authority in the case of *Vilmont* v. *Bentley* (3). That was a civil action for the recovery of stolen goods, and in the course of proceedings reference was made to the inter-relation between the injured person's civil rights in the civil courts, and his right to a restitution order. LORD ESHER, M.R., in the course of his judgment said (4):

B "The legislature, in order to stimulate persons from whom goods had been stolen to prosecute the thief, intervened between the original owner and a purchaser in market overt, who, but for the enactment, would have had an absolute property in the goods. Having to choose between the two, the legislature thought that, for the general public benefit, they ought to prefer the original owner if he prosecuted the thief to conviction, but only in that case, and if he did so, ' the property shall be restored to the owner, and the

C court shall order the restitution of the property '. Such an order can only be made against the person who has the goods in his possession at the time when it is made. But the making of such an order is left to the discretion of the court, though the previous part of the section (5) says that the property shall be restored."

D That extract demonstrates the necessity for any order being made against the person presently in possession of the goods, and also the element of discretion in making it.

Finally I think that a reference can usefully be made to the case of *Leicester & Co.* v. *Cherryman* (6), which was a case of a restitution order being made against pawnbrokers under the Pawnbrokers Act, 1872. RIDLEY, J., in the

E course of his judgment, referring to s. 100 of the Larceny Act, 1861, said (7):

"But it is the practice in courts of assize, and, I believe, in courts of quarter sessions also, not to make an order of restitution in a case where the circumstances require that there should be terms imposed unless the prosecutor consents to compensate the person who has possession of the stolen property."

F In the result I am quite satisfied, speaking for myself, that the justices had jurisdiction here so far as the matters referred to by counsel for the appellant are concerned. I think it right to add, however, that justices should hesitate before exercising this jurisdiction if the value of the goods in question is substantial, or if the application for an order is likely to raise difficult questions of law. There are many cases, and indeed this case may have been one, where the civil courts are

G really better equipped to try an issue of this kind, and I would deprecate any suggestion in the future that magistrates should be too anxious to exercise their discretion to deal with such issues. However, in simple matters it is no doubt right that they should, and there being no error of law in what was done in this case, I would not upset their decision on either of those grounds.

In passing I should mention that in the course of argument a further question

H has arisen which has been said to go to the jurisdiction of the magistrates, and that question arises from the words in s. 45 (1) of the Larceny Act, 1916, referring to an offender being prosecuted to conviction by or on behalf of the owner of the property. It has been suggested in argument that if this were a normal police prosecution, the offender would not have been prosecuted by or on behalf of the owner of the property, and that no jurisdiction to make the order would arise. I

I think that it would be quite improper for this court on this case to embark on any consideration of those matters, because, there is no finding of fact in the case as to how the prosecution was commenced. There is certainly no finding of fact which would enable us to investigate any question whether it was by or on behalf of the respondents, and it is not a question which was taken before the justices

(3) (1886), 18 Q.B.D. 332.   (4) (1886), 18 Q.B.D. at p. 327.
(5) I.e., the Larceny Act, 1861, s. 100.
(6) [1904-07] All E.R. Rep. 794; [1907] 2 K.B. 101.
(7) [1907] 2 K.B. at p. 103; [1904-07] All E.R. Rep. at p. 796.

or raised in the case at all. Accordingly, I propose not to say anything more   **A** about that issue.

The appellant's second group of submissions arose out of the provisions of the Hire-Purchase Act 1964. This is an Act which in s. 27 contains a somewhat complex provision with regard to the ownership of property which is subject to a hire-purchase agreement, and which is the subject of larceny. The appellant had contended before the magistrates that he was entitled as a matter of civil right   **B** to retain this Jaguar motor car because he was protected by s. 27 (2) which provides that where a disposition of a motor vehicle subject to a hire-purchase agreement is made to a private purchaser and he is a purchaser in good faith and without notice of the agreement

" that disposition shall have effect as if the title of the owner . . . to the vehicle had been vested in the hirer . . . immediately before that disposition."   **C**

The appellant was contending that he was a private purchaser of this car and that he was also a purchaser in good faith within the meaning of the section, but the justices have found on what counsel for the appellant admits was evidence sufficient for this purpose that the appellant was not a private purchaser and in any case did not buy in good faith. Accordingly, it is impossible for him to support   **D** any contention of ownership based on the Hire-Purchase Act 1964, and those are matters which this court need not pursue further.

For those reasons in my judgment the appeal should be dismissed.

SALMON, L.J.: I agree. I add a word on two points only. An argument was addressed to us that the restitution order was a nullity in as much as the magistrates lacked jurisdiction, since this was not a private prosecution. The   **E** argument was that the power conferred under s. 45 of the Larceny Act, 1916 depended on the prosecutor being a private prosecutor and could have no application when the police prosecuted. The short answer to that point is that there is nothing from beginning to end in this case which indicates that the prosecutor was not the respondent. The case is quite silent as to the identity of the prosecutor. If the appellant desired to avail himself of this point, it was   **F** absolutely necessary for him to show something in the case to support it; there is nothing. Had the Case Stated shown that this was a police prosecution, I am not by any means convinced that the mere fact that the point was never taken below would prevent this court from considering it, for it goes to jurisdiction. Since, however, the Case Stated says not a word about it, it is unnecessary for me to deal with the point, and I do not propose to do so.   **G**

As to discretion, the magistrates clearly had a discretion, because the cases show that whether or not a restitution order should be made is a matter of discretion. In my judgment however criminal courts should not normally exercise their discretion to make a restitution order where there are serious competing claims between third parties. There is very little risk of discretion being so exercised at assize or quarter sessions, which are overwhelmed with criminal   **H** work. It is, however, particularly important that magistrates should not exercise their discretion in the circumstances which I have described. They are not by training or experience a suitable tribunal for deciding what may be very complicated questions of law and fact. As far as the law is concerned they may have the advice of their clerk, but even so there are many questions of law and fact which are beyond the competence—I say this with no disrespect—of most   **I** benches of magistrates to decide.

In this case, there were extremely complicated questions of law and fact, but it did not matter very much which way the justices decided them because they found that the appellant was not a purchaser in good faith, so that even if all the other questions had been answered in his favour, that one finding was fatal to his case. That finding depended entirely on the view which the magistrates took of him when they heard him give evidence, and they are, I am sure, very well able to decide whether a witness is worthy of belief or whether he is not.

Another reason why it is normally undesirable that criminal courts should exercise their discretion so as to make a restitution order when there are competing claims by third parties is that there is no appeal from such an order. Large sums of money may be at stake, and it seems to me most unfortunate that the persons concerned should be deprived of an opportunity of appealing should they wish to do so.

In the ordinary case there are no competing claims and no difficulties can arise; there is no doubt about the ownership of the goods, there is no doubt that once the thief has been convicted the goods re-vest in the owner by virtue of s. 24 of the Sale of Goods Act, 1893. It matters not, as WIDGERY, J., has said, that the thief has parted with possession to another man who may be perfectly innocent. On the thief's conviction an order for restitution is usually made and properly made in favour of the true owner. Since the Hire-Purchase Act 1964, however, it is quite plain that there may be competing claims between third parties which, as I have said, may raise difficult questions of fact and law. When goods are obtained by fraud or other wrongful means not amounting to stealing, difficult questions of fact and law may arise as to who is entitled to the goods. Section 45 of the Larceny Act, 1916 by express words makes it clear that in such cases the legislature does not wish the criminal courts to decide questions of that sort. They are very much akin to the sort of questions that can now arise under s. 27 of the Hire-Purchase Act 1964.

It is not only in those cases, however, that competing claims may arise. There may be cases in which goods have undoubtedly been stolen but in which the ownership of the goods is by no means plain, as when A and B have both claimed to be the owner. It would normally be quite wrong for a criminal court to embark on an investigation to discover the true owner. Such matters are essentially for the civil courts. Sometimes it is important to have pleadings and discovery to arrive at the true result and this is not available in the criminal courts. It is only in the simple case where there is no doubt about the ownership of the goods and no question arises under the Hire-Purchase Act 1964 that normally the discretion to make a restitution order can properly be exercised.

This however is the first time that this court has had occasion to lay down the principle on which the justices' discretion should be exercised, and since I have come to the clear conclusion that no injustice has been caused by the magistrates' order I agree that this appeal should be dismissed.

LORD PARKER, C.J.: I also agree but would add only one further word on the matter of discretion. It seems to me that whenever difficult questions of law affecting title are likely to arise as, for instance—and this is only an illustration—by reason of the Hire-Purchase Act 1964, no criminal court whether assizes, quarter sessions or magistrates should embark on the consideration of making a restitution order. If that is so as regards assizes and quarter sessions, then, and with no disrespect whatever, it is all the more so in regard to magistrates, particularly when the value of the property in question, as in this case, is not even within the jurisdiction of the county court.

Appeal dismissed.

Solicitors: *Gillhams*, agents for *Norton, Peskett & Forward*, Lowestoft (for the appellant); *Edwin Coe & Calder Woods* (for the respondents)

[*Reported by* S. A. HATTEEA, ESQ., *Barrister-at-Law.*]

JOLLIFFE v. EXETER CORPORATION.

[QUEEN's BENCH DIVISION (Lawton, J.), October 17, 18, November 10, 1966.]

Compulsory Purchase—Compensation—Injurious affection—Construction of ring road—Stopping-up order of existing street made by Minister of Transport, at request of highway authority, in exercise of statutory powers under which he was not liable for compensation—Loss of frontage and access to plaintiff's garage premises fronting on existing street—Whether injurious affection— Whether highway authority liable for compensation—Lands Clauses Consolidation Act, 1845 (8 & 9 Vict. c. 18), s. 68.

The plaintiff was the owner of garage premises fronting Coombe Street, which had originally been a busy road leading off the main road at the outskirts of Exeter and providing a way round that avoided the central business area. The city corporation, which was also the highway authority, decided to construct an inner ring road which would involve the demolition of property and the blocking of the street on which the plaintiff's premises fronted. The corporation accordingly made a compulsory purchase order under the Highways Act, 1959, and the Acquisition of Land (Authorisation Procedure) Act, 1946, and this order was duly confirmed by the Minister of Transport. The corporation had themselves no power to stop up the relevant street, but they requested the Minister to exercise his powers to this effect under s. 49 of the Town and Country Planning Act, 1947, and the Minister in consequence made a stopping-up order. As a result of these orders the plaintiff's garage was left at the dead end of a cul-de-sac instead of on a fairly busy through road, and the stopping-up of the street and the construction of a pavement necessitated the loss of twenty feet of his frontage and the blocking of one entrance to his forecourt. The lack of room for turning vehicles at the end of the cul-de-sac caused difficulties of access which would have lowered the value of the premises even if used for industrial and commercial purposes other than those of a garage. The plaintiff claimed to be entitled to compensation from the corporation under the Lands Clauses Consolidation Act, 1845, s. 68*.

Held: the plaintiff was entitled to compensation because—

(i) the loss of frontage, the blocking of one of the forecourt entrances and the difficulty of access each constituted damage that amounted to injurious affection within s. 68 of the Act of 1845, although the plaintiff's damage by loss of business did not constitute injurious affection within s. 68 (see p. 261, letter F, post).

(ii) the stopping-up order was merely a step in the execution of the corporation's works for the ring road, and these works were the cause of the plaintiff's land being injuriously affected; the corporation, having counselled and procured the Minister to make the stopping-up order, were liable to pay compensation for that step in the execution of their works, notwithstanding that the Minister in making the order had exercised powers under the Town and Country Planning Act, 1947, s. 49, under which he himself was not liable for compensation (see p. 261, letter I, and p. 262, letter C, post).

Caledonian Ry. Co. v. Walker's Trustees ([1881-85] All E.R. Rep. 592) applied.

[As to compensation for injurious affection, see 10 HALSBURY's LAWS (3rd Edn.) 147, para. 256; and for cases on the subject, see 11 DIGEST (Repl.) 148-152, *271-289.*

For the Lands Clauses Consolidation Act, 1845, s. 68, see 3 HALSBURY's STATUTES (2nd Edn.) 919.

For the Town and Country Planning Act, 1947, s. 49, see 25 HALSBURY's STATUTES (2nd Edn.) 558, 559, and for the superseding provisions of s. 153, s. 156 of the Town and Country Planning Act, 1962, see 42 ibid., 1120, 1124.]

---

* Section 68, so far as material, is set out at p. 261, letter A, post.

C.A. [1967] 2 All E.R.

Reversed. 1099.

A Case referred to:

> *Caledonian Ry. Co.* v. *Walker's Trustees*, [1881-85] All E.R. Rep. 592; (1882), 7 App. Cas. 259; 46 L.T. 826; 46 J.P. 676; 11 Digest (Repl.) 149, *274.*

Action.

B This was an action, brought by writ issued on Feb. 25, 1965, whereby the plaintiff, Russell Harvey Jolliffe, sought a declaration that he was entitled to claim compensation under s. 68 of the Lands Clauses Consolidation Act, 1845, for injurious affection caused to his land and premises known as Gayton's Garage, Coombe Street, in the city of Exeter, caused by the execution of the works of construction of a highway on land acquired under the City of Exeter (Coombe Street—James Street) Compulsory Purchase Order, 1960, which was made on May 24, 1960, by the defendants. The facts are set out in the judgment.

C

A. B. Dawson for the plaintiff.

L. F. Read for the defendant corporation.

Cur. adv. vult.

Nov. 10. **LAWTON, J.,** read the following judgment: In this case the plaintiff is the owner of the freehold land and premises known as Gayton's **D** Garage, Coombe Street, in the City of Exeter. The defendants are the highway authority for the City and County of Exeter. The plaintiff submits that he is entitled to compensation under s. 68 of the Lands Clauses Consolidation Act, 1845, because his land and premises have been " injuriously affected " by the construction of an inner ring road in the City of Exeter. The defendants deny that the plaintiff's land and premises have been injuriously affected in any way which **E** could give him compensation under the Act of 1845; but say that if they have been so affected the damage has been caused by the Minister of Transport in the exercise of his powers under s. 49 of the Town and Country Planning Act, 1947, and that compensation cannot be paid for any damage caused by the Minister when acting under that section.

Before 1962 Coombe Street, Exeter, was part of a road known as B.3183. The **F** citizens of Exeter and those visiting the city probably found it a most convenient road as it led off the main A.30 road on the outskirts of Exeter on the east side, avoided the busy shopping and business areas of the city and joined the A.30 again by the Exe Bridge. The plaintiff's land and premises were situated alongside this road. For many years he had run a garage business there. The frontage on to this road was about 130 feet. Some of the buildings were contiguous with **G** the pavement of Coombe Street; the remainder were set back a little so as to form a forecourt where there were petrol pumps. There were stores, a workshop and bays for greasing. The first floor was used as a residential flat. The garage was well sited for attracting trade.

Unfortunately for the plaintiff, however good Coombe Street may have been for bringing customers to his premises, it was not adequate for keeping enough **H** traffic away from the centre of Exeter. Sometime before 1960 the defendants as the highway authority decided to construct an inner ring road for the relief of congestion. Plans were prepared which provided for the new road to cut across Coombe Street near the plaintiff's garage premises. The scheme involved the pulling down of property and the blocking of Coombe Street. It followed, the law being what it is, that nothing could be done until various statutory powers had **I** been used. The first step was to acquire compulsorily the property which was blocking the line of the new road and the second to stop up Coombe Street and other streets. Both steps required the co-operation of the Ministry of Transport. The Highways Act, 1959, s. 214, empowered the defendants to acquire land compulsorily for the construction of the proposed inner ring road, but only if the plans for it had been made or approved by the ministry. On May 24, 1960, the defendants' council resolved that a compulsory purchase order should be made for the construction of that part of the inner ring road with which I have been concerned in this case. The compulsory purchase order was duly sealed and sent to the ministry for confirmation; and it was confirmed with a few minor modifications on Feb. 27, 1962, and published on Apr. 4, 1962. This order was made under powers given by the Highways Act, 1959, and the Acquisition of Land (Authorisation Procedure) Act, 1946, and was stated to be "for the purpose of constructing a highway" and the plan envisaged the stopping-up of Coombe Street near the plaintiff's garage. The defendants themselves had no statutory powers which would have enabled them to stop up Coombe Street, but the Minister of Transport had. By letter dated Feb. 8, 1961, the defendants asked the Minister to exercise his powers which derive from s. 49 of the Town and Country Planning Act, 1947. The Minister did as he was asked and made the Stopping-up of Highways (City and County of the City of Exeter) (No. 3) Order, 1962 (1). Following the making of this order and the doing of the necessary road works to implement it the plaintiff's garage premises were no longer on a fairly busy through road: they were at the dead end of a cul-de-sac. Further, as a result of the stopping-up of Coombe Street and the defendants' construction of a pavement at the dead end the plaintiff lost about twenty feet of his frontage on to that street and one exit from his forecourt was blocked. The stopping-up of Coombe Street has had serious effects on his business. He had had a garage business in a fairly busy through road; now he had one in a dead end. Mr. King, a chartered surveyor, who gave evidence for the plaintiff, told me that the turning of Coombe Street into a cul-de-sac had affected the value of the premises as premises, apart altogether from the bad effects on the business carried on there. The reason for this was that anyone acquiring the premises for industrial or commercial purposes, which is what they were structurally fit for, would suffer inconvenience in egress and ingress. Use for commercial and industrial purposes involves nowadays comings and goings with vehicles and parking for the purpose of loading and unloading. At the dead end of the cul-de-sac there would not be much room for turning. The problem of access, said Mr. King, would affect the value of the plaintiff's premises.

After the making of this order the defendants started on the construction of the inner ring road. They built it on an embankment about seven to eight feet above the level of Coombe Street. They appreciated that their road scheme and works had had a bad effect on the plaintiff's business. They were advised that the plaintiff was not entitled to any compensation, but they did what they could to mitigate such damage as he had suffered by granting him a building lease of a plot of land on the side of the inner ring road near the dead end of Coombe Street and by allowing him to build a one way access way from this plot into his premises in Coombe Street. The Inland Revenue also recognised the bad effects which the new road had had on the plaintiff's premises by reducing their rateable value from £350 to £250. Notwithstanding what has been done by the defendants and the Inland Revenue the plaintiff contends that he is entitled in addition to be paid compensation under s. 68 of the Lands Clauses Consolidation Act, 1845: the defendants say that he is not.

The long title of the Act of 1845 is:

"An Act for consolidating in one Act certain provisions usually inserted in Acts authorising the taking of lands for undertakings of a public nature."

Section 1 provides:

"This Act shall apply to every undertaking authorised by any Act . . . which shall authorise the purchase or taking of lands for such undertaking, and this Act shall be incorporated with such Act; . . ."

The Act of 1845 contains detailed provision for the assessment of compensation for lands purchased or taken and clearly contemplated that compensation should

---

(1) S.I. 1962 No. 1276. A length of Coombe Street, and James Street, were closed permanently in 1962 pursuant to this order. The defendants pleaded that this permanent closure was made on Nov. 8, 1962, and alleged that it was effected and authorised solely by reason of the stopping-up order.

A be paid (and I quote from s. 68 omitting immaterial words) " in respect of any lands . . . injuriously affected by the execution of the works . . .". " Works " were defined by s. 2 as meaning " the works . . . of whatever nature, which shall by the special Act be authorised to be executed ". By " special Act " was meant " any Act which shall be hereafter passed which shall authorise the taking of lands for the undertaking to which the same relates ". It follows

B that the plaintiff must establish that his premises have been injuriously affected by the doing of the road works for which the defendants were authorised to take lands. The plaintiff has contended that he has established this. The defendants put forward four reasons for contending that he has not: first, because his premises have not been injuriously affected at all; secondly, that if they have been so affected, the cause was not the doing of the road works but the

C making of the stopping-up order; thirdly, that no compensation under s. 68 is payable in respect of premises injuriously affected by a stopping-up order; and fourthly, if compensation is payable, the Minister of Transport is the party responsible, not these defendants.

  The first question then for me to decide is whether there is any evidence that, in the words of s. 68, " any lands " belonging to the plaintiff have been

D " injuriously affected by the execution of the works ". If there is, he may be entitled to make a claim for compensation to the lands tribunal which nowadays has the task of assessing compensation under s. 68. In my judgment on the admitted facts and Mr. King's evidence the plaintiff has established a prima facie case that by reason of what was done in and to Coombe Street as a stage in the construction of the new inner ring road (i) the plaintiff has lost about fifteen to

E twenty feet of the frontage of his forecourt on to Coombe Street; (ii) one of the entrances to that forecourt from Coombe Street has been blocked to vehicular traffic by the pavement which has been put down by the defendants; (iii) ingress and egress into and from the plaintiff's forecourt has been made more difficult for vehicles; and (iv) he has lost business. Does any of this amount to the kind of damage for which compensation can be given? In my judgment items (i), (ii),

F and (iii) above do; item (iv) does not. My attention was called to the tangle of decisions, all nearly a hundred years old, which deal with the construction of the words " injuriously affected by the execution of the works ". The last of them was *Caledonian Ry. Co.* v. *Walker's Trustees* (2). In that case the House of Lords reviewed all the relevant earlier cases and tried to reconcile them. I will content myself with saying that I have tried to apply to this case the propositions

G formulated by LORD SELBORNE, L.C., in that case (3).

  What caused the plaintiff's premises to be injuriously affected? They were doomed when the defendants published the Minister of Transport's confirmation, with modifications, of the compulsory purchase order dated May 24, 1960. What had to be done for the construction of the inner ring road as planned by the defendants and approved with modifications by the Minister would now be done.

H The first thing to be done, was to stop up Coombe Street, because until it was closed the defendants could not start their road works on the line of the inner ring road. From the outset the defendants intended that this street should be stopped up; it was part of their plan. They asked the Minister to exercise his powers and he did so. If the Minister had not stopped up Coombe Street the plaintiff's premises would not have been injuriously affected in the way that they were—

I but there would not have been an inner ring road either.

  In my judgment the stopping-up of the highway was nothing more than a step in the execution of the authorised works—a step which the defendants counselled and procured the Minister to take. Having counselled and procured that step they must take responsibility in law for it. Part of that responsibility is to pay compensation to those whose premises have been injuriously affected. This responsibility is placed on the defendants by reason of the provisions of the

  (2) [1881-85] All E.R. Rep. 592; (1882), 7 App. Cas. 259.
  (3) [1881-85] All E.R. Rep. at p. 594; (1882), 7 App. Cas. at p. 273.

Highways Act, 1959, s. 222 and the Acquisition of Land (Authorisation Procedure) Act, 1946, the combined effect of which is to apply s. 68 of the Land
Clauses Consolidation Act, 1845. In my judgment it matters not that the Minister
himself when making the stopping-up order exercised powers under s. 49 of the
Town and Country Planning Act, 1947, with the result that he was not himself
bound to pay anyone compensation. He was doing no more than giving help
to the defendants when they asked for help. In my judgment it is wrong to chop
the sequence of events into segments and to look at the segments relating to the
stopping-up of Coombe Street by itself. I have looked at the events in the round
and have come to the conclusion that both in law and commonsense the cause of
the plaintiff's premises being injuriously affected was the execution of the
authorised works. Accordingly, the plaintiff is entitled to the declaration prayed
in the statement of claim.

Declaration accordingly.

Solicitors: *G. D. Cann & Hallett*, Exeter (for the plaintiff); *Sharpe, Pritchard &
Co.*, agents for *Town Clerk*, Exeter.

[*Reported by* MARY COLTON, *Barrister-at-Law.*]

RAEL-BROOK, LTD. *v.* MINISTER OF HOUSING AND LOCAL GOVERNMENT AND ANOTHER.

[QUEEN'S BENCH DIVISION (Lord Parker, C.J., Glyn-Jones and Widgery, JJ.),
November 10, 11, December 14, 1966.]

*Town and Country Planning—Development—Use classes—Industrial building—
Light industrial building—Building previously used by local authority as a
cooking centre for provision of school meals—Subsequent use for purpose of
making shirts—Whether use by local authority was for the purpose of a " trade
or business " within definition of " industrial building "—Town and Country
Planning (Use Classes) Order, 1950 (S.I. 1950 No. 1131) and Town and
Country Planning (Use Classes) Order 1963 (S.I. 1963 No. 708), art. 2 (2),
art. 3 (1), Schedule, class III.*

At the commencement of the Town and Country Planning Act, 1947, the
existing use of a building was as a cooking centre run by a local authority
for providing school meals. The building was acquired by the appellants
and, since 1952, had been used for making shirts. Planning permission for
such use was given and was continued until the end of 1960. On appeal
against enforcement notices in respect of continuance of the use after 1960
the appellants contended that no planning permission had been required
because their use of the building and the existing use when they acquired
the building were both uses within the same use class, viz., use as a light
industrial building* for any purpose (class III of the Town and Country
Planning (Use Classes) Order, 1950), so that the change to the appellants'
use did not, by virtue of art. 3 (1) of the order†, constitute development.

Held: in determining whether a process was carried on in the course of a
trade or business, for the purposes of coming within the definition " industrial
building " in art. 2 (2) of the Town and Country Planning (Use Classes)
Order, 1950, neither the making of profit nor any commercial activity was
essential; accordingly the activity of using the building as a cooking centre
for school meals was not excluded from the definition merely because the

---

* Article 2 (2) of the order of 1950, which contains the definition of " light industrial
building " is set out, so far as relevant, at p. 264, letter G, *post.*

† Article 3 (1) reads: " Where a building or other land is used for a purpose of any
class specified in the Schedule to this order, the use of such building or other land for
any other purpose of the same class shall not be deemed for the purposes of the Act
to involve development of the land."

Distinguished in C & E COMRS v
LORD FISHER [1981] 2 All ER 147

A   activity had been carried on by a local authority and not by commercial
caterers, and therefore, no planning permission had been required in 1952,
since the appellants' user was user within the same use class nor was their
subsequent user development (see p. 266, letters F and H, post).

Appeal allowed.

B   [**Editorial Note.** The present use classes order is the Town and Country
Planning (Use Classes) Order 1963, S.I. 1963 No. 708, which has been amended
by the Town and Country Planning (Use Classes) (Amendment) Order 1965,
S.I. 1965 No. 229. For the purposes of the decision in the present case there is
no substantial difference between the present order and the order of 1950.
Reference may also be made to the Town and Country Planning Act, 1962,
Sch. 3, para. 6 and the Town and Country Planning (Use Classes for Third
C   Schedule Purposes) Order, 1948, S.I. 1948 No. 955.

As to the use of buildings for purposes falling within the same class as the
existing use, see 37 HALSBURY'S LAWS (3rd Edn.) 375, para. 478; and as to change
of user within a use class not involving development, see ibid., pp. 264, 265,
para. 368.

D   As to the meaning of trade or business in the Town and Country Planning
legislation, see 38 HALSBURY'S LAWS (3rd Edn.) 8-10, paras. 1, 2; and for cases
on the subject, see 45 DIGEST (Repl.) 383, 384, *10-20*.

For the Town and Country Planning Act, 1962, Sch. 3, para. 6, see 42 HALS-
BURY'S STATUTES (2nd Edn.) 1191.

For the Town and Country Planning (Use Classes) Order, 1950, art. 2, art. 3 (1)
E   and Schedule, class III, see 21 HALSBURY'S STATUTORY INSTRUMENTS (1st
Re-Issue) 121, 123, 124; and for the Town and Country Planning (Use Classes
for Third Schedule Purposes) Order, 1948, S.I. 1948 No. 955, see ibid., p. 31.]

Cases referred to:

Rolls v. *Miller*, [1881-85] All E.R. Rep. 915; (1884), 27 Ch.D. 71; 53 L.J.Ch.
682; 50 L.T. 597; 45 Digest (Repl.) 383, *10*.

F   *South-West Suburban Water Co.* v. *St. Marylebone Guardians*, [1904] 2 K.B.
174; 73 L.J.K.B. 347; 68 J.P. 257; 47 Digest (Repl.) 600, *149*.

Appeal.

This was an appeal* by the appellants, Rael-Brook, Ltd., for an order that the
decision dated May 3, 1966, given by the first respondent, the Minister of Housing
and Local Government (hereinafter called " the Minister "), pursuant to s. 46 of
G   the Town and Country Planning Act, 1962, with reference, inter alia, to an enforcement notice dated Dec. 29, 1964, served on the appellants by the second
respondent, Macclesfield Rural District Council, might be declared to be erroneous
in point of law and might be remitted to the Minister on certain grounds therein
stated. These grounds are not set out in this report as the decision turned on
one point only, which is stated at p. 264, letter D, post.

H   The cases noted below† were cited during the argument in addition to those
referred to in the judgment of the court.

K. F. Goodfellow for the appellants.
Nigel Bridge for the respondents.

Dec. 14. **WIDGERY, J.,** read the judgment of the court at the invitation
I   of LORD PARKER, C.J.: This is an appeal by Rael-Brook, Ltd. under s. 180 of
the Town and Country Planning Act, 1962, against a decision of the Minister of
Housing and Local Government dated May 3, 1966 on an appeal by the appellants
against two enforcement notices served by the Macclesfield Rural District Council
and relating to the use by the appellants for industrial purposes of a building and

* Appeals to the High Court against the Minister's decisions on appeals to him against
enforcement notices lie under s. 180 of the Town and Country Planning Act, 1962;
42 HALSBURY'S STATUTES (2nd Edn.) 1147.

† *Smith* v. *Anderson*, [1874-80] All E.R. Rep. 1121; (1880), 15 Ch.D. 247; *Chester
Waterworks Co.* v. *Chester Union Guardians*, (1908), 98 L.T. 701.

land at the rear of Westfield, London Road South, Poynton. Each of the notices A
required the demolition of the building in question, but it was common ground
between the parties that this requirement was misconceived and that the planning
authority had no power to require the removal of the building. Both notices
were accordingly quashed, but the Minister took the view that the use of the
premises for industrial purposes was unauthorised and granted permission
for its continued use for light industrial purposes for a limited period of three B
years. The appellants claim an unconditional right to use the building for light
industrial purposes and accordingly contend that the Minister was wrong in
imposing a time limit on them.

The appellants have used the building on the appeal site since 1952 for the
purpose of making shirts. They applied for planning permission at the outset and
obtained permission for a period of three years expiring in 1955. In the last year C
they applied for an extension of this period and were informed by the planning
authority that the use might continue until Dec. 31, 1960. On their continuing
the use beyond that date they were served with the enforcement notices referred
to. When the appeal was before the Minister the appellants sought to justify
their claim to an unconditional right of user on several grounds but the Minister
rejected them all. This court has so far heard argument on only one of these D
grounds, namely that no planning permission was required when this use was
begun in 1952. Counsel for the Minister has conceded that if the appellants are
right on this point it may be regarded as conclusive of the appeal.

The Minister has found as a fact that in 1940 the building on the appeal site
was used by a local authority as a cooking centre for the provision of school meals.
This use continued for some six years thereafter and it is common ground that E
this may be regarded as the " existing " use for the purposes of the Town and
Country Planning Act, 1947, at the time when the appellants took possession in
1952. The appellants' contention is that this use and their own use came within
class III of the Schedule to the Town and Country Planning (Use Classes) Order,
1950, (1) namely " Use as a light industrial building for any purpose ", and that
art. 3 (1) of that Order accordingly provided that a change from one use to the F
other should not amount to development so as to require planning permission.
" Industrial building " and " light industrial building " are defined in art. 2 (2)
of the Order as follows:

" ' industrial building ' means a building . . . used for the carrying on of
any process for or incidental to any of the following purposes, [I mention
only the relevant ones] namely:—(a) the making of any article . . ., or (b) the G
altering, repairing, ornamenting, finishing, cleaning, washing, packing, or
canning, or adapting for sale . . . of any article . . . being a process carried
on in the course of trade or business . . .

" ' light industrial building ' means an industrial building . . . in which the
process carried on or the machinery installed are such as could be carried
on or installed in any residential area without detriment to the amenity of H
that area . . ."

It is common ground that the appellants' use of the building falls within class III.
It seems clear that if the building had been used in 1940 as a cooking centre
by a commercial firm of caterers it would have been an industrial building, since
the use involved the carrying on of processes for or incidental to the making of an
article as required by the definition. Further it is reasonably clear that the I
building would have been a light industrial building and counsel for the Minister
has not really sought to contest this. The real issue is whether the earlier use
by a local authority was use as an industrial building at all, having regard to the
further requirement in the definition that the processes must be " carried on in
the course of trade or business ". The Minister has decided this point against the
appellants on the short ground that an activity of a local authority providing

(1) S.I. 1950 No. 1131.

A meals under statutory powers is not carried on in the course of trade or business. There is no finding whether payment was received from the children or their parents for the meals supplied.

Counsel for the appellants contends that, while the absence of payment and of any element of profit-making prevents the activity from being a " trade ", such absence does not exclude it from the wider alternative of " business ". He

B submits that in planning legislation, which is generally more concerned with activities than with personalities, it would be absurd if two buildings used for identical activities were treated differently merely because one occupier was working for profit and the other not. Counsel accepts that the words " being a process carried on in the course of trade or business " are intended to restrict the scope of the definition of " industrial building " and to exclude from it

C workshops which are used for purposes of recreation or the pursuit of hobbies, but he contends that there is no authority which requires us to hold that profit making is an essential feature of business.

Counsel for the Minister also stresses the importance of the restriction which these words impose on the scope of the definition of " industrial building ", and contends that practical effect cannot be given to them unless the presence of

D profit making or some commercial activity is accepted as the test to distinguish between those processes which are, and those which are not, carried on in the course of trade or business. He points out that this definition of " industrial building " first appeared (2) in the Distribution of Industry Act, 1945, and was subsequently adopted (3) by s. 119 of the Town and Country Planning Act, 1947, and submits that when these statutes and the Use Classes Order are considered

E together it becomes clear that the proper distribution of industry is an object of the legislation, and that it is consequently understandable that the same activities may require different treatment when carried out by a static local authority and when undertaken by a company which is not tied to a particular locality.

We have no doubt that the restriction imposed by the words " carried on in the course of trade or business " is an important one. There are a great many

F enthusiastic amateur engineers who have workshops in which they tune motor cars and carry out all manner of processes which are concerned with the making altering repairing ornamenting or finishing of some article, and a serious proliferation of industrial activity in residential areas might follow if all such workshops could be turned over to commercial industrial activity without any control by the planning authority. Counsels' arguments in this case both recognise that the

G broad distinction desired to be drawn is that between the amateur and the professional, but it does not follow that commercial motives provide the final or only test. It is clear from authority that the making of profit is not an essential feature of carrying on a business unless the particular context so requires. In *Rolls* v. *Miller* (4) a charitable institution called a " Home for Working Girls " was held to carry on a business in breach of a covenant in a lease against use for

H business purposes and COTTON, L.J., said (5):

" There may be a great many businesses which are not trades, and although, in my opinion, receiving payment for what is done, using what you are doing as a means of getting payment with a view to profit . . . is certainly material in considering whether what was being done is, or is not, a business, yet, in my opinion, it is not essential that there should be payment in order

I to constitute a business."

LINDLEY, L.J., added (6):

---

(2) See s. 15 (1) of the Act of 1945; 25 HALSBURY'S STATUTES (2nd Edn.) 704.
(3) 25 HALSBURY'S STATUTES (2nd Edn.) 637. See now s. 221 (1) of the Town and Country Planning Act, 1962; 42 HALSBURY'S STATUTES (2nd Edn.) 1180; applying s. 21 of the Local Employment Act, 1960; 40 ibid., 1128.
(4) [1881-85] All E.R. Rep. 915; (1884), 27 Ch.D. 71.
(5) [1881-85] All E.R. Rep. at p. 918; (1884), 27 Ch.D. at p. 85.
(6) [1881-85] All E.R. Rep. at p. 920; (1884), 27 Ch.D. at p. 88.

A

" When we look into the dictionaries as to the meaning of the word ' business ', I do not think they throw much light upon it. The word means almost anything which is an occupation and not a pleasure; anything which is an occupation or duty which requires attention is a business."

We have also been referred to *South-West Suburban Water Co.* v. *St. Marylebone Guardians* (7), where the defendants as occupiers of a school demanded a supply of water for domestic purposes, but were met by the contention that " domestic purposes " did not include a supply for any trade manufacture or business and that the carrying on of the school by the defendants as part of their public duty constituted a business. BUCKLEY, J., said (8):

B

" I agree that these premises were used to carry on a business. If I were to define the business carried on I would say it is the business of providing for, maintaining, and training pauper children, and that this is none the less a business because it is carried on, not for profit, but, on the contrary, at a large expense."

C

In the present case the context in which the words " trade or business " are found is a very different one, but it is interesting to compare the definition of " industrial building " in the Use Classes Order with the definition of " factory " in s. 151 of the Factories Act, 1937 (9). Each is concerned with premises used for a process for or incidental to the making of an article or the altering repairing ornamenting finishing cleaning washing or adapting for sale of an article, and the similarity of language is such that the draftsman of the Order must have had the terms of the statute in mind, yet he appears to have discarded the qualification in the statute that the premises must be premises in which the work is carried out " by way of trade or for purposes of gain ", and substituted a qualification that the processes shall be carried on in the course of " trade or business ". This, in our view, is some indication that the purposes of gain are not an essential of the " business " referred to.

D

E

In our opinion neither the making of profit nor any commercial activity is an essential in order that a process may be carried on in the course of trade or business for the purpose of the definition of " industrial building " in the Use Classes Order. Hence the activity of a local authority which exhibits all the other possible features of a business is not excluded on that account. Even on the meagre findings of fact in the present case it can be inferred that the provision of school meals by the local authority in possession of the building from 1940 to 1946 was an occupation as opposed to a pleasure (to quote LINDLEY, L.J. (10)), that it was continuous rather than sporadic and that it was a serious undertaking earnestly pursued for the purpose of fulfilling a duty assumed by the occupier. Without attempting to decide that these features must necessarily all be present in order that an activity may amount to a business for present purposes, we are satisfied that they suffice in this case.

F

G

We shall accordingly allow this appeal and remit the matter to the Minister for reconsideration in the light of this opinion.

H

Appeal allowed. Case remitted. Leave to appeal granted.

Solicitors: *S. Buchman* (for the appellants); *Solicitor, Ministry of Housing and Local Government* (for the respondents).

[*Reported by* N. P. METCALFE, ESQ., *Barrister-at-Law.*]

I

---

(7) [1904] 2 K.B. 174.   (8) [1904] 2 K.B. at p. 180.
(9) See 9 HALSBURY'S STATUTES (2nd Edn.) 1113, and for the replacing section, s. 175 of the Factories Act, 1961, see 41 ibid., 402.
(10) [1881-85] All E.R. Rep. at p. 920; (1884), 27 Ch.D. at p. 88.

BRADFORD *v.* ROBINSON RENTALS, LTD.

[DEVON ASSIZES (Rees, J.), October 18, 19, 20, 24, 1966.]

Negligence—Cause of action—Foreseeability—Type of injury reasonably fore-seeable but precise nature of injury not reasonably foreseeable—Frostbite—Plaintiff required by employers to make long journey in unheated motor van in severe weather conditions—Some injury to health reasonably foreseeable—Plaintiff permanently injured by frostbite—Liability of employers.

The plaintiff, who was fifty-seven years of age, was employed by the defendants as a radio service engineer. He travelled over his area in a motor van and his normal daily work involved frequent stops at customers' houses and intervals spent in maintenance service in them. In January, 1963, at the time when it was known to the defendants that the weather was likely to be very severe, he was sent on a journey to change a colleague's old van; the round journey was between 450 and 500 miles and would involve about twenty hours' driving. The old van and the new van were unheated, and the radiator of the old van was defective. The plaintiff expressed the view that the journey was hazardous and ought not to be undertaken by him. He was nevertheless instructed to go. As a result of cold on the journey, and despite precautions taken by the plaintiff, he suffered injury by frostbite, which was unusual in England.

Held: the plaintiff had been called on to carry out an unusual task that would be likely to expose him to extreme cold and considerable fatigue, and thereby the defendants had exposed him to a reasonably foreseeable risk of injury; although the injury that he in fact suffered was not itself usual, yet it was an injury of the kind that was foreseeable (viz., injury from exposure to cold), and, as liability did not depend on the precise nature of the injury suffered being itself reasonably foreseeable, the defendants were liable to the plaintiff in negligence (see p. 269, letters F and G, and p. 270, letter I, post).

Hughes v. *Lord Advocate* ([1963] 1 All E.R. 705) applied.

[As to the effective cause of an accident, see 28 HALSBURY'S LAWS (3rd Edn.) 27-29, para. 25, and SUPPLEMENT; and for cases on the subject, see 36 DIGEST (Repl.) 34-39, *158-185.*

As to a master's duty not to expose his servant to unnecessary risk, see 25 HALSBURY'S LAWS (3rd Edn.) 508-510, para. 976.]

Cases referred to:

Hughes v. *Lord Advocate*, [1963] 1 All E.R. 705; [1963] A.C. 837; [1963] 2 W.L.R. 779; Digest (Cont. Vol. A) 1143, *89a.*

Overseas Tankship (U.K.), Ltd. v. *Morts Dock & Engineering Co., Ltd.*, [1961] 1 All E.R. 404; [1961] A.C. 388; [1961] 2 W.L.R. 126; Digest (Cont. Vol. A) 1148, *185a.*

Smith v. *Leech Brain & Co., Ltd.*, [1961] 3 All E.R. 1159; [1962] 2 Q.B. 405; [1962] 2 W.L.R. 148; Digest (Cont. Vol. A) 464, *155a.*

Action.

In this action Oliver Hugh Bradford, the plaintiff, claimed damages against Robinson Rentals, Ltd., the defendants, in respect of permanent injury which he suffered caused by frostbite resulting from prolonged exposure to cold during a journey in the course of his employment by the defendants in severe weather conditions on Jan. 9 and 10, 1963. The defendants denied that they were in breach of their duty of care to the plaintiff and that the plaintiff's injuries were caused in the manner alleged, and alternatively alleged contributory negligence by the plaintiff. Subject to liability, damages (including special damages) were agreed at £2,500.

In January, 1963, the plaintiff who was about fifty-seven years old and an experienced radio service engineer, was employed by the defendants in that capacity at their branch in Exeter. Between September, 1962, when he had

Distinguished in TREMAIN *v.* PIKE, [1969] 3 All E.R. 1303

joined that branch, and Jan. 8, 1963, his duties required him to travel about   A
an area allotted to him in a small Austin van and to visit the homes of customers
to repair and maintain radio and television equipment. The area extended from
Exeter to Brixham and to Okehampton and some distance beyond. He made
between twelve and twenty visits to customers' homes each day, so that his
journeys were short and he spent a substantial part of the day indoors. On
Jan. 8, 1963, the plaintiff was told (on the instructions of Mr. Jones the branch   B
manager) to drive an old Austin van, used by a colleague, to the defendants' head
office at Bedford to change it for a new one and to return in the new one. The
return journey was to be made on Jan. 9, 10, 1963, it being contemplated that
the plaintiff should reach Bedford by noon on Jan. 9, 1963. The weather at the
time was very cold throughout the country with snow and ice on the roads. It
was important for Mr. Jones, from the point of view of the branch, to effect the   C
change of vehicles quickly, or the opportunity might be lost. The plaintiff, whom
the defendants knew to be a reliable and conscientious man, protested that in the
weather conditions prevailing at the time it was utterly impossible to reach
Bedford by noon on Jan. 9 and that it might not be possible to get through to
Bedford at all. The plaintiff made enquiries about road conditions. He again
saw Mr. Buer (the defendants' senior branch engineer), who had told him to make   D
the journey, and informed him that the Automobile Association's advice was
that the proposed journey should not be made at all unless it were essential, and
that in the existing road conditions it was not possible to say whether it would be
possible to get through to Bedford on the following day. The plaintiff was told
to return at 6 p.m. to take delivery of the old Austin van. He did so, and while
waiting, told Mr. Buer the effect of a B.B.C. broadcast, viz., that road conditions   E
were such that motorists on non-essential journeys should keep off the roads;
and the plaintiff also protested to Mr. Jones against the journey. Mr. Buer then
told the plaintiff (and it was the fact) that the old van's heater had developed
a leak as a result of which it had been necessary to disconnect it, that the radiator
was leaking, that it did not contain and could not be filled with an anti-freeze
mixture and that it would be necessary for him to take (as he did in fact take)   F
a can of water to top up the radiator in the course of the journey.

    At 7 a.m. on Jan. 9, the plaintiff set out on the journey to Bedford, a distance
of some 240 miles. He took every reasonable precaution against cold. From
Honiton to Bicester road conditions were very bad indeed. In some places snow
was piled up on each side of the road to a height of fifteen feet. There were many
abandoned vehicles and few moving vehicles. The temperature inside the van was   G
" like a refrigerator ". Because there was no heater the plaintiff's breath formed
a coating of ice on the windscreen so that he was obliged to keep a window open
throughout the journey. He had to stop frequently to refill the radiator, the
water in which froze at the bottom and boiled at the top. He reached Bicester (a
distance of some two hundred miles) at about 5.30 p.m. He was shaking with cold,
his hands and feet were extremely cold and painful, and he was exhausted. After   H
describing his condition, he obtained permission from the defendants' head office
to spend the night at Bicester. He drove the forty miles to Bedford the following
morning in about 3½ hours in worse weather. The new van had no heater and
the plaintiff had, therefore, to keep a window open throughout the return journey.
Weather and road conditions were much as they had been on the previous day,
but his hands and feet became more painful and swollen. He had to stop and   I
cut a ring off his finger which due to swelling was causing him pain. The return
journey of about two hundred miles (a shorter route) took about ten hours; in
all he drove about 13½ hours that day. On arrival he could move only with
difficulty owing to pain in the soles of his feet and his hands were so painful that
he could not use them to undress himself or hold a cup. On Jan. 14, 1963, he
consulted his doctor and underwent treatment. He continued to do his normal
work, though with considerable difficulty, until Feb. 2, 1963. Except for five
days in May, 1963, the plaintiff did not work again. The medical evidence

established that the plaintiff sustained permanent injury to his hands and feet
due to cold injury, though this was probably not caused by the actual freezing
of the tissues involved.

W. G. Wingate, Q.C., and D. W. Powell for the plaintiff.
R. I. Kidwell and A. R. Tyrrell for the defendants.

REES, J., stated the nature of the proceedings and found the facts which are
summarised at p. 267, letter I, to p. 268, letter I, ante, during the course of which
he stated that he was satisfied (i) that on Jan. 8, 1963, the defendants knew that
the weather on the following day was likely to be extremely cold with many roads
covered with ice and snow and temperatures at or about freezing point and (ii)
that the cold injury sustained by the plaintiff was caused by prolonged exposure
to very low temperatures at or about freezing point, and that contributing factors
were exposure of the hands to wind admitted through the open window of the
Austin van, stagnation of the circulation owing to the necessity for prolonged
maintenance of the driving position, and extreme fatigue arising from two days'
driving over long distances in adverse conditions. REES, J., continued: So far
as the principles of law applicable to this case are concerned, they may be shortly
stated. The defendants, as the plaintiff's employers, were under a duty at common
law to take reasonable steps to avoid exposing the plaintiff to a reasonably
foreseeable risk of injury. It was strongly argued on behalf of the defendants that
injury to his health suffered by the plaintiff in this case by " frostbite " or cold
injury was not reasonably foreseeable. There was no evidence that before the
plaintiff started the journey either the plaintiff himself or the defendants'
servants, Mr. Jones or Mr. Buer, actually contemplated that the plaintiff might
suffer from " frostbite " if he were required to carry out the journey. However, I
am satisfied that any reasonable employer in possession of all the facts known to
Mr. Jones and Mr. Buer on Jan. 8, 1963, would have realised—and Mr. Jones
and Mr. Buer must have realised—that if the plaintiff was required to carry out
the journey he would certainly be subjected to a real risk of some injury to his
health arising from prolonged exposure to an exceptional degree of cold. No doubt
the kinds of injury to health due to prolonged exposure to an exceptional degree
of cold are commonly thought to include, for example, that the victim might
suffer from a common cold or in a severe case from pneumonia, or that he might
suffer from chilblains on his hands and feet. The question which I have to
consider is whether the plaintiff has established that the injury to his health
by " frostbite " (and I use the lay term for convenience), which is admittedly
unusual in this country, is nevertheless of the type and kind of injury which
was reasonably foreseeable. The law does not require that the precise nature
of the injury must be reasonably foreseeable before liability for its consequences
is attributed. The point is thus dealt with in a convenient way in SALMOND
ON TORTS (14th Edn.) at p. 719:

" (i) Type of damage must be foreseen. It has been made plain that the
precise details of the accident, or the exact concatenation of circumstances,
need not be foreseen. It is sufficient if the type, kind, degree or order of harm
could have been foreseen in a general way. The question is, was the accident
a variant of the perils originally brought about by the defendant's negligence?
The law of negligence has not been fragmented into a number of distinct
torts."

The above extract conveniently states the principle to be followed in the present
case since the decision in Overseas Tankship (U.K.), Ltd. v. Morts Dock &
Engineering Co., Ltd. (1). Valuable statements of the same principle are to be
found in the report of the Scottish Appeal to the House of Lords in Hughes v.
Lord Advocate (2). This case related not to the duty owed by an employer to his

(1) [1961] 1 All E.R. 404; [1961] A.C. 388.
(2) [1963] 1 All E.R. 705; [1963] A.C. 837.

employee but to the duty owed by the Post Office to children allured to an open manhole in a carriageway protected by a canvas shelter containing some lighted lamps. Two children played with the lamps, of which one fell into the manhole and caused an explosion, thus severely burning one of the children. It was contended that although some injury by burning might have been foreseen, yet the explosion causing the massive burning could not have been reasonably foreseen. LORD JENKINS said this (3):

> " It is true that the duty of care expected in cases of this sort is confined to reasonably foreseeable dangers, but it does not necessarily follow that liability is escaped because the danger actually materialising is not identical with the danger reasonably foreseen and guarded against. Each case much depends on its own particular facts."

LORD GUEST said (4):

> " In order to establish a coherent chain of causation it is not necessary that the precise details leading up to the accident should have been reasonably foreseeable: it is sufficient if the accident which occurred is of a type which should have been foreseeable by a reasonably careful person."

Now what were the facts which were known to the defendants through Mr. Jones and Mr. Buer which could reasonably lead them to foresee injury to the health of the plaintiff by exposure to cold? My findings of fact may be summarised thus. They knew that the weather during Jan. 9 and 10 was likely to be severe with temperatures at or about freezing point with ice and snow on the roads; that the round journey of about 450 to 500 miles in two days would be likely to involve the plaintiff in about twenty hours of driving, when the old Austin van was unheated and the new Austin van was also likely to be unheated, so that certainly the senior engineer, Mr. Buer, should know that the plaintiff would be required to drive with a window open in both directions; that the defective radiator and the lack of anti-freeze liquid in the old Austin meant that the plaintiff, on the outward journey, would be required to stop and add water at intervals which might well be frequent; that the plaintiff was being sent on a task wholly outside his normal daily duties which involved frequent stops at customers' houses. From all these facts it is plain in my judgment the defendants knew that the plaintiff was being called on to carry out an unusual task which would be likely to expose him for prolonged periods to extreme cold and considerable fatigue. They also knew that the plaintiff, then aged about fifty-seven years and whom they rightly esteemed as a sensible and conscientious man, took and vehemently expressed the view that the journey was hazardous and ought not to be undertaken by him.

I have taken into account the evidence of the expert witness called by the defendants who said that up to the year 1963 only about ten per cent. of the commercial vehicles were fitted with heaters, although about forty to fifty per cent. is the present percentage, and that during the snow-bound period, which included January, 1963, commercial vehicles did continue to use the roads.

In all these circumstances I hold that the defendants did, by sending the plaintiff out on this journey, expose him to a reasonably foreseeable risk of injury arising from exposure to severe cold and fatigue. This breach of duty caused the plaintiff to suffer from " frostbite " or cold injury with serious consequences. Even if there had been—and there is not—evidence that the plaintiff was abnormally susceptible to " frostbite " as opposed to the more common sequels of prolonged exposure to severe cold and fatigue, he would be entitled to succeed on the ground that a tortfeasor must take his victim as he finds him (see the judgment of LORD PARKER, C.J., in *Smith* v. *Leech Brain & Co., Ltd.* (5)). In so

---

(3) [1963] 1 All E.R. at p. 710; [1963] A.C. at p. 850.
(4) [1963] 1 All E.R. at p. 714; [1963] A.C. at pp. 855, 856.
(5) [1961] 3 All E.R. 1159; [1962] 2 Q.B. 405.

far as any of the allegations of contributory negligence are still persisted in by the defendants, I find that they fail. Accordingly the issue of liability is determined in favour of the plaintiff.

Judgment for the plaintiff for agreed damages of £2,500.

Solicitors: *Dixon, Ward & Co.,* agents for *A. H. Whitwam,* Seaton (for the plaintiff); *Greenwoods* (for the defendants).

[*Reported by* DEIRDRE MCKINNEY, *Barrister-at-Law.*]

G. (an infant) *v.* COLTART.

[QUEEN'S BENCH DIVISION (Lord Parker, C.J., Salmon, L.J., and Widgery, J.), November 17, 1966.]

Criminal Law—Evidence—Admissibility—Similar offences—Larceny—Evidence showing guilt of accused on charge of which she had been acquitted.

If an accused charged with a criminal offence is acquitted by a court of competent jurisdiction, the prosecution on a subsequent charge brought against that accused cannot seek to prove that he was guilty of the first charge, contrary to the verdict of the court on that charge, in order to obtain the benefit of any conclusion which might flow from such guilt (see p. 274, letter H, and p. 276, letters C and F, post).

The appellant, aged fifteen years, was employed as a domestic servant by Mr. and Mrs. T., with whom was staying Mrs. D. On Sept. 23, 1965, the appellant was told by Mrs. T. that Mrs. D. was returning to South Africa the next day. At 9 a.m. on Sept. 24, the appellant's room was searched and a considerable quantity of jewellery and articles was found there belonging to Mr. and Mrs. T. and Mrs. D. The appellant admitted to the police that she had taken all the goods, but said that she had always intended to return them to their owners. She was charged with larceny of Mrs. D.'s goods and larceny as a servant of the goods of Mr. and Mrs. T. The prosecution took the view that Mrs. D.'s case could not be proceeded with as she had left England, and the appellant was acquitted on that charge. On the charge of larceny as a servant, which was heard after the appellant had been acquitted on the first charge, the prosecution in order to negative the appellant's story that she intended to return the goods, relied on the evidence that Mrs. T. had told the appellant on Sept. 23 that Mrs. D. was returning to South Africa the next day and that, in spite of this, the appellant did not return Mrs. D.'s goods by that time. On appeal against conviction (which was based on that evidence),

Held: the evidence had been wrongly admitted for the reason stated at letter E, above and accordingly the conviction would be quashed (see p. 276, letters B, C and F, post).

Dictum of CHANNELL, J., in *R.* v. *Ollis* ([1900] 2 Q.B. at p. 783) applied.

Appeal allowed.

[As to evidence in a criminal case of similar offences by the prisoner, see 10 HALSBURY'S LAWS (3rd Edn.) 442-444, paras. 818, 819; and for cases on the subject, see 14 DIGEST (Repl.) 420-425, *4090-4125.*]

Cases referred to:
R. v. *Cokar,* [1960] 2 All E.R. 175; [1960] 2 Q.B. 207; [1960] 2 W.L.R. 836; 124 J.P. 313; 44 Cr. App. Rep. 165; Digest (Cont. Vol. A) 375, *4975a.*

R. v. *Ollis,* [1900-03] All E.R. Rep. 733; [1900] 2 Q.B. 758; 69 L.J.Q.B. 918; 83 L.T. 251; 64 J.P. 518; 14 Digest (Repl.) 422, *4104.*

Case Stated.

This was a Case Stated by the justices for the county of Dorset acting in and for the Petty Sessional Division of Blandford in respect of their adjudication as a juvenile court sitting at Blandford on Mar. 31, 1966, and Apr. 21, 1966*.

On Oct. 18, 1965, an information was preferred by the respondent, chief inspector F. Coltart, against the appellant, Truda Cynthia Gill, charging that she had committed two offences of larceny, viz., larceny from a dwelling-house between Sept. 21 and 24, 1965, of the property of Mrs. Catherine Doig, contrary to s. 13 of the Larceny Act, 1916, and larceny as a servant between Aug. 24, 1965, and Sept. 24, 1965, from her employer, Andrew Tod, contrary to s. 17 (1) of the Larceny Act, 1916. The respondent offering no evidence on the charge of larceny from Mrs. Doig contrary to s. 13 of the Larceny Act, 1916, owing to Mrs. Doig having returned to South Africa, the justices dismissed that summons. On the application of the respondent the summons under s. 17 (1) of the Larceny Act, 1916, was amended to allege that the property was that of Andrew Tod and another, and the justices then proceeded to hear the summons in respect of this offence and found the following facts. At the material time the appellant was employed by Mr. Tod as a servant. The appellant knew when Mrs. Doig was leaving Mr. and Mrs. Tod's house to return to South Africa and, accordingly, as she had not returned Mrs. Doig's property to her before she departed the appellant must have intended to and did in fact steal it. Accordingly, the justices held that they were entitled to reject, and they did reject, as untrue the explanation of the appellant on the information respecting the alleged offence in relation to the property of Mr. and Mrs. Tod that she did not intend to steal the goods but intended to replace them; and they found that the appellant was guilty of larceny as alleged, contrary to s. 17 (1) of the Larceny Act, 1916; they further found that they were entitled to hear evidence showing, or tending to show, that the appellant was guilty of stealing from Mrs. Doig notwithstanding that they had found her not guilty of that offence.

It was contended for the appellant before the justices that, as the justices had found the appellant not guilty of the charge of larceny of Mrs. Doig's property, contrary to s. 13 of the Larceny Act, 1916, and had dismissed that summons prior to hearing the second summons alleging larceny of goods the property of Mr. Tod and another, the respondent was not entitled to lead evidence to show that the appellant knew that Mrs. Doig was leaving Mr. and Mrs. Tod's house on Sept. 24, 1965, to go to South Africa, nor to allege that, as the appellant had not returned or offered to return the goods allegedly the property of Mrs. Doig and the subject of the charge under s. 13 of the Larceny Act, 1916 (on which charge they had found the appellant not guilty), before Sept. 24, 1965, that was evidence from which they could find that she intended to steal these items from Mrs. Doig, because after Mrs. Doig had left Mr. and Mrs. Tod's house to return to South Africa, the appellant would have had no opportunity to restore her goods to her. It was further contended that the respondent had no right to open the case in that way since the matter was res judicata, the court having only a few minutes previously found the appellant not guilty of the offence which the respondent was now saying that he intended to try to show that she had committed. Paragraph 1016 of ARCHBOLD'S CRIMINAL PLEADING, EVIDENCE AND PRACTICE (35th Edn.) which was cited by the respondent, could not possibly be authority for the proposition that one could call evidence tending to show the commission of an offence by an accused person which the court had found her not to have committed, and that passage from ARCHBOLD was designed to cover different circumstances, e.g., proof of conduct which had not been made the subject of a charge although it might yet be, or of previous offences which had been proved. It was contended before the justices by the respondent that para. 1016 of ARCHBOLD was authority for the view that he was entitled to open the case in the way

---

* See, for prior proceedings, *R. v. Blandford JJ., Ex p. G. (an infant)*, [1966] 1 All E.R. 1021.

A　in which he had done, and to adduce the evidence which he proposed to lead from the witnesses for the prosecution as to the appellant in fact having taken property from Mrs. Doig although the justices had earlier dismissed the summons for larceny because " the mere fact that evidence adduced tends to show the commission of other crimes does not render it inadmissible if it be relevant to an issue before the jury and it may be so relevant if it bears on the question whether the acts

B　alleged to constitute the crime charged in the indictment were designed or accidental or to rebut a defence which would otherwise be open to the accused ". The defence which the respondent indicated that he had in mind to rebut was lack of intent to steal.

The justices found the appellant guilty and placed her on probation for three years, and the appellant now appealed.

C　The authority and the case noted below* were cited during the argument in addition to the cases referred to in the judgment.

Brian Galpin for the appellant.

M. Dyer for the respondent†.

SALMON, L.J., delivered the first judgment at the invitation of LORD
D　PARKER, C.J.: This is an appeal by way of Case Stated from the Blandford justices. On Mar. 31, 1966, they convicted the appellant of larceny of certain goods belonging to her employer, Mr. Andrew Tod, and his wife; the appellant now takes the point that the justices wrongly admitted evidence against her, and, indeed based the conviction on that evidence, and that the conviction is accordingly bad. The facts of the case can be shortly stated. The appellant was a
E　girl of fifteen years of age employed as a domestic servant by Mr. and Mrs. Andrew Tod. In September, 1965, a Mrs. Doig, who was Mr. Tod's aunt, was a guest in the Tod household. On the afternoon of Sept. 23, the appellant was told by Mrs. Tod that Mrs. Doig was returning to South Africa, and would be leaving the house the following morning. At nine o'clock on the morning of Sept. 24, the appellant's room was searched and a considerable quantity of
F　jewellery and other articles were found there belonging to Mr. and Mrs. Tod, Mrs. Doig, and other members of the household. The appellant was charged on two summonses, one in respect of the alleged larceny of Mrs. Doig's goods, and the other in respect of the alleged larceny of Mr. Tod's goods. When she was seen by the police, she admitted that she had taken all the goods which had been found in her room, but said that she had no intention of stealing them; she had
G　always intended to return the goods to their owners. This is a defence which is not infrequently put forward, but which very rarely succeeds. When the appellant appeared before the magistrates, she pleaded guilty to both summonses, but it was obvious, or should have been obvious, from the documents before the magistrates that they ought not to accept the pleas because she was saying: I intended to return the goods. If she had no intention permanently to deprive
H　the owners of the goods, she could not be guilty of stealing them. An attempt was made to alter the pleas, but the justices would not have it, and she was dealt with on both summonses. Those convictions were brought to this court for review (1) and the convictions were quashed on the basis that the magistrates first of all ought not to have accepted the pleas of guilty, and, secondly, ought to have allowed her to change her pleas. So the matter went back before the
I　magistrates and they made a second attempt to deal with the case on Mar. 31, 1966, the previous attempt having taken place in the autumn of 1965.

This was a very simple case indeed, and there were only very few mistakes which it would have been possible for the prosecution to have made; they seem

---

* ARCHBOLD'S CRIMINAL PLEADING, EVIDENCE AND PRACTICE (36th Edn.), paras. 1016, 1028; *Maxwell* v. *Director of Public Prosecutions*, [1934] All E.R. Rep. 168; [1935] A.C. 309.

† Counsel for the respondent on this appeal was not the counsel acting for the prosecution in the proceedings before the magistrates.

(1) See [1966] 1 All E.R. 1021.

to have succeeded in making all of them. Mrs. Doig was in South Africa;
the prosecution took the view that that made it impossible to go on with the
summons in respect of Mrs. Doig's goods; but the appellant had admitted that
she had taken them and the only issue was—what was her intention?   I find it
difficult to understand why it should have been decided to drop that summons.
I quite agree that if the appellant, when she went into the witness box, changed
her story completely and said for the first time that Mrs. Doig had given her
permission to take the goods, or had given her the goods, the summons might have
been dismissed; but it seems to me that there was a very strong case in respect
of the charge concerning Mrs. Doig's goods, even although Mrs. Doig was absent
in South Africa.   Taking the view that Mrs. Doig's case could not be proceeded
with, the prosecution either elected or consented to that case being dealt with
first and the appellant being acquitted.   They took this course knowing that
they wanted to rely on the appellant's guilt in that case for the purposes of
obtaining a conviction in the second case.   I should have thought that it was
fairly obvious that they should have had the Tod case dealt with first, or have
asked the magistrates to keep the papers in the Doig case on the file.   It seems
very strange to me and certainly unfortunate that they agreed to the Doig
summons being dismissed, and a verdict of not guilty being entered in that case
before the Tod case was heard.

In the Tod case, in order to negative the appellant's story that she intended to
return the goods, the prosecution sought to rely on the evidence that Mrs. Tod
had told the appellant on the afternoon of Sept. 23, 1965, that Mrs. Doig was
returning to South Africa the next morning and that, in spite of this, the appellant
did not return Mrs. Doig's goods by 9 a.m. the next morning.   That said the
prosecution was very strong evidence that she intended to keep them and had
accordingly stolen them.   The prosecution said that, as she took the Tod jewellery
and the Doig jewellery at about the same time, and as it was plain that she
intended to keep the Doig jewellery, she could not have had any other intention
in respect of the Tod jewellery.   There was a discussion apparently whether
evidence along those lines was admissible.   It is plain, I think, that what the
prosecution were seeking to do was to show that the appellant was really guilty
in respect of the charge of which she had just been acquitted in order to obtain
a conviction in the Tod case.   I, for my part, am quite satisfied that this cannot
be done.   I doubt whether, if the prosecution had gone on without seeking to
rely on that evidence, they would have had very much difficulty, but I just do
not know about that.   They pressed to put the evidence in, and they succeeded in persuading the magistrates that they might do so, and indeed the
magistrates say in terms that they are satisfied that the appellant had no intention
of returning Mrs. Doig's jewellery, and, therefore, had stolen it, and accordingly,
say the magistrates, " We are satisfied that she had no intention of returning the
Tod jewellery ".

There is very little authority on this point.   I think, however, on general
principles that it would be quite wrong to allow the prosecution, in order to
obtain a conviction in case B, to seek to show that the accused was guilty in
case A, after the accused had been acquitted in case A.   I have no doubt, that,
even although the accused is acquitted in case A evidence called against
the accused in case A could be relevant in case B, for example to show what
his intent was in case B. It can never be permissible, however, in case B to
rely on the guilt of the accused in case A if he has been acquitted in case A.
In the present instance, unless the appellant was guilty of stealing Mrs. Doig's
goods, the evidence about her taking Mrs. Doig's goods and being told that Mrs.
Doig was leaving on Sept. 24, 1965, would have been quite irrelevant.   The
only relevance of the evidence tendered by the prosecution was to show that she
was in fact guilty of that offence; and I am satisfied that this is what they
cannot do.   Reliance has been placed on *R.* v. *Ollis* (2).   That was a case in

(2) [1900-03] All E.R. Rep. 733; [1900] 2 Q.B. 758.

which the accused had given one worthless cheque and had obtained a sum of £3 or thereabouts on the faith of the cheque. He was then prosecuted for having obtained the money by false pretences, viz., by putting forward this worthless cheque as a good cheque when he knew that it was worthless. He was acquitted on that charge. The next day he was tried on three more charges in respect of three other cheques on all of which he obtained money and all of which were worthless. His story apparently was that he believed that the cheques would be met because he had expectations of receiving some commission which would be paid into the bank, and would certainly be sufficient to cover the cheques and much more besides. The jury disagreed at the first trial in respect of the three cheques. When he was retried, counsel for the prosecution successfully applied to call the same evidence that had been called against the accused on his unsuccessful prosecution in respect of the first cheque. He was then convicted, and the Court of Crown Cases Reserved upheld the conviction holding that the evidence about the first cheque was relevant and admissible. It seems to me, however, that the distinction between that case and the present one is that, in the present case, the only relevance of the evidence tendered was to prove guilt in the Doig case, whereas in *R.* v. *Ollis* (3), the prosecution were able to say: we are not alleging, let alone relying on, the accused's guilt in respect of the first cheque; we are relying on the fact that the first cheque was not met only to show what the accused's knowledge or state of mind was when he gave the other three cheques. It seems to me that this is plain from the judgment of Channell, J. (4):

> " If the evidence of Ramsey were wanted to show that the prisoner had committed a fraud on Ramsey, that not being the fraud for which he was then indicted, it would be inadmissible, but it is not wanted for that purpose, but to show if possible that frauds were committed on Rawlings and Morris. Its admissibility in my opinion depends solely on whether it was relevant for that purpose. The main question on each indictment was whether the prisoner knew that the cheque he drew would not be honoured. If he did, the fraudulent intent was proved. If he drew several cheques, and knew that some of them were dishonoured, then, as to any cheques which he subsequently got cashed, there was cogent evidence of a fraudulent intent."

That, I think, is the principle; it is, perhaps, a little difficult to make it fit the facts of that particular case, but that passage from Channell, J.'s judgment clearly enunciated the principle on which the majority of the court proceeded.

There is one other case to which perhaps I ought to refer, and that is *R.* v. *Cokar* (5). That was a rather strange case of a man who was charged with entering a dwelling-house by night with intent to steal. The prosecution successfully applied to cross-examine him to show that, on a previous occasion, he had been charged (although acquitted) with being on premises by night with intent to steal. The question there turned on the true construction of proviso (f) to s. 1 of the Criminal Evidence Act, 1898:

> " A person charged and called as a witness in pursuance of this Act shall not be asked, and if asked shall not be required to answer, any question tending to show that he has committed or been convicted of or been charged with any offence other than that wherewith he is then charged, or is of bad character, unless [and then there is an absolute prohibition to which there are three exceptions, the first one being]—(i) the proof that he has committed or been convicted of such other offence is admissible evidence to show that he is guilty of the offence wherewith he is then charged."

---

(3) [1900-03] All E.R. Rep. 733; [1900] 2 Q.B. 758.
(4) [1900] 2 Q.B. at p. 783; cf. [1900-03] All E.R. Rep. at p. 742.
(5) [1960] 2 All E.R. 175; [1960] 2 Q.B. 207.

The Court of Criminal Appeal laid down that to cross-examine him solely with a view to showing that he had been charged, is not permissible. The evidence elicited by such cross-examination is not really evidence of anything, and certainly is not evidence " that he has committed or been convicted " of any other offence. If the prosecution cannot cross-examined an accused in circumstances such as those to show that he has been charged though acquitted, still less can it cross-examine him to show that he was guilty of the charge of which he was acquitted. If the prosecution may not elicit such evidence in cross-examination, clearly it may not lead such evidence.

I, for my part, feel no doubt at all that this evidence was wrongly admitted; the conviction, as the magistrates state in their Case, was based on that evidence, and should be quashed.

WIDGERY, J.: I agree. If an accused charged with a criminal offence is acquitted by a court of competent jurisdiction, it seems to me clear that the prosecution on a subsequent charge brought against that accused cannot seek to prove that he was guilty of the first charge, contrary to the verdict of the court on that charge, in order to obtain the benefit of any conclusion which might flow from such guilt. That is exactly what the prosecution sought to do here, because, as far as I can see, the incident relating to Mrs. Doig had absolutely no relevance in regard to Mrs. Tod's jewellery except on the basis that the appellant was guilty of larceny in relation to Mrs. Doig's jewellery, and must on that account have been guilty in regard to Mrs. Tod's as well. I would draw attention, however, to the concluding words of CHANNELL, J., in *R.* v. *Ollis* (6), to which reference has already been made, where he expresses his clear opinion: " That, if the evidence was otherwise admissible, it is not the less so by reason of the former acquittal." Hence, it may well happen that evidence relating to the charge giving rise to the acquittal will be called on the subsequent charge, but, if it is so called, it will be called because it has relevance to the subsequent charge quite independently of any question whether the accused was guilty or innocent on the first charge.

LORD PARKER, C.J.: I agree with both those judgments and would only add that I do so with reluctance. I say that because I think that the appellant was plainly guilty, and secondly because I think that she would in any event benefit from the supervision of the probation officer under an order which in fact the justices made.

Appeal allowed. Conviction quashed.

Solicitors: *Lovell, Son & Pitfield*, agents for *Creech, Best & Redferns*, Sturminster Newton (for the appellant); *Sharpe, Pritchard & Co.*, agents for *J. R. Pryer*, Dorchester (for the respondent).

[*Reported by* N. P. METCALFE, ESQ., *Barrister-at-Law.*]

---

(6) [1900] 2 Q.B. at p. 783.

R. *v.* WEAVER.   R. *v.* WEAVER.

[COURT OF APPEAL, CRIMINAL DIVISION (Sachs, L.J., Brabin and James, JJ.), November 18, 1966.]

Criminal Law—Evidence—Prejudicial evidence—Editing statement by accused— Evidence prejudicial to accused inadvertently let in—Whether jury should by discharged—Discretion.

The decision whether or not to discharge the jury, where evidence prejudicial to the accused has inadvertently been let in, is one for the discretion of the trial judge on the particular facts and the Court of Appeal will not lightly interfere with the exercise of that discretion; thus, every case depends on its own facts, and it is very far from being the rule that in every case where there is inadvertent admission of evidence the jury must be discharged (see p. 280, letters G and H, post).

R. v. *Firth* ([1938] 3 All E.R. 783) distinguished on the facts.

Per CURIAM: the court recognises that, according to current practice, appropriate steps are taken in certain circumstances to avoid some fact prejudicial to the accused being mentioned; thus a statement by the accused may be edited, viz., to avoid prejudicing him an effort is made to eliminate things which are part of the evidence but which it is thought to be better that the jury should not know.   The best way for this to be done is that the evidence should appear unvarnished in the depositions taken before the magistrates; then at the trial counsel can confer and the judge can, if necessary, take his part in the matter to ensure that, if any editing is done, it is done in the right way and to the right degree (see p. 279, letters E and F, post).

[As to discharging a jury during trial when prejudicial evidence is inadvertently admitted, see 10 HALSBURY'S LAWS (3rd Edn.) 427, para. 787, notes (i)-(l); and for cases on the subject, see 14 DIGEST (Repl.) 412, *4025*, 638, 639, *6473-6485*.]

Cases referred to:

R. v. *Firth*, [1938] 3 All E.R. 783; 26 Cr. App. Rep. 148; 14 Digest (Repl.) 412, *4025*.

R. v. *Palmer*, (1935), 25 Cr. App. Rep. 97; 14 Digest (Repl.) 638, *6476*.

R. v. *Parsons*, [1962] Crim. L.R. 632.

R. v. *Peckham*, [1935] All E.R. Rep. 173; 154 L.T. 275; 100 J.P. 59; 25 Cr. App. Rep. 125; 14 Digest (Repl.) 638, *6473*.

Appeals.

These were appeals by George Weaver and John Henry Weaver against their convictions at East Sussex Quarter Sessions before the deputy chairman (F. B. PURCHAS, Esq., Q.C.) and a jury, of obtaining £15 by false pretences.   The facts are set out in the judgment of the court.

The authority and case noted below* were cited during the argument in addition to those referred to in the judgment.

J. D. Alliott for the appellants.
A. D. Gavin for the Crown.

SACHS, L.J., delivered the following judgment of the court: On Aug. 11, 1966, the appellants were convicted at East Sussex Quarter Sessions of obtaining on June 15, 1966, £15 from an antique dealer called Hay by falsely pretending that the appellant George Weaver had entered into negotiations with somebody to purchase certain antiques, that he and the appellant John Weaver needed £15 to complete the purchase and that they intended after completing the purchase to sell what was acquired to Hay.   The outline of the facts as they appeared at the trial is as follows.   Mr. Hay was an antique dealer with a shop in Brighton and, according to the evidence, which was clearly accepted by the jury, on June 15

---

* ARCHBOLD'S CRIMINAL PLEADING, EVIDENCE AND PRACTICE (36th Edn.), paras. 603, 936; *R. v. Thomas*, [1957] 3 All E.R. 350.

Dictum of SACHS, L.J., *at p.* 280, *applied in* R. *v.* PALIN, [1969] 3 All E.R. 680.

one of the appellants telephoned to him in the afternoon and asked if he would
be interested in a deal which would involve him lending the appellants £15.
That was said to be required to complete the purchase of a drum table which they
were prepared, after acquiring it, to sell to him.   Mr. Hay said that he told
them that he would only advance the £15 if he could go to the vendor with them
and they agreed with that.

A few minutes later a green van arrived with three men in it and the two
appellants got out.   Mr. Hay got into the van and perhaps not unnaturally
he regarded the two appellants with what one might call a degree of caution.
Though he handed to the appellant George Weaver the £15, he had taken first
of all the precaution of marking some of the notes.   They then drove to the
bottom of the street in Hove.   There the appellant George Weaver left, saying
he would be back shortly.   Before he returned, the appellant John Weaver
went after him and the time came when they said " We have bought the table.
It is out on the pavement and George wants you [that is to say Mr. Hay] to vet
some chairs ".   So Mr. Hay got out of the van to investigate, and without further
ado the appellant John Weaver promptly drove off.   As happens on such
occasions the witness, Mr. Hay, saw no more of them until he picked them out at
an identification parade.

When the appellant George Weaver was seen by the police, he agreed that
he had had a green van on the occasion in question, but (to cut a long story
short) he denied having had anything to do with the taking of the antiques
to a dealer.   When, however, the officer took possession from him of five £1
notes they turned out to be five of those marked by Mr. Hay.   According to
the police officer, the appellant George Weaver said " I washed them notes
yesterday ".   One way or another, subject to the points which I am now about
to discuss, when one has looked at that evidence as a whole, seen the way in
which it was presented to the jury and given due weight to the considerable
number of points put forward by the appellants, the fact remains that (as the
deputy chairman said at the end when sentencing them) they were convicted on
evidence which really was overwhelming.

On this appeal, one of the appellants took a number of points relating to the
summing-up and to the evidence which it was in his notice of appeal suggested
should be put to the court.   To those no more reference will be made than to say
that counsel for the appellants, who has conducted the case with discretion
and persuasiveness, put those points as instructed and there is nothing in them.

Then one comes to the submission, presented with full force to the court by
counsel for the appellants, that, in the course of the trial, certain matters wrongly
emerged which might, according to counsel, be taken seriously against the
appellants.   These, he submitted, related to points which he described as devastating.   His submission to this court is that howsoever those particular matters
came out in evidence, once they had thus come out, it was the duty of the presiding judge, on the application which was made, to discharge the jury so that
there could be a new trial before a different jury.   The particular matters in
question were two, and counsel for the appellants very properly not only relies on
them individually, but also on the cumulative effect of both together.

The first of them arose in this way.   Obviously following something that had
similarly been done at the magistrates' court, the police officer gave certain
evidence in a form which was artificial.   He was asked:

" ' Did you say anything by way of introduction?' A. 'I cautioned him.'
The deputy chairman: ' What did you say? ' A. I said, ' You are not
obliged to say anything unless you wish to do so, but what you say will be
put in writing and may be given in evidence '."

Then a little later counsel for the prosecution proceeded in the same way with
regard to the appellant John Weaver and got the answer: " I did. I cautioned

him and said 'What is your name?'" Then, sometime later, came cross-examination. It is not clear to this court exactly what information was in the hands of cross-examining counsel and whether he had been told by the appellants all the facts or merely something which was considerably less than the full truth. The full facts according to the evidence of the police (they are facts which do not appear to have been seriously challenged) were as follows. When the police came to speak to the appellants, they proceeded, in a fashion described as light-hearted, immediately to address the police with the words of the caution. Whether they did that in chorus or not does not appear on the material before the court; but when they did recite the caution, the police officer replied "That is the caution".

Of course those being the facts, what the police had done at the magistrates' court and later at the trial was to put forward artificial evidence—evidence not strictly accurate—simply because it was thought that it might be best for the protection of the appellants somewhat to veil the facts. This arose out of a praiseworthy desire on the part of those concerned with the prosecution to act in the way most beneficial to the appellants. When, however, counsel for the appellants proceeded to cross-examine the police officer the veil came off, and when it came off, the first reaction of counsel for the appellants was "I am not making any point as to the admissibility of any of the answers on that".

Pausing there for a moment, before considering the effects of what came into evidence in this particular case, the court recognises that, according to current practice, appropriate steps are taken in certain circumstances to avoid some fact prejudicial to the accused being mentioned. Thus the statement by the accused may be edited to avoid prejudicing the accused, an effort being made to eliminate things which are part of the evidence but which it is thought better that the jury should not know. The best way for this to be done is for the evidence to appear unvarnished in the depositions taken before the magistrates; then at the trial counsel can confer and the judge can, if necessary, take his part in the matter to ensure that, if any editing is done, it is done in the right way and to the right degree. Here that does not appear to have happened; in consequence, the true facts came out in evidence, so far as counsel was concerned, by inadvertence, and it was thus that difficulties arose. Nevertheless let this be added; there is every symptom here of the inadvertence being due to his having been given untrue or inadequate instructions by the appellants themselves.

I turn to the next point, that there came a time in the proceedings when reference was made to the address 58, Cowfield Road. At that stage, counsel for the appellants put this question to a police officer: "Was the address 58, Cowfield Road, an address provided by Mr. Hay?" He answered "No", but being desirous in the first instance of telling the true facts he then started off "It is an address . . .": at that juncture he paused, realised that what he was about to say must be prejudicial to the appellants, and said "I do not know whether it is permissible for me to say". With that the chairman said "You have been asked", and counsel for the appellants, as happens on these occasions, perhaps not fully appreciating the red light which had been proffered by the police officer, stepped out with this question "How did the matter come about?" This got the answer "It is an address which is known to the police and has been circulated". Following that answer a submission was made to the deputy chairman that the jury should be discharged and the trial should continue before a fresh jury. The deputy chairman, having listened to the submissions, in his discretion decided that the trial should continue.

When it came to the summing-up, he very neatly introduced the subject of the cautions by phraseology which it is not necessary to recite in full but which included this phrase:

"... you may have heard other expressions arising which might give you an indication that the men were familiar with certain terminology, words and procedures, and if you did not consider it carefully you might say to yourselves: ' That gives me an indication that these people know a little more about criminal matters than they have made out '. But you would be utterly wrong to do that, because you must remember that nowadays with television and publicity and books, and so on, we all know such things. Even you, probably, before you came into court, knew about the administration of justice and such matters. So I direct you that you must not allow any prejudice to creep in because you may think these men behaved in a rather silly way when being interrogated.''

Pausing for a moment, in the view of this court, that was a particularly apt way for the deputy chairman in his discretion to deal with the matter. Although other passages have been criticised by counsel for the appellants, this court thinks that, taking this position as a whole, the deputy chairman did the best he could for the appellants and did it properly on this matter.

As regards the other matter, the deputy chairman took the other view and did not mention it at all. Here, again, this is completely a question of discretion and one knows from experience the difficulties which beset judges who deal with such situations. Whatever he does is submitted to be wrong. If he mentions the matter again he is accused of error in referring to it again; if he has not mentioned it again, he is accused of not having directed the jury properly. Here this court takes the view that, just as the first matter was admirably dealt with by the deputy chairman in the summing-up, equally as regards the second matter he was quite right to omit mentioning it.

Then one comes to the final question: is there anything in this case, as put forward so persuasively by counsel for the appellants, to induce the court to say that, when he declined to discharge the jury, the discretion of the deputy chairman was wrongly exercised? Cases parallel to the present one have been brought before the Court of Criminal Appeal on a considerable number of occasions in the course of the last few years and the modern practice has become well defined. In each of those cases, of course, it has been natural for counsel for the appellant or applicant to cite a trio of cases which are mentioned in ARCHBOLD'S CRIMINAL PLEADING, PRACTICE AND PROCEDURE (36th Edn.) (1), R. v. Peckham (2), R. v. Palmer (3) and R. v. Firth (4). Those cases cannot, however, be looked at in isolation. The modern practice evolved in the light of these cases is that in essence the matter now, as has often been said (see, for instance, a passage which appears in R. v. Parsons (5)) is that the decision whether or not to discharge the jury is one for the discretion of the trial judge on the particular facts, and the court will not lightly interfere with the exercise of that discretion. When that has been said, it follows, as is repeated time and again, that every case depends on its own facts. As also has been said time and time again, it thus depends on the nature of what has been admitted into evidence and the circumstances in which it has been admitted what, looking at the case as a whole, is the correct course. It is very far from being the rule that, in every case, where something of this nature gets into evidence through inadvertence, the jury must be discharged.

This particular case is a quite common type of case. The facts were brought into the cognisance of the court by questions put by counsel for the appellants. There was nothing in those particular matters which introduced such a degree of prejudice that it could not be cured by the judge acting wisely in his discretion in the later stages.

In the view of this court, accordingly, the matter was one for the discretion of the trial judge. Nothing has happened which this court feels entitled the appellants to say that what happened was devastating. After the inadvert

---

(1) Paragraphs 603, 936.   (2) [1935] All E.R. Rep. 173
(3) (1935), 25 Cr. App. Rep. 97.   (4) [1938] 3 All E.R. 783.
                    (5) [1962] Crim. L.R. 632.

admissions of evidence everything was done which should have been done, and, accordingly, the appeal is dismissed.

Appeal dismissed.

Solicitors: *Registrar of Criminal Appeals* (for the appellants); *Town Clerk,* Hove (for the Crown).

[*Reported by* N. P. Metcalfe, Esq., *Barrister-at-Law.*]

Re CYONA DISTRIBUTORS, LTD.

[Court of Appeal, civil division (Lord Denning, M.R., Danckwerts and Russell, L.JJ.), November 4, 7, 29, 1966.]

Company—Winding-up—Fraudulent trading—Creditors of insolvent company in compulsory liquidation applied for declaration that former director personally responsible for debt to creditors—Before proceedings heard payment made by third party on behalf of director—Creditors not accountable to liquidator for money so received—Companies Act, 1948 (11 & 12 Geo. 6 c. 38), s. 332.

The Commissioners of Customs and Excise, who were creditors of C.D., Ltd., a company in compulsory liquidation, brought proceedings under s. 332* of the Companies Act, 1948, the fraudulent trading section, against a former director G. and another company of his, L. & G., Ltd., alleging that they were jointly and severally liable to pay sums amounting to £25,767 17s. 3d. in respect of unpaid purchase tax. The s. 332 proceedings were stood over pending the conclusion of criminal proceedings against G., L. & G., Ltd., C., Ltd. and a third person, and had not been restored; accordingly no declaration under s. 332 had been made. On the morning of the criminal trial, three bankers orders totalling £34,000 (the money being provided by someone other than G.) had been handed over to the commissioners in the precincts of the court, thereby discharging substantially the whole of what was then their outstanding claim for purchase tax. The effect of the payment, as appropriated by the commissioners, was to extinguish C., Ltd.'s liability for purchase tax and to reduce C.D., Ltd.'s liability for purchase tax by £18,432 9s. 7d., leaving the commissioners as creditors of C.D., Ltd. in the winding-up for £7,335 7s. 8d. The liquidator of C.D., Ltd. claimed that the sum of £18,432 9s. 7d. should be paid by the commissioners to the liquidator and that the commissioners should prove in the liquidation for the amount.

Held: (i) the receipt of the £18,432 9s. 7d. had nothing to do with the claim under s. 332 of the Companies Act, 1948, but that sum was paid in order that G. might be leniently treated in the criminal proceedings; thus the payment of the £18,432 9s. 7d. was not a realisation of an asset conferred by s. 332, and the liquidator had no title to the sum (see p. 284, letter G, p. 285, letter G, and p. 288, letter G, post).

(ii) (per Lord Denning, M.R., and Danckwerts, L.J.) when a creditor applied under s. 332, as the commissioners had done, he applied on his own account and not as trustee for the liquidator, and accordingly the £18,432 9s. 7d., even if it should have been paid by reason of the s. 332 application, would not have been impressed with a trust for the liquidator or the general body of creditors (see p. 284, letter D, and p. 285, letter E, post); and (per Russell, L.J.) although a declaration under s. 332 could benefit only the company, that did not render a creditor applying under s. 332 a trustee before any declaration was made (see p. 288, letter D, post).

* Section 332 (1), so far as material, is set out at p. 283, letter I, post.

Re William C. Leitch Brothers, Ltd. (No. 2) ([1932] All E.R. Rep. 897)
considered.

Decision of PLOWMAN, J., ([1966] 1 All E.R. 825) reversed.

[As to declarations of responsibility for fraudulent trading, see 6 HALSBURY'S
LAWS (3rd Edn.) 707, 708, paras. 1406, 1407; and for cases on the subject, see
10 DIGEST (Repl.) 953, *6555-6559*.

For the Companies Act, 1948, s. 332, see 3 HALSBURY'S STATUTES (2nd Edn.)
714.]

Cases referred to:

Leitch (William C.) Brothers, Ltd., Re (No. 1), [1932] All E.R. Rep. 892; [1932]
     2 Ch. 71; 101 L.J.Ch. 380; 148 L.T. 106; 10 Digest (Repl.) 953, *6555*.

Leitch (William C.) Brothers, Ltd., Re (No. 2), [1932] All E.R. Rep. 897; [1933]
     Ch. 261; 102 L.J.Ch. 81; 148 L.T. 108; 10 Digest (Repl.) 953, *6559*.

Patrick and Lyon, Ltd., Re, [1933] All E.R. Rep. 590; [1933] Ch. 786; 102
     L.J.Ch. 300; 149 L.T. 231; 10 Digest (Repl.) 953, *6556*.

Appeal.

This was an appeal by the Commissioners of Customs and Excise from a
decision of PLOWMAN, J., dated Feb. 16, 1966, and reported [1966] 1 All E.R.
825, that the commissioners were liable to account to the liquidator of Cyona
Distributors, Ltd., for a sum of £18,432 9s. 7d., paid to them by a third party
towards discharging liability for purchase tax; at the time of the payment a
director of the company was about to stand trial on a charge of conspiracy to
defraud the commissioners of purchase tax, and the money was paid by bankers'
drafts, handed by the director's wife to his solicitor and, on the director's instructions, delivered to the commissioners in the precincts of the court. The facts
are set out in the judgment of PLOWMAN, J.*, and are summarised in the judgment
of LORD DENNING, M.R.

J. L. Arnold, Q.C., and *J. P. Warner* for the Commissioners of Customs and
Excise.

T. P. E. Curry, Q.C., and *L. J. M. Smith* for the liquidator:

Cur. adv. vult.

Nov. 29. The following judgments were read.

LORD DENNING, M.R.: Mark Godfrey was a director of three companies
in the cosmetic trade called Cyona Co., Ltd., Cyona Distributors, Ltd., and
L. & G. Godfrey, Ltd. They ought to have paid purchase tax: but evaded it.
Mr. Godfrey conspired with others to defraud the Commissioners of Customs and
Excise of the purchase tax payable by the companies: and he did in fact defraud
them. Cyona Co., Ltd. underpaid £25,567 10s. 5d. Cyona Distributors, Ltd.
underpaid £25,767 17s. 3d. In 1956 the commissioners presented a petition to
wind up Cyona Distributors, Ltd. and a winding-up order was made. In the
course of the winding-up the commissioners issued a summons under s. 332 of the
Companies Act, 1948 against Mr. Godfrey and others asking that they should be
made personally responsible for the £25,767 17s. 3d. purchase tax unpaid by Cyona
Distributors, Ltd. and/or an order that they should pay that sum to the
commissioners.

In 1960 the summons under s. 332 was adjourned. The reason was because
the commissioners had instituted criminal proceedings against Mr. Godfrey, and
a warrant had been issued for his arrest. When Mr. Godfrey got to know of the
criminal proceedings, he fled the country. He went to Paris. Conspiracy is not
an extraditable offence. So in Paris he was free; but he did not like it there. He
wanted to get back to England. Yet he did not want to go to prison. He managed
to achieve his desire. On June 13, 1960, whilst Mr. Godfrey was in Paris, his
solicitors sent a cheque for £10,000 drawn by his wife to the commissioners

---

* See [1966] 1 All E.R. at pp. 827, 828.

A " generally on account of outstanding purchase tax ". On June 17, 1960, Mr. Godfrey returned to England and surrendered to the police. He applied to the magistrates for bail. The prosecution did not object. He was granted bail. The commissioners credited this £10,000 to the purchase tax unpaid by Cyona Co., Ltd., thus leaving £15,567 10s. 5d. owing by that company.

B On Mar. 8, 1961, Mr. Godfrey was brought before the Common Serjeant, and charged together with Cyona Co., Ltd. and L. & G. Godfrey, Ltd., with conspiring fraudulently to evade purchase tax. At the door of the court Mr. Godfrey's solicitor handed to the solicitor for the commissioners three banker's drafts amounting in all to £34,000. This was the full amount stated in the depositions as purchase tax unpaid by the Godfrey companies. The commissioners accepted the drafts and regarded the purchase tax as paid up. Counsel so informed **C** the Common Serjeant. The payment played a large part in mitigation of sentence. The Common Serjeant did not send Godfrey to prison, but fined him £22,000. The commissioners appropriated the £34,000 in this way—they appropriated the sum of £15,567 10s. 5d. in discharge of the purchase tax unpaid by Cyona Co., Ltd. That left £18,432 9s. 7d. which they appropriated in part discharge of the purchase tax unpaid by Cyona Distributors, Ltd. Now the total purchase tax **D** unpaid by that company amounted to £25,767 17s. 3d. After crediting the £18,432 9s. 7d., there was £7,335 7s. 8d. unpaid. The commissioners claim to prove in the liquidation for that sum.

The question now is whether the commissioners can retain the £18,432 9s. 7d. which they appropriated in part discharge of the purchase tax unpaid by Cyona Distributors, Ltd. The liquidator says that they cannot retain it. He says that **E** the commissioners should hand it over to him, the liquidator, so that he can use it to distribute amongst the whole body of creditors: and that the commissioners should prove in the liquidation for this amount. The judge (1) has upheld the liquidator's contention. The commissioners appeal to this court.

Let me say at once that the commissioners acted with perfect propriety. They did not compound the offences committed by Mr. Godfrey. They prosecuted **F** him and let the law take its course: but, properly enough, told the court of the restitution which had been made. We do not know who provided the moneys, £10,000 and £34,000: but it must have been someone well disposed towards Mr. Godfrey. The payer did not appropriate it towards any particular indebtedness. So the commissioners were entitled to appropriate it as they thought fit; and did so. They appropriated it in discharge of the indebtedness of Cyona Co., Ltd. **G** and in part discharge of Cyona Distributors, Ltd.

If Cyona Distributors, Ltd. had not been in the course of winding-up, no one could have complained of the appropriation. Even though that company was in the course of winding-up, nevertheless if no application had been made under s. 332, no one could have complained. The appropriation made by the commissioners would have been good. It could not have been challenged by anyone. **H** It is said, however, that because an application had been made under s. 332, the commissioners were not entitled to appropriate the sum in discharge of unpaid purchase tax by Cyona Distributors, Ltd. The part so appropriated, namely, £18,432 9s. 7d., was impressed, so it is said, with a trust for the general body of creditors: and in consequence the commissioners were bound to hand it over to the liquidator. Section 332 (1) is in these terms:

I " (1) If in the course of the winding-up of a company it appears that any business of the company has been carried on with intent to defraud creditors of the company or creditors of any other person or for any fraudulent purpose, the court, on the application of the official receiver, or the liquidator or any creditor or contributory of the company, may, if it thinks proper so to do, declare that any persons who were knowingly parties to the carrying on of the business in manner aforesaid, shall be personally responsible, without any

(1) [1966] 1 All E.R. 825; [1966] Ch. 462.

limitation of liability, for all or any of the debts or other liabilities of the company as the court may direct . . ."

In my judgment, that section is deliberately phrased in wide terms so as to enable the court to bring fraudulent persons to book. If a man has carried on the business of a company fraudulently, the court can make an order against him for the payment of a fixed sum (see *Re William C. Leitch Brothers, Ltd. (No. 1)* (2)). An order can be made either at the suit of the liquidator, etc., or of *a creditor*. The sum may be compensatory; or it may be punitive. The court has full power to direct its destination. The words are quite general: " all or any of the debts or other liabilities of the company as the court shall direct ". By virtue of these words the court can order the sum to go in discharge of the debt of any particular creditor: or that it shall go to a particular class of creditors: or to the liquidator so as to go into the general assets of the company: so long as it does not exceed the total of the debts or liabilities. Of course, when an application is made by a liquidator, the court will usually order the sum to go into the general assets, as EVE, J., did in *Re William C. Leitch Brothers, Ltd. (No. 2)* (3): but I do not think that it is bound to do so. Certainly when an application is made by a creditor who has been defrauded, the court has power, I think, to order the sum to be paid to that creditor. In short, I think that the words of the section are to be given their full width. When a creditor applies, as the commissioners did here, he applies on his own account. He does not apply as being under a trust for the other creditors or for anyone else. He is the master of his own application. He can discontinue his application, if he likes, without getting the sanction of the liquidator. No doubt, however, the liquidator should always be made a party to the proceedings: so that the interests of the other creditors can be safeguarded.

Once the suggestion of a trust is discarded, this becomes a plain case. It cannot be suggested that the commissioners were doing anything in breach of trust or anything wrong in any way. No fraudulent preference or anything of that sort. The commissioners were entitled to accept this sum in part discharge of the indebtedness of the company for purchase tax: and the liquidator has no right to gainsay it.

Apart from this, it is plain that the payment of the money had nothing to do with the application under s. 332. It was not paid by Mr. Godfrey but by someone else. It was not paid so as to get rid of the application under s. 332, but so that he might be leniently treated in the criminal proceedings. I cannot see how the liquidator can have any claim to moneys which had no concern with s. 332 at all. I would allow the appeal accordingly.

DANCKWERTS, L.J.: Cyona Distributors, Ltd. is a company in compulsory winding-up, the winding-up order having been made on July 2, 1956, on the petition of the Commissioners of Customs and Excise, who were creditors of the company in respect of unpaid purchase tax. The commissioners had been deprived of sums due for purchase tax by the fraudulent trading of a director of the company, one Mark Godfrey. In the course of the winding-up the commissioners issued a summons under s. 332 of the Companies Act, 1948, against Mr. Godfrey and a company called L. & G. Godfrey, Ltd. asking that they should be made personally responsible for the sum of £25,767 17s. 3d. purchase tax unpaid by the company, and for an order that they should pay that sum to the commissioners. The commissioners also instituted criminal proceedings against Mr. Godfrey, and he fled the country. So in 1960 the summons under s. 332 was adjourned, and to this day the summons has not been restored and no order has been made on it. Mr. Godfrey was in Paris and he wanted to return to England but he did not want to go to prison. On June 13, 1960, Mr. Godfrey's solicitors sent a cheque for £10,000 drawn by his wife in favour of the commissioners. On June 17, 1960, Mr. Godfrey returned to England and surrendered to the police.

(2) [1932] All E.R. Rep. 892; [1932] 2 Ch. 71.
(3) [1932] All E.R. Rep. 897; [1933] Ch. 261.

A He applied for bail and, as the prosecution did not object, he was granted bail. On Mar. 8, 1961, Mr. Godfrey and the two companies were brought before the Common Serjeant on charges of conspiring fraudulently to evade purchase tax. At the door of the court Mr. Godfrey's solicitor handed to the solicitor for the commissioners three banker's drafts amounting in the aggregate to £34,000, so that altogether £44,000 had been received in respect of the liability of Cyona

B Co., Ltd. and Cyona Distributors, Ltd. Mr. Godfrey was not sent to prison. He was sentenced to pay a fine of £22,000, and each of the two companies was fined £1,000. As the result of the appropriations made by the commissioners, the amount owing by Cyona Co., Ltd. was satisfied in full, and the commissioners received £18,432 9s. 7d. from the £44,000 in respect of the indebtedness of Cyona Distributors, Ltd., leaving a balance owing of £7,335 7s. 8d., for which the

C commissioners proposed to prove in the winding-up of that company. In the end the commissioners amended their proof to £7,335 7s. 8d.

The present proceedings are an ordinary summons issued by the liquidator in the winding-up of Cyona Distributors, Ltd. It is claimed on behalf of the liquidator that as a summons had been issued under s. 332 of the Companies Act, 1948 (to which the liquidator had been added as a respondent), the commissioners

D were bound to account to the liquidator for the sum of £18,432 9s. 7d. for the benefit of the general body of creditors. The effect of s. 332 was fully argued before us. We were referred (amongst other things) to *Re William C. Leitch Brothers, Ltd.* (*No. 1*) *and* (*No. 2*) (4), but those cases are distinguishable from the present case because they were instances of applications by a liquidator under the section.

In the present case the application under s. 332 is by the commissioners as

E creditors of the company. So far as the effect of s. 332 is concerned, I agree with the conclusion reached by LORD DENNING, M.R., and I do not think that the commissioners are accountable for the sum obtained by them. The situation seems to me to be quite different where a creditor begins proceedings at his own expense under the section. The creditor should be entitled to his reward. I do not think that he is acting as a trustee for the general body of creditors. In any

F case, the court would appear to have a wide discretion under the section.

In fact no order in the present case has ever been made on the summons under s. 332, and the summons remains adjourned and completely dormant. I cannot see what relevance s. 332 has to the sum of £18,432 9s. 7d. That sum was not received by the commissioners by virtue of the section, and it was not paid to them by reason of the summons taken out by them. There is no evidence that the

G £44,000 represented Mr. Godfrey's money, though the moneys were produced to help Mr. Godfrey. The object of the payments was to enable Mr. Godfrey to obtain bail and to avoid a prison sentence by being able to say that all the amounts due for purchase tax had been paid to the commissioners. In my view the commissioners were completely at liberty to accept these payments, and neither the liquidator nor the general body of creditors has any enforceable claim in

H respect of the moneys.

I would allow the appeal.

RUSSELL, L.J.: Cyona Distributors, Ltd. and another company defrauded the Commissioners of Customs and Excise of large sums of purchase tax by making false returns. Mark Godfrey—the moving spirit in both the companies

I —together with others, was charged with conspiracy fraudulently to evade purchase tax. Mr. Godfrey had left the country but wanted to return to face the music. His wife paid £10,000 on account of the purchase tax liability of the companies in the hope, that was justified, that bail would not be resisted. He pleaded guilty, and before plea in mitigation and sentence, in the hope (also justified) that he might avoid imprisonment, his solicitors paid a further £34,000 to the commissioners. This involved a payment of £18,000 odd in·or towards

---

(4) [1932] All E.R. Rep. 892, 897; [1932] 2 Ch. 71; [1933] Ch. 261.

discharge of the company's purchase tax liability. The payment was by three
banker's cheques for a total of £34,000 drawn in favour of Mr. Godfrey's solicitor,
handed to the solicitor by Mr. Godfrey's wife to be dealt with on Mr. Godfrey's
instructions, on whose instructions the cheques were endorsed over to the
commissioners by the solicitor and handed to their representative at the Old
Bailey. Who actually provided the money is not known, but there was a statement in the plea in mitigation that friends had come to Mr. Godfrey's aid. This
took place in March, 1961.

It is now said, and PLOWMAN, J., has held (5), that the commissioners must
hand the sum of £18,000 odd to the liquidator of the company, which was wound
up on the petition of the commissioners in June, 1956. This contention is based
on s. 332 of the Companies Act, 1948, first introduced in the Companies Act,
1929. This section empowers the court in a winding-up to declare that any
persons knowingly parties to the carrying on of the business of the company (a)
with intent to defraud creditors of the company or creditors of anyone else, or
(b) for any other fraudulent purpose, shall be personally responsible (without any
limitation of liability) for all or any of the debts or other liabilities of the company,
as the court may direct. This jurisdiction may be invoked by application made
by the Official Receiver or by the liquidator, or by any creditor or contributory
of the company.

The first step in the liquidator's argument against the commissioners in this
case involves the proposition that the jurisdiction of the court to declare personal
responsibility is one which can only result in an accretion to the assets of the
company in the hands of the liquidator. The commissioners contend that the
section enables the court to declare the person in question personally responsible
to particular creditors—that is, to order payment to be made either to the
liquidator as part of the fund for distribution in the winding-up, or to particular
creditors of the company or both, the court having discretion not only in respect
of the personal responsibility but also in respect of its result.

Section 332 (2) provides that the court, when it makes a declaration of
responsibility, " may " give such further directions as it thinks proper for the
purpose of giving effect to that declaration, and particularises various such
directions. These include charging the declared liability of the relevant person on
anything due to him by the company, or on any charge on assets of the company
held by or vested in either that person, or another on that person's behalf, or any
assignee (widely defined) of that person unless bona fide for value without notice
of the fraudulent trading in question.

Section 332 (4) provides that a declaration of responsibility under sub-s. (1)
is deemed to be a final judgment within s. 1 (1) (g) of the Bankruptcy Act, 1914.
As was stated by MAUGHAM, J., in *Re William C. Leitch Brothers, Ltd.* (*No. 1*) (6),
this implicitly requires the declaration to be expressed in terms of a sum of
money. Additionally, however, it is necessary that there should be someone
entitled to enforce the deemed judgment and serve a bankruptcy notice based
on it: and see the final sentence of s. 1 (1) (g) of the Bankruptcy Act, 1914, (7). It
is observed that s. 332 does not envisage as essential to its working more than a
simple declaration of personal responsibility for £x, being all or part of the debts
or other liabilities of the company: no order that the person shall pay the sum
to anyone in particular is required or in terms envisaged. This is certainly consistent with the contention that the section never envisages any outcome of its
operation other than the conferring on the liquidator as such a right to enforce
the personal responsibility as an addition to the assets of the company in his
hands.

In *Re William C. Leitch Brothers, Ltd.* (*No. 1*) and (*No. 2*) (8), before MAUGHAM,

---

(5) [1966] 1 All E.R. 825; [1966] Ch. 462.
(6) [1932] All E.R. Rep. 892; [1932] 2 Ch. 71.
(7) For s. 1 (1) (g) of the Act of 1914, see 2 HALSBURY'S STATUTES (2nd Edn.) 325.
(8) [1932] All E.R. Rep. 892, 897; [1932] 2 Ch. 71; [1933] Ch. 261.

J. and EVE, J., respectively, it is I think apparent that nobody concerned thought that there could be any but two constructions of this section: one, that any declaration must swell the general assets of the company in liquidation: the other, that any declaration must benefit as a class and be apportioned among only those creditors of the company who have been defrauded (see *Leitch (No. 1)* (9) and *Leitch (No. 2)* (10)). The sum of £6,000 was ordered to be paid to the liquidator, and which of those two constructions of the section was correct was left to be dealt with on an ordinary summons in the winding-up (not under the then equivalent of s. 332), and was so dealt with by EVE, J., in *Leitch (No. 2)* (11). It is true that EVE, J., refers to an argument on the effect of the *order* made by MAUGHAM, J., but, as I understand it, his decision was on the question which of those two constructions of the *section* was correct. MAUGHAM, J., himself in *Re Patrick and Lyon, Ltd.* (12), thought that EVE, J., was dealing with the *section*.

I have no doubt that EVE, J., was correct in holding that the section was not one which conferred the benefit of any declaration exclusively on defrauded creditors of the company. The present significance of those two cases is that it did not occur to anyone that there was a discretion in the court to decide who was to benefit from the declaration and in what proportions. The most powerful argument in favour of the contention that such a discretion exists lies in the use of the phrase " personally responsible . . . for all or any of the debts or other liabilities of the company as the court may direct ", instead of a provision empowering the court in the relevant circumstances to order the person to contribute to the assets of the company a sum equivalent to all or any of the debts, etc., etc.

There are, however, it seems to me, several objections to the suggested construction. The liquidator must get on with distribution of the assets among creditors in accordance with their admitted proofs. A declaration in favour of a defrauded creditor might be made at any time, and the enforcement by him of the declaration might bear fruit at some uncertain point of time, or in driblets, or not at all: and all outside the purview of the liquidator. How is such a system to be fitted into the scheme of liquidation? Further, if declarations may be made in favour of particular creditors, perhaps on different applications, how are priorities as among them to be solved?

I have already referred to the fact that an order to pay to any particular person is not envisaged as an essential part of the scheme of the section. Moreover it seems to me that personal responsibility for a sum stated, measured by reference to all or any of the debts of the company, is a perfectly appropriate description of responsibility *to the company* which has incurred the debts without it being in any way necessary to extend it to embrace also responsibility direct to particular creditors.

I would hesitate to construe the section in a manner which never occurred to MAUGHAM, J., and EVE, J., as a possibility. In any event, however, I am of opinion that it is not the true construction, but that s. 332 can result only in an accretion to the assets of the company for distribution in due course of winding-up.

Nevertheless this conclusion does not in my judgment justify the liquidator's claim that the commissioners are accountable for the £18,000 odd. At the end of the day I was uncertain whether it was argued for the liquidator that the receipt by the commissioners lowered, by extinguishment pro tanto, the ceiling of a possible declaration under s. 332: or whether that receipt, without lowering the ceiling, diminished by £18,000 the resources of or available to Mr. Godfrey to meet any declaration under s. 332: or whether the receipt made it less likely as a practical matter that as large an order would in the court's discretion be made under s. 332 as would otherwise have been made. On any footing it was said that the

(9) [1932] All E.R. Rep. at pp. 895, 896; [1932] 2 Ch. at pp. 77, 79.
(10) [1932] All E.R. Rep. at p. 898; [1933] Ch. at p. 265.
(11) [1932] All E.R. Rep. 897; [1933] Ch. 261.
(12) [1933] All E.R. Rep. 590 at p. 593; [1933] Ch. 786 at p. 790.

commissioners, having initiated proceedings under s. 332, or (as the judge held **A**
(13)) being persons who as creditors could initiate representative proceedings
under s. 332, could not take to themselves part of the possible fruits of such
proceedings. Their interest and their duty, it was said, were in conflict, and so
they are accountable.

This, with all respect to the learned judge (13), I cannot accept. Suppose a
creditor to have a debt of the company guaranteed by a person who has been **B**
guilty of fraudulent trading. Is he accountable for sums received from the
guarantor? Surely not. The receipt would have nothing to do with the possible
liability of the guarantor under s. 332 as a person concerned with fraudulent
trading of the company. So here: the receipt of £18,000 had nothing to do with
any application or liability under s. 332: it was paid solely because the payer
wanted to say in mitigation that he had in fact paid all the unpaid purchase tax **C**
liability of the company which had been proved by the prosecution. It is said
that the right to apply under s. 332 is an asset of the company and that a creditor
applying is trustee in so doing for the company. While it is true that a declaration
under the section can only (in my view) benefit the company, that does not make
an applicant creditor a trustee either before or after he applies: still less so
when the liquidator is himself a party. I think that when Eve, J., said in *Leitch* **D**
(*No. 2*) that (14)

"... any declaration would leave the applicant a trustee for the company,
or for an unascertained body of creditors"

he was assuming that the applicant could enforce the declaration, which I do not
think he could do. Certainly Eve, J., said nothing of an applicant being trustee
before any declaration made, let alone when the liquidator was party to the **E**
proceedings.

In the end, as I see it, the point is this. The contention that any claim under
s. 332 was the property of the company, and that the commissioners as creditors
of the company were trustees of that property either before or after initiating
s. 332 proceedings, and that, therefore, they are accountable for the £18,000, **F**
breaks down at the last step: because the receipt of the £18,000 was nothing to
do with the s. 332 claim: it was not paid in recognition of the validity of any
such claim but solely for the purpose already stated. It was not the realisation
by the commissioners of an asset conferred on the company by s. 332. Indeed,
had that been so, the Common Serjeant would have been deceived when he
accepted that the proved purchase tax liability of the company had been paid. I
also would allow the appeal. **G**

Appeal allowed; Leave to appeal to the House of Lords refused.

Solicitors: *Solicitor for the Customs and Excise; Underwood & Co.* (for the
liquidator).

[*Reported by* F. Guttman, Esq., *Barrister-at-Law.*] **H**

I

---

(13) [1966] 1 All E.R. 825; [1966] Ch. 462.
(14) [1932] All E.R. Rep. at p. 898; [1933] Ch. at pp. 265, 266.

HOLM v. ROYAL BOROUGH OF KENSINGTON AND CHELSEA.

[COURT OF APPEAL, CIVIL DIVISION (Sellers, Davies and Edmund Davies, L.JJ.), November 14, 15, 1966.]

Housing—House in multiple occupation—Notice to execute works—Two residential floors, over shop, let to tenant—Tenant and wife living on first floor—Tenant's son and his family living on second floor—Separate cooking facilities—Payments equal to half rent by son to tenant's wife—No door dividing the two floors—Whether the two floors " occupied by members of more than one family "—Housing Act, 1961 (9 & 10 Eliz. 2 c. 65), s. 15 (1), s. 16 (1).

The first and top floors of premises, which consisted of a ground floor shop with these two floors over, were let to a tenant, who had lived there with his wife for over thirty years. About twelve years ago their son had married, and, with the landlord's permission, went to live on the top floor with his wife; at the material time they were still living there with their children. The tenant's son regularly paid a sum equal to half the rent of the whole two floors to his mother. The tenant and his wife lived separately on the first floor with their own cooking facilities. The son and his wife had their cooker on the landing. No door separated the two floors. The local authority served notices on the landlord, under s. 15* and s. 16† of the Housing Act, 1961, requiring him to execute certain works. The landlord contended that the first and top floors were not " occupied by members of more than one family " within the meaning of s. 15 (1) and s. 16 (1), and that the local authority were therefore not entitled to serve the notices.

Held: the tenant and his wife, their son, daughter-in-law and grandchildren were all members of one family living in one house, there were no persons living in the house who were strangers or outside that family, and so, there being only one letting of the two floors as an entirety, the house was not " occupied by members of more than one family " within the meaning of s. 15 (1) and s. 16 (1) of the Housing Act, 1961 (see p. 292, letters B and G, and p. 294, letter A, post).

Appeal dismissed.

[As to houses let as lodgings or occupied by members of more than one family, see 19 HALSBURY'S LAWS (3rd Edn.) 614, para. 992, and for cases on the subject, see 38 DIGEST (Repl.) 260-262, *680-701*, and 26 DIGEST (Repl.) 694, *86, 87, 697, 102* (clearance orders).

---

* Section 15 (1) provides: " If the condition of a house which, or a part of which, is let in lodgings, or which is occupied by members of more than one family, is, in the opinion of the local authority, so far defective with respect to any of the following matters, that is to say—natural and artificial lighting, ventilation, water supply, personal washing facilities, drainage and sanitary conveniences, facilities for the storage, preparation and cooking of food, and for the disposal of waste water, or installations for space heating or for the use of space heating appliances, having regard to the number of individuals or households, or both, accommodated for the time being on the premises, as not to be reasonably suitable for occupation by those individuals or households, the local authority may serve either—(a) on the person having control of the house (as defined by sub-s. (2) of s. 39 of the [Housing Act, 1957]), or (b) on any person to whom the house is let at a rack-rent, or on any person who, as the agent or trustee of a person to whom the house is let at a rack-rent, receives rents or other payments from tenants of parts of the house or lodgers in the house, a notice specifying the works which in the opinion of the local authority are required for rendering the premises reasonably suitable for such occupation as aforesaid, and requiring the person on whom the notice is served to execute those works."

† Section 16 (1) provides: " If it appears to a local authority that a house which, or a part of which, is let in lodgings, or which is occupied by members of more than one family, is not provided with such means of escape from fire as the local authority consider necessary, the local authority may, subject to this section, serve on any person on whom a notice may be served under s. 15 of the Act a notice specifying the works which in the opinion of the local authority are required to provide such means of escape, and requiring the person on whom the notice is served to execute those works."

For the Housing Act, 1961, s. 15, s. 16, s. 21, see 41 HALSBURY'S STATUTES (2nd Edn.) 486, 487, 493.

For the Housing Act 1964, s. 64, s. 65, see 44 HALSBURY'S STATUTES (2nd Edn.) 358, 359.]

Cases referred to:

Brock v. *Wollams*, [1949] 1 All E.R. 715; [1949] 2 K.B. 388; 31 Digest (Repl.) 664, *7641*.

Burt v. *Hellyer*, (1872), L.R. 14 Eq. 160; 41 L.J.Ch. 430; 26 L.T. 833; 49 Digest (Repl.) 803, *7551*.

Okereke v. *Borough of Brent (Town Clerk)*, [1966] 1 All E.R. 150; [1966] 2 W.L.R. 169.

Standingford v. *Probert*, [1949] 2 All E.R. 861; [1950] 1 K.B. 377; 31 Digest (Repl.) 718, *8027*.

Appeal.

The local authority, the Royal Borough of Kensington and Chelsea, by notices dated Nov. 24, 1965, and served under the Housing Act, 1961, s. 15 and s. 16, required Henry Charles Holm, the landlord and owner of 69, Golbourne Road, London, W.10, to execute certain works on the first and second (top) floors. The ground floor was used as a shop, and the second and third floors were used for residential purposes. The landlord appealed to the Marylebone County Court, where, on May 13, 1966, His Honour JUDGE ANDREW allowed the appeal and revoked the notices. The local authority now appealed against this order of JUDGE ANDREW. The facts are stated in the judgment of SELLERS, L.J.

R. A. W. Sears for the local authority.
G. H. G. Williams for the landlord.

SELLERS, L.J.: The facts of the case were not expressly found by His Honour JUDGE ANDREW as there was no conflict of testimony. At the time of the notices the whole living accommodation was let to the tenant, Mr. Allen, senior, who with his wife lived on the first floor. On the upper floor, approached by a staircase from the first floor, lived the tenant's son and daughter-in-law, Mr. and Mrs. Allen, junior, and their two daughters aged thirteen and six years.

The tenant and his wife had lived in the premises at least thirty years, originally on the top floor, and then the tenant's wife's sister and her husband occupied the first floor. After the last war the sister and her husband left and the tenant and his wife moved down to the first floor and the tenant's wife's mother and sister, it is said, " took the top floor ". The tenant's son was living with his father and mother. Eventually the tenant's wife's mother, and later her sister, left. About twelve years ago the tenant's son married and at some time went to live on the top floor, where he, his wife and children now are. There is only one rent book for the whole of the residential premises. It is in the name of the tenant and is an inclusive rental. The tenant's son pays half the rent to his mother. The tenant and his wife live separately on the first floor and have their own cooking facilities. There is no door separating the lower from the upper accommodation. There is a cooker on the landing used by the son and his wife. Mr. Freestone, the landlord, who was a predecessor of Mr. Holm, the present landlord, gave permission for the son to occupy the upper floor whenever it was that he went in—I think it was on his marriage. That seems to be the extent of the evidence and it reveals no separate tenancy of the upper floor, no sub-tenancy. It was indeed a family arrangement.

The premises as a whole seem to have been defective in some of the matters set out in s. 15 of the Housing Act, 1961, and lacked a satisfactory means of escape from fire, with which s. 16 of the Act of 1961 deals. As a consequence the local authority (the appellants to this court) on Nov. 24, 1965, served notices on the landlord requiring him to remedy the defects in the manner stated. In the schedule to the notice under s. 15 reference is made to " Top floor letting " and " First floor letting ", but in fact there was but one letting—the one of the whole premises to the tenant.   The total cost of the work was some £200 to £300 according to the manner in which it would have been carried out.   The improvements seem so desirable and in respect of the fire precautions so essential that one might have hoped that the landlord would have undertaken the work and sought some financial assistance from the tenant as he was entitled to do.   Instead of that he has challenged the local authority's right to make the orders.   Their powers lie, if at all, under the Housing Act, 1961.

Part 2 of the Act of 1961 deals with " Houses in multiple occupation ".   Section 12, s. 15 and s. 16 all apply the provisions to " a house which . . . is let in lodgings or which is occupied by members of more than one family ", and the landlord by his appeal to the county court contended that the premises are not " a house which is let in lodgings or which is occupied by members of more than one family ". It was not contended that any part was let in lodgings but the local authority contended that on the facts of this case the house was occupied by members of more than one family.

The judgment, after reviewing some authorities (1), concludes in this way:

> " Adopting that reasoning I think that I am bound to give a broad general meaning to the word ' family ' and applying that meaning I must hold that both [the tenant and his wife] and [their son and the son's wife] are members of the one family.   I think that they are members of the same family.   If Parliament had meant to provide for this situation it should have done so otherwise than in the way in which it has."

In so far as it is a question of fact that conclusion would bind us, for clearly the family relationship is established by the evidence.   It has been submitted, however, for the local authority that the judge has wrongly construed the statutory words and has misdirected himself in not enquiring whether two families are occupying the house.   The stress, it was submitted, was on multiple occupation, and here, it was said, there are two families and not one.   The argument recognised that there was the blood relationship, the father and mother on the first floor and the son and his wife and children on the second, but it is said that they constituted two separate " households ".

If " household " had been the word used, the argument might have been convincing, but the word " household " is used within the same section and can hardly have been used to replace " family ".   In so far as there is ambiguity, it is material that there is a penalty of up to £100 for wilful failure to comply with a notice (Housing Act 1964, s. 65 (1)), and I agree with the judge that the legislation should have made it clear if the provisions were to apply to such circumstances as exist here.   There is no separate letting.   It is a family arrangement.   Families can share things in common with less objection and inconvenience than can strangers.   Where strangers have rights and require facilities it is more justified for local authorities to intervene than perhaps it is for them to intrude when only members of a family are concerned, although this is an argument which hardly lies with the landlord, who has let premises so ill-equipped for user by anyone.

The expression " a house which is occupied by members of more than one family " is to be found as far back as the Public Health Act, 1875, (2), and apparently this is the first occasion when it has been sought to be relied on in circumstances such as these.   Counsel for the local authority contended that the tenant's son was occupying a separate unit in the premises.   The son had no agreement which prescribed the unit and the family may well have moved freely between one floor's accommodation and the other; assuming, however, a separate unit, the occupiers were not strangers but were members of a family.

---

(1) *Brock* v. *Wollams*, [1949] 1 All E.R. 715; [1949] 2 K.B. 388; and *Standingford* v. *Probert*, [1949] 2 All E.R. 861; [1950] 1 K.B. 377.

(2) See s. 90 of the Public Health Act, 1875.

The judge relied on *Brock* v. *Wollams* (3) and *Standingford* v. *Probert* (4). The local authority submit that these cases have no application, since they are decisions under the Rent Restrictions Acts and refer to tenants' rights and protection. They are perhaps not very helpful, but no other authority cited to us provided any guide. The relationship is clear. They are all members of one family living within the one house and there are no persons living in the house who are strangers or outside that family. I find it difficult to see that there was a defined unit or area of occupation. There is no finding to that effect in the judgment.

Like the judge I would regard the sections relied on as not applicable to the circumstances revealed here and I would dismiss the appeal to this court.

DAVIES, L.J.: I agree. I cannot help feeling that in this case the local authority were to some extent acting under some sort of misapprehension. As SELLERS, L.J., has pointed out, they appear to have thought that there were two separate lettings. For one sees in the two schedules to the notice under s. 15 of the Housing Act, 1961, that they refer more than once to a " top floor letting " and a " first floor letting ". There was, of course, only one letting. To what, if any, extent the occupation of the tenant's family and the tenant's son's family were distinct and separate we do not know, since there is no finding of fact as to that.

I turn now to s. 15 (1) of the statute, the relevant words of which are as follows:

" If the condition of a house which, or a part of which, is let in lodgings, or which is occupied by members of more than one family, is, in the opinion of the local authority, so far defective . . . "

The immediately relevant words for the purposes of this case are, of course, " If the condition of a house . . . which is occupied by members of more than one family . . . is . . . defective . . ."

The argument of counsel for the local authority, who put before us all the considerations that could properly be put forward on their behalf, is, in effect, that for the words " occupied by members of more than one family " there should be substituted the words " occupied by more than one household ". Counsel does not shrink from that. I think that he appreciates that the argument is a difficult one, particularly when later in the section one finds the words " having regard to the number of individuals or households, or both, accommodated for the time being on the premises . . ." It would, however, be straining the language of the section beyond all reason to equate (for that is what it comes to) the word " household " with the word " family "; and it seems to me that it would be quite impossible to take that course in the present case.

I would only add one word with regard to a sentence of mine in a previous case to which we were referred, *Okereke* v. *Borough of Brent* (*Town Clerk*) (5). The point at issue in that case was quite different. The question there was whether a building which was divided into three self-contained flats was " a house " within the meaning of s. 15 of the Act of 1961. In the course of discussing s. 15, I am reported as having said this:

" The next relevant words are: ' having regard to the number of . . . households . . . accommodated . . . on the premises '. The word ' households ' suggests separate and self-contained families, and, though it does not necessarily connote self-contained families in self-contained parts of the building, it is certainly not inconsistent with such a state of affairs."

The suggestion seems to be that I was saying there that " families " and " households " meant the same thing. I was not saying any such thing. I was not giving my mind at all to the problem with which we are concerned in this case. In those circumstances I do not think that, whatever value any observations

(3) [1949] 1 All E.R. 715; [1949] 2 K.B. 388.
(4) [1949] 2 All E.R. 861; [1950] 1 K.B. 377.
(5) [1966] 1 All E.R. 150 at p. 155, letter E.

A of mine might ever have, those words can have any possible relation to the question in the present case or any bearing thereon.

I agree with SELLERS, L.J., that the appeal should be dismissed.

EDMUND DAVIES, L.J.: I also agree.   The notices served on the land-lord were given pursuant to Part 2 of the Housing Act, 1961, which deals with "Houses in multiple occupation"—a phrase which, incidentally, does not
B appear in any section of that Act.

It being common ground that 69, Golborne Road is *not* " a house which, or a part of which, is let in lodgings ", the sole question that now arises for inter-pretation is whether it is " occupied by members of more than one family ". The county court judge, basing himself on certain decisions under the Rent
C Acts, and in particular *Brock* v. *Wollams* (6) and *Standingford* v. *Probert* (7) held that the two floors were occupied in their entirety by members of the same family and that, accordingly, the notices were not validly given.

The local authority deny the relevance of any decisions based on the Rent Acts. They have submitted that the only test under those Acts is whether the persons claiming to be entitled to protection are members of the tenant's family residing
D with him (see, for example, s. 12 (1) *(g)* of the Increase of Rent and Mortgage Interest (Restrictions) Act, 1920); but that the Housing Acts impose a quite different test.   It was submitted that the proper approach to adopt in the present case is not whether all who live in the premises belong to the same family, but whether two or more families *occupy* the premises.   The latter test was indeed equated to the question: Are the premises occupied by more than one
E *household*?   Applying it to the present facts, we were invited to hold that 69, Golborne Road was occupied by two distinct households (that of the tenant and his wife on the first floor and that of the son, his wife and children on the top floor) and that, accordingly, the notices were validly given.

I cannot accept this submission.   It appears to me completely to ignore the ties of blood.   Furthermore, in my judgment, it involves re-drafting s. 15 and
F s. 16 of the Act of 1961.   It necessitates substituting for the words " occupied by members of more than one family " some such words as " occupied by more than one household ".   That is not permissible, particularly when it is observed that later in s. 15 one is required to have " regard to the number of individuals or households, or both, accommodated for the time being on the premises ".   " Family " thus being employed in one part of the section and
G " household " in another part, prima facie they connote different concepts. With all respect to the zeal of counsel for the local authority, nothing that he has said has persuaded me that the interpretation which he would have placed on s. 15 is a permissible one.

As to public policy, opposing arguments can be advanced, and they are incon-clusive.   Be that as it may, it must not be overlooked that service of notices under s. 15 and s. 16 can have very burdensome, and even penal, consequences.
H If the work required to be done is not executed and has, in consequence, to be carried out by the local authority, the expense thereof becomes a charge on the premises to which the notice relates and on all estates or interests therein (see the Housing Act 1964, s. 64 (1)).   Furthermore, as has already been pointed out, wilful failure to comply with such notices renders the defaulter liable to a fine of up to £100 on a first conviction, and to a similar fine or to three months' imprison-
I ment in the case of a second or subsequent offence (see s. 65 (1)).   Having regard to such consequences, any ambiguity in the statutory provisions should be resolved by adopting that interpretation which is most benevolent to the person being proceeded against.

In my judgment, the test propounded on behalf of the local authority is not the correct one.   The Act of 1961 means what it says, and the true test must

---

(6) [1949] 1 All E.R. 715; [1949] 2 K.B. 388.
(7) [1949] 2 All E.R. 861; [1950] 1 K.B. 377.

always be: are these premises occupied by members of more than one family?
"Family", in the words of SIR JOHN WICKENS, V.-C., in *Burt* v. *Hellyer* (8),
"is a popular and not a technical expression, and may mean several things".
Much will doubtless turn on the context. Having regard to the wording of
s. 15 and s. 16 as a whole, I ask myself: is 69, Golborne Road occupied by members
of more than one family? In my judgment, the lower court, having also addressed
itself to that question, answered it correctly.

For these reasons, I too would dismiss this appeal.

Appeal dismissed. Leave to appeal to the House of Lords refused.

Solicitors: *Town Clerk, Royal Borough of Kensington and Chelsea* (for the local
authority); *Bulcraig & Davis* (for the landlord).

[*Reported by* HENRY SUMMERFIELD, ESQ., *Barrister-at-Law.*]

GREENWOOD v. WHELAN.

[QUEEN'S BENCH DIVISION (Lord Parker, C.J., Widgery and O'Connor, JJ.),
November 24, 25, 1966.]

*Medicine—Sale of medicine—" Shop "—Stall in market place—Movable structure
but retail business carried on at same place in market five days a week—
Whether stall was a shop for the purposes of Shops Act, 1912 (2 & 3 Geo. 5
c. 3), s. 19 (1) and Pharmacy and Medicines Act, 1941 (4 & 5 Geo. 6 c. 42),
s. 12 (1), s. 17 (1).*

The respondent, who had a tenancy agreement with the W. Corporation,
paid a weekly rent of £12 for a stall where he carried on a retailer's business
outside the market hall. The stall consisted of tubular steel framework
of upright supports and horizontal bearers bolted together, with a permanent
awning stretched over a tubular frame. The stall was equipped with
electric light and an illuminated sign showing the trader's name. It was
portable, inasmuch as it could be lifted bodily by two strong men and carried
to a different place. Except for two days a year when a fair was being held
and the respondent carried the stall away, it was always in the same place
which was defined by a white line painted on the ground and which could
be ascertained by reference to a book kept by the market superintendent.
Mail addressed to the respondent was delivered to the stall. He carried on
business from 9 a.m. to 5 p.m., with a staff of five except on Sundays and
Mondays, and at night he took his stock away, leaving the stall empty. On
appeal by the prosecutor against the dismissal of an information charging
the respondent with unlawfully selling an article consisting of or comprising
a substance recommended as a medicine, namely Angier's Junior Aspirin,
contrary to s. 12 (1)* of the Pharmacy and Medicines Act, 1941, he not
being one of the persons permitted under that subsection to sell such articles
unless, under s. 12 (5)† of the Act, the sale was effected at a shop (" shop "
being defined by s. 17 (1) of the Act by reference to s. 19 (1)‡ of the Shops
Act, 1912),

Held: having regard to the history of the definition of " shop " in the
consolidating Shops Act, 1912, which showed that the reason why the word
" stall " had been dropped from that definition was that under the Shops
Act, 1911, stalls were treated as places other than shops, anything which
would have been covered by the word " stall " in the Shop Hours Act, 1892,
was, under the Act of 1912, a place other than a shop; accordingly the stall
in the present case was not a " shop " within the definition of that word in
the Shops Act, 1912, and thus the defence under s. 12 (5) of the Pharmacy

(8) (1872), L.R. 14 Eq. 160 at p. 164.
* Section 12 (1), so far as material, is set out at p. 296, letter I, post.
† Section 12 (5), so far as material, is set out at p. 297, letter B, post.
‡ Section 19 (1), so far as material, is set out at p. 297, letter C, post.

A   and Medicines Act, 1941, that the sale was effected at a shop failed (see p. 298, letter D, and p. 299, letter B, post).

Summers v. *Roberts* ([1943] 2 All E.R. 757) distinguished.

Appeal allowed.

[**Editorial Note.** The Shops Act, 1912, s. 19 (1), has been repealed and replaced by s. 74 (1) of the Shops Act, 1950 (29 HALSBURY'S STATUTES (2nd Edn.)
B   246).

As to restriction of sale of medicines by unauthorised persons, see 26 HALS-BURY'S LAWS (3rd Edn.) 246-248, para. 541; and for cases on the subject, see 33 DIGEST (Repl.) 563, 564, *274-278.*

As to the meaning of shop, see 17 HALSBURY'S LAWS (3rd Edn.) 17, 18, para. 23; and for cases on the subject, see 24 DIGEST (Repl.) 1107, *518-524,* 1109, 1110,
C   *536, 537.*

For the Shops Act, 1912, s. 19, see 9 HALSBURY'S STATUTES (2nd Edn.) 943.

For the Pharmacy and Medicines Act, 1941, s. 12, s. 17, see 15 HALSBURY'S STATUTES (2nd Edn.) 306, 310.]

Cases referred to:

D   *Kahn* v. *Newberry,* [1959] 2 All E.R. 202; [1959] 2 Q.B. 1; [1959] 2 W.L.R. 650; 123 J.P. 307; Digest (Cont. Vol. A) 612, *540a.*

Summers v. *Roberts,* [1943] 2 All E.R. 757; [1944] K.B. 106; 113 L.J.K.B. 109; 170 L.T. 130; 108 J.P. 52; 33 Digest (Repl.) 564, *277.*

Case Stated.

This was a Case Stated by the justices for the county borough of Wigan in
E   respect of their adjudication as a magistrates' court sitting at Wigan on Apr. 28, 1966.   On Feb. 15, 1966, an information was preferred by the appellant, Peter Greenwood, against the respondent, David Whelan, charging that on Sept. 10, 1965, in Wigan county borough, at Wigan market, not being a person referred to in s. 12 (1) of the Pharmacy and Medicines Act, 1941, he unlawfully sold an article consisting of or comprising a substance recommended as a medicine,
F   namely, Angier's Junior Aspirin, contrary to that section. The following facts were found.   The prosecution was instituted with the prior consent of the Attorney-General.   On Sept. 10, 1965, the respondent conducted a retailer's business at a stall outside the Market Hall, Wigan, and on that day in the course of that business he sold by retail, either himself or by the hand of his servant, a container of Angier's Junior Aspirin.   The respondent was not a person to whom
G   any of the descriptions mentioned in s. 12 (1) of the Pharmacy and Medicines Act, 1941, applied.   The container of Angier's Junior Aspirin consisted of a quantity of tablets in a glass bottle and enclosed in a cardboard box, and was labelled in terms indicating that it contained a substance which could be used for the prevention or treatment of an ailment affecting the human body, and was a recommended medicine within the meaning of the Pharmacy and Medicines
H   Act, 1941.   The substance so sold was described in the edition of the British Pharmacopoeia last published before the Pharmacy and Medicines Act, 1941, was enacted, and it was sold under a title which included a word, namely aspirin, which formed part of the description in that edition of the British Pharmacopoeia. The stall from which the sale was made was within the general area known as the Wigan Market.   The Wigan Market included an enclosed market hall fur-
I   nished with fixed stalls where business was transacted in normal shopping hours, a farmers' open market where farm produce was sold on two market days in each week, and a third area outside the market hall where a small number of retail traders carried on retail business in the open air during normal shopping hours throughout the week.   The respondent's stall was in the last described area. He had a tenancy agreement with Wigan Corporation and paid a weekly rent of £12 for the stall.   The stall consisted of a tubular steel framework of upright supports and horizontal bearers bolted together with a permanent canvas awning stretched over a tubular frame.   The counter consisted of a wooden bench

bolted to the horizontal bearers. The stall was equipped with electric light and **A**
an illuminated sign showing the trader's name, but there was no evidence of the
source of power for those lights. The stall was portable inasmuch as it could be
lifted bodily by two strong men and carried to a different place. Without
breach of his tenancy agreement the respondent could have sunk the legs of the
stall into the ground or he could have bolted it to the ground for greater permanency had he desired to do so, but he had not in fact done either. The stall **B**
was always in the same place, subject to the two exceptions mentioned below,
and the place was defined by a white line painted on the ground. The place
could be ascertained by reference to a book kept by the market superintendent.
Mail addressed to the respondent had been delivered to the stall from the Post
Office. At that stall the respondent, with a staff of five assistants, conducted a
retail business in medicines and detergents. It was his practice to take his stock **C**
away at night, leaving a bare stall, and bring it back for the next day's business.
Business was conducted there between 9 a.m. and 5 p.m. every day of the week
except Sunday and Monday and subject to the further exception mentioned
below. On two occasions in each year, during the period when the Wigan fair
was being held, the respondent did not conduct this business in that place.
On each of those occasions the stall was carried bodily away and was not brought **D**
back until the fair had ended, and for two days on which in a normal week the
stall would have been open for business, the respondent did not conduct business
from this stall in this place. There was no evidence to show whether business
was transacted from the same stall elsewhere at these times.

It was contended by the appellant that the respondent was liable to be convicted because the sale was not effected at a shop. The contention that a stall **E**
of this nature did not constitute a shop for this purpose was based on several
propositions: (a) the word " shop " as used in the Act of 1941 required that,
in addition to a defined place, there should be premises consisting of a structure
at that place, and a structure created from metal tubes, an awning and a bench
clamped to tubes was not sufficient to constitute premises; (b) a structure which
was in fact portable had not the degree of permanence that the statute required; **F**
(c) a business conducted from a structure which was removed on some days when
a regular business would be conducted could not be regarded as a regular business
conducted in a permanent place; (d) the removal at the conclusion of business
hours of the entire stock and everything used in the course of the business, save
the stall itself, was inconsistent with the use of the word " shop " in the Act of
1941. It was contended by the respondent that: (i) the structure from which his **G**
business was conducted was permanent in the sense that, unlike a stall constructed of trestles and loose boards, it was never dismantled; (ii) the stall was
always to be found in the same place, which was precisely defined. The removal
of the stock for safe custody at the conclusion of the day's business was not
inconsistent with the premises being a shop. The respondent conducted a
regular business there.   **H**

The justices dismissed the information, and the appellant now appealed.

The cases noted below* were cited during the argument in addition to those
referred to in the judgment.

R. I. S. Bax, Q.C., and *J. R. Peppitt* for the appellant.
R. M. Bingham, Q.C., and *R. J. D. Livesey* for the respondent.

LORD PARKER, C.J.: Before considering the facts, it is convenient to **I**
refer to s. 12 of the Pharmacy and Medicines Act, 1941, which is dealing with the
sale of medicines by unauthorised persons, and in sub-s. (1) provides that:

" Subject to the provisions of this Act, no person shall sell by retail any
article consisting of or comprising a substance recommended as a medicine
unless he is . . ."

---

* *Eldorado Ice Cream Co., Ltd.* v. *Clark*, [1938] 1 All E.R. 330; [1938] 1 K.B. 715;
Fatstock Marketing Corpn. v. *Morgan*, [1958] 1 All E.R. 646; *Stone* v. *Boreham*, [1958]
2 All E.R. 715; [1959] 1 Q.B. 1.

A one of a number of different types of persons such as a registered medical practitioner, a registered dentist, an authorised seller of poisons, etc. It is unnecessary to go through the detail of that because no one suggests that the respondent falls into any of those categories, but by sub-s. (5) of that section it is provided that:

B " It shall also be a defence for a person charged with selling in contravention of sub-s. (1) or sub-s. (2) of this section an article consisting of or comprising a substance recommended as a medicine to prove that the sale was effected at a shop, and that the article was sold under a proprietary designation . . .",

and then a number of other conditions are provided which have to be satisfied,
C on which no point arises. Finally, by s. 17 (1), the definition section, " shop " has the same meaning as in the Shops Act, 1912. That definition is to be found in the Shops Act, 1912, s. 19 (1), which states that " The expression ' shop ' includes any premises where any retail trade or business is carried on ".

The only point, therefore, that has to be decided in this case is whether the place from which the respondent sold by retail goods comprising a substance recommended as a medicine was a shop within that definition which " includes
D any premises where any retail trade or business is carried on ". [His Lordship stated the facts, and continued:] I confess that, approaching this case, apart from any authority, I should come to the clear conclusion that a stall such as this and as described by the justices could not properly come within the expression " shop ", in that this stall was not premises where any retail trade or business is
E carried on within the meaning either of the Shops Act, 1912, or of the Pharmacy and Medicines Act, 1941. If one looks first of all at the Shops Act, 1912, itself, it is to be observed that the Act of 1912 from which this definition is taken specifically deals with retail trade or business carried on from a place which is not a shop. Thus, in s. 9, it is provided that:

F " It shall not be lawful in any locality to carry on in any place not being a shop retail trade or business of any class at any time when it would be unlawful in that locality to keep a shop open for the purposes of retail trade or business of that class . . . "

In other words, the Shops Act, 1912, is contemplating a shop, whatever that may mean, and a place from which retail trade or business is carried on which
G is not a shop. It is also clear from the decision of this court in *Kahn* v. *Newberry* (1) that retail trade or business may be carried on from something which is not even such a place. That was a case dealing with a costermonger's barrow, which was held then, in 1959, not to be a place within the equivalent of s. 9 of the Shops Act, 1912, namely, s. 12 of the Shops Act, 1950. In other words, retail trade or business may be carried on in three ways, first from a shop as defined, secondly, from a place which is not a shop, and, thirdly, as in the case
H of a costermonger's barrow or an itinerant van, in a way where there is no fixed place at all at which the business is carried on. Approaching it in that way I should say, certainly prima facie, that a stall of this kind, notwithstanding the regularity of the business, the permanency on the site and the type of the structure, was a place not being a shop. It certainly had the degree of permanence necessary to take it out of the decision in *Kahn* v. *Newberry* (1), but, in my
I judgment, it did not amount to a shop. If that is the true view of its meaning in the Shops Acts, then it seems to me that it is almost a fortiori that that must be the meaning for the purposes of the Pharmacy and Medicines Act, 1941, which is dealing, as the Act provides, with medicines and substances recommended as a medicine; it is an Act designed, amongst other things, to enhance pharmacy, and it is dealing with premises which can properly be treated as registered premises.

---

(1) [1959] 2 All E.R. 202; [1959] 2 Q.B. 1.

As it seems to me, the history of this legislation really strengthens the view that
I have expressed. It is unnecessary to go through it in very great detail, but in
the Shop Hours Act, 1892, dealing with hours of employment in shops, the
definition of shop in s. 9 was in this form:

". . . unless the context otherwise requires—' shop ' means [not includes]
retail and wholesale shops, markets, stalls, and warehouses in which assistants
are employed for hire, and includes licensed public-houses and refreshment
houses of any kind."

Quite clearly, therefore, for the purposes of the Act of 1892, this stall would be
a shop. The subsequent Acts which were all consolidated in the Shops Act,
1912, deal with the matters set out in that definition in the Act of 1892 in different
ways. Thus, wholesale shops and warehouses, when one gets to the Act of 1912,
have come out of the definition and are dealt with separately. Similarly, markets
and stalls have dropped out of the definition but have come in again as it were,
first of all in the Shops Act, 1911, s. 4, and finally in s. 9 of the Shops Act, 1912,
as places other than shops. It seems to me perfectly clear, therefore, that the
only reason that stalls have dropped out of the definition is because they are
brought in in the Act of 1911, before the consolidating Act, and, therefore, in
the consolidating Act of 1912, as places other than shops. As I have said,
approaching this matter apart from authority, I should have little doubt that a
stall such as this was not a shop within the definition either for the purposes of
the Shops Act, 1912 or the Pharmacy and Medicines Act, 1941, but a place other
than a shop.

The matter, however, is not free from authority, because in *Summers* v.
Roberts (2) the court had before them a case not altogether unlike this, a case
under the Pharmacy and Medicines Act, 1941, s. 12, of an appellant who sold
retail liniment in bottles, which was recommended as a medicine, in the uncovered
portion of a city market. He did it at a stall consisting of a board resting on, but
not fixed to, trestles, and he occupied the stall regularly on Tuesdays and Saturdays paying 10s. each day for approximately the same site. It was in those
circumstances that this court came to the conclusion, first, that this inclusive
definition meant that a shop was something more than what one might call a
shop colloquially, but that it did not, to use the words of VISCOUNT CALDECOTE,
C.J. (3),

" require [the court] to find that a place in no way limited or bounded by
any ascertainable marks or fences, with no structure on it except two
trestles and a board, with no continuity or regularity except that business
took place twice a week, is a shop . . ."

That was the decision in that case; quite clearly on the facts the present case is
completely different. I have great sympathy with the justices who really came
to the conclusion that, if the converse was shown, it would be a shop, namely, if
the site was limited, there was a structure, there was continuity and regularity
and permanency, matters of that sort. Not only do I sympathise with them, but
when one looks at the earlier part of VISCOUNT CALDECOTE's judgment, he does
say (4):

" I think that . . . the definition given by the Act must be read as including
in addition to that which would be clearly and primarily a shop, a place
defined by precise limits with some structure upon it at which a retail trade is
carried on."

If one takes those words as words of definition, and I have no doubt the magistrates did, and one cannot blame them, it is perfectly clear, in my judgment,
that the facts of this case are fully covered by that definition and that the

(2) [1943] 2 All E.R. 757; [1944] K.B. 106.
(3) [1943] 2 All E.R. at p. 759; [1944] K.B. at p. 112.
(4) [1943] 2 All E.R. at p. 758; [1944] K.B. at p. 110.

magistrates would be entitled to hold that this was a shop. Those words appear in the argument of counsel for the respondent (5) and were adopted by Viscount Caldecote, but, having regard to the actual decision in the case, they must, I think, be read as meaning that at least those requirements are necessary. I do not feel that that case was laying down an exhaustive test. What the test is I do not venture to express. It is sufficient for this case to say that anything which can generally be called a stall and which would have been covered by that expression in the Shop Hours Act, 1892, is now a place other than a shop.

In those circumstances, while sympathising with the justices, and, indeed, up to a comparatively late stage thinking that they were right, I am satisfied that they were wrong and I would allow this appeal and send the Case back to the justices with a direction to convict.

WIDGERY, J.: I agree.

O'CONNOR, J.: I agree.

Appeal allowed. Case remitted.

Solicitors: *Lamartine, Yates & Lacey* (for the appellant); *Gregory, Rowcliffe & Co.* (for the respondent).

[*Reported by* N. P. Metcalfe, Esq., *Barrister-at-Law.*]

COOK v. S.

[Court of Appeal, civil division (Lord Denning, M.R., Danckwerts and Winn, L.JJ.), November 29, 30, 1966.]

Solicitor — Negligence — Damages — Measure of damages — Nervous shock — Damages recoverable for injury to health due to nervous shock or anxiety, but only if reasonably foreseeable consequence—Defence to divorce suit negligently conducted on respondent wife's behalf—Wife peculiarly liable to nervous shock—Knowledge of this on the part of the defendant solicitor not alleged—Damage for injury to wife's health by anxiety state too remote.

Legal Aid—Costs—Payment into court—Recovery by legally assisted person of amount less than that paid in—Discretion of court—Contest as to incidence of costs, after payment in, lying substantially between legal aid fund and defendant—Action against solicitor for negligence—Costs of defendant after payment in exceeding damages recovered by plaintiff—Costs after payment in given to defendant and set-off against damages and plaintiff's costs before payment in—Legal Aid and Advice Act, 1949 (12 & 13 Geo. 6 c. 51), s. 2 (2) (e).

A solicitor acted for a wife who was respondent to a divorce suit brought by her husband on the ground of desertion. The solicitor failed to put in an answer, he failed to put forward a cross-charge of adultery when the husband amended his petition to ask for the court's discretion, and he allowed the suit to be heard as undefended although he had notice that it was in the list for hearing. After the decree nisi was pronounced counsel's advice was sought whether to try to re-open the case; counsel advised the wife to let the decree be made absolute and to apply for maintenance for the son of the marriage. The solicitor failed to apply for maintenance. It was not disputed on appeal that there was negligence on his part. The wife obtained legal aid and sued the solicitor for negligence. Her liability by virtue of an order for costs would thereafter be governed by s. 2 (2) (e) of the Legal Aid and Advice Act, 1949. Her contribution was assessed at nil. She had been earning her livelihood, but at this time she began to suffer an anxiety state and could not work. It was not pleaded that the defendant knew that she was peculiarly liable to nervous shock. At a late stage in the

---

Followed in Lockley v National Blood Transfusion Service [1992] 2 All ER 589

Distinguished in Heywood v Wellers [1976] 1 All ER 300

Distinguished in Currie & Co v The Law Society [1976] 3 All ER 832

Doubted and not followed in Mid-Land Bank v Hett, Stubbs & [1978] 3 All ER 571

action, but before briefs had been delivered, the defendant solicitor paid
£1,500 into court. The plaintiff was awarded in all £1,110 damages. These
did not include any sum for her mental distress. The defendant's costs after
the date of payment in were £1,400, and the plaintiff's costs before that date
were £698. The trial judge gave the defendant £200 only in respect of costs
since the date of payment in.

Held: (i) the plaintiff's breakdown in health owing to anxiety was not a
reasonably foreseeable consequence of the defendant's negligence, and,
although damages for reasonably foreseeable injury in health due to nervous
shock or anxiety could be recovered for breach of duty to use care and skill
where, as in the present case, the cause of action lay in contract, yet in this
case the ruling of the trial judge that the damage was too remote should
stand; accordingly the total damages recovered were £1,100 (see p. 303,
letters B, D, F and H, post).

Groom v. *Crocker* ([1938] 2 All E.R. 394) and dictum of DENNING, L.J.,
in *King* v. *Phillips* ([1953] 1 All E.R. at p. 624) applied.

(ii) there was a wide discretion on costs where a plaintiff was legally
aided, and account could be taken not only of the fact that any costs awarded
against the plaintiff would come out of the damages but also of the fact that
the legal aid fund had a charge on damages for the costs of fighting the case on
the plaintiff's behalf; the contest on costs thus lay in reality between the legal
aid fund and the defendant, and the defendant should have his costs since
the date of the payment into court, but the plaintiff would not be ordered
to pay personally any excess, and there would be a set-off of the defendant's
costs after the payment into court against the damages awarded and against
the plaintiff's costs before the payment into court, which costs were awarded
to her (see p. 304, letters E and G, post).

Decision of LAWTON, J. ([1966] 1 All E.R. 248) affirmed on (i) but reversed
on (ii).

[As to negligence of a solicitor in contentious matters, see 36 HALSBURY'S
LAWS (3rd Edn.) 101, 102, para. 137; and for cases on the subject, see 43 DIGEST
(Repl.) 103, 104, *910-922*. As to the measure of damages, see 36 HALSBURY'S
LAWS (3rd Edn.) 99, 100, para. 135, text and notes (*g*)-(*i*); and for cases on the
subject, see 43 DIGEST (Repl.) 119-121, *1082-1098*.

As to a solicitor's negligence sounding in contract, not in tort, see *Clark* v.
Kirby-Smith ([1964] 2 All E.R. 835) and 36 HALSBURY'S LAWS (3rd Edn.) 96,
para. 131, note (*f*); and for other cases on the subject, see 43 DIGEST (Repl.)
116, *1048, 1049*, 117, *1058*.

As to the remoteness of damage for breach of contract, see 11 HALSBURY'S
LAWS (3rd Edn.) 274, paras. 452, 453; and for cases on the subject, see 17 DIGEST
(Repl.) 117-121, *287-324*.

As to costs after payment into court, see 30 HALSBURY'S LAWS (3rd Edn.)
424, para. 802; and for cases on the subject, see DIGEST (Practice) 874, 875,
4158-4163.

As to the effect of a litigant being legally aided on the exercise of discretion as
to costs and as to costs being awarded against such a litigant, see 30 HALSBURY'S
LAWS (3rd Edn.) 502, 503, paras. 932, 933.

For the Legal Aid and Advice Act, 1949, s. 2 (2) (*e*), see 18 HALSBURY'S
STATUTES (2nd Edn.) 535.]

Cases referred to:
Addis v. *Gramophone Co., Ltd.*, [1908-10] All E.R. Rep. 1; [1909] A.C. 488;
    78 L.J.K.B. 1122; 101 L.T. 466; 34 Digest (Repl.) 131, *891*.
Bloomfield v. *British Transport Commission*, [1960] 2 All E.R. 54; [1960]
    2 Q.B. 86; [1960] 2 W.L.R. 693; 3rd Digest Supp.
Groom v. *Crocker*, [1938] 2 All E.R. 394; [1939] 1 K.B. 194; 108 L.J.K.B. 296;
    158 L.T. 477; 43 Digest (Repl.) 117, *1058*.

King v. *Phillips*, [1953] 1 All E.R. 617; [1953] 1 Q.B. 429; [1953] 2 W.L.R. 526; 17 Digest (Repl.) 123, *339.*

Overseas Tankship (U.K.), Ltd. v. *Morts Dock & Engineering Co., Ltd.*, [1961] 1 All E.R. 404; [1961] A.C. 388; [1961] 2 W.L.R. 126; Digest (Cont. Vol. A) 1148, *185a.*

Polemis and Furness, Withy & Co., Ltd., Re, [1921] All E.R. Rep. 40; [1921] 3 K.B. 560; sub nom. *Polemis* v. *Furness, Withy & Co., Ltd.*, 90 L.J.K.B. 1353; 126 L.T. 154; 36 Digest (Repl.) 38, *185.*

Appeal.

This was an appeal by the plaintiff from the decision of Lawton, J., dated Dec. 2, 1965, awarding £1,110* damages to her in an action brought by her against the defendant, her former solicitor, for negligence in the conduct on her behalf of a divorce suit in which she was respondent. The decision of the trial judge included, in particular, a finding that damages for injury to the plaintiff's health in consequence of mental distress caused, allegedly, by the defendant's negligent conduct of her defence to the divorce suit and his negligent failure to claim maintenance for her son, were too remote.

The defendant cross-appealed against the award of costs. The plaintiff was legally aided with a nil contribution. On Oct. 18, 1965, before briefs for the trial were delivered, the defendant paid into court £1,500. Notwithstanding that the plaintiff recovered less than this amount, the trial judge awarded the defendant only £200 costs from the date of payment in. The defendant cross-appealed against this award. The facts are set out at p. 303, letter I, to p. 304, letter A, post.

J. T. Molony, Q.C., and *A. E. Holdsworth* for the plaintiff.

B. Finlay and *C. J. Whybrow* for the defendant.

LORD DENNING, M.R.: The plaintiff, Mrs. Cook, married her husband in 1943 when she was about nineteen years of age. They had two children born in 1943 and 1944. It was not a happy marriage. They went to Ceylon and Australia, and came back to Brighton. In 1955 the husband had work in Malvern and wanted to be there; but the plaintiff wanted to be in Crawley with the children. She had her way; she stayed in Crawley. From that time onwards they were more or less separated, although he did occasionally visit her at Crawley. She wrote letters which clearly indicated a deserting mind. One was a letter of Aug. 27, 1956:

" Now you have all this in black and white, you can have proof that I will never under any conditions return as your wife."

There were subsequent visits but no reconciliation.

Eventually the husband started divorce proceedings charging the plaintiff with desertion. The plaintiff went to the defendant, a solicitor in Crawley, and asked him to defend the case. She tried to get legal aid, but for some reason did not get it. The defendant was reluctant to incur expense on the case and I fear that he neglected it badly. The judge (1) found that he was guilty of negligence, and there is no appeal from that finding. The defendant made several mistakes in the divorce suit. He did not put in an answer as he ought to have done. So it was put into the undefended list. The husband amended his petition so as to ask for the discretion of the court, thus admitting his own adultery. The defendant ought thereupon to have put in an answer and made

---

* The £1,110 damages awarded consisted of £160 damages for failing to claim maintenance for the plaintiff's son; £200 damages in respect of the unfavourable outcome of the divorce suit brought against the plaintiff by her husband, and £750 damages for the loss of her chances of protecting a future maintenance claim for herself. For the purposes of the present report nothing turns on the composition of the £1,110 damages, the aggregate amount recovered alone being relevant to the report. The Court of Appeal declined to interfere with the two awards of £160 and £200 (see p. 302, letters E and G, post), and the cross-appeal of the defendant regarding the £750 was not pursued (see p. 303, letter G, post).

(1) [1966] 1 All E.R. 248.

a cross-charge of adultery, but he did not do so. He had notice that the case was in the list for hearing at Gloucester; but he allowed it to go undefended. A decree nisi was pronounced. After decree nisi and before the decree was made absolute, the solicitor became aware of his mistakes. He went with the plaintiff to counsel. Counsel advised in conference that it would not be any good to try to re-open the decree nisi and have the matter fought out. He advised them to let the decree be made absolute and simply to apply for maintenance for the son. So the decree absolute was made on Jan. 24, 1962. The husband soon afterwards married the woman with whom he was living.

In accordance with counsel's advice, the defendant ought to have applied for maintenance for the son aged sixteen who was going to college. He did not even make that application. At length the plaintiff went to other solicitors. In 1963 she got legal aid and brought an action against the defendant for negligence in his duty to her as a solicitor. She had been earning her own living, but about this time she suffered from an anxiety state or neurosis. She was so ill that the doctor said that she could not work.

Before us the negligence has not been contested. The question is: what damages ought she to be given?

The first item is maintenance for the son. LAWTON, J., said that if the defendant had made a claim for maintenance for the son (as advised by counsel), the probabilities were that an order for £2 a week would have been made. The judge estimated that it would last for eighty weeks, making £160 loss on that account. I see no reason for disturbing his decision on that point. The £160 must stand.

The second item is the unfavourable outcome of the divorce suit. The plaintiff lost when she might have won. What damages should be obtainable? That depends on what were the prospects of a successful outcome. The judge said (2) that, even if the case had been fought, the probabilities were that the husband would still have got a divorce on the ground of desertion. That may be true; but there was quite a chance that both might have got decrees, the husband on the ground of the plaintiff's desertion and the plaintiff on the ground of the husband's adultery. There was an outside possibility of the plaintiff herself getting a decree. She is entitled to general damages for the loss of the chance of a more favourable outcome, for the simple reason that it does affect a person's standing to be found the guilty party instead of the innocent party. The judge assessed (3) the damages on this loss at £200. That was essentially a matter for him. I do not think we should interfere with the figure of £200.

The third item is loss of maintenance for the plaintiff. If she had succeeded in the divorce suit or got a cross-decree, she might have got maintenance. As it was she got nothing. The registrar treated her as the guilty party and gave her nothing. LAWTON, J., allowed (3) for her loss on that account a sum of £750. That figure is challenged, but I will defer consideration of it.

The fourth item is the claim for damages for the plaintiff's anxiety state. The judge found (3) that the plaintiff suffered a breakdown in health which led to a loss of earnings on her part. It was produced in part by the negligence of the defendant and in part by other causes. The plaintiff was also worrying about her daughter. The judge said (3) that if this item were admissible in law, he would have allowed £750; but he held that it was not admissible as a head of damage. He treated it on the same footing as injury to feelings or mental distress, and held that it could not be recovered. She appeals against his decision on this item. This raises a difficult point. The cause of action, it must be remembered, is one for breach of contract. An action against a solicitor is always one for breach of contract, as was held in *Groom* v. *Crocker* (4). The measure of damages is compensation for the consequences which follows as a natural and probable consequence of the breach; or in other words, which

_____

(2) [1966] 1 All E.R. at p. 256.   (3) [1966] 1 All E.R. at p. 257.
(4) [1938] 2 All E.R. 394; [1939] 1 K.B. 194.

could reasonably be foreseen. Special circumstances, brought home, enlarge the area of foreseeability. At one time it was thought that damages in tort were different from damages for breach of contract. Thus it was held in *Re Polemis and Furness, Withy & Co., Ltd.* (5), that in tort, damages could be recovered for all direct consequences. Since *Overseas Tankship (U.K.), Ltd.* v. *Morts Dock & Engineering Co., Ltd.* (6) it is generally accepted, however, that in tort too the measure of damages is the reasonable foreseeability of the consequences. So both in tort and in contract the measure of damages depends on what may be reasonably foreseen.

In these circumstances I think that, just as in the law of tort, so also in the law of contract, damages can be recovered for nervous shock or anxiety state if it is a reasonably foreseeable consequence. So the question became this: when a client goes to a solicitor, is it a reasonably foreseeable consequence that, if anything goes wrong with the litigation owing to the solicitor's negligence, there will be a breakdown in health? It can be foreseen that there will be injured feelings; mental distress; anger, and annoyance. But for none of these can damages be recovered. It was so held in *Groom* v. *Crocker* (7) on the same lines as *Addis* v. *Gramophone Co., Ltd.* (8). Is it reasonably foreseeable that there may be an actual breakdown in health? I do not think so. It was suggested in this case that there were special circumstances in that the plaintiff was peculiarly liable to nervous shock. I am afraid that she was. The history of her life shows one nervous breakdown after another. If this special circumstance was brought home to the defendant, it might enlarge the area of foreseeability so as to make him liable; but it was not pleaded. Moreover when counsel for the plaintiff put questions to the defendant, he did not succeed in showing that special circumstances were brought home to him. All the defendant knew was that she was a woman obviously highly strung and worried as any woman would be in the circumstances. That does not mean, however, that he should foresee that, if he was negligent, she would suffer injury to health. In all these cases of nervous shock and breakdown in mental health, it is very difficult to draw the line. In *King* v. *Phillips* (9) I asked: "Where is the line to be drawn?" I found the answer given by LORD WRIGHT (10): "Only where ' in the particular case the good sense of the . . . judge, decides '." In this present case the judge thought that the damages for the breakdown in health were too remote. I am not prepared to disturb his ruling. On this point the appeal fails.

There was a cross-appeal on the third item of £750 for loss of maintenance; but seeing that the appeal on the breakdown to health failed, counsel for the defendant did not press this cross-appeal, because there was sufficient money in court. So the order is that the appeal is dismissed and the cross-appeal (so far as it relates to damages) is also dismissed. The total sum of damages awarded to the plaintiff is £1,110.

DANCKWERTS, L.J.: I agree and I do not want to add anything.

WINN, L.J.: I also agree and do not wish to add anything.

[After argument on the cross-appeal as to costs.]

LORD DENNING, M.R.: A troublesome point arises about the costs. At a fairly late stage on Oct. 18, 1965, the defendant paid £1,500 into court. Briefs had not been delivered. The action started on Nov. 1, 1965, and went on for six days. In the result the plaintiff recovered less than £1,500. She only recovered £1,110. In these circumstances the ordinary order would be that

(5) [1921] All E.R. Rep. 40; [1921] 3 K.B. 560.
(6) [1961] 1 All E.R. 404; [1961] A.C. 388.
(7) [1938] 2 All E.R. 394; [1939] 1 K.B. 194.
(8) [1908-10] All E.R. Rep. 1; [1909] A.C. 488.
(9) [1953] 1 All E.R. 617 at p. 624; [1953] 1 Q.B. 429 at p. 442.
(10) In *Hay (or Bourhill)* v. *Young*, [1942] 2 All E.R. 396 at p. 406; [1943] A.C. 92 at p. 110.

the plaintiff should recover all her costs up to the date of payment into court (which we were told were £698) and the defendant would recover all his costs after that date (which were about £1,400); but the plaintiff was legally aided. On that account the judge only gave the defendant £200 in respect of his costs after payment in (in lieu of some £1,400 incurred by him). He was influenced by the fact that the defendant failed in the issue of liability; but that should not have influenced him over much. In nearly every case of payment into court, the defendant pays in a sum so as to avoid the cost of a contest and if that sum is enough, he ought ordinarily to be awarded the costs after making his payment into court, even though he fails on liability. No doubt there is a wide discretion in the case of a plaintiff who is legally aided. The judge can certainly take into account the fact that the plaintiff has an award of damages in her favour, and that any costs awarded against her will come out of the damages (see *Bloomfield* v. *British Transport Commission* (11)); but another matter to be taken into account is this. The legal aid fund has a charge on the damages so as to cover its costs in fighting the case on her behalf. In this case, if the whole of the damages (£1,110) are paid to the plaintiff, they will be absorbed by the costs incurred by the legal aid fund on behalf of the plaintiff after the date of payment into court. So the plaintiff will get none of the damages in any event. If the judge's order giving the defendant only £200 of his costs is correct, it will mean that out of the £1,110 damages, the defendant will retain £200 towards his costs and pay the balance of £910 to the plaintiff which will be wholly absorbed by the legal aid fund. In short, so far as the £1,110 is concerned, it is really a contest between the legal aid fund and the defendant. The £1,110 either goes to the legal aid fund for its costs (incurred on behalf of the plaintiff after the date of payment in): or it goes to the defendant (for his costs incurred by him since that date). As between the two of them, I have no doubt it should go to the defendant. The legal aid fund was maintaining this action on behalf of the plaintiff. The defendant made a payment into court which is more than the plaintiff recovered. The defendant should have all his costs from that date instead of the legal aid fund, at any rate up to the £1,110. If the defendant's costs exceed the £1,110, there should be a set-off against the costs awarded to the plaintiff. I do not think, however, that the plaintiff herself should be ordered to pay personally any of the excess. She has a nil contribution and is on national assistance. The cross-appeal (so far as it relates to costs) should, therefore, be allowed. The plaintiff is to have £1,110 with costs up to the date of payment in, but the defendant is to be awarded the costs from the date of payment in, to be set off against the £1,110 awarded as damages and against the costs awarded to the plaintiff up to payment in: but the plaintiff herself should not personally be ordered to pay anything.

DANCKWERTS, L.J.: I agree.

WINN, L.J.: I also agree.

Appeal dismissed: cross-appeal, so far as it related to costs, allowed.

Solicitors: *Lloyd & Davey* (for the plaintiff); *Gard, Lyell, Bridgman & Co.* (for the defendant).

[*Reported by* F. GUTTMAN, ESQ., *Barrister-at-Law.*]

---

(11) [1960] 2 All E.R. 54; [1960] 2 Q.B. 86.

WALLER *v.* WALLER.

[CHANCERY DIVISION (Stamp, J.), December 9, 12, 1966.]

Husband and Wife—Property—Matrimonial home—Both parties contributing to purchase—Land conveyed to husband alone—No second trustee of land—Husband entered into contract to sell matrimonial home—Injunction sought by wife to restrain sale or lease without her consent.

A cottage, the matrimonial home, was conveyed in 1965 to the husband alone, but part of the purchase price was contributed by the wife. The husband (who was thus sole trustee of the cottage on trust for sale) agreed to sell it to a purchaser, and the wife applied for an injunction to restrain any sale or lease of the cottage without her consent.

Held: the wife was in no worse position, merely because the cottage was the matrimonial home and vested in the husband, than any other equitable tenant in common of the proceeds of sale of land held on trust for sale; accordingly the injunction sought would be granted, the wife undertaking to join the purchaser as defendant and he being given liberty to apply to discharge the order (see p. 306, letter H, and p. 307, letter A, post).

[As to the protection afforded to a tenant in common, see 32 HALSBURY'S LAWS (3rd Edn.) 341, para. 535; as to receipts for purchase money by trustees on the sale of land, see 34 ibid., p. 359, para. 626; and as to the effect of the statutory trusts regarding rights of beneficiaries, see 32 ibid., pp. 342, 343, para. 537.

As to a wife's rights in the matrimonial home, see 19 HALSBURY'S LAWS (3rd Edn.) 849-851, para. 1388.

For the Trustee Act, 1925, s. 14, see 26 HALSBURY'S STATUTES (2nd Edn.) 72.

For the Law of Property Act, 1925, s. 26 (3) (as substituted), see 20 HALSBURY'S STATUTES (2nd Edn.) 472.]

Cases referred to:

Dance v. *Goldingham,* (1873), 8 Ch. App. 902; 42 L.J.Ch. 777; 29 L.T. 166; 38 J.P. 164; 47 Digest (Repl.) 417, *3733.*

Jones v. *Challenger,* [1960] 1 All E.R. 785; [1961] 1 Q.B. 176; [1960] 2 W.L.R. 695; 47 Digest (Repl.) 400, *3595.*

National Provincial Bank, Ltd. v. *Ainsworth,* [1965] 2 All E.R. 472; [1965] A.C. 1175; [1965] 3 W.L.R. 1; 3rd Digest Supp.

Rawlings v. *Rawlings,* [1964] 2 All E.R. 804; [1964] P. 398; [1964] 3 W.L.R. 294; 3rd Digest Supp.

Motion.

The wife, Monica Pamela Waller, issued a writ on Dec. 5, 1966, claiming (i) a declaration that her husband, Graeme John Joseph Waller, who was the registered proprietor at the Land Registry of the property (being their matrimonial home) known as the Railway Cottage, Lanner, Redruth, Cornwall, held the property as trustee for her; (ii) an injunction to restrain the husband from making or completing any sale or lease or other disposition of the property without her consent, and (iii) an order that such proceeds of any sale of the property as had been or should be received by the husband, being money which he held or would hold as trustee for the wife, be paid by him to the wife. This was a motion on notice dated Dec. 6, 1966, by the wife for an interlocutory injunction in the terms of (ii) above, and for an order that such proceeds of any sale of the property as had been or should be received by or on behalf of the husband be forthwith paid into court to the credit of the action. The facts are set out in the judgment.

The case noted below* was cited during the argument in addition to the cases referred to in the judgment.

D. H. Mervyn Davies for the wife.
Deborah Rowland for the husband.

---

* *Bull* v. *Bull,* [1955] 1 All E.R. 253; [1955] 1 Q.B. 234.

STAMP, J.: " Railway Cottage " was bought in the summer of 1965 in the name of the husband alone, but it is common ground for the purposes of this motion that the purchase price was provided as to a substantial part by the wife and as to a substantial part by the husband.

Had the parties not been husband and wife, the husband would on completion of the purchase have become an equitable tenant in common with the wife, of the house. He would have become a trustee of the property, holding it on a trust for sale, but since it is the policy of the law for obvious reasons (which, I think, are exemplified in this case) not to allow a single trustee to sell land which he is holding on trust for sale, and in the proceeds of sale of which other persons are interested in equity, he could not have sold the property and given a good receipt for the proceeds without first appointing an additional trustee (see the Trustee Act, 1925, s. 14 (2)). He would also have committed a breach of the trust if, having appointed an additional trustee, he had then proceeded to sell the property without ascertaining the wishes of the other beneficiary, the wife (see the Law of Property Act, 1925, s. 26 (3) as substituted (1)).

The husband, without doing either of these things, has entered into an agreement with one G. J. Jeffs to sell the property.

Subject to two points, I have no doubt that the husband ought to be restrained. The wife is entitled to be protected from what may be an improvident sale by the appointment of an additional trustee, and to have her wishes considered. What is submitted on behalf of the husband is that whatever might be the position at law and in equity as between two strangers, it is different as between husband and wife, and that where a property has been purchased by husband and wife as a matrimonial home, and the wife is no longer in possession—as, so it is submitted, is the case here—she cannot prevent the husband from selling the property.

The purpose for which the property was purchased, so the argument runs, having come to an end, it is open to the husband to sell the property without regard to the wife's wishes. In support of this proposition I was referred to *Jones* v. *Challenger* (2) and *Rawlings* v. *Rawlings* (3) and to some isolated passages in speeches in the House of Lords in *National Provincial Bank, Ltd.* v. *Ainsworth* (4).

If an additional trustee were appointed, and if then the wishes of the wife and the husband should not co-incide, it might be that on an application to resolve the differences those cases, and the submissions which have been advanced on behalf of the husband in this case, would be relevant. About that I say nothing.

Neither the authorities nor the submissions satisfy me, however, that a tenant in common in equity who is the wife of the other tenant in common in equity is in any worse a position to prevent the sale of the property by the husband, who is the sole trustee, than would be the position if the parties were complete strangers to each other. In my judgment the submission advanced on behalf of the husband in this regard is without substance.

The fact that at the time this motion was opened before me, Mr. Jeffs was not a party to the proceedings, has occasioned me more anxiety, but the general principle is that where the equities are equal, qui prior est tempore potior est jure.

Notwithstanding the fact that Mr. Jeffs has an equitable interest in the property because the husband as legal owner has entered into a contract with him to sell it, I think that the wife has made a prima facie case for restraining the husband

---

(1) By the Law of Property Amendment Act, 1926, s. 7, Schedule.
(2) [1960] 1 All E.R. 785; [1961] 1 Q.B. 176.
(3) [1964] 2 All E.R. 804; [1964] P. 398.
(4) [1965] 2 All E.R. 472; [1965] A.C. 1175.

A (see *Dance* v. *Goldingham* (5)). On the wife undertaking forthwith to join Mr. Jeffs as a defendant to the proceedings, I will grant an injunction, and give Mr. Jeffs liberty to apply to discharge it on two days' notice to the wife.

Order accordingly.

B Solicitors: *Gregory, Rowcliffe & Co.*, agents for *Peter, Bray & Harris*, Redruth, Cornwall (for the wife); *Coode, Kingdon, Cotton & Ward*, agents for *Walters & Barbary*, Camborne, Cornwall (for the husband).

[*Reported by* JENIFER SANDELL, *Barrister-at-Law.*]

C

HODGSON *v.* ARMSTRONG AND ANOTHER.

[COURT OF APPEAL, CIVIL DIVISION (Sellers, Davies and Russell, L.JJ.), June 14, 15, 16, November 15, 1966.]

D *County Court—Postal transactions—Originating application posted to county court on day before Good Friday, delivered following Tuesday—Not delivered on Saturday because of instruction by county court to Post Office not to deliver on Saturday—Post Office thus made agents for keeping mail for county court—Time for making application expired on Easter Monday—Whether application in time—C.C.R., Ord. 26, r. 1—Landlord and Tenant Act, 1954 (2 & 3 Eliz. 2 c. 56), s. 29 (3).*

E *County Court—Time—Period prescribed by statute expiring on a Sunday or holiday—Period within which application to be made to court for new business tenancy expired on Easter Monday—Application posted to court office on previous Thursday—Delivered on the Tuesday following the Easter Monday—Whether in time—C.C.R., Ord. 48, r. 10 (3)—Landlord and Tenant Act, 1954 (2 & 3 Eliz. 2 c. 56), s. 29 (3).*

F On Dec. 19, 1964, a landlord of premises comprising a dwelling-house and shop gave his tenant notice under the Landlord and Tenant Act, 1954, s. 25, terminating her tenancy. The tenant duly gave notice of unwillingness to give up possession and so entitled herself to apply to the court (the Preston County Court) for a new tenancy " not less than two and not more than four months after " Dec. 19, the period fixed by s. 29 (3)* of the Act of 1954.

G The four months therefore expired on Apr. 19, 1965, which was the Easter Monday Bank Holiday, on which the court office was closed. The office did not open on Good Friday, Apr. 16, nor on any Saturday, and after closing at noon on Thursday Apr. 15 had re-opened on Tuesday Apr. 20.

In the afternoon of Thursday Apr. 15, 1965, the tenant's solicitor posted her application for a new tenancy to the court by ordinary post. It would normally have been delivered on Saturday, Apr. 17, but the court had instructed the Post Office not to deliver mail to the court on Saturdays and to keep it until the next week-day delivery. The tenant's application was therefore kept by the Post Office, and delivered to the court on Tuesday, Apr. 20. The county court judge dismissed the tenant's application, holding that he had no jurisdiction to hear it because it had not been " made " within the four months after Dec. 19, 1965. On appeal by the tenant,

I **Held** (RUSSELL, L.J., dissenting): the tenant's application had been made in time, and so should be heard by the court, for the following reasons—

(a) since the period prescribed for the tenant to make application to the county court expired on a day when the court office was closed (Apr. 19, 1965), the application was made, by virtue of C.C.R., Ord. 48, r. 10 (3), to the court in time if it were made on the next day (Apr. 20) on which the

---

(5) (1873), 8 Ch. App. 902.
* Section 29 (3) is printed at p. 310, letter D, post.

Distinguished in KAMMINS BALL-ROOMS *v.* ZENITH INVESTMENTS. [1969] 3 All E.R. 1268

Distinguished in PRITAM KAUR *v.* RUSSELL [1972] 3 All ER 305

Considered in PRITAM KAUR *v.* RUSSELL [1973] 1 All ER 617

court office was open; in having this effect C.C.R., Ord. 48, r. 10 (3) was not extending the statutory period limited by s. 29 (3) of the Landlord and Tenant Act, 1954, but was only deeming in special circumstances an act to be done within the statutory period (see p. 315, letter A, p. 316, letter H, p. 317, letter C, and p. 318, letter H, post).

R. v. *Middlesex Justices* ((1848), 17 L.J.M.C. 111), *Mayer* v. *Harding* ((1867), L.R. 2 Q.B. 410) and *Hughes* v. *Griffiths* ((1862), 13 C.B.N.S. 324) applied.

Peacock v. *Reginam* ((1858), 4 C.B.N.S. 264) not followed.

(b) by reason of the county court's direction to the Post Office not to deliver mail to the court office on a Saturday or on Easter Monday the Post Office were constituted agents to keep for the court the mail that would otherwise have been delivered then, with the consequence in the present case that, by virtue of C.C.R., Ord. 26, r. 1*, the tenant's application to the court was made on Apr. 17 (see p. 315, letter F, and p. 319, letter E, post).

(c) (per SELLERS, L.J.), to have held that, since the court office was closed on Apr. 19, which was the last day of the statutory period, the application on the tenant's part at the court must be made before then would have been to have deprived the tenant of the full statutory period, and, the provisions of s. 29 (3) of the Landlord and Tenant Act, 1954, being procedural, the functioning of the court office was an essential factor in assessing the period of time; accordingly, on a true interpretation of the Act of 1954, the period should not be curtailed and application on the earliest subsequent day possible, Apr. 20, should be regarded as being in time (see p. 313, letter I, and p. 314, letters B and H, post).

Morris v. *Richards* ((1881), 45 L.T. 210), *Gelmini* v. *Moriggia* ([1911-13] All E.R. Rep. 1115), *Déchène* v. *City of Montreal* ([1894] A.C. 640) and *M'Niven* v. *Glasgow Corpn.* (1920 S.C. 584) not followed.

Appeal allowed.

[As to periods of time expiring on a Sunday or holiday when court offices are closed, see 9 HALSBURY'S LAWS (3rd Edn.) 228, para. 517, note (*l*) (county courts), 30 ibid., 402, para. 753, note (*s*) (Supreme Court) and 37 ibid., 98, 99, para. 173 text and notes (*t*), (*u*); and for cases on the subject, see 45 DIGEST (Repl.) 268, *349-359.*

As to the transaction of county court business by post, see 9 HALSBURY'S LAWS (3rd Edn.) 205, para. 445.

For the County Court Rules, 1936, Ord. 26, r. 1, Ord. 48, r. 10 (3), see the COUNTY COURT PRACTICE, 1966, pp. 476, 540].

Cases referred to:

Déchène v. *Montreal (City)*, [1894] A.C. 640; 64 L.J.P.C. 14; 71 L.T. 354; 45 Digest (Repl.) 258, **219.*

Dunlop v. *Higgins*, (1848), 1 H.L. Cas. 381; 9 E.R. 805; 12 Digest (Repl.) 86, *470.*

Gelmini v. *Moriggia*, [1911-13] All E.R. Rep. 1115; [1913] 2 K.B. 549; 82 L.J.K.B. 949; 109 L.T. 77; 32 Digest (Repl.) 389, *179.*

Hughes v. *Griffiths*, (1862), 13 C.B.N.S. 324; 32 L.J.C.P. 47; 143 E.R. 129; 45 Digest (Repl.) 268, *349.*

M'Niven v. *Glasgow Corpn.*, 1920 S.C. 584; 38 Digest (Repl.) 138, **541.*

Mayer v. *Harding*, (1867), L.R. 2 Q.B. 410; sub nom. *Re Mayer* v. *Harding*, 16 L.T. 429; 31 J.P. 376; 38 Digest (Repl.) 320, *1442.*

Morris v. *Richards*, (1881), 45 L.T. 210; 46 J.P. 37; 32 Digest (Repl.) 389, *178.*

Peacock v. *Reginam*, (1858), 4 C.B.N.S. 264; 27 L.J.C.P. 224; 31 L.T.O.S. 101; 22 J.P. 403; 140 E.R. 1085; 45 Digest (Repl.) 267, *342.*

R. v. *Middlesex Justices*, (1848), 17 L.J.M.C. 111; 11 L.T.O.S. 132; 12 J.P. 392; 45 Digest (Repl.) 249, *169.*

---

* Order 26, r. 1 (1) is printed at p. 322, letter D, post.

Appeal.

This was an appeal by Mrs. Mary Hodgson, the tenant of a shop at 61, Liverpool Road, Penwortham, Preston, against the ruling of His Honour Judge Ingress Bell, Q.C., at Preston County Court, on Dec. 6, 1965, on a preliminary issue whether the tenant's originating application for a new tenancy under the Landlord and Tenant Act, 1954, Pt. 2, was out of time. The county court dismissed her application for want of jurisdiction at the instance of the landlords, Kenneth Harry Armstrong and his wife Kathleen Mary Armstrong of 63, Liverpool Road. The grounds of the appeal were that the judge had misdirected himself and was wrong in law in that—(a) he directed himself that the time stipulated by s. 29 (3) of the Landlord and Tenant Act, 1954, for making an application for a new tenancy was not extended by virtue of C.C.R., Ord. 48, r. 10 (3) so as to expire on Apr. 20, 1965, notwithstanding that apart from such extension the period expired on Apr. 19, 1965, which was a day when the court office was closed; (b) he held that the application for the new tenancy was not " made " within s. 29 (3) on the posting thereof by ordinary pre-paid post on Apr. 15, 1965, and (c) he directed himself that the mere delivery of an application to the court offices would not be sufficient to constitute " the making " of an application within the meaning of s. 29 (3) and that, therefore, despite the fact that the tenant's solicitors had sent the application on Apr. 15, 1965, by ordinary pre-paid post, and that the Post Office had held the application from Apr. 16, 1965, until Apr. 20, 1965, under an express direction from the court officers not to deliver any mail to the court office until Apr. 20, 1965, the applicant had not made her application to the court within the meaning of s. 29 (3) until Apr. 20, 1965. A further ground of appeal was that, having regard to the facts stated in (c) above the judge ought to have held that the application was duly made on Apr. 16, 1965, or at the latest on Apr. 17, 1965.

The facts are stated in the judgment of Sellers, L.J., infra.

L. J. Porter for the tenant.
Gerson Newman for the landlords.

Cur. adv. vult.

Nov. 15, 1966. The following judgments were read.

SELLERS, L.J.:   The court gave leave to appeal in this case after the time for appeal had expired, as adequate grounds were shown to excuse the delay and as the case and the judgment of His Honour Judge Ingress Bell, Q.C., raised a question of undoubted importance and one which for practical reasons requires the utmost clarity. The precise point is whether an application to the court for a new lease purported to be made under Pt. 2 of the Landlord and Tenant Act, 1954, was made within the statutory time. The rateable value of the premises controls the court to which the application has to be made, either the High Court or a county court. The principle which is to govern the matter is of wide importance as the court (here the county court) which is to receive an application or a notice may on occasions be closed on the final day for the application or the notice, although less frequently closed for so many days preceding and including the final day as is the case here.

The facts are simple and undisputed. Mrs. Hodgson, the appellant tenant, occupied the premises, 61, Liverpool Road, Penwortham, Preston, comprising a dwelling-house and a shop, which she conducted, under a five-year lease dated June 24, 1958, under which she has continued in occupation up to the present time. On Dec. 19, 1964, she received a formal notice dated Dec. 15, 1964, terminating her tenancy on June 24, 1965. This was a statutory notice (1) given under s. 25 of the Landlord and Tenant Act, 1954, and it contained these paragraphs:

---

(1) The notice was in form 7 of the Appendix to the Landlord and Tenant (Notices) Regulations, 1957 (S.I. 1957 No. 1157).

"2. You are required within two months after receiving this notice to notify me in writing whether or not you will be willing to give up possession of the premises on that date. 3. I would not oppose an application to the court under Pt. 2 of the Act for the grant of a new tenancy."

It would seem that the defendants had not been the landlords long enough to oppose renewal of the tenancy at all. On Feb. 12, 1965 (within the two months) the tenant wrote a letter to the landlords giving them notice that she was not willing to give up possession of the premises in accordance with the notice served on her. The matter then, I understand, passed into the hands of solicitors then acting for her. The landlords can have been in no doubt as to the intention of the tenant to continue in the premises and of her right in the circumstances to have a new tenancy.

Section 24 of the Act of 1954 enabled the tenant to apply to the court for a new tenancy " subject to the provisions of s. 29 ". Section 29 (3) provides as follows:

" No application under sub-s. (1) of s. 24 of this Act shall be entertained unless it is made not less than two and not more than four months after the giving of the landlord's notice under s. 25 of this Act . . ."

Four months after the giving of the landlords' notice expired on Apr. 19, 1965, which in that year was the Easter Monday Bank Holiday. The Preston county court was closed that day and had been closed since the previous Thursday noon, Apr. 15, as all county courts were closed by authority from noon on Maundy Thursday until the following Tuesday morning, Apr. 20. Preston county court re-opened at 10 a.m. that day. The tenant's originating application for a new lease, county court form 335, had been prepared, properly containing all the required particulars and dated Apr. 15, 1965. On the afternoon of that day it was taken by or on behalf of the tenant's then solicitors to the Preston county court, where it had to be delivered. When delivered the court had to serve it on the landlords, but this could be done by the court within a month of its receipt (C.C.R., Ord. 40, r. 8 (1) and (1A)).

On finding the county court closed the solicitor took the originating application back to Garstang and posted it to the Preston county court by ordinary post that afternoon. The next day was Good Friday, when, we understand, no postal deliveries are normally made and in the ordinary way the document should have been delivered by post on the morning of Saturday, Apr. 17.

It was not so delivered because the Post Office, at the request of the Preston county court, do not deliver to that court on any Saturday, but keep the mail normally until the following Monday morning. This is no doubt a prudent and sensible arrangement as the court building is closed on Saturday and Sunday and payments of money are commonly made to a county court through the post. As this particular week-end was extended over the Easter Bank Holiday Monday, the mail was not delivered until the morning of Tuesday, Apr. 20, 1965. It was then that the tenant's originating application was seen by the county court which had been closed and unavailable for four and a half days. It would have been available to receive documents by post if it had not been interfered with by the county court itself in its directions to the local Post Office.

The tenant's application was accepted by the county court and duly served on the landlords, who put in an answer, dated June 1, 1965, which alleged that the court had no jurisdiction to entertain the application and relied on s. 29 (3) of the Act of 1954. Alternatively the answer pleaded objections to the terms of the new tenancy set up by the tenant. The case was heard before JUDGE INGRESS BELL on Dec. 6, 1965, and he held that he had no jurisdiction to grant a new lease as the originating application had not been received by the court on or before Apr. 19, 1965.

In the particular circumstances of the present case the court did not function at all on that day. No personal application could have been made to it, and a written application could not have received any attention though it could and probably would have been delivered to the court premises on or before that day if the court itself had not arranged for the Post Office to delay all deliveries by them until the court premises were open.

The principle to be determined here is the same whether the court was not functioning for one day, or for four and a half days as here. The judge had general but not direct authority to support his conclusion, but with great respect so to hold seems to me to bring the law into disrepute and subject it to the ridicule which is often too rapidly accorded to it. The main authorities in support of the judgment to which we were referred have been considered in the judgment to be delivered by DAVIES, L.J. I recognise the distinction of those who decided them, but the authorities are not binding on us, they relate to circumstances different from the present case and, like DAVIES, L.J., I see no reason to follow them.

It is said that this is a requirement of a statute and that the court cannot enlarge a time which a statute has specified. That, of course, must be accepted. The courts have to apply a statute in a manner which the statute can be held to have contemplated. On the face of it this would involve equal conditions for all and an application of the statute's provisions which was not fortuitous and fluctuating. If out of 101 days the court holds that one day does not count it leaves one hundred days which do. In such circumstances the court does not enlarge the one hundred days, it defines them. This seems to me to be the correct approach and function of the court which in no way would usurp the function of the legislature.

The Act of 1954 clearly gives the tenant four months and there is nothing to indicate that that period is to be in any way curtailed. The Act of 1954 requires that the originating application should be made to the court, and there would seem to be the underlying assumption that the court is functioning and available to receive it within the working hours of that date, otherwise the full statutory period may be curtailed for some by the mere mischance of dates. Further, the notification to the landlord is not regarded as a matter of urgency as the court has time in which to serve the application on the landlord, and in this case if the application had been handed in at the county court at 11.55 a.m. on Apr. 15 it is unlikely that the landlords would have been served with it any sooner than they were in fact.

In my opinion the county court officials were right in accepting the application and in sending it on to the landlords, and it would be a hardship and an injustice to the tenant and her solicitors to hold otherwise. The tenant had an undoubted claim for a new lease; only the terms remain for determination by the court, as the landlords well knew and recognised. If she has irrevocably lost this right by the mischance of the Easter Vacation falling so inconveniently, it may be that she would seek redress in a claim for damages for negligence against her then solicitors; but it might be held that it would be harsh in circumstances of this particular character to find the solicitor in negligent breach of duty to her (especially having regard to C.C.R., Ord. 48, r. 10 (3)), in which case the tenant by fortuitous circumstances completely outside her control would have lost her tenancy without redress. Against this the landlords would have a fortuitous gain. They knew that the tenant wished to have a new lease and that they could not resist one. There is no element of surprise and the landlords are not prejudiced by delay. However if the defence is legally right I suppose that it cannot be said that it is unmeritorious. It was certainly not necessary for the landlords to seize the gain of vacant possession in such unusual circumstances.

Does the law then deprive the tenant of her right and let fortune aid the undeserving? I cannot think that any Act of Parliament would intentionally so differentiate and make different limits for some than for others. Parliament has stipulated a time for applying to the court and has left it to the courts to administer this equitably and not so as to be to the prejudice of one as compared with others. If the material date had been a week later, Monday, Apr. 26, instead of the Easter Bank Holiday, no difficulty would have arisen if the solicitors had acted on the previous Thursday. Recognition of the difficulties such as have arisen here was made in the rules of both the High Court and the county court at the time the Act of 1954 was passed. The High Court rule has since been modified, as I indicate later, but the provisions seem so sensible and reasonable that one asks why they should not prevail with or without the rule.

Does the court need in each statute requiring notices to be given to a court— of which there are so many—an express stipulation about days when a court to which an application or notice is to be made or given is closed, or can it not be said that the courts are able and are intended to administer the provisions strictly but with regard to the functioning and availability of the court?

In 1858 it was held in *Peacock* v. *Reginam* (2) that an alehouse keeper, who wished to appeal from his conviction before the magistrates that he had sold beer after hours, was out of time. The conviction was on a Thursday and the statutory time for application to the justices to state a Case was within three days. The application was made on the following Monday. As the court did not sit on Sunday the decision involved that a conviction on a Thursday meant only two days in which to apply for a Case to be stated whereas a conviction on any other day but Thursday gave the three days which the statute required. It seems to me an odd discrimination against those coming to trial on a Thursday and there is nothing in the statute—or in common sense—why it should be so. I speak with deference, for over the years there have been those who have so interpreted statutory provisions as to time.

However, in a footnote to *Peacock's* case (3) there is cited *R.* v. *Middlesex Justices* (4), where a notice of appeal against an order of affiliation was required to be given " within twenty-four hours after adjudication ". It was held that in computing the twenty-four hours for that purpose, Sunday was to be excluded and consequently where the order was made on Saturday a notice of appeal given on Monday was sufficient. It was not impossible to have given a notice immediately on the making of the order, but the judgment rightly gave the party the twenty-four hours for consideration as to appeal.

In *Mayer* v. *Harding* (5) the decision turned on the impossibility of giving a notice to any time within the allotted time. The applicant, having applied to the justices to state a Case, received it from them on Good Friday and transmitted it to the proper court on the following Wednesday. It should have been transmitted by the applicant within three days after he had received it. It was held that as the court offices were closed from Friday until Wednesday the applicant had transmitted the case as soon as it was possible to do so and had sufficiently complied with the statutory requirement. It is true that in the circumstances of that case the applicant could not have transmitted the Case sooner as there were no available days within the period when the court was open. If it had so happened that the Case had been received on the Thursday the applicant would have been able to transmit it on that day, but if that was obligatory he would not have had the three days given by statute to decide whether to transmit the Case or not. One day is so obviously different from the three days allowed by statute that I cannot see how it could be read into a statute so as to defeat a notice not given within the one available day.

In either *Mayer's* case (5) or the *Peacock* case (2) one cannot visualise that Parliament, if they had intended to legislate expressly about it, would have reduced the time in respect of either litigant in circumstances where the court was closed. Such a differentiation between litigants would appear ridiculous on the face of any clause expressing it. Why then should the courts imply that Parliament intended any such curtailment of time in such fortuitous circumstances?

(2) (1858), 4 C.B.N.S. 264.   (3) (1858), 4 C.B.N.S. at p. 268.
(4) (1848), 17 L.J.M.C. 111.   (5) (1867), L.R. 2 Q.B. 410.

In 1862 a court had to consider a time limitation imposed by the Absconding Debtors Act, 1857 (see *Hughes* v. *Griffiths* (6)). A creditor to whom a debt of £20 or upwards was owing who could show probable cause for believing that such a debtor, unless he were apprehended, was about to quit England to avoid the debt could obtain a warrant for his arrest. The Act of 1857 provided expressly that every creditor who obtained such a warrant " shall forthwith cause to be issued a writ of capias " and that the debtor in custody should be served with such writ of capias " within seven days from the date of the warrant, including the day of such date ". On Apr. 12, 1862, the plaintiffs obtained a warrant. On Apr. 14 the defendant was arrested under the warrant. On Apr. 23 the plaintiffs obtained a writ of capias and served it on that day. The defendant later took out a summons to rescind that order and WILLIAMS, J., did rescind and set aside the order on the ground that it was not issued within seven days of the warrant as the statute stipulated. The seventh day was a Good Friday and no writ of capias could issue on that day or until Wednesday Apr. 23, because the court offices were closed. It was argued for the debtor that the statute did not except the Easter holidays, " its language is imperative and as it is a matter affecting the liberty of the subject it must be construed strictly "; but the court, consisting of ERLE, C.J., WILLIAMS, J., WILLES, J., and BYLES, J., reversed the order of WILLIAMS, J., and upheld the writ of capias on the ground (6) that

" the act is to be done by the court . . . the seven days limited for the issuing of a capias expired on Good Friday . . . a capias issued on the following Wednesday was in time—that being the earliest day on which it was practicable to issue the writ."

WILLES, J., referred (7) to a case where the court had held that the time allowed for the defendant's appearance might be extended to the thirteenth day where the twelfth was a Sunday. BYLES, J., said (8):

" The meaning I take to be this—the creditor shall have seven days in which to set the court in motion. Consequently, the seventh day must be one upon which the court can be set in motion; otherwise the party would not have that which the legislature contemplated that he should have."

In the present case the originating application is not a mere notice to the landlord. It is the combined act of the party and of the court. The tenant has to make the application and the court office has to receive it and itself in turn act on its receipt. It is said that the application could have been made some days before. That is true, but that would have deprived the tenant of some part of the time which the statute has prescribed. I cannot find any such differentiation between one tenant and another or between one lease and another depending on the differences of their date in relation to the time of the functioning of the appropriate court. In my view the proper construction of the statute requires that all tenants and all leases should be placed on the same basis as to time. They would be on the same footing if, in a period of months, a Saturday or a Sunday or a Bank Holiday occurring in the course of the period were to be treated for all alike as part of the month. It is only when the final day falls on a court holiday that a differentiation can arise. If the final day is a Monday and the court is open, the tenant has the complete period. If the final day is a Sunday, when the court is not open, and the necessary act cannot be done, and if it is to be held that the act must be done the day before, such a decision would deprive the party concerned of one of the days the statute stipulated. That seems to me more a usurpation of the legislature's function than to decree that the tenant should have the full period during which the combined act of the court and of the party can be performed.

Statutes and circumstances may vary widely and it may be that no principle

---

(6) (1862), 13 C.B.N.S. 324.   (7) (1862), 13 C.B.N.S. at p. 336.
(8) (1862), 13 C.B.N.S. at p. 337.

can or need be evolved to cover all circumstances, though I would prefer the approach which I have indicated to that of the decisions to the contrary in the cases to which we have been referred.. Differences have been drawn between limitation periods measured in days and those in months or years, but I do not find them convincing. The relevant provisions of the Landlord and Tenant Act, 1954, are procedural, as far as this Act is concerned the court has to play a vital part and I would hold that the functioning of the court is an essential factor in assessing the time for applications to be made.

Reference was made to the Bankruptcy Act, 1914, s. 145, which makes this express provision:

" (1) Where by this Act any limited time from or after any date or event is appointed or allowed for the doing of any act or the taking of any proceeding, then in the computation of that limited time the same shall be taken as exclusive of the day of that date or of the happening of that event, and as commencing at the beginning of the next following day; and the act or proceeding shall be done or taken at latest on the last day of that limited time as so computed, unless the last day is a Sunday, Christmas Day, Good Friday, or Monday or Tuesday in Easter Week, or a day appointed for public fast, humiliation, or thanksgiving, or a day on which the court does not sit, in which case any act or proceeding shall be considered as done or taken in due time if it is done or taken on the next day afterwards which is not one of the days in this section specified.

" (2) Where by this Act any act or proceeding is directed to be done or taken on a certain day, then, if that day happens to be one of the days in this section specified, the act or proceeding shall be considered as done or taken in due time if it is done or taken on the next day afterwards which is not one of the days in this section specified."

There may be good and perhaps historical reasons why in bankruptcy matters the position when the court was not functioning should be dealt with expressly. It makes for clarity where default might be disastrous to a man's status and trading. What conclusion has to be drawn from that? Is it to be concluded in respect of Acts which require applications and notices of like kinds that Parliament, if it had considered the matter or had thought it necessary to legislate on it, would have said that such reasonable and fair provisions in respect of bankruptcy matters should *not* apply in respect of the administration of other Acts, but that in all matters except bankruptcy there should be a differentiation so that some would have the allotted time curtailed should it chance that the dates limiting performance fell awkwardly because the courts were closed at the terminating date? It seems to me contrary to the true spirit of legislation that any such differentiation would be made, and I would not think it right that the courts in administering an Act such as the Landlord and Tenant Act, 1954, should make any such assumption.

If I am wrong in my views on a correct interpretation of the statute I would apply the County Court Rules, which in terms fit the circumstances entirely. If consulted by a solicitor they would serve to show him the provision made to meet circumstances such as arose here. The rules reflect the provision which Parliament might be held to have expressly stated if express statement had been thought necessary. They seem to me to work in conjunction with and not contrary to the statute. C.C.R., Ord. 48, r. 10 (1) and (2) deals with the circumstances " where anything is required by these rules to be done within a specified period . . .", but in contrast to those two sub-rules the third sub-rule states:

" Where the time prescribed for doing any act expires on a Sunday or any other day on which the court office is closed and by reason thereof the act cannot be done on that day, the act shall be in time if done on the next day on which the court office is open."

C.C.R., Ord. 6, r. 4 deals generally with originating applications, but Ord. 40, r. 8 deals expressly with applications for a new tenancy of business premises under the Landlord and Tenant Act, 1954. If the Act and the orders are read together, in my view Ord. 48, r. 10 (3) establishes that the originating application which the county court received and accepted on Tuesday, Apr. 20, was in time. In July, 1954, the Supreme Court Rules (9) were to the same effect. In January, 1964, an amendment came into force restricting the provisions to periods laid down by the rules themselves or by any judgment, order or direction. The reason for the amendment was not available to us, and I am not prepared to conjecture.

On the above grounds I would allow the appeal and hold that the originating application was in time and that the learned judge had both jurisdiction and an obligation to hear it.

A wholly separate point was taken on the postal delivery arrangements made by the court, without which in all probability the originating application would have been delivered on Saturday, Apr. 17. C.C.R., Ord. 26, r. 1 clearly permits delivery by post as an alternative to personal attendance. It does not make the postal authorities the agents to receive documents on behalf of the court, but a delivery to the court's office by the postal authority I would regard as delivery to the court even if the officials were not there at the time of delivery.

In the ordinary course the postal authorities would be the agents of the sender and mere postage of a sum of money or of an application or notice to the court would not normally be equivalent to delivery to the court; but here the circumstances are different. The court has expressly intervened and interfered with the ordinary postal facilities. The mail due to be delivered on Saturdays was withheld from delivery at the express request of the court. It was held at the local Post Office. For whom did the Post Office then hold the mail? Not, I think, for the sender because it was his desire that the delivery should be made in the course of post and he was no party to any postponement of delivery. It seems to me that the Post Office in these particular circumstances were made the agents of the local county court to hold on its behalf the mail which would normally have been delivered on the Saturday. It would appear that the tenant's application would have reached the court in due time but for the special arrangements which the court made, and I see no reason why the tenant should be prejudiced by them.

I would therefore further hold that the tenant's application was delivered to the court which was to receive it on Apr. 17 or was to be treated as so delivered as it was held on that date on behalf of the court. It was therefore in time.

I would allow the appeal on the above ground also and would send the case back to be heard in the Preston county court on the question of the terms of the tenancy unless in the meantime the parties agree them.

DAVIES, L.J.: The point at issue in this case is obviously a difficult one, but one cannot help feeling that the real merits of the matter are on the side of the tenant. It is true that her former solicitor could easily have made the application on her behalf at such a time as to avoid the technicality in which we are now involved; but, in view of the fact that the landlords had in the notice to quit dated Dec. 15, 1964, stated that they would not oppose an application to the court for the grant of a new tenancy, I entirely agree with SELLERS, L.J., that the ordinary layman would think it wrong that the tenant's right should be forfeited by the odd and unusual circumstances of this case, the details of which have been fully stated by SELLERS, L.J.

The tenant's application for a new tenancy under s. 24 of the Landlord and Tenant Act, 1954, has to be made by originating application (C.C.R., Ord. 40, r. 8 (1)), and must be served by the court on the landlord within one month (Ord.

---

(9) See the former R.S.C., Ord. 64, r. 3. That rule was revoked by R.S.C. (Rev.), 1962, which came into operation on Jan. 1, 1964, and replaced (with the amendment indicated) by R.S.C., Ord. 3, r. 4, and is now Ord. 3, r. 4 of the R.S.C., 1965.

40, r. 8 (1A); Ord. 8, r. 38 (1)). The method of commencing proceedings by originating application is prescribed by C.C.R., Ord. 6, r. 4; by sub-r. (2) (b) of that rule the application must be filed in the court office. By Ord. 26, r. 1 (1), however, any act that may be done by a party in the office of a county court by attendance at the office may be done by post. The period of four months prescribed by s. 29 (3) of the Landlord and Tenant Act, 1954, for the making of a tenant's application under s. 24 (1) expired at midnight on Easter Monday, Apr. 19, 1965; but, as we know, the county court office was, in accordance with the provisions of C.C.R., Ord. 1, r. 2, closed from noon on Apr. 15 (Maundy Thursday) until 10 a.m. on Tuesday, Apr. 20.

In the view that I take of this case, the decisive rule is C.C.R., Ord. 48, r. 10. That rule provides as follows:

" (1) Where anything is required by these rules to be done within a specified period of or after the happening of a particular event, the period shall be computed from the end of the day on which the event happens unless the period is expressed to be inclusive of such day.

" (2) Where anything is required by these rules to be done within a period not exceeding three days or where a period not exceeding three days is required by these rules to elapse between the doing of an act and the happening of a particular event, no Sunday and no day on which the court office is closed shall be included in the computation of that period.

" (3) Where the time prescribed for doing any act expires on a Sunday or any other day on which the court office is closed and by reason thereof the act cannot be done on that day, the act shall be in time if done on the next day on which the court office is open."

It seems to me that the contrast between the words of sub-rr. (1) and (2) on the one hand and those of sub-r. (3) on the other is most marked. The two former apply " when anything is required by these rules to be done ". The latter is quite general, videlicet, " when the time prescribed for doing any act expires ". It is pointed out for the landlords that at the date of the passing of the Landlord and Tenant Act, 1954, the relevant rules of the Supreme Court (10) were in similar terms to those of C.C.R., Ord. 48, r. 10, but that they have been subsequently altered to read as follows: " Where the time prescribed by these rules, or by any judgment, order or direction for doing any act . . . expires . . ." (R.S.C., Ord. 3, r. 4). That, it is argued, cannot afford what might be called " a day of grace " for the tenant's application under the Act of 1954 in the High Court, since in terms it does not apply to the time prescribed by any statute; and, it is said, it would be absurd if the position in this regard were different in a case which, owing to the rateable value of the premises, fell within the High Court jurisdiction from what it would be if the matter fell within the jurisdiction of the county court.

This is a powerful argument; but we do not know the reason for the change in the Rules of the Supreme Court, and we must apply the County Court Rules as they stand. On the face of C.C.R., Ord. 48, r. 10 (3) it applies to the facts of the present case. By that I mean that, as the time prescribed for making the tenant's application expired on a day on which the court office was closed and by reason thereof that act could not be done on that day, the application should be in time if done on the next day. It is said on the other side, however, that in principle and on authority the rule cannot have this effect. The principle suggested is, as I understand it, propounded in two ways. It is said that when a statute, such as s. 29 (3) of the Landlord and Tenant Act, 1954, in this case, prescribes a fixed time for the doing of any act, rules of court cannot alter that time, and that, if they purport so to do, they are ultra vires. Procedural law, it is said, cannot alter substantive law. Alternatively, it is submitted that, if a statute prescribes a time limit within which proceedings must be initiated, procedural rules such as

(10) See footnote (9), p. 315, ante.

A C.C.R., Ord. 48, r. 10 (3) can apply only to steps in the proceedings once they
have been initiated, and can have no relevance to the actual initiation of the
proceedings.

This argument is in principle difficult to follow. A statute lays down a time
within which proceedings must be commenced; but proceedings can only be
commenced in accordance with the procedural rules of the court, in this case

B C.C.R., Ord. 6, r. 4. Moreover, if that is so, any special time provisions which are
a part of the court's procedural code are necessarily incorporated. In the present
case I do not regard C.C.R., Ord. 48, r. 10 (3) as amending or altering s. 29 (3) of
the Act of 1954. It is a provision which deals with the special circumstance of the
court office being closed on the last day. It does not extend the time limited by
the statute. What it does is to provide that in such a special case the act shall

C be deemed to have been done within that time.

In principle, therefore, there appears to be no reason why full effect should not
be given to the words of C.C.R., Ord. 48, r. 10 (3). But it is submitted for the
landlords that there are authorities of long standing to the opposite effect; and,
indeed, there are such authorities. Of the most pertinent ones, the first is *Morris*
v. *Richards* (11), a decision of Mr. Commissioner WILLS, Q.C., at Shrewsbury

D Assizes. That was an action on a promissory note. The six-year period of limitation expired on a Sunday, and the writ was issued on the next day. The terms of
the then Ord. 57, r. 3 were substantially similar to those of the present C.C.R.,
Ord. 48, r. 10 (3), but the learned commissioner held that the rule did not apply
and that the writ was out of time. He said (12):

E   " I am of the opinion that the rule has no application in this case. The
      ' time for doing any act ' in this rule refers to times limited by the practice
      of the court for taking proceedings and the effect of the rule is, that in the
      cases to which it is applicable, a proceeding which but for that enactment
      would not, if taken on Monday, be duly taken in accordance with the
      practice of the court, whether established by definite enactment or other-
      wise, shall nevertheless be held to be duly taken. It certainly was never

F   intended that the provision should affect the Statute of Limitations. The
      writ in this case was ' duly issued ' on the Monday without the protection
      of Ord. 57, r. 3, and there is nothing in the enactment to alter the actual
      date of the commencement of the action."

That decision was followed by CHANNELL, J., in *Gelmini* v. *Moriggia* (13). That
again was an action on a promisory note where the six years limitation period had

G expired on a Sunday and the writ had been issued on the following day. The
rule in force was, though differently numbered, the same as that under
consideration in *Morris* v. *Richards* (11). CHANNELL, J., said (14):

      " Mr. Commissioner WILLS decided that for the purpose of anything to be
      done under the rules, the effect of [the order] was that the Monday would

H   be counted as if it was Sunday; but he decided that the rule had no effect
      on the operation of the Statute of Limitations. Although that decision was
      one at nisi prius, and therefore probably not binding on me, I think it was
      right."

The other authority to which reference was made is *Déchène* v. *City of Montreal*
(15) in the Privy Council. The proceeding there was a petition by a municipal

I elector against the City of Montreal for the annulment of a resolution of the City
Corporation on the ground of its alleged illegality. The right of so petitioning
was limited to by three months from the date of the coming into force of the
resolution. The last day of the three months was the feast of St. Peter and St.
Paul, a non-juridical day, and the petition was presented on the next day; but

---

(11) (1881), 45 L.T. 210.   (12) (1881), 45 L.T. at p. 211.
(13) [1911-13] All E.R. Rep. 1115; [1913] 2 K.B. 549.
(14) [1913] 2 K.B. at p. 552; [1911-13] All E.R. Rep. at p. 1117.
(15) [1894] A.C. 640.

it was held to be out of time. The opinion of the Judicial Committee was delivered A
by LORD WATSON, who said this (16):

"The respondents do not dispute that, when an action is depending, the
rule upon which the appellant relies is applicable to proceedings in the
litigation. But they maintain that the statutory title of the appellant to
petition the court and their own statutory immunity, which arises
immediately upon the cesser of his title, are matters of right, and not of   B
procedure; and that the prescription by which his title is cut off and their
immunity established is regulated by the provisions of the civil code.

"The rule for which the appellant contends is to be found in s. 3 of the
Code of Civil Procedure, which enacts as follows: 'If the day on which
anything ought to be done in pursuance of the law is a non-juridical day,
such thing may be done with like effect on the following juridical day.' In   C
the opinion of their lordships, that enactment refers exclusively to things
which the law has directed to be done, either by the plaintiff or the
defendant, in the course of a suit, and has no reference to the title or want
of title in the plaintiff to institute and maintain it.

"The enactment upon which the appellant chiefly relied is s. 20 of the
Quebec statute (49 & 50 Vict. c. 95). The statute did not become law until   D
Aug. 25, 1886, nearly two months after the present petition was brought,
but is said to be declaratory. Section 20 is in these terms: 'If the delay
fixed for any proceeding or for the doing of anything expires on a non-
juridical day, such delay is prolonged until the next following juridical
day.' The section appears to their lordships to be essentially a procedure
clause, and to be, in substance, a re-enactment of s. 3 of the Code of Civil   E
Procedure. Its language is not calculated to suggest that a claimant may
bring an action for recovery of land after the period of limitation has run if
he can show that the last day or days of that period were non-juridical, and
that his claim is preferred upon the first juridical day after its expiry. Yet
that would be the logical result of giving effect to the argument of the
appellant."   F

The more recent Scots case, *M'Niven* v. *Glasgow Corpn.* (17), points in the same
direction, though the question there at issue was somewhat different.

With the very greatest respect, I would not follow these authorities. As I have
said earlier, the initiation of proceedings is governed by the rules of procedure.
It is only under and in accordance with rules of court that a writ or summons   G
can be issued or an originating application can be made; and among the rules of
procedure there is to be found such a rule as C.C.R., Ord. 48, r. 10 (3), dealing as
it does with very special circumstances. There does not seem to me to be any
possible ground on which such a rule should be excluded or ignored. As I have
already said, the rule seems to me not to extend the time prescribed by the
statute but to provide that in the special circumstances the act shall be in time   H
if done on the next day. In my judgment, therefore, the rule applies, and the
application received at the county court office on Apr. 20 was in time.

An entirely different point arises under C.C.R., Ord. 26, r. 1 (1). As already
stated, that provides as follows:

"Any act that may be done by a party in the office of a county court by
attendance at the office may be done by post, subject to the condition that   I
the party shall send to the court office by prepaid post (*a*) such documents
as he would have been required to produce at the court office if he had
attended . . ."

At one stage of the argument it seemed that there might be something to be said
for the proposition that the tenant's application in this case was made when her
solicitor put it in the post, that is to say on Thursday, Apr. 15. The obvious

---

(16) [1894] A.C. at pp. 644, 645.   (17) 1920 S.C. 584.

analogy is the principle which applies to postal acceptances of an offer in the law of contract, as illustrated by the well-known line of cases such as *Dunlop* v. *Higgins* (18). On further consideration, however, it appears that to apply such a principle here would give rise to many complications and difficulties; and, as was pointed out by RUSSELL, L.J., if that principle did apply it might be thought that C.C.R., Ord. 48, r. 10 (3) would be otiose seeing that an application or other act could always be made or done by post even on a Sunday or other non-juridical day. Nevertheless it has to be observed that C.C.R., Ord. 26, r. 1 is not subject to any proviso that the sending by post must be at such a time and in such circumstances that the postal communication will in the ordinary course of post arrive at the county court office on a day when the office is open. The letter posted by the tenant's former solicitor on Thursday, Apr. 15 might reasonably be expected to have been delivered on Saturday, Apr. 17 in the ordinary course of post, the intervening day being Good Friday. If it had been so delivered, it is difficult to see how it could have been argued that the application had not been made by Apr. 17, even though the office was closed on that day and the application could not have been dealt with. Does it make any difference that the county court authorities had, for obviously good reasons, instructed the postal authorities not to make any deliveries to the county court on a Saturday or on Easter Monday? It would seem most unfair to the tenant that it should do so. Her then solicitor posted the application in time for it to be delivered on the Saturday. He must be taken to know that the office would not be open for business on that day but he might well not be aware that no letters would be delivered.

This point is also a difficult one; but on the whole it seems to me that the right conclusion is that when the county court directed that mail which would ordinarily be delivered on the Saturday should not be so delivered, but should be held by the Post Office until the following Monday, or in this particular case Tuesday, the county court were constituting the Post Office their bailees of the mail and accordingly it could rightly be said that the tenant's application was made at latest on the Saturday.

In my judgment, therefore, this appeal succeeds.

RUSSELL, L.J.: This case has two aspects. The first aspect involves in substance the question whether an application made on Tuesday, Apr. 20, 1965, under s. 24 (1) of the Landlord and Tenant Act, 1954, can be entertained notwithstanding the fact that the relevant period of four months expired on Monday, Apr. 19, a day on which, being a Bank Holiday, the relevant county court office was not functioning. (The fact that it had not functioned, owing to the Easter vacation, since some time on Thursday, Apr. 15, is not relevant to the question of law involved in this aspect of the case. Nor is it relevant to any aspect of law in this case that it happens to be one in which the landlord could dispute only the terms of a new lease if an application were made in due time. These points affect the heart, but cannot affect the head.)

The Act of 1954 is one which enables a tenant of business premises to bring legal proceedings (that is, to make application to the court) seeking an order entitling him to the grant of a new tenancy. Without such proceedings (or application) his rights as a tenant must end, unless he and the landlord voluntarily agree on a further tenancy. The Act of 1954 imposes a time limit on the ability of the tenant to initiate such proceedings by making such application to the court. Section 24 (1) says that " subject to the provisions of s. 29 . . . the tenant . . . may apply to the court for a new tenancy ". The court is either the High Court or the county court depending on rateable value: see s. 63. The Act of 1954 contains various provisions for notices by tenant and landlord which must precede the making of any such application by the tenant. Section 29 (3) so far as now relevant says:

---

(18) (1848), 1 H.L. Cas. 381.

" No application under [s. 24 (1)] shall be entertained unless it is made not less than two nor more than four months after the giving of the landlord's notice . . ."

In terms, therefore, the tenant's right to initiate proceedings by making application to the court was barred by Tuesday, Apr. 20: an application to the court then made for the first time could not be entertained by the court. The tenant had had four calendar months to think about his situation and two in which to make application. The provisions of s. 29 (3) to my mind bear clearly the character of a statutory limitation of action.

The first question is whether as a general proposition a statutory time limitation on the initiation of civil proceedings expressed in terms of calendar months or years may be construed or administered in such a way as to treat as within time a step taken outside the period, when the closing of the necessary court office makes it impossible to take the step at any time on the last available day of the period and the step is taken in fact on the first available office day outside the period. It has I think always been taken to be the law that such general proposition is not correct, and I agree with that view. If a limitation period of months or years is laid down by a statute it is speaking of periods which necessarily include days on which the initiation of proceedings is impossible owing to closure of the relevant judicial office on certain days within each such period. The proposed litigant is not given the opportunity to act on every day in the limitation period, just as he is not given every hour in every day in which to act. Suppose a proposed litigant to arrive hotfoot on the last day of the permitted period at 6 p.m., when the hours within which the judicial office functions end at 5 p.m., he must be barred. So if he arrives on the last day of the permitted period and finds that the judicial office does not function on that day, he must be barred. It is not, I think, correct to say that he is thereby deprived of the full measure of the period allowed to him by the statute, because what *is* the full measure is conditioned by the subject-matter under treatment, and the practice of closure of judicial offices.

That this is the general position was not only decided but in fact *assumed* in *Morris* v. *Richards* (19) and *Gelmini* v. *Moriggia* (20); the arguments which failed depended on an attempt to apply particular provisions of Rules of Court. It was also assumed in *Déchêne* v. *City of Montreal* (21) in the Privy Council. I am not aware that the contrary has ever been suggested or argued save in the Scottish case, *M'Niven* v. *Glasgow Corpn.* (22), where it most signally failed. These cases may not be binding on us, but I think them, for the reasons which I have given, to be right. Nor in my judgment does the rather special case of *Hughes* v. *Griffiths* (23) throw doubt on them.

I proceed then to the more limited argument on the first aspect of the case. This is based on the language of C.C.R., Ord. 48, r. 10 (3). This has already been read and the contrast between the generality of its terms and those of the preceding sub-rules has been remarked; but these rules are concerned with procedure and not with rights. At the time of *Morris* v. *Richards* (19) and *Gelmini* v. *Moriggia* (20) the relevant rule affecting the High Court was in equally general form: in both it was argued that initiation of the proceedings on the day after the expiration of the limitation period was, by force of the rule, to be considered as within the period when on the last day the judicial office was not functioning: in both cases the attempt failed, and I am not aware that any criticism has been levelled at those decisions or that they have not been universally accepted as correct. There are so many provisions in our laws having the character of statutes of limitation—in more modern times we have had examples under the Inheritance (Family Provision) Act, 1938, and s. 209 of the

---

(19) (1881), 45 L.T. 210.   (20) [1911-13] All E.R. Rep. 1115; [1913] 2 K.B. 549.
(21) [1894] A.C. 640.   (22) 1920 S.C. 584.
                    (23) (1862), 13 C.B.N.S. 324.

Companies Act, 1948—that the occasions when monthly or yearly limitation periods ended on a Saturday or Sunday or during a holiday period, and a would-be claimant awoke late to a realisation of the position, cannot have been negligible in number. The Judicial Committee in *Déchène* v. *City of Montreal* (24), when considering whether a similar provision expressed in general terms in the Code of Civil Procedure had the suggested operation in relation to a limitation period, equally confined its operation to procedural steps *in the course of* existing litigation and denied its relevance to a question of title (or want of title) to bring proceedings. Traces of a similar approach are to be found in *M'Niven* v. *Glasgow Corpn.* (25). I observe, moreover, that amendment of the relevant rule (26) of the Supreme Court in 1963 made it clear that it cannot have the effect suggested: it is now in terms restricted to periods laid down under the rules. What is to be made of this? Is it that the rule-making body for the Supreme Court wished to narrow its scope? Or is it that it accepted the construction put on it by the courts (27) (which was noted under R.S.C., Ord. 64, r. 3 in the 1963 ANNUAL PRACTICE) and thought it better to avoid a chance of a misunderstanding which could only be cleared up by inspection of authority—a step not yet taken in relation to C.C.R., Ord. 48, r. 10 (3)? The second explanation is surely preferable. The alternative is that if an action involving a period of limitation is capable of initiation in the county court one system applies: but if only capable of initiation in the High Court, since 1963 another system applies: under the Act of 1954 rateable value might make all the difference to the question whether a tenant's application was out of time.

The tenant sought further to distinguish the authorities already mentioned by saying that they dealt with the impact—or lack of impact—of rules of court on pre-existing limitation statutes: and that it would have been in those cases ultra vires the rule-making authority to affect the periods already laid down by such pre-existing statutes. The argument proceeds, as I understand it, thus: that here in 1954 is a statute which confers a right to initiate proceedings in a court (while at the same time imposing a time limit on such initiation): therefore the statute must be subjecting the operation of that time limit to the pre-existing provisions of the rules of procedure of the court in question. I cannot accept that as a true analysis of and distinction from the previous authorities. The authorities in question do not go on the question of ultra vires, but on the basis that the rules are related to procedure *in* a suit and not to title or want of title to *initiate* a suit. The argument really assumes in its favour a construction of C.C.R., Ord. 48, r. 10 (3) (and the equivalent High Court rule before amendment) which I think erroneous; and further poses, without answering, the question of the effect of the 1963 change.

On the first aspect of the case I am therefore of opinion that the application if made on Tuesday, Apr. 20 could not be entertained and was ineffective. I add only that if the legislature wishes to apply the principles found in C.C.R., Ord. 48, r. 10 (3) to periods laid down in a statute it has shown itself well able to do so in what is now s. 145 of the Bankruptcy Act, 1914: and see also the Local Government Act, 1933, s. 295 (1). I would with satisfaction hold that in all cases where

---

(24) [1894] A.C. 640.   (25) 1920 S.C. 584.
(26) See footnote (9), p. 315, ante.
(27) The note referred to, and which now appears as a note to the current R.S.C., Ord. 3, r. 4 (Supreme Court Practice 1967, p. 13), is, in part, as follows: " EFFECT OF RULE.—This rule only applies where ' by reason of ' the offices being closed the act or proceeding cannot be or taken on that day (*Re Lambert, Ex p. Saffery* (1877), 5 Ch.D. 365, C.A.). For example, when the offices are closed, a writ cannot be issued, appearance entered (*M'Kibbin* v. *M'Clelland*, [1894] 2 I.R. 65), document filed or motion moved in court (*Taylor* v. *Jones*, (1875), 34 L.T. 131); but a notice of appeal may be given (*Re Lambert, Ex p. Saffery*, supra; *Chambon* v. *Heighwey*, (1890), 54 J.P. 520). Furthermore, this rule does not, for example, serve to extend the period of limitation under a statute; and if that period expires on a Sunday, a writ issued on the following day is too late " (*Gelmini* v. *Moriggia*, [1911-13] All E.R. Rep. 1115). See also *Taylor* v. *Taylor*, (1875), 34 L.T. 131.

a statutory period for initiating proceedings expires on a dies non the next office
day should be deemed to be within the period; but this would be legislation.

I turn now to the second aspect of the case. Here the particular facts are
relevant. The application form was posted addressed to the county court office on
Thursday, Apr. 15. It is accepted that this would have been available in due
course of post on Saturday, Apr. 17: there were no deliveries on Friday, Sunday or
Monday. It is an arrangement with the Post Office that letters should not be
delivered on Saturdays, for the very good reasons that the county court office
does not function on Saturdays and no official is there to receive them. It is
argued for the tenant that " application " was " made " to the court in the
circumstances on Saturday, Apr. 17, when but for this sensible arrangement the
letter enclosing it would have been put through the letter-box of the building—
if it has one.

Reference here is made to C.C.R., Ord. 26, r. 1 (1), which is in the following
terms:

> " Any act that may be done by a party in the office of a county court by
> attendance at the office may be done by post, subject to the condition that
> the party shall send to the court office by prepaid post—(a) such documents
> as he would have been required to produce at the court office if he had
> attended; and (b) a postal or money order for any court fees payable and
> any money to be paid or tendered to a witness in accordance with Ord. 20,
> r. 8; and (c) an envelope addressed to himself and sufficiently stamped."

This rule, in my judgment, does nothing more than afford a convenient alternative
to personal attendance. What for present purposes is " the act which may be
done by a party in the office of a county court by attendance at the office "? It
is to make an application for a new lease by originating application by producing
the relevant document to the officials. This it seems to me can plainly only be
done in office hours, when the office is functioning as such. It could not have been
done on Saturday, Apr. 17 by putting the document through the letter-box (if any)
or handing it to the charwoman (if any) or pinning it to or pushing it under the
front door. Nor could any of these actions have been effective if done by the
solicitor on the afternoon of Thursday, Apr. 15 when he found the office closed and
went away. I cannot see that Ord. 26, r. 1 (1) by offering a postal alternative to
that which is otherwise required (personal attendance) permits an application to
be made to the court on a day on which personal application cannot be made.
For that reason I consider that the arrangement for non-delivery on Saturday is
irrelevant.

I would dismiss the appeal.

*Appeal allowed. Case remitted to Preston county court for terms of new tenancy to
be fixed, if not agreed. Leave to appeal to the House of Lords refused.*

Solicitors: *Bower, Cotton & Bower*, agents for *Gowling, Seddon, Taylor &
Cooper*, Preston (for the tenant); *Geoffrey Coombs & Co.*, agents for *G. W.
Hodgson & Co.*, Nottingham (for the landlords).

[*Reported by* HENRY SUMMERFIELD, ESQ., *Barrister-at-Law.*]

STICK *v.* STICK.

[DEVON ASSIZES (Karminski, J.), April 21, 22, 1966.]

Divorce—Cruelty—Provocation—Provocation must bear direct relation to acts of retaliation alleged to constitute cruelty.

The husband and wife were married in 1954, when she was twenty-eight and he was about a year younger. There were matrimonial difficulties between them. She was a woman who was very backward, and the husband must have realised when he married her that particular tolerance would be needed. The wife gradually withdrew from sexual intercourse, and during 1962 refused it altogther. Her denial of intercourse developed into disputes, the wife sometimes pinching or hitting the husband. In the summer of 1961, on the occasion of one of these disputes, the husband took the wife by the throat, and, though he said that he used very little force, frightened her. About a year later, on the occasion of another such dispute, the husband struck the wife, giving her a couple of black eyes. He apologised. After this she withdrew from sexual intercourse altogether. In August, 1963, there was a serious quarrel; the husband was at home decorating the house, the wife had not prepared lunch and proposed going out herself instead of preparing their tea. The husband, using some force, got her into the bedroom and locked her in; he did not leave the house, and entered the bedroom himself at about 10 p.m. to go to bed, but she was kept locked in for about twelve hours. On the following day she left him. On petition by the wife for divorce on the ground of cruelty,

Held: (i) in determining whether, in a divorce suit brought by a wife for cruelty, force used on her by her husband was excessive, it was essential to a defence that she was the aggressor that the provocation on her part must bear a direct relation to the husband's retaliation; moreover, in such a case, the court would have particular regard to the nature of the wife (see p. 328, letter D, post).

Waring v. *Waring* ((1813), 2 Hag. Con. 153) applied.

(ii) in the circumstances of the present case provocation by the wife was insufficient to justify the husband's retaliation; accordingly cruelty on his part was established and she was entitled to a decree nisi (see p. 328, letter H, post).

[As to provocation as a defence to a charge of cruelty, see 12 HALSBURY'S LAWS (3rd Edn.) 277, para. 532; and for cases on the subject, see 27 DIGEST (Repl.) 309, 310, *2574-2584.*]

Case referred to:

Waring v. *Waring*, (1813), 2 Hag. Con. 153; 2 Phillim. 132; 161 E.R. 699; 27 Digest (Repl.) 309, *2574.*

Petition.

This was a petition by the wife for divorce on the ground of cruelty. The particulars of cruelty included alleged acts of violence by the husband against the wife. The husband, by his defence, admitted the use of a certain degree of force but pleaded that his conduct was justified by reason of provocation by the wife. The facts are stated in the judgment.

The cases noted below* were cited during the argument in addition to the case referred to in the judgment.

Henry Summerfield for the wife.
John Hall for the husband.

---

* *King* v. *King*, [1952] 2 All E.R. 584; [1953] A.C. 124; *Gollins* v. *Gollins*, [1963] 2 All E.R. 966; [1964] A.C. 644; *Williams* v. *Williams*, [1963] 2 All E.R. 994; [1964] A.C. 698.

KARMINSKI, J.: This is a wife's petition in which she seeks dissolution of marriage from her husband, the respondent, on the grounds of his cruelty. She complains of a large number of matters, some general and some specific. Her complaint on general grounds is that the husband neglected her, that he went out a good deal in the evenings, that he gambled on horses, that he had a lot of quarrels with her and used bad language, and that on occasion he falsely accused her of going out with other men. It was also pleaded, although not advanced or supported by evidence, that his demands for sexual intercourse were excessive. The gravamen of her complaints, apart from general unkindness, however, was that on three occasions, in 1961, 1962, and in the summer of 1963, he used very considerable violence on her: in 1961 putting his hands about her throat and exercising some pressure, in 1962 hitting her and pushing her with the result that both her eyes were black, and in August, 1963, again using some violence, hitting her, forcing her into a bedroom and locking her there overnight. She says that, as a result of all that, her health has been injured.

The husband denies cruelty, but admits some things. He admits for instance, that occasionally he used what are now regarded as almost normal swear-words, not directed at her but in general conversation. He admits that he had quite a lot of bets on horses and occasionally on football pools; and he admits, too, that when his wife refused him, as she did, in his attempts to have sexual intercourse, he asked her on a number of occasions whether there was another man. So far as the acts of violence are concerned, he admits that a certain amount of force was used by himself, saying that it was provoked by his wife pinching and sometimes punching him; and he says that he did once put his hands on her throat, only for a moment, but did not exercise other than a very modest pressure. He says, too, that when provoked by his wife striking him he hit her in the dark in the bedroom, and that although he hit her with the back of his hands he blacked her eyes. He says about this that he regretted it at once and apologised. With regard to the incident in August, 1963, he admits locking his wife in the bedroom over-night but says that he was justified in that because she was spending a great deal of time away from home, that she had been out all day, leaving him to make his own mid-day meal, and had come back and then said that she was going out again. He thought that he was ill done by, and he made sure that she did not go out again by locking her in. He also admits using some force to push her into the room.

The parties separated after this incident, the wife leaving and going back to her mother. She tried to get an order on the grounds of persistent cruelty and neglect to maintain in 1963, quite soon after leaving her husband. That was heard on Nov. 4, I think, of that year, by the justices at Plymouth, and her complaint was dismissed after what appears to have been quite a full hearing at which both parties were represented by solicitors. Both counsel and I have treated those proceedings as being relevant as a matter of history, and relevant also because it is sometimes extremely helpful to see what the parties were saying in court much nearer the date of the incidents than when they are speaking now, some two and a half years later. The justices, as I have said, dismissed those complaints, but so far as this matter is concerned I treat it as a wholly new trial, and although I hope that I have proper respect for the justices, especially for the careful examination which they gave to the case when it was before them, their decision is in no way binding on me and I have to hear the matter afresh and make up my own mind. The case, as it appears to me, is very far from an easy one. The real difficulty, to my mind, is this. The husband used some degree of force on his wife from time to time, as he has freely admitted, and, indeed, as was admitted in the pleadings, and I have to decide whether he was excused from the consequences of the amount of force he used by the provocation he received from his wife. I have to ask myself the single question: has this man, the husband, treated this woman, the wife, with cruelty? Before I can answer that question, however, I have to examine the whole of the circumstances

A concerning the incidents of which evidence was given and pay particular attention to the personalities of the two principal actors, the husband and the wife.

The wife was a woman who was described by her own doctor as immature and apathetic. The doctor who was called before me, who saw her for the first time very soon after she had left her husband in 1963, was not acquainted with her formerly as her general practitioner so as to know what went on while she was

B living with her husband; but he was able, I doubt not, to form a very good judgment when he did see her, and he was not prepared to say at all that she was mentally deficient. With regard to the difficult question of what her mental age was, I heard her evidence; without being unsympathetic, she is clearly, to use a non-medical term, a woman who is now about forty years of age and extremely backward in every sense. It was thought at one time that she might

C be deaf. It is not for me, as a layman, to decide on her hearing, but she gave me the impression of a woman who heard what was being asked of her fairly well but had great difficulty in understanding sometimes the questions which were being asked, or even their subject matter. She was, from the judge's point of view, an extremely difficult witness to assess. I have no doubt that, so far as her personality is concerned, she was probably very much as she is now when

D the parties were married in 1954, and that the husband married her realising, as he must have done, that she was at least less bright than most women of her age. She was twenty-eight at the time of the marriage.

The husband himself is a quite different character. He is a man who is in fact I think about a year younger than his wife. I take the ages from the marriage certificate. He is, and has been for many years, a skilled labourer in Her Majesty's

E Dockyard at Devonport. No word has been said against his general character, and I thought that he was a man who was doing his best to be frank and honest. He never shunned the consequences of his answers. He was prepared to admit, and, I think, on the whole completely admitted, the various scuffles in which he and his wife had been engaged, and I formed the impression that he had no wish to gloss over what force he had used on his wife. I think that the husband

F was a good witness, and that he did his best to be frank and honest with the court. He was, on the other hand, a man, perhaps not surprisingly in the circumstances of this case, who was suffering from a sense of grievance, not the least of which was due to his wife's absolute refusal for about a year before she left him in 1963 to allow him to have sexual intercourse with her.

The parties were married in 1954. There are no children of the marriage.

G For quite a long time they lived with the wife's parents at Plymouth. There were, I think, difficulties from the start. The wife says that the husband went out a lot and did not take her. The husband says that he went out a lot but that the wife liked to stay at home. He did not stay out very late. He sometimes went and had a drink with his brother at a public house. The husband did indulge in a certain amount of gambling, but not to any great extent, and I cannot

H find any sort of evidence that he was giving his wife less money than she ought to have had. With regard to swearing, both parties were very much addicted in moments of stress to the use of the standard swear-words. They were probably not the only persons in Plymouth or elsewhere to use those words. I am not in the least shocked or surprised at it, because many people used such swear-words as these parties used at each other. Sometimes they were directed at inanimate

I objects, and to my mind those are unimportant matters. What was important were the differences which grew up between them. There were no doubt a good many scenes. It is extremely difficult in the context of this case, bearing in mind particularly the personalities of the parties, to decide as a general rule which spouse usually started the quarrels. I think that on the whole probably the first person to start the troubles was the wife, not because she wanted to injure the husband but because her temperamental and intellectual make-up was such that she was not always completely in control. Sexual difficulties were, I find, at the bottom of a great many of their troubles. When the parties got married

they sensibly discussed the facts of sexual behaviour between them and they
agreed that on the whole once a week was about right, except, of course, at such
times as the wife was undergoing her menstrual period. I accept that for a
good many years the parties stuck to that general arrangement. Then the
wife, perhaps because she was unhappy with the husband, perhaps because
her personality was changing, perhaps because her mind was troubled, withdrew gradually; until by the middle of 1962 or thereabouts she refused to
let the husband have any sexual intercourse at all. The husband was much
disappointed. He used the phrase that he was being denied his rights and he
made that point of view very clear to the wife. I cannot myself find that the
wife had any reason for withdrawing from cohabitation in the sexual sense.
The husband had done nothing in his sexual conduct to suggest that he should
be refused sexual intercourse. When there were discussions about this the wife
and the husband both lost their tempers. The husband suggested to the wife,
and I do not altogether blame him for it, that there might be another man in
the background. The wife denied that. The husband repeated the suggestion
on at any rate a number of occasions, and perhaps that did not help either.
What the husband says is that when he wanted intercourse it did not end only
in a denial but in a dispute which developed into the wife sometimes pinching
him and sometimes hitting him. He says that she sometimes left marks on his
forearms, but nobody seems to have seen any bruises on his forearms. That is a
part of the arm which perhaps bruises less readily than the upper arm, but be
that as it may, I think that he was provoked and on occasions he answered back
in kind. The trouble got worse, and certainly by 1961 there was some, but
little, sexual intercourse taking place between them.

Some time in 1961, probably in the summer, there was a dispute, again about
sexual matters. The parties were in bed and the wife refused and told the
husband that she was in her period. Whether she was or not, I am quite unable
to determine, but there was an argument. The husband says that he was
provoked, but what he did was to take her by the throat and to use a little, but
very little, force. The wife says that he used a deal of force. The husband
says that it was only for a moment. In any event, as I find, the effect was to
frighten the wife. She was a woman who was in emotional matters, I should
think, very delicately balanced. Nothing particularly serious happened for
about another year, during which there were quite frequently scuffles with
pinching and pushing on one side and the other. Then there was again some
dispute over intercourse, the wife saying she was in her period and refusing to
let her husband have it. She got struck by him on that occasion, as the husband
agrees, and she got as a result a couple of black eyes. That suggests to me at any
rate that he hit her fairly hard, and indeed he agrees that he lost his temper
with her and hit her with his fist. It is right to say at once that he regretted it
and recognised his loss of temper and apologised to his wife, as was indeed the
least he could do. Matters went on in this unhappy way, and from soon after
the incident when she got her black eyes the wife withdrew from sexual life with
her husband altogether. That, not surprisingly, resulted in almost constant
troubles. On both sides there were scuffles and some pushing about, but nothing
of a very serious nature until towards the end of August, 1963, when there was a
very serious quarrel which for once does not seem to have been sparked off by
sexual matters. On that occasion the husband, having a few days' leave from
the dockyard, was engaged in redecorating the home. The wife went out in the
forenoon to do shopping, or he at any rate was under the impression that she
was coming back after a not very long interval to prepare the mid-day meal
for him. In fact, she did not, and he prepared his own. It looks as if she had
left behind the necessary material, or at any rate some of it, for him to heat.
It was, I gather, eggs and bacon, and perhaps a vegetable, and he seems to
have achieved the perhaps not very difficult culinary task of frying them. Nevertheless he was aggrieved when she came back much later and when the question

A   of his having some tea was canvassed she said she was going out again.   I think
that there was some dispute whether she was going to her mother or whether
she refused to disclose her destination, but in any event the husband again
got very cross and he proceeded to manoeuvre her into the bedroom, using, as
I find, quite a bit more force than he perhaps intended.   He certainly pushed
her in, and in the process he must have used either one or two blows or some

B   pretty hard pushing.   Having got her into the bedroom—and this was at about
five o'clock in the afternoon or a little later—he locked her in, determined, as he
was, that she should not leave the house again.   He says that he locked her in
because she had a key to the front door and could have gone out, but she could
could not get out of the bedroom which he locked from the outside.   He left the
wife, a woman highly strung and of difficult temperament, in the bedroom for

C   what, I think, must have been at least twelve hours or probably a little more.
It is right to say, and I accept at once, that the husband did not leave the house,
though I do not think that he acquainted the wife of the fact that he was still
on the premises until later, perhaps at about ten o'clock or so, when she had been
locked in the bedroom for a few hours, when he unlocked it for the purpose of
going to bed himself.   That at least made her realise that she was not alone in

D   the house and locked in.   There was the position, however, and perhaps it is
not surprising to know that next day the wife withdrew from the husband and
went home to her mother and has never returned to him.   When she got back
to her mother she was in a very distressed state.   The wife's mother took her
to a doctor whose finding I have already discussed.   The mother saw on the wife's
upper arms a good deal of bruising.   Very sensibly, I think, after taking the

E   wife to the doctor, not immediately but a week or two later, she took her to the
solicitor, Mr. Howes, who saw her in September and saw that the bruises on her
upper arms were then in the very last stage of fading away.   I have no doubt,
having heard the evidence of the mother and of Mr. Howes, the solicitor, that
the bruises on her upper arms were quite extensive, and although the doctor's
attention was not called to them I think that they represented, even allowing

F   for the fact that it may be that that part of a woman bruises easily, a good deal
of force.   When the doctor examined the wife he found that she was suffering
from an anaemic condition due to diet deficiencies.   I do not attribute any
significance to that, because the dieting difficulties were probably due to her own
fault.   What is important, of course, is her mental and nervous state.

   Having dealt with the facts as I find them, I have no difficulty at all in coming

G   to the conclusion that the wife left the husband after what must have been for
her the very frightening experience of being locked in the bedroom for a long
period.   She was distraught and very anxious and unhappy.   What I have to
decide in this case is whether in all the circumstances the force which the husband
used on the wife on occasions was justified by her conduct towards him.

   It is unnecessary here to look beyond the decision of SIR WILLIAM SCOTT

H   (later LORD STOWELL) in *Waring* v. *Waring* (1) in the year 1813 in the Consistory
Court of London.   The facts of that case were very different, but the principles
remain unaffected.   SIR WILLIAM SCOTT, in introducing his findings of fact
said that complaints of cruelty (2):

   " should be supported by proof of violence and ill-treatment, endangering,

I   or at least threatening, the life, or person, or health of the complainant.
Suits of this nature are usually brought by the wife, as the more infirm party,
though they may be also brought on the part of the husband, and have
been so brought, with effect, in cases before this court.   When the wife is
the complainant, presumptions of injury may be derived from the comparative weakness of her constitution.   It is not, however, impossible, that she

---

(1) (1813), 2 Hag. Con. 153.
(2) (1813), 2 Hag. Con. at pp. 154, 155.

may have been the aggressor, and, by provocations, have brought upon herself the ill-treatment complained of: when that appears, she is not entitled
to demand relief from the court; it is the consequence of her own conduct,
and she has the remedy in her own hands, by an alteration of her conduct;
and if the law was not backward in its interference in such a case, it would
furnish the wife with a very short course to a sentence of separation, if she
wished it, for she would have nothing to do but provoke ill-treatment by
ill-behaviour.   I do not mean by this that every slight failure of duty, on
the part of the wife, is to be visited by intemperate violence on the part of
the husband.   The correction of such failings must be softened by a due
recollection of human infirmity, and of the tender relation subsisting between
such parties;   and there may be cases of that kind, provoked by the wife,
but unduly visited by the husband, in which the court would not decline to
interfere.   But if the conduct of the wife is inconsistent with the duties of
that character, and provokes the just indignation of the husband, and causes
danger to her person, she must seek the remedy for that evil, so provoked,
in the change of her own manners.   There is reason to hope that such a
remedy would not be ineffectual;   but should it prove otherwise, it may
then be the proper opportunity for application to the powers of the court.''

As I understand that passage, it is, of course, essential that the provocation by
the wife must bear a direct relation to the retaliation by the husband.

One of the matters to which I have to pay particular attention in applying that
general test is the nature of the wife.   As I have said already, when the husband
married her he must have realised that she was different in her make-up and
her inherent disposition from the ordinary run of women of her age group, and
that she would have to be treated with some particular care, and perhaps up to
a point humoured and indulged.   In that, I think, the husband fell short.   I
do not think that he was tolerant enough to her, although I sympathise with him
on several matters, particularly the refusal of sexual intercourse.   I find it
impossible, however, to find that her refusal of sexual intercourse and her
behaviour, provocative though it was, was sufficient to justify the reaction of
the husband in those circumstances in visiting undue force on her.   I am less
troubled by the exchange of pinches than by some other matters, but for a
man to put his hands about a woman's throat is a serious matter.   Though
in this case I do not think that the husband used any great force, it must have
frightened this delicate woman, delicate in the mental sense, very much indeed.
The black eyes, he admits, were caused by a flash of temper after a good deal of
provocation, and in some ways I attach less importance to that blow, serious
though it was, than to the other matters which I have already discussed, such
as putting his hands about her throat and, what is to my mind perhaps the
most important matter in this case, locking her in for a lengthy period.   I do
not think that the provocation on that occasion was anything like sufficient
to justify treating her as he did.

It is a borderline case not easy to decide;   after some anxious consideration, I
have come to the conclusion that the husband went too far in the way in which
he let fly at his wife.   As I have said, my sympathies are with him on a number
of matters on which his patience was sorely tried, but, in the end, giving full
weight to the provocation which he received from his wife from time to time, I
have come to the conclusion that, asking myself the simple question, I must
find that the husband has treated his wife with cruelty, with the result that she
succeeds, and I grant a decree nisi on the ground of cruelty.

Decree nisi.

Solicitors: *Norman E. Howes*, Plymouth (for the wife);   *Wolferstan, Snell &
Turner*, Plymouth (for the husband).

[*Reported by* DEIRDRE McKINNEY, *Barrister-at-Law.*]

Re E. (an infant).

[CHANCERY DIVISION (Cross, J.), November 25, 28, 29, 30, December 1, 2, 1966.]

Ward of Court—Jurisdiction—Alien children—Child, a girl of seven subject to custody order of foreign court, removed from jurisdiction of that court and brought to England—Custody of child previously taken from mother by foreign court and given to father—Father killed in motor accident—Child willingly making her home with father's sister in England—Temporary custody of child awarded by foreign court to mother after father's death—Comity— Special circumstances—Whether care and control of child, made a ward of court in England, should be given to father's sister.

D., a girl, was born in September, 1959, in America. Her parents were American citizens and their home was in New Mexico. Her mother had been married before and had been divorced. In 1960 the mother obtained a divorce from the father in New Mexico on the ground of incompatibility. She was given custody of D. The father, being convinced that the mother was unfit to have the custody of D., applied to the court in New Mexico and, in March, 1962, was given custody of D. in place of the mother. In August, 1962, the father signed a statement asking that, if he should meet with sudden death, D.'s custody should not be given to her mother but to some fit person, and, among others he named his sister Mrs. Z., then living in London, as having precedence. In 1965 Mrs. Z. was asked by the father to look after D., if anything happened to him, and she promised to do so. On Dec. 27, 1965, the father, whom D. adored, was killed in a motor accident in America. D. was with him in the car at the time, but her physical injuries were slight. On Dec. 30 at about the time when a conference was to take place at the judge's office in New Mexico, D. was taken from the hospital by the father's father and was flown away, ultimately being brought to England by Mrs. Z., whom D. had welcomed with open arms, willingly accepting the suggestion that she should make her home for the future in England with Mrs. Z. and her husband. On Jan. 10, 1966, the court in New Mexico made an order, reciting the removal of D., and announcing that it would award temporary custody of D. to the mother. The mother later came to London and found D. and met Mrs. Z. Mrs. Z. started proceedings making D. a ward of court on May 9, 1966. The mother remained in England and, after she had visited the school where D. was, Mrs. Z. brought on the present application to the court for care and control of D.

Held: although in general the court, when deciding questions concerning custody and wardship of children brought to England from other countries where they were the subject of custody orders or proceedings, should have regard to comity and to the order of the foreign court and should remit the child to that court's jurisdiction, unless satisfied beyond reasonable doubt that to do so would inflict serious harm on the child, yet in the present case there were special circumstances which obliged the English court to decide that D. should continue to be brought up in England in the care of Mrs. Z., subject to access to the mother; moreover in the present case the only home that D. had had in America had been her father's, that had ended with his death and she had since acquired a new home with his sister and her husband (see p. 330, letter E, p. 337, letter H, and p. 338, letters A and C, post).

Re H. (*infants*) ([1966] 1 All E.R. 866) distinguished.

[As to custody disputes affected by conflict of laws, see 7 HALSBURY'S LAWS (3rd Edn.) 126, 127, para. 227; as to infant's welfare being paramount, see 21 ibid., pp. 193, 194, para. 428; and for cases on the subject of welfare of infants, see 28 DIGEST (Repl.) 614, 615, *1205-1218*.]

Case referred to:

H. (*infants*), *Re*, [1966] 1 All E.R. 886; [1966] 1 W.L.R. 381.

Affirmed. C.A. [1967] 2 All E.R. 881.

Observations of CROSS, J., *at p.* 330, *applied in* Re T. (INFANTS), [1968] 3 All E.R. 411.

Adjourned Summons.

This was a summons by Mrs. Z., the aunt of the ward, for care and control of the ward. The mother of the ward was the defendant. The summons was heard in chambers, but judgment was delivered in open court. The facts are set out in the judgment.

S. W. Templeman, Q.C., and *A. J. Blackett-Ord* for Mrs. Z., the aunt.
J. P. Comyn, Q.C., and *V. K. Winstain* for the mother.

CROSS, J., read the following judgment: This is one of those cases which have become all too frequent of late, in which a ward of a foreign court has been brought to this country without the consent and indeed contrary to the order of that court and made a ward in this country by the person who has brought her here in order to maintain her control of the child as against the person to whom the foreign court has given custody and who is seeking to take the child back again with her. To my mind it is wrong to look at such a case solely from the point of view of the welfare of the particular child. In the western world there are thousands on thousands of children of broken homes in respect of whom courts of different countries have made custody and access orders—children who are " wards " of the courts in question. In modern conditions it is often easy and tempting for a parent who has been deprived of custody by the court of country "A" to remove the child suddenly to country " B ", and to set up home there. The courts in all countries ought, as I see it, to be careful not to do anything to encourage this tendency. The substitution of self help for due process of law in this field can only harm the interests of wards generally, and a judge should, as I see it, pay regard to the orders of the proper foreign court unless he is satisfied beyond reasonable doubt that to do so would inflict serious harm on the child. I think that a useful test is one suggested by RUSSELL, L.J., in *Re H. (infants)* (1), namely, to ask oneself: " If I were the foreign judge, what would I think of the decision which I am going to give? "

With so much by way of preface, I come to the facts of this case. The ward Diana was born on Sept. 4, 1959, and so is now seven. Her parents had been married at Albuquerque in the State of New Mexico in the United States of America on May 2, 1958. Diana is a United States citizen; and until the beginning of 1966 her home was in Albuquerque. Her father was the son of Dr. E., a Frenchman who settled in the United States in 1943 with his two children, the plaintiff, Mrs. Z., who was then unmarried and aged about twenty-five, and his son, Robert, Diana's father (referred to herein as " the father "), who was then about twenty-one. In 1945 Mrs. Z. came to England to marry Mr. Z. He is a man in a good position in this country. They have a son aged nineteen, and they are the guardians of two other children of about the same age, all three of whom are now at the university. They live here in a large flat in Kensington. The father stayed in the United States and after the war came to live at Albuquerque in New Mexico where he was employed in the forestry service. Among his friends at Albuquerque were a Mr. and Mrs. McG. Mrs. McG. is the mother of Diana's mother, Mrs. F. (herein referred to as " the mother "), who is now the wife of a Mr. F. and is the defendant in these proceedings. The father met the mother with the McG.'s in 1957, and, as I have said, they were married in 1958 and Diana was born in 1959.

I must now say something of the mother's parents and of her life before she met the father. Her father, a Mr. S., was married four times. First he married her mother, who, as I have said, is now Mrs. McG. By her he had two children, a son David and the mother herself, who was born in July, 1932, and is therefore now thirty-four. Some years later there was a divorce between Mr. S. and his first wife and he married another woman by whom he had two children—the mother's half brothers—Tony S. and Michael S. Mr. S.'s second marriage was

---

(1) [1966] 1 All E.R. 886.

A terminated by a divorce and he then re-married his first wife, the mother's mother; but this marriage was short and disastrous, and after a further divorce, he married a fourth time and died in September, 1956. After her second divorce from Mr. S., the mother's mother married, about 1950, Mr. McG., who has a good position in Albuquerque, where, as I have said, they got to know the father.

B I turn now to the mother herself. In August, 1951, being about nineteen, she married a Mr. H. and went to live with him in Illinois. There are two children of that marriage, Gregory, born on May 25, 1952, and Keven, born on Sept. 21, 1955. Her father, Mr. S.—to whom she was much attached and who was living with his third wife in Michegan, not far from Illinois—was killed in a car smash in September, 1956. This was undoubtedly a shock to the mother, and at the same time her relations with Mr. H. were becoming strained. On June 1, 1957,

C she went from Illinois to her mother's home at Albuquerque, leaving her children with Mr. H. She said that originally she meant this to be only a holiday, and that she hoped that Mr. H. would join her with the children. In fact, he instituted divorce proceedings against her based on adultery and desertion. Although she denies that she was in fact guilty of either offence, she allowed this suit to go against her by default and on Feb. 3, 1958, Mr. H. obtained a divorce decree

D and custody of the two children, aged six and 2½. The mother was given rights of access, but in fact she never exercised them. She says that Mr. H., who soon re-married, placed difficulties in her way.

On May 2, 1958, as I have said, the mother married the father. Shortly after Diana's birth on Sept. 4, 1959, relations between the father and the mother became strained, and on June 27, 1960, the mother obtained a divorce from the

E father based on incompatibility. She was given the custody of Diana, then nine months old, and the father was given rights of access, which he exercised frequently. He was ordered to pay her sixty dollars a month for maintenance of the child, but in fact paid more. Diana was at a nursery during the day while the mother went out to work. About a year later the father became convinced that the mother was unfit to have custody of Diana, and on Feb. 12, 1962, he

F applied to the court in Albuquerque to be given custody in her place. After a two-day hearing before JUDGE REIDY an order was made on Mar. 27, 1962, giving custody of Diana, then aged 2½, to the father with rights of access to the mother; but the judge indicated that he thought that this access should not extend to overnight access. The judge's findings of fact show that three matters in particular weighed with him in making this order.

G In the first place, he found that the mother had indulged in improper conduct with a man named Stone in the single room in which she was living with Diana, and had persisted in this conduct after being warned by the father that he objected to it. The mother denied and denies that her conduct with Stone was in fact improper. Secondly, the judge found that she had on a number of occasions committed adultery in her apartment with a married man named King, who was

H her employer. The mother denied this at the trial, but now admits it. Thirdly, the judge considered that certain letters passing between the mother and her half-brother, Tony S., which the father had found in her apartment, indicated an improper attachment between them. The mother denied and denies that there was anything improper in her affection for Tony.

She appealed from the decision of JUDGE REIDY to the Supreme Court of New

I Mexico, who dismissed the appeal on the general ground that the judge had seen the parties and was in a better position than the Court of Appeal to form a judgment, and that there was no ground for interfering with his discretion.

At the time of his marriage and for some time afterwards the father had been a close friend of the McG.'s; but after the custody proceedings his attitude to them not unnaturally changed. On Aug. 1, 1962, he wrote out and signed a statement containing his wishes with regard to Diana in the event of his dying while she was under age, which is in the following terms:

" To whom it may concern and specifically to the District Court,
Bernalillo County, N.M. I, Robert E., father of Diana E., desire to make
the following requests, to be considered by the proper authorities and
enforced if necessary at the expense of my estate, in case I meet with sudden
death before Diana's coming of age, said sudden death being accidental or
of any other type:

" 1.—That I do not consider [the mother], from whom Diana's custody
was taken by this court and awarded to me, to be at present a fit mother;
nor that there is any likelihood in view of her behaviour to date that she may
recognise her guilt and failings, and thereby prepare herself for acceptance of
adequate psychiatric treatment. Therefore, I entreat the authorities
responsible for the custody of Diana that this custody be not given to [the
mother], but to a suitable person or family that will give Diana a happy
and normal home.

" 2.—I do not consider as suitable for such a responsibility either of [the
mother's] parents (her mother and stepfather, Martha and Charles McG.,
respectively), nor any of her close relatives, nor . . . [he mentions another
gentleman whose name I need not mention] nor any of the other persons
involved in this case and friendly to her. The change of custody specifies
that Diana should be removed from her environment, and this agrees with
my own opinion that [the mother], [Mr. and Mrs. McG.], . . . [the mother's]
brother and half-brothers constitute an environment that is amoral,
burdened with problems of alcoholism and neurosis, and would be highly
detrimental to Diana's upbringing and mental balance.

" 3.—Among names of persons whom I consider proper for such
responsibility, but whom I have not contacted for such an eventuality, are
. . . [he gives the names of two persons in the United States, to whom I do
not think that I need refer]. Taking precedence over them would be my
own sister and brother-in-law, [Mr. and Mrs. Z.] . . . [he gives their address
in London].

" 4.—In the event that I were to meet with sudden death in any manner
that would be unexplained or suspicious in any way, I would like a thorough
investigation to be made, if necessary employing private investigators at
the expense of my estate. This is in view of the deranged and amoral
personalities of some of the parties involved, specifically [the mother],
[Michael S. and Anthony S.], her half-brothers, the last named being most
implicated.

" In the name of God and justice, and above all in the interest of my
daughter Diana, I ask that consideration be given these wishes. Robert
V. E. Albuquerque, N.M.—Aug. 1, 1962."

In all the circumstances of this case one can well understand that the father
should have formed and expressed a very unfavourable view of the mother and
her mother and stepfather, whether or not there was in fact justification for the
extremely strong language which he used; but the fact that he appears to have
been seriously apprehensive that the mother might become a party to a plot to
murder him does suggest to my mind that on this particular subject he was himself suffering from a measure of persecution mania. There is no doubt—and the
mother herself agrees—that the father was a devoted father to Diana and that
the girl herself, when he had custody of her, became very closely attached to
him. In the period of 3½ years between Mar. 27, 1962, when Diana was handed
over to the father, and the autumn of 1965, the mother saw Diana some dozen
or fifteen times for a few hours at a time with the father either present or in the
offing. She says that she would have liked to have seen more of her child, but
that the father in fact put obstacles in the way of her access. In view of the
terms of his letter this seems likely enough. On the other hand, it may be said
that if she had been really anxious to keep in touch with her child, she would
have applied to the court, if need be, to enforce her right to greater access.

After the dismissal of her appeal in 1963, the mother went to work and lived in Santa Fé, which is some sixty miles from Albuquerque, and some of the access to Diana which she enjoyed in the 3½ years period which I have mentioned was enjoyed there. On June 10, 1965, she married a Mr. F. whom she had recently met in Santa Fé. He had just been divorced from his former wife by whom he had had four children, two grown up and two younger, of whom his former wife was granted custody. In August, 1965, the father and Diana came with his father, Dr. E., now an elderly man, on a visit to this country. They were over here for some three weeks, and during most of the time they were staying with the Z.'s. While on this visit the father asked Mrs. Z. to promise that if anything happened to him she would look after Diana. She, quite naturally, readily gave the promise, though she had no reason whatever to think that the father would die before Diana grew up.

About this time Mr. F. decided to move from Santa Fé to Portland in Oregon, which is many miles from Albuquerque. Before doing so, however, he and the mother took a motor tour, through a large part of the United States, starting with a visit to Albuquerque about September, 1965, when the mother and Mr. F. saw Diana, who had just got back from England. Having regard to the distance between Portland and Albuquerque, it is clear that the mother at this time must have realised that she was very unlikely to see much more of Diana until she grew up.

On Dec. 28, 1965, the father was killed in a motor crash at Durango, a town in Colorado lying quite close to the New Mexico border. Diana was with him in his car and was taken to hospital in Durango. Her physical injuries were slight, but she had seen the father, whom she adored, killed before her eyes. There were many people eager to do their best to help her; but unfortunately they did not see eye to eye as to what should be done.

The McG.'s heard the news at Albuquerque at 7.30 on the morning of Dec. 29 and arranged to travel at once to Durango, which they reached about 12. They had telephoned to the mother in Portland and arranged with her that she should fly to meet them as soon as she could at Durango. She booked a seat in a plane to get to Durango on the morning of Dec. 30. Her attitude, of course, was that Providence had nullified the order of JUDGE REIDY and that the way was open to her to regain the custody of her child of whom she had supposed that she would see very little for many years.

Meanwhile Dr. E., who lived in New Jersey, when he heard of the father's death telephoned to the Z.'s, who were on holiday in Yugoslavia, saying that he would go to Durango and bring the child to New York, and that Mrs. Z. must fly at once to New York to collect the child from him and bring her to England to live with the Z.'s according to the father's wishes. Mrs. Z. returned at once to London to prepare for the journey to America. Mr. Z., who had meanwhile gone to Rotterdam on business, telephoned to Dr. E. from there on Jan. 3 and emphasised to him that Mrs. Z. could only bring Diana to England if it was legally proper for her to do so. Dr. E. told him that he had already brought Diana from Durango to New York and that he was satisfied that there was no legal objection to Mrs. Z. taking the child from the United States to England. Next morning Mr. Z. telephoned to Mrs. Z., who was about to leave for New York, telling her what he had heard from her father. She arrived in New York on Jan. 4.

I must now go back to say what had happened in Durango on Dec. 29 and the morning of Dec. 30. Dr. E. arrived there on Dec. 29 and was met both by the McG.'s and by Mr. M., who had been the father's attorney in the custody proceedings and a close friend of his. Dr. E. said that he had come to take Diana to New York with a view to her going to England. The McG.'s on the other hand, said that whether or not that might be to her best interests, the mother would never agree, that she was arriving next day and that the question of custody would have to be decided by the court at Albuquerque of which the child was a ward. Mrs. McG., at the request of Mr. M., telephoned the mother in the middle of the night, to confirm that that was in fact her view, and the mother said that she would not consent. In view of the conflicting views as to Diana's future, the McG.'s had mentioned the question to the local Durango judge, JUDGE EAKES, and he had very sensibly suggested that the four of them, that is, the McG.'s and Dr. E. and Mr. M. should come to a conference at his office at 9 o'clock on the morning of Dec. 30. I have no doubt that Mr. M. was perfectly well aware of this arrangement. The McG.'s attended at JUDGE EAKES' office as arranged, and at that very moment Dr. E. and Mr. M., taking advantage of their absence from the hospital, snatched Diana and drove her to Farmington, just over the New Mexico border, from where Dr. E. took her by plane to New York. Mr. and Mrs. McG. pursued them, but were unable to catch them. They therefore could do nothing but apply as soon as possible to the Albuquerque court in the mother's name for injunctions to prevent the removal of Diana to England.

On Jan. 3 JUDGE REIDY made an order on the mother's petition in the following terms:

" The court after reading the verified petition of [the mother] herein and being fully advised in the premises: Finds:

" That the child Diana . . . aged six years, is a ward of this court and subject to the jurisdiction of this court and further finds that said child has been removed from a hospital bed and is being transported from place to place and city to city within the United States. The court further finds that said child, Diana, is a dependent and neglected child within the meaning of the New Mexico statute in such cases made and provided.

" It is therefore ordered:

" 1. That the defendants and each of them [that was Mr. M., a Mrs. R., who was a friend of the father's in Albuquerque, Dr. E. and the two Z.'s] deliver custody of said child to the child's grandmother [Mrs. McG., at an address at Albuquerque, New Mexico].

" 2. That the defendants and each of them are enjoined from moving said child from the United States of America and particularly from transporting her to Canada or England."

It was further ordered that the parties should attend on Jan. 10 for a further hearing. Mr. M. was, of course, served with the order at once, and on Jan. 4 he telephoned Dr. E. and told him of it. I have no doubt that he pointed out to him that though it had not yet been served on him or his daughter, it would not be long before it would be served, and that therefore the more quickly Diana was removed from the country the better. Mrs. Z. arrived in New York on Jan. 4. Dr. E. had, of course, told Diana that her aunt, whom she had met a few months before, was to be to her in the place of the father whom she had lost and that her home was to be in England. The child accepted this with pleasure and welcomed Mrs. Z. with open arms. Dr. E. told Mrs. Z. of his telephone conversation with Mr. M. Mrs. Z. told me that she did not fully appreciate that orders had been made against her father and herself, or that there was any question of illegality or need for speed. I find that very difficult to credit, and my doubts on this head are increased by the fact that though Mrs. Z. had taken a return ticket to and from New York, when she took the child back to England, as she did on Jan. 6, she took her via Montreal. If they had flown from New York it was possible that their passports would have been checked and they themselves stopped from leaving, whereas a flight from New York to Montreal ranks as an internal flight. Dr. E. was in fact served with the injunction on Jan. 6 after his daughter and Diana had left. They had not spent the nights of Jan. 4 and Jan. 5 at his own house in New Jersey, the address of which was known to the McG.'s, but with friends.

Mrs. F.'s petition came on for hearing in Albuquerque on Jan. 10. The order made ran as follows:

" This matter coming on to be heard in open court on Jan. 10, 1966, and the court having heard testimony of the witnesses and the statements and arguments of counsel and being fully advised in the premises;

" The court finds:

" That the defendant [the father] . . . is dead; that no probate of his estate has been made in Bernalillo County and no administrator appointed; that [the father] . . . died near Durango, Colorado, on Dec. 28, 1965.

" That this court has jurisdiction over the custody of the minor child pursuant to court orders heretofore entered.

" That the child was immediately transported from Durango, Colorado, to Farmington, New Mexico, and then to Vineland, New Jersey. That said minor child is probably now in London, England, in the custody of its aunt [Mrs. Z.; and they give the address].

" That this court in open court on Jan. 10, 1966, the date of the hearing, announced that it would award temporary custody of the said infant child to the mother of the child [and they give her address in Portland, Oregon]."

I do not think that there is anything else in the order that I need read.

In awarding temporary custody to the mother, JUDGE REIDY was not, of course, deciding that on the merits of the case she ought to have custody rather than the Z.'s. His view—with which, if I may say so with respect, I entirely concur —was that the matter ought to have been brought before him, and that the action of Dr. E. and Mr. M. was grossly improper. He gave temporary custody to the mother as a weapon which she might conceivably be able to use in order to put the child back before him so that he could decide on the child's future.

In the course of the proceedings the judge asked Mr. M. how he, an officer of the court, could justify what he had done. Mr. M. argued, no doubt rightly, that the father's death did not automatically give the mother a legal right to the custody of the child. He went on to say that if the mother, the surviving parent, wanted custody, she must go to wherever the child might be and claim custody —with this corollary, I suppose, that anybody was entitled to move the child about from State to State or country to country, until she caught up with them. That argument, not surprisingly, did not appeal to the judge, and I will read his concluding exchanges with Mr. M. in full. After Mr. M. had argued in the sense which I have just indicated, the judge said:

" ' Well, you are saying that you took this step because of your friendship and because it was more or less a spur-of-the-moment something to get done because of the trouble it would be for Dr. E. to come here and argue about the custody or for Mrs. Z. to come to Albuquerque and argue about the custody, so you have taken it upon yourself, through your assistance in this matter, to get the child to England where it will certainly be very difficult for the McG.'s, if they are interested, or for the natural mother, if she is interested; and you still don't think you have done anything wrong? ' Mr. M. said: ' No, Sir, your honour, I don't.' And the judge said: ' Well, the court is not so sure '."

I must say that in his place my language would have been far less temperate than that.

The mother was now, naturally enough, filled with a burning sense of injustice. If the question of Diana's future had been brought before the court in Albuquerque, as it ought to have been, it is, of course, very far from certain that she would, in the light of her past history, have been given the custody of her daughter. Plainly a great deal would have depended on the view which the judge formed of Mr. F. The mother is a woman of great charm—dangerously great charm, I think that I may say—and of considerable intelligence; but in the past at least she has plainly lacked moral ballast. The judge in New Mexico might have taken the view, having seen the mother, that she and Mr. F. could safely be trusted with her child, Diana. On the other hand, it is equally likely that he would have thought that it was better for Diana to go and live with the Z.'s in England, as the father wished, even though that meant turning a little American girl into a little English girl and cutting her off from the mother and the mother's relatives. Conceivably as a via media he might have decided that Diana should be brought up by the McG.'s at Albuquerque, where, after all, her home had been and where she had been at school and had her friends. One cannot say what he would have decided. But difficult as the decision would have been, he was the one person in the world in a position to make it with full knowledge of all the relevant facts, and if the decision had gone against her, the mother would have had the consolation of knowing that the decision had been made by an American judge in the American courts. All that has been rendered impossible by the action of Dr. E. and Mr. M.

Now, what was the mother to do? She had no money and she knew nothing about England and its legal system. Towards the end of January she put a call through to the Z.'s flat in Kensington—which, though she did not intend it, woke up Mrs. Z. at about 2 o'clock in the morning—and asked whether Diana was there and how she was. Mrs. Z. told her that Diana was well, but that as she was asleep she could not speak to her.

Having ascertain that Diana was in fact in London with the Z.'s, the mother began to save or borrow money to enable her to come to London. She had no definite plan. She was unwilling to tell the Z.'s that she was coming because she thought that they might remove Diana to India, where, as she knew, Mr. Z. had worked for many years. I have little doubt that at the back of her mind there was the hope in some way or other to re-kidnap Diana and to pay back Dr. E. and the Z.'s in their own coin. The Z.'s on their side no doubt, as months passed and nothing happened, supposed that they would have no further trouble from that woman in Oregon. The mother arrived in London on May 3, and, in her ignorance, put up at a hotel recommended by some friend which was far beyond her very modest means. Some organisation connected with the American embassy put her in touch with a firm of solicitors; but she knew nothing of our system of legal aid and was unwilling to spend all she had on lawyers straight away. On May 6 she went to the Z.'s flat and saw Diana coming out with an Indian servant, accosted her and walked with her to the park. Diana was pleased enough to see her and asked her to come home with her. The return of Diana at tea time with the mother was, to put it mildly, a surprise for Mrs. Z.; but what must have been a very difficult meeting passed off better than might have been expected. This was largely because the mother gave Mrs. Z. to understand that she was only in London for a few days and was going to return to the United States of America on May 9. She did this because she was afraid that if she told Mrs. Z. that she meant to stay in England with a view to recapturing her child, Mrs. Z. would remove Diana to India.

After that meeting Mrs. Z., as a measure of protection, started these proceedings, making Diana a ward on May 9, and sought to serve the summons on the mother in Oregon, where she supposed her to have returned. The mother meanwhile left her expensive hotel and went to live in a cheap boarding house not very far from the Z.'s flat. She was soon reduced to serious financial straits because a money order which her mother had sent her from Albuquerque did not arrive. What she hoped to do, as I have said, was to recapture Diana, and she used to go day after day to watch outside the Z.'s flat or the high class day school in Kensington which she attended. Dr. E. and Mr. M. will I suppose to their dying day be proud of their work that morning in the hospital at Durango; but I think that if they had heard the mother giving evidence of her life in London in May and June of this year, they might have been assailed by some doubts on that score. Meanwhile the Z.'s found it impossible to serve the mother with their summons because she had not returned to Portland. Indeed it appears that a letter which the mother wrote to Mr. F. went astray and that he himself for some time did not know where she was. Diana had in fact been taken on a short holiday to Ireland in June, and this increased the mother's distress because she did not see her coming out of the Z.'s flat or going to school. Diana returned about the beginning of July and about the same time the mother received some funds from her mother which relieved her immediate necessities. On July 4 she visited Diana's school. The school mistress, who, of course, had been told by Mrs. Z. that Diana was a ward and that the mother might be attempting to kidnap her, refused to let her see her; but later that day outside the school she met Mrs. Z. The meeting was, as may be imagined, not at all a pleasant one; but it resulted in her being served with this summons and of her learning through Mrs. Z.'s solicitors of the possibility of legal aid. The solicitors to whom she was originally introduced acted for her; Mr. F. remits from Oregon the contribution fixed by the authorities; and since August the mother has been earning her living as a nanny housekeeper in Chelsea. She has had leading counsel to represent her, and I am very much indebted to him and also to leading counsel for Mrs. Z., for the help which they have given me in this difficult case.

As I have said, the question of who was to bring up Diana after her father's death ought to have been brought before the court in Albuquerque in New Mexico. Well, then, says counsel for the mother, let it be decided by that court —the proper court—now. If the court decides, as well it may, that it is best for Diana to live with the Z.'s, then they will have established a good title to her custody, to which at present they have no title at all. The court may, of course, decide that it is best for Diana to live with the mother; but if it so decides, the Z.'s cannot reasonably complain. In support of this argument counsel relies strongly on the recent case of Re H. (*infants*) (2).

Counsel for Mrs. Z. accepts to the full the general principles on which counsel for the mother's argument is based, but says that though the onus is on the Z.'s to advance reasons why Diana should not be sent back to New Mexico, yet special reasons exist in this case. Certainly the facts of this case differ considerably from those in Re H. (*infants*) (2). In the first place, though it is not the most important aspect of the matter, no such blame attaches to Mrs. Z. as attached to Mrs. H. Mrs. Z. came to America with clean hands to take charge of her niece in accordance with the father's wishes; the child, who had seen very little of the mother for $4\frac{1}{2}$ years and who had just lost the adored father, Mrs. Z.'s brother, flung herself, so to say, into her arms; Mrs. Z. shared her grief for her father and became, as it were, a mother to her and has cared for her as a mother ever since. All that can be said against Mrs. Z. personally is that she must have realised after she had got to America that so far as the law went all was not such plain sailing as her father had led Mr. Z. to understand. The mother herself was candid and generous enough to realise, however, that one could not really blame Mrs. Z. for what she did.

The second difference, and the most important difference, between Re H. (*infants*) (2) and this is that in the H. case (2) the children had had in effect two homes in America, their father's and their mother's homes, and the mother having improperly removed them to this country, the court sent them back to their father's home. Here, on the other hand, the only home which Diana had in the United States of America was destroyed by the father's death and she has acquired a fresh home in England which is her only existing home. True that home was improperly acquired. Instead of the child remaining in the hospital at Durango while the New Mexico court decided what should be done, Dr. E. took her away and as it were forced another home on her. But however much one may disapprove of his action—and I am very far indeed from condoning it—one cannot shut one's eyes to the results which have flowed from it. Having heard Mrs. Z. in the witness-box, I have no doubt whatever that she now stands in the relation of mother to Diana and that to take Diana from her would be utterly disastrous for the child.

---

(2) [1966] 1 All E.R. 886.

There are therefore, as I see it, special circumstances which oblige me to say that, despite all considerations of comity, the child must continue to be brought up here in the care of Mrs. Z. I hope JUDGE REIDY, to whom I will see that a copy of this judgment is sent, will understand my feelings in the matter. I would in fact have arrived at this conclusion even if the mother had shown herself in the past to be a responsible woman fully capable of caring properly for her child. The fact that there is, to say the least, some doubt whether she is such a person reinforces my view that Diana ought to remain with Mrs. Z. I would add, in case I should be thought to have overlooked the point, that counsel for the mother suggested that a possible solution would be for me to leave Diana here for the time being while asking the New Mexico court to decide on her future and impliedly undertaking to abide by its decision. That to my mind would be to abdicate my responsibility. In cases of this sort either the child must go back or this court must decide on the child's future. As *Re H. (infants)* (3) shows, unless there are compelling reasons to the contrary, the child ought to be sent back; but here in my judgment there are such reasons.

Finally, I come to this question of access. When the Z.'s received Diana into their care they quite naturally entertained a very unfavourable impression of the mother, since they necessarily depended on what they had heard either directly or indirectly from the father; and what they saw of the mother after the father's death until this hearing was certainly not calculated to increase their respect for her. No one who heard the mother give evidence could fail to be impressed, however, not only by her charm but by her candour and the generosity of her spirit. I have no doubt whatever that the Z.'s now feel very different towards her, and they have offered to do whatever they reasonably can to assist her to have access to Diana despite the obvious difficulties involved. I do most sincerely hope that the mother will accept this offer in the spirit in which it is made. It would be perhaps too much to hope that she will ever completely forgive Dr. E. or Mr. M.; but, as I have said, I think that she realises that Mrs. Z. is blameless and will really be a mother to Diana.

I think that on the question of access the court can now go into chambers.

Order accordingly.

Solicitors: *Roney & Co.* (for Mrs. Z., the aunt); *Crane & Hawkins* (for the mother).

[*Reported by* JACQUELINE METCALFE, *Barrister-at-Law.*]

(3) [1966] 1 All E.R. 886.

Re SELWYN'S CONVEYANCE.
HAYMAN AND OTHERS *v.* SOOLE.

[CHANCERY DIVISION (Goff, J.), November 15, 16, 1966.]

Restrictive Covenant—Restrictive covenant affecting land—Annexation—Benefit—
Covenant to " enure for the protection of the adjoining or neighbouring land
part of or lately part of the Selwyn estate " in conveyance of April, 1924—
Certainty of description of land and meaning of " lately "—Whether benefit
of covenant annexed to parts of Selwyn estate.

By a conveyance dated Apr. 16, 1924, No. 196, Kew Road, Richmond, was
conveyed to a predecessor in title of the defendant. The conveyance contained a restrictive covenant by the then purchaser " for himself and his
heirs and assigns to the intent that this covenant shall bind the hereditaments purchased by him and the owner and owners for the time being and
shall enure for the protection of the adjoining or neighbouring land part of
or lately part of the Selwyn estate " to observe and perform restrictive
covenants and provisions contained in the schedule to the conveyance. The
Selwyn Richmond estate had existed for many years, and there had been
sales in 1923 and 1924, so that at the time of the conveyance so much of the
neighbouring land as was lately part of the Selwyn estate was not all owned
by one and the same person. The plaintiffs derived title to their lands from
the same vendor as the defendant's predecessor, but by conveyances subsequent in date to his. On the question whether the benefit of the restrictive
covenant had been validly annexed to the lands of the plaintiffs, which were
adjoining properties immediately to the south of the defendant's property,
196, Kew Road.

Held: the restrictive covenant in the conveyance of Apr. 16, 1924, had
been validly annexed to each of the plaintiffs' lands so as to entitle them
severally to the benefit of it (see p. 347, letter B, post), because—

(i) the restrictive covenant was not void for uncertainty, as the description
" neighbouring land part of or lately part of the Selwyn estate " was a
description from which the land was ascertainable, and the word " lately "
merely meant " formerly " and did not import uncertainty as to how long
before (see p. 344, letters B and D, post).

Dictum of BUCKLEY, J., in *Russell* v. *Archdale* ([1962] 2 All E.R. at p. 311)
applied.

(ii) on its true construction the restrictive covenant showed by the words
land " lately part of " the estate an intention to confer its protection on
every part of such lands, and in the light of that inference showed a like
intention in regard to land then part of the estate (see p. 346, letter E, post).

Dictum of ROMER, L.J., in *Drake* v. *Gray* ([1936] 1 All E.R. at p. 376);
Russell v. *Archdale* ([1962] 2 All E.R. 305) and *Re Jeffs' Transfer (No. 2)*
([1966] 1 All E.R. 937) considered.

Per CURIAM: even if s. 56* of the Law of Property Act, 1925, did not
apply, it did not prevent valid annexation of the restrictive covenant so far as
concerned lands which the vendor did own, and if it did, this was a case in
which the restrictive covenant was severable (see p. 343, letter D, post).

[As to the annexation of the benefit of restrictive covenants to land, see 14
HALSBURY'S LAWS (3rd Edn.) 564, 565, para. 1051; and for cases on the subject,
see 40 DIGEST (Repl.) 339-343, *2764-2783.*

For the Law of Property Act, 1925, s. 56, see 20 HALSBURY'S STATUTES (2nd
Edn.) 554.]

---

* Section 56 (1) provides: " A person may take an immediate or other interest in land
or other property, or the benefit of any condition, right of entry, covenant or agreement
over or respecting land or other property, although he may not be named as a party to
the conveyance or other instrument."

Cases referred to:

Beswick v. Beswick, [1966] 3 All E.R. 1; [1966] Ch. 538; [1966] 3 W.L.R. 396.

Drake v. Gray, [1936] 1 All E.R. 363; [1936] Ch. 451; 105 L.J.Ch. 233; 155 L.T. 145; 40 Digest (Repl.) 341, 2771.

Jacobs v. London County Council, [1950] 1 All E.R. 737; [1950] A.C. 361; 114 J.P. 204; 30 Digest (Repl.) 212, 545.

Jeffs' Transfer, Re, Rogers v. Astley (No. 2), [1966] 1 All E.R. 937; [1966] 1 W.L.R. 841.

Renals v. Cowlishaw, [1874-80] All E.R. Rep. 359; (1878), 9 Ch.D. 125; 48 L.J.Ch. 33; 38 L.T. 503; affd. C.A., [1874-80] All E.R. Rep. 359; (1879), 11 Ch.D. 866; 48 L.J.Ch. 830; 41 L.T. 116; 40 Digest (Repl.) 346, 2796.

Russell v. Archdale, [1962] 2 All E.R. 305; [1964] Ch. 38; [1962] 3 W.L.R. 192; Digest (Cont. Vol. A) 1315, 2783a.

Union of London and Smith's Bank, Ltd.'s Conveyance, Re, Miles v. Easter, [1933] All E.R. Rep. 355; [1933] Ch. 611; 102 L.J.Ch. 241; 149 L.T. 82; 40 Digest (Repl.) 329, 2702.

White v. Bijou Mansions, Ltd., [1937] 3 All E.R. 269; [1937] Ch. 610; affd. C.A , [1938] 1 All E R 546; [1938] Ch 351; 104 L.J.Ch. 212; 158 L.T. 338; 38 Digest (Repl.) 881, 921.

Zetland (Marquess) v. Driver, [1938] 2 All E.R. 158; [1939] Ch. 1; 107 L.J.Ch. 316; 158 L.T. 456; 40 Digest (Repl.) 341, 2772.

Adjourned Summons.

This was an application by originating summons dated May 28, 1965, by the plaintiffs (i) John David Woodburn Hayman, and (ii) Jane Hayman his wife, the owners of No. 194, Kew Road, Richmond, in the county of Surrey, (iii) Alfred Reginald Matthiae, the owner of Nos. 190 and 192, Kew Road, aforesaid and (iv) Alexander Protheroe, the owner of No. 188, Kew Road aforesaid seeking a declaration that No. 196, Kew Road, of which the defendant, Robert David Soole, was the owner, was affected by restrictions imposed by a conveyance dated Apr. 16, 1924, and that the restrictions were enforceable by the plaintiffs. The question before the court at the hearing and the relevant facts or inferences of fact appear from the judgment of GOFF, J. The first plaintiff in his affidavit in support of the originating summons deposed the following among other matters. That Nos. 188, 190/192, 194 and 196, Kew Road formed a block of property fronting on to that road. That this block at one time formed a part of the estate known as the Selwyn Estate and was included in a conveyance dated Dec. 27, 1922, to the Reverend Stephen John Selwyn (herein called " the vendor "). That the vendor appeared to have sold off this block in four plots by four conveyances, of which the conveyance dated Apr. 16, 1924, of the site of No. 196 to a Mr. Spofforth (herein called " the sub-purchaser ") was the first; and that Sch. 1 to that conveyance contained a number of restrictive covenants of which the material one was that " not more than one such house shall be erected on the land ". That the next conveyance of property within this block was the conveyance of No. 188, dated June 11, 1924; that the next such conveyance was that of 190/192 dated Dec. 22, 1925, and that the conveyance of No. 194, under which the first plaintiff and his wife derived title, was dated Jan. 30, 1926, and was in favour of a Mr. Irons. The first plaintiff deposed that the defendant intended to develop the site of No. 196 by erecting six houses thereon.

The cases noted below* were cited during the argument in addition to those referred to in the judgment.

G. M. Godfrey (for A. J. Balcombe) for the plaintiffs.

G. H. Newsom, Q.C., Lloyd Stott and T. J. Craven for the defendant.

---

* Re Ecclesiastical Comrs. for England's Conveyance, [1934] All E.R. Rep. 118; [1936] Ch. 430; Scruttons, Ltd. v. Midland Silicones, Ltd., [1962] 1 All E.R. 1; [1962] A.C. 446.

GOFF, J.: This originating summons was issued in the matter of the freehold property known as No. 196, Kew Road, Richmond in the county of Surrey, comprised in a conveyance dated Apr. 16, 1924 and made between (i) the Reverend Stephen John Selwyn, (ii) William Thomas Allen Froude and (iii) Reginald Markham Spofforth, and in the matter of the Law of Property Act, 1925, and it was expressed to be an application made under s. 84 (2) of the Act of 1925. It asked for a declaration that

" the above-mentioned freehold property No. 196, Kew Road, Richmond is affected by the restrictions imposed by the above-mentioned conveyance dated Apr. 16, 1924, and that the said restrictions are enforceable by the plaintiffs ",

and for further relief.

The plaintiffs, however, had not taken the steps necessary in applications under that section to ascertain what persons might have a claim to the benefit of the covenant, and their counsel accordingly applied for leave to amend by deleting the reference to the Act of 1925 from the heading and the reference to s. 84, which I allowed.

It was then agreed that the matter should proceed as hostile litigation between the plaintiffs and the defendant, the result of which will be binding on them and, of course, their respective successors in title but not anybody else. It was also agreed that I cannot on the proceedings as now constituted, even if the plaintiffs be otherwise right, determine or declare that the restrictions are enforceable, if for no other reason because that involves considering the question whether when they were imposed the restrictions were capable of benefiting the land entitled to the protection thereof and possibly whether they are still so capable. The evidence relevant to that question has not been adduced before me.

The defendant's property is situate on the east side of Kew Road, Richmond with a return frontage to Walpole Avenue. The first two plaintiffs, who are husband and wife, are the owners of No. 194 which is next-door to the south. The plaintiff, Mr. Matthiae, is the owner of Nos. 190 and 192 which, I think, constitute one property, and is the next house continuing down Kew Road southwards, and the plaintiff, Mr. Protheroe, is the owner of No. 188 which comes next and lies on the corner of Kew Road and Fitzwilliam Avenue.

The conveyance of Apr. 16, 1924 is no longer extant, nor is any copy to be found, but it appears from the land registry entries relating to the defendant's title, and from the charges register, that it contained a covenant in these terms:

" The sub-purchaser for himself his heirs and assigns to the intent that this covenant shall bind the hereditaments purchased by him and the owner and owners for the time being and shall enure for the protection of the adjoining or neighbouring land part of or lately part of the Selwyn estate in the parish of Richmond hereby covenants with the vendor to observe and perform the restrictive covenants and provisions contained in Sch. 1 hereto but not so as to hold the sub-purchaser liable for any breach of the said restrictive covenants and provisions after he shall have parted with his interest in the said hereditaments."

The history of the matter begins well back in the last century. The late Sir Charles Jasper Selwyn, the Victorian lord justice of that name, who died on Aug. 11, 1869, devised all his real estate at Richmond and Kew and elsewhere in strict settlement under which his elder son, Charles William Selwyn, became tenant in tail. He died in March, 1893, and the estate tail devolved on his younger brother, Harry Jasper Selwyn, who disentailed on Oct. 17, 1893, and in turn died on Apr. 21, 1919, having by his will devised the estates on trust for sale and on beneficial trusts under which his son, the Reverend Stephen John Selwyn, was absolutely entitled. He elected to take the real estate in specie and it was conveyed to him by the trustees of that will by two separate conveyances, one of which is dated Dec. 27, 1922, and comprised all the land coloured pink, green and blue on the plan to that conveyance and the pink includes the defendant's property and the plaintiffs' properties. The other conveyance comprised other lands in separated portions to the south.

It appears from the plan to the conveyance of Dec. 27, 1922, and certain exhibits that the pink and most of the green consist of a more or less compact block which has been described in the argument as the Kew Road block. The rest of the green and the blue represent two other pieces of land tolerably near each other, but well separated from the Kew Road block, which further pieces of land have been referred to as the Sandycombe Road block. Other exhibits show that the conveyance of Dec. 28, 1922 comprised two other separate pieces of land each much further south, referred to as the lower Mortlake Road block and the Sheen Road block.

It appears from the affidavit of John William Horsford Hodgson that the aggregate of the lands comprised in those two conveyances was known as the Selwyn Richmond estate and, although various sales from time to time took place, the Reverend Stephen John Selwyn remained the estate owner of the Selwyn Richmond estate until March, 1961. The affidavit gives particulars of the sales from which it appears that there were a number in 1923, and therefore before the conveyance of Apr. 16, 1924, and others in 1924, some of which may also have been prior to that conveyance. The evidence as to these sales is somewhat meagre, but it seems to me proper to infer that the sales prior to Apr. 16, 1924, had not all been to one person only. Moreover, although the affidavit speaks of the two conveyances of December, 1922, as comprising the whole of what was known as the Selwyn Richmond estate, the Selwyn estate had obviously existed for many years prior to 1922, as is apparent from the history of the title which I have recited. I think that it is also to be inferred from the appearance of the Kew Road block that there had been sales of parts before 1923. In all the circumstances, therefore, I must proceed on the basis that so much of the adjoining or neighbouring land as was lately part of the Selwyn estate was not on Apr. 16, 1924 all owned by one and the same person.

In these circumstances the first question which has been canvassed is whether the covenant in the conveyance of that date was validly annexed to any land. It is clear that it could not be annexed to those parts of the Selwyn estate which were not then owned by the vendor, unless it be by the operation of s. 56 of the Law of Property Act, 1925, (1).

Counsel for the defendant says that s. 56 is to be narrowly construed and applies only where the covenant purports to be made with a person, though he is not named and does not execute the instrument. He relies as part of his argument on a passage in his own work (2) which reads as follows:

" By the Real Property Act, 1845, s. 5 (replaced and extended by the Law of Property Act, 1925, s. 56 (1)), the benefit of a covenant respecting land or other property may be taken by a person without his being named as a party to the deed containing it. Attempts have been made to give these sections a very wide scope, but it is now well settled that all that they do is to put an ascertainable person (who might therefore have been a party to the deed) in as good a position as if he had been a party. On the one hand, therefore, no one is entitled to invoke this statutory provision as a ground for giving him the benefit of a covenant which it would be merely convenient for him to possess.

" ' I interpret it as a section which can be called in aid only by a person in whose favour the grant purports to be made, or with whom the covenant or agreement purports to be made ' (3)."

---

(1) Section 56 (1) is printed in footnote *, at p. 339, ante.
(2) RESTRICTIVE COVENANTS AFFECTING FREEHOLD LAND (3rd Edn.) by G. H. NEWSOM, Q.C., pp. 5, 6.
(3) This quotation is from SIMONDS, J., in *White* v. *Bijou Mansions, Ltd.*, [1937] 3 All E.R. 269 at p. 277; [1937] Ch. 610 at p. 625.

Counsel relies also on *White* v. *Bijou Mansions, Ltd.*, per SIR WILFRID GREENE, M.R. (4), where he said:

"That being so, if that view be correct, it would be quite impossible to bring the matter within s. 56, because whatever else s. 56 (1) may mean, it is, I think, confined to cases where the person seeking to take advantage of it is a person within the benefit of the covenant in question, if I may use that phrase. The mere fact that somebody comes along and says ' It would be useful to me if I could enforce that covenant ', does not make him a person entitled to enforce it under s. 56 (1). Before he can enforce it, he must be a person who falls within the scope and benefit of the covenant according to the true construction of the document in question. In the present case the present appellant does not fall within the benefit of the covenant, and, in my opinion, the argument on s. 56 (1) fails."

On the other hand, views have been expressed that the section has a much wider ambit, particularly by the Court of Appeal in the recent case of *Beswick* v. *Beswick* (5). Be this as it may, it is a question which affects persons who are not parties to this action. Therefore, I will say no more about it because in my view, even if s. 56 does not apply, it does not prevent valid annexation so far as concerns the lands which the vendor did own, and if it did, this is a case in which I would sever the covenant.

Then counsel for the defendant argued that the covenant was void for uncertainty. He based this first on the words " neighbouring land " and relied on a passage in *Marquess of Zetland* v. *Driver* (6) which reads as follows:

"It is said, however, on behalf of the respondents, that this covenant is not one which can run with the land, because it is imposed, not only for the benefit of the unsold land of the vendor, but also for the benefit of the adjoining owners and the neighbourhood. If that were the true construction of the covenant, that might be so but in our judgment, reading the covenant as a whole, it cannot be so construed."

On the other hand, in *Russell* v. *Archdale* (7), BUCKLEY, J., said this:

"Counsel for the defendant contended that there is, here, no effective annexation of the covenants to any ascertainable land because the description ' the vendor's adjoining and neighbouring land ', which are the words contained in the vendor's covenants, are uncertain in their significance, and that accordingly one cannot say to what land these covenants are annexed and the attempted annexation fails for uncertainty. On the other hand, counsel for the plaintiffs said that when one comes to look at the defendant's conveyance as a whole, reading cl. 2 with the first paragraph of the schedule to that conveyance, the right conclusion to reach is that the words ' adjoining and neighbouring land ' mean the vendor's Hedgerley Park estate, and that it was to that estate, or rather to so much of it as the vendor then retained, that the vendor was alluding, in the conveyance to the defendant, for the purpose of annexation of the benefit of the covenant."

Later BUCKLEY, J., said (8):

"Having come to the conclusion that I have reached on the interpretation of cl. 2 of the conveyance, I do not feel that it leads me to the view that the description ' adjoining and neighbouring land ' is so indefinite that one cannot ascertain what the property was that was intended to be benefited. It is quite true that on the evidence before me the extent, at the date of this conveyance, of the property owned by the company outside the Hedgerley

---

(4) [1938] 1 All E.R. 546 at pp. 554, 555; [1938] Ch. 351 at p. 365.
(5) [1966] 3 All E.R. 1; [1966] Ch. 538.
(6) [1938] 2 All E.R. 158 at p. 162; [1939] Ch. 1 at p. 9.
(7) [1962] 2 All E.R. 305 at p. 310; [1964] Ch. 38 at p. 44.
(8) [1962] 2 All E.R. at p. 311; [1964] Ch. at p. 45.

Park estate has not been defined, but I see no reason for supposing that it cannot be ascertained and that it was not perfectly easy to ascertain what it consisted of at the time the conveyance was granted. So I proceed on the footing that these covenants were annexed by these words to all the adjoining and neighbouring property which was owned by the vendor at the date of the conveyance whether as part of the Hedgerley Park estate or as part of the Bulstrode Park estate, including Duke's Wood."

Here I have not got "neighbourhood" but "neighbouring land part of or lately part of the Selwyn estate". Prima facie that seems to me to be ascertained or ascertainable.

It is said that in addition to the Kew Road block there is also the Sandycombe Road block, and even more significantly the lower Mortlake Road and Sheen Road blocks which it is suggested in any case made the covenant void for uncertainty. I feel no difficulty in coming to a conclusion here. In my judgment the adjoining or neighbouring land means the Kew Road block. In my view the difficulty, if there be one, is one of construction not certainty and I resolve it in that way. Counsel for the defendant also founded his uncertainty argument on the word "lately", but in my judgment it merely means "formerly" or "heretofore" and does not import uncertainty as to how long lately may be. There may be some difficulty in ascertaining facts, but the concept is in my judgment certain.

The I turn to what is perhaps the principal battleground. Is this covenant annexed to the Selwyn estate as a whole in which case the plaintiffs plainly cannot have the benefit, whether or not anyone can now show that he is the owner of that estate so as to entitle him to the benefit of the covenant, or does the covenant, on its true construction, mean the estate or any part thereof?

In *Drake* v. *Gray* (9), either as obiter or as a second ground for his decision, ROMER, L.J., said:

"Most of the cases that have come before the courts are cases where a covenant has been entered into by a vendor for the benefit of, say, the A.B. estate for the time being. There, of course, there is no intention shown that the benefit should enure for any particular part of the estate, but where, as here, you find not 'the land coloured yellow' or 'the estate' or 'the field named so and so' or anything of that kind, but 'the lands retained by the vendor', it appears to me that there is a sufficient indication that the benefit of the covenant enures to every one of the lands retained by the vendor, and if a plaintiff in a subsequent action to enforce a covenant can say, 'I am the owner of a piece of land, or a hereditament, and that belonged to the vendor at the time of the conveyance', he is entitled to enforce the covenant."

Counsel for the plaintiffs says that here we have the words "adjoining or neighbouring land" and indeed, as the description includes land "lately part of" the estate, the description is equivalent to one containing the word "lands", and that therefore, if I adopt the views expressed by ROMER, L.J., I should find in the covenant annexation to parts of the land and not only to the whole.

In the case of *Russell* v. *Archdale* (10), however, to which I have already referred, BUCKLEY, J., after quoting this passage in the judgment of ROMER, L.J., said (11):

"I should of course wish to pay every respect to a dictum of so learned a judge as ROMER, L.J., but I must confess that I find the greatest difficulty in seeing any distinction between a case in which the benefit of a covenant is attached to something which is described as 'the land marked yellow on a plan', or the 'estate of the vendor known by such and such a name', and

(9) [1936] 1 All E.R. 363 at p. 376; [1936] Ch. 451 at p. 465.
(10) [1962] 2 All E.R. 305; [1964] Ch. 38.
(11) [1962] 2 All E.R. at p. 312; [1964] Ch. at p. 47.

a case in which the vendor, the owner of an estate part of which he is conveying away, takes the covenant from the purchaser for the benefit of his remaining land. It seems to me that his remaining land or the land he is retaining, whatever the words of description may be, is just as precise a description of the property which is to be benefited as if he had said ' the land which is shown on the plan and is marked yellow ', or, ' the land which I am retaining and which is known as my " X " estate '. No doubt every case of this kind, being one of construction, must be determined on the facts and the actual language used, but with the utmost respect to ROMER, L.J., I cannot see that the mere fact that the land intended to be benefited is described by such an expression as ' the land retained by the vendor ' is sufficient to enable the court to come to the conclusion that the covenant is intended to benefit each and every part of that land. The dictum of ROMER, L.J., was, I think, clearly obiter, for the ratio decidendi of the court was as I have stated, and in my judgment that authority does not assist counsel for the plaintiffs to say that the benefit of this covenant is annexed to each and every part of what is described by the conveyance as ' the vendor's adjoining and neighbouring land '. That being so, it must follow that the plaintiffs cannot enforce the covenant merely by reason of its annexation to the ' adjoining and neighbouring land ' of the vendor's under the conveyance of July 6, 1938 since they (the plaintiffs) have acquired part only of that land."

In *Re Jeffs' Transfer, Rogers* v. *Astley (No. 2)*, (12) STAMP, J., said:

" It is in issue whether those remarks were dicta or were a second reason for the decision of ROMER, L.J., and so binding on me (see the well-known passage in the judgment of LORD SIMONDS in *Jacobs* v. *London County Council* (13), to the effect that where a judge gives two reasons for his decision each is part of the ratio decidendi). BUCKLEY, J., in a case to which I was also referred, *Russell* v. *Archdale* (14), took the view that the remarks which I have quoted were mere dicta, and he did not feel able to accept the dicta. I do not think it necessary for me to resolve that question. ROMER, L.J.'s remarks must be read with reference to the facts of the case before him and the documents which then had to be construed, and I cannot think that those remarks were directed to laying down any principle of construction which requires me, whenever I find a covenant for the benefit of the land retained by the vendor, to hold that the benefit of the covenant is intended to be attached to each and every part of those lands or to each and every one of those lands. I have to construe this covenant as to the language used and I find nothing in the judgment of ROMER, L.J., which constrains me to construe it otherwise than in the way that I have done. My view of the construction accords with that adopted by BUCKLEY, J., in *Russell* v. *Archdale* (15) though, if I came to the conclusion that the word ' remainder ' was used in the sense submitted to me by counsel for the defendants, I could readily distinguish this case from the decision of BUCKLEY, J., in that case."

I accept the view that ROMER, L.J., was not laying down a principle of construction binding in every case where one finds words such as " adjoining " or " neighbouring land " or " lands ". Even if he was, I prefer the view expressed by BUCKLEY, J. Otherwise the passage in ROMER, L.J.'s judgment seems to me to conflict with that learned judge's own statement in *Re Union of London and Smith's Bank, Ltd.'s Conveyance, Miles* v. *Easter* (16), cited in *Jeffs'* case (17). The passage in question reads:

(12) [1966] 1 All E.R. 937 at p. 943.
(13) [1950] 1 All E.R. 737 at p. 741; [1950] A.C. 361 at p. 369.
(14) [1962] 2 All E.R. at p. 312; [1964] Ch. at p. 47.
(15) [1962] 2 All E.R. 305; [1964] Ch. 38.
(16) [1933] All E.R. Rep. 355 at p. 364; [1933] Ch. 611 at p. 628.
(17) [1966] 1 All E.R. at p. 939.

". . . that, apart from what are usually referred to as building scheme cases (and this is not a case of that sort), a purchaser from the original covenantee of land retained by him when he executed the conveyance containing the covenant will be entitled to the benefit of the covenant if the conveyance shows that the covenant was intended to enure for the benefit of that particular land. It follows that if what is being acquired by the purchaser was only part of the land shown by the conveyance as being intended to be benefited, it must also be shown that the benefit was intended to enure to each portion of that land. In such cases the benefit of the restrictive covenant will pass to the purchaser without being mentioned. It runs with the land. In all other cases the purchaser will not acquire the benefit of the covenant unless that benefit be expressly assigned to him—or, to use the words of SIR CHARLES HALL, V.-C. (18), ' it must appear that the benefit of the covenant was part of the subject-matter of the purchase '."

In the last resort, however, it seems to me that the words here, which are a hybrid, are more within the first limb of ROMER, L.J.'s dichotomy than the second.

Then it is still open to counsel for the plaintiffs to show that the words of the covenant on their true construction do mean the Selwyn estate and every part thereof, and to do this he relies on the inclusion of the words " lately part of the Selwyn estate ". The fact that it was not possible to annex a benefit to such part does not affect any inference as to intention which ought otherwise to be drawn from the attempt to include those parts.

In my judgment, and on the inference which I have drawn as to the facts, the covenant as related to the land lately part of the Selwyn estate must mean " and every part thereof ", as it was an attempt to protect all the lands sold off whoever had them.

Then ought I to allow that to colour the first part? It seems to me that I should. Counsel for the defendant says that where, as here, one has an estate owner's estate, which by and large is going to be left together, and not an estate agent's estate, which is being carved up and developed, one should prima facie construe the covenant as annexed to the estate as a whole; but that one would not normally suppose that the owner meant to allow an indefinite number of unknown persons to come in and share with him in the right to enforce or waive the covenant, and that one should not be deflected from this view by his allowing the known previous purchasers to share. He says in effect that this is a covenant for the benefit of the unsold estate as a whole on the one hand and each of the sold portions on the other. However, where, as here, it is all part of one continuous covenant and the phraseology runs straight on, it would in my judgment be strange and really doing violence to the language if I were to construe the covenant as having one meaning as to " land part of . . . the . . . estate " and another as to " land . . . lately part of the . . . estate ".

Counsel for the defendant further says that the modern tendency is to regard a covenant for the benefit of adjoining or neighbouring land, especially if it be part of a specified estate, as for the whole and not the part, and certainly that result was reached in the cases before BUCKLEY, J. (19), and STAMP, J. (20). Basically, however, it is in my judgment a question of construction of the particular covenant.

I have also considered whether it could be said that if I adopted the construction for which counsel for the plaintiffs contends I would produce a strange result in that each purchaser of a part could enforce the covenants against prior but not subsequent purchasers and would be liable to subsequent but not prior ones, so that it would all be rather fortuitous. This, however, is inherent in any

(18) In *Renals* v. *Cowlishaw*, (1878), 9 Ch.D. 125 at p. 130; [1874-80] All E.R. Rep. 359 at p. 361.
(19) I.e., *Russell* v. *Archdale*, [1962] 2 All E.R. 305; [1964] Ch. 38.
(20) I.e., *Re Jeffs' Transfer (No. 2)*, [1966] 1 All E.R. 937.

covenant expressed in terms to be for the whole or part and, as such covenants are by no means extraordinary or unusual, nor were they as far as I know in 1922, I do not feel that this is a very material consideration.

For these reasons in my judgment the plaintiffs are entitled to a declaration that the covenant is not void for uncertainty and is validly annexed to each of their respective properties, so as to entitle them severally to the benefit thereof without prejudice to any question whether it was or still is enforceable, and of course without prejudice to the rights of any other person not a party to these proceedings. I shall order accordingly.

Order accordingly.

Solicitors: *Waterhouse & Co.* (for the plaintiffs); *Hair & Co.*, agents for *Bestford & de Lattre*, Richmond, Greater London (for the defendant).

[*Reported by* JACQUELINE METCALFE, *Barrister-at-Law.*]

BARNES AND ANOTHER *v.* HILL.

[COURT OF APPEAL, CIVIL DIVISION (Lord Denning, M.R., Danckwerts and Winn, L.JJ.), November 11, 14, 1966.]

Jury—Verdict—General verdict—Question as to reasons for it should not be put to jury—Libel action—Justification and privilege pleaded—General verdict for defendant—Question as to which defence jury found to be established put to jury—New trial on ground that finding of jury must have been perverse refused.

The general secretary of a trade union of which the defendant was a member, and the secretary of a committee of the union, each brought an action for libel against the defendant in respect of an accusation by him in a circular to union members that each plaintiff had respectively approved or made false statements. The defendant pleaded justification, and, by an amendment at the trial of the consolidated actions, publication on a privileged occasion. At the trial each plaintiff gave evidence. The defendant, who appeared in person, did not cross-examine the general secretary, but put some questions to the other plaintiff. The trial judge left each case to the jury to find a general verdict. The jury found for the defendant in each case. At the instance of counsel for the plaintiffs the judge asked the jury whether their verdicts were based on the defences of justification or of privilege. Before so doing the judge told the defendant that he would not put the question to the jury unless the defendant agreed, and that their reply could not affect the verdicts. The jury's reply was that their verdicts were based on the defences of justification. The plaintiffs applied for a new trial on the ground that in the light of that reply the jury's verdicts were perverse.

Held: once a general verdict was given by a jury, the case was at an end and they should not be asked the grounds on which they gave their verdict; further, in the present case, it would be unfair to the defendant to order a new trial in view of the trial judge's statement that the jury's reply could not affect the verdicts (see p. 350, letters F and A, post).

Arnold v. *Jeffreys* ([1914] 1 K.B. 512) applied.

Newberry v. *Bristol Tramways and Carriage Co., Ltd.* ([1911-13] All E.R. Rep. 747) distinguished.

Appeal dismissed.

[As to statements by a juror as to the deliberations of the jury not being receivable, see 23 HALSBURY'S LAWS (3rd Edn.) 37, para. 71; and for cases on verdicts of juries, see 30 DIGEST (Repl.) 280, 281, *477-500*, 283, *511-520*.

As to ordering a new trial by reason of the jury's verdict, see 30 HALSBURY'S LAWS (3rd Edn.) 474, 475, para. 890.]

Cases referred to:

Arnold v. Jeffreys, [1914] 1 K.B. 512; 83 L.J.K.B. 329; 110 L.T. 253; 30 Digest (Repl.) 281, 496.

Brown v. Bristol & Exeter Ry. Co., (1861), 4 L.T. 830; 30 Digest (Repl.) 281, 495.

Newberry v. Bristol Tramways and Carriage Co., Ltd., [1911-13] All E.R. Rep. 747; (1912), 107 L.T. 801; 8 Digest (Repl.) 76, 508.

Appeal.

This was an appeal by the plaintiffs from the judgment of MILMO, J., dated June 23, 1966, in consolidated actions, whereby it was adjudged that judgment be entered for the defendant. The first action was brought by Stanley Edward Barnes against the defendant Fred Hill by writ issued Dec. 10, 1964, and the second action was brought by Ronald Gould against the same defendant by writ issued Dec. 16, 1964. In each action the plaintiff claimed damages for libel contained in a letter published by the defendant on or about Oct. 10, 1964, to one G. B. W. Hawkins and to numerous other persons, and claimed also an injunction. By notice of appeal dated July 29, 1966, in the consolidated actions the plaintiffs sought an order that the judgment of June 23, 1966, be set aside and that a new trial should be had between the parties. The grounds of the appeal were that there was no evidence on which the jury could reasonably have found for the defendant on the issue of justification, and that the verdict of the jury was perverse and ought not to be sustained. The facts are set out in the judgment of LORD DENNING, M.R.

P. H. R. Bristow, Q.C., and J. G. K. Sheldon for the plaintiffs.
The defendant appeared in person.

LORD DENNING, M.R.: Mr. Hill, the defendant, is a schoolteacher who has been a member of the National Union of Teachers for very many years. In 1956 a Bill was before Parliament concerning the superannuation of school-teachers. It proposed that the contributions of the schoolteachers should be increased by one per cent., that is, should be increased from five per cent. to six per cent. of their salaries. At that time the plaintiffs, Sir Ronald Gould, the general secretary of the National Union of Teachers, and Dr. Barnes, the secretary of the Salaries and Superannuation Committee, opposed the Bill and put forward strong reasons against it; but eventually it did go through Parliament. On July 5, 1956, an Act was passed increasing the contributions from five per cent. to six per cent. At about the same time there was a general increase in the salaries of schoolteachers. So one might think that the matter was settled. Seven years later, however, in 1963, the defendant wrote letters to Dr. Barnes about teachers' superannuation. Dr. Barnes replied in letters of Nov. 1, 1963, and May 15, 1964. The defendant questioned some of Dr. Barnes' statements in those letters. He wrote to Sir Ronald Gould about it. Sir Ronald Gould said that he had approved Dr. Barnes' letter of Aug. 15, 1964, before it was sent. There followed much correspondence. Eventually the defendant issued a circular to members of the union in which he accused Dr. Barnes of making false statements and of lying and deception. He added: " The lies have the full approval of our general secretary, Sir Ronald Gould." He accused them of deliberate false statements.

The circular was only issued to the other members of the union. It is agreed that it was a privileged occasion; but, nevertheless, Sir Ronald Gould and Dr. Barnes felt (and I can understand it) that they should do all that they could to stop such statements as these. They took, naturally enough, considerable and grave exception to them. So each of them brought an action against the defendant for libel. To which the defendant pleaded justification in the first

A instance. He said that what he said was true. Then at the trial he added by amendment a defence of privilege.

The case was put before the jury. The defendant appeared in person. Sir Ronald Gould gave evidence. The defendant did not cross-examine him. Dr. Barnes gave evidence. The defendant did ask some questions of him. Eventually the defendant addressed the jury at some length, but he did not give evidence.

B Then the judge summed up. He did not put specific questions to the jury. The judge said to counsel for both Sir Ronald Gould and Dr. Barnes, and also to the defendant:

"I was proposing to leave the issue and ask the jury to bring in their verdict in regard to each of the plaintiffs, and, if so, find what damages."

C Both agreed. So the judge left the case to the jury to find a general verdict. He told them that they had first to make up their minds whether the words were defamatory. If they did find them defamatory, they had to find whether the words were true or not. If they were true, then there would be a verdict for the defendant. Even if they were not true, nevertheless, as it was a privileged occasion, they would have to find whether there was malice or not. If there was malice, there would be verdicts for the plaintiffs. If malice was not proved,

D there would be a verdict for the defendant. No complaint is made of the summing-up. The jury retired. After a little while they came back and asked for a further explanation about malice. The judge gave it. They retired again. Then they returned. The associate asked them:

"Members of the Jury, who shall speak as your foreman? The foreman:

E I do. The associate: Are you agreed upon your verdict? The foreman: We are, my lord. The associate: In the first of these actions, *Barnes* v. *Hill,* do you find for the plaintiff Barnes or for the defendant Hill? The foreman: We find for the defendant Hill. The associate: In the second of these actions, *Gould* v. *Hill,* do you find for the plaintiff Gould or do you find for the defendant Hill? The foreman: We find for the defendant Hill. The

F associate: Is that the verdict of you all? The foreman: It is the verdict of us all."

Then the judge told the defendant he was entitled to any costs which he had incurred. The defendant said: "I do not want them, thank you". The judge said: "Well, the actions are dismissed."

So we see there was a general verdict by a jury. They found for the defendant.

G The actions were dismissed. That should have been the end of it.

Counsel for the plaintiff, however, rose and asked the judge whether he would "ask the jury as to any part of the verdict whether their decision is based on a decision of privilege or a decision of justification. It is of importance to my clients". The judge said:

"I will not ask the jury any questions at all unless you agree, Mr. Hill.

H It does not affect their verdict in any shape or form. You have won these actions. [Counsel for the plaintiffs] now wants to ask the jury a question on what grounds it is that they have found in your favour."

The defendant: "That is a very difficult question to answer, my lord. I think it might be relevant." The judge: "Have you any objection?" The defendant: "No". The judge turned to the foreman and said:

I "Mr. Foreman, I do not know whether you can answer that. Did you find for the defendant in one or other or both of these cases on the ground of justification or on the ground of no malice?"

The foreman answered: "It was on the ground of justification, my lord". The judge said: "Thank you; you are now discharged."

Counsel for the plaintiffs now complains of the verdict of the jury. He says that there was no evidence on which they could find justification, and that their finding was perverse. He asks for a new trial.

If this were right, it would not seem at all fair on the defendant. Before he
agreed to the question being put, the judge said to him: "It does not affect
their verdict in any shape or form. You have won these actions." Seeing that
the defendant received that assurance, it would not be right for us to let it affect
the verdict. No doubt counsel for the plaintiffs expected the jury to say that
they decided on the ground of no malice; but he took his chance, and cannot
complain of their answer.

I would put the matter, however, on broader grounds. Once the general
verdict was given, that was the end of the case. The judge had no right to ask
them any further questions. That has always been my understanding and I find
it confirmed by the case of *Arnold* v. *Jeffreys* (1), when a Divisional Court consisting of two very experienced judges, BRAY, J., and LUSH, J., held that where
the jury have once given a general verdict, the judge is not entitled to ask any
further question of the jury for the purpose of ascertaining whether the ground
of their verdict was one which there was evidence to support. In so holding, they
followed the view of MARTIN, B., in *Brown* v. *Bristol & Exeter Ry. Co.* (2).

Counsel for the plaintiffs argued that the decision in *Arnold* v. *Jeffreys* (1) was
contrary to a case in 1912, *Newberry* v. *Bristol Tramways and Carriage Co., Ltd.*
(3). I do not think so. In the *Newberry* case (4) CHANNELL, J., asked the jury
for a special verdict. When he summed up, he said: "I asked you if you found
there was negligence to tell us on what ground." The jury came back with a
written memorandum specifying the negligence. That was a special verdict. In
the Court of Appeal there is a passage in the report in which it appears that it
was described as a general verdict: but that is either a slip of the tongue or an
error of the reporter.

I would add this. A jury have an absolute right to give a general verdict, i.e.,
to say simply whether they find for the plaintiff or the defendant. They cannot
be required to give a special verdict or to answer specific questions. History
shows how important is this right, especially in libel actions. Once they have
given a general verdict, that is the end of the matter. The judge cannot ask them
the grounds of the verdict. In this case all the discussion after the verdict was
surplusage and is to be ignored. The action ended when the judge said: "The
actions are dismissed."

I can well understand the plaintiffs bringing these appeals, but I am afraid
that on this point of law they must fail. The appeals are dismissed.

DANCKWERTS, L.J.: I agree.

WINN, L.J.: Not without reluctance, I also agree.

Appeal dismissed.

Solicitors: *Speechly, Mumford & Soames* (for the plaintiffs).

[*Reported by* F. GUTTMAN, ESQ., *Barrister-at-Law.*]

---

(1) [1914] 1 K.B. 512.   (2) (1861), 4 L.T. 830.
(3) [1911-13] All E.R. Rep. 747; (1912), 107 L.T. 801.
(4) [1911-13] All E.R. Rep. at p. 748; (1912), 107 L.T. at p. 802.

LORD LUKE OF PAVENHAM *v.* MINISTER OF HOUSING AND LOCAL GOVERNMENT AND ANOTHER.

[QUEEN'S BENCH DIVISION (Lawton, J.), November 16, 17, December 7, 1966.]

Town and Country Planning—Development—Permission for development—Appeal—Appeal to Minister—" Findings of fact " by inspector accepted by Minister, but not inspector's " conclusions " or recommendations—No opportunity afforded to applicant to make further representations—Appeal dismissed by Minister—Application to quash Minister's decision—Whether inspector's conclusions were also findings of fact—Town and Country Planning Appeals (Inquiries Procedure) Rules, 1962 (S.I. 1962 No. 1425), r. 10 (1), (2) (b).

A planning authority's policy in regard to a characteristic village in their area was that it should remain unaltered in size and character, and accordingly that no significant new development should be permitted. The applicant applied for planning permission to build a house within an existing walled garden. This garden was on a road at the side of the village, lying on the side of the road that was free from buildings, except for the walled garden and a garden cottage within it. The planning authority refused permission, and gave as their reason that the proposal would constitute an undesirable form of isolated and sporadic development outside the limits of the village in an area where no further development should be permitted other than that which was essential for agricultural purposes. The applicant appealed and the Minister appointed an inspector to hold an inquiry. The inspector's report included findings of fact, which were followed by two paragraphs headed " conclusions ". The inspector took the view that a well-designed house within the walled garden would, far from harming the countryside, add to the existing charm of its setting. He recommended that the appeal be allowed. In the Minister's letter of decision the Minister stated that he accepted the inspector's findings of fact, but was unable to agree with the inspector's conclusions or with his recommendation. The Minister dismissed the appeal, stating that a house on the appeal site, although within a walled garden, would be sporadic development in open countryside. Before reaching his decision the Minister did not give the applicant opportunity to make further representations. The applicant applied to the court to quash the Minister's decision.

Held: in reaching his conclusion the inspector, having been correctly informed on the planning policy applicable, was applying it to observed facts and his conclusion so reached was a finding of fact within r. 10 (1)* of the Town and Country Planning (Inquiries Procedure) Rules, 1962; accordingly the Minister, on disagreeing with the inspector's recommendations, was bound by r. 10 (2) (b) to give interested parties to the appeal an

---

*Rule 10, so far as material, provides: " (1) The appointed person shall after the close of the inquiry make a report in writing to the Minister which shall include the appointed person's findings of fact and his recommendations, if any, or his reason for not making any recommendations.

" (2) Where the Minister—
  (a) differs from the appointed person on a finding of fact, or
  (b) after the close of the inquiry receives any new evidence (including expert opinion on a matter of fact) or takes into consideration any new issue of fact (not being a matter of government policy) which was not raised at the inquiry,
and by reason thereof is disposed to disagree with a recommendation made by the appointed person, he shall not come to a decision which is at variance with any such recommendation without first notifying the appellant, the local planning authority and any s. 37 party who appeared at the inquiry of his disagreement and the reasons for it and affording them an opportunity of making representations in writing within twenty-one days or (if the Minister has received new evidence or taken into consideration any new issue of fact not being a matter of government policy) of asking within twenty-one days for the reopening of the inquiry . . ."

opportunity to make further representations, and, as the Minister had not
done this, his decision would be quashed (see p. 357, letters C, E and H, post).

Dicta of DENNING, L.J., in *British Launderers' Research Assocn.* v. *Hendon
Borough Rating Authority* ([1949] 1 All E.R. at pp. 25, 26) applied.

Per CURIAM: in r. 11 of the Rules of 1962 the word " conclusions " was
apt to describe both proven and observed facts and the inferences to be
drawn from them (see p. 357, letter D, post).

[As to challenging a decision of the Minister as to the control of development,
see 37 HALSBURY'S LAWS (3rd Edn.) 331, 332, para. 437, and as to appeal to the
Minister from a decision of the local planning authority, see ibid., p. 331, para.
436; and for cases on planning permission applications, see 45 DIGEST (Repl.)
335-340, *33-55*.

For the Town and Country Planning Act, 1962, s. 23, see 42 HALSBURY'S
STATUTES (2nd Edn.) 991.

For the Town and Country Planning Act, 1959, s. 33, see 39 HALSBURY'S
STATUTES (2nd Edn.) 1208.]

Cases referred to:

Bracegirdle v. *Oxley*, [1947] 1 All E.R. 126; [1947] K.B. 349; [1947] L.J.R.
815; 176 L.T. 187; 111 J.P. 131; 45 Digest (Repl.) 86, *287.*

British Launderers' Research Association v. *Hendon Borough Rating Authority,*
[1949] 1 All E.R. 21; [1949] 1 K.B. 462; [1949] L.J.R. 416; 113 J.P.
72; 38 Digest (Repl.) 583, *627.*

Edgington v. *Fitzmaurice*, [1881-85] All E.R. Rep. 856; (1885), 29 Ch.D. 459;
55 L.J.Ch. 650; 53 L.T. 369; 50 J.P. 294; 9 Digest (Repl.) 126, *678.*

R. v. *Dent*, [1955] 2 All E.R. 806; [1955] 2 Q.B. 590; [1955] 3 W.L.R. 297;
119 J.P. 512; 15 Digest (Repl.) 1173, *11,850.*

Motion.

This was a motion by the applicant, the Right Honourable Ian St. John,
Baron Luke of Pavenham, of Odell Castle, Bedford, pursuant to s. 179 of the
Town and Country Planning Act, 1962, for an order quashing the decision of the
first respondent, the Minister of Housing and Local Government, dated Feb. 24,
1966, whereby he dismissed an appeal by the applicant against the refusal of
the second respondent, Bedford Rural District Council (acting as agent for
Bedfordshire County Council, the local planning authority) to permit the applicant to build a residential dwelling inside the walled garden attached to a house
in his ownership in the village of Pavenham, known as The Garden House. The
main ground of the application was that the Minister, while accepting what his
inspector after conducting a local inquiry had reported as his " findings of fact ",
had not agreed with the inspector's " conclusions " or recommendation that the
appeal be allowed, and that these conclusions were themselves " findings of
fact " within r. 10 (2) of the Town and Country Planning (Inquiries Procedure)
Rules, 1962, entitling the applicant to make further representations to the
Minister before the determination of the appeal, but the Minister had not given
the applicant this opportunity. The relevant facts are stated in the judgment.

A. B. Dawson for the applicant.
Nigel Bridge for the Minister.
The second respondent was not represented.

Cur. adv. vult.

Dec. 7. **LAWTON, J.,** read the following judgment: The applicant has
moved the court to quash a decision of the respondent Minister of Housing and
Local Government dated Feb. 24, 1966, whereby he dismissed the applicant's
appeal from the decision of the respondent Bedford Rural District Council
refusing the applicant planning permission for the erection of a dwelling house
on land at Garden House, Pavenham in the county of Bedford. The applicant's

main contention has been that the Minister, having differed on a finding of fact from the inspector whom he had appointed to hold an inquiry under the Town and Country Planning Act, 1962, and being disposed to disagree with the recommendation made by that inspector, came to a decision without affording the applicant an opportunity of making representations in writing. If this contention is right, the Minister's decision must be quashed, as he has failed to comply with r. 10 of the Town and Country Planning Appeals (Inquiries Procedure) Rules, 1962, now re-enacted as r. 12 of the Rules of 1965 (1). The question raised by this motion can be put more simply in these terms: what is a finding of fact under these rules?

Before 1957 the applicant had an estate in the village of Pavenham, near Bedford. In the past this village had its squire whose house was close to the church. With his house went a stable block and grounds laid out with trees. To the west of this house and grounds and on the far side of a country road which led to, and past, the church there was and still is a walled garden of about three acres which is the subject-matter of this motion. At one end of this garden there is a cottage, where in past years the squire's head gardener had probably lived. The squire's grounds separated him from villagers. Their cottages had been built along the main road which ran east to west. Anyone wishing to go from the main village street to either the squire's house or the church had to go up a country road for about three hundred yards, with the squire's grounds on one side and open fields on the other. The older part of the village was built in stone. Some of the buildings still have thatched roofs. The Bedfordshire County Council are proud of this village and, as the planning authority, want it to remain unaltered both as to size and character. They do not intend to permit any significant new development.

Since 1945 some new development has taken place. In 1957 the applicant, who had become the owner of the squire's house and grounds, sold the property; but because of his family's connexion with the village he retained the garden house and the walled garden. After the sale, the squire's house was demolished, the stable block was turned into a house and the grounds developed with a variety of detached houses. All this development was done, of course, with planning permission. The effect of it was that one side of the country road leading from the main street to the church and beyond became largely built up; but the other side of the road, save for the garden cottage and the walled garden, remained open fields as before.

On Nov. 27, 1964, the applicant applied to Bedford Rural District Council for planning permission to build a house within the walled garden. This was refused, two reasons being given. One related to the traffic conditions. The Minister disregarded this reason and I have not been concerned with it. The other reason was stated by the planning authority as follows:

" The proposal would constitute an undesirable form of isolated and sporadic development outside the limits of the village of Pavenham in an area where no further development should be permitted other than that which is essential for agricultural purposes."

The applicant appealed from this decision to the Minister, who appointed a Mr. King to hold an inquiry. This he did and in due time he sent a report dated Jan. 5, 1966, to the Minister. In this report he set out the cases of both the applicant and the planning authority and made what he described as " findings of fact ". There then followed two paragraphs which had a sub-heading " Inspector's Conclusions ". The relevant one for the purposes of this motion was in these terms:

" 39. Bearing in mind the above facts I am of the opinion that, whilst not in the built-up area of Pavenham, the site is exceptional in that it is clearly-defined by a tall and fine-looking wall and forms part of a long-established

(1) Town and Country Planning (Inquiries Procedure) Rules 1965, S.I. 1965 No. 473.

group of buildings which contribute to the attractive character of the village independent of distance. A well-designed house within the walled garden would, far from harming the countryside, add to the existing charm of its setting and could not be said to create a precedent for allowing development on farmland to the north and south."

The concluding paragraph of the report, which had the sub-heading " Recommendations ", was as follows:

" 41. I recommend that the appeal be *allowed* subject to the condition that the siting, design and external appearance of the building and the means of access thereto shall be as may be agreed with the local planning authority or, in default of agreement, as shall be determined by the Minister."

The Minister gave his decision in a letter to the applicant's solicitors dated Feb. 24, 1966. The relevant part of that letter is as follows:

" The Minister accepts the inspector's findings of fact but is unable to agree with the conclusions he draws from them or with his recommendation. The council's policy for Pavenham is that apart from the sites which have already received planning permission the village should remain substantially unaltered in size and character. The appeal site is outside the built-up area of the village and fronts the western side of a minor country road running north from the main village street. Apart from the single dwelling, ' Garden House ', immediately to the south of the site, the surrounding land on this side of the road is open and undeveloped. It is considered that a house on the appeal site, although it would be within a walled garden, would be sporadic development in open countryside on the western side of a road which apart from the existing cottage to the south is at present free of building. It would appear furthermore that there is no shortage of land suitable and approved for building to meet the housing needs of the village. For these reasons your client's proposal is considered undesirable and the Minister has decided to dismiss the appeal."

The applicant, by his counsel, has submitted that the Minister's decision should be quashed for four reasons. First, because by the reasons which he gave for his decision he showed that he had not grasped the point of the applicant's case, namely, that the granting of planning permission for building a house within the walled garden would leave the village substantially unaltered both as to its size and character and would not amount to a significant development. Secondly, because he had so misunderstood the inspector's report as to think that a house within the walled garden would be, and I quote from the Minister's decision, "sporadic development in open countryside ". Thirdly, because in stating that there is no shortage of land suitable and approved for building to meet the housing needs of the village he revealed himself as taking account of irrelevant factors. Fourthly, because the conclusions which the inspector had drawn from what he described as his " findings of fact " were themselves findings of fact to which r. 10 (2) applied.

Counsel for the Minister submitted first, that on a fair reading of the Minister's reasons he had grasped the point raised in the appeal, he had taken into account those matters to which he ought to have had regard and had not paid attention to irrelevant matters; and secondly, that in rejecting the inspector's conclusions he was not differing from the inspector on a finding of fact within the meaning of r. 10 (2). Counsel conceded that if the words, " The Minister . . . is unable to agree with the conclusions he draws from them " meant that the Minister was unable to agree with what LORD DENNING in more than one judgment has described as " conclusions from primary facts " (see, for example, *Bracegirdle* v. *Oxley* (2)), then he should have given the applicant an opportunity of making

(2) [1947] 1 All E.R. 126; [1947] K.B. 349.

representations in writing before he made his decision and that his failure to do so would entitle the applicant to an order quashing the decision.

The applicant's first three points can be dealt with shortly. The Minister's reasons must be read as a whole and in a fair minded way. Sense must be made out of them, if the sense is discoverable behind such solecisms of grammar and inaccuracies in the use of words as there may be. In my judgment the Minister did grasp the point of the appeal. Whereas the applicant was submitting that the granting of planning permission would not constitute a significant amount of new development in the village, the Minister was saying that it would because (and I quote from his decision)

> " it is considered that a house on the appeal site, although it would be within a walled garden, would be sporadic development in open countryside on the western side of a road which apart from the existing cottage to the south is at present free of building."

The applicant's second submission is nothing more than a verbal quibble arising from an inaccurate use of the word " sporadic ". In its context the words which have been criticised mean that in the Minister's opinion the building of another house on the west side of the road would start to make it look different; and this, when translated into the jargon of town and country planning, means such building would be a significant amount of new development. The reference in the Minister's reasons to other sites suitable for house building is not, in its context, irrelevant. Significant new development may have to be allowed by the Minister because of the scarcity of suitable building land for housing needs. All the Minister was saying was that in this case there was plenty of land available for houses, so that scarcity of land was not a valid reason for granting planning permission.

I turn now to the applicant's main submission, namely that the Minister differed from his inspector on findings of fact. My first task is to construe the Minister's statement that he is unable to agree with the inspector's conclusions. This takes me to those conclusions themselves; and as these had been reached on the " facts " as the inspector found them, I have to look at them too. The inspector enumerated the facts. Those numbered one to twelve were findings as to matters of topography and history. That numbered thirteen was a finding as to how the village was classified by the planning authority and what they intended to permit by way of development, which was very little (3). This finding as to the planning authority's intention was a finding of fact. That is in accord with the view expressed by BOWEN, L.J., in his well-known dictum in *Edgington* v. *Fitzmaurice* (4), and as far as I know it represents the generally accepted opinion, the only qualification being that a misstatement of intention about future conduct, whether or not it be a misstatement of existing fact, is not such a statement as will amount to a false pretence in criminal law (*R.* v. *Dent* (5)). From these findings of fact, the inspector went on to infer first, that the site for the proposed house possessed exceptional qualities and secondly, that a well designed house on that site would not alter the character of the village and would not amount to significant new development. What were these inferences? Conclusions of fact? Or, as counsel for the Minister has submitted, conclusions involving the application of planning policy? The judgment of DENNING, L.J., in *British Launderers' Research Association* v. *Hendon Borough Rating Authority* (6) helps with the solution of this problem, and I quote:

> " Counsel for the association says, however, that quarter sessions came to

---

(3) Finding thirteen was " Pavenham is classified as a village which it is intended will remain substantially unaltered both as to size and character; and where it is not expected that any significant amount of new development will be permitted."

(4) [1881-85] All E.R. Rep. 856 at p. 861; (1885), 29 Ch.D. 459 at p. 483: " There must be a mis-statement of an existing fact: but the state of a man's mind is as much a fact as the state of his digestion."

(5) [1955] 2 All E.R. 806 at p. 808; [1955] 2 Q.B. 590 at p. 595.

(6) [1949] 1 All E.R. 21 at pp. 25, 26; [1949] 1 K.B. 462 at p. 471.

a conclusion of fact in his favour with which the Divisional Court should not have interfered. On this point it is important to distinguish between primary facts and the conclusions from them. Primary facts are facts which are observed by witnesses and proved by oral testimony, or facts proved by the production of a thing itself, such as an original document. Their determination is essentially a question of fact for the tribunal of fact, and the only question of law that can arise on them is whether there was any evidence to support the finding. The conclusions from primary facts are, however, inferences deduced by a process of reasoning from them. If and in so far as those conclusions can as well be drawn by a layman (properly instructed on the law) as by a lawyer, they are conclusions of fact for the tribunal of fact and the only questions of law which can arise on them are whether there was a proper direction in point of law and whether the conclusion is one which could reasonably be drawn from the primary facts; see *Bracegirdle* v. *Oxley* (7). If and in so far, however, as the correct conclusion to be drawn from primary facts requires, for its correctness, determination by a trained lawyer—as, for instance, because it involves the interpretation of documents, or because the law and the facts cannot be separated, or because the law on the point cannot properly be understood or applied except by a trained lawyer—the conclusion is a conclusion of law on which an appellate tribunal is as competent to form an opinion as the tribunal of first instance."

Now the inspector, having been correctly informed as to the planning policy applicable to this village, looked at both the site and the village and concluded that a well-designed house on the site would not alter the character of the village and would not amount to a significant new development. He was doing no more than lining up the building proposal against the village as it existed and as the planning authority wanted it to be in the future; and having done this he came to the conclusion that all three fell into line. This conclusion was not one of law or of mixed fact and law; and it cannot be attacked for want of evidence to support it. Counsel for the Minister has submitted that, on the true construction of the rules, conclusions involving the application of planning policy are not findings of facts, the argument being that when dealing with appeals the Minister has wide powers: he may allow or dismiss the appeal, or may reverse or vary any part of the decision of the local planning authority and may deal with the application as if it had been made to him in the first instance (see the Town and Country Planning Act, 1962, s. 23 (4)). These being his powers, and the policy of the Act being to entrust the Minister with the supervision of all planning, the phrase " findings of facts " in r. 10 of the Town and Country Planning Appeal (Inquiries Procedure) Rules, 1962, should be construed, so it was submitted, as meaning facts proved by testimony or observed by the inspector, leaving to the Minister the application of planning policy to the facts so proved or observed. This argument is fortified by the provisions of s. 23 (5) of the Town and Country Planning Act, 1962, which requires the Minister to afford the parties to an appeal an opportunity of appearing before, and being heard by, an inspector appointed for the purpose. The inspector is not required by this subsection to determine anything; determination is left by s. 23 (4) to the Minister, and in most appeals that which has to be determined is the application of planning policy to proven or observed facts.

As against this argument, there stands the policy of the Tribunal and Inquiries Act, 1958, under which the rules in question were made (8). The effect of that

(7) [1947] 1 All E.R. 126; [1947] K.B. 349.

(8) The Town and Country Planning (Inquiries Procedure) Rules 1965, superseding the rules of 1962, were made (as were the rules of 1962) under s. 7A of the Tribunals and Inquiries Act, 1958, which was added by the Town and Country Planning Act, 1959, s. 33. Section 7A has been amended by s. 1 and s. 2 of the Tribunals and Inquiries Act 1966, which came into force on Dec. 13, 1966; the amendments are irrelevant to the present decision.

A Act has been to extend the supervisory powers of this court over government departments having power to make orders disposing of, or affecting, citizens' property. This court, and the Court of Appeal, have long been familiar with the exercise of supervisory powers over courts or tribunals from which there is no appeal on fact and with the problems which arise therefrom, one of which is deciding what is fact and what is not. By 1962, when the rules were made and B laid before Parliament, lawyers were familiar with the concept of a finding of fact and what it connoted. It follows, so it seems to me, that the words " finding of fact " should bear the same meaning in the Rules of 1962 as they do generally, unless there is something in the rules themselves which points against this, or their subject-matter (namely, procedure in the determination of planning appeals) is such as to make the ordinary meaning of the words inapplicable. In my C judgment under the general law the inspector's " conclusions " in this case would be findings of fact.

Rule 10 (1) provides that the inspector shall make a written report to the Minister which shall include, and I quote: " findings of fact and his recommendations, if any, or his reason for not making any recommendations ". Rule 11 requires (9) the Minister to send the interested parties either a copy of the D inspector's report or a summary of, and I quote: " [his] conclusions and recommendations ". The word " conclusions " in this context is apt to describe both proven and observed facts and the inferences to be drawn from them. As r. 10 (1) refers only to " findings of fact " and " recommendations ", it seems to me that the words " findings of fact " in that context include " conclusions " in the sense indicated above. Further, r. 10 (2) (*b*) requires the Minister to give the E interested parties to an appeal an opportunity of making further representations if, being disposed to disagree with the inspector's recommendations, he, and I quote:

" takes into consideration any new issue of fact (not being a matter of Government policy) which was not raised at the inquiry."

F This sub-rule shows that the rule contemplates that matters of policy can be issues of fact. Once they become relevant issues of fact the inspector has a duty to make findings on them. I find nothing in the Rules of 1962 themselves to support the Minister's contention that the words " findings of fact " should be construed as applying solely to proven or observed facts; they must be construed more widely than that.

G In my judgment the subject-matter of the rules provides no obstacle to a wide construction of the relevant words. The Minister is not bound by an inspector's findings of fact, whatever the meaning of these words may be; but if he differs from them, he must take the steps specified in the rules, namely to give those interested a limited right of reply. To my sense of justice this seems particularly apt when the Minister is inclined to the opinion that the inspector has gone wrong H in applying the proven planning policy to the proven and observed facts. In my judgment the Minister did differ from his inspector on findings of fact. As he did not give the applicant an opportunity of making representations in writing before determining the appeal there was a defect in procedure which deprived the applicant of his statutory rights. It follows that the Minister's decision must be quashed.

Minister's decision quashed.

I Solicitors: *Linklaters & Paines* (for the applicant);   *Solicitor, Minister of Housing and Local Government.*

[*Reported by* K. DIANA PHILLIPS, *Barrister-at-Law.*]

———

(9) See now r. 13 of the Town and Country Planning (Inquiries Procedure) Rules 1965, S.I. 1965 No. 473.

NOTE.

R. *v.* NELSON.

[COURT OF APPEAL, CRIMINAL DIVISION (Winn, L.J., Lawton and James, JJ.), December 13, 1966.]

Criminal Law—Practice—Other offences taken into consideration—Court should satisfy itself by explicit inquiry that accused admits those offences before they can be taken into consideration—Pressure on accused in regard to admission of other offences.

[**Editorial Note.** In *R. v. Davis* ([1943] 1 All E.R. 305) the Court of Criminal Appeal emphasised that the proper practice, if other offences were to be taken into consideration, was for the accused himself to admit the offences and to ask for them to be taken into consideration.

As to taking into consideration other charges, see 10 HALSBURY'S LAWS (3rd Edn.) 490, para. 892; and for cases on the subject, see 14 DIGEST (Repl.) 556-558, *5466-5500.*]

Appeal.

This was an appeal by Gerald Charles Nelson against a sentence of three years' corrective training imposed on him by the recorder (C. J. A. DOUGHTY, ESQ., Q.C.), at Brighton Quarter Sessions on Oct. 24, 1966, to which court he had been committed for sentence under s. 29 of the Magistrates' Courts Act, 1952, after he had pleaded guilty at Brighton magistrates' court on Oct. 11, 1966, to two charges of larceny for thefts of 30s. and £5 respectively. After the appellant's pleas of guilty before the magistrates' court had been put to and admitted by him at quarter sessions and the prosecution had opened the case, Detective Sergeant Simmonds gave evidence that he had served notice on the appellant under s. 23 of the Criminal Justice Act, 1948, and of the appellant's previous convictions. He had had seven previous convictions between Sept. 29, 1960, and Sept. 15, 1965. These involved larceny. He had been unemployed since July 9, 1966. The recorder then asked whether there were other offences to be taken into consideration. The witness answered that in the lower court the appellant had asked for four offences to be taken into consideration, but that the witness understood that that was no longer the appellant's wish. Counsel for the appellant then made the interpolation set out at p. 359, letter C, post. Leave to appeal was given by the single judge (FENTON ATKINSON, J.) because (a) the appellant did not appear to be a suitable corrective trainee in view of the terms of imprisonment served previously; (b) the offences charged did not appear to merit three years, and (c) the appellant had said that he did not want offences taken into consideration and the single judge took the view that pressure was brought to bear on him.

R. A. Headridge for the appellant.
The Crown was not represented.

WINN, L.J., delivered the following judgment of the court: The appellant, Gerald Charles Nelson, appeals by leave of the single judge against a sentence passed on him on Oct. 24, 1966, after he had been committed to Brighton Quarter Sessions by the Brighton Magistrates' court. He was sentenced by the recorder to three years' corrective training. He had pleaded guilty before the magistrates to two charges of larceny. Reference was made to four other offences, or alleged offences, of larceny when he was before quarter sessions.

[HIS LORDSHIP then summarised the circumstances of the offences to which the appellant had pleaded guilty, and, after referring to his criminal record, continued:] The four matters which I have already mentioned were in the end more or less clearly taken into consideration; at any rate, there is no doubt that, so far as any further proceedings against the appellant are concerned, they are to be deemed to have been taken into consideration. This court cannot, however, approve the manner in which that process of taking into consideration came about, and takes this opportunity to say that it thinks that there is nowadays an inappropriate laxity in dealing with other offences, which may or may not really be admitted by a person accused of charges established before the court. What happened was that the recorder, apparently, had knowledge that at the lower court something had been said about taking four offences into consideration; he said that he understood that that was not now the wish of the appellant. Counsel for the appellant then said:

" I have seen him and explained the nature of part of his statement. I have shown him this notice (1) and have told him that he has signed the appropriate section as having received the form. He tells me that he does not want them taken into consideration and that what he said in his statement is not true because he did not commit these offences."

The recorder then saw fit to say: " The prosecution may well want to try them." That amounts really to a threat, so it seems to this court. The recorder, pressing the appellant, then said:

" Nelson, you have heard what your learned counsel has said. You have made a statement admitting other offences; you have signed a document asking for them to be taken into consideration by me to-day, and I can do so. If you do not wish that course to be taken, the prosecution are entitled to try you for them and, if you are convicted, you will be separately sentenced in respect of those other offences. Do you want me to take into consideration the offences which you have asked on that form I should take into consideration? "

That seems to amount, in the opinion of this court, to putting pressure on the appellant of an undesirable kind. Furthermore when, after conferring with his counsel, the appellant instructed his counsel to say that he definitely did wish them to be taken into consideration, these other matters were put in the form of reference to the details by the clerk of the peace, and the question: " Is that correct? "; and that was done four times over. It seems to this court that that question: " Is that correct ? " is possibly ambiguous and may mean to the minds of some men no more than: " Have I correctly read the details of the alleged other offence of which you have already received notice? " It is essential in the opinion of this court, that in any such case the court should satisfy itself by explicit inquiry whether the accused before the court does admit his guilt of those offences before they can be properly taken into consideration.

[HIS LORDSHIP then referred to the question of sentence, and stated that the court considered corrective training to be unsuitable, but that having looked at all the circumstances the court thought that the appropriate sentence here was twenty-one months' imprisonment.]

Sentence varied.

Solicitor: *Registrar of Criminal Appeals* (for the appellant).

[*Reported by* N. P. METCALFE, ESQ., *Barrister-at-Law.*]

---

(1) Viz., the notice about further offences.

GORE *v.* VAN DER LANN (LIVERPOOL CORPORATION
intervening).

[COURT OF APPEAL, CIVIL DIVISION (Willmer, Harman and Salmon, L.JJ.),
November 7, 29, 1966.]

*Carriers—Negligence—Exclusion of liability—Free pass—Contractual animus,
not merely a licence—Holder of pass injured while boarding omnibus—
Whether condition excluding liability made void by Road Traffic Act,* 1960
(8 & 9 Eliz. 2 c. 16), *s.* 151.

*Practice—Stay of proceedings—Applicant not a party to the action—Omnibus
operator which had issued free pass on condition that operator and its servants
should not be liable to holder of pass for injury, however caused—Pass-holder
injured boarding omnibus—Action by pass-holder against servant of operator—
Whether operator entitled to stay of proceedings—Supreme Court of Judicature
(Consolidation) Act,* 1925 (15 & 16 Geo. 5 c. 49), *s.* 41, *proviso* (b).

The Liverpool Corporation issued in 1963 a " free pass " on the corporation's buses to the plaintiff, who was about seventy-nine years of age and in
receipt of a retirement pension; she made and signed a written application
whereby " in consideration of my being granted a free pass . . . I undertake
and agree that the use of such pass by me shall be subject to the conditions
overleaf . . .". These conditions included " (4) The pass is issued and
accepted on the understanding that it merely constitutes and grants a
licence to the holder to travel on the [corporation's] buses, with and subject
to the conditions that neither the [corporation] nor any of [its] servants or
agents responsible for the driving, management, control or working of their
bus system are to be liable to the holder . . . for loss of life, injury . . . or other
loss or damage to property however caused ". The pass itself bore a statement that it was " issued subject to the conditions of grant set out in the
written form of application . . . and upon the express condition that the
[corporation] and [its] servants shall be under no liability, either contractual
or otherwise, to the pass-holder when boarding, alighting from or being
carried on [the corporation's] vehicles ". Subsequently a bus which the
plaintiff was boarding moved off, and she fell and was injured. She brought
an action for damages against the conductor (who was employed by the
corporation), alleging that the accident was due to his negligence in causing
the bus to move off while she was boarding. The corporation intervened in
the action, asking the court to stay the proceedings, under proviso (b) to
s. 41* of the Supreme Court of Judicature (Consolidation) Act, 1925, on the
ground that the plaintiff was bound by the condition in her pass that its
servant, the conductor, should not be liable to her. The plaintiff contended
inter alia that the issue and acceptance of the pass constituted " a contract
for the conveyance of a passenger in a public service vehicle ", and that
condition (4) was therefore rendered void by s. 151† of the Road Traffic Act,
1960, so far as it purported " to negative or restrict the liability of a person
in respect of a claim . . . in respect of . . . bodily injury to, the passenger ".

Held: the corporation was not entitled to a stay of proceedings because—
(i) (per WILLMER and SALMON, L.JJ., HARMAN, L.J., expressing no opinion
on this point) on the facts, and having regard to the terms of the pass, its
issue and acceptance constituted a contract, not merely a licence, with the
consequence that s. 151 of the Road Traffic Act, 1960, rendered void the
condition relied on by the corporation (see p. 366, letter B, and p. 368,
letter B, post; cf., p. 367, letter G, post).

Wilkie v. *London Passenger Transport Board* ([1947] 1 All E.R. 258)
distinguished.

---

* Section 41 is printed at p. 363, letters D to G, post.
† Section 151 is printed at p. 364, letter H, post.

(ii) (per WILLMER & SALMON, L.JJ.) even if the condition was not void, it contained no express agreement not to sue an employee of the corporation and, as conditions attached to the pass should be construed against the corporation, no such agreement would be inferred (see p. 366, letters D and E, and p. 368, letter F, post).

(iii) even if the condition were not void, as the corporation was not legally liable to indemnify their servant, the conductor, against the plaintiff's claim against him in respect of his own negligence, even though in practice it might feel bound to do so, the allegation that the plaintiff's action was a fraud on the corporation, on which the corporation's application for a stay of proceedings was grounded, was not established, and the corporation had no interest entitling it to the stay that it sought under proviso (*b*) to s. 41 of the Supreme Court of Judicature (Consolidation) Act, 1925 (see p. 366, letter G, p. 367, letter F, and p. 368, letter G, post).

Cosgrove v. *Horsfall* ((1945), 175 L.T. 334) considered.

Appeal dismissed.

[**Editorial Note.** With this case should be considered also *Genys* v. *Matthews* ([1965] 3 All E.R. 24).

As to agreements to travel at own risk, see 4 HALSBURY's LAWS (3rd Edn.) 186, 187, para. 465; and for cases on the subject, see 8 DIGEST (Repl.) 111, 112, *718-724.*

As to the liability of an operator of public service vehicles to his passengers, see 33 HALSBURY's LAWS (3rd Edn.) 673, para. 1141.

As to the statutory power to stay proceedings, see 30 HALSBURY's LAWS (3rd Edn.) 406, para. 765.

For the Supreme Court of Judicature (Consolidation) Act, 1925, s. 41, see 18 HALSBURY's STATUTES (2nd Edn.) 478.

For the Road Traffic Act, 1960, s. 151, see 40 HALSBURY's STATUTES (2nd Edn.) 845.]

Cases referred to:

Cosgrove v. *Horsfall*, (1945), 175 L.T. 334; 8 Digest (Repl.) 112, *723.*

Scruttons, Ltd. v. *Midland Silicones, Ltd.,* [1962] 1 All E.R. 1; [1962] A.C. 446; [1962] 2 W.L.R. 186; Digest (Cont. Vol. A) 271, *261a.*

White v. *Harrow*, (1901), 85 L.T. 677; *on appeal* C.A., (1902), 86 L.T. 4; Digest (Practice) 975, *5092.*

Wilkie v. *London Passenger Transport Board*, [1946] 1 All E.R. 650; 175 L.T. 331; *affd.* C.A., [1947] 1 All E.R. 258; [1947] L.J.R. 864; 177 L.T. 71; 111 J.P. 98; 8 Digest (Repl.) 117, *724.*

Interlocutory appeal.

This was an appeal by Liverpool Corporation, which had applied by summons in this action, to which the corporation was not a party, for a stay of proceedings. The action was brought by the plaintiff, Mrs. Margaret Gore, widow, against the defendant, Hendrick Van der Lann, a bus conductor employed by the corporation, for damages for injuries suffered while boarding his bus. The ground of the corporation's application was a condition of a free pass on its buses issued by the corporation to the plaintiff and current at the time of the accident, which condition provided that neither the corporation nor its servants should be liable to the plaintiff for any injury however caused. The corporation's application was refused by the registrar at Liverpool county court and the corporation's appeal against the refusal was dismissed by His Honour JUDGE STANSFIELD on July 12, 1966. The facts are set out in the judgment of WILLMER, L.J.

I. H. M. Jones for Liverpool Corporation.

Rose Heilbron, Q.C., and *D. L. Bulmer* for the plaintiff.

Cur. adv. vult.

Nov. 29, 1966. The following judgments were read.

WILLMER, L.J.:   The Corporation of Liverpool has for some years been in the habit of issuing free passes for use on its buses to elderly persons in receipt of what is now called a " retirement pension ".   On Apr. 24, 1963, the plaintiff, who was a lady then nearly seventy-nine years old, applied for the issue of such a free pass, and for that purpose signed a printed form supplied by the corporation, which provided as follows:

" In consideration of my being granted a free pass for use on the buses of Liverpool Corporation, I undertake and agree that the use of such pass by me shall be subject to the conditions overleaf, *which have been read to or by me prior to signing.*"

The " conditions overleaf " included the following:

" (4) The pass is issued and accepted on the understanding that it merely constitutes and grants a licence to the holder to travel on the Liverpool Corporation's buses, with and subject to the conditions that neither the Liverpool Corporation nor any of [its] servants or agents responsible for the driving, management, control or working of their bus system, are to be liable to the holder or his or her representative for loss of life, injury or delay or other loss or damage to property however caused. (5) The pass is issued and accepted on the further understanding that the pass-holder, whenever he or she makes to board and is travelling on the corporation's buses during permitted hours or on journeys for which the pass may be used, shall be deemed on every such occasion to be making use of his or her pass and to be travelling free and subject to the conditions of travel imposed by such pass until such times as he or she tenders and pays a proper fare for the journey or in other manner expressly indicates to the conductor or other duly appointed representative of the corporation that he or she does not intend to make use of his or her free pass for the occasion or journey in question."

In response to her application the plaintiff was duly issued with a free pass, described as a pensioner's pass, on the back of which was endorsed the following clause:

" NOT TRANSFERABLE.   Issued subject to the conditions of grant set out in the written form of application previously made and signed by the pass-holder and to the bye-laws and regulations of the corporation and upon the express condition that the corporation and [its] servants shall be under no liability, either contractual or otherwise, to the pass-holder when boarding, alighting from or being carried on corporation vehicles.   W. M. Hall, General Manager."

On Nov. 7, 1965, the plaintiff was boarding a Liverpool Corporation bus at an authorised stop when, as the bus moved off, she fell and was dragged along the ground, sustaining injury.   She brought an action in the Liverpool county court against the defendant, the conductor, alleging that the accident was due to his negligence in ringing the bell and causing the bus to move off while she was in the act of boarding, and in failing to take proper precautions for her safety.

The defendant filed a defence denying negligence, and relying in the alternative on the conditions subject to which the plaintiff's free pass was issued. The material allegations were as follows:

" (7) In particular the said pass or licence was issued and accepted on the understanding that it merely constituted and granted a licence to the plaintiff to travel on the Liverpool Corporation's buses with and subject to the condition that neither the Liverpool Corporation nor any of [its] servants or agents responsible for the driving, management, control, or working of their bus system, were to be liable to the plaintiff for injury or other loss or damage however caused. (8) The defendant, the conductor of the said motor bus, was a servant of the defendants (sic) of the class referred to in the said term or condition or understanding."

I have read that paragraph of the defence as it was drafted, although it is plain that the Liverpool Corporation was not a defendant in the suit.

" (9) Further the defendant ratified the action of the Liverpool Corporation in obtaining such undertaking from the plaintiff. (10) By reason of the foregoing the plaintiff is not entitled to bring these proceedings or to succeed in these proceedings against the defendant in any circumstances whatsoever."

On the same day as the defence was filed a summons was issued on behalf of the Liverpool Corporation applying for an order that all further proceedings in the plaintiff's action be stayed. The grounds of the application were that it was a condition of the plaintiff's free pass that the servants of the corporation, including the defendant, should not be liable for injury to the plaintiff, that the corporation was obliged to meet and satisfy any judgment obtained against the defendant, and that in the premises by bringing this action the plaintiff was acting so as to defraud the corporation. The application was made in pursuance of s. 41 of the Supreme Court of Judicature (Consolidation) Act, 1925, which provides as follows:

" No cause or proceeding at any time pending in the High Court or the Court of Appeal shall be restrained by prohibition or injunction, but every matter of equity on which an injunction against the prosecution of any such cause or proceeding might formerly have been obtained, whether unconditionally or on any terms or conditions, may be relied on by way of defence thereto: Provided that—(*a*) Nothing in this Act shall disable either of the said courts, if it thinks fit so to do, from directing a stay of proceedings in any cause or matter pending before it; and (*b*) Any person, whether a party or not to any such cause or matter, who would formerly have been entitled to apply to any court to restrain the prosecution thereof, or who may be entitled to enforce, by attachment or otherwise, any judgment, decree, rule or order, in contravention of which all or any part of the proceedings in the cause or matter have been taken, may apply to the High Court or the Court of Appeal, as the case may be, by motion in a summary way, for a stay of proceedings in the cause or matter, either generally, or so far as may be necessary for the purposes of justice, and the court shall thereupon make such order as shall be just."

By s. 103 of the County Courts Act, 1959, it is provided that in any case not expressly provided for by or in pursuance of that Act, the general principles of practice in the High Court may be adopted and applied to proceedings in a county court.

The corporation's application was dismissed by the registrar, and on appeal by His Honour JUDGE STANSFIELD. No reasons appear to have been stated either by the registrar or the judge, and indeed it is complained by counsel for the corporation that he was never really given a chance to develop his argument. The corporation now appeals to this court, and we have had the benefit of a full argument.

The case for the corporation is that the plaintiff's free pass constituted no more than a licence which was granted subject to conditions. It has been contended that the plaintiff, having accepted the benefit of the licence, must also accept the conditions subject to which it was issued, and is therefore bound, as against the corporation, by the condition that neither the corporation nor its servants are to be liable for injury caused to her. The corporation is therefore entitled, under proviso (*b*) to s. 41 of the Act of 1925, to an order restraining the prosecution of the plaintiff's action against the defendant. In support of this contention we were referred to *White* v. *Harrow* (1), which was cited as an instance of a case where a person, not a party to the action, successfully

---

(1) (1901), 85 L.T. 677.

invoked his contract with the plaintiff to obtain an injunction restraining the prosecution of an action brought by the plaintiff against the defendant in breach of the terms of that contract.   We were also referred to a dictum of DU PARCQ, L.J., in *Cosgrove* v. *Horsfall* (2), where the circumstances were similar to those of the present case, in that the action was brought by the holder of a free pass against an employee of the London Passenger Transport Board.   The lord justice in that case clearly envisaged the possibility of the board applying for the very form of relief now sought by the Liverpool Corporation.   He said (2):

   " I will express no opinion on the question, which counsel for the defendant
   told us he had considered, whether the board could have applied successfully
   to stay the present action under s. 41 of the Supreme Court of Judicature
   (Consolidation) Act, 1925 (see especially proviso (b)).   We are not now
   concerned with the rights of the board, but it must not be assumed that,
   if the plaintiff caused them to suffer loss by breach of the condition they
   were without remedy and are now necessarily without redress."

Subsequent to the hearing before the judge, and for the purposes of this appeal, the following facts were agreed between the parties: (i) That the application for the free pass was the plaintiff's application, and the signature on the form was her signature; (ii) That at the time when the free pass was issued, the defendant, the conductor of the bus, was not in the employment of the corporation; (iii) That the defendant conductor's purported ratification of the action of the corporation in issuing the free pass, subject to the conditions attached thereto, was not signed till May 10, 1966, that is, after action brought.   It was conceded before us by counsel for the corporation that the conditions, subject to which the pass was issued, would be apt to afford protection against liability for injury even though the injury were caused by negligence.   It was also conceded that, having regard to the decision of this court in *Cosgrove* v. *Horsfall* (3), which was in terms approved by VISCOUNT SIMONDS in *Scruttons, Ltd.* v. *Midland Silicones, Ltd.* (4), the defendant in this action could not succeed in his defence, in so far as this is based on the conditions subject to which the free pass was issued.   It has been argued, however, that, having regard to the plaintiff's acceptance of the conditions imposed, the prosecution of the present action against the defendant amounts to a fraud on the corporation and an abuse of the process of the court, which should consequently be restrained by injunction.

   On behalf of the plaintiff it has been contended that the effect of the plaintiff's application and its acceptance by the corporation was to constitute " a contract for the conveyance of a passenger in a public service vehicle ", which is rendered void by s. 151 of the Road Traffic Act, 1960.   That section provides as follows:

   " A contract for the conveyance of a passenger in a public service vehicle
   shall, so far as it purports to negative or restrict the liability of a person
   in respect of a claim which may be made against him in respect of the
   death of, or bodily injury to, the passenger while being carried in, entering
   or alighting from the vehicle, or purports to impose any conditions with
   respect to the enforcement of any such liability, be void."

If this contention is well founded it is obvious that, assuming negligence on the part of the defendant, it effectively demolishes any possible defence to the plaintiff's claim, not only by the defendant but also by the corporation itself.   In the circumstances it is tempting to ask why the plaintiff's advisers have seen fit to adopt the tortuous procedure of suing the defendant when there would have been an equally good claim against the corporation.   Be that as it may, however, it is plain that if the plaintiff's contention be well founded, the corporation can have no possible ground for seeking to interfere with the prosecution of the present action against the defendant.

   In reply to this contention counsel for the corporation relied on the decision

---

(2) (1945), 175 L.T. 334 at p. 335.   (3) (1945), 175 L.T. 334.
        (4) [1962] 1 All E.R. 1 at p. 9; [1962] A.C. 446 at p. 471.

of LORD GODDARD, C.J. (5) and of LORD GREENE, M.R., in this court in *Wilkie*
v. *London Passenger Transport Board* (6), as authority for the proposition that
the issue by a transport authority of a free pass subject to conditions does not
constitute a contract between the holder and the authority, but amounts to no
more than the grant of a revocable licence with the condition that, while it is
being enjoyed, certain consequences are to follow.   In that case a free pass, which
was expressed to be subject to conditions similar to those in the present case,
was issued as a matter of routine by the transport board to one of its employees.
The employee had the misfortune to sustain personal injuries while attempting
to board a bus.   He thereupon brought an action against the transport board,
who relied in their defence on one of the conditions subject to which the pass
was issued.   The point was taken on behalf of the employee that the condition
attached to the pass was void under s. 97 of the Road Traffic Act, 1930, the
equivalent of s. 151 of the Act of 1960.   LORD GODDARD said (7) with regard to
this contention:

" That depends upon whether there was here a contract for the conveyance
of a passenger in a public service vehicle.   The short answer to this point is
that the pass was issued, in my opinion, as a mere privilege or licence.
It was no part of the contract of employment that a pass should be issued."

In the Court of Appeal LORD GREENE, M.R., dealt with the point as follows (8):

" I agree that the giving or receiving of this pass cannot be regarded as
a contract for the conveyance of a passenger.   It was said that the contract
for conveyance is to be found in the giving and receiving of the pass, the
contract being of this nature: ' We, the London Passenger Board,
agree to carry you free on our buses on the terms that you agree to
give up what would otherwise have been your common law rights.'   I think
the short answer to that is that the question depends on the true construction
of the pass and to regard it as having any contractual force is entirely to
misinterpret it.   There is no contractual animus to be found in relation to it.
It is clearly nothing but a licence subject to conditions, a very common
form of licence, e.g., a licence to a neighbour to walk over a field, providing
he does not go with a dog.   You cannot spell such a thing as being a contract:
' I will let you go across my field in consideration of you, as a contracting
party, agreeing not to take your dog.'   In other words, looking at this document shortly and sensibly, it contains no intention to contract.   It is the
mere grant of a revocable licence subject to a condition that, while the
licence is being enjoyed, certain consequences shall follow.   That is not
contractual, but is a term or condition of the licence, and if anyone makes
use of the licence he can do so only by being bound by the condition.   That
seems to be the short answer to the argument on s. 7."

Wilkie's case (6), being a decision of this court, is binding on us unless it is
distinguishable.   I have found the question one of no little difficulty, but I have
come to the conclusion, not without some hesitation, that the present case is to
be distinguished.   The circumstances surrounding the issue of the free pass in
the present case were quite different from those in which the pass in *Wilkie's*
case (6) was issued.   There the pass was issued to an employee of the board as a
matter of course as one of the privileges attaching to his employment.   There
was certainly nothing contractual about it;   there was, as LORD GREENE said (8),
no contractual animus.   In the present case, on the other hand, the pass was
issued, not to an employee, but to a stranger, and only in response to a written
application.   By the terms of the application which she signed the plaintiff
specifically undertook and agreed that the use of the pass should be subject

---

(5) [1946] 1 All E.R. 650.
(7) [1946] 1 All E.R. at p. 652.

(6) [1947] 1 All E.R. 258.
(8) [1947] 1 All E.R. at p. 260.

to the conditions. The very wording of that which the plaintiff signed was couched in the language of contract. It appears to me that all the elements of contract were present. By signing and submitting her application, the plaintiff, as I see it, was accepting the offer of the corporation to carry her free on its buses subject to the conditions specified. Each party gave good consideration by accepting a detriment in return for the advantages gained. Unlike *Wilkie's* case (9), the facts of the present case do in my judgment reveal a contractual animus. This conclusion is, of course, fatal to the corporation's application. If, as I think, there was a contract, it is clearly rendered void by s. 151 of the Road Traffic Act 1960. There can, therefore, be no obstacle in the way of the plaintiff prosecuting an action for negligence, whether against the corporation or against its employee. The corporation can have no possible ground for seeking to interfere with the plaintiff's right to prosecute her action.

That is sufficient to dispose of the appeal; but I think it right to add that, even if I had thought that the issue of the free pass amounted to no more than the grant of a licence subject to conditions, I should still have arrived at the same conclusion so far as this application is concerned. It is true that the conditions accepted by the plaintiff when she accepted the offer of a free pass included a provision that the employees of the corporation were not to be liable to her for any injury or loss; but I cannot construe this provision as a promise by the plaintiff not to institute proceedings against an employee. If the corporation desired such a promise from the holder of a free pass, it could have said so in clear and unambiguous terms. In my judgment the conditions are to be construed strictly against the corporation which put them forward. It is not enough to say that a promise not to sue the employee is to be implied. At the best for the corporation, the condition relied on is ambiguous, and any ambiguity must be resolved in favour of the plaintiff.

In these circumstances the corporation has not satisfied me that it has any justification for interfering with the plaintiff's prima facie right at common law to bring proceedings against the defendant whom she accuses of negligence. On this ground also I am of opinion that the judge came to the right conclusion, and that the appeal should be dismissed.

Since preparing this judgment I have had the advantage of reading the judgment of HARMAN, L.J. I should desire to express my concurrence with his view that, since it has not been shown that there was any contract between the corporation and the defendant rendering the corporation liable in law to indemnify the defendant, there is no ground on which the corporation could be held to have an interest entitling it to relief under s. 41 of the Act of 1925. On this ground, also, in addition to those which I have already set out, I am satisfied that the corporation's application was rightly dismissed.

HARMAN, L.J. (read by SALMON, L.J.): The facts of this case and the relevant documents or their effect have been fully stated by WILLMER, L.J., and I shall not repeat them. The action was one by a passenger in one of the Liverpool Corporation's buses against the conductor of the bus, who was, of course, a servant of the corporation, for damages arising out of his negligence in the conduct of the bus. In that action the corporation has intervened by motion or summons in a summary way to stay the action, and the question before us is whether such a motion can be entertained. It is based on s. 41 of the Supreme Court of Judicature (Consolidation) Act, 1925, which forbids the old practice of restraint of actions by prohibition or injunction, subject to the proviso (*b*) that any person who would formerly have been entitled to apply to any court to restrain the prosecution of an action may apply to the High Court by motion in a summary way for a stay of proceedings in the action. This section is applied to county courts by virtue of s. 103 of the County Courts Act, 1959.

The question, therefore, is whether before the Supreme Court of Judicature

(9) [1947] 1 All E.R. 258.

Act, 1873 the corporation would have been entitled to apply to restrain the action. This would have been done by a bill in Chancery. The ground stated is that the prosecution of the action would be a fraud on the corporation, and the fraud alleged apparently is that, if the action succeeded and damages were obtained against the conductor, the corporation would in some way be liable to indemnify him. It is here in my judgment that the case breaks down, for I do not see how the corporation could be liable in law for what would be a tort of its servant. The motion is said to be supported by a decision of DU PARCQ., L.J., in *Cosgrove* v. *Horsfall* (10), where the lord justice suggested that the corporation might in somewhat similar circumstances obtain redress under s. 41; but as I read the judgment that is only suggested on the footing that the corporation could be shown to have been in danger of suffering damage by the supposed breach by the plaintiff of the condition attached to her free pass. DU PARCQ, L.J., said this (11):

> " The London Passenger Transport Board may well be entitled to some redress against the plaintiff, though, before expressing a positive opinion on this matter, I should wish to know what claim they make and what answer to it the plaintiff may have. The board are not a party to these proceedings. They may be entitled to recover damages, and if they were shown to have suffered loss through the plaintiff's breach of the condition the circumstances might be such that the damages would be more than nominal. I will express no opinion on the question, which counsel for the defendant told us he had considered, whether the board could have applied successfully to stay the present action under s. 41 of the Supreme Court of Judicature (Consolidation) Act, 1925 (see especially proviso (*b*)). We are not now concerned with the rights of the board, but it must not be assumed that if the plaintiff caused them to suffer loss by a breach of the condition, they were without remedy and are now necessarily without redress. I doubt, however, whether the board are in any way affected by what the plaintiff has chosen to do."

There is no suggestion in the instant case that there is any contract between the corporation and the defendant making the corporation liable for the torts of the latter, and in its absence I cannot see that the corporation is liable at law and, if not, I think that the corporation has no interest which would entitle it to relief under the section. This seems to me to be in accordance with the opinion expressed in the passage which I have read.

In these circumstances I am of opinion that the judge below was right in refusing the corporation's application. I do not think that the question of the applicability of s. 151 of the Road Traffic Act, 1960 arises. I therefore propose to express no opinion on the difficult question whether the free pass constituted a contract between the plaintiff and the corporation, or whether it was merely a licence subject to a condition having no contractual effect.

SALMON, L.J.: I agree with both the judgments which have been delivered.

For my part I have little doubt but that there was a contract between the plaintiff and the Liverpool Corporation. The plaintiff signed an application for a pass on one of the corporation's printed forms, the very language of which is calculated to impress on an applicant that she is entering into a legally binding agreement with the corporation:

> " In consideration of my being granted a free pass for use on the buses of Liverpool Corporation, I undertake and agree that the use of such pass by me shall be subject to the conditions overleaf."

I need not repeat the conditions which have been read by WILLMER, L.J. (12); they undoubtedly negative the liability of the corporation and its servants in

---

(10) (1945), 175 L.T. 334.   (11) (1945), 175 L.T. at p. 335.
(12) See p. 362, letters C to E, ante.

respect of any injury which the passenger may sustain whilst being carried in or boarding or alighting from the corporation's buses. They clearly apply to any negligence on the part of the corporation or its servants, for there is nothing else to which they could apply. The issue of the pass depended on the applicant signing the form to which I have referred. In my judgment there was a contract between the applicant and the corporation that, in consideration of the applicant agreeing to be bound by the stated conditions, the corporation agreed to carry her free on their buses until such time as it cancelled the pass. Section 151 of the Road Traffic Act, 1960 enacts that any such conditions purporting to negative or restrict liability shall be void. The corporation relies on *Wilkie* v. *London Passenger Transport Board* (13). That no doubt is a binding authority on this court; but the facts, though apparently similar, were in reality different. Whether or not there is a contractual animus must depend largely on the true construction of the documents from which that animus is to be inferred. In *Wilkie's* case (13) the carriers did not, as here, require the passenger to sign a form which clearly indicated that the passenger was entering into an agreement by which he would be legally bound. This court found that on the facts and documents of that case there was no contractual animus. In the present case there was in my view such an animus, and accordingly s. 151 is fatal to the corporation's appeal.

Even had there been no contract in the present case, I would have come to the clear conclusion that the corporation must fail. For the corporation to obtain the relief which it claims, it would be necessary for it to show (as HARMAN, L.J., points out) that, before the Supreme Court of Judicature Act, 1873, it would have been entitled to apply to the court in Chancery to restrain the plaintiff from bringing her action against the defendant. In order to succeed, the corporation would have had to establish that the action was a fraud on the corporation either (i) because the plaintiff had agreed with the corporation for good consideration not to bring such an action, or (ii) because of some other good reason. As to (i) this presupposes a contractual promise by the plaintiff not to sue the corporation's servant. I do not think that any such promise can be implied. Even if it could, it would mean that there was a contract between the plaintiff and the defendant which, in so far as it purported to negative or restrict the plaintiff's right to sue, would be void under s. 151 of the Road Traffic Act, 1960. As to (ii), the only other reason for holding that the plaintiff's action could be a fraud on the corporation would be that the corporation would in law be obliged to indemnify its servant, the defendant, against his liability to the plaintiff in negligence. Clearly there is no such legal obligation on the corporation. I appreciate that the corporation would not wish to leave the defendant personally to bear the burden of this action, and moreover that it might face trouble with his trade union if it did so; but this is not, in my view, sufficient to stigmatise the plaintiff's action against the defendant as a fraud on the corporation.

For these reasons I agree that the appeal must be dismissed.

Appeal dismissed. Leave to appeal to the House of Lords refused.

Solicitors: *Cree, Godfrey & Wood*, agents for *Town Clerk*, Liverpool (for the Liverpool Corporation); *E. Rex Makin & Co.*, Liverpool (for the plaintiff).

[*Reported by* HENRY SUMMERFIELD, ESQ., *Barrister-at-Law.*]

---

(13) [1947] 1 All E.R. 258.

MURRAY (Inspector of Taxes) v. IMPERIAL CHEMICAL INDUSTRIES, LTD.

Affirmed. C.A. [1967] 2 All E.R. 980.

[CHANCERY DIVISION (Cross, J.), July 19, 20, 21, November 1, 1966.]

Income Tax—Profits—Computation of profits—Capital receipts—Licences for manufacture of Terylene in foreign countries—Royalty payments therefor—Covenants of licensor not to manufacture or licence manufacture there—Lump sum payments for covenants—Whether capital or income—Income Tax Act, 1952 (15 & 16 Geo. 6 & 1 Eliz. 2 c. 10), Sch. D, Case I.

The taxpayer company as exclusive licensee (outside the United States) of patents for the manufacture of Terylene granted sub-licences thereof and also licences of its own related patents for the lives of the patents to five European companies for the manufacture of equivalents of Terylene in their countries in return for the payment of agreed royalties. It undertook to supply necessary technical information as to manufacture to the companies concerned and not to supply such information to any other concern in the particular country, and to require licensees in other countries to keep the information imparted to them secret and confidential and generally not to use it in manufacturing operations in the countries where the taxpayer company granted other sub-licences and licences. It covenanted also not to manufacture or sell, nor to aid any third party to manufacture or sell, Terylene and products of a similar character, even though not made under the patents, in the particular country; that covenant* being expressly in return for a capital sum of £400,000 payable in six equal annual instalments of £66,666 13s. 4d., and not for " know how ". It also entered into similar agreements with two Japanese companies, but the " capital payment " (of £1,035,000 payable in five equal six-monthly instalments of £207,000, half by each company) was not expressly related to the covenant not to manufacture in Japan, and it was found by the Special Commissioners of Income Tax that one half of the capital sum was attributable to that covenant and one half to other terms of the licence agreement. The commissioners found that the capital sum under the European agreements, and half of that for which the Japanese agreements provided, were capital receipts in the hands of the taxpayer company and were not liable to income tax†.

Held: as the taxpayer company's rights under the patents were part of its fixed and not of its circulating capital, sums for their sale could not have been treated as trading receipts. Accordingly, since the agreements contained in substance the dispositions of the whole interest of the taxpayer company in the patents in the various countries supported by the " keep-out " covenants, the transactions were not analogous to the imparting of " know-how " for reward, and as the parties had arranged that some part of the consideration should be capital attributed to the " keep-out " covenants (which were part of the disposition of capital assets of the taxpayer company), that part of the consideration (viz., the " capital payment " of the European companies and one half the " capital payment " of the two Japanese companies) was capital also for income tax purposes (see p. 377, letters B and C, and p. 379, letter A, post).

Inland Revenue Comrs. v. *British Salmson Aero Engines, Ltd.* ([1938] 3 All E.R. 283), and *Margerison (Inspector of Taxes)* v. *Tyresoles, Ltd.* ((1942), 25 Tax Cas. 59) applied.

Per CURIAM: no view is expressed whether a lump sum payment in consideration of a " keep-out " covenant standing alone ought to be regarded as a capital payment (see p. 378, letter H, post).

---

* The terms of the covenant (art. X) are set out at p. 373, letter I, to p. 374, letter C, post; covenants are referred to as the " keep-out " covenants (see p. 374, letter D, post).

† See p. 376, letter D, post.

Appeal dismissed.

[As to capital profits not constituting profits for income tax purposes, see 20 HALSBURY'S LAWS (3rd Edn.) 149, 150, para. 263; and for cases on the subject, see 28 DIGEST (Repl.) 25-27, *105-115*, and cf. (on trading expenses) ibid., 115-124, *431-480*.

For the Income Tax Act, 1952, Sch. D, Case 1, see 31 HALSBURY'S STATUTES (2nd Edn.) 116, *122-126*.]

Cases referred to:

Higgs (Inspector of Taxes) v. *Olivier*, [1952] Ch. 311; 33 Tax Cas. 136; 28 Digest (Repl.) 156, *610*.

Inland Revenue Comrs. v. *British Salmson Aero Engines, Ltd., British Salmson Aero Engines, Ltd.* v. *Inland Revenue Comrs.*, [1937] 3 All E.R. 464; *affd.* C.A., [1938] 3 All E.R. 283; [1938] 2 K.B. 482; 107 L.J.K.B. 648; 159 L.T. 147; 22 Tax Cas. 29; 28 Digest (Repl.) 120, *461*.

Margerison (Inspector of Taxes) v. *Tyresoles, Ltd.*, (1942), 25 Tax Cas. 59; 28 Digest (Repl.) 121, *465*.

Moriarty (Inspector of Taxes) v. *Evans Medical Supplies, Ltd. Evans Medical Supplies, Ltd.* v. *Moriarty (Inspector of Taxes)*, [1957] 3 All E.R. 718; [1958] 1 W.L.R. 66; 37 Tax Cas. 540; 28 Digest (Repl.) 26, *112*.

Rolls-Royce, Ltd. v. *Jeffrey (Inspector of Taxes). Same* v. *Inland Revenue Comrs.*, [1962] 1 All E.R. 801; [1962] 1 W.L.R. 425; 40 Tax Cas. 443; Digest (Cont. Vol. A) 845, *112a*.

Ryall v. *Hoare, Ryall* v. *Honeywill*, [1923] All E.R. Rep. 528; [1923] 2 K.B. 447; 92 L.J.K.B. 1010; 129 L.T. 505; 8 Tax Cas. 521; 28 Digest (Repl.) 216, *917*.

Case Stated.

The taxpayer company appealed to the Special Commissioners of Income Tax against the following assessments to income tax under Case I of Sch. D to the Income Tax Act, 1952, in respect of its trade in fibres: 1958-59 fibres division business (man-made fibres manufacture) £2,186,000 less £1,815,000 capital allowances; and 1960-61, fibres division £4,712,000 less £2,118,000 capital allowances. It also applied under s. 341 of the Income Tax Act, 1952, for an adjustment of its liability for 1955-56 by reference to a loss claimed to have been sustained in that year. The question for decision was whether certain sums received under provisions contained in agreements or heads of agreement entered into by the taxpayer company with nine overseas concerns were sums falling to be treated as trading receipts in computing the amount of the assessments or of the loss. The commissioners held* that none of the disputed payments except one-half of those under the agreement with two Japanese concerns and those under the agreement with two Polish concerns were receipts falling to be included in the Case I computation of the taxpayer company's profits. The Crown appealed by way of Case Stated to the High Court.

The cases noted below† were cited during the argument in additkon to those referred to in the judgment.

Arthur Bagnall, Q.C., and *J. R. Phillips* for the Crown.

Heyworth Talbot, Q.C., and *N. P. M. Elles* for the taxpayer company.

Cur. adv. vult.

Nov. 1. **CROSS, J.**, read the following judgment: The question raised by this appeal is whether certain sums received by the taxpayer company,

---

* The findings of the Commissioners are set out at p. 375, letter H, to p. 376, letter G, post.

† *British Dyestuffs Corpn. (Blackley), Ltd.* v. *Inland Revenue Comrs.*, (1923), 12 Tax Cas. 586; *Vancouver Malt and Sake Brewing Co., Ltd.* v. *Vancouver Breweries, Ltd.*, [1934] All E.R. Rep. 38; [1934] A.C. 181; *Beak (Inspector of Taxes)* v. *Robson*, [1943] 1 All E.R. 46; [1943] A.C. 352; *Thompson (Inspector of Taxes)* v. *Magnesium Elektron, Ltd.*, [1944] 1 All E.R. 126; *Regent Oil Co., Ltd.* v. *Strick (Inspector of Taxes)*, [1965] 3 All E.R. 174; [1966] A.C. 295.

A   Imperial Chemical Industries, Ltd., from five European and two Japanese companies under the provisions of agreements enabling them to manufacture and sell in various foreign countries products equivalent to the products manufactured and sold by the taxpayer company here under the name " Terylene " ought to be included as trading receipts of the taxpayer company for the purpose of the Income Tax Acts.

B   The Case sets out the facts in detail and exhibits a large number of documents. In this judgment I shall refer only to so many of the facts found and to so much of the documents as seems to me to be essential in order to make my decision intelligible.   In 1941, Mr. Whinfield and Dr. Dickson, two research chemists employed by an association, the Calico Printers' Association, Ltd., invented a method of producing Terylene polymers and of so manufacturing them that

C   they could be drawn cold to yield fibres of great strength and pliability, a high melting point and a low degree of solubility in powerful solvents.   The association took out a number of patents in respect of this invention, both in the United Kingdom and in many overseas countries, but it was too small a company to undertake the development of the invention on a commercial scale.   Towards the end of the war, it was suggested that the taxpayer company might be

D   prepared to develop it and after prolonged negotiations an agreement was entered into between the two companies on Nov. 17, 1947, under which the association, in return for royalties, granted the taxpayer company for twenty years or the duration of the patents, whichever should be longer, an exclusive licence to exploit the rights of the association under its patents throughout the world, except in the United States of America, where the association had already

E   arranged for the development of the invention by others.   Clause 6 of the agreement expressly empowered the taxpayer company at its discretion to grant licence rights in respect of the patents to third parties.

In the course of the next few years, the taxpayer company expended much money and effort in the development of the invention.   As a result of its own research, it took out a number of patents ancillary to the association's master

F   patent; it established a pioneer plant at Huddersfield for the production of Terylene polymer, where output had reached some six hundred tons a year by 1952; and it also established a pioneer spinning plant at Hillhouse in Lancashire to manufacture yarn and fibre made from Terylene polymer so as to supply Terylene to the textile trade and get guidance as to the forms in which it would be suitable for use by the trade.   By the end of 1950, it was clear, not only to

G   the taxpayer company and the association, but to the textile trade both here and abroad, that Terylene had enormous commercial possibilities.   In November, 1950, the taxpayer company authorised the expenditure of £8½ million on the construction of a full-scale Terylene plant at Wilton, and, before it was completed, it was decided in April, 1953, to double its capacity so as to enable it to produce ten thousand tons a year; but even this was not more than enough to meet the

H   domestic demand and the taxpayer company was faced with the problem how best to meet the demand for Terylene outside the country.   The alternatives open appeared to be either to set up plants in foreign countries and manufacture Terylene locally itself, or to grant licences to selected foreign companies enabling them to manufacture equivalents of Terylene under the association's and taxpayer company's patents.   Even if the taxpayer company had been itself

I   prepared to face the huge capital expenditure involved in setting up sufficient Terylene plants abroad to meet the foreign demand, it was very doubtful whether at that time—1952 or 1953—Treasury approval would have been forthcoming. Accordingly, after prolonged consideration, the taxpayer company decided to grant licences to manufacture equivalents of Terylene to five European companies who were thought by reason of their competence, financial stability and enthusiasm for the project to be best fitted to make good use of the licences. These companies were Rhodiaceta in France, Montecatini in Italy, Hoechst and

Glanzstoff in Germany and A.K.U. in Holland. Heads of agreement were entered
into between the taxpayer company and these five companies in 1953 and 1954
and formal agreements implementing the heads were executed at various dates
in 1956. There are a number of minor differences between these agreements
which are referred to in detail in the Case, but neither side sought to draw any
distinction between them on the basis of these differences and I propose to neglect
them and to set out the relevant parts of one agreement as representative of all.
For this purpose, I will take that between the taxpayer company and A.K.U.,
executed on Apr. 14, 1956. That is document C.2, the relevant parts of which
I will now read.

" Article I (A). The ' agreement products ' referred to in this agreement
are: (i) flat singles continuous filament yarns, thrown singles continuous
filament yarns, tows, staple fibres and tops made of highly polymeric polymethylene terephthalates and filaments or fibres of which have when in the
drawn condition a greatest cross-sectional diameter not exceeding 2.0 mm.;
(ii) monofils made of highly polymeric polymethylene terephthalates which
have when in the drawn condition a greatest cross-sectional diameter not
exceeding 2.0 mm.; and (iii) highly polymeric polymethylene terephthalates
in basic forms, that is, in the earliest commercially saleable forms which
will normally be discrete particles such as powders or granules. [Those are
the agreement products.]

" (B) The ' manufacturing licence field ' is the processes and apparatus for
the manufacture of: (i) terephthalic acid and polymethylene terephthalate-
forming derivatives of terephthalic acid from para-xylene including all
products which are intermediate between para-xylene and polymethylene
terephthalate-forming derivatives of terephthalic acid; and (ii) the agreement
products.

" (C) The ' user licence field ' is the processes and apparatus (exclusive of
those in the manufacturing licence field) for using or treating agreement
products including the manufacture of textile articles from agreement
products . . .

" (E) ' C.P.A.' means the Calico Printers' Association, Ltd., of Manchester,
England.

" (F) The ' C.P.A. patent rights ' are the patents in The Netherlands,
Belgium, Austria, Brazil, Czechoslovakia, Hungary, Poland and Spain
owned by [the association], which are set out in Sch. 1 hereto all of which
are licensed exclusively to [the taxpayer company].

" (G) The ' I.C.I. patent rights ' are the patents in The Netherlands, Belgium,
Austria, Brazil, Czechoslovakia, Hungary, Mexico, Poland and Spain owned
by [the taxpayer company] which: (i) are set out in Sch. 2 hereto; and (ii)
have resulted or will result from any patent application in the said countries
set out in Sch. 2 hereto; and (iii) result from any patent application in the
said countries based on any British patent application having a first filing
date earlier than Jan. 1, 1954, of which the subject-matter is wholly or partly
within the manufacturing or user licence fields.

" Article II. *Grant of patent licences in the manufacturing and user licence
fields.* (1) In return for the respective royalties set out in art. III below
[the taxpayer company] hereby grants to the licensee: (A) sub-licences
under the C.P.A. patent rights; and (B) licences under the I.C.I. patent
rights. Such sub-licences and licences shall be for the respective lives of the
patents to which they relate and shall confer on the licensee the following
rights: (i) in The Netherlands and Belgium, exclusive rights for the manufacture, use, treatment, import and sale of the products of the manufacturing
and user licence fields subject however to the provisions of cll. 2 and 3 of
this article; and (ii) in Austria, Brazil, Czechoslovakia, Hungary, Mexico,
Poland and Spain, non-exclusive rights ",

and then are set out certain non-exclusive rights, to which I do not think that
I need refer in full, and I do not think that I need refer to para. (2) of the article.
Then follows art. III—

" *Royalties for sub-licences and licences granted under the C.P.A. and I.C.I.
patent rights.* (1) The consideration for the sub-licences granted under the
C.P.A. patent rights will be a royalty payable as long as The Netherlands
patent No. 60,828 is in force by the licensee to [the taxpayer company] in
sterling in London on the net invoice value of all agreement products sold or
utilised by the licensee or any authorised sub-licensee or imported under any
sub-licence granted by the licensee to any third party at the following rates—
(i) on the first 10,000,000 lb. of agreement products sold, utilised or imported
in any agreement year $5\frac{1}{4}$ per cent.; (ii) on all agreement products sold,
utilised or imported in such year in excess of 10,000,000 lb. three per cent."
I do not think that I need refer to the remainder of art. III, and then, after
arts. IV, V, VI, VII and VIII, to which I need not refer, comes art. IX—

" *Technical assistance.* (1) For the purpose of enabling the licensee to
design, erect, and operate a plant in The Netherlands, and/or Belgium for
the manufacture of agreement products [the taxpayer company] will
impart to the licensee before or as soon as practicable after Jan. 1, 1954, all
necessary technical information relating to the manufacturing licence field
which it is free to disclose. For the purpose of assisting the licensee in selling,
treating and using the agreement products, [the taxpayer company] will
impart to the licensee before or as soon as practicable after Jan. 1, 1954, all
necessary technical information relating to the user licence field which it is
free to disclose. The information to be imparted to the licensee will be all
such information which shall have come into [the taxpayer company's]
possession before Jan. 1, 1954, and it shall be imparted by [the taxpayer
company] supplying to the licensee copies of relevant existing drawings,
technical reports and data of [the taxpayer company] and by allowing
responsible members of the licensee's technical staff access to appropriate
pilot and commercial plants and laboratories of [the taxpayer company] and
giving them all facilities and advice so as to enable the licensee to put on the
market the best possible saleable products. [The taxpayer company] shall
not, however, be under any obligation itself to design the licensee's plant or
to make new drawings for the licensee.

" (2) [The taxpayer company] agrees that it will not from the date of this
agreement to Dec. 31, 1966, give such information in the manufacturing
licence field as is furnished to the licensee under this agreement to any
other person, firm or company in The Netherlands or in Belgium to enable
any such person, firm or company to manufacture agreement products in The
Netherlands or Belgium other than for use in the manufacture of films and
further [the taxpayer company] agrees that [the taxpayer company] will as
a condition of giving technical information in the manufacturing licence
field in any agreement entered into with any third party in any other country
during the said period require the licensee under any such agreement to keep
such information secret and confidential (to the extent to which the licensee
is required to keep the same secret and confidential hereunder) and not to
use it in manufacturing operations in The Netherlands or Belgium except for
the manufacture of products to be used in the manufacture of films and
except in the case of Société Rhodiaceta S.A. in Belgium for the conversion
of flat singles continuous filament yarns into thrown singles continuous
filament yarns and the conversion of tows into staple fibres or tops and the
conversion of staple fibres into tops."
Then there comes art. X—

" *Sale of manufacturing and selling rights.* (1) For the consideration
mentioned below [the taxpayer company] hereby covenants for itself and

[the association] that during the period from Feb. 2, 1954, until Dec. 31, 1966, neither [the taxpayer company nor the association] will themselves or either of them manufacture or sell nor aid any third party to manufacture or sell agreement products in The Netherlands, Belgium or Luxembourg except for use in the manufacture of films. [The taxpayer company] hereby further covenants with the licensee that it is fully authorised and entitled on behalf of [the association] to enter into the foregoing covenant on behalf of [the association].

" (2) In consideration for the above covenants by [the taxpayer company] the licensee will pay to [the taxpayer company] in sterling in London a net capital sum of £400,000. The said capital sum of £400,000 shall be payable in six equal instalments each of £66,666 13s. 4d. the first such instalment being due and payable on Feb. 2, 1954, and the remaining five instalments being due and payable on Jan. 1 in each of the five subsequent years Provided that the said capital sum of £400,000 or any outstanding part thereof shall be payable over a shorter period or in one payment at the option of the licensee which option may be exercised at any time on six months' notice to [the taxpayer company] in writing. If the licensee shall elect to exercise such option a discount will be allowed to the licensee at a rate to be agreed between the parties."

I do not think that there is anything else in that agreement.

There are two points about the agreements which merit special attention. In the first place, the covenants in art. X, which I will call the " keep-out " covenants by the taxpayer company, are not confined to manufacturing or selling under the patents, but extend to manufacturing or selling products of a Terylene character whether made under the patents or not. It was plainly essential for the licensees to have the protection of such a covenant. In the first place, some method of making Terylene without infringing the patents might have been discovered, and, secondly, the patents themselves might be held to be invalid. The second feature of the agreement is that the whole of the lump sum consideration is attributed to the covenant in art. X and no part of it to the obligation of the taxpayer company to impart " know-how " contained in art. IX. On this point, the Case (para. 32) says:

" This was not because it was agreed that such information was not of importance. [The taxpayer company], if not the European companies, considered that it was important and of substantial value but was willing to undertake in the agreements to supply the information without any express consideration therefor, bearing in mind, inter alia, that this would assist the European licensee companies and so lead to royalties becoming payable sooner than might otherwise be the case."

The taxpayer company's sales of Terylene to Japan, which were only 18,000 lb. in 1955, had risen to 135,000 lb. by 1957 and the taxpayer company came to the conclusion that the only practicable way of exploiting the Japanese market was to enter into licence agreements with Japanese companies. Accordingly, on Feb. 7, 1957, the taxpayer company entered into an agreement with two Japanese companies, Teikoku and Toyo, which is exhibited to the Case. In this case, no heads of agreement were entered into beforehand. By this agreement, the taxpayer company granted the two Japanese companies exclusive sub-licences of the association master patents and exclusive licences of the taxpayer company patents in consideration of annual royalties. It undertook that it would impart to these companies certain technical information and would not, during the period from the date of the agreement until Dec. 31, 1970, either manufacture in Japan or, subject to certain qualifications, sell in that country any agreement products. The date of the expiry of the relevant Japanese patents is Sept. 15, 1968. In the Japanese agreement, the undertaking regarding technical information and that regarding abstention from manufacture and sale appear in one

article (art. IX, the heading of which is in fact " Technical assistance ").
Article X (which is headed " Capital payment ") runs as follows:

> " The licensees will pay to [the taxpayer company] in sterling in London
> such a capital sum as after the deduction of Japanese tax will amount to
> £1,035,000. The said capital sum shall be payable in five equal instalments
> each of £207,000, the first of such instalments being due and payable within
> thirty days after the effective date of this agreement and the remaining four
> instalments being due and payable at intervals of six months thereafter. As
> regards each of the said instalments, one-half (£103,500) shall be payable
> by Teikoku and one-half (£103,500) shall be payable by Toyo."

The agreement does not contain any provision stating expressly in respect of
what consideration this capital sum is to be paid. In this connexion, the Case
says (see para. 32):

> " As regards the agreement entered into by [the taxpayer company] with
> the two Japanese companies, the technical information which [the taxpayer
> company] supplied thereunder helped them to make a quick start and was
> undoubtedly of considerable value to them. While it was the intention of
> [the taxpayer company] that the Japanese art. X payments should be
> related to the covenants contained in art. IX (9) of that agreement, it was
> not the case that there was any understanding between the parties to this
> effect. Nor did we have before us any evidence which we could regard as
> establishing that there was any understanding between the parties of any
> kind as to the allocation of art. X payments as between technical assistance
> and the art. IX (9) covenants, or as establishing the actual values of the
> consideration moving from [the taxpayer company] under those two heads
> respectively. The values which [the taxpayer company] would attribute to
> the two heads would almost certainly differ from the values which the
> Japanese companies would attribute to them, and it may well be that it
> would not be possible to find any basis for determining satisfactorily separate
> values under these heads."

The taxpayer company at all times accepted that the royalty payments under the
various agreements should be included in its accounts as trading receipts. It
contended, however, before the commissioners that the sums expressed to be
payable under the agreements with the European companies in consideration of
the sale of manufacturing and selling rights (i.e., the " keep-out " covenants) and
the sums payable under art. X of the agreement with the Japanese companies
should not be treated as trading receipts but as receipts on capital account. The
commissioners took time to consider their decision and gave it in reply on Jan. 10,
1964. After summarising the relevant facts, the decision continued, so far as is
relevant to me, as follows:

> " (3) On these facts we do not think that the sums payable to [the taxpayer
> company] in consideration of these ' keep-out ' covenants are, in whole or
> in part, sums payable, over and above amounts payable as royalties, for the
> sub-licences and licences granted by [the taxpayer company] in respect of
> the C.P.A. and I.C.I. patents: nor in our view are they payments for
> technical assistance or ' know-how '. We consider that they must, on the
> authority of the case of *Moriarty (Inspector of Taxes)* v. *Evans Medical
> Supplies, Ltd.* (1), be taken to have been paid for the consideration set out in
> the relevant clauses and for nothing else.

> " (4) In the agreement with Teikoku and Toyo there is a ' keep-out '
> covenant, contained in the ninth and last paragraph of art. IX (which is
> headed ' Technical assistance ', a matter with which the first eight para-
> graphs deal). The sums in dispute in this case are payable under a separate
> article, art. X, headed ' Capital payment ', in which it is not stated for what
> consideration these sums were paid. In these circumstances we think we must

---

(1) [1957] 3 All E.R. 718; 37 Tax Cas. 540.

try to discover what the consideration was by looking at the agreement as a whole. Royalty payments are specifically provided for elsewhere. We are satisfied on the evidence that consideration of substantial value moved from [the taxpayer company] both in respect of (i) the matters referred to in the first eight paragraphs of art. IX and (ii) the ' keep-out ' covenant in para. 9 of that article. No evidence was led before us directed to showing that there was any separate agreement, or any sort of understanding between the parties, as to any apportionment of the sums between (i) and (ii); nor had we any evidence before us as to the actual values of the consideration moving from [the taxpayer company] under these two headings respectively. There is nothing in the agreement itself to suggest that the value to Teikoku and Toyo of (i) was less than (ii) or vice versa. In these circumstances we find that the payments under art. X should be taken to have been made as to one-half in respect of the undertakings contained in the first eight paragraphs of art. IX and as to the other half in respect of the ' keep-out ' covenant in para. 9 of that article. [I omit para. (5).]

" (6) If we were to consider the Western European agreements, (and the agreements with Teikoku and Toyo, in relation to the one-half which we have held to be in respect of the undertakings contained in art. IX (9)), each separately, we would hold that the sums in dispute, being payable solely in consideration of the ' keep-out ' covenants, were not receipts falling to be included in a Case I computation of the profits of [the taxpayer company]. Under these covenants [the taxpayer company] was restrained from exercising rights to manufacture and sell: we would hold that the decision in the case of *Margerison (Inspector of Taxes)* v. *Tyresoles, Ltd.* (2), applied to the sums payable under the covenants, and that they were capital receipts in the hands of [the taxpayer company]. In thus approaching the matter we are not unmindful that agreements may need to be considered in the light of surrounding circumstances throwing light on them. We do not, however, think that the principle of the decision in the case of *Rolls-Royce, Ltd.* v. *Jeffrey (Inspector of Taxes)* (3), should be regarded as warranting our arriving at any other conclusion in the present case, even though a number of agreements are involved. The covenants here are ' keep-out ' covenants, and the transactions which were entered into seem to us to be on that account essentially different in their nature from those in question in the *Rolls-Royce* case (3)."

I think, with respect to the commissioners, that what I take to be their meaning in this paragraph would perhaps have been more clearly expressed if, instead of the words " If we were to consider " in line 1 [see letter C, above], it had read " Turning now to consider ", and if the word " would " in line 5 had been omitted. In the result, there the commissioners held that of the payments in dispute under the Western European and Japanese agreements the only payments which fell to be included in the trading receipts were one-half of the payments under art. X of the Japanese agreement.

The taxpayer company accepts the decision with regard to the half of the payments under the Japanese agreement which the commissioners attributed to technical assistance. The Crown agrees that, if the payments under art. X of the Japanese agreement have to be apportioned for tax purposes between the supply of technical assistance and the " keep-out " covenant, this apportionment made by the commissioners is the only possible one. Further, neither side contended that the lump sums payable in consideration of the " keep-out " covenants should be apportioned between capital and income for tax purposes. The dispute before me was therefore whether, as the Crown argued, they should be regarded wholly as trading receipts or, as the taxpayer company argued, they should be regarded wholly as capital receipts.

---

(2) (1942), 25 Tax Cas. 59.   (3) [1962] 1 All E.R. 801; 40 Tax Cas. 443.

The contention of the Crown before me, as before the commissioners, was that the various agreements were simply the mode in which the taxpayer company chose to exploit some of its patent rights in the course of its trade and that the lump sum payments were simply part of the total consideration for all the obligations undertaken by the taxpayer company. Even if there were no authority on the point, I, for my part, would not have accepted this argument. The rights which the taxpayer company possessed in the C.P.A. patents and its own ancillary patents were not part of its circulating capital but were fixed capital assets of its business. If it had sold those rights in different countries outright for capital sums, those sums could not have been treated as trading receipts. But the agreements in question contained in substance the dispositions of the whole interest of the taxpayer company in the patents in the various countries supported by the " keep-out " covenants. A transaction of that sort does not seem to me to be in the least like the imparting of " know-how " for reward, and, if the parties chose to arrange that part of the consideration received by the taxpayer company should take the form of a capital payment, and be attributed to the " keep-out " covenants, I do not see why that part should not be capital for tax purposes.

In fact, however, even if I had held a different opinion, I would, as I see it, have been bound to decide the matter in favour of the taxpayer company in view of the decision of the Court of Appeal in *Inland Revenue Comrs.* v. *British Salmson Aero Engines, Ltd.* (4). The assessments in question in that case were in respect of certain payments made by an English company to a French company under an agreement of Oct. 25, 1929. The English company had been incorporated shortly before, and by the agreement it acquired the exclusive right for ten years to manufacture and sell in the United Kingdom and the Commonwealth certain aeroplane engines made by the French company under certain patents. Article 2 provided that, as consideration for the licence granted to it, the English company would pay to the French company £25,000 payable as to £15,000 on the signing of the agreement, £5,000 six months thereafter and £5,000 twelve months thereafter and, in addition, would pay a royalty of £2,000 a year in each of the ten years for which the licence was to last. Article 3 provided for the French company giving the English company information and help. Article 7 provided that the French company should not, during the life of the agreement, manufacture or sell directly in the territory granted to the English company any engine of the specified type and there was a corresponding obligation imposed on the English company not to go outside its own territory. The Court of Appeal, agreeing with FINLAY, J., (5) and the commissioners, held that the English company was assessable in respect of the royalty payments but not in respect of the lump sum payments under what was then r. 21 of the All Schedules Rules. The Crown first contended that the words " any royalty or other sum paid in respect of the user of a patent " in this rule covered all sums paid in respect of the user of a patent whether or not they were in reality of a capital or income nature. The court rejected that argument. It then had to consider what was the true nature of the payments provided for under the agreement and held that the royalty payments which were recurring and were not instalments in discharge of a fixed capital sum were income payments; but that, on the other hand, the lump sum payments had, for tax purposes, the capital nature which the agreement itself gave them. In this connexion, SIR WILFRID GREENE, M.R. (6), placed reliance on the fact that the rights granted to the English company were not merely rights to use the patents, but were rights also to prevent the French company from exploiting the patents in the territory granted to the English company.

That decision was considered and applied by WROTTESLEY, J., in *Margerison*

---

(4) [1938] 3 All E.R. 283; 22 Tax Cas. 29.
(5) [1937] 3 All E.R. 464; 22 Tax Cas. 29.
(6) [1938] 3 All E.R. at pp. 286, 287; 22 Tax Cas. at p. 39.

(*Inspector of Taxes*) v. *Tyresoles, Ltd.* (7). The agreement in question there was of a very unusual and complicated nature. Tyresoles, Ltd., carried on at its own works a process for renovating old tyres—" Tyre-soles "—of which it owned the patent. It also entered into a number of agreements in the same form with motor traders which created something like a partnership between the parties, for the trader's carrying on of tyresoling in the trader's district. The trader provided suitable premises in which Tyresoles, Ltd., erected and operated plant to carry out the process—the trader paying a monthly rental for the plant. Tyresoles, Ltd., agreed by cl. 2 not to introduce another tyresoling plant nor to canvass for orders within the trader's territory. The trader agreed to supply at least 1,500 tyre casings each year by the plant installed at his premises. All tyres treated in the plant were to be invoiced by Tyresoles, Ltd., to the trader at their current list prices less a discount of forty-nine per cent. In addition to receiving its share of the price of the renovated tyre, Tyresoles, Ltd., under cl. 3 received from each trader on the signing of the agreement a lump sum payment based on the capacity of the plant installed on that trader's premises, which was expressed to be in return for the rights conferred on the trader by cl. 2—i.e., the agreement of Tyresoles, Ltd., to keep out of the trader's territory, save in so far as they operated at the plant on the trader's premises and carried out orders forwarded by the trader. The question at issue was whether those lump sum payments were trading receipts. WROTTESLEY, J., affirmed the decision of the commissioners that those lump sum payments were not trading receipts. He found support for this decision—which I gather that he would have arrived at even without such support—in the *British Salmson* case (8). After referring to passages in the judgment of SIR WILFRID GREENE, M.R., in that case, he continued (9):

" In the result I think the underlying reason for the decision of the Court of Appeal (8) was that the company in that case bought a part of the French company's patent rights, namely, the exclusive right to exploit them in the British Empire for ten years, and paid a lump sum price for it."

Counsel for the Crown submitted that the actual decision in the *Tyresoles* case (7) might possibly be supported on a ground not given by the judge, viz., that the payments in question were in the nature of premiums paid for the right of entering into this quasi-partnership; he said, however, that the reasons given by the judge for this decision—which, he conceded, would, if right, apply to the present case—were wrong and that he had misinterpreted the *British Salmson* decision (8) which simply turned on the construction of r. 21. I do not agree. I accept entirely the analysis given by WROTTESLEY, J., (9) of the *British Salmson* decision (8) and I think that it applies to this case.

There was some argument before me as to the position for tax purposes of a lump sum payment made in consideration of what I may call a " keep-out " covenant " in gross ". I would like to make it clear that I am not expressing any view—one way or the other—on the question whether a " keep-out " covenant standing alone ought to be regarded for tax purposes as the sale of a capital asset.

In *Higgs* (*Inspector of Taxes*) v. *Olivier* (10), which was referred to on this point, the Crown's claim was made under Case II of Sch. D, and failed because the covenant under which the £15,000 was paid was altogether independent of the agreement for services which had in fact been fully performed before the covenant was entered into, and because a sum paid as consideration for not exercising a man's profession cannot seriously be described as part of income coming to him from his profession. The Crown made no alternative claim under Case VI on the basis that the £15,000 was a payment for a service rendered by Sir Laurence Olivier at the request of the film company. Had it done so, then the question might well have arisen whether it was a casual profit of a revenue nature or a payment for parting with a capital asset (see the judgment of ROWLATT, J., in

---

(7) (1942), 25 Tax Cas. 59.
(9) (1942), 25 Tax Cas. at p. 70.
(8) [1938] 3 All E.R. 283; 22 Tax Cas. 29.
(10) [1952] Ch. 311; 33 Tax Cas. 136.

Ryall v. *Hoare, Ryall* v. *Honeywill* (11)). It may be—I say no more—that, had the claim been put in that way, the Crown would have succeeded.

Assuming in favour of the Crown, however, that by entering into a " keep-out " covenant one does not ipso facto part with a capital asset, that fact cannot, as I see it, make the lump sum payments with which I am concerned receipts of a revenue character, for the covenants do not stand alone. They were ancillary to the patent licences and are part and parcel of transactions which, taken as a whole, constituted dispositions by the taxpayer company of part of the fixed capital of their business.

For these reasons, I affirm the decision of the commissioners.

Appeal dismissed.

Solicitors: *Solicitor of Inland Revenue*; *J. S. Copp* (for the taxpayer company).

[*Reported by* F. A. AMIES, ESQ., *Barrister-at-Law.*]

R. *v.* KING.

[COURT OF APPEAL, CRIMINAL DIVISION (Lord Parker, C.J., Salmon, L.J., and Blain, J.), December 8, 9, 1966.]

Criminal Law — Gross indecency — Evidence — Cross-examination — Question whether accused is homosexual not improper—Accomplice—Corroboration— Untruth of accused's evidence not itself corroboration—No direction that one accomplice could not corroborate another—No miscarriage of justice.

Criminal Law—Indecent assault—Evidence—Corroboration—Summing-up.

The appellant was charged with attempting to procure acts of gross indecency, indecent assault on male persons and attempted buggery. The prosecution's evidence was that he met two boys aged thirteen and fourteen near a public lavatory on the front at Southend; that some of these offences with the boys were committed with each in turn in the lavatory; and that he met them by arrangement later that evening, and took them to his flat where the other offences occurred. After his arrest the police questioned him. At his trial the court permitted the prosecution to put to the appellant in cross-examination the question, " Are you a homosexual? ", to which he answered " Yes ". The court also allowed evidence of a question put by the police and of the appellant's answer, viz.—Q.—" Did you go to the toilets for any special purpose? ". A.—" I just went there, well to put it crudely ' didn't go there looking for trade '." The appellant denied at the trial that he was present at all on the occasion first alleged and that he had committed any offence on the second occasion alleged. In the summing-up the jury (a) were told that the appellant's admission of being a homosexual did not necessarily convey that any offence had been committed; and (b) were directed as to the need for corroboration, but were not told that the evidence of one accomplice could not corroborate the evidence of another. The jury were further directed, in reference to the first occasion, that if they thought material evidence of the appellant to be untrue, that would be capable of corroborating the evidence of the prosecution on the same subject.

Held: (i) the question, " Are you a homosexual? ", was admissible; and the jury were rightly directed that the affirmative answer did not show that the appellant had committed any offence (see p. 381, letter I, to p. 382, letters A, C and E, post).

Dictum of LORD SUMNER in *Thompson* v. *Director of Public Prosecutions* ([1918-19] All E.R. Rep. at p. 526) applied.

(ii) considered in the context of other evidence, the question, " Did you go to the toilets for any special purpose? ", was properly admitted in fairness to the appellant to show that on the occasion in question at any rate he

---

(11) [1923] All E.R. Rep. 528; 8 Tax Cas. 521.

did not go there for the alleged purpose (see p. 382, letter I, to p. 383, letter A, post).

(iii) the jury should have been directed that the boys were accomplices and could not corroborate each other (see p. 383, letter G, post).

(iv) in regard to the first occasion (as to which the appellant denied that he had been there), even if the appellant's denial were found by the jury to be untrue, that was not capable of corroborating the evidence of the boys (see p. 384, letter C, post).

(v) since, however, there was ample corroboration from the circumstances as a whole, and there had been no miscarriage* of justice, the conviction should stand (see p. 384, letter I, to p. 385, letter A, post).

Appeal dismissed.

[As to the offence of gross indecency with male persons, see 10 HALSBURY'S LAWS (3rd Edn.) 671, para. 1284, and for cases on the subject, see 15 DIGEST (Repl.) 901, 902, *8691-8701*.

As to indecent assault on male persons and as to the crime of buggery, see 10 HALSBURY'S LAWS (3rd Edn.) 669, para. 1280; and for cases on the subject, see 15 DIGEST (Repl.) 901, *8687-8689*, and 899, *8665-8672*.

As to evidence and corroboration, see 10 HALSBURY'S LAWS (3rd Edn.) 459, para. 844, and p. 462, para. 850; and for cases on the subject, see 14 DIGEST (Repl.) 682, *6966*; 15 DIGEST (Repl.) 899, 900, *8673-8680* (indecent assault), 829-832, *7936-7961* (corroboration generally).]

Cases referred to:

Jones v. *Thomas*, [1933] All E.R. Rep. 535; [1934] 1 K.B. 323; 103 L.J.K.B. 113; 150 L.T. 216; 98 J.P. 41; 30 Cox, C.C. 47; 3 Digest (Repl.) 453, *425*.

Thompson v. *Director of Public Prosecutions*, [1918-19] All E.R. Rep. 521; 87 L.J.K.B. 478; 118 L.T. 418; 82 J.P. 145; 26 Cox, C.C. 189; 13 Cr. App. Rep. 61; sub nom. *Thompson* v. *Regem*, [1918] A.C. 221; 14 Digest (Repl.) 682, *6966*.

Appeal.

This was an appeal by Dennis Arthur King against his conviction and sentence on July 15, 1966, at Southend Quarter Sessions before the deputy recorder and a jury on two counts of attempting to procure acts of gross indecency, three counts of indecent assault on males and one count of attempted buggery. The facts are set out in the judgment of LORD PARKER, C.J.

G. K. Rice for the appellant.
E. M. Hill for the Crown.

LORD PARKER, C.J.: The appellant was convicted at Southend-on-Sea Quarter Sessions in July, 1966, of various offences against two boys of thirteen and fourteen. There were two offences of attempting to procure acts of gross indecency, three of indecent assault and one (and the most serious) of attempted buggery. He was sentenced on the attempted buggery to seven years and sentences of imprisonment on the other counts, which were concurrent with that sentence. He now appeals against his conviction by leave of the court.

The facts giving rise to these charges were as follows: On Thursday, June 16, 1966, these two small boys, Smart aged fourteen and Baker, who was then thirteen though within two days of fourteen, were in Southend. They had apparently played truant from their school and homes in Birmingham, had come first to London and had then gone on to Southend. According to their evidence, they were hanging round a public lavatory on the front and they got into conversation with the appellant, who asked them if they wanted to play about with him and offered them ten shillings each. He then took each one of them in turn into a

---

* The word " substantial " in the proviso to s. 4 (1) of the Criminal Appeal Act, 1907, which formerly predicated " no substantial miscarriage of justice ", was repealed by the Criminal Appeal Act 1966, s. 4 (1).

A cubicle inside the lavatory where certain of these offences were committed. An arrangement was then made for the appellant to meet them at the same place at about 10.30 that evening and go back to his flat. They did meet that evening. The appellant took them back to his flat, one of them slept on the floor and one of them, Smart, in the bed with him; and it was there that the other offences were committed.

B The evidence of the appellant was that he had never been at the public lavatories at 7 o'clock that evening, that he had never met the boys at that time. Their story in regard to what one might call the first incident was wholly false. As regards the subsequent meeting at the lavatories between 10.30 and 11.00 that evening, his case was that he found the boys there, but not as a result of any previous arrangement; that he had gone up and talked to them, that he had asked

C them if they were alone, whether they had anywhere to stay and where they had come from. According to him, he asked them if they would like to come to his flat, and in answer to that the boys, or one of them, said " We will, provided that we don't have to do what we had to do last night ", describing how in London they had stayed with a man called Harry when certain other indecent acts took place. The appellant ended by saying " Well you don't have to come back with me unless

D you want to ". They did go back and, according to him, nothing of an indecent nature took place, and that he had only offered them a place for the night out of charity.

The jury convicted him on these offences while acquitting him on several others; and the reason why leave to appeal was given on the last occasion was in regard to certain evidence which the deputy recorder allowed to be given. Let me say at

E once that this was by no means an easy case to try. It raised a number of difficult questions of law, and the deputy recorder had to give a number of rulings.

The first point—not the first taken by counsel for the appellant, but logically the first—concerns a ruling given by the deputy recorder whereby he permitted the question to be put of the appellant in cross-examination " Are you a homosexual? ". The deputy recorder ruled that that was a question which he would

F allow to be asked, and the answer was " Yes ". Counsel for the appellant before us submits in the first instance that that question ought never to have been allowed, and he refers to the fact that there is no authority which goes so far as to say that such a question in a sexual case of this kind is permissible. He admits that in certain circumstances articles found in an accused's possession may be spoken to in evidence, as was held by the House of Lords in the case of *Thompson*

G v. *Director of Public Prosecutions* (1). The passage often referred to is a passage in the speech of LORD SUMNER. He said this (2):

" No one doubts that it does not tend to prove a man guilty of a particular crime to show that he is the kind of man who would commit a crime, or that he is generally disposed to crime and even to a particular crime but, sometimes for one reason and sometimes for another, evidence is admissible,

H notwithstanding that its general character is to show that the accused had in him the makings of a criminal, for example, in proving guilty knowledge, or intent, or system, or in rebutting an appearance of innocence, which, unexplained, the facts might wear."

Applying that principle in the case of *Thompson* (1), certain indecent photographs found on the prisoner were spoken to in evidence as corroborative of the identity

I of the man who had committed the offences. Counsel for the appellant has sought to argue that to allow this question to be put in the present case is an extension of that principle and ought not to be allowed.

In the judgment of the court it would not be an extension of the principle to allow that question to be put and answered, but that it comes plainly within the principle. It is no different to put to a man the question, " Are you a homosexual? ",

---

(1) [1918-19] All E.R. Rep. 521; [1918] A.C. 221.
(2) [1918-19] All E.R. Rep. at p. 526; [1918] A.C. at p. 232.

than to put to him certain indecent photographs of a homosexual nature **A**
found in his possession and say to him " Are these yours? ". In the judgment of
the court, following the case of *Thompson* (3), that question was prima facie
perfectly legitimate. In passing, it is to be observed that the principle laid down
by LORD SUMNER is not one of completely general application, but must be
limited to certain particular crimes, and the common one to which it has been
applied is sexual cases.   **B**

The second point under this head taken by counsel for the appellant is that that
question was objectionable in that it implied that the appellant had committed
criminal offences in the past. He says to get the answer " Yes " to the question
" Are you a homosexual? " is inviting really the jury to accept that he has been
guilty of homosexual offences.

The court is quite satisfied that the expression " I am a homosexual " does not **C**
necessarily convey that he has committed homosexual offences; but even if any
member of the jury was minded to interpret it that way there was a full direction
by the deputy recorder how they should treat the matter. In the summing-up
he referred to the fact that the jury must keep out of their minds the prejudice
that might arise from this type of case, and referred to the fact that the appellant
had admitted in cross-examination that he was a homosexual. The deputy recorder **D**
went on:

" It does not mean that he has committed this or any other offence at all.
It is a factor you must bear in mind when you come to consider the incident.
Was he going there for an innocent purpose as he has told you, or was he going
there, as the crown say, to pick up boys or men or people like that when he
could, when he knew perfectly well that is the sort of thing the place was used **E**
for and that other friends of his had used it for the same purpose."

The court sees no ground for interfering with the verdict by reason of the
prosecution being allowed to ask that question.

The second matter—and to some extent it arises out of the first, though it is
earlier in point of time—concerns the deputy recorder's ruling on certain evidence
which the police were going to give. The police interviewed this appellant, and, **F**
according to the police, he was asked:

" Q.—Did you go to the toilets for any special purpose? A.—I just went
there, well to put it crudely ' didn't go looking for trade '. Q.—Have you ever
been there looking for trade? A.—Yes, I have done."

The deputy recorder refused to allow the evidence to be given in regard to the **G**
last question and answer, but he did allow evidence to be given that the police
had asked " Did you go to the toilets for any special purpose? ", and the answer
" I just went there, well to put it crudely ' didn't go looking for trade ' ". It is
said that that was highly prejudicial, of little, if any, probative value, and ought
not to have been allowed. In this connexion it must be remembered that earlier
in the evidence given by the police officer, in answer to further questions why the **H**
appellant went to the toilets, he had said, and had been allowed to say without
objection,

" Well a lot of my mates hang around there, and I went across to see if
there was anybody I knew. Q.—Why do these friends hang around there?
A.—Most of the men that hang around there are old men and they hang
around there looking for somebody to take home and play with. Q.—And **I**
these old men are your friends? A.—Some of them aren't so old and these are
my friends."

It follows from what the court has said in regard to the question " Are you a
homosexual? " that those questions and answers were properly admitted and,
indeed, as I have said, no objection was taken to them. Once they had been
said it seems to the court that the answer which was not ruled out, namely, " I just
went there, well to put it crudely ' didn't go looking for trade ' " was something

(3) [1918-19] All E.R. Rep. 521; [1918] A.C. 221.

A which really had to be admitted in fairness to the prisoner to show that whatever he had been to the toilets for on other occasions, on this one he was not going there looking for trade. The court can see no reason to interfere with the deputy recorder's ruling on this point whereby he plainly exercised his discretion and allowed the evidence to be given.

The third matter that arises in this appeal concerns the difficult question of
B corroboration. It is quite clear that one, at any rate, of these boys was an accomplice, certainly in the offence committed with him. The deputy recorder, who gave a wholly impeccable direction to the jury as to the need for corroboration, not only because of these being young children but because of it being a sexual offence and because, at any rate, one of them was an accomplice, said this:

C " One at least of them might be regarded as an accomplice in regard to the offences in the lavatory because he told you he knew what was going to go on, or had a good idea of it, and went in there for money, that is to say in the position of a person participating knowingly and willingly in the act."

It has, however, been frankly admitted by counsel for the Crown before us that, at any rate, in the case of the lavatory incident both of these boys were clearly
D accomplices in regard to the respective offences in which they were involved; and, in those circumstances, it is to be observed that there is no warning or direction by the deputy recorder that one accomplice cannot corroborate another accomplice. The importance of that is that in directing them as to what was capable of amounting to corroboration, the deputy recorder said: " First of all you have the question of one boy corroborating the other ". In fact, if they were
E both accomplices the one could not corroborate the other. Counsel for the Crown, in answer to that submission, points out what may be true, that these two boys are not accomplices in the strict sense in law, in regard to an offence other than the one in which he was involved, and, accordingly, he would say the strict necessity for a direction that one accomplice cannot corroborate another was not needed in this case.

F This court has very grave doubt whether that is really the true position here. It seems much more likely that in regard to both the incidents, the one at the lavatory and the one at the flat, these boys were acting together as a joint enterprise and that, for instance, in regard to the lavatory incident when one went into the cubicle the other was keeping watch in case anybody came along. Be that as it may, however, it is quite clear to this court on the facts of this case that
G whatever the strict legal position the deputy recorder should have told the jury that they ought to treat these boys as accomplices and say that the one, therefore, could not corroborate the other.

Lastly, counsel for the appellant refers to another matter which the deputy recorder told the jury was capable of amounting to corroboration. The deputy recorder, in referring to the incident at the lavatories, the first incident, said
H this:

" . . . secondly there is the question of the lies to the police if you find they are lies. In other words [the appellant's] denial is, in certain circumstances which I have just narrated to you, capable of being corroboration provided you think he made that denial quite deliberately and in order to conceal what he had done and not out of fear or worry or anxiety. You see the
I situation is this, apart from A and B being present saying the offences were committed, A says that [the appellant] was there, B says that [the appellant] was there, and [the appellant] has told the police that he was not there. So if you think his denial of his presence there affords to that particular as expressed in the passage from the case I have just read to you a guilty intent that would not have been present had that lie not been told then that is is something which you are entitled to take into account."

The importance of that is that this was a matter which apparently was concerning

the jury when they retired, because they came back and asked a question, or two
questions, but the relevant one was this:

"If we consider some of the evidence to be untrue, does this corroborate
the evidence on the same subject matter on the other side?"

In answering that question the deputy recorder said:

"If you consider material parts such as I have already indicated to you in
my summing-up of the defence evidence to be untrue that is capable of
corroborating the evidence on the same subject matter on the prosecution's
case."

The court is quite satisfied that that direction was wrong, certainly as applied
to the facts of this case. The two boys were saying in regard to the first incident
that the appellant was there. The appellant was saying that he was not there at
all. His denial that he was not there, if false, if the jury thought they were unable
to accept it, does not prove that he was there, and accordingly, there was no
positive evidence that he was there which could corroborate the boys. Indeed,
if the jury, by finding that the evidence of the appellant was false in this respect,
were entitled to accept the version of the boys there would be no need for the
doctrine of corroboration at all. Accordingly, the court is satisfied that on these
two matters in regard to corroboration there was a misdirection. However, it is
to be observed that in regard to the first point under this head, although the
deputy recorder did not say that one accomplice could not corroborate the other,
he did put the matter to the jury in this way, after saying that one boy could
corroborate the other he went on:

"You will remember I have told you you must approach that with the
warning I have already given you. You must look at it with the greatest
possible care because each are victims of different counts and are the complainants in different counts, and you must only treat it as corroboration if
you are satisfied they are not collaborating to tell a false story."

The mischief aimed at, certainly in regard to a case such as this, of laying down the
principle that one accomplice cannot corroborate another is clearly because of
the danger that they have collaborated; and in the opinion of this court, though
this matter was not properly dealt with by the deputy recorder, in the result no
miscarriage could arise from that failure to direct them.

The second point, in regard to lies, is in the opinion of this court a more serious
matter; but at the same time, if one looks at this case as a whole, there was ample
corroboration to be derived from the full circumstances of the case. As was said
in *Jones* v. *Thomas* (4), by LAWRENCE, J.:

"'Mere opportunity alone does not amount to corroboration, but two
things may be said about it. One is, that the opportunity may be of such a
character as to bring in the element of suspicion. That is, that the circumstances and locality of the opportunity may be such as in themselves to
amount to corroboration'."

If one thinks of the full circumstances of this case, here is an appellant with
admittedly homosexual tendencies, who habitually goes to these lavatories knowing full well the sort of people who go there and goes there to meet them, who on
his own story when he does meet these boys makes the inquiries of them to which
I have referred, is told by them of their experiences of the previous evening with
Harry, and ends by saying "Well you don't have to come if you don't want to",
and then takes them to his flat where admittedly one of them sleeps in his bed.
If one takes that story, the story of admitted facts, it is really impossible to say
that there was not corroboration or that any jury properly directed would not

(4) [1933] All E.R. Rep. 535 at p. 538; [1934] 1 K.B. 323 at p. 330. LAWRENCE, J.,
was quoting from the judgment of LORD DUNEDIN in *Dawson* v. *McKenzie*, (1908),
45 Sc.L.R. 473 at p. 474.

have convicted this appellant. In these circumstances the appeal against conviction is dismissed. As regards the appeal against sentence, the court is quite satisfied that these little boys knew full well what they were doing. They were not
being corrupted for the first time by any means; but at the same time the
appellant aged thirty-one has already been sent to prison for six months for
attempting to procure gross indecency with a youth of fifteen, and two offences
were then taken into consideration, one of which was with a boy of nine. He has
been fined for importuning for immoral purposes; and, finally, in September,
1964, he was sentenced to twelve months' imprisonment for attempting to
procure gross indecency.

The court is quite satisfied that there is no ground on which to interfere with
this sentence, and that appeal is likewise dismissed.

Appeal dismissed. Leave to appeal to the House of Lords refused.

Solicitors: *N. R. Prevost,* Southend-on-Sea (for the appellant); *M. J. Simpson,*
Southend-on-Sea (for the Crown).

[*Reported by* S. A. HATTEEA, ESQ., *Barrister-at-Law.*]

TINGAY v. HARRIS AND ANOTHER.

[COURT OF APPEAL, CIVIL DIVISION (Davies, Russell and Salmon, L.JJ.),
November 29, 30, 1966.]

*County Court—Costs—Payment into court—Claim alleging only one cause of
action—Payment in of £75—Subsequent amendment to add additional causes
of action—Recovery by plaintiff at trial of £75 in respect of original cause
of action, plus £2 in respect of cause added after payment in of £75—Whether
plaintiff or defendant entitled to costs since payment in—C.C.R., 1936,
Ord. 11, r. 1, r. 2, r. 3, Ord. 15, r. 1 (1).*

After the defendant in a county court action by an architect for £166
remuneration for work done had paid £75 into court in satisfaction of the
claim, the plaintiff amended his particulars of claim to add claims for £400
for conversion and £25 for infringement of copyright. At the trial the
plaintiff recovered £75 on his claim for remuneration, plus £2 on his claim
for conversion. The copyright claim failed. The county court judge held
that as the plaintiff had recovered more than the amount paid in he was in
law entitled to the costs of the action. On appeal by the defendant against
this order for costs,

Held: (i) the amendment of the particulars of claim (which at the time
of amendment alleged a single cause of action) could not alter, by adding a
second cause of action, the effect of the payment into court made by the
defendant prior to the amendment, and did not cause the payment in to
relate at the trial to both causes of action; accordingly the plaintiff had not
recovered on account of remuneration more than had been paid in (see
p. 388, letters F and G, p. 389, letters E and H, and p. 390, letter G, post).

(ii) the costs relating to the £2 awarded to the plaintiff for the conversion
alleged by amendment were de minimis, and, in the circumstances, the
plaintiff should have his costs (on the appropriate scale (3)) to the date of
the payment into court and thereafter the defendant should have the costs
(on the appropriate scale (4)), no separate order being made in respect of the
costs of recovering the £2 (see p. 389, letters C and I, and p. 390, letter I,
post).

Appeal allowed.

[As to the payment into a county court of part of sum claimed, and as to
taking such payment, when not accepted, into account in awarding costs, see
9 HALSBURY'S LAWS (3rd Edn.) 231, 232, paras. 526, 528.

For the County Court Rules, 1936, Ord. 11, r. 1, r. 2, r. 3 and Ord. 15, r. 1 (1),
see COUNTY COURT PRACTICE (1966) 350, 351, 384.]

Appeal as to costs.

This was an appeal by the first defendant, Maurice Martin Harris, against so
much of the order of His Honour JUDGE GRANVILLE SMITH, made at Watford
county court on Aug. 2, 1966, as ordered him to pay the plaintiff's costs of the
action.   There was no appeal as to liability either by the first defendant, or by
the plaintiff, whose claim against the second defendant, Thomas Davies, had
been dismissed.   The facts are stated in the judgment of DAVIES, L.J.

M. P. Solomon for the first defendant.
H. J. Lloyd for the plaintiff.

DAVIES, L.J.: This is an appeal by the first defendant, whom I shall call
" the defendant ", from a judgment of JUDGE GRANVILLE SMITH at the Watford
county court given on Aug. 2, 1966.   It is an appeal as to costs only.   Such an
appeal is not normally, of course, entertained; but after the judgment the
defendant's solicitors were in communication with the county court, and there
is a letter before us from the registrar of the county court saying that the judge's
order as to costs was not made in the exercise of his discretion but purely on the
construction of the relevant county court rules.   Therefore the appeal raises a
question of law.   The judgment given by the county court judge was in favour
of the plaintiff for the sum of £77 and costs on scale 3.   The defendant appeals
from that order.

The facts can be shortly stated.   The plaintiff, who is an architect, was
instructed to advise and take various steps about licences in connexion with a
proposed extension to the defendant's house, Drummer House, Harrow.   He
did, as the judge found, a certain amount of work.   The work in respect of which
the claim was made was as follows (I am reading from the first paragraph in the
particulars of claim):

> " Aug. 5, 1965.   To taking instructions regarding extension at rear of
> Drummer House, carrying out survey of existing house, preparing and
> agreeing sketch plan, preparing final working drawings.   Submitting
> drawings to London Borough of Harrow and obtaining planning approval
> . . . . ";

and he claimed £166 odd.

That action was commenced on Dec. 15, 1965.   The particulars of defence
were filed on Dec. 29, 1965.   On Feb. 1, 1966, the defendant paid into court
the sum of £75 in satisfaction of the plaintiff's claim.   It is, of course, to be
remembered that within seven days the plaintiff could have taken out that sum
of £75 and taxed his costs in accordance with the provisions of C.C.R.,
Ord. 11, r. 9.   The plaintiff did not take out the money.   On Mar. 14,
1966, he obtained leave to add another defendant, a Mr. Davies, who was also
an architect, though, it would appear, not a qualified one.   The order provided
that the plaintiff should have leave to deliver amended particulars of claim, and,
of course, that the defendants could respectively amend or deliver particulars
of defence to the amended particulars of claim.   The amended particulars of
claim were based almost entirely on alleged breaches of copyright in respect of a
drawing which the plaintiff had prepared for this alteration to the defendant's
house.   He claimed £25 damages for infringement of copyright and £400 for
conversion—that is to say conversion in copyright law—of the drawing, and
confined his total claim to a sum within the limits of the county court jurisdiction.

As a matter of history what had happened about the drawing was this.   The
plaintiff had submitted a drawing to the defendant.   The defendant did not like
the drawing very much and he showed it to Mr. Davies, the second defendant,
pointing out to him those features of the drawing which the defendant did not

like. So Mr. Davies went away and prepared another drawing, altering the design to that which the defendant wanted.

The action came on for trial before JUDGE GRANVILLE SMITH and lasted, we were told, three days. Eventually, on Aug. 2, 1966, the judge gave judgment in favour of the plaintiff against the defendant; but he dismissed the claim against the second defendant. So far as the claim for £166 for fees and preparation of the drawing was concerned, the judge assessed the amount recoverable by the plaintiff at £75, the precise sum which the defendant had paid into court on Feb. 1; but he also gave judgment for a further sum of £2. He dismissed the plaintiff's claim in respect of infringement of copyright, or what might be conveniently called copyright conversion. There has been no appeal from that part of the judge's decision by the plaintiff, so that it is not necessary to say any more about that; but the £2 which he awarded was, as I understand it, for conversion of the drawing. There has been no appeal by the defendants against that; but I am bound to say that I find that decision a little difficult to understand. In the £75 for which judgment was given to the plaintiff against the defendant there must be included, it is to be apprehended, the fees in respect of the preparation of that drawing. It strikes me that there is some analogy here to a sale of goods. An unpaid seller of goods sold and delivered can, of course, bring an action against the buyer for the price; but it is new law to me that the seller, if he succeeds in obtaining the price of the goods, can, in addition, recover nominal or any other damages in respect of any dealing by the buyer with the goods before the price was paid or judgment was given or satisfied. The judge took the view that up to the time when, under the judgment, the defendant paid the plaintiff, any dealing by the defendant with this drawing by showing it to Mr. Davies, the other architect, amounted to a conversion. I very much doubt whether it was; but, as I say, no appeal has been brought from that finding.

The submission on behalf of the defendant, who is the appellant here, is that he is entitled to his costs on the claim for fees, in accordance with the ordinary practice, from the date of payment in, that is to say, Feb. 1. Whether or not the plaintiff is entitled to costs on the £2 which he recovered on the other cause of action, the conversion, is a matter which the defendant says is really de minimis and should not concern the court.

The relevant rules of court about this are as follows. First of all, C.C.R., Ord. 11.

" 1. A defendant in an action may at any time before judgment pay money into court—(a) in satisfaction of the claim, or, where several causes of action are joined in one action, in satisfaction of one or more of the causes of action . . .

" 2. Where the amount paid into court under the last preceding rule is less than the amount claimed, the payment shall be deemed to be made on account of the amount claimed, unless accompanied by a notice stating that it is made in satisfaction of the claim or, where several causes of action are joined in one action, a notice containing the information required in the next following rule.

" 3 (1). Where several causes of action are joined in one action and money is paid into court under r. 1 of this Order in satisfaction of one or more causes of action, the notice referred to in the last foregoing rule—(a) shall state that the money is paid in satisfaction of all the causes of action or of such of the causes of action as may be specified in the notice; (b) shall specify the sum paid in satisfaction of any cause or causes of action in respect of which the defendant desires to make a separate payment. (2) For the purposes of the foregoing paragraph money stated to be paid in satisfaction of the plaintiff's claim shall be deemed to be paid in satisfaction of all the causes of action. (3) Where a single sum of money is paid in satisfaction of two or more causes of action, and the plaintiff appears to the court to be embarrassed by the payment, the court may order the defendant to amend the notice of payment so as to specify the sum paid in respect of each cause of action."

The only other rule to which I need refer is C.C.R., Ord. 15, r. 1:

" The court may at any time (a) amend . . . [I need not read the rest of (a)] (b) add, strike out or substitute any person either as plaintiff or defendant; and all such amendments as may be necessary for the purpose of determining the real question in controversy between the parties shall be made, if duly applied for, and the proceedings shall continue in all respects as if they had been commenced in the form in which they appear after the amendment has been made."

As I have stated, at the date of the payment in by the defendant, the plaintiff had only one cause of action, that is to say, his claim for professional fees and remuneration. The payment in by the defendant then was perfectly good. The contention strenuously put forward by counsel for the plaintiff, however, is that when, in March, the plaintiff amended his particulars of claim so as to include a second cause of action, namely, that in respect of alleged infringement of copyright and conversion, the payment-in was, by the rules which I have read, deemed to have been paid in satisfaction of all the causes of action and that, therefore, the total payment in being £75 in respect of both causes of action and the plaintiff having recovered £77, the payment-in did not and should not avail the defendant.

I follow the argument; but it does seem to me to be an affront to common sense, and if something strikes one as being an affront to common sense, it is very likely that there is something wrong with the proposition. As I see it, the plaintiff, having refused to accept the £75 that was paid in in February, must, even after he had made his amendment in March, have known perfectly well to what the payment in related. It related to the claim, and the only claim, which existed at its date, namely, the claim for architect's fees. After the plaintiff had chosen to amend, there was no question whatsoever of his being misled or of his misunderstanding the position as to what the payment in had been made in respect of. To decide in any other way would, I should have thought, have meant that the making of this amendment, which of course was a concession— a proper concession—to the plaintiff, would work gravely to the prejudice of the defendant. As I see it, the payment-in of £75 in February was crystallised or earmarked in respect of the plaintiff's then claim; and, had the plaintiff been in any doubt at all, it is clear that he could have applied under C.C.R., Ord. 11, r. 3 (3) for the court to order the defendant to amend his notice of payment in, if in fact the £75 had become a payment-in in respect of all the causes of action. I do not think that it was. I think that it was a payment-in in respect of the then existing cause of action, and I cannot see that the amendment subsequently made by the plaintiff should be held to rebound to the disadvantage of the defendant.

I think that this is, despite the ingenious argument that has been put forward, really a straightforward case. In my opinion, the judge was wrong in holding himself constrained by the rules to give the plaintiff all the costs of this action. It is a very remarkable corollary to that decision that the whole of the costs of the amendment and the fresh pleadings that were necessary are under the judge's order to be paid by the defendant, although the plaintiff, as a result of all that labour and toil, has only recovered £2.

Counsel for the plaintiff finally submitted to the court that, if we were to come to the conclusion (as I have come to the conclusion) that the judge was wrong in his construction of the rules, nevertheless some mitigation of the position with regard to costs might be granted to the plaintiff. He said first of all that in this case the defendant wrongly, as the judge found, had denied that anything at all was due to the plaintiff. That is the ordinary case of a defendant who, while denying liability, makes a payment into court, is found to be liable, but has had the good fortune to pay into court a sum equal to or exceeding the amount eventually recovered by the plaintiff.

Secondly, counsel for the plaintiff says that the plaintiff was held by the judge to be an honest man. That again, as I think, has no relevance to the problem with which this court is confronted. Many honest plaintiffs have had to pay costs.

A small question arose whether or not the plaintiff should recover any costs in respect of the £2 which he recovered on his amended claim. It is perfectly plain that any costs recoverable on such a sum as that would be trifling.

I would therefore allow the appeal. The order which I would propose would be that the plaintiff should have his costs on scale 3, which is the scale appropriate to the amount recovered by him, up to the date of payment into court, and that thereafter the defendant should have the costs, on scale 4, which is the scale appropriate to the amount claimed by the plaintiff, and that there should be no separate order at all in respect of the £2.

RUSSELL, L.J.: I entirely agree.

The payment in, with its accompanying notice (1), referred exclusively to the only cause of action then asserted—that is, for fees—just as plainly as if it had expressly stated that cause of action. The language of C.C.R., Ord. 15, r. 1, expressing the general effect of amendment, certainly would not have had the effect on the payment in which is asserted by counsel for the plaintiff if the notice of payment in had expressly stated the nature of the then sole cause of action, and I cannot see why it should when the notice could not refer, when it was given, to any other cause of action.

C.C.R., Ord. 11, r. 2 and r. 3, relate to the notice which must accompany the payment in; and under those rules the question whether there is more than one cause of action must be considered at the time of payment in and the notice accompanying it. In particular, r. 3 had absolutely nothing to do with the payment in and accompanying notice in this case. Rule 3 begins with the words " Where several causes of action are joined in one action . . . the notice referred to in the last foregoing rule " . . . The " notice referred to in the last foregoing rule " is the notice accompanying the payment in. For that reason I cannot see that r. 3 has anything to do with the present case.

Counsel for the plaintiff, has sought to support the county court judge's view with an ingenious and, if I may say so, most helpful argument. He contends that the principles attending amendments (which are set out in fact in C.C.R., Ord. 15, r. 1) result in this, that at the trial the judge can look only at the language of the notice in the light not of the circumstances which obtained when the notice was given, but of the fact that by the time of the trial there were in fact here three causes of action. In my judgment, amendment does not alter the character or quality of the payment in, which must, unless there be subsequent amendment of some kind, be judged by the circumstances in relation to the number and types of causes of action obtaining at the time of the payment in.

I agree that the proper order to be made, in discretion, in this case, the county court judge being in my view wrong in his reading of the rule, is that the plaintiff will have his costs up to the date of payment in but that the defendant should have his costs thereafter. Both the sum of £2 nominal damages, awarded for a conversion which I doubt existed in law and certainly did not exist on the particulars of claim, and the amount of time taken in dealing with the conversion alleged, being de minimis, I do not think that they should carry any costs for the plaintiff.

SALMON, L.J.: I agree.

I confess that throughout the hearing of this appeal I have been oppressed

---

(1) The terms of the letter are set out at p. 390, letter F, post.

by a sense of unreality. We have had to approach this interesting question on
the basis that the county court judge's finding that the defendant converted the
piece of paper on which the plaintiff had made the working drawings was a
correct finding. The county court judge awarded 40s. in respect of that supposed
conversion, and the plaintiff therefore recovered £77. Had there been no such
conversion, he would have recovered only £75, which was the precise amount in
court; and this interesting question would never have arisen. It is perhaps
worth noting that the working drawings were sent by the plaintiff to the defendant
with a covering letter of June 28, 1965, saying: " I enclose herewith a copy
of the working drawing for your alterations and extension to Drummer House."
The judge found that there had been no infringement by the defendant of any
copyright in this drawing; but by some process of reasoning, which he did not
state and which I am unable to guess, he came to the conclusion that nevertheless
there had been a conversion of the piece of paper which was one of the things in
respect of which the plaintiff was claiming his fee. Such were counsel for the
plaintiff's powers of persuasion—and I am not surprised, having heard him
argue the case for the plaintiff so attractively in this court—that he persuaded the
judge to come to that most astonishing conclusion. There has been no appeal
from that finding and therefore we are approaching the case, as I say, on what
seems to me to be the very unreal basis that that finding was right.

On that assumption, the short point seems to me to be: is the effect of C.C.R.,
Ord. 15, r. 1, and the general practice which that embodies, such that it alters
the effect of the notice given by the defendant to the plaintiff at the date of the
payment in? At the date of the payment in, as my lords have said, there was
only one cause of action pleaded against this defendant: it was for fees of £166
and some shillings on a quantum meruit basis. When, on Feb. 1, 1966, the
money was paid into court, this letter was written to the plaintiff:

" We write to advise you that we have to-day paid into court the sum
of £75 which the defendant contends is sufficient to satisfy the plaintiff's
claim herein."

The only claim then existing was the one which I have stated.

I cannot accept the proposition that the subsequent amendment alters the
effect of that notice. One of the purposes of C.C.R., Ord. 11 is to inform the
plaintiff of the cause or causes of action in respect of which the payment into
court is being made. The plaintiff was informed on Feb. 1; and I fail entirely
to understand why, because he is later given the concession of amending his
particulars of claim by adding a claim for infringement of copyright for £25
and a claim for conversion in respect of copyright which he limits to £400, that
alters what he was plainly told in February, namely, that £75 was in court in
respect of his claim for fees.

Counsel for the plaintiff argues that on one very technical reading of C.C.R.,
Ord. 15, r. 1, it might be possible to produce the result which, as DAVIES, L.J.,
has said, offends against all common sense. There is no authority that I know
of which obliges us to achieve such a result and I think that the county court
judge was plainly wrong. The appeal should be allowed; and I agree with the
order proposed by my lords.

*Appeal allowed with costs. Plaintiff to have his costs up to date of payment in,
on scale 3; defendant to have his costs thereafter, on scale 4. Liberty to registrar
to increase scale items per C.C.R., Ord. 47, r. 21.*

Solicitors: *A. L. Bryden & Williams* (for the first defendant); *Sydney Redfern &
Co.* (for the plaintiff).

[*Reported by* HENRY SUMMERFIELD, ESQ., *Barrister-at-Law.*]

Re COCKLE'S WILL TRUSTS.

[CHANCERY DIVISION (Stamp, J.), October 27, 28, November 17, 1966.]

Will—Class gift—Period of distribution—Time of ascertainment of class—Period of distribution a misnomer—Trust for girl aged four at testator's death for life and after her death for her issue at twenty-one, etc.—Proviso that issue of deceased child of life tenant should take per stirpes—Four children born to life tenant and a number of grandchildren born in her lifetime—Issue in existence at life tenant's death intended to take beneficially but not those born afterwards—Rule in Andrews v. Partington *not applicable—Gift not void for remoteness nor for uncertainty.*

Will—Distribution—Per stirpes or per capita—Stirpital distribution by necessary implication from proviso.

A testator, who made his will on Nov. 2, 1896, died on May 30, 1900, at the age of seventy-one. After disposing of one moiety of his residuary estate, he provided by his will: " And as to the other moiety of my residuary estate hereinafter called ' the second moiety ' I declare that the trustees shall stand possessed thereof in trust for Margaret Jennie Prince Pittaway for life and after [her decease] in trust for her issue who being male shall live to attain twenty-one years or being female shall live to attain that age or marry and if more than one in equal shares Provided that the issue of any deceased child of [hers] shall take per stirpes and not per capita . . .". Miss Pittaway was born in 1896; she married a Mr. Moreland and had four children, and a number of grandchildren were born before her death in 1964. The question arose as to whom the testator intended to take the second moiety.

Held: (i) (a) the trust of the second moiety was not void for uncertainty (see p. 394, letter A, and p. 396, letter E, post).

(b) as it was unlikely that, in the circumstances, the testator could have contemplated that there would be issue of Mrs. Moreland living at his death, the intention shown by his will was that her issue in existence at her death were those intended to benefit, but that those born afterwards were not intended to benefit, and the rule in *Andrews* v. *Partington* did not apply to effect an extension of the period at which the class of beneficiaries was to close; accordingly the trust was not void for remoteness (see p. 394, letter C, p. 395, letter D, and p. 396, letter E, post).

Surridge v. *Clarkson* ((1866), 14 W.R. 979) followed.

Andrews v. *Partington* (1791), 3 Bro. C.C. 401) considered.

(ii) in the proviso the words " deceased child " referred to a child dying in the lifetime of Mrs. Moreland and the testator had shown, by necessary implication from the proviso, that he intended a distribution in which issue of a deceased child were not to take in competition with parents, viz., a stirpital distribution (see p. 396, letter G, post).

Per CURIAM: the expression " the period of distribution " is something of a misnomer; it does not denote the moment of time when the trustees will distribute the fund, but is merely descriptive of the time when the class of beneficiaries is taken finally to close (see p. 394, letter G, post).

[As to rules of convenience for ascertaining the date of distribution, see 39 HALSBURY'S LAWS (3rd Edn.) 1037-1041, paras. 1558-1561; and for cases on the subject, see 49 DIGEST (Repl.) 677-683, *6380-6443*.]

Cases referred to:

Andrews v. *Partington*, (1791), 3 Bro. C.C. 401; 29 E.R. 610; 49 Digest (Repl.) 669, *6321.*

Surridge v. *Clarkson*, (1866), 14 W.R. 979; 49 Digest (Repl.) 1212, *11136.*

Adjourned Summons.

By an originating summons dated July 16, 1904, the plaintiff, Margaret Jennie Prince Pittaway, by her next friend Charlotte Pittaway, applied, inter alia that

Applied in Re DEELEY'S SETTLE-MENT [1973] 3 All ER 1127

Applied in Re DRUMMOND'S SETTLE-MENT, FOSTER v FOSTER [1986] 3 All ER 45

the trusts declared by the will dated Nov. 2, 1896, of the testator, George Cockle, ⟋
of and concerning the one moiety of his residuary estate bequeathed to her for
her life might be carried into execution by and under the direction of the court,
and by an order dated Nov. 15, 1904, made by SWINFEN EADY, J., in such action,
it was ordered (inter alia) that an inquiry should be made of what the capital of
the second moiety in the will then consisted and that within twenty-one days
after the date of the master's certificate to be made pursuant to the order the ⟨I⟩
surviving trustees should transfer and lodge in court the moneys, stocks, funds
and securities which on making the inquiry should be found to be the capital
of the moiety after making provision for the payment of annuities, and it was
ordered that the trusts should be carried into effect by and under the directions
of the court and provision was made for taxation and payment of costs of the
action. In 1918, the plaintiff married Henry Moreland. The Public Trustee was ⟨C⟩
made a respondent in 1933 and in 1936 an order was made to carry on the proceedings against him as sole defendant, the two original defendants, Frederick James
Draffen and George Algernon Draffen, having died. Mrs. Moreland died on
May 13, 1964.

This was an application by summons dated Dec. 9, 1965, by Samuel John
Moreland, William Henry Moreland, Robert Moreland and Jane Ella Davies ⟨D⟩
who claimed to be beneficially entitled to the capital of the funds in court and
Frank Percival Risdon who with the first three applicants claimed to be the
personal representatives of Margaret Jennie Prince Moreland and entitled
as such to any interest accrued during her lifetime on the fund in court. The
summons asked whether on the true construction of the will of the testator,
George Cockle, deceased, and in the events which had happened the capital of ⟨E⟩
the fund in court (ledger credit " Re Cockle, Re Pittaway, Pittaway v. Draffen,
1904 C 2482. The share of the infant plaintiff Margaret Jennie Prince Pittaway
of the residuary estate of the testator, George Cockle, bequeathed to her for life ")
was then held (a) on trust for the applicants Samuel John Moreland, William
Henry Moreland, Robert Moreland and Jane Ella Davies in equal shares
absolutely, or (b) on trust for the applicants and for such of the children of the ⟨F⟩
applicants respectively living at the death of Margaret Jennie Prince Moreland
who being male attained the age of twenty-one years or being female had attained
that age or married in equal shares per capita, or (c) on some other and what
trusts. The facts are stated in the judgment.

The cases noted below* were cited during the argument in addition to those
referred to in the judgment.   ⟨G⟩

N. Micklem for the applicants.
T. L. Dewhurst for the grandchildren.
M. W. Cockle for the Public Trustee.
J. Monckton for those entitled to the first moiety.

Nov. 17. **STAMP, J.:** The first questions which I have to determine ⟨H⟩
in this case are questions affecting the distribution of a moiety of the residuary
estate of a testator who made his will on Nov. 2, 1896, and who died as long ago
as May 30, 1900, at the age of seventy-one. The questions became immediate
questions on the death, in 1964, of a Mrs. Moreland, who was born in the year in
which the will was made, and so was a very small girl at the date of the death.
She is, in the will, called Margaret Jennie Prince Pittaway. It is convenient to ⟨I⟩

---

* *Dick* v. *Lacy*, (1845), 8 Beav. 214; *Baldwin* v. *Rogers*, (1853), 3 De G.M. & G. 649;
Lee v. *Lee*, (1860), 1 Drew. & Sm. 85; *Jull* v. *Jacobs*, (1876), 3 Ch.D. 703; *Pearks*
v. *Moseley*, (1880), 5 App. Cas. 714; *Re Emmet's Estate*, (1880), 13 Ch.D. 484; *Re Clark*,
(1885), 31 Ch.D. 72; *Re Stephenson, Donaldson* v. *Bamber*, [1897] 1 Ch. 75; *Re Turney*,
[1899] 2 Ch. 739; *Re Rawlinson*, [1909] 2 Ch. 36; *Re Peacock*, [1957] 2 All E.R. 98;
[1957] Ch. 310; *Re Davies*, [1957] 3 All E.R. 52; *Re Taylor*, [1957] 3 All E.R. 56;
Re Hubbard's Will Trusts, [1962] 2 All E.R. 917; [1963] Ch. 275; *Re Robinson's Will
Trusts*, [1963] 1 All E.R. 777; *Re Buckton's Declaration of Trust*, [1964] 2 All E.R. 487;
[1964] Ch. 497.

say, at the outset, that Mrs. Moreland had four children and a number of grand-children born before her death, all of whom, both children and grandchildren, survived her and are parties to the present application.

The testator, after dealing with one moiety of his residuary estate, proceeded as follows:

" And as to the other moiety of my residuary estate hereinafter called ' the second moiety ' I declare that the trustees or trustee shall stand possessed thereof in trust for Margaret Jennie Prince Pittaway for life and after the decease of the said Margaret Jennie Prince Pittaway in trust for the issue of the said Margaret Jennie Prince Pittaway who being male shall live to attain twenty-one years or being female shall live to attain that age or marry and if more than one in equal shares Provided that the issue of any deceased child of the said Margaret Jennie Prince Pittaway shall take per stirpes and not per capita And in case there shall be no issue of the said Margaret Jennie Prince Pittaway who shall live to attain a vested interest in the second moiety then I declare that the trustees or trustee shall stand possessed of one moiety of the second moiety upon the trusts hereinbefore declared concerning the first moiety."

He then went on to direct the trustees to stand possessed of the remaining moiety of the second moiety on trust first of all to increase the annuities of certain annuit-ants who predeceased Mrs. Moreland and subject thereto in trust for the person or persons who became entitled to the first moiety of his residuary estate.

I will refer to the contentions advanced as to the effect of those limitations but not in the order in which they were put. Counsel for those interested in any part of the estate of which the testator was intestate, contended that the limitation to the issue of Mrs. Moreland was void ab initio for remoteness. He submits that well-known principles apply and that although the court favours a construction of a will which results in early vesting so that a gift to a class such as children, grandchildren or first cousins will vest in those members of the class, if any, who are living at the death of the testator, this is subject to the rule often referred to as the rule in *Andrews v. Partington* (1) that it will include all the children, grandchildren or first cousins who come into existence before the period of distribution: that is, in this case all those issue who being male attain twenty-one or being female attain that age or marry who are born before the first of them attains a vested interest. This being so, it follows—and indeed it does if the rule falls to be applied in the case of a gift to the issue of the tenant for life—that at the death of the testator one could not have told whether the gift to issue would take effect, if at all, within the perpetuity period. Mrs. Moreland might have died leaving a son or sons under twenty-one and no other issue, and if that son or those sons were to have died under twenty-one leaving a child or children the latter child or children would be objects of the trust but would not take a vested interest within the period allowed by the perpetuity rule. Having completed his argument that the limitation to the issue of Mrs. Moreland is void for remoteness, counsel goes on to argue that the gift over, being dependent on a limitation which is void for remoteness, is itself void for remoteness. Counsel for those entitled to the first moiety, contends that the gift to Mrs. Moreland's issue is void, not because it is too remote, but because of its uncertainty and that the gift over takes effect. Counsel on behalf of the four children of Mrs. Moreland, and counsel on behalf of her grandchildren, combine to argue that the gift to the issue of Mrs. Moreland is neither void for remoteness nor uncertainty, but part company on the question whether issue more remote than a child take in competition with their parent. It is common ground that the word issue in the limitation which I have to consider comprises issue in all degrees.

I deal first with the argument that the gift is void for uncertainty. No doubt the trust in favour of issue when read with the proviso that the issue of any

(1) (1791), 3 Bro. C.C. 401.

deceased child of Mrs. Moreland shall take per stirpes and not per capita, presents **A**
difficulties of construction; but I think that this court has solved far more
difficult problems and I am not disposed to accept the submission of counsel for
those entitled to the first moiety that the trust is void for uncertainty. Read
apart from the proviso, the original gift to the issue of Mrs. Moreland who being
male shall live to attain twenty-one years or being female shall live to attain that
age or marry and if more than one in equal shares seems, subject only to the ques- **B**
tion at what date the class of issue is closed, is tolerably clear; and it would be
a strong thing to hold the proviso so uncertain in its effect as to destroy the prior
gift. As appears later in this judgment, however, I am able to attach a meaning to
it.

Nor, in my judgment, is the gift, whether it be a gift per stirpes or per capita,
void for remoteness. The conclusion that it is void is arrived at by applying rules **C**
of construction to circumstances in which they ought not, in my judgment, to be
applied. The rules so relied on are to be found conveniently stated in ch. 7 of
HAWKINS ON WILLS (3rd Edn.). First, there is the rule that a gift to a class such
as the children of A means, prima facie, the children living at the testator's death
provided there are any in existence. Here, not only were there no such issue but
it is extremely improbable, having regard to the age of Mrs. Moreland when the **D**
testator made his will and to his own age, that he can have contemplated that
there would be any such. Furthermore, the gift is to Mrs. Moreland's issue
and it is quite impossible to suppose that the testator thought that she would have
issue remoter than a child living at his death. Two further rules are, however,
relied on: first, that where, as here, the gift is not immediate the class will
include children coming into existence before the period of distribution; and, **E**
second, that where, as here, the share of each child is made payable on attaining
a given age or marriage the period of distribution is the time when the first child
becomes entitled to receive his share and children coming into existence after
that date are excluded.

If the last stated rule, which is often referred to as the rule in *Andrews* v.
Partington (2), is applied to the facts of this case in the terms in which I have **F**
stated it, it will produce the result for which counsel for those interested on an
intestacy contends. Although conveniently so stated, however, it is to be observed
that the expression " the period of distribution " is something of a misnomer.
The period of distribution has no separate existence but is merely descriptive of
the time when the class is taken finally to close; it is not the moment of time
when the trustees will distribute the fund, because the tenant for life may still **G**
be living and there can in any event be no final distribution of the fund as a whole
until the last member of the class attains a vested interest. For present purposes,
I find it convenient to state the rule thus: where the gifts are to A for life and
after his death to such of the children of B as attain a specified age or marry
and none has attained that age or married at the death of the tenant for life,
the testator is taken to have intended to benefit all those born before, but none **H**
of those born after, the first of those children attains the specified age or marries.
If I have correctly understood the rule, I have to ask myself the question—
ought this testator to be taken to have intended that, if on Mrs. Moreland's
death there was no issue of hers who had then attained the age of twenty-one
or being female had attained that age or married, issue thereafter born to a son
of hers who was then under twenty-one were to be included among the **I**
beneficiaries, or is the prima facie rule of construction excluded?

There is one feature which distinguishes this case from the cases where *Andrews*
v. *Partington* (2) has been applied, namely, that the class consists or may consist
of more than one generation. This distinction is, I think, a material one, because
where a testator makes a bequest to the grandchildren of A, or to *all* the grandchildren of A, he has used terms consistent at least with the intention that all,

---

(2) (1791), 3 Bro. C.C. 401.

A and not only those born before some specified date, shall take: the rule in *Andrews v. Partington* (3) restricts and does not enlarge the class. In this case, however, one thing is clear beyond peradventure and that is that the testator did not intend all the generations of issue born at any time in any future age to take. The question is, accordingly, no longer one of reconciling a gift which in terms includes *all* the children or grandchildren with the presumed intention of the testator that

B the first of them to attain the qualifying age is not to be disappointed by a subsequent increase of the class; and since the testator cannot be taken to have intended all the issue to take, one must, in my judgment, ask the question, independently of the restrictive rules of construction: which of them did he intend should take? One may impute to him an intention in favour of early vesting, but not, in my judgment, an intention that those who are born before one of them

C attains the specified age are to be included. Until there is some person of whom one can say that he or she was at all events intended to take, there is no question of disappointing him by holding up distribution until he attains the qualifying age, and no ground for excluding (or including) those born after that event. The question becomes, however difficult or easy the answer may be: which of the issue of Mrs. Moreland to attain twenty-one or being female to attain that age or marry

D did the testator intend should take? Bearing in mind that at the death of this testator there were no issue of Mrs. Moreland in existence, I conclude that the issue in existence at the date of the death of Mrs. Moreland were those intended to be included, and see no good reason for including those born afterwards. So far as Mrs. Moreland's children were concerned, this must be so, because none could have been born after her death, and I see no reason to impute to the

E testator an intention that issue remoter than a child born after the death were intended to be objects of the testator's bounty. The argument that by the effect of the rule in *Andrews v. Partington* (3) the class includes not only issue born before Mrs. Moreland's death but extends to those born afterwards before one of them being male attains twenty-one or being female attains that age or marries produces, in a case such as this, the very situation which the rules in favour of

F early vesting are designed to avoid. The extension pre-supposes that at the death of Mrs. Moreland there has been no child of hers who being male has attained the age of twenty-one or being female has attained that age or married. The extension could not operate in favour of a child of Mrs. Moreland, because there could be none, and it could not operate in favour of any issue of a daughter of hers, because such issue could come into existence only after the daughter had married and had so attained a vested interest. The extension could thus only operate in favour

G of a grandchild whose parent being male failed to attain the age of twenty-one, a great grandchild whose parent and grandparent was a male who failed to attain the age of twenty-one, and so on through the generations; and if there is to be imputed to the testator an intention to bring in such a grandchild or great grand-child, and so on, there can, in my judgment, be no good reason, if the intended

H distribution is a per capita distribution, not to impute to him an intention to provide for all the issue whenever born down through the generations, which would be absurd. If, on the other hand, what is intended is a stirpital distribution it would be most remarkable if, having excluded the descendants of a daughter who married and excluded a son who died under twenty-one, the testator should have brought in the children or grandchildren of the latter by the effect of an implication

I of intention designed for quite a different purpose. Nothing could be more capricious or absurd. And by applying the rule of construction designed to limit those who are to be treated as objects of the testator's bounty one would produce the result that someone, not intended to benefit, is artificially brought in as a beneficiary. The rules of construction are, in my judgment, to be applied rationally and not in such a way as to produce an absurd or capricious result.

I have not been referred to any case where a gift to the issue of a life tenant

---

(3) (1791), 3 Bro. C.C. 401.

on a contingency personal to themselves; for example, in the present case the attaining of a given age or marriage, has been held to include issue born after the death of the life tenant. On the other hand, *Surridge* v. *Clarkson* (4), albeit an unsatisfactory case on the point which I am now considering, is, as a matter of decision, an authority in favour of the view which I have formed. In that case there was a gift in the codicil to the testator's daughter for life and after her death to her issue and in default of issue to her two surviving sisters' issue as they should arrive at the age of twenty-one. The daughter died without issue and KINDERSLEY, V.-C., having decided that the gift to the issue of the sisters was effective although both sisters predeceased the daughter, went on to decide what issue were meant. It had been argued that the gift was void for remoteness and it is to be observed that the same argument was open there as that which was advanced by counsel for those entitled on intestacy in the present case. Nevertheless KINDERSLEY, V.-C., decided that the issue to take were those alive at the testator's death or coming into being before the death of the daughter. The case is unsatisfactory because KINDERSLEY, V.-C., did not in terms address himself to the argument based on remoteness, and one does not know how the argument was put. The case was, however, decided seventy years after *Andrews* v. *Partington* (5) and I see no reason not to follow it. I have only to add that counsel for those interested in an intestacy placed no reliance on the proviso to the gift to issue as affecting the question whether the gift was void for remoteness.

Taking the view which I do that the gift is neither void for uncertainty nor for remoteness, it is not necessary for me to express any view as to the consequences if, contrary to my opinion, the gift was void on either of those grounds; and it is, I think, undesirable that I should do so.

I turn to consider the question between the children and grandchildren. Do grandchildren take in competition with their parents or is the distribution a stirpital one? It is common ground that, if the gift were read without regard to the proviso, I should have to construe it as a gift to the descendants of Mrs. Moreland of whatever degree, children taking concurrently or in competition with their parents (see HAWKINS ON WILLS (3rd Edn.), p. 113)—a per capita, and not a stirpital, distribution.

As to the proviso, it is to be noted first that it is common ground that, having regard to the ages of the testator and Mrs. Moreland at the date of the testator's will the reference to a deceased child cannot be a reference to a child of Mrs. Moreland predeceasing the testator, and, in my judgment, the reference is to a child who dies in the lifetime of Mrs. Moreland. It is also to be noted that the proviso states how issue of a deceased child are to take, but not what they are to take. In my judgment, the testator, by the proviso, has shown, by necessary implication, that what he intended was a distribution in which issue were not to take in competition with parents, namely a stirpital distribution. In the first place, if he had intended a per capita distribution it is almost impossible to suppose that he would not in the proviso have stated what it was that the children of a deceased child were to take per stirpes. Is it the sum of the shares which the issue would have taken per capita but for the proviso, and, if so, what happens to the share of the deceased child, or does it operate as a gift to the issue of the share of the deceased child, leaving them to take their original shares in addition? Whatever way the question was answered, the result would be capricious and nonsensical, operating in the former case to alter the whole basis of distribution according to whether a child or children predeceased Mrs. Moreland, and in the latter case to add a share to the shares which they took under the original gift and so favouring one family at the expense of the other. If, however, the testator intended that issue should not take in competition with parents all becomes clear. If the issue of a living child are not to take at all, the direction that the issue of a deceased child are to take per stirpes is, however inartistic, sensible and falls into

(4) (1866), 14 W.R. 979.
(5) (1791), 3 Bro. C.C. 401.

place. I must adopt the construction which produces a coherent basis of division. It is, no doubt, the fact that the words " shall take per stirpes and not per capita " in the proviso could be read as contrasting the way in which issue of a deceased child are to take under the proviso from the way in which issue are to take under the earlier substantive gift; but the words " and not per capita " are habitually used by conveyances as words of emphasis and clarification and not by way of contrast with some other gift.

Order accordingly.

Solicitors: *Gregory, Rowcliffe & Co.*, agents for *Risdon & Co.*, Taunton (for the applicants and grandchildren); *Hancock & Willis* (for the Public Trustee and those entitled to the first moiety).

[*Reported by* Jenifer Sandell, *Barrister-at-Law.*]

ROLLS RAZOR, LTD. *v.* COX.

[Court of Appeal, civil division (Lord Denning, M.R., Danckwerts and Winn, L.JJ.), November 17, 18, 21, December 8, 1966.]

Company—Winding-up—Voluntary winding-up—Creditors' voluntary winding-up—Set-off—Mutual dealings—Salesmen selling company's domestic appliances by calling on householders—Salesmen independent contractors—Proceeds of sales paid over to company—Commission paid by company to salesmen less percentage retained for salesmen in retention fund—Set-off of claim for commission and for retention fund against proceeds of sales and goods for sale in hands of salesmen—Whether salesmen had lien on such money or goods—Companies Act, 1948 (11 & 12 Geo. 6 c. 38), s. 317—Bankruptcy Act, 1914 (4 & 5 Geo. 5 c. 59), s. 31.

The plaintiff company sold washing machines and other domestic appliances, appointing salesmen, who were independent contractors. Each salesman entered into a contract with the company. He was supplied with machines and a van and he called on people in their homes, demonstrated the machines and tried to sell them on cash or hire-purchase terms. Under his contract a salesman had to pay over to the company weekly all cash that he received, without deducting commission. The company paid him weekly the commission that he had earned, but deducted a percentage to form a retention fund to be available in case a salesman should default. The fund was to be repayable to the salesman after the determination of his contract. On the determination of his contract the salesman was (by cl. 13) to deliver forthwith to the company all the goods entrusted to him by the company and to account for the value of any goods not so returned. The defendant was one of the company's salesmen. It was widely publicised that the company was in financial difficulties on about July 17, 1964. His contract was determined, it seems, at some date between July 20 and July 30, 1964. On Aug. 27, 1964, the company passed a resolution for voluntary winding-up. The defendant claimed a lien on cash and goods in his hands in respect of a sum of £245 odd, being as to £188 odd the amount held for him in the retention fund and as to £57 commission that he had previously earned. He had sold, prior to July 17, two machines, for which he had received £106 odd and in respect of which his commission was £5 10s., that sum being additional to the £57. He had possession of a table-top entrusted to him by the company for sale at a price of three guineas. Its value, however, at the date of the action was in the region of 12s. He also had

Applied in Westminster Bank v Halesowen [1972] 1 All ER 641

possession of seven tap-adaptors which were not for sale, but which he used when fitting the machines. The liquidator brought an action claiming from the defendant the £106 and the return of the table-top and tap-adaptors or their value. The defendant sought to set-off the £245 under s. 31* of the Bankruptcy Act, 1914, as applied by s. 317 of the Companies Act, 1948, and he further claimed that he had a lien on the money and goods in his hands.

Held: (i) the defendant was entitled to a set-off, by virtue of s. 31 of the Bankruptcy Act, 1914, as applied by s. 317 of the Companies Act, 1948, in respect of (a) money held by him at the time of determination of his contract and (b) (WINN, L.J., dissenting) the proceeds of goods held for sale (viz., the table top) or the value of such goods (viz., the cash value at which the defendant was authorised to sell, namely, three guineas), because the dealings between the company and the defendant were mutual dealings within s. 31, and the parties could not contract out of the statutory rule enacted in s. 31 (see p. 403, letters H and I, p. 404, letter A, p. 405, letters A and I, p. 407, letter G, p. 406, letter A, p. 408, letter H, and p. 409, letter H, post).

(ii) (per LORD DENNING, M.R., and WINN, L.J.), there was no right of set-off, however, in respect of the tap-adaptors (see p. 405, letter B, and p. 407, letter I, post).

Eberle's Hotels & Restaurant Co., Ltd. v. *Jonas* ((1887), 18 Q.B.D. 459) followed.

(iii) the defendant (per LORD DENNING, M.R.) was not a factor or (per WINN, L.J.) had not been shown by evidence to have the status of a factor, and (per CURIAM), even if he had been a factor any lien would have been excluded by cl. 13 of his contract (see p. 403, letter B, p. 405, letter F, and p. 409, letters D and E, post).

Appeal allowed on (i) and (iii) above.

[**Editorial Note.** In regard to the question of the salesmen having a lien as a factor this decision should be considered particularly with the judgment of COTTON, L.J., in *Stevens* v. *Biller* ((1883), 25 Ch.D. at p. 38).

As to the statutory right of set-off where there is insolvency, see 2 HALSBURY'S LAWS (3rd Edn.) 480, 481, para. 952; and for cases on the subject, see 4 DIGEST (Repl.) 436-444, *3859-3913*.

As to the lien of an agent, see 1 HALSBURY'S LAWS (2nd Edn.) 205, para. 466; and as to the lien of a factor, see 24 HALSBURY'S LAWS (3rd Edn.) 149, para. 272.

For the Factors Act, 1889, s. 1, see 1 HALSBURY'S STATUTES (2nd Edn.) 29.

For the Bankruptcy Act, 1914, s. 31, see 2 HALSBURY'S STATUTES (2nd Edn.) 365.

For the Companies Act, 1948, s. 317, see 3 HALSBURY'S STATUTES (2nd Edn.) 698.]

Cases referred to:

Baring v. *Corrie*, [1814-23] All E.R. Rep. 283; (1818), 2 B. & Ald. 137; 106 E.R. 317; 1 Digest (Repl.) 324, *109.*

City Equitable Fire Insurance Co., Ltd. (*No. 2*), *Re*, [1930] All E.R. Rep. 315; [1930] 2 Ch. 293; 99 L.J.Ch. 536; 143 L.T. 444; 4 Digest (Repl.) 423, *3750.*

Daintrey, Re, Ex p. Mant and Mant, [1895-99] All E.R. Rep. 657; [1900] 1 Q.B. 546; 69 L.J.Q.B. 207; 82 L.T. 239; 4 Digest (Repl.) 438, *3872.*

Deveze, Re, Ex p. Barnett, (1874), 9 Ch. App. 293; 43 L.J.Bcy. 87; 29 L.T. 858; 4 Digest (Repl.) 433, *3844.*

Eberle's Hotels & Restaurant Co., Ltd. v. *Jonas,* (1887), 18 Q.B.D. 459; 56 L.J.Q.B. 278; 4 Digest (Repl.) 442, *3903.*

French v. *Fenn,* (1783), 3 Doug. K.B. 257; 99 E.R. 642; 4 Digest (Repl.) 443, *3905.*

---

* Section 31, so far as material, is printed at p. 403, letter D, post.

Mid-Kent Fruit Factory, Ltd., Re, [1896] 1 Ch. 567; 65 L.J.Ch. 250; 74 L.T. 22;
    4 Digest (Repl.) 442, *3902.*
Naorosji v. *Chartered Bank of India,* (1868), L.R. 3 C.P. 444; 37 L.J.C.P. 221;
    18 L.T. 358; 4 Digest (Repl.) 441, *3890.*
Palmer v. *Day & Sons,* [1895] 2 Q.B. 618; 64 L.J.Q.B. 807; 4 Digest (Repl.)
    443, *3909.*
Rose v. *Hart,* (1818), 8 Taunt. 499; 129 E.R. 477; 4 Digest (Repl.) 437, *3866.*
Stevens v. *Biller,* (1883), 25 Ch.D. 31; 53 L.J.Ch. 249; 50 L.T. 36; 1 Digest
    (Repl.) 641, *2178.*
Young v. *Bank of Bengal,* (1836), 1 Moo. P.C.C. 150; 1 Moo. Ind. App. 87;
    18 E.R. 34; 4 Digest (Repl.) 442, *3893.*

Appeal.

This was an appeal by the defendant, Herbert Cox, by notice dated July 22,
1966, from so much of the judgment of His Honour JUDGE BLOCK, given on the
trial of an action brought by the plaintiff company, Rolls Razor, Ltd., then in
liquidation, by writ issued on July 21, 1965, and transferred to the Mayor's and
City of London Court by order dated Mar. 22, 1966. That court adjudged on
June 13, 1966, that the company should recover from the defendant the sum
of £106 1s. as money had and received by the defendant on behalf of the company, and that the company should recover one table-top, or its value 12s., and
seven tap-adaptors, or their value 10s. 6d., wrongfully detained by the defendant.

The facts are summarised in the judgment of LORD DENNING, M.R., at p. 401,
letter D, to p. 402, letter H, post. The agreement between the plaintiff company
and the defendant, was on a printed form and was dated Dec. 23, 1963. By
cl. 1 the plaintiff company, therein called " the company ", appointed the
defendant, therein called " the agent ", to act on behalf of the company or any
of its associated companies as agent for the sale of goods to be sold by the company
or any of its associated companies on terms and conditions thereinafter stated.
By cl. 2 the contract might be determined by either party giving written notice
thereof, and such determination should be effective from the time of the receipt
of such notice by the other party. The following are the clauses referred to in the
judgment of WINN, L.J., at p. 407, letter G, post)—

    3. (iv) On Monday of each week (or such other day as the company shall
    decide but in any case not less than once weekly) the agent shall attend
    at the company's office (or branch thereof) and pay over all moneys received
    by him on behalf of the company during the preceding week or lesser period as
    the case may be and at the same time deliver to the company the particulars
    of sale forms duly completed and a detailed record of the sales of the goods
    made by him and of all moneys received. At the same time the agent
    shall hand over to the company all hire-purchase agreements and documents
    in connexion therewith signed by customers during the preceding week or
    other period as the case may be.

    4. The agent shall at all times keep proper and sufficient accounts and
    records of all money matters and transactions whatsoever passing through
    his hands or undertaken or handled by him in the course of his appointment
    and of all details of hire-purchase transactions negotiated by him on behalf
    of the company.

    7. (i) By way of remuneration for his services as agent the company shall
    pay the agent a commission at such rate or rates as the company shall from
    time to time agree with the agent such commission to be calculated on the
    advertised cash price of the goods sold (whether by cash sale or by hire-
    purchase) PROVIDED ALWAYS that (a) the agent shall not be entitled to any
    commission on any sales by hire-purchase until the transaction shall have
    been approved by the company as provided in cl. 5 (iv) hereof; and (b) in

the event of commission having been paid in respect of a sale subsequently cancelled or not approved by the company by reason of the agent's misconduct or neglect including in particular (and without prejudice to the generality of the foregoing) any failure by the agent to comply with the regulations from time to time made by the company in relation to the completion and submission of hire-purchase agreements or of a sale being cancelled by a customer of the company for the same reason the agent shall repay the amount of such commission already paid to the agent together with such other expenses or costs incurred by the company as a result of such cancellation or non-approval from any commission payable or becoming payable by the company to the agent.

(iii) The commission shall be paid to the agent once a week on such day as the company shall decide and shall be the amount of commission earned by the agent during the preceding week and shall in no case be deductible by the agent from moneys received by him on behalf of the company. The payment of commission shall be subject to all the company's rights for deduction and/or retention whether or not expressly conferred under this agreement.

(iv) Save as otherwise separately arranged with the agent the agent shall not be entitled to any travelling hotel or out-of-pocket expenses incurred by him in the process of selling the goods.

8. (a) Out of all commission payable to the agent as aforesaid the company shall be entitled to retain an amount equal to two shillings in every £1 of such commission payable or such other amount as shall be agreed in writing between the agent and the company at all times when the amount of such moneys retained by the company shall total £100 or less, and thereafter the company shall be entitled to retain from all such commission an amount equal to one shilling in every £1 or such other sum as shall be agreed in writing between the agent and the company. The amount so retained by the company shall hereinafter be called " the retention fund " and the company shall have the right to make such retention at all times except when the retention fund in the hands of the company shall amount to £250 or more. The company shall keep an accurate record of all moneys retained under this clause and shall notify the agent of the amount retained against him at any time that the agent shall request the company to do so. The agent shall not utilise his retention fund to off-set any moneys collected by him on behalf of the company.

(b) The company may:

(i) utilise the retention fund to reimburse itself the amount of any loss damage or expenses incurred by the company arising as a result of any default negligence or fraud on the part of the agent occurring in relation to the goods or under this agreement or in respect of any moneys received by the agent on behalf of the company or in respect of any vehicle (or damage thereto) made available by the company to the agent as hereinafter stated; PROVIDED ALWAYS that the agent shall reimburse the company the amount of any loss damage or expense incurred by the company as aforesaid subject to the company's right to apply the retention fund in diminution of such amount.

(ii) deduct from the retention fund the annual insurance premium referred to in cl. 10 (a) hereof such deduction not to exceed £10 in any year.

12. IT IS HEREBY EXPRESSLY DECLARED AND AGREED between the agent and the company that for the purposes of all relevant statutes regulations and orders the agent is and shall remain a self-employed person and the agent hereby undertakes as such to make all requisite national insurance contributions and income tax returns and payment thereof.

13. On the determination of this agreement the agent shall forthwith deliver to the company all the goods/hire-purchase and other forms and agreements entrusted to him by the company and shall account for the value of any goods not so returned. The agent shall also deliver to the company the company's vehicle (if any) together with all moneys, cheques, bills of exchange or other securities he may have received as a result of sales of or hire-purchase transactions or other dealings with the goods of the company and shall transfer assign or negotiate to the company all such securities on demand.

The authorities and the cases noted below* were cited during the argument in addition to the cases referred to in the judgments.

T. P. E. Curry, Q.C., and *A. L. Figgis* for the defendant.
Muir Hunter, Q.C., and *C. H. L. Bathurst* for the plaintiff company.

Cur. adv. vult.

Dec. 8. The following judgments were read.

LORD DENNING, M.R.: This case, as the judge said, arises out of the decline and fall of the Bloom Empire. Rolls Razor, Ltd. (" the company ") was one of Bloom's companies. It sold washing machines and other domestic appliances. Its method of business was to appoint salesmen to go round to people's houses. It supplied each salesman with a stock of the company's machines: or, if he had no room to stock them, he would get machines out of a pool. It supplied each salesman with a van. (The company had got these vans on hire-purchase.) Each salesman loaded up the van with the machines. He called on people in their houses and induced them, if he could, to buy the machines, either for cash or on hire-purchase terms. Every week the salesman had to pay over to the company all the cash which he had received. He was not allowed to deduct his commission from the cash. The company paid him each week the commission which he had earned in the preceding week: but they deducted a percentage of 2s. or 1s. in the pound so as to form a " retention fund ". This was to be available in case of the salesman defaulting on cash or machines. It was repayable to the salesman only after the determination of the agreement. The salesmen were not servants of the company, but independent contractors. They paid national insurance contributions on the footing that they were " self-employed " persons. The terms of appointment were contained in a printed agreement, which is too long for me to record in full, but I will refer to relevant portions when necessary.

In the middle of July, 1964, ominous rumblings were heard. Big cracks appeared in the Bloom edifice. The salesmen were anxious about their commission, which the company had retained in the " retention fund ". They tried to save it from being lost. Some of them held on to cash in their hands or stock still unsold. The question is whether they have the right to do so. The case of Mr. Cox, the defendant, has been taken as a test case. He had been engaged in the work for two or three years, and although he had been given notice of termination in May, 1964, that had been waived and he had continued in the engagement right up to the events hereinafter mentioned.

On July 16, 1964, the board of directors of the company were advised that the company was insolvent. On July 17, 1964, they resolved that the company and its subsidiaries be voluntarily wound up. They issued a statement to the press. The banks refused to honour the company's cheques. Everyone knew that the company was " on the rocks ". The position of the defendant on that day was as follows:

---

* WILLIAMS ON LAW AND PRACTICE IN BANKRUPTCY (17th Edn.) 288; 1 HALSBURY'S LAWS OF ENGLAND (3rd Edn.) 151, para. 361; 2 HALSBURY'S LAWS OF ENGLAND (3rd Edn.) 480-482, paras. 952, 953. *Astley* v. *Gurney*, [1869] L.R. 4 C.P. 714; *Re Vaughan, Ex p. Fletcher*, [1877] 6 Ch.D. 350.

	£	s.	d.
The company held in the " rentention fund " on his behalf	188	4	11
The company owed him commission on sales during the previous week (£57 15s.) for which it issued cheques on July 16 and 17, but these were dishonoured	57	15	0
	245	19	11

On the other hand, the defendant had sold in the previous
week two machines at prices of £40 19s. and £65 2s., for
which he had received cash £106 1s. (on which he was
entitled to commission of £5 10s.)   106   1   0

In addition he had in his possession a table-top for sale at a
price of £3 3s.   He also had seven tap-adaptors (not for
sale) which he used when fitting the machines.

After July 17, 1964, the defendant, like the other salesmen, claimed a lien on the
cash and goods in his hands.   The board of directors did not insist on his handing
them over.   In the last days of July, 1964, they sent a circular to all the salesmen
in these terms:

" The board has given anxious consideration to the position of the sales
representatives.
" In the present circumstances it is the directors' duty to collect and
safeguard the assets of the company pending its liquidation.   Accordingly,
whilst the board is not in a position to admit the validity of any lien which
sales representatives may claim over goods and/or cash now in their hands,
but must reserve all the company's legal rights, the board intends to take
no immediate steps to claim payment to the company of any moneys belonging to the company held by sales representatives *up to*, but not exceeding,
the *amount claimed* to be due to sales representatives in respect of retention
moneys and commission already earned, provided that all vehicles, machines,
equipment and cash in excess of the above-mentioned amount and unpaid
cheques in respect of commission are delivered with all possible speed [to
the company].   Sales representatives are particularly warned not to dispose
of any property of the company in their hands."

The defendant acted on that circular.   He sent in his account to the company
showing what was due to him.   On July 30, 1964, pursuant to s. 293 of the
Companies Act, 1948, the company gave notice of a meeting of creditors for
Aug. 27, 1964.   On Aug. 27, 1964, an extraordinary general meeting was held
at which an extraordinary resolution was passed that the company be wound up
voluntarily.   No notice of termination was given to the defendant, but no doubt
all parties treated the agreement as determined from that time.
The liquidator now claims that the defendant must pay over to him the
£106 1s. in full and also hand over the table-top and tap-adaptors which he has
in his possession: and that the defendant cannot set off the £245 19s. 11d.
which the company owes to him.   The liquidator says that the defendant
must prove in the liquidation for the £245 19s. 11d.   That would produce very
little.   The dividend may not be as much as 6d. in the pound.

1. *Lien*

The first point is whether the salesman has any lien on the money or goods in
his hands.   It was argued that the salesman was a factor at common law and as
such entitled to a general lien in respect of all lawful claims against his principal.
Now I am quite clear that these salesmen were not factors.   The usual characteristics of a factor are these.   He is an agent entrusted with the possession of
goods of several principals, or sometimes only one principal, for the purpose of

sale in his own name without disclosing the name of his principal and he is remunerated by a commission (see *Baring* v. *Corrie* (1) per ABBOTT, C.J.; *Stevens* v. *Biller* (2) per COTTON, L.J.). These salesmen lacked one of these characteristics. They did not sell in their own names, but in the name and on behalf of their principals, the company. They were agents pure and simple, and not factors. Even if they were factors, however, there is a written agreement which is inconsistent with any lien. It expressly provides that, on the determination of the agreement, " the agent shall forthwith deliver to the company all the goods . . . and shall account for the value of any goods not so returned ".

2. *Set-off*

The second point is whether there were mutual dealings such as to give the salesman a right of set-off. In this winding-up the law of bankruptcy applies (see s. 317 of the Companies Act, 1948). So we have to apply s. 31 of the Bankruptcy Act, 1914, which provides:

" Where there have been mutual credits, mutual debts or other mutual dealings, between a debtor against whom a receiving order shall be made under this Act and any other person proving or claiming to prove a debt under the receiving order, an account shall be taken of what is due from one party to the other in respect of such mutual dealings, and the sum due from the one party shall be set off against any sum due from the other party, and the balance of the account, and no more, shall be claimed or paid on either side respectively . . ."

In this case the money claims on each side seem to me to come clearly within the section. On the one hand, the salesman owed the company £106 1s., the proceeds of goods sold on their behalf. On the other hand, the company owed the salesman £245 19s. 11d. for commission, being as to £57 15s. for commission now due, and as to £188 4s. 11d. for commission retained in the " retention fund ". The " retention fund " was not payable at once. It was payable after the determination of the agreement—one-third after three months, one-third after six months, and the remaining third after nine months—but this future payment makes no difference. It is well settled that debts due in the future can be set-off against debts due at the present time (see *Young* v. *Bank of Bengal* (3) per LORD BROUGHAM; *Re Daintrey, Ex p. Mant and Mant* (4)).

Counsel for the company argued that the salesman received the moneys for a specific purpose, namely, to pay over to the company; and that moneys so received could not be set-off. I cannot accept this contention. When moneys are received for the very purpose of being handed over to the other party, they are properly the subject of set-off under the statute, so long as the dealings are mutual. Such was the case in *Naorosji* v. *Chartered Bank of India* (5). It is only when the dealings are not mutual that there is no set-off, as in *Re Mid-Kent Fruit Factory, Ltd.* (6) and *Re City Equitable Fire Insurance Co., Ltd. (No. 2)* (7). Here the dealings were clearly mutual.

Counsel for the company also argued that the agreement expressly provided that there was to be no set-off. The agent was to " pay over all moneys received by him " on Monday of each week: his commission " shall in no case be deductible by the agent from moneys received by him ": and " the agent shall not utilise his retention fund to off-set any moneys collected by him ". I cannot accept this contention either: for the simple reason that the parties cannot contract out of the statute. Where there are mutual dealings, the statute says that " the balance of the account, and no more, shall be claimed or paid on either side ". That is an absolute statutory rule which must be observed (see

---

(1) [1814-23] All E.R. Rep. 283 at pp. 285, 286.   (2) (1883), 25 Ch.D. 31 at p. 37.
(3) (1836), 1 Moo. P.C.C. 150 at pp. 164, 165.
(4) [1895-99] All E.R. Rep. 657; [1900] 1 Q.B. 546.
(5) (1868), L.R. 3 C.P. 444.   (6) [1896] 1 Ch. 567.
           (7) [1930] All E.R. Rep. 315; [1930] 2 Ch. 293.

Re Deveze, Ex p. Barnett (8) per LORD SELBORNE, L.C.). I hold, therefore, that there is a set-off in respect of the money claims.

I turn to the question of the goods; and here I must draw a distinction between goods held by the salesman to be sold by him (such as the table-top) and goods held by him to be used or worked on by him (such as the tap-adaptors). For this is a distinction established by the cases. It goes back to 1818 when the leading case of *Rose* v. *Hart* (9) was decided. Speaking of mutual credits, GIBBS, C.J., then said (10):

"... the legislature meant such *credits* only as must in their nature terminate in *debts*, as where a debt is due from one party, and credit given by him to the other for a sum of money payable at a future day, and which will then become a debt, or where there is a debt on one side, and a delivery of property with directions to turn it into money on the other; in such case the credit given by the delivery of the property must in its nature terminate in a debt, the balance will be taken on the two debts, and the words of the statutes will in all respects be complied with: but when there is a mere deposit of property, without any authority to turn it into money, no debt can ever arise out of it, and, therefore, it is not a credit within the meaning of the statute."

This distinction is illustrated by the decided cases. In *French* v. *Fenn* (11) (quoted in *Rose* v. *Hart* (9)) Cox entrusted Fenn with a string of pearls for sale and to pay over the proceeds. Cox then became bankrupt owing Fenn money. After the bankruptcy Fenn sold the pearls. Cox's assignees claimed that the proceeds should be paid to them in full. It was held that Fenn could keep the proceeds as a set-off against the debt owing to him by Cox. The reason was because these were mutual credits. Cox was in credit with Fenn for the sum receivable on sale of the pearls. Fenn was in credit with Cox for the money owing to him by Cox. In *Rose* v. *Hart* (9) itself, Smart sent some cloth to Hart, a fuller, for the purpose of being dressed. Smart already owed money to Hart on another account. Smart went bankrupt. After the bankruptcy, Smart's assignees demanded the cloth from Hart. Hart claimed to set-off the sums due to him from Smart on other accounts. He was not allowed to do so. He had to pay over the full value of the cloth, and only prove in the bankruptcy for the money owing to him. The reason was because there were no mutual credits. The cloth was entrusted to Hart for the purpose of being dressed, and not for turning into money. There are many other illustrations in the books.

On which side of the line does this case fall? Take the table-top. The company entrusted it to the salesman for sale, with authority to receive the proceeds and pay over the proceeds to them. That was clearly a giving of credit similar to that given in *French* v. *Fenn* (11) and *Palmer* v. *Day & Sons* (12). It was a giving of credit for the expected proceeds of sale. There were thus mutual credits: on the one hand, the company gave credit to the salesman for the expected proceeds of sale: on the other hand, the salesman gave credit to the company for the retention fund. Those mutual credits gave rise to a right of set-off on insolvency. And this right could not be taken away by the insolvent person at the last moment revoking the power of sale. The statute says: " Where there *have been* mutual credits ", an account shall be taken. That means when the mutual dealings *have been* such as to give rise to mutual credits, there is a right of set-off. The insolvent person cannot, by a last minute revocation, take away that right. In this case, therefore, the circular of July 24, 1964, did not take away the right of set-off. In any case it permitted him to retain cash and goods up to the amount of his retention fund and commission, and so extended

(8) (1874), 9 Ch. App. 293 at p. 295   (9) (1818), 8 Taunt. 499.
(10) (1818), 8 Taunt. at p. 506.   (11) (1783), 3 Doug. K.B. 257.
(12) [1895] 2 Q.B. 618.

the credit up to that amount. I hold, therefore, that the defendant had a right of set-off in respect of proceeds of sale of the table-top (sold at the authorised cash price) or, if it was not sold, for the value of it, taken at the authorised sale price.

Take last the tap-adaptors. These were never entrusted to the salesman for sale or to be turned into money. There can be no set-off in such circumstances (see *Eberle's Hotels & Restaurant Co., Ltd.* v. *Jonas* (13)).

I would, therefore, uphold the order of the judge in respect of the seven tap-adaptors. The salesman ought to return these or pay their value in full. I would reverse his order, however, as to the £106 1s. and the table-top, which should be valued at £3 3s. In my opinion the salesman is entitled to retain these as a set off against the £245 19s. 11d. which the company owes to him. I would allow the appeal accordingly.

DANCKWERTS, L.J.: Rolls Razor, Ltd. went into liquidation on Aug. 27, 1964, with the prospect of a very small dividend for the creditors. The defendant was one of the company's salesmen. These salesmen were not servants or employees of the company and do not rank as preferential creditors in the company's winding-up. He was supplied with a car or van and stock (washing machines) to sell. By the terms of his agreement with the company he had to account for moneys received and have his stock checked every Monday. He was engaged on a standard form of agreement. The company has in the possession of the liquidator moneys owing to the defendant which represent commission and a retention fund retained under the terms of the agreement. The defendant has in his hands moneys, which he has not yet handed over to the company, representing sales, and a table-top worth twelve shillings. This, however, is said to be a test case, and other salesmen are said to have much larger amounts of the company's goods, as well as moneys, in their possession. His Honour JUDGE BLOCK decided against the defendant, but he was under a misapprehension as to some of the facts, it seems. For the defendant, the case has been put in three ways:

(i) It is said that the defendant had a lien on the moneys and goods in his hands. There was discussion about whether he was a factor for the purposes of the Factors Act, 1889, but whether he was a factor or not, this ground in my view must fail, because the terms of the agreement are inconsistent with and exclude any lien for the benefit of the salesman.

(ii) The second ground depends on a right of set-off under s. 31 of the Bankruptcy Act, 1914, which is applied to companies in winding up by s. 317 of the Companies Act, 1948. Section 31 of the Bankruptcy Act, 1914, provides that when there have been mutual credits, mutual debts or other mutual dealings between a debtor (i.e., the company) and any other person proving or claiming to prove a debt, an account shall be taken of what is due from the one party to the other in respect of such mutual dealings, and the sum due from the one party shall be set off against any sum due from the other party, and the balance of the account and no more shall be claimed or paid on either side respectively. In the present case, in my view, the provisions of that section plainly apply between the defendant and the company in winding-up. There have been mutual dealings between him and the company which have resulted in the company owing money to the defendant and his owing money to the company. A question was raised whether the statutory set-off could be excluded by the terms of the agreement between the parties. The authorities are meagre on this point and not very clear, but in my opinion the statutory set-off, being a matter of statute, cannot be excluded. Accordingly, in my view the defendant is entitled to the benefit of the set-off so far as moneys owed by him to the company are concerned.

(iii) The third point raised was whether such a set-off could be applied to goods in the hands of the salesman or the proceeds of such goods when they had not been sold in the ordinary course of the operations of a salesman on behalf of the com-

(13) (1887), 18 Q.B.D. 459.

pany. Though trivial in the defendant's case, the point may well be of importance in the cases of other salesmen.

The position in respect of the goods has caused me more difficulty, but in the end I find myself in agreement with LORD DENNING, M.R., on this point. It is true, of course, that an agent cannot sell his principal's goods to himself, but in the present case the agent was entrusted with the goods for sale to the public, and if he sells the goods to the public he is debited with the price of the goods in the course of the mutual dealings between the company and the agent; i.e., the result is a sum of money. Clause 13 of the agreement (14) appears to recognise that on the determination of the agreement, the salesman may not return all the goods entrusted to him for sale and is to account for the value of any goods not so returned. The salesman cannot appropriate the goods to himself, but if he sells them to the public and accounts for the value to the company, the company suffers no loss and gets the full value on the accounting. I cannot see why this is not justified by cl. 13. The fact that it may give the salesman the advantage of a set-off in the winding-up of the company is not inconsistent. It is a statutory result imposed on the mutual dealings between the company and the salesman.

As regards the tap-adaptors, apparently the value is so trivial that I am not prepared to express an opinion in respect of them; and I am not clear about the facts. Presumably they were intended to enable a sale of a washing machine to be effected, and so incidental to the selling of washing machines to the public.

Accordingly, I would allow the appeal.

WINN, L.J.: Section 31 of the Bankruptcy Act, 1914, which provides for mutual credit and set-off in a bankruptcy and is applied by s. 317 of the Companies Act, 1948, to company liquidations, relates in terms to a situation " where there have been mutual credits, mutual debts or other mutual dealings . . .". It provides that in such a situation " an account shall be taken of what is due from one party to the other in respect of such mutual dealings . . .", and that only the balance due on the taking of such an account shall be claimed.

Notwithstanding the relative order in which the section refers first to " credits ", then to " debts ", and thirdly to " dealings ", I am of the opinion that the proper construction of the section and the true guide to its applicability to any particular set of circumstances involves placing emphasis primarily on the concept of mutual dealings and consequentially regarding the debts and credits referred to as such mutual debts and mutual credits as arise from mutual dealings: by the triple use of the word " mutual ", Parliament seems to me subtly to have indicated that mutuality is the dominant characteristic of the matters in respect of which it enacted this section.

What dealings are " mutual " within the meaning of the section appears to me to be determined by the intention of the parties to those dealings, expressed to each other or to be inferred from the character of the dealings. Thus, the relationship of banker and customer on a current account implies from its very nature an intention on the part of both parties that debits and credits arising between them shall be brought into a running account on which, by reason of the customary method of keeping such account, there will at any given moment be an outstanding debit or credit balance. Similarly, producers of such commodities as fruit and vegetables, who market them through selling agents in, for example, Covent Garden, normally, if not necessarily, deal with those selling agents on a running account in which credits in their favour will arise in respect of proceeds of sales received by the agents, with related debits for commissions and sale expenses incurred by the agents in disposing of the goods or making allowances for quality deficiencies. These are only examples which could be almost indefinitely multiplied by taking into consideration such other relationships as those of a landlord and his rent collectors, or transactions of collection of outstanding debts. The common and essential characteristic of all such dealings, which I regard as the type of

(14) For cl. 13, see p. 401, letter B, ante.

mutual dealings contemplated by the section, although many others less comprehensive and of shorter continuity would also be included, is that by the intention of the parties expressed or implied, they each extend to the other credit in respect of individual sums of money until such time as such sums are brought into account and in the account set off against other sums, in totality, in respect of which the other party has given credit: to be contrasted are dealings of a kind which may occur either in isolation or within the complex of a continuous run of dealings, which are themselves mutual, of such a kind that it is clear from their character that the parties intend that the monetary outcome of them shall be separately settled between the parties and not treated as a mere item on one side or the other of a running account.

It does not seem in any way inconsistent with such a relationship on mutual running account that in some cases the parties should provide that moneys accruing due from the one to the other should become payable at different dates from the dates on which the contra items should become payable. For example, it is usual for bankers to bring in overdraft interest which has accrued on current account only at intervals of six months. It occurs to me that in some cases suppliers of commodities may require to have their revolving capital replenished by the proceeds of sales of their commodities made through their agents at shorter intervals than those acceptable to the agents for having their commission and other trading expenses paid. Therefore, for my part I do not think that a contractual provision requiring one party to a running series of dealings to pay over moneys which come into his hands on behalf of the other party so soon as or within a limited time after they are received, is inconsistent with, though undoubtedly to some extent it militates against, a view that the dealings between them are mutual dealings within the meaning of the section; nor would I regard such a state of mutual dealings as negatived by further provisions (a) that the party so bound to pay over moneys received must pay them over in full without deducting commission earned in the transaction from which those moneys were derived, or (b) that some period of credit is given in respect of payment of commission so earned plus a right of retention, by way of security for general performance of obligations, in respect of part of the commission so earned.

It is in the light of these observations that, after close consideration of the written contract made between the parties to this appeal, and in particular (15) of cl. 3 (iv), cl. 4, cl. 7 (i), (iii) and (iv), cl. 8 (a) and (b), cl. 12 and cl. 13, I have formed the opinion that the dealings between the parties pursuant to that contract were mutual dealings and gave rise to mutual debts and credits such as are required by s. 31 of the Act of 1914 to be set off, with the result required by the provisions of the section. It is, of course, plain that by force of cl. 8 (c), the debt of the respondents for moneys retained by them as a retention fund out of commission earned is a debt solvendum in futuro, but this does not exclude set-off (cf., *Re Daintrey, Ex p. Mant and Mant* (16)).

The court has had the great advantage of careful and lucid submissions from both the learned leading counsel who have appeared in this appeal. I trust that neither of them will think that I am unappreciative of their arguments or of the thorough analyses which they have made of the numerous authorities to which they referred the court, if I say that I have not found any of those decisions inconsistent with the view which I have ventured to express of the essential character of mutual dealings and of the distinction between general and specific accountability. I have endeavoured to distinguish obligations to pay over specifically moneys derived from isolated special transactions, on the one hand, and obligations generally to meet running balances, on the other.

In my judgment it is clear that there can be no right of set-off where the claim on one side is for the return of goods in specie and on the other side to pay moneys, since there is no recognition in our law of a concept of credit, properly so called,

---

(15) For the clauses referred to, see p. 399, letter G, to p. 401, letter B, ante.
(16) [1895-99] All E.R. Rep. 657; [1900] 1 Q.B. 546.

in respect of delivery of goods (cf., *Eberle's Hotels & Restaurant Co., Ltd.* v. *Jonas,* (17)). On the other hand, such a right does exist where there is a debt on one side and a delivery of property with directions to turn it into money, on the other (cf. *Naorosji* v. *Chartered Bank of India* (18)); this latter right in my opinion can exist only where the conversion of the goods into money has been effected before the authority to make it has been withdrawn.

In the instant case the company employed the defendant and a number of other men—perhaps some four hundred or more in all—as salesmen of their washing machines and other domestic utilities on terms, broadly speaking, that the employers would provide each of the agents with a stock of goods for sale and a vehicle in which they could be taken from house to house and demonstrated and offered either for cash or on hire-purchase terms. When hire-purchase transactions were entered into, the employers would, of course, deal with all resulting monetary arrangements direct with the finance company. Where, however, sales were effected for cash, paid wholly or in part to the agent, he was obliged by the contract of employment to pay over all moneys received on the Monday of the following week without deducting commission, but was entitled to be paid his commission once a week subject to the provision for retention already mentioned which is provided for in cl. 8 of the agreement. All goods in hand had to be produced for inspection and checking at a branch office once a week, and it was expressly provided by cl. 13 that on the determination of the agreement, the agent should forthwith deliver to the company all goods still in his hands. The last mentioned clause was worded, so far as relevant, as follows:

" On the determination of this agreement the agent shall forthwith deliver to the company all the goods . . . entrusted to him by the company and shall account for the value of any goods not so returned."

It was submitted by counsel for the defendant that the words quoted afforded the agent an option to retain goods on accounting for their value; for my part I am quite unable to accept this submission as a matter of construction of the words, since it seems to me they are quite incapable of conveying the meaning that he should be entitled to buy for himself goods which he had undertaken by cl. 3 (ii) of the contract to sell " only to members of the public ". It would be unusual, and in my opinion in the absence of express provision inadmissible, that an agent should buy his principal's goods for his own purposes.

Prior to the determination of the agreement between the company and the defendant, which occurred on a date not very precisely ascertainable within the period between July 20 and July 30, 1964, the defendant had sold two washing machines to customers for which he had received a total of £106 1s. If he had complied strictly with the contract, he should have paid over this sum by July 20, in fact he has never paid it over, nor did he return a table-top worth some 12s., and half-a-dozen tap-adaptors of negligible value: at the determination of the contract the appellant was entitled to commission on the two sales mentioned of £5 10s. and to other unpaid commission, in total £63 5s.

Applying the observations made earlier in this judgment to those circumstances, I am of the opinion that the sum of £106 1s. mentioned falls to be set-off against the total amount due, or falling due within the period of nine months following the determination of the contract, from the company to the defendant in respect of commission earned, whether or not retained pursuant to cl. 8 of the contract: I do not think that any set-off arises in relation to goods in the hands of the defendant at the determination of the contract or their monetary value, because, when they were delivered to him, it was not *then certain* that they would be turned into money in accordance with the contract; *a fortiori* there could be no set-off in respect of the proceeds of goods sold by any agent after the determination of the contract of that agent. These are the answers which I give to the

(17) (1887), 18 Q.B.D. 459.
(18) (1868), L.R. 3 C.P. 444.

second and third of the three questions posed by counsel for the defendant on this appeal.

Counsel for the defendant also raised a question whether the agents who were selling on behalf of the company in the manner described were factors possessing a factor's lien over goods the property of the respondents which came into their hands with authority to sell them or over the proceeds of sales made with the authority of the respondents. He referred the court to the provisions of the Factors Act, 1889, but for my part I am unable to see that the Act of 1889 has any relevance whatsoever in the present case. The Act of 1889 does not define factors, nor mercantile agents, but on its true construction refers to and gives statutory effect to dealings of a certain category of persons who, ex hypothesi, are mercantile agents. Whether or not a trader or dealer is a mercantile agent, or being a mercantile agent is also a factor, is in my opinion, as was submitted by counsel for the company, to be determined by that part of the common law which is properly to be called the law merchant. It is by custom of the business or mercantile world, established in any given case by evidence, that a court has to be informed whether a particular class of trader or dealer is a factor: no such evidence was given in this case and there is, therefore, no support for a proposition, which in any case I should have found most surprising, that travelling salesmen are, by reason of their possession of goods belonging to their employers, factors, with all the special characteristics, derived from status, not from contract, which appertain to a class of dealers to which it is relatively unlikely in modern times that there will be any additions.

Finally, I would say that even if it had been established that the defendant was a factor, a factor's lien can be negatived by contract, and I am of the opinion that the provisions of the contract in the instant case would have excluded any such lien.

For these reasons it is my view that this appeal should be allowed in part, that is to say, with respect only to the sum of money held by the defendant at the time of the determination of the contract.

C. H. L. Bathurst: It has been held by the majority that there is a right to set-off the value of the table-top against the money in hand. LORD DENNING has indicated in his judgment that the table-top was something which was for sale for £3 3s. At the time when the order for return was made against the defendant it was worth only 12s. Can your lordships indicate whether the right to set-off is a right to set-off against the present value or the value at the time at which the defendant was authorised to sell.

[The court conferred.]

LORD DENNING, M.R.: The value will be the cash value at which the defendant was authorised to sell it.

Appeal allowed in part. Leave to appeal to the House of Lords refused.

Solicitors: *Peacock & Goddard*, agents for *Willmot & East*, Poole (for the defendant); *Ashurst, Morris, Crisp & Co.* (for the plaintiff company).

[*Reported by* F. GUTTMAN, ESQ., *Barrister-at-Law.*]

WOODMAN v. WOODMAN.

[Probate, Divorce and Admiralty Division (Sir Jocelyn Simon, P., and Karminski, J.), October 4, 1966.]

Divorce—Appeal—Divisional Court—Jurisdiction—Application for re-hearing —Refusal of trial judge to grant adjournment—Whether error of court— Matrimonial Causes Rules, 1957 *(S.I.* 1957 *No.* 619)*, r.* 36 (1).

The husband, whose wife was petitioning for divorce on the ground of his adultery, applied for legal aid to defend the suit. This was refused by the local committee as was an appeal to the local area committee. The case came on as an undefended suit. The husband appeared in person at the hearing and applied for an adjournment to defend the suit. The trial judge refused the application and granted a decree nisi to the wife. On an application by the husband under r. 36 (1)* of the Matrimonial Causes Rules, 1957, to set aside the decree nisi and for a re-hearing,

Held: the application must be refused, because the Divisional Court had jurisdiction under s. 36 (1) to hear an application only where no error of the court below was alleged, and an allegation that the trial judge wrongly exercised his discretion to grant or refuse an adjournment was alleging an error of the court (see p. 411, letters B and G).

Application dismissed.

[As to applications for re-hearing, see 12 Halsbury's Laws (3rd Edn.) 425, 426, para. 954; and for cases on the subject, see 27 Digest (Repl.) 595-598, 5571-5593.

For the Matrimonial Causes Rules, 1957, r. 36, see 10 Halsbury's Statutory Instruments (2nd Re-Issue) 248.]

Case referred to:

Maxwell v. Keun, [1927] All E.R. Rep. 335; [1928] 1 K.B. 645; 97 L.J.K.B. 305; 138 L.T. 310; 30 Digest (Repl.) 149, *32.*

Application.

This was an application by the husband for an extension of time to apply under r. 36 (1) of the Matrimonial Causes Rules, 1957, to set aside a decree nisi granted to the wife by His Honour Judge Elder-Jones, sitting as a Special Commissioner, at Gloucester Assizes on July 15, 1966, and to have the suit re-heard. The facts are set out in the judgment of Sir Jocelyn Simon, P.

The husband appeared in person.

G. B. Hutton for the wife.

SIR JOCELYN SIMON, P.: This is an application by the husband, the respondent to a divorce suit, who appears before us in person, for an extension of time to apply under r. 36 (1) of the Matrimonial Causes Rules, 1957, to set aside a decree nisi obtained against him and to have the suit re-heard. All that I need say of the background of the case is this. He applied for legal aid in order to defend a divorce suit brought against him by his wife on the ground of his alleged incestuous adultery. That application for legal aid was refused by the local committee and an appeal against the refusal was rejected by the area legal aid committee. In the result the case came before His Honour Judge Elder-Jones, sitting as a special commissioner of this court, on July 15, 1966, the formal juridical position being that the petition was undefended at that stage. The husband applied for an adjournment in order that he might defend himself against the charges made against him. The commissioner, in what seems to me to be unquestionably his discretion in the matter, refused that application, proceeded to hear the wife's evidence and granted her a decree nisi.

---

* Rule 36 (1), so far as material, provides: " An application for re-hearing of a cause heard by a judge alone where no error of the court at the hearing is alleged shall be made to a Divisional Court . . ."

The husband was then officially advised to apply, if he was aggrieved, to this court under r. 36 of the Matrimonial Causes Rules, 1957 (1) for a re-hearing. Unfortunately, in my view, that advice was not correct. This court has jurisdiction under that rule to hear an application only where no error of the court below is alleged. It seems to me that an allegation that a judge wrongly exercised his discretion to grant or refuse an adjournment is alleging an error of the court: see, for example, *Maxwell* v. *Keun* (2). That being so, the jurisdiction to set aside the decree and to order a new trial lies in the Court of Appeal and not in this court; and we should be encroaching on the jurisdiction of the Court of Appeal were we to entertain such an application. Moreover, I think that it inevitably follows that the court which has jurisdiction to hear the application must be the court to grant an extension of time to hear it, if so advised. That being so this application should not have been made to this court but to the Court of Appeal.

In ordinary circumstances all I think that would be called for would be to dismiss this application. Unfortunately, the erroneous course which the husband has taken was as a result of advice given to him by an official of the court. In those circumstances, it struck me, when I first saw the papers, that, if the preliminary view which I then took of the law proved to be correct, merely to dismiss the application would, or might, amount to a denial of justice to the husband, or alternatively impose a delay on the wife in making the decree absolute which would amount to an injustice on her. I have, therefore, ascertained from Lord Denning, M.R., and Willmer, L.J., that Willmer, L.J.'s division of the Court of Appeal will hear this application at two o'clock today, if the husband wishes to make it there. Counsel for the wife has put this court in his debt by outlining very fairly the facts of this case, and it may be that he will be required to give a similar service to the Court of Appeal, as well as to indicate to them the reasons which have animated us in dismissing this application. In my view, the application must stand dismissed, the only order of this court being that the decree shall not be made absolute until the husband has had an opportunity of applying to the Court of Appeal at two o'clock today.

KARMINSKI, J.: I agree, and only want to add a few words because of the relative importance of this point. Rule 36 (1) of the Matrimonial Causes Rules, 1957, says in terms that, where no error of the court at the hearing is alleged, the application shall be made to the Divisional Court of this Division. In fact, as I understand the husband's case, his complaint is that the learned commissioner, His Honour Judge Elder-Jones, sitting at Gloucester, wrongly exercised his discretion in refusing to grant the husband an adjournment so that he could put his own case in order and defend the allegations which were made against him in the wife's petition. His complaint then is that there was an error in the court itself. Whether that complaint is well founded or not is not a matter which we have at present to consider, but I agree absolutely with Sir Jocelyn Simon, P., that the proper course here is to go to the court having jurisdiction in this case, namely, the Court of Appeal. Happily that can be done without a great loss of time, in fact later today.

I agree with the order proposed by Sir Jocelyn Simon, P.

Application dismissed accordingly.

[Later the same day, the Court of Appeal (Willmer, Harman and Salmon, L.JJ.), heard the application, gave leave to appeal out of time, rescinded the decree nisi, and ordered the suit to be re-heard.]

Solicitors: *Lapage, Norris Sons & Saleby*, Stroud (for the wife).

[*Reported by* Alice Bloomfield, *Barrister-at-Law.*]

---

(1) S.I. 1957 No. 619.
(2) [1927] All E.R. Rep. 335; [1928] 1 K.B. 645.

WALKER *v.* WALKER.

[PROBATE, DIVORCE AND ADMIRALTY DIVISION (Sir Jocelyn Simon, P., and Karminski, J.), October 5, 1966.]

Magistrates—Appeal—Conduct of proceedings in court below impugned— Affidavit tendered on appeal to establish relevant fact—Copy should be served on clerk to justices.

Magistrates—Procedure—Adjournment—Review by appellate court of exercise of discretion by justices—Summons by wife alleging cruelty and desertion— Application by husband to adjourn hearing—Husband unable to attend on date fixed, being sent abroad for twelve months on business—Adjournment refused—Finding of desertion on wife's uncontradicted evidence—Injustice to husband in that his side of case not heard—Re-hearing ordered.

Magistrates—Procedure—Evidence—Employers' letter showing arrangements for employee litigant to go abroad on business—Receivable on application for adjournment—Evidence Act, 1938 (1 & 2 Geo. 5 c. 28), s. 1.

The husband and wife finally separated on Mar. 20, 1966, after a quarrel. Only they were present together on that occasion. On Apr. 15, 1966, the wife took out a summons against the husband alleging desertion, cruelty and wilful neglect to maintain her. The return date was May 15, 1966. The husband was due to travel to India on Apr. 26, 1966, on his employers' business. He was anxious to defend the summons and before his departure sought through his solicitors to have the hearing expedited, but he failed. At the adjourned hearing on May 24, 1966, the husband's solicitors applied for an adjournment on the ground of the husband's departure on Apr. 26. The justices refused the application, the objection put forward on behalf of the wife being that the husband would be away for a year and that no provision had been made for her maintenance in his absence. On the evidence of the wife, who alone gave evidence, the justices found the husband guilty of constructive desertion.

Held: since refusal of the adjournment had resulted in serious injustice to the husband, in that his side of the case had not been heard, but an adjournment would not have prejudiced the wife as an interim order in respect of her maintenance could have been made, the court would review the justices' exercise of their discretion; a rehearing of the suit would be ordered, and in the meantime an interim order for the wife's maintenance would be made (see p. 414, letters D and I, and p. 415, letter B, post).

Maxwell v. *Keun* ([1927] All E.R. Rep. 335) applied.

Per SIR JOCELYN SIMON, P.: (a) where the conduct of proceedings by justices is impugned on appeal, a copy of an affidavit to be tendered as evidence on appeal as to a fact relevant to that aspect of the appeal and not apparent from the justices' note should be served on the clerk to the justices as well as on the respondent's solicitors (compare p. 413, letter F, post).

(b) it would have been proper for the justices to have received in evidence under s. 1 of the Evidence Act, 1938, a letter to the husband from his employers showing the arrangements made for the husband's departure to India on Apr. 26, 1966, rather than that the expense and delay of calling the export manager should have been incurred (see p. 413, letters H and I, post).

[As to justices' power of adjournment, see 25 HALSBURY'S LAWS (3rd Edn.) 198, 199, para. 360; and as to appeal against a refusal to adjourn, see 30 ibid., p. 416, para. 783, note (*f*); and for cases on adjournment, see DIGEST (Practice) 556-558, *2156-2171.*

As to interim orders for maintenance, see SUPPLEMENT to title DIVORCE, 12 HALSBURY'S LAWS (3rd Edn.) para. 1087B.

For the Evidence Act, 1938, s. 1, see 9 Halsbury's Statutes (2nd Edn.) 626. For the Matrimonial Proceedings (Magistrates' Courts) Act, 1960, s. 6, see 40 Halsbury's Statutes (2nd Edn.) 407.]

Cases referred to:

Bond v. Bond, [1964] 3 All E.R. 346; [1965] 2 W.L.R. 1008; 128 J.P. 568; 3rd Digest Supp.

Maxwell v. Keun, [1927] All E.R. Rep. 335; [1928] 1 K.B. 645; 97 L.J.K.B. 305; 138 L.T. 310; Digest (Practice) 558, *2169*.

Appeal.

This was an appeal by the husband, George Walker, against a decision of the Blackburn and Church justices, dated May 24, 1966, refusing to adjourn the hearing of a summons issued by the wife alleging desertion, persistent cruelty and wilful neglect to maintain on the part of the husband. The facts are set out in the judgment of Sir Jocelyn Simon, P.

M. R. Hickman for the husband.
J. Mulcahy and *L. Gretton* for the wife.

SIR JOCELYN SIMON, P.: The parties were married in 1955 and there are two children, aged nine and three. The parties separated after what, on the wife's evidence, was a serious quarrel on Mar. 20, 1966; and on Apr. 15, 1966, the wife took out a summons alleging that her husband had deserted her on Mar. 20, and had been guilty of persistent cruelty and of wilful neglect to maintain her. He had in fact been maintaining the two children, but had declined to maintain the wife after the separation. The return date on the summons was May 15, 1966. On receipt of the summons the husband consulted solicitors; and it is uncontroverted that he at all times desired to answer these serious charges made against him. On Mar. 28, 1966, the husband's solicitors learned that the husband was under injunction from his employers to travel to India in connexion with a contract which they (or an associated company) had there. I get that fact from an affidavit sworn by the husband's solicitor and receivable exceptionally by this court in accordance with the principles laid down in *Bond* v. *Bond*. (1). (Nevertheless, where, as here, the conduct of the court below is impugned, such an affidavit ought to be served not only on the solicitors to the respondent to the appeal but also on the clerk to the justices.) On hearing that the husband was due to go abroad, his solicitor communicated the information to the clerk to the justices and to the wife's solicitors, and tried to arrange that the hearing should be expedited. That, however, could not be done, or at least was not done; and we have no evidence before us which would enable us to review the administrative arrangements in the court appealed from, even if it were a matter for us, which I very much doubt. In the event, the hearing was adjourned from May 15 to May 24; but in the meantime, on Apr. 26, the husband left England for India, and he is still out of the jurisdiction.

When the case came on on May 24, the husband's solicitor applied for an adjournment. He produced a letter dated Apr. 19, 1966, addressed to the husband by his employers which shows at any rate that the employers had made detailed arrangements as early as that date for the husband's departure for India by air on Apr. 26. However, we are told, and it is agreed, that the justices would not look at that document; although we are given no reason why they should not have done so. In my view, they would have had the right to receive it under the Evidence Act, 1938. It is true that that would be a matter for their discretion, since the writer of the letter could have been called to give the information contained therein and, indeed, further information if required; however, I should have thought that the reasonable exercise of the court's discretion in such circumstances would be to receive a letter of that sort, rather than to incur the expense and delay of the attendance of an export manager of

(1) [1964] 3 All E.R. 346 at p. 348.

one of the leading firms of machinery makers.   The justices, as I have said, would not receive that letter, and the wife's solicitor told the justices that his instructions would not permit him to agree to an adjournment even on terms. That is slightly further spelt out in the justices' reasons.   They evidently understood that the objection of the wife's solicitor was that the husband would be abroad for about twelve months; and that, although some provision had been made for the maintenance of the children during his absence (the offer actually amounted to the same sum as the justices ultimately ordered for the children), no provision had been made for the maintenance of the wife.

It is conceded on behalf of the husband, and in my view is unquestionable, that, whether or not to grant an adjournment was at the discretion of the court asked to grant the adjournment.   However, we have authoritative guidance from the Court of Appeal in *Maxwell* v. *Keun* (2) to a two-fold effect: first, where the refusal of an adjournment would result in a serious injustice to the party requesting the adjournment, the adjournment should be refused only if that is the only way that justice can be done to the other party; and, secondly, that although the granting or refusal of an adjournment is a matter of discretion, if an appellate court is satisfied that the discretion has been exercised in such a way as would result in an injustice to one of the parties, the appellate court has both the power and the duty to review the exercise of the discretion.

I am quite satisfied that, in the present case, the refusal of the adjournment has resulted in a serious injustice to the husband, in that his side of the case has not been heard.   The justices, although not adjudicating on the charges of wilful neglect to maintain or persistent cruelty, made a finding on the wife's evidence (which was necessarily, in the circumstances that I have described, uncontradicted) that the husband had constructively deserted her.   That is a serious charge to have been found proved.   Since it was accepted that the husband had requested the wife to return to cohabitation, the justices' finding amounts to this, that the husband's misconduct has been so grave and weighty that the wife was entitled to refuse to entertain his overtures for a reconciliation. Moreover, the finding might constitute an estoppel in subsequent proceedings between the parties in a court of summary jurisdiction.

I, therefore, turn to the other limb, and ask myself whether it was necessary to refuse an adjournment because that was the only way in which justice could be done to the wife.   Counsel for the wife, in his careful argument, says that she could have been prejudiced in two ways if the justices had acceded to the husband's application: first, only an interim order for maintenance could have been made, to last only for three months, so that the wife would then have had to return to the court to have it renewed—if the husband were away for twelve months, possibly on three occasions; and secondly, her evidence might be stale when the case did come to be heard.   As for this second proposition, that was not an argument adduced to the court by the wife's solicitor in opposing the application to adjourn, and I have no reason to think that there is anything in it. In fact, the wife was the only witness to give evidence on her behalf, and the final separation, on the circumstances of which so much turned, took place with only the husband and wife present.   With regard to the first alleged ground of prejudice to the wife, nowhere in their reasons do the justices show themselves aware of their power to have made an interim order under s. 6 of the Matrimonial Proceedings (Magistrates' Courts) Act, 1960; although it appears from the solicitor's affidavit that he reminded them of it.   In my view, it was open to the justices to have acceded to the husband's application, to have received from the wife evidence of the husband's means (supplemented if necessary by evidence from his employers) and then to have made an interim order for the same amount as the final order which they made.   In those circumstances, I cannot see that the wife could have suffered any injustice from acceding to the

---

(2) [1927] All E.R. Rep. 335; [1928] 1 K.B. 645.

husband's application.   As against that, as I have said, it seems to me to be a serious injustice to the husband to have made such a finding against him when, on the material before us, he was reasonably abroad in pursuance of the terms of his employment and, indeed, to the financial advantage of the family as a whole.

Under those circumstances, I hold that we have not only the right but, as the Court of Appeal said, the duty to review the discretion of the justices and to order a re-hearing of this case, in the meantime making an interim order.

KARMINSKI, J.: I agree and only want to add a very few words of my own, because we are doing what every appellate court must be careful of doing, that is dealing with the discretion of another court on the question of an adjournment of a trial.   It has been said often that any appellate court must be very careful before it takes such a course.   In this case, however, I have not any doubt that the effect of the refusal of the justices to grant an adjournment was of the kind mentioned by Atkin, L.J., in *Maxwell* v. *Keun* (3), likely to defeat the rights of a party and to destroy them altogether.   In *Maxwell* v. *Keun* (3), the plaintiff, who was a lieutenant-colonel in command of a British battalion in India, was unable to get back in time to attend the hearing of his libel action. Lord Hewart, C.J., had refused to grant him an adjournment.   It was made clear by the Court of Appeal that, if that refusal stood, the plaintiff would be unable to prosecute his claim, with the result that there must be judgment for the defendants.   In the same way in this case, though the circumstances of the husband's sojourn in India were of a different kind, the order made by the justices refusing an adjournment made it almost certain that the uncontroverted evidence of the wife would, in all probability, prevail, as in fact it did.   I do not pretend to prophesy what may be the result if and when the husband's case is fully presented to the court.   In *Maxwell* v. *Keun* (4) it is interesting to learn from the footnote to the report that the plaintiff there, having returned in due course to the adjourned hearing, got £1,000 damages in the first action.   The second action was settled for an agreed sum.   I repeat that I have no idea whether the husband in this case is likely to be successful.   The present situation is that he has been, in my view, wrongly deprived of the opportunity of putting forward his case at all.

I agree with the order proposed by Sir Jocelyn Simon, P.

SIR JOCELYN SIMON, P.: Then we set aside the order of the justices and remit the case for re-hearing before a different panel.   Interim maintenance £2 5s. for each child and £2 a week for the wife.   Interim custody to the wife. I think that, in all the circumstances of this case, the fair order would be no order as to costs.

Order accordingly.

Solicitors: *Gamlen, Bowerman & Forward*, agents for *Simpson & Ashworth*, Accrington (for the husband); *Pritchard, Englefield, Leader & Henderson*, agents for *Reddish, Heys & Ranson*, Accrington (for the wife).

[*Reported by* Alice Bloomfield, *Barrister-at-Law.*]

---

(3) [1927] All E.R. Rep. 335;   [1928] 1 K.B. 645.
(4) [1928] 1 K.B. at p. 659.

KACZMARZ v. KACZMARZ (by her Guardian).

[PROBATE, DIVORCE AND ADMIRALTY DIVISION (Cairns, J.), October 26, 1966.]

Divorce—Desertion—Intention—Capability of respondent spouse to have animus deserendi—Delusions—Wife suffering from chronic schizophrenia—Continuance of intention—Matrimonial Causes Act 1965 (c. 72), s. 1 (2).

The parties were married on Aug. 28, 1954. There was intercourse between them for the first time on Sept. 4, 1954, in the evening. At midnight the wife became hysterical, and she was admitted to a mental hospital, where she was practically unconscious for the first few weeks. She was suffering from chronic schizophrenia. She remained in hospital for four weeks and then convalesced for about six weeks, but did not live with the husband. In November, 1954, she was re-admitted to the mental hospital and remained continuously in hospital until December, 1964. She suffered from delusions and, having religious convictions, felt that she and the husband had sinned together by having intercourse after marriage. In December, 1964, she was allowed out of hospital on leave, but did not go to live with the husband. At Christmas, 1964, when he visited her, she made it clear that she did not want him any more. She was re-admitted to a mental hospital in December, 1965, where she had been ever since. Between 1957 and 1960, she wrote several letters to the husband which showed that it was her intention to remain permanently separated from the husband. In an answer (filed on her behalf by her guardian ad litem) to a petition for divorce by the husband on the ground of her desertion, she alleged that at all material times she was suffering from a mental illness and was unable to form the necessary intention of staying with the husband or leaving him.

Held: (i) on the evidence, having regard particularly to the wife's letters between 1957 and 1960 and her conduct at Christmas, 1964, which together were sufficient to displace any presumption that there might be that a patient suffering from chronic schizophrenia was incapable of forming animus deserendi, the wife had been proved to have had the necessary intention to constitute desertion in October, 1957, and in January, 1960 (see p. 423, letters D and F, post); desertion, having once begun, continued under s. 1 (2)* of the Matrimonial Causes Act 1965 (see p. 422, letter C, post); and accordingly the court would grant a decree of divorce to the husband (see p. 423, letter H, post).

(ii) moreover, if a wife without insane delusions had reasonable cause to believe that her husband had committed a grave sin (not being a matrimonial offence) or that she had joined with him in committing such a sin, that would not constitute reasonable cause for her leaving him and thus entitle her to bring the marriage to an end, and neither, therefore, would a delusion to the same effect constitute such cause (see p. 423, letter A, post).

Perry v. *Perry* ([1963] 3 All E.R. 766) distinguished.

[As to the effect of insanity on desertion, see 12 HALSBURY'S LAWS (3rd Edn.) 255, 256, para. 478; and for cases on the subject, see 27 DIGEST (Repl.) 359, 2968-2974.

For the Matrimonial Causes Act 1965, s. 1, see 45 HALSBURY'S STATUTES (2nd Edn.) 445.]

Cases referred to:

Crowther v. *Crowther*, [1951] 1 All E.R. 1131; [1951] A.C. 723; 27 Digest (Repl.) 359, 2974.

Perry v. *Perry*, [1963] 3 All E.R. 766; [1964] 1 W.L.R. 91; Digest (Cont. Vol. A) 720, 2791a.

---

* Section 1 (2), so far as material, is set out at p. 421, letter H, post.

Petition.

This was a petition by the husband for divorce on the ground of the wife's desertion. The wife, by an answer filed on her behalf by the Official Solicitor as her guardian ad litem, denied the alleged desertion and said that, at the material times, she was suffering from mental illness, namely, chronic schizophrenia, and was unable to form the necessary intention of staying with the husband or leaving him. The facts are set out in the judgment.

F. E. Beezley for the husband.

A. B. Hollis for the wife.

CAIRNS, J.: This is a husband's petition for divorce, on the ground of his wife's desertion, the husband praying for the exercise of the court's discretion notwithstanding his own adultery. The wife, by an answer filed on her behalf by the Official Solicitor as her guardian ad litem, denies the alleged desertion and says that, at the material times, she was suffering from mental illness, namely, chronic schizophrenia, and was unable to form the necessary intention of staying with her husband, or leaving him. The sole issue that I have to try in this case is whether at the material times her mental capacity was such as to enable her to form that intention, because the position was this—she was for considerable periods in hospital, receiving treatment for mental illness and, because she was there, she was at least temporarily separated from her husband. Whilst she was there, she wrote letters expressing the wish to have nothing more to do with the husband and, after she had left the hospital, she did not return to live with him. It is accepted by counsel for the wife that, when she expressed the wish not to live with her husband any longer, if at that time she was mentally capable of forming the intention to desert, then there was desertion. The factum was present inasmuch as she was in hospital, separate from her husband; the animus was present unless by reason of mental illness the animus could not exist. As both counsel have said, it is a distressing and a difficult case. It has been argued on both sides most helpfully with moderation and good sense, and my mind has fluctuated greatly in the course of the evidence and of the arguments. I may say at this point that the conclusion which I have reached is that desertion is established, but in order to justify that conclusion, in the circumstances of this case it is, I think, necessary to deal with the evidence rather fully.

The parties were both Polish by birth. The husband came to this country in September, 1946. He has lived here ever since, working as a painter and decorator. I am satisfied that he has no intention of ever returning to Poland. He is now a naturalised Englishman and I accept that he has established a domicil in this country. He was married to the wife on Aug. 28, 1954. There are no children of the family. Before the marriage the husband had lived at a hostel at Fairford in Gloucestershire, which is a hostel for Polish people. Before the marriage he had booked hotel rooms at Weston-super-Mare for a honeymoon. However, on the wedding day the wife said that she did not want to go to Weston-super-Mare then, giving as a reason that she was menstruating, and on that first night of the marriage they both slept at the hostel, but in different rooms. The next morning, it being a Sunday, they went to church. The parties are Roman Catholics, and it is evident from what the husband told me in the witness box and from the wife's letters that she is a sincere member of that faith and, indeed, that she feels very strongly on religious matters. In some respects her attitude to religion would appear to be somewhat unbalanced, no doubt because of the mental trouble that she has had, but of the sincerity of her religious convictions there is no reason to have any doubt.

On the Sunday morning, the day after the marriage, the husband says that their conversation was normal, but in fact the wife had decided that she did not want to go to Weston-super-Mare with him and they did not have a honeymoon at all. On the following Saturday, Sept. 4, 1954, they got ready to go back to

Gloucester, where at that time the husband was employed. They went by bus, and he said that the wife was very distressed on the bus and was praying all the time. She was in doubt whether he would be a good husband. They went to his flat in Gloucester, staying there for about three hours during the evening, and there they had sexual intercourse for the first time. He said that, after it, she was shaking and said that she would not stay there any longer. He took her to another flat (I think of some friend) in Gloucester, and that night at about midnight she was hysterical and shouting, calling him " the devil " and so forth and wanting a priest. He, however, sent for a doctor, who gave her an injection. She was quiet for five or ten minutes but, after the doctor had left, she started to behave in the same way as before and the husband had her taken to Horton Road Hospital in Gloucester. There are apparently two hospitals dealing with mental patients in Gloucester, or, as I think is the correct way to put it, there is one hospital with two buildings, one being in Horton Road and the other being in Coney Hill. It was to the Horton Road branch that she first went and she was in hospital then for three or four weeks. The husband said that she was practically unconscious for the first few weeks. She stayed there until Oct. 6, 1954. During that time he visited her about twice a week and, after she had regained consciousness, she could recognise him and said to him more than once, " Why do you come here, you devil? "

After she came out of hospital in October, 1954, she went to the Fairford hostel to convalesce. She had an aunt in the hostel and stayed with her. The husband returned to Gloucester, where his work was, but he visited her about once a week, and at first he thought that she was looking better, but when he saw her she would become moody and sometimes ignore him. They did, however, have sexual intercourse more than once at the hostel. She improved in the first week that she was there but afterwards got worse and worse. He tried to re-assure her and said that he was saving money to get them a house, but she was not interested and showed a dislike of him and did not want to discuss the house at all. She was readmitted to hospital on Nov. 26, 1954. After that she stayed continuously in Horton Road to start with and afterwards Coney Hill up to December, 1964, when she was allowed out on leave to stay with her brother. She was discharged on Dec. 21, 1964, but she was re-admitted to the hospital on Dec. 17, 1965, and is still there today.

Going back to the end of 1954, when she had been readmitted to hospital, the husband said that he visited her once a week while he was working at Gloucester. She was reserved and not very pleasant, but sometimes she was better and then he tried to encourage her with promises of a better future, but she was not very interested. He said that he wrote to her about once or twice a week whilst she was in reasonably good health, but only a small number of letters that she wrote to him have been preserved and apparently none of the letters that he wrote to her. I shall be referring to her letters to him later. In August, 1955, the husband left Gloucester and went to live in London, and after that he visited her about once a month. During the last year that she was in hospital up to December, 1964, he said that she behaved oddly to him and there was no co-operation.

I now come to the letters that have survived and which are of great importance in this case. The first one was a letter which she wrote probably in 1957, but the exact date is not known, and which she began by saying,

" I am writing to you a few words to give you the news that I am in fact pregnant but the child is not yours, it will be only mine."

Then, after saying something about his parentage, she named somebody apparently as being the father of the child which she said she was carrying. The only importance of that letter is that there was no truth whatever in the suggestion that she was pregnant either by the husband or by anybody else. There had been no opportunity, indeed, for her to conceive a child at that time and it would seem probable and consistent with the doctor's evidence (to which I shall refer later) that this idea that she was pregnant was a pure delusion. Nothing more was heard of it. Then comes a very important letter from her dated Oct. 27, 1957, which the husband relies on as being the root of the desertion, and it is in these terms:

> " Wladek [that was his Christian name], the greetings which you sent me did not mean much to me, for you have written something which upset me very much. But do not let that worry you because now you do not mean much to me. The wishes should have been wedding wishes, but probably you forgot what it was about. I do not want to have anything to do with you any more and I do not care how you are doing. I wish you to have a good Christmas, preferably spent with your family. Sometimes I wonder how you manage with your new bosses. My dear brother Rysio came to see me and we had a few very pleasant moments together. I wish that the separation we obtained would last for ever and I must write again to make sure whether it is still valid or not. With this letter I must include some money for you. I do not have much, but what I have I am sending you, it will not amount to much, since you have sent me many parcels and sweets and this must have cost you a lot. So I end with this, Jula. P.S. I shall send you the money later, Jula."

Then during 1958—again the date is very uncertain—she wrote him a long letter. The greeting at the opening of this letter was merely his surname and her signature at the end was her maiden name. This is a letter in which she has a good deal to say about religious matters, and the only sentence that I think I need refer to is one which appears about half way through the letter, where she says

> " I break away from you. It was sin that I committed both before marriage and after. And I do not want to sin any more . . ."

Then on Jan. 10, 1960, she writes in this way:

> " Dear Wladek, I very much regret, but I cannot live with you in any other way. You wanted marriage and now there is no divorce. Perhaps you might get it, try to obtain it, I cannot give you a divorce although I wish for it myself. You say that I did not love you. I think I did, only in my opinion I had to act according to your behaviour. I am glad that you feel well and are in good health. This is most important. I also feel well and work now on Ward 6, I wash up the crockery and help to make beds and do the sweeping. Genia has a son, his name is Rysio Antoni. To conclude I thank you for your greetings and wish you all the best. Jula."

There are another two letters after that, of which it is only necessary to say that one of them, probably written early in 1964, addresses him by his surname and is signed by her with her maiden name, and the last one, which is a long letter, addresses him by his surname with the prefix " Mr.". That is, however, signed by her simply with her christian name, Jula.

As I have said, she was allowed out of hospital on leave in December, 1964, and she spent Christmas with her brother. I am not sure where he lived, but I think that it was probably somewhere near Swindon, and the husband was spending Christmas at Swindon and on the Boxing Day or the following day he took her a Christmas box, a parcel containing £20 in money. He handed this Christmas present to a friend—another Polish gentleman, who gave evidence—to give to the wife. At a time when a number of people were gathered together, including the husband and his Polish friend, the wife came in and, according to the evidence both of the husband and of his friend, she greeted everbody else present but ignored him. The friend thought it would be better that the husband himself should hand his wife the present and gave it to the husband to hand to her. He offered it to her and her reply was " I don't want your money ", and she either immediately continued " I don't want you ", or it may have been a little later,

in accordance with the friend's evidence, she said to the husband " I don't want
you ", and she added either " You're not my husband " or " I want a divorce ".
I accept the evidence of the husband and his friend as to what happened on that
occasion.   The exact terms of what the wife said are not important.   She was
apparently making it clear then that she did not want the husband any more and,
indeed, after that he never saw her again until the summer of 1966, which was
after the divorce proceedings had been started.

The only witness called on behalf of the wife, seeing that it was obviously
impossible for her herself to go into the witness box, was Dr. Hudson—a woman
doctor—senior medical officer at Coney Hill, who has occupied that position
since August, 1958, and since that time has been constantly looking after the
wife, except for the period when she was out of hospital.   Dr. Hudson is obviously
a lady well-qualified in this field.   She has had the best of opportunities for
studying the case of the wife from a medical point of view, and she impressed
me as a most careful and reliable witness.   She told me that according to the
records (because she, of course, knew nothing of what had happened between
1954 and 1958), the wife had been in the hospital in 1954 for a few weeks, then
out for a time, then back again, and both from those records and from Dr.
Hudson's own observation it was clear that all through the illness from which
she had suffered was chronic schizophrenia.   The doctor says that that illness
runs a variable course; patients are sometimes apparently reasonable but the
illness is always present.   In the case of the wife it was at times very acute,
especially at first, and, although she had shown marked improvement since
1954, she had never entirely recovered.   The doctor says that she experienced
many delusions, such as the delusion that the husband was a devil or that she
herself was the devil.   At first, said the doctor, she was very abnormal, noisy,
praying, misidentifying people.   That was in 1954.   The doctor said that, when
she first knew the wife, she was at times noisy and had various religious ideas
but no clear-cut delusions.   Said the doctor:

"This is not unusual.   Delusions are often clearly expressed at the
beginning, less clearly later, though always present."

She said that now the prognosis is poor.   In December, 1964, the wife was
allowed out on leave with large doses of medication, and the doctor expressed
the opinion that she could not form a rational intention whether or not to live
with the husband.   That obviously was an important answer and is, I think,
the high water mark of the evidence given in support of the answer in this case.
The doctor said that her behaviour is very variable, much affected by the
religious festivals.   She often has exaggerated ideas of religious obligations.
Once she said that she was going to write to her husband for his " name day ".
The doctor only remembered the husband having visited his wife once—that was
in 1962—but she did not say much then, except that he was very good, and, said
the doctor, it was a favourite phrase of hers to say that people were very good
or too good to her; but she thought that this was very often just a verbal expression of her wish to please.   The doctor said that the wife varied between kindness
and hostility to the staff.   In 1957 she was not very well on the whole.   She
had electro-convulsive treatment at one time in that year.   On Aug. 14, 1957,
she was described as being " now in her usual chronic state ".   On Aug. 29,
1957, it was recorded that she was having hallucinations and in September, 1957,
it was recorded that there was a suspicion of relapse and her medication was
increased.   That is of some importance, because it is the month before the
important letter written on Oct. 27, 1957.   Then in December, 1957, she was
violent.   In January, 1958, she had improved somewhat.   In January, 1960,
she was recovering from a slight setback which she had had in December, 1959.
This again is an important date because it is the date of the second letter in
which she expressed the wish not to live with the husband, and it came at a time
when, as the doctor said, she was recovering from this setback, which was not

so severe as some that she had had.   The doctor said that she would not have considered that the wife was ever capable of making a simple will, and that she was allowed to leave the hospital only because her brother asked that she should be allowed out and was willing to look after her.

In approaching the task of deciding whether desertion is established in this case, first of all I have to bear in mind the law, that there must be both the factum of separation and the animus deserendi.   As I have already indicated, however, it is not contested here—and in my opinion rightly not contested on behalf of the wife—that there was the factum of separation.   Was there the necessary animus?   And here it must be remembered that the general rule is that, to constitute desertion in the first instance, there must be the intention of permanently bringing matrimonial relations to an end, and, secondly, that that intention must continue throughout the period of alleged desertion.   It was in that state of the law that questions arose some years ago what the position was where, at some stage, a person who otherwise would be held to be in desertion could not retain the necessary intention by reason of mental illness.   The matter was considered in *Crowther* v. *Crowther* (1), in which an appeal went to the House of Lords, and it is sufficient to read the headnote (2) of that case:

" Where a divorce is sought on the ground of desertion and in the course of the three years' period immediately preceding the filing of the petition the respondent is admitted to a mental home under the Lunacy and Mental Treatment Acts, 1890-1930, there is not an irrebuttable presumption that the desertion has been terminated and the petitioner is entitled to produce evidence that the respondent remained mentally capable of an intention to desert.   Per LORD PORTER, LORD NORMAND, LORD MACDERMOTT and LORD REID: If it is not established by the petitioner that the respondent remained mentally capable of an intention to desert, or if no evidence is called, it is not open to the court to draw an inference of continued desertion from the intention displayed before and after the certification period.   Per LORD OAKSEY: once the original desertion is established the onus of proof is shifted to the deserting spouse to prove an intention to resume cohabitation."

It is clear there that the view of the majority of their lordships was that the onus was on the petitioner throughout; that if it were shown that the respondent was in a mental home, then it was for the petitioner to establish that she was mentally capable of an intention to desert and continue to desert.

It is accepted by counsel for the husband here that the onus is on him to establish an intention to desert in the first instance.   So far as a continuing intention is concerned, however, the position is materially altered by the statutory provision which is now contained in the second part of s. 1 (2) of the Matrimonial Causes Act 1965, where it is provided as follows:

". . . for the purposes of a petition for divorce, the court may treat a period of desertion as having continued at a time when the deserting party was incapable of continuing the necessary intention if the evidence before the court is such that, had that party not been so incapable, the court would have inferred that that intention continued at that time."

As I understand that provision, what it means is this, that there cannot be a beginning of desertion unless the respondent at the material time has the mental capacity to form the necessary intention, but if that intention is formed at a certain time, if the factum of separation then exists and if the factum of separation continues and if there is no conduct on the part of the respondent such that, if he or she were free from mental illness, it would put an end to the desertion, then the court may regard the desertion as continuing.

It seems to me here that, from October, 1957, onwards, the whole of the

---

(1) [1951] 1 All E.R. 1131;   [1951] A.C. 723.
(2) [1951] A.C. at p. 723.

conduct of the wife of which I have any evidence is of such a character that, leaving aside for the moment the question of her mental capacity, it points to only one conclusion, and that is the intention to desert—the intention to remain permanently separated from the husband. That appears from the letter of Oct. 27, 1957; it receives some support from the undated letter of 1958; it is firmly reiterated in the letter of Jan. 10, 1960. There is nothing to the contrary effect in the other letters contained in the bundle. The addressing of the husband by his surname in two of the letters is a slight indication of the continuance of the intention, and the behaviour of the wife after she had come out of hospital on Boxing Day, 1964, and her behaviour thereafter in never seeking to resume cohabitation with her husband is such behaviour as points to an intention to remain permanently separated from him. Therefore, if I am satisfied here that desertion once began, I have no difficulty in reaching the conclusion that it continued. I am a little puzzled by the language of the section that I have quoted where it says that " the court *may* treat a period of desertion as having continued . . ." If that is language such as to give some discretion to the court to treat it one way or the other, I am quite sure that the circumstances here are such as to make it just to treat the desertion as having continued.

So I come back to the key question in this case. Had the wife in October, 1957, or in January, 1960, or at both dates, the necessary mental capacity to form an intention to break up the marriage? In that connexion, it is certainly relevant to take into account the evidence given by the doctor that she suffered from delusions. It is clear from a judgment of LLOYD-JONES, J., in *Perry* v. *Perry* (3)—a decision with which I respectfully agree—that, if a wife is suffering from delusions by reason of mental illness and the delusions are of such a kind that, if they were true, they would justify her in refusing to live with the husband, then in refusing to live with him she cannot be said to be deserting him. The delusions in question in *Perry* v. *Perry* (3) were, among other things, to the effect that the wife believed that the husband had tried to strangle her, and it is perfectly clear that that delusion was one which was held firmly and persistently by her and which was the main motivation of her refusal to live with him. In the present case, the nature of any delusions from which the wife was suffering appear to me to be of a much vaguer character. It is true, I am told and I accept, that at times she would mistake one person for another. At times she would be hostile to somebody and then shortly afterwards friendly towards them, and it appears both from the evidence of the doctor and, indeed, from the evidence of the husband himself, that, at a very early stage of her illness, she was calling her husband " the devil ", or saying that he was " the devil ". Whether at any stage she really believed that, in the same sense as the wife in *Perry* v. *Perry* (3) believed that her husband was trying to strangle her, I very much doubt. It seems to me that, in the case of a deeply religious woman, it might mean no more than this, that she thought at the time that her husband was a very wicked man, and, indeed, it is clear from the sentence that I read from her 1958 letter that, at any rate at times, she had a deeply held feeling that both her husband and she herself had been very wicked. I refer to the sentence in which she said " I break away from you. It was sin that I committed both before marriage and after. And I do not want to sin any more . . ." I take into account also in that connexion her attitude to sexual intercourse at the time shortly after the marriage, which seems to have had an extremely upsetting effect on her. Moreover, I think that the most probable explanation of some of the wife's behaviour in this case is that she had got the idea that there was something wicked about the very act of sexual intercourse; it was a sin in which both she and her husband had taken part. It may well be that it was the effect of her illness, at least in part, that made her form a view of that kind. As that seems to me the most probable explanation of a good deal of her language and her behaviour towards

---

(3) [1963] 3 All E.R. 766.

her husband, I ask myself this question: if a wife without insane delusions had reasonable cause to believe that her husband had committed a grave sin (not being a matrimonial offence) or that she had joined with him in committing such a sin, would that enable her to leave him, bring the marriage to an end and contend that she had reasonable cause for doing so? I am quite satisfied that it would not, and I do not feel that it would be possible to base the conclusion in this case on *Perry* v. *Perry* (4), where the whole point was that, if the husband had really been trying to strangle the wife, she would have had just cause to leave him.

I have, however, to take into account the important piece of evidence given by Dr. Hudson that, in her view, the wife was not at any time from 1954 onwards able to form a rational intention whether or not to live with her husband. As to what exactly is the distinction to be drawn between an intention and a rational intention I am not quite clear, but I do not think that the doctor's evidence means anything more than this, that one could never be sure with any intention expressed by this wife that it was not affected in some way by her mental illness, unreliable and liable to be changed from time to time; and I accept that that is in general a true picture. I come back, however, to these letters which she wrote, and the letter of Oct. 27, 1957, suggests to my mind that the person who wrote it was perfectly capable of forming an intention—was quite well aware of what she was doing and was unaffected by a delusion of any kind. It seems to me that it is a sensible letter from beginning to end, the sort of letter that might well be written by any, perhaps not very highly educated, person who was explaining to her husband simply that she did not want to have any more to do with him. There is certainly nothing in that letter to my mind which indicates the sort of thing that the doctor spoke of—that the wife would at one moment be saying one thing and a few moments later saying something else. It is true that, towards the end of the letter, she speaks of sending money to her husband and then in the postscript says that she has not got the money and that she will send it later. I attach no importance to that and counsel for the wife very wisely, I think, did not invite me to do so. Moreover, the same intention to put an end to matrimonial relations is repeated in the letter of January, 1960, and is repeated by her conduct at her meeting with the husband at Christmas, 1964, and is consistent with the manner in which she addressed him in other letters which she sent to him from the hospital; and I find that there is sufficient material there to displace any presumption there may be that a patient suffering from chronic schizophrenia is incapable of forming the necessary intention. I am satisfied that she did form that intention, that she was in desertion from October, 1957, onwards, and that desertion continued up to the time of the presentation of the petition. The husband's adultery took place between March, 1958, and November, 1963, and then came to an end. The circumstances were such that the court should, I think, adopt a lenient attitude towards that adultery. This marriage has now completely broken down. I am satisfied that it is in the interests of the husband and in the public interest that it should be dissolved. I exercise my discretion and pronounce a decree nisi on the ground of desertion.

Decree nisi.

Solicitors: *Jaxa and Partners* (for the husband); *Official Solicitor.*

[*Reported by* ALICE BLOOMFIELD, *Barrister-at-Law.*]

---

(4) [1963] 3 All E.R. 766.

MURPHY v. GRIFFITHS.

[QUEEN'S BENCH DIVISION (Lord Parker, C.J., Widgery and O'Connor, JJ.), November 23, 1966.]

Road Traffic—Offence—Test certificate—Car owner found to be without test certificate—Two days later back-dated certificate issued by garage proprietor—Whether certificate false in a material particular—Road Traffic Act, 1960 (8 & 9 Eliz. 2 c. 16), s. 236.

The respondent, an authorised examiner, examined a car belonging to one D. in September, 1965, found that it complied with the prescribed statutory requirements, but failed to issue a test certificate in respect of it. On Jan. 24, 1966, D. was found using the car without having in his possession a current test certificate. On Jan. 26, 1966 D. produced a test certificate dated Jan. 19, 1966, purporting to be issued by the respondent in accordance with Sch. 4, Pt. 1*, to the Motor Vehicles (Tests) Regulations, 1960. The respondent had examined the car on Jan. 26 and back-dated the certificate to Jan. 19. On appeal by the prosecutor against the dismissal of an information against the respondent charging him with issuing a test certificate which was to his knowledge false in a material particular, contrary to s. 236† of the Road Traffic Act, 1960,

Held: the date of issue of the certificate was false to the knowledge of the respondent; and as the date of issue determined the date of expiry of the test certificate, viz., twelve months thence, it was false in a material particular (see p. 426, letters F and G, post).

Appeal allowed.

[As to vehicle tests and test certificates, see 33 HALSBURY'S LAWS (3rd Edn.) 469, 470, para. 795; and for a case on the subject, see 45 DIGEST (Repl.) 74, *225*.

For the Road Traffic Act, 1960, s. 236, see 40 HALSBURY'S STATUTES (2nd Edn.) 912.]

Case referred to:

R. v. *Stanley Evans*, [1964] 3 All E.R. 666; [1964] 1 W.L.R. 1388; 129 J.P. 29; 45 Digest (Repl.) 74, *225*.

Case Stated.

This was a Case Stated by justices for the county of Montgomery in respect of their adjudication as a magistrates' court sitting at Montgomery on Mar. 30, 1966. On Mar. 7, 1966, an information was laid by the appellant, James Buckley Murphy, against the respondent, Kenneth Edward Griffiths, charging that on Jan. 26, 1966, in the parish of Berriew in the county of Montgomery he issued a certain test certificate which was to his knowledge false in a material particular in that the certificate was dated Jan. 19, 1966, whereas it would appear to have been issued on Jan. 26, 1966, contrary to s. 236 of the Road Traffic Act, 1960. The following facts were found. The respondent was a garage proprietor and a person authorised to carry out tests and issue the required test certificate in accordance with the provision of the Road Traffic Acts. A Mr. Davies had used his vehicle, reg. no. LEP 531, on Jan. 24, 1966, and on that date Mr. Davies was not in possession of a current test certificate. On Jan. 26, 1966, Mr. Davies produced a test certificate, serial no. B 135277, which purported to have been issued by the respondent on Jan. 19, 1966. The vehicle had not been tested on Jan. 19, 1966. It had been tested in September, 1965, and also on Jan. 26, 1966, and was roadworthy at the time of these tests. The vehicle had not been tested by the respondent on any date between September, 1965, and Jan. 26, 1966. No test certificate had been issued in September, 1965, because of an oversight by the respondent and the only test certificate issued in respect of the vehicle had been issued by the respondent on Jan. 26, 1966. Although tests took place in

---

* Schedule 4, Pt. 1, so far as material, is set out at p. 426, letter B, post.

† Section 236, so far as material, is set out at p. 425, letter I to p. 426, letter A, post.

September, 1965, and on Jan. 26, 1966, and the test certificate was not in fact issued until that date, the respondent put on the test certificate Jan. 19, 1966, as the date of issue thereof thereby back-dating it to the last available entry page in the Ministry book of test certificates, namely, Jan. 19, 1966, and the respondent had not completed the required form of certificate for issue to the vehicle owner, Mr. Davies, either in September, 1965, or on Jan. 19, 1966. The respondent issued the test certificate to be valid as a test certificate between Jan. 19, 1966 (being the date of issue stated thereon by him), and Jan. 18, 1967 (being the date of expiry stated thereon by him). The respondent had not made a record of the test in the required manner, but had recorded same in his account to Mr. Davies and charged the statutory fee when entering up his ledger in September, 1965.

It was contended by the respondent that a test had been carried out in September, 1965, and that, although he had neglected to issue the required forms or complete the required records, he had not committed the offence contained in the information in that the form of certificate did not require him to state the date on which the test was carried out but only the date on which the certificate was issued. Having carried out the test in September, 1965, and again on Jan. 26, 1966, he would have been entitled to date such certificate on either of these dates but that, due to the fact that the last duplicate certificate was dated Jan. 19, 1966, he did not back-date the certificate beyond that date. It was contended by the appellant that the facts showed that the respondent did not examine the vehicle on Jan. 19, 1966. As the certificate was a certificate of roadworthiness at the time of examination and the vehicle had not in any event been examined on Jan. 19, 1966, but either in September, 1965, or on Jan. 26, 1966, the certificate was false in a material particular.

The justices dismissed the information, and the appellant now appealed.

The case noted below* was cited during the argument in addition to the case referred to in the judgment.

E. ap G. Lewis for the appellant.

The respondent did not appear and was not represented.

LORD PARKER, C.J.: Before dealing with the facts of this case, it is convenient to refer to the few relevant provisions in the statute and regulations. Section 65 of the Road Traffic Act, 1960, makes provision for the testing of motor vehicles and their accessories or equipment. By sub-s. (2):

" The Minister may by regulations make provision for the examination of vehicles submitted for examination under this section and for the issue, where it is found on such an examination that the said requirements are complied with, of a certificate (hereafter in this Act referred to as a ' test certificate ') that at the date of the examination the requirements were complied with in relation to the vehicle."

Section 66 (1) provides that:

" A person who uses on a road at any time, or causes or permits to be so used, a motor vehicle to which this section applies, and as respects which no test certificate has been issued within the appropriate period before the said time, shall be liable on summary conviction to . . ."

and the penalties are set out. By sub-s. (7):

" In this section ' appropriate period ' means a period of twelve months or such shorter period as may be prescribed."

No shorter period has been prescribed. Finally, s. 236 of the Act of 1960 provides that:

" If a person issues any such document as is referred to in paras. (*a*) or (*b*) of sub-s. (2) of the last foregoing section, or a test certificate, and the

---

* *Ocean Accident and Guarantee Corpn., Ltd.* v. *Cole*, [1932] 2 K.B. 100.

document or test certificate so issued is to his knowledge false in a material particular . . ."

he shall be guilty of an offence and liable to certain maximum penalties. The regulations made in regard to this are the Motor Vehicle (Tests) Regulations, 1960 (1). By those regulations, the form of test certificate is prescribed, and is to be found in Sch. 4, Part 1. It is headed " Test Certificate " and it reads:

" The motor vehicle, of which the registration mark is [then it has to be set out] having been examined under s. 65 of the Road Traffic Act, 1960, it is hereby certified that at the date of the examination hereof the statutory requirements prescribed by regulations made under the said s. 65 were complied with in relation to the vehicle."

Pausing there, it is to be observed that, as was stated in *R.* v. *Stanley Evans* (2), it is perhaps unfortunate that no provision is there made for the date when the examination was carried out. As I understand it, despite what was suggested by the court in that case, there have been no amending regulations to provide for the date of examination to be stated (3). The form then continues with the words " Vehicle testing station number " (4).

[HIS LORDSHIP stated the facts, and continued:] The justices, in dismissing this information, appear to have been influenced by the fact that, in *R.* v. *Stanley Evans* (5) to which I have referred, this court held that, there being no provision for the stating of the date of the examination, the test certificate could be given at any time after the examination, though of course it would imply that there had been no change in condition of the vehicle between the actual date of the examination and the date of issue of the certificate. The justices, I think, felt that there was, therefore, nothing wrong in issuing a test certificate in regard to the September, 1965, examination at any time, including Jan. 19, 1966, albeit it relates to a later examination on Jan. 26, 1966. It is quite clear that the justices felt that there were mitigating circumstances here, and that they were entitled to dismiss the information. On analysis, it is perfectly clear that they were wrong. The date of issue was false; it was clearly false to the knowledge of the respondent, and the only question was whether it was false in a material particular. One has only to realise that the date of issue is of great importance in that it determines the date of expiry of the test certificate, namely, twelve months hence, to make one realise that the date of issue is of the highest importance. In my judgment, the justices clearly came to a wrong decision, and the Case must go back to them with a direction to convict.

WIDGERY, J.: I agree.

O'CONNOR, J.: I agree.

Appeal allowed. Case remitted.

Solicitors: *T. D. Jones & Co.*, agents for *Milwyn, Jenkins & Jenkins*, Newtown, Mont. (for the appellant).

[*Reported by* N. P. METCALFE, ESQ., *Barrister-at-Law.*]

---

(1) S.I. 1960 No. 1083 as amended. A new form of test certificate was prescribed by S.I. 1963 No. 700.
(2) [1964] 3 All E.R. 666 at p. 669.
(3) A new reg. 14 (1) was, however, substituted by S.I. 1966 No. 893, the effect of which is to require that a test certificate (or notification of the refusal of a certificate) shall be issued normally on the same date as that on which the examination is completed.
(4) The test certificate then goes on ". . . Signature . . . Date of issue . . . Date of expiry . . . Serial Number of immediately preceding test certificate (to be entered when the above date of expiry is more than twelve months after the above date of issue) . . ."
(5) [1964] 3 All E.R. 666.

Re W. & M. ROITH, LTD.

[CHANCERY DIVISION (Plowman, J.), December 9, 1966.]

Company—Ultra vires—Pension—Service agreement with company's general manager and controlling shareholder, who was also a director, providing for pension to be paid to his widow—No specific amount of remuneration for director provided by the agreement—Director had controlled company for many years but had not previously had service agreement—Articles of association altered recently to allow pensions to be awarded to director's widows, among others—Director no longer in good health at date of service agreement—Director died in January, 1959—Company went into liquidation in December, 1963—Proof for capitalised value of pension rejected—Whether service agreement was reasonably incidental to the carrying on of the company's business and bona fide for the benefit of the company.

R. controlled two private companies, a manufacturing company, R., Ltd., and another company which sold the manufactured goods of R., Ltd. R. was a director and the general manager of R., Ltd., but he had had no service agreement with either company. In the summer of 1957 he consulted his solicitor concerning the continuity of the business after his death and his desire to make provision for his wife and certain other dependants without dividing the control of either company between them. By special resolution on Mar. 17, 1958, the articles of association of R., Ltd. were altered and a new article was added enabling the directors to award pensions and annuities to, among other persons, widows of directors. On Dec. 3, 1958, when R. was fifty-eight years of age and his health was no longer good, a service agreement was entered into between R., Ltd. and R. by which he was appointed general manager for the remainder of his life and agreed to devote the whole of his time and abilities to the business of the company; under the agreement he was entitled to such salary as might from time to time be agreed between him and the company. The agreement then provided, by cl. 5, " [R., Ltd.] hereby covenants with [R.] that in the event of his death occurring during his retention of [office] under this agreement [R., Ltd.] will pay to [his widow] . . . a pension at the rate of £1,040 per annum during the remainder of her life . . ."; and it provided by cl. 6 " [R.] hereby declares himself to be a trustee for [his widow] of the benefit of the covenant on the part of [R., Ltd.] . . . to pay a pension to [her] ". R. died on Jan. 30, 1959, and the pension was duly paid thereafter until R., Ltd. went into a creditors' voluntary winding-up on Dec. 10, 1963. On Oct. 13, 1964, R.'s executors lodged proof for the value of the pension. On appeal against rejection of the proof,

Held: the true inference from the circumstances was that the service agreement was not reasonably incidental to the carrying on of R., Ltd.'s business nor entered into bona fide for the benefit of and to promote the prosperity of R., Ltd.; accordingly the proof had been rightly rejected (see p. 432, letter C, post).

Re Lee, Behrens & Co., Ltd. ([1932] All E.R. Rep. 889) applied.

[As to the limits of the powers and duties of a company and its directors in regard to dealings with assets and making payments out of its funds, see 6 HALSBURY'S LAWS (3rd Edn.) 170, para. 357, and p. 294, para. 597 text and note (*r*), and as to instances of acts that are or are not ultra vires a company, see ibid., p. 415, para. 804 and p. 416, para. 805; and for cases on the subject, see 9 DIGEST (Repl.) 559, *3700*, 568, *3743-3748.*

For the Companies (Winding-up) Rules, 1949, r. 2, r. 108, see 4 HALSBURY'S STATUTORY INSTRUMENTS (1st Re-Issue) 141, 167.]

Case referred to:

Lee, Behrens & Co., Ltd., Re, [1932] All E.R. Rep. 889; [1932] 2 Ch. 46; 101 L.J.Ch. 183; 147 L.T. 348; 9 Digest (Repl.) 559, *3700.*

Considered in RE HALT GARAGE LTD
[1982] 3 All ER 1016

Doubted in Re Horsley &
Weight
1982 2H 442
JCA

Summons.

This was an application by summons dated Sept. 24, 1965, by Charles Aukin and John James Wrench, the executors of Maurice Mancini Roith, deceased, by way of appeal from the decision of Herbert William Pitt, the liquidator of W. & M. Roith, Ltd. (" the company ") and respondent to the summons, rejecting the proof for the sum of £10,400 lodged by the appellant executors; they sought an order that the liquidator's decision should be reversed and that their proof should be admitted in full. Mr. Roith, who died on Jan. 30, 1959, aged fifty-eight, was the general manager and a director of the company. The company went into a creditor's voluntary winding-up on Dec. 10, 1963. Informal proof of the debt was made by letter dated Oct. 13, 1964. The proof was for the capitalised pension payable to Mr. Roith's widow for her life under a service agreement made between him and the company dated Dec. 3, 1958. This agreement was executed by the company under seal in the manner prescribed by art. 71 of Table A to the Companies Act, 1929, which applied to the company, the relevant board minute was signed by all the directors of the company. It was common ground that, if the executors were successful on this appeal, the amount for which proof should be admitted was £9,270, not £10,400.

R. B. S. Instone for the executors.
O. R. Smith for the liquidator.

PLOWMAN, J.: The company, W. & M. Roith, Ltd., was incorporated in the year 1934 and its business was that of gown manufacturers, or manufacturers of ladies' clothing. In the year 1958, when, I am told, the company was prospering, its paid-up capital was £13,505, divided into £1 shares, all of one class, which were held as follows. Mr. Roith held 9,240, that is to say, rather more than two-thirds of the issued capital. Mrs. Roith, then his wife, now his widow, held 326. A lady whose name is Leah Roith held 3,124, and a Mrs. Lawrence held 815. Mr. Roith, Mrs. Roith and Mrs. Lawrence were the three directors of the company. Mr. Roith also controlled another company, which, I am told, was also a prosperous company, called Michael Wayne, Ltd., and the business of that company was to sell, by mail order, the output of the company with which I am concerned, W. & M. Roith, Ltd.

In August, 1957, Mr. Roith, who was then fifty-seven years old, his wife being some two years older, consulted his solicitor, Mr. Aukin, about his will and the continuity of the businesses of his two companies after his death. The evidence is that, in 1958, Mr. Roith's health was not very good and Mr. Aukin, who is one of the two appellants (the executors of Mr. Roith's will) and was Mr. Roith's solicitor, has made an affidavit in which he deposes as follows.

" The facts leading up to the execution of the service agreement are as follows. I had for many years as sole partner in the firm of Aukin & Co. (which was amalgamated with my present firm in May, 1964) acted as solicitor for Mr. Roith and for two companies which he controlled namely the company (which manufactured ladies' clothing) and Michael Wayne, Ltd. which sold the company's products by mail order. Mr. Roith consulted me in August, 1957 with regard to his will and the continuity of the businesses after his death. He informed me that he desired to make provision for his wife and for certain other dependants without dividing the control of either company between them. The two companies were at that time profitable although Mr. Roith by reason of his shareholding control had not thought it necessary in his or their interests to enter into any contract of service with either company. I advised Mr. Roith that his best course would be to enter into a contract of service with one or other of the companies whereby he undertook to serve it for the rest of his life without any specific provision for remuneration, but on the terms that if he died during such service leaving his wife surviving the company would be under a liability to pay her a pension of an amount which was within the company's capacity to pay. This would leave him free to dispose of all his shares in both companies by his will in favour of his other dependants. Mr. Roith accepted this advice and I drafted his will and the agreement forming exhibit ' A ' hereto accordingly."

I will refer to the service agreement in a moment, but before doing so I shall refer to one or two provisions of the company's memorandum and articles of association. On Mar. 17, 1958, the company, at an extraordinary general meeting, passed the following special resolution, namely:

" (a) the provisions of the memorandum of association of the company with respect of the objects of the company be and are hereby altered by deleting para. (N) of cl. 3 of such memorandum of association and substituting therefor the following new paragraph:— . . . [I need not read the whole of the new paragraph, but it includes the following:] . . . to give pensions, gratuities, or charitable aid to any person who may have served the company or its predecessors in business, or of any subsidiary allied or associated company or to the wives, children or other relatives or dependants of such persons . . . (b) the articles of association of the company be and are hereby altered by the addition after art. 21 of the following new art. 22:—' 22. The directors may give or award pensions, annuities, gratuities and superannuation or other allowances or benefits to any persons who are or have at any time been directors of or employed by or in the service of the company or of any company which is a subsidiary company of or allied or associated with the company or any such subsidiary and to the wives, widows, children and other relatives and dependants of any such persons . . . and may vote as a director in respect of the exercise of any of the powers by this article conferred upon the directors, notwithstanding that he is or may be or become interested therein '."

I should also refer to two other articles in the company's articles.

" 16. A director may hold any other office or place of profit under the company, except that of auditor, upon such terms as to remuneration, tenure of office and otherwise as may be determined by the board.

" 17. A director shall be capable of contracting or participating in the profits of any contract with the company in the same manner as if he were not a director, subject nevertheless to the following provision namely, that he shall declare the nature of his interest in any contract or proposed contract in which he is interested in manner required by s. 149 of the Companies Act, 1929, and thereupon he shall be entitled to vote in respect of the contract or proposed contract or any matter arising thereout . . ."

The service agreement which is in question in this case is dated Dec. 3, 1958, and it is made between the company of the one part and Mr. Roith of the other part and it provides as follows:

" 1. Mr. Roith is hereby appointed general manager and director of the company and as such general manager and director shall perform the duties assigned to him and exercise the powers vested in him from time to time by the directors of the company. 2. Mr. Roith shall hold the said office of general manager and director throughout the remainder of his life. 3. Mr. Roith shall unless prevented by ill health during his tenure of the said office devote the whole of his time and abilities to the business of the company and shall well and faithfully serve the company and use his best endeavours to promote the company's interests. 4. During his tenure of the said office Mr. Roith shall be entitled to such salary as may from time to time be agreed between him and the company (excluding any bonuses commissions or other similar payments). 5. The company hereby covenants with Mr. Roith that in the event of his death occurring during his retention of the said office under this agreement the company will pay to Mrs. Rosie Roith the present wife of

Mr. Roith (hereinafter called ' the wife ') if she shall survive him a pension at the rate of £1,040 per annum during the remainder of her life such pension to be payable by twelve equal monthly payments to be made on the last day of each calendar month. 6. Mr. Roith hereby declares himself to be a trustee for the wife of the benefit of the covenant on the part of the company hereinbefore contained to pay a pension to the wife."

That was on Dec. 3, 1958.

On Jan. 30, 1959, Mr. Roith died of cancer and there is some hearsay evidence that he did not know that he was suffering from that complaint, at any rate in 1958. On Oct. 13, 1964, an informal proof of debt was put in on behalf of the executors and is to be found in a letter of that date from their solicitors to the liquidator's solicitors, and that letter contains the following paragraph.

" We should be obliged therefore if your client will accept this letter as the executors' formal proof for the sum of £10,400 due under the agreement dated Dec. 3, 1958, and made between W. & M. Roith, Ltd. and the late Mr. M. M. Roith."

I have already said that it is now agreed that the appropriate amount, if any, is not £10,400, but £9,270. As that is common ground it is unnecessary to go into the reasons which led to a modification of the sum originally claimed.

That proof of debt was rejected by the liquidator on Oct. 15, 1964, on a number of grounds, only one of which, I think, is now relevant, and that is to be found in the letter of that date from the liquidator's solicitors to the executors' solicitors, which contains the following passage.

" The grounds for the rejection are as follows:— . . . [and then number three of the grounds is] The agreement was not reasonably incidental to the carrying on of the company's business and entered into bona fide for the benefit of and to promote the prosperity of the company."

That passage is an echo of what Eve, J., said in *Re Lee, Behrens and Co., Ltd.* (1), in relation to the grant of a pension by a company:

" But, whether they may be made under an express or implied power, all such grants involve an expenditure of the company's money, and that money can only be spent for purposes reasonably incidental to the carrying on of the company's business, and the validity of such grants is to be tested as is shown in all the authorities, by the answers to three pertinent questions. (i) Is the transaction reasonably incidental to the carrying on of the company's business? (ii) Is it a bona fide transaction? (iii) Is it done for the benefit, and to promote the prosperity, of the company? "

It is, I think, common ground in this case that the principle there enunciated is applicable here. Counsel for the executors, submits, however, as indeed is the fact, that Eve, J., was dealing with a gratuitous pension, and that it is in the nature of things easier to justify a transaction for value than it is a gratuitous payment.

Counsel's submissions on behalf of the executors were these. First of all, he said that a widow's pension is a normal and customary mode of remunerating a director and, therefore, the provision of a widow's pension is reasonably incidental to carrying on a company's business, and I am disposed to agree that that is so. Then, says counsel, the provision of a pension for Mrs. Roith must have been for the benefit of the company because it was for the benefit of the company that the architect of its prosperity should be tied to the company in the way in which he was tied by the service agreement, and counsel points out that the only quid pro quo for that tie was the provision of a pension for Mr. Roith's widow. Counsel points out, quite truly, that the capacity of the company to pay a pension of £1,040 a year—£20 a week—was one of the matters taken into account in

---

(1) [1932] All E.R. Rep. 889 at pp. 890, 891, [1932] 2 Ch. 46 at p. 51.

* see now Chartorbridge v Lloyds 1969 2 All ER @ 1190/1191

coming to the arrangements that were made; he submits that there is no evidence of a lack of bona fides on the part of anybody involved in the transaction on the company's part, and he relies on the fact that the liquidator has not filed evidence by either of the other directors to say otherwise.

On the other hand, counsel for the liquidator says this. He accepts that initially the onus is on the liquidator to show that this service agreement was not entered into bona fide in the interests of the company, but, while accepting that onus, he submits that he has discharged it, and he relies on the following matters. First of all, he says that Mr. Roith, as is stated in the liquidator's evidence, had been a director of the company since the year 1934 when it was incorporated and, throughout that period, had been in receipt of remuneration from the company, and he submits that there was no conceivable reason for altering the situation in the year 1958 except in order to provide for Mr. Roith's widow without leaving her his shares in the company by his will. Secondly, counsel for the liquidator points out that so long as Mr. Roith retained control the company in fact got no benefit at all from the service agreement, and he submits that the facts show that Mr. Roith intended to retain control of the company, the relevant facts being those relating to his intended testamentary disposition. Thirdly, counsel for the liquidator pointed out—and this is, I think, a significant fact—that it was regarded as immaterial which company should provide the pension, as Mr. Aukin said in his evidence:

" I advised Mr. Roith that his best course would be to enter into a contract of service with one or other of the companies."

Next, counsel for the liquidator said that the provision in the service agreement, cl. 3, which provided that

" Mr. Roith shall unless prevented by ill health . . . devote the whole of his time and abilities to the business of the company and shall well and faithfully serve the company and use his best endeavours to promote the company's interests "

was really a sham, because if one takes that at its face value he would have been precluded from devoting any of his time and abilities to the business of Michael Wayne, Ltd. Counsel for the executors suggested that there was no real evidence that Mr. Roith was in fact devoting any time and attention to Michael Wayne, Ltd. at any rate to a material extent, but it seems to me that the proper inference from the facts is that he was working to a material extent for Michael Wayne, Ltd., because both Mr. Roith and his solicitor quite clearly thought that he could justifiably call on either of those companies for a pension to his widow. Counsel for the liquidator submits that, in the light of those facts, the inference was that the real object of this scheme was not to benefit the company but was simply to provide for Mr. Roith's widow without leaving her his shares in the company and, accordingly, counsel submitted that the liquidator had discharged the onus of proof which was on him.

There was one other matter on which counsel for the liquidator relied and that was this, that there was no evidence from either of the other directors of the company explaining the purpose of the service agreement or the company's motives in entering into it; and counsel suggested that the absence of that evidence was particularly significant having regard to the fact that on Feb. 28, 1964, the liquidator's solicitors wrote to the solicitors concerned a letter which contained this paragraph:

" We have advised the liquidator to reject the claim on the grounds (a) that the covenant was ultra vires the company and (b) that it was not entered into for the benefit of and to promote the prosperity of the company. Both the deceased and Mrs. Roith were directors of the company and if either the executors or Mrs. Roith would care to indicate what evidence there is that the directors resolved to enter into the covenant with a view to benefiting the company and not Mrs. Roith, our client will consider it."

That invitation was never accepted and, as I have said, counsel for the liquidator submits that the fact that it was not accepted and that no evidence has been filed by either of the ladies who were the other directors of the company, is a matter of significance in considering what inferences it is right for me to draw from the proved facts.

I accept that submission. It seems to me that the liquidator was well justified, on the evidence, in drawing the inference which he has drawn and which is stated in para. 3 of his affidavit, in this way:

". . . as is to be inferred from the circumstances the entering into of the said agreement by the company was not reasonably incidental to the carrying on of the company's business and was not bona fide for the benefit and to promote the prosperity of the company."

I myself draw the same inferences from the facts and I have come to the conclusion that really the whole object of the plan of campaign was to benefit not the company but Mrs. Roith, and, in the circumstances, I must dismiss the appeal.

Order accordingly.

Solicitors: *Tarlo, Lyons & Aukin* (for the executors); *Nutt & Oliver* (for the liquidator).

[*Reported by* JACQUELINE METCALFE, *Barrister-at-Law.*]

PRACTICE DIRECTION.

Family Provision—Time—Extension—Practice—Family Provision Act 1966
(c. 35), s. 6.
Family Provision—Order—Interim order—Practice—Family Provision Act 1966
(c. 35), s. 6.

1. Section 5 of the Family Provision Act 1966 removes the existing restrictions on the court's discretion to extend the time for making an application beyond the expiry of a period of six months from the date of the grant of representation to the estate. A plaintiff who wishes the court to exercise its discretion in his favour should ask for its exercise as at present as a separate head of relief in his originating summons. When the evidence on this point is complete the master will adjourn this part of the summons to the judge in chambers.

2. Section 6 of the Family Provision Act 1966 enables the court to make interim orders. A plaintiff need not ask specifically for this form of relief in his originating summons. If a plaintiff wishes an interim order to be made in his favour the master on being satisfied that the state of the evidence is such as to enable the judge to decide whether or not such an order should be made will adjourn the originating summons to the judge in chambers on this point.

3. The judge will hear matters adjourned to him in chambers under 1. and 2. above on Mondays unless the estimated length of the hearing justifies a special appointment.

By direction of CROSS, J.

W. F. S. HAWKINS,
Chief Master
Jan. 24, 1967.   Chancery Division.

FRANK H. WRIGHT (CONSTRUCTIONS), LTD. AND OTHERS v. FRODOOR, LTD. AND ANOTHER.

[QUEEN'S BENCH DIVISION (Roskill, J.), November 14, 15, 16, 17, 18, 21, 22, 23, 1966.]

Moneylender—Definition of moneylender—Exception of person bona fide carrying on any business not having for its primary object the lending of money— Issuing house—Joint loans by issuing house and others—Whether unenforceable as made by unlicensed moneylender—Money-lenders Act, 1900 (63 & 64 Vict. c. 51), s. 6 (1) (d).

Valuer—Purchase price to be ascertained on balancing assets and liabilities— Independent accountants acting as experts not arbitrators—Liabilities including loans alleged to be unenforceable as made by unlicensed money- lenders—Whether accountants bound to consider whether Moneylenders Acts, 1900 to 1927, applied to loans—Accountants' report giving their reasons —Whether accountants' certificate of nil purchase price was open to challenge and should be set aside.

A private company, whose business had been built up by W. and was expanding, was in need of further capital. It consulted an issuing house, the primary object of whose business was the flotation of public companies, and who, if satisfied concerning a business, would make available capital temporarily, with a view to a flotation within a period of five years. The issuing house became interested in the company's business and growth prospects, and were prepared to make loans to it with a view to a public flotation. Between Oct. 21, 1964, and the end of October, 1965, they lent or procured to be lent to the company a total of £192,000. These loans were joint ventures by the issuing house and others; £96,000 was lent by the issuing house and the balance was contributed by one or all of three other lenders, the four lenders being described as the consortium. By the summer of 1965 the company had run into difficulties, a firm of management con- sultants was called in and their report was unfavourable. Negotiations ensued and on Feb. 9, 1966, an agreement in writing was entered into whereby the assets of the company were to be transferred to a new company, the first plaintiff, and the purchase price was to be computed by independent accountants (acting as experts, not as arbitrators) in accordance with provisions set out in Sch. 3 to the agreement. These required the accountants to value certain liabilities described in Sch. 3, which included the £192,000 loan and to value the assets there set out; the total purchase price was to be the balance found on deducting the liabilities from the assets and deducting also a sum of £5,000. The requirement in Sch. 3 was that the accountants should "physically verify the amounts outstanding as at Jan. 31, 1966 with the consortium". Independent accountants were duly appointed and, by their report which included their certificate, they certified the purchase price as nil, there being an excess of liabilities over assets. Their report gave their reasons. The assets of the transferor company included leasehold premises. These not having been assigned, but all movable assets having been handed over, to the first plaintiff, the first plaintiff and the consortium sued the transferor company and W. for specific performance of the agree- ment. The defendants did not question the validity of the agreement, but contended that the loan of £192,000 ought not to have been taken into account as a liability, on the ground that the issuing house were unlicensed moneylenders and that the loan or £96,000 part thereof was void and unen- forceable by reason of the Moneylenders Acts, 1900 to 1927, and they challenged the accountants' certificate on various other grounds.

After the accountants' report had been signed and circulated, it appeared that in one paragraph (para. 16), there was an error by including the word

Q

Applied in BURGESS v PURCHASE & CO
[1983] 2 All ER 4

Distinguished in JONES v JONES [1971] 2 All ER 676

Applied in SMITH v GALE [1974] 1 All ER 401

" not " in a sentence* which then read that future interest on capital outstanding on hire-purchase after a certain date had not been included. In fact
it had been included but the relevant figures stated were correct, so that
the error did not affect the ultimate arithmetical result.

Held: the loans by the issuing house were moneylending transactions,
but as the loans were made bona fide for the purpose of the business of an
issuing house, which was a business not having for its primary object the
lending of money but in the course of which money was lent, the loans were
brought within the exception provided by para. (d) of s. 6 (1)† of the Moneylenders Act, 1900, and were not void under that Act (see p. 449, letter D, and
p. 450, letters C and G, post).

Premor, Ltd. v. *Shaw Brothers* ([1964] 2 All E.R. 583) and *United Dominions
Trust, Ltd.* v. *Kirkwood* ([1966] 1 All E.R. 968) considered and applied.

Per CURIAM: (a) as the accountants had set out their reasons in the
report which was their certificate, it was open to the defendants to seek to
set aside the certificate; but, although the position had been difficult in
view of the faulty manner in which the company had kept records, no
mistake of a material and substantial character in the certificate had been
substantiated (see p. 454, letter G, p. 456, letter G, and p. 457, letter G,
post).

Collier v. *Mason* ((1858), 25 Beav. 200) and *Dean* v. *Prince* ([1954] 1 All
E.R. 749) applied.

(b) in valuing " liabilities " for the purposes of Sch. 3 to the agreement
the independent accountants were not bound to consider whether the
Moneylenders Acts, 1900 to 1927, did or did not apply to the £192,000 loan,
but only to put on that item in Sch. 3, as on other items therein, such value
as they thought fit (see p. 452, letter F, post).

(c) if the issuing house had been unlicensed moneylenders, the consequences of that would not have been avoided in respect of money lent by
them merely because the various acts of lending were a joint venture with
others who were not unlicensed moneylenders (see p. 452, letter H, post).

Quaere whether the totality of the loans (£192,000) would be rendered
unenforceable if the issuing house had been an unlicensed moneylender
(see p. 453, letter C, post).

[As to what constitutes the business of moneylending, see 27 HALSBURY'S
LAWS (3rd Edn.) 18, 19, para. 27; and as to the exclusion from the statutory
definition of moneylender of a person who bona fide carries on the business of
banking or certain other businesses, see ibid., p. 21, para. 31; and for cases on
the subject, see 35 DIGEST (Repl.) 232-234, *330-339.*

As to the conclusiveness of valuations to fix a contractual purchase price, see
39 HALSBURY'S LAWS (3rd Edn.) 6, para. 7; and for cases on the position of
valuers, see 47 DIGEST (Repl.) 560-562, *1-12.*

For the Money-lenders Act, 1900, s. 6, see 16 HALSBURY'S STATUTES (2nd
Edn.) 375.]

Cases referred to:
Collier v. *Mason*, (1858), 25 Beav. 200; 53 E.R. 613; 47 Digest (Repl.) 566, *49.*
Dean v. *Prince*, [1953] 2 All E.R. 636; [1953] Ch. 590; [1953] 3 W.L.R. 271;
   revsd. C.A., [1954] 1 All E.R. 749; [1954] Ch. 409; [1954] 2 W.L.R.
   538; 9 Digest (Repl.) 589, *3898.*
Edgelow v. *MacElwee*, [1918] 1 K.B. 205; 87 L.J.K.B. 738; 118 L.T. 177;
   35 Digest (Repl.) 232, *333.*
Litchfield v. *Dreyfus*, [1906] 1 K.B. 584; 75 L.J.K.B. 447; 35 Digest (Repl.)
   232, *330.*

---

* See, in regard to this, p. 457, letter D, post.
† Section 6 (1) (d) is set out at p. 443, letter C, post.

A   *Koh Hor Khoon, Bankrupt (Official Assignee of the Property of)* v. *Ek Liong Hin, Ltd.*, [1960] 1 All E.R. 440; [1960] A.C. 178; [1960] 2 W.L.R. 250; 35 Digest (Repl.) 231, *219*.

Nash v. *Layton*, [1911] 2 Ch. 71; 80 L.J.Ch. 636; 104 L.T. 834; 18 Digest (Repl.) 206, *1798*.

Newman v. *Oughton*, [1911] 1 K.B. 792; 80 L.J.K.B. 673; 104 L.T. 211;
B   35 Digest (Repl.) 233, *338*.

North Central Wagon Finance Co., Ltd. v. *Brailsford*, [1962] 1 All E.R. 502; [1962] 1 W.L.R. 1288; Digest (Cont. Vol. A) 70, *86a*.

Premor, Ltd. v. *Shaw Brothers*, [1964] 2 All E.R. 583; [1964] 1 W.L.R. 978; 3rd Digest Supp.

United Dominions Trust, Ltd. v. *Kirkwood*, [1966] 1 All E.R. 968; [1966]
C   2 Q.B. 431; [1966] 2 W.L.R. 1083.

Weekes v. *Gallard*, (1869), 21 L.T. 655; 47 Digest (Repl.) 566, *47*.

Action.

This was an action, tried in the commercial list, by five plaintiffs for specific performance of an agreement made on Feb. 9, 1966, for (inter alia) the sale by the first defendants (called in this report "the old company") to the first plaintiffs, Frank H. Wright (Constructions), Ltd. (called in this report " the new company ")
D   of certain leasehold premises described in Sch. 1 to the agreement. The agreement comprised certain other property of the old company, and the price was to be ascertained in accordance with Sch. 3 to the agreement by independent accountants and was to be certified by them. The defendants contended that loans amounting to £192,000, or £96,000 part thereof, should not be taken into con-
E   sideration as liabilities and should not be deducted in computing the purchase price, since the loans were, it was contended, void and unenforceable under the Moneylenders Acts, 1900 to 1927. The defendants also counterclaimed for a declaration that the accountants' certificate of purchase price (i.e., their report, document R.5) did not constitute an ascertainment or certification of the price pursuant to the agreement and that the purchase price should be a reasonable price deter-
F   mined by the court, and for a declaration that the loans and securities therefor were void and unenforceable by reason of the Moneylenders Acts, 1900 to 1927. The £96,000 referred to above was money lent by the second plaintiffs, an issuing house, to the old company in the circumstances hereafter stated. The following statement of facts is summarised from the judgment of ROSKILL, J.

Birmingham Industrial Trust, Ltd., the second defendants, who are referred
G   to herein as " B.I.T.", were formed in 1959, and the primary objective* of the company was to operate as an issuing house and to carry out in Birmingham all the work which an issuing house ordinarily carries out. The primary object of B.I.T. as an issuing house, stated in evidence by Mr. Rudd, who was managing director of B.I.T. and had had long experience with Erlangers, Ltd., was shown by the following passage from his evidence—

H
"Q.—How would you describe the primary objects of B.I.T.'s business? A.—The primary object is that of an issuing house, the classical description of which, I think that it is fair to say, is that it acts as an intermediary between people requiring capital and people prepared to provide it. In that sense B.I.T. find capital either from their own resources or from financial institutions or a combination of the two for British industry generally.
I   Q.—Where does the issuing part come in? A.—Private companies who are in a good trade in our opinion and have got a profit record that is suitable for flotation, and have a good management team and management succession (these are the principal yardsticks that are applied), following a complete investigation, are converted from private companies into public companies. Their articles of association are changed accordingly and an application

---

* Provisions from the memorandum of association of B.I.T. and extracts from the chairman's annual review are set out at p. 447, letter I, to p. 448, letter I, post.

is made to the appropriate stock exchange or stock exchanges for a quotation of shares. The issuing house sponsors the whole thing, draws up the proposals and agrees them with the prospective client company and its advisers, and ultimately a prospectus is published. There are various ways in which it can be done. The principal ones are a public offer for sale in which case prospectuses and application forms are made available to the public generally and they apply for such number of shares as they wish to have. When all the applications are in the board of directors of the client company and B.I.T. together decide how the allotments shall be made ... Q.—Suppose that the company which comes to you is not yet in a state that will be attractive to the public, what then? A.—We apply the same tests to it. We say: is it in a trade that we think is a progressive one? Has it got good management? Has it got a profit record that looks promising? Does it look as though it will reach a flotation standard within a period of five years? Q.—What are the factors which may affect whether it can be brought to reach a flotation standard in five years? A.—Almost always it is a common factor. If a company is in a good trade, not a declining trade, and it has a good management team and can demonstrate by its past profits record that it understands what it can do and can trade profitably, the usual requirement is an injection of further capital; the issuing house and their legal accountancy advisers and the client company's directors and their legal and accountancy advisers get together and decide how much further capital is required. We recommend what form it should take, depending on all sorts of circumstances, principally the security available, if it is to be by way of loan, and the estate duty position of the principal shareholder, if it is to be by way of a subscription of shares, and that kind of thing."

The particular aim of B.I.T., when formed in 1959, was as and when opportunity offered and client companies came their way to endeavour to float such companies, or, if they were not immediately suitable for flotation, then to take the necessary steps (necessary in B.I.T.'s view) to get those companies ready for public flotation as and when B.I.T. might judge that the moment was ripe. During the years 1960-64 there was, on the evidence, no instance of an advance of money having been made without security and some hope or expectation of an ultimate flotation; to make such an advance would have been against the policy of the board of B.I.T. By 1964 B.I.T. had become exceedingly successful.

In July, 1964, the first defendants, later called Frodoor, Ltd. and referred to herein as "the old company", were a small private company of whom the second defendant, Mr. Wright, was controlling shareholder and managing director. The old company had a business in constructional steelwork and engineering work and was expanding rapidly, the business having been successfully built up by Mr. Wright. The old company was in need of further working capital. In July Mr. Wright approached B.I.T. for advice and help; B.I.T. became interested in the old company. A letter written in July on behalf of B.I.T. to Mr. Wright included the following—

"I have now been able to consider your problems with my colleagues. On the information made available to us it seems that it would not be in your best interests to sell the whole or even a substantial part of the business to another company. There would appear every chance that your business could be floated successfully within a few years' time on a basis which would enable you to realise substantial liquid funds, while retaining a majority shareholding with voting and executive control in a prosperous and expanding business ... we recognise that, prior to flotation, your business is likely to continue and need additional capital or expansion. As part of the above scheme, provided we were satisfied with the progress of the business, we would be prepared to provide on a medium term basis that part of such future capital that could not prudently be obtained on hire-purchase or from bank facilities, up to a previously agreed limit . . ."

On Oct. 21, 1964, £120,000 was lent to the old company; this was a joint loan by B.I.T. and an insurance company, Wesleyan and General Assurance Society, Ltd. (the third plaintiffs, called herein " Wesleyan Assurance "). The loan was secured by a single charge to the lenders jointly. In fact B.I.T. contributed £80,000 and Wesleyan Assurance contributed £40,000. Further finance was provided in the following February by way of overdraft from the old company's bank, the limit of overdraft being increased from £10,000 to £40,000 and the joint lenders consenting to the old company's creating a floating charge on its assets to secure the increased overdraft. In April, 1965, two other companies, I.T.C. Pension Trust, Ltd. and I.T.C. Pension Investments, Ltd., the fourth and fifth plaintiffs (herein called " the Imperial Tobacco companies ") participated to the extent of providing £35,000; the old company received an additional £20,000 by way of loan by this means, and B.I.T.'s and Wesleyan Assurance's loans were taken over to the extent of £10,000 and £5,000 respectively by the Imperial Tobacco companies. This brought the total joint loan to £140,000. Thereafter the lenders B.I.T., Wesleyan Assurance and the Imperial Tobacco companies became known collectively as the consortium. In June, 1965, the consortium put up a further £12,000, bringing the total loan to £152,000. This extra sum was provided as to £6,000 by B.I.T., as to £3,000 by Wesleyan Assurance and as to £3,000 by the Imperial Tobacco companies. In August, 1965, the consortium consented to the old company's bank overdraft facilities being increased to £50,000. In the summer of 1965 the financial side of the old company affair was going from bad to worse. By the end of September, 1965, relations with Mr. Wright had become strained. On Nov. 1, 1965, the consortium provided a further £40,000 in addition to the £152,000, bringing the total capital advanced to the old company to £192,000; moreover £7,822 interest on the £152,000 lent was outstanding. In January, 1966, a firm of management consultants sent a long report on the old company to B.I.T. This report contained the following passage—

" The net trading profit of [the old company] is falling and we feel that it will continue to do so, unless a strong line and drastic economies are affected immediately. Under existing circumstances we do not feel that [the old company] can meet its commitment and expenses over the next few years without considerable assistance."

Negotiations between the old company and B.I.T. and other members of the consortium followed. They culminated in a meeting on Feb. 9, 1966, and in a written agreement of that date which was signed. This was the agreement on which the plaintiffs sued in the present action. Its nature was summarised by the trial judge (ROSKILL, J.) as follows. Broadly speaking the scheme of the agreement was that a shell company bearing the name of Frodoor, Ltd., was to be used. The shell company was to purchase the old company's business and assets as a going concern at the best price at which it could get them. The scheme was not that the new company should purchase the shares of the old company. To this end and in accordance with the agreement the new company bought that business and those assets and took over the old company's name and the old company thus took on itself the new company's name. The written agreement of Feb. 9, 1966, included the following—

" 1. With the consent of the consortium the vendor [the vendor being by definition the old company*] shall sell and the purchaser [the purchaser being by definition the new company†] shall purchase ALL THAT the leasehold

---

* Viz., the old company, by its then name, Frank H. Wright (Constructions) Ltd., which was taken thereafter by the new company, the first plaintiff.

† Viz., a company then called Frodoor, Ltd., which name was thereafter changed to Frank H. Wright (Constructions) Ltd., the name Frodoor, Ltd., being taken by the old company, the first defendants.

premises more particularly specified in Sch. 1 hereto (hereinafter referred to as ' the leasehold premises ').

" 2. With the consent of the consortium the vendor shall sell and the purchaser shall purchase on a going concern basis as at the close of business on Feb. 9, 1966 (hereinafter called ' the transfer date ') the following items:—

" (A) The goodwill and connexion of the business (hereinafter called ' the said business ') heretofore carried on by the vendor from the leasehold premises and

" (B) The sole and exclusive right (so far as the vendor has power to dispose of the same) to use the name ' Frank H. Wright (Constructions) ' either alone or jointly with or as part of any other name or names and to represent the purchaser as carrying on the said business in succession to the vendor and

" (C) All cranes lorries cars and vehicles plant and machinery and all fixtures and fittings in the nature of tenants and trade fixtures and fittings used in connexion with the said business as at the transfer date all of which items are hereinafter together referred to as ' plant and fixtures ' and are listed in Sch. 2 hereto and

" (D) The stock-in-trade and work in progress of the said business as at the transfer date and

" (E) The trade debtors (sic) of the said busines as at the transfer date as specified in Sch. 6 hereto (other than the loan account of Mr. Wright) and

" (F) Cash in hand as at the tran:f r date

" (G) The full benefit of all contracts engagements and orders of the vendor with customers in connexion with the said business subsisting on the transfer date

" 3. The purchase price for the property hereinbefore agreed to be sold namely:—the leasehold premises; the goodwill of the said business and the benefit of all contracts and orders; the plant and fixtures (all of which are in a state of severance and capable of passing by delivery) and the stock in trade and work in progress and book debts shall be a sum to be ascertained in accordance with the provisions contained in Sch. 3 hereto.

" 4. The sum of £50,640 shall be paid forthwith into a bank deposit account in the joint names of Messrs. Wragge & Co. (the purchaser's solicitors) and Messrs. Partridge, Nightingale & Haldenby and the said sum or such lesser amount as shall be due to the vendor pursuant to the provisions of Sch. 3 hereto shall be released to the vendor's solicitors on completion.

" 5. Completion shall take place on or before May 9, 1966, at the offices of Messrs. Partridge, Nightingale & Haldenby.

" 6. (A) The vendor shall assign its interest in the leasehold premises as beneficial owner and the title shall commence with and shall consist of the lease and tenancy agreement referred to in Sch. 1 hereto (copies of which have already been supplied to the purchaser's solicitors). The consortium shall at the request of the purchaser assign [their] interest in the leasehold premises as mortgagees . . .

" 7. The vendor hereby warrants to and covenants with the purchaser that—(A) The vendor has and will on completion date have a good and marketable title to all the assets hereby agreed to be sold. (B) All the assets hereby agreed to be sold are the sole and unincumbered property of the vendor and are free from any lien charge or incumbrances save for the hire-purchase agreements particulars whereof are set out in Sch. 4 hereto. (C) The vendor is not aware of any abnormal or onerous contracts of the vendor in connexion with the said business provided that any claim under this warranty must be delivered to the vendor within fourteen days of the transfer date . . . (F) The value of the net assets agreed to be sold shall not be materially less on the transfer date than at Jan. 31, 1966. And this agreement is entered into on the basis of such warranties.

" 8.   (A) The purchaser shall discharge all pending contracts engagements and orders taken over by it under the provisions of cl. 2 (G) of this
agreement.

" (B) The vendor hereby irrevocably appoints the purchaser as its agents
for and on behalf of the vendor to discharge out of the purchase moneys
payable hereunder the vendor's liability as at the transfer date to the consortium and to National Provincial Bank, Ltd. [the old company's bank]
and to discharge the amount owing to the trade creditors of the vendor as
specified in Sch. 5 hereto and the amount owing on the hire-purchase
agreements as specified in Sch. 4 hereto.

" (C) Save as aforesaid the vendor hereby confirms and agrees that it
will accept responsibility for all claims which may hereafter arise out of
contracts with customers completed on or before the transfer date and will
pay satisfy and discharge all of the debts liabilities expenses and outgoings
in respect of the leasehold premises and the said business down to and
including the transfer date . . .

" (D) The purchaser will pay and discharge all debts and liabilities incurred
by the purchaser in relation to the said business after the transfer date and
shall keep the vendor indemnified against all proceedings costs charges
damages claims and demands in respect thereof.

" (E) The necessary apportionments to give effect to this clause shall be
made and settled on the completion date . . .

" 14.   On or before completion the vendor shall deliver to the purchaser
a duly executed assignment of the leasehold premises and if so requested
by the purchaser an assignment of goodwill and debtors (sic) in such form as
the purchaser may reasonably require . . .

" 15.   Notwithstanding completion of the sale and purchase hereby
agreed to be made this agreement shall remain in full force and effect so far
as it remains to be implemented.

" 16.   Each party shall bear its own costs in connexion with this agreement save that the costs of the accountants shall be paid by the purchaser."

The first schedule comprised the leasehold premises. The second schedule consisted of a long list of fixed assets. Those were priced and the price totalled
£255,635 5s. 4d.   The third schedule began as follows:—

" *Computation of Purchase Price*

The price for the assets specified in cl. 3 hereof shall be ascertained
and certified by Messrs. . . . chartered accountants (hereinafter called ' the
accountants ') whose decision as to the fair value of the said items (acting as
experts and not as arbitrators) shall be final and binding on all parties.   The
price for the said assets shall be ascertained by the accountants on the
following basis . . ."

The name of the accountants was left blank when the agreement was signed;
but within a day or two the parties agreed on Messrs. Cooper Brothers as
the accountants. Clause 4 of Sch. 3, which related to pricing stock and work in
progress is set out at p. 455, letter G, post.   Schedule 3 contained also the
following clauses, among others—

" 8. *Amount owing to the consortium.*   The accountants shall physically
verify the amounts outstanding as at Jan. 31, 1966, with the consortium.

" 11. *General.*   The accountants shall compute and certify the total
purchase price payable by the [new company] to the [old company] pursuant
to the provisions of this agreement by listing the values for the assets
specified above and deducting therefrom the values for the liabilities specified above (which are to be discharged by [the new company] as agent
for [the old company]) in every case calculating such values in accordance
with the provisions of this schedule.   The balance remaining after deducting

from the assets specified above (a) the liabilities specified above and (b) a discount sum of £5,000 shall be the total purchase price payable to [the old company]. If the balance remaining is less than £50,640 such an additional amount shall be paid by [the new company] as shall bring the total balance to £50,640 provided that the additional amount so payable by [the new company] shall not exceed £5,000."

The sixth schedule contained a "draft balance sheet" for the year ending Jan. 31, 1966. On the right hand side under the heading "Fixed Assets" was the figure £287,715. Those fixed assets included the leasehold premises, which were valued in the draft balance sheet at £69,796. The fixed assets other than the leasehold premises were valued, accordingly, at a total of £217,919. On the right hand side under "Current Assets" was "stock of material £45,013. Work in progress £9,000", which together represented £54,013. On the left hand side amongst the statement of liabilities were the share capital and the various reserves, and under the heading "Long Term Finance (Debentures)" was £192,000, the figure of the total of the loan indebtedness to the four members of the consortium. These were some only of the items shown. If a balance were struck between the two sides of the draft balance sheet, immediately after the statement of trade creditors and the sum due to the old company's bank, etc.* the resulting balance was £54,675. This figure appeared in the draft balance sheet immediately above the figure for the long term finance (i.e., the loans amounting to £192,000). The figure of £54,675 thus represented, so the trial judge indicated, the estimated net equity value which was being acquired. He continued—

"I have no doubt that when this agreement was executed, Mr. Wright and those advising him hoped that that figure represented substantially what the old company would obtain when Cooper Brothers carried out the task which was entrusted to them under the third schedule."

Mr. Wright left the business on Feb. 11, 1966. Pursuant to the agreement of Feb. 9, 1966, the new company took over the physical assets of the old company; it also took over the goodwill and the business of the old company and had been running that business ever since a day or two after Feb. 9, 1966. On Feb. 16, 1966, instructions were given to Cooper Brothers on behalf of the new company by letter, with which was enclosed a copy of the agreement of Feb. 9, 1966. The instructions were as follows—

"You will see that the contract calls for an independent accountant to compute the final purchase price payable in the light of a detailed examination and verification of the principal assets and liabilities acquired. We write to confirm that we wish you to act in the capacity of such independent accounant and to report to the parties concerned . . . the purchase price payable calculated in accordance with the provisions of the third schedule to the agreement."

On June 1, 1966, formal notice to complete the agreement was given by the solicitors acting for the consortium to the solicitors acting for Mr. Wright. On June 14, 1966, the accountants sent copies of their report to all parties concerned. This report was document R.5. It is the certificate for the purposes for Sch. 3 to the agreement of Feb. 9, 1966. It showed an excess of liabilities over assets of £14,701. Paragraphs 7 and 8 of the certificate are set out at p. 455, letter H, post. Its final paragraph, para. 22, reads—

"Having regard to the excess of liabilities over assets, after including claims and counter-claims, £29,454, there is no total purchase price as defined in the third schedule, payable to the vendor. The amount of £29,454 may be either increased or decreased when the company has determined the final liability arising from claims and counter-claims."

---

* Thus excluding, it seems, share capital and reserves.

The purchase price was thus certified at nil. The parties to the action were agreed that if the certificate was not binding on them a reasonable price would become payable to the old company and that the court should determine what that reasonable price was.

Leonard Caplan, Q.C., and *Norman C. Tapp* for the plaintiffs.
G. B. H. Dillon, Q.C., and *Adrian Hamilton* for the defendants.

ROSKILL, J., having reviewed the facts and the background to the case, and having stated the terms of the agreement of Feb. 9, 1966, and that there had been no suggestion that the accountants' report (R.5) was not a certificate for the purposes of Sch. 3 to the agreement, continued: The writ in this action was issued as recently as June 28, 1966, and it is a matter for congratulation to both parties and the solicitors that it has been possible to bring a case of this complexity to trial with such rapidity, for, if one ignores the long vacation, this case has come to trial within about two months of the issue of the writ. So much for what are sometimes called the law's delays.

In their points of claim the plaintiffs rely on document R.5 (the accountant's report), and claim specific performance of the agreement. The new company (1) has already taken possession of the assets of the old company (2) to be transferred under the agreement, and the only asset to which the claim for specific performance now effectively relates is the lease. The new company seeks to obtain the legal title to that lease. Under the agreement of Feb. 9, 1966 (3) it has only the equitable title.

The defendants have never sought to say that the agreement of Feb. 9, 1966, was not a perfectly good and binding agreement. On the contrary, para. 10 of the points of defence expressly and most properly averred that it was a valid and enforceable agreement. The defendants, however, went on to challenge the certificate for a large number of reasons. They challenged it in the old phrase, " to the polls and to the array ". They say first of all that all the plaintiffs, except the new company, are or were at the material time unlicensed money-lenders. They say that the loans totalling £192,000 ought for that reason never to have been brought into account by the independent accountants, Cooper Brothers (as unquestionably Cooper Brothers did bring them into account in assessing the liabilities of the old company when they prepared document R.5). The defendants said that for that reason alone the certificate was bad.

They went on to say that it was bad for a number of other reasons, all of which are pleaded in para. 6 either in the original points of defence or by amendments made during the trial. Having sought to attack the certificate in the points of defence in that way, they then counterclaimed. They seek a declaration that the certificate being of no effect, the price payable for the assets should be a reasonable price to be determined by the court; and they also seek a declaration that the loans and the various securities relating thereto are void and unenforceable by reason of the provisions of the Moneylenders Acts, 1900 to 1927. Finally, by an amendment which was only formally made this morning (though it is right to say that it was adumbrated a few days ago) they counterclaim that by reason of certain provisions at the end of Sch. 3 to the agreement the sum of £5,000 is payable to them even if they are wrong on all other points, as a condition precedent to completion. The £5,000 point is a completely isolated point.

The objective of the defence and counterclaim is in the circumstances under-standable. The defendants seek to upset Cooper Brothers' certificate and to obtain on a determination of a reasonable price by the court that which they had hoped to obtain but have not obtained on Cooper Brothers' certificate and to this end they say that when this determination is made the old company's indebtedness in respect of these loans must be excluded from the calculations. If the pleaded

---

(1) The new company is the first plaintiff, Frank H. Wright (Constructions), Ltd.
(2) The old company are the first defendants, Frodoor, Ltd. In regard to the change of name, see p. 437, letter I, ante.
(3) The relevant terms of the agreement are set out at p. 437, letter I, et seq., ante.

counterclaim succeeds and in any recalculation either £192,000 or B.I.T.'s (4) part of that sum, namely, £96,000, fell to be excluded, the change in Mr. Wright's (5) fortunes would be dramatic, for, instead of getting little or nothing for the business which he laboured to build up, he would stand to get a very substantial sum. The suggestion that Wesleyan and General Assurance Co., Ltd. (6), the Imperial Tobacco companies, viz., I.T.C. Pension Trust, Ltd. (6) and I.T.C. Pension Investments, Ltd. (6) were unlicensed moneylenders might at first sight seem to be a little startling. Counsel for the defendants certainly appeared to find it so, because early in the case he withdrew the allegation and limited the allegation of being unlicensed moneylenders to B.I.T. He said that he could not seek to knock out the whole of the £192,000. He was content with trying to knock out the more modest sum of £96,000 together with the related interest.

The moneylending allegation is perhaps the most important and far-reaching allegation in this case, not only because of its effect on the result of this case but because of its effect on any issuing house which has not got either a banking department or a banking associated or subsidiary company and which from time to time engaged in what I would call " bridging " financial operations. The case is also of considerable importance in connexion with the nature of the obligations of accountants who are enjoined, as Cooper Brothers were enjoined in this case, to value assets and liabilities for the purposes of a take-over whether of this kind or of any other kind. Are accountants in these circumstances bound to investigate, when valuing assets and liabilities, whether a particular asset or liability is in the strict and sometimes perhaps over-rigid eyes of the law a legally enforceable asset or liability of the company or firm in question, and meticulously exclude it if it is or may be legally unenforceable even though in the case of an asset it be commercially valuable? Those are perhaps the two main points of general importance which arise for decision. I therefore propose to consider each in turn, leaving over for subsequent consideration the detailed criticisms made of Cooper Brothers' certificate, for if counsel for the defendants can succeed on the moneylending point, that is enough, and I might almost say more than enough, for his purpose.

It is worth reflecting for one moment on the effect of the argument that in valuing the assets and liabilities of the old company Cooper Brothers were bound in law to exclude the loan debt to B.I.T. on the ground that it arose from illegal moneylending. If the argument be right, it would have the effect that B.I.T., who, with the rest of the consortium (7), have bound the new company to buy the assets of the old company on a net asset value, must first of all suffer the exclusion from the calculation of that net asset value, of the amount of their own loans which ex hypothesi were illegal moneylending transactions and thus irrecoverable, and secondly, participate in buying these assets at a value which, by reason of that exclusion, is correspondingly increased, notwithstanding that part of the assets will almost certainly represent some of the proceeds of these assumedly illegal loans. The result, though perhaps correct in law, is commercially so startling that the foundations of this argument must be closely examined. The law does, from time to time, produce strange results, especially when the statute law of one generation is allowed to continue unchanged into the altered social conditions of another. That has been frequently pointed out in the courts of recent years in the case of the Moneylenders Acts, 1900 to 1927. If I may venture to borrow a phrase used in this court some years ago by DEVLIN, J., after listening without much apparent sympathy to an argument put before him, the result is one which would only appeal to the most enthusiastic lawyer.

The Moneylenders Acts, 1900 to 1927, were intended at the time when they were

---

(4) Birmingham Industrial Trust, Ltd.; they were the second plaintiffs in the action.
(5) Mr. Wright was the second defendant; he was the controlling shareholder and managing director of the old company.
(6) These three companies were joint lenders with B.I.T.; together they formed the consortium (see p. 437, letter D, ante).
(7) The members of the consortium are apparent from p. 437, letter D, ante.

passed to be a weapon of defence for the oppressed. They have become in recent years a much sought after escape route for those who seek to avoid what some might think were their just obligations. That was emphasised in a very recent decision of the Court of Appeal in *United Dominions Trust, Ltd.* v. *Kirkwood* (8), a case to which I shall have to refer in more detail hereafter; but, as the Master of the Rolls and DIPLOCK, L.J., there said, and as counsel for the defendants has rightly emphasised in this case, the law must be applied, and so long as the law is what it has been held to be in the various cases decided under those statutes, it is the duty of the court to enforce that law and apply it whatever the commercial consequences may be.

I start this part of my judgment with a reference to the Money-lenders Act, 1900, itself. The word " moneylender " is defined in s. 6, so far as material, as follows :

> " The expression ' money-lender ' in this Act shall include every person whose business is that of money-lending, or who advertises or announces himself or holds himself out in any way as carrying on that business; but shall not include . . . (*d*) any person bona fide carrying on the business of banking or insurance or bona fide carrying on any business not having for its primary object the lending of money, in the course of which and for the purposes whereof he lends money . . ."

Nobody has suggested that B.I.T. carries on the business of either banking or insurance; if, therefore, it be the fact that they have engaged in moneylending, they can escape from the consequences of having so engaged only if they can establish to my satisfaction, the burden being on them to do so, that they were bona fide carrying on a business not having for its primary object the lending of money, in the course of which and for the purposes whereof they lent money. So much for the statute.

The correct approach to the question which I have to decide was stated by the Court of Appeal in *United Dominions Trust, Ltd.* v. *Kirkwood* (8). LORD DENNING, M.R., under the rubric " Burden of Proof ", first of all set out the section which I have just read, and then went on (9):

> " The structure of the section clearly suggests that every person whose business is that of moneylending is to be regarded as a moneylender unless he can bring himself within one of the specified exceptions. It was so construed by FLETCHER MOULTON, L.J., in *Nash* v. *Layton* (10), who said that a judge would have to direct the jury that ' they must find he is a money-lender, unless he came within one of the specified exceptions '. Similarly, McCARDIE, J., in *Edgelow* v. *MacElwee* (11) said that if it appears that a ' business of moneylending is carried on, then the requirements of the definition in s. 6 of the Act of 1900 are fulfilled and the question arises whether the case falls within the exception indicated in that section '. Likewise CAIRNS, J., in *North Central Wagon Finance Co., Ltd.* v. *Brailsford* (12) said that it was for the plaintiffs, ' to show that they fell within the exception in s. 6 (*d*) of the Money-lenders Act, 1900, and they have not established this '. I am of the same opinion as those judges and hold that once the opening words of s. 6 are satisfied, the burden is on the person to bring himself within the exception on which he relies. The facts are within the knowledge of the lender and not the borrower, and he should prove them. He who affirms must prove.

> " In the present case U.D.T. sued as holder of five bills of exchange, each of £1,000. Once it produced those bills of exchange, the legal burden passed to the defendant to prove that U.D.T. was an unregistered moneylender.

---

(8) [1966] 1 All E.R. 968; [1966] 2 Q.B. 431.
(9) [1966] 1 All E.R. at p. 972; [1966] 2 Q.B. at pp. 441, 442.
(10) [1911] 2 Ch. 71 at p. 79.   (11) [1918] 1 K.B. 205 at p. 206.
(12) [1962] 1 All E.R. 502 at p. 508.

In order to discharge that burden, the defendant had to prove that the business of U.D.T. was that of moneylending. For this purpose the defendant proposed to deliver the usual interrogatories in the form settled by *Nash* v. *Layton* (13). But U.D.T.'s solicitor avoided these interrogatories by making in a letter the admission that ' our clients have for many years past made and do make numerous loans of money to customers. Such loans are made by our clients at varying rates of interest in the course of their business '. That admission was sufficient proof that U.D.T. carried on the business of moneylending. The burden then passed to U.D.T. to prove that they came within exception (*d*), i.e., that they bona fide carried on the business of banking."

HARMAN, L.J., in a dissenting judgment, said (14):

"The only point on this appeal, and indeed the only one in the court below, can be shortly stated in the form of question and answer: Q.—When is a moneylender not a moneylender? A.—When he is a banker.

"Now a moneylender is described in the Money-lenders Act, 1900, as including ' every person whose business is that of money-lending ' and that is admittedly the plaintiffs' principal business. That, as FARWELL, J., observed many years ago (*Litchfield* v. *Dreyfus* (15)) is a perfectly respectable trade, but the legislature has thought fit to enact that he who carries it on must be registered as such. Section 6 of the Act of 1900 which defines moneylenders makes certain exceptions. Relevant here is (*d*)—' any person bona fide carrying on the business of banking '."

It is against that recent statement of the law that I approach the question in this case. It follows that it is for the defendants to show that B.I.T. were money-lenders. Once the defendants do this, it is for B.I.T. to show that they come within that part of the exception in (*d*) which I have already read and on which alone they can seek to rely. There is no suggestion that B.I.T. were bankers: plainly they are not; they have never been. Therefore the present problem is different from the problem involved in *United Dominions Trust, Ltd.* v. *Kirk-wood* (16). In the present case B.I.T. say that they were not moneylenders; but they also say that if, contrary to that contention, they were, then they were bona fide carrying on the business of an issuing house which does not have for its primary object the lending of the money, and that such loans as they from time to time made (including the loans in question in the present case) were made in the course of and for the purposes of their issuing house business. It is for B.I.T. to make good that contention if they can.

It is not necessary to go through all the cases. I have referred to the *United Dominions Trust* case (16), in which reference was made to one of the earliest cases under the Act of 1900, *Litchfield* v. *Dreyfus* (17); but it is necessary to mention three of the most recent authorities. The first is *Official Assignee of the Property of Koh Hor Khoon* v. *Ek Liong Hin, Ltd.* (18). The second is *North Central Wagon Finance Co., Ltd.* v. *Brailsford* (19), the decision referred to by LORD DENNING, M.R., in his judgment in the *United Dominions Trust* case (16), approving the judgment of CAIRNS, J. The last and perhaps the most important is *Premor, Ltd.* v. *Shaw Brothers* (20).

I can consider the *Koh Hor Khoon* case (18) by reference to what was said about it in the *Premor* case (20). There is one passage in the *North Central Wagon Finance* case (21) which I should quote. CAIRNS, J., after dealing with other matters, dealt with the defendants' contentions under the Moneylenders Acts.

(13) [1911] 2 Ch. 71.   (14) [1966] 1 All E.R. at p. 981; [1966] 2 Q.B. at p. 456.
(15) [1906] 1 K.B. 584 at p. 590.   (16) [1966] 1 All E.R. 968; [1966] 2 Q.B. 431.
(17) [1906] 1 K.B. 584.   (18) [1960] 1 All E.R. 440; [1960] A.C. 178.
(19) [1962] 1 All E.R. 502.   (20) [1964] 2 All E.R. 583.
          (21) [1962] 1 All E.R. at pp. 507, 508.

A He said with reference to the argument that the North Central Wagon Finance Co. were not moneylenders (22):

" The plaintiffs have a very large business. Their turnover at the material time was to be reckoned in millions, and about 0·5 per cent. of that business, at least, consisted of what are described in their accounts as ' loans and debentures '. This is apart from any questions of whether the plaintiffs had

B other transactions like the one involved in this case, which appear in their accounts as hire-purchase, but may in truth have had the character of loans. A half of one per cent. is a small fraction but it represents business to the extent of something like £10,000 at least, and, in my opinion, a person who makes a business of lending money is not any the less a moneylender because he carries on some other business as well on a much larger scale."

C I respectfully agree with and adopt that passage.

In *Premor, Ltd.* v. *Shaw Brothers* (23) the Court of Appeal considered the problem whether what are popularly called " stocking transactions " (that is loans for the purpose of building up a stock of motor cars) made by a company who were a hire-purchase finance company were caught by the Money-lenders

D Act, 1900. The Court of Appeal, which included LORD DENNING, M.R., and DIPLOCK, L.J., held that those particular transactions were caught by the Moneylenders Acts. It is necessary to quote at some length from the judgments both of the Master of the Rolls and of DIPLOCK, L.J., because this case deals directly with the point which has been canvassed in the present case and the circumstances in which it can be said that a company carrying on a particular business and also lending money, is lending money in the course of and for the

E purposes of that business.

LORD DENNING, M.R., said (24): " Now, was the finance company a money-lender? ". His lordship then read the definition which I have read already, read what is relevant in para. (*d*) of s. 6 of the Act of 1900 for the purposes of the present case, and continued (25):

F " The question in this case is whether the finance company brings itself within that exception (*d*). The first requirement is that it should carry on a business ' not having for its primary object the lending of money '. I think that it satisfies that requirement. The primary object of this hire-purchase finance company was to enter into ordinary hire-purchase transactions. It bona fide carried on the business of a hire-purchase finance company. So far,

G so good. But the second requirement is that the lending of the money must be ' in the course of ' that business; and the third requirement is that it must be ' for the purposes of ' that business.

" Take the requirement that the lending of the money must be ' in the course of ' the business, that is, of the primary business which the person carries on. It seems to me that, in order that it should be in the course of the

H primary business, it must be associated with a transaction that business so as to be linked with it. A good illustration of such a link is found in the recent case in the Privy Council of *Official Assignee of the Property of Koh Hor Khoon, Bankrupt* v. *Ek Liong Hin, Ltd.* (26). In that case a company carried on business as rubber merchants and shipowners and warehousemen. In the course of that business they took goods into store in a ' godown ',

I and, as an ordinary commercial facility of that business, they advanced money to certain selected customers who stored goods in the godown. The lending of money was directly and immediately associated with the storage of parcels of goods in the godown. It was held that it was ' in the course of ' the business that the moneys were lent. Another illustration is when a solicitor in the course of his business lends money to a client who is in special

(22) [1962] 1 All E.R. at pp. 507, 508.   (23) [1964] 2 All E.R. 583.
(24) [1964] 2 All E.R. at p. 586.   (25) [1964] 2 All E.R. at pp. 586, 587.
(26) [1960] 1 All E.R. 440; [1960] A.C. 178.

need in regard to some particular transaction. It is a transaction which   A
the solicitor is handling at the time as a solicitor and the loan is made so as
to help the client complete that transaction.

" I ask myself: were the loans in the present case made in the course of the
primary business of the hire-purchase finance company? I am not satisfied
that they were. I can well understand that if a finance company were to lend
money to a dealer in order that the dealer could buy a specific car which was   B
to be put through on hire-purchase with the finance company, then it might
be made ' in the course of ' the hire-purchase business. It would be linked
with a specific hire-purchase transaction. But in this case many of these loans
were not linked with any specific car, and indeed, not with any hire-purchase
transaction at all. They were not made ' in the course of ' that business.

" The other requirement, in order that the finance company should bring   C
itself within the exception is that the lending must have been ' for the
purpose of ' the primary business. In other words, it must have been done
with the object of promoting the business. To satisfy this requirement,
counsel for the finance company suggested that it was sufficient if the loan
kept the customer ' sweet ', as he put it, that is, kept him well-disposed
towards the hire-purchase finance company. I do not think that that is   D
sufficient. It seems to me that the purpose of the lender in making the loan
must be directly to help the primary business as distinct from getting a
high rate of interest upon the loan. In this present case it seems pretty
clear that the purpose of the finance company was not to help their primary
business. It was simply to lend money to a customer who was ready to pay—
by way of an exchange cheque—a high rate of interest."   E

DANCKWERTS, L.J., dealt with the matter more briefly thus (27):

" It is true that it has been lending money to dealers, but, as the learned
judge . . . said, that has no real connexion with the motor trade, and it
seems to me that it is simply the lending of money on profitable terms and
has really no connexion with the main and legitimate business of a hire-   F
purchase company."

DIPLOCK, L.J., analysed the decision of the Privy Council in the *Khoon* case (28)
and sought to distinguish it (29). It is not I think necessary to discuss that in
relation to the present case. He concluded that in any event, whatever the
Privy Council had said, their decision did not represent the law of England. He
then stated what in his view the law of England is (30):   G

" The lending of money must be ' in the course of ' some business other
than that of lending money; that is to say, it must be associated with transactions entered into as part of such other business. It must also be ' for the
purposes of ' such other business; that is to say, the money must be lent with
the primary object of promoting the success of such other business and not of
obtaining profits on the loans.   H

" In my view, in order to determine whether a person who lends money
in the course of his business falls within the exception defined in para. (*d*)
of s. 6 of the Money-lenders Act, 1900, one must look (A) at the whole of the
business done by him apart from lending money, and (B) at all the loans
of money made by him, and ask whether every loan of money, apart from
mere isolated transactions (see *Newman* v. *Oughton* (31)) is (i) associated   I
with a specific transaction which forms part of the business done by him other
than such loans, and (ii) made with the primary object of promoting the
success of such other business and not of obtaining profit on the loan."

It is against that background that I turn to consider whether or not B.I.T. has

---

(27) [1964] 2 All E.R. at p. 588.   (28) [1960] 1 All E.R. 440; [1960] A.C. 178.
(29) [1964] 2 All E.R. at p. 589.   (30) [1964] 2 All E.R. at p. 590.
                    (31) [1911] 1 K.B. 792.

A   satisfied me that they are entitled to the benefit of the exemption in the relevant
part of para. (*d*) of s. 6 of the Money-lenders Act, 1900.

The British Issuing Houses Booklet (32), to which I have already referred,
states specifically and authoritatively what are the functions of an issuing house.
On p. 2 it says:

B   " Generally speaking the prime function of an issuing house is to act as an
intermediary between those who need capital and those who are willing
to provide it by investing. Before the first world war and up to the early
1930's many of the city issuing houses were primarily concerned with the
issue of bonds of foreign governments and companies. The reason for this
was that London was the financial centre of the world to which most countries
came to borrow and to which the investors of the world came to buy invest-

C   ments. At that time British industry was growing up in relatively small
units throughout the country and tended to be either self-financing or locally
financed. Gradually the business of foreign issues died away, partly because
the hazards of investing in foreign bonds became greater and partly because
for domestic reasons restrictions on their issue in London were imposed.
At the same time, by reason of expansion, amalgamations, and reorganisation

D   schemes, the capital needs of individual British companies became greater and
their problems more complex, and the use by them of the services of issuing
houses gradually increased."

I will not lengthen this judgment by reading the whole of that booklet, though
one might well incorporate the whole of it. It is extremely illuminating. It ends

E   under the heading:

" General. Most issuing houses are prepared and equipped to handle
issues of any size, large or small. Apart from the normal activities of the
issuing houses some members of the Issuing Houses Association manage
specialist organisations designed to cater for the smaller operations, without
having to disturb the status of private companies. Issuing houses are,

F   moreover, not concerned solely with operations involving stock exchange
quotations, and there are many occasions, often involving large sums of
money, on which securities are privately placed.

" Following the trend of diversification and integration within British
industry and the growing interest of overseas companies in gaining a footing
in British industry during the past fifteen years or so companies have

G   increasingly found themselves in need of financial advice regarding the
terms of mergers and take-overs. It is only natural, therefore, that companies
should have turned to issuing houses for this advice. This has become a
very important and specialist part of the issuing houses' business not only
with regard to the calculation of fair and reasonable financial terms but also
with regard to the best method by which such mergers or take-overs can be

H   effected.

" A further important consideration to the issuing house will be to foster a
continuing relationship with its client. Whether the business it has transacted is an issue of securities or a merger it is not enough that it should just
complete the business and do nothing further; the issuing house will always
try to keep up to date with its clients' developments and to continue to

I   keep in touch so as to be in a position to give advice and assistance as
needed."

I turn to B.I.T.'s memorandum and articles of association, though these are
not of great importance. As one would expect, cl. 3 (A) of the memorandum provides for B.I.T. to carry on business as an issuing house. Clause 3 (I) provides
that they may

" make advances to customers and others with or without security, and

---

(32) First published in 1950; but revised in 1965.

upon such terms as the company may approve, and generally to act as bankers for customers and others."

I turn next to the various accounts of B.I.T. which were put in evidence during the hearing. I do not propose to read more than a very few passages, but some are extremely illuminating. I begin with the report and accounts for the year ending Dec. 31, 1960, the first full year that B.I.T. had operated. The report sets out the names of the directors and the accounts follow. The chairman's review states:

" As many of our members know, the company was founded to perform the following services: (i) To advise on, and sponsor, new issues by public companies. (ii) To sponsor the flotation of suitable private companies. (iii) To provide, and find sources of, additional capital for companies not yet ready for flotation. (iv) To invest in, and find investors for, securities of suitable companies to provide funds for their shareholders."

In that first year the profit shown was a comparatively small £33,000. I will pass to the report for the next year which is perhaps the most important of all these documents. The profits had risen from £33,000 to £54,000. In the chairman's review appears this statement:

" Besides sponsoring two placings, an offer for sale, and the underwriting of a rights issue, all of which, by their nature, have been made known to you in the financial columns of the press, we have been active behind the scenes. We have made advances to and raised funds for private companies which, with our help and guidance, are likely to be floated within the next few years. A further addition has been made to the list of companies for which we act as registrars. We have also been able to fulfil our role as financial advisers to our clients both generally on everyday financial matters, and specifically in connexion with acquisitions and mergers."

I can now jump three years to 1964. In Sir Evan Norton's review as chairman one finds this statement:

" During 1964, we sponsored one offer for sale, three placings, and two rights issues. Although this represents a smaller number of issues than in the previous years, the amount of new money raised was more than fifty per cent. greater than in any previous year. We also advised on a number of acquisitions and mergers. Our greatest activity has, however, been in providing advice and finance to private companies which, under our guidance, will, we hope, be brought to the market in future years. This activity is reflected in the balance sheet by the increase in unquoted investments from £141,867 to £306,459 and by the increase in loans from £203,363 to £313,041. Much of our time towards the end of 1964 was devoted to preparing for flotations to take place during 1965."

Finally, in the accounts for 1965 one finds Sir Evan Norton saying this:

" During the year, we introduced to the stock market five companies, two by way of offers for sale and three by way of placings. In addition, we arranged the placing of two substantial debenture issues for existing clients and we handled five acquisitions or mergers involving quoted public companies. There was a satisfactory increase in our private financing operations for companies that we expect to bring to the stock market in the future. Three companies were added to the list of those for whom we act as registrars and we now carry out registration work for eighteen public companies."

The accounts for these years show by and large a steady increase in the amount of investment and in the amount of profit; and this was the position when Mr. Wright came to B.I.T. towards the end of 1964.

In the course of the trial there were put in evidence seven sets of B.I.T. documents. These are cases where advances were made by B.I.T. to various companies between May, 1964, and March, 1966; and, in addition, I was told there had been four earlier similar transactions in the years beginning with the foundation of the company at the end of 1959 and March, 1964. Clearly large sums of money have been advanced. In the course of a long cross-examination of Mr. Rudd (33) counsel for the defendants went through these documents one by one with a view to showing that these were moneylending transactions and were not transactions in the ordinary course of or for the purpose of the primary business of B.I.T. as an issuing house. Emphasis was laid on the fact that the customer was not legally bound to employ B.I.T. for the ultimate flotation and that the making of the loans was not contractually linked with the ultimate flotation of the company on the market.

Commercial considerations do not always depend on legal rights, and I have no doubt that, whatever the legal effect of clauses such as cl. 10 in B.I.T. document E may be (certainly it seems to me, as at present advised, that it had no legal effect) its commercial effect would be considerable if not conclusive.

The detailed pattern varies in each of these cases. The overall picture is broadly the same. The nature of the security varies, as it obviously will, according to the nature of the business of the company to which an advance is being made; but I think that the business throughout in the making of these loans and the taking of the securities is part of the business of an issuing house. It is not the only business. It is a part and it is only a part.

In order to give B.I.T. exemption, it is not, of course, enough that those to whom they have made advances were customers. It is not enough that advances may have been made, to use the expression quoted by LORD DENNING, M.R., in the *Premor* case (34), to keep the customer " sweet ". B.I.T. have got to show much more than that. No doubt it is true, as counsel for the defendants said and Mr. Rudd agreed, that the mere fact that B.I.T. have a loan agreement which contemplates floatation does not mean that ultimately a flotation will of necessity follow, or that if it does follow, B.I.T. will necessarily be the issuing house which makes the flotation. The expectation at the time of the loan may be defeated by a number of events. The controlling shareholder may change his mind; he may die; his management team may change; the scheme may change. There may be a score of reasons why that which was contemplated or expected at the time of the loan does not in the event ultimately materialise. All those are matters which have to be taken into account in considering what is the right conclusion on the facts as a whole.

It was said that the rate of interest was high. So it was; but I doubt whether it was higher than the rate charged by other issuing houses. There was a ceiling of ten per cent.; and in the circumstances, that can hardly be condemned as usurious or extortionate. It is perfectly clear on the evidence of Mr. Rudd—and I have no hesitation whatever in accepting his evidence on this and all other points—that the primary object of making these loans was not getting interest on the loan or making a profit on the loan. The making of the loan was merely part of the issuing house business which was done as a preliminary step to bringing the company concerned to the ultimate stage of being ripe for flotation, when all the conditions which B.I.T. regarded as essential prerequisites to successful flotation were satisfied. [HIS LORDSHIP referred to various passages in the evidence, and continued:] It is clear that B.I.T. do not look to these loans as a major source of revenue; they do not regard them as anything but one of their minor sources of revenue. An attempt was made during counsel for the defendants' cross-examination to break down the annual profits. The plaintiffs had not been asked to supply these figures before and details were not formally given in evidence; but counsel for the plaintiffs did produce a number of figures which are

---

(33) The managing director of B.I.T.   (34) [1964] 2 All E.R. at p. 587, letter E.

recorded on the transcript. I gave counsel for the defendants an opportunity of challenging them if he wished, but he wisely said that he thought that no purpose would be served by doing so. I can therefore take those figures, though not formally proved, as substantially accurate. It is clear from them that the proportion of the income of B.I.T. over the years from interest on these loans is small compared with the proportion of income which has come from other sources. They rely on their participations and flotations and on realisation of securities, for the greater part of their income. I am satisfied that these loans were not isolated moneylending transactions independent of the major part of their business.

I can best state my conclusions on this part of this case in this way: I am constrained by authority to hold that the loans of which I have been told, that is the four between 1959 and 1964, and the eight, including the present case, between March, 1964, and the present year, are in the eyes of the law moneylending transactions. I do not see what else they can be having regard to the way in which the statute has been construed over the years. Thus the burden shifts to B.I.T. to bring themselves within para. (*d*) of s. 6 of the Money-lenders Act, 1900: but only a very small part of B.I.T.'s annual profit comes from these loans. That of itself, of course, is not enough, as CAIRNS, J., pointed out in the *North Central Wagon* case (35). B.I.T., however, regularly refuse to make loans: they do not lend to all and sundry. They only lend where the loan is linked with a prospect of flotation in the future and in the eyes of B.I.T. it is necessary and desirable before a company is floated off as a public company that it should receive a temporary injection of fresh capital, just as they may take the view that such a company requires an injection of new management or financial advice.

Counsel for the defendants strenuously argued that there was no sufficient association between a loan made and a specific flotation transaction to bring the present case within the principles which LORD DENNING, M.R., and DIPLOCK, L.J., stated in the *Premor* case (36). I do not think that that is right. It must, of course, be a question of degree in each case; but in my judgment there is shown here to be in every case which has been closely examined the necessary link. There is an association in each case between the loan which was made and the anticipated flotation which it was hoped was going to be made. In no case was a loan made at large. On the contrary, in every case the loan was made " in the course of and for the purposes of " (to return to the language of the statute (37)) the very business which B.I.T. were formed to conduct, namely, the business of an issuing house.

One function of an issuing house—by no means its only function—is to get companies ready for flotation. When in the course of fulfilling that function, which involves bringing some one who needs capital to some one who has got capital, a loan is made, then in my judgment a loan so made (in the circumstances in which the loans were made by B.I.T. in the present case and in all the other cases which have been examined) is within the language of para. (*d*), that is to say, as being a loan made by a company bona fide carrying on a business of an issuing house, not having for its primary object the lending of money, in the course of which and for the purposes whereof the company lends money.

In the result, the defence raised under the Moneylenders Acts, 1900 to 1927, fails. But before I leave this matter I ought perhaps to say this. If my judgment be correct, no difficulty arises for the future where issuing houses who are not also bankers engage in this type of bridging finance; but should the view be taken that my decision is not correct, then the proposals embodied in cl. 85 of the Companies Bill (38) at present before Parliament would not put matters right. The proposals

---

(35) [1962] 1 All E.R. at p. 508.
(36) [1964] 2 All E.R. 583.
(37) See Money-lenders Act, 1900, s. 6 (1) (*d*).
(38) Bill No. (153), ordered to be printed on Nov. 21, 1966, being the Bill as amended in committee when before the House of Lords.

in that Bill, if I understand them correctly, are designed to give statutory effect to the suggestions made by LORD DENNING, M.R., in *United Dominions Trust, Ltd.* v. *Kirkwood* (39) that there should in future be a register of bankers so that the arguments which were then advanced and reluctantly accepted in HARMAN, L.J.'s dissenting judgment could not be repeated, and it could not be contended that persons carrying on business such as that of United Dominions Trust, Ltd. were not bankers. I would venture to make these observations for such considerations as they may merit. Legislation is now before Parliament for the purpose of giving effect to the view (frequently expressed in the courts in recent years) that the Moneylenders Acts, 1900 to 1927, are outdated in the light of modern financial needs. It may be thought desirable to widen the proposed provisions of cl. 85 so that the proposals relating to bankers may be extended to cover issuing houses and any other finance institutions engaging in financial operations of the kind just discussed.

My decision on the question under the Moneylenders Acts, 1900 to 1927, disposes of the first part of the defence and makes it unnecessary to deal with the other point which was argued by counsel for the defendants, namely, that Cooper Brothers ought to have struck these loans by B.I.T. out of the draft balance sheet, when making their assessment of the assets and liabilities of the old company for the purpose of arriving at the purchase price payable.

Counsel for the plaintiffs argued that even if the plaintiffs were wrong on the Moneylenders Acts point, it did not matter in the circumstances of this case having regard to the mandate which Cooper Brothers received in Sch. 3 to the agreement of Feb. 9, 1966, and the other terms of that agreement. It was said that, if these loans were unlawful moneylending transactions, Cooper Brothers were in no way bound to give effect to the strict legal position: that they were concerned to value what the parties had agreed in principle should be treated as liabilities and assets and nothing else. Although this point does not strictly arise for decision, having regard to the careful arguments on both sides, I ought to deal with the matter, for the point is of some general importance.

Schedule 3 to the agreement of Feb. 9, 1966, (40) enjoins Cooper Brothers to strike a balance. They are to value certain of the liabilities described in the third schedule and they are to value certain of the assets as therein set out; and they are told at the end of that schedule that the balance remaining after deducting from the assets (a) those liabilities and (b) a certain sum of £5,000, will be what is described at the end of the third schedule as the total purchase price payable to the vendors. The mandate of Cooper Brothers is to be found in the third schedule and nowhere else, and their letter of appointment (41) was clearly written so as to come within the framework of that mandate.

What in these circumstances is meant by " liabilities "? The word is used not only in the third schedule, but also, for example, in cl. 8 of the agreement (42). It was argued by counsel for the defendants that those " liabilities " could as a matter of construction only be the old company's legal liabilities, and, if, therefore, there were what I might call prima facie " liabilities " which on investigation proved to be caught by the Moneylenders Acts, 1900 to 1927, then the accountants were not only entitled, but also were as a matter of law bound, to strike out those liabilities when arriving at the balance and ignore them on the ground that they were irrecoverable against the old company. The argument to my mind is far reaching and not without difficulty; for one can see that in some cases if a company showed in its books a liability or an asset, for example, a gaming transaction, which plainly was irrecoverable in law, an accountant would value on that basis and it might well be his duty in assessing the value of that liability or asset to take into account the fact that it was irrecoverable and perhaps

---

(39) [1966] 1 All E.R. 968; [1960] 2 Q.B. 431.
(40) Regarding this schedule, see p. 439, letters G to I, ante.
(41) The letter of appointment is stated, so far as relevant, at p. 440, letter G, ante.
(42) For cl. 8, see p. 439, letters A to D, ante.

wholly to disregard its existence.   If counsel's argument is pressed to its logical
extreme, it involves that if one insurance company is taking over another and the
assets or liabilities of that latter insurance company include, for example, the
benefit of or liabilities under a p.p.i. policy of marine insurance which is caught by
s. 4 of the Marine Insurance Act, 1906, or before s. 23 and s. 25 of that Act were
amended by the Finance Act, 1959, the benefit of or liabilities under an unstamped
policy of marine insurance or a re-insurance treaty running for more than twelve
months, the accountants would be bound to disregard those assets or liabilities
as arising under illegal contracts, and to adjust the resulting valuation accordingly,
notwithstanding that commercially everybody would know that the fact that a
policy was p.p.i. or was unstamped, or that the treaty ran for more than twelve
months, would in no way affect its real value, because the point would never be
taken by or against the company in question.

Counsel for the plaintiffs took the argument one step further.   He asked what
would happen if accountants were directed to value the assets and liabilities of a
bookmaking business, all or virtually all the assets and liabilities of which consisted of gaming debts.   Are those all to be treated as of no value because of the
provisions of the Gaming Acts?   Is the bookmaker to be expected to plead the
Gaming Acts and risk being reported to Tattersalls?   Is the value of the business
to be assessed at virtually nothing?   It is difficult to think that an accountant's
duty can in such circumstances involve so drastic a treatment of assets and liabilities of that kind.   It must, of course, ultimately depend on the construction
of the particular agreement and the duty which is put on the accountants by
their mandate under the particular agreement.   It must be borne in mind in
relation to the present case that what the parties were referring to in the agreement
and in Sch. 3 to the agreement of Feb. 9, 1966, as liabilities included those matters
which are shown in the draft balance sheet in Sch. 6 thereto as liabilities, and those
liabilities include the debt of £192,000 (of which the B.I.T. loan was part).

In my judgment on the true construction of this mandate the accountants were
not bound when valuing those liabilities to consider whether or not the Moneylenders Act, 1900 to 1927, would apply.   Their task was to look at those liabilities
set out in the draft balance sheet and referred to in the third schedule and to
value them in accordance with the provisions of the third schedule.   They were to
put such value on them as they thought fit.   I do not think that, in a case such as
the present, it was any part of their duty to be astute to look behind those liabilities or to consider if there lay a possible defence to them.   It was for them and
them alone to consider what was the right value to place on those liabilities taking
such matters into account as they thought it right to do.

There are one or two other points with which it will be convenient to deal
before I deal with the detailed criticisms of the certificate (document R.5) (43).

Counsel for the plaintiffs sought to say that if, contrary to his submission,
the plaintiffs were engaged in unlawful moneylending, they could nevertheless
escape the consequences on the ground that they were engaged on a joint venture
with those who by concession were not unlicensed moneylenders.   He said that
there was but a single loan and a single obligation.   Of this argument I will say
only that if I had found it necessary to decide the point, I would have decided
it against the plaintiffs.   I cannot think that one who is ex hypothesi an unlicensed
moneylender can escape the consequences of being an unlicensed moneylender by
doing that which he himself cannot lawfully do in conjunction with others who
can lawfully lend money.

The other matter which deserves mention, but happily no more, is the question
debated yesterday what the position regarding the totality of the loans
would have been had I held that B.I.T. were unlicensed moneylenders.   Both
sides were at great pains to urge on me that that conclusion would not render so
much of the loans as were attributable to Wesleyan and General Assurance

_____

(43) The certificate was, or was part of, the accountants' report, which was document
R.5; see p. 440, letter I, ante.

Society, Ltd. and the Imperial Tobacco companies (44) irrecoverable. It was said by counsel for the defendants that the other members of the consortium (45) could sue the old company for their parts of the loans, joining B.I.T. (the assumedly unlicensed moneylenders) as defendants and could then recover their parts of the loan, notwithstanding the joint nature of the loan.

Counsel for the plaintiffs, on the other hand, went further. He accepted the first part of counsel for the defendants' contention that the consortium other than B.I.T. had the right to sue, joining B.I.T. as defendants, but argued that the consortium other than B.I.T. could recover the whole of the loan. When pressed to say what would happen to that part which was in fact advanced by B.I.T., he said that was recoverable by B.I.T. as a partner in the consortium from the other partners unless the latter chose to raise the defence of illegality as against B.I.T., a point which he said they would be unlikely to raise.

I confess that I find this point one of the utmost difficulty, because the loan in the first place is expressed to be a joint loan (46). Neither counsel was able to draw my attention to any authority which suggested that, if one party to the making of a joint loan is acting illegally in making that loan so that at least his part of that loan is an illegal transaction, nevertheless the other parties making that joint loan are left untainted and with full rights. Neither of the arguments put forward convinced me, and the matter can be left to arise for decision if and when the occasion arises. It may be that it would be necessary to have recourse to the as yet undeveloped law of unjustified enrichment in order to avoid the production of a somewhat remarkable result.

I now turn to deal more briefly with the remaining grounds of attack on the certificate. It must be remembered that the court is not a court of appeal from Cooper Brothers. The circumstances in which the court will interfere with a certificate of this kind are extremely restricted. The court will not and should not be astute to upset the decisions of those whom the parties have freely chosen to decide their problems for them. Any contrary approach would involve uncertainty and delay in ordinary every-day business affairs. Parties take their arbitrators and they take their experts (whether accountants or otherwise) for better or worse with the attendant risks of error which are inherent in the ordinary human weaknesses of any tribunal. But there are some occasions which are well defined when the court will and must interfere. Three cases which were referred to in the argument clearly lay down the principles. The first is *Collier* v. *Mason* (47), a decision of SIR JOHN ROMILLY, M.R. In that case the plaintiff was the owner of a house called " The Firs ". The defendant, having advertised for a house, negotiations were entered into between the defendant and the plaintiff which went on for some considerable time. Ultimately, it was agreed that Mr. Collier should sell and Mr. Mason should buy the house, " at such a price or sum as should be fixed by reference to Mr. B. A. Englehart, auctioneer and house agent ". Mr. Englehart did his task, but the result did not satisfy the plaintiff, who thought he was getting too little. SIR JOHN ROMILLY, M.R., said (47):

" It is not proved that Mr. Englehart did not exercise his judgment and discretion in the best way he could. It may have been improvident as between these parties to enter into a contract to buy and sell property at a price to be fixed by another person, but that cannot avoid the contract. Here the referee has fixed the price, which is said to be evidence of miscarriage, but this court, upon the principle laid down by LORD ELDON, must act on that valuation, unless there be proof of some mistake, or some improper motive, I do not say a fraudulent one; as if the valuer had valued something not included, or had valued it on a wholly erroneous principle, or had desired to injure one of the parties to the contract; or even, in the absence of any

(44) As to these companies, see p. 437, letter C, ante.
(45) The description " consortium " is explained at p. 437, letter D, ante.
(46) See p. 437, letter B, ante.
(47) (1858), 25 Beav. 200 at pp. 203, 204.

proof of any one of these things, if the price were too excessive or so small
as only to be explainable by reference to some such cause; in any one of these
cases the court would refuse to act on the valuation."

The second case, *Weekes* v. *Gallard* (48) was to much the same effect. I can read
LORD ROMILLY, M.R.'s judgment:

"This is a very unfortunate case, assuming the property to be valued too
low, which seems probable. But that is no defence to the plaintiff's suit. The
plaintiff and defendant agreed to be bound by the valuation of two persons
named in the agreement, and it is the duty of the court to enforce specific
performance of such agreements. The court has really no discretion in the
matter. The discretion of the court is bound, as LORD ELLENBOROUGH says,
by fixed rules. In one case of this kind a house and furniture were valued
at three times their value, and yet there was a decree for specific performance.
The only defence to such a suit would be fraud or collusion. There is no
proof here that the valuers did not value the property as fairly as they
could; there is no suggestion of fraud or collusion. There must, therefore,
be a decree for specific performance of the contract."

I can now come to more modern times, to *Dean* v. *Prince* (49). An attempt was
made here, unsuccessfully as it proved, to impeach an auditor's valuation of
shares following the death of the controlling shareholder in a small private company. The company's auditor valued the shares. The widow did not like the
valuation and sought to challenge it. The auditor wrote a letter explaining how
he had arrived at the figure, and that was made the ground for the attack.
HARMAN, J., said (50):

"It is well settled that those who have a discretion, e.g., trustees who
have powers to apply income for maintenance and directors who have
powers to admit members to a company, can maintain a silence in regard to
the reason for their decision which the court will not oblige them to break,
and that, if they do maintain silence, no action will lie against them; but if
they choose, for whatever reason, to disclose the motives which impelled them
to their decision, the plaintiff may come to the court to impeach those
motives."

In the present case, Cooper Brothers have set out their reasons in document R.5,
and it is open, therefore, to the defendants, if they can, to seek to upset that
certificate.

I turn to the report of the same case in the Court of Appeal (51) where SIR
RAYMOND EVERSHED, M.R., discussed the principle to be applied where a court
was faced with the problem of whether or not to uphold the certificate. After
quoting SIR JOHN ROMILLY, M.R.'s judgment in *Collier* v. *Mason* (52), which I
have already read, SIR RAYMOND EVERSHED, M.R., went on (53):

"There was some discussion before us of the proper meaning to be attached
to the words 'mistake', 'wholly erroneous principle' and 'miscarriage',
as used by SIR JOHN ROMILLY, M.R. I shall not attempt any exhaustive
exposition of that language or of the circumstances in which, in such a case as
the present, the court should hold a party not bound by a valuation. For
my part I think the plaintiff is prima facie entitled to succeed if she is
able to show that Mr. Jenkinson, in arriving at his figure of £7 per share, made

---

(48) (1869), 21 L.T. 655.
(49) [1953] 2 All E.R. 636; [1954] 1 All E.R. 749; [1953] Ch. 590; [1954] Ch. 409.
The decision at first instance was reversed on appeal, but there was no appeal on the
preliminary point determined at first instance, in relation to which the case is cited
here.
(50) [1954] 1 All E.R. 749; [1954] Ch. 409.
(51) [1953] 2 All E.R. at p. 638; [1953] Ch. at p. 593.
(52) (1858), 25 Beav. at p. 204.
(53) [1954] 1 All E.R. at p. 753; [1954] Ch. at p. 418.

A a mistake of a substantial character or materially misdirected himself in the course of his valuation."

DENNING, L.J., put the case rather more widely. After referring to *Collier* v. *Mason* (54), he said (55):

" For instance, if the expert added up his figures wrongly; or took some-

B thing into account which he ought not to have taken into account, or conversely: or interpreted the agreement wrongly: or proceeded on some erroneous principle. In all these cases the court will interfere. Even if the court cannot point to the actual error, nevertheless, if the figure itself is so extravagantly large or so inadequately small that the only conclusion is that he must have gone wrong somewhere, then the court will interfere in much

C the same way as the Court of Appeal will interfere with an award of damages if it is a wholly erroneous estimate. These cases about valuers bear some analogy with the cases on domestic tribunals, except of course that there need not be a hearing."

WYNN-PARRY, J., said (56):

" I accept that the principles which this court should apply in a case such

D as this are those laid down by SIR JOHN ROMILLY, M.R., in *Collier* v. *Mason* (54)."

So much for the approach to the problem. It is against that background that I turn to consider one by one the details of the criticisms which have been made. The first will be found in sub-para. (a) of para. 6 of the points of defence, which

E reads thus:

" In each of the said reports the said accountants have indicated that they have been and are unable to confirm the stock and work in progress as at Jan. 31, 1966, and have relied on a basis of valuation which is not in accordance with [Sch. 3]."

I turn, therefore, to see what is said in cl. 4 of Sch. 3 to the agreement of Feb. 9,

F 1966. It reads thus:

" Stock and Work in progress. The price for the stock and work in progress shall be the amounts for such items as shown in the draft balance sheet of the vendor as at Jan. 31, 1966, after making such adjustments as the accountants consider appropriate (if any) for slow moving and obsolete stock and in the light of an examination by the accountants of the physical check and

G inventory to be taken to the purchaser as soon as possible after the transfer date. The accountants shall confirm that such stock and work in progress was properly taken and that in their opinion the basis of valuation was reasonable."

In para. 7 and para. 8 of Cooper Brothers' certificate (document R.5) they say:

H " 7. The information available to us was as follows: (a) The valuation included in the draft balance sheet at Jan. 31, 1966. This was not substantiated by any detailed valuation. (b) Records of physical stocktaking made by the company as at Jan. 31, 1966, but not valued. (c) The physical inventory prepared by Strange, Strange & Gardner. This was made during February and March, 1966. Due to the lack of records of goods inwards and

I goods outwards, this inventory could not be related to the position as at the previous Jan. 31.

" 8. We are unable to confirm that stock and work in progress was properly taken but we believe that the combination of information available to us as described above has enabled us to arrive at a valuation which may be accepted for the purpose of the agreement, as follows:"

---

(54) (1858), 25 Beav. 200.
(55) [1954] 1 All E.R. at pp. 758, 759; [1954] Ch. at p. 427.
(56) [1954] 1 All E.R. at p. 760; [1954] Ch. at p. 430.

Then they set out the figures:

" Stock of steel and building materials, stores, small tools and lifting tackle £26,921.   Work in progress: £35,280.   Less: Invoiced on account £28,994."

Then they produce a final figure of £33,207, substantially less than the relevant figure in the draft balance sheet.

Counsel for the defendants did not seek to say that the fact that, as stated in the opening sentence of para. 8: " We are unable to confirm that stock and work in progress was properly taken " meant that they had for that reason alone gone wrong. He did not seek to say that the last sentence of cl. 4 of Sch. 3 to the agreement of Feb. 9, 1966, meant that that was a condition precedent to the provisions of the rest of the clause. What he did seek to say was that once they were unable to confirm that the stock and work in progress was properly taken, they were then thrown back on the draft balance sheet figures, and that those figures totalling £54,013 ought to have appeared without more ado in the certificate instead of £33,207.

[HIS LORDSHIP then referred to evidence given by a Mr. Maddison of Cooper Brothers, and continued:] The picture which I get from Mr. Maddison's evidence and the certificate (document R.5) is simply that Cooper Brothers were unable   L to do that which they were enjoined to do in the last paragraph of cl. 4 of Sch. 3 to the agreement of Feb. 9, 1966; but they had at least got the figures in the draft balance sheet; they had got the stocktaking records as at Jan. 31, 1966, and they had Strange, Strange & Gardner's report, for what it was worth.

What the mandate required them to do was to start from the figures in the balance sheet and then adjust; but that does not involve, as I read cl. 4, that they   E are tied for ever to those figures in the balance sheet merely because the stock-taking did not support those figures. What Mr. Maddison did, taking his evidence as a whole, was this. He had the balance sheet figures. He could use them as a starting point, but they were not much good to him as a starting point, because they were unsupported. Therefore, with those figures in the balance sheet, so to speak, in one hand, and the stocktaking in the other, and adjusting for slow   F moving and obsolescent stock, and as he was enjoined to do, examining " the physical check ", in Strange, Strange & Gardner's report, he then proceeded to arrive at the figures which are set out in para. 8 of the certificate (document R.5).

I cannot see that there is anything wrong in that. The certificate itself said this " has enabled us to arrive at a valuation which may be accepted for the purposes of the agreement "—not, it must be noted, " in lieu of that provided for by the   G agreement ".   It is clear that Mr. Maddison, taking his evidence as a whole, thought that he had complied with his mandate. While the position was no doubt difficult in view of the faulty manner in which the old company had kept records, I find nothing to criticise in para. 7 and para. 8 of the certificate; and accordingly that ground of attack on the certificate fails.

[HIS LORDSHIP then turned to other grounds of defence, on which the report of   H Cooper Brothers was challenged, but on which this case is not reported. He then turned to the ground raised by amendment in para. (6) of the points of defence and said:] Sub-paragraph (g) of para. 6 was added by amendment during the trial and raised a separate and independent point (57) with which I must now deal. On Nov. 11, 1966, Cooper Brothers' solicitors wrote to the London agents for the plaintiffs' solicitors, pointing out that there was an error in para. 16   I of their certificate, document R.5.   The certificate as signed and circulated read thus:

" *Amount Owing on Hire Purchase*. We confirmed that the capital amount

---

(57) Sub-paragraph (g) reads: " The said accountants included in the amount certified as owing on hire-purchase interest accruing after Jan. 31, 1966 (contrary to what is stated in the said reports) although required by [Sch. 3] merely to verify physic-ally the amounts outstanding as at Jan. 31, 1966.   The defendants will rely on a letter from the solicitors to the said accountants dated Nov. 11, 1966 ".

outstanding as at Jan. 31, 1966, on hire-purchase amounted to £135,610. This does not include future interest accruing after Jan. 31, 1966.''

In the letter (which has become document R.4a), Cooper Brothers' solicitors wrote:

" Paragraph 16 of the report dated June 14, 1966, (58) by our clients Messrs. Cooper Brothers states the capital amount outstanding as at Jan. 31, 1966, on hire-purchase and further states that this does not include future interest accruing after Jan. 31, 1966.

" It has now been ascertained, however, that although the figure is, in the opinion of our clients, correctly stated in the report, future interest is, in fact, included. The second sentence of para. 16 should, therefore, have stated that the figure includes future interest accruing after Jan. 31, 1966 . . .

" Our clients naturally very much regret the error in the wording, which they consider should be brought at once to the attention of the parties in this action. As stated above, our clients consider the figure stated in para. 16 to be correct, and the error does not in any way otherwise affect the report."

I take that letter to mean that Cooper Brothers made a mistake by putting in a " not " where it should not be, but that that mistake does not affect the arithmetical result at the end, namely, that there was an excess of liabilities over assets, so that the net asset value of the company is still nil. It was no doubt human if regrettable to leave a " not " where it should not have been. But there can be no doubt on the authorities that if this had been a material error, it would have entitled the defendants to have the certificate set aside without more.

Counsel for the defendants argued that I should set the certificate aside on this ground alone, even though the error did not affect the sum finally certified. On the authorities, and in particular Sir Raymond Evershed, M.R.'s judgment in *Dean* v. *Prince* (59), before the court will set aside a certificate for error, the error must be material, which means, of course, one which materially affects the ultimate result. It has long been established that the court will not set aside an award in an arbitration for an error of law or fact on its face unless that error is clearly material. Counsel for the defendants was unable to cite any case in which the court held a certificate not to be binding for error on its face where the error was not material. It seems to me, if I may say so, that the judgment of Sir Raymond Evershed, M.R., in *Dean* v. *Prince* (59) is in line with the arbitration cases. If this error had been material, it would have been enough to vitiate the whole of the certificate, small as it might be and regrettable as the consequences might be. But in my judgment, in the light of the last paragraph of document R.4a, this error is not material because it does not affect the result, and I accordingly reject the argument based on what is now sub-para. (g) of para. 6 of the points of defence.

I turn to the last point, one raised by amendment in sub-para. (h) of the points of defence, which reads thus:

" The said accountants, having verified the existence of plant and fixtures with a value at cost of £4,332, of which the [new company, i.e., the first plaintiff] had taken possession on the transfer date, ought to have included such value, or, alternatively, the written-down value of such items in the price payable to the [old company, i.e., the first defendant], but failed to do so."

I turn back to the relevant provisions in Sch. 3 to the agreement of Feb. 9, 1966, and in the certificate (document R.5). Paragraph 3 of Sch. 3 reads thus:

" *Plant and fixtures.* The accountants shall verify the existence of the plant and fixtures shown in the draft balance sheet of the vendor as at Jan. 31, 1966, including the items shown in Sch. 2 hereto which is not necessarily

(58) I.e., the certificate, document R.5.
(59) [1954] 1 All E.R. 749; [1954] Ch. 409; as to which see p. 440, letter I, ante.

complete and shall confirm that such items are in the ownership of the vendor as at the transfer date. The price for the plant and fixtures shall be the book written down values of the items as shown in the draft balance sheet of the vendor [i.e., the old company] as at Jan. 31, 1966, after making such adjustments as the accountants consider appropriate (if any) to bring the total depreciation charged in arriving at the above mentioned book values in line with the rates adopted by the vendor's auditors in auditing the accounts to Jan. 31, 1965."

The relevant passage in document R.5 is in para. 5:

" The result of our examination of plant and fixtures, shown in [Sch. 2 to the agreement of Feb. 9, 1966] as having a value at cost at Jan. 31, 1966, of £255,635 5s. 4d. is as follows . . . Verified as to existence but not as to cost and ownership—£4,332."

Counsel for the defendants argued that as the new company on or after the transfer date took over these articles which are described as " verified as to existence but not as to cost and ownership ", it thereby waived its right to insist on proof of a legal title and by the act of taking possession accepted a possessory title in lieu. He argued by analogy with contracts for the sale of land that if a vendor tenders only a possessory title and the purchaser accepts that possessory title, the purchaser has waived his right to insist on the full legal title and must rest content with the possessory title. With all respect to that argument, it has often been said that analogies from sale of land are unreliable when one is dealing with sale of goods; but, however that may be, the difficulty in the way of this argument is the relevant contractual provision. The agreement of Feb. 9, 1966, provides in terms how this matter shall be dealt with. Clause 3 of Sch. 3 directed the accountants that they should verify the existence of the plant and fixtures, warned that Sch. 2, which listed certain items, was not necessarily complete, and required them to confirm that such items were in the ownership of the old company as at the transfer date. In these circumstances, I am unable to construe this clause as providing that where ownership was not proved to the satisfaction of Cooper Brothers, the mere fact that the new company took possession of £4,332 worth of plant and fixtures from the old company to which ownership had not been proved entitled the old company as of right to have the figure included in the figure for plant and fixtures. That point therefore fails.

It may be that the result is harsh, but I also have little doubt, having seen Mr. Rudd in the witness-box, that at the end of the day this will be looked at again, and if there should be in fact any hardship involved in this result, that will be taken into account.

[HIS LORDSHIP turned then to a question of construction of the agreement of Feb. 9, 1966, in regard to the claim for payment of a sum of £5,000 on which (60) the case is not reported. HIS LORDSHIP concluded as follows:] In the result, therefore, the plaintiffs succeed, but they will have to pay £5,000 (61) in order to get specific performance. The counterclaims all fail and are dismissed.

Judgment for the plaintiffs; counterclaims dismissed.

Solicitors: *Payne, Hicks Beach & Co.*, agents for *Wragge & Co.*, Birmingham (for the plaintiffs); *Peacock & Goddard*, agents for *Partridge, Nightingale & Haldenby*, Derby (for the defendants).

[*Reported by* K. DIANA PHILLIPS, *Barrister-at-Law.*]

---

(60) This point arose on the construction of the words in cl. 11 of Sch. 3 referring to the additional £5,000 to bring the balance to £50,640; see p. 440, letter A, and p. 441, letter H, ante.

(61) This £5,000 is the sum referred to in the last sentence of cl. 11 of Sch. 3 at p. 440, letter A, ante.

LOVELIDGE *v.* ANSELM OLDLING AND SONS, LTD.

[QUEEN's BENCH DIVISION (Widgery, J.), December 15, 1966.]

Building—Construction regulations—Dangerous machinery—Powered hand-tool
—Grinding wheel driven by movable electric motor of one horse-power—
Power transmitted by flexible driving shaft approximately seven feet long—
Part of shaft unguarded—Use by mason on building site—Whether tool was
machinery requiring to be fenced—Construction (General Provisions) Regula-
tions, 1961 (S.I. 1961 No. 1580), reg. 42.

Building—Contractor—Negligence—Dress of workman using powered hand tool
unsuitable—Workman's tie becoming entangled in revolving shaft of tool—
Consequential injury to workman.

The plaintiff, an experienced mason who had worked for the defendant
employers for nearly forty years, was injured in the course of his employment
on a building site when cutting slots in a granite block. For this purpose
he was using a hand-tool comprising a cutting wheel driven by a flexible
revolving shaft which transmitted power from a one horse-power portable
electric motor. The tool was of a kind that had been in use for twenty
years. The shaft was approximately seven feet long and when running
light revolved, together with the cutting wheel with which it was connected,
at a speed of three thousand revolutions per minute. The shaft was covered
for the greater part of its length, but the covering ceased about three inches
from the site of the cutting wheel. When working on the granite block the
plaintiff had to bend, so that his face came to within about two feet of
the wheel. His tie became entangled with the exposed part of the shaft and
the tool struck him, fracturing his jaw. It was not customary for masons
on the site to wear overalls when working, and instructions had not been
given by the plaintiff's employers as to the clothing that masons should wear.
The plaintiff had always worn a jacket and tie, and had tucked his tie into
the jacket. On the occasion of the accident it was possible that the plaintiff's
tie hung out of his jacket. The plaintiff brought an action against his
employers for damages, alleging breach by them of statutory duty under
reg. 42* of the Construction (General Provisions) Regulations, 1961, that
dangerous parts of machinery should be securely fenced, and alleging
negligence at common law.

Held: (i) the defendants were in breach of their duty under reg. 42* of
the Construction (General Provisions) Regulations, 1961, because the
implement was machinery within reg. 42 and the exposed shaft was a
dangerous part of machinery within that regulation (see p. 464, letter C,
post).

Liptrot v. *British Railways Board* ([1966] 2 All E.R. 247) applied.

(ii) negligence on the part of the defendants was also established (see
p. 464, letter D, post).

(iii) the real cause of the accident was that the plaintiff was improperly
dressed, and his employers were at fault for not having corrected this earlier;
but the plaintiff was guilty of contributory negligence in not having taken
the elementary precaution of seeing that his tie was in a safe position (see
p. 464, letter I, post).

[Editorial Note. The Construction (General Provisions) Regulations, 1961,
were made under s. 76 of the Factories Act, 1961, and the requirements of reg. 42
may be compared with s. 12 (1), s. 13 (1) and s. 14 (1) of that Act, for which
sections see 41 HALSBURY'S STATUTES (2nd Edn.) 254, 256.

As to what is machinery for the purposes of the Factories Act, 1961, see 17
HALSBURY'S LAWS (3rd Edn.) 70-74, paras. 122-125; as to the determination of
what are dangerous parts of machinery, see ibid., pp. 74-77, paras. 126, 127;

---

* Regulation 42 is set out at p. 462, letter B, post.

as to building regulations, see ibid., pp. 125-128, para. 206; and for cases on the subject, see 24 DIGEST (Repl.) 1052-1055, *202-218*, DIGEST (Cont. Vol. A) 586-588, *205a-218f*, and 3rd DIGEST SUPP.

For the Construction (General Provisions) Regulations, 1961, reg. 42, see 8 HALSBURY'S STATUTORY INSTRUMENTS (First Re-Issue) 275.]

Cases referred to:

    Cherry v. *International Alloys, Ltd.*, [1960] 3 All E.R. 264; [1961] 1 Q.B. 136; [1960] 3 W.L.R. 568; Digest (Cont. Vol. A) 586, *205a*.

    Haynes v. *James Hunt & Sons, Ltd.* (Dec. 2, 1965), unreported.

    Liptrot v. *British Railways Board*, [1966] 2 All E.R. 247; [1966] 2 Q.B. 353; [1966] 2 W.L.R. 841.

Action.

This was an action for damages for negligence and breach of statutory duty brought by the plaintiff, a marble and granite mason, against his employers, who were building contractors, in respect of personal injuries received by him on Sept. 10, 1964, while he was using a power-driven hand tool in the course of his employment on a building site. The facts are set out in the judgment.

    D. J. Turner-Samuels for the plaintiff.

    R. I. Kidwell for the defendants.

WIDGERY, J.: This is a case in which Mr. Lovelidge sues his employers, Anselm Oldling & Sons, Ltd., for damages for personal injuries which he suffered on Sept. 10, 1964, as a result of an accident when at work. On that day he was working for the defendants, who are building contractors, on a building site at 10, Broadway, Westminster, and he was using an "implement"—if I may choose a neutral word—which has been described, not inaccurately, as a flexible shaft grinding tool. Whilst using this implement to cut a groove in a granite block his tie became entangled with the revolving shaft of the implement, and the implement, as it were, climbed up his tie and struck him a blow in the face which resulted in a fracture of the jaw and injury to his ear. He says that the accident was due to the negligence of his employers and also attributable to a breach by them of their duty under reg. 42 of the Construction (General Provisions) Regulations, 1961 (1). The defendants deny negligence and contend that the regulations do not apply and plead contributory negligence.

There is virtually no dispute about the circumstances of the case. The plaintiff is a very experienced marble and granite mason. He is now sixty-one years of age and he has had something like forty years with this same firm. On the day in question he was working on a granite block which was some four feet by two feet six inches by one and a half inches thick. He was, as I have said, cutting slots in these blocks to accommodate the fixing pieces which were fixed into the wall. For this purpose he was using equipment which is of a kind which has been in use by the defendants for twenty years or more and, no doubt, was extremely common in the trade. It consists of a cutting wheel some seven inches in diameter which is driven by a one horse-power electric motor. The motor can stand on the ground or on a bench and be plugged in to any convenient electrical supply, and the power from the motor is transmitted to the wheel by means of a flexible driving shaft some seven or eight feet in length. The shaft is covered for the greater part of its length, but the covering ceases about three inches from the site of the wheel and, consequently, there is exposed between the wheel and the end of the covering some three inches of shaft which revolves at the same speed as the wheel, namely above three thousand revolutions per minute when running light. The end of the covering nearest the wheel is ridged and forms a convenient holder for one of the operator's hands and his other hand is applied to a handle on the offside of the wheel, so when using the implement he holds the wheel by grasping the handles on either side. The specimen which has been brought

---

(1) S.I. 1961 No. 1580. Regulation 42 is set out at p. 462, letter B, post.

before this court includes a wheel guard. The guard is in a form which practically encloses one half of the wheel, leaving the other half exposed. The guard is attached to the outer handle and can be held in the position desired by the operator. The purpose of this guard, I am satisfied, is to protect the operator should the wheel splinter and fly, and the fact that the guard was not in use at the time of the accident seems to me to be irrelevant to the matters before me.

In his evidence the plaintiff described to me how, when using the implement in a perfectly normal way, his tie got in some way caught up in that part of the driving shaft which is uncovered, namely the three inch section of the shaft lying between the wheel and the end of the covering. He said he had to bend over when working and he demonstrated an angle which would bring his face to within two feet of the wheel, and then he went on to say:

> " It all happened in a second. My tie caught round the spindle of the machine and the machine was pulled up sharply towards my face."

It seems to me miraculous that the plaintiff did not suffer far more serious injuries than he did because in such circumstances the revolving wheel might have been brought right into contact with his face itself. However, in fact he was hit a blow behind the left ear with, I think, the outer handle of the implement and he was taken to hospital suffering quite substantial injuries. He was wearing, as he said, an ordinary jacket and tie. He was not wearing a waistcoat or pullover so that his tie was obviously capable of falling out of the front of his jacket with comparative ease. He was not wearing overalls and no overalls were issued. No instructions were given to him as to the nature of the clothing which he should wear and no-one told him to tuck his tie in. He said that masons generally do not wear overalls. It was customary, and always had been customary, for him to work dressed as he was on this day with an ordinary jacket and his tie tucked inside, and he said that notwithstanding this custom he has never had trouble of this kind before nor has any other of his fellow workmen as far as he knows.

Cross-examined by counsel for the defendants the plaintiff said " We always tuck our ties in out of the way ". Asked why he did not tuck his tie inside his shirt where it would be safer, he said that it was quicker to tuck it inside his jacket. He agreed that his tie could fall out of his jacket at any time, but he said that he never thought about tucking it inside his shirt. He said that he never used the guard to which I have referred, but I need not pursue that because that guard has no relevance to this action.

The plaintiff called an expert consultant engineer, Mr. Bright, who gave me a great deal of useful information about the implement, into which I need not go in detail. Dealing with the part of the driving shaft which is not protected by a covering, he said that it was certainly likely to cause injury particularly as it was not smooth—that is a reference to the fact that the uncovered section of the driving shaft is threaded, it being necessary, apparently, to screw a nut back along this thread in the process of changing the cutting wheel. He said there was danger to an operator's hands if his hands touched the revolving shaft when it was running at full speed, although he recognised that no very grave danger was likely to result in ordinary circumstances of this kind. He said, however, that it was dangerous to have a revolving shaft of this character in a position where it might catch on some hanging part of the operator's clothing or, indeed, any other hanging material which was secured at the other end and up which the machine might climb if it became engaged in that material. He put forward a theory—which I do not find it necessary to investigate—that the plaintiff's tie might have been blown up or attracted to the implement by the action set up by the revolving wheel, but I do not pursue that because the plaintiff's own evidence that the possibility is that his tie was hanging out in a perfectly normal way shows a very obvious possibility. Mr. Bright said that the spindle could be effectively guarded by means of a tube. He was not invited to pursue this in detail, but I understood him to mean that the unprotected portion of the shaft could be protected by means of a rubber tube without affecting its function, and I accept that evidence.

The defendants called no evidence and so the case as to liability depends on those simple facts, and it is convenient, I think, to turn first to the allegation that the defendants were in breach of reg. 42 of the Construction (General Provisions) Regulations, 1961, which is in these terms:

> " Every flywheel and every moving part of any prime mover, every part of transmission machinery and every dangerous part of other machinery (whether or not driven by mechanical power) shall be securely fenced unless it is in such a position or of such construction as to be as safe to every person employed or working on the site of the operations or works as it would be if it were securely fenced."

The argument in regard to this matter has centred on the questions, first whether the implement, as I have described it, is " machinery " at all for the purposes of this regulation, and, secondly, if it is machinery, whether the shaft is a " dangerous part " within the meaning of the regulation. It is neither pleaded nor argued that I am here concerned with transmission machinery so that it is necessary for the plaintiff, if he relies on this paragraph, to say that the unfenced part of the machine was a dangerous part.

So far as the meaning of the word " machinery " is concerned, there is a somewhat surprising lack of authority. The Factories Act and regulations contain no definition, and in those circumstances I think it right to begin with dictionary definitions. The most appropriate which has been suggested to me from the dictionary is in these terms:

> " Machinery, apparatus for applying mechanical power, consisting of a number of parts each having separate functions."

I see no reason, giving the words their ordinary meaning, why that definition should not fit the implement which I have endeavoured to describe. It is certainly —and in particular the shaft is—concerned with applying mechanical power, and the whole thing is a combination of parts each having a separate function. Although it has been argued that the word " tool " would be equally appropriate, I do not necessarily think that the words " tool " and " machine " are mutually exclusive for this purpose.

Turning to the authorities to which I have been referred, I deal first with an unreported decision of BLAIN, J., in *Haynes* v. *James Hunt & Sons, Ltd.* given on Dec. 2, 1965. BLAIN, J., was dealing with an implement very much like the present in its function except that it seems to have had this difference, that the electric motor was mounted on the side of the wheel and there was no flexible mechanical coupling, only a flexible electrical coupling. With regard to that machine, having considered the same matters that I have had to consider, he said:

> " The first question is whether this is machinery or whether it is not, there being no statutory definition. Certainly not everything operated by mechanical power is machinery and, indeed, there may be some things which constitute a machine which are not, perhaps, operated by mechanical power. I suppose a pedal cycle is a machine."

He went on to say that there was no help to be got from the authorities on the question what was machinery and what was not, and that, though this was the part of the case that gave him greatest doubt, he decided it was a tool, and that it was not machinery. Whether I would reach the same conclusion when considering the same implement as BLAIN, J., was considering is really neither here nor there but there are, I think, significant differences between that case and the present; nor, as I have already said, do I think that the expressions " tools " and " machinery " are necessarily mutually exclusive.

The next authority to which counsel for the defendants has been good enough to refer me is *Cherry* v. *International Alloys, Ltd.* (2), where the article in question was a Lister truck which was used in a factory to carry goods around and which was used both inside the factory and outside. The question arose under s. 14 of the Factories Act, 1937, and was really the same question as I have to consider now, namely, whether the engine of the truck was " machinery " for present purposes; the Court of Appeal held that it was not.   I need refer for this purpose only to the judgment of DEVLIN, L.J., where he said this (3):

" I have no doubt that a truck is a machine and its engine is machinery, but I think the full width of the words ' any machinery ' in s. 14 of the Factories Act, 1937, must be controlled by consideration of the scope and objects of the Act."

Then he goes on to quote from MAXWELL ON THE INTERPRETATION OF STATUTES (10th Edn.) at p. 60, and concludes in these terms (4):

" In my judgment the object of the Factories Act, 1937, is not to make safety provision for vehicles being things which may travel inside or outside a factory, or plant and machinery inside them. I think, therefore, that, in accordance with the principle which I have stated, the wide meaning of the words should be cut down so as to exclude vehicles."

The reference to vehicles is a reference to an earlier passage in the judgment when it was pointed out that these Lister trucks could as conveniently be called vehicles as called machinery.

Following that decision is *Liptrot* v. *British Railways Board* (5), where the article in question was a mobile crane which moved about in a factory, and in that case it was held that the mobile crane constituted machinery for the purposes of s. 14 (1) of the Factories Act, 1961. I find it unnecessary to read the judgments in detail, save to point out that they did cover (particularly the judgment of WILLMER, L.J.), matters which caused difficulty in the present case, namely such questions as whether an implement can be machinery if it can be used with equal facility in and out of the factory. In the present case, this implement might well be used in circumstances in which neither the Factories Act, 1961, nor the Construction (General Provisions) Regulations, 1961, apply and the argument that it would be strange to apply the rigour of these regulations in one case and not to apply it in another is a good one. WILLMER, L.J., recognised that argument (6), but nevertheless held that the mobile crane then in question was machinery. He also pointed out (7) that had the crane been mounted on a fixed pedestal, no one would have doubted that it was machinery, and he gave the view that its mobile condition was not enough to displace its status as machinery. Precisely the same argument can be applied to the facts of this case. If this grinding wheel derived its power from some fixed mechanical source in a factory I should have thought there was little doubt that it was " machinery " and that no-one would even dream of calling it a tool, and the fact that it derives its power from another source does not seem to me to prevent it from being machinery within the meaning of this regulation. Like those who have dealt with this point before, I do not find the case an easy one, and it may be that one day further consideration will have to be given to that whole genus of articles which are often referred to as power hand-tools. It may be that special consideration to such articles should be given by the legislature, but facing the point which I have to decide in this case I have come to the conclusion that the implement, as I have called it up to now, is machinery for the purposes of reg. 42 of the Construction (General Provisions) Regulations (8).

(2) [1960] 3 All E.R. 264; [1961] 1 Q.B. 136.
(3) [1960] 3 All E.R. at pp. 268, 269; [1961] 1 Q.B. at p. 148.
(4) [1960] 3 All E.R. at p. 269; [1961] 1 Q.B. at p. 148.
(5) [1966] 2 All E.R. 247; [1966] 2 Q.B. 353.
(6) [1966] 2 All E.R. at p. 252; [1966] 2 Q.B. at p. 363.
(7) [1966] 2 All E.R. at p. 251; [1966] 2 Q.B. at p. 362.
(8) Regulation 42 is set out at p. 462, letter B, ante.

Is the shaft, exposed as it was, a dangerous part of such machinery? This question, as counsel for the defendants submitted, must be decided by considering the foreseeability of accidents. I entirely accept Mr. Bright's view of this matter and I would hold that there is a clear foreseeability of injury in regard to contact between the operator's hand and the revolving shaft, and I would have thought also the foreseeability of entanglement between the revolving shaft and some hanging material, be it the operator's clothing or not, which risk was the greater and the more considerable by reason of the fact that this tool was a mobile tool. I can understand that a similar wheel running on a fixed base in surroundings which could be forecast and regulated might not create anything like as much of a danger as a mobile wheel which might be in proximity to a hanging tie at one moment, to a hanging piece of material on the building at another, and who knows to what other objects up which it might be tempted to climb. I therefore hold that this unfenced shaft was a "dangerous part of other machinery" within the meaning of reg. 42.

The case is put in the alternative as being a case of negligence at common law, and there again I am of the opinion that the plaintiff has made out his case. It seems to me that in this day and age every careful employer with proper regard to the safety of his workmen must realise that high speed unfenced shafts are things which will only be tolerated in circumstances where it really cannot be avoided. I am not unmindful of the fact that this machine has been used in this condition for twenty years without complaint, but that, in a sense, only explains why nothing has been done before. It may be that if these machines were designed today, matters of this kind would be taken into account because views have advanced in the last twenty years; but if a machine is made to an old design which in fact does not give serious trouble, there is the danger (into which I think the present defendants have fallen) of thinking that all is well and of not applying that enquiring mind to the machinery which a reasonably minded employer should apply.

The plaintiff, therefore, makes out his case, and the next question is to consider the allegation of contributory negligence. This is a very short and simple allegation. It is said by counsel on behalf of the defendants that anybody with any experience of working with power tools or revolving machinery must appreciate the importance of keeping such articles of clothing as his tie out of the way. Here it is said that not only was the plaintiff working with machinery of the kind I have described, but also he had to bend over in such a way that his tie was likely to fall out from the security of his jacket, and if it so fell out it would be bound to be in close proximity to the machine. It seems to me almost incredible that a man with the commonsense which I credit the plaintiff with having, and with the experience which he has had both at work and at home of hand tools, should not appreciate that the first obvious thing to do when he was working with a machine of this kind was to put his tie, not merely in the insecure confines of his jacket, but in some particularly secure place such as in the front of his shirt. Of course, he had been brought up for years to believe that masons did not wear overalls, he had been brought up for years to believe that it was perfectly normal for a mason to wear a tie, and I do not criticise him for that. The real cause of this trouble was that he was unsuitably dressed, and I should have thought that it was a fault of his employers for not having corrected it earlier, but the fault here which in the end gave rise to the accident was what I am told that I may describe as the stupidity of the plaintiff in not taking this elementary precaution of sticking his tie in a position of safety. In such circumstances it seems to me that he must certainly bear a substantial part of the blame, and I apportion the liability at fifty per cent. on either side.

[His Lordship considered the medical and other evidence relevant to the plaintiff's injuries and, on the basis of fifty per cent. contributory negligence, awarded the plaintiff £500 general damages.]

Judgment for the plaintiff accordingly.

Solicitors: *O. H. Parsons* (for the plaintiff); *Herbert Smith & Co.* (for the defendants).

[*Reported by* K. Diana Phillips, *Barrister-at-Law.*]

Re BRITISH FURNITURE MANUFACTURERS FEDERATED ASSOCIATIONS' AGREEMENT.

[Restrictive Practices Court (Buckley, J., Mr. H. F. Sherborne, Mr. P. A. Delafield and Mr. F. H. Braybrook), October 17, 1966.]

Restrictive Trade Practices—Reference—Furniture manufacturers—Agreement not to produce modern furniture of design held by committee of furniture manufacturers to be copy of that of another manufacturer—Whether restriction on descriptions of goods to be produced—Restrictive Trade Practices Act, 1956 (4 & 5 Eliz. 2 c. 68), s. 6 (1) (c).

The British Furniture Manufacturers Federated Associations (" the B.F.M.") was a group of thirteen trade associations concerned with the manufacture of furniture. The B.F.M. had itself been a member of the British Furniture Trade Confederation, which also included other bodies concerned with dealing in furniture. Until 1963 the confederation had a code of practice which included restrictions on the copying of designs by one member from another. When that code was abandoned, the B.F.M. passed a resolution providing for a procedure by which complaints of design copying between members could be investigated by a committee of the member association (where the complainant and other members were members of the same association) or of the B.F.M., and disciplinary action taken where appropriate. A standard form of consent to the complaint being investigated in accordance with the rules of the B.F.M. was prepared for signature by the parties to such a dispute, and such consent was not to operate as a bar in subsequent legal proceedings between the parties. The constitutions of the several member associations imposed a binding obligation on their constituent members to sign such a consent form. The code of procedure to be adopted on any such dispute was set out in a document headed " Procedure for dealing with cases of alleged furniture design copying "; which, the court found, referred only to cases of conscious copying of design. On a preliminary point of law whether the arrangement not to produce modern furniture of a design held under the " Procedure for dealing with cases of alleged furniture design copying " to be a copy of that of another party was a restriction to which Part 1 of the Restrictive Trade Practices Act, 1956, applied,

Held: the agreement was not a restriction of the descriptions of goods to be produced within the meaning of s. 6 (1) (c)* of the Act of 1956, since

---

* Section 6 (1), so far as material, provides: " Subject to the provisions of the two next following sections, this Part of this Act applies to any agreement between two or more persons carrying on business within the United Kingdom in the production or supply of goods, or in the application to goods of any process of manufacture, whether with or without other parties, being an agreement under which restrictions are accepted by two or more parties in respect of the following matters, that is to say:— . . . (c) the quantities or descriptions of goods to be produced, supplied or acquired; . . ."

it related only to the deliberate copying of goods by one manufacturer
from the design of another, and that could not be properly said to affect
the description of the article produced (see p. 469, letter F, post).

Dictum of MEGAW, P., in *Re Agreement between British Waste Paper
Assocn. and British Paper and Board Makers' Assocn. (Inc.)* ([1963] 2 All E.R.
at p. 429) applied.

[As to agreements subject to registration, see 38 HALSBURY'S LAWS (3rd Edn.)
98, 99, para. 126.

For the Restrictive Trade Practices Act, 1956, s. 6, see 36 HALSBURY'S
STATUTES (2nd Edn.) 937.]

Case referred to:

British Waste Paper Assocn. and British Paper and Board Makers' Assocn.
(Inc.), Re, Agreement between, [1963] 2 All E.R. 424; L.R. 4 R.P. 29;
[1963] 1 W.L.R. 540; 45 Digest (Repl.) 411, *169*.

Preliminary Point of Law.

On a reference by the Registrar of Restrictive Trading Agreements under
s. 20 (2) (*a*) of the Restrictive Trade Practices Act, 1956, of an alleged restriction
contained in an agreement between the members of the British Furniture Manufacturers' Federated Associations, it was ordered by consent that the court
should try as a preliminary point of law the issue whether the restriction alleged
to be involved in the agreement was a restriction within Part 1 of the Act of 1956.
The facts, the alleged restriction, and the question for the determination of the
court, are set out in the judgment of the court.

N. C. H. Browne-Wilkinson for the registrar.
H. A. P. Fisher, Q.C., and *W. Gumbel* for the respondent associations.

BUCKLEY, J., delivered the following judgment of the court: The respondent in this case, the British Furniture Manufacturers Federated Associations,
is a body the members of which are themselves trade associations concerned
with the manufacture of furniture. There are thirteen such members of the
respondent. The respondent itself was a member of a larger trade body known
as the British Furniture Trade Confederation, the membership of which included,
in addition to those concerned in manufacture of furniture, other bodies concerned with dealing in furniture. Until the year 1963 the last-mentioned body,
whom I will call the confederation, had a code of practice containing a number
of restrictive provisions binding on the respondent and the other members of
the confederation which in the year 1963 the confederation brought to an end.
That code included provisions amongst others restricting the copying of designs
by one member from another. When that code was brought to an end, the
respondent associations passed a resolution in terms which are set out in para. 13
of the statement of case as follows:

" The B.F.M. [that is the respondent] shall maintain and have power
from time to time to alter regulations for dealing with complaints by members
of the member associations of the B.F.M. against other members of the
same or another member association for alleged design copying by such
other member of a design or product of the complainant member. Such
regulations shall contain (inter alia) the procedure by which such complaints
may be investigated by a committee of the member association (where the
complainant and other member are members of the same member association)
or of the B.F.M., a standard form to be signed by the parties agreeing to such
investigation, and shall indicate in general terms the principles upon which
any such investigation shall be carried out, what sanctions or disciplinary
action may be imposed or taken, and by whom (including, if desirable,
publication of the findings), and any other matters which may seem to the
B.F.M. appropriate."

A For the purpose of implementing that resolution a standard form was devised intended to be signed by each party to the dispute whereby each party consented to the complaint being investigated in accordance with the rules for the time being of the respondent and agreed to accept the findings and abide by the sanctions or disciplinary action which might be imposed or taken in accordance with recommendations pursuant to such investigation by either the member

B association concerned or the B.F.M. as might be appropriate; and the party who signed the form further agreed that such consent should not operate as a bar in subsequent legal proceedings between the parties, and that the parties should not adduce the proceedings or any findings or sanctions or disciplinary action recommended to be taken in evidence in any other proceeding. It might appear from the fact that that form of consent was to be signed by the parties to a

C dispute that, unless and until the form be signed, there would be no agreement and no restriction affecting anyone; but in fact the constitutions of the several member associations imposed a binding obligation on their constituent members to sign such a form in the event of dispute arising between one of their members and another member or one of their members and a member of another member association of the respondent. So that in fact such a reference to the disciplinary

D body set up by the B.F.M. was obligatory on the parties.

   The code of procedure to be adopted on any such dispute is set out in a document which is annexed to the statement of case, that being the latest of three versions of such procedure, and we have been taken through it in some detail by counsel, but it is not, I think, necessary for me in this judgment to go through it in any detail. It is, however, of some importance, because one of the matters

E which have been debated before the court is whether this machinery is designed to deal with cases of disputes arising between persons who are within the operation of this arrangement where the similarity between their products has been merely coincidental or whether it only applies where one party has consciously and intentionally copied a design which is the original design of another party. Counsel for the registrar has been at pains to try to persuade us that the language of the

F resolution and the procedure document are such that it is at least equivocal, and that the procedure may apply to cases of purely coincidental similarity. It seems to us, reading the procedure document as a whole, that that view is one which is really untenable, for the word " copying " and " copy " is used continuously throughout, and it seems to the court that to use that word in respect of purely coincidental similarity is really a misuse of language. The document is

G itself headed " Procedure for dealing with cases of alleged furniture design copying "; and there are, just to mention a few examples of the sort of language used in the document, numerous references to the article or the design alleged to have been copied, there are references to the firm alleged to have made the copy, there are references to " the offending copy ", " the alleged copy ", " the design that has been copied ", and so on—language which, in our judgment, makes it im-

H possible to read this document as referring to anything other than cases of conscious copying of designs. There has been some suggestion in the course of the argument that the scheme may not have been operated in so restrictive a sense. With that we think that we have nothing to do. We are considering a preliminary point of law, and we must consider it on the pleadings that are before us and in the light of the documents that are before us and interpret it in accordance with

I what their language indicates as their true meaning.

   The statement of case applies to other restrictions besides the particular restriction with which we are concerned, but, by agreement between the parties, they are all to be dealt with on another reference relating to this same trade, and the only live issue left on this reference is whether the arrangement to which I have referred is one which involves restrictions of a kind to which Part 1 of the Restrictive Trade Practices Act, 1956, applies. The restriction which the registrar alleges to be involved in this arrangement is set out in the answer in these terms:

" Not to produce modern furniture of a design held under the registered
' Procedure for dealing with cases of alleged furniture design copying ' to be
a copy of that of another party."

At the hearing, counsel for the registrar has asked leave to add by way of an
amendment an alternative formulation of the restriction involved in the arrangement in these terms:

" Not to produce modern furniture so similar in appearance to products
made by another party as to be liable to be mistaken by the public the one
for the other."

The first formulation of the restriction, that is to say the one found in the answer
as originally drawn, is confined to dealing in furniture which has been held under
the design copying procedure to be a copy. The alternative which counsel for
the registrar produces now is founded on an implied agreement between the parties
that they will not produce furniture which is of a kind which would offend against
the policy or intent of the design copying regulations. The contention of counsel
for the registrar has been that that policy or intent is not confined to actual copying but to coincidental similarity, and, therefore, he has framed this alternative
restriction in the wide language which I have read; but he says that it could
be made to fit the more restricted state of affairs applicable if, as we have held,
the design copying procedure is one intended to be confined in its operation to
cases of actual copying by inserting the word " deliberately " after the word
" produce " and before " modern furniture "—" Not to produce deliberately
modern furniture so similar in appearance ", and so forth.

The matter has been referred to this court as a preliminary point of law by a
consent order which was made in these proceedings on July 28, 1966, referring
to this court this question:

" Whether by the terms set out in para. 13 and para. 14 of the statement of
case restrictions have been accepted to which Part 1 of the said Act applies."

The restrictions are the restrictions with which I have been dealing. Part 1 of
the Act of 1956 will apply if, but only if, the agreement is one which falls within
the ambit of s. 6 of the Act, which, stated shortly, provides that Part 1 of the Act
applies to any agreement under which restrictions are accepted by two or more
parties in respect of the matters set out in para. (a) to (e) inclusive of sub-s. (1)
of the section. The only paragraph of that subsection which it is suggested can
apply to the present case is para. (c); that is to say, the question is whether the
agreement is one under which restrictions are accepted in respect of descriptions
of goods to be produced, supplied or acquired. The question, therefore, is whether
the alleged restriction or restrictions can be properly described as being in respect
of the description of goods to be produced by those persons who are bound by
this design copying procedure. It has been held in this court that, in this context,
the word " description " means " kind of goods ". So that s. 6 (1) (c) is only
concerned with the restrictions of quantity or kind of goods to be produced,
supplied or acquired. That was so decided in *Re Agreement Between British Waste
Paper Assocn. and British Paper and Board Makers' Assocn. (Inc.)* (1). In the
course of the judgment in that case delivered by MEGAW, P., the court said
this (2):

" The validity of that argument depends on the meaning of the word
' descriptions ' in s. 6 (1) (c) of the Act. There is prima facie a simple charm
about the registrar's argument, because the whole provision is expressed to
relate to ' descriptions '. The first possibly relevant definition of ' description '
in the SHORTER OXFORD DICTIONARY is: ' The action of setting forth in words
by mentioning characteristics.' If this is the meaning in s. 6 (1) (c), the
registrar's argument is right. For the Association, on the other hand, it is

_____

(1) [1963] 2 All E.R. 424; L.R. 4 R.P. 29.
(2) [1963] 2 All E.R. at p. 429; L.R. 4 R.P. at p. 49.

contended that the meaning here is that which is given in the second possibly relevant definition in the same dictionary: ' The combination of qualities or features that marks out or describes a particular class: hence, a sort, kind or variety '.   In the opinion of the court that second meaning is the meaning of the word in s. 6 (1) (c)."

So that s. 6 (1) (c) is to be construed as referring to agreements under which restrictions are accepted in respect of the kind of goods to be produced or kinds of goods to be produced.

Counsel for the registrar puts the matter in two ways like this.   He says that either this is an agreement not to produce furniture of a kind which has been held under the design copying procedure to be a copy, or it is an agreement not to produce goods which are in fact copies within the meaning of that procedure, although the question whether or not they are copies has not been referred to the appropriate committee under the procedure and they have not actually been held to be copies.   He says that in either case that is a restriction by reference to the kind of goods dealt with.   Counsel for the respondent on the other hand says that the relevant description must relate to characteristics of the goods, and he says that the restriction here is not one which relates to the kind of goods to be dealt in but to the conduct of the manufacturers in producing that particular article, whatever it may be.   Counsel for the respondent is prepared to concede that an agreement not to manufacture furniture to some particular design, either a specified design or a design capable of being identified at the relevant time, would be a restriction falling within para. (c); but he says that, when questions relating to why or how the manufacturer chose or was able to adopt that particular design are introduced to the identification of the subject-matter of the restriction, this goes beyond what is meant by the words " description of goods " in s. 6 (1) (c).

It seems to us, as I have said, that the agreement here is one which relates to the deliberate copying of goods by one manufacturer from the design of another, and that the fact that the design has been deliberately copied cannot be properly said to affect the description of the article produced.   Counsel for the respondent, in the course of his argument, put the example of two substantially identical pieces of furniture, one made by manufacturer A and another by manufacturer B, manufacturer B having copied manufacturer A's design and methods of manufacture, so that the two products were virtually identical.   He says that it would be a misuse of language to say that they are not goods of the same description.   This seems to us to be a common sense view of the matter and to be right. We think that the respondent is entitled to succeed on its preliminary point of law, which will mean that, on this reference, there is no restriction still in issue to which Part 1 of the Act of 1956 applies.   That would not preclude the registrar, as we understand the position, from asserting in other proceedings that in fact there is some arrangement between the members of the respondent as the result of which this procedure was used for some wider and different purpose; but we are not concerned with that.   On the narrow issue which is before us, on the agreement as pleaded and as demonstrated by the documents annexed to the pleading, we answer the preliminary point of law which is put to us by saying that those do not disclose that there are restrictions to which Part 1 of the Act applies.

Declaration accordingly.

Solicitors: *Treasury Solicitor;   Booth & Blackwell* (for the respondent associations).

[*Reported by* MARY COLTON, *Barrister-at-Law.*]

LINDWALL v. LINDWALL.

[COURT OF APPEAL, CIVIL DIVISION (Willmer and Harman, L.JJ., and Cairns, J.), November 1, 2, 1966.]

Husband and Wife—Maintenance—Application to High Court—Wife living apart from husband—No evidence justifying wife's refusal to live in home provided by husband—Whether husband guilty of wilful neglect to maintain wife—Matrimonial Causes Act 1965 (c. 72), s. 22.

Divorce—Practice—Originating summons—Cross-examination of party on his affidavit—Wife's originating summons for maintenance—Both parties' affidavits read—Husband's submission of no case to answer—Wife's right to cross-examine husband on affidavit notwithstanding submission of no case —Submission of " no case " not applicable to proceedings on originating summons—Matrimonial Causes Rules, 1957 (S.I. 1957 No. 619), r. 58 (17).

Following the sale of the matrimonial home necessitated by financial considerations, the husband found a flat in St. John's Wood, London, which he thought would provide pleasant accommodation for his wife and son. The wife, however, chose to go with her mother to reside in Cumberland, one of her objects being to continue her business of breeding horses and pigs carried on at the old matrimonial home. The wife took out an originating summons alleging wilful neglect by the husband to maintain her, supported by an affidavit in which she said that he had failed to provide her with accommodation " and accordingly I have lived separate and apart from him ". At the trial that affidavit, the husband's affidavit, and the wife's further affidavit in reply were read by counsel for the wife and the wife was cross-examined on her affidavit. Counsel for the husband then submitted that there was no case to answer. Counsel for the wife objected, claiming the right to cross-examine the husband on his affidavit. The judge ruled that there was no right of cross-examination by reason of the provisions of the Matrimonial Causes Rules, 1957, r. 58 (17), applying the procedure of a divorce petition. In her judgment the trial judge said that the question which she had to determine was whether the wife was entitled to maintenance or whether she had lost her right thereto because she was and had been in desertion. The judge found that the wife acted reasonably in the course which she took and that she had no animus deserendi because she had no intention to remain away from the husband permanently though intending to be away from him for an indefinite period. She therefore found the husband guilty of wilful failure to maintain the wife. On appeal and cross-appeal,

Held: the case must go back for a fresh hearing because:

(i) in order to defeat a claim based on an allegation of wilful neglect to maintain a husband did not have to prove that his wife was in desertion in the sense of having separated from him with the intention of bringing cohabitation permanently to an end, for he was under no liability to maintain her in a separate establishment and, if she insisted in remaining in one without his consent, she forfeited her right to maintenance (see p. 472, letter I, p. 476, letter F, and p. 477, letter G, post).

(ii) on the evidence as it stood there was an unexplained refusal by the wife to live with the husband during any material time, and such evidence was insufficient to sustain the order pronouncing the husband guilty of wilful neglect to maintain the wife (see p. 475, letter D, p. 476, letter F, and p. 477, letter G, post).

(iii) where a party had sworn an affidavit on an application by originating summons, as the husband had done, and the affidavit had been read to the court, the other party could not be denied the right to cross-examine on it, and r. 58 (17) of the Matrimonial Causes Rules, 1957, did not render

Considered in SIMM v. SIMM, *post* p. 618.

applicable to proceedings on originating summons the procedure by sub-mission of " no case " (see p. 475, letter I, p. 476, letter F, and p. 477, letter I, post).

    Appeal and cross-appeal allowed.

[As to the husband's obligations to maintain the wife, see 19 HALSBURY'S LAWS (3rd Edn.) 817-819, paras. 1337, 1338; and for cases on the subject, see 27 DIGEST (Repl.) 80-82, *613-630.*

    As to cross-examination of deponents on their affidavits, see 15 HALSBURY'S LAWS (3rd Edn.) 464-466, paras. 838-842; and for cases on the subject, see 22 DIGEST (Repl.) 518-521, *5763-5794.*

    For the Matrimonial Causes Act 1965, s. 22, see 45 HALSBURY'S STATUTES (2nd Edn.) 476.

    For the Matrimonial Causes Rules, 1957, r. 58 (17), see 10 HALSBURY'S STATUTORY INSTRUMENTS (2nd Re-Issue) 261.]

Case referred to:
    Price v. *Price,* [1951] 2 All E.R. 580, n; [1951] P. 413; 115 J.P. 468, n.;
        27 Digest (Repl.) 85, *636.*

Appeal and cross-appeal.

    This was an appeal by the husband against an order of LANE, J., made on the trial of an action brought by the wife on May 13, 1966, whereby it was adjudged that the husband had been guilty of wilful neglect to provide reasonable main-tenance for the wife, and that the wife was entitled to receive from the husband for herself such periodical payments as might be just under the Matrimonial Causes Act 1965, s. 22. The grounds of appeal were that the judge misdirected herself and was wrong in law in so adjudging for the following reasons—(i) the wife's case as set out in her affidavit sworn on Feb. 18, 1964, was not in accordance with the subsequent evidence; (ii) the judge found on the authority of *Dunn* v. *Dunn** that the wife was not unreasonable in going to live in Cumberland when, previously in argument with the wife's counsel, she had stated that *Dunn* v. *Dunn** was not applicable to the case; (iii) the wife had formed an animus deserendi either prior to, at the time of or subsequent to her departure to Cumberland; (iv) the judge's finding that the wife's departure to Cumberland for an indefinite period did not constitute desertion was wrong in law even if in accordance with the evidence, which it was submitted it was not; (v) the judge placed reliance on the fact that the wife made some curtains for the husband's flat after the parting as being indicative of no animus deserendi and did not give adequate consideration to other indications to the contrary; (vi) the judge should not have drawn the conclusion that she did from the husband's final letters to the wife; (vii) she took into account the wife's obligations to her mother as in part justifying her refusal to live in the accommodation offered by the husband in London, and (viii) the judgment was against the weight of the evidence. The wife cross-appealed for an order, in the event of the court's coming to the conclusion that judgment should be entered for the husband, for a fresh trial of the action on the ground that the judge misdirected herself as follows. At the hearing before the judge by consent between counsel for the wife and counsel for the husband all the affidavit evidence in the case, i.e., affidavits sworn by the wife and by the husband, were read to the court by counsel for the wife. The wife was then cross-examined by counsel for the husband. At the conclusion of the wife's cross-examination counsel for the husband submitted that there was in law no case for the husband to answer. The judge was wrong in law and misdirected herself in permitting counsel for the husband to make such a submission and in ruling on the submission notwithstanding the submission to the contrary by counsel for the wife, because evidence in the shape of the husband's affidavit had been put in evidence and the husband was present in court by agreement between

---

* [1948] 2 All E.R. 822.

the solicitors for the purpose of cross-examination. Therefore the effect of the judge's ruling was to deprive the wife of the right of cross-examination of the husband.

F. J. Cridlan for the husband.
E. V. Falk for the wife.

WILLMER, L.J.: If I may begin at the end, I would say straight away that in my view both appeal and cross-appeal must be allowed, and the result of that, I think, must necessarily be that this case must be remitted for a fresh hearing. So far as the appeal is concerned, it appears to me that on the evidence as it stands the judge's finding of wilful failure to maintain the wife cannot stand. That, however, is only a provisional view based on the evidence as it stands; it in no way concludes the matters in issue between the parties, because on the cross-appeal I think that counsel for the wife is justified in his complaint that he was not accorded the right to cross-examine the husband. At the moment it is a matter of speculation how far the situation would have been altered had the husband been subjected to cross-examination. Since this has not been done, the only course for this court to take is to remit the case for re-trial. In those circumstances I will endeavour to be brief, for I naturally do not desire that anything which I may say should prejudice the issues which will have to be determined on the re-trial of the suit. I must, however, state as briefly as I can my reasons for coming to the conclusion that both appeal and cross-appeal should be allowed.

So far as the appeal is concerned, it is apparent to me (and I think that this is now accepted by counsel on both sides) that the judge asked herself the wrong question. Having asked herself the wrong question, she gave an answer which did not in my view determine the issue before her, viz., whether the husband was guilty of wilful neglect to maintain his wife. On the first page of her judgment the judge said:

" The question which I have to determine is whether the wife is entitled to maintenance or whether she has lost her right thereto because she is and has been in desertion."

In the course of her judgment the judge recited that it was the husband's case that in leaving home and going to Cumberland the wife deserted him; but she came to the conclusion that the wife acted reasonably in the course which she took, and that there was no animus deserendi because she had no intention to remain apart from her husband permanently, even though she did intend to be away from him for an indefinite period. In those circumstances the judge came to the conclusion that there had been no desertion, and she therefore answered the questions which had been put to her in favour of the wife. I do not blame the judge for dealing with the matter in this way. She was dealing with the case as it was put to her. The whole case was argued as if it were neither more nor less than a desertion case. It is fair to say that, when the appeal was opened in this court, it was opened on the same basis, and counsel for the husband said in terms that the husband's case was that the wife deserted him.

With all respect both to the judge and to those who argued the case before her, that is not the point. In order to defeat a claim based on an allegation of wilful neglect to maintain, a husband does not have to prove that his wife was in desertion, in the sense of having separated herself from him with the intention of bringing cohabitation permanently to an end. The authorities have established quite clearly that a husband is under no liability to maintain a wife in a separate establishment, even though the wife may have no intention of remaining permanently apart. So long as she remains, and insists on remaining, in a separate establishment without the consent of the husband, then on the authorities she forfeits her right to be maintained by him.

That general proposition is, of course, subject to exceptions. First, if the husband is himself in desertion (i.e., if he has expelled the wife or has refused to have her back with him), then quite clearly he must maintain her in a separate establishment. No such suggestion has so far been made in this case; may be it will be made hereafter if and when the husband is cross-examined; I do not know. Secondly, there may be a separation by consent, and it may be a term of the agreement that during the separation the husband shall maintain the wife. Again, no such agreement has so far been suggested in the present case. And, thirdly, there are cases where separation is forced on the parties by circumstances. Instances which spring to mind are where the husband is absent on war service, or is away in the course of a long voyage at sea. It has been suggested that something of the sort applies in the present case, in that the wife's removal of herself to Cumberland was something forced on her by circumstances; but, as the evidence stands at the moment, I am unable to see any circumstances that compelled this wife to remain apart. It appears to me that, whatever view one takes of its wisdom, her behaviour was the result of her own free choice.

Most of the important evidence relating to the question which has to be decided is contained in the very voluminous correspondence which passed, not only between the parties themselves, but also between their legal advisers. We start with the fact which, I think, is common ground, viz., that, having regard to the financial implications of what had taken place previously, the existing matrimonial home simply had to be sold. It is common ground now that, whether they liked it or not, the parties had to be out of the then existing matrimonial home by late August or early September, 1963. This event was foreseen for many months in advance. There was lengthy correspondence between the solicitors during the spring and early summer of 1963, in which it is fair to say that the wife's solicitors were pressing the husband's solicitors for some decision on what his plans were for accommodating the wife when the matrimonial home was lost; and it certainly appears that the husband's solicitors were inclined to stall and to evade giving any direct answer, at any rate for some considerable time. On July 26, however, they inform the wife's solicitors that the husband " is trying to fit up an unfurnished flat which will have all the accommodation for the family ". Five days later, on July 31, the solicitors for the husband write that the husband " is in negotiation with a landlord, and we cannot approve the lease until we know that your client will live with our client ". The writer goes on to say that " in the present circumstances he [the husband] is now going ahead with the negotiations, and will enter into a lease ". Then in the course of the same letter, it is said: " We may say quite definitely that we shall be asking your client to come and live with her husband together with her child ". A week later, on Aug. 6, the solicitors for the husband disclose the identity of the flat for which the husband is negotiating, " a flat at Nos. 1/5, Fairhazel Gardens, Hampstead, N.W.6 ". The letter suggests that the wife should telephone the husband, get the key, and that she " has a look at it. It would appear to be a flat which could provide suitable accommodation for the family ". Six days later, on August 12 the solicitors write and say:

> " We confirm that [the husband] has taken a flat, namely, Flat 1, Fairhazel Gardens, St. Johns Wood, N.W.6, which will afford very pleasant accommodation for his wife and son."

The only answer emanating from the wife's solicitors at this stage with regard to this offer of accommodation is that the wife " feels herself unable to vacate her present home ". Having regard to the fact, which is now accepted, that the " present home " had to be sold by the end of that month, it does not appear that the wife's attitude in putting forward that view was a very realistic one.

We can now pass to the personal correspondence between the parties, for on Aug. 20 the husband personally wrote to the wife what can only be described as an affectionate letter, in the course of which he said:

"I have settled on 1, Fairhazel Gardens as the flat I propose to take for
us, and have given instructions for the lease to be engrossed for my signature.
I shall probably have to sign today."

The letter went on to talk about the necessary administrative arrangements, the
moving of furniture, and so on. The matter was complicated by the fact that
the wife's mother had been living with her daughter, and arrangements had to
be made for her; but, so far as the wife is concerned, the letter contemplates
the removal of her things to the new flat, saying that they could all come with
the husband's belongings. The wife, however, as we know, persisted in the
intention, which she had already formed, of going with her mother to reside in
Cumberland, which she did somewhere about the end of August or early September. One of her objects in taking that course was so that she could continue to
carry on the business of breeding horses and pigs, in which she had been engaged
at the previous matrimonial home.

So the parties separated about the end of August or early September of 1963.
Letters between them in the weeks following the separation seem to be fairly
sparse, but there is one to which I should draw attention written by the husband
on Nov. 23; it is a long letter of quite a friendly nature, in which he says:

"When you said you wanted to live apart from me and go up north, I
had no power to prevent you doing what you wanted but did all I could to
persuade you to keep the home together. Left alone, not by my own choice,
I was prepared to keep on living in a bed-sitting room, until I got on my feet
again. Your solicitors saw fit to try to make my unselfishness an excuse
for your deserting me by alleging that I was failing to offer you suitable
alternative accommodation in accordance with the standards to which
you had been accustomed, etc., etc. It therefore became necessary for me
to take a house or flat which would fulfil the minimum requirements for the
law. I did a little more than that, and chose a small but very nice flat in a
good neighbourhood in preference to a larger basement flat in an over-
crowded one, a long way from open country where you might have found
accommodation for your horses."

That letter, it is true, does not contain any specific invitation to think again and
come and live with the husband, but it seems to me that that is really the implication behind it. However, a few days later, on Nov. 29, 1963, the husband says
in terms:

"On the other hand, I am again disappointed that you will not come back
to me and re-unite the family in one. Even if, from your point of view, you
only do this for Nick's sake [Nick being the child of the marriage]. Please
give it very serious thought, and tell me what you think about it."

The only answer to that letter is one written on Dec. 9, in which the wife says:
"I should like to know what you intend doing about making provision for
Nicholas and myself here", "here" meaning in Cumberland; she does not deal
at all with the invitation to go and live with the husband in London.

Finally, I should refer to the fact that in early January, 1964, the wife in fact
visited London and stayed for a week-end with the husband in the London flat.
On completion of her visit she wrote what appears to be an extremely friendly
letter to the husband, in which she said:

"I really enjoyed my very short visit to London and only wish it could
have been longer—I could have done with the change and rest and I thought
your flat charming and most comfortable."

She did, however, take the opportunity of returning the spare set of keys which
the husband had given her for use during her stay. It may be a mistake to attach
too much symbolic significance to that gesture, but it does seem to indicate that
the wife, having been to the flat and stayed in it, had made up her mind that she
was not going to live there, at any rate for the time being.

There the relevant correspondence ends, for six weeks later the wife's originating summons was on the file, and was supported by an affidavit alleging that: " My husband failed to provide me with accommodation for my child and myself and accordingly I have lived separate and apart from him ". It is recognised that that at least is an allegation which is not sustainable, but it was one which the wife was prepared to make on oath. I mention that because much reliance has been placed on the fact that, when the wife came to give evidence before the judge, she evidently made a very favourable impression on her ladyship, who said in terms in her judgment that she regarded the wife as " a careful, candid and truthful witness ". That is a view, of course, which we in this court, not having had an opportunity of seeing the wife, are bound to respect.

When this case goes back for re-trial, as I think that it must for the reason that I have given, viz., that the real point at issue has never been tried, it may well be that it will wear a very different complexion after the husband has been cross-examined and his answers have been obtained on some of the problems that arise. At the moment, however, on the evidence as it stands, largely contained in the contemporary correspondence, all that we have is a plain refusal by the wife to live with the husband during any material time, and one which I do not think was fully examined or satisfactorily explained. In such circumstances I do not think that the judge's order, pronouncing that the husband had been guilty of wilful neglect to maintain his wife, is one that can be sustained on the evidence as it stands.

With regard to the cross-appeal, that arises, as I have indicated, from the fact that the wife's counsel was denied the right to cross-examine the husband on his affidavit. What happened was that, following the usual course, proceedings were started by way of originating summons, and affidavits were filed by both parties, as required by Matrimonial Causes Rules, 1957 (1), r. 58 (2), (4) and (8), which deal respectively with the wife's affidavit, the husband's affidavit in reply, and the wife's further affidavit. What happened when the parties came to court was what frequently does happen, viz., that all three of those affidavits were read to the judge in the course of the opening of counsel for the wife. The wife was then tendered for cross-examination, and was duly cross-examined on her affidavit. At the conclusion of her evidence counsel for the husband submitted that he had no case to answer. Objection was taken by counsel for the wife, who claimed the right to cross-examine the husband on his affidavit. The judge's ruling was invited on that, and after considerable argument she ruled that counsel for the husband was justified in the course that he took, that he was entitled to submit " no case to answer ", and that therefore there was no right to cross-examine the husband.

The judge, in giving that ruling, relied on r. 58 (17), which provides:

" Subject to the provisions of this rule, these rules shall, so far as applicable, apply to an application under this rule as if—(*a*) the application were a matrimonial cause; and (*b*) the originating summons were a petition and the applicant were the petitioner, . . . ",

and there is a third para. (*c*), which is not relevant. What is said is that, since in an ordinary matrimonial case a respondent is always entitled to submit " no case ", so equally that must be so in proceedings under s. 22 of the Matrimonial Causes Act 1965, even though such proceedings are started not by petition, but by originating summons.

In reaching that conclusion, and giving that ruling, I think that the judge was in error, and was under a misapprehension as to the nature of the procedure by way of originating summons. When a party has sworn an affidavit, as the husband is required to do under the provisions of r. 58 (4), I do not think that the wife can be denied the right to cross-examine him on it, at any rate in a case where, as in the present, the affidavit has been read to the court. The judge quite evidently regarded the point as one of some difficulty, and herself expressed the hope that it was a matter which might be considered on appeal. For my part I am in no doubt, however, that, on the rules as they stand at present, the judge's ruling was erroneous, and that counsel for the wife should have been allowed to exercise his right to cross-examine the husband.

I might perhaps add this. This case has revealed what may possibly be a defect in the rules as they stand. It may well be thought that, in proceedings for maintenance under s. 22, it ought to be possible for a husband to submit " no case ", just as in an ordinary matrimonial suit. It may be that, when the rules were amended to provide for the new jurisdiction introduced by the Matrimonial Causes Act, 1950 (2), there is room for criticism of the provision that the procedure should be by way of originating summons involving, as that necessarily did, the requirement of affidavits on both sides. This is a matter which no doubt the rules committee will consider if and when any amendment of the present Matrimonial Causes Rules is in contemplation.

Be that as it may, so far as the present case is concerned, I am in no doubt that counsel for the wife was wrongly deprived of his right to cross-examine the husband. That is an additional reason why in my judgment the case must go back for a fresh trial, so that all the evidence relevant to what is the real point of the case can be before the court. What the result of such cross-examination of the husband may be remains to be seen. Counsel for the wife evidently thinks that he can do some good with the husband, and may be able to establish from his cross-examination a case of wilful neglect to maintain. I express no view about that. The case must go back for a re-hearing; but in the meantime I hope that what I have said will at least furnish some guidance to the judge who has to preside over the new trial as to what the real question for decision is.

Accordingly, as I said at the beginning of my judgment, I think that both appeal and cross-appeal must be allowed, and the case be remitted for re-trial.

HARMAN, L.J.: I agree. In the court below, and indeed in this court when the case was opened, this was treated as if it were a divorce suit with desertion as the issue. That, of course, is a wrong view and a fundamentally wrong view of this matter, which was a proceeding under s. 23 of the Matrimonial Causes Act, 1950. The issue is to be found expressed in HODSON, L.J.'s words in *Price* v. *Price* (3), when he said (4):

" A wife has no right to separate maintenance in a different home unless she can justify the fact that she is living apart from her husband,"

and that is the issue here which has never been tried. The appeal, therefore, must succeed in so far as a new trial is required.

On the cross-appeal I have felt a certain sense of unreality. The case was treated as if the originating summons procedure was the same as procedure by action, which it is far from being. The rules provide that both parties must give evidence, and where both sides have given evidence it is idle to say that one of them has no case to answer and can avoid being cross-examined. He has already given evidence and must necessarily be a person who may be cross-examined on that evidence. In this case the husband, by way of answer, gave evidence in which he denied failure to maintain his wife; if he had not said that, the wife would have succeeded. Therefore, he put the matter in issue, and on that issue he must be tendered for cross-examination; and to say that this must be treated as a witness action, and the husband withdrawn from the scrutiny of the other side because he has no case to answer is quite idle, because he has already answered, and the matter must take its course on that footing. The cross-appeal, therefore, must also be allowed, and the matter must be tried de novo. The issue will be

---

(2) Matrimonial Causes Act, 1950, s. 23. The reform was introduced by s. 5 of the Law Reform (Miscellaneous Provisions) Act, 1949.

(3) [1951] 2 All E.R. 580, n.; [1951] P. 413.   (4) [1951] P. at p. 421.

A   that which Willmer, L.J., has described, and to which I have tried in a shorter way to allude. What the answer may be, I do not know. All the opinion I can express at present is that on the material before us it is clear to me that the wife could not succeed. How it may be when the matter has been re-ventilated, I forbear to speculate. I would allow both the appeal and the cross-appeal.

B   **CAIRNS, J.:** I agree that both the appeal and the cross-appeal should be allowed. Counsel for the wife has sought to support the conclusion arrived at by the judge on the ground that she found that the wife had acted reasonably in going for the time being to live in Cumberland. Whether the judge directed her mind to the further question whether the wife, having gone to live in Cumberland, was justified in continuing to live there apart from her husband up to the date of the issue of the originating summons is not very clear to me. In any case it appears C   to me, however, that, in making her finding that the wife had acted reasonably, the judge took into account only those factors which told in favour of the separation, and did not weigh against those factors the primary duty of spouses to make their home together.

If one examines the reasons which the judge gives in her judgment for deciding that the wife behaved reasonably, those reasons appear to be divided into two, D   one that it was in the interests of the child of the marriage, and the other that the flat offered by the husband was unsuitable. So far as the unsuitability of the flat is concerned, it seems to me that no importance can be attached to this because the wife made it clear in the second of her affidavits that she was unwilling to live with the husband in any flat in London. The interests of the child were, of course, a weighty matter to be taken into account, but in looking at his interests E   the judge does not seem to have considered the importance to him of maintaining a united home, and the interests of the husband in having his wife living with him are not referred to.

I make these observations with considerable diffidence, realising that a judge often has in mind, and gives full weight to, factors which are not expressly mentioned in the judgment; but, when it is conceded (as it was here) that a case F   has been conducted throughout on wrong assumptions as to the law applicable, I do not consider that the ultimate conclusion can be upheld on a different view of the law unless the judgment makes it clear that all the relevant factors have been considered. For these reasons, in addition to those which my lords have expressed, it appears to me impossible to sustain the judgment of her ladyship on the basis argued by counsel for the wife.

G   So far as the cross-appeal is concerned, I agree entirely with what my lords have said, and would further draw attention to the fact that the judge based her decision allowing the submission of " no case " to be made on the terms of Matrimonial Causes Rules, 1957, r. 58 (17). I would point out that all that that sub-rule provides is that:

H   " Subject to the provisions of this rule, these rules shall, so far as applicable, apply to an application under this rule as if—(a) the application were a matrimonial cause; . . . "

The matter of submitting no case to answer is something which is not dealt with by the rules at all, and therefore, with respect to her ladyship, it does not appear to me that the conclusion which she reached can logically be based on the sub-I   rule. I agree that the appeal and cross-appeal must be allowed and the case must be remitted for re-hearing.

Appeal and cross-appeal allowed. Order below discharged and case remitted for re-trial.

Solicitors: *Maurice Bilmes & Co.* (for the husband); *Beckingsales & Brashiers* (for the wife).

[*Reported by* F. A. Amies, Esq., *Barrister-at-Law.*]

R. *v.* CURR.

[COURT OF APPEAL, CRIMINAL DIVISION (Lord Parker, C.J., Salmon, L.J., and Fenton Atkinson, J.), December 19, 20, 21, 1966.]

Criminal Law—Incitement to commit summary offence—Whether indictable offence—Magistrates' Courts Act, 1952 (15 & 16 *Geo.* 6 & 1 *Eliz.* 2 *c.* 55), *Sch.* 1, *para.* 20.

B

Family Allowance—Payment—Wrongful receipt—Married women lent money by appellant on security of family allowance books—Agents of appellant cashing vouchers for appellant who kept money as repayment of loans with interest—Whether knowledge of illegality by women agents necessary to establish charges of soliciting, and of conspiring to commit, offences contrary to Family Allowances Act, 1945 (8 & 9 *Geo.* 6 *c.* 41), *s.* 9 (*b*).

C

The appellant was a trafficker in family allowance books. His method was to approach married women with large families of children and lend them money on the security of their family allowance books. The women would sign some of the vouchers and hand over the book to the appellant as security. The appellant had a team of women agents whom he sent out to cash the vouchers, and he would pocket the proceeds in repayment of the loan and thereafter return the book. He admitted that he knew that he was not legally entitled to receive the family allowance payments. He was convicted, inter alia, of soliciting to commit a summary offence, contrary to s. 9 (*b*)* of the Family Allowances Act, 1945, and of conspiring to commit offences, contrary to s. 9 (*b*). In his summing-up, the trial judge did not deal with the question of the knowledge of the women agents. On appeal,

D

E

Held: (i) the convictions would be quashed, because—

(a) the appellant could be guilty of soliciting to commit an offence under s. 9 (*b*) only if the woman agent sent to collect the allowance knew that the action which she was asked to carry out amounted to an offence and the question of her knowledge had not been left to the jury for their considera- tion (see p. 481, letter I, to p. 482, letter A, and p. 482, letter E, post).

F

(b) it took two persons to make a conspiracy and, since the offence created by s. 9 (*b*) was not an absolute statutory offence, knowledge on the part of the women agents that the moneys to be drawn were not properly receivable by them had to be established before the appellant could be rightly convicted; but that knowledge had not been established (see p. 482, letters G and H, post).

G

R. v. Churchill (No. 2) ([1966] 2 All E.R. 215) distinguished.

(ii) in view of para. 20 of Sch. 1 to the Magistrates' Courts Act, 1952, incitement to commit a summary offence was an indictable offence (see p. 480, letter I, post).

Appeal allowed.

H

[**Editorial Note.** The decision in *R. v. Churchill (No. 2),* cited above, has been reversed, subsequently to the present case; see *Churchill v. Walton* (Feb. 1, 1967, H.L.) post.

The Family Allowances Act, 1945, has been repealed by the Statute Law Revision (Consequential Repeals) Act 1965, and replaced by the Family Allow- ances Act 1965. Section 9 of the Act of 1945 has been replaced by s. 9 of the Act of 1965; 45 HALSBURY'S STATUTES (2nd Edn.) 1197.

I

As to offences relating to family allowances, see 27 HALSBURY'S LAWS (3rd Edn.) 705, para. 1283.

As to incitement to commit a summary offence, see 10 HALSBURY'S LAWS (3rd Edn.) 310, para. 568, text and notes (*e*) and (*f*); and as to conspiracy to commit a summary offence, see ibid., p. 312, para. 570.

---

* Section 9, so far as material, is set out at p. 481, letter A, post.

A   For the Family Allowances Act, 1945, s. 9, see 16 HALSBURY'S STATUTES (2nd Edn.) 1016.

For the Magistrates' Courts Act, 1952, Sch. 1, see 32 HALSBURY'S LAWS (3rd Edn.) 524.

For the Family Allowances (Making of Claims and Payments) Regulation, 1946, reg. 8, reg. 12, see 15 HALSBURY'S STATUTORY INSTRUMENTS (First Re-Issue) B 413, 414.]

Case referred to:

R. v. *Churchill (No. 2)*, [1966] 2 All E.R. 215; [1966] 2 W.L.R. 1116; *reversed* H.L., sub nom. *Churchill* v. *Walton*, [1967] 1 All E.R. 497.

Appeal.

C   This was an appeal by Patrick Vincent McGinley Curr against his conviction on Sept. 29, 1966, at Salford Borough Quarter Sessions on one count (No. 1) of attempting to obtain money by false pretences, four counts (Nos. 2, 4, 5 and 7) of obtaining money by false pretences, contrary to s. 32 of the Larceny Act, 1916, one count (No. 3) of soliciting the commission of a summary offence, contrary to s. 9 (*b*) of the Family Allowances Act, 1945, and two counts (Nos. 6 and 8) of conspiring to commit an offence, contrary to s. 9 (*b*) of the Act of 1945. He D also appealed against sentence of three years' imprisonment in all. The facts are set out in the judgment of the court. The case is reported in regard to counts 3, 6 and 8. These counts were as follows. Count 3 charged soliciting to commit an offence under s. 9 (*b*) of the Family Allowances Act, 1945, in that the appellant on a day unknown between Oct. 14 and Oct. 20, 1965, in the county of Lancaster, E unlawfully solicited a woman unknown to obtain on his behalf from Her Majesty's Postmaster-General the sum of £2 18s. as on account of an allowance, knowing that it was not receivable by her. Count 6 charged conspiracy to commit an offence under s. 9 (*b*) of the Act of 1945 in that the appellant on a day unknown between Jan. 1 and Feb. 10, 1965, in the county of Lancaster conspired with Laura Kate Stone to obtain for himself the sum of £10 4s. as on account of an F allowance, knowing that the sum was not properly receivable by him. Count 8 charged the appellant with conspiracy to commit an offence under s. 9 (*b*) of the Act of 1945 in that he on a day unknown between Apr. 1 and Apr. 27, 1966, in the City of Manchester, conspired with an unknown woman to obtain for himself the sum of £3 18s. as on account of an allowance, knowing that the sum was not properly receivable by him.

G   The authority and cases noted below* were cited during the argument in addition to the case referred to in the judgment of the court.

H. A. Kershaw for the appellant.
J. Hugill for the Crown.

FENTON ATKINSON, J., delivered the judgment of the court at the invitation of LORD PARKER, C.J.: The appellant was in fact a trafficker in family H allowance books. His method was to approach some married women who had a large family of children and lend them money on the security of their family allowance books. A woman would borrow from him, let us say, £6, and would sign three of the vouchers in her family allowance book to the value of, let us say, £9, and hand over the book to him as security. He then had a team of women agents whom he sent out to cash the vouchers, and he would pocket the proceeds I in repayment of the loans and thereafter return the books. He admitted quite freely in evidence that he had done, as he put it, forty to eighty books a week, and he said that in February, 1966, he had between three and five women agents

* ARCHBOLD'S CRIMINAL PLEADING, EVIDENCE AND PRACTICE (36th Edn.), para. 4051; R. v. *Hicks*, (1618), Hob. 215; R. v. *Bacon*, (1664), 1 Lev. 146; R. v. *Higgins*, (1801), 2 East. 5; R. v. *Welham*, (1845), 1 Cox, C.C. 192; R. v. *Gregory*, (1867), L.R. 1 C.C.R. 77; R. v. *Brown*, (1899), 63 J.P. 790; R. v. *Brailsford*, [1904-07] All E.R. Rep. 240; [1905] 2 K.B. 730; *Frailey* v. *Charlton*, [1920] 1 K.B. 147; R. v. *McDonough*, (1962), 47 Cr. App. Rep. 37.

assisting him in this matter, and when he was arrested he had about eighty
family allowance books in his possession. He agreed quite frankly that he knew
that he was not legally entitled to receive these payments, and that it could be
risky; in dealing with the husband of one of the women concerned, he said:
" When you're doing business like this, you should keep your big mouth shut."
So it it quite plain that this man's dealings were highly objectionable, and the
assistant recorder who tried the case clearly had very strong views about it;
on two occasions in his summing-up he spoke of preying on these women with
large families, and he finished up his direction to the jury with words to this
effect:

> " If you are getting interest at eight hundred per cent. per annum it is
> not bad, is it? That is what the prosecution say here, that the whole system
> was corrupt,"

and the language there used was no whit too strong.

The very nature of the case was bound to arouse strong prejudice in the mind
of any right thinking juror and, for that reason it was all the more important
to put the law on each count clearly to the jury, and to make sure that the defence
was clearly put before them. [HIS LORDSHIP dealt with the false pretences
counts (Nos. 1, 2, 4, 5 and 7), in each of which the false pretence was the same,
viz., that the appellant with intent to defraud attempted to obtain, or obtained,
from Her Majesty's Postmaster-General a sum of money by pretending that it
was being received for and for the use and benefit of the women named in the
family allowance book. HIS LORDSHIP intimated that it could not be said
as a matter of law that any given sum of money received by the appellant
through his female agents from the Post Office was not received for the use and
benefit of the woman concerned, and to reach a decision on that question it
was necessary to examine the bargain between the appellant and the book-holder
concerned to see whether there was an assignment or merely an authority
to collect the allowance. The court was satisfied accordingly that there was a
possible defence which, although the matter had been raised on submission of
" no case ", was not left to the jury, and about which there was no satisfactory
direction in the summing-up. The convictions on these counts would be quashed.
HIS LORDSHIP continued:]

There remain, however, three other counts. There were three other charges
because the prosecution, very reasonably in view of the nature of this case, and
the previous record of the appellant, were not content to charge him merely with
the summary offence under s. 9 (b) of the Family Allowances Act, 1945. Count 3
was of soliciting the commission of a summary offence, contrary to s. 9 (b) of
the Act of 1945, the particulars being that on a day unknown the appellant
unlawfully

> " solicited a woman unknown to obtain on [his] behalf from Her Majesty's
> Postmaster-General the sum of £2 18s. as on account of an allowance, knowing
> that it was not properly receivable by her."

Counsel for the appellant took a preliminary point on that count that incitement
to commit a summary offence is not an indictable offence, and he referred to
some old authorities which might lend some countenance to that view. It
appears to this court, however, that Parliament in the Magistrates' Courts Act,
1952, Sch. 1, para. 20, has in fact recognised incitement of this kind as an indictable offence, and it is not necessary, therefore, to go further into that matter,
all the more because counsel for the appellant's main point is that the offence,
the commission of which the appellant is said to have solicited, is not an absolute
statutory offence, but is one requiring knowledge on the part of the female agent
that she is doing something unlawful in receiving the allowance. Section 9
is headed: " Penalty for obtaining or receiving payment wrongfully ", and
so far as material, continues:

" If any person— . . . (*b*) obtains or receives any sum as on account of an allowance, either as in that person's own right or as on behalf of another, knowing that it was not properly payable, or not properly receivable by him or her; that person shall be liable on summary conviction to imprisonment for a term not exceeding three months or to a fine not exceeding £50 or to both such imprisonment and such fine."

Counsel for the appellant's argument was that, if the woman agent in fact has no guilty knowledge, knowing perhaps nothing of the assignment, or supposing that the appellant was merely collecting for the use and benefit of the woman concerned, then she would be an innocent agent, and, by using her services in that way, the appellant would be committing the summary offence himself, but would not be inciting her to receive money knowing that it was not receivable by her. He contends that it was essential to prove, to support this charge, that the woman agent in question in this transaction affecting a Mrs. Currie, knew that the allowances were not properly receivable by her. Counsel for the Crown's answer to that submission was that the woman agent must be presumed to know the law, and, if she knew the law, she must have known, he contends, that the allowance was not receivable by her. He refers to s. 4 (2) of the Act of 1945 (1), and to the Family Allowances (Making of Claims and Payments) Regulations, 1946 (2), reg. 8 of which provides:

" Sums on account of an allowance shall become receivable at the times hereinafter prescribed and shall be paid either—(1) by means of allowance orders payable in respect of every week to a person by whom such sums are receivable . . . [that is to say the wife or husband under s. 4 (2) of the Act of 1945]; or (2) in such other special manner as the Minister may in any particular case and for any particular period determine."

Provision is made also in those regulations by reg. 12 that where any person entitled to an allowance becomes unable to act for the time being, the Minister may appoint some person to act on his behalf. Provision is made by adminis- trative direction in the case of sickness by the book-holder, and there is an instruction No. 12 on a coloured page at the end of the book:

" Payment during illness: If you are ill for a short time and cannot go to the Post Office to draw the money and, where there is a second payee, he also cannot go, someone else may cash the orders for you if you fill up and sign "

a certain form at the back of the voucher. The argument is that in no other circumstances may an agent lawfully collect for the use and benefit of the book- holder, and counsel for the Crown was ready to contend, for example, that if a mother with, say, eight children to look after at home, asks a neighbour to go and collect her allowance for her, and the neighbour does so, the neighbour would be committing an offence under s. 9 (*b*) of the Act of 1945, and the mother would be guilty of the offence of soliciting. We are by no means satisfied that any agent who collects with the full authority of the book-holder and for her use and benefit would commit an offence under this subsection. There appears to be no express prohibition, certainly we were referred to no express prohibition, in the Act or any statutory instruments making such collection unlawful. On the evidence, the Post Office in practice appear to allow this to be done in certain cases; in our view, there can be or may be situations in which an agent, however well she may know the statute and regulations, could properly suppose that her action in receiving an allowance of this kind was lawful.

In our view, the argument for the Crown here gives no effect to the word " knowing " in the section, and in our view the appellant could be guilty on

---

(1) Section 4 (2) provides: " Sums to be paid on account of an allowance for the family of a man or his wife living together shall be receivable either by the man or by the wife."

(2) S.R. & O. 1946 No. 137.

count 3 only if the woman agent sent to collect the allowance knew that the action which she was asked to carry out amounted to an offence. As has already been said, the appellant himself clearly knew that his conduct in the matter was illegal and contrary to s. 9 (*b*), but it was essential in our view for the jury to consider the knowledge, if any, of the woman agent. When the assistant recorder dealt with this count, he referred to soliciting in this way:

" Solicited means encouraged or incited another person to go and draw that money which should have been paid, you may think, to Mrs. Currie."

He then dealt with ignorance of the law being no excuse. He went on to deal with statutory offences, and read s. 4 of the Family Allowances Act, 1945, telling the jury in effect that, apart from the case of sickness, nobody else could legally receive these allowances, and then he went on to consider the position of the appellant, asking the rhetorical question whether he could be heard to say with his knowledge of this matter and his trafficking in these books that it was not known to be wrong to employ an agent to go and collect the family allowances. He never followed that, however, with the question of the knowledge of the women agents, and in the whole of the summing-up dealing with this matter he proceeded on the assumption that either guilty knowledge in the woman was irrelevant, or, alternatively, that any woman agent must be taken to have known that she was committing an offence under s. 9 (*b*). If the matter had been left on a proper direction for the jury's consideration, they might well have thought that the women agents, other than Mrs. Nicholson, whom they acquitted, must have known very well that they were doing something wrong; some of them were apparently collecting as many as ten of these weekly payments. The matter, however, was never left to them for their consideration, and here again, so it seems to this court, there was a vital matter where the defence was not left to the jury at all and there was no sufficient direction; it would be quite impossible to say that, on a proper direction, the jury must have convicted on this count.

The prosecution still had two other strings to their bow, counts 6 and 8 where they alleged conspiracy; count 6, conspiring with one of the book-holders, a certain Mrs. Stone, to commit an offence, contrary to s. 9 (*b*), count 8, conspiring with an unknown female agent to commit an offence against the same section. It seems to this court that, on the conspiracy counts, the same difficulty arises as arose in the case of the soliciting count, count 3. It takes two to make a conspiracy, and it was, therefore, necessary to show that Mrs. Stone, on count 6, or the unknown agent on count 8, agreed to do an unlawful act. It is true that there are decisions, at present subject to consideration by the House of Lords in *R.* v. *Churchill* (*No. 2*) (3), to the effect that, where one has an absolute statutory offence, a man can be convicted of conspiring to commit that offence if he agrees to do that which the law in fact forbids, even though he does not know that the act is prohibited. In that sense he is presumed to know the law. But this is not an absolute statutory offence; in our view, before either Mrs. Stone or the unknown agent may be classed as conspirators, it would have to be shown that they knew that the moneys to be drawn were not properly receivable by those who drew them, and that, in our view, was not established. Logically enough from his point of view, the assistant recorder followed his direction on count 3, and he took the view, and expressed it to the jury, that Mrs. Stone could have no possible defence to a charge under s. 9 (*b*), and similarly the woman agent under count 8. In our view, it follows that these convictions also must be quashed, a conclusion that the court has reached with regret. The appellant plainly committed a summary offence under s. 9 (*b*) many times over, and, in our view, the assistant recorder was well justified in saying that here was a case of a man preying on these women with large families and bringing hardship on many of

---

(3) [1966] 2 All E.R. 215; *reversed* on appeal, post.

them. Unfortunately, however, in our view, as the matter stands, none of the convictions can stand and they must, therefore, be quashed.

Appeal allowed. Convictions quashed.

Solicitors: *Registrar of Criminal Appeals* (for the appellant); *Solicitor, Ministry of Social Security* (for the Crown).

[*Reported by* N. P. METCALFE, ESQ., *Barrister-at-Law.*]

R. *v.* SKIVINGTON.

[COURT OF APPEAL, CRIMINAL DIVISION (Lord Parker, C.J., Winn, L.J., and Willis, J.), January 13, 1967.]

Criminal Law—Robbery—Claim of right—Whether claim of right a defence—Belief of being entitled to take the thing stolen in the way in which it was taken need not be proved—Larceny Act, 1916 (6 & 7 Geo. 5 c. 50), *s.* 23 (1).

The appellant went to the offices of the employers of himself and his wife on a Wednesday. He drew a knife and demanded his wife's wages which, according to him, he had her authority to collect. He pushed an assistant manager into an office where a safe was open and there, at the point of the knife, the appellant was given two wage packets containing money. Wages were not due until Friday. At his trial on a charge of robbery with aggravation, contrary to s. 23 (1)* of the Larceny Act, 1916, the appellant contended that he had an honest belief that he had a right to the money. The trial judge directed the jury that before the appellant could maintain a defence to the charge they must be satisfied that he had an honest belief that he was entitled to take the money in the way in which he did take it. On appeal against conviction,

Held: a claim of right was a defence to robbery or any aggravated form of robbery, and it was unnecessary to establish that the accused must have had also an honest belief that he was entitled to take the money in the way in which he did take it (see p. 485, letter G, *post*).

R. v. King-Jones and Gladdy ([1966] 1 W.L.R. 1077) overruled.

Appeal allowed in part.

[As to a claim of right as defence to a charge of robbery, see 10 HALSBURY'S LAWS (3rd Edn.) 796, para. 1538; and for cases on the subject, see 15 DIGEST (Repl.) 1061, 1062, *10,461-10,474*, 1117, *11,096.*

For the Larceny Act, 1916, s. 23, see 5 HALSBURY'S STATUTES (2nd Edn.) 1025.]

Cases referred to:

R. v. Bernhard, [1938] 2 All E.R. 140; [1938] 2 K.B. 264; 107 L.J.K.B. 449; 159 L.T. 22; 102 J.P. 282; 26 Cr. App. Rep. 137; 15 Digest (Repl.) 1125, *11,218.*

R. v. Boden, (1844), 1 Car. & Kir. 395; 174 E.R. 863; 15 Digest (Repl.) 1117, *11,096.*

R. v. Hall, (1828), 3 C. & P. 409; 172 E.R. 477; 15 Digest (Repl.) 1061, *10,462.*

R. v. Hemmings, (1864), 4 F. & F. 50; 176 E.R. 462; 15 Digest (Repl.) 1061, *10,469.*

R. v. King-Jones and Gladdy, [1966] 1 W.L.R. 1077.

Appeal.

This was an appeal by Jim Skivington against his conviction on July 20, 1966, at Nottingham City Assizes before GLYN-JONES, J., and a jury, on, among other

---

* Section 23 (1), so far as material, provides " Every person who—(*a*) being armed with any offensive weapon . . . robs . . . any person; (*b*) robs any person and, at the time of or immediately before or immediately after such robbery, uses any personal violence to any person; shall be guilty of a felony . . ."

charges, a charge (count 4) of robbery with aggravation. He had been arraigned
on an indictment containing seven counts, and had pleaded guilty to counts
3, 5, 6, and 7.   Count 1, on which he was also convicted, charged him with
wounding with intent; and count 2 charged unlawful wounding.   The counts
to which he pleaded guilty charged (by count 3) carrying an offensive weapon,
and (by counts 5, 6 and 7) three offences of common assault, the charge made by
count 5 being alternative to count 4. On July 27, 1966, he was sentenced to
six years' imprisonment in all, the sentence on count 4 being two years'
imprisonment.

The authority and cases noted below* were cited in argument in addition to
those referred to in the judgment.

J. B. R. Hazan for the appellant.
S. E. Herman for the Crown.

LORD PARKER, C.J., delivered the following judgment of the court:
The only matter with which this court is concerned is count 4, the charge of
robbery with aggravation.   That offence was alleged to have arisen out of the
following circumstances.   According to the appellant, after a particular incident,
which was the incident in count 1, his wife gave him a letter addressed to Messrs.
Drewry & Edwards, where both husband and wife worked, authorising him to
collect her wages.   When, after the incident, with which count 1 is concerned,
she left him, he sought to raise money to follow her.   He went to the employers,
Drewry & Edwards, and went into the office of the manager, a Mr. Kirk. According to Mr. Kirk the appellant produced a knife and lunged at him, whereupon
Mr. Kirk fled.   That gave rise to count 6, one of the assault counts, to which
he pleaded guilty.   When Mr. Kirk fled, however, a Mr. Thurgood, the assistant
manager, came on the scene and then, according to Mr. Thurgood, the appellant
drew a knife, grabbed him by the shoulder and said: " I want the money, I
want the money."   When asked what money, the appellant said: " My wife's
wages."   Thereupon, according to Mr. Thurgood, the appellant pushed him
into an office where there was an open safe containing a number of unissued
wage packets, and Mr. Thurgood, at the point of the knife, took out two wage
packets and handed them to the appellant.   It was his defence that albeit this
was a Wednesday and the wages for his wife and himself were not due until the
Friday, yet that he had an honest belief that he had a right to the money, and
that, accordingly, he could not be guilty of robbery with aggravation.

The point with which this appeal is concerned is the direction by the judge,
a direction given in many passages.   It is sufficient, I think, to refer to but
one of those and I take the first, where the judge said:

" So far as robbery is concerned it goes a little bit further [this is dealing
with a claim of right] because there, I think, before [the appellant] can
escape the guilt of robbery, he must honestly believe that he is entitled to
extract the money which is due to him, in the way in which he does it."

Throughout the judge was at pains to tell the jury that before they could accept
a claim of right as a defence to this charge, they must be satisfied that the appellant had an honest belief that he was entitled to take the money in the way in
which he did.   It is quite clear, and it is sufficient only to mention *R.* v. *Bernhard*
(1), that a claim of right exists whenever a man honestly believes that he has a
lawful claim, even though it may be completely unfounded in law or in fact.
The question is whether that defence to larceny applies equally when the offence
with which one is concerned is really an aggravated larceny, such as in this case
robbery, or whether the honest belief must extend to being entitled to take the
money by force.   In the opinion of the court, both on principle and on the cases,

---

* ARCHBOLD'S CRIMINAL PLEADING, EVIDENCE AND PRACTICE (36th Edn.), para. 1469;
R. v. *Farnborough*, [1895] 2 Q.B. 484; *R.* v. *Clayton*, (1920), 15 Cr. App. Rep. 45.
   (1) [1938] 2 All E.R. 140; [1938] 2 K.B. 264.

A it is clear that it can be a defence. So far as principle is concerned, it can be stated in the simple form that larceny is an ingredient of robbery, and if the honest belief that a man has a claim of right is a defence to larceny, then it negatives one of the ingredients in the offence of robbery, without proof of which the full offence is not made out. That principle simply stated as such has been upheld in case after case. Counsel for the appellant has referred us in the first instance

B to *R. v. Hall* (2) in 1828. There a gamekeeper found certain wires used for catching game and seized them for the use of the lord of the manor. The defendant, finding that the gamekeeper had these wires which he, the defendant, had set, demanded them of the gamekeeper with menaces, as a result of which the game-keeper gave them up. The jury found that the defendant acted under a bona fide impression that the game and wires were his property, and it was held that

C there was no robbery. That was followed in the case of an assault with intent to rob in *R. v. Boden* (3), and in the case, again of robbery, where violence was used to enforce the debt, *R. v. Hemmings* (4). Indeed this principle is inherent in the case of *R. v. Bernhard* (5) to which I have already referred, because in that case the claim of right arose in a case of demanding money with menaces, and a claim of right would only be a defence if the prisoner believed that he was

D entitled to take the money by these means. The same, as counsel for the appel-lant has pointed out, is true when one looks at the textbook writers. If one takes as an illustration GLANVILLE WILLIAMS' CRIMINAL LAW (2nd Edn.), THE GENERAL PART, p. 326, one finds explicitly stated:

> "Claim of right, being a defence to larceny, is also a defence to other crimes in which a charge of intent to commit larceny enters, e.g., robbery

E and burglary."

The only exception is to be found in RUSSELL ON CRIME (12th Edn.), Vol. 2, p. 855, where the editor states, without setting out any argument or reasons for the principle there stated that:

> "A creditor who assaults his debtor and compels him to pay his debt

F cannot be convicted of robbery if he does so under honest but mistaken belief that he is entitled to extract the money *in this way*."

As I said, no reasons for coming to that conclusion are given by the editor, and indeed thereafter he refers to the case of *R. v. Hemmings* (4) and the case of *R. v. Boden* (3). In the footnote on that page he, however, takes the view that because the principle is as stated by him, the judges in those cases must have

G overlooked the point. In the opinion of this court this matter is plain, namely that a claim of right is a defence to robbery or any aggravated form of robbery, and that it is unnecessary to show that the defendant must have had an honest belief also that he was entitled to take the money in the way that he did.

The only case which throws any doubt on the matter is a recent case tried at Glamorgan Assizes, by MOCATTA, J., *R. v. King-Jones and Gladdy* (6). The

H report does not indicate whether any authorities were quoted; but knowing the manner in which these matters are necessarily dealt with on Assize, it is to say the least probable that the only book available for the learned judge was Vol. 2 of RUSSELL ON CRIME (12th Edn.) and the passage to which I have already referred. This court is satisfied that that case was wrongly decided and should not be followed. The matter, however, does not rest there, because the pleader, foreseeing

I that a claim of right might be a defence, put into the indictment an alternative count of common assault on Mr. Thurgood. To that the appellant pleaded guilty, but having been convicted of the more serious offence of robbery with aggravation, he was not sentenced on that count for common assault. It is, however, open to this court to do so (7), and they will, accordingly, quash the conviction for

---

(2) (1828), 3 C. & P. 409.   (3) (1844), 1 Car. & Kir. 395.
(4) (1864), 4 F. & F. 50.   (5) [1938] 2 All E.R. 140; [1938] 2 K.B. 264.
(6) [1966] 1 W.L.R. 1077.
(7) Under s. 5 (1) of the Criminal Appeal Act, 1907.

robbery with aggravation and will sentence the prisoner to one year's imprison- **A**
ment on the count of common assault. In the result, therefore, he will serve a
total of five years' imprisonment and not six years' imprisonment.

        Appeal allowed in part. Conviction on count 4 quashed. Sentence varied.

   Solicitors: *Registrar of Criminal Appeals* (for the appellant); *Town Clerk,*
Nottingham (for the Crown).   **B**

             [*Reported by* N. P. METCALFE, ESQ., *Barrister-at-Law.*]

                                      C

R. *v.* BRITTON.

[COURT OF APPEAL, CRIMINAL DIVISION (Lord Parker, C.J., Salmon, L.J., and
   Fenton Atkinson, J.), December 19, 1966.]

*Criminal Law—Public order—Incitement to racial hatred—Distributing written
   matter likely to stir up hatred against section of the public distinguished by* **D**
   *colour—Pamphlets left in porch of private house of member of Parliament—
   Whether a distribution of the written matter—Race Relations Act* 1965
   (c. 73), *s.* 6 (1) *(a),* (2).

   A member of Parliament, when at home with his family at about 10.15 p.m.
heard the crash of the glass panel of his front door being broken. He saw
the appellant running away and pursued and caught him. On returning to **E**
his house the member of Parliament found a pamphlet, with the words on
it in large black letters, " Blacks not wanted here ", stuck on the door.
Four or five other similar pamphlets had been left in the porch, and nearby
was a beer bottle round which another pamphlet had been wrapped. The
appellant was charged with distributing written matter with intent to stir
up hatred against a section of the public in Great Britain distinguished by **F**
colour, contrary to s. 6 (1) *(a)** of the Race Relations Act 1965. In summing-
up the chairman of quarter sessions intimated that there was no contest
whether the matter was distributed, thereby withdrawing from the jury any
evidence of distribution of the matter, if there was any such evidence. On
appeal against conviction,

   Held: no distribution to the public or to a section of the public within **G**
s. 6 (1) of the Race Relations Act 1965 had been established, and moreover,
if there had been evidence of such a distribution, it had been withdrawn
from the jury; accordingly the conviction would be quashed (see p. 487,
letter I, to p. 488, letter A, and p. 488, letters C and F, post).

   Appeal allowed.

  [As to the offence of incitement to racial hatred, see SERVICE to 10 HALSBURY'S **H**
LAWS (3rd Edn.), para. 1061A.

   For the Race Relations Act 1965, s. 6, see 45 HALSBURY'S STATUTES (2nd Edn.)
35.]

Appeal.

   This was an appeal by Christopher Britton against his conviction on Oct. 17,
1966, at Middlesex Sessions on an indictment charging that on July 16, 1966, he **I**
distributed insulting written matter, namely pamphlets bearing the words
" Blacks not wanted here " being words likely and intended to stir up hatred
against a section of the public of Great Britain distinguished by colour, contrary
to s. 6 of the Race Relations Act 1965. He was seventeen years of age and was
sentenced by the chairman (E. E. S. MONTAGU, Esq., Q.C.) to undergo a period
of Borstal training. The facts are set out in the judgment of the court.

---

  * Section 6, so far as material, is set out at p. 487, letters B and C, post.

A The authorities noted below* were cited during the argument.

D. H. Wild for the appellant.

H. F. Cassel for the Crown.

LORD PARKER, C.J., delivered the following judgment of the court: It is convenient to read at once the relevant words of s. 6 of the Race Relations
B Act 1965:

" (1) A person shall be guilty of an offence under this section if, with intent to stir up hatred against any section of the public in Great Britain distinguished by colour, race, or ethnic or national origins—(*a*) he publishes or distributes written matter which is threatening, abusive or insulting; . . . being matter or words likely to stir up hatred against that section on grounds
C of colour, race, or ethnic or national origins.

" (2) . . . ' publish ' and ' distribute ' mean publish or distribute to the public at large or to any section of the public not consisting exclusively of members of an association of which the person publishing or distributing is a member . . ."

D The appellant was sentenced for the offence of distributing, not of publishing, and he was sentenced to Borstal training. Now, by leave of the single judge, he appeals against his conviction and his sentence. The short facts were that the member of Parliament for Southall lives at Hayes; he is a Mr. Bidwell, and at 10.15 p.m. on Saturday, July 16, 1966, when he was about to take his dog out for a walk, he heard a crash of glass, went to the door, found the glass panels
E broken, saw someone running away, whom he chased and with the assistance of his dog caught. The man caught was the appellant, whom Mr. Bidwell brought back to his porch. When he got there he saw stuck on the door a pamphlet, of which the court has a copy, which in large black letters said: " Blacks not wanted here ", and a big hand pictured on the poster, clearly indicating " Stop "— " Stop further Immigration " presumably. Underneath was written " Greater
F Britain Movement, London, W.C.1." There was also evidence that four or five similar pamphlets had been left in the porchway, and nearby a beer bottle round which had been wrapped another of the leaflets. Mr. Bidwell sent for the police, and various conversations took place. Apparently the appellant said: " I'll get two years for this." Mr. Bidwell said: " You are only a little weed " and the appellant replied: " So was Hitler." Finally P.C. Cargill arrived, the appellant
G would not answer any questions, and he was taken to the police station where he complained that the member of Parliament, Mr. Bidwell, was the person responsible for bringing the blacks to Britain. In his pocket, P.C. Cargill found another leaflet, this time in large letters " Do you want a black grandchild? "; that, however, had never left his pocket.

A submission was made at the end of the prosecution case that there was no
H case to answer; that was not acceded to, and thereupon the appellant did not go into the witness box. What is said by counsel for the appellant in this appeal is really twofold, first that there was no evidence, or no sufficient evidence, to leave to the jury, and secondly, that in any event the defence was not properly put, and indeed was never referred to except insofar as it was necessary to demolish it. The point which has concerned the court in this case is whether
I there can properly be said to have been distribution within the meaning of the section. Distribution has to be distribution to the public at large, or to any section of the public not consisting exclusively of members of an association of which the person publishing or distributing is a member. To take the pamphlet which was put on the door itself, that was a distribution, as it seems to this court, to the member of Parliament. It is difficult to say that that was a distribution to the public at large, even if one takes into consideration that apparently

* 5 Halsbury's Statutes (2nd Edn.) 1092; Stone's Justices' Manual (1966 Edn.), p. 2262; Gatley on Libel and Slander (5th Edn.), p. 81.

his wife was in the house, and his son-in-law and daughter.   Nor, as it seems
to this court, can one say, and indeed counsel for the Crown has not suggested
it before us, that the member of Parliament or his family were a section of the
public within the meaning of the definition clause.   The words " any section of
the public not consisting exclusively of members of an association of which the
person publishing or distributing is a member ", connote the idea of an identifiable
section of the public who, but for those words, might be said not to be members
of the public at large, in other words members of a club or of an association.
What is then said is: " Oh, but there were other pamphlets left in the porch,
and one on a beer bottle, and that that is a distribution, particularly since with
the sound of breaking glass, and the commotion, other people came on to the
scene, ordinary members of the public, and apparently walked up Mr. Bidwell's
private garden or drive or pathway to his porch."   Again, this court finds it
quite impossible to say that leaving four or five pamphlets in a porch could be a
distribution to the public.   It may be that the public would see them if Mr.
Bidwell let them come up to his front door, but it seems impossible to treat that
as a distribution by the appellant to the public at large.

It may, of course, be that by putting a pamphlet up on the door and scattering
pamphlets in the porch, members of the public might see them; there is no
suggestion that they could in this instance, because it was dark, and this was
some distance from the road.   It might amount to a publication, however, to
whoever passed along the road if they could see it; but again, this man was
charged only with distribution, not with publication.   However, the court finds it
unnecessary to come to any concluded decision as to the circumstances in which
it could be said that there was distribution to the public at large, because in the
present case that issue was wholly withdrawn from the jury.   Before the jury
retired, the chairman read to them the particulars of the indictment, and it
began: " On July 16 of this year distributed ", and the chairman then said:
" There is no contest about that."   In other words, here, even if there was any
evidence of distribution, it was withdrawn from the jury.

Finally, the court would like to say that it seems difficult to believe that
Parliament ever intended that there should be any distribution within the
meaning of this section by leaving a pamphlet of this sort with a member of
Parliament with the object of persuading him to change his policy, and fight
against allowing immigrants to come into the country.   It is difficult to think
that even if technically there was a distribution or a publication to him, that it
could be said that in those circumstances it was a distribution or publication
intended to stir up hatred.   It is the distribution which must be intended to
stir up hatred, not the words used.   In these circumstances, this court is quite
satisfied that this verdict cannot stand and the conviction must be quashed.

Appeal allowed.   Conviction quashed.

Solicitors: *Registrar of Criminal Appeals* (for the appellant); *Director of
Public Prosecutions* (for the Crown).

[*Reported by* N. P. METCALFE, ESQ., *Barrister-at-Law.*]

CROWN LODGE (SURBITON) INVESTMENTS, LTD. *v.* NALECZ.

[COURT OF APPEAL, CIVIL DIVISION (Lord Denning, M.R., Danckwerts and Winn, L.JJ.), November 10, 11, 1966.]

Rent Restriction—Long tenancy—Tenant, having purchased remainder of long lease of whole house, was in occupation of part of house on expiry of lease— Rest of house sub-let in furnished rooms—Rateable value of whole house above, part occupied by tenant below, rent restrictions limit—Whether part occupied by tenant let as a separate dwelling—Whether tenant protected by virtue of Landlord and Tenant Act, 1954 (2 & 3 Eliz. 2 c. 56), s. 2 (1), s. 3 (3), s. 22 (3).

In 1951 the tenant took an assignment of the residue of a term of ninety years from Sept. 29, 1875 of a dwelling house which consisted of a basement and five floors. The ground rent was £31 per annum. The lease contained a tenant's covenant that the premises would be used " as a private dwelling house only or as a professional residence for a physician, surgeon or a solicitor ". The tenant sub-let most of the rooms as bed-sitting rooms, himself occupying only the ground floor, the first floor and the bathroom on the second floor. The rateable value of the whole house had at all times exceeded the rent restrictions limit. The landlords had never consented to the sub-letting of the rooms. The landlords claimed possession of the whole house. The tenant contended that the portion of the house which he occupied would have, on apportionment, a rateable value below the rent restrictions limit and so was a protected tenancy by virtue of Part 1 of the Landlord and Tenant Act, 1954.

Held: where a tenant had a long lease at a low rent of a dwelling house of which the rateable value exceeded the limit for protection under the Rent Acts, he was not protected by the Landlord and Tenant Act, 1954 (see s. 2 (1), s. 3 (3) and s. 22 (3)); in the present case the house as a whole was outside the Rent Acts, the part occupied by the tenant was not let as a separate dwelling, and the tenant was not protected in respect of it (see p. 491, letters D, F and H, and p. 492, letter C, post).

Herbert v. *Byrne* ([1964] 1 All E.R. 882) distinguished.

Appeal dismissed.

[As to tenancies protected under Part 1 of the Landlord and Tenant Act, 1954, see 23 HALSBURY'S LAWS (3rd Edn.) 841-843, para. 1632; and for cases on the subject, see 3rd DIGEST (Supp.) Vols. 30, 31, *7870h*, *7870j*.

For the Landlord and Tenant Act, 1954, s. 2, s. 3 and s. 22 (3), see 34 HALSBURY'S STATUTES (2nd Edn.) 386, 388, 407.]

Cases referred to:

Amphlett v. *Dorrell*, [1948] 2 All E.R. 674; [1949] 1 K.B. 276; [1949] L.J.R. 219; 31 Digest (Repl.) 687, *7791*.

Berkeley v. *Papadoyannis*, [1954] 2 All E.R. 409; [1954] 2 Q.B. 149; [1954] 3 W.L.R. 23; Digest (Cont. Vol. A) 1073, *7616b*.

Crowhurst v. *Maidment*, [1952] 2 All E.R. 808; [1953] 1 Q.B. 23; Digest (Cont. Vol. A) 1073, *7616a*.

Herbert v. *Byrne*, [1964] 1 All E.R. 882; [1964] 1 W.L.R. 519; 3rd Digest Supp.

Skinner v. *Geary*, [1931] All E.R. Rep. 302; [1931] 2 K.B. 546; 100 L.J.K.B. 718; 145 L.T. 675; 95 J.P. 194; 31 Digest (Repl.) 659, *7612*.

Appeal.

This was an appeal by the tenant, Zygmunt Nalecz, from an order of EDMUND DAVIES, J., dated July 27, 1966, granting the landlords possession of No. 28, Ashburn Place, Kensington in the county of Greater London. The facts are set out in the judgment of LORD DENNING, M.R.

N. B. Primost for the tenant.

V. G. Wellings for the landlords.

Considered in REGALIAN SECURITIES
v RAMSDEN [1980] 2 All ER 497

LORD DENNING, M.R.: We are concerned here with a house, 28, Ashburn
Place, Kensington. It is a big house. There is a basement, ground floor and four
floors above. It was the subject of a long lease at a ground rent. The lease was
for ninety years from Sept. 29, 1875. The ground rent was £31 a year. It contained a covenant by the tenant that the premises would be used " as a private
dwelling house only or as a professional residence for a physician, surgeon or a
solicitor ". The rateable value of the house has always been very considerable.
It is so high that the whole house has never come within any of the Rent Acts.
The long lease expired on Sept. 29, 1965. The landlord sued the tenant for
possession. The tenant, Mr. Nalecz, claims to be protected by the statute, not in
respect of the whole house, but in respect of the portion which he occupies. He
occupies the ground floor, first floor and the bathroom on the second floor, and
has sub-let the rest. He says the rateable value of his portion would be sufficiently
low (if there were an apportionment) to give him the protection of the Rent
Acts. He says that by his conduct in sub-letting he has brought himself, in respect
of his own portion, within the statutory protection, although the whole house is
outside the Rent Acts. Let me make it clear that the landlords have never
consented to the sub-division of the house. The tenant took an assignment of the
lease in 1951. The then landlords in 1952 found out that the rooms were being
used mainly as bed-sitting rooms, with gas cookers there. They objected.
Nevertheless, despite their objection, it seems that the tenant has gone on living
in part of the house himself and sub-letting rooms as furnished bed-sitting rooms.
No doubt he has been making a good thing out of it.

In February, 1964, the then landlords, represented by the well-known agents,
Messrs. Cluttons, required him under the statutory provisions (1) to state and give
particulars of the sub-tenancies in the house. This is what he answered : " That
I have not a sub-tenant at 28, Ashburn Place : I have only paying guests." Now
he says quite the contrary. He says that he has sub-tenants and no paying
guests. In April, 1964, the then landlords assigned to the present landlords,
Crown Lodge Investments, Ltd. The present landlords had considerable difficulty
with the tenant as to getting entry and so forth ; but we can now put those
difficulties on one side. The lease expired on Sept. 29, 1965, and the landlords
brought these proceedings against the tenant for possession.

The tenant's case has varied from time to time in the course of the proceedings.
At first he said that he was in possession of the whole. Then he amended and said
that he was only in possession of the ground floor, first floor and bathroom on the
second floor. The landlords applied for summary judgment. The judge in
chambers ordered the tenant to give possession of the two top floors ; but he did
not do so. He went on sub-letting the rooms on those floors. Then the case
concerning the whole house came before EDMUND DAVIES, J. He held that the
tenant had no statutory protection and must go. Now the tenant appeals to
this court.

If this case were to be considered under the Rent Acts as a short lease at a
rack rent, it is plain that the tenant would not be protected in any way : for the
simple reason that the whole house was above the prescribed rateable value. In
such a case, as between the landlord and the tenant, you look at the whole house
which is let to the tenant, and not at the several parts into which he may have
sub-let it. If the whole house is outside the Rent Acts as being above the rateable
value, the tenant has no protection himself as against the landlord, see *Amphlett*
v. *Dorrell* (2), even though his sub-tenants may have protection as against the
tenant.

Counsel for the tenant argues, however, that the position is different with long
leases under the Landlord and Tenant Act, 1954. That is the Act which brought

(1) See the Landlord and Tenant Act, 1954, s. 18; 34 HALSBURY'S STATUTES (2nd
Edn.) 403.
(2) [1948] 2 All E.R. 674; [1949] 1 K.B. 276.

A long leases at a low rent within the Rent Acts. Counsel says that the tenant can in such cases sub-divide the house and gain protection for himself. I cannot accept this contention for a moment. I endeavoured to set out the effect of that statute in the case of *Herbert* v. *Byrne* (3), and I need not repeat what I then said. Applied to the present case, it comes to this. You first look at the premises as if they were let on a short lease at a rack rent; see s. 2 (1) and s. 3 (3). Then you

B look at the state of affairs at the end of the lease, and ascertain the purposes for which the premises were occupied and used at that time; see s. 22 (3). Then you ask yourself: supposing that the house were let on a short lease at a rack rent for that purpose, would it be " let as a separate dwelling " such as was protected by the old Rent Acts? That means that in the present case you are to suppose that the whole house was let on a short lease at a rack rent to the tenant for the

C purpose of his occupying it as his dwelling house with sub-tenants in furnished rooms. On that hypothesis you ask yourself: would he be protected by the old Rent Acts? The answer is clearly " No ", because the whole house was above the prescribed rateable value, and he would not be protected.

In my opinion, when a tenant has a long lease at a low rent of a house which exceeds the prescribed rateable value, he is not protected by the statutes, any

D more than he would be protected if he had a short lease of it at a rack rent. He cannot get protection for himself by sub-letting parts to others. It does not matter what his intentions are for the future, such as whether he does not intend to resume occupation of the sub-let parts (as in *Crowhurst* v. *Maidment* (4)), or does intend to resume occupation (as in *Berkeley* v. *Papadoyannis* (5)). His intentions do not matter when the whole house is outside the protection of the

E Acts as being in excess of the rateable value; but they would matter very much if the house was within the prescribed rateable value. He would then be protected if it was his home and he was living in it as his house, as in *Herbert* v. *Byrne* (6); but he would not be protected if he had given up occupation of it and had moved elsewhere, as in *Skinner* v. *Geary* (7). Seeing that this whole house was outside the Acts, I think that the tenant has no protection at all, even though he lives in

F part of it as his dwelling. Even if he had permission to sub-let parts, he would not be protected. All the more so when he had no permission.

As a last resort, counsel for the tenant sought to rely on Part 2 of the Landlord and Tenant Act, 1954. He said that the tenant was carrying on a business in the ground floor and basement, namely, the business of taking in paying guests or sub-letting furnished apartments. The judge rejected the proposed amendment,

G and I am not surprised: because a thinner case I have hardly ever seen. I think that the judge was quite right in ordering the tenant to go out. I would dismiss the appeal.

DANCKWERTS, L.J.: I agree and have nothing to add.

WINN, L.J.: I agree entirely with the judgment of Lord Denning, M.R.

H It is only out of deference to the strenuous and well-maintained submission of counsel for the tenant about what it seems to me would be a cataclysmic effect of s. 22 (3) of the Landlord and Tenant Act, 1954 that I venture to add my own view.

On construction of that subsection I am quite unable to accept his submission that the true meaning is that where the court is called on, as it is by that section, to consider whether any part of the property comprised in a tenancy—I am of

I course paraphrasing—was let as a separate dwelling, the court is to look at the purpose for which that part was used at the end of the tenancy; and having found that it was used as a dwelling house, decide the question posed by saying that it was let as a separate dwelling house. As I read the section, in accordance with, I venture to think, the ordinary meaning of simple words, it poses for the

---

(3) [1964] 1 All E.R. 882 at pp. 884, 885.
(4) [1952] 2 All E.R. 808; [1953] 1 Q.B. 23.
(5) [1954] 2 All E.R. 409; [1954] 2 Q.B. 149.
(6) [1964] 1 All E.R. 882.   (7) [1931] All E.R. Rep. 302; [1931] 2 K.B. 546.

court this question: whether the relevant part of the property let was let as a
separate dwelling, and directs the court, in approaching the decision of that question, to have regard, inter alia, to the purpose for which that part was let under the
tenancy of the whole, it being comprised in the whole of the property that was
let. In this case the purpose for which the part, as well as the whole, was let under
the original tenancy at the beginning of the ninety-year term is quite clearly
residential use. That is as far as the matter goes. The court having been directed
to accept, by the words to which I have referred, that the part in question was let
at the beginning of the long term tenancy for residential use, i.e., for the purpose
of residential use, the question remains: albeit the part was let as comprised in
the whole for the purpose of it being used residentially, was that part let
separately as a separate dwelling house? That is an entirely different question,
not determined by that subsection, since if it were thereby determined, the
question would be begged and the court would not be left free to make its own
determination of it. It is, as LORD DENNING, M.R., has said, the vital question,
since on that question depends the rateable value of the property for which
protection is claimed.

For that additional reason, as well as those which LORD DENNING, M.R., has
given, I think that it is quite impossible to bring the part used as a dwelling house
by the tenant within any of the provisions of the Landlord and Tenant Act, 1954,
Part 1. I agree that this appeal should be dismissed.

Appeal dismissed.

Solicitors: *How, Davey & Lewis* (for the tenant); *Travers Smith, Braithwaite
& Co.* (for the landlords).

[*Reported by* F. GUTTMAN, ESQ., *Barrister-at-Law.*]

R. *v.* ROE.   R. *v.* ROE.

[COURT OF APPEAL, CRIMINAL DIVISION (Lord Parker, C.J., Winn, L.J., and
Widgery, J.), October 21, 1966.]

*Criminal Law—Indictment—Election by accused, charged before magistrates
with indictable offence, to be tried by jury—New counts added on indictment
—Administration of Justice (Miscellaneous Provisions) Act, 1933 (23 & 24
Geo. 5 c. 36), s. 2 (2), proviso (i).*

*Criminal Law—Sentence—Indictable offence triable summarily—Election by
accused at summary trial for trial by jury—Graver offences added on indictment to those charged for summary trial—Sentence not limited to maximum
that justices could pass—Children and Young Persons Act, 1933 (23 Geo. 5
c. 12), s. 1 (1)—Offences against the Person Act, 1861 (24 & 25 Vict. c. 100),
s. 18, s. 20.*

An information was laid against R. and his wife charging them before a
magistrates' court with the offence of ill-treating their daughter, who at the
time was between the ages of two and five and a half months, contrary to
s. 1 (1)* of the Children and Young Persons Act, 1933. R. and his wife
elected to be tried by a jury and were committed to quarter sessions. The
indictment included also other charges. Two counts charged respectively
(i) causing grievous bodily harm with intent contrary to s. 18 of the Offences

---

* Section 1 (1), as amended by the Children and Young Persons Act 1963, s. 31, s. 64,
Sch. 3, Sch. 5, so far as material, provides: " If any person who has attained the age of
sixteen years and has the custody, charge, or care of any child or young person under
that age wilfully . . . ill-treats, neglects . . . him . . . in a manner likely to cause him unnecessary suffering or injury to health . . . that person shall be guilty of a misdemeanour
and shall be liable—(*a*) on conviction on indictment, to a fine not exceeding £100, or
alternatively, or in addition thereto, to imprisonment for any term not exceeding two
years; (*b*) on summary conviction, to a fine not exceeding £100, or, alternatively, or in
addition thereto, to imprisonment for any term not exceeding six months."

against the Person Act, 1861, and (ii) inflicting grievous bodily harm contrary to s. 20* of the Act of 1861. At the trial at assizes objection was taken that, as there had been an election in respect of an offence which was a summary offence, the charges of causing grievous bodily harm with intent and of inflicting grievous bodily harm could not be added, and that sentence was limited to what could be imposed by the magistrates. Offences under s. 1 (1) of the Act of 1933 were punishable on summary conviction or on conviction on indictment.

Held: (i) on indictment after election for trial by jury on a charge triable summarily or on indictment any count could be joined which could lawfully be added under proviso (i) to s. 2 (2)† of the Administration of Justice (Miscellaneous Provisions) Act, 1933 (see p. 496, letter E, post).

(ii) the sentence imposable on conviction on the indictment was not limited to the maximum that could have been imposed on summary conviction, the offence originally charged being a hybrid offence triable either summarily or on indictment (see p. 496, letter B, post).

R. v. *Gibbs* ([1964] 3 All E.R. 776) followed.

R. v. *Phillips* ([1953] 1 All E.R. 968), *R.* v. *Bishop* ([1959] 2 All E.R. 787) and *R.* v. *Furlong* ([1962] 1 All E.R. 656) distinguished.

Appeals dismissed.

[As to the right to trial by jury where offence charged summarily, see 25 HALSBURY'S LAWS (3rd Edn.) 177-181, paras. 327-330; and for cases on the subject, see 33 DIGEST (Repl.) 192-194, *366-372, 381-382.*

As to the offence of neglect of children, see 10 HALSBURY'S LAWS (3rd Edn.) 760-762, paras. 1470, 1471; and for cases on the subject, see 15 DIGEST (Repl.) 1033, 1034, *10,148-10,169.*

As to adding counts to an indictment after committal for trial, see 10 HALSBURY'S LAWS (3rd Edn.) 383, para. 692, text and notes (*f*)-(*i*).

For the Offences against the Person Act, 1861, s. 18, s. 20, see 5 HALSBURY'S STATUTES (2nd Edn.) 793, 795.

For the Children and Young Persons Act, 1933, s. 1 (1), see SUPPLEMENT to 12 HALSBURY'S STATUTES (2nd Edn.) para. [1468] Amended Texts.

For the Administration of Justice (Miscellaneous Provisions) Act, 1933, s. 2 (2), see 5 HALSBURY'S STATUTES (2nd Edn.) 1067.]

Cases referred to:

R. v. *Bishop,* [1959] 2 All E.R. 787; [1959] 1 W.L.R. 931; 123 J.P. 416; 43 Cr. App. Rep. 177; 37 Digest (Repl.) 444, *44.*

R. v. *Brown,* [1895] 1 Q.B. 119; 64 L.J.M.C. 1; 72 L.T. 22; 59 J.P. 485; 25 Digest (Repl.) 480, *452.*

R. v. *Furlong,* [1962] 1 All E.R. 656; [1962] 2 Q.B. 161; [1962] 2 W.L.R. 796; 12 J.P. 194; 46 Cr. App. Rep. 122; 33 Digest (Repl.) 278, *1055.*

R. v. *Gibbs,* [1964] 3 All E.R. 776; [1965] 2 Q.B. 281; [1964] 3 W.L.R. 1272; 49 Cr. App. Rep. 42; 45 Digest (Repl.) 108, *359.*

R. v. *Phillips,* [1953] 1 All E.R. 968; [1953] 2 Q.B. 14; [1953] 2 W.L.R. 868; 117 J.P. 235; 37 Cr. App. Rep. 65; 33 Digest (Repl.) 277, *1049.*

---

* Section 20 provides: " Whosoever shall unlawfully and maliciously wound or inflict any grievous bodily harm upon any other person, either with or without any weapon or instrument, shall be guilty of a misdemeanour, and being convicted thereof shall be liable to [imprisonment]."

† Section 2 (2), so far as material, provides: " Subject as hereinafter provided no bill of indictment charging a person with an indictable offence shall be prepared unless either—(*a*) the person charged has been committed for trial for the offence, . . . Provided that (i) where the person charged has been committed for trial, the bill of indictment against him may include, either in substitution for or in addition to counts charging the offence for which he was committed, any counts founded on facts or evidence disclosed in any examination or deposition taken before a justice in his presence, being counts which may lawfully be joined in the same indictment; . . ."

Appeals.

The two appellants, Terence Roe and Jeanette Roe, who were husband and wife, were convicted at Cardiff assizes in June, 1966, the first appellant of inflicting grievous bodily harm on his daughter when she was between the age of two months and five and a half months, contrary to s. 20 of the Offences against the Person Act, 1961, and of wilfully ill-treating and also of wilfully neglecting the child contrary to s. 1 (1) of the Children and Young Persons Act, 1933. He was acquitted of causing grievous bodily harm with intent, with which he had been charged in the first count. The second appellant, Jeanette Roe, was convicted only of wilfully neglecting the child. The first appellant was sentenced in all to eighteen months' imprisonment; the second appellant was placed on probation for two years. They both appealed by certificate of the trial judge. The facts are set out in the judgment of the court.

J. S. Abdela, Q.C., and *D. W. Howells* for the appellants.
J. O. Roch for the Crown.

LORD PARKER, C.J., delivered the following judgment of the court, in which, having stated the convictions and sentences, he said: It is happily unnecessary to go through the details of this horrible case, in which really grievous injuries were inflicted on this small child when she was between the ages of two months and five and a half months. They were alleged to have extended over a period from Oct. 30, 1964, to Apr. 24, 1965. It is unnecessary to do so for this reason, that the points in issue in this appeal are pure points of law depending on what took place before the magistrates, and with regard to the indictment when they were committed in the first place to quarter sessions, and then to Cardiff assizes. The history of the matter is this. An information was laid against both appellants alleging neglect and ill-treatment, two separate matters dealt with by s. 1 (1) of the Children and Young Persons Act, 1933. When the matter came before the Barry justices in April, 1966, that charge was altered in that the allegation of neglect was deleted, and the only charge was one of ill-treating, and the dates to which I have referred were inserted as the period over which the ill-treatment was said to have taken place.

One remarkable, and in the opinion of this court, lamentable feature of this case is that apparently the prosecution were prepared to have the matter dealt with summarily. The offences laid down by s. 1 (1) of the Children and Young Persons Act, 1933, are hybrid offences in the sense that proceedings can be brought for summary trial or for trial on indictment. That having been done, the appellants elected to be tried by a jury, the maximum sentence before the justices being one not exceeding six months, and in due course they were committed to quarter sessions. The indictment, however, which had been preferred expanded the charge on which they had been committed to cover the two offences under the Children and Young Persons Act, 1933, viz., wilfully ill-treating as well as wilfully neglecting, and added the two charges under the Offences against the Person Act, 1861, under s. 18 of causing grievous bodily harm with intent, and secondly under s. 20 of inflicting grievous bodily harm.

Quarter sessions had clearly no jurisdiction to deal with the first count, and the matter was then referred to Swansea assizes, and in due course came on at Cardiff assizes. At the very outset there was a motion on behalf of the appellants to quash the indictment. The argument before the judge on their behalf was that, as there had been an election in respect of an offence which was a summary offence, therefore, when the matter came on for trial on indictment, two results followed. The results were, first, that by reason of a line of cases to which reference was made, in particular *R. v. Bishop* (1) and *R. v. Furlong* (2), the court's powers of sentence were limited to the sentence that could be imposed by

---

(1) [1959] 2 All E.R. 787; 43 Cr. App. Rep. 177.
(2) [1962] 1 All E.R. 656; [1962] 2 Q.B. 161.

the justices and were not, as it were, at large; secondly, and perhaps more importantly, that as a result of the decision in *R.* v. *Phillips* (3), charges under the Offences against the Person Act, 1861, could not be added, despite the proviso to s. 2 (2) of the Administration of Justice (Miscellaneous Provisions) Act, 1933.

The answer made to those contentions by the prosecution was a reference to an older case of *R.* v. *Brown* (4). That was a case decided by the Court of Crown Cases Reserved which appears on its face to be in conflict with the later decision in *R.* v. *Phillips* (3) and also with *R.* v. *Bishop* (5) and *R.* v. *Furlong* (6), in none of which later cases had there been reference to *R.* v. *Brown* (4). The judge in those circumstances felt that the proper course was to follow this earlier case of undoubtedly a very strong court, rather than the later cases in the Court of Criminal Appeal. Following *R.* v. *Brown* (4), he refused the motion to quash the indictment, holding that these counts under the Offences against the Person Act, 1861, were properly added, and that his powers in regard to sentence were not limited to what the justices could have imposed.

Unfortunately, and I am not blaming anybody for this, there was no reference to the more recent case of *R.* v. *Gibbs* (7). That was a case in which, as in the present case, the offence was a hybrid offence, and proceedings could be taken summarily or on indictment, whereas in *R.* v. *Brown* (4), in *R.* v. *Phillips* (3), in *R.* v. *Bishop* (5) and in *R.* v. *Furlong* (6) it was a summary offence alone.

It is unnecessary to refer to all these cases. The basis of the latest decisions in the Court of Criminal Appeal, as was stated by Lord Goddard, C.J., in *R.* v. *Phillips* (3), was that to allow other counts to be added and to allow quarter sessions or assizes to impose a sentence greater than could be imposed by the justices was, as it were, a trap, and there was no provision for any warning to an accused that if he elected he might be liable to greater penalties or to additional counts being added. It was accordingly held in *R.* v. *Phillips* (3) and the later cases that, where the conviction was a conviction on indictment as a result of the election, that was a conviction on indictment by reason only of the procedure adopted, and the offence for which there was a conviction was always a summary offence, and could not be anything but a summary offence.

In *R.* v. *Gibbs* (7), as in this case, there is again a conviction on indictment, but it is not a conviction on indictment for a summary offence, but a conviction on indictment for an offence which is not merely a summary offence but also an indictable offence. In *R.* v. *Gibbs* (8), Ashworth, J., giving the judgment of the Court of Criminal Appeal, said this:

" What this court in effect has to do today is to balance the argument that this is a trap and that the principle laid down in *R.* v. *Furlong* (6) should still prevail against the principle that the plain words of the amendment in the Act of 1962 refer to conviction on indictment . . ."

Pausing there, that is a reference to s. 110 of the Road Traffic Act, 1960, dealing with driving whilst disqualified, as amended by the Road Traffic Act, 1962, which latter Act for the first time made this offence both a summary offence and an indictable offence. Ashworth, J., went on to refer to that, and said (9):

" It seems to this court that, with that alternative statutorily laid down, the matter is either a case of a summary conviction or, to use the precise words, a conviction on indictment. To give effect to counsel for the appellant's argument really means writing into the second alternative ' a conviction on indictment otherwise than a conviction reached after the accused had elected to be tried on indictment '. It is quite impossible to read those

---

(3) [1953] 1 All E.R. 968; [1953] 2 Q.B. 14.   (4) [1895] 1 Q.B. 119.
(5) [1959] 2 All E.R. 787; 43 Cr. App. Rep. 177.
(6) [1962] 1 All E.R. 656; [1962] 2 Q.B. 161.
(7) [1964] 3 All E.R. 776; [1965] 2 Q.B. 281.
(8) [1964] 3 All E.R. at p. 779; [1965] 2 Q.B. at pp. 288, 289.
(9) [1964] 3 All E.R. at p. 779; [1965] 2 Q.B. at p. 289.

words into the statute, for the words 'conviction on indictment' really admit of no qualification at all, and it is plainly unarguable that, so far as the facts go, the appellant was not convicted on indictment."

Realising that, counsel for the appellants very properly said that he could not support the second ground of appeal here, which related to the fact that the sentence imposed on the first appellant, Terence Roe, was in excess of the maximum penalty as laid down in the Children and Young Persons Act, 1933, s. 1 (1), on a summary trial.

He did, however, maintain that notwithstanding the fact that this was truly a conviction on indictment, and that under the proviso to s. 2 (2) of the Administration of Justice Act, 1933, there was power to add certain counts, yet for other reasons that could not be done in the present case. His first argument was a very wide argument to the effect that s. 1 of the Children and Young Persons Act, 1933, is in effect a self-contained code dealing with offences by parents against children, that it was exhaustive of the liabilities of an accused who was a parent, and that in those circumstances it was quite impossible to add counts by virtue of the Administration of Justice Act, 1933. This court is quite unable to accept that argument. Quite clearly it is possible to prefer an indictment against a parent for manslaughter, and indeed it is to be observed that s. 1 (4) of the Children and Young Persons Act, 1933, provides that in such a case the jury may acquit of manslaughter but convict of an offence under the Act of 1933.

Secondly, counsel for appellants says that at any rate the use of added counts under the Administration of Justice (Miscellaneous Provisions) Act, 1933, must be confined to the addition of charges which are, as he would say, similar and not wholly different. Again, this court is quite unable to accept that argument. The proviso to s. 2 (2) provides exhaustive limitations, the counts must be founded on facts or evidence disclosed in the deposition and must be counts which can lawfully be joined. Subject to those limitations, any count can be joined.

In those circumstances, this court is quite satisfied that the appeal against conviction by the first appellant entirely fails and must be dismissed.

So far as the second appellant is concerned, counsel for the appellants did have a further point which was to this effect, that she had been charged before the magistrates and committed on a charge of ill-treatment, a matter on which she desired to be tried by a jury, and that, if she had realised that she was going to be convicted of neglect, she might well not have elected and would have been dealt with summarily. The court is quite unable to accept that as any argument for quashing the conviction, and accordingly in her case also the appeal against conviction is dismissed.

The first appellant also had an application to appeal against sentence, but in the circumstances that does not arise, since there is no suggestion that, if he was properly convicted on these counts, the sentence was excessive. Indeed, having read the papers, the court feels that eighteen months' imprisonment was an extremely lenient sentence. Accordingly that application is refused.

Appeals dismissed.

Solicitors: *Registrar of Criminal Appeals* (for the appellants); *Hugh Charles & Co.*, Barry (for the Crown).

[*Reported by* S. A. HATTEEA, ESQ., *Barrister-at-Law.*]

CHURCHILL v. WALTON.

[HOUSE OF LORDS (Viscount Dilhorne, Lord MacDermott, Lord Pearce, Lord Upjohn and Lord Pearson), October 24, 25, 1966, February 1, 1967.]

Criminal Law—Conspiracy—Conspiracy to commit absolute statutory offence—Whether mens rea an element of such conspiracy—Customs and Excise Act, 1952 (15 & 16 Geo. 6 & 1 Eliz. 2 c. 44), s. 200 (2).

On a charge of conspiracy to commit a statutory offence that is an absolute offence, the question essential to the determination of the issue whether there was agreement to do an unlawful act is still, " what did the parties agree to do? ": if what they agreed to do was, on the facts known to them, an unlawful act, they are guilty of conspiracy and cannot excuse themselves by saying that, owing to their ignorance of the law, they did not realise that such an act was a crime; but if on the facts known to them what they agreed to do was lawful, they are not rendered artificially guilty of agreeing to do an unlawful act by the existence of other facts, not known to them, giving a different and criminal quality to the act agreed on (cf., p. 503, letters C and F, post).

R. v. Sorsky ([1944] 2 All E.R. 333) overruled.

Dictum of LORD GODDARD, C.J., in *Johnson v. Youden* ([1950] 1 K.B. at pp. 546, 547) approved.

Rebated heavy oil was sold for use as fuel in road vehicles without payment of an amount equal to the rebate to the Commissioners of Customs and Excise. Such use would contravene s. 200 (2) of the Customs and Excise Act, 1952. That subsection enacted an absolute offence to which an accused's state of mind was irrelevant. The appellant was charged with conspiracy to contravene s. 200 (2). The jury found that he had in fact joined in agreeing to the use of the fuel for road vehicles, but that he did not know that the fuel had not been fully taxed. Their verdicts showed that they acquitted him of dishonest intention. On appeal against conviction,

Held: the guilt of the appellant depended on whether he was party to an agreement to do an unlawful act, the unlawful act being the use of rebated fuel in road vehicles without payment of the rebate's equivalent to the commissioners; as the findings of the jury established against the appellant no more than that he had agreed to a lawful act, viz., the use of heavy oil in a road vehicle, he had been wrongly convicted, for the agreement to which he was party was not converted into an agreement to do an unlawful act merely by the fact that, unknown to him, the heavy oil being used was oil in respect of which repayment of rebate had not been made (see p. 500, letters D and E, and p. 503, letters E and F, post).

Decision of the COURT OF CRIMINAL APPEAL (sub nom. *R. v. Churchill*) (*No. 2*), [1966] 2 All E.R. 215) reversed.

[As to mens rea in common law offences, see 10 HALSBURY'S LAWS (3rd Edn.) 273, para. 507, 275, 276, para. 511; and for cases on the subject, see 14 DIGEST (Repl.) 31-33, *33-45*.

As to conspiracy, see 10 HALSBURY'S LAWS (3rd Edn.) 310, 311, para. 569; and for cases on the subject, see 14 DIGEST (Repl.) 121-125, *851-860, 870*; 128, *891, 892*.

As to rebate and heavy oils for road fuel, see 33 HALSBURY'S LAWS (3rd Edn.) 105, para. 187.

For the Customs and Excise Act, 1952, s. 200, see 32 HALSBURY'S STATUTES (2nd Edn.) 810.]

Cases referred to:

Johnson v. Youden, [1950] 1 All E.R. 300; [1950] 1 K.B. 544; 114 J.P. 136; 17 Digest (Repl.) 453, *170*.

Dictum of VISCOUNT DILHORNE at 503 applied in BELMONT FINANCE v WILLIAMS FURNITURE [1979] 1 All ER 118

R. v. *Clayton*, (1943), 33 Cr. App. Rep. 113; 17 Digest (Repl.) 475, *264*.

R. v. *Jacobs*, [1944] 1 All E.R. 485; [1944] K.B. 417; 113 L.J.K.B. 433; 171 L.T. 264; 30 Cr. App. Rep. 1; 17 Digest (Repl.) 472, *248*.

R. v. *Sorsky*, [1944] 2 All E.R. 333; 30 Cr. App. Rep. 84; 17 Digest (Repl.) 475, *263*.

R. v. *Wheat*, *R.* v. *Stocks*, [1921] All E.R. Rep. 602; [1921] 2 K.B. 119; 90 L.J.K.B. 583; 124 L.T. 830; 85 J.P. 203; 15 Cr. App. Rep. 134; 15 Digest (Repl.) 891, *8591*.

Appeal.

This was an appeal by Victor George Churchill from an order of the Court of Criminal Appeal (HINCHCLIFFE, THOMPSON and JOHN STEPHENSON, JJ.), dated Mar. 21, 1966, and reported sub nom. *R.* v. *Churchill* (*No. 2*), [1966] 2 All E.R. 215, dismissing his appeal against his conviction before THESIGER, J., and a jury at the Central Criminal Court and the Royal Courts of Justice, Strand, London, on June 3, 1965, of a conspiracy to contravene s. 200 (2) of the Customs and Excise Act, 1952. The Court of Criminal Appeal certified, under s. 1 of the Administration of Justice Act, 1960, that a point of law of general public importance was involved, namely, whether mens rea was an essential ingredient in conspiracy to commit the absolute offence charged in the count on which the appellant was convicted, and, if so, what knowledge of the facts and/or law on the part of the appellant must be established to prove the charge: and gave leave to appeal to the House of Lords. The facts are set out in the opinion of VISCOUNT DILHORNE.

Leonard Lewis for the appellant.
J. B. R. Hazan and *A. S. Troup* for the Crown.

Their lordships took time for consideration.

February 1. The following opinions were delivered.

VISCOUNT DILHORNE: My Lords, the appellant was tried with others on an indictment containing two counts, each charging conspiracy. The first count charged him with conspiracy to cheat and defraud, the particulars of the offence alleging that he and the other accused had with others conspired to cheat and defraud Her Majesty of the rebate of duty due to be repaid on diesel fuel used in road vehicles. On this count the appellant was acquitted and the other accused convicted. The second count charged conspiracy to contravene s. 200 (2) of the Customs and Excise Act, 1952, the particulars of the offence alleging that the appellant and the other accused had conspired together and with others to use in road vehicles to which s. 200 (2) of the Customs and Excise Act, 1952, applied, heavy oils in respect of which the rebate of duty had been allowed but a sum equivalent to the current rebate had not been paid to the Commissioners of Customs and Excise. The appellant was convicted on this count. As the other accused had been convicted on the first count, the jury did not return a verdict on the second count in relation to them.

A type of heavy oil can be used for domestic purposes and in road vehicles. It bears a tax of 2s. 9d. a gallon. This oil is called gas oil when it is used for domestic purposes, and it then bears a tax of 2d. a gallon. In respect of gas oil, a rebate of 2s. 7d. is therefore allowed. Since July, 1961, gas oil on which the rebate has been allowed has been coloured red. This heavy oil when used in road vehicles is called Derv and is uncoloured. The object of the conspiracy charged in the first count was the procurement of gas oil uncoloured and its sale for use in road vehicles without payment to the commissioners of a sum equivalent to the rebate allowed.

Section 200 (2) of the Customs and Excise Act, 1952, reads as follows:

" No heavy oils on the delivery of which for home use rebate has been allowed shall be used as fuel for a vehicle to which this section applies unless there has been paid to the commissioners, in accordance with regulations made for the purpose of this subsection, an amount equal to the rebate on like oils at the rate for the time being in force."

For breach of this subsection a pecuniary penalty was imposed by s. 200 (3), and by the Finance Act, 1953, s. 33, breach of it was also made a criminal offence. It is not necessary to prove that the fuel in respect of which a rebate has been allowed, and in respect of which there has been no payment to the commissioners as required, has been used in a road vehicle with any special intent or with the knowledge that such use is contrary to the law. Proof that such fuel has in fact been so used by the accused is all that is required.

The question for determination in this case is what is the proper direction to be given to a jury in relation to a charge of conspiracy to contravene s. 200 (2). The appellant complained of the direction given by Thesiger, J., in relation to the second count. He said:

" Each [count] charges a conspiracy. As you have been told, but I must repeat, a conspiracy is an agreement or arrangement between two or more men, or a man and a company, to do something unlawful. It would be unlawful, and I so direct you, first to take part in an arrangement to cheat the revenue of 2s. 7d. tax on every gallon of fuel. Secondly, it would be unlawful, and I so direct you, to take part in an arrangement, to use unmarked gas oil in road vehicles, when it had not, in fact, borne the fuel tax and was not going to do so. That is the second charge."

A little later he said:

" The second charge, the less serious charge, accuses the defendants of agreeing together . . . to do an unlawful act, and that act was to use in road vehicles fuel which, in fact, had been allowed the rebate of 2s. 7d., and therefore ought not to have been used in road vehicles, but should have been marked with dye and kept for other uses. That second charge simply involves an agreement to use such fuel in road vehicles as Derv when it had not, in fact, borne the fuel tax. It does not involve any proof of dishonest intent or of knowledge that such use would cheat the revenue out of 2s. 7d. a gallon."

The appellant's appeal to the Court of Criminal Appeal on the ground that this direction was erroneous in point of law was dismissed, but the court certified that there was a point of law of general public importance and gave leave to appeal to your lordships' House. The court stated the point of law as follows (1):

" Whether mens rea is an essential ingredient in conspiracy to commit the absolute offence charged in count 2 of the indictment, and if so, what knowledge of the facts and/or law on the part of the defendant must be established to prove the charge."

At the trial the prosecution put the case against the appellant on the second count on the basis that he should be found guilty if he was a party to an arrangement to use fuel in road vehicles and the fuel in fact used was, without his knowledge, fuel the use of which was prohibited by s. 200 (2). Thesiger, J., as the passages from his summing-up which I have quoted show, directed the jury in the same way. Hinchcliffe, J., in the course of delivering the judgment of the Court of Criminal Appeal, said (2) that the court felt that there was great force in the submission made on behalf of the appellant, but that the court felt that they were constrained by the authorities, to which I shall refer, to dismiss the appeal. By their verdicts in relation to the appellant, he said (3), the jury, in returning a verdict of not guilty on the first count, were acquitting him

" of any dishonest intention or knowledge and were convicting him merely as joining in an agreement to do an unlawful act; that is to say, to

(1) [1966] 2 All E.R. 215 at p. 221.   (2) [1966] 2 All E.R. at pp. 219, 220.
(3) [1966] 2 All E.R. at p. 218.

have fuel used in road vehicles which had not in fact (albeit not to his knowledge) been fully taxed as Derv."

As has often been said, the offence of conspiracy is the making of an agreement to do an unlawful act. It is the character and content of the agreement that matters, and the accused's knowledge of what in fact has been done is relevant if it throws light on that. Proof of a conspiracy in most cases depends on inferences to be drawn from the conduct of the parties. Proof that fuel, on which the rebate has been allowed and no repayment had been made, had been used by a number of persons acting together in a number of road vehicles could lead to the inference being drawn that they were parties to an agreement to use such fuel and so to do an unlawful act and were, therefore, guilty of conspiracy. The jury were not in this case invited either by the prosecution or the judge to consider whether such an inference could properly be drawn. They were told that it sufficed to establish guilt if such fuel was in fact so used and the accused was a party to an arrangement to use gas oil in road vehicles. The use of gas oil in road vehicles contravenes s. 200 (2) only if a rebate has been allowed on it and the amount of the rebate has not been refunded. An agreement to use in road vehicles gas oil on which a rebate has been allowed is not, therefore, per se an agreement to do an unlawful act, but it will be an agreement to do an unlawful act if the object of the agreement is so to use gas oil in respect of which no repayment has been made. An agreement which is not to do an unlawful act will not be converted into an agreement to do an unlawful act by the fact that, unknown to the accused, gas oil is used in respect of which the required repayment has not been made. If the appellant had been a party to an agreement to use fuel in road vehicles in contravention of s. 200 (2), he must have known that that would happen. The conclusion that such fuel was so used without his knowledge leads to the conclusion that he was not a party to an agreement to do an unlawful act.

The Court of Criminal Appeal felt constrained to dismiss the appeal by the decisions in three cases: *R. v. Clayton* (4); *R. v. Jacobs* (5); *R. v. Sorsky* (6). In *R. v. Clayton* (4), the indictment charged conspiracy to contravene the Limitation of Supplies (Miscellaneous) Order, 1940 (7), and the Limitation of Supplies (Miscellaneous) (No. 5) Order, 1940 (8). ASQUITH, J., delivering the judgment of the Court of Criminal Appeal, said (9):

" It was conceded that a person who sells controlled goods to unregistered persons in excess of his quota, and a fortiori if he has not any quota, commits a breach of the Orders whether or not he knows that his action amounts to such a breach, and no particular state of mind or intent on his part is a necessary ingredient in the offence, which is complete if, without more, he does what the Orders forbid. While it is admitted that that applies in the case of an individual, we are invited to say that entirely different considerations apply when persons are charged with conspiracy, that is, with an agreement to do the act which is forbidden by the Order. It was contended that in order to establish this charge, the accused must be shown not only to have agreed to the act, but to have known it was forbidden by the statutory provisions, and that mens rea in that sense is required. Now that is a proposition for which no direct authority has been cited and is one which we entirely reject ... We can find no support for the proposition that mens rea in this sense is needed in the case of conspiracy. We demur to the notion that there is anything particularly wicked attached to the word ' conspiracy '. No doubt in common speech ' conspiracy ' has a melodramatic and sinister implication, but it has been pointed out that it carries no such implications in law. The definition of it is simply an agreement to do an unlawful act ...

---

(4) (1943), 33 Cr. App. Rep. 113.   (5) [1944] 1 All E.R. 485; [1944] K.B. 417.
(6) [1944] 2 All E.R. 333.   (7) S.R. & O. 1940 No. 874.
(8) S.R. & O. 1940 No. 2031.   (9) (1943), 33 Cr. App. Rep. at pp. 118, 119.

A   It does not matter how prosaic the unlawful act may be or how ignorant the conspirators may be of the fact that the act is prohibited by the statutory provision."

In *R. v. Jacobs* (10), the accused were convicted of conspiracy to contravene the Prices of Goods Act, 1939, by reselling price regulated goods in excess of the permitted price. WROTTESLEY, J., said to the jury (11):

B

"... if you are satisfied that they were engaged in the sale and forwarding it and bringing it about, it is not necessary that you should find, in order that they should be guilty of this crime charged, that they knew exactly what the right price was or that the price in question was the wrong one. It is not necessary that every member of the conspiracy should know that. The offence is to sell at the wrong price, and in so far as they all agreed to do that, or any of them agreed to do that, they are guilty of that with which they are charged by the prosecution."

C

HUMPHREYS, J., in the course of delivering the judgment of the Court of Criminal Appeal dismissing the appeals, said (12):

D

" The unlawful act alleged to be the subject of the agreement in this case is the selling of price-regulated goods at a price in excess of the permitted price. There can be no question that the appellants did agree with Mulholland that they should buy and he should sell razor blades at 42s. a gross. What then is the answer? It appears to be that they did not know the terms of the Orders regulating the prices of the goods in which they dealt. But ignorantia juris neminem excusat."

E

In both cases the question raised on appeal was whether it had to be shown that the accused knew that the act which they had agreed to do was unlawful. In neither case was there any dispute that they had agreed to do that which was in fact unlawful.

In *R. v. Sorsky* (13) H. Bresler, H. Bresler & Sons, Ltd. and Sorsky were con-
F victed of conspiracy to supply goods in contravention of the Limitation of Supplies (Miscellaneous) Order, 1940 and of conspiracy to contravene the Limitation of Supplies (Miscellaneous) (No. 5) Order, 1940. These Orders did not prohibit dealings between registered persons in controlled goods, but made the supply of such goods by registered persons in excess of the quota held by the supplier to unregistered customers an offence. Sorsky had a stock of controlled goods but no
G quota. H. Besler & Sons, Ltd. had a quota but no goods. Sorsky and Bresler agreed that Sorsky should sell to H. Besler & Sons, Ltd. controlled goods which he would then sell as agent for that company to his customers. This agreement was lawful. The illegality arose because the quantity of goods supplied by H. Bresler & Sons, Ltd. through the agency of Sorsky to the customers exceeded the quota of H. Bresley & Sons, Ltd. The quota was a proportion of the supplies made by
H H. Bresler & Sons, Ltd. in a previous period called " the standard period ". Sorsky did not know what supplies H. Bresler & Sons, Ltd. had made in the standard period, or what was the quota of H. Bresler & Sons, Ltd. On appeal, it was argued on behalf of Sorsky that a person could not be convicted of an offence against the Order unless there was mens rea on his part, and that a charge of conspiracy to supply contrary to the Order therefore involved knowledge by the accused that the amount of the quota had been or would be exceeded. Dealing
I with this argument, HUMPHREYS, J., delivering the judgment of the court, said (14):

" The all sufficient answer to that argument is to be found in the wording of the Orders in question which makes it abundantly plain that the supply

(10) [1944] 1 All E.R. 485; [1944] K.B. 417.
(11) See [1944] 1 All E.R. at p. 486.
(12) [1944] 1 All E.R. at p. 487; [1944] K.B. at p. 420.
(13) [1944] 2 All E.R. 333.   (14) [1944] 2 All E.R. at p. 336.

of controlled goods contrary to the Order is an offence irrespective of any knowledge or state of mind of the supplier. If authority is required in support of that proposition it will be found in the judgment of this court in *R*. v. *Clayton* (15). That case is also an authority for the proposition that conspiracy to contravene the terms of these Orders does not require proof of that knowledge on the part of the accused indicated by the expression mens rea. To the same effect is *R*. v. *Jacobs* (16), in which it was contended for the appellants . . . that the conviction was wrong in that there was no evidence that the vendors were aware that the permitted price had been exceeded. That argument was rejected by this court, it being pointed out in the judgment that a criminal conspiracy consists in the agreement to do an unlawful act without reference to the knowledge on the part of the accused of its illegality."

In *R*. v. *Wheat*, *R*. v. *Stocks* (17), AVORY, J., said that the maxim " actus non facit reum, nisi mens sit rea " was " admitted to be uncertain and often misleading in its application", and that in that case the maxim was satisfied " if the evidence establishes an intention on the part of the accused to do the act forbidden by the statute ". There the accused were charged with bigamy.

That HUMPHREYS, J., was clearly right in saying that the supply of goods contrary to the Order was an offence irrespective of the state of mind of the supplier cannot be disputed. He was also clearly right in saying that it was not necessary to prove knowledge of the illegality to establish a conspiracy to contravene the Orders. He was also right in saying that a criminal conspiracy consists in an agreement to do an unlawful act without reference to the knowledge on the part of the accused of its illegality. It, however, appears to have been overlooked that the agreement between Sorsky and H. Bresler for the sale of controlled goods to H. Bresler & Sons, Ltd. and for their re-sale by Sorsky as agent for that company was not of itself an agreement to do something unlawful. The fact that, unknown to Sorsky, goods were sold in excess of the quota did not convert Sorsky's lawful agreement into a criminal conspiracy. If the conclusion had been reached that the agreement was to supply goods in excess of the quota, then the conviction of Sorsky would have been correct, for then he would have been a party to an agreement to contravene the Orders. As that was not the agreement, in my opinion the conviction of Sorsky was wrong and his appeal should have been allowed.

The unfortunate consequence of the decision in *R*. v̇. *Sorsky* (18) is that it appears to be an authority for the proposition that if in fact what was done under an agreement was unlawful, then the parties to that agreement are guilty of conspiracy, even if what was done was done without their knowledge. HINCHCLIFFE, J., followed this decision with evident reluctance (19). On this point the law is, in my opinion, the same for conspiracy as for aiding and abetting, as to which LORD GODDARD, C.J., said in *Johnson* v. *Youden* (20):

" Before a person can be convicted of aiding and abetting the commission of an offence, he must at least know the essential matters which constitute that offence. He need not actually know that an offence has been committed, because he may not know that the facts constitute an offence and ignorance of the law is not a defence. If a person knows all the facts and is assisting another person to do certain things, and it turns out that the doing of those things constitutes an offence, the person who is assisting is guilty of aiding and abetting that offence, because to allow him to say, ' I knew of all those facts but I did not know that an offence was committed ', would be allowing him to set up ignorance of the law as a defence. The reason why, in our

---

(15) (1943), 33 Cr. App. Rep. 113.   (16) [1944] 1 All E.R. 485; [1944] K.B. 417.
(17) [1921] All E.R. Rep. 602 at p. 604; [1921] 2 K.B. 119 at p. 126.
(18) [1944] 2 All E.R. 333.   (19) [1966] 2 All E.R. at p. 220.
                    (20) [1950] 1 K.B. 544; at pp. 546, 547.

A opinion, the justices were right in dismissing the informations against the first two defendants is that they found, and found on good grounds, that they did not know of the matters which in fact constituted the offence; and, as they did not know of those matters, it follows that they cannot be guilty of aiding and abetting the commission of the offence."

B In answer to the question posed by the Court of Criminal Appeal in this case, I would say that mens rea is only an essential ingredient in conspiracy insofar as there must be an intention to be a party to an agreement to do an unlawful act; that knowledge of the law on the part of the accused is immaterial, and that knowledge of the facts is only material insofar as such knowledge throws a light on what was agreed. In cases of this kind, it is desirable to avoid the use of the phrase " mens rea ", which is capable of different meanings, and to concentrate
C on the terms or effect of the agreement made by the alleged conspirators. The question is " What did they agree to do? " If what they agreed to do was, on the facts known to them, an unlawful act, they are guilty of conspiracy and cannot excuse themselves by saying that, owing to their ignorance of the law, they did not realise that such an act was a crime. If, on the facts known to them, what they agreed to do was lawful, they are not rendered artificially guilty by the
D existence of other facts, not known to them, giving a different and criminal quality to the act agreed on.

For the reasons which I have given, I think that the direction given by the judge in relation to the second count was erroneous in point of law. The guilt of the appellant did not depend on whether prohibited fuel was used in road vehicles but on whether he was a party to an agreement to use such fuel in road vehicles.
E I am of the opinion that this appeal should be allowed.

LORD MACDERMOTT: My Lords, I concur.

LORD PEARCE: My Lords, I concur.

LORD UPJOHN: My Lords, I concur.

F **LORD PEARSON:** My Lords, I concur.

Appeal allowed.

Solicitors: *Goodman, Monroe & Co.* (for the appellants); *Solicitor for the Commissioners of Customs and Excise.*

[*Reported by* Kathleen J. H. O'Brien, *Barrister-at-Law.*]

Dictum of LORD DENNING, M.R., at
p. 508, *followed in* POSTER *v.* SLOUGH
ESTATES. [1968] 3 All E.R. 257.

Applied in SHILOH v HARDING [1973]
1 All ER 90

Applied in CRABB v ARUN DC [1975]
3 All ER 865

Applied in TITO v WADDELL (No 2)
[1977] 3 All ER 129

E.R. IVES INVESTMENTS, LTD. *v.* HIGH.

[COURT OF APPEAL, CIVIL DIVISION (Lord Denning, M.R., Danckwerts and
Winn, L.JJ.), November 24, 25, 28, December 14, 1966.]

*Equity—Estoppel—Acquiescence in expenditure being made in reliance on right
over land of another—Garage erected by owner of land in reliance on right of
access over adjoining owner's land—Approved by adjoining owner—Successors in title bound although no land charge registered—Land Charges Act,
1925 (15 & 16 Geo. 5 c. 22), s. 10 (1), s. 13 (2)—Law of Property Act, 1925
(15 & 16 Geo. 5 c. 20), s. 199 (1) (i).*

*Land Charge—Equitable estoppel—Mutual benefit and burden—Right of passage
with vehicles over land of another in return for allowing trespass by the
foundations of his building—Acquiescence or estoppel giving rise subsequently
to such a right—Whether registrable as estate contract or equitable easement—
Whether invalidated as against purchaser with notice for want of registration
—Land Charges Act, 1925 (15 & 16 Geo. 5 c. 22), s. 10 (1), s. 13 (2)—Law
of Property Act, 1925 (15 & 16 Geo. 5 c. 20), s. 199 (1) (i).*

The plaintiffs' predecessor in title, W., and the defendant bought adjacent
building sites. The foundations of W.'s building trespassed under the
defendant's land. The defendant having objected, W. and he agreed in
November, 1949, that the foundations might remain where they were and
that (among other matters) the defendant should have right of access, with
or without motor vehicles, to and from his site across W.'s yard at the back
of W.'s building to a side street. Letters passed which were construed by
the court as showing a concluded agreement. W. sold his site and the flats
that he had built on it in 1950. The defendant completed his building,
and used his right of way for the purpose of the work. In 1959 the defendant
built himself a garage, so positioned that it could be entered only by access
over the yard. The then owners of W.'s building complimented the defendant on his garage. The defendant used the yard for access for his car. In
1960 he contributed one-fifth to the cost of re-surfacing the yard. In the
same year the flats were sold to the plaintiffs, the property being conveyed
subject " to the right (if any) of the owners and occupiers of " the defendant's
land " as now enjoyed to pass and repass with or without vehicles, over the
open yard at the rear " etc. No registration under the Land Charges Act,
1925, was effected at any time in regard to the defendant's rights over the
yard. The plaintiffs sought an injunction to restrain the defendant exercising
a right of passage across the yard.

Held: (i) the defendant was entitled in equity to access to and from his garage
over the yard both (a) by virtue of the principle " qui sentit commodum
sentire debet et onus ", since the benefit to the plaintiffs of the continuance
of the foundations of their building in the defendant's land was conditional
on the defendant's enjoying access to and from his garage over the yard,
and (b) by virtue of equitable estoppel or acquiescence of the plaintiffs'
immediate predecessors in title in consequence of their having stood by
when the defendant built his garage in such manner that access for a car
to and from it could be had only over the yard (see p. 507, letter G, p. 507,
letter I, to p. 508, letter A, p. 510, letter I, p. 511, letters A and B, and
p. 514, letters C and E, post).

(ii) (a) (per LORD DENNING, M.R., and DANCKWERTS, L.J.) neither of
those rights was an estate contract or equitable easement within Class C (iv) or
Class D (iii) of s. 10 (1) of the Land Charges Act, 1925, with the consequence
that neither right was invalidated for want of registration (see p. 508,
letter F, and p. 511, letter B, post), and

(b) (per WINN, L.J.) the Land Charges Act, 1925, had no impact on the
equitable estoppel that had arisen (see p. 514, letter H, post).

Considered in TAYLOR FASHIONS v
LIVERPOOL VICTORIA TRUSTEES [1981]
1 All ER 897

Hopgood v. *Brown* ([1955] 1 All E.R. 550) and *Inwards* v. *Baker* ([1965] 1 All E.R. 446) applied.

[As to estoppel by acquiescence, and estoppel as the result of standing by, see 14 HALSBURY's LAWS (3rd Edn.) 639, 640, paras. 1179, 1180, and 15 ibid., 241, 242, para. 449; and for cases on the subject, see 21 DIGEST (Repl.) 452-458, *1542-1583.*

As to the principle that one cannot both approbate and reprobate, see 15 HALSBURY's LAWS (3rd Edn.) 171, para. 340, p. 173, para. 341 text and note (*k*).

As to the position of purchasers in relation to unregistered land charges Classes C and D, see 23 HALSBURY's LAWS (3rd Edn.) 77, para. 160.

For the Land Charges Act, 1925, s. 10 (1), s. 13 (2), see 20 HALSBURY's STATUTES (2nd Edn.) 1076, 1087.

For the Law of Property Act, 1925, s. 199, see 20 HALSBURY's STATUTES (2nd Edn.) 822.]

Cases referred to:

Bonnewell v. *Jenkins*, (1878), 8 Ch.D. 70; 47 L.J.Ch. 758; 38 L.T. 581; 12 Digest (Repl.) 95, *549.*

Booker v. *Palmer*, [1942] 2 All E.R. 674; 30 Digest (Repl.) 539, *1737.*

Chillingworth v. *Esche*, [1923] All E.R. 97; [1924] 1 Ch. 97; 93 L.J.Ch. 129; 129 L.T. 808; 40 Digest (Repl.) 247, *2078.*

Errington v. *Errington*, [1952] 1 All E.R. 149; [1952] 1 K.B. 290; Digest (Cont. Vol. A) 992, *1684a.*

Halsall v. *Brizell*, [1957] 1 All E.R. 371; [1957] Ch. 169; [1957] 2 W.L.R. 123; 3rd Digest Supp.

Hopgood v. *Brown*, [1955] 1 All E.R. 550; [1955] 1 W.L.R. 213; 40 Digest (Repl.) 300, *2502.*

Inwards v. *Baker*, [1965] 1 All E.R. 446; [1965] 2 Q.B. 29; [1965] 2 W.L.R. 212; 3rd Digest Supp.

Lewisham Borough Council v. *Maloney*, [1947] 2 All E.R. 36; [1948] 1 K.B. 50; [1947] L.R.R. 991; 177 L.T. 175; 35 Digest (Repl.) 311, *281.*

May v. *Bellewille*, [1905] 2 Ch. 605; 74 L.J.Ch. 678; 93 L.T. 241; 40 Digest (Repl.) 317, *2613.*

Plimmer v. *Wellington Corpn.*, (1884), 9 App. Cas. 699; 53 L.J.P.C. 104; 51 L.T. 475; 11 Digest (Repl.) 126, *72.

Ramsden v. *Dyson*, (1866), L.R. 1 H.L. 129; 21 Digest (Repl.) 453, *1551.*

Rossiter v. *Miller*, [1874-80] All E.R. Rep. 465; (1878), 3 App. Cas. 1124; 48 L.J.Ch. 10; 39 L.T. 173; 42 J.P. 804; 40 Digest (Repl.) 29, *135.*

Von Hatzfeldt-Wildenberg v. *Alexander*, [1911-13] All E.R. Rep. 148; [1912] 1 Ch. 284; 81 L.J.Ch. 184; sub nom. *Hatzfelt* v. *Alexander*, 105 L.T. 434; 12 Digest (Repl.) 92, *523.*

Ward v. *Kirkland*, [1966] 1 All E.R. 609; [1966] 1 W.L.R. 601.

Appeal.

This was an appeal by notice dated June 24, 1966, by the plaintiffs from an order of His Honour JUDGE CAREY EVANS dated Apr. 28, 1966, at the Norwich county court, dismissing the plaintiffs' claim for damages for trespass limited to £5 and to an injunction restraining the defendant from trespassing on the plaintiffs' yard. The defendant had counterclaimed for a mandatory injunction requiring the plaintiffs to remove the foundation and footings of their building in so far as they trespassed on his land; but he claimed this relief in the event only of the plaintiffs being held validly to have ended his reciprocal right or licence for access to and from his garage. The facts are set out in the judgment of LORD DENNING, M.R.

E. I. Goulding, Q.C., and *J. H. G. Sunnucks* for the plaintiffs.
P. J. Millett for the defendant.

Cur. adv. vult.

Dec. 14. The following judgments were read.

LORD DENNING, M.R. (read by WINN, L.J.): During the war the City of Norwich was bombed by the enemy. Three houses in Earlham Road were demolished and their sites left vacant. In May, 1949, Mr. High (the defendant) bought the site of 77, Earlham Road and started to build a house on it. He was a builder and he intended to live in it himself. About the same time Mr. Westgate bought the adjoining sites of 73 and 75, Earlham Road and started to build a block of flats on the double site. In the course of the work Mr. Westgate encroached on to the defendant's site. Mr. Westgate dug down nine feet to lay the foundations of the block of flats and he put the footings and foundations twelve inches over the boundary into the defendant's land. Above ground level, the wall of the block of flats was to be on the boundary line, but below ground level, the foundations trespassed a good twelve inches over the boundary.

The defendant at once objected to the trespass. On Nov. 2, 1949, there was a meeting on the site between the defendant and Mr. Westgate, a surveyor and architect and others. Mr. Westgate admitted the trespass. The defendant could have compelled Mr. Westgate to remove the foundations; but instead of doing so, the defendant came to this agreement with Mr. Westgate. On the one hand, Mr. Westgate was to be at liberty to keep the foundations of the block of flats as they were in the defendant's land: and Mr. Westgate was to build up the wall of the flats on that side with no windows or openings on to the defendant's land. On the other hand, the defendant was to have a right of way from the back of his own house (then being built) across the yard of Mr. Westgate's block of flats so as to give access to a side road, Belvoir Street. (At that time, in November, 1949, the defendant had not got a car, but he hoped to get one some day and desired access for it).

After the agreement was made, letters passed evidencing it. There was a suggestion that the solicitors should be instructed to draw up a written agreement, but it was never done. On this account it was suggested before us that there was no concluded agreement; but the judge was satisfied there was. So am I. The agreement was complete. All that was suggested was to put it into form. Both sides acted on the agreement. Mr. Westgate went on building his block of flats with the foundations encroaching into the defendant's land, and no windows or openings on that side. The defendant built his house in such a way that the only practicable access by car was across the yard at the back of Mr. Westgate's block of flats.

In March, 1950, Mr. Westgate sold his site to Mr. and Mrs. Wright. The conveyance made no mention of the foundations or of the right of way for the defendant; but the judge inferred that the Wrights were told about the agreement. Soon afterwards the defendant finished his house. The block of flats were finished. The defendant used the way across the yard. In 1959 the defendant built a garage at the back of his house, No. 77. In doing so he relied on the right of way given him in 1949. He so constructed his garage that it could *only* be entered from the yard of the Wrights' block of flats and the car could *only* be driven in and out over that yard. The Wrights watched the garage being built and complimented the defendant on it. Next year the defendant bought a car and thereafter continually garaged it in his garage and went in and out across the Wrights' yard, which was the only means of access.

In the next year, 1960, the Wrights got the defendant to resurface the yard The cost was £14 10s. The Wrights had four garages for their flats. The defendant has his one. He paid one-fifth of the cost. Thus the Wrights recognised that he used the yard to get to and from his garage. On Nov. 27, 1962, the Wrights put up the block of flats for sale by auction. The particulars of sale stated distinctly that there was a right of way for the defendant, saying:

> " The property is also sold subject to the right of the owners and occupiers of No. 77, Earlham Road as now enjoyed to pass and repass with or without vehicles over the open yard to and from Belvoir Street."

At the auction the property was sold to E.R. Ives Investments, Ltd., the plaintiffs. During the investigation of title the purchasers' solicitors asked: " How did the right of way over the yard in favour of No. 77, Earlham Road arise? " The vendors' solicitors replied:

> " We imagine that this arose as a result of the destruction of No. 73 and No. 75 during the war. Presumably No. 77 was given a right of way over the yard in lieu of over the four feet wide passageway, but we cannot trace any document in connexion therewith."

On Jan. 1, 1963, the conveyance was made by the Wrights to the plaintiffs. It expressly stated that the property was conveyed subject

> " to the right (if any) of the owners and occupiers of No. 77, Earlham Road as now enjoyed to pass and repass with or without vehicles over the open yard at the rear of the block of flats to and from Belvoir Street."

Now here is the point. The right of way was never registered as a land charge. The plaintiffs say that it should have been registered under Class C (iv) as an estate contract, or under Class D (iii) as an equitable easement: and that, as it was not registered, it is void against them, the purchasers. Even though they had the most explicit notice of it, nevertheless they say that it is void against them. They claim to be entitled to prevent the defendant having any access to his garage across their yard: and thus render it useless to him. They have brought an action for an injunction to stop him crossing the yard at all.

One thing is quite clear. Apart from this point about the Land Charges Act, 1925, the defendant would have in equity a good right of way across the yard. This right arises in two ways:

1. *Mutual benefit and burden.*

The right arises out of the agreement of Nov. 2, 1949, and the subsequent action taken on it: on the principle that " he who takes the benefit must accept the burden ". When adjoining owners of land make an agreement to secure continuing rights and benefits for each of them in or over the land of the other, neither of them can take the benefit of the agreement and throw over the burden of it. This applies not only to the original parties, but also to their successors. The successor who takes the continuing benefit must take it subject to the continuing burden. This principle has been applied to neighbours who send their water into a common drainage system (see *Hopwood* v. *Brown* (1)) and to purchasers of houses on a building estate who had the benefit of using the roads and were subject to the burden of contributing to the upkeep (see *Halsall* v. *Brizell* (2)). The principle clearly applies in the present case. The owners of the block of flats have the benefit of having their foundations in the defendant's land. So long as they take that benefit, they must shoulder the burden. They must observe the condition on which the benefit was granted, namely, they must allow the defendant and his successors to have access over their yard (cf. *May* v. *Belleville* (3)). Conversely, so long as the defendant takes the benefit of the access, he must permit the block of flats to keep their foundations in his land.

2. *Equity arising out of acquiescence.*

The right arises out of the expense incurred by the defendant in building his garage, as it is now, with access only over the yard: and the Wrights standing by and acquiescing in it, knowing that he believed he had a right of way over the yard. By so doing the Wrights created in the defendant's mind a reasonable expectation that his access over the yard would not be disturbed. That gives rise to an " equity arising out of acquiescence ". It is available not only against the Wrights but also their successors in title. The court will not allow that expectation to be defeated when it would be inequitable so to do. It is for the court in

---

(1) [1955] 1 All E.R. 550.   (2) [1957] 1 All E.R. 371; [1957] Ch. 169.
(3) [1905] 2 Ch. 605.

each case to decide in what way the equity can be satisfied (see *Inwards* v. *Baker* (4), *Ward* v. *Kirkland* (5) and the cases cited therein). In this case it could only be satisfied by allowing the defendant and his successors to have access over the yard so long as the block of flats has its foundations in his land.

The next question is this: was that right a land charge such as to need registration under the Land Charges Act, 1925? For if it was a land charge, it was never registered and would be void as against any purchaser (see s. 13 of the Act of 1925). It would, therefore, be void against the plaintiffs, even though they took with the most express knowledge and notice of the right. It was suggested that the agreement of Nov. 2, 1949, was " an estate contract " within Class C (iv). I do not think so. There was no contract by Mr. Westgate to convey a legal estate of any kind.

It was next suggested that the right was an " equitable easement " within Class D (iii). This class is defined as

" Any easement right or privilege over or affecting land created or arising after the commencement of this Act, and being merely an equitable interest ..."

Those words are almost identical with s. 2 (3) (iii) of the Law of Property Act, 1925, and should be given the same meaning. They must be read in conjunction with s. 1 (2) (*a*), s. 2 (3) an s. 4 (1) of the Law of Property Act, 1925. It then appears that an " equitable easement " is a proprietary interest in land such as would before 1926 have been recognised as capable of being conveyed or created *at law*, but which since 1926 only takes effect as an equitable interest. An instance of such a proprietary interest is a profit á prendre for life. It does not include a right to possession by a requisitioning authority (see *Lewisham Borough Council* v. *Maloney* (6)). Nor does it include a right, liberty or privilege arising in equity by reason of " mutual benefit and burden ", or arising out of " acquiescence ", or by reason of a contractual licence: because none of those before 1926 were proprietary interests such as were capable of being conveyed or created *at law*. They only subsisted *in equity*. They do not need to be registered as land charges, so as to bind successors, but take effect in equity without registration (see an article by Mr. C. V. Davidge on " Equitable Easements " in (1937) 53 Law Quarterly Review, p. 259, and by Professor H. W. R. Wade in 1956 Cambridge Law Journal, pp. 225, 226).

The right of the defendant to cross this yard was not a right such as could ever have been created or conveyed at law. It subsisted only in equity. It therefore still subsists in equity without being registered. Any other view would enable the owners of the flats to perpetrate the grossest injustice. They could block up the defendant's access to the garage, whilst keeping their foundations in his land. That cannot be right. I am confirmed in this construction of the statute when I remember that there are many houses adjoining one another which have drainage systems in common, with mutual benefits and burdens. The statute cannot have required all these to be registered as land charges. I know that this greatly restricts the scope of Class D (iii) but this is not disturbing. A Special Committee has already suggested that Class D (iii) should be abolished altogether (see the Report of the Committee on Land Charges (1956), Cmnd. 9825, para. 16).

In these circumstances it is not necessary to consider the counterclaim. I would only say that I do not think the owners of the block of flats have acquired a " squatter's title " to the space occupied by the foundations. They were only licensees and cannot acquire a title by limitation. If they were entitled to block up the defendant's access over their yard, he would, I think be entitled to require them to remove the foundations from his land. But, fortunately for them, no such consequence will befall them. They can keep heir foundations there, but

---

(4) [1965] 1 All E.R. 446; [1965] 2 Q.B. 29.   (5) [1966] 1 All E.R. 609.
(6) [1947] 2 All E.R. 36; [1948] 1 K.B. 50.

they must not block up or impede his access across their yard, with or without vehicles.

I would therefore dismiss the appeal.

DANCKWERTS, L.J.: This appeal from the decision of His Honour Judge Carey Evans is concerned with property built on a site made vacant by war damage fronting on Earlham Road and Belvoir Street, Norwich. The defendant, Mr. High, owned the site of No. 77, Earlham Road and Mr. Westgate owned the sites of Nos. 73 and 75, Earlham Road. They were both builders. Mr. Westgate built a block of flats on his site Nos. 1 to 6, Frances Court. Unfortunately, as the defendant discovered, the foundations of this block of flats encroached some feet below ground on to the land forming part of No. 77, Earlham Road, belonging to the defendant, on which he was proposing to build a house for himself.

Both Mr. Westgate and the defendant were sensible and reasonable neighbours. They entered into negotiations and it is clear, as found by the county court judge, that they reached an oral agreement that Mr. Westgate should keep his foundations where they were, but in return the defendant should have a right of way across the yard adjoining the flats to a garage which the defendant intended to build close to the boundary of his land at the back of his house. There was a meeting on Nov. 2, 1949, on the site between the parties and there were some letters. There were letters of Dec. 6 and 12, 1949, referring to the oral agreement, and finally one on Dec. 13, 1949, from the defendant in which he said (after referring to fences):

" I shall be very glad to have the right you offer across the back of your site so that I can have access with a car to the rear of my site. Can you allow eight feet wide? Perhaps you will kindly instruct your solicitor to write to my solicitors, Daynes Keefe & Co., Castle Meadow, Norwich, with the necessary agreement."

It has been argued that this was not a binding agreement on the principle of such cases as *Chillingworth* v. *Esche* (7) (either a contract to make a contract or a conditional contract). I am satisfied, however, that the agreement was a binding contract, and the parties merely contemplated that it would be put into proper form by a solicitor in the manner recognised in such cases as *Rossiter* v. *Miller* (8) and *Bonnewell* v. *Jenkins* (9).

Unfortunately, apparently no-one told the defendant that his prudent course, by reason of the Land Charges Act, 1925, and s. 199 of the Law of Property Act, 1925, was to register a land charge either as a Class C (iv) estate contract, or a Class D (iii) equitable easement. Relying on his agreement with his neighbour, the defendant built his house with only a narrow passageway between his house and the neighbouring flats, so that he could not have had access with a car past his house that way. His house was completed nearly a year after the agreement of Nov. 2, 1949. Mr. Westgate sold his property (Nos. 73 and 75) to some people called Wright and conveyed it to them by a conveyance dated Mar. 14, 1950, which referred to the defendant's right of way.

The defendant was on good terms with the Wrights. He used the right of way without question or demur both for pedestrians and for taking rubble off his site. About the same time an eight feet wide opening was made in the wire fence separating No. 75 from No. 77 so as to allow access to No. 77 from the yard of No. 75. During the Wrights' time the wire fence was replaced with a new wall, but the eight feet gap was preserved. Mrs. Wright was consulted about this, as the wall of the defendant's garage, which he built in 1959 immediately opposite the eight feet gap, was included in this new boundary wall. The garage was constructed in such a way that it could only be entered from the yard of No. 75

(7) [1923] All E.R. Rep. 97 at p. 105; [1924] 1 Ch. 97 at pp. 113, 114.
(8) [1874-80] All E.R. Rep. 465; (1878), L.R. 3 App. Cas. 1124.
(9) (1878), 8 Ch. Div. 70.

and the defendant could only drive out over that yard. Further, the county court judge accepted the defendant's evidence that the Wrights watched the garage being built and complimented him on it. They knew that the only access to it was through the yard of No. 75. In 1960 the defendant bought a car, as he had anticipated, and thereafter used the garage and the access over the yard in connexion with it.

In 1962 the defendant tendered for and was given the job of resurfacing the yard and in his bill he deducted one-fifth of the cost, obviously because he was a user of the yard, and the bill was duly paid. Towards the end of 1962 the Wrights offered Frances Court for sale by auction and by special condition No. 9 provided for the continuance of the defendant's right of way. The property was bought by the plaintiffs, E.R. Ives Investments, Ltd. and was conveyed to them by a conveyance dated Jan. 1, 1963, in which (at the suggestion of the plaintiffs' solicitors) the conveyance was subject to the defendant's right of way " if any ". A few months later the plaintiffs challenged the defendant's right of way. The plaintiffs' solicitors changed their ground several times, but finally these pro-ceedings were started by the plaintiffs in 1965. His Honour JUDGE CAREY EVANS decided in the defendant's favour and dismissed the action. From that decision the plaintiffs appeal.

One point argued on behalf of the plaintiffs was that they had acquired title to the land occupied by the foundations under the Limitation Act, 1939. They and their predecessors in title have, of course, continued to enjoy the foundations which encroached on the defendant's land. They are still there; but it is quite clear that this occupation of the soil was permissive by reason of the oral agree-ment of Nov. 2, 1949, and not as of right. It is said, however, that the owners of Nos. 73 and 75 enjoyed the foundations under a tenancy at will and the plaintiff company claim that the statutory provisions accordingly started the time running at the end of the first year of such a tenancy and more than thirteen years have run from the beginning of such a tenancy. This in my opinion will not do. No tenancy was contemplated or created, and the statutory provisions relating to a tenancy at will have no application.

It is necessary, in connexion with the defendant's case, to consider the effect of the Land Charges Act, 1925, and s. 199 of the Law of Property Act, 1925. The effect of the provisions of the Land Charges Act, 1925, s. 10 and s. 13, is to make the defendant's right of way, so far as it ought to have been registered as an estate contract or an equitable easement, either void or unenforceable, and s. 199 of the Law of Property Act, 1925, prevents express notice of the defendant's rights being effective in any way, though the plaintiffs bought subject to the right of way and had the most positive notice of it.

That, however, is not the end of the matter. There is another equitable ground on which the defendant's rights may be protected, which has nothing whatever to do with the Land Charges Act. It is discussed in SNELL's EQUITY (26th Edn.) pp. 629-633 under the name " Proprietary estoppel ", and the comment is made (p. 633) that " the doctrine thus displays equity at its most flexible ". There are two aspects in which this equitable principle applies in the present case. First, in the present case, the defendant, in reliance on the arrangement made with Mr. Westgate, allowed the encroaching foundations to remain on his land and built his house without proper access except over the yard, and finally built his garage in such a way that it was useless unless access to it and from it could be had over the yard. Mr. Westgate acquiesced in the use of the yard for access, and the Wrights stood by and, indeed, encouraged the defendant to build his garage in these conditions and for these purposes. Could anything be more monstrous and inequitable afterwards to deprive the defendant of the benefit of what he has done?

Secondly, the Wrights had continued to enjoy the benefit of the encroaching foundations on the defendant's land. It would no doubt be quite an expensive job to remove the encroaching foundations and provide other support for the building. Equity does not allow a person who takes advantage of such a situation to deny to the other party the corresponding benefits which were the consideration for allowing the foundations to remain.

The plaintiffs bought the property subject to the defendant's equitable rights and the property was so conveyed to them. They had full knowledge of the situation, yet they continue to enjoy the benefits of the situation and wish to deny to the defendant the benefit of what he was induced to do in reliance on the mutual arrangement. As long as the plaintiffs continue to enjoy the foundations, they must accept the terms of that enjoyment. This is not a registrable charge, and s. 199 of the Law of Property Act, 1925, has no application.

I will now refer to the authorities in which support for these principles can be found. *Inwards* v. *Baker* (10) (a decision of this court) is a modern example of the protection of equity which is given to a person who is induced to expend money on land on reliance on representations by another. I would like to refer to my observations in that case (11):

"In my view, the case comes plainly within the proposition stated in the cases. It is not necessary, I think, to imply a promise. It seems to me that this is one of the cases of an equity created by estoppel, or equitable estoppel, as it is sometimes called, by which the person who has made the expenditure is induced by the expectation of obtaining protection, and equity protects him so that an injustice may not be perpetrated."

Those words apply to the present case. The principle there stated is not new. It goes back at least as far as the observations of LORD KINGSDOWN in *Ramsden* v. *Dyson* (12) which were approved by the Privy Council in *Plimmer* v. *Wellington Corpn.* (13). In the same case (*Inwards* v. *Baker* (14)) LORD DENNING, M.R., pointed out that any purchaser who took with notice would clearly be bound by the equity. The same principles were applied by UNGOED-THOMAS, J., in *Ward* v. *Kirkland* (15).

Examples of the principle that a party cannot enjoy the benefits of an arrangement without giving effect to the burden imposed on such benefits are to be found in *Hopgood* v. *Brown* (16) (a decision of this court relating to the use of drainage); and *Halsall* v. *Brizell* (17) (a decision of UPJOHN, J., holding that a successor in title could not use roads without bearing the burden of the contributions to upkeep imposed under the original terms).

In my opinion the county court judge reached the right conclusion, and I would dismiss the appeal.

WINN, L.J.: This dispute between neighbours reveals the typical characteristic of such disputes that they are imbued with a degree of acrimony unrelated to their magnitude. However, it should be said emphatically that in the instant case, the defendant in the county court, has behaved with complete propriety, albeit imprudently, inasmuch as he failed to secure his position by seeking legal advice and taking the appropriate steps to make it impregnable.

The history of the events which have called for the consideration of the court begins with a trespass on the land of Mr. High, the defendant, in the year 1949, committed by his then neighbour, a Mr. Westgate, a predecessor in title of the plaintiffs in this action. Mr. Westgate, having begun building operations for the erection of a block of flats, caused or permitted the footings forming part of the foundation of the west wall of his building to intrude to an extent of some fourteen inches over his boundary with the land of the defendant, at and below a depth of some eight feet beneath the surface. This Mr. Westgate and the defendant had acquired adjoining plots of land on a bomb site, on which plots respectively they, being builders, were minded, after clearing the ground of

(10) [1965] 1 All E.R. 446; [1965] 2 Q.B. 29.
(11) [1965] 1 All E.R. at pp. 449, 450; [1965] 2 Q.B. at p. 38.
(12) (1866), L.R. 1 H.L. 129 at p. 170.   (13) (1884), 9 App. Cas. 699, at p. 713.
(14) [1965] 1 All E.R. at p. 449; [1965] 2 Q.B. at p. 37.   (15) [1966] 1 All E.R. 609.
(16) [1955] 1 All E.R. 550.   (17) [1957] 1 All E.R. 371; [1957] Ch. 169.

the rubble from the buildings destroyed by enemy action, to build, in Mr. West-gate's case the flats referred to, and in the defendant's case a house for his own occupation: Mr. Westgate's plot lay to the eastward of the defendant's, being bounded on the east by Belvoir Street: both plots were bounded on the south by Earlham Road. In October, 1949, the defendant became aware of the intrusion of the footings and summoned Mr. Westgate to a meeting on the site which was attended by others, including a representative of the limited company controlled by Mr. Westgate which was to erect the flats. At this meeting it was established and fully accepted that the footings did so intrude into the land of the defendant and, at least tacitly, that he was entitled to have them removed; this would have been an expensive and labour-consuming task, though at the early stage of construction then reached not so grave a matter as such removal progressively would have become as and when a wall and other parts of the intended building were placed in position.

A friendly and mutually sympathetic discussion took place at which, as the county court judge found—and I have no doubt whatsoever rightly found—a concluded agreement was orally made between the defendant and Mr. Westgate. It is true that a week or two after this meeting the defendant, having become somewhat impatient, wrote a letter consistent either with an inclination to withdraw from an agreement already made or an assertion that the matter remained open for further negotiation: I take the view that the former of these two interpretations should be put on that letter and that neither its terms nor a reference to be found in the defendant's next letter, written in reply to an inter-vening letter from Mr. Westgate, to his expectation that solicitors would prepare " the necessary agreement ", puts this case into the category of cases exemplified by *Von Hatzfeldt-Wildenberg* v. *Alexander* (18); *Chillingworth* v. *Esche* (19) and many other cases. It was undoubtedly a term of the agreement so made that Mr. Westgate, whose plan for the flats to be erected would leave an open area or yard behind, that is to say, to the north of the building with an access to the eastward to Belvoir Street, would permit the defendant to exercise a right of way to and from that street across that area or yard to and from the eastern boundary of his land for use on foot or with vehicles. It is equally clear that the defendant agreed with Mr. Westgate that he would not complain of nor take any steps to secure the removal of the footings projecting under his land.

In the county court proceedings and before this court the dispute has centred on the effect in law of that agreement and the extent to which, if at all, it can operate to secure for the defendant the continued user of the right of way for which he so bargained, due regard being had to the provisions of the Land Charges Act, 1925, and of s. 199 of the Law of Property Act, 1925, in the light of the changes in ownership of the land formerly owned by Mr. Westgate which have occurred since 1949, the conduct of the parties who have held and now hold the title to the land, and the fact that the footings are still in the same position, where the plaintiffs in the present action assert that they are entitled to have them left undisturbed. The argument has involved many niceties of a somewhat technical and esoteric character.

The substance of the dispute is whether the defendant's claim to be entitled to cross the yard behind the plaintiffs' block of flats, called Frances Court, on foot and in a car, which the plaintiffs sought by their claim in this action to deny and destroy and the claim of the plaintiffs to be free in law to maintain the footings of the west wall of their flats in the defendant's land, are interdependent or, by contrast, so mutually separate and independent, in fact or in law, that the plaintiffs can both maintain their claim and bar that of the defendant. There is a subsidiary but important question whether the defendant's claim, if valid, is only a personal right; this does not fall to be now decided.

I have found it simple to decide in my own mind that the defendant and Mr. Westgate intended and mutually communicated by words or conduct the intention

(18) [1911-13] All E.R. Rep. 148; [1912] 1 Ch. 284.
(19) [1923] All E.R. Rep. 97; [1924] 1 Ch. 197.

that the defendant's plot of land should for an indefinite time (a) enjoy the adjunct of a right of way to and from Belvoir Street and the eastern boundary of the plot eight feet wide, for use on foot or in a car, (b) be subject to the detriment of the presence in the plot of such footings as existed there in November, 1949: further, such intention, by necessary inference, fixed as the event on which this arrangement would terminate any future removal of the protruding footings. It would have been wholly inconsistent with their intention, on the traditional " officious bystander " test, that it should have been left to the choice or whim of the defendant or any successor in title to his plot to require at any time the removal of the footings, even on simultaneously abandoning any claim to the right of way.

It is, however, far from a simple matter to have to envisage, as I think one must, in terms of legal concepts what effect was produced by that arrangement made with that intention. On the one hand, I accept counsel for the plaintiffs' submission that it comprised a contract by Mr. Westgate to grant a legal easement, which was equivalent in equity to an equitable easement, and his further submission that such contract or easement was by force of s. 13 (2) of the Land Charges Act, 1925, void against any subsequent purchaser for value of Mr. Westgate's property, if unregistered, despite any notice of it which such purchaser might have had before purchasing. On the other hand, I am unable to accept his submission that a tenancy at will arose in favour of Mr. Westgate in respect of the subterranean space occupied by the footings. Some legal fictions are valuable and may conveniently be used, but properly only constructively to make good lacunae in imperfectly comprehended arrangements: to impose an effect in law inconsistent with that mutually intended by the parties is, in my opinion, a function of such a device which cannot, or at least should not, if avoidable, be tolerated. In determining whether any, and if so what, tenancy has come into existence, the intention of the suggested parties is of paramount importance: cf. per DENNING, L.J., in *Errington* v. *Errington* (20):

" But, in my opinion, it is of the essence of a tenancy at will that it should be determinable by either party on demand, and it is quite clear that the relationship of these parties was not so determinable . . . It was, therefore, not a tenancy at will."

Then (21) quoting LORD GREENE, M.R., in *Booker* v. *Palmer* (22):

" To suggest there is an intention there to create a relationship of landlord and tenant appears to me to be quite impossible. There is one golden rule which is of very general application, namely, that the law does not impute intention to enter into legal relationships where the circumstances and the conduct of the parties negative any intention of the kind."

Mr. Westgate would certainly not have been willing to rely on a tenancy at will. For my part I do not envisage any tenancy of the subterranean space, but supposing, arguendo, that one is to be deemed, I would think that a tenancy at sufferance would more nearly fit the reality of the arrangement. For this reason I reject the submission that a limitation period of twelve years, running from the expiry of the first year of a tenancy at will, now bars a claim for trespass by the protruding footings; if there was a tenancy by sufferance, it was not terminated before the defendant's alleged trespass or in anticipation, of the present action.

Licence to maintain the footings is, to my mind, the concept which is far preferable: whilst recognising that a licence could not run with the land of either licensor or licensee, I have no difficulty in supposing that both intended that the licence should be, or that it was, periodically renewable and renewed between the persons from time to time concerned that it should apply. In my judgment the

(20) [1952] 1 All E.R. 149 at pp. 153, 154; [1952] 1 K.B. 290 at p. 296.
(21) [1952] 1 All E.R. at p. 154; [1952] 1 K.B. at p. 297.
(22) [1942] 2 All E.R. 674 at p. 677.

protrusion of the footings was permitted by licence until, but not after, the counterclaim in this action was filed.

During the twelve years from 1950 to 1962 purchasers from Mr. Westgate of his plot of land, a Flt. Lt. Wright and his wife managed and from time to time resided in Frances Court. They not only licensed the defendant, as had Mr. Westgate, to pass over the yard, probably motivated by their knowledge that their footings protruded, but allowed and even encouraged him when he proposed to build himself a garage on his eastern boundary so that, after he first bought a car, in about 1960, he could drive it in and out across their yard: they also accepted a contribution from him to the cost of resurfacing that yard. Thus they represented to him that he had a right so to do. A very clear equity and also an estoppel thus arose against them preventing them from denying the defendant user of the right of way (cf. per UPJOHN, J., in *Halsall* v. *Brizell* (23)). It is, however, to be observed that that case related more specifically to benefits and burdens arising under a deed and held that such benefits could not be taken without assuming also the burdens (cf. also *Inwards* v. *Baker* (24), a case of standing by with knowledge that expenditure was being incurred in reliance on conduct of the party against whom an equity was therefore held to arise). Notice of this equity, which amounted to an equitable easement, was given in para. 9 of the particulars of the auction at which the plaintiffs bought Frances Court, and the land on which it stood, and by the draft of the conveyance of the property.

In my opinion the plaintiffs as successors in title are bound by that estoppel: I do not regard myself as thereby saying anything contradictory of the proposition submitted to the court that the said equity or equitable easement, as distinct from the estoppel, was rendered void as against the plaintiffs by the statutes to which I have referred. Estoppels arising from representations made by owners of land that rights exist affecting their land will, unless in form they are limited to the duration of the interest of the representor, bind successors to his title. It is no anomaly that a person should have a legally valid answer to a claim and yet be estopped from asserting that answer against the claimant; citation of examples would be otiose and one should suffice: a tenant under a lease, in occupation, is estopped from setting up against his lessor, or an assignee, when sued by him for e.g. rent, any denial that the lessor had an estate in the demised premises entitling him to grant that lease. Where estoppel applies, the person entitled to wield it as a shield has, ex hypothesi, suffered a past detriment or other change of position: he is not asserting any positive rights, but is invoking law or equity to afford him procedural protection to avert injustice.

Such equities as arise from merely standing by whilst expenditure is incurred under a mistake of fact or law, or from attempts both to approbate and reprobate a deed, always supposing them to be capable of registration, which is I think on the whole an open question, may not survive the lethal effect of the Land Charges Act, 1925, unless they have been registered. On the other hand, I cannot see that the statute has any impact on an estoppel, nor do I think that an estoppel could be registrable under its provisions.

It follows in my judgment that the county court judge, in an admirably thorough and well reasoned judgment, came to a conclusion on the plaintiffs' claim which I would affirm. As the counterclaim is before us and counsel agree that we should deal with it, I would determine it by declaring that the footings would constitute an actionable trespass unless the defendant and his successors in title were allowed to use the right of way stipulated for in 1949. I would dismiss this appeal.

Appeal dismissed. Leave to appeal to the House of Lords refused.

Solicitors: *Jaques & Co.*, agents for *Hill & Perks*, Norwich (for the plaintiffs); *Maxwell, Batley & Co.*, agents for *Emmett & Tacon*, Norwich (for the defendant).

[*Reported by* F. GUTTMAN, ESQ., *Barrister-at-Law*.]

---

(23) [1957] 1 All E.R. at p. 377; [1957] Ch. at p. 182.
(24) [1965] 1 All E.R. 446; [1965] 2 Q.B. 29.

BENNETT v. GRIFFIN FINANCE.

[COURT OF APPEAL, CIVIL DIVISION (Lord Denning, M.R., Danckwerts and Winn, L.JJ.), December 1, 1966.]

Hire-Purchase—Re-financing arrangements—Sale of motor car by hirer whilst instalments outstanding—Fictitious sale by dealers at instance of purchaser to another finance company—Payment of settlement figure by second finance company to first finance company—Title to car accruing thereby to vendor hirer—Defendants deriving title from him through subsequent sales of car.

H., who had a car on hire-purchase, sold it to A.B. The finance company, which had let the car to H., had then to be paid the settlement figure. A.B. raised the money by means of a fictitious hire-purchase transaction arranged by dealers, who purported to sell the car to another finance company (M. Ltd.), which let it to A.B. M., Ltd. paid the settlement figure to the first finance company and paid the balance of their purchase price to the dealers, who apparently handed it to A.B., thus enabling him to pay H. A.B. later sold the car; it was re-sold and then was sold again to the defendants, who let it on hire-purchase to the plaintiff. M., Ltd. claimed the car from the plaintiff, as A.B. had defaulted on his hire-purchase agreement. The plaintiff then sued the defendants for the deposit and instalments that he had paid to them, amounting to £104 4s. 6d.

Held: when the settlement figure was paid to the first finance company, the hirer, H., thereby acquired title to the car; since he then sold it to A.B., the title to the car passed to A.B., and then passed from A.B. by successive sales to the defendants, and accordingly the defendants had a good title to the car and their letting it on hire-purchase to the plaintiff was valid, with the consequence that they were not liable to the plaintiff to repay him £104 4s. 6d. (see p. 517, letters C, E and H, post).

Appeal allowed.

[**Editorial Note.** Genuine re-financing arrangements have been upheld (see, e.g., *Stoneleigh Finance, Ltd.* v. *Phillips*, [1965] 1 All E.R. 513 at p. 527; *Eastern Distributors, Ltd.* v. *Goldring* [1957] 2 All E.R. 525; *Kingsley* v. *Industrial Securities, Ltd.* [1966] 2 All E.R. 414) and the validity of such arrangements must depend on the circumstances of the case. The present decision should be considered with *Snook* v. *West Riding Investments, Ltd.*, p. 518, post, particularly in relation to what constitutes a " sham " or fictitious transaction. Regard should also be had, in relation to sales and dealings with motor vehicles subject to hire-purchase agreements, to the provisions of s. 27 and s. 28 of the Hire-Purchase Act 1964; 44 HALSBURY'S STATUTES (2nd Edn.) 1082, 1084.

As to the effect of assignment by the hirer of the chattel hired, see 19 HALSBURY'S LAWS (3rd Edn.) 542, 543, para. 877; and for cases on the subject, see 26 DIGEST (Repl.) 669-671, *50-61*.]

Appeal.

This was an appeal by the defendants, Griffin Finance (a firm) from the judgment of the Presiding Judge of the Court of Passage of the City of Liverpool given on May 6, 1966, whereby judgment was entered for the plaintiff for £104 4s. 6d. and whereby (a) it was declared that the defendants should indemnify the plaintiff in respect of any damages and costs which the plaintiff might be adjudged liable to pay to Masterton Finance and Trading Services, Ltd., which was the owner of the motor car in question at all times, and (b) it was adjudged that the counterclaim of the defendants for £81 16s. 0½d. should be dismissed. By their counterclaim the defendants claimed outstanding moneys, viz., the hire-purchase price of the motor car less the deposit and payments made, which balance was £64 16s. 6d., together with interest to date, £16 19s. 6½d., amounting in all to £81 16s. 0½d. Clauses (5) and (8) of the terms set out in the hire-purchase agreement made by Mr. Henshaw (referred to at letter G, post) with United Dominions Trust (Commercial) Ltd. provided, so far as material, as follows:—

"(5) During the currency of this agreement the hirer shall keep the goods in his own possession and shall not take them out of the United Kingdom without the previous consent in writing of the owner and shall maintain the goods in proper repair and in good and serviceable condition (making good all damage thereto whether or not occasioned by his own act or default) and . . . shall not hold himself out as owner of the goods nor sell, offer for sale, assign or charge the goods or the benefit of this agreement nor create any lien on the goods or pledge the owner's credit either for repairs thereto or otherwise and shall not . . . attempt to do any of these things.

"(8) . . . if the hirer shall fail to observe or fulfil any term of this agreement or shall do so suffer anything whatsoever which in the owner's opinion bona fide formed upon reasonable grounds will or may have the effect of jeopardising the owner's right of property in the goods then and in each and every such case the owner may forthwith and without any notice terminate the hiring . . ."

The facts are set out in the judgment of LORD DENNING, M.R.

Mr. Georgeson, a partner in the defendants' firm, appeared in person.

H. L. Lachs for the plaintiff.

LORD DENNING, M.R.: This case raises a short but important point. The plaintiff, Mr. Bennett, took a car on hire-purchase from the defendants, a firm called Griffin Finance. It was a Humber Hawk. He paid cash down of £50. He duly paid monthly instalments amounting to another £54 4s. 6d. Then, lo and behold, another finance company called Masterton Finance and Trading Services, Ltd. wrote to him and claimed the car. Their solicitors relied on a hire-purchase document which appeared to show that it was their car which they had let on hire-purchase to a Mr. McCormack, who had defaulted. The plaintiff could see no answer to this claim. He stopped paying instalments to the defendants. Now he sues the defendants for the payments that he had made to them of £104 4s. 6d. on the ground that they had no title to the car which they had purported to let to him. The judge held in favour of the plaintiff. He gave judgment against the defendants for £104 4s. 6d., saying: "I find reluctantly that the defendants did not have title". The defendants now appeal to this court. They have appeared in person by Mr. Georgeson, one of the partners, who has put their case before us.

The history of the Humber Hawk is this. In 1957 Mr. Henshaw got it on hire-purchase from United Dominions Trust (Commercial), Ltd. The total hire-purchase price was £701 10s. Mr. Henshaw paid the deposit and duly kept up the instalments. Then in November, 1959, he decided to sell it. He agreed to sell it to a Mr. McCormack for £200. He handed over the car to Mr. McCormack who gave him a cheque for £200; but, of course, this sale would not be effective unless United Dominions Trust (Commercial), Ltd. were paid the "settlement figure" to clear off their interest. This was £87 5s. 5d. Mr. McCormack, however, had not the money in the bank to meet the cheque for £200. He raised the money in this way. He went to see some dealers, whom he knew, called J. & P. Motors. They filled in documents purporting to record a hire-purchase transaction with Masterton Finance and Trading Services, Ltd.: whereby Masterton Finance and Trading Services, Ltd., bought the car from J. & P. Motors and let it out on hire-purchase to Mr. McCormack. The judge found that the transaction was "completely fictitious". J. & P. Motors had no title to the car. They had not bought it and had no right to sell it to Masterton Finance and Trading Services, Ltd. On receiving these documents, Masterton Finance and Trading Services, Ltd. paid United Dominions Trust (Commercial), Ltd. the settlement figure of £87 5s. 5d., thus getting rid of their interest: and they paid £262 4s. 7d. to J. & P. Motors, who appear to have handed it to

Mr. McCormack, and by this means Mr. McCormack honoured his cheque to Mr. Henshaw. Thus Mr. McCormack got the car without paying a penny out of his own pocket. He kept it for a little while and then sold it to a man called Williams for £25. Mr. Williams said it looked as if it had been in a collision. He did a lot of work on the car and sold it to Georgesons Garage for £120. Then Georgesons Garage sold it to the defendants, who let it out on hire-purchase to the plaintiff.

The question is whether Masterton Finance and Trading Services, Ltd. ever got the title to the car. Counsel for the plaintiff urged before us an important proposition which the judge seems to have accepted. He said that whenever a finance company, like Masterton Finance and Trading Services, Ltd., pay off the settlement figure to another finance company, like United Dominions Trust (Commercial), Ltd., then the finance company which paid off the settlement figure became the owner. I think that proposition is entirely wrong. In my opinion when a person pays off the settlement figure to a finance company, he must be presumed to do so on behalf of the hirer. The reason is this. The hirer has the contractual right to buy the car on paying the settlement figure. No one else has that right. The hirer alone is entitled to pay it and acquire the title to the car. If anyone else pays it, he must be paying it on the hirer's behalf, for otherwise he would be acting unlawfully. No third person can be allowed to assert that he paid it on his own behalf and became the owner himself: for that would be to take advantage of his own wrong. The only permissible conclusion is that, when the settlement figure is paid, the car becomes the property of the hirer; and it is for the hirer then to dispose of as he pleases or has agreed.

Applying this proposition to the present case, when Masterton Finance and Trading Services, Ltd. paid £87 5s. 5d. to United Dominions Trust (Commercial), Ltd., they must be presumed to have done so on behalf of the hirer, Mr. Henshaw. The title to the car then passed to Mr. Henshaw. Then Mr. Henshaw could and did pass the title to Mr. McCormack, because he had sold the car to Mr. McCormack for £200. From Mr. McCormack the title passed validly to Mr. Williams, thence to Georgesons Garage, thence to the defendants, who let it out to the plaintiff. It seems to me that the claim of Masterton Finance and Trading Services, Ltd. is quite unfounded. They rely on the hire-purchase documents; but those documents cloaked a fictitious transaction. J. & P. Motors never had any title to the car and could not pass title to Masterton Finance and Trading Services, Ltd. I do not see how any finance company can acquire title through documents which are a sham.

The result, therefore, is that the defendants did have a good title to the car and validly let it on hire-purchase to plaintiff. This appeal should be allowed and judgment should be entered for the defendants with costs.

DANCKWERTS, L.J.: I agree completely with the judgment of Lord Denning, M.R., and I do not need to add anything.

WINN, L.J.: I also agree completely with Lord Denning, M.R.'s judgment. I wish to say just one thing, though it does not necessarily arise in this case, and therefore has not been argued. I wish to reserve consideration of any suggestion that, had the transaction between Mr. Henshaw and Mr. McCormack taken place *before* Mr. Henshaw's title was complete, by reason of the paying off of the £87 odd, Mr. McCormack's rights derived from that transaction could have been subsequently completed or, as is sometimes said, his " title fed " by a later payment of the balance due on the contract. That does not, as I understand the evidence here, arise in this case. I agree that this appeal should be allowed.

Appeal allowed: action dismissed. Judgment on the counterclaim for £64 16s. 6d. plus £5 3s. 6d. interest.

Solicitors: *Silverman, Livermore & Co.*, Liverpool (for the plaintiff).

[*Reported by* F. Guttman, Esq., *Barrister-at-Law.*]

SNOOK v. LONDON & WEST RIDING INVESTMENTS, LTD.

[COURT OF APPEAL, CIVIL DIVISION (Lord Denning, M.R., Diplock and Russell, L.JJ.), October 7, 10, 1966, January 17, 1967.]

Hire-Purchase—Re-financing arrangements—Estoppel—Authority given to finance company to transfer title—Minimum initial payment—Hirer desiring to obtain money on security of car that he had on hire-purchase—Value of his interest then substantial—Arrangement that settlement figure should be paid by A.F. Ltd., the new finance company, to the old finance company—New hire-purchase agreement entered into by a third finance company, defendants, with hirer by arrangement with A.F. Ltd.—Value of car inserted in documents as cash price and a figure of £500 as initial payment—Hirer obtained thus some additional finance—Default by hirer in paying instalments under new hire-purchase agreement—Car re-taken by defendants and sold—Whether new hire-purchase agreement void as unregistered bill of sale—Whether defendants able to establish title to car—Whether " actual payment " of initial payment made within Hire-Purchase and Credit Sale Agreements (Control) Order, 1960 (S.I. 1960 No. 762), art. 1 (1), Sch. 2, Pt. 1, paras. 2, 3, Pt. 2.

In September, 1963, the plaintiff bought a new motor car at the price of £935 19s. 8d.; he paid £735 19s. 8d. in cash and entered into a hire-purchase transaction with T. Ltd., whereby that finance company acquired the car and let it to him on hire-purchase terms under which he was to pay twelve monthly instalments of £17 18s. 4d. In December, 1963, when £161 approximately was outstanding the plaintiff, wanting to raise £100, approached A.F. Ltd. to carry out a re-financing operation. At their instance the plaintiff signed a letter to T. Ltd. stating that he had sold his rights in the car to A.F. Ltd.; on the bottom half of this letter was a reply ready for T. Ltd. to sign, addressed to A.F. Ltd., which would state the amount for which they would sell title to the car to A.F. Ltd. At the instance of A.F. Ltd. the plaintiff also signed a hire-purchase agreement with the defendants, who were another finance company, and signed a delivery receipt by which he acknowledged that he understood that the car was the property of the defendant. This hire-purchase agreement stated the cash price as £800 and the initial payment as £500. A.F. Ltd. forwarded to the defendants these documents together with a form by which A.F. Ltd. invoiced the car to the defendants. The defendants paid £300 to A.F. Ltd., who paid £160 to T. Ltd. in full discharge of their interests, paid £125 to the plaintiff and kept £15 for their services. The cash price and initial payment were not in fact paid in cash. After paying two instalments the plaintiff fell into arrears. A.F. Ltd. acting as agents for the defendants, re-took possession of the car, sold it for £575*, at a time when it was worth £775, paid to the defendants £280 and kept the balance of £295. In an action by the plaintiff against the defendants for conversion of the car the trial judge held that the defendants were innocent of any irregularity but that the transaction infringed the Hire-Purchase and Credit Sale Agreements Order, 1960, in that there was no " actual payment " of the initial payment (£500), and that the re-financing operation was " obviously a sham " and " nothing more than a loan of money on the security of the goods " and thus was void under the Bills of Sale Act, 1878 and 1882. The defendants had not pleaded estoppel. On appeal,

Held: (LORD DENNING, M.R., dissenting): the plaintiff's claim in conversion failed for the following reasons—

(i) as the defendants were unaware of any irregularity in the re-financing transaction and as the intention of the plaintiff in that transaction was to

---

* A. F. Ltd. had apparently offered the car to the plaintiff for £280 (see p. 532, letter B, post).

Dictum of DIPLOCK LJ at 528 applied in R v CROWN COURT AT KNIGHTS-BRIDGE [1983] 1 All ER 1148

transfer the title to the car to the hire-purchase finance company which was to provide him with the £100, the defendants had established title to the car, either because the plaintiff had authorised A.F. Ltd. to transfer it on his behalf to them, or because the plaintiff was estopped by his conduct from denying the defendants' title, and the defendants were entitled to rely on the estoppel, although they had not pleaded it, as all necessary facts had been proved (see p. 528, letters F and G, and p. 529, letters G and H, post).

Eastern Distributors, Ltd. v. *Goldring* (*Murphy, Third Party*) ([1957] 2 All E.R. 525) and *Stoneleigh Finance, Ltd.* v. *Phillips* ([1965] 1 All E.R. 513) and *Kingsley* v. *Sterling Industrial Securities, Ltd.* ([1966] 2 All E.R. 414) applied.

(ii) there was a transfer of value by the plaintiff which constituted actual payment of the amount of the initial payment (£500) on the hire-purchase arrangement with the defendants for the purposes of the Hire-Purchase and Credit Sales Agreements (Control) Order, 1960, Sch. 2, Pt. 1*, para. 3, so that the re-financing transaction was not rendered unenforceable as contravening the order (see p. 529, letter C, p. 531, letter E, and p. 532, letter A, post); nor was para. 2 of Pt. 1 of Sch. 2 to the order contravened by the fact that the cash price did not pass in cash (see p. 529, letter C, and p. 530, letter G, post).

(iii) the re-financing transaction did not mask a loan of money on the security of a chattel so as to fall within the avoidance provisions of the Bills of Sale Acts, 1878 and 1882 (see p. 528, letter D, and p. 529, letter I, post).

Per DIPLOCK, L.J.: for acts or documents to be a " sham ", with whatever legal consequences follow from this, all the parties thereto must have a common intention that the acts or documents are not to create the rights and obligations which they give the appearance of creating (see p. 528, letter I, post).

Appeal allowed.

[**Editorial Note.** The current order at the date of this report is the Hire-Purchase and Credit Sale Agreements (Control) Order 1964, S.I. 1964 No. 942, as amended by S.I. 1965 No. 1471 and 1966 No. 113. Paragraph 3 of Pt. 1, and Pt. 2, of Sch. 2 to the Order of 1964 are similar to the corresponding para. 3 and Pt. 2 of the Order of 1960.

As to the statutory control of hire-purchase agreements under emergency legislation, see 19 HALSBURY'S LAWS (3rd Edn.) 518, 519, para. 834; and for cases on the subject, see 26 DIGEST (Repl.) 663, *20, 21.*

As to the distinction between hire-purchase transactions and bills of sale, see 19 HALSBURY'S LAWS (3rd Edn.) 512, 513, para. 827; and for cases on the subject, see 7 DIGEST (Repl.) 16-19, *71-86.*]

---

* The application of Pt. 1 of Sch. 2 to the Order of 1960 is enacted by art. 1 (1). The relevant provisions are as follows. Article 1 (1) provides: "A person shall not dispose of any goods to which this Order applies in pursuance of a hire-purchase or credit sale agreement entered into after Apr. 28, 1960, unless the requirements specified in Pt. 1 of Sch. 2 hereto are or have been complied with in relation to that agreement." Part 1 of Sch. 2, so far as relevant, reads:

" 2. The agreement contains in respect of each description of goods a statement of the cash price of the goods of that description comprised in the agreement and of any amount payable by instalments under the agreement for the installation or maintenance of those goods.

" 3. Before the agreement was entered into actual payment was made in respect of each description of goods comprised in the agreement of not less than an amount equal to the percentage specified in column 2 of Pt. 1 of Sch. 1 hereto in relation to that description of goods to the aggregate of—(*a*) the cash price of the goods of that description comprised in the agreement; and (*b*) any amount payable by instalments under the agreement for the installation or maintenance of the goods of that description comprised in the agreement.

" In computing for the purposes of this paragraph the total amount to be paid before any agreement is entered into account may be taken of any allowance for any goods taken in part exchange for goods comprised in that agreement, being an allowance which is reasonable in relation to the value of the goods so taken in part exchange."

Cases referred to:

Bennett v. *Griffin Finance*, ante p. 515.

Chettiar v. *Chettiar*, [1962] 1 All E.R. 494; [1962] A.C. 294; [1962] 2 W.L.R. 548; Digest (Cont. Vol. A) 286, *2401a*.

Eastern Distributors, Ltd. v. *Goldring (Murphy, Third Party)*, [1957] 2 All E.R. 525; [1957] 2 Q.B. 600; [1957] 3 W.L.R. 237; 26 Digest (Repl.) 675, *77*.

Holman v. *Johnson*, (1775), 1 Cowp. 341; 98 E.R. 1120; 12 Digest (Repl.) 313, *2404*.

Kingsley v. *Stirling Industrial Securities, Ltd.*, [1966] 2 All E.R. 414; [1966] 2 W.L.R. 1265.

Lloyd v. *Grace, Smith & Co.*, [1911-13] All E.R. Rep. 51; [1912] A.C. 716; 81 L.J.K.B. 1140; 107 L.T. 531; 34 Digest (Repl.) 161, *1122*.

Polsky v. *S. and A. Services, Ltd.*, *S. and A. Services, Ltd.* v. *Polsky*, [1951] 1 All E.R. 185; affd., C.A., [1951] 1 All E.R. 1062, n.; 7 Digest (Repl.) 18, *79*.

Snell v. *Unity Finance, Ltd.*, [1963] 3 All E.R. 50; [1964] 2 Q.B. 203; [1963] 3 W.L.R. 559; Digest (Cont. Vol. A) 325, *929a*.

Stoneleigh Finance, Ltd. v. *Phillips*, [1965] 1 All E.R. 513; [1965] 2 Q.B. 537; [1965] 2 W.L.R. 508; 3rd Digest Supp.

Viking Hire-Purchase Co., Ltd. v. *Jordan*, (1966), 110 Sol. Jo. 51.

Wickham Holdings, Ltd. v. *Brooke House Motors, Ltd.*, ante p. 117; [1967] 1 W.L.R. 295.

Yorkshire Railway Wagon Co. v. *Maclure*, (1882), 21 Ch.D. 309; 51 L.J.Ch. 857; 47 L.T. 290; 26 Digest (Repl.) 17, *55*.

Appeal.

This was an appeal by the defendants, London and West Riding Investments, Ltd., from a judgment of His Honour Judge Ould, given on May 26, 1966 at the Sheffield county court whereby it was adjudged that the defendants had converted the plaintiff's motor car to their own use and benefit and it was ordered that the defendants do pay to the plaintiff £449 10s., its value.

By his particulars of claim, served on Apr. 5, 1966, the plaintiff pleaded, among other matters, that he was the hirer in January, 1964, under a hire-purchase agreement with Totley Investment Co., Ltd. of a motor car and, wishing to raise a loan of £300 thereon, he negotiated such a loan with Auto-Finance Services (H) Ltd. (called in this introduction " Auto-Finance "). He pleaded that the defendants were industrial bankers and that the loan of £300 was obtained from them on the security of the plaintiff's motor car. The particulars of claim continued—

" 3.   For the purpose of securing the loan the plaintiff [Auto-Finance] and the defendants executed various documents which purported to effect or evidence a purchase from the plaintiff by [Auto-Finance] of the plaintiff's rights in the motor car; the settlement of the outstanding balance of the hire-purchase agreement with Totley Investment Co., Ltd., the invoicing of the motor car to the defendants by [Auto-Finance] and the hiring back of the motor car to the plaintiff by a hire-purchase agreement dated Jan. 27, 1964.

" 4.   These documents were a sham and misrepresented the transaction which had taken place. The plaintiff never ' sold his rights ' in the motor car to [Auto-Finance], who never purchased or paid for them; all the insertions contained in the invoice of the motor car to the defendants were untrue and in particular the cash price of the motor car had not been stated to the plaintiff (the alleged cash price stated in the invoice and the initial payment being entirely bogus). The motor car was not [Auto-Finance's] absolute property, nor had they received the initial payment of £500 shown in the schedule thereto nor had they explained the terms of the agreement to the plaintiff.

" 5.   The transaction was not a hire-purchase agreement but a loan of £300 on the security of the plaintiff's motor car, and within the Bills of Sale Act, but the purported hire-purchase agreement was not registered as a bill of sale."

The plaintiff further pleaded that on June 6, 1964, when he owed the defendants approximately £325 10s. they by their servants or agents wrongfully seized and took away the motor car and converted it to their own use and benefit; that they had wrongfully sold the motor car for approximately £800 and retained the balance of £474 10s. over and above the amount which the plaintiff owed them.   The plaintiff claimed the sum of £474 10s. as damages for conversion, or alternatively as money had and received by the defendants for the plaintiff's use.

By their defence the defendants admitted the contract of hire-purchase with Totley Investment Co., Ltd. in respect of the car on Sept. 16, 1963; and admitted and alleged that the contract was terminated on or about Jan. 24, 1964, by the payment of £160 by Auto-Finance to the Totley Investment Co., Ltd., and that Auto-Finance thereafter became owners of the car.   They further pleaded—

" 3.   By an agreement made on or about Jan. 27, 1964 [Auto-Finance] sold the car to the defendants, and by an agreement made on or about the said date the plaintiff and the defendants entered into a contract of hire-purchase in respect of the same . . .

" 4   In breach of the said contract of hire-purchase with the defendants the plaintiff paid only one monthly instalment thereunder and on a date in June, 1964, the defendants re-possessed the car and sold it.

" 5.   In the premises the defendants never lent to the plaintiff the said sum of £300 or any sum at all, and never wrongfully converted the car either as alleged or at all, and they are not indebted to the plaintiff either in the sum claimed or in any sum at all."

In his judgment the county court judge, after referring to the opposing contentions, continued—

" It is essential in weighing the two opposing contentions to look at the chronology of the material events.   First of all the plaintiff had bought this car new some short time previously and had paid a cash price of £935 19s. 8d. for it.   He paid most of that in cash with his own money, but financed the balance by means of a genuine hire-purchase agreement with Totley Investment Co., Ltd.   At the material date he owed them only about £200 on that transaction, but found himself wanting some ready money and decided to try to raise a further £100 on the car, there being a substantial equity in it at that time.   He was brought into touch with [Auto-Finance] who advertised in a newspaper . . . that they can help people to re-finance cars or obtain loans on cars or hire-purchase facilities on cars.   The leading spirit in that company was their director, Mr. Hickins, with whom the plaintiff had all his dealings.   On being given particulars of the car and the transaction with Totley Investment Co., Ltd., Mr. Hickins assured the plaintiff that there would be no difficulty about obtaining a further £100 on the car, but he told him that it would have to be done by way of paying off Totley Investment Co., Ltd. and then obtaining further hire-purchase finance elsewhere. Whether or not Mr. Hickins explained matters as fully as he should have done to the plaintiff, or whether the plaintiff understood the precise mechanics of the transaction, does not seem to be very clear.   The plaintiff's attitude appears to have been that he wanted this further £100 on the security of his car, and he was leaving it to Mr. Hickins to arrange it as best he could, and he, the plaintiff, was no doubt prepared to sign any document or documents which he was assured would produce the desired results.   So, on Jan. 20, 1964, at Mr. Hickins' request the plaintiff signed the document addressed to Totley Investment Co., Ltd., saying that he had sold his rights in the car to [Auto-Finance] and requesting them to inform the latter how much they required to settle his obligations to them and to pass title to [Auto-Finance] in the vehicle. It is important to note that the statement in that document that the plaintiff had sold his rights was not true at all. He had never sold his rights to [Auto-Finance] and at all material times he had been in sole possession of the vehicle and had never parted with it to anybody. The next thing that happened was that [Auto-Finance] communicated with Totley Investment Co., Ltd. and enquired how much the latter required to release their hire-purchase interest in the vehicle. Apparently on Jan. 24, 1964, Totley Investment Co., Ltd. informed [Auto-Finance] that they were prepared to release their interest in the vehicle for a sum of £160, subject to payment within seven days. It is also important to note that Totley Investment Co., Ltd., neither then nor at any other time, executed any assignment of their ownership of this vehicle to anybody. Having obtained this information from Totley Investment Co., Ltd., Mr. Hickins then got the plaintiff to execute the pink hire-purchase form in favour of the defendants. That form contains what purports to be a suppliers' declaration and invoice under which [Auto-Finance], as purported owners of the vehicle professed to invoice it to the defendants, so that the latter may hire it back on hire-purchase terms to the plaintiff. That transaction, as the document reveals, took place on Jan. 27, 1964, and on or about the same date the defendants paid the cheque for the amount that they were advancing on hire-purchase, namely £300 to [Auto-Finance]. Having received their cheque [Auto-Finance] then paid to Totley Investment Co., Ltd. on Jan. 31, 1964, the sum due to that company, namely £160, and paid the balance to the plaintiff less a commission of fifteen guineas for their services. It is again to be noted that at that date, i.e., after the transaction with the defendants had been completed, there had been no transfer of ownership in the car from Totley Investment Co., Ltd. to [Auto-Finance]. All that had happened was that on Feb. 4 Totley Investment Co., Ltd. acknowledged receipt of the cheque for £160, the amount due to them, and confirmed that their interest in the vehicle had then been discharged. It must not be overlooked also that the hire-purchase agreement with Totley Investment Co., Ltd. contained the usual clause allowing the plaintiff to purchase the goods on completion of the payments due to that hire-purchase company. So it seems to me that, at that time, the obligation to Totley Investment Co., having been paid off, and the plaintiff's right to exercise his option under that hire-purchase agreement having arisen, he thereby became the owner of the car; but he never at any time assigned such ownership to [Auto-Finance], and I cannot see, therefore, that they could assign any title to the defendants.

" When arranging the deal with the defendants [Auto-Finance] had entered into a recourse agreement with the defendants, under which they agreed to indemnify the defendants to take over liability for the transaction if the plaintiff defaulted in any way in his obligations to the defendants. Accordingly, when the plaintiff was in arrear, the matter was reported by the defendants to [Auto-Finance] and they, as agents for the defendants, took possession of the car from the plaintiff's premises when he was away.

" [Auto-Finance] then sold the car, despite the protests of the plaintiff, who wished to pay off the arrears and carry on with the transaction, and out of the proceeds of sale [Auto-Finance] paid off the amount due to the defendants and pocketed the balance as a profit to themselves. The figures were that they sold for £575, out of which they paid the defendants £280, leaving [Auto-Finance] with a clear profit of £295 on the transaction. I should make it clear that although the defendants at all times knew that [Auto-Finance] dealt in these re-financing transactions and had had many previous deals with [Auto-Finance], there is no evidence to show that the defendants were aware of any of the irregularities in the conduct of the deal.

" On the above facts, I have come to the conclusion that there are three points on which the defence fails. Any one of which is fatal to the defence."

These three points were, briefly stated, that no title to the car ever vested in Auto-Finance nor, consequently, in the defendants; that the defendants could not rely on the documents which purported to constitute a valid hire-purchase agreement, because that would be in breach of the statutory regulations governing hire-purchase transactions and requiring the payment of a minimum deposit, whereas no deposit was, so the county court judge found, paid by the plaintiff, and (3) that the whole transaction was a sham, akin to that in the line of cases illustrated by *Polsky* v. *S. & A.S. Services**. On this third point the county court judge, in the course of his judgment said—

" The whole thing was obviously a sham and to my mind clearly falls on the side of the line represented by the *Polsky* line of cases. The facts of the present case are very like those in *Polsky's* case, except that in *Polsky's* case it was the finance company themselves who arranged the deal and there was no intervening party such as [Auto-Finance] in the present case.

" This has caused me a certain amount of hesitation, in as much as I am prepared to treat the defendants in this case as innocent parties, that is to say, innocent of any irregularity in the way in which the deal was carried through, and to that extent the case does differ from *Polsky's* case. Nevertheless, and with some hesitation, I feel that the reasoning of the *Polsky* line of cases with the accent on the protection of the borrower, in the context of the Bills of Sale Acts, 1878 and 1882, should lead me to come down on the *Polsky* side of the line and decide that the transaction was a sham and not legally enforceable."

P. M. Beard for the defendants.
S. S. Gill for the plaintiff.

Cur. adv. vult.

Jan. 17. The following judgments were read.

LORD DENNING, M.R.: In September, 1963, the plaintiff, Mr. Snook, got from a dealer a brand new M.G. car. The cash price was £935 19s. 8d. He paid most of it cash down, £735 19s. 8d., leaving only £200 outstanding. He arranged to pay off this £200 on hire-purchase terms. The dealer introduced him to a finance company called Totley Investments, Ltd. (which I will call " Totley "). On Sept. 16, 1963, Totley let him the car on these hire-purchase terms:

	£	s.	d.
Balance outstanding	200	0	0
Finance charge	15	0	0
Option fee	1	0	0
	£216	0	0

payable by twelve monthly instalments of £17 18s. 4d., the first payable on Oct. 16, 1963.

The plaintiff duly paid to Totley the first three instalments due in October, November and December, 1963, coming to £53 15s., leaving £161 5s. outstanding. Then he wanted to raise some money on the car. He saw an advertisement by another finance company called Auto-Finance, Ltd., which said:

" Auto-Finance put commonsense into credit. We can help you. Re-finance: we pay off your existing hire-purchase debt and re-finance this over a further period of twelve to thirty-six months, thus reducing monthly payments."

* [1951] 1 All E.R. 185; *affd.*, [1951] 1 All E.R. 1062, n.

The plaintiff went to Auto-Finance, Ltd. He saw a Mr. Hukins who in his presence telephoned Totley and asked for the " settlement figure ". Totley said that they would accept £160 in settlement if paid within seven days. Mr. Hukins then told Mr. Snook that they would pay out Totley and allow him a further £100.

In order to carry out this re-financing operation, Auto-Finance, Ltd. put before the plaintiff a number of documents for signature. The plaintiff signed them believing that they would produce the desired result. They turned out to be a sham. The judge so found. They dressed up the " re-financing operation " to look like a new hire-purchase transaction: whereas it was really a loan on the security of goods. The *first document* was a letter addressed to Totley. It said:

> " I have sold my rights in the above vehicle to Auto-Finance, Ltd., subject only to your lien which they will discharge. Will you please inform Auto-Finance, Ltd., how much you require to settle my obligations to you and to pass title absolutely to them in the vehicle."

On the bottom half there was a reply ready for Totley to sign. It was addressed to Auto-Finance, Ltd., and said:

> " We are prepared to sell title in the above vehicle to you absolutely for the sum of £ . . ., this amount to be received within 7/14/21 days of this date."

The plaintiff signed the top half, and left the paper with Auto-Finance, Ltd.; but it does not appear that they ever forwarded it to Totley. They seem to have kept it in their office. The bottom half was never signed by Totley. The blank figure was never filled in. Most important of all, the statement in the top half: " I have sold my rights to Auto-Finance, Ltd." was not true. The judge found that it was not true. The plaintiff had not sold his rights to them. They were worth £700 or £800 and they did not pay him a penny for them. He was in sole possession of the vehicle and had never parted with it to anyone.

It is equally important to note that Totley never sold their interest to Auto-Finance, Ltd. Nevertheless, thenceforward, in spite of having no title, Auto-Finance, Ltd. treated themselves as if they were owners of the car. They acted as if they were dealers disposing of it on hire-purchase terms to the plaintiff. They put before the plaintiff a *second document,* which was a hire-purchase form. It was not with Auto-Finance, Ltd., but with another finance company, the defendants, London and West Riding Investments, Ltd. It appears to be a company for whom Auto-Finance, Ltd., act as agents. They stock its forms and get them filled in. This form Auto-Finance, Ltd. filled in as a hire-purchase transaction for the M.G. car. They invented the figures. The cash price was filled in as £800 when it was not the price. The initial payment was put as £500 when nothing had been paid. The finance charge was put at £54. Option fee £1. The balance payable was put at £355, payable by the plaintiff over two years by monthly instalments of £14 15s. On the same form there was also a printed delivery receipt. The plaintiff signed it, as did the others. By it he acknowledged that he had accepted delivery of the car and that he understood it was the property of the defendants.

When Auto-Finance, Ltd. had got the plaintiff to sign these documents, they themselves signed another form by which they invoiced the car to the defendants, London & West Riding Investments, Ltd. They filled in the same fictitious figures, the cash price £800, initial payment of £500, balance £300. In this form they warranted that the car was their absolute property. That was not true. It was not their property. They had not bought it, nor paid a penny for it. Auto-Finance, Ltd. then sent all these documents to the defendants, who knew that Auto-Finance, Ltd. dealt in these re-financing transactions. They had had many previous deals with Auto-Finance, Ltd.; but there was no evidence that they knew of any of the irregularities in the conduct of the deal. On receiving

A the documents, the defendants paid £300 to Auto-Finance, Ltd. Auto-Finance, Ltd. paid £160 to Totley, who accepted it in full discharge and acknowledged that they had no further interest in the vehicle. Auto-Finance, Ltd. paid £125 to the plaintiff and kept £15 for themselves for their services.

The plaintiff paid the defendants the instalments of £14 15s. due on Feb. 27 and March 27, 1964, but then he was out of work and fell into arrear for the two

B months of April and May, 1964. On June 6, 1964, whilst the plaintiff had parked the car for a little while, some men seized the car and took it off. They were men from Auto-Finance, Ltd., acting as agents for the defendants. When the plaintiff discovered that they had taken it, he went to Auto-Finance, Ltd. and offered to pay off the arrears. He took the money down to them, but they refused to accept it. They resold the car. The judge found that at that time it was

C worth £775, but they sold it for £575. They paid off the defendants £280 (which satisfied them) and kept the balance of £295 for themselves. It was, they said, their " profit " in the transaction.

The plaintiff now sues the defendants for damages for conversion of the car. The defendants in their defence claim that it is their car. They say that, after the " settlement figure " was paid, Auto-Finance, Ltd. became the owners:

D and that Auto-Finance, Ltd. sold it to the defendants: and they let it on hire-purchase to the plaintiff; and that he failed to pay the instalments, whereupon " the defendants re-possessed the car and sold the same ". In considering this case there are two cardinal facts to be remembered: first, that the plaintiff was at all times in possession of the car and entitled to it as against all the world save he who could prove a better title; second, that the defendants, by their

E agents, Auto-Finance, Ltd., took possession of the car and sold it and took the proceeds. Those two facts are sufficient to give the plaintiff a prima facie case for damages for conversion. It is for the defendants to show that they were entitled to retake it, as they did.

The judge decided in favour of the plaintiff on three grounds, which I will take in the same order as he did.

F 1. *The defendants did not prove a title to the car.*

The defendants claim that they bought the car from Auto-Finance, Ltd., but they have failed to prove any title in Auto-Finance, Ltd. Immediately prior to the re-financing operation, there were two persons entitled to an interest in the car: *Totley*, who were the owners and had let it out to the plaintiff on hire-purchase; *the plaintiff*, who had the right to acquire the title by paying the

G " settlement figure " of £161; see the recent case of *Wickham Holdings, Ltd.* v. *Brook House Motors, Ltd.* (1). Seeing that the car was worth some £900, the plaintiff's contractual right (or " equity ", as it is sometimes called) was worth about £740.

In the course of the re-financing operation, Auto-Finance, Ltd. paid to Totley the " settlement figure " of £161: but that did not give Auto-Finance, Ltd. the

H title to the car. The only person who had the right to pay that " settlement figure " was the plaintiff. Auto-Finance, Ltd. must be presumed to have paid it on behalf of the plaintiff. With the result that the plaintiff became the owner of the car; see the recent case of *Bennett* v. *Griffin Finance* (2). Auto-Finance, Ltd. never bought the car from the plaintiff, nor his interest in it. They never paid him a penny for his contractual right. They did not become the owners

I of the car. The title was in the plaintiff. Seeing that Auto-Finance, Ltd. were not owners, they had nothing to transfer to the defendants. So the defendants did not become the owners. It was suggested in the course of the argument before us that they acquired a title by estoppel similar to that which the finance company acquired in *Eastern Distributors, Ltd.* v. *Goldring (Murphy, Third Party)* (3), and *Stoneleigh Finance, Ltd.* v. *Phillips* (4). I do not think that this

---

(1) Ante p. 117.   (2) Ante p. 515.
(3) [1957] 2 All E.R. 525; [1957] 2 Q.B. 600.
(4) [1965] 1 All E.R. 513; [1965] 2 Q.B. 537.

point is open to the defendants. Estoppel was not pleaded, nor was it raised in
the county court, nor found by the judge. It is not even mentioned in the notice
of appeal. Even if it were open, no evidence was given by the defendants to
support an estoppel. They do not say that they relied on any representation by
the plaintiff or on his conduct or on his signing the documents. They relied on a
sale by Totley to Auto-Finance, Ltd. and on a sale by Auto-Finance, Ltd. to
them. Their director said: " We acquired title from Auto-Finance, Ltd. and
paid them for it ". They repeated this in their defence. I would not allow them
now to change their ground.

2.   *The defendants were seeking to enforce an illegal transaction.*
    The judge held that the hire-purchase documents were in breach of the statu-
tory regulations and could not be relied on by the defendants. I think that he
was quite right. The regulations require that there should be " a statement of the
cash price of the goods ". There was here no cash price. The figure of £800
was fictitious. So there could be no statement of the cash price. The regulations
also require that there should be " actual payment " of the deposit. There
was no deposit here, and no payment of it, actual or otherwise. The figure of £500
was fictitious. The defendants relied on the recent case of *Kingsley* v. *Sterling
Industrial Securities, Ltd.* (5); but that is clearly distinguishable. The headnote
accurately states the effect of the decision. It is that the " actual payment "
need not be made in currency, but it must be a *real and genuine payment*. It
was held that a credit in account of £600 was real and genuine, and ranked as
" actual payment ". In this case, however, as the judge found,

> " no deposit was paid and no allowance by way of credit or any other
> thing which by the remotest stretch of imagination could be called a deposit
> was allowed for. The sum of £500 supposed to have been paid as a deposit
> was purely fictitious."

That finding is decisive. This hire-purchase transaction was illegal and cannot
form the basis of any claim by the defendants; see *Snell* v. *Unity Finance, Ltd.* (6)
and the recent case of *Viking Hire-Purchase Co., Ltd.* v. *Jordan* (7).
    Test it in this way. If the defendants had not taken possession of the car of their
own motion, but had recourse to the courts to recover it, it is plain that the courts
would not have assisted them. They had never been in possession and would
have perforce to rely on the illegal transaction. LORD MANSFIELD said long ago
that:

> "No court will lend its aid to a man who founds his cause of action upon an
> immoral or an illegal act " (see *Holman* v. *Johnson* (8), applied in *Chettiar* v.
> *Chettiar* (9)). In view of this illegality, the defendants could not have recovered
this car by action in the courts. It follows that they cannot justify taking it
without action. They cannot better their position by taking the law into their
own hands.

3.   *The defendants were seeking to enforce documents which were a sham.*
    The judge held that this re-financing operation was a loan; and that the docu-
ments were a sham to cover up the loan. He said that:

> " The whole thing is obviously a sham and to my mind falls clearly on the
> side of the line represented by the *Polsky* v. *S. and A. Services, Ltd.* (10) line
> of cases."

The transaction, though taking the form of a sale and reletting, was " nothing
more than a loan of money on the security of the goods " and therefore illegal
under the Bills of Sale Acts. There was ample evidence on which he could so find.
The essence of the matter was that Auto-Finance, Ltd. got the defendants to

(5) [1966] 2 All E.R. 414.   (6) [1963] 3 All E.R. 50; [1964] 2 Q.B. 203.
(7) (1966), 110 Sol. Jo. 51. Compare p. 532, letter F, post.
(8) (1775), 1 Cowp. 341 at p. 343.
(9) [1962] 1 All E.R. 494 at p. 498; [1962] A.C. 294 at p. 303.
(10) [1951] 1 All E.R. 185; *affd.*, [1951] 1 All E.R. 1062, n.

advance £300 on the security of the goods, which was applied on behalf of the plaintiff as to £160 in paying off Totley, as to £125 in making an additional loan to the plaintiff, and as to £15 in commission to Auto-Finance, Ltd. The documents were filled with fictitious figures and statements—all of which are badges of sham (see *Polksy's* case (11)).

There is this difference, however, from *Polsky's* case (11). The defendants did not themselves negotiate the transaction. They were, as the judge said, innocent of any irregularity by which the deal was carried through. Nevertheless, he thought that they could not take advantage of it. I agree with him, and for this simple reason: the real transaction, as he found, was a loan on the security of goods. I ask: who was it made this loan? The answer is plain. The defendants made it. No-one else lent any money at all. How did the defendants make it? The answer again is plain. By means of Auto-Finance, Ltd. who were their agents for this purpose. There were no other means by which the loan was made. Once it is seen that Auto-Finance, Ltd. were the agents of the defendants to make the loan, it follows inexorably that the defendants are responsible for the manner in which their agents conducted themselves therein, including the preparation of fictitious documents (see *Lloyd* v. *Grace, Smith & Co.* (12)).

It was argued that the defendants are not to be affected by this sham transaction unless they were themselves parties to it. I cannot agree with this. Although the defendants were not parties to the sham, their agents were: and that is the end of it. Every principal is answerable for the conduct of his agent in the course of his agency. The case of *Stoneleigh Finance, Ltd.* v. *Phillips* (13), is distinguishable because there was no agency.

On each of those three points the judge held that the defendants were not entitled to seize the car. As he said, any one of them is sufficient. I agree with him on all three. His judgment convinces me. The defendants are liable in damages for conversion.

Damages.

The judge held that the value of the car at the date of conversion was £775; but he did not award the plaintiff that sum. He deducted the sum which the defendants would have received if the re-financing operation had been completed, that is, £325 10s. In other words, he allowed them credit for their loan and finance charges. So he only gave judgment for £449 10s. This was right. A finance company are entitled to recoup themselves the amount owing to them, but not to take additional profit for themselves (see *Wickham Holdings, Ltd.* v. *Brook House Motors, Ltd.* (14)), and this applies not only when they sue for conversion, but also when they retake the car and sell it.

Conclusion.

Viewing the matter broadly, it comes to this. The plaintiff paid about £800 towards the purchase of this new car. It was more than three-fourths of the price. Yet after he had only had it nine months, a finance company took it from him. All because he was £30 in arrears. He offered to pay off those arrears; but they could not accept it. They insisted that the car belonged absolutely to them: and that his valuable equity was forfeited. They sold the car at a high price, recouped themselves the money they had lent, and took a large profit of £300. Seeing that he was in possession, this conduct was a plain conversion unless they could show a good title in themselves to warrant it. All that they have done is to produce documents full of fictitious entries, which the judge has found to be illegal and a sham. I do not see how the defendants can justify a conversion by reliance on illegal and sham documents. I would dismiss this appeal.

DIPLOCK, L.J. (read by RUSSELL, L.J.): It is not a presumption of law that a hire-purchase finance company cannot be innocent. It is not even a

---

(11) [1951] 1 All E.R. 185; *affd.*, [1951] 1 All E.R. 1062, n.
(12) [1911-13] All E.R. Rep. 51; [1912] A.C. 716.
(13) [1965] 1 All E.R. 513; [1965] 2 Q.B. 537.
(14) Ante p. 117.

prima facie presumption of fact. It was thus open to the county court judge to
find as he did, that the defendants were innocent in that they were unaware of
any irregularity in the way that the deal was carried through. This finding is,
in my view, crucial to the present appeal.

My sympathy, like that of LORD DENNING, M.R., is for the plaintiff. My
judgment, like that of RUSSELL, L.J., must be for the defendants. What happened
to the plaintiff was, until the Hire-Purchase Act 1965, liable to happen to any
hire-purchaser who defaulted on instalments due in respect of goods on which
he had made a large initial payment. He says that it ought not to happen to him
for three reasons: (i) the defendants never acquired title to the car; (ii) he, the
plaintiff, and Auto-Finance, Ltd., at any rate, intended the transaction to be a
sham in order to mask a loan of £300 on the security of the car; (iii) the hire-
purchase agreement was void under the Hire-Purchase and Credit Sale
Agreements (Control) Order, 1960, (15).

The plaintiff's object was to raise £100 if he could by making use of his rights
in respect of a car worth about £800, which he had on hire-purchase from Totley
under an agreement under which instalments amounting in all to £161 5s.
remained to be paid. To do this without running foul of either the Bills of Sale
Act, 1878 or the Hire-Purchase and Credit Sale Agreements (Control) Order,
1960, it was necessary to transfer the title to the car to another hire-purchase
finance company and for the plaintiff to enter into a fresh hire-purchase agreement
with that company and to make to that company actual payment of twenty-five
per cent. of the cash price of the car. He was advised by Auto-Finance, Ltd. to do
this. He took that advice and he did.

As regards transfer of the title, I do not think that it matters whether on the
true analysis of the transaction with Totley, the title to the car passed from
Totley to Auto-Finance, Ltd., on their own behalf or as trustees for the plaintiff
or passed to the plaintiff himself. In so far as the beneficial or legal title was in
him, he clearly authorised Auto-Finance, Ltd. to transfer it on his behalf to
the defendants. That Auto-Finance, Ltd. purported to act as principals in the
sale of the car to the defendants whereas they may have been acting as agents
for the plaintiff as undisclosed principal, does not in my view matter. In any
event I agree with RUSSELL, L.J., that the plaintiff is estopped by his conduct
from denying the defendants' title to the car. As the defendants were unaware
that he intended a sham, it would be a travesty of justice if he were not, and in
view of the terms in which this claim is pleaded, I do not think that the defendants
are debarred from relying, if it be necessary, on this estoppel, although it is not
expressly pleaded as such in the defence. All the facts necessary to establish it
were proved.

As regards the contention of the plaintiff that the transactions between himself,
Auto-Finance, Ltd. and the defendants were a " sham ", it is, I think, necessary
to consider what, if any, legal concept is involved in the use of this popular and
pejorative word. I apprehend that, if it has any meaning in law, it means acts
done or documents executed by the parties to the " sham " which are intended
by them to give to third parties or to the court the appearance of creating between
the parties legal rights and obligations different from the actual legal rights and
obligations (if any) which the parties intend to create. One thing I think, however, is clear in legal principle, morality and the authorities (see *Yorkshire
Railway Wagon Co.* v. *Maclure* (16); *Stoneleigh Finance, Ltd.* v. *Phillips* (17),
that for acts or documents to be a " sham ", with whatever legal consequences
follow from this, all the parties thereto must have a common intention that the
acts or documents are not to create the legal rights and obligations which they
give the appearance of creating. No unexpressed intentions of a "shammer "
affect the rights of a party whom he deceived. There is an express finding in this

(15) S.I. 1960 No. 762.   (16) (1882), 21 Ch.D. 309.
        (17) [1965] 1 All E.R. 513; [1965] 2 Q.B. 537.

case that the defendants were not parties to the alleged "sham". So this contention fails.

As regards the contention that the hire-purchase agreement was void under the Hire-Purchase and Credit Sale Agreements (Control) Order, 1960, because there was no "actual payment" of the sum of £500 credited to the plaintiff as the "initial payment" in the hire-purchase agreement, this depends on the meaning of the words "actual payment" in the Order. I agree with RUSSELL, L.J., that the words of the Order of 1960, which is penal legislation, must be construed in the light of the mischief against which the Order of 1960 is directed and also in the light of the well-known practice with respect to initial payments under hire-purchase agreements by which the hire-purchase finance company itself never receives this payment in cash from the hirer but debits it to the dealer in the purchase price and credits it to the hirer in the hire-purchase agreement. RUSSELL, L.J., in his judgment deals with this point in detail. I agree with his analysis and his conclusion. I will not try to gild his refined gold. For these reasons and for those which he will give on all three contentions of the plaintiff, I would allow this appeal.

RUSSELL, L.J.: The plaintiff's case for denying the right of the defendant to retake the car under the hire-purchase agreement is threefold. First: he says that the defendants are not shown to have acquired the title to the car. Second: he says that the whole transaction was but a dressed-up arrangement for a loan on the security of the car, and avoided by the Bills of Sale Acts. Third: he says that the hire-purchase agreement was illegal and therefore void or unenforceable because no "actual payment" was made of the £500 stated in the agreement to have been paid by way of deposit, or of any other sum, as required by the Hire-Purchase and Credit Sale Agreements (Control) Order, 1960. I will consider these contentions in that order.

First, as to the defendants' title to or ownership of the car. The county court judge analysed the sequence of events, concluded that the title never reached Auto-Finance, Ltd. and for that reason concluded that it never reached the defendants. The plaintiff, who was told, however, by Auto-Finance, Ltd. that the matter would involve paying off the existing owners (the plaintiff's existing hire-purchase company, Totley), and obtaining hire-purchase finance elsewhere, executed documents for presentation to the defendants which in terms recognised the defendants to be the owners of the car. Indeed, the plaintiff intended the title to the car to pass to the defendants, just as the defendants intended to acquire it; for only thus could the defendants hire it to the plaintiff. The plaintiff further confirmed to the defendants by letter of Feb. 17, that the details of the agreement were correct. How can it be now open to the plaintiff to assert that he became the owner of the car when Totley was paid off, that he has remained such ever since, and that the defendants never became such? One has only to look at the matter from the defendants' point of view—the defendants being, as the judge held, innocent and ignorant of any irregularities—to see that it would be quite wrong to allow the plaintiff to take this title point. He is estopped by his own conduct from denying the defendants' title to the car, and this title by estoppel is a true title. See *Eastern Distributors, Ltd.* v. *Goldring (Murphy, Third Party)* (18), and *Stoneleigh Finance, Ltd.* v. *Phillips* (19).

The plaintiff's second contention is that the substance of the transaction was the borrowing of money by the plaintiff on the security of the car, and that the defendants cannot rely on the hire-purchase agreement because of the provisions of the Bills of Sale Acts. This is not a case, however, in which the defendants were party to anything but the apparent acquisition of a car for £800 less £500, net £300, and the simultaneous hiring out of the car under a hire-purchase agreement which credited the hirer with a deposit of £500 towards ultimate purchase. The

(18) [1957] 2 All E.R. at p. 532; [1957] 2 Q.B. at p. 611.
(19) [1965] 1 All E.R. at pp. 523, 527; [1965] 2 Q.B. at pp. 571, 578.

defendants never intended to take part in any transaction by way of a loan of money on the security of the car. To enable the court to hold that a transaction was intended to mask a loan, it must find that both parties to the transaction so intended; see *Yorkshire Railway Wagon Co.* v. *Maclure* (20), and *Stoneleigh Finance, Ltd.* v. *Phillips* (21). The latter case is also authority for the proposition that even if it be correct that the substance of the whole arrangement as between the plaintiff and Auto-Finance, Ltd. was to dress up a loan on security, that intention on the part of Auto-Finance, Ltd. cannot be imputed to the defendants. I must, therefore, reject the plaintiff's contention under this head also.

Thirdly and lastly, the plaintiff says that the hire-purchase agreement on which the defendants rely is illegal under the Hire-Purchase and Credit Sale Agreements (Control) Order, 1960, and, therefore, unenforceable, because (he says) no " actual payment " was made of the required percentage of the cash price, though by the agreement he was credited with a deposit of £500 towards ultimate purchase.

The purpose of the Order of 1960 is undoubted. It is to restrict credit in the field (inter alia) of hire-purchase: in particular, the requirement of a minimum deposit of a percentage of the cash price of the goods is designed to prevent the acquisition of goods on hire-purchase without immediate and substantial reduction of the acquirer's assets. It is to be noticed that Pt. 2 of Sch. 2 of the Order of 1960 is aimed at avoiding the effect of payment when it does *not* have the effect of such reduction. On the other hand, a fair allowance for goods taken in part exchange—an operation which *does* reduce the acquirer's assets—is allowed in the calculation of the amount actually paid. It is quite clear that in the present case—for the cash price figure of £800 is not challenged as appropriate to the car— the plaintiff surrendered and the defendants acquired £500 worth of car in exchange for the same amount credited as paid towards ultimate purchase. The transaction, therefore, was one right outside the mischief of unregulated credit facilities at which the order of 1960 was aimed; the question remains whether the language of the Order of 1960 is such that its net is cast wider than the mischief and embraces also the present case. In considering the application of the Order of 1960 in this regard, I notice first that, as was remarked in *Kingsley* v. *Sterling Industrial Securities, Ltd.* (22), in the ordinary hire-purchase case, the finance company never in the strictest sense receives payment of the initial payment. This the dealer receives from the customer and retains, and the sale by dealer to finance company is carried through by a simple payment of the difference between the cash price and the deposit. It has never been thought necessary for the finance company to pay the cash price to the dealer in exchange for a payment by the dealer (on behalf of the customer hirer) of the deposit as an initial payment by the hirer to be credited to him. Nor has it been thought necessary to record the equivalent as cross entries in books. The whole process is short-circuited and the same result achieved.

Suppose a car owner wishes to raise finance (say £300) on his car which is worth £800. (Here I am not concerned with any question of invalidity on other grounds.) The transaction might take this form: the owner approaches a finance company and agrees to sell to the company for £800 on terms that it will hire back the car under a hire-purchase agreement, crediting the owner with an initial payment of £500 and providing for payment of (say) £350 by " x " equal monthly instalments. If this is carried through by a cheque from finance company to owner for £800 in exchange for a cheque the other way for £500, it could not be doubted that the owner had made an actual payment of £500. (Nor could it be said that the £500 had been " acquired " from the finance company under the Order of 1960, Sch. 2, Pt. 2—see the judgment of WINN, L.J., in the *Kingsley* case (23).) I would see no reason for denying the fact of " actual payment " in the context of the Order of 1960 if, in the example given, instead of cheques being solemnly handed across the table (or indeed currency notes handed one way and part handed back),

(20) (1882), 21 Ch.D. 309.
(22) [1966] 2 All E.R. 414.
(21) [1965] 1 All E.R. 513; [1965] 2 Q.B. 537.
(23) [1966] 2 All E.R. at p. 429.

the transaction was carried through by a cheque for £300 combined with appropriate entries in the finance company's books such as would have attended an
exchange of cheques.   I would take exactly the same view if, as a matter of
practical convenience, all that was done in order to carry out the transaction was
a cheque for £300 from the finance company accompanied by a hire-purchase
agreement in usual form stating the £800 cash price and £500 initial payment
received.   The finance company would be paying £800 for the car in part by a
cheque for £300 and in part by crediting the owner at his request with the balance
of £500 against the ultimate purchase price under the hire-purchase agreement.   I
cannot think that this would not be actual payment within the Order of 1960
when a mutual exchange of cheques, or a handing and return of £500 in notes,
would be such.   Indeed, the whole transaction could in my judgment have been
stated even more briefly with the same outcome.

" Q.—On what terms will you take over my car and hire it back to me
under a hire-purchase agreement?

" A.—Cash price £800: deposit £500: balance £300 plus finance charge
£50 by ' x ' equal monthly instalments.   Option payment £1.   Total hire-
purchase price £851."

This conversation, followed by a hire-purchase agreement signed by both declaring the finance company to be the owner of the car and containing those terms
and accompanied by a cheque to the owner for £300 would, I consider, be un-
exceptionable.   Both parties would intend the title to pass and it would pass
without any physical delivery; and in my view the owner would actually pay
the £500 within that phrase as used in the Order of 1960.   I do not think that the
Order of 1960 should be construed in such a way as to require parties to such a
transaction to take a long way round when there is a perfectly sensible short cut
to the same commercial terminus.

If in such a case " actual payment " can be achieved in this manner, what of
the case now under consideration?   The plaintiff must, I think, be taken to have
known that if the defendants were to hire the car to him on hire-purchase terms,
the title to the car must go to the defendants as purchasers: as previously stated,
he must have intended this to happen.   The £800 was a proper cash price value.
The plaintiff through Auto-Finance, Ltd. puts forward a proposition by which
the defendants will buy the car for £800, but by which, instead of paying the
cash price to him or to Auto-Finance, Ltd. on his behalf and taking £500 back
as deposit or initial payment under the hire-purchase agreement, which is an
integral part of the transaction, the procedure is short-circuited by a direct credit
given in the hire-purchase agreement.   If the defendants had paid the full £800
to Auto-Finance, Ltd., the latter would have held £500 of it for the plaintiff with
an obligation to repay it on the plaintiff's behalf as initial deposit.   If Auto-
Finance, Ltd. had exchanged their cheque for £500 with the defendants' cheque
for £800, and accounted to the plaintiff, the receipt side of such account would
have stood at £800 and the disbursement side, in addition to £160 paid to Totley,
would have included an item " £500 initial deposit paid to defendants on your
behalf ".   Clearly there would have been actual payment of the initial deposit.
I would not construe the Order of 1960 so as to destroy a transaction because
a purely formal step is not taken.   The case of *Kingsley* (24) was, of course, different; but I would borrow from the judgment of SELLERS, L.J. (25) the phrase:

" The fact that those motions were not actually gone through can make no
difference to the transaction;"

and I echo another phrase (26) by saying that here £500 was a real loss to the
plaintiff because the car was worth £800.   He had the money in the value of the

(24) [1966] 2 All E.R. 414.
(25) [1966] 2 All E.R. at p. 418, letter D.
(26) [1966] 2 All E.R. at p. 418, letter E.

car and the transaction was in no sense one where a man acquired a car when he had nothing with which to acquire it and was unable to find the deposit. Finally I agree with the statement (27) that it is not the manner of payment which the Order of 1960 affects but its reality.

For those reasons I would allow the appeal.

It is right to record that it was said in evidence for Auto-Finance, Ltd. that before the car was sold after repossession for £575, Auto-Finance, Ltd. offered it to the plaintiff for £280, the sum which Auto-Finance, Ltd. were called on to pay to the defendants under a recourse agreement: though the judge made no finding on this. If this offer were made and had the plaintiff been able or willing to accept it, his total outlay in acquiring the car from first to last would have been about £974—the retail price when he " bought " it new in September, 1963, having been £940.

I do not agree with the suggestion that Auto-Finance, Ltd. was agent of the defendants so as to validate the first two of the plaintiff's contentions. The county court judge made no such finding, and I do not think that it is any more justified than it would have been in the *Stoneleigh Finance* case (28). Particular reliance is placed on the profit made on the sale of the car and permitted by the defendants to be kept by Auto-Finance, Ltd. As to profit: this was at the relevant time a feature of any hire-purchase agreement (above certain limits of value) where there was a high percentage of initial payment and the hirer defaulted so that the finance company was entitled to repossess and sell for the true value of the car and keep the proceeds; if the plaintiff had defaulted on the Totley agreement, Totley could have repossessed and sold and made a large profit. As to the repossession being by Auto-Finance, Ltd. on behalf of the defendants, and the profit being taken by Auto-Finance, Ltd. and not by the defendants; this was presumably provided for in the recourse agreement. If anything, the profit retention by Auto-Finance, Ltd. without accounting to the defendants points away from agency.

I add that the only point for argument in the case of *Viking Hire-Purchase Co., Ltd.* v. *Jordan* (29), referred to by LORD DENNING, M.R., was whether the agreement was a hire-purchase agreement within the Order of 1960. If, as was held, it was in character such an agreement, it was conceded that it offended under the Order of 1960, because no cash price was stated therein.

Appeal allowed. Leave to appeal to the House of Lords granted.

Solicitors: *Bell, Brodrick & Gray*, agents for *Glass, Bagshawe, Miller & Co.*, Sheffield (for the defendants); *Neal, Scorah, Siddons & Co.*, Sheffield (for the plaintiff).

[*Reported by* F. GUTTMAN, ESQ., *Barrister-at-Law.*]

---

(27) [1966] 2 All E.R. at p. 420, letter D.
(28) [1965] 1 All E.R. 513; [1965] 2 Q.B. 537.
(29) (1966), 110 Sol. Jo. 51.

ADAM & HARVEY, LTD. *v.* INTERNATIONAL MARITIME SUPPLIES CO., LTD.

[COURT OF APPEAL, CIVIL DIVISION (Harman, Diplock and Winn, L.JJ.), January 11, 1967.]

Costs—Order for costs—Interlocutory appeal—Order for costs " to be taxed ", without stating " forthwith ", confers right to immediate taxation—Costs " in any event " distinguished as not conferring such a right pending trial of the action—Correction of order under slip rule—R.S.C., Ord. 62, r. 4— R.S.C., Ord. 20, r. 11.

On an interlocutory appeal the Court of Appeal intimated that there should be no immediate taxation of costs. The appeal was allowed with the appellants' costs of the appeal and before the judge. The order as drawn up provided that the costs of the proceedings before the judge should be the appellants' costs in any event and that the respondents should pay the appellants' costs of the appeal, such costs to be taxed. The appellants applied for taxation, though the action had not yet been tried. On motion under R.S.C., Ord. 20, r. 11 to amend the order so as to provide that the costs of the appeal should be the appellants' in any event,

Held: under the order as drawn up the appellants had a right to taxation, though the action had not yet come on for trial; as, however, an order enabling an immediate taxation did not express the intention of the court, the order would be amended as asked (see p. 534, letter H, post).

[As to orders for costs of appeals, see 30 HALSBURY'S LAWS (3rd Edn.) 479, 480, para. 900; and as to taxation pursuant to orders for costs, see ibid., p. 426, para. 900.

For R.S.C., Ord. 20, r. 11, Ord. 62, r. 4, see SUPREME COURT PRACTICE, 1967, Vol. 1, 309, 821.]

Motion.

By writ issued on Aug. 25, 1965, the plaintiffs claimed under a contract a sum of £5,000 with interest from the defendants. The defendants were a foreign company whose registered office was in Switzerland. By order of Master RITCHIE dated Jan. 20, 1966, the defendants were given leave to defend the action conditional on the sum of £5,000 being paid into court within twenty-eight days. An appeal from this order was dismissed by the judge in chambers on Feb. 17, 1966. On appeal to the Court of Appeal the defendants were, on Mar. 15, 1966, given unconditional leave to defend and, after discussion as to costs, the following order as to costs was drawn up—

" (i) the costs of the proceedings before [Master RITCHIE] shall be costs in the cause

" (ii) the costs of the proceedings before the judge shall be the defendants' costs in any event and

" (iii) the plaintiff shall pay to the defendants or their solicitors their costs of this appeal such costs to be taxed by a taxing master."

On Oct. 27, 1966, the plaintiffs applied for security for costs, but on Nov. 16, 1966, their application was refused. In November, 1966, the defendants took out a summons to tax the costs of the appeal to the Court of Appeal under the order of Mar. 15, 1966. The plaintiffs applied by notice of motion dated Dec. 14, 1966, under R.S.C., Ord. 20, r. 11, that so much of the order dated Mar. 15, 1966, as provided that the plaintiffs should pay to the defendants or their solicitors the costs of the appeal to the Court of Appeal, such costs to be taxed by a taxing master, be corrected so as to provide that the costs of the appeal be the defendants' costs in any event.

A. L. J. Lincoln for the plaintiffs.
T. M. Eastham, Q.C., and *J. Lloyd-Eley* for the defendants.

Followed in ALLIED COLLECTION AGENCIES v WOOD [1981] 3 All ER 176

HARMAN, L.J.: The action was an action in which defendants out of the jurisdiction were served, and they said that they had a counterclaim. The master ordered that they should have leave to defend only on the footing that they paid £5,000 into court. They appealed to the judge who affirmed the master's order. They appealed to this court, which came to the conclusion that the defendants ought to have unconditional leave to defend without payment into court.

Then there arose the question of costs. As far as I am concerned, I am quite clear what I intended to do. I said in the course of the interlocutory observations " No immediate taxation ". This was in reply to counsel for the defendants; but, as he rightly points out, it does imply that, if an order is made in this court for payment of costs, the order so made does mean that the successful party has a right to an immediate taxation and payment. I have been under the impression that the court, when it intended that result, would say expressly " Costs to be taxed and paid forthwith "; but the SUPREME COURT PRACTICE, 1967 (1) shows that I was wrong about that. It is a thing often asked for and I have made the order in that form, notwithstanding that the application was interlocutory, that payment should be made at once if the successful party chose to tax the costs. However that may be, I think it is fair to counsel for the defendants to say that in spite of the fact that he assented to my interlocutory observation, there was this difference (although I did not intend that it should be made) that he applied in a form of words which would carry, if it was assented to, an immediate taxation. That seems to have passed the court by; as far as I am concerned, perhaps by my inadvertence. It did not strike counsel for the plaintiffs, who was unaware of the difference that there is between appeal allowed with costs in any event and appeal allowed with costs, which is something of a nicety. As counsel for the defendants endorsed his brief and as the learned associate understood, it was an order which entailed the right to an immediate taxation and payment. That was in March, 1966.

The matter was next heard of in November. At that point the successful party took out a summons to tax the costs immediately and have them paid. The plaintiffs then woke up to the danger in which they were: hence this motion. It may be not unconnected with the fact that there had been an application for security, which had not succeeded. As far as I am concerned, I did not intend that there should be this exceptional order for payment of costs at once, but that costs should be in any event those of the successful appellant. That was the order which I intended to pronounce, and I thought that I had done so. I see, however, that there is some room for mistake owing to the fact that after I had made the observation which showed that I did not intend an immediate taxation, an application was made which could have had that result and was so interpreted by the learned associate. That is a slip which can be amended under R.S.C., Ord. 20, r. 11, because inadvertently the order as drawn did not express the intention of the court owing to a misunderstanding between the associate and the court which pronounced it. I am not blaming anybody for it, except perhaps myself for not being more vigilant in the matter. I am sure of what I intended and I think that we have jurisdiction to give effect to that intention, and I would so hold.

DIPLOCK, L.J.: I agree. As I am in the same white sheet as HARMAN, L.J., I have nothing to add.

WINN, L.J.: I agree. My position is precisely the same as my lords'.

Application granted.

Solicitors: *Payne, Hicks Beach & Co.* (for the plaintiffs); *Paisner & Co.* (for the defendants).

[*Reported by* F. GUTTMAN, ESQ., *Barrister-at-Law.*]

---

(1) Vol. 1, pp. 821, 822.

NASH *v.* NASH.

[PROBATE, DIVORCE AND ADMIRALTY DIVISION (Sir Jocelyn Simon, P., and Cairns, J.), November 10, 1966.]

Divorce—Re-hearing—Classes of applications—Ignorance or lack of proper advice leading to respondent's unawareness of proper procedural steps to preserve his position—Matrimonial Causes Rules, 1957 *(S.I.* 1957 *No.* 619), *r.* 36 (1).

The husband, whose wife was petitioning for divorce on the ground of cruelty and desertion, applied for legal aid to defend the suit. A legal aid certificate was ultimately granted (apparently after appeal to the appropriate area committee) but, through no fault of the husband's, reached him too late to allow him to take advantage of it. The case came on as an undefended suit, notice of setting down having been given by the wife's solicitor to the husband's solicitor, although that notice was not strictly necessary. A decree nisi was granted to the wife. The husband, having subsequently learnt of the decree, applied under r. 36 (1)* of the Matrimonial Causes Rules, 1957, to set aside the decree nisi and for a re-hearing.

Held: as the husband had at all times desired to defend and was not personally to blame that his case was not presented when the wife's petition was heard, the decree nisi would be set aside and the huband would be given leave to file an answer out of time (see p. 538, letters B and E, post).

Observations on the granting of a re-hearing in class of case additional to the two mentioned in *Stevens* v. *Stevens*, [1965] 1 All E.R. at p. 1010 (see p. 538, letter F, and p. 539, letter A, post).

[As to applications for re-hearing, see 12 HALSBURY's LAWS (3rd Edn.) 425, 426, para. 954; and for cases on the subject, see 27 DIGEST (Repl.) 595-598, *5571-5593.*

For the Matrimonial Causes Rules, 1957, r. 36, see 10 HALSBURY's STATUTORY INSTRUMENTS (second Re-Issue) 248.]

Cases referred to:

Owen v. *Owen*, [1964] 2 All E.R. 58; [1964] P. 277 and 284; [1964] 2 W.L.R. 654; 3rd Digest Supp.

Peek v. *Peek*, [1947] 2 All E.R. 578; [1948] P. 46; *affd.* C.A.; [1948] 2 All E.R. 297; 27 Digest (Repl.) 596, *5577.*

Stevens v. *Stevens*, [1965] 1 All E.R. 1003; [1965] P. 147; [1965] 2 W.L.R. 736; 3rd Digest Supp.

Tucker v. *Tucker*, [1949] P. 105; [1949] L.J.R. 76; 27 Digest (Repl.) 597, *5584.*

Winter v. *Winter*, [1942] 2 All E.R. 390; [1942] P. 151; 111 L.J.P. 95; 167 L.T. 258; 27 Digest (Repl.) 599, *5604.*

Motion.

This was a motion by the husband, respondent in a divorce suit brought by his wife, to have a decree nisi, granted to her on the suit's being heard as undefended, set aside, and that a re-hearing of the suit should be ordered.

The facts are set out in the judgment of SIR JOCELYN SIMON, P.

The husband appeared in person.

I. B. Purvis for the wife.

SIR JOCELYN SIMON, P.: This is an application by a litigant in person against whom a decree nisi of divorce was pronounced by PAYNE, J., on June 28, 1966, in an undefended suit brought by the wife on the grounds of cruelty and

---

* Rule 36 (1), so far as material, provides: " An application for re-hearing of a cause heard by a judge alone where no error of the court at the hearing is alleged shall be made to a Divisional Court of the Probate, Divorce and Admiralty Division. The application shall be by notice of motion stating the grounds on which it is based . . ."

Approved in MITCHELL v MITCHELL
[1983] 3 All ER 621

Explained in MONTAGUE *v.* MONTA-
GUE. *post* p. 802.

desertion. The application is made under r. 36 of the Matrimonial Causes Rules, 1957, which gives this court power to order a re-hearing where no error of the court below is alleged. It is not controverted that the application is rightly made to this court under r. 36, since there was ample material before PAYNE, J., which entitled him to grant the decree that he did. The essence of the husband's case is that he at all times wished to defend these proceedings; that he was not personally at fault in failing to do so; and that he believes that he had an answer to his wife's charges against him.

The history of the matter appears to be as follows; and I should like to say that, in elucidating the facts and the law, we are indebted to Mr. Purvis, counsel for the wife on this application, who has conducted his case in accordance with the best traditions of the English Bar when appearing against a litigant in person—in other words, he has clearly laid before the court the whole of the relevant material, whether or not it tells in his favour. On Nov. 8, 1963, the wife presented to the court a petition for divorce, alleging that the husband had treated her with cruelty and that the court had jurisdiction because the parties were domiciled in England. The husband obtained legal aid to defend; and the initial point that fell for decision was whether the court had jurisdiction on the ground of domicil, the husband having a domicil of origin in Jamaica which he alleged that he had never lost. That came as a preliminary issue before KARMINSKI, J., on May 11, 1965, when it was held that the husband was still domiciled in Jamaica. The petition was, therefore, dismissed for want of jurisdiction. On Sept. 29, 1965, the wife took out a summons under s. 17 of the Married Women's Property Act, 1882, in order to resolve some dispute between her and the husband as to property or possession of property. Again the husband applied for and obtained legal aid to defend. On Nov. 15, 1965, the wife presented a fresh petition for divorce. This time she founded her claim for jurisdiction on the allegation that, at the time of the presentation of the petition, she had been resident in England for three years. That petition was not served on the husband until Dec. 6, 1965. He signed an acknowledgment of service; and then he consulted a solicitor. On Dec. 8, 1965, his solicitor wrote to the wife's solicitors, advising them that the husband was applying for legal aid to defend charges made in the wife's petition. The wife's solicitor answered on the following day that they would grant an extension of time of six weeks for an answer to be filed, which, in his view, was adequate to enable the application to be made. The husband's solicitor did apply for legal aid on his behalf. Nothing further was heard, however, and on Feb. 17, 1966, the wife's solicitor wrote to the husband's solicitor that he was instructed to proceed in the matter and could wait no longer. On the following day, Feb. 18, 1966, the husband's solicitor answered that an application for legal aid had been made " some months previously ". I do not know whether the husband's solicitor was intending to refer to the application for legal aid in the divorce suit; that could hardly have been made " some months previously ". It may be, therefore, that he was confused with the application for legal aid in the s. 17 proceedings. The wife's solicitor replied, on Feb. 21, 1966, that, in his view, the husband had had time enough. It appears from the affidavit that the husband has sworn in support of this present application that, on Mar. 30, 1966, a legal aid certificate was refused to him on the ground that no sufficient grounds had been shown for defending; however, the husband, who is obviously under a disadvantage in understanding these matters, told us in his address that what he thought was that he had been offered a legal aid certificate, but at a cost beyond what he could afford. It is unnecessary to try to resolve this discrepancy, because the husband appealed to the legal aid area committee against the decision of the district committee. While that appeal was still pending, on Apr. 15, 1966, the wife's solicitor wrote to the husband's solicitor, advising him that he (the wife's solicitor) was applying for a registrar's certificate with a view to setting the case down. According to the husband's affidavit, on May 27, 1966, the legal aid area committee allowed his appeal; but the news of that decision did not reach him or his solicitor until, as he told us, June 27, 1966 (or, according to the affidavit, June 28). Again the discrepancy is quite immaterial, because the case was heard by Payne, J., on June 28, 1966, so that the husband had in any event no time to take advantage of his legal aid certificate. I should like to say at this stage that I cannot see that the wife's solicitor can be criticised in any way. He had an acknowledgment of service. No answer was filed. He gave (strictly speaking, unnecessarily) notice to the husband's solicitor that he was setting the case down; and he was fully entitled to set it down in the undefended list. The husband was in due course apprised of the decree nisi obtained against him. On Aug. 5, 1966, he filed his notice of motion under r. 36; and on Aug. 10, 1966, he was granted a limited legal aid certificate in relation to these proceedings, though he has himself appeared to argue his case.

The point for determination is whether, in these circumstances, we should set aside the decree nisi which the wife has obtained in due regularity of procedure and on evidence which was ample to satisfy Payne, J. We have particular guidance from two authorities. From *Owen* v. *Owen* (1), a decision of this court, I cite only a short passage:

" If the court is satisfied that there are substantial grounds for believing the decree to have been obtained contrary to the justice of the case, not even gross laches by the applicant, as in *Winter* v. *Winter* (2), nor deliberate suppression of documents, as in *Peek* v. *Peek* (3) will defeat the application; but, if a respondent, in possession of her faculties, with the facts of her married life in mind, and with the benefit of clear legal advice and her solicitor's explanation of the issues involved, takes a deliberate decision not to defend or not to pursue her cross-charges in circumstances which negative any suggestion of ' hoodwinking ' the court, then this court should, in our opinion, view a subsequent application for a new trial with a degree of reserve."

In *Stevens* v. *Stevens* (4), Davies, L.J., in the Court of Appeal, dealt with the principles on which the jurisdiction is exercised. Counsel for the wife, I think rightly, argued that what Davies, L.J., said was obiter dictum; nevertheless, an obiter dictum from a learned lord justice who was himself on frequent occasions a member of this court carries particular weight. What Davies, L.J., said arose in this way. It was an appeal to set aside a decree absolute. Counsel for the appellant argued that, if the circumstances on which he relied had arisen before decree absolute, the application would have been made to the Divisional Court under r. 36 and not to the Court of Appeal; and that the Divisional Court, according to its practice, would almost automatically have granted a re-hearing. Davies, L.J., dealt with that argument in a passage with which I respectfully agree. He said (5):

" As it seems to me, these applications in the Divisional Court fall into at least two classes. There is the class where the applicant comes along and says ' I was not served; I knew nothing about it ', or, ' I was deceived: all the proceedings took place behind my back '. In that sort of case the applicant gets a re-hearing almost automatically. The other class of case is the *Winter* (2) class of case, the *Tucker* (6) class of case, and this class of case, where an applicant may come along and say ' I knew all about this: I chose not to defend; but it was all wrong—let me defend now and grant me a re-hearing '. In a case of that latter kind, speaking for

(1) [1964] 2 All E.R. 58 at p. 64; [1964] P. 277 at p. 284.
(2) [1942] 2 All E.R. 390; [1942] P. 151.
(3) [1947] 2 All E.R. 578; [1948] P. 46.
(4) [1965] 1 All E.R. 1063; [1965] P. 147.
(5) [1965] 1 All E.R. at p. 1010; [1965] P. at pp. 162, 163.
(6) [1949] P. 105.

myself, I think that for an applicant to succeed he has to convince the Divisional Court, or this court if it comes before this court, that on the evidence before the court on the application as a whole it is more probable that the decree was obtained contrary to the justice of the case."

DAVIES, L.J., was expressly not purporting to be exhaustive; and it is true that this case does not fall precisely within either of the two categories to which he referred; but it does fall, in my view, close to the first class of case and a long way from the second. The husband has at all times desired to defend himself against the wife's charges. I do not think that he is personally in any way to blame that his case was not presented before the court when the wife's petition was heard. If there were to be any criticism—and I do not say for a moment that it would be justified—it might be levelled at his solicitor; but not at himself. In the ordinary way, this court requires an affidavit as to merits rather more ample than we have in the husband's here; but, speaking for myself, I think that he has dealt just sufficiently with the subject-matter of the petition and with his attitude to the wife's charges. This court, moreover, normally requires a draft answer to be exhibited to the affidavit, so that we are apprised what precisely is the defence that an applicant wishes to make and what are the issues which will arise on a rehearing. This, however, is an applicant in person—one, moreover, who is at a disadvantage even compared to an English layman when up against our legal procedures—and I think that any shortcoming in his presentation of the case is to be excused.

My conclusion, therefore, is that we ought to set aside the decree nisi and give the husband leave to file an answer out of time, so that the suit, if that answer is pursued, is tried out in the defended list.

CAIRNS, J.: I agree, and add only a few words about the passage which SIR JOCELYN SIMON, P., has cited from the judgment of DAVIES, L.J., in *Stevens v. Stevens* (7). I notice that, in that passage, DAVIES, L.J., said, " As it seems to me, these applications in the Divisional Court fall into at least two classes ". I think that there is probably at least one more class. That is the type of case where the respondent in divorce proceedings is aware that the proceedings are in progress and is anxious to defend and, although no sort of deception has occurred, nevertheless, through ignorance or lack of full advice, he is unaware of the necessity of taking procedural steps in order to preserve his position and has no knowledge of the actual hearing until after it has taken place. In such circumstances, I am of opinion that this court should not automatically, or almost automatically, grant a re-hearing, but on the other hand should not require to be satisfied that, if there were a re-hearing, a different result would be more probable than not. I think that it is necessary and sufficient that the applicant should satisfy the court that he has a case which he wishes to put forward and which, if accepted, might well lead to a different result. The court is not bound to accept the applicant's affidavit at its face value, but on the other hand should not attempt to make any such investigation of its truth as would be appropriate at the hearing of the suit. I would have preferred to have more details of the husband's case than are set out in the affidavit which he has sworn here, but, in order to avoid delay and further expense, and bearing in mind that the applicant is appearing here in person, I am content to proceed on the basis of the existing affidavit. I take the view that that affidavit is sufficient to show that the applicant has a case which he wants to put before the court and which, if accepted, might well lead to a result different from the result of the first hearing.

I agree with what SIR JOCELYN SIMON, P., has proposed.

SIR JOCELYN SIMON, P.: I should like to express my concurrence with the way that CAIRNS, J., has put the matter in his judgment. The category of

---

(7) [1965] 1 All E.R. at p. 1010; [1965] P. at pp. 162, 163.

case which he has defined is, indeed, the largest of the r. 36 applications to this court; and I also respectively agree with his definition of the attitude of the court towards it.

The order, then, is that the decree nisi should be set aside and a re-hearing ordered; leave given to the husband to present an answer within twenty-eight days.

Order accordingly.

Solicitors: *Huntley, Millard & Co.* (for the wife).

[*Reported by* ALICE BLOOMFIELD, *Barrister-at-Law.*]

BUCKLEY v. JOHN ALLEN & FORD (OXFORD), LTD.

[QUEEN'S BENCH DIVISION (Phillimore, J.), December 20, 21, 1966.]

Fatal Accident—Damages—Assessment—Deductions from damages—Re-marriage of widow—Prospects of re-marriage not adverted to in evidence—Widow aged thirty-eight with four children—Whether court should take any such prospect into consideration—Continued residence in former home as protected tenant, but widow now sub-letting three rooms—Whether income from sub-letting deductible from damages.

In July, 1964, B., aged thirty-five, was killed in a motor accident in respect of which the defendants admitted liability. B.'s widow, aged thirty-eight at the trial, brought an action for damages on behalf of herself and her four children (aged eleven, nine, six and three) under the Fatal Accidents Act, 1846, and Law Reform (Miscellaneous Provisions) Act, 1934. B.'s earnings since 1962 had been sufficient to enable him to pay a basic dependancy, including rent and holiday expenses, amounting to £1,700 per annum, and his actual and potential earnings were very considerably higher (see p. 543, letter A, post). B.'s widow continued with her children to occupy the original home as a protected tenant under the Rent Acts, but since her husband's death had sub-let three rooms at a total rental of £9 per week. She was not questioned, when giving evidence, about re-marriage, but the defendants submitted that the court should make a deduction in assessing damages for the widow's prospects of re-marriage.

Held: (i) the damages to be awarded should be of such amount as would restore the widow to the position at the deceased's death, and accordingly no deduction would be made in respect of the money received by the widow as rent for the rooms she had chosen to sub-let (see p. 542, letter B, post).

(ii) in the absence both of any evidence on the prospects of this widow's re-marriage and of any relevant statistics on the re-marriage of widows, the court would not make any deduction in respect of the widow's chances of re-marriage (see p. 542, letters H and I, post).

[**Editorial Note.** In regard to reducing the estimate of damages in view of uncertainties, e.g., re-marriage of a widow, see also per LORD WRIGHT in *Davies v. Powell Duffryn Associated Collieries, Ltd.* ([1942] 1 All E.R. at p. 665, letters A, B).

As to the reduction of damages under the Fatal Accidents Acts on account of re-marriage of the widow, see 27 HALSBURY'S LAWS (3rd Edn.) 102, para. 111, text and note (*o*), and as to deductions from damages on account of other pecuniary advantages enjoyed by the widow, see ibid., pp. 103, 104, para. 113; and for cases, see 36 DIGEST (Repl.) 221-224, *1176-1194*.

For the Fatal Accidents Acts, 1846 to 1959, see 17 HALSBURY'S STATUTES (2nd Edn.) 4, 9 and 39 ibid., 941.

Dicta of PHILLIMORE, J., at p. 542, disapproved in GOODBURN v. THOMAS COTTON. [1968] 1 All E.R. 518.

For the Law Reform (Miscellaneous Provisions) Act, 1934, s. 1, see 9 HALS-
BURY'S STATUTES (2nd Edn.) 792.]

Case referred to:

   Heatley v. *Steel Co. of Wales, Ltd.*, [1953] 1 All E.R. 489; [1953] 1 W.L.R.
      405; Digest (Cont. Vol. A) 1208, *1194a*.

Action.

This was an action for damages under the Fatal Accidents Act, 1846, and the
Law Reform (Miscellaneous Provisions) Act, 1934, by Mrs. Martha Philomena
Buckley, suing for herself and her four children as administratrix of the estate
of her deceased husband, Michael Joseph Buckley, who was killed in a motor
accident on the highway on July 16, 1964. Liability was admitted by the
defendants. The facts are set out in the judgment.

   Hugh Griffiths, Q.C., and *Patrick Bennett* for the plaintiff.
   C. J. S. French, Q.C., and *John Griffiths* for the defendants.

                                                      Cur. adv. vult.

   Dec. 21.   **PHILLIMORE, J.:** This action is brought as a result of the
death of Michael Joseph Buckley who was killed on July 16, 1964, in a road
accident. The plaintiff, who is his widow, brings it as administratrix of his estate,
on her own behalf and on behalf of her children under the Fatal Accidents Acts,
1846 to 1959. The deceased man was driving a motor vehicle along the London
Road at Ascot when a caravan, which was being towed along in front, became
detached from its trailer and slewed across the road and he ran into it. In those
circumstances the defendants admit liability. The only question that I have to
determine is how much should be awarded. In all the circumstances the sum is
bound to be substantial.

   The plaintiff and the deceased were married on Sept. 28, 1954. She was five
months older than her husband; he was thirty-five at the time of his death and
she is now thirty-eight. There are four children, three girls aged respectively
eleven, nine and six years and a boy, Michael, aged three years. In June, 1962,
they moved into a house at 66, Clarendon Drive, Putney. The house has six
bedrooms, three living-rooms and the usual offices. They were tenants under a
lease for three years granted from June 16, 1962, at a rent of £350 a year, the
tenants paying the rates. The lease granted permission to sub-let the whole or
any part of the house. As a result of the Protection from Eviction Act 1964, the
plaintiff is now occupying the house as a protected tenant.

   It is clear that the deceased was a good husband and a good father and in
addition he was a tremendous worker and a very capable man. Basically he was
a carpenter by trade, but he had a wide knowledge of the building trade, he could
read plans and supervise men and he was a man destined to get on. Apart from
his daily work he used to work many evenings and at weekends doing odd jobs
in the neighbourhood. I have had no details, but it is safe to assume that he
earned considerable sums of money a week on which he probably paid no tax.
On Nov. 11, 1963, he started work for a Mr. Gaughan who was a sub-contractor
at a site at Arborfield. Chivers, Ltd., the well-known contractors, were the main
contractors. His income tax returns show that during that winter he earned
£22 10s. a week and in addition he was paid £6 subsistence a week, that being
because the site was over thirty miles from London. From Apr. 5, 1964, onwards,
when the hours of work were increased and finished at 6 o'clock instead of 4
o'clock, Mr. Gaughan's records show that the deceased's earnings were just under
£38 and he still got the £6 a week subsistence.

   On the site was a Mr. Spiller, the surveyor agent for Chivers, Ltd., and he
observed Mr. Buckley and thought that he was an outstanding workman and
accordingly offered him a sub-contract to do concrete work, which was accepted.
On June 8, 1964, the deceased started as a sub-contractor and he worked his

gang up to about seven or eight men and carried on until his death some thirty-nine days later. Mr. Spiller has investigated the figures of the deceased's earnings and his calculations show that after paying his men and other expenses the deceased made a profit of over £94 a week. That may be too high, but I think not by much, because Mr. Gaughan told me that as a sub-contractor one reckons to make about £10 a man and I am content to accept that the deceased was making at least £70 a week gross. Mr. Spiller made it clear that as far as Chivers, Ltd. were concerned they looked on the deceased as their number one sub-contractor on outside work. Indeed, if he were alive now, Mr. Spiller said, he would be working on a similar contract at Aldershot, on similar pay. One has to remember that in the building trade the future is, to some extent, uncertain because of present economic conditions, but I think it is clear that so long as Chivers, Ltd., had this type of contract the deceased would have been in business as one of their sub-contractors. It is then clear that his earning potential was higher than his actual earnings during the winter before his death and so the potential dependancy figure of this widow is much higher than the actual dependancy derived from sums paid in the days before this man became a sub-contractor. I have to assess her dependancy figure and most of the items are undisputed.

First of all, he gave the plaintiff £14 a week housekeeping, out of which she calculates that he cost about £2 10s. because he very seldom took food with him for his lunch and only relied on her for his breakfast and his evening meal. That is about £600 a year housekeeping money, after deducting £2 a week from £14 a week. Then there is the rent of £350 and the rates and water rates; the rates used to be £70 and the water rates £4. Now the rates are £96 and the water rates £4 making £100. Then there were clothes for the plaintiff and the children; nobody quarrels with the figure of £200, which is what the plaintiff puts forward. Then there was fuel, domestic gas and hard fuel, and the total there, based largely on actual bills, is £155. Then, with the telephone at £30, and hire-purchase of the cooker at £12 (which is convenient to take at £10), the total is £1,445. In addition there are two disputed items. First of all, the cost of the annual holiday. It appears that the family used to go over to Ireland for three weeks and stay with the deceased's mother. The fares would be £60, and they used to pay the mother something but the plaintiff does not know how much, and then there would be presents and the cost of going out. For a couple with four children, it seems to me that £150 would be reasonable for this annual holiday, though counsel for the defence suggested it could be less. Finally, there is the motor car. The deceased had a Ford Consul, as well as a Dormobile, and no doubt he took the plaintiff and children out in them although he did spend a great deal of his week-ends doing these jobs. There were extra sums for housekeeping when the £14 was not quite enough—for presents, and for the expense incurred when he took the plaintiff out, and so on. These are all small items and it seems to me reasonable to assess them at £100, and that really makes a basic dependancy of £1,695, or, say, £1,700, to make a round sum. That figure is, of course, irrespective of any potential from the increase in his finances after he became a sub-contractor. I am satisfied that he had been earning sufficient to pay these sums and had paid them from June, 1962.

What deductions must I make? I have said that the plaintiff is a protected tenant. She has, however, let some of the rooms of her house; she has let two attic rooms and one room on the first floor for a total of £9 a week. Counsel for the defence says that I must take that off pound for pound. He says that the £9 a week represents the proceeds of the estate that she has inherited in the shape of the house, but counsel for the plaintiff says that I must disregard the sub-letting. He points out that I would disregard any money that she was earning, e.g., if she chose to run a boarding-house somewhere else; he submits that I must disregard anything she derives from this home because the duty of the court is to put her back in the same position as she enjoyed when she had the deceased's support, and he relies on *Heatley* v. *Steel Co. of Wales. Ltd.* (1). It seems to me that if she had not let these rooms nobody could have said that there was some notional sum that ought to be deducted on the basis that the family could occupy less accommodation than they had done before. There is a long delay between death and the award of compensation, and she and her family have to live. If, in order to survive, they double up as they have done, must the compensation be reduced? Must it be assessed on the basis that they must remain doubled up? What happens if all the lodgers leave? It seems to me that my duty is to award a sum that will put her back in the position that she enjoyed at the time of the deceased's death, and in my judgment she is not to receive less if she has taken in lodgers, any more than if she had sold this house and started a lodging-house somewhere else. Accordingly I make no deduction under this heading.

Secondly, it is said that I must take into account the prospects of the plaintiff's re-marrying, and must make a suitable deduction on the basis that she would be supported by her new husband. Counsel for the defendants did not ask her any question on this subject, an example which was naturally followed by her counsel. Having, however, abstained from asking her anything about it—and I can well understand his not doing so—counsel for the defendants now says, and it is the conventional argument, that any woman with the sum she is likely to receive is likely to re-marry. He suggested that she may not marry for perhaps seven years, but that she is likely to do so then because the children are older and largely off her hands. He says that she is an attractive woman. In this state of affairs I am wondering what is the evidence on which I must act. Am I to ask her to put on a bathing dress; because the witness box is calculated to disguise the figure? Equally, I know nothing of her temperament, I know nothing of her attitude to marriage. She may have some very good reason, perhaps a religious reason, for saying that she never will re-marry. She has had no chance to express her views. Has her marriage been an entirely happy experience? I do not know. On the other hand she may already be engaged to be married. On what do I assess the chances and fix the sum to be deducted from her compensation? After all, whatever men may like to think, women do not always want to re-marry. There are quite a lot of rich widows who prefer to remain single, and I confess that I am not sorry to avoid this problem. Is a judge fitted to assess the chance or chances or wishes of a lady about whom he knows so little and whom he has only encountered for twenty minutes when she was in the witness box, especially when no-one has broached the topic with her? Judges should, I think, act on evidence rather than guesswork. It seems to me that this particular exercise is not only unattractive but also is not one for which judges are equipped. Am I to label the plaintiff to her face as attractive or unattractive? If I have the temerity to apply the label, am I likely to be right? Supposing I say she is unattractive, it may well be that she has a friend who disagrees and has looked below the surface and found a charming character. The fact is that this exercise is a mistake. If there are statistics as to the likelihood of a widow re-marrying based on her age and the amount of her compensation, just as there are statistics on the expectancy of life, they might provide a yardstick for deduction in the absence of evidence of some special factor in the individual case. In the absence of some such yardstick I question whether, having decided what she has lost by the death of the deceased, any judge is qualified to assess whether or when she is likely to re-marry. Supposing she marries a man who is only concerned to spend her money? Is he to be treated as her new support in place of her former husband? I venture to suggest it is time judges were relieved of the need to enter into this particular guessing game. In this particular case I make no deduction for this lady's chances of re-marrying.

On top of the dependancy figure of £1,700 put forward as a basic figure by

---

(1) [1953] 1 All E.R. 489.

counsel for the plaintiff, it is said that the potential dependancy is much higher. The deceased was a man who earned about £70 a week gross in addition to what he earned by his work at night and at weekends in odd jobs in the neighbourhood. I have no doubt that he would have continued at the rate of about £70 a week. Every trade has its risks, but if anyone was set to go on earning at a high rate it was the deceased. At £70 a week he would earn over £3,500 a year. Tax on £3,500 for a man with a wife and four children would be £795, leaving him net £2,705. It is difficult in the face of these findings to doubt that the dependancy figure may have risen to £2,000 a year. However, I must bear in mind the chances of illness and gaps between contracts, and the possibility that he might not have increased his payments to his family by so very much. I have come to the conclusion that the proper figure for dependancy is £1,850 a year. I have put the figure a little lower than I was intending to do because of the dispute about the last two figures in the sum making up the basic figure of £1,700. What is the proper multiplication? This is the age group in which after due allowance has been made for such factors as the receipt of the capital sum and the chances of life the multiplier is fifteen. Counsel for the defendants suggested thirteen but I do not think that he did so with much conviction. In my judgment, therefore, the proper figure for compensation under the Fatal Accidents Act, 1846 to 1959, in this particular case is £26,750 (2). It is perhaps worth remembering that at £1,700 the widow will have to dip into the capital, since that figure would produce £25,500 at fifteen years' purchase. This at six per cent. would produce a gross sum of £1,530 a year. Taxed as unearned income she would pay £280 a year and this would only leave her £1,250 a year to spend. If the dependancy is £1,700 she would have to dip into capital at the rate of £450 per year. She will have to dip into capital at the higher figure which I have awarded. Her expectancy of life is, in fact, on the tables, about thirty-eight years. In any event a large part of the money must be divided between the children.

I have to award a sum under the Law Reform (Miscellaneous Provisions) Act, 1934. Subject to anything learned counsel may say, I would award £1,365 3s., being £1,000 for loss of expectation of life and £365 3s. the special damages. Accordingly I would award the balance of £26,750 under the Fatal Accidents Act.

It remains to consider how much of that amount should be awarded in respect of the children. [HIS LORDSHIP, after considering a submission by counsel for the plaintiff, then ordered that the eldest child should receive £1,500, the second child £1,750, the third child £2,000, and the youngest child £2,500, these amounts to be placed on trust under arrangements to be made with the court's approval.]

Judgment for the plaintiff accordingly.

Solicitors: *Russell-Cooke, Potter & Chapman* (for the plaintiff); *Stanley & Co.* (for the defendants).

[*Reported by* K. DIANA PHILLIPS, *Barrister-at-Law.*]

---

(2) I.e., calculated after deducting £1,000 awarded under the Law Reform (Miscellaneous Provisions) Act, 1934, as indicated at letter F, infra.

Dictum of Lord Denning MR a
550 applied in Tarr v Tarr [1972
2 All ER 295

BIRMINGHAM AND MIDLAND MOTOR OMNIBUS CO., LTD.
v. WORCESTERSHIRE COUNTY COUNCIL.

[CHANCERY DIVISION (Stamp, J.), November 4, 23, 1966.]

[COURT OF APPEAL, CIVIL DIVISION (Lord Denning, M.R., Danckwerts and Winn, L.JJ.), December 7, 8, 1966.]

Highway—Obstruction—Dual Carriageway—Intersections—Highway authority extending central reservation so as to block intersections at junction of carriageway with road joining it—Erection by highway authority of " dual carriageway " sign at junction—Validity of highway authority's acts—Highways Act, 1959 (7 & 8 Eliz. 2 c. 25), s. 65 (1) (a), (b).

The defendant county council were the highway authority for a new dual carriageway by-pass. Where the by-pass joined the old road, M. Lane, there was a junction which comprised an elaborate system of intersections so that traffic could pass in several directions, but that junction was found to be a danger and hindrance to traffic using it. The county council put blocks of wood across the intersections so as to make the central reservation continuous all the way down the dual carriageway with the result that traffic which used to go straight across was diverted for a distance of 1¾ miles. The county council also put up at one of the intersections* a sign of a blue circle with a white arrow and under it " Dual carriageway ", which, under the Traffic Signs Regulations and General Directions 1964, they were entitled to put up on their own authority. The county council's suggestion was that by this sign they could stop traffic going across the intersection. On appeal against an injunction granted to the plaintiffs, an omnibus company, restraining the county council from blocking up the intersections, the county council contended that they had power to do so under s. 65 (1) (a) or (b)† of the Highways Act, 1959, or alternatively by means of traffic signs,

Held: (i) the county council had no power under s. 65 (1) of the Highways Act, 1959, to close the intersections to traffic, because—

(a) section 65 (1) (a) was limited to separating two streams of traffic going in opposite directions, and did not extend to blocking a cross-stream of traffic (see p. 550, letter C, p. 551, letter G, p. 552, letter I, and p. 553, letter B, post).

(b) the diversion of the crossing traffic for a substantial distance (1¾ miles) was not " regulating the movement of traffic " within s. 65 (1) (b) (see p. 550, letter D, p. 551, letter I, and p. 553, letter A, post);

(ii) although by virtue of the traffic sign which the county council erected they could indicate to traffic the direction in which it was to go along the dual carriageway, they were not entitled by the sign to stop traffic using a highway altogether and could not, therefore, use it effectively to prohibit traffic crossing at the intersection (see p. 550, letter I, and p. 552, letters B and C, post).

Per CURIAM: by virtue of the Traffic Signs General Directions 1966, the county council might achieve their object by putting up a " No entry " sign (No. 616) with the approval in writing of the Minister (see p. 551, letter C, and p. 552, letters B and C, post; cf. p. 548, letter I, post).

Appeal dismissed.

[As to statutory powers of highway authorities affecting dual carriageways, see 19 HALSBURY'S LAWS (3rd Edn.) 214, para. 344.

For the Highway Act, 1959, s. 65, see 39 HALSBURY'S STATUTES (2nd Edn.) 486.]

---

* The sign, as viewed from the old road, Manor Lane, when approaching on it the intersection faced the approaches and by the arrow on the sign indicated the direction of the traffic on the dual carriageway, thus, in effect, intimating that the approaching traffic in Manor Lane should not cross, but that it should turn left and proceed along the dual carriageway in the same direction as the west-east traffic on that carriageway.

† Section 65 (1) is set out at p. 547, letter A, post.

Cases referred to:

Howard-Flanders v. *Maldon Corpn.*, [1926] All E.R. Rep. 110;   135 L.T. 6;
    90 J.P. 97; 26 Digest (Repl.) 454, *1492.*

Toronto (City) Municipal Corpn. v. *Virgo*, [1896] A.C. 88;   65 L.J.P.C. 4;
    73 L.T. 449; 38 Digest (Repl.) 172, *73.*

Action.

This was a motion for an interlocutory injunction in an action commenced
by writ dated Oct. 19, 1966, by Birmingham & Midland Omnibus Co., Ltd.
against Worcestershire County Council (" the county council ") whereby the
plaintiffs sought an injunction to restrain the defendants from obstructing the
public highway known as " Manor Lane, Halesowen, Nr. Birmingham " by
the erection of a central reservation at the junction between Manor Lane and
the eastern extension of Halesowen by-pass, and ordering the county council to
remove on or before Dec. 3, 1966, the central reservation erected by them at the
junction. By consent the motion was treated as the trial of the action.

The following summary of fact is taken from the judgments. At Halesowen
near Birmingham there is an old highway called Manor Lane. Towards the end
of 1965 the new motorway M.5 was brought within a mile of it. A new road was
made so as to connect up Manor Lane with the new motorway. It was called the
Halesowen by-pass, eastern extension, and was nearly a mile long. At one end
of this new road, there was a big roundabout at the point where the new road
joined the motorway. At the other end of this new road, there was a junction
where the new road joined the old road, Manor Lane. This new road was a dual
carriageway. At the end where it joined Manor Lane there was the junction,
which comprised an elaborate system of intersections so that traffic could cross in
several directions. The new road was opened in November, 1965. It was common
ground that the junction, when constructed was a dangerous one. If one were
coming from Manor Lane and going south-west to join what used to be the lower
part of Manor Lane, one came to the new double carriageway. One had first
to cross the west-east carriageway of the new road approximately at right angles,
and then, after pausing in the gap of the central reservation dividing the two
carriageways, one turned right into the east-west carriageway. There were no
traffic lights nor roundabout, and the dual carriageway was subject to no special
speed limit. There were eighteen accidents in under a year: eight of them causing
serious injuries. As early as March, 1966, the situation was causing anxiety, and
suggestions had been made that the gap in the central reservation should be
closed so as to prevent traffic from Manor Lane gaining direct access to the west-
bound carriageway of the new double carriageway road, Manor Way. The plaintiffs protested against such closure to the borough of Halesowen, which was the
authority having power to make traffic regulation orders pursuant to s. 26* of
the Road Traffic Act, 1960. The proposal had, however, been made by the county
council. Subsequently meetings took place in April and June, 1966, attended by
the Minister of Transport, the county council, the borough of Halesowen and the
plaintiffs. No decision was taken at these meetings. Then, without earlier
warning, by letter dated Oct. 11, 1966, the county council informed the plaintiffs
that the gap in the central reservation at the junction would be blocked by the
county council on or about Oct. 19, 1966. On that day the county council, who
were the highway authority for these roads, put blocks of wood across the intersections at the junctions. These blocks of wood were so placed as to make the
central reservation continuous all the way down the dual carriageway, so that
there was no longer an elaborate series of intersections but only a simple fork.
The result was that traffic which used to go straight across was now diverted.

---

* 40 Halsbury's Statutes (2nd Edn.) 732. The authority having power to make
traffic regulations is specified in sub-s. (2) of s. 26. The section has been amended by the
Road Traffic Act, 1962, s. 8, s. 51 (2), Sch. 1, Pt. 3, para. 28, Sch. 5, and by the London
Government Act, 1962, s. 15 (1), Sch. 5, Pt. 1, para. 4, but none of the amendments is
material to the present decision.

In order to get across to the other side, it had to go seven-eighths of a mile up to the roundabout on the M.5 and seven-eighths of a mile back again, making 1¾ miles to get across. The plaintiffs held road service licences under s. 134 of the Road Traffic Act, 1960*, to provide three bus services along Manor Lane. This diversion of 1¾ miles involved the plaintiffs in a great deal of extra driving and time and expense. It put their timetable out of gear. In order to overcome the difficulty, they found that they had to alter their routes altogether. This meant that the passengers on the buses were put to great inconvenience; so much so that people gave up using the buses. On Oct. 19, 1966, the plaintiffs issued their writ and moved ex parte for an injunction, which was refused. The plaintiffs alleged that the obstruction at the intersection constituted a nuisance in that the exercise of rights of passage along the public highway was prevented. It was not in issue at the hearing that the plaintiffs had sufficient interest to sustain the action without joining the Attorney-General†.

E. S. Fay, Q.C., and *N. C. H. Browne-Wilkinson* for the plaintiffs.
E. I. Goulding, Q.C., and *J. M. E. Byng* for the county council.

Cur. adv. vult.

Nov. 23, 1966. **STAMP, J.,** read the following judgment in which, having referred to the nature of the application, and having summarised the facts, he continued: There are elaborate procedures whereunder public highways may be stopped up. I do not find it necessary to examine them; but since it is under s. 65 of the Highways Act, 1959, that the defendants seek to justify the action which they have taken, I should, perhaps, refer to s. 9 of that Act (1). That section enables the Minister to make an order authorising him (inter alia) to stop up, divert or alter a highway that crosses or enters the route of a trunk road, but there are important qualifications of that power. He must, for example, be satisfied that another reasonably convenient route is available or will be provided before the highway is stopped up, and where he proposes to make an order (2) he has to advertise his proposals, serve certain persons with those proposals, consider objections and, in certain cases, cause a local inquiry to be held. The section is relevant only to this extent, that it supports the submission of counsel for the plaintiffs, which I accept, that highways are not lightly to be stopped up and a power to do so is to be found only in a section which confers clear power for the purpose in the most explicit terms and is not to be implied by mere inference. No order has been made by any competent authority stopping up Manor Lane.

Counsel for the county council is not disposed to quarrel with this approach and it is not contended that the county council, acting pursuant to s. 65 of the Highways Act, 1959, which is the section on which they rely, are entitled to obstruct the highway except to the limited extent authorised by that section. He points out that any diversion of the highway, including the construction of a roundabout contemplated by s. 65, unless duly authorised, involves an infringement of the right of the public to proceed along the highway. It follows that it is necessary to find in s. 65 in explicit terms the authority which the defendants require in order to obstruct the right of the public to proceed along the highway.

Section 65 is in Part V of the Act, which is headed "Improvement of Highways", and the section itself is immediately preceded by a cross heading: "Dual carriageways, roundabouts and cycle tracks." The section is in the following terms:

---

* 40 HALSBURY'S STATUTES (2nd Edn.) 830.

† A member of the public can maintain an action in respect of a nuisance on a highway only if he has suffered substantial injury beyond that suffered by the rest of the public, but the Attorney-General can maintain such an action without proof of damage; see 19 HALSBURY'S LAWS (3rd Edn.) 280, paras. 442, 443, text and notes (*f*), (*h*).

(1) For s. 9 and s. 65 of the Act of 1959, see 39 HALSBURY'S STATUTES (2nd Edn.) 421, 486.

(2) See the Highways Act, 1959, Sch. 1; 39 HALSBURY'S STATUTES (2nd Edn.) 722.

" (1) A highway authority may, in relation to a highway maintainable at the public expense by them, being a highway which consists of or comprises a made-up carriageway, construct and maintain works in that carriageway— (a) along any length of the highway, for separating a part of the carriageway which is to be used by traffic moving in one direction from a part of the carriageway which is to be used (whether at all times or at particular times only) by traffic moving in the other direction; (b) at cross roads or other junctions, for regulating the movement of traffic.

" (2) The powers conferred by the foregoing subsection shall include power to light any such works as aforesaid, to pave, grass or otherwise cover them or any part of them, to erect pillars, walls, rails or fences on, around or across them or any part of them, and to plant on them trees, shrubs and other vegetation either for ornament or in the interests of safety."

I need not refer to sub-ss. (3), (4) or (5), but it is to be observed that s. 66 deals with cycle tracks.

It is to para. (b) of ss. 65 (1) that the county council point as authorising what they have done. There are two features of s. 65 (1) (b) which are to be noted. In the first place, the works contemplated to be constructed and maintained are works for regulating the movement of traffic and not for stopping its movement. Secondly, the works contemplated are at cross roads or other junctions. The crossing of traffic at cross roads is a problem with which one is only too familiar and I do not doubt that on the true construction of para. (b) the works thereby authorised are works not for preventing but for enabling, facilitating and improving the movement of traffic across the cross roads to which the paragraph refers. I accept the submission of counsel for the defendants that this does involve some interference with the highway and of the right of the public to proceed along it. But whatever may be the limits or extent of the powers conferred by the paragraph they do not in my judgment extend to enable the closing of the crossing and the diversion of the traffic to a wholly different crossing point. No doubt there may be some diversion of the cross traffic to facilitate the crossing, such as there must always be when a roundabout is constructed, and where, for example, complex works are necessary to carry traffic across a complicated point of intersection, the diversion must be greater than would otherwise be the case. By no stretch of imagination, however, can the roundabout upwards of three-quarters of a mile down the east-bound carriageway of Manor Lane, which is designed for a wholly different purpose, be regarded as part of the crossing; and in my judgment the obstruction amounts to nothing less than an obstruction which prevents traffic coming from Manor Lane from crossing and proceeding in a westerly direction. The obstruction is in my judgment not a work for regulating the movement of traffic within the meaning of para. (b) because it does not assist, facilitate or improve the crossing of the cross roads but prevents traffic from using the cross-roads at all. The junction has simply ceased to be a cross-roads.

An alternative argument is advanced on behalf of the county council which seems to me, whether technically right or not, to have little merit: for the reason that if it was well founded it would cause great traffic confusion. The county council have erected and installed at the junction, pursuant to s. 52 of the Road Traffic Act, 1960, the familiar traffic sign consisting of a white arrow on a circular blue background together with a plate under it inscribed " dual carriageway ". The arrow points along the east-bound carriageway towards the roundabout. By virtue of direction 6 of the Traffic Signs General Directions 1964, as substituted (3), this combination may be used without the making of an order, regulation, by-law or notice prohibiting or restricting the use of the road by traffic. The result of this is that the drivers of traffic disobeying the arrow would commit

---

(3) A new direction 6 of the Traffic Signs General Directions 1964, which comprise Part 2 of the Traffic Signs Regulations and General Directions 1964, S.I. 1964 No. 187, was substituted by the Traffic Signs General Directions 1966, S.I. 1966, No. 489.

an offence under s. 14 of the Road Traffic Act, 1960, (4). What is said is that, if by the effect of these signs, drivers would be committing an offence if they crossed the east-bound carriageway of Manor Way at the point at which the arrow is placed in order to proceed to the west-bound carriageway of Manor Way, how can the county council be committing a nuisance by placing an obstruction across the gap which prevents them from doing so? In point of fact the traffic signs relied on are placed at a point where, but for the obstruction, the drivers of traffic emerging from Manor Lane would hardly see the signs at all; and this ground alone is in my judgment sufficient to dispose of the argument. But counsel for the plaintiffs very properly was prepared to assume for the purpose of testing the defendants' contention that there was no obstruction of the gap and that the signs were placed at a point where they would be readily visible by drivers of traffic emerging from Manor Lane. If the contention advanced by the county council is correct it clearly does enable the appropriate authority, by means of such signs as have been erected, to prevent traffic from crossing dual carriageways; and it is contended that so long as the authority acts bona fide—whatever that expression may mean in connexion with the installation of a traffic sign—the authority may divert traffic along a dual carriageway for some indefinite distance notwithstanding the existence of a road crossing the carriageway. Counsel for the plaintiffs is entitled to characterise such a state of affairs as legislation by traffic signs. He also points to the absurdity of the consequences. Approaching the standard form of roundabout from whichever of the four roads which there meet and intersect one may see one of these signs consisting of a white arrow on a blue background indicating that one should turn left, not right, and one does so. But one will not be obliged to follow the similar sign placed opposite the end of the other three approach roads, for if all drivers were to comply with all four arrows the roundabout would become a roundabout in a sense in which that word is not used in the relevant legislation. As LORD SIMONDS remarked in another context the reductio ad absurdum is sometimes a cogent argument and I accept the submission of counsel for the plaintiffs that these signs are directed only to those persons interested or concerned. If one wants to travel along a double carriageway one must comply with the sign which tells one along which side of it to proceed and must not turn round and drive against the flow of traffic. But if one wants to cross the carriageway and there is no obstruction in the way one is not required to comply with the sign that tells one how to proceed along it. If going along a road one comes to an intersection, the road on the left being marked with one of these signs with an indication that the street is a one-way street, one is not bound to turn to the left but may proceed on one's way. On the photograph M.B.G. 1 exhibited to the affidavit of Michael George Burkes, which reveals the situation as it was before the obstruction was placed across the gap in the central reservation, there is to be seen one of these white arrows on a blue background indicating that traffic emerging from Manor Lane and crossing through the gap was to proceed to the right of the post on which the sign is placed; but no-one would suppose for a single moment that this sign was directed to traffic proceeding from the west along the east-bound carriageway or that such traffic was bound to turn to the right and travel back from whence it came. The well-known " no entry " sign consisting of a white rectangular block on a red background, is the sign a driver may expect to see if he may not enter a street and it is, I think, not without significance that under direction 6 of the Traffic Signs General Directions 1964, as amended (5), which is the direction on which the county council rely, the " No entry " sign (except when placed at a site which has been approved in writing by or on behalf of the Minister or the Secretary of State), may be placed on or near a road only to indicate the effect of an order, regulation, by-law or notice which prohibits or restricts the use of the road by vehicular traffic.

---

(4) Section 14 of the Act of 1960: 40 HALSBURY'S STATUTES (2nd Edn.) 723 has been amended by the Road Traffic Act. 1962, s. 8, Sch. 1, para. 13; 42 ibid., 895, 924.
(5) See footnote (3), p. 547, ante.

Injunction for removal of obstruction within ten days; order suspended for seven days and, if notice of appeal served within that period, until disposal of appeal: inquiry as to damages.

[*Reported by* JENIFER SANDELL, *Barrister-at-Law.*]

The county council appealed. The appeal was specially expedited and on Dec. 8, 1966, their lordships delivered judgment (6).

Anthony Cripps, Q.C., and *J. M. E. Byng* for the county council.
E. S. Fay, Q.C., and *N. C. H. Browne-Wilkinson* for the plaintiffs, the omnibus company.

LORD DENNING, M.R., having summarised the facts, said: At the outset I must point out that there are two authorities who are concerned with these roads. The defendant county council are the highway authority. They are responsible for all works of construction, improvement or repair of the roads. Their activities come under the Highways Act, 1959. The Halesowen Borough Council are the traffic authority. They are the authority which makes orders prohibiting or regulating the use of the road by vehicular traffic, subject to confirmation by the Minister. Their activities come under the Road Traffic Act, 1960. One can well see that there is on occasions a conflict of interests between these two authorities. The county council have in mind the interests of this dual carriageway and the fast through traffic. Whereas the borough council have in mind the local people who want to cross the road close at hand and who do not want to go the extra 1¾ miles diversion. It would appear that the borough council could have made traffic regulations so as to stop the traffic crossing by way of these intersections, subject to confirmation by the Minister; but they have not done so, save as to a " U " turn. So the county council naturally enough felt that they must do something. That is why they blocked up the intersections with blocks of wood. According to the report of the chief inspector of police, this alteration has been successful. He said:

" I have noted that all congestion which had previously been caused to traffic, especially at peak hours, travelling down Manor Lane to Manor Way, has ceased. I have also noted there is no longer the problem and hazard created by vehicles which used to leave works premises on the north side of Manor Way and make ' U ' turns . . ."

there are no queues as before. He supports the work done by the county council and says that if the former gap was

" reopened to vehicular traffic, great confusion would be caused to motorists, and there would be a considerable and real risk that serious accidents might occur."

Still the question is: have the county council any right to block up the intersections like this? The county council claim that they have the right by reason of s. 65 (1) of the Highways Act, 1959, which provides:

" A highways authority may, in relation to a highway maintainable at the public expense by them, being a highway which consists of or comprises a made-up carriageway, construct and maintain works in that carriageway— (*a*) along any length of the highway, for separating a part of the carriageway which is to be used by traffic moving in one direction from a part of the carriageway which is to be used (whether at all times or at particular times only) by traffic moving in the other direction; (*b*) at cross roads or other junctions, for regulating the movement of traffic."

---

(6) Viz., seven weeks and one day after the obstruction was erected.

It is plain that para. (*a*) empowers the county council to make a central reservation in a dual carriageway so as to separate the line of traffic going one way from the line of traffic going the other way. Paragraph (*b*) empowers the county council to make a roundabout so as to prevent traffic going straight across and to make it go round a small circle. Although those are the obvious applications of para. (*a*) and para. (*b*), the question is whether the county council are empowered to do what they have done in this case.

Counsel for the county council relies in the first place on para. (*a*). He says that, by putting in the blocks of wood, the county council have separated the traffic in one direction from the traffic in the other direction. That is true. But at the same time the council have done much more. They have actually prevented traffic crossing by means of the intersecting portions of the highway. That is not permissible. It is one thing to separate lines of traffic. It is another thing to prevent it moving in its desired direction at all. The cross-traffic here does desire to use the intersecting portion of the highway. The county council have no right under para. (*a*) to block up those portions. Counsel for the county council next relies on para. (*b*). He says that these works were for " regulating the movement of traffic ". This paragraph would justify works which send traffic round a roundabout, or sending traffic up, say, one hundred yards in one direction and back one hundred yards in another. But does it extend to works which send the traffic seven-eighths of a mile up in one direction and seven-eighths of a mile down in another? Thus making it go an extra distance of some 1¾ miles. Does that come within the words " regulating the movement of traffic "? I think not. In *City of Toronto Municipal Corpn.* v. *Virgo* (7), LORD DAVEY said that a power to " regulate " and " govern " seems to imply the continued existence of that which is to be " regulated " or " governed ". So, here, when a highway authority simply sends the traffic round a roundabout or a short diversion, they can fairly be said to be " regulating the movement of traffic "; but if it forces the traffic to go 1¾ miles out of its way, it ceases to be " regulating " the traffic. It is equivalent to prohibiting it.

I am afraid, therefore, that, however sensible the county council have been, they have exceeded their legal powers. They have no right to block up the intersections under s. 65. I am confirmed in this view by the provisions in relation to a trunk road in s. 9 of the Highways Act, 1959. When the Minister is making or improving a trunk road and wants to divert or stop up a highway, he has to make sure that there is another reasonably convenient road, and he has to go through the machinery of public notices and local inquiry and all the rest. It would be strange if the county council could do it when the Minister could not.

Then counsel for the county council submitted that, even though the county council were not entitled to put these blocks of wood in the highway, nevertheless they were entitled to put up certain traffic signs on the highway; and he said that, by the traffic signs, they could produce the same result. At one of the intersections they have put up a sign of a blue circle with a white arrow and under it " Dual carriageway ". This is a sign which, under the traffic directions (8), the county council are entitled to put up on their own authority. It is mandatory. It must be obeyed. If it is not obeyed, the person acts unlawfully. The county council suggests that, by such a sign, they can stop people going across the intersection, even if it is not blocked up with blocks of wood. I do not think that this is correct. By virtue of this sign the highway authority can point out to traffic the direction in which it is to go along the dual carriageway; but the highway authority is not entitled by this sign to stop traffic using a highway altogether, even though it is only an intersecting highway. In order to stop traffic altogether, there should be a " no entry " sign. Until recently this needed the authority of the borough council as the traffic regulation authority. Under

(7) [1896] A.C. 88 at p. 93.
(8) The Traffic Signs Regulations and General Directions 1964 (S.I. 1964 No. 1857), as amended; cf. p. 547, footnote (3), ante.

s. 26 and s. 29 of the Road Traffic Act, 1960, and the regulations made thereunder (9), the borough council could make an order prohibiting the use of a highway. It could stop traffic from crossing this junction by means of the intersection. But they would have to give public notice and there would have to be a public inquiry; at any rate, when they are interfering with a bus service. Here the borough council have made no such order. They have not made any " No entry " order. They have applied for a " No ' U ' turn " order, but so far they do not seem to have proceeded with it. Very recently there has been a new direction which appears to authorise the county council to put up a sign " No entry " at this intersection. By the Traffic Signs General Directions 1966 (S.I. 1966 No. 489), a " No entry " sign (No. 616) can be placed on a site when it has been approved in writing by or on behalf of the Minister or by the Secretary of State. Under this new direction I think that it should be possible for the county council themselves, if the Minister or Secretary of State approved, to put up a new " No entry " sign. The county council might in that way be able to ensure the safety which they desire; but I do not think that they can do it on their own without the Minister's approval.

In my judgment, therefore, the county council were not justified in law in blocking up this junction. If there had been power in law to block it up, the only restriction on them would be that their conduct would have to be reasonable, as in *Howard-Flanders* v. *Maldon Corpn.* (10); but that does not arise as they have no power in law to block it up. I think that the plaintiff omnibus company are entitled to say that the county council have exceeded their legal powers. The injunction must go. I would dismiss this appeal.

DANCKWERTS, L.J.: I agree, but with some reluctance, because I can see that the defendants, the Worcestershire County Council, have been acting with goodwill and the best intentions to try to bring to an end the chaos at this particular junction which has resulted in so many accidents. The matter really depends on the proper construction of s. 65 (1) of the Highways Act, 1959. That section is concerned with the powers of a highway authority in connexion with a made-up carriageway. It regulates or decides the works which can be carried out by the highway authority in that carriageway. Paragraphs (*a*) and (*b*) are dealing with two things. Paragraph (*a*) seems to me to be dealing with the separation of two different streams of traffic; it does not seem to me particularly apt at all to deal with the situation at the point of junction in the present case. Paragraph (*b*) is dealing with cross roads and other junctions, and the object is given as " for regulating the movement of traffic ". It is obvious that among the things which the legislature had in mind were roundabouts, and the side-note to the section confirms that impression. What puzzles me is that roundabouts vary considerably, according to the situation of the junction with which they are intended to deal. The objection which is taken in the present case is based on the closing of established highways. It seems to me that every roundabout that is made must to some extent involve the closing of a portion of a highway, because the roundabout will be a circle. For instance, take the case of cross roads. The bits of the cross roads, being highways, where they cross each way will be shielded from use by the public and the public will be compelled to go round so much of the roundabout as is required for them to reach their proper destination. In some cases large roundabouts might include quite a substantial portion of the old highway and abolish it in that manner. As LORD DENNING, M.R., has said, it must be a question of degree. The trouble then is where to draw the line.

I have been very puzzled about this and my opinion has altered from time to time, but, on the whole, I have come to the conclusion that to send the traffic up as far as the nearest roundabout seven-eighths of a mile away is not a proper

---

(9) The Traffic Regulation Orders (Procedure) (England and Wales) Regulations, 1961 (S.I. 1961 No. 485).
(10) [1926] All E.R. Rep. 110.

exercise of the powers which are conferred in para. (*b*) of s. 65 (1). It seems clear that, if the county council had chosen to make a roundabout at the point of junction between Manor Lane and Manor Way, it would have been within their powers; but, as LORD DENNING, M.R., has said, in the circumstances they seem to have exceeded their powers and gone beyond what the section permitted in their case. Therefore, what was done was unlawful.

As regards the question of signs and so forth, I agree with the analysis and views expressed by LORD DENNING, M.R., and I do not find it necessary to add anything in respect of that point in the present case.

I also agree that the appeal must be dismissed.

WINN, L.J.: I agree with both the judgments delivered by my lords, and like DANCKWERTS, L.J., I agree specifically with all that has fallen from the lips of LORD DENNING, M.R., on the subject of the possible use and effect of installing traffic control signs. I think that it should be made clear that this court has not given, for my part at least, any expression of opinion on the reasonableness of the closure of the gap that formerly existed in this central verge. I think that we never reach that point, since it is only, as LORD DENNING has expressly said, on the hypothesis that there is a legal power to close that gap that any occasion arises for considering whether such closure, albeit lawful, might be unreasonable or reasonable. There must be many considerations properly to be explored in an inquiry where local residents and users of this bus service, as well as the plaintiffs, the Birmingham and Midlands Omnibus Co., Ltd., themselves, and persons having conflicting interests, might have a proper opportunity of presenting their views. In this court, very properly, those matters have not been fully explored. In so far as any attempt has been made to explore them, I think that it was irrelevant to the appeal.

The main question, of course, is whether or not s. 65 (1) of the Highways Act, 1959, gives power to do that which the defendants, the Worcestershire County Council saw fit to do, block up this former gap. In my opinion, one test, which in my limited experience usually proves to be a decisive test, of whether or not a purported exercise of a statutory power is within or without the power, so as to be intra or ultra vires, is to ask whether or not the person purporting to exercise that power can, applying the ordinary test of the reasonable juror, have rationally believed that he was exercising the power for the purpose for which Parliament expressly granted that power. If, with that test in mind, one looks at s. 65 (1) (*a*), the purpose stated is for separating the part of the carriageway which is to be used by traffic moving in one direction from the part which is to be used by traffic moving in the opposite direction. I emphasise: only direction 1 and the contra direction 2. The county council did not, on any view, stop up this gap in order to separate traffic moving eastwards along the one part of this main carriageway from traffic moving westwards on the other part. They cannot have had any other intention than to prevent traffic moving crossways across the carriageway, in this particular case from north to south, or to a limited extent from south to north.

The purpose of the power granted by s. 65 (1) (*a*) is limited, in my judgment, to separation of two opposite flowing lines of traffic. It is only under para. (*b*) that the power is granted to deal, to the extent stated in the subsection, with traffic which flows across the traffic using the carriageway. It is only in the carriageway and not in any side road or adjoining road that works may under this subsection be installed and maintained; and it is only under para. (*b*) that they may be installed at a junction or cross roads for the purpose of regulating the movement of traffic. That, I have no hesitation myself in saying, means traffic moving out of or into one part of a cross roads, either side of the carriageway, or moving out of an adjoining road, or a junction road, into the carriageway or into that junction road from the carriageway. The stopping up of this gap by baulks of timber laid across the mouth, in an east to west or west to east direction, could not possibly, in my judgment, be a means of regulating the movement of traffic out of Manor Lane across the carriageway on to the westbound half of that carriageway. It would be as absurd in my respectful view to regard that series of acts as " regulating " that traffic when its effect is to divert traffic, as my lord has indicated, a substantial distance to the next roundabout, as it would be to say that one is regulating a ship's chronometer if you lose your temper with it and throw it overboard.

In my judgment, this section in the Highways Act, 1959, which was not relied on so far as para. (*a*) is concerned before the learned judge, is quite incapable of justifying the action taken by the county council in this case. I agree that this appeal should be dismissed.

LORD DENNING, M.R.: I should like to say that I associate myself with what WINN, L.J. has said about reasonableness.

Appeal dismissed. Leave to appeal to the House of Lords refused.

Solicitors: *Sharpe, Pritchard & Co.*, agents for *W. R. Scurfield, clerk to Worcestershire County Council* (for the county council); *Sydney Morse & Co.* (for the omnibus company).

[*Reported by* F. GUTTMAN, ESQ., *Barrister-at-Law.*]

Re JOHNSON'S WILL TRUSTS. NATIONAL PROVINCIAL BANK, LTD. *v.* JEFFREY AND OTHERS.

[CHANCERY DIVISION (Buckley, J.), October 13, 1966.]

Will—Condition—Marriage—Public policy—Condition encouraging violation of sanctity of marriage—Small annual sum to be paid to daughter during her life out of income of residuary estate—Whole income of residuary estate payable to her if her husband died or they should be divorced or live separately—Whether condition or limitation and whether condition void.

By his will, dated Oct. 4 1961, a testator gave his residuary estate on trust to pay the income to his widow, who survived him, during her life, and ". . . from and after the death of the survivor of myself and my said wife to my daughter . . . during her life (but subject to cl. 9 and cl. 10 hereof) ". Clause 9 contained a provision whereby during the daughter's lifetime the income of the residuary estate was to be held on protective trusts for her benefit. Clause 10 provided " I further declare that notwithstanding the trusts hereinbefore contained the income payable to my said daughter under the said trusts shall not (during the period of twenty-one years after my death and during such time as my daughter is married to and living with her present husband) exceed after deduction of tax . . . the sum of £500 per annum ". After a direction for accumulation of any surplus, cl. 10 continued " I further declare that in the event of the death of my daughter's husband or if he and my said daughter shall be divorced or shall live separately during the said period of twenty-one years then the bank shall on the happening of any such event thereafter pay the whole of the income accruing from my residuary estate to my said daughter during her life as hereinbefore provided and shall also pay to her as income of the current year the whole of any of the said accumulations of income . . .". By codicil dated Oct. 25, 1962, the testator substituted in cl. 10 a figure of £50 for the figure of £500. The value of the residuary estate after his widow's death in 1965 was about £11,000.

Held: the provision in cl. 10 of the testator's will as modified by the codicil was one which would tend to encourage the daughter to separate from her husband or possibly to divorce him, and, as such, was a provision which the court could not allow; cl. 10, on the true construction of the will, would take effect as a condition by way of defeasance, not as a limitation, and was void as being contrary to public policy, with the consequence that the original gift of a life interest to the daughter took effect subject only to cl. 9 (see p. 559, letter F, post).

Re Caborne ([1943] 2 All E.R. 7) followed.

Re Thompson ([1939] 1 All E.R. 681) and *Re Lovell* ([1920] 1 Ch. 122) distinguished.

[**Editorial Note.** Evidence concerning the testator's views of his son-in-law was read de bene esse, but, as it was so read, there was no decision whether such evidence was or was not strictly admissible in law (see p. 558, letter C, post), the court determining the question before it substantially as one of construction of the will and codicil (see p. 558, letter E, post).

As to conditions subsequent contrary to public policy and the effect of their invalidity, see 39 HALSBURY'S LAWS (3rd Edn.) 916-918, paras. 1388, 1389, and as to limitations depending on marriage, see ibid., p. 922, para. 1395; and for cases on the subject, see 48 DIGEST (Repl.) 315, 316, *2736-2746.*]

Cases referred to:

Brown v. *Peck*, (1758), 1 Eden, 140; 28 E.R. 637; 48 Digest (Repl.) 315, *2737.*

Caborne, Re, *Hodge* v. *Smith*, [1943] 2 All E.R. 7; [1943] Ch. 224; 112 L.J.Ch. 210; 169 L.T. 109; 48 Digest (Repl.) 316, *2746.*

Lovell, Re, *Sparks* v. *Southall*, [1920] 1 Ch. 122; 88 L.J.Ch. 540; 122 L.T. 26; 48 Digest (Repl.) 295, *2607.*

Moore, Re, *Trafford* v. *Maconochie*, [1886-90] All E.R. Rep. 187; (1888), 39 Ch.D 116; 57 L.J.Ch. 936; 59 L.T. 681; 52 J.P. 596; 48 Digest (Repl.) 294, *2606.*

Thompson, Re, *Lloyds Bank, Ltd.* v. *George*, [1939] 1 All E.R. 681; 48 Digest (Repl.) 315, *2745.*

Adjourned Summons.

This was an application by originating summons dated July 23, 1965, by the plaintiff, National Provincial Bank, Ltd., the executor and trustee of the will dated Oct. 4, 1961, and the codicil dated Oct. 25, 1962, of the testator, Charles Leslie Johnson, deceased. The plaintiff sought the determination by the court of the questions (i) whether on the true construction of the will and codicil of the testator and in the events which had happened the provisions of cl. 10 of the will were wholly void as contrary to public policy; and (ii) if the provisions were wholly void whether the first respondent, Kathleen Mary Jeffrey, was entitled to a life interest in the whole of the income of the testator's residuary estate under cl. 7 of the will subject only to determination if she incurred a forfeiture under cl. 9 of the will, or whether the income during her lifetime was undisposed of by the will. A further question related to the disposal of the income of the residuary estate, if the provisions in cl. 10 were not wholly void. The defendants were Kathleen Mary Jeffrey, John Charles Rutherford Jeffrey, Alison Mary Jeffrey, Lucy Ann Robinson and Barry Alexander Robinson all of whom claimed to be beneficially interested under the trusts of the will and codicil (the first defendant also being interested as the only child of the testator in respect of any property undisposed of by the will and codicil), and Arthur Henry Howell (the sole personal representative of Florence Margaret Johnson, deceased, widow of the testator) who claimed as such personal representative to be interested in any property undisposed of by the will and codicil. The facts are set out in the judgment.

The case noted below* was cited during the argument in addition to those referred to in the judgment.

---

* *Hope* v. *Hope*, (1857), 8 De G. M. & G. 731.

H. *Hillaby* for the plaintiff.

J. D. *Waite* for the first defendant.

M. W. *Cockle* for the second and third defendants.

J. F. *Parker* for the fourth and fifth defendants.

BUCKLEY, J.: In this case, I have to determine the effect of a disposition of residuary estate in the will of a testator, Charles Leslie Johnson, who died on June 16, 1963, having made his will on Oct. 4, 1961, and varied it in a material respect on Oct. 25, 1962. By his will the testator, after making various other dispositions, which it is irrelevant for me to mention, disposed of his residuary estate on the usual administrative trusts and gave his net residue on trust to pay the income thereof to his widow, who survived him, during her life. She died on Feb. 16, 1965, and the testator proceeded, in his will, as follows:

". . . from and after the date of the death of the survivor of myself and my said wife to my daughter the said Kathleen Mary Jeffrey . . . during her life (but subject to cl. 9 and cl. 10 hereof)."

Kathleen Mary Jeffrey is the first defendant. Then, by cl. 8, the testator conferred on that daughter a testamentary power to appoint his residuary estate amongst her children or remoter issue and made a gift in default of and subject to any such appointment

" In trust for all or any the child or children of my said daughter who shall be living at my death or born afterwards and who being male shall attain the age of twenty-one years or being female attain that age or marry under that age and if more than one in equal shares."

He then declared that if the trusts of his residuary estate should fail then, subject to the trusts, powers and provisions declared, he gave one tenth of his residue to a Mrs. Robinson and the other nine-tenths of his residue to her son, who are the fourth and fifth defendants. Clause 9 contained a provision which converted the daughter's life interest into a protective life interest, on familiar lines and I will not pause to read it. Clause 10 is the clause on which the question arises that I have to decide.

" I FURTHER DECLARE that notwithstanding the trusts hereinbefore contained the income payable to my said daughter under the said trusts shall not (during the period of twenty-one years after my death and during such time as my said daughter is married to and living with her present husband) exceed after deduction of tax at the current rate for the time being the sum of five hundred pounds per annum and (if my daughter shall so long live) the bank shall during the said period of twenty-one years accumulate any balance of the said income in the way of compound interest by investing the same and the resulting income thereof AND I FURTHER DECLARE that in the event of the death of my said daughter's husband or if he and my said daughter shall be divorced or shall live separately during the said period of twenty-one years then the bank shall on the happening of any such event thereafter pay the whole of the income arising from my residuary estate to my said daughter during her life as hereinbefore provided and shall also pay to her as income of the current year the whole of any of the said accumulations of income AND I FURTHER DECLARE that in the event of the death of my said daughter whilst she is still married to and living with her said husband any accumulations of income shall on her death be added to the capital of my residuary estate."

By his codicil the testator, after referring to cl. 10 of his will, declared that the sum of £50 per annum should be substituted in that clause for the sum of £500 per annum and cl. 10 should be read and construed as if the sum of £50 per annum were stated therein.

It is contended, on behalf of the first defendant, the testator's daughter (herein called " Mrs. Jeffrey "), that the provisions of cl. 10 are wholly void as being contrary to public policy on the ground that they tend to encourage her to cease to cohabit with her husband, or, alternatively, to end her marriage to him by divorce. On the other side, it is contended that the object of cl. 10 of the testator's will, as modified by the codicil, was not to induce Mrs. Jeffrey to break up her marriage to her husband but was merely to make provision for her in the event of that marriage breaking up. Alternatively, it is said that even if cl. 10 is in some part bad as being contrary to public policy that consideration does not apply to the first part of cl. 10, that is to say, the part of the clause under which she is given £50 per annum net so long as she is married to and living with her husband. Nor does it affect the ultimate gift of the accumulations of the income and that, if any part of the clause is bad, it is only that part which gives her an increased benefit during the remainder of her life after her marriage or cohabitation with her husband may have come to an end as a result of separation or divorce.

I have been referred to certain authorities going back to the year 1758, when LORD HENLEY decided *Brown* v. *Peck* (1). I think that the first authority to which I shall refer is *Re Moore, Trafford* v. *Maconochie* (2), which was decide at first instance by KAY, J. (3), and was confirmed in the Court of Appeal (2). In that case the testator directed his trustee to pay to his sister, who was named in the will

". . . during such time as she may live apart from her husband, before my son attains the age of twenty-one years, the sum of £2 10s. per week for her maintenance whilst so living apart from her husband."

The testator's sister in question and her husband were married some time before the date of the will and were living together at the date of the will and at the date of the testator's death, although they did separate after the testator's death. The testator's son was an infant and it was there held that the bequest to the sister was not to be construed as a gift to her during the joint lives of herself and her husband until the testator's son attained twenty-one on a condition which might have been rejected as against public policy, but as a gift of weekly payments limited to be made during a period the commencement and duration of which were fixed in a way which the law did not allow. Consequently, the gift was void. The alternative argument was made that the gift was effective, but was subject to a condition which, being bad, should be disregarded. The gift was held to fail. In the course of his judgment COTTON, L.J. (4), mentions the fact that the testator did not like his brother-in-law, the husband of his sister in question, and that his apparent object was to induce his sister to live separate from her husband. The case turned mostly on the discussion of the question whether the gift was to be read as being a gift for a limited period, that is to say, whether the words that gave rise to the problem were words of limitation or whether there was a gift subject to a condition which could be disregarded as being contrary to public policy so that the gift was unfettered by the condition. I mention that case because, as I say, the court did seem to pay some attention to the fact as being a relevant one that the limitation was procured by the testator's dislike of his sister's husband; and that was a circumstance which was taken into account by BENNETT, J., (5) in a later case which I will mention in a minute.

The next case is a decision of P. O. LAWRENCE, J., in *Re Lovell, Sparks* v. *Southall* (6), where the testator, who was a married man but living apart from his wife, was living with a married woman to whom he made a bequest, provided she was living with him at the time of his death, of an annuity of £750

" provided and so long as she shall not return to live with her husband and provided and so long as she shall not remarry and subject to her leading a clean moral and respectable life in the opinion of my executors and trustees."

(1) (1758), 1 Eden, 140.   (2) [1886-90] All E.R. Rep. 187; (1888), 39 Ch.D. 116.
(3) (1888), 39 Ch.D. 116.
(4) [1886-90] All E.R. Rep. at p. 188; (1888), 39 Ch.D. at p. 128.
(5) I.e., *Re Thompson, Lloyds Bank, Ltd.* v. *George*, [1939] 1 All E.R. 681.
(6) [1920] 1 Ch. 122.

P. O. Lawrence, J., upheld that bequest. He held that it was a limitation and not on a condition and was therefore valid and also that it was not void as being contrary to public policy, its object being not to induce the lady to continue to live apart from her husband but to maintain her until she returned to her husband or remarried.

The next of the authorities is Bennett, J.'s decision in *Re Thompson, Lloyds Bank, Ltd.* v. *George* (7). There the testator's will contained a clause to the effect that his daughter, if still married to her present husband, whom, on the evidence— which the learned judge looked at and took into consideration—the testator disliked very much, should be entitled to no more than an annuity of £300. The will further provided that the daughter should be entitled to the income of the whole estate

> if at any time after the testator's decease she should be the widow of her present husband or married to someone other than her present husband or divorced from but not subsequently remarried to her present husband."

The question was, in those circumstances, whether the cutting down of her annuity to £300 was contrary to public policy or not, and the learned judge held that the provision was not contrary to public policy as the object of the testator's disposition was not to induce a separation of the spouses. Towards the end of the judgment, Bennett, J., said this (8):

> " It is said that, because at any time while she is married to her husband she can get free from him by means of a divorce, that increases her income from £300 per annum to the whole income, and that that is a provision for the purpose of inducing a future separation between husband and wife, and is, therefore, void. I am not satisfied that that is the purpose of the provision. The purpose of the provision is mainly to be sure that the income derived from the estate in excess of £300 will not go to the hands of, or get under the control of, a man whom the testator regarded as a spendthrift. I do not think that it can fairly be said that the object of this provision was to induce the wife either to divorce her husband or to put herself into a position in which her husband could divorce her. For these reasons, for myself, I see nothing contrary to public policy in the disposition which the testator has made of the income he has given in his will."

The last of the cases to which I shall refer is the decision of Simonds, J., in *Re Caborne, Hodge* v. *Smith* (9). There the testatrix devised and bequeathed the residue of her real and personal estate to her son absolutely. That gift was followed by a proviso that, if the son's wife should still be living and married to him, the absolute gift should be modified, but so that, if at any time during the life of the son his wife should die or the marriage should be otherwise terminated, the absolute gift should take effect as and from such event, but, if the son should die during the lifetime of the wife, the specific gifts and the residuary estate should be held on certain trusts in the nature of a gift over. After the making of the will but before the death of the testatrix, the son was, by agreement, separated from his wife. He died some years after the testatrix and his personal representatives maintained that the proviso in the testatrix's will encouraged a violation of the sanctity of marriage and was void as being contrary to public policy, so that his estate was absolutely entitled to the residuary estate of the testatrix. Simonds, J., held that the proviso was a condition which tended to encourage the violation of the sanctity of marriage, and, being contrary to public policy, was void. Amongst other authorities to which he referred in the course of his judgment was

(7) [1939] 1 All E.R. 681.
(8) [1939] 1 All E.R. at p. 684.
(9) [1943] 2 All E.R. 7; [1943] Ch. 224.

the decision of BENNETT, J., in *Re Thompson* (10), SIMONDS, J., drew attention to the fact that BENNETT, J., had looked at evidence outside the will in considering whether or not the gift in *Re Thompson* (10) was or was not a valid one, and said this (11):

" With great deference to the judge, I feel some doubt whether the decision observes the rule that, in these matters, the law looks not to the possibility of public mischief occurring in the particular instance, but to the general tendency of the disposition; but however that may be, I must regard the case as one depending on its own particular facts for which there is no parallel in the case now before me."

In the present case evidence has been filed which I have looked at and no one objected—at any rate I have read it de bene esse—which indicates that at some time before he made his will the testator had intimated to his solicitors that he was concerned to protect his daughter against her husband, as he felt the husband would probably get any money from her that she received under the trusts of the testator's will and that the testator considered that the son-in-law had a bad influence on his daughter. The fact, however, that a testator in making a provision of this kind is actuated by motives which result from his dislike of some particular person or disapproval of a particular person or distrust of that person, does not seem to me to take one very far in considering whether or not the provision in his will which one has to consider is one which should be regarded as contrary to public policy, or either on the ground of being contrary to good morals as tending to disrupt a marriage or on grounds of that kind. It seems to me that one must look at the provision itself and attempt to assess whether it is a provision of such a kind as will have results of that sort which should be regarded as undesirable. It may be that regarding the matter in that way one may come to the conclusion, as P. O. LAWRENCE, J., did in *Re Lovell* (12) that there is nothing objectionable in the disposition or one may come to the conclusion, as did SIMONDS, J., in *Re Caborne* (13), that the tendency of the disposition is such as to encourage the breaking up of a subsisting marriage, in which case that is something to which this court will not give effect, on the grounds that it is undesirable from the point of view of public policy.

In the present case it is to be observed that the testator gave to his daughter, in the first instance, an out and out life interest, qualified, it is true, by the words " but subject to cl. 9 and cl. 10 hereof ". He then engrafted on that interest the first protective trust and then these particular provisions with which I am concerned, cutting down the interest of his daughter, during the period of twenty-one years from his death and so long as she was married and living with her husband, to £50 a year. Reading cl. 10, as modified by the codicil, he goes on to declare that in the event of his son-in-law's death or if his daughter's marriage to that son-in-law should be terminated by divorce or if she should cease to live with her husband within the period or twenty-one years, then she shall receive the whole of the income and in addition, any accumulated surplus of income which has been made meanwhile. That is a provision which would tend to encourage the daughter to separate from her husband or possibly to divorce him, which it seems to me that this court cannot allow.

The value of the subject matter of this trust is upwards of £11,000 and the income of that, therefore, would be substantially greater than the £50 per year which is referred to in the codicil, and the provision is put in such a way as clearly to provide a financial incentive which might well be calculated to influence the lady's mind if she were minded to separate from her husband, or to put an end to the marriage by divorce if conditions were to arise in which that was a

(10) [1939] 1 All E.R. 681.
(11) [1943] 2 All E.R. at p. 10; [1943] Ch. at p. 231.
(12) [1920] 1 Ch. 122.
(13) [1943] 2 All E.R. 7; [1943] Ch. 224.

possibility. In fact, she has all along been living with her husband and is still living with him and there have been two children of the marriage, who are the second and third defendants; they are aged nineteen and fifteen years of age.

This is not a case in which it could be said that the testator was anxious to make provision for some woman who was already separated from her husband while she remained so separated. It is a case in which the testator, it may be said, has attempted to make considerably more liberal provisions for his daughter should she cease to live with her husband; and it is not at all an unreasonable view that the testator might have thought it was desirable to make a provision for her in those circumstances when she would not have the support of her husband to rely on, but that is not, I think, an argument which disposes of the vice in a provision of this sort. It is, as I understand it, because a provision of this sort provides an incentive to the break-up of a marriage that the court will not assist it in any way.

Reading this will as a whole, it seems to me that the right way to treat cl. 10 is to treat it as being in the nature of a condition cutting down the benefit which the daughter is to take if and so long as she remains in cohabitation with her husband. The authorities suggest that there is a distinction of substance between cases where one is dealing with a limitation and cases where one is dealing with a provision which takes effect as a condition of defeasance. Reading the will as a whole, it seems to me that, in substance, cl. 10 here is such a condition. It is true that had the same scheme been incorporated in the will in some different language and, perhaps, in a rather different order from the order in which one finds it in this will, one would have reached the conclusion that one here has a series of limited interests each confined to a period during which certain circumstances prevailed. Having regard, however, to the initial gift to the daughter of a life interest expressed to be subject to cl. 10, I think that it is right to construe this will and particularly cl. 10 in this will as operating as a condition cutting down that life interest to a benefit of £50 a year if and for so long as the daughter shall be married to and living with her husband. On that footing, the condition being one which, in my opinion, does offend public policy, it falls to be disregarded as void and the original gift takes effect, that is, the daughter is entitled to a life interest subject only to the protection of the protective trusts imposed by cl. 9.

For these reasons I shall answer the questions raised in the summons by declaring that on the true construction of the will and codicil and in the events which have happened the provisions in cl. 10 of the will are wholly void as being contrary to public policy; and that the defendant Kathleen Mary Jeffrey is entitled to a life interest in the whole of the income of the testator's residuary estate under cl. 7 of the will subject only to determination if she incurs a forfeiture under the provisions of cl. 9.

Order accordingly.

Solicitors: *Chalton, Hubbard & Co.*, agents for *Marsh & Ferriman*, Worthing (for the plaintiff); *Preston, Lane-Claypon & O'Kelly* (for the first, second and third defendants); *Hays, Roughton & Dunn* (for the fourth defendant); *Coles & Stevenson* (for the fifth defendant).

[*Reported by* Jenifer Sandell, *Barrister-at-Law.*]

Approved in POST OFFICE *v.* ESTUARY
RADIO. [1967] 3 All E.R. 663.

R. *v.* KENT JUSTICES, *Ex parte* LYE AND OTHERS.

[QUEEN'S BENCH DIVISION (Lord Parker, C.J., Salmon, L.J., and Blain, J.), December 12, 13, 1966.]

Magistrates—Jurisdiction—Implied jurisdiction from enactment creating offence —" Territorial waters "—Wireless broadcast from disused fort more than three nautical miles from low-water mark off Kent coast—Wireless Telegraphy Act, 1949 (12, 13 & 14 Geo. 6 c. 54), s. 1 (1), s. 6 (1) (a).

Since September, 1965, the appellant company (a company registered in the United Kingdom), of whom the applicants L. and A. were directors, had been broadcasting from Red Sands Tower, an old disused fort some 4·9 nautical miles from low-water mark off the Kent coast. Red Sands Tower lay less than three miles from a sand bank, Middle Sand, which was itself within three nautical miles of the low-water mark off the Kent coast and was a low-tide elevation within the meaning of art. 5 (2)* of the Territorial Waters Order in Council 1964 (implementing the Convention on the Territorial Sea and the Contiguous Zone, 1958), which laid down base lines from which the three nautical miles could be measured. The applicants were convicted before the Kent justices of unlawfully using apparatus for wireless telegraphy, namely, a transmitter, without a licence issued by the Postmaster General, contrary to s. 1 (1)† of the Wireless Telegraphy Act, 1949, the justices being of the opinion that Red Sands Tower lay in territorial waters within the meaning of s. 6 (1) (a)‡ of the Act of 1949 and that, accordingly, they had jurisdiction to try the case. On an application for certiorari to bring up and quash the convictions,

Held: the justices had jurisdiction to try the case and accordingly an order of certiorari would be refused, because—

(i) (SALMON, L.J., dissenting) in the Wireless Telegraphy Act, 1949, the expression " territorial waters ", which was not defined in the Act, meant (per LORD PARKER, C.J.) territorial waters from time to time their determination being governed by declarations of sovereignty from time to time by the Crown (see p. 565, letter A, post), or (per BLAIN, J.) waters recognised as territorial by contemporary international usage from time to time, in so far as such usage was recognised from time to time in this country (see p. 574, letter E, post).

(ii) on the true construction of the Territorial Waters Jurisdiction Act, 1878, and in particular of the definition of " territorial waters " in s. 7 thereof, the reference in the second paragraph of the definition to the three mile limit from low-water mark was ad hoc, for the purpose of the particular jurisdiction conferred by the Act of 1878 over indictable offences to persons on foreign ships, and the limits of territorial waters remained those recognised by international law; accordingly the Act of 1878 did not preclude the exercise of the prerogative by the Territorial Waters Order in Council 1964 with the consequences (SALMON, L.J., dissenting) that the limits of territorial waters applicable for the purposes of s. 6 (1) (a) of the Act of 1949 in the present case extended to three miles from Middle Sand and that Red Sands Tower lay within territorial waters (see p. 565, letter I, and p. 569, letter G, post; cf., p. 576, letter A, post).

(iii) (SALMON, L.J., concurring in the implication of jurisdiction but not that the offence as to which jurisdiction was implied extended to the present case) when s. 1 (1) of the Act of 1949 made the offence a summary offence, it impliedly created jurisdiction in the justices to try the offence, such jurisdiction being conferred by the Act of 1949 without indicating the particular court to exercise the jurisdiction, and being exercisable by the justices for

---

* Article 5 (2), so far as material, is set out at p. 563, letter H, post.
† Section 1 (1), so far as material, is set out at p. 562, letter C, post.
‡ Section 6 (1), so far as material, is set out at p. 562, letter E, post.

the county whose boundaries were thus extended to adjacent territorial waters (see p. 567, letter B, p. 570, letters A and D, and p. 576, letters C and F, post).

Cullen v. *Trimble* ((1872), L.R. 7 Q.B. 416) and *Johnson* v. *Colam* ((1875), L.R. 10 Q.B. 544) applied.

[As to meaning of territorial waters, see 10 HALSBURY'S LAWS (3rd Edn.) 319, 320, para. 583; and for a case on the subject, see 1 DIGEST (Repl.) 127, *131*.

As to legislation relating to wireless telegraphy, see 36 HALSBURY'S LAWS (3rd Edn.) 628, 629, para. 985.

As to the nature of judicial powers of magistrates, see 25 HALSBURY'S LAWS (3rd Edn.) 163, para. 297; and for cases on the subject, see 33 DIGEST (Repl.) 177, 178, *312-315*.

For the Territorial Waters Jurisdiction Act, 1878, s. 2, s. 7, see 5 HALSBURY'S STATUTES (2nd Edn.) 893, 894.

For the Wireless Telegraphy Act, 1949, s. 1, s. 6, see 24 HALSBURY'S STATUTES (2nd Edn.) 1100, 1105.]

Cases referred to:

Cullen v. *Trimble*, (1872), L.R. 7 Q.B. 416; 41 L.J.M.C. 132; 26 L.T. 691; sub nom. *Cullen* v. *Lancashire Justices*, 37 J.P. 115; 33 Digest (Repl.) 177, *314*.

Fagernes, The, [1927] P. 311; 96 L.J.P. 183; 138 L.T. 30; 17 Asp. M.L.C. 326; 11 Digest (Repl.) 579, *141*.

Johnson v. *Colam*, (1875), L.R. 10 Q.B. 544; 44 L.J.M.C. 185; 32 L.T. 725; 40 J.P. 135; 23 W.R. 697; 33 Digest (Repl.) 178, *315*.

R. v. *Keyn, The Franconia*, (1876), 2 Ex.D. 63; 2 Q.B.D. 90; 46 L.J.M.C. 17; 41 J.P. 517; 1 Digest (Repl.) 127, *131*.

Motion for certiorari.

This was an application by way of motion on behalf of a company, Estuary Radio, Ltd., and two of its directors, David Beresford Lye and Theodore Le Bouthillier Allbeury, for an order of certiorari to bring up and quash orders of convictions made by the Kent justices on Nov. 25, 1966, that, on Aug. 16, 1966, at Red Sands Tower within the jurisdiction of the county, the applicants unlawfully used apparatus for wireless telegraphy, viz., a transmitter, except under and in accordance with a licence in that behalf granted by the Postmaster General, contrary to s. 1 (1) of the Wireless Telegraphy Act, 1949. The applicant company was fined £100 and the applicant Lye and the applicant Allbeury were both given an absolute discharge, no order being made as to costs or for the confiscation of the equipment unlawfully used. The grounds for the application were that (a) Red Sands Tower lay 4·9 nautical miles from the nearest low-water mark of the county of Kent and was not in territorial waters and neither the magistrates' court nor any court had jurisdiction over acts committed on Red Sands Tower; (b) the offence alleged was a summary offence and the court had no jurisdiction, express or implied, to try a summary offence alleged to have been committed within territorial waters. The facts are set out in the judgment of LORD PARKER, C.J.

The authorities and cases noted below* were cited during the argument in addition to those referred to in the judgments.

Sir Peter Rawlinson, Q.C., and *James Harper* for the applicants.

J. H. R. Newsey and *A. O. R. Vick* for the respondents.

* OPPENHEIM, LAW OF PEACE (8th Edn.) 1954, pp. 460, 468, 490; COLUMBOS INTERNATIONAL LAW OF THE SEA (5th Edn.), 1962), p. 79, para. 97, p. 85, para. 104, p. 93, para. 114, p. 99, p. 100, paras. 120, 120A, 121; 5 HALSBURY'S STATUTES (2nd Edn.) 892, 895; 10 HALSBURY'S STATUTES (2nd Edn.) 238; 14 HALSBURY'S STATUTES (2nd Edn.) 881; 23 HALSBURY'S STATUTES (2nd Edn.) 1239; 24 HALSBURY'S STATUTES (2nd Edn.) 1100, 1105, 1114, 1115; 32 HALSBURY'S STATUTES (2nd Edn.) 424, 425; 44 HALSBURY'S STATUTES (2nd Edn.) 804, 805, 808; *R.* v. *Cunningham*, (1859), Bell C.C. 72; *Barwick* v. *South Eastern and Clapham Ry. Co.*, (1921), 124 L.T. 71; *A.-G.* v. *De Keyser's Royal Hotel*, [1920] All E.R. Rep. 80; [1920] A.C. 508; *R.* v. *Martin*, [1956] 2 All E.R. 86; [1956] 2 Q.B. 272; *R.* v. *Naylor*, [1961] 2 All E.R. 932; [1962] 2 Q.B. 527.

LORD PARKER, C.J.: This is by no means an easy case, and in the ordinary way I should have thought that it was one which justified putting one's reason's into writing, but as I, rightly or wrongly, have formed a definite view, I propose to give judgment. In these proceedings, counsel moves on behalf of three applicants, a company, Estuary Radio, Ltd., and two of its directors, David Beresford Lye and Theodore Le Bouthillier Allbeury, for an order of certiorari to bring up and quash orders of conviction made by the Kent justices sitting at Canterbury on Nov. 25, 1966. The justices found the applicants guilty on a charge of, on Aug. 16, 1966, unlawfully using apparatus for wireless telegraphy, namely, a transmitter, without a licence issued by the Postmaster General, contrary to s. 1 (1) of the Wireless Telegraphy Act, 1949. It is convenient at once to refer briefly to the relevant provisions of the Act of 1949. By s. 1 (1), it is provided that:

" No person shall establish or use any station for wireless telegraphy or instal or use any apparatus for wireless telegraphy except under the authority of a licence in that behalf granted by the Postmaster General, and any person who establishes or uses any station for wireless telegraphy or instals or uses any apparatus for wireless telegraphy except under and in accordance with such a licence shall be guilty of an offence under this Act . . ."

Section 6, so far as it is material, provides that:

" (1) Subject to the provisions of this section, the preceding provisions of this Part of this Act shall apply—(a) to all stations and apparatus in or over, or for the time being in or over, the United Kingdom or the territorial waters adjacent thereto . . ."

Finally, by s. 14 (1), which is in Part 3 of the Act, it is provided that:

" Subject to the provisions of Part 1 of this Act relating to offences committed in relation to apparatus on board foreign seagoing ships or foreign aircraft, any person committing any offences under this Act . . . (c) shall, in the case of any other offence, be liable on summary conviction to imprisonment for a period not exceeding three months or to a fine not exceeding £100 or to both such imprisonment and such a fine."

The applicant company was incorporated on June 3, 1965, and, since September, 1965, has been broadcasting from an old disused fort some 4·9 nautical miles from low-water mark off the Kent coast north of Whitstable. The fort is known as Red Sands Tower. Before the justices at the very outset the applicants objected to the justices' jurisdiction to hear the case; the justices heard argument and evidence, and finally ruled that they had jurisdiction. They stated their conclusion in these terms, which I read from para. 5 in the affidavit of Mr. Flower. They said:

" ' Red Sands Tower lies in territorial waters. The Wireless Telegraphy Act, 1949, is silent on the question of local jurisdiction. But the territorial waters in question adjoin the county of Kent and for that reason we are of the opinion that the justices have jurisdiction. On the evidence before us we find the case proved '."

The grounds of application to this court quite generally are that the justices, in coming to that conclusion, erred in law and have wrongly held that they had jurisdiction. The foundation of counsel for the applicants' argument before us, as I understand it, is that, at any rate at the time of the passing of the Wireless Telegraphy Act, 1949, it was the law of nations, by which I mean the consensus of nations, one of which was this country, that no jurisdiction could be exercised by any nation over the open seas except within three nautical miles from low-water mark, and that that law of nations had been incorporated into the municipal law of this country by the Territorial Waters Jurisdiction Act, 1878. By that Act indictable offences committed in territorial waters, whether by a British subject or a foreigner, and whether committed on a foreign ship or not, were declared to be within the jurisdiction of the Admiral, which jurisdiction had in fact been transferred to the Central Criminal Court. Thus, by s. 2 it is provided that:

" An offence committed by a person, whether he is or is not a subject of Her Majesty, on the open sea within the territorial waters of Her Majesty's dominions, is an offence within the jurisdiction of the Admiral, although it may have been committed on board or by means of a foreign ship, and the person who committed such offence may be arrested, tried, and punished accordingly."

Section 5 provides for certain savings, in that it says:

" Nothing in this Act contained shall be construed to be in derogation of any rightful jurisdiction of Her Majesty, her heirs or successors, under the law of nations, or to affect or prejudice any jurisdiction conferred by Act of Parliament or now by law existing in relation to foreign ships or in relation to persons on board such ships."

Finally, by s. 7, the interpretation section, it is provided that:

" In this Act, unless there is something inconsistent in the context, the following expressions shall respectively have the meanings herein after assigned to them; (that is to say,) . . . ' The territorial waters of Her Majesty's dominions ', in reference to the sea, means such part of the sea adjacent to the coast of the United Kingdom, or the coast of some other part of Her Majesty's dominions, as is deemed by international law to be within the territorial sovereignty of Her Majesty; and for the purpose of any offence declared by this Act to be within the jurisdiction of the Admiral, any part of the open sea within one marine league [that is, three nautical miles] of the coast measured from low-water mark shall be deemed to be open sea within the territorial waters of Her Majesty's dominions . . ."

It is, therefore, to be seen that, for certain indictable offences committed by a person within s. 2, territorial waters means three nautical miles from low-water mark.

The prosecution, on the other hand, relied on an Order in Council (1) issued under the royal prerogative on Sept. 25, 1964, which was clearly intended to implement, as it were, a convention signed at Geneva on Apr. 29, 1958, which was ratified by the United Kingdom on Mar. 14, 1960, and came into force on Sept. 10, 1964, some fourteen days before the order in council. The convention and the order in council laid down base lines, as they are called, from which the three nautical miles could be measured, and in particular provided that it could be measured from what is called any " low-tide elevation " which itself was within the three mile limit. " Low-tide elevation " was defined in art. 5 (2) of the order in these terms:

" the expression ' low-tide elevation ' means a naturally formed area of drying land surrounded by water which is below water at mean high water spring tides."

It was claimed by the prosecution that an elevation known as Middle Sand which was within three nautical miles of the low-water mark off the Kent coast was such an elevation, and it is conceded that there was evidence before the justices which entitled them to hold that Middle Sand was a low-tide elevation. It is further conceded that Red Sands Tower is less than three nautical miles from Middle Sand and, therefore, within territorial waters as measured under the terms of the order in council.

The answer made by the applicants quite generally is that such an order was ultra vires, since the Crown must be taken to have abrogated the exercise of the

_____
(1) The Territorial Waters Order in Council 1964.

prerogative powers within this field in entrusting to Parliament by the Act of 1878 the right to define territorial waters. That, it is said, is confirmed by the fact that in dealing, amongst other things, with fishing rights, it was Parliament by the Fishery Limits Act 1964 which determined those rights.

For my part, I think that the proper approach to this question is to look first at the Wireless Telegraphy Act, 1949. The real issue, as it seems to me, in the present case is what Parliament meant by the expression "territorial waters" in that Act. Does it mean "territorial waters" as, to put it quite generally, accepted by this country at that time, or does it mean territorial waters from time to time according to international law, or according to the exercise of sovereignty by the Crown? In the absence of a definition, and there is none in the Act of 1949, I have come to the conclusion that that expression "territorial waters" must mean waters over which from time to time the Crown may declare sovereignty. No doubt any declaration of sovereignty will in general, if not always, be made within the international law current at the time, though if the Crown did exercise sovereignty over a greater area, these courts would have to enforce it; but in general the exercise by the Sovereign will not be over an area greater than is permitted under international law. I have come to that conclusion in the first place because, as it seems to me, if it was intended that the expression "territorial waters" was to be confined to a precise limit, then known, it would have been perfectly easy to provide, as indeed was provided in the Act of 1878, for an express limitation of territorial waters. There is no such limitation. Secondly, as it seems to me, although as I have said it is open to the Sovereign to declare sovereignty over an area greater than is strictly permitted by international law, international law will be the framework within which that declaration of sovereignty will in general be made, and it is well known that international law on this matter has been throughout in a state of flux. This country has in general proceeded on the basis that territorial waters are limited to three nautical miles from low-water mark, but other countries have taken different views. Indeed, as I understand it, this country itself has on a number of occasions not limited territorial waters to three nautical miles from low-water mark. Accordingly, the boundaries of territorial waters must inevitably have been expected to change from time to time, and may do so in the future, although at the moment they are crystallised by the Convention of 1958 to which I have referred. Thirdly, as it seems to me, this is a matter of sovereignty; it is a matter of an extension of sovereignty over the open seas, and as such is peculiarly a matter for the Crown from time to time under the prerogative to determine. One would expect that to be done from time to time without the need for specific legislation.

I have come to that conclusion despite the forceful argument to the contrary that we are dealing with a criminal offence in which there must be certainty, and it is pointed out that a man might go to a great deal of expense to erect some structure from which broadcasting could take place just outside what were territorial waters in 1949, only to find an order in council a little later providing for base lines as a result of which that structure was then within territorial waters. I fully appreciate that, and it is perhaps unfortunate that a criminal offence is uncertain in that respect; but if one is looking at the Wireless Telegraphy Act, 1949, as a whole, it is dealing with broadcasting not only in this country, but from territorial waters and so far as territorial waters are concerned, from ships. I do not suppose Parliament had in mind, or anyone had in mind in 1949, that Red Sands Tower or any structure, a relic from the last war, would be used for broadcasting, and, if one is thinking of broadcasting in territorial waters from a ship, it matters not whether one day territorial waters are up to a certain limit, and the next day they go out a little further, because a ship can always go further away. I have come to the conclusion that, in the absence of any definition of "territorial waters", the expression in the Act of 1949 must be read as meaning "territorial waters from time to time"; and rather than to say that the determination is governed by international law, I would prefer to say that it was governed by declarations of sovereignty from time to time by the Crown.

Counsel for the applicants, however, in his forceful argument, says that Parliament in 1878 laid down a definition of territorial waters which Parliament in 1949 must have had in mind when they used the expression " territorial waters " in the Act of 1949. It is necessary, therefore, to look a little closely at that Act of 1878. The first thing to note is that it does not purport to lay down a definition of " territorial waters " for all purposes, but only for the limited purpose of that Act. The occasion of the passing of the Act of 1878 was undoubtedly the decision by a Court of Crown Cases Reserved in *R.* v. *Keyn, The Franconia* (2). Thirteen judges sat on that case, and they were divided seven to six. The seven came to the conclusion that the Admiral, and accordingly the Central Criminal Court, had no jurisdiction in the case of manslaughter by a foreigner in command of a foreign ship. They held that the Admiral had no jurisdiction to try offences by foreigners on board foreign ships, whether within or without the limit of three miles from the shore of England. The minority, on the other hand, held that the sea within three miles of the coast of England is part of the territory of England, and that the English criminal law extended over those limits. They held that the Admiral formerly had, and accordingly the Central Criminal Court then had, jurisdiction to try offences committed in territorial waters although committed on board foreign ships. The Act of 1878 was clearly intended to validate the views of the minority, and, indeed, as has been pointed out, the first recital to the Act of 1878 really says that the view of the minority had always been the law, because the first recital says that:

" Whereas the rightful jurisdiction of Her Majesty, her heirs and successors, extends and has always extended over the open seas adjacent to the coasts of the United Kingdom and of all other parts of Her Majesty's dominions to such a distance as is necessary for the defence and security of such dominions . . ."

The Act of 1878, therefore, was aimed at offences committed on a foreign ship, and declared that such offences were within the jurisdiction of the Admiral if committed within territorial waters. In other words, it was extending the jurisdiction of the Admiral, which heretofore undoubtedly existed in regard to persons on British ships anywhere on the high seas, to persons on foreign ships, provided those ships were in territorial waters. It further only dealt with indictable offences. Moreover, although the definition section, s. 7, which is not easy to construe, seems to say in its first part that, territorial waters generally are waters deemed by international law to be within the territorial sovereignty of Her Majesty, yet it goes on in its second part to say that, for the purposes of the offence under consideration, whatever international law may say, this country will limit the jurisdiction to three nautical miles. In other words, it is assuming that, whatever jurisdiction by international law this country could properly exercise, this country limited that jurisdiction for the purposes of those offences to three nautical miles.

As it seems to me, certain things emerge from the consideration of the Act. In the first place, it is not laying down a definition of " territorial waters " for all purposes; secondly, it is only dealing with indictable and not with summary offences; thirdly, it is only dealing with the jurisdiction of the Admiral, and, fourthly, it seems clear that the earlier part of the interpretation section in regard to territorial waters is dealing with territorial waters as deemed by international law to be within the territorial sovereignty of Her Majesty, which must mean deemed by international law from time to time to be within the jurisdiction of Her Majesty. That being so, I can see no reason for saying that, by the Act of 1878, the Crown has abrogated the prerogative right to lay down limits of territorial waters for purposes other than those set out in that Act. Indeed, in regard

(2) (1876), L.R. 2 Ex.D. 63.

to matters of international law covered by conventions, or in regard to treaties, or in regard to agreements between nations, the natural mode of confirming those conventions, treaties, or agreements as part of the municipal law of this country is by order in council. Indeed, reference has been made to *The Fagernes* (3), where the Attorney-General was asked by the court to say whether His Majesty claimed territorial sovereignty over a position in the Bristol Channel where a collision had taken place. ATKIN, L.J., dealt with the matter in this way (4):

"The question to be decided in this case is no less momentous than whether the Bristol Channel is part of the realm of England. What is the territory of the Crown is a matter of which the court takes judicial notice. The court has, therefore, to inform itself from the best material available; and on such a matter it may be its duty to obtain its information from the appropriate department of Government. Any definite statement from the proper representative of the Crown as to the territory of the Crown must be treated as conclusive. A conflict is not to be contemplated between the courts and the executive on such a matter, where foreign interests may be concerned, and where responsibility for protection and administration is of paramount importance to the government of the country."

I quite appreciate that there is no question of asking the Attorney-General in the present case as to the limits of sovereignty declared by Her Majesty or exercised by Her Majesty in regard to any part of the open seas; but, if it is proper for this court to treat itself as bound by any advice so tendered as in *The Fagernes* (3), it seems to me that the court is equally bound to pay attention and regard to the declaration of sovereignty which is to be found in the order in council in the present case. Moreover, it seems to me that if the reference to international law in the definition section in the Act of 1878 is to be read, as I think it must, as "international law from time to time" there is all the less reason for giving the words "territorial waters" a different meaning in the Act of 1949. In other words, it confirms the view that Parliament is dealing with territorial waters as they may be from time to time, that is as the Sovereign may declare from time to time.

Counsel for the applicants has a second point here; it is a point really not in the alternative, because in some ways it is logically his first point. It is that, even if Red Sands Tower is within territorial waters, even so the justices had no jurisdiction. He submits that, whereas the Act of 1949 creates an offence, it does not go on, either expressly or impliedly, to create a jurisdiction to try the offence; in other words, he says that there is a lacuna. He points out that, when new offences are created, as for example in the Civil Aviation Act, 1949, and the Continental Shelf Act 1964, provision is made for the jurisdiction to try the offences constituted. He says that here there is no such provision. He further points to the fact that the Magistrates' Court Act under which the justices today derive their jurisdiction is an Act of 1952, some three years after the Act under consideration, and yet there is no reference whatever to the justices having any jurisdiction in regard to offences committed in territorial waters. As is well known, in general terms the jurisdiction of a magistrates' court for a county, as for Kent, is to try all summary offences committed within the county. Further, by s. 3 (1) of that Act, provision is made for jurisdiction in the case of offences committed on the boundary between two or more local jurisdictions, and reference is made to jurisdiction in the case of an offence committed in a harbour, river, arm of the sea and so on, but not of offences committed in territorial waters. There is no reference to territorial waters. It is, as is conceded, a short point, but it seems to me that, when the Wireless Telegraphy Act, 1949, made this offence a summary offence, it was impliedly creating a jurisdiction in justices to try the case. We

---

(3) [1927] P. 311; 17 Asp. M.L.C. 326.
(4) [1927] P. at p. 324; 17 Asp. M.L.C. at p. 330.

have been referred to cases, and particularly *Cullen* v. *Trimble* (5), and to *Johnson* v. *Colam* (6). In the latter case, BLACKBURN, J., said (7):

"The case of *Cullen* v. *Trimble* (5) shows that where we can find sufficient indications of the meaning of a statute to enable us to supply an accidental defect in a particular section, we are bound to make the required amendment."

Both those cases were again dealing with a lacuna such as counsel for the applicants admits must on his argument appear in the present case. Accordingly, it seems to me that there is sufficient here by way of implication to show that, over and above the jurisdiction given to justices in the Magistrates' Court Act, 1952, there is here given a jurisdiction to justices to try offences committed in territorial waters. It does not seem to me that the fact that particular justices were not indicated as the proper persons to deal with any particular case can really affect the matter. No doubt as a matter of convenience the justices for the county whose boundaries are, as it were, extended from low-water mark to the three mile limit will be the justices to exercise jurisdiction in the particular case. It seems to me that this is a far preferable construction than to say that, in regard to all offences under the Wireless Telegraphy Act, 1949, committed in territorial waters, there is merely a declaration of an offence and no possibility of any sanction. That, as it seems to me, would render a large part of the Act of 1949 completely nugatory.

For these reasons, which I have endeavoured to express shortly, I think that this motion fails and should be dismissed. I would only add that counsel for the prosecution had further points; he contended in the first place that the Convention of 1958 had to be treated as part of the municipal law of this country, quite apart from the order in council. He also argued before the justices and contends for the respondents here, if necessary, that Red Sands Tower was within national internal waters and, therefore, by reason of s. 3 of the Magistrates' Courts Act, 1952, was clearly within the jurisdiction of the justices. In view, however, of the conclusions at which I have arrived, I find it unnecessary to deal with those further points.

SALMON, L.J.: I find this a difficult case. I agree with LORD PARKER, C.J., that everything turns on the true construction of s. 1 (1) and s. 6 (1) of the Wireless Telegraphy Act, 1949. Those sections make it an offence for any person to establish or use any station for wireless telegraphy in " the United Kingdom or the territorial waters adjacent thereto " without a licence in that behalf granted by the Postmaster General. It is an essential ingredient of the offence that it has to be committed in the United Kingdom or the territorial waters adjacent thereto. The meaning of the words " the United Kingdom " are fairly plain; they include all land within the United Kingdom down to the low-water mark. The case really turns on the true construction of the words " territorial waters " in s. 6 (1) (*a*).

I start from the point that every statute creating a criminal offence must be strictly construed. I also bear in mind that it is a principle of our courts that the criminal law should be certain. The subject ought to be able, by looking at a statute, to tell with reasonable certainty whether what he is doing or proposes to do is or is not a criminal offence. There is no definition of the words " territorial waters " in the Act of 1949. For my part, I think that that is a great pity. If there had been such a definition, and if it had been intelligibly framed, we should then have known what the legislature intended the words in their context to mean. As it is, we are left to guess. Parliament may have intended that the area covered by these words should be certain, or it may have intended that the area should be vague. There can be little doubt that, in 1949, the territorial waters adjacent to the United Kingdom were generally recognised, both by international law and the municipal law of this land as being the open sea within

---

(5) (1872), L.R. 7 Q.B. 416.   (6) (1875), L.R. 10 Q.B. 544; 23 W.R. 697.
(7) (1875), 23 W.R. at p. 697.

three nautical miles of the ordinary low-water mark along the coast line without taking account of any " low tide elevations ". Since there is no definition in this statute, I would construe the words as meaning just what they did in 1949, namely, the open sea up to three miles from the ordinary low-water mark. Looked at in another way, " territorial waters " may be defined as " waters to which the territorial sovereignty of Her Majesty extends ". If that is what they mean, then in the Act of 1949 they can mean: " waters to which the territorial sovereignty of Her Majesty *now* extends ", or " waters to which the territorial sovereignty of Her Majesty *may from time to time* extend ". Bearing in mind the principles to which I have referred that a statute creating a criminal offence should be strictly construed, and that the law should be certain, I, for my part, prefer the former construction. The other construction makes the criminal law quite uncertain. What are the waters over which territorial sovereignty may from time to time extend depends, as LORD PARKER, C.J., has said, to a very large extent on the prerogative right of the Crown to declare sovereignty, and also on the vagaries and uncertainties of international law. I cannot believe that Parliament intended to create a criminal offence which would depend on the one or the other. In order to achieve such a remarkable result, far less ambiguous language would in my view have been necessary.

Perhaps less guidance can be derived from the Territorial Waters Jurisdiction Act, 1878, than counsel for the applicants has very persuasively argued, because the definition section, s. 7, defined " territorial waters " only for the purposes of that Act. I ought first to read s. 2, which lays down that:

" An offence committed by a person, whether he is or is not a subject of Her Majesty, on the open sea within the territorial waters of Her Majesty's dominions, is an offence within the jurisdiction of the Admiral, although it may have been committed on board or by means of a foreign ship, and the person who committed such offence may be arrested, tried, and punished accordingly."

The offences to which the Act of 1878 relates are only those committed within the territorial waters of Her Majesty. That statute was passed in order to reverse the majority decision in *R.* v. *Keyn, The Franconia* (8). " Territorial waters " were defined in s. 7. The first part of the definition states that they consist of:

". . . such part of the sea adjacent to the coast of the United Kingdom, . . . as is deemed by international law to be within the territorial sovereignty of Her Majesty . . ."

I rather think that, since this country was then taking a power in relation to foreigners which according to the majority decision in *R.* v. *Keyn* (8) it never had before, namely, to try them in the courts of this country for crimes committed within territorial waters, it was thought to be politic to make it plain that this was not some autocratic assumption of power, but only that the law of England was being brought into line with the then generally accepted view of international law. That may well have been the reason for introducing into s. 7 the reference to international law. But Parliament was not content to leave it at that and allow questions of the jurisdiction of the Central Criminal Court to depend on anything so uncertain as international law. Perhaps it was alarmed by the prospects of volumes of PUFENDORF, WESTLAKE, OPPENHEIM, GROTIUS and others being carried into court whenever anyone was prosecuted under the Act of 1878, and the preliminary questions taking possibly weeks to decide. However that may be, the second part of the definition of territorial waters in s. 7 makes it plain that, for the purpose of that Act, they extend only to three nautical miles measured from low-water mark. The Act of 1878 dealt with the jurisdiction of our courts to try crimes committed in territorial waters. It did not create any offence within those waters. If it is important that it should be certain whether or not a court has jurisdiction, it seems to me to be far more important that it

(8) (1876), L.R. 2 Ex.D. 63.

should be certain whether what is done does or does not amount to a criminal offence.

The Act of 1878 may be no direct guide to the true construction of the Act of 1949. I think, however, that it is helpful to the extent to which I have indicated. It shows that, where only jurisdiction is at stake, Parliament intends to, and does, achieve certainty by precisely defining " territorial waters ". There is no such definition in the Act of 1949. It may be, as LORD PARKER, C.J., suggests, that it is to be assumed from this that the words " territorial waters " were intended to have a different meaning in the Act of 1949 from their meaning in the second part of s. 7 of the Act of 1878. I cannot accept this assumption. Why should one assume that, if there had been a definition in the Act of 1949, it would have accorded with the first part rather than the second part of the definition in s. 7 of the Act of 1878? Moreover, if one makes that assumption, it leads to the remarkable result that, of all the crimes in the calendar, the only offences committed on Red Sands for which anyone can be prosecuted are those under the Act of 1949. It is true that the legislature, when the Act of 1949 was passed, may have been thinking only of ships, and almost certainly where thinking primarily of ships, and that, therefore, the ambit of " territorial waters " was not of such vital consequence as it now is to the applicants. I cannot, however, accept that Parliament must be taken never to have had any structures of the Red Sands type in mind. However, this may be, it is still of great importance that anyone contemplating setting up in business, whether on a structure secured to the sea bed or on a ship in a certain locality, should, before embarking on the venture, be able to ascertain with reasonable certainty whether or not he will be committing a criminal offence.

If I am wrong in my construction of the words " territorial waters " in the Act of 1949, then, in my view, counsel for the applicants' contention that the order in council (9) is ultra vires is quite hopeless. If I am right in my construction, the order in council is quite irrelevant. It states, and, to my mind it states in a way which would be recognised in our courts, what, as from Sept. 30, 1964, are to be regarded as our territorial waters. It would, however, be irrelevant, because " territorial waters " for the purpose of the Act of 1949 would mean only territorial waters such as they were in 1949. On questions of sovereignty, the courts of this country will always pay the greatest attention to evidence from the executive as to what parts of the land or sea or air are within the sovereignty of Her Majesty. In *The Fagernes* (10), a statement by the Attorney-General, and I think a certificate by the Minister, were accepted by the court for the reasons given by ATKIN, L.J. (11), to which LORD PARKER, C.J., has referred. If sovereignty can thus be established, how much more easily can it be established by an order in council, which is the act of Her Majesty herself. Again, if I am wrong about the construction, I cannot accept counsel for the applicants' point about jurisdiction. It is quite true that neither the Summary Jurisdiction Act, 1879, nor the Magistrates' Courts Act, 1952, give the magistrates any power to try an offence committed in territorial waters, whereas they do give the magistrates power to try offences committed on national, internal waters, rivers, canals and so on. Counsel for the applicants argued with great persuasiveness that this shows that the magistrates have no jurisdiction in respect of offences committed in territorial waters. Section 2 (5) of the Act of 1952, however, states that:

" Nothing in this section shall affect any jurisdiction over offences conferred on a magistrates' court by any enactment not contained in this Act."

The point is: does the Act of 1949 confer such a jurisdiction on magistrates' courts? If it does, there is certainly nothing in the Act of 1952 to override it. Indeed, the Act of 1952 envisages that there may be Acts which do confer jurisdiction on a magistrates' court not conferred by that Act itself.

---

(9) The Territorial Waters Order in Council 1964.
(10) [1927] P. 311; 17 Asp. M.L.C. 326.
(11) [1927] P. at p. 324; 17 Asp. M.L.C. at p. 330.

In so far as the Act of 1949 makes it a summary offence to instal or use a wireless telegraphy station in the United Kingdom or its territorial waters without the licence of the Postmaster General, it does to my mind by necessary implication confer jurisdiction on the magistrates to try it. It would be absurd for Parliament to create an offence which is triable only by magistrates without by necessary implication giving magistrates power to try it. I am not impressed by the argument turning on the supposed difficulty of deciding which magistrates are to have jurisdiction. I should have thought that the magistrates whose jurisdiction extends over the nearest county to the point in question would have jurisdiction. It is said: what happens if the station happens to be equidistant from two counties. In such an unlikely event, help might be derived from s. 3 (1) of the Act of 1952, which reads:

" Where an offence has been committed on the boundary between two or more local jurisdictions, or within five hundred yards of such a boundary . . . the offence may be treated for the purposes of the preceding provisions of this Act as having been committed in any of those jurisdictions."

I think that a similar principle would be applied in the case of an offence committed within territorial waters.

However, on the view which I have reached about the true construction of the Act of 1949, no offence has been committed and I would, accordingly, quash the conviction.

BLAIN, J.: By this motion made pursuant to leave granted by this court on Dec. 2, 1966, one David Beresford Lye, one Theodore Edward Le Bouthillier Allbeury and a company called Estuary Radio, Ltd. apply for an order or orders of certiorari to remove into this court and quash three orders made on Nov. 25, 1966, by justices of the peace for the county of Kent sitting at Canterbury in the petty sessional division of St. Augustine in that country, whereunder each of the three applicants was respectively convicted of unlawfully using apparatus for wireless telegraphy on Aug. 16, 1966, at Red Sands Tower within the jurisdiction of the county except under and in accordance with a licence in that behalf granted by the Postmaster General, contrary to s. 1 (1) of the Wireless Telegraphy Act, 1949. It is convenient at once to consider the relevant provisions of the Act under which the charges are laid. Under s. 1 (1) of the Wireless Telegraphy Act, 1949, subject to a provision with which this court is not in these proceedings concerned:

" No person shall establish or use any station for wireless telegraphy or instal or use any apparatus for wireless telegraphy except under the authority of a licence in that behalf granted by the Postmaster General, and any person who establishes or uses any station for wireless telegraphy or instals or uses any apparatus for wireless telegraphy except under and in accordance with such a licence shall be guilty of an offence under this Act . . ."

There follow provisions as to terms and conditions, limitations of licence, fees and charges payable by licensees to the Postmaster General, provisions for the control of the use of a station for wireless telegraphy or apparatus, provisions as to experimental licences, as to misleading messages, interception of messages and so on, and the court is not presently concerned with these. Under s. 6 (1):

" Subject to the provisions of this section, the preceding provisions of this Part of this Act [that includes of course s. 1] shall apply—(a) to all stations and apparatus in or over, or for the time being in or over, the United Kingdom or the territorial waters adjacent thereto, . . ."

Subsection (1) (b) deals with the application of the provisions of the Act to British seagoing ships and aircraft; sub-s. (1) (c) to apparatus released from the areas covered by sub-s. (1) (a) or ships and aircraft covered by sub-s. (1) (b). Part 2 of the Act has no present relevance; Part 3 contains miscellaneous provisions, including s. 14. Section 14 (1), after specifying other offences in sub-s. (1) (*a*) and sub-s. (1) (*b*), reads thus:

> " Subject to the provisions of Part 1 of this Act relating to offences committed in relation to apparatus on board foreign seagoing ships or foreign aircraft, any person committing any offence under this Act . . . (*c*) shall, in the case of any other offence [that is other than in sub-s. (1) (*a*) and sub-s. (1) (*b*)], be liable on summary conviction to imprisonment for a period not exceeding three months or a fine not exceeding £100 or to both such imprisonment and such a fine."

Section 14 (2) brings in a director and other named officers in the case of an offence committed by a body corporate. Subsection (4) provides that:

> " Except as otherwise expressly provided in this Act, no criminal proceedings for an offence under this Act shall be instituted in England, Wales or Northern Ireland except with the consent of the Postmaster General."

The only other relevant section is s. 19, and it is relevant because of what it does not contain; it is the interpretation section, and it contains no definition of " territorial waters adjacent to the United Kingdom " or indeed of " territorial waters " at all.

The grounds of this application are set out in the statement filed in pursuance of R.S.C., Ord. 59, r. 3 (2); they are two in number, first, that Red Sands Tower lies 4·9 nautical miles from the nearest low-water mark of the county of Kent and is not in territorial waters and that neither the court which purported to make the orders convicting the applicants nor any other court has jurisdiction over acts committed on Red Sands Tower; secondly, that the offence alleged is a summary offence and the court has no jurisdiction to try a summary offence alleged to have been committed within territorial waters, even if it be a fact that it was in territorial waters. The facts in a nutshell are these. Red Sands Tower is a structure fixed to the bed of the sea; it lies, as I have said, 4·9 nautical miles from the nearest low-water mark of the coast of Kent. It lies less than three miles from a sandbank called Middle Sand, which sandbank is itself within three nautical miles of the nearest low-water mark of the Kent coast. The applicant Lye was at the material times, and I dare say still is, a director of the company Estuary Radio, Ltd., as is the applicant Allbeury. Estuary Radio, Ltd. is a United Kingdom registered company, and from, I think we were told, September, 1965, or thereabouts had used apparatus for wireless telegraphy, broadcasting at Red Sands Tower at least until the issue of these summonses. Such use was not under and in accordance with a licence granted by the Postmaster General; no such licence had been granted, nor, so far as the court knows, had application for such a licence been made. All three applicants were summoned for contravention of the provisions of s. 1 (1) of the Act of 1949, the prosecution being brought at the instance of the Postmaster General, as it would have to be. The justices for the petty sessional division of St. Augustine dealt with the matter on Nov. 24 and 25, 1966. Counsel for the applicants before any plea was taken, submitted that the court had no jurisdiction to hear the matter. The rights and wrongs of this matter depended in part at least on evidentiary questions, and the court decided to hear the evidence as to jurisdiction and the evidence as to the alleged offences. At the conclusion of the hearing, the court announced its decision in these terms already quoted by LORD PARKER, C.J., but I will repeat them as they are very short, for clarity's sake:

> " Red Sands Tower lies in territorial waters. The Wireless Telegraphy Act, 1949, is silent on the question of local jurisdiction. But the territorial waters in question adjoin the county of Kent and for that reason we are of the opinion that the justices have jurisdiction. On the evidence before us we find the case proved."

The applicant company were then fined £100, the applicant Lye and the applicant Allbeury were each granted an absolute discharge, and no order was made as to costs; no order was made as to confiscation of equipment.

The key question for decision, as it would appear to me, is the status in law of the waters at the spot where Red Sands Tower stands on the bed of the sea. It may have one of three statuses. Is it within the body of the county or within an arm of the sea or a river or internal waters or national waters to the landward side of a notional line joining the points of a bay? If so, jurisdiction is conceded. That possibility was negatived, however, by the decision of the justices on the facts, finding that it was in territorial waters. Is it part of the high seas beyond territorial waters? If so, then it is conceded that there was no jurisdiction. There is no evidence or suggestions to that effect. Is it in territorial waters? This raises two issues, first of all what are the boundaries of territorial waters, and, secondly, if those boundaries extend further seaward then what is loosely called the three mile limit, what jurisdiction, if any, is there beyond that three mile limit? The justices held that it was beyond the three mile limit, and that is so if the three mile limit is taken from the coast itself, the evidence being that it was, as I have stated, in reviewing the short facts, within three nautical miles of Middle Sand which itself was within three miles of low-water mark of the county proper.

I have already observed that the Wireless Telegraphy Act, 1949, fails to define what is meant by territorial waters despite the terms of s. 6 (1), namely, that

> ". . . the preceding provisions of this Part of this Act shall apply—(a) to all stations and apparatus in or over, or for the time being in or over, the the United Kingdom or the territorial waters adjacent thereto; . . . "

Indeed, I think that it is right that only in s. 6, though not only in s. 6 (1) (a), does the phrase " territorial waters " occur at all. In those circumstances, it is not surprising that the court's attention has been repeatedly directed to the definition of " territorial waters " in the Territorial Waters Jurisdiction Act, 1878, s. 7, which I will read shortly. Before considering how far that definition may be relevant to consideration of s. 6 (1) of the Wireless Telegraphy Act, 1949, it is wise to consider the context of the definition in the Act of 1878, and indeed the scope of the Act of 1878 itself. The position is that, prior to 1876, it had long been thought that the Lord High Admiral, in addition to having jurisdiction over English ships in any waters, had jurisdiction over foreigners on foreign ships whilst sailing through British territorial waters. This view was successfully challenged in *R. v. Keyn, The Franconia* (12), where a majority of seven judges to six in effect held that the realm of England extended only to the low-water mark, and that all beyond that was high seas. To be more specific, it was held that the courts had no jurisdiction to try a foreigner charged with an offence whilst on a foreign ship which was passing within three miles of the English coast. That decision evidently gave great concern to the Parliament of the day, and Parliament pretty promptly passed the Act of 1878. The courts do not look at preambles to statutes, or even, where they exist, at recitals, to interpret the wording of the statutes themselves unless ambiguity compels, and I do not find it necessary to found an interpretation on anything which can be read in the preamble or the recital here. It is, however, not uninteresting to glance at these things to see whether the strict interpretation, when one arrives at one, achieves a rational or a surprising result. Counsel for the applicants has pointed out that the Act of 1878 was described in the preamble as

> " An Act to regulate the law relating to the trial of offences committed on the sea within a certain distance of the coasts of Her Majesty's dominions."

He also points out that it is recited that:

> ". . . the rightful jurisdiction of Her Majesty, her heirs and successors, extends and has always extended over the open seas adjacent to the coasts

(12) (1876), L.R. 2 Ex.D. 63.

of the United Kingdom and of all other parts of Her Majesty's dominions to such a distance as is necessary for the defence and security of such dominions: And whereas it is expedient that all offences committed on the open sea within a certain distance of the coast of the United Kingdom and of all other parts of Her Majesty's dominions, by whomsoever committed, should be dealt with according to law."

Section 2 of that Act of 1878 reads:

" An offence committed by a person, whether he is or is not a subject of Her Majesty, on the open sea within the territorial waters of Her Majesty's dominions, is an offence within the jurisdiction of the Admiral, although it may have been committed on board or by means of a foreign ship, and the person who committed such offence may be arrested, tried, and punished accordingly."

Section 5 saves Her Majesty's existing jurisdiction in these terms:

" Nothing in this Act contained shall be construed to be in derogation of any rightful jurisdiction of Her Majesty, her heirs or successors, under the law of nations, or to affect or prejudice any jurisdiction conferred by Act of Parliament or now by law existing in relation to foreign ships or in relation to persons on board such ships."

Those, I think, are the only relevant provisions, apart from the interpretation section, s. 7. Section 7, after defining " The jurisdiction of the Admiral " and " United Kingdom ", defines " The territorial waters of Her Majesty's dominions ", a phrase which we have seen and which I have just read in precisely those words ". . . open sea within the territorial waters of Her Majesty's dominions " in s. 2. The definition is this:

" ' The territorial waters of Her Majesty's dominions ', in reference to the sea, means such part of the sea adjacent to the coast of the United Kingdom, or the coast of some other part of Her Majesty's dominions, as is deemed by international law to be within the territorial sovereignty of Her Majesty; and for the purpose of any offence declared by this Act to be within the jurisdiction of the Admiral, any part of the open sea within the marine league of the coast measured from low-water mark shall be deemed to be open sea within the territorial waters of Her Majesty's dominions."

It is to be observed that the first half of that definition before the semi-colon is general; the second part after the semi-colon in my view refers straight back to s. 2. It is directly concerned with the Admiral's jurisdiction over foreigners on foreign ships in what I may unequivocally call British waters. It cannot be too clearly emphasised that that interpretation section is introduced by the words:

" In this Act, unless there is something inconsistent in the context, the following expressions shall respectively have the meanings hereinafter assigned to them . . ."

It is, in my view, clear that the Act of 1878 by s. 2 brought within the jurisdiction of the Admiral offences committed by any person, foreign or British, on a ship within the territorial waters of Her Majesty's dominions, the phrase in s. 2 itself, that is to say, any part of the sea within one marine mile of the coast measured from low water mark, which is the phrase in the second part of the definition in s. 7. That was the ad hoc purpose of that definition in that Act in my view, and it was purely ad hoc. It is, in passing, interesting to observe that it is a definition which since has once been borrowed for and incorporated in a very limited Act of Parliament, the North Sea Fisheries Act, 1893, but has not been incorporated in any other statute. Just before leaving that section, in so far as it may be necessary to consider the general part, the first part of the definition, I do not doubt that the phrase

" Such part of the sea . . . as is deemed by international law to be within the territorial sovereignty of Her Majesty "

means such part as is deemed by international law from time to time—such part as is deemed by international law at any time in question, rather than simply—such part as is deemed as the date of the passing of this Act to be within the Sovereign's territory.

That brings one to consider the position of international law and municipal law. For many years prior to *The Franconia* (13) in 1876 and the immediately ensuing Act of 1878, and indeed for years thereafter, what in that case had been described by LUSH, J. (14) as the usage and common consent of nations which constituted international law had appropriated to the adjacent state certain waters to a limit of three miles seaward of low-water mark of the coast of that state. So that such waters were known to international law by the name of territorial waters and were regarded as being in the exclusive jurisdiction of that state. That, of course, did not and could not enlarge the area of municipal jurisdiction of that state. I have already pointed out how, in my view, the Territorial Waters Jurisdiction Act, 1878, enlarged the jurisdiction of the Lord High Admiral, and I have already referred to the key section, s. 6 (1) (*a*) of the Wireless Telegraphy Act, 1949, applying the provisions of, inter alia, s. 1 (1) of that Act, under which this prosecution was brought, to the territorial waters adjacent to the United Kingdom. I take the view that, at that time, territorial waters adjacent to the United Kingdom, in the absence of a relevant definition, because I have found the 1878 definition to be irrelevant, means waters extending by international usage to a distance of three miles seaward of low-water mark, so that Parliament by s. 6 (1) (*a*) was conferring municipal jurisdiction over those same waters, that is to say, waters regarded as territorial by contemporary international usage, contemporary international usage as recognised from time to time, in so far as such usage is recognised from time to time in this country.

That brings one to the question whether there has been a change recognised by this country since the time of the passing of the Act of 1949, for which purpose one must pass very shortly to the convention and the order in council. The Convention on the Territorial Sea and the Contiguous Zone was ratified by this country on Mar. 14, 1960; was in force as from Sept. 10, 1964, and foreshadowed the order in council (15) which was made on Sept. 25, 1964. That order in council purports to carry out the articles of the convention by exercise of the royal prerogative, and in doing so it purports to extend the limits of the waters over which the Crown has sovereignty, and the courts have jurisdiction. Counsel for the applicants submits that the prerogative to extend jurisdiction was abrogated by the Territorial Waters Jurisdiction Act, 1878, to which I have referred, and that, consequently, the order in council, as he puts it, is ultra vires and the limits could only be extended by Parliament. For myself, I would prefer to say that, if he is right, the order in council is irrelevant, ineffective to achieve this purpose; that is perhaps an academic matter. The convention, by art. 1, provides:

" The sovereignty of a state extends, beyond its land territory and its internal waters, to a belt of sea adjacent to its coast, described as the territorial sea."

Article 3 provides:

" Except where otherwise provided in these articles, the normal baseline for measuring the breadth of the territorial sea is the low-water line along the coast as marked on large-scale charts officially recognised by the coastal state."

In other words, in this context the coast of Kent itself.

---

(13) (1876), L.R. 2 Ex.D. 63.   (14) (1876), L.R. 2 Ex.D. at p. 239.
(15) The Territorial Waters Order in Council 1964.

There are two other articles, however, which qualify that or foreshadow qualifications. Article 10 provided:

" 1. An island is a naturally-formed area of land, surrounded by water, which is above water at high-tide. 2. The territorial sea of an island is measured in accordance with the provisions of these articles."

Article 11 provides:

" 1. A low tide elevation is a naturally-formed area of land which is surrounded by and above water at low-tide but submerged at high tide. Where a low-tide elevation is situated wholly or partly at a distance not exceeding the breadth of the territorial sea from the mainland or an island, the low-water line on that elevation may be used as the baseline for measuring the breadth of the territorial sea. 2. Where a low-tide elevation is wholly situated at a distance exceeding the breadth of the territorial sea from the mainland or island, it has no territorial sea of its own."

It would appear that, as between signatories to that convention, it was agreed that any one or more of them may, but not shall, decide to use for purposes of its baseline, low-tide elevations.

I pass to the order in council, first of all art. 1 and art. 2, and then two of the definitions in art. 5 are all we need be concerned with. Article 1:

" This Order may be cited as the Territorial Waters Order in Council 1964 and shall come into operation on Sept. 30, 1964."

That is the date of its operation; Sept. 25, 1964, was the date of its making. Article 2 (1):

" Except as otherwise provided in art. 3 and art. 4 of this order [which do not concern us], the baseline from which the breadth of the territorial sea, adjacent to the United Kingdom, the Channel Islands and the Isle of Man is measured shall be low-water line along the coast, including the coast of all islands comprised in those territories,"

and " island " is defined in art. 5 (1) as " a naturally formed area of land surrounded by water which is above water at mean high-water spring tides ". Article 3 (2):

" The provisions of para. (1) of this article shall be without prejudice to the operation of art. 2 of this order in relation to any island or low-tide elevation which for the purpose of that article is treated as if it were an island . . ."

The definition of " low-tide elevation " in art. 5 (1) is as follows:

" a naturally formed area of drying land surrounded by water which is below water at mean high-water spring tides."

The result is that, in this case, this low-tide elevation, which was itself within three miles of the coast to the south and within three miles, for that matter, of Red Sands Tower to its north-east, is treated as an island, and the baseline is, and can be, according to the order in council, measured from there.

What is the effect of the order in council? If it is effective for the purpose for which the court is considering, then, on admitted facts, the provisions of Part 1 of the Wireless Telegraphy Act, 1949, apply to Red Sands Tower and the offence has been committed. As I have said, if it is not effective, then it is probably irrelevant or, as it is suggested, ultra vires. It is suggested that the prerogative right to make such an order was abrogated by s. 2 and the definition s. 7 of the Territorial Waters Jurisdiction Act, 1878; I have already expressed my view that the one nautical league definition in that Act of territorial waters was purely ad hoc and the limits, therefore, are those recognised by international law. The convention recognises that they may be measured from the low-tide elevation as a baseline if the particular party to the convention decides so to do. The order in council takes advantage of that right and adopts it. That prerogative right does not, in my view, abrogate it, and Red Sands Tower, therefore, in my view, as it was in that of the justices, is within territorial waters.

That, however, is not the only point. There is the other short point taken as a second point by counsel for the applicants, which is this in a nutshell: postulating the correctness of that, namely, that Red Sands Tower is in territorial waters, it is nonetheless beyond three miles from the coast itself. This is the argument: the only offence committed is a summary offence; that was clear from the Act of 1949, the provisions which I have read. The old jurisdiction of the Lord High Admiral, the argument runs, subsequently transferred to the Central Criminal Court, was in respect only of indictable offences. The Act of 1878 gave jurisdiction in respect only of indictable offences, and there is no court with jurisdiction to try the summary offences created by the Act of 1949, and committed in what are postulated as and have been found to be territorial waters. Without going into detail, I find that argument unacceptable for the reasons given by LORD PARKER, C.J. I would merely for myself point out one thing on that aspect of the matter, that s. 14 (1) (a) of the Act of 1949 provides for penalties on summary conviction for certain offences; s. 14 (1) (b) penalties on summary conviction for other offences, and s. 14 (1) (c) penalties on summary conviction for other offences not covered by sub-s. (1) (a) or (b); and what is more pertinent to note is that s. 14 (3) provides:

" Where a person is convicted of an offence under this Act . . . the court may, in addition to any other penalty, order . . . the apparatus . . . to be forfeited . . ."

Parliament has there postulated that there is in existence, albeit that it is not in the Act of 1949 named, a court, which can only be a court of summary jurisdiction, to deal with those summary offences. This is not the first time, as *Cullen* v. *Trimble* (16) held, albeit it was before the Summary Jurisdiction Act, 1879, that Parliament has expressly created summary offences without in so many words naming the court with jurisdiction to try them.

In my view, the justices were entitled to try this matter. There is no other criticism, if they were so entitled, of the way in which they did so, and, therefore, this application fails. I would not wish to say that personally without stating that the justices clearly, from such penalties and lack of penalties as they imposed, took the view that this was not a deliberate flouting of the law, a view with which I see no possible reason to differ. One thing I would say is this. I regret feeling compelled, as I do, rightly or wrongly, to a conclusion which postulates that a man may find himself in the position where what he starts by doing lawfully suddenly becomes an offence at a stroke of the pen. If hereafter it should be held that my conclusion is wrong in the interests of the general principle of maintaining true principles of justice, I for one should be delighted.

Motion dismissed. Leave to appeal to the House of Lords granted under s. 1 of the Administration of Justice Act, 1960, the court certifying that a point of law of general public importance was involved, viz., the true construction of the expression " territorial waters " in the Wireless Telegraphy Act, 1949.

Solicitors: *Kingsford, Flower & Pain*, Ashford, Kent (for the applicants); *Solicitor, Post Office* (for the respondents).

[*Reported by* N. P. METCALFE, ESQ., *Barrister-at-Law.*]

---

(16) (1872), L.R. 7 Q.B. 416.

POST OFFICE *v.* NORWICH UNION
FIRE INSURANCE SOCIETY, LTD.

[COURT OF APPEAL, CIVIL DIVISION (Lord Denning, M.R., Harman and Salmon, L.JJ.), January 16, 17, 18, 1967.]

Insurance—Liability insurance—Public liability policy—Third persons' claims— Action by third person against insurers—Damage to Post Office cable in street by insured company digging for water main—Liability denied by company— Company went into liquidation—Post Office sued insurers direct—Liability of company not yet established and its amount not yet ascertained—Whether action maintainable—Third Parties (Rights against Insurers) Act, 1930 (20 & 21 Geo. 5 c. 25), s. 1 (1).

In May, 1964, P., Ltd. carried out work in a street and damaged a cable of the Post Office. The Post Office claimed £839 10s. 3d. damages. P., Ltd. denied liability and alleged that the damage was the fault of the Post Office, whose engineer had been consulted and had, it was alleged, not indicated correctly the site of the cable. P., Ltd. were insured under a public liability policy issued by the defendant insurance company. The policy provided that the insurance company " will indemnify [P., Ltd.] against all sums which [P., Ltd.] shall become legally liable to pay as compensation in respect of . . . loss of or damage to property ". Condition No. 3 of the policy provided that " no admission offer promise payment or indemnity shall be made or given by or on behalf of [P., Ltd.] without the written consent of [the insurance company] . . .". P., Ltd. went into liquidation. The Post Office sued the insurance company for £839 10s. 3d., claiming as statutory assignees of the insured by virtue of s. 1 (1)* of the Third Parties (Rights against Insurers) Act, 1930.

Held: the Post Office could not maintain as yet their action against the insurance company under s. 1 of the Third Parties (Rights against Insurers) Act, 1930, because—

(i) (per LORD DENNING, M.R., and SALMON, L.J.) unless P., Ltd. could have sued the insurance company the Post Office could not sue them, and until P., Ltd.'s liability was established and the amount ascertained, whether by litigation or by arbitration or by agreement, they could not sue the insurance company (see p. 579, letter G, p. 580, letters A and F, and p. 582, letter E, post); moreover, by reason of condition 3 of the policy, an admission by P., Ltd. of liability to the Post Office (if it had been made) could not have established such liability as against the insurance company and so as to entitle P., Ltd. to sue them (see p. 280, letter F, p. 282, letter F, post).

Dictum of DEVLIN, J., in *West Wake Price & Co.* v. *Ching* ([1956] 3 All E.R. at p. 825) applied.

(ii) (per HARMAN, L.J.) condition 3 of the policy would have afforded a defence to the insurance company if they were sued by P., Ltd. before liability of P., Ltd. was established and its amount was ascertained, and the Post Office, as the statutory assignees of P., Ltd., were equally barred (see p. 581, letters F and G, post).

Appeal allowed.

[As to the extent of statutory subrogation of rights under an insurance policy, see 22 HALSBURY'S LAWS (3rd Edn.) 339-342, paras. 700, 701; and for cases on the subject, see 5 DIGEST (Repl.) 726-728, *6284-6301,* and generally, 29 DIGEST (Repl.) 513-515, *3607-3623.*

For the Third Parties (Rights against Insurers) Act, 1930, s. 1 (1), see 2 HALSBURY'S STATUTES (2nd Edn.) 458.]

Cases referred to:

Harrington Motor Co., Re, Ex p. Chaplin, [1928] Ch. 105; 97 L.J.Ch. 55; 138 L.T. 185; 10 Digest (Repl.) 932, *6378.*

---

* Section 1 (1), so far as material, is set out at p. 579, letters D and E, post.

x

Approved in BRADLEY v EAGLE STAR
INSURANCE CO LTD [1989] 1 All ER 961

Hood's Trustees v. *Southern Union General Insurance Co. of Australia, Ltd.*, [1928] Ch. 793; 97 L.J.Ch. 467; 139 L.T. 536; 5 Digest (Repl.) 726, *6286*.

West Wake Price & Co. v. *Ching*, [1956] 3 All E.R. 821; [1957] 1 W.L.R. 45; 29 Digest (Repl.) 554, *3762*.

Appeal.

This was an appeal by the defendants, Norwich Union Fire Insurance Society, Ltd., from a decision of DONALDSON, J., dated Nov. 11, 1966, in favour of the plaintiffs, the Post Office, on the trial of a preliminary point of law.

The facts were that the plaintiffs had a telegraph cable laid underneath St. John's Street, Huntingdon. In May, 1963, A. J. G. Potter & Sons, Ltd. (herein called " Potters "), who were contractors, were proposing to dig a hole in the street to find a water main. On May 20, 1963, their representative met the plaintiffs' engineer on the site and discussed the position of the cable and the proposed excavation. On May 24, 1963, Potters, whilst carrying out the work, struck and damaged a cable. The plaintiffs claimed damages against Potters, being the cost of repairing the cable which amounted to £839 10s. 3d. Potters refused to pay, claiming that it was the fault of the plaintiffs' engineer, who, they alleged, had pointed out the wrong place as being the place where the telegraph cable lay. The plaintiffs learnt that Potters had taken out a public liability policy of insurance with the defendants. By this the defendants agreed to

". . . indemnify [Potters] against all sums which [Potters] shall become legally liable to pay as compensation in respect of—. . . (2) . . . damage to property . . . caused by accidents happening in connexion with [Potters'] business during the period of insurance . . ."

On June 1, 1964, Potters went into liquidation. By writ dated June 17, 1965, the plaintiffs claimed against the defendants the sum of £839 10s. 3d. pursuant to s. 8 of the Telegraph Act, 1878, and s. 1 of the Third Parties (Rights against Insurers) Act, 1930. By their defence the defendants, among other matters, raised objections in point of law. By order dated Dec. 15, 1965, an issue was ordered to be tried as a preliminary point of law. This issue was as follows—

" The plaintiffs contend that on the true construction of the Third Parties (Rights against Insurers) Act, 1930, and of the policy of insurance . . . liability of the defendants to the plaintiffs is in the events which have happened established by proof that [Potters] became liable to pay unliquidated damages to the plaintiffs.

" It is contended on behalf of the defendants that on the true construction of the Act of 1930 and of the policy of insurance, in default of agreement judgment against [Potters] is a condition precedent to liability of the defendants under the policy; and that in the premises no sum of money having been ascertained whether by judgment or agreement to be payable by [Potters] (as is admitted) the present action must fail."

DONALDSON, J., having ordered on Nov. 11, 1966, that the question of law be answered in favour of the plaintiffs, the defendants by notice of appeal dated Dec. 2, 1966, gave notice of motion that the order should be set aside and that judgment should be entered for the defendants. The grounds of the appeal were (i) that on the true construction of the policy and on the agreed facts the trial judge erred in law in holding that Potters had at any material time any right to be indemnified by the defendants under the policy; and (ii) that on the true construction of the Act of 1930 and on the agreed facts the trial judge erred in law in holding that a right to be indemnified under the policy in respect of the matters of which the plaintiffs complained had been vested in them by virtue of that Act.

The authorities and the cases noted below* were cited during the argument in addition to the cases referred to in the judgments.

Hugh Griffiths, Q.C., and *I. S. Warren* for the defendants.
Sir John Hobson, Q.C., and *J. H. R. Newey* for the Post Office.

LORD DENNING, M.R., after summarising the facts, continued: In the days before the Third Parties (Rights against Insurers) Act, 1930, when an injured person got judgment against a wrongdoer who was insured, and the wrongdoer then went bankrupt, the injured person had no direct claim against the insurance moneys. He could only prove in the bankruptcy. The insurance moneys went into the pool for the benefit of the general body of creditors (see *Re Harrington Motor Co., Ex p. Chaplin* (1) applied in *Hood's Trustees* v. *Southern Union General Insurance Co. of Australia, Ltd.* (2). That was so obviously unjust that Parliament intervened. In the Act of 1930 the injured person was given a right against the insurance company. Section 1 provides that:

" (1) Where under any contract of insurance a person (hereinafter referred to as the insured) is insured against liabilities to third parties which he may incur, then—

    (*a*) in the event of the insured becoming bankrupt . . .; or
    (*b*) in the case of the insured being a company, in the event of a winding-up . . .;

if, either before or after that event, any such liability as aforesaid is incurred by the insured, his rights against the insurer under the contract in respect of the liability shall, notwithstanding anything in any Act or rule of law to the contrary, be transferred to and vest in the third party to whom the liability was so incurred."

Under that section the injured person steps into the shoes of the wrongdoer. There is transferred to him the wrongdoer's " rights against the insurer under the contract ". What are those rights? When do they arise? So far as the " liability " of the insured is concerned, there is no doubt that his liability to the injured person arises at the time of the accident, when negligence and damage coincide; but the " rights " of the insured against the insurers do not arise at that time.

The policy in the present case provides that

" the [defendants] will indemnify the insured against all sums which the insured shall become legally liable to pay as compensation in respect of loss of or damage to property."

It seems to me that A. J. G. Potter & Sons, Ltd., acquire only a right to sue for the money when their liability to the injured person has been established so as to give rise to a right of indemnity. Their liability to the injured person must be ascertained and determined to exist, either by judgment of the court or by an award in an arbitration or by agreement. Until that is done, the right to an indemnity does not arise. I agree with the statement by Devlin, J., in *West Wake Price & Co.* v. *Ching* (3):

" The assured cannot recover anything under the main indemnity clause or make any claim against the underwriters until the assured have been found liable and so sustained a loss."

Under s. 1 of the Act of 1930 the injured person cannot sue the insurance company except in such circumstances as the insured himself could have sued the insurance

---

* 22 Halsbury's Laws (3rd Edn.) 180, 181, paras. 347, 348, Williams on Law and Practice in Bankruptcy (7th Edn.) 72, 81, 151, 160, 161, Palmer on Company Law (20th Edn.) 942, 976, Shawcross on Motor Insurance (2nd Edn.) 129. *Craig* v. *Royal Insurance Co., Ltd.*, (1914), 112 L.T. 291; *Freshwater* v. *Western Australian Assurance Co., Ltd.*, [1932] All E.R. Rep. 791; [1933] 1 K.B. 515; *McCormick* v. *National Motor and Accident Insurance Union, Ltd.*, (1934), 50 T.L.R. 528.
(1) [1928] Ch. 105.   (2) [1928] Ch. 793.
(3) [1956] 3 All E.R. 821 at p. 825.

company. Potters could have sued for an indemnity only when their liability
to the third person was established and the amount of the loss ascertained. In
some circumstances an insured might sue earlier for a declaration, e.g., if the insurance company were repudiating the policy for some reason; but where the
policy is admittedly good, the insured cannot sue for an indemnity until his own
liability to the third person is ascertained.

It appears that in *Hood's Trustees* v. *Southern Union General Insurance Company
of Australia, Ltd.* (4) it was assumed, in the course of the argument on both sides,
and by the judge, that the insured obtained a cause of action against the insurance
company at the time when the accident happened. I think that that assumption
was incorrect. The decision in *Hood's* case (4) itself can be supported on other
grounds, namely, that after the first bankruptcy there was a subsequent judgment
against the bankrupt ascertaining the amount. Once that judgment was obtained
against the bankrupt, he had a right to indemnity against the insurance company
and this right vested in the first trustee in bankruptcy under s. 38 (*a*) of the
Bankruptcy Act, 1914. Unless that judgment had been obtained, there would
have been no right to an indemnity.

There is, however, a further point. When the rights of the insured are transferred to the injured person, they are transferred on the ordinary understanding,
that is, subject to such conditions as the contract provides. Condition 3 of
this policy stipulated that:

" No admission offer promise payment or indemnity shall be made or given
by or on behalf of [Potters] without the written consent of [the defendants
who] shall be entitled if [they] so [desire] to take over and conduct in the
name of [Potters] the defence or settlement of any claim."

In the face of that condition I do not see how Potters could sue the defendants
before Potters' liability is ascertained. Potters are not at liberty to say: " We
admit we are liable and therefore we ought to recover an indemnity." They cannot
make that admission: and, therefore, cannot sue.

In these circumstances I think that the right to sue for these moneys does not
arise until the liability is established and the amount ascertained. How is this
to be done? If there is an unascertained claim for damages in tort, it cannot be
proved in the bankruptcy, nor in the liquidation of the company; but the injured
person can bring an action against the wrongdoer. In the case of a company,
he must get the leave of the court. No doubt leave would automatically be given.
The insurance company can fight that action in the name of the wrongdoer.
In that way liability can be established and the loss ascertained. Then the
injured person can go against the insurance company.

In confirmation of this view, I would remark that at the time when the Act
of 1930 was passed, the practice in these courts was to keep secret the fact that
the defendant was insured. It was misconduct on the part of counsel to indicate
to the jury that the defendant was insured. If the Act of 1930 had enabled the
injured person to sue the insurance company direct, before liability was ascertained, it would have cut right across that practice. I am sure that at that date
the legislature never contemplated any such thing. It is different now. We
assume that the defendant in an action of tort is insured unless the contrary
appears. Nevertheless, casting one's mind back to 1930, I am sure that the
legislature did not contemplate an action in tort against an insurance company
direct.

There is a further point. If a third person, who suffered personal injury, could
sue the insurance company direct, there would be a strange anomaly about the
period of limitation. The action of the injured person against the wrongdoer (for
the tort) would be barred after three years from the accident, but his action against
the insurance company (as a transferee of the rights under the contract) would
not be barred until six years from the accident.

(4) [1928] Ch. 793.

This is simply a matter of procedure. The right procedure is for the injured person to sue the wrongdoer, and having got judgment against the wrongdoer, then make his claim against the insurance company. This attempt to sue the insurance company, the defendants, direct (before liability is established) is not correct. I would, therefore, allow the appeal.

HARMAN, L.J.: The Post Office desire to sue the defendants, Norwich Union Fire Insurance Society, Ltd. direct, that is to say, to take a short-cut. The argument is that under the Third Parties (Rights against Insurers) Act, 1930, the rights of A. J. G. Potter & Sons, Ltd. (to whom I will refer as " Potters ") against the insurers vest in the third party, that is to say, the Post Office. That all sounds quite simple until one begins to think that in fact there was not an admitted liability. It was not a mere matter of quantifying the amount for which the defendants might be liable. Their allegation was that there was no liability at all because Potters had been misled by the Post Office and, therefore, had a good answer to the original claim. That seems to make it fairly clear that the kind of action contemplated is a very inconvenient form of action, to say the very least of it; for the Post Office will be suing the defendants and having to prove on the way, so to speak, what the circumstances of the accident were—the party concerned in the accident (Potters) not being a party to the suit at all.

However, it seemed to me at one time, having regard to *Hood's Trustees* v. *Southern Union General Insurance Co. of Australia, Ltd.* (5), which has been mentioned by LORD DENNING, M.R., that that was a course which could be taken, however inconvenient it might be; because I accept the view suggested in *Hood* (5) that the rights, whatever they may be, arise at the time when the wrongdoing is committed, if there is a wrongdoing. Therefore, it might be said that what is assigned to the Post Office are all those rights. I think that it may be accepted that it is so, as far as I am concerned; but even so, the contract contains not only rights, but limitations of those rights. One cannot, I think, assign to somebody part of the rights under the contract without assigning to him the condition subject to which those rights exist. Consequently, the Post Office are saddled with the inability of Potters to sue direct themselves before the liability is ascertained, because that would amount to a breach of condition 3 of the policy (6) which would in itself be a defence to the defendants.

Therefore, I would decide this case on the narrow ground that the rights assigned to the Post Office by the statute must be coupled with the rest of the particular rights and obligations which make up the contract of insurance. One cannot pick out one bit—pick out the plums and leave the duff behind. Therefore, I think that as Potters could not sue, so their statutory assignees, the Post Office, cannot sue until the amount has been ascertained and quantified.

That being so, this form of action is incompetent and ought not to be allowed, notwithstanding the inconvenience of having to get leave in the liquidation to bring the action. I suppose it is possible that such leave might be refused, but I do not think that we need contemplate that until it happens; it seems to me to be unlikely to happen. The Post Office should get leave to bring the action, and, although they cannot enforce any judgment which they get against a company in liquidation because it is an unliquidated claim, they will then be in a position to go against the defendants by reason of the help given by the statute. The statute will be quite effective in its proper place. It does not enable this particular jump to be made which the Post Office would have us allow. I would, therefore, allow the appeal.

SALMON, L.J.: On May 24, 1963, A. J. G. Potter & Sons, Ltd. admittedly damaged a telegraph cable belonging to the Post Office. Thereafter the Post Office were taking the line that they were entitled to be paid £839 10s. 3d. by Potters, which was the amount by which they stated that they were out of

---

(5) [1928] Ch. 793.   (6) For condition 3, see p. 580, letter E, ante.

pocket by reason of the damage to the cable. Potters, on the other hand, were saying that they were under no legal liability because the damage had in fact been caused owing to some wrong information which they had received from the Post Office. Potters then went into liquidation; and on June 17, 1965, the Post Office sued Potters' insurers (the defendants) claiming the sum of £839 10s. 3d. in the circumstances which I have described. The Post Office's claim against the defendants was a claim as statutory assignees of Potters' rights under Potters' policy of insurance.

The case really resolves itself into this simple question: could Potters on June 17, 1965, have successfully sued their insurers for the sum of £839 10s. 3d. which they were denying that they were under any obligation to pay to the Post Office? Stated in that way, I should have thought that the question admits of only one answer. Obviously Potters could not have claimed that money from their insurers. It is quite true that if Potters in the end are shown to have been legally liable for the damage resulting from the accident to the cable, their liability in law dates from the moment when the accident occurred and the damage was suffered. Whether or not there is any legal liability, however, and, if so, the amount due from Potters to the Post Office can, in my view, only be finally ascertained either by agreement between Potters and the Post Office or by an action or arbitration between Potters and the Post Office. It is quite unheard of in practice for any insured to sue his insurers in a money claim when the actual loss against which he wishes to be indemnified has not been ascertained. I have never heard of such an action, and there is nothing in law that makes such an action possible. I agree with the statement of DEVLIN, J., in *West Wake Price & Co.* v. *Ching* (7), to which LORD DENNING, M.R., has already referred. This statement is obiter, but I think that it correctly states the legal position, although it does not expressly point out that liability and quantum can be ascertained not only by action but also by arbitration or agreement. In any event condition 3 of the policy of insurance (8), for the reasons already stated, would have made it impossible for Potters to sue the defendants; but quite apart from condition 3, I would have thought that no such action was maintainable.

It is quite true that this is a narrow procedural point, and from one point of view it cannot matter very much whether the defendants are called Norwich Union Fire Insurance Society, Ltd. or A. J. G. Potter & Sons, Ltd. It might be said that the action would proceed in exactly the same way whoever may be the defendant because under the insurance policy the insurers are entitled to conduct the defence. That may be so; but from a broad commercial point of view I can well understand why the insurers do not want their name to appear on the record as defendants. If this Third Parties (Rights against Insurers) Act, 1930, gave third parties the right to sue insurance companies direct, it would mean that the cause lists would contain the names of many defendant insurance companies; and this could not be good for their business. If an insurance company were constantly being sued, any customer or potential customer would or might assume, quite wrongly, that the company was habitually repudiating liability under its policies with its own customers. Therefore, I can understand the reason why this case has been fought up to this court. As far as the Post Office are concerned, they cannot be in any way prejudiced by having to sue Potters. It is almost inconceivable that they would not obtain leave in the winding-up to bring the action. I can, of course, contemplate cases in which an insurance company is in a shaky position and it might be necessary for the plaintiffs to sue the insurance company after having recovered judgment against the insured. This, of course, is not such a case. Such cases would be very, very rare. I realise that it would be more convenient in such a case for the plaintiff to have the right to sue the insurers direct and thus save valuable time.

Whatever may be the rule of convenience is, however, beside the point. In law,

---

(7) [1956] 3 All E.R. at p. 825.   (8) For condition 3, see p. 580, letter E, ante.

I am satisfied that Potters had no claim in June, 1965, against the defendants. For that reason it is quite clear that the Post Office have no claim against the defendants, for they stand in Potters' shoes, and can be in no better position than Potters.

I would accordingly allow the appeal.

Appeal allowed; action dismissed. Leave to appeal to the House of Lords refused.

Solicitors: *Wm. Easton & Sons*, agents for *Mills & Reeve*, Norwich (for the insurance company); *Solicitor to Post Office*.

[*Reported by* F. Guttman, Esq., *Barrister-at-Law*.]

McARDLE v. ANDMAC ROOFING CO. AND OTHERS.

[Court of Appeal, civil division (Sellers, Davies and Edmund Davies, L.JJ.), November 15, 16, 17, 1966.]

Building—Building regulations—Roof—Opening in roof—Existing building—Temporary absence of workmen placing joists and laying boards over opening—Opening left uncovered and unprotected—Plaintiff injured by falling through opening—Whether employers liable for breach of statutory duty—Building (Safety, Health and Welfare) Regulations, 1948 (S.I. 1948 No. 1145), reg. 30 (1), (5).

Building—Construction work—Negligence—Sub-contractors liable to servant of other sub-contractors—Liability of constructional company, having conduct of work for building owner, to servant of sub-contractors—Laying of felt and bitumen on part of roof sub-contracted—Servant of sub-contractors injured by fall through opening in roof temporarily left by other sub-contractors.

The plaintiff was employed by sub-contractors (" Andmac "), who were laying felt and bitumen on the roof of an existing building which was being converted at Pontin's Holiday Camp at Blackpool. Other sub-contractors (" Newton ") were engaged to provide labour to place joists over a strip of the roof, which had been covered with glass for which new roofing was to be substituted, and to lay boards on the joists; this was, in effect, a labour only contract. Both sub-contractors were engaged by the second defendants, who were responsible for the carrying out of the structural work to the Pontin organisation. On the day of the accident the engineer of the second defendants had sent Andmac's men to work on this particular roof. Newton's men, who had been working on the roof ahead of the plaintiff, had gone for their lunch-time break leaving temporarily an aperture in the roof, some twelve feet from the ground, uncovered and unprotected. Work was to be resumed in half-an-hour. Work on laying bitumen was proceeding and the plaintiff was on the roof pouring hot bitumen from a bucket on to felt on the boards of the roof. As he moved along the roof half sideways, half backwards, holding the bucket, and having to give strict attention to his work, he reached the aperture, over-balanced fell to the ground and was injured. No arrangements had been made between the second defendants and the sub-contractors, or between the sub-contractors, for safety precautions. The plaintiff sued Andmac, the second defendants and Newton for negligence, and Andmac and the second defendants also for breach of statutory duty under reg. 30* of the Building (Safety, Health and Welfare) Regulations,

---

* Regulation 30 (1) and (5), so far as material, provide: " (1) Subject to paras. (5) and (6) of this regulation every accessible opening in a roof or in the floor of a building, working platform, gangway, or run, through which any person is liable to fall a distance of more than six feet six inches, shall be provided with—(a) a suitable guard-rail or guard-rails of adequate strength to a height of at least three feet above the edge of

(continued at foot of page 584).

Applied in R v Swan Hunter Ship-
builders Ltd [1982] 1 All ER 264

1948. The trial judge held that Andmac, the second defendants and Newton each owed in the circumstances a duty of care to the plaintiff and were liable to him for negligence, that Andmac were also liable for breach of statutory duty, that the plaintiff was not guilty of any contributory negligence, and that as between the defendants liability should be apportioned fifty per cent. to the second defendants, thirty per cent. to Andmac and twenty per cent. to Newton. On appeal by each defendant against the rejection of the allegation of contributory negligence on the plaintiff's part and against the apportionment of liability, and by the second defendants and Newton against being held liable to the plaintiff,

Held: (i) the plaintiff was not guilty of any contributory negligence, this being just the type of accident against which it was necessary to protect a man whose task required concentration (see p. 588, letters B and D, p. 589, letter H, and p. 591, letter C, post).

(ii) (a) as the second defendants were employing the other defendants, two small contractors who were to work in proximity and one of whom (Newton) was employed on a labour only basis, the second defendants assumed the duty of co-ordinating the work and thus were under a duty to see that reasonable safety precautions were taken for the contractors' men on the job;

(b) each of the defendants should have foreseen that failure to take precautions would endanger the plaintiff, each left it entirely to the others to take the necessary precautions and did nothing, so all were liable to the plaintiff (see p. 589, letters C and I, p. 590, letter G, and p. 592, letter G, post).

Clay v. *A. J. Crump & Sons, Ltd.* ([1963] 3 All E.R. 687) applied.

(iii) each of the defendants was one-third to blame and their liability to the plaintiff for damages and costs should be apportioned accordingly (see p. 589, letter F, p. 590, letter I, and p. 592, letter H, post).

Decision of CUSACK, J. ([1966] 3 All E.R. 241) affirmed, but his apportionment of liability varied.

[As to liability for the creation of dangerous conditions, see 28 HALSBURY's LAWS (3rd Edn.) 14-16, para. 13; and for cases on the subject, see 36 DIGEST (Repl.) 24, 25, *102-112.*

As to the requirement of the Building (Safety, Health and Welfare) Regulations, 1948, that openings in roofs must be protected, see 17 HALSBURY's LAWS (3rd Edn.) 127, para. 206, text to note (*k*).

For the Building (Safety, Health and Welfare) Regulations, 1948, reg. 30 (1), (5), see 8 HALSBURY's STATUTORY INSTRUMENTS (1st Re-Issue) 201, 202.]

Cases referred to:

Billings (A. C.) & Sons, Ltd. v. *Riden,* [1957] 3 All E.R. 1; [1958] A.C. 240; [1957] 3 W.L.R. 496; Digest (Cont. Vol. A) 1145, *105b.*

Clay v. *A. J. Crump & Sons, Ltd.,* [1963] 3 All E.R. 687; [1964] 1 Q.B. 533; [1963] 3 W.L.R. 866; Digest (Cont. Vol. A) 75, *486b.*

Donoghue v. *Stevenson,* [1932] All E.R. Rep. 1; [1932] A.C. 562; 101 L.J.P.C. 119; 147 L.T. 281; 36 Digest (Repl.) 85, *458.*

Donovan v. *Laing, Wharton and Down Construction Syndicate,* [1891-94] All E.R. Rep. 216; [1893] 1 Q.B. 629; 63 L.J.Q.B. 25; 68 L.T. 512; 57 J.P. 583; 34 Digest (Repl.) 24, *53.*

(continued from foot of page 583).

such opening, together with toe-boards up to a sufficient height, being in no case less than eight inches, and so placed as to prevent as far as possible the fall of persons, materials and tools through the opening; or (*b*) a covering so constructed as to prevent the fall of persons, materials and tools through the opening . . .''

" (5) Guard-rails, toe-boards, and coverings required by paras. (1), (2), (3) or (4), of this regulation may be removed or remain unerected—(*a*) where and when this is or becomes necessary in order to proceed with any permanent filling in, covering, or enclosure of the opening or open joisting; or (*b*) for the time and to the extent necessary for the access of persons or the movement of materials."

Heaven v. *Pender*, [1881-85] All E.R. Rep. 35; (1883), 11 Q.B.D. 503; 52
    L.J.Q.B. 702; 49 L.T. 357; 47 J.P. 709; 36 Digest (Repl.) 7, *10*.
London Graving Dock Co., Ltd. v. *Horton*, [1951] 2 All E.R. 1; [1951] A.C. 737;
    36 Digest (Repl.) 54, *296*.
Membery v. *Great Western Ry. Co.*, (1889), 14 App. Cas. 179; 58 L.J.Q.B. 563;
    61 L.T. 566; 54 J.P. 244; 36 Digest (Repl.) 150, *786*.
Mersey Docks and Harbour Board v. *Coggins & Griffith (Liverpool), Ltd., and
    McFarlane*, [1946] 2 All E.R. 345; [1947] A.C. 1; 115 L.J.K.B. 465;
    175 L.T. 270; 34 Digest (Repl.) 180, *1279*.
Stapley v. *Gypsum Mines, Ltd.*, [1953] 2 All E.R. 478; [1953] A.C. 663; [1953]
    3 W.L.R. 279; Digest (Cont. Vol. A) 1147, *157*.

Appeals.

These were appeals by all three defendants against the decision of CUSACK, J.,
dated June 30, 1966, and reported [1966] 3 All E.R. 241, in an action brought by
the plaintiff by writ issued on June 21, 1963, for damages for personal injuries
sustained from a fall through an aperture in the roof of a building at Pontin's
Holiday Camp at Blackpool, on which he was working in the course of his employment. The defendants were (i) his employers, (ii) Pontin's (Contractors), Ltd.
and (iii) Newton Brothers, defendants (i) and (iii) being sub-contractors of (ii).
The plaintiff's claim was based in negligence against all defendants, and also,
as against the first and second defendants, on breach of statutory duty under
reg. 30 of the Building (Safety, Health and Welfare) Regulations, 1948.

E. W. Eveleigh, Q.C., and *R. R. Leech* for the second defendants, Pontin
(Contractors), Ltd.

R. M. Bingham, Q.C., and *T. H. Pigot* for the plaintiff.

C. M. Clothier, Q.C., and *M. J. P. Macnair* for the first defendants (Andmac).

D. Hodgson, Q.C., and *G. B. H. Currie* for the third defendants (Newton).

SELLERS, L.J.: When the plaintiff's claim for damages for personal injury
and consequential loss came before CUSACK, J. (1) at the Liverpool Assizes in
June, 1966, there were three defendants in the consolidated actions. Judgment
for £19,866 2s. 2d. was entered against all the defendants and this amount and
the costs of the plaintiff were apportioned between the defendants as to thirty
per cent. to the first defendants (to whom I shall refer as " Andmac "), fifty per
cent. to the second defendants, Pontin, and twenty per cent. to the third defendants, Newton. The assessment of the damages suffered by the plaintiff was
unchallenged, and it reflects the grave injuries which the plaintiff received when he
fell in the course of his work through an open part of a roof some twelve feet to the
ground below. He has been transformed, as the learned judge said (2), ". . . from
an active, cheerful young man, who was described as loving life, into a tragic
wreck ". How easily this could have been prevented by elementary precautions
of care in a situation which so clearly demanded safety precautions!

All three defendants appeal in some measure. Each of them seeks a finding that
the plaintiff himself should be held partly liable on account of contributory
negligence. Apart from that Andmac accept the liability held against them. Both
Pontin and Newton submit, at least in form, that they owed no duty to the plaintiff and, further, that if they did owe a duty there was no breach of it by them
respectively, and in the event of some liability on them they contend that their
respective proportions are excessive. They would put the blame or the greater
part of the blame on Andmac.

A somewhat detailed statement of the facts seems to be called for on the main
legal issue raised, and once stated the facts leave little doubt of the answer.
There is a large organisation which is widely known as Pontin's whose precise
legal structure was not in evidence. Through a variety of companies it apparently
conducts holiday camps at various places throughout the country. One is at
Blackpool, which is owned by Squires Gate Blackpool Holiday Camp, Ltd.

---

(1) [1966] 3 All E.R. 241.   (2) [1966] 3 All E.R. at p. 242.

The various camps may require new buildings, extensions or structural alterations from time to time and it was to meet these requirements that the second defendant company, Pontin (Contractors), Ltd., were established by the group. They consist of only three or four employees with a Mr. Armistead, a constructional engineer, as its head. The company act for the various building owners within the group and make the arrangements necessary for the contemplated work to be done. Mr. Armistead and his associates do not seem to employ head contractors to do the work by themselves or their sub-contractors on an inclusive contract—or at least they did not on this occasion—but Pontin place contracts direct for the projects to be undertaken so that there may be, as here, a number of small contractors without any other co-ordinating or directing authority than Pontin themselves.

In the spring of 1962 considerable work was being undertaken at the Blackpool camp. In particular, as far as this case is concerned, a flat-roofed one-storey building, which had been a dining hall, was being converted into a billiard hall. On the existing roof were two parallel roof-lights just over one hundred feet long and eight feet wide, raised from the roof by a side wall or coaming eighteen inches high. The glass in those strips had to be removed and then one strip had to be completely filled in and the other similarly filled in except for some twenty-eight feet at one end which was to be left for some new skylight over some lavatories which were to be constructed below them.

The arrangements made by Pontin for this work were that Pontin were to supply the joists to be placed across the strips at intervals and the " Stramit " boards which were to be placed on top of the joists to fill in the two strips. These boards were four feet wide and approximately the size to go across, although they had to be fitted or packed. The material was, I apprehend, brought by Pontin somewhere convenient to the site where it was required for the labourers' work. Newton were a small local firm of joiners and shipwrights who had been called on to provide labour to assist in and expedite the erection of some chalets within the camp. Mr. Newton was asked to provide men to remove the glass from the two strips and to re-cover the area (except for the skylights) with the joists and " Stramit " boards provided by Pontin. This was an oral contract made between Mr. Armistead of Pontin and Mr. Newton, and for supplying the men with their own tools to do this job the price (derived from an invoice) was £27 10s. This was the price for the bare labour and nothing was said about, and no monetary provision was made for, safety precautions in a task which meant making with constant change of size a large cavity in each strip as the work of the removal of the lights took place and leaving cavities until the fitting in was completed and at the conclusion, until the skylights were erected, leaving the cavity twenty-eight feet long at the end of one strip.

Mr. Armistead of Pontin directed when and where the work of Newton was to be done, and there is some evidence that he directed the detail or manner in which it was to be done. There was no specification in writing and perhaps the work hardly needed one, and Mr. Armistead may well have stated to Newton's men where he wished nails to be put and suchlike. The men with their skill were to do the work which Pontin required. That would be the same if they had been employed individually and directly as servants with Mr. Newton as foreman. Payment by Pontin was in bulk instead of individually. It was said in argument, and I think rightly, that the Newton men were as nearly servants for the time being of Pontin, using Pontin's material and laying it as Pontin desired, as could be found short of their being held to be their temporary servants. It was not pleaded or contended that the Newton men should be treated as temporary servants of Pontin's, although so to have treated them might have fitted in much better with all the statutory provisions and regulations for safety. As counsel for Andmac said, the larger unit, as is to be seen in the case of large main contractors, employing a labour force directly of skilled and unskilled, is better able to meet the obligations as to safety and welfare which statutory provisions and reasonable care demand.

Co-ordination where there are multiple trades (even only a few) and varying activities on the one site seems essential for safety. This falls normally on the main contractor, who can allocate work and responsibility between sub-contractors.

It should be remembered that *Mersey Docks and Harbour Board* v. *Coggins & Griffith* (*Liverpool*), *Ltd. and McFarlane* (3), did not rule out the possibility that a man in the general permanent employment of one employer may be lent temporarily so as to be treated as the servant of the one whose work he was undertaking. The case only stated it to be a " heavy burden of proof ". It may be that the decision did not sufficiently recognise the advantages where there is " team-work " where an employer's own servants and " borrowed " labour work together in a joint effort or, as here, where labour alone is hired, in having responsibility placed on the employer undertaking the process or operation for which the borrowing takes place. The contract in the *Mersey Docks & Harbour Board* case (3), which provided that the cranemen provided by them should be the servants of the hirers, recognised that advantage. I do not think that it was entirely a financial arrangement. *Donovan* v. *Laing, Wharton and Down Construction Syndicate* (4) had been law for a long time, and it may be that some of the statutory provisions have been built up on the basis of that decision and do not sufficiently or clearly, therefore, deal with circumstances such as have arisen here.

The work which Newton's men were doing came under the Building (Safety, Health and Welfare) Regulations, 1948, and the employers for that work (whoever they were) were at the time of the accident in breach of reg. 30 and would have been liable if one of the Newton men had fallen and been injured. No provision had been made in the contract of hire of labour for any fence or barrier, either in the cost of labour-time or in the material to be supplied by Pontin. The injured plaintiff was employed by Andmac and any claim by him, therefore, to succeed against Pontin or Newton must be established under the common law. Before dealing with that it is necessary to turn to the work which Andmac were separately employed to do.

The " Stramit " boards, when laid, had to be covered with felt, bitumen and chippings according to Pontin's requirements and it was desirable that the boards should be covered without long exposure to the weather. Andmac is a small partnership of Mr. Anderson and Mr. McNally, who carry on a specialist business as roofing felt layers. They were engaged by Pontin to do their specialised work at the Blackpool camp including the covering of the two strips with felt, bitumen and chippings, and they employed the plaintiff and two other men for the purpose. The work was done on a time and material basis at the request and direction of Mr. Armistead of Pontin.

On Apr. 28, 1962, one strip had been completely re-roofed and the second strip was in the course of being covered in, less the twenty-eight feet which had to be left for the skylights. Newton were laying the " Stramit " boards and the plaintiff and his fellow-workmen, Mr. Roby and Mr. Weldon, were doing Andmac's work. Mr. Roby was laying the felt and the plaintiff was pouring the bitumen from a bucket somewhat ahead of Mr. Roby on his left as Mr. Roby was working down the centre. Mr. Weldon prepared the bitumen. Some time after 12 noon Newton's men left off laying the " Stramit " boards when they were still some twelve feet short of the twenty-eight feet mark. They left for a break without telling the plaintiff and Mr. Roby, who were moving along behind them, and without leaving any barrier, however temporary or improvised, to protect the large hole which still remained uncovered. This callous indifference to those whom they were leaving behind and this direct cause of the accident do not seem to me to be adequately reflected in the extent of the liability placed on Newton by the judge. The situation called for some, even elementary, care on their part to those who were so

---

(3) [1946] 2 All E.R. 345; [1947] A.C. 1.
(4) [1891-94] All E.R. Rep. 216; [1893] 1 Q.B. 629.

closely connected with their work and I find it hard to believe how the men could be so unconcerned. The plaintiff and Mr. Roby worked on and the plaintiff, who cannot have appreciated that the work ahead had ceased, walking, it would seem, half backwards while pouring out the bitumen, reached the open edge of the unfinished boarding and overbalanced, carrying the bitumen bucket three-quarters full with him, and received appalling injuries.

The first question is whether the plaintiff should have been held to have been negligent himself so as to lose some portion of the damages. The judge thought not, and I agree with him. The accident happened about 12.30 p.m. and it may be Newton's men had departed ten or fifteen minutes earlier. There was, no doubt, a duty on Andmac, in the circumstances which had arisen shortly before the accident, to comply with reg. 30 to protect the opening, once it was left with no work being done by Newton; but the plaintiff himself was throughout engaged in a duty which required strict attention, his foreman had made no provision to meet the situation, and both the plaintiff and his colleagues might have felt some assurance that Newton's men were ahead of them. As the judge said (5), this was just the type of accident against which it was necessary to protect the man concentrating on his work. With regard to the defendants' liability respectively, I agree with the judge when he said (6):

"The real trouble in this case is that each defendant left it to the others to take the necessary precautions, and that appeared to extend over the whole field of their relationship. In the result nobody gave the matter any thought, and certainly nobody took any action."

The responsibility for this would appear to lie, as the judge thought, in the first place on Pontin, who had made no arrangement whatsoever for safety in relation to this dangerous work which was being undertaken at their request. In a practical sense Pontin were conducting and organising the operations and had not, as I see it, parted with over-all responsibility to anyone. Under the conditions which changed as the work progressed there arose a continuing duty on all the defendants to take reasonable care that those who might be expected to be in the vicinity of the danger (none more obviously so than the plaintiff) were not confronted with unnecessary risks.

The seed of our present action of negligence (which must be accepted as established) was firmly planted in the dissenting judgment of SIR BALIOL BRETT, M.R., in *Heaven* v. *Pender* (7), and developed and established in *Donoghue* v. *Stevenson* (8). The prediction of LORD BUCKMASTER (9) and LORD TOMLIN (10) (who both dissented in that case) that the decision would lead to much wider application has been amply fulfilled in the many cases which have followed. Where a man (if he applied his mind properly to the matter) ought reasonably to foresee that careless acts or omissions on his part would be likely to cause physical injury to some other person, who is a person closely and directly affected by the conduct, then a duty to take reasonable care arises and a failure so to do becomes actionable at law by the person damaged by the failure. The relationship or the association of the parties may be close and proximate and so give rise to a duty, or it may be remote, and injury resulting from acts or omissions may be so unlikely that no reasonable man would have had any person in the position of the injured party in contemplation at the time of the conduct the subject of complaint.

The line between the two is frequently difficult to draw, but in this case the facts which I have already stated leave no doubt as to the duty of both Pontin and Newton to take reasonable care for the safety of the plaintiff. Andmac, too, were under a like duty; but they were also clearly in breach of statutory duty and on appeal accepted this liability. The question therefore is whether reasonable care in all the circumstances was taken by Pontin, their servants or agents, or

(5) [1966] 3 All E.R. at p. 244.   (6) [1966] 3 All E.R. at p. 245.
(7) [1881-85] All E.R. Rep. 35; (1883), 11 Q.B.D. 503.
(8) [1932] All E.R. Rep. 1; [1932] A.C. 562.
(9) [1932] All E.R. Rep. at p. 10; [1932] A.C. at pp. 577, 578.
(10) [1932] All E.R. Rep. at p. 20; [1932] A.C. at pp. 599, 600.

by Newton, their servants or agents, towards the plaintiff, and towards his colleagues working with him, who happily were not injured.

I have already expressed my views of the conduct of Newton's men towards Andmac's men working alongside them. The duty was utterly disregarded. Pontin argued more strenuously against liability, but they were directly concerned with the work in hand and they did nothing to ensure safety and had no reason to think that Newton would take any safety precautions on the contract for labour only which they made with them. It would have been apparent to them, if they had contemplated the position, that danger would arise. Ordinary care required that provision should have been made expressly by them in the particular circumstances of the two small contractors working in such close proximity. I agree with the judge that both Pontin and Newton were liable to the plaintiff under our common law.

Counsel for Pontin placed reliance mainly on *London Graving Dock Co., Ltd.* v. *Horton* (11), but the facts of that case were quite different and the decision of the majority turned on the plaintiff's knowledge of the unusual risk. In *Clay* v. *A. J. Crump & Sons, Ltd.* (12) it was decided by this court (ORMEROD, UPJOHN and DAVIES, L.JJ.) that the architect of the building owner was responsible, in part, to the plaintiff, a servant of the building contractors who came on to a site after some demolition and was injured by the collapse of a wall which had been left standing in isolation. The law to be applied in the present case is the same as that applied in the *Clay* case (12), but the facts are stronger against Pontin, who came closer to the practical work than did the architect in that case. For one thing, the material required for boarding in the strips was Pontin's concern and the labour was Newton's, and both were necessary to fulfil the task. Contrary to the argument of counsel for Pontin, I would regard the arrangement as quite different from an inclusive contract with prime cost items.

There remains the question of the apportionments. At one time this court's powers were considerably restricted by House of Lords' decisions on this matter. However since *Stapley* v. *Gypsum Mines, Ltd.* (13), when the House of Lords itself varied an apportionment, not unanimously, this court has felt less restrained, though it does not readily interfere. Here each member of the court came separately to the view that no distinction should be made between the defendants and that each should be held one-third to blame, and the liability for the damages and the costs of the plaintiff below and in the Court of Appeal should be so apportioned between them.

Each of the defendants, all of whom appealed, should bear their own costs of the appeal notwithstanding the slight variations in the apportionments. The appeals substantially fail although the order is varied.

DAVIES, L.J.: I agree. I propose not to add anything to what SELLERS, L.J., has said on the question of the liability of Andmac and Newton. Neither do I propose to say anything on the question of contributory negligence. On those matters I agree entirely with what SELLERS, L.J., has said; but I should like to add just a word or two on the liability of Pontin.

As I see it, there was here a common law duty on Pontin, who were employing these two firms of sub-contractors on a task which inevitably involved that they should work in close proximity to each other and in close proximity to this dangerous hole in the roof, to take reasonable steps, or to see that Andmac and Newton took reasonable steps, to prevent the workmen from coming to harm. That proposition was not, I think, controverted in any way by counsel for Pontin in the course of his argument. That being so, the real question was the extent of that duty or, in other words, what steps would in the circumstances have been reasonable.

One cannot help to some extent comparing the position of Pontin, as it was

(11) [1951] 2 All E.R. 1; [1951] A.C. 737.
(12) [1963] 3 All E.R. 687; [1964] 1 Q.B. 533.
(13) [1953] 2 All E.R. 478; [1953] A.C. 663.

sought to be put forward on their behalf, with the position of an ordinary private householder. If a private householder employs two firms of contractors—say roofing contractors and painters—to work together, he would of course be under a similar duty; but his duty would in the ordinary case, one apprehends, be discharged by informing the contractors of any special danger of which he knew and the contractors might not know. In the ordinary way he could probably rely on the skill and judgment of the contractors, not being himself in a position to deal with safety matters. Here, however, the position was quite different. It would be quite wrong to equate the position of Pontin with that of an ordinary private householder. It is quite impossible, in the circumstances of this case, to say that Pontin were taking reasonable steps to fulfil their duty by relying on the skill and judgment of Andmac or Newton; for it is clear that Mr. Armistead, the representative of Pontin and an engineer of some forty-two years' experience, was really personally directing operations.

It is not necessary to quote all the many passages in the evidence which make that plain, but one can give examples. Mr. Roby, who was one of Andmac's men, said that on the evening before the accident he was told by Mr. Armistead that he was to go to this billiard room to do the felting, that Mr. Armistead told him to get it done as quickly as possible and that the " Stramit " boards would be ready next morning. Mr. Size (Andmac's foreman) also said that he was given instructions by Mr. Armistead, but that no details of the job were given to him and that he (Mr. Size) did not know that the whole of this particular light was not going to be boarded over. Finally, Mr. Armistead himself in the course of his evidence said: " Andmac did anything that I suggested." So it is perfectly plain on the evidence that, as the judge concluded, it was Mr. Armistead who undertook the duty of co-ordinating the work of these various people who were employed there and directed operations. In those circumstances Mr. Armistead wholly failed in his duty. If he had given instructions about security and safety precautions to Andmac and Newton, a question might have arisen whether the mere giving of instructions was sufficient; but he gave none. He said that there were materials present on the site that could have been used as a barrier; but he never mentioned that fact to the men. Indeed, he did absolutely nothing at all. He had given instructions to Andmac; and no doubt had given instructions to Newton, though that was not specifically spoken to in the evidence, to do the fixing of the " Stramit " boards on the lights; but never at any time did he mention safety precautions to either. Being (in the shoes of Pontin) under this duty of reasonable care, he did absolutely nothing whatsoever to discharge it. In those circumstances, therefore, it is quite impossible to exculpate Pontin in this matter.

With regard to the apportionment between the defendants, a number of powerful points were submitted on behalf of Pontin: namely, that the precautions were so obvious and simple that Andmac or Newton ought to have taken them, that Mr. Armistead could not have been expected physically to erect a barrier himself, that Pontin's liability was in a sense a vicarious liability owing to the fact that Andmac and Newton failed in their duty, and that really that liability arose from a failure to see that the other two discharged their duty. Those are powerful factors. They are not sufficient to support the submission that Pontin should be completely indemnified, but they are sufficient to reduce the liability of Pontin to the proportion which SELLERS, L.J., has suggested, and to make all three defendants liable in equal shares to the plaintiff.

I agree, therefore, with the order proposed by SELLERS, L.J.

EDMUND DAVIES, L.J.: I also agree.

The liability of Andmac is, rightly, not contested in this appeal. Nevertheless, their dereliction cannot be allowed to rest there, for the nature and extent of their failure to discharge their common law and statutory duties bear directly on the issue of apportionment of liability as between the different defendants, and on the issue of contributory negligence. Andmac, the employers, were lamentably in breach of their duty to the plaintiff. They knew, or must be imputed to have known, the work that their employees were called on to perform and the conditions under which it would be performed. Furthermore, at 10.30 in the morning their foreman, Mr. Size, saw the position as it then was, with a large and entirely unprotected hole in the roof. He knew the method of work which the plaintiff and his mates would follow and, therefore, should have appreciated that the plaintiff would be obliged to move more or less backwards and ever nearer to the unprotected hole, and, furthermore, that the plaintiff would be expected to devote to his task no small degree of concentration. I have dwelt on these circumstances for two reasons. First, to indicate why in my view Andmac, the plaintiff's employers, were not only wise in conceding their liability to him, but also to indicate the circumstances which demand their sharp condemnation for contributing in a substantial degree to the disaster which befell him. Secondly, to indicate the reasons which demand, in my view, the absolution of the plaintiff from the accusation of contributory negligence. I entertain no doubt that all three defendants have completely failed to establish their counter-allegation, and it was, understandably, not vigorously pursued.

Now as to Newton. The liability of these defendants, although contested, is again, in my judgment, beyond doubt. The most superficial consideration of their position vis-à-vis the plaintiff would have brought home to them the very real possibility of his being endangered by the nature of his and their juxtaposed tasks, unless they took steps to safeguard him. They should have warned him that they were descending from the roof; in addition, or at least alternatively, they should have erected a physical barrier to prevent his backing inadvertently towards the hole in the roof. For the latter purpose, no elaborate apparatus was called for; a few planks across the " Stramit " boards, or even a couple of buckets suitably placed thereon, would have provided a sufficient warning; but they did nothing. In that respect, they were unlike another firm of joiners (Bamber's) who executed roof work on the ballroom at this camp. Their practice, we were told, was to erect a barrier in front of any hole in the roof. That Newton owed a duty to the plaintiff to take some such steps is beyond doubt. That by their breach of that duty they contributed substantially to the plaintiff's accident is not open to question.

Finally, as to Pontin. Their position gives rise to different and rather more difficult questions than those of the other two defendants. Somewhat faint-heartedly, it was submitted that they owed no duty of any kind to the plaintiff: that submission must be rejected. More substantially, it was argued that, assuming a duty existed, Pontin were not in breach of it. It is, therefore, important to consider the role played by the witness, Mr. Armistead. Although employed by Pontin (Contractors), Ltd. as a constructional engineer, he also acted on behalf of the occupiers of Pontin's Blackpool Holiday Camp, which was owned by Squires Gate Holiday Camp, Ltd. (see, for example, the letter of Jan. 29, 1962, which he sent to Andmac). His employers had at the holiday camp only three other employees—a storekeeper, a general foreman and a clerk. He not only engaged the sub-contractors but directed all the work that they were to do and when they were to do it, and in some instances gave orders how it was to be done. He conceded that he was the co-ordinating authority to bring together the various sub-contractors at the right time and the right place. With the exception of Andmac and one other, all sub-contractors (including Newton) were engaged to supply labour only, any materials needed being furnished by Pontin. Safety precautions were never discussed with any sub-contractor. Although Mr. Armistead said that he regarded the small firm of Newton as under a duty to fence off holes such as the one which caused this accident, he never indicated to them that, if for this purpose they needed any material, this was available to them on the site. He simply expected them to make such safety arrangements as they thought fit. He was perfectly aware that Newton's men would be working in close proximity to Andmac's men and that it was important that the " Stramit " boards should be covered up quickly, yet Mr. Armistead left it entirely to these sub-contractors to devise their own methods of safety. I would adopt the submission of counsel for Andmac that in the Pontin concern there was, as he put it, no horizontal organisation and no vertical management.

While Pontin (Contractors), Ltd. were a distinct legal entity from Squires Gate Holiday Camp, Ltd., the occupiers of the premises, the circumstances were such that, in my judgment, the former owed to the plaintiff a duty of care closely analogous to that owed to him by the occupiers (see *A. C. Billings & Sons, Ltd.* v. *Riden* (14)). At this stage one may profitably recall the observations of LORD HERSCHELL in *Membery* v. *Great Western Ry. Co.* (15) as to the duties there owed by the occupier to an invitee.

"... I think they were under the duty to him, having invited him upon their premises, not to permit their premises to be in such a condition that he unwittingly might fall into a trap of the existence of which he, unacquainted with their premises, would be ignorant, by which he might sustain an injury. Further than that, it might be (and I confess that I should myself be disposed to think that it was) their duty to take due and reasonable care that in the carrying on of their business they did not subject him to unreasonable risk owing to the acts which they did in the carrying on of that business. If they were carrying on a dangerous business, and one which would subject people employed upon their premises for their benefit to risk, they must take reasonable care, as it seems to me, that they do not do any act (I emphatically use the word ' act ') which would endanger the safety of the persons who thus, to their knowledge, are employed about their business upon their premises."

I apply these words to the facts of the present case in this way: never losing sight of the fact that Newton were independent contractors and not the servants or agents of Pontin, the roof work that the former were engaged to perform was such as could well involve danger to others who, to the knowledge of Pontin, would be working in close proximity to the joiners—danger, that is, unless proper safety precautions were taken. Had Newton's men been in the direct employment of Pontin there could be no doubt as to the liability of the latter. Having regard to all the circumstances, does the fact that Newton were independent contractors relieve Pontin of all responsibility? It does not. The duty of reasonable care owed by Pontin to the plaintiff necessitated their taking proper steps to see that danger was eliminated, as it so easily might have been. Having given Newton no instructions, nor specifically drawn to their attention the availability of material for constructing safety devices, it is no answer to the plaintiff's claim for Pontin to say: we left it to our independent contractors to forage around the site for such safety devices as they thought desirable to use.

For these reasons I, too, hold that Pontin are liable in the present case to the plaintiff. I would accordingly dismiss the appeals of all three defendants.

As to the apportionment of liability, I agree with my lords, and for the reasons which they have stated, in holding that this should be equally shared by all three defendants.

I would, accordingly, agree with the order proposed by my Lords.

Appeals dismissed with costs. Order below varied by substituting apportionment of plaintiff's damages, and costs in both courts, as between the three defendants of one-third each. Each defendant to bear own costs of appeal. Taxation of plaintiff's costs in Liverpool District Registry.

Solicitors: *Hewitt, Wollacott & Chown* (for Pontin); *Gregory, Rowcliffe & Co.,* agents for *Arthur D. Dean & Co.,* Manchester (for the plaintiff); *Barlow, Lyde & Gilbert* (for Andmac); *Stunt & Son,* agents for *Rawsthorn, Ambler & Brown,* Preston (for Newton)

[*Reported by* HENRY SUMMERFIELD, ESQ., *Barrister-at-Law.*]

(14) [1957] 3 All E.R. 1; [1958] A.C. 240.   (15) (1889), 14 App. Cas. 179 at p. 191.

S. *v.* E.

[QUEEN'S BENCH DIVISION (Chapman, J.) December 1, 5, 1966.]

Affiliation—Evidence—Putative father—Compellable witness at instance of mother
—Whether putative father privileged to decline to answer questions tending
to establish paternity—Whether affiliation proceedings were civil proceedings—
Foreign Tribunals Evidence Act, 1856 (19 & 20 *Vict. c.* 113), *s.* 1.

In affiliation proceedings in 1965 before a Norwegian county court a Norwegian woman, E. S., born in 1945, alleged that an Englishman was the father of her illegitimate child. It was not suggested that the intercourse took place without her consent. The Norwegian court issued letters of request asking that the putative father should be examined before the English court, and that he should be asked whether intercourse had taken place between the parties at the material time, whether he admitted paternity, and whether he had agreed to marry the mother, who had returned to England for that purpose. It was further requested that, if English law permitted, the putative father should be ordered to submit to a blood test. When he attended before the district registrar in accordance with an order under the Foreign Tribunals Evidence Act, 1856, the putative father refused to answer questions about his association with E. S., or to say whether he was willing to submit to a blood test.

Held: affiliation proceedings were civil proceedings within the meaning of the Foreign Tribunals Evidence Act, 1956, s. 1*, in which the putative father was not only a competent but a compellable witness, and there was no privilege entitling him in the present instance to refuse to answer the questions sought to be put to him (see p. 596, letter C, and p. 597, letter B, post).

Dicta of LORD CAMPBELL, C.J., in *R.* v. *Lightfoot* ((1856), 6 E. & B. at p. 827) and of CROMPTON, J., in *Parker* v. *Green* ((1862), 2 B. & S. at p. 311) applied.

[As to a defendant in affiliation proceedings being a compellable witness, see 3 HALSBURY'S LAWS (3rd Edn.) 121, para. 185; and for cases as to affiliation proceedings being civil proceedings and the defendant being compellable as a witness, see 3 DIGEST (Repl.) 454, *429-431.*

As to obtaining evidence for foreign tribunals, see 15 HALSBURY'S LAWS (3rd Edn.) 473, para. 856.

For the Foreign Tribunals Evidence Act, 1856, s. 1, see 9 HALSBURY'S STATUTES (2nd Edn.) 576.

For the Affiliation Proceedings Act, 1957, s. 1, see 37 HALSBURY'S STATUTES (2nd Edn.) 37.]

Cases referred to:

A. v. *A. and H.*, [1962] 2 All E.R. 573; [1962] P. 196; [1962] 3 W.L.R. 212; Digest (Cont. Vol. A) 767, *4546b.*

Blunt v. *Park Lane Hotel, Ltd. and Briscoe*, [1942] 2 All E.R. 187; [1942] 2 K.B. 253; 111 L.J.K.B. 706; 167 L.T. 359; 18 Digest (Repl.) 190, *1638.*

Cattell v. *Ireson*, (1858), E.B. & E. 91; 27 L.J.M.C. 167; 31 L.T.O.S. 80; 22 J.P. 672; 121 E.R. 441; 3 Digest (Repl.) 454, *430.*

Cook, Ex p., (1860), 4 All. 506; 3 Digest (Repl.) 460, *329.*

Parker v. *Green*, (1862), 2 B. & S. 299; 31 L.J.M.C. 133; 6 L.T. 46; 26 J.P. 247; 9 Cox, C.C. 169; 121 E.R. 1084; 14 Digest (Repl.) 29, *19.*

R. v. *Flavell*, (1884), 14 Q.B.D. 364; 52 L.T. 133; 49 J.P. 406; 3 Digest (Repl.) 454, *431.*

R. v. *Lightfoot*, (1856), 6 E. & B. 822; 25 L.J.M.C. 115; 27 L.T.O.S. 235; 20 J.P. 677; 119 E.R. 1070; 3 Digest (Repl.) 454, *429.*

Redfern v. *Redfern*, [1886-90] All E.R. Rep. 524; [1891] P. 139; 60 L.J.P. 9; 64 L.T. 68; 55 J.P. 37; 18 Digest (Repl.) 16, *103.*

---

* Section 1, so far as material, is set out at p. 595, letter G, post.

Rhodes v. *Cooper*, (1904), 23 N.Z.L.R. 562; 3 Digest (Repl.) 460, **330*.

Summons.

The plaintiff commenced affiliation proceedings before the Inderøy county court, Norway, which issued letters of request on Dec. 17, 1965, that the defendant should be examined before the English court. On Apr. 20, 1966, Master LAWRENCE made an order under the Foreign Tribunals Evidence Act, 1856, directing that the defendant should submit to examination before the district registrar at Plymouth. On May 3 the defendant attended before the district registrar and refused to answer the material questions. On Aug. 24 the Treasury Solicitor took out a summons pursuant to R.S.C., Ord. 39, r. 5, asking for a decision whether the defendant was entitled to object to the questions put to him, viz., (a) questions about his alleged association with the plaintiff and (b) whether he was willing to submit to a blood test, and for an order that he should answer them on his further examination before the district registrar. The summons was heard in chambers and judgment delivered in open court. The facts are set out in the judgment.

A. P. Fletcher for the plaintiff.
S. B. Thomas for the defendant.

Cur. adv. vult.

Dec. 5. **CHAPMAN, J.,** read the following judgment: This summons raises a point which has, I am told, been the subject recently of a certain amount of discussion and in some quarters apparently of debate. The point is whether in affiliation proceedings a person alleged to be the father of an illegitimate child has any, and if so what, privilege if called as a witness in relation to questions as to his alleged association with the mother of the child and as to his willingness to submit to a blood test.

The point has arisen in the following way. By petition in the Inderøy county court, Norway, the plaintiff, the unmarried daughter of a Norwegian farmer born on May 3, 1945, alleged that the defendant was the father of a male child born to her on Aug. 27, 1965. On Nov. 1, 1965, the plaintiff gave evidence to the effect that from the end of February until the end of November, 1964, she was employed as a domestic servant at a school in Shropshire; that during this period she met the defendant at a public dance and thereafter they were going steady together; that the defendant visited her in her room which she shared at first with another Norwegian girl without any sexual relations taking place before Nov. 23, 1964; that on that evening, which was her last in England, they had been out motoring together and he then stayed with her for part of the night in her room which she by then occupied alone, the other girl having left, and they there had sexual intercourse, contraceptives not being used. She said further that, having been told by her doctor that she was pregnant, she had written to the defendant to tell him this and he replied that he would come to Norway to see her; that he did this, staying at her home, and it was then arranged that she should go to England and marry the defendant there; that in March she went to England and stayed in the defendant's home (he was not there, having recently joined the army) but she found that his parents had been told nothing about the expected child or the marriage plans or even about the invitation to her to come; that his mother was opposed to the marriage and suggested that the plaintiff should have her baby adopted and she and the defendant could possibly marry later on; that she did not agree to this course and returned home to Norway. The plaintiff stressed that the defendant had admitted paternity of the child.

On Nov. 29, 1965, the Norwegian court decided that efforts should be made to have the defendant examined and his evidence taken in England. On Dec. 17, 1965, letters of request were duly issued to this end, it being requested that the defendant be particularly asked

" if he admitted he had had sexual intercourse with the plaintiff at such a time that according to the order of nature he may be the father of the child born on Aug. 27, 1965, and also if he admitted the paternity of the child and further if it was correct that they were to get married and that she had agreed to come to England for that reason."

If the defendant denied the paternity, it was further requested

" if this be possible according to English law, that he be ordered to present himself to a doctor to have a blood test taken for blood grouping tests to be made of the parties and of the child."

The translation of these letters of request was dated Jan. 10, 1966.

On Apr. 20, 1966, Master LAWRENCE made an order under the Foreign Tribunals Evidence Act, 1856, directing that the defendant should attend before the district registrar at Plymouth at his chambers at the Law Courts, Armada Way at Plymouth (where the defendant's regiment was stationed) on May 3, 1966, and there submit to be examined on oath touching the testimony required by the letters of request of Dec. 17, 1965. On May 3, 1966, the defendant attended before the said district registrar and was sworn: he gave his home address in Shropshire and went on:

" I know E. S. I refuse to answer questions about my alleged association with [her] on the grounds that I am not liable to do so under English law. I am aware of the allegations that she is making against me in proceedings in the Inderøy county court as set out in the letters of request dated [Dec. 17, 1965]. I refuse to say whether I am willing to submit to a blood test."

On Aug. 24, 1966, the Treasury Solicitor pursuant to R.S.C., Ord. 39, r. 5 took out the summons which is now before me asking for a decision whether the defendant was entitled to object to questions put to him in accordance with the letters of request, namely, (a) questions about his alleged association with the plaintiff, and (b) the question whether he was willing to submit to a blood test, and in the event of my deciding that he was not entitled to object to answer the said questions, for an order that he do answer them on his further examination as a witness.

The relevant provisions of the Foreign Tribunals Evidence Act, 1856, are as follows. Section 1 provides for the making of an order for the examination of witnesses where it appears that

" any court or tribunal of competent jurisdiction in a foreign country, before which any civil or commercial matter is pending, is desirous of obtaining the testimony in relation to such matter of any witness or witnesses within the jurisdiction of such first-mentioned court . . .' "

Section 5 provides as follows:

" Provided also, that every person examined under any order made under this Act shall have the like right to refuse to answer questions tending to criminate himself, and other questions, which a witness in any cause pending in the court by which . . . the order for examination was made would be entitled to . . .' "

The general privilege under our law in relation to incriminating questions has been summarised by GODDARD, L.J., in *Blunt* v. *Park Lane Hotel, Ltd. and Briscoe* as follows (1):

". . . the rule is that no-one is bound to answer any question if the answer thereto would, in the opinion of the judge, have a tendency to expose the deponent to any criminal charge, penalty or forfeiture which the judge regards as reasonably likely to be preferred or sued for."

It is to be observed that there is absolutely no suggestion here of intercourse having taken place against the girl's wishes or of it having been on any other grounds unlawful carnal knowledge. I can see no basis at all for any possible

(1) [1942] 2 All E.R. 187 at p. 189; [1942] 2 K.B. 253 at p. 257.

contention that answers to the questions sought to be put might expose the defendant to any criminal charge, penalty or forfeiture. Counsel for the defendant has not indeed argued that there is any such danger. He has, however, urged that the questions sought to be asked should be equated with questions as to adultery; that sexual intercourse outside wedlock has a taint or moral stigma attached to it and questions should not, therefore, be asked about it. There is, however, the direct authority of the Court of Appeal in *Redfern* v. *Redfern* (2), as explained in *Blunt* v. *Park Lane Hotel, Ltd. and Briscoe* (3), that it is only in proceedings for divorce on the ground of adultery that a privilege exists at all in relation to questions about adultery. This privilege is moreover limited to a spouse who is a party to the suit and also, in this year of grace at any rate, to matters of discovery; see *A.* v. *A. and H.* (4); CROSS ON EVIDENCE (2nd Edn., 1963) pp. 230, 231. I can see no ground for extending this privilege to other proceedings or to other persons or to questions as to other behaviour.

The crucial question which arises, therefore, is whether, within the meaning of the Foreign Tribunals Evidence Act, 1856, s. 1, these are civil proceedings. There is no dispute that according to our law the defendant is not merely a competent but also a compellable witness, even at the instance of the plaintiff if the proceedings are civil—this was enacted by s. 2 of the Evidence Act, 1851 (see also *R.* v. *Flavell* (5), per SMITH, J.). Counsel for the defendant contends that the proceedings, although not criminal in the sense of being capable of resulting in some sort of punishment, are nonetheless not civil in the sense in which that term is used in the Act of 1856. He urges that they should be regarded as quasi-criminal, although he concedes that the authorities which he has discovered, and I am greatly indebted to him for his industrious research, are against him.

There is this much to be said for the argument of counsel for the defendant, that affiliation proceedings in this country have many of the outward trappings of criminal proceedings. They are and always have been pursued in a court of summary jurisdiction and appeals lie to quarter sessions. The process, like most criminal processes in a magistrates' court, took and still takes the form of a summons (see Bastardy Laws Amendment Act, 1872, s. 1, and Affiliation Proceedings Act, 1957, s. 1). In substance, however, they are and always have been proceedings not to exact a penalty or other form of punishment but to compel payment of money towards the maintenance of the child who had been begotten (see *Cattell* v. *Ireson* (6), per LORD CAMPBELL, C.J.)). Later legislation has been at pains to make plain this essentially civil character of the proceedings. The relevant part of the Magistrates' Courts Act, 1952, was Part 2, which is headed " Civil Jurisdiction and Procedure ", and by s. 51 the application for a summons had to be by way of a complaint. This is reproduced in the legislation which is now operative, namely the Affiliation Proceedings Act, 1957, s. 1. When one turns to judicial decisions the trend of the authority is all in the same direction. Thus in *R.* v. *Lightfoot* (7) there is this statement by LORD CAMPBELL, C.J.:

" The matter here in dispute was entirely of a civil nature, viz., the obligation to maintain a child; and the defendant might have been examined as a witness on his own behalf."

See also *Cattell* v. *Ireson* (6) and *R.* v. *Flavell* (8). Counsel for the defendant added to his collection *Parker* v. *Green* (9), per CROMPTON, J.:

" It is well established that, wherever a party aggrieved is suing for a penalty, where the proceedings can be treated as the suit of the party—as, for instance, an application for an order in bastardy—the proceeding is a civil one, and the defendant is a competent witness."

(2) [1886-90] All E.R. Rep. 524; [1891] P. 139.
(3) [1942] 2 All E.R. 187; [1942] 2 K.B. 253.
(4) [1962] 2 All E.R. 573; [1962] P. 196,   (5) (1884), 14 Q.B.D. 364 at p. 367.
(6) (1858), E.B. & E. 91.   (7) (1856), 6 E. & B. 822 at p. 827.
(8) (1884), 14 Q.B.D. 364.   (9) (1862), 2 B. & S. 299 at p. 311.

He also drew my attention to two cases of persuasive authority, namely in Canada, *Ex p. Cook* (10), and in New Zealand, *Rhodes* v. *Cooper* (11), both of which decided that affiliation proceedings are civil proceedings.

The trend of the legislation and authorities, as counsel for the defendant conceded, are entirely one way. I entertain no doubt at all that affiliation proceedings are civil proceedings. This means that the defendant is not merely a competent but a compellable witness and there is no privilege which entitles him to decline to answer the questions sought to be put to him. The questions submitted by the summons must be answered in the negative and there must be an order in consequence that the defendant do answer the questions referred to.

Order accordingly.

Solicitors: *Treasury Solicitor* (for the plaintiff); *Leslie D. Tipson*, Plymouth (for the defendant).

[*Reported by* Mary Colton, *Barrister-at-Law.*]

DE ROTHSCHILD *v.* WING RURAL DISTRICT COUNCIL.

[Court of Appeal, civil division (Lord Denning, M.R., Danckwerts and Sachs, L.JJ.), December 20, 1966.]

Housing—Improvement—Notice—Farm cottage—Preliminary and immediate improvement notices—Occupier, no longer employed as farm labourer, not a tenant—Appeal by owner on ground of invalidity of notices—Whether owner substantially prejudiced—Housing Act 1964 (c. 56), *s.* 14 (1) (*a*), *s.* 16, *s.* 27 (2) (*e*), (3).

A farm cottage was situate within an area declared by the local authority to be an improvement area pursuant to s. 13 of the Housing Act 1964. The cottage was occupied by a farm labourer whose employment by the owner had been terminated, but who was allowed to stay on without paying rent. The local authority served a preliminary notice for improvement pursuant to s. 14* requiring the owner to execute improvements at an estimated cost of £375, and, notwithstanding objection by the owner that the occupier was not the tenant†, the local authority subsequently served an immediate improvement notice under s. 16‡. On appeal by the owner the county court judge purported to confirm the notice under s. 27 (3)§ on the

---

(10) (1860), 4 All. 506.   (11) (1904), 23 N.Z.L.R. 562.

* Section 14, so far as relevant, provides: " (1) At any time after publication of a notice of the declaration of an improvement area . . . the local authority, if satisfied that a dwelling in the improvement area—(*a*) is for the time being occupied by a tenant, . . . may serve a notice (in this Part of this Act referred to as ' a preliminary notice ') on the person having control of the dwelling—(i) specifying the works which in their opinion are required for the dwelling to be improved to the full standard . . ."

† The definition of " tenant " in s. 44 (2) of the Act of 1964 is, so far as material, as follows: " In this Part of this Act, unless the context otherwise requires, ' tenant '— (*b*) includes, in relation to a dwelling, a person employed in agriculture (as defined in s. 17 (1) of the Agricultural Wages Act, 1948 . . .) who occupies or resides in the dwelling as part of the terms of his employment, . . ."

‡ Section 16, so far as material, provides: " (1) If when the improvement notice is served . . . the local authority have received from the person who is then the tenant occupying the dwelling his consent to the improvement of the dwelling . . ., the local authority shall in the improvement notice require the person having control of the dwelling to carry out the works specified in the improvement notice within twelve months . . . (3) An improvement notice to which this section applies is referred to in this Part of this Act as ' an immediate improvement notice '."

§ Section 27, so far as material, provides: " (1) Within six weeks from the service on the person having control of the premises of an improvement notice, any such person . . . may appeal to the county court against the improvement notice . . .

" (2) the grounds of the appeal may be all or any of the following, that is— . . . (*e*) that the improvement notice is invalid on the ground that any requirement of this Act has not been complied with or on the ground of some informality, defect or error in or in connexion with the improvement notice ".

Subsection (3) is set out at p. 600, letter A, post.

Applied in Harrington *v.* Croydon Corpn. [1967] 3 All E.R. 929.

ground that he was not satisfied that the interests of the owner had been substantially prejudiced.

Held: the improvement notices were invalid and should be quashed because—

(i) at the time when the preliminary notice was served the occupier of the cottage was not a tenant within s. 44 (2) of the Housing Act 1964 and the notice was invalid for error within s. 27 (2) (*e*), since the condition of s. 14 (1) (*a*) for service of a preliminary notice, viz., that the dwelling was occupied by a tenant, was not satisfied, with the consequence that the preliminary notice was invalid, as also was the subsequent immediate improvement notice under s. 16 (see p. 599, letter I, and p. 600, letters F and H, post).

(ii) the court was not bound by s. 27 (3) to confirm the improvement notices, notwithstanding their invalidity, as the interests of the appellant owner had been substantially prejudiced (see p. 600, letters C, D and H, post).

Appeal allowed.

[As to improvement notices and appeals, see SUPPLEMENT to 19 HALSBURY'S LAWS (3rd Edn.), para. 1029A, items 3, 4, 9.

For the Housing Act 1964, s. 13, s. 14, s. 16, s. 27 and s. 44, see 44 HALSBURY'S STATUTES (2nd Edn.) 315, 316, 318, 330 and 341.]

Appeal.

By a preliminary notice of a local authority's proposals for improvement of a dwelling in an improvement area, dated June 29, 1965, the respondents to this appeal, Wing Rural District Council (" the local authority ") gave notice to the appellant, E. R. A. de Rothschild (" the owner ") as the person having control of the dwelling known as 8, Vicarage Lane, Wing, Leighton Buzzard, Bedford-shire, that the local authority were satisfied that this dwelling (which was situated within an improvement area declared by the local authority from June 1, 1965) " is for the time occupied by a tenant " within s. 44 (2) of the Housing Act 1964. The preliminary notice further notified the owner that the works specified in the schedule were required, in the opinion of the local authority, for the dwelling to be improved to the full standard. The cottage had been occupied by a tenant, Mr. Harold Robert Jones, as one of the terms of his employment by the owner as a farm worker. That employment was lawfully terminated on May 28, 1965, and after termination of the employment he was allowed to stay on in the cottage to give him reasonable time to find accommodation elsewhere. It was accepted by the local authority on the subsequent appeal to the county court that Mr. Jones was not a tenant within the meaning of Part 2 of the Housing Act 1964 at any time after May 28, 1965. On July 1, 1965, the following consent was signed in the name of Mr. Jones—

" *Improvements to 8, Vicarage Lane, Wing.*

" I agree to the proposed improvements being carried out while I remain in residence. But, we are under notice to leave by Nov. 1, 1965.

Date: 1/7/65.   Signed: H. R. Jones."

The consent was in fact signed by Mr. Jones' wife, but the county court judge found that she did so as agent for her husband. By an Immediate Improvement Notice in respect of Dwelling in an Improvement Area, dated Nov. 12, 1965, the local authority gave notice to the owner requiring the work specified to be carried out within twelve months. This notice stated that—" (2) the [local authority] are satisfied that the dwelling—(*a*) is occupied by a tenant: . . ."

By order of His Honour JUDGE GRANT dated July 1, 1966, on appeal by the owner to the county court at Leighton Buzzard against the immediate improvement notice, the notice was confirmed under s. 27 (3) of the Housing

Act 1964, it having been conceded on behalf of the local authority that, as Mr. Jones was not a tenant at the relevant time, not all of the requirements of the Act of 1964 had been complied with. By notice dated Aug. 11, 1966, the owner gave notice of appeal that the order of the county court should be set aside and that the improvement notice should be quashed. The grounds of appeal were, first, that the improvement notice was invalid because requirements of the Act of 1964 had not been complied with and because of defects and errors in the improvement notice, in that at no material time was H. R. Jones the tenant of 8, Vicarage Lane, Wing, within s. 44 (2) of the Act of 1964: and accordingly (*a*) at the times of service of preliminary notice of June 29, 1965, and of the immediate improvement notice respectively the dwelling was not occupied by a tenant; (*b*) copies of the preliminary notice and of the immediate improvement notice were not served on the tenant; and (*c*) when the improvement notice was served on the owner the local authority had not received from any person who was then the tenant occupying the dwelling his consent to the improvement thereof. The second ground of appeal was that the interests of the owner had been substantially prejudiced by the facts relied on by him and in particular by the fact of his having been required to carry out the works specified in the improvement notice, being works which he could not lawfully be required to carry out.

J. R. Peppitt for the owner.
R. R. F. Scott for the local authority.

LORD DENNING, M.R.: The case concerns a cottage, 8, Vicarage Lane, Wing, near Leighton Buzzard, in Bedfordshire. The owner is Mr. de Rothschild. It is a farm cottage which in 1955 he allowed one of his farmworkers to occupy. The farmworker paid no rent or rates. During his employment, he was undoubtedly a " tenant " within the meaning of the Housing Act 1964, s. 44 (2). He was a person employed in agriculture who occupied the dwelling as part of the terms of his employment; but his employment was terminated on May 28, 1965, by proper notice. Thereupon, he ceased to be a " tenant ". His " tenancy " ended on May 28, 1965. He was allowed to stay on in the cottage by the owner as a licensee until he found somewhere else to live.

After that date the local authority went through the machinery of the Housing Act 1964 to bring this house up to the standard amenities. The cottage had no proper bathroom nor basin, no hot water system nor indoor water closet. On June 1, 1965, the local authority declared that this was an " improvement area " because the dwellings were not up to standard, and published the notice to that effect required by s. 13 (2). On June 29, 1965, the local authority gave the preliminary notice which is required by s. 14 of the Act of 1964. The owner's solicitors at once contended that there was no " tenant " occupying the dwelling. The local authority did not accept that contention. They asked the occupier or his wife to sign a paper giving consent to the improvements. His wife did so. They then served an " immediate improvement notice " under s. 16. In order to give such a notice the local authority, under s. 14 (1), have to be satisfied that the dwelling: " (*a*) is for the time being occupied by a tenant." They asserted that they were so satisfied and served the notice on the owner.

The owner appealed against the notice under s. 27 (2) (*e*) of the Act of 1964. He said that the notice was invalid on the ground that there was an error in it. There was certainly an error in it. The local authority had been in error from the beginning. They thought that Mr. Jones was a " tenant ", whereas he was not a tenant at any material time. These notices can be served only when a " tenant " is there. A notice cannot be served in respect of an empty house, or an owner-occupied house, or in respect of a house where the " tenancy " has come to an end. That was prima facie a good ground of appeal; but the local authority relied on s. 27 (3), which says:

" In so far as an appeal under this section is based on the ground that the improvement notice is invalid, the court shall confirm the improvement notice unless satisfied that the interests of the appellant have been substantially prejudiced by the facts relied on by him."

The county court judge held that the owner had not been substantially prejudiced, at all, by being compelled to do these works. He said that these works would improve the house anyway.

I can sympathise with the judge's point of view, but I am afraid that I cannot agree with it. It seems to me plain that the owner's interests have been prejudiced. He has been directed to do a lot of work on this house, when it is plain that the Act of 1964 never intended that he should be liable. One of the statutory conditions is that the house should be occupied by a " tenant ", and this house was not so occupied.

It was said before the county court judge that the proper remedy of the owner was to apply for certiorari to quash the notice, or wait until the local authority took steps to enforce it. I do not think that those were the only courses open to him. He was quite entitled to appeal as he did.

This appeal should be allowed. The improvement notice is invalid. It is not binding on the owner.

DANCKWERTS, L.J.: I agree. The clerk to the local authority, concluded that Mr. Jones, who was on the premises with his wife, was the tenant. His conclusion was a mistaken one and completely wrong in the circumstances, because Mr. Jones was never the tenant at any material time. Consequently the preliminary notice could not be served on the tenant as required by s. 14 (2) of the Housing Act 1964, and the consent of the tenant could not be obtained either in writing or in any way as required by s. 16 (2). Therefore the immediate improvement notice, as well as the preliminary notice, was invalid, and the owner very properly appealed under the provisions of s. 27 (2) (e), on the ground that the improvement notice was invalid.

Then there arises this very extraordinary provision in s. 27 (3)—which is intended, I think, to deal with cases which have no merits at all—which provides that:

" In so far as an appeal under this section is based on the ground that the improvement notice is invalid, the court shall confirm the improvement notice unless satisfied that the interests of the appellant have been substantially prejudiced by the facts relied on by him."

It has been argued that the owner has not been substantially prejudiced by what has happened, but I cannot reach that conclusion. To be ordered to pay for improvements amounting to the sum of £375, which could not properly be required in accordance with the provisions of the Housing Act 1964, substantially prejudices the owner, and I agree with LORD DENNING, M.R., that this appeal should be allowed.

SACHS, J.: I agree. I do not desire to add anything.

Appeal allowed; notice quashed.

Solicitors: *Lee, Bolton & Lee*, agents for *Horwood & James*, Aylesbury (for the owner); *Moodie, Randall, Carr & Miles*, agents for *Simpson & Co.*, Leighton Buzzard (for the local authority).

[*Reported by* F. GUTTMAN, ESQ., *Barrister-at-Law.*]

TALBOT v. TALBOT.

[Chancery Court of the County Palatine of Lancaster (Burgess, V.-C.), July 19, 1966.]

Will—Option—Purchase—Gift of option to purchase land at reasonable valuation—No express reference in will to trustees fixing what the price should be—Whether option valid—Surrender of discretion by trustees to court—Inquiry to be held to fix reasonable price.

A testator directed that his son John should have the option of purchasing his farm T. and eleven acres at a reasonable valuation and his son Joseph the option of purchasing his farm P. and six acres at a reasonable valuation. There was no uncertainty as to the land affected, but there was no express provision that the trustees were to decide what the price of each property should be. The trustees surrendered their discretion as to price to the court.

Held: the mere fact that there was no express reference to the trustees' fixing the price themselves did not invalidate the rights of pre-emption given to the two sons; accordingly the options conferred by the will were valid and effectual, and a special inquiry would be directed to ascertain what was a reasonable price in regard to each option (see p. 604, letters F and H, post).

Waite v. Morland ((1866), 14 L.T. 649) and dictum of Lord Eldon, L.C., in *Earl of Radnor v. Shafto* ((1805), 11 Ves. at pp. 453, 454) applied.

[As to the creation of options to purchase by will, see 39 Halsbury's Laws (3rd Edn.) 912, para. 1383; and for cases on the subject, see 48 Digest (Repl.) 56-58, 404-417.]

Cases referred to:

Milnes v. Gery, (1807), 14 Ves. 400; 33 E.R. 574; 2 Digest (Repl.) 505, *513*.

Radnor (Earl) v. Shafto, (1805), 11 Ves. 448; 32 E.R. 1160; 48 Digest (Repl.) 56, *404*.

Vickers v. Vickers, (1867), L.R. 4 Eq. 529; 36 L.J.Ch. 946; 36 Digest (Repl.) 628, *1922*.

Waite v. Morland, (1865), 13 L.T. 91; *on appeal*, (1866), 14 L.T. 649; 12 Jur. N.S. 763, 48 Digest (Repl.) 57, *410*.

Petition.

This was a petition by the plaintiffs who were the executors and trustees of the will, dated Dec. 4, 1953, of Peter Talbot (deceased), by which he purported to give option of purchasing two farms to his sons John and Joseph. The questions for the determination of the court was whether the options were valid and effectual. The facts are set out in the judgment of Burgess, V.-C.

D. B. Mallard for the plaintiffs.

B. C. Maddocks for the first and second defendants.

P. A. Ferns for the third, fourth, fifth and sixth defendants.

BURGESS, V.-C.: This petition raises a question of construction arising under the will dated Dec. 4, 1953 of Peter Talbot, of which will the plaintiffs are the executors and trustees. The testator died on May 8, 1964. His wife predeceased him, having died on Dec. 28, 1962. The will was made on a stationers' printed form. I am told that the handwriting containing the terms of the will is not that of the testator himself. By his will he gave legacies to his executors, one of whom was his brother and the other of whom was one of his daughters. He directed that should his wife survive his decease, which did not happen, then the remainder of his real and personal estate should be held in trust by his executors for the benefit of his wife so long as she should live. He directed that on the death of his wife his son, John Talbot, who is the first defendant, should have the option of purchasing Thornbush Farm and approximately eleven acres at a reasonable valuation, " provided he allows my brother, James Talbot, to

Affirmed. C.A. [1967] 2 All E.R. 920.

reside at the farm for the remainder of his life ".   James Talbot is one of the
plaintiffs.

The testator further directed that his son, Joseph Talbot, should have the
option of purchasing part of Porch Farm and approximately six acres at a reasonable valuation. Should Joseph refuse the option, then it should be offered to his
son, John. Should he refuse, then it should be offered to his son, Ralph; and
should he refuse, then it should be offered to his son, Geoffrey. Should John
refuse the option on Thornbush Farm and the options on parts of Porch Farm,
then the testator directed that the rejected farm or farms, along with a certain
field, should be sold and the proceeds divided in equal shares between his children,
Joseph, Esther, Evette, Geoffrey, John, Ralph and Wayne and Margaret Yates,
with a proviso for substitution of issue, which in the circumstances does not
become material.

The question that I have to determine is whether or not the options purported
to be given in the first place to the son, John, and in the second place to Joseph,
on the two farms are valid and effectual. If they are valid and effectual I have
to determine what steps should be taken to ascertain what the testator has
described as a reasonable valuation, thereby fixing the price to be paid.

No difficulty arises as to the subject matter of the farms comprised in the
option. The petition sets out accurate particulars of the testator's land and property, and there is no doubt or uncertainty as to the property which he was
describing in this part of his will. What it is said to be uncertain is that the price is
in effect incapable of being reasonably fixed, and therefore the undoubted
bounty or benefit that the testator intended these two sons to have, in that they
could purchase the property on which they were resident at the time of his
death, fails. The facts disclose that valuation in this case, having regard to the
possibility of residential development and so on, may not be an easy matter, but
in my judgment, if the case is one where some valuation is to be made, the court
should not shrink, for reasons of difficulty, from giving necessary directions.

I am indebted to counsel for the first and second defendants and to counsel for
the third to sixth defendants for their industry in this matter in looking into
authorities, many of them of many years of age, and for the arguments they
have addressed to me. Counsel for the first and second defendants says that
in a will like this there is no real uncertainty. There is a direction which, read
in conjunction with the remainder of the will, must be a direction to the trustees
or executors in whom the estate of these farms vested when probate was
obtained. All that they have to do is to arrive at a reasonable valuation, and it
is solely a matter for them.

Counsel for the third to sixth defendants contends for a wider construction.
He points out that the testator in this case did not expressly state that it was for
the trustees to decide. " Reasonable valuation " covers a wide area. Was it to be
reasonable to the trustees alone, or was it to be reasonable for the person who
has the benefit of the option, or was it to be reasonable from the point of view
of those interested in residue?

For a time it seemed to me to be a point of some difficulty whether, by having
expressed himself in such general terms, there was sufficient particularity to
enable the price in this case to be ascertained. Counsel for the third to sixth
defendants pointed out, and rightly, that in agreements for the sale of land the
machinery must be fixed so that the court can order specific performance of the
agreement. If the machinery breaks down, the court cannot step in and supply
the deficiency. The parties have made their own bargains, for better for worse,
and that is an end of the matter. In support of that proposition he referred me to
Milnes v. *Gery* (1). In that case the arrangements that had been made for the
ascertaining of the price broke down because of a failure to agree on an arbitrator
or an umpire in the event of disagreement between the two valuers originally

(1) (1807), 14 Ves. 400.

appointed, and Sir William Grant, M.R., decided that in those circumstances the court could not interfere by way of a grant of specific performance, and dismissed the action. Counsel also referred me, among other cases, to *Vickers* v. *Vickers* (2), where the court did in fact enforce an agreement, although the machinery had failed. He pointed out very fairly, however, that that was a partnership case, and it is clear from the other authority which he mentioned that a failure or an attempt by one partner to seek an advantage at a later stage after the partnership has been current for some period, by taking a technical point or a point contrary to what he had agreed, is not a step that the court will countenance. Therefore, if this matter lay in contract alone, in an inter vivos contract, there might be much to be said for the argument that here the words that the testator has used are not sufficiently certain to enable a price to be fixed at which the sons could, if they wished, purchase the respective farms. Do the principles of strict inter vivos contract apply, however, in a case like the present, where the testator in his will seeks to confer a benefit or possible benefit on one of his children? In my judgment, they do not.

Counsel for the first and second defendants referred me to two cases, the first of which is *Waite* v. *Morland* (3). In that case the testatrix had given to her cousin, by codicil, a right immediately to purchase her property, the brewery, etc., at one-fourth less than its value. In the court of first instance (4) Wood, V.-C., had held that the property in question was limited to the brewery itself and did not include public houses tied to the brewery. After making that declaration there was an order of Wood, V.-C., directing an inquiry as to what was the value of the brewery and premises included in his declaration.

That judgment was appealed on the point that the property in question was more than the brewery and included tied houses, and the Court of Appeal (3) so held. Turner, L.J., in his judgment, said that (5) the question must depend on the words and the context of the codicil. It was argued on the part of some of the respondents that no certain meaning could be collected from any part of this instrument and that the whole of it ought to be held void for uncertainty; but he went on to say that some part of the instrument at least was clear. It was clear that the brewery was contained in the option. It therefore appears that the question whether the benefit sought to be given by the testamentary gift was void for uncertainty was before the Court of Appeal, and Turner, L.J.'s judgment, with which Knight Bruce, L.J., agreed, concluded with the statement (5):

" My opinion, therefore, is that the appellant is entitled to purchase all the public houses at three-fourths of their value, and I respectfully dissent from the opinion of Wood, V.-C., upon this point."

It seems to me from that case that the Court of Appeal saw no difficulty in the inquiry that Wood, V.-C., had directed, viz., " What was the value of the property comprised in the bequest? ", being carried into effect.

The second case to which counsel for the first and second defendants referred was that of the *Earl of Radnor* v. *Shato* (6). The headnote there states:

" A right to pre-emption given by will, whether at a price expressed or to be fixed by the trustees, will be executed . . ."

Lord Eldon, L.C., started his judgment by saying (7):

" Having had doubts upon this will for twenty years, there can be no use in taking more time to consider it . . ."

He then went on in the next paragraph (8):

" It is stated broadly that this court would execute a will, proposing a right of pre-emption; and there is no doubt a will may be so construed as to give a right which the court would unquestionably execute. Suppose the case

(2) (1867), L.R. 4 Eq. 529.   (3) (1866), 14 L.T. 649; 12 Jur. N.S. 763.
(4) (1865), 13 L.T. 91.   (5) (1866), 12 Jur. N.S. at p. 764.
(6) (1805), 11 Ves. 448.   (7) (1805), 11 Ves. at p. 453.
          (8) (1805), 1 Ves. at pp. 454, 455.

that has been put by the Attorney-General, a recital in the will that the estate is valued at £50,000, with a direction, that it should be offered to a particular person at £30,000: clearly this court would act. In that case, however, the testator himself has given the court the easy means of acting, and executing his purpose. The question in this case is, whether the testator having directed the trustees to offer the estate at such price and upon such terms, as they may think proper to fix, the court will, if the trustees will not act, place itself in their stead; and before the master fix a price, at which the estate shall be offered to the person, who in that way of putting it seems to be an object of the testator's favour. Upon that question there would be no difficulty or inconvenience. If the testator ordered the trustees to put a reasonable value upon the estate, and to offer it to a particular person at that value, and they die, or refuse to act, the court might direct a reference to the master to fix the value; and execute the trust by proposing the estate to him at that value; and, if he did not accept the proposal, putting it up to a public sale. If therefore there is an objection in this court to executing a will with a right of pre-emption, that must arise, not out of the general doctrine, but the terms of that will, which the court is called upon to execute. I incline upon the whole to think, first, that if the nature of the property will not alter the rule, the difficulty of executing the trust ought not to alter it; and, if it was necessary to decide upon this ground, that a reference ought to be made to the master to fix such price and terms, at which the trustees ought to have offered the estate; taking care, that the ground and information, upon which the master proceeded, should be communicated to the court; in order to ascertain, that the trust was as beneficially executed as the nature of it would allow."

I do not think that counsel for the third to sixth defendants, in his able argument, would have disputed that, if the will in this case said that a reasonable valuation would be fixed by the trustees, the matter would be at an end unless they acted wrongfully in bad faith.

In my judgment, relying on the authorities which counsel for the first and second defendants cited to me, the mere fact that there is no express reference to the trustees fixing the price themselves does not invalidate the right of pre-emption that this will gives to the two sons.

Counsel for the plaintiff executors and trustees one of whom is the brother, who would have a right to reside in one farm if the option were executed, and the other who is a daughter in whose interest, of course, it is that the highest price should be paid, very properly said that the plaintiffs desired to surrender their discretion to this court. In the circumstances, in my judgment, the proper order to make is a declaration that the options purported to be conferred by the will are valid and effectual. I shall make the usual order for administration of the estate and the execution of the trusts of the will by this court, but none of the usual accounts and inquiries in such an order are to be proceeded with except the account as to debts, and I shall direct a special inquiry as to what is a reasonable price, having regard to the terms of the will, to be paid by those to whom the right of pre-emption is given for the respective properties in question. There will be a stay automatically, until some party takes out a summons to proceed with the special inquiry.

Declaration that options are valid and effectual and order for a special inquiry what is a reasonable price.

Solicitors: *T. G. Dell*, Manchester, agents for *Thomas R. Dootson & Co.*, Leigh (for the plaintiffs); *Ackerley, Heaton & Pigot*, Wigan (for the first and second defendants); *Grundy, Kershaw & Farrar*, Manchester (for the third, fourth, fifth and sixth defendants).

[*Reported by* M. DENISE CHORLTON, *Barrister-at-Law.*]

R. *v.* CONSETT JUSTICES, *Ex parte* POSTAL BINGO, LTD.

[QUEEN'S BENCH DIVISION (Lord Parker, C.J., Winn, L.J., and Widgery, J.), November 2, 1966.]

Magistrates—Clerk—Assistant clerk—Shorthand-writer—Presence in retiring room with justices to refer to notes of points argued.

Magistrates—Clerk—Presence in retiring room while justices consider decision— Clerk cross-examining witnesses and ordering witnesses out of court—Whether conviction should be quashed.

The applicant, a company, was charged with offences under s. 42 (1) of the Betting, Gaming and Lotteries Act 1963. The case involved not only finding the primary facts, but drawing the right inferences from those facts and applying the law so far as it had been laid down in two cases. During the hearing of the case the clerk to the justices cross-examined a number of witnesses, ordered the witnesses out of court and in one instance intimated that he would not let a witness take one of the company's files away. At the end of the case the clerk retired with the justices at their request and remained with them throughout their deliberations, for two and a half hours. With the approval of the justices, the clerk invited the assistant clerk, who had taken a shorthand note of the evidence and of counsels' speeches containing the arguments on the law and the facts, to retire with the justices and he likewise remained with them throughout their deliberations. On a motion for an order of certiorari to bring up and quash the applicant's convictions on the three offences,

Held: (i) on the facts the presence of the clerk and assistant clerk with the justices when they retired did not invalidate the decision (see p. 608, letter E, and p. 610, letters C and G, post) because—

(a) law and fact being interwoven, the case was one in which the justices were entitled to have the benefit of their clerk's advice throughout (see p. 607, letter H, and p. 610, letter D, post).

(b) the assistant clerk was there only qua shorthand-writer and the case was one in which the justices were entitled to have him present throughout so that they could be reminded of the exact points in the case (see p. 608, letters A and C, post).

Practice Direction ([1953] 2 All E.R. 1306) considered.

(ii) although what happened during the hearing of the case was not a model of how a case should be conducted in a court of summary jurisdiction, the clerk in no way usurped the functions of the bench and the convictions would not be quashed (see p. 608, letter I, p. 609, letters D and E, and p. 610, letter B, post).

[As to clerk's retirement with justices, see 25 HALSBURY'S LAWS (3rd Edn.) 213, 214, para. 393; and for cases on the subject, see 33 DIGEST (Repl.) 265, 266, *919-925.*]

Cases referred to:

Armstrong v. *Director of Public Prosecutions*, [1965] 2 All E.R. 745; [1965] A.C. 1262; [1965] 3 W.L.R. 344; 129 J.P. 493; 3rd Digest Supp.

Director of Public Prosecutions v. *Regional Pool Promotions, Ltd.*, [1964] 1 All E.R. 65; [1964] 2 Q.B. 244; [1964] 2 W.L.R. 209; 128 J.P. 150; 3rd Digest Supp.

Practice Direction, [1953] 2 All E.R. 1306; 33 Digest (Repl.) 266, *922.*

R. v. *Camborne Justices, Ex p. Pearce*, [1954] 2 All E.R. 850; [1955] 1 Q.B. 41; [1954] 3 W.L.R. 415; 118 J.P. 488; 33 Digest (Repl.) 157, *106.*

R. v. *Consett Justices*, (May 13, 1960), unreported.

R. v. *East Kerrier Justices, Ex p. Mundy*, [1952] 2 All E.R. 144; [1952] 2 Q.B. 719; 116 J.P. 339; 33 Digest (Repl.) 226, *610.*

R. v. *Sussex Justices, Ex p. McCarthy*, [1923] All E.R. Rep. 233; [1924] 1 K.B.
    256; 93 L.J.K.B. 129; 88 J.P. 3; sub nom. *R.* v. *Hirst, Ex p. McCarthy*,
    130 L.T. 510; 33 Digest (Repl.) 156, *104*.

R. v. *Welshpool Justices, Ex p. Holley*, [1953] 2 All E.R. 807; [1953] 2 Q.B. 403;
    [1953] 3 W.L.R. 583; 117 J.P. 511; 33 Digest (Repl.) 265, *920*.

Motion for certiorari.

This was an application by way of motion on behalf of Postal Bingo, Ltd., for
an order of certiorari to remove into the Queen's Bench Division of the High
Court of Justice and to quash three orders and convictions made by the justices
in petty sessions at Consett in the county of Durham on Mar. 1, 1966, under
s. 42 (1) of the Betting, Gaming and Lotteries Act 1963, that the company should
pay a fine of £25 on each of three summonses. The grounds were that the orders
and convictions were not or did not appear to be the orders and convictions of the
justices, but were or appeared to be the orders and convictions of the justices and
the clerk and/or the deputy clerk, each of whom retired with the justices for
substantially the entire period of their retirement extending over a period of
two and a half hours, and that the orders and convictions were contrary to
natural justice. The facts are set out in the judgment of LORD PARKER, C.J.

G. R. F. *Morris*, Q.C., and P. J. *Crawford* for the applicant.
R. A. R. *Stroyan* for the justices.

LORD PARKER, C.J.: The broad, general ground on which this application on behalf of Postal Bingo, Ltd., is moved is, to adopt that well-known
expression, that justice must manifestly be seen to be done, and that that was
not so in the present case in that the decision appeared to be a decision not of the
justices alone but of the justices together with their clerk. It is said that there
were irregularities in the trial both before the justices retired and at the time of
retirement and during retirement. So far as the position of the retirement is
concerned, it is undoubtedly true that the clerk to the justices at their invitation
retired with them and was with them for some two and a half hours. There is a
slight dispute whether the clerk left the justices before they arrived at their
decision, or whether he proceeded out of the retiring room with the justices. For
my part, I am quite satisfied that any interval of time that there may have been
between his coming back into court and the justices coming back into court was
minimal, and to that extent I accept the account of the applicant's solicitors as
to what took place.

It has for long been recognised that the justices are entitled to have the advice
of their clerk on law but not on fact. That is all very well to state as the general
principle, but we all know that there is hardly a decision which falls to be made
which is not mixed law and fact. In 1952 and 1953 a number of cases came before
this court, beginning with the case to which reference is always made, *R.* v.
East Kerrier Justices, Ex p. Mundy (1). That was followed by further cases and,
as a result, a *Practice Direction* (2) was issued by LORD GODDARD, C.J. The
relevant passage is this (3):

" As regards the manner in which justices may consult their clerk, the
court, I think, made it clear in the *East Kerrier* case (1) that the decision of
the court must be the decision of the justices, and not that of the justices
and their clerk, and that, if the clerk retires with the justices as a matter of
course, it is inevitable that the impression will be given that he may influence
the justices as to the decision, or sentence, or both. A clerk should not retire
with his justices as a matter of course, nor should they attempt to get round
the decisions to which I have referred merely by asking him in every case to
retire with them, or by pretending that they require his advice on a point of
law. Subject to this, it is in the discretion of the justices to ask their clerk

_____

(1) [1952] 2 All E.R. 144; [1952] 2 Q.B. 719.   (2) [1953] 2 All E.R. 1306.
                (3) [1953] 2 All E.R. at p. 1307.

to retire with them if, in any particular case, it has become clear that they will need his advice. If, in the course of their deliberations, they find that they need him, they can send for him. On this matter I would stress one further point, and that is, that if the clerk does retire with the justices, or is sent for by them, he should return to his place in court as soon as he is released by the justices, leaving them to complete their deliberations in his absence and come back into court in their turn. I wish to add that the rulings this court has given on the subject derive from, and are really part of, the rule so often emphasised that justice must not only be done but must manifestly appear to be done, and, if justices bear that in mind, I feel sure they will have no difficulty in loyally following the decisions of this court."

As I have said, in the present case I am satisfied, and I find as a fact, that the justices did ask their clerk to retire with them. I also think that it is abundantly clear that they were entitled to have their clerk with them to deal with the law involved in this case.

That brings me to the nature of the case. It followed a decision of the House of Lords in *Armstrong* v. *Director of Public Prosecutions* (4), which was a decision as to when and under what circumstances there could be said to be a playing of a game of chance. It was held that certainly some active participation by the so-called players was necessary before there can be a game of chance, but the House of Lords, and indeed this court in another case, *Director of Public Prosecutions* v. *Regional Pools Promotions, Ltd.* (5), merely decided that in each case there was not sufficient participation to constitute the playing of a game and made no express definition thereof. It was undoubtedly a difficult matter for the justices. It involved not only finding the primary facts, which really were not in dispute at all, but drawing the right inferences from those facts and applying the law so far as it has been laid down in these cases. In my judgment, law and fact were so intimately interwoven that it was really impossible to say that the justices were wrong in keeping their clerk with them throughout. Indeed, there has been exhibited in this case what purports to be a note of counsel for the applicant's final speech and in that he is said to have said, amongst other things: " I do not envy your task today and those of us who have to go through the Acts ", and later:

" This step is most complicated and I do not envy your clerk his task in sifting through the law on this . . . I say that you would have to say, in rules of postal bingo, we are certain where the House of Lords are doubtful."

Counsel for the applicant has frankly said that he has no recollection of using those particular phrases, but, be that as it may, I am quite satisfied that they did represent the true position. As the chairman of the justices pointed out, to say that they could only have their clerk with them when strict law was concerned would mean that he would be in the room one moment and out the next and back again the moment afterwards. I am quite satisfied that this is a case where the justices were entitled to have the benefit of their clerk's advice throughout.

The matter does not end there because, contrary to what was stated in the *Practice Direction* (6) which I read, the clerk remained to the very end or almost the very end. That, as it seems to me, is in conflict with the *Practice Direction* (6), but for my part I do not think that that is a matter in the circumstances of this case which would call for an order of certiorari. There is one other matter in connexion with the retirement of the justices' clerk and that is that, on his own motion, he invited the assistant clerk to retire with him with the justices. That apparently was a move taken by the clerk on his own responsibility, albeit it had the approval, so the chairman says, or the subsequent approval, of the bench. The justification for that is said to be that the assistant clerk had taken a shorthand

(4) [1965] 2 All E.R. 745; [1965] A.C. 1262.
(5) [1964] 1 All E.R. 65; [1964] 2 Q.B. 244.   (6) [1953] 2 All E.R. 1306.

note of the evidence, and, indeed, a shorthand note of counsels' speeches containing the arguments on the law and the facts. It is accepted, and has been accepted by this court, that it is perfectly proper for the court to consult the shorthand-writer in any case, though the justices should come back into court and ask for the relevant passages to be read out. This is a very different case, however, from merely consulting a shorthand-writer on particular passages in the evidence. This is a case where the justices were, in my judgment, entitled to have with them the person who had taken down the arguments of counsel and could read them out to the justices, so that they could be reminded exactly of the points in the case. In so far as the clerk or the assistant clerk were concerned, the assistant clerk who was only there qua shorthand-writer and not qua assistant clerk was entitled, in my judgment, to be there and to remain there. Further, in *R.* v. *Welshpool Justices, Ex p. Holley* (7), it was said that, though the clerk was in that case entitled to retire with the justices, he had stayed longer than was purely necessary for giving advice on the law. LORD GODDARD, C.J., however, said (8):

> " But it is clear that the justices did nothing wrong in taking the clerk with them to their room as they required his advice on law, and in these circumstances we are not prepared to say, merely because he remained in the room while they were discussing the facts, that that in itself was sufficient to invalidate their decision."

Similarly, on the facts of this case, the presence of the clerk throughout and the presence of the assistant clerk throughout were not, of themselves, sufficient in my judgment to invalidate the decision of the justices.

The matter does not end there because even if, as I hold, the clerk and the assistant clerk were right to be there, it is said that the clerk hearing the case so conducted himself and took such a prominent part and was so domineering that anyone in court must have thought that the decision ultimately arrived at was really a decision influenced by the clerk. The matters complained of under this head are several in number. Quite generally it is said that the picture in court was of a silent Bench and a dominant clerk. It is said that the clerk cross-examined a number of witnesses, put questions to prosecuting counsel and generally appeared to be taking charge of the case. It is said also that he on his own motion ordered witnesses out of court, and matters of that sort. I think that it is necessary to go through the matters in a little detail. So far as cross-examining witnesses is concerned, there was apparently an unfortunate incident in the case of a prosecution witness, whom counsel for the applicant sought to cross-examine. He was interrupted by the clerk and the cross-examination by the clerk it is said continued for so long that counsel sat down and eventually begged leave to continue his cross-examination. That, indeed, is referred to by the chairman as the only discordant note in the trial. It may be, I find it unnecessary to decide whether, as stated by the chairman and I think by the clerk, that the particular witness having then been asked a simple question by the clerk, really gave a long answer and went on on his own motion without prompting by the clerk. I find it unnecessary to decide, because practice varies. There are some justices, some benches, who require their clerks to cross-examine to clear up ambiguities, and prefer that the clerk should do it rather than that they should do it themselves; there are other benches who desire to do the cross-examination themselves and for the clerk to remain silent. There is no general practice; there is no accepted practice. So far as this case is concerned, I am quite satisfied that anything which the clerk did by way of questioning was done at the implied request of the bench.

Then it is said that the clerk ordered the witnesses out of court. He certainly did, and that appears, on the affidavit of the chairman, to be the settled practice of that bench. Again it is pointed out that even when counsel on both sides

---

(7) [1953] 2 All E.R. 807; [1953] 2 Q.B. 403.
(8) [1953] 2 All E.R. at p. 809; [1953] 2 Q.B. at p. 406.

intimated that it was not necessary, certainly in the case of the managing director, a Mr. Pannett, nevertheless the clerk ordered him out. He did it, in my judgment pursuant to the general practice of that court, and no application was specifically made to the bench that he should be brought back in order to assist counsel. There was also an incident conceived with a Mr. Kelly, who produced the file of the applicant company. There again the clerk intimated that he would not let the witness take the file away; he wanted to retain it. It was only after the chairman had indicated that it might be done that Mr. Kelly was allowed to take the file away. There was an incident concerning a Mr. Armstrong. Mr. Armstrong was not going to be a witness and was allowed to be in court and he went and sat in the first instance, as I understand it, close to the applicant's solicitor and close to counsel, and the clerk intimated that he could not sit there and ordered him to the back of the court. Junior counsel for the applicant then suggested that Mr. Armstrong might bring up a chair and sit directly behind him. Again the clerk intimated that could not be done, and in effect ordered the witness to what is called the back of the court, although it was only a bench some five feet, so I understand, behind. Be that as it may, I myself think that it was for the clerk to conduct the ordinary arrangements inside the court and that he was not thereby usurping a judicial function of the bench. Again, if counsel had really required Mr. Armstrong to sit closer at hand, an application could have been made to the bench itself.

These are all matters which have given this court anxious consideration. For my part, I am satisfied that what happened here was not a model of how a case should be conducted in a court of summary jurisdiction, but to say that the conviction should be quashed is, in my judgment, a very different matter. In a more recent case, unreported, *R. v. Consett JJ.* (9), the court was dealing with a very similar application again, and this was stressed by counsel for the applicant, in the case of the same bench and the same clerk when the court was constrained to quash the conviction. The facts do not matter. The conviction was there quashed because it appeared that the clerk had used remarks to the effect that he did not consider himself bound by the *East Kerrier* case (10) any longer, and had then gone on to retire with the justices on what it was difficult to conceive could be anything but a pure question of fact. In the course of giving judgment in that case, I referred to *R. v. Camborne Justices, Ex p. Pearce* (11). The court in that case, after referring to Lord Hewart, C.J.'s well-known pronouncement in *R. v. Sussex Justices, Ex p. McCarthy* (12), that justice should not only be done, but should manifestly and undoubtedly be seen to be done, went on (13):

" [That] is being urged as a warrant for quashing convictions or invalidating orders on quite insubstantial grounds and, indeed, in some cases, on the flimsiest pretext of bias. While indorsing and fully maintaining the integrity of the principle reasserted by Lord Hewart, C.J., this court feels that the continued citation of it in cases to which it is not applicable may lead to the erroneous impression that it is more important that justice should appear to be done than that it should in fact be done."

Having referred to that, I stressed that it would require a very strong case in which this court would quash the conviction.

Counsel for the applicant submits that if regard is had to all that was done in this case—if one couples what was done by the clerk in open court with his retirement with the justices throughout and for a long period—then anyone present in court would be bound to think that this was the decision of the justices and their clerk and not of the justices alone. The spectator in court, however, must be taken to know that the justices can have the advice of their clerk and

(9) (May 13, 1960), unreported.
(10) [1952] 2 All E.R. 144; [1952] 2 Q.B. 719.
(11) [1954] 2 All E.R. 850; [1955] 1 Q.B. 41.
(12) [1923] All E.R. Rep. 233 at p. 234; [1924] 1 K.B. 256 at p. 259.
(13) [1954] 2 All E.R. at p. 855; [1955] 1 Q.B. at pp. 51, 52.

that their clerk can retire with them in certain circumstances. If I am right, they were entitled to have the clerk throughout on this occasion, and, therefore, the spectator must be taken to have known that there was nothing wrong in his retiring with the justices for two and a half hours. One then asks oneself: if the spectator merely saw what had happened in court, would he for that reason think that this was a decision other than a decision of the justices? In my judgment, this clerk may have been officious, he may have been tactless, but it is clear that he in no way usurped the functions of the bench, and I find it quite impossible to bring this case within the *Consett Justices'* case (14) in which the court felt constrained to quash the conviction.

In these circumstances, I would refuse this motion.

WINN, L.J.: I agree, and I, too, would refuse this motion feeling as I do that this court ought not, in its discretion, to grant the remedy of an order of certiorari. It is to be borne in mind that an appeal to quarter sessions could have been made. It seems to me that there was here a difficult question of mixed law and fact on which the justices needed the help of their clerk and, indeed, the very valuable assistance of being reminded from the shorthand note of the submissions made by counsel for the applicant. As I see it, it is not only pure questions of law on which justices may properly seek the assistance of their clerk, but also, there may be difficult legal concepts, as there were in this case, the definition of which in relation to the facts established by the evidence is something that lay justices may well find difficult without the assistance of their clerk.

I do not go into the details of the matters which arose in this case; I say no more about it than this, that, in *Director of Public Prosecutions* v. *Regional Pools Promotions, Ltd.* (15), LORD PARKER, C.J., and I each adumbrated it, the concept of participation in the playing of a game of chance, without thinking it necessary to develop the concept. It attracted more attention in *Armstrong* v. *Director of Public Prosecutions* (16). Counsel for the applicant submitted to the justices that the essential issue for them was what amounted to playing a game of chance and whether what was involved in the scheme under their consideration in the instant case did not amount to more than participation in the preparations for the playing of a game of chance or in the procedure required to be followed in order to collect the prizes in the game.

I agree that this motion fails.

WIDGERY, J.: I agree with the judgments and add nothing else.

Motion dismissed.

Solicitors: *Hyde, Mahon & Pascall*, agents for *Nicholson, Martin & Wilkinson*, Newcastle-upon-Tyne (for the applicant); *Director of Public Prosecutions.*

[*Reported by* KAUSHALYA PURIE, *Barrister-at-Law.*]

---

(14) (May 13, 1960), unreported.
(15) [1964] 1 All E.R. 65; [1964] 2 Q.B. 244.
(16) [1965] 2 All E.R. 745; [1965] A.C. 1262.

RYAN v. SMITH.

[QUEEN'S BENCH DIVISION (Lord Parker, C.J., Winn, L.J., and Widgery, J.), November 2, 1966.]

Road Traffic—Traffic signs—Light signals—Stop line at road junction—Vehicle crossing stop line when traffic light green stopped when half of vehicle had crossed stop line—Waited for traffic to cross in front of it—Moved forward across road when light signal had changed to red—Only rear half of vehicle crossed stop line when traffic light was red—Whether contravention of Traffic Signs Regulations and General Directions 1964 (S.I. 1964 No. 1857), reg. 34 (1) (a)—Road Traffic Act, 1960 (8 & 9 Eliz. 2 c. 16), s. 14, as amended by Road Traffic Act, 1962 (10 & 11 Eliz. 2 c. 59), s. 8 and Sch. 1, Pt. 2, para. 13.

The front part of a public service vehicle driven by the appellant crossed the stop line at a road junction when the traffic light was green. When the vehicle had gone about half its length past the traffic light by which the stop line was, the appellant stopped it to allow traffic to cross in front of him and pass into the road to his left. When this traffic had passed he drove the vehicle forward across the junction. By this time the traffic light opposite him had changed colour and was showing the red signal light. The relevant prohibition in the Traffic Signs Regulations and General Directions 1964, reg. 34 (1) (a) was that " the red signal shall convey the prohibition that vehicular traffic shall not proceed beyond the stop line ". On appeal against conviction of having unlawfully failed to comply with a traffic sign contrary to s. 14* of the Road Traffic Act, 1960,

Held: the prohibition was infringed if any part of a vehicle moved forward across the stop line; accordingly the traffic regulation was infringed when the rear part of the vehicle crossed the stop line against the red signal (see p. 613, letter H, and p. 614, letter A, post).

[As to the duty to comply with traffic directions, see 33 HALSBURY'S LAWS (3rd Edn.) 559, para. 949; and for cases on the subject, see 45 DIGEST (Repl.) 35, 36, *117-129.*

For the Road Traffic Act, 1960, s. 14, see 40 HALSBURY'S STATUTES (2nd Edn.) 723; and for the Road Traffic Act, 1962, s. 8 and Sch. 1, Pt. 2, para. 13, see 42 ibid., 895, 924.]

Case Stated.

This was a Case Stated by justices for the county of Lancaster in respect of their adjudication as a magistrates' court sitting at Prescot. On Oct. 6, 1965, an information was preferred by the respondent Ronald Smith against the appellant Phillip Ryan that he on June 15, 1965, at Prescot being the person driving a public service vehicle in a road called High Street unlawfully failed to conform to the indication given by traffic lights contrary to s. 14 of the Road Traffic Act, 1960.

The following facts were found. At about 4.50 p.m. on June 15, 1965, the appellant drove a Crosville bus in the direction of Warrington along High Street, Prescot, towards the junction with St. Helens Road, which was on his left, intending to go straight across the junction and enter Warrington Road, the continuation of High Street. The junction was controlled by traffic lights placed in accordance with the Traffic Signs Regulations and General Directions 1964.

---

* Section 14, so far as material, provides: "(1) . . . where a traffic sign . . . has been lawfully placed on or near a road, a person driving . . . a vehicle who— . . . (b) fails to comply with the indication given by the sign shall be liable . . . to a fine . . . not exceeding fifty pounds." The maximum amount of the fine for a first offence was increased to £50 by the Road Traffic Act, 1962, s. 8 and Sch. 1, Pt. 2, para. 13. By reg. 7 (b) of the Traffic Signs Regulations and General Directions 1964, s. 14 of the Act of 1960, was applied to the red signal shown by the light signals prescribed by reg. 31, by reg. 31 as varied by reg. 32, or by reg. 33.

The traffic light in High Street which faced the appellant on his left as he approached the junction was green when the appellant drove his bus past that light and the stop line to which that light related and entered the junction. As the appellant approached the junction, the witness Radcliffe drove a motor bus of the St. Helens Corporation in the opposite direction from Warrington, along Warrington Road towards the junction intending to turn to his right into St. Helens Road. The appellant stopped his bus on the junction in order to allow the St. Helens Corporation bus to be driven into St. Helens Road. The appellant when he had so stopped was at least half a bus length past the traffic light in High Street. A van being driven on the nearside of the appellants' bus was turning left from High Street into St. Helens Road. The van stopped momentarily to allow the St. Helens bus to turn, but that bus simultaneously stopped or slowed for the van. In the event the appellant's bus was delayed, the van preceding the St. Helens bus, which then passed in front of the appellant. A traffic light was situated in Warrington Road on the far side of the junction from and facing High Street, and was one of the traffic lights which controlled traffic at the junction. The traffic light in High Street and that in Warrington Road facing High Street changed simultaneously to red while the appellant was stationary in the junction. After the St. Helens Corporation bus had been driven in front of him, and after the said traffic lights had changed to red, the appellant moved his bus across the junction into Warrington Road, passing the traffic light in Warrington Road facing High Street when it was still red.

It was contended on behalf of the appellant that he was not guilty of a breach of s. 14 of the Road Traffic Act, 1960 in that he personally, although not the whole of his vehicle, had lawfully passed the traffic lights in High Street and the stop line to which the said light related when the said light was green. It was contended on behalf of the respondent that the appellant unlawfully passed the traffic light in High Street when the said light was red in spite of the fact that he (the appellant) personally, though not the whole of his bus, passed that light at green. The justices found the case proved and accordingly fined the appellant £10 and ordered that his licence should be endorsed. The appellant now appealed.

R. G. Hamilton for the appellant.
R. C. Southwell for the respondent.

WINN, L.J., delivered the first judgment at the invitation of LORD PARKER, C.J.: This is an appeal on a Case Stated by justices for the county of Lancaster sitting at Prescot against a conviction of the appellant for having unlawfully failed to comply with a traffic sign contrary to s. 14 of the Road Traffic Act, 1960, which requires that any traffic light indication shall be complied with. Regulations were made by the Minister pursuant to powers contained in the Act of 1960 providing that stop lines and traffic lights should be complied with. Those regulations are the Traffic Signs Regulations and General Directions 1964 (1), and reg. 34 (1) is conveniently set out in STONE'S JUSTICES MANUAL (1966), vol. 2, p. 3452. It provides so far as relevant, that:

" The significance of the light signals prescribed by para. (2) of reg. 31 or by reg. 33 shall be as follows:—(*a*) the red signal shall convey the prohibition that vehicular traffic shall not proceed beyond the stop line on the carriageway provided in conjunction with the signals or, if that line is not for the time being visible or there is no stop line, beyond the signals; . . ."

It is also provided, to make the matter complete, that

"(*c*) the green signal shall indicate that vehicular traffic may pass the signals and proceed straight on or to the left or to the right."

---

(1) S.I. 1964 No. 1857. The instrument has been amended by S.I. 1966 Nos. 489, 490, but the amendments are immaterial to the decision in this case.

The appellant was driving a bus at the material time. It is unnecessary to go into very much detail but what he did was to pass a traffic light which, when he came to the light short of or on the nearside of the junction he was approaching, was showing green in his favour. We are informed by counsel that the stop line was not far from the traffic light in question though it is not clear whether it was precisely level with the light or some way from it in the direction from which the appellant was coming. The appellant intended to go across the junction and enter the continuation of the street on which he was driving, which was the High Street, Prescot. There was a road on his left called St. Helens Road: as it happened, traffic was approaching him which desired to turn into St. Helens Road and the appellant courteously stopped his bus to allow that oncoming traffic to turn across the front of his bus to its right and enter St. Helens Road. He stopped, as the justices found, at least half a bus length past the traffic lights in the High Street, past the light at the nearer side of the junction that he was approaching. When the traffic which was coming from the opposite direction had turned into St. Helens Road and certain other traffic had cleared the junction, the appellant went on into the far portion of the High Street. At the time when he did that, the light facing him on the far side of the junction was showing red.

The justices found that the appellant's bus would not have caused any obstruction to traffic travelling from St. Helens Road into the High Street if it had remained stationary in the junction instead of moving on across the junction into the far side of the High Street. It was contended against the appellant that he had unlawfully passed the traffic light in the High Street when the light was red. The justices were of the opinion that the appellant had unlawfully failed to conform with the indication given by the traffic light, found the case proved and fined him £10.

The argument on what is a short point, but not an easy one, has naturally centred on the proper construction of the words " shall not proceed beyond the stop line ". It has been cogently and lucidly argued by counsel for the appellant that this bus being, it is conceded, vehicular traffic, had already proceeded beyond the stop line when the light was green, and when it subsequently started to move forward again, it could not properly then have proceeded beyond the stop line. There are matters of policy, into which I do not propose to enter, which might on one view be thought to favour the construction contended by counsel for the appellant, and on the other view to favour, for the purposes of road safety, the opposite contention of counsel for the respondent, which is that these words mean that it is prohibited to take any part of a vehicle beyond the stop line when there is a red light sign showing against it prohibiting its advance.

In my opinion the proper construction of the words is that the prohibition relates to any vehicle or any part of any vehicle and is infringed if any part of any vehicle moves forward so that that part of the vehicle crosses the line, and thereby goes from the nearer side of the line to the far side of the line, looking at the line of advance in the same sense as the line of advance of the vehicle. I think that it is a proper use of language and a proper meaning to give to these words to say that an individual or a vehicle proceeds beyond a datum or other line if, for example, one foot of the individual is moved from behind it to in front of it, or any part of the vehicle moves from hither to thither, from nearside to far side of the line. I have formed that opinion notwithstanding the recognition that one naturally holds in one's mind, that statutory prohibitions and statutory definitions of offences should always be construed strictly so as not to impose a penalty unless it is clear that the intention of Parliament and the Minister making the regulations is to constitute an offence.

I am of the opinion this appeal should be dismissed.

WIDGERY, J.: I have had some doubts about this matter in the course of argument and was much impressed by the considerations urged on us by counsel for the appellant. I can see no difficulties which might arise on either of the alternative constructions which have been argued but in the end I have come to the conclusion that the view expressed by WINN, L.J., is the correct one and I respectfully agree with his judgment.

LORD PARKER, C.J.: I have not found this an easy case but on the whole I have come to the conclusion that the appeal should be dismissed.

Appeal dismissed.

Solicitors: *Helder, Roberts & Co.* (for the appellant); *C. P. H. McCall,* Preston (for the respondent).

[*Reported by* KAUSHALYA PURIE, *Barrister-at-Law.*]

R. *v.* PLAIN.

[COURT OF APPEAL, CRIMINAL DIVISION (Winn, L.J., Lawton and James, JJ.), December 13, 1966.]

Criminal Law—No case to answer—Procedure—Successful submission of no case on one count—Charge no longer subsisting—Verdict should not subsequently be taken on that count.

Criminal Law—Trial—Withdrawal of charge by ruling on submission of no case—Alternative counts of larceny and receiving—Whether charge can be revived subsequently.

The appellant was charged at quarter sessions on an indictment containing several counts, of which one count, count 5, charged larceny of a driving licence and another count, count 6, was an alternative count charging receiving the driving licence knowing it to have been stolen. At the close of the prosecution case, counsel for the appellant made a submission that there was no case to answer on counts 5 and 6. The deputy chairman made statements to the effect that it would not be proper to leave count 5 to the jury, and that counsel need no longer concern themselves with it, but that count 6 must remain and was not withdrawn. Subsequently he exercised his discretion to permit the recall of a prosecution witness. As a result of answers given by this witness the deputy chairman reversed his former ruling on count 5. The appellant was convicted and sentenced on that count, among others.

Held: count 5 should not have been withdrawn from the jury, but, having withdrawn it, the witness should not have been permitted to be recalled on it nor should a verdict have been taken on count 5, since, once the submission of no case was upheld in regard to count 5, it was no longer to be regarded as a subsisting charge during the rest of the trial; accordingly the conviction on count 5 should be quashed (see p. 616, letter I, and p. 617, letters H and I, post).

R. v. *Meek* ((1966), 110 Sol. Jo. 867) considered.

Appeal allowed.

[As to submissions of no case to answer, see 10 HALSBURY'S LAWS (3rd Edn.) 421, para. 772; and for cases on the subject, see 14 DIGEST (Repl.) 631, 632, *6380-6394.*

As to counts for larceny and receiving joined in the same indictment, see 10 HALSBURY'S LAWS (3rd Edn.) 784, para. 1516 text and notes (*d*), (*e*); and for cases on the subject, see 14 DIGEST (Repl.) 260, 261, *2265, 2280.*

As to each count in an indictment being treated as separate for the purposes of verdict, see 10 HALSBURY'S LAWS (3rd Edn.) 391, para. 708 text and note (*a*).]

Case referred to:

R. v. *Meek,* (1966), 110 Sol. Jo. 867.

Appeal.

This was an appeal by Martin John Plain who was convicted on May 5, 1966, at Kent county quarter sessions before the deputy chairman (Sir Reginald Sharpe, Q.C.) and a jury on five counts of an indictment containing eight counts, of which one, count 5, charged him with larceny of a driving licence, value 2s. 6d. Count 5 was ultimately allowed to go to the jury after having been withdrawn from them, and the appellant was sentenced to six months' imprisonment (consecutive) on count 5. He appealed against conviction on this count, on the ground of its having been allowed to go to the jury after having been purportedly withdrawn.

G. H. Rooke for the appellant.
John A. Baker for the Crown.

WINN, L.J., delivered the following judgment of the court: The point which arises is one which the court thinks will very seldom indeed arise; and it should be emphasised that only on the extremely rare occasions when such a situation as the instant one arises would it ever cause trouble to a court of trial. Before I come to the facts of this case it should be made perfectly clear that, where there are alternative charges of larceny and receiving against the same man in respect of the same property, the proper course in almost every case will be to allow both charges to proceed and to be decided ultimately by the jury. Only in very rare cases will it be right to accede to a submission at the end of the prosecution case that there is no evidence on the larceny count, or no evidence on the receiving count which justifies that charge going to the jury. The reason is this. Very often it is only at the end of a trial that it can be seen and made the subject of the proper direction to assist the jury, and ultimately decided by the jury, whether the facts of the particular case fall into the category of larceny or the category of receiving or call for a verdict of not guilty of either. In theory at any rate, and perhaps sometimes in reality, it could be the position at the end of the prosecution case that, there being alternative charges of larceny and receiving, there was no evidence, or no evidence fit to go to the jury, to support either of those charges, e.g., for the simple reason that there was no sufficient evidence that the property in question had been stolen by anybody.

In this particular case the appellant had been charged with larceny of a driving licence, which had been the property of a man who died in August, 1965, and had been taken possession of by his son aged seventeen, not for use in driving a car but apparently because he (the son) liked to flash it round as if he were a man who was used to driving cars and had a driving licence of his own. As a result of the other matters, the subject of other counts in the indictment, this appellant was found to be in possession of this licence. It had, incidentally, been altered by someone before it was so found in his possession. At the end of the prosecution case, a submission was made by counsel who then appeared and now appears for the appellant, that there was no case to answer on this charge of larceny. This larceny charge was count 5 in the indictment, and the receiving count was count 6. The deputy chairman said:

> " Passing to counts 5 and 6, in this case a submission has been made with regard to count 6 as well as to count 5. I think, as regards count 5, that that would not be proper to leave to the jury, even in its amended form, but there is evidence of the licence being a stolen one, though not, as I have indicated, that the accused stole it. Count 6 must remain in. I cannot withdraw that from the jury. The net result is that the only count that I feel able to withdraw from the jury is count 5."

The deputy chairman then said:

> " ' I am not going to take a verdict on it.' Counsel for the appellant: ' You are not?' The deputy chairman: ' Not now. You need not concern yourselves with it. I will refer to it later on perhaps in connexion with count 6 and an

important view [that may be an error in the transcript] to returning a verdict of not guilty on count 5. ' ''

It is to be noted that the deputy chairman said to counsel for the appellant and counsel for the Crown " You need not concern yourselves with it ". It seems to this court that that is a very important declaration and an accurate one because as from that moment onwards, as soon as the submission had been accepted that there was no case to go to the jury on count 5, it became literally the truth that neither the prosecution nor, what is more important, the defence, had any concern with that count.

Instances have been given by members of the court during the hearing of this appeal, all of which are very relevant and important factual hypotheses, such as this, that after such a ruling counsel for an accused in certain circumstances might have sent away witnesses whom he had intended to call on the count, as to the invalidity of which such a submission had been accepted; they might have gone abroad as a result of being so released. Furthermore counsel for the accused would not thereafter have been concerned to lead any evidence from his own client, let alone other witnesses, on the subject matter of the particular count. It would not have been admissible because as a member of the court, said during the discussion, it would not have been relevant in relation to a count which, in the view of the court, has properly to be regarded as dead from the moment when such a ruling has been given. Furthermore it is implicit in such a situation as that that the jury having been told in plain words—" You need not concern yourselves, you need not pay any attention from now on to this count [count 5] because I have ruled it is not for your consideration "—would not feel any responsibility with regard to it. The deputy chairman said to the jury: ". . . I have decided . . . that there is no sufficient evidence in regard to count 5 . . ." Later, he said:

" I have come to the conclusion that you should in due course find the [appellant] not guilty on count 5. So that still leaves count 6. You are not finished with it; . . ."

Assuming that at least one member of the jury understood that quite simple statement it amounts to this: " You are not finished with count 6. You are finished with count 5." The deputy chairman went on to distinguish between the two counts, he told the jury what the distinction was and said: " In due course I shall direct you to bring in a verdict of not guilty on count 5." A careful and prudent juryman or foreman would then have entered up on count 5, " not guilty ", and would have forgotten it. This is a matter of principle not to be decided on the facts of this particular case; if it be not right that that count was dead, the jury would be paying no attention to what, on the contrary view, was still alive or still in suspense: it might prejudicially affect the accused man.

The court cannot understand how an accused can be effectively charged before the jury during the presentation of the prosecution case, then not charged or imperilled before that same court for a period of time until the charge is (so it is said) revived, and thereafter again effectively charged before that court. If that were possible, very dangerous traps might exist for accused persons. Furthermore a judgment of this court given on Oct. 21, 1966, in the case of *R.* v. *Meek* (1) would seem to be quite inconsistent in substance with the view of the law and practice on which the deputy chairman proceeded in this case. It is unnecessary to refer to *R.* v. *Meek* (1), where the court was presided over by LORD PARKER, C.J., beyond saying that the effect of it was to hold that after a successful submission of no case to answer had been made on a particular count in favour of one of two accused jointly charged on that count, the accused in whose favour such a submission has succeeded was no longer to be regarded as charged with the other accused on that count during the rest of the trial, albeit no formal verdict had been taken in his favour of not guilty and albeit he was almost certainly properly

---

(1) (1966), 110 Sol. Jo. 867.

to be regarded as still in the charge of the jury until a formal verdict of not guilty had been given.

That really is the main substance of this matter, but it should be stated in fairness to the deputy chairman that not only was he probably misled by passages in Archbold's Criminal Pleading, Evidence and Practice (36th Edn.), but that this case was very peculiar and exceptional in this particular aspect, namely that after the prosecution case had been closed, he exercised his discretion, and properly exercised his discretion since there was still the receiving charge which had to be answered by the appellant, in permitting the recall of a prosecution witness for further questions to be put to him. It was as a result of answers given by that prosecution witness at that stage that the deputy chairman reviewed and reversed his former ruling. Again it should be said that the deputy chairman appreciated that in so reviewing his earlier ruling, he ought not to take into account, and clearly he did not take into account, the evidence of the appellant already, in the meantime, given as far as evidence-in-chief was concerned; he limited his consideration to evidence of prosecution witnesses, including the evidence of this witness who had been recalled after the intervening period. There was logic in the approach of the deputy chairman, but in the opinion of this court it was not sound. He took the passage in Archbold's Criminal Pleading, Evidence and Practice (36th Edn.), para. 549, as governing the situation and so no doubt did counsel for the appellant who thought that he ought not to object to the court reviewing its former ruling, not having in mind the position in *R. v. Meek* (2). That passage reads:

"If a judge upholds a submission in respect of the whole indictment, he will direct the jury to return a verdict of not guilty; if he upholds the submission in respect of one or more counts only, he will inform them that when he comes to sum up he will direct them to return a verdict of not guilty in respect of such count or counts."

That is too widely expressed, in the opinion of the court. Each count in an indictment is the equivalent of a separate indictment and falls to be dealt with as though it were a separate indictment; from which it follows that where the charge is only one of larceny and there is no count of receiving, such a count should be dealt with as though it were a separate indictment: if there has been a ruling in these circumstances on a count not joined in the alternative with another count, then it is dead and finished. If on the other hand—and I am only repeating what has been said already, but it is important—there are two alternative counts of larceny and of receiving, and there may be other instances in which similar counts may be charged in the alternative, it is only if there is at the end of the prosecution case no evidence to support either count that it can be right to say the matter should be withdrawn from the jury.

Applying that test the court thinks that the deputy chairman should not have withdrawn count 5 and should not have ruled in the first place that count 5 should be removed from the jury's consideration. He did so and it is because he did so that, in the opinion of the court, he ought not to have taken a verdict of guilty on it or to have permitted a witness to be recalled to give evidence which was relevant to and capable of establishing guilt on count 5, which ought to have been regarded by that stage as dead and finished.

For these reasons the court thinks that there was a grave irregularity here and in the particular circumstances of this case it would be most unsatisfactory to allow this conviction to stand. The appeal against conviction is allowed on count 5.

Appeal allowed. Conviction on count 5 quashed.

Solicitors: *Lee, Bolton & Lee* (for the appellant); *Director of Public Prosecutions* (for the Crown).

[*Reported by* Patricia Johnston, *Barrister-at-Law.*]

(2) (1966), 110 Sol. Jo. 867.

SIMM v. SIMM.

[PROBATE, DIVORCE AND ADMIRALTY DIVISION (Sir Jocelyn Simon, P., and Cairns, J.), November 14, December 21, 1966.]

*Divorce—Appeal—Divisional Court—Appeal from order of magistrates' court—
Application for re-hearing—Divisional Court has no jurisdiction to direct
re-hearing before itself or another Divisional Court—Principles applicable
to determination of such applications for re-hearing—Fresh evidence by
husband and wife admitted on appeal by wife from dismissal of her complaint
—Evidence conflicting—Important bearing on result of case if justices were to
reject husband's explanation given in his fresh evidence—Re-hearing ordered—
Matrimonial Proceedings (Magistrates' Courts) Act, 1960 (8 & 9 Eliz.
2 c. 48), s. 11 (3)—Matrimonial Causes Rules, 1957 (S.I. 1957 No. 619),
r. 73 (7).*

On an appeal by the wife against the dismissal by justices of her complaint of cruelty, desertion and wilful neglect, the Divisional Court gave leave to her to adduce on affidavit fresh evidence, which consisted principally of communications written admittedly by the husband after the dismissal of her complaint. These communications, so she alleged, tended to show that he had given false evidence at the hearing before the justices. The husband was given leave to adduce fresh evidence in reply, and by affidavit denied that he had given false evidence, explaining that all written communications by him had been for the purpose of promoting a reconciliation with the wife*. At an adjournment of the hearing of the appeal the husband and the wife were cross-examined on their affidavits.

Held: (i) on appeal from a magistrates' court the Divisional Court had jurisdiction to direct a re-hearing by another magistrates' court either by implication from recognition of such jurisdiction in s. 11 (3)† of the Matrimonial Proceedings (Magistrates' Court) Act, 1960, and r. 73 (7)† of the Matrimonial Causes Rules, 1957, or by long standing usage, but it was not open to the Divisional Court to direct a re-hearing before a Divisional Court; accordingly two courses were open to the court, viz., either to dismiss the appeal or to direct a re-hearing by justices (see p. 621, letters A and C, post).

(ii) in deciding whether to direct a re-hearing the court should adopt the same principles as were accepted in the Court of Appeal in deciding whether to admit fresh evidence, of which the material principle was that the fresh evidence, if accepted, must be such as would have an important bearing on the result of the case (see p. 621, letters D, F and G, post).

Brown v. *Dean* ([1908-10] All E.R. Rep. 661) and *Ladd* v. *Marshall* ([1954] 3 All E.R. 745) considered.

(iii) over important parts of the evidence, both on affidavit and orally, the court was in doubt which spouse was telling the truth; some parts of the husband's written communications would, unless the justices accepted his explanation, materially affect their view of the evidence as a whole and might lead to the case being differently decided, and in such circumstances it was not for the Divisional Court to resolve the doubt, and a re-hearing before a different panel of justices would be directed (see p. 622, letter F, and p. 623, letter A, post).

Per CURIAM: answers by the spouses given in evidence to the Divisional Court to questions expressly accepted as going only to credibility could be used at the re-hearing for the different purpose of testing the evidence given on the re-hearing on the issues arising there; accordingly the Divisional Court would not give directions for any type of evidence that could normally

---

* The husband expressly waived any claim to privilege; see p. 620, letter F, post.

† The relevant words of s. 11 (3) and of r. 73 (7) are set out at p. 621, letters C and B, post.

be admissible to be excluded at the re-hearing (see p. 623, letters G and I, post).

Lindwall v. *Lindwall* (ante p. 470) considered.

[As to the powers of the court on an appeal from magistrates exercising matrimonial jurisdiction, see 12 HALSBURY'S LAWS (3rd Edn.) 510, 511, para. 1120; and for cases on the subject, see 27 DIGEST (Repl.) 732, 733, *6983-7000.*

As to the receipt of further evidence on appeal to the Court of Appeal, see 30 HALSBURY'S LAWS (3rd Edn.) 468, 469, para. 884, text and note (*p*); and for cases on the subject, see DIGEST (Practice) 775-778, *3396-3420.*

For the Matrimonial Proceedings (Magistrates' Courts) Act, 1960, s. 11, see 40 HALSBURY'S STATUTES (2nd Edn.) 415.

For the Matrimonial Causes Rules, 1957, r. 73 (7), see 10 HALSBURY'S STATUTORY INSTRUMENTS (Second Re-Issue) 273.]

Cases referred to:

Andrew v. *Andrew*, [1953] 1 W.L.R. 1453; 97 Sol. Jo. 830; 3rd Digest Supp.

Bigsby v. *Dickinson*, (1876), 4 Ch.D. 24; 46 L.J.Ch. 280; 35 L.T. 679; Digest, Practice 771, *3359.*

Braddock v. *Tillotson's Newspapers, Ltd.*, [1949] 2 All E.R. 306; [1950] 1 K.B. 47; 2nd Digest Supp.

Brown v. *Dean*, [1908-10] All E.R. Rep. 661; [1910] A.C. 373; 79 L.J.K.B. 690; 102 L.T. 661; Digest (Practice) 602, 2431.

Corbett v. *Corbett*, [1953] 2 All E.R. 69; [1953] P. 205; [1953] 2 W.L.R. 1124; Digest (Cont. Vol. A) 783, *5570b.*

Crook v. *Derbyshire*, [1961] 3 All E.R. 786; [1961] 1 W.L.R. 1360; 3rd Digest Supp.

House v. *Haughton Brothers (Worcester), Ltd.*, ante p. 39; [1957] 1 W.L.R. 148.

Ladd v. *Marshall*, [1954] 3 All E.R. 745; [1954] 1 W.L.R. 1489; 3rd Digest Supp.

Lindwall v. *Lindwall*, ante p. 470; [1967] 1 W.L.R 143.

Meek v. *Fleming*, [1961] 3 All E.R. 148; [1961] 2 Q.B. 366; [1961] 3 W.L.R. 532; 3rd Digest Supp.

Owen v. *Owen*, [1964] 2 All E.R. 58; [1964] P. 277; [1964] 2 W.L.R. 654; 3rd Digest Supp.

Theodoropoulas v. *Theodoropoulas*, [1963] 2 All E.R. 772; [1964] P. 311; [1963] 3 W.L.R. 354; Digest (Cont. Vol. A) 713, *2565a.*

W. v. *W.*, [1966] 2 All E.R. 889.

Appeal.

This was an appeal by the wife from an order made on Jan. 8, 1966, by the justices for the county borough of Blackpool, dismissing her complaints of persistent cruelty, desertion wilful neglect to maintain and adultery. The charge of adultery was abandoned in the course of the hearing.

David Wild for the wife.

P. T. H. Morgan for the husband.

Cur. adv. vult.

Dec. 21, 1966. **CAIRNS, J.**, read the following judgment of the court at the invitation of SIR JOCELYN SIMON, P.: The evidence called before the justices was that of the wife and her mother and father on one side, and of the husband and the woman named in the adultery charge on the other. The justices accepted the evidence of the husband in preference to that of the wife and her witnesses and dismissed all the charges. The grounds of appeal originally put forward were that the decision was wrong in law and against the weight of evidence; but at the opening of the hearing before us it was conceded that neither of those grounds was arguable. In any event, this court has had many occasions to remonstrate against the uninformativeness, and therefore the impropriety, of grounds of appeal couched in this way.

The appeal first came on for hearing before WRANGHAM and STIRLING, JJ., on July 21, 1966. Counsel for the wife then applied for leave to amend the notice of appeal by adding an allegation that certain letters written by the husband since the dismissal of the complaints and certain statements made by him to his wife tended to show that the husband's evidence had been false. In order to bring those letters and statements to the knowledge of the court, it was necessary to apply for the admission of fresh evidence. Accordingly leave was sought to admit for the purposes of the appeal affidavits of the wife and her mother, exhibiting the letters and stating what the husband was alleged to have said to the wife about his evidence. The husband on his side then applied for leave to put in an affidavit denying that he had given any false evidence and explaining that all the letters had been written in order to promote a reconciliation with his wife and that one (to which we shall refer as " the note ", because it is hardly a letter) was written only at the specific request of the wife. He also denied the alleged oral statements and, as these appear to us to be of little importance in comparison with the documents, we make no further reference to them. There was on the affidavits a clear conflict of testimony; both sides therefore joined in applying for an order for the deponents to all three affidavits to attend for cross-examination on a further hearing of the appeal. The court acceded to all these applications and the hearing of the appeal was adjourned. It came before us on Nov. 14, 1966.

Before we proceed further we wish to draw attention to the fact that all the letters appear on the face of them to have had as their main object the effecting of a reconciliation. This being so, it might have been open to the husband to claim privilege for them; see *Theodoropoulas* v. *Theodoropoulas* (1). If he had wished to do so, the right time for him to do it would have been at the hearing before WRANGHAM and STIRLING, JJ., and before seeking leave to put in an affidavit in answer. If, however, he had made a claim to privilege at the opening of the hearing before us we should have been prepared to consider it. No such claim was made: on the contrary, the husband's counsel expressly waived any privilege there might be and said that his client wished all the facts to be brought out. That being so we need not examine the question of privilege further.

[HIS LORDSHIP referred (i) to the notice of appeal not having been amended and intimated that, as the respondent was not embarrassed, leave to amend would be given, and (ii) to a further letter by the husband exhibited to a further affidavit of the wife's mother, and said that this letter had not been relied on as being significant. HIS LORDSHIP continued:] All the deponents to the affidavits duly attended to be cross-examined. The husband and the wife were both cross-examined, but the wife's mother was not required to go into the witness box.

Cases in which fresh evidence is admitted on appeal may be divided into two categories: first, those where the court is asked to consider the fresh evidence along with that given at first instance and to give a final decision; and, secondly, those where a re-hearing is applied for. We have found no case since 1876 (see *Bigsby* v. *Dickinson* (2) where an appellate court, on an appeal in a case heard on oral evidence, has allowed a witness to be called and has then given a final judgment based on the evidence in the court below together with the new evidence. We do not pause to consider whether there is jurisdiction for us to take such a course: it would in our view be a wholly unsatisfactory one in the present case. It was, indeed, conceded by counsel for the wife that, if he succeeded in the appeal at all, he could do no more than ask for a re-hearing. We have given some consideration to the question of whether we could order a re-hearing before ourselves or another divisional court. We realise that a re-hearing by lay justices of a case such as this, having regard to what has occurred since the original hearing, will present them with special difficulties and that a re-hearing before

---

(1) [1963] 2 All E.R. 772; [1964] P. 311.   (2) (1876), 4 Ch.D. 24.

judges of this Division might have certain advantages; but we know of no precedent for such a procedure. Moreover, the whole jurisdiction with which we
are here concerned is constituted by statute and rules made thereunder. These
legislative provisions confer the primary jurisdiction on magistrates' courts,
and merely give a right of appeal to the High Court (Matrimonial Proceedings
(Magistrates' Courts) Act, 1960, s. 11), with power to the High Court to

> " draw all inferences of fact which might have been drawn in the magis-
> trates' court and [to] give any judgment and make any order which ought
> to have been made there."

(See Matrimonial Causes Rules, 1957, r. 73 (7).) We cannot read into this language
any power to re-hear the case on fresh evidence. It is true that the statute and
the rules do not expressly confer on the Divisional Court any power to direct
a re-hearing by the magistates' court; but s. 11 (3) of the Act of 1960 clearly
contemplates such a power, referring in terms to "an order directing that a
complaint shall be re-heard by a magistrates' court ". In any event, it is a power
which has been exercised on countless occasions without any doubt being raised;
cursus curiae lex curiae. We are therefore of opinion that the two courses open
to us are either to dismiss the appeal or to direct a re-hearing by justices.

We next consider the circumstances in which an appellate court should direct
a re-hearing; and in this respect we have no doubt that this court should adopt
the same principles as are accepted in the Court of Appeal. The fundamental
issue at stake lies in the conflict and interrelationship of two considerations of
public policy: first, that adjudication (not least on matters which may, directly
or indirectly, affect matrimonial status) should be made on the fullest and most
accurately ascertained assessment of fact; and, secondly, that litigation (not
least matrimonial litigation) should not be unduly prolonged—and, in particular,
that a judgment on a question of fact which was justified by the material adduced
at the trial should not lightly be disturbed. In assessing how these conflicting
principles should be applied to the facts of the present case, we have been guided
by the authorities to which we have been referred.

All the authorities recognise that there are three rules to be observed before
the fresh evidence can be admitted, though their exact statement differs from
case to case. They may be shortly stated as follows. 1. The fresh evidence must
not have been available at the trial. 2. It must be such that, if accepted, it would
have an important bearing on the result of the case. 3. It must be credible.
Rules 1 and 3 need not detain us: the letters, written since the trial, were not
available at the trial; and there is no reason to disbelieve that they were written
—indeed, the husband admits that he wrote them. The second rule is the one
that calls for further examination here and it is the one that has been the most
variously expressed.

In *Brown* v. *Dean* (3) Lord Loreburn, L.C., said that the fresh evidence
must be conclusive, while Lord Shaw of Dunfermline accepted (4) a much
lower standard. The other two members of the House simply concurred; and,
from the order in which the speeches were made, it would seem that one agreed
with the Lord Chancellor and the other with Lord Shaw—though it may be
that each intended only to agree in the result of the appeal, as to which there
was no difference of opinion. In more recent cases the rule has usually been
stated in a form intermediate between that of Lord Loreburn and that of
Lord Shaw—that the evidence must be such as to be likely to have an important influence on the result of the case but not necessarily a conclusive one;
see *Ladd* v. *Marshall* (5), especially per Denning, L.J.; *Crook* v. *Derbyshire* (6),
especially per Ormerod, L.J., and, very recently, *House* v. *Haughton Brothers
(Worcester), Ltd.* (7), per Winn, L.J. That similar rules apply in matrimonial

(3) [1908-10] All E.R. Rep. 661 at p. 662; [1910] A.C. 373 at p. 374.
(4) [1908-10] All E.R. Rep. at p. 663; [1910] A.C. at p. 376.
(5) [1954] 3 All E.R. 745 at p. 748.   (6) [1961] 3 All E.R. 786 at pp. 788, 789.
                    (7) Ante at pp. 40, 41.

cases is clear from *Corbett* v. *Corbett* (8), approved by the Privy Council in *Andrew* v. *Andrew* (9).

Since the purpose of the wife in seeking to adduce the husband's letters is to persuade the court that his evidence at the trial was false, it might at first sight seem that what is proposed is simply to bring in matter affecting his credibility, a course which the courts are reluctant to allow (see *Braddock* v. *Tillotson's Newspapers, Ltd.* (10)); though in some very special circumstances it may be allowed (see *Meek* v. *Fleming* (11)). In the circumstances of this case, however, although the husband's credit is obviously very much in issue and the letters are such as might be used with a view to shaking it, they could, if allowed to be used at all, be used as part of the wife's case: they could, for example, be put in before the husband gave evidence and used against him even though he did not go into the witness box. They therefore not only go to credit but also bear directly on the issue of cruelty or no cruelty.

In considering whether the new material would be likely to have an important bearing on the result of the case we are in a different situation from that which usually confronts an appellate court when determining this question. In most of the reported cases the court had before it only an affidavit from the appellant (or from some proposed witness for the appellant) and had to decide only if the new material was on the face of it such as to be of substantial significance. In *Ladd* v. *Marshall* (12) there was an affidavit from the respondent, but the court took account only of the affidavits tendered by the appellant (see per HODSON, L.J. (13)). Here, in consequence of the order made by a differently constituted Divisional Court, we have before us conflicting stories both on affidavit and by way of oral evidence. If we could say that, in the light of all this evidence, we were firmly convinced that the husband had satisfactorily explained the "admissions" contained in his letters, then we consider that we ought to refuse a re-hearing. We do not find ourselves in this state of mind: over important parts of the evidence both in the affidavits and in the oral testimony we are in doubt as to which of the spouses is telling the truth. That being so, we take the view that it is not for us to resolve the doubt, but that we should examine the letters on the assumption that the wife may be speaking the truth about the circumstances in which they were written and that a desire for reconciliation may not wholly account for parts of the language used by the husband. (Cf. the approach of the Divisional Court in applications under r. 36 of the Matrimonial Causes Rules, 1957; see *Owen* v. *Owen* (14); cf. also *W.* v. *W.* (15).)

It is sufficient for us to confine ourselves to two short extracts from what the husband wrote. In one letter to the wife's mother he wrote, "I didn't really kick her and punch her as much as she makes out". In the note he wrote "I told lies at the court". The first of these statements appears to be inconsistent with the evidence that the husband had given to the justices, in the course of which he denied all the assaults of which the wife had given evidence and said: "I once struck my wife when she was hysterical, she told me to. I did not use my fist, I slapped her." In his evidence to us the husband did not suggest that in this passage of his letter he did not mean what is its apparent significance and his explanation of it was not such as to satisfy us that it was consistent with his evidence before the justices. As to the words in the note, we attach less importance to these, because (whatever may have been the circumstances in which the note was written) the "lies", if any, may well have been statements which he made about his wife's conduct rather than denials as to his own. Nevertheless, if the justices believed what he had said about his wife's behaviour, as

---

(8) [1953] 2 All E.R. 69; [1953] P. 205.   (9) [1953] 1 W.L.R. 1453.
(10) [1949] 2 All E.R. 306; [1950] 1 K.B. 47.
(11) [1961] 3 All E.R. 148; [1961] 2 Q.B. 366.   (12) [1954] 3 All E.R. 745.
(13) [1954] 3 All E.R. at pp. 750, 751.
(14) [1964] 2 All E.R. 58 at pp. 63, 64; [1964] P. 277 at p. 284.
(15) [1966] 2 All E.R. 889 at p. 892, letter F.

apparently they did, this may well have had a bearing on the view that they took of his own actions. We are of opinion, without looking further, that these parts of the husband's communications were such as could, unless the justices accepted his explanations of them, materially affect their view of the evidence as a whole and lead to the case being differently decided. For these reasons we conclude that there must be a re-hearing.

It is, we fear, inevitable that on the re-hearing (which must, in accordance with the usual practice, be before a fresh panel of justices) they will be faced with a more than usually difficult task. They will no doubt hear conflicting versions of the matrimonial history from the spouses in their evidence-in-chief and there may be other witnesses. The material available for cross-examination will be abundant. Any divergence from the evidence given in January will probably be seized upon; so will any divergence from the evidence in this court; the husband will be asked again to explain the letters on which this appeal is succeeding and if his explanation differs at all from that which he gave to us the discrepancy will be used against him. There is always a danger, when some fresh piece of evidence comes to light at a late stage, and especially when it has been made the basis of an order for re-hearing, that excessive weight may be attached to it. We have considered whether, in order to avoid this danger, we ought to impose some limit on the rights of cross-examination at the re-hearing. We considered this particularly with regard to the contents of the note (because of the suspicion that exists as to how it came to be written) and to the answers given in cross-examination in this court. As to the note, we feel that the question of how it came into existence is so much bound up with the whole question of which spouse is in general to be believed (or whether both are to some extent telling untrue stories) that it must be left to the justices to decide this issue along with the other issues of fact. As to the cross-examination here, we were concerned to ensure that it should be confined to questions about how the husband's letters came to be written and to his credibility strictly in connection therewith. This was fully accepted by counsel: it would have been quite wrong to allow questions directed to showing that the husband was guilty of cruel or expulsive conduct. Nevertheless, the matters are so intermingled that inevitably some questions, quite properly put as going to credit, produced answers which, it might be argued, tended to assist or to damage the husband's substantive case. The same might apply, though in a lesser degree, to the wife. Should counsel be allowed on the re-hearing to use answers given here to questions expressly accepted as going only to credibility in order to test the evidence which will be given there on the issues themselves? After careful consideration, we are of opinion that this must be permissible. We know of no rule that answers given in relation to credibility in one set of proceedings may not be used for a different purpose in other proceedings, whether or not they are connected with the first set. On principle we think that a person, having elected to make an affidavit, having laid himself open to cross-examination on that affidavit, and having given answers which may have a bearing on issues arising thereafter, must be prepared to face cross-examination founded on those answers (cf., *Lindwall* v. *Lindwall* (16)). Once we have reached the conclusion that the wife is entitled to a re-hearing, we do not think that it is open to us to give any direction, or to ask for any undertaking, for the exclusion of any type of evidence that would normally be admissible. Having said this, we desire to emphasise, once again, the need for the justices on the re-hearing to take a balanced and sophisticated view of the whole of the evidence which they hear and not to assume that because a party has made conflicting statements on different occasions he or she thereby automatically puts himself or herself out of court.

---

(16) Ante p. 470.

For the reasons which we have given we allow the appeal and direct a re-hearing before a fresh panel of justices.

Appeal allowed.   Re-hearing directed.

Solicitors: *Corbin, Greener & Cook*, agents for *Blackhurst, Parker & Co.*, Blackpool (for the wife); *Gibson & Weldon*, agents for *John Budd & Co.*, Blackpool (for the husband).

[*Reported by* ALICE BLOOMFIELD, *Barrister-at-Law.*]

DOLPHIN SQUARE TRUST, LTD. *v.* HARTMAN.

[COURT OF APPEAL, CIVIL DIVISION (Lord Denning, M.R., Harman and Salmon, L.JJ.), January 19, 1967.]

Rent Restriction—Tenancies excluded from being regulated tenancies—Housing association—Association becoming immediate reversioner on lease—Tenancy subsisting at date of acquisition—Rateable value of dwelling house then above Rent Act limit—Tenancy expired in October, 1965—Rent then in arrear— Action for possession brought in November, 1965—Rent Act 1965 (operative Dec. 8, 1965) extended to dwelling house—Whether housing association entitled to recover possession on ground that tenancy was free from Rent Acts under Housing Repairs and Rents Act, 1954 (2 & 3 Eliz. 2 c. 53), *s. 33* (1), (2) (b)— *Rent Act 1965 (c. 75), s. 1* (2), *s. 20* (1) (a).

On Jan. 1, 1965, the plaintiff housing association became the reversioner on a block of flats. The defendant then occupied one of the flats, of which the rateable value at the material time was £242 per annum, under a seven year lease expiring in October, 1965. At the expiry of the lease the defendant's rent was in arrear. In November, 1965, the plaintiff sued for possession. On Dec. 8, 1965, the Rent Act 1965 came into operation. If the " provision of the premises comprised in the tenancy forms part of the purposes for which [the plaintiff's] business is mainly conducted ", the letting would be excepted from the Rent Acts by the joint effect of s. 1 (2) of the Rent Act 1965 and s. 33 (2) (b)* of the Housing Repairs and Rents Act, 1954, but if not the Act of 1965 would apply by virtue of s. 20 (1) (a).

Held: although the flat was occupied by the defendant tenant when the plaintiff housing association acquired the reversion, the housing association provided it for him and for future tenants and, as that was part of the purposes for which the housing association's business was mainly conducted, the tenancy was excepted from becoming a regulated tenancy within the Rent Act 1965 (see p. 627, letters G and I, and p. 628, letter B, post).

Appeal dismissed.

[As to lettings by exempted authorities being excluded from regulated tenancies, see 23 HALSBURY'S LAWS (3rd Edn.) 759, 760, para. 1521; and for a case on the subject, see DIGEST (Cont. Vol. A) 1071, 7590a.

For the Industrial and Provident Societies Act, 1893, see 12 HALSBURY'S STATUTES (2nd Edn.) 876; and for the Act which repealed and replaced it, viz., the Industrial and Provident Societies Act 1965, see 45 ibid. 755.

For the Housing Repairs and Rents Act, 1954, s. 33, see SUPPLEMENT to 34 HALSBURY'S STATUTES (2nd Edn.) para. [392] Amended Texts.

For the Rent Act 1965, s. 1, s. 20, see 45 HALSBURY'S STATUTES (2nd Edn.) 822, 839.]

Appeal.

This was an appeal by the tenant from the judgment of His Honour JUDGE HERBERT, dated July 7, 1966, at Westminster County Court ordering the defendant to give possession of Flat 105, Keyes House, Dolphin Square, London,

---

* Section 33 (2) (b), so far as relevant, is printed at p. 626, letter H, post.

on Aug. 4, 1966, and ordering that the defendant should pay £296 11s. 2d., being the balance of arrears of rent and mesne profits after deducting a sum of £2 on or before July 21, 1966. The judgment of the county court judge included the following—

" It is submitted for the [plaintiff housing association] that the interest of the landlord belongs to it as a housing association and that by virtue of s. 33 of the [Housing Repairs and Rents Act, 1954] the defendant's tenancy was not a controlled tenancy. [His Honour read the relevant words of s. 33 (2) (*b*)* of the Act of 1954.] It is pointed out that para. (*a*) and para. (*c*) of sub-s. (2) of s. 33 of the Act of 1954 seem to refer to a past, and not a continuing, provision of the premises comprised in the tenancy, and it is submitted that, where the housing association acquires by purchase, or otherwise, the interest of the landlord who in the first instance let the premises in question, it cannot be said that it has provided, or provides, those premises. In support of this argument counsel referred to p. 110 of the latest edition of Megarry on the Rent Acts. The learned editor, to whom I pay due respects, says—' A house can hardly be said to have been provided by an association which buys it with a tenant in it '. No authority is given on the point and I think that, while the proposition may be true as regards s. 33 (2) (*a*)—' the premises were provided '—it is not true as regards s. 33 (2) (*b*), which is the subsection which governs the present case.

" Does the ' provision of the premises comprised in the tenancy (i.e., the [tenant's] flat) form part of the purposes for which the [housing association's] business is mainly conducted '? The question, as I see it, is whether the provision of the [tenant's] flat began and ended with the signing of his lease by the [housing association's] predecessors in title. In my judgment it did not. Leaving aside the devolution in title from the then landlords, can it be said that, during the currency of his lease [the housing association was] not providing him, on terms, with the possession of his flat, as well as the service that made it possible to live in. I realise that ' provision ' is an equivocal word. If I ask someone to ' provide ' me with a light for my cigarette, he provides me with a match once and for all; but that is no fair analogy for the landlord who provides me with a flat. There the mutual rights and obligations are continuous and if, rightly or wrongly, the landlord re-entered any sensible bystander would say, I think, ' the landlord has ceased to provide the tenant with a flat '.

" In my judgment the [housing association] was, at all material times, providing the [tenant] with his flat, and the services appertaining, and comes within the provisions of s. 33 (2) (*b*) of the Act of 1954.

" Another point is taken, however, by counsel for the tenant. He says that, if one looks at the [housing association's] own rules, one will see that [the housing association's] objects are ' to carry on the business—of providing housing for letting from time to time and any associated amenities '. He says that these objects do not include acting as landlord of a house (or flat) that has previously been let. If this be right, the [housing association] has been acting ultra vires in accepting rent from, and in providing service to, the [tenant]. I agree that r. 2 has not been drafted with the point raised in the present case in mind, but it seems to me to be clear, for reasons already stated, that the [housing association] is providing housing, inter alia, for the [tenant] and that is one of the objects of its business.

" In the upshot I must give judgment for the [housing association] on the claim for possession . . ."

The defendant appealed. By his notice of appeal dated Aug. 16, 1966, the grounds stated were that the county court judge misdirected himself in holding that

---

* Section 33 (2) (*b*), so far as relevant, is printed at p. 626, letter H, post.

z

(a) the premises were provided by the plaintiff housing association within the meaning of s. 33 (2) of the Act of 1954, and (b) that the plaintiff was acting as a housing association with regard to r. 2 of the Rules of the Dolphin Square Trust, Ltd. and the fact that the premises had been let to the defendant by the plaintiff housing association's predecessor in title.

D. P. Kerrigan, Q.C., J. E. S. Ricardo and *I. E. Jacob* for the defendant tenant.
G. H. Crispin, Q.C., and *D. R. Stuckey* for the plaintiff housing association.

LORD DENNING, M.R.: This raises a short but important point about the flats in Dolphin Square. These blocks of flats were originally owned by Dolphin Square Co., Ltd., which was an ordinary limited company. It let one of the flats, No. 105, Keyes House, to the tenant, Mr. Hartman. The lease was for seven years from September, 1958. It expired in October, 1965. The rent was £300 a year and the rateable value was £212 a year (1). At that time the flat was undoubtedly outside the Rent Acts. During the lease there were changes in the reversion. The Westminster City Council bought these blocks of flats from the Dolphin Square Co., Ltd. by private treaty. Then the Westminster City Council let the blocks of flats by a long lease to a new company called Dolphin Square Trust, Ltd. That company is very different from the original company. This new company is a housing association within the statutory definition of a housing association (2). It does not trade for profit.

In October, 1965, when the lease to the tenant came to an end, he was very much in arrear with his rent. The housing association (who were by this time his landlords) took proceedings for possession. They issued their proceedings in November, 1965. At that time the flat was not within the Rent Acts at all. But on Dec. 8, 1965, before any eviction took place, the new Rent Act 1965 came into operation. Under the Act of 1965 if the landlord had been a private landlord (and not a housing association) the tenant would clearly be protected. The rateable value did not exceed £400 (the figure for Greater London). The tenancy would be a regulated tenancy; and the tenant could not be evicted except on proof of the usual requirements of the Rent Acts. In particular, no order for possession could be made or enforced unless it was reasonable; see s. 1 and s. 20 of the Rent Act 1965.

The housing association say here, however, that they are in a very different position from ordinary private landlords. They claim that, because they are a housing association, the tenancy is not a controlled tenancy: and the tenant is not protected. This question depends on the true interpretation of s. 33 (1), (2) (*b*) of the Housing Repairs and Rents Act, 1954. That section provides that, where the interest of the landlord belongs to a housing association, the tenancy shall not be a controlled tenancy if this condition is fulfilled, namely, that

" (2) . . . (*b*) the housing association is registered under the Industrial and Provident Societies Act, 1893 (3) and the provision of the premises comprised in the tenancy forms part of the purposes for which its business is mainly conducted."

This housing association was formed in 1964 and registered under the Act of 1893. The objects of the society were

" to carry on the industry, business or trade of providing housing for letting from time to time and any associated amenities upon such terms and conditions as the society may determine."

The question is: did the provision of this flat form " part of the purposes for which its business was mainly conducted "? That is the whole question in the case.

---

(1) At the time of the commencement of proceedings the rateable value was £242 per annum.
(2) See the Housing Act, 1957, s. 189 (1); 37 HALSBURY'S STATUTES (2nd Edn.) 458.
(3) The Act of 1893 has been repealed and replaced by the Industrial and Provident Societies Act 1965; 45 HALSBURY'S STATUTES (2nd Edn.) 755.

Counsel for the tenant says that when the housing association bought these blocks of flats, this flat was already occupied by the tenant. The housing association did not, therefore, provide the flat for the tenant. The condition, he says, was not fulfilled, because the word " provision " in s. 33 (2) (*b*) applies only to the provision of the flat for its *future* occupation by a tenant. He supports his argument by a reference to Megarry on the Rent Acts, p. 110, where it is said:

> " These requirements exclude from the exemption houses owned by housing associations purely for investment purposes and also, apparently, those now owned but not ' provided ' by the society. A house can hardly be said to have been provided for a tenant by an association which buys it with the tenant in it [that is this case] but the Housing Act, 1957, makes it clear that a house need not be provided by new building. It seems, therefore, that a housing association letting will be exempted if the premises were first let to the particular tenant by the association."

Counsel for the housing association submits a different interpretation. He says that, in order to determine whether the condition in s. 33 (2) (*b*),

> " the provision of the premises comprised in the tenancy forms part of the purposes for which its business is mainly conducted "

is fulfilled, you must look to the objects of the housing association and to its business. You must see whether the provision of this flat is part of its main purposes. And then he says that it was so. This flat was acquired for the purpose of providing, not only the particular tenant but any future tenant, with accommodation; and that, he says, is sufficient to satisfy the section.

It is a neat point. I can see that there is much to be said on both sides. There is no help to be gained from other cases or other statutes. On the whole I agree with the county court judge. Section 33 (2) (*b*) applies to all cases where a housing association is registered under the Act of 1893 and has provided the particular premises for the purposes for which the business of the housing association was mainly conducted, namely, the provision of houses. It is not confined to the provision of an unoccupied house. It extends to the provision of an occupied house if there is a reasonable expectation of providing accommodation in the future. That is this case. Although this house was occupied by a tenant, the housing association provided it for him and for future tenants: and that was part of the purposes for which its business was mainly conducted. In my opinion, by reason of the statute, the tenancy is not a controlled tenancy. The tenant is not protected. The housing association is entitled to possession.

I would, therefore, dismiss the appeal.

HARMAN, L.J.: I agree with what Lord Denning, M.R., has said and also with the admirable judgment of the county court judge, whose judgment I should like to adopt. It seems to me there is an obvious difference in s. 33 (2) of the Housing Repairs and Rents Act, 1954, (4). Section 33 (2), para. (*a*) and para. (*c*) talk of accommodation which was provided, and to those Mr. Megarry's comments, I think, apply. When one turns to para. (*b*), these words, we must take it, were deliberately altered, and the words are: " the provision of the premises . . . forms part of the purposes for which its business is mainly conducted." It is quite clear that the provision of these premises forms part of the business of the plaintiff housing association, otherwise it would be ultra vires for the association to manage them as it is managing them, and everybody agrees that the housing association is entitled to manage them. Therefore, the housing association passes the test and qualifies for freedom from the Rent Restriction Acts and is entitled to the order for possession which the county court judge accorded to the association.

---

(4) Paragraph (*c*) was added to sub-s. (2) by the Rent Act, 1957, s. 26 (1), Sch. 6, para. 26.

SALMON, L.J.: I entirely agree. I consider that s. 33 (2), para. (*a*) and para. (*c*) relate to what the plaintiff housing association has done. Under those paragraphs the question is: has it provided accommodation? In relation to these two paragraphs it may well be that the view expressed in MR. MEGARRY'S book is correct. Paragraph (*b*), however, is not concerned with what the association has done but with its objects. To my mind this housing association quite obviously acquired the whole of Dolphin House for the purpose of conducting its main business activities, namely, the provision of accommodation in the flats which were vacant when it took possession of Dolphin House or which might became vacant in the future. I agree that the county court judge's judgment was correct, and I would accordingly dismiss the appeal.

Appeal dismissed.

Solicitors: *D. H. P. Levy & Co.* (for the tenant); *Allen & Son* (for the housing association).

[*Reported by* F. GUTTMAN, ESQ., *Barrister-at-Law.*]

THE FRITZ THYSSEN.

OWNERS OF MOTOR VESSEL MITERA MARIGO *v.* OWNERS OF MOTORSHIP OR VESSEL FRITZ THYSSEN.

[PROBATE, DIVORCE AND ADMIRALTY DIVISION (Karminski, J., assisted by Capt. R. N. Mayo and Capt. D. A. G. Dickens, Trinity Masters), November 22, 23, 24, 25, 30, 1966.]

Shipping—Collision—Damages—Causation—Novus actus interveniens—Salvage assistance declined until too late—Ship sinking in port of refuge some twenty hours after collision—Sinking not a direct result of the collision.

In a collision at sea, in respect of which the owners of the two vessels involved agreed on the respective measures of liability, the Mitera Marigo was damaged. She eventually sank and became a total loss after having been moored at Falmouth. The court found that if the Mitera Marigo, on her way to Falmouth as a port of refuge with a tug in attendance, had asked for the tug's pumping assistance earlier there was a strong possibility that the Mitera Marigo would not have sunk. On the question whether the chain of causation of damage was broken,

Held: where there was repeated and unreasonable refusal of assistance which, if accepted, might reasonably have been successful in preventing a total loss, a vessel to blame wholly or in part for a collision might be exempted from liability for the subsequent loss of the other vessel involved in the collision; in the present case the sinking of the Mitera Marigo was not a direct result of the collision (see p. 631, letter G, and p. 632, letter D, post).

The Flying Fish ((1865), 34 L.J.P.M. & A. 113) applied.

Dictum of LORD WRIGHT in *The Oropesa* ([1943] 1 All E.R. at p. 215) applied.

[As to when damage suffered by a vessel after collision is assumed to be the result of the collision, see 35 HALSBURY'S LAWS (3rd Edn.) 710, para. 1072; and for cases on the subject, see 42 DIGEST (Repl.) 893-895, *6843-6866*.

As to novus actus interveniens, see 28 HALSBURY'S LAWS (3rd Edn.) 29, 30, para. 26, particularly note (*q*); and for cases on the subject as respects collisions at sea, see 36 DIGEST (Repl.) 40, *196, 197*; 231, *1231*; 42 DIGEST (Repl.) 893, *6845*, 894, *6853*, 895, *6864*, 915, *7095*.]

Affirmed. C.A. [1967] 3 All E.R. 117.

Cases referred to:

Anderson v. Hoen, The Flying Fish, (1865), 3 Moo. P.C.C.N.S. 77; 34 L.J.P.M. &
    A. 113; 12 L.T. 619; 16 E.R. 29; 42 Digest (Repl.) 893, 6845.

Bharatkhand, The, [1952] 1 Lloyd's Rep. 470.

Guildford, The, S.S. Temple Bar (Owners) v. M.V. Guildford (Owners), [1956]
    2 All E.R. 915; [1956] P. 364; [1956] 3 W.L.R. 474; 42 Digest (Repl.)
    915, 7095.

Hendrik, The [1964] 1 Lloyd's Rep. 371.

Lord v. Pacific Steam Navigation Co., Ltd., The Oropesa, [1943] 1 All E.R. 211;
    sub nom. The Oropesa, [1943] P. 32; 112 L.J.P. 91; 168 L.T. 364;
    36 Digest (Repl.) 231, 1231.

Action.

This was an action by the plaintiffs, the owners of the m.v. Mitera Marigo, against the defendants the owners of the m.v. Fritz Thyssen, for damage suffered as result of a collision in a dense fog between the two vessels off Ushant at about 02.10 hours on May 29, 1959, solely caused, so the plaintiffs alleged in their statement of claim, by the negligence of the defendants.

The Mitera Marigo was a vessel of 8,961 gross tons, five hundred feet long with sixty-two feet beam, completed about a year before the collision. She was in the last stages of a voyage from Mormagao to Rotterdam and was fully laden with a cargo of 12,150 tons of iron ore. At the time of the collision her draught was twenty-nine feet forward and thirty feet aft. Immediately after the collision the Mitera Marigo found she had suffered considerable damage to her bows and forecastle and that water was coming in through No. 1 hold. She declined the help offered by the Fritz Thyssen and by a tug, the Englishman, stationed at Falmouth; she started to proceed to Rotterdam, but at about 05.20 hours altered course to Falmouth as water was found to be increasing in No. 1 hold. She again declined help offered by the Englishman. A tarpaulin which had been put over the hole on the starboard side was ineffective, because it could not be kept in place as the ship was moving through the water. All this time and also later the ship was using her own pumps. About 06.00 hours water was coming into No. 1 hold at about forty to fifty tons an hour. Soundings were taken and No. 2 hold was found to be dry. At 07.45 hours the Englishman tried to contact the ship but due to navigational difficulties was unable to contact her till 17.00 when they were eleven miles off Falmouth. The Mitera Marigo asked the Englishman to escort her to Rotterdam, but the Englishman advised strongly against it. Water was now coming in at the rate of sixty to seventy tons an hour into No. 1 hold. The captain stated that he was going into Falmouth and needed no further assistance; he refused the tow which the Englishman offered. Three harbour tugs met the Mitera Marigo just outside Falmouth and brought her in. By this time water was coming in faster in No. 1 hold at seventy to eighty tons an hour. Her own pumps could not keep up with what was coming in. At 20.00 hours the Mitera Marigo was moored stern first to the buoy at which she later sank. No help was sought from the Englishman or anybody else until 22.00 hours when those on board heard a noise which alarmed them and the Englishman was asked to pump. Two portable pumps and a salvage pump were put in action by the Englishman which pumped out water at the rate of four hundred tons an hour. The flow of water into the Mitera Marigo was being arrested, but it was too late. Within forty-five minutes thereafter the crisis came; the harbour master was sent for and found that her forward marks were under water. He advised beaching. The moorings were let go and she sank before she could be beached and became a total loss. A diving survey was taken a month later. The collision bulkhead was found to be in good condition though set back. No tear was observed, but the bulkhead separating No. 1 and No. 2 holds had parted at the welding. The trial judge (KARMINSKI, J.) found that what sank the Mitera Marigo was water pouring, in the later stages, from No. 1 hold into No. 2 hold, and that the breaking of the bulkhead between No. 1 and No. 2 holds occurred before the sinking of the ship, but that the collision bulkhead held until the sinking.

The apportioning of liability for the collision was agreed between the parties. There remained a single issue, raised by para. 4 of the statement of claim and para. 6 of the defence. By para. 4 of the statement of claim the plaintiffs alleged:

" As a direct result of the [collision between the Fritz Thyssen and the Mitera Marigo] the Mitera Marigo had to take salvage assistance and sank and became a total loss, whereby the plaintiffs have suffered loss and been put to expense."

By para. 6 of the defence the defendants denied para. 4 of the statement of claim and further pleaded that the sinking of the Mitera Marigo was caused by the negligence of the plaintiffs, their servants and agents. The particulars of negligence alleged by the defendants (in sub-paras. (i)-(xi) of para. 6 of the defence) in support of this allegation included—

" (ii) the plaintiffs' servants on board the Mitera Marigo and/or the plaintiffs their servants or agents instructing or directing those on board her failed to accept the proferred assistance of the salvage tug Englishman and to seek the immediately available advice of the master of the said tug as to the measures to be taken to save the Mitera Marigo from foundering.

" (v) the Mitera Marigo was not beached immediately on arrival at Falmouth, as she could and ought to have been.

" (viii) the increase in the forward draught of the Mitera Marigo remained unnoticed whilst the Mitera Marigo was proceeding to and moored at Falmouth, and thereby it was not realised that water was gaining access to No. 2 hold.

" (ix) the pumps on board the Englishman were not used to pump out the Mitera Marigo whilst proceeding to Falmouth.

" (x) the pumps of the Englishman and other tugs available at Falmouth were not used to pump out the Mitera Marigo after arrival there."

By way of counterclaim the defendants repeated the allegations in the defence and pleaded that they had suffered damage by reason of the collision. They counterclaimed for (thirdly) a declaration that the sinking of the Mitera Marigo was not a direct result of the collision as alleged in para. 4 of the statement of claim.

The trial judge accepted advice of the Elder Brethren to the following effect:— (a) that, assuming the collision bulkhead was intact until the sinking, water came into No. 1 hold through the tear in the ship's side and almost certainly through a gap below the waterline; (b) that the master of the Mitera Marigo was right in not seeking help from the Englishman until early afternoon, but after this, a prudent master would have guessed the danger and taken appropriate action; the Englishman's portable pumps could have been got on board the Mitera Marigo while the harbour tugs were making fast outside Falmouth. The Elder Brethren further advised that it would have been an additional safety precaution if the Mitera Marigo had been towed into Falmouth stern first as her injuries were at the forward end of the ship; this would have delayed the sinking. They added that they considered it possible, but not more than possible, that water had started to come into No. 2 hold before the Mitera Marigo was moored to her buoy. Lastly, the Elder Brethren advised that if the Englishman's pumps had been in full use at 20.00 hours or a little later, the Mitera Marigo would not have sunk; that meanwhile temporary repairs could have been done to prevent further water from entering her until she could have been dry-docked.

HIS LORDSHIP accordingly concluded that the Mitera Marigo should have asked for pumping assistance at 20.00 hours, and found as a fact that if she had asked for that assistance, perhaps reinforced by available pumps ashore and from the harbour tugs, there was at least a strong possibility that she would not have sunk.

The case noted below* was cited in argument in addition to those referred to in the judgment.

Gerald Darling and *N. A. Phillips* for the plaintiffs.

R. A. MacCrindle, Q.C., and *A. L. G. Stewart-Richardson* for the defendants.

Cur. adv. vult.

Nov. 30. **KARMINSKI, J.,** read the following judgment, in which, after having stated the nature of the proceedings, the single issue as previously indicated (see p. 630, letter B, ante), and after having referred to the pleadings and having stated the facts and the advice of the Elder Brethren, he continued: It is now necessary to consider the result in law of those findings of fact. There can be no doubt here that the water came into the Mitera Marigo as a result of her collision with the Fritz Thyssen. To establish para. 6 of her defence (see p. 630, letters C, D and E, ante), the Fritz Thyssen must in my view prove that the Mitera Marigo sank as a result of a novus actus interveniens following the collision. In other words, to break the chain of causation there must be a new cause. In the words of Lord Wright in *The Oropesa* (1),

"... something which I will call ultroneous, something unwarrantable, a new cause coming in disturbing the sequence of events, something that can be described as either unreasonable or extraneous or extrinsic."

The Fritz Thyssen has here to prove two matters (a) that the Mitera Marigo omitted to take some precaution which good seamanship required, and (b) that if that precaution had been taken the loss would probably have been averted (see the judgment of Willmer, J., in *The Bharatkhand* (2)).

The mere fact that the method adopted by the Mitera Marigo failed does not mean that the master's decision to adopt that method was unreasonable. In *The Guildford* (3) Lord Merriman, P., held there that the master's decision to wait for a tug was, in the circumstances of that case reasonable and seamanlike. Further a master must not be judged too harshly on a decision taken in an emergency, especially in an emergency following closely in time the collision. In these circumstances I would respectfully adopt the observations of Hewson, J., in *The Hendrik* (4), where he emphasised that a decision taken in those circumstances must not be too critically examined from an armchair. I have endeavoured to try to avoid too critical an examination of a collision in the circumstances which I have described, while myself sitting in a comfortable and warm court, and not dealing with an emergency at sea when a master had lost a good deal of the forepart of his ship. Where, however, there has been a repeated and unreasonable refusal of assistance, and of assistance which might reasonably have been successful in preventing a total loss, a vessel to blame wholly or in part for the collision may be exempted from liability for the subsequent loss (*The Flying Fish* (5)). I have to try and apply those principles to the facts of this case.

It is necessary to say a word or two about the principal actors in this case, Captain Lemos, the master of the Mitera Marigo, and Captain Hopper, the master of the Englishman. Captain Lemos as a witness gave me a very distinct impression of being vague and undecided. I have to remind myself that he was giving evidence seven and a half years after the collision, and obviously he has aged meanwhile by that measure of time. Whether he was quite as vague and unclear on the bridge of his ship in 1959 as he was in the witness-box in November, 1966, I am not prepared to say; but his actions indicate to me that in this case and at that time in 1959 he was guilty of very considerable indecision. On the other hand, I have the evidence of Captain Hopper, commanding the Englishman, who turned

* *The City of Lincoln,* [1886-90] All E.R. Rep. 272; (1889), 15 P.D. 15.
(1) [1943] 1 All E.R. 211 at p. 215; [1943] P. 32 at p. 39.
(2) [1952] 1 Lloyd's Rep. 470 at p. 479.   (3) [1956] 2 All E.R. 915; [1956] P. 364.
(4) [1964] 1 Lloyd's Rep. 371 at p. 379.
(5) (1865), 3 Moo. P.C.C.N.S. 77; 34 L.J.P.M. & A. 113.

out at any rate to be right in his assessment of the immediate danger attending
the Mitera Marigo. I bear in mind, of course, that the captain of a salvage ship
on station has a very considerable financial interest in persuading an injured
ship to accept his aid, and that on the other hand Captain Lemos was well aware
of the expense to his owners of accepting a salvage offer. I have endeavoured to
approach the matter in that way. Captain Hopper at once admitted that he had
a personal financial interest if his offer of salvage services was accepted, over and
above the considerable financial interest of his employers; but allowing for a
natural caution in the face of a salvage offer on Captain Lemos' part, I find that
his actions and his indecision were during the critical hours between 20.00 and
22.00 the disastrous cause of this sinking. I have seen photographs taken by Captain Hopper and one of his officers which show the somewhat frightening spectacle
of the Mitera Marigo in the hours before she sank. I have no doubt at all that in
this case at any rate the photographs give a realistic picture of imminent disaster.

I have to apply the principles of law which I have briefly discussed earlier in
my judgment and I have come to the conclusion here that the Mitera Marigo
omitted to take vital precautions which good seamanship required, and that if
those precautions had been taken even two hours earlier the loss would in all
probability have been averted. Having regard to that finding I do not think that
it is necessary for me to elaborate the matter further. I make the declaration
sought by the defendants in their counterclaim, viz., a declaration that the sinking
of the Mitera Marigo was not a direct result of the collision as alleged in the
statement of claim or at all.

Declaration accordingly.

Solicitors: *Constant & Constant* (for the plaintiffs); *Bentleys, Stokes & Lowless*
(for the defendants).

[*Reported by* N. P. METCALFE, ESQ., *Barrister-at-Law.*]

R. *v.* O'DRISCOLL.

[COURT OF APPEAL, CRIMINAL DIVISION (Sachs, L.J., Lawton and James, JJ.),
   December 6, 1966.]

*Criminal Law — Embezzlement — Indictment — Alternative verdict — Conviction
   upheld—Larceny Act, 1916 (6 & 7 Geo. 5 c. 50), s. 44 (2).*

*Criminal Law—Larceny—Larceny as a servant—General deficiency in employers'
   moneys—Money not banked by employee and in law in possession of employers
   —Separate counts for specific sums—Not larceny—No statutory provision
   for an alternative verdict.*

The appellant, had been employed as the manager of a garage since February, 1965; his employers' instructions were that he was to bank the takings
every working day. When he was dismissed on Jan. 13, 1966, a large sum of
money that should have been in the garage safe was not there. The case
against the appellant was dishonest conduct in relation to his employers'
money over a period from June, 1965, to his dismissal in January, 1966.
He had been failing to carry out his instructions to bank money. It appeared
that by the end of 1965 he had fallen three or four days behind in banking
his employers' money that he had received. Some of it had disappeared. In
order to cover up the deficiency, money that he received on one day was
banked the next day, but the documents were so worded as to give the
impression that the money banked related to takings on an earlier date. He
was charged on indictment on count 1 with embezzlement of a sum of £70
on June 21, 1965. He was also charged, among other offences, on three counts

under the Larceny Act, 1916, s. 17 (1) (*a*)* with larceny as a clerk or servant in respect of sums of his employers' money received on three several days in January, 1966. On appeal against conviction,

Held: (i) although the offence established in relation to count 1 was in law larceny, not embezzlement, the provisions of s. 44 (2) of the Larceny Act, 1916, were applicable and the appeal on count 1 would be dismissed (see p. 634, letter I to p. 635, letter A, and p. 635, letter G, post).

(ii) since the takings never notionally left the employers' possession until they were paid into the employers' bank account, no offence of larceny was established, although there might possibly have been maintained some other charge, e.g., of a general deficiency or of falsification of accounts; accordingly, as there was no provision in the Larceny Act, 1916, for alternative verdicts in this instance, the conviction must be quashed (see p. 635, letters E and F, post).

Appeal allowed in part.

[**Editorial Note.** Recommendations for the reform of the law of theft and related offences, together with a draft Bill, which would meet the sort of difficulty illustrated by the present decision, were put forward in the Eighth Report of the Criminal Law Revision Committee in May, 1966 (Cmnd. 2977).

As to larceny by a servant, see 10 HALSBURY'S LAWS (3rd Edn.) 781, para. 1510, and for cases on the subject, see 15 DIGEST (Repl.) 1063-1066, *10,475-10,516.*

As to the alternative verdict on a charge of embezzlement, see 10 HALSBURY'S LAWS (3rd Edn.) 789, para. 1527.

For the Larceny Act, 1916, s. 17, s. 44, see 5 HALSBURY'S STATUTES (2nd Edn.) 1021, 1039.]

Appeal.

The appellant, Andrew Vivian O'Driscoll, was convicted at Hertfordshire quarter sessions on Aug. 5, 1966, on eight counts of an indictment containing nine counts charging him with embezzlement and larceny during his employment as manager of Universal Garages (Chipperfield), Ltd.; he was acquitted only on count 3. He applied for leave to appeal, and was held entitled to appeal on counts 1, 7, 8, 9, his application for leave to appeal as regards counts 2, 4, 5 and 6 being stood over to be argued at the same time as the points of law on counts 1 and 7, 8 and 9. Count 1 charged the appellant with embezzlement, contrary to s. 17 (1) (*b*) of the Larceny Act, 1916, in that he on June 21, 1965, in the county of Hertford being clerk or servant to Universal Garages (Chipperfield), Ltd., fraudulently embezzled £70 in money received by him for or in the name of or on account of the company. Count 7 charged the appellant with larceny contrary to s. 17 (1) (*a*) of the Larceny Act, 1916, in that he on Jan. 7, 1966, in the county of Hertford, being clerk or servant to the same company, stole from the company the sum of £115 in money. Count 8 charged him with a similar offence on Jan. 8, 1966, of stealing as a clerk or servant £178 10s.; and count 9 charged a like offence on Jan. 9, 1966, of stealing as a clerk or servant the sum of £149. The facts are stated in the judgment of LAWTON, J.

L. J. Solley for the appellant.
J. W. Rogers for the Crown.

LAWTON, J., delivered the judgment of the court at the invitation of SACHS, L.J.: The appellant was employed as the manager of a garage at Chipperfield in Hertfordshire. He entered that employment in February, 1965, and was dismissed from it on Jan. 13, 1966. The Crown's case against him was that over a period starting about June, 1965, and ending with the date of his dismissal, he had behaved in a dishonest way in relation to his employers' moneys. The Crown

* Section 17 (1) so far as material, provides: " Every person who—(1) being a clerk or servant or person employed in the capacity of a clerk or servant—(*a*) steals any . . . money . . . belonging to or in the possession or power of his master or employer . . . shall be guilty of a felony and on conviction thereof be liable to penal servitude for any term not exceeding fourteen years . . ."

were faced with a difficulty and it was this; that at the end of his employment, viz., Jan. 13, 1966, when the safe at this garage was opened, it was discovered that a large sum of money, which should have represented takings for the last few days of his employment, was not there; and under the instructions given him by his employers he should have banked the takings every working day. It was clear that he had not been following his instructions.

The prosecution, at a late stage, was put into the hands of counsel for the Crown, who has appeared before us. He had the difficult task of deciding what specific counts to put in the indictment. Being an experienced prosecutor he was alive to the difficulties and inconveniences of preferring a charge based on a general deficiency; and he is to be congratulated in having decided not to prefer such a charge. Had he done so, I have no doubt the trial would have been much more complicated than it was, and it would have probably lasted a good deal longer. What he did do was to draft specific charges covering the period between June 21, 1965, and Jan. 9, 1966; and in respect of five of those charges the court has come to the conclusion that there was nothing wrong in law with them.

It was not suggested in the course of counsel for the appellant's very careful argument that so far as the facts of the case were concerned there was anything wrong in law with counts 2, 4 and 5, but it was suggested that the facts which came out at the trial did not support counts 1, 7, 8 and 9.

The facts relating to count 1 can be stated very shortly. A customer bought from the garage a Dormobile car for the sum of £75. That sum of £75 came into the possession of the appellant in his capacity as manager; he did not account for it to his employers: it disappeared. This customer, however, did not like what he had bought; he returned it to the garage and asked for the return of his money. The circumstances were such that the appellant's employers would not have hesitated to return his money. He would have been repaid by a cheque, drawn at the head office. The appellant would have been expected to put in a requisition for the repayment cheque. He did not deal with the situation in that way. Having failed to account to his employers for the £75, he then awaited an opportunity to get his hands on some more of his employers' money. About six weeks after he had had the £75 another customer paid £70 for a motor vehicle. That money came into the possession of the employers. The appellant then used that £70 to pay off the dissatisfied customer hoping thereby to cover up the fact that the £75 which he had received for the Dormobile had disappeared.

Counsel for the appellant submitted that the deputy chairman, when summing-up, omitted to put to the jury the possible defence that when using the £70 to cover up his failure to account for the £75 he was, in fact, paying off his employers' debts in an irregular way, and doing nothing more. That was an ingenious argument. Unfortunately it did not accord with the evidence at the trial: that is no fault of counsel for the appellant, because he did not represent the appellant at his trial. What the appellant had said when he was first questioned about the disappearance of the £70 was not that he had paid it on behalf of his employers, but that he had in fact banked it. That being the situation, the court has had to ask itself whether the deputy chairman did sum-up adequately to the jury on count 1 of the indictment. The deputy chairman on that count, as indeed on other counts, made it clear to the jury that the essential issue was dishonesty. He pointed out what the Crown's case was, and directed them that if they found the facts in the way which the Crown suggested they should be found, then the offence in law was larceny. The court agrees with that direction. It suffices to say that the point taken on behalf of the appellant is an entirely academic one, because on any view of the matter that £70 was employed improperly and as a fraud on the employer, since the object in applying the money in the way it was applied was to cover up fraudulently that which had happened earlier. The case would clearly have been one which came within the provisions of s. 44 (2) of the Larceny Act, 1916, (1).

The position with regard to counts 7, 8 and 9, is wholly different. Those three counts can be taken together as the point involved is substantially the same in each one. When the finances of this garage were investigated, it was discovered that the appellant had got behind in banking his employers' money. By the end of 1965 he had got three or four days behind and in order to cover up the fact that he had got behind and that the money had disappeared, moneys which were received on one day were banked the next; but the documents which came into existence contemporaneously with the banking were so worded as to give the impression that the money banked related to takings of a much earlier period. The facts relating to count 7 will suffice to illustrate the point which arises. On Jan. 1, 1966, the takings seem to have been £115. Those takings were not paid into the bank on Jan. 1, as they should have been. On Jan. 7, what was paid into the bank was £143, but the documents were made up to look as if that £143 represented the takings for Jan. 1, which they were not. The money which was paid into the bank on Jan. 7, had been received by the garage during working hours on Jan. 6. That money had gone into the safe on Jan. 6, and the appellant in his capacity as manager had taken that money to the bank on Jan. 7, and had paid it to the credit of the employers' account. It was said on behalf of the appellant that whatever offence, if any, had been committed, it was not larceny. The Crown submitted that the offence was larceny. In the judgment of this court the takings of Jan. 6 never notionally left the employers' possession until they were paid into the bank on Jan. 7. This being so, whatever other offence there may have been, larceny was not proved. It may well be that the facts relating to counts 7, 8 and 9 could have been used to support a charge based on a general deficiency (2); they might have been used to support a charge of falsification of accounts. There were no such charges. The Crown chose the wrong offence, something which it is easy to do in the present state of the law of larceny. There being no provision in the Larceny Act, 1916, for alternative verdicts in circumstances such as have arisen in this case, there is nothing this court can do but quash the conviction of larceny on count 7. The comments which I have made in detail about count 7 apply with equal force to counts 8 and 9. Those two counts must also be quashed.

[HIS LORDSHIP then referred to other points taken on behalf of the appellant in regard to the summing-up, and concluded that there was no good ground for criticising the summing-up in these respects; accordingly the appeal would be dismissed in regard to counts 1, 2, 4, 5 and 6. Although there was no appeal against sentence and this was a bad case of fraud, the sentence would, HIS LORDSHIP said, be reduced from eighteen months' to twelve months' imprisonment on each count on which conviction stood, those terms to run concurrently.]

Appeal allowed on counts 7, 8, and 9, and dismissed on counts 1, 2, 4, 5 and 6; sentence varied.

Solicitors: *Michael Shapiro,* Edgware (for the appellant); *Ottoways,* St. Albans (for the Crown).

[*Reported by* S. A. HATTEEA, ESQ., *Barrister-at-Law.*]

---

(1) Section 44 (2) provides: " If on the trial of any indictment for any offence against s. 17 of this Act (relating to embezzlement) it is proved that the defendant stole the property in question, the jury may find him guilty of stealing, and thereupon he shall be liable to be punished accordingly; and on the trial of any indictment for stealing the jury may in like manner find the defendant guilty of embezzlement or of fraudulent application or disposition, as the case may be, and thereupon he shall be liable to be punished accordingly."

(2) See, e.g., *R.* v. *Tomlin,* [1954] 2 All E.R. 272.

R. v. MERTHYR TYDFIL JUSTICES, *Ex parte* JENKINS.

[QUEEN'S BENCH DIVISION (Lord Parker, C.J., Glyn-Jones and Widgery, JJ.), November 9, 1966.]

Practice—Conduct of proceedings—Language—Welsh language—When right to use in Welsh court—Welsh Courts Act, 1942 (5 & 6 *Geo.* 6 *c.* 40), *s.* 1.

The applicant, a schoolteacher who taught in English and was well versed in it, was charged before justices in Wales on two informations of using a motor car on the road without having in force a licence under the Vehicles (Excise) Act, 1962. When he was asked to plead he said that he would not plead until the charge was put to him in the Welsh language. Pleas of not guilty having been entered, the applicant sought to cross-examine a police witness in Welsh. The justices refused to allow him to do so. When the applicant went into the witness box he was allowed to give his evidence in Welsh. He was convicted on both informations. On a motion for an order of certiorari to bring up and quash the convictions on the ground that he had been denied his right to have the proceedings conducted in Welsh under s. 1* of the Welsh Courts Act, 1942,

Held: a party or witness could avail himself of his rights under s. 1 of the Act of 1942 only if he was under a disadvantage or genuinely thought that he was under a disadvantage (see p. 637, letter H, and p. 638, letters G and H, post), and this was not a case in which the court would exercise its discretion to grant an order of certiorari (see p. 638, letter G, post).

Motion dismissed.

[As to the use of the Welsh language in court, see 9 HALSBURY'S LAWS (3rd Edn.) 346, para. 814.

For the Welsh Courts Act, 1942, s. 1, see 5 HALSBURY'S STATUTES (2nd Edn.) 421.]

Motion for certiorari.

This was a motion by the applicant, Terence Raymond Neil Jenkins, for an order of certiorari to bring up and quash two convictions by the Merthyr Tydfil justices on Dec. 7, 1965, on two informations charging him with using a motor car on the road on Oct. 26 and Oct. 29, 1965, without having in force a licence under the Vehicles (Excise) Act, 1962. He was fined £5 on each information. The facts are set out in the judgment of LORD PARKER, C.J.

The cases noted below† were cited during the argument.

T. G. Jones for the applicant.
P. Temple-Morris for the Crown.

LORD PARKER, C.J.: In these proceedings, counsel moves on behalf of the applicant, one Terence Raymond Neil Jenkins, for an order of certiorari to bring up and quash two convictions of the applicant by the justices in petty session at the Town Hall, Merthyr Tydfil. It appears that the two charges on which he was convicted were in both cases of using a motor car on a road without having in force a licence under the Vehicles (Excise) Act, 1962, one information being laid as on Oct. 26, 1965, the other as on Oct. 29, 1965. The broad general ground on which the applicant seeks an order of certiorari is that he was denied what he claims were his rights to, in effect, have the proceedings conducted in

---

* Section 1, so far as material, is set out at p. 637, letter A, post.
† *R. v. Grimsby Borough Quarter Sessions, Ex p. Fuller,* [1955] 3 All E.R. 300; [1956] 1 Q.B. 36; *Annamunthodo* v. *Oilfields Workers' Trade Union,* [1961] 3 All E.R. 621; [1961] A.C. 945; *R.* v. *Patents Appeal Tribunal, Ex p. J. R. Geigy, Société Anonyme,* [1963] 1 All E.R. 850; [1963] 2 Q.B. 728; *Ridge* v. *Baldwin,* [1963] 2 All E.R. 66; [1964] A.C. 40; *Maradana Mosque (Board of Trustees)* v. *Badi-ud-Din Mahmud,* [1966] 1 All E.R. 545.

Welsh, and he relies on s. 1 of the Welsh Courts Act, 1942. Section 1 of that Act repeals s. 17 of the Act of 27 Hen. 8 c. 26. Section 1 enacts that

> ". . . the Welsh language may be used in any court in Wales by any party or witness who considers that he would otherwise be at any disadvantage by reason of his natural language of communication being Welsh."

It is to be observed that, on its strict meaning, it is not providing for the proceedings being conducted in Welsh at the request of any party subject to a disadvantage, but is merely saying that a party or witness who considers that he would otherwise be at a disadvantage may himself use the Welsh language. No doubt, however, as a matter of natural justice, if I may use that expression, a court would in a proper case allow the proceedings to be conducted in Welsh or through an interpreter, so that the witness who claims that he would be at a disadvantage fully understands the evidence against him.

The applicant is the treasurer of the Welsh Speaking Society and he had with him and sitting next to him the secretary of that society; it is quite clear that the court or the public gallery were full of members of that society and, to put it quite bluntly, it became evident to the justices, and this no doubt accounted largely for their action, that the court was being used as a platform for propaganda, the particular propaganda in question being that the application form for an excise licence was only printed in English, whereas the society were agitating that it should also be printed in Welsh. Trouble started at once, because when the applicant was asked to plead he said that he would not plead until the charge was put to him in the Welsh language. He was probably exceeding his rights there, and moreover it appears perfectly clear that he had heard the charge before and that he knew what it was. However, and quite rightly in those circumstances, a plea of not guilty to both of these charges was entered. The next step was that a police officer in the first information went into the witness box and gave evidence of how he had found this car without an excise licence on Oct. 26, 1965, that he had asked the applicant, who was the driver, whether he had one, and that he was told: " I have not got one." When told that he would be reported, the applicant said: " Thank you, I have already written to the chief constable." All that took place in English. However, when the examination-in-chief of the police constable ended, the applicant sought to cross-examine him in Welsh, and it is undoubtedly true that the justices then refused to allow him to do so. A reference was made to the Act of 1942 and the applicant claimed that he was at a disadvantage as envisaged therein.

In my judgment, a party or a witness cannot avail himself of his rights under s. 1 of the Act of 1942 merely by asserting that he is under a disadvantage. It must be the fact that he is under a disadvantage or that he genuinely thinks that he is under a disadvantage. Here the magistrates took the view that the applicant was asserting a disadvantage merely to make a demonstration, and that he was under no disadvantage at all and could not genuinely think that he was. When one realises that the applicant was an educated man, a schoolteacher who spent seventy-five per cent. of the school time in teaching general subjects in English, and quite clearly was well versed in English, and when one considers what took place in this case, it does not surprise one that the justices took the view that this was not a genuine assertion of a disadvantage at all. Whether they were right or wrong in taking that line for my part I find it unnecessary to determine. I will assume in favour of counsel for the applicant's contention that the magistrates here, and one sympathises with them, may have acted rather precipitately, and it would have been wiser if they had allowed the applicant to proceed in Welsh, at the same time keeping him, so far as they could, to the point. I find it unnecessary to consider whether they were right or wrong in the attitude which they took up, and for this very good reason, that the writ, and now the order, of certiorari is not a writ or order as of course; it is wholly discretionary, and if ever there was a case in which the order in the discretion of the court should not go, it is this case. I say that for this very good reason, that a time came when the applicant himself went into the witness box and took the oath; it became patently clear then that he had no defence at all and that the whole thing had been engineered in order that he could draw attention to this complaint about the application form for a licence not being in Welsh. He said when he got into the witness box, and he was allowed to speak in Welsh: " May I draw the court's attention to some letters I wrote to the local taxation officer? " He went on to say that in one letter he asked for what he called an RF.1A Form in Welsh, and the chairman translated: " He says he asked for a form ", and the applicant went on again in Welsh: " I received a letter in reply from the chief constable refusing to give a Welsh form. I wrote a second letter." After interjections by the prosecution, the applicant was allowed to go on in Welsh to read a letter, and the chairman translated and the applicant went on again in Welsh reading from a second letter; and finally a time then came when the chairman pointed out that this was wholly irrelevant. According to the justices, who have sworn an affidavit here, what happened was that the applicant made an assertion in these terms: " The letter is quite relevant. It will prove that it is not my fault that my car has no licence." It was at that point that the chairman said: " We have heard enough about that. You are admitting being guilty." The applicant: " Do you refuse to allow me to explain? " The chairman: " I do, about the application form not being in Welsh." Thereupon the clerk asked the applicant whether he had anything else to say about the offence other than this statement about the form not being in Welsh. The applicant turned on his heels and left the witness box.

In the end this appears to be a case where the applicant quite clearly and in the Welsh language pleaded guilty in the sense that he plainly admitted his guilt. He was not stopped from putting forward any defence and, indeed, counsel for the applicant has quite frankly conceded that there was no defence. He was only stopped from putting forward matters which were wholly irrelevant and which it was the object of the applicant and his society to ventilate in court. Accordingly, in my judgment, even if it can be said here that the justices went too far and denied the applicant such rights as he had under the Welsh Courts Act, 1942, I am quite satisfied that it is not a case in which an order of certiorari should issue. Accordingly, I would refuse this application.

GLYN-JONES, J.: I agree.

WIDGERY, J.: I also agree and, having spent the summer on circuit in Wales where these problems have arisen, I would like to add one word as to my conclusions based on that experience of the Welsh Courts Act, 1942. I think that it is quite clear that the proper language for court proceedings in Wales is the English language. It is to my mind a complete misapprehension to believe that anybody at any time has a right to require that the proceedings be conducted in Welsh. The right which the Act of 1942 gives is the right for the individual to use the Welsh language if he considers that he would be at a disadvantage in expression if he were required to use English. That is the only right which the Act of 1942 gives, and apart from that, the language difficulties which arise in Wales can be dealt with by discretionary arrangements for an interpreter, precisely in the same way as language difficulties at the Central Criminal Court are dealt with when the accused is a Pole.

Motion dismissed.

Solicitors: *T. D. Jones & Co.*, agents for *Brinley, Richards & Huws*, Maesteg (for the applicant); *Sharpe, Pritchard & Co.*, agents for *Town Clerk*, Merthyr Tydfil (for the respondents).

[*Reported by* S. A. HATTEEA, ESQ., *Barrister-at-Law.*]

TULLEY *v.* TULLEY.

[PROBATE, DIVORCE AND ADMIRALTY DIVISION (Sir Jocelyn Simon, P.), December 8, 21, 1966.]

Divorce—Practice—Pleading—Amending answer so as to add by way of cross-petition an allegation of desertion and prayer for divorce on that ground—Desertion three years before amendment but less than three years before original answer—Jurisdiction to give leave to amend—Matrimonial Causes Rules, 1957 (S.I. 1957 No. 619), r. 3, (2) (as amended by Matrimonial Causes (Amendment) Rules, 1961 (S.I. 1961 No. 1082), r. 2).

In October, 1963, the wife, who had left the matrimonial home in June, 1963, presented a petition for divorce on the ground of cruelty. In March, 1964, the husband put in his answer, denying cruelty, cross-charging adultery with the party cited, and praying that the marriage be dissolved at his suit and for damages and costs. By their replies, the wife and the party cited denied the adultery alleged. In March, 1966, an order on the husband's application was made striking out the paragraphs in the answer alleging adultery and amending the prayer by substituting simply that the petition be dismissed. The replies of the wife and the party cited were consequently struck out and the party cited dismissed from the suit with costs. In September, 1966, the husband sought leave to re-amend his answer to ask, by way of cross-petition on the ground of desertion, that the marriage should be dissolved. On appeal against the refusal of the registrar to grant him leave,

Held: leave would be given to make the amendment requested, because, as a result of the amendment made in March, 1966, to the original answer, the position in September, 1966, was that the answer contained no prayer for substantive relief; accordingly the answer amended in the way sought was to be regarded as a petition and as the husband would not require leave, in view of the amendment* to r. 3 (2) of the Matrimonial Causes Rules, 1957, to file a fresh petition (there being no other petition by him before the court), he should be enabled, with a view to saving costs, to claim relief by cross-petition in his amended answer (see p. 642, letter F, and p. 643, letters A, B and F, post).

Robertson v. *Robertson* ([1954] 3 All E.R. 413) followed.

Blacker v. *Blacker* ([1960] 2 All E.R. 291) distinguished.

Appeal allowed.

[As to the commencement of a matrimonial suit, and as to the answer and cross-petitions or cross-prayers, and as to amendment, see 12 HALSBURY'S LAWS (3rd Edn.) 314, 315, 341, 323, para. 630, 712, 653; and for cases on the subject, see DIGEST (Cont. Vol. A) 756, *3876c*, 757, *3892c*, 762, 763, *4199b*, *4199b a*; *4221b*.

For the Matrimonial Causes Rules, 1957, r. 3, r. 19, as amended, see, 10 HALSBURY'S STATUTORY INSTRUMENTS (2nd Re-Issue) 225, 238.]

Cases referred to:

Blacker v. *Blacker*, [1960] 2 All E.R. 291; [1960] P. 146; [1960] 2 W.L.R. 800; Digest (Cont. Vol. A) 757, *3892c*.

Robertson v. *Robertson*, [1954] 3 All E.R. 413; [1954] 1 W.L.R. 1537; Digest (Cont. Vol. A) 762, *4199b*.

Appeal.

This was an appeal by the husband from an order of Mr. Registrar TOWNLEY MILLERS dated Sept. 8, 1966, refusing to grant him leave to re-amend his answer and to ask, by way of cross-petition on the ground of desertion, that the marriage should be dissolved. The appeal was heard in chambers on Dec. 8, 1966, and adjourned into open court for judgment. The facts are set out in the judgment.

---

* This amendment was made by the Matrimonial Causes (Amendment) Rules, 1961 (S.I. 1961 No. 1082), r. 2.

P. K. J. Thompson for the husband.

The wife was not represented by counsel.

Cur. adv. vult.

Dec. 21. **SIR JOCELYN SIMON, P.,** read the following judgment: This is an appeal from an order of Mr. Registrar TOWNLEY MILLERS made on Sept. 8, 1966. The learned registrar had before him a summons by a respondent husband in a divorce suit applying for leave to re-amend his answer to ask, by way of cross-petition on the ground of desertion, that the marriage should be dissolved. Notwithstanding that the wife petitioner, through her solicitors, had consented to the summons and was not represented, the learned registrar felt bound to reject it by reason of the Court of Appeal decision in *Blacker* v. *Blacker* (1). The question raised on this appeal is how far *Blacker* v. *Blacker* (1) now extends as still binding authority. The appeal from the learned registrar's decision was out of time. I was given no satisfactory explanation why this should have been so. In view, however, of the facts that the wife had given her solicitors definite instructions that she did not wish to proceed with these proceedings, that she had been in no way prejudiced by the delay, and that an important point of practice was raised by the appeal, I gave leave to the husband to proceed out of time.

The proceedings generally have been regrettably delayed at almost every stage. Their history is as follows. The marriage was in 1941. The wife left in June, 1963; and in October, 1963, she presented a petition for divorce on the ground of cruelty. In March, 1964, the husband put in his answer, denying cruelty, and cross-charging adultery with a named man. He prayed that the marriage should be dissolved at his suit and for damages and costs. Replies were in due course filed by the wife and the party cited, denying the adultery alleged. Various interlocutory proceedings then ensued, including proceedings under s. 17 of the Married Women's Property Act, 1882, in relation to the matrimonial home, which were ultimately taken to the Court of Appeal. In March, 1966, the husband applied by summons to the registrar that the allegations in his answer relating to adultery and so much of his prayer (including that for divorce) as related thereto should be struck out. His purpose in making this move was that he hoped, on the effluxion of three years from the date of the wife's departure in June, 1963, to sue for divorce on the ground of her desertion and thus avoid the cost of fighting the adultery issue; both the wife and the party cited were legally aided, whereas the husband was not. On Mar. 17, 1966, Mr. Registrar HOLLOWAY made an order, allowing the paragraphs in the answer alleging adultery to be struck out and the amendment of the prayer by substituting for the claim for dissolution, damages and costs the simple claim " that the petition be dismissed ". On this being done, the replies of the wife and the party cited were consequentially struck out and the party cited dismissed from the suit with costs. The resulting state of the suit was that there was a wife's petition alleging cruelty and an answer denying it and asking that the petition should be dismissed. On Sept. 1, 1966, the husband issued a summons for leave to re-amend his answer to add the following:

" And by way of cross petition 6. That the [wife] has without cause deserted the [husband] for a period of at least three years immediately preceding the presentation of this cross-petition, in that she on or about June 1, 1963, left the matrimonial home, intending to bring cohabitation with the [husband] to an end permanently and that she has lived apart from him ever since. 7. That this cross-petition is not presented or prosecuted in collusion with the [wife], nor is there any agreement or arrangement made or proposed to be made by or on behalf of the parties hereto in contemplation of or in connexion with these proceedings which the [husband] desires the court to consider."

---

(1) [1960] 2 All E.R. 291; [1960] P. 146.

A He further sought leave to amend the existing prayer of the answer " that the petition may be dismissed " to pray instead that the prayer of the wife might be rejected and that the marriage might be dissolved at his own suit. It was this summons that came before the learned registrar on Sept. 8, 1966, and that he felt himself to be compelled to dismiss on the authority of *Blacker* v. *Blacker* (2). The only other matter that needs to be mentioned is that, on Nov. 23, 1966, the

B solicitors for the wife, on having received the husband's summons by way of appeal from the decision of the learned registrar, wrote: " We are actually in the process of writing to the Law Society for our client's certificate to be discharged ", and adding, as I have mentioned, that they had definite instructions from their client that she did not wish to proceed with the proceedings.

In *Robertson* v. *Robertson* (3), a wife had, in August, 1952, petitioned for divorce

C on the ground of cruelty. In October, 1954, Barnard, J., allowed an amendment to the answer to allege as follows:

" By way of cross petition. 3. The [wife] has deserted the [husband] without cause for at least three years immediately preceding the presentation of this cross-petition, to wit since Apr. 6, 1950, when she left the matrimonial home with the intention of determining cohabitation with the [husband].

D She has failed to resume cohabitation thereafter ";

and to add a cross-prayer that the marriage might be dissolved. This case was considered in *Blacker* v. *Blacker* (2). There, a wife petitioned for divorce on the ground of cruelty, and her husband by his answer also sought a divorce on the ground of cruelty. At the trial neither charge of cruelty succeeded. By the time

E of the hearing the parties had been separated for three years, although they had been separated for less than three years immediately preceding the presentation of the petition or the answer. The husband was given leave by the trial court to amend his answer by way of cross-petition alleging desertion by the wife and to ask for a decree nisi of divorce on that ground; and the wife was similarly given leave to amend her reply by adding an answer to the cross-petition alleging

F desertion by the husband. However, both charges of desertion were dismissed; and, on appeal therefrom, the Court of Appeal itself took the point that the court had no jurisdiction to allow those amendments; and in considered judgments so held, on the following grounds:—first, that the allegations of desertion could not be raised merely by amendment, since that would be to defeat the plain language of s. 1 (1) (*b*) of the Matrimonial Causes Act, 1950 (now the Matri-

G monial Causes Act 1965, s. 1 (1) (*a*) (ii)), which required the period of three years to elapse not before the amendment, but before the presentation, of the petition (per Hodson, L.J. (4)); secondly, that if the amended cross-petition and the reply thereto could be regarded as separate petitions, r. 3 (2) of the Matrimonial Causes Rules, 1957, (5), had not been complied with, since the original petition and answer had not been disposed of when the amendments were made (per

H Hodson, L.J. (6), per Willmer, L.J. (7)); and, thirdly, that the procedure adopted involved that a number of procedural requirements under the rules of court had not been complied with, and that these requirements could not be dispensed with under R.S.C., Ord. 70, r. 1 (now R.S.C., Ord. 2, r. 1) (per Hodson, L.J. (8) and per Devlin, L.J., in his judgment passim (9)). Although the judgment of Devlin, L.J., proceeded on this third ground only, which he regarded (10)

I as sufficient to dispose of the appeal; he nevertheless agreed (9) " that the cross-petition and answer thereto should be declared void for the reasons given by my lords . . ."

(2) [1960] 2 All E.R. 291; [1960] P. 146.	(3) [1954] 3 All E.R. 413.
(4) [1960] 2 All E.R. at p. 293; [1960] P. at p. 150.	(5) S.I. 1957 No. 619.
(6) [1960] 2 All E.R. at p. 293; [1960] P. at p. 151.	
(7) [1960] 2 All E.R. at p. 295; [1960] P. at p. 154.	
(8) [1960] 2 All E.R. at pp. 293, 294; [1960] P. at pp. 151, 152.	
(9) [1960] 2 All E.R. at p. 296; [1960] P. at p. 156.	
(10) [1960] 2 All E.R. at p. 297; [1960] P. at p. 153.	

HODSON, L.J., stated (11) that, although desertion could not be alleged by way A
of amendment or supplemental petition where the three years had not run before
the date of the petition, this could be done by way of cross-petition, provided
the three years had expired before the presentation of the cross-petition; and
for this purpose an original answer may be regarded as a cross-petition.   He
went on (11):

> " If there is a separate cross-petition there is no obstacle to this being   B
> consolidated with the original petition; and in *Robertson* v. *Robertson* (12)
> BARNARD, J., allowed a cross-petition to be included in an answer when no
> cross-relief had been previously sought, thus avoiding the necessity of a
> separate suit and consolidation, etc.   This does not mean that where the
> respondent had already prayed for relief in his answer and thus placed
> himself in the position of a petitioner a further petition can be presented by   C
> him before the first has been disposed of."

(thereby referring to r. 3 (2) of the Matrimonial Causes Rules, 1957, as it then
stood).   Again, WILLMER, L.J., said (13),

> " If . . . as I think, the cross-petition and the answer thereto are to be
> regarded as separate proceedings from the original petition and answer,   D
> it seems to me that the effect of r. 3 (2) of the Matrimonial Causes Rules,
> 1957, is to forbid their being filed unless and until the original proceedings
> have been disposed of."

WILLMER, L.J., then referred to *Robertson* v. *Robertson* (12), and said (14),

> " . . . but I think it is possible to distinguish what was done in that case,
> on the ground that there the original answer contained no prayer for   E
> substantive relief."

In view of these observations, in my judgment *Blacker* v. *Blacker* (15) is to
be distinguished from the present case on the following grounds:—(i) In September, 1966, as a result of the amendment in the previous March, " no cross relief
had been previously sought " and the husband had not " already prayed for
relief in his answer " (cf. per HODSON, L.J. (11));   again, in such circumstances   F
" the original answer contained no prayer for substantive relief" (cf. per WILLMER,
L.J. (13));   (ii) Matrimonial Causes Rule, 1957, r. 3 (2), has been amended since
Blacker v. *Blacker* (15), so that, whereas at the time of that appeal a petition
could not be filed if there was before the court another petition by the same
petitioner which had not been dismissed or otherwise disposed of by a final
order, such a second petition may now be filed provided the leave of a judge is   G
obtained (16);   (iii) *Robertson* v. *Robertson* (12) was distinguished and, in my
view, implicitly approved in *Blacker* v. *Blacker* (15) (per HODSON, L.J. (11), per
WILLMER, L.J. (14)) and this case is indistinguishable from *Robertson* v. *Robertson*
(12);   (iv) The procedure involved in the present case does not, like that in
Blacker v. *Blacker* (15), involve disregarding or dispensing with the rules.   The
answer amended in the way sought is to be regarded as a petition (per HODSON,   H
L.J. (11); per WILLMER, L.J. (15); per DEVLIN, L.J. (17)), but as it is in fact
contained in the answer, it would merely have to be served in accordance with
such directions as are given (18) under the Matrimonial Causes Rules, 1957,
r. 19 (2); the requisite time for reply would have to be allowed; and provision
would have to be made for a stay pending renewal of the registrar's certificate.
Affidavits in support are no longer required (18) (cf. per HODSON, L.J. (19), and   I

(11) [1960] 2 All E.R. at p. 293; [1960] P. at p. 151.   (12) [1954] 3 All E.R. 413.
(13) [1960] 2 All E.R. at p. 295; [1960] P. at p. 154.
(14) [1960] 2 All E.R. at p. 295; [1960] P. at p. 155.
(15) [1960] 2 All E.R. 291; [1960] P. 146.
(16) Matrimonial Causes (Amendment) Rules, 1961 (S.I. 1961 No. 1082), r. 2.
(17) [1960] 2 All E.R. at p. 297; [1960] P. at p. 157.
(18) Rule 19 was amended and paras. (2), (3) thereof were added by Matrimonial
Causes (Amendment) Rules 1966 (S.I. 1966 No. 560).   This instrument also deleted
words from the former r. 19, thus eliminating reference to verification by affidavits.
(19) [1960] 2 All E.R. at p. 294; [1960] P. at p. 152.

A per Devlin, L.J. (20) in his judgment passim). In the present case the husband would not require the leave of a judge to file a fresh petition now, alleging that the wife had deserted him for three years immediately preceding the presentation thereof, and praying for divorce on that ground, since there is not before the court another petition *by the same petitioner* (Matrimonial Causes Rules, 1957, r. 3 (2), as amended). If this is the case, it seems to me to be manifest that, with

B a view to the saving of costs, the husband should be able to claim his relief by way of cross-petition in an answer amended for that purpose, as was done in *Robertson* v. *Robertson* (21).

In *Blacker* v. *Blacker* (22), the Court of Appeal was apprehensive that permitting the procedure there adopted might open a door to abuse, allowing a party whose only real case was one of desertion to file a petition or answer before

C the expiration of the necessary three years praying for relief on sham grounds—with the possibility, perhaps, of obtaining thereby various forms of interim relief or undue expedition of the case in priority to other litigants (see, especially, per Willmer, L.J. (23)). Certainly, the court must remain vigilant to prevent such an abuse. If the court should feel that such has been perpetrated, the party concerned is likely to find himself or herself in no favourable position when ancil-

D lary relief as a whole is finally determined. As for obtaining unfair priority, if the amendment is sought by a party who has already on the file a pleading which is (or is to be considered as) a petition, the leave of the judge is now required under the amended r. 3 (2) before any other petition is put on the file; and such leave is not likely to be forthcoming if it appears to involve an abuse of procedure. If no leave is required to present a fresh petition (as in the present case), the court,

E if it thought that its process was being abused, could either refuse leave to amend the existing pleading or to consolidate a new petition with proceedings already on the file. The discretion of the court would thus today be available in all conceivable circumstances to obviate the abuse which the Court of Appeal envisaged as being a danger if the course followed in *Blacker* v. *Blacker* (22) were allowed. In the present case, there is no reason for apprehension.

F In my view, therefore, the appeal should be allowed, and leave given to make the amendment requested.

Appeal allowed.

Solicitors: *Bernard Sheridan & Co.* (for the husband); *Nash & Co.* (for the wife).

G   [*Reported by* Alice Bloomfield, *Barrister-at-Law.*]

H

I

---

(20) [1960] 2 All E.R. at pp. 296, 297; [1960] P. at pp. 156-158.
(21) [1954] 3 All E.R. 413.
(22) [1960] 2 All E.R. 291; [1960] P. 146.
(23) [1960] 2 All E.R. at p. 294; [1960] P. at p. 153.

NORTH RIDING GARAGES, LTD. *v.* BUTTERWICK.

[QUEEN'S BENCH DIVISION (Lord Parker, C.J., Glyn-Jones and Widgery, JJ.), November 9, 10, December 21, 1966.]

*Employment—Redundancy—New management—New methods but overall require-
ments the same—Workshop manager at garage—Garage taken over by new
company with different business methods—Re-organisation transferring
rather different work to manager—Manager unable to adapt himself to new
duties—Overall requirements of business unchanged—Manager dismissed
and replaced by new manager—Whether old manager dismissed on account
of redundancy and entitled to redundancy payment—Redundancy Payments
Act 1965 (c. 62), s. 1 (2) (b).*

The respondent had been employed at a garage for thirty years, rising
to the position of workshop manager in charge of the repairs workshop.
He had given satisfactory service up to April, 1965, in which month the
business was taken over by the appellants who introduced new methods
to which the respondent could not easily adapt himself. He was having a
greater amount of work put on him than before and he was doing his best,
but was probably not as efficient as many persons in a comparable position.
The appellants were not deliberately running down the repairs side of the
business, though there was increased emphasis on the sales side. In January,
1966, the appellants dismissed the respondent by due notice given under
his contract of service. After his dismissal the appellants appointed
another workshop manager. On an application by the respondent for
redundancy payment under s. 1 (1)* of the Redundancy Payments Act
1965, the appellants claimed that the respondent was dismissed because he
was incompetent and inefficient and not by reason of redundancy. His
dismissal could have been by reason of redundancy only if under s. 1 (2) (b)†
of the Act of 1965, it was attributable wholly or mainly to the fact that the
requirements of the business for employees to carry out work of a particular
kind had ceased or diminished, or were expected to cease or diminish.
On appeal by the appellants against the finding of the Industrial Tribunal
that the respondent was entitled to redundancy payment because the
appellants had not rebutted the presumption of redundancy under s. 9 (2) (b)‡
of the Act of 1965, and that when they reorganised their system of business
as a whole their requirement for a workshop manager of the old type ceased,

Held: although an employee who remained in the same kind of work
under new management might be expected to adapt himself to new methods
and techniques, and dismissal, e.g., for inability to meet higher standards,
would not be dismissal for redundancy, yet if the new methods altered the
nature of the work the employee might be redundant because no requirement remained for work of the particular kind that he formerly did; in the
present case, since overall requirements of the business were unchanged and
it was irrelevant that the duties of the new manager were not identical with
his former duties, the respondent was not entitled to a redundancy payment
(see p. 647, letter I, and p. 648, letter D, post).

Per CURIAM: if dismissal is attributable to age, physical disability or
inability to meet the employer's standards, it is not dismissal on account of
redundancy within the meaning of the Redundancy Payments Act 1965
(see p. 647, letter H, post).

[**Editorial Note.** A question arose as to legal aid (see p. 648, letter F, post).
The availability of legal aid is based on courts, and in appropriate cases can be
obtained by litigants showing reasonable grounds for it in proceedings in those
courts. Since the Supreme Court is one of the courts specified in Part 1 of Sch. 1
to the Legal Aid and Advice Act, 1949, and a commencement order has been made

---

* Section 1 (1), so far as material, is set out at p. 645, letter G, post.
† Section 1 (2) is set out at p. 645, letter H, post.
‡ Section 9 (2), so far as material, is set out at p. 645, letter I, post.

Applied in CRESSWELL v BOARD OF
INLAND REVENUE [1984] 2 All ER 713

Dictum of WIDGERY, J., at p. 647,
explained in ARNOLD v. HARRINGTON,
LTD. [1967] 2 All E.R. 866.

in respect of that court, legal aid is available for an appeal, whether civil or criminal, to a Divisional Court, including an appeal from a tribunal though legal aid is not yet available for proceedings before tribunals.   Accordingly, an industrial tribunal not being specified in Sch. 1 to the Act of 1949, and no Regulation having been made under s. 1 (2) of that Act extending legal aid thereto, legal aid is not available in proceedings before it, but legal aid is available in respect of appeals from it to the Divisional Court.   The position is analogous to that which existed in regard to appeals from magistrates' courts, before legal aid was introduced for those courts.   Legal aid was then commonly granted on Cases Stated to a Divisional Court.   We are indebted to the Law Society for the information given in this note on legal aid.

As to dismissal of employee by reason of redundancy, see CURRENT SERVICE to HALSBURY'S LAWS (3rd Edn.), Vol. 38, title TRADE AND LABOUR, para. 808C.

For the Redundancy Payments Act 1965, s. 1, see 45 HALSBURY'S STATUTES (2nd Edn.) 290.]

Appeal.

This was an appeal by the appellants, North Riding Garages, Ltd., by notice dated June 17, 1966, from a decision of the Industrial Tribunal sitting at Harrogate, dated May 5, 1966, whereby on an application by the respondent, Alexander Ian Page Butterwick, under s. 1 of the Redundancy Payments Act 1965, the tribunal decided that the respondent had a right to a redundancy payment of £490.   The facts are set out in the judgment of the court.

Quentin Edwards for the appellants.

H. J. Byrt for the respondent.   *Cur. adv. vult.*

Dec. 21.   **WIDGERY, J.,** read the judgment of the court at the invitation of LORD PARKER, C.J.: The respondent had been employed at the Resolution Garage at Whitby for thirty years, rising to the position of workshop manager in charge of the repairs workshop.   He had given satisfactory service up to April, 1965.   In that month the business was " taken over " by the appellants who owned a number of similar establishments and, on Jan. 15, 1966, the respondent was dismissed by due notice given by the appellants under his contract of service.   Section 1 (1) of the Redundancy Payments Act 1965 provides that:

" Where on or after the appointed day an employee who has been continuously employed for the requisite period—(*a*) is dismissed by his employer by reason of redundancy, . . . then, subject to the following provisions of this Part of this Act, the employer shall be liable to pay to him a sum (in this Act referred to as a 'redundancy payment') calculated in accordance with Sch. 1 to this Act."

The " requisite period " is defined in s. 8 (1), and no question arises on it in this case, nor is there any dispute that the sum of £490 has been correctly calculated. By s. 1 (2), it is provided that

" For the purposes of this Act an employee who is dismissed shall be taken to be dismissed by reason of redundancy if the dismissal is attributable wholly or mainly to—(*a*) the fact that his employer has ceased, or intends to cease, to carry on the business for the purposes of which the employee was employed by him, or has ceased, or intends to cease, to carry on that business in the place where the employee was so employed, or (*b*) the fact that the requirements of that business for employees to carry out work of a particular kind, or for employees to carry out work of a particular kind in the place where he was so employed, have ceased or diminished or are expected to cease or diminish."

Section 9 of the Act provides for reference of disputes to the Industrial Tribunal, and by s. 9 (2):

" For the purposes of any such reference . . . (*b*) an employee who has been dismissed by his employer shall, unless the contrary is proved, be presumed to have been so dismissed by reason of redundancy."

An employee is not entitled to a redundancy payment if his employer dismisses him without notice in consequence of the employee's misconduct; that is by s. 2 (2).

It is necessary to read in full the reasons given by the tribunal for its decision, and, to avoid confusion, Mr. Butterwick is referred to as the respondent and North Riding Garages, Ltd. as the appellants throughout.

" It is agreed that the [respondent] was dismissed from his employment with the [appellants] on Jan. 15, 1966, and by the Act he is, unless the contrary is proved, presumed to have been so dismissed by reason of redundancy. By agreement between the solicitors appearing for the respective parties and with the approval of the tribunal the [appellants] called their evidence first with the object of rebutting this presumption. The [respondent] has been employed at the Resolution Garage at Whitby for thirty years. The business at this garage was taken over by the [appellants] who are a group owning several such establishments, in April, 1965. Continuity of employment was admitted. From his length of service the tribunal infer that at least up to April, 1965, he had given satisfactory service. He was workshop manager, that is he was in charge of the repairs workshop with its mechanics and other staff and in view of the comparative smallness of the staff he was expected to spend part of his time performing the mechanics' work on the vehicles. Under the [appellants'] organisation there were a garage manager for that garage (Mr. Robotham) and a garage works manager for the garage (Mr. Hodgson), who both gave evidence together with a director (Mr. Bairstow). Their contention was that the [respondent] was dismissed not by reason of redundancy but because he was inefficient and incompetent. There was no suggestion that he was wilfully inefficient, or guilty of any industrial misconduct, or any worse than he had been before April, 1965, but rather that he was doing his incompetent best. Their evidence was supported by a great deal of documentary evidence, which they said consisted merely of specimens of a larger whole, tending to show such things as slowness in dealing with jobs, lack of supervision resulting in inefficient work, faulty costing and incompetence in dealing with job cards. As regards job cards there was introduced a new system some time after the [appellants] took over. The tribunal took the view that these complaints had some substance, but the shortcomings were not uncommon in the trade generally at the present time. The [respondent] did not measure up to the standards which they expected of him and he was probably not as good as many persons in a similar position and when he was dismissed he was dismissed because they considered that he was not up to their standards. On the other hand, the [appellants] had introduced some new methods and the [respondent] was not a man who could easily adapt himself, though he was trying his best. This particular workshop was not a large one and Mr. Hodgson thought that it was the former owner who took the major decisions and decided what a job should cost, and that the [respondent] was having a greater amount of work put on him under the new management. There was an increased emphasis on the sales side, with which the [respondent] was not concerned directly, when the [appellants] took over, but the tribunal did not accept that the [appellants] were deliberately running down the repairs side, as their agencies from manufacturers depended on having certain repair facilities. When the [respondent] had been dismissed a Mr. Headlam was engaged for the post of workshop manager and he was said to be ' going along with our ideas and bringing suggestions to us '. The [appellants] contend that the post of workshop manager having been filled again there could be no redundancy. The problem is not answered as easily as that. The situation which arises when a business is taken over is becoming a familiar one with the tribunal. Inevitably the new management with new ideas and a natural desire for improved efficiency makes changes. Inevitably, ' misfits ' are found who have to be dispensed with. No general rule can be laid down as to whether these misfits come within the scope of the redundancy payments scheme. The slacker or scrounger who is weeded out may well not be redundant. On the other hand, a workshop manager under one régime may not have to fulfil the same requirements as a workshop manager under another régime. The title does not conclusively connote that the requirements of the post are constant throughout.

" The tribunal, having carefully considered the evidence proffered by the [appellants], came to the conclusion that it did not rebut the presumption of redundancy, but rather confirmed that the dismissal was in fact by reason of redundancy and that, in accordance with the Act the [respondent was] entitled to a redundancy payment. When the [appellants] took over there was a reorganisation of the system of the business as a whole and their requirement for a workshop manager of the old type ceased. They admitted that he could not very well have reverted to a mechanic. Yet he was not up to their new standards. This conclusion having been conveyed to the parties, the [respondent's] solicitors called no evidence."

The tribunal has proceeded on the assumption that the appellants' evidence is acceptable, so that the provisional findings of primary fact can be analysed as follows: (a) The respondent had given satisfactory service until April, 1965; (b) he was doing his best thereafter but was probably not as efficient as many persons in a comparable position; (c) the appellants had introduced new methods to which the respondent could not easily adapt himself, and he was having a greater amount of work put on to him than before; (d) the appellants were not deliberately running down the repairs side of the business, though there was increased emphasis on the sales side.

It is clear that this was not a case where the employer had ceased, or intended to cease, to carry on the business for the purposes of which the employee was employed within s. 1 (2) (*a*), and, accordingly, the respondent was dismissed by reason of redundancy if, but only if, his dismissal was attributable wholly or mainly to the fact that the requirements of the business for employees to carry out work of a particular kind had ceased or diminished, or were expected to cease or diminish (s. 1 (2) (*b*)).

It is, we think, important to observe that a claim under s. 1 (2) (*b*) is conditional on a change in the requirements of the business. If the requirement of the business for employees to carry out work of a particular kind increases or remains constant, no redundancy payment can be claimed by an employee, in work of that kind, whose dismissal is attributable to personal deficiencies which prevent him from satisfying his employer. The very fact of dismissal shows that the employee's services are no longer required by his employer and that he may, in a popular sense, be said to have become redundant; but if the dismissal was attributable to age, physical disability or inability to meet his employer's standards, he was not dismissed on account of redundancy within the meaning of the Act. For the purpose of the Act, an employee who remains in the same kind of work is expected to adapt himself to new methods and techniques, and cannot complain if his employer insists on higher standards of efficiency than those previously required; but if new methods alter the nature of the work required to be done, it may follow that no requirement remains for employees to do work of the particular kind which has been superseded and that they are truly redundant. Thus, if a motor manufacturer decides to use plastics instead of wood in the body-work of his cars and dismisses his woodworkers, they may well be entitled to redundancy payments on the footing that their dismissal is attributable to a cessation of the requirements of the business for employees to carry out work of a particular kind, namely, woodworking.

If one looks at the primary facts disclosed by the evidence in this case, it is difficult to see what is the particular kind of work in which a requirement for employees has ceased or diminished. The vehicle workshop remained, as did the requirement for a workshop manager, and we do not understand the tribunal to have found that the volume of repair work had diminished to such an extent as to make the respondent's dismissal wholly or mainly attributable to that fact. The only possible conclusion which appears to us to have been open to the tribunal on the evidence was that the respondent was dismissed because he could not do his job in accordance with the new methods and new standards required by the appellants. The tribunal seems to base its decision on the fact that a requirement for a workshop manager " of the old type " had ceased. This is probably a reference to the fact that the respondent had been required by the appellants to estimate costs, which the former owner had done for himself, but the mere fact that a re-organisation has transferred this work to the respondent does not show that the requirement of the business for employees to do this, or any other, kind of work has diminished. The only possible relevance of this evidence would be to show that the volume of repair work had been run down to such an extent that the respondent could no longer occupy his whole time in it, but the tribunal, on the totality of the evidence, does not seem to take that view.

We think that the tribunal has fallen into error by applying the wrong test, in that they have not looked at the overall requirements of the business but at the allocation of duties between individuals. It is irrelevant that the duties of the new manager are not identical with the duties formerly undertaken by the respondent if the overall requirements of the business are unchanged. The court will, accordingly, allow the appeal and remit the matter to the tribunal to enable the hearing to be continued in the light of this opinion.

Shelagh Morgan (for *Quentin Edwards*): I ask for the costs of the appeal.

H. J. Byrt: Legal aid does not cover either applications before the Industrial Tribunal or appeals from the tribunal in cases of this sort. Costs are not normally awarded by the tribunal in view of the statutory provision (1), though if the tribunal is of opinion that a party to the proceedings has acted frivolously or vexatiously an order in respect of costs may be made. Moreover before the tribunal the respondent never got as far as putting his case, for the tribunal's views on, apparently, a submission that there was no case to rebut the statutory presumption (2) having been conveyed to the parties, the respondent called no evidence. I submit that no order as to costs should be made.

WIDGERY, J.: I am not surprised that there is no legal aid before the tribunal, but I should have thought that legal aid would have been available on appeal to this court (3).

LORD PARKER, C.J.: I have been told that an employer has only to appeal and the employee gives up. We think that, if the appellants ask for costs of the appeal, they are entitled to them, but we would like it conveyed to them that we think that this is a case where, in all the circumstances and perhaps particularly because this is the first case that has come before this court, they ought not to enforce an order for costs.

Appeal allowed. Case remitted.

Solicitors: *Chapman & Co.* (for the appellants); *Fisher, Dowson & Wasbrough,* agents for *George Cass, Rylands & Co.,* Whitby (for the respondent).

[*Reported by* N. P. Metcalfe, Esq., *Barrister-at-Law.*]

---

(1) See Industrial Tribunals (Employment and Compensation) (England and Wales) Regulations, 1965 (S.I. 1965 No. 2018), Sch., para. 10.

(2) Redundancy Payments Act 1965, s. 1 (2) (*b*).   (3) Cf. p. 645, letter A, ante.

FRAZER *v.* WALKER AND OTHERS.

[PRIVY COUNCIL (Viscount Dilhorne, Lord Denning, Lord Hodson, Lord Wilberforce and Sir Garfield Barwick), July 4, 5, 6, 7, December 7, 1966.]

Privy Council—New Zealand—Land Registration—Indefeasibility of title of registered proprietors—Mortgage of fee simple by one joint owner forging other joint owner's signature—Memorandum of mortgage registered—Power of sale exercised by mortgagees—Memorandum of transfer registered—Mortgagees and purchaser acting in good faith—Whether purchaser and mortgagees acquired title as against the joint owner who had not known of the mortgage—Land Transfer Act, 1952 (No. 52 of 1952), s. 63, s. 85.

In 1961 the appellant and his wife were the registered owners of farm land subject to a mortgage on which £1,732 was still owing. The appellant's wife, professing to act on behalf of herself and the appellant, borrowed £3,000 from the second respondents. This was to be secured by a mortgage over the property. Having inserted in the mortgage a signature which purported to be the appellant's but was false, she took the mortgage to her solicitors where a clerk witnessed the false signature and also a genuine signature of her own. The second respondents paid the £3,000 partly in discharge of the existing mortgage and partly to her solicitors. On July 21, 1961, the mortgage memorandum was registered at the land registry office together with a discharge of the previous mortgage. No payment of principal or interest was made and on Oct. 26, 1962, the second respondents sold the property to the first respondent in exercise of their power of sale. In November, 1962, the transfer by the second respondents (the mortgagees) to the first respondent was registered. The respondents acted in good faith throughout. In an action by the first respondent for possession, the appellant counterclaimed, on the ground of forgery of his signature to the mortgage, for declarations that his interest in the land had not been affected by the mortgage and that the mortgage was a nullity; he also counter-claimed for an order to cancel the relevant entries or memorials in the land transfer register. On appeal from dismissal of his counter-claim,

Held: (i) since a mortgage of a fee simple created a charge which the Land Transfer Act, 1952, treated as an estate or interest in land, the counterclaim was an action for the recovery of land within s. 63, and, as it did not fall within any of the exceptions expressed in s. 63, it was barred by s. 63, and the power, conferred by s. 85, to cancel entries on the register was similarly excluded; accordingly the appellant's counter-claim had been rightly dismissed as against the second respondents (see p. 653, letter I, to p. 654, letter B, post).

(ii) registration was effective to vest title in a registered proprietor notwithstanding that he acquired his interest under an instrument that was void; and accordingly, as also because the counter-claim against the first respondent was a proceeding for the recovery of land and was barred by s. 63, the counter-claim failed against the first respondent (see p. 654, letter G, and p. 655, letter H, post).

Assets Co., Ltd. v. *Mere Roihi (Consolidated Appeals)* ([1905] A.C. 176) and *Boyd* v. *Wellington Corpn.* ([1924] N.Z.L.R. 1174) approved.

Gibbs v. *Messer* ([1891] A.C. 248) distinguished.

Appeal dismissed.

[As to the effect of registration of a legal charge in England, see 23 HALSBURY'S LAWS (3rd Edn.) 251, para. 557, and p. 253, para. 562.

As to rectification of the register in England, see 23 HALSBURY'S LAWS (3rd Edn.) 203, 204, para. 425, and p. 205, paras. 427, 428; and for cases on the subject, see 38 DIGEST (Repl.) 899, 900, *944-950.*]

Cases referred to:

Assets Co., Ltd. v. Mere Roihi (Consolidated Appeals), [1905] A.C. 176; 92 L.T.
397; 38 Digest (Repl.) 893, *1181.

Boyd v. Wellington Corpn., [1924] N.Z.L.R. 1174.

Gibbs v. Messer, [1891] A.C. 248; 38 Digest (Repl.) 893, *1173.

Tataurangi Tairuakena v. Mua Carr, [1927] N.Z.L.R. 688; 13 Digest (Repl.)
292, *189.

Appeal.

This was an appeal by Alan Frederick Frazer from an order of the Court of
Appeal of New Zealand (NORTH, P., TURNER and McCARTHY, JJ.) dated Nov. 15,
1965, dismissing the appellant's appeal against the judgment of the Supreme
Court of New Zealand (RICHMOND, J.) dated May 5, 1965, in an action by the
first respondent, Douglas Hamilton Walker, for possession of a farm at Kerr's
Road near Papatoetoe in New Zealand. The appellant was defendant and counterclaimed not only against the first respondent, but also against the second respondents, Edward Radomski and his wife Nellie Radomski, claiming a declaration
that the appellant's interest in the farm land had not been affected by a purported
mortgage to the second respondents or a subsequent sale by them as mortgagees
to the first respondent, a declaration that the mortgage was a nullity and a
declaration that the appellant was beneficial owner of an undivided half interest
in the farm land. The appellant further counter-claimed for an order directing
cancellation of the entries or memorials in the register relating to the land whereby
the second respondents were registered as mortgagees and the first respondent
was registered as proprietor, and substitution of an entry to restore the appellant's
name as joint owner. RICHMOND, J., gave judgment for the first respondent
on his claim in the action, and against the appellant on his counter-claim.

The facts appear in the opinion of the Judicial Committee at letter G, infra.

P. B. Temm and R. I. Barker (both of the New Zealand Bar) for the appellant.

D. S. Beattie, Q.C., and N. J. Vautier (both of the New Zealand Bar) for the
first respondent.

G. D. Speight and W. D. Baragwanath (both of the New Zealand Bar) for the
second respondents.

LORD WILBERFORCE: The appellant, Alan Frederick Frazer, and his
wife, Flora Agnes Frazer, were in 1961 the registered proprietors under the Land
Transfer Act, 1952, of a farm property in a suburb of Auckland, subject to a
mortgage to one Bailey on which £1,732 was owing. In 1961 Mrs. Frazer, professing to act on behalf of herself and the appellant, arranged to borrow £3,000
from the second respondents which sum was to be secured by a mortgage over
the property. A form of mortgage was prepared by the second respondents'
solicitors from whom it was collected by Mrs. Frazer. She took it to solicitors
acting for her and in their office a clerk witnessed her genuine signature to the
mortgage and also a signature purporting to be that of the appellant, which she
had previously inserted. The mortgage document and the certificate of title
were forwarded by these solicitors to the solicitors of the second respondents:
they paid the £3,000 partly to Mrs. Frazer's solicitors and partly on her behalf in
discharge of the existing mortgage, and in due course registered at the land registry
office, Auckland, on July 21, 1961, the memorandum of mortgage together with a
discharge of the previous mortgage. As no payment of principal or interest was
made, the second respondents exercised their power of sale, and on Oct. 26, 1962,
the property was sold by auction to the first respondent for £5,000. The second
respondents as mortgagees executed a memorandum of transfer to the first
respondent which was registered on Nov. 29, 1962. It is conceded that the
second respondents and the first respondent acted throughout in good faith and
without any knowledge of the irregularity on the part of Mrs. Frazer.

On Mar. 16, 1964, the first respondent commenced proceedings in the magistrates court at Auckland against the appellant for possession of the property, relying on his title as registered proprietor. These proceedings were removed into the Supreme Court. The appellant delivered a defence to this claim and also filed a counterclaim against the first respondent, to which he joined the second respondents as defendants, asserting that what purported to be his signature on the mortgage was a forgery and that the mortgage, the advance by the second respondents, and the sale by the mortgagees had occurred without his knowledge. He claimed a declaration that his interest in the land was not affected by the purported mortgage or by the sale to the first respondent, a declaration that the mortgage was a nullity and an order directing the district land registrar to cancel the entries or memorials in the register whereby the second respondents were registered as mortgagees and the first respondent was registered as proprietor and to restore the name of the appellant and Mrs. Frazer as joint owners of the land.

At the trial, Richmond, J., held that the appellant had given no authority to Mrs. Frazer to mortgage his interest in the land. Nevertheless he gave judgment in favour of the first respondent and dismissed the appellant's counterclaim holding that the second respondents had obtained by registration an indefeasible title and that in any event the subsequent transfer gave the first respondent an indefeasible title. On appeal to the Court of Appeal, the appellant's appeal was dismissed on the ground that the first respondent, as a bona fide purchaser, had obtained an indefeasible title. The court gave no decision as to the position of the second respondents, although certain observations as to this appeared in the judgments. Before their lordships, both the first respondent and the second respondents appeared and addressed arguments.

Their lordships will deal first with the appellant's claim against the second respondents. This raises the question whether it was open to the appellant to bring proceedings attacking the validity of the mortgage against the second respondents, whose interest as mortgagees was entered in the register, and claiming cancellation of this entry. This question must be considered by reference to the provisions of the Land Transfer Act, 1952. The relevant sections may be considered under five main headings.

I. Those sections of the Land Transfer Act, 1952, which deal with the procuring of registration, the principal of which are s. 42, s. 157 and s. 164.

Section 42 contains a prohibition against registration of any instrument except in the manner provided in the Act and unless the instrument is in accordance with the provisions of the Act. Section 157 requires every instrument, including such as charge any estate, to be signed by the registered proprietor and attested. Section 164 prohibits the registrar from receiving any instrument such as a charge unless there is endorsed thereon a certificate that it is correct for the purposes of the Act of 1952 signed by the applicant or party claiming under the instrument, a licensed land-broker or a solicitor employed by the applicant or party. The appellant invoked these sections, and reg. 24 of the Land Transfer Regulations, 1948, in support of an argument that the forged mortgage could not be received for registration or validly registered and consequently that the mortgagee never became entitled to the benefit of registration. Their lordships cannot accept this argument which would be destructive of the whole system of registration. Even if non-compliance with the Act's requirements as to registration may involve the possibility of cancellation or correction of the entry—the provisions as to this will be referred to later—, registration once effected must attract the consequences which the Act attaches to registration whether that was regular or otherwise. As will appear from the following paragraphs, the inhibiting effect of certain sections (e.g., s. 62 and s. 63) and the probative effect of others (e.g., s. 75) in no way depend on any fact other than actual registration as proprietor. It is in fact the registration and not its antecedents which vests and divests title.

II.　Those sections of the Land Transfer Act, 1952, which provide protection to the registered proprietor against claims and proceedings.

These are s. 62 and s. 63. Without attempting any comprehensive or exhaustive description of what these sections achieve, it may be said that while s. 62 secures that a registered proprietor, and consequently anyone who deals with him, shall hold his estate or interest absolutely free from encumbrances, with three specified exceptions, s. 63 protects him against any action for possession or recovery of land, with five specified exceptions. Section 63 (2) is a particularly strong provision in his favour: it provides that the register is, in every court of law or equity, to be an absolute bar to any such action against the registered proprietor, any rule of law or equity to the contrary notwithstanding. It is to be noticed that each of these sections excepts the case of fraud, s. 62 employing the words " except in case of fraud ", and s. 63 using the words " as against the person registered as proprietor of that land through fraud ". The uncertain ambit of these expressions has been limited by judicial decision to actual fraud by the registered proprietor or his agent. (See *Assets Co., Ltd.* v. *Mere Roihi* (*Consolidated Appeals*) (1).)

It is these sections which, together with those next referred to, confer on the registered proprietor what has come to be called " indefeasibility of title ". The expression, not used in the Act itself, is a convenient description of the immunity from attack by adverse claim to the land or interest in respect of which he is registered, which a registered proprietor enjoys. This conception is central in the system of registration. It does not involve that the registered proprietor is protected against any claim whatsoever; as will be seen later, there are provisions by which the entry on which he relies may be cancelled or corrected, or he may be exposed to claims in personam. These are matters not to be overlooked when a total description of his rights is required; but as registered proprietor, and while he remains such, no adverse claim (except as specifically admitted) may be brought against him.

III.　Those sections of the Land Transfer Act, 1952, which state the effect of the certificate of title. The principal section on this subject is s. 75. The certificate, unless the register shows otherwise, is to be conclusive evidence that the person named in it is seised of or as taking estate or interest [sic] in the land therein described as seised or possessed of that land for the estate or interest therein specified and that the property comprised in the certificate has been duly brought under the Act. This section is of a similar character to those last discussed; it creates another—a probative—aspect of " indefeasibility ", none the less effective though, as later provisions show, there are means by which the certificate may be cancelled or its owner compelled to hold it on trust or to deliver it up through an action in personam.

IV.　Those sections of the Land Transfer Act, 1952, which deal with correction or calling in of the certificate. The principal sections are s. 81 and s. 85.

Taking first s. 85, this gives to the court power to direct the registrar to cancel or correct certificates of title or entries in the register. But the power is carefully circumscribed. It arises on the recovery of any land, estate or interest by any proceeding in any court from the registered proprietor, but only in any case in which such a proceeding is not expressly barred. This is a clear reference to s. 63, which, as has been said, bars proceedings against a registered proprietor in all but the excepted cases. The effect is that the power of the court to cancel or correct does not extend beyond those cases in which adverse claims against the registered proprietor are admitted by the Act. (See *Assets Co., Ltd.* v. *Mere Roihi* (2).)

Section 80 and s. 81 are in a different field; they deal with the powers of the registrar. Section 80 is little more than a " slip " section and not of substantive importance, but s. 81 is evidently wider in scope. It applies in cases where it

---

(1) [1905] A.C. 176 at p. 210.　　　　　　　　(2) [1905] A.C. at p. 195.

appears to the satisfaction of the registrar that a certificate of title has been issued in error or contains a misdescription of land or boundaries or that any grant, certificate, instrument, entry or endorsement has been fraudulently or wrongfully obtained or is fraudulently or wrongfully retained. It is not a section which directly applies in the present case, though some consideration will be given to its scope later in this judgment.

V. Those sections of the Land Transfer Act, 1952, which relate to the position of third parties dealing with a registered proprietor: these are in effect, s. 182 and s. 183. Section 182 deals with notice. In all systems of registration of land it is usual and necessary to modify and indeed largely to negative the normal rules as to notice, constructive notice, or inquiry as to matters possibly affecting the title of the owner of the land. Section 182 is of no direct relevance in the present case, which does not involve any question of notice.

Section 183 is in the following terms:

" (1) Nothing in this Act shall be so interpreted as to render subject to action for recovery of damages, or for possession, or to deprivation of the estate or interest in respect of which he is registered as proprietor, any purchaser or mortgagee bona fide for valuable consideration of land under the provisions of this Act on the ground that his vendor or mortgagor may have been registered as proprietor through fraud or error, or under any void or voidable instrument, or may have derived from or through a person registered as proprietor through fraud or error, or under any void or voidable instrument, and this whether the fraud or error consists in wrong description of the boundaries or of the parcels of any land, or otherwise howsoever."

Their lordships will revert to it when they deal with the appellant's claim against the first respondent.

Before leaving the provisions of the Land Transfer Act, 1952, some reference should be made to the compensation provisions, on which each side relied in argument. The principal section is s. 172. Under para. (*b*) compensation may be claimed by any person deprived of any land, or of any estate or interest in land, by the registration of any person as proprietor of that land or by an error, omission or misdescription in any entry in the register and who by the Act is barred from bringing an action for recovery of that land, estate or interest.

Their lordships do not wish to arrive at any firm view on the possible application of this section in the present case—it would be undesirable that they should do so, since claims for compensation may have to be made. They are prepared to assume, for the purpose of argument only, that according as either failed in these proceedings, the former owner, the appellant, would, and the purported mortgagees, the second respondents, would not, be enabled to claim compensation under this section, but they cannot find in this assumed conclusion any reason for deciding that the second respondents did or did not obtain an indefeasible title. If, as the effect of the rest of the Act, they did not, it might still have been the intention of the legislature, that they should bear their own loss, which has not arisen from any fault of the registry, or even from any reliance by them on the registry, rather than that it should fall on taxpayers in New Zealand. Their lordships do not therefore feel entitled to base any argument on the manner in which the compensation sections might be operated.

The effect of these provisions on the claim of the appellant against the second respondents must now be considered. It does not in their lordships' view admit of any doubt. Although a mortgage of a fee simple does not take effect as a transfer of the fee simple (see s. 100), it does create a charge on the land which the Land Transfer Act, 1952, treats as an estate or interest in the land (see s. 2, definitions of " estate or interest " and " proprietor "). It is therefore apparent that the appellant's counter-claim against the second respondents, in so far as it sought a declaration that the appellant's interest in land was not affected by the purported mortgage and a declaration that the mortgage was a nullity, was an

action for recovery of land within the terms of s. 63. In so far as it sought cancellation by the court of the entry of the mortgage on the register, it could only be
based on s. 85. The proceeding does not fall within either the exception of fraud
or within any of the other exceptions allowed by s. 63. The power of cancellation
by the court is also excluded by the express terms of s. 85, because the proceeding
(for the recovery of land) is itself barred. No question of the invocation of the
registrar's powers under s. 80 and s. 81 arises in the case. The conclusion must
follow that the appellant's claim against the second respondents was correctly
dismissed by RICHMOND, J., and their lordships find that his judgment on this
point is supported by the authorities.

The leading case as to the rights of a person whose name has been entered on
the register without fraud in respect of an estate or interest is the decision of this
Board in *Assets Co., Ltd.* v. *Mere Roihi* (3). The Board there was concerned with
three consolidated appeals from the Court of Appeal in New Zealand, which had
decided in each case in favour of certain aboriginal natives as against the
registered proprietors. In each appeal their lordships decided that registration
was conclusive to confer on the appellants a title unimpeachable by the respondents. The facts involved in each of the appeals were complicated and not
identical one with another, a circumstance which has given rise to some difference
of opinion as to the precise ratio decidendi—the main relevant difference being
whether the decision established the indefeasibility of title of a registered
proprietor who acquired his interest under a void instrument, or whether it is
only a bona fide purchaser from such a proprietor whose title is indefeasible. In
Boyd v. *Wellington Corpn.* (4) the majority of the Court of Appeal in New Zealand
held in favour of the former view, and treated the *Assets Co.* case (3) as a decision
to that effect. The decision in *Boyd* v. *Wellington Corpn.* (4) related to a very
special situation, namely that of a registered proprietor who acquired his title
under a void proclamation, but, with certain reservations as to the case of forgery,
it has been generally accepted and followed in New Zealand as establishing, with
the supporting authority of the *Assets Co.* case (3), the indefeasibility of the title
of registered proprietors derived from void instruments generally.

Their lordships are of opinion that this conclusion is in accordance with the
interpretation to be placed on those sections of the Land Transfer Act, 1952
which they have examined. They consider that *Boyd's* case (4) was rightly
decided and that the ratio of the decision applies as regards titles derived from
registration of void instruments generally. As regards all such instruments it
established that registration is effective to vest and to divest title and to protect
the registered proprietor against adverse claims.

The appellant relied on the earlier decision of the Board in *Gibbs* v. *Messer* (5)
as supporting a contrary view, but their lordships do not find anything in the
case which can be of assistance to him. Without restating the unusual facts,
which are sufficiently well-known, it is sufficient to say that no question there
arose as to the effect of such sections as corresponded (under the very similar
Victorian Act) with s. 62 and s. 63 of the Act of 1952 now under consideration.
The Board was then concerned with the position of a bona fide " purchaser "
for value from a fictitious person, and the decision is founded on a distinction
drawn between such a case and that of a bona fide purchaser from a real registered
proprietor. The decision has in their lordships' opinion no application as regards
adverse claims made against a registered proprietor, such as came before the
courts in *Assets Co., Ltd.* v. *Mere Roihi* (3), in *Boyd* v. *Wellington Corpn.* (4)
and in the present case.

Before leaving this part of the present appeal their lordships think it desirable,
in relation to the concept of " indefeasibility of title ", as their lordships have
applied it to the facts before them, to make two further observations.

(3) [1905] A.C. 176.   (4) [1924] N.Z.L.R. 1174.

                        (5) [1891] A.C. 248.

A   First, in following and approving in this respect the two decisions in *Assets Co., Ltd.* v. *Mere Roihi* (6), and *Boyd* v. *Wellington Corpn.* (7), their lordships have accepted the general principle, that registration under the Land Transfer Act, 1952, confers on a registered proprietor a title to the interest in respect of which he is registered which is (under s. 62 and s. 63) immune from adverse claims, other than those specifically excepted. In doing so they wish to make **B** clear that this principle in no way denies the right of a plaintiff to bring against a registered proprietor a claim in personam, founded in law or in equity, for such relief as a court acting in personam may grant. That this is so has frequently, and rightly, been recognised in the courts of New Zealand and of Australia (see, for example, *Boyd* v. *Wellington Corpn.* (8) per Adams, J., and *Tataurangi Tairuakena* v. *Mua Carr* (9) per Skerrett, C.J.).

C   Their lordships refer to these cases by way of illustration only without intending to limit or define the various situations in which actions of a personal character against registered proprietors may be admitted. The principle must always remain paramount that those actions which fall within the prohibition of **s. 62** and s. 63 may not be maintained.

The second observation relates to the power of the registrar to correct entries **D** under s. 80 and s. 81 of the Land Transfer Act, 1952. It has already been pointed out (as was made clear in the *Assets Co.* case (10) by this Board) that this power is quite distinct from the power of the court to order cancellation of entries under s. 85, and moreover while the latter is invoked here, the former is not. The powers of the registrar under s. 81 are significant and extensive (see *Assets Co.* case (6)). They are not coincident with the cases excepted in s. 62 and **s. 63**. **E** As well as in the case of fraud, where any grant, certificate, instrument, entry or endorsement has been wrongfully obtained or is wrongfully retained, the registrar has power of cancellation and correction. From the argument before their lordships it appears that there is room for some difference of opinion as to what precisely may be comprehended in the word " wrongfully ". It is clear, in any event, that s. 81 must be read with and subject to s. 183 with the conse- **F** quence that the exercise of the registrar's powers must be limited to the period before a bona fide purchaser, or mortgagee, acquires a title under the latter section.

As the appellant did not in this case seek relief under s. 81, and as, if he had, his claim would have been barred by s. 183 (as explained in the next paragraph), any pronouncement on the meaning to be given to the word " wrongfully " **G** would be obiter and their lordships must leave the interpretation to be placed on that word in this section to be decided in a case in which the question directly arises.

The failure of the appeal against the second respondents entails (and it was not contended otherwise) that it must equally fail against the first respondent. Their lordships would add, however, that the action against that respondent was **H** an action for the recovery of land within the meaning of s. 63 and that it would be directly barred by that section, quite apart from the fact that it could not be maintained against the other respondents. The appellant could not bring his case against the first respondent within any of the exceptions to that section. Also their lordships would add, that, if it had been necessary for the first respondent to rely on s. 183 of the Land Transfer Act, 1952, he would by it have had a com- **I** plete answer to the claim. The appellant argued that the second respondents were not " vendors " within the meaning of the section—the suggestion being that he is only a vendor who sells the precise estate or interest of which he is the registered proprietor, so that a mortgagee does not fall within the description. It was further contended that the second respondents were not " proprietors ", because they did not own the estate or interest (i.e., the fee simple) which they

(6) [1905] A.C. 176.   (7) [1924] N.Z.L.R. 1174.
(8) [1924] N.Z.L.R. at p. 1223.   (9) [1927] N.Z.L.R. 688 at p. 702.
(10) [1905] A.C. at pp. 194, 195.

purported to transfer. Their lordships are in agreement with the Court of Appeal in holding that the section should not be so narrowly read and that it extends to the case of a mortgagee who is " proprietor " of the mortgage and who has power of sale over the fee simple. Their lordships need not elaborate on this part of the case since they concur with the conclusions agreed on by all three members of the Court of Appeal.

Their lordships will humbly advise Her Majesty that the appeal should be dismissed. The appellant must pay the respondents' costs.

Appeal dismissed.

Solicitors: *Blyth, Dutton, Wright & Bennett* (for the appellant); *Bell, Brodrick & Gray* (for the first respondent); *Mackrell & Co.* (for the second respondents).

[*Reported by* KATHLEEN J. H. O'BRIEN, *Barrister-at-Law.*]

PRACTICE DIRECTION.

CHANCERY DIVISION

Sale of Land—Vendor and purchaser summons—Lists—On adjournment to judge not to be placed in non-witness list but to be given day for hearing.

Under the Land Registration Act 1966 the voluntary registration of land is abolished. It has been suggested in some quarters that this may lead to an increase in the number of vendor and purchaser summonses which require to be promptly heard. In view of this possibility, as from Mar. 1, 1967, vendor and purchaser summonses when adjourned to the judge will not be placed in the non-witness list but will be given days for hearing as soon as possible in the same way as wardship applications.

By direction of CROSS, J.

Cancelled by PRACTICE DIRECTION
[1970] 1 All ER 671

W. F. S. HAWKINS,
Chief Master
Chancery Division.

Feb. 6, 1967.

KELLY (Widow and Administratrix of the Estate of NORMAN
KELLY *deceased*) *v.* PIERHEAD, LTD.

[COURT OF APPEAL, CIVIL DIVISION (Willmer, Harman and Salmon, L.JJ.),
November 8, 9, 10, 1966.]

*Building—Building regulations—Roof work—" Working place "—Flat roof—
Place where employee working was working place—Whole roof capable of
being working place—No guard-rail at roof's edge—Building (Safety, Health
and Welfare) Regulations, 1948 (S.I. 1948 No. 1145), reg. 24 (1).*

Roofing contractors were engaged on the construction of a flat roof on a
one-storey projection to a large main building. The roof was nearly completed. When completed it would be fifty-two feet by twenty-six feet in size
and it was twenty-three feet above the ground, one side of it resting on a
brick wall of that height. There were no guard-rails on that side. Work
had started at the end opposite that adjoining the main building and moved
towards that building, which it had nearly reached, and it consisted of fitting
concrete joists into position and putting breeze blocks between them. This
work required the workmen at times to work at the edge of the roof. One of
the contractors' employees while engaged on the work fell from the roof on
the unfenced side and was killed. On appeal from a decision that the contractors were in breach of statutory duty under reg. 24 (1)* of the Building
(Safety, Health and Welfare) Regulations, 1948, in that the employee had
been working at a working place from one side of which he was liable to
fall more than six feet six inches and which was not provided with a guard-
rail at that side,

Held: the contractors were in breach of statutory duty under reg. 24 (1),
for the whole roof, being a flat roof, could properly be regarded as a working
place (or, per SALMON, L.J., even if it could not, the part of the roof where
the deceased employee was standing at the time of the accident was his
working place), since the flat roof under construction had the same relevant
characteristics as a working platform notwithstanding the absence of precise
boundaries, these characteristics being that men would be working there for
an appreciable time, that it was flat and that its total area was sufficiently
defined and not too large (see p. 662, letters H and I, p. 633, letters G and I,
and p. 665, letters B, C and D, post).

Gill v. *Donald Humberstone & Co., Ltd.* ([1963] 3 All E.R. 180) considered
and distinguished.

Appeal dismissed.

[**Editorial Note.** There is express upholding of the decision of the trial judge.
The view that he took was that the spot at which the deceased and his mates
were working was a working place within reg. 24 (1); see p. 658, letter H, post).
The Court of Appeal took also the view that the whole roof could properly be
regarded as a working place (see p. 665, letter E, and p. 667, letter B, post).

As to the duty to provide guard-rails at working places of building operations,
see 17 HALSBURY'S LAWS (3rd Edn.) 126, para. 206; and for cases on the subject,
see 24 DIGEST 1076, *331*; 1078-1080, *341-353*.

For the Building (Safety, Health and Welfare) Regulations, 1948, reg. 24 (1),
see 8 HALSBURY'S STATUTORY INSTRUMENTS (First Re-Issue) 197.]

Cases referred to:

Ball (George) & Sons, Ltd. v. *Sill,* (1954), 52 L.G.R. 508; 24 Digest (Repl.)
1080, *352.*

Curran v. *William Neill & Son (St. Helens), Ltd.,* [1961] 3 All E.R. 108; [1961]
1 W.L.R. 1069; Digest (Cont. Vol. A) 601, *1344a.*

Field v. *Perrys (Ealing), Ltd.,* [1950] 2 All E.R. 521; 24 Digest (Repl.) 1076,
331.

---

* Regulation 24 (1) is set out at p. 660, letter D, post.

Applied in BOYTON v WILLMENT [1971] 3 All ER 624

Applied in FERGUSON v DAWSON [1976] 3 All ER 817

Gill v. *Donald Humberstone & Co., Ltd.*, [1963] 3 All E.R. 180; [1963] 1 W.L.R.
929; Digest (Cont. Vol. A) 604, *351a*.

Appeal.

The defendants appealed against the judgment of CUSACK, J., given on June 23,
1966, at Liverpool Assizes adjudging that the plaintiff recover from the defendants
damages in the sum of £9,114 13s. The grounds of appeal were: (i) that the judge
misdirected himself as to the proper construction and application of reg. 24 (1)
and (3) of the Building (Safety, Health and Welfare) Regulations, 1948; (ii) that
he was wrong in holding that the defendants were in breach of reg. 24 (1); (iii) that
there was no evidence on which the judge could properly hold that the place from
which the plaintiff's deceased husband fell was a working place within the meaning of the regulation; (iv) that there was no evidence on which any inference
could be properly drawn as to the place from which the deceased fell, and that
the judge's finding that the deceased had " set about carrying on with his work "
at the place from which he fell was against the weight of the evidence; and (v) that
the judge ought to have held that the deceased had been guilty of contributory
negligence. The plaintiff served a counter-notice that she intended to contend
that the judgment of CUSACK, J., was supportable on the following ground in
addition to or in substitution for those relied on by the judge: that the work
undertaken by the deceased could not safely be done from the building and the
defendants in breach of reg. 7 (2) of the Construction (General Provisions)
Regulations, 1961* or negligently failed to provide either scaffolds or other means
of support for the deceased while engaged in his work or at his place of work.

In the course of his judgment the trial judge, CUSACK, J., found that the
plaintiff had not established negligence at common law nor an alleged breach of
reg. 28 (1), and held further that an allegation of contributory negligence on the
part of the deceased was not made out. He took the view that the case resolved
itself on the facts to a consideration of reg. 24 (1) of the regulations of 1948, and,
as it was conceded that no guard-rail existed at the point where the deceased
fell, the question was whether the spot with which the court was concerned was a
working platform or working place. The deceased had fallen from the edge of the
wall above the entrance to a garage, there being a drop of some twenty-three feet
at that edge of the roof. The trial judge found that, in order to lay concrete
beams and to put in breeze blocks for the construction of the roof, it was necessary
for the workmen at times to go very close to the edge where there was the
twenty-three feet drop. A witness, Mr. Povey, had described how he himself
would have placed one foot on the wall and one foot on a beam in order to get a
concrete block into position at the end or edge of the flooring which was being
laid. The trial judge expressed his finding as follows—

" I take the view that I am concerned only with the spot at which the
deceased and his mates were working during the course of that day. I come
to the conclusion that it was a working place within the meaning of reg.
24 (1)."

The trial judge then turned to the authorities, *Gill* v. *Donald Humberstone & Co.,
Ltd.*† and *George Ball & Sons, Ltd.* v. *Sill*‡, and, after consideration of them, held
that there was a breach of reg. 24 (1) and that the death of the deceased was
caused by that breach.

G. W. Guthrie Jones, Q.C., and R. L. Ward for the defendants.
R. H. Forrest, Q.C., and A. M. Maguire for the plaintiff.

SALMON, L.J., delivered the first judgment at the request of WILLMER,
L.J.: In December, 1963, a large building was being erected in Glasgow at the
corner of Waterloo Street and Hope Street. One of the roofing contractors for

---

* S.I. 1961 No. 1580.
† [1963] 3 All E.R. 180.
‡ (1954), 52 L.G.R. 508.

the work was the defendant company. The plaintiff's husband was employed by that company as a concrete floor fixer. This case concerns the construction of a flat roof on a one-storey projection to the main building. The roof in question, which was also a floor in the sense that when it was completed, being flat, it would have been walked over, was fifty-two feet by twenty-six feet. It was some twenty-three feet above the ground.

There is not much evidence as to the method of construction. We know that the roof was built from concrete joists and breeze blocks. The photographs show that, as one faces the part of the main building which the one storey building adjoins, on the right there is a nine-inch brick wall which rises to a height of some twenty-three feet above a concrete ramp leading down into a subterranean garage. One side of the roof in question rested on the top of that wall. We do not know anything about the support on the other sides, and in the event that is of no importance. How the concrete joists were put in position is not explained. In as much, however, as we are told that they each weighed some three or four cwt. or more, the presumption is that they were lifted into position by a crane. It appears that, once they were roughly in position, they were manhandled by the workmen into the exact position required. In between the concrete joists, as I have said, there were the breeze blocks, which were so shaped that they fitted into the sides of the concrete joists. By Dec. 14, 1963, the roof had been nearly completed. As can be seen from the photographs, it was then very close to the main building, having been started from the side furthest away from that building. There were still two concrete joists to be put into position with breeze blocks between them; and here and there, as one can see from photograph B, some breeze blocks remained to be put into position; for example, in the forefront of the photograph there is a gap for breeze blocks very close to the brick wall to which I have referred.

On the morning of Dec. 14, 1963, the plaintiff's husband and two other men had been working on the roof. They went on working late because there was some urgency to finish the work; when I say " late ", I mean beyond the normal luncheon break. Immediately after luncheon, the plaintiff's husband and one of the other men went up on to the roof. The plaintiff's husband got on the roof by means of a ladder inside the main building, and then walked across on to the roof. There is no evidence as to precisely how he met with his accident because no one saw it occur. It is quite plain, however, that in the course of doing his work, or preparing to do his work, he slipped or tripped and fell over the side of the brick wall on to the concrete floor twenty-three feet below. Most unfortunately, as a result of the injuries which he sustained, he died. The judge's findings on this part of the case are as follows:

" Nobody saw him fall, but I hold that it was quite clear that he was intending to resume work, and that belief of mine is fortified by the fact that, when his unconscious body was found, he was wearing the gloves or mittens which were habitually worn for moving the breeze blocks, and usually, though not necessarily, worn for moving the concrete beams, and that these gloves, when he went upstairs, had been in his back pocket."

Then the judge said:

" I am satisfied that he returned to that corner [I think that there the judge is referring to the corner near the main building next to the sheer drop over the brick wall] and that he set about carrying on with his work even if he did not actually execute any work in pursuance of that intention."

The plaintiff's husband was found on the concrete ramp below, but there was no evidence as to the precise position where he was found, so it is impossible to say precisely from which point on the roof he fell.

In those circumstances, her husband being dead, the plaintiff brought this claim, basing it on common law negligence and breach of reg. 24 and reg. 28 (1) of the

Building (Safety, Health and Welfare) Regulations, 1948 (1).   It was conceded that the building regulations did apply in this case.

Common law negligence and reg. 28 really disappear from the case so far as this court is concerned. The judge found that there was no common law negligence, and that finding is not challenged. Regulation 28, which concerns the duty to keep every working platform free from unnecessary obstruction, also disappears from the case because the judge found that a steel bar (which, according to the plaintiff's case, had been an obstruction and a cause of the accident) was in reality no cause of the accident and had nothing to do with it. Again, the plaintiff does not challenge that finding of the judge.

The real and indeed only point in this appeal turns on whether or not the judge, who found in favour of the widow and awarded her a sum of upwards of £9,000 damages was justified in concluding, as he did, that the defendants were responsible for the plaintiff's husband's death by reason of a breach of reg. 24 (1), which I will now read.

" Guard-rails and toe-boards at working places.—(1) Subject to paras. (3), (4) and (5) of this regulation, every side of a working platform or working place, being a side thereof from which a person is liable to fall a distance of more than six feet six inches, shall be provided with a suitable guard-rail or guard-rails of adequate strength, to a height of at least three feet above the platform or place and above any raised standing place on the platform, and with toe-boards up to a sufficient height being in no case less than eight inches and so placed as to prevent so far as possible the fall of persons, materials and tools from such platform or place."

There was no guard-rail or toe-board along the edge of the wall on which one side of the floor rested. There was a sheer drop of twenty-three feet against which no sort of precaution or safety measure had been provided by the defendants.

The defendants' case is that the plaintiff's husband at the time of the accident was not working at a " working place ". The defendants say that neither the roof as a whole nor any part of it was a " working place " within the meaning of those words in reg. 24, and for this they rely on certain dicta in the House of Lords in *Gill* v. *Donald Humberstone & Co., Ltd.* (2), to which I will presently refer. I would start, however, by first referring to *George Ball & Sons, Ltd.* v. *Sill* (3), which is not reported in the Law Reports or in the All England Law Reports; the best report (although it is a somewhat tenuous one) is in Knight's Local Government Reports. That was a decision of the Divisional Court of the Queen's Bench Division.   In that case men had been working on a flat roof some forty feet above the ground which, like the roof in question, had no protection at all at the sides to prevent anyone falling from it. One of the workmen fell over the side and was seriously injured. The employers were prosecuted for a breach of reg. 24 of the building regulations and convicted. On a Case Stated to the Divisional Court, LORD GODDARD, C.J., in dismissing the appeal, said (4):

" I cannot see why I am not to give the words ' working place ' the ordinary meaning of the English language, that is, a place where work is being done."

A little later he said (4):

" Of course, if he is working, say, in the middle of the roof, or well away from the edges of the roof, and through some extraordinary reason, perhaps owing to a crack in a rafter or something of that sort, he falls, not off the side but through the floor on to a floor below, I do not think the mere fact that there were no guard-rails up round the edge of the roof would make any difference, because failure to put them round the edge of the building would have nothing to do with the particular accident that happened."

---

(1) S.I. 1948 No. 1145.
(3) (1954), 52 L.G.R. 508.
(2) [1963] 3 All E.R. 180.
(4) (1954), 52 L.G.R. at p. 509.

As, however, he was working on that unguarded roof and fell off the edge, LORD GODDARD had no difficulty in coming to the conclusion that there had been a breach of reg. 24, and CASSELS, J., and SLADE, J., agreed with him.

It was pointed out in *Gill* v. *Donald Humberstone & Co., Ltd.* (5) that the definition of a working place given by LORD GODDARD is not an exhaustive one, nor do I think that he intended it to be exhaustive; it was however perfectly sufficient for the purpose of the decision in that case. The House of Lords never suggested in their reference to *George Ball & Sons, Ltd.* v. *Sill* (6) that it had been wrongly decided, nor did they in any way criticise what LORD GODDARD had said save to point out that his definition was not exhaustive. It is obvious in my view that in order for a place to be a " working place " within the meaning of the regulation, it must be a place at which men work. It does not, of course, follow (and in this I entirely agree with counsel for the defendants) that every place at which a man is working is necessarily a " working place " within the meaning of the regulation. Indeed, a man may be working, as the night watchman was in *Field* v. *Perrys (Ealing), Ltd.* (7), in such circumstances that it is impossible to say that he has any " working place " at all within the meaning of reg. 24. In that case the unfortunate night watchman had a roving commission to look after the contents of a very large factory, and DEVLIN, J., held that one could not properly call any part of the factory, or the factory as a whole, the man's " working place ". In the case in the House of Lords to which I have referred (5) the plaintiff failed. He fell off a roof where there were no guard-rails. He was undoubtedly working on the roof, but the House of Lords held that he was not at a " working place " within the meaning of those words in reg. 24 at the time when he met with his accident.

In order to understand the decision in *Gill* v. *Donald Humberstone & Co., Ltd.* (5), it is, I think, necessary to consider its facts. The roof in question was not a flat roof. It was a pitched roof, i.e., a sloping roof. That is a factor of very great importance for reasons to which I will later draw attention. The plaintiff in that case was engaged with another man to paint the roof. The method employed was that one ladder was placed on one side of the roof and another ladder on the other side. They were lashed together, the lashings going over the apex of the roof with the object of preventing the ladders sliding down the sides of the roof. The plaintiff and the other man then proceeded to paint, each standing on one of the ladders, and this afforded them good hand-hold and foot-hold. After they had painted as much as they could from one position, the method adopted was for them momentarily to step off the ladders on the roof, push them along the required distance, then get back on to the ladders and go on painting. The operation was repeated until the painting of the roof was completed. I would emphasise that it took them only a moment to step off the ladders and push them along. The pitch of the roof was slight. It was, however, a large roof and the apex was a good many feet above the eaves. To my mind, the decision of the House of Lords turns very largely on the fact that this was a sloping and not a flat roof and to some extent on the fact that their work did not require the men to stand on the roof any appreciable time.

There is of course a well known rule of construction that, if a statute or regulation is capable of two meanings, one wide and one narrow, the court will adopt the narrow meaning if the wide meaning will lead to a manifest absurdity. If, of course, the provision is capable of only one meaning, that is the meaning which it must be given, however absurd the result, but the courts lean against an absurdity. LORD REID put that perhaps a little more elaborately in this way. He said (8):

" Section 60 of the Factories Act, 1937, empowered the Secretary of State to ' make such special regulations as appear to him to be reasonably practicable and to meet the necessity of the case '. So the Secretary of State, with

(5) [1963] 3 All E.R. 180.   (6) (1954), 52 L.G.R. 508.
(7) [1950] 2 All E.R. 521.   (8) [1963] 3 All E.R. at p. 183.

the wealth of experience and practical knowledge available in his department, must have thought the application of each provision to be reasonably practicable. Of course, difficulties cannot always be foreseen and it may happen that in a particular case the requirements of a regulation are unreasonable or impracticable; but if the language is capable of more than one interpretation, we ought to discard the more natural meaning if it leads to an unreasonable result, and adopt that interpretation which leads to a reasonably practicable result."

LORD DEVLIN said very much the same thing (9).

The question in *Gill* v. *Donald Humberstone & Co., Ltd.* (10) was whether the whole of the roof in question, or some part of it, was a " working place " within the meaning of the regulation. The House of Lords had no difficulty in coming to the conclusion that the answer to that question was " No ", and that as a general rule a sloping roof cannot be within reg. 24, although they did not exclude the possibility that, in some very special circumstances, it might be. The reasons given for that conclusion were as follows. The regulation requires that the railing shall be three feet above the " working platform or working place ". If the regulation applied to the whole of the sloping roof, it would mean that railings would have to be erected rising from the eaves that extended to a height of three feet above the apex of the roof. As more than one of the law lords pointed out, that would be an entirely absurd result. The other possibility was that the part of the roof on which the man was standing at the time of the accident was his " working place ". Nevertheless if a man is standing on a part of the roof near the apex, or somewhere between the apex and the eaves, and that is his working place he is not liable to fall over its sides because it has none over which he could fall. Accordingly reg. 24 could not apply. Moreover, the view expressed in that case that reg. 24 cannot, save in most exceptional circumstances, apply to any part of a sloping roof, was in the opinion of the House supported (if any support were needed) by the fact that there was an entirely separate regulation, viz., reg. 31, designed to deal with sloping roofs; and, if reg. 24 did normally apply to sloping roofs, it was extremely difficult if not impossible, as LORD DEVLIN points out (9), to reconcile the provisions of reg. 31 with the provisions of reg. 24.

I do not consider the decision, nor indeed the dicta, in *Gill* v. *Donald Humberstone & Co., Ltd.* (10), to be in any way inimical to the findings of the judge in this case. One argument that was persuasively advanced by counsel for the defendants was this. He said that reg. 24 referred to a " working platform or working place "; that anyone looking at a platform could see where it started and where it ended, i.e., could see its physical boundaries; and that, in order for any part of a roof to be a " working place " in the context of the regulation, it must have the characteristics of a working platform. In a sense I agree with that proposition. Everything, however, depends on how you define " characteristics of a working platform ". In the instant case I am by no means persuaded that the whole of this roof (which after all was only fifty-two feet by twenty-six feet) was not a " working place ". We know that at least three men were working on the roof, and that the architect and foreman and others came on to the roof in the course of the work to assist in it. I do not think that it would lead to any absurdity or place any undue burden on the defendants to require them to erect railings along the whole length of the supporting wall. Even if the whole roof was not a " working place ", however, I would have no difficulty in coming to the conclusion that that portion of it on which the plaintiff's husband was working at the time that he met with his accident was his " working place ". The fact that the precise boundaries were not marked out, does not seem to me to be of any real consequence. In *Gill* v. *Donald Humberstone & Co., Ltd.* (11), LORD DEVLIN says this:

" If these precautions are necessary on a working platform 6½ feet above the

---

(9) [1963] 3 All E.R. at p. 189.   (10) [1963] 3 All E.R. 180.
(11) [1963] 3 All E.R. at p. 190.

ground, they ought not to be dispensed with simply because an employer finds that instead of erecting a special platform he can use a similar sort of place in the building itself. To such a place the regulation can be applied as sensibly as to a platform. In my judgment in this regulation ' working place ' means and must be restricted to a place similar to a working platform and having the same characteristics."

Before I deal with the latter part of that pronouncement, let me say this. It would, I suppose, have been possible for the defendants to have erected a platform of wood or some other material, and to have placed it over the whole of the roof, or over the part where the men were actually working, and to have moved it along as the work proceeded. If that had been done, and if one of the sides of that platform adjoined the precipice to which I have already referred, no one can doubt but that the men would have been liable to fall over that precipice for a distance of twenty-three feet, and that accordingly there would then have been an obligation on the defendants to erect a guard-rail so as to protect their workman against that obvious danger. It might have been thought desirable to erect such a platform if, for example, the roof had been constructed of a substance which could have been damaged by the men's boots. The defendants, however, did not in the circumstances of this case put up any platform because none was necessary; the roof itself served in place of a platform, and the employers allowed or required their workmen to make use of it as a platform. It seems to me absurd that there should be liability to guard when the men are standing on a platform doing their work, but no liability to guard when the men are standing on the naked roof doing the same work, exposed to precisely the same danger.

Counsel for the defendants says—" that is all very well, but LORD DEVLIN has said (and his words were echoed by LORD HODSON) that the working place must have the same characteristics as a working platform ". As I have already observed, everything depends on what LORD DEVLIN meant by " the same characteristics ". Fortunately, he makes that plain in the passage immediately above that which I have already read. I think that he was there referring to three characteristics. He points out that, when a working platform is erected, it is not for a job that is going to last, for example, less than a minute, but for a job that is going to last an appreciable time. Accordingly, the " working place " must have this characteristic, that it is a place where men are going to work for an appreciable time. It must be remembered that, in the case that LORD DEVLIN was considering, the man stepped off the ladder on to the roof momentarily to push the ladder along so that the place where he stepped did not have the first characteristic of a working platform. It was not a place where the man worked for an appreciable time. In the present case there is nothing to suggest that the place where the deceased man was working was not a place where men worked for an appreciable time. Secondly, LORD DEVLIN said that the platform must be comparatively small in area so that it could be surrounded easily by guard-rails. What is " comparatively small in area " is not perhaps very easy to define; it is rather like the size of a lump of chalk. However, I cannot think that in the circumstances of this case a roof of fifty-two feet by twenty-six feet must be excluded from the category of comparatively small areas, and in any case the actual place at which the deceased was working was a comparatively small area.

Then, thirdly and most importantly, LORD DEVLIN points out that normally a characteristic of a working platform is that it is flat and not sloping, so that one can talk sensibly of a rail having to be at least three feet above it. All those characteristics were characteristics of the place where the dead man was working in this case. I can find nothing, therefore, in the speeches in the House of Lords which could lead me to hold that reg. 24 does not apply.

Before parting with the case I want to mention one other argument advanced by counsel for the defendants, which he made so attractive that at first sight I was nearly persuaded by it. He said that, applying the principle that the regulation ought not to be construed so as to work an absurdity if a sensible meaning can be given to it, this regulation would involve an absurdity if it applied to the facts of the present case for the following reason. This roof was advancing, and there was a chasm over the leading edge; whilst it is quite true that there would have been no difficulty in erecting a barrier to protect the men against the risk of falling over the side of the brick wall, how could one rail off the chasm in front of the leading edge? Counsel said that ex hypothesi this could not be done, because that was the place where men were working and laying joists. Accordingly, in as much as reg. 24 requires every side of a working place from which a man is liable to fall to be guarded by a rail, on the plaintiff's construction of reg. 24 (if it is applied here), it would be requiring an impossibility, viz., a guard-rail to be erected along the leading edge of the roof.

A convincing answer to that point, however, has been given by counsel for the plaintiff. First, he says that, although counsel for the defendants took this point in his final speech before the judge, precious little was heard of it during the course of the trial, and no real evidence was led in respect of it. He says: " For all we know, when the joists were being man-handled into position, it may be that that was done from a platform erected below." He says, I think rightly, that there is no evidence that there was no such platform, and no evidence that the drop over the leading edge was more than six feet six inches; and, if the defendants wished to rely on the argument that it would be absurd to apply the regulation to the facts of the case, the onus must be on them to establish what the facts were which made the application of the regulation absurd. There is, however, another answer to which counsel for the plaintiff also referred. He said that no such absurdity could arise because there need not have been, and may never have been, any risk of the men falling over the leading edge; a very simple precaution could and may have been taken of resting wooden planks along or beyond the leading edge. Although there is no evidence about it, it looks from the photographs that this may well have been done, because one sees from a photograph that just beyond the point to which the roof had advanced, there is in fact a wooden plank. It was not, however, for the plaintiff to establish this. It was in my judgment for the defendants to establish facts which would make the application of the regulation impracticable in this particular case, and this in my view they have failed to do.

For these reasons, I have come to the conclusion that the decision arrived at by the judge is unassailable, and I would dismiss the appeal.

WILLMER, L.J.: I have reached the same conclusion. We have had the advantage of listening to a most persuasive argument presented to us by counsel for the defendants in support of the appeal, but I am bound to say that in the event I have not been persuaded. He put in the forefront of his argument the submission that the decision of the House of Lords in *Gill* v. *Donald Humberstone & Co., Ltd.* (12), virtually compelled us to hold that this flat roof on which the deceased man was working could not be regarded as a " working place " within the meaning of reg. 24 (1) of the Building (Safety, Health and Welfare) Regulations, 1948.

The case of *Gill* v. *Donald Humberstone & Co., Ltd.* (12) was about a roof of a very different kind from that which we have in the present case. It was a sloping roof. The workman concerned, who had been working on a ladder near the apex of the sloping roof, as SALMON, L.J., has described, had occasion to step off the ladder on to the sloping roof in order to move the ladder further along. It was against that background that the House of Lords was called on to consider whether reg. 24 (1) applied. Looking at the facts of the case, and exercising some degree of common sense about it, it does not seem to me to be a very surprising result that the House of Lords decided that reg. 24 (1) had no application to such a case as that. It is fair to say, however, that the members of the House took the opportunity to consider and to express their views on what does and what does not

(12) [1963] 3 All E.R. 180.

constitute a " working place " within the meaning of this regulation. It has been argued that the views expressed by their lordships in those passages of their speeches show that a roof such as we have in the present case could not possibly be regarded as a " working place " to which the regulation applies. I am afraid that I do not agree with that submission. All that their lordships in effect said was that in this context a working place must have the same sort of characteristics as a working platform. LORD EVERSHED went perhaps into rather more detail, as did LORD DEVLIN. Both of them indicated that the expression " working place " can apply only to a limited and easily defined area. Both of them expressed the view that it could be applied only to an area which was to be used for work for an appreciable period of time.

It has been contended that the roof with which we are concerned in this case did not satisfy those conditions, and that it did not have " similar characteristics " to a working platform. The essential characteristics of a working platform, I apprehend, are that it must normally be flat and level, which this roof certainly was. It is said that the expression " working place " could not be regarded as applying to the whole of this roof, covering as it did an area said to be some 1,300 square feet. That, of course, sounds a very large area, but it was not so very large, being only some fifty feet odd in length and twenty feet odd in width. It can fairly be said to satisfy LORD EVERSHED's description of a limited and defined area. It was certainly a place in which the deceased man, and the other men with whom he was working, were called on to work for an appreciable period of time.

I do not, therefore, agree with the submission that the various dicta of the members of the House of Lords in that case are inconsistent with the view at which the judge arrived in this case, viz., that reg. 24 (1) applied to the roof in question here. I do not think that its mere size is any reason for coming to the conclusion that this flat roof was not a " working place ". I make that observation bearing in mind that the obligation to fit a guard-rail or guard-rails arises only in relation to any side of the working place from which a man is liable to fall the prescribed distance. It is not as if the whole of the roof necessarily had to be surrounded by a guard-rail, but only such part as gave rise to the risk of falling. I do not think, therefore, that the submission of counsel for the defendants as to the effect of the decision of the House of Lords precludes us from upholding the judge's view in this case.

The case nearest to this on the facts is that to which SALMON, L.J., has referred, viz., *George Ball & Sons, Ltd.* v. *Sill* (13), which was indeed a case about a flat roof. In that case LORD GODDARD, C.J., expressed the view that the expression " working place " in reg. 24 (1) means no more than a place where work is being done. It has been urged on us that that view was overruled by this court in the case of *Gill* v. *Donald Humberstone & Co., Ltd.* (14), to which I have already referred. That I do not think is quite correct; at least, the learned reporter did not think that the decision had been overruled. What this court appears to have done in *Gill* v. *Donald Humberstone & Co., Ltd.* (14) was to distinguish the case of *George Ball & Sons, Ltd.* v. *Sill* (13), which they could readily do bearing in mind that they were dealing with a sloping roof, whereas the case of *George Ball & Sons, Ltd.* v. *Sill* (13) dealt with a flat roof. It is to be observed, however, that, whatever this court may have said about *George Ball & Sons, Ltd.* v. *Sill* (13), three of the members of the House of Lords, when *Gill* v. *Donald Humberstone & Co., Ltd.* (14) reached the House, quoted and accepted as correct that which LORD GODDARD had said in *George Ball & Sons, Ltd.* v. *Sill* (13). The only quali- fication that they made was that it was not to be regarded as an exhaustive definition. As SALMON, L.J., has pointed out, it obviously cannot be considered as an exhaustive definition as, for instance, in the case of the night watchman,

---

(13) (1954), 52 L.G.R. 508.
(14) [1963] 3 All E.R. 180.

whose duties might take him to any and every part of a very large factory. It could not be said that every part of the factory was part of his " working place ", for such a result would be manifestly absurd. Subject to that, however, I see no reason to quarrel either with the decision in *George Ball & Sons, Ltd.* v. *Sill* (15), or with the observation of LORD GODDARD to which I have made reference.

I think that the applicability or otherwise of reg. 24 (1) to the facts of this case can be tested in this way, as has already been suggested by SALMON, L.J. Suppose for the sake of argument, that, instead of allowing these men to work on the naked concrete roof which had been laid, the employers had seen fit to overlay it with a wooden platform to enable the men to continue their work. I apprehend that it could not be doubted that such a platform would come within reg. 24 (1) in this sense, that, if there was a side from which a man was liable to fall for a distance of more than six feet six inches, it would have to be guarded by a guard-rail or guard-rails. Clearly there was such a side in the present case. If such a platform would call for the provision of guard-rails on the open side from which the deceased man fell, it is difficult to understand why, if no such platform is erected and men work on the flat roof itself, any different considerations should apply. By using the flat roof the men would be making use of a part of the building which, to use the expression used by LORD REID in *Gill* v. *Donald Humberstone & Co., Ltd.* (16), itself furnished a ready-made platform. It seems to me that it would be quite absurd to say that reg. 24 (1) would apply if a wooden platform was erected on top of the concrete joists, but would not apply if the men were allowed to work simply on the level surface of the roof without the provision of a platform above it.

For those reasons I am not persuaded by the argument that reg. 24 (1) had no application to the facts of this case, and in my judgment it has not been shown that the judge came to a wrong conclusion. I would accordingly dismiss the appeal.

HARMAN, L.J.: I agree with the judge's conclusions. Here was a case where men were required to work on the top of a nine-inch brick wall with a drop of twenty-three feet immediately below it, and they were bound to work at the very edge of it. One of them said that the way to do the work was to put one foot on the beam on the edge of the building and one foot on the wall, and then bend down to position the breeze blocks. In my view it would be a lamentable conclusion to reach that, if a man, without thought on his part, merely by accident fell over this precipice, no remedy could be had from the law. The judge held that there was no common law liability, and there is no appeal from that finding. I must say, however, that I felt some regret in the course of the hearing before us that it was not possible to rely on the want of care for the safety of their workmen shown by these employers.

However that may be, there being no such remedy, the workman must fall back on the regulations, and he appeals to reg. 24. We are told that that is not open either to the judge or to us because of the decision in *Gill* v. *Donald Humberstone & Co., Ltd.* (17) in the House of Lords; but, when that case is steadily confronted, it will be seen to have nothing to do with the present case. That was a case of reg. 31 or nothing. Regulation 31 deals with roof work; but the employee in *Gill's* case (17) could not bring himself within reg. 31, partly owing to the low pitch of the roof, so he had recourse to reg. 24, and the decision of this court (to which I was a party) as of their lordship's House was that reg. 24 would not do. That was not a case within reg. 24, and LORD REID explained why (18). In that case the only place where there could be a guard-rail was at the eave of the roof, which was a long way from the apex of the roof, to which the workmen had to go in order to shift the ladders with which they were doing the painting and from the place where the deceased man lost his hold and slipped. It would have been quite impossible in that case to have a guard-rail above the ridge of

---

(15) (1954), 52 L.G.R. 508.

(17) [1963] 3 All E.R. 180.

(16) [1963] 3 All E.R. at p. 183, letter A.

(18) [1963] 3 All E.R. at p. 183.

the roof, for it could start only at the eave some way below it. If Latinity were still in fashion, one would be prompted to say that decisions must be looked at secundum subjectam materiam.

In my judgment *Gill's* case (19) on its facts has really nothing at all to do with the facts of this case. In the same case LORD DEVLIN said (20) that there was no " working place " to which the regulation applied, and I think that that is the real answer to it. I can see no difficulty in holding that the whole of the roof here was a working place. It is very much less in area than that which was held to be the working place in *George Ball & Sons, Ltd.* v. *Sill* (21). I can see no reason why that part of it from which a man is likely to fall should not have a guard-rail. According to the evidence there would be no difficulty in providing one, although one of the workmen said (as workmen will say) that it would be inconvenient, as it might well be. The learned judge sought to distinguish *Gill* v. *Donald Humberstone & Co., Ltd.* (19) on the ground that that was a decision under reg. 31. In that he was mistaken. That case did not come under reg. 31; it was because reg. 31 did not apply that recourse was had to reg. 24, and their lordships decided that it was not a reg. 24 case.

One other point was taken by counsel for the defendants, and that was that the working place cannot be the place itself which is being brought into being by the work. In other words, while the roof is being made, one cannot say that the roof when half made is itself a working place. I do not accept that argument. In *Curran* v. *William Neill & Son (St. Helens), Ltd.* (22) it was held that the gutter which was itself being used as a support for making its own extension was yet a working place, and no one argued the contrary. The claim there failed, not because of its not being a working place, but because the absence of a guard-rail and the happening of the accident were not connected. I feel no difficulty, therefore, in saying that the roof on which these men were working was itself their working place, and it seems to me to be a sufficiently defined area to bring the case within the words used in their lordships' House. Consequently I see no obstacle preventing our coming to the conclusion at which I have myself arrived with satisfaction, viz., that this appeal fails.

Appeal dismissed.

Solicitors: *Norton, Rose, Botterell & Roche*, agents for *Weightman, Pedder & Co.*, Liverpool (for the defendants); *E. R. Hoskinson, Montgomery & Co.*, Liverpool (for the plaintiff).

[*Reported by* F. A. AMIES, ESQ., *Barrister-at-Law.*]

---

(19) [1963] 3 All E.R. 180.   (20) [1963] 3 All E.R. at p. 190.
(21) (1954), 52 L.G.R. 508.   (22) [1961] 3 All E.R. 108.

Re A DEBTOR (No. 17 of 1966).

[CHANCERY DIVISION (Stamp and Goff, JJ.), January 23, February 5, 1967.]

*Bankruptcy—Adjudication—Debtor's petition—Annulment of adjudication—
Damages of £2,400 awarded against infant appellant—Instalment order in
county court for payment of 25s. a week—Debtor unable to pay £2,400 but
able to pay 25s. a week and such other debts as he had—Only debts presently
payable considered in determining inability to pay debts—Annulment of
receiving order and adjudication—Bankruptcy Act, 1914 (4 & 5 Geo. 5 c. 59),
s. 6, s. 29 (1).*

As the result of being shot in the eye by an air gun held by the appellant,
the respondent lost the sight of that eye. The respondent brought an action
in the Queen's Bench Division and recovered judgment for £2,400 damages.
Both parties were infants. By consent an order was made in Reading county
court, to implement the Queen's Bench Division's order, for payment of
weekly instalments of 25s. into that court. The appellant was able to pay
all his debts presently payable, on the footing that only 25s. weekly was payable for the judgment debt. The appellant presented a petition in bankruptcy;
a receiving order was made against him and he was adjudicated bankrupt
pursuant to s. 6* of the Bankruptcy Act, 1914. On the respondent's application, pursuant to s. 29 (1)† of the Act of 1914, the receiving order was rescinded
and the adjudication was annulled on the ground that the petition was an
abuse of the process of the court.

Held: the adjudication had been rightly annulled for the following
reasons—

(i) although the judgment for £2,400 created a debt for that amount, yet,
after the instalment order was made only the instalments as they fell due
were presently payable, and, since only debts presently payable had to be
considered in determining whether there was inability to pay debts for the
purposes of s. 6 of the Bankruptcy Act, 1914, the appellant had not shown
inability to pay his debts (see p. 670, letter I, and p. 671, letter A, post); and

(ii) the appellant in the circumstances had no reasonable grounds for
alleging that he was unable to pay his debts and that he should have been
adjudicated bankrupt to protect him against liability to committal or other
harassment, since he was already protected by the instalment order (see p. 671,
letter F, and p. 672, letter B, post).

Dictum of JAMES, L.J., in *Re European Life Assurance Society* ((1869),
L.R. 9 Eq. 122) followed.

Dictum of SIR RAYMOND EVERSHED, M.R., in *Re Dunn (a Bankrupt)*,
Ex p. Official Receiver v. Dunn ([1949] 2 All E.R. at p. 392) distinguished.

Re Hancock, Ex p. Hillearys ([1904] 1 K.B. 585) and *Re Painter* ([1895]
1 Q.B. 85) distinguished.

Appeal dismissed.

[As to requisites for debtor's petition, see 2 HALSBURY'S LAWS (3rd Edn.)
300, 301, paras. 571-573; and for cases on the subject, see 4 DIGEST (Repl.)
146, 147, *1307-1316*.

For the Bankruptcy Act, 1914, s. 6, s. 29, see 2 HALSBURY'S STATUTES (2nd
Edn.) 335, 362.]

Cases referred to:

Dunn (a Bankrupt), Re, Ex p. Official Receiver v. Dunn, [1949] 2 All E.R. 388;
[1949] Ch. 640; [1949] L.J.R. 1354; 4 Digest (Repl.) 196, *1316*.
European Life Assurance Society, Re, (1869), L.R. 9 Eq. 122; 39 L.J.Ch.
324; 10 Digest (Repl.) 853, *5620*.

---

* Section 6 is set out at p. 670, letter B, post.
† Section 29, so far as material, is set out at p. 670, letters D and E, post.

Hancock, Re, Ex p. Hillearys, [1904] 1 K.B. 585; 73 L.J.K.B. 245; 90 L.T. 389; 4 Digest (Repl.) 146, *1309.*

Painter, Re, Ex p. Painter, [1895] 1 Q.B. 85; 64 L.J.Q.B. 22; 71 L.T. 581; 4 Digest (Repl.) 146, *1311.*

Appeal.

This was an appeal by notice dated Dec. 13, 1966, by the appellant Brian Ronald Josey, an infant, from the order of the registrar at Reading county court made on Nov. 29, 1966, whereby it was ordered that the adjudication in bankruptcy of the appellant be annulled; that the receiving order be rescinded; that the petition be dismissed and that the entries in the land charges register be vacated. The appellant applied that the order be set aside. The respondent was Tony Allen an infant appearing by his father and next friend, Norman Goodwin Allen.

The facts are set out in the judgment of the court.

A. L. Figgis for the appellant.
Harry Woolf for the respondent.

Cur. adv. vult.

Feb. 6.   **GOFF, J.,** read the following judgment of the court: The facts in this case are short and simple. As the result of being shot in the eye by an air gun held by the appellant Brian Ronald Josey the respondent Tony Allen unhappily lost the sight of that eye. The respondent brought an action in the Queen's Bench Division of this court and on Feb. 11, 1966, on an admission of liability recovered judgment for £2,400 damages (1). Both parties were and still are infants.

There was originally some error or inadequacy in the drawing up of the order and it was amended (2) on Oct. 13, 1966, under the slip rule after the presentation of the bankruptcy petition on which the present case arises. Counsel for the appellant has, however, conceded, and we would in any event have held, that we must decide this case on the footing that the correct order and not the wrong order was in force at all material times.

Arrangements were made for bringing the administrative machinery of the county court into operation to implement the Queen's Bench order and by consent an order was made in the Reading county court on Mar. 8, 1966, for payment of the weekly instalments of 25s. into that court. The appellant did not in fact make any payment to the county court, but he appears to have put the amount of the instalments or some part thereof aside as on adjudication he paid £10 to the Official Receiver.

On Apr. 12, 1966, on the advice of his solicitors the appellant presented his own petition in bankruptcy and on the same day a receiving order was made against him and also he was adjudicated bankrupt. In his statement of affairs

---

(1) After, having delivered judgment assessing damages, liability not being disputed, WIDGERY, J., said: " There will be judgment for the plaintiff for £2,400 with costs, but with the further order that no action shall be taken to enforce the judgment without the leave of the court . . . In this case I think on balance that the order should be one for £1 5s. a week, but I am going to give either party liberty to apply, because it is clearly possible that when [the appellant] grows up and establishes himself in life he will be able to pay larger instalments than this and perhaps dispose of his liability more quickly."

(2) The order of the Queen's Bench Division, dated Feb. 11, 1966, as amended pursuant to the order of WIDGERY, J., given on Oct. 13, 1966, provided, so far as material, as follows:—" IT IS THIS DAY ADJUDGED that [the respondent] recover from [the appellant] £2,400 and costs to be taxed, AND IT IS ORDERED that [the appellant] do have no present liability for the payment of such costs and payment thereof be not enforced without leave of the court AND IT IS FURTHER ORDERED that execution herein be stayed pending a further direction by WIDGERY, J. AND IT IS FURTHER ORDERED that the amount of the said judgment be paid to the Reading County Court by instalments of £1 5s. per week. AND IT IS FURTHER ORDERED that there be liberty to apply regarding stay of execution and as regards any variations of the said instalments . . .".

the appellant gave as his debts the £2,400 a further £34 0s. 9d. due for clothing in fact purchased through a clothing club, and £8 balance due in respect of a Moped. His assets were £10 cash in hand and £10, the estimated value of the moped. There was some question whether the Moped ought to be included at all, but it is immaterial as the asset and liability items in that regard are virtually self cancelling. The petition was presented and the appellant was adjudicated bankrupt pursuant to s. 6 of the Bankruptcy Act, 1914, which provides:

" (1) A debtor's petition shall allege that the debtor is unable to pay his debts, and the presentation thereof shall be deemed an act of bankruptcy within the previous filing by the debtor of any declaration of inability to pay his debts, and the court shall thereupon make a receiving order.

" (2) a debtor's petition shall not, after presentment, be withdrawn without the leave of the court."

Section 29 of the Bankruptcy Act, 1914, provides:

" (1) Where in the opinion of the court a debtor ought not to have been adjudged bankrupt, or where it is proved to the satisfaction of the court that the debts of the bankrupt are paid in full, the court may, on the application of any person interested, by order annul the adjudication.

" (2) Where an adjudication is annulled under this section, all sales and dispositions of property and payments duly made, and all acts theretofore done, by the official receiver, trustee, or other person acting under their authority, or by the court, shall be valid, but the property of the debtor who was adjudged bankrupt shall vest in such person as the court may appoint, or, in default of such appointment, revert to the debtor for all his estate or interest therein on such terms and subject to such conditions, if any, as the court may declare by order."

Pursuant to s. 29 of the Act of 1914 the respondent on July 28, 1966, applied to the registrar of the county court for annulment of the adjudication and rescission of the receiving order on the ground that the petition was an abuse of the process of the court and the appellant ought not to have been adjudged bankrupt. The registrar reserved his judgment and on Nov. 29 he handed out a written judgment whereby he acceded to the application. His order is dated Nov. 22, 1966, and in the circumstances there might have been some question as to the true date, but it is immaterial as this appeal was commenced in due time on any showing.

The appellant now appeals from the registrar's order. On his behalf counsel submitted that the judgment of WIDGERY, J., created a judgment debt in the full sum of £2,400 which the appellant was, and is, manifestly unable to pay, and that, therefore, he was clearly entitled to present his petition under s. 6 and the orders thereon were rightly made.

In our judgment however that short solution of the problem is not tenable. We agree that the judgment created a present debt of £2,400 but payable in future save only as to instalments of the weekly sum of 25s. from time to time actually accrued due and unpaid; and in our judgment on the true construction of s. 6 of the Bankruptcy Act, 1914, it is only debts presently payable which have to be considered for the purpose of determining inability to pay debts. Any other view would lead to absurdities. A man is not unable to pay his debts because at some future time he will have to pay a debt which he would be unable to meet if it was presently payable; and if authority were needed for that proposition it is to be found in the judgment of JAMES, L.J., in *Re European Life Assurance Society* (3) where a section similar to s. 6 was considered. We are not overlooking SIR RAYMOND EVERSHED, M.R.'s reference to prospective liability in *Re Dunn*, (*a Bankrupt*), *Ex p. Official Receiver* v. *Dunn* (4), but in our view what his lordship had in mind was not a debt payable in the future, or which might arise in the future, but a present debt not yet finally established or quantified.

(3) (1869), L.R. 9 Eq. 122.
(4) [1949] 2 All E.R. 388 at p. 392; [1949] Ch. 640 at p. 646.

Now it was clearly shown that the appellant could pay all his debts presently payable including the clothing club debt which was itself payable by instalments, and he conceded this in his evidence before the registrar. True he received an increase in pay of £1 per week in September, 1966, but, as we have said, he had already saved £10 by the time of the receiving order and he made payments to the Official Receiver from June 27, 1966.

Counsel for the appellant then said alternatively that there is no power, whether under the express terms of s. 29, or under any inherent jurisdiction, to annul adjudication or rescind the receiving order save where the adjudication order ought not to have been made or the presentation of the petition was an abuse of the process of the court.

As to the first limb of this argument he pointed out the distinction between a creditor's petition under s. 5, where the necessary allegations have to be proved, and the court has a discretion whether or not to make an order, and a debtor's petition under s. 6 where proof is not required and the section is mandatory. He said, that even if the appellant, being indeed able to pay his debts presently payable was on the true construction of s. 6 not within it, still he had reasonable grounds for alleging that he was unable to pay his debts, as he had been advised by his solicitors that the whole debt of £2,400 was relevant for this purpose and that therefore the case did not fall within s. 29.

In support of this argument counsel for the appellant relied strongly on the judgment of DENNING, L.J., in *Re Dunn* (5), and pointed out that SIR RAYMOND EVERSHED, M.R., also referred to a debtor's being entitled to go bankrupt to protect himself against possibilities (6); but these judgments must be read in their context. In that case the Court of Appeal had to deal with a claim, which at the date of the petition had not been established, and indeed in the result never was, but which was not demonstrably false, and which if valid at all created a present debt in every sense of the term. In the present case, however, there has never been any question about the facts. The only element of uncertainty lay in the construction of s. 6. We having now decided that the only relevant debts were those presently payable, it follows that the appellant had no reasonable grounds for alleging that he was unable to pay his debts and that the adjudication order ought not to have been made. He himself said in his evidence that when he presented the petition under s. 6 he understood that all he had to pay was £1 5s. a week and if he did this he would be all right and free from enforcement. The mistaken belief of his solicitors as to the true construction of the Act of 1914 cannot alter his rights or entitle him to hold an order wrongly made.

On the second limb counsel for the appellant relied on *Re Painter, Ex p. Painter* (7), and the decision of the Court of Appeal in *Re Hancock, Ex p. Hillearys* (8). The registrar sought to distinguish those cases on the ground that the original judgment was unqualified so that despite the subsequent instalment order the balance of the judgment was enforceable by any means other than committal. In our judgment that was an error, because an instalment order made on a judgment summons stays execution for the balance of the debt. *Re Painter* (7) and *Re Hancock* (8) are, however, clearly distinguishable from the present case on quite a different ground: for in none of the judgments in those cases was it considered—far less held—that a man was unable to pay his debts merely because there was a debt payable by him in future which he could not presently meet. In *Re Painter* (7) it is clear that the debtor was unable to pay even the instalments, since he had nothing but an inalienable pension so that he was unable to pay his debts presently payable. It is possible that in *Re Hancock* (8) he could have paid those, and an argument that the order was bad on that ground was foreshadowed in the notice of motion (9), but in fact it was never developed, and the point is nowhere reflected in the judgments.

(5) [1949] 2 All E.R. at p. 392; [1949] Ch. at p. 648.
(6) [1949] 2 All E.R. at p. 392, letters F, G; [1949] Ch. at p. 647.
(7) [1895] 1 Q.B. 85.   (8) [1904] 1 K.B. 585.   (9) [1904] 1 K.B. at p. 587.

The ratio decidendi of those cases was that the debtor was entitled to use the machinery of the Bankruptcy Act for his own purpose so as to shield himself from further liability to committal or other harassment. In our judgment those cases are clearly distinguishable on the facts and the points argued since here the appellant is and always has been fully protected by the terms of the original order.

It follows in our judgment that the presentation of the petition was an abuse of the process of the court, and the receiving order and adjudication ought not to have been made, and for these reasons the appeal is dismissed.

As both parties are legally aided there will be the usual taxation under the Act of 1914 of their costs, and we will make an order that the appellant do pay the respondent's party and party costs of this appeal but that he is to have no present liability for the payment of such costs and that payment thereof is not to be enforced without the leave of the court.

Appeal dismissed.

Solicitors: *Doyle, Devonshire & Co.*, agents for *Denis Berry & Co.*, Reading (for the appellant); *Richard Seymour, Aram & Co.*, Reading (for the respondent).

[*Reported by* JENIFER SANDELL, *Barrister-at-Law.*]

THE MIRAFLORES AND THE ABADESA.

OWNERS OF THE STEAM TANKER MIRAFLORES *v.* OWNERS OF THE STEAM TANKER GEORGE LIVANOS AND OTHERS

[HOUSE OF LORDS (Lord Reid, Lord Morris of Borth-y-Gest, Lord Hodson, Lord Pearce and Lord Wilberforce, assisted by Captain E. V. St. J. Morgan and Captain R. J. Galpin, nautical assessors), November 23, 24, 28, 29, 30, 1966, February 16, 1967.]

Shipping—Collision—Apportionment of liability—Two ships in collision—Third ship damaged in taking action to avoid colliding ships—Contribution to damage suffered by third ship—Method of apportionment of liability—Maritime Conventions Act, 1911 (1 & 2 Geo. 5 c. 57), s. 1 (1).

The Abadesa, proceeding against the current in the river Scheldt, and the Miraflores, approaching from the opposite direction, came into collision. The liability for the collision was apportioned as to two-thirds to the Abadesa and one-third to the Miraflores. Before the collision the Miraflores had sheered to starboard and then to port. The George Livanos, following the Miraflores, was negligently dilatory in taking action to avoid the two ships and, if she had been skilfully handled, could have avoided grounding. In an action by the George Livanos against the other two ships for damage suffered by grounding, which action was tried with the collision action between the Abadesa and the Miraflores, the trial judge treated the negligence leading to the collision as one unit and the negligence of the George Livanos as another and, finding it impossible to distinguish between the degree of fault of each of those units, he held the George Livanos to be fifty per cent. to blame, and gave judgment against the Abadesa for one-third and against the Miraflores for one-sixth of the damage sustained by the George Livanos.

Held: (i) (per LORD PEARCE, LORD REID and LORD HODSON concurring, and per LORD MORRIS OF BORTH-Y-GEST) the liability of each vessel involved must be assessed by comparison of her fault separately with the fault of each of the other vessels involved, but by treating the negligence of the Abadesa and of the Miraflores as one unit the trial judge had not weighed the negligence of the Abadesa against that of the George Livanos; accordingly (LORD MORRIS OF BORTH-Y-GEST and LORD WILBERFORCE dubitante) it was open to the appellate court to re-apportion the liability (see p. 675, letter I, p. 676, letters D, F and I, p. 679, letter A, p. 680, letter G, and p. 682, letter E, post).

Dictum of LORD PEARCE at 678 applied in FITZGERALD v LANE [1987] 2 All ER 455

Dictum of LORD PEARCE at 677 disapproved in FITZGERALD v LANE [1988] 2 All ER 961

Dictum of WILLMER, J., in *The Panther and The Ericbank* ([1957] 1 All E.R. at p. 648) disapproved.

(ii) there was no justification for altering the apportionment made by the trial judge as between the Abadesa and the Miraflores with regard to the damage but, in all the circumstances, the liability of the George Livanos in relation to the damage for grounding should not exceed that of the Abadesa, and the liability for grounding should accordingly be apportioned as to two-fifths to the Abadesa, two-fifths to the George Livanos and one-fifth to the Miraflores (see p. 676, letters H and I, p. 680, letters H and I, and p. 682, letter G, post).

Decision of the COURT OF APPEAL ([1966] 1 All E.R. 553) affirmed as to (i) and varied as to (ii).

[As to the rule of division of loss in proportion to fault, see 35 HALSBURY'S LAWS (3rd Edn.) 696-698, para. 1047; and for cases on the subject, see 42 DIGEST (Repl.) 912, 913, *7081-7086*, 915, 916, *7098-7107*.

For the Maritime Conventions Act, 1911, s. 1, see 23 HALSBURY'S STATUTES (2nd Edn.) 830.

For the Law Reform (Contributory Negligence) Act, 1945, s. 1, see 17 HALSBURY'S STATUTES (2nd Edn.) 12.]

Cases referred to:

British Fame (Owners) v. *MacGregor (Owners)*, *The MacGregor*, [1943] 1 All E.R. 33; [1943] A.C. 197; 112 L.J.P. 6; 168 L.T. 193; 42 Digest (Repl.) 913, *7085*.

Panther, The, and The Ericbank, [1957] 1 All E.R. 641; [1957] P. 143; [1957] 2 W.L.R. 432; 42 Digest (Repl.) 927, *7194*.

Appeal.

This was an appeal by the owners of the steam tanker Miraflores from a judgment of the Court of Appeal (DANCKWERTS and WINN, L.JJ., WILLMER, L.J., dissenting) dated Dec. 13, 1965 and reported [1966] 1 All E.R. 553, allowing an appeal by the first respondents, the owners of the steam tanker George Livanos and others, from a judgment of HEWSON, J., dated July 15, 1965, in a grounding action against the appellants and the second respondents, the owners of the steam tanker Abadesa.

The owners of the Miraflores brought an action (the collision action) against the owners of the Abadesa for damage suffered by collision. The owners of the George Livanos brought an action (the grounding action) against both the owners of the Miraflores and the owners of the Abadesa. These two actions were tried together before HEWSON, J. His approach and decision are concisely stated at p. 674, letters A to C, post). On appeal to the Court of Appeal in the grounding action the " unit approach " that he had adopted was held to have been wrong in principle, and liability was re-assessed by apportioning the blame as follows—to the Abadesa forty-five per cent., to the Miraflores thirty per cent., and to the George Livanos twenty-five per cent.

Mark Littman, Q.C., and *J. Franklin Willmer* for the appellants.

J. V. Naisby, Q.C., and *B. C. Sheen* for the first respondents.

Waldo Porgess, Q.C., and *James Rochford* for the second respondents.

LORD REID: My Lords, I have read the speech of my noble and learned friend, LORD PEARCE. I agree with it and I cannot usefully add to it. I, therefore, move that the appeal be allowed and that the proportion of liability should be held to be assessed at two-fifths for the Abadesa, two-fifths for the George Livanos and one-fifth for the Miraflores.

LORD MORRIS OF BORTH-Y-GEST: My Lords, there were two actions before the learned judge, and it was both convenient and desirable to try them together. The learned judge heard them over a period of six days.

He was assisted by two of the Elder Brethren of the Trinity Corporation. He delivered a judgment in which he recorded his conclusions of fact comprehensively and with great care and clarity. So far as concerns the action brought by the George Livanos his conclusion was that the damage in question in that action was occasioned by the fault or default of the vessel herself and by the fault or default of the Miraflores and by the fault or default of the Abadesa. In this House no one has sought to challenge that conclusion. The further conclusion of the learned judge was that the Miraflores should be condemned in one-sixth of the first respondents' damages as assessed and that the Abadesa should be condemned in one-third of such damages. The remaining half of the damages were held not to be recoverable by the George Livanos. That was for the reason that the learned judge held that the George Livanos was herself half to blame for her own misfortune. On appeal to the Court of Appeal (1) it was sought to vary the proportions of the apportionment of liability. An appellate court will be very slow to interfere with the decision of a judge on such a matter. The speech of LORD WRIGHT in *British Fame* (*Owners*) v. *MacGregor* (*Owners*), *The MacGregor* (2) emphasises that there would have to be a very strong case to justify any review of apportionment if an appellate court accepted the same view of the law and the facts as that taken by the learned judge. In the present case it was urged in a six day hearing in the Court of Appeal (1) (a) that the learned judge had been wrong in some of his conclusions in regard to fault and (b) that the learned judge erred in law in his approach to the question of apportionment. In his very careful judgment WILLMER, L.J. (3), fully reviewed all the facts and came to the conclusion that there was " no ground for holding that the learned judge took a wrong view of the facts of the case ". WINN, L.J. (with whose judgment DANCKWERTS, L.J. (4) expressed agreement) said (5) that he did not " entertain any markedly different view of ultimate significance on any question of fact " from those expressed by WILLMER, L.J. (6). On an acceptance, therefore, of the facts as found and as related in the judgments of the learned judge and of WILLMER, L.J. (7), the question arises whether the apportionment of the learned judge can be assailed as having been based on error of law in approach.

One view expressed in the Court of Appeal (1) was that a method of apportionment should be adopted which would achieve an assessment in respect of each ship of the overall responsibility for the occurrence of the double event of the collision and the partially consequential grounding. I do not agree with this view. In the action brought by the George Livanos the investigation concerns only the damage or loss to that vessel and it only becomes necessary to enquire as to the measure of the fault of each one of the three vessels in causing that damage or loss to that vessel.

It is to be observed that the assessors in the Court of Appeal (1) were of opinion (i) that as the George Livanos approached the area near No. 66 buoy it was not necessary for her to continue with engines at half speed; (ii) that she should have observed the sheer to starboard of the Miraflores; (iii) that she should then have stopped engines and gone astern if necessary; (iv) that had she done so and been handled skilfully grounding could have been avoided; (v) that when the Miraflores was seen to sheer to port the George Livanos should have gone full astern and let go both anchors. We addressed two questions to our assessors. Those questions with their answers were as follows:—1. Question: When Miraflores was seen to sheer to port, bearing in mind that the Caltex Manila and the Abadesa were seen to be approaching, what action by George

(1) [1966] 1 All E.R. 553; [1966] P. 18.
(2) [1943] 1 All E.R. 33 at p. 35; [1943] A.C. 197 at p. 201.
(3) [1966] 1 All E.R. at p. 556, letter H; [1966] P. at p. 34.
(4) [1966] 1 All E.R. at p. 559, letter C; [1966] P. at p. 37.
(5) [1966] 1 All E.R. at p. 557, letter F; [1966] P. at p. 35.
(6) [1966] 1 All E.R. at pp. 555-557; [1966] P. at pp. 24-35.
(7) [1966] 1 All E.R. at p. 555; [1966] P. at p. 24.

Livanos was called for? Answer: Full astern on engines. Let go both anchors as soon as sufficient way is off the ship to be able to do so without parting cables. Sound three short blasts. 2. Question: If such actions had been taken by George Livanos, would it have been likely to avoid grounding? Answer: Yes. Provided George Livanos was handled with skill she should have avoided grounding.

In his judgment at the trial the learned judge set out in turn the various ways in which each one of the three ships had been in fault. I need not attempt to summarise his full findings. The sheer to starboard of the Miraflores took place approximately four minutes before the collision. The sheer to port of the Miraflores took place approximately two minutes before the collision. The George Livanos took no action then. She took no action until approximately three minutes after the sheer to port. The learned judge said:

" Had the George Livanos reduced her speed at the first, or even second, sheer of the Miraflores she would have had much more time, opportunity and room to manoeuvre and swing round in safety with her anchors holding, for her speed by the time she dropped her anchors would have been less. In all the circumstances, therefore, I find that in part the George Livanos was the author of her own subsequent misfortune."

He gave consideration to the question whether the George Livanos should fail to recover any part of her damage on the basis that she was the sole author of her misfortune. He rejected that view. He said:

" The negligence of all the three ships is so bound up with each other to produce the ultimate result that it would be unrealistic to find the George Livanos the sole author of her misfortune."

That being so, he was undoubtedly correct in holding that s. 1 of the Maritime Conventions Act, 1911, applied. The question arises, however, whether there was any error of approach in his application of the section and, if so, whether it lead to any wrong result. Section 1 (1) and the first two provisoes are as follows:

" Where, by the fault of two or more vessels, damage or loss is caused to one or more of those vessels, to their cargoes or freight, or to any property on board, the liability to make good the damage or loss shall be in proportion to the degree in which each vessel was in fault: Provided that—(a) if, having regard to all the circumstances of the case, it is not possible to establish different degrees of fault, the liability shall be apportioned equally; and (b) nothing in this section shall operate so as to render any vessel liable for any loss or damage to which her fault has not contributed; ..."

The section calls for enquiry as to fault, and enquiry as to damage or loss, and enquiry as to causation. As applied to the claim made by the George Livanos it became necessary to decide whether the damage or loss to the George Livanos (or her cargo or freight) was *caused by* the fault of two or more vessels. The decision of the learned judge being that such loss or damage was caused by the fault of all three vessels, i.e., the fault of herself, the fault of the Miraflores and the fault of the Abadesa, it followed that the liability to make good the damage or loss had to be " in proportion to the degree in which each vessel was at fault ", which I think means the degree in which the fault of each vessel caused the loss or damage.

Consequently three enquiries were involved. To what extent as a matter of causation did the fault of the Abadesa bring about the grounding of the George Livanos? To what extent as a matter of causation did the fault of the Miraflores bring about the grounding of the George Livanos? To what extent as a matter of causation did the fault of the George Livanos bring about her grounding? The liability to make good the damage or loss caused by the grounding would be in the proportions shown by the answers to those questions.

In dealing with the matter the learned judge spoke of two " units ". It is

important to see what his two " units " were. They were not ships. One " unit "
was " the negligence leading to the collision between the Abadesa and the Miraflores ". The other " unit " was " the negligence of the George Livanos ".
Having taken those two units, the learned judge said that he found it impossible
to distinguish between the degrees of fault between the two units and he said: " It
follows therefore that I find the George Livanos was fifty per cent. to blame
for her own misfortune . . . ". That, as it seems to me, denotes that proviso (a)
was being applied, though it is only fair to say that, having referred to *The
Panther and The Ericbank* (8), the learned judge said: " Therefore I propose
in Action Folio 218 to divide the liability to make good the damage in proportion
to the degree in which each vessel was at fault."

In performing the task directed by s. 1, I think that it may lead to confusion
if it is sought to link the faults of two separate vessels into one " unit ". I think
that it is preferable to follow the wording of the section without introducing the
complication of " units ". As applicable in the present case, once it was established that there was fault in each one of the three vessels and also that the
damage or loss of the George Livanos was caused to some extent by the fault
of each one of the three vessels, then it became necessary to apportion the
liability for the damage or loss by deciding separately in reference to each one
of the three vessels what was the degree in which the fault of each one caused
the damage or loss to the George Livanos. The process necessarily involved
comparisons and it required an assessment of the inter-relation of the respective
faults of the three vessels as contributing causes of the damage or loss. If the
faults of two vessels out of three are being grouped together there may be risk
of making it difficult to make separate comparisons and assessments as between
the three.

For my part I have, however, doubted whether the approach adopted by the
learned judge led in the result to any error of assessment. There is no doubt
that his judgment contains a formidable recital of findings of fault as against
the George Livanos. So also were there formidable conclusions recorded as
against the Abadesa. The learned judge, with his specialised knowledge and
experience, set out to divide the liability to make good the damage in proportion
to the degree in which each vessel was at fault. He could not have been under
any misapprehension as to the conclusion that he recorded and he was, therefore,
well aware that he was attaching considerably more causative potency to the
fault of the George Livanos than to that of the Abadesa. He thought that the
George Livanos was fifty per cent. to blame for her own misfortune. I am
impressed also by the fact that, after his searching review of the case, WILLMER,
L.J. (9) said that he could " see nothing unfair or unjust " in that conclusion.
As, however, I understand that your lordships consider that, in view of the
approach that was adopted, it is desirable that there should be a reassessment I
will not dissent from the view that it should be on the basis that the Abadesa
should be condemned in two-fifths of the damage or loss of the George Livanos
and that the Miraflores should be condemned in one-fifth.

LORD HODSON: My Lords, I have read the speech of my noble and
learned friend, LORD PEARCE, and am in agreement with it.

LORD PEARCE: My Lords, the George Livanos grounded and suffered
damage in the river Scheldt owing to her own fault and that of the Abadesa and
the Miraflores. The Abadesa was proceeding against the current and the Miraflores was approaching the narrows from the opposite direction. The Abadesa,
instead of holding back at the narrows in order to give way to the Miraflores, as
she ought to have done, came on in mid-channel. The Miraflores, owing to a
cross-current, got into difficulties with which (largely owing to the presence of

_____

(8) [1957] 1 All E.R. 641; [1957] P. 143.
(9) [1966] 1 All E.R. at p. 557, letter E; [1966] P. at p. 35.

the Abadesa) she did not deal adequately. First, she sheered to starboard; then she sheered to port and continued to port so that she went right athwart the channel and was hit by the oncoming Abadesa. The George Livanos, following the Miraflores, was thus presented with a difficulty. She was negligently dilatory in appreciating the existence of the difficulty and taking action to avoid it. As a result she grounded.

HEWSON, J., dealt with the two actions together. The first action was concerned with the collision damage and affected only the Abadesa and the Miraflores. After a careful investigation the learned judge apportioned their respective liability at two-thirds and one-third. That decision has not been appealed. In the second action he apportioned the liability for the damage to the George Livanos by grounding. He expressed his conclusion in these words:

"I propose to treat the negligence leading to the collision between the Abadesa and the Miraflores as one unit and the negligence of the George Livanos as the other."

After citing the *Panther and The Ericbank* (10) he continued:

"Therefore I propose . . . to divide the liability to make good the damage in proportion to the degree in which each vessel was at fault. . . . I find it impossible to distinguish between the degrees of fault between the two units. It follows therefore that I find the George Livanos was fifty per cent. to blame for her own misfortune and is entitled to recover the remaining fifty per cent. from the Abadesa and the Miraflores in the proportion of two-thirds and one-third respectively."

What has been called in argument the " unit approach " was held to be wrong and the judgment was set aside by the majority of the Court of Appeal (11) on two grounds. First, it does not accord with s. 1 of the Maritime Conventions Act, 1911, which requires that liability shall be assessed " in proportion to the degree in which each vessel was at fault ". For on the " unit approach " there is not an assessment of the degree in which *each* vessel was at fault. Secondly, and in consequence, the judge assessed at too high a figure the fault of the George Livanos in proportion to the respective individual faults of the Abadesa and the Miraflores.

I agree with the majority of the Court of Appeal (11) that the unit approach is wrong. It was sought to justify it by citation of the judgment in the *Panther and The Ericbank* (10). The facts given in the reports of that case do not show with precision the exact sequence of events by which the first part of the accident, a fairly innocuous bump at the first contact, became converted into the second part of the accident whereby the negligence of the Panther in keeping her screw running holed the Trishna. I see no reason to doubt that the wise and experienced judge [WILLMER, J.] who tried that case fairly apportioned the liability for the damage on the evidence before him; but his judgment does contain words which might lead to error and which may, I think, have done so in the present case. He said (12):

"In the present case, as a matter of causation, the damage resulted from a combination of the negligence of the Trishna and the Ericbank on the one hand, in producing the contact, with the negligence of the Panther, on the other hand, in keeping her propeller working. I think that I shall not be doing any injustice if I say that these two causes operated to an equal extent. That involves that the Panther must be held in fault to the extent of one half."

If the problem were merely a question of causation, I would not criticise the last two sentences; but the investigation is concerned with " fault " which

(10) [1957] 1 All E.R. 641; [1957] P. 143.
(11) [1966] 1 All E.R. 553; [1966] P. 18.
(12) [1957]1 All E.R. at pp. 648, 649; [1957] P. at p. 150.

includes blameworthiness as well as causation; and no true apportionment can be reached unless both those factors are borne in mind.

This is most easily illustrated by taking an extreme case from a type of litigation which is tried daily in the courts. A dangerous machine is unfenced and a workman gets his hand caught in it. So far as causation alone is concerned it may be fair to say that at least half the cause of the accident is the fact that the workman put his hand into the danger; but so far as " fault " (and therefore liability) is concerned the answer may be very different. Suppose that the workman was a normally careful person who, by a pardonable but foolish reaction, wanted to save an obstruction from blocking the machine and so put his hand within the danger area. Suppose further that the factory owner had known that the machine was dangerous and ought to be fenced, that he had been previously warned on several occasions but through dilatoriness or on grounds of economy failed to rectify the fault and preferred to take a chance. In such a case the judge, weighing the fault of one party against the other, the deliberate negligence against the foolish reaction, would not assess the workman's fault at anything approaching the proportion which mere causation alone would indicate. Suppose, further, that part of the blame was that of a maintenance contractor who had been guilty of a small error of negligence contributing to the dangerous nature of the machine. It would be erroneous to put together the great negligence of the factory owner and the slight negligence of the contractor as together making up the dangerous situation and, therefore, constituting one unit of the disaster; and then to measure that unit against the negligence of the workman whose act turned a dangerous situation into an accident. For what degree of blameworthiness does one attach to such a unit? To get a fair apportionment it is necessary to weigh the fault of each negligent party against that of the others. It is or may be quite misleading to substitute for a measurement of the individual fault of each contributor to the accident a measurement of the fault of one against the joint fault of the rest.

Even had the positions of the Miraflores and the Abadesa constituted a static obstruction which had been in that position for some hours, I think that the unit approach would be wrong; but here the three ships were all moving to a situation which resulted in the grounding of the George Livanos. " The negligence of the three ships ", said the learned judge, " is so bound up with each other to produce the ultimate result that it would be unrealistic to find the George Livanos the sole author of her misfortune." The fact that there was between two of the ships an actual collision, whose resulting damage the judge was apportioning in the other action, gives a wholly fictitious unity to the colliding ships. Had they managed to lose way a few yards short of collision, their respective negligence vis-à-vis the George Livanos would have been the same and produced the same result.

It is suggested by counsel for the appellants that the Law Reform (Contributory Negligence) Act, 1945, s. 1 gives support to the reasonableness of the unit approach. In fact that Act expressly excludes s. 1 of the Maritime Conventions Act, but even if it did not, it would not give any support to the unit approach. Its intention was to allow a plaintiff, though negligent, to recover damages reduced to such an extent as the court thinks just and equitable having regard to his share in the responsibility for the damage (s. 1 (1)). That share can only be estimated, however, by weighing his fault against that of the defendant or, if there are two defendants, against that of each defendant. It is true that apportionment as between the defendants comes theoretically at a later stage (under the Law Reform (Married Women and Tortfeasors) Act, 1935); but as a matter of practice the whole matter is decided at one time and the court weighs up the fault of *each* in assessing liability as between plaintiff and defendants themselves. Moreover I see nothing in the Act of 1945 to show that it intends the court to treat the joint defendants as a unit whose joint blameworthiness could only, one presumes, be the aggregate blameworthiness of its differing components.

It follows, therefore, that I entirely agree with the observation of Winn, L.J. (13) that the liability of each vessel involved must be assessed by comparison of her fault with the fault of each of the other vessels involved individually, separately, and in no way conjunctively. I do not, however, with respect, find myself in accord with his observations in the two preceding paragraphs as to the propriety of (14)

> " an assessment in respect of each ship of the over-all responsibility for the occurrence of the double event of the collision and the partially consequential grounding."

The judge's task in the second action was to weigh and apportion only the respective faults of the three ships which led to the grounding.

In the present case the learned judge dealt carefully with the acts and omissions of each of the parties; but having, in the first action, weighed the faults of the Abadesa and Miraflores fairly against each other, he took, in the second action, a short cut which led him astray. Even on mere causation I think that it is open to question whether the respective causative effects of the Abadesa's negligence and that of the Miraflores were precisely the same in the case of the collision as in the case of the grounding; but more important is the fact that, by making a characterless " unit " of their several acts of negligence, he did not measure their respective blameworthiness against the blameworthiness of the George Livanos. In particular, he did not measure the positive initial act of negligence by the Abadesa against the resulting negligent inertia of the George Livanos in failing to realise soon enough that there was a crisis and to take timely steps to avoid it.

It is axiomatic that a person who embarks on a deliberate act of negligence should, in general, bear a greater degree of fault than one who fails to cope adequately with the resulting crisis which is thus thrust on him. This generality is subject, of course, to the particular facts, and it may be that the initial act was so slight or easily avoidable and the subsequent failure to take avoiding action so gross that the blame for the accident falls more largely or even (if the interval and opportunity for avoidance are sufficiently great) wholly on the person who failed to avoid the consequences of another's negligence. Between the extremes in which a man is either wholly excused for a foolish act done in the agony of the moment as the result of another's negligence or is wholly to blame because he had plenty of opportunity to avoid it, lies a wide area where his proportion of fault in failing to react properly to a crisis thrust on him by another must be assessed as a question of degree. Yet the driver who deliberately goes round a corner on the wrong side should, as a rule, find himself more harshly judged than the negligent driver who fails to react promptly enough to the unexpected problem thereby created. For all humans can refrain from deliberately breaking well-known safety rules; but it is not in mortals to command the perfect reaction to a crisis; and many fall short at times of that degree which reasonable care demands.

Vessels going with the current in a tricky channel are liable to greater difficulties than those going against it. For that reason there was a local rule, governing navigation in the River Scheldt (as in other places), whereby

> " When vessels are meeting in a channel where a current is running near a narrow passage . . . or bend the passage of which is so narrow that proceeding at the same time would be dangerous,"

the vessel going upstream shall hold back until the other vessel has passed the narrows. This was known to the Abadesa; but at no time did she hold back.

---

(13) [1966] 1 All E.R. at p. 558, letter H; [1966] P. at p. 37.
(14) [1966] 1 All E.R. at p. 558, letter F; [1966] P. at pp. 36, 37.

Instead she held on in mid-channel and even at the time of the collision she was proceeding at five or six knots. She never noticed the starboard sheer of the Miraflores, which was the presage of trouble. The George Livanos did notice the sheer, but did not anticipate trouble since it seemed to her only a slight sheer to which ships were often prone owing to the cross current at that spot. In this both ships alike were at fault, the Abadesa being in the circumstances certainly no less at fault than the George Livanos.

The real negligence of the George Livanos, therefore, which must be weighed against the Abadesa's initial and continuing negligence, in coming on in mid-stream when she could and should have held back, is the negligence of the George Livanos in failing to take crisis action at the time when the Miraflores sheered to port about two minutes before the collision. Your lordships asked your nautical assessors two questions with regard to the port sheer similar to those asked by the Court of Appeal (15) from their assessors with regard to the earlier starboard sheer. 1. Question. When Miraflores was seen to sheer to port, bearing in mind that the Caltex Manila and the Abadesa were seen to be approaching, what action by George Livanos was called for? Answer. Full astern on engines. Let go both anchors as soon as sufficient way is off the ship to be able to do so without parting cables. Sound three short blasts. 2. Question. If such actions had been taken by George Livanos, would it have been likely to avoid grounding? Answer. Yes. Provided George Livanos was handled with skill she should have avoided grounding.

I accept those answers. The George Livanos failed to take the action which according to those answers she should have taken. It was not until three minutes after the port sheer of the Miraflores that she took serious action. Undoubtedly she was negligent. It is urged in mitigation on her behalf that she was loth to lose steerage way in view of the cross currents and the unfortunate lie of the land; that she needed time to consider her best course of action in a difficult situation; and that time is occupied when the master takes over from the pilot in a crisis. Nevertheless, she was seriously negligent and her negligence contributed very largely to the accident; but to say that she was half as much again to blame as the Abadesa seems to me wrong. Moreover, I doubt whether the learned judge would have arrived at such an estimate had he specifically weighed the negligence of one against the negligence of the other. Owing to his " unit approach " he did not do this.

In my opinion, therefore, the majority of the Court of Appeal (15) were right in thinking that the matter was open for an appellate court; and it remains to consider whether their re-apportionment was right. I do not feel on the evidence any sufficient justification for altering, as they did, the apportionment as between the Miraflores and the Abadesa. It may be that the causation of the grounding was different from that of the collision, but I am not sufficiently sure of that matter to give effect to it. I prefer, therefore, to adhere in respect of the grounding to the same proportions of fault, as between the Abadesa and the Miraflores, which the learned judge fixed between them with regard to the collision. As against each of those ships, I think, however, that the proportion of fault attributed to the George Livanos for the grounding needs alteration. In my opinion any proportion of her fault which exceeds that of the Abadesa must be erroneous.

I would assess the proportions of liability at two-fifths to the Abadesa, two-fifths to the George Livanos and one-fifth to the Miraflores. To that extent only I would vary the order of the Court of Appeal (15) and allow the appeal.

LORD WILBERFORCE: My Lords, HEWSON, J., at the trial dealt with two actions concerning (i) the respective liabilities of the tankers Abadesa and Miraflores for damage sustained by collision, and (ii) the respective liabilities

---

(15) [1966] 1 All E.R. 553; [1966] P. 18.

of those two vessels and the tanker George Livanos for the grounding of the latter. His judgment reviews in detail the evidence concerning the navigation of all three ships, on which he had the advice of Elder Brethren of the Trinity Corporation. He decided that, as regards the collision, liability should be apportioned as to two-thirds to the Abadesa and one-third to the Miraflores. No appeal has been brought against this apportionment. As regards the George Livanos, his decision was that she was partly responsible for her own misfortune, and in the result he apportioned fifty per cent. liability to her, leaving the remaining fifty per cent. to be borne by the Abadesa and the Miraflores in the same proportions of two-thirds to one-third as had been fixed in relation to the collision. There was an appeal against this part of the learned judge's decision and the Court of Appeal (16), by a majority, deciding that he had erred in principle, revised the proportions so that forty-five per cent. was cast on the Abadesa, thirty per cent. on the Miraflores and twenty-five per cent. on the George Livanos. The owners of the Miraflores appeal to this House against this re-apportionment.

In the majority judgments, there appear to be two separate strands of argument. WINN, L.J. (17) started by taking as the object for consideration the double event consisting of the collision and the grounding. The method which he discussed, and apparently favoured in principle, was to apportion a percentage liability to each of the three ships for each of these events, attributing zero responsibility to the George Livanos for the collision and taking two alternative percentages for all three vessels as regards the grounding. He then added together these separate percentages so as to give aggregate percentages for the double event—still on an alternative basis, and finally considered what, on the alternative bases, the liability of each ship for the single events would be, on the assumption that its liability for one event should be half that for the double event. Without taking any exact mathematical figure he arrived at an approximation, midway between the two alternatives, which gave the figures which I have stated. The formula is briefly expressed in the judgment and I hope that I do justice to it if my observations on it are also brief, particularly since the respondents concentrated their defence of the re-apportionment on the second line of argument to which I shall come. I find two main difficulties in the suggested procedure: first, in the arithmetical addition of percentages, when the respective percentages are of different totals—in fact the collision damage was plainly far greater than the grounding damage; and, second, in the apparent paradox whereby the initially assumed responsibility of the George Livanos for the grounding (whether this were to be put at one hundred per cent. or fifty per cent. or any other figure) is, by the formula, reduced to half that figure for the grounding alone. That seems altogether too favourable a method for that particular ship, and I could not accept that it gives a true result.

The other line of argument, also to be found in the judgment of WINN, L.J. (18), and I think preferred by DANCKWERTS, L.J. (19), was simply to make a fresh assessment of liability on the merits. Whether this is legitimate or not must depend, first, on whether there were grounds for interfering with the judge's apportionment and, secondly, whether the new assessment is itself fair.

My lords, on the first question I am left, even after the able arguments we have heard, with much of the original predisposition, which is appropriate in an appellate court, not to disturb the apportionment made by the judge. His primary findings of fact were challenged neither in the Court of Appeal (16) nor in this House, for I think it is common ground that such further advice as has been provided by nautical assessors merely clarifies without in any way invalidating any of them. In matters of apportionment, even more than as regards findings of fact generally, the decision of the trial judge should be interfered

(16) [1966] 1 All E.R. 553; [1966] P. 18.
(17) [1966] 1 All E.R. at p. 557; [1966] P. at p. 35.
(18) [1966] 1 All E.R. at p. 559, letter B; [1966] P. at p. 37.
(19) [1966] 1 All E.R. at p. 559; [1966] P. at p. 37.

with only where some clear error of law or principle can be shown to have influenced
his decision: this was clearly laid down in the House in *British Fame (Owners)*
v. *MacGregor (Owners), The MacGregor* (20). The question is whether this test
can be satisfied here. Now, the criticism, and the only substantial criticism,
made of the judgment is that, when he came to assess the liability for the grounding of the George Livanos, the learned judge stated that he

> " proposed to treat the negligence leading to the collision between the
> Abadesa and the Miraflores as one unit and the negligence of the George
> Livanos as another."

as to which it is said that in cases of multiple fault, to apply a method known as a
unit approach is, or at least may be, mistaken. Even accepting this objection
as a general rule, it does not follow, however, that the learned judge in fact fell
into error: or that his reference to a " unit " vitiated his apportionment. To
establish that it did, it must be shown with some degree of conviction that he
failed properly to weigh the fault of the George Livanos against that of the other
vessels concerned, in the situation in which each of them were. The doubt
which I feel on this point, after reading the judgment as a whole, remains with
me after a consideration of the judgments on appeal, and in particular of the
judgment of WILLMER, L.J. (21). For he proceeded to put to himself (22) precisely
this question: whether the judge had reached a wrong result by adopting a
" unit approach ". After a detailed, and as one would expect, expert re-examination of the evidence, WILLMER, L.J., came to the conclusion (23) that the judge
had adopted a common-sense approach, had done what he was required to do by
s. 1 of the Maritime Conventions Act, 1911, and that, in reaching his decision, he
considered not only the culpability but also the causative potency in relation
to the stranding of the faults committed by each of the vessels. This concurrence
of experienced opinion is enough, without any additional attempt of my own to
review the facts, to leave me in doubt as to the existence of sufficient error at
the trial to justify a re-assessment.

The second question, which in fact arises on the view taken by your lordships,
is whether, a re-assessment being called for, the proportions fixed by the Court of
Appeal (24) are acceptable. As to this, I agree, in the first place, that no justification was given by the majority of the Court of Appeal (24), or has appeared in
argument, for disturbing the apportionment made by HEWSON, J., between the
Abadesa and the Miraflores: that should remain as 2 : 1. As to the third vessel,
the answers given by the nautical assessors, quoted (25) by my noble and learned
friend, LORD PEARCE, amply confirm the substantial responsibility for her own
grounding of the George Livanos and though, as in all such matters, there is
room for differing assessments, I would be prepared to assent to the suggested
allocation of forty per cent. to the George Livanos.

Appeal allowed.

Solicitors: *Thomas Cooper & Co.* (for the appellants); *Ince & Co.* (for the first
respondents); *Middleton, Lewis & Co.* (for the second respondents).

[*Reported by* KATHLEEN J. H. O'BRIEN, *Barrister-at-Law.*]

---

(20) [1943] 1 All E.R. 33; [1943] A.C. 197.
(21) [1966] 1 All E.R. at p. 555; [1966] P. at p. 24.
(22) [1966] 1 All E.R. at p. 556, letter B; [1966] P. at p. 33.
(23) [1966] 1 All E.R. at p. 556, letters E-G; [1966] P. at p. 33.
(24) [1966] 1 All E.R. 533; [1966] P. 18.
(25) See p. 680 letter D, ante.

R. v. HARLOW AND WINSTANLEY.

[COURT OF APPEAL, CRIMINAL DIVISION (Lord Parker, C.J., Winn, L.J., and James, J.), January 20, 1967.]

Criminal Law—Larceny—Fixtures—Floorboards in building ripped up to expose water pipes underneath—Whether an offence contrary to Larceny Act, 1916 (6 & 7 Geo. 5 c. 50), s. 8 (1) (a).

A police officer, making a routine check of derelict buildings, heard noises of scraping and knocking in the upper part of a house. Outside a bathroom on the second floor landing several floorboards had been ripped up, exposing the copper pipes underneath. Nearby various tools were lying, including a hacksaw. Both appellants were hiding behind the bathroom door, and, when asked, gave false names and addresses. In a pocket of the appellant Harlow's raincoat were two hacksaw blades which fitted the hacksaw. On appeal against conviction under s. 8 (1)* of the Larceny Act, 1916, of larceny by ripping, cutting, severing or breaking the floorboards,

Held: s. 8 (1) of the Larceny Act, 1916, dealt only with the stealing of glass or woodwork belonging to any building, or with ripping, etc., with intent to steal such glass or woodwork; in the present case no intention to steal the floorboards was shown, because the appellants were clearly seeking to obtain the pipes underneath, and accordingly the offence charged was not established and the convictions must be quashed (see p. 684, letters E and H, post).

Appeal allowed.

[As to offences of larceny of fixtures, see 10 HALSBURY'S LAWS (3rd Edn.) 776, para. 1499; and for cases on the subject, see 15 DIGEST (Repl.) 1082, 1083, *10,704-10,723.*

For the Larceny Act, 1916, s. 8 (1), see 5 HALSBURY'S STATUTES (2nd Edn.) 1017.]

Appeal.

The appellants, Allen John Harlow and Gerald Winstanley, were convicted at their trial at Brighton Quarter Sessions before the recorder (C. J. A. DOUGHTY, Q.C.) and a jury, on an indictment which included a count† charging them jointly with larceny contrary to s. 8 (1) of the Larceny Act, 1916, in that they on July 26, 1966, with intent to steal, ripped, cut, severed or broke a quantity of floorboards the property of Charles Augustus Spencer, then being woodwork belonging to a

---

* Section 8 (1), so far as material, is set out at p. 684, letter E, post.

† On arraignment of the appellants at their trial the indictment included one count alleging attempted larceny, the particulars being that the appellants attempted to steal a quantity of metal piping, the property of Charles Augustus Spencer. Before they were arraigned, counsel for the Crown made a submission, seeking to amend the indictment. He submitted that the depositions showed that there was no evidence of any offence of attempted larceny of the metal piping, and that there was the further difficulty that metal piping fixed to a house was not capable of being stolen. On the other hand there was, in his submission, a clear offence disclosed in the depositions which was not charged, viz., an offence under s. 8 (1) of the Larceny Act, 1916. Accordingly the Crown sought to amend the indictment by including a count under s. 8 (1). Leave was granted, and this became the count on which the appellants were tried, for, after the appellants had been arraigned, counsel for the Crown intimated that no evidence would be adduced by the Crown on count 1, that is, on the count of attempted larceny of a quantity of metal piping. When the case for the prosecution was closed, a submission was made on behalf of the defence in the absence of the jury. This submission was that an offence against s. 8 (1) was committed only if it were shown that the intention of the accused was to steal glass or woodwork, and that there was no evidence of such an intention. Thus the second count, which had been added by amendment, was, in the submission of the defence, bad in law. The recorder ruled that an offence under s. 8 (1) could be established, although the intended stealing was not a stealing of either glass or woodwork.

building the property of the said Charles Augustus Spencer. The appellants were sentenced to imprisonment, the appellant Harlow to imprisonment for twelve months and appellant Winstanley to imprisonment for two years. They appealed against conviction and applied for leave to appeal against sentence. The facts are stated in the judgment of LORD PARKER, C.J.

D. A. R. Bradley for the appellants.
J. B. S. Townend for the Crown.

LORD PARKER, C.J., delivered the following judgment of the court: On the morning of July 23, 1966, a police officer making a routine check of a derelict house heard noises of scraping and knocking in the upper part of the house. When he began to search the house, the noises stopped, but outside a bathroom door on the second floor landing he found that a number of floorboards had been ripped up, under which were pipes (1). Lying nearby was a case opener, a pair of tin snips, a small hacksaw, an adjustable spanner and a brass elbow-shaped pipe joint. The appellants were hiding behind the door and gave false names and addresses. When two hacksaw blades which fitted the hacksaw were found in the appellant Harlow's raincoat pocket, he claimed that he had picked them up in the house. The appellant Winstanley claimed that they were only in the house to shelter from the rain.

The only point here is whether on those facts they could be convicted of an offence contrary to s. 8 (1) of the Larceny Act, 1916, which provides as follows:

"Every person who—(1) steals, or with intent to steal, rips, cuts, severs or breaks—(a) any glass or woodwork belonging to any building . . ."

It seems to this court abundantly clear that as a matter of construction what is being dealt with here is first the stealing of any glass or woodwork belonging to a building, and second the ripping, cutting, severing or breaking with intent to steal such glass or woodwork. It is, in the opinion of the court, really impossible to give those words any other but their plain meaning. Not only does the word "steals" require an object but also this section is one of a number of sections dealing with larceny of particular objects, s. 5, larceny of dogs, s. 6, larceny of wills, s. 7, larceny of documents of title to land, and then, after this s. 8 dealing with what one might call broadly speaking fixtures and also trees and shrubs. The Act goes on in s. 9 to deal with the larceny of goods in process of manufacture and so on. Section 8 (1) is dealing only with the stealing of the specific articles there enumerated, in para. (a) glass or woodwork, in para. (b) any metal or utensil or fixture, in para. (c) anything made of metal fixed in any land being private property. It may be that this is a casus omissus in the legislature, but it is quite clear to this court that there being no evidence that there was any intention to steal the floorboards, because they were quite clearly after the pipes that were under the floorboards, they could not be held guilty of this offence. These convictions must be quashed.

Appeals allowed. Convictions quashed.

Solicitors: *Registrar of Criminal Appeals* (for the appellants); *J. Garbutt*, Brighton (for the Crown).

[*Reported by* PATRICIA JOHNSTON, *Barrister-at-Law.*]

(1) The pipes were of copper. Electric cables containing a good deal of lead were also exposed. There was evidence before the recorder that these were valuable materials that could be sold as scrap.

Re DISPLAY MULTIPLES, LTD.

[Chancery Division (Pennycuick, J.), February 6, 7, 1967.]

Company—Winding-up—Compulsory winding-up—Advertisement of petition—
Seven clear days before hearing—Saturday and Sunday excluded—Companies
(Winding-Up) Rules, 1949 (S.I. 1949 No. 330), r. 28—R.S.C., Ord. 1, r. 2 (2),
Ord. 3 r. 2 (5).

An advertisement was inserted on Friday, Jan. 27, 1967, for the hearing
of a petition for the winding-up of a company by the court on Monday, Feb. 6.
Rule 28 of the Companies (Winding-Up) Rules, 1949, provided: " Every
petition shall be advertised seven clear days before the hearing . . ."

Held: Saturdays and Sundays were to be excluded in computing the
period of seven clear days for the purposes of r. 28 of the Rules of 1949, since
R.S.C., Ord. 3, r. 2 (5)* so provided and its incorporation in the Rules of
1949 by r. 227 was not excluded by R.S.C., Ord. 2, r. 2 (2)†; accordingly
the petition had been advertised only five clear days before the hearing and
must be re-advertised (see p. 686, letter I, and p. 688, letter B, post).

Re Yeoland Consols, Ltd. ((1888), 58 L.T. 108) applied.

[As to advertisement of petition, see 6 Halsbury's Laws (3rd Edn.) 544, 545,
para. 1049; and for cases on the subject, see 10 Digest (Repl.) 884, 885, *5868-*
5877.

For the Companies (Winding-Up) Rules, 1949, r. 28, r. 227, see 4 Halsbury's
Statutory Instruments (First Re-Issue) 146, 193.

For the Matrimonial Causes Rules, 1957, r. 1 (3), see 10 Halsbury's Statutory
Instruments (Second Re-Issue) 222, 223.]

Cases referred to:

Milch v. *Frankau & Co.*, [1909] 2 K.B. 100; 78 L.J.K.B. 560; 100 L.T. 1002;
33 Digest (Repl.) 510, *88.*

Rowberry v. *Morgan*, (1854), 9 Exch. 730; 23 L.J.Ex. 191; 23 L.T.O.S. 129;
156 E.R. 313; 45 Digest (Repl.) 268, *355.*

Simpkin, Ex p., (1859), 2 E. & E. 392; 29 L.J.M.C. 23; 24 J.P. 262; 121 E.R.
148; sub nom. *R.* v. *Leicestershire Justices*, 1 L.T. 92; 45 Digest
(Repl.) 267, *343.*

Yeoland Consols, Ltd., Re, (1888), 58 L.T. 108; 10 Digest (Repl.) 890, *5949.*

Petition.

This was a petition by Bull & Son (Surrey), Ltd., who were creditors of Display
Multiples, Ltd., in the sum of £47 18s. 4d., for the compulsory winding-up of
that company on the ground that it was insolvent and unable to pay its debts.
The facts are set out in the judgment.

J. G. Monroe for the petitioners.

Allan Heyman for the company and opposing creditors.

Cur. adv. vult.

Feb. 7. **PENNYCUICK, J.:** This petition has given rise to a point as to
the length of the period of advertisement required under r. 28 of the Companies
(Winding-Up) Rules, 1949 (1). That rule, so far as material, reads as follows:
" Every petition shall be advertised seven clear days before the hearing . . .".
In the present case the advertisements were inserted on Friday, Jan. 27, 1967,
the advertisements being for hearing of the petition on Monday, Feb. 6. There
is no question as to what is meant by " clear days ". The question is whether
or not in the computation of the seven clear days Saturday and Sunday are to be
included. It will be seen here that if Saturdays and Sundays are included, there

---

* For the text of R.S.C., Ord. 3, r. 2 (5), see p. 686, letter H, post.

† For the terms of R.S.C., Ord. 1, r. 2 (2), see p. 687, letters A and B, post.

(1) S.I. 1949 No. 330.

were nine clear days. If Saturday but not Sunday are included, there were seven clear days. If Saturday and Sunday are both excluded, there were only five clear days. There is no doubt that in the absence of some provision in the relevant Act or rule, the period of seven days would include Saturdays and Sundays; see, for example, *Milch* v. *Frankau & Co.* (2), per WALTON, J.:

" I quite agree that the general rule is stated in *Ex p. Simpkin* (3), where it was very shortly put by BLACKBURN, J., thus: ' I see no reason to differ from the principle laid down by the Court of Exchequer in *Rowberry* v. *Morgan* (4), that we must adhere to the plain meaning of the Act in every case, and hold that Sunday is to be included in the computation of the number of days, if nothing is said about its exclusion.' "

The Companies (Winding-Up) Rules, 1949, themselves contain no provision as to the computation of time for this purpose. However, r. 227 of the Companies (Winding-Up) Rules, 1949, contains an incorporation of the Rules of the Supreme Court in the following terms:

" In all proceedings in or before the court, or any judge, registrar or officer thereof, or over which the court has jurisdiction under the Act and rules, where no other provision is made by the Act or rules, the practice, procedure and regulations shall, unless the court otherwise in any special case directs, in the High Court be in accordance with the Rules of the Supreme Court and practice of the High Court, and in a Palatine Court and county court in accordance, as far as practicable, with the existing rules and practice of the court in proceedings for the administration of assets by the court."

The expression " Rules of the Supreme Court and practice of the High Court " is as a matter of language open to two possible interpretations. It may mean the rule for the time being in force and the practice for the time being prevailing, or it may mean the rules in force at the date of the Companies (Winding-Up) Rules, 1949, and the practice prevailing at the date of those rules; and likewise with the county court. I think that the former must be the correct interpretation. It would be extraordinarily inconvenient to crystallise the practice in the Companies Court by reference to the rules and the practice prevailing in the High Court at Feb. 23, 1949. I understand that the former interpretation has always been acted on in practice in the companies registry. The provisions now contained in r. 227 can be traced back, with variation of language, to r. 74 of the Companies Rules, 1862.

I turn now to the Rules of the Supreme Court. R.S.C., Ord. 3, r. 2 contains the following provision:

" (1) Any period of time fixed by these rules or by any judgment, order or direction for doing any act shall be reckoned in accordance with the following provisions of this rule.

" (5) Where, apart from this paragraph, the period in question, being a period of seven days or less, would include a Saturday, Sunday or bank holiday, Christmas Day or Good Friday, that day shall be excluded . . ."

Unless there is any more to it, that seems to me to conclude the matter, that is to say, r. 227 incorporates by reference R.S.C., Ord. 3, r. 2 (5), and accordingly in the computation of the seven clear days Saturdays and Sundays are to be excluded.

Counsel for the petitioners based his argument wholly on the terms of R.S.C., Ord. 1, r. 2. That rule reads as follows:

" (1) Subject to the following provisions of this rule, these rules shall have effect in relation to all proceedings in the Supreme Court.

---

(2) [1909] 2 K.B. 100 at pp. 102, 103.   (3) (1859), 2 E. & E. 392.
      (4) (1854), 9 Exch. 730.

" (2) These rules shall not have effect in relation to proceedings of the kind specified in the first column of the following Table (being proceedings in respect of which rules may be made under the enactments specified in the second column of that Table):

TABLE

Proceedings	Enactments
. . .	. . .
2. Proceedings relating to the winding-up of companies	Companies Act, 1948, s. 365
. . .	. . .

" (3) These rules shall not, except as expressly provided by these rules, have effect in relation to any proceedings to which the Matrimonial Causes (Judgment Summons) Rules, 1952 or the Matrimonial Causes Rules, 1957 apply."

Counsel for the petitioners claims that the effect of para. (2) of r. 2 is to cancel out altogether the incorporation of the Rules of the Supreme Court into the Companies (Winding-Up) Rules, 1949.

I do not think that, even apart from para. (5) of r. 2, para. (2) of that rule would have so startling a result. It is true that by virtue of that paragraph the Rules of the Supreme Court do not of their own force have any application to winding-up proceedings; but I do not think that there is anything in para. (2) which could affect their referential incorporation by other rules. In fact, para. (2) does not stand alone. Paragraph 2 (5) provides:

" In the case of the proceedings mentioned in paras. (2), (3) and (4), nothing in those paragraphs shall be taken as affecting any provision of any rules (whether made under the Act or any other Act) by virtue of which the Rules of the Supreme Court 1965, or any provisions thereof are applied in relation to any of those proceedings."

That paragraph expressly saves the referential incorporation of the Rules of the Supreme Court into other rules if such saving were necessary. I observe the specific description of the rules of the Supreme Court as Rules of the Supreme Court 1965, but I do not think that it could be the intention of the rules to differentiate in some way between rules which refer to the Rules of the Supreme Court 1965, and those which merely refer to the rules of the Supreme Court in the sense of the rules of the Supreme Court for the time being in force. Such a differentiation would be absurd, especially bearing in mind that there are a number of existing bodies of rules which obviously could not refer to the Rules of the Supreme Court 1965.

Finally I would refer to *Re Yeoland Consols, Ltd.* (5). That was a creditors' petition for winding-up. The petition was presented on Feb. 15, 1888, which was a Wednesday, and the affidavit verifying it was filed on Feb. 20, which was the following Monday. The question was whether it had been filed within the proper time. Counsel in their argument submitted this:

" Rule 4 of the Companies Rules, 1862, no doubt, provides that the affidavit in support of a petition to wind up must be filed within four days after the presentation of the petition, but the 19th was a Sunday, so that day would not count. The Companies Rules, 1862 contain no direct provision as to whether Sunday is to be reckoned in the computation of time under those rules, but under r. 74 (a) the general practice of the court is to apply to proceedings for winding-up a company in cases not provided for by the rules or the Act; and under R.S.C., Ord. 64, r. 2 (b) Sunday is not to be reckoned in the computation of any limited time less than six days. We contend that this rule is applicable in the case of a winding-up of a company, and that the Sunday ought not to be reckoned in the computation of the four days."

(5) (1888), 58 L.T. 108.

STIRLING, J., said (6):

"The contention of the petitioner is, I think, correct. The rules seem to me to be clear, and the registrar informs me that the practice in such cases as this is not to reckon the Sunday as one of the days."

It seems to me that the principle of that case is directly applicable to the present situation, where, under the current Rules of the Supreme Court, Saturday and Sunday are both excluded. I conclude, therefore, that there was not sufficient advertisement.

It may be worth while to note that the Matrimonial Causes Rules, 1957, (7) contain in r. 82 a provision comparable to r. 227 of the Companies (Winding-Up) Rules, but that in that instance r. 1 (3) removes all doubt by express provision, namely:

"'Rules of the Supreme Court' mean the Rules of the Supreme Court, 1883, as amended by any subsequent rules."

Order for re-advertisement; the period of re-advertisement being abridged under r. 225 of the Companies (Winding-Up) Rules, 1949.

Solicitors: *Nicholson, Graham & Jones* (for the petitioners); *Kaufman & Seigal* (for the company and opposing creditors).

[*Reported by* JENIFER SANDELL, *Barrister-at-Law.*]

Re DAVIS (*deceased*).

[COURT OF APPEAL, CIVIL DIVISION (Sellers, Diplock and Russell, L.JJ.), January 16, 30, 1967.]

Coroner—Inquest—Verdict of suicide—Application for certiorari to quash— Probability of different verdict at a new inquest must be shown—Coroners Act, 1887 (50 & 51 *Vict. c.* 71), *s.* 6 (1).

Suicide—Intention—Act of self-destruction knowing the probable consequences.

To justify a verdict of suicide the act of self-destruction must be shown to be a person's intentional act, knowing the probable consequences.

Dictum of ROLFE, B., in *Clift* v. *Schwabe* ((1846), 3 C.B. at p. 464) approved.

At an inquest on a married woman who had died at a hospital five days after giving birth to a child there, the coroner, after hearing the evidence of three doctors, found that the death was caused by injuries following a jump from a second floor window at the hospital and was suicide. The widower applied for certiorari to quash the inquisition on the ground (among other grounds) that there had been insufficient inquiry. To an affidavit by the applicant there was exhibited a statement by the deceased's general medical practitioner, who had not given evidence at the inquest, that the deceased had suffered mild attacks of epilepsy and intermittent extreme anxiety while pregnant and between the birth and her death, and that in his opinion the deceased would not kill herself intentionally.

Held: certiorari must be refused because the evidence before the court did not show that there would probably be a different verdict if a new inquest were held (see p. 690, letters B, F and I, post).

[As to certiorari to quash a coroner's inquisition, see 8 HALSBURY'S LAWS (3rd Edn.) 529, para. 1002; as to the statutory power to quash, see ibid., pp. 531, 532, para. 1008; and for cases on quashing inquests, see 13 DIGEST (Repl.) 164-167, *302-339.*

As to what amounts in law to suicide, see 10 HALSBURY'S LAWS (3rd Edn.) 727, para. 1395.

---

(6) (1888), 58 L.T. at p. 108.   (7) S.I. 1957 No. 619.

Explained in R v CARDIFF CORONER [1970] 3 All ER 469

For the Coroners Act, 1887, s. 6, see 4 HALSBURY'S STATUTES (2nd Edn.) 828.]

Case referred to:

   Clift v. *Schwabe*, (1846), 3 C.B. 437;   17 L.J.C.P. 2;   7 L.T.O.S. 342;   136 E.R. 175; 29 Digest (Repl.) 396, *2988*.

Motion for certiorari.

This was a motion on notice dated Dec. 21, 1966, given on behalf of Brian Archibald Davis, the widower of Jeanette Isobel Davis, deceased, who died on Aug. 4, 1966, for certiorari to quash the verdict of suicide, found on an inquisition on Aug. 10, 1966, before C. F. J. BARON, Esq., Her Majesty's Coroner for the county of Greater London, into the cause of her death. The motion was brought with the leave of the Court of Appeal, given on Dec. 19, 1966, following the refusal by the Queen's Bench Divisional Court of an application for such leave. At the conclusion of the argument the Court of Appeal stated that the application for certiorari would be dismissed, but reserved judgment. The facts are set out in the judgment of SELLERS, L.J.

   J. M. Rankin for the applicant.
   Nigel Bridge for the coroner.

Cur. adv. vult.

Jan. 30.   **SELLERS, L.J.,** read the following judgment: The applicant is the widower of Jeanette Isobel Davis deceased, whom he married in October, 1958, and who died on Aug. 4, 1966, at the age of twenty-eight. Her Majesty's Coroner for Greater London held an inquest on Aug. 10, 1966, and after hearing evidence he found that Mrs. Davis' death was caused by "multiple injuries following jump from second floor window" at about 6.5 a.m. on Friday, July 22, 1966, at Kingston Hospital, and his conclusion as to the death was suicide.

With the authority of the Attorney-General the applicant sought leave from the Divisional Court to move for an order of certiorari in order to quash the inquisition and to obtain a new inquest.   Reliance was placed on s. 6 of the Coroners Act, 1887, and relief was sought on the grounds that (a) there was no or no sufficient evidence to support or justify the verdict, (b) there was insufficiency of inquiry, and (c) the proceedings were irregular. The Divisional Court refused the applicant leave to proceed.   Before that court the contention on behalf of the applicant seems to have been that the deceased accidentally fell out of the window whilst opening it or whilst seeking fresh air.   The Divisional Court thought that that view was untenable on the evidence, and in so far as it was raised in this court so do I.   If such a verdict had been justified I can understand the applicant seeking it, but if that is not maintainable there does not appear to be any alternative attenuating verdict.

The contention here was mainly directed to the medical evidence relating to the deceased's mental health preceding and subsequent to her entry into hospital for the purpose of inducing the birth of her child, which occurred on July 17, 1966. The applicant's affidavit, incorporating a statement of the deceased's doctor (1), showed that the deceased had suffered from mild attacks of epilepsy and with the approach of the birth of her child had suffered from extreme anxiety, and that this state of anxiety had continued at least intermittently in the five days after the child's birth.   In these circumstances this court, then constituted with

---

(1) The applicant deposed that the deceased's doctor, who was a consultant homœopathic physician and general practitioner, had had the deceased as a patient for a period of approximately five years before her death, and had seen her two days before she entered hospital; and that this doctor was not called as a witness at the inquest, although his name and address had been supplied on Aug. 4, 1966. A statement by the doctor was exhibited to this affidavit.   In it he said, among other matters, that he had visited the deceased when she was in hospital on several occasions, and had found her on July 21, 1966, which was the day before the event which caused her death, in an extremely nervous and anxious state.

DAVIES, L.J., in place of DIPLOCK, L.J., gave leave for the applicant to move for
an order of certiorari.

Counsel for the applicant sought a new inquest in order to expunge the present
finding.   The only argument ultimately relied on was that the state of the
deceased's mental health was insufficiently investigated and that it should at
least have been supplemented by the evidence of Dr. Raeside, who had attended
the deceased generally since 1961 and had seen her in hospital on several occasions
after the birth of the child, and as recently as July 20.

This court could interfere, in the circumstances of this case, only if it was of
opinion that the verdict of suicide would probably be replaced by a different
verdict if a new inquest were to be held.   It became apparent that the medical
evidence fell short of establishing this probability.   The court felt sympathy
with the applicant's desire, but notwithstanding the sustained argument of
counsel, the court came clearly to the opinion that the verdict of the coroner
ought not to be quashed and a new inquest held, and learned counsel was so
informed at the end of the argument.

Suicide is not to be presumed.   It must be affirmatively proved to justify the
finding.   Suicide requires an intention.   Every act of self-destruction is, in common
language,

"... described by the word suicide, provided it be the intentional act
of a party knowing the probable consequence of what he is about":

see per ROLFE, B., in *Clift* v. *Schwabe* (2).   A fall during a fit or delirium or
sleep-walking would justify a verdict of misadventure, but that is not this case.

The deceased was certainly in ill-health and under the stress of a disturbed
mind. This may no doubt have accounted for what she did, but on all the medical
evidence put before us, that is the evidence of Dr. Raeside in addition to that
of the three doctors whom the coroner called before him, it does not appear to
me that any coroner on a reconsideration of the cause of death would probably
find that the deceased did not know what she was doing at the time of her fall
or did not appreciate the probable consequences.   I am reluctant to say more
on this unhappy case to which this court has given most sympathetic consideration.

DIPLOCK, L.J.: I agree with the judgment which has just been delivered,
and with that which is about to be delivered by RUSSELL, L.J., and cannot
usefully add anything to either of them.

RUSSELL, L.J., read the following judgment: This case finally resolved
itself into a short point. Counsel for the coroner accepted the proposition that
" suicide " would not be a correct finding if the proper conclusion on the evidence
were that, though the deceased was aware that she was projecting herself through
an upper storey window, she was unable through a temporary defect in understanding to appreciate that death was the probable consequence of her actions,
so that she did not intend to kill herself.   In such a case the finding should be
" misadventure ": though insanity or disturbed balance of mind will justify a
finding of suicide, unless it is of such a character as to deprive the person of the
ability to appreciate the probable consequences of the act. Counsel for the coroner
also accepted that it was open to this court to consider the proposed evidence of
Dr. Raeside when deciding whether to order a new inquest; but he contended
that it would not be right to do so unless it appeared that it was probable that
in the light of that further evidence the new inquest would result in a different
finding—that is to say that it was probable that the coroner would be satisfied
that the medical condition of the deceased was such that she was at the time
unable to appreciate that the probable consequence of her action would be her
death. He submitted that this was not established, and I agree with that submission. The proposed evidence of Dr. Raeside may be thus summarised: that
he was of the opinion from his knowledge of this unfortunate lady that she would

(2) (1846), 3 C.B. 437 at p. 464.

not intentionally kill herself, and *therefore* he considered that she must have been in a temporary psychotic state such as to have deprived her of the ability to understand that the probable consequence of her deliberate act in projecting herself through this window high above the ground would be her death.

While I can well understand that the family would be more content in their minds if the evidence of Dr. Raeside had been available to the coroner, I cannot bring myself to think that it would probably have satisfied the coroner of the existence of a psychotic state having the effect in question, or that it would probably have that outcome at a further inquest. I therefore also agree that this application fails.

Application dismissed.

Solicitors: *George C. Carter & Co.* (for the applicant); *Treasury Solicitor.*

[*Reported by* HENRY SUMMERFIELD, ESQ., *Barrister-at-Law.*]

Re JENNERY (*deceased*).   JENNERY v. JENNERY.

[COURT OF APPEAL, CIVIL DIVISION (Davies and Russell, L.JJ.), November 21, 1966.]

Family Provision—Provision—Order—Effect—Enforcement—Not by four-day order—Lump sum payment order equivalent to making widow a beneficiary under will.

On an application made under the Inheritance (Family Provision) Act, 1938, as amended, an order was made for the payment of the sum of £600 to the testator's widow out of the capital of the testator's estate of about £1,100. No payment having been made under the order by the two personal representatives of the testator, who were also the sole beneficiaries under the will, the widow applied for a four-day order for payment.

Held: the rights of the widow established by the order for payment out of the testator's estate had no greater effect than to make her the equivalent of a beneficiary under the will, and bore no resemblance to an order for payment which could be made the subject of a four-day order; accordingly the application for the four-day order failed (see p. 694, letters G and H, post).

Appeal dismissed.

[As to orders making provision for the dependants of a deceased, see 16 HALSBURY'S LAWS (3rd Edn.) 463-465, paras. 926-930; and for cases on the subject, see 24 DIGEST (Repl.) 983, 984, *9800-9810.*

For the Inheritance (Family Provision) Act, 1938, s. 1, as amended by the Intestates' Estates Act, 1952, s. 8, Sch. 4, see 32 HALSBURY'S STATUTES (2nd Edn.) 139.]

Case referred to:

Pointer, Re, Shonfield v. *Edwards*, [1946] 2 All E.R. 409; [1946] Ch. 324; [1947] L.J.R. 224; 175 L.T. 309; 24 Digest (Repl.) 984, *9810.*

Appeal.

The plaintiff appealed to the Court of Appeal by notice of appeal dated Oct. 24, 1966, against an order of STAMP, J., made on Oct. 21, 1966, dismissing the plaintiff's notice of motion for an order for payment within a certain time* of a sum of £600 and interest out of the capital of the estate of the testator, Ernest

---

* By notice of motion dated Aug. 16, 1966, the plaintiff gave notice that the plaintiff would apply on Oct. 18, 1966, that the defendant administratrices might be ordered within twenty-eight days of the date of the order or subsequently within four days of service to pay the sum of £600 out of the capital of the testator's estate with interest.

Jack Jennery deceased. The grounds of appeal were that the judge erred in law in the following ways: (i) he held that the order of CROSS, J., made on July 6, 1964, put the plaintiff into the position of a pecuniary legatee with a claim in equity against the estate of the testator, but he failed to hold (as was the case) that the order put the plaintiff in the position of a pecuniary legatee and also provided for the payment by the defendants to the plaintiff of the £600 with interest thereon as recited in the order; (ii) he held that the order of CROSS, J., was not an order for the payment of money within the meaning of R.S.C., Ord. 45, r. 1*, whereas on its true construction it was such an order; (iii) he held that by reason of the decision of the Court of Appeal in *Re Oddy, Major* v. *Harness†*, the court had no power to make the order sought in the notice of motion, whereas the decision in *Re Oddy†* was limited to a judgment for the recovery of a sum of money as opposed to a judgment for the payment of such a sum, and further and in the alternative was a decision on an order of the then Rules of the Supreme Court in terms substantially different from existing orders, R.S.C., Ord. 45, r. 1; and (iv) he held that he had no power to make the order sought by the plaintiff because the effect of the order of CROSS, J., was to make the plaintiff a pecuniary legatee who could only recover her legacy by means of an administration action, her right being a mere right in equity, whereas in fact in addition to making the plaintiff a pecuniary legatee the order gave her a right to the sum of £600 which was enforceable as a debt or other claim in law.

J. H. Hames for the plaintiff.
The first defendant did not appear and was not represented.
The second defendant appeared in person.

RUSSELL, L.J., delivered the first judgment at the invitation of DAVIES, L.J.: A testator, Mr. Jennery, died on Oct. 2, 1961, and by his will, of 1954, he gave all his property to his two daughters in equal shares. He appointed executors, but they renounced. No step was taken by way of grant of letters of administration until Feb. 14, 1963, when the two beneficiaries were given a grant of letters with will annexed. The testator left a widow, with whom he had not been living for, I take it, a good many years. He also left an estate which, at the time of the present proceedings, was valued at nearly £1,100, mainly consisting of a freehold cottage valued at £1,000—in which, I assume, the testator had been living, but I do not know, and in which the two beneficiaries, his daughters, continued to live, and in which one of them, a Mrs. Ashby, with her family, still lives, her sister having subsequently married and gone to live elsewhere.

On behalf of the widow, on Mar. 1, 1963, an application was made under the Inheritance (Family Provision) Act, 1938 for reasonable provision; and an order (which I shall for the moment state very shortly) was made in her favour for provision to the tune of £600, by way of a lump sum. The parties to the proceedings were the two sisters, who were not only the sole personal representatives but also the sole beneficiaries under the will. I will come to the wording of the order in a moment. Since that order was made, the sisters—certainly the sister who is living in the cottage—have sat very tight, and the result is that the widow has not had a penny of her £600, which of course would come to her in priority to any claim by the two daughters.

---

* The R.S.C. (Revision) 1965 came into force on Oct. 1, 1966. R.S.C. Ord. 41, r. 5, to which *Re Oddy* related, was superseded, and is now replaced, so far as is relevant, by R.S.C. (Rev.) Ord. 42, r. 2 (2). In regard to four-day orders in the Chancery Division, see note to Ord. 42, r. 2 (2) in the ANNUAL PRACTICE, 1967. As to the distinction in enforcement between an order for recovery of money and an order for payment of money, see notes in the ANNUAL PRACTICE, 1967, to Ord. 45, r. 1. So far as material R.S.C. Ord. 45, r. 1, provides—" (1) Subject to the provisions of these rules, a judgment or order for the payment of money . . . may be enforced by one or more of the following means, that is to say—(a) writ of fieri facias; . . . (e) in a case in which r. 5 applies, an order for committal; . . ."
† [1906] 1 Ch. 93.

After some years' ineffective endeavour, instead of starting proceedings against the two administrators (as one would expect in the normal way) to administer the estate—in which proceedings it could be made quite sure with reasonable rapidity that the sister who is in the cottage would be forced out and the property would be realised and if necessary the sisters removed from the administrators' saddle—it occurred to the widow's advisers, or, as counsel for the widow frankly stated, it occurred to him when he was asked to advise on behalf of the widow, that a short cut might be taken, based on the order made by CROSS, J., under the Inheritance (Family Provision) Act, 1938, by getting a four-day order for payment. It was thought that the sisters, the administratrices, might be forced, under threat of imprisonment for contempt of court, into taking such steps as were necessary in order to bring the money home to the widow. So far as the one sister who is not living in the cottage is concerned, it would be difficult to do anything against her that did not result, if the other sister remained obstinate, in administration proceedings, which were sought to be avoided, because she would not be able to get the resident sister out or the property sold, if the resident sister refused to co-operate, without administration proceedings. However, STAMP, J., when application was made to him by notice of motion for a four-day order based on the order of CROSS, J., declined to make the order. He held that this was not, in any relevant sense of the word, an order for payment of money.

I think it as well to recall the form of the statutory provisions (which are now found in Sch. 4 to the Intestates' Estates Act, 1952) of the Inheritance (Family Provision) Act, 1938, s. 1, as amended. Under that statute a dependant, such as a widow, can apply to the court (I propose at the moment to leave out the amendments, which introduced cases of intestacy), if he or she considers that reasonable provision has not been made by the testator's will for her. If the court considers

" that the disposition of the deceased's estate effected by his will . . . is not such as to make reasonable provision for the maintenance of that dependant, the court may order that such reasonable provision as the court thinks fit shall, subject to such conditions or restrictions, if any, as the court may impose, be made out of the deceased's net estate for the maintenance of that dependant . . ."

Then under s. 1 (2) primarily:

" The provision for maintenance to be made by an order shall, subject to the provisions of sub-s. (4) of this section, be by way of periodical payments . . .":

and so on. Subsection (4) enables the court, in certain instances, " to make an order providing for maintenance ", i.e., of course, maintenance out of the deceased's net estate—" by way of a lump sum payment " (1), as distinct from the periodical payments which are primarily envisaged. Our attention was drawn also to sub-s. (5):

" In determining whether, and in what way, and as from what date, provision for maintenance ought to be made by an order, the court shall have regard to the nature of the property representing the deceased's net estate and shall not order any such provision to be made as would necessitate a realisation that would be improvident . . ."

Section 3 (1) is in this form:

" Where an order is made under this Act, then for all purposes, including the purposes of the enactments relating to death duties, the will or the law relating to intestacy, or both the will and the law relating to intestacy, as the case may be, shall have effect, and shall be deemed to have had effect as from

_____

(1) The words " lump sum " were inserted by amendment in 1952 (Intestates' Estates Act, 1952, s, 7 and Sch. 3).

the deceased's death, subject to such variations, as may be specified in the order for the purpose of giving effect to the provision for maintenance thereby made."

I may there refer to the statement made by WYNN-PARRY, J., in *Re Pointer, Shonfield* v. *Edwards* (2) where, having read that subsection, he continued:

"The reference to the enactments relating to death duties shows that the section proceeds on the footing that the provision made by the order is to be treated as a legacy. In my judgment, the scheme of the Act involves (i) that, assuming the necessary conditions obtain, the court may by order make provision for the dependant applying to it; (ii) if it makes such an order, the provision made thereby is to be treated for all purposes as a legacy; (iii) that the will is for all purposes to have effect as if that legacy had been contained in it when it was made."

With those words I entirely agree.

I turn then to the actual order which was made by CROSS, J. That order recites that the court

"being of opinion that the disposition of the estate of the above-named testator . . . effected by his will does not make reasonable provision for the maintenance of the plaintiff his widow [that follows exactly part of s. 1 (1)] doth pursuant to the provisions of s. 1 (4) [and I may say it is also pursuant to the provisions of s. 1 (1)] of the above-mentioned Act order that a sum of £600 be paid to the plaintiff out of the capital of the estate of the testator with interest thereon (less tax) at the rate of £4 per centum per annum from Oct. 2, 1962, until payment."

October 2, 1962, was one year from the death, from which ordinarily interest on a legacy would begin to run.

Great stress is laid on the form of that order as showing that it is an order for payment of a sum of money. I do observe in the first place that it is not an order that any person shall pay a sum of money: it is simply an order that it should be paid to the plaintiff out of the capital of the estate. That order, to my mind, follows exactly what is required and appropriate under the form of the statute, which provides that the court may order provision to be made out of the deceased's net estate and that the provision may be by way of periodical payments or it may be by way of a lump sum payment. It seems to me that what the order is doing is fulfilling the powers of the court under the statute, viz., to establish the rights of a dependant; and I consider further that those rights, when they are established by an order, have no greater effect than that of making that person the equivalent of a beneficiary under the will, with or without any special directions which might have been made in the will under which any particular legacy is to be paid out of capital or out of income, or out of one property or asset rather than another.

I can find no resemblance, except the most superficial one, between an order made in this form under the Act of 1938, as amended, and any order for payment which can be made the subject of an application for a four-day order. The proper step for a dependant to take is the ordinary step that a beneficiary in an estate has open to him if he or she is unable to get satisfaction from the trustees or personal representatives; but that is not the step that has been taken here—in search of brevity but unfortunately without that result. I entirely agree with the view of STAMP, J., and consider that the appeal should be dismissed.

Mrs. Ashby, the sitting administratrix, is present in court. It has been unnecessary for her to address us: but I must say that on the factual state of affairs I cannot see how she can ultimately be anything but the loser by declining to do what is her duty as administratrix. She has been sitting rent-free in an asset of the estate and, no doubt, in due course, in so far as it will be necessary, will be made to account for an occupation rent, among other things. She should

(2) [1946] 2 All E.R. 409 at p. 411; [1946] Ch. 324 at p. 326.

realise that she cannot successfully combat steps which are obviously bound to be taken against her on the part of the widow and which I have no doubt will now be taken with the greatest speed.

DAVIES, L.J.: I agree with everything that RUSSELL, L.J., has said on the point under discussion, and cannot usefully add anything. I would also associate myself with the warning and advice that he gave to Mrs. Ashby. The appeal will be dismissed.

Appeal dismissed.

Solicitors: *Hamlins, Grammer & Hamlin* (for the widow).

[*Reported by* F. A. AMIES, ESQ., *Barrister-at-Law.*]

PRICE v. CLAUDGEN, LTD.

[HOUSE OF LORDS (Lord Reid, Lord Morris of Borth-y-Gest, Lord Hodson, Lord Pearce and Lord Upjohn), January 17, February 16, 1967.]

Building—Building regulations — Application — Neon lighting installation—Repair of neon sign attached to cinema—Whether neon sign was part of the building for the purposes of the Building (Safety, Health and Welfare) Regulations, 1948 (S.I. 1948 No. 1145), reg. 2 (1).

The appellant, an electrician, was on the roof of a cinema, leaning over the edge and joining electric wires of a neon lighting installation, which was on the face of the building, in order to remedy a defect. The installation consisted of neon tubes outlining the features of the outside of the front of the cinema. The installation had been fixed and was maintained by the appellant's employers; it was held in place by clamps attached to pins driven into the masonry. The current was suddenly switched on from inside the building. The appellant received a shock, fell off the roof and was injured. On appeal in an action by him against his employers for alleged breach of duty under reg. 24* of the Building (Safety, Health and Welfare) Regulations, 1948,

Held: the operation on which the appellant was engaged was not repair or maintenance of a building within reg. 2 (1)† of the regulations of 1948, since the neon installation was not part of the building but was something that was on the building; accordingly the regulations did not apply and no breach of statutory duty was established (see p. 698, letters C, D and H, post).

Appeal dismissed.

[As to the application of building regulations, see 17 HALSBURY'S LAWS (3rd Edn.) 125-128, para. 206; and for cases on the meaning of building or structure, see 26 DIGEST (Repl.) 569, 570, *2342-2353.*

For the Building (Safety, Health and Welfare) Regulations, 1948, reg. 2 (1), reg. 24, see 8 HALSBURY'S STATUTORY INSTRUMENTS (First Re-Issue) 187, 197.]

Appeal.

This was an appeal against an interlocutor of the First Division of the Court of Session (The Lord President (LORD CLYDE), LORD GUTHRIE and LORD MIGDALE) dated Nov. 3, 1965, affirming an interlocutor of the Lord Ordinary (LORD MILLIGAN) dated Jan. 13, 1966, pronounced after proof, and assoilzing the respondents, who were the defenders in an action by the appellant for damages for personal injuries sustained by him on Mar. 20, 1963, while working in the respondents' employment.

I. MacDonald, Q.C., and *D. B. Robertson* (both of the Scottish Bar) for the appellant.

* Regulation 24 (1), is printed at p. 697, letter F, post.

† Regulations 2 (1) is set out at p. 697, letter H, to p. 698, letter A, post.

W. R. Grieve, Q.C., and *W. L. K. Cowie* (both of the Scottish Bar) for the respondents.

LORD REID: My Lords, I have read the speech of my noble and learned friend LORD MORRIS OF BORTH-Y-GEST. I agree with it and cannot usefully add anything. I would dismiss this appeal.

LORD MORRIS OF BORTH-Y-GEST: My Lords, the facts may be briefly stated. The appellant is an electrician. The respondents are neon sign manufacturers and repairers. On the front of the Lyceum Cinema, Govan (which was erected in about 1938) there was a neon lighting installation. That installation had been in position either from about or soon after the date when the cinema was erected. It was not established that the installation had been erected actually at the same time as the building was erected. The installation consisted of a complex of neon tubes on the face of the building and so placed as to outline the outside features of the front of the cinema. One of the tubes ran along the top of the building. The respondents were responsible for the repair and maintenance of the installation. It was they who had put it in position. According to the appellant it belonged to them, but the actual facts as to ownership were not investigated or proved. The tubing along the face of the building is held in position by sockets or clips or clamps, which were attached to the stonework by means of pins or studs driven into the masonry. The Lord Ordinary held that the installation could very easily have been removed without in any way affecting the building.

The installation was controlled by a separate lock switch which was in the switch room in the cinema and that lock switch was operated by a key. There was only one key and by means of it alone could the neon lighting installation be turned on. The key could only be removed if the lighting was off. As there was only the one key of the lock switch it followed that if it were removed the electric current to the installation could not be turned on. In the switch room near the lock switch there was a notice which read: " Before working on or near luminous tube installation remove and retain key of lock switch ". During times when the cinema was open to the public the switch room was kept locked. There were two keys to it. They were kept by the cinema operators, one of whom would be on duty when the cinema was open to the public.

The appellant was well familiar with the installation. He had taken part, as an employee of the respondents, in its repair and maintenance during a period of about eleven years before March, 1963. He had paid six or seven visits a year for the purposes of such work. Sometimes a repair or maintenance visit took place at the request of the chief cinema operator: sometimes a visit was the result of some defect having been observed by an employee of the respondents. When such an employee was sent to attend to the installation, he would normally get in touch with one of the cinema operators and obtain a key of the switch room, so as to be able to remove the key of the lock switch before going to do any adjustment to the installation. In that way he could ensure that the electric current would not be turned on while he was working.

On the evening of Mar. 19, 1963, the appellant noticed, at a time when he happened to be passing the cinema, that there was some fault in the installation. He reported this to his employers (the respondents) the next day, Mar. 20. They instructed him to go to the cinema to repair the fault. Accordingly he went. He was accompanied by a mate. He arrived there at about 4.25 p.m. The cinema was open to the public. The installation had not then been switched on. There was evidence that in the month of March it would normally be switched on some time between 4 p.m. and 5 p.m. No one at the cinema expected him, for no one at the cinema had reported the fault to the respondents and the respondents did not tell the cinema that they were sending the appellant. He went to the switch room. It was locked. He then went to the roof but he did not tell any representative of the cinema of his presence. In fact the assistant manager and a cinema operator were in the cinema. Either of them could have given the appellant the key of the switch room. The Lord Ordinary recorded that the appellant very frankly admitted that he just took a chance that the current would not be switched on. When he got to the roof the appellant readily discovered what was wrong. An insulator was bent outwards and the bell glass was broken: there was a break at the foot of the capillary tube and there was a burnt-out wire. In order to effect the repair (which for him was a relatively simple matter which would only take a matter of minutes) he had to kneel down and lean over the edge of the roof. Putting his left hand on the wall he stretched out his right hand and was in the act of joining together two wires when one of the cinema operators suddenly switched on the neon installation. The appellant had a severe shock as a result of which he fell off the edge of the roof and on to a canopy some thirty feet below. He received severe personal injuries.

Liability in the respondents was alleged on a number of grounds, but it is now only necessary to refer to one of them. It was said that the Building (Safety, Health and Welfare) Regulations, 1948 (1), applied to the operation on which the appellant was engaged, and that the respondents were in breach of reg. 24 in that there were no guard-rails and toe-boards and that such breach caused the accident to the appellant. The respondents deny that the regulations applied, and deny that the accident was caused or was materially contributed to by any breach of statutory duty. If the regulations applied, and if compliance with reg. 24 would have prevented the accident, the respondents contend that there was a very high degree of contributory negligence on the part of the appellant. If damages were recoverable it was recognised by both parties that the figure assessed by the Lord Ordinary was too low.

If, as was held by the Lord Ordinary and by their lordships in the First Division, the work on which the appellant was engaged was not an operation within the scope of the regulations, it would follow that other matters which were argued would not arise. I turn therefore to consider the regulations and whether they applied. Regulation 24 (1) is in the following terms:

" 24.—(1) Subject to paras. (3), (4) and (5) of this regulation, every side of a working platform or working place, being a side thereof from which a person is liable to fall a distance of more than six feet six inches, shall be provided with a suitable guard-rail or guard-rails of adequate strength, to a height of at least three feet above the platform or place and above any raised standing place on the platform, and with toe-boards up to a sufficient height being in no case less than eight inches and so placed as to prevent so far as possible the fall of persons, materials and tools from such platform or place."

Under reg. 4 it is the duty of every contractor and employer of workmen who is undertaking any of the operations to which the regulations apply to comply (inter alia) with such of the requirements of reg. 24 as affect any workman employed by him. To decide as to the application of the regulations consideration must be given to reg. 2 (1) which is in the following terms:

" 2.—(1) These regulations shall apply to the following operations where undertaken by way of trade or business or for the purpose of any industrial or commercial undertaking, or by or on behalf of the Crown or any municipal or other public authority, namely, the construction, structural alteration, repair or maintenance of a building (including re-pointing, re-decoration and external cleaning of the structure), the demolition of a building, and the preparation for, and laying the foundation of, an intended building whether or not the building is on or adjacent to the site of work of engineering construction within the meaning of the Factories Act, 1937, and to machinery or plant used in such operations; and Part 6 of these regulations shall apply as respects persons employed in such operations as aforesaid: Provided that the following shall not be deemed to be buildings for the purposes of this

(1) S.I. 1948 No. 1145.

regulation: Docks, harbours, wharves, quays, piers, sea defence works, lighthouses at sea, river works, canals, dams, reservoirs, aqueducts, viaducts, bridges, tunnels, sewers, pipelines, filter beds, gasholders, or pole or lattice work structures designed solely for the support of machinery, plant or electric lines.''

It is to be observed that the regulations apply to '' operations ''. The contention on behalf of the appellant was that he was engaged on the '' repair '' (or possibly the '' maintenance '') of a building or part of a building. The short point which is raised is therefore whether it can fairly be said that when the appellant was repairing (or possibly maintaining) the neon installation he was repairing (or possibly maintaining) a building or a part of a building. It was not said that the neon installation was itself a building, but that when installed or erected it had become an integral part of the building. As to this the Lord Ordinary held that it was not proved that the installation had been made a physical part of the building.

In one sense the case may be one of first impression. If it is, I confess, my lords, that mine accords with that of the Lord Ordinary and of their lordships in the First Division. If the question is posed whether the appellant was engaged in the operation of repairing a building I think that the immediate answer would be in the negative. He was engaged in the operation of repairing the neon installation. He was repairing something which was on a building. If someone replaces a burnt-out wire or mends a break in a wire in a neon installation on a building, it does not seem to me that it can reasonably be said that he is repairing a building. Both before and after such operation of replacement or repair the building will be the same: neither its structure nor its condition will be affected. Indeed, if such an installation were removed, the building as a building would (apart from any special facts and circumstances) be unaffected.

My lords, we are not here concerned with any question as to how matters would stand as between a lessor and a lessee if a neon installation were attached to a building by a lessee and then removed by him. Legal principles concerning landlords' or tenants' fixtures are not here of relevance and do not furnish guidance. Nor is it profitable to seek to formulate or to express any guiding tests as to what could be or could not be a part of a building. Decision here rests on the particular established facts. I agree with the Lord President that there may be many things, which could be attached to or hung on to or placed on to or in a building, which in no true sense would be or become a part of a building. There could be cases in which something was so fixed or installed or erected on or in a building as reasonably and properly to be regarded as a part of the building. For a determination of the present case I cannot think that a study of any authorities assists. In my view, it could not rationally be said that the operation which the appellant undertook was the repair of a building.

I would dismiss the appeal.

LORD HODSON: My Lords, I concur.

LORD PEARCE: My Lords, I concur.

LORD UPJOHN: My Lords, I concur.

Appeal dismissed.

Solicitors: *W. H. Thompson*, agents for *T. F. Russell*, Glasgow and *W. R. Courtney*, Edinburgh (for the appellant); *Martin & Co.*, agents for *Biggart, Lumsden & Co.*, Glasgow and *Campbell, Smith & Co.*, Edinburgh (for the respondents).

[*Reported by* KATHLEEN J. H. O'BRIEN, *Barrister-at-Law.*]

ESSO PETROLEUM CO., LTD. v. HARPER'S GARAGE (STOURPORT), LTD.

[HOUSE OF LORDS (Lord Reid, Lord Morris of Borth-y-Gest, Lord Hodson, Lord Pearce and Lord Wilberforce), December 5, 6, 7, 8, 12, 13, 14, 15, 19, 20, 1966, February 23, 1967.]

Trade—Restraint of trade—Agreement—Petrol filling station—Solus agreement—Agreement between owner of garage and petrol supplier for purchase and resale exclusively of supplier's products—Obligation of garage owner to carry on filling station while agreement in force—Obligation to keep station open—Obligations to be undertaken by successor—Duration of two agreements, for four years and five months and twenty-one years respectively—One agreement supported by and partly repeated in mortgage—Whether doctrine of restraint of trade applied to agreements and to mortgage—Whether agreements in unreasonable restraint of trade.

The respondents owned and operated two garages, M. garage and the C. garage, and had entered into solus agreements with the appellants. The solus agreement relating to the M. garage was for a term of four years and five months from July 1, 1963. It contained clauses for (*a*) purchase of the appellants' motor fuel at wholesale schedule prices for all requirements of the garage (" the tying covenant "); (*b*) a price maintenance clause for the sale at the appellants' retail prices, which had since become unenforceable by reason of the Retail Prices Act, 1964; (*c*) an obligation, if the garage was sold, to get the buyer to enter into a similar solus agreement (" the continuity covenant "); and (*d*) an obligation to keep the garage open at all reasonable hours (" the compulsory trading covenant ").

The appellants had a mortgage dated Oct. 6, 1962, on the C. garage to secure a principal sum of £7,000 lent to the respondents, and interest, as well as a similar solus agreement, the duration of which was for twenty-one years from July 1, 1962, which was also the period during which the mortgage money was made repayable by instalments. The mortgage charged C. garage by way of legal mortgage with repayment and payment of interest, and contained covenants for the observance and performance of stipulations; these stipulations included a tying covenant and a compulsory trading covenant on the lines previously indicated. The mortgage also contained provision that it should not be redeemed otherwise than in accordance with the covenant for repayment, viz., by instalments over twenty-one years. There was no evidence to show that a period so long as twenty-one years, or indeed exceeding five years, was reasonable.*

On appeal from a decision that the solus agreements and mortgage stipulation were unenforceable as being in unreasonable restraint of trade,

Held: (i) agreements were not excluded from the ambit of the legal doctrine regarding agreements in restraint of trade by the fact that the restriction imposed was a restriction in relation to land, nor by the fact that the agreement was by way of covenant in a mortgage of land (see p. 708, letters C and E, p. 716, letter C, p. 717, letter I, p. 721, letter D, p. 722, letter D, p. 725, letter E, and p. 736, letter A, post).

Catt v. *Tourle* ((1869), 4 Ch. App. 654; *Biggs* v. *Hoddinott* ([1895-99] All E.R. Rep. 625); *Bouchard Servais* v. *Prince's Hall Restaurant, Ltd.* ((1904), 20 T.L.R. 574); *McEllistrim* v. *Ballymacelligott Co-operative Agricultural and Dairy Society, Ltd.* ([1919] A.C. 548); *English Hop Growers, Ltd.* v. *Dering* ([1928] All E.R. Rep. 396) and *Foley* v. *Classique Coaches, Ltd.* ([1934] All E.R. Rep. 88) considered.

(ii) the solus agreements were within the category of agreements in restraint of trade (as distinct from agreements for promoting trade), and accordingly required to be justified on the ground of reasonableness; so also

* See, as regards the need for evidence, e.g., p. 723, letter H, post.

Dictum of LORD REID at 707 applied in WATSON v PRAGER [1991] 3 All ER 487

Applied in DARLINGTON [1969] 1 All E.R. 707.

Dicta of LORD PEARCE and LORD WILBERFORCE at 727, 730 doubted in INSTONE v SCHROEDER [1974] 1 All ER 171

Dicta of LORD PEARCE at 723 and of LORD WILBERFORCE at 729, 730 explained in SCHROEDER v MACAULAY [1974] 3 All ER 616

Dictum of LORD REID at 708 explained in AMOCO AUSTRALIA PTY LTD v ROCCA BROS MOTOR ENGINEERING CO PTY LTD [1975] 1 All ER 963

[1977] 1 All ER 47
DIRECTOR GEN OF FAIR TRADING
applied in RAVENSEFT PROPERTIES v
Dictum of LORD REID at 707, 708

did the stipulations in the mortgage in respect of C. garage, the loan and
mortgage being linked with the solus agreement as one transaction (see
p. 708, letter A, p. 715, letter B, p. 727, letter H, and p. 732, letter F, post).

(iii) the crucial consideration in determining reasonableness in the present
case was the length of the period for which each agreement was to last, and
in the circumstances the period of the solus agreement for the M. garage
(between four and five years) was reasonable, but the period of the restraint
in relation to the C. garage (twenty-one years) was not, with the consequence
that the M. garage agreement was valid and that, as to the C. garage, the
tying covenant was unenforceable as being in unreasonable restraint of
trade and the respondents were entitled to redeem the mortgage (see p. 710,
letter I, p. 711, letter D, p. 717, letters F and I, p. 718, letter A, p.
721, letter I, p. 722, letters F and H, p. 728, letter B, p. 733, letter I, and p.
736, letter D, post).

Petrofina (Gt. Britain), Ltd. v. *Martin* ([1966] 1 All E.R. 126) distinguished.
Dictum of SIR WILFRID GREENE, M.R., in *Knightsbridge Estates Trust, Ltd.*
v. *Byrne* ([1938] 4 All E.R. at p. 626) distinguished.

Per LORD PEARCE: the doctrine of restraint of trade does not apply to
ordinary commercial contracts for the regulation and promotion of trade
during the existence of the contract, provided that any prevention of work
outside the contract viewed as a whole is directed towards the absorption
of the parties' services and not their sterilisation (see p. 727, letter A, post).

Per LORD WILBERFORCE: the development of the law shows that judges
have been able to dispense from the necessity of justification under a public
policy test of reasonableness such contracts or provisions of contracts as,
under contemporary conditions, may be found to have passed into the
accepted and normal currency of commercial or contractual or conveyancing
relations (see p. 729, letter I, post).

Decision of the COURT OF APPEAL ([1966] 1 All E.R. 725) reversed as
regards the M. garage, affirmed as regards the C. garage.

[**Editorial Note.** Normal covenants, imposed on a sale or lease of land, are
not within the principle of this decision and their validity is not affected; see,
e.g., p. 724, letter I, post. If, however, a covenant imposed on land on such an
occasion were essentially a personal trading covenant, the principle of the
present decision would apply.

As to agreements in restraint of trade, see 38 HALSBURY'S LAWS (3rd Edn.) 20,
para. 13; and for cases on the subject, see 45 DIGEST (Repl.) 443-449, *271-297.*

As to a clog on the equity of redemption of mortgages, see 27 HALSBURY'S
LAWS (3rd Edn.) 235-239, paras. 423-430.]

Cases referred to:
Aberdeen Varieties, Ltd. v. *Donald*, 1939 S.C. 788.
Ampol Petroleum, Ltd. v. *Mutton*, (1952), 53 S.R.N.S.W. 1.
A.-G. of Commonwealth of Australia v. *Adelaide Steamship Co., Ltd.*, [1911-13]
       All E.R. Rep. 1120; [1913] A.C. 781; 83 L.J.P.C. 84; 109 L.T. 258;
       12 Asp.M.L.C. 361; 45 Digest (Repl.) 396, *119.*
B.P. Australia, Ltd. v. *Comr. of Taxation of the Commonwealth of Australia,*
       [1965] 3 All E.R. 209; [1966] A.C. 244; [1965] 3 W.L.R. 608; 3rd
       Digest Supp.
Biggs v. *Hoddinott*, [1895-99] All E.R. Rep. 625; [1898] 2 Ch. 307; 67 L.J.Ch.
       540; 79 L.T. 201; 35 Digest (Repl.) 408, *1043.*
Bouchard Servais v. *Prince's Hall Restaurant, Ltd.*, (1904), 20 T.L.R. 574;
       45 Digest (Repl.) 510, *981.*
Bradley v. *Carritt*, [1900-03] All E.R. Rep. 633; [1903] A.C. 253; 72 L.J.K.B.
       471; 88 L.T. 633; 35 Digest (Repl.) 406, *1020.*
British American Oil Co. v. *Hey*, [1941] 4 D.L.R. 725; 45 Digest (Repl.) 512,
       246.

Applied in ALEC LOBB (GARAG
LTD v TOTAL OIL LTD [1985] 1
ER 303

Applied in ALEC LOBB LTD v TOTAL
OIL GB LTD [1983] 1 All ER 944

Dictum of LORD MORRIS at 717
applied in ALEC LOBB LTD v TOTAL
OIL GB LTD [1983] 1 All ER 944

British Oxygen Co., Ltd. v. *Liquid Air, Ltd.*, [1925] Ch. 383; 95 L.J.Ch. 81; 133 L.T. 282; 45 Digest (Repl.) 458, *410.*

Broad v. *Jollyfe*, (1620), Cro. Jac. 596; 79 E.R. 509; sub nom *Jollie* v. *Broads*, 2 Roll. Rep. 201; 45 Digest (Repl.) 465, *511.*

Catt v. *Tourle*, (1869), 4 Ch. App. 654; 38 L.J.Ch. 665; 21 L.T. 188; 33 J.P. 659; 45 Digest (Repl.) 455, *371.*

Clark v. *Supertest Petroleum Corpn.*, (1958), 14 D.L.R. (2d) 454; 35 Digest (Repl.) 406, **386.*

Clegg v. *Hands*, (1890), 44 Ch.D. 503; 59 L.J.Ch. 477; 62 L.T. 502; 55 J.P. 180; 28 Digest (Repl.) 828, *717.*

Cooper v. *Twibill*, (1808), 3 Camp. 286, n.; 170 E.R. 1384; 31 Digest (Repl.) 117, *2581.*

English Hop Growers, Ltd. v. *Dering*, [1928] All E.R. Rep. 396; [1928] 2 K.B. 174; 97 L.J.K.B. 569; 139 L.T. 76; 45 Digest (Repl.) 465, *522.*

Foley v. *Classique Coaches, Ltd.*, [1934] All E.R. Rep. 88; [1934] 2 K.B. 1; 103 L.J.K.B. 550; 151 L.T. 242; 40 Digest (Repl.) 359, *2880.*

Gaumont-British Picture Corpn., Ltd. v. *Alexander*, [1936] 2 All E.R. 1686; 45 Digest (Repl.) 443, *268.*

Great Eastern Oil & Import Co. v. *Chafe*, (1956), 4 D.L.R. (2d) 310; 45 Digest (Repl.) 512, **247.*

Hartley v. *Pehall*, (1792), Peake, 178; 170 E.R. 121; 40 Digest (Repl.) 160, *1229.*

Hill v. *Regent Oil, Ltd.*, (1962), Estates Gazette Digest 452.

Hinde v. *Gray*, (1840), 1 Man. & G. 195; 9 L.J.C.P. 253; 133 E.R. 302; 45 Digest (Repl.) 489, *764.*

Horwood v. *Millar's Timber & Trading Co., Ltd.*, [1916-17] All E.R. Rep. 847; [1917] 1 K.B. 305; 86 L.J.K.B. 190; 115 L.T. 805; 45 Digest (Repl.) 441, *259.*

Knightsbridge Estates Trust, Ltd. v. *Byrne*, [1938] 4 All E.R. 618; [1939] Ch. 441; 108 L.J.Ch. 105; 160 L.T. 68; *affd.* H.L., [1940] 2 All E.R. 401; [1940] A.C. 613; 109 L.J.Ch. 200; 162 L.T. 388; 35 Digest (Repl.) 408, *1047.*

Kores Manufacturing Co., Ltd. v. *Kolok Manufacturing Co., Ltd.*, [1958] 2 All E.R. 65; [1959] Ch. 108; [1958] 2 W.L.R. 858; 45 Digest (Repl.) 447, *287.*

Lamb (W. T.) & Sons v. *Goring Brick Co.*, [1931] All E.R. Rep. 314; [1932] 1 K.B. 710; 101 L.J.K.B. 214; 146 L.T. 318; 39 Digest (Repl.) 643, *1513.*

Leather Cloth Co. v. *Lorsont*, (1869), L.R. 9 Eq. 345; 39 L.J.Ch. 86; 21 L.T. 661; 34 J.P. 328; 45 Digest (Repl.) 447, *289.*

McColl v. *Avery*, (1928), 34 O.W.N. 275.

McEllistrim v. *Ballymacelligott Co-operative Agricultural and Dairy Society, Ltd.*, [1919] A.C. 548; 88 L.J.P.C. 59; 120 L.T. 613; 45 Digest (Repl.) 462, *454.*

Mitchel v. *Reynolds*, (1711), 1 P.Wms. 181; 24 E.R. 347; 45 Digest (Repl.) 395, *110.*

Mobil Oil Australia, Ltd. v. *Comr. of Taxation of Commonwealth of Australia*, [1965] 3 All E.R. 225; [1966] A.C. 275; [1965] 3 W.L.R. 629; 3rd Digest Supp.

Mogul Steamship Co. v. *McGregor, Gow & Co.*, [1891-94] All E.R. Rep. 263; [1892] A.C. 25; 61 L.J.Q.B. 295; 66 L.T. 1; 56 J.P. 101; 45 Digest (Repl.) 393, *101.*

Morgan v. *Jeffreys*, [1910] 1 Ch. 620; 79 L.J.Ch. 360; 74 J.P. 154; 35 Digest (Repl.) 344, *530.*

Morris (Herbert), Ltd. v. *Saxelby*, [1916-17] All E.R. Rep. 305; [1916] 1 A.C. 688; 85 L.J.Ch. 210; 114 L.T. 618; 45 Digest (Repl.) 449, *296.*

Newton Abbott Co-operative Society, Ltd, v. *Williamson and Treadgold, Ltd.*, [1952] 1 All E.R. 279; [1952] Ch. 286; 40 Digest (Repl.) 353, *2839.*

Dictum of LORD REID at 708-709
applied in ALEC LOBB (GARAGES) LTD
v TOTAL OIL LTD [1985] 1 All ER 303

Nordenfelt v. *Maxim Nordenfelt Guns and Ammunition Co., Ltd.*, [1891-94] All E.R. Rep. 1; [1894] A.C. 535; 63 L.J.Ch. 908; 71 L.T. 489; 45 Digest (Repl.) 445, *275*.

North-Western Salt Co., Ltd. v. *Electrolytic Alkali Co., Ltd.*, [1914-15] All E.R. Rep. 752; [1914] A.C. 461; 83 L.J.K.B. 530; 110 L.T. 852; 45 Digest (Repl.) 394, *102*.

Peters American Delicacy Co., Ltd. v. *Patricia's Chocolates & Candies Property, Ltd.*, (1947), 21 A.L.J. 281.

Petrofina (Gt. Britain), Ltd. v. *Martin*, [1966] 1 All E.R. 126; [1966] Ch. 146; [1966] 2 W.L.R. 318.

Printing and Numerical Registering Co. v. *Sampson*, (1875), L.R. 19 Eq. 462; 44 L.J.Ch. 705; 32 L.T. 354; 45 Digest (Repl.) 499, *866*.

Regent Oil Co., Ltd. v. *J. A. Gregory (Hatch End), Ltd.*, [1965] 3 All E.R. 673; [1966] Ch. 402; [1965] 3 All E.R. 673; 3rd Digest Supp.

Regent Oil Co., Ltd. v. *Strick (Inspector of Taxes)*. *Regent Oil Co., Ltd.* v. *Inland Revenue Comrs.*, [1965] 3 All E.R. 174; [1966] A.C. 295; [1965] 3 W.L.R. 636; 3rd Digest Supp.

Rogers v. *Parrey*, (1613), 2 Bulst. 136; 80 E.R. 1012; 45 Digest (Repl.) 465, *510*.

Shell Co. of South Africa, Ltd. v. *Gerran's Garages (Pty), Ltd.*, [1954] 4 S.A.L.R. 752.

Thompson v. *Harvey*, (1688), 1 Show. 2; Comb. 121; 89 E.R. 408; 45 Digest (Repl.) 489, *768*.

U.S. v. *Standard Oil*, (1911), 221 U.S. 1; (the series of reports is the UNITED STATES REPORTS).

United Shoe Machinery Co. of Canada v. *Brunet*, [1909] A.C. 330; 78 L.J.P.C. 101; 100 L.T. 579; 45 Digest (Repl.) 398, *132*.

Warner Bros. Pictures, Inc. v. *Nelson*, [1936] 3 All E.R. 160; [1937] 1 K.B. 209; 106 L.J.K.B. 97; 155 L.T. 538; 45 Digest (Repl.) 218, *203*.

Young v. *Timmins*, (1831), 1 Cr. & J. 331; 9 L.J.O.S. Ex 68; 148 E.R. 1446; 45 Digest (Repl.) 453, *328*.

Appeal.

This was an appeal by the appellants, Esso Petroleum Co., Ltd., from the judgment of the Court of Appeal (LORD DENNING, M.R., HARMAN and DIPLOCK, L.JJ.), dated Feb. 23, 1966, and reported [1966] 1 All E.R. 725, allowing the appeal of the respondents, Harper's Garage (Stourport), Ltd., from the judgment of MOCATTA, J., dated June 15, 1965, and reported [1965] 2 All E.R. 933, given in favour of the appellants in consolidated actions.

The first action, 1964 E. No. 259, described as the " Mustow Green action ", concerned a solus agreement between the appellants and respondents, dated June 27, 1963. The respondents agreed (by cl. 2) to buy from the appellants at the appellants' wholesale schedule price to dealers ruling at the date of delivery the respondents' total requirements of motor fuels for resale at a service station known as Mustow Green garage. The agreement was (by cl. 1) to remain in force for a period of four years and five months from July 1, 1963. By cl. 3 the appellants agreed to allow the respondents a rebate of 1¼d. per gallon on all motor fuels purchased by the respondents under the agreement and to extend to the respondents the advantages of the appellants' Dealer Co-operation Plan. By cl. 4 of this solus agreement the respondents agreed, inter alia, (a) to operate the service station in accordance with the plan, which included agreement on the part of the respondents to keep the service station open at all reasonable hours for the sale of the appellants' motor fuel and motor oils; (b) not to re-sell motor fuels for use in vehicles holding private licences except in accordance with the appellants' retail schedule prices; and (c) before completing any sale or transfer of the service station premises or business to procure the prospective purchaser or transferee to enter into an agreement with the appellants and the respondents whereby such person would be substituted for the respondents for all future purposes of the agreement.

The second action, 1964 E. No. 1249, which was referred to as the " Corner garage action ", concerned another solus agreement between the appellants and the respondents in the same terms as the Mustow Green agreement save that it related to a service station known as Corner garage, was made on July 5, 1962, and was expressed to remain in force for a period of twenty-one years from July 1, 1962. Under cl. 1 of a charge by way of legal mortgage made between the respondents and the appellants on Oct. 6, 1962, the respondents covenanted to repay the appellants £7,000 with interest by quarterly instalments over a period of twenty-one years from Nov. 6, 1962; it was further provided in the mortgage deed that the respondents should not be entitled to redeem the security otherwise than in accordance with the covenant as to repayment. The respondents charged Corner garage by way of legal mortgage with payment to the appellants of all moneys thereby covenanted to be paid. The respondents further covenanted during the continuance of the mortgage to purchase exclusively from the appellants all motor fuels which the respondents might require for consumption or sale at Corner garage, so long as the appellants should be ready to supply the same at their usual list price, and not to buy, receive or sell or knowingly permit to be bought, received or sold at Corner garage any motor fuels other than such as should be purchased from the appellants.

The two actions were begun by writs issued respectively on Feb. 18 and Aug. 28, 1964, and were consolidated by order dated Mar. 17, 1965. From about the end of the year 1963 and from about August, 1964, the respondents sold at Mustow Green garage and at Corner garage respectively motor fuel that was not supplied by the appellants. On appeal to the Court of Appeal ([1966] 1 All E.R. 725) it was held, briefly stated, that the doctrine of restraint of trade applied to covenants in mortgages as well as to solus agreements; that the restrictions in the solus agreements and in the mortgage were unreasonable and void, and that the proviso in the mortgage prohibiting redemption for twenty-one years, taken with the tie of Corner garage for a like period, rendered the mortgage oppressive, and accordingly the tie was unenforceable.

R. E. Megarry, Q.C., and *A. P. Leggatt* for the appellants.
S. W. Templeman, Q.C., J. Yahuda and *E. W. H. Christie* for the respondents.

The House took time for consideration.

Feb. 23. The following opinions were delivered.

LORD REID: My Lords, the appellants are a large company whose most important product is Esso petrol, most of which is sold by them to garages and filling stations for resale to the public. The respondent company own two garages: they contracted with the appellants under what are known as solus agreements and bound themselves for the periods of those agreements, inter alia, to sell at their garages Esso petrol and no other. When cheaper " cut price " petrol came on the market they began to sell it and ceased to sell Esso petrol. The appellants then raised two actions, now consolidated, to prevent this: they sought injunctions to restrain the respondents from buying other than from them any motor fuel for resale at these garages. MOCATTA, J. (1) granted an injunction, but on appeal the Court of Appeal (2) set aside this order on the ground that the ties in these agreements were in restraint of trade and were unenforceable. The appellants now maintain first that these ties were not in restraint of trade and secondly that, if they were, they were in the circumstances valid and enforceable.

The earlier agreement related to the Corner Garage, Stourport, and was to remain in force for twenty-one years from July 1, 1962. As the case with regard

---

(1) [1965] 2 All E.R. 933; [1966] 2 Q.B. 514.
(2) The injunctions were granted on June 15, 1965, on the hearing of the actions, which had been consolidated by order dated Mar. 17, 1965, by MOCATTA, J., reported [1966] 1 All E.R. 725; [1966] 2 Q.B. at p. 555.

to it is complicated, however, by there being a mortgage as security for money lent by the appellants to the respondents, I shall first consider the second agreement which related to the Mustow Green Garage near Kidderminster. This agreement was to remain in force for four years and five months from July 1, 1963. It appears that the appellants had a similar agreement with the previous owners of that garage and that this period was chosen because it was the unexpired period of that earlier agreement.

The main provisions of the Mustow Green agreement are that while it remained in force the respondents agreed to buy from the appellants their total requirements of motor fuels for resale at that garage and agreed to keep it open at all reasonable hours for the sale of Esso motor fuels and Esso motor oils, and in return the appellants agreed to sell to the respondents at their wholesale schedule price at the time of delivery, and to allow a rebate from that price of one penny farthing per gallon payable quarterly. There were a number of other provisions with regard to advertising, service at the garage, etc., which I shall not specify because they do not appear to me to assist in determining the questions at issue; but there are two other provisions which I must notice. If the respondents wished to dispose of the garage they were not to do so except to a person who agreed to be substituted for them for all purposes of this agreement. If the agreement is otherwise unobjectionable, I do not think that this provision can invalidate it, because it was only by some such means that the appellants could ensure that their petrol would continue to be sold at this garage for the full period of the agreement. The other is a provision for retail price maintenance which the appellants at that time inserted in all their numerous tying agreements with garages and filling stations. Shortly before the present action was raised the appellants intimated that they would not enforce this clause against any of their tied customers. The respondents were in favour of retail price maintenance and their original defence was that this change of policy by the appellants entitled them to rescind the whole agreement for the tie. This defence was rejected by MOCATTA, J. (3), and it has not been maintained before your lordships.

So I can now turn to the first question in this appeal—whether this agreement is to be regarded in law as an agreement in restraint of trade. The law with regard to restraint of trade is of ancient origin. There are references to it in the YEAR BOOKS, and it seems to have received considerable attention in the time of Queen Elizabeth I. The old cases lie within a narrow compass. It seems to have been common for an apprentice or a craftsman to agree with his master that he would not compete with him after leaving his service, and also for a trader who sold his business to agree that he would not thereafter compete with the purchaser of his business. No early case was cited which did not fall within one or other of these categories. Moreover, even in recent times there have been surprisingly few reported cases falling outside these categories in which restraint of trade has been pleaded: we were informed by counsel that there are only about forty English cases which can be traced. On the other hand there is an immense body of authorities with regard to the two original categories. I have not found it an easy task to determine how far principles developed for the original categories have been or should be extended.

The most general statement with regard to restraint of trade is that of LORD PARKER OF WADDINGTON in *A.-G. of Commonwealth of Australia* v. *Adelaide Steamship Co., Ltd.* (4). He said:

" Monopolies and contracts in restraint of trade have this in common— that they both, if enforced, involve a derogation from the common law right in virtue of which any member of the community may exercise any

---

(3) [1965] 2 All E.R. at p. 944; [1966] 2 Q.B. at p. 541.
(4) [1911-13] All E.R. Rep. 1120 at p. 1123; [1913] A.C. 781 at p. 794.

trade or business he pleases, and in such manner as he thinks best in his own interests."

That cannot have been intended, however, to be a definition: all contracts in restraint of trade involve such a derogation but not all contracts involving such a derogation are contracts in restraint of trade. Whenever a man agrees to do something over a period he thereby puts it wholly or partly out of his power to " exercise any trade or business he pleases " during that period. He may enter into a contract of service or may agree to give his exclusive services to another: then during the period of the contract he is not entitled to engage in other business activities. No one has ever suggested, however, that such contracts are in restraint of trade except in very unusual circumstances, such as those in *Young v. Timmins* (5), where the servant had agreed not to work for anyone else but might have been given no work and received no remuneration for considerable periods and thus have been deprived of a livelihood: the grounds of judgment may not now be correct, but I think that the case was rightly decided.

That LORD PARKER OF WADDINGTON cannot have intended those words to be a definition is, I think, made clear by a later passage (6):

> " Contracts in restraint of trade were subject to somewhat different considerations. There is little doubt that the common law in the earlier stages of its growth treated *all* [my italics] such contracts as contracts of imperfect obligation, if not void for all purposes; they were said to be against public policy in the sense that it was deemed impolitic to enforce them . . .."

He certainly never supposed that all contracts which by obliging a man to act in one way (e.g. as a servant) prevented him from doing other things had ever been held to be of imperfect obligation or against public policy.

The leading case of *Nordenfelt* v. *Maxim Nordenfelt Guns and Ammunition Co., Ltd.* (7) fell within the old categories, and it may be misleading to take the well-known passages out of context and try to apply them to cases of quite different nature. LORD MACNAGHTEN said (8):

> " The public have an interest in every person's carrying on his trade freely; so has the individual. All interference with individual liberty of action in trading, and all restraints of trade of themselves, if there is nothing more, are contrary to public policy, and therefore void."

By " interference " he meant interference to which the individual had agreed by contract, but I am sure that he did not mean to include all cases in which one party had " interfered " with the liberty of another by getting him to agree to give his whole time to the other party's affairs. He had said (9):

> " In the age of Queen Elizabeth all restraints of trade, whatever they were, general or partial, were thought to be contrary to public policy, and therefore void."

So he only had in mind the two original kinds of case. There was no need in *Nordenfelt's* case (7) to attempt to define other classes of case to which the doctrine of retraint would apply.

If a contract is within the class of contracts in restraint of trade, the law which applies to it is quite different from the law which applies to contracts generally. In general, unless a contract is vitiated by duress, fraud or mistake, its terms will be enforced though unreasonable or even harsh and unconscionable, but here a term in restraint of trade will not be enforced unless it is reasonable. Moreover, in the ordinary case the court will not remake a contract: unless in

(5) (1831), Cr. & J. 331.
(6) [1911-13] All E.R. Rep. 1120 at p. 1123; [1913] A.C. 781 at p. 794.
(7) [1891-94] All E.R. Rep. 1; [1894] A.C. 535.
(8) [1891-94] All E.R. Rep. at p. 18; [1894] A.C. at p. 565.
(9) [1891-94] All E.R. Rep. at p. 17; [1894] A.C. at p. 564.

the special case where the contract is severable, it will not strike out one provision as unenforceable and enforce the rest. But here the party who has been paid for agreeing to the restraint may be unjustly enriched if the court holds the restraint to be too wide to be enforceable and is unable to adjust the consideration given by the other party.

It is much too late now to say that this rather anomalous doctrine of restraint of trade can be confined to the two classes of case to which it was originally applied; but the cases outside these two classes afford little guidance as to the circumstances in which it should be applied. In some it has been assumed that the doctrine applies and the controversy has been whether the restraint was reasonable; and in others, where one might have expected the point to be taken, it was not taken, perhaps because counsel thought that there was no chance of the court holding that the restraint was too wide to be reasonable.

In *McEllistrim* v. *Ballymacelligott Co-operative Agricultural and Dairy Society, Ltd.* (10) the society had changed its rules so as to prevent any member from selling (except under heavy penalty) any milk produced by him in a large area of county Kerry to anyone except the society, and a member could not terminate his membership without the society's permission. The plaintiff, who was a member, sought a declaration that the new rules were in unreasonable restraint of trade. LORD BIRKENHEAD, L.C., assumed that they were in restraint of trade and held that they were unreasonable, as did LORD ATKINSON and LORD SHAW OF DUNFERMLINE. LORD FINLAY said (11), having referred to *Herbert Morris, Ltd.* v. *Saxelby* (12):

" The present case is really governed by the principle there enunciated that ' public policy requires that every man shall be at liberty to work for himself and shall not be at liberty to deprive himself or the state of his labour, skill or talent, by any contract that he enters into '. This is equally applicable to the right to sell his goods."

I doubt whether this last sentence is quite accurate. It would seem to mean that every contract by which a man (or a company) agrees to sell his whole output (or even half of it) for any future period to the other party to the contract is a contract in restraint of trade, because it restricts his liberty to sell as he pleases, and is therefore unenforceable unless his agreement can be justified as being reasonable. There must have been many ordinary commercial contracts of that kind in the past, but no one has ever suggested that they were in restraint of trade. *McEllistrim's* case (10) at least establishes, however, that there comes a point at which such a contract can come within the doctrine of restraint of trade.

In *English Hop Growers, Ltd.* v. *Dering* (13) the defendant had agreed to sell his crop of hops to the society for five years. He failed to do so and was sued: in defence he pleaded that the contract was in restraint of trade. The restraint was held to be reasonable, but both SCRUTTON, L.J., and the other members of the court appear to have been prepared to treat this as a contract in restraint of trade. This was not just an ordinary agreement, it was rather a marketing scheme accepted by the great majority of English hop growers.

In *Foley* v. *Classique Coaches, Ltd.* (14) the purchaser of a piece of land agreed with the seller to take from him all the petrol required for the purchaser's business carried on there. The question whether this was in restraint of trade was dealt with briefly, SCRUTTON, L.J., merely saying (15) that it was not in " undue restraint of trade ". In *Bouchard Servais* v. *Prince's Hall Restaurant, Ltd.* (16). the Court of Appeal held valid a contract by which the restaurant agreed to take

(10) [1919] A.C. 548.   (11) [1919] A.C. at pp. 571, 572.
(12) [1916-17] All E.R. Rep. 305; [1916] 1 A.C. 688.
(13) [1928] All E.R. Rep. 396; [1928] K.B. 174.
(14) [1934] All E.R. Rep. 88; [1934] 2 K.B. 1.
(15) [1934] All E.R. Rep. at p. 91; [1934] 2 K.B. at p. 11.
(16) (1904), 20 T.L.R. 574.

all the burgundy sold there from the plaintiffs. It is not very clear whether they held that this was not in restraint of trade or that, though in restraint of trade, it was reasonable.

In *United Shoe Machinery Co. of Canada* v. *Brunet* (17) the company leased machinery under a condition that it should not be used in conjunction with machinery made by any other manufacturer, and it was held that this condition was not in restraint of trade. I do not think that the reasons given for the decision are very satisfactory. *Mogul Steamship Co.* v. *McGregor, Gow & Co.* (18) is relied on. There an association of shipowners agreed to use various lawful means to dissuade customers from shipping their goods by the Mogul line. It was held that this agreement was lawful in the sense that it gave the Mogul company no right to sue them; but it was recognised, at least by the majority of their lordships, that the agreement would have been unenforceable as between the members of the association. Lord Watson said (19)

"... an agreement by traders to combine for a lawful purpose and for a specified time is not binding upon any of the parties to it if he chooses to withdraw, and, consequently, cannot be enforced in invitum."

One must always bear in mind that an agreement in restraint of trade is not generally unlawful if the parties choose to abide by it: it is only unenforceable if a party chooses not to abide by it.

The main argument submitted for the appellants on this matter was that restraint of trade means a personal restraint, and does not apply to a restraint on the use of a particular piece of land. Otherwise, it was said, every covenant running with the land which prevents its use for all or for some trading purposes would be a covenant in restraint of trade and therefore unenforceable, unless it could be shown to be reasonable and for the protection of some legitimate interest. It was said that the present agreement only prevents the sale of petrol from other suppliers on the site of the Mustow Green garage: it leaves the respondents free to trade anywhere else in any way they choose. In many cases, however, a trader trading at a particular place does not have the resources to enable him to begin trading elsewhere as well, and if he did he might find it difficult to find another suitable garage for sale or to get planning permission to open a new filling station on another site. As the whole doctrine of restraint of trade is based on public policy, its application ought to depend less on legal niceties or theoretical possibilities than on the practical effect of a restraint in hampering that freedom which it is the policy of the law to protect.

It is true that it would be an innovation to hold that ordinary negative covenants preventing the use of a particular site for trading of all kinds or of a particular kind are within the scope of the doctrine of restraint of trade. I do not think that they are. Restraint of trade appears to me to imply that a man contracts to give up some freedom which otherwise he would have had. A person buying or leasing land had no previous right to be there at all, let alone to trade there, and, when he takes possession of that land subject to a negative restrictive covenant, he gives up no right or freedom which he previously had. I think that the " tied house " cases might be explained in this way, apart from *Biggs* v. *Hoddinott* (20) where the owner of a free house had agreed to a tie in favour of a brewer who had lent him money. Restraint of trade was not pleaded. If it had been the restraint would probably have been held to be reasonable; but there is some difficulty if a restraint in a lease not merely prevents the person who takes possession of the land under the lease from doing certain things there, but also obliges him to act in a particular way. In the present case the respondents, before they made this agreement, were entitled to use this land in any lawful way that they chose, and by making this agreement they agreed to restrict

(17) [1909] A.C. 330.
(18) [1891-94] All E.R. Rep. 263; [1892] A.C. 25.
(19) [1891-94] All E.R. Rep. at p. 271; [1892] A.C. at p. 42.
(20) [1895-99] All E.R. Rep. 625; [1898] 2 Ch. 307.

their right by giving up their right to sell there petrol not supplied by the
appellants.

In my view this agreement is within the scope of the doctrine of restraint
of trade, as it had been developed in English law. Not only have the respondents
agreed negatively not to sell other petrol, but also they have agreed positively
to keep this garage open for the sale of the appellants' petrol at all reasonable
hours throughout the period of the tie. It was argued that this was merely
regulating the respondent's trading and rather promoting than restraining his
trade; but regulating a person's existing trade may be a greater restraint than
prohibiting him from engaging in a new trade. Further a contract to take one's
whole supply from one source may be much more hampering than a contract to
sell one's whole output to one buyer. I would not attempt to define the dividing
line between contracts which are and contracts which are not in restraint of
trade, but in my view this contract must be held to be in restraint of trade. So it
is necessary to consider whether its provisions can be justified.

Before considering this question I must deal briefly with the other agreement
tying the Corner Garage for twenty-one years. The rebate and other advantages
to the respondents were similar to those in the Mustow Green agreement, but
in addition the appellants made a loan of £7,000 to the respondents to enable
them to improve their garage and this loan was to be repaid over the twenty-one
years of the tie. As security they took a mortgage of this garage. The agreement
provided that the loan should not be paid off earlier than at the dates stipulated;
but the respondents now tender the unpaid balance of the loan, and they say
that the appellants have no interest to refuse to accept repayment now except
in order to maintain the tie for the full twenty-one years.

The appellants argue that the fact that there is a mortgage excludes any
application of the doctrine of restraint of trade; but I agree with your lordships
in rejecting that argument. I am prepared to assume that, if the respondents
had not offered to repay the loan so far as it is still outstanding, the appellants
would have been entitled to retain the tie. As they have tendered repayment,
however, I do not think that the existence of the loan and the mortgage puts the
appellants in any stronger position to maintain the tie than they would have
been in if the original agreements had permitted repayment at an earlier date.
The appellants must shew that, in the circumstances when the agreement was
made, a tie for twenty-one years was justifiable.

It is now generally accepted that a provision in a contract which is to be
regarded as in restraint of trade must be justified if it is to be enforceable, and
that the law on this matter was correctly stated by LORD MACNAGHTEN in the
Nordenfelt case (21). He said:

"Restraints of trade and interference with individual liberty of action,
may be justified by the special circumstances of a particular case. It is a
sufficient justification, and indeed, it is the only justification, if the restriction
is reasonable—reasonable, that is, in reference to the interests of the parties
concerned and reasonable in reference to the interests of the public, so
framed and so guarded as to afford adequate protection to the party in whose
favour it is imposed, while at the same time it is in no way injurious to the
public."

So in every case it is necessary to consider, first whether the restraint went farther
than to afford adequate protection to the party in whose favour it was granted,
secondly whether it can be justified as being in the interests of the party
restrained, and thirdly whether it must be held contrary to the public interest.
I find it difficult to agree with the way in which the court has in some cases
treated the interests of the party restrained. Surely it can never be in the interest
of a person to agree to suffer a restraint unless he gets some compensating
advantage, direct or indirect; and LORD MACNAGHTEN said (21) " of course the

(21) [1891-94] All E.R. Rep. at p. 18; [1894] A.C. at p. 565.

quantum of consideration may enter into the question of the reasonableness of the contract ".

Where two experienced traders are bargaining on equal terms and one has agreed to a restraint for reasons which seem good to him, the court is in grave danger of stultifying itself if it says that it knows that trader's interest better than he does himself. There may well be cases, however, where, although the party to be restrained has deliberately accepted the main terms of the contract, he has been at a disadvantage as regards other terms: for example, where a set of conditions has been incorporated which has not been the subject of negotiation—there the court may have greater freedom to hold them unreasonable.

I think that in some cases where the court has held that a restraint was not in the interests of the parties it would have been more correct to hold that the restraint was against the public interest. For example, in *Kores Manufacturing Co., Ltd.* v. *Kolok Manufacturing Co., Ltd.* (22) the parties had agreed that neither would employ any man who had left the service of the other. From their own points of view there was probably very good reason for that; but it could well be held to be against the public interest to interfere in this way with the freedom of their employees. If the parties chose to abide by their agreement an employee would have no more right to complain than the Mogul company had in the *Mogul* case (23); but the law would not countenance their agreement by enforcing it. Moreover in cases where a party, who is in no way at a disadvantage in bargaining, chooses to take a calculated risk, I see no reason why the court should say that he has acted against his own interests: but it can say that the restraint might well produce a situation which would be contrary to the public interest.

Again, whether or not a restraint is in the personal interests of the parties, it is I think well established that the court will not enforce a restraint which goes further than affording adequate protection to the legitimate interests of the party in whose favour it is granted. This must, I think, be because too wide a restraint is against the public interest. It has often been said that a person is not entitled to be protected against mere competition. I do not find that very helpful in a case like the present. I think it better to ascertain what were the legitimate interests of the appellants which they were entitled to protect, and then to see whether these restraints were more than adequate for that purpose.

What were the appellants' legitimate interests must depend largely on what was the state of affairs in their business and with regard to the distribution and sale of petrol generally; and those are questions of fact to be answered by evidence or common knowledge. In the present case restraint of trade was not pleaded originally, and the appellants received notice that it was to be raised only a fortnight before the trial. They may have been wise in not seeking a postponement of the trial when the pleadings were amended; but the result has been that the evidence on this matter is scanty. I think, however, that it is legitimate to supplement it from the considerable body of reported cases regarding solus agreements and from the facts found in the Report of the Monopolies Commission of July, 1965 (24).

When petrol rationing came to an end in 1950 the large producers began to make agreements, now known as solus agreements, with garage owners under which the garage owner, in return for certain advantages, agreed to sell only the petrol of the producer with whom he made the agreement. Within a short time three-quarters of the filling stations in this country were tied in that way, and by the dates of the agreement in this case over ninety per cent. had agreed to ties. It appears that the garage owners were not at a disadvantage in bargaining

(22) [1958] 2 All E.R. 65; [1959] Ch. 108.
(23) [1891-94] All E.R. Rep. 263; [1892] A.C. 25.
(24) Report on the supply of petrol to retailers in the United Kingdom (chairman R. F. Levy, Q.C.), H.C. 264.

with the large producing companies as there was intense competition between these companies to obtain these ties. So we can assume that both the garage owners and the companies thought that such ties were to their advantage; and it is not said in this case that all ties are either against the public interest or against the interests of the parties. The respondents' case is that the ties with which we are concerned are for too long periods.

The advantage to the garage owner is that he gets a rebate on the wholesale price of the petrol which he buys and also may get other benefits or financial assistance. The main advantages for the producing company appear to be that distribution is made easier and more economical, and that it is assured of a steady outlet for its petrol over a period. As regards distribution it appears that there were some thirty-five thousand filling stations in this country at the relevant time, of which about a fifth were tied to the appellants. So they have to distribute only to some seven thousand filling stations instead of to a very much larger number if most filling stations sold several brands of petrol. The main reason why the producing companies want ties for five years and more instead of ties for one or two years only seems to be that they can organise their business better if on the average only one-fifth or less of their ties come to an end in any one year. The appellants make a point of fact that they have invested some £200 millions in refineries and other plant, and that they could not have done that unless they could foresee a steady and assured level of sales of their petrol. Most of their ties appear to have been made for periods of between five and twenty years; but we have no evidence as to the precise additional advantage which they derive from a five year tie as compared with a two year tie or from a twenty year tie as compared with a five year tie.

The Court of Appeal (25) held that these ties were for unreasonably long periods. They thought that, if for any reason the respondents ceased to sell the appellants' petrol, the appellants could have found other suitable outlets in the neighbourhood within two or three years. I do not think that that is the right test. In the first place there was no evidence about this, and I do not think that it would be practicable to apply this test in practice. It might happen that, when the respondents ceased to sell their petrol, the appellants would find such an alternative outlet in a very short time; but looking to the fact that well over ninety per cent. of existing filling stations are tied and that there may be great difficulty in opening a new filling station, it might take a very long time to find an alternative. Any estimate of how long it might take to find suitable alternatives for the respondents' filling stations could be little better than guesswork.

I do not think that the appellants' interest can be regarded so narrowly. They are not so much concerned with any particular outlet as with maintaining a stable system of distribution throughout the country, so as to enable their business to be run efficiently and economically. In my view there is sufficient material to justify a decision that ties of less than five years were insufficient, in the circumstances of the trade when these agreements were made, to afford adequate protection to the appellants' legitimate interests. If that is so, I cannot find anything in the details of the Mustow Green agreement which would indicate that it is unreasonable. It is true that, if some of the provisions were operated by the appellants in a manner which would be commercially unreasonable, they might put the respondents in difficulties. I think, however, that a court must have regard to the fact that the appellants must act in such a way that they will be able to obtain renewals of the great majority of their very numerous ties, some of which will come to an end almost every week. If in such circumstances a garage owner chooses to rely on the commercial probity and good sense of the producer, I do not think that a court should hold his agreement unreasonable because it is legally capable of some misuse. I would therefore allow the appeal as regards the Mustow Green agreement.

The Corner Garage agreement, however, involves much more difficulty.

(25) [1966] 1 All E.R. 725; [1966] 2 Q.B. at p. 555.

Taking first the legitimate interests of the appellants, a new argument was submitted to your lordships that, apart from any question of security for their loan, it would be unfair to the appellants if the respondents, having used the appellants' money to build up their business, were entitled after a comparatively short time to be free to seek better terms from a competing producer. There is no material, however, on which I can assess the strength of this argument, and I do not find myself in a position to determine whether it has any validity. A tie for twenty-one years stretches far beyond any period for which developments are reasonably foreseeable. Restrictions on the garage owner which might seem tolerable and reasonable in reasonably foreseeable conditions might come to have a very different effect in quite different conditions: the public interest comes in here more strongly. Moreover, apart from a case where he gets a loan, a garage owner appears to get no greater advantage from a twenty year tie than he gets from a five year tie. So I would think that there must at least be some clearly established advantage to the producing company—something to show that a shorter period would not be adequate—before so long a period could be justified; but in this case there is no evidence to prove anything of the kind. Moreover, the other material which I have thought it right to consider does not appear to me to assist the appellant here. I would therefore dismiss the appeal as regards the Corner Garage agreement.

I would add the decision in this case—particularly in view of the paucity of evidence—ought not in my view to be regarded as laying down any general rule as to the length of tie permissible in a solus agreement. I do not think that the case of *Petrofina (Gt. Britain), Ltd.* v. *Martin* (26) can be regarded as laying down a general rule. The agreement there was in unusual terms. I think that the decision was right, although I do not agree with all the reasons; but I must not be taken as expressing any opinion as to the validity of ties for periods mid-way between the two periods with which the present case is concerned.

LORD MORRIS OF BORTH-Y-GEST: My Lords, we have been concerned in this case to decide as to the application of competing principles of law. In a system of law not contained in any formal code decision is reached by applying settled or recognised principle to particular ascertained facts; but in some situations more than one principle may be relevant and important. Particularly is this so where principles have, as their foundation, the dictates of public policy. That has been so in the case of those which have been prominent in the arguments in this case. The respondent company (Harper's Garage (Stourport), Ltd.) assert, while the appellants (Esso Petroleum Co., Ltd.) deny that what is generally called the " doctrine " of restraint of trade must be considered in reference to the solus agreements: if so, then the agreements must pass a test of reasonableness before they can qualify to be enforceable. Whether the doctrine must be considered and, if so, with what result, is now the effective issue in the litigation, though it was not at first raised and, indeed, only emerged as an issue on the eve or at the commencement of the trial.

The law has for many centuries set itself against restraint of trade. Monopolies, likewise, have always been in disfavour with the law. In keeping with this, arrangements are condemned which have as their mere purpose the elimination of competition. Restraints which would result in preventing a man from pursuing his trade and earning his living may be injurious to the man himself and to a family dependent on his support, and may be detrimental to the public interest (see *Mitchel* v. *Reynolds* (27)). The abhorrence of such restraints can be strong enough to prevail over certain well accepted principles. In general the law recognises that there is freedom to enter into any contract that can lawfully be made. The law lends its weight to uphold and enforce contracts freely entered into. The law does not allow a man to derogate from his grant. If someone has sold the goodwill of his business, some restraint to enable the purchaser to have

---

(26) [1966] 1 All E.R. 126; [1966] Ch. 146.　　　　(27) (1711), 1 P.Wms. 181.

that which he has bought may be recognised as reasonable. Some restraints to ensure the protection of confidential information may be similarly regarded. The law recognises that, if business contracts are fairly made by parties who are on equal terms, such parties should know their business best. If there has been no irregularity the law does not mend or amend contracts merely for the relief of those for whom things have not turned out well; but when all this is fully recognised yet the law, in some circumstances, reserves a right to say that a contract is in restraint of trade and that to be enforceable it must pass a test of reasonableness. In the competition between varying principles possibly applicable that which makes certain covenants in restraint of trade unenforceable will in some circumstances be strong enough to prevail. Public policy will give it priority. It will have such priority because of the reasonable necessity to ensure and preserve freedom of trade. Some words spoken by SIR GEORGE JESSELL, M.R., in *Printing and Numerical Registering Co.* v. *Sampson* (28), may, however, be kept in mind. He said:

" It must not be forgotten that you are not to extend arbitrarily those rules, which say that a given contract is void as being against public policy, because if there is one thing which more than another public policy requires it is that men of full age and competent understanding shall have the utmost liberty of contracting, and that their contracts when entered into freely and voluntarily shall be held sacred and shall be enforced by courts of justice. Therefore, you have this paramount public policy to consider—that you are not lightly to interfere with this freedom of contract."

To a similar purport were some words by SCRUTTON, L.J., in his judgment in *English Hop Growers, Ltd.* v. *Dering* (29), where he said:

" I myself have always regarded it as in the public interest that parties who, being in an equal position of bargaining, make contracts, should be compelled to perform them, and not to escape from their liabilities by saying that they had agreed to something which was unreasonable."

While accepting the power and weight of these observations it can be remembered that, even if a contract is in restraint of trade, it will nevertheless be enforceable provided always that the restriction is reasonable in reference to the interest of the parties and in reference to the interest of the public. Though a person has not been under any compulsion nor has laboured under any deception when making a contract under which he agrees to a restraint in trade, yet in some circumstances the law allows him to seek to defend himself from compliance with the terms of the restraint by inviting the court to say that the contract should not be enforced.

As, therefore, the policy of the law is to uphold freedom to contract and also to uphold freedom to trade a certain adjustment is necessary. In his speech in *Herbert Morris, Ltd.* v. *Saxelby* (30) LORD SHAW OF DUNFERMLINE said:

" The delicacy of the operation of law in settling the bounds of either freedom has long been familiar. In these cases, as I have pointed out, there are two freedoms to be considered, one the freedom of trade and the other the freedom of contract: and to that I will now again venture to add that it is a mistake to think that public interest is only concerned with one. It is concerned with both."

The enquiry is raised as to what are the circumstances in which the doctrine applies. In particular in the present case the question arises whether it can be said that the solus agreements by their terms involve a restraint of trade. If they do, then it is contended by the appellants that the doctrine or principle of restraint of trade never has application to a restraint which is imposed on the trading use to be made of a particular piece of land.

(28) (1875), L.R. 19 Eq. 462 at p. 465.
(29) [1928] All E.R. Rep. at p. 400; [1928] 2 K.B. at p. 181.
(30) [1916-17] All E.R. Rep. at p. 314; [1916] 1 A.C. at p. 716.

A review of the authorities shows that in some groups of cases there has been no assertion that the doctrine or principle of restraint of trade applies. It is said, therefore, that there are classes of cases in which the doctrine does not apply, and attempt is made to define those groups of cases in which alone the doctrine does apply. For my part, I doubt whether it is possible or desirable to record any very rigid classification of groups of cases. Nor do I think that any firm inference can be made from the circumstances that in respect of certain groups of cases no one has claimed that the doctrine applies or has sought to invoke it. That might be for the reason that there are some situations in which it would not be thought by anyone that the doctrine could successfully be invoked. In some cases it matters not whether it is said that the doctrine does not apply or whether it is said that a restraint would so obviously pass the test of reasonableness that no one would be disposed even to seek to invoke the doctrine. I take the test to be as laid down by LORD MACNAGHTEN in his speech in *Nordenfelt* v. *Maxim Nordenfelt Guns and Ammunition Co., Ltd.* (31):

" All interference with the individual liberty of action in trading, and all restraints of trade of themselves, if there is nothing more, are contrary to public policy, and, therefore, void. That is the general rule. But there are exceptions. Restraints of trade and interference with individual liberty of action, may be justified by the special circumstances of a particular case. It is a sufficient justification, and indeed, it is the only justification, if the restriction is reasonable—reasonable, that is, in reference to the interests of the parties concerned and reasonable in reference to the interests of the public, so framed and so guarded as to afford adequate protection to the party in whose favour it is imposed, while at the same time it is in no way injurious to the public."

When attempt is made to define what is meant by a contract in restraint of trade, words are used which are of far-reaching application. Thus LORD DENNING, M.R., in *Petrofina (Great Britain), Ltd.* v. *Martin* (32) said:

". . . every member of the community is entitled to carry on any trade or business he chooses and in such manner as he thinks most desirable in his own interests, so long as he does nothing unlawful; with the consequence that any contract which interferes with the free exercise of his trade or business, by restricting him in the work he may do for others, or the arrangements which he may make with others, is a contract in restraint of trade. It is invalid unless it is reasonable as between the parties and not injurious to the public interest."

So DIPLOCK, L.J., in the same case said (33):

" A contract in restraint of trade is one in which a party (the covenantor) agrees with any other party (the covenantee) to restrict his liberty in the future to carry on trade with other persons not parties to the contract in such manner as he chooses . . ."

These are helpful expositions, provided they are used rationally and not too literally. Thus, if A made a contract under which he willingly agreed to serve B on reasonable terms for a few years and to give his whole working time to B, it would be surprising indeed if it were sought to describe the contract as being in restraint of trade. In fact such a contract would very likely be for the advancement of trade. Yet counsel for the respondents did not shrink from the assertion that every contract of personal service is a contract in restraint of trade. I cannot think that either authority or logic requires acceptance of so extreme a view.

I approach the present case by considering, first whether the agreements made by the respondents should, in a reasonable sense, be regarded as in restraint of

(31) [1891-94] All E.R. Rep. at p. 18; [1894] A.C. at p. 565.
(32) [1966] 1 All E.R. at p. 131; [1966] Ch. at p. 169.
(33) [1966] 1 All E.R. at p. 138; [1966] Ch. at p. 180.

trade and, if they are to be so considered, secondly the submission which was made that, since the restriction can be said to be a restriction of the trading use to be made of a particular piece of land, the doctrine of restraint of trade has no application.

The essence of the agreement of June 27, 1963, in reference to Mustow Green garage was that the respondents became tied to the appellants. The respondents agreed to buy from the appellants their total requirements of motor fuels for resale at Mustow Green garage. They agreed also to operate the garage in accordance with the Esso Dealer Co-operation Plan, one term of which was " To keep the service station open at all reasonable hours for the use of Esso motor fuels and Esso motor oils ". I cannot accept the contention that there was no positive obligation in regard to operating the garage but only an agreement as to method of operation if the garage was in fact being operated. In my view, the respondents agreed to operate the garage in a particular way and, above all, they agreed to take all their requirements of motor fuels from the appellants. Implied in this was an undertaking not to sell any other motor fuels than those of the appellants. The very basis of the agreement was restrictive. It was designed to ensure that the respondents would not sell any of the motor fuels that competed with the appellants. It restricted the manner in which the respondents could carry on their business. The supply agreement, dated July 5, 1962, in reference to the Corner Garage had in general the same features.

If the agreements are regarded, as I think that they must be, as being prima facie in restraint of trade then the question arises whether there is validity in the contention that the restriction was merely of the trading use to be made of a particular piece of land and that, as a consequence, there was exclusion of the applicability of the doctrine of restraint of trade. It was powerfully argued that it has long been accepted that a covenant in a lease of premises which prohibits the carrying-on of any trade or business on the premises is not subject to the tests of being reasonable as between parties and not injurious to the public interest: and it was argued that the reason for this can be stated to be that the doctrine of restraint of trade applies to agreements which in substance restrict the trade that a person may engage in, yet it does not apply to agreements which in substance merely restrict the use to be made of a particular piece of land. It was said that the respondents' covenants did not limit their activities anywhere else than on particular pieces of land, i.e., at their two garages.

There is a considerable difference between the covenants in the present case and covenants of the kind which might be entered into by a purchaser or by a lessee. If one who seeks to take a lease of land knows that the only lease which is available to him is a lease with a restriction, then he must either take what is offered (on the appropriate financial terms) or he must seek a lease elsewhere. No feature of public policy requires that, if he freely contracted, he should be excused from honouring his contract. In no rational sense could it be said that, if he took a lease with a restriction as to trading, he was entering into a contract that interfered with the free exercise of his trade or his business or with his " individual liberty of action in trading ". His freedom to pursue his trade or earn his living is not impaired merely because there is some land belonging to someone else on which he cannot enter for the purposes of his trade or business. In such a situation (i.e., that of voluntarily taking a lease of land with a restrictive covenant) it would not seem sensible to regard the doctrine of restraint of trade as having application. There would be nothing which could be described as interference with individual liberty of action in trading. There is a clear difference between the case where someone fetters his future by parting with a freedom which he possesses, and the case where someone seeks to claim a greater freedom than that which he possesses or has arranged to acquire. So, also, if someone seeks to buy a part of the land of a vendor and can only buy on the terms that he will covenant with the vendor not to put the land to some particular use, there would seem in principle to be no reason why the contract should not be honoured.

The agreements made by the respondents were quite different. The respondents had their garages. The appellants had no interest in them or in the land on which they were situated. By the agreements, the respondents agreed for periods of years to limit and restrict their trading activity. They agreed (in general) not to sell any motor fuels other than those of the appellants. Prima facie the agreements were in restraint of trade. They were naked covenants or covenants in gross. As covenants they seem to me to have more of a personal character than of a property character. They were concerned with the way in which the respondents would carry on their garages and their businesses. As HARMAN, L.J., said in the *Petrofina* case (34), it is a person who trades and not the land.

It is agreed that no case has been cited which lays down or upholds the wide proposition that the doctrine of restraint of trade can have no application to a covenant which is merely restrictive of the trading use to be made of a particular piece of land. If such a proposition were held to be sound then, as DIPLOCK, L.J., pointed out in the *Petrofina* case (35), there would be scope to reframe radius covenants in restraint of trade, even where the radius was very wide, as covenants not to carry on a particular trade in a particular manner on any premises in a defined area. Indeed, as most activities and enterprises take place in some way or other on or in connexion with land it would be possible, if the proposition were upheld, to frame a great many covenants so as to avoid their being open to the tests to which covenants in restraint of trade must submit. Apart from this consideration, however, there are cases in the books which point to the novelty of the proposition. Thus, in *English Hop Growers, Ltd.* v. *Dering* (36) the defendant undertook to deliver to the plaintiffs all the hops grown or produced by him in a particular year on land of a certain acreage. He contended that the agreement was not enforceable because it was in restraint of trade. The court did not say that the contention could not be advanced. They did not say that, as the defendant's undertaking was restrictive of the trading use that he was making of his land, the contention was not open to him. The court considered the contention, but held that the undertaking of the defendant was not unreasonable: accordingly it was enforced. In another case, *Bouchard Servais* v. *Prince's Hall Restaurant, Ltd.* (37), the defendants agreed (for a consideration) to give the plaintiffs the exclusive right of supplying certain wine for the defendants' restaurant. To a claim made by the plaintiffs for a breach of the agreement one plea made by the defendants was that the contract was void as being in restraint of trade and unlimited in time. SIR RICHARD HENN COLLINS, M.R., in his judgment said that, in his opinion, the case did not come within the principle by which contracts in restraint of trade were held to be invalid as being contrary to public policy. He thought that contracts such as those by which persons bound themselves to supply customers with goods obtained from a particular merchant exclusively were for the benefit of the community. He pointed out that contracts for sole agency were matters of everyday occurrence. He said that, if the contract was one of a kind which might be treated as violating the common law rule against contracts in restraint of trade, the circumstances were such as to bring in the element of reasonableness which afforded an answer to the general rule. STIRLING, L.J., in his judgment considered and gave reasons for rejecting the contention that the contract, being unlimited in point of time, was in restraint of trade. He did not suggest that, as the defendants' agreement was restrictive of the trading use that they would make of their premises, their plea was not open to them and could not be considered.

In another case, *Foley* v. *Classique Coaches, Ltd.* (38), the plaintiff agreed to sell a piece of land (adjoining other land belonging to him) to the defendants, who proposed to use the land for their business as motor coach proprietors. The sale

---

(34) [1966] 1 All E.R. at p. 136; [1966] Ch. at p. 177.
(35) [1966] 1 All E.R. at p. 141; [1966] Ch. at p. 185.
(36) [1928] All E.R. Rep. 396; [1928] 2 K.B. 174.   (37) (1904), 20 T.L.R. 574.
(38) [1934] All E.R. Rep. 88; [1934] 2 K.B. 1.

took place. The sale was made subject to the defendants entering into another agreement, which they did, to buy from the plaintiff (who had a petrol-filling station on his adjoining land) all the petrol that they needed for the running of their business as motor coach proprietors so long as the plaintiff was able to supply them. In proceedings by the plaintiff to enforce this latter agreement one contention of the defendants was that the agreement was an unreasonable and unnecessary restraint of the defendants' trade and was contrary to public policy and illegal. It was held that there was no " undue " restraint of trade. It does not appear to have been suggested that, as the defendants' agreement was restrictive of the trading use that they would make of the land which they acquired, the doctrine of restraint of trade could not possibly have application or be raised for consideration.

For the reasons which I have set out and subject to what I have said above, I am unable to accept the contention in its wide form that in no circumstances can the doctrine of restraint of trade apply to contracts or covenants regulating the trading use to be made of a particular plot of land. The agreements made in reference to the two garages of the respondents were, in my view, agreements in restraint of trade. The question, therefore, arises whether the agreements can pass the tests of reasonableness. The appellants allege that the agreements were reasonable as between the parties. The onus is on them to show that this is so. They must show that the restraint affords them no more than adequate protection for those interests which they have a right to have protected. In *Herbert Morris, Ltd.* v. *Saxelby* (39) LORD PARKER OF WADDINGTON so stated the matter. In speaking of the covenantor he added:

" As long as the restraint to which he subjects himself is no wider than is required for the adequate protection of the person in whose favour it is created, it is in his interest to be able to bind himself for the sake of the indirect advantages he may obtain by so doing."

It becomes necessary to consider separately the agreements in reference to the two respective garages. In doing so, however, the nature of the appellants' legitimate interests qualifying for protection must be remembered. There was evidence that they had expended a large sum of money in erecting refineries. They spent money in the operation of their Dealer Co-operation Plan. Following their initiative in introducing solus agreements other companies followed suit with the result that, at the time of the hearing before the learned judge, out of thirty-six thousand " outlets " in the United Kingdom at which a motorist could buy motor fuels nearly thirty-five thousand were subject to solus agreements. Of the thirty-five thousand over six thousand, six hundred were with the appellants. The circumstance that there are solus agreements in respect of so high a proportion of garages undoubtedly brings it about that delivery charges are reduced. Overall planning can affect further economies. All these and kindred considerations demonstrate that it is essential for the appellants to be able to plan ahead. In particular, in order to ensure that they will be able to sell the motor fuel that they will produce for distribution, it will be reasonable for them to have secure outlets. Moreover, as solus agreements became so much a feature of the trade and contained some features which were advantageous to garage proprietors, it was reasonable for the respondents to make arrangements in conformity with current practice. This all indicates, in my view, that from the point of view of time alone solus agreements which last for a few years are capable of being adjudged to be reasonable.

In the case of the Mustow Green garage the duration of the solus agreement was four years and five months. Though that period was arranged because it was the unexpired period under a former agreement which had been made in reference to that garage, I think that the question to be decided is whether the appellants have established that the tie as arranged for that period was reasonable as between the

---

(39) [1916-17] All E.R. Rep. at p. 316; [1916] A.C. at p. 707.

A parties. When the agreement was made (in June, 1963), price maintenance was in existence and the respondents agreed to abide by the retail schedule prices as fixed by the appellants, if they were so fixed. Though at a later date price maintenance no longer continued, it is pertinent to note that under the agreement the respondents were obliged to buy from the appellants their total requirements of motor fuels for re-sale and to buy at the appellants' wholesale schedule price.

B The respondents had a rebate from the price as fixed. The appellants could, therefore, themselves fix their schedule price from time to time. Also, there was nothing to prevent them from selling directly to some others (farmers and traders) at a price less than that which they fixed as their wholesale schedule price. In addition to being obliged to buy only from the appellants, the respondents agreed to keep the filling station open (at all reasonable hours) and agreed to sell

C or transfer only to someone who would undertake the obligations for any remaining period. Though in regard to the price that the respondents would have to pay the appellants for their motor fuel the respondents were in one sense at the mercy of the appellants, it is reasonable to assume that the appellants would wish to arrange matters in such manner as was best calculated to bring about a high volume of trade in the appellants' motor fuels. They would naturally have regard

D to the prices fixed by others, and also to the circumstance that there existed a certain number of garages not bound by any ties. From a business point of view the respondents were not being unwise in entering into a solus agreement of only a few years' duration: but, whether they were or not, they freely entered into it and it was their decision to repose a measure of confidence in the appellants. I consider, therefore, that the real problem in the case of the Mustow Green contract

E is to decide whether for a contract of its nature a duration of four years and five months makes the contract unreasonable as between the parties. Though the evidence adduced by the appellants might have been more ample, and probably would have been had the litigation been initiated on the lines along which it has later developed, I consider that the appellants did discharge the onus of showing that the contract was reasonable as between the parties.

F   In the case of the Corner garage the arrangements were very different. There was a solus agreement. There was also a loan agreement and a mortgage. The solus agreement (dated July 5, 1962), was for a period of twenty-one years. It was in similar terms to the solus agreement relating to the Mustow Green garage. The appellants lent a sum of £7,000 to the respondents for the purpose of helping the respondents to buy the Corner garage and to improve it and, by the loan

G agreement (dated July 12, 1962), the respondents agreed to purchase all their requirements of motor fuels from the appellants until the loan and interest had been repaid. Furthermore, the respondents were to grant a mortgage to the appellants as security for the loan. By the mortgage (dated Oct. 6, 1962), the respondents were to pay off the loan (with interest) over the period of twenty-one years. The respondents could only redeem in accordance with the agreement as

H to repayment—with the result that they could not redeem for twenty-one years. In the mortgage deed there was also a covenant by the respondents to occupy the garage and to conduct it and keep it open during normal business hours as retailers of motor fuels and there was a covenant to purchase motor fuels exclusively from the appellants. There were various other provisions of importance.

    A consideration of the facts and the documents leads me to the view that the

I solus agreement, the loan agreement and the mortgage can be linked together as incidents of one transaction, and that the intention was that in providing that the mortgage should be irredeemable for the period of the tie it should become a support for the solus agreement. It was the contention of the appellants that the doctrine of restraint of trade did not apply to covenants contained in mortgages of land. As to this I will content myself with expressing agreement with the Court of Appeal (40), that the doctrine of restraint of trade does apply to mortgages. In regard to the period of twenty-one years I consider that the appellants have

---

(40) [1966] 1 All E.R. 725; [1966] 2 Q.B. at p. 555.

failed to show that a period of that length was reasonable in the interests of the   A
parties. There was an unreasonable restraint of trade, and the inclusion of it in
the mortgage, which was made irredeemable for the period, went beyond what
could be justified as a protection of the appellants' interest to secure their loan. I
agree with the Court of Appeal (41) that in the circumstances the respondents
should be entitled to redeem.

In the result I would allow the appeal in regard to the Mustow Green garage   B
and I would dismiss the appeal in regard to the Corner garage.

LORD HODSON: My Lords, this appeal arises from two actions brought
by the appellants, Esso Petroleum Co., Ltd., against the respondents, Harper's
Garage (Stourport), Ltd. The appellants had at first instance been granted injunctions against the respondents and the respondents' counterclaim for certain   C
declarations had been dismissed, but the decision was reversed on appeal and
the appellants now seek to restore the judgment of the trial judge (42).

The cases concern what have come to be known as "solus agreements", by
which, in recent years, more and more garage stations in this country have tied
themselves to the big oil companies to buy all their petrol therefrom, to sell no
other petrol and to sell at prices fixed by the oil companies. Your lordships   D
were informed that at the present time of thirty-six thousand stations thirty-
five thousand were so tied.

In the cases now under consideration the tie imposed was in the one case
(action 259) four years and five months' duration and in the other (action 1249)
of twenty-one years' duration. The first question is whether or not the doctrine
of restraint of trade applies to these solus agreements and, if so, does it apply   E
equally to a mortgage which was entered into in the second case in connexion
with the solus agreement but not in the first case.

The main contention on the part of the appellants is that these agreements
relate to the use of land, and that the doctrine of restraint of trade has no application to a restriction imposed on a piece of land as opposed to a restriction imposed
on a person or corporation. Such a restriction is exemplified in contracts between   F
master and servant, vendor and purchaser of a business and combinations to
restrict output or fix prices or the like. This contention was accepted by the trial
judge (42), but has no direct authority to support it. It can be said that in many
scores of cases relating, for example, to leases of land by brewers to publicans and,
in one case, of a sale of the same sort it has been taken for granted that such
restrictive covenants on the use of land are and have been from time immemorial
imposed without objection or criticism; therefore, the doctrine has no application.   G
Thus the authorities may be said to support the proposition sub silentio, for no
attempt has been made as a rule to attack these covenants on the ground that
they are in restraint of trade. An exception is to be found in the case of *Catt* v.
Tourle (43), where a brewer had sold a piece of land to the trustees of a freehold
land society who covenanted with him that he, his heirs and assigns should
have the exclusive right of supplying beer to any public house erected on the land.   H
The defendant, also a brewer, acquired a piece of land with notice of the covenant
and erected thereon a public house which he supplied with his own beer. The
covenant was held not an unreasonable restraint of trade, although it was perpetual. SELWYN, L.J., explained the reason in the following words (44):

"... a restraint preventing a person from carrying on trade within a certain   I
limit of space, though unlimited as to time, may be good, and the limit of
space may be according to the nature of the trade... We should be introducing very great uncertainty and confusion into a very large and important trade
if we were now to suggest any doubt as to the validity of a covenant so
extremely common as this is. I think there is no ground for the distinction

(41) [1966] 1 All E.R. 725; [1966] 2 Q.B. at p. 555.
(42) [1965] 2 All E.R. 933; [1966] 2 Q.B. 514.   (43) (1869), 4 Ch. App. 654.
          (44) (1869), 4 Ch. App. at pp. 659, 660.

which has been contended for, viz. that such a covenant might be good in a lease for twenty-one, fifty or one hundred years, but is not good if entered into as part of a transaction where the fee simple of a property is conveyed."

It is to be observed that, if the appellants were right, the case could have been shortly disposed of by stating that the restriction related to the sale of a piece of land. Nevertheless, restraint of trade was dealt with by the court as if this simple answer was not available. Several cases involving indirectly, if not directly, the use of land have been decided after consideration of the doctrine of restraint of trade as being applicable. Examples are: *McEllistrim* v. *Ballymacelligott Co-operative Agriculture and Dairy Society, Ltd.* (45); *English Hop Growers, Ltd.* v. *Dering* (46) and *Foley* v. *Classique Coaches, Ltd.* (47). Apart from authority, it would appear strange if the court, as it admittedly can, were to investigate the reasonableness of a restraint of trade imposed on an area or within a radius but were to be precluded from investigating one imposed on a particular piece of land, for these two things are in substance the same in their effect in imposing a restraint of trade within a prescribed area.

One learned writer alone, the late Mr. F. A. Gare, laid down categorically that restraints on trade which arise on a sale of land are of a totally different nature from those arising on a sale of goodwill or a partnership agreement. He added that these restraints had never been treated by the courts as in any way dependent on or governed by the same rule as the other forms of restraint of trade and, later, that there can be no question of public policy involved in such a covenant as that entered into by a purchaser restraining him from carrying on his trade on a piece of ground which he has newly acquired.

My lords, I do not think that it is possible to accept this general proposition. All dealings with land are not in the same category; the purchaser of land who promises not to deal with the land he buys in a particular way is not derogating from any right he has, but is acquiring a new right by virtue of his purchase. The same consideration may apply to a lessee who accepts restraints on his use of land; on the other hand, if you subject yourself to restrictions as to the use to be made of your own land so that you can no longer do what you were doing before, you are restraining trade and there is no reason why the doctrine should not apply.

It is difficult to devise a formula relating to land which covers all cases in which the doctrine should be excluded. Counsel for the respondents submitted that the solution might be that the doctrine applied only to covenants for the benefit of the trade of the covenantee which either forbid the covenantor to carry on his trade or restrict the manner in which he does so. This solution serves the property cases to which I have referred, where restrictive covenants are given to protect property not trade but, as was pointed out in argument, does itself lead to anomalies in practice as between one property and another.

One has to remember always what is meant by restraint of trade and whence this doctrine derives. It has been said to have its origin in Magna Carta, where words are to be found wide enough to extend to freedom of trade:

" Nullus liber homo etc. disseisetur de libero tenemento vel libertatibus, vel liberis consuetudinibus suis etc."

These words are quoted by Lord Macclesfield in *Mitchel* v. *Reynolds* (48). He ended his judgment by saying (49):

" To conclude: In all restraints of trade, where nothing more appears, the law presumes them bad; but if the circumstances are set forth, that presumption is excluded, and the court is to judge of those circumstances, and determine accordingly; and if upon them it appears to be a just and honest contract, it ought to be maintained."

---

(45) [1919] A.C. 548.   (46) [1928] All E.R. Rep. 396; [1928] 2 K.B. 174.
(47) [1934] All E.R. Rep. 88; [1934] 2 K.B. 1.   (48) (1711), 1 P.Wms. at p. 188.
(49) (1711), 1 P.Wms. at p. 197.

This introduced the conception of reasonableness. LORD MACCLESFIELD had already drawn the distinction between contracts made on good consideration and those which were merely injurious and oppressive.

Before turning to reasonablness, however, I would adopt the language of DIPLOCK, L.J., in *Petrofina (Gt. Britain), Ltd.* v. *Martin* (50) where he said:

" A contract in restraint of trade is one in which a party (the covenantor) agrees with any other party (the covenantee) to restrict his liberty in the future to carry on trade with other parties not parties to the contract . . . as he chooses."

DIPLOCK, L.J., was adapting his definition from the opinion of LORD PARKER OF WADDINGTON in *A.-G. of Commonwealth of Australia* v. *Adelaide Steamship Co., Ltd.* (51). He summarised the principle thus:

" At common law every member of the community is entitled to carry on any trade or business he chooses and in such manner as he thinks most desirable in his own interests and . . . no one can lawfully interfere with another in the free exercise of his trade or business unless there exist some just cause for such interference."

When one remembers that the basis of the doctrine of restraint of trade is the protection of the public interest, it is not difficult to see how the law developed in its conception of reasonableness as the test which must be passed in order to save a contract in restraint of trade from unenforceability.

The law has developed since the days of *Mitchel* v. *Reynolds* (52), and many disputatious matters have been cleared up. For example, as LORD MACNAGHTEN pointed out in *Nordenfelt* v. *Maxim Nordenfelt Guns and Ammunition Co., Ltd.* (53), adequate consideration was formerly thought to be essential. He said (53):

" It was laid down in *Mitchel* v. *Reynolds* (52) that the court was to see that the restriction was made upon a good and adequate consideration, so as to be a proper and useful contract. But in time it was found that the parties themselves were better judges of that matter than the court, and it was held to be sufficient if there was legal consideration of value, though of course the quantum of consideration may enter into the question of the reasonableness of the contract."

Thus, a restriction as to time may be reasonable or unreasonable according to whether sufficient compensation has been given to the person restrained. The distinction between partial and general restraint is no longer alive and the courts are to-day left, I think, in the position described by LORD MACNAGHTEN earlier where he said (53):

" The true view at the present time, I think, is this. The public have an interest in every person's carrying on his trade freely; so has the individual. All interference with individual liberty of action in trading, and all restraints of trade of themselves, if there is nothing more, are contrary to public policy, and, therefore, void. That is the general rule. But there are exceptions. Restraints of trade and interference with individual liberty of action may be justified by the special circumstances of a particular case. It is a sufficient justification, and indeed, it is the only justification, if the restriction is reasonable—reasonable, that is, in reference to the interests of the parties concerned and reasonable in reference to the interests of the public, so framed and so guarded as to afford adequate protection to the party in whose favour it is imposed, while at the same time it is in no way injurious to the public."

What LORD PARKER OF WADDINGTON said in the *Adelaide Steamship Co.* case (51)

---

(50) [1966] 1 All E.R. at p. 138; [1966] Ch. at p. 180.
(51) [1911-13] All E.R. Rep. at p. 1122; [1913] A.C. at p. 793.
(52) (1711), 1 P.Wms. 181.
(53) [1891-94] All E.R. Rep. at p. 18; [1894] A.C. at p. 565.

follows naturally from this passage, which puts into prominence the interests of the public. These are mentioned before those of the individual. True it is that the interests of the individual are much discussed in the cases on restraint of trade, which seldom, if ever, have been expressly decided on public grounds. An interesting example of such a case is *Kores Manufacturing Co., Ltd.* v. *Kolok Manufacturing Co., Ltd.* (54), in which the discussion turned on whether or not the agreement in question was reasonable as between the parties, whereas it could have been, perhaps, more readily based on the public interest involved in a commercial dispute. I should add that it has been established that a covenant against competition per se will never be regarded as reasonable (see the speech of LORD BIRKENHEAD, L.C., in the *McEllistrim* case (55)).

It has been authoritatively said that the onus of establishing that an agreement is reasonable as between the parties is on the person who puts forward the agreement, while the onus of establishing that it is contrary to the public interest, being reasonable between the parties, is on the person so alleging: see *Herbert Morris, Ltd.* v. *Saxelby* (56), per LORD ATKINSON and LORD PARKER OF WADDINGTON. The reason for the distinction may be obscure, but it will seldom arise, since once the agreement is before the court it is open to the scrutiny of the court in all its surrounding circumstances as a question of law.

Having rejected, as I do, the argument that there is a special class of contract relating to land which is outside the scope of the doctrine of restraint of trade, I come now to the question whether the covenants in question here are reasonable either in the private interests of the contracting parties or in the public interest. There might be thought to be some risk of proceedings being taken in certain cases of a nuisance character where the restraint of trade is readily justifiable on the basis of long established practice in a particular sphere, such as the brewery cases on which the appellants rely, but I cannot see any practical way of hedging about the right of a party to a contract to attack it on the ground that it has been entered into in unreasonable restraint of trade. After all, a man who freely enters into a bargain will, normally, expect to be held bound by it, and I do not anticipate a spate of litigation in which contracts of, say, " sole agency " will be assailed. In the case of agreements between commercial companies for regulating their trade relations the parties are usually the best judges of what is reasonable. In such a case, as VISCOUNT HALDANE, L.C., said in *North-Western Salt Co., Ltd.* v. *Electrolytic Alkali Co., Ltd.* (57):

> ". . . the law . . . still looks carefully to the interests of the public, but it regards the parties as the best judges of what is reasonable as between themselves."

My lords, so far as the tie in the Mustow Green garage is concerned, I am in agreement with the judgments given in the Court of Appeal (58), that the vital question is whether the length of the period for which the agreement is to last is unreasonable. There is a need for the protection of continuity of outlets for the company's petrol in the area in which the station is. This is a justification of the tying covenant to which the compulsory trading and the continuity covenants are complementary, as DIPLOCK, L.J., pointed out (59). Without them the tying covenant would be insufficient for its purpose. They, therefore, stand together. I should add that I reject the argument of the appellants that the " keep open " clause in the agreement falls short of a compulsory trading clause.

I have, however, reached the conclusion that the five-year tie is not unreasonable. It is true that there does not appear to have been evidence specifically directed to this question, but I have been influenced by the number of reported cases of like nature to these, particularly from commonwealth courts, when five

---

(54) [1958] 2 All E.R. 65; [1959] Ch. 108.   (55) [1919] A.C. 548.
(56) [1916-17] All E.R. Rep. at pp. 309, 316; [1916] 1 A.C. at pp. 700, 707, 708.
(57) [1914-15] All E.R. Rep. 752 at p. 757; [1914] A.C. 461 at p. 471.
(58) [1966] 1 All E.R. 725; [1966] 2 Q.B. at p. 555.
(59) [1966] 1 All E.R. at p. 735; [1966] 2 Q.B. at p. 574.

years has been considered reasonable; compare also *Biggs* v. *Hoddinott* (60),
where a five-year tie was contained in a mortgage deed. The recommendation of
the Monopolies Commission, ordered to be printed on July 28, 1965, (61), was
that solus agreements should not normally exceed five years. HARMAN, L.J.,
pointed out (62) that the period of four years and five months in action 259 was
reached, as it were, by accident without the parties directing their minds to the
reasonableness of the period, but I am not deterred by that feature of the case
from reaching the conclusion that the period chosen, being less than five years,
is not unreasonable. I would, therefore, reverse the order of the Court of Appeal
(63) so far as the Mustow Green garage is concerned.

In the Corner garage case there was not only a solus agreement but also a mortgage as security for a loan granted by the appellants to the respondents. The mortgage was irredeemable for twenty-one years and was part and parcel of the tying
agreement and the compulsory trading agreement, so that unless ties contained
in a mortgage are outside the doctrine of restraint of trade the period of twenty-
one years is so long as to be unreasonable in the absence of evidence to justify it.
I see no reason why a tie in a mortgage is to be treated in a special way. The point
was considered in *Horwood* v. *Millar's Timber & Trading Co., Ltd.* (64), although
this was not a case of mortgage of land, and the court held that a covenant in
restraint of trade contained in a mortgage deed was bad. Reliance was placed
on *Knightsbridge Estates Trust, Ltd.* v. *Bryne* (65) for the proposition of SIR
WILFRID GREENE, M.R., that

" Equity does not reform mortgage transactions because they are unreasonable. It is concerned to see . . . that oppressive or unconscionable terms
are not enforced."

SIR WILFRID GREENE, M.R., was not dealing with covenants in restraint of trade.
These must be tested by the same criterion, whether they are contained in
mortgages or not, unless there is some exception in relation to land. I have already
expressed the view that there is no such exception. I agree, therefore, with the
opinion of the Court of Appeal (63) that the tying covenant and the compulsory
trading covenant are unenforceable. These are so closely linked with the provision
that the mortgage is to be irredeemable for twenty-one years that I would hold
that they all fall together, so that the respondents are entitled to redeem. Finally,
I should add that I do not accept the special argument based on s. 85 of the Law
of Property Act, 1925, which is based on the conception that under the Act of
1925, for conveyancing purposes, a mortgage is treated as if it were a lease.

I would rest my decision on the public interest rather than on that of the parties,
public interest being a surer foundation than the interest of private persons or
corporations when widespread commercial activities such as these are concerned.

So far as the Corner garage is concerned I would affirm the order of the Court of
Appeal (63).

LORD PEARCE: My Lords, on the assumption that the solus agreement
relating to the Mustow Green garage comes within the ambit of the doctrine of
restraint of trade and that its reasonableness is a matter which the courts must
decide, I am of opinion that it is reasonable.

The period of five years has been approved as a reasonable period for agreements of this nature in Canada (*British American Oil Co.* v. *Hey* (66); *McColl*
v. *Avery* (67); *Great Eastern Oil & Import Co.* v. *Chafe,* (68) and in South Africa

---

(60) [1895-99] All E.R. Rep. 625; [1898] 2 Ch. 307.
(61) Report on the supply of petrol to retailers in the United Kingdom (chairman,
R. F. Levy, Q.C.), H.C. 264.
(62) [1966] 1 All E.R. at p. 734; [1966] 2 Q.B. at p. 572.
(63) [1966] 1 All E.R. 725; [1966] 2 Q.B. at p. 555.
(64) [1916-17] All E.R. Rep. 847; [1917] 1 K.B. 305.
(65) [1938] 4 All E.R. 618 at p. 626; [1939] Ch. 441 at p. 457.
(66) [1941] 4 D.L.R. 725.   (67) (1928), 34 O.W.N. 275.
(68) (1956) 4 D.L.R. (2d) 310.

(*Shell Co. of South Africa, Ltd.* v. *Gerran's Garages (Pty.) Ltd.* (69)). In the courts of this country there is nothing which suggests that five years is an unreasonable length of time for a tie of this kind in a trade of this kind. In some cases the matter has passed sub silentio. Although the point was not relevant in *Regent Oil Co. Ltd.* v. *Strick (Inspector of Taxes)* (70), the language there used (per Lord Reid (71) and Lord Upjohn (72)), seems to suggest that, had the question been raised or relevant, five years would not have been considered unreasonable. So, too, in the cases of *Mobil Oil Australia, Ltd.* v. *Comr. of Taxation of the Commonwealth of Australia* (73) and *B.P. Australia, Ltd.* v. *Comr. of Taxation of the Commonwealth of Australia* (74). The facts set out in the report of the Monopolies Commission (75) and its conclusions support this view.

Since the war there has been a world-wide re-organisation of the petrol industry. The old haphazard distribution has, in the interests of economy, efficiency and finance been converted into a distribution by the respective petrol producers through their own individual (and, as a rule, improved and more efficient) outlets. Vast sums have been spent on refineries, the improvement of garages and the like. Hand-to-mouth arrangements are no longer commercially suitable to the industry, and considerable planning (involving, inter alia, the geographical spacing of the outlets) is obviously necessary. The garage proprietors were not at any disadvantage in dealing with the various competing producers of petrol. To hold that five-year periods are too long for the ties between the producers and their outlets would, in my opinion, be out of accord with modern commercial needs, would cause an embarassment to the trade and would not safeguard any public or private interest that needs protection. I would, however, regard twenty-one years as being longer than was reasonable in the circumstances.

It is important that the court, in weighing the question of reasonableness, should give full weight to commercial practices and to the generality of contracts made freely by parties bargaining on equal terms. Undue interference, though imposed on the ground of promoting freedom of trade, may in the result hamper and restrict the honest trader and, on a wider view, injure trade more than it helps it. If a man wishes to tie himself for his own good commercial reasons to a particular supplier or customer, it may be no kindness to him to subject his contract to the arbitrary rule that the court will always reserve to him a right to go back on his bargain if the court thinks fit. For such a reservation prevents the honest man from getting full value for the tie which he intends, in spite of any reservation imposed by the courts, to honour; and it may enable a less honest man to keep the fruits of a bargain from which he afterwards resiles. It may be in this respect similar to imposing on a trader the fetters of infancy; and many an upstanding infant who wishes to trade or buy a house or motorcar has found difficulty and frustration in the rule which the court has imposed for his protection. Where there are no circumstances of oppression, the court should tread warily in substituting its own views for those of current commerce generally and the contracting parties in particular. For that reason, I consider that the courts require on such a matter full guidance from evidence of all the surrounding circumstances and of relevant commercial practice. They must also have regard to the consideration. It is clear that the question of the consideration weighed with Lord Macnaghten in *Nordenfelt* v. *Maxim Nordenfelt Guns and Ammunition Co., Ltd.* (76). Moreover, although the court may not be able to weigh the details of the advantages and disadvantages with great nicety, it must appreciate the

---

(69) [1954] 4 S.A.L.R. 752.　　　　　　(70) [1965] 3 All E.R. 174; [1966] A.C. 295.
(71) [1965] 3 All E.R. at p. 186, letter D; [1966] A.C. at p. 324.
(72) [1965] 3 All E.R. at p. 199, letter F; [1966] A.C. at p. 345.
(73) [1965] 3 All E.R. 225 at p. 229, letter F; [1966] A.C. 275 at p. 293.
(74) [1965] 3 All E.R. 209 at p. 218, letter H, p. 220, letter C; [1966] A.C. 244 at pp. 265, 267.
(75) Report on the supply of petrol to retailers in the United Kingdom (chairman, R. F. Levy, Q.C.), H.C. 264.
(76) [1891-94] All E.R. Rep. at pp. 22, 23; [1894] A.C. at p. 574.

consideration at least in its more general aspects. Without such guidance they cannot hope to arrive at a sensible and up-to-date conclusion on what is reasonable. That is not to say that, when it is clear that current contracts (containing restraints), however widespread, are in fact a danger and disservice to the public and to traders, the court should hesitate to interfere.

The onus is on the party asserting the contract to show the reasonableness of the restraint. That rule was laid down in the *Nordenfelt* case (77) and in *Herbert Morris, Ltd.* v. *Saxelby* (78). When the court sees its way clearly, no question of onus arises. In a doubtful case where the court does *not* see its way clearly and the question of onus does arise, there may be a danger in preferring the guidance of a general rule, founded on grounds of public policy many generations ago, to the guidance given by free and competent parties contracting at arm's length in the management of their own affairs. Therefore, when free and competent parties agree and the background provides some commercial justification on both sides for their bargain, and there is no injury to the community, I think that the onus should be easily discharged. Public policy, like other unruly horses, is apt to change its stance; and public policy is the ultimate basis of the courts' reluctance to enforce restraints. Although the decided cases are almost invariably based on unreasonableness between the parties, it is *ultimately* on the ground of public policy that the court will decline to enforce a restraint as being unreasonable between the parties; and a doctrine based on the general commercial good must always bear in mind the changing face of commerce. There is not, as some cases seem to suggest, a separation between what is reasonable on grounds of public policy and what is reasonable as between the parties. There is one broad question: is it in the interests of the community that this restraint should, as between the parties, be held to be reasonable and enforceable?

The rule relating to restraint of trade is bound to be a compromise, as are all rules imposed for freedom's sake. The law fetters traders by a particular inability to limit their freedom of trade, so that it may protect the general freedom of trade and the good of the community; and, since the rule must be a compromise, it is difficult to define its limits on any logical basis.

The court's right to interfere with contracts in restraint of trade (by withholding their enforcement, which is the ultimate sanction of contracts and to which the parties are normally entitled) has been put in very wide words. Those words, though adequate and appropriate to the particular cases in which they were uttered, were not directed towards an exact demarcation of the line where the court will have a right to investigate whether a bargain is reasonable and will decline to enforce it if it is not. The famous passages from the opinion of LORD MACNAGHTEN in the *Nordenfelt* case (77) and the opinion of LORD PARKER OF WADDINGTON in *A.-G. of Commonwealth of Australia* v. *Adelaide Steamship Co., Ltd.* (79) are not expressly limited in any way. Since any man who sells the whole, or even a substantial part, of his services, his output, his custom or his commercial loyalty to one party is thereby restraining himself from selling them to other persons, it might be argued that the court can investigate the reasonableness of any such contract and allow the contracting party to resile subsequently from any bargain which it considers an unreasonable restraint on his liberty of trade with others. So wide a power of potential investigation, however, would allow to would-be recalcitrants a wide field of chicanery and delaying tactics in the courts. Where, then, should one draw the line?

It seems clear that covenants restraining the use of the land imposed as a condition of any sale or lease to the covenantor (or his successors) should not be unenforceable. It would be intolerable if, when a man chooses of his own free will to buy, or take a tenancy of, land which is made subject to a tie (doing so on terms more favourable to himself owing to the existence of the tie) he can then

(77) [1891-94] All E.R. Rep. 1; [1894] A.C. 535.
(78) [1916-17] All E.R. Rep. 305; [1916] 1 A.C. 688.
(79) [1911-13] All E.R. Rep. at p. 1122; [1913] A.C. at p. 793.

A repudiate the tie while retaining the benefit. I do not accept the argument of counsel for the respondents that such transactions are subject to the doctrine, but will never as a matter of fact be held unreasonable. In my view, they are not subject to the doctrine at all. Certainly public policy gives little justification for their subjection to it. This view would accord with the brewers' cases in which (after an earlier unfavourable protest by LORD ELLENBOROUGH, C.J., in *Cooper*

B *v. Twibill* (80)) the law has, for many years past, been firmly settled in allowing covenants tying the publican (as lessee or purchaser) to a particular brewer (e.g. *Clegg* v. *Hands* (81)). In one case, however, in 1869 (*Catt* v. *Tourle* (82)) a perpetual tie on a sale of land was subjected to scrutiny and was held to be reasonable; but to allow a permanent tie is not very different from holding it exempt from scrutiny.

C It may be, however, that when a man fetters with a restraint land which he already owns or occupies, the fetter comes within the scrutiny of the court.

Is one also to place mortgages in the class of cases from which the doctrine is excluded? Counsel for the appellants relies, inter alia, on the technical argument that under the mortgage he has in law a demise of three thousand years with cesser on redemption (83); that this should not be regarded as a mere notional techni-

D cality; that he is a lessee for all purposes (see *Regent Oil Co., Ltd.* v. *J. A. Gregory (Hatch End), Ltd.* (84)); that the mortgagor is a lessor in possession; and that, therefore, the covenant should bind him as on a lease. The technicalities of the position where the mortgagor has no subdemise and is only notionally a lessor in possession, however, put it on the wrong side of the line and the mortgagor cannot, therefore, come into the class of lessees to whose covenants the doctrine

E has no application.

Then, on broader grounds, does the mere fact that a restraint is embodied as an obligation under a mortgage exclude it from critical scrutiny and prevent its being unenforceable if it would have been so apart from the mortgage? I think not. In *Biggs* v. *Hoddinott* (85) the point was not raised and the case is, therefore, of little guidance. The court of equity which declines to enforce the terms of a

F mortgage, if as a matter of conscience they are harsh and oppressive, cannot be less conscientious with regard to ties which as a matter of public policy the common law courts from earliest times, and thereafter courts of equity, have consistently refused to enforce in contracts. The court has also rightly applied the doctrine against restraint of trade to a tyrannous mortgage of future earnings in *Horwood* v. *Millar's Timber & Trading Co., Ltd.* (86).

G Nevertheless, on the question whether a restraint is reasonable, the fact that it is contained as a term in a mortgage may be a determining factor in its favour. The object of a mortgage is to provide fair security for the lender; and a restraint may be reasonably necessary to protect the security, when it would not have been reasonable without that object. Moreover, it seems usually reasonable for the tie to subsist as long as there is a loan outstanding, which the borrower is

H unable or unwilling to repay. It may be that even so there must be a limit; but, if so, I would not regard twenty-one years as necessarily excessive since ex hypothesi that length of time was commercially necessary for the borrower to have the benefit of the loan for his business. If, therefore, there had been in the mortgage of the Corner garage a right to redeem either when the mortgagor wished or at any time after a reasonable term of years, say five or seven years, and

I thereby to terminate the tie I would not have regarded the tie as unreasonable, in view of the amount of the loan; but here there was no such right to redeem. Nor did the tie add anything to the protection of the security. Here, even in the most unlikely event of a shortage of petrol supplies, the supplier has a discretion

---

(80) (1808), 3 Camp. 286, n. at p. 287.   (81) (1890), 44 Ch.D. 503.
(82) (1869), 4 Ch. App. 654.   (83) See Law of Property Act, 1925, s. 87.
(84) [1965] 3 All E.R. 673; [1966] Ch. 402.
(85) [1895-99] All E.R. Rep. 625; [1898] 2 Ch. 307.
(86) [1916-17] All E.R. Rep. 847; [1917] 1 K.B. 305.

not to supply if his own sources of supply fail or go short; and in any other set of
circumstances I cannot think that a tied garage would be more valuable than, or
even as valuable as, a free garage. Moreover, if the mortgagees entered on their
security, they would have to treat it as a free garage and account on that basis.
If one regards the mortgage as a whole, the prolonged fetter on the right to
redeem seems to have been inserted merely to prolong the tie. In this case, therefore, the existence of the mortgage neither removes the tie from the area to which
the doctrine of restraint of trade applies nor, in the particular circumstances, does
it assist the appellants on the question whether the tie was reasonable.

MOCATTA, J., in his clear and careful judgment (87) held that neither tie was in
restraint of trade since it was merely restrictive of the trading use to be made of
a particular piece of land, so that the doctrine of restraint of trade had no application. I feel the force of his reasoning, but I do not feel able to accede to it. Had
the garage proprietor had no obligations to carry on his garage, I might have been
persuaded otherwise; but here there was a positive obligation to carry on the
business (or to find a transferee who must do likewise) and to purchase from none
save the appellants. The practical effect was to create a personal restraint.
Although the covenant affected only petrol sold on the particular land it did
affect the proprietor with an obligation which he or his agents could not by mere
abstention avoid. Both *English Hop Growers, Ltd.* v. *Dering* (88) and *Foley* v.
Classique Coaches, Ltd. (89), in both of which the restraint was regarded as
reasonable and *McEllistrim* v. *Ballymacelligott Co-operative Agricultural and
Dairy Society, Ltd.* (90) where it was not, lend some support to this view.

Finally, there is the important question whether this was a mere agreement for
the promotion of trade and not an agreement in restraint of it.

Somewhere there must be a line between those contracts which are in restraint
of trade and whose reasonableness can, therefore, be considered by the courts,
and those contracts which merely regulate the normal commercial relations
between the parties and are, therefore, free from the doctrine. The present case
seems near the borderline, as was the case of *Bouchard Servais* v. *Prince's Hall
Restaurant* (91), where SIR RICHARD HENN COLLINS, M.R., held that the doctrine
did not apply, while the other two lords justices apparently held that it did
apply but that the restraint was reasonable.

One of the mischiefs at which the doctrine was aimed originally was the mischief
of monopolies; but this was dealt with by legislation and the executive has from
time to time taken efficient steps to prevent it. Indeed, in the case of petrol ties
there has now been exacted (we are told) from the petrol producers an undertaking
which in practice limits these ties to five years.

When LORD MACNAGHTEN said in the *Nordenfelt* case (92) that

" in the age of Queen Elizabeth all restraints of trade, whatever they
were, general or partial, were thought to be contrary to public policy and,
therefore, void "

he was clearly not intending the words " restraints of trade " to cover any
contract whose terms, by absorbing a man's services or custom or output, in
fact prevented him from trading with others; so, too, the wide remarks of LORD
PARKER OF WADDINGTON in the *Adelaide* case (93). It was the sterilising of a
man's capacity for work and not its absorption that underlay the objection to
restraint of trade. This is the rationale of *Young* v. *Timmins* (94), where a brass
foundry was during the contract sterilised so that it could work only for a party
who might choose not to absorb its output at all but to go to other foundries, with

---

(87) [1965] 2 All E.R. at p. 936; [1966] 2 Q.B. at p. 531.
(88) [1928] All E.R. 396; [1928] 2 K.B. 174.
(89) [1934] All E.R. Rep. 88; [1934] 2 K.B. 1.
(90) [1919] A.C. 548.   (91) (1904), 20 T.L.R. 574.
(92) [1891-94] All E.R. Rep. at p. 17; [1894] A.C. at p. 564.
(93) [1911-13] All E.R. Rep. at p. 1123; [1913] A.C. at p. 794.
(94) (1831), 1 Cr. & J. 331.

the result that the foundry was completely at the mercy of the other party and might remain idle and unsupported.

The doctrine does not apply to ordinary commercial contracts for the regulation and promotion of trade during the existence of the contract, provided that any prevention of work outside the contract viewed as a whole is directed towards the absorption of the parties' services and not their sterilisation. Sole agencies are a normal and necessary incident of commerce, and those who desire the benefits of a sole agency must deny themselves the opportunities of other agencies. So, too, in the case of a film-star who may tie herself to a company in order to obtain from them the benefits of stardom (*Gaumont-British Picture Corpn., Ltd.* v. *Alexander* (95); see, too, *Warner Bros. Pictures, Inc.* v. *Nelson* (96)). Moreover, partners habitually fetter themselves to one another.

When a contract ties the parties only during the continuance of the contract, and the negative ties are only those which are incidental and normal to the positive commercial arrangements at which the contract aims, even though those ties exclude all dealings with others, there is no restraint of trade within the meaning of the doctrine and no question of reasonableness arises. If, however, the contract ties the trading activities of either party after its determination, it is a restraint of trade, and the question of reasonableness arises. So, too, if *during* the contract one of the parties is too unilaterally fettered, so that the contract loses its character of a contract for the regulation and promotion of trade and acquires the predominant character of a contract in restraint of trade. In that case the rationale of *Young* v. *Timmins* (97) comes into play and the question whether it is reasonable arises.

The difficult question in this case, as in the case of *Bouchard Servais* (98), is whether a contract regulating commercial dealings between the parties has by its restraints exceeded the normal negative ties incidental to a positive commercial transaction and has thus brought itself within the sphere to which the doctrine of restraint applies. If the appellants had assured to the respondents a supply of petrol at a reasonable price, come what may, in return for the respondents selling only the appellants' petrol, it might be that the contract would have come within the normal incidents of a commercial transaction and not within the ambit of restraint of trade; but the appellants did not do this. They hedged their liability around so that they had an absolute discretion in the event, inter alia, of a failure in their own sources of supply, whether or not the appellants should have foreseen it, to withhold supplies from the respondents (leaving them the cheerless right in such a situation to seek supplies elsewhere); and then at a later stage it would seem, if and when the appellants were prepared to supply the respondents once more, the appellants could hold the respondents to their tie with the appellants. The price was, also, to be fixed by the appellants; and for the duration of the contract the respondents owed them a contractual obligation to continue to keep the garage open (or find a successor who would do so on like terms). When these contracts are viewed as a whole the balance tilts in favour of regarding them as contracts which are in restraint of trade and which, therefore, can be enforced only if the restraint is reasonable.

I do not here find help in the well known phrases that a man is not entitled to protect himself against competition per se, or that he is only entitled to protect himself if he has an interest to protect. It is clear that a restraint which merely damages a covenantor and confers no benefit on a covenantee is as a rule unreasonable; but here the appellants had a definite interest to protect and secured a definite benefit. They wished to preserve intact their spaced network of outlets in order that they could continue to sell their products as planned over a period of years in competition with the other producers. To prevent them from doing so would be an embarrassment of trade, not a protection of its freedom. If all the other companies owned garages and the appellants were trying for the

---

(95) [1936] 2 All E.R. 1686.   (96) [1936] 3 All E.R. 160; [1937] 1 K.B. 209.
(97) (1831), 1 Cr. & J. 331.   (98) (1904), 20 T.L.R. 574.

first time to enter the market, it would stifle trading competition rather than encourage it if the appellants were prevented from being able to enter into a binding solus agreement for a sole outlet in order to compete with the others. Moreover, in a doctrine based on the wide ground of public policy the wider aspects of commerce must always be considered as well as the narrower aspect of the contract as between the parties.

Since the tie for a period of four years and five months was in the circumstances reasonable, I would allow the appeal in respect of the Mustow Green garage. Since the tie for a period of twenty-one years was not in the circumstances reasonable, I would dismiss the appeal in respect of the Corner garage.

LORD WILBERFORCE: My Lords, the main features in the solus agreements entered into by the respondent company, Harper's Garage (Stourport), Ltd., with the appellants, Esso Petroleum Co., Ltd., are that the respondents agreed to purchase from the appellants the whole of their requirements of motor fuel for resale at the relevant service stations, accepted a resale price maintenance clause, agreed to operate the relevant service stations in accordance with the Esso Dealer Co-operation Plan, which included a provision that the service station should be kept open at all reasonable hours for the sale of Esso petrol and oil and, lastly, agreed that, before completing any sale or transfer of the relevant service station, the respondents would notify the appellants and procure the intended successor to assume the respondents' obligations under the agreement.

In the case of the Mustow Green garage, the agreement, dated June 27, 1963, was expressed to operate for four years and five months from July 1, 1963, this being the residue of a longer period which was taken over by the respondents from a previous operator of the station.

In the case of the Corner garage at Stourport-on-Severn the agreement, dated July 5, 1962, was expressed to operate for twenty-one years from July 1, 1962. In addition to this solus agreement, the respondents entered into a mortgage of this station, dated Oct. 6, 1962, by which the station was charged to the appellants to secure a sum not exceeding £7,000 with interest. The principal sum was repayable—and only repayable—by instalments over twenty-one years from Nov. 6, 1962. There were certain special provisions in the mortgage deed which I need not specify at the present stage.

The first main issue is whether these agreements are to be regarded as agreements in restraint of trade so as to be exposed to the tests of reasonableness stated in *Nordenfelt* v. *Maxim Nordenfelt Guns and Ammunition Co., Ltd.* (99). It is the appellants' contention that they are not, mainly on the ground that they relate to the use of the respondents' land, and that covenants, or contracts, which so relate are by their nature incapable of being regarded as in restraint of trade. This contention has made it necessary to consider how a covenant or contract in restraint of trade is to be defined or identified.

The doctrine of restraint of trade (a convenient, if imprecise, expression which I continue to use) is one which has throughout the history of its subject-matter been expressed with considerable generality, if not ambiguity. The best known general formulations, those of LORD MACNAGHTEN in *Nordenfelt* (100) and of LORD PARKER OF WADDINGTON in *A.-G. of Commonwealth of Australia* v. *Adelaide Steamship Co., Ltd.* (101), adapted and used by DIPLOCK, L.J., in the Court of Appeal in *Petrofina (Great Britain), Ltd.* v. *Martin* (102), speak generally of all restraints of trade without any attempt at a definition. Often we find the words " restraint of trade " in a single passage used indifferently to denote, on the one hand, in a broad popular sense, any contract which limits the free exercise of trade or business, and, on the other hand, as a term of art covering those contracts

---

(99) [1891-94] All E.R. Rep. 1; [1894] A.C. 535.
(100) [1891-94] A.C. at p. 18; [1894] A.C. at p. 565.
(101) [1911-13] All E.R. Rep. at pp. 1122-1124; [1913] A.C. at pp. 793-797.
(102) [1966] 1 All E.R. at p. 138; [1966] Ch. at p. 180.

which are to be regarded as offending a rule of public policy. Often, in reported cases, we find that instead of segregating two questions (i) whether the contract is in restraint of trade, (ii) whether, if so, it is " reasonable ", the courts have fused the two by asking whether the contract is in " undue restraint of trade ", or by a compound finding that it is not satisfied that this contract is really in restraint of trade at all but, if it is, it is reasonable. A well-known text book describes contracts in restraint of trade as those which " unreasonably restrict " the rights of a person to carry on his trade or profession. There is no need to regret these tendencies: indeed, to do so, when consideration of this subject has passed through such notable minds from Lord Macclesfield onwards, would indicate a failure to understand its nature. The common law has often (if sometimes unconsciously) thrived on ambiguity and it would be mistaken, even if it were possible, to try to crystallise the rules of this, or any, aspect of public policy into neat propositions. The doctrine of restraint of trade is one to be applied to factual situations with a broad and flexible rule of reason.

The use of this expression justifies re-statement of its classic exposition by White, C.J., in *U.S.* v. *Standard Oil* (103). Speaking of the statutory words " every contract in restraint of trade " (Sherman Act, 1890), admittedly taken from the common law, almost contemporaneous with Lord Macnaghten's formula and just as wide, he said:

> " As the acts which may come under the classes stated in the first section and the restraint of trade to which that section applies are not specifically enumerated or defined, it is obvious that judgment must in every case be called into play in order to determine whether a particular act is embraced within the statutory classes, and whether if the act is within such classes its nature or effect causes it to be a restraint of trade within the intendment of the Act . . ."

Moreover, he goes on to say that to hold to the contrary would involve either holding that the statute would be destructive of all right to contract or agree or combine in any respect whatsoever, or that, the " light of reason " being excluded, enforcement of the statute was impossible because of its uncertainty. The right course was to leave it to be determined by the light of reason whether any particular act or contract was within the contemplation of the statute. One still finds much enlightenment in these words.

This does not mean that the question whether a given agreement is in restraint of trade, in either sense of these words, is nothing more than a question of fact to be individually decided in each case. It is not to be supposed, or encouraged, that a bare allegation that a contract limits a trader's freedom of action exposes a party suing on it to the burden of justification. There will always be certain general categories of contracts as to which it can be said, with some degree of certainty, that the " doctrine " does or does not apply to them. Positively, there are likely to be certain sensitive areas as to which the law will require in every case the test of reasonableness to be passed: such an area has long been and still is that of contracts between employer and employee as regards the period after the employment has ceased. Negatively, and it is this that concerns us here, there will be types of contract as to which the law should be prepared to say with some confidence that they do not enter into the field of restraint of trade at all.

How, then, can such contracts be defined or at least identified? No exhaustive test can be stated—probably no precise, non-exhaustive test. The development of the law does seem to show, however, that judges have been able to dispense from the necessity of justification under a public policy test of reasonableness such contracts or provisions of contracts as, under contemporary conditions, may be found to have passed into the accepted and normal currency of commercial or contractual or conveyancing relations. That such contracts have done so may be taken to show with at least strong prima force that, moulded under the

(103) (1911), 221 U.S. 1 at p. 63.

pressures of negotiation, competition and public opinion, they have assumed a form which satisfies the test of public policy as understood by the courts at the time, or, regarding the matter from the point of view of the trade, that the trade in question has assumed such a form that for its health or expansion it requires a degree of regulation. Absolute exemption for restriction or regulation is never obtained: circumstances, social or economic, may have altered, since they obtained acceptance, in such a way as to call for a fresh examination: there may be some exorbitant or special feature in the individual contract which takes it out of the accepted category: but the court must be persuaded of this before it calls on the relevant party to justify a contract of this kind.

Some such limitation on the meaning in legal practice of " restraints of trade " must surely have been present to the minds of LORD MACNAGHTEN and LORD PARKER OF WADDINGTON. They cannot have meant to say that any contract which in whatever way restricts a man's liberty to trade was (either historically under the common law, or at the time of which they were speaking) prima facie unenforceable and must be shown to be reasonable. They must have been well aware that areas existed, and always had existed, in which limitations of this liberty were not only defensible, but were not seriously open to the charge of restraining trade. Their language, they would surely have said, must be interpreted in relation to commercial practice and common sense.

Any attempt to trace historically the development of the common law attitude towards " restraints " of different kinds would be out of place here, and generalisations as to it are hazardous; but a few examples of comparatively modern origin show how some such rule of action, however imperfectly I have expressed it in words, has been operated. In some cases the process can be seen whereby a type of contract, initially regarded with suspicion, has later come to be accepted as not, or no longer, calling for justification.

First, there are the brewery cases. Contractual clauses tying a leased public house to the lessor's beers have been known, and commonly current, at least since the early nineteenth century (for an early case see *Hartley* v. *Pehall* (104)). In the form which they then assumed (commonly providing that if the tying covenant was broken there should be an increased rent recoverable by distress) we find them encountering some judicial criticism (*Cooper* v. *Twibill* (105), per LORD ELLENBOROUGH, C.J.). But by 1850 they had become current; the attrition of negotiation and competition may be taken to have worn them down to an acceptable shape and in *Catt* v. *Tourle* (106), the Court of Appeal in Chancery not only accepted that such covenants were outside the doctrine of restraint of trade, but were prepared to extend the exclusion to the case where the servient house was sold instead of leased. I quote SELWYN, L.J.'s words (107):

". . . with respect to this particular covenant, it seems to me that the court cannot but take judicial notice of its being extremely common. Every court of justice has had occasion to consider these brewers' covenants, and must be taken to be cognisant of the distinction between what are called free public houses and brewers' public houses which are subject to this very covenant. We should be introducing very great uncertainty into a very large and important trade if we were now to suggest any doubt as to the validity of a covenant so extremely common as this is."

GIFFARD, L.J., added (108) " it does not go beyond the ordinary brewers' covenant ". Neither of the lords justices, it will be seen, puts his decision on the ground (simple and decisive, if he had thought it appropriate) either that the covenant related to the use to be made of land, or that it was imposed on a disposition of land. That it was too late to subject such tying covenants to the test appropriate in restraint of trade was stated in 1889 by BRISTOWE, V.-C.

---

(104) (1792), Peake, 178.   (105) (1803), 3 Camp. 286, n.
(106) (1869), 4 Ch. App. 654.   (107) (1869), 4 Ch. App. at p. 659.
               (108) (1869), 4 Ch. App. at p. 662.

(*Clegg* v. *Hands* (109)), and the issue was not even debated in the Court of Appeal.

The working of the same principle can be seen even earlier in relation to covenants restricting trade in leases generally. In the normal exploitation of property, covenants are entered into, by lessee or lessor, not to trade at all or not to carry on particular trades. In 1613 (*Rogers* v. *Parrey* (110)) the issue, whether a covenant in a lease for twenty-one years not to exercise a particular trade was in restraint of trade, was still susceptible of debate, but COKE, C.J., and the judges of the King's Bench upheld its validity. By 1688 this seems to have become accepted doctrine, for in *Thompson* v. *Harvey* (111) HOLT, C.J., was able to say " it was usual to restrain a lessee from such a trade in the house let " giving as the reason " because I will choose whether to let or not ". (Cf. in relation to chattels, *United Shoe Machinery Co. of Canada* v. *Brunet* (112).)

The same has come to be true of dispositions of the freehold : for over one hundred years it has been part of the normal technique of conveyancing to impose and to accept covenants restricting the use of land, including the use for trades or for trade generally, whether of that conveyed or of that retained. A modern example of this is *Neston Abbott Co-operative Society, Ltd.* v. *Williamson and Treadgold, Ltd.* (113).

One may express the exemption of these transactions from the doctrine of restraint of trade in terms of saying that they merely take land out of commerce and do not fetter the liberty to trade of individuals ; but I think that one can only truly explain them by saying that they have become part of the accepted machinery of a type of transaction which is generally found acceptable and necessary, so that instead of being regarded as restrictive they are accepted as part of the structure of a trading society. If in any individual case one finds a deviation from accepted standards, some greater restriction of an individual's right to " trade ", or some artificial use of an accepted legal technique, it is right that this should be examined in the light of public policy. An example of this process in a lease (a lessor's covenant as to trading) may be found in *Hinde* v. *Gray* (114), and, in a conveyance, in the Scottish case of *Aberdeen Varieties, Ltd.* v. *Donald* (115).

Then there is the well-known type of case where a man sells his business and its goodwill and accepts a limitation on his right to compete. Here, too, we can see the period of scrutiny in the seventeenth century. That, on the sale of the good-will of a business, a promise might validly be given not to carry on the relevant trade was established, after debate, in *Broad* v. *Jollyfe* (116)—the covenant held void—reversed in the King's Bench (117), where DODDERIDGE, J., said that it was the usual course of men in their old age to turn over their trade to another ; general recognition was given to this type of covenant by LORD MACCLESFIELD in *Mitchel* v. *Reynolds* (118). So the rule has become accepted that, in the interest of trade itself, restrictions may be imposed on the vendor of goodwill provided that they are fairly and properly ancillary to the sale : if they exceed this limit the " doctrine " may be applied (see *Leather Cloth Co.* v. *Lorsont* (119), where JAMES, V.-C., excepted " natural " covenants from the " doctrine ").

The line of thought that restrictions may in some contexts be imposed, and upheld, where they have become part of the accepted pattern or structure of a trade, as encouraging or strengthening trade, rather than as limiting trade, is I think behind the courts' acceptance of exclusivity contracts and contracts of sole agency. So, in *Bouchard Servais* v. *Prince's Hall Restaurant, Ltd.* (120), the contract was for exclusive purchase of burgundy for the defendant's restaurant for an indefinite period. The judgments of the lords justices are based on different

(109) (1890), 44 Ch.D. 503.
(111) (1688), Comb. 121 at p. 122.
(113) [1952] 1 All E.R. 279 ; [1952] 2 Ch. 286.
(115) 1939 S.C. 788.
(117) (1620), 2 Roll. Rep. 201.
(119) (1869), L.R. 9 Eq. 345.

(110) (1613), 2 Bulst. 136.
(112) [1909] A.C. 330 at p. 343.
(114) (1840), 1 Man. & G. 195.
(116) (1620), Cro. Jac. 596·
(118) (1711), 1 P.Wms. at p. 191.
(120) (1904), 20 T.L.R. 574.

grounds and it was held, in any event, that the covenant was reasonable; but the judgment of SIR RICHARD HENN COLLINS, M.R., is instructive. He thought that the case did not come within the principle by which restraints of trade were held to be invalid as being contrary to public policy. Contracts of the same class as that now in question, viz., contracts by which persons bound themselves for good consideration to supply their customers with goods obtained from a particular merchant exclusively, were for the benefit of the community. There was need for contracts of this kind and the court must have regard to the fact that contracts for sole agency were matters of every day occurrence (see too *W. T. Lamb & Sons* v. *Goring Brick Co.* (121) where the agreement was not challenged: *British Oxygen Co., Ltd.* v. *Liquid Air, Ltd.* (122): in the *Adelaide* case (123) an agreement for exclusive purchase of a more comprehensively restrictive character was held to be in restraint of trade).

Lastly (though this is still an uncertain field) certain contracts of employment, with restrictions appropriate to their character, against undertaking other work during their currency may be acceptable (cf. *Warner Bros. Pictures, Inc.* v. *Nelson* (124); *Gaumont-British Picture Corpn., Ltd.* v. *Alexander* (125)). Here, too, however, if it is found that the restriction is purely limitative or sterilising, it may be subject to examination (see *Gaumont-British Picture Corpn., Ltd.* v. *Alexander* (126), per PORTER, J., and compare the facts in *Young* v. *Timmins* (127); the decision was mainly based on inadequacy of consideration).

These illustrations are sufficient to show that the courts are not lacking in tools which enable them to select from the whole range of those contracts which in one way or another limit freedom in trading, segments of current and recognisably normal contracts which are not currently liable to be subjected to the necessity of justification by reasonableness. Such contracts may even be listed, provisionally, in categories (see GARE, THE LAW RELATING TO COVENANTS IN RESTRAINT OF TRADE (1935); CHESHIRE & FIFOOT, LAW OF CONTRACT (6th Edn.) (1964) pp. 324, 329 ff.); but the classification must remain fluid and the categories can never be closed.

I turn now to the agreements. In my opinion, on balance, they enter into the category of agreements in restraint of trade which require justification. They directly bear on, and in some measure restrain, the exercise of the respondents' trade, so the question is whether they are to be treated as falling within some category excluded from the " doctrine " of restraint of trade. The broad test, or rather approach, which I have suggested, is capable of answering this. This is not a mere transaction in property, nor a mere transaction between owners of property: it is essentially a trade agreement between traders. It is not a mere agreement for exclusive purchase of a commodity, though it contains this element: if it were nothing more, there would be a strong case for treating it as a normal commercial agreement of an accepted type. But there are other restrictive elements. There is the tie for a fixed period with no provision for determination by notice: a combination which *McEllistrim* v. *Ballymacelligott Co-operative Agricultural and Dairy Society, Ltd.* (128) shows should be considered together: and there is the fetter on the terms on which the station may be sold. Admittedly the respondents could liberate themselves by finding a successor willing to take their place: admittedly, too, being a limited company, they could trade in several places simultaneously, so that even if they remained tied to these sites, and obliged to continue trading there, they could in theory set up business elsewhere. But just as in *McEllistrim's* case (129) the reality of the covenantor's restraint

---

(121) [1931] All E.R. Rep. 314; [1932] 1 K.B. 710.
(122) [1925] Ch. 383 at p. 392.
(123) [1911-13] All E.R. Rep. at pp. 1129, 1130; [1913] A.C. at pp. 806-808.
(124) [1936] 3 All E.R. 160; [1937] 1 K.B. 209.
(125) [1936] 2 All E.R. 1686.   (126) [1936] 2 All E.R. at p. 1692.
(127) (1831), 1 Cr. & J. 331.   (128) [1919] A.C. at p. 565.
(129) [1919] A.C. 548.

was considered more relevant than his theoretical liberty to depart, so here, in my opinion, addition of all the ingredients takes the case into the category of those which require justification.   Finally the agreement is not of a character which, by the pressure of negotiation and competition, has passed into acceptance or into a balance of interest between the parties or between the parties and their customers; the solus system is both too recent and too variable for this to be said.

The test, suggested by the appellants, seems, by comparison, artificial and unreal.   The covenant, they say, is not in restraint of trade because it relates to the use of the respondents' land.   Not only does it require an effort of mind to regard the covenant in this way, but also the comment is obvious that an opposite result would be produced by so slight an adjustment as relating the covenant to an area of land instead of to a specific property.

The view which I would take of the agreements, moreover, agrees, as that suggested by the appellants does not, with those reported cases which have been cited as bearing most directly on the present.

In *McEllistrim's* case (130) this House decided that the obligation imposed on a farmer to sell all his milk to the respondent society, a co-operative, was in restraint of trade and unreasonable on the ground that he was thereby prevented from trading both in a wide area in Western Ireland and (effectively) elsewhere and that he had no means open to him to withdraw from the agreement.   I find it impossible to extract from the case, even by an argument ex silentio, any inference that had the respondent society's obligations been limited to specified land of theirs, the restrictions would have been exempted from the doctrine.   I should be much more inclined to read into it a willingness to accept normal co-operative selling schemes and a rejection of the relevant rule, because it was an unusual and excessive fetter on the farmer's personal liberty.   *English Hop Growers, Ltd.* v. *Dering* (131) was another instance of co-operative selling.   It is one of those cases to which I have referred in which the decision was a compound one—that the agreement was not in unreasonable restraint of trade.   It being apparent that the agreement was both of a normal type (according to Romer, J., similar agreements were entered into by ninety-five per cent. of the hop growers) and inter partes reasonable, it is natural enough that the members of the Court of Appeal based their judgments in different degrees on both these factors.   Again one may add that the case lends no support to the appellants' suggestion that the decision was based on the personal character of the agreement or that it would have been any different, or differently expressed, had the agreement related more specifically to the respondent's land.   Then there is *Bouchard Servais* v. *Prince's Hall Restaurant, Ltd.* (132): I have already referred to this case; I need add here only that the decision, upholding the agreement, is not related in any way to the fact that the contract concerned the use to be made of land.

Lastly there is *Foley* v. *Classique Coaches, Ltd.* (133) where on a sale of land the purchaser agreed to take all the petrol that he needed for his coaching business from the vendor.   Scrutton, L.J. (134), with whom the other lords justices agreed, described the contract as an ordinary one to purchase petrol from a particular person and held that there was no " undue restraint of trade ", a compound finding, but the ordinary commercial character of the agreement was clearly a strand in it.   The fact that the agreement related (as it plainly did) to the use of the defendant's land played no part in the decision.

On this view of the agreements it becomes necessary to subject them to the test of reasonableness.   As regards the two solus agreements, having had the benefit of reading the opinions which precede mine, I am content to say that I am in concurrence with them in the view that the Mustow Green agreement does, and that the Corner Garage agreement does not (on account of its long duration),

(130) [1919] A.C. 548.   (131) [1928] All E.R. Rep. 396; [1928] 2 K.B. 174.
(132) (1904), 20 T.L.R. 574.   (133) [1934] All E.R. Rep. 88; [1934] 2 K.B. 1.
          (134) [1934] All E.R. Rep. at p. 91; [1934] 2 K.B. at p. 11.

satisfy the test of reasonableness in the interests of the parties. I would only add two observations. The first relates to the ground, I think the main ground, on which the Court of Appeal (135) held that even the four years and five months for which the Mustow Green agreement was to last was too long. They were faced with the difficulty (which faces us) that there was very little evidence at the trial, and because of the course which the trial took, no finding by the judge (136), of facts which would support a tie for any particular period. So the Court of Appeal (135), which had to decide the question of reasonableness for the first time, devised a special and more concrete test of their own. They asked themselves the question, how long it would take the appellants to find an alternative site if the respondents' site were liberated from the tie, and LORD DENNING, M.R., arrived (137) at a period of three years certain and thereafter subject to two year's notice. DIPLOCK, L.J., while not committing himself to any firm period, thought (138) that evidence might have justified a period of two years or so, or an indefinite period subject to two years' notice. I do not feel able to accept this way of dealing with the matter. The parties have contracted in relation to a particular site and no other: who can say what features of it they considered relevant or significant? How can one judge what site, or whether any site, would be an " alternative " or to what lengths the appellants ought to go to find one? What degree of continuity at one place are the appellants entitled to expect, or, conversely, how often may the appellants be expected to move their outlets without losing goodwill or profits? None of these questions can, in my opinion, be answered with certainty, and the question to be answered is a different question. For what the court is endeavouring to ascertain is whether it is unreasonable for the appellants, in relation to the appellants' interest in selling petrol on this location, to bind the respondents to it in the way that the respondents are bound for the period of the tie; or whether, in the public interest of preserving liberty of action to the respondents, they ought not to be held in the fetters which they have accepted. There appears to me to be enough in the evidence to show that, on the appellants' side, to secure a tie for this period was a legitimate commercial objective; and that as regards the respondents, no public policy objection existed against holding them so long bound. On this point it is, I think, legitimate to draw support from a number of decisions in various jurisdictions where restrictions of various kinds, over comparable periods, have been upheld (see *British American Oil Co.* v. *Hey* (139) (five years); *Peters American Delicacy Co., Ltd.* v. *Patricia's Chocolates & Candies Property, Ltd.* (140) (three years); *Ampol Petroleum, Ltd.* v. *Mutton* (141) (three years); *Shell Co. of South Africa, Ltd.* v. *Gerrans Garage (Pty.), Ltd.* (142) (five years); *Great Eastern Oil & Import Co.* v. *Chafe* (143) (five years)). I should add that I must not be taken either as suggesting that the periods mentioned are maximum periods, or as expressing any opinion as to the validity of ties for periods intermediate between five years and twenty-one years, such as, for example, existed in *Petrofina (Gt. Britain), Ltd.* v. *Martin* (144) (twelve years).

The second observation that I would make is this: the case has been fought exclusively on the first limb of the *Nordenfelt* (145) test of reasonableness (in reference to the interests of the parties) the respondents explicitly disclaiming any reliance on the second limb (in reference to the interests of the public). The first limb itself rests on considerations of public policy: it must do so in order to justify releasing the parties from obligations which they have voluntarily

(135) [1966] 1 All E.R. 725; [1966] 2 Q.B. at p. 555.
(136) [1965] 2 All E.R. 933; [1966] 2 Q.B. 514.
(137) [1966] 1 All E.R. at p. 729, letter E; [1966] 2 Q.B. at p. 564.
(138) [1966] 1 All E.R. at p. 737, letter A; [1966] 2 Q.B. at p. 576.
(139) [1941] 4 D.L.R. 725. (140) (1947), 21 A.L.J. 281.
(141) (1952), 53 S.R.N.S.W. 1. (142) [1954] 4 S.A.L.R. 752.
(143) (1956), 4 D.L.R. (2d) 310.
(144) [1966] 1 All E.R. 126; [1966] Ch. 146.
(145) [1891-94] All E.R. Rep. 1; [1894] A.C. 535.

accepted. In relation, however, to many agreements containing restrictions, there may well be wider issues affecting the interests of the public, than those which relate merely to the interests of the parties; these may have been the subject of enquiry, as in this case under statutory powers (Monopolies and Restrictive Practices (Inquiry and Control) Act, 1948, (146), or the subject of a finding by another court (Restrictive Trade Practices Act, 1956, (147)) or may be investigated by the court itself. In the present case no separate considerations in this wider field have emerged which are inconsistent with the validity of the Mustow Green solus agreement—on the contrary such as have appeared tend to support it, but I venture to think it important that the vitality of the second limb, or as I would prefer to put it of the wider aspects of a single public policy rule, should continue to be recognised.

Finally it is necessary to deal separately with the mortgage on the respondents' Corner garage, which the appellants contend falls in a separate category, not subject to the " doctrine " of restraint of trade at all. The submission is that, under accepted principles of equity, there is nothing to prevent a mortgage being made irredeemable for a period provided (and this is the only suggested limitation) that the terms of it are not harsh or unconscionable: for this the appellants invoke the well known judgment of Sir Wilfrid Greene, M.R., in *Knightsbridge Estates Trust, Ltd.* v. *Byrne* (148). Indeed the appellants' position is even stronger, it is claimed, because the mortgage ranks as a debenture and so may legitimately be made completely irredeemable (Companies Act, 1948, s. 89, s. 455 (1) " deben ture " (149)). The steps in this argument are coherent once its foundation is made good—that mortgages as such and restrictions in them fall totally outside the " doctrine " of restraint of trade; but is this foundation sound? I consider first the relevant authorities.

The best known of these is *Biggs* v. *Hoddinott* (150), a brewery mortgage case. The decision is conveniently summarised by Lord Davey thus: first, that stipulation for the continuance of a loan for five years was valid, and secondly, that a covenant to take beer from the mortgagee limited to the continuance of the security did not clog the equity of redemption (see *Bradley* v. *Carritt* (151)). The issue as to restraint of trade was not raised. In *Morgan* v. *Jeffreys* (152) another brewery case, where the contractual right of redemption had passed, a provision against redemption before the expiry of twenty-eight years, coupled with a tie, was held to exceed all reasonable limit, but again no question of restraint of trade was raised. *Biggs* v. *Hoddinott* (150) was recently followed by Russell, J., in *Hill* v. *Regent Oil, Ltd.* (153) where there was a mortgage, coupled with a tie, for twenty years and it was held that this was not oppressive or unconscionable. The case again was decided purely on the classical principles of equity applicable to mortgages and the judgment makes no reference to restraint of trade. A similar decision was given in Ontario in *Clark* v. *Supertest Petroleum Corpn.* (154). These authorities then establish, and to that extent I have no desire to question them, that as part of a transaction of mortgage, it is permissible, so far as the rules of equity are concerned, both to postpone the date of repayment and, at any rate during the period of the loan, to tie the mortgagor to purchase exclusively the products of the mortgagee. Such an arrangement would fall fairly

---

(146) This Act, so much of Pt. 3 of the Restrictive Trade Practices Act, 1958, as amended it, and the Monopolies and Mergers Act 1965, constitute the Monopolies and Mergers Acts 1948 and 1965; see 25 Halsbury's Statutes (2nd Edn.) 751, and 45 Halsbury's Statutes (2nd Edn.) 1691, 1711.
(147) See 36 Halsbury's Statutes (2nd Edn.) 931.
(148) [1938] 4 All E.R. 618; [1939] Ch. 441.
(149) See *Knightsbridge Estates Trust, Ltd.* v. *Byrne*, in the Court of Appeal, [1940] 2 All E.R. 401; [1940] A.C. 613.
(150) [1895-99] All E.R. Rep. 625; [1898] 2 Ch. 307.
(151) [1900-03] All E.R. Rep. 633 at p. 641; [1903] A.C. 253 at p. 267.
(152) [1910] 1 Ch. 620.
(153) (1962), Estates Gazette Digest 452.   (154) (1958), 14 D.L.R. (2d) 454.

within the principle which I have earlier suggested, as coming within a recognised and accepted category of transactions, in precisely the same manner as a lease; but just as provisions contained in a lease, affecting the lessees' (or lessors') liberty of trade, which pass beyond what is normally found in and ancillary to this type of transaction and enter on the field of regulation of the parties' trading activities, may fall to be tested as possible restraints of trade, so, in my opinion, may those in a mortgage. The mere designation of a transaction as a mortgage, however true, does not ipso facto protect the entire contents of the arrangements from examination, however fettering of trade these arrangements may be. If their purpose and nature is found not to be ancillary to the lending of money on security, as, for example, to make the lending more profitable or safer, but some quite independent purpose, they may and should be independently scrutinised. This scrutiny is called for in the present case: for it is clear, on consideration of the mortgage both taken by itself and in its relation to the solus agreement which shortly preceded it, that so far from the tie being ancillary to a predominant transaction of lending money, the mortgage, as was the solus agreement, was entered into as part of a plan, designed by the appellants, to tie the Corner garage to its products for as long as possible. As HARMAN, L.J., put it (155), after a detailed examination of the terms of the mortgage which I forbear from repeating, " the mortgage was intended to bolster up the solus agreement ". It follows, in my opinion, that it must be judged by the test of reasonableness. If this is so, I think that there can be little doubt, once a conclusion adverse to the restrictions is reached as to the solus agreement affecting the Corner garage, that the same must follow as regards the mortgage. I should add that the appellants added to their main argument on this point a subsidiary contention that the stipulations in the mortgage should be regarded in the same legal light as if they had been contained in a lease. For this they referred to s. 85 of the Law of Property Act, 1925, and *Regent Oil Co., Ltd.* v. *J. A. Gregory (Hatch End), Ltd.* (156). I cannot accept this esoteric argument. For if it be the case that inclusion of the relevant restrictions in a mortgage does not save them from examination, they surely cannot be saved because, for conveyancing purposes, the mortgage also bears the character of a lease. The relationship between the covenant and a lease of the garage site is too technical and notional to bring the case within the recognised exemption which, within limits which I have earlier stated, applies to actual leases of an accepted character.

In my opinion the appeal should be allowed as regards the Mustow Green garage and the judgment and order of MOCATTA, J. (157) so far restored. As regards the Corner garage it should be dismissed.

Appeal allowed in part, dismissed in part.

Solicitors: *Plesse & Sons* (for the appellants); *Field, Roscoe & Co.*, agents for *Frederick L. Glover*, Stourport (for the respondents).

[*Reported by* KATHLEEN J. H. O'BRIEN, *Barrister-at-Law.*]

---

(155) [1966] 1 All E.R. at p. 732, letter H; [1966] 2 Q.B. at p. 569.
(156) [1965] 3 All E.R. 673; [1966] Ch. 402.
(157) [1965] 2 All E.R. 933; [1960] 2 Q.B. 514.

PARKASHO v. SINGH.

[Probate, Divorce and Admiralty Division (Sir Jocelyn Simon, P., and Cairns, J.), November 8, 9, 1966.]

Magistrates—Husband and wife—Jurisdiction—Potentially polygamous marriage —Ceremony of marriage in India in 1942 in accordance with rites of Sikhs— Husband coming to England in 1955 and joined by wife in 1963—Whether polygamous marriage can become monogamous—Whether character of marriage to be considered at its inception or at time when proceedings taken— Whether conversion from polygamous to monogamous marriage can take place by legislation—Whether wife can obtain matrimonial relief in England —Hindu Marriage Act, 1955 (No. 25), s. 5 (i), s. 11, s. 17.

In 1942 the parties, who were Sikhs, went through a ceremony of marriage in accordance with the rites of Sikhs. That ceremony would be recognised in the courts of India as a valid marriage, but as a marriage which at the time when it was celebrated was a potentially polygamous one. In 1955 the husband came to England and he was followed by the wife in 1963. In June, 1964, they parted. In April, 1965, on a complaint by the wife that the husband had been guilty of wilful neglect to maintain her and the child of the family, a preliminary point was taken on behalf of the husband that the marriage was potentially polygamous so that there was no jurisdiction in the magistrates' court to hear the complaint. Evidence was given by two experts on Indian law, one on each side, whether or not the marriage, originally polygamous, had been rendered monogamous by an Indian Act, the Hindu Marriage Act, 1955. By s. 5 (i)* of that Act (which applied to Sikhs), a marriage might be solemnized between any two Hindus only if neither party had a spouse living at the time of the marriage; by s. 11†, any marriage solemnized after the commencement of the Act was to be null and void if it contravened s. 5 (i); and by s. 17‡, any marriage between two Hindus solemnized after the commencement of the Act was void if at the date of such marriage either party had a husband or wife living. The expert witness for the wife was wholly in favour of the view that the Act of 1955 rendered the marriage monogamous. The evidence of the expert witness for the husband was equivocal on this question. On appeal against the decision of the magistrates that the marriage was potentially polygamous in its inception and that that character had not been changed by the Act of 1955,

Held: (i) a marriage that was potentially polygamous in its inception could be changed prospectively by legislation into a monogamous one and vice versa, and the proper time to consider the nature of the union in order to see whether the magistrates' court had jurisdiction was the date of commencement of the proceedings (see p. 740, letters E and G, p. 742, letter D, p. 748, letter F, p. 749, letter B, and p. 750, letter B, post).

Cheni (otherwise Rodriguez) v. *Cheni* ([1962] 3 All E.R. 873) followed; *Sinha Peerage Case* ([1946] 1 All E.R. 348, n.) and *Starkowski* v. *A.-G.* ([1953] 2 All E.R. 1272) applied.

Dictum of Lord Merriman, P., in *Sowa* v. *Sowa* ([1960] 3 All E.R. at p. 198), and *Ali* v. *Ali* ([1966] 1 All E.R. 664) considered.

Dictum of Barnard, J., in *Mehta* v. *Mehta* ([1945] 2 All E.R. at p. 693) criticised.

(ii) the court was entitled to consider, and should consider, itself the relevant foreign statute (the Hindu Marriage Act, 1955) both in view of the court's express power by virtue of r. 73 (7)§ of the Matrimonial Causes Rules,

---

* Section 5, so far as material, is set out at p. 744, letter F, post.
† Section 11 is set out at p. 744, letter G, post.
‡ Section 17 is set out at p. 745, letter B, post.
§ Rule 73 (7), so far as material, provides: " The Divisional Court may draw all inferences of fact which might have been drawn in the magistrates' court and may give any judgment and make any order which ought to have been made . . ."

Applied in R v SAGOO [1975] 2 All ER 926

1957, to draw inferences of fact which might have been drawn in the magistrates' court and because the conflict of expert evidence justified the court in itself examining the provisions of the statute (see p. 746, letter I, **p. 748**, letter C, and p. 749, letter E, post).

Dicta of LORD WRIGHT in *Lazard Brothers & Co.* v. *Midland Bank, Ltd.* ([1932] All E.R. Rep. at pp. 576, 577), and of LORD LANGDALE, M.R., in *Earl Nelson* v. *Lord Bridport* ([1843-60] All E.R. Rep. at p. 1036) considered and applied.

(iii) accordingly, the justices had jurisdiction as the Hindu Marriage Act, 1955 had the effect of making the marriage monogamous (see p. 748, letter D, p. 749, letter H, and p. 750, letter B, post).

Appeal allowed.

[As to the general principles of validity of marriages in English law, see 7 HALSBURY'S LAWS (3rd Edn.) 88-90, paras. 161, 162; and for cases on the subject, see 11 DIGEST (Repl.) 455, 456, *906-911*, 457, 458, *918-924*.

As to examination by the court itself of documents of foreign law, see 15 HALSBURY'S LAWS (3rd Edn.) 328-330, paras. 598, text and notes (*a*), (*b*), 600.]

Cases referred to:

Ali v. *Ali*, [1966] 1 All E.R. 664; [1966] 2 W.L.R. 620.

A/S Tallinna Laevauhisus v. *Estonian State S.S. Line*, (1946), 80 Lloyd L.R. 99; 29 Digest (Repl.) 114, *587*.

A.-G. of Ceylon v. *Reid*, [1965] 1 All E.R. 812; [1965] A.C. 720; [1965] 2 W.L.R. 671; 3rd Digest Supp.

Baindail (*otherwise Lawson*) v. *Baindail*, [1946] 1 All E.R. 342; [1946] P. 122; 115 L.J.P. 65; 174 L.T. 320; 11 Digest (Repl.) 457, *921*.

Cheni (*otherwise Rodriguez*) v. *Cheni*, [1962] 3 All E.R. 873; [1965] P. 85; [1963] 2 W.L.R. 17; Digest (Cont. Vol. A.) 234, *924b*.

De Bode's Case, (1844), 8 Q.B. 208; 115 E.R. 854; *subsequent proceedings*, sub nom. *De Bode* v. *R.*, (1848), 13 Q.B. 364; (1851), 3 H.L. Cas. 449; 22 Digest (Repl.) 619, *7133*.

Hyde v. *Hyde and Woodmansee*, [1861-73] All E.R. Rep. 175; (1866), L.R. 1 P. & D. 130; 35 L.J.P. & M. 57; 14 L.T. 188; 11 Digest (Repl.) 455, *906*.

Lazard Brothers & Co. v. *Midland Bank, Ltd.*, [1932] All E.R. Rep. 571; [1933] A.C. 289; 102 L.J.K.B. 191; 148 L.T. 242; 22 Digest (Repl.) 613, *7070*.

Mehta (*otherwise Kohn*) v. *Mehta*, [1945] 2 All E.R. 690; 174 L.T. 63; 11 Digest (Repl.) 456, *910*.

Nachimson v. *Nachimson*, [1930] All E.R. Rep. 114; [1930] P. 217; 99 L.J.P. 104; 143 L.T. 254; 94 J.P. 211; 11 Digest (Repl.) 456, *911*.

Nelson (*Earl*) v. *Bridport* (*Lord*), [1843-60] All E.R. Rep. 1032; (1845), 8 Beav. 527; 8 L.T.O.S. 18; 50 E.R. 207; 22 Digest (Repl.) 614, *7080*.

Ohochuku v. *Ohochuku*, [1960] 1 All E.R. 253; [1960] 1 W.L.R. 183; Digest (Cont. Vol. A.) 234, *922b*.

Sinha Peerage Case, [1946] 1 All E.R. 348, n; 171 Lords' Journal 350.

Sowa v. *Sowa*, [1960] 3 All E.R. 196; [1961] P. 70; [1960] 3 W.L.R. 733; affd. C.A., [1961] 1 All E.R. 687; [1961] P. at p. 80; [1961] 2 W.L.R. 313; 125 J.P. 289; Digest (Cont. Vol. A.) 234, *924a*.

Starkowski (*by his next friend*) v. *A.-G.*, [1953] 2 All E.R. 1272; [1954] A.C. 155; [1953] 3 W.L.R. 942; Digest (Cont. Vol. A.) 236, *966*.

Sussex Peerage Case, [1843-60] All E.R. Rep. 55; (1844), 11 Cl. & Fin. 85; 3 L.T.O.S. 277; 8 E.R. 1034; 22 Digest (Repl.) 96, *746*.

Wellington (*Duke*), *Re, Glentanar* v. *Wellington*, [1947] 2 All E.R. 854; [1947] Ch. 506; affd. C.A., [1947] 2 All E.R. 864; [1948] Ch. 118; [1949] L.J.R. 612; 11 Digest (Repl.) 390, *494*.

Appeal.

This was an appeal by the wife from an order of the Wolverhampton Borough

A Justices dated Aug. 13, 1965, dismissing her complaint that the husband had been guilty of wilful neglect to maintain her and the child of the family on a preliminary issue that the marriage was potentially polygamous and that there was no jurisdiction in the magistrates' court to hear the complaint. The facts are set out in the judgment of CAIRNS, J.

B *F. W. Parsons* for the wife.
H. P. B. Dow for the husband.

CAIRNS, J., delivered the first judgment at the invitation of SIR JOCELYN SIMON, P.: The facts of this case are simple, but the appeal raises issues of some difficulty, and, we understand, of considerable importance to Indian people living in this country. The husband and wife are both of Indian origin, and it is

C common ground that they are Sikhs. In 1942 they went through a ceremony of marriage in accordance with the rites of the Sikhs. There was uncontradicted evidence before the magistrates that this ceremony would be recognised in the courts of India as a valid marriage, but as a marriage which at the time when it was celebrated was a potentially polygamous one. In 1955 the husband came to this country and he was followed by the wife in 1963. They lived together for

D some time at Southall, in Middlesex, but parted in June, 1964. On Apr. 23, 1965, the wife complained to the justices at Wolverhampton, where she was then living, that the husband had been guilty of wilful neglect to maintain her and the child of the marriage who had been born on Oct. 6, 1950. The hearing was fixed for June 25, 1965, but was adjourned until Aug. 13, 1965, when a preliminary point was taken on behalf of the husband, namely, that the marriage was potentially

E polygamous and that, for that reason, there was no jurisdiction in the magistrates' court to hear the complaint. The magistrates decided to try this question as a preliminary issue and they heard only the evidence of the wife as to the marriage ceremony and the subsequent movements of the parties, corroborative evidence from a relative of the wife about the ceremony, and evidence of two experts in Indian law, one on each side. The matter on which the experts gave evidence was

F whether or not the marriage, originally polygamous, had been rendered monogamous by the operation of the Hindu Marriage Act, 1955, of India. The justices, having heard this evidence and the arguments of counsel, found that the marriage was potentially polygamous in its inception and that this character had not been changed. Accordingly, they held that the wife was not entitled to the status of a married woman in this country and they dismissed her application.

G From that dismissal the wife appeals to this court.

It is clear law that only a monogamous marriage can entitle a spouse to bring proceedings under the Matrimonial Proceedings (Magistrates' Courts) Act, 1960. That was decided by the Court of Appeal in *Sowa* v. *Sowa* (1). But will proceedings lie under the Act of 1960 if the marriage was originally polygamous but has become monogamous by the time of the proceedings? Counsel for the wife has

H posed four questions to the court, which I agree are questions that we must consider. First, can a marriage be converted from one category to another; from the category of polygamous marriages to that of monogamous marriages? Secondly, if such a transmutation can take place, what is the proper time at which to consider the nature of the union in order to see whether the magistrates' court has jurisdiction? Has the character of the marriage to be considered as at its

I inception or as at the time when proceedings are taken? Thirdly, if in some circumstances a marriage can be changed from one category to the other, can such a change be effected by legislation? And fourthly, if it can, did the Hindu Marriage Act, 1955, have the effect of changing this marriage into a monogamous marriage? With regard to the first three of those questions, valuable guidance is afforded to this court by the decision of SIR JOCELYN SIMON, P., in *Cheni (otherwise Rodriguez)* v. *Cheni* (2). That case answers as a matter of direct decision forming the ratio

---

(1) [1961] 1 All E.R. 687; [1961] P. 70.   (2) [1962] 3 All E.R. 873; [1965] P. 85.

decidendi of the case the first two of counsel for the wife's questions and, incidentally, but by way of obiter dictum, it answers the third one. Admittedly, to distinguish *Cheni* v. *Cheni* (3) from the present case is a difficult task which counsel for the husband has courageously faced. Alternatively, he would have to persuade us that *Cheni* v. *Cheni* (3) was wrongly decided. That task, I think, is one of not less difficulty, and he has faced it with not less courage, and presented his argument in a most attractive manner.

In order to show to what extent this present case is governed by *Cheni* v. *Cheni* (3) it is necessary to see what the facts of that case were and what was actually decided by SIR JOCELYN SIMON, P. It will be sufficient to read the headnote and one short passage from his judgment. The headnote reads as follows (4):

" The parties, who were uncle and niece, were married in Cairo in 1924 in accordance with Jewish rites. The intention of both was to enter into a monogamous union. According to expert evidence the marriage was valid by Jewish and Egyptian law and although potentially polygamous at its inception became irrevocably monogamous on the birth of a child of the marriage in 1926. The parties continued to live in Egypt until 1957 when they settled in England where they became domiciled. In 1961 the wife filed a petition praying that the marriage be declared null and void on the ground of consanguinity or, in the alternative, that the marriage be dissolved on the ground of the husband's cruelty. On the issue of nullity:—held, (1) that the marriage was at its inception potentially polygamous and the intention of the parties that the union should be monogamous was irrelevant; but the English court had jurisdiction to adjudicate on a marriage which, although potentially polygamous at its inception, had become monogamous at the date of the commencement of the proceedings."

(The other matter that was decided, in relation to the incestuous character of the marriage in question, has no relevance to the present issues.) Thus, in *Cheni* v. *Cheni* (3), SIR JOCELYN SIMON, P., answered the first two questions posed by counsel for the wife by saying that a marriage *can* be converted from one category to another and that the proper time at which to consider the character of the marriage is at the time of the proceedings and not at the time of the inception of the marriage. Before arriving at those conclusions, SIR JOCELYN SIMON, P., made a close and careful examination of the previous law on the subject; and for my part I do not find it necessary to attempt to go through the same process of reasoning again. I am content to say that I should hesitate to put forward a different view even if I had some doubt about the matter, but I have no such doubt and I respectfully agree entirely with the decision and the grounds on which SIR JOCELYN SIMON, P., arrived at it.

When one comes to the third question—can a potentially polygamous marriage be changed into a monogamous one by legislation?—that is a question which did not arise for decision in *Cheni* v. *Cheni* (3), but there is a most illuminating and helpful paragraph in the judgment which reads in this way (5):

" This poses the question of the relevant date for examining the marriage as to its polygamous potential—the inception of the marriage or the inception of the proceedings? If the inception of the marriage, the marriage in the present case was potentially polygamous and the court has no jurisdiction over it. If the date of the proceedings, this marriage was by then monogamous and the court may proceed; but the question has significance beyond the circumstances of the present case. Two spouses may contract a valid polyga-mous union and subsequently join a monogamous sect, or go through a second ceremony in a place where monogamy is the law. Again, a marriage in its inception potentially polygamous though in fact monogamous may be

---

(3) [1962] 3 All E.R. 873; [1965] P. 85.   (4) [1965] P. at p. 85.
(5) [1962] 3 All E.R. at pp. 876, 877; [1965] P. at p. 89.

A   rendered monogamous for all time by legislative action prescribing polygamy; this, according to the evidence, has in fact happened in the State of Israel in relation to the marriages of Sephardic Jews who are her nationals. Will the English court regard such marriages as monogamous or potentially polygamous for the purpose of exercising jurisdiction? "

B   The question posed at the end of that passage is one which SIR JOCELYN SIMON, P. later in his judgment answered to the effect that the court would regard such marriages as monogamous. The result, therefore, is this, that he considered the matter as one of principle not only in the context of marriages potentially polygamous in their inception and later rendered monogamous under the operation of the law governing the parties, by events in the lives of the parties, but **C**   in various other contexts, including that of subsequent legislation. Although SIR JOCELYN SIMON, P.'s observations as to the effect of such legislation must be regarded as obiter, nevertheless it appears to me that the whole of the reasoning in the judgment applies with just as much force to a legislative change as to a change of the kind with which SIR JOCELYN SIMON, P., was immediately concerned.

D   It is not only such events as occurred in *Cheni* v. *Cheni* (6) that have been considered by the courts of this country in deciding whether a marriage could be changed from one character to another and in determining what was the appropriate date at which to test the marriage. For instance, in *Sowa* v. *Sowa* (7), in the course of his judgment LORD MERRIMAN, P., mentioned that it had been contemplated that the husband might do certain things by way of the gift of a **E**   ring and a Bible, which might have rendered the marriage monogamous, and, having said that a promise that had been made to that effect had never been carried out, he added (8):

> " However, the fact is, that that change in the nature of the marriage has never been effected, from which it follows that it comes within the class of case dealt with in *Hyde* v. *Hyde and Woodmansee* (9) . . ."

F

and so forth. So LORD MERRIMAN, P., was there clearly contemplating that there might have been things done which would have changed the character of the marriage and which would have necessitated a different attitude to it. There is nothing that I can see in the judgments in the Court of Appeal (10) that suggests that that was a wrong view. Another case where parties whose marriage was **G**   originally potentially polygamous were held to be monogamously married for the purpose of the proceedings was *Ohochuku* v. *Ohochuku* (11), a decision of WRANGHAM, J. The subsequent event in that case which changed the character of the relationship of the parties was a marriage ceremony in this country. It appears from his judgment that the way in which WRANGHAM, J., dealt with the matter was this: he took the view that the only marriage that he could consider and could **H**   dissolve was the marriage which had taken place in this country. It must, however, be recognised, because of cases such as *Baindail* (otherwise *Lawson*) v. *Baindail* (12) that even a potentially polygamous marriage must be regarded as a marriage when one is considering whether one or both of the parties to it can marry again in this country; and it may be that, on close analysis of the circumstances existing in *Ohochuku* v. *Ohochuku* (11), the right view would be that an originally **I**   potentially polygamous marriage had been converted into a monogamous marriage by a subsequent marriage ceremony in this country. A recent case in which a marriage originally potentially polygamous has been held to acquire a

---

(6) [1962] 3 All E.R. 873; [1965] P. 85.
(7) [1960] 3 All E.R. 196 at p. 197; [1961] P. at p. 72.
(8) [1960] 3 All E.R. at p. 198; [1961] P. at pp. 72, 73.
(9) [1861-73] All E.R. Rep. 175; (1866), L.R. 1 P. & D. 130.
(10) [1961] 1 All E.R. 687; [1961] P. at p. 80.
(11) [1960] 1 All E.R. 253.   (12) [1946] 1 All E.R. 342; [1946] P. 122.

monogamous character is that of *Ali* v. *Ali* (13), a decision of CUMMING-BRUCE, J. He was considering the effect in relation to a potentially polygamous marriage of a change of domicil, the parties having acquired an English domicil. He held that the effect of that circumstance was to change the character of the marriage and to give the English court jurisdiction. The case is of value, not only for the view of that learned judge on those circumstances but also for the fact that he based his decision on *Cheni* v. *Cheni* (14), and found grounds for saying that the principles of that case applied to the situation that he was considering. An important case in which it was held that the character of a marriage had changed was the *Sinha Peerage Case* (15). The proceedings were before the Committee of Privileges and the opinion reported is that of LORD MAUGHAM, L.C., concurred in by the other members of the committee. The question was whether the petitioner was entitled to succeed to the peerage, he being the fruit of a marriage which was originally potentially polygamous but which later, as was found by LORD MAUGHAM, acquired a monogamous character because of a change of sect on the part of the parties to the marriage from a sect which allowed polygamy to one which did not. The petitioner was successful, so that there again and in another different set of circumstances we have the finding that the nature of the marriage could change, and that the date at which it was material to consider the matter was a date subsequent to the inception of the marriage.

In support of the view that the court should look only to the nature of the marriage at its inception, counsel for the husband relied first on *Mehta (otherwise Kohn)* v. *Mehta* (16). That was a decision of BARNARD, J., and what he decided was that a monogamous marriage would found jurisdiction in this court notwithstanding that, if there were a change of faith on the part of the husband, the marriage might become a polygamous one. At the time of the proceedings there had been no such change of faith, and the marriage continued to be a monogamous one except in the sense which I have indicated, that a change of religion would have enabled the husband to take a further wife or wives. Having referred to those circumstances, BARNARD, J., said (17):

" Does that possibility exclude this marriage from being a marriage in the Christian sense and one which this court can adjudicate upon in its matrimonial jurisdiction? I feel satisfied that all I have to do is to look at the inception of the marriage. It is perfectly clear that this marriage was monogamous in its inception and that monogamy was the essence of the contract into which these two parties entered; and I do not think that this court can look beyond that. It may well be that such a marriage, according to the laws of different countries, can be either got rid of or altered in accordance with those laws; all this court must consider is the marriage contract in its inception; and I am fortified in that view by what ROMER, L.J., said in *Nachimson* v. *Nachimson* (18) when he was dealing with the description of marriage given in *Hyde* v. *Hyde and Woodmansee* (19) . . ."

and he quotes the well-known sentence from LORD PENZANCE's judgment and ROMER, L.J.'s comment on it, which merely indicates that the fact that a marriage is dissoluble does not prevent its being a " union for life ". In a sense, BARNARD, J., was there considering the converse of the situation that we are dealing with. He was considering whether a marriage which was monogamous in its inception but which might later become polygamous could be the foundation of jurisdiction. One possible view which has been suggested in DICEY'S CONFLICT OF LAWS (7th Edn.) at p. 272, is that it may be permissible to look at the marriage either at the date of inception or at a later date and, if it is monogamous at either date, it is sufficient to found jurisdiction. That, I think, would be consistent with the

(13) [1966] 1 All E.R. 664.   (14) [1962] 3 All E.R. 873; [1965] P. 85.
(15) [1946] 1 All E.R. 348, n.   (16) [1945] 2 All E.R. 690.
(17) [1945] 2 All E.R. at p. 693.
(18) [1930] All E.R. Rep. 114 at p. 123; [1930] P. 217 at p. 238.
(19) [1861-73] All E.R. Rep. at p. 177; (1866), L.R. 1 P. & D. at p. 133.

decision reached in *Mehta* v. *Mehta* (20). So far as concerns the passage which I have read from the judgment, however, it is to be observed that, in that case, no subsequent event had happened to change the character of the marriage. It is true that, as BARNARD, J., said, a change of faith on the part of the husband might lead to the marriage acquiring a potentially polygamous character, but, as was pointed out by SIR JOCELYN SIMON, P., in *Cheni* v. *Cheni* (21) itself:

" After all, there are no marriages which are not potentially polygamous, in the sense that they may be rendered so by a change of domicil and religion on the part of the spouses."

That sentence has not only the authority of SIR JOCELYN SIMON, P., for its validity, but was quoted with approval in the judgment that the Privy Council delivered by LORD UPJOHN in *A.-G. of Ceylon* v. *Reid* (22).

Next, counsel for the wife argued that it is only circumstances which must have been in the contemplation of the parties at the time of the marriage, the happening of which could be deemed to change its character. Thus, one could say in relation to *Cheni* v. *Cheni* (23) that the two people who married in that case knew perfectly well that, if the marriage continued, and a child was born within a certain period after the marriage, the marriage would lose its potentially polygamous character and become monogamous. I think that the answer to that argument and a strong support to the view that legislation can alter the nature of the marriage is to be found in the decision of the House of Lords in *Starkowski* (*by his next friend*) v. *A.-G.* (24). The issue in that case was whether a ceremony of marriage which had taken place in Austria in 1945, but which at that time had not the effect in Austrian law of creating a valid marriage, nevertheless could form the foundation for a valid marriage by reason of the coming into force a month later of a law which made provision for the validation of such marriages. The decision of the House of Lords was expressed briefly and accurately in the headnote in this way (25):

" Held, that the English marriage ceremony [a ceremony which had taken place at a later date] was invalid, since at the time it was celebrated the previous marriage celebrated in Austria had been already validated by the laws of that country . . . The validity of a marriage is governed by the lex loci celebrationis and, irrespective of domicil or nationality, the English courts will recognise retroactive legislation of foreign States validating informal marriages contracted within their jurisdiction."

The parties in *Starkowski* v. *A.-G.* (24) cannot be supposed to have contemplated at the time of the ceremony that the subsequent legislation would occur. Further, if legislation can bring into being a marriage originating in a ceremony which at the time was invalid, so as to make it necessary for the English courts thereafter to recognise the validity of that marriage, it seems to me illogical to say that legislation which turns a potentially polygamous marriage into a monogamous marriage cannot, in the eyes of the English courts, be deemed to have any such effect, or to say that, whereas in *Starkowski* v. *A.-G.* (24) the matter had to be considered in the light of the circumstances after the legislation, in this case the matter has to be considered only as at the inception of the marriage.

Counsel for the wife also relied on the decision of LORD PENZANCE in *Hyde* v. *Hyde and Woodmansee* (26). I do not propose to examine that well-known case again. I agree with the reasons which SIR JOCELYN SIMON, P., gave in *Cheni* v. *Cheni* (27) for distinguishing it. Finally, counsel for the wife relied on a passage

---

(20) [1945] 2 All E.R. 690.   (21) [1962] 3 All E.R. at p. 877; [1965] P. at p. 90.
(22) [1965] 1 All E.R. 812 at p. 817; [1965] A.C. 720 at p. 734.
(23) [1962] 3 All E.R. 873; [1965] P. 85.
(24) [1953] 2 All E.R. 1272; [1954] A.C. 155.
(25) [1954] A.C. at p. 156.
(26) [1861-73] All E.R. Rep. 175; (1866), L.R. 1 P. & D. 130.
(27) [1962] 3 All E.R. at p. 878; [1965] P. at pp. 91, 92.

in the judgment of HOLROYD PEARCE, L.J., in *Sowa* v. *Sowa* (28) in the Court of
Appeal, and I find it sufficient to say in relation to that that the lord justice
clearly had not this type of case in mind when he said that the English courts
could not deal with a potentially polygamous marriage.

For these reasons, I am of opinion that the justices were right in this case in
directing their attention to the status of the marriage at the time of the inception
of the proceedings before them. They were, therefore, right in considering that,
if the effect of the Hindu Marriage Act, 1955, was to change this potentially
polygamous into a monogamous marriage, they would have jurisdiction. So I
next come to the question whether they were right or wrong in holding, as they
did, that that was not the effect of the Act of 1955.

One must first observe that that Act had no effect on this marriage unless the
husband was domiciled in India at the time when it was passed: see s. 2 (1) (c)
of the Act. The evidence was that the husband came to England in 1955, though
the precise date of his coming to this country was not stated. There was, however,
no evidence that he had changed his domicil of origin before the Act came into
force on May 18, 1955, or indeed after that date. I think that the matter falls to
be approached on the same basis as it was approached before the justices, namely,
on the basis that these parties were, in 1955, subject so far as matrimonial status
was concerned, to the law of India. It seems to me that the material provisions
of the Act of 1955 were those to which attention was directed in the magistrates'
court. First, it may be noted that, by s. 2 (1) (b), the Act is to apply to a person
who is a Sikh by religion. Then s. 2 (3) provides:

" The expression ' Hindu ' in any portion of this Act shall be construed as
if it included a person who, though not a Hindu by religion, is, nevertheless,
a person to whom this Act applies by virtue of the provisions contained in
this section."

That would clearly include a Sikh. Section 5 of the Act provides that " A marriage
may be solemnized between any two Hindus, if the following conditions are
fulfilled ", and condition (i) is " that neither party has a spouse living at the
time of the marriage ". I need not read the other conditions. Section 11 provides
as follows:

" Any marriage solemnized after the commencement of this Act shall be
null and void and may, on a petition presented by either party thereto, be
so declared by a decree of nullity if it contravenes any one of the conditions
specified in clauses (i), (iv) and (v) of s. 5."

That means among other things that, if a marriage is solemnized after the coming
into force of this Act, and if at the time of such solemnization either party has a
spouse living, then that subsequent marriage is a nullity. Thus, if a potentially
polygamous marriage had been celebrated before the Act of 1955, and both
spouses were alive on May 18, 1955, and the marriage had not been dissolved, the
effect of s. 11 is that the marriage then became monogamous because any subsequent marriage of either of the parties while the marriage subsisted would be
null and void. Section 13 deals with divorce, and the important subsection is
sub-s. (2), which provides that:

" A wife may also present a petition for the dissolution of her marriage by
a decree of divorce on the ground—(i) in the case of any marriage solemnized
before the commencement of this Act, that the husband had married
again before such commencement, or that any other wife of the husband
married before such commencement was alive at the time of the solemnization
of the marriage to the petitioner: . . ."

The importance of that provision in connexion with the present case is this. The
subsection recognises that a potentially polygamous or even an actually polygamous marriage celebrated before the Act came into force would continue as a

marriage after the coming into force of the Act; would continue if there were only one wife, as a marriage between that wife and that husband. If there were two wives, each of the marriages would continue to exist, although each of the wives would have an opportunity if she so wished of petitioning for divorce, with the proviso that she could only so petition if the other wife was alive at the time of the presentation of the petition. Then s. 17 provides that:

" Any marriage between two Hindus solemnized after the commencement of this Act is void if at the date of such marriage either party had a husband or wife living; and the provisions of s. 494 and s. 495 of the Indian Penal Code shall apply accordingly."

I have looked at those sections of the penal code, and they do not carry the matter any further. They are just general provisions for the punishment of bigamy.

I have for convenience read the sections of the Act of 1955 before coming to the evidence of the expert witnesses. I will consider later the question whether and to what extent this court can put its own construction on those sections, or whether this court can use only the evidence of expert witnesses. The witness called on behalf of the wife, having stated his qualifications, said:

" I am conversant with the Hindu Marriage Act, 1955. In my view, prior to this Act, Hindu marriages were sacramental rather than contractual. They were, prior to this Act, potentially polygamous in nature. It was permitted for a Hindu to have more than one wife. The Hindu Marriage Act, 1955, transformed all existing Hindu marriages into monogamous form, and if a Hindu had more than one wife when the Act came into force the Indian Parliament did not take account of this."

There in that sentence is the clearest statement that the Hindu Marriage Act, 1955, transformed all existing Hindu marriages into monogamous form. The witness went on by way of amplification:

" If a Hindu had only one wife at the time of the Act, the marriage became of a monogamous nature because under s. 17 of the Act there is a provision relating to punishment for bigamy. If a Hindu took a second wife after this Act the marriage would not only be void but the offender would be liable to prosecution under s. 494 and s. 495 of the Indian Penal Code."

I do not think that it is necessary to read the rest of his evidence-in-chief. In cross-examination he said, " I do not agree that the Act of 1955 had the effect that from that time onwards the Hindu marriages became monogamous ". As I interpret that evidence in the light of his evidence-in-chief, what he was really saying there was that, if the man had, before 1955, married two wives, then each of those marriages would continue as a polygamous marriage; it could not be said that either of those marriages was transformed into a monogamous marriage, for the man in fact had two wives and neither marriage was automatically brought to an end by the coming into force of the Act of 1955. Later in his cross-examination he said, " The whole purpose of the Act was to turn potentially polygamous marriages into monogamous marriages ". The expert witness who was called on behalf of the husband, having stated his qualifications and dealt with some preliminary matters, said this: " The effect of the Hindu Marriage Act, 1955, has no effect on the character of the present marriage "; that would appear to be in direct conflict with what the other witness said. The witness, however, went on to say, ". . . the Act is silent about marriages before it came into operation ". That, clearly, is wrong, because s. 13 (2), if no other provision, expressly deals with marriages which were in existence before it came into operation. Later in evidence-in-chief he said, " A potentially polygamous marriage by nature before the Act remains of that nature after the Act ". So he is there reiterating the opinion which he previously expressed which was in conflict with that of the other witness. However, when we come to his cross-examination we find that his evidence conflicts with his own previous evidence, because these are some of his answers:

" After 1955 a Hindu could not take another wife whether he had one or more before that Act . . . Since the operation of the Act it is not polygamous because defendant could not take a second wife after the Act came into force. From the operation of this Act a man with one wife cannot take a second wife . . . Defendant would not have right to marry again either in India or in England."

So he is there expressing over and over again the view that the marriage had become monogamous as a result of the legislation.

Let us now look at the reasons given by the justices for their decision, to see how they dealt with the matter. They say, after setting out the history:

" For the [wife] it was argued that although the marriage ceremony was potentially polygamous at its inception this position had been completely changed by the Hindu Marriage Act, 1955, which, their expert witness contended, transformed all existing Hindu marriages into monogamous form. In support of this argument we were referred to s. 17 of that Act which made provision relating to punishment for bigamy although it was conceded that a man who had two or more wives before the Act was not liable to be prosecuted as the Act was not retrospective in its effect. It was also submitted that s. 13 of the Act of 1955 enabled a wife to obtain a divorce on the grounds that before the Act he had married more than one wife. It was contended that the whole purpose of the Act (presumably by inference) was to turn potentially polygamous marriages into monogamous marriages. The [husband's] case was that the Act of 1955 had no such effect as that put forward on behalf of the [wife] as the Act was silent as to marriages celebrated before it came into operation; that it dealt only with future marriages and did not affect the potentially polygamous nature of the marriage at present under discussion. It was submitted that there was nothing in the Act converting potentially polygamous marriages into monogamous nor that the former became invalid as a result of the Act . . . After carefully considering the arguments adduced on both sides, we were clearly of the view that this marriage was potentially polygamous at its inception and that this inherent nature had not been changed either expressly or by inference by the provisions of the Hindu Marriage Act, 1955."

We are asked by the wife to say that that decision was wrong; that the justices were wrong in their interpretation of the foreign law. The question of foreign law being a question of fact in our courts, must this court regard itself as bound by the findings of the justices on this matter? In my view, the question of foreign law, although a question of fact, is a question of fact of a peculiar kind, and the same considerations do not apply in considering whether and to what extent this court should interfere with the decision of the magistrates, as in the case of the ordinary questions of fact which come before a magistrates' court. It is not, I think, inappropriate to bear in mind that, under the provisions of s. 102 of the Supreme Court of Judicature (Consolidation) Act, 1925, it is provided that an issue of foreign law in a case which is being tried by a jury is a question of fact for the judge and not the jury. Bearing that in mind, and bearing also in mind the provisions of r. 73 (7) of the Matrimonial Causes Rules, 1957, (29) which enable this court to draw any inference of fact which might have been drawn in the justices' court, I think that it is our duty in this case to examine the evidence of foreign law which was before the justices and to decide for ourselves whether that evidence justifies the conclusion to which they came. A further matter that needs to be considered is this: must this court direct its attention solely to the oral evidence given by the expert witnesses, or are we entitled to obtain

(29) S.I. 1957 No. 619.

assistance by our own perusal of the relevant statute and our own construction of the sections of it? Guidance as to the correct approach is given in the speech of LORD WRIGHT in *Lazard Brothers & Co.* v. *Midland Bank, Ltd.* (30). It was there a question of Russian law which was being considered, and LORD WRIGHT said:

" What the Russian Soviet law is in that respect is a question of fact, of which the English court cannot take judicial cognisance, even though the foreign law has already been proved before it in another case. The court must act on the evidence before it in the actual case. The recent enactment (s. 102 of the Supreme Court of Judicature (Consolidation) Act, 1925), which provides that this question of fact must be decided by the judge alone instead of by the jury, if there be a jury, expressly treats the question as depending on the evidence given with respect to the foreign law. No earlier decision of the court can relieve the judge of the duty of deciding the question on the actual evidence given in the particular case. On what evidence of the foreign law a court can act has been often discussed. The evidence it is clear must be that of qualified experts in the foreign law. If the law is contained in a code or written form, the question is not as to the language of the written law, but what the law is as shown by its exposition, interpretation, and adjudication; so in effect it was laid down by COLERIDGE, J., in *De Bode's Case* (31). In the *Sussex Peerage Case* (32), LORD DENMAN stated his opinion to the same effect as he had done in *De Bode's Case* (33). He said that if there be a conflict of evidence of the experts ' you (the judge) must decide as well as you can on the conflicting testimony; but you must take the evidence from the witnesses '. Hence the court is not entitled to construe a foreign code itself: it has not organs to know and to deal with the text of that law (as was said by LORD BROUGHAM in the *Sussex Peerage Case* (34)). The text of the foreign law [and this is an important sentence] if put in evidence by the experts may be considered, if at all, only as part of the evidence and as a help to decide between conflicting expert testimony."

That last sentence is in accordance with what was said at a very much earlier date by LORD LANGDALE, M.R., in *Earl Nelson* v. *Lord Bridport* (35):

" If the utmost strictness were required in every case, justice might often have to stand still; and I am not disposed to say that there may not be cases in which a judge may, without impropriety, take on himself . . . to construe the words of a foreign law and determine their application to the case in question, especially if there should be a variance or want of clearness in the testimony . . ."

See also *A/S Tallinna Laevauhisus* v. *Estonian State S.S. Line* (36).

The situation as I find it here is this. The evidence of one of the two expert witnesses is wholly in favour of the view that the Act of 1955 rendered this marriage monogamous. The evidence of the other expert witness is equivocal; some of it supports the first witness, some of it contradicts that view, and, simply on the basis of considering those two witnesses and the weight of their evidence, as far as one can judge by an examination of the notes of the evidence, it would seem to me that the weight of the evidence was overwhelmingly in favour of the view that the Act of 1955 did render the marriage monogamous. The justices have given no reason for coming down on the side on which they did come down; they simply say:

(30) [1932] All E.R. Rep. 571 at pp. 576, 577; [1933] A.C. 289 at pp. 297, 298.
(31) (1844), 8 Q.B. 208 at p. 266.
(32) (1844), 11 Ch. & Fin. 85 at p. 116; [1843-60] All E.R. Rep. 55 at p. 62.
(33) (1844), 8 Q.B. 208.
(34) [1843-60] All E.R. Rep. at p. 62; (1844), 11 Ch. & Fin. at p. 116.
(35) [1843-60] All E.R. Rep. 1032 at p. 1036; (1845), 8 Beav. 527 at p. 537.
(36) (1946), 80 Lloyd L.R. 99 at p. 108.

" After carefully considering the arguments adduced on both sides we
were clearly of the view that this marriage . . . had not been changed . . . by
the provisions of the Hindu Marriage Act, 1955."

They do not say that the witness called for the wife gave his evidence in such a
way as to inspire no confidence and that the witness called on behalf of the
husband was apparently expressing his real opinion in evidence-in-chief but was
nervous in cross-examination and gave answers that he did not intend. There is
no indication at all that the conclusion to which they came was based in any way
on the preference of one of these gentlemen as a witness for the other. There
being a conflict between them, feeling as I do that much greater weight is to be
attached to the evidence given by the witness for the wife and that given in
cross-examination by the witness for the husband than to the evidence-in-chief
of the latter, I do look at the sections of the Act of 1955 myself and, applying
my own mind to the language of them, I can only say that such an examination
of those provisions on my own part strengthens and confirms the view that the
Act of 1955 did have the effect of making the marriage monogamous.

I have, therefore, come to the conclusion that the justices were wrong in
deciding to the contrary, and that it is the duty of this court in those circumstances to set aside their decision and to remit the case to the justices' court for
trial on the basis that jurisdiction is established.

SIR JOCELYN SIMON, P.: I agree. I add some words only because we
are differing from the justices and out of deference to the argument of counsel for
the husband—all the more agreeable in that it was put forward in circumstances
of some inherent delicacy.

I agree that the appeal poses the four issues which counsel for the wife set out
in his opening address, though I venture to deal with them in a different order.
First, can a marriage change from one category to another? Can it change from
being a polygamous or potentially polygamous marriage to becoming a monogamous one, or vice versa? The point fell for decision in *Cheni (otherwise Rodriguez)*
v. *Cheni* (37); and, for the reasons which I found convincing there, and particularly by reason of the cases reviewed in the judgment (38), I think that it is
unquestionable that a marriage can change in such a way. Unless that is so, the
decision of the Committee of Privileges in the *Sinha Peerage Case* (39) must have
been the other way; since the marriage there, like the marriage here, was potentially polygamous at its inception. Moreover, in *A.-G. of Ceylon* v. *Reid* (40),
LORD UPJOHN, delivering the opinion of the Judicial Committee of the Privy
Council, cited the following passage from *Cheni* v. *Cheni* (41):

" After all, there are no marriages which are not potentially polygamous,
in the sense that they may be rendered so by a change of domicil and religion
on the part of the spouses ",

adding (40),

" which recognises that the obligations assumed on undertaking a Christian
monogamous marriage may not in some circumstances be incapable of
change."

If, as is clearly suggested there, the change may be from monogamous to polygamous, a fortiori, in my view, the change may be from potentially polygamous to
monogamous.

Secondly, if the marriage can change in such a way, can the change be brought
about by legislation? I ask myself, why not? After all, in *Cheni* v. *Cheni* (37), the
change in the character of the marriage was brought about by operation of law:

(37) [1962] 3 All E.R. 873; [1965] P. 85.
(38) [1962] 3 All E.R. at pp. 877, 878; [1965] P. at pp. 90, 91.
(39) [1946] 1 All E.R. 348, n.
(40) [1965] 1 All E.R. at p. 817; [1965] A.C. at p. 734.
(41) [1962] 3 All E.R. at p. 877; [1965] P. at p. 90.

Egyptian law referred the matter to the religious law of the parties; the religious law of the parties stipulated that a potentially polygamous marriage should become monogamous for all purposes by the birth of a child. That was on ultimate analysis a provision of Egyptian law; and, being a provision of Egyptian law, it could unquestionably be altered—or, indeed, have been originally enacted —by Egyptian legislation. Similarly, as regards *Reid's* case (42) and Singhalese law. Moreover, I agree with Cairns, J., that *Starkowski (by his next friend)* v. *A.-G.* (43) is relevant here. What greater change can be effected in the character of a marriage than from void to valid? If legislation can be recognised as retro-actively changing the character of a union from void to valid marriage, I can see no reason at all why legislation may not be recognised as at least prospectively changing the character of a marriage from potentially polygamous to monogamous.

Thirdly, if the character of a marriage can be changed by legislation, did the Hindu Marriage Act, 1955, effect such a change to the present marriage? Foreign law is, it is true, regarded in English courts as a question of fact, and appellate courts are slow to interfere with trial courts on questions of fact; but that only applies with particular force as regards the assessment of relative veracity and the judgment of matters of degree. Where the inference of fact depends on the consideration of written material, an appellate court is at no particular disadvantage compared to a trial court, and will regard itself as freer to review the decision of the trial court. Moreover, as Cairns, J., has pointed out, this court is given express power by the Matrimonial Causes Rules, 1957, r. 73 (7), to draw all inferences of fact which might have been drawn in the magistrates' court. Specifically, where there is a conflict of expert evidence as to foreign law, the court may itself look at the written material of the foreign law in order to arrive at its determination: *Earl Nelson* v. *Lord Bridport* (44); *Lazard Brothers & Co.* v. *Midland Bank, Ltd.* (45); and see also the way the court dealt with questions of foreign law in *Re Duke of Wellington, Glentanar* v. *Wellington* (46). In my view, for the reasons which Cairns, J., has given, the decision of the justices here was against the weight of evidence. Moreover, I agree with Cairns, J.'s independent construction of the Hindu Marriage Act, 1955. Its relevant effect seems to me to be three-fold. First, pre-existing marriages, whether monogamous or poly-gamous, are left unaffected, unless action is taken under s. 13 (2). Secondly, under that subsection, a polygamous wife may divorce her husband on the very ground that the marriage was polygamous, notwithstanding that it was entered into before the commencement of the Act. Thirdly, by the combined effects of s. 5 (*i*), s. 11 and s. 17, no polygamous marriage can be contracted after the coming into force of the Act; indeed, any such purported marriage constitutes the crime of bigamy. It follows that any marriage which was only potentially polygamous at the time of coming into force of the Act of 1955 became thereafter for all purposes monogamous.

The fourth question, therefore, arises—namely, what is the proper time to consider the nature of the union for the purpose of determining whether the English court has jurisdiction over it? Is it the time of the marriage or is it the time of the commencement of the proceedings? In support of the former, counsel for the husband relied mainly on one or two isolated sentences in the judgment of Holroyd Pearce, L.J., in *Sowa* v. *Sowa* (47); but it is plain to my mind that Holroyd Pearce, L.J., was not directing his remarks in any way to this problem. Counsel for the husband relied, secondly, on what Barnard, J.,

---

(42) [1965] 1 All E.R. 812; [1965] A.C. 720.
(43) [1953] 2 All E.R. 1272; [1954] A.C. 155.
(44) [1843-60] All E.R. Rep. 1032; (1845), 8 Beav. 527.
(45) [1932] All E.R. Rep. 571; [1933] A.C. 289.
(46) [1947] 2 All E.R. 854; [1947] Ch. 506.
(47) [1961] 1 All E.R. 687; [1961] P. at p. 80.

said in *Mehta* (*otherwise Kohn*) v. *Mehta* (48); but, as CAIRNS, J., has pointed out, those observations were unnecessary for his decision; the marriage there was as monogamous in its inception as the *Sinha* (49) marriage was in its fulfilment, and it remained equally monogamous up to the time of the proceedings. In spite of the careful argument of counsel for the husband, I have found no reason to change the view that I formed in *Cheni* v. *Cheni* (50) that the relevant time to consider the nature of the union is the date of the inception of the proceedings.

For these reasons, as well as those put forward by CAIRNS, J., I agree that the justices here wrongly refused jurisdiction and that the case should go back to a different panel of the justices to assume jurisdiction and to adjudicate on the wife's complaint.

Appeal allowed.   Case remitted.

Solicitors: *Sharpe, Pritchard & Co.*, agents for *Norman Benton*, Wolverhampton (for the wife); *J. A. Hostettler & Co.* (for the husband).

[*Reported by* ALICE BLOOMFIELD, *Barrister-at-Law.*]

DIN v. NATIONAL ASSISTANCE BOARD.

[QUEEN'S BENCH DIVISION (Lord Parker, C.J., Salmon, L.J., and Widgery, J.), November 18, 21, 1966.]

National Assistance—Husband and wife—Polygamous marriage—Separation of husband and wife—Polygamous marriage validly entered into according to the law of the spouses' domicil—Wife and children in receipt of national assistance—Whether sums recoverable from husband towards their maintenance—National Assistance Act, 1948 (11 & 12 Geo. 6 c. 29), s. 42 (1) (a), s. 43 (1).

The wife and her children of a polygamous marriage, valid according to the law of the country of the spouses' domicile where the marriage was entered into, are the husband's wife and children for the purposes of s. 42 and s. 43 of the National Assistance Act, 1948; accordingly the husband, when in England with them, is liable to the National Assistance Board in respect of their maintenance and an order may validly be made against him under s. 43 (see p. 752, letter I, p. 754, letter G, and p. 755, letter H, post).

[**Editorial Note.** Section 42 and s. 43 of the National Assistance Act, 1948, are largely superseded by s. 22 and s. 23 of the Ministry of Social Security Act 1966. The National Assistance Board was dissolved on Nov. 28, 1966. Transitional provisions regarding legal proceedings are in para. 7 of Sch. 7 to the Act of 1966.

As to a man's liability to maintain his wife and children, see 27 HALSBURY'S LAWS (3rd Edn.) 485, para. 961; as to the recovery of the cost of assistance from persons liable for maintenance, see ibid. pp. 486, 487, para. 965; and for cases on the recovery of sums paid for national assistance, see 35 DIGEST (Repl.) 815, 816, *95-100.*

For the National Assistance Act, 1948, s. 42 (1), s. 43, see 16 HALSBURY'S STATUTES (2nd Edn.) 968, 969.

For the Family Allowances and National Insurance Act, 1956, s. 3, see 36 HALSBURY'S STATUTES (2nd Edn.) 643; the section is repealed, however, by the Family Allowances and National Insurance Act 1964, s. 6 (4) and Sch. 8.]

Cases referred to:
Baindail (*otherwise Lawson*) v. *Baindail*, [1946] 1 All E.R. 342; [1946] P. 122; 115 L.J.P. 65; 174 L.T. 320; 11 Digest (Repl.) 457, *921.*

(48) [1945] 2 All E.R. 690.   (49) [1946] 1 All E.R. 348, n.
(50) [1962] 3 All E.R. 873; [1965] P. 85.

Hyde v. *Hyde and Woodmansee*, [1861-73] All E.R. Rep. 175; (1866), L.R. 1
    P. & D. 130; 30 L.J.P. & M. 57; 14 L.T. 188; 11 Digest (Repl.) 455,
    906.
Sinha Peerage Case, [1946] 1 All E.R. 348, n.; 171 Lord's Journal 350.

Case Stated.

This was a Case Stated by the justices for the county borough of Oldham in
respect of their adjudication as a magistrates' court sitting at Oldham in the
county of Lancaster. The appellant, Iman Din, appealed from an order of the
justices that he should pay to the National Assistance Board weekly sums
totalling £6 in respect of assistance which the board had been giving his wife and
children.

On Feb. 14, 1966, the respondents, the National Assistance Board preferred
complaints against the appellant. The first complaint was that, as the husband
of Rasul Bibi Din, he was liable to maintain her pursuant to s. 42* of the National
Assistance Act, 1948, but by reference to her requirements, assistance under
Part 2 of the Act of 1948 had been given to her at the post office, King Street,
Oldham on Feb. 7, 1966, and divers other days at the weekly rate of £4 6s. and
was continuing to be given. The second complaint was that, as the father of four
children, namely Tharira Din, Parvez Din, Rashida Din and Sharhida Din, all
being children under the age of sixteen years, he was liable to maintain them
pursuant to s. 42 of the National Assistance Act, 1948, but by reference to their
requirements assistance under Part 2 of the Act of 1948 had been given at the
post office, King Street, Oldham on Feb. 7, 1966, and divers other days at the
weekly rate of £3 10s. and was continuing to be given. The following facts were
found. The appellant married Rasul Bibi Din on Mar. 14, 1948, at Gujrat in the
province of Lahore, Pakistan, both the appellant and Rasul Bibi Din being
domiciled in Pakistan. The marriage was polygamous in that at the time of its
celebration the appellant was married to one Nawaa Bibi Din and that at such
time Nawaa Bibi Din was alive. Nawaa Bibi Din died in or about 1949. The
marriage was valid according to Muslim law, this being the lex loci contractus.
There were five children of the marriage between the appellant and Rasul Bibi
Din, namely Javid, Tharira, Parvez, Rashida and Sharhida. The eldest child
resided with the appellant and the four younger children, all under the age of
sixteen years resided with Rasul Bibi Din. The appellant and Rasul Bibi Din
came to England and resided together in the county borough of Oldham until
early March, 1965, when they separated. Rasul Bibi Din had been in receipt of
national assistance benefits for the needs of herself and the four younger children
for a period of two years and was still receiving such benefits.

It was contended on behalf of the appellant that (*a*) the board's case was based
entirely on the status of the parties and that as the parties were polygamously
married, the application is analogous to matrimonial proceedings; (*b*) the word
' husband ' in s. 42 of the National Assistance Act, 1948, bore the same meaning
as it did in the Matrimonial Proceedings (Magistrates' Courts) Act, 1960, and
therefore s. 43† could not apply to parties to a marriage which was not recognised
by English law. It was contended on behalf of the respondent board that (i) the
parties to a marriage which was valid according to their personal law, were liable
to maintain each other, and were both severally liable to maintain the children of
the marriage, for the purpose of the National Assistance Act, 1948 by virtue of
s. 42 (1) notwithstanding that the marriage was actually or potentially polygamous; (ii) the term " husband " in s. 42 of the National Assistance Act, 1948,
included the husband of a polygamous or potentially polygamous marriage;
(iii) the appellant's marriage with Rasul Bibi Din being valid according to their
personal law, the appellant was liable to maintain Rasul Bibi Din and their

---

* Section 42 (1), so far as material, is set out at p. 752, letter I, post.

† Section 43 (1) is set out at p. 752, letter G, post.

children for the purposes of the National Assistance Act, 1948, by virtue of s. 42 (1) notwithstanding that the marriage was actually or potentially polygamous.

After considering all the arguments, the justices came to the conclusion that s. 42 of the National Assistance Act, 1948, conferred a power on the National Assistance Board to make a complaint for an order against persons who were liable to maintain other persons in receipt of national assistance and that the appellant was in fact and in law a person liable to maintain his wife, despite the fact that the marriage was one that was not recognised for the purposes of granting matrimonial relief, and accordingly the justices made orders pursuant to s. 43 of the National Assistance Act, 1948 that the appellant should pay to the National Assistance Board the sum of 40s. each week in respect of Rasul Bibi Din and the sum of 20s. each week for each of the four children resident with Rasul Bibi Din. The appellant now appealed.

The cases noted below* were cited during the argument in addition to those referred to in the judgment of SALMON, L.J.

A. M. Abbas and *A. M. Azhar* for the appellant.
A. E. Holdsworth for the National Assistance Board.

SALMON, L.J., delivered the first judgment at the invitation of LORD PARKER, C.J.: The facts of the case are quite short. On Mar. 14, 1948, the appellant married Rasul Bibi Din in the province of Lahore in Pakistan. Both the appellant and the woman he married were domiciled in Pakistan. The marriage was a polygamous marriage, polygamy being recognised by law of Pakistan. The marriage, therefore, was valid according to the personal law of the parties and by the lex loci celebrationis; it was indeed a polygamous marriage, because at the time the appellant had another wife living who did not die until 1949.

In 1961, the appellant brought his wife Rasul Bibi Din and the children of their marriage to this country. Sometime later he abandoned his wife and four of the children, and for about two years prior to February, 1966, which was the date on which the National Assistance Board issued the summons in this case, the board had been paying Rasul Bibi Din for her maintenance and for that of the four children a total sum of £7 16s. a week; the appellant had left them destitute. The summons was issued under the National Assistance Act, 1948. By s. 43 (1) which I will now read:

" Where assistance is given or applied for by reference to the requirements of any person (in this section referred to as a person assisted), the board or the local authority concerned may make complaint to the court against any other person who for the purposes of this Act is liable to maintain the person assisted."

So the summons goes against any person liable for the purposes of the Act to maintain the person assisted.

In order to ascertain who is liable to maintain the person assisted for the purposes of the Act of 1948, we must look back to s. 42. Section 42 (1) (a) reads as follows:

" For the purposes of this Act—(a) a man shall be liable to maintain his wife and his children— . . ."

Quite clearly, if Rasul Bibi Din is the appellant's wife and her children are his children for the purposes of s. 42, the board has a right under s. 43 to claim from him in respect of the assistance which it has given his wife and children.

The question, and the only question that arises is: is Rasul Bibi Din the appellant's wife, and are her children his children, for the purposes of the Act of 1948. The point taken by counsel for the appellant is this. He says that polygamous

* *National Assistance Board* v. *Prisk*, [1954] 1 All E.R. 400; *National Assistance Board* v. *Mitchell*, [1955] 3 All E.R. 291; [1956] 1 Q.B. 53; *Sowa* v. *Sowa*, [1960] 3 All E.R. 196; [1961] P. 70; *Cheni* v. *Cheni*, [1962] 3 All E.R. 873; [1965] P. 85; *Shahnaz* v. *Rizwan*, [1964] 2 All E.R. 993; [1965] 1 Q.B. 390; *Ali* v. *Ali*, [1966] 1 All E.R. 664.

marriages are not recognised in this country on grounds of public policy; accordingly, the word " wife " in the Act of 1948, cannot apply to a polygamously-married wife. Children referred to in a statute, being prima facie at any rate legitimate children, then since there is no marriage which the courts of this country recognise, these children cannot be " children " within the meaning of the Act of 1948. It would perhaps be as remarkable as it would be unfortunate, if a man, coming from a country where he is lawfully married to a woman and is lawfully the father of her children, may bring them here and leave them destitute, with impunity, so that when the National Assistance Board is obliged to come to their assistance, he can avoid all responsibility and thereby throw the whole burden of maintaining his wife and children on the public.

When a question arises, of recognising a foreign marriage or of construing the word " wife " in a statute, everything in my view depends on the purpose for which the marriage is to be recognised and the objects of the statute. I ask myself first of all: is there any good reason why the appellant's wife and children should not be recognised as his wife and children for the purpose of the National Assistance Act, 1948? I can find no such reason, and every reason in common-sense and justice why they should be so recognised.

Counsel for the appellant sought to derive some assistance from *Hyde* v. *Hyde and Woodmansee* (1). This case and the long stream of authority that flows from it is in my judgment of no help to the appellant. All that it lays down is that parties to a polygamous marriage, however valid that marriage may be by their personal law and the law of the country in which it was celebrated, cannot obtain matrimonial relief against each other in the courts of this country. There are perhaps many reasons for this rule, one of which may be that the matrimonial laws of this country are designed to deal only with monogamous marriages, and are not geared to polygamous marriages. It is quite plain that in *Hyde* v. *Hyde and Woodmansee* (1) and the authorities that flow from it, the courts were not laying down any wider principle than that which I have stated. Lord Penzance said (2):

" I expressed at the hearing a strong doubt whether the union of man and woman as practised and adopted among the Mormons was really a marriage in the sense understood in this, the matrimonial court of England, and whether persons so united could be considered husband and wife in the sense in which these words must be interpreted in the Matrimonial Causes Act, 1857."

Then emphasising the importance of those last words which I have read, he said (3):

" This court does not profess to decide upon the rights of succession or legitimacy which it might be proper to accord to the issue of the polygamous unions, nor upon the rights or obligations in relation to third persons which people, living under the sanction of such unions, may have created for themselves. All that is intended to be here decided is, that as between each other they are not entitled to the remedies, the adjudication, or the relief of the matrimonial law of England."

The much later case of *Baindail (otherwise Lawson)* v. *Baindail* (4), illustrates that there are purposes for which polygamous marriages are recognised in our courts. In that case a domiciled Indian married an Indian woman according to Hindu rites in India; the marriage was polygamous, valid in India, and they were both domiciled Indians at the time of the marriage. Subsequently the husband went through a form of marriage with another woman in a registry office in England, and she later petitioned for a decree of nullity on the ground that when

---

(1) [1861-73] All E.R. Rep. 175; (1866), L.R. 1 P. & D. 130.
(2) [1861-73] All E.R. Rep. at p. 176; (1866), L.R. 1 P. & D. at p. 133.
(3) [1861-73] All E.R. Rep. at p. 179; (1866), L.R. 1 P. & D. at p. 138.
(4) [1946] 1 All E.R. 342; [1946] P. 122.

the respondent took her to the registry office he was already a married man incapable in England of entering into another legitimate marriage. She succeeded. His status as a married man according to the decision in *Baindail* v. *Baindail* (5) depended on the law of his domicil and his personal law. According to that law the polygamous marriage was valid and for the purpose of ascertaining his status the courts of this country recognised the existence of the marriage. LORD GREENE, M.R., said (6):

"We are not considering in this case the question of construction of any words such as 'marriage', 'husband', 'wife', and so forth in the Divorce Acts. We are considering whether, according to what would have been the old ecclesiastical law, the existence of the Hindu marriage formed a bar. For the purpose of that consideration, what was his status on May 5, 1939? Unquestionably it was that of a married man. Will that status be recognised in this country? English law certainly does not refuse all recognition of that status. For many purposes, quite obviously, the status would have to be recognised. If a Hindu domiciled in India died intestate in England leaving personal property in this country, the succession to the personal property would be governed by the law of his domicil; and in applying the law of his domicil effect would have to be given to the rights of any children of the Hindu marriage, to the rights of his Hindu widow, and for that purpose the courts of this country would be bound to recognise the validity of a Hindu marriage so far as it bears on the title to personal property left by an intestate here; . . ."

In the *Sinha Peerage Case* (7), LORD MAUGHAM, L.C., said (8):

"On the other hand, it cannot, I think be doubted now (notwithstanding some earlier dicta by eminent judges) that a Hindu marriage between persons domiciled in India is recognised in our court; that the issue are regarded as legitimate, and that such issue can succeed to property in this country with a possible exception which will be referred to later."

That was the exception of real property. So it is plain from the authorities to which I have referred that there are purposes for which a polygamous marriage will be recognised as a valid marriage in this country, and also that in some statutes the word "wife" may be construed as covering a polygamously married wife.

The only question before us is whether, for the purposes of the National Assistance Act, 1948, this court should recognise the polygamous marriage, and hold that the woman whom the appellant married polygamously in Lahore in 1948 is his wife for the purposes of the Act of 1948. I would unhesitatingly answer that question in the affirmative.

I would stress that s. 42, which lays down that for the purposes of the Act of 1948 a man shall be liable to maintain his wife and children, does not confer any right on the man's wife and children. Section 42 has no relevance save in relation to s. 43 which gives the National Assistance Board power to recover from the man whose wife and children it has assisted: in other words s. 42 does no more than define the class to whom s. 43 (1) refers, i.e. the class from whom the board may recover. Section 43 (2) reads:

"On a complaint under this section the court shall have regard to all the circumstances and in particular to the resources of the defendant, and may order the defendant to pay such sum, weekly or otherwise, as the court may consider appropriate."

One of the circumstances no doubt which the court would take into account is whether or not some matrimonial offence has been committed by the wife which

(5) [1946] 1 All E.R. 342; [1946] P. 122.
(6) [1946] 1 All E.R. at p. 346; [1946] P. at p. 127.
(7) [1946] 1 All E.R. 348, n.
(8) [1946] 1 All E.R. at p. 349, n.

might justify her husband in not maintaining her. The circumstance which is mentioned specifically concerns the resources of the appellant. In this case the justices had no difficulty in coming to the conclusion (not challenged) that this wife had done nothing to justify the appellant leaving her and the children destitute, and that he was well able to repay the board £6 a week. It is quite clear therefore that there is no more merit in this appeal than there is substance in the point of law that had been taken on the appellant's behalf.

I wish to refer briefly to s. 3 of the Family Allowances and National Insurance Act, 1956, on which counsel for the appellant relies. That reads as follows:

" As from the appointed day, a marriage performed outside the United Kingdom under a law which permits polygamy shall be treated for any purpose of the Family Allowances Act, 1945 and 1952, the National Insurance (Industrial Injuries) Acts, 1946 to 1954, the National Insurance Acts, 1946 to 1955, and this Act as being and having at all times been a valid marriage if and so long as the authority by whom any question or claim arising in connexion with that purpose falls to be determined is satisfied that the marriage has in fact at all times been monogamous."

Counsel for the appellant says that quite clearly until that section became law, polygamous marriages were not recognised under the Family Allowances Acts, nor the National Insurance Acts, and that accordingly such marriages should not be recognised under the National Assistance Act, 1948.

That argument, however, will not bear a moment's close examination. Section 3 of the Act of 1956 was passed to mitigate the effect of certain decisions of the relevant tribunals; the decisions are No. R(G.) 18/52, No. R(G.) 11/53, and No. R(G.) 3/55 and 7/55. They decided that a polygamously married wife could not obtain a family allowance, nor when her husband died a widow's benefit. The ground of these decisions was that, as the man paid only one lot of contributions calculated on the basis of one wife at a time, the Acts applied only in case of monogamous marriages, since it would be wrong that a man who paid contributions on the basis of only one wife at a time, should be able to reap benefits in respect of perhaps three or four wives.

Section 3 was introduced because it was felt that in the case where the marriage was monogamous in fact, although polygamous in form, it was unduly harsh to deprive a contributor and his wife of all benefits under the Acts. The fact that for the reasons which I have stated a polygamously married wife was not formerly recognised as a wife for the purposes of those Acts does not, to my mind, have any bearing on whether or not she should be recognised as a wife for the purposes of the National Assistance Act, 1948. If she were not, then a man who is lawfully married to her in their own country could bring her here with their children, and leave them all destitute so that they would all be supported out of public funds without any recourse by the board against him. I can see no reason for reading the Act of 1948 in that way, and I would dismiss the appeal accordingly.

WIDGERY, J.: I, for my part, agree.

LORD PARKER, C.J.: I also agree.

Appeal dismissed (9).

Solicitors: *Adam Burn & Metson*, agents for *Conn, Goldberg & Co.*, Manchester (for the appellant); *Solicitor, Ministry of Social Security.*

[*Reported by* Kaushalya Purie, *Barrister-at-Law.*]

---

(9) The costs were being provided by the respondent board, and accordingly no order as to costs was made.

INLAND REVENUE COMMISSIONERS *v.* SAXONE, LILLEY & SKINNER (HOLDINGS), LTD.

[HOUSE OF LORDS (Lord Reid, Lord Morris of Borth-y-Gest, Lord Hodson, Lord Pearce and Lord Upjohn), January 11, February 16, 1967.]

Income Tax—Allowance—Industrial building or structure—Building used for dual purpose, one part of which was within definition and the other part of which was outside it—Warehouse used for storage of shoes—Whether warehouse an " industrial building or structure "—Some shoes manufactured by group of companies, other shoes bought from other manufacturers—Income Tax Act, 1952 (15 & 16 Geo. 6 & 1 Eliz. 2 c. 10), s. 271 (1) (d) (iii), (2).

A warehouse belonging to the respondents, a parent company, was used for storing shoes for the purposes of their trade; about one-third of the shoes stored were manufactured by a subsidiary of the respondents and the remaining two-thirds were purchased from other manufacturers. The description " industrial building or structure " was defined in s. 271 (1) (d) (iii)* of the Income Tax Act, 1952, as including one that was in use for the purposes of a trade which consisted in the storage of goods or materials which, having been manufactured in the course of a trade, had not yet been delivered   I
to any purchaser. This enactment applied by virtue of sub-s. (2) in relation to a part of a trade as it did to a trade.

Held: the warehouse was in use for that part of the respondents' trade which consisted in storing the shoes manufactured by the subsidiary, and thus was an industrial building or structure, although it was not wholly used for that purpose but was also used for storing purchased shoes (see p. 758,   F
letter A, post); moreover the test was not which use was the predominant use (see p. 758, letter G, p. 759, letter F, post).

Appeal dismissed.

[As to what are industrial buildings for the purposes of initial and other income tax allowances, see 20 HALSBURY'S LAWS (3rd Edn.) 483, para. 919,   F
paras. 947-963; and for cases on such allowances and balancing charges, see 28 DIGEST (Repl.) 310, *1356-1358*.

For the Income Tax Act, 1952, s. 271, see SUPPLEMENT to 31 HALSBURY'S STATUTES (2nd Edn.) para. [273] Amended Texts.]

Case referred to:

Inland Revenue Comrs. v. Lambhill Ironworks, Ltd., 1950 S.C. 331; 31 Tax   G
     Cas. 393; 28 Digest (Repl.) 127, *377.

Appeal.

This was an appeal from an interlocutor of the First Division of the Court of Session sitting as the Court of Exchequer in Scotland, dated Feb. 17, 1966, whereby they allowed an appeal by the respondents, Saxone, Lilley & Skinner (Holdings), Ltd., against a determination dated May 4, 1965, of the Commis-   H
sioners for the Special Purposes of the Income Tax Acts. The commissioners rejected certain claims submitted by the respondents for the years 1959-60 to 1962-63 in respect of (i) initial allowances under the Income Tax Act, 1952, s. 265 (1) and (2); (ii) investment allowances under the Finance Act, 1954, s. 16 (1) and (2); and (iii) annual allowances under the Income Tax Act, 1952, s. 266 (1) in respect of a building of the respondents in Leeds, which was let out   I
to and occupied by one of their subsidiaries, Jackson, Ltd., for the warehousing of shoes. The question on the appeal was whether the building qualified for these allowances as being an industrial building or structure within the meaning of s. 271 (1) (d) (iii) of the Income Tax Act, 1952.

The Lord Advocate (G. G. Stott, Q.C.) (of the Scottish Bar), J. R. Phillips and C. K. Davidson (of the Scottish Bar) for the Crown.

---

* Section 271, so far as material, is set out at p. 757, letter D, to p. 758, letter A, post.

H. S. Keith, Q.C. (of the Scottish Bar), *C. N. Beattie, Q.C.,* and *A. M. M. Grossart* (of the Scottish Bar) for the respondents.

Their lordships took time for consideration.

Feb. 16. The following opinions were delivered.

LORD REID: My Lords, the respondents have a number of subsidiary companies which manufacture and retail shoes. This group of companies have a large number of retail shops in various parts of Britain which sell both shoes made by one of the group at Kilmarnock and shoes bought from manufacturers outside the group. The respondents have found it convenient to have a single large warehouse in Leeds to which all their shoes are brought. They are then stored there until sent out to the retail shops. The question in this case is whether that warehouse is an industrial building within the meaning of the Income Tax Act, 1952, s. 271. If it is, the respondents are entitled to initial allowances, investment allowances, and annual allowances under that Act. The Special Commissioners rejected claims for these allowances, but the First Division (1) on Feb. 17, 1966, allowed an appeal against this decision. The relevant parts of s. 271 are (2):

" (1) Subject to the provisions of this section, in this chapter, ' industrial building or structure ' means a building or structure in use—

" (*a*) for the purposes of a trade carried on in a mill, factory or other similar premises; or

" (*b*) for the purposes of a transport, dock, inland navigation, water, electricity, hydraulic power, tunnel or bridge undertaking; or

" (*c*) for the purposes of a trade which consists in the manufacture of goods or materials or the subjection of goods or materials to any process; or

" (*d*) for the purposes of a trade which consists in the storage—(i) of goods or materials which are to be used in the manufacture of other goods or materials; or (ii) of goods or materials which are to be subjected, in the course of a trade, to any process; or (iii) of goods or materials which, having been manufactured or produced or subjected, in the course of a trade, to any process, have not yet been delivered to any purchaser; or (iv) of goods or materials on their arrival by sea or air into any part of the United Kingdom; or

" (*e*) for the purposes of a trade which consists in the working of any mine, oil well or other source of mineral deposits, or of a foreign plantation; or

" (*f*) for the purposes of a trade consisting in all or any of the following activities, that is to say, ploughing or cultivating land (other than land in the occupation of the person carrying on the trade) or doing any other agricultural operation on such land, or threshing the crops of another person, or

" (*g*) for the purposes of a trade which consists in the catching or taking of fish or shellfish . . .

" (2) The provisions of sub-s. (1) of this section shall apply in relation to a part of a trade or undertaking as they apply in relation to a trade or undertaking: Provided that where part only of a trade or undertaking complies with the conditions set out in the said provisions, a building or structure shall not, by virtue of this subsection, be an industrial building or structure unless it is in use for the purposes of that part of that trade or undertaking.

---

(1) The First Division of the Court of Session, as the Court of Exchequer in Scotland, (The Lord President (LORD CLYDE), and Lords GUTHRIE, MIGDALE and CAMERON).

(2) The enactments are printed as amended by the Finance Act, 1953, s. 17 (1), and the Finance Act, 1957, s. 17.

" (3) Notwithstanding anything in sub-s. (1) or sub-s. (2) of this section, but subject to the provisions of sub-s. (4) of this section, ' industrial building or structure ' does not include any building or structure in use as, or as part of, a dwelling-house, retail shop, showroom, hotel or office or for any purpose ancillary to the purposes of a dwelling-house, retail shop, showroom, hotel or office: . . ."

The shoes manufactured at Kilmarnock come within the scope of sub-s. (1) (d) (iii) because, when in this warehouse, they have not yet been delivered to any purchaser; but the other shoes in the warehouse have already been delivered to the respondents or one of their subsidiary companies, having been purchased from other manufacturers. During the relevant period there were generally some five hundred thousand pairs of shoes in the warehouse at any one time, of which a third or so had come from Kilmarnock and the remaining two-thirds or so from outside manufacturers. While in the warehouse these shoes were not kept separate. They were classified so that in each part of the warehouse one would generally find some of the Kilmarnock shoes and some of the others.

The trade of this warehouse keeper is storing shoes from both these sources and the contention of the respondents is that, within the meaning of sub-s. (2), storing the Kilmarnock shoes is a part of their trade. The commissioners so found and I think that this is clearly right. I reject the argument that there is no sufficient distinction between the ways in which the two kinds of shoes are treated to enable one to say that storing the one kind is one part of the trade and storing the other kind is another part. If a trader stores or sells or otherwise deals with two kinds of goods, A and B, I think that it is the ordinary use of language to say that dealing with A is one part of his trade and dealing with B is another part, and I see nothing in the context here to justify giving any other interpretation to " a part of a trade " in sub-s. (2).

The question therefore comes to be whether this warehouse is in use for the purposes of that part of the warehouseman's trade which consisted in the storing of Kilmarnock shoes. Again taking the ordinary use of language it appears to me that it clearly was. Premises can be and often are in use for more than one purpose, and I think that the whole of this warehouse was in use for both parts of the warehouseman's trade, because both kinds of shoes could generally be found stored in every part of it.

The Crown's main argument was that " in use for the purposes of a trade " or of a part of a trade means wholly or mainly in use for such purposes. But that involves writing in words which are not there, and I can see nothing in the context to make that necessary. Moreover, it requires no feat of imagination in a draftsman to see that cases may arise where the same building, or the same part of it, is being used for two purposes, and if it were intended to exclude such cases I should expect that to be made clear. The Act of 1952 does deal with the case where one part of a building is used for one purpose and another part is used for a different purpose, but it contains no machinery for dealing with dual use of the same part. Of course there can be cases where the use for a statutory purpose is only intermittent or small, and such cases could not reasonably be brought within the Act of 1952: but here the use for a statutory purpose was regular and substantial. I think that underlying the Crown's contention is the idea that it is not fair that the trader should get full allowances if the building is used in part for non-statutory purposes; but logically that would lead to the result that substantially the whole use must be for statutory purposes before allowances are due. There would still be injustice, though smaller, if even forty per cent. was non-statutory use. The Crown did not shrink from the alternative contention that substantially the whole use must be for a statutory purpose but that would mean doing still greater violence to the words of the Act of 1952.

The Crown founded on The Lord President (LORD COOPER'S) observations in *Inland Revenue Comrs.* v. *Lambhill Ironworks, Ltd.* (3). There an engineering company claimed allowances in respect of its drawing office. The main contention of the inland revenue, which failed, was that the drawing office was an " office " within the meaning of what is now s. 271 (3) of the Act of 1952. A subsidiary question arose, however, because two of a total of twenty to thirty-five men who worked there were engaged in work more akin to office work than to industrial work. Dealing with this matter LORD COOPER said (4):

". . . it is obvious that the quality or character of the drawing office as an industrial building or structure can only be determined by looking at the building as a whole, and by reference to its predominant purposes or use, and that it is quite impracticable to attempt to impart to such a building a different character or more than one character because a small proportion of the men employed in it at a given moment may be engaged in work in regard to which a different argument might be applicable."

The Crown say that the test must be the same under both sub-s. (1) and sub-s. (3), and that the *Lambhill* case (5) is therefore authority for the proposition that under sub-s. (1) it is the predominant use which determines whether allowances are due. The test could be different because sub-s. (3) refers to use " as " an office and it may be more difficult to hold that a building is in use as two different things than for two different purposes. Even if the test is the same, I think that on either view the drawing office in the *Lambhill* case (3) was not in use for non-industrial purposes. This matter must be dealt with on broad common sense lines, and I think that the presence of two men doing non-industrial work was such a relatively small matter that it could not reasonably be said that the building was being used for two purposes—one industrial and the other not. I have some doubt whether LORD COOPER would have reached the same result if a third of the men in the building had been engaged in non-industrial work because he does mention the possibility of imparting to a building more than one character. If, however, he did mean that predominant purposes or use must be the test in all cases he went farther than was necessary for the decision of that case and I would not agree with him. I would therefore dismiss this appeal.

LORD MORRIS OF BORTH-Y-GEST: My Lords, I concur.

LORD HODSON: My Lords, I concur.

LORD PEARCE: My Lords, I concur.

LORD UPJOHN: My Lords, I concur.

Appeal dismissed.

Solicitors: *Sir Charles Sopwith*, agent for *J. K. W. Dunn*, Edinburgh (for the Crown); *Titmuss, Sainer & Webb*, agents for *Steedman, Ramage & Co.*, Edinburgh (for the respondents).

[*Reported by* KATHLEEN J. H. O'BRIEN, *Barrister-at-Law.*]

---

(3) 1950 S.C. 331; 31 Tax Cas. 393.
(4) 1950 S.C. at p. 337, 31 Tax Cas. at p. 399.
(5) 1950 S.C. 331; 31 Tax Cas. 393.

MASON (Inspector of Taxes) *v.* INNES.

[CHANCERY DIVISION (Goff, J.), November 22, 23, December 9, 1966.]

*Income Tax—Profits—Author—Gift of rights in unpublished book to father—
Whether author taxable on value of rights—Income Tax Act, 1952 (15 & 16
Geo. 6 & 1 Eliz. 2 c. 10), Sch. D.*

The taxpayer, a well-known and successful author who was engaged on the
final revision of a new book, which was in typescript but had not been submitted in any form to a publisher, assigned the rights in the book valued at
£15,425 to his father by way of gift. It was found that if the taxpayer did
not write a new book within three or four years after the publication of a
previous work, the public would be less well aware of his work and the sales
of previous publications would fall, so that it was an advantage to him for the
new book to be published. The taxpayer's expenses of travelling to the
Persian Gulf to gather material for the book were allowed as a deduction
from his income for income tax purposes, and it was found that the writing of
the book and the disposal of the rights took place in the course of the
carrying on by the taxpayer of his profession as an author. The taxpayer,
whose earnings were assessed to tax on a cash basis (viz., actual receipts
less actual expenditure), was assessed to tax on the estimated value of the
rights in the book assigned to his father as if it were the taxpayer's income.

Held: the assessment must be discharged because there was no liability
to income tax in respect of income which might have been, but had not
been, received (see p. 765, letter F, post).

Sharkey (Inspector of Taxes) v. *Wernher* ([1955] 3 All E.R. 493)
distinguished.

Appeal dismissed.

[**Editorial Note.** The Revenue contended for a general principle, which they
formulated and is stated in the judgment; the importance of the present decision
lies in the rejection of its application to professional men (see p. 762, letter I, to
p. 763, letter A, and p. 765, letter B, post).

As to what constitute trade receipts for income tax purposes, see 20 HALS-
BURY'S LAWS (3rd Edn.) 149-158, paras. 262-276; 240-243, paras. 442-444; and
for cases on the subject, see 28 DIGEST (Repl.) 71-86, *268-328*; 154-158, *594-623*.]

Cases referred to:

Carson (*Inspector of Taxes*) v. *Peter Cheyney's Executor*, [1958] 3 All E.R. 573;
  [1959] A.C. 412; [1958] 3 W.L.R. 740; 38 Tax Cas. 240; 28 Digest
  (Repl.) 155, *598*.
Inland Revenue Comrs. v. *Morrison*, 1932 S.C. 638; 17 Tax Cas. 325.
Petrotim Securities, Ltd. (*formerly Gresham Trust, Ltd.*) v. *Ayres* (*Inspector of
  Taxes*), [1964] 1 All E.R. 269; [1964] 1 W.L.R. 190; 41 Tax Cas. 389;
  3rd Digest Supp.
Sharkey (*Inspector of Taxes*) v. *Wernher*, [1955] 3 All E.R. 493; [1956] A.C. 58;
  [1955] 3 W.L.R. 671; 36 Tax Cas. 275; 28 Digest (Repl.) 74, *280*.

Appeal.

The taxpayer appealed to the Special Commissioners of Income Tax against
an additional assessment to income tax under Case II of Sch. D to the Income
Tax Act, 1952, made on him for 1960-61 in the estimated amount of £17,500.
The additional assessment was in respect of the rights in his book " The Doomed
Oasis ", of which the taxpayer had executed an assignment to his father* by way
of gift in consideration of " natural love and affection " on Apr. 4, 1960. The
taxpayer contended as follows: (i) that it was not proper to assess him to income

---

* It was found in the Case Stated that the taxpayer, who published a book at approximately two-year intervals, had assigned the rights in two books, published in 1954 and
1956, to his mother and mother-in-law respectively.

Affirmed. C.A. [1967] 2 All E.R. 926.

tax in respect of profits which he did not make; (ii) that the decision of the House of Lords in *Sharkey (Inspector of Taxes)* v. *Wernher** did not apply to the carrying on by the taxpayer of his profession, but applied only to the case of a trader with stock-in-trade the value of which was required to be brought into account in computing profits for income tax purposes; (iii) that the decision in *Sharkey (Inspector of Taxes)* v. *Wernher** did not apply where profits were computed for income tax purposes by reference to actual receipts and expenditure, i.e., on a cash basis; (iv) that the carrying on by the taxpayer of his profession did not bring stock-in-trade into existence; and (v) that, as the rights in " The Doomed Oasis " were intended to be assigned by the taxpayer by way of gift to his father, the taxpayer's activities in producing the book did not take place in the course of his profession of an author. The Crown contended as follows: (i) that the effect of the decision in *Sharkey (Inspector of Taxes)* v. *Wernher* was not limited to cases in which there was a disposal of stock-in-trade by a trader; (ii) that the taxpayer in the course of his professional activities had produced and disposed of a valuable asset, viz., the rights in " The Doomed Oasis "; that the principle of the decision in *Sharkey (Inspector of Taxes)* v. *Wernher* applied to that disposal and the market value of the rights, viz., £15,425 (to which the additional assessment should be adjusted accordingly) ought to be included as a receipt in computing the taxpayer's income tax liability, and (iii) that all the taxpayer's activities in producing " The Doomed Oasis " were carried out in the course of his profession of an author.

The commissioners found as follows: (i) that the writing of the novel " The Doomed Oasis " and the disposal of the rights therein took place in the course of the carrying on by the taxpayer of his profession of an author; (ii) that in the light of the observations of LORD KEITH OF AVONHOLM in *Carson (Inspector of Taxes)* v. *Peter Cheyney's Executor†*, they were unable to regard the rights in " The Doomed Oasis " as part of the taxpayer's stock-in-trade, that a computation of the taxpayer's profits by reference to actual receipts and expenditure was an appropriate method of ascertaining his liability to income tax and that therefore the decision in *Sharkey (Inspector of Taxes)* v. *Wernher*, which was concerned with stock-in-trade valued for accounting purposes at the beginning and end of each year, could not properly be regarded as authority for treating the sum of £15,425 as a receipt of the taxpayer's profession. They allowed the appeal and discharged the assessment. The Crown appealed by way of Case Stated to the High Court.

Hubert H. Monroe, Q.C., and *J. R. Phillips* for the Crown.
R. E. Borneman, Q.C., and *R. A. Watson* for the taxpayer.

Cur. adv. vult.

Dec. 9. **GOFF, J.**, read the following judgment: The respondent taxpayer, Mr. Ralph Hammond Innes, the well-known and successful author, wrote a book called " The Doomed Oasis ". Work on this was commenced in September, 1958, and continued until the spring of 1959. There was then an interval, but the taxpayer took it up again in September, 1959, and by Apr. 4, 1960, he was engaged in the final revision of the book, which was in typescript but had not been submitted in any form to a publisher. On that day, Apr. 4, 1960, the taxpayer assigned the copyright in the work to his father by way of gift, and it is found in the Case that the market value of the rights in " The Doomed Oasis " at the date of such disposal was £15,425. This was a gift, and the taxpayer received no consideration for it; but it is stated in the Case as follows:

" If the [taxpayer] did not write a new book within three or four years after the publication of a previous work the public would become less aware of his name and the sales of previous publications would fall. It was,

---

* [1955] 3 All E.R. 493.
† [1958] 3 All E.R. at p. 584, letter I.

therefore, an advantage to him for ' The Doomed Oasis ' to be published
notwithstanding his assignment of the rights to his father."

Assessments to income tax on the taxpayer were made by reference to profit and
loss accounts of his professional activities showing the actual receipts of his
profession and the actual expenditure, and in the opinion of Mr. Pooles, a
chartered accountant who gave evidence before the commissioners, it was correct
accountancy procedure for the accounts of an author to be prepared on a " cash
basis ", and he did not think that any other method would be appropriate. In
order to obtain material for his work, the taxpayer travelled extensively about
the world, and was allowed the expenses of this travel as a deduction in the
computation of his liability to income tax. " The Doomed Oasis " was commenced as a result of material gathered by the taxpayer during a visit to the
Persian Gulf in 1953, and the expenses of this journey were included in the
deductions claimed by the taxpayer and allowed for the purposes of income tax.
Other deductions were made in respect of expenses generally without any
adjustment as regards work on " The Doomed Oasis ".

In these circumstances, the General Commissioners raised an additional assessment on the taxpayer under Case II of Sch. D for the year 1960-61. This was made
in an estimated amount of £17,500, but was in respect of the market value of the
rights in " The Doomed Oasis " at the time of the assignment, so that if the
assessment be otherwise good the amount would fall to be reduced to £15,425, as
was conceded. It was found by the commissioners that the writing of " The
Doomed Oasis " and the disposal of the rights therein took place in the course of
the carrying on by the taxpayer of his profession as an author. As, however, the
rights in question were not stock-in-trade and the " cash basis " was an
appropriate method of accounting, they did not think that the decision in *Sharkey*
(*Inspector of Taxes*) v. *Wernher* (1), on the principle of which the Crown relied
but which was concerned with stock-in-trade value for accountancy purposes at
the beginning and end of each year, could properly be regarded as authority for
treating the £15,425 as a receipt of the taxpayer's profession, and accordingly
they allowed the appeal and discharged the assessment.

The case of *Sharkey* v. *Wernher* (1) was one in which Lady Zia Wernher had
two enterprises, one a stud farm, which was taxable, and the other a string of
racehorses, which was recreational and not taxable. She transferred a number of
horses from the stud farm to the string, and the Crown claimed that she was
bound to bring the market value of those horses at the time of transfer into the
stud farm accounts. It was conceded by the respondent in that case (Lady
Zia's husband) that some figure had to be brought in, but he claimed that it
should be the cost of breeding and rearing those horses, which was a much smaller
figure. In the result, it was held that the market value was the correct figure.

Counsel for the Crown conceded that that case was different from the present,
both because it dealt with stock-in-trade—and, of course, an author such as the
present taxpayer has none—and because of the concession that something had to
be brought in, but he submitted that, despite that concession, the House of
Lords did in fact consider and decide the question of principle whether anything
at all should be brought in in respect of the transferred horses; that the principle
so decided applies equally to the case of a professional man such as the taxpayer
giving away the fruits of his efforts, particularly in view of the finding that the
writing of " The Doomed Oasis " and the disposal of the rights therein took place
in the course of the carrying on by him of his profession; and that there is no
magic in the existence or absence of stock-in-trade, or in the fact that the
accounts for tax purposes proceed on a cash rather than an earnings basis. He
stated the principle thus: " Where a trader or a professional person appropriates
value to himself by consuming or to a donee by giving away an asset (instead of
selling it and appropriating the proceeds) then his profits must be computed by

(1) [1955] 3 All E. R. 493; 36 Tax Cas. 275.

treating him as receiving the value he appropriates." He said that that applied equally where there was no stock-in-trade as such but there was an asset which, if sold, would produce cash which would be a receipt of the trade or profession. Counsel for the taxpayer argued that *Sharkey* v. *Wernher* (2) did in truth proceed on the admission that something had to be brought into the accounts in respect of the horses taken over by Lady Zia, and decided no more than how that was to be measured, whether by the cost or the market value.

I think that the House was puzzled, and at any rate Viscount Simonds clearly was, to see why the admission was made and why it was not contended that the correct answer was that nothing should be brought in at all; but I cannot say that the case turned on the admission, since Lord Simonds said (3) that he could not escape from the obvious fact that it must be determined whether, and why, a trader, who elected to throw his stock-in-trade into the sea or dispose of it in any other way than by way of sale in the course of trade, was chargeable with any notional receipt in respect of it, before it was asked with how much he should be charged; and he held (4) that the admission was rightly made. Again, Lord Radcliffe (5) clearly included an answer that nothing should be brought in as a possibility; but, when one is asked, as I am here, to extract from the case a general principle and apply it to very different facts, one must be entitled to have some regard to the fact that the particular point was not argued.

Counsel for the taxpayer, denying the Crown's contention, has further argued that the principle, whatever it be, is inapplicable in the present case because the accounts were kept for income tax purposes on a strictly cash basis as distinct from an earnings basis, and, as has been found in the Case, properly so kept. In my judgment, however, this is not conclusive, because the basis on which *Sharkey* v. *Wernher* (2) was decided is that, by consuming or giving away his stock-in-trade, a trader appropriates its value, so that there is a notional receipt; but the argument has weight since, in my judgment, it is easier to import a notional receipt into an account which necessarily involves elements of valuation of that which has not in fact been turned into money and received than it is in a purely cash account. Be this as it may, as counsel for the taxpayer has stressed, *Sharkey* v. *Wernher* (2) was an exception out of a well-settled basic principle of income tax law that income tax is a tax on what has been received or earned, not on what might have been. This was clearly recognised by Lord Simonds where he said (3):

> " My lords, I am the more puzzled by the basis on which this case has proceeded, because learned counsel for the respondent has throughout insisted on what is an elementary principle of income tax law that a man cannot be taxed on profits that he might have, but has not, made . . ."

Accordingly, I ought, in my judgment, to be very chary of extending it unless I feel compelled by logic or analogy, which I do not.

On the contrary, in my view, the case of *Carson* (*Inspector of Taxes*) v. *Peter Cheyney's Executor* (6) tends to show that there is a real distinction between the trader who has stock-in-trade and the professional man who has none. It is true that Lord Keith of Avonholm did say (7) that professional earnings were akin to the profits of a trade, but that was in a passage where he was at pains to say that, in the case of a professional man such as an author or actor, one is not concerned with the contracts under which he works or the rights in his work as an income-producing asset, but only with the receipts when they come in, whether as proceeds of sale of the rights or by those rights being retained and income

(2) [1955] 3 All E.R. 493; 36 Tax Cas. 275.
(3) [1955] 3 All E.R. at p. 496; 36 Tax Cas. at p. 296.
(4) [1955] 3 All E.R. at p. 498; 36 Tax Cas. at p. 298.
(5) [1955] 3 All E.R. at p. 504; 36 Tax Cas. at p. 306.
(6) [1958] 3 All E.R. 573; 38 Tax Cas. 240.
(7) [1958] 3 All E.R. at p. 585; 38 Tax Cas. at p. 268.

coming in therefrom. The full passage, part of which was quoted and relied on by the commissioners, is as follows (8):

"In principle, there is no difference between the case where an author sells the copyright and the case where he retains the copyright. What he has produced is not copyright but a book. Copyright is an incident attached by law to the book, fortifying that which he has produced and giving it a value which it would not have if it could be reproduced illegitimately in the shape of pirated editions. The property, then, from which the author obtains his income is the work produced by him, and the method by which that work can be turned to profit during his life is in his own hands and is but a projection of his professional activities, the means by which he earns his livelihood from his professional work. If I take the case where he retains the rights in his work and takes the profits to himself, it seems to me clear that, when he dies, any profits that come in afterwards from any issue published during his life are still the profits of what was his profession. It is not possible to say that they are mere income of property, ' pure income profit ' as it has been called. They are profits not only from writing the book but from bearing all the expenses of selling the book to the public, including the expenses of printing and publishing. They are akin to the profits of a trade, but are more properly called the profits of a profession. So it is, in my opinion, where he sells his rights in return for royalties. It is quite unreal to regard these royalties merely as a return from property. They are the reward for all he has put into his work, his labour, his thought, his skill as a writer, and the expenses incurred in creating his book. The position is materially different where rights in a book in return for royalties are granted by another than the author. The elements to which I have referred are entirely absent in such a case. The book is there already made and the idea of royalties as merely the income of property is a more intelligible conception."

A short passage on the previous page seems to me very strongly to support the commissioners' conclusion, and to point to the distinction of the *Sharkey* case (9). LORD KEITH OF AVONHOLM there said (10):

"I turn, accordingly, to consider what is involved in the professional activities of an author during his life. An author writes books generally for profit or in the hope of profit. It is only when they make a profit that any question of assessing him on the profits of a profession can arise. It is only by exploiting the work of his brain and his pen that he can make any professional income."

I would also note a passage in the speech of the Lord President (LORD CLYDE) in *Inland Revenue Comrs.* v. *Morrison* (11), where he said:

"In assessing the profits of such a professional business as this, one or other of two modes of computation are in use, which have, no doubt, been found alternatively convenient and appropriate according to particular circumstances. It is obvious that the usual mode which applies to the assessment of the profits of a trading business which buys and sells, or to a manufacturing business which buys raw material and makes it up and sells the finished product, would not be practically capable of application to an ordinary professional business in which the professional man markets nothing but his own services and ingathers nothing but his professional fees."

In *Sharkey* v. *Wernher* (9) itself, the question was much canvassed whether a man could trade with himself, and, although their lordships spoke equally of gifts as well as self-supply, had it rested there one might have found a distinction

---

(8) [1958] 3 All E.R. at pp. 584, 585; 38 Tax Cas. at p. 268.
(9) [1955] 3 All E.R. 493; 36 Tax Cas. 275.
(10) [1958] 3 All E.R. at p. 584; 38 Tax Cas. at p. 267.
(11) (1932), 17 Tax Cas. 325 at p. 330.

on that ground; but in *Petrotim Securities, Ltd.* (*formerly Gresham Trust, Ltd.*) v. *Ayres* (*Inspector of Taxes*) (12) the principle was clearly applied to gifts, since the sales there were at a gross undervalue, and therefore, although not made for reasons of bounty, were pro tanto gifts. Nevertheless, as it seems to me, so understood and carried to its logical conclusion the principle, if applied to professional men, must mean that they cannot give their services within the ambit of their profession without, in some cases at least, becoming liable to income tax on notional fees, which in my judgment is a reductio ad absurdum.

LORD RADCLIFFE gave three reasons for his conclusion in the *Sharkey* case (13). The first of these, in my judgment, was confined to the case of a self-supplying trader, since the unfairness to which his lordship referred was surely that which arises as between two traders if one sells his stock-in-trade and so attracts tax and the other consumes it himself and so does not. The other two reasons could be applied to the present case, but were directly concerned with the question of quantum, and it would not be right to take them out of their context.

Further, in the case of a trader proper accountancy practice requires that stock-in-trade shall be brought in at the beginning and end of the account of profits, and therefore raises a special problem where some of it disappears during the accounting period otherwise than in the course of a commercial transaction; and in the *Starkey* case (14) LORD SIMONDS clearly posed the problem before the House as one relating to a trader and stock-in-trade when he said:

> " The problem, therefore, in all its simplicity is whether a person, carrying on the trade of farming or, I suppose, any other trade, who disposes of part of his stock-in-trade not by way of sale in the course of trade but for his own use, enjoyment, or recreation, must bring into his trading account for income tax purposes the market value of that stock-in-trade at the time of such disposition."

For all these reasons, in my judgment the important basic principle that there is no liability to income tax in respect of income which might have been received but was not ought to prevail, and I find no sufficient grounds for treating the case of *Sharkey* v. *Wernher* (15) as laying down a principle of general application or being anything more than a particular exception applying to the particular case of a trader and stock-in-trade. Accordingly, in my judgment, the decision of the commissioners was right, and the appeal fails.

Appeal dismissed.

Solicitors: *Solicitor of Inland Revenue; Field, Roscoe & Co.* (for the taxpayer).

[*Reported by* F. A. AMIES, ESQ., *Barrister-at-Law.*]

---

(12) [1964] 1 All E.R. 269; 41 Tax Cas. 389.
(13) [1955] 3 All E.R. at pp. 504, 505; 36 Tax Cas. at p. 306.
(14) [1955] 3 All E.R. at p. 495; 36 Tax Cas. at p. 295.
(15) [1955] 3 All E.R. 493; 36 Tax Cas. 275.

NOTE.

R. *v.* HOOPER.

[COURT OF APPEAL, CRIMINAL DIVISION (Sachs, L.J., Lawton and James, JJ.),
   November 21, 1966.]

*Legal Aid—Criminal cases—Practice—Offer of legal aid, or explanation why
   legal aid not offered, should be on record of trial court even though accused
   declines legal aid.*

*Quarter Sessions—Committal to quarter sessions for sentence—Record should
   show sufficient to make clear with what charges quarter sessions were concerned,
   e.g., where there was a plea of guilty, dates of offences and sums involved.*

[As to legal aid in criminal cases, see 10 HALSBURY's LAWS (3rd Edn.) 371-373,
paras. 674, 676; and for cases on the subject, see 14 DIGEST (Repl.) 228, *1904-
1907*.

As to procedure on committal to quarter sessions for sentence, see 25 HALS-
BURY's LAWS (3rd Edn.) 228, 229, para. 423.]

Appeal.

The appellant, Anthony Francis John Hooper, pleaded guilty on Aug. 31,
1966, at Woolwich magistrates' court to seven charges of obtaining money by
fraud or false pretences. He was committed to Inner London Quarter Sessions
for sentence, where, on Sept. 15, 1966, being unrepresented, due to his own wish
he asked for fifteen similar offences to be taken into consideration and was
sentenced to three years' imprisonment in all.

V. K. Winstain for the appellant.

SACHS, L.J., in the course of delivering the judgment of the court, said:
In this case, as in a number of cases which have been committed for sentence to
quarter sessions both in London and elsewhere, the dates of the offences to which
a plea of guilty was entered in the magistrates court and the sums involved do
not appear on the transcript from the court below. It is quite essential that in
future, where there is a committal from a lower court to quarter sessions, the
matter should be so conducted at sessions that on an appeal one can find out
without undue research exactly what are the charges with which sessions were
concerned. Indeed such a procedure is really necessary in order to clarify the
position in open court at sessions for all to understand at the time.

[HIS LORDSHIP said that the appellant had pleaded guilty to certain charges
and had been committed to quarter sessions, and added:] The appellant was
not represented by counsel. That was due to his own wish; but this court repeats
that even when a prisoner does not ask for legal aid, it is advisable for there to be
on the record of the trial court an offer of legal aid or some explanation of why
none was made.

[HIS LORDSHIP referred to the circumstances and, having said that certain
further facts seemed not to have been sufficiently elicited at quarter sessions,
which also pointed to the need for a prisoner who might receive a severe sentence
to be properly represented, concluded that concurrent sentences of fifteen
months' imprisonment should be substituted for the total sentence of three
years' imprisonment.]

Solicitor: *Registrar of Criminal Appeals* (for the appellant).

[*Reported by* N. P. METCALFE, ESQ., *Barrister-at-Law.*]

TAYLOR *v.* NATIONAL UNION OF SEAMEN.

[CHANCERY DIVISION (Ungoed-Thomas, J.), October 6, 7, 10, 11, 12, 13, 14, 18, 19, 20, November 8, 1966.]

Trade Union—Domestic tribunal—Natural justice—Official of union, employed on terms of union rules, dismissed by general secretary for insubordination—Dismissal might involve disabilities as a member of union—Appeal by official in exercise of right conferred by rules to executive council—Duty of council under rules to act judicially—Consequences in issue on appeal not merely termination of employment but also ineligibility under rules to certain positions in union—Chairman of council acting as accuser and prejudicial matter introduced in plaintiff's absence—Whether declaration of continuance of employment, etc. should be made.

The plaintiff, a member and official of the defendant union, was employed by the union on the terms of the rules of the union. Under these rules the plaintiff's employment was during the will and pleasure of the executive council. On Oct. 13, 1961, having been about one year in the employment, he was summarily dismissed by the general secretary of the union for insubordination consisting in disobedience to certain instructions regarding conduct of union business, which the plaintiff said that his principles would not allow him to carry out. Dismissal on certain grounds, one or some of which might apply in the circumstances, carried ineligibility under r. 17 (5)*, r. 18 (9)* and r. 19 (2)*, for certain posts or nominations for which members of the union generally were eligible. Dismissal of the plaintiff had thus a dual aspect; on the one hand he was employed at will and pleasure, and on the other hand the consequences of dismissal might affect his eligibility for certain positions in the union. Under the rules (r. 22 (1)† read with r. 34 (7)†) a dismissed official had a right of appeal to the executive council.

---

* These rules provided that any official dismissed " for any serious misconduct or actions prejudicial to the interests of the union " should be ineligible not only for " any paid official position in the union " (r. 17, sub-r. 5) but also for " nomination to the annual general meeting " (r. 18, sub-r. 9) and " nominations to the executive council " (r. 19, sub-r. 2) for which members generally were eligible.

† The terms of the relevant rules were as follows: " 27 (1). District organisers, branch secretaries and delegates, as required, may be appointed by the General Secretary, subject to the approval or otherwise of the Executive Council, and shall hold office during the will and pleasure of the council. No member suspended from benefit shall continue to hold office or be appointed to office. The Finance and General Purposes Committee may exercise its powers with regard to branch officials, as provided in r. 21, but any action it may take shall be placed before the Executive Council for confirmation at the earliest opportunity."

" 22 (1). The General Secretary shall preside over all meetings of the Union at which he may be in attendance. He shall have power to appoint officials and also to suspend any officers who may not be giving satisfaction in the performance of their duties, or who in his opinion are acting contrary to the best interests of the Union, subject to the approval of the finance and general purposes committee and subsequent confirmation by the Executive Council. Dismissed or suspended officers shall have a right of appeal to the Executive Council at its next meeting."

" 34 (6). A special general meeting, an annual general meeting or the Executive Council, or in the interim periods between the meetings of these bodies the finance and general purposes committee, or the General Secretary may suspend or dismiss any officials elected or otherwise who may not be giving satisfaction in the performance of their duties, or who are acting contrary to the best interest of the Union, or are guilty of insubordination, or of any action likely to bring discredit on the Union or persistently act in contravention of these Rules. If any official or member or employee of the Union attempts to defraud or is found guilty of defrauding the Union he not only may be dismissed from office, but the Executive Council may, through the General Secretary bring legal action against him or her as the case may be."

" (7). In the case of an offence by an official or member under this rule, the General Secretary shall send him a statement in writing, giving full particulars of the charge against him, together with a copy of the rule under which it is brought. He shall be given an opportunity of submitting his defence at a meeting of the Executive Council

(*Continued at foot of page 768.*)

Applied in STEVENSON v UNITED ROAD TRANSPORT UNION [1976] 3 All ER 29

Rule 34 (7) premised an offence and required that the official concerned should be given a full statement of the charge against him. The plaintiff appealed. At the hearing of the appeal on Dec. 15, 1961, the plaintiff made a statement and answered questions. After the plaintiff had withdrawn, the general secretary, who was acting as chairman of the council, made a long statement in the plaintiff's absence, entering into prejudicial matters irrelevant to the charge, alleging, e.g., that the plaintiff had communist associations. The plaintiff had no opportunity to reply to these allegations. The council dismissed the appeal. The plaintiff sued for declarations that his dismissal was void and that the union should not be entitled to treat him as if dismissed for misconduct, and he claimed damages.

Held: (i) although the relationship between the union and the plaintiff was that of master and servant, that relationship was on the terms of the union's rules, under which, when hearing his appeal, the executive council were under a duty to act judicially, particularly as they were considering not only whether the plaintiff in his capacity as employee had been rightly dismissed but also whether he was guilty of misconduct carrying ineligibility for various positions in the union (see p. 774, letter B, p. 776, letter I, and p. 777, letter A, post).

(ii) the hearing of the appeal offended against the rules of natural justice in that (a) the chairman of the council hearing it acted as accuser and (b) prejudicial and irrelevant matters were introduced which the plaintiff was not given an opportunity to answer (see p. 774, letters G and I, and p. 777, letter B, post).

Dicta of COTTON, L.J., in *Leeson* v. *General Medical Council* ([1886-90] All E.R. Rep. at p. 83), and *Kanda* v. *Government of Federation of Malaya* ([1962] A.C. 322), applied.

(iii) accordingly there had been wrongful dismissal of the plaintiff, but, as the plaintiff was employed at will and pleasure, no declaration that he had continued in the employment of the union would be made; the court would make, however, an appropriate declaration so that the plaintiff's dismissal should not have the consequence of rendering him ineligible under r. 17 (5), r. 18 (9) or r. 19 (2) and would direct an inquiry as to damages (see p. 778, letters F and H, post).

Francis v. *Municipal Councillors of Kuala Lumpur* ([1962] 3 All E.R. 633) applied.

Vine v. *National Dock Labour Board* ([1956] 3 All E.R. 939) considered.

[As to the rules of natural justice, see 30 HALSBURY'S LAWS (3rd Edn.) 718, 719), para. 1368, and as to the remedies for breach of those rules, see 11 ibid., pp. 64, 65, para. 122. As to when a declaration that the employment of a wrong-fully dismissed employee has not been terminated will be made, see 25 HALSBURY'S LAWS (3rd Edn.) 519, 520, para. 991, notes (*q*), (*r*); and for cases on the subject, see DIGEST (Cont. Vol. A) 970, 971, *280aa, 280ab,* 973, *280e.*]

Cases referred to:

Francis v. *Municipal Councillors of Kuala Lumpur,* [1962] 3 All E.R. 633; [1962] 1 W.L.R. 1411; 34 Digest (Repl.) 125, *843.*

Kanda v. *Government. of Federation of Malaya,* [1962] A.C. 322; [1962] 2 W.L.R. 1153; 37 Digest (Repl.) 189, *8*.*

Law v. *Chartered Institute of Patent Agents,* [1919] 2 Ch. 276; 88 L.J.Ch. 319; 121 L.T. 50; 8 Digest (Repl.) 657, *42.*

(*Continued from page 767.*)

or a sub-committee thereof, of which meeting he shall have seven days' notice, and shall be entitled to attend in person before them. He may be accompanied or represented by one other person, who shall be a member of the Union. Whether present or not, he shall be permitted to submit such evidence in his defence as may be proper in the circum-stances. Except with the consent of the member of the Union the meeting shall not be held later than fourteen days after the date on which notice of the charge is given to him and the decision of the committee or sub-committee shall be recorded in the minutes, and a copy thereof forwarded forthwith to the member."

A   *Leeson* v. *General Medical Council*, [1886-90] All E.R. Rep. 78; (1889), 43
        Ch.D. 366; 59 L.J.Ch. 233; 61 L.T. 849; 33 Digest (Repl.) 521, *33.*
    Vine v. *National Dock Labour Board*, [1956] 3 All E.R. 939; [1957] A.C. 488;
        [1957] 2 W.L.R. 106; *varying*, [1956] 1 All E.R. 1; [1956] 1 Q.B. 658;
        [1956] 2 W.L.R. 311; Digest (Cont. Vol. A) 475, *58a.*

Action.

B   This was an action for alleged wrongful dismissal of the plaintiff by the defendants, the National Union of Seamen. The plaintiff was an official of the union
of which he was also a member, and was employed by the union on the terms of
the union's rules. He claimed first, a declaration that his purported dismissal
from his employment with the union by Mr. Scott, the general secretary of the
union, on Oct. 13, 1961, was wrongful and ought to be set aside; and secondly, a
C   declaration that the purported decision of the Executive Council of the National
Union of Seamen on Dec. 15, 1961, whereby the council purported to uphold
the said purported dismissal and dismiss the plaintiff's appeal therefrom was ultra
vires, unlawful, null and void. By amendment an alternative claim was made for
a declaration that the union should not be entitled to treat the plaintiff as if he
were dismissed for misconduct. In addition, there was a claim for damages for
D   wrongful dismissal. The union, by its defence, pleaded that the plaintiff was
justifiably dismissed for acting in defiance of an instruction of the general
secretary and that the plaintiff's appeal was properly dismissed.

The following statement of facts is summarised from the judgment of UNGOED-
THOMAS, J. On Oct. 5, 1961, the s.s. Dorrington Court arrived in London docks
after four months' trading on the West African coast, and the plaintiff, who was
E   an official of the Green Home branch of the union, visited her as part of his
routine duty. The ship was discharging her cargo in London, and most of her
crew were from the London area. They wanted to be paid off in London, but the
ship's articles provided, as normal in the case of such a cargo vessel as the Dorrington Court, that the voyage was " to end at such port in the United Kingdom as
may be required by the master ". The crew were concerned about a rumour that
F   the Dorrington Court would be going to the Tyne and that the crew would be
paid off there. The plaintiff enquired from the master about paying off and was
told of a provisional booking of a dry dock for the ship in the Tyne, and he said
that she would be going there. Mr. Spruhan, who was the Green Home branch
secretary and the plaintiff's immediate superior, and the plaintiff under him,
tried to get the crew paid off in London or alternatively, at a later stage at any
G   rate, to get " run money " (extra payment as compensation for the risk of losing
a long voyage by taking such a short voyage as from London to the Tyne) for
the crew. This was a reasonable thing to do. About half the crew reported sick,
and four were in fact found to be unfit and were discharged. Replacements
were required for these men to make good the full complement, without which
the ship could not sail. The owners were not prepared to pay run money to the
H   replacements. So when on Oct. 9 Mr. Crew, an official of the Shipping Federation,
which was the owners' organisation, asked about replacements, the plaintiff
said that there was no hope of getting them because there was no run money.
Replacements were in fact not forthcoming, partly because there was no run
money and partly because it was known amongst the seamen that the crew were
demanding to be paid off in London.

I   On the morning of Oct. 13 Mr. Spruhan requested the marine superintendent
(an official of the Board of Trade) for a ruling whether the crew should be paid
off in London, but in the end no ruling was given. That afternoon the plaintiff
went to the ship to tell the men that a ruling was awaited. When he was leaving
he saw a notice on board that the ship was sailing at 17.00 hours, and he reported
this to Mr. Spruhan. At 2.30 p.m. on Oct. 13 Mr. Scott told Mr. Hogarth, then
the London District Secretary of the Union, under whom the Green Home
branch came, that the Shipping Federation had reported to him that the Dorrington Court was due to sail for the Tyne at 5.30 p.m., that the ship was four or five

men short, that the Green Home branch had been trying to get the men paid off
in London, and that unless men were supplied in an hour or two the ship would
be held up; and that he would deal with it. Mr. Scott was concerned about the
responsibility for the ship not sailing on time, and he got the owners to agree
to pay run money to replacements, thus disposing of at any rate one obstacle to
the ship sailing.

When the plaintiff returned from the ship to the branch office, Mr. Scott
telephoned Mr. Spruhan (with whom the plaintiff was) and when Mr. Spruhan put
down the telephone he told the plaintiff " We have got to clear her. We have
got to sail ", and that there had been an agreement to pay run money. This
was the instruction which, so the judge found, the plaintiff received from the
general secretary through the branch secretary, and which was the material
instruction in defiance of which the union alleged that the plaintiff acted. It
would convey to a seaman or union official, and did convey to the plaintiff, that
financial members (that is, seamen members of the union not more than thirteen
weeks in arrear with their subscription to the Union) must be cleared, but that it
would at least be in the official's discretion not to clear others. The plaintiff and
Mr. Spruhan were, in the plaintiff's words, " flabbergasted ", " dumbfounded "
and " angry " in consequence of what Mr. Scott had said, including his
instructions to clear the ship.

A seaman then came into the branch office and said that there was trouble
aboard the Dorrington Court. Mr. Spruhan decided to go to the ship, and Mr.
Nicoll went with him to give him " moral support ". Mr. Spruhan, Mr. Nicoll
and the plaintiff thought that there might be substantial difficulty with the crew
and that trouble with the crew would be increased if replacements who were
being paid run money and enabling the ship to sail were to arrive, at any rate
before Mr. Spruhan had dealt with the crew. On leaving Mr. Spruhan gave the
plaintiff certain instructions, but they were not unmistakably plain instructions
to clear any seaman who came, and might have meant that he was to carry on
until Mr. Spruhan returned. Soon after Mr. Spruhan and Mr. Nicoll had left,
Mr. Crew (who was an official of the Shipping Federation) came to the branch
office with two seamen for clearance. The plaintiff told them of the trouble aboard
and that Mr. Spruhan and Mr. Nicoll had gone down there to clear things up.
So the men could not accept the ship. Mr. Crew went and got another two seamen
and the first two seamen spoke to them; and the plaintiff, when asked about the
difficulty, said that the branch secretary and another were there trying to sort
things out. The plaintiff then said that he was not clearing till Mr. Spruhan
returned, but that seamen must be absolutely clear (i.e., paid up to date) in
the union's book if they were to sail.

Having considered the evidence in the light of the rules of the union, by which
men over thirteen weeks in arrears with their subscriptions were not financial
members, so that the plaintiff's requirement that a member should be absolutely
clear might exclude financial members, the trial judge (UNGOED-THOMAS, J.)
found that the plaintiff, by stating that he would not clear financial members,
had acted contrary to his instructions to clear the ship, and that he perfectly well
understood this. The trial judge accordingly held that the plaintiff acted in
defiance of the instruction which he had received from the general secretary
through his branch secretary.

Mr. Spruhan dealt satisfactorily with the difficulty on board the Dorrington
Court and on his return cleared some men. At 4.30 p.m. Mr. Wright, who was
Mr. Crew's superior at the Shipping Federation, told Mr. Scott that the Green
Home branch was refusing to clear replacements. Mr. Hogarth telephoned the
Dock Street branch of the union to provide replacement for the Dorrington
Court, and when he heard that these were available he telephoned at about 4.50
p.m. Mr. Spruhan on Mr. Scott's telephone and in his presence. Mr. Hogarth
asked " What the hell is going on there? ". He was told that men had just been
cleared, and he said " Too bad, because men are going from Dock Street to her ".

A Mr. Hogarth then spoke to the plaintiff. Mr. Hogarth asked the plaintiff why he
refused to clear the men, and the plaintiff replied that his principles would not
allow it; Mr. Hogarth said that it was an instruction of the general secretary, and
the plaintiff repeated that his principles would not allow him to clear the men.

Mr. Hogarth then asked the plaintiff about a remark which the plaintiff was
supposed to have made that Mr. Scott had " sold them down the river ". Mr.
B Hogarth's evidence was that the plaintiff ultimately admitted that he had
made this remark; HIS LORDSHIP did not find the admission established, but he
found that both Mr. Scott, who was listening in, and Mr. Hogarth were convinced
by the plaintiff's answers that he was admitting having made the remark. Mr.
Scott then grabbed the telephone and remarked " So you said it ", to which the
plaintiff gave a reply inaudible to Mr. Hogarth. Mr. Hogarth said in evidence
C that Mr. Scott then said that the plaintiff had refused to clear the men and to
carry out his instructions, to which the plaintiff again said that his principles would
not allow him to do so. The conversation ended with Mr. Scott suspending the
plaintiff and then asking that Mr. Spruhan be put on the telephone and telling
Mr. Spruhan that he was suspending the plaintiff, and then amending it to dismissing the plaintiff immediately. The plaintiff was accordingly dismissed, and, in
D view of r. 27 (2) of the Union rules that an official " on being dismissed shall
receive four weeks' salary in lieu of notice ", he was paid that salary. Certain
rules* of the union provided that officials dismissed for specific cause, unlike those
dismissed at will or pleasure, were not eligible for certain positions in the union.
The relevant rules* provided for a right of appeal.

The plaintiff exercised his right under r. 22 (1) of the union's rules of appeal to
E the executive council at its next meeting. The plaintiff's case was that the union's
conduct of the appeal was contrary to the rules of natural justice and the rules
of the union. On Oct. 20, 1961, at a sitting of a meeting of the executive council
that had been adjourned from Oct. 13, before the plaintiff's dismissal, the council
purported to confirm his dismissal. It was originally submitted on his behalf
that the meeting of Oct. 20 was the next meeting of the executive council for
F the purpose of his right of appeal under r. 22 (1), but this submission was withdrawn and it was eventually conceded that the only materiality of that meeting
was its effect on the operation of the rules of natural justice at the meeting on
Dec. 15, 1961, of which an account is given at p. 772, letters D to G.

After the death of Mr. Scott in January, 1962, the plaintiff applied for nomination by branches for the post of general secretary. He was refused nomination by
G some branches in accordance with the rules on account of his dismissal. He
subsequently obtained other employment with a government department and
at the date of the hearing had been in that employment for some years.

The cases noted below† were cited during the argument in addition to those
referred to in the judgment.

H   * The terms of the relevant rules are set out in footnote †, p. 767, ante.
     † *Birmingham and District Land Co.* v. *London and North Western Ry. Co.*, [1886-90]
All E.R. Rep. 620; (1888), 40 Ch. 268; *Dickason* v. *Edwards*, (1910), 10 C.L.R. 243; *Board of
Education* v. *Rice*, [1911-13] All E.R. Rep. 36; [1911] A.C. 179; *Maclean* v. *Workers' Union*,
[1929] All E.R. Rep. 408; [1929] 1 Ch. 602; *Kilduff* v. *Wilson*, [1939] 1 All E.R. 429;
160 L.T. 103; *General Council of Medical Education and Registration of the United
Kingdom* v. *Spackman*, [1943] 2 All E.R. 337; [1943] A.C. 627; *White* v. *Kuzych*,
I [1951] 2 All E.R. 435; [1951] A.C. 585; *Abbott* v. *Sullivan*, [1952] 1 All E.R. 226; [1952]
1 K.B. 189; *Lee* v. *Showmen's Guild of Great Britain*, [1952] 1 All E.R. 1175; [1952]
2 Q.B. 329; *Bonsor* v. *Musicians' Union*, [1954] 1 All E.R. 822; [1954] Ch. 479; *Davis*
v. *Carew-Pole*, [1956] 2 All E.R. 524; *McClelland* v. *Northern Ireland General Health
Services Board*, [1957] 2 All E.R. 129; *Byrne* v. *Kinematograph Renters Society, Ltd.*,
[1958] 2 All E.R. 579; *Farmaus* v. *Film Artistes' Association*, [1963] 1 All E.R. 636;
[1963] 2 Q.B. 527; *on appeal*, [1964] 1 All E.R. 25; [1964] A.C. 925; *Ridge* v.
Baldwin, [1963] 2 All E.R. 66; [1964] A.C. 40; *Vidyodaya University Council* v. *Silva*,
[1964] 3 All E.R. 865; *Lawlor* v. *Union of Post Office Workers*, [1965] 1 All E.R. 353;
[1965] Ch. 712; *Naben* v. *National Society of Operative Printers and Assistants*, (1966),
unreported.

D. P. F. Wheatley for the plaintiff.
R. B. Gibson for the union.

Cur. adv. vult.

Nov. 8. **UNGOED-THOMAS, J.,** read the following judgment in which he stated the nature of the proceedings, found the facts, as previously summarised, and cited the relevant rules of the union (set out in footnote †, p. 767, ante). He held that the sitting of the executive council on Oct. 20, 1961, was not the next meeting of the council within r. 22 (1), because the " next meeting " referred to in r. 22 (1) was one of which the seven days' notice required by r. 34 (7) could be given and that was not possible on or after Oct. 13 for Oct. 20. HIS LORDSHIP then turned to the question whether the rules of natural justice were observed in relation to the meeting on Dec. 15. HIS LORDSHIP continued: I will now state briefly the aspects of what occurred at the meeting of the executive council on Dec. 15, 1961, relevant to the alleged breaches of the rules of the union or of natural justice. The executive council consisted of about forty-four members, of whom three-quarters, who had purported to confirm the dismissal at the meeting of Oct. 20, 1961, in the absence of the plaintiff, had heard Mr. Scott's (the general secretary's) account of the dismissal of the plaintiff and his full reasons for it. The account contained a number of material inaccuracies which Mr. Stewart said affected his attitude to the plaintiff. Mr. Scott himself presided at the Dec. 15 meeting, as at the Oct. 20 meeting, and minutes of the Oct. 20 meeting were read giving Mr. Scott's full account of the dismissal and his reasons for it and repeated his inaccuracies. The plaintiff was then given an opportunity to make a statement and to answer questions put to him by the members of the executive council, which he did. The plaintiff then withdrew and the general secretary made a long statement in the plaintiff's absence of matters completely outside the charge against him, such as that he had communist associations; and these matters, I am completely satisfied on such evidence as Mr. Stewart's and the remarks which he made near the conclusion of the meeting (see p. 775, letter I, post) affected the minds of the members of the executive council. If they were not calculated to affect their minds, why mention them at all? The decision was to dismiss the appeal, both guilt and sentence and the hearing on guilt and sentence being dealt with as one issue without distinction.

I will mention here a conflict in the evidence on one aspect of the procedure. The statement which the plaintiff made was a written statement prepared before the meeting. There was discussion on it, including quite a long intervention by the chairman, who was Mr. Scott, the general secretary, in effect reiterating his statement recorded in the October minutes. The plaintiff said that he asked for an opportunity to reply to Mr. Scott's statements but was refused it. Mr. Stewart had a hazy recollection of it, but did not know whether it happened at the beginning of the meeting or later. It does not appear in the very full shorthand note taken of the meeting, and I saw the shorthand writer, a transparently honest witness, who was positive that if there were such an intervention it would be at least indicated in her notes. It seems to me that the true explanation may be that Mr. Stewart's recollection was coloured by the statement which was made about procedure at the beginning of the meeting and by a later request by the plaintiff to read some letters which he had and which he was allowed to read despite Mr. Scott's opposition. I find that there was no request by the plaintiff to answer the statements.

For the union it was conceded in accordance with the observations of COTTON, L.J., in *Leeson* v. *General Medical Council* (1), that if this appeal were subject to the rules of natural justice applicable in the case of an expulsion of a member of a trade union, then the rules of natural justice have not been complied with.

---

(1) [1886-90] All E.R. Rep. 78 at p. 83; (1889), 43 Ch.D. 366 at p. 379.

A   There was a dual aspect to the plaintiff's position in the union, as a member and as an official, for whose appointment membership was in fact a necessary qualification. It is said on the one hand that as an official he was an employee and servant of the union subject to dismissal at will and pleasure (2) under r. 27 (1) and that the rules of natural justice are inapplicable to such a relationship; but, on the other hand, that the consequences of dismissal for misconduct affect his eligibility

B for office or position in the union for which his membership would otherwise qualify him, and that this aspect of his position attracts the rules of natural justice to his appeal. On the basis of this dual aspect it is conceded for the plaintiff that if the general secretary, who was chairman of the meeting, acted as prosecutor within the meaning of the authorities on natural justice, then a relevant requirement of natural justice was not complied with; but it is denied that he so acted.

C Did he so act?

    Cotton, L.J., in his judgment in the *Leeson* case says (3):

    " Now this appeared, that the complaint against Dr. Leeson—I will not call it indictment—was brought in the name of the Medical Defence Union, and it turns out when attention is called to the matter that two of the members of the council who were present when the case of Dr. Leeson was

D   considered were members of the Medical Defence Union; and it was said that they are to be considered in the light of prosecutors, and that as they were prosecutors they could not also sit as judges in the matter. It was, therefore, contended that any decision which the council arrived at, where these two members who were incompetent to act as judges in the matter were present, must be considered as a nullity."

E Then he goes on to deal in more general terms with the law (3):

    " Of course, the rule is very plain that no man can be plaintiff, or prosecutor, in any action, and at the same time sit in judgment to decide in that particular case—either in his own case, or in any case, where he brings forward the accusation or complaint on which the order is made. To my

F   mind it is clear here that the General Medical Council, in respect of the complaint against Dr. Leeson, were acting judicially. They were not in the ordinary sense judges, but they had to decide judicially as to whether or not the complaint against Dr. Leeson was well founded; and they could, if they found it was well founded, make an order which would be of great importance to him and remove him from the register, with very serious consequences.

G   But then we have to consider this. Ought these two gentlemen [whom Cotton, L.J., names] to be considered as complainants in this case?"

  It appears from this passage that Cotton, L.J., treats as prosecutor a person who brings forward the accusation or complaint on which the order to which the plaintiff takes exception is made, where the body before whom the complaint is brought forward have to decide judicially as to whether or not the complaint

H is well founded, and, if well founded, make an order of importance to the person against whom the complaint it made.

  The result of this appeal was indisputably of great importance to the plaintiff. His work was the work for which he was trained, and the National Union of Seamen was the organisation in which he was best qualified to pursue his career. The ground of dismissal was insubordination, with consequential disabilities

I as a member (4). The duty of the executive council was, in my view, in the words of Cotton, L.J. (5), " to decide judicially as to whether or not the complaint against [the plaintiff] was well founded ".

  The rules refer not only to the process before the executive council as " an

---

(2) For the terms of r. 27 (1) see footnote †, p. 767, ante.
(3) (1889), 43 Ch.D. at p. 379; [1886-90] All E.R. Rep. at p. 83.
(4) See rr. 17 (5), 18 (9), 19 (2), cited in footnote *, p. 767, ante.
(5) [1886-90] All E.R. Rep. at p. 83, letter D; (1889), 43 Ch.D. at p. 379.

appeal " to which the official has a " right " (6), but in the case of dismissal on
specified grounds they refer (7) also to the ground as an " offence " where full
particulars of " the charge against him " has to be given. This language is not
conclusive and may not even be appropriate for all cases in respect of which the
right of appeal exists, but it is the language commonly associated with proceedings
of a judicial nature. Their duty to act judicially appears to me to be almost beyond
dispute, and Mr. Stewart by his accepted intervention during the course of the
hearing (see p. 775, letter H, post) showed that he clearly recognised it, as indeed
did Mr. Hogarth in his evidence.

Was the general secretary (Mr. Scott) the person who (8) " brings forward the
accusation or complaint ", not in any formal or technical sense, but when one
looks to substance, substance and not technicality being the very foundation
of natural justice? The complaint against the plaintiff was exactly what Mr. Scott
did bring forward, both through the minutes of the Oct. 20 meeting and by the
course which he pursued throughout the Dec. 15 meeting. In form and in fact
his role included that of presenting the case against the plaintiff; and in fact
his role was pressing the case against the plaintiff at that meeting and, apparently,
not considering the case in any judicial sense at all. Mr. Scott, it appears, was a
strong, determined, " very dominant " and forceful person, and, as Mr. Stewart
said, " rather explosive ", and he " liked to thrust his opinions on you ". He was
angry with the plaintiff, and Mr. Hogarth said that, on the telephone to the plaintiff on Oct. 13, he " ranted and raved ". I accept the evidence, however, which
indeed was not gainsaid, that Mr. Scott was an honourable man who, Mr.
Hogarth said, believed that if there was an agreement then " it should always at
all times be honoured ". Mr. Hogarth said that at this meeting Mr. Scott " was
most certainly urging the executive council to uphold his position and dismiss the
appeal ", and Mr. Stewart said " I had no doubt what the general secretary
wanted—to endorse his action at the first meeting (that is on Oct. 20) and at the
second meeting (that is on Dec. 15) to uphold the decision of the first meeting ".
Mr. Stewart also said " The general secretary was keen to see his opinion accepted
. . . it was a forceful presentation but not an overriding one ". He stated in terms
in re-examination " The general secretary was accuser ". Mr. Hogarth stated
" The general secretary said nothing for the accused "; and then he added the
significant observation " It was not his position to do so. It was for him to make
the case against him, that is against the plaintiff ". It seems to me clear that
even before the commencement of the hearing of the appeal the role for which
Mr. Scott was cast was that of accuser, and that was certainly the role which he
most amply filled.

It was suggested at one stage of the argument that the operation of the rules
of natural justice against combining the roles of prosecutor and judge was affected
by the provision in the rules that the general secretary should preside (9).
There is, however, an express power in the rules to appoint a chairman in the
absence of the general secretary: and it was conceded that, as I was given to
understand has on occasion happened, the general secretary could leave the chair
and another could be appointed chairman in his place. Further, the objection
now under consideration is not strictly against the general secretary being in the
chair but is against the combination of membership of the tribunal, and a fortiori
chairmanship of the tribunal, with the role of prosecutor; and the rules require no
such combination. My conclusion, therefore, is, even on the basis of the union's
own submission on law, that the hearing of the appeal was contrary to the
rules of natural justice.

However, before coming to the consequences of this conclusion it may be desirable that I should refer briefly to other submissions made on the rules of natural

(6) See r. 22 (1), set out in footnote †, p. 767, ante.
(7) See r. 34 (7), set out in footnote †, pp. 767 and 768, ante.
(8) (1889), 43 Ch.D. at p. 379; [1886-90] All E.R. Rep. at p. 83.
(9) See r. 22 (1), set out in footnote †, p. 767, ante.

A justice and their alleged violation on the hearing of this appeal. It was submitted that Mr. Scott had acted in bad faith and with bias. Mr. Scott was a friend of the plaintiff and had no personal or ulterior motive whatsoever in dismissing him. I am completely satisfied that he was a most honourable man and felt outraged, with all the force of his nature, that the agreement and good faith with the owners was not being observed to the prejudice of the long term interests of the union

B and its members; and that the plaintiff was, as he saw it, violating the loyalty and discipline essential to the running of such an organisation as his union. There clearly was no mala fides on his part. His trouble was that he was not dealing with a merely administrative dismissal of an employee but with an employee entitled to an appeal of a judicial nature; and that he acted with bias, not in the sense of any personal or improper motive against the plaintiff, but in the sense

C that he was cast to act, was acting and indeed was bent on acting, as prosecutor when he was also judge.

It was also submitted that Mr. Hogarth had acted with bias. It was not suggested that he did not act in the utmost good faith, nor would there be any ground for such a suggestion. I had the advantage of seeing Mr. Hogarth in the box for a considerable time and under searching cross-examination. He was, as

D I have already indicated, a most impressive witness; solid, strong, objective and very clear-minded. It was suggested that he was biased because he took part in the events of Oct. 13. Mr. Hogarth's own evidence under cross-examination was that on the facts put forward and the telephone conversation with the plaintiff then (that is on Oct. 13) he thought it right to dismiss him; but if there were other facts he would reconsider it—that the plaintiff could hardly be not

E guilty, because of his telephone conversation with him, but that there might be other circumstances which he did not know about that might affect the case. In another part of his cross-examination he said that he would make up his mind irrespective of personalities, and spontaneously and vehemently added " It was the man's job "—conveying to my mind that the risk which the plaintiff faced of losing his job was much too serious a matter to be affected by a consideration

F of the " personalities " involved. Anyone who has had anything at all to do with trade unions will know how unmistakably true this evidence rings. There was no bias on Mr. Hogarth's part by reason of his part in the Oct. 13 events or on account of his position in the union or for any personal reasons.

So I come to the suggestion that all the executive council were biased by reason of the executive council having on Oct. 20 confirmed the dismissal. That con-

G firmation, for reasons already sufficiently canvassed, did not cause Mr. Hogarth to be biased. Mr. Stewart, when interjecting in favour of the plaintiff being allowed to read in his defence letters which had been obtained from seamen, expressed his attitude at the appeal. He said:

H " I would like to suggest that these letters be accepted or be read by him if in any way it can assist his case, because a man is in law in this country innocent until proved guilty. If you produce evidence to substantiate his innocence, I think we are entitled to hear this evidence."

This proposal, and presumably Mr. Stewart's attitude on which this proposal was based, was adopted by the executive council without any vote, despite the opposition of the general secretary. Although Mr. Stewart also said that the

I decision was based to some extent on whether the general secretary's or the plaintiff's version of what happened was accepted and great importance was attached to what the general secretary said, which naturally influenced the decision, I am satisfied that the executive council, subject only, in the case of the general secretary, to the observation which I have already made, did their best to deal with the appeal judicially and free from any possible bias.

The requirements of natural justice about bias, however, are not only that there should be freedom from actual bias but even from the appearance of bias. In

Law v. *Chartered Institute of Patent Agents* (10), EVE, J., dealt with this principle. **A**
He said (11):

"... it is this, that a person who has a judicial duty to perform is disqualified
from performing it if he has a bias which renders him otherwise than an
impartial judge, or if he has so conducted himself in relation to the matters
to be investigated as to create in the mind of a reasonable man a suspicion
that he may have such a bias."
B

Whether the Oct. 20 meeting gives that appearance of bias need not be decided
in view of the conclusion in the plaintiff's favour on other aspects of the case;
but clearly this meeting does raise a difficulty.

It was submitted for the plaintiff that the general secretary had introduced
matters of prejudice to the plaintiff, for example about alleged communist
associations, when the plaintiff had withdrawn for the executive council to **C**
discuss the case and had no opportunity of hearing or of answering them. It
was conceded for the union that this had occurred and that the appeal was in
this respect conducted contrary to the rules of natural justice if such a rule
applied to this appeal.

In *Kanda* v. *Government of Federation of Malaya* (12) LORD DENNING **D**
delivering the judgment of the Judicial Committee of the Privy Council, consisting
of himself, LORD HODSON and LORD DEVLIN, stated (13):

" If the right to be heard is to be a real right which is worth anything,
it must carry with it a right in the accused man to know the case which is
made against him. He must know what evidence has been given and what
statements have been made affecting him: and then he must be given a fair **E**
opportunity to correct or contradict them."

Then LORD DENNING referred to a number of cases and continued (14):

" It follows, of course, that the judge or whoever has to adjudicate must
not hear evidence or receive representations from one side behind the back
of the other. The court will not inquire whether the evidence or representations did work to his prejudice. Sufficient that they might do so. The court **F**
will not go into the likelihood of prejudice. The risk of it is enough. No one
who has lost a case will believe he has been fairly treated if the other side
has had access to the judge without his knowing."

For the union it was maintained that, as the plaintiff was an employee of the
union, the executive council was in the position of employer entitled to consider
what affected the continuation of the plaintiff's employment without regard to **G**
this rule of natural justice. It was argued that the plaintiff, as an official, was a
servant of the union. The words " official " and " officer " are commonly used
indiscriminately in the rules. Such an official as the plaintiff was not one of the
specified higher officials described as " executive officers " in r. 18 (6). On the
other hand, he was not one of the clerical staff referred to in the rules. He had no
identifiable or any independent sphere of responsibility, although of course his **H**
superior officer, the branch secretary, would from time to time entrust some piece
of work to him: and my impression on the evidence is that he was subject to
control, in particular of his branch secretary, not only in what he did but in how
he did it. I would conclude that his relationship with the union was that of servant
and master, but, of course, as is common ground, on the terms of the rules. I have
already concluded that the hearing of the appeal according to the rules was subject **I**
to the rules of natural justice. The executive council, when considering these
prejudicial matters irrelevant to the charge, were not sitting merely, or indeed at
all, in an administrative capacity but in a judicial capacity. When they heard

(10) [1919] 2 Ch. 276.
(11) [1919] 2 Ch. at p. 290.
(12) [1962] A.C. 322.
(13) [1962] A.C. at p. 337.
(14) [1962] A.C. at pp. 337, 338.

A them they were not even merely discussing sentence, and still less what was to be done with an employee or servant just in that capacity. They were considering guilt, whether the plaintiff was guilty of misconduct carrying ineligibility as member for various positions in the union. So the irrelevant matters were introduced to the plaintiff's substantial prejudice, not only as official but also as a member, and without being included in or covered by the charge against him and without

B his having an opportunity of being heard at all on them.

So I conclude that on this ground too the hearing of the appeal offended against the applicable rules of natural justice.

What should be the consequence of my conclusion that the hearing was against the rules of natural justice? Here it is particularly important to bear in mind the two aspects involved in rejection of the plaintiff's appeal and his dismissal:

C his position as servant of the union and his position as a member disabled in some respects by the grounds of dismissal. If the person dismissed has not a mere contract of service but has a status or can be dismissed only by specified procedure which alone confers the power to dismiss him, then the employment is not effectively terminated by wrongful dismissal. Such were the cases of *Vine* v. *National Dock Labour Board* (15), where a registered dock worker in the registered pool of

D dock workers enjoyed a status conferred by statute, and *Kanda* v. *Government of Federation of Malaya* (16), where, under the articles of the constitution of Malaya, the authority to dismiss an inspector of police was vested in the police service commission, and the commissioner of police, who had no power at all to do so, purported to dismiss an inspector. On the other hand, in *Vine* v. *National Dock Labour Board*, JENKINS, L.J. (17), in a judgment with which Lord MORTON OF

E HENRYTON (18) and LORD SOMERVELL OF HARROW (19) in the House of Lords agreed, thus stated the position about wrongful dismissal of a servant:

" But in the ordinary case of master and servant the repudiation or the wrongful dismissal puts an end to the contract, and the contract having been wrongfully put an end to a claim for damages arises. It is necessarily a claim for damages and nothing more. The nature of the bargain is such that

F it can be nothing more. In the present case we are concerned with a statutory scheme which has given a number of rights and imposed a number of obligations going far beyond any ordinary contract of service."

VISCOUNT KILMUIR, L.C., in the same case in the House of Lords said (20):

". . . if the master wrongfully dismisses the servant, either summarily

G or by giving insufficient notice, the employment is effectively terminated, albeit in breach of contract."

In *Francis* v. *Municipal Councillors of Kuala Lumpur* (21) the Judicial Committee decided, in a case where the order constituting the municipality had provided that the president of the municipal council had the power of removing a clerk, that a clerk wrongfully removed not by the president of the council but by

H the council who were his employers, was entitled to damages only and not to a declaration that his contract of service still subsisted, in the absence of special circumstances such as, for example, would, in the absence of the declaration, preclude him from working at all as a clerk. LORD MORRIS OF BORTH-Y-GEST stated (22):

I " Accepting, however, the decision of the Court of Appeal, which, as has been pointed out, has not been the subject of any cross-appeal, the position on Oct. 1 was that the removal of the appellant was a removal by the council

---

(15) [1956] 3 All E.R. 939; [1957] A.C. 488.   (16) [1962] A.C. 322.
(17) [1956] 1 All E.R. 1 at p. 8, letter I; [1956] 1 Q.B. 658 at p. 674.
(18) [1956] 3 All E.R. at p. 944; [1957] A.C. at p. 501.
(19) [1956] 3 All E.R. at p. 949; [1957] A.C. at p. 509.
(20) [1956] 3 All E.R. at p. 944, letter D; [1957] A.C. at p. 500.
(21) [1962] 3 All E.R. 633.
(22) [1962] 3 All E.R. at p. 637.

A

and not by the president. The council were his employers, but having regard to the provisions of the ordinance their termination of his service constituted wrongful dismissal. Their Lordships consider that it is beyond doubt that on Oct. 1, 1957, there was de facto a dismissal of the appellant by his employers, the respondents. On that date he was excluded from the council's premises. Since then he has not done any work for the council. In all these circum-

B

stances it seems to their Lordships that the appellant must be treated as having been wrongly dismissed on Oct. 1, 1957, and that his remedy lies in a claim for damages. It would be wholly unreal to accede to the contention that since Oct. 1, 1957, he had continued to be, and that he still continues to be, in the employment of the respondents . . . In their Lordships' view, when there has been a purported termination of a contract of service a declaration to the effect that the contract of service still subsists will rarely be made. This is a

C

consequence of the general principle of law that the courts will not grant specific performance of contracts of service. Special circumstances will be required before such a declaration is made and its making will normally be in the discretion of the court. In their Lordships' view there are no circumstances in the present case which would make it either just or proper to make such a declaration. In *Vine* v. *National Dock Labour Board* (23),

D

ORMEROD, J., had in his discretion made such a declaration and the House of Lords, adopting the view expressed by JENKINS, L.J., in his dissenting judgment in the Court of Appeal (24), were of opinion that the declaration had been rightly made. In that case, however, the circumstances were very special (25). In the circumstances of that case it was held to be right that the plaintiff—whose dismissal was shown to have been without proper

E

authority—should have the benefit of a declaration that he was still in the employment of the National Board, since, unless he was, he would be disabled from carrying on at all his chosen trade of a dock labourer."

These principles apply to any mere contract of service. In this case the plaintiff was under a contract of employment with the union, and in my view as a servant on the terms of the rules and liable to dismissal by the executive council at their

F

will and pleasure. He did in fact obtain other employment with a government department and has now been in that employment for years. In the words employed in the *Francis* case (26), it would be " wholly unreal " to make a declaration to the effect that he has continued to be in the employment of the union. His disabilities as a member by reason of the wrongful dismissal, however, are a very different matter. They affect very seriously his position as a member and his

G

prospects of a future career in the union, and here he should have the protection of a declaration, and to such a declaration I understand that the union (on the assumption, of course, that the decision on wrongful dismissal is against them) takes no objection.

So, in the exercise of my discretion on declaration, I propose to make a declaration in the alternative form asked for. As to damages, there will be an inquiry.

H

Order accordingly.

Solicitors: *J. A. Hostettler & Co.* (for the plaintiff); *Neil Maclean* (for the union).

[*Reported by* JACQUELINE METCALFE, *Barrister-at-Law.*]

I

---

(23) [1956] 3 All E.R. 939; [1957] A.C. 488.
(24) [1956] 1 All E.R. at p. 10; [1956] 1 Q.B. at p. 676.
(25) [1962] 3 All E.R. at p. 638.
(26) [1962] 3 All E.R. at p. 637, letter E.

INLAND REVENUE COMMISSIONERS *v.* BREBNER.

[HOUSE OF LORDS (Lord Reid, Lord Morris of Borth-y-Gest, Lord Hodson, Lord Pearce and Lord Upjohn), January 12, February 23, 1967.]

Income Tax—Tax advantage—Main object—Intention to obtain tax advantage—Subjective question—Two methods of carrying out commercial transactions, one involving more and the other less tax liability—Not a necessary consequence of adopting latter course that main object was to obtain tax advantage—Defeating take-over bid—Company's cash resource made available by way of return of capital, not as income—Finance Act, 1960 (8 & 9 Eliz. 2 c. 44), s. 28.

When there are two ways of carrying out a genuine commercial transaction, by one of which the maximum amount of tax would be payable and by the other of which no tax or much less tax would be payable, it is wrong to draw as a necessary consequence the inference, for the purposes of s. 28 (1)* of the Finance Act, 1960, that in adopting the latter course one of the main objects is enabling tax advantages to be obtained (see p. 784, letter F, post).

In order to defeat a take-over bid the respondent, who was a director of the company concerned, and his group made a counter-offer which, in March, 1959, was accepted by nearly all shareholders. To fulfil this counter-offer the sum of £108,000 had to be found by the respondent and his group. This was provided by a bank on terms requiring a joint and several undertaking from members of the group and early repayment. The company had £75,000 cash resources available to be distributed as to £58,500 as an ordinary dividend and as to £16,500 as a capital dividend. On the respondent's instructions a scheme for liquidating the company and forming a new company was prepared, so that the cash needed might be obtained from the company's resources. This scheme was not, however, adopted. Ultimately a scheme of reorganisation involving first increasing and then reducing the capital of the company was adopted, with the result that the £75,000 was returned to the shareholders by way of reduction of capital. It was admitted that there had been a transaction in securities and that, as a result, a tax advantage had been obtained. The Special Commissioners found that the transaction was entered into for bona fide commercial reasons and did not have as the main object or one of the main objects the enabling of tax advantages to be obtained. Further, it was not disputed on appeal that the commissioners could have found that the events were divisible into two separate chapters, one of which, consisting of the events leading to the acceptance of the counter-offer, was purely commercial, the other of which, consisting of subsequent events, had as its main object the obtaining of a tax advantage.

Held: the question whether one of the main objects was to obtain a tax advantage was a question of subjective intention; it was a question for the commissioners to decide on consideration of the relevant evidence before them and, as they had reached a reasonable conclusion on the evidence, the court would not interfere (see p. 784, letters C and G, p. 780, letters D and E, and p. 781, letter H, post).

Observations of LORD GREENE, M.R., in *Crown Bedding Co., Ltd.* v. *Inland Revenue Comrs.* ([1946] 1 All E.R. at pp. 453, 454) approved.

Appeal dismissed.

[As to the counteracting of tax advantages, see SUPPLEMENT to 20 HALSBURY'S LAWS (3rd Edn.) para. 276A.

For the Finance Act, 1960, s. 28 (1), (3), see 40 HALSBURY'S STATUTES 447, 448.]

---

* Section 28, so far as material, is printed at p. 781, letter I, to p. 782, letter B, post.

[Side notes, right margin:]

Considered in I.R. Comrs. v. Hague. [1968] 1 All E.R. 1096.

Distinguished in IRC v Goodwin [1973] 3 All ER 545

Dictum of LORD PEARCE at 781 applied in CLARK v IR COMRS [1979] 1 All ER 385

Case referred to:

Crown Bedding Co., Ltd. v. Inland Revenue Comrs., [1946] 1 All E.R. 452;
    34 Tax Cas. 107; 28 Digest (Repl.) 441, 1924.

Appeal.

This was an appeal from an interlocutor of the First Division of the Court of
Session as the Court of Exchequer in Scotland (the Lord President (LORD CLYDE),
LORD GUTHRIE, LORD MIGDALE and LORD CAMERON) dated Feb. 22, 1966, refusing
an appeal by way of Case Stated from a determination of the Commissioners
for the Special Purposes of the Income Tax Acts, dated June 16, 1964, discharging
a notice served on the respondent in accordance with s. 28 (3) of the Finance Act,
1960, that in order to counteract tax advantages obtained by the respondent,
William Brebner, certain adjustments were requisite in computing the
respondent's liability to surtax for the years 1960-61.

J. P. H. MacKay, Q.C. (of the Scottish Bar), J. R. Philips and C. K. Davidson
(of the Scottish Bar) for the Crown.

Hubert H. Monroe, Q.C., and D. A. Shirley for the respondent.

Their lordships took time for consideration.

Feb. 23. The following opinions were delivered.

LORD REID: My Lords, I have read the speech of my noble and learned
friend, LORD UPJOHN. I agree with it and have nothing to add. I would, therefore,
dismiss this appeal.

LORD MORRIS OF BORTH-Y-GEST: My Lords, I concur.

LORD HODSON: My Lords, I concur.

LORD PEARCE: My Lords, the issue before the Special Commissioners
was a question of fact. It is argued by the Crown that, as a matter of law, on a
proper analysis of the subsection (1) nobody could, on this evidence, have reasonably come to the conclusion which they reached. I cannot accept this argument.
The commissioners rightly approached the transaction as a whole from a broad
commonsense view, and there was ample evidence to justify their findings.

It was argued that their approach should have been more analytical; that
they should have isolated the later part of the transaction from the earlier;
and that the actual resolutions which finally obtained the tax advantage must
have had as their main object the tax advantage, since it was to that alone
that they (in isolation) were referable. Moreover, it was argued, the object
which was under consideration was the object of the company as such and
not of its directors or shareholders, and the company being indifferent to how
its assets were distributed cannot have a bona fide commercial reason or any
reason other than a tax advantage. In my opinion, however, such analysis and
isolation would be wrong and would destroy the opportunity of arriving at a
just and sensible conclusion which the subsection was intended to provide.

The complete series of events set out in the Case Stated was, in the view of the
Special Commissioners, one consecutive whole.

" The respondent and all other members of the group were mainly concerned, by the acquisition of additional shares to preserve the company in the
line of business which it had carried on for many years; a business, moreover,
which had good prospects of continuing profitably."

The money had to be borrowed from the bank by members of the group with a
clause providing for early repayment; and

" It had been understood from the beginning by the members of the
group that their repayments to the bank were to be effected as far as
possible by taking assets out of the company, but at this early stage there had

---

(1) Finance Act, 1960, s. 28 (1).

A   been no calculation as to how much cash could be extracted from the company, and the figure of 45s. per share was not based on any such calculation."

The resulting transaction was prepared by their auditor to carry out their main purpose.

It would be quite lacking in reality to draw a line between the first part of the

B   arrangement, namely, the purchase of the shares on a short term overdraft, and the second part of the arrangement whereby the overdraft was repaid, as initially arranged, largely out of the surplus assets of the company. The first part of the arrangement had committed them to the second part, whereby the whole original scheme was to be implemented. Unless they abandoned the whole scheme (by selling the shares to somebody who would probably wind up the

C   company), they had to go on with it.

The " object " which has to be considered is a subjective matter of intention. It cannot be narrowed down to a mere object of a company divorced from the directors who govern its policy or the shareholders who are concerned in and vote in favour of the resolutions for the increase and reduction of capital. For the company, as such, and apart from these, cannot form an intention. Thus the object

D   is a subjective matter to be derived in this case from the intentions and acts of the various members of the group; and it would be quite unrealistic, and not in accordance with the subsection, to suppose that their object has to be ascertained in isolation at each step in the arrangements.

Admittedly, an object of the carrying out of the broad scheme by way of the resolutions was a tax advantage; but that which had to be ascertained

E   was the object (not the effect) of each inter-related transaction in its actual context, and not the isolated object of each part regardless of the others. The subsection would be robbed of all practical meaning if one had to isolate one part of the carrying out of the arrangement, namely, the actual resolutions which resulted in the tax advantage, and divorce it from the object of the whole arrangement. The method of carrying it out was intended as one part of a whole which

F   was dominated by other considerations.

As the Lord President (LORD CLYDE) said:

" The material question is not what was the effect of each or all of the inter-related transactions, the question is what was the main object or objects for which any of them was adopted. Section 28 (1) of the Finance Act, 1960, draws a clear distinction between effect and object. It was to this

G   latter question that the Special Commissioners rightly directed their attention. To do so they had to consider each particular transaction in the series in its proper setting."

For those reasons, I am of opinion that the Special Commissioners came to a reasonable conclusion on the evidence before them. They could have reached a contrary conclusion, which would have been equally unassailable, had they taken

H   a different view of the evidence; but it was they who heard the witnesses, and I see no reason to suppose that their decision was not just and sensible. I entirely agree with the judgment of the Lord President.

I would dismiss the appeal.

I   **LORD UPJOHN:** My Lords, this appeal from an interlocutor of the First Division of the Court of Session as the Court of Exchequer in Scotland dated Feb. 22, 1966, is concerned with the short question, whether the Special Commissioners for Income Tax were entitled to discharge a notice dated Dec. 12, 1963, served on the respondent by the appellants under s. 28 (3) of the Finance Act, 1960. This depends entirely on the words of that section, so that I must set out its relevant parts.

" 28. Cancellation of tax advantages from certain transactions in securities.
(1) Where—

    (*a*) in any such circumstances as are mentioned in the next following
        subsection, and

    (*b*) in consequence of a transaction in securities or of the combined effect
        of two or more such transactions,

a person is in a position to obtain, or has obtained, a tax advantage, then
unless he shows that the transaction or transactions were carried out either
for bona fide commercial reasons or in the ordinary course of making or
managing investments, and that none of them had as their main object, or
one of their main objects, to enable tax advantages to be obtained, this section
shall apply to him in respect of that transaction or those transactions: . . ."

It is unnecessary to refer to the following subsections for they do not enter into
the question before your lordships.

It was admitted on behalf of the respondent that there had been a transaction
or transactions in securities within the meaning of s. 28 (1) (*b*) and that, as a result,
a tax advantage had been obtained. The only question, therefore, as stated in
para. 5 of the Case Stated by the Special Commissioners, was

    " whether s. 28 did not apply to the transactions in question because they
    were carried out for bona fide commercial reasons and none of them had as
    their main object, or one of their main objects, to enable tax advantages to
    be obtained."

The facts are set out in full in the Case Stated, and I only recapitulate some of the
leading features for the reason that the only question that your lordships have to
consider is whether on the primary facts the Special Commissioners were entitled
to draw the inferences of fact and to reach the conclusion which in fact they did,
or whether their conclusions were reached without any evidence to support them.

So, very briefly, I must state that the Aberdeen Coal and Shipping Co., Ltd.
(to which I shall refer as " the company ") was incorporated in 1900 and carried
on the business of coal merchants. It was, until the transaction presently to be
mentioned, a public company with shares quoted on the Aberdeen stock exchange.
Its capital was £60,000 divided into shares of £1 each and there were a large
number of shareholders; but the respondent and five other shareholders were the
principal and main shareholders (the group). In 1959 there was in the air what is
normally called a " take-over bid " from an outside source, and an offer was
made to all the company's shareholders to purchase the shares in the company at
a price of 40s. 6d., although the market price was only 25s. The respondent was
one of the directors of the company, and at a board meeting on Feb. 22, 1959,
the directors were unanimous that they could not allow it to be taken over and
then, as they feared, broken up, for the reasons that most of the directors had
interests in fishing companies which received favourable terms from the company
with regard to the supply of coal and they would be in difficulties about coal for
their coal-burning ships if the company ceased to operate; but, further, the
company was a happy one with good relations with its employees, who would lose
their jobs if the outside take-over bid was successful. So it was decided at this
board meeting that the only way to defeat the take-over attempt was to make a
counter offer, although at that stage the price to be offered for the shares and the
method of raising the necessary finance had not been considered.

Ultimately the respondent and his group offered all shareholders to purchase
their shares at 45s. per share. This was not based on the earning capacity of the
company, and the respondent himself thought it was too high, but the group
settled on this price in the light of another possible offer of 42s. 6d. per share from
another outside party; further, the respondent was most anxious to preserve the
company, if possible. This offer was accepted by nearly all the shareholders. This
involved the group in a total expenditure of £108,000, or about £18,000 each.
The group borrowed this from the British Linen Bank. The bank insisted on a
joint and several undertaking by the group's members with a clause providing
for early repayment. It was understood from the beginning by the members of

the group that their repayments to this bank were to be effected as far as possible by taking assets out of the company, but at this early stage there had been no calculation as to how much cash could be extracted from the company, and the figure of 45s. per share was not based on any such calculation. Putting it very briefly, the company had ample cash resources of about £75,000 part of which, as to £16,500, could have been declared as a capital dividend and the balance, as to £58,500, could have been distributed as an ordinary dividend. However, as the Special Commissioners held, to declare a dividend of £75,000 would have been a very astonishing thing indeed for a company of this size and, with the liability to surtax on the surtaxable part of the dividend, it would not have provided the required finance for repayment of bank loan; so this was never contemplated. Nor did the group ever contemplate borrowing £75,000 from the company at interest. The respondent, who appears to have been conducting matters on behalf of the group, with a view to extracting the necessary money instructed Mr. Henderson, the accountant to the company, to prepare a scheme involving the liquidation of the company and the formation of a new company. This was done, but was found by the directors to be impracticable. Had it been practicable to extract the cash in this way it was conceded that it would not have been taxable under s. 28 of the Finance Act, 1960. A second scheme was stillborn, but the third scheme, which was adopted and is the one which your lordships have to consider, was that by a scheme of reconstruction sanctioned by the Court of Session in March, 1961, the capital of the company was increased to £135,000 by capitalising the available sum of £75,000 and was then reduced by repaying to shareholders such as a sum as was necessary to put the sum of £75,000 into their pockets. This return of capital was used by members of the group to reduce the loans which they had received from the British Linen Bank for the purchase of the shares of the minority shareholders. The Special Commissioners found as a fact that the respondent and all other members of the group were mainly concerned by the acquisition of additional shares to preserve the company in the line of business that it had carried on for many years; a business, moreover, which had good prospects of continuing profitably. On the whole of this evidence the Special Commissioners came to the conclusion:

" On a consideration of all the evidence before us we found that the transactions in question had been entered into for bona fide commercial reasons. We also found that though admittedly a tax advantage had been obtained this advantage was an ancillary result of the main object, which was a bona fide commercial one, and that the transactions in question did not have as their main object, or one of their main objects, to enable tax advantages to be obtained."

As I have said earlier, the sole question for your lordships is whether that finding was made without any evidence to support it.

My lords, that finding has been attacked on this ground. It is said that the transaction which I have briefly narrated must be divided into two chapters. The first chapter dealt with the transaction down to the acceptance of the group's offer of 45s. per share in March, 1959, when it was recognised, though no plans were made, that to implement that offer the group must rely on, and extract, the cash lying in the company's coffers. As I understood the argument, down to the conclusion of this chapter, the respondent or his group would escape the net cast by s. 28. It was then said that a second chapter opened and that the group then arranged that the available money for the payment of this project should be obtained from the coffers of the company as capital. Thus, by reason of a perfectly proper scheme of arrangement, but nearly two years later, the main object of the operation in this chapter was to enable a tax advantage to be obtained because, although it would have been possible to extract the cash from the company by a dividend (subject of course to the surtax consequences as to £58,500 of that dividend), the whole object of the reduction of capital was to extract the cash without paying tax; that, it was strongly urged, showed it to be a main object. So, the argument proceeds, while the first chapter was carried out for purely bona fide commercial reasons without having as a main object the gain of a tax advantage, it must be regarded as purely introductory to the all important second chapter two years later when the scheme was devised to extract the cash by a reduction rather than the declaration of a dividend, so that it became plain that one of the main objects of the transaction was to enable a tax advantage to be obtained. Accordingly, the transaction fell within s. 28 (1) (b). Counsel for the respondent has, in my view, wisely conceded that the Special Commissioners could have found that there were two separate chapters, one of which was purely commercial, the other of which had as its main object the obtaining of a tax advantage; but this, he has urged, is a matter which must be entirely one for the commissioners. I agree that the question whether one of the main objects is to obtain a tax advantage is subjective and, as LORD GREENE, M.R., pointed out in *Crown Bedding Co., Ltd.* v. *Inland Revenue Comrs.* (2), is essentially a task for the Special Commissioners unless the relevant Act has made it objective (and that is not suggested here).

My lords, in the First Division the Lord President delivering the first judgment, with which the other Lords of Session agreed, put it in a nutshell, when he said:

" The issue raised in the case is a pure question of fact and from the facts found proved by the Special Commissioners there was ample evidence on which they could find as they did. The question which the Special Commissioners had to determine was what was the object in the mind of the respondent in entering into the transactions in question, and this is essentially a matter of fact and of inference for the commissioners."

With this I wholly agree.

My lords, I would conclude my judgment by saying only that, when the question of carrying out a genuine commercial transaction, as this was, is considered, the fact that there are two ways of carrying it out,—one by paying the maximum amount of tax, the other by paying no, or much less, tax—it would be quite wrong as a *necessary* consequence to draw the inference that in adopting the latter course one of the main objects is for the purposes of the section, avoidance of tax. No commercial man in his senses is going to carry out commercial transactions except on the footing of paying the smallest amount of tax involved. The question whether in fact one of the main objects was to avoid tax is one for the Special Commissioners to decide on a consideration of all the relevant evidence before them and the proper inferences to be drawn from that evidence.

For these reasons I would dismiss this appeal.

Appeal dismissed.

Solicitors: *Sir Charles Sopwith*, agent for *J. K. W. Dunn*, Edinburgh (for the Crown); *William A. Crump & Son*, agents for *L. Mackinnon & Son*, Aberdeen, and *Morton, Smart, MacDonald & Milligan*, Edinburgh (for the respondents).

[*Reported by* KATHLEEN J. H. O'BRIEN, *Barrister-at-Law.*]

---

(2) [1946] 1 All E.R. 452 at pp. 453, 454; 34 Tax Cas. 107 at pp. 115, 117.

EAMES (Inspector of Taxes) v. STEPNELL PROPERTIES, LTD.

[COURT OF APPEAL, CIVIL DIVISION (Willmer, Harman and Diplock, L.JJ.), December 5, 6, 7, 1966.]

Income Tax—Trade—Adventure in the nature of trade—Building company approached by council for acquisition of fields zoned for school site—Agreement to negotiate—Formation of associated company as investment company —Sale of fields by building company to associated company—Subsequent sale by associated company to council at large profit—Whether adventure in the nature of trade and taxable under Case 1 of Sch. D—Income Tax Act, 1952 (15 & 16 Geo. 6 & 1 Eliz. 2 c. 10), s. 122, s. 123 (1), s. 526 (1).

In 1955 a company, carrying on business as building contractors, purchased some fifty-three acres of agricultural land. Part of this was zoned for residential use, part was zoned for a school site and some was zoned as agricultural land. In connexion with the family affairs of the principal shareholders of the building company, two new companies were formed; one was a development company and the other, the taxpayer company, was intended to be a property investment company. The school site and agricultural land were to be vested in the taxpayer company. In April, 1959, the building company confirmed to the county architect on behalf of the acquiring authority, the county council, that the building company were prepared to negotiate on behalf of an associated company (meaning the taxpayer company which, however, had not then been formed) for the sale of two fields of the school site and enquired about a third field, which later the county architect intimated would also be the subject of negotiation for acquisition. There was uncertainty, because the county council wished also to acquire a neighbouring field, the property of Rugby School, and anticipated difficulty over that. In July the taxpayer company was formed with an issued share capital of £2. Two days later it purchased the school site and agricultural land for £2,100. Towards the end of July the district valuer wrote to the building company to negotiate a price. In August, 1959, the Town and Country Planning Act, 1959, came into operation, and the value of land for compensation purposes became its market value. In 1961 the land was acquired from the taxpayer company for £50,000. The taxpayer company having been assessed to tax under Case 1 of Sch. D on the profit of £47,900 as being profit from an adventure in the nature of trade, the Special Commissioners found, on appeal to them, that the taxpayer company was " a vehicle for investment for security ", that the school site was not its stock-in-trade and that the acquisition and subsequent sale of the site was not an adventure in the nature of the trade. On appeal from a decision over-ruling the commissioners,

Held (WILLMER, L.J., dissenting): the only true and reasonable conclusion which could have been reached on the facts was that the purchase of the school site was entered into by the taxpayer company with a view to re-sale of the land to the county council and not as an investment; accordingly it was an adventure in the nature of trade, and the profit realised from it was liable to income tax (see p. 794, letters E and F, and p. 796, letter I, post).

Appeal dismissed.

[As to what constitutes trading for income tax purposes, see 20 HALSBURY'S LAWS (3rd Edn.) 113-120, paras. 207-213, in particular p. 114, para. 207, text and notes (l) (m); and for cases on the subject, see 28 DIGEST (Repl.) 20-58, *78-225.*

For the Town and Country Planning Act, 1959, s. 2 to s. 5, see 39 HALSBURY'S STATUTES (2nd Edn.) 915, 920.]

Case referred to:

> *Edwards (Inspector of Taxes)* v. *Bairstow*, [1955] 3 All E.R. 48; [1956] A.C. 14;
> [1955] 3 W.L.R. 410; 36 Tax Cas. 207; 28 Digest (Repl.) 397, *1753*.

Case Stated.

The taxpayer company appealed to the Special Commissioners of Income Tax against an assessment to income tax made on it for 1961-62 under Case 1 of Sch. D* to the Income Tax Act, 1952, in a sum of £47,900, as profit resulting from the purchase and sale of a piece of land on the basis that the transaction was an adventure in the nature of trade. The grounds of appeal were that the taxpayer company was not engaged in the trade or business of dealing in property and that the acquisition and sale by the company of certain land near Rugby in the county of Warwickshire designated for use as a school under the Warwickshire County Council development plan was not an adventure in the nature of trade and accordingly the assessment was incompetent in law. The taxpayer company contended as follows: (i) that it was a property investment company notwithstanding the form of its memorandum and articles of association, and (ii) that the school site was not stock-in-trade nor was its acquisition and subsequent sale by the taxpayer company an adventure in the nature of trade. The Crown contended as follows: (i) that the taxpayer company was a company engaged in the trade or business of dealing in property; and (ii) that the school site was stock-in-trade of its trade or business and the acquisition and subsequent sale thereof by the taxpayer company was an adventure in the nature of trade. The Commissioners decided: (i) that when the taxpayer company was incorporated it was intended by those concerned that it should be a vehicle for investment in property notwithstanding its memorandum and articles of association, and that this intention persisted throughout the relevant period; and (ii) that the school site referred to was not stock-in-trade of the taxpayer company's business, nor was its acquisition and subsequent sale an adventure in the nature of trade. They therefore allowed the appeal. The Crown appealed by way of Case Stated to the High Court. On Mar. 22, 1966, BUCKLEY, J., allowed the appeal, holding that the acquisition and subsequent sale were an adventure in the nature of trade and that the profit made was properly taxable. The taxpayer company appealed to the Court of Appeal.

The cases noted below† were cited during the argument in addition to the case referred to in the judgments.

R. E. Borneman, Q.C., and *P. W. I. Rees* for the taxpayer company.
Heyworth Talbot, Q.C., and *J. R. Phillips* for the Crown.

WILLMER, L.J., stated the nature of the appeal and continued: I refer only to those facts which seem to me to be the salient facts of the case.

In 1955 a company of building contractors called Bosworth & Wakeford, Ltd., purchased some fifty-three acres of land on the outskirts of Rugby. The larger part of the land which it purchased was land which had been zoned for residential development. The smaller part included that with which we are immediately concerned in this case, which had been zoned for a school and playing fields. In 1957 the Bosworth company obtained planning permission in respect of that part of the land which had been zoned for residential development.

In or about 1958 Mr. Boardman, who was the solicitor to the Bosworth company, and also acted as solicitor for the Wakeford family, had occasion to give advice with regard to making provision for estate duty in relation to the Wakeford family. In the course of dealing with that problem he advised,

---

* Section 123 (1), in conjunction with s. 122 of the Income Tax Act, 1952.
† *California Copper Syndicate, Ltd.* v. *Inland Revenue (Harris, Surveyor of Taxes)*, (1904), 5 Tax Cas. 159; *Lucy & Sunderland, Ltd.* v. *Hunt (Inspector of Taxes)*, [1961] 3 All E.R. 1062; *Griffiths (Inspector of Taxes)* v. *J. P. Harrison (Watford), Ltd.*, [1962] 1 All E.R. 909; [1963] A.C. 1; *Pilkington* v. *Randall (Inspector of Taxes)*, (1965), T.R. 241; *Bishop (Inspector of Taxes)* v. *Finsbury Securities, Ltd.*, [1966] 3 All E.R. 105.

A amongst other things, the formation of two new companies, one of which should be a development company formed for the purpose of taking over and developing the land which was zoned for residential development; the other was to be a property investment company, which would take over the remainder, including the part of the land with which we are concerned, and which has been loosely, if somewhat inaccurately, described during the case as the " school site ". As

B Mr. Boardman's advice has been relied on, it is right that I should read a few lines from the Case Stated, where the effect of it is set out. It was to this effect:

"That that part of the Rokeby land which could be developed should be transferred to the new development company, and the remainder of the Rokeby land, that is, the school site together with any part of the Rokeby land zoned as agricultural land, should, when its extent was finally ascertained

C be transferred to the new investment company and form the nucleus of its property investment."

That advice was accepted and acted on, and it is the case for the taxpayer company that it was never departed from. The development company, which was called Stepnell Developments, Ltd., was in fact formed in April, 1959, and

D shortly afterwards acquired from the Bosworth company the land which had been zoned for residential development; and, as I understand it, the company set about developing that land, but we are not concerned with that.

By that time, however, certain other things had happened. From January, 1959, onwards, correspondence was taking place between the solicitor to the Bosworth company and Warwickshire County Council as to the possible acquisi-

E tion of the school site by the county council. On Jan. 21 the county architect wrote to the solicitors, and in the course of his letter he said:

"I am writing to inquire whether your clients would be prepared to sell the freehold of fields No. 269 and No. 268 shown edged red on the attached plan, and having a total area of 8.31 acres. This land would be used for playing field purposes. The remaining field, No. 286, would then be reserved

F on the town planning map as being required in the future for the erection of the new Rokeby secondary school."

As I understand it, the whole of field No. 286, and at least the major part of fields No. 268 and No. 269, were included in what I have described as the school site.

The next letter referred to in the Case is a letter from the Bosworth company

G itself, dated Apr. 3, and written to the county architect, in which it said:

"We confirm that we are prepared to negotiate on behalf of our associated company for the sale of fields No. 268 and No. 269. There is, however, the question of field No. 286, which we understand from the county planning department you may also require for educational purposes. In view of the fact that development has already started on this estate, we shall be glad if

H you will confirm that you require this field, and that you are prepared to complete the purchase."

If I may pause to comment on this letter, it is, of course, the fact that at that time the taxpayer company had not been brought into existence, and the " associated company " referred to in the letter can only have been intended

I by the writer of the letter to refer to the company which it was proposed to incorporate. It has been suggested during the course of the argument that this letter shows that the Bosworth company was pressing the county council to purchase, and reveals it as a party who was anxious to sell. For myself I do not so read that letter. To me it is more in the nature of an enquiry, directed by a party threatened with the possibility of compulsory purchase, in order to find out what it is that the county council really do want. In fact the county council seem to have had a great deal of difficulty in making up their minds. One difficulty which appears to have presented itself to them was that an adjacent

field, No. 287, which formed a vitally important part of the site for the proposed   A
new school, was land which belonged to Rugby School, and it was expected that
there might be some difficulty in the acquisition of that land.

The correspondence continued, and on May 25 we find the county architect
writing to the Bosworth company and saying this:

" I am approaching the county education officer to see whether he has any
objections to me proceeding through the district valuer with the purchase   B
of the land which you own comprising fields Nos. 268, 269 and 286 on the
plan which I previously sent to you."

That, so far as the Stated Case goes, was the last that anyone heard before
the date of incorporation of the taxpayer company. That, as I have said, took
place on July 8, 1959. A fact on which some reliance was placed at one stage in   C
the case was that the memorandum of association of the new company contained extremely wide powers, which no doubt would have been more apt for a
company engaged in development (1) than a company supposed to be only a
property investment company.

Within two days of the formation of the company (i.e., on July 10, 1959) the
Bosworth company entered into a contract with the taxpayer company to   D
transfer to the latter parts of fields Nos. 268, 269 and 286, amounting to something just under fifteen acres (which again I will refer to loosely as the " school
site ") at a price of £2,100. It is common ground that the price represented,
roughly at any rate, the agricultural value of the land. The situation thus was
that the taxpayer company was acquiring this asset in the knowledge that it
might be subject to compulsory purchase, and might accordingly have to be   E
sold. Moreover, it was an asset as to which negotiations had already been
commenced for its sale.

On July 22, 1959 (i.e., two weeks after the incorporation of the taxpayer
company) there appears on the scene for the first time the district valuer, who
started to open up negotiations as to price. On that day he wrote:

" I have been requested by the county architect to endeavour to agree   F
with you a price for the acquisition of the 14.835 acres of land or thereabouts,
as shown edged pink on the attached plan, which is required for a new
secondary school and playing fields for a nearby secondary school."

The letter goes on to record the then opinion of the county planning officer
that the only alternative use for any of this land, including the area designated,   G
would be for agricultural purposes only. The relevance of that was that about

---

(1) It was found in the Case Stated that, without careful consideration of wording,
use was made of the memorandum and articles of association prepared for Stepnell
Developments, Ltd., which was a development company, for the purpose of drafting
the memorandum and articles of association of the taxpayer company. It seemed that
initially two development companies had been contemplated. The Special Commis-   H
sioners, however, found that in fact the taxpayer company itself was always intended to
be a property investment company (see p. 789, letter F, post). The relevant clauses of
the taxpayer company's memorandum were as follows—" (A) To purchase take on
lease or in exchange or otherwise acquire any lands and buildings in the United Kingdom
and any estate or interest in and any rights connected with any such lands and buildings
and to develop and turn to account any land acquired by [the taxpayer company] or in
which [the taxpayer company] is interested and in particular by laying out and preparing
the same for building purposes constructing altering pulling down decorating maintaining   I
furnishing fitting up and improving buildings and by planting paving draining farming
cultivating letting on building lease or building agreement and by advancing money to
and entering into contracts and arrangements of all kinds with the builders tenants and
others and to carry on all or any of the following businesses namely builders and contractors decorators merchants dealers in stone sand lime bricks timber hardware and
other building requisites.
" (B) To carry on any other business (whether manufacturing or otherwise) which may
seem to [the taxpayer company] capable of being conveniently carried on in connection
with the above objects, or calculated directly or indirectly to enhance the value of or
render more profitable any of [the taxpayer company's] property."

A this time the Town and Country Planning Act, 1959, was passed and it came
into force on Aug. 16, 1959.

   Shortly after the receipt of that letter we find an application being made
on behalf of the taxpayer company under s. 5 of the Act of 1959 for a certificate
of appropriate alternative development. That was dealt with by the county
council on Jan. 5, 1960, when they refused the application except in relation
B to a small part of the land which I think is not immediately relevant to this
appeal. If that position stood, it is clear that the taxpayer company could not
expect to receive very much of a price from the county council in the event of
its entering into a contract to sell the land to the county council; indeed, on
that basis it may be that it would not have been able to get more than it had
itself paid for it. In those circumstances it took the course which I apprehend
C one would have expected it to take. It appealed to the Minister of Housing and
Local Government. The Minister's decision was not forthcoming until Mar. 22,
1961, but when it was forthcoming it was favourable to the taxpayer company.
The Minister granted a certificate that planning permission for erection of eight
houses to the acre might reasonably have been expected to be granted if the land
were not proposed to be acquired by the county council. That, of course, made a
D great deal of difference to the position of the taxpayer company, since it thereby
became entitled to expect a price on the sale of the land based on the market
value of the land with planning permission attached for residential development.
The upshot was that it did in fact conclude a contract with the county council
on Nov. 23, 1961, whereby it was able to sell this land to the county council
for the sum of £50,000, thereby securing a profit to itself of £47,900.

E   The taxpayer company then found itself assessed for income tax in respect
of this profit under Case 1 of Sch. D on the basis that it was a profit made on a
trading transaction. It appealed to the Special Commissioners, who allowed
the appeal and discharged the assessment. Their conclusion, as expressed in
the Case Stated, was:

F   " (i) That when the [taxpayer company] was incorporated it was intended
    by those concerned that it should be a vehicle for investment in property
    notwithstanding the form of its memorandum and articles of association,
    and that this intention persisted throughout the relevant period. (ii) That the
    school site referred to above was not stock-in-trade of the [taxpayer com-
    pany's] business, neither was its acquisition and subsequent sale an adventure
    in the nature of trade.   (iii) that the appeal succeeded."

G
   The matter was then taken by the Crown before BUCKLEY, J., who in turn
allowed the Crown's appeal, holding that this was indeed an adventure in the
nature of trade, so that the profit was properly taxable. I must read a part of the
judge's judgment because in the course of the hearing of this appeal it has been
much criticised, and in order to understand the criticism it is necessary to read
H certain passages. He said:

       " What I have to consider in the present case is whether, on a true view of
    the facts in this case, the acquisition of this land can properly be regarded
    as an acquisition of an investment."

The judge then dealt with that and he said:

I   " In reality one must recognise that this was land which everybody
    knew was going to be sold in the very near future to the Warwickshire
    County Council, and I cannot myself accept the view that the purchase
    of property which is on the verge of being sold can be properly regarded as an
    investment . . . It may be—I do not attempt to decide this—that to buy
    something with the expectation that at some indefinite date in the future
    it may be more valuable than it is today may properly be capable of being
    called an investment. I do not know, but to buy property which is virtually
    sold already, in respect of which negotiations are actively going on which are

manifestly going to result in a sale—to buy such property and to call it an
investment appears to me, with the utmost respect to the commissioners,
to be a misuse of language. It seems to me that perhaps the commissioners
may have been to some extent misled by their own first conclusion, which was
that the respondent company was incorporated with the intention that it
should be a vehicle for investment. I do not question, nor does counsel
for the Crown question, that it was incorporated with that intention, but it
does not follow from that that this particular transaction should be regarded
as having been an investment. On the contrary, it seems to me that the
only conclusion that one can reasonably arrive at is that the company
acquired this property with a view to its realisation and with the commercial
expectation, although not perhaps the absolute assurance, that upon such
realisation the company would make a profit.

" If that is the true view of the facts, then I think this particular transaction was one of a trading character and that the profit was one in respect
of which the company was properly assessed to tax. It is only proper for me
to take this view and to differ from the finding, or rather the conclusion, of
the commissioners, if I am satisfied that the view which I am taking is
really the true and only reasonable conclusion to draw from all the facts of
the case, and I hope I shall not be thought guilty of arrogance in saying
that I do think that that is so, notwithstanding that the commissioners
arrived at a different conclusion."

On this appeal the question is whether the judge was justified in thus reversing
the Special Commissioners' conclusion. It is agreed that if the profit made by
the taxpayer company is taxable, it can only be under Case 1 of Sch. D, i.e.,
in respect of a trade carried on in the United Kingdom. I am bound to say
that to my mind Parliament has not been very helpful in telling us what is
meant by " trade ". The only definition is contained in s. 526 of the Income
Tax Act, 1952, which says that it " includes any trade, manufacture, adventure
or concern in the nature of trade ". It seems to me that in those circumstances
it is very much a matter for the Special Commissioners to determine, in the
light of all the circumstances of the particular case, whether what was done
does or does not amount to an adventure in the nature of trade.

The power of the court to interfere with their conclusion, which is basically
a conclusion of fact, is one which is severely limited. That is a matter which was
discussed at some length in *Edwards (Inspector of Taxes)* v. *Bairstow* (2), and it is
perhaps helpful to refer once again to what was said by LORD RADCLIFFE in
that case. He said (3):

" If the Case contains anything ex facie which is bad law and which bears
on the determination, it is, obviously, erroneous in point of law. But, without
any such misconception appearing ex facie, it may be that the facts found
are such that no person acting judicially and properly instructed as to the
relevant law could have come to the determination under appeal. In those
circumstances, too, the court must intervene. It has no option but to
assume that there has been some misconception of the law, and that this
has been responsible for the determination. So there, too, there has been
error in point of law. I do not think that it much matters whether this state
of affairs is described as one in which there is no evidence to support the
determination, or as one in which the evidence is inconsistent with, and
contradictory of, the determination, or as one in which the true and only
reasonable conclusion contradicts the determination. Rightly understood,
each phrase propounds the same test. For my part, I prefer the last of the
three, since I think that it is rather misleading to speak of there being no
evidence to support a conclusion when, in cases such as these, many of the

(2) [1955] 3 All E.R. 48; 36 Tax Cas. 207.
(3) [1955] 3 All E.R. at pp. 57, 58; 36 Tax Cas. at p. 229.

facts are likely to be neutral in themselves and only to take their colour from the combination of circumstances in which they are found to occur."

At the conclusion of his speech, LORD RADCLIFFE added this (4):

"The court is not a second opinion, where there is reasonable ground for the first. But there is no reason to make a mystery about the subjects that commissioners deal with, or to invite the courts to impose any exceptional restraints on themselves because they are dealing with cases that arise out of facts found by commissioners. Their duty is no more than to examine those facts with a decent respect for the tribunal appealed from and, if they think that the only reasonable conclusion on the facts found is inconsistent with the determination come to, to say so without more ado."

The question, which was squarely faced by counsel for the Crown, is whether it can be said that the "only reasonable conclusion" on the facts as set out in the Case was that this was a trading transaction. Counsel submitted that the evidence was all one way. On the other hand, it was said in support of the appeal that this was by no means so; that there was no warrant for the judge's interfering with the decision of the commissioners, and that the highest at which it could be put was that there was evidence on which they might have decided in favour of the Crown instead of deciding in favour of the taxpayer.

In support of his appeal counsel for the taxpayer company placed much reliance on the Special Commissioners' finding as to the intention of the taxpayer company. That, he contended, was a matter of fact; moreover, the conclusion of fact arrived at was in accordance with the advice which had been tendered by Mr. Boardman back in 1958, as I have already described. Reliance was also placed on the fact that, leaving aside this particular transaction, the taxpayer company certainly never has sought to trade in property. We were informed that the proceeds of this sale were used merely for the acquisition of other property by way of investment. That was expressly conceded by counsel for the Crown. Counsel for the taxpayer company severely criticised the judgment of the judge on the basis that he had asked himself the wrong question when he said that the question was whether the acquisition of this land could properly be regarded as the acquisition of an investment. The proper question, says counsel, is whether it can properly be said that this was an adventure in the nature of trade. That no doubt is true; but I do not think that that point is one of any substance, for in the circumstances of this case the acquisition of this land by the taxpayer company was either an investment, or it was an adventure in the nature of trade. There is, so far as I can see, no possible third alternative; if it was not the one, then it was the other.

The second submission of counsel for the taxpayer company, however, was to my mind one of much greater substance, and one which in the event has persuaded me. He submitted that the judge really misdirected himself with regard to the facts as to the state of the negotiations which had taken place between the Bosworth company and the county council prior to the acquisition of this property by the taxpayer company. He submitted that it was really quite erroneous to refer to the taxpayer company as "acquiring property which is on the verge of being sold" or "property which is virtually sold already". That, he contended, was a serious exaggeration. Moreover, he complained that it was erroneous to say that the taxpayer company

"acquired this property with a view to its realisation, and with the commercial expectation (although not perhaps the absolute assurance) that upon such realisation the company would make a profit."

If, of course, that were the true state of facts, then I would agree that there would be much to be said for the view that the true and only reasonable conclusion would be that this was indeed an adventure in the nature of trade. I find it

(4) [1955] 3 All E.R. at p. 59; 36 Tax Cas. at p. 231.

impossible, however, to subscribe to the view that the evidence was all one way,   A
in the sense that it showed decisively that this property was acquired by the
taxpayer company with a view to its realisation or with any expectation that on
realisation the company would make at any rate any substantial profit.

One must, I think, start with the fact that the taxpayer company always was,
and was intended to be, a property investment company as found by the Special
Commissioners. It is perfectly true that the property which it acquired on July   B
10, 1959, was property which was at risk of being made the subject of compulsory
purchase. It is perfectly true that the Bosworth company, before the incorporation of the taxpayer company, had started negotiations with the county council;
but up to the time when the land was acquired by the taxpayer company those
negotiations had really gone no further than an expression of willingness to sell
on the part of the Bosworth company. There had been no invitation to name   C
a price. The county council were known to be in difficulties because a piece of
land essential to their scheme belonged to other persons, viz., Rugby School.
There could thus be no certainty that the county council ever would proceed
with the purchase of this land; certainly there could be no certainty that they
would be doing so in the immediately foreseeable future.

In fact, as we know now, the county council did not make up their minds to   D
purchase this land until late in 1961, two and a half years after the incorporation
of the taxpayer company. As to the possibility of a profit resulting if the land
did have to be sold to the county council, the climate prevailing in July of 1959
is illustrated by the view expressed by the planning officer as set out in the
letter of July 22, which I have already read, viz., the view that the only alternative use for this land would be use for agricultural purposes. That certainly   E
would not hold out very great hope for the taxpayer company to realise a profit
if in the event this land did come to be sold. That view of the possibilities held
the field until the decision of the Minister in 1961. In the circumstances it seems
to me that it is going too far to say that this land was land which was acquired
for the purpose of realising its value at a profit. As it appears to me, all that can
fairly be said is that the company was acquiring land which in the event might   F
or might not be sold, which the Bosworth company, it is true, had expressed its
willingness to sell, with perhaps a hope, though not necessarily with any great
expectation, of making a profit on the sale.

Counsel for the Crown in his argument before us in effect repeated the view
which had been expressed by the judge when he described this land as land
which was " predestined " for sale to the county council; but it seems to me   G
that it is going too far to say that this land was predestined for sale—the fact
is that at the time of its acquisition it was land which might or might not be sold.
In those circumstances I see difficulties in the contention that this transaction
amounted to an adventure in the nature of trade. We can disregard as quite
fortuitous and irrelevant the fact that, in the events which happened, it became
possible two years later, as we know, to sell this land at a very considerable   H
profit. This circumstance could not have the effect of converting the transaction
into an adventure in the nature of trade, if it was not already such a transaction.

In those circumstances I do not find it possible to agree with the submission
of counsel for the Crown that the evidence in this case was all one way, or that
the true and only reasonable conclusion at which the commissioners could
reasonably have arrived was a conclusion in favour of the Crown's contention.   I
It appears to me that there was a good deal to be said on both sides. In such
circumstances it is not open to the court to interfere with the conclusion of the
commissioners, to whom these matters are delegated.

It follows that in my judgment the judge erred in taking the view which he
did and in interfering with the decision of the Special Commissioners. I reach
this conclusion with regret and with a good deal of hesitation, all the more so
because I understand that both my lords take the same view as did BUCKLEY, J.
For my part, however, I find it impossible to take that view. If the matter

rested with me, I would allow this appeal and would restore the decision of the Special Commissioners.

HARMAN, L.J.: I have the misfortune to differ from Willmer, L.J., in this matter, and I can express my decision very shortly. I agree that, this being an appeal arising out of a Case Stated, we have not to decide how we should have concluded it on a balance of pro's and con's. We have to agree, if we do, with the judge that there was only one conclusion possible. I do not repeat the words of Lord Radcliffe in *Edward* (*Inspector of Taxes*) v. *Bairstow* (5) which in my judgment sum up the whole matter. I try to look at the facts as I see them.

The Rokeby estate in Warwickshire, once the home of the Rokeby Venus, came under the hammer in 1954, and in February 1955 fifty-three acres or thereabouts, being land from it, was bought by the Bosworth company. It was a building company, and a purely trading concern; and in 1957 it obtained planning permission in respect of the major portion of the land which it had bought for use for residential purposes. In the next year the family (it was a family company) were apparently concerned about the estate duty position and they took professional advice, as a result of which it was decided, as is usually done, I gather, to form two separate companies where one grew before. First, it was decided to develop the residential portion of the estate in two parts. That plan was not carried out. It was then decided to hive off the portion for which residential purposes planning permission had been obtained from that part which had not received such permission owing to the fact that it was zoned for what are very broadly called educational purposes. It was at the time agricultural land, and it was decided (and we must accept this from the commissioners) to form two companies, one to take over the immediately realisable land, and the other the less realisable land, which was the land subject to the embrace of Warwickshire County Council. That was the position in 1958.

In January, 1959, the climate begins to change, for in that month the agents for the county council write to the estate agents who were acting for the family company a letter in which they said:

" It is now intended to proceed with the acquisition of the land required for the playing fields for the Roman Catholic school, that is, fields Nos. 268 and 269 on the attached plan."

The writer of the letter, therefore, is announcing the intention of the county council of going on with what until then had been merely a project.

The answer to that comes on Apr. 3 containing this phrase: " We confirm that we are prepared to negotiate on behalf of our associated company for the sale of fields Nos. 268 and 269 ", and then the suggestion is added that field No. 286 should come into the same bargain. In fact the " associated company " did not then exist. It is the kind of phrase which, I suppose, is used by business men when they intend to form a company, but have not yet done so. So at that point they are willing in April to sell, and all that appears to be left open is the ascertainment of price. I add to that the finding of the commissioners that there was no question of the Bosworth company resisting the acquisition proposed by Warwickshire County Council. That was in April, 1959.

The formation of these two companies was not carried out until later than that. At the end of April, 1959, the development company was formed. That company bought the residential portion of the Rokeby land for £5,400, and began to develop it as a residential estate. The taxpayer company was not formed until July 8; but obviously the whole position was already crystallised, and it had by then been decided that it should take over the remaining portion of the estate from the Bosworth company, the vendors. The question is what the position of that estate was at that time. The county council had decided to buy. They had the

---

(5) [1955] 3 All E.R. at p. 59; 36 Tax Cas. at p. 231.

power to enforce their wishes. The Bosworth company had expressed their wish to sell.

This sort of property is not of any use to a building company, nor can it be considered as a form of investment of any sort, for as it was, and without purchase by the county council, it was a mere piece of agricultural land yielding about two per cent. on its price, not an investment which any family company formed for investment purposes would consider. I think, therefore, that counsel for the Crown was justified when he said that at the time when this transaction was carried out, on July 10, 1959, this land was "predestined" to be sold to the county council. The fact that it was not sold to the county council for some time was due to the vagaries of the Town and Country Planning Acts, for the chance that the taxpayer company had of getting a good price and a good profit was immensely enhanced by the Town and Country Planning Act, 1959, then already having passed its third reading in Parliament; and when the Act of 1959 reached the statute book a few days later and came into force the following month, it became possible for persons holding land to get its site value, and that must have been within the knowledge of everyone by July 10, 1959.

Therefore it seems to me that this land which was bought by the taxpayer company was land earmarked for sale, and earmarked for sale at a profit. It appears to me to matter not at all that this company had been originally projected as an investment company, and that it has since acted as an investment company; it had no assets so to act at that time, its capital being £2. Nevertheless having received £50,000 from the county council, it was in a position to have a portfolio of investments which, I understand, it has since acquired; but that does not seem to me to matter. I think that this transaction, if no other, which the taxpayer company entered into was, undertaken with a view to resale, and resale at a profit. It is to my mind flying in the face of the admitted facts to say that this could ever be regarded by the taxpayer company as an investment (and that is the alternative), when it is known that the piece of land that it was buying was subject to compulsory purchase powers by the county council if and when they decided to acquire it, and that the preson from whom the taxpayer company is buying has agreed to sell. I cannot regard this transaction as an investment. It must be regarded as one in which the taxpayer company bought to make a profit by resale. I see no other view open to the commissioners. I would uphold the judge's decision.

DIPLOCK, L.J.: But for the fact that this appeal has given rise to a difference of opinion in this court, I should not find it necessary to add anything more than that I agree with the judgment of the judge. The question before us is whether the only reasonable conclusion from the facts found by the commissioners was that the acquisition and resale of this piece of land was an adventure in the nature of trade. I think that counsel for the Crown correctly put the question which the judge and this court have to ask, viz., did the taxpayer company acquire this land on July 16, 1959, with the intention and expectation of selling it to Warwickshire County Council at a profit pursuant to the negotiations then in progress?

Before I say a word or two about how the negotiations stood at the date of acquisition of the land, there are one or two background facts as to the planning position of the land at the relevant time. Fields Nos. 269 and 268, so far as such parts as were acquired by the investment company are concerned, were on the town map for Rugby designated as a site for a secondary school, and so was a part of field No. 286, but the remainder of field No. 286 was designated as a "private open space", i.e., as agricultural land. The designation of those two portions of land with which we are concerned had important consequences under the Town and Country Planning Act, 1959, which came into force on

Aug. 16, 1959, and applied to—

"every compulsory acquisition of an interest in land in pursuance of a notice to treat served after Oct. 29, 1958."

So the Act would have applied to this purchase even if it took place before the Act came into force. As HARMAN, L.J., has said, the effect of the Act of 1959 was that, in the case of compulsory acquisition of land, the acquiring authority, instead of being able to purchase the land at the existing use value, had to purchase it at a price assessed in accordance with the Acquisition of Land (Assessment of Compensation) Act, 1919, i.e., at its value in the open market, with various assumptions as to the use to which the land would be permitted to be put.

The relevant assumptions for the purpose of this case are two. First, the assumption laid down in s. 3 (1), of the Act of 1959:

"In a case where—(a) the relevant interest is to be acquired for purposes which involve the carrying out of proposals of the acquiring authority for development of the relevant land or part thereof, and (b) on the date of service of the notice to treat there is not in force planning permission for that development, it shall be assumed that planning permission would be granted . . ."

for that purpose.

Secondly, s. 4 (1) provides:

"If the relevant land or any part thereof . . . consists or forms part of a site defined in the current development plan as the site of proposed development of a description specified in relation thereto in the plan, it shall be assumed that planning permission would be granted for that development."

In addition to these two relevant assumptions, there is a provision contained in s. 2 (3) of the Act of 1959 that:

"Nothing in these provisions shall be construed as requiring it to be assumed that planning permission would necessarily be refused for any development, notwithstanding that it is not development for which in accordance with those provisions the granting of planning permission is to be assumed; but in determining whether planning permission for any development could in any particular circumstances reasonably have been expected to be granted in respect of any land, regard shall be had to any contrary opinion expressed in relation to that land in any certificate issued . . ."

under s. 5 of the Act of 1959.

In relation to the land with which we are concerned, the effect of this legislation was that, so far as fields Nos. 269 and 268 are concerned, and that portion of field No. 286, which was included in the site of the secondary school, the owners of the land, if it were acquired, would be entitled at least to the value of the land for use as a site for a secondary school, and not merely to the agricultural value of the land. If it could be established that there was an alternative and more profitable use (for which purpose a certificate would be valuable evidence) then they would be entitled to a price higher than that obtainable for that land for use as a secondary school.

As regards that portion of field No. 286 which was designated only as agricultural land, they would, in respect of that portion, be entitled only to its value for agricultural use or as a school playing field unless they could establish a more profitable alternative use for which planning permission could be obtained. For this purpose they would need a certificate. I mention that because it is apparent from those considerations that there was a reasonable certainty that any price at which the land was acquired would be higher than its agricultural use value because of the presumption under s. 3 (1) of the Act of 1959 that planning permission would be granted for use as a school playing field.

With that background, how stood the negotiations at the time of the acquisition? As early as April, 1959, it was the common intention of those responsible for the subsequent formation of the taxpayer company and of the county council that the former should sell, and that the latter should buy, all the fields which subsequently were acquired by the taxpayer company to which I have referred. The initiative for the acquisition of fields Nos. 268 and 269 came from the county council; but in the letter in which they offered to purchase those two fields they specifically did not offer to purchase field No. 286. What they did ask was for consent of the Bosworth company to an amendment of the town plan to include field No. 286 as a site for the erection of the new Rokeby secondary school, and it was in response to that suggestion (which was not an offer to acquire it but merely a request for the company's consent to a different planning designation of the land) that the taxpayer company replied in the letter to which WILLMER, L.J., had referred (6), in which they refer to field No. 286 and ask the county council to confirm that they require the field and are prepared to complete the purchase. The initiative, therefore, for the purchase of fields Nos. 268 and 269 came from the county council. The initiative for the purchase of field No. 286 came from the Bosworth company.

That was the position, accordingly, as early as April, 1959; but at that date there were still two matters to be cleared up. One was that the county council also wanted to acquire an adjoining field, No. 287, which was the property of Rugby School; and in the letter of Apr. 8 the county architect wrote to the Bosworth company and said:

"Upon hearing from you [i.e., on hearing that you will agree with the purchase of field No. 286] I will write to the Rugby School regarding the adjacent land which is required to make up the nineteen acres, and will then refer the whole matter to the district valuer in order that he may contact you regarding the terms and compensation to be paid for the land which you own."

On May 25, Rugby School not having answered, the county architect wrote to say:

"In the absence of a reply I am approaching the county education officer to see whether he has any objections to me proceeding through the district valuer with the purchase of the land which you own."

It was at that stage, and before a reply had been received, that the taxpayer company acquired the land.

The position at that date, therefore, was that both parties were willing to purchase and sell respectively the whole of the land, and that, subject to the county education officer not objecting, the only matter left to be negotiated was the price, because it is at the price stage that the district valuer comes into the matter. That indeed is confirmed by the letter received from the district valuer twelve days after the acquisition (7) in which he says: "I have been requested by the county architect to endeavour to agree with you a price."

Thus on those facts, and on those to which my lords and the judge have referred, and bearing in mind what I have already said about the price at which the land would be acquired under s. 4 (1) of the Town and Country Planning Act, 1959, it seems to me that the only conclusion on the facts as found is that the taxpayer company acquired the land with the intention and expectation of selling it to the county council at a profit pursuant to the negotiations then in progress, and that that was an adventure in the nature of trade (8). I, too, would dismiss the appeal.

---

(6) See p. 787, letter G, ante.
(7) Viz., the letter of July 22, 1959; see p. 788, letter F, ante.
(8) The word "trade" is defined in s. 526 (1) of the Income Tax Act, 1952, as including "every trade, manufacture, adventure or concern in the nature of trade."

Appeal dismissed. Leave to appeal to the House of Lords granted.

Solicitors: *Joynson-Hicks & Co.*, agents for *Phipps & Troup*, Northampton (for the taxpayer company); *Solicitor of Inland Revenue.*

[*Reported by* F. A. AMIES, ESQ., *Barrister-at-Law.*]

R. *v.* WILSON. R. *v.* MARSHALL-GRAHAM.

[COURT OF APPEAL, CRIMINAL DIVISION (Lord Parker, C.J., Winn, L.J., and WILLIS, J.), January 17, 18, 19, 1967.]

Criminal Law—Evidence—Confession—Inducement—Person in authority—
Whether owner of house burgled and of property stolen is person in authority.

B., whose house had been burgled, approached the appellant W., told him that he was concerned to get his property back and offered a reward for information. According to B., the appellant W. said that he had the stolen property and that B. could have it back for £500. Later B. and the appellant W. met the appellant M. who handed over some of the stolen property, and B. made out a cheque for £300 to a fictitious payee and handed it to the appellant W. The rest of the stolen property not having been handed over, B. later saw the appellant M. and asked him whether he would let B. have information with regard to the missing property for a £200 reward. The appellant M. then admitted having handed the rest of the stolen property to the appellant W. who, he said, had given it to him to look after. At the trial of the appellants on a count of burglary*, the trial judge overruled objections to the oral statements of the appellants to B. being admitted in evidence. On appeal against conviction, on the question whether B. was a person in authority for the purposes of the principle that (so far as is relevant to the present case) a statement is not voluntary if it has been obtained by hope of advantage held out by a person in authority,

Held: B. being, and being known by the appellants to be, the owner of the house that had been broken into and of the property concerned, and thus being the loser and the person most interested in the matter, was a " person in authority " for the purposes of the application of the principle mentioned above; accordingly, as the prosecution had not established that the oral statements of the appellants were not made as the result of inducement by B., the convictions of burglary would be quashed (see p. 801, letters D and E, post).

Appeal allowed.

[As to who are persons in authority in relation to inducements to make confessions, see 10 HALSBURY'S LAWS (3rd Edn.) 469, 470, para. 861; and for cases on the subject, see 14 DIGEST (Repl.) 468, 469, *4508-4522.*]

Cases referred to:
Comrs. of Customs and Excise v. *Harz,* ante p. 177; [1967] 2 W.L.R. 297.
Ibrahim v. *Regem,* [1914-15] All E.R. Rep. 874; [1914] A.C. 599; 83 L.J.P.C. 185; 111 L.T. 20; 14 Digest (Repl.) 468, *4513.*
R. v. *Thompson,* [1891-94] All E.R. Rep. 376; [1893] 2 Q.B. 12; 62 L.J.M.C. 93; 69 L.T. 22; 57 J.P. 312; 14 Digest (Repl.) 468, *4521.*

Appeals.

These were appeals by David Alan Wilson and Michael Marshall-Graham against their convictions on Apr. 26, 1966, at Norfolk Assizes before MELFORD STEVENSON, J., and a jury of burglary and larceny (count 1). They also appealed

---

* The appellants were also charged with receiving, but at the trial the jury was discharged from giving verdicts on the counts of receiving; on appeal, in view of the convictions of burglary being quashed, convictions of receiving were substituted under s. 5 (2) of the Criminal Appeal Act, 1907.

Considered in DEOKINANAN *v.* R.
[1968] 2 All E.R. 346.

against their sentences of six years' imprisonment. The jury were discharged from giving a verdict on count 2 (receiving by the appellant Wilson) and count 3 (receiving by the appellant Marshall-Graham). The facts are set out in the judgment of the court.

The cases noted below* were cited during the argument in addition to those referred to in the judgment of the court.

L. K. E. Boreham, Q.C., and *F. H. L. Petre* for the appellant Wilson.
C. L. Hawser, Q.C., and *Margaret Puxon* for the appellant Marshall-Graham.
R. M. O. Havers, Q.C., and *J. G. Marriage* for the Crown.

LORD PARKER, C.J., delivered the following judgment of the court: The two appellants were convicted at Norfolk Assizes in April, 1966, of breaking into a country house during the night of Nov. 8, 1965, and stealing guns, silver snuff and tobacco boxes and other articles to a very considerable value, something over £10,500, and each was sentenced to six years' imprisonment. It is against their conviction and sentence that they now appeal to this court.

The facts need not be gone into in any great detail, nor does the court propose to give an exhaustive view on the law applicable to the real point which has been raised in the case. Had they desired to do so, they would undoubtedly have put their reasons into writing, but having formed a clear and simple view of this case, the court will now give judgment. One Captain Birkbeck was the owner of High House, Westacre, which was undoubtedly broken into on the night of Nov. 8/9, 1965. A showcase had been forced with secateurs, which were subsequently found outside the back door, and this property was stolen. The very next day one of these boxes was undoubtedly sold by the appellant Marshall-Graham to a firm in Old Bond Street. On Nov. 24, 1965, an A.A. man found in a lay-by near a place called Kentford, which was on the Bury-Newmarket Road, a sack which contained the guns and no less than thirty-four of the boxes. Police inquiries of course were started at once but, the police not having been able to trace the criminals or recover any more of the boxes, Captain Birkbeck on Dec. 10, 1965, himself decided to see what he could do. May I say at once that the court sympathises with Captain Birkbeck, but at the same time thoroughly disapproves of the exceedingly dubious transaction that thereafter he took part in. He knew that a man called Wilson had, on Oct. 30, 1965, acted as a chef and his wife as a waitress at a dance which Captain Birkbeck had given for his daughter in his house, and he decided to trace Wilson if he could. Eventually he did trace him to a flat in Hunstanton. Undoubtedly a conversation took place between Captain Birkbeck and the appellant Wilson and Mrs. Wilson, in the course of which he conveyed that he was concerned to get his property back and offered a reward for information. He said that he wanted information and that he was prepared to pay some £300 for it. I will come back in a moment to other matters which took part at the outset. According to Captain Birkbeck, the appellant Wilson immediately said: " I have got your boxes, you may have them for £500, but first I must have the money." The appellant Wilson at some period left the room and rang up the appellant Marshall-Graham. No doubt the idea was to tell the appellant Marshall-Graham what was happening, and to ask him to have the boxes available. That same evening, as an earnest of his intention, he took Captain Birkbeck down to a place called Heacham where, out of an old glove hidden nearby, one of the boxes was produced and handed over to Captain Birkbeck. The next day the appellant Wilson and his wife and Captain Birkbeck set off by car to Newmarket, and on the way, according to Captain Birkbeck, and this was to a very large extent admitted by the appellant

* *R.* v. *Croydon*, (1846), 2 Cox, C.C. 67; *R.* v. *Boughton*, (1910), 6 Cr. App. Rep. 8; *R.* v. *Murray*, [1950] 2 All E.R. 925; [1951] 1 K.B. 391; *Davies* v. *Director of Public Prosecutions*, [1954] 1 All E.R. 507; [1954] A.C. 378; *R.* v. *Golder, R.* v. *Jones, R.* v. *Porritt*, [1960] 3 All E.R. 457; *R.* v. *Thorley*, [1962] 3 All E.R. 583, n.; *R.* v. *Oliva*, [1965] 3 All E.R. 116.

Wilson, a conservation took place in which the appellant Wilson in detail explained how he and what he called his partner had in fact broken into Captain Birkbeck's house on that night, giving full details of how it had been done and how they had stolen this property. They went in the first place to Tempsford Café and continued to a public house called " Wait for the Wagon "; and a time came when—I am taking this quite shortly—the appellant Marshall-Graham arrived in a car with twenty of these boxes, handed them to the appellant Wilson, who in turn brought them in and handed them to Captain Birkbeck. They then all went off to a bank at St. Neots where in due course a cheque for £300 was made out by Captain Birkbeck to a fictitious payee and handed to the appellant Wilson. The reason why only £300 was handed over was that there were still boxes missing, and the appellant Wilson promised that, if Captain Birkbeck called at his flat the following Monday, he would have the remaining boxes available, when Captain Birkbeck would pay the balance of £200. In fact Captain Birkbeck went to the flat on the Monday morning and found pinned to the door an envelope on which was written " Coming back on Wednesday ". Finally, no message having been obtained by the Wednesday and the appellant Wilson having vanished, Captain Birkbeck went to the police. Later on he called on the appellant Marshall-Graham and told him that the appellant Wilson had let him down, and in turn asked the appellant Marshall-Graham whether he would let him have information with regard to the missing property for a £200 reward. As a result of that the appellant Marshall-Graham admitted having handed over the other boxes to the appellant Wilson at the public house, and said that he had previously been given them by the appellant Wilson to look after. In fact, not only did the appellant Marshall-Graham sell one of these boxes the very next day after the burglary to a firm in New Bond Street, but the appellant Wilson had come to London and sold another box in Chelsea. That, likewise, has been recovered, and we are told that, in effect, Captain Birkbeck has recovered almost all of the property stolen.

At the trial objection was taken to oral statements made by both the appellants to Captain Birkbeck, the objection being based on the well-known principle stated by Lord Sumner in *Ibrahim* v. *Regem* (1). It is, I think, only necessary to refer to this case on the general principle; it is to be found in a passage which only recently has been affirmed by the House of Lords in *Comrs. of Customs and Excise* v. *Harz* (2). Lord Sumner there said (3):

" It has long been established as a positive rule of English criminal law, that no statement by an accused is admissible in evidence against him unless it is shown by the prosecution to have been a voluntary statement, in the sense that it had not been obtained from him either by fear of prejudice or hope of advantage exercised or held out by a person in authority. The principle is as old as Lord Hale."

It is, of course, further a principle that it is for the prosecution to satisfy the judge if he is asked to rule on admissibility, and to satisfy the jury if the matter is admitted and left to the jury, that the statements were voluntary statements in that sense. After argument the learned judge ruled that these statements were admissible. He said this:

" First of all I am quite satisfied, particularly having heard the evidence of Mrs. Wilson herself, that what was taking place here was in the nature of a commercial transaction, perhaps of a rather dubious kind, between the [appellant] Wilson and Captain Birkbeck, the object of Captain Birkbeck manifestly being to get his property or so much of it as he could recover back, the object of [the appellant] Wilson being to get as much money as he could in respect of stolen property with which he was connected, and well knew it,

(1) [1914-15] All E.R. Rep. 874; [1914] A.C. 599.
(2) *Ante* p. 177.
(3) [1914-15] All E.R. Rep. at p. 877; [1914] A.C. at p. 609.

which was of a kind that it was practically impossible to dispose of with
safety. It was in those circumstances that this agreement was made. It may
well be that it took the form sworn to by Mrs. Wilson, that Captain Birkbeck
said he would represent to the police that the property had been returned to
him by a man whom he did not know, whom he met in the market square at
St. Neots, to whom he gave a reward to which he considered that man to be
entitled. Whether that be the true view of the facts or not, it is very
important to remember that at a very early state of the discussion between
Captain Birkbeck and [the appellant] Wilson the evidence is that Captain
Birkbeck said he was prepared to pay £300 for information leading to the
recovery of the remainder of his property, that is to say the remainder of it
after allowing for that which the A.A. man had recovered. It is not without
significance that the reward paid to the A.A. man for the property he found
in the hedgerow was expressly referred to by Captain Birkbeck, and referred
to immediately before his offer of £300 for information leading to the recovery
of the rest of the property. Then, says Captain Birkbeck, before he, Captain
Birkbeck, could say anything else, to his surprise [the appellant] Wilson
said, ' I've got your boxes and you can have them back for £500, but I must
have the money '. There clearly, if that evidence be right, is an admission by
[the appellant] Wilson that he has got the stolen property which Captain
Birkbeck is much concerned to recover, and an offer to let him have it back for
£500. [The appellant] Wilson places himself in the position of someone who is
manifestly a receiver who knows about the boxes and the fact that they are
stolen, and it seems to me that that which thereafter follows in the conversation is merely a filling in of interesting but comparatively irrelevant details
as to how the boxes came into the possession of [the appellant] Wilson. In
those circumstances, I do not think that this was a case where a voluntary
statement has been improperly induced, and I think that it is my duty to
admit this evidence, the prosecution having, as I said, satisfied me that it
was a voluntary statement. Therefore I shall disallow this objection.''

It is to be observed there that the learned judge was not dealing with what really
is the first question, whether Captain Birkbeck could properly be said to be a
person in authority within the principle, but it is quite clear that, when he came
to sum-up to the jury, he was in doubt whether Captain Birkbeck was such a
person, and really left it to the jury, indicating strongly his view that Captain
Birkbeck was not such a person.

It is to be observed, of course, that the learned judge could only rule on such
evidence as he had heard in the trial within a trial, and that he was taking the
view that this was, as he put it, a purely commercial transaction, and presumably
by that was meaning that the only inducement to hand over the property and to
make the statements which the appellant Wilson and later the appellant Marshall-
Graham made was the offer of £300. In fact, when one looks at the evidence as it
came out at the trial itself, it is clear that at some stage, probably during the car
journey on the second day, there was a discussion in the terms to which the
learned judge referred when dealing with Mrs. Wilson's evidence in that ruling.
A time did come when, it was clear, Captain Birkbeck would have to go to the
police, but he was saying that he would not, as it were, give the appellants away,
but would represent that at St. Neots in the market square some man unknown
had handed over this property. Whether that conversation took place at the
outset is, to say the least, doubtful. That it did occur at some stage, and as I
have said probably on the second day, is clear. The matter really does not rest
there, however, because it is clear on the evidence that, from the outset the
appellant Wilson was worried as to Captain Birkbeck's position. Evidence was
given that there was a car outside the flat when he arrived which the appellant
Wilson and his wife thought might be a police car. Without going into the
evidence in detail, it is clear to this court that, before anything happened, it was
conveyed to the appellant Wilson by Captain Birkbeck that all he was interested

in was the recovery of his property, and he went so far as to disparage the police and clearly conveyed to those people that he was acting and intended to act purely on his own, and that this was something quite apart from police inquiries.

The first question that arises is whether Captain Birkbeck was a person in authority. There is no authority, so far as this court knows, which clearly defines who does and who does not come within that category. It is unnecessary to go through all the cases; it is clear, however, in *R. v. Thompson* (4) that the chairman of a company whose money was said to have been embezzled by the prisoner was held to be a person in authority. It is also clear that in some cases it has been held that the prosecutor's wife is a person in authority, and in one case that the mother-in-law of a person whose house had been destroyed by arson was said to be a person in authority vis-à-vis a young girl employed by the owner of the house; in other words she was looked on as a person in authority in relation to that girl. Counsel for the appellant Marshall-Graham in the course of the argument sought to put forward the principle that a person in authority is anyone who can reasonably be considered to be concerned or connected with the prosecution, whether as initiator, conductor or witness. The court finds it unnecessary to accept or reject the definition, save to say that they think that the extension to a witness is going very much too far. On the facts of this case, however, Captain Birkbeck was, and was known to be, the owner of the house that had been broken into, and the owner of the property concerned; in other words the loser and the person most interested in the matter. It is true that in these days it would probably be impossible for him to stultify a prosecution that had been brought or to prevent a prosecution that had not yet been brought from being instituted, but nevertheless in the judgment of this court Captain Birkbeck came clearly within the principle as a person who could properly be said to be a person in authority.

[His Lordship said that, in the opinion of the court, it was not proved by the prosecution beyond reasonable doubt that the oral statements were not made as the result of an inducement from a person in authority, and therefore, the convictions of both appellants on count 1 must be quashed, but convictions of receiving would be substituted under the powers given to the court by s. 5 (2) of the Criminal Appeal Act, 1907, (5). The sentence on each appellant would be reduced to four years' imprisonment.]

Appeals allowed in part.

Solicitors: *Loynes, Son & Barow*, Kings Lynn (for the appellant Wilson); *Brignall, White & Orchard*, Stevenage (for the appellant Marshall-Graham); *Harry Pumphrey & Sons*, agents for *Metcalf, Copeman & Pettefar*, King's Lynn (for the Crown).

[*Reported by* N. P. Metcalfe, Esq., *Barrister-at-Law.*]

---

(4) [1891-94] All E.R. Rep. 376; [1893] 2 Q.B. 12.
(5) 5 Halsbury's Statutes (2nd Edn.) 930.

MONTAGUE *v.* MONTAGUE.

[PROBATE, DIVORCE AND ADMIRALTY DIVISION (Sir Jocelyn Simon, P., and Cairns, J.), January 13, 26, 27, 1967.]

Divorce—Re-hearing—Spouse lulled into false sense of security that proceedings have lapsed—Wife returning petition on ground of cruelty—Husband requesting reconciliation and wife returning no firm answer—Husband informed of hearing of petition on day before hearing—Petition heard as undefended—Wife returning to husband after decree nisi and thereafter giving no firm answer to requests for reconciliation—Matrimonial Causes Rules, 1957 (S.I. 1957 No. 619), r. 36 (1).

Divorce—Re-hearing—Time—Extension of time for applying for re-hearing—Conduct of wife entitling husband to reasonable hope of reconciliation.

On Nov. 9, 1965, the wife presented a petition for divorce on the ground of cruelty. Shortly before the petition was served, which was on Jan. 14, 1966, the wife left the matrimonial home. The husband sent in a memorandum of appearance, stating on it that he did not wish to defend, etc.; it was ineffective as an appearance, and he was informed that he would not be entitled to notice of further steps in the suit. Immediately after Jan. 14, 1966, the husband sought a reconciliation, and the wife was induced to return to the matrimonial home, where she stayed with him until June 26. On Jan. 18, 1966, the wife's solicitors wrote to the husband to the effect that they would write further after having considered the position with her. Meanwhile the husband continued to request the wife not to proceed with the divorce suit. She did not return any firm answer to these requests. She later stated in evidence that she was afraid to disclose to him her true intentions. On Sunday, June 26, 1966, the wife left the matrimonial home, leaving a note saying " Bill, you are going to get a shock ". Later on the same day, June 26, a letter dated June 20, 1966, from the wife's solicitors was delivered to the husband informing him that the petition was to be heard on June 27, 1966, but the letter did not state at which court or at what time the petition would be heard. The husband did not appear at the hearing. The petition was heard undefended, and a decree nisi was pronounced on June 27, 1966. The same evening the wife telephoned to the husband asking for money and promising to return if it was sent. He sent the money, and she came back to the matrimonial home where she continued to reside. During the period of cohabitation which followed the husband made repeated requests to her for reconciliation and that the decree should be rescinded. On Oct. 3, 1966, the husband drove her at her request to Brighton for a conference with her counsel. After the conference she told her husband that the decree nisi would stand. She left the matrimonial home on Oct. 10, 1966. The husband, having obtained legal aid, gave notice of motion on Oct. 31, 1966, for leave to apply out of time under r. 36 (1)* of the Matrimonial Causes Rules, 1957, to set aside the decree nisi and for re-hearing of the suit.

Held: the decree nisi would be set aside and there would be an order for re-hearing because—

(i) the wife had by her conduct lulled the husband into a false sense of security up to June 26, 1966, that she would not proceed with the divorce suit, and, by being informed on that day that the suit was to be heard on the following day, he had not been given reasonable opportunity to get the suit stayed; accordingly the husband, although he had had knowledge of

---

* Rule 36 (1), so far as material, reads: " An application for re-hearing of a cause heard by a judge alone where no error of the court at the hearing is alleged shall be made to a Divisional Court of the Probate, Divorce and Admiralty Division. The application shall be by notice of motion stating the ground on which it is based and the notice shall be filed in the divorce registry and served upon the opposite parties (whether they have appeared or not) within six weeks after judgment . . ."

the divorce suit, was entitled to have the decree nisi set aside, as his defence (e.g., on grounds of condonation) was not so lacking in substance that it should not be heard (see p. 809, letters D, F and H, and p. 810, letters A and E, post).

Winter v. *Winter* ([1942] 2 All E.R. 390); *Tucker* v. *Tucker* ([1949] P. 105); *Owen* v. *Owen* ([1964] 2 All E.R. 58), and *Nash* v. *Nash*, ante p. 535, considered and explained.

(ii) during the period after the decree when the wife was living with the husband, she had not made it clear to him, prior to Oct. 3, 1966, that she would not rescind the decree, and, as he had acted promptly after that date, leave would be given to make the application for re-hearing although the time for so doing had expired (see p. 809, letter I, and p. 810, letter E, post).

[As to applications to a Divisional Court for re-hearing of a matrimonial cause, see 12 HALSBURY'S LAWS (3rd Edn.) 425, 426, para. 954; and for cases on the subject, see 27 DIGEST (Repl.) 595-598, *5571-5593.*

For the Matrimonial Causes Rules, 1957, r. 36 (1), see 10 HALSBURY'S STATUTORY INSTRUMENTS (2nd Re-Issue) 248.]

Cases referred to:

Jakeman v. *Jakeman and Turner*, [1963] 3 All E.R. 889; [1964] P. 420; [1964] 2 W.L.R. 90; Digest (Cont. Vol. A) 785, *5590a.*

Nash v. *Nash*, ante p. 535.

Owen v. *Owen*, [1964] 2 All E.R. 58; [1964] P. 277; [1964] 2 W.L.R. 654; 3rd Digest Supp.

Peek v. *Peek*, [1947] 2 All E.R. 578; [1948] P. 46; *affd.* C.A., [1948] 2 All E.R. 297; 27 Digest (Repl.) 596, *5577.*

Stevens v. *Stevens*, [1965] 1 All E.R. 1003; [1965] P. 147; [1965] 2 W.L.R. 736; 3rd Digest Supp.

Tucker v. *Tucker*, [1949] P. 105; [1949] L.J.R. 76; 27 Digest (Repl.) 597, *5584.*

Winter v. *Winter*, [1942] 2 All E.R. 390; [1942] P. 151; 111 L.J.P. 95; 167 L.T. 258; 27 Digest (Repl.) 599, *5604.*

Motion.

This was a motion by the husband for leave to make an application out of time under the Matrimonial Causes Rules, 1957, r. 36 (1), and, if such leave was given, for setting aside a decree nisi pronounced on June 27, 1966, in favour of the wife on her undefended petition on the ground of the husband's cruelty, and for a re-hearing of the suit. The facts are set out in the judgment of CAIRNS, J.

A. F. B. Scrivener for the husband.

J. L. E. McManus and *T. S. G. Baker* for the wife.

CAIRNS, J., delivered the first judgment at the invitation of SIR JOCELYN SIMON, P.: The husband contends that the decree nisi was pronounced contrary to the justice of the case, no error of the court being alleged. He says that if the true facts had been known to the court the petition would have been dismissed, but that he took no part in the proceedings because he was led to believe that the wife was not going to proceed with the suit. Then, to explain the lapse of time between the granting of the decree nisi and the service of his notice of motion, he says that he was led to believe that the wife would have the decree rescinded because she was still living with him as his wife and showing every sign of being reconciled to him.

The course of the proceedings has been as follows. On Nov. 9, 1965, the wife presented her petition for divorce on the ground of cruelty. It was served on the husband on Jan. 14, 1966. He sent to the registrar the form of memorandum of appearance, stating on it that he did not wish to defend or to resist the wife's claim for ancillary relief or to make any claims for ancillary relief himself. Such a document is not under the rules an appearance at all. The registrar so informed the husband and made it clear that he was entitled to no notice of any further steps in the suit. The suit proceeded as an undefended one, was duly set down for hearing, and came for hearing as an undefended cause before a special commissioner at Brighton on June 27, 1966. He heard the evidence of the wife, was satisfied that she had established a case of cruelty, was further satisfied that the cruelty had not been condoned, and accordingly he pronounced a decree nisi. On Oct. 31, 1966, the husband gave the notice of motion which led to the present hearing. The matter came on before this court on Jan. 13, 1967, when we had before us affidavits of the husband and the wife, and we heard argument on behalf of each. We took the view that questions of fact arose which could not satisfactorily be decided on affidavit evidence and we adjourned for the parties to attend to give oral evidence. Yesterday the husband and the wife both gave evidence supplementing their affidavits and were both cross-examined: and we heard further argument from counsel. We now have to decide whether the husband should be allowed to apply for relief out of time and, if so, whether that relief should be granted.

The history of the marriage may be summarised as follows. The parties were married on July 12, 1949, and they lived together as husband and wife in the full sense up to at least December, 1965, and in some sense until several months after the decree nisi, except for two periods of about a week each. They had six children. According to the wife, the husband was guilty of considerable unkindness to her during all the latter part of the marriage and of a series of specific acts of cruelty. The husband now denies that he ever treated his wife with cruelty. An unusual feature of the married life was that in the latter years of it the parties often indulged in mutual masturbation as a substitute for normal sexual intercourse, though full sexual intercourse, with or without contraceptives, did take place from time to time. There was full sexual intercourse on an occasion in December, 1965: whether there was any later is in dispute. For about three years before the end of 1965 the parties had occupied separate bedrooms.

The wife presented her petition in November, 1965, and it was served on the husband in January, 1966, the wife having left the matrimonial home shortly before it was served on him. After the service the husband immediately sought to get his wife to return to him and, with the assistance of the local vicar, she was induced to come home after about a week for an attempt at reconciliation. For at least the next three or four weeks something like normal married life was resumed. The husband says that on two occasions during this period full sexual intercourse took place. The wife denies this but concedes that mutual masturbation occurred once. The husband says that things continued in much the same way up to June 26, 1966, with several occasions of masturbation though no more actual intercourse. The wife says that after the three or four weeks had elapsed she withdrew from the husband as much as she could, whilst still living in the same house with him and the children. She talked to him as little as possible and had no further sexual activities with him.

On Jan. 18, 1966, the wife's solicitors had written a letter to the husband in these terms:

" Dear Sir,—Divorce—With reference to your recent telephone call to our office, we have been in touch with our client and we are not in a position to see you either alone or together with your wife until such time as we have had a chance to consider the position with our client. Thereafter we will write to you further about the matter."

That the wife was undecided whether to continue with her suit is clear from two letters written to her by her solicitors on Feb. 2, 1966. The first letter reads:

" Dear Madam, Thank you for your letter of the 31st ult. and we note that you would like us to withhold any further action pending your instructions."

The second letter, of the same date, is headed " Divorce " and reads:

" Thank you for your letter received today. So far as instalments are concerned you should continue to pay these to the Law Society whilst you are deciding whether or not to proceed with the matter."

A They go on to inform her that, even if she did not proceed, she would still be liable for the payment of the instalments to the Law Society. The husband knew nothing of these letters at the time. He found them in the house some time after the date of the decree nisi. The wife says that during the period between February and June, 1966, the husband kept asking her to discontinue the divorce proceedings. Although at one stage in her evidence she denied that during this period

B she had ever weakened, at another stage she said that she would sometimes, under pressure and because she was frightened of her husband, agree to consider discontinuing. She conceded that at this time the husband might well have been under a misapprehension about her intentions and that she never said definitely that she was going on with the divorce. The husband says that during this period it was in effect agreed between them that the divorce proceedings were not to

C continue. He says that in the wife's presence some time about the end of May, 1966, he screwed up the divorce papers, saying, " We won't need these any more ". He further says that as late as the early hours of June 26 there was affectionate sexual play between himself and the wife. June 26 was a Sunday. In the morning the wife left the house and left behind a note saying amongst other things, " Bill, you are going to get a shock ". Shortly after the husband

D had read this note, an enquiry agent, instructed by the wife's solicitors, arrived at the house and handed to him a letter dated June 20, six days earlier. It read as follows:

> " Dear Sir, We send this letter to give you formal notice that the hearing of your wife's petition for divorce will be upon June 27, 1966."

E It may be noted that the letter did not state where or at what time the divorce suit was to be heard. The wife has told us in her oral evidence that she had deliberately taken steps to ensure that her husband would not be informed of the imminence of the hearing until after she had left the house. The husband, having received this letter, did nothing about it. He told us first that he had an important job to do that Monday and that it would have been very inconvenient for him to

F attend the court: secondly, that he did not know at what court or at what time the case was to be heard: and thirdly, that he did not expect his wife to get a decree because his workmates had told him that if a husband and wife lived together for more than three months, any prior matrimonial offence was thereby condoned—perhaps an unusual degree of familiarity among laymen with s. 42 of the Matrimonial Causes Act 1965. So the decree was made in the absence of

G the husband.

The wife then went to stay at Winchelsea. The same evening she rang up her husband and asked him for money and said that if he sent it, she would return to the matrimonial home. She told us that she decided to do this in order to talk things over, and because she was upset, because in the course of the telephone conversation the husband broke down and cried. He did send her some money

H and she did return to him, either immediately or within a week, and from then until October family life was resumed. There was no further full sexual intercourse: whether or not the practice of mutual masturbation was continued to any extent is in dispute. According to the wife, during this period, June to October, the husband was trying from time to time to persuade her to have the decree rescinded, and she was sometimes refusing, and at other times giving non-committal replies. On Aug. 10, 1966, the wife's solicitors wrote to the husband

I as follows:

> " We refer to our telephone conversation with you in which we made it plain to you that you had no right to remain in the matrimonial home after the decree nisi had been pronounced. [The wife] informs us that not merely have you returned to the matrimonial home [that was not accurate: the husband had never left the matrimonial home] but that you have resumed the course of conduct which was the basis of the decree. This is an intolerable position. We give you notice to leave the matrimonial home immediately

and that we are initiating proceedings for an injunction against you, and that
any further acts of cruelty, however slight, will be reported to the judge in
those proceedings.   If, after the grant of such an injunction, you acted
contrary to its terms, you could be imprisoned for contempt of court.   You
must also maintain your wife.   We suggest until the hearing of the appointment for maintenance, you pay to your wife the sum of £10 a week.   If you
fail to do this we shall once again be forced to take immediate and severe
action against you."

Shortly after receiving that letter the husband consulted solicitors.   However, no
great change took place in the relationship up to Oct. 3, when the husband, at the
wife's request, drove her to Brighton where she had a conference with her counsel.
After it she told her husband that the decree nisi was to stand.   He applied for a
legal aid certificate to bring the present application.   It was issued to him on
Oct. 18.   Meanwhile, on Oct. 10, the wife had left the matrimonial home.   On
Oct. 31 the husband's notice of motion was issued.

In approaching our consideration of this case we have the guidance of various
authorities in this court, and one in the Court of Appeal.   In *Winter* v. *Winter* (1)
a Divisional Court consisting of LANGTON and HENN COLLINS, JJ., held that if
there was good reason to believe that the matrimonial offence on which a decree
nisi had been founded had never in fact been committed, the decree nisi ought to
be set aside even if the respondent had stood by and with full knowledge of what
was happening allowed the decree to be made without any resistance.

The next case is *Tucker* v. *Tucker* (2):   another case in the Divisional Court,
consisting this time of HODSON and PILCHER, JJ.   In a sense this case is the converse of *Winter* v. *Winter* (1), because here again the respondent had stood by
and not resisted the making of the decree, but in contra-distinction from *Winter's*
case (1), the court in *Tucker's* case (2) formed the view that there was no sufficient
reason to suppose that the decree had been wrongly made.   Two short passages
from the judgments indicate the basis on which the two judges dealt with the
matter.   In *Tucker* v. *Tucker* HODSON, J., said (3):

" This court would, therefore, appear to be put into this position, that it
has to come to a conclusion whether or not there is material upon which it is
reasonable to suppose that an injustice may have been done;   that is,
material put forward by the applicant, and assuming in the applicant's favour
that all she says is accurate."

PILCHER, J., said (4):

" I do not propose to read the passages from the judgment of LANGTON, J.,
[that was the judgment in *Winter* v. *Winter* (1)] to which HODSON, J., has
already referred, but they do, I think, as he has pointed out, make it clear
that one of the matters which the court has to consider, when an application
under this rule is made to it, is whether the new matter put forward so
changes the complexion of the case as to satisfy this court that if that material
had been before the court which dealt with the matter originally the order
made would, or probably would, have been different."

A much more recent case before a Divisional Court consisting of SIR JOCELYN
SIMON, P., and SCARMAN, J., is *Owen* v. *Owen* (5).   In the judgment of the court
delivered by SCARMAN, J., (6) there is a most illuminating passage, which I
propose to read in full:

" We think that today the justification for the existence of the court's
power to order a re-hearing is the public interest and that its exercise should
be governed primarily by that consideration.   The true nature of the public

---

(1) [1942] 2 All E.R. 390; [1942] P. 151.   (2) [1949] P. 105.
(3) [1949] P. at p. 112.   (4) [1949] P. at p. 114.
(5) [1964] 2 All E.R. 58; [1964] P. 277.
(6) [1964] 2 All E.R. at pp. 63, 64; [1964] P. at pp. 284, 285.

interest is, as PILCHER, J., remarked in *Tucker* v. *Tucker* (7), to see that in matrimonial matters, where questions of status are involved, any order made by the court is made on the true facts. Certainty is not within the power of the court to achieve; but it must be satisfied that there are substantial grounds for the belief that a decree has been obtained contrary to the justice of the case before it takes the serious step of setting aside an order of the court obtained by due process of law.

" It is, we think, in this context that the conduct of the parties has to be considered. If the court is satisfied that there are substantial grounds for believing the decree to have been obtained contrary to the justice of the case, not even gross laches by the applicant, as in *Winter* v. *Winter* (8), nor deliberate suppression of documents, as in *Peek* v. *Peek* (9), will defeat the application; but, if a respondent, in possession of her faculties, with the facts of her married life in mind, and with the benefit of clear legal advice and her solicitor's explanation of the issues involved, takes a deliberate decision not to defend or not to pursue her cross-charges in circumstances which negative any suggestion of ' hoodwinking ' the court, then this court should, in our opinion, view a subsequent application for a new trial with a degree of reserve. A decision thus taken would, in our view, throw doubt on the case subsequently put forward that a decree has been obtained contrary to justice. Further, if the case sought to be advanced is cruelty (with its concomitant that the matrimonial cohabitation has become unendurable) and there is a recent history of attempts by the applicant at reconciliation, her complaints of cruel conduct must inevitably be viewed and assessed in the light of such attempts.

" The question thus arises as to the way in which it is proper for the court to deal with, and assess, evidence adduced in applications under this rule. Both members of the court touched on the subject in *Tucker* v. *Tucker* (7). Although their choice of language differed, both accepted that the court had to come to a conclusion whether or not there was material on which it was reasonable to suppose that a decree had been obtained contrary to justice. HODSON, J., after stating the test, added these words (10): ' that is, material put forward by the applicant, and assuming in the applicant's favour that all she says is accurate '. We do not think that the learned judge intended these words to be of universal application: indeed he himself disregarded them when dismissing from consideration the applicant's sworn denial of cruelty. We think that the learned judge had in mind that the hearing of the application is not the hearing of the suit, and that the Divisional Court cannot investigate or decide questions of fact which would arise on the new trial, if granted. But the Divisional Court must assess and weigh the material adduced in all its surrounding circumstances and against the background of the matrimonial history so as to reach its conclusion as to the reasonableness of believing that injustice may have been done. In our view, HODSON, J., is not to be taken to be laying down that in every matter the ipse dixit of the applicant, even when weighed as to its probability against its surrounding circumstances, must be accepted. There are some preliminary matters which of necessity lie exclusively within the province of determination of this court. For instance, in the present case the court must make up its own mind as to the nature and clarity of the explanations and advice given to the applicant by her solicitors in April and May, 1963, and as to her mental fitness to understand her problems and make her decisions at that time. Were the court undecided after reading the evidence on such questions, it would be wrong, in our view, merely to assume that the wife's version of the relevant facts was correct: the court must decide them

(7) [1949] P. 105.   (8) [1942] 2 All E.R. 390; [1942] P. 151.
(9) [1947] 2 All E.R. 578; [1948] P. 46.   (10) [1949] P. at p. 112.

for itself and may, if it thinks it necessary, order cross-examination of the deponents, as was recently done in *Jakeman* v. *Jakeman and Turner* (11)."

The wife in that case was, of course, the applicant.

The last case that I shall mention is that of *Stevens* v. *Stevens* (12), and I mention it only to quote a passage from the judgment of DAVIES, L.J., where he said (13):

" As it seems to me, these applications to the Divisional Court fall into at least two classes. There is the class where the applicant comes along and says ' I was not served: I knew nothing about it ', or, ' I was deceived: all the proceedings took place behind my back '. In that sort of case the applicant gets a re-hearing almost automatically. The other class is the *Winter* (14) class of case, the *Tucker* (15) class of case, and this class of case, where an applicant may come along and say, ' I knew all about this: I chose not to defend; but it was all wrong: let me defend now and grant me a re-hearing '. In a case of that latter kind, speaking for myself, I think that for an applicant to succeed he has to convince the Divisional Court, or this court if it comes before this court, that on the evidence before the court on the application as a whole it is more probable than not that the decree was obtained contrary to the justice of the case."

In a recent case of *Nash* v. *Nash* (16) this court has held that there is at least one other class of case intermediate between the two referred to by DAVIES, L.J., but it appears to me that the present case comes within either the first or the second of the two categories which DAVIES, L.J., mentioned: either the husband was deceived or alternatively it was a case where he stood by and allowed the decree to be made without attempting to resist it.

The effect of the cases to which I have referred in relation to this present application may, I think, be summarised as follows: We must first decide whether the husband was deceived into believing that the divorce was not going on until a moment when it was too late for him to have a reasonable chance of defending it. This is a question of fact to be decided on the evidence that we have read and heard. If he was so deceived, then he is entitled to have the decree nisi set aside and a re-hearing ordered, unless it is clear that the re-hearing would in all probability have the same result as the original hearing. If, however, he was not deceived but deliberately allowed the decree nisi to be made without any effort to resist it, then he can only have it set aside if there is a probability of a different result being achieved on a re-hearing. We should have to assess this probability on the basis of the information before us but without attempting to decide the issues of cruelty and condonation, as to which we have ruled that evidence could not be given at this stage. If on one or other of these bases it appears that the husband would, if he had applied promptly, have been entitled to a re-hearing, then we must go on to consider whether he should be allowed to apply out of time. Logically this question may be said to arise at the beginning of the enquiry instead of at the end, and indeed in many cases we so deal with it, but in a case such as the present one it is, I think, appropriate to see what merits there are in the case put forward for a re-hearing and only if these appear to be substantial to entertain the application for an extension of time.

Having considered the evidence before us I am satisfied that the husband believed for some time up to June 26, 1966, that the wife had abandoned or was abandoning the divorce proceedings. I base this conclusion first on the letter of Jan. 18, from the wife's solicitors and the absence of any further letter from them as they had promised; secondly, on the wife's continuing to reside with the husband and perform most of her wifely duties, even if intimate relations were

---

(11) [1963] 3 All E.R. 889; [1964] P. 420.
(12) [1965] 1 All E.R. 1003; [1965] P. 147.
(13) [1965] 1 All E.R. at p. 1010; [1965] P. at pp. 162, 163.
(14) [1942] 2 All E.R. 390; [1942] P. 151.
(15) [1949] P. 105.   (16) Ante, p. 535.

not continuing as in the past; thirdly, on his frequent requests to her to drop the proceedings and in the absence of any firm answer from her that she was continuing them; fourthly, on her deliberate concealment from him of the fact that the suit was shortly to be heard; and fifthly, on her acknowledgment in her parting note that her departure and the ensuing hearing of the divorce case would be a shock to him as I am satisfied that it was.

This belief of the husband was no doubt largely induced by his own reluctance to accept that his marriage was breaking up. If the belief had been wholly self-induced, I do not think that he could claim to have been deceived within the meaning of DAVIES, L.J.'s observations in *Stevens* v. *Stevens* (17), but in my view the wife had, by her behaviour, done much to bring about the husband's false sense of security. I do not say that she was to blame. She may or may not be right in saying that she was afraid to disclose to him her true intentions; but whatever may have been her motive, she did continue to reside with him and act in many day-to-day ways as a wife. She did ensure that he should not learn until the last moment that she was going to court for a divorce on June 27, and she never instructed her solicitors to let him know that the indecision which affected her in January and February had been resolved in favour of proceeding with her suit—never, that is, until the very last moment. For these reasons I am satisfied that up to June 26, the husband was lulled into a false sense of security, partly by the conduct of the wife. He cannot contend that he was unaware of the actual hearing, but notice of it reached him so late and in such circumstances that he cannot be blamed for not seeking to hold up the course of justice. It was a Sunday. He was shocked by the news he had received. He did not know in what court the case was to be heard. As an ordinary layman he did not know how to approach a court of justice to ask it to stay its hand. He had his own duties to attend to. He believed, in any case, that because of the cohabitation exceeding three months with his wife she must fail in her suit. In my view the false sense of security into which he had been drawn was dissipated, if at all, at too late a moment for him to have a reasonable opportunity to get the proceedings stayed.

In those circumstances I am of opinion that, subject to the question of whether he should be allowed to apply out of time, the husband is entitled to have the decree set aside without having to establish that there is a probability that on a re-hearing the result would be different. He is entitled to a re-hearing unless it is plain that that would be futile. The husband is denying the alleged cruelty and it is impossible for us to determine, and it would be quite wrong for us to attempt to determine at this stage, whether if the husband's evidence was heard, the finding of cruelty would still be made. Furthermore, facts have now come to light which, if they had been brought to the notice of the commissioner would certainly have necessitated a closer examination of the possibility of any cruelty having been condoned. The husband's defence may be a strong one or a weak one, but it is not a defence so lacking in substance that he could justly be deprived of the right of putting it forward.

This, however, is still subject to the question of whether the husband ought to be granted the indulgence of being allowed to bring this application forward some two and a half months later than the time prescribed by the rules. During the greater part of those two and a half months he was at least entitled to nurse some hope that, if he took no further step to get the decree set aside, his wife would herself apply to have it rescinded. According to the wife's own evidence he was repeatedly asking her to do this, and whether for fear of him or for some other reason, she never, up to Oct. 3, 1966, made it clear to him that she would take no such action. After Oct. 3, there was no undue delay by the husband in setting the machinery of the court in motion.

I am therefore of the opinion that he should be given leave for the application to be heard out of time and, for the reasons which I have stated earlier in this

(17) [1965] 1 All E.R. 1003; [1965] P. 147.

judgment, I consider that the decree nisi should be set aside and that there should
be an order for a re-hearing.

SIR JOCELYN SIMON, P.: I agree with all that CAIRNS, J., has said;
and in particular I express my concurrence with his findings of fact and with his
analysis of the juridical situation.

It is the essence of most systems of justice—certainly of the Anglo-American
system—that in litigation both sides of a dispute must be heard before decision.
" Audi alteram partem " was the aphorism of St. Augustine's which was adopted
by the courts at a time when Latin maxims were fashionable. Of course, if one
side does not wish to be heard, or deliberately stands aside while the other obtains
a judgment on uncontradicted evidence, it would generally be unjust to disturb
the judgment so obtained. Nevertheless, such is the importance which our law
attaches to matrimonial jurisdiction generally and in particular to litigation which
affects status, that even in such circumstances, when a party takes a deliberate
decision not to place his or her case before the court, that party will not in all
the circumstances be precluded from securing a re-hearing—for example, when
it is probable that the judgment has been obtained contrary to justice: that is
to say, that if the real facts had been known to the court the judgment would
have been to the contrary. That, however, is an exceptional case. On the other
hand, in the matrimonial jurisdiction, where a party's case is not put before the
court because that party was not apprised of the impending proceedings either
through some mishap or through the deceit of the other party, this court readily
orders a re-hearing. In my view this class of case extends to those where a party—
even though apprised of the inception of proceedings and even without any
deceit, in the strict legal sense, of the other party—is nevertheless lulled into a
sense of false security that the proceedings have lapsed. For the reasons given
by CAIRNS, J., I think that that is what happened here. Moreover, from June 27,
until October, 1966, the husband could reasonably hope that the decree nisi
would not be treated as effective but that instead there would be a reconciliation.

For that reason and for the other reasons given by CAIRNS, J., I think that the
husband's delay is excusable and I, therefore, agree with the order which CAIRNS,
J., has proposed.

Decree nisi rescinded. Order for re-hearing.

Solicitors: *Bosley & Co.*, Brighton (for the husband); *Mileham, Scatliffe &
Allen*, Brighton (for the wife).

[*Reported by* ALICE BLOOMFIELD, *Barrister-at-Law.*]

A

R. *v.* GASH.

[COURT OF APPEAL, CRIMINAL DIVISION (Lord Parker, C.J., Salmon, L.J., and Blain, J.), December 5, 1966.]

Criminal Law—Trial—Juror—Challenge—Jury same as had previously tried and convicted a person whom the accused called as a witness—Accused and witness had been together in car on occasion out of which charges against them arose—Court declined to empanel a new jury and intimated a challenge for cause would be disallowed—Venire de novo not sought—Whether conviction should be quashed.

On a Friday K. was tried and convicted at Inner London Sessions of assault on the police and of being in possession of a flick knife. On the following Monday the appellant came before the same court for trial on charges of possessing dangerous drugs and assaulting the police. The jury were the same as on the previous Friday. The charges arose out of an occasion when K. and the appellant had been together in a car which was stopped by the police. On the appellant's behalf counsel requested that a different jury should be empanelled. It was, in effect, intimated to counsel that challenge for cause would be disallowed. Accordingly peremptory challenge was made in respect of seven jurors, but no challenge for cause was made in respect of seven jurors, but no challenge for cause was made as regards the other five jurors. On appeal against conviction,

Held: if challenge for cause had been made, it should have been allowed and, since the impression had been created that, if challenge for cause were made on the ground indicated, it would be disallowed, the conviction would be quashed (see p. 812, letters H and I, post).

Appeal allowed.

[As to the effect of improper disallowance of challenge, see **23** HALSBURY'S LAWS (3rd Edn.) 28, para. 54; and for cases on the right of challenge, see **30** DIGEST (Repl.) 257-261, *136-239.*]

Appeal.

This was an appeal by Vincent Gash against his conviction at the Inner London Sessions in April, 1966, before the deputy chairman and a jury on a count of possessing dangerous drugs and on two counts of assaulting a police officer. The appellant was sentenced to a total of eighteen months' imprisonment. The facts are summarised in the judgment of LORD PARKER, C.J.

The authority and the cases noted below* were cited during the argument.

H. H. S. Montefiore for the appellant.

R. M. G. Simpson for the Crown.

LORD PARKER, C.J., delivered the following judgment of the court: The short facts are that on Feb. 10 in the early hours of the morning a police constable stopped a motor car in West London. In that car was a man called Kassem and also the appellant. The appellant was asked to get out of the car and to take his hands out of his anorak pockets. He complied reluctantly, but he refused to open his hand which he held tightly clenched. The police constable then ran his hands over the appellant's pockets, took out 3½d. in copper, a packet of cigarettes and a brown paper packet containing Indian hemp. He was arrested and cautioned, and he at once claimed that this Indian hemp had been planted. He said: " You have stolen 7s. 6d. from me, and you have planted this on me instead ". He became violent and kicked both police officers (there were two of them) on the legs and punched one of them in the stomach. According to the police, when he got to the police station he was

---

* BLACKSTONE'S COMMENTARIES, Vol. 3, p. 435; *Crane v. Director of Public Prosecutions,* [1921] All E.R. Rep. 19; [1921] 2 A.C. 299; *R.* v. *Williams,* (1925), 19 Cr. App. Rep. 67; *R.* v. *Gee, R.* v. *Bibby, R.* v. *Dunscombe,* [1936] 2 All E.R. 89; [1936] 2 K.B. 442; *R.* v. *Neal,* [1949] 2 All E.R. 438; [1949] 2 K.B. 590.

further searched and when his fists were forced open a second brown paper A
packet containing Indian hemp was discovered. He was charged and he said:
" I do not accept any of this ", and proceeded with some pretty abusive language.
He gave evidence at the trial that this was all a plant; he said that one of the
police officers had said when out by the car: " We'll have the one in the back,
that black bastard in the back ", and that they then grabbed hold of him. His
defence was a denial that he ever had any of the drug in his possession and that B
it had been planted. He called Kassem as a witness.

The only ground on which leave to appeal against conviction was given by the
full court concerns an alleged irregularity at the trial. It appears that Kassem
had been tried by this deputy chairman on the preceding Friday, when Kassem
had been found guilty of assault on the police, and of being in possession of a
flick knife. There had been a charge of possessing dangerous drugs, but he C
produced in evidence what was regarded as a lawful excuse for such possession.

It appears that on the Monday when this trial started, the same jury that had
tried Kassem and had dispersed over the week-end came back into court, and as
counsel for the appellant puts it, each of them went back to his seat in the jury
box. It was at that stage that counsel for the appellant made an application
to the court, pointing out that the jury was the same, or believed to be the same, D
and asking in effect that a different jury should be empanelled. There was a
discussion, and in the end the chairman indicated to counsel that he would not
take any steps in the matter, but he would leave it to counsel's remedy of
challenge.

Thereafter, the first seven jurors were challenged and that exhausted the
peremptory challenges, and thereafter no challenge was made for cause. The E
complaint made in this court is clearly two-fold: first, that had it been a different
jury, no counsel for the defence would ever have thought of calling Kassem;
indeed, there might well have been comment on the fact that there was another
person involved in the matter whom the prosecution had not called. Secondly
it is put in this way, that Kassem having to be called, and these jurors, or at
any rate five of them, knowing all about him, they would approach the matter F
with it firmly in mind that they remembered Kassem and did not believe a word
that he had said; and thus they would not come to the case with utterly unbiased
minds.

This court is quite satisfied that this undoubtedly discloses a grave irregularity.
It has been said that it was in a way counsel's fault that he did not pursue his
challenge for cause, but when one reads the argument that had taken place, it G
is quite clear that the deputy chairman was conveying to counsel that he had
his peremptory challenges, but that it was really useless for him to challenge for
cause because the deputy chairman in his discretion would refuse to allow a
challenge on this particular ground. The court thinks that it was because this
impression at any rate was conveyed that counsel for the defence did not challenge
for cause. The fact remains here that there were five members of the jury who H
had no business to be there. If a challenge for cause had been permitted, which
it was not, the deputy chairman must, in the proper exercise of the judicial
discretion, have acceded to the challenge.

This is a case where it might well be possible for the court to make an order
for a venire de novo, but counsel for the Crown very properly has not called on
us to make such an order, bearing in mind that the appellant has in effect almost I
served his sentence. Accordingly, in the result the court will merely quash the
conviction.

Appeal allowed. Conviction quashed.

Solicitors: *Registrar, Court of Appeal* (for the appellant); *Solicitor, Metropolitan
Police* (for the Crown).

[*Reported by* KAUSHALYA PURIE, *Barrister-at-Law.*]

Re SALISBURY RAILWAY & MARKET HOUSE CO., LTD.

[CHANCERY DIVISION (Buckley, J.), November 25, 28, December 21, 1966.]

Company—Memorandum of association—Objects—Alteration—Company incor-
porated by private Act of Parliament later registered as limited company—
Public utility—Undertaking largely fallen into disuse—Abandonment of
railway—Market house little used—Whether special resolution abandoning
its objects was ultra vires—Court had no power to authorise liquidator to
effect ultra vires transaction—Liberty to promote private Bill—Companies
Act, 1948 (11 & 12 Geo. 6 c. 38), s. 394 (2), (3) (c), s. 307.

A railway and market house were constructed at Salisbury by a company
incorporated by a private Act of Parliament passed in 1856, which, so the
court found, imposed on the company a statutory duty to maintain and
continue to operate the railway and market house for the benefit of the
public, subject to modifications by later legislation. The railway was on
the west of the river Avon and the market house, and certain other land of the
company, was on the east of the river. The railway fell into disuse; in July,
1964, its lines were taken up and sold, and on Nov. 9, 1966, an abandonment
order was made in relation to it. Of the original functions of the market
house only a limited use as a corn exchange continued after 1951; and in
1963 there were negotiations on behalf of the company with Salisbury
Corporation for the latter to establish a new corn market. On May 5, 1965,
the company was registered as a limited company under the Companies
Act, 1948, pursuant to Pt. 8 (s. 382-s. 397). On July 12, 1965, the company
entered into an agreement with the corporation that, on the company's
altering its objects in the manner therein specified and paying £8,500 to
the corporation, the corporation should provide a corn market in connexion
with the latter's cattle market which could take over the remaining functions
of the market house. Pursuant to this agreement the company passed a
special resolution on July 23, 1965, purporting to alter its objects to enable
it to abandon the objects of operating a railway and maintaining a market
house. On Dec. 31, 1965, the company went into a members' voluntary
winding-up. When the winding-up resolution was passed the members also
passed a special resolution authorising the liquidator to vest all or any of
the company's property in trustees for sale. The liquidator of the company
issued a summons asking whether the special resolution of July 23, 1965,
was valid, whether the agreement of July 12, 1965, was intra vires the
company, whether he, as liquidator, had power to sell any and if so what
parts of the company's land; and further that, if the agreement were ultra
vires the company, he might be at liberty to carry out its terms as if it were
binding, and that if he lacked power to sell any part of the company's lands
he might be at liberty to promote a Bill in Parliament to obtain suitable
powers.

Held: (i) Parliament, acting for the public interest, having authorised
the company, by special Act incorporating it, to construct and carry on a
public utility, the powers and duties conferred and imposed on the company
must be executed by the company and could not be transferred or delegated;
this principle applied in relation to the company's railway and market house,
but subject as regards the railway to the subsequent abandonment order
(see p. 820, letters A and D, p. 819, letter C, and p. 821, letter I, post).

Dictum of CAIRNS, L.J., in *Gardner* v. *London, Chatham & Dover Ry. Co.*
(No. 1) ((1867), 2 Ch. App. at p. 212) applied.

(ii) on the true construction of s. 394* of the Companies Act, 1948, particularly having regard to sub-s. (3) (c), (2), thereof, s. 394 did not enable a
company incorporated by a special Act, which expressly or by implication

---

* Section 394, so far as material, is set out at p. 824, letters C to G, post.

required the company to maintain a particular undertaking, to alter its objects so as to assume power to abandon that undertaking; accordingly, the special resolution of July 23, 1965, was ultra vires and invalid so far as the market house was concerned and the agreement of July 12, 1965, was ultra vires and invalid in so far as it required the company to close down its corn market at the market house, with the consequence that the liquidator had no power to sell the market house (see p. 826, letters A and G, post).

Re Nottingham General Cemetery Co., ([1955] 2 All E.R. 504) distinguished.

(iii) by reason of the abandonment order the company was no longer under a statutory obligation to maintain the railway; accordingly the company and the liquidator could sell all the company's land lying west of the river Avon and such land lying east of the river and north of the market house as was not required for the purposes of the market house (see p. 826, letter H, post).

(iv) the court had no power to authorise the liquidator to carry into effect the agreement of July 12, 1965, but the court would direct that the liquidator be at liberty to promote a Bill in Parliament to obtain the necessary powers (see p. 826, letter I, and p. 827, letter B, post).

Dictum of SIR HERBERT COZENS-HARDY, M.R., in *Re Woking Urban Council (Basingstoke Canal) Act, 1911* ([1914] 1 Ch. at p. 309) applied.

(v) the liquidator would have power to vest in trustees for sale those parts of the company's land of which the company and the liquidator were competent to dispose, if the trusts were so framed as to accord with the liquidator's statutory duties as liquidator, of which he could not relieve himself by conveying land to trustees (see p. 827, letter I, post).

[As to companies not formed under the Companies Act, 1948, which may register, and their power to alter their constitution, see 6 HALSBURY'S LAWS (3rd Edn.) 85, 89, paras. 178, 186.

As to the undertaking of a company incorporated under special Act and regulated by the Companies Clauses Act, 1845, see 6 HALSBURY'S LAWS (3rd Edn.) 43, para. 75, particularly text and note (*h*); and for cases on the power to sell such undertakings or to delegate statutory powers, see 10 DIGEST (Repl.) 1257-1259, *8858-8880.*

For the Companies Act, 1948, s. 307, s. 394, Sch. 1 (Table A), art. 135, see 3 HALSBURY'S STATUTES (2nd Edn.) 693, 750, 822, 823.]

Cases referred to:

Blaker v. *Herts & Essex Waterworks Co.*, (1889), 41 Ch.D. 399; 58 L.J.Ch. 997; 60 L.T. 776; 10 Digest (Repl.) 836, *5479.*

Gardner v. *London, Chatham and Dover Ry. Co. (No. 1)*, *Drawbridge* v. *Same*, *Gardner* v. *Same (No. 2)*, *Imperial Mercantile Credit Assocn.* v. *Same*, (1867), 2 Ch. App. 201; 36 L.J.Ch. 323; 15 L.T. 552; 31 J.P. 87; 10 Digest (Repl.) 1273, *8993.*

Marshall v. *South Staffordshire Tramways Co.*, [1895] 2 Ch. 36; 64 L.J.Ch. 481; 72 L.T. 542; 10 Digest (Repl.) 1284, *9074.*

Neate v. *Duke of Marlborough*, (1838), 3 My. & Cr. 407; 40 E.R. 983, L.C.; 30 Digest (Repl.) 187, *314.*

Nottingham General Cemetery Co., Re, [1955] 2 All E.R. 504; [1955] Ch. 683; [1955] 3 W.L.R. 61; 119 J.P. 443; Digest (Cont. Vol. A) 190, *6277a.*

Woking Urban Council (Basingstoke Canal) Act, 1911, Re, [1914] 1 Ch. 300; 83 L.J.Ch. 201; 110 L.T. 49; 78 J.P. 81; 10 Digest (Repl.) 1257, *8860.*

Adjourned Summons.

This was an application by originating summons dated Jan. 26, 1966, by Alexander Fletcher, who was the liquidator of the Salisbury Railway and Market House Co., Ltd., which was in a members' voluntary liquidation. The summons was issued pursuant to s. 307 of the Companies Act, 1948, and asked (i) whether or not and if so, to what extent special resolution (A)* passed at the extraordinary general meeting of the company held on July 23, 1965, was valid and effectual in conferring on the company the powers thereby purported to be conferred; (ii) whether or not and if so to what extent an agreement dated July 12, 1965, made between the company and Salisbury Corporation was intra vires the company and was then binding on the company in liquidation and on the applicant as liquidator; (iii) whether the applicant as liquidator had power, by virtue of some and if so which provision of the Salisbury Railway and Market House Act, 1856, and/or of the special resolution (A) and of s. 281 of the Companies Act, 1948, and/or s. 245 (2) (a) and s. 303 (1) (b) of the Companies Act, 1948, and/or of some and if so what other matter or statutory provision, to sell and to convey on sale any, and if only some, which, part or parts of the freehold property vested in the company; (iv) that it might be determined whether (a) the applicant had power pursuant to and in accordance with special resolution numbered 3 passed at the extraordinary general meeting held on Dec. 31, 1965, to convey to the trustees for sale any, and if only some, which part or parts, of the freehold property; and if so (b) in the event of the applicant conveying to the trustees for sale each and every part of the freehold property as he had power so to convey, whether such trustees would themselves have power (subject to any provisions contained in any instrument regulating the trust for sale) to sell and convey on sale each and every part of the freehold property; and if para. (ii) were answered in the negative, (v) for an order, if the court should deem it appropriate, that the applicant might be at liberty on behalf of the company to carry out the terms of the agreement to all intents as though it were binding; and if para. (iii) were answered in the negative with regard to any of the freehold property vested in the company, (vi) for an order that the applicant might be at liberty to promote a Bill in Parliament to obtain an Act empowering him to sell and convey such part or parts of the freehold property as he was not then empowered to sell and convey and to take such other steps as might be necessary for winding-up the affairs of the company. In any event the company by the summons sought (vii) that such directions as the court might consider necessary might be given regarding (a) the proposal that the applicant liquidator should convey to trustees for sale (pursuant to and in accordance with the special resolution numbered 3) the market house on the western side of the market place in the city of Salisbury (being part of the freehold premises vested in the company) with a view to the market house being eventually sold or failing this that the applicant should himself sell it; and (b) the period for which and the manner in which and the terms and conditions on which the company in voluntary liquidation or alternatively any such trustees for sale should continue to provide facilities for the use of the market house for the sale of corn. The next question raised by the summons related to the rights of the forty preference shareholders and the 536 ordinary shareholders of the company to share in the distribution of its surplus assets in the winding-up. The case is not reported on this question. The respondents were Dorothy Grace Whitty Bradshaw who held eight preference shares and Frank Donald Hicks who held eight ordinary shares and the Mayor, Aldermen and citizens of the city of New Sarum (" Salisbury Corporation "); representation orders were sought in respect of the classes of shareholders concerned. The facts are set out in the judgment (see p. 818, letter I, to letter A, post).

His Lordship (BUCKLEY, J.) reviewed the statutory provisions of the special Act of 1856 as follows, before stating his conclusion (see p. 820, letter D, post) that the principles of the decision in *Gardner* v. *London, Chatham and Dover Ry. Co. (No. 1)*† applied. He said that the company was incorporated by the

---

* Resolution A is set out at p. 823, letters D to G, post.
† (1867), 2 Ch. App. 201.

Salisbury Railway and Market House Act, 1856, of which the long title was as
follows—

"An Act for incorporating the Salisbury Railway and Market House
Company; for authorising them to make and maintain a railway and a
market house at Salisbury; and for other purposes."

The recitals to the Act of 1856 included the following:

"And whereas there is an ancient and well frequented market at Salisbury
for corn, cattle, cheese, and other articles: And whereas the market place
at Salisbury is at a considerable distance from the several railway stations
there, and the means of communication between the market place and those
railways are incommodious: And whereas there is no market house at
Salisbury, and the accommodation for persons frequenting the market,
and for the storage or shelter of goods brought for sale there, is insufficient:
and whereas if (as is anticipated) the consequence of the completion of the
several railways leading to Salisbury should be an increased resort to the
market, the present deficiencies of the market place and the approaches
thereto would be productive of much inconvenience, and the result might be
that dealers in corn, cattle, cheese, and some other articles might, after
experience of it, desert the market in favour of markets affording better
accommodation: And whereas by virtue of divers charters or prescription,
and an Act of the twenty-fifth year of George 3, c. 93, or otherwise, the
mayor, aldermen, and citizens of the city of Salisbury (in this Act called
'the corporation') are or claim to be entitled to divers tolls, stallages, and
dues payable in respect of the market: And whereas it would be of advantage
as well to the public as to the city of Salisbury, and it is expedient, that a
railway to form a communication between the Basingstoke and Salisbury
railway and the market house and stores to be erected under this Act at the
western side of the market place be made."

Section 4 incorporated the original corporators as a company

". . . with power to sue and be sued, and to purchase, take, hold, and
dispose of lands and other property for the purposes but subject to the
restrictions of this Act, and to put this Act in all respects into execution."

Section 21 referred, in the recital, to certain deposited plans relating to the
proposed works and to a book of reference containing the names of the owners
or reputed owners, lessees or reputed lessees, and occupiers of the lands in which
the same respectively were intended to be made, and provided as follows:

"Therefore, subject to the provisions of this Act, the company may make
and maintain the railway and the market house, and the works connected
therewith respectively, in the lines and upon the lands delineated on those
plans and described in that book of reference, and according to the levels
shown by those sections, and may enter upon, take, and use such of those
lands as they think expedient for the purpose."

The language of that section was permissive, but the effect of the section was
to give the company a compulsory power of acquisition.

Section 22 and s. 24 provided:

"22. The powers of the company for the compulsory purchase of lands
for the purposes of this Act shall not be exercised after the expiration of one
year after the passing of this Act.

"24. The railway and market house by this Act authorised comprise the
following: (to wit,) . . . [there followed a short description of the projected
railway and a short description of the market house, which was described as]
A market house, with stores and all suitable works and conveniences, on the
western side of the market place, and to be used for the sale of corn, cheese,
wool, meat, poultry, fish, vegetables, and general produce or merchandise."

A Section 26 was in language which clearly contemplated, the trial judge said, not that the railway might be built, but that it would be built; it was in the following terms.

"The junction or communication of the railway with the Basingstoke and Salisbury Railway shall be made by the Southwestern Co. . . . [i.e., the London and Southwestern Railway Co.] . . . at such point on the lands now
B vested in them or which they now have power to take as they approve, and by the most approved means, and shall be made, and from time to time altered, repaired, maintained, worked, and regulated by that company, so as to secure that the Basingstoke and Salisbury Railway be not prejudiced, and that the free, uninterrupted, and safe passage along the same be not impeded or interfered with."

C Section 29 provided:

"The railway, market house, and works shown on the deposited plans shall be respectively completed within two years after the opening for public traffic of the Basingstoke and Salisbury Railway, or within three years after the passing of this Act, whichever shall first happen, and on the
D expiration of that period the powers by this Act given to the company for executing the same, or otherwise in relation thereto, shall cease to be exercised except as to so much thereof as is then completed."

Section 30 made payment out of court of a sum lodged in court conditional on the company opening the railway for public traffic within a specified period. This made it clear beyond any doubt, the trial judge said, that the railway was
E intended to carry public traffic. The Act prescribed the tolls which the company were thereby authorised to demand and take for traffic carried on the railway. Section 37 related to agreements for certain purposes connected with the railway between the company, the London and Southwestern Railway Co., and the Salisbury and Yeovil Railway Co. Section 38 provided:

F "No such agreement shall be for more than ten years, and no such agreement shall have any operation until it be approved by the Board of Trade; and no such agreement shall increase, lessen, alter, or affect any of the tolls, rates, or charges which the companies parties thereto respectively are from time to time authorised to demand and take from any other person, but all other persons shall, notwithstanding any such agreement, be entitled to the user and benefit of the railways to which the agreement relates on the
G same terms and conditions, and on payment of the same tolls, rates, and charges, as if such agreement were not entered into."

This language clearly recognised, the trial judge said, that other persons, which must refer to members of the public, would be entitled to use the railway on making appropriate payments. The following sections dealt more particularly
H with the market house. Section 46:

"The company from time to time may appropriate such parts as they think fit of the market house and stores, and the works and conveniences thereof, to be used for the storing or sheltering of goods; and the company may from time to time appropriate such parts thereof as they think fit to be used for the sale and exposure for sale therein of corn, cheese, wool, meat,
I poultry, fish, vegetables, and general produce or merchandise at the usual and accustomed times for holding markets and fairs in the city of Salisbury."

In contrast with the permissive form of the language of s. 46, s. 48 read:

"The company shall from time to time appropriate part of the market house to be used as a corn exchange at such times and subject to such regulations as they think fit and appoint: provided always*, that except as by

---

* This proviso had been repealed, but BUCKLEY, J., intimated that the subsection might nevertheless be significant for the purpose of construing the Act of 1856.

A

this Act provided with respect to desks or like conveniences in the corn exchange, the company shall not make any charge for the user of the corn exchange, for the pitching of corn, and for the transaction therein of the business of buying or selling corn, and the corn exchange shall accordingly, at the times appointed by the company for the user thereof, be open free of charge to all persons desirous of transacting such business therein."

B

Section 49 provided:

" The company from time to time may alter or improve the market house and stores, and the works and conveniences thereof, and may make in the market house all such stalls, standings, and other conveniences, and in the corn exchange all such desks and other conveniences as they think fit, and from time to time may alter, improve, or discontinue the same."   C

It was clear, the trial judge said, that the last seven words of s. 49 " may alter, improve or discontinue the same " did not extend and apply to the market house itself, but only to " such stalls, standings " and so forth, as were mentioned in the section.   The Act of 1856 described what stallages, rents and tolls might be charged in respect of the market house; and s. 63 provided—

D

" And whereas the net yearly amount on the average of the five years ending with Sept. 1, 1855, of the income of the corporation for their markets and fairs in the city of Salisbury has not exceeded the sum of £100: therefore, in order to compensate the corporation for any of the tolls or stallages which may be diminished or prejudicially affected by this Act whenever in any year ending with Sept. 1, after the opening of the market house, the   E net income of the corporation arising from a public letting of their tolls and stallages from their markets and fairs in the city of Salisbury, as now charged, falls below the net sum of £100, the company shall pay to the corporation the sum required to make the net income of their markets and fairs for the same year £100."

W. F. Stubbs for the liquidator.   F
E. A. Seeley for Salisbury Corporation.
Allan Heyman for the representative preference shareholder.
J. R. Sykes for the representative ordinary shareholder.

Cur. adv. vult.

G

Dec. 21.   BUCKLEY, J., read the following judgment: I have already answered one question on this summons relating to the respective rights of the ordinary shareholders and the preference shareholders of the company, the Salisbury Railway and Market House Co., Ltd., to a share in the distribution of its surplus assets in its winding-up.   I have now to deal with the remaining question, which, stated shortly, asks whether, in the circumstances, which I   H must explain, the liquidator is competent to dispose of all or any, and if so which, parts of the land belonging to the company.

The company was incorporated in 1856 by private Act of Parliament for the purpose—and I quote from s. 4 of this private Act—". . . of making and maintaining the railway and market house by this Act authorised . . ."   In due course, the railway and market house were constructed, the railway on the west bank   I and the market house on the east bank of the river, immediately opposite.   In the course of time, circumstances and needs have changed.   The railway has ceased to be used and the market house has largely fallen into disuse.   In 1965, the company was re-incorporated as a limited company under the Companies Act, 1948.   By a special resolution passed on July 23, 1965, the company altered, or purported to alter, its objects so as to enable it expressly to abandon its objects of operating a railway and of providing and maintaining a market house. On Dec. 31, 1965, the company went into a members' voluntary winding-up

A and on Jan. 26, 1966, the liquidator presented the summons, which is now before the court, under s. 307 (1) of the Companies Act, 1948.

It has long been recognised that where a company has been incorporated by a special Act of Parliament for the purpose of providing some service, such as a railway, for the public benefit, the incorporating statute may, by inference if not expressly, impose a statutory duty on the company to establish and maintain

B the service in question, with the consequence that the company cannot properly dispose of any asset, such as part of its railway line, which is necessary for the maintenance of that service. In *Gardner* v. *London, Chatham and Dover Ry. Co. (No. 1)* (1), CAIRNS, L.J., said:

" When Parliament, acting for the public interest, authorises the con-struction and maintenance of a railway, both as a highway for the public,
C and as a road on which the company may themselves become carriers of passengers and goods, it confers powers and imposes duties and responsibilities of the largest and most important kind, and it confers and imposes them upon the company which Parliament has before it, and upon no other body of persons. These powers must be executed and these duties discharged by the company. They cannot be delegated or transferred."

D In *Marshall* v. *South Staffordshire Tramways Co.* (2), debenture holders of the defendant company were held not to be entitled to enforce a sale of the company's undertaking. The judgment of the Court of Appeal was delivered by LINDLEY, L.J., who said this (3):

" Speaking generally, the owner of an equitable charge or lien on property
E as a security for money which is due and payable has a right to a judicial sale of that property in order to satisfy the charge or lien: see *Neate* v. *Duke of Marlborough* (4). But this right does not extend to property, or what is called an undertaking, which has been acquired under statutory powers for public purposes, if those purposes will be defeated, or at all events seriously affected, by a judicial sale. This exception to the general rule is as well
F settled as the rule itself: see *Gardner* v. *London, Chatham and Dover Ry. Co. (No. 1)* (5)."

In *Blaker* v. *Herts and Essex Waterworks Co.* (6), the same principle was held to apply to a waterworks company. In *Re Woking Urban Council (Basingstoke Canal) Act, 1911*, (7), the same principle was held to apply to a canal. SIR HERBERT COZENS-HARDY, M.R., said (8):

G " Throughout the Act of 1777, in conferring rights or imposing obligations upon the company, the words ' successors or assigns ' are added. Such words are meaningless as words of limitation in a conveyance to a corporation aggregate; and in the case of a statutory company formed for the purpose of carrying on a public undertaking, I think it is clear that the company could not assign the undertaking, with its rights and obligations. The well-known
H judgment of CAIRNS, L.J., in *Gardner* v. *London, Chatham and Dover Ry. Co. (No. 1)* (9) applies; for there is, for this purpose, no distinction between a canal company and a railway company."

He later said (10):

" I think nothing passed by the conveyance, for it purported to pass
I that without which this statutory undertaking could not be carried on, and was, therefore, ultra vires the company. In saying this, I do not refer to any surplus lands, or to property which might be parted with without damage to the undertaking. The proper course for the liquidator to have taken was

---

(1) (1867), 2 Ch. App. 201 at p. 212.   (2) [1895] 2 Ch. 36.
(3) [1895] 2 Ch. at p. 50.   (4) (1838), 3 My. & Cr. 407 at p. 417.
(5) (1867), 2 Ch. App. 201.   (6) (1889), 41 Ch.D. 399.
(7) [1914] 1 Ch. 300.   (8) [1914] 1 Ch. at p. 307.
(9) (1867), 2 Ch. App. at p. 212.   (10) [1914] 1 Ch. at p. 309.

to have applied for a private Act of Parliament authorising the transfer of   A
the undertaking to the purchaser."

The first question, therefore, for consideration in the present case is whether the
principle stated by CAIRNS, L.J. (11) applies in the present circumstances.

[HIS LORDSHIP reviewed the provisions of the Salisbury Railway and Market
House Act, 1856, as set out previously (see p. 816, et seq., ante) and continued:]
The obligation under s. 63 of the Act of 1856 (12) is, apparently, one which is   B
intended to continue indefinitely. Section 48, s. 49 and s. 63 do not contemplate,
I think, the possibility of the company ceasing at any time to operate the market
house. The recitals to that Act indicate that the Act was aimed at advancing the
convenience and benefit of the public and the recitals and sections to which I
have referred together indicate that the railway and the market house were alike
intended to be maintained as public utilities. The railway, although it only   C
comprised a short length of line, was, in my judgment, in pari materia with the
railway which was under discussion in *Gardner* v. *London, Chatham and Dover
Ry. Co. (No. 1)* (13). The market house also, in my judgment, was intended as a
public utility for the benefit of the public and was intended to be carried on
indefinitely. The principles referred to in the case which I have cited, accordingly,
seem to me to apply in the present case.   D

This conclusion is, I think, reinforced by two later special Acts relating to the
company. The first of these is an Act, the short title of which is The London
and Southwestern Railway Act, 1857. The recital to that Act referred to a
number of special Acts of Parliament including the Act of 1856 with which I
have been dealing. The recitals contained the following.

" And whereas by the Market Act [that is the Act of 1856] the Market   E
Co. [and that is the company with which I am concerned] were authorised
to make and maintain a short line of railway from their market house in
Salisbury, to communicate with the authorised line of the Basingstoke and
Salisbury railway: And whereas, by reason of the line and levels of the
portion of railway by this Act authorised to be made instead of the portions   F
of railway to be abandoned by the South-western company and the Salisbury
and Yeovil Co. respectively being different from the line and levels of
the authorised Basingstoke and Salisbury railway, an alteration of the line
and levels of the market house railway will be requisite; and it is therefore
expedient that the Market Co. be authorised to abandon a part of their
authorised railway, and that the South-western Co. be authorised to make in
lieu thereof a railway, to form a line of communication between the residue   G
of the market house railway and the Basingstoke and Salisbury railway:
And whereas it is expedient that the South-western Co. and the market
company be authorised to make arrangements with respect to the making,
maintaining, managing, using, and working of the railway to be so made by
the South-western company, and the apportionment and regulation of the
tolls, rates and duties in respect of the same."   H

This clearly infers, it seems to me, if it does not state in terms, that the company
could not abandon any part of its authorised railway without statutory authority.
The Act provided that the company should abandon the making of part of its
railway, that the London and Southwestern Ry. Co. should construct a piece
of line in place of that abandoned, which, on payment of a certain sum, should   I
be vested in and henceforth maintained by the company as part of its railway
authorised by the Act of 1856.

In 1864, another special Act, entitled The Salisbury Railway and Market
House Company Act, 1864, was enacted, the recitals of which include the following.

" Whereas the Salisbury Railway and Market House Co. (herein-after

(11) (1867), 2 Ch. App. at p. 212.
(12) Section 63 is set out at p. 818, letters D and E, ante.
(13) (1867), 2 Ch. App. 201.

called the company) were incorporated by ' The Salisbury Railway and Market House Act, 1856', (herein-after called the company's Act), and were thereby empowered to establish a market house to be used for the sale of corn, cheese, wool, meat, poultry, fish, vegetables, and general produce or merchandise, and to make a short railway forming a communication between the market house and the Basingstoke and Salisbury Railway: And whereas the works connected with the market house and railway have been completed: and whereas the resort of farmers and others to the market house for the transaction of business in buying and selling of corn is large and increasing, and the market house has never been used for the sale of other commodities than corn and cheese, and could not conveniently accommodate a market for the sale of general produce and merchandise, and it is expedient that for the future the market house be used for the exclusive purpose of dealing in corn, cheese, and wool, and that the company be empowered to make reasonable charges for the use of the corn exchange established by them in the market house, as directed by the Company's Act (s. 48): And whereas the objects aforesaid cannot be effected without the authority of Parliament."

Section 4 provided:

" So much of s. 24 and s. 46 respectively of the Company's Act as directs or authorises the user or appropriation of the market house for the sale or exposure for sale therein of meat, poultry, fish, vegetables, and general produce or merchandise is hereby repealed."

By s. 6, the proviso to s. 48 of the Act of 1856 was repealed (14). This enactment of the Act of 1864 supports the view that without statutory sanction the company could not abandon any of its functions relating to the market house as envisaged by the Act of 1856. I must proceed, therefore, I think, on the footing that the Act of 1856 imposed on the company a statutory duty to construct, maintain and continue to operate for the benefit of the public the railway and market house as therein mentioned, but subject to the modifications introduced by the Acts of 1857 and 1864.

The railway and market house were constructed and used as contemplated by the Acts. In course of time the undertaking atrophied, the traffic on the railway diminished and also the use of the market house. Since about the year 1899 there has been a power station to the south of the company's railway line. The principal regular use to which the railway was put after the year 1939 (or there-abouts) was the bringing of coal along its line for consumption at this power station. No corn was brought to the market house or taken from it by rail (except perhaps very occasionally) after 1913. No cheese was brought or taken by rail after 1903. Wool sales continued until 1940 and although large quantities of wool were brought in by road only, a considerable quantity was dispatched by rail after the sales, but this use only continued for a few days annually and ceased after 1940. In about the year 1962 the power station started to use oil instead of coal and for this and other reasons the use of the railway line for this purpose ceased. It was apparent in 1962 that there was no chance of anything but sporadic and insignificant use of the railway line for any purpose, and no chance of its use for the movement of corn, cheese or wool to or from the market house at all. Since the beginning of July, 1964, the railway—that is to say, the lines—has been completely disused and it is virtually certain that it will never again be used for any purpose. The lines were sold and taken up in the year 1964 and the other fittings, gear and sleepers were then dismantled. On Nov. 9, 1966, the Minister of Transport made an abandonment order under the Transport Act, 1962, s. 83, in relation to the railway. Such an order has the effect of releasing the undertakers from any statutory obligation to maintain or operate the railway to which it relates. The lands vested in the company and lying to the west of the

---

(14) The proviso to s. 48 is set out at p. 817, letter I, to p. 818, letter A, ante.

river Avon, so far as not occupied by and used for the purposes of the company's
railway undertaking, have, from time to time, been put to various uses not connected directly or at all with the company's undertaking. They are now largely
derelict, but part of them is leased to a building material company for a term
having only a short period to run and other parts are put to more or less casual
uses.

The market house stands on the east bank of the river. Down to the year 1941,
it was put to the following uses. (a) The corn market was conducted there. (b)
Monthly cheese sales took place in the market house until the year 1903. (c)
Various items were stored therein including corn, agricultural machinery and stalls
used for the neighbouring open market. (d) The volunteers and the territorials
had regular drills and parades therein until 1935. (e) Annual wool sales lasting
several days in July each year took place until July 1940. (f) The market house
was also used from time to time for meetings, dinners, shows, sales and the like.
(g) From about 1930 onwards the game of badminton was played. In the year
1941 the market house was requisitioned by the Ministry of Food and the company had no control over it until Jan. 2, 1951, when it was derequisitioned. While
the market house was requisitioned the Corn Exchange was carried on in the
neighbouring British Legion Hall, but other uses ceased. Of the original functions
of the market house, as contemplated by the Act of 1856, the only one which was
resumed after the year 1951 and which it now discharges is that of a corn exchange
where corn is sold by sample. This corn exchange operates for a few hours on
Tuesdays and for this purpose about seventy-five firms still either rent desks from
the company or have desks of their own in the market house at which they
conduct business. These desks are situated within the central area of the market
house. There are a number of ticket-holders who are entitled to attend sessions
of the corn market on Tuesdays (desk-holders are automatically entitled to two
tickets each) and members of the public can also attend on payment of the
appropriate fee. Having regard to the very limited user of the market house at
the present time as a corn exchange, the company has attempted to gain revenue
from it in other small ways. Thus, part of the galleries is now used for storage
by a neighbouring department store. Three badminton clubs hire the market
house and play badminton on the central area throughout the winter season;
the desks are moved aside for this purpose, and it has in recent times been one of
the company's few constant sources of revenue. The market house has also been
used for various functions such as the Three Counties Cat Show, wrestling
matches, carpet sales, and so forth. A number of vehicles are permitted to park
there. The rest of the company's land to the east of the river Avon lies immediately to the north of the market house and is let and is occupied for use as a
bank, business offices and storage space.

As early as the year 1930 there were tentative negotiations with the corporation
for the purchase by the corporation either of the market house or alternatively
of the share capital of the company. These negotiations recognised that the
corporation might be better suited than the company for carrying on the activities
of the market house; and in part were motivated by a realisation on the part of
the company that the site of the market house had a considerable value even then.
However, these negotiations were fruitless. With the gradual decline in the
business carried on at the market house, and particularly after the discontinuation
of the railway in the year 1962, it became more and more apparent that the
company was ceasing to serve any useful function, except with regard to the
remaining activities, hereinbefore described, of the corn market. Accordingly
the directors of the company became more and more conscious that their duty
towards the company's shareholders might require them to explore the possibility
of realising the company's freehold properties. With a view to reconciling these
duties with such duties as they might have regarding the continuation of the corn
exchange, in about the year 1963 they entered into negotiations with the corporation with a view to the latter, in consideration of a cash payment by the company,

A establishing a new corn market at Scamells Road, Salisbury, which could take over the remaining functions of the market house. All the agricultural and cattle markets in Salisbury were moved from the market place to a new site in Scamells Road, developed for the purpose by the corporation, and where there is a restaurant and a car park and other modern facilities.

B With a view to overcoming the possible lack of power in the company to carry its scheme into effect the company was registered on May 5, 1965, as a limited company under Part 8 of the Companies Act, 1948. On July 12, 1965, the company, as so incorporated, entered into an agreement with Salisbury corporation whereby it was agreed that on the company altering its objects in the manner therein specified and paying £8,500 to the corporation the corporation should provide a corn market in connexion with the cattle market at Scamells Road

C to be carried on as nearly as possible in the same manner as the existing corn market and the company should close down its corn market at the market house. Pursuant to this agreement, on July 23, 1965, the company passed a special resolution, in the following terms:

D " (A) THAT the provisions deemed under s. 394 of the Companies Act, 1948, to be conditions and regulations of the company inserted in a registered memorandum of association of the company be altered with respect to the objects of the company so as to enable it: (a) To abandon its objects of operating a railway and providing and maintaining a market house to be used for the sale of corn cheese or wool. Provided however that the company shall not be empowered to close down the corn market now carried on by the

E company at the market house on the western side of the market place in the city of Salisbury without first making such arrangement or payments to secure to the satisfaction of the mayor aldermen and citizens of New Sarum (hereinafter called ' the corporation ') the provision of alternative facilities for a corn market in Salisbury. (b) For the purpose aforesaid to pay to the corporation the sum of £8,500 to the intent that the corporation shall

F provide facilities for and shall conduct a corn market at the corporation's cattle market in Scamells Road in the same city of Salisbury in place of the said corn market now carried on by the company aforesaid. (c) For the purpose aforesaid to assist the corporation in carrying on and promoting its said corn market. (d) To sell all or any part of the undertaking of the company."

G The company, at the same meeting, also passed a further special resolution under the letter (B); with that, I am not particularly concerned. On this resolution being presented for filing the registrar of companies questioned the power of the company to alter its objects in the manner intended to be achieved by the resolution. The resolution has, however, been filed at the registry.

On Dec. 31, 1965, the company went into a members' voluntary winding-up.

H The company and the corporation have for the time being treated the 1965 agreement as being valid, notwithstanding the views advanced on behalf of the registrar of companies. The corporation is temporarily prevented by governmental direction from proceeding with the establishment of a new corn market at the cattle market pursuant to the 1965 agreement, but intends to proceed as soon as possible and it is envisaged that this new corn market will be completed

I by about the month of August, 1967. Since the winding-up of the company, the corn exchange has continued to function in the market house as theretofore; and the other functions of the market house have also continued. The liquidator, pursuant to s. 285 (2) of the Act of 1948, has sanctioned a continuation of the powers of the directors of the company in order that they should be reponsible for ensuring and supervising the functioning of the corn market and the continuation of the other facilities provided at the market house. It is intended that the corn exchange should continue to function in the market house until the new corn exchange is completed.

The liquidator, by this summons, asks (1) whether the special resolution of July 23, 1965, was valid; (2) whether the agreement of July 12, 1965, was intra vires the company; (3) whether he as liquidator has power to sell any and if so what parts of the company's lands. He also asks (4) that, if the agreement in question were not intra vires the company, he might nevertheless be at liberty to carry out its terms as if it were binding on the company; and (6) if he lacks power to sell any part of the company's lands, that he may be at liberty to promote a Bill in Parliament to obtain suitable powers. These questions involve consideration of what seems to be a novel question of construction of the Companies Act, 1948, s. 394.

The relevant parts of that section are as follows:

" (1) When a company is registered in pursuance of this Part [i.e., Part 8] of this Act, the following provisions of this section shall have effect.

" (2) All provisions contained in any Act of Parliament or other instrument constituting or regulating the company, including, in the case of a company registered as a company limited by guarantee, the resolution declaring the amount of the guarantee, shall be deemed to be conditions and regulations of the company, in the same manner and with the same incidents as if so much thereof as would, if the company had been formed under this Act, have been required to be inserted in the memorandum, were contained in a registered memorandum, and the residue thereof were contained in registered articles.

" (3) All the provisions of this Act shall apply to the company, and the members, contributories and creditors thereof, in the same manner in all respects as if it had been formed under this Act, subject as follows: . . . (c) subject to the provisions of this section the company shall not have power to alter any provision contained in any Act of Parliament relating to the company; (d) subject to the provisions of this section the company shall not have power, without the sanction of the Board of Trade, to alter any provision contained in any letters patent relating to the company; (e) the company shall not have power to alter any provision contained in a royal charter or letters patent with respect to the objects of the company.

" (5) Nothing in this section shall authorise the company to alter any such provisions contained in any instrument constituting or regulating the company, as would, if the company had originally been formed under this Act, have been required to be contained in the memorandum and are not authorised to be altered by this Act."

Counsel for the ordinary shareholder's submissions may be put shortly thus. By virtue of s. 394 (2), every provision of the company's special Acts must be deemed to be contained either in a registered memorandum of association or in registered articles of association and with the same incidents as if they were so contained. So far as those provisions relate to the objects of the company they must be treated as contained in a notional memorandum of association, since s. 2 requires a company's memorandum to state its objects. One of the incidents of objects set out in a company's memorandum of association is that by reason of s. 4 they cannot be altered except in accordance with the provisions of the Act, but that by virtue of s. 5 they can be altered by special resolution so far as such alteration may be required to enable the company to achieve any of the ends specified in s. 5 (1). Those ends include the abandonment of any of the company's objects and the disposal of the whole or any part of its undertaking. In any event, the validity of such an alteration cannot be questioned on the ground that it was not authorised by s. 5 (1) except in proceedings brought within a limited period which has expired in the present case (see s. 5 (9)). It is thus an incident of objects contained in a company's registered memorandum of association that they may be altered in the manner in which the company has purported to alter its objects by the special resolution of July 23, 1965. Therefore, by virtue of s. 394 (2), that alteration of the company's objects was valid. Moreover, counsel for the ordinary shareholder

A submits that the application of s. 5 to the company's objects is made clear by s. 394 (3), unless it is excluded under any of the sub-paragraphs of that sub-section. The only directly relevant paragraph is para. (c) which is itself expressed to be " subject to the provisions of this section " or, in other words, except as permitted by the section. Nevertheless, says counsel, since the words " with the same incidents " in sub-s. (2) have the effect of importing the statutory power of B altering a company's objects conferred by s. 5, what was done in the present case was something permitted by s. 394, and so was not excluded by sub-s. (3) (c).

If this argument is sound it would seem necessarily to follow that, no matter how clearly Parliament might have imposed continuing statutory obligations on a company which was not originally incorporated under the Companies Act, 1948, or any of its predecessors, but which after the imposition of those obligations C registered under Part 8 of the Act of 1948, such registration would enable the company to escape altogether from its statutory obligations by adopting a course similar to that taken by the company in the present case. It seems to me im-probable that Parliament should have intended this. Moreover, if this were the intention it would render s. 394 (3) (c) inoperative, for under sub-s. (2) every statutory provision constituting or regulating the company must be treated as D contained either in the company's notional memorandum of association or in its notional articles of association. In the case of a company incorporated under the Companies Act, 1948, all provisions so contained would be capable of alteration under the Act of 1948. The consequence of the argument of counsel for the ordinary shareholder would therefore be that all the statutory provisions con-stituting or regulating a company which registered under Part 8 would be capable E of alteration. There would be no statutory provision relating to the company which the company was not, by the terms of s. 394, authorised to alter and, consequently, no statutory provision to which sub-s. (3) (c) could apply.

In my judgment, the fallacy in the argument lies in attributing too wide an effect to the words " and with the same incidents ". So long as any statutory provision constituting or regulating a company which registers under Part 8 of F the Act of 1948 remains a regulation of the company deemed to be contained in that company's notional memorandum of association it is to have the same effect as it would if the company were incorporated under the Act of 1948 and the regula-tion in question were contained in its memorandum of association. A company's power of altering the contents of its memorandum of association is not, in my judgment, an " incident " of those contents. They can only be truly said to G possess " incidents " so long as they remain operative. Death is not an incident of life, nor is alteration or abandonment of an object or regulation, nor even the right or power to alter or abandon it, an incident of that object or regulation.

The presence of the words " subject to the provisions of this section " in s. 394 (3) (c) leads one to look for something in the section authorising the alteration of statutory provisions, and if none could be found except by construing sub-s. (2) H in some other way than that which I have indicated, one might feel obliged to consider another construction, but such a power is to be found in sub-s. (4). The provisions of the Act of 1948 which are referred to in that subsection all derive from the Companies Act, 1879, when corresponding provisions first became part of the corpus of company legislation. It is, perhaps, significant that, whereas the provision in the Companies Act, 1862, namely s. 196 (3), which was the fore-I runner of the present s. 394 (3) (c), was in the unqualified terms " That no com-pany shall have power to alter any provision contained in any Act of Parliament relating to the company ", the corresponding provision of the Companies (Con-solidation) Act, 1908, namely, s. 263 (ii) (c), was couched in the same terms as the present s. 394 (3) (c). This was the first amendment of s. 196 (3) of the Act of 1862 following the enactment of the Act of 1879; but it would be right also to notice that in the meantime the Companies (Memorandum of Association) Act, 1890, had also been passed, which considerablly extended the very limited power of altering a company's memorandum of association which existed under the Act of 1862.

For these reasons, I feel unable to accept the argument presented to me. In my judgment, on the true construction of s. 394 it does not enable a company incorporated by a special Act, which expressly or by implication requires that company to maintain a particular undertaking, to alter its objects so as to assume power to abandon that undertaking.

In *Re Nottingham General Cemetery Co.* (15), WYNN-PARRY, J., had to consider whether the liquidator of a company incorporated by a special Act to establish and maintain a cemetery could disclaim the land constituting the company's cemetery. Dealing with a contention that the special Act incorporating the company implied the positive obligation to continue to carry on its undertaking indefinitely and the further obligation not to alienate that undertaking and, therefore, not to alienate its land without which the undertaking could not be carried on, and that it therefore followed that the company could alienate its land only on the authority of a further special Act of Parliament, the learned judge referred to *Re Woking Urban Council (Basingstoke Canal) Act, 1911,* (16) and said that that case bound him if it was applicable to the facts of the case before him. He went on (17):

" I take the view, however, that that case has no application to the case before me. The Act which was considered by the Court of Appeal was the act of selling land without which the undertaking could not be carried on; an act which was ultra vires the company. In the present case, the act for which authority is sought is the disposal of land because the undertaking has by force of circumstances come to an end, or is about to come to an end."

In *Re Nottingham General Cemetery Co.* (15) Parliament had, in 1923, enacted that, subject to certain limited exceptions, burials in the company's cemetery should be discontinued, in consequence of which the company's business had so far declined that it had become clear that the company could not continue to carry it on. In the present case Parliament has not in any way modified or extended the statutory obligation of the company to maintain its market house undertaking, except so far as it was modified by the Act of 1864, and, in fact, that undertaking is still being carried on, although not so actively as formerly, and could still be so carried on. In my opinion, I cannot here take the same view as was taken by WYNN-PARRY, J., in that case.

For these reasons, I am of opinion that the special resolution of July 23, 1965, was ultra vires the company and invalid so far as the market house is concerned and that the agreement of July 12, 1965, was also ultra vires and invalid insofar as it required the company to close down its corn market at the market house and to use its best endeavours to assist the corporation in promoting its new corn market. It follows from the invalidity of the resolution that the liquidator has no power to sell the market house. Nevertheless, by reason of the abandonment order the company is no longer under a statutory obligation in respect of its railway. The company and its liquidator are, in my judgment, competent to sell all the company's land lying west of the river Avon. The company's land lying to the east of the river and to the north of the market house is not required for the purposes of the market house undertaking and can be sold without in any way affecting that undertaking. In my judgment, the company and its liquidator are competent to sell this land.

This court has no power to authorise the liquidator to carry into effect any agreement which is ultra vires the company, and, accordingly, I cannot give the liquidator liberty to carry the agreement of July 12, 1965, into effect, as if those of its provisions which were ultra vires the company were nevertheless binding.

---

(15) [1955] 2 All E.R. 504; [1955] Ch. 683.
(16) [1914] 1 Ch. 300.
(17) [1955] 2 All E.R. at p. 510; [1955] Ch. at p. 694.

Counsel appearing for the corporation has suggested that the Food and Drugs Act, 1955, s. 49, may afford a solution for this difficulty. That section empowers local authorities to acquire market undertakings by agreement, but it cannot, in my judgment, clothe the company with any power that it lacks.

As regards the market house, the position is, I think, what Sir Herbert Cozens-Hardy, M.R., found to be the case in *Re Woking Urban Council (Basingstoke Canal) Act, 1911*, (18). The proper course is for the liquidator to apply for a private Act authorising the company to carry its arrangement with the corporation into effect or to dispose of its market house and market house undertaking in some other way. I will direct that the liquidator be at liberty to promote a Bill in Parliament accordingly. I regret reaching this conclusion, for a private Act is a cumbrous and expensive method of achieving an end which seems to be in the public interest or, at any rate, of reorganising the corn market in a way which should adequately protect the public interest; but, Parliament having, as I think, required the company to provide and maintain this public utility, Parliament is the proper body to decide whether, in the existing circumstances, the company should be released from this obligation and on what terms.

When the winding-up resolution was passed the company also passed a special resolution authorising the liquidator to vest all or any part of the company's property in trustees for sale. That resolution was in these terms.

" THAT the said Alexander Fletcher or other the the liquidator for the time being of the company for the purposes of its voluntary winding-up, be and he is hereby authorised, in his discretion: (a) to vest all or any part of the property and assets of the company in such trustees for sale, and by means of an instrument or instruments containing such terms and provisions (including provisions for indemnifying any such trustees), and generally in such manner, as he shall think fit, but so that the net proceeds of sale of any property or assets so vested and the net rents and profits until sale of such property or assets, subject to the payment therefrom in so far as may be requisite of the debts and liabilities of the company provable in such winding-up and the costs and expenses of such winding-up, shall be divisible amongst the shareholders of the company in such proportions as are necessary to give effect to the rights of such shareholders respectively to participate in the surplus assets of the company remaining in its winding-up after the payment of all such debts, liabilities, costs, charges and expenses as aforesaid; and (b) to execute and do, and to concur in executing and doing, all such other acts, deeds and things as may seem to him to be necessary or desirable with a view to, or in any way in relation to, any such vesting of property or assets as aforesaid."

By the summons the liquidator asks whether he has power pursuant to and in accordance with that resolution to convey any and if so what parts of the company's land to trustees for sale for the benefit of the shareholders, and whether, in the event of his doing so, such trustees could themselves sell any property so conveyed to them.

The liquidator is under a statutory duty to ensure that the liabilities of the company which are proved in the winding-up are duly discharged, to pay the expenses of the winding-up and, subject thereto, to procure the distribution of any surplus assets among the members in accordance with their rights. He cannot relieve himself of this duty by conveying any of the company's property to trustees, but if the trusts are so framed as to accord with the liquidator's duties there is, I think, no reason why he should not convey to trustees any of those parts of the company's land, of which the company is competent to dispose. Article 135 of Table A in Sch. 1 of the Companies Act, 1948, contemplates an arrangement of this kind. In the event of the company by its liquidator conveying any of the

---

(18) [1914] 1 Ch. 300.

company's land to trustees for sale the trustees will, subject, of course, to the
terms of their trust, have the same power of sale as the company has.

Order accordingly.

Solicitors: *Burchell & Ruston*, agents for *Pye-Smith, Hulbert & Kildahl*,
Salisbury (for the liquidator); *Sharpe, Pritchard & Co.*, agents for the *Town
Clerk*, Salisbury (for Salisbury Corpn.); *Field, Roscoe & Co.*, agents for *Tanner,
Vowles & Cheshire*, Bristol (for the representative preferential shareholder);
Oswald Hickson, Collier & Co., agents for *Trethowans*, Salisbury (for the repre-
sentative ordinary shareholder).

[*Reported by* JENIFER SANDELL, *Barrister-at-Law.*]

PRACTICE DIRECTION.

CHANCERY DIVISION.

*Ward of Court—Application to Chancery Division to make infant a ward of court—
Production of summons at the office of the chief master—Practice—Relationship of applicant to ward to be stated—R.S.C., Ord. 91, r. 1 (3).*

Order 91, r. 1 (3) of the Rules of the Supreme Court directs that immediately
an originating summons for wardship has been issued, the applicant MUST
produce the summons at the office of the chief master (room 169) for recording in
the register of wards.

On the production of the originating summons the applicant will be required
to state the relationship of the plaintiff to the ward. If the recording officer is
in any doubt as to the propriety of the application, he will immediately refer the
matter to the appropriate master. If the master considers that the application
for wardship is an abuse of the process of the court he may dismiss the originating
summons forthwith or refer the point to the judge.

By direction of CROSS, J.

W. F. S. HAWKINS
Chief Master
Feb. 28, 1967.   Chancery Division.

R. *v.* RICHARDS.

[COURT OF APPEAL, CRIMINAL DIVISION (Winn, L.J., MacKenna and Willis, JJ.), February 3, 1967.]

Criminal Law—Evidence—Police—Statement to police—Inducement—Trial judge to decide whether statement so obtained was voluntary.

A police officer said to the appellant, at a time when already a number of questions had been asked and he had been pressed somewhat about his movements during a certain afternoon and had made lying replies:— " I think it would be better if you made a statement and told me exactly what happened." The appellant then made a statement which amounted to a confession. The words of the police officer, coming from a person in authority, were capable of constituting an inducement to make a statement. At the trial the chairman admitted the statement de bene esse. On appeal against conviction,

Held: it was for the chairman himself to decide whether or not the appellant's statement was a voluntary one and, as he had not done so, the statement went before the jury improperly (see p. 830, letter H, to p. 831, letter A, post); further, since the court could not be sure that, if the statement had not been admitted and relied on as an integral part of the prosecution's case, the appellant would have been convicted, the conviction would be quashed (see p. 831, letter F, and p. 832, letter A, post).

Stirland v. *Director of Public Prosecutions* ([1944] 2 All E.R. 13) applied.

Appeal allowed.

[As to admissions or confessions made by a defendant before trial, see 10 HALSBURY'S LAWS (3rd Edn.) 469-470, paras. 860-862; and for cases on the subject, see 14 DIGEST (Repl.) 468, 469, *4508-4526*, 480-486, *4578-4649*.

As to the test for the applicability of the proviso, see 10 HALSBURY'S LAWS (3rd Edn.) 536, para. 985, note (*s*).]

Cases referred to:

Comrs. of Customs and Excise v. *Harz*, ante p. 177; [1967] 2 W.L.R. 297.

R. v. *Cleary*, (1963), 48 Cr. App. Rep. 116; Digest (Cont. Vol. A) 398, *6625a*.

R. v. *Priestley*, (1966), 50 Cr. App. Rep. 183.

R. v. *Smith*, [1959] 2 All E.R. 193; [1959] 2 Q.B. 35; [1959] 2 W.L.R. 623; 123 J.P. 295; 43 Cr. App. Rep. 121; Digest (Cont. Vol. A) 369, *4517a*.

Stirland v. *Director of Public Prosecutions*, [1944] 2 All E.R. 13; [1944] A.C. 315; 113 L.J.K.B. 394; 171 L.T. 78; 109 J.P. 1; sub nom. *R.* v. *Stirland*, 30 Cr. App. Rep. 40; 14 Digest (Repl.) 511, *4949*.

Appeal.

This was an appeal by Leslie Charles Richards against his conviction on Aug. 16, 1966, at South East London Sessions before the chairman (T. R. FITZWALTER BUTLER, Esq.) and a jury on two counts of housebreaking with intent to commit a felony. He was sentenced on Aug. 17, 1966, to concurrent terms of twelve months' imprisonment. He also appealed against his sentence. The facts are set out in the judgment of the court.

The authorities and cases noted below* were cited during the argument in addition to the cases referred to in the judgment of the court.

M. Waters for the appellant.

D. A. Paiba for the Crown.

WINN, L.J., delivered the following judgment of the court: The full court gave leave to appeal on one point only, which was whether in the circumstances

---

* ARCHBOLD'S CRIMINAL PLEADING, EVIDENCE AND PRACTICE (36th Edn.) para. 1115; CROSS ON EVIDENCE (2nd Edn.) 445; *Makin* v. *A.-G. for New South Wales*, [1891-94] All E.R. Rep. 24; [1893] A.C. 57; *R.* v. *Francis*, *R.* v. *Murphy*, (1959), 43 Cr. App. Rep. 174.

Dictum of WINN LJ at 830 applied in R v ISEQUILLA [1975] 1 All ER 77

of this case a certain purported confession or statement containing guilty admis- A
sions, which undoubtedly the appellant did make to a police officer, was or was
not admissible evidence against him at his trial.   The point was one which the
appellant in his application for leave to appeal not unnaturally failed himself to
take, but one which the court, in the discharge of its function to have
regard to all the possible grounds of appeal which may be possessed by a person
seeking the assistance of the court, took in his favour.   It may be stated in this B
way.   It is clear law and has been for generations in this country, for reasons
which were perhaps plainer when at one time men could not give evidence on
their own behalf than now, that no statement which has been induced or which
may have been induced by any promise or threat made by a person in authority
is admissible evidence against the maker of the statement.   It is now clear,
further, that it is immaterial, if the inducement be made by the person in authority, C
whether or not it has any reference to any pending charge, any pending prosecution, or any potential prosecution.   Whatever be the nature of the inducement
so made and however trivial it may seem to the average man to have been, such
an inducement will be at least capable of rendering the statement then made
inadmissible; it will have that effect unless in a given case it becomes plain
beyond a reasonable doubt that it did not operate at all on the mind of the D
person to whom it was made.   I refer only in passing, and without going into
the reasoning of the cases, to the decisions in *R. v. Cleary* (1), *R. v. Smith* (2)
and *Comrs. of Custom and Excise* v. *Harz* (3), recently pronounced in their lordships' House.   It is for consideration whether the decision of this court in *R. v.
Priestley* (4)—a fairly recent decision—is wholly consonant with those decisions.

Here, a police officer said to the appellant at a time when already a number of E
questions had been asked and he had been pressed somewhat about his movements during the material afternoon and had made lying replies, " I think it
would be better if you made a statement and told me exactly what happened ",
and a statement was then made.   Clearly that was something coming from a
person in authority, capable of constituting an inducement.   It does not matter
how mild may be the inducement so made, as is illustrated by *R. v. Smith* (2), F
where a sergeant-major addressed troops on parade about a theft which had been
discovered and, if my memory serves me correctly, said " None of you will go
off parade until I know the truth about this ".   This sphere of inducement is
quite separate from the sphere in which persons not in authority make promises
or threats which are alleged subsequently to have induced a statement or confession.   In that latter sphere the essential question is always what was in fact the G
effect of the inducement?   Did it go so far as to deprive the person to whom it
was made of free will and choice whether he would or would not make a statement
as he did?   For the reason that this was an inducement given by a person in
authority the court thinks that the trial within a trial which took place here
was not satisfactorily conducted.   The learned chairman, despite his great
experience and knowledge, did not apply his mind to the essential questions which H
he had to determine before ruling, as he did, that the matter should be left to
the jury to decide whether or not the appellant was induced to make the statement.   It was for the learned chairman at that stage to decide himself whether
the statement was or was not a voluntary one.   There may be grounds for
doubting what was the precise question for him to determine, but at any rate
it is clear in the opinion of the court that he did not correctly direct himself at I
the stage of the trial within a trial before admitting this statement.   He said that
he would let it go before the jury de bene esse, an expression which is not
commonly used in criminal trials and really tends to indicate some state of

(1) (1963), 48 Cr. App. Rep. 116.
(2) [1959] 2 All E.R. 193; [1959] 2 Q.B. 35.
(3) Ante, p. 177.
(4) (1966), 50 Cr. App. Rep. 183.

A confusion in the mind of the learned chairman as to what he was at that stage deciding. Furthermore, he referred to *R. v. Cleary* (5) and *R.* v. *Priestley* (6), decisions of this court which would not in the particular circumstances have given him useful guidance. So the statement went before the jury improperly. It was a deadly statement; it amounted to a confession. It is true that, in the course of his evidence, cross-examined about it, the appellant said in effect

B " Well, it is perfectly true, subject to one or two small errors, that is what I say happened ", but his evidence was not entirely in accordance with what this statement said. In his evidence he strove hard, with only very moderate success, to maintain the position that it was not until after the last offence had been committed by others that he knew what they were doing.

  The nature of the case was simply that, although he needed employment

C and was looking for a particular contract job, he in fact spent some 2½ hours at lunch-time in a public house and thereafter drove his own motor car round a residential district in what on one view was an entirely aimless progression and on the other view, suggested by the prosecution, was a course of transport of a number of men in the car with him who got out from time to time from house to house to enable them to see whether they could get in with felonious

D intent, and, if they got in, to see what they could find. It was essential, then, for the jury to decide at what stage, if any stage, of that afternoon's perambulation in his car he became aware that the motives and actions of his passengers were criminal motives and actions. Detail would only overload this judgment. It was said in his statement that at one stage, about the second of several stops that he made, he was told by one of these men, " That's an empty house; they're

E away ". Clearly at some stage a man, Brown, came to his car with his hand bleeding and told him that he had cut it when he was breaking a window to get into a house.

  The question for the jury was whether that happened early enough in the afternoon's activities to justify the conviction of the appellant as a party to a joint enterprise—as the transport man and the look-out man—of attempted or

F actual housebreaking. If that statement had not been admitted and if reliance had not thereafter naturally been placed on it to an extent which would bring it within the picturesque phrase, used by Lord Morris of Borth-y-Gest in the *Harz* case (7), of it being " woven into the fabric " of the prosecution's case, it is not altogether clear what would have happened in this trial. As Lord Morris said (8) in his speech, the test of whether the court should or should not

G apply the proviso (9) is the test laid down in *Stirland* v. *Director of Public Prosecutions* (10), that this court must make up its own mind whether, if the inadmissible evidence had not been before the jury and if a proper direction had been given to a jury whose mind had not been affected by any such inadmissible evidence, such a jury would without doubt have convicted. It is not for this court to speculate what would have happened in the trial itself, what the

H jury which was charged with the decision in that case would or would not have done. It is not sufficient that this court itself should be clear that the appellant is guilty. The court has to apply the test which I have just enunciated and ask itself whether, on the two hypotheses stated and assuming an intelligent and reasonable jury, this court can itself be sure that the appellant would have been convicted. The fact that the chances are very greatly in favour of that

I

---

(5) (1963), 48 Cr. App. Rep. 116.

(6) (1966), 50 Cr. App. Rep. 183.

(7) Ante, at p. 186, letter H.

(8) Ante, at p. 186.

(9) I.e., the proviso to s. 4 (1) of the Criminal Appeal Act, 1907; 5 Halsbury's Statutes (2nd Edn.) 929; as now amended by the Criminal Appeal Act 1966, s. 4 (1), s. 10 (2), Sch. 3.

(10) [1944] 2 All E.R. 13; [1944] A.C. 315.

having happened in the present trial is in law beside the point. It follows
that these convictions must be quashed and, so far at any rate as this matter
is concerned, the appellant is now free to go.

Appeal allowed. Convictions quashed.

Solicitors: *Leonard Kasler & Co.* (for the appellant); *Solicitor, Metropolitan
Police* (for the Crown).

[*Reported by* N. P. METCALFE, ESQ., *Barrister-at-Law.*]

PRACTICE DIRECTION.

PROBATE, DIVORCE AND ADMIRALTY DIVISION (DIVORCE).

*Divorce — Maintenance — Surviving spouse — Application — Interim order —
Extension of time for applying—Matrimonial Causes Act* 1965 (*c.* 72), *s.* 26—
Family Provision Act 1966 (*c.* 35), *s.* 6.
*Husband and Wife—Maintenance—Agreement—Variation by court—Application by surviving party after the death of the other party to the maintenance
agreement—Time—Extension of time for applying—Matrimonial Causes
Act* 1965 (*c.* 72), *s.* 25—*Family Provision Act* 1966 (*c.* 35), *s.* 5.

Section 5 of the Family Provision Act 1966 removes the existing restrictions
on the court's discretion to extend the time for making an application under
s. 25 and s. 26 of the Matrimonial Causes Act 1965 beyond the expiry of a period
of six months from the date of the grant of representation to the estate. An
applicant who wishes the court to exercise its discretion in his or her favour should
ask for its exercise as a separate head of relief in the originating summons. The
registrar may either,

     (*a*) when the evidence on this point is complete, report in writing to a
         judge, to whom the application shall be adjourned for consideration of
         this part of the summons, or
     (*b*) report to a judge upon the whole substance of the application, without
         requiring any preliminary hearing of the application for extension of
         time.

Section 6 of the Family Provision Act 1966 enables the court to make interim
orders in applications under s. 26 of the Matrimonial Causes Act 1965. An applicant need not ask specifically for this form of relief in his or her originating summons. If an applicant wishes an interim order to be made in his or her favour,
the registrar, on being satisfied that the state of the evidence is such as to enable
the judge to decide whether or not such an order should be made, will make an
interim report and adjourn the originating summons to the judge on this point.

By direction of the President.

COMPTON MILLER
Feb. 17, 1967.   Senior Registrar.

ALFRED F. BECKETT, LTD. AND ANOTHER
v. LYONS AND OTHERS.

[DURHAM CHANCERY COURT (Salt, Q.C., Chancellor), November 1, 2, 3, 4, 1965, January 24, 1966.]

[COURT OF APPEAL, CIVIL DIVISION (Harman, Russell and Winn, L.JJ.), June 29, 30, July 1, 4, 5, November 29, 1966.]

Foreshore—Rights over foreshore—Acquiring sea-borne coal—Bathing—County Palatine of Durham—Inhabitants of county alleged to have right to take sea-borne coal and for that purpose to have access to foreshore—Alleged usage based on prescription or custom—Taking as of right not the only explanation—Tolerance of owner—Whether alleged rights a profit-à-prendre.

Easement—Distinction from profit-à-prendre—Quasi-easement—Foreshore—Right to take sea-borne coal—Whether such a prescriptive or customary right capable of being acquired by inhabitants of County Palatine of Durham.

A foreshore in the County Palatine of Durham was held partly by the plaintiff company, which was purchasing from the owner under a grant made by the Crown in 1914 and at the relevant time had an equitable interest entitling it to possession, and partly by the second plaintiffs, the local authority who held under a Crown year to year lease of Aug. 18, 1934 and (after action brought) renewed in 1965, and had granted a licence of their part to the plaintiff company to collect coal in return for a rent of £3,500 a year. In an action by the plaintiffs for trespass the defendants contended that the inhabitants of the county of Durham were entitled by prescription (viz., under a presumed grant before 1189 to the Prince Bishop of the County Palatine, a corporation sole, the former owner, subject to a trust and condition laid on him and binding on his successors including the Crown) to enter on the foreshore, with or without animals or vehicles, and to collect and remove therefrom sea coal, i.e., small coals washed by the tide onto the foreshore from submarine outcrops off the Durham coast. The defendants did not raise questions of title to the foreshore or land, but set up the alleged lawful custom in favour of the inhabitants, they being inhabitants of the County Palatine. Their witnesses included two elderly residents in a nearby village since 1886 who gave evidence that people had taken bags of coal from the foreshore for their own use and for sale during the last five years of the last century, and two other witnesses who gave evidence of coal being picked up and carried away before 1914 and from 1912 to 1914. They proved that, after the closing of the beaches in the world war of 1914-18, there was increased gathering of coal particularly by unemployed miners during the strikes of 1921 and 1926, and that in 1923 the occupant of a bungalow on the beach had collected sea coal for burning it. After closure of the beaches again during the second world war of 1939-45, commerical exploitation started, coal being removed by inhabitants of the Palatinate including residents in neighbouring villages, with the aid of motor lorries over a road which gave access to and from the beaches.

Held: the defendants had no right to remove sea-borne coal from the foreshore for the following reasons—

(i) because, although inhabitants of the County Palatine of Durham would as a class of persons be capable of being constituted beneficiaries of a valid charitable gift, yet the evidence was insufficient to establish the existence of a custom supporting a right in the inhabitants of so large an area to remove sea-borne coal from the foreshore, since the evidence of such removal extended in substance only to inhabitants of villages near to the foreshore and not also to the inland area of the county (see p. 844, letter I, p. 845, letters C and G, p. 847, letter F, p. 852, letter F, and p. 853, letter C, post).

Goodman v. *Saltash Corpn.* ([1881-85] All E.R. 1076) distinguished.

Distinguished in [1991] 1 All ER 449

MILLS v SILVER

Dictum of SIR HERBERT COZENS-HARDY, M.R., in *A.-G.* v. *Horner*
(*No. 2*) ([1913] 2 Ch. at p. 169) applied.

(ii) because it was not the only reasonable conclusion from the evidence that
the practice of taking the sea-borne coal was of right and the practice was
sufficiently explained by tolerance on the part of the foreshore owner (see
p. 846, letter B, p. 847, letters A and D, and p. 853, letters H and I, post).

(iii) (per HARMAN, L.J.) because the commercial exploitation of the coal
by motor lorries was quite different from the old practice (see p. 845, letter F,
post).

(iv) (per HARMAN and WINN, L.JJ.) because the right was a profit-à-prendre
and not an easement, and a fluctuating body such as the inhabitants of a
county could not acquire by custom a right of that nature (see p. 846,
letter C, p. 851, letter E, and p. 852, letter C, post; cf., p. 847, letter G, post).

Blewett v. *Tregonning* ([1835-42] All E.R. Rep. 83 at p. 87) applied.

Semble: the public belief that there is a right of access to the foreshore
for the purpose of bathing in the sea is fallacious, the only clear rights of
the public over foreshore being for user ancillary to navigation or fishing
(see p. 842, letter I, and p. 854, letter A, post).

Appeal allowed.

[**Editorial Note.** No question of title to any part of the foreshore arose in
the action; see, e.g., p. 847, letter I, post.

As to a right to remove things from the foreshore, see 39 HALSBURY'S LAWS
(3rd Edn.) 568-572, paras. 798-805; and for cases on the subject, see 47 DIGEST
(Repl.) 714-718, *591-633*.

As to the distinction between easements and profits-à-prendre, see 12 HALS-
BURY'S LAWS (2nd Edn.) 522, 523, para. 1129; and for cases on the subject, see
19 DIGEST (Repl.) 21, 22, *76-88*.

As to prescription based on presumed grant, see 12 HALSBURY'S LAWS (3rd
Edn.) 544, 545, para. 1179; and for cases on the subject, see 19 DIGEST (Repl.)
62-66, *345-363*.

As to the rights of fluctuating bodies arising by custom, viz., quasi-easements,
see 11 HALSBURY'S LAWS (3rd Edn.) 174, 175, para. 325.

As to the prerogative rights to foreshore in the County Palatine of Durham,
see 7 HALSBURY'S LAWS (3rd Edn.) 455-457, paras. 956-958; and for a case on
the subject, see 47 DIGEST (Repl.) 708, *541*.

For the Durham (County Palatine) Act, 1836, see 5 HALSBURY'S STATUTES
(2nd Edn.) 191, and for the Durham County Palatine Act, 1858, see 4 ibid., 321.]

Cases referred to:

A.-G. v. *Antrobus*, [1905] 2 Ch. 188; 74 L.J.Ch. 599; 92 L.T. 790; 69 J.P. 141;
    19 Digest (Repl.) 66, *366*.

A.-G. v. *Horner* (*No. 2*), [1913] 2 Ch. 140; 82 L.J.Ch. 339; 108 L.T. 609;
    7 7 J.P. 257; 11 Digest (Repl.) 658, *822*.

Bagot v. *O rr*, (1801), 2 Bos. & P. 472; 126 E.R. 1391; 47 Digest (Repl.) 716, *611*.

Ball v. *He rbert*, (1789), 3 Term Rep. 253; 100 E.R. 560; 47 Digest (Repl.)
    742, *8 39*.

Blewett v. *Tr egonning*, [1835-42] All E.R. Rep. 83; (1835), 3 Ad. & El. 554;
    4 L.J.K .B. 223; 111 E.R. 524; 47 Digest (Repl.) 716, *616*.

Blundell v. *C atterall*, [1814-23] All E.R. Rep. 39; (1821), 5 B. & Ald. 268;
    106 E.R. 1 190; 47 Digest (Repl.) 715, *579*.

Brinckman v. *Natle y*, [1904-07] All E.R. Rep. 20; [1904] 2 Ch. 313; 73 L.J.Ch.
    642; 91 L.T. 429; 68 J. P. 534; 47 Digest (Repl.) 715, *610*.

Constable v. *Nicholson*, (1863), 14 C.B.N.S. 230; 32 L.J.C.P. 240; 143 E.R. 434;
    47 Digest (Repl.) 716, *618*.

Dalton v. *Angus & Co., Public Works Comrs.* v. *Angus & Co.*, [1881-85]
    All E.R. Rep. 1; (1881), 6 App. Cas. 740; 50 L.J.B.B. 689; 44 L.T.
    844; 46 J.P. 132; 19 Digest (Repl.) 8, *4*.

Fitch v. *Rawling*, (1795), 2 Hy. Bl. 393; 126 E.R. 614; 17 Digest (Repl.) 15, *165*.

Fitzhardinge (Lord) v. *Purcell*, [1908] 2 Ch. 139; 77 L.J.Ch. 529; 99 L.T. 154; 72 J.P. 276; 47 Digest (Repl.) 728, *727*.

Gardner v. *Hodgson's Kingston Brewery Co., Ltd.*, [1903] A.C. 229; 73 L.J.Ch. 558; 88 L.T. 698; 19 Digest (Repl.) 58, *317*.

Gateward's Case, (1607), 6 Co. Rep. 59b; 77 E.R. 344; 17 Digest (Repl.) 5, *18*.

Glasgow Corporation v. *Farie*, [1886-90] All E.R. Rep. 115; (1888), 13 App. Cas. 657; 58 L.J.P.C. 33; 60 L.T. 274; 11 Digest (Repl.) 163, *363*.

Goodman v. *Saltash Corpn.*, [1881-85] All E.R. Rep. 1076; (1882), 7 App. Cas. 633; 52 L.J.Q.B. 193; 48 L.T. 239; 47 J.P. 276; 19 Digest (Repl.) 61, *341*.

Grimstead v. *Marlowe*, (1792), 4 Term Rep. 717; 100 E.R. 1263; 19 Digest (Repl.) 222, *1635*.

Harris v. *Earl Chesterfield*, [1911] A.C. 623; 80 L.J.Ch. 626; 105 L.T. 453; 19 Digest (Repl.) 224, *1653*.

Hue v. *Whiteley*, [1928] All E.R. Rep. 308; [1929] 1 Ch. 440; 98 L.J.Ch. 227; 140 L.T. 531; 26 Digest (Repl.) 311, *287*.

Jones v. *Bates*, [1938] 2 All E.R. 237; 158 L.T. 507; 102 J.P. 291; 26 Digest (Repl.) 307, *262*.

Lock v. *Abercester, Ltd.*, [1939] 3 All E.R. 562; [1939] Ch. 861; 108 L.J.Ch. 328; 161 L.T. 264; 19 Digest (Repl.) 123, *765*.

Manning v. *Wasdale*, [1835-42] All E.R. Rep. 125; (1836), 5 Ad. & El. 758; 6 L.J.K.B. 59; 111 E.R. 1353; 19 Digest (Repl.) 177, *1188*.

Mellor v. *Spateman*, (1699), 1 Saund. 339; 85 E.R. 489; 11 Digest (Repl.) 32, *417*.

Mercer v. *Denne*, [1904-07] All E.R. Rep. 71; [1904] 2 Ch. 534; 74 L.J.Ch. 71; 91 L.T. 513; 68 J.P. 479; *affd.* C.A., [1904-07] All E.R. Rep. at p. 80; [1905] 2 Ch. 538; 74 L.J.Ch. 723; 93 L.T. 412; 70 J.P. 65; 17 Digest (Repl.) 4, *11*.

Potter v. *North*, (1669), 1 Vent. 383; 83 E.R. 400; 11 Digest (Repl.) 14, *146*.

R. v. *Two Casks of Tallow*, (1837), 3 Hag. Adm. 294; 166 E.R. 414; 11 Digest (Repl.) 657, *811*.

Race v. *Ward*, (1855), 4 E. & B. 702; 24 L.J.Q.B. 153; 24 L.T.O.S. 270; 19 J.P. 563; 119 E.R. 259; *subsequent proceedings*, (1857), 7 E. & B. 384; 19 Digest (Repl.) 159, *1050*.

Rangeley v. *Midland Ry. Co.*, (1868), 3 Ch. App. 306; 37 L.J.Ch. 313; 18 L.T. 69; 19 Digest (Repl.) 12, *25*.

Action.

This was an action by Alfred F. Beckett, Ltd. and Easington Rural District Council, the plaintiffs, against R. Lyons, G. Robins, J. Smith and Andrew Sanderson Softley, the defendants, for (i) injunctions restraining the defendants from entering on certain stretches of foreshore in the County Palatine of Durham and from collecting thereon or carrying away therefrom sea-borne coal; (ii) declarations that the defendants were not entitled to enter on the said stretches of foreshore or to collect thereon or carry away therefrom sea-borne coal; and (iii) damages for trespass. The foreshore in question lay between a point south of Seaham in the north and a point north of West Hartlepool in the south and extended for about nine miles. On the copy of the ordnance survey map which was annexed to the statement of claim as a plan this foreshore was divided (for the purposes of indicating title) into three stretches designated, from north to south, A to B, B to C and C to D. The map showed the foreshore between the ordinary high and low water marks. Along almost the entire stretch the foreshore was backed by cliffs or steep gradients, pierced here and there by gaps or steep gullies by which it was physically possible to obtain access to considerable lengths of foreshore. Access had in fact been so obtained over a long period at a number of points on each stretch of foreshore. One witness deposed that he had more than once made his way on foot along the entire length of the foreshore in question. With rather more difficulty one could make one's way down or up one or more of the gullies with a bicycle, perambulator or bogey or even with a pony and trap or a horse and cart. It was also possible to drive a motor vehicle to the head of a gully for the carriage inland of persons coming up from the foreshore with or without material brought therefrom. Up to 1954, there were two roads or tracks capable of taking motor traffic by which access to or near the foreshore was in practice obtained. One of these was stopped up by order in 1954. As regards the other, the Peterlee Development Corporation, who claimed an interest in the site of that part of it which had not been made up as a public highway, had in 1964 erected concrete blocks to preclude its use by lorries, and proceedings in which their right to do this was in issue were pending, the obstruction being by arrangement temporarily mitigated to allow passage by lorries in single file. A considerable amount of inferior but marketable coal was washed in (and in whole or in part also out) by the tide. It was estimated at one hundred thousand tons in 1962, though it varied considerably from year to year. This coal came partly from outcrops of coal seams out-cropping in the sea-bed east of low water mark and, since 1911, from waste and small unprofitable coal tipped into the sea from in-shore collieries. It was accepted (by the Chancellor in the Durham Chancery Court) that the undersea outcrop was the only source of sea-borne coal in the Palatine until it was augmented in the present century as indicated above.

The foreshore in the county of Durham was formerly part of the jura regalia of the Prince Bishop of Durham, a corporation sole, by prescription, viz., by a supposed grant by the Crown before the time of legal memory (1189). (See COKE, 4th Institute c. 38). It was revested in the Crown by the Durham (County Palatine) Act, 1836, and the Durham County Palatine Act, 1858. Each statute contained a saving, the former of unaffected rights of the Bishop, and the latter of estates, rights, titles and interests of all persons therefore subsisting. By a deed of settlement dated Sept. 3, 1914, the Crown for consideration relinquished all its claims, subject to a saving for Crown mines, to the stretch of foreshore B to C in favour of Richard Burdon, then lord of the manors of Horden and Little Eden. By 1934 it had become the policy of the Commissioners of Crown Lands to demise Crown foreshore to the appropriate local authority. By a lease dated Aug. 18, 1934, the Crown granted a tenancy from year to year from June 30, 1934, of the stretches A to B and C to D to the plaintiff council at an annual rent of £30 and a royalty of 4d. for every ton of sand, stone, beach, shingle or other materials taken during the tenancy. There were reservations in favour of the Crown of all mines, minerals and substrata with power to enter, work and carry away the reserved substances, and of the right of the Crown and all persons by the Crown's permission (which was to be deemed granted unless shown to have been expressly refused) to ride, drive, walk and otherwise pass to and fro over and to fish and bathe on and to gather seaweed from the demised premises and to land thereon goods and passengers from boats. The demise was (so the learned Chancellor noted) expressed to be subject to all rigths of way and other rights and easements or quasi-easements then exercisable over the demised premises. There was a covenant by the plaintiff council not without the lessor's written consent and payment of royalty to remove or permit the removal of sand, stone, beach, shingle or other materials and not to cause or permit their removal at all after notice by the lessor to that effect. After the 1939-45 war the lease dated Aug. 18, 1934, which had been mislaid, was rediscovered and the plaintiff council, under stimulus from the Commissioners of Crown Lands*, became alive to the possibility of exploiting their rights under it by sub-lease or licence. This led to an agreement dated Aug. 23, 1962, whereby the plaintiff council purported to grant to an unincorporated body called the

---

* In 1956 the commissioners were re-constituted as the Crown Estate Commissioners.

North-East Sea Coal Traders, whose members included two of the defendants, an exclusive licence to collect coal deposits from the stretches A to B and C to D for two years on payment of £6,000 per annum. This agreement was determined by the plaintiff council after a few months for default in payment. At the date of the issue of the writ the plaintiff council were holding over under the lease dated Aug. 18, 1934, and continued so to do until a new lease for fourteen years from Sept. 1, 1964, was executed on July 7, 1965, i.e., after the trespassers pleaded. By a written agreement dated Feb. 1, 1964, made in reliance on the lease of Aug. 18, 1934, and in anticipation of the lease of July 7, 1965, the plaintiff council granted the plaintiff company what purported to be an exclusive licence to collect deposits of coal on the stretches A to B and C to D for a period of five years from Jan. 1, 1964, on payment of £3,500 a year. The lease of July 7, 1965, fed this licence with retrospective effect and was relied on by the plaintiff only for that purpose. It exacted a further covenant from the lessee council to prevent motor vehicles from proceeding onto the demised foreshores A to B and C to D. By an uncompleted contract dated May 6, 1964, the plaintiff company purchased from successors in title of Richard Burdon the stretch B to C, and was accordingly entitled in equity to possession thereof.

There was evidence from two witnesses who had lived in the mining village of Easington since 1886, of people carrying up bags of coal from the beach for their own use or for sale in the village as far back as 1895. There was little evidence of this practice during the first fourteen years of the present century. The beaches were shut during the 1914-18 war, but thereafter with more coal on the beaches owing to the tipping of waste into the sea the practice increased, particularly during the coal strikes of 1913, 1921 and 1926 when unemployed miners and people from as far off as Sunderland and West Hartlepool gathered sea-borne coal. The beaches were again closed during the 1939-45 war, and with their re-opening commercial exploitation started. The practice was then carried on not only by local people, but also by operators with lorries operating by day and night.

The plaintiffs' case was of trespass, in one instance by mere entry on the foreshore and in others by entry coupled with the collection and carrying away of sea-borne coal from one or other of the stretches of foreshore. The defendants admitted the commission of the acts alleged, but pleaded that they were done lawfully and of right. They put forward three lines of defence. Their first ground was justification by common law right, but, while keeping this open, the contention was not pursued before the Palatine Court. The second ground was prescription by presumed legal origin, based on a rebuttable presumption to be drawn from evidence of enjoyment since 1895, the longest stretch of extant human memory: this contention involved the presumption of a condition or trust on the presumed grant to the Prince Bishop of Durham before 1189. The third ground was that, from the evidence of enjoyment throughout the period of living witnesses' memory (which went back to 1895), a paramount local custom in the Palatinate should be presumed.

C. A. Settle, Q.C., and *J. R. Johnson* for the plaintiffs.
E. I. Goulding, Q.C., and *F. H. Potts* for the defendants.

SALT, Q.C., Chancellor, referred to the facts and the pleadings and, having held (a) that the right of three defendants (against whom a claim for trespass only on the stretch of foreshore B–C was pleaded) stood or fell with the defence that there was a right for inhabitants of the Palatinate to collect sea-borne coal, which necessarily would include a right of entry to collect it, and (b) that the reservation of mines and minerals to the Crown expressed in the lease of Aug. 18, 1934, did not, having regard to *Glasgow Corporation* v. *Farie* (1), extend to sea-borne coal, with the consequence that the right claimed by the defendants

(1) [1886-90] All E.R. Rep. 115 at p. 120; (1888), 13 App. Cas. 657 at p. 675, per Lord Watson.

did not fail ab initio merely by reason of the reservations in the lease, stated that the defendants, while keeping open their first or common law ground of defence (2), had not pursued it before the Chancery Court of the County Palatine of Durham in the face of *Blundell* v. *Catterall* (3). THE CHANCELLOR then turned to the defendants' second defence based on *Goodman* v. *Saltash Corpn.* (4) and third defence based on local custom of the Palatinate and after referring to the evidence, continued: In my judgment the necessary substratum of fact is made out to support the defence based on *Goodman* v. *Saltash Corpn.* (4); the usage amounts to a valid right to an easement or rather quasi-easement, being immemorial, continuous, certain and reasonable.

[THE CHANCELLOR stated that he found the usage proved by wholly independent and reliable witnesses (5) back to 1895, that fluctuations in the degree to which it was exercised, e.g., in particular the increased commercial exploitation after 1947, did not affect its immemorial existence or certainty (cf., *Mercer* v. *Denne* [1904-07] All E.R. Rep. 71) and that counsel for the plaintiffs had not contended that the agreement dated Aug. 23, 1962 (6), constituted an estoppel against any of the defendants. THE CHANCELLOR intimated that there was no evidence to support an inference that the usage from 1895 could be explained by a series of implied general licences from the owners of the foreshore for the time being and that indeed it was admitted that there was no instance of permission sought or granted; but that the user had been open, notorious and unchallenged and as of right and acquiesced in throughout by the owners or lessees of the foreshore. After stating that the only de facto interruption in the usage was during the two wars when the beaches were closed or inaccessible and that it was not contended that this constituted an interruption in law in the sense of cesser or acquiescence, THE CHANCELLOR continued:] On these facts, as I have found them, I find myself constrained to hold that they disclose a situation where the decision and reasoning of the majority of the House of Lords in *Goodman* v. *Saltash Corpn.* (4) applies and governs. Whether or not one takes the view that this well-known case presents an unusual feature in our jurisprudence and a precedent not to be extended unnecessarily, it has these indubitable characteristics:—it exists; it has been followed; and it is binding on a court of first instance wherever a later situation of fact and law falls fairly within it. It has been tentatively doubted whether the inhabitants of ancient tenements in the borough of Saltash constitute such a section of the public as the law requires of the objects or beneficiaries of a condition or trust by way of charity, but no such objection can apply in the case of the inhabitants of a County Palatine. I cannot distinguish in this case the substance of the facts found and principles of law laid down in *Goodman's Case* (4). [THE CHANCELLOR considered the facts in that case, stated that it showed how powerful was the desire of the courts to find a lawful foundation for long established user as of right, and, where there were two established usages in respect of the same subject matter, to reconcile the two by presuming a grant based on prescription to the corporate owner but qualified in favour of the unincorporated users by the implication of condition or trust annexed to the descriptive title or grant on which it was founded. He cited the opinion of LORD CAIRNS ([1881-85] All E.R. Rep. 1083-1085). THE CHANCELLOR continued:] In the present case I find, among other facts, that the inhabitants of the County Palatine of Durham have from time immemorial without interruption and claiming as of right exercised the privilege of entering on the three stretches of foreshore in question and dredging for or lifting and carrying away therefrom or from the sea thereover sea-borne coal without stint for sale or otherwise. The acts complained of were done in exercise of that privilege. The present case is to all intents and purposes on all fours with *Goodman* v. *Saltash Corpn.* (4), and the

---

(2) I.e., common law right; see p. 837, letter G, ante.   (3) (1821), 5 B. and Ald. 268.
(4) [1881-85] All E.R. Rep. 1076; (1882), 7 App. Cas. 633.
(5) See, as to this evidence, p. 843, letter I, to p. 844, letter A, post.
(6) See p. 836, letter I, to p. 837, letter A, ante; cf. p. 844, letter H, post.

A facts are similar mutatis mutandis. We have the prescriptive regalia of the Bishop (a corporation sole) including the foreshores and the sea-borne coal coming and going with the tides, based on ancient grant. We have the usage which I have just described by the inhabitants. They are to be reconciled, without violating any principle of our law, in the same manner and by the same process of reasoning as the majority of the House applied in *Goodman's Case* (7).   The

B Crown is of course not a party to this action, nor bound by any decision in it. But I cannot see that the Crown, or its successors in title and its lessees and its or their licensees, stand in any better position under the nineteenth century legislation and its express savings than the bishop previously stood before 1836 or 1858, (8); or that they can shake off the condition or trust which the inhabitants of the Palatinate have established on the basis of *Goodman* v. *Saltash*

C *Corpn.* (7).   Nor is the plaintiff company, claiming through the Manors of Horden and Little Eden (9), in any better position.

Accordingly I hold that the second line of defence previously referred to has been made out in fact and in law. On that basis, without more, the plaintiffs' action for the specified alleged trespasses fails and must be dismissed.

It is not necessary for me, in view of what I have already held, to adjudicate

D on the alternative defence of ancient County Palatine custom, and I leave that question at large, observing only that I incline to the view on the evidence and on the authorities cited to me, *Race* v. *Ward* (10) and *Blewett* v. *Tregonning* (11) that the subject matter of the usage falls short of a profit-à-prendre since the sea-borne coal goes in and out with the tide and does not become integrated with the soil of the foreshore; and accordingly on the evidence I should have

E been inclined to find in the defendants' favour in the alternative on the basis of their having established a usage which does not involve a profit-à-prendre and is not on that or any other ground unreasonable, which is immemorial, uninterrupted and sufficiently certain to constitute a valid legal custom, by no means devoid of merits.

Action dismissed.

F Solicitors: *Keenlyside & Forster* (for the plaintiffs); *Richard Reed & Co.,* Sunderland (for the defendants).

[*Reported by* G. M. Smailes, Esq., *Barrister-at-Law.*]

G **Appeal.**

The plaintiffs appealed. The grounds of appeal were: (i) that the Chancellor should not have found on the evidence that the inhabitants of the County Palatine of Durham had from time immemorial without interruption and claiming of right exercised the privilege of entering on the foreshore, the subject matter of the action, and carrying away therefrom or from the sea thereover

H sea-borne coal without stint and for sale; and (ii) that the Chancellor was wrong in holding that the foreshore in question was held by the Crown and the first plaintiffs respectively subject to ingrafted condition or limit to permit the inhabitants of the County Palatine of Durham to enter on them and to carry away therefrom or from the sea thereover sea-borne coal without stint and for sale.

I *C. A. Settle*, Q.C., and *R. A. Percy* for the plaintiffs.
E. I. Goulding, Q.C., and *F. H. Potts* for the defendants.

Cur. adv. vult.

Nov. 29.   The following judgments were read.

---

(7) [1881-85] All E.R. Rep. 1076; (1882), 7 App. Cas. 633.
(8) See the Acts of these dates cited at p. 836, letter E, ante.
(9) I.e., through the deed of settlement dated Sept. 3, 1914;   see p. 836, letter F, ante.
(10) (1855), 4 E. & B. 702.
(11) [1835-42] All E.R. Rep. 83; (1835), 3 Ad. and El. 534.

HARMAN, L.J.: The plaintiffs sue the defendants in trespass seeking *A*
injunctions to restrain their entry on parts of the foreshore in the County Palatine
of Durham and from collecting thereon or from carrying away therefrom sea-
washed coal. The strip of foreshore in question lies between Seaham and Hartlepool, both in the county, and extends for about nine miles. As a matter of title
it is divided into a northern section A to B on the map and a southern section
marked C to D.   Between these is a strip marked B to C held under a different *B*
title. The whole of the foreshore in the county was formerly part of the property
of the Prince Bishop of Durham held by that prelate by a supposed grant from the
Crown before the time of living memory. The foreshore in the county was revested
in the Crown by the Durham County Palatine Act, 1858. The intervening strip
B–C was purchased of the Crown by a deed made in 1914 containing a grant
of the foreshore saving to the Crown mines and so forth within or under the *C*
foreshore. The plaintiff company traces its equitable title under that deed having
purchased from certain personal representatives, which purchase will not be
completed by the transfer of the legal estate until the year 1969, though the
equitable estate entitles the company to possession.

At the time when the writ was issued in this action the foreshore from A–B and
C–D was held by the plaintiff council under a Crown lease from year to year *D*
made on Aug. 18, 1934. That lease excepted from the demise the mines and
substrata and the right for licensees of the lessor to ride, drive, walk or pass over
and fish and bathe and gather seaweed or ware (a species of seaweed) and to land
goods and embark them: also the right to lay sewers and to maintain two aerial
roadways. The habendum of this deed was made " subject to easements or
quasi-easements now exercisable " and the reddendum consisted of a rent of £30 *E*
a year and a royalty per ton of sand, stone, beach shingle " or other materials "
taken off the demised premises. There were covenants by the lessees not to
remove or permit to be removed such materials without the consent of the
Crown, to use their best endeavours to prevent unlawful acts, and not to sublet.
The plaintiff council held over under this lease until July 7, 1965, when a new lease
was executed containing a demise by the Crown to the plaintiff council of the *F*
foreshore between A and B, and C and D, mines and minerals being excepted
for a term of fourteen years subject to public rights of navigation and fishing
" and all other rights or easements or quasi-easements and privileges now exercisable ". The rent was £85 a year plus a royalty on sand, stone, beach shingle
or other materials removed, and there were lessees' covenants not to remove such
materials without consent and to prevent unauthorised removal and to permit the *G*
public to resort on foot for private recreational purposes but not to allow anyone
to drive mechanical vehicles on the foreshore. The defendants do not rely on any
of the exceptions in the instruments above referred to, but deny that they are
trespassers and allege that, as members of the public or alternatively as inhabitants
of the county of Durham, they are entitled to enter on the foreshore with or
without animals or vehicles and to collect and remove therefrom sea-coal. They *H*
justify this right by a prescription from time immemorial either by common law
or by custom or by lost grant or declaration of trust.

" Sea coal " has not in this case what I should have taken to be its ordinary
meaning, which was coal transported by sea in Newcastle bottoms and landed in
London, where Sea Coal Lane still exists. A proclamation was issued by Edward I
against burning this sea coal, but it had become a common fuel by the time of *I*
Elizabeth I and it will be remembered that according to Mistress Quickly
when Falstaff promised to marry her he was (12)

> " sitting in my dolphin-chamber, at the round table, by a sea-coal fire,
> on Wednesday in Whitsun week, when the prince broke thy head for
> liking his father to a singing man of Windsor."

The expression " sea coal " in this district meant, until the present century, small

_____

(12) Shakespeare's *Henry IV*, Pt. 2. Act 2, sc. 1.

coals washed by the tide on the beach from the submarine outcrops off the Durham coast. During the present century this supply has been largely augmented because the local collieries which come down to the sea have since the year 1911 been in the habit of depositing their coal dirt into the sea by aerial railways or otherwise. This coal is washed by the tide and a great deal of it gets back on the beach and drifts back and forth as the tides ebb and flow.

The action was heard by the Chancellor of the Court of the County Palatine of Durham and evidence over the time of living memory satisfied him that it was right to assume the practice of entering on the foreshore and there gathering the sea-coal whether above or below low water mark and carrying it away for use or sale to be immemorial and one to which a legal origin ought if possible to be attributed. This he found himself able to do on the authority of the well-known case of *Goodman* v. *Saltash Corpn.* (13). He supposed a presumed grant before 1189 to the Prince Bishop of Durham, a corporation sole, subject to a trust or condition laid on him and binding on his conscience and on that of his successor the Crown to allow to the inhabitants of the county the free right to take coal from this strip of foreshore. The main question in this action, in my judgment, is whether the evidence called before the Chancellor supports the glittering structure so raised on it.

Now there is no doubt that from time to time back to about 1895 people from the locality have gone down on to the beach and picked up and taken away coal for their own domestic use. The way down to the shore was steep and until fairly recently there was no road, let alone a highway, down on to the foreshore. Wheeled vehicles used to wait at the top of the cliff and take bags of coal from people struggling up from the shore. The amount of coal on the shore increased very much after 1911, when the colliery tipping started. On the other hand people who lived in the vicinity were mostly miners who got free coal as part of their wages and therefore did not worry about collecting sea coal except when out of employment. Evidence was given of a great increase in coal-gathering over the strikes of 1921 and 1926, and some evidence of bags of coal having been sold as far afield as Seaham in the north and Hartlepool in the south around those times.

The beaches were shut during both wars, but after 1946 there was a resumption of the practice, and it was now possible to get motor vehicles down on to the beach apparently by two roads, one of which was closed by the local authority after a public inquiry, and the other of which is still the subject-matter of an action in the Court of the County Palatine of Durham. It seems that after the last war the local authority at the instance of the Crown rediscovered the lease of 1934, which had been lost, and made an attempt to put its terms into effect by preventing unauthorised access to the foreshore. This culminated in an agreement made in 1962 with certain individuals representing what was called the Coal Traders' Association, whereby the plaintiff council licensed the association " to take and carry away deposits of coal " on the A–B and C–D strips of the foreshore for a term of two years at a rent of no less than £6,000 a year. There was a covenant by the licensees to use only " the recognised road to the beach at Dene Holm ". That is by point C on the map, the northern point of the C–D strip. The rent was far more than the association could pay and the agreement was abortive. The plaintiff council then, on Feb. 1, 1964, relying on the lease of 1934 and the promise of a further lease (which has in fact been granted as I have mentioned), licensed the plaintiff company for five years to collect coal on the foreshore at a rent of £3,500 a year, using as before only the recognised road. The title, therefore, of the two plaintiffs to maintain the action is not in doubt, the plaintiff company being the owner of the B–C strip and licensee of the A–B and C–D strips, and the plaintiff council being the lessee from the Crown of the last two strips.

---

(13) [1881-85] All E.R. Rep. 1076; (1882), 7 App. Cas. 633.

The decision of the Chancellor really began and ended with the case of *Goodman* v. *Saltash Corpn.* (14). That case started on an entirely different footing from the present. There the House of Lords was confronted with an agreed set of facts and felt constrained to find an explanation of them in consonance with the law. The agreed facts were set out in a Special Case and included the following. First, that the respondent, the mayor and corporation of Saltash as a corporation by royal charter, was the owner by prescriptive right of the bed and soil and a several oyster fishery in the estuary of the River Tamar; second (15), that

" The free inhabitants of the ancient tenements in the borough of Saltash have from time immemorial, without interruption and claiming as of right, exercised the privilege of dredging for oysters in "

the same parts of the river in which the corporation had its several fishery from Candlemas to Easter (i.e., about half the oyster season), a usage which did in fact tend to the destruction of the fishery. Confronted with these two rival sets of facts, the House of Lords found itself able, by what was afterwards described as a splendid effort of equitable imagination (see LORD ASHBOURNE'S observations in *Harris* v. *Earl of Chesterfield* (16); see also HAMILTON, L.J., in *A.-G.* v. *Horner* (*No. 2*) (17)), to reconcile the two conflicting rights, that of the corporation to the several fishery, and that of the free inhabitants to take oysters, by supposing that the grant to the corporation of the soil and the oyster fishery, which must be taken to have been a grant before legal memory, was made by the Crown or the Duchy of Cornwall subject to a trust or condition binding on the grantee, the corporation, to allow the owners of ancient tenements within the borough this limited right to dredge for oysters notwithstanding that the right might lead to the destruction of the fishery. In the instant case none of the facts assumed as the basis of the decision in the *Saltash* case (14) is established; all have to be proved. The first of them may be taken to be proven, viz., that the grant of the foreshore to the Bishop of Durham was before the time of legal memory; but the next step is the difficult one, viz., to show that a section of the public, at least during the time of living memory and under a claim of right, have exercised the privilege. This depends on the facts proved. The Chancellor made a finding as follows (18):

" There has been open, notorious, unchallenged user as of right or under claim of right and acquiescence in it throughout [i.e., throughout living memory] by the owners or lessees of the foreshore."

The Chancellor was apparently under the impression that the plaintiffs by their counsel admitted at the Bar that the user was not " precarious " in the sense of being permissive. The plaintiffs' counsel before us denied that he made any such concession and I think that the shorthand note justifies him. All that he conceded was that he had no evidence of permission being asked or refused, but this as it seems to me is very far from showing that the exercise of the privilege was under a claim of right. It is notorious that many things are done on the sea-shore by the public which they have no legal right to do. The only clear right of the public on the foreshore is the right to pass over it in boats when it is covered with water for the purpose of fishing. Bathing, for instance, is not a public right but goes on by tolerance: see *Brinckman* v. *Matley* (19), a decision of the Court of Appeal following *Blundell* v. *Catterall* (20).

I cannot find any clear decision that the public has the right to walk on the foreshore when the tide is out, nor of landing from boats or embarking except in cases of emergency. It seems also clear enough that there is no public highway along the foreshore. It is on the other hand notorious that in many, and indeed

---

(14) [1881-85] All E.R. Rep. 1076; (1882), 7 App. Cas. 633.
(15) (1882), 7 App. Cas. at p. 634.   (16) [1911] A.C. 623 at p. 633.
(17) [1913] 2 Ch. 140 at p. 190.   (18) See p. 838, letter D, ante.
(19) [1904-07] All E.R. Rep. 20; [1904] 2 Ch. 313.
(20) [1814-23] All E.R. Rep. 39; (1821), 5 B. & Ald. 268.

A most, places the use of the foreshore by the public for purposes of recreation and bathing is tolerated. For instance, it appears by the lease of 1934 already recited that on the foreshore here in question the Crown reserves for its licensees (which word is defined so that it means all persons not expressly forbidden) the comparatively extensive rights there specified, viz., to ride, drive, walk or pass over and fish and bathe and gather seaweed and land and embark goods from

B boats. It seems clear that all these enumerated acts when done by members of the public are done by licence of the Crown and not under a claim of right. Why, then, it may be asked, should the further privilege of taking away coal be treated as a right rather than as a matter of permission?

The authorities seem to show that, when the law talks of something being done as of right, it means that the person doing it believes himself to be exercising a

C public right: *Jones* v. *Bates* (21). So far as I can see no witness was asked whether in picking up coal he believed himself to be exercising a right or was merely doing something which he felt confident that the owner would not stop but would tolerate because it did no harm. Indeed, as carried on up to the last war the practice was (except perhaps during the exceptional weeks of the strikes of 1921 and 1926) on so small a scale as to be a matter of indifference to the owner.

D Here I may cite the words of Holroyd, J., in *Blundell* v. *Catterall* (22), quoted by Parker, J., in *Lord Fitzhardinge* v. *Purcell* (23). That was a case about a right of fowling in a manor, claimed by the defendant. It was held (24):

" On the evidence, that the plaintiff had proved his title to the foreshore as part of the manors, and also to a several fishery in the Severn. The public have no rights over the foreshore of a tidal navigable river, when

E not covered by the tide, except such as are ancillary to their rights of fishing and navigation in the sea. When covered by the tide the foreshore is part of the sea, and the only rights of the public in or over it are the rights of navigation and fishing and rights ancillary thereto. The right claimed to kill and carry away wild duck is . . . a profit-à-prendre and cannot be claimed by custom . . . Held, also, that there was not sufficient evidence

F of user to enable the court to presume the existence of a trust . . ."

The passage which I wish to cite from Parker, J.'s decision is this (25):

" What was said by Holroyd, J., in *Blundell* v. *Catterall* (22) with regard to the alleged right of bathing on the foreshore may, I think, be said with equal truth of the alleged right to kill wild fowl in the channel of navigable rivers—' Where the soil remains the King's, and where no mischief or

G injury is likely to arise from the enjoyment or exercise of such a public right, it is not to be supposed that an unnecessary and injurious restraint upon the subjects would, in that respect, be enforced by the King, the parens patriae '—and I think what is thus said of the King may with equal truth be said of those subjects of the King to whom beds of navigable rivers have

H been granted. At any rate I am satisfied in the present case that the defendant's sport would never have been interfered with had he not persistently asserted a right to shoot wild fowl, and that, too, in the immediate neighbourhood of the plaintiff's decoys."

In other words, if one pushes a privilege into a right one will find it opposed which it never would be so long as one admits that it is a privilege.

I Turning now to the evidence on this subject, there were only two witnesses whose recollections went beyond the present century, a Mr. Hirst and his sister who had lived at Easington, a mining village lying just inshore of a part of the A–B strip, since about 1886. These two old people testified to people going on the beach and carrying up coal in bags. Mr. Hirst remembered people carrying

(21) [1938] 2 All E.R. 237 at p. 241.
(22) [1814-23] All E.R. Rep. at p. 46; (1821), 5 B. & Ald. at p. 300.
(23) [1908] 2 Ch. 139 at p. 168.
(24) [1908] 2 Ch. at p. 139.   (25) [1908] 2 Ch. at pp. 168, 169.

bags of coal along the road on which his father's house stood and damaging the
house gate by leaning bags on it.   This was on the way to the village; and his
sister said she had seen people bringing bags of coal up from Hawthorne Hive,
a bay a little to the north of the village where there was a way, both for their
own use and for sale in the village of Easington. This evidence goes back to the
last five years of the last century. There was very little evidence to cover the
first fourteen years of this century. A witness called Mr. Hewitt from Easington
saw coal picked up on the beach before 1914, but only near the village and
apparently by local people. A Mr. Richardson had seen people daily on the beach
between 1912 and 1914 picking up coal and carrying it away with buckets and
bags.   The beaches were shut during the 1914-18 war, but after that was over
there was much more coal on the beaches owing to the practice of tipping from
the collieries, and an increased activity particularly during the strikes of 1921
and 1926 when large numbers of unemployed miners from the collieries, and
indeed people from as far off as Hartlepool, gathered coal on the beach while the
strikes lasted. Mr. Humphreys had once collected coal in a bag in or about 1923
and had a bungalow on the beach where the tide rolled coal almost to the door
and he picked it up and burned it in the house. The impression that I get from
the evidence is that before 1939 there was no activity which could be called
commercial. It was merely the practice of local people getting a bag or two of
coal for their own fires and perhaps obliging a friend.

The shore was again closed in the second war and it was after it was
reopened that commercial exploitation started. It was still carried on by people
from neighbouring villages, but the motor lorry made a great change. These could
be got on to the sea shore itself at one time by two roads and later by one, and the
attention of the local council was really drawn to what was going on because of
the use of the roads and the complaints of the inhabitants of the villages through
which the lorries passed both by day and by night. These are Easington, already
mentioned, and Horden and Black Hall, two colliery villages adjacent to the
shore on the B–C and C–D strips.   From both these collieries dirt was tipped
directly into the sea. There was evidence that the second plaintiffs knew of the
practice of coal-taking by 1946 but at that time the existence of the lease of 1934
was overlooked and they were concerned with the use of the roads. No royalty
was claimed by the Crown under that lease until 1962 and it was not till about
that period that the plaintiff council were stirred into activity the result of which
was the abortive agreement (already mentioned) of that year with the Coal
Traders' Association. Two of the defendants in this action were members of that
body, and it seems clear enough that at that time neither they nor the other
members of the association conceived themselves to have rights, but they were
willing to be parties to a licence.   I agree with the Chancellor (26) that this
document does not constitute an estoppel against members of the association or
anybody else which can preclude them now from setting up a claim of right, but
it is nevertheless in my judgment at least some evidence that the persons who were
exploiting this privilege at that time had no belief that they were doing it as a
matter of right.

Another difficulty for the defendants is the class of persons alleged to be the
beneficiaries under the trust said to have been imposed on the bishop. No doubt
there could be a charitable gift in favour of the inhabitants of the County Palatine,
though that is a very large and indeterminate body of persons. The County
Palatine extends, as I understand, many miles inland and to several isolated
districts north of the Tyne where the administrative county boundary is. In my
judgment the evidence led to prove the custom was quite insufficient so far as
area was concerned; it really went no further than the parish of Easington, or
perhaps the neighbouring villages of Horden and Black Hall, and it is of course
obvious that, so long as the privilege, so to call it, was exercised by people with

---

(26) See p. 838, letter C, ante.

bags and buckets and wheelbarrows, it could only be purely local in extent. I agree that it would not be necessary to prove exercise of the privilege from every part of the county, but it would at least be necessary to show that the coal-gatherers supposed themselves to be gathering coal in right of their inhabitancy of the county, and of this I see no sign. If they considered it at all, I take it that a man bringing a bag of coal up from the beach to burn in his fire in Easington village would not have dreamed that he was exercising a right open to anyone in the county, even if he got as far as thinking of it as a right at all. At most he might suppose it to be a right in the parishioners of Easington. No alternative claim of this sort was set up, perhaps because the immemorial trustee was the Bishop of Durham, who could not be supposed to be concerned with any area but his County Palatine.

In my judgment, therefore, the defendants have wholly failed to show that the conditions existed in this area which confronted their lordships' House in the *Saltash* case (27). It follows, in my judgment, that there is no room to argue a supposed charitable trust. The practice may be sufficiently explained by tolerance of the foreshore owner, who would have been churlish indeed if he had stopped a poor man climbing up the cliff with a bag of small coals picked up on the shore to nourish his evening fire.

It is true that an ancient right, like a custom, alters with the times. This is well illustrated by the case of *Mercer* v. *Denne* (28). In that case the custom alleged was for local fishermen to dry nets on the land of a private owner and it was held good though the number of people engaged in fishing and the methods of drying the nets, and the fishing seasons themselves, had altered with the lapse of time. FARWELL, J., (29) deals with this argument by saying that a custom is not uncertain because it is not invariable in every part, and he illustrates this by, among others, the case of *Fitch* v. *Rawling* (30), where the custom to play all kinds of games justified the playing of cricket, a game unknown in the time of Richard I and indeed illegal in the much later reign of Henry VIII. I do not think that this line of reasoning applies here. The commercial exploitation of what is said to amount to one hundred thousand tons a year of this coal by means of motor lorries is a thing quite different from the old practice such as it was and not I think justified by it.

In my judgment, the usage claimed must be justified by the evidence and is bad if it goes beyond it, and the evidence here does not show a right exercised by or on behalf of the inhabitants of the whole county. Compare *A.-G.* v. *Horner* (*No. 2*) (31). I do not think it necessary to consider whether the coal when it lands on the beach or lies in pools above low water mark is or is not the property of the owners of the foreshore. All I think that we need say is that as owners or possessors of the foreshore they have the right to reduce it into possession, whereas the defendants have no such right because they have no right to go on to the foreshore for that purpose. It is as if a man who had a right of way over his neighbour's close should use his right of passage to shoot his neighbour's pheasants.

A right of this sort can be established only if no other explanation is forth-coming; see LORD LINDLEY's observations in *Gardner* v. *Hodgson's Kingston Brewery Co., Ltd.* (32). He says:

"A title by prescription can be established by long peaceable open enjoyment only; but in order that it may be so established the enjoyment must be inconsistent with any other reasonable inference than that it has been as of right in the sense above explained. This, I think, is the proper inference

---

(27) [1881-85] All E.R. Rep. 1076; (1882), 7 App. Cas. 633.
(28) [1904-07] All E.R. Rep. 71; [1904] 2 Ch. 534.
(29) [1904-07] All E.R. Rep. at p. 75; [1904] 2 Ch. at p. 552.
(30) (1795), 2 Hy. Bl. 393.   (31) [1913] 2 Ch. 140.
            (32) [1903] A.C. 229 at p. 239.

to be drawn from the authorities discussed in the court below. If the enjoyment is equally consistent with two reasonable inferences, enjoyment as of right is not established; and this, I think, is the real truth in the present case. The enjoyment is equally open to explanation in one of two ways, namely, by a lost grant of a right of way in consideration of a rentcharge . . . or by a succession of yearly licences not, perhaps, expressed every year, but implied and assumed and paid for."

If it be clear that the usage has long been practised under a claim of right then the court will be astute to find a legal origin for it, but where another explanation is equally possible this principle does not prevail. Here I think toleration is a sufficient explanation.

So far as the claim was made under a plea of custom, it must, I think, fail for the additional reasons that the taking of coal off the beach is not an easement but a profit-à-prendre and it is well settled that a fluctuating body such as the inhabitants of the county cannot acquire a prescriptive right of this nature: *Blewett* v. *Tregonning* (33). The Chancellor, though he did not decide it, inclined to the view (34) that this was not a profit-à-prendre in alieno solo. In this the Chancellor was I think influenced by the *Saltash* case (35), but that is quite different, for the class of persons claiming the right did so by right of property in the borough and were thus members of the corporation. Here the bishop is a corporation sole in which the inhabitants of the county had no part. I think that the taking of coal must be as much a profit as the taking of fish. I would therefore hold that, even if the facts permitted, this could not be a good custom and that this line of defence is not open to the defendants. I would allow the appeal.

RUSSELL, L.J. (read by WINN, L.J.): My lords have dealt so fully with the matters in debate in this appeal that I will state my views briefly. The Chancellor based his decision on analogy with the case of *Goodman* v. *Saltash Corpn.* (35). That was a case in which it was admitted that the practice, which was asserted in the proceedings to be a legal right, had from time immemorial been exercised openly and as of right, without resistance by the corporation to which an ancient grant of the fishery was presumed. The practice admittedly thus exercised was one which was highly detrimental to the corporation's fishery, and indeed was said by the corporation to be potentially destructive of it. It was not in those circumstances reasonable to account for the admitted immemorial practice as being attributed to mere tolerance or otherwise than ascribable to a legal right with a legal origin, if such were possible. Had the right alleged not been of the character of a profit-à-prendre it would plainly have been ascribed to custom, i.e., to local common law: but that was not possible. It was however found possible to conceive a legal origin in the form of a trust or condition imposed and accepted on the occasion of a (presumed) ancient grant by the Crown to the corporation of the fishery as a whole: this was possible (a) because the corporation being such was capable of being a grantee subject to a trust or condition, and (b) because there was no objection in point of perpetuity in that (or so it was considered) the persons claiming the right alleged were a sufficient section of the public to enable the trust to be treated as charitable.

In the present case an ancient grant is presumed in favour of the Bishop of Durham, a corporation, of the jura regalia of the County Palatine including the soil of the foreshore, and it is asserted that the evidence justifies a finding that a trust or condition was imposed and accepted on the occasion of that grant whereby the inhabitants of the County Palatine were given the right to go on this foreshore for the purpose of removing sea coal therefrom and making it their property, those inhabitants being a sufficient section of the public to avoid any problem of perpetuity.

(33) [1835-42] All E.R. Rep. 83 at p. 87; (1835), 3 Ad. & El. 554 at p. 575.
(34) See p. 839, letter D, ante.
(35) [1881-85] All E.R. Rep. 1076; (1882), 7 App. Cas. 633.

In my judgment this assertion is not on the facts of this case justified. In the first place the evidence does not establish that the gathering of sea coal was from the earliest living memory done as of right as distinct from being merely a de facto practice which the gatherers rightly thought no one would find objectionable and which the owner of the foreshore in fact tolerated as unobjectionable. It is true that according to the ENCYCLOPAEDIA BRITANNICA " charbon de roche " (sea coal) was by 1200 A.D. being exported from England to Bruges in appreciable quantities. The evidence of earliest living memory in the present case, however, is wholly inadequate to suggest that the sea coal available and taken on this foreshore in those days, washed in from outcrops in the sea bed, was of any value or significance to any except the poorer inhabitants of the immediate neighbourhood. Any presumption therefore that it was gathered to the same extent from time immemorial cannot serve to found an origin in a legal right. It is a well-known aspect of English law that in relation to the foreshore a great many activities have been generally tolerated without giving rise to any legal right to continue them. It has never been established in English law that beachcombing can give rise to a legal right to frequent the foreshore for the purpose of beachcombing or require a presumption of a legal origin; and the early evidence in this case to my mind amounts to no more than beachcombing.

For the same reasons it does not seem to me that the only reasonable conclusion from the evidence is that the practice must have had a legal origin; here the factual contrast with *Goodman* v. *Saltash Corpn.* (36) is most marked. I think that the only reasonable conclusion is mere tolerance of the unimportant; nor am I in any way persuaded of the contrary by the later history of gathering sea coal on this foreshore as it developed with tipping of mine waste into the sea below low water mark. Further, a notional trust or condition of the character suggested, imposed on the occasion of a presumed ancient grant of the jura regalia, does not seem to me to be a reasonably probable additional fiction. Why should it be thought that the Crown, on making the bishop in some respects the local Crown, would wish to make the rights of the inhabitants of that local kingdom over the foreshore (or this part of it) more extensive than they had been or were in other parts of the realm? Moreover, the only right asserted is a right in all the inhabitants of the County Palatine; not in the inhabitants of any particular parish or parishes; but the evidence of early user by no means suffices, in my judgment, to embrace so wide a field.

The alternative suggestion that a custom to the same effect is established equally fails. I will accept (without deciding) that the custom alleged, viz., a right to go on the foreshore for the purpose of taking into possession chattels not owned by anyone in the form of this sea coal, whether floating or deposited and awaiting the next tide, is not a profit. Nevertheless considerations to which I have drawn attention as making *Goodman* v. *Saltash Corpn.* (36) inapplicable apply also under this head; in particular I see no sufficient ground for holding that it is part of the local common law of the whole County Palatine that its inhabitants should have the alleged right to indulge in this particular kind of beachcombing. I would allow the appeal.

WINN, L.J.: The pleadings in this action raise issues of very considerable difficulty but of comparatively narrow scope. It should be emphasised that no question of title to the foreshore of the beaches in question was raised for decision. The second plaintiffs, the Easington Rural District Council, affirmed by para. 1 of the statement of claim that they were the lessees from the Crown, acting by the Commissioners of Crown Lands, of those parts of the foreshore near Horden in the county of Durham which lay between points marked A and B and points marked C and D on a plan a copy of which was exhibit 11 in the action. The plaintiff company asserted that it had been granted by the plaintiff council an exclusive licence to collect such deposits of coal as might be found on those parts of the

(36) [1881-85] All E.R. Rep. 1076; (1882), 7 App. Cas. 633.

said foreshore. The plaintiff company further alleged by para. 2 of the statement of claim that it had agreed to buy all that part of the same foreshore which lay between the points marked B and C on the said plan from the former owners thereof and that, although the said purchase had not been completed, it was entitled to exclusive possession of that part of the foreshore. By their defence the defendants admitted all the aforesaid averments. It follows that nothing decided in this action or this appeal could have any bearing on any question of title in respect of any part of the said foreshore, and it is, of course, plain a fortiori that no rights of persons not parties to this action can in any way be affected.

Merely as a passing comment I note that, notwithstanding the transfer to the Crown of the jura regalia of the Bishop of Durham by statutes of 1836 and 1858, in a book published in 1888 entitled A HISTORY OF THE FORESHORE AND THE LAW RELATING THERETO by STUART A. MOORE, F.S.A., barrister (at pp. 24, 25), there is to be found the following passage:

" By the end of the reign of King John the Crown had parted with and granted out almost every manor situate upon the sea coast and the tidal rivers of the kingdom: very few remained in the Crown . . . The County of Durham, which extends from the mid-stream of the Tyne to the mid-stream of the Tees, had been given to the see of Durham as a county palatine: the foreshore passed with it, and is claimed by the Ecclesiastical Commissioners, as against the tenants of the Bishopric, to this day."

No indication is given of any foundation for such a claim.

The action was fought and the appeal has turned on the contention raised by the defendants in para. 6 of their defence that, in so far as any of them entered the said foreshore, they did so " lawfully and as of right ". Particulars were requested and given of the said plea by which it was asserted that the defendants

" and all of the other inhabitants of the County Palatine of Durham or alternatively . . . the public at large, are entitled to enter upon the said foreshore, with or without animals or vehicles, and thence to take and carry away sea-washed coal [and that] the said inhabitants, or alternatively the public at large, have entered and taken coal as aforesaid from time immemorial. These defendants will submit that a lawful origin may and should be inferred for such usage either at common law or by custom or by lost grant or declaration of trust."

The said pleas of right of the public at large and of usage at common law were not pursued at the trial and it was expressly conceded by counsel for the defendants that there could not be any right common to all the inhabitants of the kingdom or recognised as part of the common law of England which justified the actions of the defendants, of which the plaintiffs complained as constituting trespasses against their possessory rights in the foreshore.

The real subject-matter of this dispute is the right commercially to exploit the coal which for reasons peculiar to the locality is found in very considerable and valuable quantities on this foreshore. It was made plain to the court that neither of the plaintiffs would have any objection to local inhabitants helping themselves to such relatively negligible quantities of coal as they might choose by the expenditure of their own physical effort to collect and carry away to their homes for burning there, or for supplying, out of kindness, or for some small remuneration, to their neighbours who lacked the strength or inclination to fetch and carry such coal for themselves. The dispute is not of negligible consequence, since the court was informed that the harvest of coal if fully exploited could reach one hundred thousand tons a year; if this be so it might be worth something of the order of £1/2 million or even more. The coal is brought to the shore by the sea partly from outcrops of coal seams in the sea bed and partly from dirt rejected from the in-shore collieries and dumped from overhead ropeways running out from the shore. I think it proper to take judicial notice of the notorious fact that no such conditions productive of coal deposits exist generally around the coasts of the

A United Kingdom, whether or not there are other areas where some coal is brought
on to the beaches by the action of the sea. It follows, in my judgment, that
counsel for the defendants rightly appreciated that he was compelled to concede
that there could not be any common law right to come on foreshores and collect
coal brought there by the sea. LORD KENYON, C.J., in *Ball* v. *Herbert* (37) said:

B " Now common law rights are either to be found in the opinion of lawyers,
delivered as axioms, or to be collected from the universal and immemorial
usage throughout the country."

In 1830 there was published an essay by a MR. HALL entitled AN ESSAY ON THE
RIGHTS OF THE CROWN IN THE SEASHORES OF THE REALM, which is reproduced
with notes in MOORE'S HISTORY OF THE FORESHORE. In this essay I find a
C similar view expressed in a passage of MOORE'S HISTORY (p. 888):

" It may, it is conceived, be ' collected from universal and immemorial
usage ' that the seashore has been resorted to for the purposes in question
(for obtaining natural products useful as manures) not in a few places or in
two counties only (viz., Cornwall and Devon) but generally throughout the
realm. It is a custom quite in contrast with that of towage: it is, in fact,
D essentially and in its nature general; as agricultural is general and the
manuring of land is general the products of the shore are also as generally
applicable and available in one part of the kingdom as another . . . A general
common law custom cannot be lost by local disuse; it may at any time be
revived into use for the public good. Such is the case with ' fishery '; and
nationally speaking, so it should be with the custom in question."

E In this context and generally for the purposes of this appeal the observations made
by FARWELL, J., on the subject of general public rights in *A.-G.* v. *Antrobus* (38)
are of very special importance. He said:

" The public as such cannot prescribe; nor is jus spatiandi [which was
the relevant topic in the case] known to our law as a possible subject-matter
F of grant or prescription; ' and for such things as can have no lawful
beginning, nor be created at this day by any manner of grant, or reservation,
or deed that can be supposed, no prescription is good ' [cf. a quotation from
Sir Francis North's argument in *Potter* v. *North* (39), quoted by LORD
SELBORNE, L.C., in *Dalton* v. *Angus & Co., Public Works Comrs.* v. *Angus
& Co.* (40)]. It is true that in some cases in the books the courts have pre-
G sumed trusts, but they have been cases where corporations holding the fee
of an area have been held to be trustees for some of their corporators, or of
the inhabitants, to the exclusion of the others. *Goodman* v. *Saltash Corpn.* (41)
is a good illustration of this . . ."

The decision in the case was that the general public cannot acquire by user a
right to visit a public monument, such as Stonehenge, or other object of interest
H on private property, and that there can be no public right of way to such a
monument or object acquired by mere user.

It is, I think, a minor but not uninteresting feature of the instant case that the
coal which is found in, on and off the beaches of the part of the county of Durham
to which this action relates is probably not the property of any person until any
particular piece of it has been reduced into possession or has at least become fixed
I on the shore (cf., per SIR JOHN NICHOLL in *R.* v. *Two Casks of Tallow* (42) in 1837).
That, at any rate, seems to me to be the position, though no argument was
addressed to the point or any authority on it cited to the court. I express that
view without overlooking the decisions establishing that gravel, stones and sand

(37) (1789), 3 Term Rep. 253 at p. 261.   (38) [1905] 2 Ch. 188 at pp. 198, 199.
(39) (1669), 1 Vent. 383 at p. 387.
(40) [1881-85] All E.R. Rep. 1 at p. 8; (1881), 6 App. Cas. 740 at p. 795.
(41) [1881-85] All E.R. Rep. 1076; (1882), 7 App. Cas. 633.
(42) (1837), 3 Hag. Adm. 294 at p. 297.

washed on to a foreshore are the property of the owner of the foreshore: cf., *A*
Blewett v. *Tregonning* (43). However, it is not important for the purposes of this
appeal to decide whether that view is correct, since what is more particularly and,
indeed, specifically in issue is whether the defendants have any right to go on this
foreshore and go about on it for the purpose of collecting coal and taking it away.
If, as I think, they cannot have that right merely because they are inhabitants or
citizens of the United Kingdom by virtue of its common law, their other claims **B**
of right must be considered.

First, however, it is convenient, I think, to refer to two particular facts: (i)
that, so far as the evidence in this case reveals, it is quite impossible that the
defendants never dug into the beach to take coal from it or took coal which was
wholly or partially embedded: the plea in their defence may be correct inasmuch
as they denied " removing . . . sea-washed coal then adhering to the foreshore "; **C**
(ii) that some, at any rate, of the coal which had been taken by the defendants
and others was found by them on rocks or in pools or afloat below the low tide
mark of ordinary tides, viz., not on the foreshore.

In my judgment the first of these facts is not, for the purposes of this case, of
significance since, although consideration requires to be given to the question
whether the defendants by asserting that they are entitled to take coal from the **D**
foreshore have thereby sought to set up a right which in its true nature is a
profit-à-prendre, I do not think that the answer will depend on any circumstance
of the coal being embedded in or adhering to the soil of the foreshore. As I
understand the meaning of the term " profit-à-prendre in solo alieno ", the latter
words " in solo alieno " are not equivalent to " ex solo alieno " but refer only to
something which is taken within the bounds of the land of another. It is, however, **E**
relevant to recall that the case of *Bagot* v. *Orr* (44) related to the taking and carrying away of shellfish and shells on the foreshore of a manor in Morecambe Bay.
It was argued for the defendants that ownership of the foreshore would not exclude
the public right to fish and that the statute (1609), 7 Jac. 1 c. 18 which related
specifically to the taking of sand in Devon and Cornwall was a full recognition of
the right of the subject to use the shore of the sea in every way in which it could **F**
be serviceable to him, and that his right was not confined to the privilege of taking
shellfish left on the shore by the ebbing of the tides, but that he might also take
the fish shells, and even the sand of the shore. The court held that this plea
succeeded so far only as it related to the taking of fish but observed that, as no
authority had been cited to support the claim to take shells, they should pause
before they established a general right of that kind. Although no judgment **G**
appears to have been given as to the right to take fish shells, the court evidently
leaned against such a claim, apparently attaching importance to the fact that
such shells might be wholly or partly *in* the soil of the shore.

With regard to the second fact just mentioned, it was, I gather, accepted by
counsel in this appeal that the plaintiffs could not restrain anybody from coming
in a boat from seaward and taking coal wherever it might be found below low **H**
tide mark. I desire only to comment that I think that it does not follow that the
Crown might not be entitled to prevent this being done, either by asserting a
proprietary right in the soil of the sea or possibly in Her Majesty's capacity as
Lord High Admiral of England. It would be outside the proper scope of this
judgment to consider the rights of the Crown in the sea adjoining the United
Kingdom, and it suffices to say that there is considerable authority that, apart **I**
from a few special cases of express grant, the Crown has ever since the Conquest
been the owner of the soil of the sea below low tide mark to a seaward extent which
may be somewhat uncertain. Thus SIR MATTHEW HALE in his TREATISE DE
JURE MARIS, ch. 4, states:

" The narrow sea, adjoining to the coast of England, is part of the wast and
demesnes and dominions of the King of England, whether it lie within the

---

(43) [1835-42] All E.R. Rep. 83; (1835), 3 Ad. & El. 554.
(44) (1801), 2 Bos. & P. 472.

a township to take gravel, etc., for the cultivation and improvement of their land and repair to the highways of the parish were bad in law because, inter alia,

" if the claim were founded in prescription it would be bad inasmuch as it was a claim by persons who not being a corporation were incapable of taking by grant and were not claiming in a que estate."

In so far as the concept of a trust or condition is invoked it seems to me that this objection to its validity in the circumstances of the instant case must prevail: the objects are too vague and perpetual.

With regard to the evidence which was given in this case, I do not propose to discuss the details of it, and content myself with saying that, after carefully considering its scope and effect, I do not think that either in relation to the period 1895 to 1900 or in relation to more modern times did it establish a usage exercised by and in the capacity of inhabitants of the whole county of Durham as distinct from inhabitants or occupiers of land or houses in and around Easington and other villages lying close to the shore of the North Sea.

In *A.-G.* v. *Horner* (*No. 2*) (59) Sir Herbert Cozens-Hardy, M.R., said:

" I am not prepared to make a presumption not in accordance with rights claimed. Long user not explained may justify the court and, indeed, in some circumstances, may almost compel the court, to presume what is necessary to give validity to the usage. When, however, the right claimed cannot be established on the ground claimed, an incidental portion of the right claimed cannot be established on the mere ground of long usage. In other words, a presumption to support a right claimed may be reasonable, but a presumption to support a mere fragment of a right claimed and never exercised apart from the right claimed is a wholly different proposition."

I venture to think that it is equally right to say, where the difference between the right claimed and the usage established consists in excess of the former over the latter rather than in the fact that the right claimed is less extensive than the usage, that even if a presumption to support the usage may be reasonable a presumption to support a more extensive right is a wholly different proposition. I am therefore of the opinion that, even if it is reasonable to presume from the usage proved by the evidence in this case the existence of a right in favour of the category of persons who lived near or had houses near the shore, it is an entirely different proposition to suggest that there should be a presumption of a lost grant in favour of any wider or more widely dispersed category of persons.

Finally, I would state a reason which is fundamental to my conclusion that the judgment of the Chancellor upholding the right asserted by the defendants is erroneous and should be set aside. The evidence does not seem to me to establish that those who were used to come on the foreshore at any time within living memory to collect coal there and take it away did so in the belief that all the inhabitants of the county of Durham were entitled so to do. In so far as any of them, acting as they did openly and peacefully and without first seeking permission, are to be presumed to have believed that they had a right so to act, this conduct appears to me to be consistent with and therefore to establish no more than either a traditional understanding that all who lived close to the shore might resort there and take coal from it as of right, i.e., without being liable to be lawfully prevented by anyone from so doing; or with a similar belief that a practice which had been long permitted would continue to be permitted, and that it was safe to assume that the owner of the foreshore, whoever that might be, would not suddenly withdraw permission without prior notification. After fairly considerable research and reading I have failed to find elsewhere than in Hall's Essay—which in this respect is partisan and argumentative and commented on critically by Moore—any support for the view that there has ever been a right in the inhabitants of the United Kingdom or any county or town or district

---

(59) [1913] 2 Ch. at p. 169.

comprised in it, to have access to any foreshore, elsewhere than in Devon and Cornwall, to collect what may be found there by a process described in the course of this appeal as beachcombing. It seems to be clear that there has for long been a common—though it may be no less fallacious—belief entertained fairly generally by the public that there is a right of access to the foreshore for the purpose of bathing; it would be outside the scope of this appeal to pronounce on the existence or non-existence of any right to bathe from the foreshore, but it is at least clear that the only well-established rights of user of the foreshore are those ancillary to fishing and navigating. I would allow this appeal.

Appeal allowed. Declaration and injunctions in terms of statement of claim. Leave to appeal to the House of Lords refused.

Solicitors: *Lewin, Gregory, Mead & Sons*, agents for *Keenlyside & Forster*, Newcastle-on-Tyne (for the plaintiffs); *Ward, Bowie & Co.*, agents for *Richard Reed & Co.*, Sunderland (for the defendants).

[*Reported by* F. A. AMIES, ESQ., *Barrister-at-Law.*]

Re PAULET'S WILL TRUSTS.

[CHANCERY DIVISION (Buckley, J.), November 23, 24, 1966.]

Estate Duty—Incidence—Property not passing to executor as such—Recovery of duty from person entitled to sum charged on property—Jointures—Appointments of jointures to full amounts—Supplemental deed executed subsequently providing for payment of jointures free of all death duties—Whether jointures payable subject to deduction for estate duty—Finance Act, 1894 (57 & 58 Vict. c. 30), s. 14 (1).

A tenant for life had two powers of jointuring over settled property, one was for appointing a sum of £500 per annum under a will made in 1891 by a testator who died in 1893, and the other was for appointing a sum of £1,500 under a will made in 1899 of a testator who died in that year. Neither power expressly referred to making the appointment free from duty. In June, 1952, the tenant for life exercised each of these powers. He appointed to his wife a jointure of the maximum amount in each case, and in each case the jointure was charged on the settled party. In December, 1952, he executed a supplemental deed purporting to appoint that the two jointures of £500 and £1,500 per annum should be free of all death duties. He died in 1962.

Held: the entitlement of the widow to " any sum charged on the inheritance " within the meaning of those words in s. 14 (1)* of the Finance Act, 1894, arose wholly under the deeds of appointment of June, 1952, which dispositions did not contain any provision excluding the liability imposed by s. 14 (1) on the jointress to bear a rateable part of the estate duty exigible in respect of the settled properties; accordingly the jointures were payable subject to deduction in respect of estate duty (see p. 860, letters B and D, post).

Re Lonsdale's Will Trusts ([1959] 3 All E.R. 679) distinguished.

[As to the recovery of a rateable part of the estate duty from a person entitled to a sum charged on the property, see 15 HALSBURY'S STATUTES (3rd Edn.) 136, 137, para. 281; and for cases on the subject, see 21 DIGEST (Repl.) 85-88, *385-400*.

For the Finance Act, 1894, s. 14 (1), see 9 HALSBURY'S STATUTES (3rd Edn.) 375.]

Cases referred to:
Smith-Bosanquet, Re, Smith v. *Smith-Bosanquet*, [1940] 3 All E.R. 519; [1940] Ch. 954; 109 L.J.Ch. 440; 164 L.T. 267; 21 Digest (Repl.) 86, *391.*

* Section 14 (1) is set out at p. 857, letter B, post.

Lonsdale's Will Trusts, Re, Lowther v. *Lowther*, [1959] 3 All E.R. 679; [1960]
Ch. 288; [1959] 3 W.L.R. 879; 21 Digest (Repl.) 87, *395*.

Adjourned Summons.

This was an application by originating summons dated Mar. 30, 1966, by the
plaintiffs Roger Edward Thompson and Cyril Petersen who were the trustees of
the will of Lord William Paulet, deceased, dated Aug. 24, 1891, and of the
will of the fifteenth Marquis of Winchester, deceased, dated Sept. 29, 1899. The
application was to determine (i) whether on the true construction of the wills and
of three deeds of appointment of jointures (dated June 30, 1952, June 30, 1952,
and Dec. 5, 1952), the jointures of £500 and £1,500 payable to the first defendant
out of the estates of the respective testators were payable (a) free of estate duty,
or (b) subject to deductions in respect of the proper proportions attributable to the
jointures of the estate duty payable on the death of the sixteenth Marquis of
Winchester on the property on which such jointures were respectively charged:
(ii) if the answer to (i) were in the terms of para. (b) thereof, then (a) whether the
jointures or either of them should be reduced by the effective rates at which estate
duty was paid in respect of the property on which the jointures were charged on
the death of the sixteenth Marquis, and if not (b) how the proportions of estate
duty attributable to the jointures should be calculated and at what rate interest
should be charged thereon against the jointures or in what other manner the
proper proportions of estate duty should be borne by the jointures.

The third question raised by the summons was not material to this report.
The defendants were Bapsi, Marchioness of Winchester and the seventeenth
Marquis of Winchester. The facts are set out in the judgment.

The cases noted below* were cited during the argument in addition to those
referred to in the judgment.

M. W. Cockle for the plaintiffs.

J. A. Brightman, Q.C., and *Martin Roth* for the first defendant.

E. J. A. Freeman for the second defendant.

BUCKLEY, J.: The first point which arises in this case relates to the effect
of s. 14 (1) of the Finance Act, 1894, in the circumstances of the case. By his will,
which was dated Aug. 24, 1891, the late Field Marshal Lord William Paulet
settled certain property described as " the settled estate ", a settlement under
which the fifteenth Marquis of Winchester took a life interest, with remainders
to his issue, which failed to take effect. Subject thereto, the sixteenth Marquis of
Winchester was given a life interest, with remainders over, under which, in the
events which have happened, the seventeenth Marquis, the second defendant in
these proceedings is now tenant in tail possession. By the terms of his will the
Field Marshal provided that

> " each tenant for life of full age may (subject to preceding estates interests
> and charges) by deed or will appoint to any wife any jointure out of the
> settled estate for her life not exceeding £500 a year . . ."

By his will dated Sept. 29, 1899, the fifteenth Marquis also settled property
described in his will as " the settled estate " on similar trusts, so far as they are
now relevant, with power contained in cl. 12 of his will for

> " each tenant for life of full age . . . (subject to preceding estates interests
> and charges) by deed or will [to] appoint to any wife any jointure out of the
> settled estate or any part thereof for her life of not exceeding £1,500 a
> year . . ."

Field Marshal Lord William Paulet died on May 9, 1893, and the fifteenth Marquis
died on Dec. 11, 1899, whereupon the sixteenth Marquis became the tenant for

---

* *Hervey* v. *Hervey*, (1739), 1 Atk. 561; *Lady Londonderry* v. *Wayne*, (1763), Amb. 424;
Re Parker-Jervis, [1895-99] All E.R. Rep. 439; [1898] 2 Ch. 643; *Re Viscount Portman*,
[1924] 2 Ch. 6; *Re Sebright*, [1944] 2 All E.R. 547; [1944] Ch. 287; *Re Keele Estates*
(*No. 2*), [1952] 2 All E.R. 164; [1952] Ch. 603.

life in possession of those settled estates. On July 9, 1927, disentailing deeds
(one in respect of each settled estate) were executed and the entails were barred
by the second defendant, with the consent of the sixteenth Marquis, so that,
subject to the life interest of the sixteenth Marquis and his power of jointure, the
seventeenth Marquis, the second defendant, became absolutely entitled to the
settled property.

By the terms of each disentailing deed the sixteenth Marquis covenanted
with the now seventeenth Marquis that the power of appointing jointures, in the
one case not exceeding £500 and in the other not exceeding £1,500 a year, so far
as regards any future wife of his, the sixteenth Marquis, should only be exercisable
and exercised by him by an appointment of a jointure not exceeding £500

"... to arise out of and be charged on such part of the settled estate as
shall consist of securities representing capital moneys of the nature authorised
by law for the investment of trust moneys (other than railway preference
stocks) and as shall suffice by the income thereof at the time such jointure
shall arise and take effect to produce eleven-tenths (or a margin of ten per
cent. in excess) of any such jointure in favour of any such future wife that
may hereafter be created or appointed by the present Marquis To the intent
that such power of jointuring shall be so restricted and operate accordingly
And that the settled estate of Lord William Paulet ... (other than and
except capital moneys represented by securities of the nature and to the
amount or extent aforesaid) shall stand and be released and discharged
from the power of the present Marquis to create or appoint any jointure
in favour of any future wife of the present Marquis."

That covenant is not relevant to the point which I am at present considering, but
may become relevant to matters which may have to be considered hereafter, if I
decide this question in a particular way.

On June 30, 1952, the sixteenth Marquis executed two deeds of appointment.
By one, after reciting that the marriage was intended shortly to be solemnised
between the sixteenth Marquis and the lady who subsequently became his wife
(the first defendant in these proceedings), it states that the sixteenth Marquis as
settlor in exercise of the power vested in him by the said will (of Lord William
Paulet) and of every other power appointed to her from his own death (in case the
marriage should be solemnised) during the residue of her life a jointure or yearly
rent charge of £500 to be payable out of and charged on the securities (other than
railway preference stocks) for the time being subject to the will of Lord William
Paulet. By the second deed of appointment, on the same day, the Marquis made
a similar appointment, in this case in exercise of the power vested in the fifteenth
Marquis, of a jointure or yearly rent charge of £1,500. It is substantially in the
same form.

On Dec. 5, 1952, the sixteenth Marquis executed a deed which gives rise to the
question that I am at present concerned with. It is called a deed of appointment
made between the sixteenth Marquis of the one part and the Marchioness of the
other part and expressed to be supplemental to the two deeds of appointment
which I have mentioned and it recites that the marriage was solemnised on July 2,
1952, and the operative part of the deed is in these terms:

" Now THIS DEED WITNESSETH that the husband as settlor in exercise of
the powers vested in him by the will dated Aug. 24, 1891, of Field Marshal
Lord William Paulet, G.C.B., and the will dated Sept. 29, 1899, of the Most
Honourable Augustus John Henry Beaumont (Fifteenth) Marquis of
Winchester and of every other power enabling him in that behalf hereby
appoints and directs that the jointures or yearly rent charges of £500 and
£1,500 respectively appointed by the husband to the wife by the said two
deeds of appointment dated June 30, 1952, to which this deed is supplemental
shall be free of all death duties."

The sixteenth Marquis died on June 28, 1962, and the Marchioness thereupon

became entitled to the jointures appointed to her, and the second defendant
became entitled to the settled estates subject to the jointures.

Section 14 (1) of the Finance Act, 1894, provides:

" In the case of property which does not pass to the executor as such, an
amount equal to the proper rateable part of the estate duty may be recovered
by the person, who being authorised or required to pay the estate duty in
respect of any property has paid such duty, from the person entitled to any
sum charged on such property (whether as capital or as an annuity or otherwise), under a disposition not containing any express provision to the
contrary."

On the death of the sixteenth Marquis the settled estates, comprised in the wills
of the Field Marshal and the fifteenth Marquis, passed, but not to the executor
of the sixteenth Marquis as such and, accordingly, the case is one to which this
subsection is applicable, and the question is whether, in the circumstances which
I have mentioned, the Marchioness is entitled to receive her annuity without
being liable to have recovered from her by the person who has paid duty in respect
of the property a rateable part of the duty appropriate to be attributed to her
jointures.

The question as posed by counsel for the first defendant is this: whether the
Marchioness is entitled to her jointures under a disposition or dispositions containing an express provision barring the person who pays the duty from recovering
a part of it from her.   The only question that arises in this case is this, whether
the contrary intention can be expressed in some document other than that which
in fact creates the charge of the jointure on the inheritance, or whether one
must find the contrary intention expressed in the document itself or in some
way associated directly with the disposition creating the charge on the inheritance.

At one time, it was thought that the power to take advantage of this subsection was one which must have been, in some way or other, conferred by the
document which conferred the power of appointment, but that view was negatived
by the decision of BENNETT, J., in *Re Smith-Bosanquet, Smith* v. *Smith-Bosanquet*
(1).   It is now clear, from the decision of the Court of Appeal in *Re Lonsdale's
Will Trusts, Lowther* v. *Lowther* (2), that the power to relieve the jointress or
portioner or anyone else, who would, unless relieved, be subject to having some
part of the duty recovered from them under s. 14 (1), is a statutory power and is
something quite distinct from powers conferred by the document containing the
power of appointment under which the interest arises which gives rise to, or
would give rise to, the primary application of s. 14 (1).   In *Re Lonsdale's Will
Trusts* (2) the court was concerned with powers to jointure which were contained
in the will of the second Earl of Lonsdale, who died in 1872, long before the Finance
Act, 1894, was enacted, and the will of the third Earl, who died in 1876, also long
before the statute had been enacted.   In exercise of those powers of jointure, the
sixth Earl had appointed the jointures to be paid without any deduction, except
for succession duty, if any, and it was held that if in an appointment of a jointure
the formula " free of duty ", or similar words, were used that was " an express
provision to the contrary " within the last words of s. 14 (1) of the Finance Act,
1894 and, accordingly, that the appointments by the sixth Earl in that case
was apt to bring the exempting provisions of s. 14 (1) into operation.   It was
held that the appointment made by the sixth Earl was a disposition within
s. 14 (1) and that he had power to exempt the jointress from liability to contribute
to the estate duty, notwithstanding, as I say, that the wills in question under
which the power to jointure arose had been made long before the Act of 1894 and
long before the existence of estate duty and long before the existence of the
power conferred by s. 14 (1), so that the testators could have had no such idea in
their minds.

(1) [1940] 3 All E.R. 519; [1940] Ch. 954.
(2) [1959] 3 All E.R. 679; [1960] Ch. 288.

That case is authority, counsel for the first defendant has submitted, for the contention that, notwithstanding that the document that created the appointment is silent as to estate duty, the right of dispensation under s. 14 (1) is available to the donee of the power; and it is also authority for the view that the dispensing power is a separate and distinct power from the power of appointment, in that the power of appointment is a power conferred by the donor of the power, and the power of dispensing is a power conferred by the legislature on the person who is capable of exercising the power of appointment. SELLERS, L.J., said this (3):

" This seems to give a right to the person making the disposition to provide that the capital or annuity of which he is making a disposition should not bear the burden of the tax. His right with regard to the incidence of the tax is, therefore, given and recognised by statute and is independent of any prior deed or authority which gave the power to charge any property, at least where the deed placed no express restrictions to the contrary."

HARMAN, L.J., said this (4):

" The effect of the section is to give a dispensing power to the disposer who created the charge. The disposer in this case, as in others of the sort, seems to me necessarily to be the person who exercises the power, be it a jointure or a portion, because it is he, after all, who makes the power effective. If he does not exercise the power, no charge is thrown on the inheritance. He may exercise the power up to the limit of the figure he is given. When he adds the words ' free of duty ' or similar words he is not exercising the power at all. It is, in my judgment, a fallacy to treat it as if he were exercising further the power. It is true that he burdens the inheritance and frees the jointress; but that is a right given to him by the statute. It is not necessary to refer to the power at all."

At the end of his judgment he said (4):

" It is a mistake, I think, to treat the exercise of the statutory dispensing power as a further exercise of the power of appointment."

The question which I have to consider did not arise at all in *Re Lonsdale's Will Trusts* (5) because the words " free of duty ", or whatever the actual words used in that case were, were to be found in the deeds of appointment. It is contended, on behalf of the Marchioness, that if a person has two distinct powers, as in *Re Lonsdale's Will Trusts* (5) the power of appointment and the dispensing power under the section, then, prima facie, he can exercise them either in the same instrument or in consecutive instruments: there is no necessity to exercise them in one and the same instrument. Indeed, counsel for the first defendant says that it was irrational to suppose that both powers must be exercised in the same instrument.

One has to look at the terms of the section and construe the language to see what it says may be done. If Parliament said that something must be done in a particular way it is not for me to say that that is an irrational view. The question must turn in the end on the construction of the language of the subsection. The contention of counsel for the first defendant is that having exercised the powers of appointment of June 30, 1952, the sixteenth Marquis had not exhausted his powers, because he still had up his sleeve, as it were, a dispensing power under s. 14 (1). Counsel for the first defendant calls *Re Lonsdale's Will Trusts* (5) to his aid in this way. LORD EVERSHED, M.R., in the course of his judgment in *Re Lonsdale's Will Trusts* (6), called attention to the fact that Parliament, in 1894, when the Act was passed, must surely have known that there would be many outstanding settlements which would not have conferred such a dispensing

(3) [1959] 3 All E.R. at p. 691; [1960] Ch. at p. 311.
(4) [1959] 3 All E.R. at p. 692; [1960] Ch. at p. 312.
(5) [1959] 3 All E.R. 679; [1960] Ch. 288.
(6) [1959] 3 All E.R. at p. 691; [1960] Ch. at p. 310.

A power on the person having the right to appoint a jointure. He was concerned with the question whether one must find something in the original settlement or instrument creating the power to make the dispensing power available to the donee of a power of appointment. LORD EVERSHED, M.R., used this argument to say that that was not so: all that was needed was to see whether the donee's power of appointment, when he disposed of the property, disclosed an intention

B to the contrary of s. 14 (1).

Counsel for the first defendant says that Parliament must also have been aware that there would have been, at the passing of the Finance Act, 1894, many appointments already made under pre-existing powers which had not yet come into operation, appointments of portions and appointments of jointures, which were awaiting the death of the donee of the power to take effect. And he said that

C Parliament cannot have intended to leave these cases outside the operation of s. 14 (1) and that it is reasonable to suppose that Parliament would have intended that in such cases the persons who had appointed portions or jointures, as the case may be, should be able to exercise this dispensing power, relieving the objects in whose favour they made the appointment, of the burden first placed on them in 1894 of bearing some part of the new duty then first invented. There is a great

D force in that argument and I have to look at the language of the section to see whether it is one to which one can give effect. On the other hand, counsel who appears for the seventeenth Marquis, the second defendant, has contended that when the sixteenth Marquis exercised the powers of appointment of June 30, 1952, he exercised them to the full permissible extent, in the one case to the extent of £500 a year and in the other to the extent of £1,500 a year, and that he had

E thereby exhausted his power of appointment. Those appointments were irrevocable and the argument of counsel is that the sixteenth Marquis' powers of appointment of jointure in favour of his wife were thereby exhausted and spent. He says that the statutory power of dispensing must, on the true construction of s. 14 (1), be exercised in the document creating the charge on the inheritance, that is to say, in the present case it must be found to have been exercised in the appoint-

F ments of June 30, 1952, notwithstanding that it is a separate and distinct power from the power of appointment, and for that he relied on the language of the section. He submits that the statutory power of dispensing is a power, not to appoint any further benefit to the jointress, but a power to shift the incidence of the duty; and he says that the supplemental deed, although it is in fact called a deed of appointment and is framed in language suitable to an exercise

G of a power of appointment and, indeed, refers to the powers vested in the sixteenth Marquis under the wills of the Field Marshal and the fifteenth Marquis, nevertheless is not in truth an appointment at all and does not dispose of any property at all.

Now the effect of the appointments was undoubtedly to charge the jointures on the two settled estates and these jointures became charged on the settled

H estates under the deeds of appointment of June 30, 1952, and the Marchioness is a person entitled to those jointures charged on those settled estates under those deeds of appointment. Unless, the Marchioness is in some sense entitled to a sum or sums charged on the settled estates under the supplemental deed, or under the combined effect of the supplemental deed and the appointments, it is difficult to bring the case within the language of s. 14 (1) of the Act of 1894.

I I have, in the course of the argument, been rather attracted by the idea that, having regard to the provisions of the Finance Act, 1894, the effect of the appointment of the jointures was to confer on the Marchioness the right to a benefit which was subject to something in the nature of an encumbrance, that is to say, the obligation to contribute to the duty and that the direction that the jointures should be free of duty could be, perhaps, regarded as a disposition in this sense, that it relieved the jointress of the obligation to make that contribution and relieved her of that encumbrance and so could be regarded as being a disposition.

When I come to read the language of the subsection, however, I do not feel
really that I can get away from this, that the question which I have to ask
myself is—under what disposition is she entitled to " any sum charged on " the
inheritance? The sum which is charged on the inheritance is the amount of
the jointures, and she is entitled to the jointures under the deeds of appointment
of June 30, 1952. But the fact that someone else has a statutory right to recover
something from her under this subsection does not alter the fact that what is
charged on the inheritance is the jointures and the jointures are something to
which she is entitled under the appointments of June 30, 1952. It seems to me
that the idea which rather favourably impressed me at one stage, that one could
look on the supplemental deed as being a further disposition or as being, if taken
in conjunction with the deeds of appointment, a disposition of something greater,
by reason of the direction that the jointures should be free from duty, than the
Marchioness would otherwise have been entitled to, does not make it possible
for me to come to the conclusion that the supplemental deed is a disposition
under which she is entitled to any sum charged on the inheritance.

With considerable regret, therefore, I feel compelled to come to the conclusion
that this is a case which cannot be brought within the language of the subsection
so far as it confers the dispensing power, and I must answer the first question
on the summons in the sense that on the true construction of the wills and deeds
of appointment the jointures of £500 and £1,500 payable to the first defendant
out of the estates of Lord William Paulet and the fifteenth Marquis respectively
are payable subject to deductions in respect of the proper proportions attributable
to the said jointures of the estate duty payable on the death of the sixteenth
Marquis on the property on which such jointures are respectively charged.

Order accordingly.

Solicitors: *Garrard, Wolfe & Co.* (for the plaintiffs); *Theodore Goddard & Co.*
(for the first defendant); *Rooper & Whately* (for the second defendant).

[*Reported by* JENIFER SANDELL, *Barrister-at-Law.*]

A

MURPHY v. VERATI.

[QUEEN'S BENCH DIVISION (Lord Parker, C.J., Winn, L.J., and Willis, J.), February 7, 1967.]

Railway—Offences by passengers—Fare—Intent to avoid payment of fare of
B　*co-passenger—Whether co-passenger in process of travelling when at ticket*
barrier after alighting from train—London Transport Board Bye-laws, No.
8 (1) made under Transport Act, 1962 (10 & 11 Eliz. 2 c. 46), s. 67.

The respondent and a woman companion arrived at the exit barrier of Stockwell station on the London underground, both without tickets. The respondent gave the ticket inspector 2s., saying—" Two from Kennington
C　station ". In fact, both the respondent and the woman had come from King's Cross station, for which the journey fare payable was more than the fare from Kennington. The respondent was charged before a magistrates' court, inter alia, with contravening Bye-law No. 8 (1) of the London Transport Bye-laws in that he " tendered to an authorised person [the inspector] money on behalf of another person [the woman] with intent to enable the
D　person on whose behalf the money was tendered to travel on the railway without having previously paid [her] fare ". The magistrate dismissed the information on the ground that there was no offence unless the money was tendered before the traveller travelled. On appeal by the prosecutor,

Held: a traveller on the underground was still travelling when at the exit or terminus of the arrival platform, not having yet left the arrival platform;
E　accordingly, in the present case when the respondent tendered a sum of money on behalf of the woman companion he was seeking to enable her to continue travelling, so as to complete her process of travelling by leaving the arrival platform, and the case would be remitted with a direction to convict (see p. 863, letters G to I, post).

Bremme v. *Dubery* ([1964] 1 All E.R. 193) considered.

F　　Appeal allowed.

[As to the offence of travelling on a railway with intent to avoid payment of fare, see 31 HALSBURY'S LAWS (3rd Edn.) 670, 671, para. 1047; and for cases on the subject, see 8 DIGEST (Repl.) 119, 120, *761-775*.]

Case referred to:
G　*Bremme* v. *Dubery*, [1964] 1 All E.R. 193; [1964] 1 W.L.R. 119; 128 J.P. 148;
　　3rd Digest Supp.

Case Stated.

This was a Case stated by A. H. G. CRASKE, ESQ., one of Her Majesty's stipendiary magistrates for the county of London, in respect of his adjudication as a magistrate's court sitting at Lavender Hill, Battersea, on May 19, 1966.
H　　On Apr. 27, 1966, two informations were laid by the appellant, Myles Murphy, a duly authorised officer of the British Transport Police of and for and on behalf of the London Transport Board against the respondent, Gianorio Verati, charging that he on Feb. 28, 1966, at Stockwell Station: (a) did unlawfully travel on a railway without having previously paid his fare and with intent to avoid payment thereof, contrary to s. 5 (3) of the Regulation of Railways Act, 1889, and s. 84 (2)
I　of the Transport Act, 1962; (b) with intent that the London Transport Board should be defrauded tendered to an authorised person money on behalf of another person with intent to enable the person on whose behalf the money was tendered to travel on the railway without having previously paid her fare, contrary to Bye-law No. 8 (1) of the Bye-laws of the London Transport Board relating to railways in that behalf duly made, approved and published.

The respondent pleaded " guilty " to both charges. The magistrate directed that a plea of " not guilty " to the information set out at para. (b) ante be entered and found the following facts. On Feb. 28, 1966, the respondent who

was then accompanied by a Miss Catherine Smith, travelled on the railway, **A**
arriving with her at the railway station at Stockwell but without any tickets.
On arrival at the way out barrier at Stockwell station the respondent tendered a
2s. piece to one Phelps, a duly authorised ticket inspector then and there on duty,
saying—" Two from Kennington station ". The inspector gave the respondent
eightpence change (the correct fare from Kennington station to Stockwell
station being eightpence per passenger). The respondent and Miss Smith, in each **B**
other's presence, said that they had travelled only from Kennington, but later
both similarly admitted having travelled by railway from King's Cross Station (for
which journey the correct fare was 1s. 6d. per passenger). Both the respondent
and Miss Smith admitted, in each other's presence, that they had never had
tickets for their journeys. The respondent was thereupon cautioned by the
inspector and told that the facts would be reported with a view to his being **C**
prosecuted.

It was contended on behalf of the appellant that: (i) since a passenger had not
in law finished travelling on a railway until he left the railway's premises he
might evince a fraudulent intention at the way-out barrier of a station; (ii) on
the uncontradicted evidence of the inspector the information set out at (b) ante
was proved.   **D**

No contention was advanced by or on behalf of the respondent, who did not
give evidence or call witnesses on his own behalf.

The magistrate was of opinion that on a proper construction of the wording
of Bye-law 8 (1) expecially in view of the words " to enable . . . to travel " there
could only be an offence if it were proved that a person tendered money before
the person on whose behalf the aforesaid money was tendered travelled. He, **E**
accordingly, dismissed the information set out at (b), p. 861, letter I, ante.

B. L. *Leary* for the appellant.
The respondent did not appear and was not represented.

WINN, L.J., delivered the first judgment at the invitation of LORD PARKER,
C.J.: The appellant, a duly authorised officer of the British Transport police, **F**
prosecuted the respondent, Gianorio Verati, charging him with two alleged
offences. To the first of them, as well indeed to the second, he pleaded guilty,
but the magistrate directed that a plea of not guilty should be entered in respect
of the second charge. The first charge was that he unlawfully travelled on the
railway without having previously paid his fare—I emphasise " his fare "—and
with intent to avoid payment thereof, contrary to s. 5 (3) of the Regulation of **G**
Railways Act, 1889, and s. 84 (2) of the Transport Act, 1962. Nothing more
need be said about that information.

The second was that he, with intent that the London Transport Board should
be defrauded, tendered to an authorised person money on behalf of another
person with intent to enable the person on whose behalf the money was tendered
to travel on the railway without having previously paid her fare, contrary to **H**
Bye-law No. 8 (1) of the Bye-Laws of the London Transport Board relating
to railways in that behalf duly made, approved and published. I pause to say
that counsel for the appellant has referred the court to the provisions of s. 67
of the Transport Act, 1962, under the powers granted by which these bye-laws
were made. The court is satisfied that those powers comprised power to make
that bye-law. The magistrate set out the facts, which need not be detailed, **I**
but include a finding that it was at the way-out barrier at the railway station
at Stockwell that the incident occurred. Both the respondent and a lady with
him arrived at that barrier without any tickets. At that barrier, the way-out
barrier of the station, the respondent tendered a 2s. piece to the inspector and
said to him:—" Two from Kennington station ". Both the respondent and his
friend admitted later, as was the fact, that they had come so far as from King's
Cross station. A larger fare was payable for the journey which they had in fact
made. It was the opinion of the magistrate, as he states in the Case, that on a

A proper construction of the wording of the bye-laws, having regard to the words
" to enable that other person on whose behalf the ticket or money is tendered
to travel ", that the offence could be committed only before the person on whose
behalf the money was tendered had travelled. For the reason that he so construed
the bye-law, he dismissed the information.

B The question for this court is whether he is right in so construing it. There is
some authority on the matter which is not direct authority in the present case,
but certainly is extremely relevant, in the case of *Bremme* v. *Dubery* (1). The case
was one where the charge was brought against a man who had himself, as he
was charged, unlawfully travelled without having previously paid his fare with
intent to avoid payment thereof, contrary to certain regulations, and to a certain
section of the Transport Act, 1962. The court held that although the words
C " with intent to avoid payment of the fare " in s. 5 (3) (a) of the Act of 1889
referred to a point of time when an accused was still travelling on a railway,
yet as a person did not cease to travel on a railway when he alighted on a station
platform, the appellant had been rightly convicted.

Lord Parker, C.J., gave the judgment of the court, and in his judgment he
said this (2):

D   " The matter is in a very short compass; it is to be observed that the
Act of 1889 is to be read with the Regulation of Railways Acts from 1840
onwards, and by the Act of 1873, s. 3, the term ' railway ' is defined as
including every station, siding, wharf or dock of or belonging to any railway
in the United Kingdom constructed or carried on under an Act of Parliament
and used for the purposes of public traffic. In my judgment a man who
E has been physically conveyed on a railway does not cease to travel on that
railway merely when he alights on the platform."

The point is of course, that when still on the arrival platform, and not having yet
left the arrival platform, the traveller is, as Lord Parker said, still travelling. In
that case it was not necessary to decide at precisely what point the traveller
ceases to travel, nor indeed is it necessary precisely to decide it in the present case.
F Whether he continues to travel until he has left the railway premises or ceases
to travel when he leaves that part of the railway premises which is devoted to
travel user, as distinct from a general concourse hall with shops and booths in
it, is something which may sooner or later have to be specifically considered
and decided. So long as the person is in the process of arriving, however, having
come by a railway conveyance, at the exit or terminus from the arrival platform,
G he is in my judgment still travelling; and applying that to the facts of the present
case, it must be equally clear as a matter of logic that a companion, on whose
behalf he tenders a sum of money, is still in the process of travelling when that
companion has not himself or herself arrived at the point of having left the
arrival platform. It is, therefore, clear in this case on the facts found by the
magistrate that the intent, of which indeed a plea of guilty was the best evidence,
H was, by paying this sum of money, to enable the companion to continue to travel
and complete the process of travelling up to the point of leaving the arrival
platform, that is to say, after passing through the barrier where tickets were
to be shown before leaving that platform. In my opinion the magistrate's
decision was wrong in law, and this case should go back with a direction that he
should convict.

I   **WILLIS, J.:** I agree.

LORD PARKER, C.J.: I also agree.

Appeal allowed.   Case remitted.

Solicitor: *Stephen G. Jones* (for the appellant).

[*Reported by* N. P. Metcalfe, Esq., *Barrister-at-Law.*]

(1) [1964] 1 All E.R. 193.   (2) [1964] 1 All E.R. at pp. 194, 195.

QUISTCLOSE INVESTMENTS, LTD. *v.* ROLLS RAZOR, LTD. A
AND ANOTHER.

[CHANCERY DIVISION (Plowman, J.), February 1, 2, 3, 6, 7, 17, 1967.]

Bank—Account—Separate account—Trust—Money lent to company to meet its
declared dividend and paid by company into separate account with bank—
Creditors' voluntary winding-up supervening before dividend paid—Company B
indebted to bank in sum exceeding amount of loan—Lender seeking to recover
money lent from bank on alleged resulting trust—Whether resulting trust
arose on failure of specific purpose for which loan was made.

A company was lent money by the plaintiffs for the specific purpose of
enabling it to meet a dividend that it had declared. There was no express
obligation to pay the money into a separate account at the company's bank,   C
but the company in fact did so. At all material times the company was
indebted to the bank for substantially more than the amount of the loan.
Before the dividend was paid the company went into a creditors' voluntary
winding-up. The plaintiffs sought to recover the money lent from the bank
under an alleged resulting trust.

Held: as the money had been lent, there was a contractual obligation to   D
repay it, and an additional equitable obligation by way of resulting trust to
refund it would not be implied; accordingly, even assuming that there had
been a fiduciary duty to apply the money in paying the dividend, there was no
resulting trust and the bank was not a trustee of the money in the separate
account for the plaintiffs (see p. 868, letter H, and p. 869, letters A and G,
post).

Moseley v. Cressey's Co. ((1865), L.R. 1 Eq. 405) applied.   E
Toovey v. Milne ((1819), 2 B. & Ald. 683) considered.
Re Nanwa Gold Mines, Ltd. ([1955] 3 All E.R. 219) distinguished.

[As to a bank being bound by notice of a trust, see 2 HALSBURY'S LAWS (3rd
Edn.) 168, 169, para. 314; and for cases on trust accounts with bankers, see 3
DIGEST (Repl.) 195-201, *385-413*.   F

As to a banker's lien or set-off, see 2 HALSBURY'S LAWS (3rd Edn.) 213, para.
395. As to property in possession of a bankrupt for a specific purpose, see
ibid., p. 437, para. 862; and for cases on this subject, see 5 DIGEST (Repl.)
756-762, *6493-6533*.

As to a resulting trust on the failure of the purpose of a gift ostensibly beneficial,
see 38 HALSBURY'S LAWS (3rd Edn.) 865, para. 1459.]   G

Cases referred to:

Drucker (No. 1), Re, Ex p. Basden, [1902] 2 K.B. 55; *on appeal* C.A., [1902]
    2 K.B. 237; 71 L.J.K.B. 686; sub nom. *Re Drucker, Ex p. Trustee* v.
    Birmingham District & Counties Banking Co., Ltd., 86 L.T. 785; 5 Digest
    (Repl.) 757, *6503*.

Edwards v. *Glyn*, (1859), 2 E. & E. 29; 28 L.J.Q.B. 350; 33 L.T.O.S. 236;   H
    121 E.R. 12; 5 Digest (Repl.) 763, *6542*.

Moseley v. *Cressey's Co.*, (1865), L.R. 1 Eq. 405; 35 L.J.Ch. 360; 14 L.T. 99;
    9 Digest (Repl.) 721, *4786*.

Nanwa Gold Mines, Ltd., Re, Ballantyne v. *Nanwa Gold Mines, Ltd.*, [1955]
    3 All E.R. 219; [1955] 1 W.L.R. 1080; Digest (Cont. Vol. A) 165, *866a*.

Rogers, Re, Ex p. Holland & Hannen, (1891), 8 Morr. 243; 5 Digest (Repl.)   I
    757, *6502*.

Toovey v. *Milne*, (1819), 2 B. & Ald. 683; 106 E.R. 514; 5 Digest (Repl.)
    757, *6501*.

Action.

This was an action commenced by writ issued on Oct. 1, 1964 by the plaintiffs,
Quistclose Investments, Ltd., against the defendants, Rolls Razor, Ltd. (in
voluntary liquidation) and Barclays Bank, Ltd. By their statement of claim,

Reversed, C.A. [1968] 1 All E.R. 313.

served on Oct. 26, 1964, the plaintiffs claimed (i) a declaration that the plaintiffs were the absolute beneficial owners of the sum of £209,719 8s. 6d. standing to the credit of Rolls Razor, Ltd., in a separate account with Barclays Bank, Ltd.; (ii) a declaration that the defendants were express or alternatively constructive trustees of the said sum of money for the plaintiffs; (iii) payment of the said sum of money with interest thereon at the rate of five per cent. per annum, and (iv) an injunction restraining the defendants and each of them whether by their servants or agents or otherwise from paying or applying or dealing with the said sum of money or any part thereof otherwise than by payment thereof to the plaintiffs or as the plaintiffs might direct.

By their defence dated Jan. 15, 1965, the first defendants, Rolls Razor, Ltd. (the company) did not admit that the sum representing the proceeds of the cheque drawn by the plaintiffs on their bank account in favour of the company was at any time trust money; and alternatively, if it should be held to be trust money, did not admit that it was held in trust for the plaintiffs as the beneficial owners thereof.

By their amended defence dated Nov. 18, 1964, the second defendants, Barclays Bank, Ltd., denied that the said sum of £209,719 8s. 6d. was trust money or was held by them on trust for the plaintiffs and denied that the plaintiffs had any claim against it in relation to the said sum of money or at all. The facts are set out in the judgment.

The cases noted below* were cited during the argument in addition to those referred to in the judgment.

Arthur Bagnall, Q.C., and *M. D. Sherrard* for the plaintiffs.
Muir Hunter, Q.C., and *David Graham* for the company.
J. L. Arnold, Q.C., and *Allan Heyman* for the bank.

Cur. adv. vult.

Feb. 17.   **PLOWMAN, J.**, read the following judgment: In 1964 the plaintiffs lent the defendant, Rolls Razor, Ltd. (which I will call " the company "), £209,719 8s. 6d. to enable it to pay a dividend which it had already declared. The company paid the money into a separate account at the defendant bank, Barclays Bank, Ltd. (hereinafter referred to as " the bank "). Before the dividend was paid, the company went into liquidation and the plaintiffs now seek to recover the money from the bank. The question is whether they are entitled to do so.

The plaintiffs put their case in this way: they say first, that the company took the money as trustee, on trust to pay the dividend; secondly, that this trust having failed by reason of the liquidation, there is a resulting trust of the money for the plaintiffs, and thirdly, that the money came into the hands of the bank with notice of the trusts affecting it and accordingly that the bank is a constructive trustee of the money for the plaintiffs.

The bank's answer is this: that even if the plaintiffs are right in saying that the money lent became impressed with the trust to pay the dividend (which is disputed), they are wrong in saying that on the failure of that trust there was any resulting trust; that the company's obligation to repay the money to the

---

* *Ward* v. *Lant*, (1701), Prec. Ch. 182; *Birch* v. *Blagrave*, (1755), Amb. 264; *Platamone* v. *Staple*, (1815), Coop. G. 250; *Cecil* v. *Butcher*, (1821), 2 Jac. & W. 565; *Childers* v. *Childers*, (1857), 1 De G. & J. 482; *Gray* v. *Johnston*, (1868), L.R. 3 H.L. 1; *Symes* v. *Hughes*, (1870), L.R. 9 Eq. 475; *Re Gross, Ex p. Kingston*, (1871), 6 Ch. App. 632; *Taylor* v. *Bowers*, [1874-80] All E.R. Rep. 405; (1876), 1 Q.B.D. 291; *Barclay* v. *Pearson*, [1893] 2 Ch. 154; *Union Bank of Australia, Ltd.* v. *Murray-Aynsley*, [1898] A.C. 693; *Sharp* v. *Jackson*, [1895-99] All E.R. Rep. 755; [1899] A.C. 419; *Hermann* v. *Charlesworth*, [1905] 2 K.B. 123; *Re Hooley, Ex p. Trustee*, [1915] H.B.R. 181; *British America Elevator Co., Ltd.* v. *Bank of British North America*, [1919] A.C. 658; *Cunningham* v. *Northern Banking Co., Ltd.*, [1928] N.I. 112; *Latchford Premier Cinema, Ltd.* v. *Ennion*, [1931] All E.R. Rep. 55; [1931] 2 Ch. 409; *Re Cleadon Trust, Ltd.*, [1938] 4 All E.R. 518; [1939] Ch. 286; *Re Kent & Sussex Sawmills, Ltd.*, [1946] 2 All E.R. 638; [1947] Ch. 177; *Re Eros Films, Ltd.*, [1963] 1 All E.R. 383; [1963] Ch. 565.

plaintiffs is no more than the contractual obligation of a borrower to repay his lender and accordingly that the question of notice does not arise, but that, if it does, the bank did not have notice. Since the company was indebted to the bank in a sum in excess of the amount in the separate account, the bank (subject to the result of this action) has exercised its right to set-off the money standing to the credit of that account against the company's indebtedness and says that the only right of the plaintiffs is to prove in the liquidation.

In a little more detail, the events which seem to me to be relevant to the question whether the company took the money as trustee were as follows. On May 14, 1964, the directors of the company approved the accounts for the year ending Dec. 31, 1963, and resolved to recommend a final dividend of 120 per cent., making a total dividend of two hundred per cent. for the year 1963. The sum required to pay the final dividend after deduction of tax was the said sum of £209,719 8s. 6d. At the annual general meeting on July 2, 1964, the payment of the final dividend was approved. The company itself had not got the money to pay the dividend, but it managed to borrow it from the plaintiffs, and the loan was effected by a cheque drawn by the plaintiffs on July 15, 1964, in favour of the company. The arrangements which the plaintiffs made to obtain the money to lend to the company do not seem to me to throw any light on the problem with which I am concerned and I pass over them. On the same day the company sent the cheque to the bank and asked the bank to open a No. 4 ordinary dividend share account and credit the cheque to that account. The plaintiffs' bank account was debited with the amount of the cheque on July 16, and the company's new account credited with it on July 17. I am satisfied that the loan was offered to and accepted by the company on the condition that it was used to pay the company's final dividend. It was not, however, a term of the loan that the company should place the money to the credit of a separate account and there was no obligation on it to do so.

On Aug. 27, 1964, the company passed a special resolution to wind up, and since no declaration of solvency was filed, the winding-up became a creditors' voluntary winding-up. It is common ground that as the dividend was not paid prior to the liquidation, the shareholders' debt, arising from the declaration of dividend, became converted into a right to prove in the liquidation and any trust for their benefit failed. As I understand the position, the shareholders' right of proof is in fact worthless since they rank as deferred creditors and the company's assets will be swallowed up by creditors ranking ahead of them.

Counsel's submission on behalf of the plaintiffs that the money was impressed with a trust in the hands of the company for payment of the final dividend was based on a series of bankruptcy cases consisting of *Toovey* v. *Milne* (1); *Edwards* v. *Glyn* (2); *Re Rogers, Ex p. Holland & Hannen* (3) and *Re Drucker (No. 1), Ex p. Basden* (4). All four cases were proceedings by a trustee in bankruptcy to recover from the defendant money paid to him by an insolvent debtor. In the first two cases, *Toovey* v. *Milne* (1) and *Edwards* v. *Glyn* (2), the defendant had originally advanced money to the debtor for a specific purpose which was not carried out and the debtor had repaid the money to the defendant. In the last two cases, *Re Rogers* (3) and *Re Drucker (No. 1)* (4), the defendant had received from the debtor money advanced to him by a third person for a specific purpose and in pursuance of that purpose the debtor had paid the defendant. In all four cases the question was whether the repayment to the defendant was a fraudulent preference, and in all four cases the trustee in bankruptcy's action failed.

I propose to refer to only one of those cases in greater detail, namely *Toovey* v. *Milne* (1), which was the corner-stone of counsel's argument on behalf of the plaintiffs and is the case from which the other cases stem. The side-note to that case is as follows (5):

---

(1) (1819), 2 B. & Ald. 683.   (2) (1859), 2 E. & E. 29.
(3) (1891), 8 Morr. 243.   (4) [1902] 2 K.B. 55.
(5) (1819), 2 B. & Ald. at p. 683.

" Act of bankruptcy by lying two months in prison. During the imprison-ment A. advanced to the bankrupt money for the purpose of settling with his creditors. The purpose failing, a part of the money was repaid to A. by the bankrupt: Held that this repayment was protected, and that the assignees could not recover the money so repaid."

Referring to the facts in more detail, it is stated as follows (6):

" The act of bankruptcy was a lying in prison two months. During the continuance of the imprisonment, the bankrupt being desirous of settling with his creditors, sent his wife to borrow of the defendant, his brother-in-law, £120 for that purpose. The money was accordingly lent, but the purpose failing, £95 was afterwards repaid to the defendant by the bankrupt, who still remained in prison. It did not appear that the individual notes com-posing the £95 were any part of the notes originally advanced by the defendant, nor was there at the time of the advance any express stipulation, that if the object was not attained the money should be restored. ABBOTT, C.J., thought that this was money advanced for a special purpose, and that it did not pass to the assignee, and that therefore the repayment was protected, and nonsuited the plaintiff. And now [counsel] moved for a new trial."

The judgment of ABBOTT, C.J., was as follows (7):

" I thought at the trial, and still think, that the fair inference from the facts proved was that this money was advanced for a special purpose, and that being so clothed with a specific trust, no property in it passed to the assignee of the bankrupt. Then the purpose having failed, there is an implied stipulation, that the money shall be repaid. That has been done in the present case; and I am of opinion that that repayment was lawful, and that the nonsuit was right."

That case shows, as do the other three, that where money is paid by one person to another for a specific purpose, the obligation to carry out that purpose may be fiduciary, and I am content to assume for the purposes of the present case that the company received the money from the plaintiffs subject to a fiduciary obligation or trust to pay the final dividend. It does not, however, in my judg-ment, necessarily follow from that that when the purpose for which a loan has been made has failed, the obligation to repay the money is anything more than the ordinary obligation of a borrower to repay his lender, that is to say, contractual.

In the four cases to which I have referred the question of the nature of this obligation did not arise because in none of them (unlike the present case) did the money remain in the hands of the debtor. I was, however, referred to two cases where money which had been paid for a purpose which failed remained in the hands of the payee and the payer sought to recover it on the basis of a trust. The first was *Moseley* v. *Cressey's Co.* (8). In that case the promoters of a company issued a prospectus inviting applications for shares and stating that deposits would be returned if no allotment of shares was made. A number of people applied for shares and paid their deposits and the promoters paid these into the company's bank account. No allotment of shares was, however, made. The action was a representative action in which the depositors sought to restrain certain creditors of the company who were threatening to attach the moneys standing to the credit of the company at the bank from attaching those moneys. The plaintiff's bill contained the following allegation (9):

" ' But the said deposits never belonged to or formed assets of the company, but were specially appropriated to a particular purpose in the event which happened; namely, if no allotment of shares in the company was made, they were to be returned to the persons who paid them. And such

---

(6) (1819), 2 B. & Ald. at pp. 683, 684.   (7) (1819), 2 B. & Ald. at p. 684.
(8) (1865), L.R. 1 Eq. 405.   (9) (1865), L.R. 1 Eq. at p. 406.

moneys were paid into the account of the company with their said bankers as a trust fund specifically applicable to the purpose aforesaid; and the same never belonged to the company, or to any of the seven persons who constituted the company.' That ' part of the said deposits, amounting to about £80, was paid to the defendant, the secretary of the company, to be held by him upon trust for the company if any allotment of shares was made, in which case the deposits would belong to the company, but to be returned to the persons who paid the same respectively in the event which happened of there being no such allotment ', and that the secretary ought to have retained the same moneys as a trust fund, and that he ought to repay and make good the same."

The defendants demurred to the bill and the report is of the proceedings on the demurrer which SIR WILLIAM PAGE WOOD, V.-C., allowed. In the course of his judgment he said (10):

" The plaintiffs say not only that these promoters are liable as for money had and received, but that they have no authority to deal with it otherwise than upon the trust by which it was to be returned to the depositors. But if the object had been to create a lien of this kind, the obvious way of doing so would have been to have said in the prospectus that there would be a lien on the deposits until the company was established, or that it was to be set apart as a trust fund in the names of trustees, to be returned in the event of the company not being established. Nothing of that kind was done; nor was that the contract. The contract was—' You are to pay so much per share when you apply for shares, and your deposits will be returned if no allotment is made '—not that the actual thing so deposited was to be paid back; for payment to the company's bankers to the account of the company made the moneys ipso facto part of the company's assets . . . The cases cited by [counsel for the plaintiffs] show that the plaintiffs have a legal remedy for the return of their deposits. They paid their money on the faith that it should be returned if not required. Upon the faith of these payments the company gets credit, and people trust them. But, says [counsel], these moneys were not the moneys of the company until the plaintiffs got their shares. But that is not so; they were not retained by the promoters, they were paid into the credit of the company at their bankers. What was intended to have been done seems to have been done; and there was no trust created, it was merely a debt."

It is to be noted that in that case, as in the present, there was no obligation on the company to pay the money which it obtained into a separate, or indeed any, bank account. As far as it goes therefore, that case is against the plaintiffs' contentions.

There appear, however, to be two possible relevant grounds of distinction between that case and this and the question is whether either of them makes any difference. The first is that in *Moseley* v. *Cressey's Co.* (11) there was an express undertaking to repay the money if the purpose failed. In my view that is not material. In a contract of loan, an obligation to repay is implied. Both are contractual.

The second is that in *Moseley* v. *Cressey's Co.* (11) it was held that no trust was created, whereas I have said that I am willing to assume that in this case the company was under a fiduciary duty to apply the loan in payment of the final dividend. In my view, however, that makes no difference. Counsel for the plaintiffs argued that where there is a primary trust which fails there automatically arises a resulting trust for the person providing the fund, but I know of no authority to that effect and none was cited to me. The doctrine of resulting trusts is founded on the unexpressed but presumed intention of the settlor and I see no reason for imputing the intention that there shall be some additional or

---

(10) (1865), L.R. 1 Eq. at pp. 409, 410.   (11) (1865), L.R. 1 Eq. 405.

A other obligation to refund money in a case where a legal obligation to do so already exists. More specifically, I see no reason why, if a lender pays money to a borrower for a specific purpose which fails, the borrower's contractual obligation to repay the money should have engrafted on it some additional equitable obligation. If there had been no contract of loan in this case the position might have been different, but it is with the lending and borrowing of money that I am **B** primarily concerned.

The second case, where money paid for a purpose which failed remained in the hands of the payee, was *Re Nanwa Gold Mines, Ltd., Ballantyne* v. *Nanwa Gold Mines, Ltd.* (12). In that case the application form sent out by a company when inviting subscriptions for a further issue of capital contained a statement that if certain conditions were not fulfilled " application moneys will be refunded and **C** meanwhile will be retained in a separate account ". A circular letter sent out with the form was to the same effect. The response to the application was inadequate, and shortly after the list was closed a debenture-holders' action was started and a receiver appointed. The question to be determined on the summons was whether the money subscribed, which was held in a separate account, formed part of the general assets of the company, so that the subscribers ranked with the **D** other creditors of the company, or whether it was returnable to the subscribers. It was conceded that the mere fact that money was kept in a separate account did not of itself create a trust. It was held that, on the true construction of the application form, and in the circumstances, the moneys were returnable to the subscribers, and did not form part of the general assets of the company. *Moseley* v. *Cressey's Co.* (13) was distinguished. HARMAN, J., said this (14):

E
   " The point is a short one: is the relationship of the subscriber and the company that of creditor and debtor, or has the subscriber a lien on this fund or an equity against it so as to be able to attach it for the payment of his debt without allowing other creditors of the company to share with him? That depends, as I say, on whether the relationship is that of debtor and creditor or of bailor and bailee; and in effect, it all turns on these words in the **F** form of application, ' and meanwhile will be retained in a separate account '."

He then went on (14) to distinguish the case of *Moseley* v. *Cressey's Co.* (13) on the ground that in that case there was no promise to keep the money in a separate account. That was not, in my judgment, a case of a resulting trust. In that case, **G** unlike the present, the company was under an obligation to place the moneys in a separate account and that fact, coupled with the express undertaking to refund the money in the events which happened, created what amounted to an express trust for the repayment of the money. I do not think that the *Nanwa* case (12) really assists.

The plaintiffs have therefore failed, in my judgment, to establish any resulting **H** trust in their favour and it follows that I am not concerned with the further question whether the bank had notice.

In the result I dismiss the action.

Action dismissed.

Solicitors: *D. J. Freeman & Co.* (for the plaintiffs); *Ashurst, Morris, Crisp & Co.* (for the company); *Durrant Cooper & Hambling* (for the bank).

I
[*Reported by* JACQUELINE METCALFE, *Barrister-at-Law.*]

---

(12) [1955] 3 All E.R. 219.   (13) (1865), L.R. 1 Eq. 405.
            (14) [1955] 3 All E.R. at p. 222.

M. *v.* M. (No. 1).

E. *v.* E. AND R.   B. *v.* B. AND T.

B. *v.* B. AND D.   M. *v.* M. (No. 2).

W. *v.* W. (No. 2).

[PROBATE, DIVORCE AND ADMIRALTY DIVISION (Sir Jocelyn Simon, P.), December 19, 1966, February 7, 1967.]

Divorce—Collusion—Agreements and arrangements—Consideration by court— Observations on the court's approach to determination of applications for directions as to agreements and arrangements—Maintenance—Financial arrangements—Matrimonial Causes Act 1965 (c. 72) s. 5 (2).

Machinery was established by virtue of s. 4 of the Matrimonial Causes Act 1963 (re-enacted in s. 5* of the Act of 1965) and r. 2A added to the Matrimonial Causes Rules, 1957, in 1963† whereby agreements or arrangements (whether or not collusive or potentially collusive) relating to subjects of contention in a matrimonial suit could be brought before the court for consideration. This jurisdiction is exercised in chambers. General observations (see p. 872, letter C, post) on the exercise of the court's discretion under this jurisdiction and six specific instances of the exercise of the discretion (see p. 873, letter F, et seq., post) are made public by the President (SIR JOCELYN SIMON) for the guidance of practitioners.

[As to what agreements amount to collusion, see 12 HALSBURY'S LAWS (3rd Edn.) 301, 302, para. 597; and for cases on the subject, see 27 DIGEST (Repl.) 388-395, *3206-3253.*

For the Matrimonial Causes Act 1965, s. 5, see 45 HALSBURY'S STATUTES (2nd Edn.) 452.

For the Matrimonial Causes Rules, 1957, r. 2A, see 10 HALSBURY'S STATUTORY INSTRUMENTS (Second Re-Issue) 225.]

Cases referred to:

Head (formerly Cox) v. *Cox (Smith cited),* [1964] 1 All E.R. 776; [1964] P. 228; [1964] 2 W.L.R. 358; 3rd Digest Supp.

Mulhouse (formerly Mulhausen) v. *Mulhouse (formerly Mulhausen),* [1964] 2 All E.R. 50; [1966] P. 39; [1964] 2 W.L.R. 808; 3rd Digest Supp.

Nash v. *Nash,* [1965] 1 All E.R. 480; [1965] P. 266; [1965] 2 W.L.R. 317; 3rd Digest Supp.

O'Brien v. *O'Brien,* [1950] W.N. 330; 94 Sol. Jo. 486; 27 Digest (Repl.) 429, *3591.*

Sydenham v. *Sydenham and Illingworth,* [1949] 2 All E.R. 196; [1949] L.J.R. 1424; 27 Digest (Repl.) 612, *5737.*

Summonses.

These were six summonses under s. 5 (2) of the Matrimonial Causes Act 1965, adjourned into open court for judgment. The facts are set out in the judgment. The representation of the parties was as follows:

[M. v. M. (No. 1)] *J. A. P. Hazel* for the wife.

F. J. M. Mars-Johnson for the husband.

[E. v. E. and R.] *E. S. Cazalet* for the husband.

The wife was represented in chambers by her solicitors.

B. Garland for the co-respondent.

---

* Section 5 (2) provides: " Provision may be made by rules of court for enabling the court, on application made either before or after the presentation of the petition, to take into consideration for the purposes of this section any agreement or arrangement made or proposed to be made between the parties and to give such directions on the matter as the court thinks fit; but nothing in the subsection affects any duty of the parties to disclose to the court any agreement or arrangement made between the parties in contemplation of or in connexion with the proceedings."

† S.I. 1963 No. 1990.

Considered in GOSLING *v.* GOSLING.
[1967] 2 All E.R. 510.

Applied in DEAN v DEAN [1978] 3 All ER 758

Considered in MINTON v MINTON [1979] 1 All ER 79

A   [B. *v.* B. and T.] *P. Sheridan* for the husband.
     The wife appeared in person.
     J. J. Davis for the co-respondent.
     [B. *v.* B. and D.] *J. D. A. Fennell* for the husband.
     The wife and the co-respondent did not appear and were not represented.
     [M. *v.* M. (No. 2)] *J. A. P. Hazel* for the wife.
B   *M. H. Jackson-Lipkin* for the husband.
     [W. *v.* W. (No. 2)] *W. H. Dunn* for the wife.
     D. J. Stinson for the husband.

                                                        Cur. adv. vult.

C   Feb. 7. **SIR JOCELYN SIMON, P.**, read the following judgment:
     Periodically Parliament (either directly in statute or by rules made subject to
     its approval) enjoins that judicial proceedings should take place in chambers
     or closed court or otherwises impose limitations on the publicity of the proceedings.
     Sometimes the greater informality or the obviation of publicity is indicated by
     the nature of the judicial business—for example, where the welfare of children
     falls for determination. Sometimes—as with some interlocutory business—the
     comparative informality and the freedom from the full publicity attendant on
D   suits in open court makes it easier for parties to compromise their differences
     at this stage. In still other cases the business may be deemed not to be of
     sufficient public concern as to merit publicity. In a few cases it is difficult to
     determine why it is that the particular business is enjoined to be transacted in
     chambers. Even where the reason for the privacy of the litigation is apparent,
     there may be concomitant disadvantages. Parliament and public may be left
E   uninstructed by the organs of information and opinion how the relevant part
     of the constitution is functioning and on what principles and practice the courts
     are exercising the jurisdiction conferred by Parliament. Practitioners especially
     need such information in order to be able to give authoritative advice to their
     clients. The courts can help to mitigate any such disadvantages by indicating
     from time to time in public judgments how a chambers jurisdiction, particularly
F   a new one, has been exercised. Not least is this desirable in the sphere of matri-
     monial jurisdiction, which is a matter of more than purely private concern.
     Most of all it is desirable when Parliament has given wide discretionary powers to
     the judiciary or appears to be relying on the judiciary to any significant extent
     for the adaptation and development of the law to accord with changing social
     conditions.
G   By s. 4 of the Matrimonial Causes Act 1963, an important change was made in
     the matrimonial law. Collusion ceased to be an absolute bar to divorce in the
     suit in which it had taken place; and machinery was provided whereby arrange-
     ments or agreements (whether or not collusive or potentially collusive) relating
     to any of the subject-matters of contention in a matrimonial suit could be brought
     before the court for its consideration. On the face of the statute the judges
H   were given so unfettered a discretion that, theoretically, divorce by consent
     might thereafter have been sanctioned (at least in the sense of a valid defence
     to a divorce suit being bought off). *Mulhouse (formerly Mulhausen)* v. *Mulhouse
     (formerly Mulhausen)* (1) established that any such construction of the law
     would go far beyond the proper sphere of judicial law-making and, indeed, that
     there were a number of indications that that was not the way in which Parlia-
I   ment intended the discretion to be exercised. That case established, so to speak,
     a negative delimitation—a line beyond which practitioners thereafter knew they
     must not trespass. But it still left practitioners uncertain in respect of what
     agreements or arrangements the court's discretion was likely to be favourably
     exercised. With the object of providing further guidance on these lines, an
     unselected series of summonses under the subsection were put into the list of
     Scarman, J., with the intent that he should deliver a formal judgment on them.

_____

(1) [1964] 2 All E.R. 50; [1966] P. 39.

Students of the constitution and of the modern judicial process are entitled to   **A**
know that, before doing so, he had the advantage of attendance at a general
discussion by the judges of the Division on the operation of the section, though
of course without reference to any of the cases with which SCARMAN, J., was
concerned, of which the other judges knew nothing. The resulting series of
judgments that he delivered is reported under the title of *Nash* v. *Nash* (2). It
is to be presumed that it was in the light of *Mulhouse* v. *Mulhouse* (3) and *Nash*   **B**
v. *Nash* (2) that Parliament repealed s. 4 of the Matrimonial Causes Act 1963
and re-enacted it verbatim in s. 5 of the Matrimonial Causes Act 1965.

It is in the hope of providing further and closer guidance how at least one of the
judges of the Division has exercised his discretion under this subsection that I
propose now to indicate publicly how I dealt with a number of summonses that
came before me under the subsection in the normal course of judicial business on   **C**
Dec. 19, 1966.

Before I come to deal with the individual cases, there are six general observations which I wish to make. First, as to the use of s. 5 (2). In 1966 there were
310 summonses under it in London alone, in the overwhelming majority of
which the agreement or arrangement was allowed to go forward without substantial amendment. But this did not exhaust the usefulness of s. 5 (2); under   **D**
it judges were on occasion able to assist parties actually involved in a contest
before the court to come to a reasonable accommodation of their various disputes.

Secondly, when an agreement or arrangement under s. 5 (2) comes before me in
chambers or court, I invariably ask the counsel or solicitors appearing before
me whether, in their view, the decree which the court will be asked, or is likely,
to make in consequence of the agreement or arrangement is what would be the   **E**
likely result of the case were it to be fought out on the pleadings as they might be
constituted by the actual instructions to the legal representatives of the respective
parties. The resulting duty placed on the legal representative is not always
one easy of performance; it involves a critical, a judicial, attitude towards
one's own case. It is a characteristic example of the way in which the administration of justice is a co-operative proceeding and how the court has to a sub-   **F**
stantial extent to rely on the legal representatives of the parties in its performance
of the duty laid on it by Parliament.

Thirdly, as to provisions for a wife's maintenance. Where the result of the
agreement or arrangement is likely to be the grant of a decree to a wife, I do
not, in other than quite exceptional circumstances, sanction a term providing
for the dismissal for all time of a wife's claim to maintenance. When I do dismiss   **G**
a wife's claim for maintenance, it is intended as an indication to a judge dealing
subsequently with an application by the wife for leave to make a claim for maintenance out of time or to a registrar dealing subsequently with a wife's claim for
maintenance that I have been satisfied either that the wife's conduct has been
such that it would be unjust that her husband should be ordered to provide
maintenance for her or that her support has been adequately and reasonably   **H**
provided for in some other way. Even so, the tribunal dealing with the matter
subsequently is not concluded by my order; it is intended as no more than an
indication of the view to which I have come on the material before me. Again
with the aim of giving some guidance to the registrar, where I have sufficient
material before me to indicate that the wife would be entitled to a substantial
maintenance were it not for her own actual or potential income at the time, I   **I**
make a nominal order in her favour. Where I have insufficient evidence before
me, whether going to conduct or means, to be able to form any view as to what
extent the wife should be maintained by the husband, my order is silent as to
maintenance; this, once more, is intended as no more than an indication to the
registrar that I have not had sufficient material to come to a concluded view on the

(2) [1965] 1 All E.R. 480; [1965] P. 266.
(3) [1964] 2 All E.R. 50; [1966] P. 39.

A　matter, and it does not preclude the wife from subsequently claiming maintenance.

Fourthly, the discretion given by Parliament is finally the responsibility of the trial judge; and the machinery provided by the rules is intended as no more than a convenience to the parties. If the agreement or arrangement presents any difficulty on its investigation in chambers, I make it my practice to reserve the trial of the suit to myself, in order to avoid the expense of time involved in a

B　double investigation and possible embarrassment arising out of any difference of view between the chambers and the trial judge.

Fifthly, it is not infrequent that arrangements or agreements are negotiated and submitted for the consideration of the court under s. 5 (2) because a wife wishes to be assured of her financial security before starting divorce proceedings. In many cases this is entirely reasonable—where, for example, a divorce will

C　entail the loss of financial rights on widowhood. Other cases will require close scrutiny by the court to ensure that its procedures are not being used as an instrument for extortion. The issue in each such case will be whether the provision proposed to be made for the wife is a reasonable one in all the circumstances. Particularly in such cases, but also generally in adjudication under s. 5 (2), the court will need to be apprised of the respective means of the parties.

D　Sixthly, in *Head (formerly Cox)* v. *Cox (Smith cited)* (4), Wrangham, J., emphasised as a consideration which the court will weigh, together with the primary—and overriding (see *Mulhouse* v. *Mulhouse* (5))—consideration that the result of the agreement or arrangement should not be a decree contrary to the justice of the case, the welfare of any children of the marriage, infants in particular. In this connexion I have had, on occasion, to weigh the desirability

E　of sparing children of a marriage the bitterness and publicity liable to be attendant on contested proceedings. Moreover (particularly when there has been a history of mental instability), I have also on occasion taken into consideration the advantage of sparing the parties themselves the strain of contested proceedings—even though they may themselves be said to have voluntarily invoked the jurisdiction of the court.

F　I turn now to the particular summonses that I heard on Dec. 19, 1966.

M. *v.* M. (No. 1)

The parties were married in 1954, the wife now being over fifty years of age. There are no children of the family now living. On Mar. 16, 1966, the wife presented a petition for divorce on the ground that the husband had committed

G　adultery with a named woman from about November, 1962. The wife prayed that the decree should be granted to her in the exercise of the court's discretion, and asked in addition for maintenance and a secured provision. The husband had been a farmer at the time of the marriage; but the farm had now been sold and at the time of the summons he had free capital of about £50,000. In addition, he had recently bought for over £4,000 the house in which the wife was living.

H　The parties themselves had not been in personal contact but the following agreement as to maintenance and security had been negotiated between their solicitors, subject to the consideration of the court:—(a) The house, together with £5,000 cash, to be transferred to trustees to be held on the following principal trusts:— (i) the wife to be entitled to occupy it during her lifetime; (ii) the income from the trust sum of £5,000 to be paid to the wife during her lifetime until re-

I　marriage; (iii) if the wife should remarry, she should continue to enjoy half the income of the trust sum of £5,000, the capital of the other half reverting to the husband. (b) The husband to pay the wife £180 to enable her to complete the furnishing of the house. (c) The husband to pay to the wife during joint lives or until the wife's remarriage £500 a year less tax. There was a further term which was not entirely clear; but I recorded that it was agreed between counsel that it meant that the arrangements as to maintenance and security

(4) [1964] 1 All E.R. 776 at p. 777; [1964] P. 228 at p. 230.
(5) [1964] 2 All E.R. at p. 55; [1966] P. at p. 47.

which I have recited should not be varied merely by reason of the fact that either   A
party or both should hereafter enjoy an earned income.

This agreement seemed to me an entirely reasonable way to dispose of the
wife's claim for maintenance and I so indicated. Nothing which took place
before me, of course, affects in any way the obligation of the wife to prove the
contents of her petition or to satisfy the court that it is a proper case for
discretionary relief.   B

E. v. E. and R.

The parties were married on Nov. 10, 1960. There were two children of the
marriage, boys born in 1961 and 1963 respectively. On Nov. 2, 1966, the husband
presented a petition for divorce on the ground of the wife's adultery since
November, 1965. Paragraph 8 of the petition read: C

"That the court will be asked to approve the financial arrangements
agreed by the petitioner, the respondent and co-respondent and if the same
be collusive asked to exercise its discretion in respect of the said arrangements."

However, the prayer of the petition, in addition to dissolution of the marriage,
only asked for custody of the children and costs against the co-respondent. I   D
was told by counsel that the intention was that the co-respondent should pay a
specified sum by way of damages, or in lieu of the same, to be settled on the
children. An agreement as to quantum of damages, standing by itself, would not
be regarded by the court as collusive; though the court may direct in what
manner any damages (whether agreed or the subject of contested judgment)
should be paid or applied: see Matrimonial Causes Act 1965 s. 41 (3). But   E
on the appearance before me, it appeared that the parties were not, after all,
ad idem; the petition had not been amended to claim damages; there was no
draft before the court of any deed of trust in favour of the children, as would
plainly be desirable. At the request of all parties I, therefore, adjourned the
summons sine die.

In the event, the summons was restored before LLOYD-JONES, J., on Jan. 31,   F
1967. A proper trust deed had been drawn up; and he was satisfied that the
proposed arrangement was a satisfactory one.

B. v. B. and T.

The parties were married in 1947. There is one child of the family, born in
1948, now self-supporting. The husband is a proprietor of a public house in   G
Soho. The marriage broke up in April, 1958—according to the wife, owing to
the husband's ill-treatment; according to the husband, owing to incompata-
bility. The husband then bought for the wife, for a sum between £5,000 and
£10,000, a house for her to live in. In addition, he paid her maintenance at the
rate of £1 a week. On Dec. 7, 1959, the husband and wife entered into a deed
providing for maintenance, but not separation. Among other provisions (all   H
usual) it made provision for the maintenance of the child and of the wife (the
latter at £1 a week, again). The husband covenanted to allow the wife to
reside in the house he had bought during her life until the marriage should be
dissolved. He made her a gift of the equipment of the house. On July 23, 1965,
the husband presented a petition for divorce on the ground that the wife had
committed adultery at the beginning of 1965 with a named co-respondent. He   I
desired the court to take into consideration the deed of maintenance of Dec. 7,
1959 (which, of course, presented no difficulty). He prayed for a divorce in the
exercise of the court's discretion, he having admittedly himself committed
adultery. He claimed costs against both the wife and the co-respondent. On
Aug. 20, 1965, the wife entered an appearance, indicating that she intended to
defend the petition. However, no answer was filed; and I was given to understand that she did not intend to file an answer if the court raised no objection to
a further agreement between the parties. Her counsel told me that the adultery

alleged against her could not be denied; but she had contemplated making cross-charges of adultery and cruelty. Both counsel considered that, if the suit were fought out on the instructions they had received, the likely result would be cross-decrees on the ground of adultery. This seemed to me, too, to be highly probable, in view of the fact that both parties admitted having committed adultery and that any charge of cruelty by the wife would be at least eight years stale. The husband's income was just short of £2,000 a year, but likely to be reduced. He had investments producing about £200 a year. The wife had an earned income of about £300 a year.

The proposed further agreement which it was desired that the court should take into consideration was as follows:—(i) The husband should pay off the balance of the mortgage (amounting to just short of £3,000) on the house where the wife was living (this would involve his selling a substantial part of his investments). (ii) The house should be conveyed to the wife to become her property absolutely. (iii) The husband should pay the wife £500 a year maintenance less tax. (iv) The husband should pay the wife £75 as a contribution towards her costs of the suit and of the making of the proposed agreement. (v) The husband would make no claim for costs against the wife or against the co-respondent. (vi) The deed of Dec. 7, 1959, should be discharged. Financially, this arrangement seemed to me to accord with the justice of the case. It was, of course, implicit that the husband would, if the trial court were satisfied, obtain a decree of divorce in the exercise of the court's discretion; whereas if the case were fought out the estimated likely result would be cross-decrees. But cross-decrees do not necessarily imply that the parties are equally to blame (see *Sydenham* v. *Sydenham and Illingworth* (6); *O'Brien* v. *O'Brien* (7)). I was satisfied that the course proposed held no risk of a miscarriage of justice; and I allowed the case to go forward for trial on the basis of the agreement proposed.

B. *v.* B. AND D.

The parties were married in 1934. They appear to be in quite modest circumstances. The three children of the marriage are all grown up. By his petition dated Aug. 27, 1966, the husband alleged that the wife had deserted him in 1958 and had thereafter lived in adultery with the co-respondent. He prayed for a divorce in the exercise of the discretion of the court and that the co-respondent should be ordered to pay the costs of the suit. Only the husband was represented before me. The wife and co-respondent had received no notice of the application, though the agreement between the parties was clearly proved by correspondence passing between the respective solicitors. It provided for the co-respondent depositing with the husband's solicitors the sum of £125 to go towards the cost of the proceedings. It was, however, further provided that such sum would be payable to the husband's solicitors whether or not an order for costs was obtained against the co-respondent. At this stage I thought it right to inspect the husband's discretion statement, which had been lodged pursuant to r. 28 of the Matrimonial Causes Rules, 1957 (8). According to it the husband had first committed adultery a number of years after the inception of the wife's alleged desertion and adultery.

I expressed the view that the agreement arrived at between the solicitors was unobjectionable, save for the provision that the sum of £125 should be payable to the husband's solicitors whether or not the court ordered costs against the co-respondent; I was not prepared to countenance such a term as it pre-empted the court's discretion as to costs. Since the wife and co-respondent were not before the court, the term could not simply be deleted. I, therefore, gave liberty to apply further, if the parties were so advised.

(6) [1949] 2 All E.R. 196.
(7) [1950] W.N. 330; 94 Sol. Jo. 486.
(8) S.I. 1957 No. 619, as amended.

M. v. M. (No. 2)

The marriage was in 1946.   The husband has a salary of about £3,500 a year and capital assets in excess of £250,000.   The wife has free capital amounting to about £21,000; moreover, she resides in a house which the husband had bought in her name worth about £20,000.   There are two living children of the family, daughters, aged eighteen and thirteen.   They have an equal interest in two trust funds, one set up by the husband and one by his mother; these amount to £27,000 in all, and are held on trusts for accumulation until the age of twenty-one, when the capital becomes payable.   The wife is forty-two years of age, in poor health and crippled with poliomyelitis. The marriage finally broke down in 1965. In February, 1966, the wife learnt from her solicitors that the husband had committed adultery at an hotel in London with a woman whose name he had disclosed to them.   The agreement, in the form of a draft deed, provides as follows:—(i) Within seven days of decree absolute the husband should transfer to the wife as a lump sum payment by way of maintenance the sum of £25,000.   (ii) Within seven days of decree absolute the husband should transfer the sum of £60,000 in money and/or investments as might be agreed to trustees on trust to pay the income to the wife for her life, and thereafter to the children in equal shares.   (iii) The husband acknowledged that the house where the wife lived was her sole property, and the wife that the contents thereof were the husband's sole property.   (iv) The husband agreed notwithstanding that the wife should have the use of the contents (other than some specified items) so long as she should live there.   (v) The husband agreed to pay the reasonable fees of the elder child in respect of further education and/or vocational training and to pay her £180 a year net from decree absolute until she should marry or attain the age of thirty years, whichever was the earlier.   (vi) The husband agreed to pay the fees of the younger child at her present public school, and to pay her £180 a year from her leaving school until she should marry or attain the age of thirty years, whichever was the earlier. (vii) The wife agreed that out of the foregoing provisions she would support and maintain herself and the children and make no further financial claims against the husband on her own or her daughter's behalf and would indemnify the husband against any such claims or debts however arising.

This seemed to me to be a case where it was entirely proper for the wife to be reassured as to her own and the children's financial position before starting divorce proceedings.   I was satisfied that the provisions made were reasonable in the circumstances and that the court would not be condoning any element of extortion.   Moreover, it seemed to me to be one of those exceptional cases where it would be wrong to demur to the wife, in consideration of the ample other provision made for her, covenanting to abandon any future claim to maintenance.

W. v. W. (No. 2)

This was yet another case where the wife wished to be assured as to her financial position before starting divorce proceedings.   She is aged fifty-seven and she has virtually no means.   She has never worked during the marriage, which took place in 1931.   The only child, a son, of full age, lives with the wife and contributes a small sum towards her support.   The husband left the wife in 1961, since when he has been living with the woman proposed to be named in the wife's petition; he has, however, signed a confession to adultery since 1958.   A child has been born to the woman proposed to be named.   The wife continued living at the former matrimonial home, the property of the husband, which is today of an approximate value of £7,000, subject to a mortgage the outstanding amount of which is about £2,500.   Since leaving her in 1961, the husband has been paying the wife £3 a week maintenance plus £4 a week in respect of outgoings on the matrimonial home.   He has in addition discharged the mortgage repayments of £26 a month.   In June, 1962, a divorce petition was drawn up and sworn to on the ground of the husband's adultery, but it was not filed owing to negotiations between the parties' solicitors relating to the former matrimonial home; such negotiations, however, proved abortive. The husband is now fifty-six years of age. He had sworn no affidavit of means, but counsel were agreed as to his income and capital. Although he had in recent years enjoyed an income before tax in excess of £3,000, his future income was estimated at about £1,400. Apart from the former matrimonial home, his capital assets were about £26,750, including free capital of £22,600, against which, however, there was a contingent liability of £3,000 or £4,000.

The essence of the agreement submitted for the consideration of the court was as follows. The husband should pay off the mortgage on the former matrimonial home and transfer it free of encumbrance to the wife. The wife intended then either to take in lodgers, or to sell the house and buy a smaller one, living on the profit of the sale (which she estimated at about £3,000). In consideration of the provision so made for her, she would expressly abandon for all time any further claim to maintenance or security. At this stage I made it plain that I was not prepared to countenance the dismissal of the wife's claim to maintenance and that, if the matter came before me on trial, I would not exercise my discretion favourably to grant a divorce. Counsel thereupon took instructions from their clients and were instructed to agree to a nominal order for the wife's maintenance. With that term substituted, the agreement seemed to me to be unobjectionable.

Solicitors:

[M. *v.* M. (No. 1)] *Monckton Son & Collis*, Maidstone (for the wife); *F. B. Jevons, Riley & Pope*, Tonbridge (for the husband).

[E *v.* E. and R.] *Withers Nicholl, Manisty & Co.* (for the husband); *Gordon Dadds & Co.* (for the wife); *Lee & Pembertons* (for the co-respondent).

[B. *v.* B. and T.] *Newburn, Walker & Cato* (for the husband); *Berger, Oliver & Co.*, (for the co-respondent).

[B. *v.* B. and D.] *Joynson-Hicks & Co.*, agents for *R. A. C. Symes & Co.*, Scunthorpe (for the husband); *J. C. Llewellen & Co.*, Usk (for the wife).

[M. *v.* M. (No. 2)] *Bischoff & Co.* (for the wife); *Groos, Guest, Lowden & Hazell* (for the husband).

[W. *v.* W. (No. 2)] *Hardcastle, Sanders & Armitage* (for the wife); *Owen L. Blyth* (for the husband).

[*Reported by* Alice Bloomfield, *Barrister-at-Law.*]

Re SAINSBURY'S SETTLEMENT.
SAINSBURY *v*. FIRST C.B. TRUSTEE, LTD. AND OTHERS.

[CHANCERY DIVISION (Goff, J.), October 19, 20, 1966.]

Trust and Trustee—Variation of trusts by the court—Arrangement in view of prospective incidence of capital gains tax—Shares in private company forming trust fund—Acceleration of entitlement—Insurance policies to be effected— Variation of Trusts Act, 1958 (6 & 7 Eliz. 2 c. 53), s. 1 (1).

[As to the jurisdiction to vary trusts under the Act of 1958, see 38 HALSBURY'S LAWS (3rd Edn.) 1029, 1030, para. 1772; and for cases on the subject, see 47 DIGEST (Repl.) 332-338, *2993-3018*.

As to the charge to capital gains tax and chargeable assets, and as to that tax in relation to settled property, see SUPPLEMENT to 20 HALSBURY'S LAWS (3rd Edn.) paras. 3003, 3006, 3061.

For the Variation of Trusts Act, 1958, s. 1, see 38 HALSBURY'S STATUTES (2nd Edn.) 1130.

For the Finance Act, 1965, ss. 19, 20, 22, 25, see 45 HALSBURY'S STATUTES (2nd Edn.) 530, 531, 535, 540.]

Adjourned summons.

By originating summons, dated Dec. 16, 1965, the plaintiffs, who were the three sons, John, Simon and Timothy, of the Rt. Hon. Alan John, Lord Sainsbury, applied to the court under s. 1 of the Variation of Trusts Act, 1958, for approval of an arrangement, hereinafter mentioned, on behalf of the infant defendants* (viz., Paulette, the daughter of Lord Sainsbury, Sarah, daughter of John Sainsbury, and Timothy and Camilla, children of Timothy Sainsbury) and of all persons unborn or unascertained who might thereafter become entitled under a settlement made on Jan. 15, 1953, between Lord Sainsbury of the one part, and First C. B. Trustee, Ltd., Frederick William Salisbury, James Arthur Sainsbury and Edward Albert Farrell (the original trustees) of the other part, to any property from time to time subject to the trusts of the settlement. The principal beneficiaries under the settlement were Lord Sainsbury's four children and their respective issue. By the settlement moneys paid or to be paid to the trustees by Lord Sainsbury were to be invested in the purchase of " A " ordinary £1 shares of J. Sainsbury, Ltd., or as otherwise authorised by the settlement, and the moneys and investments for the time being representing the same (" the trust fund ") were to be held on certain trusts for Lord Sainsbury's sons, John, Simon and Timothy, each of whom became indefeasibly entitled to a share in two-fifths of the trust fund (" the directorship fund ") when he had attained thirty years and become a director of the company, and to a share in the remaining three-fifths of the trust fund (" the personal fund ") when he had attained thirty-eight years. In the meantime, each of the three sons on attaining thirty-five years or previously marrying was to be entitled to a share of the income from the personal fund. For five years from the date of the settlement, the income of the trust fund not otherwise payable under the trusts of the settlement was to be invested as an addition to the corpus of the directorship fund or the personal fund, as the case might be, and the income thereafter arising from the corpus of these funds and not for the time being payable to any of the sons (" the interim income ") was to be held by the trustees until Lord Sainsbury's daughter Paulette attained twenty-one or until her earlier marriage on trust for providing a portion for her, or was to be held, in the event of her death, on discretionary trusts for the sons or their wives, widows and issue. The three sons had each attained an absolutely vested interest in the directorship fund, which had been distributed. John had attained thirty-eight on Nov. 2, 1965, and had attained an absolutely vested

---

* Another child of John Sainsbury, a boy, John Julian Sainsbury, born in March, 1966, was added as defendant by order dated Mar. 23, 1966.

interest in his one-third share of the personal fund. Simon had attained thirty-five years and had become absolutely entitled to the income of his presumptive one-third share of the personal fund and would become indefeasibly entitled to the capital of his share on attaining thirty-eight years on Mar. 1, 1968. On his marriage Timothy had become absolutely entitled to one-half of the income of his presumptive one-third share of the personal fund and would become entitled to the other half on attaining thirty-five on June 11, 1967. He would become indefeasibly entitled to the capital of his share on attaining thirty-eight on June 11, 1970. Paulette would attain twenty-one on Mar. 2, 1967. Neither Simon nor Paulette had married.

Simon and Timothy, the two younger sons, had been advised that when each became absolutely entitled (in 1968 and 1970 respectively) to his respective one-third share in the personal fund, a charge to capital gains tax under the Finance Act, 1965 was likely to arise on the assets of their respective shares if the value, particularly that of the " A " ordinary shares of the company, should then be higher than on Apr. 6, 1965. That likelihood, and the probable insufficiency of their respective liquid resources to meet the charge to capital gains tax, made it desirable that the dates on which they became entitled each to his respective one-third share of the personal fund should if possible be accelerated so as to reduce the likelihood of a liability to capital gains tax. For that purpose, an arrangement varying the trusts of the settlement relating to the personal fund had been prepared, the principal proposals of which may be summarised as follows:

A. In regard to Simon.

(i) Certain of his " A " ordinary shares of the company (Simon's reversioners' fund) were to be held on trusts principally for the benefit of his future born children, subject to which the whole of his one-third share would be held in trust for him absolutely.

(ii) In the event of his marriage before attaining thirty-eight years, he would pay certain sums out of his free estate to be held by the trustees on the trusts of Simon's reversioners' fund.

(iii) In the event of his death before attaining thirty-eight years without having married, his personal representatives would pay to the trustees a capital sum (without deduction of estate duty) to be held on the trusts of Timothy's reversioners' fund.

(iv) He would effect a single premium policy (Simon's reversioners' policy) for payment to the trustees, in the event of his death within five years of the arrangement becoming effective, of sums equal to the amounts of estate duty prospectively payable on his death in respect of Simon's reversioners' fund.

The purpose of Simon's reversioners' fund and the arrangements in the event of his marriage or death was to compensate Simon's future born children (and the other beneficiaries interested if he had no child who attained a vested interest) for the loss of their contingent interest in Simon's share of the personal fund (which would fall into possession if he should die under the age of thirty-eight years).

B. In regard to Timothy.

(i) Certain of his " A " ordinary shares of the company (Timothy's reversioners' fund) were to be held on trusts principally for the benefit of his children, and other ordinary shares (Timothy's portioners' compensation fund) on the trusts of Paulette Sainsbury's portion fund, subject to which the whole of his one-third share would be held in trust for him absolutely.

(ii) He would effect a single premium policy (Timothy's reversioners' policy) providing for payment to the trustees, in the event of his death within five years of the arrangement becoming effective, of sums equal to the amounts of estate duty prospectively payable on his death in respect of Timothy's reversioners' fund.

(iii) He would effect a further single premium policy (Timothy's first portioners' policy) providing for payment to the trustees, in the event of his death within five years of the arrangement becoming effective, of sums equal to the amounts of estate duty prospectively payable on his death in respect of Timothy's portioners' compensation fund.

The purpose of Timothy's reversioners' fund was to compensate Timothy's children (and the other beneficiaries interested if Timothy should leave no child attaining a vested interest) for the loss of their contingent interest in his share of the personal fund (which would fall into possession if he should die under the age of thirty-eight years).

The purpose of Timothy's portioners' compensation fund was to compensate persons interested in the portion fund under the settlement for the loss of one-half of the income from Timothy's share of the personal fund accruing up to his thirty-fifth birthday (which income fell to be accumulated for the benefit of the portion fund under the settlement).

C. *Further proposals.*

Further proposals were that Simon should take out a single premium policy (Simon's portioners' policy) providing for payment of certain sums to the trustees (on the trusts of the portion fund) in the event of his death under thirty-eight years and on every anniversary of his death occurring before Timothy's thirty-eighth birthday; and that Timothy would take out a single premium policy (Timothy's second portioners' policy) for payment of certain sums to the trustees (on the trusts of the portion fund) in the event of his death under thirty-eight years and on every anniversary of his death occurring before Simon's thirty-eighth birthday. The purpose of Simon's portioners' policy and Timothy's second portioners' policy was to compensate the persons interested in the interim income of the personal fund for the loss of their possible interests.

Moreover, all powers conferred on Simon or Timothy by the settlement, to appoint any beneficial interest to a widow, should be released; further, on any marriage of John, Simon or Timothy before June 11, 1970 (the date when the youngest of the sons would attain thirty-eight years), nominal sums were to be paid by Simon and Timothy to the trustees on trust for the wife of any such marriage absolutely, in compensation for any benefit such wife might have received under the discretonary trust of income in the settlement.

C. J. Slade, Q.C., and *P. M. F. Horsfield* for the plaintiffs.

J. A. Brightman, Q.C., and *M. P. Nolan* for the present trustees*, and the eleventh defendant, the settlor.

Harold Lightman, Q.C., and *J. Maurice Price* for the fifth, eighth, ninth, tenth and twelfth defendants, infants.

J. E. Vinelott for the sixth and seventh defendants (wives of John and Timothy).

GOFF, J.: It is quite clear that the motive of the scheme of arrangement to vary the trusts of the settlement of Jan. 15, 1953, is that it may place certain members of the Sainsbury family in a better position so far as capital gains tax is concerned, but it is a perfectly legitimate motive for seeking the court's sanction of the arrangement and, so long as I am satisfied that the scheme is for the benefit of infants and unborn persons, it is my duty to sanction it. I am satisfied that the scheme is for the benefit of infants and unborn persons on whose behalf I am asked to sanction it and that it is a completely fair scheme. I have raised a number of points because it is my duty to scrutinise the proposed arrangement. I will make the order as asked.

Arrangement approved accordingly.

Solicitors: *Herbert Oppenheimer, Nathan & Vandyk* (for all parties).

[*Reported by* JENIFER SANDELL, *Barrister-at-Law.*]

---

* The fourth defendant, a trustee, died in October, 1966; he was represented by counsel for the trustees.

MURGATROYD (Inspector of Taxes) v. EVANS-JACKSON.

[CHANCERY DIVISION (Plowman, J.), November 29, 1966.]

Income Tax—Deduction in computing profits—Medical expenses—Nursing home charges—Expenses not being money " wholly and exclusively . . . expended for the purpose of the . . . profession "—Trade mark agent—Charges for treatment in private nursing home—Need of office facilities to maintain business— Charges not exclusively expended for purposes of profession—Income Tax Act, 1952 (15 & 16 Geo. 6 & 1 Eliz. 2 c. 10), s. 137 (a), (b).

The taxpayer exercised his profession as a trade mark agent partly at his London office where he had a staff of eight to ten people and partly in Dublin. As a result of an accident he ruptured a disc in his spine and was advised to receive electrical treatment. He was unable to take advantage of the offer of a bed in a hospital under the national health service because it would have been impossible for him to conduct his business owing to restricted hours of visiting, lack of a telephone and inability to hold conferences with clients and staff. Instead, he entered a nursing home as a private patient, he was provided with a room and all necessary facilities for carrying on his business and for five weeks, while receiving treatment, held conferences with clients and staff who visited him every morning and afternoon with his correspondence and were given instructions to pass on to clients. He claimed to deduct, on assessment under Sch. D to the Income Tax Act, 1952, sixty per cent. of the total nursing home charges of £270 12s. 7d. (including £13 11s. telephone rent and calls for which a total of £15 was conceded) as a business expense incurred in respect of the use of the room as an office,

Held: apart from the telephone charges no deduction could be made in respect of the nursing home charges because—

(i) implicit in a claim of only sixty per cent. of the nursing home charges as an expense of the taxpayer's profession was an admission that they served a dual purpose, viz., as to forty per cent. some purpose other than a professional purpose; and the deduction claimed was, therefore, prohibited by s. 137 (a)* of the Income Tax Act, 1952, as the sum expended was not " wholly and exclusively laid out or expended for the purposes of the . . . profession " (see p. 887, letter F, post).

(ii) the charges were " expenses of maintenance of the [taxpayer] . . . or sums expended for any other domestic or private purpose as distinct from the purposes of the [taxpayer's] profession ", within s. 137 (b)*, by which, accordingly, deduction was prohibited (see p. 885, letter I, to p. 886, letter A, post).

Norman v. *Golder (Inspector of Taxes)* ([1945] 1 All E.R. 352) applied.

Appeal allowed.

[As to expenses deductible in computing the profits of a trade, profession or vocation, see 20 HALSBURY'S LAWS (3rd Edn.) 158, 159, paras. 277, 278 and 166-172, paras. 286-297; and for cases on the subject, see 28 DIGEST (Repl.) 87-101, *329-401.*

For the Income Tax Act, 1952, s. 137 (a), (b), see 31 HALSBURY'S STATUTES (2nd Edn.) 134.]

Cases referred to:

Bentleys, Stokes and Lowless v. *Beeson (Inspector of Taxes)*, [1952] 2 All E.R. 82; 33 Tax Cas. 491; 28 Digest (Repl.) 98, *387.*

Bowden (Inspector of Taxes) v. *Russell and Russell,* [1965] 2 All E.R. 258; [1965] 1 W.L.R. 711; 42 Tax Cas. 301; 3rd Digest Supp.

Morgan (Inspector of Taxes) v. *Tate & Lyle, Ltd.,* [1953] 2 All E.R. 162; [1953] Ch. 601; [1953] 3 W.L.R. 1; *affd.* H.L., [1954] 2 All E.R. 413; [1955] A.C. 21; [1954] 3 W.L.R. 85; 35 Tax Cas. 367; 28 Digest (Repl.) 91, *345.*

---

* Section 137, so far as material, is set out at p. 884, letter F, post.

Norman v. *Golder (Inspector of Taxes)*, [1944] 1 All E.R. 632; *affd.* C.A.,
[1945] 1 All E.R. 352; 114 L.J.K.B. 108; 171 L.T. 369; 26 Tax Cas.
293; 28 Digest (Repl.) 90, *342.*

Case Stated.

The taxpayer appealed to the General Commissioners of Income Tax for St.
Margaret and St. John in the county of London against an assessment of £4,790
made on him under Sch. D to the Income Tax Act, 1952, in respect of the profits
of his profession as a trade mark agent. The question at issue was whether, in
computing such profits, the taxpayer was entitled to deduct £162, being a proportion of expenses incurred by him whilst receiving treatment in a nursing home.
The taxpayer contended before the commissioners that sixty per cent of the
£270 12s. 7d. charged by the nursing home, i.e., the £162 in issue, in respect of
the use of his room in the nursing home as an office should be allocated to business
expenses. The Crown contended before the commissioners as follows. (i) That
the Income Tax Acts did not specify what expenditure could be deducted in
arriving at the amount of the assessable profit, but they did contain in s. 137
of the Income Tax Act, 1952, a list of items which could not be deducted. In
referring to para. (*a*) and para. (*b*) of that section the taxpayer's claim failed on
both counts. The expenditure of £270 12s. 7d. (except for telephone rent and
calls for which £15 was conceded to be a proper deduction) was incurred
primarily to enable the taxpayer to recover his health and could not be said to be
wholly and exclusively incurred for the purpose of his profession; alternatively it
was incurred for the maintenance of the taxpayer or other domestic or private
purposes distinct from the purposes of his profession. (ii) That the commissioners
were entitled to consider whether a man in the taxpayer's position who chose to
pay for medical advice would not also have chosen to have treatment in a nursing
home for personal reasons. (iii) That in any case the Income Tax Act, 1952, and
the cases, made it clear that expenditure which had a dual purpose could not be
apportioned and should be disallowed in full. (iv) That the items in the account,
with the exception of the item of £15 for telephone charge (conceded), were either
admittedly private or had a mixed purpose. (iv) That the assessment should be
determined at £4,775, less capital allowances £74.

The commissioners were of opinion that the £162 was a deductible expense,
and determined the assessment at £4,628 less capital allowance of £74.

The cases noted below* were cited during the argument in addition to those
referred to in the judgment.

J. R. Phillips for the Crown.
The taxpayer appeared in person.

PLOWMAN, J.: This is an appeal by the inspector of taxes from the decision
of the General Commissioners of Income Tax for the division of St. Margaret and
St. John, Westminster, reducing the taxpayer's assessment under Case II of
Sch. D for the year 1963-64. The original amount of the assessment was £4,790,
but a deduction of £15 from that figure for the use of the telephone, to which I
will refer further in a moment, has been accepted, and from the revised assessment of £4,475 the commissioners allowed a further deduction of £147, and it is in
relation to that sum of £147 that the inspector appeals.

Paragraph 2 of the Case Stated reads—

" The sole question raised by this appeal was whether in computing the
profits of the [taxpayer's] said profession for the purpose of assessment to
income tax he was entitled to deduct £162, being a proportion of expenses
incurred by him whilst receiving treatment in a nursing home."

The profession in question is that of a trade mark agent. Then the facts are stated
in para. 3 which is as follows:

---

* *Copeman* v. *William Flood & Sons, Ltd.*, [1941] 1 K.B. 202; *Edwards (Inspector of
Taxes)* v. *Bairstow*, [1955] 3 All E.R. 48; [1956] A.C. 14; *Ellwood (Inspector of Taxes)*
v. *Utilz*, (1964), 42 Tax Cas. 482.

" The [taxpayer] gave evidence before us and the following facts were admitted or proved—(i) The [taxpayer] exercises his profession as a trade mark agent partly at his office in Albert Hall Mansions, London, where he employs a routine staff of eight to ten people, and partly from Dublin where a firm of accountants provide him with a permanent office and secretary. (ii) In August, 1962, as the result of an accident, the [taxpayer] ruptured a disc in his spine and was advised by a neurologist that he should receive electrical treatment. (iii) The [taxpayer] was offered a bed in a hospital under the national health service, but was unable to take advantage of this offer as it would have been impossible for him to conduct his business owing to the restricted hours of visiting and a telephone not being available to him; also, he would not have been able to hold conferences with his clients and staff. (iv) On Aug. 20, 1962, the [taxpayer] entered a nursing home as a private patient and was provided with a room and all the necessary facilities to enable him to carry on his business. He stayed in the nursing home for five weeks during which period he received treatment, held conferences with his clients and members of his staff who called every morning and afternoon with his correspondence which he dealt with, and gave them instructions to pass on to his clients. (v) The [taxpayer's] account with the nursing home amounted to £270 12s. 7d., made up as follows: nursing home fees £209 5s.; drugs and dressing £6 3s. 7d.; treatment £34 13s.; television £7; telephone rent and calls £13 11s."

That telephone account is the amount which I mentioned earlier on as being not in dispute. In fact, the taxpayer has been allowed £15 in respect of the telephone and not merely that figure of £13 11s. The Case Stated goes on:

" No special charge was made by the nursing home for giving access to the [taxpayer's] staff and clients. (vi) The [taxpayer] is unmarried and lives in a flat in Kensington with a married sister. He has no resident domestic staff, but employs a daily cleaner and a cook in the evenings.

" 4. It was contended by the [taxpayer] that sixty per cent. of the said £270 12s. 7d., i.e., £162, in respect of the use of the room in the nursing home as an office should be allocated to business expenses."

The taxpayer tells me that he claims the figure of sixty per cent. because, on the occasion of an earlier accident to his back where he had made similar provision for carrying on his practice during his incapacity, he had in fact been allowed sixty per cent. of the expenses incurred by him as a deduction, and, therefore, he claims a similar proportion in this case. The Case Stated continues:

" The [taxpayer] said that, although he had been offered and was willing to take advantage of the national health service he was compelled to receive treatment in a nursing home in order to obtain all the necessary facilities to enable him to pursue his professional activities. If he had not been able to have a room as an office together with the use of a telephone which he used considerably, his business would have suffered as his clients would not have waited for him to recover but would have gone to another agent. As a result of these arrangements he earned profits and these profits were included in his accounts and he was paying tax on them. If he had not been in a nursing home he would not have earned profits, and therefore it was reasonable to allocate sixty per cent. of the total cost of his stay in the nursing home to business expenses and that £162 should therefore be deducted in arriving at the amount of his assessable profit. In cross-examination he said that he paid fees to his medical adviser in preference to having a national health service doctor because, like his clients, he wanted prompt and expert service. This would not have prevented him from having national health service treatment."

Then the determination of the commissioners is set out in para. 8 of the Case Stated in this way:

" We, the commissioners who heard the appeal, were of opinion that the sum of £162 was a deductible expense. The inspector of taxes having agreed that the amount of £15 for the use of a telephone included in the sum of £162 was a deductible expense, we reduced the assessment of £4,790 for the year 1963-64 to £4,775. From the revised assessment of £4,775 we deducted £147 and determined the assessment at £4,628, less capital allowances of £74."

I pause there to say that the form in which that determination is stated is not very satisfactory. It is a form which has been criticised in other cases, and in particular by LORD MORTON OF HENRYTON, in *Morgan (Inspector of Taxes)* v. *Tate & Lyle, Ltd.* (1), who said this about a finding in a similar form:

" The commissioners are the judges of fact, but they have not found for what purpose or purposes the sum in question was, in fact, laid out. Accordingly, your lordships have first to decide this question, and have then to decide, as a question of law, whether expenditure for that purpose is, or is not, deductible for income tax purposes."

What the taxpayer says is this: " I am not asking to be allowed the costs of medical treatment or anything like that; what I am asking is to be allowed my expenses of an office in which I can carry on my practice." He says that he was in a position where he would suffer severely in his business if he were not able to see his clients and carry on his business to the best of his ability whilst he was ill. During that period he was earning profits on which he was paying tax, and he says that it is only right that he should be allowed the expenses of that office, as he put it. This is an argument which deserves sympathy, but the question which I have to consider is whether those expenses are expenses which can be allowed him under the provisions of the Income Tax Act, 1952.

There are two sections of the Act of 1952 to which I should refer:

" 126. The tax under Cases I and II of Sch. D shall be charged without any other deduction than is by this Act allowed.

" 137. Subject to the provisions of this Act, in computing the amount of the profits or gains to be charged under Case I or Case II of Sch. D, no sum shall be deducted in respect of—(*a*) any disbursements or expenses, not being money wholly and exclusively laid out or expended for the purposes of the trade, profession or vocation; (*b*) any disbursements or expenses of maintenance of the parties, their families or establishments or any sums expended for any other domestic or private purposes distinct from the purposes of such trade, profession or vocation; . . ."

Now I am concerned with Case II of Sch. D. The submission which was made by counsel for the Crown is this. First of all, he said, the sum in question, even if expended for the purposes of the taxpayer's business, was not wholly and exclusively so expended; part of it, he said, was spent for the purpose of receiving treatment and therefore he submitted such expenditure was excluded by para. (*a*) of s. 137. Secondly, counsel submitted that this expenditure was for domestic or private purposes and so was excluded by para. (*b*) of s. 137. Counsel referred me to certain authorities. First, he referred to the case which I have already cited of *Morgan (Inspector of Taxes)* v. *Tate & Lyle, Ltd.* (2), where JENKINS, L.J., in the Court of Appeal explained (3) the general principle of the Act of 1952 in regard to permitted deductions for the purposes of Cases I and II of Sch. D, a passage which was subsequently approved by LORD MORTON OF HENRYTON in the House of Lords. JENKINS, L.J., said this (3):

" Accordingly, it has long been well settled that the effect of these provisions as to deductions is that the balance of the profits and gains of a

(1) [1954] 2 All E.R. 413 at p. 416; 35 Tax Cas. 367 at p. 407.
(2) [1954] 2 All E.R. 413; 35 Tax Cas. 367.
(3) [1953] 2 All E.R. 162 at p. 175; 35 Tax Cas. at p. 393.

trade must be ascertained in accordance with the ordinary principles of commercial trading, by deducting from the gross receipts all expenditure properly deductible from them on those principles, save in so far as any amount so deducted falls within any of the statutory prohibitions contained in the relevant rules, in which case it must be added back for the purpose of arriving at the balance of profits and gains assessable to tax: . . ."

Then counsel referred me to *Norman* v. *Golder* (*Inspector of Taxes*) (4). In that case, which related to matters which happened before the national health service came into being, the appellant, a shorthand writer, appealed against an assessment to income tax (Sch. D) in respect of his professional earnings. He had suffered from a severe illness and had incurred expenses—doctor's bills, etc. He stated that his illness was the direct result of working in unfavourable conditions. He contended that the expenses should be deducted in computing the liability to tax in respect of his earnings as being expenditure wholly and exclusively incurred in connexion with his professional work, and not domestic expenditure. Alternatively, he contended that the expenditure should be allowed as an allowance for wear and tear. The case went to the Court of Appeal, and LORD GREENE, M.R., said this (5):

" The next point relates to the deduction of his doctor's bills. It is much to be regretted that he had to incur those bills, and I may perhaps be permitted to say that I am glad to see that the trouble from which he suffered is now apparently passed and that he is restored to health, but his argument there is that they are permissible deductions on one of two grounds— one on general grounds; the other under the wear and tear clauses."

After dealing with the question of wear and tear, LORD GREENE said this (5):

" The appellant says that the medical expenses are deductible on general grounds. The answer there, to my mind, is quite conclusive. The rules about deductions are to be found in r. 3 of the rules applicable to Sch. D, Cases I and II, in which deduction is prohibited in respect of 'any disbursements or expenses, not being money wholly and exclusively laid out or expended for the purposes of the trade, profession, employment or vocation.' It is quite impossible to argue that doctor's bills represent money wholly and exclusively laid out for the purposes of the trade, profession, employment or vocation of the patient. True it is that if you do not get yourself well and so incur expenses to doctors you cannot carry on your trade or profession, and if you do not carry on your trade or profession you will not earn an income, and if you do not earn an income the Revenue will not get any tax. The same thing applies to the food you eat and the clothes that you wear. But expenses of that kind are not wholly and exclusively laid out for the purposes of the trade, profession or vocation. They are laid out in part for the advantage and benefit of the taxpayer as a living human being. Paragraph (*b*) of the rule equally would exclude doctor's bills, because they are, in my opinion, expenses of maintenance of the party, his family, or a sum expended for a domestic or private purpose, distinct from the purpose of the trade or profession."

Counsel for the Crown very fairly points out that an argument was not open to Mr. Norman in that case which might be open to the taxpayer in this, viz., that the taxpayer's treatment, unlike Mr. Norman's, is treatment that he might have had for nothing, and counsel therefore concedes that *Norman* v. *Golder* (*Inspector of Taxes*) (4) is not conclusive in favour of the Crown on the facts of the present case. Nevertheless, so far as concerns what LORD GREENE said about what is now para. (*b*) of s. 137, I find it impossible to draw any distinction between that case and the present case. It seems clear that LORD GREENE took the view

(4) [1945] 1 All E.R. 352; 26 Tax Cas. 293.
(5) [1945] 1 All E.R. at p. 354; 26 Tax Cas. at p. 298.

that the medical expenses in question were excluded from deduction by para. (*b*), because, as he said, they are " expenses of maintenance of the party, his family, or a sum expended for a domestic or private purpose ".

Then, again, in regard to the question of whether the expenses claimed by the taxpayer were wholly and exclusively laid out for the purpose of his trade, profession or vocation, counsel for the Crown referred me to *Bowden* (*Inspector of Taxes*) v. *Russell and Russell* (6). The respondents in that case were a firm of solicitors, of which in 1960 T. was sole partner. Its practice was not of an international nature. In August, 1960, T. visited America and Canada with his wife to attend, in an unofficial capacity, the annual meeting of the American Bar Association in Washington and the Empire Law Conference in Ottawa. He intended to have a holiday at the same time. He attended five conference sessions, only one of which contained an exposition of English law. On appeal against an assessment to income tax under Case II of Sch. D for the year 1961-62, the respondents claimed that the cost of the visit, which amounted to £573 excluding the wife's expenses, should be deducted. It was contended for the respondents that the visit was necessary to maintain the firm's efficiency, to obtain new clients and to improve its organisation. For the Crown it was contended, inter alia, first, that the subject matter of the two conferences was remote from the work carried out by the firm, and second, which is the relevant contention, that the purposes of T.'s visit were not exclusively to enable him to attend the conferences but substantially included holiday and social purposes. The General Commissioners found that £448 of the expenses claimed were expended wholly and exclusively for the purpose of the profession of the firm. It was held that the respondents were not entitled to the deduction claimed. PENNYCUICK, J., after referring to the passage in the judgment of JENKINS, L.J., in *Morgan* v. *Tate & Lyle* (7) which I have already read, said this (8):

" I confess that the more I read s. 137 (*a*) the greater difficulty I find in the expression ' money wholly and exclusively laid out or expended for the purposes of the trade, profession or vocation '. However, this paragraph has received authoritative analysis in the recent case of *Bentleys, Stokes and Lowless* v. *Beeson* (*Inspector of Taxes*) (9). Beyond citing the judgment of ROMER, L.J., who delivered the judgment of the Court of Appeal in that case, I am not concerned to go further into the matter. ROMER, L.J., states the principle as follows (10): ' The relevant words of para. 3 (*a*) of the Rules Applicable to Cases I and II—" wholly and exclusively laid out or expended for the purposes of the . . . profession "—appear straightforward enough. It is conceded that the first adverb—" wholly "—is in reference to the quantum of the money expended and has no relevance to the present case. The sole question is whether the expenditure in question was " exclusively " laid out for business purposes, that is: What was the motive or object in the mind of the two individuals responsible for the activities in question? It is well established that the question is one of fact: and again, therefore, the problem seems simple enough. The difficulty, however, arises, as we think, from the nature of the activity in question. Entertaining involves inevitably the characteristic of hospitality; giving to charity or subscribing to a staff pension fund involves inevitably the object of benefaction; an undertaking to guarantee to a limited amount a national exhibition involves inevitably supporting that exhibition and the purposes for which it has been organised. But the question in all such cases is: Was the entertaining, the charitable subscription, the guarantee, undertaken solely for the purposes of business, that is, solely with the object of promoting the business or its profit earning

(6) [1965] 2 All E.R. 258; 42 Tax Cas. 301.
(7) [1953] 2 All E.R. at p. 175; 35 Tax Cas at p. 393.
(8) [1965] 2 All E.R. at pp. 262, 263; 42 Tax Cas. at pp. 305, 306.
(9) [1952] 2 All E.R. 82; 33 Tax Cas. 491.
(10) [1952] 2 All E.R. at pp. 84, 85; 33 Tax Cas. at p. 503.

capacity? It is, as we have said, a question of fact. And it is quite clear that the purpose must be the sole purpose. The paragraph says so in clear terms. If the activity be undertaken with the object both of promoting business and also with some other purpose, for example, with the object of indulging an independent wish of entertaining a friend or stranger or of supporting a charitable or benevolent object, then the paragraph is not satisfied, though in the mind of the actor the business motive may predominate. For the statute so prescribes. Per contra, if, in truth, the sole object is business promotion, the expenditure is not disqualified because the nature of the activity necessarily involves some other result, or the attainment or further-ance of some other objective, since the latter result or objective is necessarily inherent in the act.'

"Then ROMER, L.J., gives a number of examples. As appears from that judgment it may often be difficult to determine whether the person incurring the expense has in mind two distinct purposes or a single purpose which will or may produce some secondary consequence; but, once it is found that the person has a distinct purpose other than that of enabling him to carry on and earn profits in his trade or profession, s. 137 (*a*) prohibits deduc-tion of the expense. In the present case, the commissioners said, in para. 4 of the Case Stated which I have read, that Mr. Taylor gave evidence before them that ' it was also his intention to have a holiday with his wife at the same time '. It seems to me that this statement by Mr. Taylor represents an unequivocal admission by him that the expenses of the American visit were incurred for a dual purpose, viz., (i) the advancement of his profession and (ii) the enjoyment of a holiday. This being the case, para. (*a*) of s. 137 and also para. (*b*) of the same section apply and prohibit the deduction of the expenses."

The claim by the taxpayer for sixty per cent. of his expenses is really fatal to his case, because implicit in a claim for only sixty per cent. of the expenses must be an admission that the expenses involved a dual purpose, viz., as to sixty per cent. expenses of conducting an office and as to forty per cent. something else. More plausible, I think, would have been the taxpayer's claim had he claimed the whole of his expenses in the nursing home and not merely sixty per cent. of them. Even had he claimed the whole of the expenses, however, it seems to me that it would not really be a rational view of the situation to conclude that the whole of his expenses in the nursing home were incurred wholly and exclusively for the purposes of his business. The whole object of going into the nursing home in the first place was to receive treatment for the injury which he had sustained, and it seems to me that it would offend common sense to say that at any rate one of his motives or purposes in going into the nursing home was not to receive treatment for that injury—treatment which would enure to his benefit, not merely during the time when he was carrying on his business, but, as LORD GREENE said in the passage which I have already read from *Norman* v. *Golder* (11) " as a living human being ".

In those circumstances, both on the ground that the deduction is prohibited by para. (*a*) of s. 137 of the Act of 1952 and on the ground that it is prohibited by para. (*b*) of the same section, I must allow this appeal.

Appeal allowed.

Solicitor: *Solicitor of Inland Revenue.*

[*Reported by* F. A. AMIES, ESQ., *Barrister-at-Law.*]

---

(11) [1945] 1 All E.R. at p. 354; 26 Tax Cas. at p. 299.

Re LANDSOWNE'S WILL TRUSTS. MARQUIS OF LANSDOWNE v. EARL OF SHELBURNE AND OTHERS.

[CHANCERY DIVISION (Buckley, J.), January 25, 26, February 9, 1967.]

Trust and Trustee—Variation of trusts by the court—Settlement of shares in company on trust for sale and conversion into land—Proceeds settled as in a settlement of land—Second son an infant and tenant in tail—Arrangement involving execution of disentailing deed—Person appointed to execute disentailing deed—Proposed arrangement for benefit of infant, of those with interests subsequent to his and of future male issue of eldest son—Trustee Act, 1925 (15 & 16 Geo. 5 c. 19), s. 53—Variation of Trusts Act, 1958 (6 & 7 Eliz. 2 c. 53), s. 1.

Under the will of the seventh Marquis of Lansdowne shares of an estate company were settled on trust for sale and conversion into land.   The land was settled on trusts under which the plaintiff was entitled to a life interest, the remainder to the first defendant (the plaintiff's eldest son) for life, with a remainder to his sons successively in tail male, with remainders to the second son of the plaintiff and any future sons of the plaintiff successively in tail male with remainders over.   The second son was an infant.   An arrangement, affecting some but not all of the property subject to the will, was proposed which involved the execution of a disentailing deed under the authority of the court by virtue of s. 53* of the Trustee Act, 1925, to bar the second son's entail, since there were many interests under the settlement affected by the will ranking in priority to the estate tail of the only tenant in tail who was of full age.   The plaintiff's life interest in certain properties was to be enlarged to an absolute interest; other properties were to be held in trust for the first defendant absolutely, a third group of properties was to be held on discretionary trusts of which the second son and others would be objects, and, last, the remainder of the properties (referred to as " the reversioners' share " and consisting entirely of agricultural land) were to be held on trust for sale, the proceeds of sale being settled on trusts including trusts for accumulation and under which the beneficiaries would include the sons of the first defendant and in default a discretionary trust of which the objects would include the second son, and subject thereto, trusts for the second son for life contingently on attaining twenty-one and thereafter for his sons successively in tail male with the remainders over, a power of appointment in his own favour being reserved to the second son if he attained twenty-one.   There was thus no certainty that the second son would ever receive anything under the trusts of the proposed arrangement.   The value of the reversioners' share was considerably greater than the combined reversionary interests of the second son and of all whose interests ranked after his estate tail under the existing settlement.   The arrangement would be beneficial also to future issue of the first defendant.   The plaintiff sought an order under s. 53 of the Trustee Act, 1925, for the execution of the proposed disentailing deed, and an order under s. 1 of the Variation of Trusts Act, 1958, approving the proposed arrangement on behalf of the second son and future mail issue of the first defendant.

Held: re-settlement of the reversioners' share amounted, for the purposes of s. 53 of the Trustee Act, 1925, to an " application of the capital " of so much of the settled land as was comprised in the proposed arrangement;

---

* Section 53 provides: " Where an infant is beneficially entitled to any property the court may, with a view to the application of the capital or income thereof for the maintenance, education, or benefit of the infant, make an order—(a) appointing a person to convey such property; or (b) in the case of stock, or a thing in action, vesting in any person the right to transfer or call for a transfer of such stock, or to receive the dividends or income thereof, or to sue for and recover such thing in action, upon such terms as the court may think fit."

and, since the proposed disentailing deed was a necessary and integral part of the scheme for carrying the proposed arrangement into effect, and in view of the value of the reversioners' share, the proposed arrangement would benefit the second son and those whose interests under the existing will were subsequent to his, the court would order execution of the proposed disentailing deed and would approve the arrangement on behalf of the second son and of future male issue of the first defendant (see p. 893, letter I, p. 894, letter B, and p. 895, letter A, post).

Re Meux's Will Trusts ([1957] 2 All E.R. 630) applied.

[**Editorial Note.** This case should be considered with *Re Bristol's Settled Estates* ([1964] 3 All E.R. 939).

As to the court's jurisdiction to appoint a person to convey the property of an infant, see 21 HALSBURY'S LAWS (3rd Edn.) 176, para. 382; and for cases on the subject see 47 DIGEST (Repl.) 331, 332, *2986-2992.*

As to the jurisdiction under the Variation of Trusts Act, 1958, see 38 HALS-BURY'S LAWS (3rd Edn.) 1029, 1030, para. 1772; and for cases on the subject see 47 DIGEST (Repl.) 332-338, *2993-3018.*

For the Trustee Act, 1925, s. 53, see 26 HALSBURY'S STATUTES (2nd Edn.) 134.

For the Variation of Trusts Act, 1958, see 38 HALSBURY'S STATUTES (2nd Edn.) 1130.]

Cases referred to:

Gower's Settlement, Re, [1934] All E.R. Rep. 796; [1934] Ch. 365; 103 L.J.Ch. 169; 150 L.T. 449; 47 Digest (Repl.) 228, *1973.*

Heyworth's Settlements, Re, [1956] 2 All E.R. 21; [1956] Ch. 369; [1956] 2 W.L.R. 1044; 47 Digest (Repl.) 330, *2975.*

Meux's Will Trusts, Re, Gilmour v. *Gilmour,* [1957] 2 All E.R. 630; [1958] Ch. 154; [1957] 3 W.L.R. 377; 47 Digest (Repl.) 332, *2988.*

Adjourned Summons.

This was an application by originating summons dated June 27, 1966, by the plaintiff the Most Hon. George John Charles, Marquis of Lansdowne, who was beneficially interested under the trusts of the will dated Nov. 16, 1938, of the Most Hon. Charles Hope, Marquis of Lansdowne, deceased. The plaintiff sought (i) an order under s. 53* of the Trustee Act, 1925, that the Hon. John Astor, M.P. or some other suitable person might be appointed to execute, with the consent of the plaintiff as protector of the settlement created by the trusts of the will, a disentailing assurance (in the terms of a draft disentailing assurance which was exhibited to an affidavit sworn in support of the summons by the plaintiff) barring the interest in tail male under the trusts, of the second defendant, the Hon. Lord Robert Harold Mercer Nairne in the property specified in the draft disentailing assurance, with a view to the application of the capital and income thereof for his benefit in the manner specified in an arrangement under the Variation of Trusts Act, 1958. (ii) An order pursuant to the Variation of Trusts Act, 1958, approving an arrangement on behalf of the infant defendant, Lord Robert, and all male issue as yet unborn of the first defendant the Right Hon. Charles Maurice Petty Fitzmaurice, Earl of Shelburne who might become beneficially interested under the trusts of the will. The third defendant was the Hon. Lady Georgina Elizabeth Petty Fitzmaurice who, together with the first and second defendants, was beneficially interested under the trusts of the will. The fourth defendant was Charles Edgar Matthews Hardie and the fifth was Baring Brothers & Co., Ltd., who were trustees of the will. The facts are set out in the judgment.

J. E. Vinelott for the plaintiff.

N. C. H. Browne-Wilkinson for the first defendant.

M. J. Fox for the second defendant.

R. A. R. Evans for the third defendant.

D. K. Rattee for the fourth and fifth defendants.

---

* See footnote *, at p. 888, ante.

Cur. adv. vult.

Feb. 9. **BUCKLEY, J.,** read the following judgment: This is an application under the Trustee Act, 1925, s. 53 and under the Variation of Trusts Act, 1958, to effect a variation of the trusts of the will of the late seventh Marquis of Lansdowne, whom I will call the testator, who died on active service on Aug. 20, 1944. He was not survived by any brother nor by any issue of any brother. On his death the title to the peerage passed to his first cousin, the plaintiff, as the eighth Marquis of Lansdowne. The plaintiff is married and has had issue two sons, namely the defendants the Earl of Shelburne and Lord Robert Mercer Nairne. The latter was born on Feb. 16, 1947, and consequently is still an infant. The plaintiff has also had two daughters of whom the elder died in 1956 without issue, and the younger is the defendant Lady Georgina Fitzmaurice, who was born in 1950. Lord Shelburne is aged twenty-six, is married and has had issue one child only, a daughter.

By his will dated Nov. 16, 1938, the testator by cl. 2 bequeathed all his shares, stocks and debentures in a family estate company called " Bowood Estate Co.", which I will call the company, on trust for sale and conversion and investment of the proceeds in land as if such proceeds were capital moneys under the Settled Land Act, 1925, and directed that the land so purchased should be settled on the trusts and with and subject to the powers therein contained. The will then contained a strict and elaborate settlement of this subject-matter under which in the events which have occurred it is now held on trust (*a*) for the plaintiff for life with remainder (*b*) for Lord Shelburne for life with remainder (*c*) for Lord Shelburne's sons successively according to seniority in tail male with remainder (*d*) for Lord Robert and any future sons of the plaintiff successively according to seniority in tail male with remainder (*e*) for Lady Georgina and any future daughters of the plaintiff successively according to seniority in tail male with remainder (*f*) for Lord Shelburne's daughters successively according to seniority in tail male with remainder (*g*) for Lord Shelburne's sons successively according to seniority in tail general with remainder (*h*) for Lord Shelburne's daughters successively according to seniority in tail general with remainder (*i*) for Lord Robert and any future sons of the plaintiff successively according to seniority in tail general with remainder (*j*) for Lady Georgina and any future daughters of the plaintiff successively according to seniority in tail general with numerous remainders over, under which the first existing adult with an entailed interest takes subject to the interests of some sixty persons with prior life or entailed interests.

All but three of the 44,793 issued shares of the company are comprised in the settlement. At the death of the testator the company owned the Bowood Estate which included extensive agricultural lands. In 1954 by agreement between the trustees of the will and the company the Bowood Estate was conveyed to the trustees in consideration of the cancellation of some of the shares in the company then held by the trustees. The estate is itself now subject to the trusts of the settlement. Its value in August, 1965, apart from the principal mansion house and other property excluded from the arrangement to which this application relates, exceeded £1,000,000 of which approximately £770,000 was the value of agricultural land.

The plaintiff has free estate of a considerable value, and Lord Shelburne has substantial expectations in the form of contingent reversionary in trusts under certain American settlements. In these circumstances, if matters remain as at present, heavy death duties will be payable on the settled estate on the death of the plaintiff, and also on the death of Lord Shelburne if he survives the plaintiff.

The arrangement of which the approval of the court is now sought is designed to reduce this fiscal burden, to make some immediate provision out of the settled estate for the plaintiff's issue and to make some part of the capital of the settled estate available to the plaintiff out of which he intends to make further provision inter vivos for his own issue which, if he lives long enough, will escape duty at his death. The arrangement does not affect the whole of the settled property. The principal mansion house and other property valued at some £200,000, the shares in the company and certain heirlooms are excluded from it and will continue to be held on the trusts of the will. The rest of the settled property consisting wholly of real estate, and including all the agricultural land, is included in the arrangement.

Having regard to the very large number of persons with interests under the settlement which rank in priority to the estate tail of the only tenant in tail in remainder who is of age, it would be impracticable to carry such an arrangement into effect without the assistance of this court under the Trustee Act, 1925, s. 53 to enable Lord Robert's estate in tail male expectant on the deaths of the plaintiff and Lord Shelburne and failure of the estates in tail male of any son or sons of Lord Shelburne, to be barred. That section empowers the court, where an infant is beneficially entitled to any property, to appoint a person to convey such property " with a view to the application of the capital or income thereof for the maintenance education or benefit of the infant ". Under this section the court has power in a proper case to appoint a person to bar an infant's estate tail (*Re Gower's Settlement* (1)). It is proposed that the court shall appoint a named person to execute, with the consent of the plaintiff as protector of the settlement, a disentailing assurance in respect of the property comprised in the arrangement barring Lord Robert's estate therein in tail male with the result that the arrangement can proceed without regard to any more remote interests at present subsisting under the trusts.

The arrangement then provides that the plaintiff's life interest in certain specifically-appropriated properties, defined as " Lord Lansdowne's share ", shall be enlarged to an absolute interest, so that those properties shall henceforth belong to him absolutely. Other specifically appropriated properties, defined as " Lord Shelburne's absolute share ", are to be held in trust for Lord Shelburne absolutely.

A third group of specifically appropriated properties, defined as " Lord Shelburne's settled share ", are to be held on trusts under which it is sufficient for present purposes to say that Lord Robert will take no interest except as a member of a large class of objects of certain discretionary trusts and powers.

Finally, the remainder of the properties comprised in the arrangement, defined as " the reversioners' share ", consisting entirely of agricultural land, are to be held on trust for sale with the usual power to postpone sale, the proceeds and the rents and profits until sale being settled on trusts which, stated shortly, are proposed to be as follows: (a) on trust for Lord Shelburne's sons who attain twenty-one or marry successively according to seniority in tail male, such estate being cut down to a life estate in the case of any such son who may die before a defined perpetuity date in which case, expectant on the death of such son, his sons are to take successively in tail male; (b) on trust to accumulate the income during any period or periods falling within a defined accumulation period when there is no male issue of Lord Shelburne alive entitled to a vested or contingent interest under the preceding trust and no such male issue has died, after barring his entailed interest, but with power for the trustees notwithstanding the trust for accumulation to pay or apply any of the income to or for the benefit of, as things stand at present, Lord Robert; (c) after the end of the accumulation period during the remainder of a defined discretionary period, when there is no male issue of Lord Shelburne alive entitled to a vested or contingent interest under the foregoing trust and no such male issue has died after barring his entailed interest, on discretionary trusts for a class of objects which includes Lord Robert with a precatory direction that as things now stand, prior regard shall be had to his interests; (d) subject as aforesaid on trust for Lord Robert for life on his attaining twenty-one years and so that this trust shall, subject as aforesaid,

(1) [1934] All E.R. Rep. 796; [1934] Ch. 365.

carry the intermediate income whenever there is no male issue of Lord Shelburne
alive entitled to a vested or contingent interest under the foregoing trust and no
such male issue has died after barring his entailed interests; (e) on trust for Lord
Robert's sons successively according to seniority in tail male contingently on
attaining twenty-one or marrying or surviving the perpetuity date and so as to
carry the intermediate income in a similar manner as before mentioned; (f) on
trust for any future sons of the plaintiff successively according to seniority in tail
male contingently on their attaining twenty-one or marrying and so as to carry
the intermediate income in a similar manner; (g) on trust for the plaintiff's
daughters successively according to seniority in tail male contingently on their
attaining twenty-one or marrying and so as to carry the intermediate income in
a similar manner; (h) on the trusts declared by the will of the testator in respect
of the settled estate to take effect in remainder after the interest in tail male
thereby given to the plaintiff's daughters, but freed and discharged from the
prior trusts declared by the will, and so as to carry the intermediate income in a
similar manner.

There follows a proviso that any son of Lord Shelburne who becomes entitled
to a life interest under the first above-mentioned trust shall have power at any
time before the perpetuity date by deed or will to appoint the whole or part of
the reversioners' share in his own favour, or so as to form part of his estate, but
so that, except with the consent of the trustees, he shall not exercise this power
by deed in respect of more than a quarter of the fund while under twenty-five,
nor in respect of more than half the fund while under thirty.

There follows a further proviso that Lord Robert shall have power at any time
after attaining his majority and after the death of Lord Shelburne, but before the
perpetuity date, to appoint by deed the whole or part of the reversioners' share
in his own favour absolutely, subject to the trusts in favour of Lord Shelburne's
sons and their sons but in priority to all the other foregoing trusts.

Lord Shelburne's settled share and the reversioners' share will be protected
against the risk of a charge to estate duty in the event of the plaintiff dying within
five years by a policy of assurance in a suitable amount to be effected at the
plaintiff's expense.

Comparing the trusts of the settled estate subsisting under the will with the
proposed trusts of the reversioners' share under the arrangement, the plaintiff's
life interest in possession and Lord Shelburne's reversionary life interest are
omitted from the latter. The interests in tail male of Lord Shelburne's sons are
made contingent on attaining twenty-one and are cut down until the perpetuity
date in the case of any son who does not survive that date to a life interest with
remainder in tail male for the sons of that son; but in conjunction with his life
interest any son of Lord Shelburne whose estate tail is so cut down is given the
power of appointing capital in his own favour contained in the first proviso which
I have mentioned. The trust for accumulation during the accumulation period
and the discretionary trust thereafter during the remainder of the discretionary
period are introduced in priority to any interest given to Lord Robert, but with a
discretionary power during the earlier period to apply income for his benefit and
a precatory direction that during the latter period prior regard shall be had to his
interests in the exercise of the trustee's discretion. There follows, in lieu of his
existing interest in tail male in remainder, a life interest for Lord Robert contingent on his attaining twenty-one, so framed that he will receive the income so
long as and whenever there is no male issue of Lord Shelburne in the male line
alive and the entail of Lord Shelburne's male issue in the male line has not been
barred; and in remainder expectant on Lord Robert's death his sons are given
successive contingent interests in tail male framed in a similar manner. In
conjunction with his life interest Lord Robert is given, in the event of his attaining
twenty-one and surviving Lord Shelburne, the power to appoint capital in his
own favour contained in the second proviso which I have mentioned. The

A interests in tail male of any future sons of the plaintiff or of his daughters, including Lady Georgina, are restored but made contingent on their attaining twenty-
one or marrying, and all the remoter interests under the will are restored without
modification.

   The first question for consideration is whether in the circumstances the proposed
disentailing deed can properly be said to be with a view to the application of
B capital or income for the maintenance, education or benefit of Lord Robert within
s. 53 of the Trustee Act, 1925. In *Re Heyworth's Settlements* (2) UPJOHN, J., was
concerned with a proposed sale for cash to a tenant for life of an infant's reversionary interest which was contingent on the infant surviving the tenant for life. The
bargain was undoubtedly beneficial to the infant for the price she would have
received would have been substantially in excess of the actuarial value of her
C reversion and, moreover, substantially in excess of the sum which would have been
receivable by the reversioner at the death of the life tenant, unless there were
some wholly unexpected change in rates of estate duty. There was, however, no
present need of the cash for the infant. In these circumstances the judge reached
the conclusion that the proposed sale was not with a view to the application of, or
for the purpose of applying, any capital or income of the infant for her benefit.

D   In the present case there is no indication of any need for any money or property
to be applied for Lord Robert's benefit; nor indeed is there any certainty that he
will ever receive anything, whether income or capital, under the trusts of the
arrangement or that any money or other property will be applied for his benefit
under those trusts.

   In *Re Meux's Will Trusts, Gilmour* v. *Gilmour* (3) property was settled on trust
E for a life tenant for life with remainder to his first and other sons successively in
tail male. The life tenant's eldest son was an infant. The life tenant applied to the
court for a person to be appointed under s. 53 of the Trustee Act, 1925, to bar his
eldest son's entailed interest with the life tenant's consent as protector by conveying that interest to the life tenant in consideration of a purchase price to be
paid to the trustees of a settlement virtually on the same trusts as those sub-
F sisting under the original settlement, except for the elimination of the life interest
of the life tenant. WYNN-PARRY, J., held that the proposed transfer of the
purchase price to the trustees of the new settlement amounted to an " application " of that fund within the meaning of s. 53. The benefit to the infant in that
case arose from the saving resulting from avoidance of estate duty consequent on
the sale of the reversionary interest. It was contended that the new settlement,
G per se, did not benefit the infant and that this application of the purchase price
consequently did not clothe the court with jurisdiction under s. 53. As I understand his judgment, which at this point seems to be imperfectly reported,
WYNN-PARRY, J., would have accepted this contention had he thought that the
arrangement, properly regarded, consisted of two separate transactions, (i) the
sale and (ii) the settlement. He considered, however, that the arrangement con-
H stituted one indivisible transaction, which was overwhelmingly favourable to the
infant reversioner. He consequently came to the conclusion that the proposed
conveyance of the reversionary interest was with a view to an application for the
benefit of the infant reversioner within s. 53.

   In the present case the proposed disentailing deed is clearly a necessary and
integral part of the scheme for carrying the arrangement into effect and is to be
I made with that object in view and for that purpose. The legal estate in the
properties comprised in the arrangement is at present vested in the plaintiff as
tenant for life. Lord Lansdowne's share will remain so vested but will become his
absolute property. The plaintiff will convey the properties constituting Lord
Shelburne's absolute share to Lord Shelburne or as he shall direct. The plaintiff
will convey the properties constituting Lord Shelburne's settled share to the

(2) [1956] 2 All E.R. 21; [1956] Ch. 364.
(3) [1957] 2 All E.R. 630; [1958] Ch. 154.

trustees of the testator's will as statutory owners for the purposes of the Settled
Land Act, 1925, on the trusts set out in the arrangement in respect of that share.
Finally the plaintiff will convey the properties constituting the reversioners' share
to the same trustees on trust for sale, with power to postpone, and to stand
possessed of the proceeds and of the rents and profits until sale on the trusts set
out in the arrangement in respect of that share.

This resettlement of the reversioners' share is in my judgment an " application " within the meaning of s. 53 of the capital of that part of the settled land
comprised in the arrangement (*Re Meux's Will Trusts* (4)), so also in my judgment
are the proposed dealings with the other three shares under the arrangement.

The value of the reversioners' share is considerably greater than the value of the
combined reversionary interests of Lord Robert and all whose interests rank after
his estate tail under the existing settlement. It is also considerably higher than
the value of the property to which Lord Robert as first tenant in tail in remainder
could expect to succeed after payment of estate duty if the existing settlement
were to continue in operation and, as is most probable, Lord Shelburne survives
the plaintiff.

The beneficial interest in the reversioners' share differ as regards their organisation from the beneficial interests under the existing settlement, but broadly they
may be said to correspond to and be commensurate with the latter, except for the
significant improvement of the reversioners' position by the exclusion of the life
interests of the plaintiff and Lord Shelburne.

Under the existing trusts Lord Robert has no possibility of becoming entitled
to the settled property in possession until after the death of the survivor of the
plaintiff and Lord Shelburne and failure of Lord Shelburne's male issue. As Lord
Shelburne is a young man not yet twenty-six years of age Lord Robert's expectations are at present remote and speculative, but under the arrangement he will,
so long as there is no male issue of Lord Shelburne in existence, be an immediate
object of the power to apply income for his benefit during the accumulation
period, which will continue for twenty-one years from today's date or until such
earlier date after Lord Shelburne's death as the trustees may appoint. The
discretionary period will continue from the end of the accumulation period until
the perpetuity date (i.e. twenty-one years less one day after the death of the last
survivor of the issue of George V living on Aug. 21, 1944, when the testator died)
or until such earlier date after Lord Shelburne's death as the trustees may
appoint. During this discretionary period Lord Robert will, so long as there is no
male issue of Lord Shelburne in existence, be by virtue of the precatory discretion
the prime object of the discretionary trust of income. If he survives Lord Shelburne Lord Robert will have the power of appointing capital (including any
accumulations) in his own favour contained in the second proviso previously
referred to.

In view of the relative values of Lord Robert's existing expectations and of the
reversioners' share, I am satisfied that the proposed resettlement of the latter
will benefit Lord Robert. The appropriation and resettlement of the reversioners'
share has been negotiated as part of the arrangement as a whole. That benefit
could not have been obtained for him without agreement as to the appropriation
and application of the other shares under the arrangement. I am consequently
satisfied that the proposed disentailing deed is to be executed with a view to the
application not only of the reversioners' share but indeed of the whole of the
properties to be affected by it in manners beneficial to Lord Robert.

Not only will the arrangement benefit Lord Robert; it will likewise benefit the
persons interested under the existing settlement in remainder after Lord Robert's
entailed interest. There is consequently no reason why on their account I should
refuse to exercise the jurisdiction under s. 53.

I therefore reach the conclusion that the case is one in which I have jurisdiction

(4) [1957] 2 All E.R. 630; [1958] Ch. 154.

A under s. 53 to facilitate the barring of Lord Robert's entail and that it is a proper case in which to do so. I have been taken through this elaborate scheme by counsel with great care, and I have been satisfied that the arrangement is beneficial not only to Lord Robert but also to any male issue in the male line of Lord Shelburne who may be born. I will accordingly appoint the gentleman named in the minute of order to execute the proposed disentailing deed and I will approve the arrange-

B ment which will be scheduled to the order on behalf of Lord Robert and of all such male issue of Lord Shelburne as aforesaid.

The arrangement as set out in the exhibited minutes of order calls for some amendment in respect of matters raised in the course of the argument which I need not mention in detail. I will make the order in the form of an amended minute to be signed by the plaintiff's counsel and approved by counsel for all

C other parties.

Order accordingly.

Solicitors: *Freshfields* (for the plaintiff and the first, second and third defendants); *Penningtons and Lewis & Lewis* (for the fourth and fifth defendants).

[*Reported by* JENIFER SANDELL, *Barrister-at-Law.*]

D

R. *v.* GARDINER.

E [COURT OF APPEAL, CRIMINAL DIVISION (Lord Parker, C.J., Winn, L.J., and Willis, J.), January 24, 1967.]

Criminal Law—Sentence—Hospital order—Restriction order—Secretary of State's powers—Mentally sub-normal person—Indecency—Conviction—Three years' imprisonment—Transfer to mental hospital and restriction imposed for

F *period of sentence—Guidance in regard to convicted prisoners suffering from mental disorder—Mental Health Act, 1959 (7 & 8 Eliz. 2 c. 72), s. 60, s. 65, s. 72.*

The observations of the Court of Appéal on the effect of hospital orders and restriction orders and on matters to be borne in mind by courts in dealing with prisoners under the Mental Health Act, 1959, for which this case is reported, are set out at p. 897, letter G, et seq., post).

G The appellant, a mentally subnormal person, had been convicted at the Hampstead magistrates' court of indecent assault on one boy and of inciting two others to commit acts of indecency. He was committed for sentence to Inner London Sessions. The chairman of sessions felt that it was a case in which there should be a restriction order (viz., an order under s. 65 of the Mental Health Act, 1959) but, on being informed that there was no secure

H hospital that would take the appellant, a sentence of three years' imprisonment was imposed. The appellant was granted leave to appeal against sentence. On Jan. 5, 1967, the Secretary of State directed (under s. 72) that the appellant should be transferred to a mental hospital and that he be subject to the restrictions set out in s. 65. The restrictions thus imposed would operate only for the period of the appellant's sentence. The appellant

I accordingly sought leave to abandon his appeal.

Held: leave to abandon the appeal would be granted (see p. 897, letter F, post).

Per CURIAM: since in most cases the prognosis cannot be certain, the safer course is to make any restriction order unlimited in point of time (see (p. 898, letter I, post).

[**Editorial Note.** In regard to inquiring, before a hospital order is made, whether a mental hospital will receive a prisoner, and whether it has facilities for keeping prisoners in safe custody, see *R.* v. *Higginbotham* ([1961] 3 All E.R. at p. 620, letter F).

As to hospital orders, see 29 HALSBURY'S LAWS (3rd Edn.) 524, 525, para. 985; as to orders restricting discharge, see ibid., pp. 527, 528, para. 990; and as to the powers of the Secretary of State in respect of the transfer to hospital of persons serving sentences of imprisonment, see ibid., pp. 550-552, para. 1024.

For the Mental Health Act, 1959, s. 60, s. 65, s. 72, see 39 HALSBURY'S STATUTES (2nd Edn.) 1013, 1019, 1027.]

Application.

This was an application by Alistair George Cecil Gardiner for leave to abandon his appeal against a sentence of three years' imprisonment passed on him at the Inner London Sessions on Sept. 15, 1966. The facts are summarised in the judgment.

W. F. C. Thomas for the appellant.

LORD PARKER, C.J., delivered the following judgment of the court: This case illustrates the difficulties under which courts act when they wish to deal with a prisoner under the Mental Health Act, 1959. Although this is a case which really involves leave to abandon the appeal, the court feels it right to give a judgment in the matter.

On July 26, 1966, three boys under fourteen, two of them brothers aged eight and ten, went on to Hampstead Heath and there met another boy of fourteen, and all went to the fair ground where they met the appellant, who was employed there. During the course of the day the appellant gave the boys money to spend at the fair, bought them tea and cakes, and about 7.30 p.m. he offered to see them on their way home. As they walked across the heath he suggested to the boys that they should partake in a form of indecency; it is unnecessary to go through the details of what then occurred. It so happened, however, that a park keeper was near the scene and hearing the scream of one of the boys aged eight, he chased the appellant, and after half a mile caught him. Those matters gave rise to a charge against him before the Hampstead magistrates' court of indecent assault on one boy, and of inciting the other two to commit acts of indecency. He was then committed for sentence to Inner London Sessions where, in the end, he was sentenced to three years' imprisonment.

At the first hearing before Inner London Sessions, namely on Aug. 19, the chairman had before him medical reports; he had a report from Dr. Finn, a psychiatrist and approved (1) medical practitioner of the Leavesden Hospital of Hertfordshire, and also of a Dr. Pollitt, an approved medical practitioner, who is medical officer of Her Majesty's Prison at Brixton. Both doctors expressed the opinion that the appellant was suffering from subnormality and that the subnormality warranted his detention in hospital for treatment. They recommended that he should go to Leavesden Hospital where he had already been as a voluntary patient, and where he was known and where a place was available.

The chairman, no doubt with good reason, felt that this was a matter in which there should be a restriction order; he was unable to make a restriction order without having one of the medical experts present. Accordingly, he adjourned the case for three days to Aug. 22. On Aug. 22 he learned that the appellant while a voluntary patient at Leavesden Hospital had discharged himself, and, rightly or wrongly, the chairman took the view that if merely a hospital order and a restriction order were made, and if the appellant were sent to an ordinary mental hospital, then, though not able to discharge himself, he might walk out. Accordingly the chairman was minded to send the appellant,

---

(1) I.e., approved for the purposes of s. 28 of the Act of 1959 as having special experience in the diagnosis or treatment of mental disorders; see s. 62 (1) of the Act, 39 HALSBURY'S STATUTES (2nd Edn.) 1016.

A if that were possible, to one of the special hospitals, a secure hospital, and he adjourned the matter again to Sept. 15.

On Sept. 15 the chairman was advised of the position, which constantly comes before the courts, of there being no secure hospital that would take him. He had the report from a doctor who said that he did not think that it was a case for a secure hospital, and he had before him a letter from the Ministry of Health

B saying that no place would be made available in a secure hospital for this man. It was in those circumstances that the chairman, and again I say rightly or wrongly, decided that, as he could not send the appellant to a secure hospital, he had better send him to prison instead of making a hospital order and restriction order.

It was in those circumstances that he sentenced the appellant to three years'

C imprisonment. In due course the appellant applied for leave and was granted leave to appeal against that sentence. The court had in mind that perhaps this was not a case for a secure hospital, anyhow no place was available, and that perhaps the better course was to make a hospital order and a restriction order. Meanwhile, the Secretary of State on Jan. 5, 1967, by a direction made under s. 72 of the Act of 1959, in fact transferred the appellant to a mental hospital and

D further directed that he be subject to the restrictions set out in s. 65 of that Act. Accordingly it is in those circumstances, he now being in a mental hospital and subject to the restrictions of a restriction order, that the appellant, perhaps wisely for him, asks leave to abandon the appeal. I say " wisely for him " because under the Secretary of State's order the s. 65 restrictions will operate for a period of only three years, the period of his sentence. Then, unless he

E can be detained on medical grounds, he must be freed; whereas, if the matter had come before this court, it is at least likely that a restriction order would have been made unlimited in point of time.

The court grants the appellant leave to abandon his appeal. This case, however, does give this court an opportunity of dealing with rather more general matters which should be borne in mind by courts dealing with prisoners under

F the Mental Health Act, 1959. A number of cases concerning hospital orders under s. 60 and restriction orders under s. 65 of the Mental Health Act, 1959, have come to the attention of the court from which it would clearly appear that some courts do not fully appreciate the advisability in some cases of making a restriction order.

G It must be borne in mind that when only a hospital order is made:—

1. It is only authority for the patient's detention for one year in the first instance. This authority can be renewed if the medical practitioner in charge of the treatment of the patient (whom I will call the " responsible medical officer ") reports to the hospital managers that it appears to him that further detention is necessary in the interests of the patient's health or safety or for the protection

H of others. The hospital managers, however, are not bound to act on such a report and may refuse to extend the period and accordingly discharge the patient. Further, if the patient is sixteen or over he or his nearest relative can apply, at certain intervals to a mental health review tribunal who may in any case direct the patient's discharge and must do so if satisfied that he is no longer suffering from a mental disorder or that his further detention is not necessary.

I 2. The patient can be discharged at any time by the hospital managers whose power is unlimited or by the responsible medical officer whose power is also unlimited or by a mental health review tribunal as already stated.

3. Once discharged the patient is no longer liable to recall.

4. A patient who is absent without leave cannot be re-taken into custody and indeed ceases to be liable to be detained (a) if he is over twenty-one and is classified as psychopathic or subnormal, after six months' absence, (b) in any other case, after twenty-eight days' absence.

If, however, a restriction order is made in addition to a hospital order: (i) there A
is authority to detain the patient for at any rate the duration of that order,
though the Secretary of State may terminate it at any time if satisfied that it is
no longer required for the protection of the public; (ii) the patient can only
be discharged with the consent of the Secretary of State or by the Secretary of
State himself; (iii) the Secretary of State has power in discharging the patient
himself to make the discharge conditional, in which case the patient remains B
liable to recall during the period up to the expiration of the restriction order.
This power is particularly useful as a means of keeping a discharged patient
under the supervision of a probation officer or mental welfare officer for a longer
period than would be possible if there were no restriction order; lastly a patient
who is absent without leave may be taken into custody again at any time.

Accordingly it will be seen from the above that a restriction order enables the C
Secretary of State to exercise the function (as recommended by the Royal
Commission on the Law relating to Mental Illness and Mental Deficiency (2))
of a central authority which pays special regard to the protection of the public
in controlling the discharge of dangerous patients. Apart from a restriction order
it is inevitable that the hospital's first concern is the welfare of the patient and
this does result in some cases in a patient who is subject to a hospital order alone D
securing his discharge earlier than he would do if he were also subject to a restriction order. The Secretary of State might well feel that although the patient was
apparently no longer in need of medical treatment a further period in hospital
under observation was advisable and was required to guard against the possibility of relapse leading to further crime.

This is not meant to suggest that restriction orders should be made in every E
case, but it is very advisable that they should be made in all cases where it is
thought that the protection of the public is required. Thus in, for example, the
case of crimes of violence and of the more serious sexual offences, particularly
if the prisoner has a record of such offences, or if there is a history of mental
disorder involving violent behaviour, it is suggested that there must be compelling reasons to explain why a restriction order should not be made. F

Nevertheless experience has shown that there are an alarming number of
cases in which in such circumstances no restriction order has been made. As an
example, a woman with a history of mental disorder attacked a neighbour with
an iron bar and was made the subject of a hospital order alone. Four months
later she obtained her discharge and within less than a year she killed a man with
an axe, was found unfit to plead and removed to Broadmoor. Again, a thirty-two G
year old man, with previous convictions for assault and attempted rape, followed
a seventy year old woman, who was not known to him, and without provocation
struck her violently in the face and knocked her over a stone wall. This occurred
only two months after his release from hospital following detention under a
hospital order alone, made as a result of a conviction for assault.

There have also been cases in which a court has decided that the prisoner H
must be detained under conditions of special security in one of the special hospitals and yet no restriction order has been made. In the result he may well be
able to secure his discharge on application to a mental health review tribunal (3)
on the ground that he is not at the time suffering from mental disorder, even
though relapses may be expected.

Finally, since in most cases the prognosis cannot be certain the safer course is I
to make any restriction order unlimited in point of time. The only exception is
where the doctors are able to assert confidently that recovery will take place
within a fixed period, when the restriction order can properly be limited to that
period.

---

(2) May, 1957, CMND. 169.
(3) In regard to applications to mental health review tribunals, see 29 HALSBURY'S
LAWS (3rd Edn.) 457, para. 878.

A The court has thought it proper to make these observations in the light of experience, and it is hoped that they will be of some use to courts throughout the country, and particularly to magistrates' courts which, of course, cannot make restriction orders themselves but must commit to quarter sessions before such orders can be made.

B Solicitors: *T. V. Edwards & Co.* (for the appellant).

[*Reported by* KAUSHALYA PURIE, *Barrister-at-Law.*]

MARTIN *v.* PUTTICK.

C [QUEEN'S BENCH DIVISION (Lord Parker, C.J., Winn, L.J., and Willis, J.), February 6, 1967.]

Criminal Law—Larceny—Asportation—Supermarket—Customer obtaining meat from assistant, and failing to pay for it at cash counter, allowed to leave store after manager had seen meat in customer's bag—Whether customer had per-
D *mission to take away meat—Whether larceny—Larceny Act, 1916 (6 & 7 Geo. 5 c. 50), s. 1 (1).*

The respondent, having taken various articles from the shelves at a supermarket and put them into the wire basket provided for that purpose, went to the meat counter where she selected two pork chops. The shop assistant wrapped them up in paper, marked the price on the paper and
E handed the parcel to the respondent. As the chops were damp and the wrapping paper was not capable of retaining the moisture, the respondent placed them in a shopping bag which she was carrying. When she went to the cash desk, she produced the articles from the wire basket and paid for them, but she did not produce the chops from her shopping bag. The shop manager, who was helping her to put the articles for which she had paid into her
F shopping bag, saw the package containing the chops in the shopping bag. The manager, thinking that he was bound to let the respondent leave the supermarket before he could detain or charge her, did not move the chops but allowed the respondent to leave carrying her shopping bag and, very shortly afterwards, spoke to her and detained her. The respondent con-sistently protested that she had no intention of dishonestly taking the chops.
G It was found that the respondent intended to avoid payment when she was at the cash desk, but had not intended to avoid payment when she placed the chops in her shopping bag. On appeal by the prosecutor against the dismissal of a charge against the respondent of feloniously stealing the chops, contrary to s. 1* of the Larceny Act, 1916,

Held: (i) when a customer picked up goods from shelves or other display
H stands in a shop which conducted itself as a supermarket store, the customer did not then become entitled to any form of property in the goods, nor did the customer acquire any exclusive possession of the goods (see p. 902, letter B, and p. 904, letter H, post).

(ii) as the chops were not at the material time in the manager's power nor were they released by him into the respondent's possession, there was nothing
I in his conduct which prevented the actual carrying of the chops by the respon-dent out of the shop from being an asportation against the will of the owner with the criminal intention to deprive the owner, without any claim of right, permanently, at the time when the carrying away took place, and accordingly theft was established (see p. 904, letters E, G and H, post).

---

* Section 1, so far as material, provides: " For the purposes of this Act—(1) a person steals who, without the consent of the owner, fraudulently and without claim of right made in good faith, takes and carries away anything capable of being stolen with intent, at the time of such taking, permanently to deprive the owner thereof . . ."

R. v. *Turvey* ([1946] 2 All E.R. 60) distinguished.

Appeal allowed.

[**Editorial Note.** In regard to the analysis of purchase of goods in a self-service shop this case may be considered with *Pharmaceutical Society of Great Britain* v. *Boots Cash Chemists (Southern), Ltd.* ([1953] 1 All E.R. 482).

As to asportation, see 10 HALSBURY's LAWS (3rd Edn.) 767, 768, para. 1484; and for cases on the subject, see 15 DIGEST (Repl.) 1053-1055, *10,372-10,393.*

For the Larceny Act, 1916, s. 1, see 5 HALSBURY's STATUTES (2nd Edn.) 1012.]

Cases referred to:

Coggs v. *Bernard*, (1703), 2 Ld. Raym. 909; 92 E.R. 107; 3 Digest (Repl.) 71, *106.*

R. v. *Miller, R.* v. *Page*, (1965), 49 Cr. App. Rep. 241.

R. v. *Turvey*, [1946] 2 All E.R. 60; 175 L.T. 308; 110 J.P. 270; 31 Cr. App. Rep. 154; 15 Digest (Repl.) 1056, *10,403.*

Thompson v. *Nixon*, [1965] 2 All E.R. 741; [1966] 1 Q.B. 103; [1965] 3 W.L.R. 501; 129 J.P. 414; 3rd Digest Supp.

Case Stated.

This was a Case Stated by justices for the city of Cardiff in respect of their adjudication as a magistrates' court sitting at the Law Courts, Cardiff, on Apr. 7 and 28, 1966.

On Apr. 7, 1966, a charge was preferred by the appellant, Gillian Martin, who was a police woman, against the respondent, Mary Puttick, charging that at Cardiff on Mar. 10, 1966, she feloniously stole two pork chops valued at 4s. 11d. the property of Crowleys Stores (Cardiff), Ltd. The following facts were found: Crowleys Stores (Cardiff), Ltd., were proprietors of a grocery and provision shop in Cardiff. In that shop customers took articles they required (except greengrocery and meat) from shelves and display stands and produced them to a cashier at a cash desk placed near the exit door of the shop. The cashier made up the bill for the goods produced and the customer paid for them there. A customer requiring meat selected it at the meat counter which was attended by a shop assistant. That shop assistant wrapped the meat selected by the customer and wrote the price of it on the wrapping paper. The meat was then handed to the customer who should have produced it and paid for it at the cash desk at the exit. The same procedure applied to purchases of greengrocery. Wire baskets were provided at the entrance to the shop for customers' use in carrying goods to the cash desk. On Mar. 10, 1966, the respondent entered the shop, took various goods from shelves and put them in the wire basket she had taken on entering the shop. The respondent was also carrying a shopping bag. The respondent eventually went to the meat counter and asked the shop assistant for two pork chops. When the respondent had selected them, the shop assistant wrapped the chops in paper, marked the price of them on the wrapping paper and handed the parcel to the respondent. The respondent walked towards the greengrocery counter at the other side of the shop. At that time the respondent held the parcel containing the chops in her hand. The chops were damp and the wrapping paper around them was not capable of retaining the moisture, and for that reason she did not place the parcel in the wire basket with the other goods. The shop assistant, having seen the respondent place the parcel in her shopping bag, spoke to the shop manager who immediately went to the cash desk. Later the respondent went to the cash desk where she produced to the cashier the articles from the wire basket. She did not produce the meat from her shopping bag. The shop manager asked the respondent if he could have her shopping bag in order to put in it the articles she had paid for. The respondent handed her bag to the shop manager. The manager looked inside the bag and saw a package covered by some advertising paper. He knew that the package contained the chops and that the respondent had not produced them to the cashier. Thinking that he was not allowed to take the chops until the respondent had left the shop, the manager put the goods the respondent had paid for

A into the shopping bag and returned it to her. The respondent left the shop. She was followed by the shop manager who asked her if he could check the goods in her bag. She consented and the package containing the chops was in the bag. When the shop manager showed the respondent the chops, she replied " The cashier couldn't have taken for them ". The manager said " No, because they were not in the basket ". The respondent replied " I wouldn't do anything like that ".

B The appellant was called to the shop and, in the presence of the respondent, was told by the manager " One of my assistants saw [the respondent] put pork chops in her own shopping bag, and not in the firm's basket. As a result of what she told me I waited by the check-out for the goods to be counted and paid for. A number of items were counted but not the chops and I followed the woman out of the store ". The appellant asked the respondent what she wanted to say and

C cautioned her. She replied " I thought I put it on the counter but I must have put it in my bag and forgotten all about it. It wasn't done intentionally ". The respondent was arrested and taken to a police station where, after having been formally charged and cautioned, she replied " Well, there's nothing to say, is there? ". The respondent had £1 8s. 11½d. in her possession when she was arrested. The value of the pork chops was 4s. 11d.; they were the property of Crowleys

D Stores (Cardiff), Ltd.

It was contended on behalf of the appellant that, in the meat department, it was manifestly impossible for the customer to select, cut, wrap and price meat. An assistant was provided for this function by the shop proprietor to act as the customer's agent, and there was no question of the assistant being in that position on behalf of her employer. Also the placing of the chops in the appellant's hand

E bag was evidence of animus furandi. It was contended on behalf of the respondent that (a) there was no animus furandi at the time the chops were handed over to the respondent by the meat counter attendant; (b) the receipt of the goods was innocent and devoid of any tortious element. Thus, even if the respondent had subsequently decided to steal there could be no relating back of the animus furandi; and (c) permitting the respondent to leave the store with the chops, the manager

F had set a trap for the respondent and, if the court should perchance be against the respondent on all points of fact and law argued earlier, the proper conviction, if any, was of attempted larceny only.

The justices were of opinion that: (i) there was no taking of the meat to constitute larceny, because (a) although the respondent purposely did not produce the chops to the cashier, it was improbable that she intended to avoid payment

G when the shop assistant handed them to her: and (b) the transfer of the meat by the shop assistant to the respondent was not inconsistent with the transfer of the owner's property to the respondent; and (ii) assuming that the property in the meat had not been transferred to the respondent by the shop assistant, the shop manager, by handing the respondent the meat and allowing her to leave, knowing that she had not paid for it, consented to the passing of possession of the meat to

H the respondent. They accordingly, dismissed the charge, and the appellant now appealed.

The authority and cases noted below* were cited during the argument in addition to the cases referred to in the judgment of Winn, L.J.

N. C. Lloyd-Davies for the appellant.

D. G. Knight for the respondent.

I

WINN, L.J., delivered the first judgment at the invitation of LORD PARKER, C.J. The appellant is a police woman and the respondent a shopper, shopping at the material time at a grocery and provision shop in Cardiff belonging to Messrs. Crowleys Stores (Cardiff), Ltd. The method of business at this store

---

* Archbold's Criminal Pleading, Evidence and Practice (36th Edn.), paras. 1452, 1515; *R. v. Slowly and Humphrey*, (1873), 12 Cox, C.C. 269; *Pharmaceutical Society of Great Britain* v. *Boots Cash Chemists (Southern), Ltd.*, [1952] 2 All E.R. 456; [1952] 2 Q.B. 795.

appears from the Case Stated to be clearly that which nowadays is usually called
a supermarket store business. It is found that in this shop customers take articles
which they require, except greengrocery and meat, from shelves and display
stands and produce them to a cashier at a cash desk placed near the exit door of
the shop. The cashier then makes up the bill for the goods produced and the
customer pays for them there. Pausing there for a moment before coming to the
more special facts of this case, it seems to me that, when a customer does so
pick up goods from shelves or other display stands in a shop which conducts its
business as a supermarket store, the customer does not then become entitled to
any form of property in the goods, nor does the customer acquire any exclusive
possession of the goods. The basic understanding of persons trading in this way
and inviting purchases of their goods, and of the shoppers who go to such stores
must, it seems to me, be that in the interval between the moment of picking up
any such article and the point of time and of place (i.e., of position in terms of
space) when the customer is at the cash desk and is transacting with the cashier
the completion of the purchases by obtaining from the cashier the total price and
paying that price, the customer is holding the goods and carrying them by
permission of the proprietor of the store for the purposes of the transaction.
Whether it is strictly right to speak of the relationship of the customer to the goods
during that interval as one of bailment or of licence or of custody, may not be
very clear. Such a situation is one where plainly the proprietor of the store, by
implication, has given a limited permission to handle and carry goods which are
still his property. It may be that the result is bailment in the sense of the judg-
lent of SACHS, J., in *Thompson* v. *Nixon* (1), even though it is not within any of the
defined categories in the form of *Coggs* v. *Bernard* (2). It really is unnecessary to
pronounce on the academic point, whether or not there is a bailment. It is clearly,
in my view, a licence, possibly custody subject to an overriding course of control
and continuing right of termination remaining in the proprietor. At any rate no
property has passed and no right has been conceded or granted by the proprietor
to retain exclusive possession beyond the moment when the customer presents
himself or herself to the cashier; and it is subject to a condition subsequent that
any such possession shall terminate unless the amount which is found to be due is
paid by the customer to the cashier. As counsel for the respondent has said
in a submission to which I should like myself to pay tribute as helpful, lucid
and very carefully thought out, the customer does in a physical sense take
the article by picking it up and putting it into a basket or shopping bag: that
is not such a taking as is contemplated by or relevant to the purposes of the
Larceny Act, 1916, in the definition of theft.

In this particular case there was a special feature not to be found in the more
general situations to which I have already adverted, which, however, does not
alter the analysis of the general legal position that I have given, inasmuch
as the article in relation to which the respondent was charged with theft was
one of meat. It was a couple of chops worth rather less than five shillings.
That meat was obtained by her at the meat counter and, because of the general
characteristics of such meat articles, there was an assistant there to wrap up
the meat and it may well be to weigh it, though that, I think, is not expressly
found. The assistant did wrap up these two chops and hand them to the respondent. The respondent held them for a while in her hand but, noticing
that they tended to drip with moisture, there may even have been blood, she
thought it unsuitable to put them into the wire basket with which she had
been provided for the carriage of the rest of the articles which she was acquiring
that day in that store, so she put them into a shopping bag of her own which
she had taken to the store. The respondent went over to the cashier's desk
and placed the wire basket on the desk. In the ordinary way, the cashier

(1) [1965] 2 All E.R. 741; [1966] 1 Q.B. 103.   (2) (1703), 2 Ld. Raym. 909.

A checked over all the articles in that basket totalling up the price of them, told
the respondent what it was and the respondent duly paid that price. She did not
produce to the cashier the chops which were still in her shopping bag.

The magistrates have found in their opinion, which is perhaps not the most
convenient place in which to state it, that she purposely did not produce the chops
to the cashier. There can be no doubt, as counsel for the respondent conceded,
B that the magistrates did find in so stating their " opinion " that, when dealing
with the cashier and by the time, at the latest, when the transaction was completed, the respondent had formed the criminal intention of avoiding payment for
those chops. The magistrates found, and this can be put aside quite quickly, that,
on the balance of probabilities, the respondent did not intend to avoid payment
at the moment when the shop assistant at the meat counter handed the chops to
C her. They further expressed the opinion that it was not unreasonable to take the
view that the shop assistant who was handling the meat at the meat counter had
transferred the owner's property in the chops to the respondent. That is, in my
view, quite an untenable proposition. The limit of the authority of the meat
counter assistant is clearly merely to hand over and wrap up the meat and not to
deal in any way with any transfer of property from the owner of the shop to the
D customer. So one has the respondent at the cashier's desk with a criminal mind
and with the two chops still in her bag. At that stage, of course, she has carried
them no further than the point to which she was, in my view, permitted by licence
of the proprietor of the shop to carry them.

The manager of this shop happened by chance to be standing by and, as a
courteous man and no doubt in the course of his duty to make the customers feel
E that they were at home and receiving good service in the shop, he invited the
respondent to allow him to help her pack the goods into her shopping bag, since
of course the wire basket would have remained behind in the store. She handed
him her shopping bag, he looked into it and in it he saw these two chops wrapped
up and apparently he was able to recognise they had been wrapped up in the store
and that they had been acquired in the store, but, as he then well knew, not paid
F for in the transaction between the respondent and the cashier. The manager, it
seems, did not remove the chops from the bag. It seems also that the respondent
at no time took them out of the bag and put them on to the counter. The manager,
so far as the Case Stated finds, did not move the chops; he did not put them into
the bag since, as I have said, they were never out of the bag. What he did was to
leave them where they were, putting the other purchases into the bag and handing
G the bag politely to the respondent, thinking, as the Case informs the court, that
he was bound to let the respondent leave the store before he could safely charge
her, or indeed safely detain her with a view to charging her with any offence as
regards these chops; so he let her go out of the store, carrying the shopping bag
including the chops, and very shortly afterwards outside the exit of the store he
went up to her, spoke to her, asked her to come to his office and the usual inter-
H view followed. The respondent consistently protested that she had no intention
of dishonestly taking the chops.

The point which ultimately presents itself is so fine and academic that I myself
venture to hope that it will never present itself again in identical form, and it is
this: whether there was any asportation of these chops by the respondent such
as is required as an essential element in an offence of larceny, in carrying away
I of the chops. There can be no doubt in one sense that the respondent did carry
the chops away from the cashier's desk to the door of the store and a few yards
down the street but, though that may be so, it cannot stand by itself as a sufficient
asportation if that carrying was not committed against the will of the owner of
the chops, invito domino. If the true view of what happened is, or may reasonably be held to be, that the manager on behalf of the owners of the chops, and
with their authority, consented to the respondent carrying the chops out of the
shop, then there would be no sufficient asportation. That in itself depends on

whether as a matter of law, resting on the decision in *R*. v. *Turvey* (3), it was *f*
necessary to hold that there was here a handing of the property to the respondent.
In *R*. v. *Turvey* (3), where a servant acting on his master's instructions had handed
certain property of the master's over to the appellant, it was held that the appellant could not be convicted of larceny because there was no sufficient asportation
against the will of the master. The court, however, said that an instruction by the
master to the servant merely to facilitate the commission of the crime by the   *F*
appellant would not have prevented the property being taken invito domino.
That doctrine has been more recently applied in *R*. v. *Miller*, *R*. v. *Page* (4).
There, a lorry driver, who had reported to his master that thieves had approached
him and asked him to arrange that they should be able to steal a lorry load of
bales of woollen rag, was told by the master to take the lorry to an appointed
place.   He did so and, at that place, helped the appellants to unload it.   There   *C*
again it was held that there had been no taking against the will of the master.

   In the light of those two decisions, the question here is, as a matter of law and
principle: did the manager here consent to the taking away of the goods?   At
the moment when he became aware that the respondent had these goods and had
taken them, though not taken them away, with intent to avoid payment for them,
the chops were not in the physical possession or the control of the manager. He   *D*
could only have taken them into his hands by obtaining permission from the
respondent to do so, or by snatching the bag from her. They were then in her
physical possession though she had not yet taken them away. He did not thereafter, as owner of the goods, hand them to the respondent or give her any permission to take them away, except for the limited purpose that he had in his own
mind of being able to charge her. What is significant is not so much the restriction   *E*
on his own intent as the fact that they were never then in his power nor were
they released from his power into her possession. That seems to me to distinguish
this case from those cases to which I have referred. I would accept at once any
criticism to the effect that that distinction is a very fine distinction indeed. It
may, perhaps, be that some day *R*. v. *Turvey* (3) will need, itself, to be considered
but, whilst it stands, the duty of the court is to see whether or not any given   *F*
fact brings the case which is being considered within the principle enunciated in
R. v. *Turvey* (3). In my opinion, although the distinction is a very fine one, the
facts of the present case do not fall within *R*. v. *Turvey* (3), and there was nothing
here which prevented the actual carrying away of these chops from being an
asportation against the will of the owner with criminal intention to deprive
the owner, without any claim of right, permanently, at the time when that   *G*
carrying away took place.

   I would allow this appeal.

   WILLIS, J.: I agree.

   LORD PARKER, C.J.: I also agree.

                                            Appeal allowed. Case remitted.   **H**

   Solicitors: *Theodore Goddard & Co.*, agents for *D. A. Roberts Thomas*, Cardiff
(for the appellant); *Myer Cohen & Co.*, Cardiff (for the respondent).

                            [*Reported by* N. P. METCALFE, ESQ., *Barrister-at-Law.*]

                                                                                    I

---

(3) [1946] 2 All E.R. 60.
(4) (1965), 49 Cr. App. Rep. 241.

SINCLAIR (FORMERLY STEINBOCK) *v.* SINCLAIR (FORMERLY STEINBOCK).

Reversed. C.A. [1967] 3 All E.R. 882.

[PROBATE, DIVORCE AND ADMIRALTY DIVISION (Ormrod, J.), January 11, 12, 13, 27, 1967.]

Divorce—Judicial separation—Jurisdiction—Residence—Husband returning to United States, leaving wife and children in England—Husband pressing for reconciliation and for wife and children to go to United States—Ultimatum by husband to wife to go or he would not support her—Refusal by wife—After petition filed by wife, husband terminated his lease of house where wife and children living—Whether husband had sufficient residence in England at date when petition filed to confer jurisdiction on court.

In 1945, the parties married in England where they lived until 1947; the husband was born in Poland of Polish parents and the wife was English. In 1947 the husband emigrated to Canada, the wife following him shortly afterwards. In 1954 they moved to the United States where they lived until June, 1964, when the wife and the two children of the family came to England, in the first place on holiday. From September, 1964, onwards, the husband took a series of furnished houses in England on short tenancies. He sold the house in the United States. From then he had no other place which could be called a home or residence anywhere in the world. In the autumn of 1965 a contract on which the husband was working, which involved travel to Iran, came abruptly to an end and he returned to the United States in search of other contracts or employment. He still visited England and his family. After an incident in March, 1966, in England, which formed the basis of a charge of adultery, he returned to the United States. The parties did not thereafter live in the same house as husband and wife, and the husband remained continuously in the United States apart from a short visit to England in September, 1966. After his return to the United States, he repeatedly pressed the wife for a reconciliation and did everything he could to persuade the wife to come back to the United States with the children, but the wife's replies were non-committal. In May, 1966, she issued an originating summons in the Chancery Division making the children wards of court, and in June, 1966, her solicitors wrote to the husband saying that they had instructions to file a petition for judicial separation and that the wife had no intention of going to the United States on a visit. In July, 1966, the husband wrote sending air tickets to the United States and saying that, if the wife did not return to the United States, he would no longer support her and would take all the consequential steps, such as cancelling the lease on the furnished house where she was living. This he did from the end of September, 1966, the wife having refused to go to the United States. On Aug. 1, 1966, she filed a petition for divorce or alternatively for judicial separation, one of the allegations being constructive desertion from Mar. 24, 1966. It was common ground that the wife could not establish three years' residence for the purpose of founding jurisdiction in divorce until June, 1967, and that her alternative prayer for judicial separation rested solely on proof that the husband was resident in England on Aug. 1, 1966.

Held: (i) the date or stage of the proceedings at which residence within the territorial jurisdiction of the court must be proved for the purposes of a suit for judicial separation was the date on which the petition was filed (see p. 908, letter F, post).

Ward v. *Ward* ((1923), 39 T.L.R. 440) explained and distinguished.
Milligan v. *Milligan* ([1941] 2 All E.R. 62) not followed.
Graham v. *Graham* ([1922] All E.R. Rep. 149) applied.

(ii) the husband had not retained a sufficient degree of residence in England

at the date when the petition was filed to enable the court to have jurisdic- *f*
tion, because the family as a unit had ceased to exist, either on the wife's
case from the end of March, 1966, or on the rest of the evidence from at the
latest the rejection by her of the proposals in the husband's letter of July,
1966, and the continuing tenancy of the house in England at the relevant
date (Aug. 1, 1966) was not sufficient to constitute residence by him (see
p. 912, letters F and H, post); accordingly the petition would be dismissed. *F*
    Raeburn v. *Raeburn* ((1928), 138 L.T. 672) distinguished.

[As to jurisdiction of the English courts to hear petitions for judicial separation,
see 7 HALSBURY'S LAWS (3rd Edn.) 105, 106, para. 188; and for cases on the
subject, see 11 DIGEST (Repl.) 475, 476, *1051-1060*.]

Cases referred to: *C*
    Armytage v. *Armytage*, [1895-99] All E.R. Rep. 377; [1898] P. 178; 67 L.J.P.
        90; 78 L.T. 689; 27 Digest (Repl.) 268, *2151*.
    Collett v. *Collett*, (1843), 3 Cur. 726; 163 E.R. 881; 27 Digest (Repl.) 468, *4031*.
    Eustace v. *Eustace*, [1923] All E.R. Rep. 281; [1924] P. 45; 93 L.J.P. 28;
        130 L.T. 79; 11 Digest (Repl.) 476, *1056*.
    Firebrace v. *Firebrace*, (1878), 4 P.D. 63; 47 L.J.P.C. 41; 39 L.T. 94; 11 *D*
        Digest (Repl.) 342, *127*.
    Graham v. *Graham*, [1922] All E.R. Rep. 149; [1923] P. 31; 92 L.J.P. 26;
        128 L.T. 639; 11 Digest (Repl.) 475, *1054*.
    Matalon v. *Matalon*, [1952] 1 All E.R. 1025; [1952] P. 233; 11 Digest (Repl.)
        476, *1058*.
    Milligan v. *Milligan*, [1941] 2 All E.R. 62; [1941] P. 78; 110 L.J.P. 49; *E*
        166 L.T. 46; 11 Digest (Repl.) 477, *1064*.
    Niboyet v. *Niboyet*, (1878), 4 P.D. 1; 48 L.J.P. 1; 39 L.T. 486; 43 J.P. 140;
        11 Digest (Repl.) 469, *1021*.
    Raeburn v. *Raeburn*, (1928), 138 L.T. 672; 11 Digest (Repl.) 476, *1055*.
    Ross-Smith v. *Ross-Smith* (*otherwise Radford*), [1962] 1 All E.R. 344; [1963]
        A.C. 280; [1962] 2 W.L.R. 388; Digest (Cont. Vol. A) 243, *1067b*. *F*
    Simonin v. *Mallac*, [1843-60] All E.R. Rep. 68; (1860), 2 Sw. & Tr. 67; 29
        L.J.P.M. & A. 97; 2 L.T. 327; 164 E.R. 917; 11 Digest (Repl.) 478, *1065*.
    Ward v. *Ward*, (1923), 39 T.L.R. 440; 11 Digest (Repl.) 342, *123*.

Petition.
This was a petition by the wife for divorce or alternatively for judicial separa- *G*
tion. An issue was ordered to be tried on the question of whether the husband
was domiciled or resident in England at the date of the alleged desertion and/or
of the date of the filing of the petition.
    The husband was born in Poland of Polish parents. When he was nineteen
years of age he came to England as a student. That was in 1939 and he remained
in England until 1947, becoming a naturalised British subject. On Nov. 27, *H*
1945, he married the wife, who was an English woman, in England. In 1947
he went to Canada on an immigrant visa, and the wife followed him shortly
afterwards. They lived in Canada until 1952, and then for two years in South
America. In December, 1954, they moved to the United States where they
established their home in the State of New Jersey. Both children of the marriage
were born there. For most of the period between 1954 and August, 1966, the *I*
husband was working on his own account, using his home as his business address
until 1964. His work involved him in a great deal of travel mostly in the western
hemisphere. In June, 1964, the husband having obtained a long-term contract
which would involve frequent visits to Iran, the wife and the children came to
England. In September, 1964, the husband took accommodation in England;
and the house in New Jersey was sold. In October or November, 1965, the
Iranian contract came abruptly to an end. The husband returned to the United
States to try to find other employment. Thereafter he was frequently in England,

but only for short visits, until the end of March, 1966. The facts regarding the issue of residence are set out in the judgment at p. 911, letters D to G, post.

H. S. Law for the husband.

S. Goldblatt for the wife.

Cur. adv. vult.

Jan. 27.   **ORMROD, J.,** read the following judgment: This is essentially an issue as to the jurisdiction of this court to entertain a petition by Mrs. Nancy Sinclair, whom I will call " the wife ", for divorce from her husband, Samuel Robert Sinclair, whom I will call " the husband ", on the various grounds set out in her petition which was filed on Aug. 1, 1966, or alternatively for judicial separation. As formulated, the issue states that the wife avers that the husband was domiciled or resident in England at the date of the alleged desertion (that is Mar. 19, 1966) and/or of the date of the filing of the petition.

It is common ground that the only basis of jurisdiction to entertain the wife's suit for a decree of dissolution of marriage is the domicil of the parties, because the wife was not in a position to avail herself of the provisions of the Matrimonial Causes Act 1965, s. 40 (1) (*b*), at the date when the petition was filed. She will not be able to establish the necessary three years' residence in England until June, 1967. Consequently, if she fails on the issue of domicil, her present suit for a decree of dissolution cannot proceed. It is now, I think, common ground that the jurisdiction of this court to entertain the wife's alternative prayer for judicial separation rests solely on proof by her that the husband was resident in England on Aug. 1, 1966. At one stage, counsel for the wife indicated that he would rely in the alternative on the fact that the husband was resident in England when cohabitation between the parties ceased. This submission was based on a statement in DICEY'S CONFLICT OF LAWS (7th Edn.), p. 335, where it appears as the second limb of DICEY'S r. 46 (3) as to jurisdiction. In the end counsel, I think, conceded that this statement cannot be supported by the authorities. I shall nonetheless have to deal with it in due course.

[HIS LORDSHIP, having reviewed the facts relevant to the question of the husband's domicil, having referred to the evidence, and having intimated that as a consequence of the wife's answers to questions put to her in evidence, the attempt to prove that the husband had an English domicil was abandoned. HIS LORDSHIP said that he had thought it right to set out briefly matters relevant to that issue, but that how, on the facts, it could possibly be supposed that the husband had acquired a domicil of choice in England in or after 1964, or how he could be said to have retained a domicil in England after November, 1965, it was difficult to see. HIS LORDSHIP concluded:] In my judgment, the husband was clearly domiciled in the United States at all material times and, consequently, the wife's petition for dissolution is incompetent.

The second part of the issue, namely, whether at the material time the husband was resident in England to an extent sufficient to give this court jurisdiction to entertain the alternative prayer for judicial separation is much more difficult. In my judgment, it is now clearly established by authority that jurisdiction in proceedings for judicial separation depends exclusively on either residence of the respondent in England (*Armytage* v. *Armytage* (1)) or domicil in this country (*Eustace* v. *Eustace* (2)).

The jurisdiction of the High Court in matrimonial causes other than suits for dissolution was exhaustively examined and considered by the House of Lords in *Ross-Smith* v. *Ross-Smith* (*otherwise Radford*) (3). That was in fact a nullity suit, but the basis of the ecclesiastical court's jurisdiction in matrimonial matters before the Matrimonial Causes Act, 1857, was fully investigated. The conclusion

---

(1) [1895-99] All E.R. Rep. 377; [1898] P. 178.
(2) [1923] All E.R. Rep. 281; [1924] P. 45.
(3) [1962] 1 All E.R. 344; [1963] A.C. 280.

is to be found in LORD REID's speech (4), and is to the effect that this jurisdiction *A* was founded on the residence of the respondent within the diocese of the court, subject only to his right to waive objection to jurisdiction. This principle of the canon law is the old principle of the civil law, namely, actor sequitur forum rei, reinforced by the Statute of Citations of Henry VIII. This jurisdiction was transferred to the High Court by the Matrimonial Causes Act, 1857, s. 2, and by s. 22 of that Act the High Court was required to act on principles and rules as nearly as *B* may be conformable to the principles and rules of the ecclesiastical courts. Pursuant to this requirement, the basis of jurisdiction of the High Court in matrimonial causes other than suits for dissolution has been adapted by the decisions to which I have referred from residence of the respondent in the diocese of the court from which the citation issued, to residence in England and later to domicil in England. In the case of a suit by a wife, this jurisdiction has been enlarged by *C* statute to enable the wife to rely on the domicil at the date of desertion or deportation and, in the case of suits for nullity only, on her own residence in England for three years, immediately preceding the institution of the suit (Matrimonial Causes Act 1965 s. 40).

In these circumstances, it is unnecessary for me to re-examine the ecclesiastical cases which were so fully considered by the House of Lords in *Ross-Smith* v. *D* *Ross-Smith* (5) except to observe in passing that, in a number of the old cases often referred to in this connexion, the proceedings were ex parte and, consequently, the court was without the advantage of hearing argument on both sides. The unfortunate results which may ensue from placing too much reliance on such cases is vividly illustrated by the fate which befell *Simonin* v. *Mallac* (6) in that case. *E*

It remains to consider two important points of law, the date or stage of the proceedings at which residence within the territorial jurisdiction of this court must be proved and the extent and quality of the residence on which jurisdiction to entertain the proceedings is founded. The crucial date and stage of the suit for this purpose is, in my judgment, the inception of the suit, which means, in our current practice, the date on which the petition is filed. This must follow *F* if the principles of the ecclesiastical courts are the foundation on which this jurisdiction depends.   The Statute of Citations prohibited the citation of a person who was not inhabiting or dwelling within the diocese. DR. LUSHINGTON in *Collett* v. *Collett* (7) specifically based jurisdiction on this statute. GORELL BARNES, J., in *Armytage* v. *Armytage* (8), which is the locus classicus on this topic, said: *G*

> " In my opinion, if the parties had a matrimonial home, but were not
> domiciled within the jurisdiction of an ecclesiastical court, that court would
> have interfered, if the parties were within the jurisdiction at the commence-
> ment of the suit, to protect the injured party against the other party in
> respect of the adultery or cruelty of the latter, and I can find no authority
> for the suggestion made by the husband's counsel that such interference *H*
> could be limited to cases where the offence complained of was committed
> within the jurisdiction."

Graham v. *Graham* (9) and *Raeburn* v. *Raeburn* (10) are to the same effect. Indeed, but for the passage in DICEY'S CONFLICT OF LAWS, p. 335, which I mentioned earlier, I would have thought that the contrary was unarguable. The learned *I* editor of that invaluable book, however, suggests that the court has jurisdiction to entertain a suit for judicial separation or restitution of conjugal rights when the parties had a matrimonial home in England when the events

---

(4) [1962] 1 All E.R. at p. 350; [1963] A.C. at p. 297.
(5) [1962] 1 All E.R. 344; [1963] A.C. 280.
(6) [1843-60] All E.R. Rep. 68; (1860), 2 Sw. & Tro. 67.
(7) (1843), 3 Cur. 726.
(8) [1895-99] All E.R. Rep. at p. 384; [1898] P. at p. 194.
(9) [1922] All E.R. Rep. 149; [1923] P. 31.　　　　　　(10) (1928), 138 L.T. 672.

A occurred on which the claim for separation was based, or when their cohabitation ceased. This proposition appears to be directly contrary to the decision
of SIR JAMES HANNEN, P., in *Firebrace* v. *Firebrace* (11), and I have not
been able to find any suggestion of such a basis for jurisdiction in the earlier
cases. Two cases are cited in support of the proposition, *Ward* v. *Ward* (12)
and *Milligan* v. *Milligan* (13), but neither of them appears to me in fact to support

B it. *Ward* v. *Ward* (12) was an ex parte decision made after the minimum of
discussion or argument and is based on the proposition that the respondent,
who was temporarily in India on Army service, could properly be regarded as
retaining a sufficient residence in England. The decision was actually made when
Eustace v. *Eustace* (14) was under appeal, and the question whether domicil
could be relied on to found jurisdiction was sub judice. Since *Eustace* v. *Eustace*

C (14) jurisdiction on the facts in *Ward* v. *Ward* (12) would be taken on the basis
of domicil.

   Milligan v. *Milligan* (13) is not an easy decision to interpret. It was a restitution suit in which the husband respondent challenged the jurisdiction on the
grounds (i) that he was domiciled in Scotland; (ii) that the parties were not
both resident within the jurisdiction; (iii) that the parties did not have a matri-

D monial home in England when cohabitation ceased. It was conceded that the
husband was neither domiciled nor resident in England at the institution of the
suit, and the court ordered that an issue be tried to determine the facts on the
third ground. The learned judge, HENN COLLINS, J., decided that the parties
in fact had had a matrimonial home within the jurisdiction when cohabitation
ceased. Throughout his judgment, however, he seems to accept that the crucial

E test of jurisdiction is the residence in England of the wrongdoer. This appears
from his comment (15) on a passage which he had cited (16) from the judgment
of JAMES, L.J., in *Niboyet* v. *Niboyet* (17), and from his remarks where he said (18):

   " Having regard to the principles upon which the ecclesiastical courts
   acted, would they have refused jurisdiction merely because the wrongdoing

F husband, having for some good reason left a joint home within the jurisdiction, had elected to live alone elsewhere within the jurisdiction, and had
   failed there to provide a home for his wife? Let me take an extreme case.
   Suppose a married couple, of foriegn domicil but living in England, left their
   home in one town to go to a new one a few miles away, and that, on the way,
   the husband deserted his wife. Has she no remedy in England? Is she

G relegated to the tribunals of her husband's domicil? I answer that she is not,
   if only for the reason that the husband cannot be allowed to take advantage
   of his own wrong."

   Finally HENN COLLINS, J., stated his conclusion in these words (19):

   " In my judgment, therefore, the phrase ' matrimonial home ' extends, in
   relation to jurisdiction, to the husband's residence in England in such

H circumstances that any husband similarly circumstanced and not estranged
   from his wife would set up his home in England. Judged by that rule,
   the parties had a matrimonial home in or convenient to Blackdown when
   cohabitation ceased, and I answer the question propounded accordingly."

   I have some difficulty in understanding precisely the effect of that passage.

I It is, perhaps, enough to say that, if the facts are correctly stated in the report
   and that the husband was not in fact resident somewhere in England at the

---

(11) (1878), 4 P.D. 63.   (12) (1923), 39 T.L.R. 440.
(13) [1941] 2 All E.R. 62; [1941] P. 78.
(14) [1923] All E.R. Rep. 281; [1924] P. 45.
(15) [1941] 2 All E.R. at p. 65; [1941] P. at p. 82.
(16) [1941] 2 All E.R. at p. 65; [1941] P. at p. 81.
(17) (1878), 4 P.D. 1 at p. 6.
(18) [1941] 2 All E.R. at p. 66; [1941] P. at pp. 83, 84.
(19) [1941] 2 All E.R. at pp. 66, 67; [1941] P. at p. 84.

date of the institution of the proceedings, the decision cannot be reconciled
with *Firebrace* v. *Firebrace* (20) which was not apparently cited. Indeed, no
argument seems to have been directed to the relevance of the facts which were
in dispute to the issue of jurisdiction. In these circumstances, if the learned
judge was in fact deciding that the existence of a matrimonial home within the
jurisdiction at the date when cohabitation ceased is sufficient to found jurisdiction
in a suit for restitution or judicial separation, I must respectfully decline to
follow him. It remains only to observe that the fact that service was effected
on the respondent in England is irrelevant to the issue of jurisdiction in a matrimonial cause.

The question of fact which I have to decide, therefore, is whether the husband
was resident in England on Aug. 1, 1966, when the wife's petition was filed.
This brings me to the second point of law, namely, the extent and quality of
residence which must be proved. Two classes of case may be distinguished,
those in which the respondent was actually in England when the proceedings
were instituted and those in which he was out of the jurisdiction at the critical
time but is said to have retained a sufficient degree of residence to give jurisdiction to this court. The first class is represented by *Armytage* v. *Armytage* (21)
and *Matalon* v. *Matalon* (22). These cases show that something more than
mere casual presence on a visit or in itinere is necessary. How much more is
not easy to determine. In both these cases the husband had come to England
primarily in order to obtain custody of his children. Both had started proceedings
in England in relation to the children. Mr. Matalon had been in England for
about two months when the proceedings began, Mr. Armytage for perhaps
rather longer (the date of the petition is not stated in the report). In both
cases it was held that there was sufficient residence to found jurisdiction. In
both cases some emphasis was placed on the fact that the husband had already
subjected himself to the jurisdiction of the courts of this country in relation to
the children, but this is not the basis of either decision. The ratio of both cases
is probably to be found in the words of GORELL BARNES, J., in *Armytage* v.
Armytage (23), where he said:

"... no valid reason can be urged against the courts of a country in
which a husband and wife are actually living pronouncing a decree which
will protect the one against the other as long as they remain within the
jurisdiction."

This passage was sited with approval by HODSON, L.J., in *Matalon* v. *Matalon* (24).

The present case, however, belongs to the second class, because it is common
ground that the husband was in the United States on Aug. 1, 1966, when the
petition was filed and had not been in England at all since the end of March,
1966. The only case cited to me which bears on this situation is *Raeburn* v.
Raeburn (25), a decision of LORD MERRIVALE, P. In that case, on facts which
resemble those in the present case, LORD MERRIVALE, P., held that sufficient residence
was established to found jurisdiction. It is, therefore, necessary to examine the
facts of that case carefully. The husband was a business man, presumably
domiciled in Scotland, who had been a member of Parliament. His principal
home was in Scotland at a house called Wood End. Some years before the
proceedings began he bought a house at Woking called Overdale primarily as a
place to stay at when in London on Parliamentary duties. The marriage had
not been happy for some years and, after he ceased to be a member of Parliament, the pattern of living developed in such a way that he came to live almost
exclusively at the house in Scotland and the wife exclusively at the house
in Woking. In 1923 he put the house in the market for sale but did not

---

(20) (1878), 4 P.D. 63.   (21) [1895-99] All E.R. Rep. 377; [1898] P. 178.
(22) [1952] 1 All E.R. 1025; [1952] P. 233.
(23) [1895-99] All E.R. Rep. at p. 386; [1898] P. at p. 196.
(24) [1952] 1 All E.R. at p. 1029; [1952] P. at p. 239.
(25) (1928), 138 L.T. 672.

A proceed with the sale in the hope of effecting a reconciliation with his wife. He had only slept in the house on three occasions in the two years preceding the filing of the petition. In July, 1926, a suspension of disputes for a year was agreed on in the hope of saving the marriage. In April, 1927, differences became acute, and the husband informed the wife's solicitors that he would be closing the Woking home at midsummer and asking the wife to join him in

B Scotland. In fact he did not close the house. Discussions continued and Lord Merrivale, P., held that at this stage " the petitioner as the respondent's wife remained mistress of the house at Overdale ". On Oct. 3, 1927, the wife's petition was issued for service. On Oct. 24, 1927, three weeks after the proceedings had commenced, the husband wrote to his wife saying that he was " still the owner of Overdale and head of the house ". On Nov. 18, 1927, he was at Overdale

C to discuss whether there was any way out of their difficulties. On those findings, Lord Merrivale, P., held that the husband was sufficiently resident in England on Oct. 3 to found jurisdiction in this court. In the course of his judgment, Lord Merrivale, P., considered the alternative suggestion that residence could be derived from the fact that the husband was the tenant of a flat in London, where his daughter lived and where he stayed from time to time, but rejected

D this as a sufficient residence for the purposes of that case.

    The facts of the present case are strikingly similar in many respects. From September, 1964, onwards the husband had taken a series of furnished houses on short tenancies where his wife and sons had lived and in which he had stayed when he was in London. He had spent more time with his wife in London at this stage than had the husband in *Raeburn* v. *Raeburn* (26), and he had no

E other place which could be called a home or residence anywhere in the world. Some of his personal belongings were kept in the house in England, including a filing cabinet containing some of his business files. It is clear from the correspondence that, after November, 1965, he had not given up all hope of getting a contract which would enable the wife and children to continue to live in England and he to join them at intervals. Following *Raeburn* v. *Raeburn* (26), I would be

F prepared to hold on the facts of this case that, at any rate up to the end of March, 1966, the husband was resident in this country for present purposes. At the end of March, 1966, however, an incident occurred during a brief visit by the husband to his family in London which forms the basis of a charge of adultery against him with an au pair girl which appears in the petition. Very shortly afterwards the husband left England and returned to the United States. This was in fact the

G last time that they lived in the same house on the footing of husband and wife. The husband has remained in the United States continuously apart from a short visit to England in September, 1966, and is plainly for all purposes now resident in that country. In September, 1966, also, he started divorce proceedings in New Jersey which are still pending.

    Accordingly, if he is to be found to have been resident in England for the

H purposes of jurisdiction on Aug. 1, 1966, on these facts, it can only be on the basis that he was still residing at that date at 12, Dover Park Drive, S.W.15, where the wife and children were living. This pre-supposes that the family still existed as a unit consisting of husband and wife and children and as a family continued to live at 12, Dover Park Drive. If, on the other hand, the family had, in fact, ceased to exist as a unit and had become wife and children on the one

I hand and husband on the other, I find it impossible to derive even the most formal residence in England of the husband from the continued residence here of the wife and children. In my judgment, the basis of Lord Merrivale, P.'s, decision in *Raeburn* v. *Raeburn* (26) is that, however attenuated it may have been, the relation of the husband and wife in that case still subsisted at the date of the petition and the marital relationship had not completely broken down, so that it was justifiable to hold that there was sufficient residence by the husband in the house occupied by the wife.

---

(26) (1928), 138 L.T. 672.

What are the facts in the present case? It is plain from the correspondence
that, after the return of the husband to the United States in March or April,
1966, he was repeatedly pressing for a reconciliation and doing everything he
could to persuade his wife to come back with the children to the United States.
On the wife's side the replies were non-committal. On May 20, 1966, she issued
an originating summons in the Chancery Division making the children wards of
court. On June 15, 1966, her solicitors wrote saying that they had instructions
to file a petition for judicial separation and that the wife had no intention of
going to the United States on a visit. On July 21, 1966, the husband wrote what
is, in effect, an ultimatum, sending air tickets to the United States and saying
that, if she did not return to the United States, he would no longer support her
and would take all the consequential steps, such as cancelling the lease on 12,
Dover Park Drive. The wife refused to come to the United States. Whether
or not he actually gave notice to the landlords at this time was not proved,
but it is common ground that the lease was terminated by him as from the end
of September, 1966. In my judgment, it is not possible to suggest that, after the
wife's rejection of the husband's proposals in his letter of July 21, 1966, any kind
of cohabitation in any sense continued. From that date, if not from an earlier
stage, this family had ceased to exist as a unit. This view is fully confirmed
by the wife herself who, in her petition, alleges that she withdrew from cohabitation from her husband immediately after Mar. 24, 1966, from which date she
alleges constructive desertion. To make doubly sure, she has included in her
petition the very unusual averment that the husband " will not be permitted
by her to return to the said matrimonial home ", and again the assertion that
she " has made it plain to him that she is not prepared to allow him so to return "
(i.e., to the matrimonial home). I have not been referred to anything in the
correspondence which goes as far as those remarkably bold averments, but I
must assume that what the wife says in her petition she means. In my judgment,
by her own pleading she has confirmed that she has no case on the issue of
jurisdiction. In my view, this case is to be distinguished from *Raeburn* v.
Raeburn (27) by the fact that, in this case, the married life had ended before
the petition was filed and that the family as a unit had ceased to exist on the
wife's case from the end of March, 1966, and on the rest of the evidence from
at the latest the rejection by her of the proposals in the letter of July 21, 1966.

If, in these circumstances, I were to hold that there was jurisdiction to hear
this suit, I would in fact be basing jurisdiction on the wife's residence alone
which is clearly insufficient. The only alternative would be to regard the continuing tenancy in the husband's name of 12, Dover Park Drive as sufficient
to constitute residence by him. I prefer to follow LORD MERRIVALE, P., and reject
this as a sufficient degree of residence. I accordingly hold that the husband was
not resident in England at the date of the institution of these proceedings.

I have reached this conclusion with less regret in this case than I might have
felt in another. Proceedings are pending for divorce in the courts of New Jersey,
and it would be expensive and inconvenient to try the issues between these
parties twice over on opposite sides of the Atlantic, more particularly when any
relief given by this court would be replaced or cancelled by the court of the
domicil in the near future. Moreover, if the proceedings in New Jersey are
unduly protracted, it will be open to the wife in June, 1967, to rely on her three
years' residence and present a new petition for divorce.

Petition dismissed.

Solicitors: *M. A. Jacobs & Sons* (for the husband); *Lewis Cutner & Co.* (for
the wife).

[*Reported by* ALICE BLOOMFIELD, *Barrister-at-Law.*]

---

(27) (1928), 138 L.T. 672.

DAVIES JENKINS & CO., LTD. v. DAVIES (Inspector of Taxes).

[HOUSE OF LORDS (Viscount Dilhorne, Lord MacDermott, Lord Morris of Borth-y-Gest, Lord Guest and Lord Upjohn), January 30, 31, March 15, 1967.]

Income Tax—Deductions in computing profits—Subvention payments—Payments to meet deficits of associated company—Associated company no longer trading—Whether trading expenses of payor company—Finance Act, 1953 (1 & 2 Eliz. 2 c. 34), s. 20 (1), (9), (10).

The fact that when a recipient company receives a subvention payment it has ceased to trade does not exclude the associated company that made the subvention payment from being entitled under s. 20 (1)* of the Finance Act, 1953, to deduct it as a trading expense for the purposes of assessment to income tax (so held by the majority, LORD GUEST dissenting, see p. 917, letter D, p. 919, letter D, p. 921, letter A, p. 922, letter E, and p. 927, letter H, post).

Decision of the COURT OF APPEAL (sub nom. *Davies (Inspector of Taxes)* v. *Davies Jenkins & Co., Ltd.*, [1966] 2 All E.R. 930) reversed.

Per LORD MORRIS OF BORTH-Y-GEST: it is well settled that the beliefs and assumptions of those who frame Acts of Parliament cannot make the law; accordingly the fact that when Parliament enacted s. 18 of the Finance Act, 1954, it must have proceeded on the basis that it was not necessary that the recipient company should have been trading at the time of receipt of the subvention payment did not relieve the court from giving untrammelled consideration to the interpretation of s. 20 of the Finance Act, 1953, and did not furnish material for guidance of the court in interpreting s. 20 (see p. 922, letter D, post; cf. p. 915, letter H, and p. 927, letter I, to p. 928, letter A, post).

[**Editorial Note.** In regard to the relevance of s. 18 of the Finance Act, 1954, to the construction of s. 20 of the Act of 1953, and to the question of deriving guidance on the interpretation of an Act by referring to a subsequent statute, see also *Camille and Henry Dreyfus Foundation, Inc.* v. *Inland Revenue Comrs.* ([1954] 2 All E.R. 466).

As to income tax treatment of subvention payments between associated companies in respect of deficits, for income tax purposes, see 20 HALSBURY'S LAWS (3rd Edn.) 154, 155, para. 270.

For the Finance Act, 1953, s. 20, see 33 HALSBURY'S STATUTES (2nd Edn.) 121.]

Cases referred to:

Bullock (Inspector of Taxes) v. *Unit Construction Co., Ltd.*, [1958] 3 All E.R. 186; 38 Tax Cas. 712; 28 Digest (Repl.) 258, *1138.*

Kirkness (Inspector of Taxes) v. *John Hudson & Co., Ltd.*, [1955] 2 All E.R. 345; [1955] A.C. 696; [1955] 2 W.L.R. 1135; 36 Tax Cas. 28; 28 Digest (Repl.) 310, *1356.*

Appeal.

This was an appeal by the taxpayer company, Davies Jenkins & Co., Ltd., from an order of the Court of Appeal (DIPLOCK and WINN, L.JJ., HARMAN, L.J., dissenting), dated May 6, 1966, and reported [1966] 2 All E.R. 930, affirming an order of the Chancery Division (STAMP, J.), dated Dec. 21, 1965, and reported [1966] 1 All E.R. 716, allowing an appeal by the Crown by way of Case Stated from a determination of the Income Tax Commissioners in respect of assessments to income tax made on the taxpayer company for the years of assessment 1959-60 and 1960-61 in the amounts of £5,000 and £20,000 respectively. The question in issue was whether the taxpayer company in computing, the amount of its profits for the purpose of those assessments, was entitled under s. 20 of the Finance Act, 1953, to make deductions in respect of subvention payments made

---

* Section 20 (1), (9) and (10) are printed at p. 924, letter G, to p. 925, letter C, post.

by it to Wood Brothers (Glossop), Ltd., of which company the taxpayer company
was a subsidiary.

Heyworth Talbot, Q.C., R. E. Borneman, Q.C., and *P. W. I. Rees* for the taxpayer
company.

Sir George Honeyman, Q.C., J. R. Phillips and *J. P. Warner* for the Crown.

Their lordships took time for consideration.

Mar. 15.   The following opinions were delivered.

VISCOUNT DILHORNE: My Lords, in this case the Crown contend that
the taxpayer company is not entitled by virtue of s. 20 of the Finance Act, 1953,
as amended by s. 23 of the Finance Act, 1958, when computing profits or losses
for the purposes of income tax, to deduct two payments that it had made to
Wood Brothers (Glossop), Ltd. as if they were trading expenses.   The Crown
contend that the taxpayer company cannot do so, as at the time when the
payments were made Wood Brothers (Glossop), Ltd. had ceased to carry on a
trade.   They maintain that s. 20 of the Act of 1953 applies only to companies
which at all relevant times and at the time of receipt of the payment come
within sub-s. (9) of that section, that is to say, companies resident in the United
Kingdom and carrying on a trade wholly or partly in the United Kingdom.   Such
a company can conveniently be referred to as a " trading company ".   Section
20 (9) further provides that a company " whose business consists mainly in
the making of investments and the principal part of whose income is derived
therefrom " is for the purposes of s. 20 to be treated as a trading company.
When considering s. 20, therefore, all references to a trading company must be
taken to include what may conveniently be called an " investment company ".

It is further provided by s. 20 (10) that to avail themselves of the rights given
by the section, both the paying company and the receiving company must at
all material times, including in particular the time at which the payment is
made, have either been subsidiaries within the meaning of s. 42 of the Finance
Act, 1938, of a third company or one the subsidiary of the other.

The taxpayer company was at all material times, including the time of the
making of the payments in question, a subsidiary of Wood Brothers (Glossop),
Ltd.

Section 20 (2) provides that such a payment is to be treated as a subvention
payment within the meaning of the section only if it is made

" . . . under an agreement providing for the paying company to bear or
share in losses or a particular loss of the payee company, and is not a payment
which (apart from this section) would be taken into account in computing
profits or gains or losses of either company or on which (apart from this section
and from any relief from tax) the payee company would be liable to bear
tax by deduction or otherwise . . . ."

The payments made by the taxpayer company were made pursuant to such an
agreement and were not payments which apart from the section would be taken
into account in computing profits or losses or on which the payee company
would be liable to bear tax by deduction or otherwise.   Section 20 (1) reads as
follows:

" Subject to the provisions of this section, where a company has a deficit
for tax purposes during any accounting period of the company, and receives
a subvention payment in respect of that period from an associated company
having a surplus for tax purposes in the corresponding period, then in
computing for the purposes of income tax the profits or gains or losses of
those companies the payment shall be treated as a trading receipt receivable
by the one company on the last day of the accounting period during which
it has the deficit, and shall be allowed as a deduction to the other company
as if it were a trading expense incurred on that day."

The provisions to which I have referred were not altered by the Finance Act,
1958.

A   Wood Brothers (Glossop), Ltd. had deficits for tax purposes in two of its accounting periods and the taxpayer company had surpluses for tax purposes in its corresponding periods.   They were both trading companies within the meaning of sub-s. (10), but Wood Brothers (Glossop), Ltd. ceased to trade towards the end of its second accounting period and had ceased to trade when it received the payments from the taxpayer company.   From the beginning of the

B   relevant accounting periods, and at the time of the making of the payments, one was the subsidiary of the other.

The taxpayer company contends that the payments which it made are to be treated as trading receipts received by Wood Brothers (Glossop), Ltd. on the last day of each of the respective accounting periods and are to be allowed as a deduction to the taxpayer company as if they were trading expenses incurred on

C   those days.

It is only after the end of an accounting period that it can be ascertained that one company has a deficit for tax purposes and another a surplus in the corresponding period.   Then, if a payment is made pursuant to an agreement which comes within sub-s. (2) and one company is the subsidiary of the other or both are subsidiaries of a third company, the payment can be treated as a trading

D   receipt of one company and a trading expense of the other.   The proviso to s. 20 (2) of the Act of 1953 provided that the payment had to be made within or before the year of assessment following that in which the period ends.   This was extended by the Finance Act, 1958, to require it to be made in or before the second year of assessment (1) following that in which the period ends.   Thus it is possible for a payment made a considerable time after the end of the accounting

E   period to come within the section and to be treated as a payment received on the last day of the payee company's accounting period and, if the other requirements of the section are satisfied, to be treated as a trading receipt and a trading expense of the companies.

Provided that the payment is made within the prescribed time and provided that then one company is still the subsidiary of the other or that both are sub-

F   sidiaries of a third company, nothing appears to turn on the actual date of payment; but the Crown contend that the section only applies if at the actual date of payment the company which receives it is carrying on a trade.   There appears to be no good reason for so restricting the application of the section. The Crown was not able to suggest one, but they contended that, on its true construction, the section had that effect.

G   They concede that Parliament, when s. 18 and para. 1 and para. 3 of Sch. 4 to the Finance Act, 1954, were enacted, proceeded on the basis that the provisions of s. 20 did not cease to apply if the company which received the payment had at the time of receipt ceased to trade, but they rightly say that the contents of subsequent legislation affords no reliable guide to the interpretation of an earlier statute as Parliament may have proceeded on an erroneous view on the

H   law (see *Kirkness (Inspector of Taxes)* v. *John Hudson & Co., Ltd.* (2)).

It is, however, inconceivable that the government of the day would have introduced a Finance Bill containing what are now s. 18 of and para. 1 and para. 3 of Sch. 4 to the Finance Act, 1954, if the Crown had not at that time held the view that cessation of trading by the receiving company did not affect the application of s. 20.   Indeed, the Crown admitted that it was not until after the decision

I   in *Bullock (Inspector of Taxes)* v. *Unit Construction Co., Ltd.* (3), a case on the meaning to be attached to the word " resident " in s. 20 (9), that it occurred to them that the scope of s. 20 was limited as they now suggest and that it ought to be given the construction for which they now contend.

Whatever be the result of this case, one cannot help but feel some sympathy

---

(1) Finance Act, 1958, s. 23 and Sch. 6, Part 1, para. 2 (*e*).
(2) [1955] 2 All E.R. 345; 36 Tax Cas. 28.
(3) [1958] 3 All E.R. 186; 38 Tax Cas. 712.

with the unfortunate taxpayer company, which no doubt acted in the belief, as
originally the Crown thought was the case, that it was entitled if it made the
payments in question to treat them as trading expenses, and which now finds
itself involved in this litigation with the result so far that it had been held not
entitled to do so.   The Crown now seek, not by securing parliamentary approval
of an amendment to s. 20, to make it clear that the section is to be so limited, but
by litigation with a taxpayer to establish that it is.

If the section properly construed has to be interpreted as the Crown now
suggest, then although that was not the view of the Crown originally or of
Parliament when the Finance Act, 1954, was enacted, that is the end of the
matter so far as your lordships are concerned.   The Crown's argument depends
on the application of sub-s. (9) to the rest of s. 20.   They say that in consequence
of this subsection the company which receives the payment referred to in sub-s.
(10) must at the time of the receipt have been a trading company; and, secondly,
that in construing sub-s. (10) one must apply sub-s. (9), with the result that
both companies must be subsidiaries of a third company or one the subsidiary
of the other and both must be trading companies within sub-s. (9) at the time
the payment is received.

It will be convenient to consider the second argument first.

There are obvious reasons for requiring that at all times down to the making
of the payment or payments the companies concerned should be members of
the same group.   That is secured by sub-s. (10).   There are obvious reasons for
defining, if the section is not to apply to all companies, the class of companies
to which it is to apply.   That is done by sub-s. (9).   But there is no reason why
companies which qualify for the benefits given by the section should be deprived
of them if the company receiving the payment has at the time of its receipt
ceased to trade.

Both sub-s. (9) and sub-s. (10) begin with the words " For the purposes of
this section " and the Crown therefore contends that sub-s. (9) must be applied
to sub-s. (10).   That contention appears to me to depend on the fact that the
contents of the two subsections were not included in one subsection or indeed
in a separate section of the Finance Act, 1953.   If, for instance, instead of there
being two subsections there had been one commencing with the words " For
the purposes of this section " containing two paragraphs (a) and (b), and (a) contained what is now in sub-s. (9) and (b) what is in sub-s. (10), it would not be
right as a matter of construction to interpret the contents of (b) in the light of
the contents of (a) and it would, in my opinion, be clear that (a) and (b) were
each intended to apply to the other subsections of the section, which one might
call the operative part.   Similarly, if the contents of sub-s. (9) and sub-s. (10)
were included in a separate section commencing with the words " For the purposes
of s. 20 ", it would be clear that they were only intended to apply to that section.

I refuse to infer that the effect of these two subsections is different from that
which their contents would have if in one subsection or in a separate section, and
I am therefore of the opinion that this contention advanced by the Crown should
be rejected.

In sub-s. (1) every reference to a company has to be treated, inter alia, as a
reference to a trading company coming within sub-s. (9).   Bearing this in mind,
sub-s. (1) appears to me to require the following conditions to be satisfied for
the section to apply:

First, a trading company must have a deficit for tax purposes in one of its
accounting periods;
Secondly, it (that is the company) must have received a payment in respect
of that period from an associated trading company which has a surplus for
tax purposes for the corresponding period.

If the words " the company " appeared before the word " receives " in the
subsection, then one would be compelled to the conclusion that at the time of the

receipt of the payment the company must have been carrying on a trade for the section to apply.   On the other hand, if the word " it " appeared before the word " receives ", one would not have to apply to that word sub-s. (9).   I see no reason to read into sub-s. (1) the word " company " when it does not appear, so as to attract sub-s. (9).   The application of that subsection to the word " company " where it appears in the subsection is apt to define the class of companies which can if they have respectively a deficit and a surplus for tax purposes in corresponding accounting periods avail themselves of the section. Reading the subsection as if the word " company " appeared before the word " receives " imports a further condition into the second condition stated above by the inclusion of the words " while carrying on a trade " after the word " must ".   I do not think that the language of the subsection read with sub-s. (9) requires this to be done or that it has this meaning.   As I have said, there is no valid reason for imposing such a requirement.

If company A has a deficit for tax purposes at a time when it is carrying on a trade, then one has to look to see whether company A has received a subvention payment from an associated trading company.   One is not, in my opinion, required to consider whether company A was carrying on a trade when it received the payment.   If it had been intended that this should be done, then one would have expected that to have been made clear, either by the insertion of the words " the company " before " receives " or in some other way.

In my opinion, HARMAN, L.J., was right (4) in rejecting the Crown's contentions and the section should be held to have the meaning that the Crown originally thought that it had and which Parliament attached to it when the Finance Act, 1954, was passed.

I would therefore allow the appeal.

LORD MACDERMOTT: My Lords, I have had the advantage of reading the opinions prepared by my noble and learned friends, LORD MORRIS OF BORTH-Y-GEST and LORD UPJOHN.   I agree with their conclusion that this appeal should be allowed and with their reasoning for that conclusion and their description of the material circumstances.   I do not, therefore, propose to burden your lordships with any detailed exposition of the relevant facts and enactments, and only wish to add some observations of my own on the main issue because of the acute divergence of judicial opinion on that issue which this litigation has revealed.

The essence of the case made against the taxpayer company, and accepted in the courts below, was that its claim to relief under s. 20 (1) of the Finance Act, 1953, in respect of the subvention payments which it had made to another company of which it was a subsidiary (and which for brevity I will call " Glossop ") failed because at the time when these payments were made Glossop (as was admitted) had ceased to trade.   This contention was based, in turn, on s. 20 (9) which says that:

> " (9) For the purposes of this section . . . references to a company shall be taken to apply only to a company resident in the United Kingdom and carrying on a trade wholly or partly in the United Kingdom . . ."

Section 20 (1) sets out the conditions on which the relief it provides for is to be granted.   The first two of these appear, separated by the second comma, in the opening words of the subsection which read:

> " (1) Subject to the provisions of this section, where a company has a deficit for tax purposes during any accounting period of the company, and receives a subvention payment in respect of that period . . ."

It was not disputed, and there can be no doubt, that the word " company " as it is used twice in this part of the subsection means, by virtue of sub-s. (9), a resident and trading company.   Glossop had a deficit during an accounting

---

(4) [1966] 2 All E.R. 930 at pp. 932-934.

period while thus qualified and the first condition of sub-s. (1) was accordingly satisfied. The second condition begins with the words " and receives ", and here it is that the main issue emerges. On the one hand, the Crown say, in effect, that these words mean " and the company receives " and so invoke sub-s. (9), as it were de novo, with the result that they must be read as referring to a receiving company which is still, at the time of the receiving, a resident trading company; and, on the other hand, the taxpayer company submits that the reference is simply to a company which has been brought over the threshold of sub-s. (1) by complying with its first condition, and that the trading qualification need not, therefore, continue to exist until the time when the subvention payment is eventually made.

My lords, of these contentions that of the Crown seems to me to place more weight on sub-s. (9) than it was intended to bear. It is a form of definition that must be applied with caution, for it involves characteristics or qualifications which may not be constant, and it relates to a situation which, however sub-s. (1) may be read, is bound to develop over, and can only be completed after, the lapse of an appreciable period of time. In my opinion, however, two things at least are reasonably clear. In the first place, if s. 20 is read as a whole it is evident that sub-s. (9) cannot be interpreted as requiring that, in every instance where the word " company " is used or referred to, the reference must be to a resident trading company. The proviso to sub-s. (9) furnishes one example of this, as STAMP, J., has already observed (5); and another may, I think, be found in that part of sub-s. (1) which comes after the conditions for relief have been stated and provides that " then in computing . . . the profits or gains or losses of those companies . . ." the payment shall be treated as a trading receipt and a trading expense of the payee and paying companies respectively. A company might well cease trading after receipt of a subvention payment and before the accounts had allowed the necessary computation to begin. Applied indiscriminately sub-s. (9) would appear to bar the computation and therefore the relief in that event, but the Crown did not contend for such an irrational result and I do not think that a construction which produced it could be supported. If, then, " those companies " in this context may include companies which were but are no longer qualified under sub-s. (9), why should the taxpayer company's submission on the words " and receives " be excluded merely on the language of the enactment? Secondly, there is nothing, at any rate that I can discern, in the language of s. 20 to preclude, on this issue of construction, a consideration of the policy and purpose of the legislature as revealed in the enactment itself. STAMP, J., (6) at first instance and DIPLOCK, L.J., (7) and WINN, L.J., (7) in the Court of Appeal seem to have taken a different view on the ground that the words of the statute were plain and unequivocal and offered no possible alternative to the interpretation contended for by the Crown. My lords, with the greatest respect, I am unable to agree. The submission of the taxpayer company seems to me to ride not less but rather more easily than that of the Crown on the grammar and wording of the section, and I can find nothing in any of the subsections, including sub-s. (10), which comes near to making the Crown's submission the only possible or even the more likely interpretation. It is, of course, trite to say that statutory definitions can, on occasion, produce unexpected results that seem to work against the apparent tenor of a particular context; but I do not think that the language of sub-s. (9), which as HARMAN, L.J., pointed out (8) is rather odd, can be said to have this kind of draconian effect. If I am right in the view already expressed, it has to be applied with some degree of selectivity and, in any event, it begins with the words " For the purposes of this section . . ." Those words may mean much or little in different contexts, but with them present here it would be strange

(5) [1966] 1 All E.R. 716 at p. 721, letter A.
(6) [1966] 1 All E.R. at p. 718.
(7) [1966] 2 All E.R. at p. 934.
(8) [1966] 2 All E.R. at p. 932, letter I.

indeed if a court of construction could not ask, with relevance to the issue now before your lordships, what the purposes of the section were.

My lords, these considerations lead me to the view that the proper construction is that for which the taxpayer company has argued. To my mind, it is the view to be preferred on the terms of the statute and, beyond that, it is the view best calculated to give effect to the policy of s. 20. That policy has been described by HARMAN, L.J., (9) in the Court of Appeal and by my noble and learned friends in the opinions to which I have already referred and I need not describe it again. It is not in dispute and is readily conveyed to the informed mind by the terms of the section. Suffice it to say that the taxpayer company's contention accords entirely with the intendment of the section, whereas that of the Crown would mean, in effect, that relief thereunder could not be granted in respect of a deficit incurred in a company's last accounting period—an anomalous result for which no explanation was forthcoming.

The Crown also based an argument on sub-s. (10), but as it cannot prevail if that based on sub-s. (9) fails, I need say no more about it, except to add that I share the view favoured by those of your lordships who consider that sub-s. (9) and sub-s. (10) are independent of each other and should be read and applied accordingly.

For these reasons I think that HARMAN, L.J., (9) was right and I would allow the appeal.

LORD MORRIS OF BORTH-Y-GEST: My Lords, at all relevant times all the ordinary shares in Davies Jenkins & Co., Ltd., the taxpayer company, were beneficially held by a company called Wood Brothers (Glossop), Ltd. At all relevant times all the ordinary shares in that latter company were beneficially held by Wood Brothers (Glossop) Holdings, Ltd. There are two accounting periods of Wood Brothers (Glossop), Ltd. which are relevant for present purposes. The first is the accounting period from Apr. 1, 1958, to Mar. 31, 1959. That company was resident in England and carried on the trade of cotton spinners in England throughout the whole of that period. It is not in dispute that it had " a deficit for tax purposes " (within the meaning of s. 20 of the Finance Act, 1953), during that accounting period. It is not in dispute that the taxpayer company had " a surplus for tax purposes " (within the meaning of s. 20) in the corresponding period. In respect of that period the taxpayer company made a subvention payment of £13,327 to Wood Brothers (Glossop), Ltd. The payment was made on Feb. 24, 1960. Wood Brothers (Glossop), Ltd. had ceased to trade on Dec. 21, 1959. Their deficit for the accounting period was such as to absorb the £13,327.

The second relevant accounting period of Wood Brothers (Glossop), Ltd. is the period from Apr. 1, 1959, to Mar. 31, 1960. That company was resident in England and it carried on the trade of cotton spinners in England until Dec. 21, 1959. It is not in dispute that it had a deficit for tax purposes during the accounting period, nor is it in dispute that in the corresponding period the taxpayer company had a surplus for tax purposes. The taxpayer company made a subvention payment of £12,395 in respect of that period to Wood Brothers (Glossop), Ltd. It was made on Mar. 28, 1961. The deficit of Wood Brothers (Glossop), Ltd. absorbed £6,669 of the £12,395. The two subvention payments were made pursuant to a subvention agreement which was dated Mar. 17, 1955, and was an agreement which satisfied the requirements of s. 20 (2).

The question which has arisen is whether the Special Commissioners were right in holding that the subvention payments should be treated as trading expenses of the taxpayer company under the provisions of s. 20 (1). In ordinary circumstances a subvention payment will be made after the end of the accounting period of the receiving company. It will be made to such company after it is ascertained that it has a deficit for tax purposes. That will only be ascertained

---

(9) [1966] 2 All E.R. at p. 932.

after the end of the accounting period. A payment will be made by the paying company after it is ascertained that it has a surplus for tax purposes. In computing for the purposes of income tax the profits or gains or losses of the respective companies a payment is " treated " as a trading receipt receivable by the receiving company " on the last day of the accounting period during which it has the deficit " and is to be " allowed as a deduction to the other company as if it were a trading expense incurred on that day " (see sub-s. (1).) It would seem to follow that from a practical point of view the actual date of the subvention payment is of no materiality save that regard must be had to the proviso to sub-s. (2) which lays it down that a payment in respect of any accounting period of the payee company is not to be treated as a subvention payment unless made in or before the second year of assessment (10) following that in which the period ends. There would seem to be no necessity that trading should be continuing at the time of a payment though association must be continuing.

The result of the provisions to which I have referred would seem to be that (when considering, for example, the first payment) the sum of £13,327 paid by the taxpayer company to Wood Brothers (Glossop), Ltd. on Feb. 24, 1960, is, in computing for the purposes of income tax the profits or gains or losses of the companies, to be " treated " as a trading receipt receivable by the latter company on Mar. 31, 1959, and as a trading expense of the taxpayer company incurred on Mar. 31, 1959. It is said, however, by the Crown that the words of s. 20 (1) preclude this result for the reason that on the date of receipt by Wood Brothers (Glossop), Ltd. that company had ceased to carry on trade. If this contention is correct, it produces an anomaly. It would mean that, in respect of the final trading year of a subsidiary company which has a deficit, a subvention payment cannot ordinarily be received. If this is what the section provides, then of course its provisions must be faithfully followed.

I pass therefore to consider the words of sub-s. (1) of s. 20 of the Finance Act, 1953. The important words are:

" Subject to the provisions of this section, where a company has a deficit for tax purposes during any accounting period of the company, and receives a subvention payment in respect of that period from an associated company having a surplus for tax purposes in the corresponding period, then . . .''

The word " where " clearly does not refer to a place. It is used in the sense of " if " or " whenever ". The word " then " is not used as referring to time. It prescribes results or consequences which are to follow. The word " company " must be read having regard to the provisions of sub-s. (9). For the purposes of the section the word " company " includes any body corporate " but references to a company shall be taken to apply only to a company resident in the United Kingdom and carrying on a trade wholly or partly in the United Kingdom ". In regard to the meaning of an associated company it is necessary to have regard to sub-s. (10).

Applying the provisions of sub-s. (9) to sub-s. (10) and applying both to sub-s. (1), the consequence is that, if a company resident in the United Kingdom and carrying on a trade wholly or partly in the United Kingdom has a deficit for tax purposes during an accounting period and receives a subvention payment in respect of that period from a company resident in the United Kingdom and carrying on a trade wholly or partly in the United Kingdom, and if at all times between the beginning of the payee company's accounting period in respect of which the payment is made and the making of the payment one of them is a subsidiary (within the meaning of s. 42 of the Finance Act, 1938) of the other, then the payment is to be treated as a trading receipt receivable by the one company on the last day of the accounting period during which it has the deficit and is to be allowed as a deduction to the other company as if it were a trading expense incurred on that day.

---

(10) See footnote (15), p. 924, post.

I see no reason why the words " and receives " should not be read perfectly naturally and literally. The section does not stipulate that there must be receipt at some particular time. It would be surprising if it did. The time of receipt is unimportant save that there is a late date limit as laid down by the proviso to sub-s. (2). I see no need to read in or to insert words so as to require that receipt must be before a company has discontinued trading.

On the facts of the present case the application of s. 20 may be considered by posing and answering certain questions. Was Wood Brothers (Glossop), Ltd. a company resident in the United Kingdom and carrying on a trade wholly or partly in the United Kingdom during the two accounting periods? The answer is in the affirmative. Did Wood Brothers (Glossop), Ltd. have a deficit for tax purposes during the two accounting periods? The answer again is in the affirmative. (It was common ground that the fact that the cessation of trade was before the end of the second accounting period does not affect the issues now arising.) Did Wood Brothers (Glossop), Ltd. receive subvention payments in respect of those periods? The answer is in the affirmative. At all times between Apr. 1, 1958, (the beginning of the payee company's accounting period) and Mar. 28, 1961 (the date of the second payment) was one of the two companies the subsidiary of the other? The answer is in the affirmative.

In sub-s. (1) it is made clear that the receiving company must be a company that comes within certain descriptions. The descriptions are to be found in sub-s. (9). The deficit for tax purposes during an accounting period must be that of a company resident in and trading in the United Kingdom during the account-ing period. It is only receipt of a payment by such a company that can be regarded as a subvention receipt. The date of receipt seems, however, to be of no particular importance provided that it is not too long delayed. There is the further require-ment which is prescribed in sub-s. (10). In order that the paying company shall be treated as an associated company of the other, one of them must have been the subsidiary of the other (or both of them subsidiaries of a third company) at all times between the beginning of the payee company's accounting period and the making of the payment. That additional requirement was satisfied. The fact that the payee company ceased to trade did not affect the " subsidiary " relationship.

It seems to me that the purpose of sub-s. (10) was to provide that both the paying and the receiving company should continue to be, so to speak, members of the family down to the time of payment. There is force, therefore, in the contention that sub-s. (9) and sub-s. (10) should be read as imposing separate independent qualifications and that sub-s. (9) should not be infused into sub-s. (10). If, however, sub-s. (9) is to be applied to sub-s. (10), then I think that in that event what is being provided for as between the two companies is as follows. One of them that was resident in and carrying on trade in the United Kingdom during an accounting period will have had a deficit for tax purposes during the accounting period. The other that also was resident in and carrying on trade in the United Kingdom during the corresponding period will have had a surplus for tax purposes in the corresponding period. There having been a subvention agreement between them the latter company at some stage will make a payment pursuant to the agreement to the former. The paying company will be " treated " as the other's " associated company " for the purposes of sub-s. (1) provided that one continues to be the subsidiary of the other down to the time of payment. Subject to that, the date of making the payment is immaterial. The word " making " in the phrase " a company making a subvention payment to another " denotes no more than that as between one company that could be described as above and another company that could be described as above there will at some time have been a subvention payment. In a subsection clearly designed for a particular purpose I cannot think that from the word " making " there should be extracted the requirement that the receiving company must be continuing to trade at the moment of receipt.

At the time when s. 20 is being applied and administered the events being considered will all be in the past. So the words " where a company has a deficit for tax purposes " will denote a company (as specified in sub-s. (9)) which had a deficit during an accounting period; but such a company will only look to sub-s. (1) if it has received a subvention payment. The word " receives " in the sub-section bears the meaning " has received ". I agree with the view expressed by HARMAN, L.J., in his dissenting judgment in the Court of Appeal (11) that the use of the word " receives " does not denote the present tense in a temporal sense. The receipt of a payment will almost inevitably be made at some future time after the end of the accounting period which has resulted in a deficit for tax purposes. After the receipt of a payment it may be treated as a trading receipt receivable for the past period. It will be the fact of receipt that will be of importance and not its date. To insist on a requirement that the receipt must be before a company ceases to trade involves reading into the subsection some words that are not there; but at the date of payment the subsidiary relationship must be existing. As to that it is clear that one company does not cease to be a subsidiary of another merely because one or other of them ceases to trade.

I understand that it is accepted that when Parliament enacted s. 18 of the Finance Act, 1954, it must have proceeded on the basis that it was not necessary for the purposes of s. 20 of the Finance Act, 1953, that the recipient company should be trading at the time of receipt of a subvention payment. This, in my view, neither relieves the courts from giving free and untrammelled consideration to the interpretation of s. 20, nor does it furnish material for their guidance in so giving it. It is well accepted that the beliefs and assumptions of those who frame Acts of Parliament cannot make the law.

For the reasons which I have set out, and agreeing as I do with the approach of HARMAN, L.J., (12) I would allow the appeal.

LORD GUEST: My Lords, I have the misfortune to differ from the rest of your lordships, and, although I regard this case as a difficult one of statutory construction, I can express my views quite shortly. The short question, by no means easy of answer, is—whether in order to obtain the benefit of what has been described as the subvention procedure available to associated companies under s. 20 of the Finance Act, 1953, it is necessary that the company receiving the subvention payment should be resident and trading in the United Kingdom at the date when the subvention payment is received. It must obviously be trading during the chargeable accounting period when the deficit occurs, and it is agreed that the company making the payment and the company receiving the payment must be associated within the meaning of s. 20 (10) from the beginning of the payee company's accounting period to the date of making the payment, but the recipient company, it is argued, need not be resident and trading when the payment is received.

There are thirteen subsections to s. 20 of the Finance Act, 1953, but it is only necessary to quote sub-ss. (1), (9) and (10). [His LORDSHIP read the relevant terms of those subsections, which are set out at p. 924, letter G, to p. 925, letter C, post, and continued:] Subsection (1) prescribes the conditions necessary before a subvention payment can be allowed as a deduction for income tax purposes. (First) the company must have a deficit for tax purposes; (second) the company must be what has been compendiously described as a " resident and trading company " within the meaning of sub-s. (9); (third) the company must receive a subvention payment from an associated company within the meaning of sub-s. (10). If these conditions are satisfied, " then ", and only then, do the results follow.

The Crown contend that in interpreting sub-s. (1) in order to give effect to the importation of the definition of " company " in sub-s. (9), the grammatical con-struction of sub-s. (1) requires that, in order to qualify, the company must be resident and trading not only during the accounting period, but that it must also

---

(11) [1966] 2 All E.R. at p. 933, letter G.   (12) [1966] 2 All E.R. at p. 932.

be resident and trading when the subvention payment is received. The company in question, the Crown says, cannot " receive a subvention payment " under sub-s. (1) unless it is a company within sub-s. (9). The taxpayer company would read sub-s. (1) so that the company in question, having qualified as a resident and trading company when the deficit is incurred under the first limb of the section, becomes a " designated company " as it is called, for the rest of the subvention procedure and, having so qualified, it matters not that it has ceased to be resident and to trade when the subvention payment is received. I cannot so read the subsection. This interpretation flies in the very face of the grammatical construction of sub-s. (1). It would result in the two verbs " has " and " receives " in the first and second limbs of the section being controlled by two different subjects, in the first limb a company which is resident and trading and in the second limb a company which need be neither. It is said that there is a marked distinction between the words used in sub-s. (9) to define a " company " and the words used in sub-s. (10) to define an " associated company ". In the latter case the company must have been associated " at all times " between the beginning of the accounting period and the making of the payment, whereas in the former case nothing is said about the period during which the company must be resident and trading. I can see no force in this distinction and I would point out that for the purposes of sub-s. (10) it was necessary to provide the period during which association had to exist. Merely to have provided for association simpliciter would have been meaningless. The necessity for the company being resident and trading up to the date of payment is implicit in the definition of company. The subvention procedure never begins until the company qualifies as resident and trading. Moreover, if the words of sub-s. (9) are taken with the words of sub-s. (10) there can be no association between one company and another unless both companies fulfil the qualifications of sub-s. (9). I regard residence and trading as an essential preliminary to the operation of sub-s. (1).

I realise that this interpretation of s. 20 may run counter to what may be supposed to have been the intention of Parliament; but the intention of Parliament can only be deduced from the words used. These words are, in my view, quite clear. It is also said that this interpretation may result in the anomaly that the subvention procedure can never be available during the terminal period of the company's trading life. I recognise this anomaly but, if it is an anomaly, it is for the legislature to correct it, not the courts. Although it may not matter that the company in question has ceased trading at the date of payment, it may be of importance, the Crown said, if the company has ceased to be resident and trading in the United Kingdom at that date. Residence and trading are inseparably linked together. However this may be, I cannot see that there is any ambiguity in the words of s. 20 or that if they are interpreted according to their natural and grammatical meaning they can lead to any other result than that for which the Crown contends. There is no room, in my view, for what would amount, in my view, to judicial legislation.

I find the judgment of Stamp, J., (13) entirely satisfactory and I would dismiss the appeal.

LORD UPJOHN: My Lords, this appeal is concerned with a very short point of construction on s. 20 of the Finance Act, 1953. This section was introduced in 1953 to meet the development by the commercial community of the use of subsidiary and associated companies to carry out large enterprises usually under the umbrella of a parent company controlling the group. The practice had long grown up whereby if one subsidiary or associated company made a loss and another a profit, agreements were made within the group for a profitable subsidiary to make a subvention payment to a less successful subsidiary making a loss in any trading year. This was obviously a fair and sensible practice

---

(13) [1966] 1 All E.R. at p. 718.

but the Income Tax Acts made no provision for bringing subvention payments
or receipts into the well understood basis of computation on income tax principles
for the purpose of making annual assessments of profits or losses of companies.
To remedy this state of affairs and in justice to the taxpayer Parliament enacted
s. 20 whereby, putting it generally, within the group and for income tax purposes
the profitable company could claim an allowance for its payments to the company
making the loss but, in justice to the Crown, this had to be taken into account as
part of the trading receipts of the company having the loss, with the corollary (so
we are told) that if the company making the loss subsequently made a profit it
could not claim to set off its earlier losses, at all events to the extent to which
they had been met in earlier years by a subvention payment.

The scheme of s. 20 was rightly and properly conditioned for its application,
and the sole question is whether the taxpayer company has satisfied those
conditions. The facts are of the simplest. The taxpayer company was a wholly
owned subsidiary of Wood Brothers (Glossop), Ltd. (I shall call it " Glossop ")
which latter was a subsidiary of the parent company, Wood Brothers Holdings,
Ltd. By virtue of a subvention agreement made between the member companies
of the group in 1955 the taxpayer company made two payments to Glossop—
(i) in respect of the accounting period Apr. 1, 1958, to Mar. 31, 1959, the sum of
£13,327 on Feb. 24, 1960; (ii) in respect of the accounting period Apr. 1, 1959,
to Mar. 31, 1960, the sum of £12,395 on Mar. 28, 1961. No difficulty would have
arisen about these payments which would have qualified to be brought into
computation as a deduction for the purposes of income tax by the taxpayer
company under s. 20, apart from the fact that Glossop ceased to trade on Dec. 21,
1959.

I should mention here that the Crown and the taxpayer company have expressly
disclaimed any reliance on the fact that in respect of the second accounting period
Glossop ceased to trade before the end of that period.

The sole question, therefore, is whether the taxpayer company is unable to
claim the benefit of s. 20 by reason only of the fact that Glossop ceased to trade
before the dates of payment of the sums payable under the subvention agreement.

I must now set out the relevant terms of the Finance Act, 1953, s. 20, on which
alone this question is to be determined. While it is a long and involved section
with many subsections, it is agreed that, as STAMP, J., said, (14) sub-s. (1) is the
enacting part of the section. This subsection, however, must be construed in the
light of the all important sub-ss. (9) and (10). So I need set out little more than
these subsections:

" 20.—(1) Subject to the provisions of this section, where a company has
a deficit for tax purposes during any accounting period of the company and
receives a subvention payment in respect of that period from an associated
company having a surplus for tax purposes in the corresponding period, then
in computing for the purposes of income tax the profits or gains or losses of
those companies the payment shall be treated as a trading receipt receivable
by the one company on the last day of the accounting period during which
it has the deficit, and shall be allowed as a deduction to the other company as
if it were a trading expense incurred on that day.

" (2) . . . Provided that a payment in respect of any accounting period of the
payee company shall not be treated as a subvention payment unless made
in or before the second (15) year of assessment following that in which the
period ends.

. . . .

" (9) For the purposes of this section, ' company ' includes any body

---

(14) [1966] 1 All E.R. at p. 721, letter D.
(15) The word " second " was inserted by Finance Act, 1958, s. 23 and Sch. 6
Part 1, para. 2 (e). Part 1 of of Sch. 6 was deemed to have come into force on Apr. 5,
1958 (see ibid., para. 3).

A   corporate, but references to a company shall be taken to apply only to a company resident in the United Kingdom and carrying on a trade wholly or partly in the United Kingdom: Provided that this section shall apply in relation to a company whose business consists mainly in the making of investments and the principal part of whose income is derived therefrom as if that business were the carrying on of a trade, and in the case of such a company,

B   any payment which is directed by this section to be treated as a trading receipt or a trading expense shall be treated as a payment chargeable under Case VI of Sch. D or as an expense of management, as the case may be.

    " (10) For the purposes of this section, a company making a subvention payment to another shall be treated as the other's associated company if, but only if, at all times between the beginning of the payee company's

C   accounting period in respect of which the payment is made and the making of the payment one of them is the subsidiary of the other, or both are subsidiaries of a third company, and for this purpose ' subsidiary ' has the meaning assigned to it for certain purposes of the profits tax by s. 42 of the Finance Act, 1938."

D   The Special Commissioners reached the conclusion, based to some extent on the provisions of the Finance Act, 1954, that a subvention payment made to Glossop after it had ceased to trade still qualified under s. 20. The Crown appealed from their decision. Stamp, J., (16) reversed the decision of the commissioners and held that the taxpayer company were not entitled to any allowance in respect of their payments to Glossop as at the moment of payment Glossop was not trading and, therefore, was not qualified as payee by sub-s. (9); nor was it qualified as an

E   associated company at that moment of time (as he held that it must be) by sub-s. (10). On appeal Diplock, L.J., (17) and Winn, L.J., (17) in very brief judgments agreed with Stamp, J., (16) and with his reasons without adding any of their own. Harman, L.J., dissented (18) and would have allowed the appeal.

    The argument of the Crown before your lordships followed closely and relied on the reasons given by Stamp, J., in his judgment (19), though for my part I

F   think that Stamp, J., (19) while agreeing with those arguments in principle, reached the same conclusion by a slightly different route, which I shall examine later.

    The Crown's argument is that one must fasten on the definition of " company " in sub-s. (9) and so that in the enacting sub-s. (1), where the word " company " first occurs, one must read it as a company " resident in the United Kingdom

G   and carrying on a trade wholly or partly in the United Kingdom ", which qualification for brevity in argument was referred to as a resident trading company, a phrase which, for the like reason, I shall adopt. So far this proposition could not be disputed. The argument then proceeds that where the word " company " follows " during any accounting period of the company " one must again read in the words of the definition and, so reading on " and receives ", one finds that

H   to qualify for the benefit the company must be a resident trading company which receives—i.e., a company which at the moment of receipt is a resident trading company. Stamp, J., expressed this point of view very clearly when he said (20):

    " Subsection (9) requires one to ' take ' (note the words ' shall be taken ') the reference to a company in sub-s. (1) as applying only to a company

I   (note the present tense) ' resident in the United Kingdom and carrying on ' (note again the present tense) a trade there; and before sub-s. (1) can apply one must find the case to be one where, reading sub-s. (9) into sub-s. (1) ' a company resident in the United Kingdom ' and carrying on a trade there,

---

(16) [1966] 1 All E.R. 716.
(17) [1966] 2 All E.R. at p. 934.
(18) [1966] 2 All E.R. at p. 932.
(19) [1966] 1 All E.R. at p. 718.
(20) (1966) 1 All E.R. at p. 721, letter F.

has such a deficit as is there described and receives a subvention payment.   **A**
In this case no such company did receive a subvention payment."

The Crown superadded to this view an argument based on reading sub-ss. (9)
and (10) together, and again I think that STAMP, J., has expressed this view
concisely in a passage in his judgment following on that which I have just
quoted (21):

                                                   B

" Similarly, in the absence of some contrary indication, I would conclude
that the paying company must have the qualification of being an associated
company at the moment of receipt and payment. Subsection (10), however,
requires that qualification to subsist as well over the whole period between
the beginning of the payees' accounting period and the payment."

My lords, I find myself quite unable to accept these views of the matter which seem **C**
to me to do complete violence to the words of the section and to all normal canons
of construction. Looking at sub-s. (1), the enacting part, it is quite clear that the
only relevant period is the relevant accounting period of the payee company
(Glossop). Of course there must be a paying company (the taxpayer company)
for that is a causa sine qua non; without that the section does not bite. But the
actual moment of payment is utterly irrelevant to any matter mentioned in **D**
sub-s. (1). It is relevant only to the proviso in sub-s. (2), i.e., the payment must
be made within two years, and to sub-s. (10) where it must be established that at
the moment of payment the companies must be associated.

So I approach the enacting sub-s. (1) with this in mind, that the moment of
payment does not seem to be of any importance provided it has been made. Had
Parliament thought that the moment of payment was vital to claim the benefit **E**
of the section in the sense that the company must then be a resident trading
company, I note that Parliament knew how to do that in sub-s. (10) and it has
signally failed to do so in sub-s. (9); I would suppose because it thought that
consideration to be irrelevant when construing sub-s. (1), as indeed it does to me.
So I fail to understand why STAMP, J., placed such emphasis (22) on the time of
payment.   **F**

Apart from this consideration, however, it seems to me that, assuming sub-s.
(9) to be in truth a definition section, a matter to which I shall return, it is quite
a wrong method of construction slavishly to read in the definition whenever and
wherever the word so defined occurs. Regard must be had to the context. The
" company " in s. 20 (1), where it first occurs, is plainly defined as a resident
trading company. Having been so defined, as a matter of construction of that **G**
subsection it is perfectly plain that where the word secondly occurs the word
" company " refers back to the company already defined, i.e., it must be read as
" that company " and to introduce again the words of the definition is a misuse
of language. The construction of the subsection seems to me plain. It should be
read and construed in this way:

                                                   H

". . . where a resident trading company has a deficit for tax purposes
during any accounting period of that company and it receives . . ."

The matter, however, does not end there for, if one has to read in the definition of
company as a resident trading company after the word where it secondly occurs,
it gives what is, to my mind, a wholly misleading construction to the section, for
it introduces, sub silentio (on the Crown's argument already mentioned), the **I**
further condition that the company must be a resident trading company not only
during the relevant accounting period but also at the moment of time of payment
of the subvention, which for the reasons that I have already mentioned seems
utterly irrelevant to this matter. Therefore, construing this subsection in the
ordinary way and giving each word in the section its ordinary meaning and

---

(21) [1966] 1 All E.R. at p. 721, letter H.
(22) [1966] 1 All E.R. at p. 721.

A applying the so-called definition sections in the ordinary way in which such sections should be employed, I reach, with all respect to STAMP, J., (23) and the majority of the Court of Appeal (24), the clear conclusion that to qualify for the benefit of s. 20 the taxpayer company does not have to prove that Glossop, the payee company, continued trading until the moment of payment.

So much for the Crown's argument; but I must turn to the first reason given
B by STAMP, J., in his judgment for reaching his conclusion, and in fairness to him I set it out in full (25):

" Moreover, it is to be noted that it is the word ' payment ' which is grammatically the subject of the sentence which one finds in sub-s. (1), and it is the payment which is to receive the treatment prescribed; and, if the question be asked, at what moment of time is the company which receives
C the payment to have the qualification required by sub-s. (9), I would . . . conclude that it was at the time of the payment, that it was payment at that moment of time which brings sub-s. (1) into operation."

My lords, while as a matter of substance or grammar I cannot exalt the time of payment to the significance given to it by the learned judge, I think that he posed to himself the right question which I shall answer later. This leads me to a closer
D examination of sub-ss. (9) and (10). Subsection (9) has been referred to as a definition section and so, in a sense, it is, but as it applies in the same subclause to an investment trust company as though it was a resident trading company, as a matter of construction it is loose and, in my view, it was intended as no more than a " qualification " section. It merely defines those companies who are
E qualified to obtain the benefits of sub-s. (1). This consideration is an additional or, indeed, independent ground for disposing of the Crown's claim, in their main argument. To my mind, also, sub-ss. (9) and (10) are quite independent of each other and cannot be read as a whole so as to produce the result already mentioned and accepted by STAMP, J., (26). Subsection (9) sets out the qualifications which companies within a group must satisfy to claim the benefit of the section. Sub-
F section (10) is dealing and dealing only with the question whether companies are associated or subsidiary. For the first and only relevant time, apart from the proviso to sub-s. (2), sub-s. (10) rightly brings in the element of the importance of the time of payment. If at the moment of payment the payor company is no longer within the group or family there is no reason why it should be entitled to the benefit of the section.

So I pose to myself the question posed by STAMP, J., (26). I answer it by saying
G that for the reasons which I have already stated I cannot see any relevance in the *time* of payment. I look for the purposes of the enacting sub-s. (1) to the relevant accounting period and to no other, for that is the only relevant consideration; sub-ss. (2) and (10) being out of the way. During the relevant accounting period the taxpayer company satisfied all the conditions of the section and with all respect to the judgment of the Court of Appeal (24) to the contrary
H I would regard this as a clear case, as I think did HARMAN, L.J., (27). I reach this conclusion without any reference to arguments based on ambiguity, anomalies or later statutes.

My lords, I am disturbed, as I have been disturbed in another case very recently, at the conduct of the Board of Inland Revenue in respect of these matters. Until 1958 they very rightly accepted the interpretation which I have
I placed on this section without question; they caused an Act to be passed in 1954 on the footing of this interpretation (they now say that was all a mistake), and so the matter remained until in 1958 some question arose, not on trading but on residence. This led, so your lordships were informed, to a reappraisal of the

---

(23) [1966] 1 All E.R. 716.
(25) [1966] 1 All E.R. at p. 721, letter E.
(26) [1966] 1 All E.R. at p. 721.
(27) [1966] 2 All E.R. at p. 932.

(24) [1966] 2 All E.R. 930.

section and the Board then adopted a construction which, in my opinion, is quite   A
untenable and incidentally introduced anomalies. If the Board want to change
the basis of taxation from the clear words which Parliament has used and to alter
a clearly settled practice understood by Crown and subject alike, surely they
should seek statutory powers to do so and not, by an internal change of practice,
try to alter well settled law.

I would allow this appeal and restore the decision of the commissioners.   B

Appeal allowed.

Solicitors: *Sir Charles Sopwith* (for the Crown); *Coward, Chance & Co.* (for the
taxpayer company).

[*Reported by* KATHLEEN J. H. O'BRIEN, *Barrister-at-Law.*]

C

C. *v.* C.

[PROBATE, DIVORCE AND ADMIRALTY DIVISION (Sir Jocelyn Simon, P.), April 20,
November 28, December 21, 1966.]

*Divorce—Petition—Petition within three years of marriage—Discretion to allow—
Matters for court to consider—Failure to seek reconciliation after adjournment*   D
for that purpose—Matrimonial Causes Act 1965 (c. 72), *s.* 2 (2).

On an application under s. 2 (2)* of the Matrimonial Causes Act 1965, for
leave to present a petition for divorce before the expiration of the period of
three years from the date of the marriage, the court must not only have
regard to the matters which the enactment has specifically indicated—the
interests of any relevant child and the question whether there is reasonable   E
probability of a reconciliation between the parties within the three years—
but may also consider all other circumstances (see p. 931, letter E, and
p. 933, letter B, post).

The parties were married on Jan. 23, 1965, and separated on Aug. 29, 1965.
There were no children. The wife applied under s. 2 (2) of the Matrimonial
Causes Act 1965, for leave to present a petition of divorce within three   F
years of the marriage, on the grounds that the case was one of exceptional
hardship suffered by her and of exceptional depravity on the part of the
husband. Some of her allegations were comparative trivialities, but others,
in relation to the sexual life of the parties, amounted to sexual aberrations,
if not sexual perversions. The judge was of the opinion that the wife had
made out a prima facie case of exceptional depravity on the part of the hus-   G
band; but because of the husband's expressed wish for a reconciliation, the
triviality of some of the wife's allegations and, with regard to the more
serious allegations, what was said by LORD MERRIMAN, P., in *Holborn* v.
Holborn†, the very short marriage and the fact that there had been no real
attempt at reconciliation though the wife refused to consider one, he
adjourned the application for a serious attempt to be made at reconciliation.   H
No attempt was made at reconciliation and on the restoration of the application the wife filed affidavits from two doctors who said that, in their view,
reconciliation was not to be considered, and the husband said that he was
no longer willing for a reconciliation.

Held: the wife would be given leave to present her petition under s. 2 (2)
of the Act of 1965 because reconciliation was no longer a possibility and,   I
in view of the medical evidence, it could not be held that she had behaved
so unreasonably in making no positive approach to the husband for a
reconciliation that the court's discretion should not be exercised (see p. 933,
letter G, post); further, the marriage was beyond repair and it would be
adverse to the wife's psychological health that she should be kept for a further
year with proceedings in contemplation (see p. 933, letter H, post).

---
* Section 2 (2) is set out at p. 929, letter G, post.
† [1947] 1 All E.R. 32.

A   [As to principles on which leave to petition within three years of marriage is granted, see 12 Halsbury's Laws (3rd Edn.) 235, para. 442; and for cases on the subject, see 27 Digest (Repl.) 373, *3077-3081*.

For the Matrimonial Causes Act 1965, s. 2, see 45 Halsbury's Statutes (2nd Edn.) 449.]

Cases referred to:

B   *Holborn* v. *Holborn*, [1947] 1 All E.R. 32; 176 L.T. 57; 111 J.P. 36; 27 Digest (Repl.) 703, *6719*.

Jamieson v. *Jamieson*, [1952] 1 All E.R. 875; [1952] A.C. 525; 116 J.P. 226; Digest (Cont. Vol. A) 709, *2506a*.

Owen v. *Owen*, [1964] 2 All E.R. 58; [1964] P. 277; [1964] 2 W.L.R. 654; 3rd Digest Supp.

C   *W.* v. *W.*, [1966] 2 All E.R. 889.

Winter v. *Winter*, [1944] P. 72; 113 L.J.P. 49; 171 L.T. 111; 27 Digest (Repl.) 373, *3077*.

Application.

This was an application by the wife under s. 2 (2) of the Matrimonial Causes

D   Act 1965, for leave to present a petition for divorce notwithstanding that three years had not expired since the date of marriage. The facts are set out in the judgment.

The judgment was delivered in chambers and is reported by permission of Sir Jocelyn Simon, P.

B. Garland for the wife.

E   *Sir Graeme Finlay* for the husband.

SIR JOCELYN SIMON, P.: This is an application by a wife under s. 2 of the Matrimonial Causes Act 1965, asking for leave to present a petition for divorce notwithstanding that three years have not expired since the marriage. By sub-s. (1) of that section, no petition for divorce shall be presented to the court before the expiration of the period of three years from the date of the

F   marriage (thereinafter referred to as " the specified period "). By sub-s. (2), however,

" A judge of the court may, on an application made to him, allow the presentation of a petition for divorce within the specified period on the ground that the case is one of exceptional hardship suffered by the petitioner or of exceptional depravity on the part of the respondent; but in determining the

G   application the judge shall have regard to the interests of any relevant child and to the question whether there is reasonable probability of a reconciliation between the parties during the specified period."

The marriage here was on Jan. 23, 1965. The parties separated on Aug. 29, 1965. So there was an effective cohabitation of only some seven months. There are no

H   children. On Mar. 25, 1966, the wife issued her summons for leave to file her petition, and swore and filed an affidavit on the same day exhibiting her draft petition. She puts her case on the grounds of both exceptional hardship and exceptional depravity.

I do not propose to read in detail the allegations which she makes. Some are comparative trivialities. When I say comparative trivialities, I mean in relation

I   to some of the other allegations. She complains, for example, of such matters as that the husband criticised her, and denigrated her, and told her that she was too young to be of any use to him. Those sort of allegations can hardly now be excluded from a pleading in view of the decision in *Jamieson* v. *Jamieson* (1). The day has gone when Lord Merrivale, P., could say robustly that twenty black rabbits do not make one black ram. There are, however, three things to be said about those sort of allegations. First, unless they can be said to be the last straw which leads to a breakdown in cohabitation or in health, they do not

(1) [1952] 1 All E.R. 875; [1952] A.C. 525.

really add very much to serious allegations. Secondly, they often seem to reflect A
the sort of difficulties in adjustment which many spouses experience in the early
stages of a marriage and which, if the parties cannot surmount them by their
own good sense, consideration, tolerance and increasing maturity are often
susceptible of being overcome with the help of friends and relatives bent on
sustaining, rather than encouraging the disruption of, so solemn and momentous
a union as marriage. And thirdly, they are rarely capable of constituting, or B
advancing in any significant way, a case of exceptional depravity or exceptional
hardship. If anything, the inclusion of such allegations rather derogates from
it.

The wife, however, makes other allegations which are more serious. I refer
to allegations which she makes in relation to the sexual life of the parties. Some,
certainly, seem to reflect the difficulties in sexual adjustment which many C
spouses experience in the early years of matrimony; but others really amount
to sexual aberrations, if not sexual perversions. I have, however, in mind what
LORD MERRIMAN, P., with his great experience, said in *Holborn* v. *Holborn* (2):

> " No-one can sit here as long as I have sat without realising that there is
> the greatest diversity of standards between one set of spouses and another
> as to what is or what is not a normal standard of sexual intercourse.   What D
> will be regarded as grossly excessive demands by one wife (or by the husband,
> as the case may be) will be regarded as quite normal and reasonable by
> another wife or husband. I go further. There are things strictly outside what
> may be called normal sexual intercourse which will be regarded by one wife
> (or one husband, as the case may be) as so revolting as to be unmentionable,
> whereas other couples will regard them as nothing more than natural, normal E
> love-making.   Anyone who is familiar with the class of evidence and the
> class of controversies which arise in this court will know exactly what I
> mean."

Nevertheless, some of the allegations made by the wife, if accepted, would, in my
view, constitute exceptional depravity on the part of the husband and exceptional hardship suffered by her. I say " if accepted ", because I have in mind F
a passage in the judgment of *W.* v. *W.* (3), where it was said:

> " On what material should the court form a judgment whether the case is
> one of exceptional hardship or exceptional depravity? I think that the
> approach of the court here is similar to that of the Divisional Court in
> applications under r. 36 of the Matrimonial Causes Rules, 1957, (4). In G
> other words, the court cannot at this stage try whether the case is one of
> exceptional hardship or exceptional depravity, since this would involve
> deciding whether the allegations in the proposed petition are true: all that
> the court can do is to come to a conclusion that the allegations made in the
> affidavits filed on the application are such that, if true, they would amount
> to exceptional hardship or depravity; see GODDARD, L.J., in *Winter* v. H
> *Winter* (5).   Nevertheless the court is not bound to accept such evidence
> uncritically: it can consider it against the general background of the marriage
> as disclosed at this stage, and against any evidence filed in opposition.   The
> court can also take into account, if such be the case, that the charges are
> inherently improbable, or that the conduct complained of seems to have been
> provoked, or that there is a self-inconsistency in the evidence filed (cf., *Owen* I
> v. *Owen* (6)). As in the r. 36 application, the court can, if necessary, order a
> deponent to be cross-examined on his affidavit: see SCOTT, L.J., in *Winter*
> v. *Winter* (7): though this will be done only in exceptional circumstances."

(2) [1947] 1 All E.R. 32, letters G and H.   (3) [1966] 2 All E.R. 889 at p. 892.
(4) S.I. 1957 No. 619. For r. 36, see 10 HALSBURY'S STATUTORY INSTRUMENTS (Second
Re-Issue) 248.
(5) [1944] P. 72 at p. 75.
(6) [1964] 2 All E.R. 58 at p. 64; [1964] P. 277 at pp. 284, 285.
(7)[1944] P. at p. 74.

A   The husband, the respondent to this application, has in fact filed an affidavit. He denies generally that he has been guilty of exceptional depravity or that the wife has suffered exceptional hardship. He denies some of the wife's allegations, and says as to others that they are a gross exaggeration of admitted events, giving one or two examples. As to the sexual allegations, he says that the wife was at all times a willing participant. That indicates that some of the more

B   serious of the wife's allegations have some foundation of fact at any rate; even though it may not constitute in law corroboration of them, since the contest would seem to be whether the wife consented. However, I also have in mind that those allegations would seem to be generally incapable of corroboration. Nevertheless, considering the matter as best I can in the way indicated in *W.* v. *W.* (8), at this stage it seems to me that the wife has made out a sufficient prima facie

C   case of exceptional depravity on the part of the husband, and exceptional hardship suffered by her, to give the court a discretion to allow her to present a petition notwithstanding that three years have not elapsed since the marriage. Of course, if she did not establish such a prima facie case, the court would have no discretion in the matter at all and a petition could not be presented, though she could present a petition for judicial separation and could petition

D   for divorce at the end of the three year period, if she were so advised, in relation to the matters arising within the specified period: see s. 2 (3) of the Act of 1965. If a prima facie case of exceptional depravity or exceptional hardship is shown, there is still, therefore, no right to present the petition; it is a matter of discretion; and the court has to have regard to specific matters which the legislature has indicated—the interest of any relevant child, and the question whether there

E   is a reasonable probability of a reconciliation between the parties during the specified period.

    When the matter came before me first on Apr. 20, 1966, there being no child, and I having formed the view that a prima facie case was made out, what troubled me was whether there was a reasonable probability of reconciliation. The husband then, through his counsel, expressed the wish for a reconciliation, and I gathered

F   indeed that he had made overtures for it. I had in mind, secondly, the triviality of some of the allegations, and as to the more serious, what was said by Lord Merriman, P., in *Holborn* v. *Holborn* (9). Thirdly, this was a very short marriage; and there had been no real attempt at reconciliation. I was told, though it was not on affidavit, that the wife had invited the husband to see a psychiatrist. Whether that would amount to an attempt at reconciliation would certainly

G   depend on how it was said. I suppose that it might be put in some such way as " You ought to have your head looked at ". On the other hand, if it were a serious suggestion that both parties should see some experienced psychiatrist with a view to resolving their problems and establishing the marriage on a reasonable and mutually satisfactory basis, that would be another thing. But, fourthly, the wife at the hearing before me, adamantly refused, through her

H   counsel and in her affidavit, to consider a reconciliation. Under those circumstances I was unable to say affirmatively that there was a reasonable probability of reconciliation; but it seemed to me consistent with the intention of the legislature to grant an adjournment to give the opportunity of exploring the possibility of reconciliation. I, therefore, adjourned the application for a *serious* attempt—and I emphasised that word—to be made at reconciliation.

I   In the event, not only was no serious attempt made at reconciliation, but no attempt was really made at all. The matter was restored before me by the wife on Nov. 28, 1966. She then filed two further affidavits. Their dates, and the dates of the matters referred to therein, are to my mind significant. The first affidavit was from a Dr. R. That was sworn on July 15, 1966, although it was not filed until Sept. 16, 1966. He had met the wife as a secretarial colleague in June, 1964. She had had a professional consultation with him on Oct. 27, 1965. It is significant

---

that that was two months after the separation. He found that she was complaining of tension, headaches, sleep-walking and sleeping badly. She had lost a lot
of weight since he had last seen her and looked very strained and nervous and
was near to tears throughout. He listened to the story of her marriage, and concluded that it was clear that she could not think of returning to her husband.
He avers: " I, as a doctor, could not have recommended her to consider a
reconciliation. " He prescribed tranquilisers and sleeping pills. He obviously
formed the view that what he found was consistent with a history of matrimonial
ill-treatment; on the other hand, he did not appear to have considered in any way
whether the husband had a case in the matter. It would seem to a layman that,
although what Dr. R. found was consistent with matrimonial ill-treatment, it
might also be consistent with worry about the breakdown of the marriage after
so short a time and a possible strain of conflicting loyalties. It seems to me, again,
of some significance that, on Nov. 10, 1965, the wife again consulted Dr. R.;
and his evidence suggests that she was then worse rather than better. He says:

> " I again discussed her marriage and was again satisfied that there neither
> could be or should be any question of suggesting a reconciliation [and] I
> have since read her petition and her affidavit. Her condition, both on
> Oct. 27, 1965, and Nov. 10, 1965, was consistent with her having been
> treated as described in those two documents."

He does not say whether it was consistent with any other matter. He goes on to
say that a little later in November, 1965, the wife, started work for him on a
part-time basis:

> " She felt she ought to have a job and I encouraged it not for my sake but
> for hers. There has over the past month been a marked improvement in her
> health."

He does not say to what that marked improvement could be ascribed; it might
be, of course, that it was now a longer period since she had been subjected to
matrimonial strain; it might be that a conflict of loyalties had now been resolved;
it might be that she had settled down by now to a new life; or it might be, I
suppose, a combination of all three. However, there was his view that a
reconciliation was not to be considered.

The second affidavit that was put in on the re-hearing before me was from a
Dr. M., a woman gynaecologist and endocrinologist. She has a specialist practice
with particular reference to fertility problems and psycho-sexual difficulties.
She is a medical adviser to two organisations concerned with matrimonial problems. She had first met the wife professionally before the marriage on Nov. 23,
1964, when the wife consulted her with a view to pre-marital contraceptive
advice. What she says about that consultation has no direct bearing on the matter
that I have to consider; though there is one detail which tends marginally to
make me feel that there is no reason to hold that the wife's story as told in her
affidavit, in the face of the husband's denial contained in his, should be taken
as prima facie unacceptable. The wife again consulted Dr. M. on May 16, 1966.
That was within a month after the first hearing before me. The wife consulted
Dr. M. as to whether a reconciliation was possible. It does not appear that Dr. M.
was shown the husband's affidavit, or that she considered in any way that he
might have some case to be weighed. Dr. M. clearly formed, on the material
that was laid before her, an adverse view of the husband's character. Dr. M.
concluded that her patient has developed an invincible repugnance as a result of
his (the husband's) treatment of her, and that reconciliation was not possible
under the circumstances. I cannot help feeling that it might have been possible to
have found another psychiatrist, or even Dr. M. herself under different circumstances, who might have regarded the husband less censoriously or even have contemplated that he might benefit from psycho-therapy, or some other treatment,
rather than merely be deserving of obloquy. The other new factor that I had
before me was that the husband, through his counsel, indicated that he was no

A longer willing for a reconciliation, ostensibly in view of the further affidavits which had been filed.

The upshot is that I am now affirmatively satisfied that there is no reasonable prospect of a reconciliation; and the question then arises; how my discretion should be exercised. If, of course, the two matters to which, by statute, I must have regard are exclusive of any others, that is an end of the matter; there are

B no children, and I am satisfied that there is now no reasonable prospect of a reconciliation. However, I do not think that those considerations are exclusive of any others. The wording of s. 2 (2) of the Act of 1965 does not suggest that; and, in my view, the court can consider all other circumstances.

I must first of all consider the matter in relation to the adjournment. I gave no injunction as to any particular course to be followed; indeed, in my view,

C there is no power in the court to do any such thing. I was merely giving an opportunity to the parties to seek reconciliation if it were possible, with an implicit warning as to the risk to the application if the wife behaved unreasonably. Being satisfied, as I am, that the considerations expressly referred to in s. 2 (2) are not exclusive of all others, it seems to me that, if an applicant unreasonably refuses to entertain any overtures for reconciliation (so that there is, indeed, no reason-

D able probability of reconciliation), then that is a matter which the court is entitled to weigh in deciding how to exercise its discretion. So, finally, the question comes down to this: has the wife behaved so unreasonably in making no approach to the husband, either directly or through a qualified conciliation agency, at a time when he was apparently anxious for a reconciliation, that that should be weighed against her in considering how the discretion of the court should be

E exercised? I have tried to put out of my mind the consideration that the wife must realise that she has done considerably less than I envisaged, and, indeed, might be said to have shown scant respect to the court in the course that she has pursued. On the other hand, there are certain matters which, to my mind, weigh in her favour. There are, first, not only Dr. M.'s medical qualifications, but also that she acts in an advisory capacity to the agencies to which I have referred. Secondly,

F the wife consulted her with a view to seeing whether a reconciliation was possible. Thirdly, there is the advice of both Dr. R. and Dr. M. that reconciliation is not to be considered. It is true, as I have said, that neither seems to have weighed in any way the husband's case, or apparently considered whether, assuming that what the wife says is true, the husband might nevertheless be helped by treatment. On the other hand, they have both come to a clear opinion, having considered the

G wife as their patient; and in view of that I do not think that I can hold that the wife has behaved so unreasonably in making no positive approach to the husband for a reconciliation that I should on that ground refuse to exercise discretion to allow presentation of the petition. In favour of an affirmative exercise of the discretion there are two further matters that weigh with me. First, although this marriage was of very short duration and I have a feeling that, with proper

H guidance and help, it might at one time have been saved, I can have no such hope in the events which have now occurred; and it does seem to me that this marriage is now unhappily beyond repair. Secondly, although I have no specific medical evidence to this effect, I think that it is implicit in what Dr. R. and Dr. M. say, that it would be adverse to the wife's psychological health that she should be kept for a further year with proceedings in contemplation, so that all her memories

I remain raw and she is tied with a bond which has become practically meaningless.

Therefore, although I have had considerable doubts about this case at times, my conclusion is that the wife should be given leave to present her petition under s. 2 (2) of the Act of 1965, notwithstanding that three years have not elapsed since the date of the marriage. *Leave granted.*

Solicitors: *Charles Russell & Co.* (for the wife); *Rowley, Ashworth & Co.* (for the husband).

[*Reported by* Alice Bloomfield, *Barrister-at-Law.*]

LIBERIAN SHIPPING CORPORATION
v. A. KING & SONS, LTD.

[COURT OF APPEAL, CIVIL DIVISION (Lord Denning, M.R., Harman and Salmon,
L.JJ.), January 18, 19, 1967.]

*Arbitration—Commencement—Extension of time fixed by agreement—Charterparty
in Centrocon form—Cross-claims—Parties negotiating for a settlement and
unaware of expiry of time limit—Substantial claim by owners—Meeting
with a view to settlement on day after expiry of time limit—No settlement
reached—Nine days after expiry of time limit owners sought extension of time
by consent—Charterers had not contributed to delay, but were not prejudiced
by it—Whether " undue hardship " would be caused to owners if time were
not extended—Arbitration Act, 1950 (14 Geo. 6 c. 27), s. 27.*

A vessel was let on a voyage charterparty in Centrocon form containing an
arbitration clause under which any claim had to be made in writing and the
claimant's arbitrator had to be appointed within three months of final discharge. A fire occurred on board the vessel during loading. The vessel was
delayed. Both the owners and the charterers had claims against each other.
The time limit was to expire on June 26, 1966. The parties were negotiating
and, after considerable correspondence, a meeting between both parties was
arranged for June 27, 1966, with a view to settlement. Neither party appreciated that time had expired. The meeting did not result in a settlement. The
charterers first realised that time had expired when the owners sought an
extension of it by consent, nine days after the expiry. The charterers had not
contributed to delay on the part of the owners in relation to the arbitration
clause. The charterers did not consent to the time being extended. The
owners applied under s. 27* of the Arbitration Act, 1950, for an extension of
time on the ground that " undue hardship " would otherwise be caused to
them. Their claim amounted to about £33,000. The master granted an
extension of time, but on appeal the judge refused it. On further appeal,

Held (HARMAN, L.J., dissenting): in the circumstances the charterers
would not be prejudiced by time being extended, but, if time were not
extended, undue hardship would be caused to the owners since they would
be deprived of what might be a valid claim for £33,000 by a delay of only
a few days due to excusable inadvertence; accordingly the court would
exercise the discretion conferred by s. 27 of the Arbitration Act, 1950, and
would extend the time for fourteen days from the date of judgment (see
p. 938, letters E and G, p. 943, letters F and G, and p. 944, letter A, post).

Dictum of SINGLETON, L.J., in *Watney, Combe, Reid & Co., Ltd.* v. *E. M.
Dower & Co., Ltd.* ([1956] 2 Lloyd's Rep. at p. 330) applied.

Jajasan Urusan Bahan Makanan v. *Compania de Navegacion Geamar
Sociedade de Responsabilidad, Ltda.* ([1953] 1 Lloyd's Rep. 499) not followed.

F. E. Hookway & Co., Ltd. v. *H. W. Hooper & Co.* ([1950] 2 All E.R. 842, n.)
applied.

Appeal allowed.

[As to the extension of time by the court, see 2 HALSBURY's LAWS (3rd Edn.)
19, 20, para. 47; and for cases on the subject, see 2 DIGEST (Repl.) 421, 7, 8.

For the Arbitration Act, 1950, s. 27, see 29 HALSBURY's STATUTES (2nd Edn.)
113.]

Cases referred to:

Hookway (F. E.) & Co., Ltd. v. *H. W. Hooper & Co.*, (1950), 84 Lloyd L.R. 335;
    affd. C.A., [1950] 2 All E.R. 842, n.; 84 Lloyd L.R. 443; 2 Digest (Repl.)
    421, 7.

Hughes v. *Metropolitan Ry. Co.*, [1874-80] All E.R. Rep. 187; (1877), 2 App.
    Cas. 439; 46 L.J.Q.B. 583; 36 L.T. 932; 42 J.P. 421; 31 Digest (Repl.)
    556, 6557.

* Section 27 is printed at p. 936, letter B, post.

A   *Jajasan Urusan Bahan Makanan* v. *Compania de Navegacion Geamar Sociedade de Responsabilidad, Ltda.*, [1953] 1 Lloyd's Rep. 511; *on appeal*, [1953] 1 Lloyd's Rep. 499; 3rd Digest Supp.

      Sigalas (G.) Sons v. *Man Mohan Singh & Co.*, [1958] 2 Lloyd's Rep. 298; 3rd Digest Supp.

      Steamship Co. of 1912 & Steamship Co. Svendborg v. *Anglo-American Grain*

B   *Co., Ltd., The Leise Maersk*, [1958] 2 Lloyd's Rep. 341.

      Ward v. *James*, [1965] 1 All E.R. 563; [1966] 1 Q.B. 273; [1966] 2 W.L.R. 455; [1965] 1 Lloyd's Rep. 145; 3rd Digest Supp.

      Watney, Combe, Reid & Co., Ltd. v. *E. M. Dower & Co., Ltd.*, [1956] 2 Lloyd's Rep. 129; *affd.* C.A., [1956] 2 Lloyd's Rep. 325.

Appeal.

C   This was an appeal by notice dated Nov. 25, 1966, by the ship owners, Liberian Shipping Corporation, from an order of Donaldson, J., dated Nov. 3, 1966, allowing an appeal from an order of Master Lawrence, dated July 27, 1966. Master Lawrence had ordered that the time for giving notice of arbitration, appointing an arbitrator and otherwise commencing an arbitration under an arbitration clause contained in a charterparty dated Nov. 15, 1965, between the owners and

D A. King & Sons, Ltd., the defendant charterers, should be extended until fourteen days from the date of the order, the extension of time being granted under s. 27 of the Arbitration Act, 1950. Donaldson, J., ordered that this order should be set aside, and the owners appealed, seeking that Donaldson, J.'s order should be set aside and that the order of Master Lawrence should be restored. The grounds of appeal were—(i) that the judge erred, or exercised his discretion wrongly, in

E that he failed to take into account, or failed to attach sufficient weight to the fact, that the charterers invited the owners to travel to England to attend a meeting at which a settlement of the disputes between the parties was to be discussed, such meeting to take place after the three months' time limit for commencing arbitration had previously expired, or that the charterers thereby caused or contributed to a misunderstanding resulting in the failure to commence an

F arbitration within the three months' period; (ii) that the judge misdirected himself, or exercised his discretion wrongly, in that he ought to have held that by reason of the matters set out at (i) above the charterers were estopped from relying on the three months' limitation provisions contained in the arbitration clause; (iii) that the judge erred or exercised his discretion wrongly in that he failed to attach sufficient weight to the fact that the owners' claim for damage to the

G vessel amounted to a substantial sum, estimated to be more than £25,000, and that the existence or the extent of the bottom damage to the vessel was not known to the owners during the three months' period, and (iv) that the judge ought to have found that in all the circumstances of the case having regard to the reasons for the delay and the amount at stake, undue hardship would be caused to the owners if the time for giving notice of arbitration and appointing an arbitrator

H under the arbitration clause were not extended.

    The case mentioned below* was cited during the argument in addition to those referred to in the judgments.

    A. E. J. Diamond for the owners.
    Brian Davenport for the charterers.

I   **LORD DENNING, M.R.:** The question here is whether the owners of a ship are barred by a time limit. The charterparty contained an arbitration clause in the Centrocon form. It imposed a three months' time limit. The owners were nine days out of time in demanding an arbitration. They seek to have the time extended under s. 27 of the Arbitration Act, 1950, on the ground that it would be undue hardship for them to be time-barred. The clause in this charterparty is this:

---

    * *Bulgaris* v. *La Plata Cereal Co., S.A.*, (1947), 80 Lloyd L.R. 455.

" Any claim must be made in writing and claimant's arbitrator appointed   A
within three months of final discharge, and where this provision is not
complied with, the claim shall be deemed to be waived and absolutely barred."

Section 27 of the Arbitration Act, 1950, provides:

" Where the terms of an agreement to refer future disputes to arbitration
provide that any claims to which the agreement applies shall be barred unless   B
notice to appoint an arbitrator is given or an arbitrator is appointed or some
other step to commence arbitration proceedings is taken within a time fixed
by the agreement, and a dispute arises to which the agreement applies, the
High Court, if it is of opinion that in the circumstances of the case undue hardship would otherwise be caused, and notwithstanding that the time so fixed
has expired, may, on such terms, if any, as the justice of the case may require,   C
but without prejudice to the provisions of any enactment limiting the time for
the commencement of arbitration proceedings, extend the time for such period
as it thinks proper."

The facts are these. The owners of the motor vessel " Pegasus " on Nov. 15,
1965, let it out on a voyage charterparty whereby the vessel was to load a cargo
of scrap and turnings at Great Yarmouth and carry it to Italy to be discharged   D
at La Spezia as the first port and Portici as the second port. On Jan. 15, 1966,
the " Pegasus " was at Great Yarmouth and started loading. After Nos. 1 and 2
holds had been loaded with this swarf, as it is sometimes called, there was spon-
taneous combustion. It went up in flames. The fire brigades, after considerable
efforts, managed to put out the fire in those two holds. The swarf was discharged.
Other cargo was loaded. The loading was finished on Feb. 17, 1966. The vessel   E
left Great Yarmouth and went out to La Spezia. There was some delay. The
ship went on to Portici. She could not enter because the depth of water was not
sufficient. So she had to go on to a nearby port called Pozzuoli. Eventually
the cargo was discharged on Mar. 26, 1966. That is the important date. Under
the Centrocon clause either party had three months in which to make a claim
and appoint an arbitrator. So the three months would expire on June 26, 1966.   F

There were claims on both sides. The owners claimed £2,000 demurrage for
the delay caused to their vessel by the fire at Great Yarmouth. They asserted
a lien for it and it was paid. They also asserted that the vessel itself was damaged
by the fire. The inside of the vessel was damaged. They indicated also that the
outside was damaged. In a letter they said that, as a result of the fire-fighting,
" the ship broke her mooring wires, and it is highly possible that the rudder, pro-   G
peller and ship's structure below waterline also suffered damage ". In addition,
the owners claimed for delay at La Spezia and Pozzuoli. On the other hand, there
were cross-claims by the charterers. They said that they were put to expense by
reason of the failure to discharge at Portici, and having to arrange transport from
Pozzuoli.

In view of the cross-claims, a meeting was suggested. The owners' represent-   H
ative, Mr. Krapp, who was at Rotterdam, offered to come over from Rotterdam
to discuss the matter with the charterers' representives here. On May 23, 1966,
the charterers wrote:

" We feel very strongly that both ourselves and owners have been victims
of this most unfortunate fire. It has cost us something like £30,000, most of
which may never be recovered. We do not doubt that for owners it has like-   I
wise been a misfortune. Therefore, whilst maintaining adamantly our position
as indicated in this and previous letters, we have no objection to meeting Mr.
Krapp in London or Norwich and seeing if we cannot put our heads together,
as companions in misfortune, to dispose of all these troubles without further
endless correspondence."

There were one or two further letters. Eventually a letter was written by the
charterers on June 10, in these terms:

A   " Finally, we would again repeat that we are all victims of the tragic fire on the ' Pegasus '. We are anxious to show goodwill where possible and are quite happy to meet Mr. Krapp in England to see if we cannot settle everything amicably. Please try and arrange such an appointment, but you must make it clear to Mr. Krapp that his present bulldozing arguments will not influence us favourably."

B   That was on June 10. The three months would be up on June 26. Under the Centrocon clause the party had to appoint his arbitrator by that time or be barred absolutely. After June 10, there were telephone conversations, culminating on June 23, a Thursday, with an arrangement by telephone that Mr. Krapp should come over to London and discuss the matter with the charterers' representatives on Monday, June 27. That would be one day after the three months had expired.

C The meeting was in fact held on that day. There was a discussion for some three hours at which the various claims and counterclaims were discussed. No settlement was reached. The owners suggested arbitration, but the charterers said that they did not like arbitration as it was an expensive process. At the end of the meeting it was left that the charterers might make a proposal to settle the outstanding disputes. That meeting was held on June 27, one day after the three

D months had expired. Both sides had, it appears, overlooked the point about the time. No offer was forthcoming. The owners became anxious. On July 6, they put the matter before the Protection and Indemnity Association, who immediately were aware of the time limit. On the same day, that is about nine days after the time limit expired, their representative telephoned the charterers asking that the time limit be extended by agreement. It was not extended by agreement. At

E once the owners' solicitors applied to the court for an extension of time under s. 27 of the Arbitration Act, 1950. It was heard by Master LAWRENCE on July 27. He extended the time. The charterers appealed to DONALDSON, J., who is very experienced in commercial matters. He considered the authorities and held that owing to the restricted manner in which the courts have interpreted s. 27 (about undue hardship), the time should not be extended. He said:

F
    " I accept that there is hardship but within the narrow meaning of ' undue hardship ', this case does not come within a mile of it."

If his judgment stands, it means that the claim is absolutely barred because the owners were nine days out of time. After Master LAWRENCE had extended the time, the ship was in dry dock for an annual overhaul. It was discovered that

G there was a great deal of damage to the bottom, costing about £25,000 to £30,000 to put right. The owners say that it is due to the grounding during the fire, and seek to claim for it. They also claim for the damage to the inside of the vessel which they put at £5,000. They have, in addition, the claims for delay. Are these claims all barred, or can the time be extended?

  We have been referred to the cases on this subject. The courts have on occasion

H given a narrow meaning to " undue hardship ". Thus in *G. Sigalas Sons* v. *Man Mohan Singh & Co.* (1), LORD PARKER, C.J., said: " The powers of this court to extend the time, though discretionary, are only exercised in very restricted cases ". In that case the owners were only two days late, but the court did not extend the time.

  Counsel for the charterers, in his excellent argument, supported these cases

I by saying that commercial men must know where they stand; and that, as soon as the three months are up, they are entitled to consider that all claims are barred save in very exceptional circumstances. He said that exceptional circumstances would exist when the claimant was not at fault at all, as, for instance, where the claimant did not know that he had a claim within three months and could not reasonably be expected to know: for example, goods afterwards discovered not to be up to sample; or late claims by third parties. If, however, the claimant

---

(1) [1958] 2 Lloyd's Rep. 298 at p. 301.

was at fault himself in not reading the clause, or forgetting about it, or over- **A** looking it, the time should not be extended.

It does appear that in the past the courts have been inclined to emphasise the word " undue ", and to say that if a man does not read the contract and is a day or two late, it is a " hardship "; but it is not an " undue hardship ", because it is his own fault. I cannot accept this narrow interpretation of the statute. These time-limit clauses used to operate most unjustly. Claimants used to find their **B** claims barred when, by some oversight, they were only a day or two late. In order to avoid that injustice, the legislature intervened so as to enable the courts to extend the time whenever " in the circumstances of the case undue hardship would otherwise be caused ". " Undue " there simply means excessive. It means greater hardship than the circumstances warrant. Even though a claimant has been at fault himself, it is an undue hardship on him if the consequences are out **C** of proportion to his fault.

Applying this test, it seems to me that if a claimant makes a mistake which is excusable, and is in consequence a few days out of time, then if there is no preju- dice to the other side, it would be altogether too harsh to deprive him of all chance for ever of coming and making his claim. All the more so if the mistake is con- tributed to or shared by the other side. That indeed is this very case. I am quite **D** prepared to accept that the charterers, when they went to the meeting of June 27, did not intend to mislead the owners. They were both under a misapprehension. Neither of them realised that the time had already expired; but it is pretty plain that the conduct of the charterers put the owners off their guard. The owners would not contemplate that they would be barred whilst negotiations were still going on. As soon as they realised that the negotiations were not going to be **E** fruitful, they at once took the necessary steps. They were only nine days late. In these circumstances it seems to me it would be undue hardship to hold that the owners are barred absolutely. The case has a resemblance to *Hughes* v. *Metro-politan Ry. Co.* (2), where there were negotiations for a settlement and it was held that pending those negotiations, the strict rights of the parties did not apply.

It was said that this was a matter for the judge's discretion. True enough. **F** We have, however, said time and again that we will interfere with a judge's discretion if satisfied that the discretion was wrongly exercised. In any case the judge was not exercising an unfettered discretion. He felt himself fettered by the trend of the authorities to give the words " undue hardship " a narrow meaning. I think that we should reverse that trend and give the words their ordinary mean- ing, as Parliament intended. It would be " undue hardship " on the owners to **G** hold them barred by the clause. I would allow the appeal and restore the order of the master.

HARMAN, L.J.: I find myself constrained to take the opposite view. I should like very much to feel that these people were not shut out of what really they may have by the terms of the contract into which they entered. I do not **H** think, however, that we are at liberty, consistently with the view which our predecessors have taken of these matters, to be indulgent because we feel sym- pathy with people who have made a blunder. That is all it is. Where I depart from LORD DENNING, M.R., is where he says that the mistake was " contributed to or shared by " the other parties. Now I do not find any authority for those last words " or shared by " in the cases. It is said, and rightly said, that in **I** matters of this sort, which are questions of construction depending on the exact circumstances of the case, as the section shows, one case is not binding on another, for there always is some difference between one case and another.

Nevertheless, it is the duty of a court of construction to try and produce a consistent body of doctrine, so that people should know where they stand and not be at the whim of the particular court before whom they come. Borderline

---

(2) [1874-80] All E.R. Rep. 187; (1877), 2 App. Cas. 439.

A   cases may seem hard. *G. Sigalas Sons* v. *Man Mohan Singh & Co.* (3) before
LORD PARKER, C.J., to which LORD DENNING, M.R., referred, was a very hard
case because they were only two days out of time. Nevertheless LORD PARKER,
C.J., felt himself bound to hold that one could not deprive the other side of their
rights under the contract simply because one thought that two days was not a very
long time. A very little mistake is just as bad as a very big one, as far as I can
B   see, unless it is contributed to by the other side or caused by the other side, or
unless there is some other circumstance, for instance, a letter going astray in
the post or where an agent is negligent in performing his clear instructions or
where there is a sample which has not been seen. There must be some circumstance, however, which entitles the person who overstays his time to say: " That
is an undue hardship on me ".

C   In my judgment LORD DENNING, M.R., has construed those words as if
they were " hardship ". They are not " hardship ": they are " undue hardship ",
and that is something very different. In *Steamship Co. of 1912 & Steamship
Co. Svendborg* v. *Anglo-American Grain Co., Ltd., The Leise Maersk* (4), LORD
PARKER, C.J., had another instance of this in which he decided the other way.
He said (5):

D   " It has been said, over and over again by this court, that there must be
    very special circumstances for extending the time. Of course, if a valid claim
    is barred, there is hardship, but that is not what is provided for by the
    clause, and before this court can extend the time they must be satisfied that
    the hardship amounts in the particular case to undue hardship. This is very
    different from the case (6) which came before us earlier these sittings [the
E   case referred to by LORD DENNING, M.R., in his judgment] and, for myself,
    I am perfectly satisfied that the circumstances of this case come within the
    well known principle on which this court will extend the time, namely, that
    the failure to appoint the arbitrator was due to a misunderstanding, which
    misunderstanding, if not caused, was at least contributed to, by the other
    side."

F
One sees the distinction very clearly there. In this case there was no contribution
as I see it, and it is really hardly suggested that there was, by the other side. The
truth is that there had been negotiations and both parties had overlooked the
fact that time was running by them: but neither the owners nor the charterers
misrepresented the matter. When they arranged the meeting of June 27, they
G   overlooked the fact that the limiting date was June 26. They would not have
arranged a meeting on that day if either of them had thought of it. There is a
good warning, however, because, if one looks at the correspondence, already by
May 23, the charterers were writing in this way:

    " Therefore, whilst maintaining adamantly our position as indicated in
    this and previous letters, we have no objection to meeting Mr. Krapp in
H   London or Norwich and seeing if we cannot put our heads together, as
    companions in misfortune, to dispose of all these troubles without further
    endless correspondence."

They then go on to say that Mr. Krapp must not think that they are being weak
because they are being friendly. It may be that Mr. Krapp, by reason of the
tendency attributed to people of his nation, was giving too little and asking too
I   much in matters of business. The parties were miles apart. Mr. Krapp did not
get that letter for some time and did not answer it for some further time. Then
he rang up and asked for a meeting which was arranged for June 27.
    It does not seem to me that those circumstances, which are the only circum-
stances suggested as disentitling the charters to stand on their rights, do come up
to the kind of circumstances referred to by LORD PARKER, C.J., and referred to at

---

(3) [1958] 2 Lloyd's Rep. 298.   (4) [1958] 2 Lloyd's Rep. 341.
(5) [1958] 2 Lloyd's Rep. at p. 344.
(6) *G. Sigalas Sons* v. *Man Mohan Singh & Co.*, [1958] 2 Lloyd's Rep. 298.

length in his former judgment, where he quotes (7) LORD GODDARD, C.J., in **A**
Watney, Combe, Reid & Co., Ltd. v. *E. M. Dower & Co., Ltd.* (8) in which LORD
GODDARD, C.J., said this:

> " I desire to say in the clearest possible terms that the mere fact that the
> claimant is barred cannot be held to be an undue hardship, which is what the
> section requires to be found by the court before it extends the time. The
> section does not mean that this court can take out of the contract the **B**
> provision which will bar the claim if it is not pursued in time. They have no
> power to do that. The only thing they have power to do is to extend the time
> if undue hardship is caused. One can visualise certain cases of undue hard-
> ship."

HUMPHREYS, J., in another case (9) said: **C**

> " From all that, while no one attributes any blame to anyone at all, the
> fact appears that it was the laudable desire to save expense which principally
> accounted for the delay, and that saving of expense was the result of the
> action of the agents of the applicants, for whom, of course, they are respon-
> sible. This is not a case in which it can be said that there was any misunder-
> standing by anyone at all; still less can it be said that it was in any shape or **D**
> way the fault of the respondents that this sampling did not take place within
> the fourteen days allowed."

Therefore, one must find some fault or some misunderstanding, as I see it, on the
part of the person who is to suffer, before his vested rights, so to call them, are
taken away from him by the power of the court to extend the time. I quite agree
that the limit of so many days is to be read subject to the section of the Arbitration **E**
Act, 1950; and the court always has power to extend the time. We cannot do so
simply because there is hardship. In this case there is in my judgment no more.
The judge was quite right in what he said in his short judgment which was read to
us by counsel:

> " The learned master said that neither party was relying on the charter-
> party and that therefore the hardship was undue. But if this was his decision, **F**
> it is contrary to the whole trend of the authorities. I accept that there is
> hardship, but within the narrow meaning of undue hardship this case does
> not come within a mile of it."

I agree with that statement and I would dismiss the appeal.

      G

      SALMON, L.J.: I entirely agree with HARMAN, L.J., that everything in
this appeal turns on the true construction of the words " undue hardship ". I
further agree that it is not enough for the owners to show mere hardship. They
must show undue hardship. I am, however, unable to accept HARMAN, L.J.'s
construction of s. 27 of the Arbitration Act, 1950: nor that which has been
placed on it in several cases by the Divisional Court. The section, in so far as it **H**
is relevant, states that in relation to arbitration clauses such as the one we have
to consider,

> ". . . the High Court, if it is of opinion that in the circumstances of the
> case undue hardship would otherwise be caused, and notwithstanding that
> the time so fixed has expired, may, on such terms, if any, as the justice of the
> case may require . . . extend the time for such period as it thinks proper." **I**

That section seems to me to state quite plainly that if, having considered all
the circumstances of the case, the court comes to the conclusion that the hardship
imposed by the form of the arbitration clause on the claimant is greater than
that which, in justice, he should be called on to bear, the time within which to
appoint an arbitrator may be extended by the court. I do not believe that the

---

(7) [1958] 2 Lloyd's Rep. at p. 301.   (8) [1956] 2 Lloyd's Rep. 129 at p. 131.
(9) *F. E. Hookway & Co., Ltd.* v. *H. W. Hooper & Co.*, (1950), 84 Lloyd L.R. 335 at
p. 338.

A courts are entitled to read words into this section which are not there and which
would have the effect of cutting down the power given to the courts by the plain
language of the section itself.   Prior to this enactment, which was first introduced
into the law in 1934 (10), the commercial community—and not only the commercial community, but also those who practised and administered commercial
law—were shackled by the form, sometimes the printed form, of this type of
B arbitration clause.   It put it out of the power of the court to grant any relief to
a claimant who had allowed perhaps a day or two to run beyond the period
(sometimes only ten days) specified in the clause, even although the delay could
have caused no conceivable harm to the other side.   Commercial men and those
who practised and administered the commercial law had spent their working lives
with the law in this state.   They had no doubt experienced many cases in which
C a man with a perfectly good claim for thousands of pounds worth of damage
for breach of contract inadvertently allowed a day or two to go by and was
thereby deprived of the right to be compensated for the loss which he had suffered.
The other party, who had not been in any way affected by this slight delay and
who perhaps had been guilty of a deliberate breach of contract, was relieved
from liability to pay compensation for the heavy loss which he had caused.

D It was no doubt to remedy this hardship and injustice that the legislature
intervened to alter the law.   This enactment was a beneficent reform, liberalising
the law in an admittedly narrow sector of the commercial field.   I have heard
it said that when people have spent their lives in chains and the shackles are
eventually struck off, they cannot believe that their chains are no longer there.
They still feel bound by the shackles to which they have so long been accustomed
E To my mind, that factor may explain the court's approach in some of the cases
to the problem with which we are now faced. *Jajasan Urusan Bahan Makanan* v.
Compania de Navegacion Geamar Sociedade de Responsabilidad, Ltda., (11) was
decided by a very strong Divisional Court. LYNSKEY, J., said this (12):

F " I do not propose to define what undue hardship is in s. 27 of the Arbitration Act, 1950, but in my view it certainly does not apply to a case where
the whole cause of the trouble has been the applicants' own negligence or
failure to read their documents.   If that is the cause of their failure to
make a claim or to appoint an arbitrator in time, in my opinion that does not
amount to undue hardship within the meaning of the section, and I would
refuse the application for extension of time."

G He was concurring with LORD GODDARD, C.J., and PARKER, J., also agreed.
This case, which was followed by the Divisional Court in *G. Sigalas & Sons* v.
Man Mohan Singh & Co. (13), which seems to lay down that if the failure to
appoint an arbitrator within the time limit specified in the clause is due to any
fault on the part of the claimant, then whatever the circumstances of the case
may be, the court has no power to extend the time.   With very great respect,
H I profoundly disagree with that view.   There is nothing in s. 27 of the Act of
1950 to support it.   I cannot accept that when a man, who by reason of a breach
of contract has suffered perhaps thousands of pounds worth of damage
and due to some trivial inadvertence, but nevertheless due to his fault,
has failed to appoint an arbitrator until a few days after he should have
done so—even although that delay could not conceivably have done the other
side any harm—the court has no power to say: " In all the circumstances
I £33,000 is too big a price to pay for this inadvertence.   It would cause undue
hardship to deprive him of the chance of recouping the loss of that sum ".   The
contrary view would no doubt have been acceptable to those who argued for
the retention of capital punishment for theft.   It might have been said: " This
boy of fifteen stole the sheep.   How can you say that there is any undue hardship
in his being hanged?   The hardship cannot be undue hardship because it is

(10) The Arbitration Act, 1934, s. 16 (6).   (11) [1953] 1 Lloyd's Rep. 511.
(12) [1953] 1 Lloyd's Rep. at p. 513.   (13) [1958] 2 Lloyd's Rep. 298.

caused by his own fault ''. I certainly cannot see anything in the Act of 1950 which compels me to say that whatever the circumstances, a penalty of thousands of pounds should be exacted for a trivial piece of inadvertence which has done no one any harm.

It is to be observed that when this court considered the problem in *F. E. Hookway & Co., Ltd.* v. *H. W. Hooper & Co.* (14), it did not say that if there was any fault in the claimant that automatically put him out of court on an application for an extension of time. What SOMERVELL, L.J., said (and DENNING, L.J., who was the other member of the court, agreed) was that the fact that the delay was the fault of the person asking for the extension of time was a relevant circumstance for the court to take into account. So of course it is, but there is a vast difference between saying this is one of the relevant circumstances to take into account and saying, as it was said in the *Jajasan* case (15), that it is an absolute bar. I infinitely prefer, and indeed I am bound by, the approach of this court in *F. E. Hookway & Co., Ltd.* v. *H. W. Hooper & Co.* (14). It is true that in that case there was a refusal to extend the time, but that refusal turned on the facts of the case. It is interesting to note that in that case there was a very real chance that the delay had prejudiced the sellers. The buyers were seeking to reject and asking for arbitration out of time on the ground that the goods did not correspond with the sample, the goods having then been in the warehouse for some three weeks longer than they should have been. One of the objects of the clause in that case was that if the goods were rejected on those grounds, they should be rejected immediately after delivery so that the seller would know what their condition then was and would not be subjected to the risk of a further deterioration in the goods being laid at his door.

Counsel for the charterers in the course of his very able argument pointed out that in the *Jajasan* case (15) leave to appeal was refused by this court (16) and argued that if that case had been wrongly decided, leave to appeal would have been granted. It is worth noting, however, that by the time the application for leave to appeal was made to this court, the claimants had arrested the respondents' ship in New York and there was an action pending between the respondents and the claimants in the courts of the United States. It was argued on behalf of the respondents that not only was it not an undue hardship on the claimants to refuse to extend the time, but an extension of the time would impose a very real hardship on the respondents because they would then be faced simultaneously with an arbitration in England and with an action in the United States in respect of the same subject matter. Moreover, in 1953 the exercise of discretion by the court below was regarded as perhaps more sacrosanct than it is now since the decision of this court in *Ward* v. *James* (17). In *Watney, Combe, Reid & Co., Ltd.* v. *E. M. Dower & Co., Ltd.* (18), in the Divisional Court, LORD GODDARD, C.J., said in effect that he felt that there could be undue hardship only in cases where a man had been led by his opponent to believe something was happening which was not happening or if, through no fault of his own, he was unable to get some necessary information in time; but on the whole LORD GODDARD thought that what Parliament really had in mind was the type of case in which, if time were not extended, the claimant might be made bankrupt.

Those views were not, however, accepted by this court (19). SINGLETON, L.J., said (20):

"What, then, is the meaning of ' undue hardship ' ? ' Undue ', it is said by [counsel for the respondents] means something which is not merited by the conduct of the claimant. That may be right. If the result of claimants being perhaps a day late is so oppressive, so burdensome, as to be

---

(14) [1950] 2 All E.R. 842, n.; 84 Lloyd L.R. 443.
(15) [1953] 1 Lloyd's Rep. 511.   (16) [1953] 1 Lloyd's Rep. 499.
(17) [1965] 1 All E.R. 563; [1966] 1 Q.B. 273.
(18) [1956] 2 Lloyd's Rep. 129.   (19) [1956] 2 Lloyd's Rep. 325.
(20) [1956] 2 Lloyd's Rep. at p. 330.

altogether out of proportion to the fault, I am inclined to think that one may well say that there is undue hardship.   Both the amount at stake and the reasons for the delay are material considerations."

That appeal was dismissed on its facts and also on the ground that the Divisional Court had exercised its discretion.

In the present case I, for my part, agree with Harman, L.J., that it cannot be said that the charterers contributed to the delay.   The delay was solely caused by what I regard as the minor inadvertence by the owners.   It is quite obvious from the letters, which Lord Denning, M.R., has read, that although both sides were breathing fire against each other in the correspondence, they were both also expressing a willingness to meet and see whether, as ordinary sensible business men, they could not compose their differences.   Indeed on two occasions the charterers proposed a meeting in London for this purpose.   It is obvious from the fact that the charterers suggested June 27 as the day on which the conference should take place in London, that the charterers were quite unaware that time expired on June 26.   Counsel for the charterers says, and I naturally accept, that they had no idea that time expired on that day.   It would appear that the reason why they did not know that the time had expired was because they too had not looked at the arbitration clause.   They apparently did not do so until the delay had been pointed out to them in a telephone conversation on July 6, by the owners' representative when he asked for an extension of time.   The importance of that fact is that it shows conclusively that the charterers did not do anything or fail to do anything as a result of the time for appointing an arbitrator having expired.   They had not appreciated that the time for appointing an arbitrator had gone by, and indeed it has not been suggested and it could not be suggested that they have been in any way prejudiced by the delay.   I cannot find anything in s. 27 which in these circumstances compels me to say that it would not impose undue hardship on the claimants to hold they must forfeit their claim to some £33,000 because of this small delay which has had no effect at all on the charterers.   It is said rightly that commercial men enter into contracts such as the present on the basis of the arbitration clause.   They must be presumed, however, to read it in the light of s. 27.   I have no doubt at all that if two ordinary business men entering into this contract had been asked if it would cause undue hardship to refuse to extend the time should circumstances such as the present occur, they would both unhesitatingly have answered " Yes ".   I am not prepared to hold that the court's powers under the section should be very rarely exercised.   Still less that they should be exercised freely.   The question whether those powers should or should not be exercised must turn exclusively on the particular facts of each case in which the question arises.

In considering this question the court must take all the relevant circumstances of the case into account: the degree of blameworthiness of the claimants in failing to appoint an arbitrator within the time; the amount at stake, the length of the delay; whether the claimants have been misled, whether through some circumstances beyond their control it was impossible for them to appoint an arbitrator in time.   In the last two circumstances which I have mentioned, which do not arise here, it is obvious that normally the power would be exercised; but those are not the only circumstances and they are not, to my mind, necessary circumstances for the exercise of the power to extend time.   I do not intend to catalogue the circumstances to be taken into account, but one very important circumstance is whether there is any possibility of the other side having been prejudiced by the delay.   Of course, if there is such a possibility, it might be said that it is no undue hardship on the owners to refuse an extension of time because, if the hardship is lifted from their shoulders, some hardship will fall on the shoulders of the charterers, and, after all, the delay is the owners' fault.

There is, however, no such possibility in this case.   This is a simple case of a few days delay, caused by an excusable piece of inadvertence which has done the charterers no conceivable harm and which, unless we exercise the powers which in my view we undoubtedly have, will deprive the owners of what may turn out to be a valid claim for £33,000 and lift the liability off the shoulders of the charterers. I have no doubt but that this would cause the owners undue hardship. There is nothing in this Act of 1950 which obliges me to come to the conclusion that in these circumstances time should not be extended. Nor do I believe that I am bound by any of the cases to reach such a conclusion. The learned judge thought rightly that he was so bound and accordingly refused to extend the time. For the reasons that I have indicated, I would, however, allow the appeal.

Appeal allowed. Time extended for fourteen days from the date of judgment. Leave to appeal to the House of Lords granted.

Solicitors: *Holman, Fenwick & Willan* (for the owners); *Bentleys, Stokes & Lowless* (for the charterers).

[*Reported by* F. GUTTMAN, ESQ., *Barrister-at-Law.*]

RADZIEJ (otherwise SIERKOWSKA) *v.* RADZIEJ.

[PROBATE, DIVORCE AND ADMIRALTY DIVISION (Baker, J.), January 27, February 14, 1967.]

Variation of Settlement (Matrimonial Causes)—Post-nuptial settlement—House purchased to provide matrimonial home—Conveyance to spouses as joint tenants on trust for sale—Decree nisi of nullity to wife—Notice of severance to husband transforming equitable joint tenancy in proceeds of sale into tenancy in common—Right of wife to apply for variation of settlement to extinguish husband's rights in property—Matrimonial Causes Act 1965 (c. 72), s. 17, s. 19.

The parties, who were Polish, purported to marry in East Africa in 1947. In 1951, they came to England, and in 1958 bought a house in Leeds as their matrimonial home. This was conveyed to them as joint tenants on trust for sale, the proceeds of sale being declared to be on trust for them jointly. The wife, having discovered in 1964 that the husband had another wife who was living and three children, was granted a decree nisi of nullity on Feb. 21, 1966, which was made absolute on Nov. 10, 1966. On June 13, 1966, the wife's solicitor sent the husband a notice of severance, by which the equitable joint tenancy in the proceeds of sale was converted into a tenancy in common. The district registrar, on a summons by the wife under s. 17 and s. 19 of the Matrimonial Causes Act 1965, ordered the post-nuptial settlement to be varied so as to extinguish the husband's rights in the matrimonial home, subject to the wife paying him £205. The husband was also ordered to give up possession. On appeal by the husband,

Held: (i) the conveyance originally constituted a post-nuptial settlement, and the nuptial element was not lost by the giving of a notice of severance after the decree nisi (see p. 946, letter D, and p. 947, letter A, post; *Young v. Young*, [1961] 3 All E.R. 695, distinguished); moreover, although the beneficial interest in the proceeds of sale of the land conveyed had been severed, the legal estate remained unaffected, and the conveyance retained the attributes of a settlement, the creation of an equitable tenancy in common not being inconsistent with a post-nuptial settlement (see p. 946, letter I, post).

(ii) although the severance might have made it impossible for the wife to proceed under s. 17 of the Married Women's Property Act, 1882, or to maintain a denial in such proceedings, or on a sale by mutual consent or by order of the Chancery Division, that the husband was entitled to an equal

share, yet she was not estopped from applying under s. 17 and s. 19 of the
Act of 1965 to vary the post-nuptial settlement (see p. 947, letter C, post);
and, on the merits of the case the court would not interfere with the district
registrar's decision (see p. 947, letter I, post).

Appeal dismissed.

[As to the meaning of settlement for the purposes of the Matrimonial Causes
legislation, see 12 HALSBURY'S LAWS (3rd Edn.) 451, 452, paras. 1015-1017;
and for cases on the subject, see 27 DIGEST (Repl.) 645-649, *6089-6111*; DIGEST
(Cont. Vol. A) 799, 800, *6101a, 6101b, 6106c.*

For the Married Women's Property Act, 1882, s. 17, see 11 HALSBURY'S
STATUTES (2nd Edn.) 804.

For the Matrimonial Causes Act 1965, s. 17, s. 19, see 45 HALSBURY'S STATUTES
(2nd Edn.) 470, 473.]

Cases referred to:

Bedson v. *Bedson*, [1965] 3 All E.R. 307; [1965] 2 Q.B. 666; [1965] 3 W.L.R.
891; 3rd Digest Supp.

Brown v. *Brown*, [1959] 2 All E.R. 266; [1959] P. 86; [1959] 2 W.L.R. 776;
Digest (Cont. Vol. A) 799, *6101a.*

Cook v. *Cook*, [1962] 2 All E.R. 262; [1962] P. 235; [1962] 2 W.L.R. 963;
affd. C.A., [1962] 2 All E.R. 811; [1962] P. 235; [1962] 3 W.L.R. 441;
Digest (Cont. Vol. A) 799, *6101b.*

Tomkins v. *Tomkins*, [1948] 1 All E.R. 237; [1948] P. 170; [1948] L.J.R. 1028;
27 Digest (Repl.) 235, *1893.*

Young v. *Young*, [1961] 3 All E.R. 695; [1961] 3 W.L.R. 1109; sub nom.
Young v. *Young (No. 1)*, [1962] P. 27; Digest (Cont. Vol. A) 800, *6106c.*

Appeal.

This was an appeal by the husband from an order of Mr. District Registrar
LAWTON varying the terms of a post-nuptial settlement. The facts are set out in
the judgment.

J. Hampton for the husband.
S. Morris for the wife.

BAKER, J.: This matter came before me at Leeds Assizes on an application
to consider the district registrar's report on the wife's summons, under s. 17 and
s. 19 of the Matrimonial Causes Act 1965, to vary a post-nuptial settlement.
When it was discovered that the district registrar had in fact given a decision
(as he was entitled to do under (1) the Matrimonial Causes Rules, 1957, r. 52) and
that an order had been drawn up and published to both parties, counsel very
sensibly agreed to treat the hearing as an appeal from the order and thereby save
costs. Fear was expressed that the legal aid certificates might be prejudiced; the
arguments have been the same, the parties were not at fault and I trust that such
fears are groundless. The district registrar's order is

" that the terms of settlement in respect of the property described as 64,
Savile Place, Leeds, be varied so as to extinguish the rights of the [husband]
in the said property subject to the payment by the [wife] to the [husband]
of the sum of £205 payable on or before Jan. 20, 1967, [and] that the
[husband] do deliver up possession of the said property to the [wife] one
month after payment of the said sum of £205."

The husband, who is the appellant, contends: (i) there is now no settlement; (ii)
there is no nuptial element; (iii) if there is a post-nuptial settlement, it is no
longer susceptible to variation by the court; (iv) in any event the district
registrar's order is unjust and insupportable on the evidence.

The parties are Poles. They purported to marry on Oct. 24, 1947, in East

(1) S.I. 1957 No. 619. For r. 52, as amended, see 10 HALSBURY'S STATUTORY
INSTRUMENTS (Second Re-Issue) 256.

Africa where they were in a refugee settlement. There are no children. They came
to England in 1951, lived in a hostel until 1958, then bought 64, Savile Place,
Leeds, as their matrimonial home. They are living there to this day. In 1964 the
wife discovered that the husband had a living wife and three children. She
started proceedings for nullity in January, 1965. On Feb. 21, 1966, there was a
decree nisi which was made absolute on Nov. 10, 1966. The conveyance of 64,
Savile Place states that:

"in consideration of the sum of £600 paid by the purchasers to the
vendors . . . the vendors as trustees hereby convey to the purchasers . . .
No. 64 . . . to hold the same unto the purchasers in fee simple as joint
tenants."

Then cl. 3 (a) provides:

"The purchasers shall hold the said property upon trust to sell the same
with power to postpone the sale thereof and shall hold the net proceeds of sale
and other moneys applicable as capital and the net rents and profits thereof
until sale upon trust for themselves as joint tenants."

This conveyance was a post-nuptial settlement: see *Brown* v. *Brown* (2) and
Bedson v. *Bedson* (3), per LORD DENNING, M.R. On June 13, 1966, that is between
decree nisi and decree absolute, the wife's solicitor sent the husband a notice of
severance in the following terms:

"I Genevieve Radziej also called Genowefa Radziej of 64, Savile Place in
the city of Leeds hereby give you notice that as from the date hereof shall
treat (sic) the joint tenancy created by the conveyance dated Aug. 22, 1958
. . . as severed and converted in a tenancy (sic) in common as to one-half equal
share belonging to myself the said Genevieve Radziej also called Genowefa
Radziej and as to the other-half equal share to the said Wlodzimierz Radziej."

In his affidavit of Dec. 6, 1966, the husband, who is a registered blind person,
swore that he had not been served with the notice of severance. His counsel now
relies on it as putting an end to the post-nuptial settlement. Somebody, I can
only assume that he was the wife's solicitor, has endorsed a memorandum on the
conveyance as follows:

"By notice dated June 13, 1966 . . . the joint tenancy created by the
within written conveyance was severed and transformed into a tenancy in
common as to one-half share belonging to (Genowefa Radziej) . . . and to
other half share belong to (Wlodzimierz Radziej)."

The purpose of this notice of severance was, I am told, to sever the beneficial
joint tenancy and destroy the right of survivorship. LORD DENNING, in *Bedson*
v. *Bedson* (4), says that there can be no severance of the equitable interest so long
as the husband and wife are in possession as joint tenants, but I do not think that
this necessarily applies after decree nisi, and, in any event, RUSSELL, L.J.,
disagreed (5).

I think that the notice of severance here transformed the equitable joint
tenancy into an equitable tenancy in common leaving untouched the legal joint
tenancy held on trust for sale. The creation of an equitable tenancy in common is
not inconsistent with a post-nuptial settlement: see *Cook* v. *Cook* (6). It follows
that, although the beneficial interest has been severed and transformed, the
legal interest remains as it was originally created by the conveyance, which
retains the attributes of a settlement.

(2) [1959] 2 All E.R. 266; [1959] P. 86.
(3) [1965] 3 All E.R. 307 at p. 312; [1965] 2 Q.B. 666 at p. 679.
(4) [1965] 3 All E.R. at p. 311; [1965] 2 Q.B. at p. 678.
(5) [1965] 3 All E.R. at p. 319; [1965] 2 Q.B. at p. 690.
(6) [1962] 2 All E.R. 262, 811; [1962] P. 181, 235.

A   The conveyance was entered into on the footing that the marriage was to
continue, and I cannot accept that the nuptial element was lost by the giving of
a notice of severance after decree nisi. The facts in *Young* v. *Young* (7) were very
different. No settlement existed before decree nisi. There was never a nuptial
settlement.

The husband's third contention, however, is the most compelling. Counsel for
B   the husband says that, even if there is still a post-nuptial settlement, the wife
has made her choice. Having said by the severance " one-half equal share
belonging to myself ", she has settled her interest for all time at one-half equal
share, no more and no less, and from that moment it became irrelevant in what
proportion the parties had initially contributed. It may be that the severance
has made it impossible for here to proceed under s. 17 of the Married Women's
C   Property Act, 1882, or to deny that the husband is entitled to an equal share in
such proceedings, or on a sale by mutual consent or by order of the Chancery
Division, but I cannot find any justification or support for the contention that
she is estopped from applying to this court under s. 17 and s. 19 of the Matrimonial Causes Act 1965, to vary the post-nuptial settlement. Put shortly in the
language of the statute, where there is a post-nuptial settlement, this court can,
D   under s. 17 (1) (*b*),

> " make such orders as the court thinks fit as respects the application, for
> the benefit of . . . the parties to the marriage, of the whole or any part of the
> property settled."

It would be a catastrophe if the wife, by the endeavours of her legal advisers to
E   end the right of survivorship of a man who had never been her husband, but who
had secured the survivorship right on the assumption that he was, had lost her
statutory right to have the merits enquired into by this court.

What are the merits? The district registrar who heard oral evidence has said
that he accepts her evidence without hesitation where the parties differ. She is
reliable and the husband is not. He was dishonest and stole her £95. The main
F   facts are: (i) she provided £350 and he put up £300 for the purchase (both appear
to agree that £50 more than the purchase price of £600 was required); (ii) she
worked and took lodgers. The husband has been unemployed because of his lack
of sight since 1954. She has substantially maintained him and the house since
then, believing that she was married to him and that it was her duty; (iii) he
stole her savings of £95; (iv) he has used physical violence over a long period;
G   (v) he deceived her for seventeen years. LORD GREENE, M.R., said in *Tomkins*
v. *Tomkins* (8):

> " If a judge were to make an order based on the idea of punishing a person
> as being a guilty spouse, that order could not stand."

No such order is being made here and, indeed, one must have some sympathy
for the husband, however badly he has behaved, because of his disability and the
H   obvious hardship of life in an unknown dwelling. The wife has also to be considered. It is said that she will be able to use his room for another lodger and will
have a substantial income if she is given possession of the house, and that there
was no evidence of the present value of the house. These are matters which I
think that the district registrar must have had well in mind when exercising his
discretionary jurisdiction, and I should not interfere with his decision. I think
I   that his is the right order.

There is a final point. Counsel for the husband suggests that the £205 will be
subject to the Law Society's charge under s. 3 (4) of the Legal Aid and Advice
Act, 1949, which will result in the husband receiving little or nothing. No words
of mine can or should influence the Law Society who have a statutory duty to

---

(7) [1961] 3 All E.R. 695; [1962] P. 27.
(8) [1948] 1 All E.R. 237 at p. 240; [1948] P. 170 at p. 175.

perform, but I understand that this sum would probably be treated as the husband's share of the property and not subject to a lien or charge by them. If so, there is no further hardship.

The appeal fails.

Appeal dismissed.

Solicitors: *Lovell, White & King,* agents for *Denis Lyth,* Leeds (for the husband); *B. B. Fielding,* Leeds (for the wife).

[*Reported by* ALICE BLOOMFIELD, *Barrister-at-Law.*]

CHAN WAI-KEUNG *v.* REGINAM.

[PRIVY COUNCIL (Lord Hodson, Lord Pearce and Lord Pearson), October 6, 10, November 7, 1966.]

Privy Council—Hong Kong—Criminal law—Evidence—Confession—Admissibility determined by judge—Whether summing-up should include direction to disregard confession unless jury satisfied beyond all reasonable doubt as to its voluntary character.

In regard to confessions and admissions by persons accused of crime, the question of admissibility, viz., whether the statement was voluntarily made, is for the judge, who for this purpose must decide independently of the jury both the relevant facts and the law; if the statement is admitted, then the question of its probative value or effect, which is a different question from its admissibility, is for the jury, and in order to determine this it may be necessary to go over before the jury testimony that the judge has heard when deciding whether the statement was voluntary (see p. 953, letters B and H, post).

Basto v. *Reginam* ((1954), 91 C.L.R. 628 at p. 640) adopted; *R.* v. *Murray* ([1950] 2 All E.R. 925) applied.

Dictum of BYRNE, J., in *R.* v. *Bass* ([1953] 1 All E.R. at p. 1065) not followed.

At the trial of the accused for murder the evidence against him consisted of two written statements or confessions made by him to the police after caution. The admissibility of these was challenged and, in the absence of the jury, the trial judge ruled that they were admissible. Whether the statements were voluntary was again challenged subsequently in the evidence given before the jury. The trial judge did not add to his direction on the onus of proof of the crime a further direction that the jury must be satisfied that the statements were voluntary and, if not so satisfied, should give no weight to them.

Held: the trial judge's directions to the jury were not open to objection on the ground that he did not add the further specific direction that the jury must be satisfied beyond reasonable doubt as to the voluntariness of the statements before giving them consideration (see p. 954, letter B, post).

Appeal dismissed.

[As to the functions of the trial judge in regard to questions of admissibility of confessions, see 10 HALSBURY'S LAWS (3rd Edn.) 470, para. 863; and for cases on confessions made to the police, see 14 DIGEST (Repl.) 474-477, *4528-4577*.]

Cases referred to:

Bartlett v. Smith, (1843), 11 M. & W. 483; 12 L.J.Ex. 287; 1 L.T.O.S. 149; 152 E.R. 895; 22 Digest (Repl.) 29, *90.*

Basto v. Reginam, (1954), 91 C.L.R. 628.

Cornelius v. Regem, (1936), 55 C.L.R. 235; [1936] V.L.R. 222; 10 A.L.J. 118; 14 Digest (Repl.) 471, *3032.*

Adopted in R. *v.* OVENELL. [1968] 1 All E.R. 933.

Ibrahim v. *Regem*, [1914-15] All E.R. Rep. 874; [1914] A.C. 599; 83 L.J.P.C.
    185; 111 L.T. 20; 24 Cox, C.C. 174; 14 Digest (Repl.) 468, *4513.*

Lau Hoi v. *Regem*, (1948), 32 H.K.L.R. 49.

Minter v. *Priest*, [1930] All E.R. 431; [1930] A.C. 558; 99 L.J.K.B. 391;
    143 L.T. 57; 22 Digest (Repl.) 405, *4351.*

R. v. *Bass*, [1953] 1 All E.R. 1064; [1953] 1 Q.B. 680; [1953] 2 W.L.R. 825;
    117 J.P. 246; 37 Cr. App. Rep. 51; 14 Digest (Repl.) 476, *4568.*

R. v. *Czerwinski*, [1954] V.L.R. 483; [1954] A.L.R. 621; 14 Digest (Repl.)
    460, **2910.*

R. v. *Francis, R.* v. *Murphy*, (1959), 43 Cr. App. Rep. 174; Digest (Cont. Vol.
    A) 368, *4448a.*

R. v. *McAloon*, (1959), 124 Can. Crim. Cas. 182; [1959] O.R. 441; [1959]
    O.W.N. 203; 30 C.R. 305; Digest (Cont. Vol. A) 358, **1935a.*

R. v. *McLaren*, [1949] 2 D.L.R. 682; [1949] 1 W.W. R. 529; 93 Can. Crim. Cas.
    296; 7 C.R. 402; 14 Digest (Repl.) 470, **3009.*

R. v. *Murray*, [1950] 2 All E.R. 925; [1951] 1 K.B. 391; 114 J.P. 609; 34 Cr.
    App. Rep. 203; 14 Digest (Repl.) 469, *4523.*

Sparks v. *Reginam*, [1964] 1 All E.R. 727; [1964] A.C. 964; [1964] 2 W.L.R.
    566; 3rd Digest Supp.

Appeal.

This was an appeal in forma pauperis, by special leave, from a judgment and
order of the Supreme Court of Hong Kong in its appellate jurisdiction (RIGBY, J.
MACFEE and HUGGINS, A.JJ.) dated Oct. 8, 1965, whereby the appellant's appeal
against his conviction on a charge of murder and sentence of death before the
Supreme Court of Hong Kong in its criminal jurisdiction (BRIGGS, J., and a jury)
was dismissed.

S. P. Khambatta, Q.C., and *G. L. D. de Silva* for the appellant.
J. G. Le Quesne, Q.C., and *F. Addison* (of the Hong Kong Bar) for the Crown.

LORD HODSON: This is an appeal from the judgment of the Court of
Appeal of the Supreme Court of Hong Kong (RIGBY, J., MACFEE and HUGGINS,
A.JJ.) dated Oct. 8, 1965, whereby the appellant's appeal against his conviction
of murder and sentence of death in the Supreme Court of Hong Kong on Aug. 11,
1965, was dismissed.

The trial took place before BRIGGS, J., and a jury and the question on the
appeal is whether or not the judge's direction to the jury was adequate or not
in the following circumstances. The evidence for the Crown included the following:

The deceased Leung Pui-chuen was employed as a night watchman at the
Bonnie Hair Products Factory, 95A, Ha Heung Road, on the ninth floor. Above
that, on the roof top, the appellant was employed until May 10, 1965. He left
the premises, having spent the night there, on May 11, 1965. The deceased
was last seen alive at 11.05 p.m. on May 11, 1965, and his body was discovered at
8.30 a.m. on May 12, 1965, lying on a canvas bed inside his employer's premises.
Dr. Lee Fuk-Kee said that the cause of death was shock and haemorrhage from
multiple injuries to the head which were consistent with an attack with an iron
rod similar to that found on the premises.

The appellant was seen on May 25 and on that evening agreed to go to the
Hung Hom Police Station. On arrival there at 9.10 p.m. he was questioned
and made a statement describing his movements on the night of May 11/12, 1965,
and on the succeeding night, claiming to have been in the company of certain
persons. On May 25 he was confronted with four of these persons, who denied in
his presence that they had seen him on May 11/12, 1965. After the fourth of
those persons had left the room where the confrontation took place, the appellant
said words to the effect that the officer need not ask him so many questions:
he was bored with them and would tell what really happened. He was cautioned
and made two written statements confessing to the murder of the deceased.

The case for the prosecution rested entirely on these two statements. The admissibility of the statements was challenged. After hearing evidence in the absence of the jury, BRIGGS, J., ruled that these statements were voluntary and, therefore, admissible. The voluntary character of the statements was again challenged in the course of evidence subsequently given in the presence of the jury.

The appellant's contention is that the judge failed to direct the jury adequately, because, although the judge's general direction to the jury that they must be satisfied beyond reasonable doubt of the guilt of the appellant was not open to criticism, yet, he should have added a further direction that the jury must be satisfied whether the confessions were made voluntarily and, if not so satisfied, they should give no weight to them and disregard them. This, it is said, he did not do, and the majority of the Court of Appeal would have allowed the appeal on this ground but for a technical difficulty which need not now be discussed.

The law of Hong Kong is the same as the law of England as it existed on Apr. 5, 1843, with any modifications made by local statutes. The Criminal Procedure Ordinance, 1899, s. 60, provides:

" If on a trial by jury of a person accused of an offence, a statement alleged to have been made by such accused person is admitted in evidence, all evidence relating to the circumstances in which the alleged statement was made shall be admissible for the purpose of enabling the jury to decide upon the weight (if any) to be given to the statement; and, if any such evidence has been taken in the absence of the jury before the admission of the statement, the Crown and such accused person shall have the right to have any such evidence retaken in the presence of the jury."

This section appears to have been brought into existence in 1949 to correct the effect of a decision of the previous year, namely *Lau Hoi* v. *Regem* (1). However this may be, in their lordships' opinion, there is no inconsistency between this section and the law of England. There is no doubt that the question whether a confession is voluntary is determined by the judge on the voir dire in order to decide whether it is admissible or not and that at this stage the accused may give evidence himself as well as call witnesses.

In the civil case of *Bartlett* v. *Smith* (2) the admissibility of a bill of exchange was objected to. LORD ABINGER, C.B., said (3) categorically that all questions respecting the admissibility of evidence are to be determined by the judge, who ought to receive that evidence and decide on it without any reference to the jury. PARKE, B., was of the same opinion (4) and recollected the case of Major Campbell who was indicted for murder in Ireland. On a dying declaration being tendered in evidence, the judge left it to the jury to say whether the deceased knew, when he made it, that he was at the point of death. The question as to the propriety of the course adopted was sent over for the opinion of the English judges, who returned for answer that the course taken was not the right one, and that the judge ought to have decided the question himself. ALDERSON, B., was of the same opinion and said (4):

" Where a question arises as to the admissibility of evidence, the facts upon which its admissibility depends are to be determined by the judge, and not by the jury. If the opposite course were adopted, it would be equivalent to leaving it to the jury to say whether a particular thing were evidence or not. It might as well be contended that a judge ought to leave to the jury the question, whether sufficient search had been made for a document so as to admit secondary evidence of its contents."

ROLFE, B., concurred (4).

(1948), 32 H.K.L.R. 49.   (2) (1843), 11 M. & W. 483.
843), 11 M. & W. at p. 485.   (4) (1843), 11 M. & W. at p. 486.

In *Minter* v. *Priest* (5) the House of Lords had to determine a question as to the admissibility of evidence and LORD ATKIN put the matter succinctly in these words (6):

" The question is one of admissibility of evidence; and on all such questions it is for the judge to decide after hearing if necessary evidence on both sides bearing on any contested question of fact relevant to the question. Thus the question whether a confession is voluntary or a deposition admissible as a dying deposition are questions to be determined by the judge and not the jury. Cf. *Bartlett* v. *Smith* (7)"

The truth of the confession is not directly relevant at the voir dire, although it will be a crucial question for the jury if the judge admits it. This is well illustrated by a decision of the Court of Criminal Appeal, *R.* v. *Murray* (8). There the only evidence against the prisoner on an indictment for felony was a confession signed by him but not, as he alleged, voluntarily made. The recorder having heard evidence from the police and the prisoner held that it had been properly obtained and was admissible. He, however, refused to allow counsel for the accused to cross-examine the police again in the presence of the jury as to the manner in which the confession had been obtained, and in his summing-up he told the jury that they must accept from him that the confession was a voluntary one obtained from the prisoner without duress, bribe or threat. LORD GODDARD, C.J., delivered (9) the judgment of the court, consisting of himself, BYRNE and McNAIR, JJ., which allowed the appeal and used these words (10):

" It has always, as far as this court is aware . . . been the right of counsel for the defence to cross-examine again before the jury the witnesses who have already given evidence in the absence of the jury, because, if he can induce the jury to think that the confession has been obtained by some threat or promise, its value is enormously weakened. The weight of the evidence, and value of the evidence, is always for the jury."

This gives the accused a second chance of attacking the confession, but it is a, long way from saying that the jury must be directed specifically that the Crown must satisfy them beyond reasonable doubt that the confession is voluntary and that otherwise they must disregard it. This would be to disregard the fact that voluntariness is a test of admissibility not an absolute test of the truth of the statement.

Their lordships have been referred to a recent decision of the Privy Council, *Sparks* v. *Reginam* (11) where the question of admissibility of confessions arose. LORD MORRIS OF BORTH-Y-GEST in delivering the judgment of the Board (12) cited the words of LORD SUMNER in an earlier case before the Privy Council, *Ibrahim* v. *Regem* (13) where he said:

" It has long been established as a positive rule of English criminal law, that no statement by an accused is admissible in evidence against him unless it is shown by the prosecution to have been a voluntary statement in the sense that it has not been obtained from him either by fear of prejudice or hope of advantage exercised or held out by a person in authority."

Their lordships will refer to this citation again, but draw attention at this point to the fact that LORD SUMNER (14) was dealing with the admissibility of evidence

(5) [1930] All E.R. Rep. 431; [1930] A.C. 558.
(6) [1930] All E.R. Rep. at p. 440; [1930] A.C. at p. 581.
(7) (1843), 11 M. & W. 483.
(8) [1950] 2 All E.R. 925; [1951] 1 K.B. 391.
(9) [1950] 2 All E.R. at p. 926; [1951] 1 K.B. at p. 392.
(10) [1950] 2 All E.R. at p. 927; [1951] 1 K.B. at p. 393.
(11) [1964] 1 All E.R. 727; [1964] A.C. 964.
(12) [1964] 1 All E.R. at p. 735; [1964] A.C. at p. 981.
(13) [1914-15] All E.R. Rep. 874 at p. 877; [1914] A.C. 599 at p. 609.
(14) [1914-15] All E.R. Rep. at p. 877; [1914] A.C. at p. 609.

and not its truth or weight. In the *Sparks* case (15) LORD MORRIS referred to
the admissibility of statements made by the appellant, saying (16):

> " If they were held by the learned judge to be admissible, it was still open
> to the prosecution and the defence to allow the jury to hear the testimony
> as to the circumstances under which they came into being so that the jury,
> forming their own opinion as to the testimony, could decide what weight
> to give to the statements or could decide not to give any weight at all to
> them for the reason that they (the jury) were not satisfied that they were
> voluntary statements. An accused person is, however, entitled in the first
> place to have evidence excluded if, on the view of the facts which is accepted
> by the learned judge at the trial, it is not shown that the evidence is legally
> admissible."

True that the point now under consideration did not arise (indeed the reference
(17) to the case of *R.* v. *Francis, R.* v. *Murphy* (18) indicates that it did not),
yet the passage which has been cited from the *Sparks* case (16) is consistent with
the distinction which can be drawn from the cited cases, between voluntariness
as a test of admissibility and as a matter to be considered by the jury in arriving
at the truth.

The contention of the appellant to which their lordships now turn derives
from a decision of the Court of Appeal in *R.* v. *Bass* (19) where BYRNE, J., speaking
(20) for himself and LORD GODDARD, C.J., and PARKER, J., used language
which has made it appear that one question for the jury is whether they are
satisfied that the statements are voluntary and that they should be so told.
The full passage reads (21):

> " It is to be observed, as this court pointed out in *R.* v. *Murray* (22), that,
> while it is for the presiding judge to rule whether the statement is admissible,
> its for the jury to determine the weight to be given to it if he admits it, and
> thus, when a statement has been admitted by the judge, he should direct the
> jury to apply to their consideration of it the principle as stated by LORD
> SUMNER [in *Ibrahim* v. *Regem* (23)] and he should further tell them that, if
> they are not satisfied that it was made voluntarily, they should give it no
> weight at all and disregard it."

The passage from LORD SUMNER's judgment (23) has been referred to already
and deals with admissibility and the meaning of the word voluntary. The
language of BYRNE, J. (21) may have been intended to go no further than the
decision in *R.* v. *Murray* (22) for the former judgment was given by LORD GOD-
DARD, C.J. (24), who was a party to the *Bass* case (19), but it is susceptible of
the construction that a jury must always be told to disregard a confession which
was not in their view made voluntarily even if they should consider it to be true.
The difficulties of accepting the language of BYRNE, J. (21) literally have led
the High Court of Australia to doubt this part of the judgment in *R.* v. *Bass* (19).
In *Basto* v. *Reginam* (25), where the court consisted of DIXON, C.J., WEBB,
FULLAGAR, KITTO and TAYLOR, JJ., after a reference to *R.* v. *Murray* (22),
the court said (26):

> " The jury is not concerned with the admissibility of the evidence; that is

(15) [1964] 1 All E.R. 727; [1964] A.C. 964.
(16) [1964] 1 All E.R. at p. 736; [1964] A.C. at p. 983.
(17) [1964] 1 All E.R. at p. 736; [1964] A.C. at pp. 982, 983.
(18) (1959), 43 Cr. App. Rep. 174.
(19) [1953] 1 All E.R. 1064; [1953] 1 Q.B. 680.
(20) [1953] 1 All E.R. at p. 1065; [1953] 1 Q.B. at p. 683.
(21) [1953] 1 All E.R. at p. 1066; [1953] 1 Q.B. at p. 684.
(22) [1950] 2 All E.R. 925; [1951] 1 K.B. 391.
(23) [1914-15] All E.R. Rep. at p. 877; [1914] A.C. at p. 609.
(24) [1950] 2 All E.R. at p. 926; [1951] 1 K.B. at p. 392.
(25) (1954), 91 C.L.R. 628.
(26) (1954), 91 C.L.R. at p. 640.

for the judge, whose ruling is conclusive upon the jury and who for the purpose of making it must decide both the facts and the law for himself independently of the jury.   Once the evidence is admitted the only question for the jury to consider with reference to the evidence so admitted is its probative value or effect.   For that purpose it must sometimes be necessary to go over before the jury the same testimony and material as the judge has heard or considered on a voir dire for the purpose of deciding the admissibility of the accused's confessional statements as voluntarily made.   The jury's consideration of the probative value of statements attributed to the prisoner must, of course, be independent of any views the judge has formed or expressed in deciding that the statements were voluntary.   Moreover the question what probative value should be allowed to the statements made by the prisoner is not the same as the question whether they are voluntary statements nor at all dependent upon the answers to the latter question. A confessional statement may be voluntary and yet to act upon it might be quite unsafe; it may have no probative value.   Or such a statement may be involuntary and yet carry with it the greatest assurance of its reliability or truth.   That a statement may not be voluntary and yet according to circumstances may be safely acted upon as representing the truth is apparent if the case is considered of a promise of advantage being held out by a person in authority.   A statement induced by such a promise is involuntary within the doctrine of the common law, but it is plain enough that the inducement is not of such a kind as often will be really likely to result in a prisoner's making an untrue confessional statement."

Later commenting on *R.* v. *Bass* (27) the court said (28):

" Unfortunately, in *R.* v. *Bass* (27) BYRNE, J., speaking for himself and LORD GODDARD, C.J., and PARKER, J., used language (29) which makes it appear that the question for the jury is whether the statements are voluntary and that they must be so told. 'When a statement has been admitted by the judge, he should direct the jury to apply to their consideration of it the principle as stated by LORD SUMNER (in *Ibrahim* v. *Regem* (30)) and he should further tell them that if they are not satisfied that it was made voluntarily they should give it no weight at all and disregard it.'   With all respect, this cannot be right. The admissibility of evidence is not for the jury to decide, be it dependent on fact or law: and voluntariness is only a test of admissibility: see *Cornelius* v. *Regem* (31).   The true view is expressed by the Supreme Court of Victoria in a judgment delivered by GAVAN DUFFY, J., in *R.* v. *Czerwinski* (32)."

In an earlier passage (33) the court referred to the case of *R.* v. *Murray* (34) as being in accord with their view.

Their lordships have been referred to other cases in Australia and to the Canadian cases of *R.* v. *McAloon* (35) and *R.* v. *McLaren* (36).   The commonwealth decisions are all in line with the judgment of LORD GODDARD in *R.* v. *Murray* (34) and in their lordships' opinion they correctly express the law as to the admissibility of evidence and direction to the jury after evidence has been admitted.

R. v. *Bass* (27) on its literal interpretation has led the Court of Criminal Appeal in several cases, apparently without hearing argument, to restate the necessity of a separate direction to the jury to the effect that they must be satisfied beyond

(27) [1953] 1 All E.R. 1064; [1953] 1 Q.B. 680.
(28) (1954), 91 C.L.R. at pp. 640, 641.
(29) [1953] 1 All E.R. at p. 1066; [1953] 1 Q.B. at p. 684.
(30) [1914-15] All E.R. Rep. at p. 877; [1914] A.C. at p. 609.
(31) (1936), 55 C.L.R. 235 at pp. 246, 248, 249.
(32) [1954] V.L.R. 483.   (33) (1954), 91 C.L.R. at p. 640.
(34) [1950] 2 All E.R. 925; [1951] 1 K.B. 391.
(35) [1959] O.R. 441.   (36) [1949] 1 W.W.R. 529; [1949] 2 D.L.R. 682.

reasonable doubt as to the voluntariness of statements notwithstanding their admission after a decision has been given as to admissibility by the judge. Many of the cases are to be found only in newspaper reports but one, namely *R.* v. *Francis, R.* v. *Murphy* (37) was reported and was noticed in the judgment delivered by LORD MORRIS in *Sparks* v. *Reginam* (38).

Their lordships are of opinion that the judge's direction to the jury is not open to criticism on the ground that he did not follow the course of giving a specific direction that the jury must be satisfied beyond reasonable doubt as to the voluntariness of the confessions before giving them any consideration.

It should be added that the Crown contended that if such a course were necessary the learned judge's direction, when read as a whole, was sufficient to comply with the need for a specific direction of this kind. It is unnecessary to pursue this matter in detail for their lordships are in agreement with the judges in the appellate court, that, had it been necessary for the jury to decide as a separate issue whether the appellant's statements had been voluntarily made, the direction was insufficient.

Their lordships have accordingly humbly advised Her Majesty that this appeal be dismissed.

Appeal dismissed.

Solicitors: *T. L. Wilson & Co.* (for the appellant); *Charles Russell & Co.* (for the Crown).

[*Reported by* KATHLEEN J. H. O'BRIEN, *Barrister-at-Law.*]

COMMISSIONER OF INCOME TAX
v. HANOVER AGENCIES, LTD.

[PRIVY COUNCIL (Lord Guest, Lord Upjohn and Lord Pearson), November 7, 8, December 14, 1966.]

Privy Council—Jamaica—Income Tax—Business—Carrying on business—Acquisition and letting of premises—Wear and tear allowance—Whether acquisition and letting of premises was a business—Whether building let was used by owner for the purpose of acquiring income from a business carried on by him—Income Tax Law (No. 59 of 1954), s. 8 (o).

In 1944 a business, one of whose objects was the acquiring and letting of property, was purchased by predecessors of the respondent company, and in 1947 the business was vested in the respondent company which was formed to carry it on. The business included that of merchants dealing in hardware and lumber, and that of operating a wharf, as well as that of letting premises. In 1945 three buildings were purchased by the business. One of these buildings (" Bank Building ") was subsequently pulled down, rebuilt and leased. On appeal from an order upholding the respondent company's claim to an allowance for wear and tear in respect of bank building under s. 8 (o)* of the Income Tax Law, 1954, of Jamaica,

Held: s. 8 (o) of the Income Tax Law, 1954, was satisfied in regard to Bank Building, and the respondent company were accordingly entitled to an allowance for wear and tear in respect of it for the following reasons—

(i) because the respondent company were in fact carrying out their object of acquiring and leasing properties and accordingly were carrying on that business, and profits on which the respondent company were assessed arose from the business, viz., the acquisition and renting of Bank Building (see p. 956, letter G, and p. 957, letter H, post).

---

(37) (1959) 43 Cr. App. Rep. 174.
(38) [1964] 1 All E.R. at p. 736; [1964] A.C. at pp. 982, 983.
* The relevant terms of s. 8 (o) are set out at p. 956, letter B, post.

Dictum of SIR ERNEST POLLOCK, M.R., in *Inland Revenue Comrs. v. West-leigh Estates Co., Ltd.* ([1924] 1 K.B. at pp. 408, 409) followed.

(ii) because, since the respondent company carried on a business of letting premises, they were " using " Bank Building for the purpose of acquiring the income from that business within s. 8 (*o*) of the Law of 1954 (see p. 958, letters A and B, post).

Dictum of FURNESS, C.J., in *Hendriks* v. (*Income Tax*) *Assessment Committee* ((1941), 4 J.L.R. 60) disapproved.

Appeal dismissed.

[As to the question, in English income tax law, of whether there is a trade being one of fact, see 20 HALSBURY'S LAWS (3rd Edn.) 114, para. 207; cf. ibid., p. 110, para. 202; and for cases on the subject, see 28 DIGEST (Repl.) 395-397, *1740-1752.*]

Cases referred to:

Fry v. *Salisbury House Estate, Ltd.; Jones* v. *City of London Real Property Co., Ltd.,* [1930] All E.R. Rep. 538; [1930] A.C. 432; 99 L.J.K.B. 403; 143 L.T. 77; 15 Tax Cas. 266; 28 Digest (Repl.) 33, *148.*

Hendriks v. (*Income Tax*) *Assessment Committee,* (1941), 4 J.L.R. 60.

Inland Revenue Comrs. v. *Westleigh Estates Co., Ltd.,* [1924] 1 K.B. 390; 93 L.J.K.B. 289; 130 L.T. 538; 12 Tax Cas. 657; 28 Digest (Repl.) 450, *1940.*

Appeal.

This was an appeal by the Commissioner of Income Tax from a judgment and order of the Court of Appeal of Jamaica (DUFFUS, P., HENRIQUES and WADDING-TON, JJ.) dated Dec. 18, 1964, allowing an appeal by the respondents Hanover Agencies, Ltd. from an order made by SHELLEY, J., dated Oct. 18, 1963, whereby the respondents' appeal from a decision of the Income Tax Appeal Board of Jamaica dated May 1, 1963, upholding an assessment to income tax made on the respondents in respect of the year of assessment 1960, was dismissed.

In the Case for the appellant the following reasons for appeal were given: (a) that the Income Tax Appeal Board misdirected themselves in law in deciding that the respondents were carrying on a business of renting premises in that the negotiation of leases and the collection of rents could not constitute the carrying on of a business within the meaning of s. 5 (*a*) (ii)* of the Income Tax Law, 1954, and that there was no evidence on which the board could properly arrive at their decision in this respect; and (b) that the premises owned and let by the respondents were not used by their owners for the purpose of acquiring income from a business and so did not qualify for an allowance under s. 8 (*o*) of the Law of 1954. The facts are summarised in the opinion of LORD GUEST, at p. 956, letters C to F, post.

Hubert H. Monroe, Q.C., and *M. P. Nolan* for the appellant.
David Coore, Q.C. (of the Jamaican Bar) and *S. T. Bates* for the respondents.

LORD GUEST: This is an appeal from a judgment of the Court of Appeal of Jamaica allowing an appeal by the respondents from an order made by SHELLEY, J., by which order the respondents' appeal against a decision of the Income Tax Appeal Board of Jamaica was dismissed. By this decision the Income Tax Appeal Board upheld an assessment to income tax, dated Jan. 5, 1962, made on the respondents for the year of assessment 1960.

---

* Section 5 of the Income Tax Law, 1954, provides, so far as is material: " Income Tax shall, subject to the provisions of this Law, be payable by every person at the rate or rates specified hereafter for each year of assessment in respect of all income, profits or gains respectively described hereunder—(*a*) the annual profits or gains arising or accruing—(i) to any person residing in the Island from any kind of property whatever, whether situate in the Island or elsewhere; and (ii) to any person residing in the Island from any trade, business, profession, employment or vocation whether carried on in the Island or elsewhere; . . (*b*) profits or gains accruing in or derived from the Island or elsewhere, and whether received in the Island or not in respect of—. . . (ii) rents, royalties, premiums and any other profits arising from property; . . ."

The respondents unsuccessfully appealed to the Income Tax Appeal Board against the determination of the appellant as to the assessment on the company for the year of assessment of 1960 claiming to be entitled under s. 8 (o) of the Income Tax Law of Jamaica to an allowance for wear and tear in respect of a building known as the " Bank Building ". Section 8 (o) of the Income Tax Law, 1954, so far as relevant is in the following terms:

" For the purpose of ascertaining the chargeable income of any person there shall be deducted all disbursements and expenses wholly and exclusively incurred by such person in acquiring the income . . . and such disbursements and expenses may include . . .

" (o) a reasonable amount for exhaustion, wear and tear of any building or structure used by the owner thereof for the purpose of acquiring the income from a trade, business, profession or vocation carried on by him; . . ."

The facts may be summarised as follows. The respondents were incorporated as a limited liability company in 1947 for the purpose of taking over a business carried on under the name or style of Kirkconnell Brothers Successors; it had as one of its objects the acquiring of freehold property and the leasing of all or part of the company's property. That business which, up to 1944, was carried on and known as Kirkconnell Brothers was purchased in 1944 by the principal shareholders of the respondents. The business of Kirkconnell Brothers included that of merchants dealing in hardware and lumber, that of operating a wharf and of letting premises to tenants. Their successors added to the range of businesses that of dry goods merchants, picture house proprietors, building blocks, manufacturers, wholesale provision merchants and insurance sub-agency. In 1945 Kirkconnell Brothers Successors purchased three buildings, one of them was subsequently pulled down and rebuilt in accordance with designs and plans submitted by Barclays Bank D.C.O., to whom the building was leased and who still occupy the " Bank Building " as tenants of the respondents. After the acquisition of the business of Kirkconnell Brothers Successors, the respondents continued to rent the premises acquired from Kirkconnell Brothers Successors and acquired six additional premises which they also rented out.

The question whether they were carrying on business is primarily a question of fact. There are concurrent findings of fact in the courts below to this effect and there was in their lordships' opinion ample evidence on which such a conclusion could be reached.

As the respondents' claim depends on their satisfying the requirements of s. 8 (o), it may be convenient to consider this section first. In order to qualify for the deduction the building must be used for the purpose of acquiring income from a trade or business carried on by the respondents. The word " business " is of wide import and must be given its ordinary meaning, unless the context otherwise requires. The respondents' objects include inter alia acquiring of freehold property and the leasing of all or any of the company's property. If a company's objects are business objects and are in fact carried out, it carries on business (*Inland Revenue Comrs.* v. *Westleigh Estates Co., Ltd.* (1) per SIR ERNEST POLLOCK, M.R.). The respondents are engaged in negotiating leases and collecting rents from their properties. This would prima facie indicate that they were carrying on business so as to bring them within the terms of s. 8 (o).

The appellant, however, submitted that in order to ascertain whether the respondents were carrying on business the terms of s. 5 of the Income Tax Law must be looked at in order to see whether they were carrying on a business on the profits of which they were taxed. This, it was said, was the proper question which arose. The scheme of the Income Tax Law as a whole must be looked at. Section 5 defines chargeable incomes. The classes of income profits or gains are respectively described as income profits or gains arising or accruing (a) (i)

---

(1) [1924] 1 K.B. 390 at pp. 408, 409; 12 Tax Cas. 657 at p. 686.

A from any kind of property, (ii) from any trade, business, profession, employment or vocation and (*b*) (ii) rents, royalties, premiums and any other profits arising from property.   It was submitted that the charge to income tax on the respondents was in respect of the rent arising from the " Bank Building ". Thus, it was argued, they were not carrying on business on the profits of which they were taxed, but the profits on which they were taxed arose from

B the rent.   Counsel attempted to draw an analogy from the case of *Fry* v. *Salsibury House Estate, Ltd.* (2).   This company, formed to acquire and manage a block of buildings, let out the rooms as unfurnished offices to tenants. The company also provided services at an additional charge. They were assessed under Sch. A to income tax on the gross annual value of the building. The Revenue claimed, in making an assessment under Sch. A, to include the rents of the offices

C as part of the receipts of the trade, making allowance for tax assessed under Sch. A. This claim failed, the House of Lords holding that the assessment under Sch. A was exhaustive.   There are expressions of opinion in some of the speeches that the company were not carrying on a trade, but these expressions must be taken in the context of the British Income Tax Law and particularly in the context of Sch. D.   The real ratio decidendi is contained in the speech of Lord Atkin (3),

D when he says that annual income from the ownership of land can be assessed only under Sch. A and that the option of the Revenue to assess under whatever schedule they prefer does not exist.   The schedules are mutually exclusive.   In their lordships' opinion the decision in the *Salisbury House* case (2) has no bearing on the construction of the provisions of the Income Tax Law of Jamaica, where there is no parallel to the division of the charge to income tax into various separate

E and distinct Schedules. Section 5 already referred to is an omnibus section which treats all profits and gains together whether arising from property or from a trade, business, employment or profession, or in respect of rent or emoluments, salaries or wages. These are all treated as profits or gains. There is no heading corresponding to Sch. A and there is no provision for income tax in respect of the ownership of lands and hereditaments, it is only the rent of leased property which is

F charged. There is in fact in Jamaica a separate property tax on the capital value of all property shown in the valuation roll and imposed on the person in possession of the property (Property Tax Law c. 212).   The question, therefore, reverts to whether the respondents were carrying on a business.   It was not seriously disputed by the appellant that they were. If so, then it appears to their lordships indisputable that the profits on which they were assessed under s. 5 (*a*) (ii) were

G the profits arising from that business. If, of course, there was a case of an individual or a company which did not carry on a business of letting property, then they would be assessed in respect of the rent of the property under s. 5 (*b*) (ii), but this provision cannot preclude the assessment of a company engaged in the business of letting property on the rents obtained as the profits of that business. Their lordships agree with the opinion formed by the Court of Appeal on this

H branch of the case.

   The second requirement under s. 8 (*o*) is that the building must be used by the respondents for the purpose of acquiring the income from the business carried on. Discussion took place on the meaning to be attributed to the word " used ". Here again the word must be given its ordinary meaning in the absence of any indication to the contrary.   In the ordinarily accepted meaning of the word a building is

I " used " for the purpose of acquiring income if rents are derived from it.   The appellant argued that, if this meaning were given to the word " used ", then there might in view of the definition of " owner " in para. 7 (*a*) of Sch. 2 be two claims for wear and tear, one from the lessor and one from the lessee.   However this may be, it cannot control the meaning to be attributed to the word " used ", if it is capable of being applied both to the lessor and the lessee. The appellant's

---

(2) [1930] All E.R. Rep. 538; [1930] A.C. 432.
(3) [1930] All E.R. Rep. at p. 551; [1930] A.C. at p. 454.

contention really amounted to saying that " used " must mean " occupied ",   A
but this is not what the section says, although it would have been simple for the
legislation so to provide.   Their lordships adopt with approval the view of
WADDINGTON, J., to this effect:

> " It is my view that an owner of premises who leases them is making use
> of these premises by employing or applying them for the purpose of letting,
> and it follows therefore, that if he carries on a business of letting premises   B
> then he is using the premises for the purpose of acquiring any income which
> he may derive therefrom.   It is with regret therefore that I find myself in
> respectful disagreement with the decision, on this aspect of the case, of the
> learned judges in *Hendriks* v. *(Income Tax) Assessment Committee* (4), and I
> would accordingly answer the second question posed above in the affirmative."

Support for this view is to be obtained from sub-s. (c) and sub-s. (g) of s. 8.   C
Section 8 (c) provides for the purpose of ascertaining a chargeable income for a
deduction in respect of sums expended for repair of buildings employed in acquiring the income and s. 8 (g) provides for deduction of fire insurance premiums on
property used in acquiring the income on which the tax is payable.   The legislation
accordingly treats the owner of property as employing or using the property in   D
acquiring the income whether he does it as part of a business or not.   These
deductions, their lordships were informed, are in practice given to property
owners irrespective of whether they carry on a business of letting the property or
not.

The Income Tax Appeal Board, while reaching the conclusion that the respondents were carrying on the business of letting premises, felt themselves bound by   E
the decision in the case of *Hendriks* v. *(Income Tax) Assessment Committee* (4)
and dismissed the appeal.   That case concerned the same provision of the Income
Tax Law as this case.   The Court of Appeal in that case held that on the facts of
that case the individual taxpayer who rented service properties was not carrying
on a business within the meaning of s. 8 (o).   They did, however, reserve the case
of a company formed and organised expressly for the purpose of acquiring and   F
letting property.   FURNESS, C.J., who gave the opinion of the court proceeded to
deal, on the assumption that the appellant was carrying on a business, with the
question whether it could be said that the premises were being used for the purpose
of acquiring the income in this way (5):

> " That business would be carried on—not on the premises in question but
> elsewhere—at the appellant's office or home.   It would be the appellant's   G
> office or home that would be used for the purpose of acquiring the income
> from the business—not the premises themselves.   The premises were used
> by the various tenants.   The appellant, having parted with possession of
> them, could no longer be said to be using them within the meaning of s. 5 (c)
> though it is true, as Mr. Manley urged, that they in fact produced the income."

There is some question whether these observations were obiter, but whether they   H
were or not, their lordships have reached the conclusion that they are not well
founded.

Their lordships will humbly advise Her Majesty that this appeal should be
dismissed.   The appellant must pay the costs of the appeal.

Appeal dismissed.

Solicitors: *Charles Russell & Co.* (for the appellant); *Linklaters & Paines* (for   I
the respondents).

[*Reported by* KATHLEEN J. H. O'BRIEN, *Barrister-at-Law.*]

---

(4) (1941), 4 J.L.R. 60.   (5) (1941), 4 J.L.R. at p. 65.

A
Re SPENBOROUGH URBAN DISTRICT COUNCIL'S AGREEMENT.
SPENBOROUGH CORPORATION *v.* COOKE SONS & CO., LTD.

[CHANCERY DIVISION (Buckley, J.), January 27, 30, 31, March 6, 1967.]

B
Contract—Duration—Whether determinable by reasonable notice—Contract regulating the discharge of trade effluent into the public sewer.

The defendant owned a factory where carpet yarn was scoured and dyed. The processes produced trade effluents which was discharged into the plaintiff corporation's sewer. The consent of the corporation, or its predecessor the urban district council, to discharge of the trade effluent into its sewer was not necessary, by virtue of s. 4 of the Public Health (Drainage of Trade Premises) Act, 1937, if effluent of the same nature was lawfully so discharged during the year ending Mar. 3, 1937, subject to certain limits of quantity. The defendant did so discharge effluent during that year, but at that time the effluent was treated to reduce grease. On Apr. 17, 1947, the defendant entered into an agreement with the plaintiff's predecessor relating to the discharge of effluents into the public sewer. This agreement was expressly made terminable on three months' notice by either party, and terminable immediately by the urban district council for breach by the defendant. The agreement was superseded by a new agreement made on Aug. 3, 1951, which contained no provision for termination by notice. The 1951 agreement did not limit the amount to be discharged, and did not require effluent to be treated; it did not oblige the defendant to continue to discharge effluent (and thus to pay for so doing), with the consequence that, by ceasing to discharge effluent the defendant could bring the agreement to an end, but the agreement did provide for revision of the corporation's charges on three months' notice. There was an increase in the amount of effluent discharged, and, faced with the prospect of heavy capital expenditure to instal plant to treat the effluent, the corporation decided to terminate the 1951 agreement and to negotiate a new one. By letter dated Jan. 26, 1966, the corporation gave twelve months' notice to the defendant to determine the 1951 agreement on Jan. 26, 1967. The defendant did not accept that the 1951 agreement could be determined on reasonable notice unilaterally, but did not dispute that, if the 1951 agreement were so terminable, the period of notice was reasonable.

G
Held: (i) where an agreement did not in terms confer on the parties or one of them the power to determine it, the question whether such a power should be inferred was one of construction in a broad sense, viz., of ascertaining in the light of all admissible evidence and of what the parties had said or omitted to say in the agreement, what their common intention was (see p. 962, letters E and F, post).

H
Dictum of LORD MACDERMOTT in *Winter Garden Theatre (London), Ltd.* v. *Millenium Products, Ltd.* ([1947] 2 All E.R. at p. 343) applied.

(ii) the defendant's rights under the 1951 agreement differed from the statutory rights under s. 4, or the rights which the defendant might obtain under s. 1 or s. 2 of the Act of 1937, and the court would infer that the 1951 agreement was negotiated for commercial reasons and on a commercial basis (see p. 965, letter H, and p. 965, letter I, to p. 966, letter A, post); having regard to all the circumstances, the 1951 agreement on its true construction was terminable by reasonable notice and was effectively determined by the corporation's notice as at Jan. 26, 1967 (see p. 967, letter A, post).

I
Crediton Gas Co. v. *Crediton Urban District Council* ([1928] Ch. 174), and *Martin-Baker Aircraft Co., Ltd.* v. *Canadian Flight Equipment, Ltd.* ([1955] 2 All E.R. 722) applied.

[As to determination of contracts indefinite as to time, see 8 HALSBURY'S LAWS (3rd Edn.) 156, 157, para. 267; and for cases on the subject, see in addition

Applied in STAFFS AREA HEALTH V S STAFFS WATERWORKS [1973] 3 All ER 769

to those cited in the judgment, 12 DIGEST (Repl.) 162, *1042*, 707, *5399*; 30 DIGEST A
(Repl.) 540, *1742*, *1747*; 47 DIGEST (Repl.) 582, *43*.

As to agreements with traders relating to the discharge of effluents, see 31
HALSBURY'S LAWS (3rd Edn.) 218, para. 318.

For the Public Health (Drainage of Trade Premises) Act, 1937, s. 1, s. 4, s. 7,
see 19 HALSBURY'S STATUTES (3rd Edn.) 510, 513, 517; and for the amending
Public Health Act, 1961, see 41 ibid., pp. 859, et seq.]   B

Cases referred to:

Crediton Gas Co. v. *Crediton Urban District Council*, [1928] Ch. 174; *affd.* C.A.,
    [1928] Ch. 447; 97 L.J.Ch. 184; 138 L.T. 723; 92 J.P. 76; 25 Digest
    (Repl.) 529, *69*.

Llanelly Ry. & Dock Co. v. *London & North Western Ry. Co.*, (1875), L.R. 7 H.L.
    550; 45 L.J.Ch. 539; 32 L.T. 575; *affg.* (1873), 8 Ch. App. 942; 42 C
    L.J.Ch. 884; 29 L.T. 357; 38 Digest (Repl.) 367, *415*.

Martin-Baker Aircraft Co., Ltd. v. *Canadian Flight Equipment, Ltd., Martin-
    Baker Aircraft Co., Ltd.* v. *Murison*, [1955] 2 All E.R. 722; [1955] 2
    Q.B. 556; [1955] 3 W.L.R. 212; Digest (Cont. Vol. A) 1250, *1872b*.

Winter Garden Theatre (London), Ltd. v. *Millenium Productions, Ltd.*, [1947]
    2 All E.R. 331; [1948] A.C. 173; [1947] L.J.R. 1422; 177 L.T. 349; 45 D
    Digest (Repl.) 201, *83*.

Adjourned Summons.

This was an application by originating summons dated Feb. 16, 1966, by which
the plaintiff corporation, the mayor, aldermen and burgesses of the borough of
Spenborough, sought, against the defendant, Cooke Sons & Co., Ltd., the following
declarations: (i) that on its true construction the agreement dated Aug. 3, 1951, E
made between the urban district council of Spenborough of the one part and the
defendant, Cooke Sons & Co., Ltd., of the other part, was determinable at any
time by either party thereto giving reasonable notice to the other of them; (ii)
that twelve months' notice to determine the agreement was reasonable notice;
alternatively that it might be determined what was a reasonable length of notice
to determine the agreement, and (iii) that the notice dated Jan. 26, 1966, served F
by the plaintiff corporation on the defendant under cover of a letter of the same
date addressed to the defendant by the plaintiff corporation was effective to
determine the agreement at the expiration of the period mentioned in the notice.
The facts are set out in the judgment.

The cases noted below* were cited during the argument in addition to those G
referred to in the judgment.

Sir Andrew Clark, Q.C., and *E. A. Seeley* for the plaintiff corporation.
J. L. Arnold, Q.C., and *M. Mann* for the defendant.

                                                Cur. adv. vult.

Mar. 6. **BUCKLEY, J.,** read the following judgment: The plaintiff corporation, whom I will refer to as " the corporation ", seek a declaration that an agree- H
ment dated Aug. 3, 1951, and made between the corporation's predecessor, the
urban district council of Spenborough, of the one part and the defendant
company of the other part, is determinable by either party on reasonable notice.
If this is so, the defendant does not dispute that the agreement has been effectively
determined by twelve months' notice in writing given on Jan. 26, 1966.

The defendant owns a factory called the Spen Valley Carpet Mills within the I
borough of Spenborough, where carpet yarn is scoured and dyed. The processes
carried on by the defendant at this factory produce trade effluent consisting of
dye liquor and wool scouring liquor, which are discharged into the corporation's
sewer. This wool scouring liquor contains considerable amounts of grease, which

* *Re Berker Sportcraft, Ltd.'s Agreements*, (1947), 177 L.T. 420; *Birtley and District
Co-operative Society, Ltd.* v. *Windy Nook and District Industrial Co-operative Society,
Ltd.*, [1959] 1 All E.R. 43; *Australian Blue Metal, Ltd.* v. *Hughes*, [1962] 3 All E.R. 335;
[1963] A.C. 74.

A give rise to special difficulties in the operation of the corporation's sewage system. Effluents of this nature were, during the year ended Mar. 3, 1937, being discharged from the factory into the public sewer of the urban district council, which was then the sewage disposal authority for this area. It seems that at this time, and until the second world war, the defendant used to carry out some form of treatment of the wool scouring liquor directed to the partial elimination of the grease.

B During that war the defendant discontinued its operations at the factory, which was put to other uses, but resumed them at the end of hostilities. It seems that from this time the defendant has carried out no treatment of the wool scouring liquor before its discharge into the sewer. This is certainly true of the period since early in August, 1951, although the position before that time is not entirely clear.

C On July 1, 1938, the Public Health (Drainage of Trade Premises) Act, 1937, came into force. Section 1 of the Act of 1937 entitles the occupier of any trade premises within the district of a local authority with the consent of that authority to discharge trade effluent into such authority's public sewers. Section 4 provides that the consent of the local authority shall not be necessary if any trade effluent of the same nature or composition as that to be discharged into the public sewers

D was lawfully so discharged from the trade premises in question into the sewer in question at some time during the year ended Mar. 3, 1937. During that year the defendant was discharging effluents of the kind that I have mentioned from the Spen Valley Carpet Mills into the public sewer of the urban district council and the defendant is accordingly entitled, without the corporation's consent, to discharge effluents of the same nature and composition into that same sewer, which

E is now the corporation's sewer, subject to the limits as to quantity and rate of discharge imposed by s. 4.

Section 7 of the Act of 1937 authorises a local authority to enter into an agreement with the owner or occupier of trade premises for the reception and disposal of trade effluent. On Apr. 17, 1947, the urban district council entered into an agreement in writing with the defendant, which I will call " the 1947

F agreement ", regulating the discharge of the defendant's trade effluents into the public sewer. The defendant was required by this agreement to eliminate certain constituents from the effluent which were likely to injure or obstruct the sewers or make the treatment or disposal therefrom of the sewage difficult or expensive. It is not altogether clear whether this term of the agreement was implemented. Limits were placed by the 1947 agreement on the maximum quantities of effluent

G to be discharged in a year, in a day and in an hour. A limit was also placed on the temperature of the effluent discharged. The defendant was to pay 3d. per one thousand gallons discharged. The 1947 agreement was expressly made terminable by either party on three months' notice and the urban district council was authorised to terminate it immediately on a breach of the agreement by the defendant.

H Subsequently, for reasons into which I need not go, a new agreement was negotiated between the urban district council and the defendant. This agreement, which is dated Aug. 3, 1951, which I will call " the 1951 agreement ", no longer required the elimination of the objectionable constituents referred to in the 1947 agreement. It imposed no limits on quantities or temperatures. The charge to the defendant was increased to 6d. per one thousand gallons. Provision was made

I for either party on three months' notice to require a revision of this charge, but, notably, no express provision was made for the determination of the agreement on notice, although the urban district council was authorised to terminate it immediately on breach. The rights of the defendant under s. 4 of the Act of 1937 were expressly preserved. On May 23, 1955, the corporation obtained its charter and thereupon the benefit of the 1951 agreement vested in the corporation as successor to the urban district council.

Since the date of the 1951 agreement the amount of effluent discharged from the defendant's factory has greatly increased. The discharge of wool scouring

liquor is now at the rate of about fifteen thousand gallons daily, compared with
a maximum daily discharge of ten thousand gallons of trade effluent of any kind
permitted by the 1947 agreement. To remove the grease from the liquor at source
would require the installation of plant costing upwards of £45,000 to provide and
about £2,000 a year to operate and maintain. The defendant is unwilling to instal
such plant and the corporation consider that expenditure of this order by the
corporation to deal only with the defendant's effluent cannot be justified in the
absence of any obligation on the defendant to continue for any definite period to
pay any annual charge. The corporation, however, is under pressure from the
Yorkshire Ouse and Hull River Authority to produce from the corporation's
main sewage disposal works a final effluent conforming to the authority's
requirements.

In these circumstances the corporation decided to determine the 1951 agreement with a view to negotiating a new agreement with the defendant. Accordingly
by letter dated Jan. 26, 1966, the corporation gave twelve months' notice to the
defendant determining or purporting to determine the 1951 agreement. The
defendant does not accept that the 1951 agreement can be unilaterally determined
otherwise than for breach. The question for decision is whether the corporation
was competent to determine the 1951 agreement on reasonable notice as it
purported to do.

Authority establishes that, where an agreement does not in terms confer on the
parties or one of them a power to determine the agreement, whether such a power
should be inferred is a question of construction of the agreement to be determined
in accordance with the ordinary principles applicable to such a question (*Wintergarden Theatre (London), Ltd.* v. *Millenium Productions, Ltd.* (1), per LORD
MacDERMOTT, with whose opinion VISCOUNT SIMON and LORD SIMONDS concurred). Since ex hypothesi such an agreement contains no provision expressly
dealing with determination by the party who asserts that this should be inferred,
the question is not one of construction in the narrow sense of putting a meaning
on language which the parties have used, but in the wider sense of ascertaining,
in the light of all the admissible evidence and in the light of what the parties have
said or omitted to say in the agreement, what the common intention of the parties
was in the relevant respect when they entered into the agreement.

It is of the nature of this problem that he who asserts that the parties intended
something which they omitted to state expressly must demonstrate that this was
so. Counsel for the corporation accepts this. The court does not, however, in
my judgment, lean one way or the other. LORD SELBORNE in *Llanelly Ry. &
Dock Co.* v. *London & North Western Ry. Co.* (2) and JAMES, L.J., in the same case
in the Court of Appeal (3) said, I think, nothing inconsistent with this (see per
LORD MacDERMOTT in *Wintergarden Theatre (London), Ltd.* v. *Millenium Productions, Ltd.* (4)). An agreement which is silent about the determination will not
be determinable unless the facts of the case, such as the subject-matter of the
agreement, the nature of the contract or the circumstances in which the agreement was made, support a finding that the parties intended that it should be
determinable, but there is, in my judgment, no presumption one way or the
other.

In the present case the corporation contends that the nature of the 1951 agreement is such that the parties could not reasonably be taken to have intended that
the corporation should be powerless to bring it to an end. They point out that
under the 1951 agreement no limit is placed on the amount of effluent which the
defendant may discharge into the corporation's sewer, however obnoxious it may
be. The defendant's statutory rights under s. 4 of the Act of 1937 on the other
hand are limited both as regards quantity and character by reference to what

(1) [1947] 2 All E.R. 331 at p. 343; [1948] A.C. 173 at p. 203.
(2) (1875), L.R. 7 H.L. 550 at p. 567.
(3) (1873), 8 Ch. App. 942 at pp. 949, 950.
(4) [1947] 2 All E.R. at p. 343; [1948] A.C. at p. 203.

happened in the year ended Mar. 3, 1937. They point out that they are under statutory duties to accept and dispose of sewage from other properties in their area, which they might have difficulty in performing if the defendant's discharge became excessive. They point out that they are under obligations to the river authority about the character and quality of the sewage effluent which the corporation ultimately discharges into the river Ouse, which it might become very difficult or very expensive for them to perform if the defendant's effluent were of a very obnoxious kind or became excessive in amount.

These are all, counsel for the corporation submits, circumstances pointing in favour of the view that the parties contemplated and intended that the corporation should have power to bring the agreement to an end on reasonable notice; but he says that there are other and weightier considerations which point the same way. One is that, as he contends, this is an agreement of a commercial character, a contract for a facility to be provided by the corporation of a kind which is necessary to the defendant in connexion with its trade and to be provided in consideration of periodical payments by the defendant to the corporation related in amount to the extent to which the defendant uses the facility. To such a contract, counsel for the corporation says, the remarks of McNAIR, J., in *Martin-Baker Aircraft Co., Ltd.* v. *Canadian Flight Equipment, Ltd.* (5) apply. The judge there said:

" Accordingly it appears to me that I have to approach the determination of this question without any presumption in favour of permanence; and indeed, if there is any presumption at all, it would seem to me to be a presumption the other way. It is to be borne in mind that this agreement is one in a commercial or mercantile field. No case was cited to me where it has been held that this doctrine of irrevocability applies to a contract in the commercial or mercantile field, and I do not feel that the law merchant would normally look at such an agreement as this as being an agreement intended to constitute permanent relationships. For example, I have little doubt that the law merchant would regard a contract for sale of a hundred tons of coal monthly at a fixed price, no period being specified, as a contract determinable on reasonable notice. The common law, in applying the law merchant to commercial transactions has always proceeded, when filling up the gaps in a contract which the parties have made, on the basis of what is reasonable, so far as that does not conflict with the express terms of the contract, rather than on the basis of rigidity."

The judge went on (6):

" It is, of course, true that this kind of consideration can in many cases be excluded by express provision; but, where the contract leaves the matter open, I think that the common law approach would be to provide a solution which is reasonable. At the same time I bear in mind that it is not the function of the court to make a reasonable contract between the parties, and, in so far as the matter is one of implying terms, one can only imply terms which are reasonable to give business efficacy to the contract. To my mind, however, the question whether a contract such as this is permanent or revocable does not depend on the insertion of an implied term, but depends on the true construction of the language used. This is certainly the view expressed by LORD MACDERMOTT in the *Winter Garden Theatre* case (7). Accordingly, subject to there being anything in the agreements . . . which is inconsistent with their being revocable, I would favour the view that they are revocable."

Further or alternatively, counsel for the corporation contends that the 1951 agreement is a licence agreement and that a licence is prima facie determinable.

(5) [1955] 2 All E.R. 722 at pp. 732, 733; [1955] 2 Q.B. 556 at p. 577.
(6) [1955] 2 All E.R. at p. 733; [1955] 2 Q.B. at p. 578.
(7) [1947] 2 All E.R. 331; [1948] A.C. 173.

He relies on *Winter Garden Theatre (London), Ltd.* v. *Millenium Productions, Ltd.* (8), per LORD PORTER and on *Martin-Baker Aircraft Co., Ltd.* v. *Canadian Flight Equipment, Ltd.* (9). Where, therefore, the contract under consideration is a licence agreement counsel for the corporation contends that a burden rests on the licensee to demonstrate that the circumstances are such as to displace a presumption that the parties intended the agreement to be determinable at least on reasonable notice, if not peremptorily. If, as in *Llanelly Ry. & Dock Co.* v. *London & North Western Ry. Co.* (10), the consideration moving from the licensee, or a substantial part of it, consists of an immediate benefit conferred on the licensor, this may afford a strong reason for inferring that the licensor was not intended to have a right to determine the licence. On the other hand, where the consideration given by the licensee takes the form of periodic payments, as in the *Winter Garden* case (11) and the *Martin-Baker* case (9), this and other relevant circumstances may lead to the conclusion that an intention should be attributed to the parties that the licence should be terminable.

LORD PORTER was, I think, the only one of the noble lords who decided the *Winter Garden* case (11) to rely on the suggested rule of law that a licence is prima facie determinable. The majority treated the question as purely one of construction, but LORD MACDERMOTT (12) was careful to avoid formulating any such general proposition. In the *Martin-Baker* case (13) MCNAIR, J., went no further than to say that it appeared to him that he had to approach the determination of that question without any presumption in favour of permanence: and, indeed, if there was any presumption it would seem to him to be a presumption the other way. I propose to approach the question before me on the footing that there is no presumption either way.

Counsel for the defendant naturally lays great stress on the presence in the 1947 agreement of an express provision of determination on notice and the absence of any similar provision in the 1951 agreement. A comparison of the language of the two agreements, I think, makes it clear that either the draftsman of the 1951 agreement worked with the 1947 agreement before him as a precedent, or both agreements derive from some unidentified common precedent. I think that counsel for the defendant is justified in describing the absence of such a provision from the 1951 agreement as a conscious departure from the earlier agreement.

He points to the fact that the defendant's statutory rights under s. 4 of the Act of 1937 would continue indefinitely and contends that if the defendant sought the consent of the corporation under s. 1 and s. 2 of the Act of 1937, the corporation could not impose a condition limiting the period of the discharge for which consent was sought or reserving a right to withdraw consent. Nor, he submits, could the Minister on an appeal under s. 3 impose such a condition (14). Counsel for the defendant consequently contends that, just as in the *Llanelly* case (15) the fact that the London & North Western Ry. Co. could under compulsory statutory powers have secured perpetual running powers over the applicant company's line was an important consideration, so in the present case the fact that such statutory rights as his clients have would lead to perpetual rights to discharge effluent into the corporation's sewers supports the view that the 1951 agreement was intended to confer perpetual rights except so far as expressly otherwise provided.

Counsel for the defendant says that, although the 1951 agreement is in a sense a commercial contract, it is, because of this statutory background, not one that

---

(8) [1947] 2 All E.R. at p. 339; [1948] A.C. at p. 195.
(9) [1955] 2 All E.R. 722; [1955] 2 Q.B. 556.
(10) (1875), L.R. 7 H.L. 550;   (11) [1947] 2 All E.R. 331; [1948] A.C. 173.
(12) [1947] 2 All E.R. at p. 344; [1948] A.C. at p. 204.
(13) [1955] 2 All E.R. at p. 732; [1955] 2 Q.B. at p. 577.
(14) As to the Minister's powers on an appeal under s. 3 of the Act of 1937, see the Public Health Act, 1961, s. 61; 41 HALSBURY'S STATUTES (2nd Edn.) 910.
(15) (1875), L.R. 7 H.L. 550.

A   was negotiated in normal commercial conditions and that consequently the observations of McNAIR, J., which I have cited (16) are not applicable. He places reliance on the fact that the 1951 agreement contains an express provision for summary determination by the corporation in the event of a breach of covenant by the defendant, saying that in none of the reported cases where a power to determine a contract has been inferred has there been any express power of

B   determination given to the party in whose favour the inference has been made. He places reliance on the provision for the revision of charges, saying first that, if the corporation can determine the agreement, there is the less reason for this provision, since the corporation could always procure a revision by putting an end to the contract and re-negotiating, and secondly that the inclusion of this provision makes it possible for the corporation to meet unforeseen hazards, such

C   as the cost of complying with the requirements of the river authority, by an appropriate adjustment of the charges, which, he suggests, weakens the case for regarding a power for the corporation to determine the agreement as something which ought reasonably to be inferred.

   Approaching the problem before me as one of construction to be determined in accordance with the ordinary principles applicable to such a question, without

D   leaning one way or the other, I must have regard to the following circumstances. Under the agreement the defendant is restricted to discharging wool scouring and dye liquor, but, apart from the exclusion of condensing and surface water, the defendant is not under any obligation to extract any ingredient of such liquor or to treat it in any way. In this respect the defendant's rights under the agreement differ materially from its statutory rights under s. 4, which only extend to

E   effluent of the same nature and composition as that discharged in the year ended Mar. 3, 1937. At that time the defendant was discharging treated effluent. Under the agreement the defendant is unrestricted as to the amount it may discharge. In this respect also the rights under the agreement differ from the statutory rights which are restricted to a daily maximum not exceeding the maximum discharged in any one day in the year ended Mar. 3, 1937. It would seem from the

F   recitals to the 1951 agreement that in the present case this maximum may have been forty thousand gallons, which is probably considerably more than the current maximum daily discharge, but it remains true that the defendant could, if it chose, exceed that limit. The defendant is not under any obligation to continue to discharge any effluent into the corporation's sewer. It can discharge as little or as much as it likes. It can thus suspend the operation of the agreement

G   at any time and for as long as it chooses. Should the defendant permanently cease to discharge effluent into the corporation's sewer it is bound at its own expense to disconnect its drains from the sewer. The defendant has thus an effective power to bring the agreement to an end by its own unilateral act.

   The defendant's rights under the agreement differ from its statutory rights under s. 4 in the ways that I have already mentioned, and they also, I think, differ

H   from any rights which the defendant might obtain under s. 1 and s. 2, for I feel entitled to assume that, if the corporation's consent was sought under those sections, the corporation would certainly impose conditions (17) as to the nature or composition of the defendant's effluent which would involve the defendant's treating its effluent before its discharge into the public sewer, and I see no reason to suppose that the Minister on an appeal would take a different view.

I   In the present case, therefore, I do not feel that the existence of these statutory rights assists me in construing the agreement in the way that counsel for the defendant suggests. On the contrary, the fact that the defendant, rather than rely on such statutory rights, preferred to negotiate an agreement for rights of a different kind seems to me to indicate that the 1951 agreement was negotiated

---

(16) See p. 963, letter E, ante.
(17) As to the conditions which may be attached to such a consent and their variation, see the Public Health Act, 1961, s. 59, s. 60; 41 HALSBURY'S STATUTES (2nd Edn.) 908, 909.

for commercial reasons and on a commercial basis. In *Crediton Gas Co.* v. *Crediton* A
Urban District Council (18), the fact that the gas company was under a statutory
duty to supply gas to the urban district council was not regarded by RUSSELL, J.
(19) as preventing an agreement between the parties from having a commercial
character.

If at this point I pause to ask myself whether in the light of these circumstances
it is commercially sensible to suppose either that the corporation, when it entered B
into the 1951 agreement, intended to assume obligations to which it would
have no power to put an end except on a breach by the defendant, or that the
defendant, when it entered into the agreement, thought that the corporation
intended to assume such obligations, I think that the answer should be " No ".
The most cogent indication of this is, I think, the capacity of the defendant
unilaterally and at any moment to suspend or put an end to the operation of the C
agreement. Somewhat similar considerations weighed with the Court of Appeal
in *Crediton Gas Co.* v. *Crediton Urban District Council* (20). It is the cumulative
effect, however, of the considerations which I have mentioned, all of which, in
my opinion, point the same way, that make me think that a negative answer
should be given to the question.

I cannot, however, have regard to these indications without at the same time D
taking into consideration the provision for the variation of charges, the presence
in the 1951 agreement of the express provision for determination by the corporation on a breach by the defendant, and the conscious departure from the terms of
the 1947 agreement in omitting from the 1951 agreement any provision enabling
either party to bring the agreement to an end on notice.

As regards the revision of charges, it is true that the inclusion of this clause E
would have made it unnecessary for the corporation to determine the agreement
for the purpose of negotiating a new rate of charge; but it does not provide the
corporation with any satisfactory means of recouping any heavy capital expenditure which it might have to incur as the result of accepting the defendant's
effluent, for the amount of money which the corporation would receive would
always be dependent on the amount of effluent discharged, so that the corpor- F
ation could never know over what period or at what rate they could hope to
amortise capital expenditure out of future receipts from the defendant, if, indeed,
they could do so at all.

The clause permitting determination of the agreement on a breach is not, in
my judgment, significant. It is of so different a character from a term permitting
determination on notice without any breach that its presence in the 1951 agree- G
ment, to my mind, has really no bearing on the question whether, apart from
any breach of contract by the defendant, the corporation's obligations under the
agreement were intended to continue indefinitely. The clause in the 1947 agreement permitting either party to terminate the agreement on giving three months'
notice cannot, I think, be regarded as equivalent to a provision for determination
on reasonable notice, for it seems to me that reasonable notice on the part of the H
corporation would in the nature of these agreements need to be considerably
longer than three months. This clause in the 1947 agreement permitted
determination on shorter notice than would otherwise be considered reasonable.
The omission of this clause from the 1951 agreement is consequently not irrecon-
cilable with an intention that the 1951 agreement should be determinable on
reasonable notice. The fact that the 1947 agreement contained an express I
provision for determination on notice and that the 1951 agreement contained
none is, in my judgment, certainly proper to be taken into account along with
the other relevant considerations in deciding whether the parties intended the
latter agreement to be terminable by notice, but for the reasons which I have
indicated it is not, in my judgment, even when considered in conjunction with
the other matters relied on by the defendant, a sufficiently clear and strong

(18) [1928] Ch. 174; on appeal, [1928] Ch. 447.
(19) [1928] Ch. at p. 178.   (20) [1928] Ch. 447.

A indication of a contrary intention to negative the indications pointing the other way to which I have referred.

I consequently reach the conclusion that on the true construction of the 1951 agreement it was determinable by the corporation on the corporation giving reasonable notice to the defendant. The defendant not contending that the notice which the corporation has given was other than reasonable notice, I will

B declare that the 1951 agreement was effectively determined as at Jan. 26, 1967.

Declaration that agreement of Aug. 3, 1951, was determinable by either party giving reasonable notice to the other, followed by a recital that defendant did not contend that the notice was not reasonable and a declaration that the agreement was effectively determined as at Jan. 26, 1967.

C Solicitors: *Sharpe, Pritchard & Co.*, agents for *Town Clerk*, Spenborough, Cleckheaton (for the plaintiff corporation); *Vizard, Oldham, Crowder & Cash* (for the defendant).

[*Reported by* JENIFER SANDELL, *Barrister-at-Law.*]

D # MARSDEN v. MARSDEN.

[PROBATE, DIVORCE AND ADMIRALTY DIVISION (Sir Jocelyn Simon, P., and Cairns, J.), January 13, 16, 1967.]

Divorce—Desertion—Constructive desertion—Adultery—Alleged belief by one spouse in other spouse's adultery—Duty of spouse in possession of evidence

E *leading to reasonable belief to afford other spouse opportunity to give explanation—Whether, if opportunity not given within reasonable time, defence of such reasonable belief can be maintained.*

If evidence comes into the possession of a spouse which raises a suspicion of adultery, then (unless the evidence points to adultery beyond reasonable doubt) it is incumbent on the spouse in possession of that evidence to give to

F the other spouse an opportunity to explain it; if such an opportunity is not given within a reasonable time, the spouse in possession of the evidence cannot thereafter maintain, as a defence to a charge of constructive desertion, a contention of reasonable belief that the other spouse had committed adultery (see p. 972, letter A, post).

Dicta of DAVIES, J., in *Forbes* v. *Forbes* ([1954] 3 All E.R. at p. 465 and of

G WILLMER, J., in *Fishburn* v. *Fishburn* ([1955] 1 All E.R. at pp. 233, 234) applied.

Observations on the limitations to be placed on the court's exercise of the wide discretionary power conferred by Matrimonial Causes Rules, 1957, r. 73 (7) (see p. 968, letter B, et seq., post).

H [As to reasonable belief in the other spouse's adultery as a defence to a charge of desertion, see 12 HALSBURY'S LAWS (3rd Edn.) 257, 258, paras. 484-486; and for cases on the subject, see 27 DIGEST (Repl.) 365-367, *3018-3042*.]

Cases referd to:
Beer v. *Beer (Neilson cited), Beer* v. *Beer and Neilson*, [1947] 2 All E.R. 711; [1948] P. 10; [1948] L.J.R. 743; 112 J.P. 50; 27 Digest (Repl.) 367,

I *3041.*
Bond v. *Bond*, [1964] 3 All E.R. 346; [1965] 2 W.L.R. 1008; 128 J.P. 568; 3rd Digest Supp.
Buchler v. *Buchler*, [1947] 1 All E.R. 319; [1947] P. 25; [1947] L.J.R. 820; 176 L.T. 341; 111 J.P. 179; 27 Digest (Repl.) 350, *2899.*
Fishburn v. *Fishburn*, [1955] 1 All E.R. 230; [1955] P. 29; [1955] 2 W.L.R. 236; 119 J.P. 86; Digest (Cont. Vol. A) 815, *6654a.*
Forbes v. *Forbes*, [1954] 3 All E.R. 461; [1954] 1 W.L.R. 1526; 119 J.P. 30; Digest (Cont. Vol. A) 731, *3039a.*

Lang v. *Lang*, [1954] 3 All E.R. 571; [1955] A.C. 402; [1954] 2 W.L.R. 762; **A**
    119 J.P. 368; Digest (Cont. Vol. A) 724, *2899a*.

Wood v. *Wood*, [1947] 2 All E.R. 95; [1947] P. 103; [1948] L.J.R. 784; 111
    J.P. 428; 27 Digest (Repl.) 320, *2667*.

Appeal.

This was an appeal by the wife against a decision of the justices of Stoke-on-
Trent given on June 30, 1966, dismissing three complaints of the wife of (i) per- **B**
sistent cruelty, (ii) constructive desertion and (iii) wilful neglect thereafter to
provide reasonable maintenance for her.   The facts are set out in the judgment
of SIR JOCELYN SIMON, P.

E. F. Monier-Williams for the wife.
The husband did not appear and was not represented.

                                                        C

    SIR JOCELYN SIMON, P.: This is an appeal by a wife against a decision
of the justices of Stoke-on-Trent on June 30, 1966. They had before them three
complaints by the wife: first, that her husband had treated her with persistent
cruelty up to Dec. 19, 1965; secondly, that he had deserted her on that date, the
desertion being constructive desertion since it was she who left, so that she was
asserting that he drove her out; and, thirdly, that he had thereafter wilfully **D**
neglected to provide reasonable maintenance for her. It has been clear on this
appeal, as it must have been below, that the charge of wilful neglect depended on
the establishment by the wife of either persistent cruelty or desertion; since,
unless she had good cause for leaving, the husband was not bound to maintain her.
The appeal was out of time, but we were satisfied that the delay was excusable
and we gave leave to appeal out of time. **E**

    By r. 73 (7) of the Matrimonial Causes Rules, 1957, (1), the Divisional Court
may draw all inferences of fact which might have been drawn in the magistrates'
court and may give any judgment and make any order which ought to have been
made. That is a clear indication by statutory authority of the way that we should
exercise our jurisdiction—so far as I know unparalleled in relation to any other
appellate institution—and as to the responsibility which this court may properly **F**
assume. It is, moreover, understandable, when it is appreciated that the matrimonial courts of summary jurisdiction are courts of immediate relief manned by
laymen (advised, it is true, by their clerk), from whom there is no appeal on fact to
quarter sessions, as there is in respect of their criminal jurisdiction; and that a
re-hearing may involve hardship to the parties. Nevertheless, this court is bound
to recognise some limitation of the very wide powers accorded by the rule. In **G**
the first place, the decision below may be based on an assessment of the veracity
of witnesses; and it is virtually impossible for us, having only a written note of
evidence, to review such an assessment. Moreover, the note of evidence, even
when (as in the present case) it is copious, does not give the questions and answers,
such as the Court of Appeal gets by way of transcript in an appeal from a decision
of the High Court. Secondly, very frequently these cases fall into what ASQUITH, **H**
L.J., in *Buchler* v. *Buchler* (2) described as a " no man's land " of fact and degree
within which it is impossible to say that any reasonable tribunal must have found
the charge proved or unproved—where it would be open to a reasonable tribunal,
seeing the witnesses and in the light of its peculiar knowledge of the local mores,
to come to one decision or the other. Where the point of issue lies in such a " no
man's land ", we are very reluctant indeed to interfere with the decision. It **I**
inevitably follows that, in spite of r. 73 (7), there may be occasions when this
court, although inclined to feel that it might itself have come to a different decision
from that at which the justices have arrived, must leave it undisturbed. There
are other cases where we are satisfied that the court below was in error but are,
nevertheless, convinced that only a court seeing and hearing the witnesses can

    (1) S.I. 1957 No. 619. For r. 73 (7), see 10 HALSBURY'S STATUTORY INSTRUMENTS
(Second Re-Issue) 273.
    (2) [1947] 1 All E.R. 319 at p. 326; [1947] P. 25 at p. 46.

A come to a decision; in such circumstances, it is our practice to order a re-hearing rather than ourselves attempting to make the final decision. There is, however, a third class of case (where, for example, there is a discrepancy in the justices' findings or where the decision depends on a finding of secondary fact, in other words on an inference of fact from those findings of fact dependent on the assessment of the witnesses' veracity) where this court can sometimes assume the

B responsibility that seems to be indicated by r. 73 (7). I mention these points because, although I find myself differing in one respect from the conclusions to which the justices came, that difference arises out of a difficulty which I have found in relating that conclusion to one of their own findings. It is, nevertheless, clear that the justices have taken great trouble with this case, and the notes of evidence seem to give a faithful impression of all the evidence that was given

C before the justices—indeed, they have not sought to supplement the notes of evidence in their findings: cf. *Bond* v. *Bond* (3). We have had two further advantages. In the first place the grounds of appeal are most informative and, secondly, this case has been well argued by counsel for the wife. The husband has not appeared; and under such circumstances an exceptional burden lies on counsel.

D   The background of the appeal is as follows. The marriage was on Aug. 30, 1947. There is one daughter, a girl called Mary, born in 1948. The wife had left the husband on two occasions previous to Dec. 19, 1965. It appears that those were some time ago, and she did not allege that she had any good cause for leaving him then; on the other hand, the matter was, understandably, not explored. It seems to have been accepted on both sides that the marriage was reasonably

E happy until the summer of 1965. Just before that, about May, 1965, a young man called John Tams came to live at the matrimonial home, 23, Albert Street, Sandford Hill, Longton. That arose out of a disagreement which he had had with his own parents. It may be—I should think that it was—that he was at the time courting the daughter Mary, but they were not yet formally engaged to marry. Mr. Tams was at all material times an apprentice mechanic. He was attending

F what I believe are called " sandwich classes " at the local technical college, once a week on Thursdays. He had a car which he used when it was serviceable (which was not always) to get to the technical college; and he kept that on a piece of waste ground near the matrimonial home. Occasionally he missed his " sandwich course " owing to indisposition. In about August, 1965, the husband was taken to hospital with some trouble with his eyes, and when he came out his attitude to

G the wife, according to the finding of the justices (which was based on the evidence of the wife, the daughter and Mr. Tams), had somewhat changed. He became more reserved. Mr. Tams said that the wife tried to speak to him but that he was reluctant to reply; and he went out on his own to play darts at a club. At about this time Mr. Tams became formally engaged to Mary. The sleeping arrangements when Mr. Tams first came to the house were that the husband and wife were

H sleeping in one bedroom, the daughter in the second and Mr. Tams in the third. However, something went wrong at some time which was not ascertained with the ceiling of one of the rooms; and thereafter Mr. Tams occupied one room, and the husband, wife and daughter the second available room, the wife and daughter sleeping in one bed. Some time in the autumn of 1965 the wife had some trouble with her wrist, and was confined to the house.

I   On Oct. 21, 1965, occurred the first event to which the husband attached significance. He says that he returned on that day, a Thursday, at dinner time, at about 12.40 p.m. That was not his practice, but at odd times he did so. He came to the front door, but he found that his key would not turn in the lock. He tried it several times but still with no success. There was a door in the " entry " —I think a side door—which he also tried without success. He knocked and shouted and got no answer, and was unable to get into the house; so he went back

---

(3) [1964] 3 All E.R. 346 at p. 348.

to work. Before he did so, he noticed that Mr. Tams' car was on the waste piece A
of ground. However, as he said, he thought no more about the matter at the time.
But a week later, on Oct. 28, 1965, something of the same sort happened.   He
went home at mid-day for his meal and again tried the key in the door without
success. He knocked and shouted but obtained no answer. During the intervening
week he had used the front door from time to time but without any difficulty.
He noticed again on Oct. 28, that Mr. Tams' car was on the waste land. This time B
he was suspicious—so much so that, when he got home in the evening about 6.30
p.m., he went up to the matrimonial bedroom, turned the blankets down on the
bed which was occupied by his wife and daughter, and found a wet patch on it
which he concluded was semen. He seems to have been strongly suspicious that
this indicated that his wife and Mr. Tams had committed adultery together;
and as a result he consulted a solicitor and obtained certain advice. There were C
other occasions when something of the same sort happened. It is not at all certain
when they were. Possible dates were Nov. 16, 18, 20 and 22, 1965. (Those various
dates were either mentioned in evidence or in a letter by way of particulars before
the hearing.) The only specific date given by the husband in evidence was Nov. 20
(which is unlikely to be right, since he thought that it was a Thursday (4)). Again
he came home from work and looked at the blankets and found a patch on them D
which indicated to him, after he had tested it, that it was semen; and the same
thing happened a week later, which might have been Nov. 30. On that occasion
he got home about 4.30 or 4.50 p.m. He did not try the front door on that occasion,
but the entry door. He heard a key turn and the bolt being lifted, and Mr. Tams
opened the door to him. The husband went upstairs, inspected the bed again, and
again found a wet patch on it, which he concluded was semen. His attitude to his E
wife was becoming more and more reserved; and there was a considerable body
of evidence from her, the daughter and Mr. Tams, that this was, understandably,
causing the wife considerable disturbance.   The upshot was that, on Dec. 19,
1965—I think that was the date, though the husband was inclined to put it as
Dec. 12—the wife was contemplating leaving the husband.   Mr. Tams was
evidently trying to dissuade her, and had his arm round her for that object. F
Unfortunately, the husband came in at this moment, and a fight started between
him and Mr. Tams. The daughter and the wife tried to separate the husband
and Mr. Tams and, in the course of that, the wife became slightly injured. It
is not suggested that it was an intentional blow that she received, or that it
was in any way a grave one.   It is not clear whether it was before or after or
during the course of the fight that a colloquy took place between the husband G
and Mr. Tams, in which Mr. Tams said, " She [meaning the wife] has been
in hospital; you were too mean to go and see her ". That was an unfair and
impertinent remark; the wife had only been three days in hospital, and had
come out unexpectedly early. The husband replied, or may have replied,
" I was going to, but she came out early "; he certainly said something to
this effect, " It's nothing to do with you. What makes you so interested? H
Why are you thinking so much about my wife? "   That was obviously a reflection of the suspicions which the husband had come to harbour in relation to
his wife and Mr. Tams. Mr. Tams said that he thought of her with respect
as a prospective mother-in-law; the husband said, " Is that all? " to which
Mr. Tams replied, equally offensively, " The trouble with you is that you've
got a dirty mind ". It ended by the husband telling Mr. Tams to leave the I
house. Mary then said that, if Mr. Tams left, she would too; and the wife said
that, if her daughter left, she would go as well. In fact all three of them left;
and it was that departure that the wife relied on as constituting desertion on the
part of her husband. That was on a Sunday. The parties met the following day,
but there was no clear offer of reconciliation on either side. The husband said
that he had seen a solicitor and suggested that the wife had better see one too.

---

(4) Nov. 20, 1965, was a Saturday.

A He did not put to the wife the suspicions which he had formed; and, therefore, still gave her no opportunity to dispel them. They met once more some weeks later, again inconclusively. The husband asked if the wife had now been to see a solicitor, but there was no discussion about reconciliation; if anything, it was on the basis that they were going to part and related to the division of the home.

B On May 10, 1966, the wife issued her summons with the three complaints that I have rehearsed; and on a date (which I think must be June 24, 1966, although the letter is incorrectly dated), the husband's solicitor wrote to the wife's solicitor saying,

C " We are writing to inform you that [the husband] will give evidence at the hearing that he believes that the [wife] committed adultery with one John Tams at 23, Albert Street, Sandford Hill, Longton, on Oct. 28, 1965, Nov. 18, 1965, Nov. 22, 1965, and Nov. 30, 1965."

On June 30, 1966, the matter came before the justices. The wife gave evidence and called Mary and Mr. Tams to support her case. Mary and Mr. Tams were both asked in cross-examination whether they had had sexual intercourse together, D but denied it. The wife and Mr. Tams specifically denied that they had themselves committed adultery. The husband gave evidence on his side. Both husband and wife indicated, unhappily, that, so far as each was concerned, the marriage was at an end. The justices dismissed all three charges. They have given us, very helpfully, their reasons for doing so; and I propose to read the relevant passages, starting at para. 3:

E " 3. When the husband expelled the witness Tams from his home, it was the wife who made her own decision to leave; the husband said nothing. Indeed she was, on her own evidence, contemplating leaving before the fight took place. 4. With regard to the events since, the wife had not specifically asked to return, although she had approached her husband and all that he had done (in effect) was to refer her to a solicitor, but the wife appeared to F have done nothing further except to arrange for a division of the furniture and to take out the summons. 5. The husband's attitude had changed on his return from hospital in August, 1965, for an unexplained reason, but by Oct. 28, 1965, he suspected his wife of committing adultery and this suspicion was enhanced by subsequent events. 6. Sexual intercourse had taken place (as agreed on both sides) up to the end of October, and in circumstances G of some difficulty [that refers, of course, to the shared bedroom] indicating that the real weight of the complaint against the husband did not arise until after the incident on Oct. 28. 7. Whilst there was no conduct on the part of the wife herself giving rise to suspicion, the discoveries made by the husband (which we believed) were such as to raise good grounds for suspicion in the mind of any ordinary husband and to call for some explanation. H 8. Unfortunately the husband (apparently acting on advice) sought no explanation but adopted a cool attitude towards his wife—'did not speak to her much ' or take her out. 9. The wife's health had deteriorated but there was no medical evidence in support of her own statement that she had had a ' nervous breakdown '. She had had an accident and been under the doctor, and we were not satisfied that her deterioration in health was due I to her husband's attitude towards her. 10. Considering cruelty, we were (in view of our findings) of opinion that the conduct of the husband was not of a nature nor of a degree to be fairly classed as cruelty, nor were we satisfied that it had in fact seriously injured the wife's health, or was likely to do so. 11. Considering desertion and neglect to maintain, we came to the conclusions: (a) that the wife left the home without just and reasonable cause; (b) that the husband had reasonable grounds for suspecting that she had committed adultery; (c) that although the husband had prior to the court hearing apparently not revealed the basis of his suspicion, the wife must have known

at the time of her leaving (from the remarks made) that he suspected her of   A
misconduct; (d) that unless and until the husband's suspicions (which we
considered to be reasonable) were discussed and found to be groundless, he
was justified in not specifically asking her to return and in not maintaining
her. We accordingly dismissed the complaint."

[HIS LORDSHIP considered the appeal against dismissal of the charge of persistent cruelty and held that the finding of the justices dismissing the charge was   B
unimpugnable. He continued:] I turn then to the charge of desertion, which
presents more difficulty. I think that it depends on whether the husband had a
reasonable belief in his wife's adultery. If a spouse reasonably believes that the
other is committing adultery, the former is entitled to withdraw from cohabitation.
It seems to me to follow that the former is equally entitled, without force, to
expel the latter from cohabitation. On the other hand, an unreasonable accusa-   C
tion of adultery may afford the spouse against whom it is made good cause for
withdrawal from cohabitation; equally, it may constitute constructive desertion
on the part of the spouse making such an unreasonable charge. That, I think,
follows inevitably from the decision of the Privy Council in *Lang* v. *Lang* (5).
If a husband must know that his wife, if she acts like any reasonable woman in
her position, would in all probability withdraw from cohabitation as a result   D
of his conduct, he is guilty of constructive desertion if she does so. If, therefore
(as seems to me to be unquestionable) a reasonable wife, unreasonably accused
of adultery, would in consequence withdraw from cohabitation, it follows that,
where a husband unreasonably makes an accusation of adultery, he may be
guilty of constructive desertion. Three questions, therefore, arise: first, was the
husband's belief in his wife's adultery reasonable?; secondly, if it was not, did he   E
evince his suspicion to his wife?; and thirdly, if so, did it cause the wife's departure? In spite of the fact that the justices' reasons are full, I have found some
difficulty in understanding what they mean exactly in para. 7 of their reasons:
" Whilst there was no conduct on the part of the wife herself giving rise to
suspicion . . ." That could mean one of two things: either that there was reasonable ground for suspicion but that it was not caused by any conduct of the wife   F
(*Beer* v. *Beer* (*Neilson cited*), *Beer* v. *Beer and Neilson*, (6); *Wood* v. *Wood* (7));
or that the wife did not commit adultery. I think that counsel for the wife is
right in conceding (and it was of course against him) that the former could hardly
be what the magistrates meant; clearly, if a husband discovers semen on a bed
which his wife occupies, at a time when she is alone in the house with another man,
it cannot be said that, if he reasonably concludes from that that she has committed   G
adultery, it is not due to conduct on her part. I, therefore, think that what the
justices must have meant was that the husband did make the " discoveries "
that he said he did, that they gave him reasonable grounds for suspicion, but that
the wife had not in fact committed adultery. In any case, these are the conclusions
of fact that I should myself draw; since I do not think that sufficient evidence
was adduced to establish adultery to the requisite standard of proof.   H

The justices finally say the husband's " discoveries " were such as to raise
good cause for suspicion in the mind of any ordinary husband and to call for some
explanation. Although they note that no explanation was in fact called for, they
draw no inference from that fact. In my view, there is a rule of law which can be
stated as follows. If evidence comes into the possession of a spouse which raises
a suspicion of adultery, then (unless the evidence points to adultery beyond   I
reasonable doubt) it is incumbent on the spouse in possession of that evidence to
give the other an opportunity to explain it; if the former does not do so within
a reasonable time, he or she cannot thereafter claim that the belief in adultery
was reasonable. Like most propositions of law, I think that this one is really
founded on the requirements of justice and of good sense. If authority were

(5) [1954] 3 All E.R. 571; [1955] A.C. 402.
(6) [1947] 2 All E.R. 711 at p. 712; [1948] P. 10 at p. 13.
(7) [1947] 2 All E.R. 95; [1957] P. 103.

needed, however, it is, in my view, to be found sufficiently in *Forbes* v. *Forbes* (8), where DAVIES, J., said:

" It is plain therefore, in my judgment, that it must not be assumed that because at the moment of parting, or at whatever other date it is alleged that desertion commenced, the respondent may have induced in the petitioner the belief that adultery had been committed, the petitioner is necessarily entitled, without further inquiry and by mere inactivity to assert that such belief subsisted throughout the statutory triennium up to the presentation of the petition."

See also *Fishburn* v. *Fishburn* (9), per WILLMER, J. The justices believed, as they were entitled to, that the husband made the " discoveries " that he stated. That is to say, first, that the door was jammed; however, that might have been accidental. Secondly, that the car of Mr. Tams was on the vacant space of ground; that again did not point unequivocally or beyond reasonable doubt to adultery. And thirdly—and this was the gravamen—that there were fresh semen stains on the bed. It must, however, be remembered that that bed was not only the wife's but the daughter's also. It is true that both the daughter and Mr. Tams denied that they had had sexual intercourse together; but there is no finding by the justices as to that matter, and counsel for the wife rightly points out that what was said is possibly consistent with some form of sexual commerce less than full intercourse, which might, of course, if true, exonerate the wife. I do not lose sight of the fact that the husband said that at least on one of the occasions to which he referred the daughter was not in the house at the relevant time; but that came out for the first time in cross-examination, and the husband accepted that, although the daughter generally had lunch at her place of work, she did sometimes return at mid-day. Speaking for myself, I accept the primary finding of fact of the justices. On the other hand, I do not think that it was sufficient to satisfy any reasonable husband beyond reasonable doubt that the wife had committed adultery; as, indeed, it did not, I think, so satisfy the magistrates. I fully agree with the justices that what had been found called for some explanation; but the fact is that the husband never gave the wife a chance to explain the matters which aroused his suspicions. He had an opportunity to do so, more than one opportunity; and, if I am right in the rule of law which I have just stated, it was not open to the husband thereafter to allege that his belief in his wife's adultery was a reasonable one.

The second question, therefore, arises: did the wife understand that she was being accused of adultery? The justices, rightly in my view, say that that must have been apparent to her at the time of leaving. She had seemingly contemplated leaving before that, though it does not appear that she had finally determined to, and it may well be that it was the fact that her daughter (10) and Mr. Tams were being arbitrarily turned out that finally made up her mind. But clearly she knew that something was seriously wrong between herself and her husband before Dec. 19, 1965; and it is difficult to believe that the husband's attitude, prompted as it was by these suspicions, did not manifest itself to the wife and make her miserable. There is abundant evidence that it did so. Moreover, and this answers the third question which I have posed, it seems to me unavoidable that the husband's final manifestation of his suspicion must have clinched the wife's decision to leave.

In those circumstances, I think that she was entitled to treat herself as dismissed from the matrimonial home. I think that, once the justices had found that there was no adultery on the part of the wife and Mr. Tams, and that what was " discovered " called for an explanation but that in fact no explanation was asked for, they ought to have found that the husband was in desertion; and it would follow

---

(8) [1954] 3 All E.R. 461 at p. 465, letter E; see also p. 466, letter D.
(9) [1955] 1 All E.R. 230 at pp. 233, 234; [1955] P. 29 at p. 37.
(10) As to the circumstances of the daughter's departure, see p. 970, letter I, ante.

that there should also have been a finding of wilful neglect to maintain. On the principles that I tried to state at the outset of this judgment, it seems to me, therefore, that we ought to substitute for the finding of the justices a finding that the husband was in desertion and guilty of wilful neglect to maintain and to remit the case to a fresh panel of justices for assessment of maintenance. I desire only to add that such a finding is not necessarily the end of the marriage. It was of long subsistence, and seems during most of the time to have been of reasonable satisfaction to both spouses. It is open to the husband at any time to make appropriate overtures to his wife and, if he does so, it is her duty to give them consideration. There are unofficial agencies which might assist these parties to come together again. In any event, since there has to be a re-hearing on quantum of maintenance, it may well be that the justices would think it appropriate to make their own probation service available. I sincerely trust so.

The result, therefore, in my view, is that the appeal should be dismissed so far as it complains of the justices' dismissal of the complaint of persistent cruelty, but that it should be allowed so far as it complains of the dismissal of the complaints of desertion and wilful neglect; that we should ourselves make a finding of desertion and wilful neglect to maintain; and that we should remit the case for the assessment of maintenance.

CAIRNS, J.: I agree. [HIS LORDSHIP discussed the matters relied on in support of the wife's charge of persistent cruelty and concluded that he agreed that the justices' finding that persistent cruelty was not established could not be challenged. He continued:] Desertion is much more difficult. I think that the following questions arise for consideration: (i) Was the husband's conduct over the weeks up to Dec. 19, 1965, and on that day such that any reasonable man would know, and the husband must have known, that it was likely to cause the wife to leave him? (ii) Was his conduct justified? This involves four subsidiary questions: (a) Did the husband make the discoveries which he said that he made? (b) If so, did he in consequence believe that the wife had committed adultery? (c) If so, was it a reasonable belief? (d) If so, did that belief entitle him to behave as he did towards his wife without further enquiry? (iii) Did the husband's conduct in fact cause the wife to depart? (iv) Whether or not the wife left the matrimonial home without just cause, did the husband's subsequent behaviour prevent her from returning? (v) If so, was that subsequent behaviour justified? (vi) If the wife was unjustly expelled by the husband, did anything occur to terminate his constructive desertion of her? I have posed these questions as questions of fact, but they have to be answered on the basis that, if the justices have themselves supplied answers to any of them, those answers must stand unless they were answers that the justices were not entitled to reach on the evidence before them.

(i) It was common ground that, for at least some six weeks before the wife left, the husband had not treated her in an ordinary husbandly manner. There had been no sexual intercourse. The wife, the daughter and Mr. Tams described how the husband was silent and withdrawn, never asked his wife to go out and, as the wife put it, the atmosphere in the house was completely terrible. They put the commencement of this behaviour on the husband's part in about August, 1965, and said that it got progressively worse as time went on. The husband disagreed only about the date. He said that it began only about the end of October, 1965. In my view, this conduct of the husband, without more, would be such that he must have known that his wife would not put up with it indefinitely. Whether it had gone on so long and reached such a degree by Dec. 19, 1965, that it had by then become intolerable may be open to doubt. The culmination of events came on the Sunday evening, Dec. 19, when the husband accused Mr. Tams of an improper interest in his wife and told Mr. Tams to go. As a judge of facts, I might have taken the view that the husband's accusation meant no more than that Mr. Tams was making improper advances to the wife. The husband's own case, however, was that he then believed that adultery had actually occurred, and the justices have found that the wife must have known at the time of her leaving, from remarks then made, that the husband suspected her of misconduct. I do not consider that this court can reject that finding. At any rate the husband has not challenged it. Coming on top of the husband's attitude to her over the previous weeks, I consider that these remarks, interpreted as the justices have interpreted them, were expulsive in character.

(ii) (a) The justices have found that the husband made the discoveries of which he gave evidence. I think that these must include the jammed door, the semen stains in the bed and the presence of Mr. Tams' car in the vicinity. I see no reason for rejecting this finding. It was a pure question of primary fact and there is no reason to suppose that the justices did not take full account of the matters relied on by counsel for the wife as tending to render the husband's account unacceptable. I do not include among the discoveries the alleged absence of the daughter from the house at material times. This could not properly be called a " discovery ", and I do not think that the justices are to be taken as including it under that term. So they made no finding about it—and I consider that the tenor of their reasons suggests that they did not accept this part of the husband's evidence, otherwise I do not see how they could have found that there was no conduct on the part of the wife herself giving rise to suspicion. The husband's own evidence about the absence of his daughter was not of a convincing character, and neither the daughter nor any other witness was asked about it. In my view, the husband had not established the absence of the daughter.

(b) There is no finding by the justices that the husband *believed* that the wife had committed adultery. In their reasons they use five times the word " suspicion " or its cognates, but never the word " belief ". Nor can I find in the husband's evidence any statement that he believed that his wife had committed adultery, though in cross-examination and in re-examination he said, " I thought she had committed adultery " or words to the same effect. Most of the time he spoke only as having *suspected* it. It am not satisfied that he believed in it in the sense of being convinced that it had occurred. In this connexion, it is right to take into account that the husband has at no time in these proceedings or otherwise made a formal charge of adultery against the wife; this is a relevant matter to take into account: see *Forbes* v. *Forbes* (11), and *Fishburn* v. *Fishburn* (12). That the husband had strong suspicion of adultery I do not doubt.

(c) The justices have held that the husband's suspicion was reasonable. In my view, that finding must stand. Once the husband's discoveries are accepted, even supposing that he could not be sure that his daughter had not been in the house, I think that he could reasonably suspect adultery; but I do not regard this as equivalent to reasonable belief.

(d) A reasonable belief in her adultery may entitled a husband to treat his wife as an adulteress. A reasonable suspicion no doubt entitles him to withhold full matrimonial relations until his suspicion is allayed, but not to behave towards his wife as a guilty wife until he has made such inquiries as are open to him to confirm or remove his suspicion. I can well understand the husband's reluctance to approach the wife or the daughter or Mr. Tams about his unpleasant discoveries, but it was certainly open to him to make inquiries of them, and if he was unwilling to do so, then he was not justified in behaving over some six or seven weeks as a man who wanted no more to do with his wife or in making remarks which implied an accusation of adultery. The justices have expressed the opinion that the husband's discoveries call for some explanation and that he unfortunately sought no explanation. In my opinion, as a matter of law, they should have gone on to hold that, unless and until he sought an explanation or found some more convincing evidence of adultery, he ought not to have behaved as though adultery were already established. I agree with the proposition of law that SIR JOCELYN SIMON, P., has enunciated in this connexion.

(11) [1954] 3 All E.R. at p. 466.
(12) [1955] 1 All E.R. at pp. 233, 234; [1955] P. at p. 37.

(iii) The justices have found that the wife was contemplating leaving before
the fight took place, and that, after the fight, she made her own decision to leave.
I accept these findings, but they do not conclude the issue of whether the wife
left because of the husband's conduct towards her. In my view, the fact that the
wife contemplated leaving before the fight is rather against the husband's case
than favourable to it. There is no suggestion that the wife had contemplated
leaving for any other cause than the husband's unkindness to her. The idea
that she might have left to carry on an affair with Mr. Tams was never canvassed.
While the fact that Mr. Tams was being expelled and that the daughter had
elected to accompany him may well have been the matters which led immediately
to her departure, I cannot doubt that the whole of the husband's recent behaviour,
culminating in his accusation of adultery, had a causal connexion with her
leaving. Her evidence was that she said to her daughter, " Well, I am leaving
with you. I am not standing this any longer ". I see no reason for not believing
that she did say this, that it represented the true state of her feelings, and that
what she was not willing to stand any longer was her husband's treatment of her.

(iv) Whether or not the wife did leave without just cause, it seems to me
improbable that she had any intention when she left of remaining away permanently. She had twice left her husband before and afterwards returned to him, and
her evidence was that she had it in mind that the same thing would happen on
this occasion. This evidence was not challenged. When she saw her husband again
to discuss the future, all that he had to say to her was that he had consulted a
solicitor and that he would advise her to do the same. This, taken in conjunction
with what had gone before, was a clear indication that he did not want her back
at any time. The wife so interpreted it, because she said in evidence, " I gathered
that he just did not want me any longer and that the marriage was squashed ".
The justices have not dealt with this, and I would draw the inference on the evidence that it was this attitude of the husband which made the separation
permanent.

(v) The justices say that, unless and until the husband's suspicions were
discussed and found to be groundless, he was justified in not specifically asking
her to return. He did more than not ask her to return, however, in effect he asked
her to stay away and, in my view, it was for him and not her to initiate the
discussions to see if the suspicions were groundless. As he failed to do anything
of the kind, I consider that his conduct at this stage was unjustified.

(vi) There is no evidence that the husband ever asked the wife to return, or did
anything else to end his desertion of her if it had once begun.

For these reasons, I am of the opinion that the justices' conclusion that the
husband was not in desertion cannot stand, and that on this complaint the appeal
must be allowed. There is nothing to refer back to the justices on the issue of
desertion. On the evidence, and accepting their findings as to the primary facts,
the right inference is that the husband deserted the wife. It follows that there
was also wilful neglect by him to provide reasonable maintenance for her. Accordingly, I agree that the case should be remitted to a fresh panel of justices only
for the amount of maintenance to be assessed. I also respectfully agree with SIR
JOCELYN SIMON, P., that this is a case where the husband might, by a proper offer
of reconciliation, with assurances as to his future conduct, put an end to his
desertion, and I join with my lord in expressing the hope that, by further
discussions between them, possibly with the assistance of an appropriate reconciliation officer, this marriage may again become an effective marriage.

*Appeal as to persistent cruelty dismissed. Appeal as to desertion and wilful
neglect to maintain allowed. Case remitted.*

Solicitors: *Wedlake, Letts & Birds*, agents for *Kent, Jones & Done*, Stoke-on-
Trent (for the wife).

[*Reported by* ALICE BLOOMFIELD, *Barrister-at-Law.*]

Re MACK TRUCKS (BRITAIN), LTD.

[CHANCERY DIVISION (Pennycuick, J.), February 15, 16, 1967.]

Master and Servant—Contract of service—Termination—Notice—Receiver and manager appointed by debenture holder—Contracts of employees of company forthwith terminated by receiver and employees re-employed—Company subsequently ceasing business and employee given nine days' notice—Whether continuity of employment with company notwithstanding the appointment of the receiver, the termination of service and the re-employment—Length of notice required—Whether receiver liable personally for wrongful dismissal—Companies Act, 1948 (11 & 12 Geo. 6 c. 38), s. 369 (2)—Contracts of Employment Act 1963 (c. 49), s. 1 (1).

By a mortgage a company charged its property and undertaking as security for moneys advanced. The mortgage gave the mortgagee power to appoint a receiver and manager (who would be the agent of the company) at any time after the principal moneys thereby secured became payable. On Nov. 27, 1964, the mortgagee duly appointed a receiver and manager of the company. On the same day a managing clerk employed by the receiver's firm of chartered accountants went, on instruction from the receiver, to the company's premises and addressed the assembled employees. He informed them of the appointment of the receiver and that he was, on the latter's behalf, terminating their employment and offered re-employment by the receiver on the same terms as before. Every employee accepted and continued to work as before. In November, 1964, the employees were not given particulars of terms of employment but on Apr. 1, 1965, the receiver sent all the employees, including the first respondent, a notice stating that he was about to apply to the High Court for determination of questions arising under the Contracts of Employment Act 1963. The company continued to trade until July, 1965. A letter dated July 14, 1965, signed on behalf of the receiver's firm was sent to the first respondent informing him that the company would cease to trade on July 23, and terminating his employment on that date. The first respondent had been employed continuously since 1956.

Held: (i) existing contracts of service were not determined by the appointment out of court of a receiver who was an agent of the company (see p. 982, letter D, post).

Dictum of PLOWMAN, J., in *Re Foster Clark, Ltd.'s Indenture Trusts* ([1966] 1 All E.R. at p. 48) applied.

(ii) the contract offered on behalf of the receiver and accepted by the first respondent was a contract between the company, acting through the receiver, and the first respondent, and was not a contract between the receiver as principal and the first respondent (see p. 982, letter F, post).

(iii) the continuity of the employment of the first respondent for the purposes of s. 1 (1)* of the Contracts of Employment Act 1963 was nevertheless not broken by the termination of his contract on Nov. 27, 1964, followed by his re-engagement, for s. 1 (1) did not predicate that the period of continuous employment should be under one single contract; accordingly the first respondent had been entitled to four weeks' notice under s. 1 (1) in July, 1963, on the footing that his employment had continued from 1956 (see p. 983, letters A, C and I, post).

(iv) the receiver, having entered into a new contract with the first respondent, was himself personally liable on that contract by virtue of s. 369 (2)† of the Companies Act, 1948, and having determined it on insufficient notice (nine days instead of four weeks) was liable in damages to the respondent (see p. 983, letter H, and p. 984, letter A, post).

---

* Section 1 (1) is set out at p. 981, letter E, post.

† Section 369 (2), so far as material, is set out at p. 983, letter G, post.

Applied in GRIFFITHS v SEC OF STATE [1973] 3 All ER 1184

Quaere what the position is where a receiver, appointed out of court,   A
merely continues the employment of the company's employees during his
receivership, without making a new contract (see p. 983, letter I, post).

[As to the effect of the appointment of a receiver on contracts of service,
see 6 HALSBURY'S LAWS (3rd Edn.) 325, para. 641, p. 515, para. 1000, notes (*i*)
and (*k*); and for cases on the subject, see 10 DIGEST (Repl.) 830, *5427-5432.*   B

For the Companies Act, 1948, s. 369 (2), see 3 HALSBURY'S STATUTES (2nd
Edn.) 737.

For the Contracts of Employment Act 1963, s. 1, s. 2, s. 3, s. 4, Sch. 1, see
43 HALSBURY'S STATUTES (2nd Edn.) 276, 277, 278, 284.]

Case referred to:

    Foster Clark, Ltd.'s Indenture Trusts, Re, Loveland v. *Horscroft*, [1966] 1 All E.R.   C
    43; [1966] 1 W.L.R. 125.

Adjourned Summons.

This was an application by originating summons dated May 6, 1966, by Walter
Thomas Wells Tickler, who was the receiver and manager of Mack Trucks
(Britain), Ltd., appointed on Nov. 27, 1964, by Molton Finance, Ltd., pursuant   D
to a mortgage and general charge, dated June 11, 1964, and made between the
company of the one part and Molton Finance, Ltd. (" the mortgagee ") of the
other part. By that deed the company charged, with payment to the mortgagee
of all such sums of money as were or should become owing to the mortgagee from
the company, all its undertaking, goodwill, property assets and rights present
and future, such charge being by way of floating security. The clause conferring   E
power to appoint a receiver (cl. 5) is set out, so far as material, at p. 979, letters
F to I, post. By appointment under the seal of the mortgagee, the mortgagee in
pursuance of the said power appointed Mr. Tickler to be receiver and manager of
the premises charged by " the debenture ", viz., the mortgage and general
charge of June 11, 1964, on the terms and with and subject to the powers and
provisions of the debenture.   F

The originating summons sought directions on the following matters—(i)
Whether on the appointment of the applicant as receiver and manager and by
virtue of such appointment all the employees of the company were automatically
dismissed from their subsisting employment by the company; or alternatively
continued in their employment until dismissed by the applicant. (ii) On the
footing that on and by virtue of the applicant's appointment, all the company's   G
employees were dismissed from their employment with the company whether the
applicant was obliged to give to such of the dismissed employees as was employed,
(alternatively re-employed) by him in his capacity as receiver and manager
particulars of the terms of that employment (or re-employment) as prescribed
by s. 4 (1)* of the Contracts of Employment Act 1963. (iii) On the like footing,
whether the applicant with regard to each one of the dismissed employees as was   H
employed (alternatively re-employed) by him as aforesaid, was obliged to treat
their employment (alternatively re-employment) by him as a continuation of their
previous employment with the company for the purpose of s. 1 of the Act of 1963.
(iv) Whether on such dismissal of such employees of the company either on or
by virtue of such appointment (alternatively by such specific dismissal), the
employees so dismissed became entitled by virtue of the provisions of s. 1 of the   I
Act of 1963 to periods of statutory notice or to wages in lieu thereof, which wages
the applicant was obliged to treat as preferential for the purposes of s. 94 and
s. 319 of the Companies Act, 1948. (v) Whether after and by virtue of such
employment (alternatively re-employment) by him the applicant had become
personally liable, whether by virtue of s. 369 of the Companies Act, 1948, or
otherwise for any wages payable to employees in lieu of notice. The respondents

---

* Section 4 (1), so far as material, is set out at p. 981, letter G, post.

A were William Alan Heard, a former employee of the company, and Molton Finance, Ltd.

In the course of argument at the hearing a further question was added by amendment between questions (iv) and (v), viz.—(a) whether employees who ceased to be employed on July 23, 1965*, were then entitled to statutory notice on the footing that their employment by the company continued down to that

B date or to payments in lieu of such notice and if so (b) whether the applicant should be directed or alternatively was at liberty to offer payments in lieu of notice to such employees as were not given appropriate statutory notice and (c) whether payments made by the applicant in lieu of notice ranked as expenses of or incidental to the exercise of his powers as receiver and manager under the debenture. The cases noted below† were cited during the argument in addition

C to the cases referred to in the judgment.

Muir Hunter, Q.C., and *David Graham* for the applicant.
J. W. Mills, Q.C., and *J. F. Parker* for the first respondent.
Gavin Lightman for the second respondent.

PENNYCUICK, J.: This summons is issued by Mr. Walter Thomas Wells

D Tickler, the receiver and manager of Mack Trucks (Britain), Ltd., to which I will refer as " the company ", for directions on his liability, if any, towards the first respondent William Alan Heard, a former employee of the company, in the circumstances hereinafter mentioned. The second respondent to the summons is Molton Finance, Ltd., to which I will refer as " the mortgagee ".

The company was incorporated in 1939 and carried on the business of motor

E and general engineers. By a mortgage dated June 11, 1964, the company charged its property and undertaking as security for moneys from time to time owing by it to the mortgagee. Clause 5 of the mortgage contains, so far as now material, the following provisions:

" (1) At any time after the principal moneys hereby secured shall have become payable the [mortgagee] may from time to time appoint by writing

F any person or persons to be a receiver or receivers of the property hereby charged or any part thereof . . . (2) A receiver or receivers so appointed shall be the agent or agents of the [company] and the [company] shall be solely responsible for his or their acts and defaults and remuneration. Such receiver or receivers shall have power: . . . (ii) To carry on or concur in carrying on the business of the [company] . . . (4) The net profits of carrying on the

G said business and the net proceeds of sale and all other money received by the receiver or receivers shall be applied by him or them subject to the claims of all secured and unsecured creditors (if any) ranking in priority to this security: First in payment of all costs, charges and expenses of and incidental to the appointment of the receiver or receivers and the exercise of all or any of the powers aforesaid and of all outgoings properly paid by him or them.

H Secondly in payment of remuneration to the receiver or receivers . . . Thirdly in or towards payment to the [mortgagee] of all moneys and interest due in respect of this security. Fourthly any surplus shall be paid to the [company] . . . (6) In respect of an appointment of a receiver or receivers by the [mortgagee] . . . under its statutory powers the provisions of the Law of Property Act, 1925, in that behalf shall be and they are hereby extended or

I varied in manner following, viz.: (i) So as to authorise any receiver appointed under the said provisions . . . to manage and carry on or concur in carrying on the business for the time being carried on upon the property in respect whereof the appointment is made . . ."

---

* July 23, 1965, was the date on which the company ceased to trade. Notices of termination of contracts of employment were given for that date (see p. 981, letter B, post).
† *Reid* v. *Explosives Co., Ltd.*, (1887), 19 Q.B.D. 264; *Re Newdigate Colliery, Ltd.*, [1912] 1 Ch. 468; *Parsons* v. *Sovereign Bank of Canada*, [1913] A.C. 160; *Nokes* v. *Doncaster Amalgamated Collieries, Ltd.*, [1940] 3 All E.R. 549; [1940] A.C. 1014.

On Nov. 27, 1964, the mortgagee duly appointed the applicant to be the receiver and manager of the company. The receiver is a chartered accountant and a partner in the firm of Messrs. W. H. Cork, Gully & Co. On the same date Mr. H. C. Clarry, a managing clerk employed by the receiver's firm, went on instructions from the receiver to the company's premises and collected together practically all the employees of the company, about forty-nine in all, including Mr. Heard. Mr. Clarry's account of what happened on that occasion is set out in the receiver's affidavit, and confirmed by Mr. Clarry, in the following terms:

" I am informed by the said Mr. Clarry and verily believe that on that day, in accordance with my instructions, he went to the company's said premises and immediately organised a ' pay parade ' of the employees, which was attended by all or practically all those persons who were then employed by the company. Mr. Clarry in my name informed each of those present individually of my appointment as receiver and manager and that he was on my behalf terminating the employment of each one of the company's employees, and he there and then for the purposes of my said receivership and managership offered employment by myself as receiver and manager personally to each employee at the ' parade ' at the same remuneration and on the same terms as they had previously enjoyed. No employee present declined to accept this offer of re-employment. The employees so ' re-employed ' thereafter continued to work for and to be paid by the company acting by myself as receiver and manager. A few left the employment from time to time, but the majority continued until July 23, 1965 . . ."

Mr. Heard in his affidavit gives the following account. He states that he has been employed by the company since June, 1956, on a weekly basis and that he was still employed on Nov. 27, 1964 and then he deposes:

" Nov. 27, 1964, was a Friday and I and my co-employees had been waiting for our wages for some time. At about 6.30 p.m. someone, who said he had been appointed by the receiver, told each of us that as from that evening our employment with the company was terminated but that if we reported for work as usual at 8 a.m. the following morning we would be re-engaged under new management or words to that effect. I took this as meaning that I would still be employed by the company but that the company would be under different management. I asked the gentleman in question whether my length of service would be taken into account and he said ' We will have to go into that later '. I did not say that I accepted the offer made by the gentleman, but I felt I had no alternative but to report back for work next morning. Work carried on as though nothing had happened and the company continued to trade under its own name. My cards were never returned to me, so I thought I was still employed by the company. Also, I took the view that I would be breaking my agreement with the company if I did not report for work."

There was no cross-examination on the affidavits and I doubt if there is any real difference between the accounts given by Mr. Clarry through the applicant and by Mr. Heard. I will return to that point later on.

The receiver did not in November, 1964, give to Mr. Heard or the other employees any particulars of terms of employment of the nature specified in the Contracts of Employment Act 1963, but on Apr. 1, 1965, he sent to Mr. Heard and the other employees a document in the following terms:

" Contracts of Employment Act 1963—Important Notice—The enclosed notice is sent to you without prejudice to the question (1) whether any and, if so, what form of notice by me, as receiver and manager of the company, should be served upon you under the Contracts of Employment Act 1963; and (2) as to the length of notice to which, under that Act, you are entitled,

A as to which questions I am about to make an application to the High Court of Justice for its directions."

Attached is a form of " Particulars of Terms of Employment ".

In many instances the transactions which I am about to mention were common to Mr. Heard and the other employees, but for convenience I will refer hence-forward only to Mr. Heard himself. The company continued to trade until July,

B 1965, i.e., some eight months. By a letter dated July 14, 1965, a signatory on behalf of Messrs. W. H. Cork, Gully & Co., described as the receiver of the company, wrote to Mr. Heard in the following terms:

" The above business will be ceasing to trade on July 23, 1965. This notice is to inform you that your employment with the company will be

C terminated on that date."

The company did in fact cease to trade on July 23 and the employment of Mr. Heard was in fact terminated on the same day. Mr. Heard was paid his current wages up to July 23, 1965.

The present question results from a provision as to notice contained in the Contracts of Employment Act 1963. I will read certain provisions from that

D Act.

" 1.—(1) The notice required to be given by an employer to terminate the contract of employment of a person who has been continuously employed for twenty-six weeks or more—(a) shall be not less than one week's notice if his period of continuous employment is less than two years, and (b) shall be not less than two weeks' notice if his period of continuous employment is two

E years or more but less than five years, and (c) shall be not less than four weeks' notice if his period of continuous employment is five years or more . . .

" (5) Schedule 1 to this Act shall apply for the purposes of this and the next following section for ascertaining the length of an employee's period of employment and whether that period of employment has been continuous."

F Section 2 prescribes certain rights of the employee in the period of notice. Section 3 provides that

" If an employer fails to give the notice required by s. 1 of this Act the rights conferred by the last foregoing section (with Sch. 2 to this Act) shall be taken into account in assessing his liability for breach of the contract."

G Section 4 (1) reads:

" Not later than thirteen weeks after the beginning of an employee's period of employment with an employer, the employer shall give to the employee a written statement identifying the parties, specifying the date when the employment began, and giving the following particulars of the terms of employment as at a specified date not more than one week before

H the statement is given, that is . . .",

and there follow the prescribed particulars. Finally, I will read Sch. 1, which is headed " Computation of Period of Employment ". So far as is material that provides:

" 1.—(1) The employee's period of employment shall be computed in weeks in accordance with this schedule, and the periods of two and five years

I mentioned in s. 1 of this Act shall be taken as 104 and 260 weeks respectively . . . 2. Except so far as otherwise provided by the following provisions of this schedule, any week which does not count under paras. 3 to 6 of this schedule breaks the continuity of the period of employment. 3. Any week in which the employee is employed for twenty-one hours or more shall count in computing a period of employment."

It will be remembered that Mr. Heard had been in the employment of the company from 1956 until the appointment of the receiver on Nov. 27, 1964. He then

continued, to use a neutral expression, to be employed under the receiver until
July 23, 1965. The receiver gave him nine days' notice to expire on that date.
The first question is whether this notice was sufficient under s. 1 of the Contracts
of Employment Act 1963. It was sufficient if his period of continuous employment is to be treated as having begun on Nov. 27, 1964, but not if it is to be
treated as having begun in 1956.

The first matter which was discussed in argument on this question was whether
Mr. Heard's employment was automatically determined by the appointment of
the receiver. I see no reason in principle why the appointment of a new managing
agent on behalf of a company should determine existing contracts of service,
unless of course the terms of service are such as to be inconsistent with the
appointment of a new managing agent, e.g., a contract for employment of
a manager. This point has been considered in many cases in relation to receivers
appointed by the court, and the decisions are not easy to reconcile. There appears
to be no actual decision in relation to a receiver appointed out of court who is the
agent of the company, but I was referred to the dictum of PLOWMAN, J., in *Re
Foster Clark, Ltd.'s Indenture Trusts, Loveland* v. *Horscroft* (1), and also to a
number of textbook statements all to the effect that the appointment of a receiver
out of court does not of itself bring about the determination of current service
contracts. I have no hesitation in reaching the same conclusion myself. I do not
propose to elaborate this point since it is in the present case rendered largely, if
not entirely, academic by the events of Nov. 27, 1964.

I turn next to consider the last-mentioned events. It seems to me that the only
legitimate inference to be drawn from the accounts given by the receiver and
Mr. Clarry on the one hand, and by Mr. Heard on the other hand, is that on that
occasion the receiver in his capacity as receiver offered to continue the employment of Mr. Heard on the same terms as theretofore and that Mr. Heard by his
conduct accepted that offer. When Mr. Clarry used the word " personally " after
the words " as receiver and manager " he did not mean, and cannot have meant,
as principal. The receiver was, as such, the agent of the company. Mr. Heard's
services continued to be rendered to the company and his wages continued to be
paid by the company. In these circumstances the contract, offered and accepted
by Mr. Heard, was a contract between the company acting through the receiver and
Mr. Heard and not a contract between the receiver as principal and Mr. Heard. That
corresponds to Mr. Heard's own understanding of the matter as set out in his
affidavit. So the position was this : the receiver as the new managing agent of
the company first determined Mr. Heard's employment by the company and
then as such managing agent, expressing himself to act as receiver, offered
new employment by the company to Mr. Heard on the same terms, and Mr.
Heard accepted that offer. It is necessary to consider the effects of these proceedings in two different relations, namely first of all as between the company
and Mr. Heard and secondly as between the receiver and Mr. Heard.

So far as the relation between the company and Mr. Heard is concerned, it
seems to me that the operations carried out on Nov. 27, 1964, made no substantial
difference to the contractual relation between the company and Mr. Heard. It is
always open, I suppose, to two parties to a subsisting contract to enter into a new
agreement under which they express themselves to determine the existing agreement and bind themselves by a new agreement in identical terms. Where they do
that, the substantial relation between them continues exactly as before. Nor, as
it seems to me, was there any breach in the continuity of Mr. Heard's employment
for the purpose of s. 1 of the Contracts of Employment Act 1963. Section 1 (1)
predicates that the person whose contract of employment is terminated shall
have been continuously employed, which for the present purpose means continuously employed by the same employer, though there are one or two qualifications,

(1) [1966] 1 All E.R. 43 at p. 48.

A for a specified period. The enactment does not require that the period of continuous employment should be under a single contract, i.e., the contract of employment which is terminated by the notice. Nor, can such a provision be implied into the subsection. It must frequently happen in the case of a long period of service with a single employer that employer and employee enter into a whole succession of new contracts, e.g., on promotion or for other reasons. In ordinary

B speech one would in such circumstances treat the period of employment as dating from the commencement of the first of these contracts and not from the commencement of the contract currently in force at the date of its termination. Nor, as it seems to me, is any such limitation required by the context of the subsection. On the contrary, such a limitation would be quite inappropriate, e.g., if a man had thirty years' continuous service with his employer but had

C entered into a new contract a month before its termination, then he would only be entitled to one weeks' notice. I must give effect to what I think is the plain meaning of the words in s. 1 and treat the period of continuous employment as running from the date when Mr. Heard was first employed, i.e., 1956.

It may be that there was a break of minutes or hours between the formal termination of the existing contract in November, 1964, and the formation

D of a new contract which, it may be, did not happen until Mr. Heard presented himself for work the next morning. However, any difficulty on this point appears to be obviated by the provisions which I have read out from Sch. 1 to the Act of 1963. In the relevant week Mr. Heard was employed for " twenty-one hours or more ", and it appears accordingly that the relevant week must be counted in computing his period of employment, even if there was a break of

E minutes or hours between the termination of the old contract and the formation of the new contract.

The relation between the receiver and Mr. Heard gives rise to a different question, and here what was done by the receiver is of major importance. It will be remembered that the receiver in terms expressed himself as terminating the existing employment and offering employment by himself as receiver and

F manager. On the face of what was then said on his behalf, the receiver made a new contract as receiver. This is no accident but precisely what the receiver expressed himself to do, and bound himself to do. The new contract, it seems to me, falls squarely within the terms of s. 369 (2) of the Companies Act, 1948. That subsection is in these terms :

G " A receiver or manager of the property of a company appointed as aforesaid [i.e., appointed under the power contained in any instrument] shall, to the same extent as if he had been appointed by order of a court, be personally liable on any contract entered into by him in the performance of his functions, except in so far as the contract otherwise provides, and entitled in respect of that liability to indemnity out of the assets . . ."

H So here the receiver having entered into a new contract of service with Mr. Heard rendered himself personally liable under that contract, and, having determined the contract without proper notice to Mr. Heard, the receiver incurred a personal liability in damages to Mr. Heard. I will interject at this stage that the debenture holder concedes that the receiver is entitled to be indemnified against this liability out of the assets in his hands as receiver. So no question arises as between the

I debenture holder and the receiver. I need, therefore, not pursue the questions which might otherwise arise in that connexion.

I have based my conclusions on what took place on Nov. 27, 1964. I deliberately express no view one way or the other, and do not intend to imply a view one way or the other, as to what would be the position where a receiver without express termination of an old contract and the making of a new contract merely continues during his receivership to employ servants of the company. Having reached the conclusion which I have expressed, I propose to make a declaration that Mr. Heard, who ceased to be employed on July 23, 1965, was then entitled to four weeks' notice on the footing that his employment by the company had continued **A** from 1956 down to that date, and that the receiver is liable to Mr. Heard in damages for his failure to give the proper notice. It is not possible on the material before me to assess the damages and I will formally direct an inquiry as to the damages. I imagine that there will be very little difficulty in agreeing them. The order should, I think, incorporate in some words the agreement of the debenture holder that the receiver should be indemnified against those damages out of the **B** assets of the company.

Order accordingly.

Solicitors: *Gouldens* (for the applicant and the second respondent); *Douglas Wiseman, Karsberg & Collyer*, Barking (for the first respondent).

[*Reported by* JENIFER SANDELL, *Barrister-at-Law.*]   **C**

STEVENS *v.* SERVICES WINDOW & GENERAL CLEANING CO., LTD.

[QUEEN'S BENCH DIVISION (Chapman, J.), November 30, December 5, 1966.]   **D**

Writ—Extension of validity—Cause of action statute-barred—Writ issued before cause of action statute-barred, but writ not served—Extension granted within twelve months of issue of writ—Writ served after limitation period had expired—Conditional appearance entered by defendants—Application to set aside service of writ—Burden on applicant to show good cause for renewal of writ—R.S.C., Ord. 6, r. 8 (2).

  E

The plaintiff sustained an accident on Nov. 9, 1961, giving rise to an alleged claim in negligence against his employers. On Dec. 13, 1963 the first intimation of claim was given to the employers who denied liability on Jan. 10, 1964. On Nov. 5 the writ was issued, but it was not served. The three years available for bringing the action expired on Nov. 8, 1964. On Sept. 8, 1965, the plaintiff informed the employers that a writ had been issued and would   **F** be served shortly. On Oct. 26/27, 1965, the district registrar in Birmingham granted the plaintiff on his ex parte application an extension of the validity of the writ under R.S.C., Ord. 6, r. 8 (2)*. On July 7, 1966, the writ and statement of claim were sent to the solicitors of the employers in Birmingham for acceptance of service. On July 28, the employers' London solicitors accepted service and entered conditional appearance, and on July 29 they took out a   **G** summons to set aside service.

Held: the fact that at the date when an extension of the validity of the writ was granted it had not expired did not render inapplicable the principle that good cause, viz., good reason to excuse the delay, must be shown in order to justify the granting of an extension; in the present case good cause had not been shown, and the extension granted by the registrar would be   **H** set aside (see p. 988, letter H, and p. 989, letter C, post).

[As to the renewal of a writ of summons, see 24 HALSBURY'S LAWS (3rd Edn.) 199, 200, para. 357, and 30 ibid., p. 303, para. 558; and for cases on the subject, see 32 DIGEST (Repl.) 623, 624, *2001-2013*, DIGEST (Practice) 311, 312, *358-368*, and 3rd DIGEST SUPP.

For the Limitation Act, 1939, s. 2 (1), see 13 HALSBURY'S STATUTES (2nd Edn.)   **I** 1160.

For the Law Reform (Limitation of Actions, &c.) Act, 1954, s. 2 (1), see 34 HALSBURY'S STATUTES 464.]

---

* The relevant rule at the time was R.S.C., Ord. 6, r. 8 (2). The rule was formerly enacted by R.S.C. (Rev.), 1962, which came into force on Jan. 1, 1964. Its terms were the same as those set out at p. 987, letter H, post. The revised R.S.C. came into operation on Oct. 1, 1966, and the present appeal was decided under the revised rules.

Cases referred to:

Baker v. *Bowketts Cakes, Ltd.*, [1966] 2 All E.R. 290; [1966] 1 W.L.R. 861.

Battersby v. *Anglo-American Oil Co., Ltd.*, [1944] 2 All E.R. 387; [1945] K.B. 23; 114 L.J.K.B. 49; 171 L.T. 30; 2nd Digest Supp.

Heaven v. *Road and Rail Wagons, Ltd.*, [1965] 2 All E.R. 409; [1965] 2 Q.B. 355; [1965] 2 W.L.R. 1249; 3rd Digest Supp.

Sheldon v. *Brown Bayley's Steelworks, Ltd.*, [1953] 2 All E.R. 894; [1953] 2 Q.B. 393; [1953] 3 W.L.R. 542; 3rd Digest Supp.

Appeal.

This was an appeal from an order of Master Clayton dated Oct. 11, 1966, on a summons, taken out on July 29, 1966, by the defendants, Services Window & General Cleaning Co., Ltd., in an action brought by the plaintiff, George Stevens, for damages for personal injury sustained on Nov. 9, 1961, in the course of his employment by the defendants. The summons was for an order to set aside the service of the writ, which was issued on Nov. 5, 1964, service of which was accepted and conditional appearance entered on July 28, 1966. On Oct. 26 or 27, 1965, the writ had been renewed by the district registrar in Birmingham on an application made by the plaintiff ex parte. The master adjourned the summons generally, taking the view that he had no jurisdiction and that the summons should go back to the district registrar. The facts are set out in the judgment.

Michael Lewis for the plaintiff.
M. Stuart-Smith for the defendants.

Cur. adv. vult.

Dec. 5.   **CHAPMAN, J.**, read the following judgment: This case raises once again the much litigated question as to the circumstances in which renewal of a writ may or should be granted when a defendant has accrued or accruing rights under the Limitation Act, 1939. The writ was issued in time (just, by four days) and an ex parte order was then made before the expiration of this writ for an extension of it, no service having been effected meantime.

It is convenient to set out the basic timetable at the outset. On Nov. 9, 1961, there happened, so it is alleged, an accident to the plaintiff in circumstances giving rise to a common law claim in negligence against the defendants, his employers. A long gap intervened and then, on Dec. 13, 1963, the first intimation of a claim was given to the defendants; on Jan. 10, 1964, liability was denied by the defendants; on Feb. 11, 1964, a legal aid certificate was issued to the plaintiff limited to all steps up to but excluding the issue of a writ; on Feb. 11, 1964, the defendants were notified of the issue of a legal aid certificate. Another considerable gap intervened and then on Nov. 5, 1964, the writ was issued, without any legal aid cover, but nothing was done so far as the defendants were concerned; on Nov. 8, 1964, the three years available for bringing action against the defendants expired; on Aug. 31, 1965, a further legal aid certificate was issued limited to all steps up to but excluding renewal of the writ; on Sept. 8, 1965, the defendants were told that a writ had been issued and would be served shortly. This was the first intimation that the defendants had received since Feb. 11, 1964; on Sept. 9, 1965, the defendants requested that the writ should be sent to their solicitors in Birmingham for acceptance of service; on Oct. 19, 1965, a further legal aid certificate was issued up to and including renewal of the writ and for obtaining further opinion from counsel; on Oct. 21, 1965, the affidavit of Mr. Coles in support of the application for renewal of the writ was sworn; on Oct. 26 or 27, 1965 (the first date being the one given above the registrar's signature, the second being the one which was given in the affidavits) the writ was renewed by the district registrar in Birmingham; on Jan. 25, 1966, an unlimited legal aid certificate was issued " to permit service of the writ "; on Apr. 20, 1966, the draft statement of claim was received from the plaintiff's counsel; on July 7, 1966, the writ and statement of claim were sent to the Birmingham solicitors for acceptance of service; on July 28, 1966, the defendants' London solicitors accepted service and entered conditional appearance in the central office in London; on July 29, 1966, the London solicitors took out a summons to set aside the service; on Oct. 11, 1966, the summons came before Master CLAYTON who took the view that the matter should have been taken back to the district registrar and that he had no jurisdiction to consider it. He ordered that the matter be adjourned generally; the costs were reserved. His view was contested at the time by counsel for the plaintiff and he does not now contend, having regard to the provisions of R.S.C., Ord. 4, r. 6 (3) that it is supportable. It seemed to me that this decision amounted, in substance, to a refusal to grant the relief claimed and that I could and should embark on a consideration of the merits of the matter without putting the parties to the expense of a further hearing in Birmingham from which, in any case, an appeal would have been necessary.

The legal principles which are basically material have been under consideration recently in two important judgments. In *Heaven* v. *Road and Rail Wagons, Ltd.* (1) MEGAW, J., examined with great care the decisions which had been given under the old R.S.C., Ord. 8, r. 1 (or R.S.C., Ord. 64, r. 7) and then proceeded to consider the question whether any alteration had been effected by the new wording contained in R.S.C., Ord. 6, r. 8 (2). His conclusion was that the principles of the old decisions, in so far as they stressed the importance of preserving a defendant's rights under the Limitation Act, 1939, remained unimpaired. In *Baker* v. *Bowketts Cakes, Ltd.* (2) this decision was considered by the Court of Appeal (LORD DENNING, M.R., HARMAN and WINN, L.JJ.). WINN, L.J., who dissented, did not think (3) that the reference in the headnote of *Heaven's* case (4) to " exceptional circumstances " was justified, although he regarded the decision in substance as sound, in particular that part of it which held that the change of wording in the rules did not effect a change of emphasis so far as principles were concerned.

It is perhaps important to observe the timetable in these two cases. In *Heaven's* case (1) it was as follows: on Mar. 31, 1961, was the alleged accident; on Dec. 20, 1963, the writ was issued; on Mar. 30, 1964, the time limited under the Limitation Act, 1939, expired; on Sept. 15, 1964, the negotiations for a settlement broke down; on Dec. 19, 1964, the writ expired; on Jan. 26, 1965, an order extending validity of the writ for three months was made ex parte; on Jan. 29, 1965, the writ was served; on Feb. 22, 1965, an application to set aside writ and service was dismissed by Master RITCHIE; on Apr. 9, 1965, MEGAW, J., gave judgment on appeal from Master RITCHIE. That case was, therefore, one in which before the renewal order was made (the date of the application is not in fact recorded but it would seem to have been after Dec. 19, 1964) not only had the writ died but also the maturity date for the defendants' rights under the Limitation Act, 1939, had passed.

In *Baker's* case (2) the timetable was as follows: in January, 1962, the plaintiff left the employment to which he alleged his industrial disease was due; in April, 1962, the claim was intimated to the defendants; in October, 1962, the last meeting at which the claim was discussed with the defendants' insurers was held; on May 11, 1964, legal aid was granted to cover the issue of the writ; on May 28, 1964, the writ was issued; in January, 1965, the time limited under the Limitation Act, 1939, expired; on May 25, 1965, the district registrar at Ramsgate adjourned the plaintiff's application for extension of time to serve the writ; on May 27, 1965, the writ expired; on Aug. 16, 1965, BROWNE, J., ex parte renewed the writ for four months from May 28, 1965, until Sept. 27, 1965; on Sept. 10, 1965, the writ was served; on Feb. 14, 1966, BROWNE, J., ordered that the renewal of the writ on Aug. 16, 1965 and its service on Sept. 10, 1965 be set aside.

The distinction, therefore, is that although the maturity date of the defendants'

---

(1) [1965] 2 All E.R. 409; [1965] 2 Q.B. 355.   (2) [1966] 2 All E.R. 290.
(3) [1966] 2 All E.R. at p. 294.   (4) [1965] 2 W.L.R. 1249 at p. 1250.

A rights under the Limitation Act, 1939, had occurred during the life of a valid writ, steps had been taken, although not with any result, to secure the renewal of the writ before it expired. Notwithstanding this, the Court of Appeal (5) upheld the decision of BROWNE, J., setting aside the renewal and subsequent service. This also should perhaps be stressed as regards the old rules. If the plaintiff, not having served his writ during the twelve months of its prima facie life, applied

B within that period for its renewal, the matter was governed by R.S.C., Ord. 8, r. 1 and the court or a judge could order renewal for six months from the date of the renewal and so on from time to time during the currency of the renewed writ, provided the court or a judge was satisfied either that reasonable efforts had been made to serve the defendant or that other good reasons existed for the renewal. If no application was made for renewal within the original twelve month period,

C the matter came within the general enlargement of time rule, R.S.C., Ord. 64, r. 7, which provided that—

"A court . . . shall have power to enlarge . . . the time appointed by these rules . . . and any such enlargement may be ordered although the application for the same is not made until after the expiration of the time appointed or allowed."

D
It was mainly in cases coming within the latter category that courts had consistently laid it down that,

"The court will not normally exercise its discretion in favour of the renewal of a writ after the period of service has expired if the effect of doing so will be to deprive a defendant of the benefit of a limitation which has

E accrued."

See *Sheldon* v. *Brown Bayley's Steelworks, Ltd.* (6), per SINGLETON, L.J., and per DENNING, L.J., (7). In *Battersby* v. *Anglo-American Oil Co., Ltd.* (8) LORD GODDARD, giving the judgment of the court, thought it right to mention cases within the other category. He said (9):

F "We conclude by saying that even when an application for renewal of a writ is made within twelve months of the date of issue, the jurisdiction given by R.S.C., Ord. 64, r. 7, ought to be exercised with caution. It is the duty of a plaintiff who issues a writ to serve it promptly, and renewal is certainly not to be granted as of course, on an application which is necessarily made ex parte. In every case care should be taken to see that the renewal will not prejudice any right of defence then existing, and in any case it should only

G be granted where the court is satisfied that good reasons appear to excuse the delay in service, as, indeed, is laid down in the order."

The order referred to was R.S.C., Ord. 8, r. 1. Now both categories are dealt with together in the new R.S.C., Ord. 6, r. 8 (2) which provides:

"Where a writ has not been served on a defendant, the court may by order

H extend the validity of the writ from time to time for such period, not exceeding twelve months at any one time, beginning with the day next following that on which it would otherwise expire, as may be specified in the order, if an application for an extension [of time] is made to the court before that day or such later day (if any) as the court may allow."

I It was in relation to this new rule that LORD DENNING, M.R., laid down the test in the recent decision in *Baker* v. *Bowketts Cakes, Ltd.* (10), where he said:

"In seeing whether the discretion should be exercised under that rule, we must remember the Limitation Act, 1939. A plaintiff in an action for

(5) [1966] 2 All E.R. 290.
(6) [1953] 2 All E.R. 894 at p. 895; [1953] 2 Q.B. 393 at p. 398.
(7) [1953] 2 All E.R. at p. 897; [1953] 2 Q.B. at p. 401.
(8) [1944] 2 All E.R. 387; [1945] K.B. 23.
(9) [1944] 2 All E.R. at p. 391; [1945] K.B. at p. 32.
(10) [1966] 2 All E.R. at p. 292.

personal injuries has three years to issue his writ. If he issues it within those three years, he has another twelve months within which he can serve the writ. If he requires to extend it for a further time before service, he ought to show sufficient reason for an extension of time. That follows from what LORD GODDARD said in *Battersby* v. *Anglo-American Oil Co., Ltd.* (11), and from what MEGAW, J., said in *Heaven* v. *Road and Rail Wagons, Ltd.* (12). In particular, when the Limitation Act, 1939, has run or is running in favour of a defendant, as here, the plaintiff who desires a further extension must show sufficient reason for an extension. These cases ought to be brought on for trial as soon as reasonably may be, while facts are fresh in people's minds and while medical evidence and so forth can be obtained. If the plaintiff delays until the very last minute, he has only himself to thank. If it is his solicitors' fault, he can blame them; but he ought not to get an extension, to the prejudice of the defendants, except for good cause."

Has good cause or sufficient reason been shown here? I must not allow myself to be affected by comings and goings between the plaintiff and the legal aid committee or by delays which may have occurred on the part of the latter—it would not be right that a defendant's position should be prejudiced by matters of that kind (see *Baker's* case (13)). What I must look for primarily, although not perhaps exclusively, is good reason to excuse the delay in service (see *Battersby's* case (11)). Examples of excuses which might well be valid are set out in detail by MEGAW, J., in *Heaven's* case (14). Yet nothing on these lines was put before the district registrar at all. What was said in Mr. Coles' affidavit of Oct. 21, 1965, was this:

" Since the issue of the said writ further enquiries have been instituted and expert opinions and evidence obtained, but owing to the complexities of certain aspects of the case it has not been possible to complete the preparation of the case to enable service of the writ to be effected."

What can be attributed in the way of expert opinions to a prima facie very uncomplex case of a man who slips on a roof and in falling breaks his wrist is very difficult to see, and no solicitor would really expect at the date either of issue or of service of this writ to have the case in the apple pie order necessary for trial. By the time when the matter came before Master CLAYTON, a fuller picture of what was happening was deposed to by Mr. Coles, but the stress was all on delay in obtaining counsel's opinion, supplementing the medical reports, to-ings and fro-ings with the legal aid committee, getting further opinions from counsel, getting a statement of claim drafted and so on. The final assertion in para. 16 was

" on the facts and for the reasons stated above it was not possible for the writ to be served before it expired ",

but not a single fact or reason was given substantiating the alleged impossibility.

Counsel for the plaintiff has stressed the speciality which exists here, that, when the matter came before the district registrar in October, 1965, the writ was still alive so that it was not a case where rights under the Limitation Act, 1939, had come to full maturity, as would be the case if a writ had died after the expiration of the limitation period and before any extension had been made. In my view this cannot affect the principle of the matter. If a person issues a writ on the last day or within the last week before the falling of the guillotine under the Limitation Act, 1939, he gets the benefit of a full year, less a day or a week, before he need serve his writ; but it is all along a writ which he ought to realise will not be renewable unless good cause for the renewal can be shown. This, I think, is

---

(11) [1944] 2 All E.R. at p. 391; [1945] K.B. at p. 32.
(12) [1965] 2 All E.R. 409; [1965] 2 Q.B. 355.
(13) [1966] 2 All E.R. at p. 292.
(14) [1965] 2 All E.R. at p. 415; [1965] 2 Q.B. at p. 365.

A implicit in the stress which LORD DENNING, M.R., in *Baker's* case (15) lays on the position where " the Limitation Act, 1939 has run, or is running in favour of a defendant ". Counsel for the plaintiff has urged with great force what he has described as " the intolerable injustice to the plaintiff " if the district registrar's order were set aside. If, he says, it had never been made, there would have been still time to effect service and the plaintiff's solicitors were prepared to act **B** without legal aid backing, as was shown by their initial issue of the writ. Counsel for the defendants has urged that this is tantamount to saying that if the court can be persuaded to make an order without there being adequate materials for it, the order should nevertheless be regarded as unassailable once it is too late to make good the deficiency. I think that counsel for the defendants is right about this. I must look at the matter on the basis of the material which has been put before the court and if no good and sufficient reason has been shown for a renewal **C** I am bound to say so and to make the order which necessarily follows. It is my conclusion here that no good or sufficient reason has been shown, and I must therefore set aside the renewal which was allowed by the district registrar and the ensuing service of the writ on the defendants.

Renewal and service of writ set aside.

D Solicitors: *Burton, Yeates & Hart*, agents for *Edge & Ellison*, Sutton Coldfield (for the plaintiff); *L. Bingham & Co.* (for the defendants).

[*Reported by* MARY COLTON, *Barrister-at-Law.*]

E

R. *v.* TREGEAR.

[COURT OF APPEAL, CRIMINAL DIVISION (Davies, L.J., Fenton Atkinson and Cantley, JJ.), February 17, 1967.]

Criminal Law—Evidence—Witness—Court calling witness not called by prosecu-
F   *tion or defence—Defence having sought that prosecution should call two*
   witnesses—Prosecution having declined to call both witnesses on ground of
   their unreliability, defence called one only—Case for defence closed—Matter
   not arising ex improviso—Judge seeking to ascertain truth called the other
   witness—Whether irregular and unjust to accused that court should call this
   witness—Conviction upheld.

G Two men, C. and J., saw a third man tampering with cars, including one belonging to C. They threatened to take him to the local police station. The next day the man whom C. and J. thought that they had accosted called at the house where they were, and, shortly afterwards, two car loads of men arrived and attacked the occupants of the house, including J. The appellant was arrested and charged with riot and wounding with intent to do grievous **H** bodily harm. The only real evidence against him was oral statements which he had made to the police. Both C. and J. made statements to the police and were witnesses for the prosecution in the committal proceedings. They proved unreliable witnesses and one of them was treated as hostile. At the trial counsel for the Crown intimated to the trial judge that he did not propose to call them, as they could not be put forward as truthful witnesses. The **I** judge, in his discretion, overruled a submission on behalf of the appellant that the Crown were bound to call C. and J. C. was called as a witness by counsel for the appellant. C. told the jury that the appellant was not the person whom he and J. had accosted, but that that person was an eighteen-year-old lad. When the evidence for the defence had been concluded, the trial judge called J., telling both counsel that they would have an opportunity to cross-examine him. No objection was made by counsel for the appellant. J., who was serving a sentence of imprisonment, also told the jury that the

(15) [1966] 2 All E.R. at p. 292.

Distinguished in R. *v.* CLEGHORN, *post* p. 996.

appellant was not the man whom he and C. had seen, but that that person was an eighteen-year-old lad. On appeal against conviction,

Held: the appellant had been rightly convicted, because—

(i) the trial judge was right in assenting to the course, rightly proposed by counsel for the Crown, not to call either C. or J. as witnesses on the ground that their evidence was wholly unreliable (see p. 992, letter G, post).

Dictum of LORD PARKER, C.J., in *R. v. Oliva* ([1965] 3 All E.R. at p. 122) applied.

(ii) the case did not fall within the ambit of the general rule of practice that a trial judge should not call a witness after the close of the case for the defence except on a matter which arose ex improviso and which no human ingenuity could have foreseen, since (a) the trial judge in calling J. was seeking to ascertain the truth, not to supplement the evidence for the prosecution, and (b) in the present case the defence had sought that both C. and J. should be called as witnesses for the prosecution and had raised no objection to J.'s being called by the court (see p. 993, letter E, and p. 995, letter B, post).

Dicta of AVORY, J., in *R. v. Harris* ((1927), 20 Cr. App. Rep. at p. 89) and of LORD HEWART, C.J., in *R. v. McMahon* ((1933), 24 Cr. App. Rep. at p. 97) distinguished.

Appeal dismissed.

[**Editorial Note:** This case should be compared with *R. v. Cleghorn*; see particularly at p. 998, letters G and H, post.

As to the powers of the judge in a criminal case to call witnesses, see 10 HALSBURY'S LAWS (3rd Edn.) 423, para. 778; and for cases on the subject, see 14 DIGEST (Repl.) 298, *2776-2782*.]

Cases referred to:

R. v. Frost, [1835-42] All E.R. Rep. 106; (1839), 9 C. & P. 129; 4 State Tr.N.S. 85; 169 E.R. 56; 14 Digest (Repl.) 192, *1578*.

R. v. Harris, [1927] All E.R. Rep. 473; [1927] 2 K.B. 587; 96 L.J.K.B. 1069; 137 L.T. 535; 91 J.P. 152; 20 Cr. App. Rep. 86; 14 Digest (Repl.) 298, *2777*.

R. v. Haynes, (1859), 1 F. & F. 666; 175 E.R. 898; 14 Digest (Repl.) 323, *3127*.

R. v. Liddle, (1928), 21 Cr. App. Rep. 3; 14 Digest (Repl.) 298, *2778*.

R. v. McMahon, (1933), 24 Cr. App. Rep. 95; 32 Digest (Repl.) 237, *2643*.

R. v. Oliva, [1965] 3 All E.R. 116; [1965] 1 W.L.R. 1028.

R. v. Sullivan, [1922] All E.R. Rep. 431; [1923] 1 K.B. 47; 91 L.J.K.B. 927; 126 L.T. 643; 86 J.P. 167; 16 Cr. App. Rep. 121; 14 Digest (Repl.) 323, *3129*.

Appeal.

This was an appeal by Terence William Tregear, by leave of the single judge, against his conviction on Sept. 15, 1966, at the Central Criminal Court before His Honour JUDGE CLARKE, Q.C., and a jury, of riot and of wounding with intent to do grievous bodily harm. He also appealed against his sentence of two years' imprisonment consecutive on each count. The facts are set out in the judgment of the court.

The cases noted below* were cited during the argument in addition to those referred to in the judgment.

D. P. F. Wheatley for the appellant.
M. D. L. Worsley for the Crown.

DAVIES, L.J., delivered the following judgment of the court: On May 23, 1966, two men called Chown and Jarman were near a club called Smith's Club in Rushey Green when they saw another man apparently tampering with motor

---

* *R. v. Day*, [1940] 1 All E.R. 402; *R. v. Browne*, (1943), 29 Cr. App. Rep. 106; *Harris v. Director of Public Prosecutions*, [1952] 1 All E.R. 1044; [1952] A.C. 694.

cars, including one car which belonged to Mr. Chown. They went up to him and pulled him about in some sort of way which does not really matter; and they threatened to take him to the police station, it being suggested that they were pretending to be police officers. On the following morning a telephone call was received at the Lewisham police station from a man who gave his name as Terry; and the policeman who took the call thought that it might possibly be the voice of the appellant. Whoever it was at the end of the telephone said that he had been pulled up at Rushey Green the previous evening by two people who said that they were policemen, and he wanted to know whether in fact there were policemen at that place at that time. On the evening of May 24, Mr. Chown and Mr. Jarman were at a house at 12, Lanier Road, Lewisham, with a number of people, including a Mr. and Mrs. Drew, a Mr. and Mrs. Hampsheir and a Mr. Orgles, watching television. There came a knock on the door, and a man appeared and then went away. He was apparently seen at his first visit both by Mr. Jarman and Mr. Chown. Mr. Chown and Mr. Jarman thought that it was the man whom they had accosted on the previous evening; and, in some trepidation for his motor car, Mr. Chown with Mr. Drew went and drove it away a short distance to safety. Shortly afterwards two car loads of men arrived and attacked the occupants of the house, including Mr. Jarman and Mr. Hampsheir, who was quite severely injured. At about 5 o'clock in the morning of May 28 a policeman went to the appellant's house and told him that he was making inquiries into the serious assault at 12, Lanier Road; and according to the policeman the appellant said " It's down to me then ". It is right, I think, that I should refer to the police evidence as to the oral statements made by the appellant; for in the event that really was the only evidence against him at his trial. He was taken to the police station and the detective sergeant said to him:

> " Mr. Roots has told me that he has cautioned you and that you have admitted being at 12, Lanier Road the other night when a man was seriously assaulted."

And according to the police the appellant replied: " Yes. I've told him its down to me." The sergeant said:

> " You may not know this, but the man who is in the Brook Hospital with a fractured skull was only visiting 12, Lanier Road. Why was he sorted out by you and others in this violent attack? "

The appellant is alleged to have said:

> " You know what it's all down to, Sarge, them two giving me a pull and saying they were law men. I found out where this fellow's car was. I took some blokes up there, right. We got in. There was a fight inside and outside."

The sergeant then said: " One man in the house named Jarman says you hit him with a chair "; and the appellant said: " Right, he was one of them I wanted squared up." The sergeant:

> " Yes, I can understand that to some extent, but the people who were injured are in fact innocent parties who got badly beaten up. One finished with his skull fractured. The other was hit with bricks on the hands and hit over the head with what he thinks was a guitar. Why did this happen to them? They had done nothing to you? "

The appellant is alleged to have replied:

> " As I've said, there was a fight inside and outside, everybody went potty. It's down to me. I took them up there, so that's it. I can't be a grass so I'll have to do the bird."

The sergeant said: " The man with a fractured skull was hit with a brick once or more. Who did that? " The appellant is alleged to have replied: " It could have been any of us. By the way, I'm not putting anything in writing." He was

told he would be charged; he was cautioned, and he said: " O.K. Down to me.
How do you think it will go? "

That obviously is an extremely formidable case on the facts. If the jury
accepted the police evidence about those oral statements, there could be only
one result; but it has been submitted forcefully by counsel on behalf of the
appellant that there was a serious error in the conduct of the trial. What is relied
on is this. These two men, Mr. Jarman and Mr. Chown, made statements to the
police and were called as witnesses for the prosecution before the magistrates.
They turned out to be very unsatisfactory witnesses, and one of them was
permitted by the committing court to be treated as hostile. They were very
unsatisfactory and unreliable witnesses because it was thought that they would
identify the appellant as being the man whom they had accosted on the evening
of May 23 and who had come to Lanier Road on the evening of May 24, but they
were going back on that. So when it came to the Old Bailey, counsel for the
Crown intimated to the learned judge that he did not propose to call either of
them because they were not witnesses whom the prosecution could possibly put
forward as truthful witnesses. An argument then took place, with counsel for the
appellant contending strenuously that the Crown were bound to call these two
witnesses. No doubt counsel for the appellant had a good idea what they were
likely to say when they went into the witness box. Counsel for the Crown on the
other hand stated, for the reasons which I have indicated, that he did not propose
to call the witnesses. The learned judge heard the arguments on either side and
came to the conclusion, in his discretion, that counsel for the Crown was perfectly
entitled to take the course proposed by him. We have been referred to *R. v.
Oliva* (1) and there has been read to us a substantial quotation from that case.
For the purposes of this judgment it is unnecessary to read any more than a
short passage where LORD PARKER, C.J., said (2):

" This is a case where the prosecution were abundantly entitled to form
the view that, to say the very least, these two witnesses were wholly
unreliable and that the interest of justice would not be furthered by calling
such witnesses. That is sufficient to dispose of perhaps the most important
point in this appeal."

So far as concerns the point with which I am presently dealing (which is not
the most important point in this appeal), that applies in every respect to the
present case. We are of opinion that the learned judge was perfectly right in
assenting to the course proposed by counsel for the Crown and that counsel was
right in taking that course.

The other ground of appeal also concerns the two men, Mr. Chown and Mr.
Jarman. The prosecution having refused to call them, counsel for the appellant,
having called the appellant, called Mr. Chown. To the surprise of no-one Mr.
Chown, who had formerly said that the appellant was the man whom they had
accosted on May 23, told the jury on oath that the appellant was not the man.
He said that the man who had been accosted on May 23 and had appeared on
May 24 was an eighteen-year-old lad and was not the appellant. When the
evidence for the defence had been concluded, the judge said to counsel for the
Crown:

" ' I have been considering this matter very carefully and it is now clear
in this case that the prosecution, for reasons which seem to be good to them,
decided not to call either of the witnesses Chown or Jarman, but to make
available, if necessary, for anyone to call, both these witnesses; and as a
result of this availability, the defence have called the witness Chown. We
have now reached the stage where both the prosecution and defence have
called all the evidence that they intend to put before the court and there is
one witness who is in this building at the moment whom neither side has

called, and that is Jarman.' Counsel for the Crown: ' Yes, my lord.' JUDGE
CLARKE: 'I understand that it is within the discretion of the judge, if
necessary, to call any witness that he wants to, quite apart from the prosecution or the defence?' Counsel for the Crown: ' That is so, my lord.' JUDGE
CLARKE: ' Then I call the witness Robert Alfred Jarman. Let him be brought
up, please.' "

He was sworn, and the judge said to counsel:

> " This means that both of you will have an opportunity of examining and
> cross-examining this witness. I don't think the jury should be kept in the
> dark in respect of any witness who was present on this particular occasion."

Two matters, before I proceed further are, perhaps, to be observed. First,
apart from the second question put by the judge to Mr. Jarman, namely

> " And so that there is no mystery about this, you are at present serving
> a sentence of imprisonment for a criminal offence? A.—Yes ",

no question as to the records of either of these men was put. In the submissions
as to the calling of these two witnesses, it was rightly pointed out by counsel for
the appellant that, if either of those witnesses was called by the defence instead
of by the prosecution, then counsel for the Crown would have the opportunity
of discrediting them by asking questions about their criminal records; and they
each had one. Counsel for the Crown tells us, however, that he undertook that
he would not ask such questions, unless it was sought to be put before the jury
that they were of good character; and no such question was in fact asked.
Secondly, counsel for the appellant having strenuously, as I have pointed out,
demanded that these two witnesses should be called for the prosecution, took
no sort of objection at all when the learned judge at the end of the defence
evidence indicated his intention to call Mr. Jarman. It is perhaps difficult
sometimes for counsel effectively to interfere with the course which a judge is
proposing to take; but there would have been no difficulty at that stage for
counsel for the appellant to have said: " I have called Mr. Chown but I do not
think that you ought to call Mr. Jarman." However, that was not done.
Mr. Jarman went into the witness box and having at first made rather a hash
of his evidence by using the name of the appellant as the man whom he saw on
May 23/24, went back on that and said that he only heard the name of the
appellant at the magistrates' court and that the appellant, the man in the dock,
was not the man. He said both in examination-in-chief to the judge, and under
cross-examination by counsel for the Crown and by counsel for the appellant,
that the appellant was not the man who had been accosted by him and by Mr.
Chown on the evening of May 23 and who had come to Lanier Road on the
evening of May 24. He, too, said that that man was an eighteen-year-old lad.
Counsel for the appellant suggests that that evidence had a disastrous effect on
the jury from the point of view of the defence.

What is submitted is that there is an inflexible rule that in no circumstances
whatever may a judge call a witness after the close of the case for the defence.
That proposition is supported by a citation of a number of authorities which at
first sight do lend support to the existence of such a general rule. I would only
refer to two of them, the first being *R.* v. *Harris* (3), and I will refer to the
judgment of AVORY, J. (4):

> " The two questions for this court are, was the course taken of calling
> Benton at the stage at which he was called in accordance with the recognised
> rules, and, assuming that it was, was there a proper direction on the corro-
> boration of accomplices? It is clear from the cases that only in a criminal
> case may the judge call a witness at all, but in no case is there a definite
> rule at what stage he may do so. But it is obvious that injustice may be

---

(3) [1927] All E.R. Rep. 473; 20 Cr. App. Rep. 86.
(4) (1927), 20 Cr. App. Rep. at p. 89; [1927] All E.R. Rep. at p. 475.

done to a defendant unless some limitation is put on the power, and for this case we adopt the words of TINDAL, C.J. cited in *R.* v. *Sullivan* (5) from *R.* v. *Frost* (6): ' Where the Crown begins its case like a plaintiff in a civil suit, they cannot afterwards support their case by calling fresh witnesses because they are met by certain evidence that contradicts it. They stand or fall by the evidence they have given. They must close their case before the defence begins; but if any matter arises ex improviso, which no human ingenuity can foresee, on the part of a defendant in a civil suit, or a prisoner in a criminal case, there seems to me no reason why that matter which so arose ex improviso may not be answered by contrary evidence on the part of the Crown.' That passage only applies to the Crown, but it should also apply to the judge who calls a witness, i.e., after the close of the case for the defence fresh evidence is limited to something arising ex improviso. BRAM-WELL, B., acted on this principle in *R.* v. *Haynes* (7). A further objection in this case [and this seems to me to be a most important point in the decision in *R.* v. *Harris* (8)] is that Benton was present in the dock throughout, and no doubt understood that he was asked to supplement the case against this appellant; moreover he was then unsentenced, and therefore had everything to expect from the judge. In these circumstances [and mark these words] and without laying it down that in no circumstances may an additional witness be called by the judge after the close of the defence, we think that in this case it was irregular, and calculated to do an injustice to this appellant.''

That, as indicated by the judgment, was an odd case. The man Benton had pleaded guilty but for some reason had not been sent down to the cells and had remained sitting in the dock listening to all the evidence. Then, after the defence was closed, the recorder himself called him as a witness for the prosecution; and, being unsentenced, the witness probably thought that the better the evidence he gave for the prosecution the lighter the sentence that he would get from the court. While appreciating the weight of the observations there and in other cases, that case is not one (indeed the last words of the judgment which I have read indicate this) which says that in all circumstances and in all cases a judge may not call a witness. The only other case I would refer to is *R.* v. *McMahon* (9). I will quote a passage from that case because it refers back to another authority. This is from HEWART, C.J.'s judgment (10):

" As was said by this court in *R.* v. *Liddle* (11): ' A judge at a criminal trial has the right to call a witness not called by either the prosecution or the defence, without the consent of either the prosecution or the defence, if in his opinion that course is necessary in the interests of justice, but in order that injustice should not be done to an accused person, a judge should not call a witness in a criminal trial after the case for the defence is closed, except " in a case where a matter arises ex improviso, which no human ingenuity can foresee, on the part of the prisoner, otherwise injustice would ensue." ' Now in our opinion those conditions were not fulfilled with regard to these witnesses, and it follows that the evidence of these six witnesses was, in our view, wrongly admitted.''

That is applying a general approach to the matter without any reference to any particular circumstances of any particular case.

In our view the present case does not fall within the ambit of the general rule. Here the defence, who had been insisting on the calling of these two witnesses, had called the witness Mr. Chown, but chose not to call Mr. Jarman. The judge, I suppose, if he had wanted to avoid calling Mr. Jarman at the close of the

(5) [1922] All E.R. Rep. 431; [1923] 1 K.B. 47.
(6) (1839), 4 State Tr. N.S. 85 at p. 386; [1835-42] All E.R. Rep. 106 at p. 116.
(7) (1859), 1 F. & F. 666.   (8) [1927] All E.R. Rep. 473; 20 Cr. App. Rep. 86.
(9) (1933), 24 Cr. App. Rep. 95.   (10) (1933), 24 Cr. App. Rep. at p. 97.
(11) (1928), 21 Cr. App. Rep. 3 at p. 11.

defence, could have taken one of two courses. He could have interrupted the evidence of the appellant and then, or else immediately the last question had been put to Mr. Chown and before the defence had closed its case, he could have called Mr. Jarman; but he did not. In our view, this case falls outside the application of the general rule owing to the fact that here, as is, I think, apparent, the learned judge was not seeking to supplement the prosecution by calling this witness, Mr. Jarman. Mr. Chown had been called by the defence, who had submitted that both should be called as witnesses for the prosecution. The judge considered it right, not in order to supplement the evidence for the prosecution but to ascertain the truth and put all the evidence before the jury, that this witness should be called by him and subjected to cross-examination by counsel for the Crown and for the appellant. In the event cross-examination by counsel for the appellant was more in the nature of re-examination, since this witness was wholly favourable to the appellant. Thus, Mr. Chown and Mr. Jarman were both called and the jury rejected their evidence. It is difficult, I think, in the circumstances of this case to accept the submission of counsel for the Crown that this was a matter ex improviso, the surprise being that Mr. Jarman was not called by the defence; but we accept his contention that, in the circumstances of this case, there was no objection to the calling of Mr. Jarman by the judge. Therefore, in our judgment, the second contention on the part of the appellant with regard to his conviction fails like the first. FENTON ATKINSON, J., reminds me that I might add to what I have already said, in expressing the view of the court about this appeal against conviction, that, even if we had come to another conclusion on these technical points—I do not use the word technical in any offensive sense—which have been raised in support of the appeal, this, in our view, is a case which would clearly fall within the proviso (12) to s. 4 (1) of the Criminal Appeal Act, 1907, that is to say, a case in which there was no miscarriage of justice.

I turn now to sentence. This was a very bad case. The appellant has five previous convictions, including one for robbery with violence for which he received twelve months. There was obviously some altercation between Mr. Jarman and Mr. Chown and the appellant on the evening of May 23 and, on the evidence, the appellant on May 24 summoned a gang and went round to find Mr. Chown and Mr. Jarman who had done whatever they had done to him. He missed Mr. Chown, because Mr. Chown went away; but he and his gang broke into this house and there was a riotous assembly there, in the course of which a number of innocent people suffered most unpleasant injuries. The learned judge took the view that the proper sentence was two years on the charge of riot and two years on the charge of wounding with intent to do grievous bodily harm. What is said on behalf of the appellant is that that is really sentencing him twice for one offence because it was all one affair. We can see the force of that argument. On the other hand it appears to this court that the overall sentence of four years is completely justified on the serious facts of this case. An appropriate sentence might well have been four years on each count concurrent. The learned judge took the view that the machinery of sentence should be two years on each, consecutive. With that total sentence we see no ground for interfering. Accordingly, the appeals both against conviction and sentence are dismissed.

Appeal dismissed.

Solicitors: *Registrar of Criminal Appeals* (for the appellant); *Solicitor, Metropolitan Police* (for the Crown).

[*Reported by* N. P. METCALFE, ESQ., *Barrister-at-Law.*]

---

(12) The proviso to s. 4 (1) of the Act of 1907 (5 HALSBURY'S STATUTES (2nd Edn.) 929) is amended by s. 4 (1) (c) of the Criminal Appeal Act 1966.

R. *v.* CLEGHORN.

[COURT OF APPEAL, CRIMINAL DIVISION (Lord Parker, C.J., Diplock, L.J., and Ashworth, J.), February 20, 1967.]

Criminal Law—Evidence—Witness—Court calling witness not called by prosecution or defence—Defence not having sought that prosecution should call witness—Case for defence closed—Matter not arising ex improviso—Trial taking on different aspect—Whether irregular and unjust to accused that court should call witness—Conviction quashed.

The appellant was charged with rape. The case for the prosecution was that a French au pair girl and her girl friend met the appellant and one T. at a club. They all went to the appellant's flat where the appellant raped the au pair girl, while the friend was with T. in another room. Early in the trial the judge said that if T. was not called to give evidence for the defence or the prosecution, he, the judge, would have to decide whether to call him himself. T. was called by the court as a witness after the close of the case for the defence. Both prosecution and defence counsel were allowed to cross-examine T., the defence then having to recall the appellant and to call two other witnesses who would not otherwise have been called. On appeal against conviction,

Held: the conviction would be quashed, because in the circumstances of this case there was no sufficient ground for departing from the general rule of practice that evidence should only be called after the defence case has been closed where some matter arises ex improviso (see p. 998, letter I, post).

Dictum of AVORY, J., in *R.* v. *Harris* ([1927] All E.R. Rep. at p. 476) applied.

R. v. *Tregear* (ante, p. 989) distinguished.

Appeal allowed.

[As to the power of the judge in a criminal case to call witnesses, see 10 HALSBURY'S LAWS (3rd Edn.) 423, para. 778; and for cases on the subject, see 14 DIGEST (Repl.) 298, *2776-2782.*]

Cases referred to:

R. v. *Edwards, Underwood and Edwards,* (1848), 3 Cox, C.C. 82; 11 L.T.O.S. 50; 12 J.P. 795; 14 Digest (Repl.) 306, *2902.*

R. v. *Frost,* [1835-42] All E.R. Rep. 106; (1839), 9 C. & P. 129; 4 State Tr.N.S. 85; 169 E.R. 56; 14 Digest (Repl.) 192, *1578.*

R. v. *Harris,* [1927] All E.R. Rep. 473; [1927] 2 K.B. 587; 96 L.J.K.B. 1069; 137 L.T. 535; 91 J.P. 152; 20 Cr. App. Rep. 86; 14 Digest (Repl.) 298, *2777.*

R. v. *Liddle,* (1928), 21 Cr. App. Rep. 3; 14 Digest (Repl.) 298, *2778.*

R. v. *McMahon,* (1933), 24 Cr. App. Rep. 95; 32 Digest (Repl.) 237, *2643.*

R. v. *Oliva,* [1965] 3 All E.R. 116; [1965] 1 W.L.R. 1028.

R. v. *Tregear,* ante, p. 989.

Appeal.

This was an appeal by John Robert Cleghorn against his conviction at the Central Criminal Court on July 15, 1966, before His Honour JUDGE CLARKE, Q.C., and a jury of rape. He was sentenced to six years' imprisonment.

The cases noted below* were cited during the argument in addition to those referred to in the judgment.

Sir Lionel Thompson for the appellant.
H. J. Leonard for the Crown.

LORD PARKER, C.J., delivered the following judgment of the court: The case for the prosecution was that a young French au pair girl of nineteen

---

* *R.* v. *Cain,* (1936), 25 Cr. App. Rep. 204; *R.* v. *Day,* [1940] 1 All E.R. 402; *R.* v. *Browne,* (1943), 29 Cr. App. Rep. 106.

A called Martine had been raped by the appellant on the evening of Mar. 5, 1966. The case against him rested on the evidence of Martine and of a friend of hers, another girl called Thérèse. According to them they had been to a club called The Europa Club in Finchley Road, they met the appellant and a man called Geoff Thompson, and after some time there they had gone away in a car and had finally ended up at the appellant's flat. As to what took place there, Martine

B and the other girl maintained that the appellant's manner changed, that he started making obscene jokes, that he ordered Mr. Thompson and Thérèse into another room, producing a gun which later proved to be a toy gun, that he then made Martine undress and raped her twice. At an early stage in the case the judge was clearly concerned whether any of the parties were going to call Mr. Thompson, and before the prosecution case had ended he said this:

C "I shall wait with interest to see what evidence the defence call and whether Geoff is called, but if, at the end of the case for the prosecution and the defence, Geoff is not called by either side, I shall have to consider whether I, as the judge presiding over this court, should not exercise my undoubted right to have Geoff in the witness box . . ."

D In due course the defence opened and closed their case, the appellant alone being called; the judge meanwhile had issued a subpoena to Mr. Thompson. Finally the judge said:

"In the circumstances, as neither the prosecution nor the defence have seen fit to call Thompson, I think in the interests of justice it is only right that the witness Thompson should be called to give evidence, so the jury can form

E some conclusion as to his reliability."

Thereupon Mr. Thompson was called and examined by the court, and was cross-examined by both the prosecution and the defence. His evidence, if believed, strongly supported the prosecution's case.

The first and main ground of appeal, and the only one with which the court finds it necessary to deal, is the submission that the learned judge should not

F have called this witness, as he did, at the end of the appellant's case. It is abundantly clear that it is the right of a judge in a criminal case where the liberty of the subject is at stake and where the sole object of the proceedings is to make certain that justice should be done as between the subject and the state, that he should have a right to call a witness who has not been called by either party. It is clear, of course, that the discretion to call such a witness should be

G carefully exercised and, indeed, as was said in *R.* v. *Edwards, Underwood and Edwards* (1) by Erle, J.:

"There are, no doubt, cases in which a judge might think it a matter of justice so to interfere; but, generally speaking, we ought to be careful not to overrule the discretion of counsel, who are, of course, more fully aware of

H the facts of the case than we can be."

There clearly are, however, cases in which the judge is justified in calling a witness. In *R.* v. *Oliva* (2), dealing with the failure of the prosecution to call or to tender for cross-examination a witness whose name was on the back of the indictment, the court said this:

"If the prosecution appear to be exercising that discretion improperly, it

I is open to the judge of trial to interfere and in his discretion in turn to invite the prosecution to call a particular witness, and if they refuse there is the ultimate sanction in the judge himself calling that witness."

However, when dealing with a case such as this, in which the witness is called only at the end of the defendant's case, the court has sought to ensure that that should only be done in cases where no injustice or prejudice could be caused to a

(1) (1848), 3 Cox, C.C. 82 at p. 83.
(2) [1965] 3 All E.R. 116 at p. 122.

defendant, and for that purpose laid down a rule of practice that in general it should only be done where some matter arises ex improviso. The first case dealing with this matter is *R.* v. *Harris* (3), where AVORY, J., in giving the judgment of the court said:

> " It is true that in none of the cases has there been laid down any definite rule limiting the point in the proceedings at which the judge may exercise that right; but it is obvious that, unless some limitation is put on the exercise of that right, injustice may be done to an accused person, and, for the purposes of this case, we adopt the words of TINDALL, C.J., in *R.* v. *Frost* (4) . . .''

The passage that AVORY, J., then read was concerned with the right of a plaintiff to call evidence at the end of the defendant's case, which, of course, is permissible only where a matter does arise ex improviso which no human ingenuity could foresee. AVORY, J., went on to say (5):

> " That [rule] applies only to a witness called by the Crown or on behalf of the Crown. We think that [the] principle should apply to a case where the judge himself calls a witness in a criminal trial after the close of the case for the defence—namely, that the right of the judge should be limited to cases where a matter has arisen ex improviso, which no human ingenuity could have foreseen. Otherwise, as it appears to us, injury may be done to an accused person . . .''

That rule of practice has been adopted and approved, first of all in *R.* v. *Liddle* (6) and, finally in *R.* v. *McMahon* (7). It is to be observed that AVORY, J., in *R.* v. *Harris* (8) went on to say this:

> " In these circumstances, without laying down that in no case can an additional witness be properly called by the judge . . . after the close of the case for the defence, we are of opinion that in this particular case the course adopted was irregular and calculated to do injustice to the appellant Harris.''

There may, as AVORY, J., said there, be cases where it would not be right to be bound by the general practice to which he had referred, and in a recent case before another court of the Criminal Division of the Court of Appeal as recently as Feb. 17, 1967, *R.* v. *Tregear* (9), the court held that, in the particular circumstances of that case, they ought not to treat themselves as bound by that general rule of practice. The special circumstances of that case were that the defence had been urging that the prosecution should call two witnesses; the prosecution did not call those two witnesses and the defence in fact called one and only one of them. It was in those circumstances that the judge, who incidentally was the same judge as in the present case, felt that it was right that he should call the other witness as a witness of the court. The Court of Appeal in that case upheld his conduct in calling that witness, but upheld it on the basis, as this court understands it, that it was really at the request of the defence that the witness was to be called. It is to be noted in that connexion that, in those circumstances, there was no question whatever of the trial having been continued by the calling of or recalling of witnesses. The court, however, in the present case, can find no sufficient ground for departing from the general rule of practice laid down in the cases to which I have referred. In particular, it is to be observed that, once the learned judge in this case had called Mr. Thompson, it became necessary for much more to be done; the appellant himself had to be recalled, counsel had to

(3) [1927] All E.R. Rep. 473 at p. 475; [1927] 2 K.B. 587 at p. 594.
(4) (1839), 4 State Tr.N.S. 85 at p. 386; [1835-42] All E.R. Rep. 106 at. p. 116.
(5) [1927] All E.R. Rep. at p. 475; [1927] 2 K.B. at p. 595.
(6) (1928), 21 Cr. App. Rep. 3.   (7) (1933), 24 Cr. App. Rep. 95.
(8) [1927] All E.R. Rep. at p. 476; [1927] 2 K.B. at p. 596.
(9) Ante, p. 989.

take further instructions, in fact two further defence witnesses were called who otherwise would not have been called, and the trial took on a completely different aspect.

While recognising that this rule of practice is only a general rule, and that there may be occasions to depart from it, this court can see no ground in the present case for so departing. Accordingly, the court has come to the conclusion, though it confesses with some reluctance, that this is a case in which the conviction must be quashed. So far, therefore, as this case is concerned at any rate, the appellant is discharged.

Appeal allowed. Conviction quashed.

Solicitors: *Lincoln & Lincoln* (for the appellant); *Director of Public Prosecutions* (for the Crown).

[*Reported by* N. P. Metcalfe, Esq., *Barrister-at-Law.*]

RATTAN SINGH *v.* COMMISSIONER OF INCOME TAX.

[Privy Council (Lord Guest, Lord Upjohn and Lord Pearson), November 28, 29, 30, 1966, February 2, 1967.]

Privy Council—Eastern Africa—Statute—Retrospective operation—Taxing Act repealing previous Act—Provisions of new Act applicable as if incorporated in previous Act—Proviso that no party to any " legal proceedings " pending on certain date to be prejudiced—Appeal by taxpayer lodged on following day —Notice of objection to assessments and of refusal of Commissioner to amend assessments had been previously given—Statutory discretion of judge on appeal to reduce assessment had not been re-enacted in the new Act—Whether legal proceedings were pending on the relevant date—Whether court's discretion under the previous Act remained applicable to the appeal—Income Tax (Management) Act, 1952, s. 78 (6)—Income Tax (Management) Act, 1958, s. 152, Sch. 5, para. 1.

On Dec. 30, 1958, the relevant provisions of the East African Income Tax (Management) Act, 1958, took effect and were deemed to have come into operation on Jan. 1, 1958, subject to the provisions of Sch. 5, and the previous Act, the East African Income Tax (Management) Act, 1952, was repealed subject also to Sch. 5. On Dec. 31, 1958, the appellant taxpayer, who in September, 1958, had given notice of objection (under s. 74 (2) of the Act of 1952) to additional assessments made on him by the respondent for the years 1946 to 1953, gave notice of intention to appeal to the court against a refusal by the respondent by notice dated Dec. 4, 1958, to amend the assessments. These assessments were subsequently upheld by the court on the footing that the taxpayer had made fraudulent returns. In such circumstances there would have been under the Act of 1952, s. 78 (6)*, a discretion in the court to reduce or increase the assessments; but under the Act of 1958, there was no corresponding discretion. Schedule 5, para. 1† of the Act of 1958 provided that the Act of 1952, notwithstanding the repeal, should continue to apply to tax in respect of the years of income up to and including 1957. This was made subject to a proviso that as from Dec. 30, 1958, the relevant provisions of the Act of 1958 should apply as if they had been contained in the Act of 1952 " so, however—(*a*) that no party to any legal proceedings by or against the [respondent] which are pending on [Dec. 30, 1958] shall be prejudicially affected by this paragraph; . . .". The question arose whether

* Section 78, so far as material, provides: " (1) Any person who, being aggrieved by an assessment . . . may appeal against the assessment to a judge upon giving notice in writing to the commissioner . . . (6) The judge may confirm, reduce, increase, or annul the assessment or make such order thereon as to him may seem fit."
† Schedule 5, para. 1 is printed at p. 1002, letters E to G, post.

the Act of 1952 or the Act of 1958 was applicable in regard to the taxpayer's appeal.

Held: (i) the provisions of para. 1 of Sch. 5 to the Act of 1958 overrode the corresponding provisions of the Act of 1952 unless the taxpayer could obtain protection under sub-para. (*a*) of the proviso to para. 1 (see p. 1003, letter G, post).

(ii) the taxpayer was not a " party to any legal proceedings against the respondent which were pending on Dec. 30, 1958 " within para. (*a*) of the proviso, because his notice of intention to appeal to the court against the assessments was given on Dec. 31, 1958, and neither the previous service by the taxpayer of notice of objection under s. 74 (2) of the Act of 1952 nor the respondent's notice of refusal to amend the assessments was sufficient to constitute pending legal proceedings (see p. 1004, letters A and D, post); consequently the taxpayer had not brought himself within the proviso and the court's former discretion under s. 78 (6) of the Act of 1952 to amend an assessment did not apply.

Appeal dismissed.

[As to fiscal statutes being construed strictly, see 36 HALSBURY'S LAWS (3rd Edn.) 416, 417, para. 633, and as to the operation of savings provisions in repealing enactments, see ibid., pp. 469, 470, para. 714; and for cases on the construction of fiscal statutes, see 44 DIGEST (Repl.) 331-334, *1656-1687*, and for cases on the effect of repeals, see ibid. pp. 371, 372, *2098-2117*.]

Appeal.

This was an appeal from a judgment and order of the Court of Appeal for Eastern Africa at Nairobi, Kenya (GOULD, A.P., CRAWSHAW, A.V.-P., and EDMONDS, J.), dated Aug. 24, 1963, which substantially dismissed the appellant's appeal from a judgment and order of the Supreme Court of Kenya at Nairobi (MAYERS, J.), dated July 31, 1961, dismissing eight appeals against the decisions of the respondent, the Commissioner of Income Tax, relating to assessments of income tax on the appellant for the years of income 1946 to 1953 inclusive. The facts and statutory enactments are set out in the judgment of the Board.

P. M. B. Rowland and *B. G. C. Webb* for the appellant.
Hubert H. Monroe, Q.C., and *M. G. Muli* (of the Kenya Bar) for the respondent.

LORD UPJOHN: On May 28, 1958, the respondent, acting under the powers conferred on him by s. 72 of the East African Income Tax (Management) Act, 1952 which was then in force, made additional assessments on the appellant for the years of income 1946-1953 inclusive. The appellant challenges the correctness of those assessments.

Section 72 provided that where it appeared to the respondent that a taxpayer had been assessed at a less amount than that which ought to have been charged he might, within seven years after the expiration of the year of income, raise additional assessments on him; but there was a proviso in these terms: -

" (*a*) where any fraud or wilful default has been committed by or on behalf of any person in connexion with or in relation to tax for any year of income, the commissioner may, for the purpose of making good to the revenue of the territories any loss of tax attributable to the fraud or wilful default, assess that person at any time; "

Section 40 of the Act of 1952 provided that any person who omitted from his return for any year of income any amount which should have been included should be charged with an amount of tax equal to treble the difference between the tax as calculated in respect of the total income returned by him and the tax properly chargeable after including the amount omitted. Section 40 (2) and (3) were in these terms;

A

" (2) If the commissioner is satisfied that the default in rendering the return or any such omission was not due to any fraud, or gross or wilful neglect, he shall remit the whole of the said treble tax and in any other case may remit such part or all of the said treble tax as he may think fit.

" (3) The additional amounts of tax for which provision is made under this section shall be chargeable in cases where tax has been assessed by the

B

commissioner under the provisions of s. 72 as well as in cases where such income or any part thereof is determined from returns furnished."

The respondent made the additional assessments on the footing that for each of the relevant years 1946-1953 the appellant was guilty of fraud or gross or wilful neglect, and so he claimed treble tax in respect of each year. However exercising

C

the discretion vested in him by s. 40 (2) he remitted parts of such additional tax in each year. The rate of remission varied from year to year but it is material, for the reasons which will appear later in their lordships' judgment to note that he never charged as much as twice the basic tax by way of additional tax; the overall average additional tax for the relevant years was 152 per cent. of the basic tax.

D

The appellant under s. 74 (2) of the Act of 1952, lodged notices of objection against these additional assessments, but by a notice dated Dec. 4, 1958, the respondent, acting under s. 74 (4), refused to amend the assessments or any of them and from such refusal the appellant, by notice dated Dec. 31, 1958, appealed to the judge under s. 78 (1). Section 78 (6) provided that the judge might confirm, reduce, increase or annul the assessment.

E

The appeal came on for hearing before MAYERS, J., on June 6, 1960: it lasted nineteen days spread over many months and in a reserved judgment delivered on July 31, 1961, he reached the clear conclusion that the appellant had made fraudulent returns in respect of each of the relevant years of assessment and he dismissed the appeal. The appellant appealed to the Court of Appeal (GOULD, A.P., CRAWSHAW, A.V.-P., and EDMONDS, J.), who dismissed the appeal, with an immaterial variation in respect of some years of income. The trial judge's finding

F

of fraud was challenged in the Court of Appeal but the acting president, who delivered the leading judgment of that court, expressly upheld the judge's finding of fraud in each and every relevant year, and this finding has not been challenged before their lordships.

Had the matter rested there two points of construction of the Act of 1952 would have arisen, neither of them, as their lordships think, of great difficulty; to these

G

points their lordships will briefly return later. The major difficulty has been created, however, by the provisions contained in a new Income Tax Act entitled the East African Income Tax (Management) Act, 1958 and published in the Gazette on Dec. 30, 1958. Their lordships must refer to a number of sections and to Sch. 5 to the Act of 1958. Section 101 (1) (*a*) provided that on default in making a return the taxpayer should be charged with double the normal tax. Section

H

101 (1) (*b*) corresponded with s. 72, proviso (*a*) of the Act of 1952 and was in these terms:

" Any person who . . . (*b*) omits from his return of income for any year of income any amount which should have been included therein shall, where such omission was due to any fraud or to any gross neglect, be charged for

I

such year of income with an amount of tax equal to double the difference between the normal tax chargeable in respect of the income returned by him and the normal tax chargeable in respect of his total income; "

Section 101 (5) is in these terms:

" (5) Notwithstanding anything in Part 13, where in any appeal against any assessment which includes additional tax one of the grounds of appeal relates to the charge of such additional tax, then the decision of the local committee or judge in relation to such ground of appeal shall be confined to the question as to whether or not the failure, default, or omission which gave rise to the charge under sub-s. (1) was due to any fraud or to any gross neglect; and where it is decided that such failure, default or omission was not so due, then the whole of the additional tax so charged shall be remitted."

It is to be noted, and is the chief reason for this appeal, that while under the former s. 78 (6) the judge could, in effect, vary the remission by the respondent of the treble tax, no longer has he such power under this subsection, and that in that respect the decision of the respondent is final.

Section 151 of the Act of 1958 is important:

" (1) The transitional provisions contained in Sch. 5 shall, notwithstanding anything in this Act, have effect for the purposes of the transition from the provisions of the enactments repealed by this Act to the provisions of this Act.

" (2) If any difficulty should arise in bringing into operation any of the provisions of this Act or in giving effect to such provisions, the High Commission may by order amend Sch. 5 in such respect as appears necessary or expedient for the purpose of removing such difficulty: Provided that no order under this section shall be made later than Dec. 31, 1959, and every such order shall be laid before the assembly at the next meeting after the publication of such order."

By s. 152 subject to Sch. 5 the Act of 1952 (inter alia) was repealed.

This brings their lordships to the provisions of Sch. 5 which give rise to the great difficulty in this case.

" 1. Subject to this Schedule, the repealed enactment shall, notwithstanding its repeal, continue to apply to income tax chargeable, leviable, and collectable, under such enactment in respect of the years of income up to and including the year of income 1957, as if such enactment had not been repealed: provided that, as from the date of the publication of this Act in the Gazette, the provisions contained in Parts 10 to 17 inclusive of this Act shall apply as if such provisions had been contained in the repealed enactment, so, however—(a) that no party to any legal proceedings by or against the commissioner which are pending on the date of such publication shall be prejudicially affected by this paragraph; (b) that Part 13 of the repealed enactment shall, in relation to any act or omission which took place before the date of such publication, continue to have effect to the exclusion of Part 15, other than s. 135, of this Act."

In the courts below the major issue was that of fraud, which does not arise here, and before their lordships the main arguments were addressed to the effect of Sch. 5, para. 1 on the assessments made on the appellant which were still outstanding when the Act of 1958 was published on Dec. 30, of that year.

Two distinct points arise: (i) What is the effect of the proviso that the provisions contained in Parts 10-17 of the Act of 1958 should apply " as if such provisions had been contained in the " Act of 1952? (ii) Can the appellant claim the benefit of para. (a) on the footing that legal proceedings were pending on Dec. 30, 1958?

As to the first point, it seems to have been assumed in the courts below that the necessary consequence of the incorporation of the stated provisions of the Act of 1958 into the Act of 1952 was to override the provisions of the latter Act where there was any inconsistency, and only the second point was seriously argued. Before their lordships, however, it was strenuously argued that the 1952 code remained in existence and continued to run parallel to the 1958 code, and that the latter was a supplement only to fill in any gaps in the former code. Some examples were referred to, the first three by way of argument or illustration only for they do not arise for decision in this case, and the last being directly in point, to show that the legislature cannot have intended retroactively to have affected

A the vested rights of the taxpayers under the Act in force during the relevant years of income. First, under the Act of 1952 the taxpayer had sixty days within which to appeal from a refusal of the respondent to amend an assessment; under the Act of 1958 he only had forty-five days; secondly, there was no power under the Act of 1958 corresponding to the provisions of s. 77 (5) of the Act of 1952 which entitled the taxpayer, in cases where the tax involved was 200s. or under,

B to elect to treat the hearing before the local committee as final. Thirdly, the additional tax chargeable under the Act of 1958 was double tax compared to treble tax under the Act of 1952 (incidentally an alteration to the taxpayer's benefit). Finally, while under the Act of 1952 the judge was entitled to exercise his own discretion as to the remission of additional tax, it is perfectly clear that he has no such power under the Act of 1958. Minor inconsistencies were also

C relied on, which their lordships do not think it necessary to mention. It was said that these inconsistencies and injustices to the taxpayer made it necessary to treat the provisions of the Act of 1952 as remaining applicable to assessments made in respect of years of income up to 1957 inclusive.

Their lordships cannot agree with this argument. In the first place, although the drafting may be inelegant, the legislature in introducing by Sch. 5, para. 1

D certain parts of the Act of 1958 into the Act of 1952 thereby repealed, must have intended that they should supersede and, where inconsistent, control and override the former provisions, for in that way only is it possible to give sensible effect to the scheme of legislation. Furthermore, it seems clear that the legislature realised that such retroactive alterations to the Act of 1952 in respect of past years of income might prejudice and act unfairly to taxpayers where their tax affairs

E remained unsettled on Dec. 30, 1958. This is evident from the terms of s. 151 of the Act of 1958 and particularly sub-s. (2) which has already been set out. This system of legislating is not new to Kenya for it copied the same procedure when the Act of 1952 superseded the Kenya Ordinance c. 204 of 1940. This is further supported by the provisions of para. 1 (*a*) which clearly contemplated that the introduction of the Act of 1958 provisions might prejudicially affect taxpayers

F retroactively where their tax affairs remained outstanding on Dec. 30, 1958, for an exception was made to such prejudice if legal proceedings were then pending; finally, para. (*b*) made it quite plain that the new scales of penalties were not to apply to offences committed during the pre-1958 years of income.

In their lordships' judgment, therefore, in respect of pre-1958 assessments outstanding on Dec. 30, 1958, the provisions of the Act of 1958 introduced by

G Sch. 5, para. 1 supersede, override and control the corresponding provisions in the Act of 1952, unless the taxpayer can claim the protection of paras. (*a*) or (*b*) of para. 1. Accordingly, their lordships agree that in the courts below it was rightly held that there was no discretionary power of remission of additional tax any longer vested in the trial judge.

However, before turning to consider the second point their lordships would

H mention that (though it does not arise for decision now), as they are at present advised, the relevant provisions of the Act of 1958 which are incorporated into the Act of 1952 must act both in favour of and against the Crown; thus, had the respondent charged the appellant with additional tax of more than double tax for any of the relevant years of income, such charge could not have stood in respect of assessments outstanding on Dec. 31, 1958. Their lordships did not

I understand counsel for the respondent to dissent from this general proposition.

As to the second point, the appellant appealed on Dec. 31, 1958, against the refusal of the respondent to amend the relevant assessments. The question which their lordships have to consider is whether there were any legal proceedings by or against the commissioner which were properly described as " pending " on Dec. 30, 1958. Their lordships have some sympathy with the appellant for, had he appealed one day or at any rate two days earlier, undoubtedly there would have been pending proceedings, though they do not overlook the fact that MAYERS, J., would have had power 'had the Act of 1952 remained operative not

merely to remit but also to increase the additional tax. It was argued that for **A**
the purposes of this paragraph proceedings could properly be described as pending,
either from the service by the appellant of notice of objection under s. 74 (2) of
the Act of 1952 or, at latest, from the refusal by the notice given on Dec. 4, 1958,
whereby the respondent refused to amend his assessments. It was not seriously
suggested that the negotiations and correspondence between the appellant's
advisers and the respondent were technically legal proceedings for, clearly, they **B**
were not. As GOULD, A.P., pointed out in his judgment the respondent was then
merely finalising the assessment. It was argued, however, that in a broader sense
which should be adopted in justice to the taxpayer whose liabilities were being
retroactively affected they were pending in the sense that legal proceedings were
then imminent and that the next step would initiate legal proceedings, that is an
appeal from the refusal of the respondent, and this was the inevitable consequence **C**
of the negotiations and correspondence down to date. A number of authorities
was cited to their lordships, but they do not really touch on this short point.

   Their lordships have reached the clear conclusion that it cannot be said with
any sense of legal accuracy that there were legal proceedings pending on Dec. 30.
On this point they agree with the judgments given in both courts below and do
not think that they can usefully add anything thereto.   **D**

   Though counsel for the appellant did not dispute or challenge the finding of
fraud in the courts below, he raised one point where he said the trial judge misdirected himself for he said that it was the duty of the judge to make up his mind
as a separate question in relation to each year of income what was a proper
estimate of the appellant's income of that year and then to consider whether
the discrepancy between the figures return by the appellant and the figures **E**
which the judge thought to be a fair estimate of his income was sufficient to infer
fraud, and the onus it was said, was on the respondent to prove that in respect of
each year. As the learned judge did not do this, therefore the matter must go
back for him to reconsider the whole matter. This argument seems to be based
on a fallacy. If the respondent wants to reopen an otherwise time barred year of
income the onus is on him to prove fraud or gross or wilful neglect (s. 105 (1) of **F**
the Act of 1958). This question is not to be determined on making estimates of
income but on the facts of each particular case, which the judge assesses as a jury
question: was the taxpayer in respect of the relevant year fraudulent or not?
The respondent discharged this onus in respect of each relevant year. Then that
tax year being reopened for consideration the usual rule applies; the onus is on **G**
the taxpayer to show that respondent's assessment is excessive. This he signally
failed to do in any year of income.

   It only remains to notice two points argued before their lordships arising under
the provisions of the Act of 1952, but which in fact are now academic, as they do
not arise under the incorporated provisions of the Act of 1958. First it was said
that under s. 72 of the Act of 1952 tax lost could be recovered only once and not **H**
three times. Their lordships think that this point is fully answered in the concise
judgment of MAYERS, J., where he said that the argument was fully disposed of
by the provisions of s. 40 (3). Their lordships do not desire to add anything to that.
Then it was said that under s. 72 an additional (post six year) assessment is
confined to income fraudulently omitted, though it is conceded that this is not so
under the relevant provision of the Act of 1958, where the words on which the **I**
argument was founded namely " for the purpose of making good any loss of tax
attributable to the fraud or wilful default " do not occur. Even if, however,
s. 72 was still operative the onus would be on the appellant to prove that some
income was omitted innocently from his return, and this he failed to do.
Accordingly their lordships do not have to consider whether, had the facts been
otherwise, on the true construction of s. 72 he would have escaped any assessment
in respect of any sum innocently omitted.

For these reasons their lordships will dismiss the appeal. The appellant must pay the cost of the appeal.

Appeal dismissed.

Solicitors: *T. L. Wilson & Co.* (for the appellant); *Charles Russell & Co.* (for the respondent).

[*Reported by* Kathleen J. H. O'Brien, *Barrister-at-Law.*]

BOARD OF GOVERNORS OF THE HOSPITAL FOR SICK CHILDREN *v.* WALT DISNEY PRODUCTIONS, INC.

[Court of Appeal, civil division (Lord Denning, M.R., Harman and Salmon, L.JJ.), January 24, 25, 26, February 14, 1967.]

Copyright—Assignment—Licence—Exclusive licence assignable only with author's consent—Death of author—Whether consent to assignment could be given by his assigns.

Copyright—Licence—Exclusive licence to produce author's literary and dramatic works in cinematograph or moving picture films—Licence granted in 1919— Sound track films not then produced commercially—Whether licence extended to sound motion pictures or only to silent films.

Injunction—Jurisdiction—Foreign corporation—Breach of contract—Submission to English jurisdiction—No evidence of assets within jurisdiction—Whether remedy by injunction available to restrain its agents from further breaches of contract.

The author of a play, " Peter Pan ", granted by an agreement made in 1919 (the " agreement of 1919 ") a licence to make films of the play. The agreement of 1919 granted " the sole and exclusive licence to produce all [the author's] literary and dramative works existing and future of whatsoever nature for the terms of the respective copyrights thereof in cinematograph or moving picture films ". This agreement did not provide that references to the author should include his assigns or that references to the assignee company should include the company's assigns; but it provided that the company should not assign the benefit of the agreement without the author's consent. In 1925 the company with the author's consent assigned the benefit of the agreement to an American film corporation. A silent film of the play was produced and released in 1925. In 1932 the assignee corporation re-assigned to the author the film rights in all his works not already produced, except only works from which motion pictures had been made. By an assignment made in 1929 the author had assigned to the plaintiff (the " hospital ") all of his copyright in specified works, including " Peter Pan ", together with the benefit of the agreement of 1919. He died in 1937 having bequeathed to the hospital all his performing rights in " Peter Pan ". In October, 1938, there was an assignment by the American film corporation to a newly formed Californian corporation in which a corporation of the same name as the defendant was consolidated; this constituent corporation was thus merged in the new corporation. The new corporation, which later changed its name, was the defendant. The hospital's consent was given to an assignment of the agreement of 1919 to the constituent corporation of the same name as the defendant, but not to an assignment to the defendant itself. On Jan. 11, 1939, the hospital entered into an agreement (the " agreement of 1939 ") with the defendant which recited that the defendant had acquired the film rights granted by the agreement of 1919; the agreement of 1939 author-ised the defendant to make an animated cartoon of " Peter Pan ". By the agreement of 1939 the defendant agreed that after ten years (which expired in 1963) it would not object to " the hospital or its assigns or licensees making an ordinary sound motion picture exclusively with living actors ". The agreement of 1939 was expressed to be subject to the law of Great Britain and the jurisdiction of the English courts. In 1964 the hospital was in negotiation with a view to authorising the making of a sound film of " Peter Pan ", when the defendant objected. As a consequence of this objection the hospital lost the prospect of a valuable contract. The hospital sued the defendant for damages and obtained an inquiry as to damages and an injunction restraining the defendant from making statements calculated to lead to the belief that the hospital was not entitled to make sound films based on " Peter Pan ". On appeal the breach of contract was not disputed, but the defendant contended that the injunction should not have been granted and sought the decision of the Court of Appeal on (a) whether the agreement of 1919 licensed the making of sound films as well as silent films and (b) whether the defendant was validly the assignee of that licence. No evidence was adduced whether the defendant had assets in England.

Held: an injunction could properly be granted against the defendant, although it was a foreign corporation, to stop its agents from doing acts in breach of contract either in England or abroad, and notwithstanding that there was no evidence before the court that the foreign corporation had assets within the jurisdiction, for it was for the defendant to produce evidence of the absence of such assets if it wished an injunction to be refused on that ground (see p. 1011, letter G, p. 1012, letter I, to p. 1013, letter B, and p. 1016, letter H, post).

Semble: the wording of the licence granted by the agreement of 1919 was wide enough to licence the making of sound films as well as silent films (see p. 1014, letter G, p. 1017, letter D, and cf. p. 1009, letter G, post).

L. C. Page & Co. v. *Fox Film Corpn.* ((1936), 83 F. (2d) 196) and *J. C. Williamson, Ltd.* v. *Metro-Goldwyn-Mayer Theatres, Ltd.* ((1937), 56 C.L.R. 567) applied.

Per CURIAM: in the circumstances, however, the agreement of 1919 licensed only the making of silent films because (a) (per LORD DENNING, M.R.) having regard to other terms in the agreement of 1919, to its date and the facts that sound films were not then in contemplation and that a silent film was produced in 1925 in accordance with the agreement, the licence given by the agreement of 1919 did not extend to making sound films of " Peter Pan " and (b) (per HARMAN, L.J.) the film producing rights conferred by the agreement of 1919 were spent as from the re-assignment of 1932 (see p. 1009, letter H, p. 1010, letter A, p. 1014, letter E, and p. 1017, letter G, post).

Per LORD DENNING, M.R., and SALMON, L.J. (HARMAN, L.J., dissenting): in the agreement of 1919 the references to the author and to the company should be construed as including their respective assigns (see p. 1010, letters C and E, and p. 1017, letter H, post; cf., p. 1013, letter C, post).

Decision of BUCKLEY, J., ([1966] 2 All E.R. 321) affirmed as to the grant of the injunction.

[As to the rights granted by copyright licences, see 8 HALSBURY'S LAWS (3rd Edn.) 408, para. 741, and as to assignment of such licences, see ibid., pp. 408, 409, para. 744; and for cases on the subject, see 13 DIGEST (Repl.) 94, 95, *359-366.*

As to the persons against whom an injunction may be granted, see 21 HALSBURY'S LAWS (3rd Edn.) 408, para. 856; and cf. ibid., p. 346, para. 725.]

Cases referred to:

Page (L. C.) & Co. v. *Fox Film Corpn.*, (1936), 83 F. (2d) 196. The series of reports is FEDERAL REPORTER, second series.

Williamson (J. C.), Ltd. v. *Metro-Goldwyn-Mayer Theatres, Ltd.*, [1937] V.L.R. 67, 140; *on appeal* (1937), 56 C.L.R. 567; 11 A.L.J. 112; 13 Digest (Repl.) 96, *88.*

Appeal.

On notice of appeal, as amended, the defendant appealed from parts of the judgment of BUCKLEY, J., dated Mar. 10, 1966, and reported [1966] 2 All E.R. 321, in an action brought by the plaintiff hospital against the defendant, a Californian corporation. The appeal was against (i) the granting of the injunction restraining the defendant by its officers or by its servants or agents or any of them, or otherwise howsoever in breach of an agreement (referred to as the " agreement of 1939 ") from objecting to the hospital or its assignees or licencees making or exhibiting a film with living actors based on the play " Peter Pan " by J. M. Barrie under the title of " Peter Pan " and from threatening Mr. George Cukor and Mr. Mel Ferrer or any other person in respect of the production and release of a film starring Audrey Hepburn or any other well known actors and entitled " Peter Pan "; and (ii) the inquiry whether any and if any what damages had been sustained by the hospital by reason of the breach by the defendant of the agreement of 1939. The defendant sought that the order for the injunction should be set aside, and that as regards any inquiry as to damages, the Court of Appeal should declare that it should be taken on the basis (a) that the agreement of 1919 was effective to grant sound and silent film rights in the works mentioned in that agreement; and (b) that the agreement of 1938 was effective to pass the rights granted by the agreement of 1919. The grounds of appeal were that the trial judge was wrong in deciding that the agreement of 1919 was only effective to grant silent film rights in the works mentioned in the agreement of 1919; that he was wrong in deciding that the agreement of 1938 was ineffective to pass the rights granted by the agreement of 1919 because of the absence of any consent under cl. 11 of the agreement of 1919, and that he improperly exercised his discretion in granting an injunction as the defendant was an American corporation. There was no appeal against the decision of the trial judge that the defendant was in breach of contract and that damages were recoverable.

The cases noted below* were cited during the argument in addition to those referred to in the judgments.

Frank Whitworth, Q.C., and *E. P. Skone James* for the defendant.
Sir Milner Holland, Q.C., and *A. D. Russell-Clarke* for the plaintiff hospital.

Cur. adv. vult.

Feb. 14. The following judgments were read.

LORD DENNING, M.R.: This case is full of detail but it arises in this way. The copyright in " Peter Pan " is now vested in the plaintiffs, the Hospital for Sick Children, Great Ormond Street (whom I will call " the hospital "). The defendant, a Californian corporation, called Walt Disney Productions, Inc., has a licence to make animated cartoons of " Peter Pan ". In June 1964 the hospital were in negotiations with two gentlemen called George Cukor and Mel Ferrer. The hospital proposed to grant them the right to make a sound film of " Peter Pan " with Miss Audrey Hepburn as the principal boy. The hospital was to get £45,000 out of it. When the defendant got to know of this proposal, it objected to it. It said that the hospital had no right to use the title " Peter Pan " for a sound film or to authorise Mr. Cukor or Mr. Ferrer to use it. In consequence

---

* *Kalem Co.* v. *Harper Brothers*, (1911), 222 U.S. 55; *Serra* v. *Famous Lasky Films Service, Ltd.*, (1922), 127 L.T. 109; *Messager* v. *British Broadcasting Co., Ltd.*, [1927] 2 K.B. 543; *Macloon* v. *Vitagraph Inc.*, (1929), 30 F. (2d) 634; *Kirke La Shelle Co.* v. *Paul Armstrong Co.*, (1932), 257 N.Y.S. 38; (1933), 188 N.E. 163; *Cinema Corp. of America* v. *De Mille*, (1933), 267 N.Y.S. 327, 959; *Pathé Pictures, Ltd.* v. *Bancroft*, (1933), MacG. Cop. Case (1928-35) 403; *Rosenberg* v. *Wright*, (1934), 20 Cop. Cas. 599; *Murphy* v. *Warner Brothers Pictures, Inc.*, (1940), 112 F. (2d) 746; *Ricordi & Co.* v. *Paramount Pictures, Inc.*, (1956), 92 F. Supp. 537.

the negotiations fell through. The hospital now sues the defendant for causing this loss. BUCKLEY, J. (1) has decided in favour of the hospital. He made a declaration that the defendant has no right to object to the hospital or its licensees making a sound film under the title " Peter Pan ". He granted an injunction restraining the defendant from objecting to it; and he ordered an inquiry as to damages.

The defendant appeals to this court. In its original notice of appeal it complained of the whole order of the judge; however it afterwards amended the notice. It admits now that it was wrong in objecting to the film. It admits that the declaration was properly made against it. It admits that the judge properly ordered an inquiry as to damages. It contends, however, that he ought not to have granted an injunction against it. It contends also that some of the findings (contained in his stated reasons) were wrong. We had some discussion whether we were entitled to consider in this court the defendant's complaint about the judge's findings because they found no place in his order; but both sides invited us to do so; and I think that we should. For this reason. The gist of the complaint is that the judge, in ordering an inquiry as to damages, ought to have given certain directions, and failed to do so. It is a complaint of an omission from the order. Such a complaint can properly be made the subject of appeal. These are the two points:—1. The defendant claims that under an agreement of 1919 Sir James Barrie granted a licence to make both silent and sound films of " Peter Pan ". 2. The defendant claims that it is validly the assignee of that licence. Such being the points, I will state the facts concerning them.

James Barrie was born in 1860. In 1904, when he was forty-four, he wrote a fairy-tale. He called it " Peter Pan or The Boy Who Never Grew Up ". He wrote it as a play to be performed on the living stage. It was first produced on Dec. 27, 1904, and was a great success. It has been produced many times since. Barrie had, of course, the copyright in the work, because he was the author. That gave him the sole right to authorise its performance, not only as a play, but also to turn it into a book, or to make a film of it. That right lasted for his life and for fifty years after his death. He had the right to assign it, or any part of it, during his lifetime for the period of his life and twenty-five years after his death: and he had the right to make a will disposing of the remaining twenty-five years.

In 1919 Sir James Barrie granted a licence to make films of " Peter Pan ". I shall have to consider in a few moments whether this was a right only to make a *silent* film or whether it covered both *silent* and *sound* films. That was the only grant which he made out of the copyright. He afterwards transferred all the rights he retained to the hospital. He did it by an assignment dated Aug. 14, 1929, followed up by his will dated June 14, 1937. He died on June 19, 1937. So the hospital is the owner of the entire copyright in " Peter Pan " save for the grant of 1919. The question is: what did that grant comprise? Was it only silent films? Or sound films as well?

1. *The Agreement of 1919*

The agreement was dated Aug. 19, 1919, and was made between Sir James Barrie and the Famous Players Film Co., Ltd. At that time the only films on the market were silent films. People had been trying for years to find a way to make talking films. Edison had experimented in 1896; but no-one had succeeded in making it a practical proposition. The break-through came with the discovery of the thermionic valve in 1923. This paved the way for commercial development. In 1927 talking films were introduced to the public. In a few years they entirely ousted silent films. By the agreement of 1919 Barrie granted to the company

" the sole and exclusive licence to produce all his literary and dramatic works existing and future of whatsoever nature for the terms of the respective copyrights thereof *in cinematograph or moving picture films*."

(1) [1966] 2 All E.R. 321.

A There is no useful authority in England on the meaning of those words, such as to show whether they comprehend a sound film as well as a silent film. There are, however, two valuable cases from overseas. The first is the decision of the United States Court of Appeals for the Second Circuit in *L. C. Page & Co.* v. *Fox Film Corpn.* (2). The court was a strong one, consisting of JUDGES LEARNED HAND, SWAN and AUGUSTUS HAND. It had to consider an agreement made in

B 1923 reserving the " exclusive moving picture rights " at a time when sound motion pictures were in the contemplation of one of the parties, but not both of them. The court said (3):

> " We can entertain no doubt that the words used, ' the exclusive moving picture rights ', were sufficient to embrace not only motion pictures of the sort then known, but also such technical improvements in motion pictures
C > as might be developed during the term of the licence, namely, the term of the copyright. The development of mechanism making it possible to accompany the screen picture with the sound of spoken words was but an improvement in the motion picture art. As the plaintiff well says, ' talkies ' are but a species of the genus motion pictures; they are employed by the same theatres, enjoyed by the same audiences, and nothing more than a
D > forward step in the same art. Essentially the form and area of exploitation were the same. The mere fact that the species ' talkies ' may have been unknown and not within the contemplation of the parties in their description of the generic ' moving pictures ' does not prevent the latter from comprehending the former."

E The second was a case before the High Court of Australia—*J. C. Williamson, Ltd.* v. *Metro-Goldwyn-Mayer Theatres, Ltd.* (4). That court had to consider an agreement made in 1924 when only silent films were being produced but sound films were imminent, and the parties knew it. The majority of the court (which included that great lawyer, DIXON, J.) held that a reservation of " the motion picture film rights " included the right to make both silent and sound
F films. They said that (5):

> " The simultaneous oral and visual mechanical reproduction of the play . . . could not be regarded as so entirely different from the exhibition of motion pictures as then commercially practised that it would altogether fall outside the reservation . . . the only alternative is that the agreement divides the right to exhibit sound films between the parties to it. That they
G > entertained an actual intention to do so seems to us to be very unlikely."

Those authorities show that, even before sound films were a commercial proposition, a grant or reservation of moving picture film rights was capable of carrying the right to make, not only a silent film, but also a sound film. When I come to study the agreement of 1919, however, I am satisfied that in this particular
H case the words did not comprehend sound films. This agreement was made in 1919 when sound films were very remote. Neither of the parties had them in mind. They only envisaged that one film of " Peter Pan " should be made, and that it should be a silent film of the then current variety, with titles and sub-titles. The company was to prepare a scenario for the film and submit it to Sir James Barrie for approval. He was also to approve the actress taking the part of " Peter Pan ". The company were to be at liberty to take lines or excerpts
I from the play for the titles and sub-titles, but otherwise they had no permission to use the words of the play. After the film was made, the company were not to release the film except with the written permission of Sir James Barrie. They were to pay him $100,000 on the signing of the agreement and another $100,000 on the release of the film. Every word of that agreement was fulfilled. " Peter Pan " was first made as a film in 1924. It was a silent film and was first shown

---

(2) (1936), 83 F. (2d) 196. (3) (1936), 83 F. (2d) at pp. 198, 199.
(4) (1937), 56 C.L.R. 567. (5) (1937), 56 C.L.R. at p. 579.

in London on Jan. 14, 1925. Seeing that the agreement was fully implemented A
within six years, in accordance with the intention of the parties, I see no reason
for extending it to cover sound films, which were not then in contemplation at all.
Nearly fifty years have passed since 1919: and no-one, so far as I know, claimed
till now that the licence included the right to make a sound film. It is far too
late to make the suggestion.

2. *The Validity of the Assignment to Walt Disney Productions, Inc.* B

The agreement of Aug. 19, 1919, was made between Sir James Barrie (hereinafter called " the author ") and Famous Players Film Co., Ltd. (hereinafter
called " the company "). The agreement did not expressly say that " the author "
included his assigns: or that " the company " included the company's assigns;
but I am clearly of opinion that assigns are included by implication. The rights
under this contract were not personal to the author and the company. They were C
assignable just like the rights under any other contract of a non-personal nature.
The company was entitled to assign its right to make a sound film just as any
owner of partial copyright is entitled to assign it. The statute so provides, and
an assignee from the company was in turn entitled to assign it to a new assignee.
Save, of course, for the contractual restriction contained in cl. 11, which says
that D

" the benefit of this agreement . . . shall not be assignable by the company
without the written permission of the author."

That means that it is not to be assigned by the company *or its assigns* without
the written permission of the author *or his assigns*. I do not accept the contention
of the defendant that, after the first assignment, no further consent was necessary. E

The first assignment was on June 1, 1925, Famous Players Film Co., Ltd. to
Famous Players-Lasky Corpn. Sir James Barrie gave his written consent to
this assignment on Oct. 10, 1919.

The second assignment took place in these circumstances. In September
1938 the hospital was asked for its consent to an assignment to a Californian
corporation called Walt Disney Productions, Inc. It gave its consent on Sept. F
13, 1938, to an assignment by Famous Players-Lasky Corpn. (which had by that
time changed its name to Paramount Pictures, Inc.) to Walt Disney Productions,
Inc. Before any assignment took place, however, that Californian corporation
became merged with two other Californian corporations so as to form one consolidated corporation called Walt Disney Enterprises: and all its assets were
transferred to the consolidated corporation. The new consolidated corporation G
was formed on Sept. 29, 1938. Then on Oct. 10, 1938, Paramount Pictures, Inc.
assigned its rights in " Peter Pan " under the agreement of 1919 to the new
consolidated corporation, Walt Disney Enterprises. Technically this assignment
was out of order. The hospital had only authorised an assignment to the constituent company, Walt Disney Productions, Inc. It had not authorised the
assignment to the consolidated corporation, Walt Disney Enterprises. The judge H
so held (6): and thus far I agree with him. Nevertheless it appears to me possible
(though the point was not taken before us) that afterwards the hospital waived
that irregularity or consented to it ex post facto: because on Jan. 11, 1939,
they entered into an agreement with the new consolidated company, Walt
Disney Enterprises, which recited that under the agreement of 1919 the film
rights I

" became vested in Paramount Pictures, Inc. or its predecessors, *which
rights have since been acquired by Walt Disney Enterprises.*"

That may be regarded as a recognition of the assignment to Walt Disney Enterprises. On Dec. 22, 1938, Walt Disney Enterprises changed its name to Walt
Disney Productions, and that has remained its name ever since. It is the
defendant in this action.

---

(6) [1966] 2 All E.R. at p. 331.

A   It looks to me, therefore, that the defendant became validly entitled to the benefit of the agreement of 1919: but it does not matter whether it did or not. In any case the agreement of 1919 did not give it the right to make a sound film of " Peter Pan ": because it only covered the right to make a *silent* film.

3. *The Agreement of 1939*

B   In 1939 the defendant wished to make an animated cartoon of " Peter Pan ". If it had the right (which it now claims) to make a sound film, one would have thought that in 1939 it would have the right to make an animated cartoon: for an animated cartoon is a moving picture film made up of drawings instead of photographs. The defendant did not, however, assert any such right. By the agreement dated Jan. 11, 1939, the hospital granted to the defendant the right to make an animated cartoon: and the defendant paid the hospital £5,000 for

C   the privilege. The defendant did not wish its cartoon to be met with competition from an ordinary sound film: so it asked the hospital to agree, and the hospital did agree, that it would not exhibit an ordinary sound film of " Peter Pan " till ten years after the world première of the animated cartoon; but the hospital stipulated that after the ten years it should have the right to do so. The defendant in turn agreed that, after the ten years, it would not

D
" object to [the hospital] or its assigns or licensees making . . . an ordinary sound motion picture exclusively with living actors."

Owing to the war the animated cartoon was delayed. The defendant did not produce it until 1953. The ten years expired in 1963. So from that time onwards the hospital was entitled to make a sound film, or to authorise the making of it:

E   and the defendant was contractually bound " not to object to it ".

In 1964 the hospital proposed to authorise the making of a sound film, as the agreement entitled it to do. The defendant had promised not to object: but in breach of its contract it did object: and hence the hospital lost the prospect of a valuable contract. That is the breach for which the defendant is liable for damages.

F 4. *The Injunction*

The defendant is a company incorporated in California and it sought to say that on that account the court should not grant an injunction against it. I cannot accept this contention. It is admitted that the court can make a declaration: and, if this is so, I do not see why the court should not grant an injunction. An injunction is a remedy granted in personam. Even though the defendant

G   is a company abroad, an injunction can be granted so as to stop its agents from doing acts in breach of contract either here or abroad. If they disobey the injunction, it can be enforced by sequestration against its assets here. There is no evidence that it has any assets here today: but that does not matter. It may have assets here tomorrow.

5. *Conclusion*

H   At the hearing before this court, the defendant admitted it had broken its contract. It had objected to the hospital producing, or authorising the production, of a sound film under the title of " Peter Pan ": and it had no right so to object. It has sought to limit the damages by claiming that it has a right to make a sound film itself of " Peter Pan ". I do not think that it has any such right. I would dismiss this appeal.

I
HARMAN, L.J.: Of all the dream-children who people the whimsical country of J. M. Barrie's fantasy, none is better known, none dearer to his father's heart, nor, one may add, to his father's pocket than " the boy who wouldn't grow up ". Now what every woman knows about this character is and always has been that his name is " Peter Pan ". It was, therefore, a surprise to find this case started and carried on because of a claim by the defendant, Walt Disney Productions, Inc., to be entitled to prevent the plaintiff hospital, the present owner of the copyright in the work, from using that name as

the title of a motion picture which the plaintiff was admittedly entitled itself to A
make or authorise to be made by others. The defendant in the court below (7)
maintained that it was entitled to adopt this attitude as assignee under a deed
made in 1938 of rights then vested in Paramount Pictures derived under an
agreement made between the author and an English company called Famous
Players Film Co., Ltd. in 1919.

The first argument for the plaintiff was that by cl. 4 of an agreement of Jan. B
11, 1939, made between the plaintiff's predecessors and the defendant's predecessors, the latter expressly agreed that it or its assignees or licensees would
not object to the hospital or its assignees or licensees " making and exhibiting
an ordinary sound motion picture exclusively with living actors based on ",
among others, " Peter Pan ", after an interval of ten years from the release of
the animated cartoon licensed by the plaintiffs under that agreement, which C
period expired in 1963. By the same clause the defendant's predecessors granted
a licence to the hospital in respect of such of the rights acquired in 1938, as I
have mentioned, as should be necessary to give effect to the provisions of that
clause. Having regard to the clause last recited, it is not surprising that the
judge (8) reached the conclusion that the defendant had no right to object to the
use of the name " Peter Pan " in connexion with the projected motion picture. D
Evidence was given that there was some form of registration of title by the
defendant in the United States and in this country under which the title " Peter
Pan " was registered in the defendant's name, but the judge held that any
restriction thus imposed was not obligatory on the defendant as between itself
and the plaintiff and that the defendant was bound under the recited licence to
take no such objection. The judge, moreover, held (9) that the defendant's acts E
constituted a breach of contract, that is a breach of the 1939 agreement, for which
the defendant was liable in damages, and he directed an inquiry on that subject,
and, moreover, granted an injunction to restrain a repetition of the wrongful
acts complained of.

An appeal was entered against the whole judgment, but by the time of the
hearing before us every complaint against the order of the court below had been F
abandoned except the complaint of the granting of an injunction. On the hearing
of the appeal nearly the whole time was occupied with a different plea sought
to be introduced by amendment of the notice. This arose out of the fact that the
learned judge rested his conclusion (10) not only on cl. 4 of the 1939 agreement,
but on the construction of the 1919 agreement, holding, first, that the benefit of
that agreement had not been validly assigned to the defendant, and, second, G
that anyhow it did not extend beyond a licence to make silent films and that,
therefore, the defendant had no locus standi to object to the making of a talking
film by, or by the licensees of, the plaintiff, even apart from the agreement of
1939. These last matters are not reflected in the order of the court below and it is
against this order alone, strictly speaking, that the defendant has a right to
appeal. It is said, however, that the judge based his decision on two grounds, H
not only the obligations of the defendant under the 1939 agreement, but also
on the lack of title under the agreement of 1919, and that if the inquiry as to
damages be proceeded with as the matter stands at present the defendant will
be at a disadvantage because it will not be open to it to rely on the rights derived
under the 1919 agreement which would have the effect, if properly construed,
so it says, of mitigating the amount of damages. As we have heard full argument I
on this subject, we decided to take the unusual course of expressing an opinion,
although in my view this expression is obiter and not binding, because it does not
directly arise out of the order as pronounced.

I must deal first with the injunction point, and I say at once that I find no
substance in it. It is said that an injunction ought not to be granted against a
foreign corporation, as the defendant is, being incorporated in California, because

(7) [1966] 2 All E.R. 321.   (8) [1966] 2 All E.R. at p. 337.
(9) [1966] 2 All E.R. at p. 338.   (10) [1966] 2 All E.R. at pp. 336, 337.

A allegedly there is some lack of comity involved, and also because the defendant has or may have no assets in this country against which an injunction may be enforced. As to the former point, the 1939 agreement was made expressly subject to the law of Great Britain and the jurisdiction of the English courts —see cl. 7. A writ was properly served out of the jurisdiction and appearance was entered by the defendant here without protest, and as the breach of contract **B** was insisted on generally, even though it should be committed in England, I see no reason why an injunction should not be granted. As to the point about the defendant's assets in England, if that was to be pressed, it was for the defendant to show that it had no assets here, which seems to me in fact very unlikely, but anyhow the burden of showing this was on the defendant and it made no attempt to do so. I would, therefore, affirm the grant of the injunction.

C It was expressly provided by the 1919 agreement between the author and Famous Players Film Co., Ltd., that its benefit should not be assignable by the company " without the written permission of the author ". In my opinion the word " author " means Sir James Matthew Barrie and no-one else. It is so defined at the head of the agreement, and where the personal representatives are intended to be included, the agreement says so; for instance, in the proviso **D** that the company should not release films of " Peter Pan " or two other specified plays " without the written permission of the author during his lifetime and after his death on payment to his executors administrators and assigns of a sum of $100,000 ". Moreover, in cl. 4 the licensee is bound to prepare a scenario founded on " Peter Pan "

E " for the purpose of producing a film thereof and shall submit the ms. thereof to the author and such ms. shall be subject to the author's approval. No film of " Peter Pan " shall be made except with the previous written approval by the author of the actress taking the part of ' Peter Pan '."

I cannot suppose that this last clause can refer to anyone other than the author personally. It is odd, but characteristic, that Barrie assumed that the part would **F** be played by a female. It will be remembered that the first exponent on the stage was Miss Cissie Loftus, a male impersonator. Barrie always had a special interest in the leading ladies appearing in his plays. An example of this is seen in his will in the legacy " to my loved Elizabeth Bergner the sum of £2,000 for the best performance ever given in any play of mine ". This was the last play, " The Boy David ", written especially for her, but there were earlier instances. **G** There is the dream-child herself (in the person of Miss Faith Celli); there is a review called " Rosie Rapture " written as a vehicle for the art of Miss Gaby Deslys. There is also a play written for Madame Karsavina.

The defendant's argument on this point was based on the fact that in October, 1919, Barrie did authorise the assignment of the licensee's rights under the 1919 agreement to Famous Players-Lasky Corpn., a New York company, under **H** whom by various mesne assignments the defendant claims. It was said that the consent once given the obligation to obtain consent was exhausted and no further consent was required. I do not accept this. The assignee must take the assignment of the benefit of the agreement with all its obligations, and one of these is the obligation to obtain the author's consent to assigning its benefit. It is common ground that no further consent was ever given by the author **I** personally, and accordingly it was open in my judgment to the plaintiff hospital to say that the assignment was ineffective. This point, however, was not taken by the hospital because in September, 1938, the hospital as assign of the author did give a written consent, but it was common ground that this consent was given to the wrong person and was, therefore, ineffective, so that unless no consent was necessary, no rights under the 1919 agreement have been assigned to the defendant.

If this be wrong and the assignment of the benefit of the 1919 agreement has been effective to vest in the defendant all the benefits which that agreement

conferred, it remains to consider what they are. The agreement starts by granting
exclusive licence to the grantee to produce all existing and future works of the
author, with certain immaterial exceptions, for the terms of the copyrights
" in cinematograph or moving picture films ". The meaning of these last words
was the chief point of discussion in the court below and I shall refer to it again,
but that is by no means the end of the agreement so far as films of " Peter Pan "
are concerned. There is an initial payment of $100,000 for the general rights
payable on the signing of the agreement, but a further $100,000 " before the
release " of " Peter Pan ", which is not to be brought about without the written
permission of the author during his lifetime.

Under cl. 4 of the agreement the company is under a duty to prepare a scenario

> " founded upon ' Peter Pan ' for the purpose of producing a film thereof
> and shall submit the ms. thereof to the author and such ms. shall be subject
> to the author's approval."

There follows the provision about approving of the actress to take the part.
In fact a scenario was prepared in accordance with this clause and approved
by the author and released in his lifetime in 1925. This was, of course, a silent
film. In 1932 rights in all the works not already produced were re-assigned to
Barrie except only such works from which motion pictures had already been
made. This exception would clearly cover the 1925 version of " Peter Pan ".
No further scenario was produced or submitted to the author in his lifetime,
and it seems to me to follow that so far as that activity is concerned, the agreement is spent. It would, I suppose, be possible to re-issue the silent 1925 film,
but this seems highly improbable and I do not see how under the 1919 agreement
any further version of " Peter Pan " (talking or silent) could be made.

This makes the question debated below academic. The judge (11) came to the
conclusion that the phrase " cinematograph or moving picture films " appearing
in an agreement of 1919 was confined to silent films, because no others could
have been in the mind of the parties at the time. I do not think that this is
the right way to construe such a document. To construe a document rightly,
the court must seek not merely what it thinks to be the intention of the parties,
it must seek that intention in the words the parties have used. Now the words
here are very wide. They are to be applied to works existing and future and
of whatever nature for the terms of their copyrights, and there is a covenant
not to grant any other licence in respect of cinematograph or moving picture
films to anyone whatsoever. These are, it seems to me, words wide enough to
cover talking films with living actors and I incline to the view, though having
regard to what I have said I do not think it necessary to come to a concluded
opinion, that the judge took somewhat too narrow a view and that the better
opinion would accord with the decision in the Australian case cited to him—
J. C. Williamson, Ltd. v. *Metro-Goldwyn-Mayer Theatres, Ltd.* (12).

It follows from what I have said that the inquiry as to damages now pending
should not be taken on either of the bases proposed in the amended notice of
appeal, and I do not think that our formal order should make any pronouncement
on either of these points.

SALMON, L.J.: At the beginning of 1939 the defendant wished to make
an animated cartoon of the well known play by Sir James Barrie called " Peter
Pan ". Sir James, who died in 1937, had made a gift to the plaintiff hospital by
deed and by will of all his rights in that play. By an agreement between the
hospital and the defendant, Walt Disney Productions, Inc., dated Jan. 11,
1939, the defendant acquired from the hospital for £5,000 the sole and exclusive
licence to exploit in any part of the world all the rights in " Peter Pan " which
might be vested in the hospital so far as they related to the making, reproduction
or exhibition of animated cartoons. Although a silent film of " Peter Pan "
had been produced in 1925, by 1939 no ordinary talking picture of the play

---

(11) [1966] 2 All E.R. at p. 336.   (12) (1937), 56 C.L.R. 567.

A had yet been made. Clearly the hospital's right to grant a licence to produce such a talking picture was and would be likely to remain a very valuable asset. On the other hand, equally clearly, if the hospital were to realise this asset fairly soon after the production of the animated cartoon, this might hurt the defendant since an ordinary talking picture might well compete with the animated cartoon. The parties accordingly agreed that the hospital would make

B no use of the asset to which I have referred until the expiration of a period of ten years from the "world première" of the animated cartoon, but thereafter might make such use of the asset as it wished. This is the effect of cl. 3 and cl. 4 of the agreement of Jan. 11, 1939. Clause 4 is of particular importance and I must read the relevant parts of it.

C "[The defendant] hereby agrees that it will not object to [the hospital] or its assigns or licensees making and exhibiting an ordinary sound motion picture . . . based on the literary and dramatic works provided that such ordinary sound motion picture is not exhibited in public in any part of the world prior to the expiration of ten years from the date of the world première of (the animated cartoon) . . ."

D The literary and dramatic works there referred to are defined in the agreement as including the play "Peter Pan".

The world première of the defendant's animated cartoon of this play took place in January, 1953. Accordingly the ten year period referred to in the 1939 agreement expired in January, 1963. It is quite evident that thereafter the hospital was free to realise the very valuable asset to which I have referred, and that the

E defendant had pledged its word not to object to the hospital's doing so. Neither of the parties to the 1939 agreement, nor anyone else, could have supposed that when the ordinary talking motion picture of "Peter Pan" came to be made, its title would be anything other than "Peter Pan". I have no doubt but that the defendant must at all times have realised that it had pledged its word not to object after the expiration of the ten year period to the production of an

F ordinary talking motion picture bearing the title "Peter Pan".

After January, 1963, Mr. Mel Ferrer and Mr. George Cukor, both prominent in the film industry, were minded to produce an ordinary talking motion picture of "Peter Pan" with the famous actress, Miss Audrey Hepburn, in the title role. Accordingly, they entered into negotiations with the hospital to acquire the rights to carry out this project. By June, 1964, these negotiations had

G reached a very advanced stage and apparently a draft agreement was about to be signed under which the hospital would have received £45,000, ten per cent. of certain receipts in respect of merchandising rights, and five per cent. of the producers' share of the net profit derived from the exploitation of the film. The news that Mr. Ferrer and Mr. Cukor had acquired or were about to acquire the talking film rights in "Peter Pan" from the hospital appeared in the film

H trade papers of June 1, 1964. On June 5, 1964, the defendant, with a cynical disregard for its pledged word not to object, wrote to Mr. Cukor and Mr. Ferrer objecting to their producing any film entitled "Peter Pan", and threatening them with an action should they do so. As a result of this letter Mr. Ferrer and Mr. Cukor resiled from their negotiations with the hospital and the contract fell through. Anyone might well be daunted at the prospect of

I being involved in litigation with such a large and powerful corporation as the defendant. No doubt the defendant realised this and for this reason wrote the letter of objection of June 5. No doubt the defendant also realised that it had promised not to object and that by breaking its promise it would be causing very serious financial loss to a hospital for sick children. Nevertheless the defendant deliberately broke its promise. It did so in order to secure a possible financial advantage for itself, in case (as stated in its letter of June 5) the production of the ordinary talking motion picture of "Peter Pan" might coincide with a possible re-issue of the defendant's animated cartoon. To the aphorism that

" all is fair in love and war ", the defendant apparently would add the words A "and big business ". It seems to me, however, that by deliberately breaking its agreement with the hospital, the defendant fell far below the generally accepted standards of commercial propriety. I cannot believe that the man whose name it bears approved of this conduct.

The hospital brought this action claiming (i) a declaration that the defendant had by its letter of June 5, 1964, breached the contract of January, 1939: (ii) an B injunction to restrain further breaches, and (iii) an inquiry as to damages.

Before the judge, the defendant put forward an elaborate but highly artificial argument to support a supposed defence based on a ridiculous construction of the agreement of January, 1939, and also on the alleged effect of certain assignments to which I shall presently refer. In a very careful judgment, the judge found against the defendant and granted the hospital the relief for which it C prayed. The defendant appealed against the whole judgment although, of course, it never had had any real defence on liability. This the defendant acknowledged by withdrawing its appeal except in so far as it relates to the injunction. The defendant now admits that it has broken its contract with the hospital and that the hospital is entitled to a declaration to that effect and to an inquiry as to damages; but the defendant says that no injunction should have been granted. Whilst D stating in this court that it has no intention of again breaking its pledged word to the hospital, it objects to being ordered not to do so. In a case such as the present, an injunction is normally granted if it appears that the breach of contract may be repeated. I can think of no clearer indication of such a likelihood than the defendant's conduct in June, 1964. If it was then prepared, as obviously it was, to break its contract with the hospital in order to secure a commercial advantage E for itself, there is no reason to suppose that, unless restrained, it would not be prepared to commit a similar breach in the future. It was further argued on the defendant's behalf that since it is a company incorporated and situated in the U.S.A., it would be contrary to the comity of nations for the courts of this country to grant an injunction. I cannot accept this argument, nor indeed understand how, in the circumstances of this case, it can have any foundation. F I have no doubt at all but that, if this action had been brought in the courts of the U.S.A., they would have recognised that the defendant ought to be subjected to an injunction and would have granted it with no less hesitation than did the judge.

Then it was argued on the defendant's behalf that as the courts of this country cannot enforce an injunction against the defendant, it would be contrary to G their dignity, and therefore to their practice, to grant such an injunction. This argument, in the mouth of the defendant had a particularly hollow ring. An injunction can be enforced against any company by attaching its assets within the jurisdiction of the courts which grant the injunction. No-one knows better than the defendant whether or not it has any assets in this country. It has produced no evidence that it has none. Nor is there any reason to suppose that H it has no assets here or any intention of acquiring or bringing any assets within our jurisdiction. In these circumstances the appeal against the granting of the injunction must clearly be dismissed. This is the only question that arises for decision in this court.

We have, however, been asked by the defendant to decide whether the hospital has the exclusive right to grant a licence for the production of a talking I motion picture of " Peter Pan " because, so it is said, the answer to this question may affect the damages. Whether or not this factor will affect the damages depends on evidence which has not yet been given and about the nature of which I am not prepared to speculate. Counsel for the hospital has pointed out the difficulties inherent in this court expressing opinions which must necessarily be obiter about questions relating to damage which are not before it. He has indicated, however, that he has no real objection to this court doing so—especially if these opinions are in his favour. I have the gravest doubts as to whether we ought to express any such opinions.

These question depend largely on the true construction of certain assignments on which the defendant unsuccessfully relied before the judge to negative the breach of contract which it now admits. On Aug. 19, 1919, Sir James Barrie entered into a contract with Famous Players Film Co., Ltd. by which Sir James Barrie granted to that company

> " the sole and exclusive licence to produce all his literary and dramatic works existing and future (including ' Peter Pan ') . . . for the terms of the respective copyrights thereof in cinematograph or moving picture films."

The defendant asserts that these rights include the rights to make a talking picture of " Peter Pan "; that these rights have been lawfully assigned to the defendant by the successors in title of the original licensees and that accordingly, although the defendant cannot, because of the agreement of 1939, properly, object to the hospital's exercising the talking picture rights of " Peter Pan " the hospital do not own these rights exclusively. In my view, such words as those which I have cited from the agreement of 1919 are capable of passing, and indeed would normally pass, the talking picture rights even though commercial talking pictures were not in existence and therefore not in the minds of the parties to the contract at the time it was written. At that time there were only three ways in which plays could be presented to the public—in book form, in the living theatre and in the cinema. Talking picture films are but a species of the genus " cinematograph or moving picture films ". They are an improvement on the silent films which, for all practical purposes, they have replaced in the cinema. The words " cinematograph or moving picture films " would not normally in my view have been intended to exclude any improvements that might thereafter be invented in the cinematographic technique and methods of production. This point has hardly been considered by the courts of this country, but it is the subject of a number of decisions in the Commonwealth and U.S.A. which support the view that I have expressed; see e.g., *L. C. Page & Co.* v. *Fox Film Corpn.* (13), and *J. C. Williamson, Ltd.* v. *Metro-Goldwyn-Mayer Theatres, Ltd.* (14). My lords, while accepting that the words cited from the agreement of 1919 are in themselves capable of including talking picture rights, I take the view that there is other language in the contract which shows that the respective parties intended it to apply only to one silent film. I am not so confident as my brothers that this view is correct but I do not dissent. I prefer to express no concluded opinion on it.

I incline to the view expressed by LORD DENNING, M.R., and for the reasons which he gives, that the words " the company " and " the author " in each case by implication include assigns. The author is unlikely to have intended to prevent the production of the film after his death. The company is equally unlikely to have intended that it should be prevented from producing the film in the event of the author dying. I agree, therefore, with LORD DENNING, M.R., that the prohibition contained in cl. 11 of the agreement of 1919 against assignment " by the company without the written permission of the author " means that there can be no assignment by the company or its assigns without the written permission of the author or his assigns. The author assented to the assignment in 1925, to which my lords have referred. There was, however, no formal assent by the hospital (the author's assign) to the assignment to the defendant on Oct. 10, 1938, and this assignment was accordingly, prima facie, ineffective. I am not at all sure, however, that the hospital is estopped by the recital in the agreement of 1939 from denying that it assented to the assignment of 1938 or must be taken to have agreed to it ex post facto. The relevant recital states that

> " [The defendant] *claims* that [pursuant to certain instruments] . . . cinematograph or moving picture film rights (in " Peter Pan ") became vested

(13) (1936), 83 F. (2d) 196.   (14) (1937), 56 C.L.R. 567.

in Paramount Pictures Inc. . . . which rights have since been acquired by
[the defendant]."

I incline to the view that the words " [the defendant] claims " cover the whole
of the recital, and that accordingly the hospital in signing the agreement acknowledged merely that the defendant claimed that the rights had been acquired by it.
This, however, is perhaps of little importance. Since both LORD DENNING, M.R.,
and HARMAN, L.J., are satisfied that the agreement of 1919 passed nothing
but the right to make one silent film, the inquiry as to damages will presumably,
in any event, be taken on the basis that the exclusive talking picture rights
remain vested in the hospital. I confess that I have expressed such opinions as I
have on questions which may affect damages only with hesitation and reluctance,
since in my view these questions do not really arise on this appeal.

Frank Whitworth, Q.C.: I troubled your lordships only with five pages out of over
two hundred pages of correspondence, all of which was gone through before
the trial judge. In my submission the correspondence would have shown that
the hospital and the defendant had at an earlier stage concluded what was in
law a binding agreement, from which the hospital resiled, which may have
affected the views taken by the defendant. If there had been occasion to go
through the whole bundle of correspondence, I venture to think that some
comments that have been made on my clients might have been less derogatory
of them.

Appeal dismissed. Leave to appeal to the House of Lords refused.

Solicitors: *Warren, Murton & Co.* (for the defendant); *Waterhouse & Co.*
(for the plaintiff hospital).

[*Reported by* F. GUTTMAN, ESQ., *Barrister-at-Law.*]

ANGEL v. H. H. BUSHELL & CO., LTD. AND ANOTHER.

[QUEEN'S BENCH DIVISION (Milmo, J.), January 16, 17, 18, 19, 20, 26, 1967.]

*Libel—Privilege—Qualified privilege—Occasion—Privilege ordinarily attribut-
able to communications between persons in a particular relationship not lost
merely by absence of duty or common interest to make the particular communication that was made—Malice—Damages—Statement that plaintiff not
conversant with normal business ethics—Communicated by letter to mutual
friend who had introduced plaintiff to the writer with a view to business—
Letter written unnecessarily and in anger.*

The defendant company, which was controlled by the second defendant,
carried on business as general merchants, in the course of which they sometimes bought aircraft that were sold for scrap. The plaintiff dealt in second-
hand air-frame parts. W., a mutual friend, introduced the plaintiff to the
second defendant, as a trustworthy man who had extensive contacts for
air-frame spare parts, suggesting that if the second defendant were prepared
to hold some air-frame parts selected by the plaintiff, the latter might be
able to sell them to their mutual advantage. On the plaintiff's advice the
second defendant kept at his farm some Vampire air-frame components and,
in April, 1962, components of Meteor aircraft which the defendants had
bought for scrap. The components, however, were not sold as spare parts.
Meantime the price of scrap fell. In anger the second defendant wrote, on
behalf of the defendant company, to W. on July 9, 1962, a letter containing
the words " I fear that [the plaintiff] is not conversant with normal business
ethics ", and saying that he would be obliged if W. would pass the contents
of the letter on to the plaintiff. W. sent a copy of the letter to the plaintiff,
who brought an action against the defendants for libel. The defendants
pleaded, among other defences, qualified privilege.

Held: (i) a communication from the defendants to W. stating the reasons
for the ending of business relations between the defendants and the plaintiff

A would, if normally made, be made on an occasion of qualified privilege and, notwithstanding that the letter of July 9, 1962, was not sent to discharge any duty or to further any common interest, the occasion remained one of qualified privilege (see p. 1025, letter I, to p. 1026, letter A, post).

(ii) nevertheless, the second defendant having written the letter in anger and unnecessarily had, in the circumstances, been actuated by malice and,

B as the words complained of were defamatory, the plaintiff was entitled to damages for defamation (see p. 1023, letter B, and p. 1026, letter G, post) which, as the letter was published only to W. and in fact had had no permanent ill-effects on the plaintiff's reputation with W., would be assessed at £250 (see p. 1026, letter I, post).

Dicta of PEARSON, L.J., in *McCarey* v. *Associated Newspapers, Ltd.* ([1964]

C 3 All E.R. at p. 957) applied.

[As to what occasions are occasions of qualified privilege, see 24 HALSBURY'S LAWS (3rd Edn.) 54-56, paras. 97-99, p. 61, para. 105; and for cases on the subject, see 32 DIGEST (Repl.) 137, *1576*, 153, 154, *1703-1718*.

As to malice as avoiding qualified privilege, see 24 HALSBURY'S LAWS (3rd

D Edn.) 79-80, paras. 138-142; and for cases on the subject, see 32 DIGEST (Repl.) 186, 187, *1988-1998*, 189, *2011-2027*.]

Case referred to:

McCarey v. *Associated Newspapers, Ltd.*, [1964] 2 All E.R. 335, n.; [1964] 1 W.L.R. 855; *revsd. on other grounds*, C.A., [1964] 3 All E.R. 947; [1965] 2 Q.B. 86; [1965] 2 W.L.R. 45; 3rd Digest Supp.

E **Action.**

This was an action by the plaintiff, Norman William Angel, claiming damages from H. H. Bushell & Co., Ltd., and Herbert Henry Bushell, for libel alleged to be contained in a letter dated July 9, 1962, sent by the second defendant on behalf of the first defendant, a company controlled by him, to a Mr. White and a company then owned and controlled by Mr. White, viz., Phillips & White, Ltd.

F The words complained of were " I fear that Mr. Angel [the plaintiff] is not conversant with normal business ethics ".

The following statement of the matters leading up to the sending of the letter is summarised from the judgment of MILMO, J. The plaintiff was a pilot officer in the R.A.F. during the war and also a fully qualified flight engineer. He left the service in 1947 and since 1952 had been dealing in aircraft com-

G ponents and spare parts, mostly second-hand. In 1962 he had launched out in this business on his own but owing to his limited resources could not carry any appreciable quantity of stocks. He dealt mostly in parts from military aircraft and had useful contacts with foreign governments and their air attachés in London embassies. Without them he could scarcely carry on any business at all in components of military aircraft. He relied for supplies almost exclusively

H on government sales of R.A.F. surplus or obsolete stocks of spares and components from military aircraft. Only infrequently did he deal in any parts other than air-frame components. He did not deal in engines, engine parts, instruments or anything of that kind. The second defendant (Mr. Bushell) managed and controlled the defendant company. The company carried on the business of general merchants, prepared to deal in almost any goods if there

I were a reasonable prospect of profit. At the material time his trading activities fell into two main categories. He had four retail shops in the Birmingham area where he sold ex-government surplus stocks ranging from clothing to mechanical equipment. He also dealt in a very large way in scrap metal. In 1961-62 his principal source of supply for scrap metal was the purchase of R.A.F. surplus or obsolete aeroplanes sold by the Air Ministry as they were on the airfield. The defendants dismantled and removed them. The bulk of the material would be delivered by the defendants direct from the airfield to customers but a proportion of it, such as engines and cables which could not be conveniently dismantled, stripped and sorted out on the site would be sent to the defendants' factory in Birmingham where this work would be carried out. From time to time some of the components of dismantled aircraft would be found suitable for retail trade in the defendants' shops; others might be sold to persons interested in such things; and components sold in such ways realised a very much higher price than scrap. This method of sale accounted for a small proportion of the defendants' sales, the vast bulk being sold for scrap. The defendants were not "stockists" of aircraft components, though occasionally they had on their hands for relatively short periods aircraft components which they could sell at a greatly enhanced profit if they knew of a likely purchaser but which they would dispose of as scrap if no purchaser turned up.

In late 1961 or early 1962 the plaintiff and the second defendant were introduced by Mr. White, a mutual friend, at a government sale at Hatherley. He thought it would be to the mutual business advantage of the plaintiff and the second defendant if they were brought together. Mr. White himself not infrequently made purchases from the second defendant, but was interested principally in aircraft instruments while the plaintiff was solely interested in aircraft frames. Occasionally he used to ask the second defendant to look out for some article or component which he wanted, and at times when the second defendant came across something in an aircraft which he thought might be of interest to Mr. White he would inquire of Mr. White if he wanted it. In making the introduction Mr. White thought that the same sort of business relationship might develop between the plaintiff and the second defendant. At Hatherley Mr. White introduced the plaintiff as a trustworthy man who had extensive contacts for air-frame parts and who had recently launched out on his own. Mr. White suggested that if the second defendant was prepared to hold on to some aircraft parts as selected by the plaintiff, the plaintiff would be able to sell them to their mutual advantage. The plaintiff himself explained to the second defendant that he was not in a position to hold any stock himself or to buy complete aircraft, but that there were certain types of aircraft, and in particular Vampires and Meteors, for certain parts of which he, the plaintiff, got enquiries from time to time. He made it quite plain that immediate sales were not to be expected and that parts might have to be held for some time before being sold. No specific time was mentioned on either side. In the end the matter was left in this way. A Mr. Woodward, one of the defendants' staff, was to telephone the plaintiff when the defendants had succeeded in purchasing aircraft for scrap and to enquire of the plaintiff whether any, and if so what, parts might be of interest to him. If the plaintiff indicated the parts which it might be possible to re-sell as components, the second defendant was prepared to hold them giving the plaintiff an option on them, though not an enforceable legal option, to sell them if and when he got a customer, to their mutual benefit. The second defendant said in evidence that even at that stage he already had it in mind to store any such material on his farm. There was, in fact, no committal on the part of the plaintiff to purchase in course of time all or any of the parts so obtained. Before the plaintiff was called on to state whether any parts were potentially saleable as components the defendants would already have purchased them as scrap. The plaintiff erroneously felt that the defendants were proposing to extend their activities as "stockists" in aircraft components and spares.

Mr. Woodward, who at the time of the trial was no longer employed by the defendant company, was at the relevant time in their employment as a foreman, though described as their outside manager. The first meeting between him and the plaintiff was in February, 1962, at Halton R.A.F. station where the defendants had purchased and were dismantling some Meteor aircraft. Mr. Woodward had telephoned him to enquire if he was interested in any parts of the aircraft. The plaintiff went and found the aircraft were of no interest. In the course of conversation the plaintiff mentioned his contacts with foreign embassies and air attachés and also said that he was on the look out for a new

A   wing for a Vampire, though he did not mention this matter with the possibility in mind that the defendants would come by such an aircraft. What the plaintiff required and obtained shortly afterwards was a new wing, which was something which would not come the defendants' way. Further, a complete second-hand wing for a Vampire would not be saleable for use as a wing unless accompanied by its log, which was something which the defendants would not be likely to

B   obtain; but component parts of a second-hand wing could be sold without a log. Shortly afterwards the defendants made a successful tender to the Air Ministry for certain aircraft at St. Athan in Glamorgan, and these included the air-frame of a Vampire aircraft. Mr. Woodward, remembering his conversation with the plaintiff, informed him about it. After being supplied with relevant data, the plaintiff told Mr. Woodward that there were good prospects of being able to re-sell

C   some, if not all, of the components as spares. Accordingly Mr. Woodward got into touch with the second defendant and arrangements were made for the parts to be taken to the second defendant's farm to be kept there until the plaintiff had the opportunity to find customers, if he could. The plaintiff did not appreciate that it was only because he might be able to find a customer that this was done; but the second defendant in not selling them as scrap was relying solely

D   on the possibility of the plaintiff finding a customer and thus substantially increasing his profit. The Vampire air-frame reached the farm about the middle of March, 1962.

On a day prior to Mar. 31, 1962, the defendants had purchased from the Air Ministry ten Meteor aircraft at Kimble, Gloucestershire. After the plaintiff had inspected them, he suggested to Mr. Woodward that it would be worthwhile

E   keeping certain parts with a view to their re-sale as spares. These parts included a certain number of cockpits and tail pieces. After suggesting that the Meteor parts should be taken into store the plaintiff made a remark to Mr. Woodward that they would be able to pick from them like a Christmas tree. To Mr. Woodward, however, it appeared that the plaintiff would not be able to dispose of all the parts which he was suggesting should be taken into stock and that there

F   was an element of speculation about the whole enterprise. In a rough profit and loss account which the second defendant drew up, the purchase and sale of the ten Meteor aircraft showed a small profit even on the basis that the sale of the parts put aside at the farm on the recommendation of the plaintiff were saleable only as scrap. The second defendant was already committed on this contract before the plaintiff was ever asked whether any of the material

G   was likely to be saleable as spare parts. The Meteor parts were taken to the second defendant's farm in the first half of April, 1962. This was the last business transaction of the defendants with which the plaintiff was in any way involved. There were thereafter numerous telephone conversations between Mr. Woodward and the plaintiff asking whether the plaintiff had managed to interest anyone in the parts which were stored. The plaintiff invariably replied that these things

H   took time and the defendants must be patient. There was prior to July 9, 1962, no communication oral or written by or on behalf of the defendants to the plaintiff for an explanation as to why he had not sold any material which had been stored and still less that he had behaved towards the defendants in any unethical, discreditable or dishonourable manner.

I   *R. Millner*, Q.C., and *D. J. Turner-Samuels* for the plaintiff.
David Hurst, Q.C., and *R. J. S. Harvey* for the defendants.

MILMO, J.: In this action the plaintiff, Mr. Norman William Angel, claims damages from the defendants, H. H. Bushell & Co., Ltd. and Mr. Hubert Henry Bushell, for libel alleged to be contained in a letter dated July 9, 1962, sent by Mr. Bushell on behalf of the defendant company to a Mr. White and to a company then owned and controlled by Mr. White, namely Phillips & White, Ltd. The actual words in the letter of which complaint is made are: " I fear that Mr. Angel "—meaning the plaintiff—" is not conversant with normal

business ethics." The defendants, by their amended defence, deny that the **A**
offending words bore, or were capable of bearing, any meaning defamatory of the
plaintiff. They further plead justification and qualified privilege.

[HIS LORDSHIP reviewed the circumstances leading up to the position in
April, 1962, when the second defendant had stored parts of a Vampire air-frame
and parts of the Meteor aircraft on his farm with a view to the plaintiff's effecting
sales of them. The course of events is summarised at pp. 1019, letter G, ante, et **B**
seq. HIS LORDSHIP continued:] On July 9, 1962, out of the blue and without any
prior warning or notification to the plaintiff that anything was amiss, the second
defendant wrote to Mr. White the letter complained of in this action, which reads
as follows:

"Dear Mr. White, It is most unfortunate that we do not have [the
plaintiff's] address, but I should be obliged if you could pass the contents of **C**
this letter on to him, as he expressed interest in Vampire and Meteor
material, and some aircraft jacks, and it will interest you to know that we
have held quantities of Vampire and Meteor material, and since holding it
the price has dropped £30 per ton and apart from the transport and storage
this has given us a loss of over £200, without the courtesy of a letter or
telephone call from this gentleman, and although you and I have done **D**
satisfactory business together [and these are the actual words complained of]
I fear that [the plaintiff] is not conversant with normal business ethics, and
unless I hear something fairly positive within the course of the next seven
days I shall have no further wish to try and transact any business with this
gentleman. I am sorry this letter has had to come through you, but it is the
only way of contacting him . . . Yours sincerely, p.p. H. H. Bushell & Co., **E**
Ltd. (Signed) managing director."

Mr. White, the addressee and recipient of that letter, was called as a witness by
the defendants. I am satisfied that his immediate reaction on receipt of the
letter was very hostile towards the plaintiff, who he considered had let him down.
He at once picked up the telephone, got in touch with the plaintiff and asked him
what the devil he had been doing. He caused his secretary to make a copy of **F**
the letter and sent it with a compliments slip to the plaintiff. The plaintiff stated
that he was minded to reply himself, but before doing so went to his solicitors,
and on July 18, 1962, his solicitors wrote this letter to the defendant company:

"We act for [the plaintiff], who has handed us a letter addressed by you
to a Mr. W. A. L. White of Messrs. Phillips & White, Ltd., 61, Queen's
Gardens, Paddington, W.2. In your letter to Mr. White, among other things **G**
you state: ' I fear that [the plaintiff] is not conversant with normal business
ethics.' In our opinion this statement is libellous. We must, therefore, ask
you forthwith to let us have a letter withdrawing this statement together
with an undertaking to write to Mr. White apologising for the libellous
statement made by you concerning our client, and, finally, with a proposal **H**
to compensate our client for this damaging statement."

The second defendant himself replied on behalf of his company, the first
defendant, on July 23, in these terms:

"We are in receipt of your letter of 18th inst. of above reference. We are
passing this on to our solicitors from whom you will no doubt be hearing in
due course." **I**

In fact, the plaintiff's solicitors did not hear anything " in due course "; but the
plaintiff, on his side, was equally passive, and nothing was done until June 26,
1964, which was almost two years later. Then his solicitors wrote again as follows:

"On July 23, 1962 you wrote to us concerning the libellous statement made
by you and you then advised us that you were sending the papers to your
solicitors from whom we would no doubt be hearing. We have heard nothing
further and we have now been instructed by our client to submit the papers
to counsel to settle the proceedings against you for libel."

A   Again, there was no reply to that letter; but on July 1, 1964, a further letter was sent by the plaintiff's solicitors saying that, not having heard, they were instituting proceedings. The writ was issued on July 17, 1964. The writ was followed by the statement of claim, which bears the date Oct. 1, 1964, the long vacation having intervened, and it complains of the words to which I have referred as being a libel, and claims damages from both defendants.

B   The first issue with which I have to deal is whether the words complained of are defamatory. In my judgment, they plainly are defamatory. Indeed, it was conceded that they had a defamatory meaning, though there was a difference as to the severity of meaning. I think that it is a serious imputation to say of a businessman that he is not conversant with business ethics. There is a very real difference between an allegation of failure to comply with etiquette and a failure

C   to conform with ethical standards, and it is the latter imputation which, in my view, is made by this letter. Ethics involve a moral standard, and, in my judgment, a breach of ethics connotes at a minimum dishonourable behaviour. The words complained of, in the context in which they appear, meant that the plaintiff had failed to act honourably in accordance with the standards which respectable businessmen observe in their dealings with one another.

D   I now pass to the defence of justification, and I will say at once that the defendants have, in my judgment, wholly failed to justify the words complained of in the above sense or, indeed, in any other sense. It is to be observed that in the particulars of justification contained in the amended defence it is asserted that the purchase by the defendants of the Vampire at St. Athan and the ten Meteors was made at the plaintiff's request. At the trial it was conceded that this was not

E   so. In each case the purchase was made before the plaintiff was informed. Then the further and better particulars of the defence in relation to the plea of justification, which were delivered on Aug. 13, 1965, contain two further allegations against the plaintiff which were eventually thrown overboard in the course of the trial and are conceded to be without foundation. I refer to the particulars delivered pursuant to the order of Master JACOB dated Apr. 22, 1965. Sub-

F   paragraph (1) of the particulars under head (h) reads as follows:

"The plaintiff should have given to the defendants his own name and address if he is in business on his own account, or (if not in business on his own account) the name and address of his employers, so that the defendants could communicate with him in writing and effectively enforce against him or his employers (as the case might be) any contractual liability arising in

G   the transaction."

The defendants admitted that the plaintiff had given them both his home and his office telephone numbers, and that there would have been no difficulty in ascertaining his address; and further, that there was no question of his ever being under any contractual obligation to them at all. That has gone. If, however, there had been any substance in that allegation that he withheld his address in the

H   manner suggested, that item afforded some support for the charge of a failure to observe, or a failure to be conversant with (which, in my judgment, comes to the same thing), normal business ethics. But the next sub-paragraph is perhaps more eloquent in this connexion. It reads as follows:

"The plaintiff having specially requested the defendants to take into

I   stock the aircraft parts referred to in the particulars of justification, and knowing that the defendants had in fact purchased them pursuant to such request, should have himself purchased them from the defendants, or at least offered to accept responsibility for the loss suffered by the defendants as a result of the transaction."

It was said by the second defendant in the witness box that not only was this allegation completely unfounded, but also that he had never thought that the plaintiff was under any such obligation. He said this in relation to this particular paragraph:

" I am not charging the plaintiff with being blameworthy in not purchasing   A
the goods or offering to accept responsibility for the loss."

He said earlier that there was no question of the plaintiff being under any
contractual liability to him whatsoever. When the second defendant was asked
in examination-in-chief what he understood by the phrase " normal business
ethics " he gave this answer. He said that this phrase related to his code of
business in his particular sphere, which revolves basically on four principles: (1)   B
You call a spade a spade; (2) you honour your word; (3) you do not sell something
twice—that is to say, if someone comes along with a better offer for something
that you have sold at a lower price, you still sell it at the lower price; (4) you do
not take advantage of another man's personal introduction, whether in buying or
selling—that is to say, you do not go behind his back. He stated that there had
never been any question of the plaintiff not honouring his word or of the defen-   C
dants thinking that he had not honoured his word. Equally, he said that there was
no question of his selling anything twice, or of the plaintiff having gone behind
anybody's back. It emerged that the only complaint that the second defendant
wished to make and intended to make against the plaintiff in writing that letter
saying that he was not conversant with normal business ethics was that the
plaintiff had not called a spade a spade. He said that the plaintiff had messed him   D
about by not giving him word as to what progress he had made, and that this was
a failure to call a spade a spade. In my judgment no conduct was proved against
the plaintiff which begins to justify this imputation that he was not conversant
with normal business ethics. The second defendant was well aware from the start
that any sales by the plaintiff were likely to take time. The prospect of the
greatly increased profit which would result to the second defendant from such   E
sales was attractive, and he was prepared to wait. His only complaint against the
plaintiff was that the plaintiff omitted to volunteer a full disclosure of his business
activities at the time in question, with whom he had been in contact and what
prospects, if any, he had. I am satisfied that at no time did the second defendant
or anyone on his behalf ask the plaintiff to reveal to the defendants any such
details as to his, the plaintiff's, business activities.   F

Turning now to the defence of qualified privilege, in the defence, and for some
time throughout the trial, the privilege was alleged to arise in two different ways.
In the first place, it was said that the plaintiff had omitted to supply the defendants with his address, and the only way in which they were able to get in touch
with him was by letter written to Mr. White. Secondly, it was said that in the
light of the circumstances in which Mr. White had introduced the plaintiff to the   G
defendants, the defendants and Mr. White had a common and corresponding
interest to have the information contained in the letter communicated in the way
it was communicated to Mr. White. The first of these grounds is manifestly
unsustainable and it is not surprising that it was abandoned in the course of the
trial. Nevertheless, I think it right to say something about it. If the defendants
had genuinely wanted to obtain the plaintiff's address they had only to ask him   H
for it, and I have not the slightest doubt that he would have given it to them. I
am equally satisfied that they knew perfectly well that he would have done so.
Alternatively, they could have asked Mr. White to let them have the address,
and there is no conceivable reason for them to think that Mr. White would not
have let them have it if they had asked for it. Even if one assumes, however, that
they had bona fide objections to both of these courses, there was nothing whatever   I
to prevent them from putting the offending letter into a sealed envelope with a
stamp on it and sending this to Mr. White with a request that he should re-address
it to the plaintiff. The defendants significantly refrained from taking any of these
courses, and I listened in vain for any acceptable explanation from the lips of
the second defendant. Before looking at the offending letter itself, it is pertinent
to observe that the second defendant stated in evidence that he regarded it as a
basic principle of business ethics that one should, to use his own expression, " call
a spade a spade ". Looking at the first and last sentences of the opening para-

A graph of the letter, these statements are a piece of window dressing and not calling a spade a spade. I refer to the sentence: " It is most unfortunate that we do not have [the plaintiff's] address . . .", and the last sentence of that paragraph: " I am sorry this letter has had to come through you, but it is the only way of contacting him." It was, to the second defendant's knowledge, wholly unnecessary to use this device to communicate with the plaintiff, and the reason which he was there

B giving for troubling Mr. White with the matter at all was a completely bogus one.

I have already dealt with the plaintiff's interest in Vampire and Meteor material, matters referred to in the letter, but I have omitted to mention the aircraft jacks which are also referred to. At the original and only meeting between the plaintiff and the second defendant—that is to say, the meeting at Hatherley, where Mr. White was present—the second defendant had asked

C whether there were any particular items in which the plaintiff or Mr. White were currently interested. Both Mr. White and the plaintiff replied that they were then interested in some five ton aircraft jacks. In fact, they had a joint interest in this equipment, which was required by Mr. White, who had commissioned the plaintiff to procure such jacks for him and to put them into serviceable condition before delivery. The second defendant stated that he had some jacks in stock, but,

D having no technical knowledge, was unable to say whether they were of the type that was required. Accordingly, it was arranged that he should send a photograph to Mr. White. This he did, and on being shown the photograph by Mr. White the plaintiff immediately told Mr. White that they were not the type that was wanted. So far as the plaintiff was concerned, that was an end of the matter of the jacks. There follows in the letter a reference to a loss on the Meteor and

E Vampire material put at over £200 (probably a somewhat exaggerated figure), and alleged to be attributable to a fall in scrap values. I am satisfied that there was a considerable drop in scrap values between January and August, 1962, and that in consequence the second defendant, if he were going to make any worthwhile profit on the Meteor transaction, had to rely on it being possible to sell as spares the parts which were removed to his farm. It is true that the plaintiff never wrote

F a letter to the defendants; but I am satisfied that it was never suggested that he should do so, and that no occasion had arisen for him to do so. It is equally true that the plaintiff never received any sort of letter from the defendants. The suggestion in the letter that there had never been any telephone communications with the plaintiff is completely unfounded. True, he does not appear to have telephoned them himself, but it was part of their case, and accepted as a fact, that

G Mr. Woodward was very frequently speaking to the plaintiff over the telephone. On the face of it, the offending letter does not purport to be written for the purpose of communicating to Mr. White any information which the second defendant had any duty or any interest to communicate, and, having observed the second defendant in the witness box, I am unable to believe that this was in fact his purpose in writing the letter. He said that if he had written direct to the

H plaintiff his letter would have been in stronger terms and he would have sent a copy of such letter for information to Mr. White. I am unable to accept this. I do not believe that the second defendant ever gave the matter of Mr. White's interest a thought; nor, indeed, did the second defendant ever give the matter of any duty on his own side a thought. Moreover, since the second defendant conceded that his only complaint against the plaintiff was that the plaintiff had

I failed to call a spade a spade, it is not easy to see in what stronger terms a letter sent direct to the plaintiff could have been couched. In view of Mr. White's introduction of the plaintiff to the second defendant and what he, Mr. White, said to the second defendant concerning the plaintiff having good contacts in aircraft circles and being a fully trustworthy individual, I think that a communication from the second defendant to Mr. White stating the reasons for termination of relations with the plaintiff would in the ordinary way be an occasion of qualified privilege. The question arises, however, whether this remained so as a matter of law, despite my finding that the letter does not purport to be sent, and was not in fact sent, with the view to discharging any duty or furthering any common interest. I have come to the conclusion that the correct analysis is that the occasion remains prima facie privileged, and that these other matters to which I have referred go to malice only, which, if established, would destroy the privilege.

I now have to pass to the reply. The reply is in the usual form when one gets a plea of privilege in the defence in an action for defamation. It denies that the occasion was privileged and then continues in para. 2:

" Further, and in the alternative, the plaintiff says that the defendants and each of them published the words complained of with actual malice."

Then follow the particulars:

" The defendants and each of them bore resentment (although wholly unreasonable and undeserved resentment) against the plaintiff by reason of the fact that they did not succeed in selling any aircraft parts to him."

In the course of the trial, on more than one occasion counsel for the defendants pointed out that this was the sole allegation of malice with which he had to deal. Half way through the final speech on behalf of the plaintiff an application was made to me to give leave to add to these particulars. I declined to do so at that late stage, when all the evidence had been completed and counsel for the defendants had concluded his address.

I am satisfied that, when the second defendant wrote that letter, he was not in fact concerned to discharge any duty or further any interest. He said that he was not well that day. I am satisfied that he was an angry man. The price of scrap had fallen, and unless the plaintiff contrived to sell the spare parts which were at the second defendant's farm, as such, and thereby, to use the second defendant's own phrase, " turn up trumps ", the Meteor transaction was going to be a relative failure. The second defendant laid the blame for all this, I am satisfied, on the plaintiff, and on the plaintiff unreasonably, because trumps were not turned up, and when he did so he knew that the plaintiff had never pledged himself to sell anything within any specified limit of time. I find it impossible to accept the second defendant's statement that when he wrote this letter he bore no personal hostility or bitterness towards the plaintiff. I am driven to the conclusion that he did, and that what he was doing was taking it out on the plaintiff because the plaintiff had failed to ensure that trumps turned up in the manner indicated by the entry on the profit and loss account to which I have already made reference, and, frankly, he vented his spleen on the plaintiff in this way by writing this letter, wholly unnecessarily, so as to pass through Mr. White's hands. For these reasons, I find that when the second defendant wrote this letter he was in fact actuated by malice. The plaintiff is, therefore, entitled to recover damages.

I have now to assess the amount of those damages. While I have no doubt that initially the second defendant's letter came as an ugly shock to Mr. White and unquestionably reduced the plaintiff in the esteem of Mr. White, in the long term I am satisfied that it has had no permanent ill-effect on the plaintiff's reputation with Mr. White. Further, I am satisfied that it has not affected their business relations in any shape or form. What effect it had on Mr. White's secretary, I do not know, but I do not suppose it would have had very much. My task, therefore, is to assess the damages in a case where the libel itself has, in my view, been an ugly one, and one which if it had received more extensive circulation could have been very serious indeed; but it was only published to Mr. White and, so far as Mr. White is concerned, no permanent damage has been done. Taking everything into consideration, and applying the principles which have been laid down by PEARSON, L.J., in *McCarey* v. *Associated Newspapers, Ltd.* (1), I assess the damages at £250.   *Judgment for the plaintiff for £250.*

Solicitors: *Seifert, Sedley & Co.* (for the plaintiff); *Nash, Field & Co.* (for the defendants).   [*Reported by* K. DIANA PHILIPPS, *Barrister-at-Law.*]

---

(1) [1964] 3 All E.R. 947 at p. 957; [1965] 2 Q.B. 86 at p. 104.

NOTE.

A

MILLER *v.* BRITISH ROAD SERVICES, LTD. AND OTHERS.

[QUEEN'S BENCH DIVISION (Waller, J.), November 30, December 1, 1966.]

B

Fatal   Accident—Damages—Assessment—Measure   of   damages—Inflation— Prospect of constant inflation a relevant factor.

[As to the basis of assessment of damages in fatal accident cases, and as to apportionment of such damages, see 28 HALSBURY'S LAWS (3rd Edn.) 101, para. 111, and p. 105, para. 115; and for cases on the subject, see 36 DIGEST (Repl.) 221-224, *1176-1194*, pp. 225, 226, *1195-1200*.]

C   **Action.**

This was an action by Mrs. Elsie Lilian Miller, the widow and administratrix of Mr. Ernest Edward Miller, claiming damages under the Fatal Accidents Acts, 1846 to 1959, and the Law Reform (Miscellaneous Provisions) Act, 1934, in respect of her husband's death in a motor accident, which took place on Feb. 17, 1964.   At the time of the accident the deceased was a passenger in a car driven

D   by Mr. Evans, who was employed by the second defendants, Keystone Press Agency, Ltd.   The car was in collision with a lorry driven by the third defendant, George William Price, who was employed by the first defendants, British Road Services, Ltd.   The trial judge, WALLER, J., found that the accident was wholly due to the fault of the driver of the lorry, Mr. Price, in attempting to pass a tractor at a time when the car driven by Mr. Evans was approaching; the trial

E   judge found that Mr. Evans' driving was in no way responsible for the accident. Accordingly the plaintiff was entitled to recover damages in full from the first and third defendants.   The case is reported only on the assessment of damages and, in particular, on the view that inflation must be taken into account in assessing them.

F   *D. C. Calcutt* for the plaintiff.
   John D. Stocker, Q.C., and *Patrick Bennett* for the first and third defendants.
   Hugh Griffiths, Q.C., and *G. B. Best* for the second defendants.

   WALLER, J., having reviewed the facts and the evidence and reached the conclusions previously stated, continued: The deceased was employed by the second defendants, as a press photographer, and he was obviously a conscientious

G   and good photographer, who had on one occasion won a special prize at an exhibition at the Hague.   He had however reached the highest grade that he was likely to reach in the employment of the second defendants and in that grade his weekly wage was £21 17s. gross or £19 7s. 5d. net, but by now the net wage which the deceased would have been earning would be £21 7s. 9d. per week. The plaintiff has described how her husband gave her £13 per week out of which

H   she paid the rent, how there were hire-purchase payments of £1 a week, how he paid for the electricity and half her clothes and half the children's clothes and how he paid for a holiday.   She estimated that the only difference as a result of this disaster that has arrived in her life, is something of the order of £2 a week and, as counsel for the plaintiff says, the additional saving that there would be on the holiday which they used to have.   It seems to me that the appropriate depen-

I   dancy which I should take is one of £16 per week, after having made all these various adjustments including an adjustment for the increase which has now taken place, and that the final award of damages should be based on that figure.

   I do not propose to set out the precise method of arriving at a final figure. I have to take into account on the one hand the risks which existed for the deceased.   The probability is that he would have continued to work until he was sixty-five.   He would now be forty-three.   I have to take that into account, but on the other hand, there are the ordinary risks of life which must be borne in mind.   I also have to take into account the fact that there is constant inflation which goes on, and, I think that that is a relevant factor which ought to be borne in mind. On the other hand I have to take into account the possibility that the plaintiff, who is a very good looking woman, might re-marry although, as she has said, she has no intention of doing so. All of these have to be taken into account and given some effect in the final figure which I award. In my view, taking all these matters into account, a proper figure to award is one of £11,000 (1), and £120 special damages. I award accordingly against the first and third defendants. Of that £11,120, £1,000 are damages under the Law Reform (Miscellaneous Provisions) Act, 1934.

Judgment for the plaintiff accordingly.

Solicitors: *Avery & Wolverson* (for the plaintiff); *G. Howard & Co.* (for the first and third defendants); *C. Bingham & Co.* (for the second defendants).

[*Reported by* MARY COLTON, *Barrister-at-Law.*]

ADCOCK AND OTHERS v. WILSON.

[QUEEN'S BENCH DIVISION (Winn, L.J., Ashworth and Widgery, JJ.), February 9, 10, 1967.]

Gaming—Lawful and unlawful gaming—Clubs—Bingo—Golden Scoop—1s. stake purchased at first game of each session—Half stake used for ordinary club game and balance retained by club as a contribution to national Golden Scoop game in which five hundred affiliated clubs participated—No communication between players of different affiliated clubs—Whether individuals playing in local bingo game were at relevant time playing in a second game, a national Golden Scoop game—Betting, Gaming and Lotteries Act 1963 (c. 2), s. 32 (1) (b), (4).

At a local bingo club players bought a bingo ticket for 1s. at the first game of each session. Sixpence of this was paid by way of stake on the house game, which was conducted in the club, and sixpence was retained by the club as a contribution to prizes in the National Golden Scoop Club game. The alleged national game was run by Golden Scoop, Ltd., about five hundred affiliated clubs participating in it nightly. In playing bingo at any club, the players were not in communication with the players at any other club. Each club notified the head office of Golden Scoop, Ltd. by telephone of the amount retained as Golden Scoop prize money, of the name of the winner of the ordinary club game and of the total number of calls made before the game was won. All prize money contributed to Golden Scoop, Ltd. was returned as prize money in accordance with a certain formula. On appeal against conviction of the owners of the local club (and others) for an offence against s. 32 (4)* of the Betting, Gaming and Lotteries Act 1963 in that the sixpences retained for the alleged national game were disposed of otherwise than by payment to a player as winnings,

Held: the conviction should stand because—

(i) (per WINN, L.J. and WIDGERY, J.) the players playing bingo in the local club did not become players in any national bingo game, for the game at which they were playing in their club was not a game in which persons at other clubs were also playing (see p. 1035, letter I, to p. 1036, letter A, and p. 1037, letter D, post).

---

(1) There were two children of the marriage, a girl and a boy. £1,000 was apportioned to the girl and £1,500 to the boy. On the application of the plaintiff £1,120 was directed to be paid to the plaintiff or her solicitor, and the whole of the remainder, £10,000, was directed to be paid into Southwark county court.

* Section 32 (4), so far as material, reads " If any gaming takes place on any premises— (a) which is by virtue of sub-s. (1) of this section . . . unlawful gaming . . . any person concerned in the organisation or management of the gaming . . . shall be guilty of an offence . . ."

Affirmed, H.L. [1968] 1 All E.R. 929.

(ii) (per ASHWORTH, J., WIDGERY, J., concurring) no national game was being played, but what was being played was the local house game on which national benefits were superimposed (see p. 1036, letter I, and p. 1037, letter G, post).

Dictum of LORD PEARSON in *Armstrong* v. *Director of Public Prosecutions* ([1965] 2 All E.R. at p. 750) applied.

Appeal dismissed.

[As to lawful and unlawful gaming, see SUPPLEMENT to 18 HALSBURY'S LAWS (3rd Edn.) title Gaming and Wagering, para. 369A, 2.

For the Betting, Gaming and Lotteries Act 1963, s. 32, see 43 HALSBURY'S STATUTES (2nd Edn.) 343.]

Case referred to:

Armstrong v. *Director of Public Prosecutions*, [1965] 2 All E.R. 745; [1965] A.C. 1262; [1965] 3 W.L.R. 344; 129 J.P. 493; 3rd Digest Supp.

Case Stated.

This was a Case Stated by D. N. O'SULLIVAN, ESQ., stipendiary magistrate for the city and county of Kingston-upon-Hull, sitting at Hull on Jan. 31, Feb. 1, 2 and 3, 1966. On Dec. 23, 1965, informations were laid by the respondent, Leslie Vincent Wilson, against the appellants, Ronald Adcock, John Xavier Prendergast, Kenneth Wheatley, William Edward Underwood, Albert Walter Underwood, James Thomas Guthrie, Golden Scoop, Ltd. and Astoria Cinemas (Hull), Ltd., charging that, on Sept. 16, 1965, they were concerned in the organisation of unlawful gaming (the Golden Scoop) at the premises of the Waterloo Bingo Club, Hull, in that money which players put down as stakes was disposed of otherwise than by payment to a player as winnings, contrary to s. 32 (4) of the Betting, Gaming and Lotteries Act 1963. The following facts were found. The appellants W. E. Underwood and Guthrie were proprietors of the Waterloo Bingo Club, Hull. The appellant A. W. Underwood was the manager of that club jointly with the appellant Guthrie. The appellants Prendergast, Wheatley and Guthrie were directors of Golden Scoop, Ltd., a company which organised bingo on a national scale and operated through administrative sub-controls in various parts of the country. The appellant Adcock was the manager of the Astoria Bingo and Social Club, Hull, and was employed by its owners, Astoria Cinemas (Hull), Ltd., of which the appellant Prendergast was managing director. The premises of the Astoria Bingo and Social Club were used as the sub-control in the Hull area of the national Golden Scoop, Ltd. The operation of that sub-control was the responsibility of the appellant Adcock which he was required to carry out by his employers. The game of bingo was played for winnings in money at the premises of the Waterloo Bingo Club at regular nightly sessions, including one held on Sept. 16, 1965. At each session several rounds or hands were played, each hand constituting a separate game of Bingo. Each game necessitated the use by a player of a ticket. Those were sold on the premises and a player could purchase any number of tickets for a particular game. Each ticket had printed on it a different selection of numbers from one to ninety-nine. An official known as a caller would select numbers between one and ninety-nine in a random manner, calling out each number as he selected it. If a number was called which appeared on a player's ticket, the player would cancel it. The first player to cancel all the numbers on his ticket would be the winner of a cash prize, paid to him forthwith. Each game as so played was a "game of chance", and the playing of it constituted "gaming" within the definitions of those terms in s. 55 (1) of the Betting, Gaming and Lotteries Act 1963. The Golden Scoop involved participation by a plurality of bingo clubs. An aim was to increase the attractions of bingo by providing large prizes. Facts hereinafter set out indicate its nature and scope and how it operated. At the time relevant to these charges there were about five hundred bingo clubs throughout the country participating in the Golden Scoop. The proprietor of each individual club was connected to

Golden Scoop, Ltd. by a standard form of contract. The Waterloo Bingo Club was connected to Golden Scoop, Ltd. in that way. The schedule of membership of the Waterloo Bingo Club referred to in cl. 8 of the contract was never attached to the contract or required to be supplied to Golden Scoop, Ltd. The Golden Scoop was organised and run by the National Golden Scoop Club. That club was owned by Golden Scoop, Ltd. When a person applied to become a member of a club affiliated to the National Golden Scoop Club, he applied at the same time to become a member of the National Golden Scoop Club. That club, however, kept no separate list or record of persons purporting to be members. The only way in which the membership of the club could be discovered would be by consulting the individual records of membership of the affiliated clubs. There was no committee of the National Golden Scoop Club nor did it have any premises on which bingo was played. The Golden Scoop was operated by all the five hundred affiliated clubs on every night of the year except Christmas, and its profits and expenses were obtained by charging each affiliated bingo club proprietor the sum of one guinea per night. The Golden Scoop was operated at the bingo sessions of the Waterloo Bingo Club, including that held on Sept. 16, 1965, in the manner hereinafter described. For the first bingo game of the session a player bought a bingo ticket for 1s. One side of the ticket set out the selection of numbers and the other side bore the words:

" NATIONAL GOLDEN SCOOP CLUB.
Church Bank House, Bradford 1.
National Golden Scoop Club Game.

The price of this ticket (1s.) consists of 6d. by way of stake in the house game and 6d. by way of stake in the National Golden Scoop Club game."

Had a player wished to compete for prizes in the Golden Scoop only, his bingo ticket would have cost him 6d. and he would have been charged no admission fee. No one ever so wished at the Waterloo Club. The game was played in the ordinary way, as described above. The winner received one-half of the shilling stakes. The other half was retained by the club to contribute, in due course, to prizes in the Golden Scoop for that date. The name of the winner of the club bingo game, the total number of calls made before the game was won and the total amount of money retained by the club for the Golden Scoop was notified by telephone to the head office of Golden Scoop, Ltd. in Bradford through the sub-control at the Astoria Cinema, Hull. Subsequently a return was forwarded by the club to the head office in accordance with cl. 3 of the contract. The Golden Scoop was similarly operated by the other affiliated clubs. In the playing of the relevant bingo game, the players in any one club were not in communication with the players in any other club. At the head office the returns from individual clubs were checked by a qualified accountant and prizes in the Golden Scoop awarded in accordance with a certain formula. All the money received from individual clubs for prizes in the Golden Scoop was disposed of in that way. On Sept. 16, 1965, no prize in the Golden Scoop was won by any of the players of the Waterloo Bingo Club. On that date the Waterloo Bingo Club had sold 690 1s. tickets for the relevant bingo game and contributed half the proceeds, namely, £17 5s. to the Golden Scoop for that date.

On behalf of the appellants it was contended that (a) the Golden Scoop was lawful gaming; (b) the physical separation of some of the participants was irrelevant; (c) people taking part in it regarded it as a game; (d) there was a sufficient degree of participation by the players to warrant it gaming; (e) all the stakes were returned to the players as winnings and, therefore, no offence was committed. On behalf of the respondent it was contended that (a) the Golden Scoop was not a game but a series of games each played in the individual local clubs followed by a mere lottery, in that the game played locally served only to select those ticket holders who had a chance in the Golden Scoop; (b) as the stake money put down by the players in the game in an individual local club was not returned to those players, but was distributed as aforesaid to other players in other local clubs, the condition laid down by s. 32 (1) (b)* of the Betting, Gaming and Lotteries Act 1963, was broken and the gaming was, therefore, unlawful.

The stipendiary magistrate found the charges proved and imposed the following penalties: the appellant Adcock, £75 fine or three months and fifty guineas costs; the appellant Prendergast, £100 fine or three months and one hundred guineas costs; the appellant Wheatley, £100 fine or three months and fifty guineas costs; the appellant W. E. Underwood, £75 fine or three months and twenty-five guineas costs; the appellant A. W. Underwood, £75 fine or three months and fifty guineas costs; the appellant Guthrie, £75 fine or three months and twenty-five guineas costs; the appellant Golden Scoop, Ltd., £100 fine and one hundred guineas costs; and the appellant Astoria Cinemas (Hull), Ltd., £100 fine and one hundred guineas costs. The appellants now appealed. No point was taken on the appeal of differentiation between the positions of the appellants shown by the varying fines imposed.

The authority and cases noted below† were cited during the argument in addition to the case referred to in the judgments.

Leonard Caplan, Q.C., and *G. Gray* for the appellants.
R. H. Hutchinson for the respondent.

Cur. adv. vult.

Feb. 10. **WINN, L.J.**, stated the nature of the appeal and continued: So far as this appeal is concerned the question is the simple one: guilty or not guilty on the Case Stated in regard to each of the appellants, without distinction. The terms of the summons charged the appellants that they were

" concerned in the organisation of gaming, namely the Golden Scoop, which took place at premises known as the Waterloo Bingo Club . . . which was unlawful, in that money which players put down as stakes was disposed of otherwise than by payment to a player as winnings, contrary to s. 32 (4) of the Betting, Gaming and Lotteries Act 1963."

[HIS LORDSHIP summarised the facts which were found by the magistrate (see p. 1029, letter F, to p. 1030, letter H, ante), and continued:] I turn to the exhibit which sets out the formula for distribution of all the moneys contributed from the individual bingo clubs in accordance with the procedure set out in this Case Stated. This shows that there were set prizes and other prizes which together would absorb all the money contributed by the clubs as a result of any particular Golden Scoop activity. There are six altogether, and it is right to emphasise that provision is made for distribution in the form of prizes of all the money which came in the manner indicated from the holding of the totality of Golden Scoop activities throughout the country on any one night. Oddly enough, the set prizes are smaller than the prizes to be derived, at any rate on the night in question, from the balance of moneys over and above the set prizes. Thus the lowest number of calls, that is to say the case where " bingo " was called or " house " was called on a complete card produced anywhere in the country, the lowest number of calls nationally, was no more than £100. There was a booby prize of £50 for the worst result, that is to say the completion of a bingo card on the highest number of calls anywhere in the country on that occasion; and there was a £400 set prize for the completion of a card on what is called the clickety click which may or may not be a synonym for sixty-six, but at any rate is the card which was completed on exactly sixty-six calls. Then the balance was distributed as to sixty per cent. to the second lowest, twenty per cent. to the third lowest and

* Section 32 (1) (b), so far as material, is set out at p. 1033, letter B, post.
† EDDY AND LOEWE'S NEW LAW OF BETTING AND GAMING ((2nd Edn.) 1964), pp. 125, 126, 127, 236, 237, 238, 258; *Smith* v. *Wyles*, [1958] 3 All E.R. 279; [1959] 1 Q.B. 164; *Rogers* v. *Cowley*, [1962] 2 All E.R. 683; *Director of Public Prosecutions* v. *Regional Pools Promoters, Ltd.*, [1964] 1 All E.R. 65; [1964] 2 Q.B. 244.

twenty per cent. to what is called the golden number, i.e., the holder of a completed card who completed his card on that number of calls which coincided with the golden number, which for every Monday was fifty-six, and thereafter for every day up to Sunday rose by one to sixty-two, and then started again at fifty-six. On the evening in question in these proceedings the total amount of money available for distribution in accordance with that formula was £4,128. The first of the set prizes which I have mentioned was £100 fixed as such prize, but the major percentage, called the major prize of the balance moneys, amounted to so much as £2,148. It is further found in the Case that, on the relevant date, Sept. 16, 1965, no prize in the Golden Scoop was won by any of the players of the Waterloo Bingo Club; that does not seem to me to affect the position in law at all.

The parties' contentions are set out; and the magistrate gave his opinion which he based on various grounds, the essential one of which is that there was no National Scoop game which in fact or in law could be regarded as a game in which all the persons who took part in the gaming on that evening during the first hand of the bingo games played in the respective clubs could be held to be players. It is right to say, since this attracted criticism from counsel for the appellants, that, as part of his opinion, the magistrate expressed himself thus: " In my opinion, however, ' the National Golden Scoop Club game ' was not in any respect a game. It was simply and solely a lottery." In so expressing himself, it seems to me with all due respect to the learned magistrate that he was using an elliptical, and it may be an inaccurate, expression; he was not concerned with whether or not there was here a lottery. Let it be conceded that there was a lottery, since clearly moneys were being distributed by chance under this formula, but it may nevertheless be perfectly possible and acceptable that the activity was lawful gaming. However, I do not myself think that the fact that he said that it was simply and solely a lottery militates against the validity of his opinion, if in other respects it is sound, that the National Golden Scoop game was *not* a game, which is the essential basis of his opinion. By way of analogy, it might be said that if, in any given case, there were an essential question of fact whether a particular colour was or was not white, it would not destroy a finding that it was not white if the tribunal went on to say that in its view the colour was blue or yellow or red. It might, of course, lead to a rational suggestion that the tribunal was colour-blind, or that there had been some confusion of reasoning. Ultimately the question must be: *was* there a National Scoop game?

The position with regard to lotteries and to gaming is really quite clear under the Betting, Gaming and Lotteries Act 1963, which provides by s. 41 that, " Subject to the provisions of this Act, all lotteries are unlawful ", but also provides by s. 38 (2):

" Nothing in s. 41 of this Act shall make unlawful any gaming conducted in such circumstances that no offence under this Part of this Act is committed."

Section 32 (1) (*b*) is the relevant provision for the purposes of this case. Section 32 (1) provides that:

" Subject to the provisions of this Act, any gaming shall be lawful if, but only if, it is conducted in accordance with the following conditions . . .",

and then some are set out. That is equivalent to saying that gaming is unlawful unless the conditions specified are complied with. " Gaming ", by the definition in s. 55 (1) of the Act of 1963, means " the playing of a game of chance for winnings in money or money's worth ". By reference to the definition of " game of chance " in s. 55 (1) that means the playing of

" a game of chance and skill combined and a pretended game of chance or of chance and skill combined, but does not include any athletic game or sport."

It is and had to be common ground between the parties to this appeal that gaming was conducted at the relevant time in the Waterloo Bingo Club. The question is whether or not there was an infringement or failure to comply in respect of the gaming that did take place at that time in those premises with the requirements of s. 32 (1) (*b*)

> " that no money . . . which any of the players puts down as stakes . . . is disposed of otherwise than by payment to a player as winnings."

There cannot, I think, be any doubt that that is equivalent to saying that it is a requirement that no money which any player who is entering a game puts down as stakes for that game shall be disposed of otherwise than by payment to some player in that game as winnings. There was a game played in these premises at the relevant time which has been conveniently referred to in the course of the hearing of the appeal as the house game. No one suggests that there was any illegality whatsoever, or any failure to comply in respect of that game with the requirement to which I have referred, which is the only requirement suggested by the respondent to have been not complied with in this case. Sixpence was taken as the purchase price of, if I may use the expression, that part of the ticket which was understood to relate to the house game, though of course there was only one ticket which bore on its face reference to the house game and also to the Golden Scoop game. All the moneys collected from *those* sixpences, which totalled £17 5s., was duly returned to the winner, being one of the players in that house game. The question is whether or not the balance over those sixpences to which I have referred, i.e., the rest of the totality of the shillings paid for the tickets which were used during the first hand of bingo that night in that club, was returned to players in any game or to players in a game in respect of which that other half of each shilling was paid as a stake?

In my own opinion, none of the decided cases have any sufficient relevance to the problem now before the court to merit reference to them in this judgment. Counsel for the appellants referred the court to everything in any of the cases which have already been decided which could have relevance, but I think that he shared the view which I am expressing that little if any assistance was to be derived from any of those reported decisions. It may be right to say, as counsel for the appellants urged before the court, that one can by any given set of activities play two games simultaneously. I do not myself think that it is necessary that I should, nor do I wish to, express any firm opinion about that. I am content to accept solely for the purposes of this judgment that his submission in that respect is correct. He gave instances, some perhaps from his own experience, some possibly from what he has read or been told about, of respects in which it might well be right to regard variants of the game of golf and variants of the game of billiards as resulting in the playing simultaneously, by the same set of activities on the part of the players, of two games. It is quite clear that there was participation here sufficient in itself to amount to playing a game. This case does not turn on any question of participation or absence of sufficient participation; it turns on the question whether or not those individuals who were playing bingo at the material time at the premises of this club were playing in a National Golden Scoop game. As I have said, I am content for the purposes of this judgment to accept counsel for the appellants' submission; he knows at any rate far more about the activities mentioned than I myself do. Nevertheless, I would say this about it, that, in the case of his golf illustration, it is clear that there would be no competitor in the sense of anybody who was playing simultaneously on the same course in such a way as to affect his own endeavour to obtain the result that he was envisaging, the longest drive achieved on the same day in any golf club down a straight course and so on; whereas, of course, if one were playing bingo as bingo was played in this club, there would be competition in the sense that relative alertness, quickness of ear, quickness of eye to identify a number that has been called, and quickness of reaction to call out " house " or " bingo " do enter into the bingo game. One has grown quite old enough in the courts to know that more often than not analogies tend to mislead rather than point a clear direction, but one has occurred to me and so I just mention it. Were there ever a scheme or plan or enterprise by which it was provided that, on a given summer Saturday, or on successive Saturdays in the summer, in this country when cricket is being played by clubs, a prize should be given nationally to the winner of those clubs who chose to enter based on the greatest number of runs scored by any individual batsman or the greatest number of runs nationally scored by any club playing on that day, one would at once appreciate very clearly that the conditions in which the individual batsman and the respective teams were playing would be wholly diverse on one cricket ground compared with those on another, throughout the country. I do not want to labour the point, but clearly the success of a batsman in making a large score must depend not only on his own skill but on the skill of the bowlers whom he encounters, the quickness of the fielders to stop his runs being scored, on the pitch, the state of the ball and the state of the light; and I use this analogy merely to point to what ultimately I feel is the right question of fact in this case, namely: what would an ordinary sensible man say if he were asked in the case of such a contest as I have envisaged: was that a game in which all the clubs and all the players were playing in a national game? Here, of course, there were five hundred clubs playing at the same time, different groups of competitors, no doubt differing in number and possibly to some extent in those qualities of alertness that I have mentioned; but what is far more important as I see it, looking at the matter factually, is that in each of these separate bingo clubs the coincidence, dependent purely on luck, between the sequence of numbers drawn by the caller (or otherwise chosen) for the purposes of the game and the numbers present on one or more of the cards held by the players were necessarily in fact different; and that is the essential element of bingo apart from the participation and competitive qualities which I have not overlooked.

One comes in the ultimate analysis to this question: as a matter of fact, or of mixed fact and law—since in this sphere I fully recognise that certain findings of fact might not be compatible with the legal principles which are relevant—were those individuals who participated during the first hand of the bingo session at the Waterloo Club at the relevant time playing in a game which was a national countrywide Golden Scoop game? Even accepting that they might, at any rate in their own understanding, have been playing two games simultaneously, it would still be, in my view, correct to say that, whereas one of those games was the house game which calls for no further consideration, the other " game " was no more than a game played with a view to having a share or chance of a share in the prizes in the national Golden Scoop game. One way of posing the question, and I think that it is the essential criterion, is whether the notional second game, which for this purpose I am accepting as having been played, as well as the house game, by the same activities of those who participated in the first hand, was part of the national game as the appellants contend that it was, or whether it was only one of a series of like games held simultaneously throughout the country. In my own view, once that question is posed, it can only be answered in the negative, that is to say it can only be answered by saying that the game that they were notionally playing at the same time as and in addition to the house game was a separate game with the opportunity that I have indicated, but was not a playing of any Golden Scoop game which itself was a game played throughout the country at that time. The difference is between something which is separate from, though interconnected by motive, opportunity and advantage with, the Golden Scoop—I avoid saying " Golden Scoop game " as I avoid saying " Golden Scoop lottery "—and on the other hand the concept that, by playing to the extent that they did play and in the manner that they did play in the club at the material time, they were playing in a game in which all other players in all these other bingo clubs, totalling five hundred, were also at the same time playing.

A   I cannot myself accept the fact that they were playing in any national game which is the contention and the essential contention of the appellants.

The learned magistrate himself stressed certain matters of fact which he thought pointed to the conclusion that the players in the bingo club in Hull were not playing in any national game. He said:

B   ". . . the ' national Golden Scoop Club game ' . . . involved the playing of numerous bingo games each played under separate management on separate premises by separate groups of players with no communication between the groups."

C   I fully appreciate that it is not as a matter of law in any sense conclusive that individuals with regard to whom the question arises whether they were playing the same game were doing that which they did by way of intended participation in premises separate the one from the other. I have in mind LORD PEARSON'S judgment in the latter part of his speech in *Armstrong* v. *Director of Public Prosecutions* (1), where he said—I do not stop to quote precisely—that the fact that the supposed players were found to be carrying on their activities in separate places was something which had impact on and tended to strengthen a general argument that they were not participating in the same game. The learned

D   magistrate mentioned separate management; I take him by that to mean that there would be quite a different caller in each place. He does not expressly refer to the point that I have made as to the luck of the run of numbers that would come out, he does not expressly refer to the luck relating to the cards and the requisite coincidence between the numbers on the cards and the numbers called. The Case Stated does not find whether an identical batch of cards

E   would be available in each of these clubs, from which again as a matter of luck any particular player might or might not draw a card which would be made up, in terms of presentation of the numbers in various squares, in precisely the same form as some card or cards which would have been drawn by purchasers of cards in other clubs. He stressed also " separate groups of players "; that is relevant to the degree of competition which would be met by a player in any particular

F   club. " No communication between the groups "; in my own mind I do not attach so much importance to that, since I think that communication is relevant only where the game is of a kind which, in order that it may proceed regularly and in accordance with the rules, requires one player or one group of players to know what has happened, what success has been achieved, or what choice has been made by the opposed player or group of players.

G   In my own view, this decision of the learned magistrate is correct in fact and in law. I would only like to say before parting from the matter that it is clearly a very well thought out scheme; there is no reason whatsoever, nor has it been suggested, to suppose that it has not been operated with complete integrity and with due regard and attempted loyalty for the law. It is a fact that the turnover is really very great; the revenue of the club, not of course their profit,

H   would be as much, on the experience of this particular night, as five hundred guineas multiplied by 364 in any one year—though, no doubt, the numbers playing would fluctuate; the amount of money paid out by the players in this particular club in order to enter, as no doubt they thought they were entering, as players in the Golden Scoop game was £17 5s.; £4,128 was taken from all the clubs together. If that be multiplied by forty, since it was all derived from

I   sixpences, it can be seen how many sixpences were paid in order to join in this " game ".

In my opinion, the ultimate question is as simple as this: whatever the players thought, did they, by such participation in bingo as they gave that evening during the first hand, become players in any national game, in the national Golden Scoop game so called? I think not, because that which they were doing was not playing in any game in which all the others, or indeed any of the

(1) [1965] 2 All E.R. 745 at p. 750; [1965] A.C. 1262 at p. 1284.

others, present in different clubs were also participating as players. The result, of course, is that in the gaming which was admittedly conducted at the material time in this club a sum of £17 5s. derived from the excess over 6d. as part of the shillings which were paid for the bingo tickets was not distributed as winnings to players in that game, if there was one, which consisted of the notional additional game. It was paid away, not paid to any of them, but paid away in accordance with the formula to those who by force of that formula were entitled to receive it. I think that this appeal must be dismissed.

ASHWORTH, J.: I agree, and I only intend to add a few words of my own. The heart of the argument presented to this court by counsel for the appellants can be put in this way: there were on the first hand at the Waterloo Club two games taking place, a local game and a national game. He derives support for that from the endorsement on the ticket which in terms stated that the participant in that hand was by his ticket paying 1s., 6d. by way of stake in the house game and 6d. by way of stake in the national Golden Scoop club game. It is common ground that the local house game was indeed a game, and all those who were taking part in it could be identified and seen in the Waterloo Club. But in order to take part in a game, it seems to me that one of the features is that there should be some means, so to speak, of identifying a competitor and knowing who is taking part. It is true that, as the result of *Armstrong* v. *Director of Public Prosecutions* (2) it would not be right to say that there must be an assembly of all the players in any one place, but it is, I venture to think, worth citing what LORD PEARSON said (3):

" I should mention that on behalf of the respondent a further argument was put forward to the effect that there cannot be ' gaming '—the playing of a game—within the meaning of Part 2 of the Act of 1960 (4), unless there is an assembly of players playing a game in each other's presence. Undoubtedly that is the normal way of playing a game."

A little later he said (5):

" I think it is doubtful whether this argument can succeed, and I am not basing my opinion on it. On the other hand, the facts that there is no assembly of players, and that the alleged players are not in each other's presence nor in communication with each other, may well have considerable weight in any case as evidence in favour of a more general argument that there is no playing of a game."

In my view, the learned stipendiary magistrate approached this matter correctly by asking himself: what were the participants of the Waterloo Club doing; were they playing in one game or were they playing, as counsel for the appellants argues, in two? For my part, I still feel that, while it is common ground that they were playing in the local game, I do not think that it would be right to hold that from any realistic point of view they were taking any part in any other game at all. Language is apt to be misleading, but I think that what they were doing was playing one game locally which had twofold consequences; the winner of the local game became eligible for a wider prize, not by having taken part in a wider or national game, but by an arrangement made by the proprietors of the national Golden Scoop that those who took part in multiple local games might qualify for possible distribution to them of the national prizes. It was a local game on which there were superimposed, so to speak, national benefits, but the notion that a person taking part in bingo, the first hand at the Waterloo Club, was playing a game at the same time with any, whatever the number may be, of the five hundred other clubs is to my mind

(2) [1965] 2 All E.R. 745; [1965] A.C. 1262.
(3) [1965] 2 All E.R. at pp. 749, 750; [1965] A.C. at p. 1284.
(4) The Betting and Gaming Act, 1960.
(5) [1965] 2 All E.R. at p. 750; [1965] A.C. at p. 1284.

A putting forward a concept that is quite divorced from reality A much simpler approach is the one which I have endeavoured to express, and which I think does accord with reality in this case. I agree with Winn, L.J., that the real essence of this is that there was no national game played in that first hand, and that was the basis of the learned stipendiary magistrate's decision.

B   **WIDGERY, J.:** In the course of argument I also had inclined to the view that the proper interpretation of the facts in this case was that those playing in the Golden Scoop were playing a single game of bingo, and that on that single game of bingo they had the opportunity of winning two prizes, first a cash prize payable there and then and representing one half of the shilling which they had staked, and the other an opportunity to take part in what on this view would

C be a simple lottery run by the National Golden Scoop Club. If I were satisfied on the learned magistrate's finding that that was the reality of the matter, I should not be deterred from looking at the case in that way by the fact that the ticket specifically apportions the sum of 1s. between the house game and the national Golden Scoop game separately. There is a feeling left on reading this Case that in fact no one who went to the Waterloo Club ever took advantage of

D the opportunity presented of playing in one part of the game only, and it may well be that the reality, as Ashworth, J., has said, is that this was one game. However, it seems to me fairer to the appellants in the present case that one should adopt on the magistrate's finding the view expressed by Winn, L.J., and treat this as two games, but so treating it I come to precisely the same conclusion as that to which he came.

E   The only other matter on which I would wish to add a word is in relation to the observation of Winn, L.J., that, in deciding whether persons are playing a game, one should have regard to the ordinary meaning which an ordinary man would give to those words. I think that an ordinary man, when talking of playing a game, is talking of something which involves entertainment, he is talking of something which involves excitement and fun in the common pursuit

F by a number of competitors of a similar and known object, and it seems to me exceedingly difficult to produce those elements which the common man would ascribe to a game if the participants are in separate places with no communication between them whilst the activity is going on, and thus no sort of opportunity of seeing how their competitors are progressing and, I would have thought, none of the excitement and entertainment which any true game can provide.

G   I agree with both judgments which have been delivered, and I am of the opinion that this appeal should be dismissed.

Appeal dismissed. Leave to appeal to the House of Lords granted under s. 1 of the Administration of Justice Act, 1960, the court certifying that a point of law of general public importance was involved, viz., whether all the persons playing the first hand of a bingo session in each of about five hundred bingo clubs could in law

H *be playing a game of bingo with each other.*

   Solicitors: *Ward, Bowie & Co.*, agents for *David Yablon & Co.*, Bradford (for the appellants); *T. D. Jones & Co.*, agents for *David Morgan*, Kingston-upon-Hull (for the respondent).

              [*Reported by* N. P. Metcalfe, Esq., *Barrister-at-Law.*]

HILL *v.* ARCHBOLD.   A

[QUEEN'S BENCH DIVISION (MacKenna, J.), January 24, 25, 26, 27, 1967.]

Maintenance of Action—Common interest—Nature of interest—Trade union
employing full-time salaried officials—Action by officials against union
member for defamation in respect of their conduct in course of their duties—
Union executive supporting legal action in good faith, reasonably believing   B
that officials were unjustly defamed—Whether this constituted maintenance
—Express authority to defray costs of officials not given by union's rules—
Whether power to do so implied.

A union's rules included among its objects (r. 2 (*l*)*) that of affording
assistance to individual members in legal cases of a professional nature.
The general fund of the union was made applicable (r. 39, r. 40 (*a*)) for the   C
purpose of attaining the objects of the union, as defined by, and subject to,
the rules. A separate rule (r. 46*) governed the administration of legal
assistance. The court construed this separate rule as confined to the giving
of legal assistance to subscribing members of the union.

Two whole-time salaried officials of the union, who were no longer subscribing members, were the subject of letters which were capable of being   D
defamatory and were written by the plaintiff, a member of the union. The
union in good faith supported actions by the officers to vindicate their reputations. Their libel actions were dismissed, the jury finding that the defence
of justification had been made out, and appeals on the ground that the
verdict was perverse were dismissed for the reason that the jury should
not have been allowed to state the grounds on which they based their verdicts. E
The plaintiff, having successfully defended the actions, sought to restrain
the union's treasurer from using the union's funds to pay the costs of the two
officials.

Held: (i) the union did not commit the offence of maintenance by supporting the litigation brought to vindicate its servants' reputation (see p. 1041,
letter I, post).   F

Hickman v. *Kent or Romney Marsh Sheep Breeders' Association* ((1921),
37 T.L.R. 163; affirming (1920), 36 T.L.R. 528) followed.

Oram v. *Hutt* ([1911-13] All E.R. Rep. 376) considered and distinguished.

(ii) the power to support such litigation on behalf of the union's servants
was to be implied in the union's rules, and the expense of so doing could
properly be defrayed out of the general fund of the union (see p. 1041, letter G
A, and p. 1043, letters A and F, post).

[As to liability for maintenance of actions, what amounts to maintenance,
and the exceptions to the rule that it is illegal, see 1 HALSBURY's LAWS (3rd Edn.)
39-41, paras. 80-82; and for cases, see 1 DIGEST (Repl.) 80-84, *607-634*, 96-101,
710-768.]
                                                                                 H
Cases referred to:

Alfin v. *Hewlett*, (1902), 18 T.L.R. 664; 45 Digest (Repl.) 549, *1268*.
Baker v. *Jones*, [1954] 2 All E.R. 553; [1954] 1 W.L.R. 1005; 1 Digest (Repl.)
    97, *714*.
Greig v. *National Amalgamated Union of Shop Assistants, Warehousemen &*
    Clerks, (1906), 22 T.L.R. 274; 1 Digest (Repl.) 100, *755*.
Hickman v. *Kent or Romney Marsh Sheep Breeders' Association*, (1920), 36   I
    T.L.R. 528; *affd.* C.A. (1920); 37 T.L.R. 163; 1 Digest (Repl.) 83, *624*.
Martell v. *Consett Iron Co., Ltd.*, [1955] 1 All E.R. 481; [1955] Ch. 363; [1955]
    2 W.L.R. 463; Digest (Cont. Vol. A) 125, *110a*.
Oram v. *Hutt*, [1911-13] All E.R. Rep. 376; [1914] 1 Ch. 98; 83 L.J.Ch. 161;
    110 L.T. 187; 78 J.P. 51; 1 Digest (Repl.) 82, *620*.

---

* The terms of r. 2 (*l*) and r. 46, so far as relevant, are stated at p. 1042, letters B and
F, post.

A   *Scott* v. *National Society for Prevention of Cruelty to Children and Parr*, (1909), 25 T.L.R. 789; 1 Digest (Repl.) 82, *619.*

Action.

In this action, commenced by specially endorsed writ dated July 26, 1966, the plaintiff, Fred Hill, a schoolteacher and a member of the National Union of Teachers, sought an injunction to restrain the defendant John Archbold,

B   the treasurer of the union, from using the funds of the union to pay the whole or part of the costs incurred by two officials of the union who were the plaintiffs in unsuccessful libel actions against the plaintiff (consolidated and intituled *Barnes and Gould* v. *Hill*) which were heard before MILMO, J., and a jury in the High Court in June, 1966.   The writ and statement of claim (dated July 27, 1966) also asked that the treasurer be restrained from using union funds to further

C   the actions of the two officials by appeal or retrial.   Notice of appeal in the actions was filed on July 29, 1966, and on Nov. 14, 1966, the Court of Appeal dismissed the appeals*.   The facts in the former actions, so far as here relevant, and the facts in the present action are set out in the judgment.

The cases noted below† were cited during the argument in addition to those referred to in the judgment.

D   The plaintiff appeared in person.
Owen Stable, Q.C., and *J. M. Rankin* for the defendant.

MacKENNA, J.: In 1963 and 1964 Dr. Barnes was the secretary of the Superannuation and Salaries Committee of the National Union of Teachers, and Sir Ronald Gould was the union's general secretary.   Both were whole-time

E   salaried servants of the union.   They had been, but were no longer, subscribing members of the union.   In those two years Mr. Hill wrote letters to Dr. Barnes in his official capacity raising points on the working of the Teachers (Superannuation) Act, 1956, which had imposed a liability on teachers to contribute an extra one per cent. of their salaries to a superannuation fund established by an earlier Act (1).   Dr. Barnes, with Sir Ronald Gould's approval, given by him

F   as general secretary of the union, replied to Mr. Hill's letters expressing the view that the teachers had not been treated unjustly.   Mr. Hill thereupon published to several members of the union a circular accusing Dr. Barnes of having knowingly made false statements with intent to deceive in his replies to Mr. Hill's letters, and accusing Sir Ronald Gould of having been a party to the deceptions. The circular meant that both officials were unfit to be employed by the union.

G   Mr. Hill threatened to repeat these statements.   The defamed officials applied to their employer, the union, for assistance in defending their reputations against Mr. Hill's attack.   On Nov. 6, 1964, the Law and Tenure Committee of the executive passed the following resolution: (1) That authority be given for legal assistance to be extended to the general secretary and Dr. Barnes as employees of the union and when so acting in the course of their duties, in any action to

H   be taken against Mr. Hill.   (2) That approval be given to such legal assistance being rendered to the general secretary and Dr. Barnes by an outside firm of solicitors.   Before passing this resolution the committee had been referred to an opinion of counsel dated Oct. 22, 1964, advising as follows:

I   * See *Barnes* v. *Hill*, ante p. 347.
† *Findon* v. *Parker*, [1843-60] All E.R. Rep. 876; *Elborough* v. *Ayres*, (1870), L.R. 10 Eq. 367; *A.-G.* v. *Gt. Eastern Ry. Co.*, (1880), 5 App. Cas. 473; *Plating Co.* v. *Farquharson*, [1881-85] All E.R. Rep. 303; (1881), 17 Ch.D. 49; *Bradlaugh* v. *Newdegate*, (1883), 11 Q.B.D. 1; *Small* v. *Smith*, (1884), 10 App. Cas. 119; *Harris* v. *Brisco*, [1886-90] All E.R. Rep. 564; (1886), 17 Q.B. 504; *Alabaster* v. *Harness*, [1891-94] All E.R. Rep. 817; [1895] 1 Q.B. 339; *British Cash and Parcels Conveyors, Ltd.* v. *Lamson Store Service Co., Ltd.*, [1908-10] All E.R. Rep. 146; [1908] 1 K.B. 1006; *Cyclists' Touring Club* v. *Hopkinson*, [1910] 1 Ch. 179; *Neville* v. *London Express Newspaper, Ltd.*, [1918-19] All E.R. Rep. 61; [1919] A.C. 368; *Wimbledon and Putney Commons Conservators* v. *Tuely*, [1931] 1 Ch. 190.
(1) The Teachers (Superannuation) Act, 1925, s. 9.

" (a) That the statements made by Mr. Hill in the circular in question are   **A**
defamatory both of Sir Ronald Gould and Dr. Barnes; (b) that it would be
impossible for Mr. Hill to justify such defamatory allegations; (c) that
there is ample evidence of malice on his part to defeat any defence of qualified
privilege that might be raised."

On Dec. 5, 1964, this resolution was confirmed by the executive committee.

In seeking to protect their servants' reputations which had been attacked   **B**
because of letters written by them in the course of their employment, these
committees acted in good faith, reasonably believing that their servants had
been unjustly defamed, and as good employers. They believed that what they
were doing was in their union's interest. The success of Mr. Hill's campaign,
if it were successful, might have made it impossible for the union to retain the
services of Dr. Barnes and Sir Ronald Gould.   **C**

On Dec. 10, 1964, a writ was issued by Dr. Barnes against Mr. Hill, claiming
damages for libel and an injunction. On Dec. 16, 1964, a writ making similar
claims was issued by Sir Ronald Gould. The purpose of these actions was to
vindicate the reputations of these two gentlemen and to stop the threatened
further publication of the circular. Mr. Hill was in no position to pay substantial
damages. The union did not instigate this litigation. They supported actions   **D**
which both they and the two officers reasonably thought were necessary to
vindicate the officers' reputations and to protect them against further attacks.
Outside solicitors were instructed in accordance with the resolution, and the
union did not intermeddle in the litigation which followed the issue of the writs.
Mr. Hill defended each of the actions pleading justification and later, by
amendment, privilege.   **E**

In June, 1966, the two actions were tried before MILMO, J., and a jury, who
returned a general verdict in Mr. Hill's favour. At the instance of counsel for
Dr. Barnes and Sir Ronald Gould, the judge asked the jury whether they had
found for Mr. Hill on the ground of privilege or because the defamatory statements were justified. The foreman answered: on the ground of justification.
The unsuccessful plaintiffs appealed to the Court of Appeal (2), complaining that   **F**
the jury's verdict was perverse. There was (it was said) no evidence on which
justification could properly be found. Their appeal was dismissed. As I understand the judgment of the Court of Appeal (2), the reason was that the jury
ought not to have been asked to give the grounds of their verdict. The foreman's
answer should, therefore, be ignored, and, without that answer the verdict could
as well be supported by Mr. Hill's plea of privilege, which was not assailable,   **G**
as on the more questionable ground of justification. The costs in question here
are those incurred by Dr. Barnes and Sir Ronald Gould in these unsuccessful
actions and appeals. Mr. Hill did not ask for any costs in either court and was
awarded none.

There are two questions to be considered by me:—(i) Is it the offence of
maintenance for an employer to support his servant's action for libel brought   **H**
in the circumstances of this case, where the defamed servants were accused of
misconduct in the course of their employment by the union, where the defamatory
statements had been circulated to many members of the union and were likely
to be circulated to many more, and where the purpose of the action was to
vindicate the reputation of the defamed servants and to protect them against
further attacks of the same kind? If it is not, (ii) Can a power to give such   **I**
support be implied in the union's constitution as a power reasonably necessary
for the attainment of the union's objects?

If it is to be held that the union's funds are expendable for this purpose,
the first question must be answered negatively and the second affirmatively;
as regards the first question, because there can be no power to spend the funds
for an illegal purpose; as regards the second question, because if the power is

---

(2) See *Barnes* v. *Hill*, ante p. 347.

A　to exist at all it must be implied, for there is no express power to spend the union funds in supporting a servant's action—moreover no power can be implied unless it is reasonably necessary for the attainment of the union's objects. I would answer the first question negatively and the second affirmatively.

On the first question, I have read all the cases to which I have been referred by Mr. Hill and by counsel for the defendant, as well as the passage in WIN-

B　FIELD'S PRESENT LAW OF ABUSE OF LEGAL PROCEDURE (1921 Edn.) pp. 34-39, and the case of *Hickman* v. *Kent or Romney Marsh Sheep Breeders' Association* (3) which was affirmed on appeal (4). I do not propose to discuss these many cases at length. Most of them were considered in the judgment of JENKINS, L.J., in *Martell* v. *Consett Iron Co., Ltd.* (5). I summarise my conclusions on this part of the case in two propositions:

C　(i) The right of a master to support his servant's litigation is an exception to the general rule prohibiting the maintenance of other men's actions.

(ii) No modern case decides that this exception is obsolete or that it is inapplicable to an action for libel whose object is to protect a servant's reputation attacked by reason of acts done by him in the course of his employment. The exception was applied in *Hickman's* case (6), which was one of libel. BRAY, J., refused

D　to apply the exception to the master's maintenance of his servant's action for slander in *Scott* v. *The National Society for Prevention of Cruelty to Children and Parr* (7), for reasons which are inapplicable to the present case. The judgment of BRAY, J., apparently assumed that the exception was still alive and that it applied to actions for slander. *Oram* v. *Hutt* (8) in the Court of Appeal is not against my second proposition. Although it was argued in that case that it fell

E　within the exception of master and servant, and although the indemnity given to the union's official was held to be obnoxious to the law of maintenance and therefore ultra vires, LORD SUMNER, one of the three judges of the Court of Appeal, stated (9) that the relations between the maintained official and the union excluded the application of any of the recognised exceptions of the rule as to maintenance, notably those relating to master and servant. He gave no

F　reasons for the view that the maintained official was not a servant of the union. A possible explanation is that the union's officials in that case were unpaid. This may also be the reason why in *Baker* v. *Jones* (10) the union's claim to support its officials was not based on the relation of master and servant. LYNSKEY, J.'s dictum (11), so far as it relates to servants, is not, in my opinion, supported by the two cases which he cites, *Oram* v. *Hutt* (12) and *Alfin* v. *Hewlett* (13). I

G　have already mentioned *Oram* v. *Hutt* (12). As to *Alfin* v. *Hewlett* (13), it does not appear from the report that the relations between the official and the union which maintained him was that of servant and master. Furthermore, the maintained official alleged in his defence that he was acting on his own behalf at the material time, and his defence was supported by his union only because they wished to prove that he was not acting on their behalf. Another case relied on

H　by Mr. Hill was *Greig* v. *National Amalgamated Union of Shop Assistants, Warehousemen and Clerks* (14). There, too, there was no relation of master and servant between the union and the maintained litigant.

As it seems to me reasonable that a master should be allowed to support such litigation as that between Dr. Barnes, Sir Ronald Gould and Mr. Hill, and as there is, in my opinion, no authority deciding that he may not do so, I shall hold

I　that a master does not commit the offence of maintenance by supporting such litigation.

(3) (1920), 36 T.L.R. 528.　　　　　　　　　(4) (1920), 37 T.L.R. 163.
(5) [1955] 1 All E.R. 481; [1955] Ch. 363.
(6) [1920], 36 T.L.R. 528; (1920), 37 T.L.R. 163.
(7) (1909), 25 T.L.R. 789.　　　(8) [1911-13] All E.R. Rep. 376; [1914] 1 Ch. 98.
(9) [1911-13] All E.R. Rep. at p. 380; [1914] 1 Ch. at p. 107.
(10) [1954] 2 All E.R. 553.　　　　　　　　(11) [1954] 2 All E.R. at p. 560.
(12) [1911-13] All E.R. Rep. 376; [1914] 1 Ch. 98.
(13) (1902), 18 T.L.R. 664.　　　　　　　　(14) (1906), 22 T.L.R. 274.

The question remains whether the power to give such support to a servant can **A** be implied in the union's constitution. Before considering this question I shall state those provisions of the union's rules to which I have been referred as bearing on this question. Rule 2 sets out the objects of the union, including under (*l*),

" to afford advice and assistance to individual members in educational **B** and professional matters, and in legal cases of a professional nature."

Rule 3 provides that Conference is the supreme authority of the union, and r. 4 that the affairs of the union shall be managed by the executive, and that all decisions of the executive involving the salary policy of the union as approved by Conference must be in accord with that policy subject to an exception which I need not mention. Rule 5 deals with the qualifications for membership of the **C** union: no one can be a member of the union who is not a teacher with the necessary qualifications (15). Rule 18 provides that the officials of the union shall be the general secretary and all other officials whose offices have been sanctioned by the annual conference, and that the power to appoint or dismiss any official of the union shall be vested in the executive. Rule 39 provides that there shall be established a number of funds including a general fund and that those funds shall **D** be applicable for the purposes of attaining the objects of the union as defined by, and subject to, the provisions of the rules. Rule 40 provides that annual subscriptions shall be paid into this fund and that all expenditure other than expenditure on account of sustentation, or of disbursements chargeable to the building fund, shall be made from the general fund. I am told that this fund is not treated as covered by the provisions of r. 43 relating to trustees, and Mr. Hill has **E** not contended that this practice is wrong.

Rule 46 is, for present purposes, an important rule. Paragraph (*a*) of the rule is as follows:

" 46.   *Administration of legal assistance.*—(*a*) *General.*—No payments shall be made out of the funds of the union except for the purposes of cases of professional conduct, cases under sections (*f*) and (*o*), and for the purposes **F** of affording legal assistance or support to members, in accordance with the resolution of the Newcastle Conference."

There follow the provisions of that resolution which stipulate for legal assistance to members involved in cases affecting the rights and interests of teachers, and the support of teachers who may have suffered through legitimate action taken **G** in defence of professional objects. Section (*f*) deals with cases not involving proceedings in court, and section (*o*) deals with arbitration. It is clear from these and other provisions of the rule that it deals only with the giving of legal assistance to subscribing members of the union. As I said earlier in this judgment, neither Sir Ronald Gould nor Dr. Barnes was, at any time material to these proceedings, a subscribing member of the union. Other provisions of r. 46, notably section (*i*) **H** and section (*j*) regulate the manner in which this legal assistance shall be given.

The defendant (16) concedes that there is no express provision conferring the necessary power, but argues that it is to be implied. His argument may be summarised in these five propositions:

(i) The union has express power to employ servants such as Sir Ronald Gould and Dr. Barnes for the purpose of attaining the union's objects; **I**

_____

(15) The terms of r. 5, so far as material, were as follows: " (*a*) The union shall consist of such local and central associations of teachers (hereinafter referred to   collectively as ' constituent associations ') as may be affiliated by the executive.   (*b*) . . . (*c*) . . . a constituent association shall admit to membership teachers recognised by the Ministry of Education as qualified teachers, or possessing such alternative qualifications as may be accepted by the executive: and also teachers recognised by the Ministry of Education as temporary teachers provided that any such temporary teacher shall cease to be eligible for membership immediately his recognition as a temporary teacher expires."

(16) The defendant was the treasurer of the union.

A   (ii) As incidental to this power, there must be implied a further power to do such things as a good employer would reasonably do for the benefit of his servants, having regard, among other things, to his own interest;

(iii) This general implied power includes the power to support the servant's litigation in cases like the present;

(iv) Such an implied power is not inconsistent with the express provisions of
B   r. 46. If it were, the implication would of course be impossible. Rule 46 (*a*), read literally, would forbid the use of the union's funds for any purpose except the provision of legal assistance in accordance with the rule, which would be absurd. The provision of legal assistance is only one of the union's many objects, and its funds must be expendable for other purposes. It follows that r. 46 must be read with some limitation. There are three conceivable limitations. One is to read
C   the rule as dealing exclusively with the matter of legal expenses: " No payments shall be made out of the funds of the union except for the purposes of cases of professional conduct . . .", etc. That, however, would preclude the union from litigating in protection of its property or interests either as plaintiff or as defendant, which would be equally absurd. An alternative is to read the rule as dealing exclusively with the matter of legal assistance to persons or bodies other than
D   the union itself. The third and, it is argued, the more reasonable alternative is to read it as dealing with the matter of providing legal assistance in performance of the objects described in r. 2 (*l*), viz., to afford advice and assistance to individual members in educational and professional matters, and in legal cases of a professional nature. Read in this way, there is, it is said, no inconsistency between the implication of a power to support the union's servant's action in a proper case
E   and an express power to provide legal assistance to its members in accordance with the provisions of r. 46.

(v) If it is within the union's power to support a servant's litigation, expense incurred in exercising the power can be defrayed out of the general fund, which is available for that and any other expenditure for attaining the union's objects.

In my opinion, the argument succeeds. I do not consider that the observations
F   of Lord Parker of Waddington in *Oram* v. *Hutt* (17) are inconsistent with this argument. He was dealing with the possibility of implying a power to give legal assistance to a union's members. Because it is impossible to imply a power of that kind it does not follow that it is impossible to imply a power to give legal assistance to a union's servants in any case where a good employer would give that assistance acting reasonably and having regard to his own interests. I have
G   found some difficulty in accepting the fourth step of the argument which seeks to reconcile the implied power with the express provisions of r. 46, but in the end I was convinced by the argument of counsel for the defendant. The action fails. There will be judgment for the defendant.

Judgment accordingly.

H   Solicitor: *Kenneth Wormald* (for the defendant).

[*Reported by* K. Diana Phillips, *Barrister-at-Law.*]

I

---

(17) [1911-13] All E.R. Rep. at pp. 378, 379; [1914] 1 Ch. at p. 105.

WATTS v. SEYMOUR.

A

[QUEEN'S BENCH DIVISION (Winn, L.J., Ashworth and Widgery, JJ.), February 15, 1967.]

Firearms—Rifle—Sale to person under seventeen years who was not entitled to purchase rifle—Payment made in cash but possession of rifle retained by dealer —Whether contravention of Firearms Act—Conditional contract to sell and property to pass at some future time—Whether such agreement for sale is within Firearms Act, 1937 (1 Edw. 8 & 1 Geo. 6 c. 12), s. 11 (1), s. 19 (1)— Sale of Goods Act, 1893 (56 & 57 Vict. c. 71), s. 1 (3).

B

S., a youth under seventeen years old, asked the respondent, a registered firearms dealer, if he could purchase a rifle, both he and the respondent being members of the same rifle club. S. was invited to inspect the rifles on the respondent's premises. He selected a rifle and paid for it in cash and received a receipt which stated that the rifle was in the possession of the respondent's firm and " taken to range for use by us ". The respondent refused to let S. take the rifle away without a permit, but said that he would keep it and bring it down to the range for S. to use there. He also endorsed the receipt to that effect. On appeal by the prosecution against the dismissal of charges against the respondent of contravening s. 19 (1)* of the Firearms Act, 1937, in that he sold the rifle to a person whom he knew or had reasonable grounds for believing to be under the age of seventeen, and of selling the rifle to a person not being a registered firearms dealer who did not produce to him a firearms certificate authorising him to purchase or acquire the rifle nor show any other exemption, contrary to s. 11 (1)† of the Act of 1937,

C

D

E

Held: it was not an essential element of a sale that an immediate right to possession should pass by the transaction and, as the respondent had entered contractually into a transaction the effect of which was to transfer the property in the rifle to S., there had been a sale of the rifle to S.; accordingly the case would be remitted to the justices with a direction to convict (see p. 1047, letters D and G, and p. 1048, letter A, post).

F

Per CURIAM: an agreement to sell, as defined by s. 1 (3) of the Sale of Goods Act, 1893 (viz., where the transfer in the property in the goods is to take place at a future time or subject to some condition thereafter to be fulfilled), would not amount to a selling within the meaning of the Firearms Act, 1937, though it would mature into a sale on a subsequent passing of the property; any transaction, however, by which property was transferred or by which it was agreed that following on, e.g., some adaptation of the firearm, property would automatically pass, would be an infringement of the Act of 1937 (see p. 1047, letter I, and p. 1048, letter B, post).

G

Appeal allowed.

[As to the purchase and possession of firearms by young persons, see 10 HALSBURY'S LAWS (3rd Edn.) 599, 600, para. 1115; and as to the restrictions in dealing with firearms, see ibid., pp. 596, 597, para. 1109.

For the Sale of Goods Act, 1893, s. 1, s. 17, s. 18, see 22 HALSBURY'S STATUTES (2nd Edn.) 986, 995, 996.

For the Firearms Act, 1937, s. 11, s. 19, see 5 HALSBURY'S STATUTES (2nd Edn.) 1103, 1109.]

H

I

* Section 19 (1), so far as material, provides: " No person under the age of seventeen years shall purchase or hire any firearm . . . and no person shall sell or let on hire any firearm . . . to any other person whom he knows or has reasonable ground for believing to be under the age of seventeen years."

† Section 11 (1), so far as material, provides: " No person shall sell or transfer to any other person in the United Kingdom, other than a registered firearms dealer, any firearm . . . to which this Part of this Act applies, unless that other person produces a firearm certificate authorising him to purchase or acquire it or shows that he is by virtue of the Act entitled to purchase or acquire it without holding such a certificate."

A   **Case Stated.**

This was a Case Stated by the justices for the county borough of Southend-on-Sea in respect of their adjudication as a magistrates' court sitting at the Court House, Victoria Avenue, Southend-on-Sea on June 17, 1966. On June 7, 1966, informations were laid by the appellant, Frederick Thomas William Watts, against the respondent, George Seymour Seymour, alleging that he had: (i) on

B   Apr. 1, 1966, in the county borough of Southend-on-Sea sold a certain firearm, namely, a ·303 Lee Enfield rifle No. 65524, to Christopher Robin Stacey (hereinafter called " Stacey "), a person whom he knew or had reasonable grounds for believing to be under the age of seventeen years—contrary to s. 19 (1) of the Firearms Act, 1937; (ii) on Apr. 1, 1966, in the county borough of Southend-on-Sea sold to Stacey a certain firearm, namely, a ·303 Lee Enfield Rifle No. 65524 to

C   which Part 1 of the Firearms Act, 1937, applied, Stacey not being a registered firearms dealer and not producing a firearms certificate authorising him to purchase or acquire the firearm and not showing that he was by virtue of the Act of 1937 entitled to purchase or acquire the firearm without holding such a certificate, contrary to s. 11 (1) of the Firearms Act, 1937. The following facts were found: (a) Stacey was a person under the age of seventeen years and that was known to

D   the respondent; (b) Stacey was not a registered firearms dealer; (c) Stacey did not produce a firearms certificate authorising him to purchase or acquire the firearm or show that he was by virtue of the Act of 1937 entitled to purchase or acquire the firearm without holding such a certificate; (d) the respondent was a registered firearms dealer carrying on business from his premises 41, Broadway, Thorpe Bay, within the county borough; (e) during March, 1966, Stacey asked the respondent

E   if he could purchase a rifle. The respondent said, " Come down and have a look ". On Friday, Apr. 1, 1966, Stacey went to the premises of the respondent and examined the rifles displayed there. He selected a Lee Enfield rifle, No. 65524, and asked the price. The respondent told him £7 12s. 6d. He then told the respondent that he would purchase the rifle and paid him £7 12s. 6d. cash. The respondent gave him a receipt for that amount on which he wrote " This rifle in possession

F   of S. & G. Arms Co. kept by us and take to range for use by us ". Stacey then said to the respondent " May I take it away with me? " The respondent replied " No, you must have a permit. It's a bit difficult so I'll keep it and bring it down to the range for you to use." The respondent then endorsed the receipt to that effect; (g) Stacey used the gun after Apr. 1, 1966, at the Southend Rifle and Pistol Club, of which he and the respondent were members; (h) the rifle was not in Stacey's

G   possession other than at the premises of the Southend Rifle and Pistol Club. It was contended by the appellant that: (a) the Firearms Acts make it an offence to sell a firearm in certain circumstances. The offence was, therefore, committed when the sale was completed and the time of the giving of possession was irrelevant; (b) for the purpose of the Firearms Acts, a sale took place when the contract was made; (c) once the rifle had been chosen, agreement reached and the purchase price paid, a contract was in existence. For the purposes of the Firearms

H   Acts, 1937 and 1965, that sale took place and the offence was committed on Apr. 1, 1966; (d) even if for these purposes a sale was not complete when a contract was made, it must be complete when the property in the subject-matter of the contract passed or would have passed in the absence of any illegality; (e) s. 18, r. 1, of the Sale of Goods Act, 1893, provided that

I   " Where there is an unconditional contract for the sale of specific goods, in a deliverable state, the property in the goods passes to the buyer when the contract is made, and it is immaterial whether the time of payment or the time of delivery, or both, be postponed."

The sale was, therefore, complete as the property in the goods would, in the absence of any illegality, have passed; (f) the contract was not a conditional contract as the endorsement as to possession was not made at the time the contract was made but afterwards when the question of possession was raised;

(g) if there had been no sale, or a sale conditional on Stacey reaching the age of A
seventeen and obtaining a permit, there would have been no need for the respondent to endorse on the receipt the reservation as to the possession as he would
have been entitled to possession by virtue of his ownership.   It was contended
by the respondent that: (a) the provisions of s. 1 (3) of the Sale of Goods Act,
1893, should apply to the transaction in that the property in the rifle was to be
transferred at some future time on the fulfilment of two conditions, namely, B
(i) when Stacey attained the age of seventeen years; (ii) that he should obtain a
firearms certificate, and that until that time the contract was an agreement to sell
and not a sale. In accordance with sub-s. (4) of that section, the agreement to sell
did not become a sale until the time had elapsed and the conditions had been
fulfilled; (b) the provisions of s. 17 of the Sale of Goods Act, 1893, should apply
to this transaction for the purpose of ascertaining the intentions of the parties C
as to the time of transfer of the property; (c) the contract was legal, but any
attempt by Stacey to enforce the same before fulfilment of the two conditions
hereinbefore mentioned must fail because the respondent could legally refuse
to deliver the rifle on the ground that such action would convert a legal contract
into an illegal contract and it was, therefore, unenforceable and the property in
those circumstances would not pass; (d) the evil that the Firearms Acts sought to D
prevent was a firearm coming into the hands of a person under seventeen years
of age, and the respondent's action was calculated to prevent that mischief.

The justices considered that the property in the goods did not pass to Stacey.
They dismissed the charges and ordered the prosecution to make a contribution of
£10 10s. towards the costs of the respondent. The appellant now appealed.

E. M. Hill for the appellant.   E
P. Temple-Morris for the respondent.

WINN, L.J.: Two charges were brought which both related to the same
transaction. The respondent, George Seymour, was charged on the first information that he sold in April, 1966, a Lee Enfield rifle to a young man called Stacey,
being a person whom he knew or had reasonable grounds for believing to be F
under the age of seventeen years, contrary to s. 19 (1) of the Firearms Act, 1937.
It is convenient to say that he did not dispute that he knew that Stacey was
under the age of seventeen. The second charge was that, on the same day, with
regard to the same person and the same rifle, he sold it to a person not being a
registered firearms dealer who did not produce to him a firearms certificate
authorising him to purchase or acquire the firearm, nor show any other exemption, G
contrary to s. 11 (1) of the Act of 1937.

The essential facts are simple, and shortly stated by the magistrates in para.
2 (e) and (f) of the Case. During the previous month of March, 1966, Stacey asked
the respondent if he could purchase a rifle. It appears, and it is right to make this
plain, that the respondent and Stacey were members of the same rifle club, and
that in fact there is no reason to suppose that Stacey has ever unlawfully used H
the rifle in question, though he has used it at this rifle club. It is further right to
say that the respondent was properly concerned to ensure so far as it lay in his
power that Stacey did not illegally use the rifle. The respondent replied to his
enquiry, " Come down and have a look ". So on Apr. 1, 1966, Stacey went to the
respondent's premises and examined certain rifles displayed there. He selected
a particular Lee Enfield rifle, the number of which is given, and asked the price.   I
The respondent told him £7 12s. 6d. He then told the respondent that he would
purchase the rifle and he paid him that amount in cash. The respondent gave him
a receipt for that amount, referring to the rifle by number, and on that receipt
the respondent wrote: " This rifle in possession of S. & G. Arms Co. [which is the
firm of the respondent] kept by us and taken to range for use by us." When that
transaction had been completed to the extent that I have indicated, Stacey,
said to the respondent, " May I take it away with me? ". The respondent replied:
" No, you must have a permit. It's a bit difficult so I'll keep it and bring it down

A to the range for you to use." He then endorsed the receipt to that effect. Taking
those two findings together, it seems clear to me that what the respondent had in
mind was that he would take the rifle to the range, keep it under his control there,
but would allow Stacey to use it only at the range. As I have said, it was in no
sense wicked conduct on the part of the respondent. The question is whether it
was a breach of s. 19 (1) and, so far as the lack of certificate and absence of regis-
B tration of a firearms dealer was concerned, against s. 11 (1) of the Act of 1937.
Each of those subsections makes it an offence to sell any firearm subject to the
conditions that I have indicated.

The magistrates took a very great deal of trouble over this case. They applied
themselves assiduously and, if I may be allowed to say so, with considerable
application and intelligence, to a number of provisions of the Sale of Goods Act,
C 1893, and they formed their opinion on the basis of their understanding of the
provisions of that Act and the application of those provisions to the circumstances which they found and which I have narrated. I regret to have to say that
I cannot accept their opinion, partly—by no means principally—because neither
s. 35 of the Sale of Goods Act, 1893, nor any question of avoidability of infants'
contracts, nor whether or not goods are necessaries nor of illegality making a
D contract voidable, if not wholly void, has any relevance to this case. What is
relevant and essential is whether or not the respondent did sell this rifle to Stacey.
In my opinion, the answer to that question is plainly yes, since he entered contractually into a transaction the effect of which was to transfer the property in
the rifle to Stacey, notwithstanding that a restriction was imposed on possession,
and the right to demand delivery, by that same transaction itself or by an
E immediately following variation of it in the form which is set out in para. 2 (f) of
the Case. In my opinion, it is not an essential element of a sale, or of a transaction
of which it can properly be said that by it " A " sold an article to " B " and it
can be said of " A " that he infringed a prohibition to sell, that any immediate
right to possession should be passed by the contract. There must be many
hypothetical cases, which could be envisaged, in which parties agree for money or
F money's worth that one will there and then transfer property to the other but will
retain, even against the will of the purchaser, possession of the article for a period
of time or until some condition has been satisfied. Possession is something quite
different from property in this context, though normally, of course, the right to
possession will follow ownership. It is not an essential element of a sale that an
immediate right to possession should be transferred by the transaction. I think
G that there can only be one answer to the acid test, as I see it; after the transaction
in question could Stacey have validly sold so as to transfer property in the rifle
to somebody else? I think that he clearly could. That means that he had acquired
property by the payment he made in the course of this transaction and strengthens,
in my opinion, my view that the respondent here did sell, and did sell in contravention of each of the subsections of the Act of 1937 to which I have referred.

H   I would allow this appeal.

The court was invited to decide a further point, unnecessary for the purposes
of the present appeal, and that is whether or not such an agreement to sell as is
referred to in s. 1 (3) of the Sale of Goods Act, 1893, if made, would amount to
selling in contravention of the subsections to which I have referred (1) in the Act
of 1937. Put in that form, I should myself say that an agreement to sell as there
I defined, namely, where the transfer of the property in the goods is to take place
at a future time or subject to some condition thereafter to be fulfilled, would
not amount to selling within the meaning of the Firearms Act, 1937; but any
transaction by which property was transferred or by which it was agreed that
following on, e.g., some adaptation of the firearm, property would automatically

---

(1) The subsections are s. 11 (1) and s. 19 (1), which are printed, so far as relevant, in
the footnotes on p. 1044, ante. Other provisions of the Firearms Act, 1937, also contain
prohibitions on sale, e.g., s. 17 (1), s. 20 (1) and s. 21 (4).

pass would, I think myself, be an infringement: but this last part of my judg- **A**
ment is obiter and academic, and I am only giving it in response to the invitation
which counsel for the appellant addressed to the court.

ASHWORTH, J.: I agree.

WIDGERY, J.: I also agree. I agree with WINN, L.J.'s view that we should
not venture on an opinion in general terms about whether an agreement to sell **B**
amounts to selling for the purposes of the Firearms Act, 1937. I would merely
add that, on any view, an agreement to sell would subsequently mature into
a sale on the passing of the property. It would unquestionably be selling at that
time.

WINN, L.J.: I would like to associate myself with what WIDGERY, J., has **C**
said.

Appeal allowed. Case remitted.

Solicitors: *Sharpe, Pritchard & Co.*, agents for *M. J. Simpson*, Southend-on-
Sea (for the appellant); *Maxwell Lewis*, Southend-on-Sea (for the respondent).

[*Reported by* N. P. METCALFE, ESQ., *Barrister-at-Law.*] **D**

JAMES *v.* CAVEY.

[QUEEN'S BENCH DIVISION (Winn, L.J., Ashworth and Widgery, JJ.), February **E**
15, 1967.]

*Road Traffic—Traffic sign—Parking—Unilateral waiting—Parking prohibited
on east side of road from 9.0 a.m. on Monday falling on odd day in month—
Appellant parking car on east side of road at 6.0 a.m. on such Monday—
Car remaining until after 9.0 a.m.—No traffic signs erected in road to indicate
that the prohibition depended on whether Monday fell on odd day in month—* **F**
*Whether offence committed—Traffic Regulation Orders (Procedure) (England
and Wales) Regulations, 1961 (S.I. 1961 No. 485), reg. 15 (c)—Brighton
Corporation (Various Roads) (No. 3) (Unilateral Waiting) Order 1965.*

At 6.0 a.m. on Monday, Nov. 15, 1965, the appellant parked his car on
the east side of a road in Brighton, and it remained there until 1.30 p.m.
By the Brighton Corporation (Various Roads) (No. 3) (Unilateral Waiting) **G**
Order 1965, made in exercise of the powers conferred by s. 26 of the Road
Traffic Act, 1960, and which applied to the road in question, parking on the
east side of the road was prohibited from 9.0 a.m. on Monday to the following
Sunday at 6.0 p.m. if the Monday fell on an odd day of the month. By
reg. 15 (c)* of the Traffic Regulation Orders (Procedure) (England and Wales)
Regulations, 1961, where a traffic regulation order was made by a local **H**
authority, the local authority had to take all such steps as were reasonably
practicable to cause to be erected on or near such a road traffic signs requisite
for the purpose of securing that adequate information as to the effect of the
order was given to persons using the road. There was nothing on any of
the traffic signs erected in the road in question to indicate that the prohibition on parking on the east side of the road depended on whether a **I**
Monday fell on an odd day of the month or an even day of the month.
Between 6.0 a.m. and 9.0 a.m. on Nov. 15, 1965, the signs in the road were
altered so as to indicate that parking was not allowed on the east side of the
road. On appeal by the appellant against a conviction of unlawfully causing
his car to wait in the road from 10.10 a.m. to 11.35 a.m.,
Held: the local authority had not taken such steps as they were required

---

* Regulation 15, so far as material, is set out at p. 1051, letter F, post.

Distinguished in COOPER *v.* HALL.
[1968] 1 All E.R. 185.

A　to take by reg. 15 (*c*) of the regulations of 1961, since on neither side of the road was there any traffic sign indicating the importance of whether the current period of parking regulation began with a Monday whose date was an even-numbered or an odd-numbered day in the month; and accordingly the conviction would be quashed (see p. 1051, letters H and I, and p. 1052, letter A, post).

B　　*Macleod* v. *Hamilton* ([1965] S.L.T. 305) applied.

　　Appeal allowed.

　　[As to the power to make orders relating to the use of parking places, see 33 HALSBURY'S LAWS (3rd Edn.) 526, 527, para. 897.

　　For the Road Traffic Act, 1960, s. 26, s. 27, s. 29, see 40 HALSBURY'S STATUTES (2nd Edn.) 732, 734, 736; and for the relevant amendments, see notes (3), (4),
C　post.]

　　Case referred to:

　　MacLeod v. *Hamilton*, [1965] S.L.T. 305.

　　Case Stated.

　　This was a Case Stated by justices for the county borough of Brighton in
D　respect of their adjudication as a magistrates' court sitting at Brighton on Apr. 26, 1966. On Jan. 11, 1966, an information was preferred by the respondent, William Cavey, against the appellant, David Alfred Morgan James, charging that on Nov. 15, 1965, at the county borough, he unlawfully, except on the direction of or with the permission of a police constable in uniform, caused a motor car to wait from 10.10 a.m. to 11.35 a.m. in Queens Gardens otherwise than on
E　the west side of the road, contrary to the Brighton Corporation (Various Roads) (No. 3) (Unilateral Waiting) Order 1965, duly made by the council of the county borough in exercise of the powers conferred on them by s. 26 of the Road Traffic Act, 1960, and of all other powers enabling them in that behalf. The following facts were proved or admitted. The appellant was at all material times the driver of a Morris 1000 motor car, index number 977 GPL. On Monday, Nov.
F　15, 1965, at about 6.0 a.m. the appellant parked the Morris motor car on the east side of Queens Gardens in the county borough of Brighton. The Morris motor car remained parked as aforesaid until about 1.30 p.m. the same day. At all material times there was in force the Brighton Corporation (Various Roads) (No. 3) (Unilateral Waiting) Order 1965, which order had been duly made by the council of the county borough in the exercise of the powers conferred on
G　them by s. 26 of the Road Traffic Act, 1960. The order applied to Queens Gardens and was found to be in force at all material times. At all material times there were the following signs erected in Queen's Gardens: (i) Yellow plates ten inches wide and twelve inches high bearing a replica of diagram No. 636 (in Part 2 of Sch. 1 to the Traffic Signs Regulations and General Directions, 1964*) in the top centre and bearing the words " Continuous 9 a.m. Monday until
H　6 p.m. Sunday next " and bearing an arrow pointing south on the sign at the northern end of the road and pointing north on all other signs; (ii) a broken yellow line was showing on the road surface on both east and west sides of the road similar to those indicated by diagram 1015 (in Part 2 of Sch. 2 to the regulations of 1964); (iii) plain blue plates ten inches wide and twelve inches high on the side of the road on which waiting was unrestricted. These signs did not bear any
I　legend. At all material times there were no signs in the form as indicated by diagram 636 in Part 2 of Sch. 1 to the regulations of 1964, erected in or at the end of Queens Gardens. At 6.0 a.m. on Nov. 15, 1965, when the appellant parked his Morris car in Queens Gardens, the traffic signs erected in Queens Gardens indicated that waiting was restricted between the hours of 9.0 a.m. on Monday until 6.0 p.m. the following Sunday continuously on the west side of Queens Gardens. Between the hours of 6.0 a.m. and 9.0 a.m. on that day the signs were altered so as to indicate that the aforesaid restriction applied to the east side of Queens

* S.I. 1964 No. 1857.

Garden and not to the west side. At 6.0 a.m. on Nov. 15, 1965, when the appellant A
parked his Morris motor car in Queens Gardens he was entitled to do so under
the provisions of the Brighton Corporation (Various Roads) (No. 3) (Unilateral
Waiting) Order 1965.   At all material times there was nothing on any of the
traffic signs erected in Queens Gardens to indicate that the prohibition on causing
or permitting vehicles to wait on the east side of Queens Gardens or on the west
side depended on whether a Monday fell on a day of the month which bore an B
odd number or on a day of the month which bore an even number.

It was contended for the appellant that (i) the signs did not comply with the
regulations of 1964 in that: (a) there were no signs as indicated in diagram 636;
(b) those signs in Queens Gardens which purported to comply with diagram 639
should have been of dimensions of nine inches long by six inches high, but were
in fact ten inches long by twelve inches high; and that variation from the C
prescribed dimensions exceeded the five per cent. variation permitted by reg. 8
nor was the variation within the variations permitted by reg. 12; (ii) at the time
the appellant parked his motor car in Queens Gardens he so parked the motor
car in compliance with the direction then displayed by the traffic signs.   The
signs ought correctly to have displayed the extent and nature of the restrictions
at all times throughout Monday, Nov. 15, 1965, and the signs failed to do so; D
(iii) signs complying with the regulations of 1964 must be displayed to show the
the effect of the order and unless that be done, no offence was committed. It was
contended for the respondent that (i) a sign in the form of diagram 636 was not
necessary because the sign would indicate an absolute prohibition against waiting
in the street at all; (ii) the signs erected in Queens Gardens complied with the
regulations of 1964; (iii) at all material times, namely from 9.0 a.m. on Nov. 15, E
1965, onwards, the signs correctly indicated the nature and extent of the
restrictions on waiting; (iv) in any event the offence was an offence against the
order and not an offence against the signs;   and it was not an essential prerequisite to the validity of the order that traffic signs be erected as indicated
by the regulations of 1964.

The justices convicted the appellant and fined him £2, and the appellant now F
appealed.

A. D. Gavin for the appellant.
R. A. Headridge for the respondent.

WINN, L.J., having stated the nature of the appeal and reviewed the facts, G
continued: The argument in the magistrates' court proceeded on several grounds
which are no longer submitted in this court. It was said there that a sign in the
form of a diagram which is to be found in regulations (1) which relate to the
dimensions and shape of traffic signs, diagram 636, was necessary and was not
displayed. That has been abandoned by counsel for the appellant very properly
in this court and no more need be said about it. There was a further contention H
in the magistrates' court that the signs which were exhibited in Queens Gardens,
either side of the road, did not comply with another diagram, No. 639, in the
regulations because the dimensions were different.   That again has been
abandoned in this court very properly by counsel for the appellant on a further
study of all the regulations. The abandonment of those two contentions has been
very acceptable to and has caused considerable relief to counsel for the respondent. I
To change the signs would have cost a lot of money.

What remains is one point alone, a point on which there is fortunately authoritative guidance, though not any binding decision, viz., a case in Scotland,
MacLeod v. *Hamilton* (2). Counsel for the respondent is, in my view, quite right

---

(1) Traffic Signs Regulations and General Directions 1964 (S.I. 1964 No. 1857),
Sch. 1, Part. 2.
(2) [1965] S.L.T. 305.

A   in saying that the facts of that case were not identical with the facts of this case. That case was, compared with the present case, an a fortiori case since there were no proper signs exhibited in a street in Edinburgh, but nevertheless it is, in my opinion, quite clear that the basic ratio of the Scots decision is that, unless an authority which makes a traffic control order complies with the requirements imposed on the making of such an order and the publication of the order is
B   adequate, then any offence which it purports to create cannot be effectively prosecuted.

I do not desire to dwell on the statutory provisions, and I hope that it will suffice if I say that, under the Road Traffic Act, 1960, s. 26, authority is given to make orders for controlling traffic in various respects. A local authority is empowered by s. 27 of the Act of 1960 to make, without any requirement of
C   confirmation by the Minister, as is provided by s. 27 (4), as amended (3) any order containing no provisions other than certain specified provisions including, under para. (*c*), the prohibiting or restricting the waiting of vehicles on a road. Where an order is validly made—and it is not doubted in this court that there was power validly to make the order to which I have referred—s. 26 (7) of the Road Traffic Act, 1960, as amended (4), makes it an offence for any person to contravene
D   such a traffic regulation order and makes him liable on summary conviction to a fine not exceeding £20. By s. 29 (2) of the Act of 1960, it is provided that

" Where a traffic regulation order is made by a local authority . . . the local authority shall publish, in such manner as may be prescribed by regulations made by the appropriate Minister, notice of the making and effect of the
E   order."

The manner of publication was prescribed by reg. 15 of the Traffic Regulation Orders (Procedure) (England and Wales) Regulations, 1961 (5). Paragraphs (*a*) and (*b*) of reg. 15 provide for publication in the ordinary sense, e.g., publication of notice in newspapers, and then it is provided that the local authority shall

F   " (*c*) forthwith take all such steps as are reasonably practicable to cause to be erected on or near to the said roads traffic signs in such positions as the local authority may consider to be requisite for the purpose of securing that adequate information as to the effect of the order is given to persons using the said roads: . . ."

The authority must take all such steps as are reasonably practicable—and the
G   following are the operative words in my opinion—" for the purpose of securing that adequate information as to the effect of the order is given to persons using the said roads ".

The reason, shortly stated, which requires, in my view, that this appeal should be allowed, is that the local authority did not take such steps as they were required to take under that regulation. They did not take steps which clearly could have
H   been taken, and which clearly would have been practicable, to cause adequate information to be given to persons using the road by the signs which they erected. On neither side of the road was there any sign referring to the importance, for the purpose of control of parking in Queens Gardens, of whether the day on which someone desired to park was within a period beginning with a Monday which itself fell on an odd day in the month or was within a period beginning with a
I   Monday which itself fell on an even day in the month. I do not think that really the matter is more complex than that when it has been analysed. The court would

---

(3) I.e., by the Road Traffic Act, 1962, s. 51 (1), Sch. 4, Part 1; 42 HALSBURY'S STATUTES (2nd Edn.) 922, 934.

(4) I.e., by the Road Traffic Act, 1962, s. 8, Sch. 1, Part 3, para. 28; 42 HALSBURY'S STATUTES (2nd Edn.) 895, 927.

(5) S.I. 1961 No. 485.

like to pay tribute to the lucidity of the analysis which counsel for the appellant **A** has given to this matter before the court today. I am of the opinion that the appeal should be allowed.

ASHWORTH, J.: I agree.

WIDGERY, J.: I agree also.

Appeal allowed. **B**

Solicitors: *J. B. Izod* (for the appellant); *Town Clerk*, Brighton (for the respondent).

[*Reported by* N. P. METCALFE, ESQ., *Barrister-at-Law.*]

C

NOTE.

R. *v.* CRAIG.

[COURT OF APPEAL, CRIMINAL DIVISION (Lord Parker, C.J., Winn, L.J., and **D** Widgery, J.), October 7, 1966.]

Criminal Law—Appeal—Sentence—Conviction quashed on one count of indictment—Power of Court of Appeal to increase sentence on other part of indictment in substitution for sentence passed at trial—Criminal Appeal Act, 1907 (7 Edw. 7 c. 23), s. 5 (1), as amended by Criminal Appeal Act 1966 (c. 31), s. 4 (2).

E

[As to the power of the Court of Appeal* to vary sentences, see 10 HALSBURY'S LAWS (3rd Edn.) 539, 540, para. 990.

For the Criminal Appeal Act, 1907, s. 5, see 5 HALSBURY'S STATUTES (2nd Edn.) 930.]

Appeal and application.   **F**

The appellant, Edward Malcolm Craig, was convicted of robbery with violence (count 3) and assault occasioning actual bodily harm (count 4) in an indictment containing six counts. He was acquitted on the first two counts, pleaded guilty to two other counts and asked for six other offences to be taken into consideration. He was sentenced to five years' imprisonment on count 3, to three years' imprisonment on count 4, and to nine months' imprisonment on the two counts to which **G** he pleaded guilty, all the sentences to run concurrently. He appealed against conviction on count 3 by leave of the single judge, who also gave leave to appeal generally against sentence.

D. M. Sumner for the appellant.
D. D. Brown for the respondent.

H

LORD PARKER, C.J., in delivering the judgment of the court said that the conviction of robbery with violence must be quashed because there had been a misreception of evidence and a misdirection and, accordingly, the sentence of five years' imprisonment fell to the ground. He continued: Under s. 5 (1) of the Criminal Appeal Act, 1907, it is provided that:

"If it appears to the Court of Criminal Appeal that an appellant, though **I** not properly convicted on some count or part of the indictment, has been properly convicted on some other count or part of the indictment, the court may either affirm the sentence passed on the appellant at the trial, or pass such sentence in substitution therefor as they think proper, and as may be warranted in law by the verdict on the count or part of the indictment on which the court consider that the appellant has been properly convicted."

* Viz., the Criminal Division of the Court of Appeal; see the Criminal Appeal Act 1966, s. 1 (1), (2).

A Pausing there, there was, therefore, power under the Criminal Appeal Act, 1907, in a case such as this to increase the sentence on the assault count (count 4) against which there is no appeal and which stands. That sentence is three years' imprisonment, and it would be possible for this court under s. 5 (1) of the Act of 1907 to increase that sentence, and to increase it to any extent within the range applicable to the particular crime. By the Criminal Appeal Act 1966, s. 4 (2),

B however, a limitation is made to increasing sentences. In general, no sentence of any greater severity may be passed, and in a case contemplated by s. 5 (1) of the Act of 1907 it is provided that, if the sentence is increased on the part or parts of the indictment which stand, it cannot be increased to a greater extent than the sentence passed on the indictment as a whole. The position, therefore, is that the court can increase the sentence of three years on the assault count, but

C not beyond the five years which was the totality of the sentence passed on the whole indictment.

[His Lordship said that the court had given the matter anxious consideration, referred to the seriousness of the offences and continued:] In all the circumstances of this case, the court feels that there is real ground for increasing the sentence of three years imposed on the assault count; they will not increase it to the

D maximum of five years, but they will substitute a sentence of four years' imprisonment on that count.

Appeal allowed in part. Sentence varied.

Solicitors: *Registrar of Criminal Appeals* (for the appellant); *O. G. Ogden*, Manchester (for the Crown).

E   [*Reported by* N. P. Metcalfe, Esq., *Barrister-at-Law.*]

PIONEER PLASTIC CONTAINERS LTD. v. COMMISSIONERS
F ## OF CUSTOMS AND EXCISE.

[Chancery Division (Buckley, J.), February 21, 22, 1967.]

Evidence—Point of law in issue on pleadings—Defence containing admission of facts alleged in statement of claim but raising objection in point of law—Claim for declaration that plastic closures for tins were not chargeable to
G *purchase tax—Whether leave should be given to adduce evidence by affidavit.*

The plaintiffs issued a writ against the Commissioners of Customs and Excise asking for a declaration that certain plastic closures or lids manufactured and sold by them were not chargeable within Group 11 (*a*) in Sch. 1, Pt. 1, to the Purchase Tax Act 1963. By their statement of claim the plaintiffs stated the alleged purpose of the plastic lids and the object of their design

H (viz., to close sealed tins of ground coffee after the tins had been opened), and that the commissioners claimed that the lids were chargeable under Group 11 (*a*). Group 11 (*a*) comprised " furniture, hardware, ironmongery, turnery, table-ware, kitchen-ware and toilet-ware, being articles of a kind used for domestic or office purposes ". Paragraph (*a*) of the group included " articles not comprised below in this group ". The commissioners by their

I defence admitted the facts alleged in the statement of claim, but objected in point of law that on the true construction of Group 11 (*a*) it included the plastic lids. The plaintiffs sought leave to adduce evidence by two affidavits, drafts of which had been submitted to the commissioners. One matter to which the affidavits were directed was whether the plastic closures or lids were designed for any after-use.

Held: since all the facts were admitted on the pleadings, leaving only the question of law raised thereon to be decided, the plaintiffs would not be allowed to adduce affidavit evidence (see p. 1056, letter G, post).

The Hardwick ((1884), 9 P.D. 32) considered.   A

[As to objections in point of law, see 30 HALSBURY'S LAWS (3rd Edn.) 17,
para. 35, p. 392, para. 731; and as to a party being bound by his pleadings, see
ibid., p. 4, para. 4; and for cases on points of law, see DIGEST (Pleading) 48-53,
390-427.]

Cases referred to: -   B
    A.-G. v. *Milliwatt, Ltd.,* [1948] 1 All E.R. 331; 39 Digest (Repl.) 349, *827.*
    Hardwick, The, (1884), 9 P.D. 32; 53 L.J.P. 23; 50 L.T. 128; 5 Asp. M.L.C.
        199; Digest (Pleading) 213, *1781.*

Procedure Summons.

An action was brought by the plaintiffs, Pioneer Plastic Containers, Ltd., by
writ issued on Apr. 26, 1966, against the Commissioners of Customs and Excise C
for a declaration that the plastic lids manufactured and sold by the plaintiffs to
J. Lyons & Co., Ltd., were not (and never had been) chargeable goods within
Group 11 (*a*) of Sch. 1, Pt. 1, to the Purchase Tax Act 1963. This was a summons
dated Dec. 20, 1966, taken out in the action by the plaintiffs for leave to file two
affidavits to be admitted in evidence in support of the plaintiffs' case.

By their statement of claim the plaintiffs pleaded, among other allegations, D
as follows—

    " 3. In the course of [their trade] the [plaintiffs manufacture and supply]
    to J. Lyons & Co., Ltd. a plastic lid. J. Lyons & Co., Ltd. fixes these
    lids to the half-pound sealed tins of pure ground coffee which it sells as part
    of its trade. The purpose of the lid is to enable the coffee to be kept fresh
    after the tin is opened. The lid is specifically designed to fit the tin in which E
    the coffee is sold and for this purpose only. The [plaintiffs are] precluded
    by contract with J. Lyons & Co., Ltd. from selling [the lids] elsewhere . . .
    the lids are supplied in bulk . . . and are fitted by J. Lyons & Co., Ltd.'s
    staff to the individual tins before the tins are sold through the retail shop.
    The price of the tin includes the lid for which no separate charge is made."

                                                      F
By their defence the commissioners pleaded that they admitted the facts alleged
in the statement of claim, but would object in point of law that on the true
construction of Group 11 (*a*) in Part 1 of Sch. 1 to the Purchase Tax Act 1963 that
group included the plastic lids mentioned in the statement of claim. The
affidavit evidence which the plaintiffs sought to adduce was contained in an
affidavit of Richard Clark and an affidavit of Barry Henry Silverman. The G
affidavit of Mr. Clark, who was and had been a director of the plaintiffs for
twelve years, included by para. 9 thereof—

    " 9. The plastic caps manufactured to the order of J. Lyons & Co., Ltd.
    hereinbefore referred to, were not designed for any after-use, nor were they
    in my opinion capable of being offered to the public for any defined use."

The affidavit of Mr. Silverman, who was employed by J. Lyons & Co., Ltd. as H
senior marketing executive, included by para. 5 the following—

    " 5. I have seen the affidavit of [Mr. Clark] sworn herein . . . and confirm
    . . . that the plastic caps . . . there referred to were and are, in my opinion,
    suitable only for the purpose for which my company ordered them, namely
    as a means of ensuing that the coffee in each tin remained fresh during the
    normal period of use."   I

The cases noted below* were cited during the argument in addition to those
referred to in the judgment.

---

    * *The Rothbury,* (1893), 10 T.L.R. 60; *The Buteshire,* [1909] P. 170; *Stephenson
Brothers, Ltd.* v. *Comrs. of Customs and Excise,* [1953] 1 All E.R. 469; *Esso Petroleum
Co., Ltd.* v. *Southport Corpn.,* [1956] 3 All E.R. 864; [1956] A.C. 218; *Betterways Panels,
Ltd.* v. *Comrs. of Customs and Excise,* [1964] 1 All E.R. 948; *Comrs. of Customs and
Excise* v. *H. G. Kewley, Ltd.,* [1965] 1 All E.R. 929.

A   *D. C. Miller*, Q.C., and *S. I. Simon* for the plaintiffs.
    J. P. Warner for the commissioners.

BUCKLEY, J.: This action, which is concerned with the question whether
or not a particular article falls within a particular charge to purchase tax, was
commenced by the plaintiffs by writ asking for a declaration that the article
B   in question, a plastic lid manufactured and sold by them to J. Lyons & Co., Ltd.,
is not chargeable within Group 11 (*a*) in Part 1 of Sch. 1 to the Purchase Tax
Act 1963. The plaintiffs served a statement of claim in which they allege what
they say the purpose of the lid is and what the object of its design is. They say, as
is the fact, that the defendant Commissioners of Customs and Excise claim that
these lids are chargeable under Group 11 (*a*) of Part 1 of Sch. 1 to the Purchase
C   Tax Act 1963, but the plaintiffs maintain that the lids in question are not, and
never have been, chargeable under that head. The commissioners by their defence
admitted all the allegations in the statement of claim, but say that they will
object in point of law that on the true construction of the relevant part of Sch. 1
to the Act of 1963 that Group 11 (*a*) includes the plaintiffs' plastic lids.
    The allegations of fact having been all admitted in that way, the parties
D   considered that the hearing of their action would be expedited if the matter were
transferred into the non-witness list in the Chancery Division, the action having
been commenced in this Division, rather than wait to take its place in the witness
list. That circumstance is not material to the point to be decided. The plaintiffs have
sought leave to adduce evidence in the form of two affidavits, drafts of which
they submitted to the commissioners, and which are before the court. The
E   commissioners object to the admission of any evidence on the ground that there
are no issues of fact raised on the pleadings at all, all the facts alleged in the
statement of claim having been admitted. In those circumstances they say that
it would be wrong to allow the plaintiffs to introduce evidence—and it matters
not if it is evidence given orally or evidence on affidavit—because if it does no
more than establish what is alleged in the statement of claim such evidence is
F   unnecessary; if it goes further than that and introduces matters of fact not
alleged in the statement of claim then it ought not to be admitted as relating to
something which is not an issue between the parties.
    It seems to me that the question which the court has to decide in this action is
partly one of law and partly one of fact. The interpretation of the provisions
of the Purchase Tax Act 1963, is a matter of law pure and simple. The nature
G   of the article, the plastic lid, with which the action is concerned, and the uses for
which it is designed and to which it can be put are questions of fact. So far as
those facts are relevant to the determination of the case, it is for the plaintiffs
to plead the facts in their statement of claim, and if, the plaintiffs having pleaded
them in the statement of claim, the commissioners admit all those facts, then there
is no issue between the parties on that part of the case which is concerned with
H   matters of fact. Where there is no issue to be decided there is no purpose to be
served by admitting any evidence. Indeed, as counsel for the commissioners has
pointed out, where a defendant admits all the facts alleged against him by a
plaintiff, but says that nevertheless he disputes the plaintiff's right to relief, the
case is analogous to demurrer under the old practice. In those circumtances
the plaintiff ought not to be allowed to elaborate his case in any way by way of
I   admitting evidence which may embroider the facts alleged in the statement of
claim.
    Counsel for the plaintiffs has referred me to one purchase tax case, *A.-G.* v.
Milliwatt, Ltd. (1), as supporting his contention that evidence is relevant in a
case which raises considerations, such as are involved in the decision of the
present case, and that evidence had been admitted as to matters of the kind on
which he now seeks the admission of evidence, i.e., evidence relating to such things

---

(1) [1948] 1 All E.R. 331.

A

as the design of the goods in question, their possible use, the way in which they are marketed and so on. No doubt that is perfectly true. In an action in which there are issues of fact the court will of course hear evidence directed to resolving those issues of fact; but that was not a case, I think, in which the facts were admitted by the defendant company. The defendant company were, it seems clear from the report, asserting that the goods there in question, which were electric blankets and the like, were not goods for use for domestic purposes but were goods used for medical purposes; that was the issue which the court had to decide, and it was therefore relevant to investigate matters of the kind which I have mentioned and evidence would be properly adduced to deal with those issues between the parties. But that evidence is accepted by the court in a case where there are issues of fact between the parties is no reason for holding that evidence should be admitted where all the facts alleged by the plaintiff are admitted by the defendant.

B

C

Counsel for the plaintiffs has also referred me to *The Hardwick* (2), a case in which the defendants admitted all the facts pleaded in the statement of claim. SIR JAMES HANNEN, P., did not see fit to admit evidence in that case. He made observations, however, leading to the conclusion that he thought that the court could admit evidence in a special case and in the exercise of its discretion, notwithstanding that all the alleged facts were admitted on the pleadings. That was, as has been pointed out, a salvage case. In salvage cases questions arise for the decision of the court and the exercise of the court's discretion which may require the court to be informed of matters that are not strictly in issue between the parties. The court has, in the exercise of its discretionary power, to assess the proper amount of salvage reward and remuneration, which can only be done on some investigation of the facts. Even in *The Hardwick* (2), however, the application to admit evidence was unsuccessful. I have been shown no case in any way near the present case in which evidence has been admitted notwithstanding that there is no issue of fact between the parties. Indeed, I have been shown no case in which that course has been taken at all.

D

E

In these circumstances it seems to me that this is not a case in which, on the pleadings as they stand, any evidence ought properly to be admitted. The matter should be heard and determined on the pleadings and on the admissions contained in the pleadings. Consequently I think that the commissioners are right in their submissions that the plaintiffs ought not to be permitted to put in affidavit evidence, or indeed to seek to adduce oral evidence. Accordingly I shall direct that no evidence be admitted and that the case should come on on the pleadings as they stand.

F

G

Order that affidavits should not be admitted.

Solicitors: *Bartlett & Gluckstein* (for the plaintiffs); *Solicitor, Customs and Excise.*

[Reported by JENIFER SANDELL, *Barrister-at-Law.]*

H

I

[END OF VOLUME ONE.]

---

(2) (1884), 9 P.D. 32.